Encyclopedia of Multi-Attribute Decision-Making (MADM)

Encyclopedia of Multi-Attribute Decision-Making (MADM)

Edited by

Gholamreza Haseli
School of Engineering and Sciences, Tecnologico de Monterrey, Monterrey, Mexico

Muhammet Deveci
Department of Industrial Engineering, Turkish Naval Academy, National Defence University, Istanbul, Türkiye

Mostafa Hajiaghaei-Keshteli
School of Engineering and Sciences, Tecnologico de Monterrey, Monterrey, Mexico

ELSEVIER

MK MORGAN KAUFMANN

Morgan Kaufmann is an imprint of Elsevier
50 Hampshire Street, 5th Floor, Cambridge, MA 02139, United States

ISBN: 978-0-443-33275-3

For Information on all Morgan Kaufmann publications
visit our website at https://www.elsevier.com/books-and-journals

Publisher: Mara Conner
Acquisitions Editor: Chris Katsaropoulos
Editorial Project Manager: Asmi Bharati
Production Project Manager: Aishwarya R.
Cover Designer: Gopalakrishnan Venkatraman

Printed in England by CPI Group (UK) Ltd
Croydon CR0 4YY
United Kingdom

Typeset by MPS Limited, Chennai, India
Last digit is the print number: 10 9 8 7 6 5 4 3 2 1

Contents

Section 2
Extensions for the MADM methods

99. ORESTE: Organization Rangement et synthese de ronnees relationnelles for multi-attribute decision-making

Ibrahim Yilmaz and Babek Erdebilli

100. GLDS: Gained and lost dominance score for multi-attribute decision-making

Xingli Wu and Huchang Liao

List of contributors

Andrés Esteban Acero-López School of Engineering and Sciences, Tecnológico de Monterrey, Monterrey, Nuevo León, Mexico

Abdullah Alamoodi MEU Research Unit, Middle East University, Amman, Jordan; META, UPSI, Tanjung Malim, Malaysia

Ahmed Shihab Albahri Technical Engineering College, Imam Jafar Alsadiq University, Baghdad, Iraq; University of Information Technology and Communication (IJOITC), Baghdad, Iraq

Osamah Albahri Institute of Innovation, Science and Sustainability, Federation University Australia, Melbourne, VIC, Australia; Computer Techniques Engineering Department, Mazaya University College, Nasiriyah, Iraq

Moslem Alimohammadlou Department of Management, Shiraz University, Shiraz, Iran

Yousaf Ayub Department of Industrial and Systems Engineering, The Hong Kong Polytechnic University, Hong Kong SAR, P.R. China

Ibrahim Badi Libyan Academy, Misrata, Libya

Parmida Bahreini Department of Industrial Engineering, Ankara Yıldırım Beyazıt University, Ankara, Turkey

George Baryannis School of Computing and Engineering, University of Huddersfield, Huddersfield, United Kingdom

Mahmut Baydaş Faculty of Applied Sciences, Necmettin Erbakan University, Konya, Türkiye

Enes Emre Başar Faculty of Economics and Administrative Sciences, Faculty of Economics and Administrative Sciences, Anadolu University, Eskisehir, Türkiye

Sanjib Biswas Amity Business School, Amity University Kolkata, Kolkata, West Bengal, India

Jurica Bosna Department of Economics, University of Zadar, Zadar, Croatia

Mouhamed Bayane Bouraima International School of Technical Education, Sichuan University of Architectural Technology, Deyang, P.R. China

Darko Božanić Military Academy, University of Defence in Belgrade, Belgrade, Serbia

Yushuo Cao College of Economics and Management, Nanjing University of Aeronautics and Astronautics, Nanjing, P.R. China

Prasenjit Chatterjee Department of Mechanical Engineering, MCKV Institute of Engineering, Howrah, West Bengal, India

Yu Chen School of Economics and Management, Anhui Normal University, Wuhu, Anhui Province, P.R. China

Shuping Cheng School of Business Administration, Chaohu University, Hefei, Anhui Province, P.R. China

Chiara Colombaroni Department of Civil, Constructional and Environmental Engineering, Sapienza University of Rome, Rome, Italy

Saeed Sadeghi Darvazeh School of Engineering and Sciences, Tecnológico de Monterrey, Monterrey, Mexico

Hakan Ayhan Dağıstanlı Industrial Engineering, National Defense University, Ankara, Çankaya, Türkiye

Gülay Demir High School of Health Vocational Services, Sivas Cumhuriyet University, Sivas, Türkiye

Zeynep Kizilkan Demir Industrial Engineering Department, Istanbul Technical University, Istanbul, Türkiye

Muhammet Deveci Department of Industrial Engineering, Turkish Naval Academy, National Defence University, Istanbul, Türkiye

Szabolcs Duleba Department of Transport Technology and Economics, Faculty of Transportation and Vehicle Engineering, Budapest University of Technology and Economics, Budapest, Hungary; Institute of Mathematics and Informatics, University of Nyíregyháza, Nyíregyháza, Hungary

Cem Niyazi Durmuş Department of Business Administration, Faculty of Economic, Administration, and Social Sciences, Kadir Has University, Istanbul, Türkiye

Şeyma Duymaz Department of Industrial Engineering, Turkish Naval Academy, National Defence University, Tuzla, İstanbul, Türkiye

Fatih Ecer Sub-Department of Operations Research, Faculty of Economics and Administrative Sciences, Afyon Kocatepe University, Afyonkarahisar, Turkey

Maryam Eghbalizarch Department of Industrial and Systems Engineering, Southern Polytechnic College of Engineering and Engineering Technology, Kennesaw State University, Marietta, GA, United States

Elham Elmi Department of Industrial management, Islamic Azad University Science and Research Branch, Tehran, Iran

Babek Erdebilli Department of Industrial Engineering, Ankara Yıldırım Beyazıt University, Ankara, Turkey; Department of Industrial Engineering, Ankara Yıldırım Beyazıt University, Ankara, Turkiye; Department of Industrial Engineering, Ankara Yıldırım Beyazıt University, Ankara, Türkiye; School of Business, Worcester Polytechnic Institute, Worcester, MA, United States

Yeşim Erdebilli Department of Industrial Engineering, Ankara Yıldırım Beyazıt University, Ankara, Turkey

Nazlı Ersoy Osmaniye Korkut Ata University, Osmaniye, Türkiye

Hamidreza Eskandari Department of Business Analytics, Swansea University, United Kingdom

Gaetano Fusco Department of Civil, Constructional and Environmental Engineering, Sapienza University of Rome, Rome, Italy

Chong Gao Department of Economics and Management, North China Electric Power University, Baoding, Hebei, P.R. China

Diego García-Zamora Department of Mathematics, University of Jaén, Jaén, Spain

Nazanin Ghaemi-Zadeh Department of Industrial Engineering, Faculty of Engineering, Sharif University of Technology, Tehran, Iran

Ömer Faruk Görçün Department of Business Administration, Faculty of Economic, Administration, and Social Sciences, Kadir Has University, Istanbul, Türkiye

Bartu Güneri Department of Industrial Engineering, Turkish Naval Academy, National Defence University, Tuzla, İstanbul, Türkiye

Ashkan Hafezalkotob Department of Management and Marketing, La Trobe University, Melbourne, VIC, Australia

Mostafa Hajiaghaei-Keshteli School of Engineering and Sciences, Tecnologico de Monterrey, Monterrey, Mexico

Aliakbar Hasani Department of Industrial Engineering and Management, Shahrood University of Technology, Shahroud, Iran

Gholamreza Haseli School of Engineering and Sciences, Tecnologico de Monterrey, Monterrey, Mexico

Shide Sadat Hashemi Department of Management, Behin Avina co, MST Park, Tehran, Iran

Eldina Huskanović Faculty of Transport and Traffic Engineering, University of East Sarajevo, Doboj, Bosnia and Herzegovina

Mehtap Isik Department of International Trade, Bogazici University, Bebek, Istanbul, Türkiye

Cengiz Kahraman Industrial Engineering Department, Istanbul Technical University, Istanbul, Türkiye

Karahan Kara Department of Data Science and Analytics, Faculty of Economics and Administrative Sciences, İzmir Katip Çelebi University, İzmir, Türkiye; Department of Business, Faculty of Economics and Administrative Sciences, OSTIM Technical University, Ankara, Türkiye; Department of Business, Faculty of Economics and Administrative Sciences, İzmir Katip Çelebi University, İzmir, Türkiye

Çağlar Karamaşa Department of Quantitative Methods, Faculty of Economics and Administrative Sciences, Anadolu University, Eskişehir, Türkiye

Mustafa Kavacık Necmettin Erbakan University, Konya, Türkiye

Salar Keshavarz Hedayati Department of Management, Faculty of Management and Financial Sciences, Khatam University, Tehran, Iran

Mehdi Keshavarz-Ghorabaee Department of Management, Faculty of Humanities (Azadshahr Branch), Gonbad Kavous University, Gonbad Kavous, Iran

Moein Khazaei School of Engineering and Sciences, Tecnologico de Monterrey, Monterrey, Mexico

Reza Kia Department of Operations Management and Business Statistics, Sultan Qaboos University, Muscat, Oman

Mustafa Kocaoğlu Necmettin Erbakan University, Konya, Türkiye

Nikola Komatina Faculty of Engineering, University of Kragujevac, Kragujevac, Serbia

Dimitri Konstantas Geneva School of Economics and Management, University of Geneva, Geneva, Switzerland

Hande Küçükönder Department of Business, Faculty of Economics and Administrative Sciences, Bartın University, Bartın, Turkey

Kemal Gürol Kurtay Industrial Engineering, National Defense University, Ankara, Çankaya, Türkiye

Álvaro Labella Department of Computer Sciences, University of Jaén, Jaén, Spain

Huchang Liao Business School, Sichuan University, Chengdu, Sichuan Province, P.R. China

Sheng-Wei Lin Department of Financial Management, Management College, National Defense University, Taipei, Taiwan

Xiaodi Liu School of Microelectronics and Data Science, Anhui University of Technology, Ma'anshan, Anhui, P.R. China

Huai-Wei Lo Department of Industrial Engineering and Management, National Yunlin University of Science and Technology, Douliu City, Taiwan

Miloš Madić Faculty of Mechanical Engineering, University of Niš, Niš, Serbia

Amir H. Malekijoo Information Sciences and Technology, George Mason University, Fairfax County, VA, United States

Reyhane Malekijoo Department of Physics and Energy Engineering, AmirKabir University of Technology, Tehran, Iran

Farzaneh MansooriMooseloo School of Engineering and Sciences, Tecnológico de Monterrey, Monterrey, Mexico

Neda Mansouri School of Industrial Engineering, Iran University of Science and Technology, Tehran, Iran

Dragan Marinković Faculty of Mechanical Engineering and Transport Systems, TU Berlin, Berlin, Germany; Mechanical Science Institute, Vilnius Gediminas Technical University-VILNIUS TECH, Vilnius, Lithuania; University College, Korea University, Seoul, Korea; Department of Structural Analysis, Technical University of Berlin, Berlin, Germany; University College, Korea University, Seongbuk-gu, Seoul, Republic of Korea; Department of Structural Analysis, Technical University Berlin, Berlin, Germany; Department of Structural Analysis, Faculty of Mechanical and Transport Systems, TU Berlin, Berlin, Germany; Institute of Mechanical Science, Vilnius Gediminas Technical University, Vilnius, Lithuania; University College, Korea University, Seoul, Republic of Korea

Luis Martínez Department of Computer Sciences, University of Jaén, Jaén, Spain

Amir Mehdiabadi Department of Industrial Management, Islamic Azad University, Semnan, Iran

Maryam Mehrparvar Department of mathematics, Bozorgmehr University of Qaenat, Qaen, Iran

Fatemeh Mirsaeedi School of Industrial Engineering, College of Engineering, University of Tehran, Tehran, Iran; Department of Industrial Engineering, University of Tehran, Tehran, Iran

Mostafa Mohammadi Department of Industrial Economics and Technology Management, Norwegian University of Science and Technology, Trondheim, Trøndelag, Norway

Zahra Mohemmi College of Business, Government and Law, Flinders University, Adelaide, SA, Australia

Md. Abdul Moktadir Department of Industrial and Systems Engineering, The Hong Kong Polytechnic University, Hong Kong SAR, P.R. China

Homa Molavi School of Business, Operations and Strategy, University of Greenwich, London, United Kingdom

Sarbast Moslem Department of Civil, Structural and Environmental Engineering, Trinity College Dublin, Dublin, Ireland; Civil Engineering Department, Faculty of Engineering and Natural Sciences, Istinye University, Istanbul, Turkey

Amirhossein Mostofi Department of Management, Technology and Organization, Auckland University of Technology, New Zealand

Emine Nur Nacar Department of Industrial Engineering, Ankara Yıldırım Beyazıt University, Ankara, Türkiye

Javad Nazarian-Jashnabadi Department of Management, Faculty of Economic, Management and Social Science, Shiraz University, Shiraz, Iran

Miroslav Nedeljković Institute of Agricultural Economics, Belgrade, Serbia

Amir Hossein Nobil School of Engineering and Sciences, Tecnolo gico de Monterrey, Mexico

Sezi Cevik Onar ReTech Center, Ecole des Ponts, ParisTech, Paris, France

Yavuz Selim Özdemir Department of Industrial Engineering, Ankara Bilim University, Ankara, Turkiye

Basar Oztaysi Industrial Engineering Department, Istanbul Technical University, Istanbul, Türkiye

Dragan Pamucar Department of Operations Research and Statistics, University of Belgrade, Belgrade, Serbia; UNEC Applied Artificial Intelligence Research Center, Azerbaijan State University of Economics (UNEC), Baku, Azerbaijan; Faculty of Engineering, Dogus University, Istanbul, Türkiye

Bartosz Paradowski National Institute of Telecommunications, Warsaw, Poland

Mahsa Pashang Department of Management, Faculty of Management and Financial Sciences, Khatam University, Tehran, Iran

Goran Petrović Faculty of Mechanical Engineering, University of Niš, Niš, Serbia

Nikola Petrović Faculty of Mechanical Engineering, University of Niš, Niš, Serbia

Mahsa Pishdar Management and Accounting Faculty, College of Farabi, University of Tehran, Qom, Iran

Adis Puška Department of Public Safety, Government of the Brcko District of BiH, Brčko, Bosnia and Herzegovina

Golman Rahmanifar Department of Industrial Engineering & Innovation Sciences, Eindhoven University of Technology, Eindhoven, North Brabant, Netherlands

Shabnam Rahnamay Bonab Department of Management, Monash University, Melbourne, VIC, Australia

Mohammad Ramezani Industrial Management, Tarbiat Modares University, Tehran, Iran

Seyed Hossein Razavi Hajiagha Department of Management, Faculty of Management and Financial Sciences, Khatam University, Tehran, Iran

Jingzheng Ren Department of Industrial and Systems Engineering, The Hong Kong Polytechnic University, Hong Kong SAR, P.R. China

Hossein Reyhani Yamchi La Trobe Business School, La Trobe University, Melbourne, VIC, Australia

Rosa M. Rodríguez Department of Computer Sciences, University of Jaén, Jaén, Spain

Aparajita Sanyal Amity Business School, Amity University Kolkata, Kolkata, West Bengal, India

Irem Ucal Sari Industrial Engineering Department, Baskent University, Ankara, Türkiye

Wojciech Sałabun National Institute of Telecommunications, Warsaw, Poland; West Pomeranian University of Technology in Szczecin, Szczecin, Poland

Tapan Senapati Saveetha School of Engineering, Saveetha Institute of Medical and Technical Sciences, Chennai, Tamil Nadu, India

Soheila Senfi Faculty of Industrial Management and Administration, Shahrood University of Technology, Shahrood, Iran

Tahereh Sepahi Department of Management, Faculty of Management and Accounting, Shahid Beheshti University, Tehran, Iran

Vahideh Shahin Department of Management, Shiraz University, Shiraz, Iran

Iman Mohamad Sharaf Department of Basic Sciences, Higher Technological Institute, Tenth of Ramadan City, Egypt

Reza Sheikh Faculty of Industrial Management and Administration, Shahrood University of Technology, Shahrood, Iran

Andrii Shekhovtsov National Institute of Telecommunications, Warsaw, Poland; West Pomeranian University of Technology in Szczecin, Szczecin, Poland

Ali Sibevei University of Torbat Heydarieh, Torbat Heydarieh, Iran

Vladimir Simic Faculty of Transport and Traffic Engineering, University of Belgrade, Belgrade, Serbia; Faculty of Engineering, Dogus University, Istanbul, Türkiye

Alireza Sotoudeh-Anvari Department of Industrial Engineering, Science and Research Branch, Islamic Azad University, Tehran, Iran

Željko Stević Department of Mobile Machinery and Railway Transport, Faculty of Transport Engineering, Vilnius Gediminas Technical University, Vilnius, Lithuania; Faculty of Transport and Traffic Engineering, University of East Sarajevo, Doboj, Bosnia and Herzegovina

Anđelka Štilić The College of Tourism, Academy of Applied Studies Belgrade, Belgrade, Serbia

Mahmoud Tajik School of Industrial Engineering, Iran University of Science and Technology, Tehran, Iran

Jing Tang School of Digital Commerce and Trade, Zhejiang Polytechnic University of Mechanical and Electrical Engineering, Hangzhou, Zhejiang, P.R. China; School of Economics and Management, Southeast University, Nanjing, Jiangsu, P.R. China

Erfan Babaee Tirkolaee Department of Industrial Engineering, Istinye University, Istanbul, Türkiye

Hana Tomaskova Faculty of Informatics and Management, University of Hradec Kralove, Hradec Králové, Czech Republic

Ayşe Topal Department of Business Administration, Faculty of Business and Economics Sciences, Nigde Omer Halisdemir University, Nigde, Turkiye

Bengü Tosun Department of Economics, Istanbul Nişantaşı University, İstanbul, Türkiye

Alptekin Ulutaş Department of International Trade and Logistics, Faculty of Economics and Administrative Sciences, Inonu University, Malatya, Turkiye

Gül Uslu Department of Occupational Health and Safety, Sinop University, Sinop, Türkiye

Mahsa Valipour Concordia Institute for Information Systems Engineering, Concordia University, Montréal, QC, Canada

Haifeng Wang Department of Economics and Management, North China Electric Power University, Baoding, Hebei, P.R. China

Weizhong Wang School of Economics and Management, Anhui Normal University, Wuhu, Anhui Province, P.R. China

Xingli Wu Business School, Sichuan University, Chengdu, Sichuan Province, P.R. China

Osman Yakıt Akdeniz University, Antalya, Türkiye

Galip Cihan Yalçın Department of Business, Faculty of Economics and Administrative Sciences, OSTIM Technical University, Ankara, Türkiye

Zhengyan Yang School of Economics and Management, Anhui Normal University, Wuhu, Anhui Province, P.R. China

Morteza Yazdani European University of Madrid, Villaviciosa de odon Campus, Madrid, Spain; Institute of Dynamic Management, Vilnius Gediminas Technical University, Vilnius, Lithuania

Ibrahim Yilmaz Department of Industrial Engineering, Ankara Yıldırım Beyazıt University, Ankara, Turkey

Samuel Yousefi Department of Mechanical and Manufacturing Engineering, Ontario Tech University, Oshawa, ON, Canada

Ali Aygün Yürüyen Department of Transportation Services, Ardahan University, Göle, Ardahan, Turkiye; Department of Transportation Services, Nihat Delibalta Göle Vocational School, Göle, Ardahan, Turkiye; Department of Transportation Services, Ardahan University, Göle, Ardahan, Turkey

Shervin Zakeri Geneva School of Economics and Management, University of Geneva, Geneva, Switzerland

Edmundas Kazimieras Zavadskas Department of Construction Management and Real Estate, Vilnius Gediminas Technical University, Vilnius, Lithuania

Ling Zhang College of Economics and Management, Nanjing University of Aeronautics and Astronautics, Nanjing, P.R. China

Shiji Zhang School of Microelectronics and Data Science, Anhui University of Technology, Ma'anshan, Anhui, P.R. China

Shitao Zhang School of Microelectronics and Data Science, Anhui University of Technology, Ma'anshan, Anhui, P.R. China

Yajing Zhang School of Economics and Management, Anhui Normal University, Wuhu, Anhui Province, P.R. China

Qiaohong Zheng Department of Economics and Management, North China Electric Power University, Baoding, Hebei, P.R. China

Preface

Decision-making is a fundamental activity across science, engineering, management, and social systems. In many real-world problems, decisions are rarely based on a single factor but rather on multiple, often conflicting, attributes. The field of multi-attribute decision-making (MADM) provides a structured framework for addressing such complexity, enabling decision-makers to evaluate, compare, and rank alternatives based on diverse quantitative and qualitative criteria. Over the past decades, MADM has evolved into one of the most vibrant and widely applied areas within operations research, management science, and applied mathematics.

Despite the rapid advancement of MADM theory and its extensive application in various domains, no comprehensive reference work has previously integrated all existing MADM methods in a single volume. This book aims to fill that gap. This encyclopedia serves as the first complete and authoritative source that systematically compiles, categorizes, and explains the entire spectrum of MADM methodologies. The *Encyclopedia of Multi-Attribute Decision-Making (MADM)* collects and describes the methods that practitioners and researchers use. Our goal was not only to summarize methods but also to present them in a way that helps readers choose and apply the right technique for a given problem.

For clarity and practical use, the encyclopedia is arranged into four sections:

1. Weighting methods, covering subjective and objective ways to determine criteria importance.
2. Developments in MADM, which review extensions to combine with MADM methods.
3. Ranking methods, describing algorithms for ordering alternatives.
4. Outranking methods, which deal with pairwise comparisons and preference relations.

Each method gives the necessary theory, the mathematical formulation, step-by-step procedures, and representative applications so that both newcomers and experienced users can follow and implement the methods.

We hope this encyclopedia will serve multiple audiences, such as researchers seeking a rigorous reference, practitioners needing practical guidance, and students learning the foundations and variations of MADM techniques.

Acknowledgments

The preparation of this encyclopedia depended on the broad participation of the international multi-attribute decision-making community. The 145 authors from 102 universities in 35 countries prepared the 100 chapters. Combined efforts of an inclusive mix of Full/Associate/Assistant Professors, early-career researchers, and industry experts cover both theoretical foundations and practical applications. We extend our heartfelt thanks to each author for their scholarly rigor and the time invested in writing and revising their contributions.

We also acknowledge Elsevier's editorial and production teams for their support throughout the publication process. Finally, we are grateful to the universities that supported this work and to the families of the editors and contributors, whose patience and encouragement made this project possible. This encyclopedia is the product of a true international collaboration, and we thank everyone involved.

Section 1

Weighting methods

Chapter 1

AHP: Analytic hierarchy process for multi-attribute decision-making

Cengiz Kahraman[1], Irem Ucal Sari[2], Sezi Cevik Onar[3], Basar Oztaysi[1], and Zeynep Kizilkan Demir[1]
[1]*Industrial Engineering Department, Istanbul Technical University, Istanbul, Türkiye,* [2]*Baskent University, Industrial Engineering Department, Ankara, Türkiye,* [3]*ReTech Center, Ecole des Ponts, ParisTech, France*

1.1 Introduction

Multi-criteria decision-making (MCDM) methods provide a set of approaches to support complex decision problems characterized by uncertainty and conflicting objectives. Such problems typically require the evaluation of multiple alternatives against a combination of quantitative and qualitative criteria. In the literature, MCDM methods can be classified into two groups, one of them is multi-attribute decision-making (MADM), which deals with a limited number of alternatives and is also called discrete MCDM, and the other one is multiobjective decision-making (MODM), which deals with numerous alternatives and is also called continuous MCDM. The objective of MCDM methods is to maximize the obtained benefit of the decision-makers at the end of the process by modeling the decision process according to criteria. MCDM methods are designed to identify the best alternative, classify alternatives in a small number of categories, and/or rank alternatives in subjective order of preference.

The literature presents numerous methods proposed in the field of MCDM. These methods can be classified into four main groups (Çebi et al., 2022), namely outranking methods, distance-based methods, value/utility function-based methods, and pairwise comparison-based methods. Outranking methods, such as ÉLimination Et Choix Traduisant la REalité (ELECTRE) and Preference Ranking Organization Method for Enrichment Evaluation (PROMETHEE), compare alternatives to determine whether one 'outranks' another based on their performance across multiple criteria. Distance-based methods, including the technique of order preference similarity to the ideal solution (TOPSIS), VlseKriterijumska Optimizacija I Kompromisno Resenje (VIKOR), and Evaluation based on Distance from Average Solution (EDAS), focus on ranking alternatives according to their distance from the ideal solutions. Value/utility-based approaches, such as Simple Additive Weighting (SAW), Weighted Product Method (WPM), and Multi-Attribute Utility Theory (MAUT), evaluate alternatives by calculating their scores through a value or utility function. Finally, the pairwise comparison approaches, including analytic hierarchy process (AHP), analytical network process (ANP), and best-worst method, rely on pairwise comparisons of alternatives with respect to one another.

AHP, proposed by Saaty (1986), is one of the most widely used MCDM methods. The method is based on a decision matrix constructed through pairwise comparison evaluations of the alternatives. These comparisons are conducted using a 1–9 scale, where 1 represents equal importance, and 9 represents the absolute importance of one alternative over another. Once the decision matrix is completed with expert evaluations, the steps of the method can be applied to derive the weights (importance scores) of the alternatives, which are then used to rank them.

AHP has attracted considerable attention due to several key features. One of these is its ability to address both tangible and intangible criteria simultaneously. Tangible criteria refer to those whose values can be objectively measured, such as the price of a product. In contrast, intangible criteria require subjective judgment, for example, the aesthetics of a product. By employing a 1–9 scale for pairwise comparisons, the method enables decision-makers to evaluate alternatives on the basis of both tangible and intangible criteria.

Another feature of AHP is the consistency ratio (*CR*), which was proposed to measure the consistency of evaluations in a decision matrix. A pairwise decision matrix is composed of pairwise comparisons; let a_{ij} denote the comparison of the ith alternative with respect to the jth alternative. The value a_{ij} represents the ratio between the two compared alternatives.

Encyclopedia of Multi-Attribute Decision-Making (MADM). DOI: https://doi.org/10.1016/B978-0-443-33275-3.00004-X

In other words, for each set of alternatives, the relation $a_{ij} = a_{ik} \times a_{kj}$ should hold, where i, j, and k represent different criteria. However, due to cognitive limitations or constraints of the scale being used, it is often not possible to fully maintain these equalities. To address this, Saaty (1986) introduced the concept of the *CR* to assess the acceptability of the decision matrix, thereby helping decision-makers achieve more consistent and realistic results.

One final feature of AHP is its ability to decompose complex problems into smaller and more manageable subproblems. In this method, a complex problem is modeled in the form of a hierarchy, where smaller matrices can be constructed at each level of the hierarchy. This has two main advantages in decision-making problems. First, it has been suggested that cognitive limitations allow decision-makers to compare up to nine alternatives at a time; therefore, in cases with more than nine alternatives, the decision matrix may not function properly. Second, the number of pairwise comparisons increases exponentially with the number of alternatives. For instance, to construct a decision matrix with five criteria, a decision-maker needs to perform 20 pairwise comparisons. As the number of comparisons increases, decision-makers may lose concentration, which can negatively affect the decision-making process. Consequently, the ability to structure the problem hierarchically reduces the number of required evaluations and supports more effective decision-making.

As a result of the aforementioned characteristics, AHP has been extensively applied in the literature and has gained significant popularity. While many studies focus on applying AHP to different problem domains, another stream of research aims to enhance the method through the integration of fuzzy logic. In these studies, the classical representation of pairwise comparisons with crisp numbers between 1 and 9 is replaced by fuzzy numbers. Fuzzy logic, proposed by Zadeh (1965), provides a mathematical framework for representing data under uncertainty and vagueness. Traditional fuzzy set theory introduces the concept of membership degree, which takes values between zero and one. This concept enables the partial membership of an element in a set and thus offers a more accurate representation of uncertainty. Early studies in this field combined traditional fuzzy sets with AHP, employing fuzzy numbers for evaluations and fuzzy set operations to integrate these into the AHP methodology (Buckley, 1985a; Cheng, 1997; Van Laarhoven & Pedrycz, 1983). In the broader context of fuzzy logic, several novel extensions of fuzzy sets have been proposed, including type-2 fuzzy sets (Zadeh, 1975), intuitionistic fuzzy sets (IFSs) (Atanassov, 1986), fuzzy multisets (Yager, 1986), hesitant fuzzy sets (Torra, 2010), Pythagorean fuzzy sets (PFSs) (Yager, 2013), spherical fuzzy sets (SFSs) (Kutlu & Kahraman 2019b, 2019a), and proportional fuzzy sets (Kahraman, 2024).

Based on the developments in the field of fuzzy logic, AHP has been further extended through the incorporation of these novel fuzzy set theories. This chapter aims to present the state-of-the-art studies on fuzzy AHP (FAHP). The rest of this chapter is structured as follows: Section 1.2 provides a brief literature review of AHP studies, highlighting the comparison between classical and FAHP. Section 3 presents the theory and practices of classical AHP and FAHP. Section 4 includes an application of classical AHP. Section 5 gives two applications of the FAHP approaches. Finally, the conclusion is presented in the last section

1.2 Literature review

The AHP introduced by Thomas L. Saaty (1980) is a powerful multicriteria decision-making (MCDM) method that has been widely used in the literature. AHP enables breaking down complex problems into hierarchies of goals, criteria, and alternatives and using pairwise comparisons, making it easily applicable to many decision-making problems. AHP also enables decision-makers to evaluate both qualitative and quantitative criteria. Due to these advantages, over the years, AHP has been widely used in various fields, including engineering, management, economics, and the social sciences.

To examine the development and usage of AHP in the literature, a bibliometric analysis is conducted. In this search, we have used the Scopus database since it has broad coverage of peer-reviewed journals (Mongeon & Paul-Hus, 2016). We have used this Boolean string for the search Title-Abstract-Keywords (TITLE-ABS-KEY) (“AHP” OR “analytic hierarchy process” OR “analytical hierarchy process”) on August 19, 2025. The time span covered publications from 1988 through August 19, 2025. The initial Scopus search showed 70,570 documents. In order to see the general trends, we conducted descriptive analytics on these documents. For the thematic analysis, we limited the scope to titles for thematic analysis, which resulted in 20,298 results. After data collection, keyword cooccurrence networks were analyzed using VOSviewer (Van Eck & Waltman, 2010). Fig. 1.1 shows the change in the number of studies over the years according to the literature. In order to see the trend, we limited the timeframe from 1998 to 2025.

Fig. 1.1 shows a constant and accelerated increase, especially after 2003. This shows the usefulness and capacity of AHP. Along with its extensions, the studies on AHP are increasing every year. Fig. 1.2 shows the top 20 sources, including the conferences that have published the most studies on AHP.

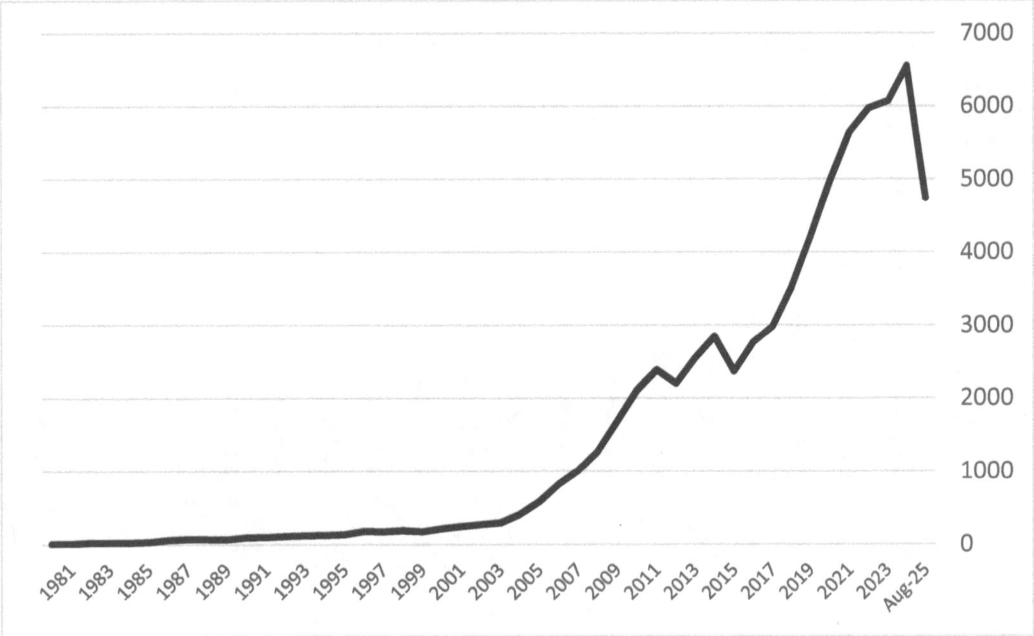

FIGURE 1.1 Number of analytic hierarchy process studies per year (Scopus database).

Sustainability Switzerland, Iop Conference Series: Earth and Environmental Science, Advanced Materials Research, Applied Mechanics and Materials, Journal of Physics Conference Series, Association for Computing Machinery (ACM) International Conference Proceeding Series, Lecture Notes in Computer Science Including Subseries Lecture Notes in Artificial Intelligence and Lecture Notes in Bioinformatics, Journal of Cleaner Production, Aip Conference Proceedings, Lecture Notes in Electrical Engineering, Proceedings of SPIE the International Society for Optical Engineering, Expert Systems with Applications, Advances in Intelligent Systems and Computing, E3S Web of Conferences, Lecture Notes in Networks and Systems, Applied Sciences Switzerland, Energies, Water Switzerland, Institute of Electrical and Electronics Engineers (IEEE) Access, are the top publications that publish FAHP. The top 20 journals that publish the most AHP involve both the practical applications and methodological advancements. Fig. 1.3 presents the keyword cooccurrence analysis for ANP research, conducted in VOSViewer with a minimum occurrence threshold of fifty keywords with full counting.

The keyword cooccurrence map for AHP in Fig. 1.3 highlights three main directions in the literature. At its core, the method remains closely tied to decision-making and multicriteria evaluation, often extended through fuzzy sets, fuzzy logic, and risk analysis. Another strong stream of research connects AHP with optimization and comparative methods, such as TOPSIS, particularly in applications, such as supplier selection, product design, and location planning. A third prominent area shows the method's integration with GIS and remote sensing, where it is widely used in land-use planning, water and climate studies, and hazard assessment, such as floods and landslides. Smaller clusters also point to social and human-centered applications, often based on questionnaires and survey data. Together, these themes show that AHP has evolved into a versatile tool, bridging methodological innovation with diverse applications in sustainability, engineering, and decision support.

Although AHP has been widely accepted for its simplicity, it has been criticized for requiring precise judgments that do not always capture the vagueness and imprecision of human reasoning and for problems in the rank reversal process (Buckley, 1985a). To overcome these limitations, fuzzy extensions of AHP have been developed. Van Laarhoven and Pedrycz (1983) used triangular fuzzy numbers and a square-logarithmic approach for FAHP. Buckley, (1985a, 1985b) used trapezoidal fuzzy numbers for FAHP. Chang (1996) developed the extent analysis method, with its simplicity in computation, Chang's FAHP became very popular. These extensions of AHP enabled capturing the ambiguity of expert judgments more effectively. Although FAHP has also been broadly used in literature, the consistency and accuracy of some computational approaches, such as extent analysis, have been questioned in the literature (Chang, 1996). The increasing mathematical complexity has sometimes been seen as a barrier for practitioners (Buckley, 1985a). Although

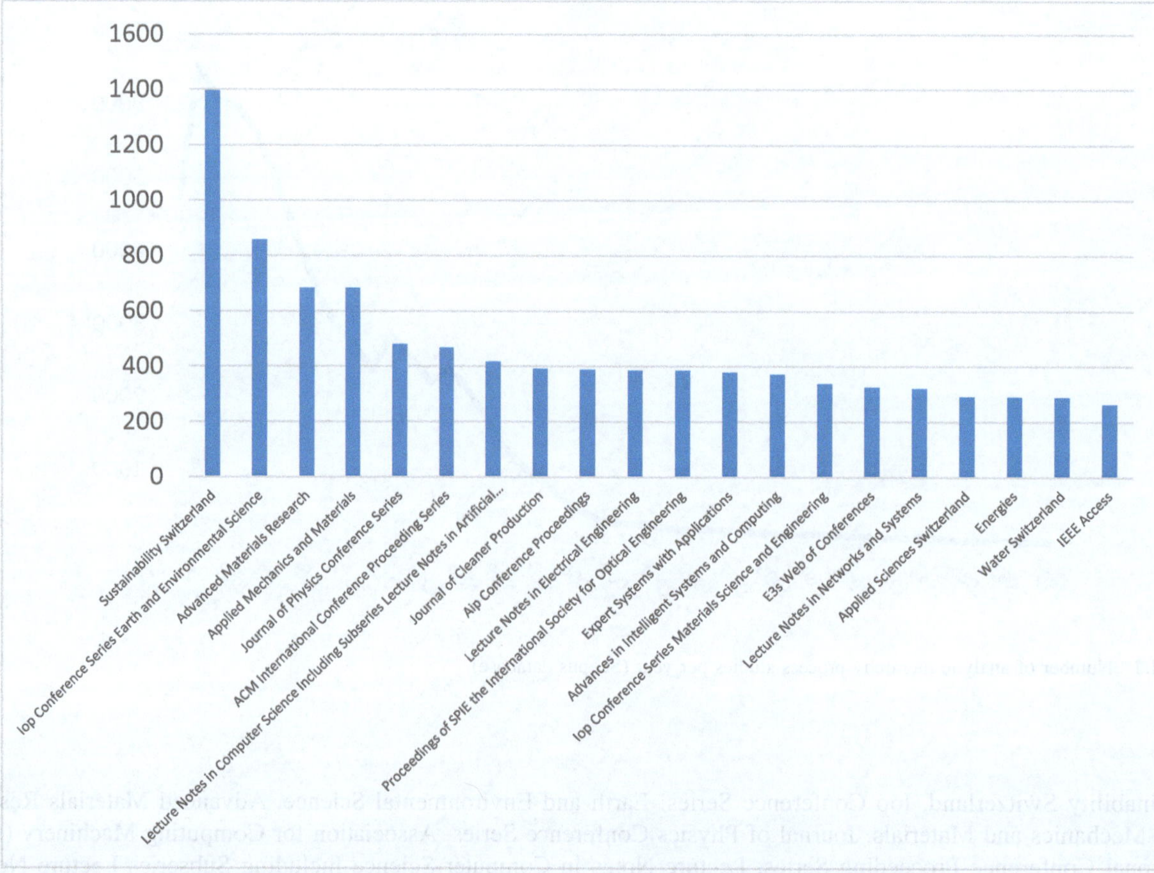

FIGURE 1.2 Top sources that have published the most studies on analytic hierarchy process (Scopus database).

FAHP has these limitations, it is still one of the most widely used MCDM methods. It provides flexibility for the decision-makers (Chang, 1996; Van Laarhoven & Pedrycz, 1983).

To examine the development and usage of FAHP in the literature, a bibliometric analysis is conducted. We have used this Boolean string for the search TITLE-ABS-KEY ("fuzzy AHP" OR "fuzzy analytic hierarchy process" OR "fuzzy analytical hierarchy process" OR "FAHP") on August 19, 2025. The time span covered publications from 1988 through August 19, 2025. The initial Scopus search showed 10,595 documents. After restricting the results to only english-language publications, 9904 remained. We limited the scope to journal articles, books, and book chapters; the final dataset that is used in the bibliometric analysis consisted of 6997 documents. After data collection, keyword cooccurrence networks were analyzed using VOSviewer (Van Eck & Waltman, 2010). Fig. 1.4 shows the change in the number of studies over the years according to the literature. In order to see the trend, we limited the timeframe from 1998 to 2024.

Fig. 1.1 shows the annual publication trend of FAHP studies indexed in Scopus between 1986 and 2024. We see a steady but limited increase until the mid-2000s, and after 2010, we see an accelerated growth. Around 800 in 2024 shows the acceptance and usefulness of FAHP in various fields. This exponential growth is also in line with the methodological extensions of FAHP, such as type-2 fuzzy AHP (Cevik et al., 2014), intuitionistic fuzzy AHP (Sadiq & Tesfamariam, 2009), Pythagorean fuzzy AHP (Ilbahar et al., 2018), and hesitant fuzzy AHP (Cevik Onar et al., 2016). Fig. 1.5 shows the top 10 journals that have published the most of the studies on FAHP.

The top 10 journals that publish the most FAHP involve both the practical applications and methodological advancements. Sustainability (Switzerland) comes first, with 239 papers, and is an application journal. The following journals, Expert Systems with Applications (149) and the Journal of Intelligent and Fuzzy Systems (102), are more toward methodological journals. Journal of Cleaner Production (99), Environmental Science and Pollution Research (64), and Energies (44) show how FAHP is applied to various problems. Technical and methodological journals, such as IEEE Access (67), Mathematical Problems in Engineering (59), Mathematics (52), Applied Soft Computing (45), and Soft

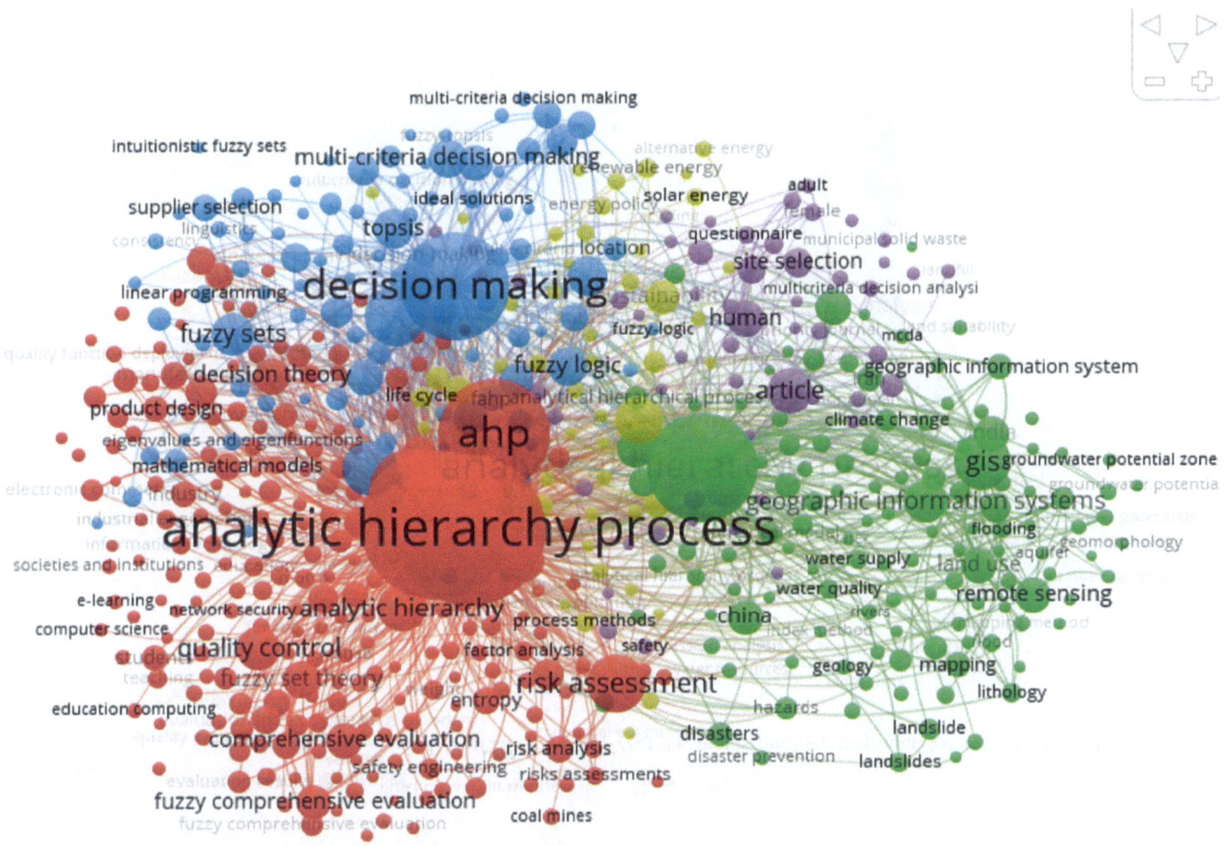

FIGURE 1.3 Analytic hierarchy process keyword cooccurrence VOSviewer network visualization.

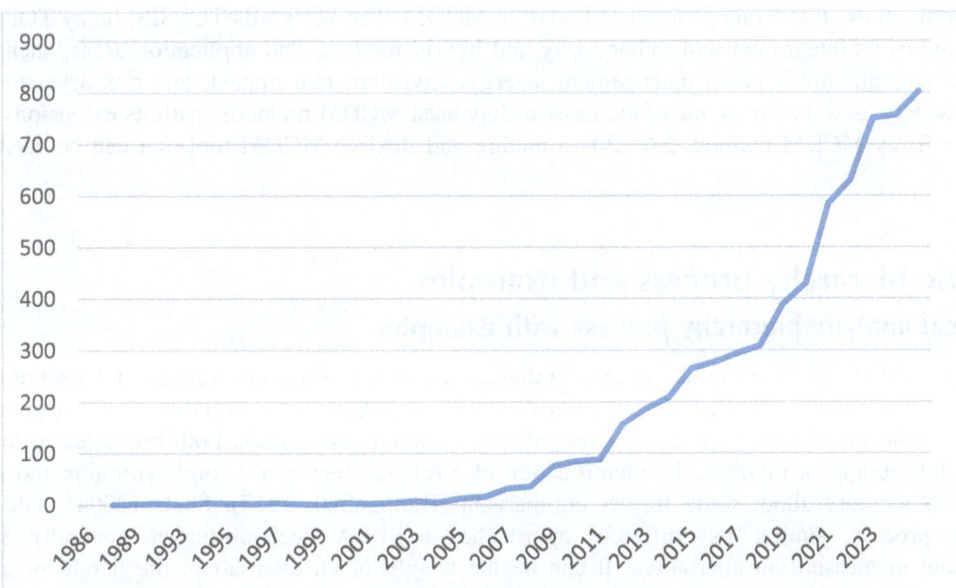

FIGURE 1.4 Number of fuzzy analytic hierarchy process studies per year (Scopus database from 1986 to 2024).

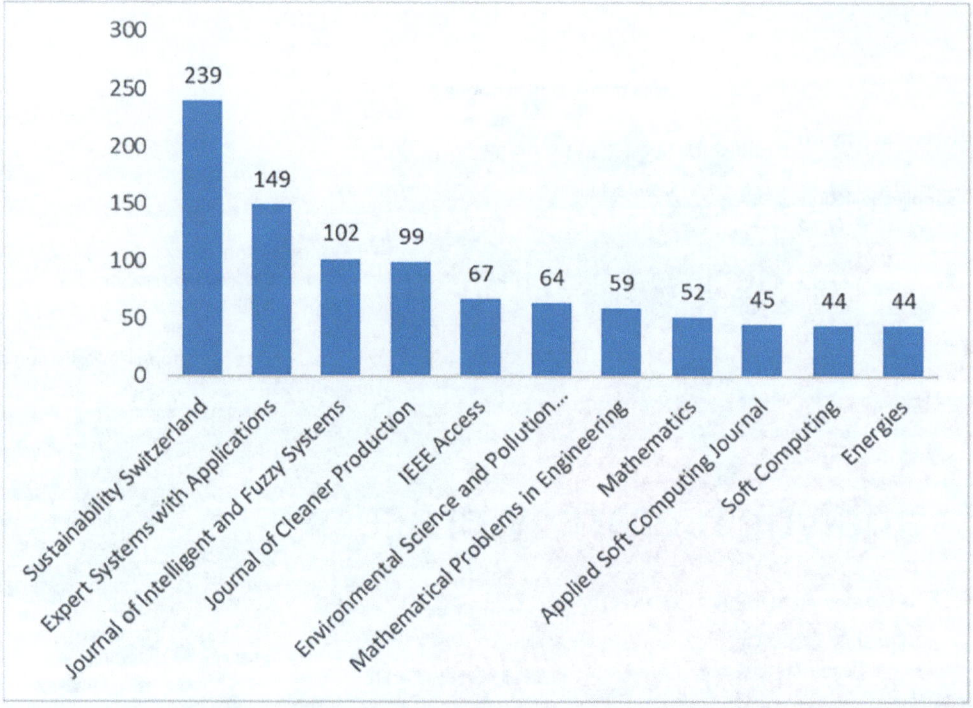

FIGURE 1.5 Top journals that have published the most studies on fuzzy analytic hierarchy process (Scopus database)

Computing (44), show the importance of methodological and theoretical aspects. Fig. 1.6 presents the keyword cooccurrence analysis for Fuzzy Analytic Network Process (FANP) research, conducted in VOSviewer with a minimum occurrence threshold of fifty keywords in order to filter out less frequent keywords and use fractional counting.

The VOSviewer density visualization in Fig. 1.3 shows similar results with the journals, the research on FAHP are clustered around both methodology and applications. The most used keywords, decision making, FAHP, AHP, and hierarchical systems shows the strong position of FAHP in MCDM. The keywords TOPSIS, fuzzy TOPSIS, VIKOR, and PROMETHEE shows its integration with other fuzzy and hybrid models. The application areas, such as sustainability, sustainable development, supply chain management, energy, environmental impact, and risk assessment, are the areas where FAHP is widely used. FAHP is one of the most widely used MCDM methods, with its extensions it still remains as the most popular fuzzy MCDM method. FAHP is a mature and flexible MCDM tool that can be used to solve various problems.

1.3 Analytic hierarchy process and examples

1.3.1 Classical analytic hierarchy process with examples

Decision-making problems involve evaluation criteria that generally have different weights and a set of alternatives, from which one must be selected or ranked. There are two kinds of judgments, comparative and absolute judgments. In comparative judgment, the observer identifies some relation between two stimuli, both presented to him or her. On the other hand, absolute judgment involves the identification of a relation between a single stimulus and some information held in short-term memory about some former comparison (Blumenthal, 1977). Saaty (2004) states that during the decision-making process, similar but different approaches exist. A decision-maker generally seeks a physical measurement scale to measure an alternative. It can be the weight of an alternative, the height of an alternative, the price of an alternative, or other physical measurement values. A decision-making approach based on such measurement scales is called absolute decision-making. On the other hand, Saaty also states that, in cases where such absolute measurement scales exist, a human being makes a comparison between alternatives. In some cases, such an absolute measurement may not be applicable, for example "price of a car" can be an absolute measurement, but a criterion, such as

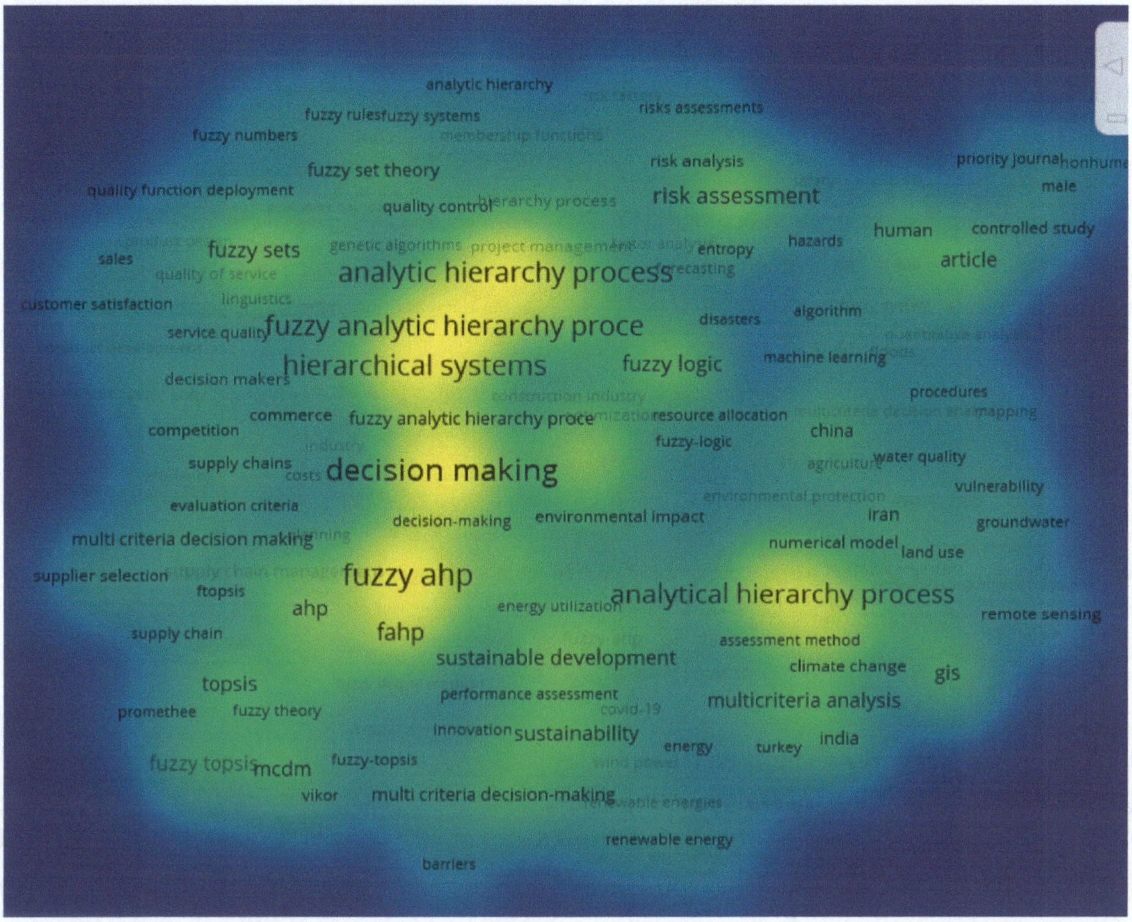

FIGURE 1.6 Keyword cooccurrence VOSviewer density visualization.

"virtual appearance of a car," does not have a physical measurement scale. So, the decision-maker must make a subjective evaluation, and most probably this process involves comparisons between the alternatives.

AHP is a method proposed to divide complex decision-making problems into small problems and solve them by using pairwise comparison matrices. A pairwise comparison matrix is a matrix that holds comparison judgments of a decision-maker about the objects (either alternatives or criteria) to be compared.

1.3.1.1 Comparison and scale

The AHP method is based on decision-maker's comparison judgment between two objects. Mathematically, a scale is defined as a set of numbers, a set of objects, and a mapping of the objects to the numbers. In the AHP methodology, the ratio scale is used for comparisons. A ratio scale is a similarity transformation, which can be represented as $y = ax$, $a > 0$ (Saaty, 2004). In other words, the decision-maker is asked to compare two objects in a ratio scale. When two objects are to be compared, the question is "How many times more dominant is one element than the other with respect to a certain criterion or attribute?" For example, in a car selection problem a question can be asked as "How many times more CarA is dominant than CarB with respect to the beauty criterion". A mathematical formulation for this question can be represented as $CarA_{\text{beauty}} = ? \times CarB_{\text{beauty}}$.

Decision-makers need a scale to provide the judgments that can be later used in the method. To this end, Saaty, (1977, 1980) proposes a fundamental scale of absolute numbers ranging from 1 to 9 (Table 1.1).

The scale given in Table 1.1 involves numeric values and linguistic definitions to direct decision-makers to better represent their judgments. Since the ratio scale is defined as $y = ax$ one can derive the equation $x = \frac{1}{a}y$, so the reciprocals of the integer values given in the scale can also be used for comparisons.

TABLE 1.1 Fundamental scale of absolute numbers (Saaty, 1980).

Intensity of importance	Definition	Explanation
1	Equal importance	Two activities contribute equally to the objective
2	Weak or slight	
3	Moderate importance	Experience and judgment slightly favor one activity over another
4	Moderate plus	
5	Strong importance	Experience and judgment strongly favor one activity over another
6	Strong plus	
7	Very strong or demonstrated importance	An activity is favored very strongly over another; its dominance is demonstrated in practice
8	Very, very strong	
9	Extreme importance	The evidence favoring one activity over another is of the highest possible order of affirmation
Reciprocals of above	If activity i has one of the above nonzero numbers assigned to it when compared with activity j, then j has the reciprocal value when compared with i	

TABLE 1.2 Structure of pairwise comparison matrix.

Affordability comparison	 **CAR A**	 **CAR B**	 **CAR C**
 **CAR A**	S_1/S_1	S_1/S_2	S_1/S_3
 **CAR B**	S_2/S_1	S_2/S_2	S_2/S_3
CAR C 	S_3/S_1	S_3/S_2	S_3/S_3

1.3.1.2 Decision matrix

In the AHP method, the complex decision problems are divided into smaller problems and during the solution phase, different decision matrices are formed, and weights are calculated. A pairwise comparison matrix, or decision matrix, is defined as a matrix of judgments $A = (a_{ij})$ which is constructed with respect to a particular property the elements have in common (Saaty, 2004). Table 1.2 shows the structure of pairwise comparison matrix.

As shown in Table 1.2, the value 1 is assigned to the comparison of an element with itself, and one judgement is enough to represent the inverse of the relation $\left(\frac{S_1}{S_2} = \frac{1}{S_2/S_1}\right)$. So $\frac{n(n-1)}{2}$ judgments are required for a matrix with n elements.

1.3.1.3 Calculation of weights

The mathematical representation of a pairwise comparison matrix is given in Table 1.3. In this figure, three alternative cars are compared with respect to the affordability criterion.

TABLE 1.3 An example of a pairwise comparison matrix.

	Car 1	Car 2	Car 3
Car 1	1	3	5
Car 2	1/3	1	3
Car 3	1/5	1/3	1

After a pairwise comparison matrix is formed, relative weights of the elements can be calculated. There are different ways of calculating the weight of each element in the literature. Most commonly adopted methods are as follows (Oztaysi et al., 2023):

- Approximate method: The row averages are calculated and then normalized to find the weights of the criteria.
- Inverse of column max: Sum of values in each column is calculated, then the values are inverted, and finally the inverse values are normalized to find the weights of the criteria.
- Mean of normalized values: Each column is normalized, then row averages are calculated to find the weights.
- Geometric mean: The geometric mean of each row is calculated, then the geometric mean values are normalized to find the weights.
- Power method: The pairwise comparison matrix is raised to a sufficiently large power, then the row averages of the new matrix are calculated. The process ends when the weight values converge.

Here, the calculation details of some of the above-mentioned methods are given. Assume we have a pairwise comparison matrix as given in Eq. 1.1.

$$P = \begin{pmatrix} 1 & 3 & 5 \\ 1/3 & 1 & 3 \\ 1/5 & 1/3 & 1 \end{pmatrix} \tag{1.1}$$

According to the approximate method, the weights are calculated as follows:

$$r_1 = \frac{1 + 3 + 5}{3} = 2.67$$

$$r_2 = \frac{1/3 + 1 + 3}{3} = 1.45$$

$$r_3 = \frac{1/5 + 1/3 + 1}{3} = 0.51$$

$$w_1 = \frac{2.67}{2.67 + \quad 1.45 + \quad 0.51} = 0.60 \tag{1.2}$$

The weight of each element is obtained by normalizing the row average values given by Eq. (1.2).

In geometric mean approach, the geometric mean of each row is calculated.

$$r_1 = \sqrt[3]{1 \times 3 \times 5} = 2.46$$

$$r_2 = \sqrt[3]{1/3 \times 1 \times 3}1$$

$$r_3 = \sqrt[3]{1/5 \quad \times 1/3 \times 1} = 0.40$$

$$w_1 = \frac{2.46}{2.46 + 1 + 0.4} = 0.63 \tag{1.3}$$

In power method, the matrix is raised to its powers, and the row averages are calculated in each step. After each raise, the row averages are calculated, and the final result is obtained if the weights converge. The second power of the given pairwise comparison matrix is given in Eq. 1.3

$$P^2 = \begin{pmatrix} 3 & 7.67 & 19 \\ 1.27 & 3 & 7.67 \\ 0.51 & 1.27 & 3 \end{pmatrix}, \text{Row Avg.} = \begin{pmatrix} 3 \\ 1.44 \\ 0.51 \end{pmatrix}, \text{Weights} = \begin{pmatrix} 0.605 \\ 0.291 \\ 0.104 \end{pmatrix}$$

In a similar approach, the pairwise comparison matrix is raised to its powers. Table 1.4 shows the calculated weights of different powers.

As shown in Table 1.4, the weights converge when the power is five, and this converged weights are the final weights obtained from the process.

1.3.1.4 Consistency check

In AHP, it is crucial to verify whether the decision-maker's judgments are consistent. For instance, if a decision-maker states that "A is twice as important as B, and B is three times as important as C," then logically "A should be six times as important as C." If this logical chain does not hold, inconsistency arises.

In AHP, after a pairwise comparison is constructed and the weights are calculated, the consistency check can be done. The basis of the consistency check lies in finding the maximum eigenvalue (λ_{max}) of the pairwise comparison matrix. In order to obtain λ_{max}, first P (pairwise comparison matrix) is multiplied by the weight vector.

$$Pw = y \tag{1.4}$$

Then the elements of obtained y value is divided by the associated weights.

$$\Theta_i = \frac{y_i}{w_i} \tag{1.5}$$

λ_{max} can be obtained by calculating the average of Θ_i values.

$$\lambda_{max} = \frac{1}{n}\sum_{i=1}^{n} \Theta_i \tag{1.6}$$

where n is the number of elements in P.

Based on λ_{max}, the consistency index (CI) can be calculated using Eq. 1.7.

$$CI = \frac{\lambda_{max} - \mathrm{n}}{n - 1} \tag{1.7}$$

CI is later used to calculate CR which can be used to assess the acceptability of the decision matrix.

$$CR = \frac{CI}{RI} \tag{1.8}$$

where RI represents the random index.

The pairwise comparison matrix is consistent if $CR \le 0.10$ and inconsistent if $CR \ge 0.10$.

The RI values for different pairwise comparison matrices are shown in Table 1.5.

TABLE 1.4 Calculated weights for different powers of the matrix.

	P	P^2	P^3	P^4	P^5
W1	0.6053	0.6396	0.6373	0.6370	0.6370
W2	0.2914	0.2573	0.2578	0.2583	0.2583
W3	0.1031	0.1030	0.1047	0.1047	0.1047

TABLE 1.5 Random index.

n	1	2	3	4	5	6	7	8	9	10
Random Index	0	0	0.52	0.89	1.11	1.25	1.35	1.40	1.45	1.49

A sample calculation for the given P, w can be calculated.

$$P = \begin{pmatrix} 1 & 3 & 5 \\ 1/3 & 1 & 3 \\ 1/5 & 1/3 & 1 \end{pmatrix}, \quad w = \begin{pmatrix} 0.6370 \\ 0.2583 \\ 0.1047 \end{pmatrix}$$

when the values are multiplied

$$y = \begin{pmatrix} 1 & 3 & 5 \\ 1/3 & 1 & 3 \\ 1/5 & 1/3 & 1 \end{pmatrix} \times \begin{pmatrix} 0.6370 \\ 0.2583 \\ 0.1047 \end{pmatrix} = \begin{pmatrix} 1.9353 \\ 0.7847 \\ 0.31818 \end{pmatrix}$$

The elements of y are divided by the associated w value to find θ_i values. $\lambda_{\max}$ is obtained by calculating the average of θ_i values.

$$\theta_1 = \frac{1.9353}{0.6370} = 3.038, \quad \theta_2 = \frac{0.7847}{0.2583} = 3.0379, \quad \theta_1 = \frac{0.31818}{0.1047} = 3.03896$$

$$\lambda_{\max} = \frac{3.038 + 3.0379 + 3.03896}{3} = 3.0385$$

Using $\lambda_{\max}$, CI and CR values can be calculated.

$$CI = \frac{3.0385 - 3}{3 - 1} = 0.01925$$

$$CR = \frac{0.01925}{0.52} = 0.03703$$

The RI value is obtained from Table 1.5, since n = 3 the RI value is selected as 0.52. The obtained CR value is less than 0.10, so the pairwise matrix is consistent.

1.3.1.5 Constructing the decision hierarchy and finding overall results

AHP method is based on weighing the relative weights/priorities of the criteria and alternatives by using pairwise comparison matrices. Using a scale based on ratios enable decision-makers to model the decisions as a hierarchy. This approach helps dividing complex problems into smaller parts and solve them easily. A sample hierarchy is shown in Fig. 1.7.

Fig. 1.7 represents a hierarchy with three levels. At the top, the final decision takes place, at the second level involves the criteria, which will be used in decision-making and at the final level, alternatives exist. A sample decision model about car selection problem is shown in Fig. 1.8. Here, there are three criteria namely, affordability, design, and comfort. The decision-maker wants to select among four different cars namely, Car 1, Car 2, Car 3, and Car 4.

According to the hierarchy, pairwise comparison matrices are formed. At first, a pairwise comparison matrices for comparing the criteria are formed. Then, three different pairwise comparison matrices are formed comparing the alternative cars with respect to associated criterion. At this level a sample comparison question can be written as: "At what degree Car 1 is dominant over Car 2 with respect to Comfort".

After the weights of the elements are calculated, the decision-maker can reach to an overall result. Assume that the weights of the criteria are 0.4, 0.35, and 0.25, respectively, and the weights of the alternatives with respect to different criterion are given in Table 1.6.

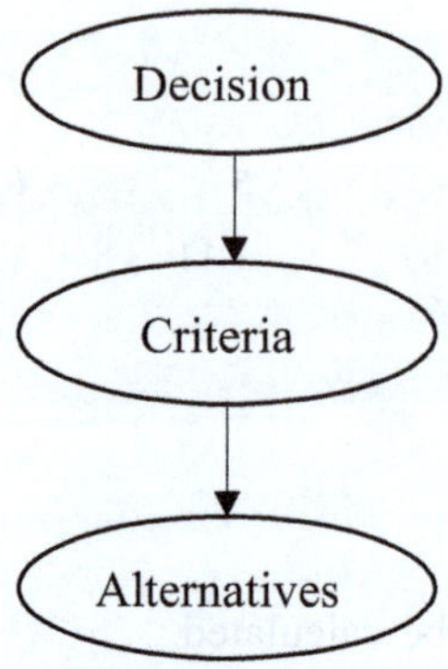

FIGURE 1.7 Abstract representation of a hierarchy.

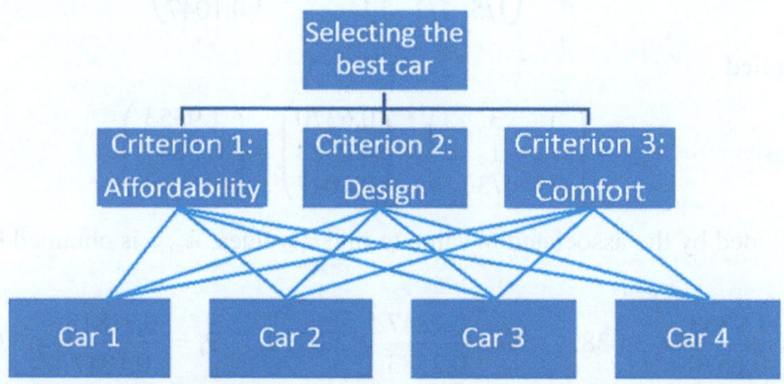

FIGURE 1.8 A decision model for best car selection problem.

TABLE 1.6 Weights of the alternatives with respect to criteria.

	Weight w.r.t criterion 1	Weight w.r.t criterion 2	Weight w.r.t criterion 3
Car 1	0.2	0.25	0.40
Car 2	0.15	0.25	0.20
Car 3	0.4	0.25	0.20
Car 4	0.25	0.25	0.20

TABLE 1.7 Total weights of the alternatives.

	Overall weight w.r.t criterion 1	Overall weight w.r.t criterion 2	Overall weight w.r.t criterion 3	Total weight
Car 1	0.08	0.0875	0.1	0.2675
Car 2	0.16	0.0875	0.05	0.2975
Car 3	0.08	0.0875	0.05	0.2175
Car 4	0.08	0.0875	0.05	0.2175

The final decision is reached by obtaining the total overall weight of each alternative. In order to find it, the alternative weights are multiplied with the criteria weights, and total overall weight is obtained. Table 1.7 presents the overall weights and total weights of the alternative.

The weight of Car 1 with respect to Criterion 1 is 0.2, and the weight of Criterion 1 is 0.4. In order to find the overall weight the values are multiplied. After this is applied to each alternative and criterion, the total overall weight of an alternative can be calculated. For example, for Car 1, the calculation is: 0.08 + 0.0875 + 0.1 = 0.2675. The decision-maker can select the best car by comparing the total weights. In this example, Car 2 is selected since it has the highest total weight.

1.3.2 Fuzzy analytic hierarchy process and its extensions

FAHP methods, which are commonly employed to model uncertainties inherent in linguistic evaluations within decision-making problems, have been progressively developed with numerous variations over time. Particularly, through the development of different fuzzy number extensions that vary in their approaches to handling uncertainty, various FAHP extensions have been proposed by utilizing these advanced fuzzy extensions, resulting in their widespread application across diverse fields. In this section, the classification of FAHP methods is first presented, after which different fuzzy number-based FAHP extensions will be examined in terms of their fundamental distinctions. FAHP methods can be classified according to three basic dimensions: the structure of the decision-making process, the extension of the fuzzy numbers used, and the areas of application.

Regarding decision-making structure, FAHP methods can be classified into three primary categories. The first and most basic form is individual decision-making, which relies exclusively on evaluations from a single decision-maker through a single fuzzy pairwise comparison matrix, making it suitable for relatively simple problems where expert consensus is unnecessary. For more complex scenarios requiring multidisciplinary input, the consensus-based group approach brings multiple experts together to deliberate and produce a single fuzzy evaluation matrix representing their collective judgment. In the third category, aggregated multiexpert decision-making, individual assessments of several experts are combined using mathematical operators, such as weighted averaging or ordered weighted averaging. Aggregated decision-making permits differential weighting of experts based on their demonstrated reliability, proficiency, or expertise level. This classification provides researchers and practitioners with a framework for selecting the most appropriate decision matrix for FAHP procedure based on their specific decision-making requirements and problem complexity.

1.3.2.1 Ordinary fuzzy analytic hierarchy process

The conventional FAHP approach, which forms the foundation for all subsequent extensions, is presented in this section. Chang's Extent Analysis method (1996) and Buckley's Geometric Mean method (1987) are the two principal methodologies developed for ordinary FAHP. While Chang's approach has been widely adopted due to its computational simplicity, it has been criticized in the literature for several limitations. First, its normalization procedure has been shown to produce mathematically inconsistent results, particularly when incomplete comparison matrices are used. Second, the priority derivation method has been demonstrated to occasionally generate illogical weight distributions that contradict expert judgments. Third, the approach has been proven unreliable when dealing with extreme fuzzy number comparisons, where weights may be improperly distributed. These theoretical flaws have been experimentally verified in multiple comparative studies, where Chang's method was found to rank alternatives incorrectly in approximately 15%–20% of test cases according to Wang et al. (2008).

Buckley's method, which employs the geometric mean for fuzzy weight calculation, is presented as an alternative approach that addresses some of these limitations. Since most of the FAHP extensions utilize Buckley's FAHP, the fundamental steps of this approach are summarized as follows:

Step 1. Problem definition and construction of the hierarchical structure. In the first step, the decision problem is determined, and a hierarchy including goal, criteria, subcriteria, and alternatives is constructed.

Step 2. Linguistic scales determination: Define fuzzy linguistic scales and their corresponding equivalences using triangular fuzzy numbers. Table 1.8 could be used for the linguistic statements and related triangular fuzzy scales.

Step 3. Construction of pairwise comparison matrices: Experts compare criteria using the linguistic scale determined in Step 2. Then the corresponding fuzzy scale is used to determine fuzzy pairwise comparison matrices in the form of (1.9).

$$\widetilde{A} = \begin{vmatrix} 1 & \widetilde{a}_{12} & \cdots & \widetilde{a}_{1n} \\ \widetilde{a}_{21} & 1 & \cdots & \widetilde{a}_{2n} \\ \vdots & \vdots & \ddots & \vdots \\ \widetilde{a}_{m1} & \widetilde{a}_{m2} & \cdots & 1 \end{vmatrix} \tag{1.9}$$

TABLE 1.8 Ordinary fuzzy scale for linguistic statements (Bozbura et al., 2007).

Linguistic scale	Triangular fuzzy numbers
Just equal (E)	(1, 1, 1)
Almost equally important (AE)	(1/2, 1, 3/2)
Weakly more important than (WM)	(1, 3/2, 2)
Strongly more important than (SM)	(3/2, 2, 5/2)
Very strongly more important than (VSM)	(2, 5/2, 3)
Certainly more important than (CM)	(5/2, 3, 7/2)
If factor *i* has one of the above linguistic variables assigned to it when compared with factor *j*, then *j* has the reciprocal value when compared with *i*	Reciprocals of above

Step 4. Consistency Check: The pairwise comparison matrices are defuzzified and the *CR* is calculated using defuzzified matrices as in crisp AHP (Saaty, 1980). If *CR* is less then 0.1, the matrix is determined as consistent, otherwise the comparisons should be renewed.

Step 5. Aggregation of Expert Judgments: Expert opinions are combined using the geometric mean method for each fuzzy comparison and a single decision matrix is constructed.

Step 6. Calculation of geometric mean of fuzzy comparisons: For each parameter of $\tilde{a}_{ij}$ in the n dimensional pairwise comparison matrix geometric means are calculated. If $(\tilde{r}_i)$ is geometric mean of each row of $\widetilde{A} = [\tilde{a}_{ij}]$ then it is calculated as follows:

$$\tilde{r}_i = [\tilde{a}_{i1} \otimes \ldots \quad \otimes \tilde{a}_{in}]^{1/n} \tag{1.10}$$

Step 6. Calculation of fuzzy weights: The fuzzy weights are generated by normalization. The fuzzy weight $(\widetilde{w}_i)$ of the ith criterion is calculated as follows:

$$\widetilde{w}_i = \tilde{r}_i \otimes [\tilde{r}_1 \oplus \ldots \oplus \tilde{r}_i \oplus \ldots \oplus \tilde{r}_n]^{-1} \tag{1.11}$$

Step 7. Defuzzification: Eq. (1.4) can be used for the defuzzification of the normalized weights vector $A = (a_l, a_m, a_r)$:

$$\alpha = \frac{a_l + 2a_m + a_r}{4} \tag{1.12}$$

1.3.2.1.1 A numerical example: supplier selection problem by using Buckley's fuzzy analytic hierarchy process

Supplier selection problem refers to the decision-making process of identifying, evaluating, and choosing the most suitable supplier(s) among alternatives. FAHP is commonly used for supplier selection problem since it involves both tangible and intangible criteria.

Assume that a producer company aims to select the most appropriate supplier. The decision-makers propose five criteria to be considered in this evaluation process:

1. Cost (C1): Product/service price, payment terms, and overall cost structure.
2. Quality (C2): Compliance with quality standards, defect rates, and certifications.
3. Delivery performance (C3): Lead time, on-time delivery rate, and flexibility.
4. Reliability and reputation (C4): Financial stability, past performance, and market reputation.
5. Communication and collaboration (C5): Customer support, problem-solving capability, and openness to long-term cooperation.

The producer company wants to evaluate five alternative suppliers namely, A1, A2, A3, A4, and A5. According to the hierarchical structure of FAHP, the decision matrices must be formed first. The first decision matrix focuses on pairwise comparison of the criteria with respect to the goal. The result of this matrix is to determine the weights of the criteria. Then, five other pairwise comparison matrices must be formed. These matrices involve pairwise comparison of the

TABLE 1.9 Triangular fuzzy comparisons of the criteria

	C1	C2	C3	C4	C5
C1	(1, 1, 1)	(1.5, 2, 2.5)	(1.5, 2, 2.5)	(0.5, 1, 1.5)	(1, 1.5, 2)
C2	(0.4, 0.5, 0.67)	(1, 1, 1)	(1, 1, 1)	(0.29, 0.33, 0.4)	(0.67, 1, 2)
C3	(0.4, 0.5, 0.67)	(1, 1, 1)	(1, 1, 1)	(1, 1.5, 2)	(0.67, 1, 2)
C4	(0.67, 1, 2)	(2.5, 3, 3.5)	(0.5, 0.67, 1)	(1, 1, 1)	(0.5, 1, 1.5)
C5	(0.5, 0.67, 1)	(0.5, 1, 1.5)	(0.5, 1, 1.5)	(0.5, 1, 1.5)	(1, 1, 1)

TABLE 1.10 Geometric means, fuzzy weights, and crisp weights.

	Geometric means	Fuzzy weights	Crisp weights
C1	(1.02, 1.43, 1.8)	(0.15, 0.28, 0.47)	0.269858
C2	(0.6, 0.7, 0.88)	(0.09, 0.14, 0.23)	0.136427
C3	(0.77, 0.94, 1.22)	(0.11, 0.18, 0.32)	0.184554
C4	(0.84, 1.15, 1.6)	(0.12, 0.22, 0.42)	0.22981
C5	(0.57, 0.92, 1.28)	(0.08, 0.18, 0.34)	0.179351

alternatives with respect to each criterion. Table 1.9 presents the pairwise comparisons of the criteria with respect to the goal.

In the next step, the geometric means for each row are calculated. In Table 1.10, the geometric means, fuzzy weights, and crisp weights are presented.

The geometric mean of the first row is (1.02,1.43,1.8), which is calculated by the geometric mean of the same level parameters separately. For the first parameter, the calculation is $\sqrt[5]{1 \times 1.5 \times 1.5 \times 0.5 \times 1} = 1.02$

In order to find the fuzzy weights, first the sum of geometric means is calculated, and the value (3.8, 5.14, 6.77) is obtained. Then the geometric mean value of each row is divided by the sum of geometric means to find the fuzzy weight before normalization.

$$w_{C1} = \frac{(1.02,\ 1.43,\ 1.8)}{(3.8,\ 5.14,\ 6.77)} = (0.15,\ 0.28,\ 0.47)$$

The fuzzy weights are later defuzzified and normalized to find the crisp weights. The crisp weights for this pairwise comparison matrix are given in Table 1.10. The same steps are applied to the pairwise comparison matrices of the alternatives with respect to each criterion, and the resulting weights are obtained as given in Table 1.11.

In order to find the overall ranking of the alternatives, the obtained weights should be combined. To do this, global weight (GW) of each alternative with respect to each criterion is computed by multiplying the alternative's weight with the weight of the associated criterion. For example, the weight of A1 with respect to C1 is 0.233 and the weight of C1 is 0.269858. To find the GW of A1 with respect to C1, we multiply 0.233 by 0.269858.

Table 1.12 presents the GW of each alternative with respect to each criterion. The overall score of each alternative can be calculated by summing up the GWs. According to the results, the highest overall score is 0.214. The results show that A1 is the best alternative, which is followed by A3, A5, A2, and A4, respectively.

TABLE 1.11 Local weights of the alternatives with respect to the criteria.

	w.r.t C1	w.r.t C2	w.r.t C3	w.r.t C4	w.r.t C5
A1	0.233	0.237	0.221	0.190	0.194
A2	0.178	0.195	0.184	0.200	0.204
A3	0.205	0.177	0.194	0.220	0.204
A4	0.182	0.195	0.187	0.188	0.204
A5	0.202	0.195	0.214	0.202	0.194

TABLE 1.12 Global weights of the alternatives and the rankings.

	GW w.r.t C1	GW w.r.t C2	GW w.r.t C3	GW w.r.t C4	GW w.r.t C5	Total	Ranking
A1	0.063	0.032	0.041	0.044	0.035	0.214	1
A2	0.048	0.027	0.034	0.046	0.037	0.191	4
A3	0.055	0.024	0.036	0.051	0.037	0.202	2
A4	0.049	0.027	0.035	0.043	0.037	0.19	5
A5	0.055	0.027	0.039	0.046	0.035	0.202	3

1.3.2.2 Type-2 fuzzy analytic hierarchy process

Zadeh (1975) introduced the concept of a type-2 fuzzy set as an extension of ordinary fuzzy sets. In type-2 fuzzy sets, the membership degrees are ordinary fuzzy sets, making this extension particularly valuable in situations where defining a precise membership function is challenging.

Kahraman et al. (2014) proposed type 2 FAHP which is an extension of Buckley's fuzzy AHP method. The main difference of this extension is the use of interval type 2 fuzzy numbers to quantify the linguistic evaluations of experts. In this paper, fuzzy scales that are given in Table 1.13 are developed using both triangular and trapezoidal interval type-2 fuzzy sets, enabling a more comprehensive representation of uncertainty.

There are several significant features of this extension. First, criteria weights are obtained as type-2 fuzzy numbers, with the fuzziness being maintained throughout all calculations. Then, the evaluation of alternatives is carried out while this inherent fuzziness is preserved in all operations. Finally, defuzzification is performed only at the last step, when the final ranking of alternatives needs to be determined. This approach ensures that uncertainty is properly handled at every stage, with simplification being avoided until absolutely necessary. The method's effectiveness has been demonstrated by its widespread adoption in multicriteria decision-making, with over 500 citations.

1.3.2.3 Intuitionistic fuzzy analytic hierarchy process

IFSs were introduced by Atanassov (1986) as an extension of ordinary fuzzy sets, where not only the degree of membership but also the degree of nonmembership is considered for each element. Unlike traditional fuzzy sets, where the nonmembership is simply the complement of membership, in IFSs, these two degrees are independent, allowing for a more flexible representation of uncertainty. In IFSs, the sum of the membership and nonmembership degrees is constrained to be no greater than one, thereby introducing a hesitation margin that quantifies the degree of uncertainty or indeterminacy associated with an element. This characteristic differentiates IFSs from traditional fuzzy sets, where nonmembership is merely the complement of membership.

In the literature, numerous extensions of the Intuitionistic Fuzzy Analytic Hierarchy Process (IF-AHP) have been developed, each differing in methodological approaches, computational complexity, and application contexts

TABLE 1.13 Type-2 fuzzy scale for linguistic statements (Kahraman et al., 2014).

Linguistic variables	Triangular interval type-2 fuzzy numbers	Trapezoidal interval type-2 fuzzy numbers
Absolutely strong (AS)	(7.5,9,10.5;1) (8.5,9,9.5;0.9)	(7,8,9,9;1,1) (7.2,8.2,8.8,9;0.8,0.8)
Very strong (VS)	(5.5,7,8.5;1)(6.5,7,7.5;0.9)	(5,6,8,9;1,1) (5.2,6.2,7.8,8.8;0.8,0.8)
Fairly strong (FS)	(3.5,5,6.5;1)(4.5,5,5.5;0.9)	(3,4,6,7;1,1) (3.2,4.2,5.8,6.8;0.8,0.8)
Slightly strong (SS)	(1.5,3,4.5;1)(2.5,3,3.5;0.9)	(1,2,4,5;1,1) (1.2,2.2,3.8,4.8;0.8,0.8)
Exactly equal (E)	(1,1,1;1)(1,1,1;1)	(1,1,1,1;1,1) (1,1,1,1;1,1)
If factor *i* has one of the above linguistic variables assigned to it when compared with factor *j*, then *j* has the reciprocal value when compared with *i*	Reciprocals of above	Reciprocals of above

(Alimohammadlou et al., 2023). The first IF-AHP method was introduced by Sadiq and Tesfamariam (2009) which proposed a distinctive method for converting linguistic evaluations into intuitionistic fuzzy (IF) judgments within an IF-AHP framework. Unlike traditional FAHP, which relies on triangular fuzzy numbers to capture vagueness, this approach integrates the decision-maker's confidence level directly into the membership function, forming a subnormal fuzzy set. The lower bound of membership reflects the stated belief (e.g., partial confidence in the evaluation), while the upper bound assumes full membership in the absence of explicit nonbelief.

Among the various IF-AHP methods proposed in the literature, the approach introduced by Xu and Liao (2013) stands out as one of the most widely cited. A key contribution of their work is the introduction of a novel consistency-checking mechanism for intuitionistic preference relations, along with an automated procedure to rectify inconsistencies without requiring additional input from the decision-maker—a feature that enhances efficiency compared to conventional AHP methods. Additionally, they proposed a normalized rank summation method to derive priority vectors from intuitionistic preference relations, forming the basis for hierarchical prioritization in IFAHP. While Xu and Liao (2013) provided a detailed step-by-step procedure and demonstrated their method through a case study on global supplier development, they did not explicitly define an IF scale for linguistic evaluations.

For practical implementation, alternative IF scales from the literature may be employed, such as the one proposed by Onar et al. (2015), where linguistic terms are systematically mapped to specific interval-valued IF numbers, as given in Table 1.14.

To address the computational challenges of handling extremely small or large numbers in IF algebraic operations, Onar et al. (2015) introduced an IF-AHP approach that modifies the conventional AHP framework by incorporating a structured sequence of calculations, including the derivation of a score judgment matrix, an interval multiplicative matrix, and a possibility degree matrix, prior to the final weight prioritization.

1.3.2.4 Pythagorean fuzzy analytic hierarchy process

PFSs, introduced by Yager (2013), extend the concept of IFSs to better capture complex uncertainty in decision-making. While traditional fuzzy sets rely solely on membership and nonmembership degrees, PFSs offer greater flexibility by allowing the squared sum of these degrees to exceed 1, provided their squared sum remains within bounds. This expanded framework enables a richer representation of ambiguity, making PFSs especially valuable in where human judgments involve hesitation or conflicting information. PFSs have found widespread use in MCDM, risk assessment, and other domains requiring sophisticated handling of imprecise information. Building upon these advantages, the Pythagorean Fuzzy Analytic Hierarchy Process (PF-AHP) integrates PFSs with the classic AHP method, providing a more robust and adaptable approach to handling uncertainty in hierarchical decision problems.

Ilbahar et al. (2018) developed a novel approach to risk assessment for occupational health and safety using Pythagorean fuzzy AHP and fuzzy inference system. This AHP extension proceeds by calculating a differences matrix, derived from the discrepancies between the lower and upper values of the membership (μ) and nonmembership (v) functions for each pairwise comparison. Subsequently, an interval multiplicative matrix is formed, and the determinacy

TABLE 1.14 Interval-valued intuitionistic fuzzy scale for linguistic statements. (Onar et al., 2015).

Linguistic statements	Membership and nonmembership
Absolutely less important than	([0, 0.2], [0.5, 0.8])
Much less important than	([0.1, 0.3], [0.4, 0.7])
Less important than	([0.2, 0.4], [0.3, 0.6])
Slightly less important than	([0.3, 0.5], [0.2, 0.5])
Equal importance	([0.4, 0.6], [0.2, 0.4])
Slightly more important than	([0.5, 0.7], [0.1, 0.3])
More important than	([0.6, 0.8], [0, 0.2])
Much more important than	([0.7, 0.9], [0, 0.1])
Absolutely more important than	([0.8, 1.0], [0, 0])

TABLE 1.15 Pythagorean fuzzy scale for linguistic statements (Ilbahar et al., 2018).

Linguistic statements	Interval-valued intuitionistic fuzzy numbers
Absolutely less important than	([0, 0], [0.9, 1])
Much less important than	([0.1, 0.2], [0.8, 0.9])
Less important than	([0.2, 0.35], [0.65, 0.89])
Slightly less important than	([0.35, 0.45], [0.55, 0.65])
Equal importance	([0.45, 0.55], [0.45, 0.55])
Slightly more important than	([0.55, 0.65], [0.35, 0.45])
More important than	([0.65, 0.8], [0.2, 0.35])
Much more important than	([0.8, 0.9], [0.1, 0.2])
Absolutely more important than	([0.9, 1], [0, 0])

value is computed. The weights are then obtained by multiplying the determinacy degrees by the interval multiplicative matrix, ensuring that uncertain judgments are appropriately weighted. Finally, the prioritization weights are normalized to derive the final criteria or alternative rankings. As an example, Table 1.15 presents the fuzzy Pythagorean scale for linguistic evaluations.

1.3.2.5 *Picture fuzzy analytic hierarchy process*

Picture fuzzy sets (PicFS), introduced by Cuong and Kreinovich in 2014 as an extension of IFSs, incorporate an additional parameter to account for the refusal degree in decision-making processes. This enhancement allows PicFS-based methods to effectively capture diverse expert opinions, including acceptance, neutrality, rejection, and indecision. Due to their ability to model uncertainty more comprehensively, PicFS-based approaches have proven to be highly effective in various applications, such as cluster analysis and pattern recognition, where handling ambiguous or incomplete information is crucial.

Picture fuzzy (PicF) AHP, introduced by Gündoğdu et al. (2021), offers a novel approach to MCDM, particularly demonstrated in a public transport development case study. This method stands out from other AHP extensions due to its computational efficiency and structured methodology. The process begins with the construction of a PicF decision matrix, followed by the calculation of local weights for each criterion using the PicF weighted average mean operator. To

TABLE 1.16 Picture fuzzy scale for linguistic statements (Kahraman et al., 2022).

Linguistic statements	Abbreviation	Picture fuzzy numbers
Absolutely more important than	AMI	(0.9, 0, 0.05)
Much more important than	MMI	(0.8, 0.05, 0.15)
more important than	MI	(0.7, 0.1, 0.2)
Slightly more important than	SMI	(0.6, 0.05, 0.35)
Equal importance	EI	(0.5, 0, 0.5)
Slightly less important than	SLI	(0.35, 0.05, 0.6)
less important than	LI	(0.2,0.1,0.7)
Much less important than	MLI	(0.15,0.05, 0.8)
Absolutely less important than	ALI	(0.05,0,0.9)

determine GWs, the local weights are defuzzified through a modified score function and then normalized. The final PicF weights for criteria and subcriteria are derived by multiplying the GWs at the first level with the corresponding subcriterion weights. This simplified approach enhances decision-making under uncertainty while maintaining practical applicability. Table 1.16 presents an example PicF scale for linguistic evaluations.

1.3.2.6 Spherical fuzzy analytic hierarchy process

SFSs, introduced by Kutlu Gündoğdu and Kahraman in 2018, represent a recent advancement in the evolution of IFSs. Such as PicFS and neutrosophic sets, SFSs belong to the category of three-parameter fuzzy set extensions, defined by membership, nonmembership, and hesitancy (indeterminacy) degrees. A distinctive feature of SFSs is the requirement that the squared sum of these three parameters must not exceed 1, with the difference from 1 representing the squared refusal degree. This framework places SFSs within a broader family of fuzzy set extensions that offer an expanded domain for assigning membership and nonmembership degrees, thereby enhancing their flexibility in modeling uncertainty.

Kutlu and Kahraman (2020) developed spherical fuzzy (SF) AHP method and applied it to a renewable energy location selection problem. This extension utilizes the fuzzy scale given in Table 1.6 that converts linguistic evaluations into SF numbers. The SF-AHP methodology involves constructing SF pairwise comparison matrices and determining alternative weights for each criterion using the weighted arithmetic mean. The SF weights are then aggregated hierarchically, from the bottom level to the top level to derive final rankings of alternatives. At this stage, two approaches are proposed. In the first approach, the criteria weights are defuzzified using the score function, and then multiplied using SF arithmetic. The final SF-AHP score for each alternative is obtained by aggregating the global preference weights through SF addition. In the second approach, the SF global preference weights are computed directly, and the final scores are derived without defuzzification. Table 1.17 gives the SF linguistic scale.

1.3.2.7 A proportional picture fuzzy analytic hierarchy process approach

Here, we first present the preliminaries of the proportional PicFS.

Consider the PicFS $\widetilde{T} = \{\langle x;\mu_{\widetilde{T}}(x),\ \pi_{\widetilde{T}}(x),\ \vartheta_{\widetilde{T}}(x)\rangle | x \epsilon X\}$. Assume that the expert judges the proportions between $\mu_{\widetilde{T}}(x)$, $\vartheta_{\widetilde{T}}(x)$ and $\pi_{\widetilde{T}}(x)$ as in Eqs. (1.13–1.15) (Kahraman, 2024):

$$\mu(x) = k_1 r_{\widetilde{T}}(x) \tag{1.13}$$

$$\pi(x) = k_2 r_{\widetilde{T}}(x) \tag{1.14}$$

and

$$\vartheta(x) = k_3 r_{\widetilde{T}}(x) \tag{1.15}$$

TABLE 1.17 Spherical fuzzy scale for linguistic statements (Kutlu and Kahraman (2020)).

Linguistic statements	Spherical fuzzy numbers
Absolutely more important than	(0.9, 0.1, 0.0)
Much more important than	(0.8, 0.2, 0.1)
more important than	(0.7, 0.3, 0.2)
Slightly more important than	(0.6, 0.4, 0.3)
Equal importance	(0.5, 0.4, 0.4)
Slightly less important than	(0.4, 0.6, 0.3)
less important than	(0.3, 0.7, 0.2)
Much less important than	(0.2, 0.8, 0.1)
Absolutely less important than	(0.1, 0.9, 0.0)

satisfying

$$r_{\widetilde{T}}(x) + k_1 r_{\widetilde{T}}(x) + k_2 r_{\widetilde{T}}(x) + k_3 r_{\widetilde{T}}(x) = 1 \tag{1.16}$$

The refusal degree can be given by (1.9)

$$r_{\widetilde{T}}(x) = \frac{1}{1 + k_1 + k_2 + k_3} \tag{1.17}$$

Then, each element in the set $\widetilde{T}$ can be represented by the following:

$$\widetilde{T} = \left\{ \left\langle x; k_1 \frac{1}{1 + k_1 + k_2 + k_3}, k_2 \frac{1}{1 + k_1 + k_2 + k_3}, k_3 \frac{1}{1 + k_1 + k_2 + k_3} \right\rangle \middle| x \in X \right\} \tag{1.18}$$

Let $\widetilde{A}$ and $\widetilde{B}$ be two proportional PicFS: $\widetilde{A} = \{\langle x;\mu_{\widetilde{A}}(x), \pi_{\widetilde{A}}(x), \vartheta_{\widetilde{A}}(x)\rangle | x \epsilon X\}$ and $\widetilde{B} = \{\langle x;\mu_{\widetilde{B}}(x), \pi_{\widetilde{B}}(x), \vartheta_{\widetilde{B}}(x)\rangle | x \epsilon X\}$. Addition and multiplication operations are defined as in Eqs. (1.19–1.20), respectively.

$$\begin{aligned}\widetilde{A} + \widetilde{B} = \Bigg(x,\ & k_{A1}\frac{1}{1 + k_{A1} + k_{A2} + k_{A3}} + k_{B1}\frac{1}{1 + k_{B1} + k_{B2} + k_{B3}} - k_{A1}\frac{1}{1 + k_{A1} + k_{A2} + k_{A3}} \\ & \times k_{B1}\frac{1}{1 + k_{B1} + k_{B2} + k_{B3}}, k_{A2}\frac{1}{1 + k_{A1} + k_{A2} + k_{A3}} \\ & \times k_{B2}\frac{1}{1 + k_{B1} + k_{B2} + k_{B3}}, k_{A3}\frac{1}{1 + k_{A1} + k_{A2} + k_{A3}} \times k_{B3}\frac{1}{1 + k_{B1} + k_{B2} + k_{B3}} \Bigg| x \in X \Bigg)\end{aligned} \tag{1.19}$$

$$\begin{aligned}\widetilde{A} \times \widetilde{B} = \Bigg(x,\ & k_{A1}\frac{1}{1 + k_{A1} + k_{A2} + k_{A3}} \times k_{B1}\frac{1}{1 + k_{B1} + k_{B2} + k_{B3}}, k_{A2}\frac{1}{1 + k_{A1} + k_{A2} + k_{A3}} \\ & + k_{B2}\frac{1}{1 + k_{B1} + k_{B2} + k_{B3}} - k_{A2}\frac{1}{1 + k_{A1} + k_{A2} + k_{A3}} \\ & \times k_{B2}\frac{1}{1 + k_{B1} + k_{B2} + k_{B3}}, k_{A3}\frac{1}{1 + k_{A1} + k_{A2} + k_{A3}} \\ & + k_{B3}\frac{1}{1 + k_{B1} + k_{B2} + k_{B3}} - k_{A3}\frac{1}{1 + k_{A1} + k_{A2} + k_{A3}} \times k_{B3}\frac{1}{1 + k_{B1} + k_{B2} + k_{B3}}\ | x \in X \Bigg)\end{aligned} \tag{1.20}$$

The multiplication by a constant and power operation are given by Eqs. (1.21–1.22), respectively.

$$\lambda\cdot\widetilde{A} = \left\langle 1-\left(1-k_{A1}\frac{1}{1+k_{A1}+k_{A2}+k_{A3}}\right)^{\lambda}, \left(k_{A2}\frac{1}{1+k_{A1}+k_{A2}+k_{A3}}\right)^{\lambda}, \left(k_{A3}\frac{1}{1+k_{A1}+k_{A2}+k_{A3}}\right)^{\lambda}\right\rangle \quad (1.21)$$

$$\widetilde{A}^{\lambda} = <\left(k_{A1}\frac{1}{1+k_{A1}+k_{A2}+k_{A3}}\right)^{\lambda}, 1-\left(1-k_{A2}\frac{1}{1+k_{A1}+k_{A2}+k_{A3}}\right)^{\lambda}, 1-\left(1-k_{A3}\frac{1}{1+k_{A1}+k_{A2}+k_{A3}}\right)^{\lambda}> \quad (1.22)$$

A pairwise comparison matrix of n criteria whose Proportional Picture Fuzzy (PPicF) elements are $x_{ij} = (k_{1ij}, k_{2ij}, k_{3ij})$, $i = 1, 2, \ldots, n$; $j = 1, 2, \ldots, n$ is given by (1.23) by using the proportion triplets:

$$\widetilde{P}(k_1, k_2, k_3) = \begin{bmatrix} 1 & \cdots & (k_{11n}, k_{21n}, k_{31n}) \\ \vdots & (k_{1ij}, k_{2ij}, k_{3ij}) & \vdots \\ (k_{31n}, k_{21n}, k_{11n}) & \cdots & 1 \end{bmatrix} \quad (1.23)$$

where there is a relation between reciprocal values such that $(k_{11n}, k_{21n}, k_{31n}) \rightarrow (k_{31n}, k_{21n}, k_{11n})$. The matrix in (1.23) is transformed to (1.24):

$$\widetilde{P}_P(k_1, k_2, k_3) = \begin{bmatrix} 1 & \cdots & \left(k_{11n}\frac{1}{1+k_{11n}+k_{21n}+k_{31n}}, k_{21n}\frac{1}{1+k_{11n}+k_{21n}+k_{31n}}, k_{31n}\frac{1}{1+k_{11n}+k_{21n}+k_{31n}}\right) \\ \vdots & \ddots & \vdots \\ \left(k_{31n}\frac{1}{1+k_{11n}+k_{21n}+k_{31n}}, k_{21n}\frac{1}{1+k_{11n}+k_{21n}+k_{31n}}, k_{11n}\frac{1}{1+k_{11n}+k_{21n}+k_{31n}}\right) & \cdots & 1 \end{bmatrix} \quad (1.24)$$

Then, by computing the score function as in Eq. (1.25), we obtain the crisp pairwise comparison matrix P given as in Eq. (1.26). In (1.17), the comparison of x_{ij} with x_{ji} is realized. When $i \neq j$, use the second row if it gives a positive value; but if it gives zero or a negative value, compute the reciprocal value by using the same formula for the comparison of x_{ji} with x_{ij}. (5, 5, 5) indicates that the comparison value equals 1.

$$S(k_1, k_2, k_3) = \begin{cases} 1, & if\ i = j \\ 10 \times k_{11n}\frac{1}{1+k_{11n}+k_{21n}+k_{31n}} + \left(k_{21n}\frac{1}{1+k_{11n}+k_{21n}+k_{31n}}\right)/\left(2-k_{31n}\frac{1}{1+k_{11n}+k_{21n}+k_{31n}}\right), & \text{if positive} \end{cases} \quad (1.25)$$

$$P = \begin{bmatrix} 1 & \cdots & S_{1n}(k_1, k_2, k_3) \\ \vdots & \ddots & \vdots \\ S_{n1}(k_1, k_2, k_3) & \cdots & 1 \end{bmatrix} \quad (1.26)$$

Consistency of a crisp decision matrix is measured by Eq. (1.27) (Saaty, 1980), and the matrix is corrected if the consistency ratio (CR) is larger than 0.10.

$$CR = \left(\frac{\lambda_{\max} - n}{n-1}\right)/RI \quad (1.27)$$

where $\lambda_{\max}$ is the eigenvalue; n is the dimension of the square matrix; and RI is the random index for the considered square matrix. Table 1.18 shows the PPF linguistic scale.

1.3.2.8 Proportional intuitionistic fuzzy analytic hierarchy process approach

Here, we first present the preliminaries of the proportional IFSs.

Consider the intuitionistic fuzzy set $\widetilde{T} = \{\langle x; \mu_{\widetilde{T}}(x), \vartheta_{\widetilde{T}}(x)\rangle | x \in X\}$. Assume that the expert judges the proportions between $\mu_{\widetilde{T}}(x)$ and $\vartheta_{\widetilde{T}}(x)$ with respect to the hesitancy degree $h_{\widetilde{T}}(x)$ as in Eqs. (1.28–1.29) (Kahraman, 2024):

$$\mu(x) = k_1 h_{\widetilde{T}}(x) \quad (1.28)$$

TABLE 1.18 PPF linguistic scale.

Linguistic terms (l)	PPF values ($\tilde{x}_{ij}$)	Corresponding picture fuzzy set (μ, π, ϑ)
Absolutely less important than	(1, 1, 9)	(0.08333, 0.08333, 0.75000)
Much less important than	(2, 2, 8)	(0,16667, 0.16667, 0.66667)
Less important than	(3, 3, 7)	(0.25000, 0.25000, 0.58333)
Slightly less important than	(4, 4, 6)	(0.33333, 0.33333, 0.50000)
Equal importance	(5, 5, 5)	(0.41667, 0.41667, 0.41667)
Slightly more important than	(6, 4, 4)	(0.50000, 0.33333, 0.33333)
More important than	(7, 3, 3)	(0.58333, 0.25000, 0.25000)
Much more important than	(8, 2, 2)	(0.66667, 0.16667, 0.16667)
Absolutely more important than	(9, 1, 1)	(0.75000, 0.08333, 0.08333)

$$\vartheta(x) = k_2 h_{\widetilde{T}}(x) \tag{1.29}$$

satisfying

$$h_{\widetilde{T}}(x) + k_1 h_{\widetilde{T}}(x) + k_2 h_{\widetilde{T}}(x) = 1 \tag{1.30}$$

The hesitancy degree can be given by (1.31)

$$h_{\widetilde{T}}(x) = \frac{1}{1 + k_1 + k_2} \tag{1.31}$$

Then, each element in the set $\widetilde{T}$ can be represented by the following:

$$\widetilde{T} = \left\{ \left\langle x; k_1 \frac{1}{1 + k_1 + k_2}, k_2 \frac{1}{1 + k_1 + k_2} \right\rangle | x \in X \right\} \tag{1.32}$$

Let $\widetilde{A}$ and $\widetilde{B}$ be two proportional IFSs: $\widetilde{A} = \{\langle x; \mu_{\widetilde{A}}(x), \vartheta_{\widetilde{A}}(x)\rangle | x \in X\}$ and $\widetilde{B} = \{\langle x; \mu_{\widetilde{B}}(x), \vartheta_{\widetilde{B}}(x)\rangle | x \in X\}$. Addition and multiplication operations are defined as in Eqs. (1.33–1.34), respectively.

$$\begin{aligned}\widetilde{A} + \widetilde{B} = \Bigg(& x,\ k_{A1}\frac{1}{1 + k_{A1} + k_{A2}} + k_{B1}\frac{1}{1 + k_{B1} + k_{B2}} - k_{A1}\frac{1}{1 + k_{A1} + k_{A2}} \\ & \times k_{B1}\frac{1}{1 + k_{B1} + k_{B2}},\ k_{A2}\frac{1}{1 + k_{A1} + k_{A2}} \times k_{B2}\frac{1}{1 + k_{B1} + k_{B2}} \Bigg| x \in X \Bigg)\end{aligned} \tag{1.33}$$

$$\begin{aligned}\widetilde{A} \times \widetilde{B} = \Bigg(& x,\ k_{A1}\frac{1}{1 + k_{A1} + k_{A2}} \times k_{B1}\frac{1}{1 + k_{B1} + k_{B2}},\ k_{A2}\frac{1}{1 + k_{A1} + k_{A2}} \\ & + k_{B2}\frac{1}{1 + k_{B1} + k_{B2}} - k_{A2}\frac{1}{1 + k_{A1} + k_{A2}} \times k_{B2}\frac{1}{1 + k_{B1} + k_{B2}}\ | x \in X \Bigg)\end{aligned} \tag{1.34}$$

The multiplication by a constant and power operation are given by Eq. (1.35–1.36), respectively.

$$\lambda \cdot \widetilde{A} = \left(1 - \left(1 - k_{A1}\frac{1}{1 + k_{A1} + k_{A2}} \right)^{\lambda}, \left(k_{A2}\frac{1}{1 + k_{A1} + k_{A2}} \right)^{\lambda} \right) \tag{1.35}$$

$$\widetilde{A}^{\lambda} = \left(\left(k_{A1}\frac{1}{1 + k_{A1} + k_{A2}} \right)^{\lambda}, 1 - \left(1 - k_{A2}\frac{1}{1 + k_{A1} + k_{A2}} \right)^{\lambda} \right) \tag{1.36}$$

A pairwise comparison matrix of n criteria whose Proportional Intuitionistic Fuzzy (PIF) elements are $x_{ij} = (k_{1ij}, k_{2ij})$, $i = 1, 2, \ldots, n$; $j = 1, 2, \ldots, n$ is given by (1.37) by using the proportion pairs:

$$\widetilde{P}(k_1, k_2) = \begin{bmatrix} 1 & \cdots & (k_{11n}, k_{21n}) \\ \vdots & (k_{1ij}, k_{2ij}) & \vdots \\ (k_{21n}, k_{11n}) & \cdots & 1 \end{bmatrix} \tag{1.37}$$

where there is a relation between reciprocal values such that $(k_{11n}, k_{21n}) \rightarrow (k_{21n}, k_{11n})$. The matrix in (1.37) is transformed to (1.38):

$$\widetilde{P}_P(k_1, k_2) = \begin{bmatrix} 1 & \cdots & \left(k_{11n}\frac{1}{1+k_{11n}+k_{21n}}, \; k_{21n}\frac{1}{1+k_{11n}+k_{21n}} \right) \\ \vdots & \ddots & \vdots \\ \left(k_{21n}\frac{1}{1+k_{11n}+k_{21n}}, \; k_{11n}\frac{1}{1+k_{11n}+k_{21n}} \right) & \cdots & 1 \end{bmatrix} \tag{1.38}$$

Then, by computing the score function as in (1.31), we obtain the crisp pairwise comparison matrix P given as in Eq. (1.40). In Eq. (1.39), the comparison of x_{ij} with x_{ji} is realized. When $i \neq j$, use the second row if it gives a positive value; but if it gives zero or a negative value, compute the reciprocal value by using the same formula for the comparison of x_{ji} with x_{ij}. (5, 5) indicates that the comparison value equals 1.

$$S(k_1, k_2) = \begin{cases} 1, & \textit{if } i = j \\ 10 \times \left(k_{11n}\frac{1}{1+k_{11n}+k_{21n}} - k_{21n}\frac{1}{1+k_{11n}+k_{21n}} \right), & \textit{if positive} \end{cases} \tag{1.39}$$

$$P = \begin{bmatrix} 1 & \cdots & S_{1n}(k_1, k_2) \\ \vdots & \ddots & \vdots \\ S_{n1}(k_1, k_2) & \cdots & 1 \end{bmatrix} \tag{1.40}$$

Consistency of a crisp decision matrix is measured by Eq. (1.27) (Saaty, 1980) and the matrix is corrected if the consistency ratio (CR) is larger than 0.10. Table 1.19 presents the linguistic PIF scale.

TABLE 1.19 Linguistic PIF scale

Linguistic terms (l)	PIF values ($\tilde{x}_{ij}$)	Corresponding intuitionistic fuzzy set (μ, ϑ)
Absolutely less important than	(1, 9)	(0.0909, 0.8182)
Much less important than	(2, 8)	(0.1818, 0.7273)
Less important than	(3, 7)	(0.2727, 0.6364)
Slightly less important than	(4, 6)	(0.3636, 0.5455)
Equal importance	(5, 5)	(0.4545, 0.4545)
Slightly more important than	(6, 4)	(0.5455, 0.3636)
More important than	(7, 3)	(0.6364, 0.2727)
Much more important than	(8, 2)	(0.7273, 0.1818)
Absolutely more important than	(9, 1)	(0.8182, 0.0909)

1.4 Numerical example for classical analytic hierarchy process

A student who has reached university age has identified three alternative universities. To choose the most suitable one among them, the student has determined six criteria. The criteria are as follows: The process of university selection involves the evaluation of multiple criteria that collectively influence the decision-making outcome. Within the framework of the AHP, six primary criteria can be identified:

1. **Campus and physical facilities (C1):** The quality and availability of infrastructure, such as libraries, laboratories, dormitories, sports complexes, and social spaces, are important determinants of both academic performance and student well-being.
2. **Cost and scholarship opportunities (C2):** Financial considerations constitute a critical aspect of the selection process. Tuition fees, living expenses, and the availability of scholarships or financial aid programs determine the economic feasibility of attending a particular institution.
3. **Academic quality and reputation (C3):** This criterion refers to the overall scholarly standing of the institution, including faculty qualifications, research output, accreditation status, and performance in national and international rankings. A strong academic profile enhances the perceived value of the education provided.
4. **Career and post-graduation opportunities (C4):** Employability prospects and career support mechanisms provided by the university are central to long-term outcomes. Indicators include internship opportunities, collaboration with industry, graduate employment rates, and the strength of alumni networks.
5. **Location and social environment (C5):** The geographical context of the university influences accessibility, safety, cultural life, and cost of living. The social environment also shapes the overall quality of the student experience.
6. **International opportunities (C6):** In the context of globalization, international opportunities have become increasingly significant. Student exchange programs, partnerships with foreign institutions, and a diverse international community contribute to cross-cultural competencies and global perspectives.

Fig. 1.9 presents the hierarchy of the problem.

In order to solve the problem, first, a pairwise decision matrix is formed to compare the six criteria. Table 1.20 represents the pairwise comparison matrix, as well as the CI and criteria weights calculated as explained in the methodology section.

In a similar way, the three alternatives are pairwise compared with respect to each criterion. The pairwise comparison matrices are given in Table 1.21.

In order to find the overall weights of the alternatives, first, the alternative weights are multiplied by the weight of the associated criterion. Then these weights are summed up to find the overall weights. The results are given in Table 1.22.

According to the overall weights given in Table 1.22, the best university is A2, and it is followed by A3 and A1.

1.5 Numerical examples with fuzzy analytic hierarchy process

1.5.1 Car selection

This example is presented to show the application of proportional picture FAHP. The goal of the application problem is the purchase of the best car. The best car will be selected among five alternatives based on the considered five evaluation criteria. Fig. 1.10 shows the hierarchy of the problem. Table 1.23 gives the pairwise comparison matrix of the criteria,

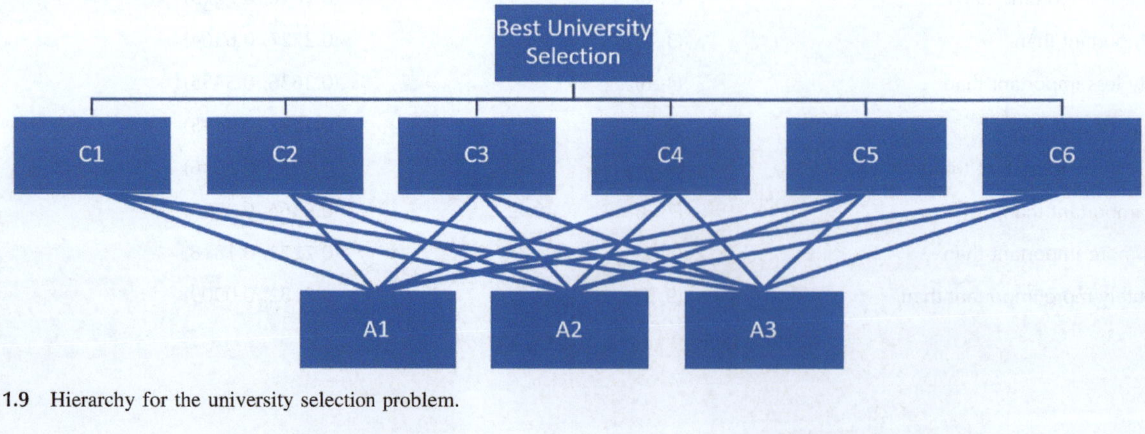

FIGURE 1.9 Hierarchy for the university selection problem.

TABLE 1.20 Pairwise comparison of the criteria with respect to the goal.

	C1	C2	C3	C4	C5	C6	Weights
C1	1	1/2	1/3	3	5	3	0.187
C2	2	1	1/2	4	6	3	0.267
C3	3	2	1	2	4	3	0.321
C4	1/3	1/4	1/2	1	3	1	0.094
C5	1/5	1/6	1/4	1/3	1	1/3	0.042
C6	1/3	1/3	1/3	1	3	1	0.089
				Consistency ratio:			0.057

TABLE 1.21 Alternative comparisons with respect to each criterion.

wrt C1	A1	A2	A3	Weights
A1	1	3	1	0.429
A2	1/3	1	1/3	0.143
A3	1	3	1	0.429
		C. R.:		0

(a) Alternative comparisons w.r.t C1

wrt C2	A1	A2	A3	Weights
A1	1	1/4	1/3	0.121957
A2	4	1	2	0.558425
A3	3	1/2	1	0.319618
		C. R.:		0.015771

(b) Alternative comparisons w.r.t C2

wrt C3	A1	A2	A3	Weights
A1	1	1/2	1/3	0.1692
A2	2	1	1	0.387371
A3	3	1	1	0.443429
		C. R.:		0.015771

(c) Alternative comparisons w.r.t C3

wrt C4	A1	A2	A3	Weights
A1	1	5	3	0.636986
A2	1/5	1	1/3	0.104729
A3	1/3	3	1	0.258285
		C.R.:		0.033199

(d) Alternative comparisons w.r.t C4

wrt C5	A1	A2	A3	Weights
A1	1	1/7	1/5	0.071927
A2	7	1	3	0.649118
A3	5	1/3	1	0.278955
		C. R.:		0.055938

(e) Alternative comparisons w.r.t C5

wrt C6	A1	A2	A3	Weights
A1	1	1/7	1/5	0.4
A2	7	1	3	0.4
A3	5	1/3	1	0.2
		C. R.:		0

(f) Alternative comparisons w.r.t C6

whereas Tables 1.13 presents the pairwise comparison matrices of alternatives for each of the criteria. The *CR*s of the matrices have been checked and found that they are all lower than 0.1.

Applying Eq. (1.25), Table 1.24 is obtained, and the weights of the criteria are computed by following the classical AHP method.

TABLE 1.22 Criteria weights, alternative weights, and the global weights.

	C1 (0.187)	C2 (0.267)	C3 (0.321)	C4 (0.094)	C5 (0.042)	C6 (0.089)	Overall weights
A1	0.429	0.122	0.169	0.637	0.072	0.4	0.265
A2	0.143	0.559	0.387	0.105	0.649	0.4	0.373
A3	0.429	0.319	0.444	0.258	0.279	0.2	0.362

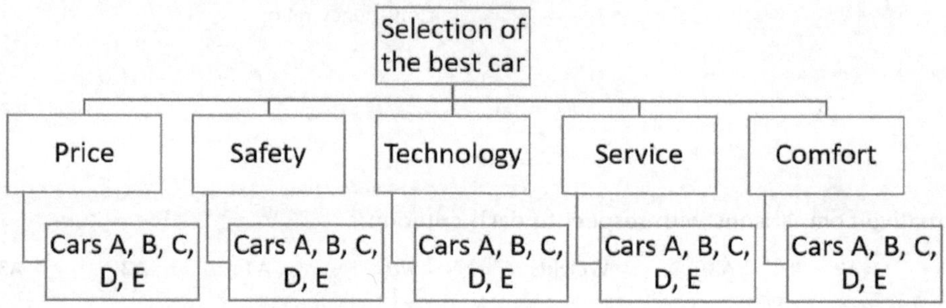

FIGURE 1.10 Hierarchy of the car selection problem.

TABLE 1.23 Pairwise comparison matrix of the criteria.

With respect to the goal	Technology	Safety	Service	Comfort	Price
Technology	(5, 5, 5)	(6, 4, 4)	(7, 3, 3)	(7, 3, 3)	(3, 3, 7)
Safety	(4, 4, 6)	(5, 5, 5)	(6, 4, 4)	(6, 4, 4)	(2, 2, 8)
Service	(3, 3, 7)	(4, 4, 6)	(5, 5, 5)	(5, 5, 5)	(1, 1, 9)
Comfort	(3, 3, 7)	(4, 4, 6)	(5, 5, 5)	(5, 5, 5)	(1, 1, 9)
Price	(7, 3, 3)	(8, 2, 2)	(9, 1, 1)	(9, 1, 1)	(5, 5, 5)

TABLE 1.24 Classical pairwise comparison matrix of the criteria.

With respect to the goal	Technology	Safety	Service	Comfort	Price
Technology	1	2.67	3.93	3.93	0.25
Safety	0.375	1	2.67	2.67	0.186
Service	0.254	0.375	1	1	0.141
Comfort	0.254	0.375	1	1	0.141
Price	3.93	5.385	7.08	7.08	1

From Table 1.24, we obtain the weights of the criteria as $w_{technology} = 0.218$, $w_{safety} = 0.136$, $w_{service} = 0.058$, $w_{comfort} = 0.058$, and $w_{price} = 0.537$. Similarly, the set of alternatives' weights is computed with respect to each criterion as in Table 1.25.

TABLE 1.25 **Pairwise comparison matrices of alternatives with respect to each criterion.**

With respect to technology	**A**	**B**	**C**	**D**	**E**
A	(5, 5, 5)	(8, 2, 2)	(6, 4, 4)	(4, 4, 6)	(7, 3, 3)
B	(2, 2, 8)	(5, 5, 5)	(3, 3, 7)	(1, 1, 9)	(4, 4, 6)
C	(4, 4, 6)	(7, 3, 3)	(5, 5, 5)	(3, 3, 7)	(6, 4, 4)
D	(6, 4, 4)	(9, 1, 1)	(7, 3, 3)	(5, 5, 5)	(8, 2, 2)
E	(3, 3, 7)	(6, 4, 4)	(4, 4, 6)	(2, 2, 8)	(5, 5, 5)
Weights	$w_A = 0.275$	$w_B = 0.050$	$w_C = 0.171$	$w_D = 0.466$	$w_E = 0.102$
With respect to safety	A	B	C	D	E
A	(5, 5, 5)	(6, 4, 4)	(8, 2, 2)	(4, 4, 6)	(7, 3, 3)
B	(4, 4, 6)	(5, 5, 5)	(7, 3, 3)	(3, 3, 7)	(6, 4, 4)
C	(2, 2, 8)	(3, 3, 7)	(5, 5, 5)	(1, 1, 9)	(4, 4, 6)
D	(6, 4, 4)	(7, 3, 3)	(9, 1, 1)	(5, 5, 5)	(8, 2, 2)
E	(3, 3, 7)	(4, 4, 6)	(6, 4, 4)	(2, 2, 8)	(5, 5, 5)
Weights	$w_A = 0.255$	$w_B = 0.151$	$w_C = 0.045$	$w_D = 0.443$	$w_E = 0.085$
With respect to service	A	B	C	D	E
A	(5, 5, 5)	(2, 2, 8)	(3, 3, 7)	(4, 4, 6)	(1, 1, 9)
B	(8, 2, 2)	(5, 5, 5)	(6, 4, 4)	(7, 3, 3)	(4, 4, 6)
C	(7, 3, 3)	(4, 4, 6)	(5, 5, 5)	(6, 4, 4)	(3, 3, 7)
D	(6, 4, 4)	(3, 3, 7)	(4, 4, 6)	(5, 5, 5)	(1, 1, 9)
E	(9, 1, 1)	(6, 4, 4)	(7, 3, 3)	(9, 1, 1)	(5, 5, 5)
Weights	$w_A = 0.059$	$w_B = 0.321$	$w_C = 0.210$	$w_D = 0.124$	$w_E = 0.534$
With respect to comfort	A	B	C	D	E
A	(5, 5, 5)	(3, 3, 7)	(4, 4, 6)	(6, 4, 4)	(7, 3, 3)
B	(7, 3, 3)	(5, 5, 5)	(6, 4, 4)	(8, 2, 2)	(9, 1, 1)
C	(6, 4, 4)	(4, 4, 6)	(5, 5, 5)	(7, 3, 3)	(8, 2, 2)
D	(4, 4, 6)	(2, 2, 8)	(3, 3, 7)	(5, 5, 5)	(6, 4, 4)
E	(3, 3, 7)	(1, 1, 9)	(2, 2, 8)	(4, 4, 6)	(5, 5, 5)
Weights	$w_A = 0.122$	$w_B = 0.334$	$w_C = 0.220$	$w_D = 0.061$	$w_E = 0.029$
With respect to price	A	B	C	D	E
A	(5, 5, 5)	(7, 3, 3)	(1, 1, 9)	(6, 4, 4)	(2, 2, 8)
B	(3, 3, 7)	(5, 5, 5)	(2, 2, 8)	(4, 4, 6)	(2, 2, 8)
C	(9, 1, 1)	(8, 2, 2)	(5, 5, 5)	(8, 2, 2)	(5, 5, 5)
D	(4, 4, 6)	(6, 4, 4)	(2, 2, 8)	(5, 5, 5)	(1, 1, 9)
E	(8, 2, 2)	(8, 2, 2)	(5, 5, 5)	(9, 1, 1)	(5, 5, 5)
Weights	$w_A = 0.161$	$w_B = 0.050$	$w_C = 0.497$	$w_D = 0.092$	$w_E = 0.463$

TABLE 1.26 Overall scores of the alternatives with PPF analytic hierarchy process.

Alternatives	Technology w = 0.218	Safety w = 0.136	Service w = 0.058	Comfort w = 0.058	Price w = 0.537	Overall scores
A	0.275	0.255	0.059	0.122	0.161	0.191585
B	0.050	0.151	0.321	0.334	0.050	0.096276
C	0.171	0.045	0.210	0.220	0.497	0.335227
D	0.466	0.443	0.124	0.061	0.092	0.221970
E	0.102	0.085	0.534	0.029	0.463	0.315081

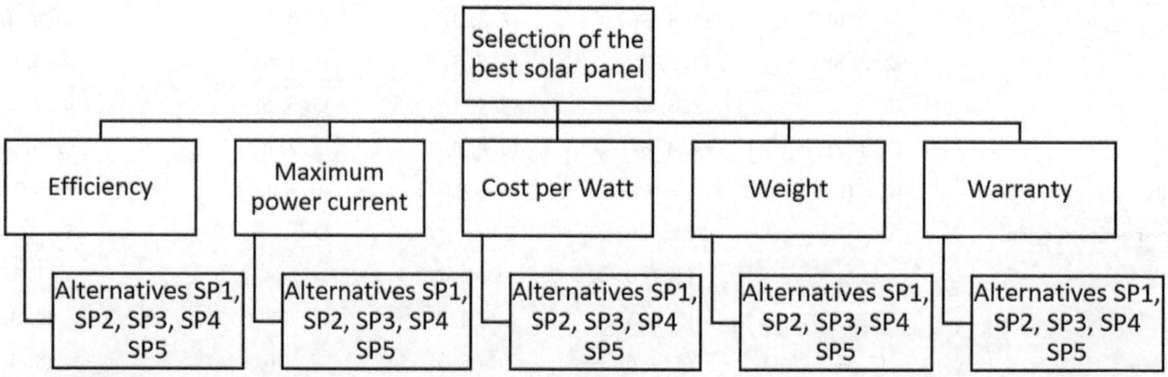

FIGURE 1.11 Hierarchy of the solar panel selection problem.

TABLE 1.27 Pairwise comparison matrix of the criteria.

With respect to the goal	Efficiency	Max. power current	Cost per Watt	Weight	Warranty
Efficiency	(5, 5)	(6, 4)	(7, 3)	(7, 3)	(3, 7)
Max. power current	(4, 6)	(5, 5)	(6, 4)	(6, 4)	(2, 8)
Cost per Watt	(3, 7)	(4, 6)	(5, 5)	(5, 5)	(1, 9)
Weight	(3, 7)	(4, 6)	(5, 5)	(5, 5)	(1, 9)
Warranty	(7, 3)	(8, 2)	(9, 1)	(9, 1)	(5, 5)

TABLE 1.28 Classical pairwise comparison matrix of the criteria

With respect to the goal	Efficiency	Max. power current	Cost per Watt	Weight	Warranty
Efficiency	1.000	1.818	3.636	3.636	0.275
Max. power current	0.550	1.000	1.818	1.818	0.183
Cost per Watt	0.275	0.550	1.000	1.000	0.138
Weight	0.275	0.550	1.000	1.000	0.138
Warranty	3.636	5.455	7.273	7.273	1.000

TABLE 1.29 Pairwise comparison matrices of alternatives with respect to each criterion.

With respect to technology	A	B	C	D	E
A	(5, 5)	(8, 2)	(6, 4)	(4, 6)	(7, 3)
B	(2, 8)	(5, 5)	(3, 7)	(1, 9)	(4, 6)
C	(4, 6)	(7, 3)	(5, 5)	(3, 7)	(6, 4)
D	(6, 4)	(9, 1)	(7, 3)	(5, 5)	(8, 2)
E	(3, 7)	(6, 4)	(4, 6)	(2, 8)	(5, 5)
Weights	$w_A = 0.275$	$w_B = 0.050$	$w_C = 0.139$	$w_D = 0.464$	$w_E = 0.072$
With respect to safety	A	B	C	D	E
A	(5, 5)	(6, 4)	(8, 2)	(4, 6)	(7, 3)
B	(4, 6)	(5, 5)	(7, 3)	(3, 7)	(6, 4)
C	(2, 8)	(3, 7)	(5, 5)	(1, 9)	(4, 6)
D	(6, 4)	(7, 3)	(9, 1)	(5, 5)	(8, 2)
E	(3, 7)	(4, 6)	(6, 4)	(2, 8)	(5, 5)
Weights	$w_A = 0.269$	$w_B = 0.149$	$w_C = 0.049$	$w_D = 0.452$	$w_E = 0.082$
With respect to service	A	B	C	D	E
A	(5, 5)	(2, 8)	(3, 7)	(4, 6)	(1, 9)
B	(8, 2)	(5, 5)	(6, 4)	(7, 3)	(4, 6)
C	(7, 3)	(4, 6)	(5, 5)	(6, 4)	(3, 7)
D	(6, 4)	(3, 7)	(4, 6)	(5, 5)	(1, 9)
E	(9, 1)	(6, 4)	(7, 3)	(9, 1)	(5, 5)
Weights	$w_A = 0.048$	$w_B = 0.262$	$w_C = 0.146$	$w_D = 0.076$	$w_E = 0.468$
With respect to comfort	A	B	C	D	E
A	(5, 5)	(3, 7)	(4, 6)	(6, 4)	(7, 3)
B	(7, 3)	(5, 5)	(6, 4)	(8, 2)	(9, 1)
C	(6, 4)	(4, 6)	(5, 5)	(7, 3)	(8, 2)
D	(4, 6)	(2, 8)	(3, 7)	(5, 5)	(6, 4)
E	(3, 7)	(1, 9)	(2, 8)	(4, 6)	(5, 5)
Weights	$w_A= 0.149$	$w_B= 0.452$	$w_C= 0.269$	$w_D= 0.082$	$w_E = 0.049$
With respect to price	A	B	C	D	E
A	(5, 5)	(7, 3)	(1, 9)	(6, 4)	(2, 8)
B	(3, 7)	(5, 5)	(2, 8)	(4, 6)	(2, 8)
C	(9, 1)	(8, 2)	(5, 5)	(8, 2)	(5, 5)
D	(4, 6)	(6, 4)	(2, 8)	(5, 5)	(1, 9)
E	(8, 2)	(8, 2)	(5, 5)	(9, 1)	(5, 5)
Weights	$w_A = 0.104$	$w_B = 0.051$	$w_C = 0.390$	$w_D = 0.067$	$w_E = 0.388$

TABLE 1.30 Overall scores of the alternatives with PIF analytic hierarchy process.

Alternatives	Efficiency w = 0.204	Max. power current w = 0.111	Cost per Watt w = 0.064	Weight w = 0.064	Warranty w = 0.556	Overall scores
A	0.275	0.269	0.048	0.149	0.104	0.1564
B	0.050	0.149	0.262	0.452	0.051	0.1008
C	0.139	0.049	0.146	0.269	0.390	0.2772
D	0.464	0.452	0.076	0.082	0.067	0.1922
E	0.072	0.082	0.468	0.049	0.388	0.2726

Table 1.26 presents the overall scores of the alternatives.
The overall ranking is as follows: C > E > D > A > B.

1.5.2 Solar panel selection

This example is presented to show the application of proportional intuitionistic fuzzy AHP. The best solar panel will be selected among five alternatives based on the considered five evaluation criteria. The goal of the application problem is the selection of the best solar panel type. The best solar panel type will be selected among five alternatives (polycrystalline, monocrystalline, thin-film, transparent, and solar tiles) based on the considered five evaluation criteria (efficiency, maximum power current, cost per Watt, weight, and warranty). Fig. 1.11 shows the hierarchy of the problem. For comparative purposes, we use the same linguistic evaluations of the PPF car selection problem. Table 1.27 gives the pairwise comparison matrix of the criteria, whereas Table 1.28 presents the pairwise comparison matrices of alternatives for each of the criteria. The *CR*s of the matrices have been checked and found that they are all lower than 0.1.

Applying Eq. (1.39), Table 1.28 is obtained, and the weights of the criteria are computed by following the classical AHP method.

From Table 1.28, we obtain the weights of the criteria as $w_{\text{efficiency}} = 0.204$, $w_{\text{max.powercurrent}} = 0.111$, $w_{\text{costperWatt}} = 0.064$, $w_{\text{weight}} = 0.064$, and $w_{\text{price}} = 0.556$. Similarly, the set of alternatives' weights is computed with respect to each criterion as given in Table 1.29.

Table 1.30 presents the overall scores of the alternatives.

The overall ranking is as follows: C > E > D > A > B.

This ranking is the same as PPF AHP. The overall scores with PIF AHP are closer to each other than PPF AHP.

1.6 Conclusions

In this chapter, both the classical AHP and its fuzzy extensions have been systematically reviewed within the framework of MCDM. Beginning with the fundamental structure of AHP, the chapter emphasized its ability to decompose complex decision problems into a hierarchy of manageable subproblems and to combine different types of criteria within a unified framework. AHP is one of the most widely used MCDM methods since it has a higher ability to structure complex decision problems into a hierarchy of criteria, alternatives, or goals by deriving priorities using pairwise comparisons. This supports decision-makers in breaking down problems into understandable and controllable levels while utilizing both qualitative and quantitative data. By using a 1–9 scale for comparisons and eigenvalue-based weight calculations, AHP ensures that the judgments of decision-makers can be composed into consistent and coherent outputs.

The classical AHP offers several methodological advantages. First, it is adaptable to both qualitative and quantitative values, which permits corporation of measurable indicators along with subjective judgments. Second, the *CR* check provides the coherence and reliability of the decision-making model. These properties lead to extensive adoption of this method across engineering, management, economics, and social sciences. Its clear and transparent logic has made AHP a preferred decision-making method both in academic studies and practical applications.

At the same time, AHP has been critiqued for certain theoretical and practical limitations. Because it requires precise numerical judgments, it can struggle to reflect the vagueness and partial preferences that characterize human reasoning. The method is also sensitive to rank reversal, where the introduction or removal of an alternative can change the relative ranking of existing options. These discussions have enriched the theoretical foundation of AHP and motivated a variety of new research directions.

While the classical AHP has become one of the most widely applied MCDM techniques, its reliance on crisp pairwise comparisons can limit its capacity to reflect human judgment under vagueness and uncertainty. This gap has motivated the integration of fuzzy numbers into the AHP methodology, enabling decision-makers to provide linguistic assessments that are directly translated into fuzzy numbers.

The integration of fuzzy set theory into AHP has been an important step in decision science. Early FAHP approaches, such as Buckley's and Chang's, made it possible to use fuzzy numbers in pairwise comparison matrices. These approaches were widely applied but also faced some methodological problems, such as issues with normalization, consistency, and ranking accuracy. To overcome such problems, researchers developed new FAHP extensions by using different types of fuzzy sets. These include type-2 fuzzy sets, IFSs, PFSs, PicFS, SFSs, and proportional fuzzy sets. Each extension was designed to model different kinds of uncertainty, for example, by adding hesitation, refusal, or more flexible membership functions. Over time, AHP has been extended by using a wide family of fuzzy numbers that can handle complex decision problems under uncertainty.

From a methodological perspective, the extensions of FAHP show both the flexibility of the original AHP framework and the potential of fuzzy logic to provide better representations of uncertainty. Maintaining fuzziness throughout the decision-making process by postponing defuzzification to the final stage, these approaches reduce information loss and improve the credibility of the obtained rankings. Together, these developments have improved both the academic rigor and the practical usability of AHP in areas such as energy planning, supply chain management, healthcare, and risk analysis.

In addition to the methodological discussion, this chapter also presents a bibliometric analysis of the development and applications of FAHP in the literature. The results of this analysis clearly demonstrate the growing acceptance and maturity of FAHP as one of the most popular fuzzy MCDM methods. The bibliometric trends reveal a steady increase in publications until the mid-2000s, followed by a sharp acceleration. Keyword cooccurrence analysis further confirms that FAHP research is positioned at the intersection of methodological development and practical implementation, often in combination with other fuzzy MCDM methods, such as TOPSIS, VIKOR, and PROMETHEE. Taken together, these findings highlight FAHP as a mature, flexible, and widely accepted tool that continues to evolve both theoretically and practically, ensuring its strong position in the MCDM literature.

The practical benefits of FAHP are also clear. Experts can give their judgments in linguistic form, which is easier for real human reasoning. This reduces the cognitive load of the decision-maker and leads to more reliable evaluations. The different extensions of FAHP allow practitioners to choose the most suitable method for their needs. For example, type-2 fuzzy AHP can represent uncertainty when membership functions are not precisely known, intuitionistic and Pythagorean fuzzy AHP can capture hesitation in expert opinions, while picture and spherical fuzzy AHP add further flexibility by including refusal and multidimensional uncertainty. These features show that FAHP is not only a theoretical contribution but also a practical decision support tool with wide applications.

At the same time, FAHP still has some limitations. A major problem is the lack of universally accepted consistency measures that are fully defined in the fuzzy domain. Many studies adapt crisp consistency indices by defuzzifying the fuzzy matrices, but this does not fully reflect the nature of fuzzy evaluations. Another challenge is that higher-order fuzzy extensions may increase computational complexity, which makes it difficult to use them in very large or real-time problems. Finally, since many different fuzzy AHP variants exist, there is no standard approach, which complicates the comparison of results across studies.

Future research of AHP can focus on developing more robust priority-derivation and consistency-checking procedures that reduce sensitivity to rank reversal and improve mathematical soundness. The integration of AHP with artificial intelligence, optimization, and machine learning techniques could enable automated pairwise comparisons and enhance large-scale decision analyses. Moreover, future research on FAHP can focus on several directions. One important goal is to create consistency indices that work directly in the fuzzy domain and to establish threshold values similar to those in crisp AHP. Another research direction is to compare different FAHP extensions under the same conditions to clarify their relative strengths and weaknesses. Combining FAHP with other MCDM methods and optimization techniques is another promising line of research, as it could produce hybrid models for complex decision problems. In addition, the development of open-source software tools will help practitioners apply FAHP more easily and transparently.

In conclusion, the chapter shows that AHP has evolved from a crisp hierarchical model into a broad methodological family that integrates fuzzy logic and other extensions to meet the challenges of real-world decision problems.

Its combination of conceptual clarity, practical flexibility, and continuous methodological development ensures that both classical AHP and its fuzzy variants will remain essential tools for decision analysts and practitioners in engineering, management, and many other disciplines.

References

Alimohammadlou, M., Khoshsepehr, Z., & Alinejad, S. (2023). Single-valued intuitionistic fuzzy AHP and interval-valued intuitionistic fuzzy AHP. In *Analytic hierarchy process with fuzzy sets extensions: Applications and discussions*. Cham: Springer International Publishing, 121–152.

Atanassov, K. T. (1986). Intuitionistic fuzzy sets. *Fuzzy Sets and Systems, 20*(1), 87–96.

Blumenthal, A. L. (1977). *The process of cognition*. Prentice Hall/Pearson Education.

Bozbura, F. T., Beskese, A., & Kahraman, C. (2007). Prioritization of human capital measurement indicators using fuzzy AHP. *Expert Systems with Applications, 32*(4), 1100–1112.

Buckley, J. J. (1985a). Fuzzy hierarchical analysis. *Fuzzy Sets and Systems, 17*(3), 233–247.

Buckley, J. J. (1985b). Ranking alternatives using fuzzy numbers. *Fuzzy Sets and Systems, 15*(1), 21–31.

Cevik, O. S., Oztaysi, B., & Kahraman, C. (2014). Strategic decision selection using hesitant fuzzy TOPSIS and interval type-2 fuzzy AHP: A case study. *Int J Comput Intell Syst, 7*(5), 1002–1021. https://doi.org/10.1080/18756891.2014.964011.

Cevik, O. S., Büyüközkan, G., Öztaysi, B., & Kahraman, C. (2016). A new hesitant fuzzy QFD approach: An application to computer workstation selection. *Appl Soft Comput J, 46*, 1–16.

Chang, D. Y. (1996). Applications of the extent analysis method on fuzzy AHP. *European Journal of Operational Research, 95*(3), 649–655.

Cheng, C. H. (1997). Evaluating naval tactical missile systems by fuzzy AHP based on the grade value of membership function. *European Journal of Operational Research, 96*(2), 343–350.

Gündoğdu, F. K., Duleba, S., Moslem, S., & Aydın, S. (2021). Evaluating public transport service quality using picture fuzzy analytic hierarchy process and linear assignment model. *Applied Soft Computing, 100*, 106920.

Ilbahar, E., Karaşan, A., Cebi, S., & Kahraman, C. (2018). A novel approach to risk assessment for occupational health and safety using Pythagorean fuzzy AHP & fuzzy inference system. *Safety science, 103*, 124–136.

Kahraman, C. (2024). Proportional fuzzy set extensions and imprecise proportions. *Informatica, 35*(2), 311–339.

Kahraman, C., Öztayşi, B., Sarı, İ. U., & Turanoğlu, E. (2014). Fuzzy analytic hierarchy process with interval type-2 fuzzy sets. *Knowledge-Based Systems, 59*, 48–57.

Kahraman, C., Ucal Sari, I., & Çevik Onar, S. (2022). Strategic multi-criteria decision-making against pandemics using picture and spherical fuzzy AHP and TOPSIS. In *New perspectives in operations research and management science: Essays in honor of Fusun Ulengin*. Cham: Springer International Publishing, 385–422.

Kutlu, G., F., & Kahraman, C. (2019a). Spherical fuzzy sets and spherical fuzzy TOPSIS method. *Journal of Intelligent & Fuzzy Systems, 36*(1), 337–352.

Kutlu, G., F., & Kahraman, C. (2019b). Extension of WASPAS with spherical fuzzy sets. *Informatica, 30*(2), 269–292.

Kutlu, G., F., & Kahraman, C. (2020). A novel spherical fuzzy analytic hierarchy process and its renewable energy application. *Soft Computing, 24*(6), 4607–4621.

Mongeon, P., & Paul-Hus, A. (2016). The journal coverage of web of science and scopus: A comparative analysis. *Scientometrics, 106*(1), 213–228.

Onar, S. C., Oztaysi, B., Otay, İ., & Kahraman, C. (2015). Multi-expert wind energy technology selection using interval-valued intuitionistic fuzzy sets. *Energy, 90*, 274–285.

Oztaysi, B., Onar, S. C., & Kahraman, C. (2023). An initial research on comparison of fuzzy AHP and classical AHP methods. In *International conference on intelligent and fuzzy systems*. Cham: Springer Nature Switzerland, 382–388.

Saaty, T. L. (1977). A scaling method for priorities in hierarchical structures. *Journal of Mathematical Psychology, 15*(3), 234–281.

Saaty, T. L. (1980). *The analytic hierarchy process*. New York: McGraw-Hill.

Saaty, T. L. (1986). Axiomatic foundation of the analytic hierarchy process. *Management Science, 32*(7), 841–855.

Saaty, T. L. (2004). Decision making—the analytic hierarchy and network processes (AHP/ANP). *Journal of Systems Science and Systems Engineering, 13*(1), 1–35.

Sadiq, R., & Tesfamariam, S. (2009). Environmental decision-making under uncertainty using intuitionistic fuzzy analytic hierarchy process (IF-AHP). *Stochastic Environmental Research and Risk Assessment, 23*(1), 75–91.

Torra, V. (2010). Hesitant fuzzy sets. *International Journal of Intelligent Systems, 25*(6), 529–539.

Van Eck, N. J., & Waltman, L. (2010). Software survey: VOSviewer, a computer program for bibliometric mapping. *Scientometrics, 84*(2), 523–538.

Van Laarhoven, P. J. M., & Pedrycz, W. (1983). A fuzzy extension of Saaty›s priority theory. *Fuzzy Sets and Systems, 11*(1), 199–227.

Wang, Y. M., Luo, Y., & Hua, Z. (2008). On the extent analysis method for fuzzy AHP and its applications. *European Journal of Operational Research, 186*(2), 735–747.

Xu, Z., & Liao, H. (2013). Intuitionistic fuzzy analytic hierarchy process. *IEEE Transactions on Fuzzy Systems, 22*(4), 749–761.

Yager, R. R. (1986). On the theory of bags. *International Journal of General System, 13*(1), 23–37.

Yager, R. R. (2013). Pythagorean fuzzy subsets. *Joint IFSA World Congress and NAFIPS Annual Meeting (IFSA/NAFIPS)*, 24–28 June, Edmonton, AB, Canada (pp. 57–61).

Zadeh, L. (1965). Fuzzy Sets. *Information and Control, 8*, 338–353.
Zadeh, L. A. (1975). The concept of a linguistic variable and its application to approximate reasoning—I. *Information Sciences, 8*(3), 199–249.
Çebi, S., Onar, S.Ç., Öztayşi, B., & Kahraman, C. (2022). Integration of analytic hierarchy process with other MCDM methods: A literature review. *In International Symposium on the Analytic Hierarchy Process, ISAHP,* 1–6.

Further reading

Cường, B. C. (2014). Picture fuzzy sets. *Journal of computer science and cybernetics, 30*(4), 409 -409.
Saaty, T. L., & Wind, Y. (1980). Marketing applications of the analytic hierarchy process. *Management science, 26*(7), 641–658.

Chapter 2

ANP: Analytic network process for multi-attribute decision-making

Cengiz Kahraman[1], Irem Ucal Sari[2], Sezi Cevik Onar[3], Basar Oztaysi[1], and Zeynep Kizilkan Demir[1]
[1]*Industrial Engineering Department, Istanbul Technical University, Istanbul, Türkiye,* [2]*Industrial Engineering Department, Baskent University, Ankara, Türkiye,* [3]*ReTech Center, Ecole des Ponts, ParisTech, Paris, France*

2.1 Introduction

Multicriteria decision-making (MCDM) methods provide systematic approaches to support complex decisions that involve uncertainty, conflicting objectives, and both quantitative and qualitative criteria. The main purpose of these methods is to model the decision process according to criteria in order to identify the best option, rank alternatives, or classify them into categories. In the literature, MCDM techniques are often grouped into four categories: outranking methods (e.g., elimination and choice translating reality [ELECTRE], preference ranking organization method for enrichment evaluation), distance-based methods (e.g., technique for order preference by similarity to ideal solution [TOPSIS], VlseKriterijumska Optimizacija I Kompromisno Resenje [VIKOR], evaluation based on distance from average solution), value/utility-based methods (e.g., simple additive weighting [SAW], weighted product method [WPM], multi-attribute utility theory [MAUT]), and pairwise comparison-based methods (e.g., analytic hierarchy process [AHP], analytic network process [ANP], best–worst method).

Among the above-mentioned methods, AHP has gained wide attention due to its ability to handle both tangible and intangible criteria, allowing decision-makers to evaluate alternatives using a 1–9 pairwise comparison scale. In the AHP method, the consistency ratio is also proposed to measure the logical coherence of the decision matrix and to help ensure more reliable results. Finally, AHP structures complex problems into a hierarchy of smaller subproblems, reducing the cognitive burden of comparisons and making the decision process more manageable and effective.

Despite its favorable features and frequent use, the AHP method has a limitation concerning the structure of its decision model, criteria, and alternatives. Specifically, it relies on the assumption that criteria are mutually independent, alternatives are mutually independent, and that both criteria and alternatives are independent of each other within the decision model. These assumptions can be restrictive for real-world problems, as criteria and alternatives may exhibit interdependencies. This situation narrows the range of problem domains where AHP can be effectively applied. Therefore, as an extension of AHP, Saaty (1975) proposed the ANP.

Saaty (1975) identifies different dependencies in decision-making problems. In AHP, the decision problem is modeled as a hierarchy, which means criteria, subcriteria, and alternatives are defined at different levels of the hierarchy. In the ANP method, Saaty states that there can be inner dependencies or outer dependencies in a hierarchy. Inner dependency refers to dependencies among the elements of a cluster (i.e., subcriteria under a specific criterion). Outer dependency, on the other hand, refers to dependencies between the elements of different clusters (i.e., the dependency of a criterion on an alternative). Saaty also states that an element in a hierarchy can be affected by another element and, at the same time, it can affect other elements, which creates feedback within the hierarchy. As a result, the term network is used instead of hierarchy to represent these complex dependencies in a decision problem. To solve problems with such complex structures, the ANP method was developed.

The ANP method is based on the pairwise comparison matrices, similar to AHP. While it preserves the basic application steps such as decomposing complex problems and conducting consistency checks, it additionally allows for the identification and quantitative representation of the interdependencies present in the decision model. After the interdependencies in the decision model are identified, they are pairwise compared regarding to their effects on the decision matrix. As a result, a matrix called the supermatrix is obtained, which represents the pairwise comparisons of the criteria, alternatives, and interdependencies.

Encyclopedia of Multi-Attribute Decision-Making (MADM). DOI: https://doi.org/10.1016/B978-0-443-33275-3.00027-0

In the next step, the powers of the supermatrix are computed in order to capture the effects of interdependencies on the outcome. When the supermatrix converges to a limit, the final solution is obtained. In this way, the ranking and selection of alternatives are carried out based on this matrix. ANP method has been used in different decision-making problems such as health, safety, and environmental management; hydrology and water management; business and financial management; human resources management; tourism; logistics and supply chain management; design, engineering, and manufacturing systems; and energy management (Kheybari et al., 2020).

Another branch of ANP studies focuses on extending the method by using fuzzy set theory. In these studies, the conventional method of expressing pairwise comparisons using exact values from 1 to 9 is substituted with fuzzy numbers. Introduced by Zadeh in 1965, fuzzy logic establishes a mathematical basis for handling imprecision and uncertainty in data. Unlike classical logic, fuzzy set theory brings forward the idea of a membership degree, which varies continuously between 0 and 1. The term membership degree enables partial membership of an element to a set so it enables better numerical representation of uncertainty in decision-making problems. The extension of the ANP method using fuzzy numbers has emerged as a significant area of interest in the literature, and the method has been enhanced through the incorporation of various novel fuzzy set extensions (Büyüközkan et al., 2024; Ma & Lin, 2025; Yang et al., 2020; Zhang et al., 2024; Zheng et al., 2018).

The aim of this chapter is to present the state-of-the-art studies on fuzzy analytic network process (FANP). The remainder of the chapter is structured as follows: Section 2.2 provides a comparative literature review of ANP studies. Section 2.3 summarizes the ANP method and FANP methods. In this section, a new proportional picture FANP model is presented, and its application is given. In Section 2.4, an application of classical ANP is presented. Section 2.5 includes the application of the developed proportional picture FANP. Finally, the conclusion is presented in the last section.

2.2 Literature review on analytic network process

2.2.1 Classical analytic network process

The ANP is a generalization of AHP that can model the interdependence and feedback loops among decision criteria (Saaty, 1996). In order to see the usage and evolution of ANP literature, we conducted a bibliometric analysis using the Scopus database. Scopus was selected since it offers a broad coverage of journals, especially in engineering, management, and applied sciences (Mongeon & Paul-Hus, 2016).

We have used this Boolean string for the search "analytic network process" OR "analytical network process" on August 19, 2025. The result is 4845 papers. In order to ensure the relevance of the studies, we have limited it to titles, abstracts, and keywords. After data collection, keyword cooccurrence networks were analyzed using VOSviewer (van Eck & Waltman, 2010). Fig. 2.1 shows the change in the number of studies over the years according to the bibliometric analysis.

Although its wide usage, ANP studies show a fragmented increase, where for some periods the usage has remained stable or decreased. Each year, many studies are conducted for ANP, which show the usefulness of ANP. Fig. 2.2 shows the top twenty sources that have published the most studies on ANP.

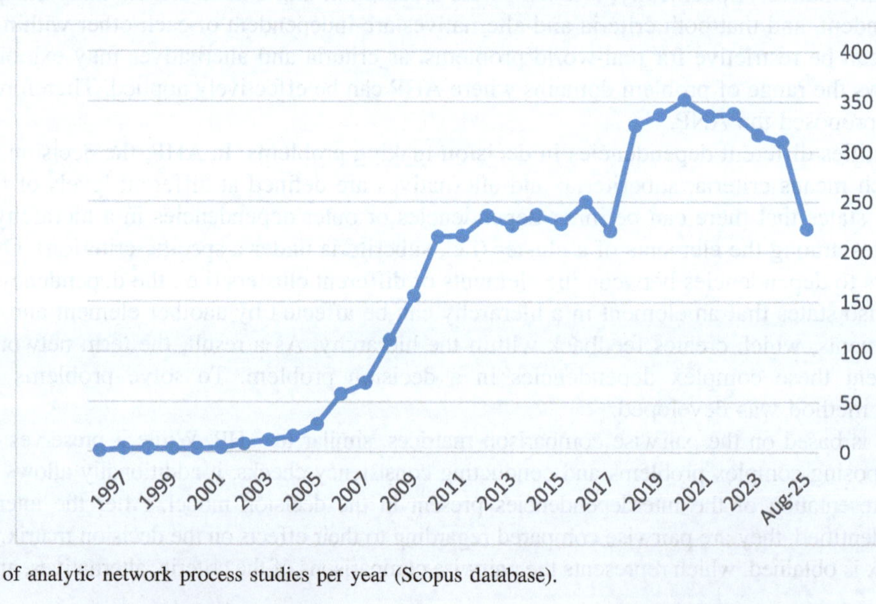

FIGURE 2.1 Number of analytic network process studies per year (Scopus database).

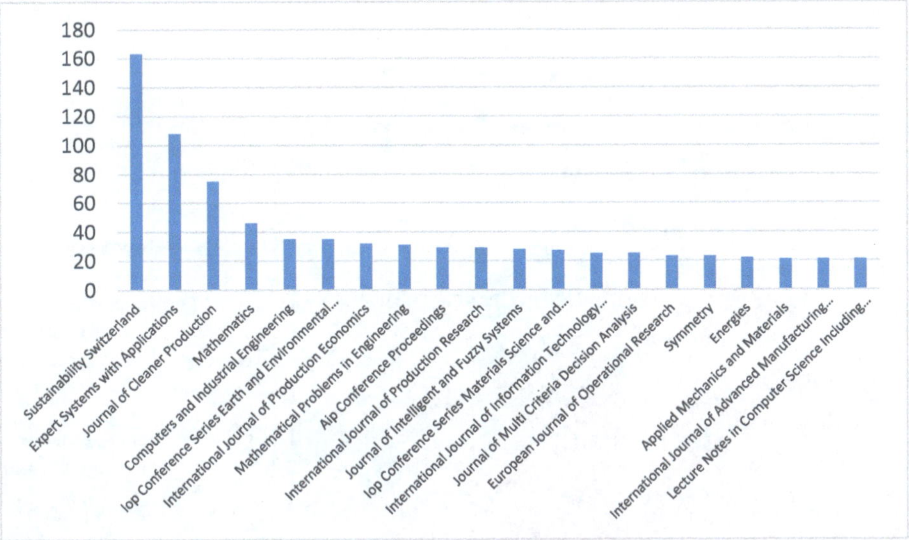

FIGURE 2.2 Top sources that have published the most studies on analytic network process (Scopus database).

The ANP research highlights its wide usage across interdisciplinary studies. Sustainability Switzerland leads with 163 papers, reflecting ANP's strong alignment with sustainable development. Expert Systems with Applications (108 papers) underlines the method's role in decision support systems and intelligent applications. Journal of Cleaner Production (75 papers) further emphasizes the importance of ANP in environmental management. Mathematical and methodological contributions are represented by Mathematics (46 papers), Mathematical Problems in Engineering (31 papers), and Symmetry (23 papers), which provide theoretical and computational frameworks. Industrial and engineering applications appear in Computers and Industrial Engineering (35 papers), International Journal of Production Economics (32 papers), International Journal of Production Research (29 papers), and International Journal of Advanced Manufacturing Technology (21 papers). ANP has become a multipurpose tool and is applied to various fields. Fig. 2.3 presents the keyword cooccurrence analysis for ANP research, conducted in VOSviewer with a minimum occurrence threshold of twenty keywords. The objective of this analysis was to highlight the dominant research themes in ANP studies.

The cooccurrence map for ANP in Fig. 2.3 shows that research in this area has developed along two main lines: methodological advances and applied domains. At the core, ANP is strongly tied to decision theory, fuzzy logic, and fuzzy set theory, often extended through hybrid approaches like decision-making trial and evaluation laboratory (DEMATEL) or VIKOR to handle interdependencies and uncertainty in complex decisions. It is widely used for quality control, supplier selection, product development, and competition in industrial and management contexts.

2.2.2 Fuzzy analytic network process

The ANP is a generalization of AHP that can model the interdependence and feedback loops among decision criteria (Saaty, 1996). In order to deal with vagueness, imprecision, and hesitancy in expert judgments, the FANP was developed (Mikhailov & Singh, 1999). Both ANP and FANP are widely used in literature (Huang, 2012: Kaytez, 2022). Kahraman et al. (2004) utilized FANP in supplier selection. Promentilla (2008) used FANP in environmental remediation. Ali et al. (2024) applied FANP in evaluating societal impacts of virtual reality. Chen et al. (2023) used FANP in healthcare logistics. FANP has also been combined with various methods, including mathematical programming (Huang, 2012), strengths, weaknesses, opportunities, and threats (SWOT)–FANP (Kaytez, 2022), and FANP–fuzzy regression model (Amiri et al., 2024).

Although FANP has several benefits and has been used widely in literature, the mathematical soundness of FANP has been questioned by various researchers. Saaty (2006) himself claimed that the eigenvalue foundation of the original models is questionable in fuzzy extensions. The mathematical inconsistencies, especially the fuzzy scales, defuzzification, and priority derivations, have been discussed in several studies (Senturk, 2016; Zhü, 2014). Brunelli (2017) claimed that the defuzzification step often involves subjectivity, the benefit of fuzzification is diminished at this step. For large-scale decision problems, since fuzziness increases computational complexity, it is harder to deal with FANP (Taherdoost & Madanchian, 2023).

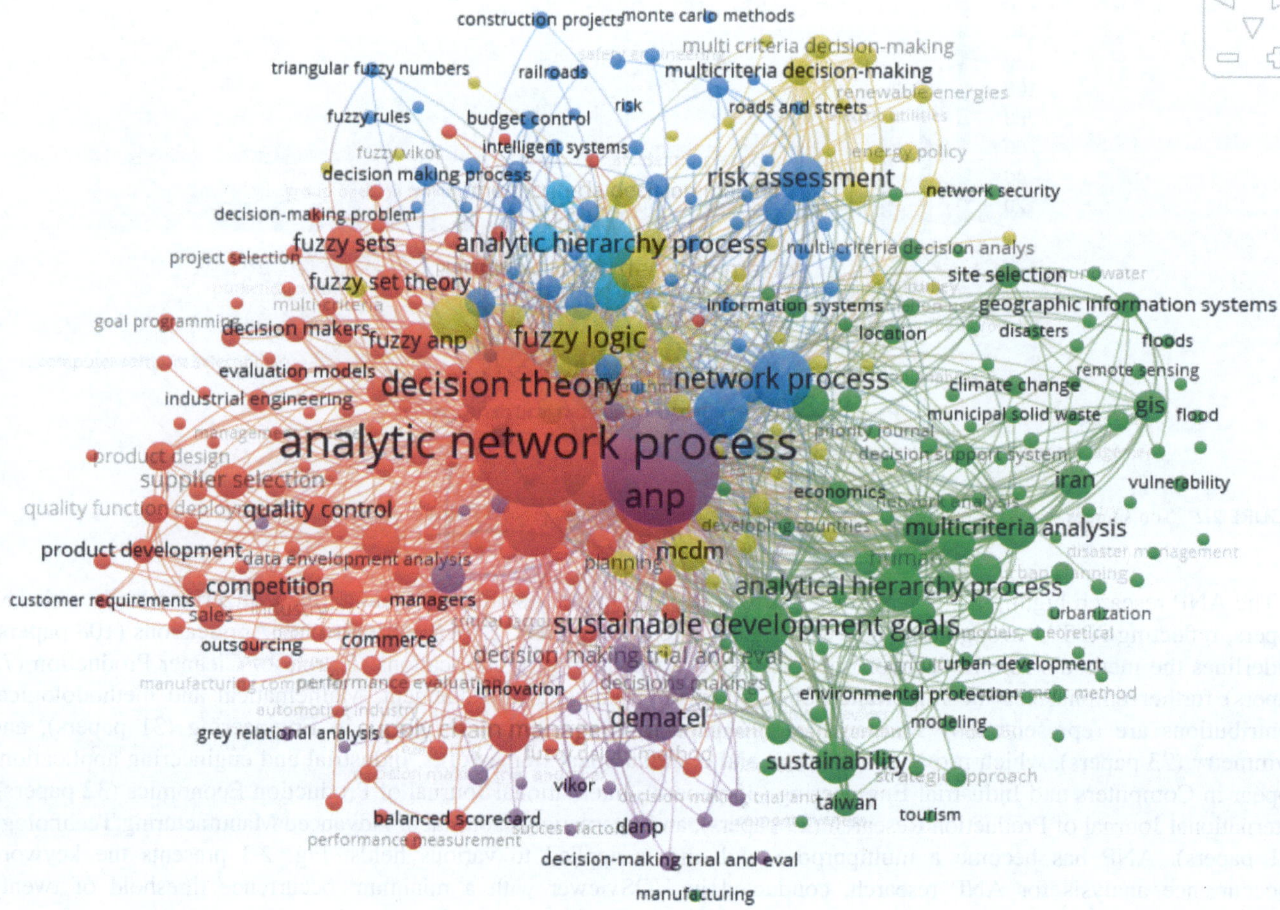

FIGURE 2.3 Keyword cooccurrence analysis for analytic network process.

Despite the criticisms, FANP has continued to be used in the literature since it enables handling complex interdependencies and uncertain judgments. The linguistic assessments in FANP enable easy modeling of feedback effects among decision criteria. For example, FANP has been used in quality function deployment to better match customer needs with technical solutions, making the prioritization process more realistic (Kahraman et al., 2006). Especially in the emerging areas where flexibility is the key for successful decision-making, FANP has been used widely. Pereira and Sousa (2023) showed the benefits of FANP in airborne wind energy system selection, where site-dependent variables are combined with fuzzy expert judgments.

In order to see the usage and evolution of FANP literature, we conducted a bibliometric analysis using the Scopus database. Scopus was selected since it offers a broad coverage of journals, especially in engineering, management, and applied sciences (Mongeon & Paul-Hus, 2016). We have used this Boolean string for the search "fuzzy analytic network process" OR "fuzzy ANP" OR "FANP" on August 19, 2025. In order to ensure the relevance of the studies, we have limited it to titles, abstracts, and keywords. After data collection, keyword cooccurrence networks were analyzed using VOSviewer (van Eck & Waltman, 2010). Fig. 2.4 shows the change in the number of studies over the years according to the bibliometric analysis since 2003.

According to Fig. 2.1, the studies that use FANP were very limited until 2007. From 2008, the number of studies began to increase. Especially from 2010 to 2018, the number of studies increased dramatically. Yet, after 2021, we see a constant drop. This drop can be the reflection of the usage of new methods in decision-making problems. Despite the recent decline, the number of studies using FANP each year remains significant, showing that researchers continue to recognize and be convinced by its benefits. Fig. 2.5 shows the top nine journals that have published the most studies on FANP.

Expert Systems with Applications is the leading journal for FANP studies, with nearly 30 papers. This shows a strong link between ANP and applied decision-making methods. Many studies in Sustainability (Switzerland) and the Journal of

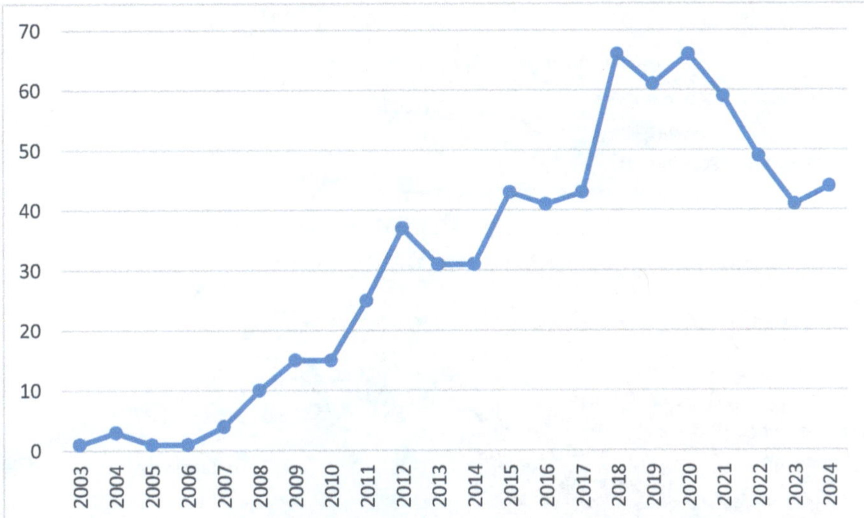

FIGURE 2.4 Number of fuzzy analytic network process studies per year (Scopus database from 2003).

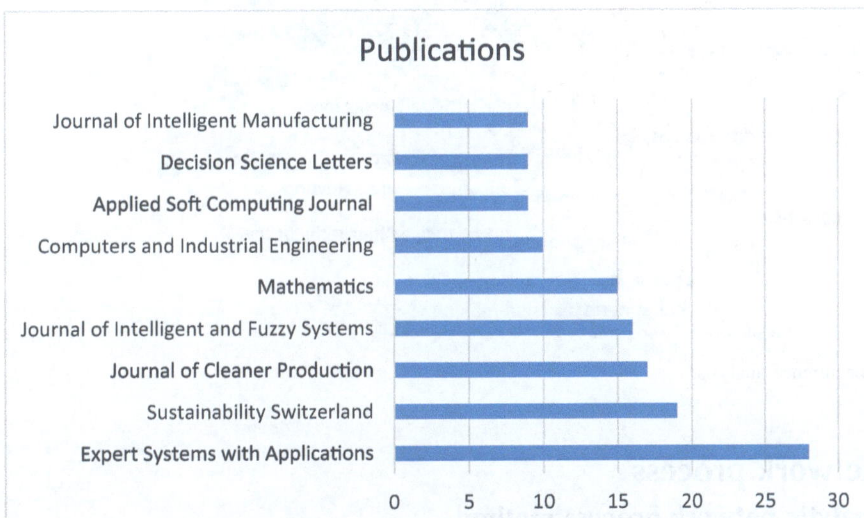

FIGURE 2.5 Top journals that have published the most studies on fuzzy analytic network process (Scopus database).

Cleaner Production are using FANP to solve problems involving sustainability, energy, and environmental management. The other journals, such as Journal of Intelligent and Fuzzy Systems, Mathematics, Journal of Intelligent Manufacturing, Decision Science Letters, and Computers and Industrial Engineering, show that FANP is used both in methodological developments and domain-specific applications. Fig. 2.6 presents the keyword cooccurrence analysis for FANP research, conducted in VOSviewer with a minimum occurrence threshold of ten keywords in order to filter out less frequent keywords and using fractional counting. The objective of this analysis was to highlight the dominant research themes in FANP studies.

Fig. 2.6 shows how research on FANP is clustered around several major themes. The main themes are located at the center. Decision-making, fuzzy logic, and ANP are the main themes, which reflect the methodological core of the field. Various fuzzy MCDM methods, such as fuzzy AHP, fuzzy DEMATEL, fuzzy VIKOR, and fuzzy TOPSIS, are used along with FANP. There are also strong connections with application-oriented keywords such as supply chain management, risk assessment, sustainability, product development, and energy policy. The analysis shows that FANP is a widely used multi-criteria decision-making approach. It has been used in various fields ranging from supplier selection and healthcare to sustainability and energy management.

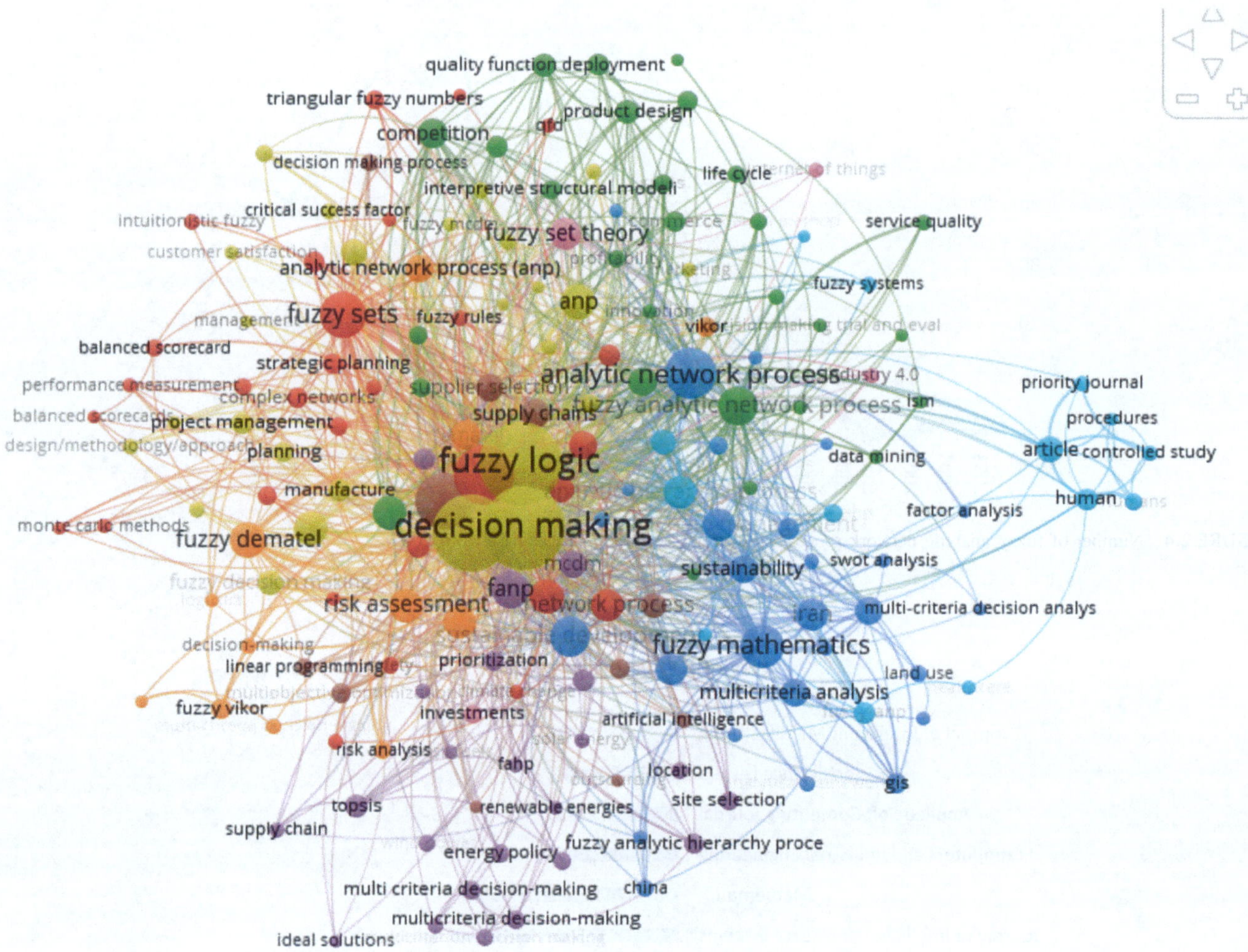

FIGURE 2.6 Keyword cooccurrence analysis.

2.3 Analytic network process

2.3.1 Classical analytic network process method

Saaty (2004) introduced the ANP as an advanced extension of the AHP, specifically designed to address decision-making problems where criteria demonstrate interdependencies. Unlike the hierarchical structure of the AHP, ANP employs a networked model to capture both inner dependencies (within clusters) and outer dependencies (between clusters), offering a more realistic framework for real-world problems.

The difference between hierarchy and network is given in Fig. 2.7. In Fig. 2.7a an abstract representation of hierarchy is given, in Fig. 2.7b a network structure is shown. In Fig. 2.7a, the loop indicates that each element depends only on itself. Fig. 2.7b, represents a feedback network with components having inner and outer dependence among their elements. The arc from C4 to C2 indicates the outer dependence of elements in C2 on the elements in C4 with respect to a common property. A loop in a component indicates inner dependence of the elements in that component with respect to a common property.

We can explain the need for a network structure by using an example. Let us consider the problem of selecting a service provider for a university cafeteria. In this case, cost, quality, variety, health and hygiene, and student satisfaction can be regarded as the criteria to be used in the selection of the company. When this problem is addressed using AHP, a three-level hierarchy can be established: company selection, criteria, and alternatives. In this approach, it is assumed that all criteria are independent of one another. However, the performance of an alternative in the area of health and hygiene may affect its performance in the quality criterion. Moreover, the performance in the quality criterion may influence student satisfaction. Considering the existence of these interactions, solving the problem by establishing a network structure instead of a hierarchical one will provide a more accurate result.

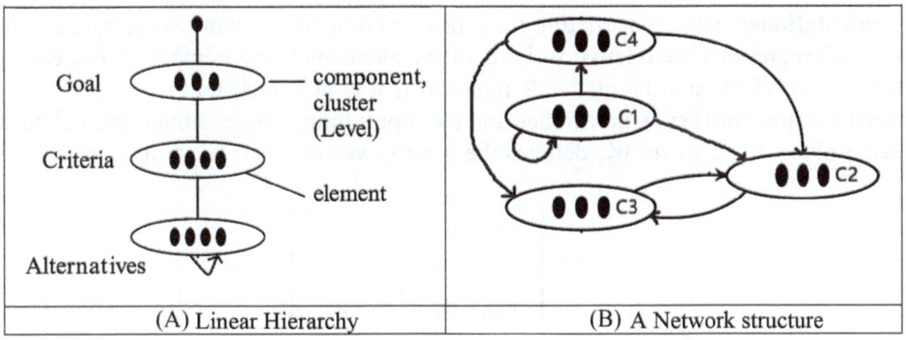

FIGURE 2.7 A: Linear hierarchy. B: A network structure.

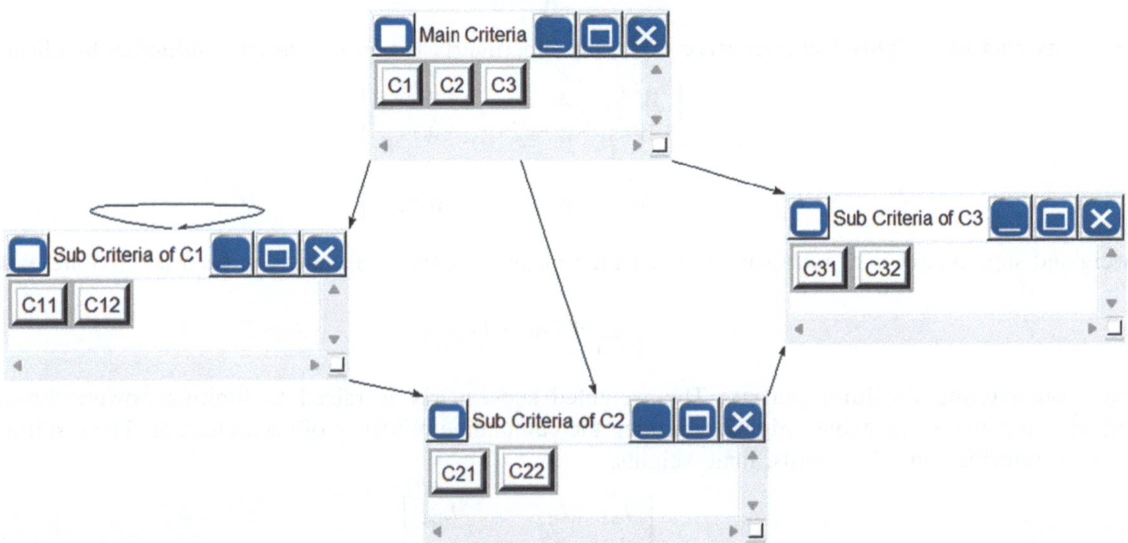

FIGURE 2.8 A network example.

Similar to the AHP method, the core unit in ANP methodology is the pairwise comparison matrix, which is based on the comparison evaluation of the decision makers. The operations on pairwise comparison matrices are identical to those in AHP, and the priorities of the elements are obtained after the consistency check. But the difference between AHP and ANP is in the formulation of the decision and formation of pairwise comparison matrices for each dependency in ANP.

The main stages of the ANP methodology are as follows:

Step 1. Network construction: The problem is decomposed into clusters such as main criteria, subcriteria, and alternatives, and the interactions among elements are identified. In the graphical representation, the dependencies are shown via directed arrows, where an arrow from cluster X to cluster Y indicates dependence (subcriteria may influence main criteria and other subcriteria). As an example, the decision-making problem consists of three main criteria (C1, C2, and C3 as top-level decision factors), and two subcriteria for each main criterion (C11, C12, C21, C22, C31, C33) is presented in Fig. 2.8. A feedback loop connects C11 and C12, indicating mutual influence between these subcriteria under C1. Arrows link subcriteria of C1-C2 and C2-C3 represent intercriteria interactions.

Step 2. Pairwise comparisons: Pairwise comparisons are conducted to evaluate the relative influence of elements within and between clusters using Saaty's 1–9 scale and the pairwise comparison matrix given in Eq. 2.1 is constructed:

$$A = \begin{bmatrix} 1 & a_{12} & \cdots & a_{1n} \\ 1/a_{12} & 1 & \cdots & a_{2n} \\ \vdots & \vdots & \ddots & \vdots \\ 1/a_{1n} & 1/a_{2n} & \cdots & 1 \end{bmatrix} \tag{2.1}$$

Step 3. Priority calculations: After constructing the pairwise comparison matrix (A), the next step is to compute the priority vector (w), which represents the relative weights of the elements being compared. For each pairwise comparison matrix, the consistency is checked, and the matrix is renewed if it is not consistent.

Step 4. Constructing supermatrix: A partitioned matrix representing these influences, called the "supermatrix", is constructed in the form of Eq. (2.3) where W_{11} denotes the priority vector of elements in cluster i influenced by cluster j.

$$S = \begin{bmatrix} W_{11} & W_{12} & \dots & W_{1m} \\ W_{21} & W_{22} & \dots & W_{2m} \\ \vdots & \vdots & \ddots & \vdots \\ W_{m1} & W_{m2} & \dots & W_{mm} \end{bmatrix} \tag{2.2}$$

$$W_{ij} = \begin{bmatrix} w_1 \\ w_2 \\ \vdots \\ w_n \end{bmatrix} \tag{2.3}$$

Step 5. Constructing weighted supermatrix: Then the supermatrix is normalized and multiplied by cluster weights.

$$S^w = \begin{bmatrix} W^w{}_{11} & W^w{}_{12} & \dots & W^w{}_{1m} \\ W^w{}_{21} & W^w{}_{22} & \dots & W^w{}_{2m} \\ \vdots & \vdots & \ddots & \vdots \\ W^w{}_{m1} & W^w{}_{m2} & \dots & W^w{}_{mm} \end{bmatrix} \tag{2.4}$$

The weighted supermatrix is a stochastic matrix, which means that the total values in each column are equal to 1.

$$\sum_{k=1}^{m} W^w{}_{mk} = 1 \tag{2.5}$$

Step 6. Constructing the limit matrix: The weighted supermatrix is raised to limiting powers through matrix exponentiation to converge to stable weights, reflecting the cumulative influence of each element. The resulting columns provide global priorities, in other words, final weights.

$$L = \begin{bmatrix} L_{11} & L_{12} & \dots & L_{1m} \\ L_{21} & L_{22} & \dots & L_{2m} \\ \vdots & \vdots & \ddots & \vdots \\ L_{m1} & L_{m2} & \dots & L_{mm} \end{bmatrix} \tag{2.6}$$

The part of the limit matrix showing the weights of the alternatives is used as the final result of the process.

The criteria of the service provider selection problem for the university cafeteria case are cost (C1), quality (C2), variety (C3), health and hygiene (C4), and student satisfaction (C5), and there are three alternatives: A1, A2, and A3. The network regarding the problem is shown in Fig. 2.9. The arrows show the dependencies between the criteria.

The structure of the supermatrix for the given case is shown in Table 2.1. The empty cells show the cells with a value 0.

In Table 2.1, the cells with values w_{21}, w_{31}, to w_{61} show the weight vectors resulting from pairwise comparison of the criteria with respect to the goal. The cells, w_{72}, w_{82}, and w_{92} shows the weight vectors resulting from pairwise comparison of the alternatives with respect to Criterion 1. The values w_{23} and w_{53} represent the relative weight of dependence degrees of C1 and C4 on C2. In order to find these values, a pairwise comparison matrix is constructed, and the decision maker is

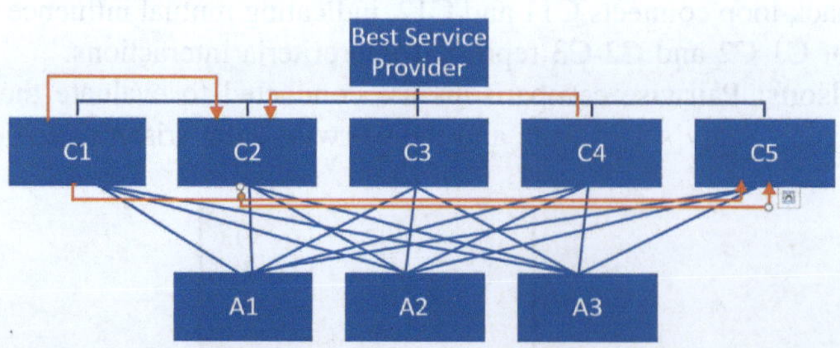

FIGURE 2.9 The decision model for service provider selection for a university cafeteria.

TABLE 2.1 Structure of the supermatrix.

		Goal	Criteria					Alternatives		
		G	**C1**	**C2**	**C3**	**C4**	**C5**	**A1**	**A2**	**A3**
Goal	G									
Criteria	C1	w_{21}		w_{23}			w_{26}			
	C2	w_{31}					w_{36}			
	C3	w_{41}								
	C4	w_{51}		w_{53}						
	C5	w_{61}								
Alternatives	A1		w_{72}	w_{73}	w_{74}	w_{75}	w_{76}			
	A2		w_{82}	w_{83}	w_{84}	w_{85}	w_{86}			
	A3		w_{92}	w_{93}	w_{94}	w_{95}	w_{96}			

TABLE 2.2 Supermatrix for the service provider selection case.

		Goal	Criteria					Alternatives		
		G	**C1**	**C2**	**C3**	**C4**	**C5**	**A1**	**A2**	**A3**
Goal	G	0	0	0	0	0	0	0	0	0
Criteria	C1	0.58	0	0.27	0	0	0.5	0	0	0
	C2	0.099	0	0	0	0	0.5	0	0	0
	C3	0.034	0	0	0	0	0	0	0	0
	C4	0.137	0	0.75	0	0	0	0	0	0
	C5	0.146	0	0	0	0	0	0	0	0
Alternatives	A1	0	0.16	0.33	0.46	0.75	0.25	1	0	0
	A2	0	0.59	0.33	0.09	0.06	0.5	0	1	0
	A3	0	0.25	0.33	0.46	0.19	0.25	0	0	1

asked to compare the degree of dependencies. In the same manner, w_{26} and w_{36} show the relative weight of dependence levels of C1 and C2 on C5. Table 2.2 represents the supermatrix for the service provider selection problem.

After the supermatrix is formed, the next step is to derive the weighted supermatrix. In order to calculate the weighted supermatrix, the weight values are normalized so that the sum of the values in each column equals 1. Table 2.3 shows the weighted supermatrix for service provider selection.

In order to obtain the final results, the weighted supermatrix is raised to its powers. The raising process ends when the matrix converges. In Table 2.4, the limit matrix for the service provider selection case is given.

According to the results given in Table 2.4, Alternative 1 has a weight of 0.30, Alternative 2 has a weight of 0.45, and Alternative 3 has a weight of 0.25. The results reveal that Alternative 2 is the best alternative.

2.3.2 Fuzzy analytic network process approaches

FANP has emerged as a powerful tool for modeling uncertainties in linguistic evaluations, particularly in complex decision-making problems characterized by interdependent criteria. Over time, significant advancements have been made

TABLE 2.3 Weighted supermatrix for the service provider selection case.

		Goal	Criteria					Alternatives		
		G	C1	C2	C3	C4	C5	A1	A2	A3
Goal	G	0	0	0	0	0	0	0	0	0
Criteria	C1	0.58	0	0.13	0	0	0.25	0	0	0
	C2	0.1	0	0	0	0	0.25	0	0	0
	C3	0.03	0	0	0	0	0	0	0	0
	C4	0.14	0	0.37	0	0	0	0	0	0
	C5	0.15	0	0	0	0	0	0	0	0
Alternatives	A1	0	0.16	0.16	0.46	0.75	0.13	1	0	0
	A2	0	0.59	0.16	0.09	0.06	0.25	0	1	0
	A3	0	0.25	0.16	0.46	0.19	0.13	0	0	1

TABLE 2.4 Limit matrix for the service provider selection case.

		Goal	Criteria					Alternatives		
		G	C1	C2	C3	C4	C5	A1	A2	A3
Goal	G	0	0	0	0	0	0	0	0	0
Criteria	C1	0	0	0	0	0	0	0	0	0
	C2	0	0	0	0	0	0	0	0	0
	C3	0	0	0	0	0	0	0	0	0
	C4	0	0	0	0	0	0	0	0	0
	C5	0	0	0	0	0	0	0	0	0
Alternatives	A1	0.3	0.16	0.47	0.46	0.75	0.28	1	0	0
	A2	0.45	0.59	0.27	0.09	0.06	0.46	0	1	0
	A3	0.25	0.25	0.27	0.46	0.19	0.25	0	0	1

in this field, leading to the development of various FANP extensions. These extensions employ different types of fuzzy numbers, each offering distinct approaches to handling uncertainty. While the ANP method represents a generalized form of the AHP, the fuzzy version of ANP has not achieved the same level of popularity as fuzzy AHP, primarily due to its more complex computational procedures. Despite this, FANP remains a well-researched methodology in the literature, with numerous extensions incorporating various fuzzy number types to enhance its flexibility and applicability. As a result, FANP has found widespread application across multiple domains, including risk assessment, supply chain management, and strategic decision-making.

This section first presents the fundamental steps of crisp ANP (which serves as the basis for fuzzy extensions), followed by an analysis of various FANP extensions and their distinguishing characteristics.

2.3.2.1 Ordinary fuzzy analytic network process

The FANP extends the traditional ANP by incorporating fuzzy set theory to handle linguistic uncertainties in decision-making. Mikhailov and Singh (2003) proposed a fuzzy extension of the ANP to handle uncertain and imprecise human judgments in decision-making. Unlike classical ANP, which relies on crisp pairwise comparisons and the eigenvector method, their approach incorporates fuzzy logic to model interval-based or fuzzy preference inputs, enhancing the method's robustness in real-world scenarios where human judgments are inherently vague. One of the earliest and most influential FANP methodologies was proposed by Büyüközkan et al. (2004), who applied triangular fuzzy numbers (TFNs) to prioritize design requirements in the house of quality. This approach was groundbreaking at the time, as it allowed decision-makers to express judgments using linguistic terms (e.g., "very important," "moderate," "weak") and then convert them into fuzzy numbers for computation. However, this method relied on Chang's extent analysis (1996) for fuzzy pairwise comparisons, a technique that has since been widely criticized for its mathematical inconsistencies. Despite its limitations, Büyüközkan et al.'s approach laid the foundation for many subsequent FANP extensions. The steps of this algorithm are summarized below (Büyüközkan et al., 2024):

- Step 1. Identify the main criteria and relevant subcriteria
- Step 2. Calculation of the initial criterion weight vector (w_1): Assuming no dependence among main criteria, determine their importance degrees using linguistic data.
- Step 3. Calculation of subcriteria weight relative to each main criterion (W_2): Assuming no dependence among subcriteria, determine the importance degrees with respect to each main criterion using linguistic data.
- Step 4. Calculation of the main criteria interdependence matrix (W_3): Determine the inner dependence matrix of the main criteria with respect to each main criterion using linguistic data, based on the schematic representation of inner dependence among main criteria.
- Step 5. Calculation of subcriteria interdependence matrix (W_4): Determine the inner dependence matrix of the subcriteria with respect to each subcriterion using linguistic data, based on the schematic representation of inner dependence among subcriteria.
- Step 6. Calculate the interdependent priorities of the main criteria (w_C): Initial criterion weight vector multiplied by the main criteria interdependence matrix:

$$w_C = W_3 \times w_1 \tag{2.7}$$

Step 7. Calculate the interdependent priorities of the sub criteria (W_A): multiplication of sub criteria interdependence matrix with sub criteria weight

$$W_A = W_2 \times W_4 \tag{2.8}$$

Step 8. Determine the overall priorities of the sub criteria (W_{ANP}): Multiply the interdependent priorities of the sub criteria with the interdependent priorities of the main criteria:

$$W_{ANP} = W_A \times w_C \tag{2.9}$$

In the studies employing ordinary FANP methodologies, Wu et al. (2008) proposed a fuzzy extension of the ANP that incorporates uncertain human preferences as input data for decision-making. Their approach replaces the classical Eigenvector prioritization method used in the standard ANP with a novel fuzzy preference programming technique, which derives precise priority weights from inconsistent interval and fuzzy judgments. Tadić et al. (2014) introduced an advanced FANP methodology that employs logarithmic fuzzy preference programming for deriving priority weights from pairwise comparison matrices. Zečević et al. (2017) proposed a fuzzy Delphi-based ANP methodology in which the fuzzy Delphi method was used to aggregate individual expert assessments.

2.3.2.2 Advanced fuzzy extensions of analytic network process

As new fuzzy number extensions emerge, several advanced FANP extensions have been introduced. Some of the advanced FANP methodologies are summarized below:

2.3.2.3 Type-2 fuzzy analytic network process

Wu and Liu (2016) proposed a FANP method with interval type-2 fuzzy sets to evaluate enterprise technology innovation ability. In this paper, an interval type-2 trapezoidal fuzzy scale is used for the linguistic variables, and fuzziness is preserved until the final stages. After the fuzzy weighted supermatrix is defuzzified, the limit supermatrix is obtained using the eigenvalue method. A linguistic scale that could be used in type-2 FANP is given in Table 2.5. The defuzzification of the fuzzy numbers given in the scale is generally the preferred way in the application of type-2 FANP.

TABLE 2.5 Linguistic scales of type-2 fuzzy analytic network process.

Linguistic variables	Interval type-2 trapezoidal fuzzy sets
Absolutely more important than	(7, 8, 10, 11; 1) (7.5, 8.5, 9.5, 10.5; 0.9)
Much more important than	(5, 6, 8, 9; 1) (5.5, 6.5, 7.5, 8.5; 0.9)
more important than	(3, 4, 6, 7; 1) (3.5, 4.5, 5.5, 6.5; 0.9)
Slightly more important than	(1, 2, 4, 5; 1) (1.5, 2.5, 3.5, 4.5; 0.9)
Equal importance	(1, 1, 1, 1; 1)(1, 1, 1, 1; 1)
Slightly less important than	$(\frac{1}{5}, \frac{1}{4}, \frac{1}{2}, 1; 1)(\frac{10}{45}, \frac{10}{35}, \frac{10}{25}, \frac{10}{15}; 0.9)$
less important than	$(\frac{1}{7}, \frac{1}{6}, \frac{1}{4}, \frac{1}{3}; 1)(\frac{10}{65}, \frac{10}{55}, \frac{10}{45}, \frac{10}{35}; 0.9)$
Much less important than	$(\frac{1}{9}, \frac{1}{8}, \frac{1}{6}, \frac{1}{5}; 1)(\frac{10}{85}, \frac{10}{75}, \frac{10}{65}, \frac{10}{55}; 0.9)$
Absolutely less important than	$(\frac{1}{11}, \frac{1}{10}, \frac{1}{8}, \frac{1}{7}; 1)(\frac{10}{105}, \frac{10}{95}, \frac{10}{85}, \frac{10}{75}; 0.9)$

TABLE 2.6 Linguistic scales of intuitionistic fuzzy analytic network process.

Linguistic variables	Intuitionistic fuzzy numbers
Absolutely more important than	(0.90, 0.10)
Much more important than	(0.80, 0.15)
More important than	(0.70, 0.25)
Slightly more important than	(0.60, 0.35)
Equal importance	(0.50, 0.50)
Slightly less important than	(0.35, 0.60)
less important than	(0.25, 0.70)
Much less important than	(0.15, 0.80)
Absolutely less important than	(0.10, 0.90)

2.3.2.4 *Intuitionistic fuzzy analytic network process*

Saeedi et al. (2008) developed an intuitionistic FANP method that employs triangular intuitionistic fuzzy (IF) numbers for pairwise comparisons. In the proposed method, the decision-maker specifies vagueness using TFNs, along with their belief degree and nonbelief degree for the pairwise comparisons. Based on these degrees, a fuzzification factor is introduced, and an IF decision matrix is obtained. The upper and lower bounds of the comparisons are aggregated by introducing an optimism index, enabling the algorithm to incorporate the decision-maker's attitude toward judgment fuzziness. The supermatrix is then constructed using α-cuts. An example of a linguistic scale for IF-ANP is given in Table 2.6.

2.3.2.5 *Neutrosophic analytic network process*

Abdel-Basset et al. (2018) introduced a neutrosophic ANP methodology for supplier selection problems, integrating it with the TOPSIS approach. In their proposed framework, pairwise comparisons are expressed using interval-valued neutrosophic numbers. A de-neutrosophication function is then applied to convert these neutrosophic values into crisp equivalents, meaning that defuzzification occurs at the initial stage of the methodology. The linguistic scale that can be used for neutrosophic ANP evaluations is provided in Table 2.7.

TABLE 2.7 Linguistic scales of neutrosophic analytic network process.

Linguistic variables	Neutrosophic numbers
Absolutely more important than	(1, 0.1, 0.1)
Much more important than	(0.9, 0.1, 0.2)
more important than	(0.8, 0.2, 0.3)
Slightly more important than	(0.7, 0.3, 0.4)
Equal importance	(0.5, 0.5, 0.5)
Slightly less important than	(0.4, 0.3, 0.7)
less important than	(0.3, 0.2, 0.8)
Much less important than	(0.2, 0.1, 0.9)
Absolutely less important than	(0.1, 0.1, 1)

TABLE 2.8 Linguistic scales of Pythagorean fuzzy analytic network process.

Linguistic variables	Pythagorean fuzzy numbers
Absolutely more important than	(0.95, 0.15)
Much more important than	(0.90, 0.20)
More important than	(0.85, 0.25)
Slightly more important than	(0.80, 0.35)
Equal importance	(0.50, 0.50)
Slightly less important than	(0.35, 0.80)
less important than	(0.25, 0.85)
Much less important than	(0.20, 0.90)
Absolutely less important than	(0.15, 0.95)

2.3.2.6 Pythagorean fuzzy analytic network process

Yaman (2020) extended the ANP methodology using interval-valued Pythagorean fuzzy numbers and applied it to the warehouse location selection problem. In this study, prior to constructing the supermatrix, the fuzzy interval multiplicative matrix is computed, and the corresponding weight matrix is normalized into a crisp form. An example of linguistic scales that can be used in Pythagorean FANP is given in Table 2.8.

2.3.2.7 Picture fuzzy analytic network process

Although their application has not been widely documented in existing literature, picture fuzzy numbers hold potential for integration into the FANP. As illustrated in Table 2.9, a linguistic scale based on picture fuzzy numbers is provided to facilitate such implementations.

2.3.2.8 Spherical fuzzy analytic network process

Erdoğan et al. (2021) introduced a spherical FANP extension and applied it to the risk assessment of autonomous vehicle driving systems, integrating DEMATEL and VIKOR methods. Prior to constructing the supermatrix, they defuzzified the spherical fuzzy numbers. Linguistic scales for spherical FANP is provided in Table 2.10.

TABLE 2.9 Linguistic scales of picture fuzzy analytic network process.

Linguistic variables	Picture fuzzy numbers
Absolutely more important than	(0.9, 0.05, 0.05)
Much more important than	(0.8, 0.1, 0.1)
More important than	(0.7, 0.05, 0.2)
Slightly more important than	(0.6, 0.05, 0.3)
Equal importance	(0.5, 0, 0.5)
Slightly less important than	(0.3, 0.05, 0.6)
less important than	(0.2, 0.05, 0.7)
Much less important than	(0.1, 0.1, 0.8)
Absolutely less important than	(0.05, 0.05, 0.9)

TABLE 2.10 Linguistic scales of spherical fuzzy analytic network process.

Linguistic variables	Spherical fuzzy numbers
Absolutely more important than	(0.9, 0.1, 0.1)
Much more important than	(0.8, 0.2, 0.2)
More important than	(0.7, 0.3, 0.3)
Slightly more important than	(0.6, 0.4, 0.4)
Equal importance	(0.5, 0.5, 0.5)
Slightly less important than	(0.4, 0.4, 0.6)
less important than	(0.3, 0.3, 0.7)
Much less important than	(0.2, 0.2, 0.8)
Absolutely less important than	(0.1, 0.1, 0.9)

2.3.2.9 Fermatean fuzzy analytic network process

Lo et al. (2025) developed an Interval Fermatean fuzzy DEMATEL-based ANP methodology to assess the sustainability and risk resilience of international airports. This hybrid methodology integrates the group judgment integration technique and DEMATEL-based ANP to handle uncertainty and aggregate expert judgments. The Fermatean fuzzy scale that can be used in Fermatean FANP is given in Table 2.11.

2.3.2.10 A proportional picture fuzzy analytic network process approach

2.3.2.10.1 Proportional picture fuzzy sets

Consider the picture fuzzy set $\widetilde{T} = \{\langle x; \mu_{\widetilde{T}}(x), \ \pi_{\widetilde{T}}(x), \ \vartheta_{\widetilde{T}}(x)\rangle | x \epsilon X\}$. Assume that the expert judges the proportions between $\mu_{\widetilde{T}}(x)$, $\vartheta_{\widetilde{T}}(x)$, and $\pi_{\widetilde{T}}(x)$ as in Eqs. (2.10–2.12) (Kahraman et al., 2004):

$$\mu(x) = k_1 r_{\widetilde{T}}(x) \tag{2.10}$$

$$\pi(x) = k_2 r_{\widetilde{T}}(x) \tag{2.11}$$

TABLE 2.11 Linguistic scales of Fermatean fuzzy analytic network process.

Linguistic variables	Fermatean fuzzy numbers
Absolutely more important than	(0.95, 0.25)
Much more important than	(0.90, 0.30)
More important than	(0.85, 0.35)
Slightly more important than	(0.80, 0.40)
Equal importance	(0.50, 0.50)
Slightly less important than	(0.40, 0.80)
less important than	(0.35, 0.85)
Much less important than	(0.30, 0.90)
Absolutely less important than	(0.25, 0.95)

and

$$\vartheta(x) = k_3 r_{\widetilde{T}}(x) \tag{2.12}$$

satisfying

$$r_{\widetilde{T}}(x) + k_1 r_{\widetilde{T}}(x) + k_2 r_{\widetilde{T}}(x) + k_3 r_{\widetilde{T}}(x) = 1 \tag{2.13}$$

The refusal degree can be given by (2.14)

$$r_{\widetilde{T}}(x) = \frac{1}{1 + k_1 + k_2 + k_3} \tag{2.14}$$

Then, each element in the set $\widetilde{T}$ can be represented by

$$\widetilde{T} = \left\{ \left\langle x; k_1 \frac{1}{1 + k_1 + k_2 + k_3}, k_2 \frac{1}{1 + k_1 + k_2 + k_3}, k_3 \frac{1}{1 + k_1 + k_2 + k_3} \right\rangle | x \in X \right\} \tag{2.15}$$

Let $\widetilde{A}$ and $\widetilde{B}$ be two proportional picture fuzzy sets: $\widetilde{A} = \{\langle x;\mu_{\widetilde{A}}(x), \pi_{\widetilde{A}}(x), \vartheta_{\widetilde{A}}(x)\rangle | x \epsilon X\}$ and $\widetilde{B} = \{\langle x;\mu_{\widetilde{B}}(x), \pi_{\widetilde{B}}(x), \vartheta_{\widetilde{B}}(x)\rangle | x \epsilon X\}$. Addition and multiplication operations are defined as in Eqs. (2.16–2.17), respectively.

$$\widetilde{A} + \widetilde{B} = \left(\begin{array}{l} x, \quad k_{A1}\frac{1}{1+k_{A1}+k_{A2}+k_{A3}} + k_{B1}\frac{1}{1+k_{B1}+k_{B2}+k_{B3}} - k_{A1}\frac{1}{1+k_{A1}+k_{A2}+k_{A3}} \times k_{B1}\frac{1}{1+k_{B1}+k_{B2}+k_{B3}}, k_{A2}\frac{1}{1+k_{A1}+k_{A2}+k_{A3}} \\ \times k_{B2}\frac{1}{1+k_{B1}+k_{B2}+k_{B3}}, \\ \qquad k_{A3}\frac{1}{1+k_{A1}+k_{A2}+k_{A3}} \times k_{B3}\frac{1}{1+k_{B1}+k_{B2}+k_{B3}} \Big| x \in X \end{array} \right) \tag{2.16}$$

$$\begin{aligned} \widetilde{A} \times \widetilde{B} = \Big(x, & k_{A1}\frac{1}{1 + k_{A1} + k_{A2} + k_{A3}} \times k_{B1}\frac{1}{1 + k_{B1} + k_{B2} + k_{B3}}, k_{A2}\frac{1}{1 + k_{A1} + k_{A2} + k_{A3}} \\ & + k_{B2}\frac{1}{1 + k_{B1} + k_{B2} + k_{B3}} - k_{A2}\frac{1}{1 + k_{A1} + k_{A2} + k_{A3}} \\ & \times k_{B2}\frac{1}{1 + k_{B1} + k_{B2} + k_{B3}}, k_{A3}\frac{1}{1 + k_{A1} + k_{A2} + k_{A3}} \\ & + k_{B3}\frac{1}{1 + k_{B1} + k_{B2} + k_{B3}} - k_{A3}\frac{1}{1 + k_{A1} + k_{A2} + k_{A3}} \times k_{B3}\frac{1}{1 + k_{B1} + k_{B2} + k_{B3}} | x \in X \Big) \end{aligned} \tag{2.17}$$

The multiplication by a constant and power operation is given by Eqs. (2.18–2.19), respectively.

$$\lambda \cdot \widetilde{A} = \left\langle 1 - \left(1 - k_{A1}\frac{1}{1 + k_{A1} + k_{A2} + k_{A3}}\right)^{\lambda}, \left(k_{A2}\frac{1}{1 + k_{A1} + k_{A2} + k_{A3}}\right)^{\lambda}, \left(k_{A3}\frac{1}{1 + k_{A1} + k_{A2} + k_{A3}}\right)^{\lambda} \right\rangle \tag{2.18}$$

$$\begin{aligned} \widetilde{A}^{\lambda} = &< \left(k_{A1}\frac{1}{1 + k_{A1} + k_{A2} + k_{A3}}\right)^{\lambda}, 1 - \left(1 - k_{A2}\frac{1}{1 + k_{A1} + k_{A2} + k_{A3}}\right)^{\lambda}, 1 \\ &- \left(1 - k_{A3}\frac{1}{1 + k_{A1} + k_{A2} + k_{A3}}\right)^{\lambda} > \end{aligned} \tag{2.19}$$

2.3.2.10.2 Proportional picture fuzzy pairwise comparison matrix and calculation of weights

A pairwise comparison matrix of n criteria whose proportional picture fuzzy (PPF) elements are $x_{ij} = (k_{1ij}, k_{2ij}, k_{3ij})$, $i = 1, 2, \ldots, n$; $j=1,2,\ldots,n$ is given by Eq. (2.20) by using the proportion triplets:

$$\widetilde{P}\,(k_1, k_2, k_3) = \begin{bmatrix} 1 & \cdots & (k_{11n}, k_{21n}, k_{31n}) \\ \vdots & (k_{1ij}, k_{2ij}, k_{3ij}) & \vdots \\ (k_{31n}, k_{21n}, k_{11n}) & \cdots & 1 \end{bmatrix} \tag{2.20}$$

where there is a relation between reciprocal values such that $(k_{11n}, k_{21n}, k_{31n}) \rightarrow (k_{31n}, k_{21n}, k_{11n})$. The matrix in Eq. (2.20) is transformed to Eq. (2.21):

$$\widetilde{P}_P\,(k_1, k_2, k_3) = \begin{bmatrix} 1 & \cdots & \left(\begin{array}{c} k_{11n}\frac{1}{1+k_{11n}+k_{21n}+k_{31n}}, k_{21n}\frac{1}{1+k_{11n}+k_{21n}+k_{31n}}, \\ k_{31n}\frac{1}{1+k_{11n}+k_{21n}+k_{31n}} \end{array} \right) \\ \vdots & \ddots & \vdots \\ \left(\begin{array}{c} k_{31n}\frac{1}{1+k_{11n}+k_{21n}+k_{31n}}, k_{21n}\frac{1}{1+k_{11n}+k_{21n}+k_{31n}}, \\ k_{11n}\frac{1}{1+k_{11n}+k_{21n}+k_{31n}} \end{array} \right) & \cdots & 1 \end{bmatrix} \tag{2.21}$$

Then, by computing the score function as in Eq. (2.22), we obtain the crisp pairwise comparison matrix P given as in Eq. (2.23). In Eq. (2.22), the comparison of x_{ij} with x_{ji} is realized. When $i \neq j$, use the second row if it gives a positive value; but if it gives zero or a negative value, compute the reciprocal value by using the same formula for the comparison of x_{ji} with x_{ij}. (5, 5, 5) indicates that the comparison value equals 1.

$$S\,(k_1, k_2, k_3) = \begin{cases} 1, \; if \; i = j \\ 10 \times \left(k_{11n}\frac{1}{1+k_{11n}+k_{21n}+k_{31n}} + \left(k_{21n}\frac{1}{1+k_{11n}+k_{21n}+k_{31n}} \right) / 2 - k_{31n}\frac{1}{1+k_{11n}+k_{21n}+k_{31n}} \right) \end{cases} \tag{2.22}$$

$$P = \begin{bmatrix} 1 & \cdots & S_{1n}\,(k_1, k_2, k_3) \\ \vdots & \ddots & \vdots \\ S_{n1}\,(k_1, k_2, k_3) & \cdots & 1 \end{bmatrix} \tag{2.23}$$

Consistency of a crisp decision matrix is measured by Eq. (2.24) (Saaty, 1980), and the matrix is corrected if the consistency ratio (CI) is larger than 0.10.

$$CR = \left(\frac{\lambda_{max} - n}{n - 1} \right) / RI \tag{2.24}$$

where λ_{max} is the eigenvalue; n is the dimension of the square matrix; and RI is the random index for the considered square matrix.

2.4 Numerical example 1: classical analytic network process

Let's consider the network given in Fig. 2.8. The goal is to select the most suitable device for a graduate student who will use it for data analysis and research. The student determined the six most important criteria for the selection as display quality (C11), processing speed (C12), and battery life (C13), storage capacity (C14), build quality (C15), and weight (C16) in Cluster 1. The six alternatives are given in Cluster 2. The inner and outer relations are also illustrated in Fig. 2.10. The influence matrix is given in Table 2.12.

The linguistic scale is given in Table 2.13. Decision makers can assign the numeric or linguistic terms in the pairwise comparison matrices.

The pairwise comparison matrices based on the influence matrix are constructed as in Table 2.14.

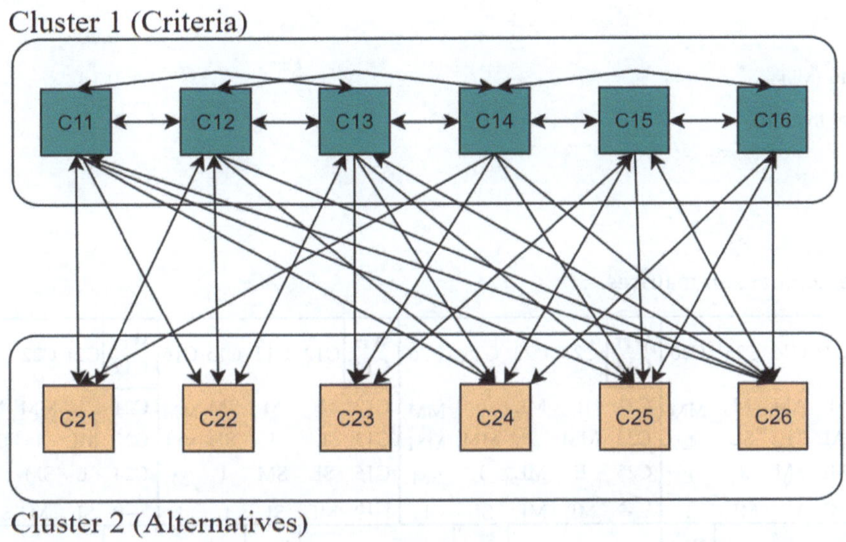

FIGURE 2.10 Network.

TABLE 2.12 Influence matrix.

		Cluster 1(criteria)						Cluster 2(alternatives)					
		C11	C12	C13	C14	C15	C16	C21	C22	C23	C24	C25	C26
Cluster 1(criteria)	C11	0	1	1	0	0	0	1	0	0	0	0	1
	C12	1	0	1	1	0	0	1	1	0	0	0	0
	C13	1	1	0	1	0	0	0	1	0	0	0	1
	C14	0	1	1	0	1	1	0	0	0	0	0	0
	C15	0	0	0	1	0	1	0	0	1	1	0	1
	C16	0	0	0	1	1	0	0	0	0	0	1	0
Cluster 2 (alternatives)	C21	1	1	0	1	0	0	0	0	0	0	0	0
	C22	1	1	1	0	0	0	0	0	0	0	0	0
	C23	0	0	1	1	1	0	0	0	0	0	0	0
	C24	1	1	1	0	1	1	0	0	0	0	0	0
	C25	1	0	1	1	1	1	0	0	0	0	0	0
	C26	1	1	1	1	1	1	0	0	0	0	0	0

TABLE 2.13 Linguistic scale.

Linguistic variables	Crisp numbers
Absolutely more important than (AM)	9
Much more important than (MM)	7
More important than (M)	5
Slightly more important than (SM)	3
Equal importance (E)	1
Slightly less important than (SL)	0.33
Less important than (L)	0.20
Much less important than (ML)	0.14
Absolutely less important than (AL)	0.11

TABLE 2.14 Pairwise comparison matrices.

Wrt C15	C23	C24	C25	C26
C23	1	AM	M	MM
C24	AL	1	SL	L
C25	ML	SM	1	L
C26	ML	ML	ML	1

Wrt C14	C21	C23	C25	C26
C21	1	ML	E	MM
C23	MM	1	MM	MM
C25	E	ML	1	SM
C26	ML	ML	SL	1

Wrt C14	C12	C13	C15	C16
C12	1	M	SM	MM
C13	L	1	SL	SM
C15	SL	SM	1	M
C16	ML	SL	L	1

Wrt C12	C21	C22	C24	C26
C21	1	MM	M	SM
C22	ML	1	SL	L
C24	L	SM	1	SL
C26	SL	M	SM	1

Wrt C12	C11	C13	C14
C11	1	SM	M
C13	SL	1	SM
C14	L	SL	1

Wrt C13	C11	C12	C14
C11	1	M	MM
C12	L	1	SM
C14	ML	SL	1

Wrt C26	C11	C13	C15
C11	1	SM	MM
C13	SL	1	M
C15	ML	L	1

Wrt C16	C24	C25	C26
C24	1	M	AM
C25	SL	1	M
C26	ML	L	1

Wrt C15	C14	C16
C14	1	ML
C16	MM	1

Wrt C11	C12	C13
C12	1	AM
C13	AL	1

Wrt C16	C14	C15
C14	1	SL
C15	SM	1

Wrt C21	C11	C12
C11	1	M
C12	L	1

Wrt C22	C12	C13
C12	1	E
C13	E	1

Wrt C11	C21	C22	C24	C25	C26
C21	1	SM	M	MM	AM
C22	SL	1	SM	MM	MM
C24	L	SL	1	SM	M
C25	ML	L	SL	1	SM
C26	AL	ML	L	SL	1

Wrt C13	C22	C23	C24	C25	C26
C22	1	MM	AM	AM	AM
C23	L	1	SM	M	MM
C24	AL	SL	1	SM	M
C25	AL	L	SL	1	SM
C26	AL	ML	L	SL	1

Table 2.15 gives the corresponding numbers of the linguistic terms.

The consistency check was made before further processing. Table 2.16 presents the computed priorities for the super matrix from Table 2.15.

Table 2.17 gives the weighted supermatrix.

The limit supermatrix is computed by raising the weighted supermatrix to powers until it converges. Table 2.18 gives the limit supermatrix when the 64th power is applied.

TABLE 2.15 Values of pairwise comparison matrices.

Wrt C15	C23	C24	C25	C26
C23	1	9	5	7
C24	0.11	1	0.33	0.2
C25	0.14	3	1	0.2
C26	0.14	0.14	0.14	1

Wrt C14	C21	C23	C25	C26
C21	1	0.14	1	7
C23	7	1	7	7
C25	1	0.14	1	3
C26	0.14	0.14	0.33	1

Wrt C14	C12	C13	C15	C16
C12	1	5	3	7
C13	0.2	1	0.33	3
C15	0.33	3	1	5
C16	0.14	0.33	0.2	1

Wrt C12	C21	C22	C24	C26
C21	1	7	5	3
C22	0.14	1	0.33	0.2
C24	0.2	3	1	0.33
C26	0.33	5	3	1

Wrt C12	C11	C13	C14
C11	1	3	5
C13	0.33	1	3
C14	0.2	0.33	1

Wrt C13	C11	C12	C14
C11	1	5	7
C12	0.2	1	3
C14	0.14	0.33	1

Wrt C26	C11	C13	C15
C11	1	3	7
C13	0.33	1	5
C15	0.14	0.2	1

Wrt C16	C24	C25	C26
C24	1	5	9
C25	0.33	1	5
C26	0.14	0.2	1

Wrt C15	C14	C16
C14	1	0.14
C16	7	1

Wrt C11	C12	C13
C12	1	9
C13	0.11	1

Wrt C16	C14	C15
C14	1	0.33
C15	3	1

Wrt C21	C11	C12
C11	1	5
C12	0.2	1

Wrt C22	C12	C13
C12	1	1
C13	1	1

Wrt C11	C21	C22	C24	C25	C26
C21	1	3	5	7	9
C22	0.33	1	3	7	7
C24	0.2	0.33	1	3	5
C25	0.14	0.2	0.33	1	3

Wrt C13	C22	C23	C24	C25	C26
C22	1	7	9	9	9
C23	0.2	1	3	5	7
C24	0.11	0.33	1	3	5
C25	0.11	0.2	0.33	1	3

TABLE 2.16 Priorities for the super matrix.

		Cluster 1(criteria)						Cluster 2(alternatives)					
		C11	**C12**	**C13**	**C14**	**C15**	**C16**	**C21**	**C22**	**C23**	**C24**	**C25**	**C26**
Cluster 1(criteria)	C11	0	0.634	0.724	0	0	0	0.833	0	0	0	0	0.644
	C12	0.9	0	0.193	0.559	0	0	0.167	0.5	0	0	0	0
	C13	0.1	0.26	0	0.122	0	0	0	0.5	0	0	0	0.282
	C14	0	0.106	0.083	0	0.124	0.249	0	0	0	0	0	0
	C15	0	0	0	0.263	0	0.751	0	0	1	1	0	0.073
	C16	0	0	0	0.056	0.876	0	0	0	0	0	1	0
Cluster 2 (alternatives)	C21	0.494	0.559	0	0.176	0	0	0	0	0	0	0	0
	C22	0.275	0.056	0.595	0	0	0	0	0	0	0	0	0
	C23	0	0	0.204	0.652	0.753	0	0	0	0	0	0	0
	C24	0.13	0.122	0.11	0	0.058	0.696	0	0	0	0	0	0
	C25	0.066	0	0.059	0.12	0.127	0.24	0	0	0	0	0	0
	C26	0.034	0.263	0.032	0.051	0.063	0.065	0	0	0	0	0	0

TABLE 2.17 Weighted supermatrix.

		Cluster 1(criteria)						Cluster 2(alternatives)					
		C11	C12	C13	C14	C15	C16	C21	C22	C23	C24	C25	C26
Cluster 1(criteria)	C11	0	0.317	0.362	0	0	0	0.833	0	0	0	0	0.645
	C12	0.45	0	0.097	0.28	0	0	0.167	0.5	0	0	0	0
	C13	0.05	0.13	0	0.061	0	0	0	0.5	0	0	0	0.282
	C14	0	0.053	0.042	0	0.062	0.124	0	0	0	0	0	0
	C15	0	0	0	0.132	0	0.375	0	0	1	1	0	0.073
	C16	0	0	0	0.028	0.438	0	0	0	0	0	1	0
Cluster 2 (alternatives)	C21	0.247	0.28	0	0.088	0	0	0	0	0	0	0	0
	C22	0.138	0.028	0.298	0	0	0	0	0	0	0	0	0
	C23	0	0	0.102	0.326	0.376	0	0	0	0	0	0	0
	C24	0.065	0.061	0.055	0	0.029	0.348	0	0	0	0	0	0
	C25	0.033	0	0.03	0.06	0.063	0.12	0	0	0	0	0	0
	C26	0.017	0.132	0.016	0.026	0.031	0.032	0	0	0	0	0	0

From Table 2.19, the set of computed weights are normalized. First, the computed weights of alternatives are summed as $0.052 + 0.028 + 0.11 + 0.073 + 0.04 + 0.027 = 0.33$. Then, each weight is divided by the sum. The final weights of the alternatives are $w_{C21} = 0.158$, $w_{C22} = 0.086$, $w_{C23} = 0.331$, $w_{C24} = 0.221$, $w_{C25} = 0.122$, $w_{C26} = 0.81$. The ranking is obtained as C23 > C24 > C21 > C25 > C22 > C26. The graduate student should select C23.

2.5 Numerical example 2: proportional picture fuzzy analytic network process

Let's consider the network given in Fig. 2.5. The goal is to select the best solar panel alternative based on some predetermined criteria. There are three criteria in Cluster 1 whereas there are four alternatives in Cluster 2. The influence matrix is given in Fig. 2.6. The solar panel alternatives in this network are polycrystalline (C21), monocrystalline (C22), transparent (C23) and thin-film (C24). The considered criteria are efficiency (C11), maximum power current (C12), and cost per watt (C13). The inner and outer relations are also illustrated in Fig. 2.5. The influence matrix is given in Table 2.19.

The linguistic proportional picture fuzzy scale is given in Table 2.20. Experts can assign these terms or intermediate terms such as "between equal importance and slightly more important than" in the pairwise comparison matrices (Fig. 2.11).

The pairwise comparison matrices based on the influence matrix are constructed as in Table 2.21.

Table 2.22 gives the corresponding PPF numbers of the linguistic terms.

The consistency check was made before further process. Table 2.23 presents the computed priorities for the supermatrix from Table 2.22.

Table 2.24 gives the weighted supermatrix.

The limit supermatrix is computed by raising the weighted supermatrix to powers until it converges. Table 2.25 gives the limit supermatrix when the 50th power is applied.

From Table 2.25, the set of computed weights is normalized. First we sum the computed weights $0.0329 + 0.0514 + 0.0759 + 0.1732 = 0.3334$. Then, each weight is divided by the sum. The final weights of the solar panel alternatives are $w_{C21} = 0.0987$, $w_{C22} = 0.1542$, $w_{C23} = 0.2277$, and $w_{C24} = 0.5195$. The ranking is obtained as C24 > C23 > C22 > C21.

TABLE 2.18 Limit supermatrix.

		Cluster 1(criteria)						Cluster 2(alternatives)					
		C11	**C12**	**C13**	**C14**	**C15**	**C16**	**C21**	**C22**	**C23**	**C24**	**C25**	**C26**
Cluster 1(criteria)	C11	0.102	0.102	0.102	0.102	0.101	0.101	0.102	0.102	0.101	0.101	0.101	0.102
	C12	0.084	0.084	0.084	0.084	0.083	0.083	0.084	0.084	0.083	0.083	0.083	0.084
	C13	0.04	0.04	0.04	0.04	0.04	0.04	0.04	0.04	0.04	0.04	0.04	0.04
	C14	0.04	0.04	0.04	0.04	0.04	0.04	0.04	0.04	0.04	0.04	0.04	0.04
	C15	0.246	0.246	0.246	0.245	0.244	0.244	0.246	0.246	0.244	0.244	0.244	0.246
	C16	0.149	0.149	0.149	0.149	0.148	0.148	0.149	0.149	0.148	0.148	0.148	0.149
Cluster 2(alternatives)	C21	0.052	0.052	0.052	0.052	0.052	0.052	0.052	0.052	0.052	0.052	0.052	0.052
	C22	0.028	0.029	0.029	0.028	0.028	0.028	0.029	0.029	0.028	0.028	0.028	0.028
	C23	0.11	0.11	0.11	0.109	0.109	0.109	0.11	0.11	0.109	0.109	0.109	0.11
	C24	0.073	0.073	0.073	0.073	0.072	0.073	0.073	0.073	0.073	0.073	0.073	0.073
	C25	0.04	0.04	0.04	0.04	0.04	0.04	0.04	0.04	0.04	0.04	0.04	0.04
	C26	0.027	0.027	0.027	0.027	0.027	0.027	0.027	0.027	0.027	0.027	0.027	0.027

TABLE 2.19 Influence matrix of solar panel network.

		Cluster 1 (criteria)			Cluster 2 (alternatives)			
		C_{11}	C_{12}	C_{13}	C_{21}	C_{22}	C_{23}	C_{24}
Cluster 1 (criteria)	C_{11}	0	1	0	1	1	1	0
	C_{12}	1	0	1	1	0	1	1
	C_{13}	1	1	0	1	1	0	1
Cluster 2 (alternatives)	C_{21}	1	0	1	0	0	0	0
	C_{22}	0	1	1	0	0	0	0
	C_{23}	1	0	1	0	0	0	0
	C_{24}	1	1	1	0	0	0	0

TABLE 2.20 Proportional picture fuzzy (PPF) linguistic scale.

Linguistic terms (l)	**PPF values** ($\tilde{x}_{ij}$)	**Corresponding PFS** (μ, π, ϑ)
Absolutely less important than (AL)	(1, 1, 9)	(0.08333, 0.08333, 0.75000)
Much less important than (ML)	(2, 2, 8)	(0,16667, 0.16667, 0.66667)
Less important than (L)	(3, 3, 7)	(0.25000, 0.25000, 0.58333)
Slightly less important than (SL)	(4, 4, 6)	(0.33333, 0.33333, 0.50000)
Equal importance (E)	(5, 5, 5)	(0.41667, 0.41667, 0.41667)
Slightly more important than (SM)	(6, 4, 4)	(0.50000, 0.33333, 0.33333)
More important than (M)	(7, 3, 3)	(0.58333, 0.25000, 0.25000)
Much more important than (MM)	(8, 2, 2)	(0.66667, 0.16667, 0.16667)
Absolutely more important than (AM)	(9, 1, 1)	(0.75000, 0.08333, 0.08333)

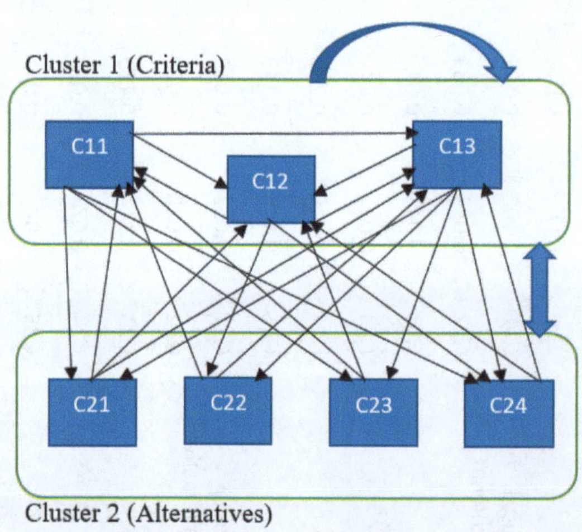

FIGURE 2.11 Network.

TABLE 2.21 Pairwise comparison matrices.

Wrt C11	C12	C13	Wrt C12	C11	C13	Wrt C22	C11	C13
C12	1	MM	C11	1	M	C11	1	SM
C13	ML	1	C13	L	1	C13	SL	1
Wrt C24	C12	C13	Wrt C12	C22	C24	Wrt C23	C11	C12
C12	1	AL	C22	1	ML	C11	1	SL
C13	AM	1	C24	MM	1	C12	SM	1
Wrt C21	C11	C12	C13	Wrt C11	C21	C23	C24	
C11	1	AM	L	C21	1	E	L	
C12	AL	1	SL	C23	E	1	SL	
C13	M	SM	1	C24	M	SM	1	
Wrt C13	C21	C22	C23	C24				
C21	1	ML	AL	AM				
C22	MM	1	SL	M				
C23	AM	SM	1	MM				
C24	AL	L	ML	1				

TABLE 2.22 Proportional picture fuzzy values of pairwise comparison matrices.

Wrt C11	C12	C13	Wrt C12	C11	C13	Wrt C22	C11	C13
C12	1	(8, 2, 2)	C11	1	(7, 3, 3)	C11	1	(6, 4, 4)
C13	(2, 8, 8)	1	C13	(3, 3, 7)	1	C13	(4, 4, 6)	1
Wrt C24	C12	C13	Wrt C12	C22	C24	Wrt C23	C11	C12
C12	1	(1, 1, 9)	C22	1	(2, 2, 8)	C11	1	(4, 4, 6)
C13	(9, 1, 1)	1	C24	(8, 2, 2)	1	C12	(6, 4, 4)	1
Wrt C21	C11	C12	C13	Wrt C11	C21	C23	C24	
C11	1	(9, 1, 1)	(3, 3, 7)	C21	1	(5, 5, 5)	(3, 3, 7)	
C12	(1, 1, 9)	1	(4, 4, 6)	C23	(5, 5, 5)	1	(4, 4, 6)	
C13	(7, 3, 3)	(6, 4, 4)	1	C24	(7, 3, 3)	(6, 4, 4)	1	
Wrt C13	C21	C22	C23	C24				
C21	1	(2, 2, 8)	(1, 1, 9)	(9, 1 ,1)				
C22	(8, 2, 2)	1	(4, 4, 6)	(7, 3, 3)				
C23	(9, 1, 1)	(6, 4, 4)	1	(8, 2, 2)				
C24	(1, 1, 9)	(3, 3, 7)	(2, 2, 8)	1				

TABLE 2.23 Priorities for the supermatrix.

		Cluster1 (Criteria)			Cluster2 (Alternatives)			
		C_{11}	C_{12}	C_{13}	C_{21}	C_{22}	C_{23}	C_{24}
Cluster1 (Criteria)	C_{11}	0	0.797	0	0.337	0.727	0.273	0
	C_{12}	0.843	0	1	0.117	0	0.727	0.124
	C_{13}	0.157	0.203	0	0.546	0.273	0	0.876
Cluster2 (Alternatives)	C_{21}	0.180	0	0.152	0	0	0	0
	C_{22}	0	0.157	0.271	0	0	0	0
	C_{23}	0.204	0	0.517	0	0	0	0
	C_{24}	0.616	0.843	0.060	0	0	0	0

TABLE 2.24 Weighted supermatrix.

		Cluster1 (Criteria)			Cluster2 (Alternatives)			
		C_{11}	C_{12}	C_{13}	C_{21}	C_{22}	C_{23}	C_{24}
Cluster1 (Criteria)	C_{11}	0	0.3985	0	0.337	0.727	0.273	0
	C_{12}	0.4215	0	0.5	0.117	0	0.727	0.124
	C_{13}	0.0785	0.1015	0	0.546	0.273	0	0.876
Cluster2 (Alternatives)	C_{21}	0.09	0	0.076	0	0	0	0
	C_{22}	0	0.0785	0.1355	0	0	0	0
	C_{23}	0.102	0	0.2585	0	0	0	0
	C_{24}	0.308	0.4215	0.03	0	0	0	0

TABLE 2.25 Limit supermatrix.

		Cluster1 (Criteria)			Cluster2 (Alternatives)			
		C_{11}	C_{12}	C_{13}	C_{21}	C_{22}	C_{23}	C_{24}
Cluster1 (Criteria)	C_{11}	0.1754	0.1754	0.1754	0.1754	0.1754	0.1754	0.1754
	C_{12}	0.2667	0.2667	0.2667	0.2667	0.2667	0.2667	0.2667
	C_{13}	0.2245	0.2245	0.2245	0.2245	0.2245	0.2245	0.2245
Cluster2 (Alternatives)	C_{21}	**0.0329**	0.0329	0.0329	0.0329	0.0329	0.0329	0.0329
	C_{22}	**0.0514**	0.0514	0.0514	0.0514	0.0514	0.0514	0.0514
	C_{23}	**0.0759**	0.0759	0.0759	0.0759	0.0759	0.0759	0.0759
	C_{24}	**0.1732**	0.1732	0.1732	0.1732	0.1732	0.1732	0.1732

2.6 Conclusions

This chapter has presented a comprehensive state-of-the-art literature review on both the classical ANP and the FANP, highlighting their theoretical foundations, methodological developments, and diverse application areas. Through the use of clusters, feedback loops, and the supermatrix limit matrix procedure, ANP provides a systematic way to represent and quantify interdependencies and feedback effects within complex decision problems. Its ability to capture both inner and outer dependencies makes ANP particularly suitable for contexts where relationships between decision elements are dynamic and strongly interconnected.

Classical ANP retains distinctive methodological advantages that continue to justify its wide application. By allowing criteria and subcriteria to influence one another, ANP offers a more realistic model than the purely hierarchical AHP. The supermatrix framework captures both direct and indirect influences, while the limit matrix provides stable global priorities after iterative convergence. This network-based representation is well suited to areas such as project management, supply chain design, energy planning, and technology selection, where criteria frequently interact. Moreover, the eigenvalue-based consistency analysis and the pairwise comparison procedure preserve the transparency and interpretability that characterize the AHP family.

At the same time, classical ANP presents theoretical and practical challenges that invite future investigation. The construction and manipulation of large supermatrices can become computationally complex, especially when the number of clusters and elements grows. Consistency evaluation of interdependent clusters is more complex than in a pure hierarchy, and sensitivity to inconsistent judgments can affect final priorities. Furthermore, as the number of dependencies increase, the derivation of expert judgments can become time-consuming and cognitively demanding. These motivate efforts to refine computational algorithms, improve data elicitation strategies, and develop software tools that support larger and more dynamic decision networks.

The FANP effectively extends the classical ANP by incorporating fuzzy set theory to capture vagueness, hesitancy, and imprecision in expert judgments. While FANP has been applied to a broad range of domains such as supply chain management, healthcare, environmental management, and energy systems, its use is still accompanied by challenges related to mathematical consistency, computational complexity, and the subjectivity of defuzzification procedures.

The analysis of FANP extensions—including type-2 fuzzy, IF, neutrosophic, Pythagorean fuzzy, picture fuzzy, spherical fuzzy, and Fermatean fuzzy approaches—demonstrates the continuous effort of researchers to enhance its flexibility and realism in modeling complex decision problems. Each extension offers unique ways to represent uncertainty, enriching the decision-making process and broadening the scope of application. The PPF-ANP introduced and applied to solar panel selection illustrates the practical advantages of these advanced models in capturing nuanced expert evaluations and delivering robust results.

Regardless of these achievements, both classical ANP and FANP face open challenges. For classical ANP, computational burden and the elicitation of a large number of pairwise comparisons remain limiting factors. For classical ANP, priorities include improving algorithms for supermatrix convergence, developing dynamic or real-time network models that can adapt to changing decision environments, and creating open-source, user-friendly software that supports large-scale applications.

Despite criticisms, the persistent and widespread use of FANP underlines its value as a robust multicriteria decision-making tool in contexts where uncertainty and interdependencies are central. Future research should focus on improving the mathematical soundness of fuzzy extensions, developing more efficient computational algorithms, and integrating FANP with emerging decision-support technologies such as artificial intelligence, machine learning, and big data analytics.

Such advancements will strengthen the position of FANP as a practical and versatile methodology for addressing increasingly complex real-world decision-making problems.

References

Abdel-Basset, M., Mohamed, M., & Smarandache, F. (2018). A hybrid neutrosophic group ANP-TOPSIS framework for supplier selection problems. *Symmetry, 10*(6), 226.

Ali, M., Rehman, S. U., Naseem, S., & Zubair, S. (2024). Identifying social concerns in virtual reality technology through integrated fuzzy analytic network process. *Computers and Industrial Engineering, 187*, 109011.

Amiri, M., Yazdani, M., & Chatterjee, P. (2024). An integrated fuzzy analytic network process and fuzzy regression model for Bitcoin price prediction. *Internet of Things, 26*, 101065.

Brunelli, M. (2017). *Introduction to the Analytic Hierarchy Process*. Springer.

Büyüközkan, G., Ertay, T., Kahraman, C., & Ruan, D. (2004). Determining the importance weights for the design requirements in the house of quality using the fuzzy analytic network approach. *International Journal of Intelligent Systems, 19*(5), 443–461.

Büyüközkan, G., Karabulut, Y., & Göçer, F. (2024). Spherical fuzzy sets based integrated DEMATEL, ANP, VIKOR approach and its application for renewable energy selection in Turkey. *Applied Soft Computing, 158*, 111465.

Chen, Z., Wang, Y., & Liu, J. (2023). Medicine shelf matching strategy based on Bayesian convolutional neural network and fuzzy analytic network process. *Expert Systems with Applications, 222*, 119798.

van Eck, N. J., & Waltman, L. (2010). Software survey: VOSviewer, a computer program for bibliometric mapping. *Scientometrics, 84*(2), 523–538.

Erdoğan, M., Kaya, I., Karaşan, A., & Çolak, M. (2021). Evaluation of autonomous vehicle driving systems for risk assessment based on three-dimensional uncertain linguistic variables. *Applied Soft Computing, 113*, 107934.

Huang, J. J. (2012). Mathematical programming for fuzzy analytic hierarchy and network processes. *European Journal of Operational Research, 223*(3), 865–872.

Kahraman, C., Cebeci, U., & Ruan, D. (2004). Multi-criteria supplier selection using fuzzy AHP. *Logistics Information Management, 16*(6), 382–394.

Kahraman, C., Ertay, T., & Büyüközkan, G. (2006). A fuzzy optimization model for QFD planning process using analytic network approach. *European Journal of Operational Research, 171*(2), 390–411.

Kaytez, F. (2022). Evaluation of priority strategies for the expansion of installed wind power capacity in Turkey: A SWOT–FANP model. *Renewable Energy, 190*, 524–537.

Kheybari, S., Rezaie, F. M., & Farazmand, H. (2020). Analytic network process: An overview of applications. *Applied Mathematics and Computation, 367*, 124780.

Lo, H. W., Chen, T. H., Fang, T. Y., & Lin, S. W. (2025). Airport sustainability and risk assessment using interval-valued fermatean fuzzy MCDM network analysis. *Research in Transportation Business & Management, 62*, 101454.

Ma, Y. Y., & Lin, C. L. (2025). Key influencing service quality index evaluation and ranking for online physics teaching in the post-COVID-19 era: A hybrid fuzzy ANP-GRA approach. *Evaluation and Program Planning, 111*, 102590.

Mikhailov, L., & Singh, M. G. (1999). Fuzzy analytic network process and its application to decision making. *International Journal of Systems Science, 30*(9), 1021–1032.

Mikhailov, L., & Singh, M. G. (2003). Fuzzy analytic network process and its application to the development of decision support systems. *IEEE Transactions on Systems, Man, and Cybernetics, Part C (Applications and Reviews, 33*(1), 33–41.

Mongeon, P., & Paul-Hus, A. (2016). The journal coverage of Web of Science and Scopus: A comparative analysis. *Scientometrics, 106*(1), 213–228.

Pereira, A. F. C., & Sousa, J. M. M. (2023). Assisted site-dependent selection of the most suitable airborne wind energy system via fuzzy analytic network process. *Energy Reports, 9*, 2881–2899. https://doi.org/10.1016/j.egyr.2023.10.070.

Promentilla, M. A. B. (2008). A fuzzy analytic network process for evaluating remedial countermeasures. *Journal of Environmental Management, 88*(3), 479–495.

Saaty, T. L. (1996). *Decision Making With Dependence And Feedback: The Analytic Network Process*. Pittsburgh: RWS Publications.

Saaty, T. L. (2004). Fundamentals of the analytic network process—multiple networks with benefits, costs, opportunities and risks. *Journal of Systems Science and Systems Engineering, 13*(3), 348–379.

Saaty, T. L. (2006). Rank from comparisons and from ratings in the analytic hierarchy/network process. *European Journal of Operational Research, 168*(2), 557–570.

Saeedi, S., Malek, M. R., Delavar, M. R., & Tayyebi, A. (2008). An intuitionistic fuzzy analytical network process for parking site selection. *In Computational Intelligence in Decision and Control,* 1033–1038.

Senturk, S. (2016). Critical evaluation of fuzzy analytic hierarchy and network processes. *Journal of Multi-Criteria Decision Analysis, 23*(1-2), 25–36.

Tadić, S., Zečević, S., & Krstić, M. (2014). A novel hybrid MCDM model based on fuzzy DEMATEL, fuzzy ANP and fuzzy VIKOR for city logistics concept selection. *Expert Systems with Applications, 41*(18), 8112–8128.

Taherdoost, H., & Madanchian, M. (2023). A systematic review of fuzzy multi-criteria decision-making methods. *Expert Systems with Applications, 213*, 119208.

Wu, C. R., Chang, C. W., & Lin, H. L. (2008). A fuzzy ANP-based approach to evaluate medical organizational performance. *Information and Management Sciences, 19*(1), 53–74.

Wu, T., & Liu, X. (2016). An interval type-2 fuzzy ANP approach to evaluate enterprise technological innovation ability. *Kybernetes, 45*(9), 1486–1500.

Yaman, T. T. (2020). Pythagorean fuzzy analytical network process (ANP) and its application to warehouse location selection problem. In *2020 15th Conference on Computer Science and Information Systems (FedCSIS*. IEEE, 137–140.

Yang, Y., Li, H., Zhang, Z., & Liu, X. (2020). Interval-valued intuitionistic fuzzy analytic network process. *Information Sciences, 526*, 102–118.

Zečević, S., Tadić, S., & Krstić, M. (2017). Intermodal transport terminal location selection using a novel hybrid MCDM model. *International Journal of Uncertainty, Fuzziness and Knowledge-Based Systems, 25*(06), 853–876.

Zhang, Y., Wang, S., Liu, J., Liu, D., Li, T., & Wu, W. (2024). A corrosion assessment methodology based on triangular intuitionistic fuzzy comprehensive evaluation (TIFCE) with analytic network process (TIFANP): An application to external corrosion of the storage tank floor. *Expert Systems with Applications, 238*, 121896.

Zheng, Y., He, Y., Xu, Z., & Pedrycz, W. (2018). Assessment for hierarchical medical policy proposals using hesitant fuzzy linguistic analytic network process. *Knowledge-Based Systems, 161*, 254–267.

Zhü, K. (2014). Fuzzy analytic hierarchy process: Fallacy of the popular methodology. *European Journal of Operational Research, 236*(1), 209–217.

Chapter 3

DEMATEL: Decision-making trial and evaluation laboratory for multi-attribute decision-making

Andrés Esteban Acero-López
School of Engineering and Sciences, Tecnológico de Monterrey, Monterrey, Mexico

3.1 Introduction

Many decisions in practice involve multiple criteria that must be considered simultaneously. The multi-attribute decision-making (MADM) addresses such problems by providing a structured framework to evaluate and compare alternatives across different factors. In the MADM problems, alternatives represent the possible options in the decision problems (Haseli, Yaran Ögel, et al., 2023). Additionally, criteria are the measurable factors used to judge those alternatives. Determining how much weight or importance each criterion has is an important part of the MADM methods. This part involves evaluating the alternatives, enabling the decision-maker to rank the alternatives and select the optimal option (Haseli, Ranjbarzadeh, et al., 2023). One of the common approaches to compare the criteria is the use of pairwise comparisons. Using pairwise comparisons, decision-maker(s) compare each pair of criteria to assess their relative importance. Decision-maker(s) might judge whether criterion *A* is more important than criterion *B*, and if so, by how much (Hasani et al., 2025). There are different numerical scales to gather these judgments of the decision-makers. Pairwise comparison underpins several classic MADM methods, like decision-making trial and evaluation laboratory (DEMATEL; Andre & Fontela, 1972), analytic hierarchy process (AHP; Saaty, 1990), analytic network process (ANP; Saaty & Vargas, 2013), best worst method (BWM; Rezaei, 2015), and base criterion method (BCM; Haseli et al., 2020; Haseli & Sheikh, 2022), enabling systematic quantification of preferences.

While the concepts of alternatives, criteria, and pairwise evaluation form the foundation of MADM, traditional methods often assume that criteria are independent factors. For example, in MADM methods such as AHP, BWM, and BCM, the criteria are considered independent factors. In some real-world problems, this assumption is not logical. Therefore, the influence of the criteria on each other should be considered in complex systems. Recognizing the influence between the criteria is important to understand the complexity of decision problems (Du & Li, 2021). The DEMATEL method is one of the MADM methods that can address the interdependence issue between criteria (Lee et al., 2013). The primary purpose of the DEMATEL method is to quantify and model the causal relationships among criteria in a system. In the context of MADM, DEMATEL is used to uncover how different criteria influence each other and incorporate these interdependencies into the decision analysis.

According to the concept of DEMATEL, this method constructs a network of criteria with directed links that represent the strength and direction of influence between criteria. These directed links are visualized as a directed graph (Zhang et al., 2025). In the mentioned graph, an arrow from criterion *A* to criterion *B* signifies that *A* has an impact on *B*. Therefore, decision-makers can know which criteria have a strong influence on other criteria and which criteria are primarily influenced by others. Based on the mentioned features of explicitly modeling feedback and interactions among criteria, the DEMATEL method is different from some other MADM approaches. By transforming qualitative expert judgments into a formal, structured model, DEMATEL enables decision-makers to see the big picture of their multicriteria problem. The resulting causal network highlights which criteria are the most influential drivers. Improving a driver criterion will indirectly improve many other criteria. Subsequently, the DEMATEL method helps to focus on the criteria

Encyclopedia of Multi-Attribute Decision-Making (MADM). DOI: https://doi.org/10.1016/B978-0-443-33275-3.00045-2

that improve the overall impact on the system. By explicitly modeling the network of influences among criteria, DEMATEL provides a richer understanding of the decision context and system dynamics.

In this regard, the aim of this chapter is to provide details about DEMATEL and its applicability. Therefore the rest of this chapter is designed as follows. The summary of the previous works on DEMATEL is provided in Section 3.2. All steps of DEMATEL for solve a decision problem are mentioned in Section 3.3. Then, two numerical examples are provided in Sections 3.4 and 3.5, respectively. Finally, the conclusion of DEMATEL for this chapter is provided in Section 3.6.

3.2 Literature review

The DEMATEL has been successfully applied in various scientific fields to analyze complex interrelationships. These studies in various scientific fields highlight DEMATEL's ability to disentangle complex interrelationships among criteria in decision-making. In this regard, a summary of the most widely cited applications of DEMATEL across different disciplines, offering a snapshot of how the method has been utilized in practice, is provided in Table 3.1.

In addition to the direct applications, the DEMATEL method has also been extended through integration with fuzzy set theory. The fuzzy extensions of DEMATEL are better suited to capture uncertainty and vagueness in expert judgments. In recent years, numerous fuzzy extensions of DEMATEL have been introduced. Table 3.2 outlines major developments in fuzzy and hybrid DEMATEL approaches, illustrating the diversity of methodological advancements in this research stream.

3.3 Methodology

As mentioned before, DEMATEL is used to identify the influence between the criteria in the decision problems. Suppose there are n criteria $C = \{C_1, \ldots, C_n\}$ for a selected decision problem. A directed influence from criterion C_i to criterion C_j is quantified by a nonnegative real number a_{ij}. The numerical scale provided in Table 3.3 is designed to assign directed influence between the criteria by decision-makers.

TABLE 3.1 Summarizes some of the most widely cited of decision-making trial and evaluation laboratory (DEMATEL) across different disciplines.

Related works	Methods	Application
Wu (2008)	ANP and DEMATEL	Knowledge management strategies selection
Lin and Tzeng (2009)	DEMATEL	A value-created system of science–technology park
Shieh et al. (2010)	DEMATEL	Hospital service quality
Wang et al. (2012)	SIA and DEMATEL	Performance improving in a matrix organization
Gölcük and Baykasoğlu (2016)	ANP and DEMATEL	Criteria interaction handling
Yazdi et al. (2020)	DEMATEL	Effective safety management
Asadi et al. (2022)	DEMATEL	Barriers and enablers of using electric vehicles
Bagherian et al. (2024)	ISM, MICMAC, and DEMATEL	Energy sustainability and digitalization
Du and Shen (2024)	DEMATEL	Large-scale group decision approach for automatic consensus
Li and Lu (2025)	ISM, ANP, and DEMATEL	Smart city resilience enablers
Li and Fei (2025)	BWM and DEMATEL	Barriers to the use of UAVs in emergency rescue operations
He et al. (2025)	ISM and DEMATEL	Resilient behavior of flight crew
Kabra and Mukerjee (2025)	DEMATEL	Design thinking adoption in organizations
Chi et al. (2025)	ISM and DEMATEL	Metaverse in the service industry

TABLE 3.2 **Summarizes fuzzy extensions of the decision-making trial and evaluation laboratory (DEMATEL).**

Related works	Methods	Fuzzy sets	Application
Wu and Lee (2007)	DEMATEL	Ordinary fuzzy sets	Developing global managers' competencies
Chang et al. (2011)	DEMATEL	Ordinary fuzzy sets	Supplier selection
Govindan et al. (2015)	DEMATEL	Intuitionistic fuzzy sets	Green supply chain
Zhang et al. (2020)	DEMATEL	Interval-valued intuitionistic hesitant fuzzy	Youth unemployment
Kilic and Yalcin (2021)	DEMATEL and TOPSIS	Neutrosophic fuzzy sets	Comparison of municipalities
Kilic et al. (2021)	DEMATEL	Neutrosophic fuzzy sets	Leanness assessment
Karasan et al. (2022)	AHP, QFD, and DEMATEL	Neutrosophic fuzzy sets	Designing customer-oriented products
Giri et al. (2022)	DEMATEL	Pythagorean fuzzy sets	Supplier selection
Zheng et al. (2022)	AHP and DEMATEL	Gray theory and fuzzy set theory	Inundation risk assessment
Zhang et al. (2023)	DEMATEL	Alpha level fuzzy sets	Proposing a novel approach
Tsai et al. (2023)	DEMATEL	Interval-valued hesitant fuzzy	Blockchain technology adoption
Irfan et al. (2024)	DEMATEL	Ordinary fuzzy sets	Metaverse in the construction industry
Büyüközkan et al. (2024)	DEMATEL, ANP, and VIKOR	Spherical fuzzy sets	Renewable energy selection
Trivedi et al. (2025)	DEMATEL	Gray theory	Addressing the challenges of India's transition to green hydrogen
Haseli et al. (2026)Haseli et al., 2026	DEMATEL and FCM	Fuzzy ZE-numbers	Cloud Supply Chain as a Service implementation

TABLE 3.3 **Numerical scale for decision-making trial and evaluation laboratory (Gutiérrez et al., 2023).**

Numerical values	Linguistic variables	Abbreviations
0	No influence	NI
1	Very low influence	VLI
2	Low influence	LI
3	High influence	HI
4	Very low influence	VHI

In this regard, a pairwise comparison matrix should be considered for the n criteria. Therefore, the pairwise comparison matrix for DEMATEL is as follows.

$$A = [a_{ij}]_{n*n} \tag{3.1}$$

Where $a_{ij} = 0$ represents no influence, and a_{ij} more than zero represents the influence of criterion C_i to criterion C_j.

Step 1. Constructing the direct-relation matrix

Collecting the pairwise influence judgments for every pairwise comparison between criteria (C_i, C_j) to construct the direct-relation matrix.

Step 2. Normalizing the direct-relation matrix

To guarantee convergence of the subsequent series expansion, the direct-relation matrix A should be normalized. In the normalization mode, the largest row sum does not exceed 1. Eq. (3.2) indicates the normalization formula for DEMATEL. In this regard, the sum of each row X is ≤1.

$$S = \max \sum_{j=1}^{n} a_{ij}, \quad 1 < i < n$$

$$X = \frac{1}{S}A \tag{3.2}$$

Step 3. Computing the total-relation matrix

The DEMATEL method considers both direct and indirect influences. Therefore, the total-relation matrix T collects the cumulative influence transmitted through paths of all lengths.

$$T = X + X^2 + X^3 + \ldots = X(I - X)^{-1} \tag{3.3}$$

Where I is the $n \times n$ identity matrix. The convergence of the infinite sum is guaranteed when $\rho(X) < 1$. In this regard, the closed form $X(I - X)^{-1}$ is numerically stable once $I - X$ is nonsingular.

Step 4. Deriving prominence and relation indices

Computing two scalar indices for each criterion r_i and c_i from the total-relation matrix $T = [t_{ij}]$. Eq. (3.4) represents the influence given (sum of the rows), and Eq. (3.5) indicates the influence received (sum of the columns), respectively.

$$r_i = \sum_{j=1}^{n} t_{ij} \tag{3.4}$$

$$c_i = \sum_{j=1}^{n} t_{ji} \tag{3.5}$$

After computing r_i and c_i scalar indices for each criterion, two compound measures are defined based on the values of r_i and c_i. In this regard, the first compound measure is prominence, which is defined as $p_i = r_i + c_i$. Additionally, the second compound measure is net relation, which is defined as $s_i = r_i - c_i$. Regarding the outcomes of the net relation compound measure, if $s_i > 0$, the criterion is a net cause, and if $s_i < 0$, the criterion is a net effect.

Note: Prominence compound measure orders criteria by their centrality in the influence structure, while the sign and magnitude of s_i reveal whether a criterion predominantly drives the system or is driven by it.

Step 5. Selecting a threshold and constructing the causal diagram

To produce a readable causal digraph, a threshold α should be applied to the entries of T. (3.6) represents a calculation process for the threshold α.

$$\alpha = \frac{1}{n^2} \sum_{i=1}^{n} \sum_{j=1}^{n} t_{ij} \tag{3.6}$$

To show the application of the DEMATEL method based on the mentioned steps, two numerical examples are provided in the next sections.

3.4 Numerical example 1

The first numerical example is a decision problem to prioritize barriers that impede the implementation of a new information system in an organization. In this regard, five barriers are identified for the implementation of a new information system. The identified barriers are the lack of top management support (C1), inadequate technical skills (C2), high implementation cost (C3), resistance to change among staff (C4), and poor IT infrastructure (C5).

According to the first step of DEMATEL, a direct-relation matrix should be constructed based on the judgment of the decision-maker. In this regard, the decision-makers should assign values for the comparisons based on the scale provided in Table 3.3. The result of the direct-relation matrix based on the comparisons is provided in Table 3.4. In this matrix, the

TABLE 3.4 Result of the direct-relation matrix.

	C1	C2	C3	C4	C5
C1	0	3	1	0	2
C2	2	0	3	1	0
C3	0	1	0	4	2
C4	1	0	2	0	3
C5	3	2	0	1	0

TABLE 3.5 Result of the normalized relation matrix.

	C1	C2	C3	C4	C5
C1	0	0.4286	0.1429	0.0000	0.2857
C2	0.2857	0	0.4286	0.1429	0.0000
C3	0.0000	0.1429	0	0.5714	0.2857
C4	0.1429	0.0000	0.2857	0	0.4286
C5	0.4286	0.2857	0.0000	0.1429	0

TABLE 3.6 Result of the total-relation matrix.

	C1	C2	C3	C4	C5	Sum
C1	1.3719	1.6905	1.4334	1.2952	1.6423	7.4334
C2	1.5620	1.3558	1.6648	1.5122	1.5700	7.6648
C3	1.5620	1.5781	1.4426	1.9011	1.9589	8.4426
C4	1.5041	1.3756	1.4591	1.2916	1.8287	7.4591
C5	1.6777	1.5941	1.2984	1.3145	1.4137	7.2984
Sum	7.6777	7.5941	7.2984	7.3145	8.4137	7.4334

elements related to the comparison of pairs of barriers that affect each other are marked with numbers from 1 to 4. Also, the value of zero in each element indicates that there is no relationship between the corresponding barriers.

After constructing the direct-relation matrix, all its values are normalized based on Eq. (3.2) of Step 2. The result of the normalized relation matrix is presented in Table 3.5.

In Step 3, the total-relation matrix values are computed based on Eq. (3.3) on the values of the normalized direct-relation matrix. In this regard, the total-relation matrix values are presented in Table 3.6. All values of the total-relation matrix are rounded to four significant digits.

Based on the provided results in Table 3.6, the values of the $I - X$ matrix and its inverse are calculated and presented in Tables 3.7 and 3.8, respectively.

TABLE 3.7 Results for values of the $I - X$ matrix.

	C1	C2	C3	C4	C5
C1	1	-0.4286	-0.1429	0.0000	-0.2857
C2	-0.2857	1	-0.4286	-0.1429	0.0000
C3	0.0000	-0.1429	1	-0.5714	-0.2857
C4	-0.1429	0.0000	-0.2857	1	-0.4286
C5	-0.4286	-0.2857	0.0000	-0.1429	1

TABLE 3.8 Results for values of the $(I - X)^{-1}$ matrix.

	C1	C2	C3	C4	C5
C1	2.3719	1.6905	1.4334	1.2952	1.6423
C2	1.5620	2.3558	1.6648	1.5122	1.5700
C3	1.5620	1.5781	2.4426	1.9011	1.9589
C4	1.5041	1.3756	1.4591	2.2916	1.8287
C5	1.6777	1.5941	1.2984	1.3145	2.4137

TABLE 3.9 Results for values of the prominence and relation indices.

	r_i	c_i	$r_i + c_i$	$r_i - c_i$
C1	7.4334	7.6777	15.1111	-0.2443
C2	7.6648	7.5941	15.2590	0.0707
C3	8.4426	7.2984	15.7410	1.1442
C4	7.4591	7.3145	14.7736	0.1446
C5	7.2984	8.4137	15.7121	-1.1152

In Step 4, the prominence and relation indices are calculated using Eqs. (3.4) and (3.5). In this regard, the results of two r_i and c_i scalar indices for each criterion are presented in Table 3.9. Additionally, the values of the $r_i + c_i$ and $r_i - c_i$ for each criterion are presented in Table 3.9.

Based on the calculated results for each of the barriers, Fig. 3.1 presents a causal diagram of the identified barriers for the implementation of a new information system in an organization.

Based on the position of each barrier in the cause-and-effect diagram, the C2, C3, and C4 barriers are in the cause group. Furthermore, the C1 and C5 barriers are in the effect group. In this regard, the C3 has the most impact on the barriers, and the C5 has received more effects than other barriers.

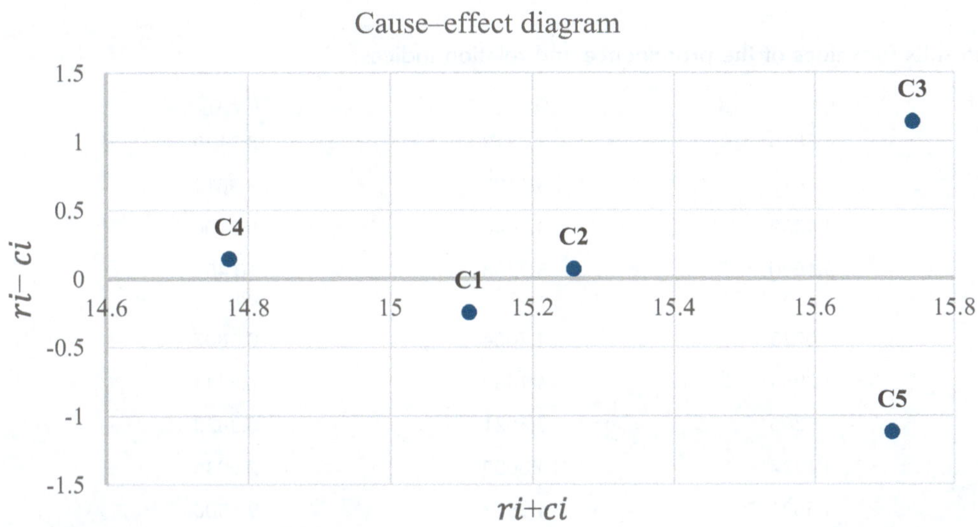

FIGURE 3.1 Cause and effect diagram for identified barriers.

TABLE 3.10 Result of the direct-relation matrix for the renewable energy system barriers.

	C1	C2	C3	C4	C5	C6	C7	C8	C9
C1	0	3	1	2	1	2	0	1	1
C2	2	0	2	1	1	1	2	1	2
C3	1	2	0	1	0	1	1	1	1
C4	1	1	1	0	3	2	1	2	2
C5	0	1	0	2	0	1	2	1	2
C6	1	1	1	2	1	0	1	1	1
C7	2	2	1	1	2	1	0	1	1
C8	1	1	1	2	1	1	1	0	2
C9	1	2	1	2	2	1	1	1	0

3.5 Numerical example 2

The second numerical example is a decision problem to prioritize barriers to implementing a new renewable energy system. In this regard, nine barriers are identified for the implementation of a new renewable energy system. The identified barriers are the lack of management commitment (C1), financial constraints (C2), regulatory uncertainty (C3), technical skills shortage (C4), poor infrastructure (C5), stakeholder resistance (C6), supply chain limitations (C7), data quality and availability (C8), and high implementation complexity (C9).

According to the first step of DEMATEL, a direct-relation matrix should be constructed based on the judgment of the decision-maker. In this regard, the decision-makers should assign values for the comparisons based on the scale provided in Table 3.3. The result of the direct-relation matrix based on the comparisons is provided in Table 3.10. In this matrix, the elements related to the comparison of pairs of barriers that affect each other are marked with numbers from 1 to 4, the same as the provided results in numerical example 1.

After constructing the direct-relation matrix, all its values are normalized based on Eq. (3.2) of Step 2. The results of the normalized relation matrix, total-relation matrix, I-X matrix, and its inverse are calculated in a manner similar to the process in the first numerical example. Based on the calculated results, the prominence and relation indices are calculated

TABLE 3.11 Results for values of the prominence and relation indices.

	r_i	c_i	$r_i + c_i$	$r_i - c_i$
C1	4.5810	3.7319	8.3129	0.8491
C2	4.8617	5.1195	9.9812	-0.2578
C3	3.4259	3.3846	6.8106	0.0413
C4	5.1620	5.2388	10.40-08	-0.0767
C5	3.8723	4.7084	8.5807	-0.8361
C6	3.7954	4.1389	7.9343	-0.3435
C7	4.5206	3.8621	8.3828	0.6585
C8	4.1927	3.8009	7.9936	0.3918
C9	4.5621	4.9887	9.5508	-0.4265

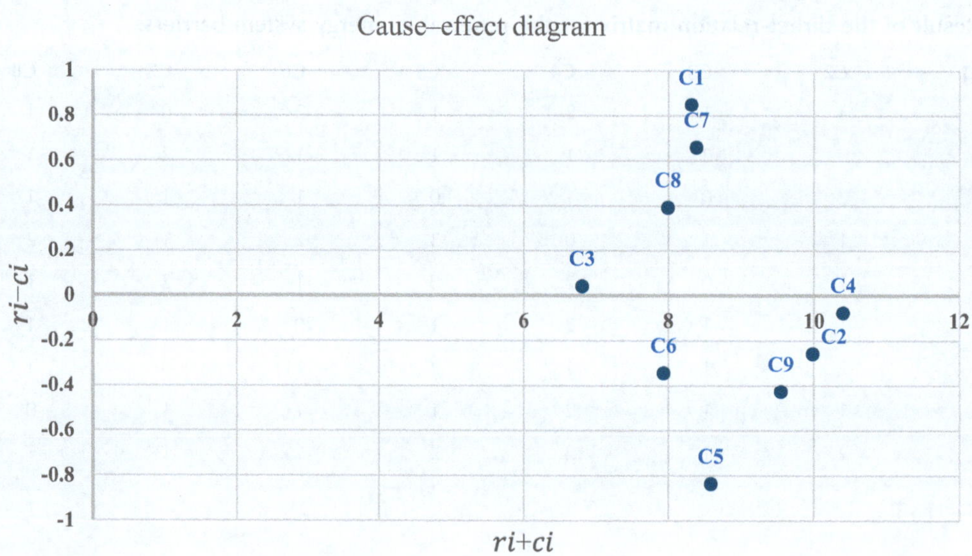

FIGURE 3.2 Cause and effect diagram for identified barriers.

using Eqs. (3.4) and (3.5). In this regard, the results of two r_i and c_i scalar indices for each criterion are presented in Table 3.11. Additionally, the values of the $r_i + c_i$ and $r_i - c_i$ for each criterion are presented in Table 3.11.

Based on the calculated results of the $r_i + c_i$ and $r_i - c_i$ for each of the barriers, Fig. 3.2 presents a causal diagram of the identified barriers for the implementation of a new renewable energy system.

Based on the position of each barrier in the cause-and-effect diagram, the C1, C3, C4, C7, and C8 barriers are in the cause group. Furthermore, the C2, C5, C6, and C9 barriers are in the effect group. In this regard, the C1 has the most impact on the barriers, and the C5 has had more effect than other barriers.

3.6 Conclusion

DEMATEL offers a distinct and practically valuable perspective within the MADM toolbox by shifting attention from isolated criterion weights to the pattern of causal interdependence among factors. Its central contribution is methodological: it converts qualitative expert judgments about direct influences into a quantitative, network-style representation that explicitly captures both direct and indirect effects. The resulting indices' prominence and net relation allow analysts to separate criteria that act as systemic drivers from those that are primarily dependents, and to prioritize interventions that will produce cascading improvements across the decision system. In applied settings, this causal clarity helps decision-makers move beyond single-criterion. Despite the strengths of DEMATEL, this method is not a panacea and should be used with careful attention to implementation choices. The method depends on the quality of expert judgments, the chosen influence scale, aggregation rules, normalization approach, and the threshold for graph construction; each of these choices affects the computed network and thus the interpretation. Therefore it is better to combine DEMATEL with good elicitation practice (clear scenarios) and conduct sensitivity checks on key parameters.

Despite wide applicability and effectiveness of DEMATEL in modeling complex cause–effect relationships, the DEMATEL method has several limitations. One key limitation is its reliance on expert judgments, which can introduce subjectivity and bias into the results. Additionally, DEMATEL typically requires a predefined set of criteria, making it less flexible when new or evolving factors emerge. The method also assumes linear relationships among variables, which may not fully capture nonlinear dynamics in real-world systems.

References

Andre, G., & Fontela, E. J. B. G. R. C. (1972). World problems, an invitation to further thought within the framework of DEMATEL. *Battelle Geneva Research Center, 1*(8), 12–14.

Asadi, S., Nilashi, M., Iranmanesh, M., Ghobakhloo, M., Samad, S., Alghamdi, A., Almulihi, A., & Mohd, S. (2022). Drivers and barriers of electric vehicle usage in Malaysia: A DEMATEL approach. *Resources, Conservation and Recycling, 177*, 105965. https://doi.org/10.1016/j.resconrec.2021.105965.

Bagherian, A., Gershon, M., Kumar, S., & Kumar Mishra, M. (2024). Analyzing the relationship between digitalization and energy sustainability: A comprehensive ISM-MICMAC and DEMATEL approach. *Expert Systems with Applications, 236*, 121193. https://doi.org/10.1016/j.eswa.2023.121193.

Büyüközkan, G., Karabulut, Y., & Göçer, F. (2024). Spherical fuzzy sets based integrated DEMATEL, ANP, VIKOR approach and its application for renewable energy selection in Turkey. *Applied Soft Computing, 158*, 111465. https://doi.org/10.1016/j.asoc.2024.111465.

Chang, B., Chang, C.-W., & Wu, C.-H. (2011). Fuzzy DEMATEL method for developing supplier selection criteria. *Expert Systems with Applications, 38*(3), 1850–1858. https://doi.org/10.1016/j.eswa.2010.07.114.

Chi, M., Ren, S., Xu, Y., Chen, Y., & Wu, Y. (2025). Critical success factors for metaverse implementation in the service industry: A hybrid ISM-DEMATEL approach. *Journal of Retailing and Consumer Services, 87*, 104424. https://doi.org/10.1016/j.jretconser.2025.104424.

Du, Y.-W., & Li, X.-X. (2021). Hierarchical DEMATEL method for complex systems. *Expert Systems with Applications, 167*, 113871. https://doi.org/10.1016/j.eswa.2020.113871.

Du, Y.-W., & Shen, X.-L. (2024). Large-scale group hierarchical DEMATEL method with automatic consensus reaching. *Information Fusion, 108*, 102411. https://doi.org/10.1016/j.inffus.2024.102411.

Giri, B. C., Molla, M. U., & Biswas, P. (2022). Pythagorean fuzzy DEMATEL method for supplier selection in sustainable supply chain management. *Expert Systems with Applications, 193*, 116396. https://doi.org/10.1016/j.eswa.2021.116396.

Gölcük, İ., & Baykasoğlu, A. (2016). An analysis of DEMATEL approaches for criteria interaction handling within ANP. *Expert Systems with Applications, 46*, 346–366. https://doi.org/10.1016/j.eswa.2015.10.041.

Govindan, K., Khodaverdi, R., & Vafadarnikjoo, A. (2015). Intuitionistic fuzzy based DEMATEL method for developing green practices and performances in a green supply chain. *Expert Systems with Applications, 42*(20), 7207–7220. https://doi.org/10.1016/j.eswa.2015.04.030.

Gutiérrez, L. E., Samper, J. J., Jabba, D., Nieto, W., Guerrero, C. A., Betts, M. M., & López-Ospina, H. A. (2023). Combined framework of multicriteria methods to identify quality attributes in augmented reality applications. *Mathematics, 11*(13), 2834. https://doi.org/10.3390/math11132834.

Hasani, A., Haseli, G., & Deveci, M. (2025). Analyzing operational risks of digital supply chain transformation using hybrid ISM-MICMAC method. *OPSEARCH, 62*(2), 583–607. https://doi.org/10.1007/s12597-024-00792-y.

Haseli, G., Ranjbarzadeh, R., Hajiaghaei-Keshteli, M., Jafarzadeh Ghoushchi, S., Hasani, A., Deveci, M., & Ding, W. (2023). HECON: Weight assessment of the product loyalty criteria considering the customer decision's halo effect using the convolutional neural networks. *Information Sciences, 623*, 184–205. https://doi.org/10.1016/j.ins.2022.12.027.

Haseli, G., & Sheikh, R. (2022). *Base Criterion Method (BCM)*. doi: 10.1007/978-981-16-7414-3_2.

Haseli, G., Sheikh, R., & Sana, S. S. (2020). Base-criterion on multi-criteria decision-making method and its applications. *International Journal of Management Science and Engineering Management, 15*(2), 79–88. https://doi.org/10.1080/17509653.2019.1633964.

Haseli, G., Yaran Ögel, İ., Ecer, F., & Hajiaghaei-Keshteli, M. (2023). Luxury in female technology (FemTech): Selection of smart jewelry for women through BCM-MARCOS group decision-making framework with fuzzy ZE-numbers. *Technological Forecasting and Social Change, 196*. https://doi.org/10.1016/j.techfore.2023.122870.

Haseli, G., Hajiaghaei-Keshteli, M., Deveci, M., & Tomaskova, H. (2026). Cloud supply chain as a service: overcoming barriers in the fashion retail industry by developing a new cognitive map model. *Transportation Research Part E: Logistics and Transportation Review, 206*, 104554. 10.1016/j.tre.2025.104554.

He, P., Lu, F., Sun, R., & Zhang, Z. (2025). Examining influencing factors and their hierarchical relationships in flight crew resilient behavior through a hybrid ISM-DEMATEL approach. *Scientific Reports, 15*(1), 1606. https://doi.org/10.1038/s41598-025-85990-4.

Irfan, M., Rauniyar, A., Hu, J., Singh, A. K., & Chandra, S. S. (2024). Modeling barriers to the adoption of metaverse in the construction industry: An application of fuzzy-DEMATEL approach. *Applied Soft Computing, 167*, 112180. https://doi.org/10.1016/j.asoc.2024.112180.

Kabra, G., & Mukerjee, H. S. (2025). Analyzing barriers to design thinking adoption within organizations: A DEMATEL approach. *International Journal of Productivity and Performance Management, 74*(3), 915–939. https://doi.org/10.1108/IJPPM-12-2023-0670.

Karasan, A., Ilbahar, E., Cebi, S., & Kahraman, C. (2022). Customer-oriented product design using an integrated neutrosophic AHP & DEMATEL & QFD methodology. *Applied Soft Computing, 118*, 108445. https://doi.org/10.1016/j.asoc.2022.108445.

Kilic, H. S., & Yalcin, A. S. (2021). Comparison of municipalities considering environmental sustainability via neutrosophic DEMATEL based TOPSIS. *Socio-economic Planning Sciences, 75*, 100827. https://doi.org/10.1016/j.seps.2020.100827.

Kilic, H. S., Yurdaer, P., & Aglan, C. (2021). A leanness assessment methodology based on neutrosophic DEMATEL. *Journal of Manufacturing Systems, 59*, 320–344. https://doi.org/10.1016/j.jmsy.2021.03.003.

Lee, H.-S., Tzeng, G.-H., Yeih, W., Wang, Y.-J., & Yang, S.-C. (2013). Revised DEMATEL: Resolving the Infeasibility of DEMATEL. *Applied Mathematical Modelling, 37*(10–11), 6746–6757. https://doi.org/10.1016/j.apm.2013.01.016.

Li, R., & Lu, Y. (2025). Toward a resilient and smart city: Analysis on enablers for smart city resilience using an integrated DEMATEL–ISM–ANP method. *Technological Forecasting and Social Change, 215*, 124081. https://doi.org/10.1016/j.techfore.2025.124081.

Li, T., & Fei, L. (2025). Exploring obstacles to the use of unmanned aerial vehicles in emergency rescue: A BWM-DEMATEL approach. *Technology in Society, 81*, 102863. https://doi.org/10.1016/j.techsoc.2025.102863.

Lin, C.-L., & Tzeng, G.-H. (2009). A value-created system of science (technology) park by using DEMATEL. *Expert Systems with Applications, 36*(6), 9683–9697. https://doi.org/10.1016/j.eswa.2008.11.040.

Rezaei, J. (2015). Best-worst multi-criteria decision-making method. *Omega, 53*, 49–57. https://doi.org/10.1016/j.omega.2014.11.009.

Saaty, T. L. (1990). How to make a decision: The analytic hierarchy process. *European Journal of Operational Research, 48*(1), 9–26. https://doi.org/10.1016/0377-2217(90)90057-I.

Saaty, T. L., & Vargas, L. G. (2013). *The Analytic Network Process*. doi: 10.1007/978-1-4614-7279-7_1.

Shieh, J.-I., Wu, H.-H., & Huang, K.-K. (2010). A DEMATEL method in identifying key success factors of hospital service quality. *Knowledge-Based Systems, 23*(3), 277–282. https://doi.org/10.1016/j.knosys.2010.01.013.

Trivedi, A., Trivedi, V., & Singh, R. (2025). Road to decarbonization: Navigating India's green hydrogen transition challenges through grey DEMATEL. *Journal of Cleaner Production, 486*, 144502. https://doi.org/10.1016/j.jclepro.2024.144502.

Tsai, J.-F., Tran, D.-H., Nguyen, P.-H., & Lin, M.-H. (2023). Interval-valued hesitant fuzzy DEMATEL-based blockchain technology adoption barriers evaluation methodology in agricultural supply chain management. *Sustainability, 15*(5), 4686. https://doi.org/10.3390/su15054686.

Wang, W.-C., Lin, Y.-H., Lin, C.-L., Chung, C.-H., & Lee, M.-T. (2012). DEMATEL-based model to improve the performance in a matrix organization. *Expert Systems with Applications, 39*(5), 4978–4986. https://doi.org/10.1016/j.eswa.2011.10.016.

Wu, W.-W. (2008). Choosing knowledge management strategies by using a combined ANP and DEMATEL approach. *Expert Systems with Applications, 35*(3), 828–835. https://doi.org/10.1016/j.eswa.2007.07.025.

Wu, W.-W., & Lee, Y.-T. (2007). Developing global managers' competencies using the fuzzy DEMATEL method. *Expert Systems with Applications, 32*(2), 499–507. https://doi.org/10.1016/j.eswa.2005.12.005.

Yazdi, M., Khan, F., Abbassi, R., & Rusli, R. (2020). Improved DEMATEL methodology for effective safety management decision-making. *Safety Science, 127*, 104705. https://doi.org/10.1016/j.ssci.2020.104705.

Zhang, G., Zhou, S., Xia, X., Yuksel, S., Bas, H., & Dincer, H. (2020). Strategic mapping of youth unemployment with interval-valued intuitionistic hesitant fuzzy DEMATEL based on 2-tuple linguistic values. *IEEE Access, 8*, 25706–25721. https://doi.org/10.1109/ACCESS.2020.2971102.

Zhang, Z.-X., Wang, L., Wang, Y.-M., & Martínez, L. (2023). A novel alpha-level sets based fuzzy DEMATEL method considering experts' hesitant information. *Expert Systems with Applications, 213*, 118925. https://doi.org/10.1016/j.eswa.2022.118925.

Zhang, Z.-X., Wang, L., Xie, X., Wu, Q., Wang, Y.-M., & Rodriguez, R. M. (2025). Dynamic critical factors identification: A novel fuzzy DEMATEL method considering heterogeneous information. *Expert Systems with Applications, 265*, 125957. https://doi.org/10.1016/j.eswa.2024.125957.

Zheng, Q., Shen, S.-L., Zhou, A., & Lyu, H.-M. (2022). Inundation risk assessment based on G-DEMATEL-AHP and its application to Zhengzhou flooding disaster. *Sustainable Cities and Society, 86*, 104138. https://doi.org/10.1016/j.scs.2022.104138.

Chapter 4

DANP: DEMATEL-based ANP for multi-attribute decision-making

Huai-Wei Lo[1] and Sheng-Wei Lin[2]
[1]*Department of Industrial Engineering and Management, National Yunlin University of Science and Technology, Douliu City, Taiwan,* [2]*Department of Financial Management, Management College, National Defense University, Taipei, Taiwan*

4.1 Introduction

In multi-criteria decision-making (MCDM), deriving reliable weights for dimensions/criteria is central to any evaluation system (Aydın, 2025; Dağıstanlı, 2025; Gokasar & Okur, 2025). The analytic hierarchy process (AHP) remains one of the most widely used approaches, as it decomposes a decision into hierarchical levels and assumes local independence among factors within each level (Saaty & Vargas, 1987). To accommodate the interdependence and feedback often observed in practice, the analytic network process (ANP) extends AHP by modeling criteria as a network. Global priorities are obtained by constructing a (weighted) supermatrix and raising it to a sufficiently large power until convergence, yielding stable weights (Saaty, 1996). In practice, however, the inter and intra-cluster priority blocks that populate the ANP supermatrix are still elicited via AHP-style pairwise comparisons, thereby inheriting the AHP's local judgment burden and consistency diagnostics. Moreover, the conventional supermatrix normalization typically assumes equal cluster weights, an expedient that is often at odds with the asymmetric and heterogeneous influence patterns observed across clusters in real settings. Because network links and cluster weights are usually specified from expert opinion, these assumptions can bias the resulting priorities.

To address these issues, the decision-making and trial evaluation laboratory-based ANP (DANP) framework has been proposed. DANP first uses the decision-making and trial evaluation laboratory (DEMATEL) to estimate the direct and indirect influence structure among criteria and clusters. It then uses these empirically derived influence intensities to normalize and weight the supermatrix, which removes the equal-cluster assumption. The resulting influential network relation map (INRM) and DANP-weighted supermatrix produce global priorities that better reflect real interdependencies and their magnitudes (Chiu et al., 2013; Yang et al., 2008; Yang et al., 2013).

Recent work positions DANP as a versatile core for problems where interdependence among criteria is substantive and traceable priorities are needed across energy, manufacturing, urban services, logistics, platforms, and public organizations. In renewable and urban energy planning, DANP variants have identified leverage points for sustainable wind development in remote regions by highlighting interactions among technological, economic, social, environmental, and market-demand factors under an interval-neutrosophic design (Shao & Lo, 2025). Aparisi-Cerdá et al. (2024) prioritized positive energy districts using a Delphi-based DANP protocol that aligns retrofitting potential with economic and social acceptance across city districts (Aparisi-Cerdá et al., 2024). In green transformation and industrial management, rough–fuzzy DANP stabilizes noisy expert judgments to identify the pivotal role of green value realization and its links to value capture and proposition in machinery manufacturing (Shao et al., 2024); complementary applications combine DANP with modified gray relation to improve outsourcing provider selection by focusing on criterion-to-aspiration gaps rather than mere ranking (Hsu et al., 2013). Public service and mobility studies have integrated DANP with modified VlseKriterijumska Optimizacija I Kompromisno Resenje (VIKOR) and grey theory to evaluate and improve bike-sharing service quality. Applications to Taipei's systems led to targeted managerial policies (Hsu et al., 2018).

In supply chain and logistics settings, DANP has been embedded upstream of optimization and reliability modules: a DANP and binary goal programming scheme supports joint decisions on packaging postponement and supplier selection, quantifying trade-offs between packaging and transportation costs (Gunawan et al., 2025); a DANP–combined

Encyclopedia of Multi-Attribute Decision-Making (MADM). DOI: https://doi.org/10.1016/B978-0-443-33275-3.00070-1

compromise solution (COCOSO)–Federal Emergency Management Agency (FMEA) pipeline identifies reliable and greener routes in a multimodal cement network by coupling influence-based weights with criticality-driven reliability assignment (Rashidian et al., 2024). Digital platforms and organizational capability studies likewise deploy fuzzy/grey DANP: platform selection work pairs fuzzy DANP with technique of order preference similarity to the ideal solution (TOPSIS) to reveal the centrality of transaction volume, relationship stability, and dependence in China's intelligent engineering B2B platforms (Zhang et al., 2023); a grey-DANP framework, grounded in dynamic capability theory, elicits and weights critical success factors for logistics small and medium-sized enterprises digital transformation, using weight-variance analysis to diagnose capability gaps and phase implementation (Areerakulkan & Sumrit, 2025). Methodological hybrids continue to expand DANP's frontier, for example, a hermeneutic–fuzzy–DANP model that first enlarges the factor universe via text-driven hermeneutics, then quantifies cause–effect strengths to rank key influencers for soft-science institutes (Du & Li, 2023).

Across these studies, three themes recur. First, causal transparency: DEMATEL's INRM renders inter and intra-cluster effects auditable before weighting (e.g., Shao and Lo (2025), Aparisi-Cerdá et al. (2024)). Second, uncertainty accommodation: rough, fuzzy, gray, and neutrosophic DANP variants temper sparse or noisy expertise and yield more stable priorities (Areerakulkan & Sumrit, 2025; Shao et al., 2024; Zhang et al., 2023). Third, the method is actionable. DANP is routinely combined with VIKOR, TOPSIS, or COCOSO, with goal programming or FMEA used where appropriate, so that influence-consistent weights translate into specific selections, improvements, and policy levers (Gunawan et al., 2025; Hsu et al., 2013; Hsu et al., 2018; Rashidian et al., 2024). Collectively, this corpus underscores DANP's maturity and adaptability as a weighting engine for interdependent criteria, with hybridizations providing a clear pipeline from causal structure to priorities and implementable decisions across sectors.

The remainder of this chapter is organized as follows. Section 2 presents the DANP methodology and reporting conventions. Section 3 applies the approach to case 1 (semiconductor alliance partner selection) and interprets the findings. Section 4 reports case 2 (digital manufacturing platform selection) with managerial implications. Section 5 offers a comparative discussion of DANP, AHP, Best-worst method (BWM), ANP, DEMATEL, and interpretive structural modeling (ISM). Section 6 concludes with key takeaways and notes directions for future work.

4.2 Methodology

The DEMATEL constructs a structural model of causal relations among criteria by eliciting direct influence scores, propagating them to capture indirect effects, and visualizing the resulting system as an INRM (Lo et al., 2025). In the INRM, nodes denote criteria (or factors), directed arcs encode the direction of influence, and arc weights (or labels) indicate the intensity of effects. The procedure can be summarized as follows.

4.2.1 Step 1. Elicit and aggregate the direct-relation matrix

Design a survey in which domain experts assess how strongly criterion i directly influences criterion j on an ordinal scale (e.g., 0, 1, 2, 3, 4, meaning "no influence" to "very high influence"). For each respondent $k = 1, 2,..., K$, this yields a direct-relation matrix:

$$\mathbf{D}^{(k)} = \begin{bmatrix} d_{11}^{(k)} & \cdots & d_{1j}^{(k)} & \cdots & d_{1n}^{(k)} \\ \vdots & \ddots & \vdots & \ddots & \vdots \\ d_{i1}^{(k)} & \cdots & d_{ij}^{(k)} & \cdots & d_{in}^{(k)} \\ \vdots & \ddots & \vdots & \ddots & \vdots \\ d_{n1}^{(k)} & \cdots & d_{nj}^{(k)} & \cdots & d_{nn}^{(k)} \end{bmatrix}, i, j = 1, 2, \ldots, n; k = 1, 2, \ldots, K. \tag{4.1}$$

Aggregate across respondents to obtain the average direct-relation matrix:

$$\mathbf{D} = \begin{bmatrix} d_{11} & \cdots & d_{1j} & \cdots & d_{1n} \\ \vdots & \ddots & \vdots & \ddots & \vdots \\ d_{i1} & \cdots & d_{ij} & \cdots & d_{in} \\ \vdots & \ddots & \vdots & \ddots & \vdots \\ d_{n1} & \cdots & d_{nj} & \cdots & d_{nn} \end{bmatrix}, i, j = 1, 2, \ldots, n; k = 1, 2, \ldots, K \tag{4.2}$$

4.2.2 Step 2. Calculation of the normalized matrix

To propagate influences safely in later steps, the group direct-relation matrix $\boldsymbol{D}$ is rescaled to a normalized direct-relation matrix $\boldsymbol{X}$, whose magnitude guarantees convergence of the Neumann series used to compute total effects.

$$\boldsymbol{X} = c \cdot \boldsymbol{D} \tag{4.3}$$

where,

$$c = \min\left\{\frac{1}{\max_i \sum_{j=1}^{n} d_{ij}}, \frac{1}{\max_j \sum_{i=1}^{n} d_{ij}}\right\} \tag{4.4}$$

4.2.3 Step 3. Derive the total-influence matrix

With the normalized direct-relation matrix $\boldsymbol{X}$ in hand (diagonal fixed at zero), indirect effects are propagated through successive powers of $\boldsymbol{X}$. The term $\boldsymbol{X}^h$ captures the cumulative impact transmitted along all paths of length h from each criterion to every other. Under the normalization in Step 2, and with a small damping to ensure $\rho(X) < 1$, the higher-order powers decay, so $\boldsymbol{X}^h = [0]_{n\times n}$ as $h \to \infty$. The total-influence matrix at the criterion level is thus obtained by summing direct and all indirect effects via the matrix geometric series:

$$T^h = X + X^2 + \ldots + X^h = X(I - X)^{-1}, \textit{ in which } X^h = [0]_{nxn}, \tag{4.5}$$

where $\boldsymbol{T} = [t_{ij}]_{n\times n}$, for i, $j = 1, 2, \ldots, n$, and $(\boldsymbol{I}\text{-}\boldsymbol{X})(\boldsymbol{I}\text{-}\boldsymbol{X})^{-1} = \boldsymbol{I}$, where $\boldsymbol{I}$ represents the identity matrix. Additionally, we calculate each row sum and column sum of matrix $\boldsymbol{T}$.

$$\boldsymbol{r} = (r_1, \ldots, r_i, \ldots, r_n)' = [r_i]_{n\times 1} = \left[\sum_{j=1}^{n} t_{ij}\right]_{n\times 1} \tag{4.6}$$

$$\boldsymbol{s} = (s_1, \ldots, s_j, \ldots, s_n) = [s_j]_{nx1} = (s_j)'_{1\times n} = \left[\sum_{i=1}^{n} t_{ij}\right]_{1\times n} \tag{4.7}$$

where r_i is the row sum of the ith row of matrix $\boldsymbol{T}$ and indicates the sum of the total effects of criterion i on the other criteria. Similarly, s_j is the column sum of the jth column of matrix $\boldsymbol{T}$ and indicates the sum of total effects received by criterion j from the other criteria. A larger $r_i + s_i$ indicates that criterion iii is more central to the network (it both sends and receives substantial influence). The sign of $r_i - s_i$ classifies its causal role: $r_i - s_i > 0$ implies a causal criterion (it influences others more than it is influenced), while $r_i - s_i < 0$ implies an affected criterion (it is influenced more than it influences). Values of $r_i - s_i$ near zero suggest a mediating/balancing role. Plotting the pairs $(r_i + s_i,\ r_i - s_i)$ yields the INRM; for readability, arcs are often drawn only for entries t_{ij} above a chosen threshold α.

To determine criterion weights under interdependence, we adopt DANP. In our design, DEMATEL first quantifies the direct and indirect influences among criteria and clusters; these empirically estimated influence intensities then serve as the normalization basis for the ANP supermatrix. In doing so, DANP dispenses with the equal-cluster assumption of classical ANP and produces global priorities consistent with the observed causal structure. The method is summarized below.

4.2.4 Step 4. Partition the total-influence matrix and build the unweighted supermatrix

Let the total-influence matrix from DEMATEL be $\boldsymbol{T}$. Partition $\boldsymbol{T}$ into a cluster (dimension) level matrix $\boldsymbol{T_D}$ and a criterion level matrix $\boldsymbol{T_C}$, arranged in blocks according to the cluster assignment of criteria.

$$T_C = \begin{array}{c} \\ \\ D_1\ c_{11} \\ D_2\ c_{12} \\ \vdots\ \ \vdots \\ D_3\ c_{1m_1} \end{array} \begin{array}{c} \begin{array}{cccc} D_1 & D_2 & \cdots & D_n \\ c_{11}\ldots c_{1m_1} & c_{21}\ldots c_{2m_2} & \cdots & c_{n1}\ldots c_{nm_n} \end{array} \\ \begin{bmatrix} T_C^{11} & T_C^{12} & \cdots & T_C^{1n} \\ \vdots & \vdots & & \vdots \\ T_C^{21} & T_C^{22} & \cdots & T_C^{2n} \\ \vdots & \vdots & \ddots & \vdots \\ T_C^{n1} & T_C^{n2} & \cdots & T_C^{nn} \end{bmatrix} \end{array} \tag{4.8}$$

Following ANP conventions, the unweighted supermatrix is obtained by blockwise column-normalizing the criterion-level influence matrix and then transposing it so that each row sums to one (i.e., the supermatrix is row-stochastic). For example, submatrix T_C^{12} (Eq. 4.9) from matrix T_C, normalized into $T_C^{\alpha 12}$, can be derived from a normalized T_C with a total degree of effect to obtain T_C^{α}, as shown in Eq. (4.10).

Following the foundational principles of ANP methodology, the construction of the unweighted supermatrix involves a transposition procedure whereby columnar elements are reconfigured as row vectors, with subsequent normalization ensuring that each row's elements sum to unity.

$$T_c^{12} = \begin{array}{c} \\ c_{11} \\ \vdots \\ c_{1i} \\ \vdots \\ c_{1m_1} \end{array} \begin{array}{c} \begin{array}{ccccc} c_{21} & \cdots & c_{2j} & \cdots & c_{2m_2} \end{array} \\ \begin{bmatrix} t_{11}^{12} & \cdots & t_{1j}^{12} & \cdots & t_{1m_2}^{12} \\ \vdots & & \vdots & & \vdots \\ t_{i1}^{12} & \cdots & t_{ij}^{12} & \cdots & t_{im_2}^{12} \\ \vdots & & \vdots & & \vdots \\ t_{m_1 1}^{12} & \cdots & t_{m_1 j}^{12} & \cdots & t_{m_1 m_2}^{12} \end{bmatrix} \end{array} \begin{array}{l} \rightarrow t_1^{12} = \sum_{j=1}^{m_2} t_{1j}^{12} \\ \quad \vdots \\ \rightarrow t_i^{12} = \sum_{j=1}^{m_2} t_{ij}^{12}, \\ \quad \vdots \\ \rightarrow t_{m_1}^{12} = \sum_{j=1}^{m_2} t_{m_1 j}^{12} \end{array} \tag{4.9}$$

where $t_i^{12} = \sum_{j=1}^{m2} t_{ij}^{12}$, $I = 1, 2, \ldots, m_1$,

$$T_c^{\alpha 12} = \begin{array}{c} \\ c_{11} \\ \vdots \\ c_{1i} \\ \vdots \\ c_{1m_1} \end{array} \begin{array}{c} \begin{array}{ccccc} c_{21} & \cdots & c_{2j} & \cdots & c_{2m2} \end{array} \\ \begin{bmatrix} t_{11}^{12}/t_1^{12} & \cdots & t_{1j}^{12}/t_1^{12} & \cdots & t_{1m_2}^{12}/t_1^{12} \\ \vdots & & \vdots & & \vdots \\ t_{i1}^{12}/t_i^{12} & \cdots & t_{ij}^{12}/t_i^{12} & \cdots & t_{im_2}^{12}/t_i^{12} \\ \vdots & & \vdots & & \vdots \\ t_{m_1 1}^{12}/t_{m_1}^{12} & \cdots & t_{m_1 j}^{12}/t_{m_1}^{12} & \cdots & t_{m_1 m_2}^{12}/t_{m_1}^{12} \end{bmatrix} \end{array} = \begin{bmatrix} t_{11}^{\alpha 12} & \cdots & t_{1j}^{\alpha 12} & \cdots & t_{1m_2}^{\alpha 12} \\ \vdots & & \vdots & & \vdots \\ t_{i1}^{\alpha 12} & \cdots & t_{ij}^{\alpha 12} & \cdots & t_{im_2}^{\alpha 12} \\ \vdots & & \vdots & & \vdots \\ t_{m_1 1}^{\alpha 12} & \cdots & t_{m_1 j}^{\alpha 12} & \cdots & t_{m_1 m_2}^{\alpha 12} \end{bmatrix} \tag{4.10}$$

4.2.5 Step 5. Formation of an unweighted matrix

The DANP methodology incorporates influence measures derived from DEMATEL analysis to establish the relative significance among evaluation criteria. Within this framework, the supermatrix assumes the general formulation $W_{21} = T_C^{\alpha 12'}$, in which the prime notation' signifies matrix transposition. To illustrate this operation, the element W_{21} is generated through the transposition of the normalized influence matrix $T_C^{\alpha 12}$.

$$\mathbf{W} = (T_c^{\alpha})' = \begin{array}{cc} & \\ C_1 & \begin{array}{c} c_{11} \\ c_{12} \\ \vdots \\ c_{1m_1} \end{array} \\ C_2 & \begin{array}{c} c_{21} \\ c_{22} \\ \vdots \\ c_{2m_2} \end{array} \\ \vdots & \vdots \\ C_n & \begin{array}{c} c_{n1} \\ c_{n2} \\ \vdots \\ c_{nm_n} \end{array} \end{array} \begin{array}{c} \begin{array}{cccc} C_1 & C_2 & & C_n \\ c_{11}\ldots c_{1m_1} & c_{21}\ldots c_{2m_2} & \cdots & c_{n1}\ldots c_{nm_n} \end{array} \\ \begin{bmatrix} W_{11} & W_{12} & \cdots & W_{1n} \\ W_{21} & W_{22} & \cdots & W_{2n} \\ \vdots & \vdots & \vdots\vdots\vdots & \vdots \\ W_{n1} & W_{n2} & \cdots & W_{nn} \end{bmatrix} \end{array}, \tag{4.11}$$

$$\mathbf{W}_{21} = \begin{array}{c} \\ c_{21} \\ \vdots \\ c_{2j} \\ \vdots \\ c_{2m_2} \end{array} \begin{array}{c} \begin{array}{ccccc} c_{11} & \cdots & c_{1j} & \cdots & c_{1m_1} \end{array} \\ \begin{bmatrix} t_{11}^{\alpha 12} & \cdots & t_{i1}^{\alpha 12} & \cdots & t_{m_1 1}^{\alpha 12} \\ \vdots & & \vdots & & \vdots \\ t_{1j}^{\alpha 12} & \cdots & t_{ij}^{\alpha 12} & \cdots & t_{m_1 j}^{\alpha 12} \\ \vdots & & \vdots & & \vdots \\ t_{1m_2}^{\alpha 12} & \cdots & t_{im_2}^{\alpha 12} & \cdots & t_{m_1 m_2}^{\alpha 12} \end{bmatrix} \end{array} \tag{4.12}$$

In this framework, the notation C_n denotes the nth dimension (alternatively termed a cluster), while C_{nm} signifies the mth criterion within that particular dimension. The term $\boldsymbol{W}_{ij}$ designates the principal eigenvector derived from the criterion matrix when comparing the jth dimension against the ith dimension. It should be noted that when dimension j exerts no influence over dimension i, the corresponding weight vector $\boldsymbol{W}_{ij}$ equals the null vector *[0]*.

Traditional ANP methodology employs a normalization approach wherein values within each dimension are scaled by the total number of dimensions, thereby ensuring unit column sums. This normalization strategy implicitly assumes uniform significance across all dimensions, suggesting equivalent levels of influence throughout the system. Such an assumption proves problematic, as interdimensional influence relationships inherently exhibit varying degrees of strength. The premise of homogeneous weighting across dimensions lacks validity in constructing the weighted supermatrix, particularly given the heterogeneous nature of dimensional interactions.

To address this limitation, the present research integrates DEMATEL findings to quantify differential influence relationships within the matrix $\boldsymbol{T}_C$ across the n-dimensional space. Consequently, the aggregate influence relationships for each dimension can be expressed through the normalized total influence matrix, designated as $\boldsymbol{T}_{\boldsymbol{D}}^{\alpha}$.

where $d_i = \sum t_{ij}^{D}$, $i = 1,2,\ldots,n$,

$$\boldsymbol{T}_D^{\alpha} = \begin{bmatrix} t_{11}^{D}/d_1 & \cdots & t_{1j}^{D}/d_1 & \cdots & t_{1n}^{D}/d_1 \\ \vdots & & \vdots & & \vdots \\ t_{i1}^{D}/d_i & \cdots & t_{ij}^{D}/d_i & \cdots & t_{in}^{D}/d_i \\ \vdots & & \vdots & & \vdots \\ t_{n1}^{D}/d_n & \cdots & t_{nj}^{D}/d_n & \cdots & t_{nn}^{D}/d_n \end{bmatrix} = \begin{bmatrix} t_{11}^{D_\alpha} & \cdots & t_{1j}^{D_\alpha} & \cdots & t_{1n}^{D_\alpha} \\ \vdots & & \vdots & & \vdots \\ t_{i1}^{D_\alpha} & \cdots & t_{ij}^{D_\alpha} & \cdots & t_{in}^{D_\alpha} \\ \vdots & & \vdots & & \vdots \\ t_{n1}^{D_\alpha} & \cdots & t_{nj}^{D_\alpha} & \cdots & t_{nn}^{D_\alpha} \end{bmatrix}, \tag{4.13}$$

Next, we combine $\boldsymbol{T}_D^{\alpha}$ (hereafter referred to as "the normalized matrix by dimensions") with the $\boldsymbol{W}$ to find the weighted supermatrix $\mathbf{W}_w$ as in Eq. (4.13) below,

$$\mathbf{W}_w = \boldsymbol{T}_D^{\alpha} \times \boldsymbol{W} = \begin{bmatrix} t_{11}^{D_\alpha} \times \mathbf{W}_{11} & t_{21}^{D_\varepsilon} \times \mathbf{W}_{12} & \cdots & \cdots & t_{n1}^{D_\alpha} \times \mathbf{W}_{1n} \\ t_{12}^{D_\alpha} \times \mathbf{W}_{21} & t_{22}^{D_\alpha} \times \mathbf{W}_{22} & \vdots & & \vdots \\ \vdots & \cdots & t_{ji}^{D_\alpha} \times \mathbf{W}_{ij} & \cdots & t_{ni}^{D_\alpha} \times \mathbf{W}_{in} \\ \vdots & & \vdots & & \vdots \\ t_{1n}^{D_\alpha} \times \mathbf{W}_{n1} & t_{2n}^{D_\alpha} \times \mathbf{W}_{n2} & \cdots & \cdots & t_{nn}^{D_\alpha} \times \mathbf{W}_{nn} \end{bmatrix}. \tag{4.14}$$

4.2.6 Step 6. Derivation of the global weights

The weighted supermatrix can be obtained by raising the power of the supermatrix until the supermatrix becomes stable; each row represents the influential weight as:

$$\lim_{\rho\to\infty} (\otimes \mathbf{W}_w)^{\rho}. \tag{4.15}$$

The above steps can be used to derive a limiting supermatrix for calculating the global influential weights $w = (w_1,\ldots, w_j,\ldots, w_n)$. The local weights can be aggregated and normalized from the global weights.

4.3 Numerical example 1—selecting strategic alliance partners for a semiconductor packaging and testing firm

A leading outsourced semiconductor assembly and test (OSAT) company is preparing to establish a strategic alliance intended to enhance technology access, capacity flexibility, and market reach over the next three to five years. Because alliance performance in this industry is shaped not only by traditional economic fit but also by environmental and social expectations set by global customers and financiers, the firm adopts an Environmental, social, and governance (ESG)-oriented evaluation frame and seeks network-consistent criterion weights rather than treating criteria as independent. The assessment architecture comprises three dimensions: economic (D_1), environmental (D_2), and social (D_3). Each dimension contains three operational criteria. On the economic side, the company considers a partner's company size (c_1) (installed capacity and asset base), market share (c_2) (competitive position and breadth of the customer base), and product selling price (c_3) (price levels for comparable services or inputs). The environmental dimension captures the use of recyclable materials (c_4) (design-for-recyclability and recycled content), compliance with environmental regulations (c_5) (formal certifications and audit history), and renewable energy utilization (c_6) (share of electricity sourced via on-site generation or power purchase agreements). The social dimension reflects gender equality (c_7) (representation and pay parity), protection of disadvantaged groups (c_8) (inclusive hiring and community engagement), and employee rights (c_9) (freedom of association, safety performance, and credible grievance mechanisms).

The firm's methodological choice follows from the observed entanglement among these attributes. In practice, market share often comoves with price discipline; environmental compliance serves as a gateway to Tier-1 customers and international procurement lists; robust employee rights support yield stability and on time delivery; and long-term renewable energy contracts can alter the cost structure in ways not captured by one-shot price benchmarks. Such reciprocal influences argue against hierarchical models that assume local independence and motivate the use of DANP, which calibrates analytic network priorities with empirically estimated causal influence intensities. In this case, judgments are provided by a five-member expert panel spanning operations and packaging engineering, strategic procurement, ESG leadership, corporate finance/strategy, and an external adviser with long experience in the OSAT ecosystem. Each expert supplies direct-influence ratings for ordered criterion pairs on a five-point ordinal scale (0 denoting no influence and 4 denoting very high influence). Individual direct-relation matrices are aggregated into a group matrix after a short calibration discussion to align interpretations. The same panel also reviews interactions among the three dimensions to support cluster-level analysis.

Table 4.1 reports the direct-relation matrix provided by expert 1 for case 1. Rows denote the source criterion (the factor exerting an effect) and columns denote the target criterion (the factor being affected). For illustration, the self-influence of c_1 on itself is not elicited; therefore, the entry is set to 0 (i.e., $d_{11} = 0$). If c_1 exerts a strong direct effect on c_2, the corresponding entry is rated 4 on the 0–4 scale ("no influence" to "very high influence"). All experts completed the DEMATEL questionnaire in this manner. Their individual matrices were then aggregated element-wise using the arithmetic mean to obtain the average direct-relation matrix, as reported in Table 4.2.

By applying the normalization procedure, we obtain the normalized matrix (Table 4.3), in which all elements lie between 0 and 1 (i.e., $0 \le x_{ij} \le 1$; the diagonal remains $x_{ii} = 0$). Accounting for both direct and indirect effects, the total-influence matrix is obtained by summing the higher-order powers of the normalized matrix, as reported in Table 4.4.

Table 4.5 summarizes the DEMATEL results. For each criterion i, the row sum $r_i = \sum_{j=1}^{n} t_{ij}$ measures the total effect it dispatches to the rest of the system, while the column sum $s_i = \sum_{i=1}^{n} t_{ij}$ captures the total effect it receives. As an example, criterion c_1 (company size) sends out $r_1 = 8.423$ units of influence and receives $s_1 = 8.757$; its prominence is therefore $r_1 + s_1 = 17.181$, and its net relation is $r_1 - s_1 = -0.334$. By construction, $\sum_{i=1}^{n} (r_i - s_i) = 0$, because the sum of all row totals equals the sum of all column totals in $\boldsymbol{T}$; the figures in Table 4.5 satisfy this identity exactly. Prominence ($r + s$) is highest for the economic criteria (c_1 [17.181] and c_2 [16.974]) followed by c_7 (16.610) and c_3 (16.418). These nodes are the most central in the network, participating intensely in the system's influence flows. At the other end, c_8 (12.335) is the least prominent, indicating a more peripheral position despite its directional role discussed below. The net-relation index ($r - s$)

TABLE 4.1 The direct-relation matrix provided by expert 1 for case 1 (Eq. 4.1).

		D_1			D_2			D_3		
		c_1	c_2	c_3	c_4	c_5	c_6	c_7	c_8	c_9
D_1	c_1	0	4	4	4	3	3	3	1	4
	c_2	4	0	4	4	3	3	3	2	4
	c_3	4	4	0	4	3	3	2	2	4
D_2	c_4	4	4	4	0	3	3	2	2	3
	c_5	3	3	3	4	0	4	4	4	2
	c_6	3	3	3	3	4	0	4	3	2
D_3	c_7	3	3	3	3	4	4	0	4	1
	c_8	3	3	3	3	3	3	3	0	1
	c_9	4	4	4	3	3	3	2	1	0

TABLE 4.2 The average direct-relation matrix for case 1 (Eq. 4.2).

		D_1			D_2			D_3		
		c_1	c_2	c_3	c_4	c_5	c_6	c_7	c_8	c_9
D_1	c_1	0	4	4	4	2.6	3	3.4	1.4	3.8
	c_2	4	0	4	4	2.4	2.6	3.4	1.8	3.8
	c_3	4	4	0	4	2	2.6	3	1.8	3.8
D_2	c_4	4	4	3.8	0	2	2.6	3	1.6	3.4
	c_5	2.6	2.8	2.6	2.4	0	3.6	4	2.8	2
	c_6	3.2	3	2.6	2.2	3.6	0	4	2.6	2
D_3	c_7	3.2	3.2	3	3	4	3.8	0	3.8	2
	c_8	2.6	2.2	2.2	2.2	3.2	3.2	3.2	0	1.6
	c_9	3.8	3.6	3.4	3.2	2.2	2.4	2.4	1.6	0

TABLE 4.3 The normalized matrix for case 1 (Eqs. 4.3–4.4).

		D_1			D_2			D_3		
		c_1	c_2	c_3	c_4	c_5	c_6	c_7	c_8	c_9
D_1	c_1	0.000	0.146	0.146	0.146	0.095	0.109	0.124	0.051	0.139
	c_2	0.146	0.000	0.146	0.146	0.088	0.095	0.124	0.066	0.139
	c_3	0.146	0.146	0.000	0.146	0.073	0.095	0.109	0.066	0.139
D_2	c_4	0.146	0.146	0.139	0.000	0.073	0.095	0.109	0.058	0.124
	c_5	0.095	0.102	0.095	0.088	0.000	0.131	0.146	0.102	0.073
	c_6	0.117	0.109	0.095	0.080	0.131	0.000	0.146	0.095	0.073
D_3	c_7	0.117	0.117	0.109	0.109	0.146	0.139	0.000	0.139	0.073
	c_8	0.095	0.080	0.080	0.080	0.117	0.117	0.117	0.000	0.058
	c_9	0.139	0.131	0.124	0.117	0.080	0.088	0.088	0.058	0.000

TABLE 4.4 The total-influence matrix for case 1 (Eq. 4.5).

		D_1			D_2			D_3		
		c_1	c_2	c_3	c_4	c_5	c_6	c_7	c_8	c_9
D_1	c_1	0.950	1.063	1.027	1.011	0.848	0.919	1.014	0.665	0.927
	c_2	1.071	0.928	1.020	1.004	0.836	0.901	1.006	0.671	0.921
	c_3	1.046	1.031	0.869	0.981	0.803	0.878	0.971	0.654	0.901
D_2	c_4	1.022	1.008	0.969	0.831	0.784	0.858	0.948	0.633	0.869
	c_5	0.912	0.904	0.867	0.846	0.670	0.836	0.920	0.635	0.764
	c_6	0.945	0.926	0.882	0.855	0.799	0.733	0.935	0.638	0.778
D_3	c_7	1.028	1.013	0.972	0.955	0.878	0.928	0.887	0.728	0.848
	c_8	0.830	0.806	0.778	0.764	0.709	0.754	0.819	0.489	0.683
	c_9	0.955	0.936	0.899	0.879	0.741	0.799	0.873	0.593	0.707

TABLE 4.5 The DEMATEL results for case 1 (Eqs. 4.6–4.7).

		r	s	$r+s$	$r-s$
D_1	c_1	8.423	8.757	17.181	-0.334
	c_2	8.359	8.615	16.974	-0.256
	c_3	8.135	8.283	16.418	-0.148
D_2	c_4	7.921	8.126	16.048	-0.205
	c_5	7.354	7.068	14.423	0.286
	c_6	7.490	7.606	15.097	-0.116
D_3	c_7	8.238	8.372	16.610	-0.135
	c_8	6.631	5.704	12.335	0.926
	c_9	7.381	7.399	14.780	-0.018

TABLE 4.6 The T_c^α matrix for case 1 (Eq. 4.8).

		D_1			D_2			D_3			Sum
		c_1	c_2	c_3	c_4	c_5	c_6	c_7	c_8	c_9	
D_1	c_1	0.313	0.350	0.338	0.364	0.305	0.331	0.389	0.255	0.356	3
	c_2	0.355	0.307	0.338	0.366	0.305	0.329	0.387	0.258	0.355	3
	c_3	0.355	0.350	0.295	0.368	0.302	0.330	0.384	0.259	0.357	3
D_2	c_4	0.341	0.336	0.323	0.336	0.317	0.347	0.387	0.258	0.355	3
	c_5	0.340	0.337	0.323	0.360	0.285	0.355	0.397	0.274	0.330	3
	c_6	0.343	0.336	0.320	0.358	0.335	0.307	0.398	0.271	0.331	3
D_3	c_7	0.341	0.336	0.323	0.346	0.318	0.336	0.360	0.295	0.344	3
	c_8	0.344	0.334	0.322	0.343	0.318	0.339	0.411	0.245	0.343	3
	c_9	0.342	0.336	0.322	0.363	0.306	0.330	0.402	0.273	0.325	3

divides the criteria into drivers (positive values) and receivers (negative values). Two criteria emerge as net causes: c_8 (protection of disadvantaged groups) with a strong positive score of 0.926, and c_5 (environmental compliance) with 0.286. Their positive balances mean they transmit more influence than they absorb, so improvements here are expected to propagate widely through the system. Nearly all remaining criteria are net effects: the three economic criteria c_1, c_2, and c_3 exhibit small negative balances (−0.334, −0.256, −0.148), suggesting that, in the experts' view, economic performance is shaped by social and environmental practices rather than driving them. The same pattern holds for c_4 (−0.205), c_6 (−0.116), and c_7 (−0.135). Criterion c_9 (employee rights) is essentially balanced at −0.018, acting neither as a strong source nor sink of influence and thus behaving as a mediator.

Table 4.6 reports the $\boldsymbol{T}_c^\alpha$ matrix. Starting from the total-influence matrix $\boldsymbol{T}$, criteria belonging to the same dimension are blockwise normalized so that the entries within each dimension sum to 1. Because there are three dimensions (economic, environmental, social), the row totals of $\boldsymbol{T}_c^\alpha$ equal 3 for every criterion. Each row contributes one normalized unit to each dimension block (see the rightmost "3" column). Table 4.7 presents the transpose of the $\boldsymbol{T}_c^\alpha$ (i.e., $\boldsymbol{T}_c^{\alpha'} = \boldsymbol{W}$). This is the form used in DANP as the unweighted supermatrix at the criterion level, obtained by transposing the block-normalized criterion-to-criterion influence matrix reported in Table 4.6.

TABLE 4.7 The transpose of T_c^α matrix (W) for case 1 (Eqs. 4.9–4.12).

		D_1			D_2			D_3		
		c_1	c_2	c_3	c_4	c_5	c_6	c_7	c_8	c_9
D_1	c_1	0.313	0.355	0.355	0.341	0.340	0.343	0.341	0.344	0.342
	c_2	0.350	0.307	0.350	0.336	0.337	0.336	0.336	0.334	0.336
	c_3	0.338	0.338	0.295	0.323	0.323	0.320	0.323	0.322	0.322
D_2	c_4	0.364	0.366	0.368	0.336	0.360	0.358	0.346	0.343	0.363
	c_5	0.305	0.305	0.302	0.317	0.285	0.335	0.318	0.318	0.306
	c_6	0.331	0.329	0.330	0.347	0.355	0.307	0.336	0.339	0.330
D_3	c_7	0.389	0.387	0.384	0.387	0.397	0.398	0.360	0.411	0.402
	c_8	0.255	0.258	0.259	0.258	0.274	0.271	0.295	0.245	0.273
	c_9	0.356	0.355	0.357	0.355	0.330	0.331	0.344	0.343	0.325
	Sum	3	3	3	3	3	3	3	3	3

TABLE 4.8 The T_D^α matrix for case 1 (The process of Eq. 4.13).

	D_1	D_2	D_3	Sum
D_1	1.001	0.909	0.859	2.769
D_2	0.937	0.802	0.791	2.530
D_3	0.913	0.823	0.736	2.472

TABLE 4.9 The normalized T_D^α matrix for case 1 (The process of Eq. 4.13).

	D_1	D_2	D_3	Sum
D_1	0.361	0.328	0.310	1
D_2	0.370	0.317	0.313	1
D_3	0.369	0.333	0.298	1

Table 4.8 reports $\boldsymbol{T}_D^\alpha$ (unnormalized), the dimension-level aggregation of the total-influence matrix $\boldsymbol{T}$. For example, the value $D_1 \rightarrow D_1 = 1.001$ is the mean of the nine elements formed by rows c_1, c_2, $c_3$and columns c_1, c_2, c_3 in $\boldsymbol{T}$ (i.e., $c_1 \rightarrow c_1$ through $c_3 \rightarrow c_3$). This procedure is applied analogously to all cross-dimension blocks to obtain the complete $\boldsymbol{T}_D^\alpha$. Table 4.9 shows the row-normalized version of Table 4.8, that is, the normalized dimension influence matrix $\boldsymbol{T}_D^\alpha$. Each row is scaled so that its horizontal sum equals 1, yielding the proportion with which a given dimension distributes its total influence across all dimensions. This step replaces the equal-cluster assumption in classical ANP with empirically estimated influence shares. Table 4.10 is the transpose of Table 4.9 (i.e., $\boldsymbol{T}_D^{\alpha'}$).

Table 4.11 presents the weighted supermatrix $\boldsymbol{W}_w$. It is obtained by weighting the criterion-level unweighted supermatrix $\boldsymbol{W}$ with the row-normalized dimension influence matrix $\boldsymbol{T}_D^\alpha$'. Each column of $\boldsymbol{W}_w$ is stochastic (the bottom "Sum" row equals 1), which ensures the existence of a limiting supermatrix when $\boldsymbol{W}_w$ is raised to large powers; the

TABLE 4.10 The transpose of the normalized T_D^{α} matrix for case 1 (Eq. 4.13).

	D_1	D_2	D_3
D_1	0.361	0.370	0.369
D_2	0.328	0.317	0.333
D_3	0.310	0.313	0.298
Sum	1	1	1

TABLE 4.11 The weighted supermatrix for case 1 (Eq. 4.14).

		D_1			D_2			D_3		
		c_1	c_2	c_3	c_4	c_5	c_6	c_7	c_8	c_9
D_1	c_1	0.113	0.128	0.128	0.126	0.126	0.127	0.126	0.127	0.126
	c_2	0.126	0.111	0.127	0.125	0.125	0.125	0.124	0.123	0.124
	c_3	0.122	0.122	0.107	0.120	0.120	0.119	0.119	0.119	0.119
D_2	c_4	0.119	0.120	0.121	0.106	0.114	0.114	0.115	0.114	0.121
	c_5	0.100	0.100	0.099	0.100	0.090	0.106	0.106	0.106	0.102
	c_6	0.109	0.108	0.108	0.110	0.113	0.097	0.112	0.113	0.110
D_3	c_7	0.121	0.120	0.119	0.121	0.124	0.124	0.107	0.123	0.120
	c_8	0.079	0.080	0.080	0.081	0.086	0.085	0.088	0.073	0.081
	c_9	0.110	0.110	0.111	0.111	0.103	0.104	0.103	0.102	0.097
	Sum	1	1	1	1	1	1	1	1	1

resulting limit yields the global criterion weights reported in Table 4.12. Fig. 4.1 shows the DANP criterion weight results for case 1.

Table 4.12 reports the limiting supermatrix of the DANP procedure and, therefore, the global priorities. Reading the rank column and the corresponding weights, the final ordering from highest to lowest is:

c_1 (0.125) > c_2 (0.123) > c_7 (0.120) > c_3 (0.118) > c_4(0.116) > c_6 (0.109) > c_9 (0.106) > c_5 (0.101) > c_8 (0.082).

Aggregating by dimension yields economic (D_1) = 0.366, environmental (D_2) = 0.326, and social (D_3) = 0.308. Thus while the ESG emphasis is relatively balanced, economic considerations are marginally predominant, followed closely by environmental, with social factors only slightly lower in aggregate.

Substantively, the dominance of company size (c_1) and market share (c_2) indicates that alliance viability in the OSAT context is first and foremost scale- and market-led. These capabilities underpin ramp-up speed, bargaining power, and supply assurance, and they should therefore anchor key performance indicator (KPI) weighting and shortlisting. Gender equality (c_7) ranks third. This indicates that social governance has measurable salience for partner differentiation. The result is consistent with buyer audits and with talent-retention concerns in global electronics supply chains. The next tier, product price (c_3) and recyclable materials (c_4), suggests that cost competitiveness and circular-materials programs jointly shape perceived partner quality; both should feature in negotiation targets and improvement roadmaps. The mid-ranking items, renewable energy use (c_6) and employee rights (c_9), are well suited to staged covenants, such as progressive power purchase agreements and labor-rights KPIs. These commitments shape the alliance's long-term risk and cost profile while not dominating the initial screen. Finally, environmental compliance (c_5) and protection of disadvantaged groups (c_8) have the smallest weights; in practice, they function as gatekeeping requirements rather than differentiators and are best enforced through pre qualification thresholds and periodic audits.

TABLE 4.12 The DANP results for case 1 (Eq. 4.15).

		D_1			D_2			D_3			Rank
		c_1	c_2	c_3	c_4	c_5	c_6	c_7	c_8	c_9	
D_1	c_1	0.125	0.125	0.125	0.125	0.125	0.125	0.125	0.125	0.125	1
	c_2	0.123	0.123	0.123	0.123	0.123	0.123	0.123	0.123	0.123	2
	c_3	0.118	0.118	0.118	0.118	0.118	0.118	0.118	0.118	0.118	4
D_2	c_4	0.116	0.116	0.116	0.116	0.116	0.116	0.116	0.116	0.116	5
	c_5	0.101	0.101	0.101	0.101	0.101	0.101	0.101	0.101	0.101	8
	c_6	0.109	0.109	0.109	0.109	0.109	0.109	0.109	0.109	0.109	6
D_3	c_7	0.120	0.120	0.120	0.120	0.120	0.120	0.120	0.120	0.120	3
	c_8	0.082	0.082	0.082	0.082	0.082	0.082	0.082	0.082	0.082	9
	c_9	0.106	0.106	0.106	0.106	0.106	0.106	0.106	0.106	0.106	7
	Sum	1	1	1	1	1	1	1	1	1	

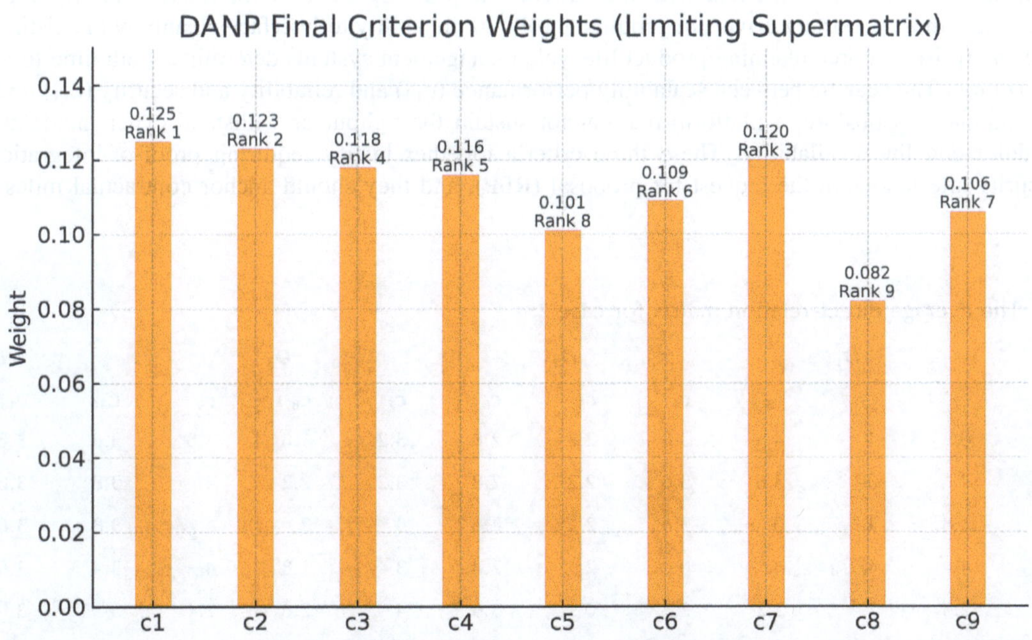

FIGURE 4.1 The DANP criterion weight results for case 1.

This revised interpretation aligns with the earlier DEMATEL diagnosis. Some social and environmental items act as net drivers in the causal map, yet their equilibrium weights in Table 4.12 are lower once influence is distributed across the full network. This outcome is expected for the limiting supermatrix in DANP.

4.4 Numerical example 2—selecting a digital manufacturing platform partner

A multinational electronics manufacturer set out to standardize its shop-floor digital infrastructure across multiple plants. The program required a single digital manufacturing platform (covering manufacturing execution system, data integration, and analytics) to be sourced from an external partner and rolled out in waves. Because the success of such programs depends as much on technology and operations as on commercial fit, compliance, and user adoption, the firm evaluated candidates across four dimensions, each represented by three criteria (12 in total):

(i) Commercial viability (D_1): total cost of ownership (c_1), vendor market maturity/installed base (c_2), pricing flexibility (c_3).
(ii) Compliance and sustainability (D_2): environmental and regulatory conformance (c_4), audit track record and certifications (c_5), supply-chain transparency/traceability (c_6).
(iii) People and adoption (D_3): training and change management (c_7), external/community acceptance (c_8), usability and operator experience (c_9).
(iv) Technology and operations (D_4): system interoperability/integration (c_{10}), reliability and security/uptime (c_{11}), scalability and performance (c_{12}).

An eight-member panel comprising experts from operations, IT, procurement, environmental, health, and safety, plant leadership, and an external systems integrator provided direct-influence judgments on a 0 to 4 DEMATEL scale. Table 4.13 shows the average direct-relation matrix across experts.

Rather than detailing the intermediate matrices, we report the final DANP priorities in Table 4.14. The weights and ranks are:

c_{10} (0.093) > c_2 (0.090) > c_{12} (0.089) ≥ c_{11} (0.089) > c_7 (0.088) > c_9 (0.087) ≥ c_1 (0.087) > c_3 (0.085) ≥ c_4 (0.085) > c_6 (0.079) > c_5 (0.066) > c_8 (0.062).

Aggregated by dimension, the priorities are $D_4 = 0.271$, $D_1 = 0.262$, $D_3 = 0.237$, and $D_2 = 0.230$. Technology and operations considerations are marginally dominant, commercial fit is a close second, and people/adoption and compliance form a solid but secondary foundation. Fig. 4.2 shows the DANP criterion weight results for case 2.

The ordering in Table 4.14 is consistent with the structure implied by Table 4.13. Interoperability/integration (c_{10}) emerges as the single most important driver. In a multisite rollout, the ability to interface cleanly with existing equipment, historians, and enterprise resource planning/product lifecycle management systems determines both time-to-value and the cost of customization. The near-tie between scalability/performance (c_{12}) and reliability and security (c_{11}) underscores the program's operational risk posture: a platform that cannot sustain throughput or withstand cyber incidents jeopardizes ramp-up schedules and line availability. These three criteria together justify requiring proof-of-integration, reference loads, and security attestations in the request for proposal (RFP), and they should anchor contractual milestones.

TABLE 4.13 The average direct-relation matrix for case 2.

		D_1			D_2			D_3			D_4		
		c_1	c_2	c_3	c_4	c_5	c_6	c_7	c_8	c_9	c_{10}	c_{11}	c_{12}
D_1	c_1	0	4	4	3.8	2.2	2.8	3.2	1.8	3.8	3.8	3.8	3.6
	c_2	4	0	3.8	3.8	2.2	2.8	3.2	2.2	4	3.8	3.8	3.4
	c_3	3.8	4	0	3.8	2	2.6	3	2	4	3.8	3.6	3.4
D_2	c_4	4	4	4	0	2	2.8	3	1.8	4	3.4	3.6	3.4
	c_5	2.6	2.4	2.2	2.2	0	3.6	4	2.6	2.4	3	3	3.2
	c_6	2.8	3	2.4	2.4	3.2	0	4	3.2	2.4	3.4	3	3.6
D_3	c_7	3	3	3	3	3.4	3.8	0	3.4	2.6	3.6	3.2	3.4
	c_8	1.6	2.2	2	2.2	2.8	3.2	3.8	0	2.2	2.6	2.6	2.8
	c_9	3.8	3.8	3.6	3.2	2	2.6	2.6	2	0	3.8	3.4	3.2
D_4	c_{10}	3.4	3.6	3.4	3.6	2.6	2.4	2.8	2.2	3.6	0	3.4	3.4
	c_{11}	3.4	3.8	3.2	3.4	2	2.6	3.4	2	3.6	3.8	0	3.6
	c_{12}	3	3.2	3.2	3.2	2.4	3.6	3.8	2.2	3.2	3.4	3.4	0

TABLE 4.14 The DANP results for case 2.

Dimension	Criterion	Weight	Rank
D_1	c_1	0.087	7
	c_2	0.090	2
	c_3	0.085	8
D_2	c_4	0.085	9
	c_5	0.066	11
	c_6	0.079	10
D_3	c_7	0.088	5
	c_8	0.062	12
	c_9	0.087	6
D_4	c_{10}	0.093	1
	c_{11}	0.089	4
	c_{12}	0.089	3

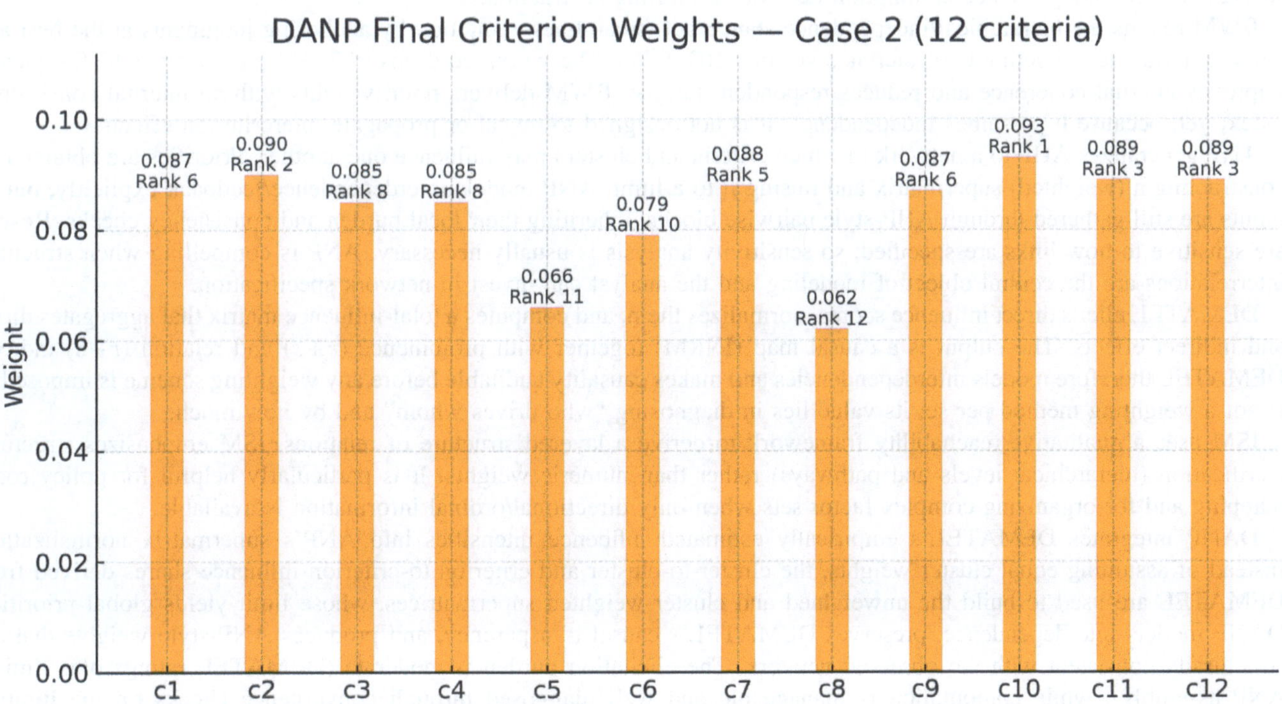

FIGURE 4.2 The DANP criterion weight results for case 2.

The second position of vendor market maturity (c_2) reflects a pragmatic commercial lens: a provider with a broad installed base offers richer implementation playbooks, a more resilient support ecosystem, and better leverage in codeveloping features. Meanwhile, training and change management (c_7) and usability (c_9) occupy the middle ranks, highlighting that adoption quality is a meaningful differentiator even when technology leads; pilots should therefore include operator-facing user experience (UX) tests and formal change-management deliverables. Total cost of ownership

(c_1) and pricing flexibility (c_3) remain important but are not decisive once integration and reliability are validated. This allocation helps avoid short-term cost savings that undermine long-term value.

At the lower end, audit/certification history (c_5) and external/community acceptance (c_8) have the smallest weights. The firm interprets these as hygiene factors rather than differentiators: they are enforced as prequalification thresholds (must-have certifications, audit readiness, and community engagement policies), while higher-weight criteria drive ranking among vendors that clear the bar. Supply-chain transparency (c_6) occupies a mid-low position. It is treated as a roadmap commitment, with targets for traceability modules and supplier data connectivity specified in the alliance governance plan.

Taken together, the DANP results provide a coherent narrative for decision and execution. The selection should prioritize platforms with demonstrated integration, reliability/security, and scalable performance, backed by a vendor with a mature installed base.

4.5 Discussion

Methods for multicriteria modeling can be situated along two practical axes: how faithfully they represent interrelationships among criteria and how much judgmental and computational effort they require. The comparison in Table 4.15 condenses these trade-offs by reporting, for each method, (i) the structural paradigm it adopts, (ii) whether it assumes independence or models interdependence/feedback, (iii) the judgment format and workload, (iv) the nature of the outputs, and (v) diagnostic tools and typical use. The narrative below interprets Table 4.15, clarifying what each method actually computes and when it is best deployed.

AHP represents the problem as a hierarchy and assumes local independence among criteria within a level. Preferences are elicited via pairwise comparisons, yielding eigenvector-based priorities. The judgment load grows as $[n(n-1)]/2$ per level, which explains AHP's strong transparency but rising cognitive burden as the criterion set expands. Its hallmark consistency index/consistency ratio diagnostic is a practical strength; however, when cross-criterion influences are substantive, the independence assumption becomes a limiting abstraction.

BWM retains the hierarchical/independence stance but streamlines elicitation by anchoring judgments at the best and worst criteria and collecting two reference vectors (BO, OW). The workload drops to $2n-3$ judgments, which typically improves internal coherence and reduces respondent fatigue. BWM delivers point weights with an internal consistency index; yet, because it presumes independence, it is not designed to reveal or propagate intercriterion effects.

ANP generalizes AHP to a network in which criteria and clusters may influence one another. Priorities are obtained by constructing a (weighted) supermatrix and raising it to a limit. ANP models interdependence/feedback explicitly, but its inputs are still gathered through AHP-style pairwise blocks, inheriting their local burden and consistency checks. Results are sensitive to how links are specified, so sensitivity analysis is usually necessary. ANP is compelling when structural interrelations are the central object of modeling and the analyst can invest in network specification.

DEMATEL elicits direct influence scores, normalizes them, and computes a total-influence matrix that aggregates direct and indirect effects. The output is a causal map (INRM) together with prominence ($r+s$) and relation ($r-s$) indices. DEMATEL therefore models interdependencies and makes causality auditable before any weighting scheme is imposed. It is not a weighting method per se; its value lies in diagnosing "who drives whom" and by how much.

ISM uses a qualitative reachability framework to derive a layered structure of relations. ISM emphasizes structural clarification (hierarchical levels and pathways) rather than numeric weights. It is particularly helpful for policy roadmapping and for organizing complex factor sets when only directional/ordinal information is available.

DANP integrates DEMATEL's empirically estimated influence intensities into ANP's supermatrix normalization. Instead of assuming equal cluster weights, the cluster-to-cluster and criterion-to-criterion influence shares derived from DEMATEL are used to build the unweighted and cluster-weighted supermatrices, whose limit yields global priorities. DANP models interdependence, preserves DEMATEL's causal transparency, and produces ANP-style weights that are structurally consistent with the observed network. The elicitation burden is moderate (DEMATEL ratings plus limited ANP assembly), while computation is manageable and well diagnosed through convergence checks on the limiting supermatrix.

Read against Table 4.15, DANP occupies a distinctive middle ground: it inherits DEMATEL's visibility into causality and produces actionable weights without imposing ANP's equal-cluster assumption. This alignment between causal structure and priority derivation is valuable when: (i) interdependence and feedback are substantive (e.g., technology adoption ecosystems, energy and urban systems, supply-chain strategy, service quality architectures); (ii) stakeholders require traceability from judgments to weights (governance and auditability); and (iii) weights must feed directly into downstream ranking or optimization (e.g., TOPSIS/VIKOR/COCOSO, goal programming), closing the loop from "structure → weights → decisions." In short, when independence is tenable and speed is paramount, AHP/BWM remains

TABLE 4.15 Method comparisons.

Method	Structural model	Criterion independence vs. interdependence	Primary judgment format	Typical of judgments (for n criteria)	Principal output
Analytic hierarchy process (AHP)	Hierarchy	Assumes independence (within each level)	Pairwise comparisons (ratio scale)	$[n(n-1)]/2$	Local/global weights
Best-worst method BWM	Hierarchy with best/worst anchors	Assumes independence	Two reference vectors: *best-to-others* (BO) and *others-to-worst* (OW)	$2n-3$	Local/global weights
Analytic network process (ANP)	Network (clusters with feedback)	Models interdependence/feedback	Pairwise comparisons (multiple interlinked matrices)	≥ AHP	Weights
DEMATEL	Causal network (direct/indirect effects)	Models interdependence	Direct-influence ratings (e.g., 0–4)	$n(n-1)$	Total-influence matrix and influential network relation map (INRM)
Interpretive structural modeling (ISM)	Interpretive reachability hierarchy	Models interrelations (reachability)	Binary/qualitative relations	$\leq [n(n-1)]/2$	Hierarchical structure/levels
DANP	Decision-Making and Trial Evaluation Laboratory-informed ANP	Models interdependence	DEMATEL + ANP-style supermatrix	$n(n-1)$	Total-influence matrix, INRM, and weights

attractive; when structural effects dominate and resources permit, ANP is justifiable; but when one needs both causal clarity and defensible weights calibrated to that causality, DANP is the method of choice.

4.6 Conclusions

This chapter has argued that DANP offers a coherent route from causal structure to actionable priorities in decisions where criteria influence one another. DANP combines DEMATEL's influence propagation with ANP's supermatrix calculus. It then weights the supermatrix using empirically observed cluster-to-cluster effects. This procedure removes the equal-cluster simplification and aligns the final priorities with observed system behavior. Because the INRM and the intermediate matrices are retained, the analysis is not a black box: stakeholders can audit who drives whom, by how much, and how those relationships are reflected in the final weights.

The OSAT alliance case is an appropriate testbed because partner suitability is shaped jointly by economic capacity and market access, environmental practices, and social governance. These elements are mutually reinforcing (e.g., compliance affects access to key customers; workforce practices influence yield and delivery reliability), and a method that assumes independence would be mis-specified. DANP allows the firm to (i) map and discuss the causal backbone with experts from operations, procurement, finance, and ESG; (ii) translate that backbone into priorities without imposing equal cluster weights; and (iii) carry those priorities forward into partner screening, contract KPIs, and audit/remediation plans. The approach distinguishes threshold items, defined as criteria that must be met for eligibility, from differentiating items that should drive selection among eligible candidates. It does so without relying on a bare list of ranks.

The digital manufacturing-platform case is likewise well suited because program success depends simultaneously on technology (interoperability, reliability, scalability), adoption (training and usability), compliance (certifications, traceability), and commercial fit. Here, the INRM clarifies why certain technology attributes have system-wide reach, while DANP ensures that these influence patterns calibrate the priorities used in procurement and rollout planning. The analysis supports concrete actions: structure RFP evidence (proofs of integration and security attestations), stage change management and UX validation in pilots, and specify roadmap commitments for compliance and transparency. All steps remain traceable from expert judgments to final weights.

Limitations include reliance on expert judgment, sensitivity to normalization and thresholding, and a static influence model. These can be mitigated through robust aggregation, outlier screening, and sensitivity analyses; they also motivate extensions such as fuzzy/gray/neutrosophic DANP for uncertainty, dynamic DANP for time-varying systems, and Bayesian treatments that would attach credible intervals to weights.

In sum, the two applications show that DANP is fit for purpose wherever interdependence is intrinsic and governance demands a transparent link from expert knowledge to defensible priorities. The method enables decision makers to align selection criteria, KPIs, and improvement roadmaps with the system's causal mechanics, while avoiding independence assumptions and opaque weighting rules.

References

Aparisi-Cerdá, I., Ribó-Pérez, D., Gómez-Navarro, T., García-Melón, M., & Peris-Blanes, J. (2024). Prioritising positive energy districts to achieve carbon neutral cities: Delphi-DANP approach. *Renewable and Sustainable Energy Reviews, 203*, 114764.

Areerakulkan, N., & Sumrit, D. (2025). Elucidating critical success factors for digital transformation in logistics service providers using a grey-DANP approach: Insights from the Thai SMEs road freight transportation sector. *Journal of Open Innovation: Technology, Market, and Complexity*, 100549.

Aydın, Y. (2025). A hybrid multi-criteria decision-making model for performance assessment in the banking industry. *Knowledge and Decision Systems with Applications, 1*, 234–256.

Chiu, W.-Y., Tzeng, G.-H., & Li, H.-L. (2013). A new hybrid MCDM model combining DANP with VIKOR to improve e-store business. *Knowledge-Based Systems, 37*, 48–61.

Dağıstanlı, H. A. (2025). Prioritizing design criteria for unmanned helicopter systems under uncertainty using fuzzy best worst method approach. *Journal of Intelligent Decision Making and Granular Computing, 1*(1), 1–12.

Du, S., & Li, X. (2023). A new hybrid hermeneutic-fuzzy-DANP model based key influencing factors evaluation and ranking of soft science institute. *International Journal of Fuzzy Systems, 25*(8), 3016–3035.

Gokasar, I., & Okur, I. (2025). A multi-criteria utility approach to bridge maintenance prioritization. *Knowledge and Decision Systems with Applications, 1*, 35–56.

Gunawan, I., Trihastuti, D., Kumar, A., & Tan, K. H. (2025). Integrated DANP and binary goal programming model in generating joint-decision making for packaging postponement and supplier selection. *Annals of Operations Research, 346*(2), 981–1010.

Hsu, C.-C., Liou, J. J., & Chuang, Y.-C. (2013). Integrating DANP and modified grey relation theory for the selection of an outsourcing provider. *Expert Systems with Applications, 40*(6), 2297–2304.

Hsu, C.-C., Liou, J. J., Lo, H.-W., & Wang, Y.-C. (2018). Using a hybrid method for evaluating and improving the service quality of public bike-sharing systems. *Journal of Cleaner Production, 202*, 1131–1144.

Lo, H.-W., Li, K.-Y., & Lin, S.-W. (2025). Multi-year performance evaluation and trend tracking of sustainable suppliers: An application of a hybrid decision analysis model. *Journal of Intelligent Decision Making and Granular Computing, 1*(1), 89–105.

Rashidian, F., Eydi, A., & Roghanian, E. (2024). Reliable and green road-rail routing using a hybrid procedure of DANP, COCOSO, and FMEA criticality methods: A case study of cement transportation network in Iran. *Journal of Cleaner Production, 447*, 141250.

Saaty, T. L. (1996). *Decision making with dependence and feedback: The analytic network process*. RWS publications Pittsburgh.

Saaty, T. L., & Vargas, L. G. (1987). Uncertainty and rank order in the analytic hierarchy process. *European Journal of Operational Research, 32*(1), 107–117.

Shao, Q., & Lo, H.-W. (2025). Advancing renewable energy technologies in remote areas: Exploring key success factors and interdependencies for sustainable wind energy development. *Sustainable Energy Technologies and Assessments, 79*, 104367.

Shao, Q., Lo, H.-W., Liu, S., Jiang, C., & Su, P. (2024). Using a rough-fuzzy DANP technique for analysis of the key factors affecting the development of a green business in the machinery manufacturing sector. *Journal of Cleaner Production, 480*, 144089.

Yang, Y.-P. O., Shieh, H.-M., Leu, J.-D., & Tzeng, G.-H. (2008). A novel hybrid MCDM model combined with DEMATEL and ANP with applications. *International Journal of Operations Research, 5*(3), 160–168.

Yang, Y.-P. O., Shieh, H.-M., & Tzeng, G.-H. (2013). A VIKOR technique based on DEMATEL and ANP for information security risk control assessment. *Information Sciences, 232*, 482–500.

Zhang, Z., Jiang, H., Shao, T., & Shao, Q. (2023). Understanding the selection of intelligent engineering B2B platform in China through the fuzzy DANP and TOPSIS techniques: A multi-study analysis. *Applied Soft Computing, 141*, 110277.

Hsu, C.-W., Liou, J. J. H., & Chuang, Y.-C. (2013). Integrating DANP and modified grey relation theory for the selection of an outsourcing provider. *Expert Systems with Applications*, *40*(6), 2297–2304.
Huo, C.-H., Liou, J. J. H., Lo, H.-W., & Wang, Y.-C. (2018). Using a hybrid method for evaluating and improving the service quality of public bike-sharing systems. *Journal of Cleaner Production*, *202*, 1132–1144.
Lo, H.-W., Lu, K.-Y., & Lin, S.-W. (2025). Multi-year performance evaluation and trend analysis of sustainable suppliers: An application of a hybrid decision analysis model. *Journal of Intelligent Decision Making and Granular Computing*, *1*(1), 89–105.
Rashidian, ..., A., & Rouhbakhsh, E. (2024). Reliable and green road-rail routing using a hybrid procedure of DANP, COCOSO, and FMEA criticality methods: A case study of cement transportation network in Iran. *Journal of Cleaner Production*, *447*, 141269.
Saaty, T. L. (1996). *Decision making with dependence and feedback: The analytic network process*. RWS publications, Pittsburgh.
Saaty, T. L., & Vargas, L. G. (1987). Uncertainty and rank order in the analytic hierarchy process. *European Journal of Operational Research*, *32*(1), 107–117.
Shao, Q., & Lo, H.-W. (2024). Advancing renewable energy technologies in remote areas: Exploring key success factors and interdependencies for sustainable wind energy development. *Sustainable Energy Technologies and Assessments*, *73*, 104159.
Shao, Q., Lo, H.-W., Jiang, S., Hang, C., & Chen, P. (2024). Using a three-way DANP technique for analysis of the key factors affecting the development of green business in the machinery manufacturing sector. *Journal of Cleaner Production*, *480*, 144089.
Yang, Y.-P. O., Shieh, H.-M., Leu, J.-D., & Tzeng, G.-H. (2008). A novel hybrid MCDM model combined with DEMATEL and ANP with applications. *International Journal of Operations Research*, *5*(3), 160–168.
Yang, Y.-P. O., Shieh, H.-M., & Tzeng, G.-H. (2013). A VIKOR technique based on DEMATEL and ANP for information security risk control assessment. *Information Sciences*, *232*, 482–500.
Zhang, Z., Tian, H., Shao, T., & Shao, Q. (2023). Understanding the selection of intelligent engineering B2B platform in China through the fuzzy DANP and TOPSIS techniques: A multi-study analysis. *Applied Soft Computing*, *142*, 110277.

Chapter 5

WINGS: Weighted influence nonlinear gauge system for multi-attribute decision-making

Md. Abdul Moktadir, Yousaf Ayub, and Jingzheng Ren

Department of Industrial and Systems Engineering, The Hong Kong Polytechnic University, Hong Kong SAR, P.R. China

5.1 Introduction

Multicriteria decision-making (MCDM) is a major part of operations research and management science, providing structured approaches to evaluate the importance and intertwined relationships among decision criteria and supporting alternative selection characterized by multiple, often conflicting criteria (Dash et al., 2025; Huang et al., 2025; Moktadir et al., 2025). Traditional MCDM methods, such as the weighted sum model (WSM), best–worst method (BWM), and the analytical hierarchy process (AHP), often rely on an assumption: that the decision criteria are independent (Malakar & Rai, 2023; Otay et al., 2024). In real-life situations, decision-making criteria often interact, influence each other, and exhibit complex interdependencies that, if ignored, can lead to inaccurate results. To avoid the drawback of classical MCDM, the decision-making trial and evaluation laboratory (DEMATEL) technique was found to be useful for interactions assessment, which can divide the decision criteria into two groups: causal and effect groups (Gabus & Fontela, 1973).

However, the DEMATEL approach is limited to interaction assessment and is unable to address the strength of the decision criteria. To deal with this issue, Michnik (2013) proposed the weighted influence nonlinear gauge system (WINGS) for capturing strength-intertwined relationships among decision-making elements. More specifically, the WINGS enhances the computational efficiency of its predecessor DEMATEL by integrating two fundamental features of any system component: its internal strength (inherent importance or power) and its external influence (the intensity of its effect on other components) (Tavana et al., 2023; Wang et al., 2024). This integration enables the WINGS model to more accurately model the complex, nonlinear relationships within a system, whether that system is a set of evaluation criteria, a network of risk factors, or a branch of strategic objectives (Michnik, 2013). WINGS cannot only model the complex problem but also provide more robust and consistent results. Due to these numerous advantages, it is now gaining popularity among scholars for analyzing various socioeconomic and policy-related issues. The various studies utilized the WINGS model individually or advanced the classical model by integrating it with other models to achieve the best results. For instance, the classical WINGS has been applied in analyzing barriers to blockchain technology adoption (Govindan and Nasr, 2023), policymaking research for undergraduate elective courses (Hashemkhani Zolfani et al., 2022), sustainable partner selection for green partnerships (Tavana et al., 2022), etc. Additionally, the advanced WINGS model, such as grey WINGS (Wang & Zhang, 2022), fuzzy WINGS (Wang et al., 2023), interval type-2 trapezoidal fuzzy set (IT2TrFS)-WINGS (Moktadir & Ren, 2023), decomposed fuzzy set (DFS)-WINGS (Moktadir & Ren, 2024a), etc., are also used for addressing various decision-making problems. Therefore, to facilitate an understanding of the WINGS model among industrial decision-makers (DMs), policymakers, students, and scholars, this chapter provides practical guidance by presenting two numerical examples of the WINGS model, encompassing both a hypothetical case example and a complex real-life decision problem. In addition, a Python-based graphical user interface (GUI) application for the WINGS model has been developed and deployed on the Streamlit platform, integrated with a GitHub repository, providing easy access to analyze complex, intertwined, and real-world decision-making problems while avoiding computational

Encyclopedia of Multi-Attribute Decision-Making (MADM). DOI: https://doi.org/10.1016/B978-0-443-33275-3.00029-4

difficulties. The WINGS app is further capable of handling real data-driven decision-making, where scholars/practitioners/students/academics can input real data directly to examine the complex, strength-intertwined relationship among system components. Additionally, the WINGS application can be further used for advanced WINGS models such as crisp score-based IT2TrFS-WINGS, DFS-WINGS, interval valued Fermatean fuzzy sets WINGS, intuitionistic fuzzy WINGS, 2-tuple linguistic WINGS, etc., which are the most significant contributions of this chapter.

The rest of the chapter is organized into the following ways: Section 5.2 provides the literature review on the WINGS model, and the methodological stepwise procedure for the WINGS model is depicted in Section 5.3. Section 5.4 shows a hypothetical case example to understand the WINGS model. In addition, a complex real-life decision-making problem is formulated in Section 5.5, and the WINGS model is implemented to provide in-depth insight into the complex modeling of WINGS. Finally, the conclusions of this chapter are given in Section 5.6. An example implementation process of the WINGS model on a Python-based GUI application platform is depicted in Appendix A (the numerical example 1 is used to present the implementation process as well for verification).

5.2 Literature review

The WINGS model is gaining popularity among scholars and DMs for its superiority over the classical DEMATEL method. The literature review on WINGS reveals that numerous studies have been conducted to evaluate the strength-interaction relationship among system factors, as well as to use the WINGS model to determine the weight of factors for selecting the best alternative. Since the WINGS method has been applied across various domains to address complex decision problems involving interdependencies, a summary of its trends and advancements is presented in Table 5.1.

The growing trend of applying the WINGS model, along with its advancements, demonstrates its superiority. Therefore, this chapter will also make a significant contribution to the existing literature in two ways: first, it demonstrates how the WINGS model works by providing two comprehensive numerical examples by showing a step-by-step computational process that will support scholars/decision-makers/policymakers/students in understanding how the WINGS model applies to real-life decision-making. Second, it develops a dynamic, Python-based GUI application for the WINGS model, enabling the real-time implementation of the WINGS method. In this application software, several interactive options have been integrated, allowing for comprehensive strength-interactions analysis among elements without encountering any computational difficulties. This web-based application software will also allow users to select a suitable model, as we have developed both an individual linguistic model that utilizes linguistic input and a data-driven model that utilizes real data. The web-based Python application software will also support adjusting the expert's weight and be able to handle a larger number of decision-making factors and experts, which is crucial for the decision-making process, rather than giving equal importance to decision-makers. Although we presented the computational process step-by-step, the analysis was performed both in Excel-based software and Python-based GUI WINGS application software to confirm its reliability in the computation process. The next section shows the complete methodology.

5.3 Methodology

In many decision science and socioeconomic problem analyses, various types of weighting models, such as the AHP, BWM, and entropy, are widely used (Carnero, 2026; Otay et al., 2024). However, the weighting models are unable to capture the complex and intertwined relationships among the decision-making components. In this sense, the DEMATEL model was invented by the Geneva Research Center of the Battelle Memorial Institute (Gabus & Fontela, 1973), which is recognized as a powerful tool for capturing intertwined relationships in a structural manner and has received greater attention in the literature (Huang et al., 2025; Pinto et al., 2025). However, the classical DEMATEL only provides a cause-and-effect relationship, rather than a strength-interaction relationship. To fill these gaps, Michnik (2013) first invented the WINGS method, which is able to assess both strength-interaction relationships among system elements. To better understand the classical WINGS model, the stepwise computational algorithm is explained below, based on the original study offered by Michnik (2013):

Step 1: Identification of evaluation components (e.g., criteria, elements, factors)

In this step, a set of evaluation components, such as decision-making criteria, factors, or elements, is identified from experts' consultation/literature review/field survey/social network analysis/large language model (LLM)/a combination of these approaches. It is also noted that applying this model requires confirming that the evaluation components are greater than or equal to two.

TABLE 5.1 Various applications of the weighted influence nonlinear gauge system (WINGS) model and its extension in different domains.

Author(s)	Application domain	Key method
Michnik (2013)	Methodological foundation	Introduced the WINGS method as an extension of DEMATEL.
Michnik (2013)	Innovation projects selection	Classical WINGS
Kaviani et al. (2020)	Barriers to reverse logistics implementation in the automotive industry	BWM-WINGS
Tavana et al. (2021)	Technology project evaluation at NASA	Fuzzy WINGS
Wang et al. (2021)	Influencing factor evaluation for green building development.	Radial basis function neural network-based WINGS
Hashemkhani Zolfani et al. (2022)	Policy making for an undergraduate elective course	Classical ordinal priority approach-WINGS
Wang et al. (2023)	Agricultural supply chain decision-making	Fuzzy D-number WINGS-MICMAC
Tavana et al. (2023)	Assessment of criteria and mission architecture at NASA	Fuzzy preference programming and classical WINGS
Olorvida et al. (2023)	Evaluation of barriers to circular economy implementation for refurbished mobile	Grey WINGS
Tian and Zhang (2023)	Factor analysis for green technology innovation	Bipolar neutrosophic WINGS
Gao et al. (2024)	Equipment evaluations	Intuitionistic fuzzy WINGS
Lu et al. (2024)	Interactions mechanism assessment among the driving factors for energy poverty	Backpropagation neural network and WINGS
Kannan et al. (2024)	Barriers analysis of blockchain integration in the circular economy and the Industry 4.0 era.	Fuzzy WINGS
Moktadir and Ren (2024b)	Barriers and strategies analysis for tannery solid waste management, focusing on environment, social, and governance practices.	IVFFSs Delphi, WINGS, and novel IVFFSs-TODIM approach
Wu et al. (2024)	Repair for loss of social trust factor analysis considering public health emergency	2-tuple linguistic WINGS and regret theory
Wang et al. (2024)	Critical success factors analysis in collaborative emergency management	Multigranularity extended probabilistic linguistic WINGS-ISM
Kumar and Shukla (2025)	Analyzing key impediments focusing on the e-waste supply chain systems	Delphi and fuzzy WINGS
Shamekhi Amiri et al. (2025)	Classical comparisons of DEMATEL and WINGS	DEMATEL and WINGS
Zhang et al. (2025)	Analyzing factors that include agricultural carbon emissions	Fermatean neutrosophic set WINGS, AHP, and entropy
Liu et al. (2025)	Performance shaping factors analysis in standardized plant analysis, risk human reliability analysis	WINGS-based adversarial interpretive structure modeling
Moktadir and Ren (2025)	Carbon reduction strategies analysis focusing leather supply chain	Machine learning based novel trapezoidal fuzzy WINGS-ISM model

Step 2: Determine the internal strength and interactions to form an initial strength-influence relation matrix (ISIRM) among decision-making criteria/factors/elements using linguistic terms

DMs and industrial managers can use linguistic terms to assess both the internal strength and the influential relations of decision-making criteria/factors/elements. The following linguistic terms, shown in Table 5.2, or user-defined linguistic

TABLE 5.2 Classical linguistic scale for strength interactions assessment (authors defined).

Linguistic attribute for strength	Linguistic attribute for influence	Rating value
Absolute strength (AS)	Absolute influence (AI)	9
Extreme strength (ExS)	Extreme influence (ExI)	8
Very strong strength (VSS)	Very strong influence (VSI)	7
Strong strength plus (SSP)	Strong influence plus (SIP)	6
Strong strength (SS)	Strong influence (SI)	5
Moderate strength plus (MSP)	Moderate influence plus (MIP)	4
Moderate strength (MS)	Moderate influence (MI)	3
Weak strength (WS)	Weak influence (WI)	2
Equal strength (EqS)	Equal influence (EqI)	1
No strength (NS)	No strength/influence (NS)	0

FIGURE 5.1 Strengths and interactions of two criteria/factors/elements in the classical weighted influence nonlinear gauge system environment.

terms, can be used to assess the strength-interaction relationship. During the assessment process, the diagonal terms represent the strength, and other linguistic terms denote the influential relationship. It is also recommended to construct a map to understand how strength-interaction is assessed in the WINGS platform. In the map, nodes represent the criteria/factors/elements, and the interactive relationships between two criteria/factors/elements are represented by arrows.

For a better understanding, we can refer to the example in Fig. 5.1 below. Assume an expert is requested to evaluate the strength and interactions of two components, such as "Sun Light (CI1)" and "Plant Growth (CI2)." Based on his evaluation, it is shown that the strengths of the factors "CI1" and "CI2" are assigned to "ExS" and "MS," respectively, while factor "CI1" can only influence the factor "CI2" at the "VSI" level.

Step 3: Develop final direct strength-influence relation matrices (DSIRMs) and a weighted aggregated DSIRM

To form the DSIRM (P^k) for the k-th expert/decision maker/scholar, the user-defined linguistic terms shown in Table 5.2 are converted into linguistic values. Alternatively, the real data can be used directly to determine the DSIRMs (P), and for this, there is no need to form an aggregated DSIRM. It is also noted that the strength/intensity of criteria/factors/elements is provided following that $i \neq j$. For the linguistic model, the DSIRM (P^k) for the k-th expert/decision maker/scholar is formed as follows:

$$(P^k) = (p_{ij}^k) = \begin{bmatrix} p_{11}^k & \cdots & p_{1n}^k \\ p_{21}^k & \cdots & p_{2n}^k \\ \ddots & \ddots & \ddots \\ & \cdots & \\ p_{n1}^k & & p_{nn}^k \end{bmatrix} \tag{5.1}$$

where p_{ij}^k presents the numeric value for the k-th expert/decision maker/scholar. It is also an $n \times n$ matrix with n evaluation criteria/factors/elements. For a real data-driven model, there will be a single DSIRMs (P).

Therefore, the final weighted aggregated DSIRM (Q)/data-driven is formed from the DSIRMs obtained from all experts/decision-makers/scholars. In this case, $\omega = (\omega_1, \omega_2, ..., \omega_l)^T$ is the weight vector of the expert/decision maker/

scholar with $\omega_k \in [0,1]$ and $\sum_{k=1}^{l} \omega_k = 1\,(k = 1,2, ...,l)$. The simple averaging technique shown in Eq. (5.2) is used to form the final weighted aggregated DSIRM (Q) as follows:

$$Q = (\tilde{q}_{ij}) = \begin{bmatrix} q_{11} & \cdots & q_{1n} \\ q_{21} & \cdots & q_{2n} \\ \ddots & \ddots & \ddots \\ q_{n1} & \cdots & q_{nn} \end{bmatrix} = \begin{bmatrix} \frac{\sum_{k=1}^{l} \omega_k \cdot p_{11}^{k}}{l} & \cdots & \frac{\sum_{k=1}^{l} \omega_k \cdot p_{1n}^{k}}{l} \\ \frac{\sum_{k=1}^{l} \omega_k \cdot p_{21}^{k}}{l} & \cdots & \frac{\sum_{k=1}^{l} \omega_k \cdot p_{2n}^{k}}{l} \\ \ddots & \ddots & \ddots \\ \frac{\sum_{k=1}^{l} \omega_k \cdot p_{n1}^{k}}{l} & \cdots & \frac{\sum_{k=1}^{l} \omega_k \cdot p_{nn}^{k}}{l} \end{bmatrix} \tag{5.2}$$

Step 4: Determine the normalized DSIRM (R)

The normalized DSIRM (R) is constructed from the final aggregated DSIRM (Q) using the following Equations (5.3) and (5.4).

$$R = \frac{1}{\lambda} Q \tag{5.3}$$

The calibrating factor (λ) for normalization is determined by the summation of all elements in the final aggregated DSIRM (Q) shown in Eq. (5.4) as follows:

$$\lambda = \sum_{i=1}^{n} \sum_{j=1}^{n} q_{ij} \tag{5.4}$$

Step 5: Determine the total DSIRM (S) from the normalized DSIRM (R)

The total DSIRM (S) is determined using the following Eq. (5.5):

$$S = R + R^2 + R^3 + ... = R(I - R)^{-1} \tag{5.5}$$

In Eq. (5.5), I represents the identity matrix.

Step 6: Determine total impact ($\mathbf{TI_i}$), total receptivity ($\mathbf{TR_j}$) of criteria/factors/elements

To determine the total impact (TI_i) and total receptivity (TR_j), the following Equations (5.6)–(5.8) are utilized. The total impact (TI_i) and total receptivity (TR_j) denote the row sum and column sum, respectively.

$$S = [s_{ij}]_{n \times n};\ i, j = 1,\ 2,\ \ldots,\ n \tag{5.6}$$

$$TI_i = \left[\sum_{j=1}^{n} s_{ij} \right]_{n\times 1 = [t_i]n\times 1} \tag{5.7}$$

$$TR_j = \left[\sum_{i=1}^{n} s_{ij} \right]_{1\times n = [t_i]1\times n} \tag{5.8}$$

Step 7: Calculate total engagement ($\mathbf{TI_i + TR_i}$) and role (position) ($\mathbf{TI_i - TR_i}$) of system components

Finally, the total engagement ($TI_i + TR_i$) and role (position) ($TI_i - TR_i$) of criteria/factors/elements are calculated. It is also noted that the positive and negative values of the role (position) ($TI_i - TR_i$) indicate components belong to the influencing (cause) and influenced (effect/result) groups, respectively. The infographic of the engagement-role map is plotted based on a dataset of ($TI_i + TR_i$) $vs.$ ($TI_i - TR_i$).

5.4 Numerical example 1

To demonstrate the WINGS model presented in Section 5.3, a simple hypothetical decision-making problem based on the paper Moktadir and Ren (2024c) is formulated, where only five components are considered. The decision-making problem and the full implementation process, along with the mathematical computational procedure of the WINGS model, are given below:

Assume the management team in the transportation sector would like to understand the strength-interaction relationship among barriers instead of the ranking of barriers to the development of zero-emission transportation modes (ZETM). Therefore, the higher-level management team asks one senior manager (SM) to provide the insightful findings on barriers to ZETM for policy-making purposes. Therefore, the SM began brainstorming about the problem and concluded that SM needed to identify the strength-interaction relationship among the barriers so that policymaking would be easier. For this purpose, SM first identified a set of barriers that could hinder the development of a ZETM through a scholarly literature search. SM planned to implement the WINGS model, as it has the capability to determine the strength-interaction relationship among these barriers, whereas classical DEMATEL does not. Based on this problem, the full implementation process of the conventional WINGS model is given below with a stepwise procedure:

Step 1: Identify the critical barriers to the development of ZETM

One SM identified/selected the following five barriers from the previous study conducted by Moktadir and Ren (2024c) to determine the strength-interaction relationship among them.

CL1: Absence of policies and law enforcement for carbon emissions
CL2: Deficiency of preparedness to transform and redesign the existing supply chain
CL3: Nonexistence of accessibility of charging stations for electric vehicles
CL4: Lack of affordability of clean technologies
CL5: Absence of split incentives

Step 2: Define linguistic terms and construct the ISIRM

After finalizing the key barriers, to assess the strength-interaction relationship among them, the linguistic terms defined in Table 5.2 (which can be varied) are used to rate the internal strength of barriers and the influential relationship among them. In this example application, a single expert is considered (one SM). It is also noted that the linguistic scale given in diagonal and off-diagonal refer to internal strength and influences, respectively. In addition, to understand the internal strength and influences, the graphical approach shown in Fig. 5.1 is also used. Finally, the hypothetical linguistic data computed by the expert (SM) is given in Table 5.3.

Step 3: DSIRMs from ISIRM

Construct the final DSIRM (*P*) from ISIRM by transforming linguistic terms into numerical values using Eq. (5.1). The final DSIRM is given below.

$$P = \begin{bmatrix} 8 & 7 & 6 & 5 & 6 \\ 2 & 5 & 5 & 2 & 2 \\ 3 & 3 & 3 & 2 & 2 \\ 2 & 2 & 2 & 7 & 5 \\ 2 & 2 & 2 & 2 & 6 \end{bmatrix}$$

As a single expert (SM) is involved in this process, there is no need to use Eq. (5.2) to form the final weighted aggregated DSIRM (*Q*).

Step 4: Normalize the final DSIRM (R)

To determine the normalized DSIRM (*R*), first compute the normalizing factor (λ) using Eq. (5.4) and then the normalized DSIRM (*R*) is constructed using Eq. (5.3) with the support of a normalizing factor (λ).

$$\lambda = \sum_{i=1}^{n} \sum_{j=1}^{n} p_{ij} = 8+7+6+5+6+2+5+5+2+2+3+3+3+2+2+2+2+2+7+5+2+2+2+2 + 6 = 93.$$

TABLE 5.3 Initial strength-influence relation matrix.

Barrier	CL1	CL2	CL3	CL4	CL5
CL1	**ExS**	VSI	SIP	SI	SIP
CL2	WI	**SS**	SI	WI	WI
CL3	MI	MI	**MS**	WI	WI
CL4	WI	WI	WI	**VSS**	SI
CL5	WI	WI	WI	WI	**SSP**

Note: Diagonal linguistic terms (i.e., CL1: extreme strength [ExS]) represent internal strength, and off-diagonals (i.e., CL1 → CL2: very strong influence) represent influence.

$$R = \frac{1}{\lambda}P = \begin{bmatrix} \frac{8}{93} & \frac{7}{93} & \frac{6}{93} & \frac{5}{93} & \frac{6}{93} \\ \frac{2}{93} & \frac{5}{93} & \frac{5}{93} & \frac{2}{93} & \frac{2}{93} \\ \frac{3}{93} & \frac{3}{93} & \frac{3}{93} & \frac{2}{93} & \frac{2}{93} \\ \frac{2}{93} & \frac{2}{93} & \frac{2}{93} & \frac{7}{93} & \frac{5}{93} \\ \frac{2}{93} & \frac{2}{93} & \frac{2}{93} & \frac{2}{93} & \frac{2}{93} \end{bmatrix} = \begin{bmatrix} 0.086 & 0.075 & 0.065 & 0.054 & 0.065 \\ 0.022 & 0.054 & 0.054 & 0.022 & 0.022 \\ 0.032 & 0.032 & 0.032 & 0.022 & 0.022 \\ 0.022 & 0.022 & 0.022 & 0.075 & 0.054 \\ 0.022 & 0.022 & 0.022 & 0.022 & 0.065 \end{bmatrix}$$

Step 5: Determine the total DSIRM (S) from the normalized DSIRM (R)

The total DSIRM (S) is determined using Eq. (5.5) by using software such as Python, MATLAB, and Excel. In this example, an Excel-based platform has been used and verified through our Python-based WINGS application software. During calculation, it is also necessary to consider the 5×5 identity matrix (I). The identity matrix (I), final total DSIRM (S), and the computational process are shown below:

$$I = \begin{bmatrix} 1 & 0 & 0 & 0 & 0 \\ 0 & 1 & 0 & 0 & 0 \\ 0 & 0 & 1 & 0 & 0 \\ 0 & 0 & 0 & 1 & 0 \\ 0 & 0 & 0 & 0 & 1 \end{bmatrix}$$

$$S = R(I - R)^{-1} = \left(\begin{bmatrix} 0.086 & 0.075 & 0.065 & 0.054 & 0.065 \\ 0.022 & 0.054 & 0.054 & 0.022 & 0.022 \\ 0.032 & 0.032 & 0.032 & 0.022 & 0.022 \\ 0.022 & 0.022 & 0.022 & 0.075 & 0.054 \\ 0.022 & 0.022 & 0.022 & 0.022 & 0.065 \end{bmatrix} \right)$$

$$\times \left(\begin{bmatrix} 1 & 0 & 0 & 0 & 0 \\ 0 & 1 & 0 & 0 & 0 \\ 0 & 0 & 1 & 0 & 0 \\ 0 & 0 & 0 & 1 & 0 \\ 0 & 0 & 0 & 0 & 1 \end{bmatrix} - \begin{bmatrix} 0.086 & 0.075 & 0.065 & 0.054 & 0.065 \\ 0.022 & 0.054 & 0.054 & 0.022 & 0.022 \\ 0.032 & 0.032 & 0.032 & 0.022 & 0.022 \\ 0.022 & 0.022 & 0.022 & 0.075 & 0.054 \\ 0.022 & 0.022 & 0.022 & 0.022 & 0.065 \end{bmatrix} \right)^{-1} = \begin{bmatrix} 0.103 & 0.094 & 0.082 & 0.070 & 0.084 \\ 0.029 & 0.063 & 0.062 & 0.029 & 0.029 \\ 0.039 & 0.040 & 0.039 & 0.028 & 0.029 \\ 0.029 & 0.029 & 0.029 & 0.086 & 0.066 \\ 0.028 & 0.028 & 0.028 & 0.028 & 0.074 \end{bmatrix}$$

Step 6: Determine total impact ($\mathbf{TI_i}$), total receptivity ($\mathbf{TR_j}$) of barriers from the total DSIRM (S)

Using Equations (5.7) and (5.8), total impact (TI_i) and total receptivity (TR_j) of barriers can be determined and shown in Table 5.4.

TABLE 5.4 Total impact (TI_i), total receptivity (TR_j), total engagement ($TI_i + TR_i$) and role (position) ($TI_i - TR_i$) of barriers.

Barrier	*Total impact* (TI_i)	*Total receptivity* (TR_j)	($TI_i + TR_i$)	($TI_i - TR_i$)	*Group*
CL1	0.433	0.227	*0.660*	*0.207*	**Cause**
CL2	0.211	0.254	*0.465*	*-0.043*	*Effect*
CL3	0.175	0.241	*0.416*	*-0.065*	*Effect*
CL4	0.239	0.241	*0.480*	*-0.001*	*Effect*
CL5	0.185	0.282	*0.467*	*-0.097*	*Effect*

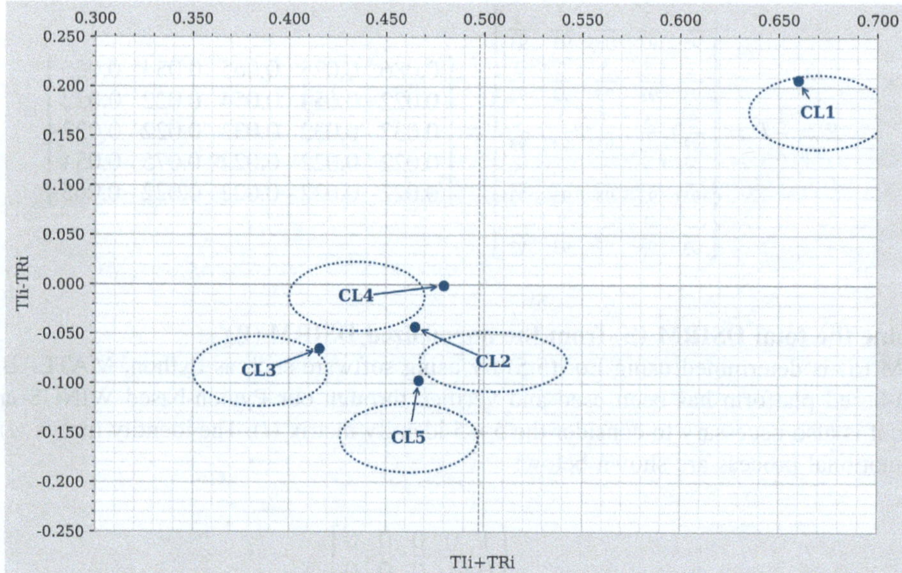

FIGURE 5.2 Infographic of the engagement-role of barriers.

The computational process of total impact (TI_i) and total receptivity (TR_j) of barrier (CL1) is given below for better understanding:

$$TI_i = \left[\sum_{j=1}^{n} s_{ij}\right]_{n\times1=[t_i]n\times1} = TI_{CL1} = 0.103 + 0.094 + 0.082 + 0.070 + 0.084 = 0.433$$

$$TR_j = \left[\sum_{i=1}^{n} s_{ij}\right]_{1\times n=[t_i]1\times n} = TR_{CL1} = 0.103 + 0.029 + 0.039 + 0.029 + 0.028 = 0.227$$

Step 7: Determine the total engagement and role (position) of barriers

The total engagement ($TI_i + TR_i$) and role (position) ($TI_i - TR_i$) of barriers are determined based on the total impact (TI_i) and total receptivity (TR_j) shown in Table 5.4. The cause-effect group was also determined based on the positive and negative values of the role (position) ($TI_i - TR_i$). The total engagement and role (position) of barriers is given in Table 5.4. Finally, the infographic of the engagement role is constructed based on a dataset of $(TI_i + TR_i) vs. (TI_i - TR_i)$ and shown in Fig. 5.2.

According to this analysis, it is shown that the most prominent barrier among the five is "Lack of policies and law enforcement for carbon emissions (CL1)," which received the highest engagement ($TI_i + TR_i$) score of 0.660. It is also noticed that the barrier "(CL1)" comes under the causal group, whereas the other four barriers come under the influenced group. It means that if policymakers or governmental agencies work to mitigate one barrier (CL1), the other barriers will be mitigated automatically. According to these findings, top management can reform policies to support the development of ZETM. This example can clarify deeply how the WINGS model works in the decision-making process. In addition, we have developed a comprehensive WINGS application software to deploy the WINGS model, which can be accessed through https://wings-app.streamlit.app/ freely and verified with manually computation process done in Excel-based software. The app is very comprehensive, as it can be considered for a group decision-making approach, and users can assign a direct importance level to experts who may participate in the decision-making process. In addition, real data can also be used in the WINGS app.

5.5 Numerical example 2

Another complex practical decision-making problem is also presented in this section to demonstrate the application of the WINGS model in a real-life, complex decision-making process, as outlined in the paper by Moktadir et al. (2025).

TABLE 5.5 Selected barriers to safe and sustainable by design implementation in waste-to-energy process for tannery solid waste management (Cefic, 2024; Moktadir et al., 2025).

Code	Barriers
CI1	Environmental and health hazards
CI2	Complexity of pollution prevention
CI3	Low energy efficiency and resource optimization
CI4	Skills gap
CI5	Complexity of stakeholder engagement
CI6	Challenges of financial viability and cost-effectiveness
CI7	Complexity in collaboration within the value chain
CI8	Emissions during energy production
CI9	Criticality for risk management of energy products
CI10	Consumers' affordability and competitiveness

The previous study employed a weighting model (trapezoidal fuzzy BWM), which cannot effectively handle the complex strength-intertwined relationship between barriers to safe and sustainable by design (SSbD) practices for waste-to-energy (WtE). Therefore, it is also necessary to understand the strength-intertwined relationship among barriers for ensuring safe and sustainable WtE process, particularly for tannery solid waste (TSW) management, in line with the SSbD principles. This understanding will help policymakers prioritize mitigation efforts and allocate resources more effectively. Therefore, to address this problem, we have formed a panel of four experts with diverse backgrounds (including researchers, academics, and practitioners) for the purpose of group decision-making to assess the strength and interaction relationships between the barriers. The research group would also like to consider the 10 most pressing barriers based on the previous study by Moktadir et al. (2025). Therefore, the WINGS model depicted in Section 5.3 is utilized to determine the strength-interaction relationship and is provided below.

Step 1: Identification of evaluation components

Based on the previous study conducted by Moktadir et al. (2025), the 10 most critical barriers (elements) shown in Table 5.5 are selected purposively by the research team for strength and interaction relationships evaluation. These selections represent all four dimensions (safety, environmental, social, and economic).

Step 2: Determine internal strength and interactions using linguistic terms to form ISIRM

After selecting a set of barriers to SSbD practices for TSW management, the four DMs (DM1, DM2, DM3, DM4) are invited to evaluate these barriers using the linguistic scale shown in Table 5.2 to assess the internal strength (diagonal) and influential relationships (off-diagonal) between the 10 barriers. In this evaluation, the two academicians who are working as assistant professor and lecturer with 10+ and 4+ years of professional teaching and research experience, as well as two practitioners from two different waste treatment plants, along with 5+ and 14+ years of experience, are invited to the evaluation process using linguistic terms shown in Table 5.2. Their linguistic assessment is given in Table 5.6. It is also noted that the research team establishes the interaction relationships among barriers based on consensus among DMs before collecting linguistic data from them. However, it can be individually collected from the experts. In this study, it is prefixed to avoid any bias in the decision-making process, which is not mandatory for the group decision-making process through WINGS.

Additionally, for a better understanding of the assessment process using linguistic terms, the graphical approach provided in Fig. 5.1 is also used. For this purpose, the graphical approach for DM1 is presented below, with Fig. 5.3 (created using Python), which facilitates DM1's understanding of the complex strength-intertwined relationship among barriers. It is also noted that to simplify this graph, the keywords present in the barriers list are intentionally used to represent the original barrier. Other DMs also constructed this graph to demonstrate the strength-intertwined relationship.

TABLE 5.6 Initial strength-influence relation matrix for DM1-DM4.

	CI1	CI2	CI3	CI4	CI5	CI6	CI7	CI8	CI9	CI10
CI1	ExS,ExS,ExS,VSS	MI,MIP,MI,SI	NI,NI,NI,NI	NI,NI,NI,NI	NI,NI,NI,NI	NI,NI,NI,NI	NI,NI,NI,NI	MI,MIP,SI,MI	SI,MIP,ExI,MIP	NI,NI,NI,NI
CI2	NI,NI,NI,NI	VSS,SSP,VSS,VSS	VSI,SIP,VSI,VSI	NI,NI,NI,NI	NI,NI,NI,NI	SI,MIP,SI,SI	NI,NI,NI,NI	ExI,VSI,SIP,VSI	NI,NI,NI,NI	NI,NI,NI,NI
CI3	NI,NI,NI,NI	NI,NI,NI,NI	SS,SSP,SS,SSP,SS	NI,NI,NI,NI	NI,NI,NI,NI	WI,MI,WI,WI	NI,NI,NI,NI	NI,NI,NI,NI	NI,NI,NI,NI	MI,MIP,SI,MI
CI4	NI,NI,NI,NI	NI,NI,NI,NI	NI,NI,NI,NI	MSP,SS,MSP,SS	SIP,VSI,SIP,SIP	NI,NI,NI,NI	MIP,MI,MIP,MI	NI,NI,NI,NI	NI,NI,NI,NI	NI,NI,NI,NI
CI5	NI,NI,NI,NI	NI,NI,NI,NI	NI,NI,NI,NI	VSI,SIP,ExI,VSI	MS,MS,WS,WS	MI,MI,MI,MI	VSI,VSI,VSI,SI	NI,NI,NI,NI	NI,NI,NI,NI	NI,NI,NI,NI
CI6	NI,NI,NI,NI	NI,NI,NI,NI	SI,MIP,SI,SI	NI,NI,NI,NI	NI,NI,NI,NI	VSS,VSS,ExS,VSS	AI, ExI,SIP,VSI	NI,NI,NI,NI	NI,NI,NI,NI	SI,SI,MI,MI
CI7	NI,NI,NI,NI	WI,MI,WI,WI	NI,NI,NI,NI	NI,NI,NI,NI	NI,NI,NI,NI	MI,WI,WI,WI	SS,MSP, MSP, SS	NI,NI,NI,NI	NI,NI,NI,NI	NI,NI,NI,NI
CI8	MI,MIP,MI,MIP	SIP,SI,VSI,SI	NI,NI,NI,NI	NI,NI,NI,NI	NI,NI,NI,NI	NI,NI,NI,NI	NI,NI,NI,NI	SSP, MSP, SSP,SS	NI,NI,NI,NI	NI,NI,NI,NI
CI9	SI,MIP,SI,VSI	NI,NI,NI,NI	NI,NI,NI,NI	MIP,SI,SIP,MIP	NI,NI,NI,NI	NI,NI,NI,NI	NI,NI,NI,NI	NI,NI,NI,NI	MS, WS,SSP,SS	NI,NI,NI,NI
CI10	NI,NI,NI,NI	NI,NI,NI,NI	NI,NI,NI,NI	NI,NI,NI,NI	WI,WI,WI,WI	WI,MI,MI,WI	NI,NI,NI,NI	NI,NI,NI,NI	NI,NI,NI,NI	WS,MS,WS,WS

Note: For DM1 data, diagonal linguistic terms (i.e., CI1: ExS) represent internal strength, and off-diagonals (i.e., CI1 → CI2: moderate influence) represent influence.

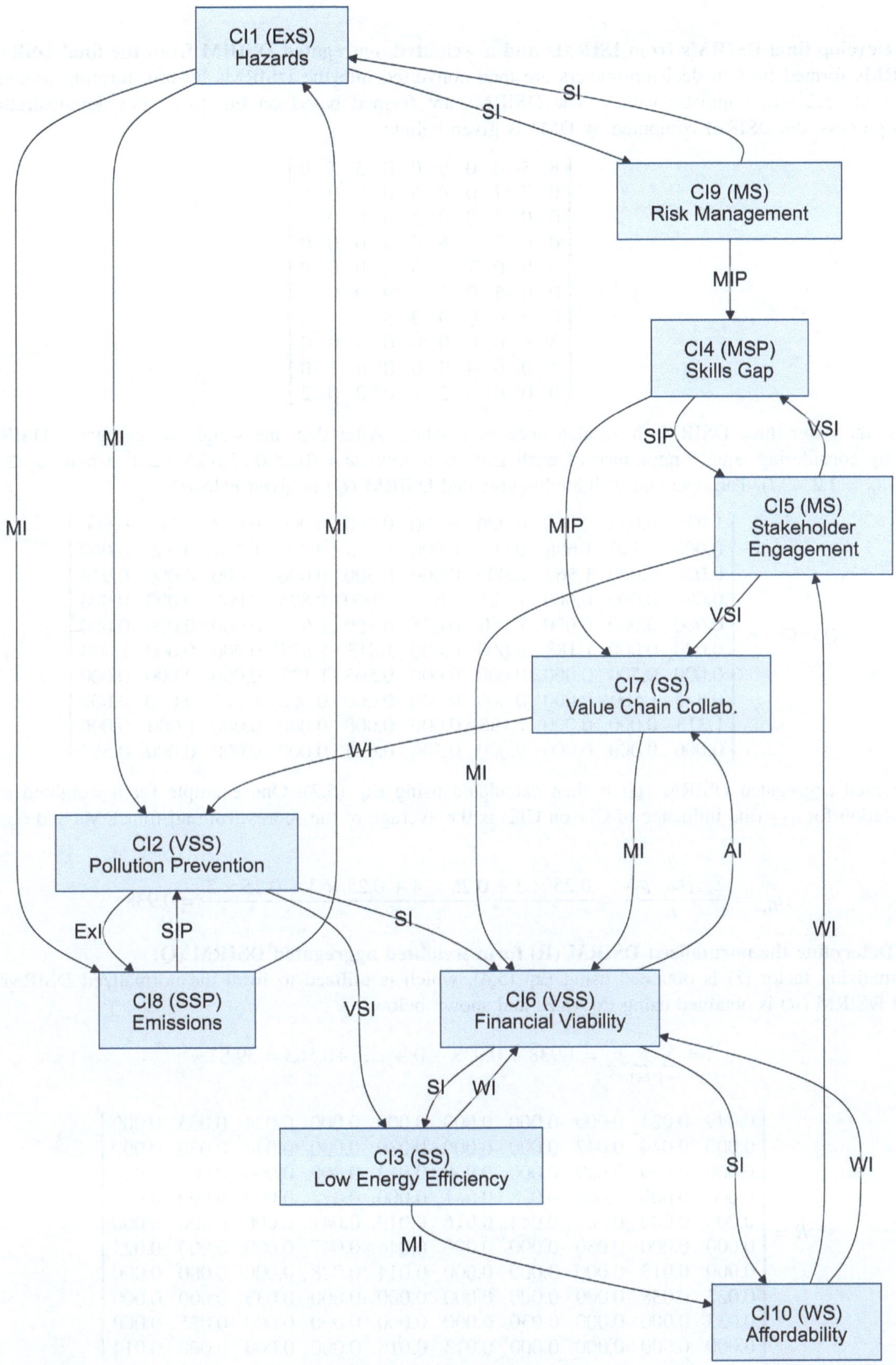

FIGURE 5.3 Strengths and interactions of barriers in the classical weighted influence nonlinear gauge system environment, determined by DM1.

Step 3: Develop final DSIRMs from ISIRMs and a weighted aggregated DSIRM from the final DSRMs

The ISIRMs formed by k-th decision-makers are then converted into the DSIRMs by transforming linguistic terms shown in Table 5.2 into linguistic values. The DSIRMs are formed based on Eq. (5.1). For demonstration of the calculation process, the DSIRM computed by DM1 is given below:

$$P^1 = \begin{bmatrix} 8 & 3 & 0 & 0 & 0 & 0 & 0 & 3 & 5 & 0 \\ 0 & 7 & 7 & 0 & 0 & 5 & 0 & 8 & 0 & 0 \\ 0 & 0 & 5 & 0 & 0 & 2 & 0 & 0 & 0 & 3 \\ 0 & 0 & 0 & 4 & 6 & 0 & 4 & 0 & 0 & 0 \\ 0 & 0 & 0 & 7 & 3 & 3 & 7 & 0 & 0 & 0 \\ 0 & 0 & 5 & 0 & 0 & 7 & 9 & 0 & 0 & 5 \\ 0 & 2 & 0 & 0 & 0 & 3 & 5 & 0 & 0 & 0 \\ 3 & 6 & 0 & 0 & 0 & 0 & 0 & 6 & 0 & 0 \\ 5 & 0 & 0 & 4 & 0 & 0 & 0 & 0 & 3 & 0 \\ 0 & 0 & 0 & 0 & 2 & 2 & 0 & 0 & 0 & 2 \end{bmatrix}$$

Similarly, the other three DSIRMs have also been established. After that, the weighted aggregated DSIRM (Q) is developed by considering equal importance of each DM as follows $\omega = (0.25,0.25,0.25,0.25)^T$ where $\omega_k \in [0,1]$ and $\sum_{k=1}^{l} \omega_k = 1$ $(k = 1,2, ...,l)$. The resultant weighted aggregated DSIRM (Q) is given below:

$$Q = (\tilde{q}_{ij}) = \begin{bmatrix} 1.938 & 0.938 & 0.000 & 0.000 & 0.000 & 0.000 & 0.000 & 0.938 & 1.313 & 0.000 \\ 0.000 & 1.750 & 1.688 & 0.000 & 0.000 & 1.188 & 0.000 & 1.750 & 0.000 & 0.000 \\ 0.000 & 0.000 & 1.563 & 0.000 & 0.000 & 0.500 & 0.000 & 0.000 & 0.000 & 0.938 \\ 0.000 & 0.000 & 0.000 & 1.125 & 1.625 & 0.000 & 0.875 & 0.000 & 0.000 & 0.000 \\ 0.000 & 0.000 & 0.000 & 1.750 & 0.625 & 0.750 & 1.625 & 0.000 & 0.000 & 0.000 \\ 0.000 & 0.000 & 1.188 & 0.000 & 0.000 & 1.813 & 1.875 & 0.000 & 0.000 & 1.000 \\ 0.000 & 0.500 & 0.000 & 0.000 & 0.000 & 0.563 & 1.125 & 0.000 & 0.000 & 0.000 \\ 0.875 & 1.500 & 0.000 & 0.000 & 0.000 & 0.000 & 0.000 & 1.313 & 0.000 & 0.000 \\ 1.313 & 0.000 & 0.000 & 1.188 & 0.000 & 0.000 & 0.000 & 0.000 & 1.000 & 0.000 \\ 0.000 & 0.000 & 0.000 & 0.000 & 0.500 & 0.625 & 0.000 & 0.000 & 0.000 & 0.563 \end{bmatrix}$$

The weighted aggregated DSIRM (**Q**) is then calculated using Eq. (5.2). One example for a weighted aggregated value calculation for $q_{1,2}$ (the influence of CI1 on CI2) is the average of the scores from all four DMs and computed as follows:

$$q_{1,2} = \frac{\sum_{k=1}^{l} \omega_k \cdot p_{12}^{k}}{l} = \frac{0.25 \times 3 + 0.25 \times 4 + 0.25 \times 3 + 0.25 \times 5}{4} = 0.938$$

Step 4: Determine the normalized DSIRM (R) form weighted aggregated DSIRM (Q)

The normalizing factor (λ) is obtained using Eq. (5.4), which is utilized to form the normalized DSIRM (R). The normalized DSIRM (R) is obtained using Eq. (5.3) and shown below.

$$\lambda = \sum_{i=1}^{n} \sum_{j=1}^{n} p_{ij} = 1.938 + 0.938 + 0 + ,\ldots, +0.563 = 39.813.$$

$$R = \begin{bmatrix} 0.049 & 0.024 & 0.000 & 0.000 & 0.000 & 0.000 & 0.000 & 0.024 & 0.033 & 0.000 \\ 0.000 & 0.044 & 0.042 & 0.000 & 0.000 & 0.030 & 0.000 & 0.044 & 0.000 & 0.000 \\ 0.000 & 0.000 & 0.039 & 0.000 & 0.000 & 0.013 & 0.000 & 0.000 & 0.000 & 0.024 \\ 0.000 & 0.000 & 0.000 & 0.028 & 0.041 & 0.000 & 0.022 & 0.000 & 0.000 & 0.000 \\ 0.000 & 0.000 & 0.000 & 0.044 & 0.016 & 0.019 & 0.041 & 0.000 & 0.000 & 0.000 \\ 0.000 & 0.000 & 0.030 & 0.000 & 0.000 & 0.046 & 0.047 & 0.000 & 0.000 & 0.025 \\ 0.000 & 0.013 & 0.000 & 0.000 & 0.000 & 0.014 & 0.028 & 0.000 & 0.000 & 0.000 \\ 0.022 & 0.038 & 0.000 & 0.000 & 0.000 & 0.000 & 0.000 & 0.033 & 0.000 & 0.000 \\ 0.033 & 0.000 & 0.000 & 0.030 & 0.000 & 0.000 & 0.000 & 0.000 & 0.025 & 0.000 \\ 0.000 & 0.000 & 0.000 & 0.000 & 0.013 & 0.016 & 0.000 & 0.000 & 0.000 & 0.014 \end{bmatrix}$$

Step 5: Determine the total DSIRM (S) from the normalized DSIRM (R)

Similar to the first example, the total DSIRM (S) is developed using Eq. (5.5) in an Excel-based platform and verified through our Python-based WINGS web-application (https://wings-app.streamlit.app/) developed by the authors. The final total DSIRM ***(S)*** is shown below:

$$S = \begin{bmatrix} 0.053 & 0.027 & 0.001 & 0.001 & 0.000 & 0.001 & 0.000 & 0.027 & 0.036 & 0.000 \\ 0.001 & 0.048 & 0.047 & 0.000 & 0.000 & 0.033 & 0.002 & 0.048 & 0.000 & 0.002 \\ 0.000 & 0.000 & 0.041 & 0.000 & 0.000 & 0.014 & 0.001 & 0.000 & 0.000 & 0.025 \\ 0.000 & 0.000 & 0.000 & 0.031 & 0.043 & 0.001 & 0.025 & 0.000 & 0.000 & 0.000 \\ 0.000 & 0.001 & 0.001 & 0.046 & 0.018 & 0.021 & 0.045 & 0.000 & 0.000 & 0.001 \\ 0.000 & 0.001 & 0.033 & 0.000 & 0.000 & 0.049 & 0.051 & 0.000 & 0.000 & 0.028 \\ 0.000 & 0.014 & 0.001 & 0.000 & 0.000 & 0.016 & 0.030 & 0.001 & 0.000 & 0.000 \\ 0.024 & 0.041 & 0.002 & 0.000 & 0.000 & 0.001 & 0.000 & 0.037 & 0.001 & 0.000 \\ 0.036 & 0.001 & 0.000 & 0.032 & 0.001 & 0.000 & 0.001 & 0.001 & 0.027 & 0.000 \\ 0.000 & 0.000 & 0.001 & 0.001 & 0.013 & 0.017 & 0.001 & 0.000 & 0.000 & 0.015 \end{bmatrix}$$

Steps 6 and 7: Calculate total impact (TI_i), total receptivity (TR_j), total engagement ($TI_i + TR_i$), and role (position) ($TI_i - TR_i$) of barriers

Using Equations (5.6)–(5.8), total impact (TI_i) (row sum) and total receptivity (TR_j) (column sum) from the total DSIRM *(S)* are determined, as well as the total engagement ($TI_i + TR_i$) and role (position) ($TI_i - TR_i$) are computed from (TI_i) and (TR_j) values. The resultant total impact (TI_i), total receptivity (TR_j), total engagement ($TI_i + TR_i$) and role (position) ($TI_i - TR_i$) are given in Table 5.7.

According to the engagement ($TI_i + TR_i$) score, the two most central and active barriers are "Challenges of financial viability and cost-effectiveness (CI6)" and "Complexity of pollution prevention (CI2)," as these two barriers receive the highest ($TI_i + TR_i$) scores of 0.315 and 0.313, respectively. These findings suggest that these barriers are highly interconnected, both influencing (causal barriers) and influencing other barriers (result/effect group). Addressing these barriers has significant and widespread ripple effects for TSW management through the implementation of the WtE process. Therefore, policymakers must be aware of these barriers to take the necessary actions (Fig. 5.4).

TABLE 5.7 Total impact (TI_i), total receptivity (TR_j), total engagement ($TI_i + TR_i$) and role (position) ($TI_i - TR_i$) of barriers.

Barriers	(TI_i)	(TR_j)	Engagement ($TI_i + TR_i$)	Role ($TI_i - TR_i$)	Group
CI1	0.146	0.114	0.260	0.032	Cause
CI2	0.181	0.132	0.313	0.049	Cause
CI3	0.082	0.127	0.208	-0.045	Effect
CI4	0.101	0.110	0.211	-0.010	Effect
CI5	0.131	0.076	0.207	0.056	Cause
CI6	0.161	0.154	0.315	0.008	Cause
CI7	0.061	0.155	0.217	-0.094	Effect
CI8	0.106	0.113	0.219	-0.007	Effect
CI9	0.098	0.063	0.162	0.035	Cause
CI10	0.047	0.071	0.118	-0.023	Effect

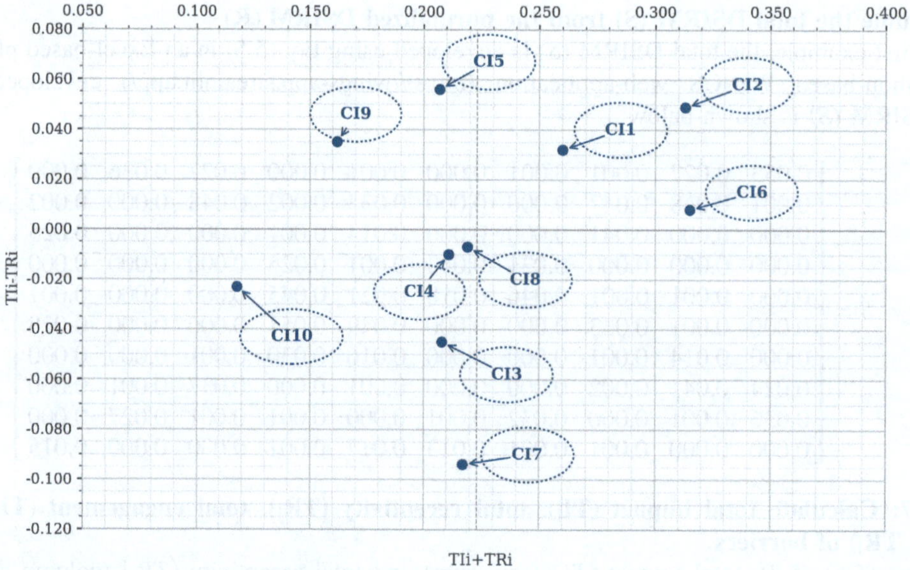

FIGURE 5.4 Infographic of the engagement-role of barriers.

In addition, according to the positive values of role ($TI_i - TR_i$), the most influential barrier is "Complexity of stakeholder engagement (CI5)" that received the highest score of 0.056. It suggests that improving stakeholder engagement can positively impact many other barriers, particularly those within the effect group. The other causal group barriers are "Complexity of pollution prevention (CI2)," "Criticality for risk management of energy products (CI9)," "Environmental and health hazards (CI1)," and "Challenges of financial viability and cost-effectiveness (CI6)". These barriers are net drivers in the system, which means addressing them can directly and indirectly support the mitigation of other result/effect group barriers.

In addition, according to the negative values of role ($TI_i - TR_i$), the effect/result group barriers are determined, and the most dependent barrier is "Complexity in collaboration within the value chain (CI7)," which cannot be fixed without first addressing its causes, likely "Complexity of stakeholder engagement (CI5)." Similarly, other effect group barriers can be fixed by improving causal group barriers to implement and ensure SSbD practices in the WtE plant. According to these findings, it can be suggested that policymakers and governmental agencies should focus first on the cause elements, especially "Complexity of stakeholder engagement (CI5)" and "Criticality for risk management of energy products (CI9)," as improving these will naturally alleviate pressures on the effect/result group elements, such as "Low energy efficiency and resource optimization (CI3)" and "Complexity in collaboration within the value chain (CI7)."

5.6 Comparative and sensitivity analysis

For the real case set in numerical example 2, a comparative and a sensitivity analysis are also conducted to demonstrate how to investigate the robustness of the WINGS model in relation to other models and the weight variation of DMs (Moktadir & Ren, 2025). To perform a comparative analysis, first, the classical DEMATEL model is considered. In the DEMATEL model, the strength values of all barriers are now set to zero, and the DEMATEL model is run. According to the findings, the results show variation, especially in engagement and the position of barriers. The variation can be observed in Table 5.8. According to the analysis, the ranking order of barriers based on the ($TI_i + TR_i$) score has been significantly changed in the DEMATEL analysis due to the inability to handle the strength of elements in the DEMATEL model. In addition, the cause-effect/result group barriers are also changed in the DEMATEL model. Therefore, it is vital to consider the internal strength of elements to get the most reliable result, which can only be handled via the WINGS model. This proves the superiority of WINGS over classical DEMATEL.

TABLE 5.8 Comparative analysis with classical decision-making trial and evaluation laboratory (DEMATEL).

Barriers	WINGS				DEMATEL			
	$(TI_i + TR_i)$	Rank	$(TI_i - TR_i)$	Group	$(TI_i + TR_i)$	Rank	$(TI_i - TR_i)$	Group
CI1	0.260	3	0.032	**Cause**	2.720	6	0.972	**Cause**
CI2	0.313	2	0.049	**Cause**	3.666	1	0.687	**Cause**
CI3	0.208	7	-0.045	**Effect**	2.258	8	-1.071	**Effect**
CI4	0.211	6	-0.010	**Effect**	2.455	7	0.163	**Cause**
CI5	0.207	8	0.056	**Cause**	2.832	5	0.854	**Cause**
CI6	0.315	1	0.008	**Cause**	3.372	2	-0.518	**Effect**
CI7	0.217	5	-0.094	**Effect**	2.938	3	-1.660	**Effect**
CI8	0.219	4	-0.007	**Effect**	2.891	4	0.247	**Cause**
CI9	0.162	9	0.035	**Cause**	1.932	9	0.869	**Cause**
CI10	0.118	10	-0.023	**Effect**	1.812	10	-0.542	**Effect**

TABLE 5.9 Weight scenarios of decision-makers.

Scenarios	DM1	DM2	DM3	DM4
Base	0.25	0.25	0.25	0.25
Trail_1	**0.30**	0.23	0.23	0.23
Trail_2	0.23	**0.30**	0.23	0.23
Trail_3	0.23	0.23	**0.30**	0.23
Trail_4	0.23	0.23	0.23	**0.30**

A sensitivity analysis is also conducted for the real case set in numerical example 2 by creating different weight scenarios for the experts involved in the group decision-making process. The archetypal sensitivity analysis is considered, where on the diagonal the expert's weight is fixed as 0.3, and the remaining 0.7 is assigned to the other three experts equally, to observe the ranking variation (Moktadir & Ren, 2025). The weight scenarios of DMs are given in Table 5.9.

The results presented in Table 5.10 confirm that there is no significant difference in the ranking order of the barriers when considering the engagement $(TI_i + TR_i)$ score. Particularly, there are a few minor variations observed in the ranking order for Trail_1, Trail_2, and Trail_4 scenarios. Furthermore, there is no difference in the role/position of barrier for all four scenarios compared to the base case, which ensured the robustness of the model. The complete results of the sensitivity analysis can be observed in Table 5.10.

TABLE 5.10 Sensitivity analysis by varying decision-makers weights.

Barrier	Base			Trial_1			Trial_2			Trial_3			Trial_4		
	$(TI_i - TR_i)$ Rank	$(TI_i - TR_i)$	Group	$(TI_i - TR_i)$ Rank	$(TI_i - TR_i)$	Group	$(TI_i - TR_i)$ Rank	$(TI_i - TR_i)$	Group	$(TI_i - TR_i)$ Rank	$(TI_i - TR_i)$	Group	$(TI_i - TR_i)$ Rank	$(TI_i - TR_i)$	Group
CI1	3	0.032	**Cause**	3	0.032	**Cause**	3	0.032	**Cause**	3	0.034	**Cause**	3	0.031	**Cause**
CI2	2	0.049	**Cause**	2	0.050	**Cause**	2	0.048	**Cause**	2	0.049	**Cause**	1	0.048	**Cause**
CI3	7	-0.045	**Effect**	7	-0.045	**Effect**	7	-0.044	**Effect**	7	-0.044	**Effect**	7	-0.046	**Effect**
CI4	6	-0.010	**Effect**	6	-0.009	**Effect**	6	-0.009	**Effect**	6	-0.011	**Effect**	6	-0.010	**Effect**
CI5	8	0.056	**Cause**	7	0.056	**Cause**	7	0.055	**Cause**	8	0.056	**Cause**	8	0.055	**Cause**
CI6	1	0.008	**Cause**	1	0.009	**Cause**	1	0.008	**Cause**	1	0.006	**Cause**	1	0.007	**Cause**
CI7	5	-0.094	**Effect**	4	-0.095	**Effect**	5	-0.095	**Effect**	5	-0.094	**Effect**	5	-0.093	**Effect**
CI8	4	-0.007	**Effect**	4	-0.007	**Effect**	4	-0.006	**Effect**	4	-0.007	**Effect**	4	-0.006	**Effect**
CI9	9	0.035	**Cause**	9	0.034	**Cause**	9	0.035	**Cause**	9	0.034	**Cause**	9	0.036	**Cause**
CI10	10	-0.023	**Effect**	10	-0.024	**Effect**	10	-0.024	**Effect**	10	-0.023	**Effect**	10	-0.023	**Effect**

5.7 Conclusions

The WINGS method represents a significant advancement in the MCDM domain, offering a robust and reliable framework for addressing the complex interdependencies inherent in real-world decision problems. Its key strength lies in its simultaneous consideration of the internal importance of components and the external influences between them, all within a single, mathematically sound model. The method is both mathematically well-grounded, powerful, and accessible. Its flexibility is evidenced by its ability to reduce to the simple WSM, AHP, and BWM models when dependencies are absent, ensuring backward compatibility with classical methods. In addition, to make the implementation process easy, this study also develops a Python-based GUI application software which can handle numerous issues, such as allowing real data for interaction assessment, permitting the use of a number of DM for group decision-making, facilitating to assign a level of importance of DM, and a more flexible rating scale, making it practical for researchers and practitioners.

A hypothetical analysis, as shown in numerical example 1, and a real-world complex decision-making problem, as presented in numerical example 2, clearly illustrate the implementation process, which can also help students, researchers, practitioners, and policymakers easily understand the computational process of the WINGS model. Furthermore, this chapter provides comparative and sensitivity analyses for students, researchers, practitioners, and policymakers to understand how to assess the robustness and superiority of the model.

Though the classical WINGS model is an interactive strength-interactions assessment model, it has some drawbacks. In real-life situations, the problem may be vague and ambiguous, requiring consideration of uncertainty that cannot be handled by the conventional WINGS model. However, to address these issues, several extensions of WINGS are already in the literature, as reported in Table 5.1. However, it is rarely noticed that AI/LLM/ML/social network analysis, combined with WINGS, to extract the elements that need to be investigated to understand the strength-interactions relationship. Therefore, in the future, the integration of AI, ML, LLM, and social network analysis with WINGS/advanced fuzzy-based WINGS will be a future direction for the advancement of this model. Despite these potential extensions, WINGS in its current form stands as a highly valuable and intuitive tool for deciphering the complexity of interconnected systems and making more informed, reliable decisions.

Acknowledgments

The work described in this paper was supported by a grant from the research committee of The Hong Kong Polytechnic University under student account code RKHB (PolyU Presidential PhD Fellowship awardee to **Md. Abdul Moktadir**).

A statement of contribution for authors

Md. Abdul Moktadir: Conceptualization, data curation, methodology, formal analysis, writing – original draft, writing – review and editing. **Yousaf Ayub**: Conceptualization, methodology, writing – review and editing; **Jingzheng Ren**: Conceptualization, supervision, methodology, project administration, funding acquisition, writing – review and editing.

Appendix A

User Guidelines for Python-based WINGS Software (Deployed on Streamlit Platform)

Web-Application Software Link: https://wings-app.streamlit.app/

User Interface:

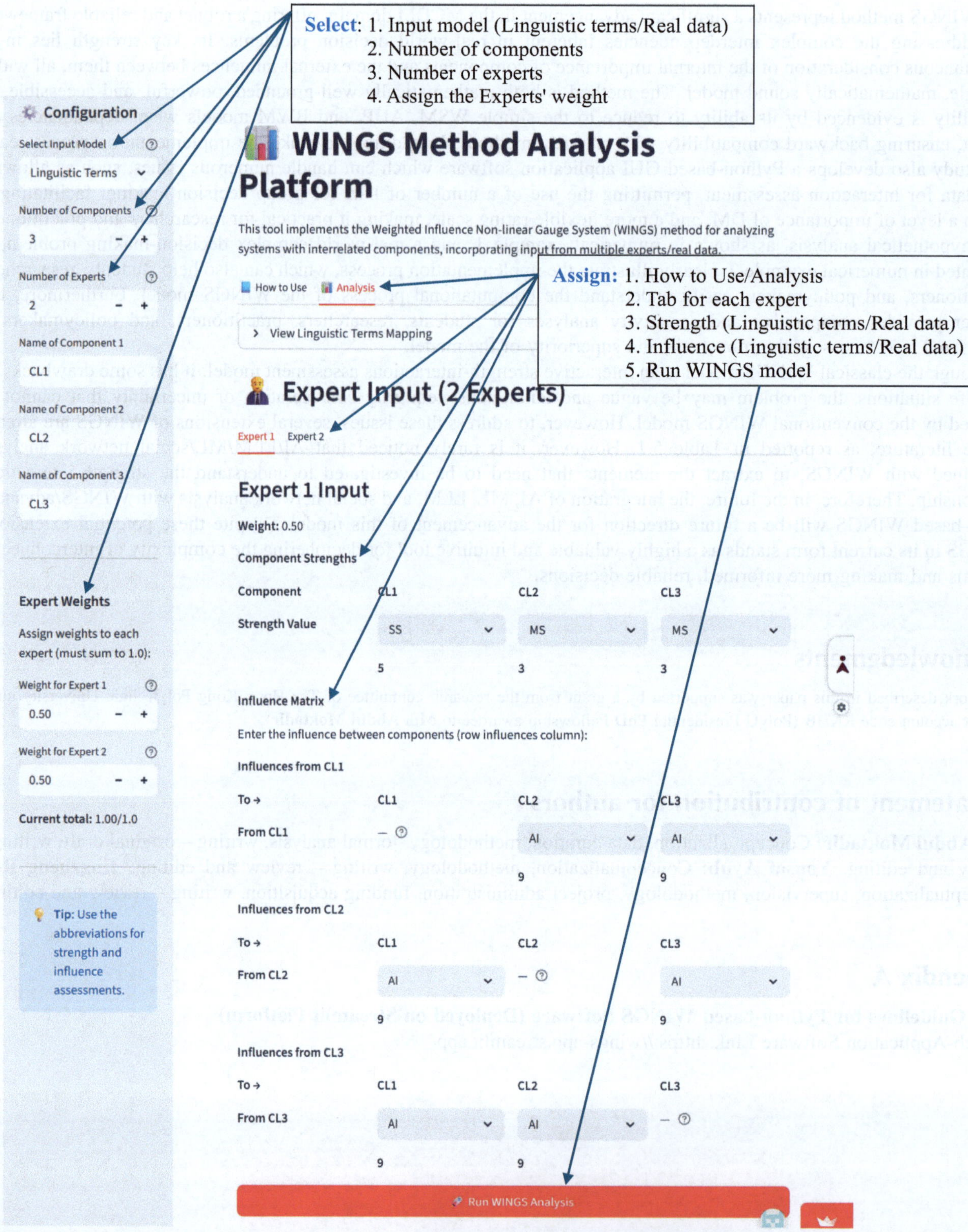

Sample analysis (numerical example 1 see Section 5.4)

Step 1: Input data like the following image

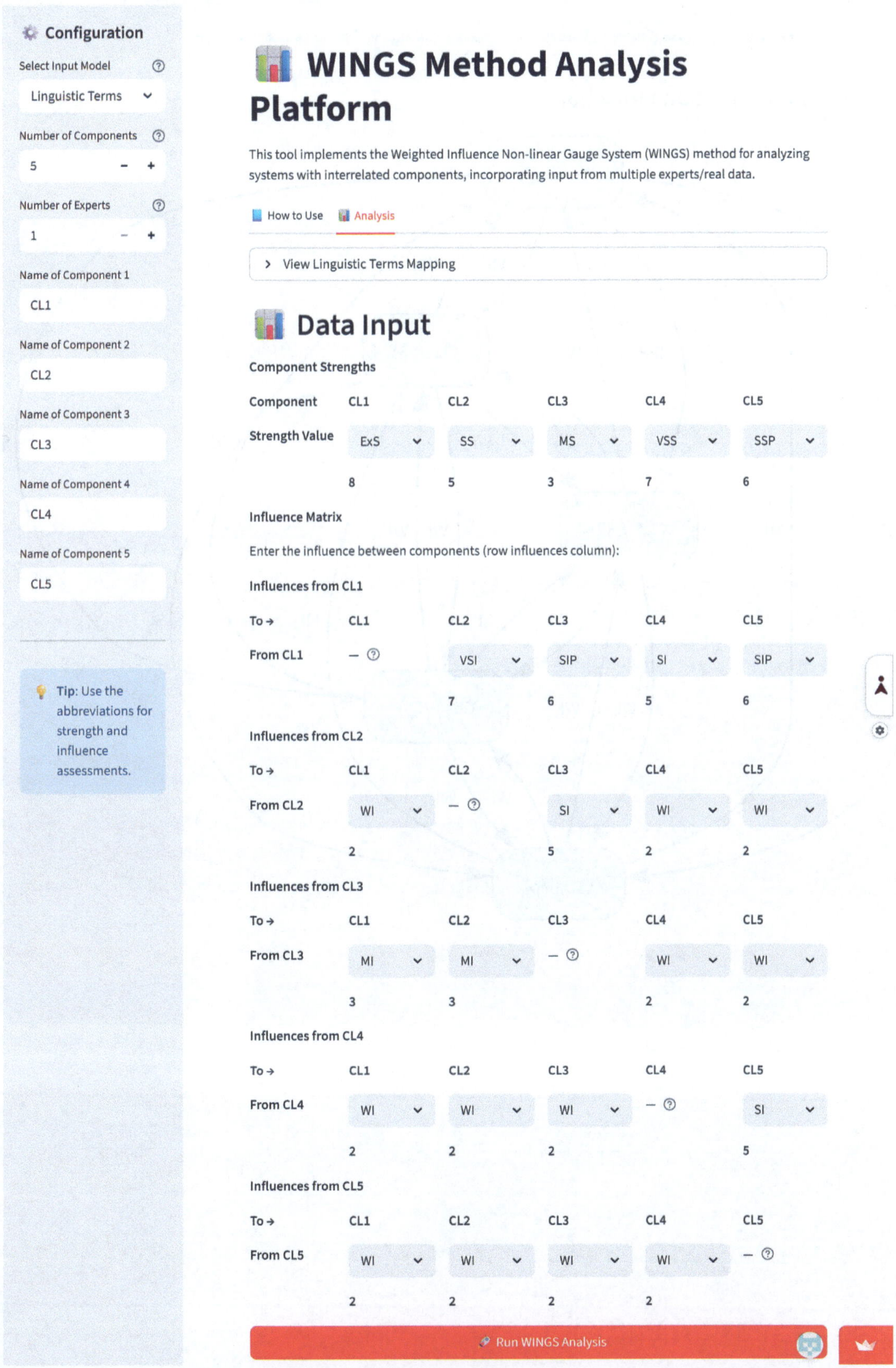

Step 2: Click "Run WINGS Analysis." Results will show below under different tabs as follows

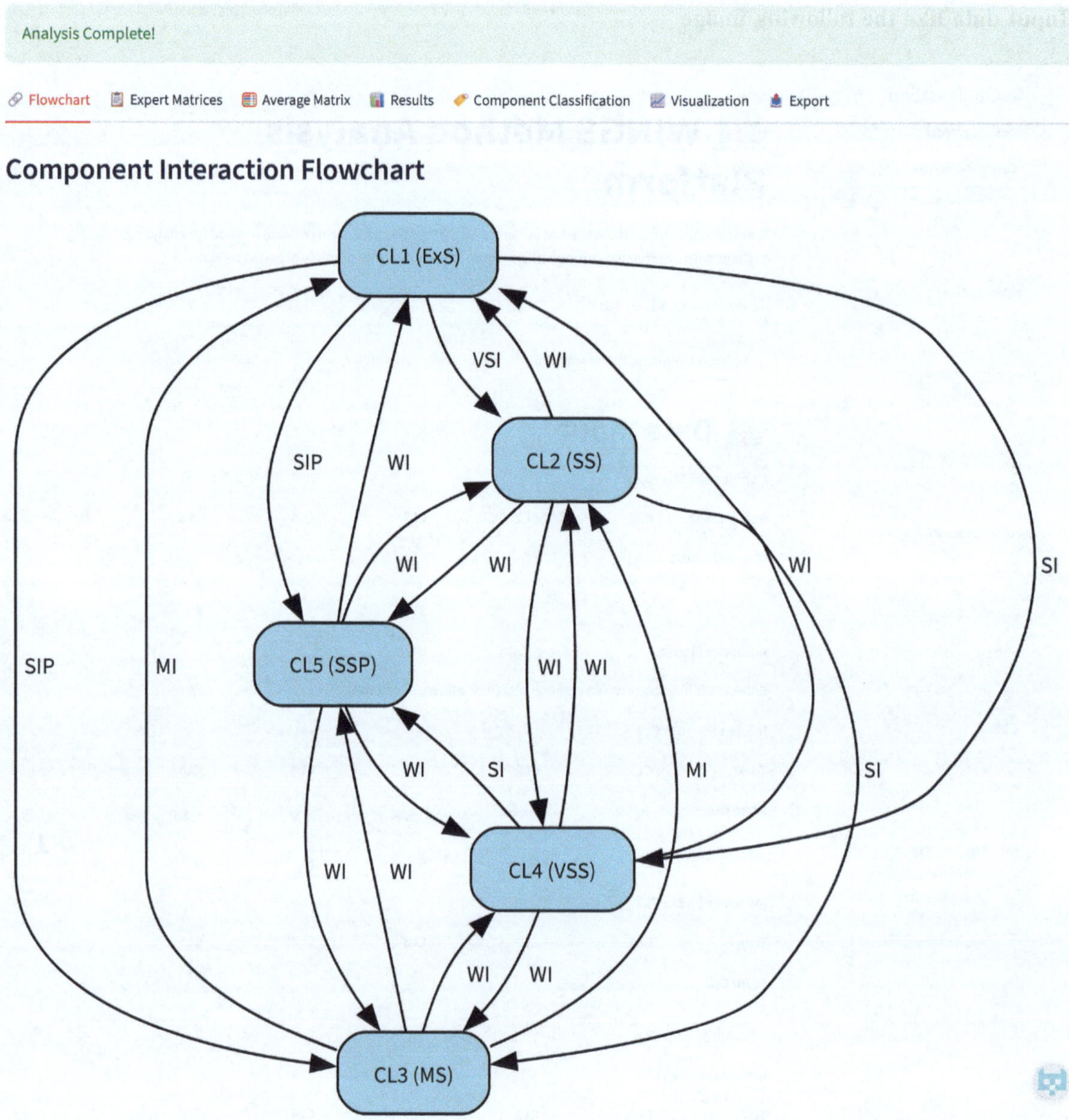

Analysis Complete!

Flowchart | Expert Matrices | Average Matrix | Results | Component Classification | Visualization | Export

Direct Matrix D

	CL1	CL2	CL3	CL4	CL5
CL1	8.000	7.000	6.000	5.000	6.000
CL2	2.000	5.000	5.000	2.000	2.000
CL3	3.000	3.000	3.000	2.000	2.000
CL4	2.000	2.000	2.000	7.000	5.000
CL5	2.000	2.000	2.000	2.000	6.000

Analysis Complete!

Flowchart | Expert Matrices | Average Matrix | Results | Component Classification | Visualization | Export

Average Direct Matrix D_avg

	CL1	CL2	CL3	CL4	CL5
CL1	8.000	7.000	6.000	5.000	6.000
CL2	2.000	5.000	5.000	2.000	2.000
CL3	3.000	3.000	3.000	2.000	2.000
CL4	2.000	2.000	2.000	7.000	5.000
CL5	2.000	2.000	2.000	2.000	6.000

Calibrated Matrix C

	CL1	CL2	CL3	CL4	CL5
CL1	0.086	0.075	0.065	0.054	0.065
CL2	0.022	0.054	0.054	0.022	0.022
CL3	0.032	0.032	0.032	0.022	0.022
CL4	0.022	0.022	0.022	0.075	0.054
CL5	0.022	0.022	0.022	0.022	0.065

Total Strength-Influence Matrix T

	CL1	CL2	CL3	CL4	CL5
CL1	0.103	0.094	0.082	0.070	0.084
CL2	0.029	0.063	0.062	0.029	0.029
CL3	0.039	0.040	0.039	0.028	0.029
CL4	0.029	0.029	0.029	0.086	0.066
CL5	0.028	0.028	0.028	0.028	0.074

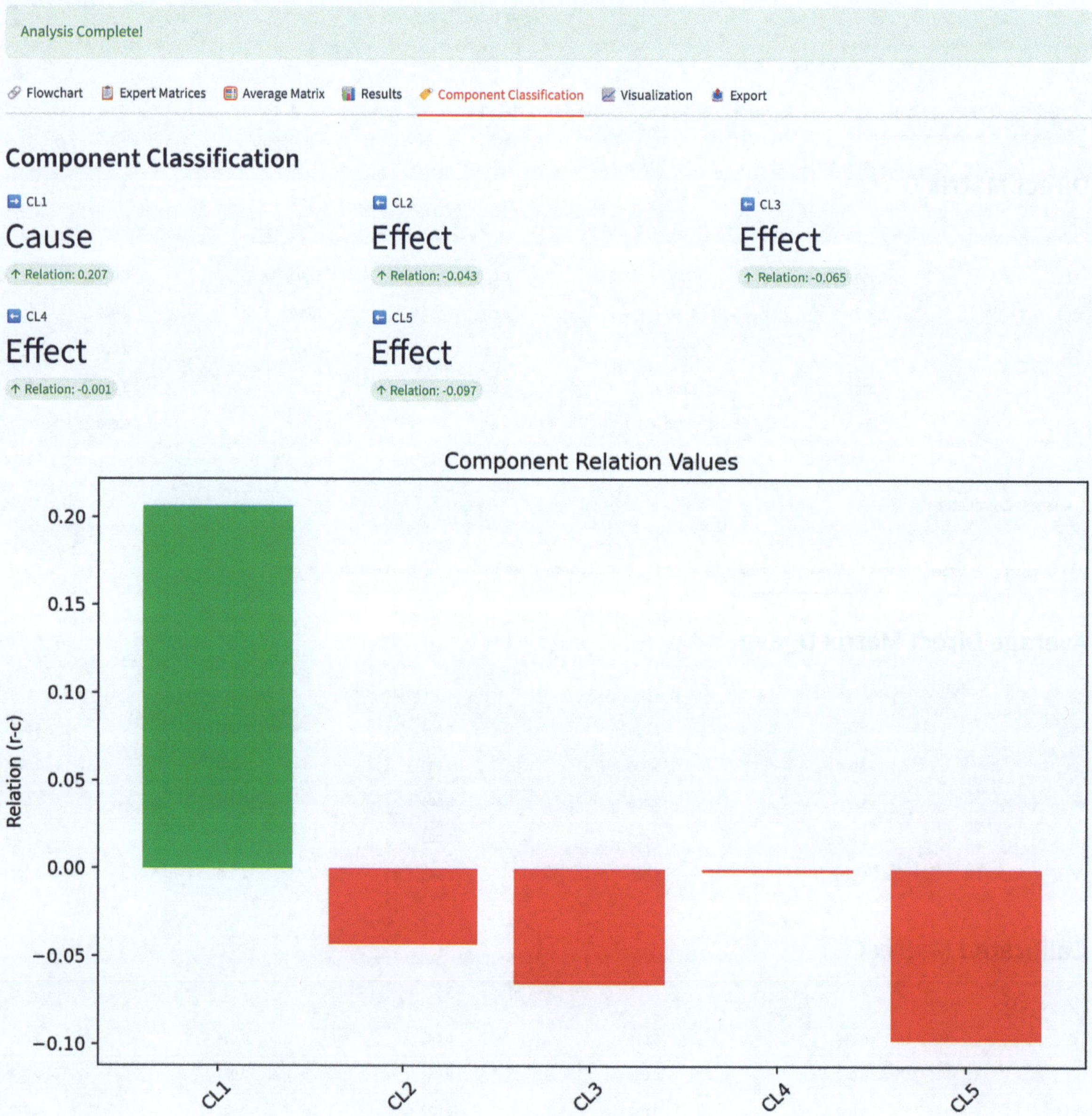
Analysis Complete!
Flowchart
Expert Matrices
Average Matrix
Results
Component Classification
Visualization
Export
Component Classification
CL1
Cause
Relation: 0.207
CL2
Effect
Relation: -0.043
CL3
Effect
Relation: -0.065
CL4
Effect
Relation: -0.001
CL5
Effect
Relation: -0.097
Component Relation Values
Relation (r-c)
0.20
0.15
0.10
0.05
0.00
−0.05
−0.10
CL1
CL2
CL3
CL4
CL5

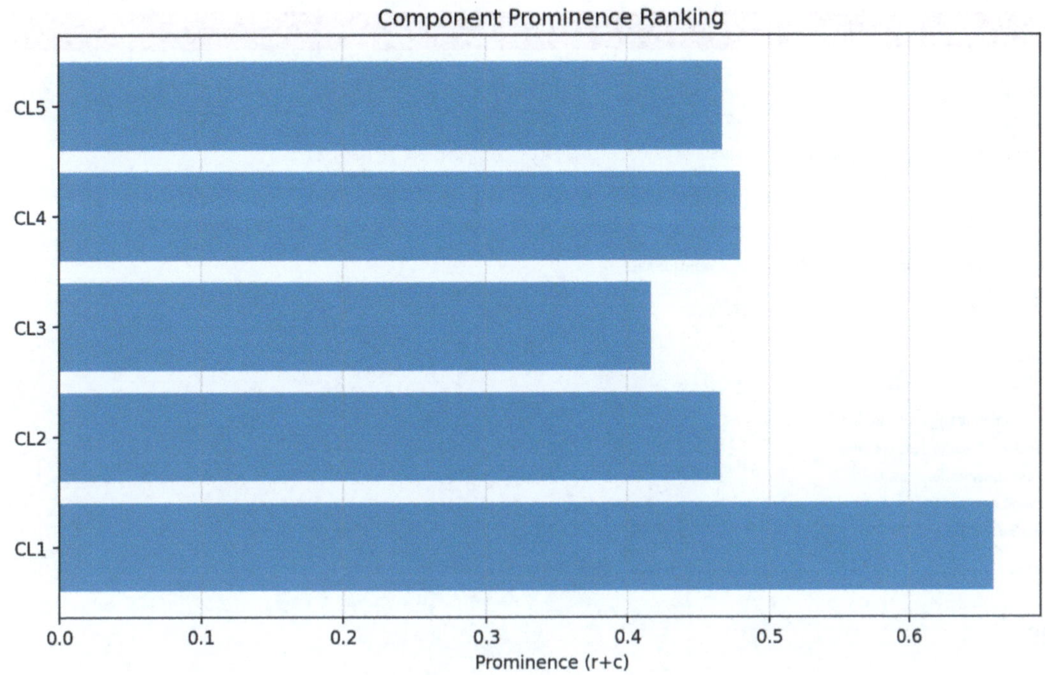
Component Prominence Ranking
CL5
CL4
CL3
CL2
CL1
0.0
0.1
0.2
0.3
0.4
0.5
0.6
Prominence (r+c)

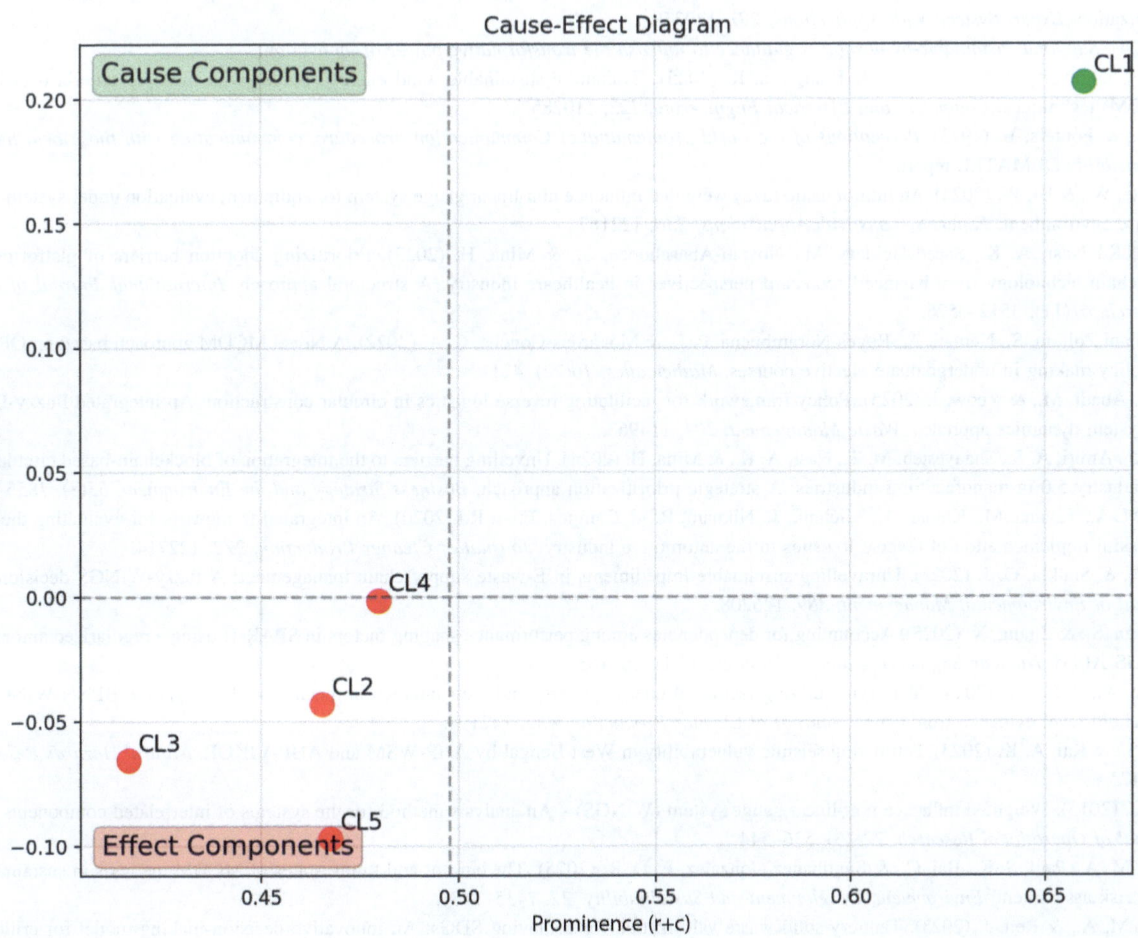
Cause-Effect Diagram
Cause Components
Effect Components
CL1
CL4
CL2
CL3
CL5
0.20
0.15
0.10
0.05
0.00
−0.05
−0.10
Relation (r-c)
0.45
0.50
0.55
0.60
0.65
Prominence (r+c)

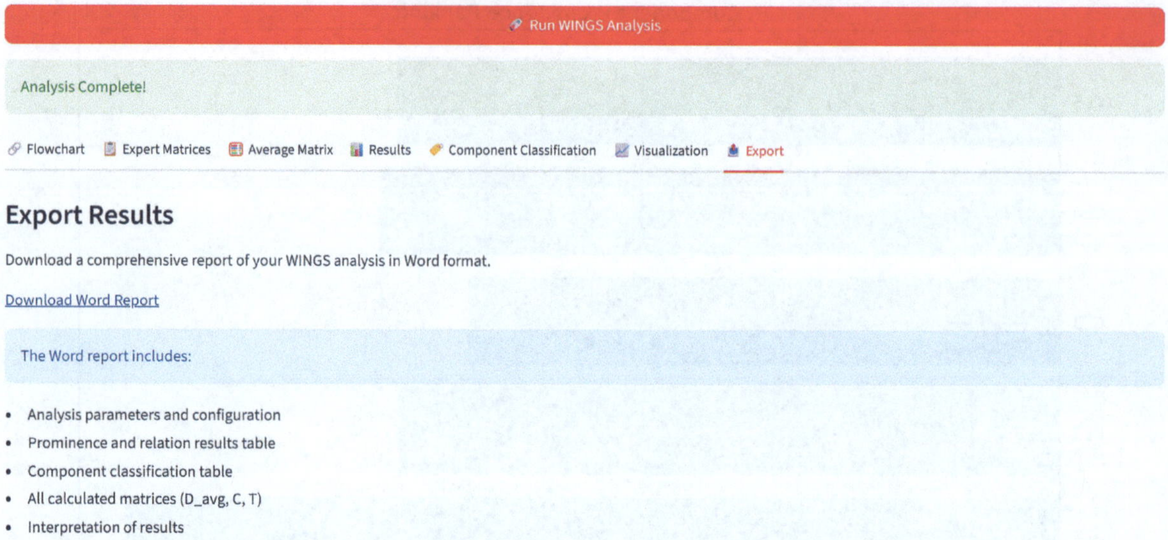

References

Carnero, M. C. (2026). A modified IF-AHP intuitionistic fuzzy FMEA methodology to prioritize maintenance management deficiencies in a health care organization. *Expert Systems with Applications, 297*, 129370.

Cefic (2024). *Safe and sustainable-by-design: A guidance to unleash the transformative power of innovation.*

Dash, S., Chakravarty, S., Giri, N. C., & Khargotra, R. (2025). Evaluating sustainable wind energy sources with multiple criteria decision-making (MCDM) techniques. *Computers and Electrical Engineering, 123*, 110285.

Gabus, A., & Fontela, E. (1973). *Perceptions of the world problematique: Communication procedure, communicating with those bearing collective responsibility* DEMATEL report.

Gao, F., He, W., & Bi, W. (2024). An intuitionistic fuzzy weighted influence non-linear gauge system for equipment evaluation under system-of-systems warfare environment. *Expert Systems with Applications, 238*, 122187.

Govindan, K., Nasr, A. K., Saeed Heidary, M., Nosrati-Abarghooee, S., & Mina, H. (2023). Prioritizing adoption barriers of platforms based on blockchain technology from balanced scorecard perspectives in healthcare industry: A structural approach. *International Journal of Production Research, 61*(11), 3512–3526.

Hashemkhani Zolfani, S., Nemati, A., Reyes-Norambuena, P. J., & Monardes-Concha, C. A. (2022). A Novel MCDM approach based on OPA-WINGS for policy making in undergraduate elective courses. *Mathematics, 10*(22), 4211.

Huang, J., Abadi, M., & Yeow, J. (2025). Policy framework for facilitating reverse logistics in circular construction: An integrated Fuzzy-DEMATEL and system dynamics approach. *Waste Management, 204*, 114963.

Kannan, D., Amiri, A. S., Shaayesteh, M. T., Nasr, A. K., & Mina, H. (2024). Unveiling barriers to the integration of blockchain-based circular economy and Industry 5.0 in manufacturing industries: A strategic prioritization approach. *Business Strategy and the Environment, 33*(8), 7855–7886.

Kaviani, M. A., Tavana, M., Kumar, A., Michnik, J., Niknam, R., & Campos, E. A. Rd (2020). An integrated framework for evaluating the barriers to successful implementation of reverse logistics in the automotive industry. *Journal of Cleaner Production, 272*, 122714.

Kumar, V., & Shukla, O. J. (2025). Unravelling sustainable impediments in E-waste supply chain management: A fuzzy-WINGS decision approach. *Journal of Environmental Management, 389*, 126208.

Liu, X., Yan, S., & Zhang, X. (2025). Accounting for dependencies among performance shaping factors in SPAR-H using a regularized autoencoder and WINGS-AISM. *Nuclear Engineering and Technology, 57*(1), 103165.

Lu, S., Yu, X., & Ren, J. (2024). Identifying driving factors of energy poverty and their interaction mechanism based on the BPNN-WINGS method: Household-level evidence from China. *Journal of Cleaner Production, 452*, 142194.

Malakar, S., & Rai, A. K. (2023). Estimating seismic vulnerability in West Bengal by AHP-WSM and AHP-VIKOR. *Natural Hazards Research, 3*(3), 464–473.

Michnik, J. (2013). Weighted influence non-linear gauge system (WINGS) – An analysis method for the systems of interrelated components. *European Journal of Operational Research, 228*(3), 536–544.

Moktadir, M. A., Paul, S. K., Bai, C., & Santibanez Gonzalez, E. D. R. (2025). The current and future states of MCDM methods in sustainable supply chain risk assessment. *Environment, Development and Sustainability, 27*, 7435–7480.

Moktadir, M. A., & Ren, J. (2023). Tannery solid waste valorization for achieving SDGs: An innovative decision-making model for critical success factors analysis and sustainable technology selection. *Process Safety and Environmental Protection, 177*, 1272–1293.

Moktadir, M. A., & Ren, J. (2024a). Global semiconductor supply chain resilience challenges and mitigation strategies: A novel integrated decomposed fuzzy set Delphi, WINGS and QFD model. *International Journal of Production Economics, 273*, 109280.

Moktadir, M. A., & Ren, J. (2024b). Leveraging environmental, social, and governance strategies for sustainable tannery solid waste management towards achieving sustainable development goals. *Sustainable Development, 32*(4), 2869–2898.

Moktadir, M. A., & Ren, J. (2024c). Towards green logistics: An innovative decision support model for zero-emission transportation modes development. *Transportation Research Part E: Logistics and Transportation Review, 189*, 103648.

Moktadir, M. A., & Ren, J. (2025). Carbon reduction strategies for the leather supply chain: Implications for climate change mitigation policy toward carbon neutrality. *Sustainable Development, 33*(6), 9279–9302.

Moktadir, M. A., Zhou, J., Ren, J., & Toniolo, S. (2025). A decision support framework for safe and sustainable by-design practices promoting circularity in waste-to-energy supply chains. *Sustainable Production and Consumption, 54*, 487–501.

Olorvida, R. C., Bande, R. A., Ngalot, D., Lacaba, R., Codilla, J., Arcuino, L. A., Egloso, N., Aro, J. L., Maturan, F., & Ocampo, L. (2023). Grey weighted influence non-linear gauge systems (WINGS) for evaluating consumption barriers of refurbished mobile phones for a circular economy. *Cleaner and Responsible Consumption, 8*, 100091.

Otay, İ., Çevik Onar, S., Öztayşi, B., & Kahraman, C. (2024). Evaluation of sustainable energy systems in smart cities using a multi-expert pythagorean fuzzy BWM & TOPSIS methodology. *Expert Systems with Applications, 250*, 123874.

Pinto, G. D., Cassânego, V. M., Zanon, L. G., Ferraz, D., & Rebelatto, D. Ad. N. (2025). Strengthening short food supply chains: Prioritizing obstacles and opportunities with PROMETHEE, Fuzzy DEMATEL, and Fuzzy TOPSIS class. *International Journal of Production Economics, 289*, 109732.

Shamekhi Amiri, A., Torabi, S. A., & Tavana, M. (2025). An assessment of the prominence and total engagement metrics for ranking interdependent attributes in DEMATEL and WINGS. *Omega, 130*, 103176.

Tavana, M., Heidary, M. S., & Mina, H. (2023). A fuzzy preference programming and weighted influence non-linear gauge system for mission architecture assessment at NASA. *Applied Soft Computing, 145*, 110572.

Tavana, M., Khalili Nasr, A., Mina, H., & Michnik, J. (2022). A private sustainable partner selection model for green public-private partnerships and regional economic development. *Socio-Economic Planning Sciences, 83*, 101189.

Tavana, M., Mousavi, H., Khalili Nasr, A., & Mina, H. (2021). A fuzzy weighted influence non-linear gauge system with application to advanced technology assessment at NASA. *Expert Systems with Applications, 182*, 115274.

Tian, Y., & Zhang, K. (2023). Bipolar neutrosophic WINGS for green technology innovation. *Scientific Reports, 13*(1), 19159.

Wang, M., Tian, Y., & Zhang, K. (2023). The fuzzy weighted influence nonlinear gauge system method extended with D numbers and MICMAC. *Complex & Intelligent Systems, 9*(1), 719–731.

Wang, M., & Zhang, K. (2022). Improving agricultural green supply chain management by a novel integrated fuzzy-delphi and grey-WINGS model. *Agriculture (Switzerland), 12*(10).

Wang, M., Zhang, Y., Tian, Y., & Zhang, K. (2023). An integrated rough-fuzzy WINGS-ISM method with an application in ASSCM. *Expert Systems with Applications, 212*, 118843.

Wang, W., Tian, Z., Xi, W., Tan, Y. R., & Deng, Y. (2021). The influencing factors of China's green building development: An analysis using RBF-WINGS method. *Building and Environment, 188*, 107425.

Wang, X., Li, X., Liang, X., & Zhu, C. (2024). An improved WINGS-ISM approach with consensus model in group decision-making for addressing critical success factors of collaborative emergency management. *Expert Systems with Applications, 248*, 123217.

Wu, J., Wang, Z., Luo, P., Li, X., Zhang, W., & Wu, W. (2024). Which factors affect the repair for loss of social trust after public health emergency? An approach integrating 2-tuple linguistic WINGS and regret theory. *Expert Systems with Applications, 250*, 123870.

Zhang, K., Chen, Z., & Wang, Y. (2025). A novel approach for agricultural carbon emission reduction by integrating fermatean neutrosophic set with WINGS and AHP-EWM. *Scientific Reports, 15*(1), 391.

Chapter 6

CRITIC: Criteria importance through intercriteria correlation for multi-attribute decision-making

Babek Erdebilli[1] **and Emine Nur Nacar**[2]

[1]*School of Business, Worcester Polytechnic Institute, Worcester, MA, United States,* [2]*Department of Industrial Engineering, Ankara Yıldırım Beyazıt University, Ankara, Türkiye*

6.1 Introduction

In complex real-world decision problems, decision-makers are often required to evaluate multiple alternatives based on several conflicting criteria. This situation arises in a wide range of domains, including supplier selection, environmental management, project evaluation, personnel recruitment, energy planning, and technology assessment (Wu et al., 2021; Zolfani & Aghdaie, 2024; Zolfani et al., 2019). Such problems fall under the umbrella of Multicriteria decision-making (MCDM), which provides systematic approaches for ranking or selecting alternatives when multiple, and often incommensurable, criteria are involved (Hwang & Yoon, 1981; Saaty, 2008).

MCDM methods are generally structured into two main phases: the weighting of criteria and the aggregation of alternatives based on those weights. The determination of criteria weights is a crucial step because the relative importance assigned to each criterion directly influences the final decision. Weighting methods can be broadly categorized into subjective and objective approaches (Hashemkhani Zolfani et al., 2023). Subjective methods, such as analytic hierarchy process (AHP) or Delphi, rely on expert judgments and preferences, which may introduce personal bias and inconsistency. Objective methods, on the other hand, derive weights from the structure and characteristics of the data itself, making them particularly suitable when expert opinions are unavailable or when a transparent, data-driven approach is desired (Rajabi et al., 2022; Zavadskas & Turskis, 2011).

Among the objective weighting techniques, the criteria importance through the intercriteria correlation (CRITIC) method, introduced by Diakoulaki et al. (1995), has gained popularity due to its ability to simultaneously consider two essential aspects: the contrast intensity of each criterion and the conflict among criteria. Specifically, CRITIC calculates the standard deviation of each criterion to reflect its ability to discriminate between alternatives and analyzes the correlation between criteria to capture redundancy. A criterion with high variability and low correlation with others is considered more informative and is therefore assigned a higher weight. Recent applications of CRITIC in energy, environment, construction, and supplier evaluation problems demonstrate its robustness and growing significance (Li et al., 2020; Wu et al., 2021; Zhang et al., 2022; Zhong et al., 2023).

The CRITIC method presents several advantages. It is entirely objective and data-driven, avoiding subjective influence. It also provides a more balanced weighting by penalizing highly correlated (i.e., redundant) criteria (Pamucar et al., 2023; Zhou et al., 2022). However, it also has some limitations. Since it relies on correlation coefficients, it assumes linear relationships between criteria and may not fully capture nonlinear dependencies. Moreover, its effectiveness depends on the quality and representativeness of the data matrix (Fujimoto & Guo, 2018; Rajabi et al., 2022). Nevertheless, its simplicity, transparency, and mathematical rigor have made CRITIC a widely used method in academic and practical decision-making studies.

In this study, the CRITIC method is applied to a realistic supplier selection problem involving 12 evaluation criteria. The aim is to demonstrate how the method can objectively determine the importance of each criterion, contributing to a rational and justifiable selection process.

Encyclopedia of Multi-Attribute Decision-Making (MADM). DOI: https://doi.org/10.1016/B978-0-443-33275-3.00081-6

6.2 Literature review

The literature on MCDM has seen substantial growth, particularly in the development of objective weighting methods. Traditional approaches such as the AHP (Saaty, 2008) and simple additive weighting (Hwang & Yoon, 1981) have been widely used but are limited by their reliance on subjective judgments. This has led to increased interest in objective weighting techniques, which assign weights based on inherent data characteristics rather than expert opinions.

The CRITIC method (Diakoulaki et al., 1995) is one of the most prominent objective approaches, balancing contrast intensity and intercriteria correlation. Numerous studies have extended or applied CRITIC to different domains. For example, Zhong et al. (2023) used an improved CRITIC method for thermal coal supplier evaluation, demonstrating its ability to handle conflicting value ranges of indicators (Zhong et al., 2023). Similarly, Wu et al. (2021) applied CRITIC in environmental policy analysis, highlighting its effectiveness in comparing sustainable energy strategies (Wu et al., 2021). In agriculture, CRITIC has been employed to evaluate sustainability criteria, integrating both environmental and economic perspectives (Puska et al., 2022).

Recent advancements have focused on integrating CRITIC with other techniques. Pamucar et al. (2023) proposed a fuzzy-rough CRITIC variant to address uncertainty in decision environments (Pamucar et al., 2023). Zolfani and colleagues have compared CRITIC with indifference threshold-based attribute ratio analysis and method based on the removal effects of criteria, providing a comprehensive understanding of objective weighting methods and their applicability across various fields, such as urban resilience and industrial management (Zolfani & Aghdaie, 2024). In addition, hybrid models combining CRITIC with fuzzy logic and rough set theory have been developed to capture uncertainty and enhance robustness in decision-making (Zhou et al., 2022).

Applications of CRITIC span multiple areas. In supply chain and supplier evaluation, it has been used to assess performance under dynamic conditions (Zhong et al., 2023). In energy systems, CRITIC helps prioritize technologies and strategies for sustainable planning (Li et al., 2020; Wu et al., 2021). In finance and healthcare, it assists in performance assessment, risk analysis, and resource allocation (Rajabi et al., 2022). These applications underline the versatility and growing significance of the CRITIC method in solving real-world multicriteria problems.

6.3 Methodology: the criteria importance through intercriteria correlation method

The CRITIC method is an objective weighting technique used in MCDM problems. Unlike subjective methods that rely on expert judgments, CRITIC determines the weights of criteria solely based on the structure of the decision matrix, utilizing both the contrast intensity (standard deviation) and the conflict (correlation) among criteria (Diakoulaki et al., 1995).

The steps of the CRITIC method are as follows:

Step 1: Construction of the normalized decision matrix

Let $X=[x_{ij}]$ be the original decision matrix where $i=1, 2, \ldots, m$ alternatives and $j=1, 2, \ldots, n$ criteria. The matrix is normalized to ensure comparability among different scales. For a benefit-type criterion, normalization is performed as:

$$r_{ij} = \frac{x_{ij} - \min(x_j)}{\max(x_j) - \min(x_j)} \tag{6.1}$$

For a cost-type criterion, the formula is:

$$r_{ij} = \frac{\max(x_j) - x_{ij}}{\max(x_j) - \min(x_j)} \tag{6.2}$$

The resulting matrix $R=[r_{ij}]$ is the normalized decision matrix.

Step 2: Calculation of standard deviations

For each criterion j, the standard deviation σ_j of the normalized values is computed:

$$\sigma_j = \sqrt{\frac{1}{m}\sum_{i=1}^{m}\left(r_{ij} - \bar{r}_j\right)^2} \tag{6.3}$$

where $\bar{r}_j$ is the mean value of the normalized values for criterion j. The standard deviation indicates the contrast intensity, reflecting the discriminating power of each criterion.

Step 3: Correlation and conflict matrix

The correlation coefficient r_{jk} is calculated between every pair of criteria j and k using Pearson's correlation:

$$r_{jk} = \frac{\sum_{i=1}^{m}\left(r_{ij} - \bar{r}_j\right)(r_{ik} - \bar{r}_k)}{\sqrt{\sum_{i=1}^{m}\left(r_{ij} - \bar{r}_j\right)^2 \sum_{i=1}^{m}(r_{ik} - \bar{r}_k)^2}} \tag{6.4}$$

The conflict between criteria is computed as:

$$c_{jk} = 1 - r_{jk}, \quad c_{jj} = 0 \tag{6.5}$$

A higher c_{jk} value indicates greater disagreement (conflict) between criteria j and k.

Step 4: Computation of the information content (C_j)

The information content of each criterion j is calculated as:

$$C_j = a_j \cdot \sum_{k=1}^{n}\left(1 - r_{jk}\right) \tag{6.6}$$

This step integrates both contrast intensity and intercriteria conflict, effectively capturing the importance of a criterion from a systemic perspective.

Step 5: Determination of criteria weights

The normalized importance values (weights) of each criterion are determined by:

$$w_j = \frac{C_j}{\sum_{j=1}^{n} C_j}, \quad \sum_{j=1}^{n} w_j = 1 \tag{6.7}$$

These weights w_j are then used in subsequent decision-making models such as technique for order preference by similarity to ideal solution (TOPSIS), VlseKriterijumska Optimizacija I Kompromisno Resenje (VIKOR), or utility-based ranking.

The CRITIC method is particularly useful in complex decision environments where subjective weighting is either infeasible or unreliable. It allows analysts to derive criterion weights based solely on the underlying structure of data, enhancing objectivity and reproducibility.

Note on traceability: Tables in the numerical examples directly correspond to the above equations.

For example 1, Table 6.3 comes from (6.4); Table 6.4 from (6.5); Table 6.5 from Eqs. (6.3) and (6.6); and Table 6.6 from (6.7). For example 2, Tables 6.9 and 6.10 correspond to Eqs. (6.4) and (6.5), while Tables 6.11 and 6.12 correspond to Eqs. (6.3)–(6.7).

6.4 Numerical example 1: facility location selection using the criteria importance through the intercriteria correlation method

This section presents a simple numerical example to illustrate the application of the CRITIC method. The objective is to determine the weights of decision criteria based on the contrast intensity and correlation among them. The context of the problem is facility location selection, where a company must choose among three potential sites.

6.4.1 Problem definition

A company plans to establish a new manufacturing facility and considers three candidate locations: A1 (Ankara), A2 (Konya), and A3 (Eskisehir). The decision-making process is based on the evaluation of four criteria:

- C1: Land cost (£/m^2) – to be minimized
- C2: Transportation accessibility (score from 1 to 10) – to be maximized
- C3: Labor accessibility (score from 1 to 10) – to be maximized
- C4: Energy cost (£/kWh) – to be minimized

The raw decision matrix is provided in Table 6.7. These values reflect realistic differences among the locations and are intentionally selected to demonstrate meaningful differentiation in criterion weights (Table 6.1).

TABLE 6.1 Raw decision matrix.

Alternative	C1	C2	C3	C4
A1	240	7.5	8.0	0.72
A2	195	6.5	6.0	0.85
A3	310	9.2	5.5	0.65

TABLE 6.2 Normalized decision matrix.

Alternative	C1 (cost)	C2 (benefit)	C3 (benefit)	C4 (cost)
A1	0.6087	0.3704	1.0000	0.6500
A2	1.0000	0.0000	0.2000	0.0000
A3	0.0000	1.0000	0.0000	1.0000

TABLE 6.3 Correlation coefficient matrix.

	C1	C2	C3	C4
C1	1.000	-0.981	0.762	-0.999
C2	-0.981	1.000	-0.949	0.975
C3	0.762	-0.949	1.000	-0.777
C4	-0.999	0.975	-0.777	1.000

Step 1: Normalization of the decision matrix

The raw data are normalized using min-max normalization. For benefit criteria (C2 and C3), higher values are better, while for cost criteria (C1 and C4), lower values are better. The normalized matrix is shown in Table 6.2.

Step 2: Correlation coefficient matrix

Next, the Pearson correlation coefficient matrix is calculated to determine the interdependencies among criteria. The values in Table 6.3 indicate how strongly each pair of criteria is correlated. High absolute values indicate redundancy, while low values suggest uniqueness.

Step 3: Construction of the 1 – r_{jk} matrix

The correlation matrix is transformed by computing $1 - r_{jk}$ to quantify the contrast or conflict between criteria. This matrix is provided in Table 6.4.

Step 4: Standard deviations

Standard deviations of each criterion from the normalized matrix are calculated as:

$\sigma_{C1} = 0.4117$,
$\sigma_{C2} = 0.4131$,
$\sigma_{C3} = 0.4320$,
$\sigma_{C4} = 0.4144$.

Step 5: Information content calculation

The CRITIC information content scores are obtained by multiplying each standard deviation by the sum of its corresponding row in the $1 - r_{jk}$ matrix: Table 6.5.

TABLE 6.4 $1 - r_{jk}$ matrix.

	C1	C2	C3	C4
C1	0.000	1.981	0.238	1.999
C2	1.981	0.000	1.949	0.025
C3	0.238	1.949	0.000	1.777
C4	1.999	0.025	1.777	0.000

TABLE 6.5 Information content values (C_j).

Criterion	Row sum	C_j
C1	4.218	1.7369
C2	3.955	1.6333
C3	3.964	1.7125
C4	3.801	1.5751

TABLE 6.6 Final criteria importance through intercriteria correlation weights (w_j).

Criterion	Weight
C1 (Land cost)	0.2609
C2 (Transportation access)	0.2453
C3 (Labor access)	0.2573
C4 (Energy cost)	0.2364

Step 6: Final criteria importance through intercriteria correlation weights

Each C_j value is normalized to determine the relative weight of each criterion: Table 6.6.

6.4.8 Discussion and interpretation

The results demonstrate that all four criteria have relatively balanced but distinct contributions to the decision-making process. Land cost (C1) and labor accessibility (C3) received slightly higher weights, indicating their greater influence. Transportation (C2) and energy cost (C4) are still important but slightly less impactful in this specific context.

This weighting scheme, obtained objectively from the data using the CRITIC method, can now be applied in any subsequent multiple attribute decision-making ranking method such as TOPSIS, VIKOR, or weighted aggregated sum product assessment.

6.5 Numerical example 2: supplier selection using the criteria importance through intercriteria correlation method

This section presents a more complex and realistic application of the CRITIC method. The goal is to select the most appropriate supplier among eight candidates based on 12 evaluation criteria. The selected criteria reflect operational, financial, environmental, and technological considerations. This example demonstrates the full potential of the CRITIC method by handling high-dimensional and varied data.

6.5.1 Problem definition

A manufacturing company seeks to establish long-term partnerships with reliable suppliers. Eight suppliers are evaluated across 12 distinct criteria:

- C1: Unit cost (£) [cost] – The purchase price per unit offered by the supplier.
- C2: Delivery time (days) [cost] – The average number of days to deliver an order.
- C3: Quality score (0–10) [benefit] – The quality level of supplied materials based on inspection results.
- C4: Delivery reliability (%) [benefit] – The percentage of on-time and complete deliveries.
- C5: Financial strength (0–100) [benefit] – A score reflecting financial health and solvency.
- C6: Communication speed (hours) [cost] – Average time to respond to queries or resolve issues.
- C7: Environmental certifications (count) [benefit] – Number of recognized environmental certifications.
- C8: Flexibility (response speed) [benefit] – The ability to accommodate urgent or changing de- mands.
- C9: Enterprise resource planning (ERP) compatibility (1 = Yes, 0 = No) [benefit] – Whether the supplier's system is compatible with the firm's ERP.
- C10: Distance from plant (km) [cost] – Proximity to the manufacturing facility.
- C11: Payment conditions (score 0–10) [benefit] – Flexibility and favorability of payment terms.
- C12: Monthly supply capacity (tons) [benefit] – The supplier's monthly maximum supply volume.

The suppliers under evaluation are: Table 6.7:

- A1: Delta industrial
- A2: Nova materials
- A3: Orion components
- A4: Vertex supplies
- A5: Altay machine
- A6: ZenTek solutions
- A7: Elmas group
- A8: ArgePlus Ltd.

Step 1: Normalized decision matrix
The raw data matrix is normalized using min-max normalization. Table 6.8 presents the normalized values, considering each criterion's type (cost or benefit).
Step 2: Correlation and conflict matrix
Tables 6.9 and 6.10.
Step 3: Standard deviation and C_j values
The standard deviation of each criterion is calculated from the normalized matrix. These values are then multiplied by the sum of the corresponding row in the $1 - r_{jk}$ matrix to compute the information content C_j. Table 6.11.

TABLE 6.7 Raw decision matrix for the supplier selection problem.

	C1	C2	C3	C4	C5	C6	C7	C8	C9	C10	C11	C12
A1	7.5	3	8	85	80	2	3	6	1	60	8	30
A2	8.2	2	6	70	60	3	2	4	1	50	4	20
A3	6.1	4	5	90	90	2.5	4	9	1	65	6	45
A4	9.0	1	9	95	95	4	5	8	1	35	8	50
A5	5.0	0	4	40	40	5	1	2	0	30	2	15
A6	8.5	2.5	5.5	80	75	2.5	3	4	1	55	6	35
A7	10.0	5	10	100	100	1	6	10	1	70	10	60
A8	5.8	0.5	3	30	30	4.5	0	0	0	75	0	10

TABLE 6.8 Normalized decision matrix (min-max method).

	C1	C2	C3	C4	C5	C6	C7	C8	C9	C10	C11	C12
A1	0.492	0.667	0.682	0.636	0.636	0.833	0.50	0.60	1.00	0.538	0.80	0.545
A2	0.630	0.333	0.455	0.409	0.341	0.500	0.33	0.40	1.00	0.385	0.40	0.364
A3	0.275	0.833	0.273	0.727	0.727	0.667	0.67	0.90	1.00	0.615	0.60	0.818
A4	0.800	0.167	0.864	0.909	0.909	0.333	0.83	0.80	1.00	0.154	0.80	0.909
A5	0.000	0.000	0.136	0.227	0.114	0.000	0.17	0.20	0.00	0.000	0.20	0.273
A6	0.738	0.500	0.318	0.591	0.568	0.667	0.50	0.40	1.00	0.462	0.60	0.636
A7	1.000	1.000	1.000	1.000	1.000	1.000	1.00	1.00	1.00	0.692	1.00	1.000
A8	0.377	0.083	0.000	0.000	0.000	0.167	0.00	0.00	0.00	0.923	0.00	0.000

TABLE 6.9 Correlation matrix among criteria.

	C1	C2	C3	C4	C5	C6	C7	C8	C9	C10	C11	C12
C1	1.000	0.453	0.775	0.673	0.694	0.638	0.691	0.525	0.676	0.226	0.698	0.611
C2	0.453	1.000	0.518	0.695	0.715	0.943	0.705	0.773	0.688	0.448	0.739	0.687
C3	0.775	0.518	1.000	0.869	0.862	0.639	0.861	0.783	0.695	-0.102	0.908	0.787
C4	0.673	0.695	0.869	1.000	0.995	0.716	0.991	0.955	0.821	-0.097	0.965	0.986
C5	0.694	0.715	0.862	0.995	1.000	0.739	0.988	0.954	0.824	-0.011	0.964	0.978
C6	0.638	0.943	0.639	0.716	0.739	1.000	0.703	0.715	0.798	0.420	0.811	0.667
C7	0.691	0.705	0.861	0.991	0.988	0.703	1.000	0.959	0.770	-0.037	0.941	0.986
C8	0.525	0.773	0.783	0.955	0.954	0.715	0.959	1.000	0.771	0.006	0.898	0.955
C9	0.676	0.688	0.695	0.821	0.824	0.798	0.770	0.771	1.000	0.020	0.832	0.778
C10	0.226	0.448	-0.102	-0.097	-0.011	0.420	-0.037	0.006	0.020	1.000	-0.039	-0.112
C11	0.698	0.739	0.908	0.965	0.964	0.811	0.941	0.898	0.832	-0.039	1.000	0.919
C12	0.611	0.687	0.787	0.986	0.978	0.667	0.986	0.955	0.778	-0.112	0.919	1.000

TABLE 6.10 Conflict matrix $1 - r_{jk}$.

	C1	C2	C3	C4	C5	C6	C7	C8	C9	C10	C11	C12
C1	0.000	0.547	0.225	0.327	0.306	0.362	0.309	0.475	0.324	0.774	0.302	0.389
C2	0.547	0.000	0.482	0.305	0.285	0.057	0.295	0.227	0.312	0.552	0.261	0.313
C3	0.225	0.482	0.000	0.131	0.138	0.361	0.139	0.217	0.305	1.102	0.092	0.213
C4	0.327	0.305	0.131	0.000	0.005	0.284	0.009	0.045	0.179	1.097	0.035	0.014
C5	0.306	0.285	0.138	0.005	0.000	0.261	0.012	0.046	0.176	1.011	0.036	0.022
C6	0.362	0.057	0.361	0.284	0.261	0.000	0.297	0.285	0.202	0.580	0.189	0.333
C7	0.309	0.295	0.139	0.009	0.012	0.297	0.000	0.041	0.230	1.037	0.059	0.014
C8	0.475	0.227	0.217	0.045	0.046	0.285	0.041	0.000	0.229	0.994	0.102	0.045
C9	0.324	0.312	0.305	0.179	0.176	0.202	0.230	0.229	0.000	0.980	0.168	0.222
C10	0.774	0.552	1.102	1.097	1.011	0.580	1.037	0.994	0.980	0.000	1.039	1.112
C11	0.302	0.261	0.092	0.035	0.036	0.189	0.059	0.102	0.168	1.039	0.000	0.081
C12	0.389	0.313	0.213	0.014	0.022	0.333	0.014	0.045	0.222	1.112	0.081	0.000

TABLE 6.11 Standard deviations and C_j values.

Criterion	C1	C2	C3	C4	C5	C6	C7	C8	C9	C10	C11	C12
Std. Dev	0.299	0.341	0.331	0.316	0.336	0.317	0.311	0.328	0.433	0.276	0.312	0.321
C_j	1.300	1.480	1.436	1.371	1.461	1.375	1.352	1.422	1.880	1.197	1.356	1.392

TABLE 6.12 Final criteria importance through intercriteria correlation weights.

Criterion	C1	C2	C3	C4	C5	C6	C7	C8	C9	C10	C11	C12
w_j	0.076	0.087	0.084	0.081	0.086	0.081	0.079	0.084	0.110	0.070	0.080	0.082

Step 4: Final weights w_j
The final CRITIC weights are obtained by normalizing the C_j values. Table 6.12.

6.5.6 Interpretation

The final weights indicate the relative importance of each criterion. Notably, ERP compatibility (C9) has the highest weight (0.110), suggesting that it provides the most unique and influential information in the dataset. In contrast, distance from the plant (C10) has the lowest weight (0.070), likely due to its strong correlation with other cost-related factors.

Overall, the CRITIC method has successfully revealed the internal structure of the decision data, quantifying both variability and interdependence among criteria. These weights can now be used in multicriteria ranking methods such as TOPSIS or VIKOR for final supplier selection.

6.6 Conclusions

This chapter has presented a comprehensive application of the CRITIC method to support objective decision-making in multicriteria environments. Through two numerical examples of increasing complexity—facility location selection and supplier evaluation—the versatility and analytical power of the CRITIC approach have been illustrated in detail.

The CRITIC method provides a systematic and transparent mechanism for determining objective criteria weights by incorporating both the variability of each criterion and the degree of correlation among them. This dual consideration enables the method to identify criteria that are both discriminative and nonredundant, thus yielding more informative weighting schemes. In both case studies, the method successfully differentiated between criteria, avoided redundancy, and offered rational support for selecting the most suitable alternatives.

The first example demonstrated how CRITIC can be applied to a relatively simple problem with only four criteria and three alternatives, making it suitable for educational and illustrative purposes. The second example extended the application to a real-world problem involving 12 criteria and eight suppliers, highlighting the method's scalability and practical relevance in operational decision contexts. Despite its benefits, the CRITIC method has certain limitations. Since it relies on correlation coefficients, it assumes linear relationships between criteria and may not fully account for complex or nonlinear interactions. Additionally, it is sensitive to data quality and scale, emphasizing the need for appropriate normalization prior to weight computation.

Future studies may explore hybrid approaches where CRITIC is combined with other MCDM methods—such as TOPSIS, VIKOR, or elimination and choice translating reality—for enhanced decision support. Furthermore, incorporating fuzzy sets or interval-valued data could improve robustness in cases with uncertainty or imprecise information. CRITIC can also be embedded into group decision-making settings, where weights must reflect consensus or disagreement among multiple decision-makers.

From a practical standpoint, CRITIC has already been deployed across diverse real-world settings, which underscores its external validity and transferability. Recent studies report successful use in construction project risk management

(Mirjalili et al., 2023), aerospace selection problems (Majumder et al., 2023), investment portfolio construction (Silva et al., 2023), and product design in immersive (virtual reality/metaverse) environments (Sleem et al., 2023). The supplier-selection case examined in this chapter is aligned with these deployments and further illustrates how data-driven weighting can support transparent, auditable, and defensible decisions in operational contexts.

In conclusion, CRITIC stands out as a valuable tool in the MCDM toolkit, particularly in scenarios where objectivity, consistency, and data-driven insight are critical. Its continued development and integration with other decision-making frameworks hold strong potential for addressing complex, high-stakes decisions in industrial, environmental, and strategic management contexts.

References

Diakoulaki, D., Mavrotas, G., & Papayannakis, L. (1995). Determining objective weights in multiple criteria problems: The CRITIC method. *Computers & Operations Research, 22*(7), 763–770.

Fujimoto, Y., & Guo, M. (2018). On the properties of the CRITIC method in objective decision weighting. In *Proceedings of the 35th International Conference on Machine Learning* (PMLR 80), pp. 1324–1332.

Hashemkhani Zolfani, S., Rajabi, M., & Yazdani, M. (2023). Objective vs. subjective weighting in MCDM: A systematic review. *Journal of Multi-Criteria Decision Analysis, 30*(1-2), 45–60.

Hwang, C. L., & Yoon, K. (1981). *Multiple attribute decision making: methods and applications*. Berlin: Springer.

Li, X., Zhou, Y., & Huang, J. (2020). CRITIC-based evaluation of renewable energy technologies for sustainable development. *Energy Reports, 6*, 2202–2211. https://doi.org/10.1016/j.egyr.2020.08.043.

Majumder, A., Kaur, G., Dhara, A., Sandhu, B. S., Puhan, A., & Adhikari, M. S. (2023). A CRITIC-TOPSIS MCDM technique under the neutrosophic environment with application on aircraft selection. *Contemporary Mathematics, 4*(4), 1180–1203. https://doi.org/10.37256/cm.4420232963.

Mirjalili, S., Lork, A., & Amin Nejad, B. (2023). Risk assessment in construction projects portfolio management by CRITIC MCDM method. *Journal of Structural and Construction Engineering, 10*(12), 5–17. https://doi.org/10.22065/jsce.2023.357970.3030.

Pamucar, D., Yazdani, M., & Suzić, Z. (2023). A fuzzy-rough CRITIC method for determining criteria weights in uncertain decision environments. *Applied Soft Computing, 138*, 110210. https://doi.org/10.1016/j.asoc.2023.110210.

Puska, A., Suzić, Z., Stankovi´c, M., Jovanovi´c, S., & Tanackov, I. (2022). Evaluation of pear market sustainability using fuzzy CRITIC and MABAC methods. *Agriculture, 12*(1), 139. https://doi.org/10.3390/agriculture12010139.

Rajabi, M., Ghorabaee, M. K., & Amiri, M. (2022). Objective weighting methods in healthcare decision-making: A comparative study of CRITIC, entropy, and SD. *Operations Research in Health Care, 34*, 100345. https://doi.org/10.1016/j.orhc.2022.100345.

Saaty, T. L. (2008). Decision making with the analytic hierarchy process. *International Journal of Services Sciences, 1*(1), 83–98.

Silva, N. F., dos Santos, M., Gomes, C. F. S., & de Andrade, L. P. (2023). An integrated CRITIC and grey relational analysis approach for investment portfolio selection. *Decision Analytics Journal, 8*, 100285. https://doi.org/10.1016/j.dajour.2023.100285.

Sleem, A., Mostafa, N., & Elhenawy, I. (2023). Neutrosophic CRITIC MCDM methodology for ranking factors and needs of customers in product design in the virtual reality metaverse. *Neutrosophic Systems with Applications, 2*, 55–67. https://doi.org/10.5281/zenodo.8196024.

Wu, Y., Guo, X., & Zhang, B. (2021). Application of CRITIC method in environmental policy assessment: A case of sustainable energy strategies. *Sustainability, 13*(9), 4098. https://doi.org/10.3390/su13094098.

Zavadskas, E. K., & Turskis, Z. (2011). Multiple criteria decision making (MCDM) methods in economics: An overview. *Technological and Economic Development of Economy, 17*(2), 397–427.

Zhang, J., Li, X., & Wang, Y. (2022). Rock burst intensity evaluation based on CRITIC-cloud model coupling. *Mathematics, 13*(2), 240. https://doi.org/10.3390/math13020240.

Zhong, R., Chen, Y., & Li, H. (2023). An improved CRITIC method for thermal coal supplier evaluation. *Scientific Reports, 13*, 27495. https://doi.org/10.1038/s41598-023-27495-6.

Zhou, J., Liu, H., & Wang, C. (2022). Modification of the CRITIC method using fuzzy rough numbers. *Expert Systems with Applications, 203*, 117429. https://doi.org/10.1016/j.eswa.2022.117429.

Zolfani, S. H., & Aghdaie, M. H. (2024). Comparison of CRITIC, ITARA, and MEREC weighting methods in MCDM: Insights from urban resilience applications. *Decision Making: Applications in Management and Engineering, 1*(1), 105–120.

Zolfani, S. H., Yazdani, M., & Torkayesh, A. E. (2019). An extended CRITIC method using FUCOM approach for sustainable supplier selection. *Sustainability, 11*(12), 3376. https://doi.org/10.3390/su11123376.

Further reading

Krishnan, A. R., Kasim, M. M., Hamid, R., & Ghazali, M. F. (2021). A modified CRITIC method to estimate the objective weights of decision criteria. *Symmetry, 13*(6), 973. https://doi.org/10.3390/sym13060973.

Mukhametzyanov, I. Z. (2021). Specific character of objective methods for determining weights of criteria in MCDM problems: Entropy, CRITIC, SD. *Decision Making: Applications in Management and Engineering, 4*(2), 76–105. https://doi.org/10.31181/dmame210402076i.

Chapter 7

REGIME: Ranks and evaluation by guide indices and matrices for multi-attribute decision-making

Yajing Zhang and Weizhong Wang
School of Economics and Management, Anhui Normal University, Wuhu, Anhui Province, P.R. China

7.1 Introduction

The REGIME method was first proposed by Hinloopen et al. (1983) to address multiattribute decision-making (MADM) problems. It is a compensatory decision-making method designed to handle both qualitative and quantitative attributes, making it particularly suitable for complex decision problems under uncertainty (Haktanır & Kahraman, 2022; Massei et al., 2014). The REGIME method ranks alternatives based on pairwise comparisons of their performance under multiple criteria, offering a simple and flexible approach. The REGIME method possesses several distinctive features: (1) It does not require normalization of the original data, which enhances its robustness in handling uncertainty in decision-making. (2) It utilizes pairwise comparisons to rank alternatives, which reflects the flexibility of the method. (3) It is applicable to both qualitative and quantitative data and enhances its effectiveness in practical decision-making contexts. Due to these characteristics, the REGIME method has been widely applied in various domains, including policy analysis (Akgün et al., 2012), spatial planning (Massei et al., 2014), medical treatment selection (Camgoz Akdag & Menekse, 2023), and site selection (Akram, Ahmad, et al., 2024). These applications demonstrate that the REGIME method has matured into a reliable decision-support approach across diverse disciplines. Its capacity to integrate qualitative judgments with quantitative assessments underscores its value in addressing complex and multifaceted real-world decision-making problems.

The remainder of this paper is organized as follows. Section 2 reviews the literature on the REGIME method. Section 3 introduces the fundamental concepts and procedural steps of REGIME. Sections 4 and 5 present a simple and a complex numerical example, respectively, to demonstrate its applicability. Section 6 provides a comparative analysis between REGIME and other existing MADM methods. Finally, Section 7 outlines the conclusions and future research directions.

7.2 Literature review

The REGIME method, first introduced by Hinloopen et al. (1983), has been widely applied to address a variety of MADM problems (Hinloopen & Nijkamp, 1990). For instance, Akgün et al. (2012) employed the REGIME method to address regional policy selection problems involving multiple attributes. Massei et al. (2014) integrated REGIME with geographic information systems to solve spatial decision-making problems. Uncertain environments have been extensively studied in decision-making research, with various types of fuzzy sets employed to model such uncertainty (Demir, 2025a, b; Nwokoro et al., 2025; Wang & Zhao, Liu, et al., 2025). The REGIME method focuses on pairwise comparisons, which enhances its applicability to qualitative and uncertain contexts. For instance, integration with Pythagorean fuzzy sets (Oztaysi et al., 2021) and T-spherical fuzzy sets (Chen, 2021b). Chen (2021a) further enhanced the T-spherical fuzzy REGIME approach by incorporating the Minkowski-type distance measure and Gaussian preference function. Esangbedo et al. (2021) pioneered the integration of the REGIME method with gray system theory to solve human resource system selection problems. Oztaysi et al. (2022) applied the REGIME method within a T-spherical fuzzy set environment to address the waste disposal site selection problem. (Haktanır & Kahraman, 2022) extended the REGIME method to single-valued picture fuzzy sets. Fetanat et al. (2023) applied the REGIME model in a Fermatean fuzzy environment to support optimal technology selection. Integrating REGIME with different types of fuzzy sets

Encyclopedia of Multi-Attribute Decision-Making (MADM). DOI: https://doi.org/10.1016/B978-0-443-33275-3.00075-0

significantly improves its applicability to more complex and imprecise evaluation environments, thereby enhancing the reliability of decision outcomes (Dağıstanlı, 2025; Wang & Liu, 2025).

In addition, the reliability of REGIME-based decisions can be improved by assigning appropriate weights to criteria. A common approach involves integrating REGIME with the criteria importance through intercriteria correlation (CRITIC) method (CRITIC–REGIME), which provides an objective way to determine criterion weights based on contrast intensity and correlation (Haktanır & Kahraman, 2022). Camgoz Akdag and Menekse (2023) applied the CRITIC–REGIME method to the selection of medical treatment alternatives. Akram, Zahid, et al. (2024) used the same hybrid approach to investigate sustainable supply chain issues in public transportation. Moreover, entropy-based weighting has also been utilized to enhance the objectivity of the REGIME method. Akram, Ahmad, et al. (2024) combined entropy weights with the REGIME method to address complex site selection problems. Akram et al. (2025) extended the CRITIC–REGIME method into the T-spherical fuzzy environment and applied it to support optimal process selection.

7.3 Methodology

The REGIME method performs pairwise comparisons of alternatives based on their performance under each criterion and captures their relative superiority. These pairwise comparisons are combined with the weights of the criteria to rank the alternatives. The REGIME method involves the following steps:

Step 1. Construct the decision matrix.

For a MADM problem with m alternatives $A_i (i = 1, 2, \ldots, m)$ and n criteria $C_j (j = 1, 2, \ldots, n)$. Construct a decision matrix $D = (d_{ij})_{m \times n}$ as follows:

$$D = \begin{bmatrix} d_{11} & d_{12} & \cdots & d_{1n} \\ d_{21} & d_{22} & \cdots & d_{2n} \\ \vdots & \vdots & \ddots & \vdots \\ d_{m1} & d_{m2} & \cdots & d_{mn} \end{bmatrix} \tag{7.1}$$

where d_{ij} represents the evaluation score of alternative A_i under criterion C_j.

Step 2. Calculate the superiority index.

The superiority index S represents the degree to which one alternative A_i is superior to another alternative A_i' with respect to the evaluation criteria. The superiority index for each pair of alternatives under a given criterion is defined as follows:

$$S_{ii'} = \begin{Bmatrix} \textit{set of critria } C_i, \textit{ for which } A_i \textit{ is at least as good as } A_i', \ j \in B; \\ \textit{set of critria } C_i, \textit{ for which } A_i \textit{ is at most as good as } A_i', \ j \in C. \end{Bmatrix} \tag{7.2}$$

where B indicates the subset of criteria to be the benefit type, and C is the subset of criteria to be the cost type.

Step 3. Determine the superiority identifier.

Based on the weights, the superiority identifier is calculated by the following formula.

$$\tilde{S}_{ii'} = \sum_{j \in S_{ii'}} w_j \tag{7.3}$$

where $w_j (j = 1, 2, \ldots, n)$ represents the weight of criteria C_j.

Step 4: Construct the impacts matrix.

The impact matrix $R = (r_{ij})_{m \times n}$ is generated by ranking the values in the decision matrix $D = (d_{ij})_{m \times n}$.

$$R = \begin{bmatrix} r_{11} & r_{12} & \cdots & r_{1n} \\ r_{21} & r_{22} & \cdots & r_{2n} \\ \vdots & \vdots & \ddots & \vdots \\ r_{m1} & r_{m2} & \cdots & r_{mn} \end{bmatrix} \tag{7.4}$$

where $r_{ij} \in \{1, 2, \cdots, m\}$ indicates the rank of alternative $A_i (i = 1, 2, \ldots, m)$ with respect to criterion $C_j (j = 1, 2, \ldots, n)$. Higher values receive a rank of 1 for benefit-type criteria, while lower values receive a rank of 1 for cost-type criteria.

Step 5: Construct the REGIME matrix.

The REGIME matrix $\Im$ is constructed based on the impact matrix $R = (r_{ij})_{m \times n}$, and the REGIME vector $\Im_{ii'} = (\Im_{ii',1}, \Im_{ii',2}, \cdots, \Im_{ii',n})$ is defined as follows:

$$\Im_{ii',j} = \begin{cases} +1, & \text{if } r_{ij} > r_{ij}'; \\ 0, & \text{if } r_{ij} = r_{ij}', \\ -1, & \text{if } r_{ij} < r_{ij}'. \end{cases} \tag{7.5}$$

where $\mathfrak{I}_{ii'}$ refers to a comparison between any two alternatives A_i and A_i', conducted by evaluating their ranks r_{ij} under each criterion under each criterion $C_j (j = 1, 2, \ldots, n)$.

Step 6. Ranking of alternatives.

Two methods can be used to rank the alternatives:

Method 1: Calculate the guide index $\widetilde{\mathfrak{I}}_{ii'}$, which is defined as:

$$\widetilde{\mathfrak{I}}_{ii'} = \sum_{j=1}^{n} \mathfrak{I}_{ii',j} \times w_j \tag{7.6}$$

where greater the guide index $\widetilde{\mathfrak{I}}_{ii'}$, the better the alternative is ranked.

Method 2: The ranking is determined based on the differences in the superiority indicators. A positive value of $\widetilde{S}_{ii'} - \widetilde{S}_{i'i}$ indicates that alternative A_i is better than alternative A_i', while a negative value implies that A_i' is better than A_i.

7.4 Numerical example 1

This section presents a simple numerical example to illustrate the application of the REGIME method. In real-world store location decisions, companies are often confronted with multiple alternative sites, each with various advantages and drawbacks. As market dynamics and consumer preferences continue to evolve rapidly, selecting an optimal store location requires careful consideration of multiple factors, such as rent costs, customer foot traffic, and safety conditions. MADM methods provide a structured framework to evaluate alternative sites by weighing diverse attributes. This enables decision-makers to identify the most suitable location, improving operational effectiveness and competitive advantage.

In this example, a retail company is planning to open a new store and must choose among three potential locations: A_1, A_2, and A_3. The selection is based on five criteria: rent (C_1), foot traffic (C_2), transportation accessibility (C_3), spending power (C_4), and competitor Density (C_5), detailed definition is shown in Table 7.1. (C_1) and (C_5) are cost-type criteria, where lower values indicate more preferred alternatives. The remaining indicators are benefit-type criteria.

Step 1. Construct the decision matrix.

In this step, data on the alternatives for each criterion are collected. The detailed data is presented in Table 7.2.

Step 2. Calculate the superiority index.

As shown in Table 7.1, for each criterion, the superiority index between every pair of alternatives is calculated by Eq. (7.2). The superiority index is shown in Table 7.3.

Step 3. Determine the superiority identifier.

According to Eq. (7.3), the superiority identifier can be calculated, which is shown in Table 7.4.

Step 4: Construct the impacts matrix.

The evaluation values of each alternative are compared under the same criterion to obtain the impact matrix using Eq. (7.4). The result is shown in Table 7.5.

Step 5: Construct the REGIME matrix.

Construct the REGIME matrix based on the impact matrix by using Eq. (7.5), which is shown in Table 7.6.

TABLE 7.1 The evaluation criteria.

	Description	Type
C_1	Monthly rent	Cost
C_2	Traffic volume on a nonholiday day	Benefit
C_3	Number of public transportation stops	Benefit
C_4	Per capita income of the region	Benefit
C_5	Number of physical stores of similar competitors	Cost

TABLE 7.2 The decision matrix.

	C_1	C_2	C_3	C_4	C_5
A_1	1000	80	10	1200	20
A_2	650	120	5	800	10
A_3	800	200	2	500	2
Wight	0.105	0.175	0.250	0.350	0.120

TABLE 7.3 The superiority index.

S_{12}	S_{13}	S_{21}	S_{23}	S_{31}	S_{32}
C_3	C_3	C_1	C_1	C_1	C_2
		C_2	C_3	C_2	C_4
		C_4		C_4	C_5
		C_5		C_5	

TABLE 7.4 The superiority identifier.

$\tilde{S}_{12}$	$\tilde{S}_{13}$	$\tilde{S}_{21}$	$\tilde{S}_{23}$	$\tilde{S}_{31}$	$\tilde{S}_{32}$
0.250	0.250	0.75	0.355	0.75	0.645

TABLE 7.5 The impact matrix.

	C_1	C_2	C_3	C_4	C_5
A_1	3	3	1	3	3
A_2	1	2	2	2	2
A_3	2	1	3	1	1

Step 6. Ranking of alternatives.

Method 1: Calculate the guide index according to Eq. (7.6). According to the results presented in Table 7.7, the final ranking of the alternatives is as follows: $A_3 > A_2 > A_1$.

Method 2: Determine the ranking of alternatives based on the differences in their superiority indicators. The ranking of the alternatives is $A_3 > A_2 > A_1$, as shown in Table 7.8.

TABLE 7.6 The REGIME matrix.

	C_1	C_2	C_3	C_4	C_5
$\mathfrak{I}_{12}$	-1	-1	+1	-1	-1
$\mathfrak{I}_{13}$	-1	-1	+1	-1	-1
$\mathfrak{I}_{21}$	+1	+1	-1	+1	+1
$\mathfrak{I}_{23}$	+1	-1	+1	-1	-1
$\mathfrak{I}_{31}$	+1	+1	-1	+1	+1
$\mathfrak{I}_{32}$	-1	+1	-1	+1	+1

TABLE 7.7 The guide index.

	$\tilde{\mathfrak{I}}_{12}$	$\tilde{\mathfrak{I}}_{13}$	$\tilde{\mathfrak{I}}_{21}$	$\tilde{\mathfrak{I}}_{23}$	$\tilde{\mathfrak{I}}_{31}$	$\tilde{\mathfrak{I}}_{32}$
Guide index	-0.5	-0.5	0.5	-0.290	0.5	0.290
Ranking						$A_1 < A_2$
$A_1 < A_3$						$A_2 > A_1$
$A_2 < A_3$				$A_3 > A_1$		$A_3 > A_2$

TABLE 7.8 The subtraction of the superiority identifier.

	Subtraction of the superiority identifier	Ranking
$\tilde{S}_{12} - \tilde{S}_{21}$	$0.75–0.25 > 0$	$A_2 > A_1$
$\tilde{S}_{23} - \tilde{S}_{32}$	$0.355–0.645 < 0$	$A_3 > A_2$

7.5 Numerical example 2

To better demonstrate the practical applicability of the REGIME method in a real-world scenario, a comprehensive numerical example concerning supplier selection for industrial equipment is presented. In practice, supplier selection represents a complex and high-stakes decision-making problem, particularly in the context of globalized manufacturing and technological advancement.

In this case, a multinational industrial equipment manufacturer is preparing to expand its global production capacity. To support this strategic initiative, the company intends to procure a new batch of high-precision robotic arms for integration into its next-generation automated assembly lines. Therefore the company will identify the most suitable supplier from a list of eight prequalified suppliers. The selection process must consider a variety of conflicting criteria, encompassing both quantitative metrics (e.g., cost, lead time, financial stability) and qualitative judgments (e.g., service quality, integration compatibility, partnership potential).

As introduced above, the supplier selection problem can be modeled as a MADM framework. To illustrate the method's practical implementation, this study examines the selection of suppliers based on ten evaluation criteria and eight alternatives $A_1, A_2, A_3, A_4, A_5, A_6, A_7, A_8$, combining objective data with subjective expert assessments. The evaluation criteria are shown in Table 7.9. To ensure a comprehensive and professional evaluation, three experts with distinct

TABLE 7.9 The evaluation criteria.

Code	Criterion	Type	Description	Source	Weight
C_1	Total acquisition cost (USD)	Cost	Quoted price including delivery, installation, and taxes.	Objective	0.18
C_2	Delivery lead time (weeks)	Cost	Time from purchase order to final acceptance test.	Objective	0.12
C_3	Product quality	Benefit	Measures the overall reliability, precision, and defect rate of the product.	Expert	0.15
C_4	Technical compatibility	Benefit	Assesses the degree of integration with existing systems and production lines.	Expert	0.1
C_5	After-sales service	Benefit	Evaluates the responsiveness, coverage, and comprehensiveness of support services.	Expert	0.1
C_6	Delivery capability	Benefit	Reflects the supplier's ability to deliver products on time and in full.	Expert	0.08
C_7	Cooperation history	Benefit	Considers past collaboration effectiveness, trust, and conflict management.	Expert	0.07
C_8	Brand reputation	Benefit	Represents the supplier's market image, recognition, and industry credibility.	Expert	0.07
C_9	Product quality	Benefit	Measures the overall reliability, precision, and defect rate of the product.	Expert	0.07
C_{10}	Technical compatibility	Benefit	Assesses the degree of integration with existing systems and production lines.	Expert	0.06

backgrounds were engaged in the assessment process: a senior mechanical engineer (E_1), a procurement manager (E_2), and a senior financial analyst (E_3). The positive integers {1, 2, 3, 4, 5} are used to represent the evaluation information.

Step 1. Construct the decision matrix.

In this step, objective data for each alternative were collected and are presented in Table 7.10. The evaluation scores $Sc_j^{E_i}$ provided by the expert E_i are shown in Tables 7.11-7.13.

The decision matrix of subjective factors is obtained by taking a weighted average of the evaluation scores provided by the experts. Each expert has the same weight, and the final score is calculated according to $d_{ij} = \sum_{i=1}^{3} Sc_j^{Ei}/3$. The decision matrix summarizing objective and subjective indicators is presented in Table 7.14.

Step 2. Calculate the superiority index.

As shown in Table 7.14, for each criterion, the superiority index between every pair of alternatives is calculated using Eq. (7.2). The superiority indices are shown in Tables 7.15-7.16.

Step 3. Determine the superiority identifier.

According to Eq. (7.3), the superiority identifier can be calculated, which is shown in Table 7.17.

Step 4: Construct the impacts matrix.

The evaluation values of each alternative are compared under the same criterion to obtain the impact matrix using Eq. (7.4). The result is shown in Table 7.18.

TABLE 7.10 The objective index decision matrix.

	C_1	C_2
A_1	480,000	10
A_2	400,000	8
A_3	520,000	9
A_4	510,000	11
A_5	460,000	9
A_6	470,000	7
A_7	530,000	10
A_8	420,000	8

TABLE 7.11 The evaluation information of expert E_1.

	C_3	C_4	C_5	C_6	C_7	C_8	C_9	C_{10}
A_1	4	5	3	3	4	3	4	5
A_2	5	4	3	4	3	4	5	4
A_3	5	5	4	5	5	4	5	5
A_4	4	3	2	3	4	2	4	3
A_5	3	4	3	4	3	3	3	4
A_6	4	5	4	4	4	4	4	5
A_7	3	3	2	3	3	2	3	3
A_8	4	4	3	5	4	3	4	4

TABLE 7.12 The evaluation information of expert E_2.

	C_3	C_4	C_5	C_6	C_7	C_8	C_9	C_{10}
A_1	4	4	4	5	3	3	4	4
A_2	4	3	5	5	3	4	4	3
A_3	5	5	5	5	4	5	5	5
A_4	3	3	3	4	2	3	3	3
A_5	4	4	4	4	3	3	4	4
A_6	5	5	5	5	4	4	5	5
A_7	3	2	2	3	2	2	3	2
A_8	4	3	4	4	3	4	4	3

TABLE 7.13 The evaluation information of expert E_3.

	C_3	C_4	C_5	C_6	C_7	C_8	C_9	C_{10}
A_1	3	4	4	5	4	4	3	4
A_2	4	4	4	4	3	4	4	4
A_3	5	5	5	5	5	5	5	5
A_4	3	3	3	3	3	3	3	3
A_5	3	4	3	4	3	4	3	4
A_6	5	5	4	5	4	5	5	5
A_7	2	2	3	3	2	2	2	2
A_8	4	4	4	4	4	4	4	4

TABLE 7.14 The decision matrix.

	C_1	C_2	C_3	C_4	C_5	C_6	C_7	C_8	C_9	C_{10}
A_1	480,000	10	3.667	4.333	3.667	4.333	3.667	3.333	3.667	4.333
A_2	400,000	8	4.333	3.667	4.000	4.333	3.000	4.000	4.333	3.667
A_3	520,000	9	5.000	5.000	4.667	5.000	4.667	4.667	5.000	5.000
A_4	510,000	11	3.333	3.000	2.667	3.333	3.000	2.667	3.333	3.000
A_5	460,000	9	3.333	4.000	3.333	4.000	3.000	3.333	3.333	4.000
A_6	470,000	7	4.667	5.000	4.333	4.667	4.000	4.333	4.667	5.000
A_7	530,000	10	2.667	2.333	2.333	3.000	2.333	2.000	2.667	2.333
A_8	420,000	8	4.000	3.667	3.667	4.333	3.667	3.667	4.000	3.667

TABLE 7.15 The superiority index.

	$S_{i'1}$	$S_{i'2}$	$S_{i'3}$	$S_{i'4}$
$S_{1i'}$	-	$\{C_4, C_6, C_7, C_{10}\}$	$\{C_1\}$	$\{C_1, C_2, C_3, C_4, C_5, C_6, C_7, C_8, C_9, C_{10}\}$
$S_{2i'}$	$\{C_1, C_2, C_3, C_5, C_6, C_8, C_9\}$	-	$\{C_1, C_2\}$	$\{C_1, C_2, C_3, C_4, C_5, C_6, C_7, C_8, C_9, C_{10}\}$
$S_{3i'}$	$\{C_2, C_3, C_4, C_5, C_6, C_7, C_8, C_9, C_{10}\}$	$\{C_3, C_4, C_5, C_6, C_7, C_8, C_9, C_{10}\}$	-	$\{C_1, C_2, C_3, C_4, C_5, C_6, C_7, C_8, C_9, C_{10}\}$
$S_{4i'}$		$\{C_7\}$	$\{C_1\}$	-
$S_{5i'}$	$\{C_1, C_2, C_8\}$	$\{C_4, C_7, C_{10}\}$	$\{C_1, C_2\}$	$\{C_1, C_2, C_3, C_4, C_5, C_6, C_7, C_8, C_9, C_{10}\}$
$S_{6i'}$	$\{C_1, C_2, C_3, C_4, C_5, C_6, C_7, C_8, C_9, C_{10}\}$	$\{C_2, C_3, C_4, C_5, C_6, C_7, C_8, C_9, C_{10}\}$	$\{C_1, C_2, C_4, C_{10}\}$	$\{C_1, C_2, C_3, C_4, C_5, C_6, C_7, C_8, C_9, C_{10}\}$
$S_{7i'}$	$\{C_2\}$			$\{C_2\}$
$S_{8i'}$	$\{C_1, C_2, C_3, C_5, C_6, C_7, C_8, C_9\}$	$\{C_2, C_4, C_6, C_7, C_{10}\}$	$\{C_1, C_2\}$	$\{C_1, C_2, C_3, C_4, C_5, C_6, C_7, C_8, C_9, C_{10}\}$

TABLE 7.16 The superiority index.

	$S_{i'5}$	$S_{i'6}$	$S_{i'7}$	$S_{i'8}$
$S_{1i'}$	$\{C_3, C_4, C_5, C_6, C_7, C_8, C_9, C_{10}\}$		$\{C_1, C_2, C_3, C_4, C_5, C_6, C_7, C_8, C_9, C_{10}\}$	$\{C_4, C_5, C_6, C_7, C_{10}\}$
$S_{2i'}$	$\{C_1, C_2, C_3, C_5, C_6, C_7, C_8, C_9\}$	$\{C_1\}$	$\{C_1, C_2, C_3, C_4, C_5, C_6, C_7, C_8, C_9, C_{10}\}$	$\{C_1, C_2, C_3, C_4, C_5, C_6, C_8, C_9, C_{10}\}$
$S_{3i'}$	$\{C_2, C_3, C_4, C_5, C_6, C_7, C_8, C_9, C_{10}\}$	$\{C_3, C_4, C_5, C_6, C_7, C_8, C_9, C_{10}\}$	$\{C_1, C_2, C_3, C_4, C_5, C_6, C_7, C_8, C_9, C_{10}\}$	$\{C_3, C_4, C_5, C_6, C_7, C_8, C_9, C_{10}\}$
$S_{4i'}$	$\{C_3, C_7, C_9\}$		$\{C_1, C_3, C_4, C_5, C_6, C_7, C_8, C_9, C_{10}\}$	
$S_{5i'}$	-	$\{C_1\}$	$\{C_1, C_2, C_3, C_4, C_5, C_6, C_7, C_8, C_9, C_{10}\}$	$\{C_4, C_{10}\}$
$S_{6i'}$	$\{C_2, C_3, C_4, C_5, C_6, C_7, C_8, C_9, C_{10}\}$	-	$\{C_1, C_2, C_3, C_4, C_5, C_6, C_7, C_8, C_9, C_{10}\}$	$\{C_2, C_3, C_4, C_5, C_6, C_7, C_8, C_9, C_{10}\}$
$S_{7i'}$			-	
$S_{8i'}$	{12356789}	$\{C_1\}$	$\{C_1, C_2, C_3, C_4, C_5, C_6, C_7, C_8, C_9, C_{10}\}$	-

TABLE 7.17 The superiority identifier.

	$\tilde{S}_{i'1}$	$\tilde{S}_{i'2}$	$\tilde{S}_{i'3}$	$\tilde{S}_{i'4}$	$\tilde{S}_{i'5}$	$\tilde{S}_{i'6}$	$\tilde{S}_{i'7}$	$\tilde{S}_{i'8}$
$\tilde{S}_{1i'}$	-	0.310	0.180	1.000	0.700	0.000	1.000	0.410
$\tilde{S}_{2i'}$	0.770	-	0.300	1.000	0.840	0.180	1.000	0.930
$\tilde{S}_{3i'}$	0.820	0.700	-	0.820	0.820	0.700	1.000	0.700
$\tilde{S}_{4i'}$	0.000	0.070	0.180	-	0.290	0.000	0.880	0.000
$\tilde{S}_{5i'}$	0.370	0.230	0.300	1.000	-	0.180	1.000	0.160
$\tilde{S}_{6i'}$	1.000	0.820	0.460	1.000	0.820	-	1.000	0.820
$\tilde{S}_{7i'}$	0.120	0.000	0.000	0.120	0.000	0.000	-	0.000
$\tilde{S}_{8i'}$	0.840	0.430	0.300	1.000	0.840	0.180	1.000	-

TABLE 7.18 The impact matrix.

	C_1	C_2	C_3	C_4	C_5	C_6	C_7	C_8	C_9	C_{10}
A_1	5	6	5	3	4	3	3	5	5	3
A_2	1	2	3	5	3	3	5	3	3	5
A_3	7	4	1	1	1	1	1	1	1	1
A_4	6	8	6	7	7	7	5	7	6	7
A_5	3	4	6	4	6	6	5	5	6	4
A_6	4	1	2	1	2	2	2	2	2	1
A_7	8	6	8	8	8	8	8	8	8	8
A_8	2	2	4	5	4	3	3	4	4	5

Step 5: Construct the REGIME matrix.

Construct the REGIME matrix based on the impact matrix by using Eq. (7.5), which is shown in Table 7.19.

Step 6. Ranking of alternatives.

Method 1: Calculate the guide index according to Eq. (7.6). According to the results presented in Table 7.19, the final ranking of the alternatives is as follows: $A_3 > A_6 > A_2 > A_8 > A_1 > A_5 > A_4 > A_7$.

Method 2: Determine the ranking of alternatives based on the differences in their superiority indicators. The results are presented in Table 7.20.

7.6 Comparative analysis

This section presents a comparative analysis between the REGIME method and two classical MADM approaches, technique for order preference by similarity to ideal solution (TOPSIS) and VlseKriterijumska Optimizacija I Kompromisno Resenje (VIKOR), in order to verify the effectiveness and rationality of the REGIME method. These methods are applied to numerical example 2 in Section 5 for comparative analysis. The ranking results of the alternatives derived from the three methods are illustrated in Fig. 7.1.

TABLE 7.19 The REGIME matrix and guide index.

	C_1	C_2	C_3	C_4	C_5	C_6	C_7	C_8	C_9	C_{10}	$\tilde{\Im}_{ii'}$
$\Im_{12}$	-1	-1	-1	1	-1	0	1	-1	-1	1	-0.46
$\Im_{13}$	1	-1	-1	-1	-1	-1	-1	-1	-1	-1	-0.64
$\Im_{14}$	1	1	1	1	1	1	1	1	1	1	1.00
$\Im_{15}$	-1	-1	1	1	1	1	1	0	1	1	0.33
$\Im_{16}$	-1	-1	-1	-1	-1	-1	-1	-1	-1	-1	-1.00
$\Im_{17}$	1	0	1	1	1	1	1	1	1	1	0.88
$\Im_{18}$	-1	-1	-1	1	0	0	0	-1	-1	1	-0.43
$\Im_{21}$	1	1	1	-1	1	0	-1	1	1	-1	0.46
$\Im_{23}$	1	1	-1	-1	-1	-1	-1	-1	-1	-1	-0.40
$\Im_{24}$	1	1	1	1	1	1	0	1	1	1	0.93
$\Im_{25}$	1	1	1	-1	1	1	0	1	1	-1	0.61
$\Im_{26}$	1	-1	-1	-1	-1	-1	-1	-1	-1	-1	-0.64
$\Im_{27}$	1	1	1	1	1	1	1	1	1	1	1.00
$\Im_{28}$	1	0	1	0	1	0	-1	1	1	0	0.50
$\Im_{31}$	-1	1	1	1	1	1	1	1	1	1	0.64
$\Im_{32}$	-1	-1	1	1	1	1	1	1	1	1	0.40
$\Im_{34}$	-1	1	1	1	1	1	1	1	1	1	0.64
$\Im_{35}$	-1	0	1	1	1	1	1	1	1	1	0.52
$\Im_{36}$	-1	-1	1	0	1	1	1	1	1	0	0.24
$\Im_{37}$	1	1	1	1	1	1	1	1	1	1	1.00
$\Im_{38}$	-1	-1	1	1	1	1	1	1	1	1	0.40
$\Im_{41}$	-1	-1	-1	-1	-1	-1	-1	-1	-1	-1	-1.00
$\Im_{42}$	-1	-1	-1	-1	-1	-1	0	-1	-1	-1	-0.93
$\Im_{43}$	1	-1	-1	-1	-1	-1	-1	-1	-1	-1	-0.64
$\Im_{45}$	-1	-1	0	-1	-1	-1	0	-1	0	-1	-0.71
$\Im_{46}$	-1	-1	-1	-1	-1	-1	-1	-1	-1	-1	-1.00
$\Im_{47}$	1	-1	1	1	1	1	1	1	1	1	0.76
$\Im_{48}$	-1	-1	-1	-1	-1	-1	-1	-1	-1	-1	-1.00
$\Im_{51}$	1	1	-1	-1	-1	-1	-1	0	-1	-1	-0.33
$\Im_{52}$	-1	-1	-1	1	-1	-1	0	-1	-1	1	-0.61
$\Im_{53}$	1	0	-1	-1	-1	-1	-1	-1	-1	-1	-0.52
$\Im_{54}$	1	1	0	1	1	1	0	1	0	1	0.71
$\Im_{56}$	1	-1	-1	-1	-1	-1	-1	-1	-1	-1	-0.64
$\Im_{57}$	1	1	1	1	1	1	1	1	1	1	1.00
$\Im_{58}$	-1	-1	-1	1	-1	-1	-1	-1	-1	1	-0.68

(*Continued*)

TABLE 7.19 (Continued)

	C_1	C_2	C_3	C_4	C_5	C_6	C_7	C_8	C_9	C_{10}	$\tilde{\mathfrak{I}}_{ii'}$
$\mathfrak{I}_{61}$	1	1	1	1	1	1	1	1	1	1	1.00
$\mathfrak{I}_{62}$	-1	1	1	1	1	1	1	1	1	1	0.64
$\mathfrak{I}_{63}$	1	1	-1	0	-1	-1	-1	-1	-1	0	-0.24
$\mathfrak{I}_{64}$	1	1	1	1	1	1	1	1	1	1	1.00
$\mathfrak{I}_{65}$	-1	1	1	1	1	1	1	1	1	1	0.64
$\mathfrak{I}_{67}$	1	1	1	1	1	1	1	1	1	1	1.00
$\mathfrak{I}_{68}$	-1	1	1	1	1	1	1	1	1	1	0.64
$\mathfrak{I}_{71}$	-1	0	-1	-1	-1	-1	-1	-1	-1	-1	-0.88
$\mathfrak{I}_{72}$	-1	-1	-1	-1	-1	-1	-1	-1	-1	-1	-1.00
$\mathfrak{I}_{73}$	-1	-1	-1	-1	-1	-1	-1	-1	-1	-1	-1.00
$\mathfrak{I}_{74}$	-1	1	-1	-1	-1	-1	-1	-1	-1	-1	-0.76
$\mathfrak{I}_{75}$	-1	-1	-1	-1	-1	-1	-1	-1	-1	-1	-1.00
$\mathfrak{I}_{76}$	-1	-1	-1	-1	-1	-1	-1	-1	-1	-1	-1.00
$\mathfrak{I}_{78}$	-1	-1	-1	-1	-1	-1	-1	-1	-1	-1	-1.00
$\mathfrak{I}_{81}$	1	1	1	-1	0	0	0	1	1	-1	0.43
$\mathfrak{I}_{82}$	-1	0	-1	0	-1	0	1	-1	-1	0	-0.50
$\mathfrak{I}_{83}$	1	1	-1	-1	-1	-1	-1	-1	-1	-1	-0.40
$\mathfrak{I}_{84}$	1	1	1	1	1	1	1	1	1	1	1.00
$\mathfrak{I}_{85}$	1	1	1	-1	1	1	1	1	1	-1	0.68
$\mathfrak{I}_{86}$	1	-1	-1	-1	-1	-1	-1	-1	-1	-1	-0.64
$\mathfrak{I}_{87}$	1	1	1	1	1	1	1	1	1	1	1.00

TABLE 7.20 The subtraction of the superiority identifier.

	Subtraction of the superiority identifier	Ranking
$\tilde{S}_{74} - \tilde{S}_{47}$	0.12–0.88 < 0	$A_7 < A_4$
$\tilde{S}_{45} - \tilde{S}_{54}$	0.29–1 < 0	$A_4 < A_5$
$\tilde{S}_{51} - \tilde{S}_{15}$	0.37–0.7 < 0	$A_5 < A_1$
$\tilde{S}_{18} - \tilde{S}_{81}$	0.41–0.84 < 0	$A_1 < A_8$
$\tilde{S}_{82} - \tilde{S}_{28}$	0.43–0.93 < 0	$A_8 < A_2$
$\tilde{S}_{26} - \tilde{S}_{62}$	0.18–0.82 < 0	$A_2 < A_6$
$\tilde{S}_{63} - \tilde{S}_{36}$	0.46–0.7 < 0	$A_6 < A_3$

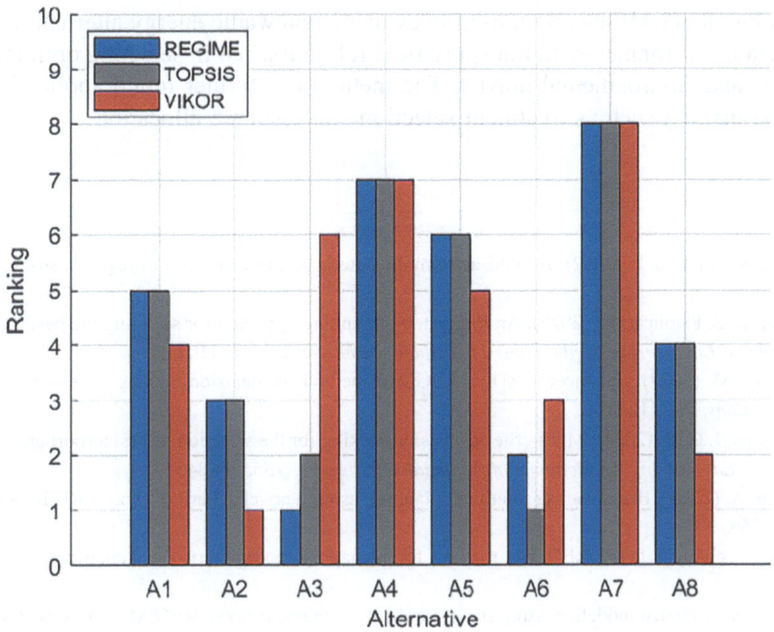

FIGURE 7.1 The ranking results obtained by different methods.

As shown in the figure, the rankings of most alternatives are consistent across all three methods, indicating a high degree of correlation and coherence between REGIME, TOPSIS, and VIKOR. For example, alternatives A_4 and A_7 receive the same rankings from all three methods, suggesting that REGIME produces results similar to well-established methods and therefore demonstrates strong reliability.

However, differences in the rankings of certain alternatives, such as A_3 and A_6. These differences arise from the distinct theoretical foundations and ranking mechanisms employed by each method. The REGIME method models the relative relationships among multiple attributes, emphasizing consistency and global ranking stability. This approach improves robustness in scenarios involving high variability in attribute values and reduces the influence of extreme values on the final decision.

By contrast, the TOPSIS method evaluates alternatives based on their Euclidean distance from an ideal solution and an antiideal solution. It tends to favor alternatives that are relatively balanced and closer to the ideal point. VIKOR places emphasis on achieving a compromise solution by maximizing group utility and minimizing individual regret, and is therefore more sensitive to conflicts among attributes. Moreover, the REGIME method does not rely on a fixed normalization procedure, which enhances its flexibility when dealing with diverse data types. Compared with VIKOR, REGIME shows greater stability in rankings and is less affected by local inconsistencies, thereby avoiding abrupt ranking changes when individual attribute values vary slightly.

In conclusion, the REGIME method demonstrates both consistency with traditional MADM approaches and distinct advantages in terms of ranking stability and adaptability to heterogeneous data. The observed differences in some cases also suggest that method selection or integration should be context-specific, with careful consideration of the decision environment and evaluation priorities to support decision-making.

7.7 Conclusions

This chapter introduced the REGIME method as an effective approach in MADM. Its theoretical foundations and implementation steps were clearly explained, followed by two case studies that demonstrated its practical application, including both a basic example and a complex supplier evaluation scenario. A comparative analysis with classical methods such as TOPSIS and VIKOR revealed that REGIME provides stronger ranking stability, better adaptability to diverse data, and greater robustness against extreme values. These findings indicate that REGIME is a reliable and flexible tool for addressing complex decision-making problems. The method has also been widely applied in real-world contexts. For example, in energy planning, REGIME has been used to evaluate renewable energy alternatives and prioritize sustainable technologies under uncertain environments. In transportation, it has assisted in selecting optimal infrastructure projects by balancing cost, efficiency, and environmental impact. The method has further found applications in healthcare, where it supports medical decision-making such as treatment selection and resource allocation.

References

Akgün, A. A., van Leeuwen, E., & Nijkamp, P. (2012). A multi-actor multi-criteria scenario analysis of regional sustainable resource policy. *Ecological Economics, 78*, 19–28.

Akram, M., Azam, S., Mustafa, G., & Pamucar, D. (2025). An integrated outranking approach for selecting the best waste water treatment process with spherical fuzzy rough numbers. *Engineering Applications of Artificial Intelligence, 144*, 110115.

Akram, M., Zahid, S., & Deveci, M. (2024). Enhanced CRITIC-REGIME method for decision making based on Pythagorean fuzzy rough number. *Expert Systems with Applications, 238*, 122014.

Akram, Z., Ahmad, U., & Alcantud, J. C. R. (2024). Multi-criteria decision-making for the selection of best airport ground access mode with a new fuzzy rough-entropy based method. *Engineering Applications of Artificial Intelligence, 135*, 108843.

Camgoz Akdag, H., & Menekse, A. (2023). Breast cancer treatment planning using a novel spherical fuzzy CRITIC-REGIME. *Journal of Intelligent & Fuzzy Systems, 44*, 8343–8356.

Chen, T.-Y. (2021a). A novel T-spherical fuzzy REGIME method for managing multiple-criteria choice analysis under uncertain circumstances. *Informatica, 33*, 437–476.

Chen, T. Y. (2021b). Multiple criteria choice modeling using the grounds of T-spherical fuzzy REGIME analysis. *International Journal of Intelligent Systems, 37*, 1972–2011.

Dağıstanlı, H. A. (2025). Prioritizing design criteria for unmanned helicopter systems under uncertainty using fuzzy best worst method approach. *Journal of Intelligent Decision Making and Granular Computing, 1*, 1–12.

Demir, G. (2025a). Fuzzy multi-criteria decision-making based security management: Risk assessment and countermeasure selection in smart cities. *Knowledge Decision Systems with Applications, 1*, 70–91.

Demir, G. (2025b). The synergy of fuzzy logic and multi-criteria decision-making: Application areas and global trends. *Journal of Intelligent Decision Making Information Science, 2*, 429–455.

Esangbedo, M. O., Bai, S., Mirjalili, S., & Wang, Z. (2021). Evaluation of human resource information systems using grey ordinal pairwise comparison MCDM methods. *Expert Systems with Applications, 182*, 115151.

Fetanat, A., Tayebi, M., & Mofid, H. (2023). Water-energy-carbon nexus and sustainability-oriented prioritization of negative emissions technologies for the oil & gas industry: A decision support system under Fermatean fuzzy environment. *Process Safety and Environmental Protection, 179*, 462–483.

Haktanır, E., & Kahraman, C. (2022). A novel picture fuzzy CRITIC & REGIME methodology: Wearable health technology application. *Engineering Applications of Artificial Intelligence, 113*, 104942.

Hinloopen, E., & Nijkamp, P. (1990). Qualitative multiple criteria choice analysis. *Quality and Quantity, 24*, 37–56.

Hinloopen, E., Nijkamp, P., & Rietveld, P. (1983). The regime method: A new multicriteria technique. In P. Hansen (Ed.). *Essays and surveys on multiple criteria decision making* (pp. 146–155). Berlin, Heidelberg: Springer Berlin Heidelberg.

Massei, G., Rocchi, L., Paolotti, L., Greco, S., & Boggia, A. (2014). Decision support systems for environmental management: A case study on wastewater from agriculture. *Journal of Environmental Management, 146*, 491–504.

Nwokoro, C. O., & Ejegwa, P. A. (2025). A decade of picture fuzzy sets in multi-criteria decision-making: A comprehensive review of trends, gaps, and future directions. *Decision Science and Web Applications*, 1, 145–164.

Oztaysi, B., Kahraman, C., & Onar, S. C. (2022). Spherical fuzzy REGIME method waste disposal location selection. In C. Kahraman, S. Cebi, S. Cevik Onar, B. Oztaysi, A. C. Tolga, & I. U. Sari (Eds.). *Intelligent and fuzzy techniques for emerging conditions and digital transformation* (pp. 715–723). Cham: Springer International Publishing.

Oztaysi, B., Onar, S. C., & Kahraman, C. (2021). Waste disposal location selection by using pythagorean fuzzy REGIME method. *Journal of Intelligent & Fuzzy Systems, 42*, 401–410.

Wang, H., & Liu, J. (2025). Some spherical uncertain linguistic aggregation operators and their application in multi-attribute decision-making. *Journal of Intelligent Decision Making and Granular Computing, 1*, 106–126.

Wang, H., Zhao, W., Liu, J., Feng, L., Mahmood, T., & Kumar, K. (2025). Novel hamy mean aggregation operators based on advanced operations for T-spherical fuzzy group decision-making. *Journal of Intelligent Decision Making and Information Science, 2*, 332–365.

Chapter 8

PAPRIKA: Potentially all pairwise rankings of all possible alternatives for multi-attribute decision-making

Adis Puška[1], Miroslav Nedeljković[2], and Jurica Bosna[3]

[1]*Department of Public Safety, Government of the Brcko District of BiH, Brčko, Bosnia and Herzegovina,* [2]*Institute of Agricultural Economics, Belgrade, Serbia,* [3]*Department of Economics, University of Zadar, Zadar, Croatia*

8.1 Introduction

Decisions are continuously made in daily life (Akbulut, 2024), encompassing both routine choices and intricate decisions that are infrequently encountered. The significance of decision-making within corporate environments is particularly pronounced (Ullah and Yow, 2025). A single decision can profoundly influence the trajectory of a company (Tomić, 2025). Consequently, the choices made during the decision-making process affect the operations of the company (Hoque et al., 2024). It is crucial to make decisions that will enhance competitiveness and support the company's long-term viability. The significance of decision-making has increased due to the limited resources available to companies (Sarfraz & Božanić, 2024), necessitating their rational utilization (Lukić, 2024). Furthermore, it is essential to respond appropriately and promptly to the changes that arise in the market (Ofori et al., 2025). To arrive at a decision, one must find a balance between often conflicting objectives (Topal & Ulutaş, 2024). It is not always possible to produce a high-quality product while keeping resource consumption to a minimum. Therefore, a balance is struck between the set decision criteria (Mohammed et al., 2024) in order to make a decision on the choice of the alternative that best meets the set criteria.

The evolution of the decision-making process in practice has led to the development of various techniques for addressing multicriteria decision-making challenges. These techniques are designed to assist the decision maker (DM) in assessing criteria and alternatives to arrive at a decision that aids in achieving the established objectives. One such technique is potentially all pairwise ranKings of all possible alternatives (PAPRIKA). This technique serves as an effective decision-making tool where the decision-making occurs through a sequence of pairwise comparisons. This approach was initially implemented in practice by Hansen & Ombler (2008) in the context of prioritizing patients for heart surgery in New Zealand.

The significance of employing the PAPRIKA method lies in its flexibility and its capacity to identify the optimal alternative through DM assessment. The PAPRIKA method enables the assessment of the significance of the criteria weights. To elucidate this method and demonstrate its practical application, examples pertaining to agribusiness will be utilized. Decision-making within agribusiness is marked by the presence of incomplete information and uncertainty. Consequently, the objective of this chapter is to showcase the application of the PAPRIKA method through agribusiness examples. This will advocate for the method as a valuable decision-making tool.

8.2 Literature review

The utilization of the PAPRIKA method has proven to be highly impactful in practice thus far, as it was first implemented in 2009. Consequently, this section of the paper will present several studies in which this method has been applied. Hansen & Ombler (2008) were the pioneers in employing this method to assess the significance of criteria through pairwise comparisons in a novel manner. Brock et al. (2023) explored public sentiment regarding the implementation of measures

Encyclopedia of Multi-Attribute Decision-Making (MADM). DOI: https://doi.org/10.1016/B978-0-443-33275-3.00035-X

aimed at reducing CO_2 emissions, utilizing the PAPRIKA method as part of a conjunctive analysis to accurately rank alternatives, thereby gaining insight into the compromises that citizens are willing to make when adopting these measures. Isihara et al. (2020) applied the PAPRIKA method to validate criteria pertinent to decision-making in the context of humanitarian assistance.

Molnar et al. (2017) conducted a comparison of various methods for assessing the weight of criteria, revealing that the PAPRIKA method provides a comprehensive analysis; however, it necessitates a larger sample size to ascertain the significance of the criteria, which poses a limitation to this approach. Liberman et al. (2019) utilized the PAPRIKA method through the 1000minds platform to evaluate clinical decisions regarding thrombolysis in patients who have experienced minor strokes. Baggott et al. (2020) employed the PAPRIKA method to investigate patients suffering from mild asthma, concluding that the criteria most valued by these patients were the absence of shortness of breath and a minimal risk of disease exacerbation. Balogun et al. (2022) applied the PAPRIKA method in the context of cassava breeding, where distinct preference typologies among respondents were identified, thereby enhancing the alignment of priorities in the breeding process.

Chan et al. (2024) examined citizens' perceptions of vaccines utilizing the PAPRIKA method. Their study revealed that the primary criteria include the risk of side effects, vaccine effectiveness, and the duration of protection. Mirzaee et al. (2019) conducted a comparison between the PAPRIKA and simple multiattribute rating technique methods in the realm of designing resilient and sustainable buildings. During this analysis, the PAPRIKA method facilitated a comprehensive mapping of the relative significance of the criteria. Carnero (2020) implemented the PAPRIKA method within a risk evaluation model for the segregation of medical waste. The PAPRIKA method was utilized alongside fuzzy logic, enabling the identification of the weights of the criteria for accurately ranking the most significant errors. Liberman et al. (2019) employed the PAPRIKA method to explore the criteria for thrombolysis in mild stroke cases. The objective of their chapters was to ascertain which clinical criteria hold the greatest weight.

Sullivan et al. (2025) demonstrated through the PAPRIKA method that it is both acceptable and feasible for adolescents to assess conditions, including those deemed "worse than death". Ismail et al. (2023) employed the PAPRIKA method as a component of the MCDA (Multi-Criteria Decision Analysis) approach to determine the optimal hybrid energy configuration aimed at reducing CO_2 emissions. Patel et al. (2023) explored the acceptance of commercialization for 3D surgical video technology. Payini et al. (2020) examined the wine preferences among Indian women. The PAPRIKA method pinpointed essential criteria: type, taste, price, brand, and origin. Roy et al. (2021) created a tool for the prioritized referral of patients infected with the COVID-19 virus to intensive care, utilizing the PAPRIKA method.

The PAPRIKA method has proven to be flexible and applicable across various fields, ranging from healthcare and energy to public opinion and product design. The capability of the PAPRIKA method lies in its ability to determine precise weights for criteria based on pairwise comparisons. This approach facilitates a deeper understanding of expert reasoning. Although this method may require more time and resources due to the increased number of comparisons, its methodological approach renders it a reliable tool for decision support in complex contexts.

8.3 Methodology

The PAPRIKA method assesses the alternatives by assigning scores through the additive multiattribute model, which evaluates the criteria values via pairwise comparisons of the alternatives. This approach identifies all potential solutions for the alternatives, and the corresponding values for these solutions are derived from pairwise comparisons of the possible outcomes. For a comprehensive explanation of this method, reference will be made to the paper by Hansen & Ombler (2008), in which this method was initially applied in practice.

Step 1. Formulation of the value-added model: In the process of developing this decision-making model, the potential outcomes of the alternatives are initially identified, which are characterized by several criteria, and the values are assigned for each criterion. If we consider three criteria labeled A, B, and C, which are assessed using two categories, for instance, the values of small denoted by 1 and large denoted by 2, it becomes feasible to derive eight outcomes for the examined alternatives (23). Concurrently, the alternatives can assume one of the following value combinations: (1,1,1), (1,1,2), (1,2,1), (1,2,2), (2,1,1), (2,1,2), (2,2,1), (2,2,2). Following the assessment of these alternatives, a scoring process is conducted, leading to the establishment of a ranking for the alternatives. The best value for a particular alternative would be (2,2,2), while the worst value would be (1,1,1). Depending on the evaluation of the DM alternative, it can take on any of the listed values.

Step 2. Identification of nondominated pairs of alternatives: This is the most important step in the PAPRIKA method. In this step, it is determined which criterion or alternative is given priority if the values are quite the same, so that there is no dominance. An alternative is considered nondominant if it possesses at least one superior criterion and at least one inferior criterion in comparison to another alternative, while the remaining criteria are identical to those of the other alternative. Conversely, an alternative is deemed dominant if it has at least one criterion value that is higher than that of another alternative, while the other criterion values are either higher or equal to those of the other alternative. For instance, if one alternative has the values 1, 1, 2, and the other alternative has the values 1, 2, 1, this represents a nondominant pair of alternatives. In this case, the value of the first criterion remains the same, while the values of the second and third criteria differ. Consequently, the DM must ascertain which is preferable, whether the value of the second criterion or the value of the third criterion is greater. Based on this assessment, the DM can conclude whether B > C, B < C, or B = C. If one alternative has the values 1, 1, 2, and the other alternative has the values 2, 1, 2, we assert that the second alternative dominates the first. In this step, the main task of the DM is the decision-making process. He decides which criteria or alternatives he will prioritize and influences the final selection. When it is the dominant solution, it has no influence, because priority is automatically given to one criterion or alternative.

The process of decision-making utilizing the PAPRIKA method is conducted as follows:

- Identification of nondominated pairs of alternatives occurs.
- Exclusion of dominant pairs of alternatives takes place.
- Uniquely nondominant pairs are recognized by eliminating duplicate comparisons and discarding identical pairs. The exclusion of pairs is based on initial comparisons. For instance, if 2, 2, 1 > 1, 2, 1, and 1, 2, 1 > 1, 1, 2, then it follows that 2, 2, 1 > 1, 1, 2. This approach effectively reduces the number of comparisons.

This procedure is based on the application of the 1000minds program, which was created by the authors of this method, Hansen & Ombler (2008). All authors later used this program because it automatically excludes pairs and gives an indication of how consistent the decision is. If this procedure were to be done mechanically, it would be very complicated for the DM, especially when the number of criteria or alternatives increases. This is due to the fact that with this method, all pairs should be compared, and then determine which are the dominant pairs and which are not. Therefore, in this chapter, the explanation of this method is based on this program.

Step 3. Establishing a system of inequations: In this phase, nondominated pairs of alternatives are transformed into inequations. Therefore, in the earlier example, the inequations A2 + B2 + C1 > A1 + B2 + C1 are generated.

Step 4. Solving a system of inequations: The solving of these systems of inequations is achieved through linear programming to identify alternative points.

Step 5. Consistency verification: This step is conducted to assess whether the decision-making regarding the selection of nondominant pairs was consistent or inconsistent.

To elucidate the application of this method in greater detail, a table will be constructed to illustrate how to identify which solutions are dominant and which are nondominant, as well as how a system of inequations is established (see Table 8.1).

TABLE 8.1 Dominant and nondominant pairs of alternatives.

Alternatives	222	221	212	122	112	121	211	111
222		X	X	X	X	X	X	X
221			1) B2+C1 vs B1+C2	2) A2+C1 vs A1+C2	4) A2+B2+C1 vs A1+B1+C2	X	X	X
212				3) A2+B1 vs A1+B2	X	5) A2+B1+C2 vs A1+B2+C1	X	X
122					X	X	6) A2+B1+C1 vs A1+B2+C2	X
112						B1+C2 vs B2+C1	A1+C2 vs A2+C1	X
121							A1+B2 vs A2+B1	X
211								X
111								

If the value of alternative 221 is analyzed in relation to the other alternative values, it can be concluded that the alternative with the value 222 dominates this particular alternative. The value of the second alternative, 221 is identical to that of the first, indicating that this pair is equivalent. In conjunction with three additional values, a nondominant solution arises, specifically with the values of the second alternative 212, 122, and 112, leading to the formation of inequations where the DM must evaluate which is more significant: (1) B2+C1 versus B1+C2, (2) A2+C1 versus A1+C2, and (3) A2+B2+C1 versus A1+B1+C2. Through these inequations, the DM is tasked with determining whether an alternative dominates, does not dominate, or is equivalent to another alternative. Regarding the values of the other alternatives 121, 211, and 111, it can be asserted that the value of alternative 221 dominates these values. The remaining set of comparisons is elucidated in the same manner.

If additional criteria can be assessed with a greater number of options, the quantity of dominant and nondominant pairs of alternatives increases, thereby complicating the decision-making process. Consequently, when three criteria are evaluated with three options each, there are 27 potential evaluations of alternatives (3^3). Nevertheless, the required comparisons of alternatives are diminished, as they are conducted by identifying the dominant alternatives and the same comparisons, thus simplifying the decision-making task. For instance, if there are eight criteria, each with four options, the total number of evaluations for alternatives reaches 65,536 (4^8), but this figure is reduced to approximately 95 evaluations of pairs. In this manner, the decision-making process is streamlined. If it were to be done manually, DMs would first have to identify dominant and nondominant pairs out of 65,536 pairs, then exclude the same and similar pairs, and finally make a choice among these pairs. However, the decision-making process becomes increasingly intricate with the introduction of additional criteria and options for those criteria. This complexity poses challenges for the DM and hinders the ability to be succinct in decision-making.

In the subsequent sections, the utilization of this method with the 1000minds application will be detailed, as this application has been employed in all prior studies. This is because the complexity of decision-making increases with the increase in the number of criteria and alternatives. In addition, it is possible that the valuation values have several levels, which would further complicate this decision-making process. This is why this program is used in practice.

8.4 Numerical example 1

When executing their responsibilities, agribusiness firms encounter a multitude of decisions that require their attention. A pivotal decision for every firm is the selection of a supplier. Suppliers play a crucial role in the operations of any business. They ought to act as partners to the company (Waghmare et al., 2025) and provide assistance, particularly when they deliver punctually and in the necessary quantities. The selection of a supplier represents the initial step in the entire supply chain of any organization, including agribusiness firms. To illustrate the supplier selection process, four criteria will be applied, and four suppliers will be evaluated. The objective of this decision-making process is to identify the supplier with whom the company will forge a partnership and who will contribute to enhancing the company's operations. The following criteria will be utilized in the supplier selection process:

- The price denotes the financial value associated with the cost of the products acquired from the supplier.
- The delivery time indicates the duration necessary for the supplier to transport the goods from the date the order is placed.
- Product quality signifies the capacity of the goods to meet customer requirements.
- The payment time refers to the timeframe within which the customer is obligated to settle the payment for the received goods.

The evaluation of these criteria will involve three options: low, medium, and high. For the criteria concerning price and delivery time, a low grade is preferred, whereas for quality and payment time, a high grade for the supplier is desirable. Four suppliers will be assessed based on these grades. The selection of suppliers will be conducted using the 1000minds program.

The first step in implementing this program involves creating a decision-making model. This model is structured in such a manner that both the criteria and alternatives are established. When specifying options for the criteria, it is essential that the options for the first two criteria are inverted; specifically, the lowest value is considered high, while the highest value is regarded as low. This inversion is necessitated by the unique nature of these criteria. Once the decision-making model is established, the subsequent phase is Trade-offs, where it is assessed which option is preferable for the DM among nondominant pairs of alternatives. The first question is which is preferable: a medium delivery time with a certain product quality, or a low delivery time with low product quality, which may yield equivalent outcomes. In this scenario, preference will be given to medium delivery time and product quality (refer to Fig. 8.1). The second question posed by the DM is

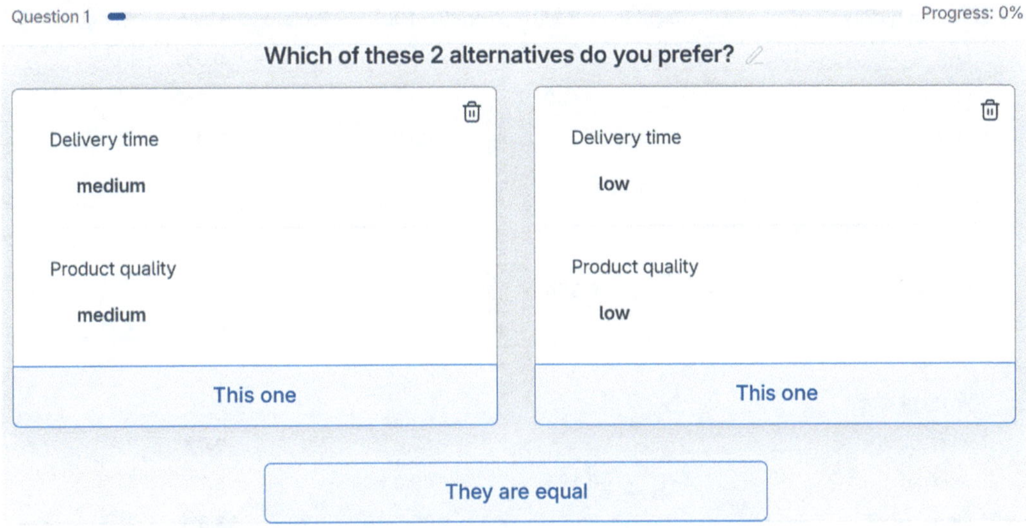

FIGURE 8.1 First question to the decision maker.

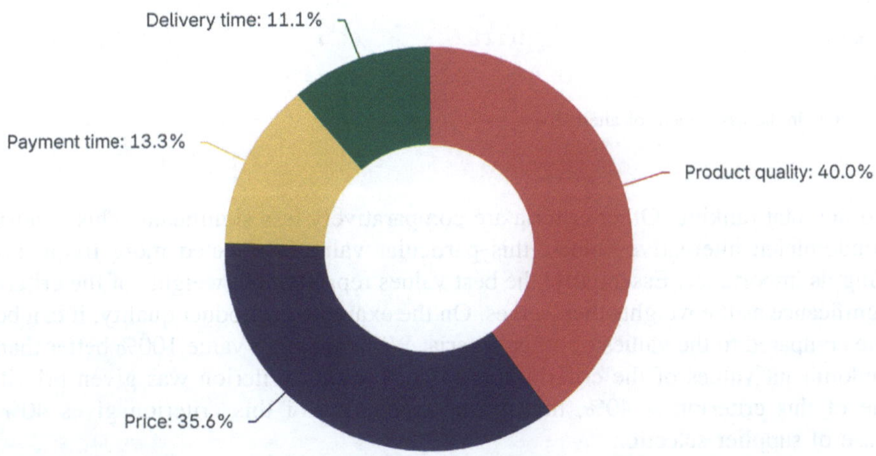

FIGURE 8.2 Value of criteria weights.

whether it is more advantageous for the price to be low with medium product quality, or for the price to be medium with high product quality. The latter option will be chosen in this case. The selection process persists until the values for the nondominant alternatives are established. The DM had a total of 18 questions to address. Within this decision-making scenario, a conflict arises between the criteria that must be defined for nondominant alternatives. It is impossible for the product quality to be high while the price is low, and vice versa. This principle is applicable to the other criteria as well. Consequently, the level of conciseness achieved was 77%.

Once the responses to all 18 questions were selected, the criteria weights were established (see Fig. 8.2). From these findings, it can be inferred that for the DM, the most significant criterion is product quality (40.0%), followed by price (35.6%), whereas the least significant criterion is delivery time (11.1%). Therefore, it can be deduced that the DM aims to maximize quality, minimize price, and is indifferent to the cost incurred or the manner in which the goods are obtained.

When the nondominant values of the alternatives were analyzed to establish the weight of the criteria, the weight assigned to each option within the criteria was also identified (see Fig. 8.3). Consequently, for all criteria, there is no option with the lowest value (0.0%). Simultaneously, these values hold no significance when ranking the alternatives. The medium and highest values are crucial for the ranking process. Therefore, the criterion with the greatest significance in the medium ranking is delivery time, which contributes 8.9% to the overall ranking, whereas the highest (but low) value

Product quality	Weight (sum = 1)		Score (0-100)	Preference value	Bar graph
low		×	0.0 =	0.0%	
medium	0.400	×	55.6 =	22.2%	
high		×	100.0 =	**40.0%**	
Price					
high		×	0.0 =	0.0%	
medium	0.356	×	56.2 =	20.0%	
low		×	100.0 =	**35.6%**	
Payment time					
low		×	0.0 =	0.0%	
medium	0.133	×	50.0 =	6.7%	
high		×	100.0 =	**13.3%**	
Delivery time					
high		×	0.0 =	0.0%	
medium	0.111	×	80.0 =	8.9%	
low		×	100.0 =	**11.1%**	

FIGURE 8.3 Value of options in the assessment of alternatives.

contributes 11.1% to the total ranking. Other criteria are comparatively less significant. This is attributed to the fact that when comparing nondominant alternative values, this particular value is selected more frequently than other average values, thus enhancing its importance. Essentially, the best values represent the weights of the criteria, meaning they hold the same level of significance as the weights themselves. On the example of product quality, it can be seen that 55.6% had a better median value compared to the values of other criteria. While the high value 100% better than other criteria. When determining the nondominant values of the criteria, the product quality criterion was given priority over other criteria. Therefore, the value of this criterion is 40%, that is, the evaluation of this criterion gives 40% of the value of the alternative in this case of supplier selection.

When determining the importance of criteria, we started by comparing nondominant solutions. The DM had to determine whether it is more important, say, that the quality is medium or that the delivery is low. Would he prefer to wait a few days for the goods and get them of better quality, or would he prefer the goods to arrive faster and be of lower quality. Due to the importance of quality for DM, in the largest number of nondominant solutions, they chose that quality is more important than other criteria. In this way, product quality is 1.1 times better than price, 3.0 times better than payment time, while it is 3.6 times better than delivery time (see Table 8.2). The weight of the criteria is calculated on the basis of this ratio. This is done in such a way that all the values for one criterion are added up. For the product quality criterion, it is calculated as follows:

$$sum = 1.0 + 1.1 + 3.0 + 3.6 = 8.7$$

In this way, the sum for all individual criteria is calculated, and finally the sum for all criteria is calculated. The individual sum is then divided by the total, and the weight value of the criteria is calculated. It should be noted that these values are generated by the 1000minds program based on the comparison of nondominant solutions, so these values are rounded to one decimal place. Therefore, the calculated value in this example differs from the actual value because rounded values are used. Thus, the importance of the weight of the product quality criterion is obtained as follows:

$$w_1 = \frac{8.7}{21.8} = 0.399$$

The ultimate ranking of the alternatives was established by utilizing the values of the evaluation criteria for the alternatives along with the rankings assigned to these alternatives (see Fig. 8.4). According to these assessments, supplier

TABLE 8.2 Relative importance of criteria for example 1.

	Product quality	Price	Payment time	Delivery time	Sum
Product quality	1.0	1.1	3.0	3.6	8.7
Price	0.9	1.0	2.7	3.2	7.8
Payment time	0.3	0.4	1.0	1.2	2.9
Delivery time	0.3	0.3	0.8	1.0	2.4
	40.0%	35.6%	13.3%	11.1%	sum 21.8

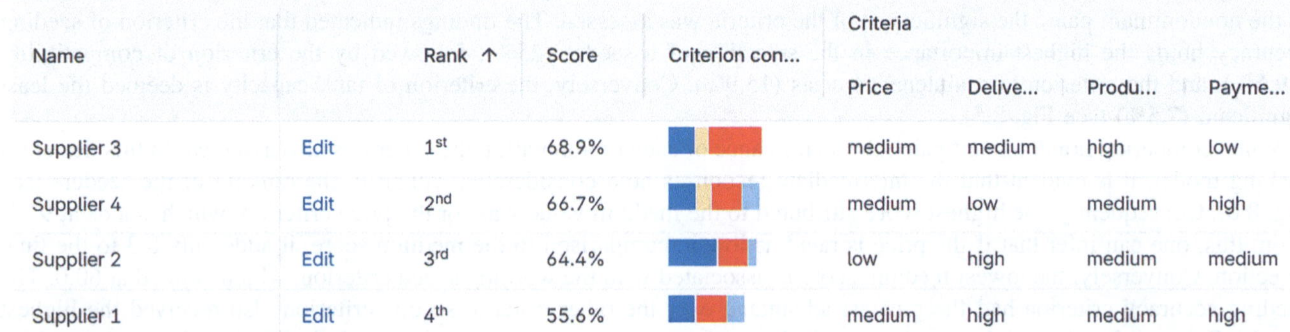

Name		Rank ↑	Score	Criterion con...	Criteria: Price	Delive...	Produ...	Payme...
Supplier 3	Edit	1st	68.9%		medium	medium	high	low
Supplier 4	Edit	2nd	66.7%		medium	low	medium	high
Supplier 2	Edit	3rd	64.4%		low	high	medium	medium
Supplier 1	Edit	4th	55.6%		medium	high	medium	high

FIGURE 8.4 Determining supplier ranking.

3 emerged as the top choice, characterized by moderate pricing and delivery durations, superior product quality, and minimal payment periods. Using this supplier as an example, the score was calculated in percentage form as follows:

$$R1 = 20.0\% + 8.9\% + 40.0\% + 0.0\% = 68.9\%$$

Supplier 3 is followed by supplier 4, which achieved a score of 66.7%, followed by supplier 2 with a score of 64.4%. The lowest-ranked supplier is Supplier 1, which received a score of 55.6%. From these findings, it can be inferred that the company ought to select Supplier 3 as a partner to enhance its competitiveness.

8.5 Numerical example 2

The fundamental responsibilities of every agribusiness that each farmer undertakes annually include sowing and harvesting. When sowing a specific agricultural crop, it is essential to consider the method of sowing that was employed. To perform this task correctly, the use of agricultural machinery, particularly a seeder, is required. The choice of any agricultural machinery represents an investment decision due to the financial commitment involved in acquiring such equipment. Consequently, it is imperative to analyze various alternatives in the form of seed drills available in the market and select one accordingly. Seed drills are crucial in agricultural production as they help to balance costs and revenues. It is vital to ensure uniform seed distribution during planting to achieve consistent yields across the plot. When selecting a seeder, farmers aim to choose one that facilitates more uniform sowing while minimizing seed losses. Therefore, this example seeks to identify a seeder that will contribute to improved yields. However, it is important to note that yield is influenced by numerous factors, making the seeder just one of the elements affecting the overall yield. In this instance, seven distinct seed drills will be examined and assessed based on seven specific criteria. These criteria are as follows:

- The working area denotes the width that the seeder is capable of sowing in a single pass.
- Seeding accuracy indicates the capacity to modify the seed quantity and the proficiency in achieving an even sowing distribution.

– Tank capacity refers to the volume of seed that the seeder can accommodate.
– Compatibility signifies the capability to utilize various types of seeds during planting.
– Maintenance costs encompass the overall expenses associated with the operation of the seeder.
– Price reflects the financial value assigned to this seeder.
– Working speed illustrates the extent of area that the seeder can cover within a specified timeframe.

Similar to the earlier example, three alternatives will be utilized here to assess the options: low, medium, and high. To employ these alternatives, it is essential first to ascertain whether the value of a specific criterion should be lower or higher, which will guide the formation of these options. Only in two criteria is it preferable to have a lower value, specifically in the areas of maintenance costs and price. Once the criteria and alternatives have been established, a decision-making model will be created within the 1000minds program, and the seed drill will be chosen through this program.

Once the criteria and their corresponding options have been established, the nondominant pairs that require evaluation are identified. Throughout this decision-making process, a total of 36 comparisons were conducted, achieving a comparison rate of 81%. It is important to note that the program itself facilitates the further identification of nondominant pairs, thereby enhancing the precision of this model; however, this improvement necessitates additional time for the decision-making process. An increase in the number of criteria results in a greater number of comparisons, making it challenging to maintain consistency in selection due to the increased options available. After selecting the options related to the nondominant pairs, the significance of the criteria was assessed. The findings indicated that the criterion of seeding accuracy holds the highest importance in the selection of a seeder (25%), followed by the criterion of compatibility (19.6%), and the criterion of maintenance costs (15.9%). Conversely, the criterion of tank capacity is deemed the least significant (7.5%) (see Fig. 8.5).

When comparing nondominant pairs, the significance of each option within the criteria is also assessed. In this decision-making model, it is evident that the intermediate responses hold considerable weight in the ranking of the seeders (see Fig. 8.6). Consequently, the highest score attributed to the medium value was for the price criterion, which stands at 91.7. From this, one can infer that if the price is rated as low in comparison to the medium score, it adds only 8.3 to the final selection. Conversely, the lowest medium score is associated with the working speed criterion, which is rated at 60.0. The seeding accuracy criterion had the greatest advantage over the other criteria, so this criterion also received the highest weight. Determining the weight was done on the basis of a comparison of nondominant solutions, where it was determined that this criterion was better than other criteria for a certain percentage (see Table 8.3).

When selecting nondominant values of the seeding accuracy criterion, more advantages were given compared to other criteria. Thus, this criterion was the most significant. This criterion was 1.3 times better than the compatibility criterion, while it was 1.6 times better than maintenance costs (see Table 8.3). The process of obtaining these criteria values is done in such a way that the values for how much each criterion was better or worse than the other criterion in order are added,

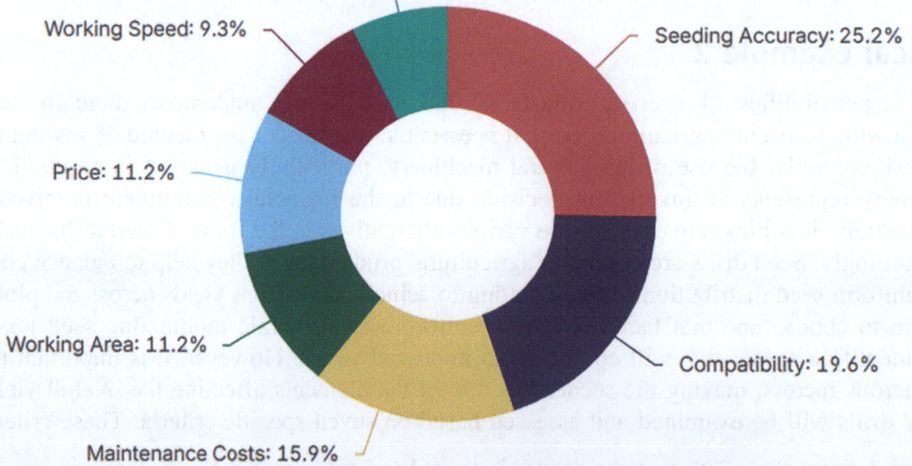

FIGURE 8.5 Significance of criteria in the selection of a seeder.

Seeding Accuracy	Weight (sum = 1)		Score (0-100)	Preference value	Bar graph
low		×	0.0 =	0.0%	
medium	0.252	×	81.5 =	20.6%	
high		×	100.0 =	25.2%	
Compatibility					
low		×	0.0 =	0.0%	
medium	0.196	×	85.7 =	16.8%	
high		×	100.0 =	19.6%	
Maintenance Costs					
high		×	0.0 =	0.0%	
medium	0.159	×	76.5 =	12.1%	
low		×	100.0 =	15.9%	
Working Area					
low		×	0.0 =	0.0%	
medium	0.112	×	83.3 =	9.3%	
high		×	100.0 =	11.2%	
Price					
high		×	0.0 =	0.0%	
medium	0.112	×	91.7 =	10.3%	
low		×	100.0 =	11.2%	
Working Speed					
low		×	0.0 =	0.0%	
medium	0.093	×	60.0 =	5.6%	
high		×	100.0 =	9.3%	
Tank capacity					
low		×	0.0 =	0.0%	
medium	0.075	×	75.0 =	5.6%	
high		×	100.0 =	7.5%	

FIGURE 8.6 Value of criteria options.

and then the sum of that criterion is divided by the total sum. Since the figures are rounded here, there is a slight deviation from the actual weights. Thus, when the sum for the seeding accuracy criterion is divided by the total sum (14.4/56.3 = 25.6%), an amount of 25.6% is obtained, which differs from the actual one by 0.4%. The difference is that the values were rounded up to a higher value.

Ultimately, a ranking of the observed seeders is established based on specific scores. The highest-rated seeder was seeder 6, followed by seeder 2, whereas the least favorable option according to DM rankings is seeder 5 (see Fig. 8.7). It can be seen that seeder 6 dominates by far in comparison to other seeders and is the first choice for purchasing agricultural machinery.

TABLE 8.3 Relative importance of criteria for example 2.

	Seeding accuracy	Compatibility	Maintenance costs	Working area	Price	Working speed	Tank capacity	Sum
Seeding accuracy	1.0	1.3	1.6	2.2	2.2	2.7	3.4	14.4
Compatibility	0.8	1.0	1.2	1.7	1.7	2.1	2.6	11.3
Maintenance costs	0.6	0.8	1.0	1.4	1.4	1.7	2.1	9.0
Working area	0.4	0.6	0.7	1.0	1.0	1.2	1.5	5.4
Price	0.4	0.6	0.7	1.0	1.0	1.2	1.5	6.4
Working speed	0.4	0.5	0.6	0.8	0.8	1.0	1.3	5.4
Tank capacity	0.3	0.4	0.5	0.7	0.7	0.8	1.0	4.4
	25.2%	19.6%	15.9%	11.2%	11.2%	9.3%	7.5%	Sum 56.3

Name		Rank ↑	Score	Criterion contribution	Criteria						
					Working A...	Seeding A...	Tank capa...	Compatibi...	Maintena...	Price	Working S...
Seeders 6	Edit	1st	92.5%		medium	high	medium	medium	low	medium	high
Seeders 2	Edit	2nd	73.8%		low	high	medium	medium	low	medium	low
Seeders 1	Edit	3rd	72.0%		medium	high	medium	low	medium	medium	high
Seeders 7	Edit	4th	67.3%		medium	medium	low	high	medium	high	medium
Seeders 3	Edit	5th	57.0%		medium	medium	low	medium	high	medium	low
Seeders 4	Edit	6th	55.1%		low	medium	low	medium	medium	high	medium
Seeders 5	Edit	7th	53.3%		medium	low	medium	medium	medium	high	high

FIGURE 8.7 Ranking of seeders.

8.6 Conclusions

In practical decision-making, various methods are employed to assist the DM in making a decision. This chapter utilized the PAPRIKA method for decision-making within the agribusiness sector. This method serves as an effective and adaptable tool that facilitates decision-making when multiple criteria must be considered. The strength of this method lies in its approach to determining the weight of the criteria and evaluating alternatives through pairwise comparisons of different criteria. In the process of ranking scores, a set of potential solutions is established, necessitating the identification of dominant solutions and those that are not. When one solution is found to dominate another, such instances are excluded from the decision-making process. Therefore, it is essential to ascertain whether it is evident that one solution surpasses the others, particularly when one or more criteria exhibit superior rankings while the remaining criteria are equivalent to those of the alternative solution. Consequently, the PAPRIKA method focuses solely on nondominant pairs, requiring a decision on what is preferable for the DM: whether the value of one criterion should be lower while the other is higher, or vice versa, with the possibility of criteria holding equal significance. Based on this, inequations are established and resolved through linear programming, yielding results.

These practical scenarios were addressed utilizing the 1000minds software solution. A distinctive feature of this program is its ability to automatically identify and minimize the total number of comparisons of nondominant pairs, thereby streamlining the decision-making process. By employing this software, the number of comparisons is significantly reduced, resulting in a figure that is considerably lower than the theoretical number of comparisons. The exclusion process is based on logical reasoning and certain repetitions of pairs. The decision itself is derived from a score that incorporates the weight of the criteria and the respective grades. This method assesses the significance of each criterion and subsequently evaluates how much each criterion's grade impacts the final decision. By applying this approach in practical examples, it was demonstrated that supplier 3 exhibits the most favorable indicators, while seeder 6 stands out in the second instance.

This chapter was conducted to promote and demonstrate the application of the PAPRIKA method through practical examples, illustrating how decisions can be made utilizing this approach. The significance of this method lies in its ability to enhance the decision-making process, as the software solution assesses the conciseness of the decision and identifies areas for further improvement. Consequently, it allows for the adjustment of the DM's preferences and enhances the accuracy of the established decision-making model, thereby facilitating the formulation of a more precise and comprehensive decision. This is crucial for the DM, as it leads to an improved decision-making process that ultimately contributes to the enhancement of the company's operations. Nevertheless, alongside the notable strengths of the PAPRIKA method, it also presents certain limitations when compared to alternative methods. The primary drawback of this method is that as the number of criteria and options within each criterion increases, the quantity of comparisons involving nondominant pairs also rises. This issue was addressed through the implementation of the 1000minds software solution, which was utilized in this chapter.

References

Akbulut, O. Y. (2024). Assessing the environmental sustainability performance of the banking sector: A novel integrated grey multi-criteria decision-making (MCDM) approach. *International Journal of Knowledge and Innovation Studies, 2*(4), 239–258. https://doi.org/10.56578/ijkis020404.

Baggott, C., Hansen, P., Hancox, R. J., Hardy, J. K., Sparks, J., Holliday, M., Weatherall, M., Beasley, R., Reddel, H. K., Fingleton, J., & PRACTICAL discrete choice experiment study team (2020). What matters most to patients when choosing treatment for mild-moderate asthma? Results from a discrete choice experiment. *Thorax, 75*(10), 842–848. https://doi.org/10.1136/thoraxjnl-2019-214343.

Balogun, I., Garner, E., Amer, P., Fennessy, P., Teeken, B., Olaosebikan, O., Abolore, B., Madu, T., Okoye, B., Santos, B., Byrne, T., Martin-Collado, D., Egesi, C., Kulakow, P., & Tufan, H. A. (2022). From traits to typologies: Piloting new approaches to profiling trait preferences along the cassava value chain in Nigeria. *Crop Science, 62*, 259–274. https://doi.org/10.1002/csc2.20680.

Brock, A., Williams, I., & Kemp, S. (2023). I'll take the easiest option please". Carbon reduction preferences of the public. *Journal of Cleaner Production, 429*, 139398. https://doi.org/10.1016/j.jclepro.2023.139398.

Carnero, M. C. (2020). Waste segregation FMEA model integranking intuitionistic fuzzy set and the PAPRIKA method. *Mathematics, 8*(8), 1375. https://doi.org/10.3390/math8081375.

Chan, A. H. Y., Tao, M., Marsh, S., & Petousis-Harris, H. (2024). Vaccine decision making in New Zealand: A discrete choice experiment. *BMC Public Health, 24*(1), 447. https://doi.org/10.1186/s12889-024-17865-8.

Hansen, P., & Ombler, F. (2008). A new method for scoring additive multi-attribute value models using pairwise rankings of alternatives. *Journal of Multi-Criteria Decision Analysis, 15*(3-4), 87–107. https://doi.org/10.1002/mcda.428.

Hoque, M. J., Islam, M. S., & Mohtasim, S. A. (2024). Optimizing decision-making through customer-centric market basket analysis. *Journal of Operational and Strategic Analytics, 2*(2), 72–83. https://doi.org/10.56578/josa020201.

Isihara, P., Shi, C., Ward, J., O'Malley, L., Laney, S., Diedrichs, D., & Flores, G. (2020). Identifying most typical and most ideal attribute levels in small populations of expert decision makers: Studying the Go/No Go decision of disaster relief organizations. *Journal of Choice Modelling, 35*, 100204. https://doi.org/10.1016/j.jocm.2020.100204.

Ismail, M., Alham, M. H., & Ibrahim, D. K. (2023). A novel approach for optimal hybrid energy decarbonization using multi-criteria decision analysis: Abu Rudeis, Egypt as a case study. *Energy Conversion and Management, 290*, 117199. https://doi.org/10.1016/j.enconman.2023.117199.

Liberman, A. L., Pinto, D., Rostanski, S. K., Labovitz, D. L., Naidech, A. M., & Prabhakaran, S. (2019). Clinical decision-making for thrombolysis of acute minor stroke using adaptive conjoint analysis. *The Neurohospitalist, 9*(1), 9–14. https://doi.org/10.1177/1941874418799563.

Lukić, R. (2024). Evaluation of trade performance dynamics in Serbia using ARAT and rough MABAC methods. *Oeconomica Jadertina, 14*(2), 34–44. https://doi.org/10.15291/oec.4559.

Mirzaee, S., Fannon, D., & Ruth, M. (2019). A comparison of preference elicitation methods for multi-criteria design decisions about resilient and sustainable buildings. *Environment Systems & Decisions, 39*(4), 439–453. https://doi.org/10.1007/s10669-019-09726-2.

Mohammed, U., Karataev, T., Oshiga, O., Oghorada, O., Adeshina, S. A., Hussein, S. U., Abualigah, L., Galadima, Ah., Abubakar, D., & Sanusi, J. (2024). ICSOMPA: A novel improved hybrid algorithm for global optimisation. *Evolutionary Intelligence, 17*(5-6), 3337–3440. https://doi.org/10.1007/s12065-024-00937-4.

Molnar, A., Nemeth, B., Inotai, A., & Kaló, Z. (2017). Comparison of Weighting methods used during the construction of multiple-criteria decision analysis tool for repeated use in lower income countries. *Value in Health, 20*(9), A776. https://doi.org/10.1016/j.jval.2017.08.2240.

Ofori, B. S., Padi, A., & Musah, A. (2025). Corporate governance effectiveness, operational risk and financial performance of banks: The role of firm size. *Economics, 13*(2), 71–93. https://doi.org/10.2478/eoik-2025-0031.

Patel, P. C., Stenmark, M., Parida, V., & Tran, P.-K. (2023). A socio-institutional perspective on the reluctance among the elderly concerning the commercialization of 3D surgical video technology in Sweden. *Journal of Innovation & Knowledge, 8*(2), 100361. https://doi.org/10.1016/j.jik.2023.100361.

Payini, V., Mallya, J., & Piramanayagam, S. (2022). Indian women consumers' wine choice: a study based on conjoint analysis. *International Journal of Wine Business Research, 34*(4), 469–494. https://doi.org/10.1108/ijwbr-05-2021-0031.

Roy, M., Hansen, P., Sullivan, T., Ombler, F., Kiore, M., Stapleton, A., & Carr, C. (2021). Rapid development of a tool for prioritizing patients with coronavirus disease 2019 for intensive care. *Critical Care Explorations, 3*(3), e0368. https://doi.org/10.1097/CCE.0000000000000368.

Sarfraz, M., & Božanić, D. (2024). Optimization of market risk via Maclaurin symmetric mean aggregation operators: An application of interval-valued intuitionistic fuzzy sets in multi-attribute group decision-making. *Journal of Engineering Management and Systems Engineering, 3*(2), 100–115. https://doi.org/10.56578/jemse030205.

Sullivan, T. A., Wyeth, E. H., Turner, R. M., Hansen, P., Ombler, F., Devlin, N. J., & Derrett, S. (2025). Can adolescents value the EQ-5D-Y-5L and EQ-5D-5L, and how do the values compare? A feasibility study. *Value in Health: The Journal of the International Society for Pharmacoeconomics and Outcomes Research, 28*(6), 936–944. https://doi.org/10.1016/j.jval.2025.02.013.

Tomić, D. (2025). Strategic decision-making, marketing investments, and game theory: Optimal competitive strategies between Coca-Cola and Pepsi. *Oeconomica Jadertina, 15*(1), 22–39. https://doi.org/10.15291/oec.4734.

Topal, A., & Ulutaş, A. (2024). Evaluating the logistics performance of G8 nations using multi-criteria decision-making models. *Journal of Intelligent Management Decision, 3*(3), 150–158. https://doi.org/10.56578/jimd030302.

Ullah, I., & Yow, K. S. (2025). Automated vehicle dent detection using hybrid image processing and fuzzy decision making. *Mechatronics and Intelligent Transportation Systems, 4*(1), 49–60. https://doi.org/10.56578/mits040105.

Waghmare, G., Dash, P., Jogalekar, J., Killedar, M., Rao, M. S., & Biswas, M. (2025). Corporate social responsibility: Economic impacts on consumer loyalty and brand value in the digital era. *Economics, 13*(2), 507–527. https://doi.org/10.2478/eoik-2025-0045.

Chapter 9

QFD: Quality function deployment for multi-attribute decision-making

Vahideh Shahin[1], Morteza Yazdani[2], and Moslem Alimohammadlou[1]
[1]*Department of Management, Shiraz University, Shiraz, Iran,* [2]*Institute of Dynamic Management, Vilnius Gediminas Technical University, Vilnius, Lithuania*

9.1 Introduction

Quality function deployment (QFD) is a well-established quality management methodology that emphasizes the *voice of the customer* by translating needs and preferences into specific product or service requirements (Chadly et al., 2024; Li et al., 2023). Its core framework, the house of quality (HoQ), systematically links customer demands (the *WHATs*) with engineering characteristics or design measures (the *HOWs*), thereby enabling organizations to optimize design, improve process quality, reduce costs, and enhance customer satisfaction (Chan & Wu, 2002; Li et al., 2025). Since its development in Japan during the late 1960s, QFD has evolved beyond its original application in product design and has been successfully applied across diverse domains such as supply chain management, energy systems, and service design (Tavana et al., 2017; Yazdani et al., 2017; Yazdani et al., 2016). Initially, it has been developed for product development to assess customer requirements, after that QFD was utilized in diverse projects as a distinguished organizational tool and its suitability, capacity and adaptability has been demonstrated in hundreds of researches under diverse domains such as supply chain management, energy systems, and design (García-León et al., 2021; Haiyun et al., 2021; Moktadir & Ren, 2024).

Despite its strengths, traditional QFD faces challenges when dealing with multilevel decision structures, interdependencies, and subjective judgments. Defining accurate relationships between customer requirements and technical attributes often becomes a bottleneck, particularly under conditions of uncertainty. To overcome these limitations, scholars have increasingly integrated QFD with multicriteria decision-making (MCDM) techniques. Approaches such as

analytic hierarchy process (AHP), analytic network process (ANP), step-wise weight assessment ratio analysis (SWARA), best-worst method (BWM), decision-making trial and evaluation laboratory (DEMATEL), technique for order preference by similarity to ideal solution (TOPSIS), and VlseKriterijumska Optimizacija I Kompromisno Resenje (VIKOR),and their fuzzy extensions have been used to strengthen QFD's analytical rigor, improve the weighting of criteria, and capture complex interrelationships in decision problems (Fazeli & Peng, 2023; Li et al., 2014; Wu et al., 2017). This synergy has transformed QFD into a dynamic decision-support tool capable of bridging subjective preferences with structured evaluation.

Building on this progress, the present study contributes to the literature by proposing an integrated framework that combines BWM, DEMATEL, and the Combined Compromise for Ideal Solution (CoCoFiSo) method within the QFD structure. The framework enhances the precision and consistency of weighting processes, models causal interdependencies among decision factors, and provides robust prioritization of alternatives. To demonstrate its applicability, the study applies the proposed methodology to the problem of green supplier (GS) selection, where economic, environmental, and social dimensions must be simultaneously considered. This application illustrates not only the methodological contributions of the integrated approach but also its practical relevance in addressing real-world sustainability challenges.

The order of the chapter is followed by a literature review in section 2 that explores the recent studies of QFD. Then, in section 3, the methodology is released. Section 4 presents the case study, model implementation, and results generation. At the end conclusion is provided in section 5.

Encyclopedia of Multi-Attribute Decision-Making (MADM). DOI: https://doi.org/10.1016/B978-0-443-33275-3.00067-1

9.2 Literature review

Recent studies reveal an emerging paradigm of integrating QFD with MCDM approaches to enhance its analytical robustness. This development is examined in detail in the subsequent discussion, while Table 9.1 provides a structured overview of the reviewed QFD integrations and their respective configurations.

A significant contribution by Wudhikarn and Pongpatcharatorntep (2022) saw the ANP combined with QFD to rectify limitations in traditional intellectual capital management. Their model used two interlinked HoQs. In the first, key success factors were the "Whats" and key performance indicators (KPIs) were the "Hows". The output from this phase, the prioritized KPIs, then became the "Whats" in the second HoQ. These were correlated with specific action plans as the "Hows". This cascading approach effectively turns strategic goals into executable initiatives. The inclusion of ANP was crucial for managing the complex interdependencies among criteria, resulting in a more coherent framework. Similarly, Li et al. (2022) proposed a four-phase QFD model integrated with DEMATEL and TOPSIS under a picture fuzzy rough sets (PFRs). They evaluated innovative financing solutions for renewable energy. Their model began with customer needs as the initial "Whats." Financial innovation priorities served as the final "Hows" in the fourth HoQ. Intermediary elements, like technical characteristics and competencies, functioned as both "Hows" in one phase and "Whats" in the next. This created a continuous translation of requirements. The PFR-DEMATEL method determined the weights of the "Whats", while PFR-TOPSIS was used to rank the alternative solutions ("Hows"). The application of cascading HoQs to supply chain vulnerabilities is explored in the work of Hsu et al. (2022), who applied a two-tiered QFD approach for a new energy materials supply chain. Ripple effect factors served as "Whats" and supply chain agility indicators (SCAIs) as "Hows" in the first HoQ. The resulting SCAIs then became the "Whats" in the second HoQ, which were linked to Industry 4.0 enablers as "Hows". Their method used DEMATEL to weight the "Whats" and Grey-VIKOR to analyze the relationships, offering a way to model complex dependencies under uncertainty.

In the context of cultural heritage preservation, Li et al. (2023) adopted an AHP–QFD framework to guide innovative commercial renovations of traditional dwellings. They used the AHP technique to determine the weights of renovation objectives ("Whats"). These were then deployed in QFD to derive specific design features ("Hows") based on expert feedback. Notably, their model incorporated the standard HoQ components: customer requirements, quality characteristics, their relationships, a correlation matrix, and competitive analysis. Advancing the integration of fuzzy set theories for handling imprecise data, Lu et al. (2023) developed a hybrid model for renewable energy technology selection aimed at alleviating energy poverty. They applied the interval-valued intuitionistic fuzzy BWM (IVIF-BWM) to determine the weights of energy poverty reduction requirements ("Whats" in the first HoQ), integrating these weights into a matrix where IVIF numbers defined the relationships between the "Whats" and technical selection criteria ("Hows"). Subsequently, they used the output weights to prioritize the renewable energy technology alternatives which functioned as the "Hows" in the second HoQ, using IVIF-VIKOR analysis.

In another context, Chadly et al. (2024) adopted AHP, fuzzy TOPSIS (FTOPSIS), preference selection index (PSI), and QFD to determine optimal dust cleaning techniques for solar panels, implementing these methods separately and comparing their results. Their AHP method was applied to determine criteria weights and prioritize cleaning alternatives, while FTOPSIS assessed these alternatives using the weighted criteria from AHP. The PSI method was used separately to assess alternatives without requiring predetermined criteria weights. Their QFD approach structured two HoQs: in the first HoQ, customer needs ("Whats") were mapped to engineering criteria ("Hows") previously used in AHP/FTOPSIS, with customer importance weights assigned on a 1–10 scale and relationship strengths rated on a 1–3 point scale to calculate relative weights; interrelations between "Hows" were also assessed using this scale and incorporated into technical target values. In the second HoQ, the weighted criteria from the first HoQ became the new "Whats" to evaluate the cleaning alternative technologies ("Hows"). Extending QFD integration with advanced fuzzy techniques, Zhang and Zhang (2024) devised a Fermatean fuzzy (FF) framework to assess smart Industry 4.0 technologies for agri-food waste valorization. The study first determined the initial weights of the challenges ("Whats") using the FF-SWARA method. These weights were subsequently refined by analyzing the causal interrelationships among the challenges via FF-DEMATEL. Leveraging the total relation matrix from FF-DEMATEL, the authors then constructed an initial reachability matrix for the Interpretive Structural Modeling approach to further elucidate the hierarchical and interactional structure of the challenges. The refined weights of the challenges ("Whats"), combined with FF assessments of the relationships between these "Whats" and the smart technology solutions ("Hows"), were used to compute initial relative importance values. These values were ultimately adjusted using a correlation matrix to account for interdependencies among the "Hows", yielding their absolute importance weights.

In a recent study, Puzovic et al. (2025) developed a robust model for new product development (NPD) analysis. They used interval type-2 fuzzy AHP to prioritize customer attributes ("Whats"). The interval type-2 fuzzy EDAS

TABLE 9.1 Recent integrations of quality function deployment (QFD) with multicriteria decision-making methods.

Method used	Application	HoQ(s) Structure			Reference
		# of house of quality (HoQs)	WHATs	HOWs	
ANP-QFD	Prioritizing action plans (APs) for improved intellectual capital management	2	HoQ-I: key success factors HoQ-II: key performance indicators (KPIs)	HoQ-I: KPIs HoQ-II: APs	Wudhikarn and Pongpatcharatorntep (2022)
PFR-DEMATEL–TOPSIS–QFD	Evaluating innovative financing solutions for renewable energy inverstors	4	HoQ-I: customer needs HoQ II: technical characteristics HoQ III: Competencies HoQ IV: prioritized KPIs	HoQ I: technical characteristics HoQ II: competencies HoQ III: KPIs HoQ IV: financial innovation priorities	Li et al. (2022)
DEMATEL–Grey-VIKOR–QFD	Mitigating supply chain vulnerabilities for new energy materials	2	HoQ-I: ripple effect factors HoQ-II: supply chain agility indicators (SCAIs)	HoQ-I: SCAIs HoQ-II: industry 4.0 enablers	Hsu et al. (2022)
AHP–QFD	Guiding innovative commercial renovations of traditional dwellings	1	Renovation objectives	Design features	Li et al. (2022)
IVIF-BWM- QFD-VIKOR	Renewable energy technology selection to alleviate energy poverty	2	HoQ-I: energy poverty reduction requirements HoQ-II: technical criteria	HoQ-I: technical criteria HoQ-II: technology alternatives	Lu et al. (2023)
AHP, FTOPSIS, PSI, and QFD	Determining optimal dust cleaning techniques for solar panels	2	HoQ-I: customer needs HoQ-II: weighted criteria	HoQ-I: engineering criteria HoQ-II: cleaning alternatives	Chadly et al. (2024)
FF-SWARA–DEMATEL–ISM–QFD	Assessing smart Industry 4.0 technologies for agri-food waste valorization	1	Challenges	Smart technologies	Zhang and Zhang (2024)
IT2F-AHP-evaluation based on distance from average solution (EDAS)-QFD	New product development (NPD) analysis	1	Customer attributes	NPD practices	Puzovic et al. (2025)
FF-SWARA-QFD	Risk management and mitigation strategy development	1	Risk factors	Mitigation strategies	Sumrit and Keeratibhubordee (2025)
TFAHP-QFD-VIKOR	Optimal design selection for modern Tibetan furniture	2	HoQ-I: user demands HoQ-II: technical features	HoQ-I: technical features HoQ-II: design alternatives	Li et al. (2025)

(IT2F-EDAS) method calculated initial weights for the NPD practices ("Hows") which were then refined through an autocorrelation-based weighting computation to yield the final, absolute weights. For risk management, Sumrit and Keeratibhubordee (2025) combined SWARA with QFD within a FF framework, drawing on the earlier model proposed by Zhang and Zhang (2024). Using FF-SWARA, they derived the weights of risk factors ("Whats"), which were then incorporated into a QFD matrix to map their relationships with mitigation strategies ("Hows"). The relational matrix was further refined to account for correlations among the "Hows," leading to the calculation of the final absolute importance weights of the strategies. This approach provides the advantage of effectively handling high degrees of uncertainty and subjective expert judgments in risk assessment through the FF set, while systematically translating prioritized risks into actionable, ranked strategic responses. Concluding this progression, Li et al. (2025) addressed the conflict between cultural heritage and modern functionality in Tibetan furniture design by integrating Triangular Fuzzy AHP (TFAHP), QFD, and VIKOR. Their methodology first used TFAHP to determine the weights of user demands ("Whats"). These were then input into a QFD matrix, where relationships to technical features ("Hows") were assessed on a 6-point scale to calculate the final importance of the "Hows". Crucially, these QFD-derived weights served as the criteria weights in a subsequent VIKOR analysis to select the optimal design from three scheme options.

The above discussion highlighst QFD's adaptability in structuring complex problems and its synergistic potential with MCDM to transform subjective requirements into prioritized, actionable decisions. A deeper analysis identifies the main reasons for diversity in QFD-MCDM approaches:

- Number of HoQs: Determined by the specific research problem's structure and complexity.
- Weighting of "WHATs": Use of different techniques, from simple rating scales to advanced MCDM methods (e.g., SWARA, AHP, BWM).
- Linking "WHATs" and "HOWs": Various methods to establish relationships and calculate the importance of "HOWs", from a basic three-point scale to advanced MCDM techniques like TOPSIS or MARCOS.
- Analyzing the "Roof" (HOWs correlations): Differing approaches to assess the interrelationships between technical characteristics ("HOWs"') and their subsequent impact on the final prioritized weights.

9.3 Methodology

The QFD method provides a comprehensive, multistep framework for aligning customer needs with engineering design measures. Its core structure, as shown in Fig. 9.1, is defined by six key elements: (a) the "WHATs" matrix (customer requirements/customer attributes), (b) the "HOWs" matrix (technical requirements/design measures/engineering characteristics), (c) the relative importance weights of the "WHATs", (d) the relationship matrix correlating "WHATs" and "HOWs" (forming the central body of the HoQ), (e) the interrelationship matrix between the HOWs (the "roof" of the HoQ), and (f) the resulting priority weights of the HOWs (Sumrit & Keeratibhubordee, 2025; Wudhikarn & Pongpatcharatorntep, 2022; Yazdani et al., 2016).

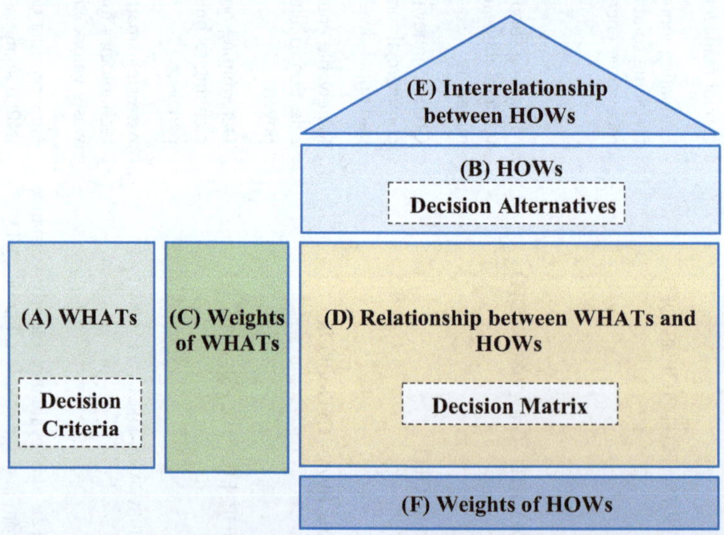

FIGURE 9.1 The standard structure of the quality function deployment–multicriteria decision-making model (own elaboration).

The integrated QFD-MCDM approach commonly treats customer requirements (*WHATs*) as criteria and design measures (*HOWs*) as alternatives. This framing allows the relationship matrix to act as the primary decision matrix. The specific points of MCDM integration, highlighted by dotted-line boxes in Fig. 9.1, occur at these stages to quantify relationships and priorities.

To elucidate the standard process for developing an integrated QFD-MCDM model, this section delineates the procedural steps, as conceptually outlined in Fig. 9.1.

Step 1: Definition of "WHATs" (decision criteria): The initial phase involves identifying and defining the set of customer requirements or strategic objectives, termed "WHATs." These constitute the decision criteria and are positioned in section (a) of the HoQ matrix.

Step 2: Definition of "HOWs" (decision alternatives): Subsequently, the engineering characteristics, design attributes, or potential solutions required to fulfill the "WHATs" are defined. These "HOWs" function as the decision alternatives and are detailed in section (b) of the HoQ.

Step 3: Determining the importance weights of "WHATs": A critical step involves evaluating the relative importance of each i-th criterion (C_i), where the weight vector ($\Sigma C_i = 1$, $C_i \in [0,1]$) is established (section [c]). While the classical QFD approach employs direct expert rating and weighted averaging, integrated QFD-MCDM methodologies preferentially utilize robust MCDM techniques (e.g., AHP, SWARA, BWM) for this purpose. This integration enhances precision by effectively capturing expert judgment and managing subjectivity and uncertainty (Puzovic et al., 2025; Sumrit & Keeratibhubordee, 2025).

Among the various methods for determining criteria weights, the BWM, originally proposed by Rezaei (2015), has gained prominence for its efficiency in MCDM. Compared with the AHP, it requires substantially fewer pairwise comparisons, thereby reducing cognitive burden and improving consistency of judgments, while also demonstrating flexibility across diverse decision contexts and the capacity to incorporate group preferences (Shahin et al., 2024).

Step 3.1: Identification of the decision criteria set: In this step, the decision criteria are defined as a set $\{c1, c2, c3, \ldots, cm\}$.

Step 3.2: Selecting the best and worst criteria: The decision-maker identifies the most significant (best) and the least significant (worst) criterion in general terms.

Step 3.3: Executing the best-to-others (BO) Comparison: The preference of the best criterion (B) over all other criteria is determined using a numerical scale ranging from 1 to 9. This results in the (BO) vector, $A_B = (a_{B1}, a_{B2}, \ldots, a_{Bm})$, where a_{Bj} indicates the preference of the B over criterion j, and $a_{BB} = 1$.

Step 3.4: Executing the others-to-worst (OW) comparison: The preference of all other criteria over the worst criterion (W) is determined, again using a scale of 1 to 9. This yields the OW vector, $A_W = (a_{1W}, a_{2W}, \ldots a_{mW})^T$, where a_{jW} represents the preference of criterion j over the W, with $a_{WW} = 1$.

Step 3.5: Formulating and solving the optimization model: A linear programming model (Eq. 9.1) is formulated to determine the optimal weights for the criteria. The model, aimed at minimizing the maximum absolute difference for consistency, is presented as follows:

$$\min \xi \tag{9.1}$$

s.t.

$$|w_B/w_i - a_{Bi}| \le \xi \quad for\ all\ i$$

$$|w_j/w_w - a_{iw}| \le \xi \ for\ all\ i$$

$$\sum_i w_i = 1,\ w_i \ge 0 \quad for\ all\ i$$

Solving this model yields the optimal weights $(w_1^*, w_2^*, \ldots, w_m^*)$ and the optimal value of the consistency index (ξ^*).

Step 3.6: Consistency ratio calculation: The value of ξ^* is utilized to calculate a Consistency Ratio (CR), as indicated in Eq. 9.2.

$$\text{ConsistencyRatio (CR)} = \xi/\text{Consistency Index(CI)}_* \tag{9.2}$$

The maximum possible value of ξ for a given preference structure, known as the consistency index (CI), can be referenced from Table 9.2. This table maps values of a_{BW} to their corresponding CI values.

Step 4: Establishment of the relationship matrix: The core of the HoQ is the relationship matrix (section [d]), which maps the interactions between "WHATs" and "HOWs." Expert evaluations are typically collected using predefined scales. In conventional QFD applications, a three-point scale is often adopted—1 (weak, ▲), 3 (moderate, ■), and

TABLE 9.2 Consistency indices in the best-worst method.

a_{BW}	1	2	3	4	5	6	7	8	9
CI	0.00	0.44	1.00	1.63	2.30	3.00	3.73	4.47	5.23

9 (strong, ●)—with blank cells indicating no relationship (Chadly et al., 2024; Wudhikarn & Pongpatcharatorntep, 2022). For integration with MCDM approaches, however, evaluations may be captured using crisp Likert scales or fuzzy-based linguistic terms, allowing a more nuanced representation of expert judgments.

Step 5: Establishment of the correlation matrix (roof of house of quality): This optional step involves analyzing the interrelations (synergies or trade-offs) among the "HOWs" themselves, documented in the correlation matrix or "roof" of the HoQ (section [e]). The correlations are generally rated as strongly positive (++), positive (+), neutral (blank), negative (–), or strongly negative (—) (Chadly et al., 2024). While this step enriches the analysis by highlighting synergies or trade-offs among design attributes, it is not compulsory in QFD practice. Some studies have incorporated this analysis to refine "HOW" weights (He et al., 2021; Hsu et al., 2022; Puzovic et al., 2025; Wudhikarn & Pongpatcharatorntep, 2022), while others have either omitted it altogether (Li et al., 2025; Yazdani et al., 2016) or considered it without integrating it into the computation of relative weights (Chadly et al., 2024).

In the integration of QFD and MCDM frameworks, the DEMATEL method stands as a robust technique for analyzing the complex interdependencies among the "Hows." DEMATEL excels in modeling both direct and indirect influences, thereby clarifying causal relationships and enabling effective prioritization within decision-making structures. Its reliance on expert input ensures practical validity, while its methodological flexibility permits seamless combination with other MCDM approaches, enhancing overall analytical rigor (Shahin et al., 2025).

The DEMATEL procedure comprises the following steps:

Step 5.1: Constructing the direct-relation matrix (*X*): Experts assess pairwise influences among *nn* factors using an integer scale (0–4), where 0 denotes no influence and 4 very high influence, resulting in a nonnegative matrix $X = [xij]_{n\times n}$ with null diagonal:

$$X = \begin{bmatrix} x_{11} & \cdots & x_{1n} \\ \vdots & \ddots & \vdots \\ x_{n1} & \cdots & x_{nn} \end{bmatrix} \tag{9.3}$$

For multiple experts, the arithmetic mean of their matrices is used.

Step 5.2: Forming the normalized direct-relation matrix (*N*): The direct-relation matrix is normalized by multiplying each element by *k*, using:

$$N = k \times X,\ k = \min\left(\frac{1}{\max\ \sum_{j=1}^{n} xij} \cdot \frac{1}{\max\ \sum_{i=1}^{n} xij}\right) \tag{9.4}$$

Step 5.3: Total-relation matrix (T) calculation: The total-influence matrix *T*, incorporating direct and indirect effects, is derived as:

$$T = [t_{ij}]_{n\times n} = N(I - N) - 1 \tag{9.5}$$

where *I* is the identity matrix.

Step 5.4: Evaluating the "prominence" and "relation" values calculation: Determine the row and column sums of the total influence matrix (T), as $D = [\sum_{j=1}^{n} t_{ij}]_{n\times 1}$, and $R = [\sum_{i=1}^{n} t_{ij}]_{1\times n}$, respectively. Then, the values of $d_i + r_i$ and $d_i - r_i$ are computed to determine the "prominence" and "relation" of each factor, respectively. "Prominence" signifies the overall influence and centrality of a factor within the system, whereas relation distinguishes causal factors (positive values) from effect factors (negative values).

Step 5.5: Computing the influence importance values: Based on the computed prominence and relation values, the influence-importance (*FIwj*) for each factor *j* is determined using the Euclidean distance formula: (He et al., 2021; Shahin et al., 2025).

$$FIw_j = \sqrt{(d_i + r_i)^2 + (d_i - r_i)^2} \tag{9.6}$$

Subsequently, the normalized influence-importance value (*FIWj*) is derived as:

$$FIW_{\mathrm{j}} = \frac{FIw_j}{\sum_{j=1}^{n} FIw_j} \tag{9.7}$$

Step 6: Computing the relative weights of HOWs: The final step (Section [f]) calculates the priority weights for the "HOWs" In classical QFD, for m "WHATs" and n "HOWs," the overall importance weight (w_j) for the *j-th* "HOW" is computed as the sum of its weighted relationships:

$$w_j = \sum_{i=1}^{m} R_{ij} C_i, \tag{9.8}$$

where, for $i = 1....m$ and, $j = 1....n$ R_{ij} denotes the relationship rating between the *i-th* "WHAT" and *j-th* "HOW," and and C_i represents the weight of *i-th* factor. The normalized weight of each "How" variable $\widetilde{w}_j$, also known as relative weight, is then derived as (Chadly et al., 2024):

$$\widetilde{w}_j = \frac{w_j}{\sum_{j=1}^{n} w_j} \tag{9.9}$$

Although these formulations remain generic to any QFD-based analysis (Wudhikarn & Pongpatcharatorntep, 2022), the integration with MCDM methods enhances this step considerably. Instead of relying solely on formulaic computations, advanced prioritization techniques (e.g., TOPSIS, VIKOR) can be employed, depending on the research problem. This provides a more rigorous and context-sensitive prioritization of HOWs (Sumrit & Keeratibhubordee, 2025).

The CoCoSo method, introduced by Yazdani et al. (2019), is a compromise-based MCDM approach offering advantages such as stability, integrability, and efficiency. To overcome its limitations, Rasoanaivo et al. (2024) proposed the improved CoCoFiSo method, which demonstrates higher stability and accuracy across all scenarios. Given its reliability and superiority, CoCoFiSo is suggested to be applied in the present step of the QFD-MCDM approach. The implementation steps of the method are as follows:

Step 6.1: Constructing the decision matrix (*D*): Initially, a decision matrix consisting of mm alternatives and nn criteria is formed, as expressed in the following equation. This matrix serves as the foundation for all subsequent calculations.

$$\mathrm{D} = \begin{bmatrix} d_{11} & \cdots & d_{1n} \\ \vdots & \ddots & \vdots \\ d_{n1} & \cdots & d_{mn} \end{bmatrix}, \ \mathrm{i} = \{1,\ 2,\ \ldots,\ \mathrm{m}\},\ \mathrm{j} = \{1,\ 2,\ \ldots,\ \mathrm{n}\} \tag{9.10}$$

Step 6.2: Normalizing the decision matrix: Normalization of the decision matrix. In this step, the decision matrix is normalized. Similar to the TOPSIS method, Euclidean normalization is applied, which, unlike the original CoCoSo approach, does not differentiate between benefit and cost criteria.

$$\mathrm{r_{ij}} = \frac{x_{ij}}{\sqrt{\sum_{i=1}^{m} {x_{ij}}^2}} \tag{9.11}$$

Step 6.3: Calculating the additive and multiplicative aggregated values: At this stage, the additive aggregated values (S_i) and multiplicative aggregated values (P_i) for each alternative are computed using specific formulas, incorporating the weights of each criterion.

$$\mathrm{S_i} = \sum_{j=1}^{n} w_j\, r_{ij} = 1 \tag{9.12}$$

$$\mathrm{P_i} = \sum_{j=1}^{n} {r_{ij}}^{w_j} = 1 \tag{9.13}$$

Step 6.4: Determining the initial scores of alternatives: In this step, alternatives are evaluated using three different strategies. These strategies are implemented through specific formulas representing arithmetic mean calculations and alternative comparisons. Additionally, a compromise relationship between two different criteria is considered.

$$\mathrm{ki}_a = \frac{S_i + P_i}{\sum_{i=1}^{m} (S_i + P_i)} \tag{9.14}$$

$$\mathrm{ki_b} = \frac{S_i + P_i}{1 + \frac{S_i}{1+\ S_i} + \frac{P_i}{1+\ P_i}} \tag{9.15}$$

$$\mathrm{ki}_c = \frac{\lambda S_i + (1-\lambda)P_i}{\lambda \max_i S_i + (1-\lambda)\max_i P_i}, \quad \lambda \epsilon [0.\ 1] \tag{9.16}$$

Step 6.5: Calculating the final score and ranking alternatives: At this stage, the final score for each alternative is calculated, and the final ranking is determined accordingly. This ranking is based on the arithmetic mean of the three previous evaluation strategies, which determine the score of each alternative. The alternative with the highest score is considered the best (Yazdani et al., 2019).

$$k_i = (k_{ia}k_{ib}k_{ic})^{\frac{1}{3}} + \frac{1}{3}(k_{ia} + k_{ib} + k_{ic}) \tag{9.17}$$

9.4 Case study and results

This section elucidates the proposed BWM-DEMATEL-CoCoFiSo-QFD approach through a hypothetical case study designed for GS selection. The illustrative example employs two interlinked HoQs, the structure of which is depicted in Fig. 9.2. In this process, three decision makers (DMs) are engaged across all stages that require expert judgment and feedback.

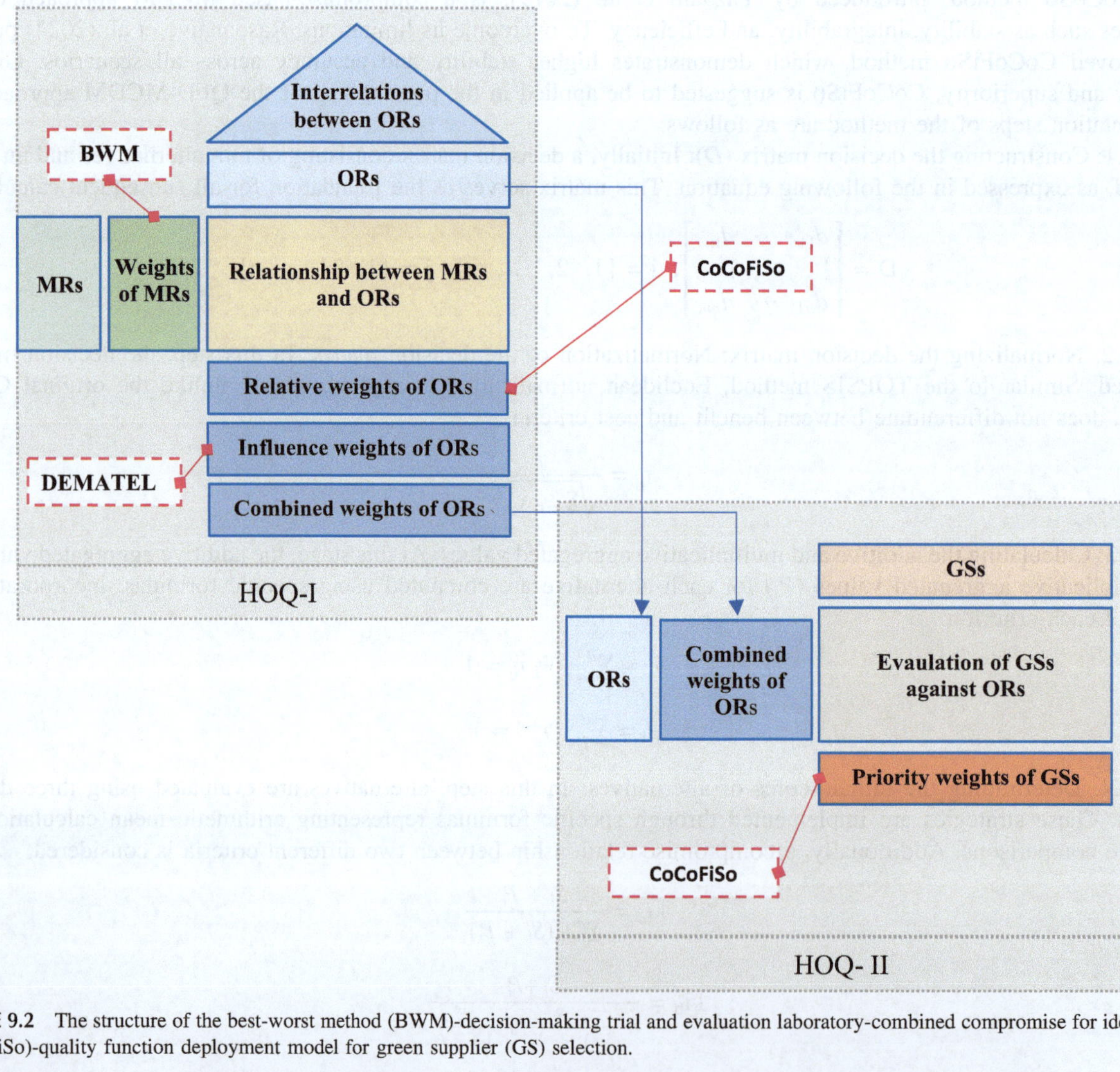

FIGURE 9.2 The structure of the best-worst method (BWM)-decision-making trial and evaluation laboratory-combined compromise for ideal solution (CoCoFiSo)-quality function deployment model for green supplier (GS) selection.

As illustrated in Fig. 9.2, the first HoQ (HoQ-I) translates the management requirements (MRs) into operational requirements (ORs), while the second HoQ (HoQ-II) evaluates the GS alternatives based on the ORs. In line with the procedure outlined in the previous section, the outcomes of applying the model are reported below.

Steps 1 and 2: The factors acting as the "whats" and the "hows" are listed in Table 9.3.

Step 3: The final weights for the MRs were derived by applying the BWM, utilizing the evaluative inputs from the three DMs presented in Table 9.4.

By applying steps 3.1 to 3.6 and using Eqs. 9.1–9.2, the weights of the whats in HoQ-I were obtained (Table 9.5). As an illustration, we present the procedure for calculating the values in this table. First, a linear model was formulated based on the response of DM1. In this model, according to Eq. 9.1, the ξ value and the weights of the MRs (w_j) are treated as unknowns, while the given data, a_{Bj} and a_{jw}, are provided in the first column of the BO and OW sections of Table 9.4,

TABLE 9.3 Factors defined in the proposed model.

Code	"WHATs" in HoQ-I	Code	"HOWs" in HoQ-I "WHATS" in HoQ-II	Code	"HOWs" in HoQ-II
MR1	Quality	**OR1**	Product reliability and quality assurance	**GS1**	Company A
MR2	Service delivery	**OR2**	Delivery and service performance	**GS2**	Company B
MR3	Cost	**OR3**	Cost efficiency	**GS3**	Company C
MR4	Environment friendly	**OR4**	Environmental sustainability	**GS4**	Company D
MR5	Social responsibility	**OR5**	Transparency and compliance		
		OR6	Occupational health and safety		

TABLE 9.4 Input data for best-worst method analysis of MRs.

Best-to-others	DM1	DM2	DM3	Others-to-worst	DM1	DM2	DM3
	MR3	**MR1**	**MR3**		**MR5**	**MR4**	**MR5**
MR1	2	1	2	**MR1**	4	4	4
MR2	3	3	3	**MR2**	2	2	2
MR3	1	2	1	**MR3**	5	3	5
MR4	4	4	3	**MR4**	3	1	2
MR5	5	4	5	**MR5**	1	1	1

TABLE 9.5 Results of the best-worst method for determining the MRs' weights.

MRs' weights	MR1	MR2	MR3	MR4	MR5	ξ^*	CR
DM1	0.2426	0.1618	0.4081	0.1213	0.0662	0.0772	0.0336
DM2	0.4122	0.1527	0.2290	0.0916	0.1145	0.0458	0.0281
DM3	0.2267	0.1512	0.4012	0.1512	0.0698	0.0523	0.0228
Final	0.2939	0.1552	0.3461	0.1214	0.0835		

respectively. In this case, MR3 was identified as the best factor and MR5 as the worst. The constructed model is expressed as follows:

$$\min \xi$$

s.t.

$$|w_3/w_1 - 2| \leq \xi$$

$$|w_3/w_2 - 3| \leq \xi$$

$$|w_3/w_4 - 4| \leq \xi$$

$$|w_3/w_5 - 5| \leq \xi$$

$$|w_1/w_5 - 4| \leq \xi$$

$$|w_2/w_5 - 2| \leq \xi$$

$$|w_3/w_5 - 5| \leq \xi$$

$$|w_4/w_5 - 3| \leq \xi$$

$$w_1 + w_2 + w_3 + w_4 + w_5 = 1$$

$$w_1,\ w_2,\ w_3,\ w_4,\ w_5 \geq 0$$

By solving this model in excel, the weight vector was obtained as $[w_1, w_2, w_3, w_4, w_5] = [0.242, 0.1618, 0.4081, 0.1213, 0.0662]$ with $\xi^* = 0.0772$, as reported in the first row of Table 9.5. To assess the CR in this model, Eq. 9.2 was applied, and the corresponding result is also presented in the first row of Table 9.5. Since the relative importance of the best factor compared to the worst was rated as 5 by DM1 (Table 9.4), the CI was determined as 2.30 based on Table 9.2. Consequently, the CR value was determined as follows:

$$CR = \frac{0.0772}{2.30} = 0.0336$$

As evidenced by the results, the CRs for all three solved models are approximately zero, indicating a high degree of consistency in the expert evaluations. The final weight for each MR was subsequently calculated by taking the arithmetic mean of the individual results derived from each DM.

Step 4: To assess the ORs as decision alternatives against the weighted MRs, a relationship matrix was constructed. This matrix utilized a five-point Likert scale to denote the strength of correlations, ranging from very weak to very strong. The interrelationships within the HoQ-I, as captured by (9.10), are presented in Table 9.6. This table provides the aggregated feedback from the three DMs, with each cell containing a triple evaluation element corresponding to the inputs from DM1, DM2, and DM3.

Step 5: The interrelationships among the ORs were evaluated using the DEMATEL method, following the established procedure (Steps 5.1 to 5.5). Table 9.7 presents the initial direct-relation matrices (Eq. 9.3) provided by the DMs, listing

TABLE 9.6 Relationship matrix in house of quality -I based on the decision makers' feedback.

"'How" "What"	OR1	OR2	OR3	OR4	OR5	OR6
MR1	5, 5, 5	4, 3, 4	4, 3, 4	0, 2, 3	0, 0, 2	1, 0, 0
MR2	1, 0, 1	5, 5, 5	1, 0, 0	0, 0, 0	3, 4, 2	0, 0, 0
MR3	1, 2, 1	2, 2, 3	5, 5, 5	0, 1, 0	0, 0, 0	0, 0, 0
MR4	0, 0, 2	0, 0, 0	2, 1, 0	5, 5, 5	4, 3, 2	3, 1, 0
MR5	2, 2, 1	0, 2, 0	0, 0, 1	5, 5, 3	5, 5, 3	4, 4, 5

TABLE 9.7 Interrelationship matrix among ORs as decision-making trial and evaluation laboratory input by decision makers.

X	OR1		OR2		OR3		OR4		OR5		OR6	
OR1	0, 0, 0	0	2, 1, 3	2	3, 3, 4	3.333	3, 1, 2	2	2, 3, 1	2	1, 0, 0	0.333
OR2	3, 2, 4	3	0, 0, 0	0	4, 2, 4	3.333	2, 0, 0	0.667	1, 0, 1	0.667	0, 1, 0	0.333
OR3	3, 3, 2	2.667	2, 1, 2	1.667	0, 0, 0	0	0, 0, 0	0	0, 0, 0	0	0, 2, 0	0.667
OR4	2, 4, 3	3	0, 0, 0	0	3, 2, 2	2.333	0, 0, 0	0	4, 3, 4	3.667	2, 0, 0	0.667
OR5	4, 3, 2	3	2, 2, 4	2.667	0, 0, 0	0	0, 2, 1	1	0, 0, 0	0	3, 4, 4	3.667
OR6	2, 1, 3	2	3, 2, 4	3	0, 1, 0	0.333	1, 2, 1	1.333	4, 4, 4	4	0, 0, 0	0

TABLE 9.8 Normalized matrix in decision-making trial and evaluation laboratory analysis.

N	OR1	OR2	OR3	OR4	OR5	OR6
OR1	0.0000	0.1463	0.2439	0.1463	0.1463	0.0244
OR2	0.2195	0.0000	0.2439	0.0488	0.0488	0.0244
OR3	0.1951	0.1220	0.0000	0.0000	0.0000	0.0488
OR4	0.2195	0.0000	0.1707	0.0000	0.2683	0.0488
OR5	0.2195	0.1951	0.0000	0.0732	0.0000	0.2683
OR6	0.1463	0.2195	0.0244	0.0976	0.2927	0.0000

the three values assigned to each relation. The arithmetic mean of those three values is shown in an adjacent column (second column under each factor); these mean values were used as the input for the subsequent analysis.

Subsequently, the normalized direct-relation matrix N was computed using Eq. 9.4 and is shown in Table 9.8. An example of how the values in Table 9.8 are derived from Table 9.7 is provided below. The scaling factor is determined as:

$$k = \min\left(\frac{1}{13.6667}, \frac{1}{10.6667}\right) = 0.07317$$

Accordingly, the entries in the first row of Table 9.8 are computed as follows:

$$0.07317 \times [0,\ 2,\ 3.333,\ 2,\ 2,\ 0.333] = [0,\ 0.1463,\ 0.2439,\ 0.1463,\ 0.1463,\ 0.0244]$$

The total relation matrix T was constructed employing Eq. 9.5, yielding the "prominence" and "relation" values. Specifically, the matrix $(I-N)$ was inverted in excel using the MINVERSE function and subsequently multiplied by the N matrix using the MMULT function. As an example, the prominence and relation values for OR1 (first row in Table 9.9) were calculated as follows:

$$R = 0.3127 + 0.3454 + 0.4507 + 0.2483 + 0.3227 + 0.1611 = 1.8410$$

$$D = 0.3127 + 0.4337 + 0.3337 + 0.5163 + 0.5462 + 0.5057 = 2.6484$$

$$R + D = 4.4893$$

$$R - D = -0.8074$$

These derived measures subsequently served as the basis for calculating the final influence-importance weights (FIW_j) via Eqs. 9.6–9.7. The comprehensive results of this analysis are compiled in Table 9.9. To clarify how the values in this table were obtained, the FIW_1 value in the first row was calculated using (9.6) as follows:

$FIw_1 = \sqrt{(4.4893)^2 + (-0.8074)^2} = 4.5613$

In a similar manner, the remaining values were computed, and their sum was used to evaluate FIw_1. Accordingly, the normalized influence-importance value (FIW_j) was derived as follows:

$$FIW_1 = \frac{4.5613}{4.5613 + 3.4685 + 3.1979 + 3.2092 + 4.0910 + 3.5828} = 0.2063$$

Step 6: The CoCoFiSo method was utilized to determine the relative importance of the ORs, which function as the "hows" within HoQ-I. Specifically, the relationship matrix of HoQ-I (Table 9.6), aggregated via the arithmetic mean of the DMs' judgments, was normalized via (9.11). To illustrate, the first element of the matrix in Table 9.10 corresponds to the interaction between MR1 and MR2, which the three DMs rated identically as (5, 5, 5). The aggregated score for this relation in the decision matrix is calculated as: $\frac{5+5+5}{3} = 5$

Analogously, the remaining entries in the first column were processed, yielding the normalized value through (9.11):

$$5/(5^2 + 0.6667^2 + 1.3333^2 + 0.6667^2 + 1.6667^2) = 0.9062$$

The resulting normalized matrix is indicated in Table 9.10.

Following this, the required CoCoFiSo computations were performed by incorporating the criterion weights from Table 9.5 along with (9.12)–18. The resulting values, reflecting the relative importance of the ORs, are summarized in Table 9.11. The calculation procedure is exemplified using the first row of this table. According to (9.12), the SUMPRODUCT function in excel was applied, combining the two necessary vectors: the MRs' weights and the first column of Table 9.10. The corresponding manual computation is:

$$S1 = 0.2939 \times 0.9062 + 0.1552 \times 0.1208 + 0.3461 \times 0.2416 + 0.1214 \times 0.1208 + 0.0835 \times 0.3021 = 0.4086$$

TABLE 9.9 Total relation matrix and influence-importance of ORs.

T	OR1	OR2	OR3	OR4	OR5	OR6	*R+D*	*R-D*	FIW_j
OR1	0.3127	0.3454	0.4507	0.2483	0.3227	0.1611	4.4893	-0.8074	0.2063
OR2	0.4337	0.1792	0.4214	0.1469	0.1954	0.1195	3.4396	-0.4473	0.1569
OR3	0.3337	0.2343	0.1545	0.0786	0.1118	0.1040	3.0365	-1.0030	0.1446
OR4	0.5163	0.2601	0.3898	0.1429	0.4583	0.2167	3.0853	0.8828	0.1451
OR5	0.5462	0.4518	0.2930	0.2340	0.2799	0.3934	4.0786	0.3181	0.1850
OR6	0.5057	0.4727	0.3104	0.2505	0.5122	0.1886	3.4234	1.0568	0.1620

TABLE 9.10 The normalized relationship matrix of house of quality-I.

"Hows" "Whats"	OR1	OR2	OR3	OR4	OR5	OR6
MR1	0.9062	0.5507	0.5822	0.2440	0.1093	0.0733
MR2	0.1208	0.7509	0.0529	0.0000	0.4917	0.0000
MR3	0.2416	0.3504	0.7939	0.0488	0.0000	0.0000
MR4	0.1208	0.0000	0.1588	0.7319	0.4917	0.2933
MR5	0.3021	0.1001	0.0529	0.6343	0.7103	0.9532

TABLE 9.11 Relative importance of ORs using combined compromise for ideal solution method.

"Hows'"in house of quality (HoQ)-I	*S*	*P*	k_a	k_b	k_c	*k*	C_j
OR1	0.4086	3.9822	0.2019	2.1015	0.9823	1.8422	0.1979
OR2	0.4080	3.3166	0.1713	1.8097	0.8332	1.5749	0.1692
OR3	0.4777	3.9923	0.2056	2.1055	1.0000	1.8601	0.1999
OR4	0.2304	2.9378	0.1457	1.6387	0.7088	1.3842	0.1487
OR5	0.2274	3.3067	0.1625	1.8095	0.7906	1.5358	0.1650
OR6	0.1367	2.3217	0.1131	1.3514	0.5500	1.1095	0.1192

TABLE 9.12 The combined weights of ORs.

"Hows" in house of quality (HoQ)-I "Whats" in HoQ-II	C_j	FIW_j	*Combined Weight*
OR1	0.1979	0.2063	0.2021
OR2	0.1692	0.1569	0.1630
OR3	0.1999	0.1446	0.1723
OR4	0.1487	0.1451	0.1469
OR5	0.1650	0.1850	0.1750
OR6	0.1192	0.1620	0.1406

The remaining values in this row were calculated similarly.

$$P_I = 0.2939^{0.9062} + 0.1552^{0.1208} + 0.3461^{0.2416} + 0.1214^{0.1208} + 0.0835^{0.3021} = 3.9822$$

$$S_1 + P_1 = 4.3907$$

$$k1_a = \frac{4.3907}{4.3907 + 3.7246 + 4.4700 + 3.1682 + 3.5341 + 2.4584} = 0.2019$$

$$k1_b = \frac{4.3907}{1 + \frac{0.4086}{1+0.4086} + \frac{3.9822}{1+3.9822}} = 2.1015$$

The λ parameter in (9.16) was assigned a value of 0.5 based on the DMs' consensus.

$$k1_c = \frac{0.5 \times \quad 0.4086 + (1 - 0.5) \times 3.9822}{0.5 \times \max(0.4086,\ 0.4080,\ 0.4777,\ 0.2304,\ 0.2274,\ 0.1367) + (1 - 0.5) \times \max(3.9822,\ 3.3166,\ 3.9923,\ 2.9378,\ 3.3067,\ 2.3217)} = 0.9823$$

$$k_1 = (0.20192.10150.9823)^{(1/3)} + (0.2019 + 2.1015 + 0.9823)/3 = 1.8422$$

$$C_1 = \frac{4.3907}{1.8422 + 1.5749 + 1.8601 + 1.3842 + 1.5358 + 1.1095} = 0.1979$$

To determine the combined weights of the ORs, the arithmetic mean was calculated between the normalized relative weight (C_j) obtained from CoCoFiSo and the influence-importance value (FIW_j) derived from DEMATEL for each OR. The resulting values, presented in Table 9.12, serve as the weights for the new "WHATs" in HoQ-II. For instance, the combined weight of OR1 was calculated as follows:

$$Combined\ Weight = \frac{0.1979 + 0.2063}{2} = 0.2021$$

Following the procedure applied for HoQ-I, the analysis for HoQ-II was carried out. In this step, the decision matrices provided by the DMs (Table 9.13) were collected, where the GSs as alternatives were evaluated against the ORs serving as decision criteria.

Next, using the combined weights of ORs and applying (9.11)–18, the priority weights of the green suppliersgreen suppliers (GSs) were determined, as summarized in Table 9.14. Although the procedure to determine the values in this table mirrors that used for Table 9.11, the numerical calculations for the first row are presented here for clarity.

$$S_1 = 20.2021 + 20.1630 + 40.1723 + 10.1469 + 1.33330.1750 + 0.33330.1406 = 1.8465$$

$$P_1 = 2^{0.2021} + 2^{0.1630} + 4^{0.1723} + 1^{0.1469} + 1.3333^{0.1750} + 0.3333^{0.1406} = 6.4482$$

$$S_1 + P_1 = 8.2947$$

$$k1_a = \frac{8.2947}{8.2947 + 8.8062 + 7.5286 + 8.5359} = 0.2501$$

$$k1_b = \frac{8.2947}{1 + \frac{1.8465}{1+1.8465} + \frac{6.4482}{1+6.4482}} = 3.2989$$

The λ parameter in (9.16) was designated as 0.5 based on the DMs' agreement.

$$k1_c = \frac{0.5 \times 1.8465 + (1 - 0.5) \times 6.4482}{0.5 \times \max(1.8465,\ 2.0736,\ 1.5058,\ 1.9673) + (1 - 0.5) \times \max(6.4482,\ 6.7326,\ 6.0229,\ 6.5686)}$$
$$= 0.9419$$

$$k_1 = (0.25013.29890.9419)^{(1/3)} + (0.2501 + 3.2989 + 0.9419)/3 = 2.4163$$

TABLE 9.13 Relationship matrix in house of quality-II based on the decision makers' feedback.

HOW WHAT	GS1		GS2		GS3		GS4	
OR1	2, 1, 3	2	4, 2, 2	2.667	3, 2, 4	3	4, 2, 2	2.6667
OR2	1, 3, 2	2	3, 2, 3	2.667	0, 0, 1	0.3333	0, 0, 2	0.6667
OR3	5, 4, 3	4	2, 0, 3	1.667	5, 3, 2	3.3333	3, 1, 2	2.0000
OR4	0, 1, 2	1	4, 2, 2	2.667	1, 0, 0	0.3333	0, 1, 1	0.6667
OR5	2, 1, 1	1.3333	2, 2, 0	1.333	1, 1, 1	1	3, 2, 2	2.3333
OR6	1, 0, 0	0.3333	2, 1, 1	1.333	0, 0, 1	0.3333	3, 3, 4	3.3333

TABLE 9.14 The priority weights of GSs using combined compromise for ideal solution method.

T	*S*	*P*	k_a	k_b	k_c	*k*	*Rank*
GS1	1.8465	6.4482	0.2501	3.2989	0.9419	2.4163	3
GS2	2.0736	6.7326	0.2655	3.4597	1.0000	2.5472	1
GS3	1.5058	6.0229	0.2270	3.0623	0.8549	2.2221	4
GS4	1.9673	6.5686	0.2574	3.3727	0.9693	2.4772	2

Therefore employing the integrated BWM-DEMATEL-CoCoFiSo-QFD framework, the prioritization of GSs was established, incorporating both marketing and operational perspectives throughout the analytical process. These findings provide valuable insights for scholars and practitioners, demonstrating the applicability of this comprehensive methodology for addressing complex real-world decision-making challenges.

9.5 Conclusion

The collective body of research demonstrates a clear and sophisticated evolution in the application of QFD, moving beyond its traditional role to function as the central, integrative engine within complex MCDM frameworks. These hybrid models consistently leverage QFD's cascading HoQ structure to systematically translate high-level strategic objectives, customer needs, or risk factors into prioritized actionable initiatives, technical features, or technology solutions. A critical advancement across these studies is the strategic pairing of QFD with a diverse suite of MCDM techniques,such as ANP, DEMATEL, SWARA, AHP, BWM, and VIKOR,and their fuzzy set extensions, which are specifically employed to accurately weight criteria and capture intricate interdependencies under conditions of hybrid uncertainty and subjective judgment. This powerful integration provides a robust, analytically coherent, and mathematically rigorous decision-making framework capable of navigating the complexities inherent in modern strategic planning across a vast spectrum of disciplines, from supply chain management and energy policy to product development and cultural heritage preservation.

The illustrative case study on GS selection further validated the applicability of the proposed BWM–DEMATEL–CoCoFiSo–QFD framework. By cascading two interlinked Houses of Quality, the model systematically translated market and operational requirements into supplier evaluation criteria and ultimately prioritized alternative suppliers. The results highlighted the framework's capability to balance economic, environmental, and social dimensions while handling subjective judgments and interdependencies among factors. This practical demonstration not only confirmed the robustness of the integrated methodology but also emphasized its potential for addressing complex decision-making problems in real-world contexts where sustainability and stakeholder considerations are critical.

Building on the insights from recent contributions, future research should focus on advancing methodological rigor in QFD–MCDM integrations. One promising avenue is the adoption of advanced MCDM techniques rather than relying on conventional weighted averaging, as this would yield more precise and reliable prioritizations of quality attributes relative to customer and stakeholder expectations (Sumrit & Keeratibhubordee, 2025). Another important direction involves leveraging more sophisticated fuzzy set frameworks, such as spherical or circular fuzzy sets (Puzovic et al., 2025). These advanced fuzzy environments enable the HoQ to incorporate linguistic expressions and explicitly account for hesitation in customer or expert evaluations, thereby reflecting the inherent imprecision of human judgments. By embedding linguistic assessments into fuzzy set-based numerical analyses, future studies can strengthen the descriptive and analytical capacity of QFD, expanding its applicability across complex and uncertainty-prone contexts (Zhang & Zhang, 2024). Besides, as noted in the illustrative example, considering the interactions among "Hows" when determining technical targets or the absolute weights of "Hows," following approaches suggested in prior research (He et al., 2021), can further enrich the methodology by capturing interdependencies and improving the robustness of decision outcomes.

References

Chadly, A., Aldayyani, H. Y., Hamasha, M. M., Amer, S., Maalouf, M., & Mayyas, A. (2024). Selection of optimal strategy for managing decentralized solar PV systems considering uncertain weather conditions. *Scientific Reports, 14*(1). https://doi.org/10.1038/s41598-024-62891-6 Article 12269.

Chan, L.-K., & Wu, M.-L. (2002). Quality function deployment: A literature review. *European journal of operational research, 143*(3), 463–497. https://doi.org/10.1016/S0377-2217(02)00178-9.

Fazeli, H. R., & Peng, Q. (2023). Integrated approaches of BWM-QFD and FUCOM-QFD for improving weighting solution of design matrix. *Journal Of Intelligent Manufacturing, 34*(3), 1003–1020. https://doi.org/10.1007/s10845-021-01832-w.

García-León, R. A., Jaimes-Gonzalez, W., Becerra, L. D., Flórez-Solano, E., Cabellos-Martínez, M., & Meneses-Torres, D. (2021). Application of the QFD method to the design of a cocoa pulping machine. *International Journal of System Assurance Engineering and Management, 12*(6), 1199–1220. https://doi.org/10.1007/s13198-021-01416-0.

Haiyun, C., Zhixiong, H., Yüksel, S., & Dinçer, H. (2021). Analysis of the innovation strategies for green supply chain management in the energy industry using the QFD-based hybrid interval valued intuitionistic fuzzy decision approach. *Renewable and Sustainable Energy Reviews, 143*, 110844. https://doi.org/10.1016/j.rser.2021.110844.

He, L., Wu, Z., Xiang, W., Goh, M., Xu, Z., Song, W., Ming, X., & Wu, X. (2021). A novel Kano-QFD-DEMATEL approach to optimise the risk resilience solution for sustainable supply chain. *International Journal Of Production Research, 59*(6), 1714–1735. https://doi.org/10.1080/00207543.2020.1724343.

Hsu, C. H., He, X., Zhang, T. Y., Chang, A. Y., Liu, W. L., & Lin, Z. Q. (2022). Enhancing supply chain agility with industry 4.0 enablers to mitigate ripple effects based on integrated QFD-MCDM: An empirical study of new energy materials manufacturers. *Mathematics, 10*(10). https://doi.org/10.3390/math10101635 Article 1635.

Li, J. J., Peng, X. B., Li, C., Luo, Q., Peng, S. A., Tang, H. C., & Tang, R. M. (2023). Renovation of traditional residential buildings in Lijiang based on AHP-QFD methodology: A case study of the Wenzhi village. *Buildings, 13*(8). https://doi.org/10.3390/buildings13082055 Article 2055.

Li, M., Jin, L., & Wang, J. (2014). A new MCDM method combining QFD with TOPSIS for knowledge management system selection from the user's perspective in intuitionistic fuzzy environment. *Applied Soft Computing, 21*, 28–37. https://doi.org/10.1016/j.asoc.2014.03.008.

Li, W., Yüksel, S., & Dinçer, H. (2022). Understanding the financial innovation priorities for renewable energy investors via QFD-based picture fuzzy and rough numbers. *Financial Innovation, 8*(1). https://doi.org/10.1186/s40854-022-00372-3 Article 67.

Li, X. L., Wang, J., & Tang, N. (2025). A multi-criteria decision-making framework for Tibetan furniture design driven by the needs of users: Integration and evaluation via TFAHP-QFD-VIKOR. *Bioresources, 20*(4), 8566–8590. https://doi.org/10.15376/biores.20.4.8566-8590.

Lu, S. F., Zhou, J. Z., & Ren, J. Z. (2023). Alleviating energy poverty through renewable energy technology: An investigation using a best-worst method-based quality function deployment approach with interval-valued intuitionistic fuzzy numbers. *International Journal Of Energy Research, 2023*. https://doi.org/10.1155/2023/8358799 Article 8358799.

Moktadir, M. A., & Ren, J. (2024). Global semiconductor supply chain resilience challenges and mitigation strategies: A novel integrated decomposed fuzzy set Delphi, WINGS and QFD model. *International Journal Of Production Economics, 273*, 109280. https://doi.org/10.1016/j.ijpe.2024.109280.

Puzovic, S., Vasovic, J. V., Tadic, D., & Milanovic, D. D. (2025). An integrated new product development evaluation model in an interval type-2 fuzzy environment for PLM strategy setting. *Applied Sciences-Basel, 15*(9). https://doi.org/10.3390/app15095025 Article 5025.

Rasoanaivo, R. G., Yazdani, M., Zaraté, P., & Fateh, A. (2024). Combined compromise for ideal solution (CoCoFISo): A multi-criteria decision-making based on the CoCoSo method algorithm. *Expert Systems With Applications, 251*, 124079. https://doi.org/10.1016/j.eswa.2024.124079.

Rezaei, J. (2015). Best-worst multi-criteria decision-making method. *Omega, 53*, 49–57. https://doi.org/10.1016/j.omega.2014.11.009.

Shahin, V., Alimohammadlou, M., & Abbasi, A. (2024). Identifying and prioritizing the barriers to green innovation in SMEs and the strategies to counteract the barriers: An interval-valued intuitionistic fuzzy approach. *Technological Forecasting And Social Change, 204*, 123408. https://doi.org/10.1016/j.techfore.2024.123408.

Shahin, V., Pamucar, D., & Alimohammadlou, M. (2025). Developing a hybrid circular intuitionistic fuzzy framework to assess tourism 5.0 challenges. *Applied Soft Computing*113769. https://doi.org/10.1016/j.asoc.2025.113769.

Sumrit, D., & Keeratibhubordee, J. (2025). An integrated SWARA-QFD under Fermatean fuzzy set approach to assess proactive risk mitigation strategies in recycling supply chain: Case study of plastic recycling industry. *Journal Of Engineering Research, 13*(2), 492–510. https://doi.org/10.1016/j.jer.2023.11.007.

Tavana, M., Yazdani, M., & Di Caprio, D. (2017). An application of an integrated ANP–QFD framework for sustainable supplier selection. *International Journal of Logistics Research and Applications, 20*(3), 254–275. https://doi.org/10.1080/13675567.2016.1219702.

Wu, S.-M., Liu, H.-C., & Wang, L.-E. (2017). Hesitant fuzzy integrated MCDM approach for quality function deployment: A case study in electric vehicle. *International Journal Of Production Research, 55*(15), 4436–4449. https://doi.org/10.1080/00207543.2016.1259670.

Wudhikarn, R., & Pongpatcharatorntep, D. (2022). An improved intellectual capital management method for selecting and prioritizing intangible-related aspects: A case study of small enterprise in Thailand. *Mathematics, 10*(4). https://doi.org/10.3390/math10040626.

Yazdani, M., Chatterjee, P., Zavadskas, E. K., & Zolfani, S. H. (2017). Integrated QFD-MCDM framework for green supplier selection. *Journal Of Cleaner Production, 142*, 3728–3740. https://doi.org/10.1016/j.jclepro.2016.10.095.

Yazdani, M., Hashemkhani Zolfani, S., & Zavadskas, E. K. (2016). New integration of MCDM methods and QFD in the selection of green suppliers. *Journal of Business Economics and Management, 17*(6), 1097–1113. https://doi.org/10.3846/16111699.2016.1165282.

Yazdani, M., Zarate, P., Kazimieras Zavadskas, E., & Turskis, Z. (2019). A combined compromise solution (CoCoSo) method for multi-criteria decision-making problems. *Management decision, 57*(9), 2501–2519. https://doi.org/10.1108/MD-05-2017-0458.

Zhang, Q., & Zhang, H. J. (2024). Assessing agri-food waste valorization challenges and solutions considering smart technologies: An integrated fermatean fuzzy multi-criteria decision-making approach. *Sustainability, 16*(14). https://doi.org/10.3390/su16146169 Article 6169.

Chapter 10

SMART: Simple multi-attribute rating technique for multi-attribute decision-making

Babek Erdebilli and Parmida Bahreini
Department of Industrial Engineering, Ankara Yıldırım Beyazıt University, Ankara, Turkey

10.1 Introduction

In the field of decision sciences, multicriteria decision-making (MCDM) is typically divided into two main categories: multi-attribute decision-making (MADM) and multiobjective decision-making (MODM). The primary distinction between them lies in the nature and structure of the alternatives (Soltanifar et al., 2023; Triantaphyllou et al., 1998). MADM addresses problems where a finite and predefined set of alternatives exists, each evaluated based on a series of often conflicting criteria or attributes. The task is to select, rank, or classify these alternatives based on decision-maker preferences and performance data (Feng et al., 2022). In contrast, MODM is applied when alternatives are not explicitly listed but instead need to be generated by optimizing several objectives simultaneously. These objectives are generally modeled using continuous functions, making the solution space theoretically infinite. MODM typically involves finding a set of optimal solutions (Pareto front) from which a final choice may be made based on trade-offs (Taherdoost & Madanchian, 2023). Real-world decision-making rarely occurs in a perfectly defined or deterministic environment. In many cases, the objectives, criteria, and constraints are vague, imprecise, or subjectively interpreted. To address this ambiguity, fuzzy set theory, introduced by Zadeh (1965), provides a flexible mathematical framework for modeling such complexity. Unlike traditional Boolean logic, which enforces binary classifications, fuzzy logic allows partial membership in sets, enabling more nuanced reasoning. This makes it well-suited to problems involving linguistic variables, human judgment, or incomplete data. Among the branches of MCDM, MADM is widely used in operational and strategic decision-making. It involves assessing alternatives characterized by multiple measurable attributes and integrating this information along with the decision-maker's judgments to arrive at a final evaluation. Solving a MADM problem typically includes processes of scoring, weighting, ranking, and selection, often using structured techniques that combine data from a decision matrix with subjective input from stakeholders.

Problems within the scope of MADM typically involve several key components: one or more objectives to be achieved, an individual or group of decision-makers, a collection of evaluation criteria, a finite set of decision alternatives, a number of unknown or decision variables, and the comparative results derived from assessing pairs of alternatives (Martino Neto et al., 2023). Compatibility and correlation of MADM: a case of industrial relocation. At the core of this framework lies the decision matrix, which organizes information in a tabular format, where rows represent the alternatives and columns denote the evaluation attributes. This matrix serves as the foundation for analyzing and comparing decision options based on their performance across multiple criteria (Zavadskas et al., 2014). Beyond its theoretical foundations, the multi-attribute rating technique (SMART) method has proven valuable across a wide range of real-world decision contexts. For example, Akmaludin et al. (2023) apply SMART (together with analytical hierarchy process [AHP] and multi-attribute utility theory [MAUT]) to selecting employee promotions, demonstrating how consistent intervals and utility conversion can yield the same ranking outcomes under different methods. Hybrid data envelopment analysis (DEA)-SMART approaches have also been developed to address Industry 4.0 supply chains, improving supplier evaluation in digital manufacturing environments (Bahreini & Erdebilli, 2024). Broader reviews confirm that SMART and similar multi-criteria decision analysis (MCDA) techniques are increasingly used in healthcare prioritization, renewable energy planning, transportation systems, and environmental management (Więckowski et al., 2023; Taherdoost &

Encyclopedia of Multi-Attribute Decision-Making (MADM). DOI: https://doi.org/10.1016/B978-0-443-33275-3.00039-7

Mohebi, 2024). These examples highlight SMART's versatility and practical relevance for decision-makers confronting complex, multicriteria trade-offs.

The SMART, introduced by Edwards in 1971, is a well-established method within the family of MCDM techniques. As a compensatory approach, SMART was designed to offer a straightforward application of the core principles of MAUT (Ghadimi et al., 2019). It has gained popularity for its ease of use in evaluating alternatives based on several attributes or criteria. In the SMART framework, the decision-maker first determines the relevant evaluation criteria, then assigns weights to each criterion according to their perceived importance. Each alternative is scored against every criterion, and the final evaluation is obtained by calculating the weighted sum of these scores. This linear additive model ensures that each attribute's performance is multiplied by its assigned weight, and the sum of these products represents the overall value of the alternative (Ghobakhloo, 2020). The method relies heavily on the decision-maker's judgment in assigning these weights, which establishes the relative importance of the criteria (Hwang & Yoon, 1981).

This chapter demonstrates the effectiveness of the SMART approach through numerical examples, including applications in manufacturing industries and electronic marketplaces, where decision support systems rely on structured supplier evaluation.

10.2 Literature review

In recent years, the field of MCDM has seen renewed attention, especially in supplier selection, sustainable procurement, and decision support systems. The SMART method, although simpler than some alternatives, fits well in this growing literature because of its clarity, ease of implementation, and transparent weighting procedure. Mustajoki et al. (2005) introduced interval SMART and SWING weighting to accommodate imprecise judgments and recommended sensitivity analysis to examine ranking stability. Building on SMART's core principles, Chou and Chang (2008) developed a fuzzy SMART model for supplier selection, demonstrating how incorporating fuzzy sets can improve robustness when decision criteria involve uncertainty. Patel et al. (2017) presented a planning case using SMART to rank alternatives for a nuclear waste site selection problem, highlighting the method's transparency in environmental and spatial planning contexts. Similarly, Rahim (2017) analyzed SMART's procedural steps and compared its performance with alternative MCDM methods, reinforcing its suitability for quick, interpretable decisions in decision-support settings.

Taherdoost and Mohebi (2024) surveyed SMART's broad applications and critiqued its sensitivity to weight assignment and normalization choices, offering a balanced view of its strengths and weaknesses. Taylor and Love (2014) applied SMART to prioritize renewable energy investments, illustrating its value in energy planning where transparent decision support is essential for stakeholder buy-in. In human resources, Fahlepi (2020) employed SMART in a decision-support system to classify employee discipline issues, showing its flexibility beyond industrial contexts. Mahdiana and Kusumawardhany (2020) combined AHP with SMART to select the best lecturer candidate, evidencing SMART's compatibility with other methods in educational evaluations. In supply chain and Industry 4.0 contexts, Bahreini and Erdebilli (2024) combined DEA efficiency analysis with SMART scoring to evaluate suppliers, demonstrating how SMART can be hybridized to address modern manufacturing and digitalization challenges. Broader MCDM developments also influence SMART's ecosystem: Haseli et al. (2021) proposed the group best–worst method for supply chain decisions, and Haseli et al. (2024) introduced the spherical fuzzy best–worst method, reflecting a shift toward collaborative weighting and advanced uncertainty handling. Collectively, these studies confirm that SMART is a flexible and practical tool for multicriteria decision problems across diverse fields, ranging from supplier selection and renewable energy planning to healthcare, human resources, and educational evaluations. They also show that researchers have expanded SMART through fuzzy extensions, hybrid frameworks (e.g., DEA-SMART or AHP-SMART), and group decision-making adaptations to handle uncertainty and evolving industrial requirements. Despite these advances, relatively few works provide a step-by-step, transparent demonstration of SMART calculations, including normalization, weight assignment, and aggregation within a single cohesive example suitable for teaching or practitioner reference. Additionally, most studies focus on specialized or hybrid methods, leaving a need for clear, accessible demonstrations of the standard SMART technique and its real-world applicability in straightforward decision contexts. This chapter addresses that gap by presenting detailed numerical examples and discussing practical applications in procurement and educational technology.

10.3 Methodology

In this section, we show how the SMART can be used to support a real decision problem. The idea behind SMART is straightforward: we take several alternatives, look at them through a set of meaningful criteria, and then translate the decision-makers' judgments into numerical scores that can be compared. Each criterion reflects an aspect of performance that matters in practice, and decision-makers indicate how important these criteria are by assigning weights. Using these inputs, the method normalizes the performance values, converts them into utilities, and then combines them into an overall score for each alternative. In this way, SMART turns scattered opinions and qualitative impressions into a clear and transparent ranking. In the following, we present the procedure step by step, starting from defining the problem and building the decision matrix, and then moving through weighting, normalization, utility calculation, and final ranking.

***Step 1:* Decision Matrix** At the outset, a decision matrix is constructed, organizing the alternatives and their corresponding attributes based on information provided by the decision maker. This matrix, typically represented as $X = [r_{ij}]$, consists of m rows and n columns, where each row i corresponds to an alternative and each column j represents an attribute. The element r_{ij}, denotes the performance score or rating of the *i-th* alternative with respect to the *j-th* criterion.

At the outset, a decision matrix is established to systematically represent the alternatives and their associated evaluation criteria, based on input from the decision-maker. This matrix, denoted as:

$$X = \begin{bmatrix} r_{11} & r_{12} & \cdots & r_{1n} \\ \vdots & & \ddots & \vdots \\ r_{m1} & r_{m2} & \cdots & r_{mn} \end{bmatrix} \tag{10.1}$$

Note: In this application of the SMART method, a correlation coefficient matrix was not computed, as the three criteria, quality, delivery time, and price were deliberately selected for their distinct and independent nature. Preliminary consideration indicated no significant redundancy among these attributes; therefore, assessing intercriteria correlations was deemed unnecessary for this analysis.

Step 2: Weight assignment

In the second phase of the SMART methodology, each evaluation criterion is assigned a weight that reflects its relative importance in the decision-making process. The decision-maker allocates numerical values typically ranging from 1 to 100 to each criterion, with higher values indicating greater importance. This weighting process allows subjective preferences to be systematically incorporated into the analysis and ensures that more critical attributes exert a stronger influence on the final evaluation of alternatives.

Step 3: Normalization of weights

Once the weights have been assigned to all criteria, the next step involves normalizing these values to ensure proportional consistency across the decision model. This is achieved by dividing the weight of each individual criterion by the total sum of all weights. The normalization process ensures that the weights are converted into relative proportions that sum to one, allowing for fair and meaningful aggregation of performance scores.

The normalization formula is expressed as:

$$\textbf{Normalization} = \frac{w_j}{\sum w_j} \tag{10.2}$$

where:

- w_j represents the weight assigned to criterion j,
- $\sum w_j$ denotes the total weight across all criteria.

This step is essential for enabling the aggregation of scores in a way that accurately reflects the prioritized importance of each attribute in the final decision-making process.

Step 4: Calculating utility values

After normalization, the next stage involves determining the utility values for each alternative across all criteria. This step is crucial in translating the raw attribute data into a common performance scale that facilitates direct comparison among alternatives. The utility function standardizes the performance of each alternative relative to the observed range of the criterion.

The utility value for each attribute is computed using the following equation:

$$U_i(a_i) = \frac{C_{out} - C_{\min}}{C_{\max} - C_{\min}} \tag{10.3}$$

where:

- $U_i(a_i)$ denotes the utility value for the *i-th* alternative on a specific criterion,
- C_{out} represents the observed (raw) criterion value for the alternative,
- C_{min} and C_{max} indicate the minimum and maximum values of the criterion across all alternatives, respectively.

This linear scaling approach ensures that the performance of each alternative is mapped between 0 and 1, with higher values indicating more desirable performance. The use of utility values standardizes the raw data and enables the application of weighted aggregation techniques in the subsequent decision-making step.

Step 5: Aggregating utility scores to determine final rankings

In the final stage of the SMART method, the overall score for each alternative is calculated by integrating the normalized weights and the corresponding utility values obtained in the previous steps. This is achieved through a weighted summation process, where each utility score is multiplied by the relative importance (weight) of its corresponding criterion.

The final utility score for each alternative is computed using the following formula:

$$\mathbf{U(ai)} = \sum_{j=1}^{m} w_j .u_i(a_i), \quad \text{i} = 1,\ 2,\ \ldots,\ m \tag{10.4}$$

where:

- $U(a_i)$ denotes the aggregated utility score of the *i-th* alternative,
- w_j is the normalized weight assigned to the *j-th* criterion,
- $u_i(a_i)$ is the utility value of the *i-th* alternative with respect to *the j-th* criterion,
- m represents the total number of criteria considered in the decision-making process.

This step yields a single scalar value for each alternative, representing its overall desirability. The alternatives can then be ranked in descending order of their final scores, with the highest-scoring alternative identified as the most preferred option. The SMART technique thus enables a clear and systematic comparison of alternatives, grounded in both quantitative performance and subjective preference.

10.4 Numerical example 1

10.4.1 Supplier selection for a regional electronics distributor

This section illustrates the application of the SMART method for supplier selection in a regional electronics distribution company. Supplier selection is a critical challenge, particularly in dynamic markets where *quality, delivery reliability, and cost* are key factors influencing procurement decisions. In this example, we consider three evaluation criteria: quality, delivery time, and price, applied to four potential suppliers (alternatives). The decision-maker aims to prioritize suppliers by evaluating each alternative across these criteria. The SMART technique is employed to assign weights to the criteria based on their relative importance and to compute an overall score for each supplier. This approach facilitates a transparent and systematic ranking of suppliers, helping the company to identify the most suitable option for its procurement needs. A numerical example demonstrates how the SMART method processes the criteria weights and utility values to derive a final ranking, enabling a clear comparison of alternatives.

To ensure comparability among criteria measured in different units (for example, quality scored on a 1–10 scale, delivery time expressed in days, and price in USD), the raw scores from Table 10.1 are normalized before weighting. The normalization procedure described in Eq. (10.3) is applied to each criterion using the benefit-type form for quality and the cost-type form for delivery time and price. This transformation produces the normalized values reported in Tables 10.3, where higher values consistently represent better performance across all criteria. Converting the original scores into a common scale prevents any single criterion from dominating the decision because of its numerical range and ensures a fair, transparent comparison of supplier alternatives.

- Three criteria: **quality, delivery time, price**
- Four alternatives: **supplier A, supplier B, supplier C, supplier D**

Description of criteria:

C1: quality: Reflects the overall performance and reliability of the products supplied.

C2: delivery time: Captures how quickly and reliably each supplier can deliver orders.

C3: price: Represents the total purchasing cost associated with each supplier.
Step 1: Assign weights to criteria
Suppose the decision-maker assigns importance weights as follows:

- Quality: 70
- Delivery time: 20
- Price: 10

Step 2: Normalize weights
Table 10.2
Step 3: Calculate utility values for each criterion using Eq. (10.3)
For quality (higher is better)
Where $C_{max} = 9$, $C_{min} = 6$
Table 10.3

TABLE 10.1 Evaluation matrix of alternatives with respect to criteria.

Supplier	*Quality (score out of 10)*	*Delivery time (days)*	*Price (USD per unit)*
Supplier A	8	5	50
Supplier B	7	4	55
Supplier C	9	6	48
Supplier D	6	3	52

TABLE 10.2 Weight values of criteria derived from the SMART method.

$wQuality = \frac{70}{70+20+10} = \frac{70}{100}$	*0.70*
$wDelivery = \frac{20}{70+20+10} = \frac{20}{100}$	*0.20*
$wPrice = \frac{10}{70+20+10} = \frac{10}{100}$	*0.10*

TABLE 10.3 Normalized criteria weights.

Supplier	Quality	Utility U_i for quality
A	8	$\frac{8-6}{9-6} = \frac{2}{3} \approx 0.67$
B	7	$\frac{7-6}{9-6} = \frac{1}{3} \approx 0.33$
C	9	$\frac{9-6}{9-6} = \frac{3}{3} \approx 1.00$
D	6	$\frac{6-6}{9-6} = \frac{0}{3} \approx 0.00$

For delivery time (lower is better)
Where C_{max} ***= 6,*** C_{min} ***= 3***
Table 10.4
For price (lower is better)
Where C_{max} ***= 55,*** C_{min} ***= 48***
Table 10.5
Step 4: Calculate final scores for each supplier
The final ranking of suppliers is determined using the SMART aggregation formula described in (10.4), where each criterion's normalized utility value is multiplied by its corresponding weight and summed to obtain the overall score for each alternative.
Table 10.6
Step 5: Ranking of suppliers
Based on the final scores, the suppliers are ranked as follows:
Table 10.7

10.5 Numerical example 2

A university procurement committee consisting of three decision-makers must select the most suitable learning management system (LMS) platform for university-wide implementation. Given the rise of digital education, especially post-COVID, universities are under pressure to provide highly effective, scalable, and user-friendly platforms. The decision-makers come from:

1. The IT department
2. The academic senate
3. The finance office

TABLE 10.4 Normalized criteria weights.

Supplier	Delivery time	Utility U_i for delivery time
A	5	$\frac{1}{3} \approx 0.33$
B	4	$\frac{2}{3} \approx 0.67$
C	6	$\frac{0}{3} \approx 0.00$
D	3	$\frac{3}{3} \approx 1.00$

TABLE 10.5 Normalized criteria weights.

Supplier	Price	Utility U_i for price
A	50	$\frac{5}{7} \approx 0.71$
B	55	$\frac{0}{7} \approx 0.00$
C	48	$\frac{7}{7} \approx 1.00$
D	52	$\frac{3}{7} \approx 0.43$

TABLE 10.6 Utility values of each alternative per criterion.

Supplier	Calculation	Score $U(a_j)$
A	0.70. 0.67 + 0.20. 0.33 + 0.10. 0.71 = 0.469 + 0.066 + 0.071 = 0.606	0.606
B	0.70. 0.33 + 0.20. 0.67 + 0.10. 0.00 = 0.231 + 0.134 + 0 = 0.365	0.365
C	0.70. 1.00 + 0.20. 0.00 + 0.10 + 1.00 + 0.70 + 0 + 0.10 = 0.80	0.80
D	0.70. 0.00 + 0.20. 1.00 + 0.10. 0.43 = 0 + 0.20 + 0.043 = 0.243	0.243

TABLE 10.7 Final rankings of alternatives based on SMART scores.

1	Supplier C	0.80
2	Supplier A	0.61
3	Supplier B	0.37
4	Supplier D	0.24

They aim to evaluate seven LMS platforms using seven criteria, applying SMART to assign weights and make a final decision.

Step 1: Define alternatives and criteria

Alternatives (seven learning management system platforms):

In this step, there are seven alternatives, including EduFlow (A1), Moodle (A2), Canvas (A3), Blackboard (A4), TalentLMS (A5), D2L Brightspace (A6), and Sakai (A7). Mentioned alternatives should be evaluated based on the seven criteria, including cost (C1), user interface (UI) (C2), integration capability (C3), technical support (C4), mobile compatibility (C5), data security (C6), and customizability (C7).

Description of criteria:

C1- cost: This criterion covers the overall financial burden of adopting and operating the LMS.

C2- user interface: The UI criterion reflects how intuitive, clear, and user-friendly the platform is for students, instructors, and administrators.

C3- integration capability: Captures how easily the LMS can connect with existing university systems and tools, such as student information systems, authentication services, video-conferencing tools, and content repositories.

C4- technical support: Reflects the quality and responsiveness of vendor (or community) support. It includes availability of help desks, response times, documentation quality, training materials, and the presence of active user communities.

C5- mobile compatibility: Assesses how well the LMS performs on smartphones and tablets, across different operating systems.

C6- data security: Concerns the platform's ability to protect sensitive information, such as student records, grades, and learning materials.

C7- customizability: Captures how easily the LMS can be adapted to the institution's specific needs.

Step 2: Assign weights using simple multi-attribute rating technique

Each decision-maker assigns values from 1–100 to each criterion. The average of their scores is used for final weights.

Table 10.8

Total average score: **544.00**

Normalized weights using Eq. (10.2)

Table 10.9

TABLE 10.8 Decision makers' weights for each criterion.

Criteria	*D1 score*	*D2 score*	*D3 score*	*Average score*
Cost	90	80	85	85.00
UI	75	90	80	81.67
Integration	85	70	90	81.67
Support	80	60	70	70.00
Mobile	70	85	65	73.33
Security	95	95	90	93.33
Customizability	60	55	65	60.00

TABLE 10.9 Aggregated weights of criteria.

Criteria	*Average score*	*Normalized weight (w_j)*
Cost	85.00	0.1563
UI	81.67	0.1501
Integration	81.67	0.1501
Support	70.00	0.1287
Mobile	73.33	0.1348
Security	93.33	0.1715
Customizability	60.00	0.1103

Step 3: Prepare raw data for each learning management system platform (C1 to C7)

*Note: Some criteria (like cost) are **cost-type** (lower is better), while others are **benefit-type** (higher is better). We will normalize accordingly.*

Table 10.10

Step 4: Normalize raw data to utility values

For each criterion:

- If **benefit-type** (e.g., UI, Integration):
  $U_i(a_i) = \frac{C_{out} - C_{min}}{C_{max} - C_{min}}$
- If **cost-type** (Cost):
  $U_i(a_i) = \frac{C_{max} - C_{out}}{C_{max} - C_{min}}$

Table 10.11

Step 5: Calculate final simple multi-attribute rating technique ***score for each learning management system***

We will now multiply each utility value by its corresponding weight and sum across the criteria:

Table 10.12

Final calculation of simple multi-attribute rating technique scores

Table 10.13

Final* learning management system *ranking based on simple multi-attribute rating technique scores

Table 10.14

TABLE 10.10 Matrix of alternatives with respect to criteria.

LMS alternatives	*Cost (USD/ user/year) ↓*	*UI (rating/ 10) ↑*	*Integration (score/10) ↑*	*Support (24/7=10) ↑*	*Mobile (app rating/10) ↑*	*Security (score/10) ↑*	*Customizability (score/10) ↑*
A1: EduFlow	25	8.5	7	9	8.8	9	7.5
A2: Moodle	15	7.5	6	7	8.2	8	9
A3: Canvas	20	9	9	10	9.4	9.5	8.2
A4: Blackboard	30	8	8	6	7.9	8.5	6.8
A5: TalentLMS	18	7.8	7.5	8	8.5	8.7	7.1
A6: Brightspace	22	8.2	8	9	9.1	9.2	8.6
A7: Sakai	16	6.9	6	7	7.4	7.5	6.9

TABLE 10.11 Utility values of each alternative per criterion.

LMS	*C1: cost*	*C2: UI*	*C3: integration*	*C4: support*	*C5: mobile*	*C6: security*	*C7: customizability*
EduFlow	0.167	0.8	0.5	0.75	0.636	0.857	0.458
Moodle	0.833	0.4	0.0	0.25	0.364	0.357	1.000
Canvas	0.500	1.0	1.0	1.0	1.000	1.000	0.733
Blackboard	0.000	0.6	0.75	0.0	0.227	0.643	0.250
TalentLMS	0.600	0.52	0.75	0.5	0.545	0.786	0.392
Brightspace	0.267	0.68	0.75	0.75	0.818	0.929	0.867
Sakai	0.767	0.0	0.0	0.25	0.000	0.000	0.283

TABLE 10.12 Criteria's weight.

Criteria	*Weight*
C1: cost	0.10
C2: user interface	0.20
C3: integration ease	0.15
C4: support availability	0.15
C5: mobile compatibility	0.10
C6: security features	0.20
C7: customizability	0.10

TABLE 10.13 Final simple multi-attribute rating technique scores for each alternative.

LMS	*C1: cost*	*C2: UI*	*C3: integration*	*C4: support*	*C5: mobile*	*C6: security*	*C7: customizability*
EduFlow	0.017	0.160	0.075	0.112	0.064	0.171	0.046
Moodle	0.083	0.080	0.000	0.038	0.036	0.071	0.100
Canvas	0.050	0.200	0.150	0.150	0.100	0.200	0.073
Blackboard	0.000	0.120	0.113	0.000	0.023	0.129	0.025
TalentLMS	0.060	0.104	0.113	0.075	0.055	0.157	0.039
Brightspace	0.027	0.136	0.113	0.112	0.082	0.186	0.087
Sakai	0.077	0.000	0.000	0.038	0.000	0.000	0.028

TABLE 10.14 Ranking of alternatives based on simple multi-attribute rating technique scores.

LMS	*Total score*	*Ranking*
Canvas	0.923	1
Brightspace	0.743	2
EduFlow	0.645	3
TalentLMS	0.603	4
Blackboard	0.410	5
Moodle	0.408	6
Sakai	0.143	7

Based on the SMART analysis, **Canvas** emerges as the most suitable LMS among the seven alternatives, achieving the highest aggregate score of **0.923**. This indicates that Canvas performs exceptionally well across the most critical criteria, including functionality, user satisfaction, integration capabilities, and scalability. **Brightspace** and **EduFlow** follow with scores of **0.743** and **0.645**, respectively, reflecting strong performance in multiple dimensions, though not as uniformly high as Canvas. In contrast, **Sakai** ranks the lowest with a score of **0.143**, suggesting that it lacks competitiveness in several key areas, especially in integration and technical support. These results help decision-makers prioritize LMS solutions that align best with institutional or organizational needs, particularly in complex educational environments requiring high flexibility, robust features, and seamless user experience.

10.6 Conclusion

In this chapter, we explored the application of the Simple SMART) as a straightforward and efficient method for solving MCDM problems. By breaking down complex decisions into a series of weighted criteria and corresponding utility scores, SMART enables decision-makers to evaluate alternatives transparently and logically. Two numerical examples, one basic and one complex, demonstrated how the method could be employed in real-world contexts ranging from supplier evaluation to educational software selection. The results from both cases highlighted SMART's flexibility, ease of implementation, and suitability for decision problems where stakeholder judgment plays a central role. The ability to adapt the method for group decision-making and its compatibility with both quantitative and qualitative criteria underscore its practical value in industrial, educational, and service-oriented settings. The evidence from recent studies underscores that SMART is not only a theoretically sound technique but also an effective tool in practice. Its applications, ranging from pharmaceutical supply chain management and Industry 4.0 supplier evaluation to renewable energy site selection, healthcare resource allocation, and smart city planning, highlight its ability to guide complex decisions where multiple objectives must be balanced. Incorporating these practical insights strengthens the chapter's relevance for practitioners and researchers seeking robust decision-support frameworks. However, despite its strengths, SMART has limitations in dealing with highly uncertain environments or when preferences are fuzzy or imprecise. In such cases, extending the model using fuzzy logic or integrating with other techniques (such as AHP or technique for order preference by similarity to ideal solution [TOPSIS]) could improve robustness and credibility.

10.6.1 Future directions

Looking ahead, several directions can further strengthen the SMART methodology and its applications. One promising avenue is the development of fuzzy SMART extensions that use fuzzy sets to better capture ambiguity in expert evaluations and criterion weights. Another is the refinement of group decision-making procedures, with more systematic aggregation techniques for multistakeholder settings. In addition, hybrid frameworks that integrate SMART with advanced tools such as machine learning algorithms or optimization models can help automate and enhance decision support systems. Finally, there is considerable potential in tailoring SMART to specific sectors, for example, by designing domain-focused variants for healthcare resource allocation, smart city planning, or renewable energy project evaluation, so that the method can more directly respond to the unique needs and constraints of particular application areas. Overall, this chapter reaffirms SMART as a valuable decision-support tool and lays the foundation for future methodological innovations in the field of multicriteria analysis.

References

Akmaludin, A., Sihombing, E. G., Dewi, L. S., & Arisawati, E. (2023). Comparison of selection for employee position recommended MCDM-AHP, SMART and MAUT method. *Sinkron: jurnal dan penelitian teknik informatika, 7*(2), 603–616.

Bahreini, P., & Erdebilli, B. (2024). Supplier selection in the context of industry 4.0 using hybrid DEA-SMART method. *International Journal of Supply & Operations Management, 11*(2).

Chou, S. Y., & Chang, Y. H. (2008). A decision support system for supplier selection based on a strategy-aligned fuzzy SMART approach. *Expert Systems with Applications, 34*(4), 2241–2253.

Fahlepi, R. (2020). Decision support systems employee discipline identification using the simple multi attribute rating technique (SMART) method. *Journal of Applied Engineering and Technological Science (JAETS, 1*(2), 103–112.

Feng, J., Yan, Y., Huang, M., Du, Y., Lu, Z., & Li, B. (2022). A study on the multi-attribute decision theory and methods. *Procedia Computer Science, 214*, 544–551.

Ghadimi, P., Wang, C., Lim, M. K., & Heavey, C. (2019). Intelligent sustainable supplier selection using multi-agent technology: Theory and application for Industry 4.0 supply chains. *Computers & Industrial Engineering, 127*, 588–600.

Ghobakhloo, M. (2020). Industry 4.0, digitization, and opportunities for sustainability. *Journal of cleaner production, 252*, 119869.

Haseli, G., Sheikh, R., Ghoushchi, S. J., Hajiaghaei-Keshteli, M., Moslem, S., Deveci, M., & Kadry, S. (2024). An extension of the best–worst method based on the spherical fuzzy sets for multi-criteria decision-making. *Granular Computing, 9*(2), 40.

Haseli, G., Sheikh, R., Wang, J., Tomaskova, H., & Tirkolaee, E. B. (2021). A novel approach for group decision making based on the best–worst method (G-bwm): Application to supply chain management. *Mathematics, 9*(16), 1881.

Hwang, C. L., & Yoon, K. (1981). Methods for multiple attribute decision making. *Multiple attribute decision making: methods and applications a state-of-the-art survey* (pp. 58–191). Berlin, Heidelberg: Springer Berlin Heidelberg.

Mahdiana, D., & Kusumawardhany, N. (2020). The combination of analytical hierarchy process and simple multi-attribute rating technique for the selection of the best lecturer. In *2020 International Conference on Smart Technology and Applications (ICoSTA*. IEEE, 1–5.

Martino Neto, J., Salomon, V. A. P., Ortiz-Barrios, M. A., & Petrillo, A. (2023). Compatibility and correlation of multi-attribute decision making: A case of industrial relocation. *Annals of Operations Research, 326*(2), 831–852.

Mustajoki, J., Hämäläinen, R. P., & Salo, A. (2005). Decision support by interval SMART/SWING—incorporating imprecision in the SMART and SWING methods. *Decision Sciences, 36*(2), 317–339.

Patel, M. R., Vashi, M. P., & Bhatt, B. V. (2017). SMART-multi-criteria decision-making technique for use in planning activities. *New Horizons in Civil Engineering (NHCE, 2017*, 1–6.

Rahim, R. (2017). *Study of the simple multi-attribute rating technique for decision support.*

Soltanifar, M., Tavana, M., Santos-Arteaga, F. J., & Sharafi, H. (2023). A hybrid multi-attribute decision-making and data envelopment analysis model with heterogeneous attributes: The case of sustainable development goals. *Environmental Science & Policy, 147*, 89–102.

Taherdoost, H., & Madanchian, M. (2023). Multi-criteria decision making (MCDM) methods and concepts. *Encyclopedia, 3*(1), 77–87.

Taherdoost, H., & Mohebi, A. (2024). Using SMART method for multi-criteria decision making: Applications, advantages, and limitations. *Archives of Advanced Engineering Science, 2*(4), 190–197.

Taylor, J. M., Jr, & Love, B. N. (2014). Simple multi-attribute rating technique for renewable energy deployment decisions (SMART REDD). *The Journal of Defense Modeling and Simulation, 11*(3), 227–232.

Triantaphyllou, E., Shu, B., Sanchez, S. N., & Ray, T. (1998). Multi-criteria decision making: An operations research approach. *Encyclopedia of Electrical and Electronics Engineering, 15*(1998), 175–186.

Więckowski, J., Sałabun, W., Kizielewicz, B., Bączkiewicz, A., Shekhovtsov, A., Paradowski, B., & Wątróbski, J. (2023). Recent advances in multi-criteria decision analysis: A comprehensive review of applications and trends. *International Journal of Knowledge-based and Intelligent Engineering Systems, 27*(4), 367–393.

Zadeh, L. A. (1965). Fuzzy sets. *Information and Control, 8*(3), 338–353.

Zavadskas, E. K., Turskis, Z., & Kildienė, S. (2014). State of art surveys of overviews on MCDM/MADM methods. *Technological and Economic Development of Economy, 20*(1), 165–179.

Chapter 11

COMET: Characteristic objects method for multi-attribute decision-making

Andrii Shekhovtsov[1,2] and Wojciech Sałabun[1,2]
[1]National Institute of Telecommunications, Warsaw, Poland, [2]West Pomeranian University of Technology in Szczecin, Szczecin, Poland

11.1 Introduction

Multicriteria decision analysis (MCDA) is a domain that provides a set of methods and approaches designed to support decision-making when multiple, often conflicting, criteria must be considered (Cinelli et al., 2014). MCDA offers a structured way to evaluate alternatives by taking into account both quantitative and qualitative aspects, and helps decision makers reach consistent and transparent choices. It is widely used in fields such as engineering (Nabavi et al., 2023), management (Rayhan & Bhuiyan, 2025), public policy (Danielson et al., 2022), and environmental planning (Junyent et al., 2024), where complex decisions require careful analysis of trade-offs (Yalcin, 2025).

The characteristic objects method (COMET) is an MCDA approach originally designed as an improved alternative to the technique for order of preference by similarity to ideal solution (TOPSIS) (Salabun et al., 2019). The COMET method uses expert knowledge while maintaining a reliable and robust evaluation of decision alternatives. It builds a full-domain decision model identified through the matrix of expert judgment (MEJ), which captures the expert's preferences. The expert compares different characteristic objects (COs) to construct the MEJ. These judgments are then aggregated and used to assign preference values to all characteristic objects, forming a fuzzy rule base that is later used to evaluate the alternatives (Wątróbski et al., 2022).

This approach allows each alternative to be evaluated independently using fuzzy inference (Magdalena, 2015), producing a robust ranking of the alternatives. One of COMET's key strengths is that it is rank reversal free, meaning that the evaluation of one alternative does not affect the ranking of others, as long as it is performed within the same decision model (Salabun et al., 2019). By constructing a full-domain decision model based on pairwise comparisons, COMET provides a rigorous yet practical framework that combines expert knowledge with systematic problem analysis. Its ability to create a complete decision model from expert knowledge makes it a significant tool in MCDA practice and research.

Despite its advantages, COMET has certain limitations. The number of pairwise comparisons required grows exponentially with the number of criteria and characteristic values. This makes it difficult, or even impossible, for a single expert to fully assess large models. To address this challenge, various techniques have been developed to reduce the complexity of the MEJ identification process, enabling the application of COMET to large, real-world decision problems (Shekhovtsov & Salabun, 2023; Kizielewicz et al., 2025).

The rest of the paper is structured as follows. Section 11.2 provides a literature review of the COMET applications and extensions. Section 11.3 is devoted to the COMET algorithm and explains how the method works. Sections 11.4, 11.5 present two numerical examples. The first is a synthetic example intended to illustrate the calculations step by step, while the second is a more complex case demonstrating how to apply the COMET method in a practical study. Finally, Section 11.6 summarizes the chapter and outlines directions for the future development of the COMET method.

11.2 Literature review

In recent years, the COMET method has been applied to a wide range of decision-making problems in fields such as energy (Paradowski & Salabun, 2021), agriculture (Habeeb et al., 2022), and engineering (Shekhovtsov et al., 2022). It has been used to optimize the development of sustainable electricity technologies, alongside other MCDA methods such as

Encyclopedia of Multi-Attribute Decision-Making (MADM). DOI: https://doi.org/10.1016/B978-0-443-33275-3.00092-0

multiattributive ideal-real comparative analysis and Stable Preference Ordering Towards Ideal Solution (SPOTIS), providing a structured evaluation of alternatives under multiple criteria (Tran, 2024). The COMET method has also been employed to enhance the analytic hierarchy process by eliminating the rank reversal phenomenon and ensuring more reliable rankings (Yulistia et al., 2023). In the field of renewable energy, it has supported the assessment of solar panel evolution to maximize energy efficiency and reduce material costs under a neutrosophic model (Sleem & Elhenawy, 2023). In agriculture, the COMET method has been applied to regional crop yield assessments, enabling systematic comparison of different scenarios (Habeeb et al., 2022).

Methodologically, many extensions and improvements of the COMET method have been developed. Some of them address uncertainty and the handling of fuzzy data, while others focus on the curse of dimensionality, aiming to reduce the time and effort required to identify the model. In the following part of this section, we briefly discuss several of these extensions and related paradigms.

To adapt the COMET method to uncertain data, several extensions have been developed. Notably, in 2017, Faizi et al. introduced a COMET extension based on hesitant fuzzy sets (Faizi et al., 2018), which was later applied to the evaluation of electric city bus development (Salabun et al., 2018). Another extension by Faizi incorporated intuitionistic fuzzy sets into COMET to address group decision-making problems (Faizi et al., 2020).

Since the problem of identifying the preferences of characteristic objects can itself be formulated as an MCDA problem, another MCDA method can be used to solve it. This approach has been demonstrated in several studies on the evaluation of renewable energy sources, showing practical applications of the VlseKriterijumska Optimizacija I Kompromisno Resenje-COMET (Wątróbski, Bqczkiewicz, et al., 2022) and the combinative distance-based assessment-COMET (Wątróbski et al., 2022) methods. The main advantage of this combination, compared to the standalone COMET method, is that the resulting hybrid approach retains the key properties of COMET, including resistance to rank reversal and the creation of a full-domain decision model.

Expected solution point (ESP)-COMET extension was proposed as an easier alternative for COMET model identification, using only an ESP that defines the expert's expectations (Shekhovtsov et al., 2023). It proved useful in analyzing customer preferences for the hydrogen car market (Shekhovtsov et al., 2024), showing good performance and accuracy compared to other extensions.

The compromise COMET extension was proposed to adapt the classical COMET method for generating compromise rankings by introducing a voting mechanism into the model identification procedure (Kizielewicz et al., 2024c). The practical application of this approach was demonstrated through the evaluation of forest products for trade economics.

The structural COMET approach was adopted to reduce the computational burden and time effort associated with identifying large COMET models. It was first introduced in (Shekhovtsov et al., 2020), demonstrating a significant reduction in the number of pairwise comparisons, and was later practically applied in (Shekhovtsov et al., 2024) for the evaluation of hydrogen cars.

The triad support algorithm was proposed to reduce the number of manual pairwise comparisons relying on transitivity and consistency rules, partially filling the MEJ matrix based on previous answers (Shekhovtsov & Salabun, 2023). This approach allows for even a 90% reduction in pairwise comparisons for larger matrices.

There were also propositions to combine the COMET method with machine learning algorithms, for the purpose of expert substitution or model reidentification. For example, such extensions as Intelligent COMET (INCOME) (Kizielewicz et al., 2024b), Support Vector Regression COMET (SVR-COMET) (Kizielewicz et al., 2024a), or Lasso COMET (LA-COMET) (Kizielewicz et al., 2025) are purposed to identify the model based on the available data, while the Stochastic Identification of Models (SITCOM) (Kizielewicz, 2022) method was proposed to reidentify the models based on previously evaluated alternatives.

The continuous development of the COMET method demonstrates its flexibility and growing importance in decision-making research. Over time, it has evolved from a single MCDA tool into a versatile framework capable of addressing uncertainty, high dimensionality, and expert-based or data-driven model identification. Altogether, these advancements show that COMET is an active and evolving method, continuously adapted to meet the complex requirements of modern multicriteria decision-making.

11.3 Methodology

The characteristic objects method was proposed by (Salabun et al., 2019) as a first MCDA method that is completely resistant to the rank reversal problem. Another advantage of that method is that it approximates a decision function based on expert preferences in the complete domain of the decision problem, allowing for independent evaluation of any alternatives that lie within problem boundaries. In the following part of this section, we will present and explain the consequent steps that are required to apply this method.

Step 1. Define the space of the problem—first, the expert or decision-maker should formally define the decision problem. It consists of r criteria $C_1,\ C_2,\ \ldots,\ C_r$, which define the dimensionality of the problem. The decision alternatives can also be selected at this step. Finally, the set of fuzzy numbers $\{\widetilde{C}_{i1},\ \widetilde{C}_{i2},\ \ldots,\ \widetilde{C}_{ic_i}\}$ for each criterion C_i is selected as shown in (11.1), based on the characteristic values:

$$\begin{aligned} C_1 &= \left\{\widetilde{C}_{11}, \widetilde{C}_{12}, \ldots, \widetilde{C}_{1c_1}\right\} \\ C_2 &= \left\{\widetilde{C}_{21}, \widetilde{C}_{22}, \ldots, \widetilde{C}_{2c_2}\right\} \\ &\ldots \\ C_r &= \left\{\widetilde{C}_{r1}, \widetilde{C}_{r2}, \ldots, \widetilde{C}_{rc_r}\right\} \end{aligned} \tag{11.1}$$

where $c_1,\ c_2,\ \ldots, c_r$ are the numbers of the fuzzy numbers for each criterion.

Step 2. Generate characteristic objects. The *COs* are generated by using the Cartesian product of fuzzy numbers cores for each criterion as follows (2):

$$CO = C(C_1) \times C(C_2) \times \ldots \times C(C_r) \tag{11.2}$$

As a result of the Cartesian product, an ordered set of all CO is obtained as shown in (11.3):

$$\begin{aligned} CO_1 &= \langle C(\widetilde{C}_{11}),\ C(\widetilde{C}_{21}),\ \ldots,\ C(\widetilde{C}_{r1})\rangle \\ CO_2 &= \langle C(\widetilde{C}_{11}),\ C(\widetilde{C}_{21}),\ \ldots,\ C(\widetilde{C}_{r1})\rangle \\ &\ldots \\ CO_t &= \langle C(\widetilde{C}_{1c_1}),\ C(\widetilde{C}_{2c_2}),\ \ldots,\ C(\widetilde{C}_{rc_r})\rangle \end{aligned} \tag{11.3}$$

The number of resulting CO t depends on the number of triangular fuzzy number (TFN) values for each criterion, as shown in Eq. (11.4).

$$t = \prod_{i=1}^{r} c_i \tag{11.4}$$

Step 3. Rank the characteristic objects. The expert or decision-maker now determines the *MEJ*. The *MEJ* matrix is a pairwise comparison matrix that contains the results of the expert's comparison of characteristic objects. Values of *MEJ* denoted as α_{ij} are the result of the comparison of CO_i and CO_j by the expert. The function f_{exp} denotes the mental function of the expert preferences (which usually cannot be formulated mathematically). It depends solely on the knowledge of the expert and can be presented as (5). Notice that because α_{ii}=0.5 and $\alpha_{ij} = \alpha_{ji}$, only the upper triangle of the *MEJ* should be identified, resulting in $\frac{t(t-1)}{2}$ pairwise comparisons.

$$\alpha_{ij} = \begin{cases} 0.0, & f_{exp}(CO_i) < f_{exp}(CO_j) \\ 0.5, & f_{exp}(CO_i) = f_{exp}(CO_j) \\ 1.0, & f_{exp}(CO_i) > f_{exp}(CO_j) \end{cases} \tag{11.5}$$

After the full *MEJ* matrix is identified, the vertical vector of the summed judgments (SJ) is obtained as follows (6).

$$SJ_i = \sum_{j=1}^{t} \alpha_{ij} \tag{11.6}$$

Finally, values of preference are approximated for each characteristic object. As a result, the vertical vector P is obtained, where $i-th$ row contains the approximate value of preference for CO_i. Values of P are determined by assignment of uniformly distributed values in the range [0,1] to each of the unique values of SJ. To better understand the mechanism, consider the following examples:

$$SJ=\{0.5,1.5,2.5,3.5\} \rightarrow P=\{0.0,0.3(3),0.6(6),1.0\} \tag{11.7}$$

$$SJ=\{0.5,2.0,2.0,3.5\} \rightarrow P=\{0.0,0.5,0.5,1.0\} \tag{11.8}$$

Step 4. The rule base—Next, each characteristic object CO_i and its preference values P_i are converted to a fuzzy rule as follows (9):

$$IF\ C(\widetilde{C}_{1i})\ AND\ C(\widetilde{C}_{2i})\ AND \ldots THEN\ P_i \tag{11.9}$$

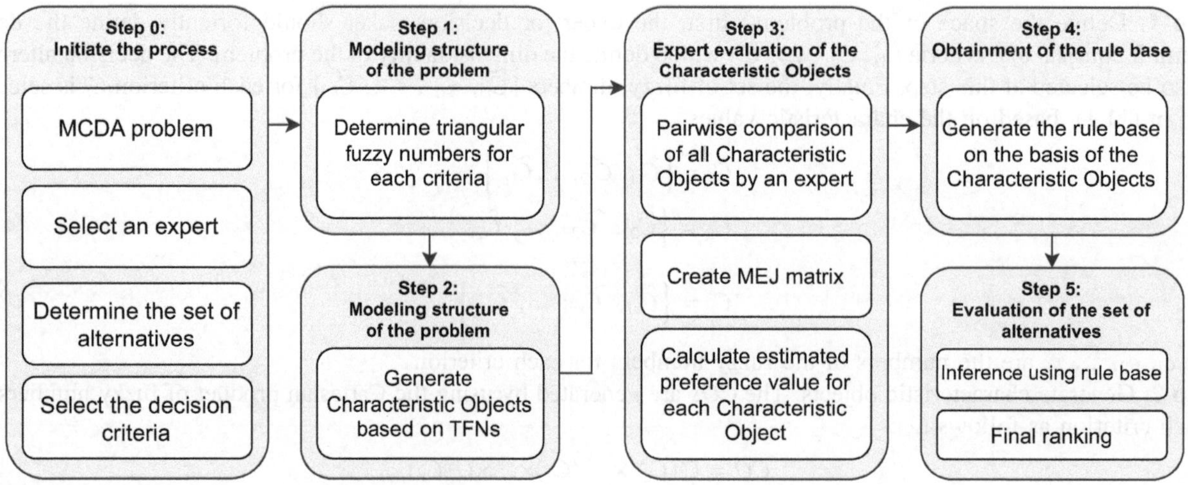

FIGURE 11.1 Framework of the characteristic objects method.

In this way, the complete fuzzy rule base is obtained.

Step 5. Inference and final ranking. Each alternative A_i should be defined as a set of crisp numbers $A_i = \{a_{1i}, a_{2i}, \ldots, a_{ri}\}$, according to the selected criteria $\{C_1, C_2, \ldots, C_r\}$. Then, Mamdani's fuzzy inference method is used to calculate the preference of the i-th alternative. The rule base guarantees that the obtained results are robust and not influenced by the other alternatives. This property makes the COMET method completely free of the rank reversal paradox.

The aforementioned algorithm can be summarized in the form of the flowchart presented in Fig. 11.1, starting with initiation of the decision process, modeling the problem's structure, and evaluation of the CO and construction of the fuzzy rule base. Finally, the constructed rule base is used to evaluate the alternatives and create a final ranking.

To apply the COMET method without implementing it, the pymcdm library can be used (Kizielewicz et al., 2023; Kizielewicz, Shekhovtsov, et al., 2023). Besides a large number of different MCDA methods, it contains a vast toolkit related to the COMET method and its extensions, which can be easily used in practical applications.

11.4 Numerical example 1

In this section, we describe a simple synthetic example to demonstrate how to solve the decision problem with the COMET method step by step. This example is a two-criterion problem, in which we want to rank alternatives with regard to profit on a 0–10 scale and cost in USD.

After selecting the criteria, the characteristic values for each criterion must be defined. These values will be used to construct the characteristic objects and then create a fuzzy rule base. Extreme characteristic values should define the minimum and maximum bounds of the decision problem domain. Next, zero or more characteristic values can be defined between the minimum and maximum values. Usually, three characteristic values (minimum, maximum, and the point between them) are enough for most problems. However, a larger number can be selected. The in-between points can be chosen according to different strategies. They can be uniformly distributed, selected based on statistics, or based on the ESP.

In this example, we selected three characteristic values, namely [0,8,10] for the profit criterion and [0,50,100] for the cost criterion. This can be formally written as follows:

$$CV_1 = \{CV_{11}, CV_{12}, CV_{13}\} = [0, 8, 10]$$

$$CV_2 = \{CV_{21}, CV_{22}, CV_{23}\} = [0, 500, 100]$$

These characteristic values will result in three TFNs presented in Fig. 11.2. The Cartesian product of these TFNs results in a set of characteristic objects presented in Table 11.1. These TFNs will be used later to evaluate the alternatives.

Characteristic objects then should be evaluated by the expert, or in one of the other ways described in Section 11.2. In the original COMET method, evaluation of the CO is achieved through the pairwise comparison matrix MEJ, which is

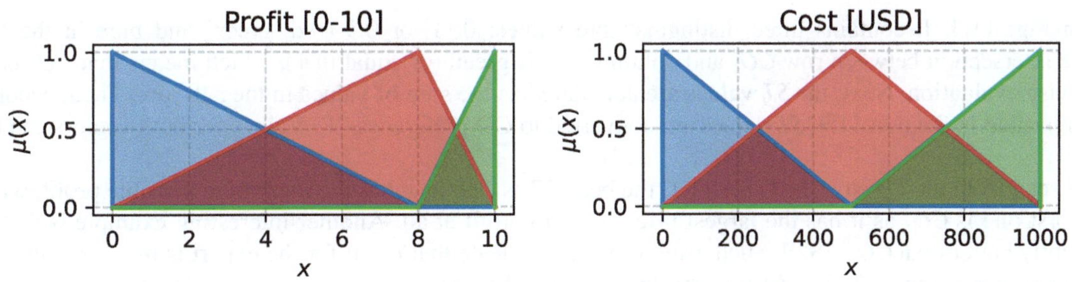

FIGURE 11.2 Triangular fuzzy numbers that were generated based on selected characteristic values.

TABLE 11.1 Characteristic objects, criteria values, and evaluation results.

CO_i	C_1	C_2	SJ_i	P_i
CO_1	0	0	2.5000	0.2500
CO_2	0	500	1.5000	0.1250
CO_3	0	1000	0.5000	0.0000
CO_4	8	0	6.5000	0.7500
CO_5	8	500	5.5000	0.6250
CO_6	8	1000	3.5000	0.3750
CO_7	10	0	8.5000	1.0000
CO_8	10	500	7.5000	0.8750
CO_9	10	1000	4.5000	0.5000

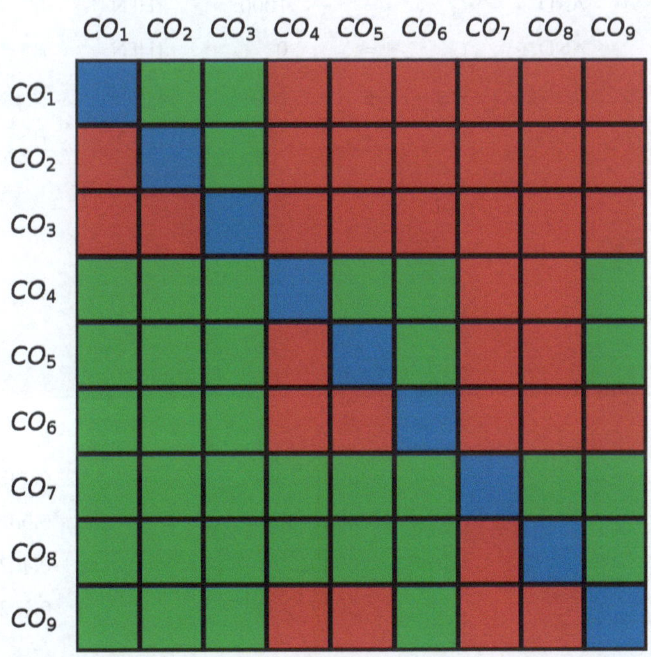

FIGURE 11.3 Matrix of expert judgments.
Red, green, and blue colors represent 0, 1, or 0.5, respectively.

presented in Fig. 11.3. It contains three distinguishable values: 0, 1, or 0.5 (red, green, and blue in the figure). For example, the intersection between row CO_1 and column CO_2 is green (or equal to 1), which means that CO_1 is better than CO_2 in pairwise evaluation. Next, the SJ_i values are calculated as the sum of values in the i-th row. Then, according to the algorithm presented in Section 11.3, SJ_i values are converted to CO preferences P_i. Values for both vectors can be found in Table 11.1.

As can be seen from the P_i values in Table 11.1, the best CO is CO_7 as it has the maximum possible profit, with no costs, while the worst one is CO_3 as it has the largest price with no profit at all. Another interesting example is CO_8=[10,500], which is slightly better than CO_4=[8,0]. Such a situation can indicate that profit for the expert is more important than cost, as we are ready to pay more (500 vs 0) for marginal profit (10 vs 8).

After the COs are evaluated based on manual pairwise comparisons or any other available method, and P_i values are computed, a fuzzy rule base for alternative evaluation is required. For this example, the rule base can be presented as shown in Table 11.2. Because of the Mamdani inference mechanism, it is possible to evaluate any alternative within the defined decision problem domain, as each of the rules is represented by TFNs (only cores are provided for clarity).

To illustrate how the COMET method evaluates the alternative, we select four synthetic alternatives presented in Table 11.3. None of these alternatives is dominated or dominant; therefore, we cannot easily choose which one is the best or worst one. Mamdani's fuzzy inference is utilized to evaluate alternatives and obtain the final preference values in the range [0,1], where 1 indicates the best alternative and 0 the worst. As can be seen in Table 11.3, the resulting alternatives order is $A_2 \succ A_4 \succ A_3 \succ A_4$. As A_2 has the biggest profit from all the alternatives, the method evaluates it as the best one.

In Fig. 11.4, we present a visualization of the decision function, which can be calculated at each point inside the defined decision problem domain. Alternatives $A_1 - A_4$ are also presented in this visualization, and it can be seen that they fall

TABLE 11.2 Fuzzy rule base for the current decision problem.

IF	C_1	=	0	AND	C_2	=	0	THEN	P_i	=	0.2500
IF	C_1	=	0	AND	C_2	=	500	THEN	P_i	=	0.1250
IF	C_1	=	0	AND	C_2	=	1000	THEN	P_i	=	0.0000
IF	C_1	=	8	AND	C_2	=	0	THEN	P_i	=	0.7500
IF	C_1	=	8	AND	C_2	=	500	THEN	P_i	=	0.6250
IF	C_1	=	8	AND	C_2	=	1000	THEN	P_i	=	0.3750
IF	C_1	=	10	AND	C_2	=	0	THEN	P_i	=	1.0000
IF	C_1	=	10	AND	C_2	=	500	THEN	P_i	=	0.8750
IF	C_1	=	10	AND	C_2	=	1000	THEN	P_i	=	0.5000

TABLE 11.3 Alternative data and calculation results.

A_i	C_1	C_2	P_i	R_i
A_1	3	200	0.3875	4
A_2	9	600	0.6875	1
A_3	5	400	0.4625	3
A_4	7	500	0.5625	2

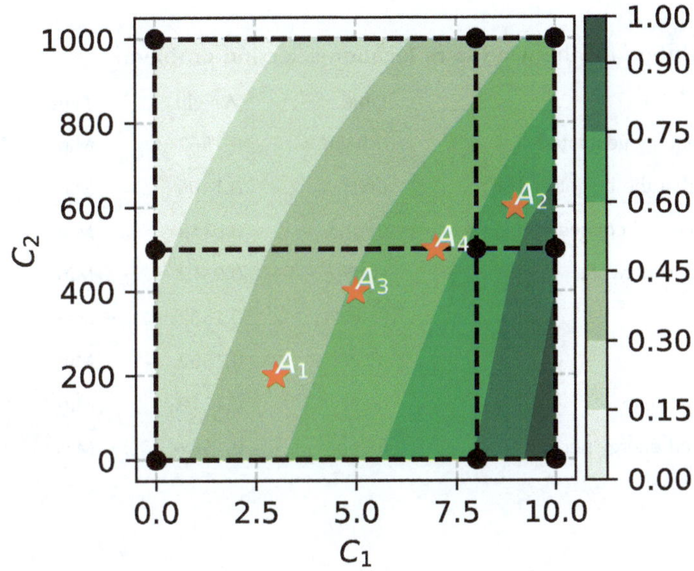

FIGURE 11.4 Modeled decision function in the decision problem domain.

within different levels of preference. The ability to evaluate alternatives independently based on the fuzzy rules base ensures that the COMET method is completely resistant to the rank reversal paradox.

An additional step that can be included in the analysis is the computation of the global weights based on the algorithm presented in (Kizielewicz, Shekhovtsov, et al., 2023). This algorithm utilizes linear regression on CO values and their preferences, approximating the weights of the criteria. This algorithm works under the assumption that the expert preference function is linear, which is not always true; therefore, the accuracy of the results may vary. Applying the algorithm for global weights calculation, we obtain the result **W**=[0.6436, 0.3564], which confirms the previous observations on profit importance over the cost.

11.5 Numerical example 2

In this Section, we demonstrate a more complex example of the COMET method application. We select the problem of evaluation of wind farm location selection based on the data provided in the literature (Kizielewicz et al., 2020). We select this specific topic for the case study, as the MCDA methods are often used to evaluate alternatives in the different aspects of renewable energy (Badi et al., 2023; Boskovic et al., 2025). The problem is summarized in Table 11.4. From the available data, we choose criteria such as the yearly amount of energy, average speed of wind, distances from power and road, social acceptance, and costs of the investment, as well as yearly operational costs and yearly profits from generated energy. Table 11.4 indicates units of the criteria and their types, as well as proposed characteristic values. In this specific problem, characteristic values were selected based on data, with a small margin, which allows for the introduction of new alternatives if needed, without the necessity to reevaluate the entire model. The criteria weights shown in the table were obtained using the Raning Comparison method (Więckowski et al., 2023).

Usually, the COMET method can be applied without knowledge about types or weights, but in the considered problem, we will obtain $t=3^8=6561$ COs, resulting in 21 million pairwise comparisons. Therefore, we decided to use the TOPSIS method with min-max normalization for COs evaluation. In this case, the downsides of the TOPSIS method are not noticeable, as the set of the CO is constant for the current problem, and distances between synthetically generated objects are bigger than usual distances between alternatives, allowing for easier ordering. This way, instead of pairwise comparison, the COs will be evaluated using the TOPSIS method, with the weights and types provided in Table 11.4, and the results of this evaluation will be used to generate preferences P_i for characteristic objects.

In Table 11.5, we present the alternative locations for the wind farm, sourced from (Kizielewicz et al., 2020). As we can see, the data is pretty diverse, and considering all the criteria at once, it is not easy to choose which alternative is the best one. Therefore, the MCDA method can be applied here to aid the decision-making process.

TABLE 11.4 Criteria description for the wind farm location selection problem.

C_i	Criterion name	Unit	Weight	Type	CV_1	CV_2	CV_3
C_1	Yearly amount Of energy generated	(MWh)	0.1562	Max	45	75	110
C_2	Average wind speed at the height of 100 m	(m/s)	0.1406	Max	6	6.5	8
C_3	Distance from power grid connection	(km)	0.0312	Min	0	20	70
C_4	distance from the road network	(km)	0.0312	Min	0	6	10
C_5	Social acceptance	(%)	0.1562	Max	20	40	60
C_6	Investment cost	(PLN)	0.1562	Min	270	390	460
C_7	Operational costs per year	(PLN)	0.1719	Min	4.5	6.5	9
C_8	Profits from generated energy per year	(PLN)	0.1562	Max	15	25	40

TABLE 11.5 Decision matrix for the wind farm location selection problem.

A_i	C_1	C_2	C_3	C_4	C_5	C_6	C_7	C_8
A_1	106.78	6.75	2.00	6.00	52.00	455.50	8.90	36.80
A_2	86.37	7.12	3.00	10.00	20.00	336.50	7.20	29.80
A_3	104.85	6.95	60.00	7.00	60.00	416.00	8.70	36.20
A_4	46.60	6.04	1.00	3.00	50.00	277.00	6.30	17.11
A_5	69.18	7.05	33.16	8.00	35.49	364.79	5.39	33.71
A_6	66.48	6.06	26.32	6.53	34.82	304.02	4.67	27.07
A_7	74.48	6.81	45.25	4.76	44.19	349.45	4.93	28.89
A_8	73.67	6.06	19.54	3.19	46.41	354.65	6.01	21.00
A_9	100.58	6.37	39.27	8.43	22.07	449.42	7.89	17.62
A_{10}	94.81	6.13	50.58	4.18	21.14	450.88	5.12	17.60
A_{11}	48.93	7.12	21.48	5.47	55.72	454.71	8.39	19.16
A_{12}	74.75	6.58	7.08	9.90	26.01	455.17	4.78	18.44

As mentioned previously, we chose to evaluate the COs with the TOPSIS method. However, it is not possible to show all the results for this evaluation. Instead, we decided to show and compare how the results obtained with only the TOPSIS method are comparable with TOPSIS-COMET results. Table 11.6 contains four vectors, including preferences and ranking for the TOPSIS method ($P_i^{(T)}$, $R_i^{(T)}$) and preferences and ranking for the COMET method ($P_i^{(C)}$, $R_i^{(C)}$). It can be seen that preferences in both cases lie within the [0,1] range, and rankings are pretty similar (weighted Spearman r_w correlation between the rankings is equal to 0.9796).

There are some differences in the middle of the rankings; however, the first and last positions are the same. This is possible, as the regular TOPSIS method directly evaluates the alternatives that can be close to themselves. Additionally,

TABLE 11.6 Results of the calculation for the TOPSIS method ($P_i^{(T)}$, $R_i^{(T)}$), and the COMET method $P_i^{(C)}$, $R_i^{(C)}$.

A_i	$P_i^{(T)}$	$R_i^{(T)}$	$P_i^{(C)}$	$R_i^{(C)}$
A_1	0.5321	4	0.5485	5
A_2	0.5310	6	0.4816	6
A_3	0.5841	3	0.6739	2
A_4	0.4534	8	0.4308	8
A_5	0.6149	2	0.6671	3
A_6	0.5314	5	0.6141	4
A_7	0.6423	1	0.7365	1
A_8	0.4641	7	0.4484	7
A_9	0.3310	12	0.1546	12
A_{10}	0.4031	10	0.2849	10
A_{11}	0.4028	11	0.2236	11
A_{12}	0.4197	9	0.2916	9

positive and negative ideal solutions are derived from the data and can change if the set of alternatives changes. The COMET method, on the other hand, builds the complete decision model in the defined bounds, providing robust evaluation of the alternatives with no regard to changes in the number of alternatives.

11.6 Conclusions

In this chapter, we explain how to apply the COMET and provide a review of its different extensions and selected application scenarios. The first numerical example explained the method step by step with additional visualization of the resulting preference function. As the second numerical example, the problem of wind farm location selection was adopted. As the problem was bigger and included more characteristic objects, we decided to evaluate them using the TOPSIS method, as well as compare the results for the classical TOPSIS method with the obtained TOPSIS-COMET hybrid method. While the results are similar, the COMET method has several advantages over the classical MCDA method, such as being resistant to rank reversal and building a complete domain model.

In future research, we want to concentrate on extensions and other modifications of the COMET method, reducing its complexity while maintaining the accuracy and other advantages.

References

Badi, I., Stevie, Z., & Bayane Bouraima, M. (2023). Overcoming obstacles to renew-able energy development in Libya: An MCDM approach towards effective strategy formulation. *decision making Advances, 1*(1), 17–24.

Boskovic, S., et al. (2025). A new criteria importance assessment (Cimas) method in multi-criteria group decision-making: Criteria evaluation for supplier selection. *Facta Universitatis) Series: Mechanical Engineering, 23*(2), 335–349.

Cinelli, M., Coles, S. R., & Kirwan., K. (2014). Analysis of the potentials of multi criteria decision analysis methods to conduct sustainability assessment. *Ecological Indicators, 46*, 138–148.

Danielson, M., et al. (2022). A participatory MCDA approach to energy transition policy formation. In *Multicriteria and optimization models for risk, reliability, and maintenance decision analysis: Recent advances*. Springer, 79–110.

Faizi, S., et al. (2018). Decision making with uncertainty using hesitant fuzzy sets. *International Journal of Fuzzy Systems, 20*(1), 93–103.

Faizi, S., et al. (2020). Intuitionistic fuzzy sets in multi-criteria group decision making problems using the characteristic objects method. *Symmetry, 12*(9), 1382.

Habeeb, R., et al. (2022). A proposed comparative algorithm for regional crop yield assessment: An application of characteristic objects method. *Mathematical Problems in Engineering, 2022*(1), 8224953. https://doi.org/10.1155/2022/s224953 ISSN: 1563-5147.

Junyent, I. A., et al. (2024). Planning shared mobility hubs in European cities: A methodological framework using MCDA and GIS applied to Barcelona. *Sustainable Cities and Society, 106*, 105377.

Kizielewicz, B. (2022). Towards the identification of continuous decisional model: The accuracy testing in the SITCOM approach. *Procedia Computer Science, 207*, 4390–4400.

Kizielewicz, B., Shekhovtsov, A., & Salabun, W. (2023). Pymcdm-the universal library for solving multicriteria decision-making problems. *SoftwareX, 22*, 101368.

Kizielewicz, B., Wątróbski, J., & Salabun, V. (2020). Identification of relevant criteria set in the MCDA process-wind farm location case study. *Energies, 13*(24), 6548.

Kizielewicz, B., et al. (2023). Determination of local and global decision weights based on fuzzy modeling. In *International conference on neural information processing*. Springer, 188–200.

Kizielewicz, B., et al. (2024a). Comparative analysis of re-identification methods of multi-criteria decision analysis models. *IEEE Access*.

Kizielewicz, B., et al. (2024b). Intelligent characteristic objects method (INCOME): a data knowledge-based multi-criteria decision analysis. *Artificial Intelligence Review, 57*(10), 266.

Kizielewicz B. et al. (2024c). The Compromise-COMET method for identifying an adaptive multi-criteria decision model. In: IEEE Access.

Kizielewicz B. et al. (2025). LA-COMET: Toward reducing redundant criteria in multi-criteria decision analysis.

Magdalena, L. (2015). Fuzzy rule-based systems. In *Springer handbook of computational intelligence*. Springer, 203–218.

Nabavi, S. R., Wang, Z., & Rangaiah, G. P. (2023). Sensitivity analysis of multi-criteria decision-making methods for engineering applications. *Industrial 8 Engineering Chemistry Re-search, 62*(17), 6707–6722.

Paradowski, B., & Salabun, W. (2021). Are the results of MCDA methods reliable? Selection of materials for thermal energy storage. *Procedia Computer Science, 192*, 1313–1322.

Rayhan, D. S. A., & Bhuiyan, I. U. (2025). A framework for evaluation of construction and demolition waste management alternatives using MCDA techniques in the context of Dhaka City. *International Journal of Construction Management, 25*(4), 481–493.

Salabun, W., Karczmarczyk, A., & Wątróbski, J. (2018). Decision-making using the hesitant fuzzy sets COMET method: An empirical study of the electric city buses selection. In *2018 IEEE symposium series on computational intelligence (SSCI)*. IEEE, 1485–1492.

Salabun, W., et al. (2019). The COMET method: The first MCDA method completely resistant to rank reversal paradox. *European Working Group Series, 3*.

Shekhovtsov, A., et al. (2022). Towards reliable decision-making in the green urban transport domain. *Facta Universitatis Series: Mechanical Engineering, 20*(2), 381–398.

Shekhovtsov, A., & Salabun, W. (2023). The new algorithm for effective reducing the number of pairwise comparisons in the decision support methods. In *European conference on artificial intelligence*. Springer, 243–254.

Shekhovtsov, A., et al. (2024). Analyzing customer preferences for hydrogen cars: A characteristic objects method approach. *Artificial Intelligence Review, 58*(2), 52.

Shekhovtsov, A., Kizielewicz, B., & Salabun, W. (2023). Advancing individual decision-making: An extension of the characteristic objects method using expected solution point. *Information Sciences, 647*, 119456.

Shekhovtsov, A., Kolodziejczyk, J., & Salabun, W. (2020). Fuzzy model identification using monolithic and structured approaches in decision problems with partially incomplete data. *Symmetry, 12*(9), 1541.

Sleem, A., & Elhenawy, I. (2023). Energy efficiency and material cost savings by evolution of solar panels used in photovoltaic systems under neutrosophic model. *Neutrosophic Systems with Applications, 5*(1), 36–43. https://doi.org/10.61356/j.nswa.2023.31 ISSN: 2993-7159.

Tran, N.-T. (2024). Application of the multi-criteria analysis method MAIRCA, SPOTIS, COMET for the optimisation of sustainable electricity technology development. *EUREKA: Physics and Engineering, (11)*, 180–188. https://doi.org/10.21303/2461-4262.2024.003133.

Wątróbski, J., et al. (2022). Green electricity generation assessment using the CODAS-COMET method. *Ecological Indicators, 143*, 109391.

Wątróbski, J., Bqczkiewicz, A., & Salabun, W. (2022). New multi-criteria method for evaluation of sustainable RES management. *Applied Energy, 324*, 119695.

Więckowski, J., et al. (2023). RANCOM: A novel approach to identifying criteria relevance based on inaccuracy expert judgments. *Engineering Applications of Artificial Intelligence, 122*, 106114.

Yalcin, G. C. (2025). Development of a fuzzy-based decision support system for sustainable tractor selection in green ports. *Facta Universitatis, Series: Mechanical Engineering*.

Yulistia, et al. (2023). New AHP improvement using COMET method characteristic to eliminate rank reversal phenomenon. *International Journal of Advanced Computer Science and Applications, 14*(11), ISSN: 21565570, 2158107X https://doi.org/10.14569/IJACSA.2023.0141190, http://thesai.org/Publications/ViewPaper?Volume=14&Issue=11&Code=IJACSA&SerialNo=90.

Chapter 12

DIBR: Defining interrelationships between ranked for multi-attribute decision-making

Galip Cihan Yalçın[1] **and Karahan Kara**[1,2]
[1]*Department of Business, Faculty of Economics and Administrative Sciences, OSTIM Technical University, Ankara, Türkiye,* [2]*Department of Business, Faculty of Economics and Administrative Sciences, İzmir Katip Çelebi University, İzmir, Türkiye*

12.1 Introduction

The defining interrelationships between ranked criteria (DIBR) method, developed by Pamucar et al. (2021), has emerged as a robust approach for determining criteria weights in multi-attribute decision-making (MADM) processes. This method relies on the ranking of criteria by experts and the analysis of relationships among these ranked criteria, facilitating the identification of weight coefficients and the calculation of reliable criterion weights. Additionally, the use of two control variables to compute the reliability index (RI) value further enhances the method's reliability, making it a consistent tool for complex decision-making problems.

Over recent years, the DIBR method has been widely applied across diverse domains, highlighting its versatility and robustness. For instance, Pamucar et al. (2021) employed DIBR to prioritize circular economy concepts while integrating the fuzzy Dombi-based combined compromise solution (CoCoSo) method for ranking alternatives. Similarly, Deveci et al. (2022) utilized DIBR for determining criteria weights in urban freight transportation, implicating the type-2 neutrosophic CoCoSo method to identify optimal management alternatives. In defense and security applications, Tešić and Marinković (2023) demonstrated the use of DIBR and its extended variants to derive reliable criterion weights for complex combat system selection, whereas Tešić et al., (2023a, 2023b, 2023c) applied rough DIBR and DIBR for earthquake risk assessment, drone selection, and strategic management, respectively, each time pairing DIBR with complementary MADM methods to ensure robust alternative ranking and decision-making under uncertainty.

The application of DIBR has also expanded to energy, transportation, and economic sectors. For example, Kara et al. (2024) utilized the spherical fuzzy (SF)-DIBR II method to evaluate the sustainable performance of wind energy power plants, while implicating the spherical fuzzy-alternative ranking order method accounting for two-step normalization (SF-AROMAN) method for ranking alternatives. Ecer et al. (2025) applied the fuzzy defining interrelationships between ranked criteria method (F-DIBR) to select electric vehicle charging station sites, complemented by the fuzzy rough numbers mixed aggregation by comprehensive normalization technique (FRN-MACONT) method for ranking. Similarly, Ayough et al. (2023) emphasized DIBR for supplier selection, implicating the base criterion and utility additive (BCUA) method to simultaneously determine criteria weights and alternative rankings. In the rural development and economic performance domains, Ayough et al., 2023; Dündar, 2024 and Lukić (2023) highlighted DIBR for prioritizing rural development programs and analyzing the economic performance of Bosnia and Herzegovina, respectively, while employing the ranking of alternatives with weights of criterion (RAWEC) and the multiatributive ideal-real comparative analysis (MAIRCA) methods to rank alternatives effectively.

Overall, these applications demonstrate the versatility of the DIBR method in capturing decision-makers' preferences, enhancing consistency, and providing a reliable basis for MADM analyzes across multiple sectors. The remainder of this chapter is structured as follows: Section 2 provides a detailed description of the DIBR method; Sections 3 and 4 present

Encyclopedia of Multi-Attribute Decision-Making (MADM). DOI: https://doi.org/10.1016/B978-0-443-33275-3.00007-5

numerical examples and applications of the DIBR framework; and Section 5 concludes the study with key findings, managerial implications, and directions for future research.

12.2 Methodology

The DIBR method is a procedure that ranks the criteria according to their levels of importance and, based on this ranking, assigns weights to the criteria through weight coefficient values (Pamucar et al., 2021). The method demonstrates the robustness and reliability of the resulting criterion weight vector by employing an RI calculation derived from two control vectors. The DIBR method consists of six steps, which are as follows:

Step 1: In the first phase of the DIBR method, the set of criteria $C = \{C_1,\ C_2,\ \ldots,\ C_j,\ \ldots,\ C_N\}\,(j = 1, 2,\ \ldots, N)$ and the panel of experts $E = \{E_1, E_2, \ldots, E_k, \ldots, E_M\}\,(k = 1,2,\ \ldots, L)$ are established. Each expert (E_k) then ranks the criteria (C_j) according to their perceived level of importance, thereby generating individual priority orderings of the criteria.

Step 2: In the second phase of the DIBR method, each expert assigns values between 0 and 1 to reflect the differences in importance among the criteria in their respective rankings. In this way, both an ordered list and a pairwise comparison matrix of the criteria are obtained. For example, let us consider a set of criteria $C = \{C_1, C_2, \ldots, C_j, \ldots, C_N\}\,(j = 1,2,\ \ldots, N)$ with an importance ranking of $C_1 > C_2 > \ldots > C_j > \ldots > C_N$ (It is assumed that all experts provide the same priority ordering of the criteria). Based on this example, the pairwise comparison matrix $(X = [X_{j-1,j}^{E_k}]_{LN})$ for experts is presented in Eq. (12.1).

$$X = \begin{bmatrix} X_{1,2}^{E_1}, X_{2,3}^{E_1}, \cdots X_{j-1,j}^{E_1} \cdots X_{N-1,N}^{E_1} \\ \vdots \cdots \vdots \cdots \vdots \\ X_{1,2}^{E_k}, X_{2,3}^{E_k}, \cdots X_{j-1,j}^{E_k} \cdots X_{N-1,N}^{E_k} \\ \vdots \cdots \vdots \cdots \vdots \\ X_{1,2}^{E_L}, X_{2,3}^{E_L}, \cdots X_{j-1,j}^{E_L} \cdots X_{N-1,N}^{E_L} \end{bmatrix};(k = 1,\ 2,\ \ldots, L; j = 1,\ 2,\ \ldots, N). \tag{12.1}$$

Step 3: In the third stage of the DIBR method, the weight coefficient matrix $(Y = [Y_j^{E_k}]_{LN})$ is derived using Eqs. (12.3–12.7) and represented as shown in Eq. (12.2):

$$Y = \begin{bmatrix} Y_1^{E_1}, Y_2^{E_1}, \cdots Y_j^{E_1} \ldots Y_N^{E_1} \\ \vdots \cdots \vdots \cdots \vdots \\ Y_1^{E_k}, Y_2^{E_k}, \cdots Y_j^{E_k} \ldots Y_N^{E_k} \\ \vdots \cdots \vdots \cdots \vdots \\ Y_1^{E_L}, Y_2^{E_L}, \cdots Y_j^{E_L} \ldots Y_N^{E_L} \end{bmatrix};(k = 1,\ 2,\ \ldots, L; j = 1,\ 2,\ \ldots, N). \tag{12.2}$$

$$Y_2^{E_k} = \frac{X_{1,2}^{E_k}}{(1 - X_{1,2}^{E_k})} * Y_1^{E_k}. \tag{12.3}$$

$$Y_3^{E_k} = \frac{X_{1,2}^{E_k}}{(1 - X_{1,2}^{E_k})} * \frac{X_{2,3}^{E_k}}{(1 - X_{2,3}^{E_k})} * Y_1^{E_k}. \tag{12.4}$$

$$Y_j^{E_k} = \frac{X_{1,2}^{E_k}}{(1 - X_{1,2}^{E_k})} * \frac{X_{2,3}^{E_k}}{(1 - X_{2,3}^{E_k})} * \ldots * \frac{X_{j-1,1}^{E_k}}{(1 - X_{j-1,1}^{E_k})} * Y_1^{E_k}. \tag{12.5}$$

$$Y_N^{E_k} = \frac{X_{1,2}^{E_k}}{(1 - X_{1,2}^{E_k})} * \frac{X_{2,3}^{E_k}}{(1 - X_{2,3}^{E_k})} * \ldots * \frac{X_{j-1,1}^{E_k}}{(1 - X_{j-1,1}^{E_k})} * \ldots * \frac{X_{N-1,N}^{E_k}}{(1 - X_{N-1,N}^{E_k})} * Y_1^{E_k} \tag{12.6}$$

$$Y_1^{E_k} = \left(1 + \frac{Y_2^{E_k}}{Y_1^{E_k}} + \frac{Y_3^{E_k}}{Y_1^{E_k}} + \ldots + \frac{Y_j^{E_k}}{Y_1^{E_k}} + \ldots + \frac{Y_N^{E_k}}{Y_1^{E_k}}\right)^{-1}. \tag{12.7}$$

Step 4: In the fourth stage of the DIBR method, the weight coefficient matrix is integrated with the expert weight vector $w = \{w_1, w_2, \ldots, w_k, \ldots, w_L\}\,(k = 1,2,\ \ldots, L)$ through a multiplicative operation, as formulated in Eq. (12.8). This procedure

TABLE 12.1 The algorithm illustrates the steps of defining interrelationships between ranked criteria (DIBR) weighting method.

Algorithm:	The purpose of this algorithm is to present the procedural steps of the DIBR method.	
Input	A set of experts: $E = \{E_1, E_2, \ldots, E_k, \ldots, E_L\} (k = 1,2, \ldots, L)$, a set of criteria: $C = \{C_1, C_2, \ldots, C_j, \ldots, C_N\} (j = 1,2, \ldots, N)$, and an expert weight vector: $w = \{w_1, w_2, \ldots, w_k, \ldots, w_L\} (k = 1,2, \ldots, L)$.	
Step-1:	Determine the priority orderings of the criteria by each expert.	$C_1 > C_2 > \ldots > C_j > \ldots > C_N f$
Step-2:	Generate the pairwise comparison matrix ($X = [X^{E_k}_{j-1,j}]_{LN}$) by employing Eq. (12.1).	$X = \begin{bmatrix} X^{E_1}_{1,2}, X^{E_1}_{2,3}, \cdots X^{E_1}_{j-1,j} \cdots X^{E_1}_{N-1,N} \\ \vdots \cdots \vdots \cdots \vdots \\ X^{E_k}_{1,2}, X^{E_k}_{2,3}, \cdots X^{E_k}_{j-1,j} \cdots X^{E_k}_{N-1,N} \\ \vdots \cdots \vdots \cdots \vdots \\ X^{E_L}_{1,2}, X^{E_L}_{2,3}, \cdots X^{E_L}_{j-1,j} \cdots X^{E_L}_{N-1,N} \end{bmatrix}$
Step-3:	Calculate the weight coefficient matrix ($Y = [Y^{E_k}_j]_{LN}$) by employing Eq. (12.2-12.7).	$Y^{E_k}_2 = \frac{X^{E_k}_{1,2}}{(1 - X^{E_k}_{1,2})} * Y^{E_k}_1 \; Y^{E_k}_3 = \frac{X^{E_k}_{1,2}}{(1 - X^{E_k}_{1,2})} * \frac{X^{E_k}_{2,3}}{(1 - X^{E_k}_{2,3})} * Y^{E_k}_1 \; Y^{E_k}_j = \frac{X^{E_k}_{1,2}}{(1 - X^{E_k}_{1,2})} * \frac{X^{E_k}_{2,3}}{(1 - X^{E_k}_{2,3})} * \ldots * \frac{X^{E_k}_{j-1,1}}{(1 - X^{E_k}_{j-1,1})} * Y^{E_k}_1$ $Y^{E_k}_N = \frac{X^{E_k}_{1,2}}{(1 - X^{E_k}_{1,2})} * \frac{X^{E_k}_{2,3}}{(1 - X^{E_k}_{2,3})} * \ldots * \frac{X^{E_k}_{j-1,1}}{(1 - X^{E_k}_{j-1,1})} * \ldots * \frac{X^{E_k}_{N-1,N}}{(1 - X^{E_k}_{N-1,N})} * Y^{E_k}_1 \; Y^{E_k}_1 = \left(1 + \frac{Y^{E_k}_2}{Y^{E_k}_1} + \frac{Y^{E_k}_3}{Y^{E_k}_1} + \ldots + \frac{Y^{E_k}_j}{Y^{E_k}_1} + \ldots + \frac{Y^{E_k}_N}{Y^{E_k}_1}\right)^{-1} \; Y = \begin{bmatrix} Y^{E_1}_1, Y^{E_1}_2, \cdots Y^{E_1}_j \ldots Y^{E_1}_N \\ \vdots \cdots \vdots \cdots \vdots \\ Y^{E_k}_1, Y^{E_k}_2, \cdots Y^{E_k}_j \ldots Y^{E_k}_N \\ \vdots \cdots \vdots \cdots \vdots \\ Y^{E_L}_1, Y^{E_L}_2, \cdots Y^{E_L}_j \ldots Y^{E_L}_N \end{bmatrix}$
Step-4:	Calculate weighted matrix ($D = [D_{kj}]_{LN}$) by employing Eq. (12.8).	$D_{kj} = w_k * Y^{E_k}_j$
Step-5:	Calculate the criteria weight vector ($R = [R_j]_N$) by employing Eq. (12.9).	$R_j = \Sigma^L_{k=1} D_{kj}$
Step-6:	Construct the first control vector ($\lambda = [\lambda^{E_k}_{1,N}]_{LN}$) and the second control vector ($\mu = [\mu^{E_k}_{1,N}]_{LN}$) and reliability index (RI) vector ($RI = [RI^{E_k}_{1,N}]_{LN}$) by employing Eq. (12.10-12.12)	$\lambda^{E_k}_{1,N} = \left(\frac{Y^{E_k}_1}{Y^{E_k}_N} + 1\right)^{-1} \; \mu^{E_k}_{1,N} = \left(\frac{Y^{E_k}_N}{Y^{E_k}_N + Y^{E_k}_1}\right) RI^{E_k}_{1,N} = \lvert \mu^{E_k}_{1,N} - \lambda^{E_k}_{1,N} \rvert$
Output	A criteria weight vector: $R = \{R_1, R_2, \ldots, R_j, \ldots, R_N\} (j = 1,2, \ldots, N)$.	

generates the weighted matrix ($D = [D_{kj}]_{LN}$), in which the relative importance of each expert is systematically embedded into the evaluation process:

$$D_{kj} = w_k * Y_j^{E_k}; (k = 1, 2, \ldots, L; j = 1, 2, \ldots, N). \tag{12.8}$$

herein, $\sum_{k=1}^{L} w_k = 1$.

Step 5: In the fifth step of the DIBR method, the application of the sum calculation yields the criteria weight vector ($R = [R_j]_N$) presented in Eq. (12.9):

$$R_j = \sum_{k=1}^{L} D_{kj}; (k = 1, 2, \ldots, L; j = 1, 2, \ldots, N). \tag{12.9}$$

Step 6: In the seventh (checking) step of the DIBR method, the RI vector ($RI = [RI_{1,N}^{E_k}]_{LN}$) (Eq. (12.12)) between the elements of the first control vector ($\lambda = [\lambda_{1,N}^{E_k}]_{LN}$) (Eq. (12.10)) and the second control vector ($\mu = [\mu_{1,N}^{E_k}]_{LN}$) (Eq. (12.11)) must be less than 0.10. Otherwise, the experts are required to re-evaluate the pairwise comparisons of the criteria, and the steps of the method must be repeated:

$$\lambda_{1,N}^{E_k} = \left(\frac{Y_1^{E_k}}{Y_N^{E_k}} + 1 \right)^{-1}; (k = 1, 2, \ldots, L; j = 1, 2, \ldots, N). \tag{12.10}$$

$$\mu_{1,N}^{E_k} = \left(\frac{Y_N^{E_k}}{Y_N^{E_k} + Y_1^{E_k}} \right); (k = 1, 2, \ldots, L; j = 1, 2, \ldots, N). \tag{12.11}$$

$$RI_{1,N}^{E_k} = |\mu_{1,N}^{E_k} - \lambda_{1,N}^{E_k}|; (k = 1, 2, \ldots, L; j = 1, 2, \ldots, N). \tag{12.12}$$

TABLE 12.2 The rankings provided by the experts.

X_{kj}	Rank
E_1	$C_3 > C_1 > C_2$
E_2	$C_2 > C_1 > C_3$
E_3	$C_3 > C_2 > C_1$
E_4	$C_3 > C_1 > C_2$

TABLE 12.3 The pairwise comparison matrix.

	$C_{3,1}$	$C_{1,2}$
E_1	0.75	0.75
	$C_{2,1}$	$C_{1,3}$
E_2	0.80	0.75
	$C_{3,2}$	$C_{2,1}$
E_3	0.80	0.70
	$C_{3,1}$	$C_{1,2}$
E_4	0.85	0.75

The algorithm of the DIBR method is presented in Table 12.1.

12.3 Numerical example 1

For numerical example 1, the essential inputs required to implement the DIBR algorithm, as presented in Table 12.1, consist of a set of experts $E = \{E_1, E_2, E_3, E_4\}(i = 1,2,3,4)$, a set of criteria $C = \{C_1, C_2, C_3\}(j = 1,2,3)$, and an expert weight vector $w = \{0.20,0.30,0.25,0.25\}$. Based on these inputs, the procedural steps of the DIBR method were systematically executed in the following order:

Step 1: Each expert ranked the criteria according to their level of importance. The rankings provided by the experts are presented in Table 12.2.

TABLE 12.4 The weight coefficient matrix.

	C_2	C_3	C_1
E_1	0.6923	0.2308	0.0769
	C_2	C_1	C_3
E_2	0.7500	0.1875	0.0625
	C_3	C_2	C_1
E_3	0.7368	0.1842	0.0789
	C_2	C_3	C_1
E_4	0.8095	0.1429	0.0476

TABLE 12.5 The weighted matrix.

	C_2	C_3	C_1
E_1	0.1385	0.0462	0.0154
	C_2	C_1	C_3
E_2	0.1500	0.0375	0.0125
	C_3	C_2	C_1
E_3	0.1474	0.0368	0.0158
	C_2	C_3	C_1
E_4	0.1619	0.0286	0.0095

TABLE 12.6 The criteria weight vector.

	C_1	C_2	C_3
R_j	0.0782	0.4872	0.2346
Rank	3	1	2

Step 2: The pairwise comparison matrix ($X = [X_{j-1,j}^{E_k}]_{LN}$) derived from Eq. (12.1), is provided in Table 12.3.

Step 3: By using Eq. (12.2–12.7), the weight coefficient matrix ($Y = [Y_j^{E_k}]_{LN}$) was calculated and presented in Table 12.4.

Step 4: The weighted matrix ($D = [D_{kj}]_{LN}$) was calculated by employing Eq. (12.8). It is also shown in Table 12.5.

Step 5: The criteria weight vector ($R = [R_j]_N$) was computed by employing Eq. (12.9). It is also presented in Table 12.6.

Step 6: The first control vector ($\lambda = [\lambda_{1,N}^{E_k}]_{LN}$), and the second control vector ($\mu = [\mu_{1,N}^{E_k}]_{LN}$), and the RI vector ($RI = [RI_{1,N}^{E_k}]_{LN}$) were calculated by employing Eqs. (12.10–12.12) and shown in Table 12.7. All RI values are below 0.10, indicating that the criterion weight vector is reliable.

12.4 Numerical example 2

For numerical example 2, the essential inputs required to implement the DIBR algorithm, as presented in Table 12.1, consist of a set of experts $E = \{E_1, E_2, E_3, E_4, E_5, E_6\} (i = 1,2, \ldots,6)$, a set of criteria $C = \{C_1, C_2, C_3, C_4, C_5, C_6\} (j = 1,2, \ldots,6)$, and a experts weight vector $w = \{0.10,0.20,0.15,0.20,0.15,0.20\}$. Based on these inputs, the procedural steps of the DIBR method were systematically executed in the following order:

Step 1: Each expert ranked the criteria according to their level of importance. The rankings provided by the experts are presented in Table 12.8.

Step 2: The pairwise comparison matrix ($X = [X_{j-1,j}^{E_k}]_{LN}$) derived from Eq. (12.1), is provided in Table 12.9.

Step 3: By using Eq. (12.2–12.7), the weight coefficient matrix ($Y = [Y_j^{E_k}]_{LN}$) was calculated and presented in Table 12.10.

Step 4: The weighted matrix ($D = [D_{kj}]_{LN}$) was calculated by employing Eq. (12.8). It is also shown in Table 12.11.

Step 5: The criteria weight vector ($R = [R_j]_N$) was computed by employing Eq. (12.9). It is also presented in Table 12.12.

TABLE 12.7 The first and second control vectors and reliability index vectors.

Y_{kj}	$\lambda_{1,N}^{E_k}$	$\mu_{1,N}^{E_k}$	$RI_{1,N}^{E_k}$
E_1	0.1000	0.1880	*0.0880*
E_2	0.0769	0.1458	*0.0689*
E_3	0.0968	0.1861	*0.0893*
E_4	0.0556	0.1064	*0.0509*

TABLE 12.8 The rankings provided by the experts.

X_{kj}	*Rank*
E_1	$C_2 > C_3 > C_1 > C_5 > C_4 > C_6$
E_2	$C_2 > C_1 > C_3 > C_5 > C_6 > C_4$
E_3	$C_3 > C_2 > C_5 > C_1 > C_4 > C_6$
E_4	$C_2 > C_3 > C_5 > C_1 > C_4 > C_6$
E_5	$C_2 > C_1 > C_3 > C_4 > C_5 > C_6$
E_6	$C_2 > C_3 > C_5 > C_4 > C_1 > C_6$

TABLE 12.9 The pairwise comparison matrix.

	$C_{2,3}$	$C_{3,1}$	$C_{1,5}$	$C_{5,4}$	$C_{4.6}$
E_1	0.52	0.80	0.55	0.53	0.60
	$C_{2,1}$	$C_{1,3}$	$C_{3,5}$	$C_{5,6}$	$C_{6.4}$
E_2	0.60	0.65	0.58	0.62	0.55
	$C_{3,2}$	$C_{2,5}$	$C_{5,1}$	$C_{1,4}$	$C_{4.6}$
E_3	0.70	0.60	0.65	0.60	0.55
	$C_{2,3}$	$C_{3,5}$	$C_{5,1}$	$C_{1,4}$	$C_{4.6}$
E_4	0.55	0.58	0.62	0.60	0.56
	$C_{2,1}$	$C_{1,3}$	$C_{3,4}$	$C_{4,5}$	$C_{5.6}$
E_5	0.54	0.51	0.53	0.55	0.75
	$C_{2,3}$	$C_{3,5}$	$C_{5,4}$	$C_{4,1}$	$C_{1.6}$
E_6	0.58	0.60	0.55	0.56	0.80

TABLE 12.10 The weight coefficient matrix.

	C_2	C_3	C_1	C_5	C_4	C_6
E_1	0.3814	0.3521	0.0880	0.0720	0.0639	0.0426
	C_2	C_1	C_3	C_5	C_6	C_4
E_2	0.3883	0.2589	0.1394	0.1009	0.0619	0.0506
	C_3	C_2	C_5	C_1	C_4	C_6
E_3	0.4867	0.2086	0.1391	0.0749	0.0499	0.0408
	C_2	C_3	C_5	C_1	C_4	C_6
E_4	0.3119	0.2552	0.1848	0.1133	0.0755	0.0593
	C_2	C_1	C_3	C_4	C_5	C_6
E_5	0.2388	0.203	0.195	0.173	0.142	0.047
	C_2	C_3	C_5	C_4	C_1	C_6
E_6	0.3345	0.2422	0.1615	0.1321	0.1038	0.0260

Step 6: The first control vector ($\lambda = [\lambda_{1,N}^{E_k}]_{LN}$), and the second control vector ($\mu = [\mu_{1,N}^{E_k}]_{LN}$), and the RI vector ($RI = [RI_{1,N}^{E_k}]_{LN}$) were calculated by employing Eqs. (12.10–12.12) and shown in Table 12.13. All RI values are below 0.10, indicating that the criterion weight vector is reliable.

TABLE 12.11 The weighted matrix.

	C_2	C_3	C_1	C_5	C_4	C_6
E_1	0.0381	0.0352	0.0088	0.0072	0.0064	0.0043
	C_2	C_1	C_3	C_5	C_6	C_4
E_2	0.0777	0.0518	0.0279	0.0202	0.0124	0.0101
	C_3	C_2	C_5	C_1	C_4	C_6
E_3	0.0730	0.0313	0.0209	0.0112	0.0075	0.0061
	C_2	C_3	C_5	C_1	C_4	C_6
E_4	0.0624	0.0510	0.0370	0.0227	0.0151	0.0119
	C_2	C_1	C_3	C_4	C_5	C_6
E_5	0.0358	0.0305	0.0293	0.0260	0.0213	0.0071
	C_2	C_3	C_5	C_4	C_1	C_6
E_6	0.0669	0.0484	0.0323	0.0264	0.0208	0.0052

TABLE 12.12 The criteria weight vector.

	C_1	C_2	C_3	C_4	C_5	C_6
R_j	0.1457	0.3122	0.2649	0.0915	0.1388	0.0469
Rank	3	1	2	5	4	6

TABLE 12.13 The first and second control vectors and reliability index vectors.

Y_{kj}	$\lambda_{1,N}^{Ek}$	$\mu_{1,N}^{Ek}$	$RI_{1,N}^{Ek}$
E_1	0.1004	0.1542	*0.0538*
E_2	0.1153	0.1810	*0.0657*
E_3	0.0774	0.1248	*0.0473*
E_4	0.1598	0.2495	*0.0897*
E_5	0.1652	0.2452	*0.0800*
E_6	0.0720	0.1035	*0.0315*

12.5 Conclusion

This chapter presented the DIBR method for criteria weighing and alternative ranking, demonstrating its application through two numerical examples. The study highlights several key advantages of the DIBR method. First, by focusing on the relationships between adjacent ranked criteria, the method reduces the complexity and number of pairwise comparisons, enhancing consistency in the results. Second, the method provides a systematic and transparent approach for determining weight coefficients based on expert judgments, making it particularly suitable for decision-making scenarios involving subjective assessments. Third, its straightforward mathematical framework allows for easy implementation and adaptation across various MADM problems.

Despite these strengths, certain limitations of the DIBR method should be noted. The method relies heavily on expert rankings, which may introduce bias or inconsistency if the expert group is not sufficiently diverse or experienced. Additionally, the approach primarily addresses relationships between adjacent criteria, potentially overlooking indirect influences among nonadjacent criteria. Furthermore, while the method effectively determines criteria weights, the ranking of alternatives may still require integration with complementary MADM techniques for enhanced robustness under uncertainty.

For future research, several directions are suggested. The DIBR method could be extended by incorporating fuzzy sets (Wang et al., 2025), rough sets (Dinçer et al., 2025), or neutrosophic (Önden et al., 2024) sets to better handle uncertainty and vagueness in expert judgments. Hybridizing DIBR with other ranking approaches, such as the deviation-based pairwise assessment ratio technique (DEPART) (Yalçın et al., 2025), ERUNS (Babaçoğlu et al., 2025), best-worst method (BMW) (Jorshary et al., 2025), or the alternative ranking using two-step logarithmic normalization method (ARLON) (Kara et al., 2025), could improve the accuracy and reliability of alternative rankings in complex decision-making contexts. Additionally, empirical studies across diverse application domains, including energy, transportation, and defense, would help to further validate and generalize the method's effectiveness. Finally, exploring automated or software-supported implementations of DIBR could enhance its practicality for large-scale decision problems.

In conclusion, the DIBR method provides a reliable, efficient, and transparent framework for criteria weighting and decision-making, and its integration with advanced MADM techniques offers promising avenues for future research and application.

References

Ayough, A., Shargh, S. B., & Khorshidvand, B. (2023). A new integrated approach based on base-criterion and utility additive methods and its application to supplier selection problem. *Expert Systems with Applications, 221*, 119740. https://doi.org/10.1016/j.eswa.2023.119740.

Babaçoğlu, S., Yalçın, G. C., Kara, K., Turen, U., Simic, V., Polat, M., & Pamucar, D. (2025). Promoting benchmarking and best practices in education: An interval-valued spherical fuzzy model for assessing sustainable digital transformation maturity. *Technology in Society, 81*, 102850. https://doi.org/10.1016/j.techsoc.2025.102850.

Deveci, M., Pamucar, D., Gokasar, I., Delen, D., Wu, Q., & Simic, V. (2022). An analytics approach to decision alternative prioritization for zero-emission zone logistics. *Journal of Business Research, 146*, 554–570. https://doi.org/10.1016/j.jbusres.2022.03.059.

Dinçer, H., Abadi, B., Yüksel, S., & Eti, S. (2025). Multi-perspective strategic analysis of wind energy projects via AI-integrated quantum fuzzy recommender approach. *Journal of Intelligent Decision Making and Granular Computing, 1*(1), 13–28. https://doi.org/10.31181/jidmgc1120253.

Dündar, S. (2024). Performance evaluation of IPARD-II rural development programs with integrated DIBR-RAWEC methods. *Pamukkale Üniversitesi Mühendislik Bilimleri Dergisi, 31*(3), 339–350. https://dergipark.org.tr/tr/pub/pajes/issue/92855/1727829.

Ecer, F., Pamucar, D., & Demir, G. (2025). Decision-analytics-based electric vehicle charging station location selection: A cutting-edge fuzzy rough framework. *Energy Reports, 14*, 711–735. https://doi.org/10.1016/j.egyr.2025.06.035.

Jorshary, K. M., Sassani, M., Raoufi, S., & Khamoushi, S. (2025). Ranking of AI-driven strategies for optimizing the health tourism supply chain using stratified BWM. *Knowledge and Decision Systems with Applications, 1*, 295–315. https://doi.org/10.59543/kadsa.v1i.15051.

Kara, K., Ergin, E. A., Yalçın, G. C., Çelik, T., Deveci, M., & Kadry, S. (2025). Sustainable brand logo selection using an AI-supported PF-WENSLO-ARLON hybrid method. *Expert Systems with Applications, 260*, 125382. https://doi.org/10.1016/j.eswa.2024.125382.

Kara, K., Yalçın, G. C., Simic, V., Yıldırım, A. T., Pamucar, D., & Siarry, P. (2024). A spherical fuzzy-based DIBR II-AROMAN model for sustainability performance benchmarking of wind energy power plants. *Expert Systems with Applications, 253*, 124300. https://doi.org/10.1016/j.eswa.2024.124300.

Lukić, R. (2023). Application of DIBR and MAIRCA methods in the evaluation of the economic performance of the economy of Bosnia and Herzegovina. *Economic Review: Journal of Economics and Business, 21*(1), 53–64. https://doi.org/10.51558/2303-680X.2023.21.1.53.

Önden, A., Kara, K., Önden, İ., Yalçın, G. C., Simic, V., & Pamucar, D. (2024). Exploring the adoption of the metaverse and chat generative pre-trained transformer: A single-valued neutrosophic Dombi Bonferroni-based method for the selection of software development strategies. *Engineering Applications of Artificial Intelligence, 133*, 108378. https://doi.org/10.1016/j.engappai.2024.108378.

Pamucar, D., Deveci, M., Gokasar, I., Işık, M., & Zizovic, M. (2021). Circular economy concepts in urban mobility alternatives using integrated DIBR method and fuzzy Dombi CoCoSo model. *Journal of Cleaner Production, 323*, 129096. https://doi.org/10.1016/j.jclepro.2021.129096.

Tešić, D., Bozanic, D., Puška, A., Štilić, A., & Milić, A. (2023a). *Application of MCDM model rough DIBR-fuzzy LBWA-BONFERRONI and decision support system DEXi for the improvement of earthquake risk level assessment*. https://doi.org/10.21203/rs.3.rs-3248793/v1.

Tešić, D. Z., Božanić, D. I., & Miljković, B. D. (2023b). Application of MCDM DIBR-rough MABAC model for selection of drone for use in natural disaster caused by flood. In *Serbian International Conference on Applied Artificial Intelligence*. Springer International Publishing, 151–169 https://doi.org/10.1007/978-3-031-29717-5_11.

Tešić, D., Božanić, D., Stojković, D., Puška, A., & Stojanović, I. (2023c). DIBR–DOMBI–FUZZY MAIRCA model for strategy selection in the system of defense. *Discrete Dynamics in Nature and Society, 2023*(1), 4961972. https://doi.org/10.1155/2023/4961972.

Tešić, D., & Marinković, D. (2023). Application of fermatean fuzzy weight operators and MCDM model DIBR-DIBR II-NWBM-BM for efficiency-based selection of a complex combat system. *Journal of Decision Analytics and Intelligent Computing, 3*(1), 243–256. https://doi.org/10.31181/10002122023t.

Wang, D., Letchmunan, S., Liao, J., Qiu, H., & Liu, Z. (2025). Construction of new similarity measures for complex pythagorean fuzzy sets and their applications in decision-making problems. *Journal of Intelligent Decision Making and Information Science, 2*, 156–173. https://doi.org/10.59543/jidmis.v2i.11737.

Yalçın, G. C., Kara, K., Işık, G., Tekeli, E. S., Simic, V., Ballı, A., & Pamucar, D. (2025). Promoting sustainability-oriented brand activist campaigns: A spherical fuzzy decision support framework for evaluating activist advertising videos. *Engineering Applications of Artificial Intelligence, 162*, 112349. https://doi.org/10.1016/j.engappai.2025.112349.

Chapter 13

SWARA: Stepwise weight assessment ratio analysis for multi-attribute decision-making

Shabnam Rahnamay Bonab
Department of Management, Monash University, Melbourne, VIC, Australia

13.1 Introduction

Decision-making is a critical ability that affects both individual habits and organizational effectiveness. Individuals and organizations are confronted daily with problems that require careful analysis and action, and the implications of those decisions reach far into personal development, career advancement, and general societal or cultural contexts (Mahmudah et al., 2024; Haseli et al., 2023a). To successfully resolve these challenges, choosing a systematic and sound decision-making process is of key concern. Multi-criteria decision-making (MCDM) is today a powerful methodology that helps decision-makers to take into account a group of factors collectively instead of depending upon any single measure (Haseli et al., 2020). This combined process enables balanced thinking and minimizes the possibilities of biased decisions centered on emotional responses or subconscious prejudices (Ashofteh & Dougaheh, 2024; Haseli et al., 2025). In addition, MCDM is needed in a group setting, where it harmonizes various judgments and treats each criterion according to its relative significance (Haseli & Sheikh, 2022). By structuring decisions into systematic parts such as alternatives, criteria of evaluation, weight assignment, and stakeholders' participation, MCDM enhances the consistency and reasonableness of decisions made under complicated or uncertain situations (Haseli et al., 2023b; Jafarzadeh Ghoushchi et al., 2023).

The stepwise weight assessment ratio analysis (SWARA) is a technique used in MCDM processes to evaluate and assign significance to both criteria and subcriteria. Originally proposed by Turskis et al. (2010), SWARA involves ranking the criteria in order of importance, with the highest priority item placed at the top and the least significant at the bottom. Expert input is essential in this method, as it provides the judgments that guide the weighting process (Karakuş, 2023). One of the strengths of the SWARA method is its ease of use, making it accessible to professionals across different disciplines who can intuitively grasp its purpose (Deveci et al., 2023).

The SWARA method enables decision-makers and policymakers to set priorities according to prevailing environmental and economic conditions. A core feature of this approach is its reliance on expert assessments to determine the relative significance of each criterion (Turskis et al., 2010; Mahmudah et al., 2024). Moreover, SWARA facilitates the organization and synthesis of expert input, making it an effective tool for structured data collection. Due to its simplicity, professionals from various fields can engage with the method with ease (Bouraima et al., 2023). One of SWARA's key strengths is that, in certain contexts, priorities are preestablished by organizational or national policies, eliminating the need for additional evaluation or ranking of criteria (Prajapati et al., 2019). As a result, SWARA proves valuable in scenarios where decision priorities are already aligned with recognized conditions and has been recommended for use in such structured decision-making settings (Stanujkic et al., 2015; Moslem et al., 2023). According to these features, SWARA can be effectively applied in different real-world problems such as assessing indicators of energy systems, prioritizing barriers and solutions in e-waste management, evaluating supplier performance in sustainable supply chains, and selecting renewable energy projects. It has also been used in healthcare decision-making, for example, in ranking medical equipment procurement or preventive strategies, as well as in urban planning for assessing smart city infrastructure. These diverse applications highlight SWARA's flexibility and relevance in both environmental and economic decision-making contexts.

Encyclopedia of Multi-Attribute Decision-Making (MADM). DOI: https://doi.org/10.1016/B978-0-443-33275-3.00020-8

13.2 Literature review

In recent years, with the growing complexity of decision-making problems and the uncertain environment, the use of decision-making methods in very important issues such as energy, transportation, logistics, and sustainability has become very common and important (Haseli et al., 2023c; Stanujkic et al., 2015). Researchers use MCDM methods for structured and logical evaluation. The SWARA method has attracted the attention of researchers in many fields to assign the weight of criteria based on its high applicability and simple calculations.

Researchers have also improved its accuracy and applicability by combining the SWARA method with other decision-making methods such as multiobjective optimization by ratio analysis, the technique for order preference by similarity to ideal solution, and fuzzy logic. As shown in Table 13.1, researchers have benefited from this method in various fields.

TABLE 13.1 Literature review related to the stepwise weight assessment ratio analysis (SWARA) method.

Author(s)	Research objective/focus	Methodology
(Stanujkic et al., 2015)	Selection of a packaging design	SWARA
(Blagojević et al., 2021)	Evaluation of the railway management model	SWARA-MABAC
(Hashemkhani Zolfani et al., 2018)	Extending the SWARA method to improve decision-making quality	SWARA
(Bouraima et al., 2023)	Railway transportation system assessment	SWARA-CoCoSo
(Vrtagić et al., 2021)	Determining weight coefficients for ranking road sections' safety	SWARA-MARCOS
(Sivageerthi et al., 2022)	Prioritizing coal supply chain risks in power plants	SWARA
(Moslem et al., 2023)	Determining key criteria for improving public transport quality	SWARA
(Prajapati et al., 2019)	Identifying and prioritizing solutions for reverse logistics barriers	SWARA-WASPAS
(Karabašević et al., 2016)	Optimizing personnel selection	SWARA-WASPAS
(Deveci et al., 2023)	Identifying and prioritizing risks impeding sustainable mining	Fuzzy SWARA
(Ayyildiz, 2022)	Prioritizing Sustainable Development Goal 7: Affordable and Clean Energy indicators for accessible and clean energy achievement	Fermatean fuzzy SWARA
(Stanujkić et al., 2021)	Proposing grey extension of SWARA and PIPRECIA for group decision-making	SWARA-PIPRECIA
(Yücenur & Ipekçi, 2021)	Proposing location selection model for marine current energy plant	SWARA-WASPAS
(Ulutaş et al., 2020)	Proposing integrated Geographic Information System -based MCDM model for logistics center selection	SWARA-CoCoSo
(Soltani & Mirzaei Aliabadi, 2023)	Evaluating firefighting job risks, identifying key hazards	Fuzzy SWARA-ARAS
(Dinçer et al., 2022)	Ranking microgeneration energy investments, prioritizing photovoltaic systems for efficiency	SWARA-TOPSIS
(Haghnazar Kouchaksaraei et al., 2015)	Glasshouse location selection	SWARA-COPRAS
(Ghenai et al., 2020)	Assessing sustainability indicators of renewable energy systems	SWARA-ARAS
(Seikh & Chatterjee, 2024)	Evaluating attribute weights effectively for renewable energy decision-making	SWARA-ARAS
(Rahnamay Bonab & Osgooei, 2022)	Identification of environmental threats in wastewater treatment operations	SWARA-COPRAS
(Alrasheedi et al., 2023)	Determining criteria weights under intuitionistic fuzzy information for renewable energy evaluation	SWARA-MARCOS
(Ghoushchi et al., 2022)	Assessment of failure mechanisms in wind turbines	SWARA-CoCoSo

13.3 Methodology

This section provides a comprehensive step-by-step explanation of the SWARA method, with each stage supported by corresponding mathematical equations to ensure clarity and facilitate understanding of the computational procedure. The first step in this method is to identify and determine the criteria that will be applied to assess the alternatives. These criteria can include various characteristics such as cost, quality, delivery time, etc.

13.3.1 Step 1: List and rank the criteria

In this approach, each expert initially ranks the criteria in order of importance, assigning the top position to the most significant and the bottom to the least significant. The final ranking is then established by averaging the individual rankings provided by all experts.

13.3.2 Step 2: Calculate the comparative importance (S_j)

From the second criterion onward, the expert determines how much less important each criterion is compared to the one just above it.

13.3.3 Step 3: Calculate the coefficient (K_j)

(13.1) is applied to compute the coefficient (K_j) of a feature for each criterion.

$$K_j = \begin{cases} 1 & if j = 1 \\ S_j + 1 & if j > 1 \end{cases}; \quad j = 1, \ \ldots, \ n \tag{13.1}$$

13.3.4 Step 4: Calculate the recalculated weights (q_j)

In this step, (13.2) is used to compute the preliminary weight of each attribute as assigned by individual decision-makers.

$$q_j = \begin{cases} 1 if j = 1 \\ \frac{q_{j-1}}{k_j} if j > 1 \end{cases}; \quad j = 1, \ \ldots, \ n \tag{13.2}$$

13.3.5 Step 5: Normalize the weights

In this step, by Eq. (13.3), the normalized and final weights for each criterion are calculated.

$$W_j = \frac{q_j}{\sum_{j=1}^{n} q_j} \tag{13.3}$$

13.3.6 Step 6: The final ranking of criteria

Finally, based on the weights obtained from the previous stage, the values are arranged in descending order to establish the final ranking.

13.4 Numerical example 1: select a partner company

The first problem is considered relatively simple. Suppose a company wants to make a decision to select a partner company. For this purpose, five criteria, including quality (C_1), cost (C_2), delivery time (C_3), efficiency (C_4), and appropriate behavior (C_5) need to be weighted.

Initially, experts in the relevant domain rank the criteria according to their importance, assigning the highest rank to the most critical criterion and the lowest rank to the least significant one. In this case study, the quality criterion has received the first rank (the most important criterion), and the cost has received the last rank (the least important criterion). The other criteria have also been ranked according to Table 13.2.

Then, the comparative importance scores (S_j) are computed for each criterion, the results of which are shown in Table 13.3. Each criterion from the second to the last is compared to the one before it to determine its relative importance.

Then, based on (13.1), the coefficient (K_j) are computed, and the results are displayed in Table 13.4.

TABLE 13.2 Related criteria.

Ran-k	Criteria	Symbol
1	Quality	C_1
2	Delivery time	C_3
3	Appropriate behavior	C_5
4	Efficiency	C_4
5	Cost	C_2

TABLE 13.3 The comparative importance scores

Criteria	Compare to....	S_j
C_1		-
C_3	C_1	0.3
C_5	C_3	0.2
C_4	C_5	0.4
C_2	C_4	0.5

K_i calculation:

$$K_3 = S_j + 1 = 0.3 + 1 = 1.3$$

$$K_5 = S_5 + 1 = 0.2 + 1 = 1.2$$

$$K_4 = S_4 + 1 = 0.4 + 1 = 1.4$$

$$K_2 = S_2 + 1 = 0.5 + 1 = 1.5$$

In this stage, using (13.2), q_i values are computed as below: Table 13.5.

$q_1 = 1$ (C_1 is the most important)

Now compute each subsequent q_i:

$$q_3 = \frac{q_1}{K_3} = \frac{1}{1.3} \approx 0.769$$

$$q_5 = \frac{q_3}{K_5} = \frac{0.769}{1.2} \approx 0.641$$

$$q_4 = \frac{q_5}{K_4} = \frac{0.641}{1.4} \approx 0.458$$

$$q_2 = \frac{q_4}{K_2} = \frac{0.458}{1.5} \approx 0.305$$

TABLE 13.4 The coefficient (K_j) values.

Criteria	Compared to...	S_j	K_j
C_1		-	1.0
C_3	C_1	0.3	1.3
C_5	C_3	0.2	1.2
C_4	C_5	0.4	1.4
C_2	C_4	0.5	1.5

TABLE 13.5 q_i values.

	q_j
C_1	1.000
C_3	0.769
C_5	0.641
C_4	0.458
C_2	0.305

Finally, using Eq. (13.3), the final weight for each criterion is computed and shown in Table 13.6.
Final weight for

$$C_i = \frac{q_i}{\Sigma q}$$

$$W_1 = \frac{1.000}{3.173} = 0.315$$

$$W_3 = \frac{0.769}{3.173} = 0.242$$

$$W_5 = \frac{0.641}{3.173} = 0.202$$

$$W_4 = \frac{0.458}{3.173} = 0.144$$

$$W_2 = \frac{0.305}{3.173} = 0.096$$

Fig. 13.1 shows that the C_1 criterion holds the greatest significance, with a weight of 0.315. Following this, criteria C_3, C_5, and C_4 occupy the second, third, and fourth positions, having weights of 0.242, 0.202, and 0.144, respectively. Criterion C_2 is ranked last, with a weight of 0.096.

TABLE 13.6 The criteria and their description.

Criteria	Symbol	Description
Product quality	C_1	Quality refers to the degree to which a product conforms to customer needs, standards, and expectations.
Delivery time	C_2	This criterion refers to the supplier's ability to deliver orders on time.
Contract flexibility	C_3	This measure assesses the degree of cooperation and flexibility of the supplier in the face of changes in contract conditions, order volumes, prices, or special needs.
Sustainability	C_4	Sustainability refers to observing environmental principles and optimal utilization of resources in the production process.
Social responsibility	C_5	This criterion shows how much the supplier cares about social issues such as workers' rights, workplace safety, the absence of child labor, and positive engagement with the community.
Price	C_6	This criterion refers to the economic feasibility of purchasing from the supplier,
After-sales service	C_7	This criterion includes technical support, maintenance, parts replacement, training, and other services provided after the sale of the product.
Technical capability & innovation	C_8	This criterion evaluates a supplier's ability to use advanced technologies, develop new solutions, and continuously improve their products, services, or processes.

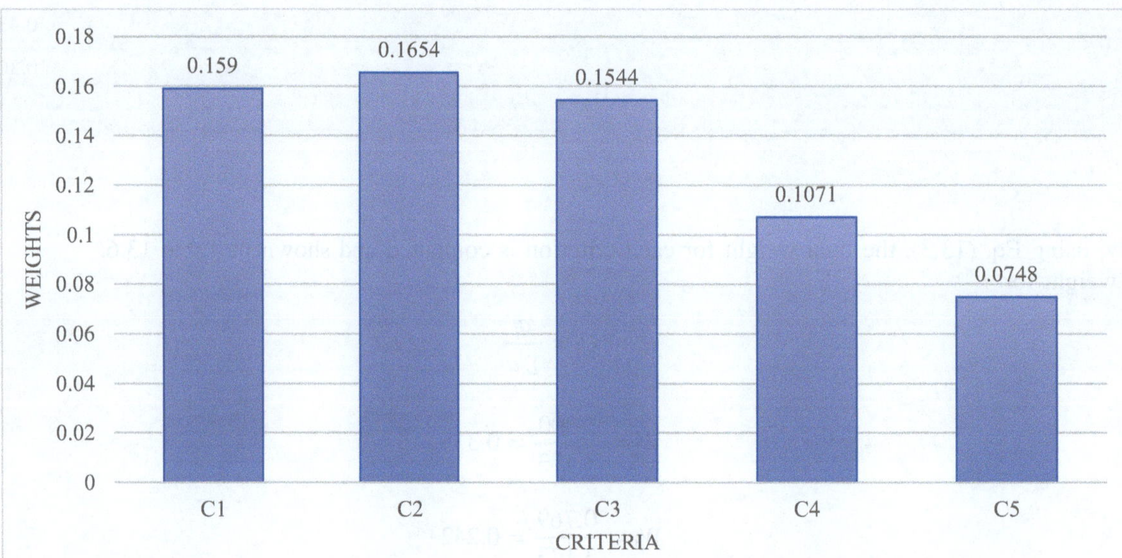

FIGURE 13.1 The normalized final weights for each criterion.

13.5 Numerical example 2: supplier selection

The second case study examined in this study is relatively complex. Suppose an electronics manufacturing company is facing challenges in the supplier selection process and decides to use the SWARA method to solve this problem.

In this regard, relevant experts have identified seven key criteria for evaluating suppliers, including the following: Product quality (C_1), delivery time (C_2), contract flexibility (C_3), sustainability (C_4), social responsibility (C_5), price(C_6), after-sales service(C_7), technical capability & innovation(C_8). The information related to the criteria is shown in Table 13.6.

TABLE 13.7 The preferences of all experts.

The preferences of first expert		The preferences of second expert		The preferences of third expert	
Rank	**Criteria**	**Rank**	**Criteria**	**Rank**	**Criteria**
1	C_8	1	C_8	1	C_8
2	C_2	2	C_3	2	C_1
3	C_3	3	C_2	3	C_2
4	C_1	4	C_1	4	C_3
5	C_4	5	C_4	5	C_4
6	C_5	6	C_5	6	C_6
7	C_7	7	C_7	7	C_7
8	C_6	8	C_6	8	C_5

TABLE 13.8 The comparative importance scores.

Expert 1			Expert 2			Expert 3		
Criteria	Compare to....	S_j	C_8	Compare to....	S_j	Criteria	Compare to....	S_j
C_8		-	C_3		-	C_8		-
C_2	C_8	0.1	C_2	C_8	0.2	C_1	C_8	0.14
C_3	C_2	0.2	C_1	C_3	0.15	C_2	C_1	0.27
C_1	C_3	0.15	C_4	C_2	0.18	C_3	C_2	0.20
C_4	C_1	0.25	C_5	C_1	0.23	C_4	C_3	0.19
C_5	C_4	0.2	C_7	C_4	0.3	C_6	C_4	0.22
C_7	C_5	0.3	C_{76}	C_5	0.35	C_7	C_6	0.35
C_6	C_7	0.2	C_{76}	C_6	0.19	C_5	C_7	0.25

In this problem, the opinions of three experts, including a technical expert, a financial manager, and a purchasing manager, have been used to make the process of selecting the right supplier for the company more accurate and comprehensive. Because multiple decision-makers participate in the process, this matter can be addressed as a group decision-making problem.

In the first step of the SWARA method, the criteria are ranked based on the opinions of each expert. The ranking of the criteria from the perspective of each expert is presented in Table 13.7.

The highest priority criterion is assigned the top rank, while the least important one is placed last. In this case study, the technical capability and innovation (C_8) criterion has received the first rank (the most important criterion), and the social responsibility (C_5) has received the last rank (the least important criterion) based on the opinion of the first expert.

Then, the comparative importance scores (S_j) are computed for each criterion, the results of which are presented in Table 13.8. Each criterion from the second to the last is compared to the one before it to determine its relative importance.

Then, based on (13.1), the coefficient (K_i) are calculated, and the results are displayed in Table 13.9.

TABLE 13.9 The coefficient (K_j) values

Criteria	K_j (expert 1)	K_j (expert 2)	K_j (expert 3)
C_8	1.00	1.00	1.00
C_2	1.10	1.15	1.27
C_3	1.20	1.20	1.20
C_1	1.15	1.18	1.14
C_4	1.25	1.23	1.19
C_5	1.20	1.30	1.25
C_7	1.30	1.35	1.35
C_6	1.20	1.19	1.22

TABLE 13.10 q_i values.

Criteria	q_j (expert 1)	q_j (expert 2)	q_j (expert 3)
C_8	1.000	1.000	1.000
C_2	0.9091	0.724	0.690
C_3	0.7576	0.833	0.575
C_1	0.6588	0.613	0.877
C_4	0.5270	0.498	0.483
C_5	0.4392	0.383	0.234
C_7	0.3378	0.284	0.293
C_6	0.2815	0.239	0.396

In this stage, using (13.2) q_i , values are computed as below (for first expert): Table 13.10.

$$q_8 = 1 \quad (C_8 \textit{ is the most important})$$

Now compute each subsequent q_i:

$$q_2 = \frac{q_8}{K_2} = \frac{1}{1.10} \approx 0.909$$

$$q_3 = \frac{q_2}{K_3} = \frac{0.909}{1.20} \approx 0.757$$

$$q_1 = \frac{q_3}{K_1} = \frac{0.757}{1.15} \approx 0.658$$

$$q_4 = \frac{q_1}{4} = \frac{0.658}{1.25} \approx 0.527$$

TABLE 13.11 The normalized final weights for each criterion.

Criteria	Final weigh (expert 1)	Final weigh (expert 2)	Final weigh (expert 3)
C_8	0.2036	0.218	0.219
C_2	0.1851	0.158	0.151
C_3	0.1542	0.182	0.126
C_1	0.1341	0.133	0.192
C_4	0.1073	0.108	0.106
C_5	0.0894	0.083	0.051
C_7	0.0688	0.062	0.064
C_6	0.0573	0.052	0.087

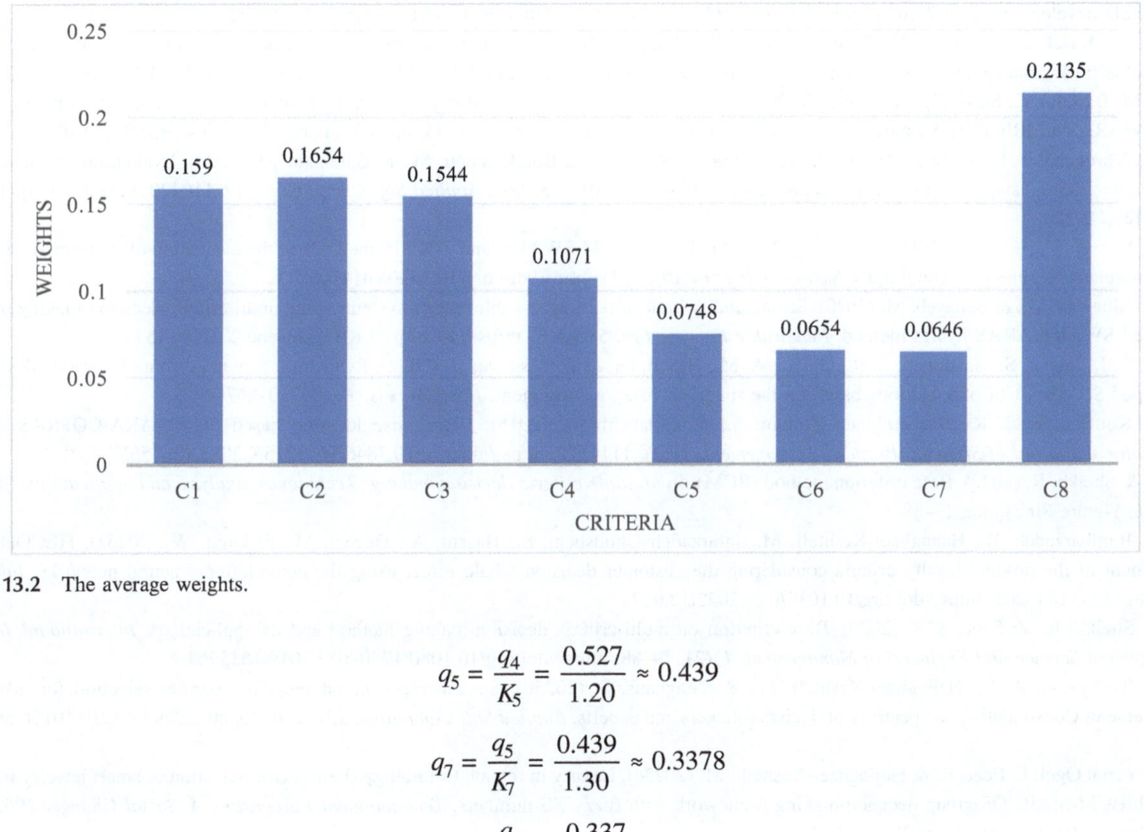

FIGURE 13.2 The average weights.

$$q_5 = \frac{q_4}{K_5} = \frac{0.527}{1.20} \approx 0.439$$

$$q_7 = \frac{q_5}{K_7} = \frac{0.439}{1.30} \approx 0.3378$$

$$q_6 = \frac{q_7}{K_6} = \frac{0.337}{1.20} \approx 0.281$$

Finally, using Eq. (13.3), the final weight for each criterion is calculated and shown in Table 13.11.

To determine the final weights, given the input from three experts, the average of the individual expert weights was calculated using the following formula:

$$\textit{Average weights} = \frac{\textit{Weight (Expert} \quad 1) + \textit{Weight (Expert} \quad 2) + \textit{Weight (Expert} \quad 3)}{3}$$

According to Fig. 13.2, criterion C_8 holds the highest importance with a value of 0.2135, while criterion C_7 is the least significant, having a value of 0.0646.

13.6 Conclusion

In this chapter, we have comprehensively reviewed the SWARA method, which is a MCDM method for weighting criteria. This approach has seen extensive application across diverse disciplines. This chapter begins with an introduction to the SWARA method and then reviews studies that have used the SWARA method. Subsequently, a detailed explanation of the SWARA process is presented. Finally, two case studies are presented to further explain and provide practical application. The purpose of these case studies is to demonstrate the flexibility and provide valuable insights into the strengths and limitations of this method. The purpose of this chapter is to provide a complete understanding of the SWARA method and its potential to address difficult and complex problems in various decision-making fields.

References

Alrasheedi, A. F., Mishra, A. R., Rani, P., Zavadskas, E. K., & Cavallaro, F. (2023). Multicriteria group decision making approach based on an improved distance measure, the SWARA method and the WASPAS method. *Granular Computing (Internet), 8*(6), 1867–1885. https://doi.org/10.1007/s41066-023-00413-x.

Ashofteh, P. S., & Dougaheh, M. P. (2024). Ranking the optimal combination of low-impact urban development systems under climate change with the TODIM multi-criteria decision-making method. *Journal of Cleaner Production, 434*, 140108.

Ayyildiz, E. (2022). Fermatean fuzzy step-wise weight assessment ratio analysis (SWARA) and its application to prioritizing indicators to achieve sustainable development goal-7. *Renewable Energy, 193*, 136–148. https://doi.org/10.1016/j.renene.2022.05.021.

Blagojević, A., Kasalica, S., Stević, Ž., Tričković, G., & Pavelkić, V. (2021). Evaluation of safety degree at railway crossings in order to achieve sustainable traffic management: A novel integrated fuzzy MCDM model. *Sustainability, 13*(2), 832. https://doi.org/10.3390/su13020832.

Bouraima, M. B., Qiu, Y., Stević, Ž., & Simić, V. (2023). Assessment of alternative railway systems for sustainable transportation using an integrated IRN SWARA and IRN CoCoSo model. *Socio-Economic Planning Sciences, 86*, 101475. https://doi.org/10.1016/j.seps.2022.101475.

Deveci, M., Varouchakis, E. A., Brito-Parada, P. R., Mishra, A. R., Rani, P., Bolgkoranou, M., & Galetakis, M. (2023). Evaluation of risks impeding sustainable mining using Fermatean fuzzy score function based SWARA method. *Applied Soft Computing, 139*, 110220. https://doi.org/10.1016/j.asoc.2023.110220.

Dinçer, H., Yüksel, S., Aksoy, T., & Hacıoğlu, Ü. (2022). Application of M-SWARA and TOPSIS methods in the evaluation of investment alternatives of microgeneration energy technologies. *Sustainability, 14*(10), 6271. https://doi.org/10.3390/su14106271.

Ghenai, C., Albawab, M., & Bettayeb, M. (2020). Sustainability indicators for renewable energy systems using multi-criteria decision-making model and extended SWARA/ARAS hybrid method. *Renewable Energy, 146*, 580–597. https://doi.org/10.1016/j.renene.2019.06.157.

Ghoushchi, S. J., Jalalat, S. M., Bonab, S. R., Ghiaci, A. M., Haseli, G., & Tomaskova, H. (2022). Evaluation of wind turbine failure modes using the developed SWARA-CoCoSo methods based on the spherical fuzzy environment. *IEEE Access, 10*, 86750–86764.

Haghnazar Kouchaksaraei, R., Hashemkhani Zolfani, S., & Golabchi, M. (2015). Glasshouse locating based on SWARA-COPRAS approach. *International Journal of Strategic Property Management, 19*(2), 111–122. https://doi.org/10.3846/1648715X.2015.1004565.

Haseli, G., & Sheikh, R. (2022). Base criterion method (BCM). In *Multiple criteria decision making: Techniques, analysis and applications*. Singapore: Springer Nature Singapore, 17–38.

Haseli, G., Ranjbarzadeh, R., Hajiaghaei-Keshteli, M., Jafarzadeh Ghoushchi, S., Hasani, A., Deveci, M., & Ding, W. (2023a). HECON: Weight assessment of the product loyalty criteria considering the customer decision's halo effect using the convolutional neural networks. *Information Sciences, 623*, 184–205. https://doi.org/10.1016/j.ins.2022.12.027.

Haseli, G., Sheikh, R., & Sana, S. S. (2020). Base-criterion on multi-criteria decision-making method and its applications. *International Journal of Management Science and Engineering Management, 15*(2), 79–88. https://doi.org/10.1080/17509653.2019.1633964.

Haseli, G., Torkayesh, A. E., Hajiaghaei-Keshteli, M., & Venghaus, S. (2023b). Sustainable resilient recycling partner selection for urban waste management: Consolidating perspectives of decision-makers and experts. *Applied Soft Computing, 137*, 110120. https://doi.org/10.1016/j.asoc.2023.110120.

Haseli, G., Yaran Ögel, İ., Ecer, F., & Hajiaghaei-Keshteli, M. (2023c). Luxury in female technology (FemTech): Selection of smart jewelry for women through BCM-MARCOS group decision-making framework with fuzzy ZE-numbers. *Technological Forecasting & Social Change, 196*, 122870. https://doi.org/10.1016/j.techfore.2023.122870.

Haseli, G., Yazdani, M., Shaayesteh, M. T., & Hajiaghaei-Keshteli, M. (2025). Logistic hub location problem under fuzzy extended Z-numbers to consider the uncertainty and reliable group decision-making. *Applied Soft Computing, 171*, 112751. https://doi.org/10.1016/j.asoc.2025.112751.

Hashemkhani Zolfani, S., Yazdani, M., & Zavadskas, E. K. (2018). An extended stepwise weight assessment ratio analysis (SWARA) method for improving criteria prioritization process. *Soft Computing (Berlin, Germany), 22*(22), 7399–7405. https://doi.org/10.1007/s00500-018-3092-2.

Jafarzadeh Ghoushchi, S., Garg, H., Rahnamay Bonab, S., & Rahimi, A. (2023). An integrated SWARA-CODAS decision-making algorithm with spherical fuzzy information for clean energy barriers evaluation. *Expert Systems with Applications, 223*, 119884. https://doi.org/10.1016/j.eswa.2023.119884.

Karabašević, D., Stanujkić, D., Urošević, S., & Maksimović, M. (2016). An approach to personnel selection based on SWARA and WASPAS methods. *Bizinfo Blace, 7*(1), 1–11.

Karakuş, C. B. (2023). Groundwater potential assessment based on GIS-based best–worst method (BWM) and step-wise weight assessment ratio analysis (SWARA) method. *Environmental Science and Pollution Research International, 30*(11), 31851–31880. https://doi.org/10.1007/s11356-022-24425-3.

Mahmudah, R. S., Putri, D. I., Abdullah, A. G., Shafii, M. A., Hakim, D. L., & Setiadipura, T. (2024). Developing a multi-criteria decision-making model for nuclear power plant location selection using fuzzy analytic hierarchy process and fuzzy VIKOR methods focused on socio-economic factors. *Cleaner Engineering and Technology, 19*, 100737.

Moslem, S., Stević, Ž., Tanackov, I., & Pilla, F. (2023). Sustainable development solutions of public transportation: An integrated IMF SWARA and fuzzy bonferroni operator. *Sustainable Cities and Society, 93*, 104530. https://doi.org/10.1016/j.scs.2023.104530.

Prajapati, H., Kant, R., & Shankar, R. (2019). Prioritizing the solutions of reverse logistics implementation to mitigate its barriers: A hybrid modified SWARA and WASPAS approach. *Journal of Cleaner Production, 240*, 118219. https://doi.org/10.1016/j.jclepro.2019.118219.

Rahnamay Bonab, S., & Osgooei, E. (2022). Environment risk assessment of wastewater treatment using FMEA method based on Pythagorean fuzzy multiple-criteria decision-making. *Environment, Development and Sustainability,* 1–31.

Seikh, M. R., & Chatterjee, P. (2024). Determination of best renewable energy sources in India using SWARA-ARAS in confidence level based interval-valued Fermatean fuzzy environment. *Applied Soft Computing, 155*, 111495. https://doi.org/10.1016/j.asoc.2024.111495.

Sivageerthi, T., Bathrinath, S., Uthayakumar, M., & Bhalaji, R. K. A. (2022). A SWARA method to analyze the risks in coal supply chain management. *Materials Today: Proceedings, 50*, 935–940. https://doi.org/10.1016/j.matpr.2021.06.338.

Soltani, E., & Mirzaei Aliabadi, M. (2023). Risk assessment of firefighting job using hybrid SWARA-ARAS methods in fuzzy environment. *Heliyon, 9*(11). https://doi.org/10.1016/j.heliyon.2023.e22230 e22230–e22230.

Stanujkic, D., Karabasevic, D., & Zavadskas, E. K. (2015). A framework for the selection of a packaging design based on the SWARA method. *Inžinerinė Ekonomika, 26*(2), 181–187. https://doi.org/10.5755/j01.ee.26.2.8820.

Stanujkić, D., Karabašević, D., Popović, G., Stanimirović, P. S., Saračević, M., Smarandache, F., Katsikis, V. N., & Ulutaş, A. (2021). A new grey approach for using SWARA and PIPRECIA methods in a group decision-making environment. *Mathematics (Basel), 9*(13), 1554. https://doi.org/10.3390/math9131554.

Turskis, Z., Keršulienė, V., & Zavadskas, E. K. (2010). Selection of rational dispute resolution method by applying new step-wise weight assessment ratio analysis. *Journal of Business Economics and Management, 11*(2), 243–258. https://doi.org/10.3846/jbem.2010.12.

Ulutaş, A., Karakuş, C. B., & Topal, A. (2020). Location selection for logistics center with fuzzy SWARA and CoCoSo methods. *Journal of Intelligent & Fuzzy Systems, 38*(4), 4693–4709. https://doi.org/10.3233/JIFS-191400.

Vrtagić, S., Softić, E., Subotić, M., Stević, Ž., Dordevic, M., & Ponjavic, M. (2021). Ranking road sections based on MCDM model: new improved fuzzy SWARA (IMF SWARA). *Axioms, 10*(2), 92. https://doi.org/10.3390/axioms10020092.

Yücenur, G. N., & Ipekçi, A. (2021). SWARA/WASPAS methods for a marine current energy plant location selection problem. *Renewable Energy, 163*, 1287–1298. https://doi.org/10.1016/j.renene.2020.08.131.

Further reading

Jafarzadeh Ghoushchi, S., Garg, H., Rahnamay Bonab, S., & Rahimi, A. (2023). An integrated SWARA-CODAS decision-making algorithm with spherical fuzzy information for clean energy barriers evaluation. *Expert Systems with Applications, 223*, 119884. https://doi.org/10.1016/j.eswa.2023.119884.

Chapter 14

BWM: Best–worst method for multi-attribute decision-making

Gholamreza Haseli
School of Engineering and Sciences, Tecnologico de Monterrey, Monterrey, Mexico

14.1 Introduction

Human decisions in all fields rarely depend on a single criterion. Whether selecting a supplier, prioritizing infrastructure projects, or evaluating technology options, decision-makers routinely face a set of criteria. It means each human decision-making problem must be judged across multiple criteria (Haseli, Ranjbarzadeh, et al., 2023). multi-attribute decision-making (MADM) methods provide structured ways to aggregate heterogeneous information into a ranking or choice approach. Therefore, the MADM methods can consider and process both qualitative and quantitative data that comes from human judgment (Torkayesh et al., 2021). In most MADM approaches, some general common elements include a set of alternatives and criteria, a rule for bringing measurements onto a comparable scale, and a procedure for combining criterion importance. The best–worst method (BWM) (Rezaei, 2015) is one of the methods that is designed to propose a rule for bringing measurements onto a comparable scale. This method enables the measurement of criterion importance. The BWM is designed to make weight elicitation both efficient and consistent while remaining easy to communicate to decision-makers during data gathering. This method departs from fully populated pairwise comparison matrices (as used in methods such as the analytic hierarchy process (Saaty, 2013) by relying on two focused vectors of judgments (Haseli et al., 2020; Moslem, 2025). These two compact preference strings suffice to recover an entire weight vector by solving a small optimization problem that seeks the most consistent weights compatible with the supplied comparisons. The logic behind the BWM is straightforward. Asking fewer, targeted questions reduces cognitive burden and tends to produce more coherent judgments, while the optimization step enforces consistency across the partial assessments (Rezaei, 2016).

There are several practical features that explain the rapid adoption of BWM in applied research. The number of pairwise comparisons grows linearly with the number of criteria ($2n-3$), instead of quadratically as in full pairwise matrices (Haseli & Sheikh, 2022). For moderate to large criteria sets, this is a significant efficiency gain. Another positive feature is that the BWM produces a quantifiable consistency indicator that informs decision-makers whether the preferences are mutually compatible (F. Liang et al., 2020). This transparency helps the decision-makers diagnose. Therefore, if necessary, decision-makers can re-assign values for the inconsistent judgments. The last feature proposes a simple numerical scale for comparisons. The BWM uses an integer scale (1–9) that can be replaced with the linguistic variables. The proposed numerical scale can integrate readily with other MADM methods.

Methodologically, BWM strikes a balance between parsimony and mathematical rigor. The optimization model that underpins weight recovery is typically expressed as a linear or linear-fractional program. It minimizes the maximum absolute deviation between the ratios implied by the weight vector and the decision-maker's pairwise ratio judgments. The resulting weight vector guarantees that the worst inconsistency, across both best-to-others and others-to-worst comparisons, is as small as possible. This minimax characterization has two useful consequences. It yields a single, objective solution rather than an arbitrary averaging of inconsistent judgments, and it permits a principled assessment of robustness by examining how the optimal objective value responds to small perturbations in the input judgments. BWM's interpretability makes it especially well-suited to real-world decision contexts where expert time is scarce or where many criteria must be considered. It has been used in supply-chain management, healthcare prioritization, renewable-energy planning, supplier selection, and many other domains where structured expert judgment is essential.

Encyclopedia of Multi-Attribute Decision-Making (MADM). DOI: https://doi.org/10.1016/B978-0-443-33275-3.00053-1

This chapter presents BWM in depth. We first present a brief literature review of the previous studies in Section 2. Then, we formalize the mathematical model for weight derivation and consistency diagnostics in Section 3. Two worked numerical examples are presented in Sections 4 and 5, respectively. This chapter closes by discussing general conclusions, limitations, and proposing future methodological refinement. In this regard, the emphasis of this chapter is on clarity and reproducibility. Therefore, readers can apply BWM confidently in both research and practice.

14.2 Literature review

The BWM has gained significant attention in MADM due to its efficiency, consistency, and simplicity compared to other weighting methods. Over the years, numerous studies have extended and applied BWM across diverse fields, addressing both methodological enhancements and practical applications. This section provides a comprehensive review of the literature, highlighting the key developments, fuzzy extensions, and the main domains where BWM has been successfully utilized.

In this regard, Table 14.1 summarizes the main methodological developments of BWM. These extensions of BWM illustrate how researchers have refined and extended the original approach. These developments include adaptations that improve the method's flexibility, accuracy, and applicability in complex decision-making scenarios. By presenting these contributions in a structured manner, the table provides a clear overview of how BWM has evolved over time.

TABLE 14.1 Summarizes the main methodological developments for the best–worst method (BWM).

Extensions	Year	Contributions	References
Group BWM	2017	Extends the original method to handle multiple experts' opinions, aggregating their judgments to derive consensus weights while preserving consistency across the group.	Hafezalkotob and Hafezalkotob (2017); Safarzadeh et al. (2018); Haseli et al. (2021)
Multiplicative BWM	2019	Extends the BWM by using a multiplicative approach to calculate criteria weights, which can improve consistency and better reflect proportional differences between the best and worst criteria.	Brunelli and Rezaei (2019); Ratandhara and Kumar (2024)
Bayesian BWM	2020	Treats BWM comparisons probabilistically to aggregate multiple decision-makers and redesigns BWM as a Bayesian hierarchical model.	Mohammadi and Rezaei (2020); Chauhan et al. (2022); Gul et al. (2022); Aslam et al. (2025)
Stratified BWM	2021	The stratified BWM advances the method by dividing criteria into stratified levels, allowing decision-makers to handle complex, multilayered decision problems more systematically.	Torkayesh et al. (2021); Asadabadi et al. (2023); Ecer and Torkayesh (2024); Johny et al. (2025)
Best–worst tradeoff	2022	Enhances the BWM by explicitly incorporating tradeoffs between the best and worst criteria, improving the realism and robustness of weight derivation in decision-making.	Liang et al. (2022)
Nonadditive BWM	2022	Extends the BWM by allowing for nonadditive aggregation of criteria weights, which enables the BWM to capture interactions and dependencies among criteria more effectively.	Liang et al. (2023)
Parsimonious BWM	2023	Improves the BWM by reducing the number of pairwise comparisons required, making the weighting process more efficient while maintaining accuracy and consistency.	Moslem (2023, 2025); Corrente et al. (2024)
Stochastic general BWM	2024	Proposes a scenario-based stochastic approach for the BWM to better handle uncertainty and provides flexible criteria weights.	Tavana et al. (2024)

TABLE 14.2 Fuzzy extensions of the best–worst method (BWM).

Fuzzy extensions	Contributions	References
Triangular fuzzy BWM	Contributes by incorporating triangular fuzzy numbers into BWM, allowing decision-makers to better capture vagueness and imprecision in pairwise comparisons.	Amoozad Mahdiraji et al. (2018); Ghoushchi et al. (2019); Guo and Zhao (2017)
Hesitant fuzzy BWM	Uses hesitant fuzzy multiplicative preference relations and defines a new consistency ratio.	Ali and Rashid (2019); Heidary-Dahooie et al. (2022); Li et al. (2021); Liao et al. (2019)
Intuitionistic fuzzy BWM	This model enforces multiplicative consistency on intuitionistic fuzzy comparisons and defines an Intuitionistic fuzzy consistency ratio.	Cheng and Chen (2024); Dong and Wan (2024); Liu et al. (2023); Wan and Dong (2022)
Neutrosophic BWM	Provides a triple of membership, indeterminacy, and nonmembership degrees for each comparison.	Ambilkar et al. (2024); Vafadarnikjoo et al. (2020); Yucesan and Gul (2021)
Interval type-2 fuzzy BWM	Criteria are compared using interval type-2 fuzzy numbers and linguistic terms. This feature allows handling more ambiguity than ordinary fuzzy BWM.	Alimohammadlou and Sharifian (2023); Altay et al. (2023); Celik et al. (2021)
Grey BWM	Integrates grey system theory into BWM to enable the method to effectively handle incomplete or uncertain preference information in decision-making.	Mahmoudi et al. (2020); Ulutaş et al. (2022)
Rough BWM	Pairwise judgments are represented as rough intervals, and BWM's optimization is adjusted for interval data.	Chang et al. (2019); Liu et al. (2020); Mei and Chen (2021)
Pythagorean fuzzy BWM	Combinates the BWM with Pythagorean fuzzy sets to offer greater flexibility in modeling hesitation and uncertainty in expert judgments.	Otay et al. (2024)
Spherical fuzzy BWM	Provides membership, nonmembership, and hesitancy degrees for each comparison in BWM.	Deniz and Aydin (2024); Haseli et al. (2024)
Fuzzy Z-numbers BWM	Fuzzy Z-numbers allow BWM not only to represent uncertain information but also to reflect the degree of confidence in the provided assessments.	Aboutorab et al. (2018); Zhang et al. (2023)
Fuzzy D-numbers BWM	It uses fuzzy D-numbers to represent uncertain and incomplete information in the BWM process, making the results more consistent.	Hadi Mousavi-Nasab and Sotoudeh-Anvari (2020); Navaei et al. (2025); Pamučar et al. (2021)
Fuzzy ZE-numbers BWM	This method enables simultaneous treatment of uncertainty, reliability, and the restriction level of expert judgments in decision-making.	Haseli et al. (2025); Haseli et al. (2023)

Table 14.2 presents the various fuzzy extensions of BWM, reflecting efforts to handle uncertainty, imprecision, and hesitation in expert judgments. These extensions incorporate different types of fuzzy sets, including triangular, Pythagorean, D-numbers, Z-numbers, and ZE-numbers, among others. The table highlights how these fuzzy adaptations enhance the method's capability to model real-world decision-making under ambiguous and uncertain conditions.

Table 14.3 lists 10 major domains where BWM has been widely applied, demonstrating its versatility and practical relevance. These domains range from supply-chain management and sustainability to healthcare, energy, and human resources. The table provides a concise overview of the fields in which BWM has been effectively used to support structured and consistent decision-making.

14.3 Methodology

This section gives a self-contained statement of the classical BWM (with crisp values). We introduce notation, set out the mathematical optimization used to infer criterion weights from the decision-maker's best/worst comparisons, and show the standard linear programming formulation.

TABLE 14.3 Top 10 major domains where the best–worst method (BWM) has been frequently used.

Topic	Description	References
Supply-chain management	BWM contributes by systematically prioritizing criteria and strategies, helping organizations optimize supplier selection, risk management, and overall supply-chain performance.	Kampalasiri et al., (2021; Kumar et al. (2021; Kampalasiri et al. (2025)
Sustainability and sustainable development	BWM aids decision-making by ranking environmental, social, and economic criteria, enabling more effective sustainability strategies.	Khan (2022); Zhang and Chen (2024); kharayat and Gupta (2025)
Healthcare and waste management	Helps prioritize critical factors supporting more efficient resource allocation and environmentally responsible practices.	Haseli et al. (2023); Beheshtinia et al., (2024; Beheshtinia et al. (2025)
Risk assessment and management	BWM contributes toweighting and ranking risk factors and improving the accuracy and consistency of risk evaluation.	Aghabegloo et al. (2024); Ju et al. (2024); Tanaji and Roychowdhury (2024); Wang et al. (2025)
Energy planning and renewable energy	Assists in evaluating and prioritizing energy options and criteria, supporting more informed and sustainable energy policy and investment decisions.	Balezentis et al. (2021); Kang et al. (2023); F. Mohammadi et al. (2023)
Transportation and logistics	Helps in prioritizing key factors, enabling more efficient route planning, resource allocation, and overall operational performance.	Rezaei et al. (2017); Moktadir and Ren (2024); Haseli et al. (2025)
Project management and evaluation	Contributes by systematically enhancing project selection, ranking project criteria and alternatives, and resource allocation.	Khan et al., Kusi-Sarpong, et al. (2022, 2023); Alsharkawy et al. (2025)
Information technology and systems selection	Aids in evaluating and selecting IT options, leading to more effective and reliable technology adoption decisions.	Sabilla Ajrina et al. (2018); Hashemizadeh et al. (2020); Koohathongsumrit and Luangpaiboon (2024)
Manufacturing and production systems	BWM supports the identification and prioritization of key operational and process criteria, improving efficiency, quality, and decision-making in production planning.	Malek and Desai (2019); Mathiyazhagan et al. (2021); Ghadimi et al. (2022)
Human resources and performance evaluation	Used to assess and rank employee performance criteria, enabling fairer evaluations and more informed HR decisions.	Dwivedi et al. (2021); James et al. (2022); Ergülen and Çalık (2024)

About the notion of the elements in BWM, suppose there are n criteria $C = \{C_1, C_2, \ldots, C_n\}$. The decision-maker supplies the best and worst criteria as inputs: a best criterion index $B \in \{1, \ldots, n\}$ such that C_B is judged most important. A worst criterion index $W \in \{1, \ldots, n\}$ such that C_W is judged least important. In this regard, the best and worst criteria are not the same ($B \neq W$). A set of best-to-others comparison scores a_{Bj} for every $j = 1, \ldots, n$. Each a_{Bj} quantifies how strongly the best criterion dominates criterion j. By convention $a_{BB} = 1$. Additionally, a set of others-to-worst comparison scores a_{jW} for every $j = 1, \ldots, n$. Each a_{jW} quantifies how strongly the criterion j dominates the worst criterion. By convention, a_{BB} and a_{WW} are equal to 1.

Comparison scores are positive real numbers taken from a bounded numerical preference scale (typical practice uses integer scales such as 1, …,9 where 1 means "equal importance" and 9 means "extremely more important"). For consistency with the literature, we require $a_{Bj} \geq 1$ when C_B is at least as important as C_j on the chosen scale. Similarly, $a_{jW} \geq 1$ when C_j is at least as important as C_W. Our goal is to compute a nonnegative weight vector $w = (w_1, w_2, \ldots, w_n)$ that reflects the supplied comparisons as closely as possible, subject to $\sum_{j=1}^{n} w_j = 1$ and $w_j \geq 0$.

According to the mentioned details for the notation and definitions, the steps of the BWM are as follows:

Step 1: Preparing the criteria list for the decision problem.

List the n criteria $C = \{C_1, C_2, \ldots, C_n\}$ clearly and ensure the decision-maker(s) understand each criterion's meaning and measurement. Keep criteria mutually exclusive and collectively exhaustive for the decision scope.

Step 2: Selecting the best and worst among the set of criteria.

As mentioned before, BWM uses the values of two vectors instead of requiring the values of the full matrix. Therefore, ask the decision-maker to identify the single best criterion index B (most important) and the single worst criterion index W (least important). If the decision maker hesitates, provide examples and encourage a decisive choice; BWM requires a unique best and worst for the canonical workflow.

Step 3: Obtaining best-to-others comparisons a_{Bj}.

For every best-to-others comparison, record a_{Bj} answering on a mentioned 1 to 9 scale (how much more important is criterion C_B than C_j?). In this regard, use an anchored verbal description for scale integers (1 = equal, 3 = moderate, 5 = strong, 7 = very strong, 9 = extreme) to ensure consistent interpretation. (1) indicates the vector of the best-to-others comparisons.

$$a_{Bj} = a_{B1},\ a_{B2},\ a_{B3},\ \ldots,\ a_{Bn} \tag{1}$$

Step 4: Obtaining others-to-worst comparisons a_{jW}.

For every others-to-worst comparison, record a_{jW} answering on a mentioned 1 to 9 scale (how much more important is criterion C_j than C_W?). In this regard, the scale is the same as the provided values for step 3. Similarly, (2) indicates the vector of the others-to-worst comparisons.

$$a_{jw} = a_{1w},\ a_{2w},\ a_{3w},\ \ldots,\ a_{nw} \tag{2}$$

Step 5: Formulating the minimax optimization problem based on the values of the comparisons.

The BWM optimization is stated as a minimax problem to find weights and the smallest possible scalar $\xi \geq 0$ such that all ratio deviations are bounded by ξ. In this way, Eq. (3) defines the optimal weight of n criteria.

$$\min \xi$$

Subject to:

$$\left| \frac{w_B}{w_j} - a_{Bj} \right| \leq \xi,\ \ \mathrm{j} = 1, 2, 3, \ldots, \mathrm{n}.$$

$$\left| \frac{w_j}{w_w} - a_{jW} \right| \leq \xi,\ \ \mathrm{j} = 1, 2, 3, \ldots, \mathrm{n}.$$

$$\sum_{j=1}^{n} w_j = 1,\quad w_j \geq 0$$

$$\xi \geq 0 \tag{3}$$

The ξ is the maximum absolute deviation between the decision-maker's ratios and the ratios implied by the candidate weight vector. The smaller the optimal ξ^*, the more consistent the judgments with a single weight vector.

The absolute values in Eq. (3) can be rewritten as the following linear equations.

$$w_B - a_{Bj} w_j \leq \xi w_j$$

$$w_B - a_{Bj} w_j \geq -\xi w_j$$

$$w_j - a_{jw} w_w \leq \xi w_w$$

$$w_j - a_{jw} w_w \geq -\xi w_w \tag{4}$$

Therefore, the optimization problem provided in Eq. (3) can be converted to Eq. (5).

$$\min \xi$$

Subject to:

$$w_B - a_{Bj} w_j \leq \xi w_j$$

$$w_B - a_{Bj} w_j \geq -\xi w_j$$

$$w_j - a_{jw} w_w \leq \xi w_w$$

$$w_j - a_{jw} w_w \geq -\xi w_w$$

$$\sum_{j=1}^{n} w_j = 1, \quad w_j \geq 0$$

$$\xi \geq 0 \tag{5}$$

Multiplying through by weights linearizes the absolute ratio deviations and yields a standard linear programming problem solvable by any solver. The final weight for each criterion is calculated after solving Eq. (5) based on the values of the pairwise comparisons between the criteria. Additionally, the value for ξ is computed, which is used to calculate the pairwise comparisons.

14.3.1 Consistency ratio

In practice, decision-maker judgments are not perfectly consistent. Therefore, exact equalities are typically impossible. In this way, BWM seeks a weight vector that minimizes the maximum deviation between the ratios implied by w and the reported pairwise scores. This minimax approach yields a single objective that controls the worst inconsistency across all supplied comparisons. Ideally, the exact relationships implied by the weights should satisfy $\frac{w_B}{w_j} = a_{Bj}$ and $\frac{w_j}{w_w} = a_{jW}$ for all j.

BWM uses an optimization model that finds a weight vector w minimizing the maximum deviation ξ between the implied ratios and the expressed comparisons. The scalar ξ is therefore the raw consistency measure. It quantifies the worst absolute inconsistency across all supplied comparisons. Lower ξ indicates higher internal consistency. To produce a scale-free indicator analogous to the consistency ratio (CR), a CR of BWM is computed by normalizing ξ by an expected inconsistency level obtained under random (uninformative) judgments for the same problem size. This yields a relative measure of how inconsistent the actual judgments are compared. To calculate the final CR value, we need to have values of the ξ and consistency index (CI). As proposed by Rezaei (2015), the CI value can be chosen from the scale provided in Table 14.4. The scale of CI is defined based on the values of a_{BW}. Therefore, if the decision-maker assigns the value of 9 for the pairwise comparison of best to the worst criterion, the value of 5.23 should be selected as the CI value.

The final CR value is calculated using the ξ and CI values according to Eq. (6). In this regard, $CR = 0$ indicates perfect consistency. $CR < 0.1$ is often deemed highly consistent. $CR \approx 1$ suggests inconsistency comparable to random judgments. $CR > 1$ implies judgments are worse than random, and re-elicitation is recommended.

$$CR = \frac{\xi}{CI} \tag{6}$$

TABLE 14.4 Consistency index (CI) for the best– worst method (Rezaei, 2015).

a_{BW}	CI values
1	0.00
2	0.44
3	1.00
4	1.63
5	2.30
6	3.00
7	3.73
8	4.47
9	5.23

TABLE 14.5 Pairwise comparison vectors for the best-to-others and others-to-worst.

Index		C-1	C-2	C-3	C4
Best-to-others	C-3	4	9	1	5
Others-to-worst	C-2	3	1	9	2

14.4 Numerical example 1

For the first numerical example, we consider a simple decision problem with four criteria for a logistics assessment. At the first step, our criteria were determined as cost effectiveness (C1), delivery time (C2), reliability (C3), and operational flexibility (C4). At the second step, according to the steps of the BWM, the best and worst criteria were selected by the decision-maker. In this regard, C3 is determined as the best and C2 as the worst criterion. As the third step, the decision-maker performed best-to-others comparisons. The results of the comparisons between C3 and other criteria are provided in Table 14.5.

Similarly, the decision-maker performed others-to-worst comparisons according to step 4 of the BWM. The results of the comparisons between all criteria and C2 (as the worst criterion) are provided in Table 14.5. Based on the presented results in Table 14.5, the optimization problem to solve the BWM model should be as Eq. (7):

$$\min \xi$$

Subject to:

$$\left|\frac{w_3}{w_1} - a_{31}\right| \leq \xi$$

$$\left|\frac{w_3}{w_2} - a_{32}\right| \leq \xi$$

$$\left|\frac{w_3}{w_4} - a_{34}\right| \leq \xi$$

$$\left|\frac{w_1}{w_2} - a_{12}\right| \leq \xi$$

$$\left|\frac{w_4}{w_2} - a_{42}\right| \leq \xi$$

$$w_1 + w_2 + w_3 + w_4 = 1$$

$$w_j \geq 0$$

$$\xi \geq 0 \tag{7}$$

As mentioned in section 3, the above optimization problem can be rewritten as follows:

$$\min \xi;$$

Subject to:

$$w_3 - a_{31}w_1 \leq \xi w_1;$$

$$w_3 - a_{31}w_1 \geq -\xi w_1;$$

$$w_3 - a_{32}w_2 \leq \xi w_2;$$
$$w_3 - a_{32}w_2 \geq -\xi w_2;$$
$$w_3 - a_{34}w_4 \leq \xi w_4;$$
$$w_3 - a_{34}w_4 \geq -\xi w_4;$$
$$w_1 - a_{12}w_2 \leq \xi w_2;$$
$$w_1 - a_{12}w_2 \geq -\xi w_2;$$
$$w_1 - a_{42}w_2 \leq \xi w_2;$$
$$w_1 - a_{42}w_2 \geq -\xi w_2;$$
$$w_1 + w_2 + w_3 + w_4 = 1;$$
$$w_j \geq 0;$$
$$\xi \geq 0; \quad (8)$$

In this step, the assigned values for comparisons by the decision-maker should be added to the optimization problem. Therefore, Eq. (9) presents the optimization problem of the BWM based on the judgment of the decision-maker.

$$\min \xi;$$

Subject to:

$$w_3 - 4w_1 \leq \xi w_1;$$
$$w_3 - 4w_1 \geq -\xi w_1;$$
$$w_3 - 9w_2 \leq \xi w_2;$$
$$w_3 - 9w_2 \geq -\xi w_2;$$
$$w_3 - 5w_4 \leq \xi w_4;$$
$$w_3 - 5w_4 \geq -\xi w_4;$$
$$w_1 - 3w_2 \leq \xi w_2;$$
$$w_1 - 3w_2 \geq -\xi w_2;$$
$$w_1 - 2w_2 \leq \xi w_2;$$
$$w_1 - 2w_2 \geq -\xi w_2;$$
$$w_1 + w_2 + w_3 + w_4 = 1;$$
$$w_1 \geq 0;$$

TABLE 14.6 Results for the numerical example 1.

Variabl-es	w1	w2 (best)	w3 (worst)	w4	ξ	Consistency index	Consistency ratio
Results	0.1806-2	0.07225	0.6322	0.114-9	0.-5	5.23	0.0956

$$w_2 \geq 0;$$

$$w_3 \geq 0;$$

$$w_4 \geq 0;$$

$$\xi \geq 0; \tag{9}$$

By solving the above problem using a linear programming solver like Lingo, the weight of each criterion plus ξ value can be calculated. Table 14.6 presents the final criteria weights and ξ value for the numerical example 1.

As presented in Table 14.6, the weights of the second and third criteria have the highest and lowest values, respectively. Additionally, the calculated value for the ξ is 0.5. To calculate the CR value, we need the value of CI in addition to the ξ. As the decision-maker has assigned a value of 9 for the a_{BW}, the CI value should be 5.23 according to the mentioned indexes in Table 14.4. Therefore, the CI value is calculated as Eq. (10).

$$CR = \frac{\xi}{CI} = \frac{0.5}{5.23} = 0.0956, \ (0.0956 \geq 0.1) \tag{10}$$

The final calculated value for the CR indicates the acceptable consistency for the results. Therefore, using BWM had some advantages, such as requiring fewer comparisons, a simple data gathering process, and acceptable consistency.

14.5 Numerical example 2

For the second numerical example, we consider a decision problem for the selection of an optimal strategic solution for a large-scale project. Such decisions are inherently complex. Therefore, we should consider multiple criteria simultaneously. In this example, we considered seven criteria, including quality (C1), cost (C2), time (C3), flexibility (C4), reliability (C5), security (C6), and scalability (C7). The objective is to minimize risks and maximize organizational value by identifying the alternative that offers the best overall balance across these dimensions. Accordingly, we aim to determine the optimal weight for each criterion before evaluating the alternatives using the BWM. Alternatives can be evaluated using ranking or outranking MADM methods that are presented in the rest of this book.

As mentioned, the first step was identifying the set of criteria. At the second step, according to the steps of the BWM, the best and worst criteria were selected by the decision-maker. In this regard, C1 is determined as the best, and C2 as the worst criterion. As the third step, the decision-maker performed best-to-others comparisons. The results of the comparisons between C1 and other criteria are provided in Table 14.7.

Similarly, the decision-maker performed others-to-worst comparisons according to step 4 of the BWM. The results of the comparisons between all criteria and C2 (as the worst criterion) are provided in Table 14.7. Based on the presented results in Table 14.7, the optimization problem to solve the BWM model should be as Eq. (11):

$$\min \xi$$

Subject to:

$$\left| \frac{w_1}{w_2} - a_{12} \right| \leq \xi$$

TABLE 14.7 Pairwise comparison vectors for the best-to-others and others-to-worst for numerical example 2.

Index		C-1	C-2	C-3	C-4	C-5	C-6	C7
Best-to-others	C-1	1	9	5	3	4	4	2
Others-to-worst	C-2	9	1	2	4	3	3	6

$$\left|\frac{w_1}{w_3} - a_{13}\right| \le \xi$$

$$\left|\frac{w_1}{w_4} - a_{14}\right| \le \xi$$

$$\left|\frac{w_1}{w_5} - a_{15}\right| \le \xi$$

$$\left|\frac{w_1}{w_6} - a_{16}\right| \le \xi$$

$$\left|\frac{w_1}{w_7} - a_{17}\right| \le \xi$$

$$\left|\frac{w_3}{w_2} - a_{32}\right| \le \xi$$

$$\left|\frac{w_4}{w_2} - a_{42}\right| \le \xi$$

$$\left|\frac{w_5}{w_2} - a_{52}\right| \le \xi$$

$$\left|\frac{w_6}{w_2} - a_{62}\right| \le \xi$$

$$\left|\frac{w_7}{w_2} - a_{72}\right| \le \xi$$

$$w_1 + w_2 + w_3 + w_4 + w_5 + w_6 + w_7 = 1$$

$$w_j \ge 0$$

$$\xi \ge 0 \tag{11}$$

As mentioned in section 3, the above optimization problem can be rewritten as follows:

$$\min \xi;$$

Subject to:

$$w_1 - a_{12}w_2 \le \xi w_2; \quad w_1 - a_{12}w_2 \ge -\xi w_2;$$

$$w_1 - a_{13}w_3 \le \xi w_3; \quad w_1 - a_{13}w_3 \ge -\xi w_3;$$

$$w_1 - a_{14}w_4 \le \xi w_4; \quad w_1 - a_{14}w_4 \ge -\xi w_4;$$

$$w_1 - a_{15}w_5 \le \xi w_5; \quad w_1 - a_{15}w_5 \ge -\xi w_5;$$

$$w_1 - a_{16}w_6 \le \xi w_6; \quad w_1 - a_{16}w_6 \ge -\xi w_6;$$

$$w_1 - a_{17}w_7 \le \xi w_7; \quad w_1 - a_{17}w_7 \ge -\xi w_7;$$

$$w_3 - a_{32}w_2 \le \xi w_2; \quad w_3 - a_{32}w_2 \ge -\xi w_2;$$

$$w_4 - a_{42}w_2 \le \xi w_2; \quad w_4 - a_{42}w_2 \ge -\xi w_2;$$

$$w_5 - a_{52}w_2 \le \xi w_2; \quad w_5 - a_{52}w_2 \ge -\xi w_2;$$

$$w_6 - a_{62}w_2 \le \xi w_2; \quad w_6 - a_{62}w_2 \ge -\xi \quad w_2;$$

$$w_7 - a_{72}w_2 \le \xi w_2; \quad w_7 - a_{72}w_2 \ge -\xi \quad w_2;$$

$$w_1 + w_2 + w_3 + w_4 + w_5 + w_6 + w_7 = 1;$$

$$w_1 \ge 0; \; w_2 \ge 0; \; w_3 \ge 0; \; w_4 \ge 0; \; w_5 \ge 0; \; w_6 \ge 0; \; w_7 \ge 0;$$

$$\xi \ge 0; \tag{12}$$

In this step, the assigned values for comparisons by the decision-maker should be added to the optimization problem. Therefore Eq. (12) presents the optimization problem of the BWM based on the judgment of the decision-maker.

$$\min \xi;$$

Subject to:

$$w_1 - 9*w_2 \le \xi w_2; \quad w_1 - 9*w_2 \ge -\xi \quad w_2;$$

$$w_1 - 5*w_3 \le \xi w_3; \quad w_1 - 5*w_3 \ge -\xi \quad w_3;$$

$$w_1 - 3*w_4 \le \xi w_4; \quad w_1 - 3*w_4 \ge -\xi \quad w_4;$$

$$w_1 - 4*w_5 \le \xi w_5; \quad w_1 - 4*w_5 \ge -\xi \quad w_5;$$

$$w_1 - 4*w_6 \le \xi w_6; \quad w_1 - 4*w_6 \ge -\xi \quad w_6;$$

$$w_1 - 2*w_7 \le \xi w_7; \quad w_1 - 2*w_7 \ge -\xi \quad w_7;$$

$$w_3 - 2*w_2 \le \xi w_2; \quad w_3 - 2*w_2 \ge -\xi \quad w_2;$$

$$w_4 - 4*w_2 \le \xi w_2; \quad w_4 - 4*w_2 \ge -\xi \quad w_2;$$

$$w_5 - 3*w_2 \le \xi w_2; \quad w_5 - 3*w_2 \ge -\xi \quad w_2;$$

$$w_6 - 3*w_2 \le \xi w_2; \quad w_6 - 3*w_2 \ge -\xi w_2;$$

$$w_7 - 6*w_2 \le \xi w_2; \quad w_7 - 6*w_2 \ge -\xi w_2;$$

$$w_1 + w_2 + w_3 + w_4 + w_5 + w_6 + w_7 = 1;$$

$$w_1 \ge 0; \; w_2 \ge 0; \; w_3 \ge 0; \; w_4 \ge 0; \; w_5 \ge 0; \; w_6 \ge 0; \; w_7 \ge 0;$$

$$\xi \ge 0; \tag{13}$$

By solving the above problem using a linear programming solver like Lingo, the weight of each criterion plus ξ value can be calculated. Table 14.8 presents the final criteria weights and ξ value for the numerical example 2.

As presented in Table 14.8, the weights of the second and third criteria have the highest and lowest values, respectively. Additionally, the calculated value for the ξ is 0.3944. To calculate the CR value, we need the value of CI in addition to the ξ. As the decision-maker has assigned a value of 9 for the a_{BW}, the CI value should be 5.23 according to the mentioned indexes in Table 14.4. Therefore, the CI value is calculated as Eq. (14).

$$CR = \frac{\xi}{CI} = \frac{0.3944}{5.23} = 0.0754, \; (0.0754 \ge 0.1) \tag{14}$$

TABLE 14.8 Results for the numerical example 2.

Variabl-es	w1 (best)	w2 (worst)	w3	w4	w5	w6	w7
Results	0.3505	0.0373	0.649-7	0.134-5	0.097-2	0.097-2	0.2183

The final calculated value for the CR indicates the acceptable consistency for the results. Therefore using BWM had some advantages, such as requiring fewer comparisons, a simple data gathering process, and acceptable consistency.

14.6 Conclusion

The analyses and numerical examples presented in the chapter demonstrate that the BWM delivers a pragmatic and mathematically grounded approach for eliciting criterion weights. By asking experts to identify the single most important and the single least important criteria, and then to provide two compact vectors of comparisons, BWM reconstructs a full weight vector by solving a small optimization problem that minimizes the maximum deviation between implied ratios and stated preferences. The two numerical examples in the chapter illustrate this behavior concretely. Both numerical examples produce interpretable weight vectors and an associated consistency metric (ξ), thereby quantifying the coherence of elicited judgments. These results confirm that BWM can produce defensible, easily communicated weighting solutions with substantially fewer elicitation questions than full pairwise comparison methods.

Beyond its parsimony in the pairwise comparisons, BWM has several methodological strengths that make it attractive for research and practice. The minimax optimization underpinning weight recovery yields a unique objective solution rather than ad hoc averaging, and the explicit consistency indicator provides decision makers with diagnostic feedback that can guide re-elicitation when judgments conflict. Because the required comparisons grow linearly with the number of criteria ($2n-3$), BWM is especially useful in contexts where expert time is limited or cognitive load must be minimized. Using a simple 1–9 scale and related linguistic variables to numerical values enhances usability across domains. Therefore, the BWM strikes a productive balance between rigor and operational feasibility.

At the same time, decision-makers should be aware of the limitations of this method. The method hinges on the correct identification of the best and worst criteria. The misidentification or ambiguous judgments can bias the resulting weights. Additionally, while the number of comparisons is small, that does not eliminate the possibility of inconsistency. Indeed, the method provides diagnostics precisely because inconsistency can and does occur. BWM also presumes that a single decision-maker or an integrated group judgment can supply coherent best/worst choices; in multistakeholder settings, it may be necessary to aggregate multiple BWM runs via consensus protocols or to adopt group-elicitation extensions. In other words, in group decision settings, simple aggregation of individual BWM runs can obscure heterogeneity of views. Consequently, special aggregation protocols or consensus mechanisms are often necessary but nontrivial to implement. Additionally, the consistency metric ξ is informative, but its interpretation depends on chosen normalization procedures (CI/CR tables) and on the judgment scale. Therefore, thresholds for "acceptable" inconsistency are somewhat heuristic and may require calibration for different application areas.

To advance both the theory and practice of BWM, future research should pursue methodological refinements and robust application guidelines. Promising directions include approaches that explicitly model uncertainty in expert judgments. Fuzzy sets or fuzzy numbers and their combination with group decision-making can be a reliable way to extend the BWM. Work is also needed on principled calibration of the CI and on automated inconsistency-resolution procedures that suggest minimal changes to elicited comparisons to restore acceptable ξ levels. Applied research should benchmark BWM against alternative weighting methods across diverse domains, develop open-source software toolboxes for reproducible elicitation and sensitivity analysis, and produce practitioner-oriented protocols that reduce cognitive bias and improve interexpert agreement. Implementing these advances will broaden BWM's reliability and uptake in both scholarly and industrial decision contexts.

References

Aboutorab, H., Saberi, M., Asadabadi, M. R., Hussain, O., & Chang, E. (2018). ZBWM: The Z-number extension of best worst method and its application for supplier development. *Expert Systems with Applications, 107*, 115–125. https://doi.org/10.1016/j.eswa.2018.04.015.

Aghabegloo, M., Rezaie, K., Torabi, S. A., & Yazdani, M. (2024). Integrating business impact analysis and risk assessment for physical asset criticality analysis: A framework for sustainable operations in process industries. *Expert Systems with Applications, 241*, 122737. https://doi.org/10.1016/j.eswa.2023.122737.

Ali, A., & Rashid, T. (2019). Hesitant fuzzy best-worst multi-criteria decision-making method and its applications. *International Journal of Intelligent Systems, 34*(8), 1953–1967. https://doi.org/10.1002/int.22131.

Alimohammadlou, M., & Sharifian, S. (2023). Industry 4.0 implementation challenges in small- and medium-sized enterprises: An approach integrating interval type-2 fuzzy BWM and DEMATEL. *Soft Computing, 27*(1), 169–186. https://doi.org/10.1007/s00500-022-07569-9.

Alsharkawy, M., Hamdy, A., & Marzouk, M. (2025). Developing a new sustainable rating system for assessing construction projects using BWM. *Cleaner Engineering and Technology, 25*, 100920. https://doi.org/10.1016/j.clet.2025.100920.

Altay, B. C., Celik, E., Okumus, A., Balin, A., & Gul, M. (2023). An integrated interval type-2 fuzzy BWM-MARCOS model for location selection of e-scooter sharing stations: The case of a university campus. *Engineering Applications of Artificial Intelligence, 122*, 106095. https://doi.org/10.1016/j.engappai.2023.106095.

Ambilkar, P., Verma, P., & Das, D. (2024). Sustailient supplier selection using neutrosophic best–worst approach: A case study of additively manufactured trinkets. *Benchmarking: An International Journal, 31*(5), 1515–1547. https://doi.org/10.1108/BIJ-02-2023-0122.

Amoozad Mahdiraji, H., Arzaghi, S., Stauskis, G., & Zavadskas, E. K. (2018). A hybrid fuzzy BWM-COPRAS method for Analyzing key factors of sustainable architecture. *Sustainability, 10*(5), 1626. https://doi.org/10.3390/su10051626.

Asadabadi, M. R., Ahmadi, H. B., Gupta, H., & Liou, J. J. H. (2023). Supplier selection to support environmental sustainability: The stratified BWM TOPSIS method. *Annals of Operations Research, 322*(1), 321–344. https://doi.org/10.1007/s10479-022-04878-y.

Aslam, J., Lai, K., Hanbali, A. A., & Khan, N. T. (2025). Blockchain solution for supply chains & logistics challenges: An empirical investigation. *Transportation Research Part E: Logistics and Transportation Review, 198*, 104134. http://doi.org/10.1016/j.tre.2025.104134.

Balezentis, T., Siksnelyte-Butkiene, I., & Streimikiene, D. (2021). Stakeholder involvement for sustainable energy development based on uncertain group decision making: Prioritizing the renewable energy heating technologies and the BWM-WASPAS-IN approach. *Sustainable Cities and Society, 73*, 103114. https://doi.org/10.1016/j.scs.2021.103114.

Beheshtinia, M. A., Safarzadeh, M. S., Fathi, M., Ghobakhloo, M., Al-Emran, M., & Tseng, M. L. (2025). Enhancing healthcare waste management: a novel hybrid multi-criteria decision-making method. *Management of Environmental Quality: An International Journal, 36*(5), 1095–1124. https://doi.org/10.1108/MEQ-09-2024-0368.

Brunelli, M., & Rezaei, J. (2019). A multiplicative best–worst method for multi-criteria decision making. *Operations Research Letters, 47*(1), 12–15. https://doi.org/10.1016/j.orl.2018.11.008.

Celik, E., Yucesan, M., & Gul, M. (2021). Green supplier selection for textile industry: A case study using BWM-TODIM integration under interval type-2 fuzzy sets. *Environmental Science and Pollution Research, 28*(45), 64793–64817. https://doi.org/10.1007/s11356-021-13832-7.

Chang, T.-W., Lo, H.-W., Chen, K.-Y., & Liou, J. (2019). A novel FMEA model based on rough BWM and rough TOPSIS-AL for risk assessment. *Mathematics, 7*(10), 874. https://doi.org/10.3390/math7100874.

Chauhan, A., Jakhar, S. K., & Jabbour, C. J. C. (2022). Implications for sustainable healthcare operations in embracing telemedicine services during a pandemic. *Technological Forecasting and Social Change, 176*, 121462. https://doi.org/10.1016/j.techfore.2021.121462.

Chen, Z., Wu, D., Luo, W., & Cheng, X. (2024). A hybrid heterogeneous framework for medical waste disposal evaluation by fusing group BWM and regret-rejoice MABAC. *Expert Systems with Applications, 249*, 123514. https://doi.org/10.1016/j.eswa.2024.123514.

Cheng, X., & Chen, C. (2024). Decision making with intuitionistic fuzzy best-worst method. *Expert Systems with Applications, 237*, 121215. https://doi.org/10.1016/j.eswa.2023.121215.

Corrente, S., Greco, S., & Rezaei, J. (2024). Better decisions with less cognitive load: The Parsimonious BWM. *Omega, 126*, 103075. https://doi.org/10.1016/j.omega.2024.103075.

Deniz, R., & Aydin, N. (2024). Sustainable and smart electric bus charging station deployment via hybrid spherical fuzzy BWM and MULTIMOORA framework. *Neural Computing and Applications, 36*(25), 15685–15703. https://doi.org/10.1007/s00521-024-09788-7.

Dong, J.-Y., & Wan, S.-P. (2024). Interval-valued intuitionistic fuzzy best-worst method with additive consistency. *Expert Systems with Applications, 236*, 121213. https://doi.org/10.1016/j.eswa.2023.121213.

Dwivedi, R., Prasad, K., Mandal, N., Singh, S., Vardhan, M., & Pamucar, D. (2021). Performance evaluation of an insurance company using an integrated Balanced Scorecard (BSC) and Best-Worst Method (BWM). *Decision Making: Applications in Management and Engineering, 4*(1), 33–50. https://doi.org/10.31181/dmame2104033d.

Ecer, F., & Torkayesh, A. E. (2024). A stratified fuzzy decision-making approach for sustainable circular supplier selection. *IEEE Transactions on Engineering Management, 71*, 1130–1144. https://doi.org/10.1109/TEM.2022.3151491.

Ergülen, A., & Çalık, A. (2024). F-BWM-MARCOS approach for performance evaluation of Türkiye's top 500 industrial enterprises in the pre-pandemic and pandemic era. *Benchmarking: An International Journal*. https://doi.org/10.1108/BIJ-05-2023-0336.

Ghadimi, P., Donnelly, O., Sar, K., Wang, C., & Azadnia, A. H. (2022). The successful implementation of industry 4.0 in manufacturing: An analysis and prioritization of risks in Irish industry. *Technological Forecasting and Social Change, 175*, 121394. https://doi.org/10.1016/j.techfore.2021.121394.

Ghoushchi, S. J., Yousefi, S., & Khazaeili, M. (2019). An extended FMEA approach based on the Z-MOORA and fuzzy BWM for prioritization of failures. *Applied Soft Computing, 81*, 105505. https://doi.org/10.1016/j.asoc.2019.105505.

Gul, M., Yucesan, M., & Ak, M. F. (2022). Control measure prioritization in Fine – Kinney-based risk assessment: A Bayesian BWM-Fuzzy VIKOR combined approach in an oil station. *Environmental Science and Pollution Research, 29*(39), 59385–59402. https://doi.org/10.1007/s11356-022-19454-x.

Gunduz, M. A., Demir, S., & Paksoy, T. (2021). Matching functions of supply chain management with smart and sustainable tools: A novel hybrid BWM-QFD based method. *Computers & Industrial Engineering, 162*, 107676. https://doi.org/10.1016/j.cie.2021.107676.

Guo, S., & Zhao, H. (2017). Fuzzy best-worst multi-criteria decision-making method and its applications. *Knowledge-Based Systems, 121*, 23–31. https://doi.org/10.1016/j.knosys.2017.01.010.

Hadi Mousavi-Nasab, S., & Sotoudeh-Anvari, A. (2020). An extension of best-worst method with D numbers: Application in evaluation of renewable energy resources. *Sustainable Energy Technologies and Assessments, 40*, 100771. https://doi.org/10.1016/j.seta.2020.100771.

Hafezalkotob, A., & Hafezalkotob, A. (2017). A novel approach for combination of individual and group decisions based on fuzzy best-worst method. *Applied Soft Computing, 59*, 316–325. https://doi.org/10.1016/j.asoc.2017.05.036.

Haseli, G., Ranjbarzadeh, R., Hajiaghaei-Keshteli, M., Jafarzadeh Ghoushchi, S., Hasani, A., Deveci, M., & Ding, W. (2023). HECON: Weight assessment of the product loyalty criteria considering the customer decision's halo effect using the convolutional neural networks. *Information Sciences, 623*, 184–205. https://doi.org/10.1016/j.ins.2022.12.027.

Haseli, G., & Sheikh, R. (2022). *Base Criterion Method (BCM),* 17–38. https://doi.org/10.1007/978-981-16-7414-3_2.

Haseli, G., Sheikh, R., Ghoushchi, S. J., Hajiaghaei-Keshteli, M., Moslem, S., Deveci, M., & Kadry, S. (2024). An extension of the best–worst method based on the spherical fuzzy sets for multi-criteria decision-making. *Granular Computing, 9*(2), 40. https://doi.org/10.1007/s41066-024-00462-w.

Haseli, G., Sheikh, R., & Sana, S. S. (2020). Base-criterion on multi-criteria decision-making method and its applications. *International Journal of Management Science and Engineering Management, 15*(2), 79–88. https://doi.org/10.1080/17509653.2019.1633964.

Haseli, G., Sheikh, R., Wang, J., Tomaskova, H., & Tirkolaee, E. B. (2021). A novel approach for group decision making based on the best–worst method (G-BWM): Application to supply chain management. *Mathematics, 9*(16), 1881. https://doi.org/10.3390/math9161881.

Haseli, G., Torkayesh, A. E., Hajiaghaei-Keshteli, M., & Venghaus, S. (2023). Sustainable resilient recycling partner selection for urban waste management: Consolidating perspectives of decision-makers and experts. *Applied Soft Computing, 137*, 110120. https://doi.org/10.1016/j.asoc.2023.110120.

Haseli, G., Yazdani, M., Shaayesteh, M. T., & Hajiaghaei-Keshteli, M. (2025). Logistic hub location problem under fuzzy Extended Z-numbers to consider the uncertainty and reliable group decision-making. *Applied Soft Computing, 171*, 112751. https://doi.org/10.1016/j.asoc.2025.112751.

Hashemizadeh, A., Ju, Y., & Dong, P. (2020). A combined geographical information system and best–worst method approach for site selection for photovoltaic power plant projects. *International Journal of Environmental Science and Technology, 17*(4), 2027–2042. https://doi.org/10.1007/s13762-019-02598-8.

Heidary-Dahooie, J., Rafiee, M., Mohammadi, M., & Meidute-Kavaliauskienė, I. (2022). Proposing a new LSGDM framework based on BWM with hesitant fuzzy information for prioritizing blockchain adoption barriers in supply chain. *Technology in Society, 71*, 102146. https://doi.org/10.1016/j.techsoc.2022.102146.

James, A. T., Kumar, G., Tayal, P., Chauhan, A., Wadhawa, C., & Panchal, J. (2022). Analysis of human resource management challenges in implementation of industry 4.0 in Indian automobile industry. *Technological Forecasting and Social Change, 176*, 121483. https://doi.org/10.1016/j.techfore.2022.121483.

Johny, D., Padhi, S. S., & Cheng, T. C. E. (2025). Drone selection for disaster responses: An application of the stratified-best-worst method. *Management Decision*. https://doi.org/10.1108/MD-07-2024-1658.

Ju, Y., Zhao, Q., Luis, M., Liang, Y., Dong, J., Dong, P., & Giannakis, M. (2024). A novel framework for FMEA using evidential BWM and SMAA-MARCOS method. *Expert Systems with Applications, 243*, 122796. https://doi.org/10.1016/j.eswa.2023.122796.

Kampalasiri, C., Pitiruek, K., & Sureeyatanapas, P. (2025). An enhanced TOPSIS method for resilient supplier selection under data uncertainty. *International Journal of Management Science and Engineering Management,* 1–16. https://doi.org/10.1080/17509653.2025.2544569.

Kang, D., Manirathinam, T., Geetha, S., Narayanamoorthy, S., Ferrara, M., & Ahmadian, A. (2023). An advanced stratified decision-making strategy to explore viable plastic waste-to-energy method: A step towards sustainable dumped wastes management. *Applied Soft Computing, 143*, 110452. https://doi.org/10.1016/j.asoc.2023.110452.

Khan, S. (2022). Barriers of big data analytics for smart cities development: A context of emerging economies. *International Journal of Management Science and Engineering Management, 17*(2), 123–131. https://doi.org/10.1080/17509653.2021.1997662.

Khan, S. A., Kusi-Sarpong, S., Naim, I., Ahmadi, H. B., & Oyedijo, A. (2022). A best-worst-method-based performance evaluation framework for manufacturing industry. *Kybernetes, 51*(10), 2938–2963. https://doi.org/10.1108/K-03-2021-0202.

Khan, S. A., Ojiako, U., Marshall, A., Dalalah, D., Ceylan, S., Ali Shabani, N. N., & Al Sharqawi, S. I. (2023). The critical risk factors that influence production-oriented projects in the United Arab Emirates: A 'best-worst method' (BWM) analysis. *Engineering Management Journal, 35*(2), 144–160. https://doi.org/10.1080/10429247.2022.2041963.

kharayat, T. S., & Gupta, H. (2025). Assessment of circular economy strategies for climate change mitigation": A forecast on India's path to a net zero future. *Technological Forecasting and Social Change, 220*, 124294. https://doi.org/10.1016/j.techfore.2025.124294.

Koohathongsumrit, N., & Luangpaiboon, P. (2024). Strategic marketing information system planning: An integrated BWM–ELECTRE approach. *Group Decision and Negotiation, 33*(2), 267–289. https://doi.org/10.1007/s10726-023-09861-x.

Kumar, A., Mangla, S. K., Kumar, P., & Song, M. (2021). Mitigate risks in perishable food supply chains: Learning from COVID-19. *Technological Forecasting and Social Change, 166*, 120643. https://doi.org/10.1016/j.techfore.2021.120643.

Li, J., Niu, L., Chen, Q., & Wang, Z. (2021). Approaches for multicriteria decision-making based on the hesitant fuzzy best–worst method. *Complex & Intelligent Systems, 7*(5), 2617–2634. https://doi.org/10.1007/s40747-021-00406-w.

Liang, F., Brunelli, M., & Rezaei, J. (2020). Consistency issues in the best worst method: Measurements and thresholds. *Omega, 96*, 102175. https://doi.org/10.1016/j.omega.2019.102175.

Liang, F., Brunelli, M., & Rezaei, J. (2022). Best-worst tradeoff method. *Information Sciences, 610*, 957–976. https://doi.org/10.1016/j.ins.2022.07.097.

Liang, Y., Ju, Y., Tu, Y., & Rezaei, J. (2023). Nonadditive best-worst method: Incorporating criteria interaction using the Choquet integral. *Journal of the Operational Research Society, 74*(6), 1495–1506. https://doi.org/10.1080/01605682.2022.2096504.

Liao, H., Mi, X., Yu, Q., & Luo, L. (2019). Hospital performance evaluation by a hesitant fuzzy linguistic best worst method with inconsistency repairing. *Journal of Cleaner Production, 232*, 657–671. https://doi.org/10.1016/j.jclepro.2019.05.308.

Liu, L., Song, W., & Han, W. (2020). How sustainable is smart PSS? An integrated evaluation approach based on rough BWM and TODIM. *Advanced Engineering Informatics, 43*, 101042. https://doi.org/10.1016/j.aei.2020.101042.

Liu, W., Du, Y., & Chang, J. (2023). A new intuitionistic fuzzy best worst method for deriving weight vector of criteria and its application. *Artificial Intelligence Review, 56*(10), 11071–11093. https://doi.org/10.1007/s10462-023-10439-x.

Mahmoudi, A., Mi, X., Liao, H., Feylizadeh, M. R., & Turskis, Z. (2020). Grey best-worst method for multiple experts multiple criteria decision making under uncertainty. *Informatica,* 331–357. https://doi.org/10.15388/20-INFOR409.

Malek, J., & Desai, T. N. (2019). Prioritization of sustainable manufacturing barriers using best worst method. *Journal of Cleaner Production, 226,* 589–600. https://doi.org/10.1016/j.jclepro.2019.04.056.

Mathiyazhagan, K., Agarwal, V., Appolloni, A., Saikouk, T., & Gnanavelbabu, A. (2021). Integrating lean and agile practices for achieving global sustainability goals in Indian manufacturing industries. *Technological Forecasting and Social Change, 171,* 120982. https://doi.org/10.1016/j.techfore.2021.120982.

Mei, M., & Chen, Z. (2021). Evaluation and selection of sustainable hydrogen production technology with hybrid uncertain sustainability indicators based on rough-fuzzy BWM-DEA. *Renewable Energy, 165,* 716–730. https://doi.org/10.1016/j.renene.2020.11.051.

Mohammadi, F., Nabi Bidhendi, G., & Aslani, A. (2023). Designing an energy security index with a sustainable development approach for energy-exporting countries using fuzzy BWM method. *Environmental Science and Pollution Research, 30*(3), 7427–7445. https://doi.org/10.1007/s11356-022-22631-7.

Mohammadi, M., & Rezaei, J. (2020). Bayesian best-worst method: A probabilistic group decision making model. *Omega, 96,* 102075. https://doi.org/10.1016/j.omega.2019.06.001.

Moktadir, M. A., & Ren, J. (2024). Towards green logistics: An innovative decision support model for zero-emission transportation modes development. *Transportation Research Part E: Logistics and Transportation Review, 189,* 103648. https://doi.org/10.1016/j.tre.2024.103648.

Moslem, S. (2023). A novel Parsimonious best worst method for evaluating travel mode choice. *IEEE Access, 11,* 16768–16773. https://doi.org/10.1109/ACCESS.2023.3242120.

Moslem, S. (2025). Evaluating commuters' travel mode choice using the Z-number extension of Parsimonious best worst method. *Applied Soft Computing, 173,* 112918. https://doi.org/10.1016/j.asoc.2025.112918.

Navaei, J., Sardar, S., & Saati, S. (2025). How to implemented knowledge management in supply chain management best-worst with D-number. *IEEE Access, 13,* 120709–120716. https://doi.org/10.1109/ACCESS.2023.3253785.

Otay, İ., Çevik Onar, S., Öztayşi, B., & Kahraman, C. (2024). Evaluation of sustainable energy systems in smart cities using a multi-expert Pythagorean fuzzy BWM & TOPSIS methodology. *Expert Systems with Applications, 250,* 123874. https://doi.org/10.1016/j.eswa.2024.123874.

Pamučar, D., Puška, A., Stević, Ž., & Ćirović, G. (2021). A new intelligent MCDM model for HCW management: The integrated BWM–MABAC model based on D numbers. *Expert Systems with Applications, 175,* 114862. https://doi.org/10.1016/j.eswa.2021.114862.

Ratandhara, H. M., & Kumar, M. (2024). An analytical framework for the multiplicative best-worst method. *Journal of Multi-Criteria Decision Analysis, 31*(5–6). https://doi.org/10.1002/mcda.1840.

Rezaei, J. (2015). Best-worst multi-criteria decision-making method. *Omega, 53,* 49–57. https://doi.org/10.1016/j.omega.2014.11.009.

Rezaei, J. (2016). Best-worst multi-criteria decision-making method: Some properties and a linear model. *Omega, 64,* 126–130. https://doi.org/10.1016/j.omega.2015.12.001.

Rezaei, J., Hemmes, A., & Tavasszy, L. (2017). Multi-criteria decision-making for complex bundling configurations in surface transportation of air freight. *Journal of Air Transport Management, 61,* 95–105. https://doi.org/10.1016/j.jairtraman.2016.02.006.

Saaty, T. L. (2013). Analytic hierarchy process. In *Encyclopedia of operations research and management science*. Boston, MA: Springer US, 52–64. http://doi.org/10.1007/978-1-4419-1153-7_31.

Sabilla Ajrina, A., Sarno, R., & Hari Ginardi, R. V. (2018). Comparison of AHP and BWM methods based on geographic information system for determining potential zone of Pasir Batu mining. *2018 International Seminar on Application for Technology of Information and Communication,* 453–457. https://doi.org/10.1109/ISEMANTIC.2018.8549818.

Safarzadeh, S., Khansefid, S., & Rasti-Barzoki, M. (2018). A group multi-criteria decision-making based on best-worst method. *Computers & Industrial Engineering, 126,* 111–121. https://doi.org/10.1016/j.cie.2018.09.011.

Tanaji, B. A., & Roychowdhury, S. (2024). BWM Integrated VIKOR method using Neutrosophic fuzzy sets for cybersecurity risk assessment of connected and autonomous vehicles. *Applied Soft Computing, 159,* 111628. https://doi.org/10.1016/j.asoc.2024.111628.

Tavana, M., Sorooshian, S., Rezaei, H., & Mina, H. (2024). A novel fuzzy scenario-based stochastic general best-worst method. *Expert Systems with Applications, 252,* 124246. https://doi.org/10.1016/j.eswa.2024.124246.

Torkayesh, A. E., Malmir, B., & Rajabi Asadabadi, M. (2021). Sustainable waste disposal technology selection: The stratified best-worst multi-criteria decision-making method. *Waste Management, 122,* 100–112. https://doi.org/10.1016/j.wasman.2020.12.040.

Ulutaş, A., Topal, A., Pamučar, D., Stević, Ž., Karabašević, D., & Popović, G. (2022). A new integrated multi-criteria decision-making model for sustainable supplier selection based on a novel grey WISP and grey BWM methods. *Sustainability, 14*(24), 16921. https://doi.org/10.3390/su142416921.

Vafadarnikjoo, A., Tavana, M., Botelho, T., & Chalvatzis, K. (2020). A neutrosophic enhanced best–worst method for considering decision-makers' confidence in the best and worst criteria. *Annals of Operations Research, 289*(2), 391–418. https://doi.org/10.1007/s10479-020-03603-x.

Wan, S., & Dong, J. (2022). A novel extension of best-worst method with intuitionistic fuzzy reference comparisons. *IEEE Transactions on Fuzzy Systems, 30*(6), 1698–1711. https://doi.org/10.1109/TFUZZ.2021.3064695.

Wang, D., Deng, W., Hu, L., Huang, Z., Lu, Y., & Zhang, H. (2025). Safety assessment of intelligent vehicles considering drivers' risk perception information under interval 2-tuple q-rung orthopair fuzzy sets. *Applied Soft Computing, 175,* 112919. https://doi.org/10.1016/j.asoc.2025.112919.

Yucesan, M., & Gul, M. (2021). Failure prioritization and control using the neutrosophic best and worst method. *Granular Computing, 6*(2), 435–449. https://doi.org/10.1007/s41066-019-00206-1.

Zhang, C., Hu, Z., Qin, Y., & Song, W. (2023). Performance evaluation of technological service platform: A rough Z-number-based BWM-TODIM method. *Expert Systems with Applications, 230*, 120665. https://doi.org/10.1016/j.eswa.2023.120665.

Zhang, K., & Chen, Z. (2024). Promoting agricultural sustainable development by a novel integrated pythagorean neutrosophic and WINGS-BWM model. *Scientific Reports, 14*(1), 29043. https://doi.org/10.1038/s41598-024-80463-6.

Chapter 15

Stratified BWM: Stratified best–worst method for multi-attribute decision-making

Çağlar Karamaşa[1] **and Fatih Ecer**[2]

[1]*Department of Quantitative Methods, Faculty of Economics and Administrative Sciences, Anadolu University, Eskişehir, Türkiye,* [2]*Sub-Department of Operations Research, Faculty of Economics and Administrative Sciences, Afyon Kocatepe University, Afyonkarahisar, Turkey*

15.1 Introduction

One of the critical parts related to the process of multicriteria decision-making (MCDM) is the determination of the weights for the criteria. Stratified MCDM, which is based on the concept of stratification (CST), considers the sets of criteria weights in different states, and these weights are acquired in each state when taking an event that can happen in the future into account, unlike classical MCDM methods. Stratified best–worst method (SBWM) considers the uncertainty in terms of the occurrence of events that have an impact on the weights of criteria and provides the consideration of a set of states in each of which an event or combination occurs. Following this, an expert group gives weights to the criteria for each state separately. Then the optimal weights related to the criteria are computed by taking the probability of occurrence of these states into account. The expert group has the capability to identify the criteria for various states. The weights of the criteria, as determined by an expert group, are subjective and differ from those of other groups, which can impact optimal weights (Torkayesh et al., 2021; Ecer & Torkayesh, 2024). This paper shows the applicability of the SBWM as a recently developed MCDM method for real-world case studies, such as municipal waste infrastructure selection and sustainable waste disposal site selection.

The application of SBWM is particularly salient in the context of complex, multistakeholder logistics systems such as seaports. Port operations are inherently dynamic and are subject to a multitude of uncertain future events, including fluctuations in global trade volumes, geopolitical instability, technological disruptions, and stringent new environmental regulations. Traditional MCDM methods, which often rely on static weight assignments, fail to capture this volatility, potentially leading to suboptimal strategic decisions. The stratified approach of SBWM allows decision-makers to proactively model these potential future "states of the world," thereby creating a more resilient and robust framework for evaluation. This capability to incorporate strategic foresight directly into the weighting calculus makes SBWM a superior tool for long-term infrastructure and technology investment decisions, where adaptability to change is a critical success factor (Santos et al., 2025; Parker et al., 2019)

The remainder of this paper is stated as follows. Methodology, including the application steps of the best–worst method (BWM) and SBWM, is presented in Section 2. Two real-world case studies for Eskişehir municipality are explained, and the results are given in Section 3. Conclusions, managerial and practical implications, and future suggestions for each case study are presented in Section 4.

15.2 Methodology

The methodology section consists of two parts. While BWM and its application steps are presented in the first part, the SBWM is defined in the second part.

Encyclopedia of Multi-Attribute Decision-Making (MADM). DOI: https://doi.org/10.1016/B978-0-443-33275-3.00019-1

15.2.1 Best–worst method

BWM, which was proposed by Rezaei (2015) as one of the novel, innovative, and robust subjective criteria weighting MCDM methods. According to this method, the best (e.g., the most important, the most desirable) and the worst (e.g., the least important, the least desirable) criteria are determined by experts respectively. Following that, the best criterion is compared with all the criteria, and all the criteria are compared with the worst criterion, and two vectors, namely best-to-others and others-to-worst, are acquired (Ecer, 2024; Arman & Kundakcı, 2023). As a result, a nonlinear maximin model that aims to minimize the maximum absolute difference between criteria-related weight ratios and pairwise comparisons is constructed for acquiring the criterion weights (Kocak et al., 2018; Zolfani et al., 2020; Arman & Kundakcı, 2023; Ecer, Murat, et al., 2024). BWM produces more consistent and reliable outcomes as compared to its counterparts, such as the analytic hierarchy process (AHP) and step-wise weight assessment ratio analysis (SWARA) (Pamucar et al., 2020; Zolfani et al., 2022; Yaran Ögel et al., 2023). BWM eliminates the weaknesses of some of the methods, like AHP, SWARA, full consistent method (FCM), level based weight assessment (LBWA), and pairwise relative criteria importance assessment, due to having a short and understandable processing time (Fazlollahtabar & Kazemitash, 2021; Ecer, 2021; Yaran Ögel et al., 2023).

The steps of BWM can be summarized as follows (Yaman et al., 2024):

Step 1: The decision criteria $\{dc_1, dc_2, \ldots, dc_n\}$ and their related subcriteria are determined via literature review and the views of experts.

Step 2: The best and the worst criteria are determined in terms of both the main criteria and subcriteria.

Step 3: The preference of the best criterion (subcriterion) over all the criteria (subcriteria) is determined via a scale of 1 to 9 from Table 15.1 by each expert and then the best-to-others vector is acquired as $A_B = (a_{B1}, a_{B2}, \ldots, a_{Bn})$ where the preference of the best criterion over the jth criterion ($j = 1, 2, \ldots, n$) is shown by a_{Bj} and $a_{BB} = 1$.

Step 4: The preference of all the criteria (subcriteria) over the worst criterion (subcriterion) is determined via a scale of 1 to 9 from Table 15.1 by each expert, and then the others-to-worst vector is acquired as $A_W = (a_{1W}, a_{2W}, \ldots, a_{nW})$, where the preference of the jth criterion ($j = 1, 2, \ldots, n$) over the worst criterion is shown by a_{jW} for $j = 1, 2, \ldots, n$ and $a_{WW} = 1$.

Step 5: Optimal criteria weights ($w^* = w_1^*, w_2^*, \ldots, w_n^*$) are calculated. In terms of obtaining the optimal criteria weights, where for each pair w_B/w_j and w_j/w_W, we have $\frac{w_B}{w_j} = a_{Bj}$ and $\frac{w_j}{w_W} = a_{jW}$. In order to satisfy the aforementioned conditions for all j, a solution needs to be acquired where the maximum absolute gaps $\left|\frac{w_B}{w_j} - a_{Bj}\right|$ and $\left|\frac{w_j}{w_W} - a_{jW}\right|$ for all j are minimized (Rezaei, 2015; Guo & Zhao, 2017; Arman & Kundakcı, 2023). The nonnegativity and sum conditions related to the weights are taken into account, and the problem can be written as follows:

$$\min_j \max \left\{ \left| \frac{w_B}{w_j} - a_{Bj} \right|, \left| \frac{w_j}{w_W} - a_{jW} \right| \right\},$$

TABLE 15.1 Linguistic terms for pairwise comparison according to Saaty's scale.

Saaty scale	Linguistic term
1	Equally important (EI)
2	Value between EI and SI
3	Slightly important (SI)
4	Value between SI and STI
5	Strongly important (STI)
6	Value between STI and VSI
7	Very strongly important (VSI)
8	Value between VSI and AI
9	Absolutely important (AI)

TABLE 15.2 Consistency index (CI) values related to best–worst method (Rezaei, 2015.

a_{BW}	1	2	3	4	5	6	7	8	9
CI	0.00	0.44	1.00	1.63	2.30	3.00	3.73	4.47	5.23

s.t

$$\sum w_j = 1 \tag{15.1}$$

$$w_j \geq 0 \quad for\ all\ j.$$

This problem is converted as follows:

$$\min \xi,$$

s.t

$$\left| \frac{w_B}{w_j} - a_{Bj} \right| \leq \xi \ for\ all\ j,$$

$$\left| \frac{w_j}{w_W} - a_{jW} \right| \leq \xi \ for\ all\ j,$$

$$\sum w_j = 1 \tag{15.2}$$

$$w_j \geq 0 \quad for\ all\ j.$$

After solving Eq.(15.2), the optimal weights ($w_1^*, w_2^*, \ldots, w_n^*$) and ξ^* are obtained. The consistency ratio (CR) is calculated via ξ^* and consistency index (CI) according to Eq.(15.3). The CI values for different numbers of criteria are shown in Table 15.2.

$$CR = \frac{\xi^*}{CI} \tag{15.3}$$

The smaller CR values provide more consistent comparisons and evaluations.

15.2.2 The stratified best–worst method

The CST in which several states are placed in various strata and a system receives inputs based on which it transitions to the states is proposed by Zadeh (2016) and is the basis for stratified MCDM methods. Stratified MCDM takes sets of criteria weights in various states into account, and these weights are obtained in each state when considering an event that can happen. The steps of the SBWM are summarized below (Torkayesh et al., 2021):

Step 1: The criteria set is defined and selected.

Step 2: States that can occur in the future and have an impact on the criteria weights are determined.

Step 3: Probabilities related to transitions between the states are defined, and the transition probability matrix is structured. The likelihood related to the occurrence of each event is provided by experts, referring to the historical data and information.

Step 4: Pairwise comparisons between criteria for each state are made via BWM.

Step 5: Weights of the states are multiplied by the transition probability matrix, and the optimal criteria weights are acquired.

15.3 Case study

Real-world case studies, including municipal waste infrastructure selection and sustainable waste disposal site selection, are presented in this section.

15.3.1 Case study I

The first case study is related to selecting municipal waste infrastructure for Eskişehir in Türkiye. To select the municipal waste infrastructure for Eskişehir, five criteria were determined by considering a literature review, expert opinions, and relevant authorities. The criteria, their descriptions, and related references are given in Table 15.3.

The selection of an optimal waste management system is a classic MCDM problem, characterized by conflicting economic, environmental, and social objectives alongside inherent data uncertainty. Traditional cost-benefit analysis is often insufficient to capture this complexity. Therefore, this study employs the SBWM (Torkayesh et al., 2021) to determine criteria weights under different strategic scenarios or "states." This approach is particularly justified here, as the importance of a criterion like proximity to water sources (C1) could drastically increase in a future state with higher environmental regulatory pressures, or Local economic benefits (C5) could become more critical under a state of economic downturn. The SBWM allows for the modeling of these probabilistic future events, providing a more robust and dynamic decision-making framework for Eskişehir's long-term infrastructure planning than static weighting methods.

According to the Case study I, two events that can occur in the future, which have an impact on the importance of the aforementioned five criteria, are identified by an expert group related to waste management. While Event 1 is the occurrence of the eco-city compliance, consisting of high greenhouse gas (GHG) reduction and water protection, Event 2 is related to the urban pragmatism, composed of minimizing transport and public resistance. These two events generate the four different states, including the occurrence of events separately or in combination. The generated various states related to selecting municipal waste infrastructure are stated below:

1. State 1: No events (the current status)
2. State 2: Event 1 occurs (cost efficiency focus)
3. State 3: Event 2 occurs (environmental sustainability focus)
4. State 4: Event 1 and 2 (both events occurred)

An expert group consisting of managers and authorities experienced in waste management is interviewed in order to estimate the probability of Events 1 and 2. A group consensus is reached, and the probability of the current status is estimated to be 10%. Additionally, while the expert group determined the probability of the occurrence of Event 1 to be 45%, it defined the probability of Event 2 to be 55%. The probability related to the occurrence of states based on the lowest provided probability is taken into account. For example, the probability of State 1 occurring is stated with P_1. Additionally, the probability of occurrence related to States 2 and 3 is $4.5P1$ and $5.5P1$, respectively. In terms of independence of the events, the probability of occurrence of State 4 is obtained by multiplying the probability of occurrence of States 2 and 3 that contribute to creating State 4, and is equal to $24.75P_1^2$. The sum of these probabilities should be equal to 1, so P_1 can be computed as below:

$$24.75P_1^2 + 11P_1 = 1$$

$$P_1 = 0.0774$$

TABLE 15.3 Criteria and their related information for case study I.

Criteria	Description	Reference
Proximity to water sources and flood risk (C1)	Eskişehir's Porsuk River and groundwater resources must be protected from leachate contamination.	Nong et al. (2024); Başeğmez (2025)
Distance from residential areas (C2)	Avoid public backlash (e.g., Odunpazarı or Tepebaşı districts may resist nearby facilities).	Fataei and Mohammadian (2015); Yaman (2024)
Existing waste composition (C3)	Eskişehir's waste has ~50% organic content (high composting potential) and ~20% recyclables.	Mujtaba et al. (2024); Kharat et al. (2020)
Integration with municipal waste collection routes (C4)	Current collection logistics (e.g., compactors, transfer stations) influence transport cost efficiency.	Rafiquee and Shabbiruddin (2024); Ayyildiz and Erdogan (2024)
Local economic benefits (C5)	Social sustainability: waste-to-energy plants create skilled jobs; landfills employ low-skilled labor	Fauzi et al. (2025); Tahir et al. (2024)

Therefore, the transition probabilities are found as 0.0774, 0.3483, 0.4257, and 0.1482 for the States 1, 2, 3, and 4, respectively.

Graphical CST related to the Case Study I is presented in Fig. 15.1.

Following this, best-to-others vectors for Case Study I are constructed as shown in Table 15.4. The values in each column show the preference of the best criterion over all the criteria in each state. After that, others-to-worst vectors related to Case Study I are generated as presented in Table 15.5. The values in each column show the preference of all the criteria over the worst criterion for each state.

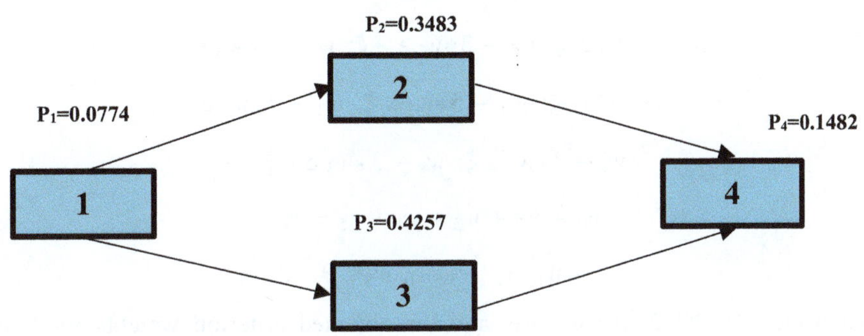

FIGURE 15.1 Graphical concept of stratification for Case Study I.

TABLE 15.4 Best-to-others vectors for Case Study I.

	Best criterion			
States	S1	S2	S3	S4
Criteria	C5	C1	C4	C5
C1	7	1	9	7
C2	5	7	3	5
C3	9	3	3	9
C4	3	5	1	5
C5	1	9	5	1

TABLE 15.5 Others-to-worst vectors for Case Study I.

	Worst criterion			
States	S1	S2	S3	S4
Criteria	C3	C5	C1	C3
C1	5	9	1	3
C2	5	3	3	5
C3	1	5	5	1
C4	3	7	9	7
C5	9	1	3	9

Following that, nonlinear models are formed to obtain the weights of the criteria for each state. For example, a nonlinear model for determining the weights of the criteria for State 1 is presented below:

$$\min \xi$$

s.t

$$w_5 - 7*w_1 \le \xi;\ w_5 - 7*w_1 \ge -\xi;\ w_5 - 5*w_2 \le \xi;$$

$$w_5 - 5*w_2 \ge -\xi;\ w_5 - 9*w_3 \le \xi;\ w_5 - 9*w_3 \ge -\xi;$$

$$w_5 - 3*w_4 \le \xi;\ w_5 - 3*w_4 \ge -\xi;\ w_1 - 5*w_3 \le \xi;$$

$$w_1 - 5*w_3 \ge -\xi;\ w_2 - 5*w_3 \le \xi;\ w_2 - 5*w_3 \ge -\xi;$$

$$w_4 - 3*w_3 \le \xi;\ w_4 - 3*w_3 \ge -\xi;$$

$$w_1 + w_2 + w_3 + w_4 + w_5 = 1;$$

$$w_1, w_2, w_3, w_4, w_5 \ge 0$$

The model is solved using LINGO 21.0 software, and the obtained criterion weights for State 1 are as follows: $w_1 = 0.0923$, $w_2 = 0.1292$, $w_3 = 0.0437$, $w_4 = 0.2153$, $w_5 = 0.5196$, and $\xi = 0.1263$, respectively. According to Eq. (15.3), CR is found to be 0.024 (0.1263/5.23), indicating that the obtained weights have high consistency. Similar calculations are made for other states.

The weightings of the criteria are acquired via SBWM for each state and presented in Table 15.6.

The optimal weights related to the criteria are computed by multiplying the weights of the states presented in Table 15.6 with the obtained transition probability values shown in Fig. 15.1. For example, the optimal weight of C1 is obtained as follows:

$$w_{C1} = 0.0923*0.0774 + 0.5122*0.3483 + 0.0474*0.4257 + 0.1037*0.1482 = 0.2210$$

Similar calculations are performed to determine the optimal weights for the remaining criteria.

According to the optimal weights of the criteria as shown in Table 15.7, while integration with municipal waste collection routes (C4) is found as the most important criterion for Case Study I, distance from residential areas (C2) is

TABLE 15.6 Weights of the states according to the best–worst method for Case Study I.

Criteria	S1	S2	S3	S4
C1	0.0923	0.5122	0.0474	0.1037
C2	0.1292	0.0945	0.1803	0.1452
C3	0.0437	0.2206	0.1803	0.0442
C4	0.2153	0.1324	0.4839	0.1452
C5	0.5196	0.0403	0.1082	0.5618
Ksi	0.1263	0.1496	0.0569	0.1641

TABLE 15.7 Optimal weights related to the criteria via stratified best–worst method for Case Study I.

Criteria	C1	C2	C3	C4	C5
Weight	0.2210	0.1411	0.1635	0.2902	0.1835

acquired as the least essential criterion for the sustainable municipal waste infrastructure determination problem in Eskişehir. Ranking of criteria can be stated as C4 > C1 > C5 > C3 > C2, respectively.

15.3.2 Case study II

The second case study is related to the selection of a sustainable waste disposal site for the Eskişehir municipality in Türkiye. To select the sustainable waste disposal site for Eskişehir, nine criteria were determined by considering a literature review, expert opinions, and relevant authorities. The criteria, their descriptions, and related references are given in Table 15.8.

The task of selecting a final disposal site represents a high-stakes, strategic decision fraught with uncertainty and conflicting stakeholder priorities. A change in municipal policy, economic conditions, or environmental regulations could significantly alter the importance of the defined criteria over the long lifespan of a waste disposal site. The SBWM is therefore employed to account for this dynamism. For instance, under a future "state" of stringent environmental regulation, the weight of criteria like groundwater contamination risk (C6) and GHG emissions (C4) would increase. Conversely, in a future state of economic constraint, *land acquisition cost (C1)* and *operational cost (C2)* might become disproportionately important. By calculating optimal weights across these different stratified states, the SBWM provides a more resilient and forward-looking decision-making framework than static models, ensuring the chosen site remains viable and sustainable under various plausible future scenarios (Torkayesh et al., 2021).

According to Case Study II, two events that can occur in the future, which have an impact on the importance of the aforementioned five criteria, are identified by an expert group related to waste management and explained as follows:

Event 1: Cost-efficiency focus (short-term budget constraints): Minimizing immediate financial burdens while maintaining basic sustainability standards.

Event 2: Environmental sustainability focus (long-term green policy): Reducing carbon footprint, aligning with the EU and Türkiye's 2053 net-zero goals.

TABLE 15.8 Criteria and their related information for Case Study II.

Criteria	Description	Reference
Land acquisition cost (C1)	Site selection must consider the cost of acquiring land, which varies across urban and rural zones.	Özbekler and Akgül (2025)
Operational cost (C2)	Ongoing expenses influence sustainability and feasibility. The article emphasizes cost-efficiency as a short-term priority in decision-making.	Moeis and Al Makmur (2024); Wang et al. (2025)
Transportation cost (C3)	Proximity to waste generation centers affects logistics and operational efficiency.	Günay and Dere (2024); Khan et al. (2022)
Greenhouse gas emissions (C4)	Emissions are a major concern in municipal solid waste (MSW) management. The article highlights incineration and landfilling as high-emission options.	Florindo et al. (2018); Chusi et al. (2025)
Proximity to protected areas (C5)	Avoiding ecological zones and agricultural lands is essential for long-term sustainability.	Deribew et al. (2022); Yaman (2024)
Groundwater contamination risk (C6)	Eskişehir's geological structure necessitates careful evaluation of leachate risks.	Lima et al. (2019); Moussaoui et al. (2025)
Public acceptance (C7)	Social resistance can hinder implementation. The article notes this as a critical factor, especially for incineration and landfilling.	Zakeri et al. (2024); Sadabadi et al. (2024)
Job creation (C8)	Employment opportunities contribute to socioeconomic development. mechanical biological treatment (MBT) and recycling-based systems are highlighted for their labor intensity.	Zhang et al. (2015); Karipoğlu et al. (2023)
Health and safety risks (C9)	Exposure to pollutants and operational hazards affects community well-being. Technologies with lower emissions and better containment are preferred.	Liu et al. (2020); Jimenez-Delgado et al. (2020)

These two events generate the four different states, including the occurrence of events separately or in combination. The various states generated related to selecting a sustainable waste disposal site are stated below:

1. State 1: No events (the current status)
2. State 2: Event 1 occurs (cost efficiency focus)
3. State 3: Event 2 occurs (environmental sustainability focus)
4. State 4: Event 1 and 2 (both events occur): Trade-offs between cost and environmental impact

An expert group consisting of managers and authorities experienced in waste management is interviewed in order to estimate the probability of Events 1 and 2. A group consensus is reached, estimating the probability of 10% that neither of these two events occurs. Additionally, while the expert group determined the probability of Event 1 occurring to be 40%, it defined the probability of Event 2 occurring to be 30%. The probability related to the occurrence of states based on the lowest provided probability is taken into account. For example, the probability of State 1 occurring is stated with P_1. Additionally, the probability of occurrence related to States 2 and 3 is $4P1$ and $3P1$, respectively. In terms of independence of the events, the probability of occurrence of State 4 is obtained by multiplying the probability of occurrence of States 2 and 3 that contribute to creating State 4, and is equal to $12P_1^2$. The sum of these probabilities should be equal to 1, so P_1 can be computed as below:

$$12P_1^2 + 8P_1 = 1$$

$$P_1 = 0.1076$$

Therefore, the transition probabilities are found as 0.1076, 0.4304, 0.3228, and 0.1389 for the States 1, 2, 3, and 4, respectively.

Graphical CST related to Case Study II is presented in Fig. 15.2.

Following this, best-to-others vectors for Case Study II are constructed as shown in Table 15.9. The values in each column show the preference of the best criterion over all the criteria in each state. After that, others-to-worst vectors related to Case Study II are generated as presented in Table 15.10. The values in each column show the preference of all the criteria over the worst criterion for each state.

After that, nonlinear models are formed to obtain the weights of the criteria for each state. For example, a nonlinear model for determining the weights of the criteria for State 1 is presented below:

$$\min \xi$$

s.t

$$w_1 - 3*w_2 \le \xi;\ w_1 - 3*w_2 \ge -\xi;\ w_1 - 3*w_3 \le \xi;$$

$$w_1 - 3*w_3 \ge -\xi;\ w_1 - 5*w_4 \le \xi;\ w_1 - 5*w_4 \ge -\xi;$$

$$w_1 - 5*w_5 \le \xi;\ w_1 - 5*w_5 \ge -\xi;\ w_1 - 7*w_6 \le \xi;$$

$$w_1 - 7*w_6 \ge -\xi;\ w_1 - 7*w_7 \le \xi;\ w_1 - 7*w_7 \ge -\xi;$$

$$w_1 - 9*w_8 \le \xi;\ w_1 - 9*w_8 \ge -\xi;\ w_1 - 7*w_9 \le \xi;$$

$$w_1 - 7*w_9 \ge -\xi;\ w_2 - 8*w_8 \le \xi;\ w_2 - 8*w_8 \ge -\xi;$$

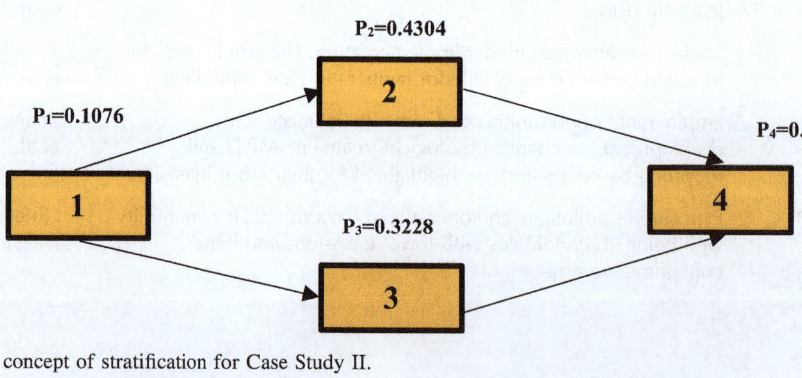

FIGURE 15.2 Graphical concept of stratification for Case Study II.

TABLE 15.9 Best-to-others vectors for Case Study II.

	Best criterion			
States	S1	S2	S3	S4
Criteria	C1	C1	C6	C2
C1	1	1	3	3
C2	3	2	7	1
C3	3	3	7	3
C4	5	9	2	5
C5	5	7	2	5
C6	7	7	1	7
C7	7	5	5	9
C8	9	5	9	3
C9	7	5	3	7

TABLE 15.10 Others-to-worst vectors for Case Study II.

	Worst criterion			
States	S1	S2	S3	S4
Criteria	C8	C4	C8	C7
C1	9	9	5	7
C2	8	7	2	9
C3	6	7	3	3
C4	3	1	4	7
C5	5	2	4	7
C6	5	3	9	7
C7	4	3	5	1
C8	1	5	1	3
C9	5	5	3	5

$$w_3 - 6*w_8 \le \xi;\ w_3 - 6*w_8 \ge -\xi;\ w_4 - 3*w_8 \le \xi;\ w_4 - 3*w_8 \ge -\xi;$$

$$w_5 - 5*w_8 \le \xi;\ w_5 - 5*w_8 \ge -\xi;\ w_6 - 5*w_8 \le \xi;\ w_6 - 5*w_8 \ge -\xi;$$

$$w_7 - 4*w_8 \le \xi;\ w_7 - 4*w_8 \ge -\xi;\ w_9 - 5*w_8 \le \xi;\ w_9 - 5*w_8 \ge -\xi;$$

$$w_1 + w_2 + w_3 + w_4 + w_5 + w_6 + w_7 + w_8 + w_9 = 1;$$

$$w_1, w_2, w_3, w_4, w_5, w_6, w_7, w_8, w_9 \ge 0$$

The model is solved via LINGO 21.0 software, and the obtained criteria weights for State 1 are written as $w_1 = 0.3387$, $w_2 = 0.1411$, $w_3 = 0.1411$, $w_4 = 0.0846$, $w_5 = 0.0846$, $w_6 = 0.0604$, $w_7 = 0.0604$, $w_8 = 0.0282$, $w_9 = 0.0604$, and $\xi = 0.0846$,

TABLE 15.11 Weights of the states according to the best–worst method for Case Study II.

Criteria	S1	S2	S3	S4
C1	0.3387	0.3155	0.1117	0.1336
C2	0.1411	0.1910	0.0478	0.3014
C3	0.1411	0.1273	0.0478	0.1336
C4	0.0846	0.0276	0.1552	0.0802
C5	0.0846	0.0545	0.1552	0.0802
C6	0.0604	0.0545	0.2786	0.0572
C7	0.0604	0.0764	0.0670	0.0224
C8	0.0282	0.0764	0.0246	0.1336
C9	0.0604	0.0764	0.1117	0.0572
Ksi	0.0846	0.0664	0.0564	0.0996

TABLE 15.12 Optimal weights related to the criteria via stratified best–worst method for Case Study II.

Criteria	C1	C2	C3	C4	C5	C6	C7	C8	C9
Weight	0.2268	0.1546	0.1039	0.0822	0.0937	0.1278	0.0641	0.0624	0.0833

respectively. According to Eq. (15.3), CR is found to be 0.016 (0.0846/5.23), indicating that the obtained weights exhibit high consistency. Similar calculations are made for other states. Then the weightings of the criteria are acquired via SBWM for each state and presented in Table 15.11.

The optimal weights related to the criteria are computed by multiplying the weights of the states presented in Table 15.11 by the obtained transition probability values shown in Fig. 15.2. For example, the optimal weight of C1 is obtained as follows:

$$w_{C1} = 0.3387*0.1076 + 0.3155*0.4304 + 0.1117*0.3228 + 0.1336*0.1389 = 0.2268$$

Similar calculations are made for acquiring the optimal weights related to the remaining criteria.

According to the optimal weights of the criteria as presented in Table 15.12, while land acquisition cost (C1), operational cost (C2) and groundwater contamination risk (C6) are found as the most important three criteria for Case Study II, job creation (C8) is obtained as the least essential criterion for sustainable waste disposal site selection problem in Eskişehir municipality. Ranking of criteria can be written as C1 > C2 > C6 > C3 > C5 > C9 > C4 > C7 > C8 respectively.

15.4 Conclusion

This section consists of conclusions related to Case Studies I and II, respectively.

15.4.1 For case study I

The SBWM analysis conducted for Case Study I of Eskişehir municipality's sustainable waste infrastructure planning reveals a distinct prioritization of criteria, markedly different from Case Study II. Here, logistical integration and operational efficiency emerge as dominant considerations, surpassing traditional concerns such as land acquisition costs or groundwater protection. The optimal weights (Table 15.7) identify integration with municipal waste collection routes (C4, 29.02%) as the most influential criterion, followed by proximity to water sources and flood risk (C1, 22.10%) and waste composition (C5, 18.35%), while distance from residential areas (C2, 14.11%) ranks lowest. This hierarchy—C4 > C1 > C5 > C3 > C2—underscores Eskişehir's emphasis on minimizing transport costs and streamlining existing logistics, consistent with urban waste system studies in compact cities like Istanbul (Akdaş et al., 2021). Although land cost remains significant, its secondary position relative to logistical efficiency reflects a preference for proximity to infrastructure over inexpensive rural land, paralleling findings from EU cities with high transport expenditures. Local economic benefits (C5) also surpass waste composition (C3) and distance from residential areas (C2), suggesting a prioritization of technology compatibility, such as anaerobic digestion for organic-rich waste, over carbon mitigation or public opposition. The low weight assigned to C2 contrasts with studies emphasizing odor and community resistance, potentially indicating a centralized planning model that marginalizes participatory input.

Based on these insights, key recommendations include optimizing facility placement near existing transfer stations, particularly in the northern industrial zone to enhance C4, leveraging waste composition data to deploy modular technologies (e.g., mechanical–biological treatment systems), and addressing GHG emissions through strategic interventions such as electric compactor trucks that preserve logistical efficiency. Nonetheless, limitations persist. Rapid urban expansion may elevate the relevance of C2 over time, and the current weighting scheme may underestimate potential community backlash if residential proximity concerns are neglected.

In conclusion, Case Study I illustrates Eskişehir's urban-centric, efficiency-driven waste management paradigm, where integration with existing collection networks takes precedence over environmental and social considerations. This reflects a broader trend among mid-sized municipalities favoring operational pragmatism over normative ideals. Future research should explore the real-world trade-offs, particularly between cost and emissions at selected sites and incorporate participatory multicriteria frameworks to capture stakeholder perspectives more effectively.

15.4.2 For case study II

The SBWM analysis for Eskişehir municipality's sustainable waste disposal site selection revealed critical insights into the prioritization of decision-making criteria. The optimal weights (Table 15.12) highlight that land acquisition cost (C1, 22.68%), operational cost (C2, 15.46%), and groundwater contamination risk (C6, 12.78%) are the three most influential factors, while job creation (C8, 6.24%) was deemed the least significant. The final ranking of criteria follows the order:

C1 (land cost) > C2 (operational cost) > C6 (groundwater risk) > C3 (transportation cost) > C5 (proximity to protected areas) > C9 (health and safety risks) > C4 (GHG emissions) > C7 (public acceptance) > C8 (job creation).

The key findings from the Eskişehir waste management scenario analysis reveal a strong dominance of economic factors, particularly land and operational costs (C1, C2), which aligns with similar studies in developing municipalities where budget constraints heavily shape decision-making, such as Ülengin et al.'s (2022) study on Turkish waste systems. In contrast to wealthier EU cities like Copenhagen that prioritize circular economy principles, Eskişehir's approach reflects a pragmatic emphasis on short-term financial feasibility. Environmental risks, especially groundwater protection (C6), were prioritized over social benefits like job creation (C8), echoing patterns observed in water-scarce regions such as India (Kumari et al., 2017), and likely influenced by the city's reliance on the Porsuk River. The relatively low ranking of job creation diverges from socially driven waste initiatives seen in contexts like Brazilian favelas, suggesting Eskişehir's focus leans more toward infrastructure than labor market development. Proximity to protected areas (C5) and health and safety risks (C9) held moderate importance; while NIMBY concerns were notable scoring higher than GHG emissions (C4), they remained secondary to cost and environmental considerations, consistent with urban Turkish waste management trends (Hoşoğlu, 2022). The mid-tier ranking of waste composition implies that although Eskişehir's waste stream contains approximately 50% organic material, technological adaptability is necessary but not the primary driver of site selection.

Comparative analysis with existing literature highlights a broad consensus on the priority of economic and environmental criteria in sustainable waste management. Similar studies, such as the selection of the Istanbul landfill by Beskese et al. (2015), have also emphasized land cost and pollution concerns, with a greater GHG emissions weight (C4) due to compliance with European Union standards. However, a notable difference emerges in the treatment of social criteria; studies conducted in socially focused contexts such as South Africa tend to prioritize employment creation more prominently, highlighting Eskişehir's economic orientation. Based on these findings, strategic recommendations for Eskişehir include prioritizing low-cost, low-risk sites, particularly in rural or peri-urban areas characterized by inexpensive land (C1) and minimal aquifer vulnerability (C6). Furthermore, considering the balance between operating costs (C2) and the city's health and safety risks (C9), which contains approximately 50% organic matter, intermediate waste treatment technologies such as anaerobic digestion or modular landfill systems are considered appropriate. To mitigate potential public opposition (C5), proactive engagement with residents in districts such as Tepebaşı and Odunpazarı, and learning from similar waste infrastructure projects in Ankara, is recommended. The study acknowledges limitations, particularly the potential bias inherent in assuming municipal priorities in criteria weighting; future research should include public opinion surveys to recalibrate social dimensions (C5, C8). Furthermore, dynamic factors such as climate change-induced flood risks and evolving regulatory frameworks, particularly Türkiye's Zero Waste Law, may necessitate revisions to existing prioritizations. Ultimately, the findings confirm that Eskişehir's landfill selection reflects a pragmatic balance between economic viability and environmental protection, offering valuable insights for medium-sized municipalities facing the dilemma of fiscal austerity and sustainable development. Future research should evaluate participatory MCDM approaches to better integrate community perspectives into planning processes.

SBWM, as based on CST, states how the uncertainty that decision makers (DMs) have regarding the future can be examined for constructing reliable long-term decisions. This paper shows how uncertainty can be examined in relation to obtaining criteria weightings via SBWM with two real-world case studies. There are some limitations related to the proposed model. One of them is that the results depend on the probabilities assigned to future events. The second limitation is related to ignoring the interdependencies between criteria. The third limitation is based on utilizing CST only for the weight determination process. The last limitation is associated with the application area, consisting of two case studies. For future studies, DM's subjective judgments can be considered using fuzzy set theory, which may be combined with SBWM. Besides other weighting MCDM methods, such as AHP, analytic network process, decision-making trial and evaluation laboratory (DEMATEL), and SWARA, can be integrated with the CST for future applications.

References

Akdaş, H.Ş., Demir, Ö., Doğan, B., Bas, A., & Uslu, B.Ç. (2021). Vehicle route optimization for solid waste management: A case study of maltepe, Istanbul. In *2021 13th International Conference on Electronics, Computers and Artificial Intelligence (ECAI)* (pp. 1-6). IEEE. https://doi.org/10.1109/ECAI52376.2021.9515129

Arman, K., & Kundakcı, N. (2023). A fuzzy best worst method based prioritization of solar panel selection criteria. In J. Rezaei, M. Brunelli, & M. Mohammadi (Vol. Eds.), *Advances in best-worst method. BWM: 2022*Cham: Lecture Notes in Operations Research. Springer https://doi.org/10.1007/978-3-031-24816-0_9.

Ayyildiz, E., & Erdogan, M. (2024). Literature analysis of the location selection studies related to the waste facilities within MCDM approaches. *Environmental science and pollution research,* 1–22. https://doi.org/10.1007/s11356-024-34370-y.

Başeğmez, M. (2025). Strategic multi-criteria framework for nuclear plant siting: Integrating AHP, EWM, and Game Theory with GIS. *Progress in Nuclear Energy, 188*, 105897. https://doi.org/10.1016/j.pnucene.2025.105897.

Beskese, A., Demir, H. H., Ozcan, H. K., & Okten, H. E. (2015). Landfill site selection using fuzzy AHP and fuzzy TOPSIS: A case study for Istanbul. *Environmental Earth Sciences, 73*(7), 3513–3521. https://doi.org/10.1007/s12665-014-3635-5.

Chusi, T. N., Qian, S., Więckowski, J., Bouraima, M. B., & Qiu, Y. (2025). Revolutionizing Africa's carbon footprint through innovative technology dissemination strategies for greenhouse gas emission reduction: An MCDM approach. *Journal of Fuzzy Extension & Applications (JFEA), 6*(2), 216. https://doi.org/10.22105/jfea.2024.474476.1596.

Deribew, K. T., Mihretu, Y., Abreha, G., & Gemeda, D. O. (2022). Spatial analysis of potential ecological sites in the northeastern parts of Ethiopia using multi-criteria decision-making models. *Asia-Pacific Journal of Regional Science, 6*(3), 961–991. https://doi.org/10.1007/s41685-022-00248-5.

Ecer, F., & Torkayesh, A. E. (2024). A stratified fuzzy decision-making approach for sustainable circular supplier selection. *IEEE Transactions on Engineering Management, 71*, 1130–1144. https://doi.org/10.1109/TEM.2022.3151491.

Ecer, F. (2021). Sustainability assessment of existing onshore wind plants in the context of triple bottom line: A best-worst method (BWM) based MCDM framework. *Environmental Science and Pollution Research, 28*(16), 19677–19693. https://doi.org/10.1007/s11356-020-11940-4.

Ecer, F. (2024). A state-of-the-art review of the BWM method and future research agenda. *Technological and Economic Development of Economy, 30*(4), 1165–1204. https://doi.org/10.3846/tede.2024.20761.

Ecer, F., Murat, T., Dinçer, H., & Yüksel, S. (2024). A fuzzy BWM and MARCOS integrated framework with Heronian function for evaluating cryptocurrency exchanges: A case study of Türkiye. *Financial Innovation, 10*(1), 31. https://doi.org/10.1186/s40854-023-00543-w.

Fataei, E., & Mohammadian, A. (2015). Industrial state site selection using MCDM method and GIS in Germi, Ardabil, Iran. *Journal of Industrial and Intelligent Information Vol, 3*(4), 324–329. https://doi.org/10.12720/jiii.3.4.324-329.

Fauzi, R. A., Saputra, Y. M., Ma'mun, A., & Nuryadi, N. (2025). Analysis of sports tourism potential in sumedang: An Implementation of MSPDM (Marketability, Sustainability, Participatory, Disaster Mitigation). *ACTIVE: Journal of Physical Education, Sport, Health and Recreation, 14*(1), 11–20. https://doi.org/10.15294/active.v14i1.14485.

Fazlollahtabar, H., & Kazemitash, N. (2021). Green supplier selection based on the information system performance evaluation using the integrated Best-Worst Method. *Facta Universitatis, Series: Mechanical Engineering, 19*(3), 345–360. https://doi.org/10.22190/FUME201125029F.

Florindo, T. J., Florindo, G. D. M., Talamini, E., Da Costa, J. S., De Léis, C. M., Tang, W. Z., Schultz, G., Kulay, L., Pinto, A. T., & Ruviaro, C. F. (2018). Application of the multiple criteria decision-making (MCDM) approach in the identification of Carbon Footprint reduction actions in the Brazilian beef production chain. *Journal of Cleaner Production, 196*, 1379–1389. https://doi.org/10.1016/j.jclepro.2018.06.116.

Günay, E. E., & Dere, S. (2024). Hazardous solid waste landfill site selection for İstanbul, Türkiye using multi-criteria decision-making methods and GIS data. *Journal of Advanced Research in Natural and Applied Sciences, 10*(2), 446–463. https://doi.org/10.28979/jarnas.1416814.

Guo, S., & Zhao, H. (2017). Fuzzy best-worst multi-criteria decision-making method and its applications. *Knowledge-Based Systems, 121*, 23–31. https://doi.org/10.1016/j.knosys.2017.01.010.

Hoşoğlu, F. (2022). Urban waste management: The case of Turkey and Istanbul. In *The Elgar Companion to Urban Infrastructure Governance*. Edward Elgar Publishing, 218–237 https://doi.org/10.4337/9781800375611.00021.

Jimenez-Delgado, G., Senior-Naveda, A., Marín-Gonzalez, F., García-Guiliany, J., Fontalvo-Molina, L., Ruiz-Muñoz, M., Hernandez-Palma, H., & Santos-Hernandez, B. (2020). Improving the performance in occupational health and safety management in the electric sector: An integrated methodology using fuzzy multicriteria approach. In *International Conference on Human-Computer Interaction* (pp. 130-158). Cham: Springer International Publishing. https://doi.org/10.1007/978-3-030-49907-5_10

Karipoğlu, F., Ozturk, S., & Efe, B. (2023). A GIS-based FAHP and FEDAS analysis framework for suitable site selection of a hybrid offshore wind and solar power plant. *Energy for Sustainable Development, 77*, 101349. https://doi.org/10.1016/j.esd.2023.101349.

Khan, S. A., Radi, R. M., Ali, S. M., Zahran, E. H., Sahtout, A. H. A., & Esam, S. A. (2022). An analysis of third party logistic selection criteria in oil and gas sector: An integrated SWOT-AHP approach. *International Journal of Logistics Systems and Management, 43*(1), 20–47. https://doi.org/10.1504/IJLSM.2022.125660.

Kharat, M. G., Murthy, S., Kamble, S. J., & Kharat, M. G. (2020). Selecting sustainable technologies for municipal solid waste treatment and disposal: An expert based MCDM approach. *The Journal of Solid Waste Technology and Management, 46*(1), 44–57. https://doi.org/10.5276/JSWTM/2020.44.

Kocak, H., Caglar, A., & Oztas, G. Z. (2018). Euclidean best-worst method and its application. *International Journal of Information Technology & Decision Making, 17*(5), 1587–1605. https://doi.org/10.1142/S0219622018500323.

Kumari, P., Gupta, N. C., & Kaur, A. (2017). A review of groundwater pollution potential threats from municipal solid waste landfill sites: Assessing the impact on human health. *Avicenna Journal of Environmental Health Engineering, 4*(1), 11525. https://doi.org/10.5812/ajehe.11525.

Lima, M. L., Romanelli, A., Calderon, G., & Massone, H. E. (2019). Multi-criteria decision model for assessing groundwater pollution risk in the urban-rural interface of Mar del Plata City (Argentina). *Environmental Monitoring and Assessment, 191*(6), 347. https://doi.org/10.1007/s10661-019-7485-1.

Liu, R., Hou, L. X., Liu, H. C., & Lin, W. (2020). Occupational health and safety risk assessment using an integrated SWARA-MABAC model under bipolar fuzzy environment. *Computational and Applied Mathematics, 39*(4), 276. https://doi.org/10.1007/s40314-020-01311-7.

Moeis, A.O., & Al Makmur, O.J. (2024). Determining indicators of international container terminal selection using the analytical hierarchical process. In *AIP Conference Proceedings* (Vol. 3215, No. 1, p. 090006). AIP Publishing LLC. https://doi.org/10.1063/5.0237149

Moussaoui, Z., Abdelkarim, B., Brahim, F. B., Antunes, M., Hamed, Y., & Bouri, S. (2025). Advancing sustainable water resources management in central tunisia: An innovative groundwater vulnerability assessment using K-SOM and MCDM. *Earth Systems and Environment*, 1–23. https://doi.org/10.1007/s41748-025-00671-6.

Mujtaba, M. A., Munir, A., Imran, S., Nasir, M. K., Muhayyuddin, M. G., Javed, A., Mehmood, A., Habila, M. A., Fayaz, H., & Qazi, A. (2024). Evaluating sustainable municipal solid waste management scenarios: A multicriteria decision making approach. *Heliyon, 10*(4), e25788. https://doi.org/10.1016/j.heliyon.2024.e25788.

Nong, D.H., Nguyen, T.T., Vu, X.T., Ngo, S.T., Vo, C.H., & Tran, P.T. (2024). A systematic review of GIS-based and AHP approaches for identifying suitable locations for livestock farms. In *IOP Conference Series: Earth and Environmental Science* (Vol. 1345, No. 1, p. 012003). IOP Publishing. https://doi.org/10.1088/1755-1315/1345/1/012003

Özbekler, T. M., & Akgül, A. K. (2025). A GIS-based multi-criteria decision-making approach for location selection of urban micro-consolidation centers under sustainability. *Journal of Turkish Operations Management, 9*(1), 158–180. https://doi.org/10.56554/jtom.1615906.

Pamucar, D., Ecer, F., Cirovic, G., & Arlasheedi, M. A. (2020). Application of improved best worst method (BWM) in real-world problems. *Mathematics, 8*(8), 1342. https://doi.org/10.3390/math8081342.

Parker, R., Barnes, R. Y., & Jelsma, J. (2019). Improvements in health-related quality of life and function in middle-aged women with chronic diseases of lifestyle after participating in a non-pharmacological intervention programme: A pragmatic randomised controlled trial. *African Journal of Disability, 8*(1), 1–14.

Rafiquee, A., & Shabbiruddin (2024). Optimal selection and challenges of municipal waste management system using an integrated approach: A case study. *Energy Sources, Part A: Recovery, Utilization, and Environmental Effects, 46*(1), 1996–2023. https://doi.org/10.1080/15567036.2023.2298285.

Rezaei, J. (2015). Best-worst multi-criteria decision-making method. *Omega, 53*, 49–57. https://doi.org/10.1016/j.omega.2014.11.009.

Sadabadi, A. A., Mohamadi Etergeleh, F., Fartash, K., & Shahi, N. (2024). An analysis of social acceptance of energy in Iran: Case study of fossil, nuclear, solar and wind energy. *International Journal of Energy Sector Management, 18*(6), 2045–2058. https://doi.org/10.1108/IJESM-03-2021-0027.

Santos, P. A. S., Cortez, B., & Carvalho, M. T. M. (2025). Integrating GIS and BIM with MCDM for infrastructure planning: A comprehensive framework. *Engineering, Construction and Architectural Management, 32*(6), 4197–4226. https://doi.org/10.1108/ECAM-08-2023-0830.

Tahir, F., Rasheed, R., Mahmood, S., Chohan, K., & Ahmad, S. R. (2024). REDD+ framework and forest sustainability in Pakistan versus other South Asian countries: A multi-criteria-based analysis. *Environment, Development and Sustainability, 26*(3), 6471–6492. https://doi.org/10.1007/s10668-023-02971-1.

Torkayesh, A. E., Malmir, B., & Asadabadi, M. R. (2021). Sustainable waste disposal technology selection: The stratified best-worst multi-criteria decision making method. *Waste Management, 122*, 100–112. https://doi.org/10.1016/j.wasman.2020.12.040.

Wang, J., Setiawansyah, S., & Isnain, A. R. (2025). Multi-criteria decision support system for best warehouse performance selection using combined compromise solution method. *Bulletin of Data Science, 4*(2), 86–93. https://doi.org/10.47065/bulletinds.v4i2.7196.

Yaman, A. (2024). A GIS-based multi-criteria decision-making approach (GIS-MCDM) for determination of the most appropriate site selection of onshore wind farm in Adana, Turkey. *Clean Technologies and Environmental Policy, 26*(12), 4231–4254. https://doi.org/10.1007/s10098-024-02866-3.

Yaman, F., Zavadskas, E. K., Medetoğlu, B., & Ecer, F. (2024). Parsimonious BWM (BWM-P) for prioritizing ad appeals in the Metaverse world. *International Journal of Computers Communications & Control, 19*(2).

Yaran Ögel, İ., Aygün Özgöz, A., & Ecer, F. (2023). Prioritizing causes and drivers of retail food waste through a fuzzy Dombi-Bonferroni operators-based best–worst approach: An emerging economy perspective. *Environmental Science and Pollution Research, 30*, 4899–4916. https://doi.org/10.1007/s11356-022-22553-4.

Zadeh, L. A. (2016). Stratification, target set reachability and incremental enlargement principle. *Information Sciences, 354*, 131–139. https://doi.org/10.1016/j.ins.2016.02.047.

Zakeri, S., Konstantas, D., Sorooshian, S., & Chatterjee, P. (2024). A novel ML-MCDM-based decision support system for evaluating autonomous vehicle integration scenarios in Geneva's public transportation. *Artificial intelligence review, 57*(11), 310. https://doi.org/10.1007/s10462-024-10917-w.

Zhang, L., Zhou, P., Newton, S., Fang, J. X., Zhou, D. Q., & Zhang, L. P. (2015). Evaluating clean energy alternatives for Jiangsu, China: An improved multi-criteria decision making method. *Energy, 90*, 953–964. https://doi.org/10.1016/j.energy.2015.07.124.

Zolfani, S. H., Bazrafshan, R., Ecer, F., & Karamaşa, Ç. (2022). The suitability-feasibility-acceptability strategy integrated with Bayesian BWM-MARCOS methods to determine the optimal lithium battery plant located in South America. *Mathematics, 10*(14), 2401. https://doi.org/10.3390/math10142401.

Zolfani, S. H., Ecer, F., Pamučar, D., & Raslanas, S. (2020). Neighborhood selection for a newcomer via a novel BWM-based revised MAIRCA integrated model: A case from the Coquimbo-La Serena conurbation, Chile. *International Journal of Strategic Property Management, 24*(2), 102–118. https://doi.org/10.3846/ijspm.2020.11543.

Further reading

https://doi.org/10.15837/ijccc.2024.2.6421, (no.date).

Chapter 16

Bayesian BWM: Bayesian best–worst method for multi-attribute decision-making

Huai-Wei Lo[1] and Sheng-Wei Lin[2]

[1]*Department of Industrial Engineering and Management, National Yunlin University of Science and Technology, Douliu City, Taiwan,* [2]*Department of Financial Management, Management College, National Defense University, Taipei, Taiwan*

16.1 Introduction

The best–worst method (BWM), originally proposed by Rezaei (2015), was developed to overcome two key limitations of the analytic hierarchy process (AHP): the excessive number of pairwise comparisons and the relatively low consistency of results. Unlike AHP, BWM requires decision-makers to provide only a limited set of structured pairwise comparisons, resulting in two reference vectors, namely the best-to-others (BO) and others-to-worst (OW) vectors. This structured elicitation process reduces the cognitive burden on experts and improves the accuracy and reliability of the derived weights. Over the past few years, BWM has been successfully applied across various domains, including supply chain management, risk assessment, technology evaluation, and energy planning, due to its efficiency and robustness.

Despite its advantages, the classical BWM is primarily designed for a single decision-maker. In group decision-making contexts, where multiple experts are involved, the common practice has been to aggregate individual weight vectors using simple operators such as the arithmetic mean. While computationally straightforward, this approach has notable drawbacks: it ignores the dispersion of opinions, is sensitive to outliers, and often distorts results when there is substantial disagreement among experts. Such limitations make traditional aggregation unsuitable for complex group decision-making problems where diverse perspectives must be faithfully represented (Mohammadi & Rezaei, 2020).

To address these challenges, Mohammadi and Rezaei (2020) introduced the Bayesian BWM. This probabilistic extension meaningfully reinterprets the BWM framework through a Bayesian hierarchical model. In Bayesian BWM, the BO and OW vectors are modeled as multinomial distributions, while the final weights are modeled using the Dirichlet distribution. This formulation not only enables simultaneous estimation of both individual and aggregated group weights but also provides richer information by quantifying the confidence associated with the ranking of criteria. Specifically, a novel concept known as credal ranking is introduced, whereby each pairwise comparison between criteria is associated with a confidence level. This allows decision-makers to assess not only which criterion is more important but also the degree of certainty underlying that judgment.

From the perspective of multiple criteria decision-making (MCDM), the weight vector must satisfy two fundamental conditions: the weights must be nonnegative ($w_j \geq 0$), and their sum must equal 1 ($\sum w_j = 1$). This naturally aligns with the probabilistic interpretation of criteria weights. Specifically, each criterion c_j ($j = 1, 2, \ldots, n$) can be regarded as a random event, while its corresponding weight w_j represents the probability of that event occurring. Thus, extending BWM into a probabilistic framework not only ensures theoretical consistency but also enhances its applicability in real-world group decision-making scenarios where uncertainty and disagreement are inevitable. In summary, Bayesian BWM represents a significant advancement in preference elicitation and weight determination for group MCDM. By shifting from deterministic aggregation to probabilistic modeling, it provides decision-makers with deeper insights into both consensus and disagreement, thereby enabling more informed and reliable strategic decisions.

In recent years, Bayesian BWM has been widely adopted in diverse application domains, demonstrating its flexibility and robustness in handling group decision-making under uncertainty. For instance, Huang et al. (2021) applied Bayesian

Encyclopedia of Multi-Attribute Decision-Making (MADM). DOI: https://doi.org/10.1016/B978-0-443-33275-3.00011-7

BWM to develop an airport resilience assessment model, illustrating its effectiveness in capturing the relative importance of resilience factors in complex transportation systems. Yao et al. (2023) integrated Bayesian BWM with the preference ranking organization method for enrichment evaluation (PROMETHEE) method to evaluate mobile commerce service quality, using a food delivery platform as a case study. Their findings highlighted the ability of Bayesian BWM to generate consistent and representative weights even in highly competitive and dynamic service environments. Similarly, (Yanilmaz et al., 2021) extended Federal Emergency Management Agency and seriousness manageability urgency growth models by incorporating Bayesian BWM to improve disaster risk reduction strategies, thereby showcasing its potential in high-stakes decision-making contexts. Moreover, Munim et al. (2022) employed Bayesian BWM to assess blockchain adoption in the Norwegian oil and gas industry, providing a structured approach to evaluate technological and organizational factors in an uncertain environment.

Expanding on these applications, the method has also found significant traction within the supply chain and manufacturing management literature for identifying critical factors and optimizing operational decisions. In this vein, researchers have utilized Bayesian BWM to identify and prioritize key drivers and success factors for enhancing sustainability and circularity. For example, Debnath et al. (2023) applied the method to assess the critical success factors for implementing sustainable lean manufacturing in the furniture industry of an emerging economy. Their study underscored the method's advantage in aggregating expert opinions with less information loss and providing a credal ranking that reflects the certainty of the criteria's hierarchy. Similarly, Salman et al. (2025) employed Bayesian BWM to explore lean manufacturing drivers that enhance circular economy performance within the pharmaceutical industry, noting its superiority over other methods in handling the inherent uncertainty and subjective judgments of decision-makers.

The application of Bayesian BWM also extends to optimizing specific supply chain processes, such as supplier selection. Modares et al. (2025) developed a framework that integrates blockchain technology with Bayesian BWM to determine optimal weights for supplier evaluation criteria, which were then used in a fuzzy technique for order preference by similarity to ideal solution model for ranking. This approach proved effective in modeling decision-maker preferences and managing qualitative uncertainties, particularly in the communication between suppliers and retailers. Furthermore, related Bayesian principles have been used to create more holistic evaluation frameworks. Patel & Chang (2024) integrated subjective weights from the traditional BWM with objective weights from the entropy method using Bayes' theorem to construct a comprehensive port competitiveness index. Collectively, this body of work illustrates that Bayesian BWM is a robust tool for addressing complex decision problems in operations and supply chain management, offering a probabilistic approach that enhances the reliability and transparency of strategic decision-making.

Collectively, these studies not only validate the methodological soundness of Bayesian BWM but also demonstrate its adaptability to different decision-making contexts. Today, Bayesian BWM can be regarded as a well-established and versatile MCDM method, offering both theoretical rigor and practical utility for addressing decision problems characterized by uncertainty, diversity of opinion, and strategic complexity.

The remainder of this chapter is organized as follows. Section 16.2 introduces the computational steps and theoretical foundations of Bayesian BWM, providing the essential concepts required to apply the model. Section 16.3 presents a simple illustrative example in which Bayesian BWM is applied to evaluate decision factors for selecting electric vehicles (EVs), demonstrating the method's applicability to a basic problem setting. Section 16.4 extends the analysis to a complex real-world case study involving a larger number of experts and criteria, where Bayesian BWM is employed to assess the relative importance of strategic alliance partner selection criteria in the semiconductor industry. Section 16.5 provides a comparative discussion, examining the similarities and differences between Bayesian BWM and several related MCDM methods, highlighting its advantages and limitations. Finally, Section 16.6 concludes the chapter by summarizing key insights and outlining potential directions for future research.

16.2 Methodology

The Bayesian BWM is an extension of the classical BWM, proposed by Mohammadi & Rezaei (2020), which incorporates Bayesian principles to address group decision-making issues. The Bayesian BWM applies probabilistic modeling and Bayesian inference to derive a set of optimal group weights. The computational procedure is outlined as follows.

Step 1. Establish the evaluation criteria

Through literature review and expert consultation, a set of n criteria is identified, denoted as:

$$c_j = \{c_1, c_2, \ldots, c_n\}$$

Step 2. Select the best and worst criteria

Among the n criteria, the most important criterion (Best, c_B) and the least important criterion (Worst, c_W) are determined by the decision-makers.

Step 3. Construct the best-to-others vector

The best criterion c_B is compared pairwise with each of the other criteria using a scale from 1 to 9, where 1 indicates equal importance and 9 indicates absolute dominance. The resulting BO vector is:

$$A_{Bj} = (a_{B1}, a_{B2}, \ldots, a_{Bn})$$

where a_{Bj} represents the relative importance of the best criterion c_B over criterion c_j.

Step 4. Construct the others-to-worst vector

Similarly, each criterion is compared with the worst criterion c_W. The OW vector is:

$$A_{jW} = (a_{1W},\ a_{2W},\ \ldots,\ a_{nW})^T$$

where a_{jW} denotes the relative importance of criterion c_j compared to the worst criterion c_W. By definition, self-comparisons satisfy $a_{BB} = 1$ and $a_{WW} = 1$.

Step 5. Derivation of optimal weights of the criteria

The BO and OW vectors form the foundation for constructing a multinomial probability distribution model. The probability mass function of the multinomial distribution for the OW vector is:

$$P\left(A_{jW}\middle|w_j\right) = \frac{\left(\sum_{j=1}^{n} a_{jW}\right)!}{\prod_{j=1}^{n} a_{jW}\,!} \prod_{j=1}^{n} w_j^{a_{jW}} \tag{16.1}$$

where w_j represents the probabilistic weight of criterion c_j. Since the weight probabilities are proportional to a_{jW}, we obtain:

$$w_j \propto \frac{a_{jW}}{\sum_{j=1}^{n} a_{jW}},\ j = 1,\ 2,\ \ldots, n \tag{16.2}$$

$$w_W \propto \frac{a_{WW}}{\sum_{j=1}^{n} a_{jW}} = \frac{1}{\sum_{j=1}^{n} a_{jW}} \tag{16.3}$$

which yields:

$$\frac{w_j}{w_W} \propto a_{jW},\ j = 1,\ 2,\ \ldots, n \tag{16.4}$$

Similarly, the weight probability of the best criterion is derived as:

$$\frac{1}{w_B} \propto \frac{a_{BB}}{\sum_{j=1}^{n} a_{Bj}} = \frac{1}{\sum_{j=1}^{n} a_{Bj}} \Rightarrow \frac{w_B}{w_j} \propto a_{Bj},\ j = 1,\ 2,\ \ldots, n \tag{16.5}$$

And the Dirichlet distribution is then applied to estimate the optimal weight values w_j:

$$Dir\,(w_1, w_2, \ldots, w_n|\alpha) = \frac{1}{B(\alpha)} \prod_{j=1}^{n} w_j^{\alpha_j - 1} \tag{16.6}$$

where α is the parameter vector, typically set to 1, subject to the conditions:

$w_j \geq 0,\ \sum w_j = 1$

Step 5.1. Construct the joint probability distribution

Suppose there are K experts, indexed as $k = 1, 2, \ldots, K$. Each expert provides individual weights w_j^k, which can be aggregated into group weights w_j^{agg}. Let $A_{Bj}^{1:K}$ and $A_{jW}^{1:K}$ denote the BO and OW vectors of all experts. The joint probability distribution for the group decision is expressed as:

$$P\left(w_j^{agg},\ w_j^{1:K} \middle| A_{Bj}^{1:K},\ A_{jW}^{1:K}\right) \tag{16.7}$$

Step 5.2. Bayesian hierarchical modeling

Each individual weight vector w_j^k is dependent on the corresponding A_{Bj}^k and A_{jW}^k, while the aggregated group weight vector w_j^{agg} is derived from all w_j^k. Following the Bayesian hierarchical structure, the joint probability model is:

$$P\left(w_j^{agg},\ w_j^{1:K} \middle| A_{Bj}^{1:K},\ A_{jW}^{1:K}\right) \propto P\left(A_{Bj}^{1:K},\ A_{jW}^{1:K} \middle| w_j^{agg},\ w_j^{1:K}\right) P\left(w_j^{agg},\ w_j^{1:K}\right) \tag{16.8}$$

This can be further expanded as:

$$P\left(A_{Bj}^{1:K},\ A_{jW}^{1:K} \middle| w_j^{agg},\ w_j^{1:K}\right) P\left(w_j^{agg},\ w_j^{1:K}\right) = P\left(w_j^{agg}\right) \prod_{k=1}^{K} P\left(A_{jW}^k \middle| w_j^k\right) P\left(A_{Bj}^k \middle| w_j^k\right) P\left(w_j^k \middle| w_j^{agg}\right) \tag{16.9}$$

The distributions of A_{Bj}^k and A_{jW}^k conditioned on w_j^k follow multinomial distributions:

$$A_B^k \middle| w_j^k \sim Multinomial\left(\frac{1}{w_j^k}\right),\ A_{jW}^k \middle| w_j^k \sim Multinomial\left(w_j^k\right),\ k = 1, 2, \ldots, K \tag{16.10}$$

Given w_j^{agg}, the individual expert weights w_j^k follow a Dirichlet distribution:

$$w_j^k \middle| w_j^{agg} \sim Dir\left(\gamma \cdot w_j^{agg}\right),\ k = 1, 2, \ldots, K \tag{16.11}$$

where w_j^{agg} is the mean of the Dirichlet distribution, and γ is a nonnegative parameter controlling the concentration, modeled as:

$$\gamma \sim gamma\ (a, b) \tag{16.12}$$

With shape a and scale b parameters. Finally, the group optimal weights follow a Dirichlet prior:

$$w_j^{agg} \sim Dir\ (\alpha)$$

where α is typically set to 1.

Step 6. Estimation via Markov chain Monte Carlo

Once all probability distributions are specified, the Bayesian BWM employs Markov chain Monte Carlo (MCMC) simulation to generate q samples. The posterior distribution of the aggregated weights w_j^{agg} is then obtained, providing an optimal and probabilistically robust solution for group decision-making.

16.3 Numerical example 1—evaluating strategic alliance partners in the semiconductor supply chain

To demonstrate the basic application of the Bayesian BWM, we begin with a simple example focusing on consumer preferences for EVs. The motivation for this case study stems from the growing importance of sustainable transportation and the increasing demand for electric mobility worldwide. For many consumers, the decision to purchase an EV depends on balancing economic, technical, and lifestyle considerations.

In this illustrative study, a group of 14 potential customers who expressed interest in purchasing an EV were surveyed. These individuals were asked to evaluate the relative importance of four key criteria commonly considered in EV adoption:

(i) Price (c_1): The affordability of the EV, including purchase cost and long-term financial implications.
(ii) Performance (c_2): Driving experience and technical specifications, such as acceleration, handling, and safety.
(iii) Driving range (c_3): The distance the vehicle can travel on a single charge, representing a critical factor for usability and convenience.
(iv) Design and appearance (c_4): Aesthetic aspects and exterior styling, which influence consumer appeal and lifestyle fit.

Each respondent completed a structured questionnaire to provide their preferences. Specifically, they identified the most important criterion (best) and the least important criterion (worst), and then performed pairwise comparisons to generate the BO vector (see Table 16.1) and the OW vector (see Table 16.2). In the BO vector, the entry of 1 indicates the most important criterion (as the best criterion is always compared to itself with a value of 1), whereas larger numbers correspond to less important criteria relative to the best one. Conversely, in the OW vector, the entry of 1 indicates the least important criterion (as the worst criterion is always compared to itself with a value of 1), while larger numbers represent greater importance relative to the worst criterion.

The robustness of the ranking outcomes was further examined through the credal ranking procedure developed by Mohammadi and Rezaei (2020). In this example, the analysis produced an average confidence level of 83.99%, which demonstrates that the experts' judgments were highly consistent and dependable. Table 16.3 summarizes the confidence levels associated with all pairwise comparisons between the criteria. To illustrate, the confidence that c_1 is more important than c_2 was 91.52%, whereas the reverse confidence of c_2 over c_1 was only 8.48%. This asymmetry highlights that most respondents consistently ranked c_1 higher than c_2. Only those comparisons with confidence levels above 50% are retained in the table, since they represent the prevailing preferences within the group. A higher average confidence score indicates that the experts reached a stronger consensus on the relative importance of criteria. In this chapter, the 83.99% average suggests that the elicited rankings are both reliable and representative of the group.

Table 16.4 presents the individual and aggregated weights derived from the Bayesian BWM analysis. Each row corresponds to the weights assigned by a single respondent, while the last row reports the aggregated group weights. The results reveal a clear prioritization among the four criteria. Specifically, criterion "driving range (c_3)" achieved the highest aggregated weight of 0.309, ranking first overall. This indicates that most potential EV buyers place the greatest emphasis on the vehicle's driving range when making purchasing decisions. The second most important factor was "price (c_1)" with a weight of 0.269, highlighting the critical role of affordability. "Design and appearance (c_4)" followed with a weight of 0.225, suggesting that although aesthetics matter, they are secondary to performance-related attributes. Finally, performance (c_2) was assigned the lowest aggregated weight of 0.197, which implies that while vehicle performance

TABLE 16.1 Best-to-others vectors of the case 1.

	c_1	c_2	c_3	c_4
No. 1	1	2	1	2
No. 2	2	2	1	1
No. 3	1	1	1	1
No. 4	1	1	1	1
No. 5	1	1	1	1
No. 6	3	2	1	2
No. 7	1	1	1	1
No. 8	1	2	1	1
No. 9	1	1	1	1
No. 10	1	1	1	2
No. 11	1	4	4	2
No. 12	2	4	1	4
No. 13	2	4	1	2
No. 14	1	1	1	2

TABLE 16.2 Others-to-worst vectors of the case 1.

	c_1	c_2	c_3	c_4
No. 1	2	1	2	1
No. 2	1	1	2	2
No. 3	1	1	1	1
No. 4	1	1	1	1
No. 5	1	1	1	1
No. 6	1	2	3	2
No. 7	1	1	1	1
No. 8	2	1	2	2
No. 9	1	1	1	1
No. 10	2	2	2	1
No. 11	4	1	1	2
No. 12	2	1	4	1
No. 13	2	1	4	2
No. 14	2	2	2	1

TABLE 16.3 Credal ranking results of the case 1.

	c_1	c_2	c_3	c_4
c_1	-	91.52%		78.15%
c_2		-		
c_3	73.05%	97.39%	-	91.48%
c_4		72.32%		-
Average	83.99%			

remains a relevant consideration, it is less decisive compared to cost, range, and appearance in shaping consumer preferences (see Fig. 16.1).

Overall, the aggregated results underscore that buyers are primarily concerned with practical usability (range and price), rather than technical specifications alone. This reflects a demand-driven perspective where consumers prioritize value-for-money and everyday functionality over purely mechanical performance.

16.4 Numerical example 2—evaluating strategic alliance partners in the semiconductor supply chain

The semiconductor industry is characterized by its high complexity, global interdependencies, and rapid pace of technological innovation. To remain competitive, firms often rely on strategic alliances with reliable partners across the supply chain, including wafer foundries, integrated circuit (IC) design houses, packaging and testing firms, and upstream material and equipment suppliers. Selecting appropriate partners requires a systematic evaluation framework that captures both technical and operational considerations. In this case study, the Bayesian BWM is applied to determine the relative

TABLE 16.4 Bayesian best–worst method analysis results of case 1.

	c_1	c_2	c_3	c_4
No. 1	0.200	0.154	0.144	0.078
No. 2	0.275	0.194	0.312	0.219
No. 3	0.257	0.194	0.312	0.237
No. 4	0.267	0.201	0.304	0.227
No. 5	0.267	0.201	0.304	0.227
No. 6	0.267	0.201	0.304	0.227
No. 7	0.248	0.204	0.319	0.229
No. 8	0.267	0.201	0.304	0.227
No. 9	0.271	0.190	0.307	0.232
No. 10	0.267	0.201	0.304	0.227
No. 11	0.271	0.207	0.307	0.214
No. 12	0.298	0.188	0.280	0.235
No. 13	0.271	0.187	0.332	0.209
No. 14	0.265	0.181	0.326	0.228
w^{agg}	0.269	0.197	0.309	0.225
Rank	2	4	1	6

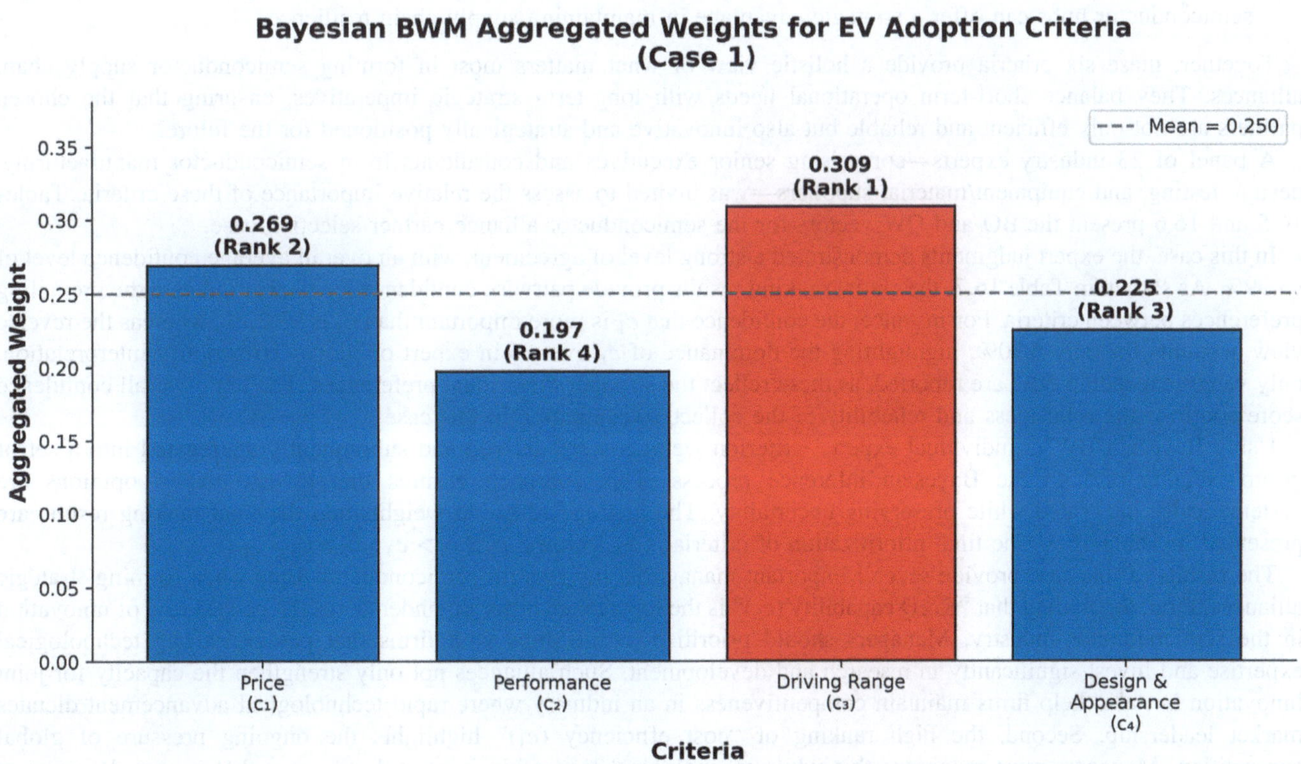

FIGURE 16.1 Bayesian best–worst method (BWM) aggregated weights for electric vehicle (EV) adoption criteria (case 1).

importance of key criteria for partner selection, integrating the judgments of multiple experts into a coherent group decision.

When semiconductor firms consider forming strategic alliances, the choice of partners is rarely straightforward. Decision-makers must weigh multiple dimensions that influence not only operational efficiency but also long-term competitiveness. In this case study, six evaluation criteria were selected based on extensive discussions with industry experts and a review of the strategic needs of semiconductor supply chains.

(i) First and foremost, cost efficiency (c_1) remains a decisive factor. In an industry where margins are often underpressure due to global competition, a partner's ability to control manufacturing and operating costs directly affects the profitability of the alliance. Firms are naturally drawn to collaborators who can offer competitive pricing without sacrificing reliability.
(ii) Equally critical is delivery reliability (c_2). Semiconductor production is highly sensitive to disruptions, and any delay in component delivery can cascade through the supply chain, causing costly downtime. Therefore, a partner's track record of on-time delivery and stable supply performance is essential for building trust in the collaboration.
(iii) Another indispensable dimension is quality assurance (c_3). Semiconductor products must adhere to extremely stringent quality standards. Partners with strong quality control mechanisms and rigorous inspection systems ensure that defective products are minimized, protecting both the integrity of the supply chain and the reputation of the firms involved.
(iv) In today's volatile market, flexibility and responsiveness (c_4) also play a significant role. Demand for semiconductor products often fluctuates due to shifts in consumer electronics, automotive requirements, or geopolitical events. A partner that can adapt quickly to sudden changes, whether by adjusting production capacity or reallocating resources, provides a critical buffer against uncertainty.
(v) However, operational concerns are only part of the equation. Long-term success in the semiconductor industry is heavily tied to R&D capability (c_5). As technology nodes continue to shrink and advanced manufacturing processes become more complex, innovation is the key driver of competitive advantage. Partners that invest in research and development not only bring new technologies to the table but also enhance the overall innovative capacity of the alliance.
(vi) Finally, geographic location (c_6) cannot be overlooked. In a globally interconnected yet geopolitically fragile industry, the location of partners' manufacturing sites and facilities significantly influences logistics efficiency, lead times, and even risk exposure to trade restrictions. Proximity to key markets or integration within regional semiconductor hubs can offer a strategic advantage in maintaining supply chain resilience.

Together, these six criteria provide a holistic view of what matters most in forming semiconductor supply chain alliances. They balance short-term operational needs with long-term strategic imperatives, ensuring that the chosen partners are not only efficient and reliable but also innovative and strategically positioned for the future.

A panel of 23 industry experts—comprising senior executives and consultants from semiconductor manufacturing, design, testing, and equipment/material suppliers—was invited to assess the relative importance of these criteria. Tables 16.5 and 16.6 present the BO and OW vectors for the semiconductor alliance partner selection case.

In this case, the expert judgments demonstrated a strong level of agreement, with an overall average confidence level of 93.99%. As shown in Table 16.7, the credal ranking results provide pairwise confidence levels that indicate the prevailing preferences between criteria. For instance, the confidence that c_1 is more important than c_2 is 93.30%, whereas the reverse view accounts for only 6.70%, highlighting the dominance of c_1 over c_2 in expert opinions. To simplify interpretation, only values exceeding 50% are reported, as these reflect the stronger directional preferences. The high overall confidence score confirms the robustness and reliability of the collective evaluation in this case.

Using Bayesian BWM, individual experts' criterion weights were derived and subsequently aggregated into a set of group weights through the Bayesian inference process. This approach ensures that diverse expert opinions are systematically integrated while preserving uncertainty. The aggregated group weights and the final ranking results are presented in Table 16.8. The final prioritization of criteria is as follows: $c_5 > c_1 > c_3 > c_2 > c_6 > c_4$.

The results of this case provide several important managerial insights for semiconductor firms when forming strategic alliances. First, the finding that "R&D capability (c_5)" is the top-ranked criterion underscores the central role of innovation in the semiconductor industry. Managers should prioritize partnerships with firms that possess strong technological expertise and invest significantly in research and development. Such alliances not only strengthen the capacity for joint innovation but also help firms maintain competitiveness in an industry where rapid technological advancement dictates market leadership. Second, the high ranking of "cost efficiency (c_1)" highlights the ongoing pressure of global competition. Managers must recognize that while technological leadership is critical, alliances that cannot deliver cost

TABLE 16.5 Best-to-others vectors of the case 2.

	c_1	c_2	c_3	c_4	c_5	c_6
No. 1	2	3	4	8	1	5
No. 2	2	4	3	4	1	3
No. 3	3	3	5	5	1	5
No. 4	3	2	3	6	1	7
No. 5	5	8	7	9	1	3
No. 6	3	4	2	5	1	6
No. 7	2	7	4	5	1	6
No. 8	2	3	4	5	1	6
No. 9	3	2	4	7	1	8
No. 10	1	4	1	2	1	3
No. 11	5	1	3	7	2	9
No. 12	3	3	4	8	1	6
No. 13	1	3	3	2	1	3
No. 14	2	7	4	5	1	9
No. 15	4	3	2	6	1	5
No. 16	4	3	2	5	1	6
No. 17	8	5	7	1	9	4
No. 18	1	3	3	2	1	3
No. 19	2	2	2	4	1	3
No. 20	2	2	5	6	1	3
No. 21	5	2	3	7	1	2
No. 22	2	3	1	6	4	5
No. 23	3	9	5	7	1	4

advantages are unlikely to be sustainable. Thus, partner selection should emphasize both innovation and cost control to strike a balance between long-term advancement and short-term profitability. Third, the emphasis on "quality assurance (c_3)" reflects the stringent standards and low tolerance for defects in semiconductor production. Managers should view quality systems as a prerequisite for partnership. Collaborators with robust inspection and quality management systems can reduce risks of supply chain disruptions, costly recalls, and reputational damage. Fourth, "delivery reliability (c_2)," although ranked slightly lower, remains a vital consideration. In practice, even the most innovative and cost-efficient partners can cause significant losses if they fail to deliver on time. Managers should evaluate the historical delivery performance of potential partners and, where possible, design contractual safeguards or redundancy mechanisms to mitigate risks. Interestingly, "geographic location (c_6)" and "flexibility and responsiveness (c_4)" were ranked lower. This suggests that in semiconductor alliances, strategic and technical considerations outweigh geographical convenience or short-term adaptability. While location and flexibility should not be ignored, managers may view them as secondary factors once the core pillars of R&D, cost, and quality have been satisfied.

Overall, these findings highlight that semiconductor supply chain alliances must be strategically oriented toward long-term technological innovation while simultaneously ensuring cost competitiveness and product quality. Managers should

TABLE 16.6 Others-to-worst vectors of the case 2.

	c_1	c_2	c_3	c_4	c_5	c_6
No. 1	6	4	3	1	8	2
No. 2	2	1	2	1	4	2
No. 3	3	3	1	5	5	5
No. 4	3	6	3	2	7	1
No. 5	2	1	2	1	9	4
No. 6	3	3	5	2	6	1
No. 7	5	1	3	2	7	2
No. 8	3	2	2	2	6	1
No. 9	4	5	3	2	8	1
No. 10	4	1	4	3	4	2
No. 11	2	9	4	2	5	1
No. 12	4	3	3	1	8	2
No. 13	3	1	1	2	3	1
No. 14	7	2	3	2	9	1
No. 15	2	3	5	1	6	2
No. 16	3	4	5	1	9	2
No. 17	1	2	2	9	1	3
No. 18	3	1	1	2	3	1
No. 19	3	3	3	1	4	2
No. 20	5	5	2	1	6	3
No. 21	2	4	3	1	7	6
No. 22	4	3	6	1	2	2
No. 23	4	1	2	2	9	3

TABLE 16.7 Credal ranking results of the case 2.

	c_1	c_2	c_3	c_4	c_5	c_6
c_1	-	93.30%	87.85%	99.99%		99.97%
c_2		-		99.56%		98.23%
c_3		62.98%	-	99.81%		99.28%
c_4				-		
c_5	100.00%	100.00%	100.00%	100.00%	-	100.00%
c_6				68.81%		-
Average	93.99%					

TABLE 16.8 Bayesian best–worst method analysis results of case 2.

	c_1	c_2	c_3	c_4	c_5	c_6
No. 1	0.200	0.154	0.144	0.078	0.321	0.104
No. 2	0.181	0.131	0.152	0.100	0.316	0.120
No. 3	0.180	0.156	0.131	0.106	0.317	0.110
No. 4	0.171	0.178	0.153	0.094	0.318	0.087
No. 5	0.164	0.117	0.133	0.089	0.350	0.146
No. 6	0.173	0.142	0.177	0.101	0.314	0.093
No. 7	0.201	0.113	0.151	0.106	0.325	0.104
No. 8	0.187	0.147	0.144	0.103	0.325	0.095
No. 9	0.180	0.172	0.147	0.092	0.325	0.085
No. 10	0.192	0.117	0.172	0.117	0.296	0.107
No. 11	0.153	0.213	0.164	0.095	0.292	0.083
No. 12	0.182	0.152	0.150	0.083	0.331	0.103
No. 13	0.196	0.134	0.139	0.117	0.307	0.107
No. 14	0.212	0.119	0.149	0.106	0.332	0.083
No. 15	0.159	0.151	0.179	0.089	0.317	0.105
No. 16	0.160	0.152	0.172	0.092	0.329	0.096
No. 17	0.144	0.150	0.141	0.200	0.223	0.141
No. 18	0.196	0.134	0.139	0.117	0.307	0.107
No. 19	0.179	0.154	0.160	0.093	0.303	0.111
No. 20	0.192	0.168	0.128	0.085	0.308	0.120
No. 21	0.145	0.161	0.150	0.081	0.314	0.150
No. 22	0.192	0.153	0.198	0.091	0.259	0.107
No. 23	0.187	0.106	0.140	0.099	0.342	0.127
w^{agg}	0.180	0.146	0.153	0.101	0.311	0.109
Rank	2	4	3	6	1	5

approach partner selection not merely as a transactional decision but as a strategic investment that shapes the future competitiveness of the entire supply chain.

16.5 Discussion

This section contrasts five widely used weighting and prioritization approaches—AHP, analytic network process (ANP), BWM, modified BWM, and Bayesian BWM—from conceptual, computational, and practical standpoints. We then reflect on what these differences mean in light of our two case studies (EV adoption and semiconductor alliance partner selection).

AHP begins from a hierarchical abstraction that presumes independence among criteria; priorities are obtained from pairwise comparison matrices via eigenvector methods with a consistency ratio to diagnose judgmental coherence. Its chief limitation is structural and operational: as the number of criteria grows, the number of required comparisons

TABLE 16.9 Method comparisons.

Method	Structure	Pairwise inputs (typical)	Core computation	Built-in consistency	Uncertainty in outputs
AHP	Hierarchy, independent criteria	$n(n-1)/2$	Eigenvector	CR (CI/RI)	Not modeled (point weights)
ANP	Network with interdependence/ feedback	> AHP (multiple linked matrices)	Weighted supermatrix	CR (CI/RI)	Not modeled (point weights)
BWM	Best–worst vectors, independent criteria	$2n-3$	Min–max/LP	BWM consistency index	Not modeled (point weights)
Modified BWM	Variants of BWM objective/ constraints, independent criteria	$2n-3$	Min–max/LP	BWM consistency index	Not modeled (point weights)
Bayesian BWM	Bayesian hierarchical on BO/OW, independent criteria	$2n-3$	MCMC for Dirichlet-multinomial	Posterior diagnostics + credal confidence	Posterior means/intervals + credal ranking

increases quadratically, which amplifies respondent fatigue and the risk of inconsistency. ANP relaxes the independence premise by admitting interdependencies and feedback among criteria and clusters. It thereby offers a richer representation of causally entangled decision spaces, but at the cost of greater modeling effort—links must be justified and parameterized—and heavier computation through the construction and powering of a weighted supermatrix, with results often necessitating post hoc sensitivity analysis to probe specification risk. However, in practice, the inter- and intra-cluster priorities that populate the ANP supermatrix are still elicited via AHP-style pairwise comparisons, thereby inheriting AHP's local judgment burden and consistency diagnostics.

BWM reframes elicitation around two anchors—the most and the least important criteria—so that only two reference comparison vectors (BO and OW) are needed. This reduces the elicitation load to $2n–3$ judgments for n criteria, which in practice leads to higher internal consistency and markedly lower cognitive burden relative to hierarchical pairwise matrices. The basic formulation, however, is typically deterministic: in group settings, it is common to aggregate individual priorities by averaging, a practice that may suppress dispersion and mask meaningful disagreement across experts. Modified BWM variants address these concerns at the optimization layer by refining the objective and constraints to improve uniqueness, numerical stability, and consistency diagnostics, or by supplying closed-form solutions in special cases; these refinements preserve the economical input structure of BWM while strengthening its solution properties, provided that the precise variant and diagnostic checks are transparently reported.

Bayesian BWM pushes the framework into a probabilistic domain. By modeling BO/OW judgments with multinomial likelihoods and placing a Dirichlet prior on the weight vector within a hierarchical structure, it integrates multiple experts without collapsing heterogeneity into a single point estimate. The posterior distribution delivers not only aggregated weights but also credible intervals that quantify estimation uncertainty, alongside credal ranking that assigns confidence levels to pairwise dominance relations among criteria. Consequently, the primary trade-off shifts from human effort to computation: the number of judgments remains $2n–3$, but estimation requires MCMC or variational inference with appropriate convergence diagnostics. In governance-intense or high-stakes contexts, the additional information—posterior dispersion and confidence in the ordering—can be decisive for auditability and consensus building.

The two case studies illustrate how these contrasts play out in practice. In the EV adoption case (few criteria, many respondents), Bayesian BWM delivered clear group weights with quantified confidence while keeping respondent effort minimal—exactly the setting where low cognitive load and communicable uncertainty add value. In the semiconductor alliance case (more criteria, expert heterogeneity), Bayesian BWM exposed both central tendencies (R&D and cost) and the strength of agreement via credal confidence, supporting key performance indicator (KPI) weighting, contract design, and board-level justification. Were strong intercriteria feedbacks the dominant concern, an ANP workflow—fed by AHP-style inputs—would be the appropriate alternative; where speed and simplicity outweigh uncertainty quantification, (modified) BWM is a pragmatic choice.

In short, selecting AHP for a well-understood, independent structure with standard diagnostics; ANP when interdependence is substantively central, and you can afford modeling/sensitivity work; (modified) BWM when expert time is scarce but consistent weights are needed quickly; and Bayesian BWM when multiexpert integration, explicit uncertainty, and consensus transparency are mission-critical. This alignment between method characteristics, elicitation/computation costs, and evidentiary needs should guide method selection across contexts, as summarized in Table 16.9.

16.6 Conclusions

This chapter has positioned Bayesian BWM as a mature, actionable approach for group multicriteria weighting under uncertainty. Building on the economy and internal consistency of classical BWM, the Bayesian formulation adds a principled probabilistic layer: BO/OW judgments are modeled through multinomial likelihoods; criterion weights follow Dirichlet posteriors; and credal ranking quantifies how confidently one criterion dominates another. The result is a method that preserves low elicitation burden while returning richer, audit-ready evidence about both central tendencies and dispersion in expert opinion.

The two case studies demonstrated this dual value in contrasting settings. In the EV adoption example (four criteria, 14 respondents), Bayesian BWM produced clear group weights—driving range > price > appearance > performance—with an average credal confidence of ~84%, indicating a solid but not unanimous consumer consensus. In the semiconductor alliance partner example (six criteria, 23 experts), the method highlighted a strategy-centric ordering—R&D capability > cost efficiency > quality assurance > delivery reliability > location > flexibility—and a higher overall confidence of ~94%, reflecting tighter agreement in an expert community. Across both studies, managers can translate results directly into action: EV makers should prioritize range–cost trade-offs and messaging to mitigate range anxiety; semiconductor firms should weight R&D and quality in partner KPIs and contract design, with cost as a disciplined second pillar.

The comparative discussion clarified when to use which tool. AHP remains a transparent baseline when independence is acceptable; ANP is preferable when interdependencies are central (though its inputs still rely on AHP-style pairwise judgments); (modified) BWM is ideal when expert time is scarce yet consistent weights are needed quickly; and Bayesian BWM is most informative when multiexpert integration, explicit uncertainty, and consensus transparency are mission-critical. Practically, the trade-off shifts from human effort to computation: Bayesian BWM keeps the 2n–32n–32n–3 judgment economy of BWM but asks for posterior inference and convergence diagnostics in return for posterior intervals and confidence in the ranking itself.

Limitations arise from modeling and computation. Posterior summaries depend on prior choices (e.g., Dirichlet concentration) and MCMC/variational inference (VI) settings; reporting priors, diagnostics (R-hat, effective sample size), and sensitivity checks is essential. Moreover, Bayesian BWM infers weights for independent criteria; when feedback and network effects are substantively important, analysts should complement it with ANP/decision-making trial and evaluation laboratory based analytic network process (DANP) or first map interrelations (e.g., decision-making trial and evaluation laboratory) and then weight with Bayesian BWM. Future directions include: (i) integration with DANP to propagate interdependencies while retaining Bayesian uncertainty quantification; (ii) scalable inference (variational Bayes) for large expert panels; (iii) hierarchical/mixed models to capture expert subgroups; (iv) dynamic (time-varying) Bayesian BWM for drifting preferences; and (v) hybrid pipelines that couple Bayesian BWM weights with outranking/ranking methods (e.g., PROMETHEE, VlseKriterijumska Optimizacija I Kompromisno Resenje) for alternative evaluation.

In sum, Bayesian BWM now stands as a well-established component of the MCDM toolkit: it is light to elicit, rich to interpret, and ready for governance. When paired judiciously with network-aware methods such as DANP, it offers a coherent pathway from expert judgments to transparent, defensible managerial decisions.

References

Debnath, B., Shakur, M. S., Bari, A. M., & Karmaker, C. L. (2023). A Bayesian best–worst approach for assessing the critical success factors in sustainable lean manufacturing. *Decision Analytics Journal, 6*, 100157.

Huang, C.-N., Liou, J. J., Lo, H.-W., & Chang, F.-J. (2021). Building an assessment model for measuring airport resilience. *Journal of Air Transport Management, 95*, 102101.

Modares, A., Emroozi, V. B., Roozkhosh, P., & Modares, A. (2025). A Bayesian best-worst approach with blockchain integration for optimizing supply chain efficiency through supplier selection. *Supply Chain Analytics, 9*, 100100.

Mohammadi, M., & Rezaei, J. (2020). Bayesian best-worst method: A probabilistic group decision making model. *Omega, 96*, 102075.

Munim, Z. H., Balasubramaniyan, S., Kouhizadeh, M., & Hossain, N. U. I. (2022). Assessing blockchain technology adoption in the Norwegian oil and gas industry using Bayesian best worst method. *Journal of Industrial Information Integration, 28*, 100346.

Patel, H., & Chang, C.-T. (2024). Beyond throughput: Evaluating maritime port competitiveness using MABAC and Bayesian methods. *Computers & Industrial Engineering, 192*, 110248.

Rezaei, J. (2015). Best-worst multi-criteria decision-making method. *Omega, 53*, 49–57.

Salman, S., Morshed, S. M., Karim, M. R., Rahman, R., Hasanat, S., & Ahsan, A. (2025). Exploring lean manufacturing drivers for enhancing circular economy performance in the pharmaceutical industry: A Bayesian best–worst approach. *International Journal of Industrial Engineering and Operations Management, 7*(1), 68–96.

Yanilmaz, S., Baskak, D., Yucesan, M., & Gul, M. (2021). Extension of FEMA and SMUG models with Bayesian best-worst method for disaster risk reduction. *International Journal of Disaster Risk Reduction, 66*, 102631.

Yao, K.-C., Yang, J.-J., Lo, H.-W., Lin, S.-W., & Li, G.-H. (2023). Using a BBWM-PROMETHEE model for evaluating mobile commerce service quality: A case study of food delivery platform. *Research in Transportation Business & Management, 49*, 100988.

Chapter 17

Nonadditive BWM: Nonadditive best-worst method for multi-attribute decision-making

Javad Nazarian-Jashnabadi[1], Gholamreza Haseli[2], Mostafa Hajiaghaei-Keshteli[2], Muhammet Deveci[3], and Hana Tomaskova[4]

[1]*Department of Management, Faculty of Economic, Management and Social Science, Shiraz University, Shiraz, Iran,* [2]*School of Engineering and Sciences, Tecnologico de Monterrey, Monterrey, Mexico,* [3]*Department of Industrial Engineering, Turkish Naval Academy, National Defence University, Istanbul, Türkiye,* [4]*Faculty of Informatics and Management, University of Hradec Kralove, Hradec Králové, Czech Republic*

17.1 Introduction

Multi-attribute decision-making (MADM), a branch of Multicriteria decision-making, is an approach to decision-making in situations where multiple criteria with different attributes are involved in the decision-making process. MADM methods enable more accurate and transparent decision-making due to their systematic structure and ability to manage multiple criteria (Zhang et al., 2026). By providing a coherent framework for analyzing complex problems, these methods help decision-makers (DMs) make choices based on data and logic (Haseli et al., 2020). MADM is divided into two categories: compensatory and noncompensatory methods. In compensatory methods, the DM can compensate for the weakness of one criterion with the advantage of another criterion, while in noncompensatory methods, the criteria are evaluated independently of each other (Banihabib et al., 2017). An important part of the MADM methods deals with the weighting of criteria, which includes techniques such as analytic hierarchy process (AHP) (Saaty, 1977), analytic network process (Saaty, 1996), and best–worst method (BWM) (Rezaei, 2015), which use pairwise comparisons to determine the weights of criteria. By determining the relative importance of criteria, weighting methods increase the accuracy and flexibility in decision-making and allow objective comparison of criteria (Ahemad et al., 2025). Despite the multitude of weighting methods, choosing the appropriate weighting method is a key factor in validating the results, because the nature of the problem is considered the most important criterion in choosing the appropriate methodology.

Classic additive methods, such as AHP, are efficient in problems with independent criteria, but in cases where criteria interaction exists, the application of additive methods will affect the results. For example, the use of additive methods in vehicle selection (with affiliative criteria like price, fuel consumption, and efficiency), in addition to ignoring the effect of the negative interaction of price and fuel consumption, does not calculate the positive synergy of price and efficiency, and ultimately leads to risky decisions. Therefore, it is a prerequisite for valid outputs in strategic decision-making to match the method with the problem structure (dependence or autonomy of the criteria, level of complexity, and data type) (Jiang et al., 2021).

Due to the remarkable advantages of BWM, which make it a privileged choice in MADM, this method has simplified implementation by reducing the number of paired comparisons to traditional methods, and on the other hand, by providing a consistency index, it is possible to evaluate the reliability of the preferences of the DM. Another key advantage of BWM is the reduction of cognitive biases, such as "Anchoring Bias" and "Equalizing Bias" that are common in paired comparisons (Tahura et al., 2025). Furthermore, its flexible mathematical modeling, in addition to computational complexity management, guarantees the stability of the results against the volatility of the data. These features have turned BWM into a basic framework that has wide applications in operational areas such as supplier selection, resource management, and resource allocation (Luo & Li, 2025).

Encyclopedia of Multi-Attribute Decision-Making (MADM). DOI: https://doi.org/10.1016/B978-0-443-33275-3.00065-8

However, a major limitation in all the original and modified versions still stands. All of them assume that the criteria are independent and additive. This assumption in real-world decision-making problems in which the criteria are mutually dependent is often violated. To overcome this challenge, Liang et al. (2023) attempted to develop a new and efficient framework called "Nonadditive BWM". This method combines the criteria interactions systematically by integrating the Choquet integral (Choquet, 1954) and the 2-additive fuzzy measures. This approach calculates the individual importance of the criteria in addition to the degree of paired interaction and evaluates the performance of the alternatives by considering the interdependencies of the criteria. Thus, the nonadditive BWM, while retaining key advantages of classic BWM such as reduction of paired comparisons, evaluation of preference consistency, and stability of results, provides the fundamental limitation of previous methods in neglecting the criteria interactions.

The rest of this chapter is organized as follows. Section 2 provides a comprehensive review of the existing literature. In this section, first, studies related to BWM are reviewed, and then the nonadditive approach in MADM problems is analyzed. Section 3 describes the six steps of nonadditive BWM and calculating the consistency ratio (CR), which is a key indicator in conducting pairwise comparisons. Section 5 illustrates the proposed approach through a numerical case study related to the ranking of health tourism destinations. Finally, Section 6 summarizes the main findings of this chapter and discusses their implications.

17.2 Literature review

A review of the studies shows that BWM has been used in a wide range of scientific and applied fields and has expanded significantly in terms of subject matter and methodological diversity (see Table 17.1). In the field of sustainability and environment, this method has been used to evaluate the efficiency of container terminals (Hsu et al., 2025), select medical waste management technology (Gao et al., 2024), and locate solar-wind systems (Aghaloo et al., 2023). In materials and energy engineering, BWM has been used in the design of cold patching asphalt binder (Chen et al., 2025) and the optimization of heat transfer in solar systems (Khargotra et al., 2024). In education, it has also been used to compare the effectiveness of online and offline learning (Tahura et al., 2025), and in digital marketing, it has helped analyze the marketing of tourist attractions on social networks such as TikTok (Luo & Li, 2025). BWM has also been widely used in supply chain management and supplier selection (Haseli et al., 2023; Vaezi et al., 2024; Zhang et al., 2024). It has also been used in the field of urban management to assess the sustainable development of a city (Foroozesh et al., 2022). In addition, several methodological developments have been made to improve BWM, including ensemble models (Haseli et al., 2021) and spherical fuzzy (SF) models (Haseli et al., 2024). This diversity shows that BWM has high performance in MADM problems.

In recent studies, the use of BWM in combination with other MADM methods has been increasingly widespread, and these combinations have been recognized as novel approaches to solving complex decision-making problems. One of the reasons for this trend is the simplicity and high accuracy of BWM in the criteria weighting stage, while at the same time requiring complementary methods for ranking options or analyzing uncertainties. For example, Chen et al. (2025) combined BWM with technique for order preference by similarity to ideal solution to rank different asphalt options in addition to weighting performance criteria. Similarly, Gao et al. (2024) proposed a hybrid BWM-Vlse Kriterijumsk Optimizacija Kompromisno Resenje (VIKOR) to achieve optimal selection of medical waste management technologies. In the field of risk and uncertainty analysis, BWM has been combined with Dempster–Shafer theory, stochastic multiobjective acceptability analysis, and measurement alternatives and ranking according to compromise solution (MARCOS) to provide a more accurate failure modes and effects analysis model (Ju et al., 2024). Additionally, a hybrid approach combining the BWM and MARCOS methods was employed for mineral potential modeling (Roshanravan et al., 2025).

New methods such as picture fuzzy numbers BWM (Luo & Li, 2025), SF BWM (Haseli et al., 2024), and scenario-varying Z-numbers BWM (Zhang et al., 2024) have been developed, which reflect the efforts of researchers to improve the accuracy, consistency, and reliability of BWM under uncertainty. Furthermore, in application areas such as supply chain, BWM has been used as a core component in hybrid frameworks with MULTIMOORA (Vaezi et al., 2024) to determine the weights of criteria with high accuracy on the one hand and to rank the final decision alternatives more accurately on the other. Also, the integration of BWM with the Multi-attribute border approximation area comparison (MABAC) approach under extended Z-numbers has been applied to logistic hub location selection to address uncertainty in global operations (Haseli et al., 2025). This study highlights the importance of cost and infrastructure in logistics decision-making. These combinations have made BWM-based hybrid methods a dominant paradigm in complex, multilevel decision-making. Overall, the combined use of BWM with other methods has increased the accuracy of the analysis and increased its adaptability to real-world conditions and uncertainties. This trend was very pronounced in the studies from

TABLE 17.1 Summary of related studies.

	Author(s) and year	Research objective	Fuzzy approach	Methodology	Research area
1	Hsu et al. (2025)	Assessing container terminals' efficiency from a sustainable development perspective	–	Integration of BWM–GRA[a] with SBM[a] model	Sustainable transportation/port operations
2	Chen et al. (2025)	Optimizing cold-patching asphalt composition using performance-based criteria	–	Integrated BWM + TOPSIS + Taguchi method	Material science/pavement engineering
3	Roshanravan et al., 2025	Enhancing mineral potential modeling using a hybrid MCDM approach	–	BWM–MARCOS	Geoscience/ mineral exploration
4	Tahura et al. (2025)	Comparing online and offline learning effectiveness in developing regions	–	BWM	Education/E-learning strategies
5	Luo and Li (2025)	Evaluate TikTok marketing performance of tourist attractions in China	PFN	PFN–BWM	Tourism marketing/social media analytics
6	Haseli et al. (2025)	Modeling a logistics hub location problem under uncertainty	ZE-numbers	MABAC + BWM	Logistics and supply chain management
7	Gao et al. (2024)	Select optimal treatment technologies for medical waste management	Fermatean fuzzy Sets	BWM + VIKOR	Healthcare/waste management
8	Ju et al. (2024)	Prioritize failure modes in automobile manufacturing using uncertainty-based FMEA	–	BWM + SMAA + MARCOS	Reliability engineering/ risk assessment
9	Vaezi et al. (2024)	Integrate blockchain and sustainability in supplier selection and order allocation	–	BWM + MULTIMOORA + bi-objective MILP[a] model	Supply chain/ blockchain/ sustainability
10	Khargotra et al. (2024)	Optimize flow and performance of system	–	Hybrid BWM–CODAS[a]	Thermal systems/ energy engineering
11	Haseli et al. (2024)	Extend BWM to address MCDM problems under uncertainty	SF	SF–BWM	Decision science/ uncertainty modeling
12	Zhang et al. (2024)	Prioritize GRID-based[a] suppliers under dependent uncertain events	SVZ	Enhanced BWM + TOPSIS + SVZ	Supply chain/ sustainable procurement
13	Aghaloo et al. (2023)	Select optimal sites for solar-wind hybrid renewable energy systems	Fuzzy logic	GIS-based[a] BWM + fuzzy logic + sensitivity analysis	Renewable energy/site selection
14	Foroozesh et al. (2022)	Assess the sustainable urban development of Karaj city	Group fuzzy sets	Group fuzzy BWM + AHP + GIS + WLC[a] + TOPSIS	Urban planning/ sustainability assessment
15	Haseli et al. (2021)	Develop a democratic group decision-making model based on BWM	–	Group BWM	Group decision-making/supply chain management

[a] *GRA: grey relational analysis; SBM: slacks-based measure; MILP: mixed-integer linear programming; CODAS: combinative distance-based assessment; GRID: green, resilient, and embrace inclusive development; GIS: geographic information system; WLC: weighted linear combination.*

2023 to 2025, establishing BWM as a central core in modern decision-making frameworks. Table 17.1 presents a summary of the literature in this field.

The nonadditive approach in MADM methods has received attention in recent years because it considers interactions and interdependencies between criteria, unlike classical models. For example, an efficient identification technique for 2-additive fuzzy measures has been proposed to capture both importance and interaction indices among decision criteria. This approach reduces the complexity of monotonicity constraints and adjusts for subjective biases through decision parameters, leading to more reliable evaluations in green material selection tasks (Guan et al., 2024). Similarly, in the context of sustainability assessment of carbon capture utilization and storage technologies, a Choquet integral-based MADM framework was developed, utilizing a 2-additive fuzzy measure to account for complementary and redundant relationships between economic, environmental, and technical criteria (He et al., 2024). Another notable application is the development of the nonadditive BWM, which integrates the Choquet integral to accommodate interaction effects among criteria, demonstrating improved performance in the selection of battery-powered electric vehicles (Liang et al., 2023). Furthermore, the concept of nonadditivity has been extended to rough set theory, where a nonadditive grey tolerance rough set classifier was introduced. By incorporating interaction and interdependencies through grey relational analysis and decision-making trial and evaluation laboratory, the classifier achieved higher accuracy compared to traditional models (Jiang et al., 2021).

This modeling approach has also been applied in healthcare decision-making, where the incorporation of expert knowledge and interaction among medical factors is critical. For instance, a healthcare decision support system based on nonadditive measures and the Choquet integral was proposed for cardiovascular risk evaluation, showing its usefulness in diagnosis and insurance pricing when data are scarce or expert judgment is central (Anzilli & Giove, 2020). Beyond healthcare, the nonadditive robust ordinal regression (NAROR) method has been applied in urban planning problems, offering a flexible decision support mechanism where preference information is uncertain or incomplete. NAROR handles interactions through fuzzy measures, providing robust recommendations based on both necessary and possible preferences (Angilella et al., 2016). In vendor selection, where interdependencies among evaluation criteria are common, and data uncertainty prevails, a hybrid fuzzy MADM model incorporating interpretive structural modeling and nonadditive fuzzy integrals was developed. The approach successfully captured interrelations among subcriteria and outperformed traditional additive models in selecting the most suitable vendor (Yang et al., 2008). Similarly, in evaluating environmental investment strategies, the nonadditive fuzzy integral method has demonstrated its ability to model stakeholder preferences across dependent and fuzzy criteria. Using triangular fuzzy numbers and an AHP-based structure, the method aggregated sustainability indicators more effectively than additive techniques, particularly under criteria interdependence (Chiou et al., 2005). Table 17.2 reports an overview of studies related to the nonadditive approach.

17.3 Methodology

In this section, an extended version of BWM is presented, which aims to weight criteria by considering interactions and dependencies between them. Unlike the classic versions of BWM, which mainly focused on comparing criteria with respect to the best and worst criteria, this new version also attempts to consider the interactions between criteria. This improvement makes the obtained weights a more accurate reflection of the real decision-making structure. The steps of implementing this method are described below (Liang et al., 2023).

Step 1. A set of decision criteria $C = \{c_j, \quad j = 1, 2, \ldots, n\}$ is determined by the DM. In this step, the focus is on fully and accurately identifying the key criteria that play a decisive role in the evaluation process. The correct selection of these criteria will be the basis for conducting future comparisons.

Step 2. The DM selects the most important criterion as the "best" (C_B) and the least important criterion as the "worst" (C_W) from the set of specified criteria. After determining these two reference criteria, pairwise comparisons are made between the best criterion and the other criteria (BO), as well as between the other criteria and the worst criterion (OW). These comparisons are made using a numerical scale from 1 to 9. The results of these comparisons are denoted in the form of two preference vectors as Eqs. 17.1 and 17.2:

$$BO = (a_{B1}, \ a_{B2}, \ \ldots, \ a_{Bn}) \tag{17.1}$$

$$OW = (a_{1W}, \ a_{2W}, \ \ldots, \ a_{nW})^T \tag{17.2}$$

TABLE 17.2 Research literature in the nonadditive approach.

	Author and Year	Research objective	Fuzzy approach	Methodology	Research area
1	Guan et al. (2024)	Developing a technique for identifying 2-additive fuzzy measures	2-additive fuzzy measures	DEMATEL	Feature interaction analysis in MADM
2	He et al. (2024)	Proposing a Choquet integral-based framework for CCUS sustainability assessment	2-additive fuzzy measure	Choquet integral-based MCDM; TOPSIS	Sustainability assessment of CCUS technologies
3	Liang et al. (2023)	Extending BWM to a nonadditive model using Choquet integral	–	Nonadditive BWM with Choquet integral	MADM model development
4	Jiang et al. (2021)	Incorporating interdependencies into tolerance rough set classifiers	Nonadditive fuzzy measures	Nonadditive GRA + DEMATEL + genetic algorithm	Pattern classification
5	Anzilli and Giove (2020)	Designing a healthcare decision support system based on nonadditive measures	–	Choquet integral, MCDM, expert-based evaluation, error estimation	Healthcare decision support
6	Angilella et al. (2016)	Applying NAROR for interaction-aware urban planning decisions	Nonadditive fuzzy measures	NAROR	Urban and territorial planning
7	Yang et al. (2008)	Integrating fuzzy MCDM methods for interdependent vendor selection	Triangular fuzzy numbers	ISM[a], fuzzy AHP, nonadditive fuzzy integral	Vendor selection under uncertainty
8	Chiou et al. (2005)	Evaluating sustainable investment strategies using nonadditive fuzzy integrals	Nonadditive fuzzy integral with triangular fuzzy numbers	Factor analysis + AHP + fuzzy integral aggregation	Sustainable development evaluation

[a] *ISM*

Step 3. The interactions between the criteria are provided by the DM. To do this, the DM provides qualitative assessments for the relationships among the criteria, such as positive, negative, no interaction, or unknown. The result of this assessment will be the formation of a symmetric interaction matrix ($D = (t_{ij})_{n \times n}$ *and* $t_{ij} = t_{ji}$, $i \neq j, i, j = 1, 2, \ldots, n$) in which each cell represents the type of relationship between the two criteria.

$$D = \begin{array}{c} \\ c_1 \\ c_2 \\ \vdots \\ c_n \end{array} \begin{array}{c} \begin{array}{cccc} c_1 & c_2 & \cdots & c_n \end{array} \\ \begin{bmatrix} / & t_{12} & \cdots & t_{1n} \\ t_{21} & / & \cdots & t_{2n} \\ \vdots & \vdots & \ddots & \vdots \\ t_{1n} & t_{2n} & \cdots & / \end{bmatrix} \end{array} \tag{17.3}$$

Where $t_{ij} \in \{+, \; -, \; \Delta, \text{u'}\}$, $i \neq j, i, j = 1, 2, \ldots, n$ and "+" means positive interaction between two criteria, "−" means the two criteria interact negatively, "Δ" indicates that the two criteria act independently and have no interaction and finally "u" is used when the DM cannot make a definitive statement about the type of relationship between the two criteria.

Step 4. According to the values of the interaction matrix, the degree of criteria interaction I_{ij}, $i \neq j$, $i, j = 1, 2, \ldots, n$ is determined as Eq. 17.4. It should be noted that since $I_{ij} = I_{ji}$, $i \neq j, i, j = 1, 2, \ldots, n$, only I_{ij}, $i < j; i, j = 1, 2, \ldots, n$ is considered.

$$\begin{cases} I_{ij} > 0, & if \;\; t_{ij} = +; \\ I_{ij} < 0, & if \;\; t_{ij} = -; \\ I_{ij} = 0, & if \;\; t_{ij} = \Delta; \\ I_{ij} \in [-1, 1], & if \;\; t_{ij} = \text{u}'; \end{cases} \tag{17.4}$$

(17.5) shows the criteria interaction I_{ij} which is equivalent to the Mobius representation m_{ij} (Angilella et al., 2004):

$$I_{ij} = m_{ij}, \; i \neq j \tag{17.5}$$

Next, I_j represents the relative importance of each criterion c_j, and it can be obtained using the Shapley value (Shapley, 1953). The relative importance of each criterion is obtained using (17.6).

$$I_j = m_j + \sum\nolimits_{c_i \in C \;\; \{c_j\}} \frac{m_{ij}}{2}, \quad j = 1, 2, \ldots, n \tag{17.6}$$

Step 5. The goal of this step is to calculate the relative importance of the criteria in such a way that the maximum absolute difference between the presented pairwise comparisons and their associated weight ratios is minimized. For this purpose, a linear model is created using (17.7).

$$\begin{aligned} & \min \max_j \left\{ \left| \frac{I_B}{I_j} - a_{Bj} \right|, \left| \frac{I_j}{I_W} - a_{jW} \right| \right\} \\ & \text{subject to } \; m(\theta) = 0; \; \sum\nolimits_{c_j \in C} m_j + \sum\nolimits_{c_i, c_j \in C} m_{ij} = 1; \\ & \quad m_j + \sum\nolimits_{c_i \in T} m_{ij} \geq 0, \; i, j = 1, 2, \ldots, n \text{ and } T \subseteq C\{c_j\}, \; T \neq \theta; \\ & \quad I_{ij} = m_{ij}, \; i \neq j, \; i, j = 1, 2, \ldots, n; \\ & \quad I_j = m_j + \sum\nolimits_{c_i \in C \{c_j\}} \frac{m_{ij}}{2}, \; i \neq j; \\ & \quad I_{ij} > 0, \;\; if \;\; t_{ij} = +, i < j; \\ & \quad I_{ij} < 0, \;\; if \;\; t_{ij} = -, i < j; \\ & \quad I_{ij} = 0, \;\; if \;\; t_{ij} = \Delta, \; i < j; \\ & \quad I_{ij} \in [-1, 1], \;\; if t_{ij} = \text{u}', \; i < j; \end{aligned} \tag{17.7}$$

Model 7 can be transferred into Model 8 as follows:

$$\begin{aligned}
&\min \quad \xi \\
&\text{subject to} \quad m(\Theta) = 0;\ \Sigma_{c_j \in C} m_j + \Sigma_{c_i, c_j \in C} m_{ij} = 1; \\
&m_j + \Sigma_{c_i \in T} m_{ij} \geq 0,\ i, j = 1, 2, \ldots, n \ \text{and}\ \mathrm{T} \subseteq \mathrm{C}\{c_j\},\ \mathrm{T} \neq \Theta; \\
&\mathrm{I}_{ij} = m_{ij},\ \ i \neq j; \\
&\mathrm{I}_j = m_j + \Sigma_{c_i \in C\{c_j\}} \frac{m_{ij}}{2},\ \ i \neq j; \\
&\left| \frac{\mathrm{I}_B}{\mathrm{I}_j} - a_{Bj} \right| \leq \xi,\ j = 1, 2, \ldots, n; \\
&\left| \frac{\mathrm{I}_j}{\mathrm{I}_W} - a_{jW} \right| \leq \xi,\ j = 1, 2, \ldots, n; \\
&\mathrm{I}_{ij} > 0,\ \ if\ \ t_{ij} = +, i < j; \\
&\mathrm{I}_{ij} < 0,\ \ if\ \ t_{ij} = -, i < j; \\
&\mathrm{I}_{ij} = 0,\ \ if\ \ t_{ij} = \Delta,\ \ i < j; \\
&\mathrm{I}_{ij} \in [-1, 1],\ \ if\ \ t_{ij} = \mathrm{u}',\ \ i < j;
\end{aligned} \tag{17.8}$$

Model 8 contains nonlinear constraints, which make it difficult to solve using standard optimization techniques like linear programming or mixed-integer linear programming. Additionally, inconsistencies between the qualitative preferences for criterion interactions and the pairwise comparison data can lead to situations where the model either has no feasible solution or produces multiple optimal ones. This complicates both interpretation and practical use. To overcome these challenges, the model is reformulated as Model 9, where all constraints are linear.

$$\begin{aligned}
&\min \quad \xi \\
&\text{subject to} \quad m(\Theta) = 0;\ \Sigma_{c_j \in C} m_j + \Sigma_{c_i, c_j \in C} m_{ij} = 1; \\
&m_j + \Sigma_{c_i \in T} m_{ij} \geq 0,\ i, j = 1, 2, \ldots, n \ \text{and}\ \mathrm{T} \subseteq \mathrm{C}\{c_j\},\ \mathrm{T} \neq \Theta; \\
&\mathrm{I}_{ij} = m_{ij},\ i \neq j,\ i, j = 1, 2, \ldots, n; \\
&\mathrm{I}_j = m_j + \Sigma_{c_i \in C\{c_j\}} \frac{m_{ij}}{2},\ i \neq j; \\
&\mathrm{I}_B - a_{Bj}\mathrm{I}_j \leq \xi, j = 1, 2, \ldots, n;\ \mathrm{I}_B - a_{Bj}\mathrm{I}_j \geq -\xi,\ j = 1, 2, \ldots, n; \\
&\mathrm{I}_j - a_{jW}\mathrm{I}_W \leq \xi, j = 1, 2, \ldots, n;\ \mathrm{I}_j - a_{jW}\mathrm{I}_W \geq -\xi,\ j = 1, 2, \ldots, n; \\
&\mathrm{I}_{ij} > 0,\ \ if\ \ t_{ij} = +, i < j; \\
&\mathrm{I}_{ij} < 0,\ \ if\ \ t_{ij} = -, i < j; \\
&\mathrm{I}_{ij} = 0,\ \ if\ \ t_{ij} = \Delta,\ \ i < j; \\
&\mathrm{I}_{ij} \in [-1, 1],\ \ if\ \ t_{ij} = \mathrm{u}',\ \ i < j;
\end{aligned} \tag{17.9}$$

Step 6. Using the results of solving the model in the previous step, in this step the final score of the alternatives is calculated, and their ranking is performed. For this purpose, first each of the alternatives is evaluated separately based on each of the criteria determined by the DM. This evaluation can be done based on quantitative or qualitative criteria, and positive or negative. We denote a set of alternatives as $A = \{a_p, p = 1, 2, \ldots, q\}$, and a set of criteria as $C = \{c_j, j = 1, 2, \ldots, n\}$. Then the performance of the alternative a_p under the criterion c_j is represented by $g_j(a_p)$. Since different criteria have different measurement scales, normalization is necessary. Various methods can be used for this. Here, the common method according to (17.10) is used.

$$v(g_j(a_p)) = \begin{cases} \dfrac{g_j(a_p) - l_j}{h_j - l_j}, & if\ \ c_j \ \text{is a benefit criterion;} \\ \dfrac{h_j - g_j(a_p)}{h_j - l_j}, & if\ \ c_j \ \text{is a cost criterion;} \end{cases} \tag{17.10}$$

Where h_j and l_j represent the maximum and minimum scores determined by the DM among different alternatives under the criterion c_j, respectively. So $v(g_j(a_p))$ is the normalized value of $g_j(a_p)$ and $v(g_j(a_p)) \in [0,1]$. Finally, the score of each alternative based on the Choquet integral ($C_\mu(a_p)$) is obtained using Eq. (17.11). The higher $C_\mu(a_p)$, the better the performance of the alternative a_p and the higher it is ranked.

$$C_\mu(a_p) = \sum_{c_j \in C} m_j v(g_j(a_p)) + \sum_{c_i, c_j \in C} m_{ij} \min\{v(g_i(a_p)), v(g_j(a_p))\} \tag{17.11}$$

17.3.1 Consistency ratio

When performing pairwise comparisons, the consistency of comparisons is important. A comparison is fully consistent when (17.12) holds for all j (Rezaei, 2015).

$$a_{Bj} \times a_{jW} = a_{BW} \tag{17.12}$$

Where a_{Bj}, a_{jW} , and a_{BW} are the preference of the best criterion over the criterion j, the preference of the criterion j over the worst criterion, and the preference of the best criterion over the worst criterion, respectively. Since some comparisons may not be consistent, the concept of CR was introduced and is calculated using Eq. 17.13.

$$\text{Consistency Ratio}(CR) = \frac{\xi^*}{\text{Consistency Index (CI)}} \tag{17.13}$$

The values of the consistency index for different values of a_{BW} are given in Table 17.3.

The smaller the CR value, the higher the consistency of the pairwise comparisons. To determine whether the CR value is acceptable, it should be compared with the threshold value presented in Table 17.4 (Liang et al., 2020). If the CR is less than the threshold, the pairwise comparisons are considered to have an acceptable level of consistency.

17.4 Numerical example: health tourism destination selection

Health tourism, as one of the new and strategic branches of the tourism industry, plays an important role in improving the quality of life, generating income, and promoting sustainable development. With the growth of emerging technologies, especially artificial intelligence, unique opportunities have been provided to improve the patient experience, optimize medical services, and increase the trust of health tourists. Meanwhile, countries that can efficiently utilize the capabilities of artificial intelligence will have a significant competitive advantage in this industry.

Given the diversity of countries' conditions in areas such as the quality of medical services, the level of technological infrastructure, interactions between medical and tourism institutions, and the capabilities of doctors, choosing the best destination for investing or guiding health tourists has become a complex and multicriteria problem. This decision requires careful consideration of several key criteria simultaneously and evaluating different alternatives based on them. Interactions between criteria can also influence decision-making, as some criteria reinforce each other, while others may conflict.

It is essential to use a structured decision-making method such as the nonadditive BWM to scientifically evaluate the performance of alternatives (see Table 17.5) by identifying and correctly weighting the criteria.

The goal is to select a country that, while having real competitive advantages, is most consistent with the success criteria in the field of AI-based health tourism. This analysis can be a key guide for policymakers, investors, and health tourism professionals to make targeted decisions. Table 17.6 presents the list of criteria and their brief definition.

TABLE 17.3 Consistency index (CI) (Rezaei, 2015).

a_{BW}	1	2	3	4	5	6	7	8	9
CI	0.00	0.44	1.00	1.63	2.30	3.00	3.73	4.47	5.23

TABLE 17.4 Threshold for consistency measurement (Liang et al., 2020).

	Criteria						
Scale	**3**	**4**	**5**	**6**	**7**	**8**	**9**
3	0.2087	0.2087	0.2087	0.2087	0.2087	0.2087	0.2087
4	0.1581	0.2352	0.2738	0.2928	0.3102	0.3145	0.3273
5	0.2111	0.2848	0.3019	0.3309	0.3479	0.3611	0.3741
6	0.2164	0.2922	0.3565	0.3924	0.4061	0.4168	0.4225
7	0.2090	0.3313	0.3734	0.3931	0.4035	0.4108	0.4298
8	0.2267	0.3409	0.4029	0.4230	0.4379	0.4543	0.4599
9	0.2122	0.3653	0.4055	0.4225	0.4445	0.4587	0.4747

TABLE 17.5 Features of various alternatives.

Code	Alternatives	Positive features	Negative features
A1	Country A	Abundant natural healing resources, expert doctors	Weak IT infrastructure, inadequate access to medical information
A2	Country B	High variety of medical services, low cost	Low quality of hospital services, limited equipment
A3	Country C	Advanced medical equipment, convenient access to information	Poor interaction between health tourism institutions
A4	Country D	Strong advertising, effective branding, high security	High cost of medical services, expensive tariffs
A5	Country E	Compliance with medical standards, internationally accredited doctors	Low attractiveness for nonmedical and cultural tourism
A6	Country F	Quality accommodations, efficient transportation	Weak diversity of medical services, limited IT infrastructure
A7	Country G	Highly advanced infrastructure, data and service integration, excellent service quality	High costs, complicated health tourist entry processes

As mentioned in step 3, the interaction between criteria must be considered. To do this, the DM has provided the type of interaction for the pairs of criteria according to Eq. 17.14. For further explanation, Table 17.7 describes some of these interactions.

$$c_1 \quad c_2 \quad c_3 \quad c_4 \quad c_5 \quad c_6 \quad c_7 \tag{17.14}$$

TABLE 17.6 Features of various alternatives.

Code	Criteria	Definition
C1	Medical services quality	The level of treatment standards and treatment outcomes in destination medical centers
C2	Physicians' reputation	The level of experience, expertise, and international reputation of doctors
C3	Hospital equipment and facilities	The level of modernity of equipment, up-to-date technologies, and technical facilities
C4	Medical information accessibility	The possibility of quick, accurate, and reliable access to medical records and information by tourists
C5	Medical services diversity	Types of medical services (preventive, surgical, rehabilitation, etc.)
C6	Infrastructures (information technology, transportation, and residential facilities)	Availability of fast internet, safe transportation, suitable accommodations for patients
C7	Health tourism companies interaction	Level of cooperation and information exchange between agencies, medical centers, and hotels

TABLE 17.7 Some of the criteria interactions.

	Criterion pair	Interaction type	Interaction description
1	C1 and C2	+	Skilled physicians improve the quality of care.
2	C1 and C3	+	Good equipment improves the quality of care.
3	C1 and C4	Δ	Quality of care is not necessarily dependent on access to information.
4	C1 and C5	−	Too much variation may reduce focus on quality.

$$D = \begin{matrix} c_1 \\ c_2 \\ c_3 \\ c_4 \\ c_5 \\ c_6 \\ c_7 \end{matrix} \begin{bmatrix} / & + & + & \Delta & - & \Delta & + \\ + & / & + & \Delta & \Delta & \Delta & - \\ + & + & / & + & \Delta & - & u' \\ \Delta & \Delta & + & / & + & + & + \\ - & \Delta & \Delta & + & / & u' & + \\ \Delta & \Delta & - & + & u' & / & \Delta \\ + & - & u' & + & + & \Delta & / \end{bmatrix}$$

Considering a set of criteria and their interactions, the final model was determined based on a linear model, which is described in the methodology section. This model reflects the logical structure of the relationships between variables, the solution of which shows the importance of the criteria. It should be noted that, based on the opinion of the DM, "Medical Services Quality" (C1) was determined as the best and "Health Tourism Companies Interaction" (C7) as the worst criterion. In the following, the form of the linear model is presented. Table 17.8 gives *BO* and *OW* pairwise comparisons vectors.

TABLE 17.8 Pairwise comparisons vectors.

	C1	C2	C3	C4	C5	C6	C7
BO	1	2	3	5	4	6	9
OW	9	8	7	6	7	5	1

$$
\begin{array}{ll}
\min & \xi \\
\text{subject to} & m(\theta) = 0; \Sigma_{c_j \in C}\, m_j + \Sigma_{c_i, c_j \in C}\, m_{ij} = 1; \\
& m_j + \Sigma_{c_i \in T}\, m_{ij} \geq 0,\ i, j = 1,2,\ldots,7 \text{ and } T \subseteq C\{c_j\},\ T \neq \theta; \\
& I_{ij} = m_{ij},\ i \neq j,\ i, j = 1,2,\ldots,7; \\
& I_j = m_j + \Sigma_{c_i \in C\{c_j\}} \frac{m_{ij}}{2},\ i \neq j,\ i, j = 1,2,\ldots,7; \\
& I_1 - 2I_2 \leq \xi; \quad I_1 - 2I_2 \geq -\xi; \\
& I_1 - 3I_3 \leq \xi; \quad I_1 - 3I_3 \geq -\xi; \\
& I_1 - 5I_4 \leq \xi; \quad I_1 - 5I_4 \geq -\xi; \\
& I_1 - 4I_5 \leq \xi; \quad I_1 - 4I_5 \geq -\xi; \\
& I_1 - 6I_6 \leq \xi; \quad I_1 - 6I_6 \geq -\xi; \\
& I_1 - 9I_7 \leq \xi; \quad I_1 - 9I_7 \geq -\xi; \\
& I_2 - 8I_7 \leq \xi; \quad I_2 - 8I_7 \geq -\xi; \\
& I_3 - 7I_7 \leq \xi; \quad I_3 - 7I_7 \geq -\xi; \\
& I_4 - 6I_7 \leq \xi; \quad I_4 - 6I_7 \geq -\xi; \\
& I_5 - 7I_7 \leq \xi; \quad I_5 - 7I_7 \geq -\xi; \\
& I_6 - 5I_7 \leq \xi; \quad I_6 - 5I_7 \geq -\xi; \\
& I_{12} > 0;\ I_{13} > 0;\ I_{14} = 0;\ I_{15} < 0;\ I_{16} = 0;\ I_{17} > 0; \\
& I_{23} > 0;\ I_{24} = 0;\ I_{25} = 0;\ I_{26} = 0;\ I_{27} < 0; \\
& I_{34} > 0;\ I_{35} = 0;\ I_{36} < 0;\ I_{37} \in [-1,1]; \\
& I_{45} > 0;\ I_{46} > 0;\ I_{47} > 0; \\
& I_{56} \in [-1,1];\ I_{57} > 0; \\
& I_{67} = 0.
\end{array} \tag{17.15}
$$

Solving Model 15 of nonadditive BWM, the optimal solution is obtained as follows: $\xi^* = 0.089$ and $I_1 = 0.344$, $I_2 = 0.217$, $I_3 = 0.144$, $I_4 = 0.086$, $I_5 = 0.108$, $I_6 = 0.072$, $I_7 = 0.028$, $I_{12} = 0.015$, $I_{13} = 0.025$, $I_{14} = 0$, $I_{15} = -0.015$, $I_{16} = 0$, $I_{17} = 0.015$, $I_{23} = 0.015$,
$I_{24} = 0$, $I_{25} = 0$, $I_{26} = 0$, $I_{27} = -0.01$, $I_{34} = 0.02$, $I_{35} = 0$, $I_{36} = -0.01$, $I_{37} = 0$, $I_{45} = 0.01$, $I_{46} = 0.015$, $I_{47} = 0.02$, $I_{56} = 0$, $I_{57} = 0.015$, $I_{67} = 0$, $m_1 = 0.324$, $m_2 = 0.207$, $m_3 = 0.119$ $m_4 = 0.054$, $m_5 = 0.103$, $m_6 = 0.069$, $m_7 = 0.008$.

According to (17.16), the CR value is obtained as follows:

$$CR = \frac{0.089}{5.23} = 0.017 \tag{17.16}$$

Since the obtained CR value is less than its associated threshold of 0.4445 (see Table 17.4), the pairwise comparisons have acceptable consistency.

TABLE 17.9 Evaluation of alternatives in each attribute.

	C1	C2	C3	C4	C5	C6	C7
A1	6	9	6	3	5	3	5
A2	3	5	3	5	9	5	5
A3	6	6	9	8	5	5	3
A4	5	6	6	6	6	6	8
A5	8	9	9	6	4	6	5
A6	6	6	6	5	3	8	5
A7	9	9	10	10	9	10	9
h_j	10	10	10	10	10	10	10
l_j	2	2	2	2	2	2	2

To assign numerical scores to each alternative in each of the criteria, a qualitative content analysis of the advantages and disadvantages of each country was first used. Then, based on the intensity of the strength or weakness in each criterion, a score of 1 to 10 was assigned to that alternative. For example, if a country has advanced medical equipment and a high level of access to medical information, it would receive high scores such as 9 or 10 in C3 (hospital equipment and facilities) and C4 (medical information accessibility). Conversely, if there is a specific weakness in the IT infrastructure or interaction between health tourism institutions, a low score, such as 3 or 4, would be assigned to the corresponding criteria (C6 and C7). In cases where the data was neutral or ambiguous (neither a direct strength nor a weakness), a middle score (4 to 6) has been assigned. In this way, by combining qualitative data and quantitative structure, a precise and numerically analyzable table has been created for decision-making in the field of comparing health tourism destination countries (see Table 17.9).

Based on the results of the linear model and considering the scores of each alternative, whose normalized values are presented in Table 17.10, the final ranking of the alternatives was derived. This ranking represents a comprehensive assessment of the performance of each alternative with respect to a set of weighted criteria, interactions between them, and the examination of each alternative in the criteria obtained. The ranking of alternatives is A7 > A5 > A3 > A1 > A4 > A6 > A2.

Based on the nonadditive BWM method, Country G (A7, 1.012225) secured the first rank. Despite challenges such as high costs and complex entry processes for health tourists, this country achieved the highest score due to its highly advanced infrastructure, seamless data and service integration, and exceptional service quality. Country E (A5, 0.753975) ranked second. Although it has limited appeal for nonmedical and cultural tourism, its compliance with medical standards and the presence of internationally accredited physicians bolstered its strong position. Country C (A3, 0.570988) took the third rank, benefiting from advanced medical equipment and easy access to information, though weak interaction between health tourism institutions remains its primary challenge.

Continuing the ranking, Country A (A1, 0.5323) placed fourth. Abundant therapeutic natural resources and specialized physicians are its strengths, but weak IT infrastructure and insufficient access to medical information pose limitations. Country D (A4, 0.50905) ranked fifth, recognized for strong advertising, effective branding, and high security, yet high medical service costs and expensive tariffs hinder its performance. Country F (A6, 0.506013) came in sixth, offering high-quality accommodations and efficient transportation, but limited diversity in medical services and constrained information technology infrastructure prevent better performance. Finally, Country B (A2, 0.326375) ranked last. Despite offering a wide variety of medical services and low costs, poor hospital service quality and limited equipment significantly impact its operational efficiency.

TABLE 17.10 Final ranking of the alternatives.

	$V(g_1(a_p))$	$V(g_2(a_p))$	$V(g_3(a_p))$	$V(g_4(a_p))$	$V(g_5(a_p))$	$V(g_6(a_p))$	$V(g_7(a_p))$	Choquet integral	Final ranking
A1	0.5	0.875	0.5	0.125	0.375	0.125	0.375	0.5323	4
A2	0.125	0.375	0.125	0.375	0.875	0.375	0.375	0.326375	7
A3	0.5	0.5	0.875	0.75	0.375	0.375	0.125	0.570988	3
A4	0.375	0.5	0.5	0.5	0.5	0.5	0.75	0.50905	5
A5	0.75	0.875	0.875	0.5	0.25	0.5	0.375	0.753975	2
A6	0.5	0.5	0.5	0.375	0.125	0.75	0.375	0.506013	6
A7	0.875	0.875	1	1	0.875	1	0.875	1.012225	1

17.5 Conclusion

The purpose of this chapter is to introduce the nonadditive BWM as a novel approach to solving MADM problems with dependent criteria. This method combines the advantages of the efficient structure of BWM and the capabilities of the Choquet integral in modeling the interactions of criteria through the 2-additive fuzzy measure, and eliminates the fundamental limitation of previous methods in the neglect of the criteria interactions. The key advantage of nonadditive BWM is the simultaneous calculation of the individual importance of the criteria and the interactions between the criteria.

The widespread applications of this method include areas in which criteria have an inherent entanglement, such as selecting complex technologies (hybrid vehicles with price and energy interaction), evaluation of suppliers (with the interaction of quality and cost), and allocation of strategic resources (agricultural water resources with economic-environmental dimensions). In this way, by presenting linear and nonlinear models, nonadditive BWM guarantees analytical precision in complex environments in real decisions.

In order to investigate the nonadditive BWM in practice, a case study was conducted to select the most optimal destination for "artificial intelligence-based health tourism." Seven key criteria, including "Medical Services Quality," "Physicians' Reputation," "Hospital equipment and facilities," "Medical Information Accessibility," "Medical Services Diversity," "Infrastructures (Information technology, transportation, and residential facilities)," and "Health Tourism Companies Interaction" were obtained from the review of previous literature.

After determining the weight of the criteria using nonadditive BWM, the available alternatives were evaluated, and Country G (A7) was selected as the best alternative. Enjoying a highly developed infrastructure, data integrity and services, and the high quality of medical services, this alternative achieved a better score than others. Although high costs and relatively complex entry processes are among the disadvantages, the strengths of Country G in key areas such as information technology infrastructure, quality of medical services, and integrated interactions between health tourism companies have caused these weaknesses to be less important. In contrast, Country F (A6) and Country B (A2) ranked sixth and seventh, respectively. Although Country F enjoys efficient transportation and quality residences, weaknesses in medical services diversity and the infrastructure limitation of information technology make it impossible for the key criteria to be achieved. On the other hand, Country B, despite low cost and variety of medical services, has gained the last rank due to low quality of medical services and severe limitations in medical equipment.

Finally, the results of this case study showed that the nonadditive BWM could clearly reveal the differences between the alternatives with close scores and, in the face of the interactions of the criteria, show exact performance. Nonadditive BWM was able to distinguish between strong and weak alternatives in terms of nonlinear interactions between criteria with high accuracy. This method, as an innovative and flexible method, has a high capacity for application in various fields such as health policy making, technological resources management, and strategic planning. Using this method can increase the accuracy of analysis and, by modeling real relations between criteria, provide better support for decision-making processes.

References

Aghaloo, K., Ali, T., Chiu, Y. R., & Sharifi, A. (2023). Optimal site selection for the solar-wind hybrid renewable energy systems in Bangladesh using an integrated GIS-based BWM-fuzzy logic method. *Energy Conversion and Management, 283*, 116899.

Ahemad, F., Gupta, P., Mehlawat, M. K., Deveci, M., & Jin, L. (2025). A multi-criteria decision-making approach using bipolar fuzzy numbers for optimizing two-sided matching in technology transfer decisions. *Applied Soft Computing,* 113633.

Angilella, S., Bottero, M., Corrente, S., Ferretti, V., Greco, S., & Lami, I. M. (2016). Nonadditive robust ordinal regression for urban and territorial planning: An application for siting an urban waste landfill. *Annals of Operations Research, 245*(1), 427–456.

Angilella, S., Greco, S., Lamantia, F., & Matarazzo, B. (2004). Assessing non-additive utility for multicriteria decision aid. *European Journal of Operational Research, 158*(3), 734–744.

Anzilli, L., & Giove, S. (2020). Multi-criteria and medical diagnosis for application to health insurance systems: A general approach through non-additive measures. *Decisions in Economics and Finance, 43*(2), 559–582.

Banihabib, M. E., Hashemi-Madani, F. S., & Forghani, A. (2017). Comparison of compensatory and non-compensatory multi criteria decision making models in water resources strategic management. *Water Resources Management, 31*(12), 3745–3759.

Chen, L., Yu, W., Zhang, B., Wang, W., Dai, G., Zhu, J., & Zhao, X. (2025). A BWM-TOPSIS based multi-criteria decision-making framework for design of cold patching asphalt binder. *Case Studies in Construction Materials,* e04806.

Chiou, H. K., Tzeng, G. H., & Cheng, D. C. (2005). Evaluating sustainable fishing development strategies using fuzzy MCDM approach. *Omega, 33*(3), 223–234.

Choquet, G. (1954). Theory of capacities. In *Annales de l'institut Fourier*131–295 Vol. 5.

Foroozesh, F., Monavari, S. M., Salmanmahiny, A., Robati, M., & Rahimi, R. (2022). Assessment of sustainable urban development based on a hybrid decision-making approach: Group fuzzy BWM, AHP, and TOPSIS–GIS. *Sustainable Cities and Society, 76*, 103402.

Gao, F., Han, M., Wang, S., & Gao, J. (2024). A novel Fermatean fuzzy BWM-VIKOR based multi-criteria decision-making approach for selecting health care waste treatment technology. *Engineering Applications of Artificial Intelligence, 127*, 107451.

Guan, X., Guo, K., & Tian, H. (2024). Efficient identification technique for 2-additive fuzzy measures with consideration of objective relationships among features. *International Journal of Machine Learning and Cybernetics, 15*(11), 5217–5237.

Haseli, G., Sheikh, R., Ghoushchi, S. J., Hajiaghaei-Keshteli, M., Moslem, S., Deveci, M., & Kadry, S. (2024). An extension of the best–worst method based on the spherical fuzzy sets for multi-criteria decision-making. *Granular Computing, 9*(2), 40.

Haseli, G., Sheikh, R., & Sana, S. S. (2020). Base-criterion on multi-criteria decision-making method and its applications. *International Journal of Management Science and Engineering Management, 15*(2), 79–88.

Haseli, G., Sheikh, R., Wang, J., Tomaskova, H., & Tirkolaee, E. B. (2021). A novel approach for group decision making based on the best–worst method (G-BWM): Application to supply chain management. *Mathematics, 9*(16), 1881.

Haseli, G., Torkayesh, A. E., Hajiaghaei-Keshteli, M., & Venghaus, S. (2023). Sustainable resilient recycling partner selection for urban waste management: Consolidating perspectives of decision-makers and experts. *Applied Soft Computing, 137*, 110120.

Haseli, G., Yazdani, M., Shaayesteh, M. T., & Hajiaghaei-Keshteli, M. (2025). Logistic hub location problem under fuzzy Extended Z-numbers to consider the uncertainty and reliable group decision-making. *Applied Soft Computing, 171*, 112751.

He, Q., Ren, X., Li, W., Dong, L., & Hu, X. (2024). Sustainability prioritization of CCUS systems with consideration of criteria interaction: A fuzzy multi-criteria decision-making framework based on 2-additive fuzzy measure and Choquet integral method. *Environment, Development and Sustainability*, 1–25.

Hsu, W. K., Huang, S. H., Le, T. N. N., Huynh, N. T., & Wang, D. J. (2025). Assessing container terminals' efficiency from the sustainable development perspective: The BWM-GRA-SBM model. *Transport Policy, 162*, 443–455.

Jiang, P., Wang, W., Hu, Y. C., Chiu, Y. J., & Tsao, S. J. (2021). Pattern classification using tolerance rough sets based on non-additive grey relational analysis and DEMATEL. *Grey Systems: Theory and Application, 11*(1), 166–182.

Ju, Y., Zhao, Q., Luis, M., Liang, Y., Dong, J., Dong, P., & Giannakis, M. (2024). A novel framework for FMEA using evidential BWM and SMAA-MARCOS method. *Expert Systems with Applications, 243*, 122796.

Khargotra, R., Alam, T., Thu, K., András, K., & Singh, T. (2024). Optimization of design parameter of V-shaped perforated blocks in rectangular duct of solar air heater by using hybrid BWM-CODAS technique. *Solar Energy Materials and Solar Cells, 264*, 112627.

Liang, F., Brunelli, M., & Rezaei, J. (2020). Consistency issues in the best worst method: Measurements and thresholds. *Omega, 96*, 102175.

Liang, Y., Ju, Y., Tu, Y., & Rezaei, J. (2023). Nonadditive best-worst method: Incorporating criteria interaction using the Choquet integral. *Journal of the Operational Research Society, 74*(6), 1495–1506. https://doi.org/10.1080/01605682.2022.2096504.

Luo, S., & Li, Q. (2025). Influencing factor analysis and marketing performance evaluation of tourist attractions on China TikTok: A PFN-BWM approach. *Journal of Travel & Tourism Marketing, 42*(2), 248–266.

Rezaei, J. (2015). Best-worst multi-criteria decision-making method. *Omega, 53*, 49–57.

Roshanravan, B., Kreuzer, O. P., & Buckingham, A. (2025). BWM-MARCOS: A new hybrid MCDM approach for mineral potential modelling. *Journal of Geochemical Exploration, 269*, 107639.

Saaty, T. L. (1977). A scaling method for priorities in hierarchical structures. *Journal of Mathematical Psychology, 15*(3), 234–281. https://doi.org/10.1016/0022-2496(77)90033-5.

Saaty, T. L. (1996). *Decisions with the analytic network process (ANP)*. University of Pittsburgh (USA), ISAHP, 96.

Shapley, L. S. (1953). A value for n-person games. In H. W. Kuhn, & A. W. Tucker (Eds.). *Contributions to the theory of Games II* (pp. 307–317). Princeton University Press.

Tahura, S. S., Shabur, M. A., & Nuva, T. J. (2025). BWM analysis of online and offline learning effectiveness in Bangladesh. *Scientific Reports, 15*(1), 8377.

Vaezi, A., Rabbani, E., & Yazdian, S. A. (2024). Blockchain-integrated sustainable supplier selection and order allocation: A hybrid BWM-MULTIMOORA and bi-objective programming approach. *Journal of Cleaner Production, 444*, 141216.

Yang, J. L., Chiu, H. N., Tzeng, G. H., & Yeh, R. H. (2008). Vendor selection by integrated fuzzy MCDM techniques with independent and interdependent relationships. *Information Sciences, 178*(21), 4166–4183.

Zhang, X., Goh, M., Bai, S., & Wang, Q. (2024). Green, resilient, and inclusive supplier selection using enhanced BWM-TOPSIS with scenario-varying Z-numbers and reversed PageRank. *Information Sciences, 674*, 120728.

Zhang, Y., Kong, M., Wang, W. Z., Deveci, M., Bilican, M. S., & Delen, D. (2026). A multi-criteria decision-making framework for metaverse adoption: Evidence from higher education systems. *Expert Systems with Applications, 296*, 129132.

Chapter 18

BWT: Best-worst tradeoff for multi-attribute decision-making

Gholamreza Haseli[1], Javad Nazarian-Jashnabadi[2], Mostafa Hajiaghaei-Keshteli[1], Muhammet Deveci[3], and Hana Tomaskova[4]

[1]*School of Engineering and Sciences, Tecnologico de Monterrey, Monterrey, Mexico,* [2]*Department of Management, Faculty of Economic, Management and Social Science, Shiraz University, Shiraz, Iran,* [3]*Department of Industrial Engineering, Turkish Naval Academy, National Defence University, Istanbul, Türkiye,* [4]*Faculty of Informatics and Management, University of Hradec Kralove, Hradec Králové, Czech Republic*

18.1 Introduction

Decision-making in complex and multidimensional fields has become more important than ever. In managerial, economic, technological, and social issues, multicriteria decision-making (MCDM) and one of its subcategories, called multi-attribute decision-making, have emerged as key tools for weighting criteria and evaluating alternatives based on these different criteria (Oubrahim, 2025). Since methodology represents a set of implementation tools and a conceptual framework for designing and guiding the entire process of understanding and decision-making, failing to select an appropriate methodology can lead to semantic ambiguity in the data and undermine the scientific validity of conclusions (Zhang et al., 2026). Therefore, choosing a methodology that is appropriate to the characteristics of the problem at hand is of great importance.

Considering the significant advantages of best—worst method (BWM) (Rezaei, 2015) and tradeoff (Raiffa & Keeney, 1975) methods, Liang et al. (2022) attempted to design a new and efficient framework called best–worst tradeoff (BWT) by combining the strengths of these two approaches. In this new approach, on the one hand, the advantages of the BWM method, such as reducing the number of pairwise comparisons compared to traditional methods such as analytic hierarchy process (AHP) (Haseli et al., 2020; Saaty, 1977), the ability to examine the consistency of decision-maker's (DM) preferences through the consistency index (Tahura et al., 2025), simplicity and ease of implementation through the use of two reference points (best and worst) (Roshanravan et al., 2025), the possibility of mathematical modeling and optimization solutions (Otay et al., 2024), and high stability against input data fluctuations, have been taken into account.

On the other hand, BWT also includes the key advantages of the tradeoff method, including careful attention to the range of changes of attributes in the weighting process, foundation based on multi-attribute value theory (MAVT), appropriate application in scenarios with minor differences between alternatives, and also increased cognitive accuracy through a more explicit assessment of the preferences of the DM (Liang et al., 2022). Recent developments in the methodological space have also made it necessary to pay attention to the integration of methods. With the expansion of decision-making problems with features such as uncertainty, conflict of interests, or interdependence of attributes, the need for methods that have both a rigorous structure and cognitive flexibility has increased.

Accordingly, the main objective of Liang et al. (2022) in developing the BWT method was to provide a comprehensive framework that could systematically account for the impact of attribute ranges in weighting, while also leveraging the coherent and reduced pairwise comparison mechanism of BWM. As a result, this method seeks to minimize cognitive distortions and biases arising from fixed reference points, while maintaining the internal consistency of the DM's preferences. In this chapter, an attempt will be made to present the theoretical foundations of the BWT method, introduce its step-by-step structure, and provide a practical example to apply this method in real scenarios.

The rest of this chapter is structured as follows: in Section 18.2, a review of the literature and previous studies is provided. In this section, previous studies are reviewed based on two approaches. The first approach analyzes studies

Encyclopedia of Multi-Attribute Decision-Making (MADM). DOI: https://doi.org/10.1016/B978-0-443-33275-3.00043-9

related to the BWM method, and in the second approach, the literature related to the tradeoff method is reviewed. Section 18.3 is dedicated to the description of the research method. The steps of BWT are given in this section. In Section 18.4, consistency measurement is discussed, and two types of consistency, ordinal and cardinal, are defined. A numerical example is provided in Section 18.5 to examine the efficiency of the model, and finally, Section 18.6 is dedicated to the conclusion.

18.2 Literature review

The BWM introduced by Rezaei (2015) has been widely accepted in applied studies. It has been used in various fields in recent years, such as supply chain (Haseli et al., 2021) and sustainable supplier selection (Gupta & Barua, 2017), waste management (Haseli et al., 2023), logistics and transportation (Li & Fei, 2025; Rezaei et al., 2018), renewable energy, emerging technologies, assessing projects (Alsharkawy et al., 2025), and performance evaluation (Kumar et al., 2020).

In a study by Li, and Zhong, & Fei (2025), the BWM was combined with the criteria importance through an intercriteria correlation model, which was used to select fire trucks with a lift and was able to improve their performance in critical conditions. Also, Raed et al. (2025) used the BWM with the technique for order preference by similarity to the ideal solution model to select the optimal dispatch method in offshore projects, which led to better risk management and improved project performance. Amiri et al. (2021) applied the fuzzy BWM model to evaluate suppliers in the supply chain and were able to introduce the most sustainable supplier by increasing the analytical accuracy. The study by Rezaei et al. (2018) showed that using BWM in evaluating service quality in the air transportation system can accurately identify the most important service dimensions, such as reliability.

Badi et al. (2023) used BWM integrated with AHP and measurement alternatives and ranking according to a compromise solution to select a wind farm location in Libya, and "safety and quality" was identified as the most important attribute. In the study of Mendes et al. (2022), it was used to identify factors affecting sustainable entrepreneurship in small and medium-sized enterprises. Dehshiri et al. (2022) improved versions of the group BWM to evaluate the attributes for implementing blockchain technology in the automotive industry supply chain, and its high accuracy was confirmed. In healthcare, Torkayesh et al. (2021) used the combined model of BWM and a constrained combined compromise solution to evaluate the performance of health systems in Europe, which led to improved performance analysis in Eastern European countries. Table 18.1 presents a summary of the related studies.

A review of the research background shows that various MCDM methods, such as AHP, analytic network process (Saaty, 1996), and especially the BWM, have been used to weight criteria, but there are still gaps in combining analytical accuracy with computational efficiency and realism in evaluating attributes. Accordingly, the present study, using the new BWT method, has attempted to provide an answer to these challenges by combining the advantages of BWM and tradeoff methods and introducing a more efficient approach for decision-making in dynamic, complex, and close-to-reality conditions.

The tradeoff approach in MCDM seeks to create a balance between competing criteria. This approach has been considered in various studies. Some studies have integrated it with other methods, such as integrating the BWM with the tradeoff method (Liang et al., 2022). Also, its combination with holistic and decomposition paradigms has improved flexibility in preference modeling (de Almeida et al., 2021). Using this approach in determining upper and lower expectation levels to prevent poor choices (Kheybari, 2021), supporting mapping in geographic information systems and assisting in spatial decision-making (Jankowski et al., 2019), and also its fuzzy matching using triangular fuzzy numbers (Jaini & Utyuzhnikov, 2017a) are other applications of this approach in studies. Furthermore, interactive versions for extracting criteria weights have simplified comparisons and reduced the burden on DMs (de Almeida et al., 2016).

Previous studies have provided the basis for these developments. Some have examined the effects of loss aversion and scale compatibility on the tradeoff process (Bleichrodt & Pinto, 2002), while others have identified common mistakes in making value tradeoffs and suggested strategies to avoid them (Keeney, 2002). Some research on behavioral factors influencing criterion weight judgments (Weber & Borcherding, 1993) and comparisons of different weighting methods (Borcherding et al., 1991) have emphasized the need to improve the internal consistency of this approach. Fundamental decision-making frameworks for managing conflicting objectives have also formed the theoretical basis of this field (Raiffa & Keeney, 1975). Table 18.2 shows a summary of studies related to the tradeoff method.

18.3 Methodology

In this section, the BWT method is introduced and explained. The process of weighting criteria in this method is completed by implementing six steps, which are described below (Liang et al., 2022).

TABLE 18.1 Summary of related studies on best--worst method (BWM).

	Author(s) and year	Research objective	Methodology	Research area/case study
1	Li, and Zhong, & Fei (2025)	Selection of fire trucks with a lift for urban emergency preparedness	CRITIC – BWM	Urban emergency preparedness
2	Raed et al. (2025)	Determining the optimal dispatch method for offshore projects	BWM – TOPSIS	Offshore platform construction
3	Gupta and Barua (2017)	Selection of suppliers among SMEs based on green innovation capability	BWM – fuzzy TOPSIS	Green supplier selection
4	Rezaei et al. (2018)	Evaluation of the quality of the air cargo transportation system with a focus on passenger satisfaction	BWM	Service quality assessment, airport baggage handling systems
5	Amiri et al. (2021)	Evaluation and selection of sustainable suppliers in the supply chain	fuzzy BWM	Sustainable supplier selection, automotive industry (Iran Khodro Company)
6	Mendes et al. (2022)	Identification of factors affecting sustainable entrepreneurship in SMEs	BWM – cognitive mapping	Sustainable entrepreneurship assessment
7	Dehshiri et al. (2022)	Evaluation of criteria for implementing blockchain technology in the automotive industry supply chain	Group BWM	Automotive industry
8	Badi et al. (2023)	Selection of wind farm sites in Libya	BWM – AHP – MARCOS	Wind farm site selection, Libya
9	Kumar et al. (2020)	Evaluation of the green performance of airports	BWM – VIKOR[a]	Evaluation of green performance criteria for airports
10	Huang et al. (2022)	Evaluation and selection of design options considering multiple uncertainties in experts' perceptions	BWM – MABAC[a]	Product development
11	Torkayesh et al. (2021)	Evaluation of the performance of healthcare sectors in Europe with a focus on sustainable development	BWM – CoCoSo	Performance evaluation
12	Corrente et al. (2024)	Reducing the cognitive load of decision-makers in problems with a large number of options	Parsimonious BWM	MCDM model development
13	Ghoushchi et al. (2019)	Prioritization of failure modes considering uncertainty and reliability	Fuzzy BWM – Z-MOORA[a]	Risk management – failure analysis in the automotive spare parts industry
14	Bahrami et al. (2019)	Mapping the potential of copper deposits through integrating multisource geological data	BWM – ARAS[a]	Mineral prospectivity mapping
15	Haseli et al. (2024)	Develop an extension of BWM using spherical fuzzy sets (SFS) to handle uncertainty in MCDM problems	BWM – SFS	MCDM model development
16	Haseli et al. (2025)	To model a logistics hub location selection problem using a group decision-making model under uncertainty	Extended Z-numbers – BWM – MABAC	Logistic hub location selection

[a] *VIKOR: Vlse Kriterijumsk Optimizacija Kompromisno Resenje; MABAC: multiattributive border approximation area comparison; MOORA: multiobjective optimization by ratio analysis; ARAS: additive ratio assessment.*

TABLE 18.2 Summary of related studies on the tradeoff method.

	Author(s) and year	Research objective	Methodology	Research area/case study
1	Liang et al. (2022)	Develop a new MADM method to improve consistency and account for attribute ranges.	BWM and tradeoff	General MADM applications
2	Kheybari (2021)	Propose a framework for controlling tradeoffs	Expectation Levels approach in MCDM	General MCDM applications
3	de Almeida et al. (2021)	Enhance the FITradeoff method by combining holistic and decomposition paradigms	FITradeoff method	General MCDM applications
4	Jankowski et al. (2019)	Apply a multiple-criteria tradeoff approach to spatial alternative screening	MCDM + GIS	Spatial decision-making
5	Jaini and Utyuzhnikov (2017a)	Present fuzzy tradeoff ranking method	Fuzzy tradeoff, fuzzy TOPSIS, fuzzy VIKOR	Fuzzy MCDM problems
6	Jaini and Utyuzhnikov (2017b)	Develop a tradeoff ranking method to automatically rank Pareto solutions	Tradeoff ranking method in MCDM; directed search domain algorithm	Pareto frontier analysis
7	de Almeida et al. (2016)	Propose the FITradeoff method to reduce decision-maker effort in eliciting criteria weights.	FITradeoff method	Supplier selection
8	Bleichrodt and Pinto (2002)	Examine loss aversion and scale compatibility in tradeoffs	Experimental study; utility measurement	Medical decision-making
9	Keeney (2002)	Identify common mistakes in making value tradeoffs	Prescriptive analysis	General MCDM applications
10	Weber and Borcherding (1993)	Review behavioral influences on weight judgments in multi-attribute decision-making.	Literature review	General MADM applications
11	Borcherding et al. (1991)	Compare four weighting methods for multi-attribute utility measurement	Ratio method, Swing weighting, tradeoff method, pricing out method	Nuclear waste repository site evaluation
12	Raiffa and Keeney (1975)	Present theory and procedures for decision analysis with multiple conflicting objectives.	MAVT; tradeoff methods	Various applied contexts

Step 1. Determine alternatives and attributes

The first step in the BWT implementation process is to determine the alternatives and attributes for decision-making. In this step, a set of alternatives to be analyzed and compared is first identified. In parallel, the attributes are also determined, which can include cost or benefit factors and, depending on the nature of the problem, can be quantitative or qualitative. Also, in this step, initial data related to the performance of each alternative concerning the determined attributes is collected.

Step 2. Determine the value function for each attribute

It is necessary to define a value function (vj) for each attribute that reflects the way that DM values the different levels of that attribute. In other words, these functions show how much the DM attaches importance to changes in the attribute values. Here, in order to simplify the valuation process, a technique called "Mid-Value Splitting" was used, which was first introduced by Raiffa and Keeney (1975).

- First, we consider the value of the lowest attribute level (x_0) as 0 and the value of the highest attribute level (x_1) as 1.
- We calculate the midpoint of the interval $[x_0, x_1]$ and call it $x_{0.5}$. We consider the value of this point as 0.5.
- Then we obtain the midpoint of the interval $[x_0, x_{0.5}]$ and call it $x_{0.25}$ and determine its value as 0.25.
- Next, we calculate the midpoint of the interval $[x_{0.5}, x_1]$ and call it $x_{0.75}$. For this point, the value of 0.75 is considered.
- To ensure the consistency of the DM's preferences, it should be checked whether $x_{0.5}$ is actually in the middle of $x_{0.25}$ and $x_{0.75}$; if not, the values should be modified.
- Finally, using the five determined points, namely $(x_0,0)$, $(x_{0.25}, 0.25)$, $(x_{0.5}, 0.5)$, $(x_{0.75}, 0.75)$, and $(x_1,1)$, the value function corresponding to that attribute can be estimated. This value function is an important basis for subsequent analyses in the decision-making process.

Step 3. Identify the best and worst attributes

The DM, based on their specialized knowledge and personal perspective, selects one attribute as the "best" (C_B) and another one as the "worst" (C_W) from the set of available attributes. This selection is made based on the importance, impact, or desirability of the attribute in the decision-making problem. In other words, the DM identifies the attribute that has the most impact or desirability as the best, and the attribute that has the least importance or desirability as the worst. The tradeoff method is employed for this purpose. In this way, n hypothetical consequences $x^j (j = 1,2, \ldots,n)$ are constructed. Each represents the best performance level for the jth attribute, with all other attributes at their worst level. The DM compares and ranks these hypothetical consequences $x^1, \ldots, x^j, \ldots, x^n$ to identify which attribute is the best (C_B) and which is the worst (C_W).

Step 4. Compare best to others tradeoff

In this step, the goal is to determine the preference for the best attribute (C_B) compared to other attributes. For a given comparison between C_B and another attribute C_k ($k \neq B$), two auxiliary hypothetical consequences are constructed:

- In the first consequence ($x^{B,k}$), the value of the best attribute (C_B) is yet to be specified, and the other attributes are set to their lowest performance level ($v_j(\underline{x}_j) = 0$).
- In the second consequence (x^k), the kth attribute (C_k) is at the highest level ($v_k(\overline{x}_k) = 1$), and the other attributes remain at the lowest level ($v_j(\underline{x}_j) = 0$).

The DM is then requested to indicate the performance score of C_B in $x^{B,k}$ such that the consequences $x^{B,k}$ and x^k are equivalent or indifferent. In other words, the DM must determine what the performance level of the best attribute should be so that these two consequences are the same ($x^{B,k} \sim x^k$ where $\sim$ indicates indifference between the two consequences). Using the additive value function, this level corresponds to the ratio between the weights w_k and w_B. These comparisons are repeated for all attributes and are represented by a_{bk}. In this way, a "Best-to-Others" vector (A^{BO}) is created, which reflects the degree of preference of the best attribute over the other attributes and provides a basis for calculating the final weight of the attributes. Therefore, the A^{BO} vector is defined as follows:

$$A^{BO} = (a_{b1}, a_{b2}, \ldots, a_{bn}) \tag{18.1}$$

Each element a_{bk} in A^{BO} can be interpreted either as the multiplier required to convert w_k into w_B, or as the ratio w_B/w_W.

Step 5. Compare others to the worst tradeoff

The inverse comparison is made to the previous step, and the DM is asked to determine the degree of preference of the other attributes over the worst attribute. In other words, after determining the worst attribute (C_W), each of the remaining attributes is compared to it individually. For this purpose, first, for each attribute C_k ($k \neq W$), two auxiliary hypothetical consequences are designed.

- The first consequence ($x^{k,W}$), where the level of C_k is left to be determined, and the other attributes are set to their lowest level ($v_j(\underline{x}_j) = 0$).
- The second consequence (x^W) where the worst attribute (C_W) is at the highest level ($v_W(\overline{x}_W) = 1$), and the other attributes are set to their lowest level ($v_j(\underline{x}_j) = 0$).

As in the previous step, the DM must determine the level of C_k in $x^{k,W}$, such that the consequences $x^{k,W}$, and x^W are equivalent or indifferent. Based on the additive value model, this level represents the ratio between the weights w_W and w_k. Finally, the "Others-to-Worst" vector (A^{OW}) is defined as follows:

$$A^{OW} = (a_{1W},\ a_{2W},\ \ldots,\ a_{nW}) \tag{18.2}$$

Each element a_{kW} can be interpreted as the factor needed to express w_k in terms of w_W, or as the ratio w_k/w_W.

Step 6. Obtain the optimal weights

After completing the pairwise comparisons and constructing the A^{BO} and A^{OW} vectors, the weights of the attributes are derived from the system of equations below.

$$\begin{cases} W_k a_{Bk} = W_B, & \forall\ k \neq B \\ W_k = a_{kW} W_W, & \forall\ k \neq W \\ W_1 + W_2 + \ldots + W_n = 1 \end{cases} \tag{18.3}$$

In general, this system of equations may be inconsistent due to the subjective judgments of the DM, so it is essential to apply appropriate methods to obtain reliable estimates of the weights. In line with the BWM formulation (Rezaei, 2015), an optimization model is proposed to find the weight vector that minimizes the maximum absolute deviation from the set of equations using (18.4).

$$\begin{aligned} &\min\ \max_j \{|W_j a_{Bj} - W_B|,\ |W_W a_{jW} - W_j|\} \\ &\textit{subject to}\quad W_1 + W_2 + \ldots + W_n = 1 \\ &W_j \geq 0, \quad j = 1, 2, \ldots, n \end{aligned} \tag{18.4}$$

The Model 4 can be rewritten as the Model 5:

$$\begin{aligned} &\min\ \xi \\ &\textit{subject to}\quad \left|W_j a_{Bj} - W_B\right| \leq \xi, \quad \forall\ \mathrm{j} \neq \mathrm{B} \\ &\left|W_W a_{jW} - W_j\right| \leq \xi, \quad \forall\ \mathrm{j} \neq \mathrm{W} \\ &W_1 + W_2 + \ldots + W_n = 1 \\ &W_j \geq 0, \quad j = 1, 2, \ldots, n \end{aligned} \tag{18.5}$$

18.4 Consistency measurement

In the decision-making process, one of the most important issues is that the DM's judgments are consistent. If the judgments are inconsistent, the weights obtained for the attributes may not be reliable. In the framework of the BWT method, assessing the consistency of the DM's preferences is of particular importance, since inconsistency can reduce the validity of the results obtained from the weighting of the attributes. In this regard, two distinct types of consistency are defined (Liang et al., 2022).

18.4.1 Ordinal consistency

This consistency refers to the consistency of the relative order of comparisons in the two vectors (A^{BO} and A^{OW}). If the relative priorities between the attributes are preserved in both vectors, the DM's preferences are considered to be ordinal consistent. A set of pairwise comparisons is said to be ordinally consistent if, for any three attributes i, j, and k, the preference direction is logically preserved. Specifically, if attribute i is preferred to attribute j, and attribute j is preferred to attribute k, then attribute i must also be preferred to attribute k. This condition is shown in (18.6) (Kendall, 1938):

$$(a_{Bk} - a_{Bj}) \times (a_{jW} - a_{kW}) > 0 \text{ or } (a_{Bk} = a_{Bj} \text{ and } a_{jW} = a_{kW}), \ \forall \text{ k and j} \tag{18.6}$$

To quantify this consistency, an index called the ordinal consistency ratio (OR) is defined, which is calculated using (18.7):

$$OR = \max_j OR_j \tag{18.7}$$

Where

$$OR_j = \frac{1}{n-1} \sum_{k=1}^{n} F((a_{Bk} - a_{Bj}) \times (a_{jW} - a_{kW})) \tag{18.8}$$

And

a_{Bk} is the preference value of the attribute C_B over the attribute C_k (in the A^{BO} vector)
a_{Bj} is the preference value of the attribute C_B over the attribute C_j
a_{jW} is the preference value of the attribute C_j over the attribute C_W (in the A^{OW} vector)
a_{kW} is the preference value of the attribute C_k over the attribute C_W
n is the number of attributes
$F(\gamma, \delta)$ is a discrete function defined to identify ordinal inconsistencies as defined in Eq. 18.9:

$$F(\gamma, \delta) = \begin{cases} 1, & \text{if } \gamma \times \delta < 0, \\ 0.5, & \text{if } \gamma \times \delta = 0 \text{ and } (\gamma \neq 0 \text{ or } \delta \neq 0) \\ 0 & \text{otherwise.} \end{cases} \tag{18.9}$$

The local ordinal consistency ratio, denoted as OR_j , represents the extent of consistency in relation to the jth attribute. OR is called the global ordinal consistency ratio and reflects the ordinal consistency of the pairwise comparison system provided by the DM. The OR value ranges between 0 and 1. $OR = 0$ indicates complete ordinal consistency between the two vectors, and $OR = 1$ indicates the highest level of preference inconsistency. This index can be used as a tool to review the DM's preferences. If the OR value is high, it is suggested that the DM re-examine the judgments to improve ordinal consistency.

18.4.2 Cardinal consistency

This type of consistency is related to the agreement of the numerical values obtained from pairwise comparisons with the final weights of the attributes. If the numerical ratios obtained from the judgments are consistent with the calculated weights, then numerical consistency can be ensured. Ideally, the DM's numerical judgments should be such that Eq. 18.10 holds for each attribute.

$$a_{Bj} a_{jW} = a_{BW}, \ \forall j. \tag{18.10}$$

To assess the deviation from complete cardinal consistency, the cardinal consistency ratio (CR) is formulated in (18.11).

$$CR = \max_j CR_j \tag{18.11}$$

$$CR_j = \begin{cases} \dfrac{|a_{Bj} a_{jW} - a_{BW}|}{a_{BW} a_{BW} - a_{BW}}, & a_{BW} > 1, \\ 0, & a_{BW} = 1 \end{cases} \tag{18.12}$$

CR_j denotes the local consistency level corresponding to attribute Cj, which allows us to identify the attribute with the highest inconsistency. Meanwhile, CR refers to the global consistency ratio across all attributes, reflecting the overall consistency of the preferences. The CR value also varies between 0 and 1. If the DM's preferences are completely consistent, the value of this index will be 0. The closer it is to 1, the greater the inconsistency in preferences.

18.4.3 Consistency thresholds

To assess whether the degree of consistency in the DM's preferences is acceptable, it is necessary to compare it with certain threshold values. These thresholds are defined to determine the tolerable level of inconsistency in subjective preferences. A large set of hypothetical preferences and the obtained threshold values in different combinations of the number of attributes (n) and the best-to-worst attribute preference value (a_{BW}) is generated. The results of these analyses are presented in Table 18.3.

If the index value is less than the threshold ($CR < CR_{threshold}$), the judgments are acceptable, and if the index value is greater than the threshold ($CR > CR_{threshold}$), the judgments need to be revised.

18.5 Numerical example: optimal selection of business intelligence system using the best–worst tradeoff method

Given the increasing spread of business intelligence (BI) systems and their key role in data-driven decision-making, organizations face several challenges in selecting the right system. These systems have various features and capabilities such as analytical power, data security, ease of use, scalability, cost, and quality of support, which are of different importance to organizations. The main issue is to rank existing BI systems based on a set of quantitative and qualitative attributes to determine which system is most suitable for organizational needs.

Step 1. In the first step, different BI systems are determined by the DM and form the set of alternatives, which are listed in Table 18.4.

Next, seven attributes, including "Integration Capability," "User Interface," "Analytical and Predictive Power," "Security," "Scalability," "System Downtime Frequency," and "Implementation and Maintenance Cost," have been considered as evaluation attributes. Table 18.5 presents the list of attributes along with their type and definition.

Step 2. According to the second step in the BWT method, it is necessary to define a value function for each attribute. To do this, we use the mid-value splitting method. Table 18.6 reports the mid-value points for each attribute.

Step 3. According to the procedure described in step 3, the DM identified "Analytical and Predictive Power" (C3) and "System Downtime Frequency" (C6) as the best and worst attributes, respectively.

TABLE 18.3 The thresholds of the consistency ratios in different combinations (Liang et al., 2022).

a_{BW}	n					
	4	5	6	7	8	9
2	0.34	0.35	0.36	0.38	0.39	0.39
3	0.31	0.33	0.35	0.37	0.38	0.39
4	0.32	0.34	0.36	0.37	0.39	0.4
5	0.31	0.35	0.37	0.38	0.4	0.4
6	0.32	0.35	0.37	0.38	0.4	0.41
7	0.33	0.35	0.37	0.39	0.4	0.41
8	0.32	0.35	0.37	0.39	0.4	0.41
9	0.33	0.36	0.37	0.39	0.4	0.41

TABLE 18.4 Different types of business intelligence systems.

Description	Alternatives	No.
Focusing on advanced analytics and providing diverse predictive models. With high security and a relatively simple user interface, suitable for medium and large organizations.	System A	1
Suitable for businesses that need high scalability and advanced security. The main focus of this system is on ease of use and large data management.	System B	2
A system with strong integration capabilities with existing systems. Although the maintenance cost is relatively low, its user interface is more complex than other options.	System C	3
Has the highest score in ease of use and user interface. Suitable for organizations that attach great importance to user training and user experience.	System D	4
Focus on scalability and fast support services. A suitable option for organizations with rapid growth and the need to develop human resources and technology.	System E	5
It is the most economical option in terms of implementation cost. It is suitable for small to medium businesses with limited budgets. It has acceptable analytical power.	System F	6
A balanced combination of features with a focus on strong support services and appropriate security. It is a desirable option for organizations that value performance stability and after-sales service.	System G	7

TABLE 18.5 List of evaluation attributes.

Description	Attribute type	Attributes	Code
The system's ability to connect and coordinate with other organizational systems, such as enterprise resource planning (ERP), customer relationship management (CRM), and various databases. This feature plays an important role in data productivity and reducing rework.	Benefit	Integration capability	C1
User experience, simple menus, appropriate graphics, and the ability to learn quickly by users. A user-friendly system increases acceptance and reduces training costs.	Benefit	User interface	C2
The power of the system to process data, run data mining models, analyze trends, and provide decision-based predictions. This attribute is considered one of the most important competitive advantages of BI.	Benefit	Analytical and predictive power	C3
Includes access control capabilities, encryption, support for multifactor authentication, and dealing with cyber threats. High security helps organizations protect sensitive data.	Benefit	Security	C4
The system's ability to respond to an increase in users, data, and processes without reducing performance. This feature is very critical for organizations with rapid growth or high data volumes.	Benefit	Scalability	C5
The number of times a system becomes unavailable or inactive in a given period. An increase in this metric indicates a decrease in system stability and reliability.	Cost	System downtime frequency	C6
Includes the costs of purchasing, installing, training, supporting, and updating the system throughout the year. A vital metric for organizations with budget constraints.	Cost	Implementation and maintenance cost	C7

TABLE 18.6 The mid-value points for each attribute.

Value assignment	Max (100%)	75%	50%	25%	Min (0%)	Attribute	Code
Range of 50 to 95; linear division of the range into four equal parts for normalization	95.00	83.75	72.50	61.25	50.00	Integration capability	C1
Range of 40 to 90 based on software quality; linear and equal division of the range for better analysis	90.00	77.50	65.00	52.50	40.00	User interface	C2
Range of 65 to 98; linear division to show analytical and predictive power levels	98.00	89.75	81.50	73.25	65.00	Analytical and predictive power	C3
Range of 60 to 100; 25–50–75 percentile points defined linearly between minimum and maximum	100.00	90.00	80.00	70.00	60.00	Security	C4
Range of 45 to 95; linear scaling of values for normalizing the system scalability	95.00	82.50	70.00	57.50	45.00	Scalability	C5
Range of 2 to 12 times per month; linear percentile points used for system downtime frequency	2.00	4.50	7.00	9.50	12.00	System downtime Frequency	C6
Range of 3 to 10 million; linear scaling for normalizing the implementation and maintenance cost	3.00	4.75	6.50	8.25	10.00	Implementation and maintenance cost	C7

Step 4. To determine the tradeoff between the best attribute C3 to the other attributes, consequence ($x^{B,k}$) and x^k were generated as follows:

$$x^{3,1} \sim x^1 \leftrightarrow (50,\ 40,\ x^{3,1},\ 60,\ 45,\ 12,\ 10) \sim (95,\ 40,\ 65,\ 60,\ 45,\ 12,\ 10)$$

$$x^{3,2} \sim x^2 \leftrightarrow (50,\ 40,\ x^{3,2},\ 60,\ 45,\ 12,\ 10) \sim (50,\ 90,\ 65,\ 60,\ 45,\ 12,\ 10)$$

$$x^{3,4} \sim x^4 \leftrightarrow (50,\ 40,\ x^{3,4},\ 60,\ 45,\ 12,\ 10) \sim (50,\ 40,\ 65,\ 100,\ 45,\ 12,\ 10)$$

$$x^{3,5} \sim x^5 \leftrightarrow (50,\ 40,\ x^{3,5},\ 60,\ 45,\ 12,\ 10) \sim (50,\ 40,\ 65,\ 60,\ 95,\ 12,\ 10)$$

$$x^{3,6} \sim x^6 \leftrightarrow (50,\ 40,\ x^{3,6},\ 60,\ 45,\ 12,\ 10) \sim (50,\ 40,\ 65,\ 60,\ 45,\ 2,\ 10)$$

$$x^{3,7} \sim x^7 \leftrightarrow (50,\ 40,\ x^{3,7},\ 60,\ 45,\ 12,\ 10) \sim (50,\ 40,\ 65,\ 60,\ 45,\ 12,\ 3)$$

The DM was then asked to assign values to these comparisons based on the scale of the best attribute. These values were provided in such a way that the given pairwise consequences were considered equivalent or indifferent. After evaluation, the DM proposed the following values.

$$(x^{3,1},\ x^{3,2},\ x^{3,3},\ x^{3,4},\ x^{3,5},\ x^{3,6},\ x^{3,1}) = (81,\ 75,\ 98,\ 85,\ 72,\ 69,\ 70)$$

These values were normalized based on the value function of C3, resulting in vector A^{BO}. Fig. 18.1 shows the value function of C3.

$$A^{Bo} = (0.4848,\ 0.3030,\ 1,\ 0.6061,\ 0.2121,\ 0.1212,\ 0.1515)$$

Step 5. After determining C6 as the worst attribute, consequence ($x^{k,W}$) and x^W were structured, and the following indifference relations can be satisfied:

$$x^{1,6} \sim x^6 \leftrightarrow (x_1,\ 40,\ 65,\ 60,\ 45,\ 12,\ 10) \sim (50,\ 40,\ 65,\ 60,\ 45,\ 2,\ 10)$$

$$x^{2,6} \sim x^6 \leftrightarrow (50,\ x_2,\ 65,\ 60,\ 45,\ 12,\ 10) \sim (50,\ 40,\ 65,\ 60,\ 45,\ 2,\ 10)$$

$$x^{3,6} \sim x^6 \leftrightarrow (50,\ 40,\ x_3,\ 60,\ 45,\ 12,\ 10) \sim (50,\ 40,\ 65,\ 60,\ 45,\ 2,\ 10)$$

$$x^{4,6} \sim x^6 \leftrightarrow (50,\ 40,\ 65,\ x_4,\ 45,\ 12,\ 10) \sim (50,\ 40,\ 65,\ 60,\ 45,\ 2,\ 10)$$

$$x^{5,6} \sim x^6 \leftrightarrow (50,\ 40,\ 65,\ 60,\ x_5,\ 12,\ 10) \sim (50,\ 40,\ 65,\ 60,\ 45,\ 2,\ 10)$$

$$x^{7,6} \sim x^6 \leftrightarrow (50,\ 40,\ 65,\ 60,\ 45,\ 12,\ x_7) \sim (50,\ 40,\ 65,\ 60,\ 45,\ 2,\ 10)$$

After evaluation, the DM proposed the following values.

$$(x_1,\ x_2,\ x_3,\ x_4,\ x_5,\ x_6,\ x_7) = (81,\ 75,\ 69,\ 70,\ 72,\ 12,\ 3.5)$$

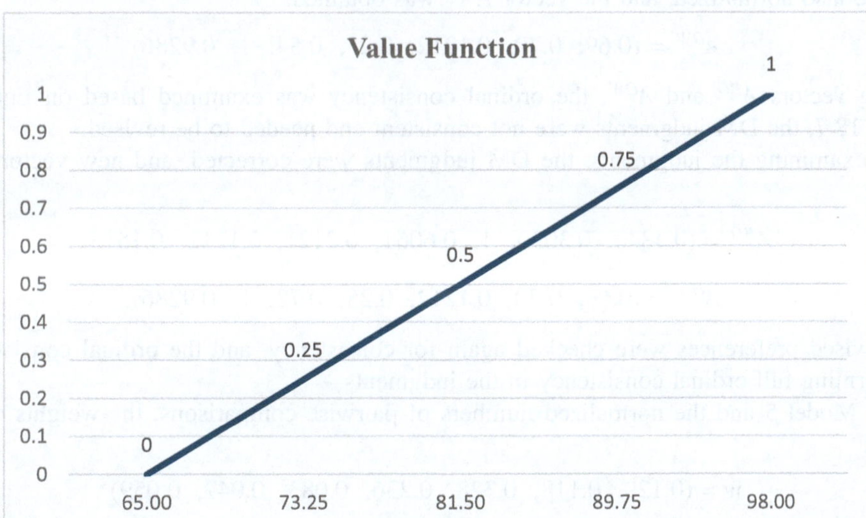

FIGURE 18.1 Value function for C3.

TABLE 18.7 The ordinal consistency check table.

	C1	C2	C3	C4	C5	C6	C7	OR_j
C1	0	0	0	0	1	0	0	0.17
C2	0	0	0	0	1	0	0	0.17
C3	0	0	0	0	0	0	0	0
C4	0	0	0	0	0	0	0	0
C5	1	1	0	0	0	0	0	0.33
C6	0	0	0	0	0	0	0	0
C7	0	0	0	0	0	0	0	0

TABLE 18.8 Evaluation of alternatives in each attribute.

0.059	0.047	0.083	0.236	0.328	0.118	0.129	Weight
C7	C6	C5	C4	C3	C2	C1	Attributes BI systems
6	5	6	4	7	5	6	A
5	4	6	7	5	6	5	B
5	6	4	5	6	5	7	C
6	5	5	6	5	7	6	D
6	5	7	6	4	6	5	E
6	7	4	5	6	5	4	F
7	4	6	6	5	5	6	G

These values were also normalized, and the vector A^{OW} was obtained.

$$A^{OW} = (0.69,\ 0.70,\ 0.1212,\ 0.25,\ 0.54,\ 1,\ 0.9286)$$

After determining vectors A^{BO} and A^{OW}, the ordinal consistency was examined based on Equations 18.6 to 18.9. According to Table 18.7, the DM judgments were not consistent and needed to be revised.

Therefore, by re-examining the judgments, the DM judgments were corrected, and new vectors A^{BO} and A^{OW} were obtained as follows:

$$A^{BO} = (0.4848,\ 0.3030,\ 1,\ 0.6061,\ 0.2121,\ 0.1212,\ 0.1515)$$

$$A^{OW} = (0.69,\ 0.70,\ 0.1212,\ 0.25,\ 0.72,\ 1,\ 0.9286)$$

Afterward, the revised preferences were checked again for consistency, and the ordinal consistency ratio (OR) was found to be 0, confirming full ordinal consistency in the judgments.

Step 6. Based on Model 5 and the normalized numbers of pairwise comparisons, the weights of the attributes were obtained as follows.

$$w = (0.129,\ 0.118,\ 0.328,\ 0.236,\ 0.083,\ 0.047,\ 0.059)$$

The cardinal consistency ratio is also less than the associated threshold (0.39), as shown in Table 18.3, which means the judgments are acceptable.

TABLE 18.9 Final ranking of alternatives.

Ranking	Final score	C7	C6	C5	C4	C3	C2	C1	BI systems
1	5.691	0.354	0.235	0.498	0.944	2.296	0.59	0.774	A
3	5.626	0.295	0.188	0.498	1.652	1.64	0.708	0.645	B
4	5.55	0.295	0.282	0.332	1.18	1.968	0.59	0.903	C
2	5.66	0.354	0.235	0.415	1.416	1.64	0.826	0.774	D
7	5.251	0.354	0.235	0.581	1.416	1.312	0.708	0.645	E
6	5.269	0.354	0.329	0.332	1.18	1.968	0.59	0.516	F
5	5.519	0.413	0.188	0.498	1.416	1.64	0.59	0.774	G

In Table 18.8, each of the alternatives (BI systems) under consideration is analyzed based on the seven evaluation attributes. For this end, DM was asked to assign a score of 1 to 10 to each alternative in each attribute. Also, the final weights of the attributes, which are given through the mathematical model, are given. These weights help quantitatively to evaluate and compare the systems.

In Table 18.9, the final ranking of the alternatives is obtained based on the sum of their weights in each of the evaluation attributes. For this purpose, first, the score of each alternative in each attribute is multiplied by the final weight of that attribute, and then the sum of these values is calculated for each alternative. This final weight represents the overall and relative value of each alternative, taking into account the different importance of the attributes, and is the main basis for the final ranking of the systems. Therefore, the alternative that obtains the highest final score (System A) is considered the most appropriate choice.

Based on the ranking results, System A (A1) ranked first with the highest score (5.691). This system is considered an ideal option for medium and large organizations with its focus on advanced analytics, providing diverse predictive models, high security, and a relatively simple user interface. System D (A4), with a score of 5.66 and second place, has the most focus on ease of use, superior user interface, and user training, and for this reason, it performed significantly in indicators related to user experience, although it was slightly lower than System A in some technical criteria. After that, System B (A2) ranked third with a score of 5.626 and a focus on high scalability, advanced security, and ease of use.

In fourth place, System C (A3) with a score of 5.55 performed well due to its high integration with existing systems and low maintenance costs, but its more complex user interface prevented it from reaching higher ranks. System G (A7) with a score of 5.519 offers a balanced combination of capabilities, adequate security, and strong support services, but performed weaker than its competitors in innovation indicators and some technical capabilities, and ranked fifth. In sixth place, System F (A6) with a score of 5.269 is recognized as the most cost-effective option for small and medium-sized businesses with limited budgets, although its analytical power and some technical capabilities are more limited. Finally, System E (A5) with a score of 5.251 ranked last; despite its high scalability and fast support services, this system performed worse in criteria such as user experience and security.

18.6 Conclusion

The purpose of this chapter is to describe the BWT method, which is a novel hybrid approach in the field of MCDM. BWT combines the BWM and tradeoff methods and has been able to collect the key advantages of both methods while covering many of their shortcomings. By combining the advantages of these two methods, BWT reduces the number of pairwise comparisons on the one hand and, on the other hand, assigns weights in a more realistic and sensitive way to environmental changes by considering the range of real changes of the attributes.

The BWT method has significant advantages in MCDM problems, especially in dynamic, complex, and ambiguous environments, which makes it a valuable tool for analyzing real problems. In such environments, the DM needs tools that, while maintaining simplicity and efficiency in the decision-making process, can record subjective preferences with high accuracy and enable their compatibility analysis. These features have made BWT widely used in the analysis of decisions related to risk management, emerging technologies, adaptive policymaking, and resource allocation in changing conditions, and it is a suitable and flexible approach for research designed in the context of unstable and future-oriented environments. This method will be efficient, especially in situations where DM are faced with relatively similar alternatives or minor differences in attributes are important.

To examine the practical application of the BWT method, a case study of selecting a BI system was conducted. In this analysis, seven key attributes, including "Integration Capability," "User Interface," "Analytical and Predictive Power," "Security," "Scalability," "System Downtime Frequency," and "Implementation and Maintenance Cost," were considered as decision-making attributes. After determining the weight of these attributes using the BWT method, the available alternatives were evaluated.

The results showed that System A, with the highest score (5.691), was identified as the best option, which was most aligned with organizational priorities due to its focus on advanced analysis and provision of diverse predictive models, high security, and a relatively simple user interface. This study showed that the BWT method, in addition to reducing the cognitive load of DM and increasing the accuracy of weighting by considering real changes in the range of attributes, can also be highly effective for ranking alternatives that are close to each other. Overall, the BWT method, by balancing implementation simplicity and analytical accuracy, has been able to provide an innovative framework that can be exploited in both theoretical research and practical applications.

References

Alsharkawy, M., Hamdy, A., & Marzouk, M. (2025). Developing a new sustainable rating system for assessing construction projects using BWM. *Cleaner Engineering and Technology, 25*, 100920.

Amiri, M., Hashemi-Tabatabaei, M., Ghahremanloo, M., Keshavarz-Ghorabaee, M., Zavadskas, E. K., & Banaitis, A. (2021). A new fuzzy BWM approach for evaluating and selecting a sustainable supplier in supply chain management. *International Journal of Sustainable Development & World Ecology, 28*(2), 125–142.

Badi, I., Pamučar, D., Stević, Ž., & Muhammad, L. J. (2023). Wind farm site selection using BWM-AHP-MARCOS method: A case study of Libya. *Scientific African, 19*, e01511.

Bahrami, Y., Hassani, H., & Maghsoudi, A. (2019). BWM-ARAS: A new hybrid MCDM method for Cu prospectivity mapping in the Abhar area, NW Iran. *Spatial Statistics, 33*, 100382.

Bleichrodt, H., & Pinto, J. L. (2002). Loss aversion and scale compatibility in two-attribute trade-offs. *Journal of Mathematical Psychology, 46*(3), 315–337.

Borcherding, K., Eppel, T., & Von Winterfeldt, D. (1991). Comparison of weighting judgments in multiattribute utility measurement. *Management Science, 37*(12), 1603–1619.

Corrente, S., Greco, S., & Rezaei, J. (2024). Better decisions with less cognitive load: The Parsimonious BWM. *Omega, 126*, 103075.

de Almeida, A. T., de Almeida, J. A., Costa, A. P. C. S., & de Almeida-Filho, A. T. (2016). A new method for elicitation of criteria weights in additive models: Flexible and interactive tradeoff. *European Journal of Operational Research, 250*(1), 179–191.

de Almeida, A. T., Frej, E. A., & Roselli, L. R. P. (2021). Combining holistic and decomposition paradigms in preference modeling with the flexibility of FITradeoff. *Central European Journal of Operations Research, 29*(1), 7–47.

Dehshiri, S. J. H., Emamat, M. S. M. M., & Amiri, M. (2022). A novel group BWM approach to evaluate the implementation criteria of blockchain technology in the automotive industry supply chain. *Expert Systems with Applications, 198*, 116826.

Ghoushchi, S. J., Yousefi, S., & Khazaeili, M. (2019). An extended FMEA approach based on the Z-MOORA and fuzzy BWM for prioritization of failures. *Applied Soft Computing, 81*, 105505.

Gupta, H., & Barua, M. K. (2017). Supplier selection among SMEs on the basis of their green innovation ability using BWM and fuzzy TOPSIS. *Journal of Cleaner Production, 152*, 242–258.

Haseli, G., Sheikh, R., & Sana, S. S. (2020). Base-criterion on multi-criteria decision-making method and its applications. *International Journal of Management Science and Engineering Management, 15*(2), 79–88.

Haseli, G., Sheikh, R., Ghoushchi, S. J., Hajiaghaei-Keshteli, M., Moslem, S., Deveci, M., & Kadry, S. (2024). An extension of the best–worst method based on the spherical fuzzy sets for multi-criteria decision-making. *Granular Computing, 9*(2), 40.

Haseli, G., Sheikh, R., Wang, J., Tomaskova, H., & Tirkolaee, E. B. (2021). A novel approach for group decision making based on the best–worst method (G-bwm): Application to supply chain management. *Mathematics, 9*(16), 1881.

Haseli, G., Torkayesh, A. E., Hajiaghaei-Keshteli, M., & Venghaus, S. (2023). Sustainable resilient recycling partner selection for urban waste management: Consolidating perspectives of decision-makers and experts. *Applied Soft Computing, 137*, 110120.

Haseli, G., Yazdani, M., Shaayesteh, M. T., & Hajiaghaei-Keshteli, M. (2025). Logistic hub location problem under fuzzy Extended Z-numbers to consider the uncertainty and reliable group decision-making. *Applied Soft Computing, 171*, 112751.

Huang, G., Xiao, L., Pedrycz, W., Pamucar, D., Zhang, G., & Martínez, L. (2022). Design alternative assessment and selection: A novel Z-cloud rough number-based BWM-MABAC model. *Information Sciences, 603*, 149–189.

Jaini, N. I., & Utyuzhnikov, S. V. (2017a). A fuzzy trade-off ranking method for multi-criteria decision-making. *Axioms, 7*(1), 1.

Jaini, N., & Utyuzhnikov, S. (2017). Trade-off ranking method for multi-criteria decision analysis. *Journal of Multi-Criteria Decision Analysis, 24*(3-4), 121–132.

Jankowski, P., Lotov, A. V., & Gusev, D. (2019). Application of a multiple criteria trade-off approach to spatial decision making. In *Spatial multicriteria decision making and analysis*. Routledge, 127–148.

Keeney, R. L. (2002). Common mistakes in making value trade-offs. *Operations Research, 50*(6), 935–945.

Kendall, M. G. (1938). A new measure of rank correlation. *Biometrika, 30*(1-2), 81–93.

Kheybari, S. (2021). Adjusting trade-offs in multi-criteria decision-making problems. *International Journal of Information Technology & Decision Making, 20*(05), 1499–1517.

Kumar, A., Aswin, A., & Gupta, H. (2020). Evaluating green performance of the airports using hybrid BWM and VIKOR methodology. *Tourism Management, 76*, 103941.

Li, T., & Fei, L. (2025). Exploring obstacles to the use of unmanned aerial vehicles in emergency rescue: A BWM-DEMATEL approach. *Technology in Society, 81*, 102863.

Li, T., Zhong, M., & Fei, L. (2025). Selection of high-arm fire trucks for urban emergency preparedness based on evidential linguistic CRITIC-BWM approach. *Expert Systems with Applications,* 128064.

Liang, F., Brunelli, M., & Rezaei, J. (2022). Best-worst tradeoff method. *Information Sciences, 610*, 957–976.

Mendes, A. C., Ferreira, F. A., Kannan, D., Ferreira, N. C., & Correia, R. J. (2022). A BWM approach to determinants of sustainable entrepreneurship in small and medium-sized enterprises. *Journal of Cleaner Production, 371*, 133300.

Otay, I., Onar, S.Ç., Öztayşi, B., & Kahraman, C. (2024). Evaluation of sustainable energy systems in smart cities using a Multi-Expert Pythagorean fuzzy BWM & TOPSIS methodology. *Expert Systems with Applications, 250*, 123874.

Oubrahim, I. (2025). Multi-criteria decision-making frameworks for sustainable supply chain management: a systematic literature review. In *International Conference Interdisciplinarity in Engineering* (pp. 204-223). Springer, Cham.

Raed, L., Mahdi, I., Ibrahim, H. M. H., Tolba, E. R., & Ebid, A. M. (2025). Innovative BWM–TOPSIS-based approach to determine the optimum delivery method for offshore projects. *Scientific Reports, 15*(1), 13340.

Raiffa, H., & Keeney, R.L. (1975). Decision analysis with multiple conflicting objectives, preferences and value tradeoffs. IIASA Working Paper. IIASA, Laxenburg, Austria: WP-75-053.

Rezaei, J. (2015). Best-worst multi-criteria decision-making method. *Omega, 53*, 49–57.

Rezaei, J., Kothadiya, O., Tavasszy, L., & Kroesen, M. (2018). Quality assessment of airline baggage handling systems using SERVQUAL and BWM. *Tourism Management, 66*, 85–93.

Roshanravan, B., Kreuzer, O. P., & Buckingham, A. (2025). BWM-MARCOS: A new hybrid MCDM approach for mineral potential modelling. *Journal of Geochemical Exploration, 269*, 107639.

Saaty, T. L. (1977). A scaling method for priorities in hierarchical structures. *Journal of Mathematical Psychology, 15*(3), 234–281. https://doi.org/10.1016/0022-2496(77)90033-5.

Saaty, T. L. (1996). *Decisions with the analytic network process (ANP).* University of Pittsburgh (USA), ISAHP, 96.

Tahura, S. S., Shabur, M. A., & Nuva, T. J. (2025). BWM analysis of online and offline learning effectiveness in Bangladesh. *Scientific Reports, 15*(1), 8377.

Torkayesh, A. E., Pamucar, D., Ecer, F., & Chatterjee, P. (2021). An integrated BWM-LBWA-CoCoSo framework for evaluation of healthcare sectors in Eastern Europe. *Socio-Economic Planning Sciences, 78*, 101052.

Weber, M., & Borcherding, K. (1993). Behavioral influences on weight judgments in multiattribute decision making. *European Journal of Operational Research, 67*(1), 1–12.

Zhang, Y., Kong, M., Wang, W. Z., Deveci, M., Bilican, M. S., & Delen, D. (2026). A multi-criteria decision-making framework for metaverse adoption: Evidence from higher education systems. *Expert Systems with Applications, 296*, 129132.

Chapter 19

IDOCRIW: Integrated determination of objective criteria weights for multi-attribute decision-making

Maryam Eghbalizarch[1] and Nazanin Ghaemi-Zadeh[2]
[1]*Department of Industrial and Systems Engineering, Southern Polytechnic College of Engineering and Engineering Technology, Kennesaw State University, Marietta, GA, United States,* [2]*Department of Industrial Engineering, Faculty of Engineering, Sharif University of Technology, Tehran, Iran*

19.1 Introduction

Decision-making in complex environments requires the simultaneous consideration of multiple, and often conflicting, criteria. Multi-attribute decision-making (MADM) techniques provide structured frameworks for this purpose, yet their effectiveness critically depends on the accurate determination of criteria weights. Weighting reflects the relative importance of attributes in shaping outcomes, and thus influences the ranking of alternatives and the final decision (Ji et al., 2024; Zavadskas & Podvezko, 2016). The literature emphasizes that relying solely on subjective expert judgment may introduce bias, while purely statistical measures may overlook contextual significance. To overcome these limitations, integrated approaches to objective weighting have been developed, among which the integrated determination of objective criteria weights (IDOCRIW) method has gained particular prominence (Zavadskas & Podvezko, 2016; Zavadskas et al., 2017).

The IDOCRIW method combines two complementary objective weighting techniques: the entropy method, which captures internal data variability, and the criterion impact loss (CILOS) method, which assesses external comparative importance based on performance loss. The entropy method identifies criteria with higher informational content by analyzing the dispersion of data across alternatives, while the CILOS method quantifies the influence of each criterion by evaluating the impact lost when it assumes its optimal value. The integration of these two perspectives ensures that neither statistical dispersion nor contextual importance dominates the outcome. In this sense, IDOCRIW offers a balanced framework—one that reflects both the discriminatory power of the data and the practical significance of each criterion. This dual-perspective aggregation mitigates the limitations of each method when used independently and produces a more stable and representative weighting scheme. IDOCRIW is especially suitable for compensatory decision-making environments involving independent criteria and has been successfully applied across various domains. Ultimately, its balanced structure enhances the robustness of MADM applications by aligning data-driven insights with performance-oriented considerations.

Since its introduction, IDOCRIW has attracted considerable attention across diverse application areas. In urban sustainability, Zavadskas et al. (2017) assessed healthy and safe built environments in Vilnius by integrating IDOCRIW with classical MADM methods such as complex proportional assessment (COPRAS), simple additive weighting, technique for order preference by similarity to ideal solution (TOPSIS), and evaluation based on distance from average solution. In the construction industry, Eghbali-Zarch et al. (2021) utilized a fuzzy-enhanced IDOCRIW–weighted aggregated sum product assessment hybrid to prioritize strategies for construction and demolition waste management. Their findings highlighted IDOCRIW's effectiveness in capturing the uncertainty and fuzziness inherent in real-world decision-making environments. The method has also been hybridized with emerging decision-making models. Parthasarathy et al. (2024) combined fuzzy IDOCRIW with the combined compromise solution (COCOSO) method to develop an advanced MADM structure for optimizing electric vehicle battery recycling. Similarly, Luo et al. (2021)

Encyclopedia of Multi-Attribute Decision-Making (MADM). DOI: https://doi.org/10.1016/B978-0-443-33275-3.00093-2

applied a probabilistic linguistic term set-based IDOCRIW–COCOSO model to select tourism attractions by analyzing sentiment in online user reviews. In energy management, Alao et al. (2021) adopted an IDOCRIW–TOPSIS hybrid to select optimal waste-to-energy technologies in South Africa, demonstrating the model's scalability to large urban infrastructure projects. Meanwhile, Ji et al. (2024) incorporated IDOCRIW with cloud models and game theory for decision-making in agrivoltaic energy storage investments. Beyond environmental and energy applications, IDOCRIW has been instrumental in road safety management. Naz et al. (2024) proposed a 2TLq-ROF-based IDOCRIW–QUALItative FLEXible (QUALIFLEX) framework to evaluate accident prediction models in Pakistan. In the water quality domain, Das (2025) employed an IDOCRIW–COPRAS model to assess drinking water sources in India's Brahmani River basin.

Collectively, these applications confirm the adaptability of IDOCRIW to environmental, energy, industrial, and social contexts, underscoring its role as a robust and reliable method for real-world decision-making. By addressing both data variability and performance loss, IDOCRIW provides a stable weighting structure that enhances the credibility of MADM outcomes.

19.2 Methodology

The IDOCRIW method provides an integrated framework for objectively determining criteria weights in MADM problems. It combines two objective techniques, entropy and CILOS, to capture both data variability and the relative impact of attributes. The methodology follows a structured sequence of normalization, entropy computation, impact loss evaluation, and weight aggregation. Each step ensures a more reliable and accurate weighting process. The following subsections describe the IDOCRIW procedure in detail. Moreover, the flowchart of this method is shown in Fig. 19.1.

Constructing the decision matrix: The initial step in the IDOCRIW method involves constructing a decision matrix that captures the performance evaluations of multiple alternatives across various criteria. Let n represent the number of alternatives and m the number of criteria. Each element r_{ij} of the decision matrix denotes the performance rating of the i-th alternative (A_i) with respect to the j-th criterion (c_j). The set of alternatives is defined as $A = \{A_1, A_2, \ldots, A_n\}$, and the set of criteria is given by $C = \{c_1, c_2, \ldots, c_m\}$. In this matrix, r_{ij} represents the input data needed to initiate the IDOCRIW weighting procedure. The matrix R is structured as follows (Alinezhad & Khalili, 2019; Zavadskas et al., 2017):

$$R = \begin{bmatrix} r_{11} & \cdots & r_{1j} & \cdots & r_{1m} \\ \vdots & \vdots & \vdots & \vdots & \vdots \\ r_{i1} & \cdots & r_{ij} & \cdots & r_{im} \\ \vdots & \vdots & \vdots & \ddots & \vdots \\ r_{n1} & \cdots & r_{nj} & \cdots & r_{nm} \end{bmatrix}_{n\times m}; \; i \in \{1, 2, \ldots, n\}, \quad j \in \{1, 2, \ldots, m\} \tag{19.1}$$

19.2.1 Entropy framework

The entropy method, originally introduced by Shannon (1948), is employed to determine objective criteria weights based on the diversity of information within the decision matrix.

Normalizing the decision matrix: This step involves normalizing the criteria values, as shown in (19.2):

$$\tilde{r}_{ij} = r_{ij} / \sum_{i=1}^{n} r_{ij}; \; j = 1, 2, \ldots, m \tag{19.2}$$

Calculating entropy values: Subsequently, the entropy value for each criterion j is calculated using (19.3):

$$E_j = -\frac{1}{\ln n} \sum_{i=1}^{n} \tilde{r}_{ij} . \ln \tilde{r}_{ij}; \; (j = 1, 2, \ldots, m; 0 \leq E_j \leq 1) \tag{19.3}$$

Calculating degree of diversification: The degree of diversification for each criterion is then determined by Eq. (19.4):

$$d_j = 1 - E_j \tag{19.4}$$

Deriving entropy weights: Finally, the entropy weight W_j for each criterion is obtained by normalizing the diversification degrees as shown in Eq. (19.5):

$$W_j = d_j / \sum_{j=1}^{m} d_j \tag{19.5}$$

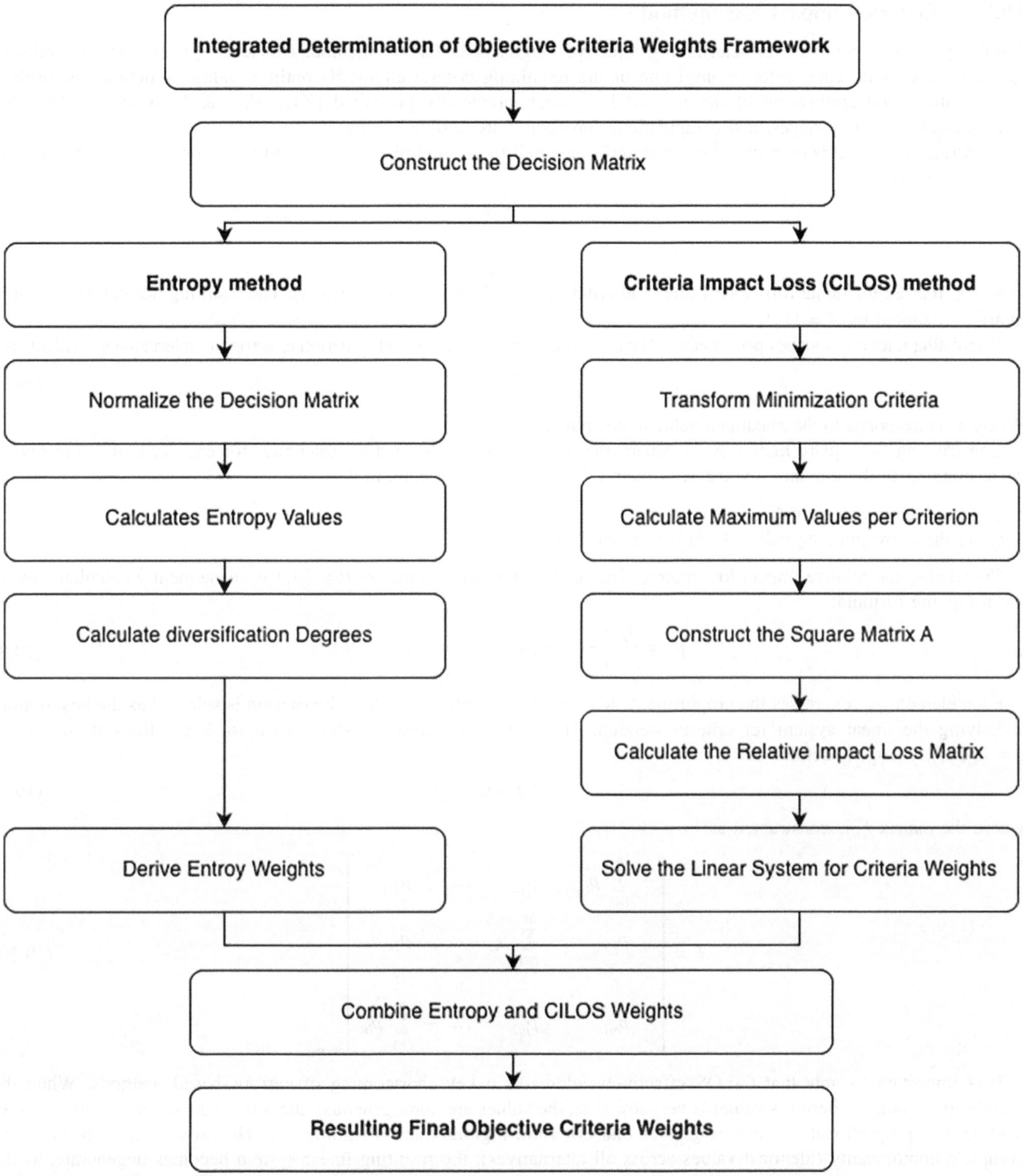

FIGURE 19.1 Flowchart of integrated determination of objective criteria with weights method.

The entropy weights reflect the informational structure and heterogeneity of the dataset. Criteria with minimal variability among their values tend to receive near-zero weights, indicating a lower influence on the overall evaluation. Conversely, criteria with greater dispersion are assigned higher entropy weights, emphasizing their greater discriminative power within the decision-making process.

19.2.2 Criterion impact loss method

Another promising approach for determining objective weights is the CILOS method. This technique evaluates the relative loss associated with each criterion until one of the remaining criteria attains its optimal value. A detailed algorithm, formalization, and application of the method have been previously presented (Zavadskas & Podvezko, 2016). The fundamental logic, key stages, and computational procedure are outlined below.

Transforming minimization criteria: For criteria intended to be minimized, a transformation into maximizing form is performed using:

$$\bar{r}_{ij} = \frac{\min_i r_{ij}}{r_{ij}} \tag{19.6}$$

Where r_{ij} represents the performance value of alternative A_i with respect to criterion c_j. The resulting normalized decision matrix is denoted by $X = \{x_{ij}\}$.

Calculating maximum values per criterion: Next, the maximum value for each criterion c_j across all alternatives is calculated:

$$x_j = \max_i r_{ij} \tag{19.7}$$

Where x_j corresponds to the maximum value in column j.

Constructing the square matrix A: A square matrix $A = \{a_{ij}\}$ is formed by selecting, for each criterion, the row k_j corresponding to the maximum value x_j in matrix X. Thus, for each column j:

- $a_{jj} = x_j$ (diagonal elements),
- a_{ij} are the corresponding values from the selected rows.

Calculating the relative impact loss matrix: The relative impact loss matrix $P = \{p_{ij}\}$ is subsequently calculated using the following formula:

$$p_{ij} = \frac{x_j - a_{ij}}{x_j}; (p_{jj} = 0; i, j = 1, 2, \ldots, m) \tag{19.8}$$

Each element p_{ij} expresses the proportionate loss in the j-th criterion if the i-th criterion is selected as the best option.

Solving the linear system for criteria weights: The system of linear equations used to derive the criteria weight $q = (q_1, q_2, \ldots, q_m)$ is defined as:

$$Fq = 0 \tag{19.9}$$

where the matrix F is constructed as:

$$F = \begin{bmatrix} -\sum_{i=1}^{n} p_{i1} & p_{12} & \cdots & p_{1m} \\ p_{21} & -\sum_{i=1}^{n} p_{i2} & \cdots & p_{2m} \\ \vdots & \vdots & \ddots & \vdots \\ p_{m1} & p_{m2} & \cdots & -\sum_{i=1}^{n} p_{im} \end{bmatrix}_{m \times m} \tag{19.10}$$

It is important to note that CILOS effectively addresses a key shortcoming of entropy-based methods. When the variability among a criterion's values is very low (i.e., the values are homogeneous), the relative losses p_{ij} approach zero, leading to a proportionally larger weight for that criterion, highlighting its significance. However, if a criterion shows complete homogeneity (identical values across all alternatives), the resulting linear system becomes degenerate, as the associated column in matrix P will be zero.

19.2.3 Aggregate objective weights: integrated determination of objective criteria with weights method

Combining entropy and criterion impact loss weights into aggregate weights: The integration of different significance weights into a single overall weighting system can enhance the objectivity of decision-making (Zavadskas & Podvezko, 2016). In the IDOCRIW method, the entropy-based weights W_j and the CILOS weights q_j are combined to form a unified set of aggregate weights ω_j according to the following formula:

$$\omega_j = q_j W_j / \sum_{i=1}^{n} q_j W_j \tag{19.11}$$

This aggregation approach simultaneously accounts for the dispersion of criterion values (captured through entropy) and the relative importance of criteria based on impact loss. While the entropy component emphasizes the variation among criteria, the impact loss component adjusts for the diminishing effect caused by potential losses in other criteria. The resulting aggregate weights are then applied in the multi criteria assessment process to prioritize the alternatives and identify the most favorable option.

19.3 Numerical example 1: building location selection (simple real case)

In the case study presented by Alinezhad and Khalili (2019), an organization is planning to construct a new administrative building and is evaluating four possible options. The company's decision-makers aim to assess and rank various criteria—including cost (C_1), building size (C_2), proximity to the organization's current location (C_3), and construction quality (C_4)—based on expert evaluations. The corresponding decision matrix is provided in Table 19.1. To determine the objective importance of each criterion and guide the final selection of the optimal building alternative, the IDOCRIW method is applied to the decision matrix in Table 19.1. This approach integrates both entropy and CILOS techniques to calculate robust and comprehensive criteria weights.

The entropy framework. The decision matrix is first normalized using (19.2), where the criteria are normalized accordingly to transform them into a uniform scale. This step ensures comparability across different units.

Using the normalized matrix as shown in Table 19.2, the degree of entropy and diversification for each criterion is calculated as follows:

$$E_1 = -\frac{1}{\ln 4}\begin{pmatrix} 0.316 \times \ln 0.316+ \\ 0.263 \times \ln 0.263+ \\ 0.189 \times \ln 0.189+ \\ 0.232 \times \ln 0.232 \end{pmatrix} = 0.988 \rightarrow d_1 = 1 - 0.988 = 0.012$$

TABLE 19.1 Decision matrix.

Alternatives	C_1^-	C_2^+	C_3^-	C_4^+
A_1	3.00	100	10	7
A_2	2.50	80	8	5
A_3	1.80	50	20	11
A_4	2.20	70	12	9

TABLE 19.2 Normalized decision matrix.

Alternatives	C_1^-	C_2^+	C_3^-	C_4^+
A_1	0.316	0.333	0.200	0.219
A_2	0.263	0.267	0.160	0.156
A_3	0.189	0.167	0.400	0.344
A_4	0.232	0.233	0.240	0.281

$$E_2 = -\frac{1}{\ln 4}\begin{pmatrix} 0.333 \times \ln 0.333+ \\ 0.267 \times \ln 0.267+ \\ 0.167 \times \ln 0.167+ \\ 0.233 \times \ln 0.233 \end{pmatrix} = 0.979 \rightarrow d_2 = 1 - 0.979 = 0.021$$

$$E_3 = -\frac{1}{\ln 4}\begin{pmatrix} 0.200 \times \ln 0.200+ \\ 0.160 \times \ln 0.160+ \\ 0.400 \times \ln 0.400+ \\ 0.240 \times \ln 0.240 \end{pmatrix} = 0.955 \rightarrow d_3 = 1 - 0.955 = 0.045$$

$$E_4 = -\frac{1}{\ln 4}\begin{pmatrix} 0.219 \times \ln 0.219+ \\ 0.156 \times \ln 0.156+ \\ 0.344 \times \ln 0.344+ \\ 0.281 \times \ln 0.281 \end{pmatrix} = 0.971 \rightarrow d_4 = 1 - 0.971 = 0.029$$

The entropy values calculated for each criterion reflect the degree of information uncertainty or uniformity in the normalized data. Criterion C_1 has the highest entropy value ($E_1 = 0.988$), resulting in a very low diversification degree ($d_1 = 0.012$), indicating that the values for cost are highly uniform across alternatives and thus contribute the least to distinguishing among them. C2 also shows relatively high entropy ($E_2 = 0.979$; $d_2 = 0.021$), suggesting a low, but slightly better, discriminatory power. In contrast, C_3 ($E_3 = 0.955$; $d_3 = 0.045$) exhibits the highest degree of diversification, implying the most variation in distance among options and therefore the most informational value. C_4 ($E_4 = 0.971$; $d_4 = 0.029$) shows moderate variability. Overall, these results indicate that C_3 (distance) plays the most significant role in differentiating alternatives, while C_1 (cost) is the least influential in terms of data diversity. Finally, the entropy weights can be calculated as follows:

$$w_1 = \frac{0.012}{0.012 + 0.021 + 0.045 + 0.029} = 0.115$$

$$w_2 = \frac{0.021}{0.012 + 0.021 + 0.045 + 0.029} = 0.198$$

$$w_3 = \frac{0.045}{0.012 + 0.021 + 0.045 + 0.029} = 0.418$$

$$w_4 = \frac{0.029}{0.012 + 0.021 + 0.045 + 0.029} = 0.269$$

These weights demonstrate that criterion C_3 (distance) is the most influential in the decision-making process, followed by C_4 (quality) and C_2 (building area), whereas C_1 (cost) has the least impact based on the data variability captured by the entropy method. This objective weighting scheme thus prioritizes criteria according to their information content, providing a solid foundation for subsequent multi criteria decision analysis.

The criterion impact loss framework. In the following sections, the CILOS method will be applied to further determine the objective weights of the criteria. The first step involves transforming all criteria that are to be minimized into a maximizing form. This transformation is necessary because the CILOS method requires benefit-oriented data to properly evaluate the relative impact loss. Therefore, the minimum values for the cost (C_1) and distance (C_3) criteria, which are 1.8 and 8 respectively, are used in the transformation process to normalize these criteria into a benefit format for subsequent analysis.

To prepare the transformed decision matrix for further analysis using the CILOS method, the data must be normalized using (19.2) to ensure all criteria values are on a comparable scale, typically between 0 and 1. This normalization helps eliminate the effect of differing units and magnitudes among criteria. Additionally, the maximum amount of each column is specified as shown in Table 19.3 and Table 19.4.

From this matrix, the diagonal elements corresponding to the maximum values of each criterion are:

$$a_{11} = 0.319, \quad a_{22} = 0.333, \quad a_{33} = 0.349, \quad a_{44} = 0.344$$

Finally, the square matrix A is constructed by selecting the rows corresponding to the maximum normalized values for each criterion, as shown in Table 19.5. This matrix serves as the basis for calculating the relative impact loss.

TABLE 19.3 Transformed decision matrix.

Alternatives	C_1^+	C_2^+	C_3^+	C_4^+
A_1	0.600	100	0.800	7
A_2	0.720	80	1.000	5
A_3	1.000	50	0.400	11
A_4	0.818	70	0.667	9

TABLE 19.4 Normalized transformed decision matrix.

Alternatives	C_1^+	C_2^+	C_3^+	C_4^+
A_1	0.191	0.333	0.279	0.219
A_2	0.229	0.267	0.349	0.156
A_3	0.319	0.167	0.140	0.344
A_4	0.261	0.233	0.233	0.281
max	0.319	0.333	0.349	0.344

TABLE 19.5 Square matrix.

Alternatives	C_1^+	C_2^+	C_3^+	C_4^+
A_3	0.319	0.167	0.140	0.344
A_1	0.191	0.333	0.279	0.219
A_2	0.229	0.267	0.349	0.156
A_3	0.319	0.167	0.140	0.344

Using matrix A, the relative impact loss matrix, P, is computed according to (19.8). This matrix reflects the proportional loss in each criterion if a particular criterion is chosen as the best reference, with zero losses along the diagonal. Table 19.6 presents the resulting relative impact loss matrix.

Using the relative impact loss matrix from Table 19.6, the weights system matrix, F, is constructed as defined in Eq. (19.10). This matrix is formed by placing the negative sums of each column's impact losses on the diagonal, and the off-diagonal elements correspond to the relative losses between criteria. Solving the system allows us to derive the criteria weights vector, q, which reflects the relative importance of each criterion based on their impact losses. Table 19.7 displays the weights system matrix used for this purpose.

At this stage, the system of linear equations derived from the weights matrix, F, is represented as follows:

TABLE 19.6 Relative impact loss matrix.

Alternatives	C_1^+	C_2^+	C_3^+	C_4^+
A_3	0.000	0.500	0.600	0.000
A_1	0.400	0.000	0.200	0.364
A_2	0.280	0.200	0.000	0.545
A_3	0.000	0.500	0.600	0.000
sum	0.680	1.200	1.400	0.909

TABLE 19.7 Weights system matrix.

Alternatives	C_1^+	C_2^+	C_3^+	C_4^+
A_3	-0.680	0.500	0.600	0.000
A_1	0.400	-1.200	0.200	0.364
A_2	0.280	0.200	-1.400	0.545
A_3	0.000	0.500	0.600	-0.909

$$\begin{cases} -0.680q_1 + 0.500q_2 + 0.600q_3 = 0 \\ 0.400q_1 - 1.200q_2 + 0.200q_3 + 0.364q_4 = 0 \\ 0.280q_1 + 0.200q_2 - 1.400q_3 + 0.545q_4 = 0 \\ 0.500q_2 + 0.600q_3 - 0.909q_4 = 0 \end{cases}$$

Solving this system yields the weight vector $q = (q_1,\ q_2,\ \ldots, q_m)$, representing the relative importance of each criterion:

$$q_1 = 0.334, \quad q_2 = 0.220, \quad q_3 = 0.196, \quad q_4 = 0.250$$

These weights reflect the contribution of each attribute to the overall decision, as determined by the CILOS impact loss approach.

The integrated determination of objective criteria weights framework. The aggregate weight (ω_j) for each attribute is computed by combining the weights derived from the CILOS method (q_j) and the entropy weights (W_j) using Eq. (19.11).

$$\omega_1 = \frac{(0.334 \times 0.115)}{(0.334 \times 0.115) + (0.220 \times 0.198) + (0.196 \times 0.418) + (0.250 \times 0.269)} = 0.166$$

$$\omega_2 = \frac{(0.220 \times 0.198)}{(0.334 \times 0.115) + (0.220 \times 0.198) + (0.196 \times 0.418) + (0.250 \times 0.269)} = 0.189$$

$$\omega_3 = \frac{(0.196 \times 0.418)}{(0.334 \times 0.115) + (0.220 \times 0.198) + (0.196 \times 0.418) + (0.250 \times 0.269)} = 0.354$$

$$\omega_4 = \frac{(0.250 \times 0.269)}{(0.334 \times 0.115) + (0.220 \times 0.198) + (0.196 \times 0.418) + (0.250 \times 0.269)} = 0.291$$

These values indicate that Criterion 3 holds the greatest combined significance, followed by Criterion 4. Criteria 1 and 2 have lower aggregate importance, reflecting their comparatively smaller contributions both in terms of variability and impact loss. This integrated weighting confirms that the decision-making process should prioritize the criteria with higher aggregate weights for a more robust and data-driven evaluation.

19.4 Numerical example 2: optimal photovoltaic thermal selection (complex real case)

In the case study presented by Hosouli et al. (2024), the selection of an optimal photovoltaic thermal (PVT) collector is addressed using an MCDM approach. Ten commercially available PVT modules are evaluated based on six key criteria that encompass both technical performance and economic considerations. The first three benefit-type criteria to be maximized include electrical efficiency at standard test conditions (C_1), zero-loss efficiency (C_2), and maximum working temperature (C_5). Conversely, the remaining three are cost-type criteria to be minimized, namely the first-order heat loss coefficient (C_3), second-order heat loss coefficient (C_4), and relative price (C_6). The decision matrix formed from this dataset includes crisp numerical values extracted from manufacturer specifications, reflecting real-world complexity and variability across alternatives. The corresponding decision matrix is provided in Table 19.8.

To objectively assess the significance of each criterion and support the final decision in selecting the optimal building alternative, the IDOCRIW method is employed using the decision matrix in Table 19.8. This method combines the entropy and CILOS techniques to derive reliable and well-rounded weights for the criteria.

The entropy framework. The decision matrix is initially normalized using (19.2), which adjusts the criteria values to a common scale. This normalization process ensures that the data are comparable despite differences in their original units.

Based on the normalized matrix presented in Table 19.9 and Table 19.10, the entropy values and diversification degrees for each criterion are calculated as follows:

$$E_1 = -\frac{1}{\ln 10}\begin{pmatrix} 0.108 \times \ln 0.108 + 0.073 \times \ln 0.073+ \\ 0.104 \times \ln 0.104 + 0.091 \times \ln 0.091+ \\ 0.078 \times \ln 0.078 + 0.115 \times \ln 0.115+ \\ 0.123 \times \ln 0.123 + 0.104 \times \ln 0.104+ \\ 0.093 \times \ln 0.093 + 0.111 \times \ln 0.111 \end{pmatrix} = 0.9947 \rightarrow d_1 = 1 - 0.9947 = 0.0053$$

$$E_2 = -\frac{1}{\ln 10}\begin{pmatrix} 0.131 \times \ln 0.131 + 0.088 \times \ln 0.088+ \\ 0.095 \times \ln 0.095 + 0.089 \times \ln 0.089+ \\ 0.091 \times \ln 0.091 + 0.100 \times \ln 0.100+ \\ 0.127 \times \ln 0.127 + 0.091 \times \ln 0.091+ \\ 0.103 \times \ln 0.103 + 0.088 \times \ln 0.088 \end{pmatrix} = 0.9953 \rightarrow d_2 = 1 - 0.9953 = 0.0047$$

TABLE 19.8 Decision matrix.

Alternatives	C_1^+	C_2^+	C_3^-	C_4^-	C_5^+	C_6^-
A_1	17.8	0.700	5.980	0.001	126	7.440
A_2	12.0	0.470	3.780	0.014	180	8.270
A_3	17.2	0.510	11.40	0.001	74.7	16.46
A_4	15.1	0.475	8.370	0.586	101	9.580
A_5	12.9	0.486	4.030	0.067	134	9.670
A_6	19.0	0.534	8.370	0.586	93.0	9.130
A_7	20.4	0.680	10.04	0.001	83.0	8.520
A_8	17.1	0.487	5.770	0.009	95.0	10.08
A_9	15.3	0.550	6.300	0.080	85.0	12.02
A_{10}	18.4	0.470	9.500	0.001	85.0	8.830

TABLE 19.9 Normalized decision matrix.

Alternatives	C_1^+	C_2^+	C_3^-	C_4^-	C_5^+	C_6^-
A_1	0.108	0.131	0.081	0.001	0.119	0.074
A_2	0.073	0.088	0.051	0.010	0.170	0.083
A_3	0.104	0.095	0.155	0.001	0.071	0.165
A_4	0.091	0.089	0.114	0.435	0.096	0.096
A_5	0.078	0.091	0.055	0.050	0.127	0.097
A_6	0.115	0.100	0.114	0.435	0.088	0.091
A_7	0.123	0.127	0.137	0.001	0.079	0.085
A_8	0.104	0.091	0.078	0.007	0.090	0.101
A_9	0.093	0.103	0.086	0.059	0.080	0.120
A_{10}	0.111	0.088	0.129	0.001	0.080	0.088

TABLE 19.10 Transformed decision matrix.

Alternatives	C_1^+	C_2^+	C_3^+	C_4^+	C_5^+	C_6^+
A_1	17.80	0.70	0.63	1.000	126.00	1.00
A_2	12.00	0.47	1.00	0.071	180.00	0.90
A_3	17.20	0.51	0.33	1.000	74.70	0.45
A_4	15.10	0.48	0.45	0.002	101.00	0.78
A_5	12.90	0.49	0.94	0.015	134.00	0.77
A_6	19.00	0.53	0.45	0.002	93.00	0.81
A_7	20.40	0.68	0.38	1.000	83.00	0.87
A_8	17.10	0.49	0.66	0.111	95.00	0.74
A_9	15.30	0.55	0.60	0.013	85.00	0.62
A_{10}	18.40	0.47	0.40	1.000	85.00	0.84

$$E_3 = -\frac{1}{\ln 10}\begin{pmatrix} 0.081 \times \ln 0.081 + 0.051 \times \ln 0.051 + \\ 0.155 \times \ln 0.155 + 0.114 \times \ln 0.114 + \\ 0.055 \times \ln 0.055 + 0.114 \times \ln 0.114 + \\ 0.137 \times \ln 0.137 + 0.078 \times \ln 0.078 + \\ 0.086 \times \ln 0.086 + 0.129 \times \ln 0.129 \end{pmatrix} = 0.9754 \rightarrow d_3 = 1 - 0.9754 = 0.0246$$

$$E_4 = -\frac{1}{\ln 10}\begin{pmatrix} 0.001 \times \ln 0.001 + 0.010 \times \ln 0.010 + \\ 0.001 \times \ln 0.001 + 0.435 \times \ln 0.435 + \\ 0.050 \times \ln 0.050 + 0.435 \times \ln 0.435 + \\ 0.001 \times \ln 0.001 + 0.007 \times \ln 0.007 + \\ 0.059 \times \ln 0.059 + 0.001 \times \ln 0.001 \end{pmatrix} = 0.4966 \rightarrow d_4 = 1 - 0.4966 = 0.5034$$

$$E_5 = -\frac{1}{\ln 10}\begin{pmatrix} 0.119 \times \ln 0.119 + 0.170 \times \ln 0.170+ \\ 0.071 \times \ln 0.071 + 0.096 \times \ln 0.096+ \\ 0.127 \times \ln 0.127 + 0.088 \times \ln 0.088+ \\ 0.079 \times \ln 0.079 + 0.090 \times \ln 0.090+ \\ 0.080 \times \ln 0.080 + 0.080 \times \ln 0.080 \end{pmatrix} = 0.9834 \rightarrow d_5 = 1 - 0.9834 = 0.0166$$

$$E_6 = -\frac{1}{\ln 10}\begin{pmatrix} 0.074 \times \ln 0.074 + 0.083 \times \ln 0.083+ \\ 0.165 \times \ln 0.165 + 0.096 \times \ln 0.096+ \\ 0.097 \times \ln 0.097 + 0.091 \times \ln 0.091+ \\ 0.085 \times \ln 0.085 + 0.101 \times \ln 0.101+ \\ 0.120 \times \ln 0.120 + 0.080 \times \ln 0.080 \end{pmatrix} = 0.9883 \rightarrow d_6 = 1 - 0.9883 = 0.0117$$

The entropy analysis shows that among the six criteria, the second-order heat loss coefficient (C_4) has the lowest entropy (0.497) and highest diversification (0.503), indicating it provides the most discrimination between alternatives. The first-order heat loss coefficient (C_3) and relative price (C_6) show moderate variability, contributing some differentiation. In contrast, the benefit-type criteria—electrical efficiency (C_1), zero-loss efficiency (C_2), and maximum working temperature (C_5)—have very high entropy values and low diversification degrees, meaning their values are fairly uniform across alternatives and less effective in distinguishing them. Overall, the cost-type criteria, especially C_4, play a stronger role in differentiating options in this evaluation. Finally, the entropy weights can be calculated as follows:

$$w_1 = \frac{0.0053}{0.0053 + 0.0047 + 0.0246 + 0.5034 + 0.0166 + 0.0117} = 0.0093$$

$$w_2 = \frac{0.0047}{0.0053 + 0.0047 + 0.0246 + 0.5034 + 0.0166 + 0.0117} = 0.0083$$

$$w_3 = \frac{0.0246}{0.0053 + 0.0047 + 0.0246 + 0.5034 + 0.0166 + 0.0117} = 0.0435$$

$$w_4 = \frac{0.5034}{0.0053 + 0.0047 + 0.0246 + 0.5034 + 0.0166 + 0.0117} = 0.8889$$

$$w_5 = \frac{0.0166}{0.0053 + 0.0047 + 0.0246 + 0.5034 + 0.0166 + 0.0117} = 0.0293$$

$$w_6 = \frac{0.0117}{0.0053 + 0.0047 + 0.0246 + 0.5034 + 0.0166 + 0.0117} = 0.0207$$

The weights show that C_4 (second-order heat loss) is by far the most important criterion with 89% weight, reflecting its strong ability to differentiate alternatives. C_3 has moderate importance (4.4%), while the other criteria (C_1, C_2, C_5, C_6) have very low weights below 3%, indicating limited impact on decision-making.

The criterion impact loss framework. In the subsequent sections, the CILOS method is employed to further refine the objective weighting of the criteria. The first step involves converting all cost-type (minimization) criteria into benefit-type (maximization) form. This transformation is essential, as the CILOS approach evaluates criteria based on their relative impact loss, which requires all inputs to be in a benefit-oriented format. Accordingly, the minimum values of the cost-type criteria—namely C_3, C_4, and C_6, with minimum values of 3.78, 0.001, and 7.44, respectively—are used to normalize these criteria into a comparable maximizing scale for further analysis.

To facilitate further analysis with the CILOS method, the decision matrix must first be normalized using (19.2), ensuring that all criteria are scaled uniformly—typically within the range of 0 to 1. This normalization process is crucial for eliminating the influence of varying units and magnitudes across different criteria. The maximum value for each criterion column, required for this normalization, is presented in Table 19.11.

From this matrix, the diagonal elements corresponding to the maximum values of each criterion are:

$$a_{11} = 0.123, \quad a_{22} = 0.131, \quad a_{33} = 0.171, \quad a_{44} = 0.237, \quad a_{55} = 0.170, a_{66} = 0.128$$

Finally, the square matrix A is constructed by selecting the rows corresponding to the maximum normalized values for each criterion, as shown in Table 19.12. In cases where multiple alternatives share the same maximum value for a given criterion, a consistent selection strategy must be applied to ensure reproducibility and methodological rigor. Three common approaches include: (1) selecting the first occurrence of the maximum value (e.g., A_1), (2) choosing the

TABLE 19.11 Normalized transformed decision matrix.

Alternatives	C_1^+	C_2^+	C_3^+	C_4^+	C_5^+	C_6^+
A_1	0.108	0.131	0.108	0.237	0.119	0.128
A_2	0.073	0.088	0.171	0.017	0.170	0.116
A_3	0.104	0.095	0.057	0.237	0.071	0.058
A_4	0.091	0.089	0.077	0.000	0.096	0.100
A_5	0.078	0.091	0.161	0.004	0.127	0.099
A_6	0.115	0.100	0.077	0.000	0.088	0.105
A_7	0.123	0.127	0.065	0.237	0.079	0.112
A_8	0.104	0.091	0.112	0.026	0.090	0.095
A_9	0.093	0.103	0.103	0.003	0.080	0.080
A_{10}	0.111	0.088	0.068	0.237	0.080	0.108
max	0.123	0.131	0.171	0.237	0.170	0.128

TABLE 19.12 Square matrix.

Alternatives	C_1^+	C_2^+	C_3^+	C_4^+	C_5^+	C_6^+
A_7	0.123	0.127	0.065	0.237	0.079	0.112
A_1	0.108	0.131	0.108	0.237	0.119	0.128
A_2	0.073	0.088	0.171	0.017	0.170	0.116
A_4	0.108	0.131	0.108	0.237	0.119	0.128
A_2	0.073	0.088	0.171	0.017	0.170	0.116
A_1	0.108	0.131	0.108	0.237	0.119	0.128

alternative with the best overall performance across all criteria, typically measured by the total sum or average of normalized values, and (3) applying a deterministic rule, such as lexicographic order or the alternative with the minimum index. For criterion C_4, four alternatives (A_1, A_3, A_7, A_{10}) exhibited the same maximum value (0.237). Based on the overall performance rule, A_1, having the highest aggregate normalized score (0.831), was selected to represent C_4. This ensures that the square matrix captures not only the peak value but also the most representative alternative for each criterion. The resulting matrix serves as the basis for calculating relative impact loss within the CILOS framework.

Based on matrix A, the relative impact loss matrix (P) is calculated using (19.8). This matrix quantifies the proportionate loss associated with each criterion when another criterion is considered the optimal reference. By design, the diagonal elements are zero, as no loss occurs when a criterion is compared to itself. The resulting values are presented in Table 19.13.

Using the relative impact loss matrix from Table 19.13, the weights system matrix, F, is constructed as defined in Eq. (19.10). This matrix is formed by placing the negative sums of each column's impact losses on the diagonal, and the off-diagonal elements correspond to the relative losses between criteria. Solving the system allows us to derive the criteria weights vector, q, which reflects the relative importance of each criterion based on their impact losses. Table 19.14 displays the weight system matrix used for this purpose.

TABLE 19.13 Relative impact loss matrix.

Alternatives	C_1^+	C_2^+	C_3^+	C_4^+	C_5^+	C_6^+
A_7	0.000	0.031	0.620	0.000	0.535	0.125
A_1	0.122	0.000	0.368	0.000	0.300	0.000
A_2	0.407	0.328	0.000	0.928	0.000	0.094
A_4	0.122	0.000	0.368	0.000	0.300	0.000
A_2	0.407	0.328	0.000	0.928	0.000	0.094
A_1	0.122	0.000	0.368	0.000	0.300	0.000
Sum	1.179	0.687	1.725	1.857	1.435	0.313

TABLE 19.14 Weight system matrix.

Alternatives	C_1^+	C_2^+	C_3^+	C_4^+	C_5^+	C_6^+
A_7	-1.179	0.031	0.620	0.000	0.535	0.125
A_1	0.122	-0.687	0.368	0.000	0.300	0.000
A_2	0.407	0.328	-1.725	0.928	0.000	0.094
A_4	0.122	0.000	0.368	-1.857	0.300	0.000
A_2	0.407	0.328	0.000	0.928	-1.435	0.094
A_1	0.122	0.000	0.368	0.000	0.300	-0.313

At this stage, the system of linear equations derived from the weights matrix, F, is represented as follows:

$$\begin{cases} -1.179q_1 + 0.122q_2 + 0.407q_3 + 0.122q_4 + 0.407q_5 + 0.122q_6 = 0 \\ 0.031q_1 - 0.687q_2 + 0.328q_3 + 0.328q_3 + 0.328q_5 + 0.328q_3 = 0 \\ 0.620q_1 + 0.368q_2 - 1.725q_3 + 0.368q_4 + 0.368q_4 + 0.368q_6 = 0 \\ 0.620q_1 + 0.500q_2 + 0.928q_3 - 1.857q_4 + 0.928q_5 + 0.928q_3 = 0 \\ 0.535q_1 + 0.300q_2 + 0.300q_1 + 0.300q_4 - 1.435q_5 + 0.300q_6 = 0 \\ 0.125q_1 + 0.300q_2 + 0.094q_3 + 0.300q_2 + 0.094q_5 - 0.313q_6 = 0 \end{cases}$$

Solving this system yields the weight vector $q = (q_1, q_2, \ldots, q_m)$, representing the relative importance of each criterion:

$$q_1 = 0.1703, \quad q_2 = 0.1582, \quad q_3 = 0.1207, \quad q_4 = 0.0585, \; q_5 = 0.1451, \; q_6 = 0.3473$$

These weights reflect the contribution of each attribute to the overall decision, as determined by the CILOS impact loss approach.

The integrated determination of objective criteria weights framework. The aggregate weight (ω_j) for each attribute is computed by combining the weights derived from the CILOS method (q_j) and the entropy weights (W_j) using Eq. (19.11).

$$\omega_1 = \frac{(0.1703 \times 0.0093)}{\begin{pmatrix}(0.1703 \times 0.0093) + (0.1582 \times 0.0083)+ \\ (0.1207 \times 0.0435) + (0.0585 \times 0.8889)+ \\ (0.1451 \times 0.0293) + (0.3473 \times 0.0207)\end{pmatrix}} = 0.022$$

$$\omega_2 = \frac{(0.1582 \times 0.0083)}{\begin{pmatrix}(0.1703 \times 0.0093) + (0.1582 \times 0.0083)+ \\ (0.1207 \times 0.0435) + (0.0585 \times 0.8889)+ \\ (0.1451 \times 0.0293) + (0.3473 \times 0.0207)\end{pmatrix}} = 0.018$$

$$\omega_3 = \frac{(0.1207 \times 0.0435)}{\begin{pmatrix}(0.1703 \times 0.0093) + (0.1582 \times 0.0083)+ \\ (0.1207 \times 0.0435) + (0.0585 \times 0.8889)+ \\ (0.1451 \times 0.0293) + (0.3473 \times 0.0207)\end{pmatrix}} = 0.073$$

$$\omega_4 = \frac{(0.0585 \times 0.8889)}{\begin{pmatrix}(0.1703 \times 0.0093) + (0.1582 \times 0.0083)+ \\ (0.1207 \times 0.0435) + (0.0585 \times 0.8889)+ \\ (0.1451 \times 0.0293) + (0.3473 \times 0.0207)\end{pmatrix}} = 0.727$$

$$\omega_5 = \frac{(0.1451 \times 0.0293)}{\begin{pmatrix}(0.1703 \times 0.0093) + (0.1582 \times 0.0083)+ \\ (0.1207 \times 0.0435) + (0.0585 \times 0.8889)+ \\ (0.1451 \times 0.0293) + (0.3473 \times 0.0207)\end{pmatrix}} = 0.059$$

$$\omega_6 = \frac{(0.3473 \times 0.0207)}{\begin{pmatrix}(0.1703 \times 0.0093) + (0.1582 \times 0.0083)+ \\ (0.1207 \times 0.0435) + (0.0585 \times 0.8889)+ \\ (0.1451 \times 0.0293) + (0.3473 \times 0.0207)\end{pmatrix}} = 0.100$$

The results show that Criterion 4 dominates the weighting with an aggregate weight of 0.727, indicating it has the highest overall significance in the decision-making process. This confirms its critical role, consistent with its high diversification and impact loss values. The next most important criteria are Criterion 6 (0.100) and Criterion 3 (0.073), followed by Criterion 5 (0.059). Meanwhile, Criteria 1 and 2 have the lowest combined weights (0.022 and 0.018, respectively), reflecting their limited influence due to lower variability and smaller impact loss. This integrated weighting approach effectively balances the contribution of each criterion from both statistical dispersion and impact perspectives, emphasizing the criteria that should be prioritized for a more robust and data-driven evaluation.

19.5 Conclusion

This chapter has presented the theoretical foundations, methodological steps, and practical applications of the IDOCRIW method. By integrating the entropy method, which captures variability and informational diversity in data with the CILOS method, which measures the relative importance of attributes through comparative loss analysis—IDOCRIW offers a robust solution to the persistent challenge of assigning objective weights in MADM. This dual perspective ensures that attributes are evaluated not only on the basis of their statistical variability but also in terms of their contextual impact, resulting in a more balanced, stable, and reliable weighting system. The numerical case studies demonstrate that criteria with both high variability and significant impact loss are assigned appropriately higher weights, ensuring that the decision framework prioritizes the most critical attributes. This integration of data-driven and performance-oriented perspectives enables decision-makers to obtain results that are both statistically rigorous and practically meaningful. Despite these strengths, IDOCRIW is not without limitations. Its current formulation assumes independence among criteria, an assumption that may not always hold in interdependent systems. Furthermore, its reliance on crisp data restricts its applicability in environments characterized by uncertainty, fuzziness, or linguistic ambiguity. Addressing these challenges represents a promising direction for future research. Potential extensions include adapting the method to fuzzy, interval-valued, hesitant, or probabilistic environments; integrating it with machine learning models for dynamic weighting in large-scale datasets; and developing domain-specific modifications. Ultimately, IDOCRIW bridges data-driven dispersion analysis and context-driven performance evaluation, equipping decision-makers with a transparent and adaptable tool for multi-criteria analysis. Beyond its theoretical contributions, it has also demonstrated value in various domains, highlighting its potential as a versatile decision-support instrument in complex and uncertain environments.

References

Alao, M. A., Popoola, O. M., & Ayodele, T. R. (2021). Selection of waste-to-energy technology for distributed generation using IDOCRIW-Weighted TOPSIS method: A case study of the City of Johannesburg, South Africa. *Renewable Energy, 178*, 162–183.

Alinezhad, A., & Khalili, J. (2019). IDOCRIW method. In *New methods and applications in multiple attribute decision making (MADM)*. Springer International Publishing, 133–141 Vol. 277.

Das, A. (2025). Assessment of surface water quality modelling for drinking purposes in Brahmani River Basin (BRB), Odisha, using geographical information system (GIS), IDOCRIW (I) and COPRAS (Ui) techniques. In *Surface, sub-surface hydrology and management: Application of geospatial and geostatistical techniques*. Cham: Springer Nature Switzerland, 185–217.

Eghbali-Zarch, M., Tavakkoli-Moghaddam, R., Dehghan-Sanej, K., & Kaboli, A. (2021). Prioritizing the effective strategies for construction and demolition waste management using fuzzy IDOCRIW and WASPAS methods. *Engineering, Construction and Architectural Management*.

Hosouli, S., Gaikwad, N., Qamar, S. H., & Gomes, J. (2024). Optimizing photovoltaic thermal (PVT) collector selection: A multi-criteria decision-making (MCDM) approach for renewable energy systems. *Heliyon, 10*(6), e27605.

Ji, Z., Li, W., & Niu, D. (2024). Optimal investment decision of agrivoltaic coupling energy storage project based on distributed linguistic trust and hybrid evaluation method. *Applied Energy, 353*, 122139.

Luo, Y., Zhang, X., Qin, Y., Yang, Z., & Liang, Y. (2021). Tourism attraction selection with sentiment analysis of online reviews based on probabilistic linguistic term sets and the IDOCRIW-COCOSO model. *International Journal of Fuzzy Systems, 23*(1), 295–308.

Naz, S., Shafiq, A., Butt, S. A., Mazhar, S., Martinez, D. J., & De La Hoz Franco, E. (2024). Decision analysis with IDOCRIW-QUALIFLEX approach in the 2TLq-ROF environment: An application of accident prediction models in Pakistan. *Heliyon, 10*(6).

Parthasarathy, T. N., Narayanamoorthy, S., Thilagasree, C. S., Marimuthu, P. R., Salahshour, S., Ferrara, M., & Ahmadian, A. (2024). An enhanced fuzzy IDOCRIW-COCOSO multi-attribute decision making algorithm for decisive electric vehicle battery recycling method. *Results in Engineering, 22*.

Shannon, C. E. (1948). A mathematical theory of communication. *Bell System Technical Journal, 27*(3), 379–423.

Zavadskas, E., Cavallaro, F., Podvezko, V., Ubarte, I., & Kaklauskas, A. (2017). MCDM assessment of a healthy and safe built environment according to sustainable development principles: A practical neighborhood approach in Vilnius. *Sustainability, 9*(5), 702.

Zavadskas, E. K., & Podvezko, V. (2016). Integrated determination of objective criteria weights in MCDM. *International Journal of Information Technology & Decision Making, 15*(2), 267–283.

Chapter 20

PIPRECIA: Pivot pair-wise relative criteria importance assessment method for multi-attribute decision-making

Ayşe Topal[1], Alptekin Ulutaş[2], and Ali Aygün Yürüyen[3]
[1]*Department of Business Administration, Faculty of Business and Economics Sciences, Nigde Omer Halisdemir University, Nigde, Turkiye,* [2]*Department of International Trade and Business, Faculty of Economics and Administrative Sciences, Inonu University, Malatya, Turkiye,* [3]*Department of Transportation Services, Nihat Delibalta Göle Vocational School, Göle, Ardahan, Turkiye*

20.1 Introduction

Decision-making problems require a complicated cognitive process that assesses diverse facets of a problem to find an optimal solution to the problem. These problems can involve precise or imprecise assumptions that are affected by various criteria such as economic, environmental, and social (Ananda & Herath, 2009; Saaty, 2005; Stević et al., 2018; Yalcin & Gul, 2017). For these reasons, decision-making becomes a highly complex process. Therefore, they are attempted to be solved by using several analytical approaches such as mathematical formulations, statistics, and economic theories (Ananda & Herath, 2009; Stević et al., 2018). One of them is multicriteria decision-making (MCDM). MCDM is mostly defined by a set of various criteria (Vincke, 1992; Zavadskas & Turskis, 2011). They are developed to deal with real-life issues that involve inconsistent and conflicting criteria (Bakır et al., 2020). They simply assess the alternatives that are presented to solve the decision problem, with the criteria that are developed specifically for determining the performance of alternatives (Bakır et al., 2021; Stanujkić, Karabasevic, & Popovic, 2021; Stanujkić, Karabasevic, Popovic, & Sava, 2021). MCDM techniques differ from other techniques, such as statistical analysis, because they are able to assess all criteria regardless of objective or nonobjective (Karamaşa, 2021).

Various MCDM techniques have been presented to deal with decision issues in various sectors over the last few decades, such as health, engineering, logistics, transportation, and energy (Kumar & Pamucar, 2025). These techniques distinguish from each other with the quantity and quality of criteria, the mathematical approach followed, the ease of method, and the sensitivity analysis employed (Zavadskas & Turskis, 2011).

Weight determination of criteria is a significantly important step in MCDM because criteria weights identify the relative significance of each criterion and enable the decision-making process (Ayan et al., 2023; Pamučar et al., 2018; Žižović & Pamucar, 2019). Also, they directly affect the precision and reliability of the ranking results of alternatives (Singh & Pant, 2021). Several MCDM methods have been proposed to determine the importance level of the criteria weights. Table 20.1 summarizes the criteria weighing MCDM techniques used in the literature.

The pairwise relative criteria importance assessment (PIPRECIA) technique was developed as a step-wise weight assessment ratio analysis (SWARA)-based model to reveal the mental tendencies and evaluation approaches of decision makers (Dm) in a more systematic way (Bakır et al., 2021; Stanujkić et al., 2017). It handles the restriction of the SWARA technique (Stanujkić, Karabasevic, & Popovic, 2021; Stanujkić, Karabasevic, Popovic, & Sava, 2021). The criteria weights are calculated solely based on comparisons of relative importance levels among criteria rather than on the decision maker's personal judgments (Truong & Thinh, 2022). The PIPRECIA technique may have some benefits, as it does not need the use of an ordered list of evaluation criteria (Stanujkić et al., 2017). The main benefit of the PIPRECIA technique is that it allows the evaluation of criteria without prior ranking of importance, which the SWARA technique does not (Stević et al., 2018). However, the absence of a consistency index in the calculation structure of the SWARA technique

Encyclopedia of Multi-Attribute Decision-Making (MADM). DOI: https://doi.org/10.1016/B978-0-443-33275-3.00021-X

TABLE 20.1 The review of criteria weighing multicriteria decision-making techniques.

Methods	Developed by	Used by
Analytic hierarchy process	Saaty (1977, 1980)	Dutta and Deka (2024), Hamidah et al. (2022), Kang et al. (2024)
CRITIC	Diakoulaki et al. (1995)	Du et al. (2024), Hassan et al. (2023), Mukhametzyanov (2021)
SWARA	Keršuliene et al. (2010)	Karamaşa (2021), Kumar and Rajak (2025), Seker and Aydin (2022)
PSI	Maniya and Bhatt (2011)	Mahesh et al. (2021), Obeidat and Beliah (2024), Van Dua (2025)
Best–worst method	Rezaei (2015)	Aryafar and Roshanravan (2021), Mostafa (2021), Shakeri et al. (2023)
CILOS	Zavadskas and Podvezko (2016)	Chatterjee and Chakraborty (2024), Das (2025), Naz et al. (2024)
IDOCRIW	Zavadskas and Podvezko (2016)	Alao et al. (2021), Luo et al. (2021), Wang et al. (2024)
FUCOM	Pamučar et al. (2018)	Abdullah et al. (2022), Gökler (2024), Khazaelpour and Zolfani (2024)
MEREC	Keshavarz-Ghorabaee et al. (2021)	Fan et al. (2024), Kara et al. (2024), Ulutaş et al. (2023)
LOPCOW	Ecer and Pamucar (2022)	Ecer et al. (2023), Riaz et al. (2024), Sharma et al. (2025)
SIWEC	Puška et al. (2024)	Katrancı et al. (2026), Nedeljković et al. (2024), Puška et al. (2025)

creates limitations in terms of questioning the reliability of Dm's opinions. In response to this deficiency, the PIPRECIA technique provides the opportunity to test the consistency of Dm's ranking-based evaluations with Kendall's Tau or Spearman's ranking correlation coefficient (Bakır et al., 2020; Stanujkić et al., 2019). The PIPRECIA technique is effective in group-based decision-making processes involving a large number of criteria or expert opinions, as it significantly reduces the cognitive load of Dm by reducing the number of pairwise comparisons (Bakır et al., 2021; Stanujkić et al., 2017). Table 20.2 shows the studies using the PIPRECIA method.

20.2 Methodology

The weights of criteria are calculated using the PIPRECIA as shown below (Stanujkić et al., 2017):

Step 1: The criteria are determined, and Dm assess the relative significance of each criterion compared to the next criterion. However, it is not mandatory to order the criteria in a hierarchical manner, and this step can be skipped optionally.

Step 2: Beginning from the second criterion, relative significance levels are established in line with the structural framework presented below.

$$s_j = \begin{cases} >1 & \text{if } C_j > C_{j-1} \\ =1 & \text{if } C_j = C_{j-1} \\ <1 & \text{if } C_j < C_{j-1} \end{cases} \tag{20.1}$$

Here, C_j represents the significance of criterion j, while C_{j-1} represents the significance of the previous criterion $j-1$.

Step 3: The k_j coefficient is obtained by Eq. (20.2).

$$k_j = \begin{cases} 1 & \text{if } j = 1 \\ 2 - s_j & \text{if } j > 1 \end{cases} \tag{20.2}$$

TABLE 20.2 The review of studies using PIPRECIA.

Studies	Methods		Decision problem
	Criteria weighting	Alternative ranking	
Stanujkic et al. (2018)	PIPRECIA	Weighted sum preferred levels of performances	Evaluation of website quality in the hotel industry
Tomašević et al. (2020)	Fuzzy PIPRECIA	-	Prioritization of high-performance computing criteria
Đalić et al. (2020)	Fuzzy PIPRECIA	Interval rough saw	Green supplier selection
Ulutaş et al. (2020)	PIPRECIA-G	OCRA-G	Personnel selection
Özdağoğlu et al. (2021)	PIPRECIA	COPRAS, MOPA, MOOSRA, ROV, SAW, and WPM	Motorbike selection
Stanujkić, Karabasevic and Popovic (2021), Stanujkić, Karabasevic, Popovic and Sava (2021)	PIPRECIA	PIPRECIA	Website assessment
Aytekin (2022)	PIPRECIA-S	-	Prioritization of transportation criteria
Truong and Thinh (2022)	PIPRECIA	FUCA	Lathe selection
Mladenovic et al. (2023)	PIPRECIA-S	PIPRECIA-S	Platform assessment
Arshad and Rahmanto (2024)	PIPRECIA	TOPSIS	Hotal assessment
Setiawansyah et al. (2024)	PIPRECIA-S	MABAC	Leader selection
Stanujkić et al. (2024)	PIPRECIA-S	MULTIMOORA	Employee assessment
Yildirim et al. (2024)	Fermatean fuzzy PIPRECIA	FF-VIKOR	Location selection for electric vehicle sharing stations
Sarbat (2024)	PIPRECIA-S	-	Prioritizing psychosocial risks in job satisfaction
Vikas and Mishra (2024)	Fuzzy PIPRECIA	-	Prioritization of total productive maintenance criteria
Mirčetić et al. (2024)	CRITIC and PIPRECIA-S	COBRA	Innovative human resource management selection
Alnoor et al. (2025)	Z-cloud rough fuzzy-based PIPRECIA	Z-cloud rough fuzzy-based CoCoSo	Evaluation of agricultural decision support tools.
Popović et al. (2025)	PIPRECIA-S	-	Prioritizing criteria for AI Algorithm Selection
Marinović et al. (2025)	PIPRECIA	Net worth analysis	Operating system selection

Step 4: The recalculated weight q_j is obtained by Eq. (20.3).

$$q_j = \begin{cases} 1 & if\ j = 1 \\ \frac{q_{j-1}}{k_j} & if\ j > 1 \end{cases} \tag{20.3}$$

Step 5: Relative weights of evaluation criteria are calculated by Eq. (20.4). n represents the number of criteria.

$$w_j = \frac{q_j}{\sum_{k=1}^{n} q_k} \tag{20.4}$$

Here w_j indicates the relative weight of criterion j.

Step 6: If there is more than one decision maker, the weights are determined with Eqs. (20.5) and (20.6). p demonstrates the pth decision maker, and Z represents the number of Dm.

$$w'_j = \left(\prod_{p=1}^{Z} w_j^p \right)^{1/Z} \tag{20.5}$$

$$w_j = \frac{w'_j}{\sum_{j=1}^{n} w'_j} \tag{20.6}$$

20.3 Numerical examples

In this chapter, two separate applications were carried out to demonstrate the applicability of the PIPRECIA method.

20.3.1 Numerical example 1

In this chapter, two separate applications were carried out to show the applicability of the PIPRECIA technique. The first application includes a simple problem scenario that allows understanding of the basic operating logic of the method. Five criteria were evaluated in the analysis. Of these criteria, CRT1, CRT2, and CRT3 are benefit criteria, while CRT4 and CRT5 are cost criteria. The data used in the chapter were obtained with the help of a Monte Carlo simulation. The results obtained after completing the steps of the technique systematically are presented in Table 20.3. How to calculate an element of a matrix

k_3, q_3 and w_3 are explained below.

$$k_3 = 2 - 0.38 = 1.6200$$

$$q_3 = \frac{0.5291}{1.6200} = 0.3266$$

$$w_3 = \frac{0.3266}{2.6137} = 0.1250$$

20.3.2 Numerical example 2

The decision matrices used in this section were created using Monte Carlo simulation, taking into account the opinions of four Dm. In this application, the criterion weights were calculated for a more difficult decision problem involving more criteria and alternatives than in application 1. The individual decision matrices of the expert opinions and the PIPRECIA method results are presented in Table 20.4 (Dm1), Table 20.5 (Dm2), Table 20.6 (Dm3), and Table 20.7 (Dm4), respectively. How to calculate an element of a matrix

k_3, q_3 and w_3 are explained below.

TABLE 20.3 PIPRECIA calculations.

		s_j	k_j	q_j	w_j	**Ranking criteria**
CRT2	1		1	1	0.3826	1
CRT4	2	0.1100	1.8900	0.5291	0.2024	2
CRT1	3	0.3800	1.6200	0.3266	0.1250	4
CRT5	4	1.3400	0.6600	0.4948	0.1893	3
CRT3	5	0.1200	1.8800	0.2632	0.1007	5

The findings present that the criteria weights are ranked as CRT2 > CRT4 > CRT5 > CRT1 > CRT3.

TABLE 20.4 PIPRECIA calculations for decision makers1.

		s_j	k_j	q_j	w_j	Ranking criteria
CRT12	1		1	1	0.0214	9
CRT15	2	0.7500	1.2500	0.8000	0.0171	13
CRT11	3	0.9600	1.0400	0.7692	0.0165	14
CRT3	4	1.0400	0.9600	0.8013	0.0172	12
CRT6	5	1.1300	0.8700	0.9210	0.0197	11
CRT10	6	1	1	1	0.0214	9
CRT5	7	0.1300	1.8700	0.5348	0.0115	15
CRT9	8	1.5600	0.4400	1.2155	0.0261	8
CRT8	9	1.7200	0.2800	4.3411	0.0931	5
CRT7	10	0.5900	1.4100	3.0788	0.066	7
CRT14	11	1.5700	0.4300	7.1600	0.1535	2
CRT1	12	0.4300	1.5700	4.5605	0.0978	4
CRT4	13	1.5700	0.4300	10.6058	0.2273	1
CRT13	14	0.1100	1.8900	5.6115	0.1203	3
CRT2	15	0.6800	1.3200	4.2511	0.0911	6

According to the PIPRECIA method result for Dm1, the priority order according to the weight of the criteria is CRT4 > CRT14 > CRT13 > CRT1 > CRT8 > CRT2 > CRT7 > CRT9 > CRT10 = CRT12 > CRT6 > CRT3 > CRT15 > CRT11 > CRT5.

TABLE 20.5 PIPRECIA calculations for decision makers2.

		s_j	k_j	q_j	w_j	Ranking criteria
CRT15	1		1	1	0.0292	6
CRT7	2	0.65	1.35	0.7407	0.0217	11
CRT11	3	1.2900	0.7100	1.0432	0.0305	5
CRT8	4	0.8700	1.1300	0.9232	0.0270	9
CRT3	5	1.1200	0.8800	1.0491	0.0307	4
CRT10	6	0.1500	1.8500	0.5671	0.0166	14
CRT4	7	0.3600	1.6400	0.3458	0.0101	15
CRT12	8	1.6200	0.3800	0.9100	0.0266	10
CRT5	9	1.1500	0.8500	1.0706	0.0313	3
CRT14	10	0.3800	1.6200	0.6609	0.0193	12
CRT9	11	0.9600	1.0400	0.6355	0.0186	13
CRT2	12	1.3300	0.6700	0.9485	0.0277	7
CRT1	13	1	1	0.9485	0.0277	7
CRT6	14	1.8400	0.1600	5.9281	0.1733	2
CRT13	15	1.6600	0.3400	17.4356	0.5097	1

According to the PIPRECIA method result for Dm2, the priority order according to the weight of the criteria is CRT13 > CRT6 > CRT5 > CRT3 > CRT11 > CRT15 > CRT1 = CRT2 > CRT8 > CRT12 > CRT12 > CRT7 > CRT14 > CRT9 > CRT10 > CRT4.

TABLE 20.6 PIPRECIA calculations for decision makers3.

		s_j	k_j	q_j	w_j	Ranking criteria
CRT3	1		1	1	0.0853	5
CRT8	2	1.0600	0.9400	1.0638	0.0908	2
CRT12	3	1.1500	0.8500	1.2515	0.1068	1
CRT6	4	0.4800	1.5200	0.8234	0.0703	7
CRT7	5	0.7500	1.2500	0.6587	0.0562	10
CRT15	6	1.0200	0.9800	0.6721	0.0573	9
CRT11	7	1.3500	0.6500	1.0340	0.0882	4
CRT10	8	0.3200	1.6800	0.6155	0.0525	12
CRT5	9	0.6400	1.3600	0.4526	0.0386	13
CRT2	10	0.9300	1.0700	0.4230	0.0361	14
CRT13	11	1.5300	0.4700	0.9000	0.0768	6
CRT9	12	1.1500	0.8500	1.0588	0.0903	3
CRT14	13	0.5200	1.4800	0.7154	0.0610	8
CRT1	14	0.8800	1.1200	0.6388	0.0545	11
CRT4	15	0.4500	1.5500	0.4121	0.0352	15

According to the PIPRECIA method result for Dm3, the priority order according to the weight of the criteria is CRT12 > CRT8 > CRT9 > CRT11 > CRT3 > CRT13 > CRT6 > CRT14 > CRT15 > CRT7 > CRT1 > CRT10 > CRT5 > CRT2 > CRT4.

TABLE 20.7 PIPRECIA calculations for decision makers4.

		s_j	k_j	q_j	w_j	Ranking criteria
CRT6	1		1	1	0.0329	10
CRT10	2	0.1900	1.8100	0.5525	0.0182	15
CRT5	3	1.1100	0.8900	0.6208	0.0204	14
CRT12	4	1.3300	0.6700	0.9266	0.0305	12
CRT8	5	1.3600	0.6400	1.4478	0.0476	7
CRT3	6	1.1900	0.8100	1.7874	0.0588	6
CRT11	7	0.5800	1.4200	1.2587	0.0414	8
CRT9	8	0.7300	1.2700	0.9911	0.0326	11
CRT14	9	1.1000	0.9000	1.1012	0.0362	9
CRT1	10	0.6200	1.3800	0.7980	0.0262	13
CRT13	11	1.8800	0.1200	6.6500	0.2187	1
CRT15	12	0.4900	1.5100	4.4040	0.1448	2
CRT7	13	0.2700	1.7300	2.5457	0.0837	5
CRT2	14	1.1600	0.8400	3.0306	0.0997	4
CRT4	15	1.0800	0.9200	3.2941	0.1083	3

According to the PIPRECIA method result for Dm4, the priority order according to the weight of the criteria is CRT13 > CRT15 > CRT4 > CRT2 > CRT7 > CRT3 > CRT8 > CRT11 > CRT14 > CRT6 > CRT9 > CRT12 > CRT1 > CRT5 > CRT10.

TABLE 20.8 Combined criteria weights.

	CRT1	CRT2	CRT3	CRT4	CRT5	CRT6	CRT7	CRT8
w_j	0.0443	0.0549	0.0403	0.0544	0.0231	0.0530	0.0509	0.0574
Rank	9	3	10	4	15	5	6	2
	CRT9	**CRT10**	**CRT11**	**CRT12**	**CRT13**	**CRT14**	**CRT15**	
w_j	0.0346	0.0241	0.0368	0.0369	0.1791	0.0506	0.0451	
Rank	13	14	12	11	1	7	8	

The order of the craters formed according to the combined criteria weights is CRT13 > CRT8 > CRT2 > CRT4 > CRT6 > CRT7 > CRT14 > CRT15 > CRT1 > CRT3 > CRT12 > CRT11 > CRT9 > CRT10 > CRT5.

$$k_3 = 2 - 0.9600 = 1.0400$$

$$q_3 = \frac{0.8000}{1.0400} = 0.7692$$

$$w_3 = \frac{0.7692}{46.6506} = 0.0165$$

The PIPRECIA method results obtained from four different Dm were combined with the geometric mean method, and the resulting combined criterion weights are presented in Table 20.8.

20.4 Conclusion

There are several methods utilized for finding the criteria weights in MCDM; PIPRECIA is one of these methods. The main distinguishing feature of PIPRECIA is that it does not require ranking the priority of criteria. Therefore, it provides an easily applicable and understandable way for the criteria weights.

PIPRECIA is applied to two different cases (numerical example 1 and numerical example 2) with different difficulty levels to provide the accuracy and feasibility of the technique. The criteria weights in a simple decision problem are calculated in the first example, while in the second example, the criteria weights in a more difficult and complicated decision problem are found. The findings show that in the first example, the criteria weights in Table 20.3 are ranked as follows: CRT2 > CRT4 > CRT5 > CRT1 > CRT3. In the second example, the combined weights of criteria (see Table 20.8) are ordered as CRT13 > CRT8 > CRT2 > CRT4 > CRT6 > CRT7 > CRT14 > CRT15 > CRT1 > CRT3 > CRT12 > CRT11 > CRT9 > CRT10 > CRT5. These results show that the PIPRECIA method can be successfully applied to both simple and difficult decision problems, as it provides reliable results.

While the PIPRECIA method is discussed in detail in this chapter, it has two limitations. First, it does not include expert opinions from companies operating in a specific industry to assess the applicability of PIPRECIA in real cases. Therefore, future studies can use expert opinions from industry to make PIPRECIA produce more reliable results. Second, it has a low number of criteria. Future studies can expand by increasing the number of criteria evaluated. Also, the PIPRECIA can be extended using fuzzy, rough, or gray theories to handle uncertainty. Furthermore, it can be integrated with other MCDM methods to develop a comprehensive decision-making approach.

References

Abdullah, A., Ahmad, S., Athar, M. A., Rajpoot, N., & Talib, F. (2022). Healthcare performance management using integrated FUCOM-MARCOS approach: The case of India. *The International Journal of Health Planning and Management, 37*(5), 2635–2668. https://doi.org/10.1002/hpm.3488.

Alao, M. A., Popoola, O. M., & Ayodele, T. R. (2021). Selection of waste-to-energy technology for distributed generation using IDOCRIW-Weighted TOPSIS method: A case study of the city of Johannesburg, South Africa. *Renewable Energy, 178*, 162–183. https://doi.org/10.1016/j.renene.2021.06.031.

Alnoor, A., Muhsen, Y. R., Husin, N. A., Chew, X., Zolkepli, M. B., & Manshor, N. (2025). Z-cloud rough fuzzy-based PIPRECIA and CoCoSo integration to assess agriculture decision support tools. *International Journal of Fuzzy Systems, 27*(1), 190–203. https://doi.org/10.1007/s40815-024-01771-7.

Ananda, J., & Herath, G. (2009). A critical review of multi-criteria decision making methods with special reference to forest management and planning. *Ecological Economics, 68*(10), 2535–2548. https://doi.org/10.1016/j.ecolecon.2009.05.010.

Arshad, M. W., & Rahmanto, Y. (2024). Combination of TOPSIS method and PIPRECIA weighting for best hotel selection. *International Journal of Informatics and Data Science, 1*(2), 46–54.

Aryafar, A., & Roshanravan, B. (2021). BWM-SAW: A new hybrid MCDM technique for modeling of chromite potential in the Birjand district, east of Iran. *Journal of Geochemical Exploration, 231*, 106876. https://doi.org/10.1016/j.gexplo.2021.106876.

Ayan, B., Abacıoğlu, S., & Basilio, M. P. (2023). A comprehensive review of the novel weighting methods for multi-criteria decision-making. *Information, 14*(5), 285. https://doi.org/10.3390/info14050285.

Aytekin, A. (2022). Determining criteria weights for vehicle tracking system selection using PIPRECIA-S. *Journal of Process Management and New Technologies, 10*(1-2), 115–124. https://doi.org/10.5937/jpmnt10-38145.

Bakır, M., Akan, Ş., Kiraci, K., Karabasevic, D., Stanujkić, D., & Popovic, G. (2020). Multiple-criteria approach of the operational performance evaluation in the airline industry: Evidence from the emerging markets. *Romanian Journal of Economic Forecasting, 23*(2), 149–172.

Bakır, M., Akan, Ş., & Özdemir, E. (2021). Regional aircraft selection with fuzzy PIPRECIA and fuzzy MARCOS: A case study of the Turkish airline industry. *Facta Universitatis, Series: Mechanical Engineering, 19*(3), 423–445. https://doi.org/10.22190/FUME210505053B.

Chatterjee, S., & Chakraborty, S. (2024). A study on the effects of objective weighting methods on TOPSIS-based parametric optimization of non-traditional machining processes. *Decision Analytics Journal, 11*, 100451. https://doi.org/10.1016/j.dajour.2024.100451.

Đalić, I., Stević, Ž., Karamasa, C., & Puška, A. (2020). A novel integrated fuzzy PIPRECIA–interval rough SAW model: Green supplier selection. *Decision Making: Applications in Management and Engineering, 3*(1), 126–145. https://doi.org/10.31181/dmame2003114d.

Das, A. (2025). Water pollution and water quality assessment and application of criterion impact loss (CILOS), geographical information system (GIS), artificial neural network (ANN) and decision-learning technique in river water quality management: An experiment on the Mahanadi catchment, Odisha, India. *Desalination and Water Treatment, 321*, 100969. https://doi.org/10.1016/j.dwt.2024.100969.

Diakoulaki, D., Mavrotas, G., & Papayannakis, L. (1995). Determining objective weights in multiple criteria problems: The critic method. *Computers & Operations Research, 22*(7), 763–770. https://doi.org/10.1016/0305-0548(94)00059-H.

Du, X., Wang, Y., & Chen, F. (2024). Evaluation of coal-resource-based cities transformation based on CRITIC-TOPSIS model. *Sustainable Cities and Society, 103*, 105271. https://doi.org/10.1016/j.scs.2024.105271.

Dutta, P., & Deka, S. (2024). A novel approach to flood risk assessment: Synergizing with geospatial based MCDM-AHP model, multicollinearity, and sensitivity analysis in the Lower Brahmaputra Floodplain, Assam. *Journal of Cleaner Production, 467*, 142985. https://doi.org/10.1016/j.jclepro.2024.142985.

Ecer, F., Küçükönder, H., Kaya, S. K., & Görçün, Ö. F. (2023). Sustainability performance analysis of micro-mobility solutions in urban transportation with a novel IVFNN-Delphi-LOPCOW-CoCoSo framework. *Transportation Research Part A: Policy and Practice, 172*, 103667. https://doi.org/10.1016/j.tra.2023.103667.

Ecer, F., & Pamucar, D. (2022). A novel LOPCOW-DOBI multi-criteria sustainability performance assessment methodology: An application in developing country banking sector. *Omega, 112*, 102690. https://doi.org/10.1016/j.omega.2022.102690.

Fan, J., Lei, T., & Wu, M. (2024). MEREC-MABAC method based on cumulative prospect theory for picture fuzzy sets: Applications to wearable health technology devices. *Expert Systems with Applications, 255*, 124749. https://doi.org/10.1016/j.eswa.2024.124749.

Gökler, S. H. (2024). Optimal site selection for electric vehicle charging stations: Analysis with hybrid FUCOM and geographic information systems. *Energy, 307*, 132659. https://doi.org/10.1016/j.energy.2024.132659.

Hamidah, M., Hasmadi, I. M., Chua, L. S. L., Yong, W. S. Y., Lau, K. H., Faridah-Hanum, I., & Pakhriazad, H. Z. (2022). Development of a protocol for Malaysian important plant areas criterion weights using multi-criteria decision making-analytical hierarchy process (MCDM-AHP). *Global Ecology and Conservation, 34*, e02033. https://doi.org/10.1016/j.gecco.2022.e02033.

Hassan, I., Alhamrouni, I., & Azhan, N. H. (2023). A CRITIC–TOPSIS multi-criteria decision-making approach for optimum site selection for solar PV farm. *Energies, 16*(10), 4245. https://doi.org/10.3390/en16104245.

Kang, Y. O., Yabar, H., Mizunoya, T., & Higano, Y. (2024). Optimal landfill site selection using ArcGIS multi-criteria decision-making (MCDM) and analytic hierarchy process (AHP) for Kinshasa City. *Environmental Challenges, 14*, 100826. https://doi.org/10.1016/j.envc.2023.100826.

Kara, K., Yalçın, G. C., Acar, A. Z., Simic, V., Konya, S., & Pamucar, D. (2024). The MEREC-AROMAN method for determining sustainable competitiveness levels: A case study for Turkey. *Socio-economic Planning Sciences, 91*, 101762. https://doi.org/10.1016/j.seps.2023.101762.

Karamaşa, Ç. (2021). Ranking service quality using multi-criteria decision-making methods: Example of Erzurum province. *Journal of Process Management and New Technologies, 9*(3-4), 1–12. https://doi.org/10.5937/jpmnt9-33449.

Katrancı, A., Kundakcı, N., & Arman, K. (2026). Fuzzy SIWEC and fuzzy RAWEC methods for sustainable waste disposal technology selection. *Spectrum of Operational Research*, 87–102. https://doi.org/10.31181/sor31202633.

Keršuliene, V., Zavadskas, E. K., & Turskis, Z. (2010). Selection of rational dispute resolution method by applying new step-wise weight assessment ratio analysis (SWARA). *Journal of Business Economics and Management, 11*(2), 243–258. https://doi.org/10.3846/jbem.2010.12.

Keshavarz-Ghorabaee, M., Amiri, M., Zavadskas, E. K., Turskis, Z., & Antucheviciene, J. (2021). Determination of objective weights using a new method based on the removal effects of criteria (MEREC). *Symmetry, 13*(4), 525. https://doi.org/10.3390/sym13040525.

Khazaelpour, P., & Zolfani, S. H. (2024). FUCOM-optimization based predictive maintenance strategy using expert elicitation and Artificial Neural Network. *Expert Systems with Applications, 238*, 121322. https://doi.org/10.1016/j.eswa.2023.121322.

Kumar, A., & Rajak, S. (2025). Selection of bio-implant materials based on metal additive manufacturing using integrated SWARA and WASPAS MCDM technique. *Journal of Materials Engineering and Performance*, 1–21. https://doi.org/10.1007/s11665-024-10545-z.

Kumar, R., & Pamucar, D. (2025). A comprehensive and systematic review of multi-criteria decision-making (MCDM) methods to solve decision-making problems: Two decades from 2004 to 2024. *Spectrum of Decision Making and Applications, 2*(1), 178–197. https://doi.org/10.31181/sdmap21202524.

Luo, Y., Zhang, X., Qin, Y., Yang, Z., & Liang, Y. (2021). Tourism attraction selection with sentiment analysis of online reviews based on probabilistic linguistic term sets and the IDOCRIW-COCOSO model. *International Journal of Fuzzy Systems, 23*(1), 295–308. https://doi.org/10.1016/j.rineng.2024.102272.

Mahesh, V., Joladarashi, S., & Kulkarni, S. M. (2021). Development and mechanical characterization of novel polymer-based flexible composite and optimization of stacking sequences using VIKOR and PSI techniques. *Journal of Thermoplastic Composite Materials, 34*(8), 1080–1102. https://doi.org/10.1177/0892705719864619.

Maniya, K. D., & Bhatt, M. G. (2011). An alternative multiple attribute decision making methodology for solving optimal facility layout design selection problems. *Computers & Industrial Engineering, 61*(3), 542–549. https://doi.org/10.1016/j.cie.2011.04.009.

Marinović, M., Viduka, D., Lavrnić, I., Stojčetović, B., Skulić, A., Bašić, A., Balaban, P., & Rastovac, D. (2025). An intelligent multi-criteria decision approach for selecting the optimal operating system for educational environments. *Electronics, 14*(3), 514. https://doi.org/10.3390/electronics14030514.

Mirčetić, V., Popović, G., Vukotić, S., Mihić, M., Kovačević, I., Đoković, A., & Slavković, M. (2024). Navigating the complexity of HRM practice: A multiple-criteria decision-making framework. *Mathematics, 12*(23), 3769. https://doi.org/10.3390/math12233769.

Mladenovic, M., Đukić, T., & Popovic, G. (2023). Analysis of financial reporting platforms based on the PIPRECIA-S Method. *Journal of Process Management and New Technologies, 11*(3-4), 95–104. https://doi.org/10.5937/jpmnt11-48186.

Mostafa, A. M. (2021). An MCDM approach for cloud computing service selection based on best-only method. *IEEE Access, 9*, 155072–155086. https://doi.org/10.1109/ACCESS.2021.3129716.

Mukhametzyanov, I. (2021). Specific character of objective methods for determining weights of criteria in MCDM problems: Entropy, CRITIC and SD. *Decision Making: Applications in Management and Engineering, 4*(2), 76–105. https://doi.org/10.31181/dmame210402076i.

Naz, S., Shafiq, A., & Butt, S. A. (2024). CILOS-WASPAS approach based on Schweizer–Sklar power operators for evaluating cosmetic brands in a group decision-making environment. *Granular Computing, 9*(3), 59. https://doi.org/10.1007/s41066-024-00481-7.

Nedeljković, M., Papović, Z., & Krstić, S. (2024). Assessment of the weight of factors influencing food losses using fuzzy multi-criteria analysis. *Economics of Agriculture, 71*(4), 1313–1324. https://doi.org/10.59267/ekoPolj24041313N.

Obeidat, M. S., & Beliah, M. K. (2024). The reliability of green supply chain management practices in the printing industry based on the PSI and IPA approaches. *International Journal of Logistics Systems and Management, 49*(2), 240–254. https://doi.org/10.1504/IJLSM.2024.141699.

Özdağoğlu, A., Keleş, M. K., Altınata, A., & Ulutaş, A. (2021). Combining different MCDM methods with the Copeland method: An investigation on motorcycle selection. *Journal of Process Management and New Technologies, 9*(3-4), 13–27. https://doi.org/10.5937/jpmnt9-34120.

Pamučar, D., Stević, Ž., & Sremac, S. (2018). A new model for determining weight coefficients of criteria in MCDM models: Full consistency method (FUCOM). *Symmetry, 10*(9), 393. https://doi.org/10.3390/sym10090393.

Popović, S., Viduka, D., Bašić, A., Dimić, V., Djukic, D., Nikolić, V., & Stokić, A. (2025). Optimization of artificial intelligence algorithm selection: PIPRECIA-S model and multi-criteria analysis. *Electronics, 14*(3), 562. https://doi.org/10.3390/electronics14030562.

Puška, A., Božanić, D., Štilić, A., Nedeljković, M., & Khalilzadeh, M. (2025). Application of fuzzy-rough methodology to the selection of electric tractors for small farms in Semberija. *Journal of Fuzzy Extension and Applications*e212931. https://doi.org/10.22105/jfea.2025.482890.1663.

Puška, A., Nedeljković, M., Pamučar, D., Božanić, D., & Simić, V. (2024). Application of the new simple weight calculation (SIWEC) method in the case study in the sales channels of agricultural products. *MethodsX, 13*, 102930. https://doi.org/10.1016/j.mex.2024.102930.

Rezaei, J. (2015). Best-worst multi-criteria decision-making method. *Omega, 53*, 49–57. https://doi.org/10.1016/j.omega.2014.11.009.

Riaz, M., Qamar, F., Tariq, S., & Alsager, K. (2024). AI-driven LOPCOW-AROMAN framework and topological data analysis using circular intuitionistic fuzzy information: Healthcare supply chain innovation. *Mathematics, 12*(22), 3593. https://doi.org/10.3390/math12223593.

Saaty, T. L (1977). A scaling method for priorities in hierarchical structures. *Journal of mathematical psychology, 15*(3), 234–281.

Saaty, T. L. (1980). *The Analytic Hierarchy Process*. New York: McGraw-Hill.

Saaty, T. L. (2005). *Theory and applications of the analytic network process: Decision making with benefits, opportunities, costs, and risks*. RWS publications.

Sarbat, I. (2024). A MCDM-based measurement proposal of job satisfaction comprising psychosocial risks. *Ergonomics, 67*(12), 1909–1924. https://doi.org/10.1080/00140139.2024.2361301.

Seker, S., & Aydin, N. (2022). Assessment of hydrogen production methods via integrated MCDM approach under uncertainty. *International Journal of Hydrogen Energy, 47*(5), 3171–3184. https://doi.org/10.1016/j.ijhydene.2021.07.232.

Setiawansyah, S., Hadad, S. H., Aldino, A. A., Palupiningsih, P., Laxmi, G. F., & Megawaty, D. A. (2024). Employing PIPRECIA-S weighting with MABAC: A strategy for identifying organizational leadership elections. *Bulletin of Electrical Engineering and Informatics, 13*(6), 4273–4284. https://doi.org/10.11591/eei.v13i6.7713.

Shakeri, R., Alijani, F., & Nassery, H. R. (2023). Comparison of the DRASTIC+ L and modified VABHAT models in vulnerability assessment of Karaj aquifer, central Iran, using MCDM, SWARA, and BWM methods. *Environmental Earth Sciences, 82*(4), 97. https://doi.org/10.1007/s12665-023-10773-x.

Sharma, P., Nila, B., Pamucar, D., & Roy, J. (2025). Integrating LOPCOW-DOBI method and possibilistic programming for two-stage decision making in resilient food supply chain network. *Journal of Industrial Information Integration*100847. https://doi.org/10.1016/j.jii.2025.100847.

Singh, M., & Pant, M. (2021). A review of selected weighing methods in MCDM with a case study. *International Journal of System Assurance Engineering and Management, 12*, 126–144. https://doi.org/10.1007/s13198-020-01033-3.

Stanujkic, D., Karabasevic, D., & Cipriana, S. A. V. A. (2018). An application of the PIPRECIA and WS PLP methods for evaluating website quality in hotel industry. *Quaestus, 12*, 190–198.

Stanujkić, D., Karabasevic, D., & Popovic, G. (2021). Ranking alternatives using PIPRECIA method: A case of hotels' website evaluation. *Journal of Process Management and New Technologies, 9*(3-4), 62–68. https://doi.org/10.5937/jpmnt9-34506.

Stanujkić, D., Karabasevic, D., Popovic, G., & Sava, C. (2021). Simplified pivot pairwise relative criteria importance assessment (PIPRECIA-S) method. *Romanian Journal of Economic Forecasting, 24*(4), 141.

Stanujkić, D., Karabasevic, D., Zavadskas, E. K., Florentin Smarandache, F., & Cavallaro, F. (2019). An approach to determining customer satisfaction in traditional Serbian restaurants. *Entrepreneurship and Sustainability Issues, 6*(3), 1127–1138. https://doi.org/10.9770/jesi.2019.6.3(5).

Stanujkić, D., Zavadskas, E. K., Karabasevic, D., Smarandache, F., & Turskis, Z. (2017). The use of the pivot pairwise relative criteria importance assessment method for determining the weights of criteria. *Romanian Journal of Economic Forecasting, 20*(4), 116–133.

Stanujkić, M., Popović, G., Karabašević, D., Šarčević, M., Stanujkić, D., & Novaković, S. (2024). Approach to the personnel selection in a group decision-making environment based on the use of the MULTIMOORA and PIPRECIA-S methods. *BizInfo Blace, 15*(1), 19–26. https://doi.org/10.5937/bizinfo2401019S.

Stević, Ž., Stjepanović, Ž., Božičković, Z., Das, D. K., & Stanujkić, D. (2018). Assessment of conditions for implementing information technology in a warehouse system: A novel fuzzy PIPRECIA method. *Symmetry, 10*(11), 586. https://doi.org/10.3390/sym10110586.

Tomašević, M., Lapuh, L., Stević, Ž., Stanujkić, D., & Karabašević, D. (2020). Evaluation of criteria for the implementation of high-performance computing (HPC) in Danube Region countries using fuzzy PIPRECIA method. *Sustainability, 12*(7), 3017. https://doi.org/10.3390/su12073017.

Truong, N. X., & Thinh, H. X. (2022). Combined PIPRECIA method and modified FUCA method for selection of lathe. *Journal of Applied Engineering Science, 20*(4), 1355–1365. https://doi.org/10.5937/jaes0-39335.

Ulutaş, A., Balo, F., & Topal, A. (2023). Identifying the most efficient natural fibre for common commercial building insulation materials with an integrated PSI, MEREC, LOPCOW and MCRAT model. *Polymers, 15*(6), 1500. https://doi.org/10.3390/polym15061500.

Ulutaş, A., Popovic, G., Stanujkic, D., Karabasevic, D., Zavadskas, E. K., & Turskis, Z. (2020). A new hybrid MCDM model for personnel selection based on a novel grey PIPRECIA and grey OCRA methods. *Mathematics, 8*(10), 1698. https://doi.org/10.3390/math8101698.

Van Dua, T. (2025). Application of the PSI method in selecting sustainable energy development technologies. *Engineering, Technology & Applied Science Research, 15*(1), 19596–19601. https://doi.org/10.48084/etasr.9317.

Vikas, & Mishra, A. (2024). Evaluation of TPM adoption factors in manufacturing organizations using fuzzy PIPRECIA method. *Journal of Quality in Maintenance Engineering, 30*(1), 101–119. https://doi.org/10.1108/JQME-11-2020-0115.

Vincke, P. (1992). *Multicriteria Decision Aid*. New York: Wiley.

Wang, J., Wen, J., Pajić, V., & Andrejić, M. (2024). Optimizing cross-dock terminal location selection: A multi-step approach based on CI-DEA–IDOCRIW–MABAC for enhanced supply chain efficiency—A case study. *Mathematics, 12*(5), 736. https://doi.org/10.3390/math12050736.

Yalcin, M., & Gul, F. K. (2017). A GIS-based multi criteria decision analysis approach for exploring geothermal resources: Akarcay basin (Afyonkarahisar). *Geothermics, 67*, 18–28. https://doi.org/10.1016/j.geothermics.2017.01.002.

Yildirim, B., Ayyildiz, E., & Aydin, N. (2024). Optimal location selection for electric vehicle car-sharing stations using Fermatean fuzzy decision-making methodology. *Journal of Cleaner Production, 485*, 144400.

Zavadskas, E. K., & Podvezko, V. (2016). Integrated determination of objective criteria weights in MCDM. *International Journal of Information Technology & Decision Making, 15*(02), 267–283. https://doi.org/10.1142/S0219622016500036.

Zavadskas, E. K., & Turskis, Z. (2011). Multiple criteria decision making (MCDM) methods in economics: An overview. *Technological and Economic Development of Economy, 17*(2), 397–427. https://doi.org/10.3846/20294913.2011.593291.

Žižović, M., & Pamucar, D. (2019). New model for determining criteria weights: Level based weight assessment (LBWA) model. *Decision Making: Applications in Management and Engineering, 2*(2), 126–137. https://doi.org/10.31181/dmame1902102z.

Chapter 21

FUCOM: Full consistency method for multi-attribute decision-making

Dragan Pamucar[1,2,3], Ibrahim Badi[4], Mouhamed Bayane Bouraima[5], and George Baryannis[6]

[1]*Department of Operations Research and Statistics, University of Belgrade, Belgrade, Serbia,* [2]*UNEC Applied Artificial Intelligence Research Center, Azerbaijan State University of Economics (UNEC), Baku, Azerbaijan,* [3]*Faculty of Engineering, Dogus University, Istanbul, Türkiye,* [4]*Libyan Academy, Misrata, Libya,* [5]*International School of Technical Education, Sichuan University of Architectural Technology, Deyang, P.R. China,* [6]*School of Computing and Engineering, University of Huddersfield, Huddersfield, United Kingdom*

21.1 Introduction

The use of criterion weights in multi-attribute decision-making (MADM) is critical in making decisions and maintaining legitimacy (Ayan et al., 2023). MADM addresses decision problems with multiple, often conflicting criteria, and weights determine the relative importance of each criterion, in a given context (Chachi & Kazemifard, 2024; Mardani, Jusoh, Zavadskas, Khalifah et al., 2017). The weighting process has a substantial impact in the validity and reliability of the final decision (Ishizaka & Siraj, 2018).

Research on MADM has continued to show that changes in criterion weights can significantly alter decision outcomes, therefore it is paramount to have a robust, transparent, and justifiable weighting process (Kumar et al., 2017). Deciding on what this process will entail has a knock-on effect on the validity, robustness, and transparency of the decision-making process itself (Zavadskas et al., 2014). Several factors should be considered when selecting a weighting method:

1. Suitability: is the method appropriate for the specific decision problem at hand?
2. Data compatibility: what type of data is available, and how can its features and measurement scales be incorporated into the weighting process?
3. Criterion independence: are the criteria independent, or are there known interdependencies?

Because different weighting methods can yield different results, it is often advisable to apply more than one method or conduct a sensitivity analysis to verify the robustness of the decision (Şahin, 2021).

Weighting methods are generally grouped into three categories: subjective, objective, and hybrid (Singh & Pant, 2021). Subjective approaches rely on expert judgment to derive weights, often including contextual or experiential knowledge, but can be prone to bias and inconsistency (Odu, 2019). Objective approaches derive weights mathematically from data through decision matrices, reducing human error but often lacking context sensitivity in terms of the decision being made and the importance of factors relevant to making that decision (Mukhametzyanov, 2021). Hybrid or integrated approaches aim to combine the advantages of both by synthesizing expert assessment with empirical data (Taherdoost & Madanchian, 2023a). Selecting an appropriate weighting method in MADM is not merely a technical task; it is a strategic decision that significantly impacts the credibility and legitimacy of the entire decision-making process (Aruldoss et al., 2013).

As MADM methodologies evolve, there is a growing demand for approaches that strike a balance between consistency and simplicity. Traditional approaches, such as the analytic hierarchy process (AHP), offer robust frameworks for pairwise comparisons and consistency checking, but they often require a large number of pairwise comparisons, especially as the number of criteria increases (Saaty, 2013). This leads to cognitive overload that may, in turn, lead to increased risk of inconsistency and error. Inconsistent judgments can undermine the reliability of outcomes and obscure genuine preferences, making it difficult to defend or replicate decisions.

Other established methods include Measuring attractiveness by a categorical based evaluation technique (Ferreira & Santos, 2021), decision-making trial and evaluation laboratory (Si et al., 2018), criteria importance through intercriteria

Encyclopedia of Multi-Attribute Decision-Making (MADM). DOI: https://doi.org/10.1016/B978-0-443-33275-3.00002-6

correlation (Diakoulaki et al., 1995), and entropy (Dasgupta et al., 2025), while more recent developments comprise methods such as the best–worst method (BWM) (Mi et al., 2019), criterion impact loss (Podvezko et al., 2020), Cubic effect-based measurement (Altıntaş, 2023), level-based weight assessment (Žižović & Pamucar, 2019), and method based on the removal effects of criteria (Keshavarz-Ghorabaee et al., 2021). Despite the growing body of research, comprehensive comparative studies specifically focused on weighting techniques remain limited. Some review works have addressed selected methods, including AHP (Russo & Camanho, 2015), analytic network process (ANP) (Taherdoost & Madanchian, 2023b), BWM (Ecer & Demir, 2024), and SWARA (Mardani et al., 2017).

In parallel, there is an increasing appreciation for simpler, more intuitive methods that have fewer steps, require fewer inputs, and follow more natural logic. These methods support more straightforward and practical decision processes, while preserving analytical integrity. The full consistency method (FUCOM) (Pamučar & Stević, 2018) is one such method, reducing the amount of comparisons needed, while retaining, or improving, consistency in expert judgments. Its simplicity enhances usability and credibility, and supports more effective translation of decision models into action.

The remainder of this chapter is structured as follows. Section 2 provides a comprehensive review of FUCOM applications in the literature. Section 3 outlines the theoretical foundations and algorithmic formulation of FUCOM, and presents an illustrative example of its application. Section 4 presents a detailed case study that applies FUCOM to decision-making in the context of developing railway infrastructure in Libya. Section 5 offers a comparative analysis of FUCOM against widely used MADM approaches, AHP, BWM, and step-wise weight assessment ratio analysis (SWARA), and Section 6 presents concluding remarks.

21.2 Literature review

FUCOM enables decision-makers to derive consistent weights for evaluation criteria using a minimal number of pairwise comparisons. By embedding transitivity conditions into a linear optimization model, the method guarantees full consistency across derived priorities (Božanić et al., 2019).

Since its introduction, FUCOM has attracted increasing attention in both theoretical and applied MADM research. Its ability to reduce the cognitive burden on experts while maintaining analytical rigor makes it especially valuable in time-sensitive or data-scarce decision environments (Radovanović et al., 2023; Stević, Bašić, et al., 2023). The versatility of the method has facilitated many extensions and hybridizations, reinforcing its relevance across a growing number of application areas (Pajić et al., 2025).

FUCOM has been widely adopted in real-world decision-making contexts due to its conceptual simplicity and consistent weighting logic. Notably, the transportation and logistics sectors are among its most frequent adopters (Derse, 2024; Mitrović Simić et al., 2020; Pamučar et al., 2021). Applications in this area include optimizing freight distribution channels by balancing cost, speed, and traceability considerations (Popović et al., 2022). FUCOM has also been applied to the evaluation of sustainable urban mobility plans in order to assess and prioritize sustainable transport initiatives (Gökler, 2024). In military contexts, FUCOM has been used in the analysis of tactical vehicle options through performance, safety, and maintenance assessments (Božanić et al., 2020; Duško & Božanić, 2023). Environmental planning has also seen increased uptake of FUCOM (Badi, Muhammad, et al., 2022; Durmić et al., 2020; Ildoromi & Spehri, 2023). This has included selecting site options for waste management, sustainable land management, and construction decision-making within sustainable development frameworks (Feizi et al., 2021).

Beyond transport and environmental engineering, FUCOM has been employed across diverse sectors, including healthcare (Abdullah et al., 2022), industry (Çelik & Aka, 2023), education (Baki, 2022; Öztaş & Öztaş, 2023), telecommunication (Çodur et al., 2024), and construction (Božanić et al., 2021). In healthcare, it has been used to evaluate selecting waste treatment alternatives by balancing environmental, economic, and operational dimensions (Saha et al., 2022). In education, FUCOM has helped assess institutional resilience through the evaluation of preparedness indicators, particularly during crises such as the COVID-19 pandemic (Almacen et al., 2023). In construction, FUCOM has informed the prioritization of sustainable strategies for managing construction and demolition waste (Alossta et al., 2024). The method has also been applied in geo-risk analysis, such as the ranking of landslide hazard indicators to inform land use planning (Ildoromi & Spehri, 2023).

To better accommodate uncertainty in expert judgment, several methodological extensions of FUCOM have been proposed (Dey et al., 2023; Nemati et al., 2023; Torrisi et al., 2025). Fuzzy FUCOM (F-FUCOM), the fuzzy extension of FUCOM (Majumder, 2023; Pamucar & Ecer, 2020; Sofuoğlu, 2020), has been used to evaluate barriers to environmental education and performance in urban mobility (Milinković et al., 2025). Other notable extensions include q-rung orthopair fuzzy FUCOM, designed to model deeper uncertainty, particularly in complex domains like healthcare waste management (Saha et al., 2022). Additional variants include neutrosophic FUCOM and intuitionistic fuzzy FUCOM. FUCOM extensions strengthen its ability to address challenges arising from dynamic information environments, ambiguous inputs, and complex decision scenarios involving multiple stakeholders (Erceg et al., 2019; Kayişoğlu et al., 2024).

In addition to its fuzzy variants, FUCOM has been integrated with a range of other MCDM methods to form hybrid decision-making models. These include combinations of FUCOM with: measurement alternatives and ranking according to compromise solution (MARCOS) (Stević & Brković, 2020; Stević, Mujaković, et al., 2023); combinative distance-based assessment (CODAS) (Badi & Kridish, 2020); simple additive weighting (SAW) (Mahendra, 2021; Tenodi et al., 2025) combined compromise solution (CoCoSo) (Demir et al., 2022) Visekriterijumska Optimizacija i kompromisno resenje) (Ong et al., 2021) evaluation based on distance from average solution multiattributive ideal-real comparative analysis (MAIRCA) (Tešić et al., 2023) axial-distance-based aggregated measurement (ADAM) (Andrejić et al., 2023) and weighted aggregated sum product assessment (WASPAS) (Fazlollahtabar et al., 2019). These hybrid frameworks have been applied across sectors such as infrastructure planning, logistics, sustainable product development, and healthcare. For example, FUCOM–MARCOS has been applied to examine green supplier performance and regional priorities for infrastructure (Badi, Muhammad, et al., 2022), FUCOM–CoCoSo has been used for selecting sites for fire stations (Badi, Jibril, et al., 2022), FUCOM–CODAS has been employed for landfill site selection (Badi & Kridish, 2020), and FUCOM–ADAM has supported the choices for ranking distribution models in logistics and supply networks (Andrejić et al., 2023).

These integrated approaches capitalize on FUCOM's ability to generate consistent, nonredundant weights, while also leveraging the analytical strengths of established ranking techniques, enabling more robust, flexible, and context-sensitive decision support. As the field of MADM continues to evolve, hybrid FUCOM methods are likely to remain a central focus of both research and practice, offering powerful tools for addressing complex, multicriteria problems across a wide array of application domains.

21.3 Full consistency method: theoretical foundations and algorithmic formulation

FUCOM is a relatively recent addition to the family of MADM techniques and was developed to address key limitations of conventional pairwise comparison techniques, such as AHP and BWM (Mardani, Jusoh, Zavadskas et al., 2017). Specifically, FUCOM is designed to reduce cognitive burden, minimize redundancy, and ensure full consistency in judgments made by decision-makers. The theoretical foundations of FUCOM are based upon the application of criteria prioritization with a fully consistent relationship through linear programming. FUCOM is primarily designed to address two key challenges, which are discussed next: the cognitive and computational burden associated with a large number of pairwise comparisons, and the inconsistencies in weight attribution that arise from subjective judgment.

In contrast to AHP, which requires $\frac{n(n-1)}{2}$ pairwise comparisons for n criteria, or BWM, which entails identifying and comparing the best and worst criteria against all others, FUCOM significantly reduces the required comparisons to just $n-1$. This is accomplished by asking decision-makers to rank the criteria in descending order of importance and specify the relative significance of each criterion with respect to its immediate successor. This alleviates cognitive load and input redundancy, improving simplicity and usability.

In real decision-making contexts, pairwise comparison values, represented as $a_{ij} = w_i/w_j$, indicating the relative significance of criterion i compared to criterion j, are seldom obtained from objective measurements. Rather, they are generally founded on subjective assessments, which are intrinsically susceptible to inconsistency. Such assessments frequently diverge from the optimal ratios established by the foundational weight vector, wherein the ideal ratio w_i signifies the genuine relative significance of the criterion. An instance of contradiction occurs when a decision-maker assesses criterion A as more significant than B, B as more significant than C, and C as more significant than A. This form of transitivity violation compromises the dependability of the results and becomes progressively troublesome as the quantity of criteria and comparisons increases. FUCOM mitigates this issue by minimizing inconsistency through the aforementioned approach that necessitates just $n-1$ comparisons, and by integrating consistency constraints into a linear programming model to ascertain optimal weight values. Furthermore, FUCOM facilitates the confirmation of the solution's internal consistency by calculating the deviation from full consistency (DFC) index.

FUCOM offers an efficient and reliable instrument for criterion weighting by integrating low redundancy, computational transparency, and mathematical rigor, making it particularly applicable to real-world issues where consistency and simplicity are paramount. FUCOM's methodological framework is explicitly crafted to maintain logical coherence with minimal input, providing a more systematic and economical means of determining dependable criterion weights. A detailed, step-by-step algorithmic formulation of FUCOM is presented in the remainder of this section.

Step 1: Ranking the criteria

The set of evaluation criteria $C_j = \{C_1, C_2, ..., C_n\}, j = 1, ...n$ is first ranked in descending order based on their perceived importance. The ranking is conducted based on criteria importance, beginning with the criterion anticipated to possess the largest weight coefficient and concluding with the criterion of minimal significance. Consequently, the criteria are sorted based on the anticipated values of the weight coefficients. Let k denote the position of a criterion in the ranking, as follows:

$$C_{j(1)} > C_{j(2)} > ... > C_{j(k)} \tag{21.1}$$

If two or more criteria are judged to be equally important, equality signs are used in place of inequality signs.

Step 2: Determining comparative priorities

Next, the decision-maker evaluates the relative importance of each criterion $C_{j(k)}$ with respect to its immediate successor $C_{j(k+1)}$, resulting in a set of comparative priority values:

$$\Phi = (\varphi_{1/2}, \varphi_{2/3}, ..., \varphi_{k/(k+1)}) \tag{21.2}$$

where $\varphi_{k/(k+1)}$ represents the significance (priority) that the criterion of the k rank has compared to the criterion of the $k+1$ rank.

These comparative values can be derived in two ways. First, decision-makers may rely on their own preferences and experience to judge the relative importance of criteria. For example, if one criterion is believed to be more important than another based on professional intuition or contextual understanding, the decision-maker can express this preference using a qualitative or linguistic scale. These judgments reflect how much more significant one criterion is compared to another, without requiring exact numerical values. Second, a predefined linguistic or numerical scale can be used to support consistent comparisons. In this approach, all other criteria are compared to the most important one, which serves as a reference point. The goal is to express how much less important each criterion is compared to this top-ranked criterion. Because the most important criterion is always compared with itself, it is assigned a baseline value, and only $n-1$ comparisons are needed for n criteria. This structured approach ensures that the prioritization of criteria is both consistent and logically sound, enabling more reliable decision-making outcomes.

For example, suppose a given decision problem involves three criteria C_1, C_2, and C_3 ranked as $C_2 > C_1 > C_3$. Suppose that the scale $w_{C_{j(k)}} \in [1,9]$ is used to determine the priorities of the criteria and that, based on the decision-maker's preferences, the following are the obtained priorities of criteria $w_{C_2} = 1$, $w_{C_1} = 3.5$ and $w_{C_3} = 6$. On the basis of the obtained criteria priorities and condition $\frac{w_k}{w_{k+1}} = \varphi_{k/(k+1)}$, we perform the following calculations: $\frac{w_2}{w_1} = \frac{3.5}{1}$ that is, $w_2 = 3.5 \cdot w_1$, $\frac{w_1}{w_3} = \frac{6}{3.5}$ that is, $w_1 = 1.714 \cdot w_3$. In this way, the following comparative priorities are calculated: $\varphi_{C_2/C_1} = 3.5/1 = 3.5$ and $\varphi_{C_1/C_3} = 6/3.5 = 1.714$.

As we can see from the example, FUCOM facilitates pairwise comparison of criteria using integer, decimal values, or values from a preset scale.

Step 3: Deriving final weights via linear programming

The final step is to compute the weight coefficients for the evaluation criteria: $(w_1, w_2, ..., w_n)^T$. These weights must satisfy two key conditions:

1. The ratio between consecutive weights must reflect the comparative priorities established in step 2, as expressed by the following:

$$\frac{w_k}{w_{k+1}} = \varphi_{k/(k+1)} \tag{21.3}$$

2. The weights must satisfy transitivity, that is, that $\varphi_{k/(k+1)} \otimes \varphi_{(k+1)/(k+2)} = \varphi_{k/(k+2)}$. Since $\varphi_{k/(k+1)} = \frac{w_k}{w_{k+1}}$ and $\varphi_{(k+1)/(k+2)} = \frac{w_{k+1}}{w_{k+2}}$, then it should be that $\frac{w_k}{w_{k+1}} \otimes \frac{w_{k+1}}{w_{k+2}} = \frac{w_k}{w_{k+2}}$. Thus, the following needs to be satisfied:

$$\frac{w_k}{w_{k+2}} = \varphi_{k/(k+1)} \otimes \varphi_{(k+1)/(k+2)} \tag{21.4}$$

Full consistency that is, minimum DFC is satisfied only if transitivity is fully respected, that is, when these two conditions are met. In order for the conditions to be met, it is necessary that the values of the weight coefficients

$(w_1, w_2, ..., w_n)^T$ meet the condition of $\left|\frac{w_k}{w_{k+1}} - \varphi_{k/(k+1)}\right| \le \chi$, and $\left|\frac{w_k}{w_{k+2}} - \varphi_{k/(k+1)} \otimes \varphi_{(k+1)/(k+2)}\right| \le \chi$, with the minimization of the value χ, which represents DFC.

To formalize this, FUCOM formulates a linear programming problem as described below:

$$\min \chi \text{s.t.}$$

$$\left|\frac{w_{j(k)}}{w_{j(k+1)}} - \varphi_{k/(k+1)}\right| \le \chi, \ \forall j$$

$$\left|\frac{w_{j(k)}}{w_{j(k+2)}} - \varphi_{k/(k+1)} \otimes \varphi_{(k+1)/(k+2)}\right| \le \chi, \ \forall j$$

$$\sum_{j=1}^{n} w_j = 1, \ \forall j$$

$$w_j \ge 0, \ \forall j \tag{21.5}$$

By solving these models, the final values of the evaluation criteria $(w_1, w_2, ..., w_n)^T$, and the degree of DFC (χ) are generated.

An illustrative example is presented next to demonstrate the step-by-step application of the FUCOM method. The objective is to clarify the core principles and computational logic underlying the approach. The example involves four evaluation criteria, with the goal of deriving consistent weights based on expert input.

Step 1: the decision-maker initially ranks the four criteria in descending order of importance as follows: $C_1 > C_3 > C_4 > C_2$. The decision-maker designates C_1 as the most important criterion.

Step 2: next, the decision-maker performs pairwise comparisons among the criteria established in step 1. Each criterion is compared to the most important one, C_1 , as a reference point. The subjective judgments provided are as follows:

- C_1 is three times more important than C_3
- C_1 is five times more important than C_4
- C_1 is eight times more important than C_2

The comparison was based on the scale [1,9] and is shown in Table 21.1.

The comparative priorities of the criteria are determined based on the given priorities as follows: $\varphi_{C_1/C_3} = 3/1 = 3.0$, $\varphi_{C_3/C_4} = 5/3 = 1.67$, $\varphi_{C_4/C_2} = 8/5 = 1.6$.

Step 3: the final weights must satisfy the following requirements, that is, that $\frac{w_1}{w_3} = 3.0$, $\frac{w_3}{w_4} = 1.67$, $\frac{w_4}{w_2} = 1.6$.

Furthermore, the final values of the weight coefficients must satisfy the principle of transitivity, that is, that $\frac{w_1}{w_4} = 3.0 \times 1.67 = 5.01$, $\frac{w_1}{w_2} = 3.0 \times 1.67 \times 1.6 = 8.01$. So, the linear programming model for determining the weight coefficients can be defined as:

$$\min \chi$$

$$s.t. \begin{cases} & \left|\frac{w_1}{w_3} - 3,0\right| \le \chi, \quad \left|\frac{w_3}{w_4} - 1,67\right| \le \chi, \quad \left|\frac{w_4}{w_2} - 1.6\right| \le \chi, \quad \left|\frac{w_1}{w_4} - 5,01\right| \le \chi, \\ & \left|\frac{w_1}{w_2} - 8,01\right| \le \chi, \\ & \sum_{j=1}^{4} w_j = 1, \quad w_j \ge 0, \ \forall j \end{cases}$$

TABLE 21.1 Priorities of criteria.

Criteria	C_1	C_3	C_4	C_2
$w_{C_{j(k)}}$	1	3	5	8

The model is solved using Microsoft Excel Solver, yielding the final weight coefficients $(0.603, 0.201, 0.121, 0.075)^T$ and a DFC of the findings $\chi = 0.000$. This indicates perfect consistency between the decision-maker's judgments and the final weights. The results confirm that C1 is the most significant criterion, followed by C3, C4, and C2.

21.4 Case study: prioritizing barriers to railway infrastructure development in Libya

Libya has a long history of challenges with respect to the national transportation infrastructure due to political and economic instability and prolonged institutional fragmentation. One of the most notable gaps in the country's transport system is the absence of a railway. Although plans for the development of a railway system were originally discussed in the 1980s, including initiatives by engineers and specialists in Western countries, no operational railway exists to date. In this context, it is important to systematically investigate the barriers that continue to exist as a hindrance towards implementation. This case study seeks to systematically identify and prioritize the key barriers to railway infrastructure development in Libya. The analysis is based on the knowledge and views of the four domain experts who have experience with transportation planning, infrastructure development, and regional policy.

An initial set of criteria was formulated through a comprehensive review of the literature on transportation infrastructure and railway development. These initial criteria incorporate the technical and contextual aspects impacting the feasibility of railway projects in Libya. The criteria were then reviewed by the experts to ensure they were consistent with the national context and current challenges. According to their suggestions, revisions were made which resulted in the final evaluation criteria shown in Table 21.2.

FUCOM was applied to derive relative weights for the eight criteria. The process started with each expert ranking the criteria in descending order of importance. Subsequently, each expert provided crisp values for the comparative priority (Φ) between adjacent criteria in their ranking. The collected rankings and comparative priorities of the four experts are shown in Table 21.3.

Let's look at Expert E1 in more detail. E1 provided the following ranking: C1 > C2 > C4 > C6 > C5 > C7 > C3 > C8. After establishing this order, they evaluated the relative importance between the top-ranked criterion C1 and all others, assigning the numerical priority values 1, 2, 3, 3, 4, 5, and 7. For example, the numerical priority between C1 and C4 is 2, indicating that C1 is considered twice as important as C4.

The vector of comparative priorities of the criteria, denoted as Φ, is derived from these initial relative importance values by calculating the ratio of the importance of each criterion to the importance of the criterion ranked immediately below it. This process was repeated for each successive pair of criteria, producing the following comparative priority values for E1: $\varphi_{C_1/C_2} = 1/1 = 1.0$, $\varphi_{C_2/C_4} = 2/1 = 2.0$, $\varphi_{C_4/C_6} = 3/2 = 1.5$, $\varphi_{C_6/C_5} = 3/3 = 1.0$, $\varphi_{C_5/C_7} = 4/3 = 1.33$, $\varphi_{C_7/C_3} = 5/4 = 1.25$, $\varphi_{C_3/C_8} = 7/5 = 1.4$. This process transforms the expert's static assessment relative to the most important criterion into a set of pairwise comparison values between adjacent ranks.

The final weights for the direct constraints must satisfy the following requirements, that is, that $\frac{w_1}{w_2} = 1.0$, $\frac{w_2}{w_4} = 2.0$, $\frac{w_4}{w_6} = 1.5$, $\frac{w_6}{w_5} = 1.0$, $\frac{w_5}{w_7} = 1.33$, $\frac{w_7}{w_3} = 1.25$, $\frac{w_3}{w_8} = 1.4$

TABLE 21.2 Criteria used in the assessment.

Criterion	Description
C1	Political instability
C2	Insufficient government funding
C3	Lack of foreign investment
C4	Weak institutional and legal framework
C5	Inadequate technical expertise
C6	Land acquisition and resettlement issues
C7	Corruption and bureaucratic inefficiency
C8	Topographical and geological challenges

TABLE 21.3 Ranking and numerical priorities by different experts.

Expert	Ranked order of criteria	Numerical priorities
E1	C1 > C2 > C4 > C6 > C5 > C7 > C3 > C8	1, 1, 2, 3, 3, 4, 5, 7
E2	C2 > C6 > C1 > C3 > C7 > C4 > C5 > C8	1, 1, 2, 4, 4, 5, 7, 8
E3	C1 > C2 > C6 > C4 > C5 > C3> C8 > C7	1, 2, 2, 4, 4, 5, 6, 8
E4	C1 > C7 > C2 > C6 > C4 > C7 > C8 > C3	1, 2, 2, 2, 5, 6, 7, 8

TABLE 21.4 Final weights for Expert 1.

Criterion	E1 weight
C1	0.280
C2	0.280
C4	0.140
C6	0.093
C5	0.093
C7	0.070
C3	0.056
C8	0.040

Furthermore, the final values of the weight coefficients must satisfy the mathematical principle of transitivity to ensure full multiplicative consistency in the pairwise comparisons. This principle dictates that the derived relationship between any two nonadjacent criteria must be equivalent to the product of the consecutive relationships linking them. These values are calculated as follows: $\frac{w_1}{w_4} = 1.0 \times 2.0 = 2.0$, $\frac{w_2}{w_6} = 2.0 \times 1.5 = 3.0$, $\frac{w_4}{w_5} = 1.5 \times 1.0 = 1.5$, $\frac{w_6}{w_7} = 1.0 \times 1.33 = 1.33$, $\frac{w_5}{w_3} = 1.33 \times 1.25 = 1.66$, $\frac{w_7}{w_8} = 1.25 \times 1.4 = 1.75$, $\frac{w_1}{w_6} = 1.0 \times 2.0 \times 1.5 = 3.0$, $\frac{w_2}{w_5} = 2.0 \times 1.5 \times 1.0 = 3.0$, $\frac{w_4}{w_7} = 1.5 \times 1.0 \times 1.33 = 1.99$, $\frac{w_6}{w_3} = 1.0 \times 1.33 \times 1.25 = 1.66$, $\frac{w_1}{w_5} = 1.0 \times 2.0 \times 1.5 \times 1.0 = 3.0$, $\frac{w_2}{w_7} = 2.0 \times 1.5 \times 1.0 \times 1.33 = 3.99$, $\frac{w_4}{w_3} = 1.5 \times 1.0 \times 1.33 \times 1.25 = 2.49$, $\frac{w_1}{w_7} = 1.0 \times 2.0 \times 1.5 \times 1.0 \times 1.33 = 3.99$, $\frac{w_2}{w_3} = 2.0 \times 1.5 \times 1.0 \times 1.33 \times 1.25 = 4.99$, $\frac{w_1}{w_3} = 1.0 \times 2.0 \times 1.5 \times 1.0 \times 1.33 \times 1.25 = 4.99$, and $\frac{w_1}{w_8} = 1.0 \times 2.0 \times 1.5 \times 1.0 \times 1.33 \times 1.25 \times 1.4 = 6.99$.

So, the linear programming model for determining the weight coefficients can be defined as:

$$\min \chi$$

$$s.t. \begin{cases} \& \left|\frac{w_1}{w_2} - 1,00\right| \le \chi, \quad \left|\frac{w_2}{w_4} - 2,00\right| \le \chi, \quad \left|\frac{w_4}{w_6} - 1.50\right| \le \chi, \quad \left|\frac{w_6}{w_5} - 1,00\right| \le \chi, \quad \left|\frac{w_5}{w_7} - 1,33\right| \\ \& \left|\frac{w_7}{w_3} - 1,25\right| \le \chi, \quad \left|\frac{w_3}{w_8} - 1,40\right| \le \chi \;, \left|\frac{w_1}{w_4} - 2,00\right| \le \chi, \left|\frac{w_2}{w_6} - 3,00\right|, \left|\frac{w_4}{w_5} - 1,50\right| \\ \left|\frac{w_6}{w_7} - 1,33\right|, \left|\frac{w_5}{w_3} - 1,66\right|, \left|\frac{w_7}{w_8} - 1,75\right|, \left|\frac{w_1}{w_6} - 3,00\right|, \left|\frac{w_2}{w_5} - 3,00\right|, \left|\frac{w_4}{w_7} - 1,99\right| \\ \left|\frac{w_6}{w_3} - 1,66\right|, \left|\frac{w_1}{w_5} - 3,00\right|, \left|\frac{w_2}{w_7} - 3,99\right|, \left|\frac{w_4}{w_3} - 2,49\right|, \left|\frac{w_1}{w_7} - 3,99\right|, \left|\frac{w_2}{w_3} - 4,99\right| \\ \left|\frac{w_1}{w_3} - 4,99\right|, \left|\frac{w_1}{w_8} - 6,99\right| \\ \& \sum_{j=1}^{8} w_j = 1, \quad w_j \ge 0, \forall j \end{cases}$$

The model is solved using Microsoft Excel Solver, yielding the final weight coefficients provided in Table 21.4, and a DFC of the findings $\chi = 0.000$. This indicates perfect consistency between the decision-maker's judgments and the final weights. The results confirm that C1 is the most significant criterion, followed by C2 and C4.

The formulated linear programming model, following the identical procedure detailed for Expert 1, was applied to calculate the precise local weight values for the evaluation criteria based on the individual crisp assessments provided by all four experts. Each model was solved using Microsoft Excel Solver, which computed the optimal weight sets that minimized the DFC for each expert. Subsequently, the final aggregated weights were determined by calculating the geometric mean of the individual weights for each criterion across all experts, providing a robust group consensus. The final ranking of the criteria, along with individual and aggregated weights, is presented in Table 21.5.

TABLE 21.5 Final weights and ranking for criteria.

	E1	E2	E3	E4	Aggregated	Rank
C1	0.280	0.160	0.261	0.278	0.241	1
C2	0.280	0.320	0.131	0.139	0.208	2
C3	0.056	0.080	0.052	0.035	0.054	8
C4	0.140	0.064	0.065	0.056	0.079	5
C5	0.093	0.046	0.065	0.046	0.061	6
C6	0.093	0.320	0.131	0.139	0.159	3
C7	0.070	0.080	0.032	0.139	0.075	4
C8	0.040	0.040	0.043	0.040	0.041	7

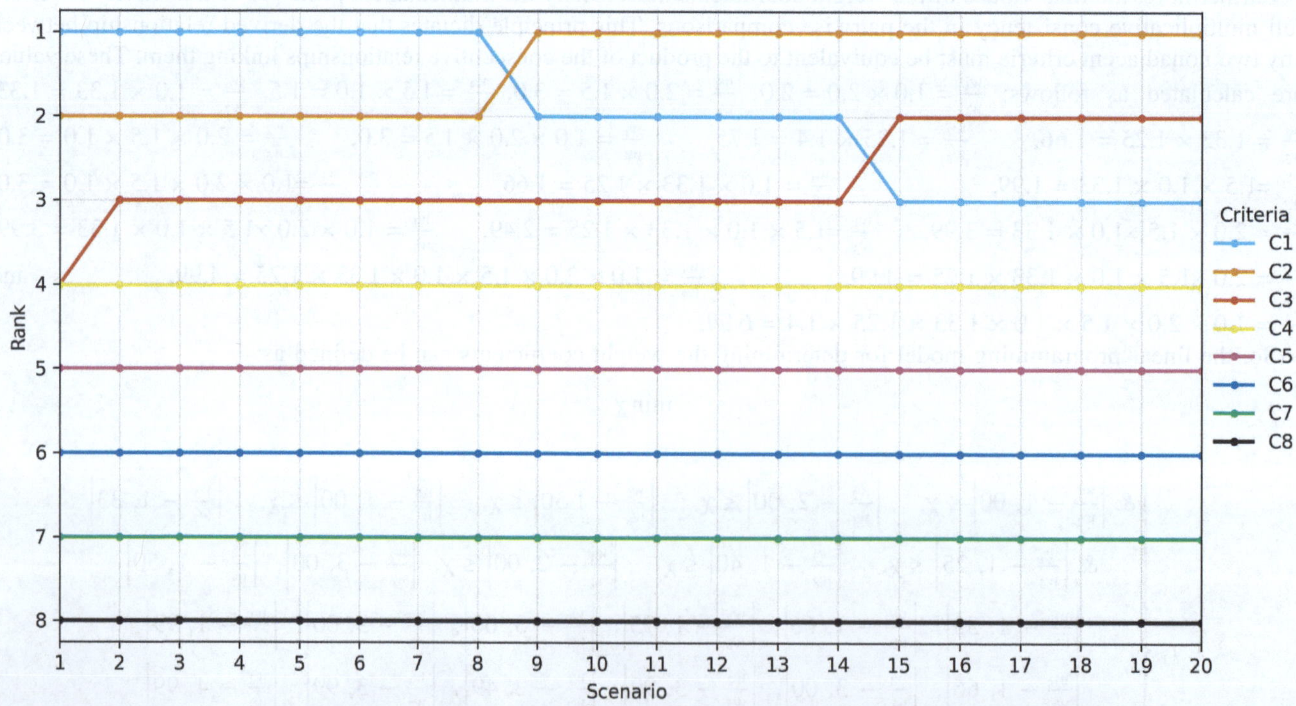

FIGURE 21.1 Sensitivity analysis of full consistency method weights under 20 case scenarios.

TABLE 21.6 Comparison of full consistency method (FUCOM) against analytical hierarchy process (AHP), best–worst method (BWM), and step-wise weight assessment ratio analysis (SWARA).

Feature	FUCOM	AHP	BWM	SWARA
Input type	Pairwise comparisons w.r.t. most important criterion	Full pairwise comparisons between all criteria	Best-to-others and others-to-worst comparisons	Ranked criteria with relative importance
Number of comparisons required	$n-1$	$n(n-1)/2$	$2n-3$	$n-1$
Consistencycheck	Full consistency enforced through nonlinear optimization	Consistency ratio	Consistency index	No formal consistency check
Handling expert subjectivity	Fuzzy logic supported; multiexpert aggregation possible	Moderate; group consensus supported	Moderate; requires consensus on best/worst	High subjectivity in coefficient assignment
Mathematical complexity	Moderate (requires solver-based optimization)	Low to moderate	Moderate	Low
Ease of use	High, especially with structured input and software tools	User-friendly with software support	Requires understanding of BWM formulation	Very simple to implement
Support for fuzzy extension	Well-developed	Available (F-AHP)	Available (F-BWM)	Available (fuzzy SWARA)
Output	Consistent, optimized fuzzy weights	Priority vector (normalized weights)	Optimized weights based on best/worst distances	Weighted scores based on relative importance

The aggregated results, derived from the individual FUCOM models of the four experts, support the relative rank-order of the barriers to railway infrastructure development in Libya. As Table 21.5 shows, political instability (C1) and inadequate government funding (C2) have the two largest weights (0.241 and 0.208 respectively), by an order of magnitude in this analysis. Clearly, there is a consensus from the experts that the necessary macro-level governance and economic enabling conditions are the major impediments, compared to other factors. The third-ranked barrier, land acquisition and resettlement issues (C6), reinforces the confusion around the socio-political landscape facing large-scale infrastructure projects. The barriers ranked fourth to sixth, corruption and bureaucratic inefficiency (C7), weak institutional and legal framework (C4), and inadequate technical capabilities (C5), are significant but secondary, and are also associated with the operational capacity of the Libyan state. Finally, topographical and geological issues (C8) and lack of foreign investment (C3) were reported to have the least importance, indicating that if there are difficult terrains, and that investment may be needed, these cannot be addressed without the more fundamental and pressing political and governance issues being addressed (C1, C2, C4, C7). The high level of agreement on this rank order, despite variations in individual expert judgments, underscores the robustness of the findings and highlights the areas where intervention is most urgently required.

A comprehensive sensitivity analysis was conducted by simultaneously varying the weights of the top three criteria (C1, C2, and C6) by ±30% across 20 test scenarios, while proportionally adjusting the remaining criteria to maintain a total weight of 1.0. This approach provides a rigorous test of FUCOM's robustness under more complex variations in expert judgments. The results, shown in Fig. 21.1, demonstrate that the rankings of the lower five criteria (C3, C4, C5, C7, C8) remained completely stable throughout all scenarios, indicating strong resilience in the overall ranking structure. There were only minor rank shifts in the top three criteria, with occasional swaps between C1, C2, and C6, reflecting natural sensitivity at the highest influence levels. These findings indicate that FUCOM exhibits a high degree of rank-order stability, suggesting that its outputs are not unduly sensitive to moderate changes in initial assumptions. Such robustness is particularly valuable in complex policy settings where expert inputs are inherently uncertain.

21.5 Comparative analysis

This section compares FUCOM with three widely used MADM techniques: AHP, BWM, and SWARA. As shown in Table 21.6, FUCOM stands out in its methodological efficiency and internal consistency.

The most notable feature of FUCOM is that it requires only $n-1$ pairwise comparisons, all structured with respect to the most important criterion selected by the decision-maker. This reduces the cognitive load significantly, especially when compared with AHP, which requires $\frac{n(n-1)}{2}$ comparisons, and BWM, which requires $2n-3$. SWARA, although comparably efficient in terms of comparison volume, relies on purely subjective coefficient assignment without any formal consistency mechanism.

FUCOM further distinguishes itself by embedding consistency directly into its nonlinear optimization model. In contrast, AHP and BWM apply post hoc checks (consistency ratio and consistency index, respectively), while SWARA provides no consistency verification at all. Additionally, FUCOM supports fuzzy extensions natively, allowing it to incorporate uncertainty and imprecision in expert judgment, an increasingly important consideration in complex decision environments. This methodological rigor, combined with practical usability, makes FUCOM a strong candidate for high-stakes, expert-driven decision contexts.

21.6 Conclusion

The FUCOMrepresents a significant advancement in MADM by offering an elegant balance between methodological simplicity and mathematical rigor. Unlike traditional pairwise comparison techniques, FUCOM requires only $n-1$ pairwise comparisons, significantly reducing the cognitive and computational burden on decision-makers. An additional strength of FUCOM lies in its ability to maintain consistency without sacrificing analytical robustness. The method's consistency is quantified using the DFC index, which provides a structured and transparent validation of expert input. This feature is especially valuable in high-stakes decision contexts where defensibility and repeatability are essential.

This study illustrated the advantages of FUCOM's in systematically identifying and ranking the important barriers to railway infrastructure development in Libya. The method was effective at distilling reliable, consistent weights from expert judgments, and clearly illustrated the political stability and limited government funding were the most pressing barriers to railway infrastructure development in Libya. The advantages of FUCOM range from a theoretical innovation to a real-world, cognitively efficient, and consistency-enforced method to support MADM. The ability to gain reliable measures from limited available data and expert effort adds to the relevance of its applicability to real-world decision contexts.

FUCOM's advantages extend beyond theoretical innovation, offering a practical, cognitively efficient, and consistency-enforced approach to MADM. Its ability to produce reliable results with limited data and expert effort makes it highly relevant for real-world decision contexts. As the broader MADM literature evolves to address increasingly complex and data-intensive problems, there is a growing interest in integrating MADM techniques with emerging technologies such as artificial intelligence and machine learning (Wyrembek & Baryannis, 2024). This convergence reflects a shared aim: to develop decision support systems that are both analytically rigorous and accessible to nontechnical users. FUCOM's methodological clarity and potential for hybridization make it a promising candidate for such integrated, intelligent decision-support frameworks. As decision-makers increasingly seek methods that combine rigor with practical usability, FUCOM is well-placed to become a core component of the contemporary MADM toolkit.

References

Abdullah, A., Ahmad, S., Athar, M. A., Rajpoot, N., & Talib, F. I. (2022). Healthcare performance management using integrated FUCOM-MARCOS: A case study from India. *International Journal of Health Planning Management, 2022*, 2635–2668.

Almacen, R. M., Balanay, M. A., Papa, C. A., & Garcia, M. (2023). Preparedness indicator system for education 4.0 with FUCOM and rough sets. *Systems, 11*(6), 288.

Alossta, A., Eltariki, I., Elmansouri, O., & Badi, I. J. (2024). Optimizing construction and demolition waste management strategies in Libya: A FUCOM–EDAS multi-criteria decision-making approach. *Journal of Green Economy and Low-Carbon Development, 3*(4), 258–272.

Altıntaş, F. F. J. (2023). A novel approach to measuring criterion weights in multiple criteria decision-making: Cubic effect-based measurement (CEBM). *Nicel Bilimler Dergisi, 5*(2), 151–195.

Andrejić, M., Pajić, V., & Kilibarda, M. J. (2023). Distribution channel selection using FUCOM-ADAM: A novel approach. *Sustainability, 15*(19), 14527.

Aruldoss, M., Lakshmi, T. M., & Venkatesan, V. P. (2013). A survey on multi-criteria decision-making methods and their applications. *Asian Journal of Information Systems, 1*(1), 31–43.

Ayan, B., Abacıoğlu, S., & Basilio, M. P. (2023). A comprehensive review of novel weighting methods for multi-criteria decision-making. *Information, 14*(5), 285.

Badi, I., & Kridish, M. (2020). Landfill site selection using a novel FUCOM-CODAS model: A case study in Libya. *Scientific African, 9*, e00537.

Badi, I., Muhammad, L., Abubakar, M., & Bakır, M. S. T. (2022). Measuring sustainability performance indicators using FUCOM-MARCOS methods. *Operational Research in Engineering Sciences Theory and Applications, 5*(2), 99–116.

Badi, I., Jibril, M., & Bakır, M. S. T. (2022b). A composite approach for site optimization of fire stations. *Journal of Intelligent Management Decision, 1*(1), 28–35.

Baki, R. (2022). Evaluation of barriers to implementation of environmental education with Fuzzy FUCOM. *International Journal of Social Sciences Perspectives, 10*(1), 17–25.

Božanić, D., Tešić, D., & Kočić, J. (2019). Multi-criteria FUCOM-Fuzzy MABAC model for the selection of location for construction of a single-span Bailey bridge. *Decision Making: Applications in Management and Engineering, 2*(1), 132–146.

Božanić, D., Milić, A., Tešić, D., & Pamučar, D. P. (2020). Multicriteria decision-making model with Z-numbers based on FUCOM and MABAC model. *Decision Making: Applications in Management and Engineering, 3*(2), 19–36.

Božanić, D., Milić, A., Tešić, D., & Pamučar, D. (2021). D-numbers–FUCOM–fuzzy RAFSI model for selecting construction machinery for enabling mobility. *Facta Universitatis, Series: Mechanical Engineering, 19*(3), 447–471.

Çodur, S., Aydın, H., & Öztürk, F. (2024). Application of the full consistency method (FUCOM)–cosine similarity framework in 5G infrastructure investment planning: An approach for telecommunication quality improvements. *Heliyon, 10*(9).

Çelik, D., & Aka, İ. (2023). Evaluation of the effects of Industry 4.0 on organizational agility with FUCOM: Implementation in the textile industry. *International Journal of Economic and Administrative Studies, 40*(2), 33–48.

Chachi, J., & Kazemifard, A. (2024). A novel extended approach to evaluate criteria weights in MADM problems in fuzzy framework. *International Journal of Fuzzy Systems, 21*(4), 101–122.

Dasgupta, A., Sen, B., Dutta, P., et al. (2025). Entropy-TOPSIS-based material selection for sustainable polymer composite: An MCDM framework promoting circular economy. *Journal of Elastomers & Plastics*.

Demir, G., Damjanović, M., Matović, B., & Vujadinović, R. S. (2022). Toward sustainable urban mobility by using fuzzy-FUCOM and fuzzy-CoCoSo methods: The case of the SUMP Podgorica. *Sustainability, 14*(9), 4972.

Derse, O. J. (2024). Prioritizing solutions of green reverse logistics barriers with fuzzy DEMATEL–FUCOM–SWARA methods. *Ecological Indicators, 165*, 112198.

Dey, S., Smarandache, F., Debbarma, R., & Majumder, P. (2023). A hybrid IF-FUCOM-GRA approach and its application to determine optimal bacterial concentrations on mortar at optimal curing day. *Informatica: An International Journal of Computing and Informatics, 34*(2), 223–248.

Diakoulaki, D., Mavrotas, G., & Papayannakis, L. C. (1995). Determining objective weights in multiple criteria problems: The CRITIC method. *Computers & Operations Research, 22*(7), 763–770.

Durmić, E., Stević, Ž., Chatterjee, P., Vasiljević, M., & Tomašević, M. (2020). Sustainable supplier selection using combined FUCOM–Rough-SAW model. *Reports in Mechanical Engineering, 27*(1), 34–43.

Duško, T., & Božanić, M. (2023). Optimizing military decision-making: Application of the FUCOM–EWAA–COPRAS-G MCDM model. *Acadlore Transactions on Applied Mathematics and Statistics, 2023*(3), 148–160.

Ecer, F. J. T., & Demir, E. (2024). A state-of-the-art review of the Best–Worst Method and future research agenda. *Technological and Economic Development of Economy, 30*(4), 1165–1204.

Erceg, Ž., Starčević, V., Pamučar, D., Mitrović, G., Stević, Ž., & Žikić, S. (2019). A new model for stock management in order to rationalize costs: ABC-FUCOM-interval rough CoCoSo model. *Symmetry, 11*(12), 1527.

Fazlollahtabar, H., Smailbašić, A., & Stević, Ž. (2019). FUCOM method in group decision-making: Selection of forklift in a warehouse. *Decision Making: Applications in Management and Engineering, 2*(1), 49–65.

Feizi, F., Karbalaei-Ramezanali, A., & Farhadi, S. A. S. (2021). FUCOM–MOORA and FUCOM–MOOSRA methods for mineral potential mapping. *SN Applied Sciences, 3*, 1–19.

Ferreira, F. A., & Santos, S. P. (2021). Two decades of the MACBETH approach: A bibliometric analysis. *Annals of Operations Research, 296*, 901–925.

Gökler, S. H. J. (2024). Optimal site selection for electric vehicle charging stations: Analysis with hybrid FUCOM and geographic information systems. *Energy, 307*, 132659.

Ildoromi, A., & Spehri, M. H. (2023). Accuracy of landslide hazard mapping of Kurdistan dam watershed using FUCOM, BWM, and AHP. *Hydrogeomorphology, 10*(37) 80–63.

Ishizaka, A., & Siraj, S. (2018). Are multi-criteria decision-making tools useful? An experimental comparative study of three methods. *European Journal of Operational Research, 264*(2), 462–471.

Kayişoğlu, G., Güneş, B., & Bolat, P. (2024). ECDIS cyber security dynamics analysis based on the fuzzy-FUCOM method. *Transactions on Maritime Science, 13*(1).

Keshavarz-Ghorabaee, M., Amiri, M., Zavadskas, E. K., Turskis, Z., & Antucheviciene, J. (2021). Determination of objective weights using a new method based on the removal effects of criteria (MEREC). *Symmetry, 13*(4).

Kumar, A., Kumar, M., & Bhardwaj, S. (2017). A review of multi-criteria decision-making (MCDM) towards sustainable renewable energy development. *Renewable and Sustainable Energy Reviews, 69*, 596–609.

Mahendra, G. S. (2021). Implementation of the FUCOM-SAW method on e-commerce selection DSS in Indonesia. *Technology Electronic, 5*(1), 75–85.

Majumder, P. (2023). An integrated trapezoidal fuzzy FUCOM with single-valued neutrosophic fuzzy MARCOS and GMDH method to determine the alternatives weight and its applications in efficiency analysis of water treatment plant. *Expert Systems with Applications, 225*, 120087.

Mardani, A., Jusoh, A., Zavadskas, E. K., Khalifah, Z., Zakuan, N., Jusoh, A., Md Nor, Z., & Khoshnoudi, M. (2017). A review of multi-criteria decision-making applications to solve energy management problems: Two decades from 1995 to 2015. *Renewable and Sustainable Energy Reviews, 71*, 216–256.

Mardani, A., Jusoh, M., & Zavadskas, E. K. (2017). A systematic review and meta-analysis of SWARA and WASPAS methods: Theory and applications with recent fuzzy developments. *Applied Soft Computing, 57*, 265–292.

Mi, X., Tang, M., Liao, H., Shen, W., & Lev, B. (2019). The state-of-the-art survey on integrations and applications of the best-worst method in decision making: Why, what, what for and what's next? *Omega, 87*, 205–225.

Milinković, A., Brkljač, D., Škorić, S., Stević, Ž., Danilevičius, A., & Das, D. K. B. (2025). Evaluation of potentials for urban planning using the fuzzy FUCOM-IMF SWARA-fuzzy OPARA model. *Buildings, 15*(5), 803.

Mitrović Simić, J., Stević, Ž., Zavadskas, E. K., Bogdanović, V., Subotić, M., & Mardani, A. (2020). A novel CRITIC–fuzzy FUCOM–DEA–fuzzy MARCOS model for safety evaluation of road sections based on geometric parameters. *Symmetry, 12*(12), 2006.

Mukhametzyanov, A. (2021). Specific character of objective methods for determining weights of criteria in MCDM problems: Entropy, CRITIC and SD. *International Journal of Decision Making and Risk Engineering, 4*(2), 76–105.

Nemati, A., Zolfani, S. H., & Khazaelpour, P. (2023). A novel grey FUCOM method and its application for better video game experiences. *Expert Systems with Applications, 234*, 121041.

Odu, G. (2019). Weighting methods for multi-criteria decision-making technique. *Journal of Management, 23*(8), 1449–1457.

Ong, M. C., Leong, Y. T., Wan, Y. K., & Chew, I. M. L. (2021). Multi-objective optimization of integrated water system by FUCOM-VIKOR approach. *Process Integration and Optimization for Sustainability, 5*(1), 43–62.

Öztaş, T., & Öztaş, G. Z. (2023). A comparative analysis of factors affecting the selection of English grammar checkers with FUCOM and BWM. *Journal of the Faculty of Economics and Administrative Sciences, 13*(3), 1026–1051.

Pajić, V., Andrejić, M., & Kilibarda, M. J. (2025). Procurement optimization by selecting efficient suppliers using DEA-FUCOM-CoCoSo approach and solving order allocation problem. *Facta Universitatis, Series: Mechanical Engineering, in press*, 109–125.

Pamucar, D., & Ecer, F. (2020). Prioritizing the weights of the evaluation criteria under fuzziness: The fuzzy full consistency method–FUCOM-F. *Facta Universitatis, Series: Mechanical Engineering, 18*(3), 419–437.

Pamučar, D., Ecer, F., & Deveci, M. J. S. (2021). Assessment of alternative fuel vehicles for sustainable road transportation of United States using integrated fuzzy FUCOM and neutrosophic fuzzy MARCOS methodology. *Science of the Total Environment, 788*, 147763.

Pamučar, Ž., & Stević, S. (2018). Sremac, A new model for determining weight coefficients of criteria in MCDM models: Full Consistency Method (FUCOM). *Symmetry, 10*(9), 393.

Podvezko, V., Zavadskas, E. K., Podviezko, A., & Studies, E. C. (2020). An extension of the new objective weight assessment methods CILOS and IDOCRIW to fuzzy MCDM. *Economic Computation and Economic Cybernetics Studies and Research, 54*(2).

Popović, V., Pamučar, D., Stević, Ž., Lukovac, V., & Jovković, S. J. S. (2022). Multicriteria optimization of logistics processes using a grey FUCOM–SWOT model. *Symmetry, 14*(4), 794.

Radovanović, M., Božanić, D., Tešić, D., Puška, A., Hezam, I. M., & Jana, C. (2023). Application of hybrid DIBR-FUCOM-LMAW-Bonferroni-grey-EDAS model in multicriteria decision-making. *Facta Universitatis, Series: Mechanical Engineering, 21*(3), 387–403.

Russo, R. De. F. S. M., & Camanho, R. (2015). Criteria in AHP: A systematic review of literature. *Procedia Computer Science, 55*, 1123–1132.

Saaty, T. L. (2013). Analytic hierarchy process. In S. I. Gass, & C. Harris (Eds.). *Encyclopedia of Operations Research and Management Science* (pp. 52–64). Springer.

Saha, A., Mishra, A. R., Rani, P., Hezam, I. M., & Cavallaro, F. J. (2022). A q-rung orthopair fuzzy FUCOM double normalization-based multi-aggregation method for healthcare waste treatment method selection. *Sustainability, 14*(7), 4171.

Şahin, M. (2021). A comprehensive analysis of weighting and multi-criteria methods in the context of sustainable energy. *International Journal of Energy Sector Management, 18*(6), 1591–1616.

Si, S.-L., You, X.-Y., Liu, H.-C., & Zhang, P. (2018). DEMATEL technique: A systematic review of methodologies and applications. *Mathematical Problems in Engineering, 2018* Article ID 3696457.

Singh, M., & Pant, A. (2021). A review of selected weighting methods in MCDM with a case study. *International Journal of Systems Assurance Engineering and Management, 12*, 126–144.

Sofuoğlu, M. A. (2020). Fuzzy applications of FUCOM method in manufacturing environment. *Journal of Polytechnic, 23*(1), 189–195.

Stević, Z., Mujaković, N., Goli, A., & Moslem, S. (2023). Selection of logistics distribution channels for final product delivery: FUCOM-MARCOS model. *Journal of Intelligent Management Decision, 2*, 172–178.

Stević, Ž., & Brković, N. (2020). A novel integrated FUCOM-MARCOS model for evaluation of human resources in a transport company. *Logistics, 16*(1), 4.

Stević, Ž., Bašić, A., Moslem, S., & Zhong, K. (2023). An integrated ABC-FUCOM model for product classification. *Spectrum of Engineering and Management Sciences, 1*(1), 83–91.

Taherdoost, H., & Madanchian, M. (2023a). Multi-criteria decision-making (MCDM) methods and concepts. *Journal of Engineering and Management, 3*(1), 77–87.

Taherdoost, H., & Madanchian, M. (2023b). Analytic network process (ANP) method: A comprehensive review of applications, advantages, and limitations. *Journal of Decision Systems, 1*(1), 12–18.

Tenodi, S., Plavšić, T., Vuković, D., & Stević, Ž. (2025). Application of the FUCOM-SAW model for comprehensive risk assessment of contaminated sediments: A case study of the Great Bačka Canal and Begej River. *Journal of Contaminant Hydrology, 104644*.

Tešić, D., Delibašić, B., Božanić, D., Lojić, R., Pamučar, D., & Balassa, B. E. (2023). Application of the FUCOM-FUZZY MAIRCA model in human resource management. *Acta Polytechnica Hungarica, 20*(3), 231–249.

Torrisi, V., Camporeale, R., Moslem, S., & Campisi, T. (2025). FUCOM–Kendall model for evaluating e-scooter adoption: A case study in Catania, Italy. *Transportation Research Procedia, 86*, 1–8.

Wyrembek, M., & Baryannis, G. (2024). Using MCDM methods to optimise machine learning decisions for supply chain delay prediction: A stakeholder-centric approach. *LogForum, 20*(2), 175–189.

Zavadskas, E. K., Turskis, Z., & Kildienė, S. (2014). State-of-the-art surveys of overviews on MCDM/MADM methods. *Technological and Economic Development of Economy, 20*(1), 165–179.

Žižović, M., & Pamucar, D. (2019). New model for determining criteria weights: Level Based Weight. *Assessment (LBWA) model, decision making: Applications in management and engineering, 2*(2), 126–137 D.

Chapter 22

LBWA: Level-based weight assessment for multi-attribute decision-making

Sanjib Biswas[1], Prasenjit Chatterjee[2], and Dragan Pamucar[3,4,5]

[1]*Amity Business School, Amity University, Kolkata, West Bengal, India,* [2]*Department of Mechanical Engineering, MCKV Institute of Engineering, Howrah, West Bengal, India,* [3]*Department of Operations Research and Statistics, University of Belgrade, Belgrade, Serbia,* [4]*UNEC Applied Artificial Intelligence Research Center, Azerbaijan State University of Economics (UNEC), Baku, Azerbaijan,* [5]*Faculty of Engineering, Dogus University, Istanbul, Türkiye*

22.1 Introduction

Decision-making in complex problem-solving environments involves the consideration of multiple factors that may not always align with one another. Decision-makers are typically confronted with a variety of criteria that must be evaluated simultaneously. Some of these criteria are quantitative, which can be measured with precision, while others are qualitative and depend on expert judgment or preferences. Because of this complexity, decision-making processes often require a structured methodology that allows for a rational and systematic comparison among alternatives. Multicriteria decision-making (MCDM) methods have emerged to fulfill this need by offering techniques that account for diverse indicators and enable balanced judgments (Zavadskas & Turskis, 2011). In an MCDM environment, the distribution of weights across criteria is a fundamental step that shapes the validity and acceptability of final outcomes. Criteria weights reflect the degree of importance attributed to each criterion and act as a bridge between the decision context and the mathematical model. When weights are inaccurately assigned or determined without sufficient justification, the evaluation process may generate misleading rankings, affecting both the transparency and reliability of the decision. Over several decades, numerous methods have been proposed for determining criteria weights, which are generally divided into objective and subjective categories. Objective methods rely entirely on available data to compute weights through mathematical models, thereby removing individual biases but often overlooking contextual realities (Mukhametzyanov, 2021; Ucar, 2024).

Subjective methods, on the other hand, involve experts or decision-makers directly, capturing human knowledge, preferences, and experience (Chatterjee & Chakraborty, 2024; Rezaei, 2015). This variability can extend beyond identifying the best alternative, reshaping the entire preference structure and altering the positions of intermediate and lower-ranked alternatives as well. Decision-makers should carefully consider factors like complexity of the problem, type and quality of data, measurement scales used, and possible connections among criteria before selecting a weighting method (Ayan et al., 2023). While subjective weighting is often more relevant to real-world decisions, it is not without limitations. Decision-makers can become overwhelmed by the extensive number of comparisons required, especially when the problem involves a large set of criteria. In addition, inconsistencies in judgments are difficult to avoid when many comparisons are involved, leading to unstable or unreliable results. These limitations have encouraged researchers to design techniques that are simple for experts to apply and capable of producing reliable and interpretable outcomes. A significant development in this context is level-based weight assessment (LBWA) method, which offers a structured yet less demanding process for assigning weights.

The LBWA method, developed by Žižović and Pamucar (2019), is a subjective criteria weighting method in MCDM that offers an efficient way of determining the significance of criteria compared to many well-established techniques. Traditional weighting methods like analytic hierarchy process (AHP) or best–worst method (BWM) often require a large number of comparisons, which can place a considerable burden on decision-makers. The most significant advantage of the LBWA method lies in its lower number of pairwise comparisons. LBWA requires only $(n-1)$ number of comparisons compared to its popular counterparts, like AHP (Saaty, 1980) $(n(n-1)/2)$, decision-making trial and

Encyclopedia of Multi-Attribute Decision-Making (MADM). DOI: https://doi.org/10.1016/B978-0-443-33275-3.00084-1

evaluation laboratory (Gabus & Fontela, 1972) ($n(n-1)$), or BWM (Rezaei, 2015) ($2n-3$). In real-life situations, when the number of criteria is high, this feature helps in withstanding subjective bias and inconsistencies.

LBWA classifies criteria into hierarchical levels according to their importance, as established by expert consultation. Criteria at a given level are seen as equally significant, whilst those at higher levels are deemed progressively more essential. This logical division enables decision-makers to express their preferences systematically and clearly, thereby preventing contradictions that arise from complex numerical scales. This ordered structure is then transformed into quantitative weights using a simple mathematical model. One of the strengths of LBWA is that its functionality does not deteriorate when the number of criteria increases. Whether the decision problem involves a smaller or larger set of criteria, the structure remains stable and adaptable (Ecer et al., 2021). Another advantage lies in the fact that LBWA reduces inconsistencies that commonly occur in expert evaluations. In methods like AHP, the large volume of pairwise comparisons often leads to contradictions in judgments, which can affect the validity of results. As LBWA requires fewer comparisons, it minimizes such contradictions and tends to generate more reliable weight distributions across criteria. A distinctive element of LBWA is the elasticity coefficient (EC), which allows decision-makers to perform sensitivity analysis. This feature makes it possible to explore how changes in the relative weight of one or more criteria may alter the ranking of alternatives (Pamučar et al., 2022). Through this process, practitioners can assess the stability of their decisions and identify which criteria exert the strongest influence on the results.

The remaining part of this chapter is organized as follows. In Section 22.2, the findings of the literature review of various extensions and applications of the LBWA method are outlined. Section 22.3 outlines the methodological steps of the LBWA method. Sections 22.4 and 22.5 present the case studies, accompanied by a demonstration of the findings and their implications. Section 22.6 exhibits the validation testing. Section 22.7 concludes and highlights some of the future scopes.

22.2 Literature review

LBWA and its fuzzy extensions have been serving as effective models for criteria weighting under different application contexts. Researchers have combined LBWA with various ranking methods, entropy measures, simulation techniques, and compromise solutions to enhance robustness, address ambiguity, and ensure reliable decision outcomes. A chronological overview of applications of the LBWA method is presented below.

Ecer et al. (2021) proposed an extended LBWA-based framework using interval rough number-based combinative distance-based assessment (CODAS) method to evaluate renewable energy resources in Turkey. Pamučar et al. (2021) proposed a hybrid LBWA-weighted aggregated sum product assessment (WASPAS) framework enhanced with weighted power Heronian and weighted geometric power Heronian functions to evaluate energy consumption and renewable energy potential in Iran's Caspian Sea region. Torkayesh et al. (2021) developed an integrated MCDM framework combining BWM-LBWA for healthcare indicator weighting and combined compromise solution (CoCoSo) for performance evaluation. Adali et al. (2022) proposed a hybrid grey-based MCDM framework integrating LBWA and evaluation based on distance from average solution to benchmark the smartness levels of European cities. Yazdani et al. (2021) proposed a two-phase sustainable multitier supplier selection model for food supply chains by integrating SWARA-LBWA with D-numbers for criteria weighting and measurement of alternatives and ranking according to compromise solution (MARCOS)-D for ranking suppliers. Božanić et al. (2023) proposed a hybrid MCDM framework integrating LBWA with the modified Z-number multiattributive border approximation area comparison method to support oil spill emergency management.

Demir (2023) proposed a Fuzzy LBWA (FLBWA)-based framework to evaluate and rank sustainability indicators for green building production in Turkey. Korucuk et al. (2022) proposed a hybrid MCDM framework using picture FLBWA and PFCoCoSo methods to evaluate green transportation indicators and select smart network strategies in logistics companies. Ogundoyin and Kamil (2023) proposed a hybrid MCDM framework for fog gateway selection in fog computing, integrating fuzzy best worst method (FBWM), FLBWA, and vector-normalized FCoCoSo with later defuzzification for weighting and ranking alternatives. Pamučar et al. (2023) proposed a hybrid MCDM framework combining stratified FLBWA and fuzzy rough Hamacher CoCoSo to prioritize the integration of unmanned aerial vehicles in transportation systems. Sharma et al. (2023) proposed a hybrid MCDM framework integrating BWM, LBWA, and CoCoSo to analyze barriers to adopting digital technologies for sustainable production and consumption in food supply chains. Yu et al. (2023) developed a hybrid fuzzy LBWA-WASPAS-H model integrating weighted Heronian mean (WHM) and weighted geometric Heronian mean functions to evaluate airport ground access modes for Istanbul Airport.

Wang, and Chen, Wang, et al. (2024) proposed a hybrid decision-making framework integrating LBWA, criteria importance through intercriteria correlation, WHM aggregation, and ranking of alternatives through Functional mapping of criterion subintervals into a single interval with Fermatean cubic fuzzy sets to evaluate barriers to digital transformation in energy transitions. Bachari and Iranfar (2025) proposed a hybrid MCDM framework for project risk management in engineering, procurement, and construction projects, integrating the Delphi method, FLBWA, and FCoCoSo to identify, weight, and rank risks. Dündar and Karadağ (2025) proposed a hybrid MCDM framework to identify optimal investment locations among 47 African countries for a cosmetics company. Işık et al. (2025) proposed a two-phase fuzzy MCDM framework combining FLBWA, fuzzy logarithm methodology of additive weights, and MARCOS methods for evaluating bank performance. Karbalaeiramezanali et al. (2025) applied a hybrid MCDM approach integrating Monte Carlo simulation-based LBWA with MARCOS method to enhance mineral prospectivity mapping for W-Mo-Sb-Au deposits. Pei et al. (2025) proposed an integrated framework for evaluating fighter cockpit ergonomics during the preliminary design stage. Sumrit and Maneelok (2025) proposed a hybrid MCDM framework for implementing civil helicopter emergency medical services via public-private partnerships in low- and middle-income countries. Yu et al. (2025) proposed an improved failure mode and effects analysis framework for liquefied natural gas storage safety by combining interval-valued spherical fuzzy set with CODAS. Zorlu et al. (2025) proposed a FMCDM framework to quantify the degradation risk of geosites by integrating multi-attribute ideal-real comparative analysis method with LBWA. Table 22.1 presents a chronological summary of studies that have employed LBWA-based MCDM frameworks across various application domains.

22.3 Methodology: level-based weight assessment

The procedural steps of the LBWA method (Žižović & Pamucar, 2019) are delineated below.

Suppose $\vartheta_j (j = 1, 2, ..., n)$ represents the variables or criteria whose weights are calculated using the LBWA method.

Step 1. Identify the most important criterion

The criteria are sorted in order of importance. It is done in two ways: (a) comparing the contributions or significance; (b) using the rating of the criteria (based on a predetermined scale) by the experts or decision-makers. Assume that $\vartheta_k \in V = \{\vartheta_1, \vartheta_2, ..., \vartheta_n\}$ is any criterion that is most important among others.

Step 2. Compare the other criteria with the most significant one and formulate level-wise subsets of criteria

All other criteria are compared with the most significant one, and according to their relative positions, several levels are created. Each such level indicates a subset of criteria. The formulation of the subsets is explained below.

Level L_1: It contains a subset consisting of the criteria whose relative contributions or importance are equal to or up to half compared with the most significant criterion, ϑ_k.

Level L_2: It contains the subset that consists of the criteria for which the most significant criterion, ϑ_k is found to be two times or up to three times more important.

Level L_3: It contains a subset that consists of the criteria whose relative contributions or importance are equal to three times or up to four times less compared with the most significant criterion, ϑ_k.

This way, the level partitioning continues until all criteria are exhausted and comparisons are completed. In general,

Level L_p: It contains the subset that consists of the criteria whose relative contributions or importance are equal to p times or up to $(p + 1)$ times less compared with the most significant criterion, ϑ_k.

Therefore, collectively, we can write $V = L_1 \cup L_2 \cup L_3 \cup ....\cup L_p$

If $S\left(\vartheta_j\right)$ is the significance of the ϑ_j compared to the most significant one, then we can mathematically express the subset contained by L_p as follows.

$$L_p = \left\{\vartheta_j \in V \middle| p \leq S\left(\vartheta_j\right) < p + 1\right\} \tag{22.1}$$

Of course, the leveling is subject to the satisfaction of the following condition, which states

$$L_g \cap L_h = \varnothing; \quad g \neq h; \quad g, \ h \in \{1, 2, ..., p\} \tag{22.2}$$

It means the levels should be distinct, and there should not be any overlap of elements across the subsets.

Step 3. Intra-group comparisons

Within a subset, the criteria are compared in accordance with their significance. Each criterion, $\vartheta_j \in L_p$ is assigned with an integer value, $\Delta_j \in \{0, 1, ... ,r\}$. The maximum value on the scale of comparison, r is the maximum of the cardinal values of the levels, that is,

$$r = Max\left\{|L_1|, \ |L_2|, \ ..., \ \left|L_p\right|\right\} \tag{22.3}$$

TABLE 22.1 Literature review of LBWA-based MCDM frameworks.

Authors	Framework	Application/case study
Ecer et al. (2021)	Extended LBWA with IRN-based CODAS	Renewable energy resource evaluation in Turkey
Pamučar et al. (2021)	Hybrid LBWA-WASPAS with WPHA & WGPHA	Energy consumption & renewable potential in Caspian Sea, Iran
Torkayesh et al. (2021)	Integrated BWM-LBWA and CoCoSo	Healthcare system performance in Eastern Europe
Adali et al. (2022)	Hybrid grey LBWA-EDAS (LBWA-G + EDAS-G)	Smartness benchmarking of European cities
Yazdani et al. (2021)	Two-phase SWARA-LBWA with D-numbers + MARCOS-D	Sustainable multitier supplier selection in Spanish wine industry
Božanić et al. (2023)	LBWA + modified Z-number MABAC	Oil spill emergency management, Libya (El Sharara oil field)
Demir (2023)	FLBWA-based framework	Sustainability indicators in Turkish green building production
Korucuk et al. (2022)	PFLBWA + PFCoCoSo	Green transportation indicators in logistics companies
Ogundoyin and Kamil (2023)	FBWM + FLBWA + V-Fuzzy-CoCoSo-LD	Fog gateway selection in fog computing
Pamučar et al. (2023)	Stratified FLBWA + fuzzy rough Hamacher CoCoSo	UAV integration in transportation systems
Sharma et al. (2023)	BWM + LBWA + CoCoSo	Barriers to adopting digital technologies in food supply chains
Yu et al. (2023)	Hybrid FLBWA-WASPAS-H with WHM & WGHM	Airport ground access mode selection (Istanbul airport)
Wang, and Chen, Wang, et al. (2024)	LBWA + CRITIC + WHM aggregation + RAFSI with Fermatean cubic fuzzy sets	Barriers to digital transformation in energy transitions
Bachari and Iranfar (2025)	Delphi + FLBWA + FCoCoSo	Project risk management in EPC projects
Dündar and Karadağ (2025)	FLBWA + IRAWEC	Investment location selection across 47 African countries
Işık et al. (2025)	FLBWA + FLMAW + MARCOS	Bank performance evaluation in Pakistan
Karbalaeiramezanali et al. (2025)	Monte Carlo simulation-based LBWA + MARCOS	Mineral prospectivity mapping (W-Mo-Sb-Au deposits)
Pei et al. (2025)	FLBWA + fuzzy entropy + FCoCoSo (Bonferroni)	Fighter cockpit ergonomics evaluation
Sumrit and Maneelok (2025)	LBWA + IDOCRIW + CRADIS + IVq-ROFS	PPP strategies for civil helicopter EMS in LMICs
Yu et al. (2025)	IVSFS + CODAS with LBWA and MEREC	LNG storage safety risk (Chinese LNG tanks)
Zorlu et al. (2025)	Fuzzy MAIRCA + LBWA	Geosite degradation risk assessment

Conditions:

- The integer value of the most important criterion is zero, that is, $\Delta_k = 0$
- If $\vartheta_g > \vartheta_h$ then $\Delta_g < \Delta_h$. It means the higher the significance, the lesser the integer value.
- Two criteria are assigned with the same integer value, that is, $\Delta_g = \Delta_h$, if they are equally significant.

Step 4. Obtain the EC

EC is any real number that is greater than r, that is, $r_0 > r$

Step 5. Compute the influence function values (IFVs) for each criterion

IFV of the criterion $\vartheta_j \in L_p$ is obtained as follows.

$$\xi_j = f\left(\vartheta_j\right): L \to R = \frac{r_0}{pr_0 + \Delta_j} \tag{22.4}$$

Step 6. Calculate the weights of the criteria

The weight of the most important criterion is obtained as

$$w_k = \frac{1}{1 + \xi_1 + \xi_2 + ..+\xi_n} \tag{22.5}$$

Here, $k \in j\,(j = 1, 2, ..,n)$

The weights of the other criteria are computed as follows.

$$w_{j \neq k} = \xi_j w_k \tag{22.6}$$

22.4 Numerical example 1

22.4.1 Case study 1: challenges of first-generation entrepreneurs in Industry 5.0

This case study addresses various challenges faced by the first-generation entrepreneurs (FGEs) in Industry 5.0. Industry 5.0 represents a pivotal transition in industrial advancement, emphasizing human-centric innovation, sustainability, and resilience (Rame et al., 2024). It integrates advanced technologies, including artificial intelligence, the Internet of Things, virtual/augmented reality, digital twins, blockchain, and robotics. FGEs face distinct hurdles, including substantial initial investments in technology and skills, financial constraints, managing supply chains, and the challenge of scaling innovative potential (Ali et al., 2025; Ghag et al., 2025; León et al., 2025).

Industry 5.0 emphasizes the synergistic partnership between humans and machines, particularly through collaborative robots (cobots). Establishing trust among employees and consumers is challenging for newcomers who lack a proven track record of organizational flexibility. The dynamic capabilities perspective (Teece et al., 1997) emphasizes the need for rapid development and adaptation of unique organizational processes, presenting a challenge for FGEs who are building skills from scratch (Benghouala & Benamirouche, 2025; Gamberini & Pluchino, 2024; Ghobakhloo et al., 2023).

Researchers have highlighted the challenges of upgrading labor skills to meet the demands of emerging technologies, social sustainability concerns, and the threat of technological unemployment. Security issues and legal ambiguities in automation and AI subject first-generation entrepreneurs to novel vulnerabilities in cyber-physical systems (Adel, 2022; Zare et al., 2025). Socio-technical systems theory (Trist, 1981) emphasizes the interplay between social and technological subsystems in Industry 5.0, presenting significant challenges. To address these challenges, robust organizational methods, proactive workforce management, and creative policies are essential for fostering resilient and fair growth in the emerging period (Ali et al., 2025; Gamberini & Pluchino, 2024; León et al., 2025).

Some scholars (for instance, Anne et al., 2025; Sudaryanto & Sylvana, 2024; Suhara & Sopyan, 2024; Taş, 2024; Zare et al., 2025) have attempted to address various issues related to entrepreneurship in Industry 5.0. However, the body of literature lacks extensive investigations into the concerns for FGEs. The current work bridges the gap in the literature by presenting a case study to discern key issues of FGEs in Industry 5.0. Table 22.2 presents the challenges identified through a review of related past contributions.

22.4.2 Data collection

This study evaluates the challenges (Table 22.2) based on the opinions of experts. We followed a snowball approach through referrals. Ultimately, a group of 30 experts agreed to participate in this study. The focused group of experts showcases a balanced mix of entrepreneurs, government officials, industry experts, and academic professors (Table 22.3).

The experts were contacted both in person and by telephone. The ratings of the challenging factors were conducted using a 7-point Likert scale (7: extremely critical; 1: least critical). The experts' ratings of various challenges are exhibited in Table 22.4.

TABLE 22.2 Barriers to FGEs in Industry 5.0.

Barriers	Description
C1	Constraints in investment
C2	Trust and reliability in human-machine collaboration
C3	Data management, security, and privacy concerns
C4	Difficulty in adapting the business model transformation
C5	Skill gaps and knowledge management
C6	Uncertain regulatory and legal framework

TABLE 22.3 Profile of the experts involved in case study 1.

Education		Sector		Experience	
PhD	5	Industry	8	10 to 15 years	20
Masters	16	Academia	5	More than 15 years	10
Bachelors	9	Entrepreneurs	12		
		Others	5		
Total	30	Total	30	Total	30

22.4.3 Analysis and results

In this section, we demonstrate the application of the LBWA method in prioritizing the barriers faced by FGEs in Industry 5.0. For this case study, we have $n = 6$ barriers (Table 22.2).

Step 1. Identify the most important barrier

We calculate the total weighted rating scores for the barriers to sort them. To this end, first, we calculate the weights of the experts. The experts are weighted based on their education level and experience, utilizing the Heron mean (Bošković et al., 2025; Kara et al., 2024) as outlined below.

$$\omega_i^{Edu} = \frac{\gamma_i^{Edu}}{\sum_{i=1}^{m} \gamma_i^{Edu}} \tag{22.7}$$

$$\omega_i^{Exp} = \frac{\gamma_i^{Exp}}{\sum_{i=1}^{m} \gamma_i^{Exp}} \tag{22.8}$$

$$\omega_i = \lambda\left(\omega_i^{Edu}\omega_i^{Exp}\right)^{1/2} + (1-\lambda)\left(\frac{\omega_i^{Edu} + \omega_i^{Exp}}{2}\right) \tag{22.9}$$

Here, γ_i^{Edu} = Score value based on education level (1: bachelor's, 2: master's, 3: PhD)

γ_i^{Exp} = Score value based on experience level = number of years of experience

$\lambda \in [0, 1]$ is a scalar coefficient, used to examine the sensitivity of the model to decision-makers' experience and education levels. For the initial case, we set $\lambda = 0.5$. The calculation of expert weights is demonstrated in Table A1 (Appendix A).

TABLE 22.4 Evaluation of the challenges by experts.

Expert ID	C1	C2	C3	C4	C5	C6	Expert ID	C1	C2	C3	C4	C5	C6
1	7	5	3	6	4	2	16	6	6	2	6	6	2
2	6	7	3	7	4	1	17	7	4	3	6	3	4
3	7	6	3	6	3	1	18	7	7	3	7	7	3
4	6	5	2	6	5	2	19	7	5	3	7	3	2
5	7	4	5	6	5	4	20	7	5	2	6	5	2
6	6	6	6	6	5	3	21	7	7	4	7	4	3
7	7	5	2	5	5	2	22	7	6	5	6	5	3
8	7	5	4	6	4	2	23	7	5	3	5	5	3
9	7	6	5	6	4	2	24	7	4	4	7	4	2
10	6	4	4	6	4	3	25	7	4	2	7	4	1
11	6	5	3	5	5	2	26	7	6	6	6	6	6
12	7	4	3	6	3	2	27	7	5	2	5	5	2
13	6	4	2	6	3	1	28	7	6	5	5	5	1
14	7	5	5	5	5	3	29	7	5	2	6	2	1
15	6	5	4	7	4	2	30	7	6	2	6	3	1

Next, we multiply the expert weights by the corresponding ratings of the barriers (Table 22.4). The weighted rating scores for ϑ_j are obtained as follows.

$$\zeta_{ji} = \varphi_{ji}\omega_i \tag{22.10}$$

Where

φ_{ji} is the rating of the jth barrier by the ith expert (Table 22.4).

For instance,

$$\zeta_{11} = \varphi_{11}\omega_1 = 7 \times 0.0339 = 0.237; \;\; \zeta_{12} = \varphi_{12}\omega_2 = 6 \times 0.0350 = 0.210;$$
$$\zeta_{41} = \varphi_{41}\omega_1 = 6 \times 0.0339 = 0.2031; \;\; \zeta_{54} = \varphi_{54}\omega_4 = 5 \times 0.0302 = 0.151$$

Similarly, the weighted rating score values for all barriers, as assessed by all experts, are calculated (See Table 22.5).

We then derive the overall score values for all barriers using Eq. (22.11) as follows. The overall score value is the geometric mean of all weighted rating scores. The geometric mean provides a smoother effect than the arithmetic average and is less susceptible to the outlier effect. In this case, there is no possibility of a zero or negative value in the weighted rating score matrix; therefore, the use of the geometric mean poses no potential issues.

$$\alpha_j = \left(\prod_{i=1}^{m} \zeta_{ji}\right)^{\frac{1}{m}} \tag{22.11}$$

Next, the criteria are sorted using their α_j values. The alternative with the highest α_j value is treated as the most significant barrier. For example,

$$\alpha_1 = (0.237 \times 0.210 \times 0.3136 \times \ldots.\times 0.2202)^{\frac{1}{30}} = 0.2158$$

$$\alpha_4 = (0.203 \times 0.245 \times 0.2688 \times \ldots.\times 0.1887)^{\frac{1}{30}} = 0.1927$$

Step 2. Compare the other barriers with the most significant one and formulate level-wise subsets

TABLE A.1 Calculation of expert weights (at $\lambda = 0.5$) (case study 1).

Expert ID	Exp. (years)	Edu	Edu code	Weight (exp)	Weight (edu)	Final weight	Expert ID	Exp. (years)	Edu	Edu code	Weight (exp)	Weight (edu)	Final weight
1	14	Masters	2	0.0320	0.0357	0.0339	16	10	Masters	2	0.0229	0.0357	0.0289
2	15	Masters	2	0.0343	0.0357	0.0350	17	11	Bachelors	1	0.0252	0.0179	0.0214
3	24	Masters	2	0.0549	0.0357	0.0448	18	14	Bachelors	1	0.0320	0.0179	0.0244
4	11	Masters	2	0.0252	0.0357	0.0302	19	16	Masters	2	0.0366	0.0357	0.0362
5	12	Masters	2	0.0275	0.0357	0.0315	20	15	Masters	2	0.0343	0.0357	0.0350
6	18	PhD	3	0.0412	0.0536	0.0472	21	15	Masters	2	0.0343	0.0357	0.0350
7	10	Bachelors	1	0.0229	0.0179	0.0203	22	15	Bachelors	1	0.0343	0.0179	0.0254
8	11	PhD	3	0.0252	0.0536	0.0380	23	14	Masters	2	0.0320	0.0357	0.0339
9	17	PhD	3	0.0389	0.0536	0.0459	24	20	Masters	2	0.0458	0.0357	0.0406
10	16	Bachelors	1	0.0366	0.0179	0.0264	25	18	Masters	2	0.0412	0.0357	0.0384
11	10	Bachelors	1	0.0229	0.0179	0.0203	26	17	Masters	2	0.0389	0.0357	0.0373
12	12	Bachelors	1	0.0275	0.0179	0.0224	27	15	Bachelors	1	0.0343	0.0179	0.0254
13	19	Bachelors	1	0.0435	0.0179	0.0293	28	13	Masters	2	0.0297	0.0357	0.0327
14	16	Masters	2	0.0366	0.0357	0.0362	29	12	PhD	3	0.0275	0.0536	0.0394
15	15	PhD	3	0.0343	0.0536	0.0434	30	12	Masters	2	0.0275	0.0357	0.0315

TABLE 22.5 Weighted rating values of the challenges.

Weight	0.0339	0.0350	0.0448	0.0302	0.0315	0.0472	0.0203	0.0380	0.0459	0.0264
Expert ID/ barriers	1	2	3	4	5	6	7	8	9	10
C1	0.237	0.21	0.314	0.181	0.22	0.283	0.142	0.266	0.322	0.158
C2	0.169	0.245	0.269	0.151	0.126	0.283	0.101	0.19	0.276	0.106
C3	0.102	0.105	0.134	0.06	0.157	0.283	0.041	0.152	0.23	0.106
C4	0.203	0.245	0.269	0.181	0.189	0.283	0.101	0.228	0.276	0.158
C5	0.135	0.14	0.134	0.151	0.157	0.236	0.101	0.152	0.184	0.106
C6	0.068	0.035	0.045	0.06	0.126	0.142	0.041	0.076	0.092	0.079
Weight	0.0203	0.0224	0.0293	0.0362	0.0434	0.0289	0.0214	0.0244	0.0362	0.0350
Expert ID/ barriers	11	12	13	14	15	16	17	18	19	20
C1	0.122	0.157	0.176	0.253	0.26	0.174	0.15	0.171	0.253	0.245
C2	0.101	0.09	0.117	0.181	0.217	0.174	0.085	0.171	0.181	0.175
C3	0.061	0.067	0.059	0.181	0.174	0.058	0.064	0.073	0.108	0.07
C4	0.101	0.134	0.176	0.181	0.304	0.174	0.128	0.171	0.253	0.21
C5	0.101	0.067	0.088	0.181	0.174	0.174	0.064	0.171	0.108	0.175
C6	0.041	0.045	0.029	0.108	0.087	0.058	0.085	0.073	0.072	0.07
Weight	0.0350	0.0254	0.0339	0.0406	0.0384	0.0373	0.0254	0.0327	0.0394	0.0315
Expert ID/ barriers	21	22	23	24	25	26	27	28	29	30
C1	0.245	0.178	0.237	0.284	0.269	0.261	0.178	0.229	0.276	0.22
C2	0.245	0.153	0.169	0.162	0.154	0.224	0.127	0.196	0.197	0.189
C3	0.14	0.127	0.102	0.162	0.077	0.224	0.051	0.163	0.079	0.063
C4	0.245	0.153	0.169	0.284	0.269	0.224	0.127	0.163	0.237	0.189
C5	0.14	0.127	0.169	0.162	0.154	0.224	0.127	0.163	0.079	0.094
C6	0.105	0.076	0.102	0.081	0.038	0.224	0.051	0.033	0.039	0.031

We now proceed to level partitioning. We find that α_1 is the highest value, suggesting that ϑ_1 (i.e., Ch 1) is the most significant barrier. The other barriers are sorted in accordance with their corresponding α_j values (Table 22.6).

Then, we compare ϑ_1 with all the others and determine its relative importance compared to the others. For instance, the relative importance value of ϑ_1 over ϑ_4 is given by

$$\frac{\alpha_1}{\alpha_4} = \frac{0.2158}{0.1927} = 1.1202$$

Similarly, we have $\frac{\alpha_1}{\alpha_2} = \frac{0.2158}{0.1656} = 1.3036$; $\frac{\alpha_1}{\alpha_5} = \frac{0.2158}{0.1347} = 1.6026$; $\frac{\alpha_1}{\alpha_3} = \frac{0.2158}{0.1021} = 2.1139$; $\frac{\alpha_1}{\alpha_6} = \frac{0.2158}{0.0653} = 3.3067$

TABLE 22.6 Level partitioning and calculation of weights of the barriers.

Barrier	Score		Level	Function	Weight	Rank
C1	0.2158		0	1.0000	0.2538	1
C4	0.1927	1.1202	1	0.8333	0.2115	2
C2	0.1656	1.3036	2	0.7143	0.1813	3
C5	0.1347	1.6026	3	0.6250	0.1586	4
C3	0.1021	2.1139	1	0.4545	0.1154	5
C6	0.0653	3.3067	1	0.3125	0.0793	6

Therefore, we notice that $\{\vartheta_1, \vartheta_4, \vartheta_2, \vartheta_5\} \in L_1$; $\{\vartheta_3\} \in L_2$; $\{\vartheta_6\} \in L_3$

Thus, we partition the barriers into three levels for this case study.

Step 3. Intra-group comparisons

Now, inside each group, that is, at each level, we assign the integer values to the constituent elements. For instance, for L_1, the values assigned are $\Delta_1 = 0$((most significant), $\Delta_4 = 1$; $\Delta_2 = 2$; $\Delta_5 = 3$. The integer values of all other elements at L_2 and L_3 are 1, that is, $\Delta_3 = 1$; $\Delta_6 = 1$.

Step 4. Obtain the EC

We notice that $r = 4$ because L_1 has the maximum number of elements, that is, 4. Therefore, the value of EC is obtained as $r_0 > r \Rightarrow r_0 = 5$.

Step 5. Compute the IFVs for each barrier.

The IFVs are obtained by applying Eq. (22.4).

For instance,

$$\xi_1 = \frac{r_0}{pr_0+\Delta_1} = \frac{5}{1\times 5+0} = 1$$

$$\xi_4 = \frac{r_0}{pr_0+\Delta_4} = \frac{5}{1\times 5+1} = 0.833$$

Step 6. Calculate the weights of the barriers

The weights of the barriers are obtained by using Eqs. (22.5) and (22.6).

For instance, the weight of the most important barrier, ϑ_1 is obtained as

$$w_1 = \frac{1}{1+\xi_2+\xi_3+\xi_4+\xi_5+\xi_6} = \frac{1}{1+0.7143+0.4545+0.8333+0.6250+0.3125} = 0.2538$$

The weights of the other criteria are computed by using Eq. (22.6). For example,

$$w_4 = \xi_4 w_1 = 0.8333 \times 0.2538 = 0.2115$$
$$w_2 = \xi_2 w_1 = 0.7143 \times 0.2538 = 0.1813$$
$$w_5 = \xi_5 w_1 = 0.6250 \times 0.2538 = 0.1586$$
$$w_3 = \xi_3 w_1 = 0.4545 \times 0.2538 = 0.1154$$
$$w_6 = \xi_6 w_1 = 0.3125 \times 0.2538 = 0.0793$$

Accordingly, the barriers are ranked based on their calculated weights. Table 22.6 exhibits the calculations at steps 2 to 6 and the ranking of the barriers.

22.4.4 Discussion

The analysis reveals that investment (C1) is a significant concern (rank 1) for FGEs. Modern technologies require a high initial outlay, and thereafter, they necessitate operational and maintenance costs. FGEs often face difficulties in arranging capital. Limited capital allocation hinders experimentation and extensive implementation, thereby obstructing substantial transformation. Digital transformations require a massive-scale reengineering of conventional processes; structural inertia and resistance to change hinder strategic realignment for adapting to business model transformations (C4). The implementation of advanced digital technologies requires a seamless collaboration between humans and machines. Trust and dependability play a crucial role. The barrier (C2) at the third position highlights persistent concerns over the accountability of autonomous systems and their acceptance by stakeholders.

The results obtained from this case study exhibit some significant implications.

- Managers must confront investment limitations by carefully strategizing and selecting activities that yield the highest return on investment. Confronting problems in business model transition necessitates proactive change management, fostering organizational agility and strategic flexibility. Confidence in human-machine collaboration is essential, necessitating transparency in AI-generated assessments and human oversight when required. Investing in continuous training programs is crucial to rectifying skill shortfalls and promoting knowledge transfer within the firm.
- Overcoming challenges in automation can enhance employee adaptability and resilience. Trust difficulties in human-machine contact might improve acceptance, mitigate job displacement apprehensions, and promote inclusive partnerships. The cultivation of digital literacy skills enhances employees and communities, promoting societal acceptability. Comprehensive security mechanisms mitigate privacy concerns, preserving public confidence in digital systems and protecting stakeholder interests.
- Governments and regulatory bodies ought to establish comprehensive legislation that harmonizes innovation with ethical safeguards. Investment by the public sector in digital infrastructure, combined with the incentivization of private innovation, can reduce expenses and enhance uptake. Policymakers ought to promote national reskilling efforts to maintain a competitive workforce. Comprehensive data governance frameworks augment trust, safeguard privacy, and facilitate digital transformation.

22.5 Numerical example 2

22.5.1 Case study 2: critical criteria for renewable energy technology selection

Over the years, there has been a continuing effort on environmental sustainability. In line with the emphasis on climate protection, green entrepreneurship has emerged as a strategic area for future investment. Green entrepreneurship involves the creation and management of enterprises that offer ecologically sustainable solutions, aiming to mitigate environmental harm and promote social change through responsible economic practices (Demirel et al., 2019). The generation and use of renewable energies has been one of the key action areas for green entrepreneurship to achieve the target of net zero (Haldar, 2019; Juarez-Rojas et al., 2023).

Besides environmental sustainability, the inclusive development of rural regions has been a priority for the nation's economic growth. Green entrepreneurship plays a crucial role in revitalizing the rural sector, promoting sustainable development (Chandel, 2022; Wang & Ye, 2024). Scholars (Dobrovolska et al., 2024; Karimi et al., 2024; Li & Shen, 2019; Romero-Castro et al., 2022; Vernet et al., 2019; Zaman, 2025) have advocated for rapid electrification through renewable energy sources to drive rural growth and have recognized the role of green entrepreneurship, though selecting technology for renewable energy generation in rural electrification is a complex and critical decision (Li et al., 2024).

The current case study presents a multicriteria group decision-making approach using the LBWA method, enabling entrepreneurs to identify the critical factors influencing the selection of renewable energy technology for rural electrification. The criteria are delineated for evaluating renewable energy technologies based on the review of related past contributions. The selection of renewable energy technology for rural electrification requires a thorough evaluation methodology that encompasses technical, economic, environmental, and socio-political considerations (Sumarliah & Olebogeng Makgetho, 2025). The efficacy, stability, scalability, and compatibility of renewable energy sources with local infrastructure are essential.

Economic considerations, including initial capital investment, operations and maintenance expenses, and the levelized cost of electricity, are essential for rural electrification initiatives. Payback periods and financial methodologies are crucial, whereas incentives, subsidies, and novel financing structures, like solar bonds, significantly affect technical adoption. Environmental considerations, including life-cycle emissions, resource depletion potential, and ecological effects, are also significant. Biomass and small hydro alternatives should be assessed for their carbon neutrality and ecological impacts. Socio-political elements, including community backing, legislative support, and socioeconomic effects, are crucial for project sustainability and social equality (El-Maaroufi et al., 2024; Husain et al., 2024; Kassem et al., 2024; Kumar et al., 2024; Mandal et al., 2025)

The integration of these criteria provides a holistic viewpoint for decision-making, reflecting the growing trends in sustainable energy research. This case study demonstrates how a systematic, expert-driven evaluation can guide rural electrification initiatives, aligning technological choices with environmental and socioeconomic objectives throughout India's energy transition. The criteria are outlined in Table 22.7.

22.5.2 Data collection

Likewise, in the previous case study, we followed a snowball approach through referrals. Ultimately, a group of 20 experts agreed to participate in this study. The focused group of experts comprises a balanced mix of industry experts, technocrats, scientists, and academic professors (Table 22.8).

The experts were contacted both in person and by telephone. The ratings of the challenging factors were conducted using a 7-point Likert scale (7: extremely critical; 1: least critical). The experts' ratings of various challenges are exhibited in Table 22.9.

22.5.3 Analysis and results

The evaluation of the criteria based on their calculated weights using the LBWA method is carried out step-by-step as demonstrated in section 22.4.3. First, expert weights are determined using Eqs. (22.7) to (22.9). In this case, we have 20 experts. The calculated expert weights are reported in Table A2.

The ratings of the experts are recorded in Table 22.9. The weighted rating scores of the criteria are calculated using Eq. (22.10), as given in Table 22.10. In this case, $n = 8$.

The overall scores of the criteria are derived using Eq. (22.11), as shown in Table 22.11. The criteria are then partitioned based on their overall scores, as demonstrated in Section 22.4.3. In this case, ϑ_5(i.e., Cr-5) is the most

TABLE 22.7 Criteria for evaluating renewable energy technologies for rural electrification.

Criteria	Description
Cr-1	Installation cost
Cr-2	Operation and maintenance cost
Cr-3	Energy efficiency
Cr-4	Reliability
Cr-5	Environmental impact
Cr-6	Social acceptance
Cr-7	Government policy support
Cr-8	Scalability

TABLE 22.8 Profile of the experts involved in case study 2.

Education		Sector		Experience	
PhD	8	Industry	8	10 to 15 years	6
Masters	9	Academia	5	15 to 20 years	10
Bachelors	3	Environmental scientists	4	More than 20 years	4
		Others	3		
Total	20	Total	2-0	Total	20

TABLE 22.9 Evaluation of the criteria for renewable energy technology selection.

Expert ID	Cr-1	Cr-2	Cr-3	Cr-4	Cr-5	Cr-6	Cr-7	Cr-8
1	7	5	6	3	7	2	2	3
2	5	5	7	4	6	2	3	3
3	5	5	6	5	7	3	3	5
4	6	6	5	6	7	2	2	4
5	7	6	5	4	7	3	2	4
6	6	4	6	5	6	3	3	3
7	6	5	5	3	6	3	2	3
8	7	4	5	4	7	2	3	4
9	7	4	5	4	7	2	2	3
10	6	3	6	7	7	3	5	4
11	7	6	4	4	6	2	2	4
12	5	7	7	4	5	3	5	5
13	6	5	7	5	6	3	5	5
14	6	5	5	4	5	2	4	4
15	5	4	6	4	7	3	3	3
16	6	3	4	4	7	2	3	3
17	5	3	7	3	7	2	2	2
18	5	4	5	3	7	2	3	3
19	5	5	5	5	6	2	2	3
20	6	6	5	3	6	3	2	3

important criterion, as rated by the experts. Accordingly, two distinct levels are identified, L_1 and L_2. The EC value is $r_0 = 7$.

Accordingly, integer values are assigned to the criteria at different levels and compute their IFVs. Finally, by applying Eq. (22.5), the weight of Cr-5 is computed. The weights of the other criteria are calculated using Eq. (22.6). Table 22.11 presents the calculation of the criterion weights and their ranking.

22.5.4 Discussions

Table 22.11 illustrates a prioritization of determinants that influence the adoption of technology. The environmental impact is paramount, underscoring the need for sustainable methods. The installation cost is the second most critical aspect, particularly in budget-constrained scenarios. Energy efficiency is the third aspect, emphasizing operational performance and cost reductions. Operational and maintenance expenses, together with reliability, have intermediate importance, with ongoing financial and technical performance being secondary to original investment and environmental impacts. Scalability, governmental policy support, and societal acceptance are crucial yet often overlooked factors for enduring integration and widespread adoption. The findings suggest that MCDM for technology adoption should prioritize sustainability, cost structure, and efficiency, while also considering policy, social, and scaling factors to ensure resilient and future-oriented judgments.

Case study 2 highlights several implications.

- Managers must emphasize sustainability by reducing environmental impact in technology selection and deployment, controlling installation and operational costs, and enhancing energy efficiency. There is a need to augment

TABLE A2 Calculation of expert weights (at $\lambda = 0.5$) (case study 2).

Expert ID	Exp. (years)	Edu	Edu code	Weight (exp)	Weight (edu)	Final weight	Expert ID	Exp. (years)	Edu	Edu code	Weight (exp)	Weight (edu)	Final weight
1	16	Masters	2	0.0441	0.0541	0.0489	11	18	Bachelors	1	0.0496	0.0270	0.0375
2	25	Masters	2	0.0689	0.0541	0.0612	12	17	Bachelors	1	0.0468	0.0270	0.0363
3	13	Masters	2	0.0358	0.0541	0.0445	13	13	Bachelors	1	0.0358	0.0270	0.0313
4	25	Masters	2	0.0689	0.0541	0.0612	14	20	Masters	2	0.0551	0.0541	0.0546
5	17	Masters	2	0.0468	0.0541	0.0504	15	18	PhD	3	0.0496	0.0811	0.0644
6	16	PhD	3	0.0441	0.0811	0.0612	16	17	Masters	2	0.0468	0.0541	0.0504
7	15	Bachelors	1	0.0413	0.0270	0.0338	17	12	Bachelors	1	0.0331	0.0270	0.0300
8	22	PhD	3	0.0606	0.0811	0.0705	18	22	Bachelors	1	0.0606	0.0270	0.0421
9	24	PhD	3	0.0661	0.0811	0.0734	19	24	Masters	2	0.0661	0.0541	0.0599
10	13	Bachelors	1	0.0358	0.0270	0.0313	20	16	Masters	2	0.0441	0.0541	0.0489

TABLE 22.10 Weighted rating values of the criteria for technology selection.

Weight	0.0489	0.0612	0.0445	0.0612	0.0504	0.0612	0.0338	0.0705	0.0734	0.0313
Expert ID/ criteria	1	2	3	4	5	6	7	8	9	10
Cr-1	0.3426	0.3062	0.2223	0.3674	0.3526	0.3671	0.2028	0.4933	0.5139	0.1876
Cr-2	0.2447	0.3062	0.2223	0.3674	0.3023	0.2447	0.1690	0.2819	0.2936	0.0938
Cr-3	0.2936	0.4287	0.2668	0.3062	0.2519	0.3671	0.1690	0.3524	0.3670	0.1876
Cr-4	0.1468	0.2450	0.2223	0.3674	0.2015	0.3059	0.1014	0.2819	0.2936	0.2189
Cr-5	0.3426	0.3674	0.3113	0.4287	0.3526	0.3671	0.2028	0.4933	0.5139	0.2189
Cr-6	0.0979	0.1225	0.1334	0.1225	0.1511	0.1835	0.1014	0.1409	0.1468	0.0938
Cr-7	0.0979	0.1837	0.1334	0.1225	0.1008	0.1835	0.0676	0.2114	0.1468	0.1563
Cr-8	0.1468	0.1837	0.2223	0.2450	0.2015	0.1835	0.1014	0.2819	0.2202	0.1251
Weight	0.0375	0.0363	0.0313	0.0546	0.0644	0.0504	0.0300	0.0421	0.0599	0.0489
Expert ID/ criteria	11	12	13	14	15	16	17	18	19	20
Cr-1	0.2622	0.1813	0.1876	0.3274	0.3219	0.3023	0.1498	0.2107	0.2997	0.2936
Cr-2	0.2247	0.2538	0.1563	0.2729	0.2575	0.1511	0.0899	0.1686	0.2997	0.2936
Cr-3	0.1498	0.2538	0.2189	0.2729	0.3862	0.2015	0.2098	0.2107	0.2997	0.2447
Cr-4	0.1498	0.1450	0.1563	0.2183	0.2575	0.2015	0.0899	0.1264	0.2997	0.1468
Cr-5	0.2247	0.1813	0.1876	0.2729	0.4506	0.3526	0.2098	0.2950	0.3596	0.2936
Cr-6	0.0749	0.1088	0.0938	0.1091	0.1931	0.1008	0.0599	0.0843	0.1199	0.1468
Cr-7	0.0749	0.1813	0.1563	0.2183	0.1931	0.1511	0.0599	0.1264	0.1199	0.0979
Cr-8	0.1498	0.1813	0.1563	0.2183	0.1931	0.1511	0.0599	0.1264	0.1798	0.1468

TABLE 22.11 Level partitioning and calculation of weights of the criteria for technology selection.

Criteria	Score		Level	Function	Weight	Rank
Cr-5	0.3063		0	1.000	0.1826	1
Cr-1	0.2795	1.0962	1	0.875	0.1598	2
Cr-3	0.2615	1.1715	2	0.778	0.1420	3
Cr-2	0.2207	1.3882	3	0.700	0.1278	4
Cr-4	0.1951	1.5700	4	0.636	0.1162	5
Cr-8	0.165	1.8534	5	0.583	0.1065	6
Cr-7	0.131	2.3423	1	0.467	0.0852	7
Cr-6	0.1147	2.6717	2	0.438	0.0799	8

organizational readiness by cultivating an innovation-centric culture, emphasizing reliability, planning for scalability, and implementing supporting leadership for swift adoption.

- Social acceptability is essential for the transmission of technology, engaging stakeholders through awareness campaigns and educational efforts. It fosters adoption by alleviating concerns, ensuring equitable access to benefits, and addressing environmental challenges, thereby bolstering community trust in sustainable development.
- Policymakers have to enhance mechanisms for investing in sustainable technology and offer subsidies or tax incentives for energy-efficient solutions. Steady governmental assistance can enhance scalability and mitigate unpredictability. Collaborations between public and private sectors, together with training, can alleviate cost and societal acceptance challenges. Comprehensive methods that include economic, ecological, and social elements can facilitate technological adoption and advance sustainable development.

22.6 Validation

MCDM models often exhibit vulnerability in their results due to variations in the underlying conditions, like changes in parameter values, weighting conditions, normalization schemes, experts' preferences, mathematical formulations, and aggregations (Biswas, Bhattacharjee, et al., 2025). Thus, it is necessary to validate the results. This research follows a two-step approach to validate the results.

- First, it employs several other MCDM methods to determine the weights of the barriers (Case 1) and criteria (Case 2), and compares them with LBWA. This is a recommended approach in the literature to ensure the generalizability of a specific MCDM model under varying conditions (Biswas, Sanyal, et al., 2025; Tufan & Ulutaş, 2026).
- Secondly, the values of ES are deliberately varied to examine its sensitivity to the external condition. Sensitivity analysis is a widely used approach to examine the stability of a model (Biswas, Biswas, et al., 2025; Sanyal et al., 2025).

At the first step, the weights of the barriers and criteria are computed using alternative MCDM models, and the barriers are ranked accordingly. Subsequently, the Spearman rank correlation test is conducted to assess the statistical significance of correlations among the different MCDM models. Table 22.12 highlights the statistically significant, very high associations between the LBWA model and other renowned MCDM methods for Case 1.

The validity of LBWA for equitable decision-making is affirmed in Fig. 22.1, as it reduces bias and prioritizes method sensitivity. Comparison research confirms its reliability, especially in multidisciplinary situations where equity and transparency in ranking obstacles are crucial academic issues.

Similarly, statistically significant and high correlations are observed among the various methods in Case 2 (Table 22.13), indicating that LBWA is a reliable approach for calculating weights and ranking (Fig. 22.2).

A sensitivity analysis is conducted to examine the impact of variations in the EC on the calculated weights and the ranking of the barriers in Case 1 (Figs. 22.3 and 22.4) and renewable technology selection criteria in Case 2 (Figs. 22.5 and 22.6). Fig. 22.3 illustrates that fluctuations in EC consistently affect the weights assigned to each barrier. As r_0 rises, the importance of C1 (constraints in investment) decreases, whilst C2 (trust and reliability) and C5 (skill gaps) exhibit considerable increases. Additional criteria, such as C3 (data management) and C4 (business model transformation), exhibit relative stability, indicating diminished susceptibility to variations in r_0. The robustness of the model is demonstrated by the stable ranking of C1 (constraints in investment) and C6 (uncertain regulatory and legal framework), regardless of parameter variations (Fig. 22.4). This illustrates the structural stability of barrier rankings, affirming its trustworthiness for policy analysis and resource allocation across many scenarios, including sensitivity adjustments.

Fig. 22.5 signifies the impact of fluctuations in the EC on the weights of evaluation criteria in case study 2. Ecological Consequences and implementation costs initially exert a substantial influence, but their significance wanes as r0 increases. Operations and maintenance cost, reliability, and scalability exhibit increasing tendencies, but government policy support and social acceptance demonstrate reduced sensitivities. This study confirms the weighted model's capacity to differentiate and withstand challenges in assessing barriers to technology adoption in sustainability-oriented operations. Fig. 22.6

TABLE 22.12 Spearman's rank correlation test (comparison of MCDM methods used in case study 1).

Method	FUCOM	COBRAC	SWARA	BWM	DIBR-II
LBWA	1.000	1.000	0.943	0.829	0.943

(All values are significant at the 0.05 level, two-tailed).

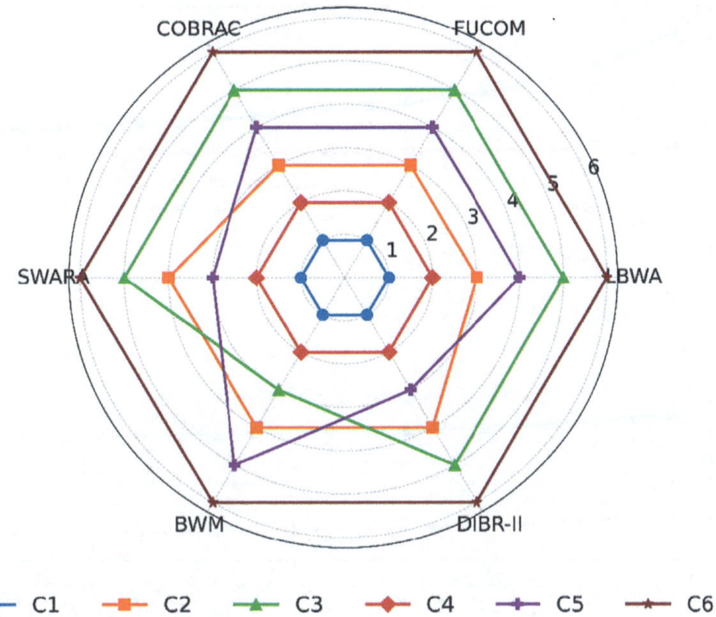

FIGURE 22.1 Comparison of MCDM methods (case study 1).

TABLE 22.13 Spearman's rank correlation test (comparison of MCDM methods used in case study 2).

Method	FUCOM	COBRAC	SWARA	BWM	DIBR-II
LBWA	1.000	1.000	0.905	0.976	0.929

(All values are significant at the 0.05 level, two-tailed).

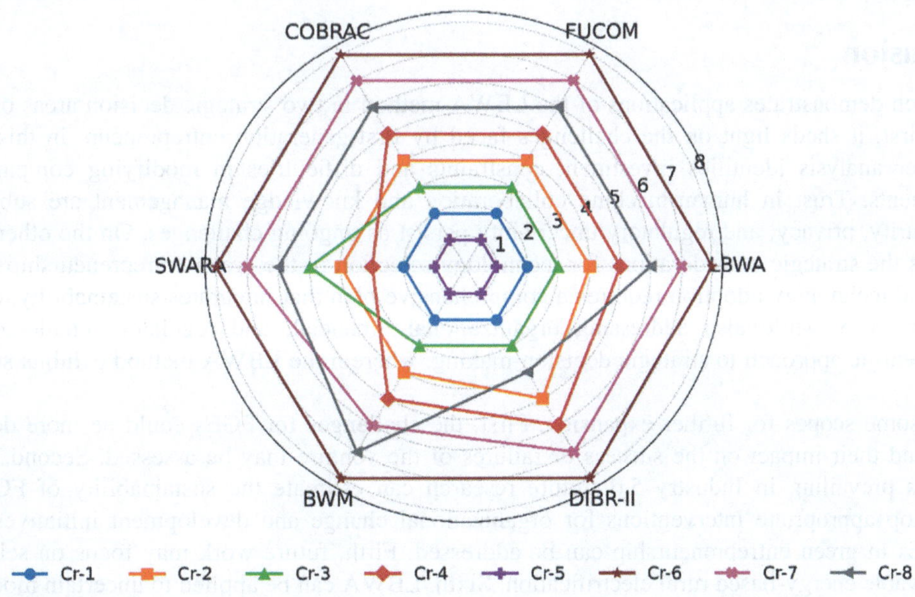

FIGURE 22.2 Comparison of MCDM methods (case study 2).

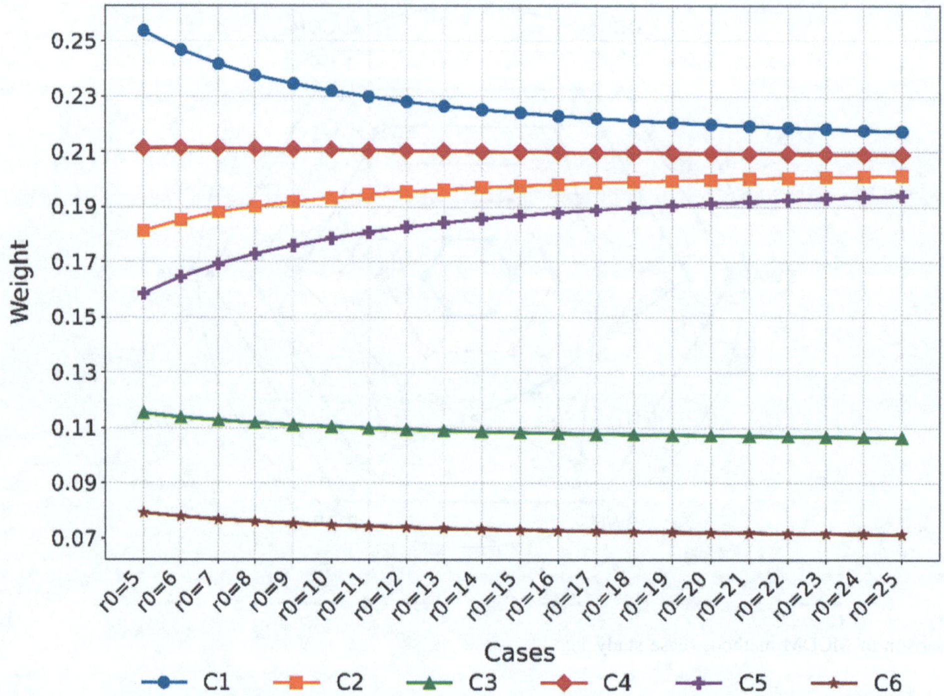

FIGURE 22.3 Effect of variations in the elasticity coefficient values on the criteria weight (case study 1).

shows the impact of variations in the EC on the rankings of criteria in case study 2. The environmental impact and installation cost regularly receive the highest rankings, whilst government policy support and social acceptance are ranked the lowest. Criteria like operation and maintenance cost, energy efficiency, reliability, and scalability are situated in stable intermediate layers, affirming the robustness of the ranking method.

The LBWA method demonstrates stability and resilience in MCDM, yielding balanced outcomes despite fluctuations in parameters. The mathematical simplicity and elasticity parameter provide accurate modifications without adding complexity, enabling reliable criteria weighting in both individual and collective decision-making contexts. This approach is appropriate for dynamic and transdisciplinary decision-making environments, minimizing inconsistencies among experts.

22.7 Conclusion

The current research demonstrates applications of the LBWA method in two strategic decision areas of entrepreneurship in Industry 5.0. First, it sheds light on the challenges faced by first-generation entrepreneurs in this era of AI-driven digitization. Barrier analysis identifies investment constraints and difficulties in modifying company models as the principal impediments. Trust in human-machine collaboration and knowledge management are substantial obstacles; however, data security, privacy, and regulatory uncertainty persist as ongoing challenges. On the other hand, the current research highlights the strategic considerations for technology selection in the green entrepreneurship space. It becomes clear that successful technology adoption requires a comprehensive plan that integrates sustainability, cost-effectiveness, and optimal energy use, while also addressing organizational, financial, and regulatory challenges. This research demonstrates a scientific approach to strategic decision-making, wherein the LBWA method exhibits substantial stability and reliability.

There are also some scopes for further expansion. First, the challenges for FGEs could be more deeply introspected at the sublevels, and their impact on the success or failures of the venture may be assessed. Second, given the context of various barriers prevailing in Industry 5.0, future research can estimate the sustainability of FGEs. Third, future studies may develop appropriate interventions for organizational change and development initiatives. Fourth, specific challenges of FGEs in green entrepreneurship can be addressed. Fifth, future work may focus on selecting technology suppliers for renewable energy-based rural electrification. Sixth, LBWA can be applied to uncertain models that use fuzzy and rough numbers.

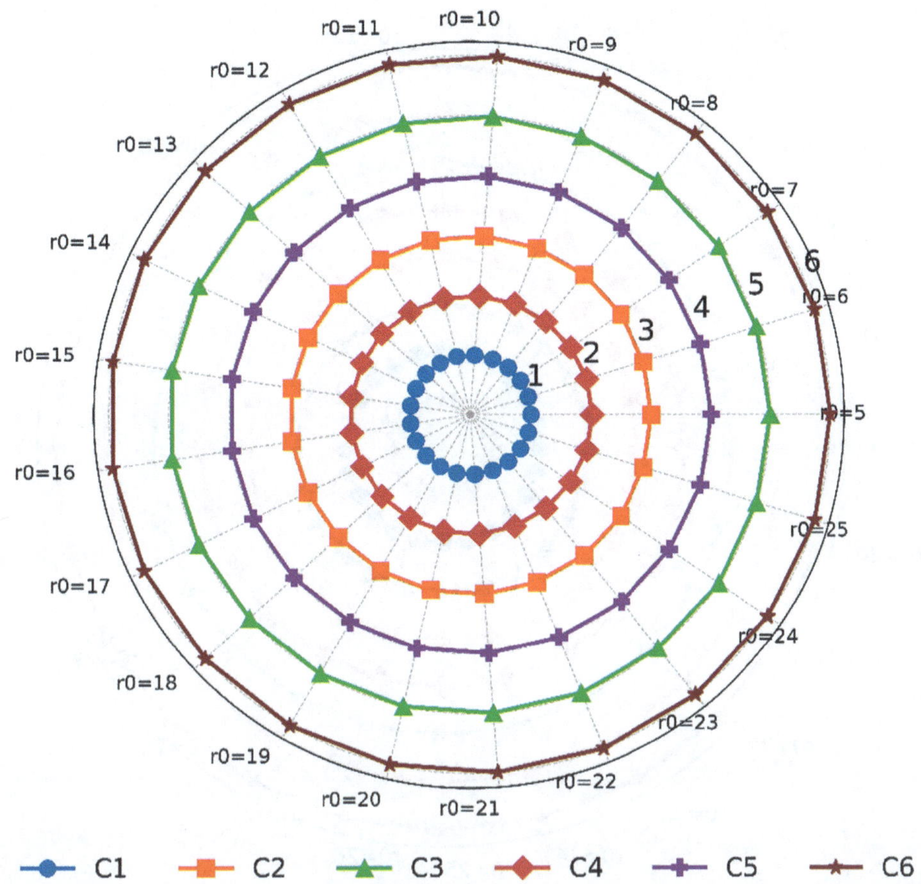

FIGURE 22.4 Effect of variations in the elasticity coefficient values on the criteria ranking (case study 1).

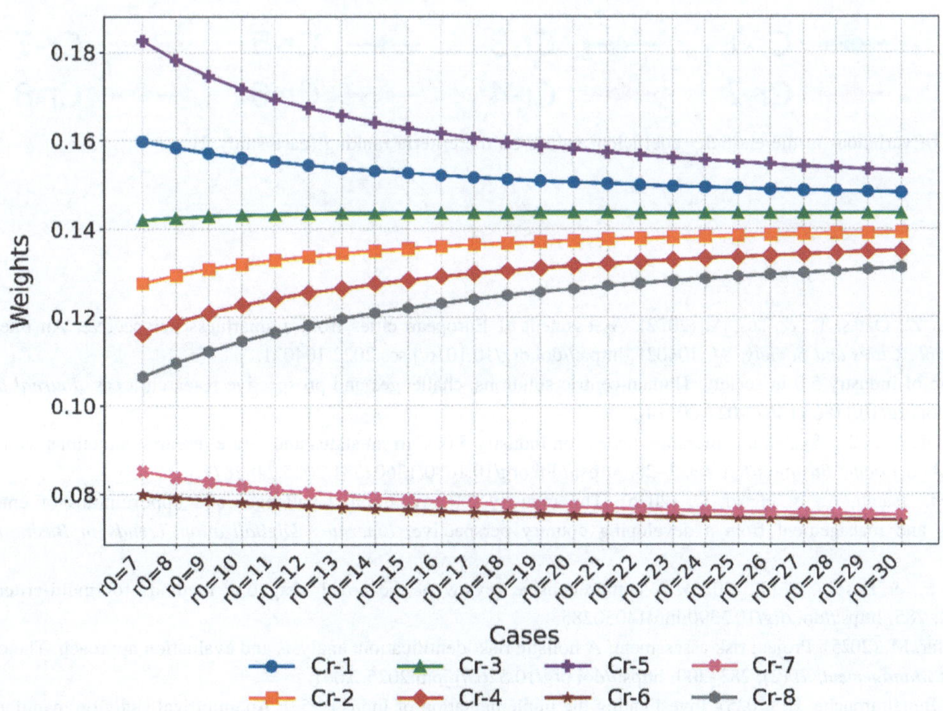

FIGURE 22.5 Effect of variations in the elasticity coefficient values on the criteria weight (case study 2).

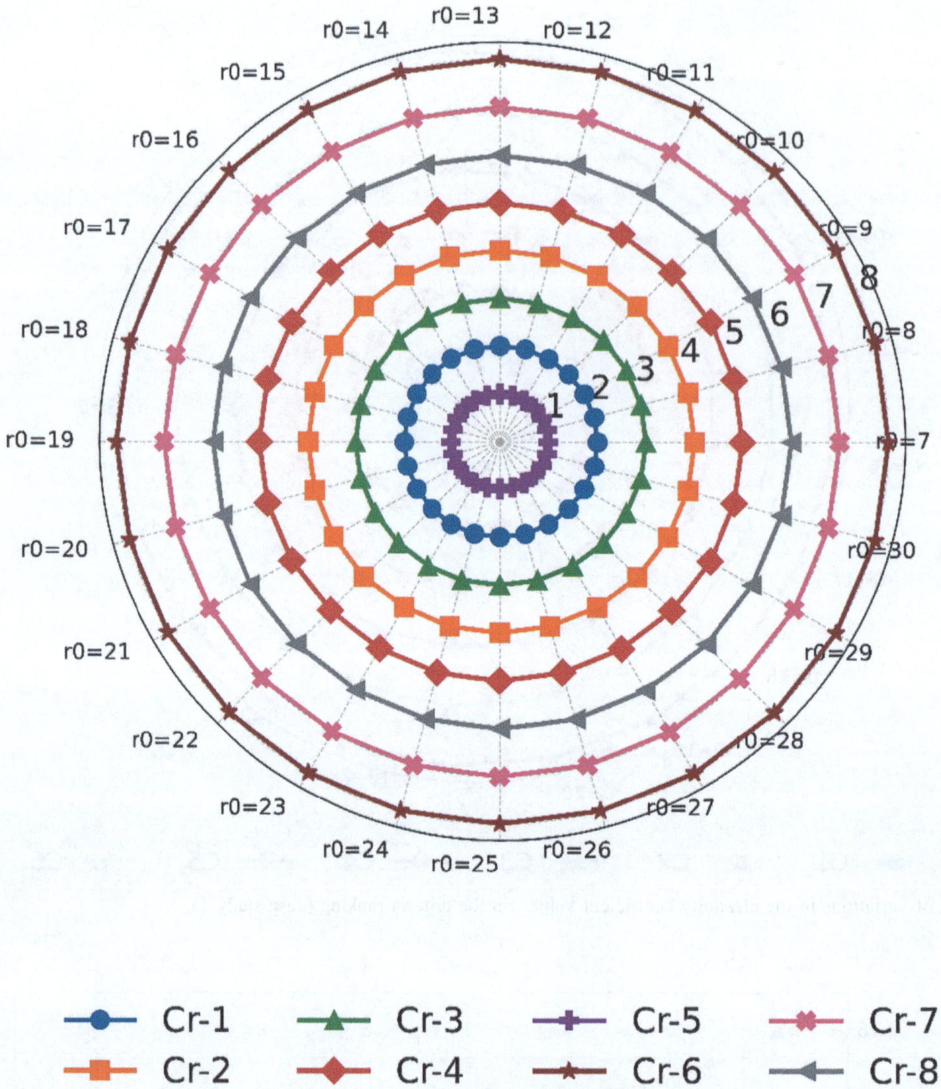

FIGURE 22.6 Effect of variations in the elasticity coefficient values on the criteria ranking (case study 2).

References

Adali, E. A., Öztaş, G. Z., Öztaş, T., & Tuş, A. (2022). Assessment of European cities from a smartness perspective: An integrated grey MCDM approach. *Sustainable Cities and Society, 84*, 104021. https://doi.org/10.1016/j.scs.2022.104021.

Adel, A. (2022). Future of industry 5.0 in society: Human-centric solutions, challenges and prospective research areas. *Journal of Cloud Computing, 11*(1), 40. https://doi.org/10.1186/s13677-022-00314-5.

Ali, I., Nguyen, K., & Oh, I. (2025). Systematic literature review on Industry 5.0: Current status and future research directions with insights for the Asia Pacific countries. *Asia Pacific Business Review,* 1–28. https://doi.org/10.1080/13602381.2025.2452877.

Anne, O., Adenike, M., Isaiah, A., & Ngozi, C. (2025). The industry 5.0 revolution: Challenges and opportunities of emerging digitalization trends in business and management from a developing country perspective. *Emerging Digitalization Trends in Business and Management,* 77–108.

Ayan, B., Abacıoğlu, S., & Basilio, M. P. (2023). A comprehensive review of the novel weighting methods for multi-criteria decision-making. *Information, 14*(5), 285. https://doi.org/10.3390/info14050285.

Bachari, M. S., & Iranfar, M. (2025). Project risk assessment: A holistic risk identification, analysis and evaluation approach, The case of EPC projects. *Journal of Project Management, 10*(2), 283–300. https://doi.org/10.5267/j.jpm.2025.2.001.

Benghouala, M. A., & Benamirouche, H. (2025). Investigating the implementation of Industry 5.0: An empirical study on manufacturing companies in Algeria. *Sustainable Futures, 10*, 101111. https://doi.org/10.1016/j.sftr.2025.101111.

Biswas, S., Bhattacharjee, S., Biswas, B., Mitra, K., & Khawas, N. (2025). An expert opinion-based soft computing framework for comparing nanotechnologies used in agriculture. *Spectrum of Operational Research,* 1–39. https://doi.org/10.31181/sor4156.

Biswas, S., Biswas, B., & Mitra, K. (2025). A novel group decision making model to compare online shopping platforms. *Spectrum of Decision Making and Applications, 2*(1), 1–27. https://doi.org/10.31181/sdmap2120259.

Biswas, S., Sanyal, A., & Pamucar, D. (2025). Students' perceptions about the webinars: An intuitionistic fuzzy force field analysis. *Spectrum of Operational Research, 2*(1), 113–133. https://doi.org/10.31181/sor21202513.

Bošković, S., Jovčić, S., Simic, V., Švadlenka, L., Dobrodolac, M., & Bacanin, N. (2025). A new criteria importance assessment (Cimas) method in multi-criteria group decision-making: Criteria evaluation for supplier selection. *Facta Universitatis, Series: Mechanical Engineering, 23*(2), 335–349. https://doi.org/10.22190/FUME230730050B.

Božanić, D., Pamucar, D., Badi, I., & Tešić, D. (2023). A decision support tool for oil spill response strategy selection: application of LBWA and Z MABAC methods. *Opsearch, 60*(1), 24–58.

Chandel, T. A. (2022). Green entrepreneurship and sustainable development. In *International perspectives on value creation and sustainability through social entrepreneurship.* IGI Global Scientific Publishing, 173–208.

Chatterjee, S., & Chakraborty, S. (2024). A study on the effects of objective weighting methods on TOPSIS-based parametric optimization of non-traditional machining processes. *Decision Analytics Journal, 11,* 100451. https://doi.org/10.1016/j.dajour.2024.100451.

Demir, G. (2023). Evaluation of sustainable green building indicators by fuzzy multi-criteria decision making. In *Studies in Fuzziness and Soft Computing* (pp. 333–350). https://doi.org/10.1007/978-981-19-4929-6_16

Demirel, P., Li, Q. C., Rentocchini, F., & Tamvada, J. P. (2019). Born to be green: New insights into the economics and management of green entrepreneurship. *Small Business Economics, 52*(4), 759–771. https://doi.org/10.1007/s11187-017-9933-z.

Dobrovolska, O., Ortmanns, W., Podosynnikov, S., Halynskyi, D., & Miniailo, A. (2024). Start-ups and entrepreneurship in renewable energy: Investments and risks. *Financial Markets, Institutions and Risks, 8*(2), 213–240. https://doi.org/10.61093/fmir.8(2).213-240.2024.

Dündar, S., & Karadağ, İ. (2025). Selection of a facility location for a cosmetics company by integrated F-LBWA and I-RAWEC methods. *International Journal of Fuzzy Systems.* https://doi.org/10.1007/s40815-024-01960-4.

Ecer, F., Pamucar, D., Mardani, A., & Alrasheedi, M. (2021). Assessment of renewable energy resources using new interval rough number extension of the level based weight assessment and combinative distance-based assessment. *Renewable Energy, 170,* 1156–1177. https://doi.org/10.1016/j.renene.2021.02.004.

El-Maaroufi, A., Daoudi, M., & Laamara, R. A. (2024). Techno-economic analysis of a PV/WT/biomass off-grid hybrid power system for rural electrification in northern Morocco using HOMER. *Renewable Energy, 231,* 120904. https://doi.org/10.1016/j.renene.2024.120904.

Gabus, A., & Fontela, E.J.B.G.R.C. (1972)World problems, an invitation to further thought within the framework of DEMATEL1Geneva, Switzerland: Battelle Geneva Research Center, 12–14. 8.

Gamberini, L., & Pluchino, P. (2024). Industry 5.0: A comprehensive insight into the future of work, social sustainability, sustainable development, and career. *Australian Journal of Career Development, 33*(1), 5–14. https://doi.org/10.1177/10384162241231118.

Ghag, N., Sonar, H., Sawant, R., & Bankapalli, K. (2025). Examining industry 5.0 and supply chain performance: An empirical study for managing supply chain complexity. *Production & Manufacturing Research, 13*(1), 2501181. https://doi.org/10.1080/21693277.2025.2501181.

Ghobakhloo, M., Iranmanesh, M., Tseng, M. L., Grybauskas, A., Stefanini, A., & Amran, A. (2023). Behind the definition of Industry 5.0: A systematic review of technologies, principles, components, and values. *Journal of Industrial and Production Engineering, 40*(6), 432–447. https://doi.org/10.1080/21681015.2023.2216701.

Haldar, S. (2019). Green entrepreneurship in the renewable energy sector-a case study of Gujarat. *Journal of Science and Technology Policy Management, 10*(1), 234–250. https://doi.org/10.1108/JSTPM-12-2017-0070.

Husain, A. M., Hasan, M. M., Khan, Z. A., & Asjad, M. (2024). A robust decision-making approach for the selection of an optimal renewable energy source in India. *Energy Conversion and Management, 301,* 117989. https://doi.org/10.1016/j.enconman.2023.117989.

Işık, Ö., Shabir, M., Demir, G., Puska, A., & Pamucar, D. (2025). A hybrid framework for assessing Pakistani commercial bank performance using multi-criteria decision-making. *Financial Innovation, 11*(1). https://doi.org/10.1186/s40854-024-00728-x.

Juarez-Rojas, L., Alvarez-Risco, A., Campos-Dávalos, N., de las Mercedes Anderson-Seminario, M., & Del-Aguila-Arcentales, S. (2023). Effectiveness of renewable energy policies in promoting green entrepreneurship: A global benchmark comparison. In *Footprint and entrepreneurship: Global green initiatives.* Singapore: Springer Nature Singapore, 47–87. https://doi.org/10.1007/978-981-19-8895-0_3.

Kara, K., Yalçın, G. C., Simic, V., Baysal, Z., & Pamucar, D. (2024). The alternative ranking using two-step logarithmic normalization method for benchmarking the supply chain performance of countries. *Socio-economic Planning Sciences, 92,* 101822. https://doi.org/10.1016/j.seps.2024.101822.

Karbalaeiramezanali, A., Parsa, M., Lentz, D. R., & Thorne, K. G. (2025). Prospectivity modeling of devonian intrusion-related W-MO-SB-AU deposits in the Pokiok Plutonic Suite, West-Central New Brunswick, Canada, using a Monte Carlo-based framework. *Natural Resources Research.* https://doi.org/10.1007/s11053-024-10437-y.

Karimi, M. S., Doostkouei, S. G., Shaiban, M., Easvaralingam, Y., & Khan, Y. A. (2024). Investigating the role of entrepreneurship in advancing renewable energy for sustainable development: Evidence from a System-GMM panel data approach. *Sustainable Development, 32*(4), 3329–3343. https://doi.org/10.1002/sd.2847.

Kassem, R., Mahmoud, M. M., Ibrahim, N. F., Alkuhayli, A., Khaled, U., Beroual, A., & Saleeb, H. (2024). A techno-economic-environmental feasibility study of residential solar photovoltaic/biomass power generation for rural electrification: A real case study. *Sustainability, 16*(5), 2036. https://doi.org/10.3390/su16052036.

Korucuk, S., Aytekin, A., Ecer, F., Pamucar, D. S. S., & Karamaşa, Ç. (2022). Assessment of ideal smart network strategies for logistics companies using an integrated picture fuzzy LBWA-CoCoSo framework. *Management Decision, 61*(5), 1434–1462. https://doi.org/10.1108/md-12-2021-1621.
Kumar, P. H., Gopi, R. R., Rajarajan, R., Vaishali, N. B., Vasavi, K., & Kumar, S. (2024). Prefeasibility techno-economic analysis of hybrid renewable energy system. *e-Prime-Advances in Electrical Engineering, Electronics and Energy, 7*, 100443. https://doi.org/10.1016/j.prime.2024.100443.
León, O., Puente, J., Fernandez, I., & Luna, M. (2025). Challenges in transitioning from Industry 4.0 to Industry 5.0: A multicriteria analysis. *Journal of Industrial Integration & Management, 10*(1), 109–151. https://doi.org/10.1142/S2424862224500192.
Li, C., & Shen, B. (2019). Accelerating renewable energy electrification and rural economic development with an innovative business model: A case study in China. *Energy Policy, 127*, 280–286. https://doi.org/10.1016/j.enpol.2018.12.009.
Li, T., Wang, H., & Lin, Y. (2024). Selection of renewable energy development path for sustainable development using a fuzzy MCDM based on cumulative prospect theory: The case of Malaysia. *Scientific Reports, 14*(1), 15082. https://doi.org/10.1038/s41598-024-65982-6.
Mandal, N., Sarkar, P., & Petrović, N. (2025). Multi-criteria decision-making for ranking renewable energy sources: A case study from the Republic of Serbia. *Journal of Engineering Management and Systems Engineering, 4*(2), 109–121. https://doi.org/10.56578/jemse040203.
Mukhametzyanov, I. (2021). Specific character of objective methods for determining weights of criteria in MCDM problems: Entropy, CRITIC and SD. *Decision Making Applications in Management and Engineering, 4*(2), 76–105. https://doi.org/10.31181/dmame210402076i.
Ogundoyin, S. O., & Kamil, I. A. (2023). An integrated fuzzy-BWM, fuzzy-LBWA and V-fuzzy-CoCoSo-LD model for gateway selection in fog-bolstered internet of things. *Applied Soft Computing, 143*, 110393. https://doi.org/10.1016/j.asoc.2023.110393.
Pamučar, D., Behzad, M., Božanić, D., & Behzad, M. (2021). Decision making to support sustainable energy policies corresponding to agriculture sector: Case study in Iran's Caspian Sea coastline. *Journal of Cleaner Production, 292*, 125302.
Pamučar, D., Gokasar, I., Torkayesh, A. E., Deveci, M., Martínez, L., & Wu, Q. (2022). Prioritization of unmanned aerial vehicles in transportation systems using the integrated stratified fuzzy rough decision-making approach with the hamacher operator. *Information Sciences, 622*, 374–404. https://doi.org/10.1016/j.ins.2022.11.143.
Pamucar, D., Gokasar, D., Torkayesh, A. E, Deveci, M., Martínez, L., & Wu, Q. (2023). Prioritization of unmanned aerial vehicles in transportation systems using the integrated stratified fuzzy rough decision-making approach with the hamacher operator. *Information Sciences, 622*, 374–404.
Pei, H., Chen, Y., Bai, Z., Sun, J., Wang, Z., & Cao, J. (2025). A multi-criteria evaluation framework for fighter cockpit ergonomics based on integrated fuzzy combination weighting and fuzzy CoCoSo with Bonferroni functions. *International Journal of Information Technology & Decision Making*, 1–32. https://doi.org/10.1142/s0219622025500634.
Rame, R., Purwanto, P., & Sudarno, S. (2024). Industry 5.0 and sustainability: An overview of emerging trends and challenges for a green future. *Innovation and Green Development, 3*(4), 100173. https://doi.org/10.1016/j.igd.2024.100173.
Rezaei, J. (2015). Best-worst multi-criteria decision-making method. *Omega, 53*, 49–57. https://doi.org/10.1016/j.omega.2014.11.009.
Romero-Castro, N., Miramontes-Viña, V., & López-Cabarcos, M.Á. (2022). Understanding the antecedents of entrepreneurship and renewable energies to promote the development of community renewable energy in rural areas. *Sustainability, 14*(3), 1234. https://doi.org/10.3390/su14031234.
Saaty, T. L. (1980). *The Analytic Hierarchy Process: Planning, Priority Setting, Resource Allocation*. New York, NY: McGraw-Hill.
Sanyal, A., Biswas, S., & Sur, S. (2025). An integrated full consistent LOPCOW-EDAS framework for modelling consumer decision making for organic food selection. *Yugoslav Journal of Operations Research, 35*(2), 331–364. https://doi.org/10.2298/YJOR240315022S.
Sharma, M., Joshi, S., & Govindan, K. (2023). Overcoming barriers to implement digital technologies to achieve sustainable production and consumption in the food sector: A circular economy perspective. *Sustainable Production and Consumption, 39*, 203–215. https://doi.org/10.1016/j.spc.2023.04.002.
Sudaryanto, M. A., & Sylvana, A. (2024). Generation Z and entrepreneurship: Understanding the character of entrepreneurs in the midst of industrial revolution 5.0. *Innovative: Journal Of Social Science Research, 4*(6), 4344–4351. https://doi.org/10.31004/innovative.v4i6.16775.
Suhara, S., & Sopyan, A. (2024). Entrepreneurship in the era of society 5.0: Navigating digitalization for innovation and growth, 6(1), 1-13. https://doi.org/10.35912/joste.v6i1.2224
Sumarliah, E., & Olebogeng Makgetho, A. (2025). Assessing solar-biomass system for rural electrification in Botswana using the integrated multi-objective optimization and TOPSIS. *Journal of Renewable and Sustainable Energy, 17*(4), 046304. https://doi.org/10.1063/5.0268253.
Sumrit, D., & Maneelok, S. (2025). An analytical framework for prioritizing barriers and public-private partnership solutions in civil helicopter emergency medical services. *Decision Analytics Journal, 16*, 100617. https://doi.org/10.1016/j.dajour.2025.100617.
Taş, A. (2024). An entrepreneurial perspective on industry 4.0 and industry 5.0. In *Empowering Entrepreneurial Mindsets With AI*. IGI Global, 187–208.
Teece, D. J., Pisano, G., & Shuen, A. (1997). Dynamic capabilities and strategic management. *Strategic Management Journal, 18*(7), 509–533. https://doi.org/10.1002/(SICI)1097-0266(199708)18:7%3C509::AID-SMJ882%3E3.0.CO;2-Z.
Torkayesh, A. E., Pamucar, D., Ecer, F., & Chatterjee, P. (2021). An integrated BWM-LBWA-CoCoSo framework for evaluation of healthcare sectors in Eastern Europe. *Socio-economic Planning Sciences, 78*, 101052. https://doi.org/10.1016/j.seps.2021.101052.
Trist, E.L. (1981The evolution of socio-technical systems2Toronto: Ontario Quality of Working Life Centre, 1981.
Tufan, D., & Ulutaş, A. (2026). Supplier selection in the food sector: An integrated approach using LODECI and CORASO methods. *Spectrum of Decision Making and Applications, 3*(1), 40–51. https://doi.org/10.31181/sdmap31202631.
Ucar, M. G. (2024). Integrated entropy-based MCDM methods for investigating the effectiveness of Turkey's energy policies. *Energy Systems*. https://doi.org/10.1007/s12667-024-00688-2.
Vernet, A., Khayesi, J. N., George, V., George, G., & Bahaj, A. S. (2019). How does energy matter? Rural electrification, entrepreneurship, and community development in Kenya. *Energy Policy, 126*, 88–98. https://doi.org/10.1016/j.enpol.2018.11.012.

Wang, W., Chen, Y., Wang, Y., Deveci, M., Moslem, S., & Coffman, D. (2024). Unveiling the implementation barriers to the digital transformation in the energy sector using the Fermatean cubic fuzzy method. *Applied Energy, 360*, 122756. https://doi.org/10.1016/j.apenergy.2024.122756.

Wang, Y., & Ye, D. (2024). Enhancing rural revitalization in China through digital economic transformation and green entrepreneurship. *Sustainability, 16*(10), 4147. https://doi.org/10.3390/su16104147.

Yazdani, M., Pamucar, D., Chatterjee, P., & Torkayesh, A. E. (2021). A multi-tier sustainable food supplier selection model under uncertainty. *Operations Management Research, 15*(1-2), 116–145. https://doi.org/10.1007/s12063-021-00186-z.

Yu, N., Gao, C., Wang, X., Li, D., & You, W. (2023). Evaluating the derivative value of smart grid investment under dual carbon target: A hybrid multi-criteria decision-making analysis. *Energy Engineering, 120*(12), 2879–2901. https://doi.org/10.32604/ee.2023.029426.

Yu, Y., Yang, Y., Yu, J., Wu, S., Zeng, Q., Ding, H., Ma, J., & Duan, Q. (2025). An improved FMEA approach based on interval-valued spherical fuzzy sets and CODAS method for LNG tank safety analysis. *Journal of Loss Prevention in the Process Industries*105679. https://doi.org/10.1016/j.jlp.2025.105679.

Zaman, A. U. (2025). Green energy entrepreneurship: Emerging business models for decentralized renewable power in developing economies. *Pacific Journal of Business Innovation and Strategy, 2*(3), 60–71. https://doi.org/10.70818/pjbis.v02i03.090.

Zare, L., Ali, M. B., Rauch, E., & Matt, D. T. (2025). Navigating challenges of small and medium-sized enterprises in the era of industry 5.0. *Results in Engineering*106457. https://doi.org/10.1016/j.rineng.2025.106457.

Zavadskas, E. K., & Turskis, Z. (2011). Multiple criteria decision making (MCDM) methods in economics: An overview. *Technological and Economic Development of Economy, 17*(2), 397–427. https://doi.org/10.3846/20294913.2011.593291.

Žižović, M., & Pamucar, D. (2019). New model for determining criteria weights: Level based weight assessment (LBWA) model. *Decision Making: Applications in Management and Engineering, 2*(2), 126–137. https://doi.org/10.31181/dmame1902102z.

Zorlu, K., Polat, S., Dede, V., & Yılmaz, A. (2025). Measuring degradation risk levels of resources in sustainable geotourism development: A multi-criteria decision making (MCDM) approach under spherical fuzzy environments. *International Journal of Geoheritage and Parks, 13*(2), 250–273. https://doi.org/10.1016/j.ijgeop.2024.11.011.

Further reading

Pamučar, D., Behzad, M., Božanić, D., & Behzad, M. (2020). Decision making to support sustainable energy policies corresponding to agriculture sector: Case study in Iran's Caspian Sea coastline. *Journal of Cleaner Production, 292*, 125302. https://doi.org/10.1016/j.jclepro.2020.125302.

Chapter 23

OPA: Ordinal priority approach in multi-attribute decision-making

Aliakbar Hasani
Department of Industrial Engineering and Management, Shahrood University of Technology, Shahroud, Iran

23.1 Introduction

In today's complex and uncertain business environments and social systems, decision-making has become one of the most important and challenging tasks for managers, policymakers, and researchers (Haseli et al., 2026). Key decisions in such environments are usually influenced by multiple, sometimes conflicting factors that are difficult to evaluate and weigh without using scientific and structured methods to do so (Pilla et al., 2026). Multicriteria decision-making (MCDM), one of the most widely used branches of operations research and decision management, provides tools for the systematic analysis of complex problems (Hasani & Darayi, 2026a; 2026b). These methods help decision-makers choose the best or most appropriate option by considering a set of quantitative criteria.

Classical and widely used methods such as the analytic hierarchy process (AHP), analytic network process (ANP), technique for order preference by similarity to ideal solution (TOPSIS), and VlseKriterijumska Optimizacija I Kompromisno Resenje have been instrumental in effectively solving multicriteria problems over the last few decades. These methods typically require precise quantitative data, extensive pairwise comparisons, and the determination of numerical weights. Despite the high accuracy of these approaches, collecting accurate and reliable data often encounters significant practical limitations. These limitations include incomplete data, high costs and time associated with the evaluation process, mental errors resulting from complex calculations, and experts' inability to accurately convey their judgments. Furthermore, in many real-world problems, decision-makers' knowledge is more intuitive and qualitative, making it challenging to express it in precise quantitative terms. In response to these limitations, researchers have sought to develop simpler and more flexible approaches that utilize ordinal data instead of quantitative data. In these approaches, decision-makers are not required to specify exact values; only the order of importance of the criteria and options is obtained from them. This reduces cognitive load, increases ease of use, and maintains the validity of decision-making.

One of the innovative methods introduced in recent years is the ordinal priority approach (OPA), first proposed by Aghdaie et al. (2019). OPA utilizes rank information to create a linear programming (LP) model that aims to determine the weight of criteria and calculate the final scores of options in a manner that aligns as closely as possible with decision-makers' rank preferences while minimizing inconsistencies. One of the important advantages of the OPA method is that the evaluation process relies solely on rankings rather than precise numerical comparisons. Decision-makers simply rank the criteria in order of importance, the options under each criterion, and, if necessary, the relative importance of the decision-makers. The OPA mathematical model then calculates the weights and final results using LP. This makes the OPA method highly effective in environments where quantitative information is insufficient or unavailable, and decisions must be made based on subjective judgments.

Simplifying the decision-making process, reducing the time and cost of evaluation, minimizing the likelihood of inconsistent errors in judgment, and the potential for use in both individual and group decision-making are among the most significant reasons for the popularity of this method. Numerous studies have shown that OPA can perform efficiently and reliably in various areas, such as selecting and evaluating suppliers, ranking investment projects, formulating organizational strategies, risk management, and even prioritizing macro policies. This article aims to provide a comprehensive introduction to the OPA method by considering its features and advantages. The theoretical foundations and necessity of using this method in MCDM are first reviewed. The structure of the mathematical model and its

Encyclopedia of Multi-Attribute Decision-Making (MADM). DOI: https://doi.org/10.1016/B978-0-443-33275-3.00033-6

implementation algorithm are described. By presenting a real case study, the capabilities and practical advantages of this method compared with classical decision-making methods are analyzed. Finally, suggestions for future research and the development of the application of this method in different fields are presented in the conclusion.

23.2 Literature review

The concept of using ordinal data in MCDM was developed in response to challenges related to collecting and ensuring the accuracy of numerical data (Zavadskas & Turskis, 2011). Aghdaie et al. (2019) introduced the OPA method, which relies on LP and the ordinal order of criteria, options, and decision-makers to calculate weights and scores simultaneously (Ataei et al., 2020). Their initial study, which applied OPA to machinery selection, highlighted the significance of the method in solving real-world problems (Aghdaie et al., 2019). In a theoretical expansion, Mahmoudi and Javed (2023a) introduced two versions of OPA: OPA-S (hard) and OPA-W (soft), which differentiate between hard and soft ordinal relationships, respectively. They demonstrated that the original OPA model represents the hard form and introduced new features to the OPA theory (Mahmoudi & Javed, 2023a). Mahmoudi and Javed (2023b) introduced an Interval OPA to assess group decision-making quality under uncertainty. In a more recent development, Wang (2024a) introduced the generalized OPA model with a two-stage estimate-then-optimize framework that allows for the use of incomplete preference information. This model involves extracting preference distributions, weighting experts, criteria, and options simultaneously, and evaluating the confidence and consistency of the results (Wang, 2024a). Wang (2024b) also introduced the Preference Robust OPA (OPA-PR) and the Preference Robust Satisficing OPA (OPA-PRS) versions, which aim to address the ambiguity of preferences in decision-making (Wang, 2024b).

OPA has been implemented in various studies at the application and fuzzy development levels. Abdel-Basset et al. (2022) introduced a nitrosophic version of OPA for high-uncertainty decision-making problems. Majumdar and Selvarajan (2024) developed a hybrid OPA-IF-GRA (OPA under Intuitionistic Fuzzy and the Grey relational analysis) method that performed better in engineering problems. Additionally, the picture fuzzy OPA version has been used in the fields of sustainable transportation and carbon emission reduction (Liu et al., 2022).

From an application perspective, OPA has been implemented in several studies. OPA has been used in contractor selection for construction projects, and combining OPA with Delphi research and principal component analysis has been shown to provide reliable results (Alkaabi & Raoof Mahjoob, 2023). In the prioritization of emergency recovery programs, the DGRA-POPA model, combined with dynamic gray relation analysis, is more flexible in group decision-making. Additionally, the OPA solver tool was designed as web-based software (JavaScript) to facilitate the modeling process, weight estimation, and validation of group decisions (Mahmoudi et al., 2023).

Future studies can focus on combining OPA with other multi-attribute decision-making methods (e.g., TOPSIS, data envelopment analysis, and evaluation based on distance from average solution), developing large-scale solution algorithms, conducting sensitivity analyses of rank values, and practical implementation in software decision aids.

23.3 Methodology

In the following, the MCDM method OPA is explained in detail based on the mathematical model proposed by Aghdaie et al. (2019) and subsequent developments.

23.3.1 The main idea of the ordinal priority approach

The goal of the OPA is to calculate the weights of criteria and the scores of options using ranking information (order of importance) instead of precise quantitative data in a way that is most consistent with the decision-maker's preferences. This method was implemented using LP. Main inputs of the OPA decision-making method are the ranking of decision-makers (if there are multiple decision-makers), the ranking of criteria by each decision-maker, and the ranking of options in each criterion by each decision-maker. Then, the key output of applying the OPA method is the weight of each decision-maker, the weight of each criterion, and the final score of each option.

23.3.2 Notation

The following sets, variables, and parameters are considered. Considered sets in the proposed mathematical modeling are K (i.e., number of decision-makers), N (i.e., criteria number), and M (i.e., alternative number). In addition, regarded variables are W_k (i.e., weight of decision-maker k), V_{jk} (i.e., weight of criterion j from the decision-maker k), S_{ijk} (i.e., score of alternative i in terms of criteria j from the perspective of decision-maker k), and P (i.e., considered the objective function that should be maximized, such as the overall satisfaction value). Finally, the considered input values are $R_k^{(D)}$ (i.e., rank of decision-maker k), $R_k^{(C)}$ (i.e., rank of criteria j from the perspective of n decision-maker k), and $R_{ijk}^{(A)}$ (i.e., rank of alternative i in terms of criteria j from the perspective of n decision-maker k). It should be mentioned that all of the aforementioned data is ordinal.

23.3.3 Mathematical model idea

Instead of strict scoring, the OPA defines a system of weight constraints to ensure that the final weights are consistent with the following given ranking features. The better ranking of a criterion or option is presented with the larger the weight. To avoid inconsistency, an auxiliary variable is defined to ensure that the difference between the weights is minimal. The mathematical model seeks to maximize the minimum consistency between rankings and weights. Finally, the steps of the OPA method are presented as follows:

- Step 1: Form the ranking matrix: For each decision-maker k, record the ranking of the criteria and alternatives in the criteria and option ranking matrices. Eq. (23.1) presents the criteria ranking matrix. Eq. (23.2) shows the option ranking matrix for each criterion.

$$R_k^{(C)} = [r_{jk}^{(C)}] \tag{23.1}$$

$$R_{jk}^{(A)} = [r_{ijk}^{(C)}] \tag{23.2}$$

- Step 2: Define preference relations: For each ranking, the following constraints are regarded:
- If criterion j_1 has a better ranking than criterion j_2 (Eq. 23.3):

$$\epsilon + v_{j2,k} \leq v_{j1,k} \tag{23.3}$$

- Similarly for alternatives (Eq. 23.4):

$$\epsilon + s_{i2,j,k} \leq s_{i1,j,k} \tag{23.4}$$

Where ϵ is the minimum distance and is defined as a free variable in the model.

- Step 3: OPA LP model: Eq. (23.5) presents the objective function of the OPA LP model. The objective is to maximize the minimum difference consistent with the ranks. (23.6) presents the weights normalization constraint. Arrangement of decision-makers is presented by Eq. (23.7). Criteria are sorting by Eq. (23.8). Order of options are determined by Eq. (23.9). Finally, Eq. (23.10) shows the non-negative weights and scores.

$$Max\epsilon \tag{23.5}$$

$$1 = \sum_{i=1}^{m} s_{ijk}, \quad 1 = \sum_{j=1}^{n} v_{jk}, \quad 1 = \sum_{k=1}^{K} w_k \tag{23.6}$$

$$r_{k_2}^{(D)} > \epsilon_{k_1}^{(D)}, \qquad \forall\, r + w_{k_2} \leq w_{k_1} \tag{23.7}$$

$$r_{j_2,k}^{(C)} > \epsilon_{j_1,k}^{(C)}, \qquad \forall\, r + v_{j_2,k} \leq v_{j_1,k} \tag{23.8}$$

$$r_{i_2 j,k}^{(A)} > \epsilon_{i_1 j,k}^{(A)} \quad \forall\, r + s_{i_2 j,k} \leq s_{i_1 j,k} \tag{23.9}$$

$$\in \geq 0, \qquad W_k, V_{jk}, S_{ijk} \geq 0 \tag{23.10}$$

- Step 4: Solve the model: The above model is a LP problem and can be solved with software such as LINGO, GAMS, or MATLAB®. The solution output includes the values of W_k, V_{jk}, and S_{ijk}.

- Step 5: Calculating the final score of the options: After obtaining the weights, the final score of the options is calculated as in Eq. (23.11). The alternative with the highest Score (i) value is introduced as the best choice.

$$Score\ (i) = \sum_{j=1}^{n} \sum_{k=1}^{K} W_k.\ V_{jk}.\ S_{ijk} \tag{23.11}$$

Features and advantages of the OPA method could be classified in terms of simplicity, consistency, applicability, and flexibility. Simplicity focuses on the required ordinal data instead of precise quantitative data. Consistency mentions that the LP model ensures the greatest consistency with preferences. Applicability indicate on suitability for group and individual decision-making, and flexibility presents the possibility of expansion to fuzzy, nitrosophic, robust versions, etc.

23.4 Numerical example 1

Suppose we want to select the best city to build a new factory based on various criteria. The location of a factory is a strategic decision that directly impacts transportation costs, market access, and raw material supply. Choosing the right location can significantly increase productivity, competitiveness, and supply chain sustainability. Conversely, choosing the wrong location can lead to increased costs, reduced service quality, and missed growth opportunities. This numerical example, which will be implemented with the OPA MCDM method, includes six alternatives and six decision criteria. In addition, the opinions of three experts were used for the analysis. The decision alternatives are A_1–A_6. The key decision criteria are C_1 (market access), C_2 (land cost), C_3 (human resources), C_4 (transportation infrastructure), C_5 (economic stability), and C_6 (environmental pollution). The experts are indicated by the symbols E_1 to E_3.

Step 1: Ranking of criteria by experts: Decicion making criteira are ranked based on the experts' openions (see Table 23.1).

Step 2: Ranking the options against each criterion by each expert: For example, the option with a rank of 1 is the best option in terms of the criterion. The following table presents the evaluation information for criterion C_1 for each expert. This assessment should be conducted by experts for all the criteria (see Table 23.2).

To summarize, we assume that all rankings are given as in the matrix above, and the results of the solution using the OPA method will be presented.

Step 3: Define the OPA mathematical model: The main objective of this method is to find the weight of each option such that the sum of the weights of the better alternative (based on rank) is greater than that of the worse alternatives. OPA solves the following model using a LP technique:

- Variables: The mathematical mode varibles rae W_j (i.e., weight of alternative j), W_c (i.e., weight of criteria c), W_e (i.e., weight of expert e) and Z (i.e., optimization variable for minimization).
- Objective function: Objecyive of the mathematical model is presented by (23.12).

$$\text{Max z} \tag{23.12}$$

TABLE 23.1 Criteria ranking by experts for example 1.

Criteria	Experts		
	E_1	E_2	E_3
C_1	1	2	1
C_2	3	3	2
C_3	2	1	3
C_4	4	4	4
C_5	5	5	5
C_6	6	6	6

TABLE 23.2 Expert's evaluation for criterion 1 for example 1.

Criteria	Expert's evaluation for each criterion C_1		
	E_1	E_2	E_2
A_1	2	1	1
A_2	1	2	3
A_3	3	4	2
A_4	4	3	4
A_5	5	5	5
A_6	6	6	6

TABLE 23.3 Average ranks of evaluated criteria for example 1.

Criteria	Average rank	Weight
C_1	1.33	0.25
C_2	2.66	0.19
C_3	2.00	0.22
C_4	4.00	0.14
C_5	5.00	0.11
C_6	6.00	0.09

- Constraints:

The OPA uses ranks; therefore for any rank between two alternatives, if A_i has a better rank than A_k, we should have (Eq. 23.13):

$$z + w_k \leq w_i \tag{23.13}$$

Similarly, for the weights of the criteria and experts, the normalized weights are as in Eq. (23.14):

$$\sum_e w_e = 1, \quad \sum_c w_c = 1, \quad \sum_j w_j = 1 \tag{23.14}$$

And all of the variables are non-negative (Eq. 23.15):

$$w_e \geq 0, \quad w_c \geq 0, \quad w_j \geq 0 \tag{23.15}$$

Step 4: Solve the model (i.e., equations 23.12–23.15) with optimization software

For simplicity, we used direct weighting based on ranks (inverse weighting with rank) (see Eq. 23.16). For each expert, we will have a criterion and an alternative.

$$Alternative\ weight\ A_{ij} = \frac{1}{Rank\ of\ A_{ij}} \tag{23.16}$$

Finally, the weighted average for each option is calculated for each criterion. In addition, the weight of each criterion and expert is also taken similarly from the inverse ranking. For example, the final weight of an option is calculated as

TABLE 23.4 Final average and reverse ranks of evaluated criteria for example 1.

Criteria	Rank (average of three experts' opinions)	Reverse the weight of rank
C_1	1.33	0.75
C_2	2.00	0.50
C_3	2.66	0.38
C_4	3.00	0.33
C_5	4.00	0.25
C_6	5.00	0.20

follows: the normalized weights of the criteria are assumed to be calculated from the inverse rank by equations (23.12–23.15) (see Table 23.3).

The weight calculation for alternative A_1 is performed according to the following rankings of the criteria according to the experts' opinions via Eq. (23.16) (see Table 23.4).

The final weight of alternative A1 is calculated as follow $A_1 = (0.75 \times 0.25) + (0.50 \times 0.19) + (0.38 \times 0.22) + (0.33 \times 0.14) + (0.25 \times 0.11) + (0.20 \times 0.09) = 0.469$. This process was performed for alternatives A_2–A_6. The final rankings for alternatives are as follows: A_1 (0.469), A_2 (0.422), A_3 (0.401), A_4 (0.387), A_5 (0.310), and A_6 (0.267). Therefore alternative A_1 is the best option for establishing a manufacturing facility.

23.5 Numerical example 2

An investment firm is looking to select the best investment option from ten startups. Choosing the best investment option among ten startups is crucial for an investment firm as it can guarantee long-term financial returns and portfolio growth. This decision also helps in managing financial and operational risks, reducing the chances of investment failure. Furthermore, making the right choice can enhance the company's competitive position in the innovative investment market. This decision will be based on ten criteria and will be carried out by a team of three experts. The evaluation will utilize the OPA MCDM method. The options considered are labeled A_1 to A_{10}, while the evaluation criteria include C_1 (product innovation), C_2 (market growth potential), C_3 (management team), C_4 (business model scalability), C_5 (projected profitability), C_6 (financial structure), C_7 (competitive advantage), C_8 (readiness to attract capital), C_9 (social responsibility), and C_{10} (legal and regulatory risks). The research experts involved were E_1 (investment manager), E_2 (market analyst), and E_3 (legal advisor).

Step 1: Ranking of criteria by experts: Decicion making criteira are ranked based on the experts' openions (see Table 23.5)

Calculating criteria weights based on inverse rank and normalization (see Eq. 23.17):

$$Weight\ of\ C_i = \frac{1/Average\ weight\ C_i}{\Sigma_i\ 1/Average\ weight\ C_i} \tag{23.17}$$

Average rating of each criterion (see Table 23.6) via solving optimization model (12–15):

Step 2: Ranking the options against each criterion by experts: For brevity, we assume that the average ranking of the three experts for each option in each criterion is as follows: Information for criterion C_1 is provided as an example. This process was repeated for the other criteria via Eq. (23.17) (see Table 23.7). For simplicity, we assume that the results of the other evaluations are similar to those of criterion C_1.

Step 3: Calculate the final score for each option (see Eq. 23.18):

$$Final\ weight\ of\ alternative\ A_j = \sum_{i=1}^{10} (weight\ of\ criteria\ c_i) \times \frac{1}{Rank\ of\ criteria\ is\ for\ alternative\ j} \tag{23.18}$$

For example, the calculations related to the rank of the A_1 alternative in various criteria are as follows (see Table 23.8).

TABLE 23.5 Experts' opinions for example 2.

	Experts		
	E_1	E_2	E_3
C_1	1	2	1
C_2	2	1	2
C_3	3	3	3
C_4	4	5	4
C_5	5	4	5
C_6	6	6	6
C_7	7	7	7
C_8	8	8	8
C_9	9	9	9
C_{10}	10	10	10

TABLE 23.6 Average and reverse ranks of evaluated criteria for example 2.

Criteria	Average rank	Inverse	Normal weight
C_1	1.33	0.75	0.193
C_2	1.66	0.60	0.154
C_3	3.0	0.33	0.085
C_4	4.33	0.23	0.060
C_5	4.66	0.21	0.054
C_6	6.0	0.16	0.041
C_7	7.0	0.14	0.036
C_8	8.0	0,125	0.032
C_9	9.0	0.111	0.029
C_{10}	10.0	10.0	0.027
Sum			1

Final weight A_1=0.2613 (Sum of calculated shares). The final result of evaluating all options is as follows (see Table 23.9):

As a result, alternative A_2 has been selected as the preferred alternative.

23.6 Conclusion

In this study, the MCDM method, the OPA, was introduced and investigated as a novel and efficient framework for analyzing complex decisions with ranked data. By relying on ordinal data and modeling it as a LP problem, the OPA method provides a structured and mathematically based approach to prioritizing options and determining the weights of

TABLE 23.7 Final average and reverse ranks of evaluated criterion C_1 for example 2.

Alternative assessment in terms of C_1	Rank	Inverse rank
A_1	2	0.5
A_2	1	1.0
A_3	4	0.25
A_4	5	2.0
A_5	3	0.33
A_6	6	0.166
A_7	7	0.142
A_8	8	0.125
A_9	9	0.111
A_{10}	10	0.10

TABLE 23.8 Final criteria rank for example 2.

Criteria	Rank	Inerse	Criteria rank	Share
C_1	2	0.5	0.193	0.0965
C_2	3	0.33	0.154	0.0508
C_3	2	0.5	0.085	0.0425
C_4	4	0.25	0.060	0.015
C_5	3	0.33	0.054	0.0178
C_6	5	0.2	0.041	0.0082
C_7	4	0.25	0.036	0.009
C_8	6	0.166	0.032	0.0053
C_9	4	0.25	0.029	0.0073
C_{10}	3	0.33	0.027	0.0089

criteria, without the need for precise quantitative data or pairwise comparison scales that are necessary in many classical methods, such as AHP and ANP. One of the key advantages of OPA is the simplicity of data collection and the increased validity of decisions in the presence of multiple experts. Instead of precise comparisons or determining definitive weights, decision-makers only need to provide the relative rankings of the criteria and options. This feature facilitates the application of OPA in real-world environments with data limitations, subjective ambiguities, or diverse expert knowledge. In addition, this method allows for the integration of multiple expert opinions and their weighting into a unified structure, which increases the coverage of different stakeholders and reduces individual bias in the decision-making process. The results of solving the OPA model are prioritization of options based on a clear mathematical objective function that can be implemented in optimization software and decision-support tools. Overall, the OPA method, by combining conceptual simplicity, mathematical clarity, and compatibility with qualitative data, can be used as an effective and flexible tool in a wide range of MCDM problems in the fields of management, engineering, policy-making, and social sciences. In future

TABLE 23.9 Final weights of evaluated alternatives for example 2.

Alternatives	Final weight
A_2	0.289
A_1	0.261
A_3	0.244
A_4	0.210
A_5	0.198
A_6	0.186
A_7	0.174
A_8	0.169
A_9	0.162
A_{10}	0.150

research, an empirical comparison between OPA and other MCDM decision-making methods, such as TOPSIS, preference ranking organization method for enrichment evaluation, and best–worst method, should be conducted, and the capabilities of the OPA method under different conditions (such as data instability, uncertain weighting, and sensitivity analysis) should be comprehensively evaluated.

References

Abdel-Basset, M., Mohamed, R., & Chang, V. (2022). A novel neutrosophic OPA for multi-criteria decision-making problems. *Complex & Intelligent Systems, 8*(3), 1757–1774.

Aghdaie, M. H., Zolfani, S. H., & Zavadskas, E. K. (2019). Decision making in machine tool selection: An integrated approach of OPA and WASPAS methods. *Applied Soft Computing, 86*, 105893.

Alkaabi, S. A. M., & Raoof Mahjoob, A. M. (2023). Using the ordinal priority approach for selecting the contractor in construction projects. *Organization, technology & management in construction: an international journal, 15*(1), 136–156.

Ataei, Y., Mahmoudi, A., Feylizadeh, M. R., & Li, D. F. (2020). Ordinal priority approach (OPA) in multiple attribute decision-making. *Applied Soft Computing, 86*, 105893.

Hasani, A., & Darayi, M. (2026a). Decision support reliability under fuzzy ZE-numbers in urban climate change policy for transportation activities. In *Reliable decision-making for sustainable transportation*. Academic Press, 97–110.

Hasani, A., & Darayi, M. (2026b). Fuzzy ZE-VIKOR for estimating sustainable mobility system. In *Reliable decision-making for sustainable transportation*. Academic Press, 147–167.

Haseli, G., Hajiaghaei-Keshteli, M., & Moslem, S. (2026). An overview of group decision-making reliability for sustainable transportation. *Reliable Decision-Making for Sustainable Transportation,* 1–21.

Liu, H., Liao, H., Wu, X., & Xu, Z. (2022). Sustainable transport strategy selection with picture fuzzy OPA. *Computers & Industrial Engineering, 168*, 108259.

Mahmoudi, A., & Javed, S. A. (2023a). Strict and weak ordinal relations for estimating the criteria weights in Ordinal Priority Approach (OPA). *MethodsX, 11*, 102389.

Mahmoudi, A., & Javed, S. A. (2023b). Uncertainty analysis in group decisions through interval ordinal priority approach. *Group Decision and Negotiation, 32*, 807–833.

Mahmoudi, A., Sadeghi, M., Deng, X., & Pan, P. (2023). OPA solver: A web-based software for ordinal priority approach in multiple criteria decision analysis using JavaScript. *SoftwareX, 24*, 101546.

Majumdar, A., & Selvarajan, R. (2024). An integrated intuitionistic fuzzy OPA-GRA approach for engineering decision-making problems. *Mathematics, 12*(19), 3156.

Pilla, F., Yazdani, M., Hasani, A., & Tomaskova, H. (2026). Citizen participation and transport sustainability: A reliable analytic hierarchy process model under fuzzy ZE-numbers. In *Reliable decision-making for sustainable transportation*. Academic Press, 23–37.

Wang, R. (2024a). *Generalized ordinal priority approach: An estimate–then–optimize framework for incomplete preferences.* arXiv preprint arXiv:2407.17099*.

Wang, R. (2024b). *Preference robust ordinal priority approach and its satisficing extension for multi-attribute decision-making with incomplete information* *arXiv preprint arXiv:2412.12690*.

Zavadskas, E. K., & Turskis, Z. (2011). Multiple criteria decision making (MCDM) methods in economics: An overview. *Technological and Economic Development of Economy, 17*(2), 397–427.

Chapter 24

RAFSI: Ranking of alternatives through functional mapping of criterion sub-intervals into a single interval for multi-attribute decision-making

Hakan Ayhan Dağıstanlı[1] **and Kemal Gürol Kurtay**[2]

[1]*Industrial Engineering, National Defense University, Ankara, Çankaya, Türkiye,* [2]*Industrial Engineering, National Defense University, Ankara, Çankaya, Türkiye*

24.1 Introduction

Multicriteria decision-making (MCDM) methods are highly useful tools frequently employed in the solution and analysis of complex problems involving multiple criteria (Pamučar & Deliktaş, 2025). The use of these methods provides a mathematical approach to ensuring the effective and efficient use of resources (Toktaş & Can, 2023). Resource allocation often involves objectives that are conflicting, overlapping, or require trade-offs (Li et al., 2023; Metin & Bulkan, 2019). In situations where there are multiple goals or objectives, decision-makers can determine the importance, or in other words, the weights of these objectives, calculate the weights of available alternatives using an MCDM method, rank them according to their importance and decide which options to choose in line with the desired capabilities (Badi et al., 2025; Gokasar & Okur, 2025; Lo et al., 2025; Yardım et al., 2025).

In defense planning, determining expenditure requires consideration of a wide range of factors such as various threat scenarios, resource constraints, strategic priorities, and objectives (Aksoy et al, 2024). Such defense expenditure management constitutes a complex, multidimensional decision-making process involving numerous constraints and criteria. Each weapon system encompasses multiple criteria, including varying levels of effectiveness, costs, maintenance requirements, and capacity (Dağıstanlı, 2025).

Given that decision-makers in defense planning processes often rely on intuitive approaches, in today's security environment where capability determination has become increasingly challenging, the use of digitized decision-support methods is essential for enhancing decision effectiveness (Correia, 2019; Taliaferro et al., 2019). Studies and applications on the subject indicate that in identifying and prioritizing critical sensitivities, needs, and capabilities, the use of scientific decision-support methods such as Bayesian probability theory, MCDM, mathematical modeling, and simulation can be highly beneficial (Altundaş et al., 2025; Ercan & Gencer, 2018; Karadayi et al., 2019; Kurtay, 2024).

MCDM is particularly valuable for solving complex problems that take multiple criteria into account (Demir, 2025; Zare et al., 2025). For accurate prioritization of ongoing projects and effective decision-making, analytical methods must be applied (Dağıstanlı et al., 2024). When there are multiple objectives or attributes, the decision maker can adjust their relative importance and determine the weight of the alternatives using any MCDM technique (Deliktaş & Ustun, 2023).

The aim of this study is to introduce one of the most recent methods developed in literature: ranking of alternatives through functional mapping of criterion subintervals into a single interval (RAFSI). To enhance understanding of the method, two applications are presented in the field of military decision-making. The methodology proposed in this study can be applied to a greater number of alternatives and criteria, and can also be effectively used for the selection of other weapon systems or systems requiring evaluation.

Encyclopedia of Multi-Attribute Decision-Making (MADM). DOI: https://doi.org/10.1016/B978-0-443-33275-3.00076-2

Security occupies the second tier right after physiological needs in Maslow's hierarchy of needs. From this perspective, defense is an indispensable public function for nations to sustain their existence and independence. Global uncertainties, instability, risks, multidimensional threats, and advancements in weapons technologies drive the need for policies and strategies that ensure national security and allocate a significant share of the budget to defense expenditures (Scharre, 2018). Defense planning and management is a process that includes determining how defense forces will be used to achieve strategic objectives and identifying the necessary defense assets (Boyuan et al., 2019). Possessing the right and effective weapon system is one of the most critical decisions a country must make. The weapon system selection process involves various factors such as threat analysis, operational requirements, and cost–benefit assessments (Dağdeviren et al., 2009).

While past conflicts relied heavily on manpower and ground forces, modern warfare is characterized by tactical and ballistic missiles, unmanned aerial vehicles (UAVs), and satellite-based weapons (Zikidis, 2017). Armed forces must be prepared to counter multiple and diverse threats simultaneously. Procuring the "best" weapon system does not necessarily mean it can be used in every military mission; rather forming the most effective group of weapon systems capable of executing planned operations is indispensable in today's hybrid warfare concept (Reichborn-Kjennerud & Cullen, 2022).

A notable example is found in the ongoing Russia–Ukraine war, where multiple launch rocket systems (MLRS) and first-person view (FPV) drones a subset of kamikaze UAVs have played critical roles (Arisoy & Gokasar, 2025; Chow et al., 2024; Molloy, 2024). MLRS missile systems are used in various missions such as striking critical targets, neutralizing air defense systems, providing fire support, and demoralizing the enemy (Bondarenko et al., 2024). Selecting a system capable of delivering superior performance for these and other tasks is of vital importance for national defense. Similarly, kamikaze drones UAVs that destroy themselves by striking targets are increasingly influential on modern battlefields (Kunertova, 2023). Known in military literature as "loitering munitions," these systems can hover over a designated area for extended periods, wait for the optimal moment to strike, and then dive into the target, detonating upon impact. This capability places kamikaze drones in a hybrid weapon category that combines the tactical advantages of traditional missile systems and UAVs.

In the MCDM framework, performance measurement requires identifying the system that can deliver optimal results across various criteria (Konur Bilgen et al., 2025; Yüksel & Dinçer, 2025). Here, the goal is to ensure that the chosen system maximizes the operational effectiveness of the armed forces. Numerous factors influence the deployment of these systems in conflict environments, depending on the needs and doctrines of the armed forces. Determining which criteria are important, assigning weights to each, and selecting weapon systems accordingly are critical for cost-effectiveness and benefit maximization.

The ongoing Russia–Ukraine war provides a significant testing ground for assessing the strengths and weaknesses of these weapon systems. Interpreting the lessons learned and selecting new weapon systems based on predefined criteria is essential for enhancing a nation's defense capabilities.

The second section of this study presents the RAFSI method. The third section outlines the application steps for the MLRS example. The fourth section applies the method to the selection of FPV drones. The final section presents the conclusions.

24.2 Ranking of alternatives through functional mapping of criterion subintervals into a single interval

The RAFSI method systematically converts the entries in the decision matrix into a standardized range, using the ideal and antiideal values specified by the decision maker as reference points. Through this process, all criteria are normalized irrespective of their original measurement units, enabling straightforward comparison across different dimensions. The approach supports both benefit criteria and cost criteria. After this initial conversion, the criterion values are further normalized by applying statistical measures such as arithmetic and harmonic means. In the final stage, these normalized values are multiplied by the corresponding criterion weights, and the resulting products are summed to generate the RAFSI score for each alternative. This score reflects the overall performance of the alternatives, which are subsequently ranked in order. The main procedural steps of the method are as follows (Altıntaş, 2025):

Step 1: Construction of the decision matrix and definition of ideal and anti-ideal values.

$$N = [n_{ij}]_{mxn} = \begin{bmatrix} n_{11} & n_{12} & \cdots & n_{1n} \\ n_{21} & n_{22} & \cdots & n_{2n} \\ \vdots & \vdots & \vdots & \vdots \\ n_{m1} & n_{m2} & \cdots & n_{mn} \end{bmatrix} \tag{24.1}$$

$i = 1, 2, 3, \ldots m$; where m denotes the number of descision alternatives, N represents the decision matrix and n_{ij} indicates the value of the ith decision alternative with respect to the jth criterion component.

Subsequently, the decision matrix defined by Eq. (24.1) is constructed by satisfying the condition $\sum_{j=1}^{n} W_j = 1$, where $C_j (j = 1, 2, \ldots, n)$ represents the criteria, and the benefit and cost directions of the components are taken into account. In the process of determining the ideal and antiideal values for each C_j component $C_j (j = 1, 2, \ldots, n)$, the decision maker determines two values: a_{Ij} (ideal value of criterion C_j) and a_{Nj} (antiideal value of criterion C_j). For benefit type criteria, $a_{Ij} > a_{Nj}$, and for cost type criteria, $a_{Nj} > a_{Ij}$.

Step 2: Association of decision matrix values with component weights (presentation of the standardized decision matrix).

The formulations presented in Eqs. (24.2) and (24.3) are employed to handle benefit-oriented and cost-oriented components, respectively.

(24.2) is applied for benefit-type components.

$$C_j \in [a_{Nj},\ a_{Ij}] \tag{24.2}$$

(24.3) is applied for cost-type components.

$$C_j \in [a_{Ij},\ a_{Nj}] \tag{24.3}$$

In order to transform all the criteria of the initial decision matrix into the interval $[n_1,\ n_{2k}]$, a sequence of k values is generated by inserting $k - 1$ points between the maximum and minimum values of the criteria interval.

$$n_1 < n_2 \le n_3 < n_4 \le n_5 < n_6 \ldots \le n_{2k-1} < n_{2k} \tag{24.4}$$

All components have fixed points and weights. The value n_{2k} represents the maximum for benefit-oriented components (a_{Ij}) and cost-oriented components (a_{Nj}). Conversely, n_l represents the minimum for cost-oriented components (a_{Ij}) and benefit-oriented components (a_{Nj}). In this context, it is recommended that the ideal or antiideal value be six times better than the alternative; therefore, $n_l = 1$ and $n_{2k} = 6$ should be used. However, it is also suggested that the method can be applied with $n_l = 1$ and $n_{2k} = 9$, depending on the decision-maker's preference. Subsequently, a function $f_s(x)$ is constructed to map the subinterval component weight to the interval $[n_l, n_{2k}]$. Eq. (24.5) defines the corresponding $f_s(x)$ function.

$$f_s(x) = \frac{n_{2k} - n_l}{n_{Ij} - a_{Nj}} \cdot x + \frac{a_{Ij} \cdot n_l - a_{Nj} \cdot n_{2k}}{a_{Ij} - a_{Nj}} \tag{24.5}$$

Eq. (24.5) presents the relationship indicating the extent to which the ideal value is preferred over the antiideal value, represented by n_{2k} and n_l. To define the values of a_{Ij} and a_{Nj}, the criterion weights and their boundary values can be used. In this study, the boundary values of the criterion weights were utilized to determine a_{Ij} and a_{Nj}. All values in the matrix are provided by the standardized decision matrix $S = [s_{ij}]_{mxn}$, where $i = 1, 2, \ldots, m$ and $j = 1, 2, \ldots, n$. The functional mapping of the initial decision matrix (N) values to the criterion weight interval $[n_l, n_{2k}]$ implies that for each " i " and " j ", the condition $n_l < S_{ij} < n_{2k}$ must be satisfied.

$$S = [S_{ij}]_{mxn} = \begin{bmatrix} S_{11} & S_{12} & \cdots & S_{1n} \\ S_{21} & S_{22} & \cdots & S_{2n} \\ \vdots & \vdots & \vdots & \vdots \\ S_{m1} & S_{m2} & \cdots & S_{mn} \end{bmatrix} = 1,\ 2,\ \ldots,\ mj \tag{24.6}$$

The values of the matrix S, as shown in (24.6), are obtained through the expression $S_{ij} = f_{A_i}(C_j)$. For benefit-oriented components, there exists a value a_{xj} such that $a_{xj} > a_{ij}$. In this case, $f(a_{xj}) = f(a_{ij})$. Similarly, for cost-oriented components, when there exists a value $a_{xj} < a_{ij}$, the condition $f(a_{xj}) = f(a_{ij})$ is again satisfied.

Step 3: Measuring arithmetic and harmonic means.

For the maximum and minimum sequence of n_{2k} and n_l values, Eq. (24.7) is applied for the arithmetic mean, and Eq. (24.8) is applied for the harmonic mean.

$$A = \frac{n_l + n_{2k}}{2} \tag{24.7}$$

$$H = \frac{2.\ n_{2k} \cdot n_l}{n_{2k} + n_l} \tag{24.8}$$

Step 4: The normalized decision matrix (S) is constructed.

The values of the matrix S are normalized to the interval [0, 1] by applying Eq. (24.9) for benefit-oriented components and Eq. (24.10) for cost-oriented components. Subsequently, the matrix S is represented by (24.11).

$$\hat{S}_{ij} = \frac{s_{ij}}{2A} \tag{24.9}$$

$$\hat{S}_{ij} = \frac{H}{2s_{ij}} \tag{24.10}$$

$$(\hat{S}) = [\hat{S}_{ij}]_{mxn} = \begin{bmatrix} \hat{S}_{11} & \hat{S}_{12} & \cdots & \hat{S}_{1n} \\ \hat{S}_{21} & \hat{S}_{22} & \cdots & \hat{S}_{2n} \\ \vdots & \vdots & \vdots & \vdots \\ \hat{S}_{m1} & \hat{S}_{m2} & \cdots & \hat{S}_{mn} \end{bmatrix}, \quad i = 1,\ 2,\ \ldots,\ m = 1,\ 2,\ \ldots, n \tag{24.11}$$

Eq. (24.12) applies to benefit-oriented components, while Eq. (24.13) applies to cost-oriented components.

$$0 < \frac{n_l}{2A} \le \hat{s}_{ij} \le \frac{H}{2n_l} < 1 \tag{24.12}$$

$$0 < \frac{H}{2n_{2k}} \le \hat{s}_{ij} \le \frac{H}{2n_l} < 1 \tag{24.13}$$

Step 5: Alternative criterion functions [V(Ai)] are determined.

The sum of the normalized and weighted values, given by Eq. (24.14), represents the total performance of the alternative. Based on this score, the performance of decision alternatives is ranked in descending order from the best to the worst (Rezaei, 2015).

$$V(A_i) = w_1 \times \hat{S}_{i1} + w_2 \times \hat{S}_{i2} + \ldots + w_n \times \hat{S}_{in} \tag{24.14}$$

The RAFSI method has been the subject of a limited number of studies in the literature. The RAFSI method, introduced by Žižović et al. (2020) as a novel MCDM ranking approach, transforms criterion values in a decision matrix into a unified range based on proximity to ideal and antiideal points, enabling comparability across different measurement scales and addressing rank reversal issues. Its versatility has been demonstrated in diverse fields, including logistics (Alosta et al., 2021), military decision-making (Güngör, 2021), process optimization (Do Duc Trung et al., 2022), port planning (Pamucar et al., 2022), and performance evaluations of G7 countries (Altıntaş, 2023; Altıntaş, 2025), as well as in financial sustainability assessments (Ali et al., 2024). Extensions of the method, such as method based on the removal effects of criteria–RAFSI, Full Consistency Method–RAFSI, and fuzzy-based integrations, further expand its applicability to decision-making under uncertainty (Görçün et al., 2026; Wang et al., 2025). This study fills the gap in the literature in terms of the RAFSI method's guidance in two important military problems.

24.3 Application: multiple launch rocket system selection

MLRS constitute a critical component of contemporary artillery doctrine, functioning as force multipliers within combined arms operations (Gamble & Jenkins, 2000). These systems represent a distinct category of indirect fire support platforms, characterized by their capacity to deliver concentrated firepower across expansive target areas through the simultaneous or rapid sequential launch of multiple projectiles. Unlike conventional tube artillery systems that typically engage point targets through sustained fire missions, MLRS are engineered to achieve area saturation effects, thereby enabling commanders to suppress, neutralize, or destroy dispersed enemy formations and installations within compressed timeframes. This fundamental operational distinction positions MLRS as particularly efficacious instruments for shaping the battlefield environment during both defensive and offensive phases of military operations. The complexity of MLRS design necessitates sophisticated analytical approaches to optimize system performance, with recent research emphasizing multibody dynamics modeling and mechanical system analysis to enhance operational effectiveness (Li et al., 2021).

The selection, procurement, and operational deployment of MLRS platforms present multifaceted decision-making challenges that necessitate systematic evaluation of competing design alternatives and performance trade-offs. Contemporary MLRS development involves complex engineering considerations including guidance system accuracy, fire control optimization, launch platform stability, and munitions versatility. Research has demonstrated that control system design significantly influences MLRS operational performance, with advanced methodologies such as fuzzy adaptive sliding mode control proving effective in managing the dynamic complexities of mobile firing operations (Qu et al., 2023). Furthermore, the integration of intelligent control architectures, including neural network predictive systems, has emerged as a promising approach to compensate for actuator delays and enhance fire mission responsiveness under operational uncertainties (Li et al., 2020). These technological considerations introduce multiple, often conflicting criteria that must be systematically evaluated when assessing MLRS alternatives, factors that inherently align with MCDM frameworks.

The evolution of MLRS technology since the early 2000s has fundamentally transformed these systems from area saturation weapons into precision strike platforms capable of servicing strategic targets with high accuracy. This transformation has been facilitated by the integration of precision-guided munitions incorporating global positioning system (GPS) guidance technologies, which have substantially improved delivery accuracy while reducing collateral effects (Gamble & Jenkins, 2000). The development of cost-effective guidance solutions for MLRS munitions exemplifies the engineering optimization challenges inherent in military system design, where competing objectives of precision, affordability, and operational flexibility must be balanced through systematic trade-off analysis (Tu et al., 2022). Modern MLRS platforms exhibit considerable versatility in munitions employment, with contemporary systems such as the M142 high mobility artillery rocket system capable of launching both conventional unguided rockets with ranges of 30–40 kilometers and precision-guided Army Tactical Missile System projectiles with operational ranges exceeding 300 kilometers. However, the adoption of precision-guided capabilities introduces complex strategic considerations regarding the appropriate balance between massed area fires and discrete precision engagement, with recent scholarship questioning certain assumptions underlying precision strike doctrine and highlighting unintended operational consequences (Fox, 2024).

The proliferation of diverse MLRS platforms across global armed forces, coupled with rapid technological advancement in guidance systems, propulsion technologies, and fire control architectures, has created increasingly complex procurement and capability development decisions for defense planners. This multidimensional evaluation problem is further complicated by the need to assess system performance under diverse operational scenarios, threat environments, and doctrinal employment concepts. Consequently, MLRS selection and capability assessment represent paradigmatic applications for MCDM methodologies, which provide structured analytical frameworks for synthesizing disparate evaluation criteria, accommodating stakeholder preferences, and supporting defensible resource allocation decisions within complex defense acquisition contexts. The application of MCDM techniques to MLRS evaluation enables systematic comparison of alternative systems while explicitly accounting for the inherent trade-offs between competing performance attributes and operational requirements.

For this case study, six primary criteria commonly considered in the literature on weapon selection problems were determined for evaluating alternative MLRS platforms:

1. **Range:** Missile range and accuracy have become fundamental parameters defining the effectiveness and reliability of modern weapon systems. Range refers to the maximum distance a missile can travel while still delivering its payload effectively (Abbasi & Sarabadan, 2015). This parameter plays a vital role in determining the operational capabilities of missile systems and is influenced by factors such as missile design, propulsion system, and guidance/targeting technologies.
2. **Accuracy:** Accuracy in missile performance refers to the precision with which a missile can strike its intended target (Mon et al., 1994). It encompasses elements such as guidance systems, targeting algorithms, and real-time data integration. High accuracy significantly increases mission success probability. Accuracy is determined by how close the missile can strike to the designated aim point and is affected by similar factors to those influencing range, namely, design, propulsion, and guidance technologies.
3. **Speed:** Missiles can achieve extremely high speeds, posing significant challenges to defensive systems designed to intercept them. The higher the missile speed, the more difficult interception becomes (Cheng, 1997). For this reason, missile velocity is a critical factor in MLRS selection. In the battlefield, missiles must be fast, highly maneuverable, and capable of evading enemy air defense systems.
4. **Warhead:** The warhead refers to the explosive payload carried by the missile. High-explosive warheads are essential for target destruction, and the amount of explosive contained directly affects the likelihood of neutralizing the target (Abbasi & Sarabadan, 2015). Therefore, larger explosive payloads are a desirable attribute in missile systems.
5. **Launch preparation time:** This is the time required to prepare a missile for launch (Cheng, 1997). The shorter this duration, the faster the system can become operationally ready.
6. **Cost:** Missile systems are often high-cost assets. Given budget constraints, it is important that defense expenditures be as cost-effective as possible. Procuring lower-cost systems allows for greater numbers to be acquired within the same budget, which is advantageous for national defense planning (Mon et al., 1994).

Table 24.1 presents the criteria values for various MLRS platforms developed by different countries, based on open-source research. For confidentiality and generalizability, the names of the countries and weapon system models are omitted. The weights of the criteria were assigned by subject matter experts. In practice, weighting methods from MCDM methodologies could be applied to compute and integrate these weights into the evaluation process.

Step 1: Creating the decision matrix and defining ideal and antiideal values.

The decision matrix shown in Table 24.1 was created by obtaining consensus from expert evaluations.

Step 2: Associating decision matrix values with component weights.

Since the optimal value in the RAFSI method is at least six times superior to the antioptimal value, all criteria are normalized in the range of 1–6. The values normalized in the range of 1–6 are shown in Table 24.2.

Sample calculation: For A_1 and C_1 values;

$$f = 1 + (5 - 3)/(5 - 3)*5 = 6$$

Step 3: Measuring arithmetic and harmonic means.

$$A = \frac{n_1 + n_{2k}}{2} = 1 + \frac{6}{2} = 3.5$$

$$H = \frac{2n_{2k}*n_1}{n_{2k} + n_1} = 2*6*1/7 = 1.71$$

Step 4: Creating the normalized decision matrix (S).

For the values of the S matrix, equality (9) was considered for the benefit-oriented components and equality (10) for the cost-oriented components. The values in Table 24.2 were used to obtain Table 24.3. The S matrix obtained as a result of the calculations is shown in Table 24.3.

Sample calculation: For A1 and C1 values;

$$\hat{S}_{ij} = \frac{Sij}{2A} = \frac{6}{7} = 0.857$$

Step 5: Alternative criterion functions [V(Ai)] are found.

TABLE 24.1 Results of expert opinions.

w	0.30	0.25	0.10	0.15	0.05	0.15
System name	C_1	C_2	C_3	C_4	C_5	C_6
A_1	5	5	4	2	5	4
A_2	3	1	3	5	2	3
A_3	3	3	4	3	4	4
A_4	4	3	5	4	2	2

TABLE 24.2 Standardized decision matrix.

	C_1	C_2	C_3	C_4	C_5	C_6
A_1	6.00	6.00	3.50	1.00	6.00	6.00
A_2	1.00	1.00	1.00	6.00	1.00	3.50
A_3	1.00	3.50	3.50	2.67	4.33	6.00
A_4	3.50	3.50	6.00	4.33	1.00	1.00

TABLE 24.3 The matrix that is normalized.

	C_1	C_2	C_3	C_4	C_5	C_6
A_1	0.857	0.143	0.500	0.143	0.143	0.143
A_2	0.143	0.855	0.143	0.857	0.855	0.244
A_3	0.143	0.244	0.500	0.381	0.197	0.143
A_4	0.500	0.244	0.857	0.619	0.855	0.855

TABLE 24.4 Final version of the criterion—alternative matrix.

	C_1	C_2	C_3	C_4	C_5	C_6	Sum	Rank
A_1	0.26	0.04	0.05	0.02	0.01	0.02	0.39	3
A_2	0.04	0.21	0.01	0.13	0.04	0.04	0.48	2
A_3	0.04	0.06	0.05	0.06	0.01	0.02	0.24	4
A_4	0.15	0.06	0.09	0.09	0.04	0.13	0.56	1

Criteria weights were initially assigned based on expert opinion. The calculated criteria weights are shown in Table 24.1. The performances of the decision alternatives are ranked according to the scores obtained from Eq. (24.14) shown in Table 24.4.

Sample application: For A_1;

$$V(A_i) = w_1 \times \hat{S}_{i1} + w_2 \times \hat{S}_{i2} + \ldots + w_n \times \hat{S}_{in}$$

As seen in Table 24.4, according to the values obtained, the best alternative was MLRS defined with A_4 (0.56 total score).

24.4 Application: first-person view drone selection

The type of FPV drone examined in this case study is a subcategory of the kamikaze drone family, equipped with explosive payloads (Khudov et al., 2025). Inspired by the kamikaze attacks carried out by Japanese pilots during World War II, this technology removes the human element from the battlefield, thereby reducing operational risk and offering armed forces a strategic advantage in terms of cost-effectiveness. The integration of GPS, high-resolution optical and infrared sensors, compact explosive warheads, and secure data transmission systems has significantly improved the precision and operational capabilities of kamikaze drones. They play a key role in achieving area dominance and weakening enemy defenses.

In asymmetric warfare, their small and agile platforms make them highly suitable for strategic and surprise attacks by guerrilla or irregular forces. Kamikaze drones have transformed the nature of modern warfare with their low cost, high operational flexibility, and elimination of personnel casualties. However, they also face limitations such as vulnerability to GPS jamming, electronic countermeasures, and weather conditions.

Since 2015, FPV drones have emerged as force multipliers in asymmetric conflict environments. The Russia–Ukraine war, which began in 2022, has seen the most extensive and diverse use of kamikaze drones to date. In the early months of the conflict, both sides primarily relied on UAVs for reconnaissance and surveillance. As the war progressed, kamikaze drones became central to both strategic and tactical operations. Their low production cost and small radar cross-section allow them to be deployed in swarms against air defense systems, forcing the depletion of expensive interceptor munitions before launching a second wave of attacks with more sophisticated weapons to strike enemy targets. These drones have also played an important role in targeting critical infrastructure. In the Russia–Ukraine war, they have been used against energy facilities such as power plants, substations, and transmission lines.

A major challenge for these drones on the battlefield is electronic warfare (EW). Both Ukraine and Russia have deployed powerful jammers to disrupt kamikaze drone signals. In response, UAV operators have developed countermeasures such as flying at shorter ranges, incorporating automatic dive modes to mitigate signal loss, and using alternative communication frequencies. Additionally, kamikaze drones have been used to create psychological pressure on civilians, as well as to conduct pinpoint strikes against artillery batteries, ammunition depots, armored vehicles, and radar systems. Ukraine has further developed maritime kamikaze drones, posing an unexpected threat to the Russian Navy in the Black Sea.

FPV drones demonstrate operational effectiveness at both tactical and strategic levels. On the front line, they have expanded maneuvering space for ground forces by destroying enemy artillery and armored vehicles. At the strategic level, they have influenced the tempo of warfare by targeting energy infrastructure and logistics hubs. This pattern of use strongly indicates that the prevalence of kamikaze drones in conventional warfare will continue to increase in the future.

The selection of FPV drones for military use depends on the combination of technical capacity, operational requirements, and logistical factors. Lessons from the Russia–Ukraine war suggest that the following six criteria commonly found in the literature on weapon selection problems are most relevant for evaluating FPV drone systems (Altundaş et al., 2022):

1. **Remote control range**
The ability to destroy targets without entering the enemy's engagement zone offers a significant advantage. Guiding drones from the longest possible distance reduces risk to the operator and increases the UAV's coverage area. While fully operator-controlled systems provide flexibility, autonomous or tethered systems are more resistant to electronic jamming. A greater remote-control range is therefore desirable.
2. **Payload capacity**
Payload capacity refers to the number of explosives the UAV can carry, which is crucial for target destruction. The required payload depends on the nature of the target; lighter warheads are suited for mobile targets, while heavier warheads are preferred for infrastructure or fortified positions. A higher payload increases the probability of target neutralization (Abbasi & Sarabadan, 2015).
3. **Cost**
Cost is critical for enabling the acquisition of large numbers of drones and ensuring cost-effectiveness. Procuring lower-cost UAVs helps preserve national defense budgets (Cheng and Mon, 1994). Economical models also support high-volume production and swarm attack concepts.
4. **Endurance**
Endurance refers to the maximum time a UAV can remain airborne without returning to base. Longer endurance increases operational flexibility, allowing drones to loiter while searching for targets or to reach more distant objectives.
5. **Operational altitude**
A higher operational altitude enhances target detection and tracking capabilities, enabling wider area surveillance and easier monitoring of enemy movements within the coverage zone.
6. **Maximum speed**

Although UAVs generally cannot match the speeds of missiles, higher velocity offers a significant advantage against defense systems designed to intercept them. Low speed can allow targets to evade incoming UAVs, whereas higher speed reduces the likelihood of interception and increases strike success (Chen, 1996). Speed is therefore a key criterion in UAV selection.

Step 1: Creating the decision matrix and defining ideal and antiideal values.

Table 24.5 below shows the various FPV drone systems developed by various countries and their associated criteria, based on open-source research. These candidate weapon systems are ranked.

Step 2: Associating decision matrix values with component weights.

Since the optimal value in the RAFSI method is at least six times superior to the antioptimal value, all criteria are normalized in the range of 1–6. The values normalized in the range of 1–6 are shown in Table 24.6.

Sample calculation: For A_1 and C_1 values;

$$f = 1 + (3 - 2)/(5 - 2)*5 = 2.67$$

Step 3: Measuring arithmetic and harmonic means.

$$A = \frac{n_1 + n_{2k}}{2} = 1 + \frac{6}{2} = 3.5$$

$$H = \frac{2n_{2k}*n_1}{n_{2k} + n_1} = 2*6*1/7 = 1.71$$

TABLE 24.5 Results of expert opinions.

w	0.30	0.25	0.05	0.25	0.10	0.05
	C_1	C_2	C_3	C_4	C_5	C_6
A_1	3	2	3	5	2	4
A_2	5	3	3	4	5	4
A_3	4	2	1	3	5	4
A_4	3	1	5	2	2	4
A_5	4	5	1	4	2	5
A_6	2	1	4	1	2	4
A_7	2	1	4	2	2	4

TABLE 24.6 Standardized decision matrix.

	C_1	C_2	C_3	C_4	C_5	C_6
A_1	2.67	2.25	3.50	6.00	1.00	1.00
A_2	6.00	3.50	3.50	4.75	6.00	1.00
A_3	4.33	2.25	1.00	3.50	6.00	1.00
A_4	2.67	1.00	6.00	2.25	1.00	1.00
A_5	4.33	6.00	1.00	4.75	1.00	6.00
A_6	1.00	1.00	4.75	1.00	1.00	1.00
A_7	1.00	1.00	4.75	2.25	1.00	1.00

TABLE 24.7 The matrix that is normalized

	C_1	C_2	C_3	C_4	C_5	C_6
A_1	0.381	0.321	0.244	0.857	0.857	0.143
A_2	0.857	0.500	0.244	0.679	0.679	0.143
A_3	0.619	0.321	0.855	0.500	0.500	0.143
A_4	0.381	0.143	0.143	0.321	0.321	0.143
A_5	0.619	0.857	0.855	0.679	0.679	0.857
A_6	0.143	0.143	0.180	0.143	0.143	0.143
A_7	0.143	0.143	0.180	0.321	0.321	0.143

Step 4: Creating the normalized decision matrix (S).

For the values of the S matrix, equality (9) was taken into account for the benefit-oriented components and equality (10) for the cost-oriented components. The S matrix obtained as a result of the calculations is shown in Table 24.7.

TABLE 24.8 Final version of the criterion—alternative matrix.

	C_1	C_2	C_3	C_4	C_5	C_6	Sum	Rank
A_1	0.11	0.08	0.01	0.21	0.09	0.01	0.51	3
A_2	0.26	0.13	0.01	0.17	0.07	0.01	0.64	2
A_3	0.19	0.08	0.04	0.13	0.05	0.01	0.49	4
A_4	0.11	0.04	0.01	0.08	0.03	0.01	0.28	5
A_5	0.19	0.21	0.04	0.17	0.07	0.04	0.72	1
A_6	0.04	0.04	0.01	0.04	0.01	0.01	0.14	7
A_7	0.04	0.04	0.01	0.08	0.03	0.01	0.21	6

Sample calculation: For A1 and C1 values;

$$\hat{S}_{ij} = \frac{Sij}{2A} = \frac{2,67}{7} = 0.381$$

Step 5: Alternative criterion functions [V(Ai)] are found.

Criteria weights were initially determined based on expert opinion. The calculated criteria weights are shown in Table 24.5. The performances of the decision alternatives are ranked according to the scores obtained from Eq. (24.14) shown in Table 24.8.

Sample application: For A1;

$$V(A_i) = w_1 \times \hat{S}_{i1} + w_2 \times \hat{S}_{i2} + \ldots + w_n \times \hat{S}_{in}$$

As seen in Table 24.8, the best alternative, based on the obtained values, is the FPV Drone, designated A_5 (0.72 total score). With their low-cost, high-impact, and flexible use, FPV drones have created a new paradigm on the battlefield. With technological advances and tactical innovations, it seems inevitable that these systems will become more widespread and effective in the inventories of both conventional armies and irregular forces.

24.5 Conclusion

In today's asymmetric combat environment, many military experts are developing new doctrines that incorporate weapon systems such as kamikaze drones and MLRS, which are promoted as effective solutions. Nations make substantial expenditures to meet their defense needs, and due to their high costs, weapon systems constitute a significant share of these budgets. This makes it essential to evaluate them according to multiple criteria during the selection or development phase. These criteria vary depending on the mission objective, the enemy's weapons and defensive equipment, and the operational environment.

In this study, the RAFSI method was presented for ranking MLRS and FPV drone systems that are, and will continue to be, indispensable on the modern battlefield. Using RAFSI, a relatively new method for weapon system selection, six different MLRS widely deployed in world militaries were evaluated against six criteria based on open-source data. In a similar application, seven alternative FPV drone systems were assessed according to six criteria. The results obtained are sensitive to changes in the weights of these criteria, meaning that altering the weight distribution will lead to different rankings. Thus, by applying an up-to-date methodology that incorporates current technological advancements, emerging warfare concepts, and technical specifications, the resulting criterion weights can provide valuable guidance to military decision-makers.

This research demonstrates that the weapon system selection problem can be analyzed using a novel analytical method. The same approach can also be applied to other combat platforms and systems (e.g., armored personnel carriers, howitzers, helicopters), allowing for the selection of optimal systems tailored to specific missions. In this context, the RAFSI method, as presented here, offers significant potential within the scope of MCDM methodologies for enhancing diverse operational capabilities.

Looking ahead, developments such as AI-assisted target recognition, real-time coordination with UAVs, autonomous fire planning, and integration with unmanned carrier platforms will make these systems more lethal and adaptable. MLRS have evolved beyond being merely traditional area-fire weapons, transforming into highly mobile, precision-strike, high-value fire-support platforms capable of meeting the multidimensional demands of modern warfare.

Similarly, FPV drones are expected to benefit from advances in AI-driven target identification, coordinated swarm attacks, and longer-range platforms factors that will amplify the impact of kamikaze drones. This evolution will create both new risks and opportunities in battlespace and the broader international security environment. The proliferation of kamikaze drones is also driving the advancement of EW countermeasures, sophisticated radar systems, and antidrone technologies. As a result, future battlefields will likely see more frequent "drone-versus-drone" and "drone-versus-EW" engagements. All these developments will inevitably open new problem domains that can be addressed using MCDM approaches.

References

Abbasi, S., & Sarabadan, S. (2015). Evaluating tactical missile systems by using fuzzy ahp and topsis technique. *Journal of Management and Information Science, 3*(2), 28–36. https://doi.org/10.17858/jmisci.69912.

Aksoy, S., Begenirbaş, M., & Kurtay, K. G. (2024). Yetenek temelli risk tabanli savunma planlaması için Bulanık AHP-TOPSIS ile Silah Seçimi. *Savunma Bilimleri Dergisi, 20*(2), 363–387. https://doi.org/10.17134/khosbd.1494965.

Ali, J., Naser Hussain, K., Alnoor, A., Muhsen, Y. R., & Atiyah, A. G. (2024). Benchmarking methodology of banks based on financial sustainability using CRITIC and RAFSI techniques. *Decision Making: Applications in Management and Engineering, 7*(1), 315–341. https://doi.org/10.31181/dmame712024945.

Alosta, A., Alsyouf, I., & Al-Tahat, M. D. (2021). Resolving a location selection problem by means of an integrated AHP-RAFSI approach. *Decision Making: Applications in Management and Engineering, 4*(2), 1–15. https://doi.org/10.31181/rme200102135a.

Altıntaş, F. F. (2023). Kırılganlık performanslarının MEREC tabanlı RAFSI yöntemi ile analizi: G7 grubu ülkeleri. *Karamanoğlu Mehmetbey Üniversitesi Sosyal ve Ekonomik Araştırmalar Dergisi, 25*(44), 464–490. https://doi.org/10.58620/fbujoss.1313949.

Altıntaş, F. F. (2025). Analysis of climate change performances of G7 group countries: An application using the MEREC-based RAFSI method. *Journal of Mehmet Akif Ersoy University Economics and Administrative Sciences Faculty, 12*(1), 214–245. https://doi.org/10.30798/makuiibf.1489592.

Altundaş, A., Arıkan, M., & Erol, S. (2025). Routing and payload planning of multi-base, heterogeneous fleet unmanned aerial vehicles to time-windowed missions. *Journal of the Faculty of Engineering and Architecture of Gazi University, 40*(3). https://doi.org/10.17341/gazimmfd.1559891.

Altundaş, A., Kurtay, K. G., & Erol, S. (2022). Sınır güvenliği ve müdahale görevi yapan İHA'ların ÇKKV yöntemleri ile değerlendirilmesi. *Savunma Bilimleri Dergisi,* (42), 155–185. https://doi.org/10.17134/khosbd.1049863.

Arisoy, A., & Gokasar, I. (2025). The logistics conjuncture of the middle corridor trade route and Turkey's strategic role. *Journal of Intelligent Decision Making and Granular Computing, 1*(1), 143–150. https://doi.org/10.31181/jidmgc1120259.

Badi, I., Bayane Bouraima, M., & Zonon, B. I. P. (2025). A multi-criteria decision-making model for prioritizing the causes of inflation in libya using the best-worst method and analytic hierarchy process. *Knowledge and Decision Systems With Applications, 1*, 165–176. https://doi.org/10.59543/kadsa.v1i.14259.

Bondarenko, M., Habrinets, V., & Vorobei, M. (2024). Evolution of multiple launch rocket systems from early rockets to HIMARS and beyond. *Challenges and Issues of Modern Science, 3*, 23–34.

Boyuan, X. I. A., Qingsong, Z. H. A. O., Kewei, Y. A. N. G., Yajie, D. O. U., & Zhiwei, Y. A. N. G. (2019). Scenario-based modeling and solving research on robust weapon project planning problems. *Journal of Systems Engineering and Electronics, 30*(1), 85–99. https://doi.org/10.21629/JSEE.2019.01.09.

Chen, S. M. (1996). Evaluating weapon systems using fuzzy arithmetic operations. *Fuzzy sets and systems, 77*(3), 265–276.

Cheng, C. H. (1997). Evaluating naval tactical missile systems by fuzzy AHP based on the grade value of membership function. *European Journal of Operational Research, 96*(2), 343–350. https://doi.org/10.1016/S0377-2217(96)00026-4.

Cheng, C. H., & Mon, D. L. (1994). Evaluating weapon system by analytical hierarchy process based on fuzzy scales. *Fuzzy sets and systems, 63*(1), 1–10.

Chow, T. E., Sanchez, D. P., Amatya, P., & Tanzir, M. T. (2024). Modelling the suitability of multiple launch rocket system in the war in Ukraine. *Applied Geography, 164*, 103206. https://doi.org/10.1016/j.apgeog.2024.103206.

Correia, J. (2019). Military capabilities and the strategic planning conundrum. *Security and Defence Quarterly, 24*(2), 21–50. https://doi.org/10.35467/sdq/108667.

Dağdeviren, M., Yavuz, S., & Kılınç, N. (2009). Weapon selection using the AHP and TOPSIS methods under fuzzy environment. *Expert systems with applications, 36*(4), 8143–8151. https://doi.org/10.1016/j.eswa.2008.10.016.

Dağıstanlı, H. A. (2025). Weapon system selection for capability-based defense planning using lanchester models integrated with fuzzy MCDM in computer assisted military experiment. *Knowledge and Decision Systems With Applications, 1*, 11–23. https://doi.org/10.59543/kadsa.v1i.13601.

Dağıstanlı, H. A., Altundaş, A., Kurtay, K. G., & Gökmen, Y. (2024). The optimization of long-term dynamic defense industry project portfolio management with a mixed and holistic project prioritization approach. *Dynamic Games and Applications,* 1–30. https://doi.org/10.1007/s13235-024-00602-6.

Deliktaş, D., & Ustun, O. (2023). Multi-objective genetic algorithm based on the fuzzy MULTIMOORA method for solving the cardinality constrained portfolio optimization. *Applied Intelligence, 53*(12), 14717–14743. https://doi.org/10.1007/s10489-022-04240-6.

Demir, G. (2025). The synergy of fuzzy logic and multi-criteria decision-making: Application areas and global trends. *Journal of Intelligent Decision Making and Information Science, 2*, 429–455. https://doi.org/10.59543/jidmis.v2i.14157.

Do Duc Trung, D., Van Hung, P., Nguyen, T. H., & Bui, T. D. (2022). Comparison of the RAFSI and PIV method in multi -criteria decision making: Application to turning processes. *International Journal of Metrology and Quality Engineering, 13*(7). https://doi.org/10.1051/ijmqe/2022014.

Ercan, C., & Gencer, C. (2018). A decision support system for dynamic heterogeneous unmanned aerial system fleets. *Gazi University Journal of Science, 31*(3), 863–877.

Fox, A. C. (2024). Precision paradox and myths of precision strike in modern armed conflict. *The RUSI Journal, 169*(1–2), 62–74. https://doi.org/10.1080/03071847.2024.2343717.

Gamble, A. E., & Jenkins, P. N. (2000). Low cost guidance for the multiple launch rocket system (MLRS) artillery rocket. In *IEEE 2000. Position location and navigation symposium (Cat. No. 00CH37062)*. IEEE, 193–199 https://doi.org/10.1109/PLANS.2000.838302.

Gokasar, I., & Okur, I. (2025). A multi-criteria utility approach to bridge maintenance prioritization. *Knowledge and Decision Systems with Applications, 1*, 35–56. https://doi.org/10.59543/kadsa.v1i.13625.

Görçün, Ö. F., Küçükönder, H., & Çalık, A. (2026). Prioritizing sustainable energy strategies using multi -criteria decision -making models in type -2 neutrosophic environment. *Optimization in Sustainable Energy: Methods and Applications*, 113–182. https://doi.org/10.1002/9781394242139.ch4.

Güngör, M. (2021). The relationship between military expenditures and fragility in the greater black sea region: A panel data analysis. *Journal of International Security and Terrorism, 3*(2), 45–60.

Karadayi, M. A., Ekinci, Y., & Tozan, H. (2019). A fuzzy MCDM framework for weapon systems selection. In *Operations research for military organizations*. IGI Global Scientific Publishing, 185–204 https://doi.org/10.4018/978-1-5225-5513-1.ch009.

Khudov, H., Khudov, R., Khizhnyak, I., Makoveichuk, O., & Khudov, V. (2025). Image segmentation methods for kamikaze FPV drones targeting to aid critical energy national infrastructure assets protection. In *Systems, decision and control in energy VII: Volume I: Energy informatics and transport*. Cham: Springer Nature Switzerland, 139–151 https://doi.org/10.1007/978-3-031-90462-2_7.

Konur Bilgen, M., Guneri, B., & Baldıran, S. (2025). Integrated fermatean fuzzy SWARA and Q-ROF-EDAS methodology for supplier evaluation in the shipyard industry. *Journal of Intelligent Decision Making and Granular Computing, 1*(1), 48–75. https://doi.org/10.31181/jidmgc1120257.

Kunertova, D. (2023). The war in Ukraine shows the game-changing effect of drones depends on the game. *Bulletin of the Atomic Scientists, 79*(2), 95–102. https://doi.org/10.1080/00963402.2023.2178180.

Kurtay, K. G. (2024). Selection of military armored vehicle using fuzzy EDAS method. *Computer and Decision Making: An International Journal, 1*, 134–150. https://doi.org/10.59543/comdem.v1i.10413.

Li, B., Rui, X., Tian, W., & Cui, G. (2020). Neural-network-predictor-based control for an uncertain multiple launch rocket system with actuator delay. *Mechanical Systems and Signal Processing, 141*, 106489. https://doi.org/10.1016/j.ymssp.2019.106489.

Li, B., Rui, X., Wang, G., Zhang, J., & Zhou, Q. (2021). On modeling and dynamics of a multiple launch rocket system. *Proceedings of the Institution of Mechanical Engineers, Part G: Journal of Aerospace Engineering, 235*(10), 1182–1197. https://doi.org/10.1177/0954410020982243.

Li, L., Xiao, B., Su, S., Zhang, H., Wu, X., & Guo, Y. (2023). Attack-defense differential game to strength allocation strategies generation. *Optimal Control Applications and Methods, 44*(6), 3219–3236. https://doi.org/10.1002/oca.3035.

Lo, H. W., Chen, W. Y., & Lin, S. W. (2025). Using Bayesian BWM to analyze elevator performance requirements for collaborative product innovation design. *Journal of Intelligent Decision Making and Information Science, 2*, 218–232. https://doi.org/10.59543/jidmis.v2i.11503.

Metin, M. G., & Bulkan, S. (2019). Optimization in military planning: Resource allocation problems. In *Operations research for military organizations*. IGI Global Scientific Publishing, 111–130 https://doi.org/10.4018/978-1-5225-5513-1.ch006.

Molloy, D. O. (2024). Drones in modern warfare: Lessons learnt from the War in Ukraine. *Australian Army Research Centre*. https://doi.org/10.61451/267513.

Mon, D. L., Cheng, C. H., & Lin, J. C. (1994). Evaluating weapon system using fuzzy analytic hierarchy process based on entropy weight. *Fuzzy Sets and Systems, 62*(2), 127–134. https://doi.org/10.1016/0165-0114(94)90052-3.

Pamučar, D., & Deliktaş, D. (2025). Decision-analytics-based stock selection: A fuzzy Aczel–Alsina ordinal priority approach. *International Journal of Fuzzy Systems*, 1–25. https://doi.org/10.1007/s40815-025-02034-9.

Pamucar, D., Badi, I., & Stevic, Z. (2022). An integrated fucom -rafsi model for assessing the potential of a new gateway port in libya for some african landlocked countries. *International Journal for Quality Research, 16*(2). https://doi.org/10.24874/IJQR16.02-17.

Qu, P., Sun, Z., Li, Q., Zhang, J., Liu, P., & Zhou, D. (2023). Dynamic simulation of multiple launch rocket system marching fire based on the fuzzy adaptive sliding mode control. *Machines, 11*(4), 427. https://doi.org/10.3390/machines11040427.

Reichborn-Kjennerud, E., & Cullen, P. (2022). What is hybrid warfare?. Norwegian Institute for International Affairs (NUPI).

Rezaei, J. (2015). Best-worst multi-criteria decision-making method. *Omega, 53*, 49–57. https://doi.org/10.1016/j.omega.2014.11.009.

Scharre, P. (2018). *Army of none: Autonomous weapons and the future of war*. WW Norton & Company.

Taliaferro, A.C., Gonzalez, L.M., Tillman, M., Ghosh, P., Clarke, P., & Hinkle, W. (2019). Defense Governance and Management: Improving the Defense Management Capabilities of Foreign Defense Institutions-A Guide to Capability-Based Planning (CBP).

Toktaş, P., & Can, G. F. (2023). A three-stage holistic risk assessment approach proposal based on KEMIRA-M and DEMATEL integration. *Knowledge and Information Systems, 65*(4), 1735–1768. https://doi.org/10.1007/s10115-022-01809-y.

Tu, T., Wang, G., Miao, Y., & Rui, X. (2022). Sensitivity analysis of multiple launch rocket system based on the response surface method. In *Proceedings of the 1st International Conference on Mechanical System Dynamics (ICMSD 2022)* (pp. 403–408). https://doi.org/10.1049/icp.2022.1784

Wang, W., Chen, Y., Wang, Y., Deveci, M., Al-Hinai, A., & Kadry, S. (2025). Analyzing the barriers to blockchain adoption in supply chain finance using an integrated interval -valued Fermatean fuzzy RAFSI model. *Financial Innovation, 11*(1), 9. https://doi.org/10.1186/s40854-024-00670-y.

Yardım, M. F., Yüksel, S., & Dinçer, H. (2025). Development of optimal investment strategies for electric vehicle charging stations with a novel decision-making technique. *Journal of Operations Intelligence, 3*(1), 67–73. https://doi.org/10.31181/jopi31202534.

Yüksel, S., & Dinçer, H. (2025). A decision-making framework for the development of molten-salt reactors: Prioritizing environmental and technological factors. *Journal of Soft Computing and Decision Analytics, 3*(1), 18–25. https://doi.org/10.31181/jscda31202547.

Zare, Z., Ashrafzadeh, M., & Karatas, M. (2025). A hybrid fuzzy AHP and fuzzy TOPSIS approach for warehouse location selection. *Computer and Decision Making: An International Journal, 2*, 613–632. https://doi.org/10.59543/comdem.v2i.14239.

Zikidis, K. C. (2017). Early warning against stealth aircraft, missiles and unmanned aerial vehicles. In *Surveillance in action: Technologies for civilian, military and cyber surveillance*. Cham: Springer International Publishing, 195–216 https://doi.org/10.1007/978-3-319-68533-5_10.

Žižović, M., Pamučar, D., Albijanić, M., Chatterjee, P., & Pribićević, I. (2020). Eliminating rank reversal problem using a new multi-attribute model—The RAFSI method. *Mathematics, 8*(6), 1015. https://doi.org/10.3390/math8061015.

Wang, W., Chen, Y., Wang, Y., Deveci, M., Al-Hinai, A., & Kadry, S. (2023). Analyzing the barriers to blockchain adoption in supply chain finance using an integrated interval-valued Fermatean fuzzy CAPSI model. *Financial Innovation*, 11(1), 9. https://doi.org/10.1186/s40854-024-00703-y.
Yadım, M. B., Yüksel, S., & Dinçer, H. (2023). Development of optimal investment strategies for electric vehicle charging stations with a novel decision-making technique. *Journal of Operations Intelligence*, 1(1), 67–73. https://doi.org/10.31181/jopi1120233.
Yüksel, S., & Dinçer, H. (2023). A decision-making framework for the development of nuclear reactors: Preventing environmental and technological failures. *Journal of Soft Computing and Decision Analytics*, 1(1), 15–25. https://doi.org/10.31181/jscda11202347.
Zare, Z., Abdollahzadeh, M., & Kashefi, M. (2024). A hybrid fuzzy AHP and fuzzy TOPSIS approach for ... location selection. *Computer and Decision Making: An International Journal*, 1, 61–67. https://doi.org/10.59543/comdem.v1i.10279.
Zhou, K. C. (2017). Early warning against stealth attacks, missiles and unmanned aerial vehicles. In *Surveillance ... technologies for defense and ...*. Cham: Springer International Publishing. https://doi.org/10.1007/978-3-319-...
Žižović, M., Pamučar, D., Albijanić, M., Chatterjee, P., & Pribićević, I. (2020). Eliminating rank reversal problem using a new multi-attribute model—The RAFSI method. *Mathematics*, 8(6), 1015. https://doi.org/10.3390/math8061015.

Chapter 25

ITARA: Indifference threshold-based attribute ratio analysis for multi-attribute decision-making

Moein Khazaei[1], Hamidreza Eskandari[2], and Mohammad Ramezani[3]

[1]*School of Engineering and Sciences, Tecnologico de Monterrey, Monterrey, Mexico,* [2]*Department of Business Analytics, Swansea University, United Kingdom,* [3]*Industrial Management, Tarbiat Modares University, Tehran, Iran*

25.1 Introduction

Assigning appropriate weights to attributes is a fundamental requirement in multiple attribute decision-making (MADM) (Bonakdari et al., 2025), since the importance attached to each criterion directly shapes the final ranking and selection outcomes (Khazaei, Gholian-Jouybari, Dolatabadi, et al., 2025). Although a broad range of subjective, semiobjective, and fully objective weighting methods has been proposed in the literature, the challenge persists in situations where the decision maker is unable or unwilling to provide explicit preference information (Pena et al., 2020). In many practical contexts, especially when attributes are numerous, complex, or nonmonetary, subjective elicitation becomes unreliable or inconsistent, which increases the need for robust data-driven approaches (Anawar & Adnan, 2024). This has motivated the development of several dispersion-based weighting techniques that quantify the level of contrast within the decision matrix and assign higher weights to attributes exhibiting greater variability across alternatives (Nguyen & Gigliarano, 2025).

Despite these advances, dispersion-based approaches often rely solely on statistical spread without considering the decision maker's tolerance for small or negligible differences in attribute values (Mohammadi et al., 2023). In real decision settings, many deviations between alternatives may fall within a zone of indifference and therefore should not influence the weighting structure (Jovanović et al., 2024). The absence of this behavioral element can lead to oversensitive weights, particularly when the decision matrix contains minor fluctuations that lack meaningful discriminating power (Bovkir et al., 2025). Addressing this gap requires a weighting mechanism capable of integrating both the objective dispersion of data and the notion of insignificant differences (Fuentes et al., 2022). The indifference threshold-based attribute ratio analysis (ITARA) method, is introduced to fulfill this purpose (Hatefi, 2019). ITARA incorporates the classical logic of dispersion while embedding the concept of an indifference threshold, which determines whether the observed difference between two adjacent performance scores is substantial enough to influence the weight of an attribute (Liu et al., 2022). By filtering out variations falling below the threshold, the method avoids artificial inflation of weights and provides a more behaviorally aligned measurement of importance. This design makes ITARA particularly suitable for conditions involving incomplete preference information, cognitive limitations, or time-constrained decision-making (Sofuoğlu, 2019).

In addition to its conceptual contribution, ITARA offers a structured computational procedure that is simple, transparent, and adaptable to different problem scales (Ahmadi Pargo & Hashemkhani Zolfani, 2025). The method follows a sequential process including normalization, ordering, deviation measurement, and threshold adjustment before aggregating the significant deviations into a final weight for each attribute (Vafaei et al., 2022). Simulation-based evidence reported in the foundational study demonstrates that ITARA surpasses well-known dispersion-based techniques such as entropy, standard deviation, ideal point, and maximizing deviation across several performance criteria, including hit ratio, rank order correlation, and robustness (Zolfani, 2024). These findings highlight the strong practical value of ITARA as a reliable semi-objective weighting tool within the broader MADM framework (Ulutaş et al., 2020).

Encyclopedia of Multi-Attribute Decision-Making (MADM). DOI: https://doi.org/10.1016/B978-0-443-33275-3.00071-3

In light of these theoretical and empirical developments, the remainder of this paper provides a comprehensive and implementable formulation of the ITARA method, followed by illustrative numerical examples that demonstrate its behavior in realistic decision settings. The methodological section elaborates each computational stage in a transparent and reproducible manner, emphasizing the role of threshold-adjusted deviations in capturing meaningful attribute dispersion. The numerical examples then show how ITARA operates in both small-scale and larger, multidimensional decision matrices, highlighting the influence of aspiration levels, threshold selection, and lp-metric aggregation on the resulting weights. By combining conceptual clarity with practical rigor, the paper aims to provide decision analysts, researchers, and practitioners with a clear understanding of how ITARA can be applied to derive stable, behaviorally grounded weights in contexts where subjective preference elicitation is difficult or incomplete.

25.2 Literature review

Recent advancements in multicriteria decision-making have increasingly incorporated the ITARA method as a core weighting mechanism, reflecting its growing acceptance as a semi-objective and behaviorally sensitive approach for attribute weighting. Early integrations of ITARA with classical MADM techniques, such as the technique for order preference by similarity to ideal solution (TOPSIS) demonstrated its ability to refine risk assessment models, particularly by capturing meaningful deviations while ignoring insignificant differences. For instance, (Lo et al., 2021) developed an ITARA-TOPSIS framework for identifying system and product risks within the Federal Emergency Management Agency, showing that ITARA yielded more reliable factor weights while gray-based TOPSIS improved the discrimination of failure modes. Subsequent studies applied similar hybrid models to sustainability and institutional assessment, including university sustainability risk analysis using neutrosophic ITARA and aspiration-level TOPSIS (Lin & Lo, 2024) and corporate sustainability performance evaluation via trapezoidal fuzzy ITARA reference ideal method (ITARA-RIM) (Hsu et al., 2024).

Beyond classical fuzzy environments, ITARA has been expanded into higher-order representations of uncertainty, resulting in hybrid frameworks capable of addressing complex, ambiguous, or qualitative decision information. In this trajectory, Simić et al. (2023) introduced a type-2 neutrosophic ITARA-evaluation based on distance from the average solution model for sustainable petroleum route selection, demonstrating clear performance advantages over alternative neutrosophic MADM tools (Khan et al., 2023). Advanced the field by combining ITARA with VlseKriterijumska Optimizacija I Kompromisno Resenje under 2-tuple linguistic q-rung picture fuzzy sets, thereby leveraging linguistic expressiveness and q-rung flexibility to better capture expert hesitation. Other enhancements include probabilistic hesitant fuzzy environments, where Liu et al. (2022) combined the best–worst method and ITARA within a probabilistic hesitant fuzzy taxonomy framework, enabling integration of subjective and objective weights. Parallel developments such as fuzzy ITARA-R-number TOPSIS (RTOPSIS) and spherical fuzzy ITARA integrated with Élimination et Choix Traduisant la Réalité (ELECTRE) III and three-way decision mechanisms underscore ITARA's adaptability across distinct fuzzy settings and decision architectures (Wu et al., 2023).

Applications of ITARA have also expanded across diverse operational domains, including logistics, financial analysis, Internet of Things (IoT) hardware design, and pandemic-related facility planning. Ulutaş et al. (2020) used correlation coefficient and the standard deviation (CCSD) and ITARA jointly to establish semiobjective criteria weights for measurement alternatives and ranking according to compromise solution (MARCOS) in stacker selection, confirming the hybrid model's stability through comparative analysis. In financial performance assessment, Katrancı et al. (2025) integrated ITARA with the COmprehensive Distance Based Ranking (COBRA) method to evaluate Borsa Istanbul 100 firms, demonstrating reliable rankings validated through Spearman correlation tests and sensitivity analysis. Gray and Fermatean fuzzy variants further extended ITARA's applicability: Ahmadi Pargo & Hashemkhani Zolfani (2025) implemented a gray ITARA-COBRA system for IoT hardware selection, while Simic et al. (2023) used Fermatean fuzzy ITARA-MARCOS with machine learning–based feature elimination to locate COVID-19 disinfection facilities. These studies collectively confirm ITARA's versatility, robustness, and growing methodological significance across modern MADM research.

25.3 Methods and materials

The ITARA method determines attribute weights by combining dispersion logic with an indifference threshold that filters out minor, noninfluential differences between alternatives (Lo et al., 2021). The core premise is that attributes with highly similar performance scores across alternatives should receive lower weights, while attributes with clear and significant discriminating power should be emphasized. To achieve this, ITARA introduces two fundamental concepts: dispersion logic and the indifference threshold.

Dispersion logic implies that if an attribute exhibits minimal variation among alternatives, its importance should be small because it provides limited discriminatory information. Conversely, attributes with larger performance differences hold more influence in the evaluation. The indifference threshold refines this idea by specifying a minimum difference that must be exceeded for a variation to be considered meaningful. If the gap between two performance values is less than or equal to the threshold, that gap is ignored because it does not reflect a perceptible difference to the decision maker. This concept is directly rooted in classical MADM constructs such as lexicographic semiorder and outranking models. Following these principles, ITARA proceeds through six computational stages.

Symbol	Description
m	Number of alternatives in the decision problem.
n	Number of attributes or criteria.
a_{ij}	Performance value of alternative i under attribute j.
IT_j	Indifference threshold for attribute j in its raw (unnormalized) scale. Represents the smallest meaningful difference for that attribute.
a_{rj}, a_{sj}	Performance values of two alternatives r and s for attribute j, used to evaluate indifference.
α_{ij}	Normalized performance value of alternative i under attribute j, computed using ratio normalization.
NIT_j	Normalized indifference threshold for attribute j, computed as IT_j divided by the column sum Σa_{ij}.
β_{ij}	Sorted normalized values of attribute j, arranged in ascending order.
γ_{ij}	Consecutive difference between adjacent ordered values for attribute j, computed as $\beta(i+1)_j$ minus βij.
δ_{ij}	Threshold-adjusted difference for attribute j after applying the indifference threshold rule.
p	Parameter of the lp-metric used for aggregation (1 = Manhattan, 2 = Euclidean, $p \to \infty$ = Chebyshev).
v_j	Aggregated meaningful deviation for attribute j, computed using the lp-metric.
w_j	Final weight of attribute j, computed by normalizing V_j across all attributes.

Stage 1. Construct the decision matrix and determine indifference thresholds

Consider a set of m alternatives and n attributes, forming a decision matrix a_{ij} where each element denotes the performance of alternative i under attribute j:

$$A = [a_{ij}]_{m \times n} \tag{25.1}$$

Assign an indifference threshold IT_j for each attribute C_j. A pair of performance scores a_{rj} and a_{sj} is considered indifferent if:

$$|a_{rj} - a_{sj}| \leq IT_j \tag{25.2}$$

The threshold reflects the smallest meaningful difference for that attribute.

Stage 2. Normalize attribute values and normalize the indifference threshold

Normalize each attribute column using ratio normalization:

$$\alpha_{ij} = \frac{a_{ij}}{\sum_{i=1}^{m} a_{ij}} \tag{25.3}$$

Normalize the indifference threshold in the same manner:

$$NIT_j = \frac{IT_j}{\sum_{i=1}^{m} a_{ij}} \tag{25.4}$$

The normalized threshold NIT_j allows consistent comparison across scaled values.

Stage 3. Sort normalized values in ascending order

For each attribute C_j, sort the normalized scores α_{ij} ascending to obtain ordered values β_{ij}:

$$\beta_{1j} \leq \beta_{2j} \leq \ldots \leq \beta_{mj} \tag{25.5}$$

Sorting ensures that distance calculations in the next step are monotonic and comparable.

Stage 4. Compute ordered distances between adjacent values

For each attribute, compute the consecutive differences:

$$\gamma_{ij} = \beta_{(i+1)j} - \beta_{ij} \quad i = 1,\ 2,\ \ldots,\ m-1 \tag{25.6}$$

These represent local dispersion within the sorted series of normalized scores.

Stage 5. Apply the indifference threshold to extract meaningful differences

The indifference threshold determines whether a difference γ_{ij} contributes to the attribute weight. Define the adjusted difference δ_{ij} as:

$$\delta_{ij} = \begin{cases} \gamma_{ij} - NIT_j, & if\ \gamma_{ij} > NIT_j \\ 0, & if\ \gamma_{ij} \leq NIT_j \end{cases} \quad (25.7)$$

If the gap is not large enough to exceed the threshold, it is excluded from weight computation.

Mixed case: only gaps above the threshold contribute.

Stage 6. Aggregate meaningful differences and compute attribute weights

To unify the adjusted differences into a single dispersion score for each attribute, ITARA uses an lp-metric aggregation:

$$v_j = \left(\sum_{i=1}^{m-1} \delta_{ij}^p \right)^{\frac{1}{p}} \quad (25.8)$$

where the parameter $p \in [1, \infty]$ determines the metric:

p = 1: Manhattan metric,

p = 2: Euclidean metric,

p→∞: Chebyshev metric.

Finally, compute attribute weights as:

$$w_j = \frac{v_j}{\sum_{j=1}^{m} v_j} \quad (25.9)$$

These weights reflect only the meaningful dispersion beyond the threshold, capturing the relative discriminatory power of each attribute.

The ITARA approach integrates dispersion logic with human perceptual thresholds, producing objective yet behaviorally grounded weights. By eliminating insignificant differences and emphasizing only meaningful attribute variability, the method offers a robust alternative to entropy, standard deviation, and similar purely statistical weighting schemes.

25.4 Numerical example 1

To illustrate the computational procedure of the ITARA method, a numerical example involving supplier evaluation is presented. The decision problem considers the selection of the most suitable supplier based on multiple performance attributes (Foukolaei et al., 2024). Four criteria, denoted as C1 to C4, represent key dimensions of supplier performance such as cost, quality, delivery reliability, and sustainability (Ghaedi et al., 2024; Gholian-Jouybari et al., 2024). Six potential suppliers are assessed, and each criterion is associated with an aspiration level indicating the desired target, as well as an indifference threshold reflecting the minimum meaningful difference between alternatives under that criterion. These thresholds play a central role in ITARA by filtering out insignificant variations that should not influence the weighting process.

Table 25.1 presents the initial decision matrix that includes the raw performance values of each supplier across the four criteria. The aspiration levels and the corresponding IT_j for each criterion are also provided. The last row shows the total sum of each column, which is later used for normalization.

In the next step, the raw values, aspiration levels, and indifference thresholds are normalized by dividing each entry by the column total. This step ensures proportional comparability across criteria and rescales all data to the [0,1] interval. Table 25.2 displays the resulting normalized decision matrix, along with normalized aspiration values and normalized IT thresholds.

After normalization, the ITARA procedure requires sorting the normalized values of each criterion in ascending order, including the aspiration point treated as an additional reference level. Table 25.3 reports the sorted values for each criterion.

The next step involves calculating the ordered differences between consecutive sorted values. These differences represent the gaps in performance among alternatives. Table 25.4 presents these consecutive differences for all criteria.

TABLE 25.1 Initial decision matrix, aspiration levels, and IT values.

	C1	C2	C3	C4
Supplier 1	9.000	5.000	6.000	4.000
Supplier 2	3.000	4.000	7.000	5.000
Supplier 3	4.000	3.000	6.000	8.000
Supplier 4	1.000	2.000	5.000	9.000
Supplier 5	5.000	9.000	8.000	3.000
Supplier 6	9.000	5.000	3.000	4.000
Aspire	1	1	1	1
IT_j	0.3	0.5	0.4	0.6
Sum	32.000	29.000	36.000	34.000

TABLE 25.2 Normalized decision matrix, normalized aspiration levels, and normalized IT values.

	C1	C2	C3	C4
Supplier 1	0.2813	0.1724	0.1667	0.1176
Supplier 2	0.0938	0.1379	0.1944	0.1471
Supplier 3	0.1250	0.1034	0.1667	0.2353
Supplier 4	0.0313	0.0690	0.1389	0.2647
Supplier 5	0.1563	0.3103	0.2222	0.0882
Supplier 6	0.2813	0.1724	0.0833	0.1176
Aspire	0.0313	0.0345	0.0278	0.0294
IT_j	0.0094	0.0172	0.0111	0.0176

TABLE 25.3 Sorted normalized performance values for each criterion.

	C1	C2	C3	C4
Sort 1	0.0313	0.0345	0.0278	0.0294
Sort 2	0.0313	0.0690	0.0833	0.0882
Sort 3	0.0938	0.1034	0.1389	0.1176
Sort 4	0.1250	0.1379	0.1667	0.1176
Sort 5	0.1563	0.1724	0.1667	0.1471
Sort 6	0.2813	0.1724	0.1944	0.2353
Sort 7	0.2813	0.3103	0.2222	0.2647

TABLE 25.4 Consecutive differences between sorted normalized values.

	C1	C2	C3	C4
Sort 2-1	0.0000	0.0345	0.0556	0.0588
Sort 3-2	0.0625	0.0345	0.0556	0.0294
Sort 4-3	0.0313	0.0345	0.0278	0.0000
Sort 5-4	0.0313	0.0345	0.0000	0.0294
Sort 6-5	0.1250	0.0000	0.0278	0.0882
Sort 7-6	0.0000	0.1379	0.0278	0.0294

ITARA applies the indifference threshold to determine which differences are meaningful. If a difference is smaller than or equal to the threshold, it is set to zero; otherwise, the difference is reduced by the threshold. Table 25.5 shows the adjusted gaps δ_{ij} that remain after applying the indifference threshold.

These adjusted values form the basis for computing the attribute weight indicators V_j using the lp-metric (here, the Euclidean norm). The resulting V_j values, along with the coefficient of variation and the final normalized weights W_j, are summarized in Table 25.6. The ranking of the criteria indicates the relative importance derived through the ITARA procedure.

The calculation begins by normalizing the performance values of criterion C1. The sum of the raw scores is 32, and each value is divided by this total to obtain the normalized matrix. The aspiration level, originally equal to 1, is normalized in the same manner, resulting in 1 divided by 32, which gives 0.0313. Likewise, the indifference threshold IT_j for C1 is rescaled by dividing 0.3 by 32, producing a normalized threshold of 0.0094.

$$9 + 3 + 4 + 1 + 5 + 9 = 32$$

Supplier	C1 normalized
S1	0.2813
S2	0.0938
S3	0.1250
S4	0.0313
S5	0.1563
S6	0.2813

Aspire = 1 becomes:

$$\frac{1}{32} = 0.0313$$

IT_j normalized:

$$\frac{0.3}{32} = 0.0094$$

After normalization, the values associated with C1, including the aspiration point, are arranged in ascending order. This sorted list captures the distribution of performance across all alternatives and forms the basis for computing meaningful performance gaps. The ordered values for C1 range from 0.0313 to 0.2813, reflecting increasing levels of supplier performance under this criterion.

$$[0.0313,\ 0.0313,\ 0.0938,\ 0.1250,\ 0.1563,\ 0.2813,\ 0.2813]$$

TABLE 25.5 Threshold-adjusted differences δ_{ij} for each criterion.

	C1	C2	C3	C4
1	0.0000	0.0172	0.0444	0.0412
2	0.0531	0.0172	0.0444	0.0118
3	0.0219	0.0172	0.0167	0.0000
4	0.0219	0.0172	0.0000	0.0118
5	0.1156	0.0000	0.0167	0.0706
6	0.0000	0.1207	0.0167	0.0118

TABLE 25.6 Attribute scores V_j, final weights W_j, and criterion ranking.

	C1	C2	C3	C4
V_j	0.1310	0.1255	0.0692	0.0842
W_j	0.3245	0.2954	0.1645	0.2156
RANK	1	2	4	3

The next step involves determining the consecutive differences between these sorted values. These differences represent the incremental performance improvements from one ordered level to the next. For C1, the differences vary from 0.0000, indicating equal values, to 0.1250, reflecting the largest performance jump between two adjacent entries in the sorted sequence.

Difference	Value
Sort 2 − Sort 1	0.0000
Sort 3 − Sort 2	0.0625
Sort 4 − Sort 3	0.0313
Sort 5 − Sort 4	0.0313
Sort 6 − Sort 5	0.1250
Sort 7 − Sort 6	0.0000

Once the differences are obtained, the indifference threshold is applied. Differences that are less than or equal to the normalized IT value of 0.0094 are considered insignificant and are therefore set to zero. Differences exceeding this threshold are reduced by subtracting the IT value. This adjustment removes negligible fluctuations and retains only meaningful performance gaps that should contribute to the importance of the criterion. The resulting δ values for C1 reflect exactly this logic, with several small gaps eliminated and larger differences preserved in adjusted form.

Rule:

- If difference ≤ IT → 0
- If difference > IT → difference − IT
- $IT_j = 0.0094$

Applying:

1. ≤ 0.0094 → 0

2. 0.0625 − 0.0094 = 0.0531
3. 0.0313 − 0.0094 = 0.0219
4. 0.0313 − 0.0094 = 0.0219
5. 0.1250 − 0.0094 = 0.1156
6. ≤ 0.0094 → 0

Final δ values for C1:

Row	δ(C1)
1	0.0000
2	0.0531
3	0.0219
4	0.0219
5	0.1156
6	0.0000

These adjusted δ values are then aggregated using the Euclidean metric to obtain V1, the ITARA measure of the significance of criterion C1. Squaring and summing the nonzero δ values yields 0.01714, and taking the square root results in V1 equal to 0.1310. This value quantifies the extent of meaningful dispersion in the performance of alternatives under C1.

$$V_1 = \sqrt{0^2 + 0.0531^2 + 0.0219^2 + 0.0219^2 + 0.1156^2 + 0^2}$$

Square each:

- $0.0531^2 = 0.00282$
- $0.0219^2 = 0.00048$
- $0.0219^2 = 0.00048$
- $0.1156^2 = 0.01336$

Sum:

$$0.00282 + 0.00048 + 0.00048 + 0.01336 = 0.01714$$

$$V_1 = \sqrt{0.01714} = 0.1310$$

Finally, the weight of C1 is obtained by normalizing V1 with respect to the sum of the V_j values of all criteria. With a total dispersion value of 0.4099 across all criteria, dividing 0.1310 by this total results in a final weight of 0.3245 for C1. This confirms that C1 is the most influential criterion in this example, receiving the highest rank among all criteria.

$$V_{total} = 0.1310 + 0.1255 + 0.0692 + 0.0842 = 0.4099$$

Weight:

$$W_1 = \frac{0.1310}{0.4099} = 0.3245$$

25.5 Numerical example 2

In this example, a purchasing manager seeks to identify the most influential criteria in evaluating renewable energy suppliers within a sustainable procurement program (Ghaedi et al., 2024; Khazaei, Gholian-Jouybari, Ramezani, et al., 2025). The organization is assessing nine potential suppliers based on seven criteria that reflect economic, environmental, technical, and operational considerations. Since the decision environment involves varying sensitivity to performance differences across criteria, the ITARA method is applied to determine the relative weights. Each supplier is evaluated against criteria C1 to C7, and an aspiration level is introduced to anchor the analysis. An indifference threshold is also specified for each criterion to distinguish between meaningful and negligible performance gaps.

The goal of this numerical example is not to choose the best supplier but to illustrate how ITARA computes the weights of the criteria. This is done by normalizing raw values, sorting them, extracting adjacent differences, applying threshold adjustments, aggregating adjusted gaps using the Euclidean metric, and finally computing the weight of each criterion (see Table 25.7).

TABLE 25.7 Raw decision matrix, aspiration levels, indifference thresholds, and column sums for example 2.

	C1	C2	C3	C4	C5	C6	C7
Supplier 1	5	9	6	8	5	7	7
Supplier 2	4	4	7	5	7	5	5
Supplier 3	6	3	6	7	4	1	2
Supplier 4	9	2	5	2	2	2	3
Supplier 5	8	9	4	3	1	3	5
Supplier 6	7	5	3	4	6	5	4
Supplier 7	5	1	8	8	5	7	7
Supplier 8	4	2	9	7	8	8	8
Supplier 9	2	3	5	2	9	8	6
Aspire	1	1	1	1	1	1	1
IT_j	0.4	0.5	0.2	0.7	0.5	0.4	0.5
Sum	51.000	39.000	54.000	47.000	48.000	47.000	48.000

TABLE 25.8 Normalized supplier scores, normalized aspiration levels, and normalized IT values.

	C1	C2	C3	C4	C5	C6	C7
Supplier 1	0.0980	0.2308	0.1111	0.1702	0.1042	0.1489	0.1458
Supplier 2	0.0784	0.1026	0.1296	0.1064	0.1458	0.1064	0.1042
Supplier 3	0.1176	0.0769	0.1111	0.1489	0.0833	0.0213	0.0417
Supplier 4	0.1765	0.0513	0.0926	0.0426	0.0417	0.0426	0.0625
Supplier 5	0.1569	0.2308	0.0741	0.0638	0.0208	0.0638	0.1042
Supplier 6	0.1373	0.1282	0.0556	0.0851	0.1250	0.1064	0.0833
Supplier 7	0.0980	0.0256	0.1481	0.1702	0.1042	0.1489	0.1458
Supplier 8	0.0784	0.0513	0.1667	0.1489	0.1667	0.1702	0.1667
Supplier 9	0.0392	0.0769	0.0926	0.0426	0.1875	0.1702	0.1250
Aspire	0.0196	0.0256	0.0185	0.0213	0.0208	0.0213	0.0208
IT_j	0.0078	0.0128	0.0037	0.0149	0.0104	0.0085	0.0104

After presenting the raw matrix, each value is normalized by dividing it by the corresponding column sum. The aspiration level for each criterion, originally set equal to 1, is normalized in the same way. The indifference thresholds are also transformed by dividing their raw values by the total of each criterion. These normalized values serve as the foundation of the ITARA procedure (see Table 25.8).

Once normalization is complete, the values for each criterion, including the aspiration point, are sorted in ascending order. This step reorganizes the distribution of performance across suppliers, making it possible to detect how performance progresses as we move from the lowest to the highest score. The sorted lists for all seven criteria reveal where major and minor transitions occur (see Table 25.9).

The next step computes the consecutive differences between each pair of adjacent values in these sorted sequences. These differences reflect the incremental performance improvements that take place from one ordered level to the next. Some differences are small, indicating almost identical performance among suppliers, while others are much larger and reflect substantive improvement (see Table 25.10).

After the differences are calculated, the indifference thresholds are applied. For each criterion, differences that are less than or equal to the corresponding normalized IT value are considered insignificant and are therefore reduced to zero. Conversely, differences that exceed the threshold are reduced by subtracting the normalized IT value. This operation eliminates noise from the decision data and ensures that only meaningful performance gaps contribute to the importance of each criterion (see Table 25.11).

TABLE 25.9 Sorted normalized values for each criterion.

	C1	C2	C3	C4	C5	C6	C7
Sort 1	0.0196	0.0256	0.0185	0.0213	0.0208	0.0213	0.0208
Sort 2	0.0392	0.0256	0.0556	0.0426	0.0208	0.0213	0.0417
Sort 3	0.0784	0.0513	0.0741	0.0426	0.0417	0.0426	0.0625
Sort 4	0.0784	0.0513	0.0926	0.0638	0.0833	0.0638	0.0833
Sort 5	0.0980	0.0769	0.0926	0.0851	0.1042	0.1064	0.1042
Sort 6	0.0980	0.0769	0.1111	0.1064	0.1042	0.1064	0.1042
Sort 7	0.1176	0.1026	0.1111	0.1489	0.1250	0.1489	0.1250
Sort 8	0.1373	0.1282	0.1296	0.1489	0.1458	0.1489	0.1458
Sort 9	0.1569	0.2308	0.1481	0.1702	0.1667	0.1702	0.1458
Sort 10	0.1765	0.2308	0.1667	0.1702	0.1875	0.1702	0.1667

TABLE 25.10 Adjacent differences between sorted values.

	C1	C2	C3	C4	C5	C6	C7
Sort 2-1	0.0196	0.0000	0.0370	0.0213	0.0000	0.0000	0.0208
Sort 3-2	0.0392	0.0256	0.0185	0.0000	0.0208	0.0213	0.0208
Sort 4-3	0.0000	0.0000	0.0185	0.0213	0.0417	0.0213	0.0208
Sort 5-4	0.0196	0.0256	0.0000	0.0213	0.0208	0.0426	0.0208
Sort 6-5	0.0000	0.0000	0.0185	0.0213	0.0000	0.0000	0.0000
Sort 7-6	0.0196	0.0256	0.0000	0.0426	0.0208	0.0426	0.0208
Sort 8-7	0.0196	0.0256	0.0185	0.0000	0.0208	0.0000	0.0208
Sort 9-8	0.0196	0.1026	0.0185	0.0213	0.0208	0.0213	0.0000
Sort 10-9	0.0196	0.0000	0.0185	0.0000	0.0208	0.0000	0.0208

TABLE 25.11 Adjusted δ values after applying indifference thresholds.

	C1	C2	C3	C4	C5	C6	C7
1	0.0118	0.0000	0.0333	0.0064	0.0000	0.0000	0.0104
2	0.0314	0.0128	0.0148	0.0000	0.0104	0.0128	0.0104
3	0.0000	0.0000	0.0148	0.0064	0.0313	0.0128	0.0104
4	0.0118	0.0128	0.0000	0.0064	0.0104	0.0340	0.0104
5	0.0000	0.0000	0.0148	0.0064	0.0000	0.0000	0.0000
6	0.0118	0.0128	0.0000	0.0277	0.0104	0.0340	0.0104
7	0.0118	0.0128	0.0148	0.0000	0.0104	0.0000	0.0104
8	0.0118	0.0897	0.0148	0.0064	0.0104	0.0128	0.0000
9	0.0118	0.0000	0.0148	0.0000	0.0104	0.0000	0.0104

TABLE 25.12 Euclidean distances V_j, final weights W_j, and ranking of criteria.

	C1	C2	C3	C4	C5	C6	C7
V_j	0.0426	0.0933	0.0493	0.0311	0.0403	0.0530	0.0276
W_j	0.1239	0.2541	0.1293	0.1114	0.1314	0.1565	0.0935
RANK	5	1	4	6	3	2	7

Once the δ values have been determined, ITARA aggregates them using the Euclidean metric to generate a single measure of dispersion, V_j, for each criterion. This value captures how much meaningful separation exists among suppliers when evaluated under a particular criterion. Higher V_j values indicate greater discriminatory power and therefore higher importance (see Table 25.12).

The computation for criterion C3 begins with the raw performance values, which range from 3 to 9 across the nine suppliers. With the aspiration level equal to 1, the total sum for this criterion is 54. Each value is then normalized by dividing by this total, producing values that match exactly the normalized scores in the second table. The aspiration level becomes 1 divided by 54, or 0.0185, and the raw indifference threshold of 0.2 becomes 0.0037 after normalization.

$$a_{1,3} = 6, \quad a_{2,3} = 7, \; a_{3,3} = 6, \; a_{4,3} = 5, \; a_{5,3} = 4, \; a_{6,3} = 3, \; a_{7,3} = 8, \; a_{8,3} = 9, \; a_{9,3} = 5$$

Aspire = 1

- Indifference threshold for C3: IT3 = 0.2
  Sum of scores for C3 (including Aspire):

$$\sum a_{i3=54}$$

- Supplier 1: 6/54 = 0.1111
- Supplier 2: 7/54 = 0.1296
- Supplier 3: 6/54 = 0.1111
- Supplier 4: 5/54 = 0.0926
- Supplier 5: 4/54 = 0.0741

- Supplier 6: 3/54 = 0.0556
- Supplier 7: 8/54 = 0.1481
- Supplier 8: 9/54 = 0.1667
- Supplier 9: 5/54 = 0.0926
- Aspire: 1/54 = 0.0185

After normalization, the values are sorted in ascending order to obtain the ordered series β1,3 to β10,3. This sorted sequence reflects the full distribution of performance for C3, beginning at 0.0185 and ending at 0.1667. Adjacent differences are then computed, with values ranging from zero to 0.0370. These differences indicate where performance jumps occur between successive suppliers.

- β1,3 = 0.0185
- β2,3 = 0.0556
- β3,3 = 0.0741
- β4,3 = 0.0926
- β5,3 = 0.0926
- β6,3 = 0.1111
- β7,3 = 0.1111
- β8,3 = 0.1296
- β9,3 = 0.1481
- β10,3 = 0.1667

The indifference threshold plays a critical role in determining which of these performance gaps matter. Differences less than or equal to 0.0037 are considered negligible and are set to zero. Differences greater than this value are reduced by subtracting the threshold. As a result, the adjusted δ values for C3 reflect only meaningful transitions, and these match the table precisely:

- γ1,3 = 0.0556 − 0.0185 = 0.0370
- γ2,3 = 0.0741 − 0.0556 = 0.0185
- γ3,3 = 0.0926 − 0.0741 = 0.0185
- γ4,3 = 0.0926 − 0.0926 = 0
- γ5,3 = 0.1111 − 0.0926 = 0.0185
- γ6,3 = 0.1111 − 0.1111 = 0
- γ7,3 = 0.1296 − 0.1111 = 0.0185
- γ8,3 = 0.1481 − 0.1296 = 0.0185
- γ9,3 = 0.1667 − 0.1481 = 0.0185

These adjacent differences correspond to the values presented in the "Sort 2-1" through "Sort 10-9" rows for C3, and the next step applies the normalized indifference threshold NIT3 equal to 0.0037. Differences greater than this threshold, such as 0.0370 and 0.0185, are reduced by subtracting the threshold, yielding adjusted values of approximately 0.0333 and 0.0148. Differences equal to zero fall below the threshold and therefore remain zero. This process produces the final adjusted distances δk,3, which reflect only the meaningful performance gaps for criterion C3.

- δ1,3 = 0.0333
- δ2,3 = 0.0148
- δ3,3 = 0.0148
- δ4,3 = 0
- δ5,3 = 0.0148
- δ6,3 = 0
- δ7,3 = 0.0148
- δ8,3 = 0.0148
- δ9,3 = 0.0148

To obtain the aggregated indicator V3, the Euclidean measure is applied to the δ values. Squaring and summing the nonzero δ values yields approximately 0.00243, and taking the square root produces V3 equal to 0.0493. This value represents the magnitude of meaningful dispersion among suppliers under C3. Finally, the weight of C3 is computed by dividing V3 by the total of all V_j values, which assigns C3 its relative importance in the overall decision model:

$$\sqrt{0.00243} = 0.0493$$

If we use ITARA alone for weighting, the weight of C3 is obtained by normalizing V3 across all criteria:

$$w_3 = \frac{0.0493}{0.3372} = 0.146$$

25.6 Conclusion

The ITARA method provides a rigorous yet behaviorally informed approach to attribute weighting in MADM by integrating dispersion-based logic with an explicit indifference threshold that suppresses negligible differences. Through its sequential process of normalization, ordering, threshold filtering, and lp-metric aggregation, ITARA generates weights that reflect only meaningful performance variation among alternatives. The two numerical examples presented in this work demonstrate that the method effectively differentiates between criteria with genuine discriminatory power and those with minimal impact, providing a more stable and interpretable weighting structure compared with traditional statistical approaches. By incorporating aspiration levels and allowing the decision maker to define tolerance for insignificant deviations, ITARA enhances both methodological transparency and practical realism, making it suitable for complex decision contexts where subjective judgments are limited or inconsistent.

Beyond its computational strengths, ITARA offers a flexible foundation for hybrid integration within broader MADM frameworks. Its threshold-based logic aligns well with linguistic evaluation, fuzzy uncertainty, and incomplete preference information, and its metric-based aggregation supports adaptation to different sensitivity requirements. The examples affirm that ITARA maintains ranking robustness even when applied to high-dimensional matrices, which underscores its usefulness in sustainability assessment, supplier selection, risk evaluation, and strategic planning.

Future studies may explore adaptive or data-driven mechanisms for determining indifference thresholds, allowing thresholds to vary dynamically across criteria or decision environments. Another promising direction involves integrating ITARA with advanced fuzzy, probabilistic, or belief-structure representations to better capture human hesitation and vagueness in complex systems. Comparative studies using large-scale datasets could also investigate ITARA's performance relative to emerging weighting methods, including metaheuristic-based and machine-learning-assisted schemes. Finally, developing automated software tools or decision-support modules that implement ITARA could enhance its practical accessibility for analysts and policymakers working in fields such as sustainability, energy systems, healthcare, and supply chain management.

References

Ahmadi Pargo, T., & Hashemkhani Zolfani, S. (2025). Developing an expert system for hardware selection in internet of things-based system design: Grey ITARA-COBRA approach (with an example in the agricultural domain). *Information, 16*(6), 425.

Anawar, S., & Adnan, W. A. W. (2024). Non-monetary incentives for participatory sensing data collection: A sequential explanatory design. *IEEE Access*.

Bonakdari, H., Khazaei, M., Gholian-Jouybari, F., & Hajiaghaei-Keshteli, M. (2025). Sustainable wastewater-to-hydrogen systems in Canada: A scenario-based decision support analysis. *Renewable Energy*, 124308.

Bovkir, R., Moslem, S., & Pilla, F. (2025). GIS-based fuzzy multi-criteria decision-making for selecting optimal parcel lockers location: A case study in Dublin, Ireland. *Land Use Policy, 158*, 107771.

Foukolaei, P. Z., Asari, F. A., Khazaei, M., Gholian-Jouybari, F., & Hajiaghaei-Keshteli, M. (2024). From responsible sourcing of wastes to sustainable energy consumption in the blue hydrogen supply chain: Case of nearshoring in Nuevo Leon. *International Journal of Hydrogen Energy, 77*, 1387–1400.

Fuentes, A., Lüdtke, O., & Robitzsch, A. (2022). Causal inference with multilevel data: A comparison of different propensity score weighting approaches. *Multivariate Behavioral Research, 57*(6), 916–939.

Ghaedi, M., Foukolaei, P. Z., Asari, F. A., Khazaei, M., Gholian-Jouybari, F., & Hajiaghaei-Keshteli, M. (2024). Pricing electricity from blue hydrogen to mitigate the energy rebound effect: A case study in agriculture and livestock. *International Journal of Hydrogen Energy, 84*, 993–1003.

Gholian-Jouybari, F., et al. (2024). Developing environmental, social and governance (ESG) strategies on evaluation of municipal waste disposal centers: A case of Mexico. *Chemosphere, 364*, 142961.

Hatefi, M. A. (2019). Indifference threshold-based attribute ratio analysis: A method for assigning the weights to the attributes in multiple attribute decision making. *Applied Soft Computing, 74*, 643–651.

Hsu, W.-C. J., Lin, K.-Y., Lo, H.-W., & Yang, J.-J. (2024). Assessing corporation sustainability performance towards achieving sustainable development goals using a novel trapezoidal fuzzy ITARA-RIM approach. *Annals of Operations Research,* 1–28.

Jovanović, B., Šarac, D., & Čačić, N. (2024). Performance benchmarking of European postal incumbents with TOPSIS and BMW-TOPSIS. *Utilities Policy, 91,* 101845.

Katrancı, A., Kundakcı, N., & Pamucar, D. (2025). Financial performance evaluation of firms in BIST 100 index with ITARA and COBRA methods. *Financial Innovation, 11*(1), 34.

Khan, A., Ahmad, U., & Shahzadi, S. (2023). A new decision analysis based on 2-tuple linguistic q-rung picture fuzzy ITARA–VIKOR method. *Soft Computing,* 1–24.

Khazaei, M., Gholian-Jouybari, F., Dolatabadi, M. D., Alamdari, A. P., Eskandari, H., & Hajiaghaei-Keshteli, M. (2025). Renewable energy portfolio in Mexico for industry 5.0 and SDGs: Hydrogen, wind, or solar? *Renewable and Sustainable Energy Reviews, 213,* 115420.

Khazaei, M., Gholian-Jouybari, F., Ramezani, M., & Hajiaghaei-Keshteli, M. (2025). Environmental, social, and governance enablers of the hydrogen supply chain: Application of community operational research using STRIDES framework. *Journal of Environmental Management, 389,* 126092.

Lin, S.-W., & Lo, H.-W. (2024). An FMEA model for risk assessment of university sustainability: Using a combined ITARA with TOPSIS-AL approach based neutrosophic sets. *Annals of Operations Research, 342*(3), 2119–2145.

Liu, P., Wu, Y., & Li, Y. (2022). Probabilistic hesitant fuzzy taxonomy method based on best–worst-method (BWM) and indifference threshold-based attribute ratio analysis (ITARA) for multi-attributes decision-making. *International Journal of Fuzzy Systems, 24*(3), 1301–1317.

Lo, H.-W., Hsu, C.-C., Huang, C.-N., & Liou, J. J. (2021). An ITARA-TOPSIS based integrated assessment model to identify potential product and system risks. *Mathematics, 9*(3), 239.

Mohammadi, M., Tamburri, D. A., & Rezaei, J. (2023). Unveiling and unraveling aggregation and dispersion fallacies in group MCDM. *Group Decision and Negotiation, 32*(4), 779–806.

Nguyen, V. D., & Gigliarano, C. (2025). Sensitivity-based weighting method for composite indicators. *Annals of Operations Research,* 1–33.

Pena, J., Nápoles, G., & Salgueiro, Y. (2020). Explicit methods for attribute weighting in multi-attribute decision-making: A review study. *Artificial Intelligence Review, 53*(5), 3127–3152.

Simic, V., Ebadi Torkayesh, A., & Ijadi Maghsoodi, A. (2023). Locating a disinfection facility for hazardous healthcare waste in the COVID-19 era: A novel approach based on Fermatean fuzzy ITARA-MARCOS and random forest recursive feature elimination algorithm. *Annals of Operations Research, 328*(1), 1105–1150.

Simić, V., Milovanović, B., Pantelić, S., Pamučar, D., & Tirkolaee, E. B. (2023). Sustainable route selection of petroleum transportation using a type-2 neutrosophic number based ITARA-EDAS model. *Information Sciences, 622,* 732–754.

Sofuoğlu, M. A. (2019). Development of an ITARA-based hybrid multi-criteria decision-making model for material selection. *Soft Computing, 23*(15), 6715–6725.

Ulutaş, A., Karabasevic, D., Popovic, G., Stanujkic, D., Nguyen, P. T., & Karaköy, Ç. (2020). Development of a novel integrated CCSD-ITARA-MARCOS decision-making approach for stackers selection in a logistics system. *Mathematics, 8*(10), 1672.

Vafaei, N., Ribeiro, R. A., & Camarinha-Matos, L. M. (2022). Assessing normalization techniques for simple additive weighting method. *Procedia Computer Science, 199,* 1229–1236.

Wu, M., Yang, J., & Fan, J. (2023). An extended ITARA-TOPSIS method for multi-criteria group decision-making problems based on R-number. *Journal of Intelligent & Fuzzy Systems, 45*(5), 8889–8905.

Zolfani, S. H. (2024). Objective weighting in mcdm: A comparative study of critic, itara, merec, and beyond. *Decision Making and Artificial Intelligence Trends, 1*(1), 105–120.

Chapter 26

BCM: Base-criterion method for multi-attribute decision-making

Gholamreza Haseli
School of Engineering and Sciences, Tecnologico de Monterrey, Monterrey, Mexico

26.1 Introduction

Decision problems in engineering, management, and policy commonly require simultaneously weighing many factors. When a problem depends on multiple criteria, ranking those criteria correctly is a necessary precursor to any robust choice among alternatives. In these situations, we need multicriteria decision-making (MCDM) methods (Hajiaghaei-Keshteli et al., 2023). MCDM methods have been categorized into two main areas, including multi-attribute decision-making (MADM) and multiobjective decision-making (MODM). The MADM arises when a decision-maker must choose among alternatives based on several factors simultaneously. MODM approaches that treat objectives as continuous vectors to be optimized by mathematical programming (Haseli and Sheikh, 2020). However, MADM typically assumes a discrete set of alternatives and focuses on eliciting preference information that allows direct ranking of those alternatives (Bonab et al., 2023).

A common architecture in MADM methods is to separate (1) the acquisition of criterion importance (weights) and (2) the evaluation of alternatives against those criteria (Gabriel Rasoanaivo et al., 2024). For decades, pairwise-comparison methods have been the dominant approach to convert expert judgments into numerical criterion weights. Traditional methods, such as the analytic hierarchy process (AHP) (Saaty, 2013), ask decision-makers to compare each pair of criteria using a scale with a range of 1/9 to 9. While intuitive, full pairwise comparison grows quadratically with the number of criteria and often produces inconsistent judgments when human raters become fatigued or confused. Several alternatives, most notably the best–worst method (BWM) (Rezaei, 2015), reduce the number of comparisons and improve stability. However, they still evaluate consistency indirectly through the outputs of comparisons rather than by proactively controlling the inputs.

The base criterion method (BCM) (Haseli & Sheikh, 2022; Haseli and Sheikh, 2020) was introduced to address these two practical problems: (1) reduce the number of required pairwise judgments, and (2) avoid inconsistent results by controlling the inputs to the comparison system rather than only checking its outputs. In BCM, an expert selects a single criterion as a base (reference) and performs pairwise comparisons of every other criterion against that base only. Because every comparison is referenced to the same anchor, BCM needs only $n-1$ judgments for n criteria instead of the $n(n-1)/2$ demands of a full AHP matrix. Compared with BWM, BCM is also simpler because it requires only one reference criterion rather than choosing both best and worst items. These features make BCM particularly attractive for problems where speed, clarity, and consistency are paramount.

26.1.1 Inconsistency in pairwise comparisons: direction versus strength

In pairwise-comparison frameworks, it is helpful to separate two different failure modes. Two kinds of inconsistency commonly appear in pairwise matrices: directional (i.e., conflicting preference directions) and strength (i.e., inconsistent magnitudes). Both inconsistencies may arise in MADM methods that employ the pairwise-comparison approach. Each of the inconsistency mode is presented in detail in the next sections (Haseli & Sheikh, 2022).

Encyclopedia of Multi-Attribute Decision-Making (MADM). DOI: https://doi.org/10.1016/B978-0-443-33275-3.00098-1

26.1.1.1 Inconsistency in direction

Directional inconsistency arises when preference directions conflict. For the three criteria C_1, C_2, and C_3, directional inconsistency occurs if the pairwise inputs imply. For example, suppose $C_1 > C_2$ and $C_2 > C_3$, but the decision-maker nevertheless states $C_3 > C_1$,. This is a reversal of implied ordering and is qualitatively severe because it contradicts transitive structure. Directional inconsistency is typically more obvious. In many decision contexts, it is more damaging to credibility. Concrete numeric example of strength inconsistency. Consider the same three criteria with pairwise judgments on a 1/9 to 9 scale. If a decision-maker states $a_{12} = 3$ (so C_1 preferred to C_2) and $a_{23} = 3$ (so C_2 preferred to C_3), transitivity suggests that C_1 should be preferred to C_3 by a factor of around nine. But if the decision-maker then reports $a_{13} = 1/2$ (i.e., directly saying C_3 is twice as important as C_1), the directional relationship is reversed, and the matrix contains a logical contradiction. In AHP, such patterns produce very high inconsistency ratios and often force the analyst to re-elicit judgments or to accept unstable weight estimates.

26.1.1.2 Inconsistency in strength

Strength inconsistency refers to a numeric mismatch of intensities. It means the implied numerical ratio between two criteria (via a third criterion) disagrees with the directly stated value. Both types reduce the reliability of derived weights and can lead to irrational or unstable rankings of alternatives. MADM methods differ in how prone they are to each kind. For example, AHP's independent pairwise elicitation can show both direction and strength inconsistencies, whereas reference-anchored methods like BWM tend to eliminate directional inconsistency by construction and only leave strength variability to be controlled. Concrete numeric example of strength inconsistency. Consider the same three criteria with pairwise judgments on a 1/9 to 9 scale. Suppose the decision-maker reports $a_{12} = 5$ (meaning C_1 is five times more important than C_2), and reports $a_{23} = 1$ (meaning C_2 and C_3 are judged equal). Under multiplicative consistency, the implied value for a_{13} must be $a_{12} \times a_{23} = 5 \times 1 = 5$. If instead of five, the decision-maker enters $a_{13} = 4$ or 6, an inconsistency in strength exists. In this condition, the direction $C_1 > C_3$ is preserved, but the magnitudes disagree. Such discrepancies produce nonzero residuals when one solves for weights and inflate inconsistency indices used in AHP-style diagnostics. Therefore, calculated weights become a best-fit compromise rather than an exact reflection of the stated ratios, and small numerical perturbations can change rank order among closely scored alternatives.

26.1.2 Advantages of the base-criterion method in inconsistency and pairwise comparisons

AHP's full-pairwise approach allows both to appear. Methods that reference comparisons to one or two anchors reduce directional conflicts automatically; BCM takes this further by imposing simple input bounds that keep indirectly computed comparisons (those not directly assessed) inside the allowable scale. By bounding base comparisons so that any derived comparison also remains within the standard 1/9 to 9 scale, BCM prevents values that would otherwise fall outside the scale and thereby removes sources of later inconsistency. When the base comparisons respect these input bounds, the optimization that recovers the weights produces full consistency (zero error) in the BCM framework.

Besides improved consistency and fewer comparisons, BCM has two other noteworthy practical advantages. First, a complete pairwise matrix can be reconstructed from the base comparisons using simple multiplicative relations, so missing or lost entries can be recovered under full-consistency assumptions. Second, BCM admits straightforward fuzzy extensions (e.g., triangular fuzzy numbers) to handle vagueness in human judgments when crisp numbers are insufficient, which expands its applicability to qualitative criteria. At the same time, BCM is simple to explain to nonexperts and easy to implement with off-the-shelf solvers. The method is therefore well-suited for applied research and industry practitioners who need defensible criterion weights without heavy elicitation overhead.

The remainder of this chapter is structured to guide the reader from foundational concepts to practical implementation of the BCM. First, a detailed literature review synthesizes prior applications and methodological extensions of BCM. Next, the methodological section elaborates the theoretical formulation of BCM, including input-control rules, variable-scale logic, and the optimization model used to derive fully consistent weights in Section 26.3. Sections 26.4 and 26.5 are followed by two numerical examples that demonstrate step-by-step application of BCM to real-world sustainability-related decision problems. A comparative analysis section then contrasts BCM with AHP and BWM in terms of comparison, consistency, and scalability. Finally, the by summarizing the main insights, advantages, and practical contributions of BCM.

26.2 Literature review

Over the past few years, the BCM has attracted growing attention in the MADM community due to its ability to generate consistent and interpretable weights with minimal pairwise judgments. BCM's reliance on a single base-comparison vector, its capability to reconstruct complete pairwise matrices, and its potential for achieving zero inconsistency have positioned it as a promising alternative to traditional approaches such as AHP and BWM. Consequently, several studies have applied BCM in diverse domains, highlighting both its versatility and its methodological advantages.

In this regard, the literature on BCM can be categorized into two main streams. The first stream consists of application-focused studies where BCM is employed as the primary weighting tool for solving real-world decision problems. The second stream includes methodological contributions that extend BCM's theoretical foundations, propose hybrid models, integrate BCM with other MCDM methods, or enhance its ability to handle missing or inconsistent judgments. Reviewing these studies provides essential insights into how BCM has evolved, in what contexts it has been effectively utilized, and what gaps remain for future research. Table 26.1 summarizes representative contributions, their methodological features, and key innovations, offering a structured overview for readers and helping frame the relevance of BCM in contemporary decision-making research.

TABLE 26.1 Summarizes previous works on the base-criterion method (BCM).

Studies	Application domain	Fuzzy extension	Combination with other methods
Haseli et al. (2020)b	Extension of BCM	Fuzzy sets	-
Narang et al. (2021)	Stock portfolio selection	Fuzzy sets	COPRAS
Bisht and Kumar (2022)	Stock portfolio selection	Fuzzy sets and evidence theory	-
Narang, Joshi, Pal, et al. (2022)	Extension of BCM	Hesitant fuzzy multiplicative	-
Haseli and Jafarzadeh Ghoushchi (2022)	Waste management	Spherical fuzzy sets	-
Narang, Joshi, Bisht, et al. (2022)	Portfolio analysis	Heronian mean	CoCoSo
Bisht and Pal, 2023	Automobile sector	Fuzzy sets	DEMATEL, VIKOR
Haseli et al. (2023)	Luxury in FemTech	Fuzzy ZE-numbers	MARCOS
Narayanan and Paul (2023)	Twin chain	-	OB-DNB
Zafaranlouei et al. (2023)	Waste management	Fuzzy Z-numbers	CoCoSo
Ayough et al. (2023)	Supplier selection	-	Utility additive
Haseli, Nazarian-Jashnabadi, et al. (2024)	Circular supply chain	Fuzzy ZE-numbers	MABAC
Imran et al. (2024)	Electric vehicles	Trapezoidal fuzzy numbers	-
Phulara and Kumar (2024)	Over the top platforms	Grey information	-
Debalki et al. (2024)	Distributed relay selection	Fuzzy sets	-
Wu et al. (2024)	Product upgrading	-	QFD-FMEA, CoCoSo
Haseli, Rahnamay Bonab, et al. (2024)	Urban transportation	Fuzzy ZE-numbers	CoCoSo
Sun et al. (2025)	Supplier selection and order allocation	Single-valued neutrosophic	TODIM, U-NSGA-III, TOPSIS
Apiecionek et al. (2025)	Yoga therapy in physiotherapy	-	AHP, BWM, RANCOM
Liu and Tan (2025)	Habitat selection of Arabica coffee	GIS-based	BWM
Abdollahi et al. (2026)	Solar energy supply chain	Fuzzy ZE-numbers	DNMA
Wu et al. (2026)	Quality function deployment	-	QFD and CoCoSo

26.3 Methodology

As mentioned earlier, the structure of the BCM is designed on selecting a base criterion. This is one of the advantages of the BCM in reducing the required pairwise comparisons. To better understand how base comparisons work, Figs. 26.1 and 26.2 show how the pairwise comparisons are done in the AHP, BWM, and BCM methods. As mentioned before, we need a pairwise-comparison matrix for the AHP. Fig. 26.1 shows that each of the criteria must be compared with all the other criteria in the AHP. It means that at least $n(n-1)/2$ comparisons must be done between the criteria by the decision-maker under the AHP. On the other side, the BWM needs two pairwise-comparison vectors instead of a full matrix based on the best and worst criteria. As presented in Fig. 26.1, the green flags are for the comparisons between the best and other criteria. Also, the red flags indicate the comparisons between the criteria and the worst criterion. This method has advantages over AHP. However, BWM also requires more pairwise comparisons $(2n-3)$.

In addition to the mentioned advantages of the BCM on the consistency ratio rather than AHP and BWM, this method also requires fewer comparisons $(n-1)$. In BCM, instead of performing pairwise comparisons between all the criteria or selecting the best and worst criteria, one of the criteria is selected as a base criterion. This selection is totally dependent on the preference of the decision-maker. For example, criterion C5 is selected as a base criterion in Fig. 26.2. However, the decision-maker can select each of the other criteria as the base criterion. After selecting the base criterion, the pairwise comparisons should be done between the base criterion and the other criteria.

26.3.1 Steps of the base-criterion method

The BCM workflow is compact and can be described as four stages: (1) define the criteria, (2) select a base criterion, (3) elicit base comparisons (with input control), and (4) solve an optimization problem to obtain the weights. Below each stage is presented with the mathematical relations, implementation advice, and practical checks.

Step 1. Define the criteria

Let the criteria be $C_1, C_2, C_3, \ldots, C_n$. Denote by a_{ij} the usual pairwise-comparison value expressing the importance of criterion i relative to criterion j on the standard 1/9 to 9 Saaty scale (******).

Step 2. Select a base criterion

Choose one criterion as the base (C_{base}). The base criterion should be selected totally dependent on the preference of the decision-maker. It means that the decision-maker can select one of the best, worst, or other simple criteria.

Step 3. Elicit base comparisons (with input control)

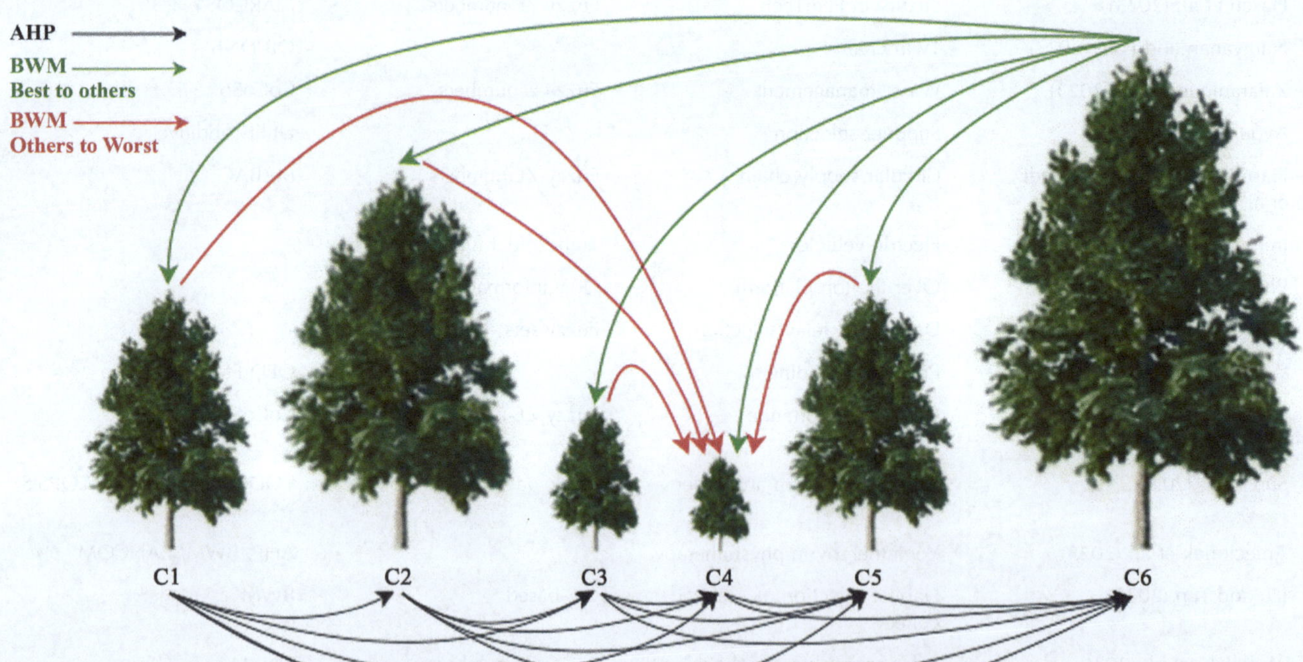

FIGURE 26.1 Pairwise comparisons approach of the analytic hierarchy process (AHP) and best–worst method (BWM).

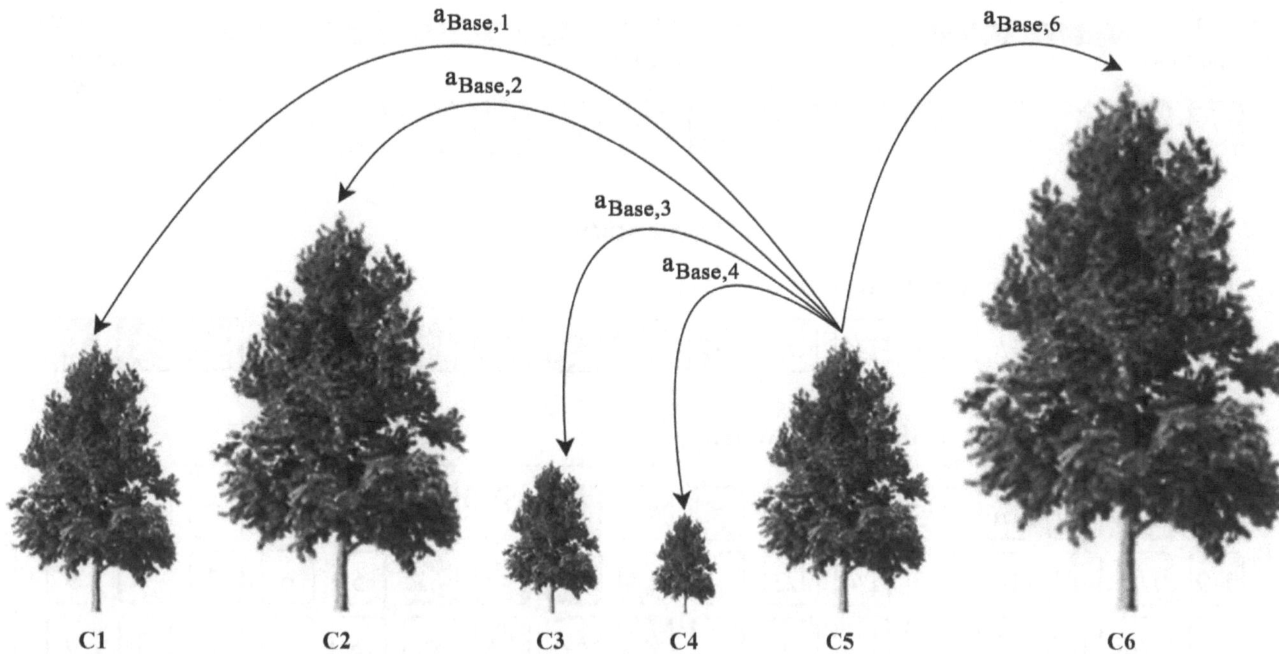

FIGURE 26.2 Pairwise comparisons approach of the base-criterion method.

The base-comparisons should be done as presented in Fig. 26.2. The mathematical form of the base-comparison vector should be as follows:

$$a_{base} = \left(a_{base,1},\ a_{base,2},\ a_{base,3},\ \ldots,\ a_{base,n}\right) \tag{26.1}$$

In this regard, the $a_{base,base} = 1$.

Definition: Input-control rule. To prevent derived comparisons from exceeding the allowable scale, an enforcement for every base comparison should be like (26.2).

$$\frac{1}{9} \le \frac{a_{base,j}}{a_{base,i}} \le 9,\ \forall j = 2,\ \ldots, n,\ \forall i = 1,\ \ldots, j-1 \tag{26.2}$$

This simple bound is the primary mechanism by which BCM prevents the derivation of invalid values. The BCM proposes the variable numerical scales to support this input control for the pairwise comparisons.

Definition: Unlike the AHP and BWM, the BCM uses variable numerical scales based on the selected base comparisons. As mentioned before, the BCM uses a 1/9 to 9 numerical scale. However, decision-makers can consider part of this scale based on the states of the selected base criterion. There are three states in all decision problems based on the framework of the BCM. Fig. 26.3 indicates three states that exist in the BCM framework. If the selected criterion as the base is the best criterion, then the decision-maker should use the 1 to 9 part of the provided numerical scale. If the selected criterion as the base is the worst criterion, then the decision-maker should use 1/9 to 1 part of the provided numerical scale. If the selected criterion as the base is not the best or worst criterion, then the decision-maker should use the variable numerical scale by considering (26.2). In this regard, meaning of variable numerical scale for state two is that if decision-maker assigns 1/2 to a base comparison, then cannot use number more than five to assign for the other base comparisons. As shown in Fig. 26.3, this process of selecting a variable numerical scale continues in this manner.

Step 4. Solve an optimization problem to obtain the weights

After collecting the base vector, BCM finds criterion weights $w_1,\ w_2,\ \ldots,\ w_n$ that are as fully consistent with the base ratios. BCM formulates a min–max problem as (26.3) that minimizes the maximum deviation between the implied ratios w_b/w_j and the elicited base ratios a_{bj}.

$$\begin{aligned} & Min\ \xi \\ & s.\ t. \\ & |(W_{Base}/W_j) - a_{Base,j}| \le \xi \\ & \Sigma_{j=1}^{n}\,(W_j) = 1 \\ & W_j \ge 0,\ for\ all\ j \end{aligned} \tag{26.3}$$

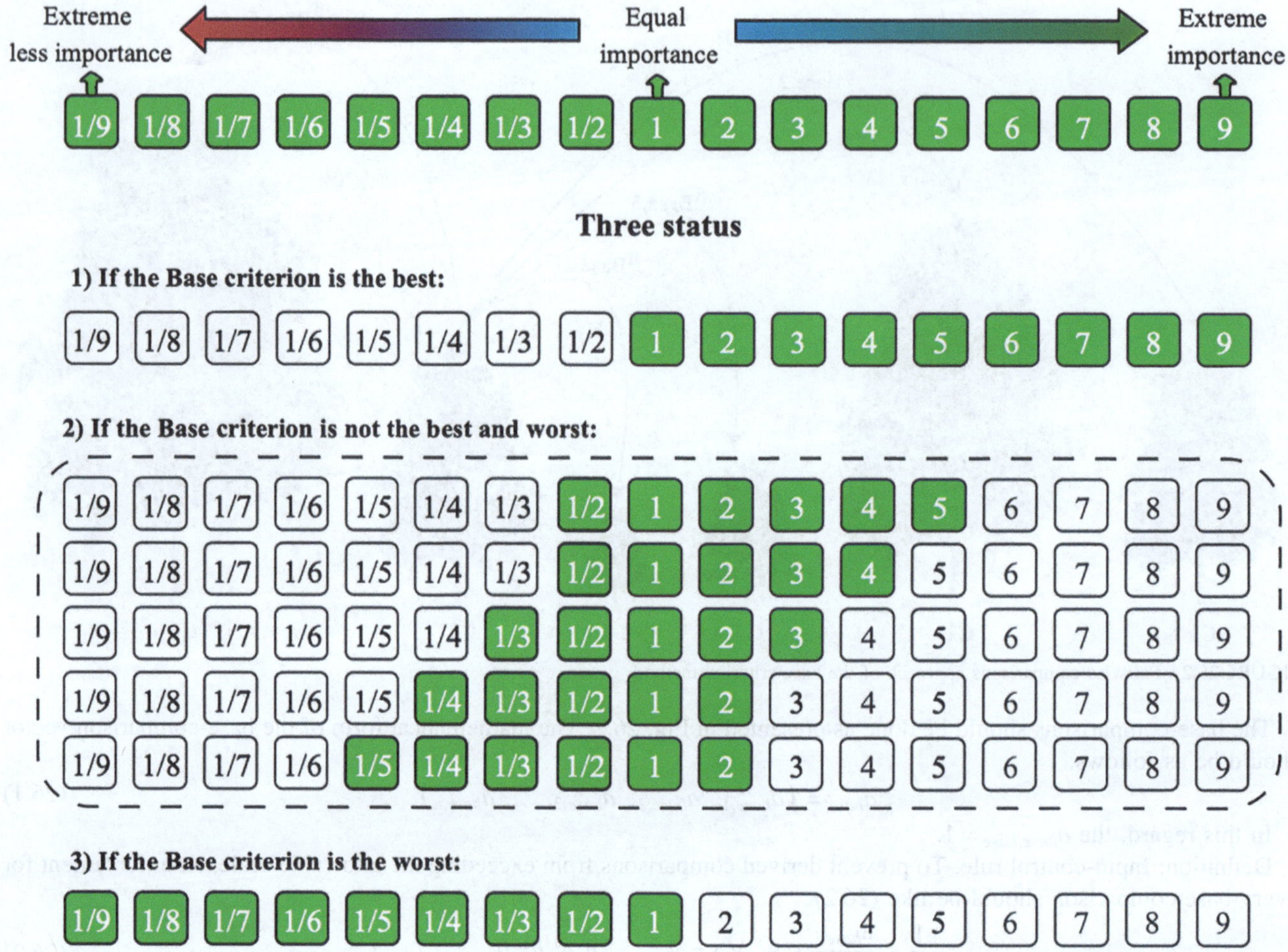

FIGURE 26.3 Variable numerical scale for the base-criterion method.

Here, ξ is the worst-case deviation. If the base inputs respect the input-control rule and are coherent, the optimization often attains $\xi = 0$, that is, full consistency.

26.4 Numerical example 1

In many developing and even developed cities, optimizing the urban transport network is a policy priority because it has a direct impact on the quality of life. The problem in this numerical example is that an urban entity (e.g., a transport department or a municipality) wants to know which criteria are most important when designing or optimizing a transport program. For example, choosing between a dedicated bus line, increasing the frequency of the metro, or designing a regional bike-sharing system. Therefore, subsequent decision-making can be based on those weights. The selected criteria represent three key dimensions of sustainability: time efficiency (reduction in travel time, which affects the value of citizens' time and economic productivity), the economic dimension (cost of travel, which determines the financial burden), and the environmental/social dimension (CO_2 emissions and accessibility/equity, which indicates the distribution of benefits across classes and neighborhoods). These criteria are chosen so that decision-makers can clearly weigh the trade-offs between travel time (C_1), travel cost (C_2), CO_2 emissions per passenger (C_3), and accessibility/equity (C_4).

In this regard, an expert group (or policy team) is assumed to select the base criterion and estimate the relative importance of each base comparison. According to the second step of the BCM, the "travel time (C_1)" is selected as the

TABLE 26.2 Base comparisons result for the transportation criteria.

Base criterion	Travel time (C_1)	Travel cost (C_2)	CO_2 emissions per passenger (C_3)	Accessibility/equity (C_4)
Travel time (C_1)	1	3	5	2

base criterion. The purpose of this tutorial is to show how the BCM method, by entering only n – 1 base comparisons (here, three judgments relative to the basic criterion), can quickly, consistently, and interpretably extract criterion weights. Therefore, n – 1 base comparisons should be done by the experts based on the third step of the BCM. The results of the base comparisons for the criteria of this numerical example are provided in Table 26.2.

After collecting the base comparisons vector, the assigned values by the experts should be considered in (26.3). (26.4) presents the mode of (26.3) with the assigned values for the base comparisons.

$$
\begin{aligned}
&Min\ \xi \\
&s.\ t. \\
&|(W_1/W_2) - 3| \le \xi; \\
&|(W_1/W_3) - 5| \le \xi; \\
&|(W_1/W_4) - 2| \le \xi; \\
&W_1 + W_2 + W_3 + W_4 = 1; \\
&W_1 > 0; \\
&W_2 > 0; \\
&W_3 > 0; \\
&W_4 > 0; \\
&\xi \ge 0;
\end{aligned}
\tag{26.4}
$$

We should convert the above nonlinear problem to a linear programming problem for solving in some software like Lingo. Therefore, (26.4) should be converted to Eq. (26.5). In this regard, we use k instead of the symbol ξ.

```
min=k;
w1 - 3*w2 < =k*w2;
w1 - 3*w2 > =-k*w2;
w1 - 5*w3 < =k*w3;
w1 - 5*w3 > =-k*w3;
w1 - 2*w4 < =k*w4;
w1 - 2*w4 > =-k*w4;                    (26.5)
w1 + w2 + w3 + w4 = 1;
w1 > 0;
w2 > 0;
w3 > 0;
w4 > 0;
k > =0;
```

After calculating using the Lingo software, the results show that the weight of the criteria includes: $W_1 = 0.4918$, $W_2 = 0.1639$, $W_3 = 0.0984$, and $W_4 = 0.2459$. The results show that the value of k or ξ is zero. It means all calculated weights are fully consistent. Additionally, the summation of the weights is equal to one.

TABLE 26.3 Base comparisons result for the renewable energy technologies criteria.

Base criterion	C_1	C_2	C_3	C_4	C_5	C_6	C_7
Scalability of manufacturing (C_5)	1/3	1/2	2	3	1	1/2	1

26.5 Numerical example 2

With the accelerating global push toward decarbonization and the rising demand for clean electricity in the mid-2020s, selecting the most appropriate renewable energy technology has become a complex policy and investment decision. In this example, it is assumed that a project developer or an energy planning authority must compare several renewable technologies, such as ground-mounted solar PV, floating PV, onshore or offshore wind, and hybrid systems, to determine which one offers the best balance of sustainable performance. The evaluation must consider multiple dimensions like reliable and consistent energy output (C_1), levelized cost of energy (C_2), land-use and ecological impact (C_3), lifecycle carbon footprint (C_4), scalability of manufacturing (C_5), socio-economic benefits (C_6), and the complexity of grid integration (C_7). A wrong decision could lead to long-term challenges such as grid instability, excessive operational costs, or loss of biodiversity in sensitive areas, highlighting the need for a structured multicriteria approach.

According to the second step of the BCM, the criterion "reliable and consistent energy output (C_1)" is chosen as the base criterion because, from both operational and economic perspectives, predictable and stable power generation is the cornerstone of revenue estimation and energy security. Using the BCM, the experts only need to express the relative importance of each of the other criteria compared to this base one. The results of the base comparisons for the criteria of this numerical example are provided in Table 26.3.

After collecting the base comparisons vector, the assigned values by the experts should be considered in (26.3). (26.6) presents the mode of (26.3) with the assigned values for the base comparisons.

$$
\begin{aligned}
& Min\ \xi \\
& s.\ t. \\
& |(W_5/W_1) - 1/3| \le \xi; \\
& |(W_5/W_2) - 1/2| \le \xi; \\
& |(W_5/W_3) - 2| \le \xi; \\
& |(W_5/W_4) - 3| \le \xi; \\
& |(W_5/W_6) - 1/2| \le \xi; \\
& |(W_5/W_7) - 1| \le \xi; \\
& W_1 + W_2 + W_3 + W_4 + W_5 + W_6 + W_7 = 1; \\
& W_1 > 0; \\
& W_2 > 0; \\
& W_3 > 0; \\
& W_4 > 0; \\
& W_5 > 0; \\
& W_6 > 0; \\
& W_7 > 0; \\
& \xi \ge 0;
\end{aligned}
\tag{26.6}
$$

Similar to the numerical example 1, we should convert the above nonlinear problem to a linear programming problem for solving in some software like Lingo. Therefore, (26.6) should be converted to Eq. (26.7). In this regard, we use k instead of the symbol ξ same as the numerical example 1.

```
min=k;
w5 - 0.3333*w1 < =k*w1;
w5 - 0.3333*w1 > =-k*w1;
w5 - 0.5*w2 < =k*w2;
w5 - 0.5*w2 > =-k*w2;
w5 - 2*w3 < =k*w3;
w5 - 2*w3 > =-k*w3;
w5 - 3*w4 < =k*w4;
w5 - 3*w4 > =-k*w4;
w5 - 0.5*w6 < =k*w6;
w5 - 0.5*w6 > =-k*w6;
w5 - 1*w7 < =k*w7;
w5 - 1*w7 > =-k*w7;
w1 + w2 + w3 + w4 + w5 + w6 + w7 = 1;
w1 > 0;
w2 > 0;
w3 > 0;
w4 > 0;
w5 > 0;
w6 > 0;
w7 > 0;
k > =0;
```
(26.7)

After calculating using the Lingo software, the results show that the weight of the criteria includes: $W_1 = 0.3051$, $W_2 = 0.2034$, $W_3 = 0.0509$, $W_4 = 0.3390$, $W_5 = 0.1017$, $W_6 = 0.2034$, and $W_7 = 0.1017$. The results show that the value of k or ξ is zero. It means all calculated weights are fully consistent. Additionally, the summation of the weights is equal to one.

26.6 Comparative analyses

The AHP, BWM, and BCM are all widely used approaches for deriving criterion weights in MCDM problems. While they share a common foundation in pairwise comparisons of criteria, their data requirements, computational complexity, and consistency behavior differ significantly. Understanding these differences is crucial when selecting an appropriate method for real-world applications that involve limited expert input or large numbers of criteria.

A quantitative comparison of the three methods is summarized in Table 26.4, which lists the number of pairwise comparisons required for problems ranging from 3 to 10 criteria. As seen from the table, AHP requires a rapidly increasing number of judgments. In AHP, 45 comparisons for only 10 criteria, while BWM requires 17, and BCM only nine. This contrast highlights the scalability advantage of BCM and, to a lesser extent, BWM, particularly for complex decision models with many evaluation criteria.

The implications of these differences extend beyond computational simplicity. Because AHP involves a quadratic number of comparisons, the likelihood of inconsistent or conflicting judgments rises sharply as n grows. In contrast, both BWM and BCM, by relying on linear numbers of comparisons, naturally enhance judgmental consistency. The BCM achieves mathematical consistency by construction when all base comparisons adhere to the multiplicative transitivity condition. Moreover, BCM can handle incomplete or missing comparisons more flexibly, as the base vector can be used to regenerate the missing elements in the pairwise matrix.

Regarding the BCM advantage in handling incomplete or missing comparisons, (26.8) is introduced to calculate all elements of the decision matrix using the base comparisons vector.

$$a_{Base,i} * a_{ij} = a_{Base,j} \tag{26.8}$$

If we want to have a full decision matrix based on the base comparisons vector, (26.8) can help to calculate all elements of the matrix. For example, in Fig. 26.4, two simple examples are provided to show how we can calculate the incomplete parts of the matrix using the proposed framework of the BCM. As presented in Fig. 26.4, we can calculate the value of $a_{3,2}$

TABLE 26.4 Comparative analyses between the analytic hierarchy process (AHP), best–worst method (BWM), and base-criterion method (BCM).

	AHP	BWM	BCM
Required pairwise comparisons	$n(n-1)/2$	$2n-3$	$n-1$
Decision problem with 3 criteria	3	3	2
Decision problem with 4 criteria	6	5	3
Decision problem with 5 criteria	10	7	4
Decision problem with 6 criteria	15	9	5
Decision problem with 7 criteria	21	11	6
Decision problem with 8 criteria	28	13	7
Decision problem with 9 criteria	36	15	8
Decision problem with 10 criteria	45	17	9
Fully consistent feature	X	X	✓
Input control	X	X	✓

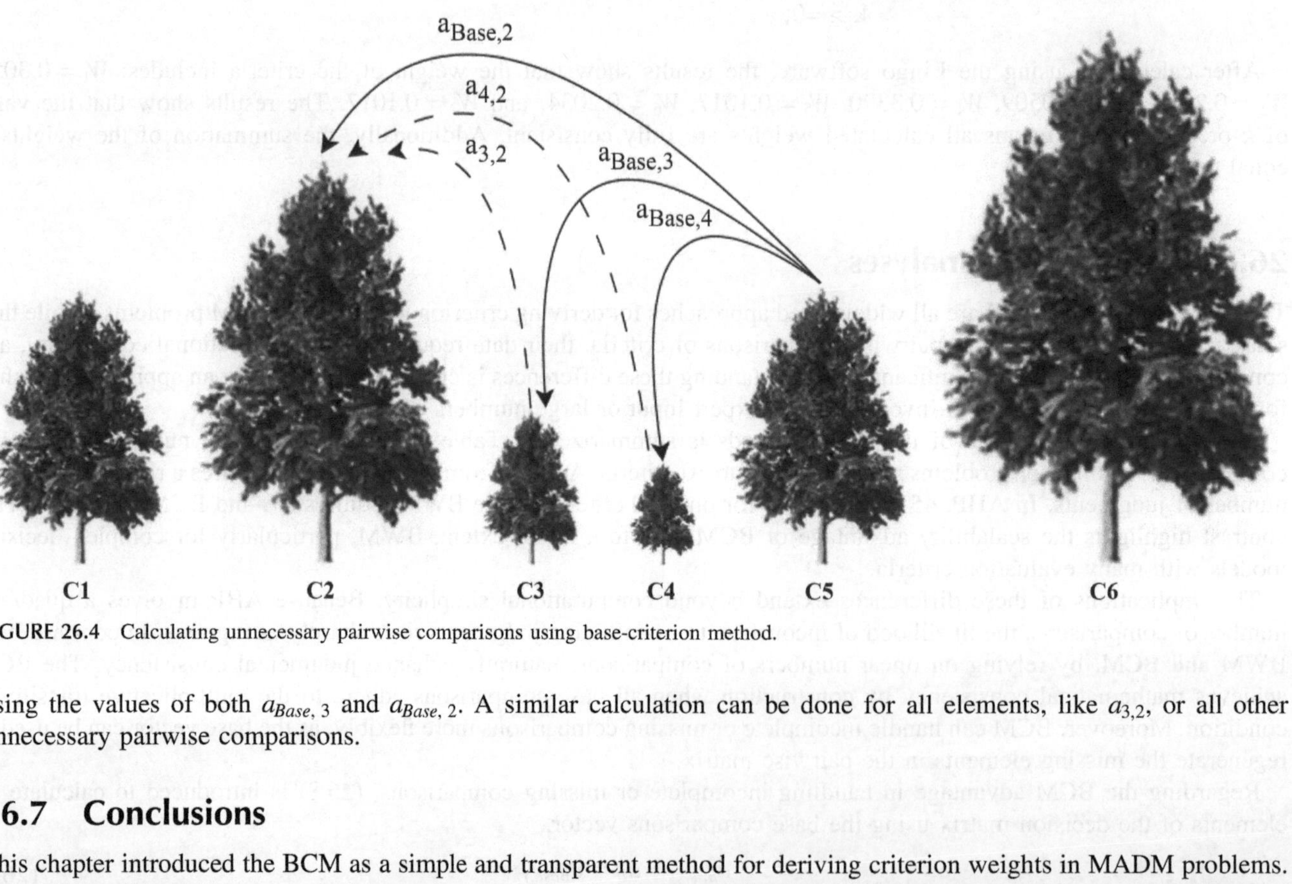

FIGURE 26.4 Calculating unnecessary pairwise comparisons using base-criterion method.

using the values of both $a_{Base,\,3}$ and $a_{Base,\,2}$. A similar calculation can be done for all elements, like $a_{3,2}$, or all other unnecessary pairwise comparisons.

26.7 Conclusions

This chapter introduced the BCM as a simple and transparent method for deriving criterion weights in MADM problems. Through two illustrative numerical examples, one related to transportation and the other to renewable energy technology selection, it was demonstrated how only n − 1 pairwise judgments can be used to construct a complete pairwise-comparison matrix and compute consistent weights. The main objective of the chapter was to provide a practical framework that can be applied by both researchers and policymakers in rapidly evolving scientific contexts. The examples were presented step-by-step to ensure conceptual clarity, reproducibility, and pedagogical value for readers using BCM for the first time.

The key advantage of BCM over traditional methods such as AHP and BWM lies in its significant reduction in the number of required judgments and its inherently higher level of consistency. This feature makes BCM particularly suitable for real-world policy applications and technical evaluations where expert time is scarce or data collection is constrained. Furthermore, the method's algebraic reconstruction of the full comparison matrix from a single base vector allows for straightforward sensitivity analysis, efficient completion of missing comparisons, and transparent reporting of all underlying assumptions. As a result, BCM-based models are easier to validate, compare, and replicate, an important quality in academic peer review and sustainability-related decision-making frameworks. Therefore, while all three methods provide systematic ways to derive criterion weights, BCM offers the most efficient balance between simplicity, consistency, and computational clarity. It reduces the number of required comparisons to the theoretical minimum (n – 1), ensures zero inconsistency in ideal conditions, and maintains analytical transparency, thereby addressing some of the key limitations inherent in both AHP and BWM.

References

Apiecionek, O., Listewnik, B., & Kizielewicz, B. (2025). Is it possible to standardize diagnostic decision-making in yoga therapy for LBP? A study using AHP, BWM, RANCOM, and BCM. *Procedia Comput Sci, 270*, 5865–5875. https://doi.org/10.1016/j.procs.2025.10.055.

Abdollahi, S., Ghoushchi, S. J., & Haseli, G. (2026). Evaluation of sustainable strategies for implementing blockchain technology in the solar energy supply chain under fuzzy ZE-numbers. *Applied Soft Computing, 189*, 114522. https://doi.org/10.1016/j.asoc.2025.114522.

Ayough, A., Shargh, S. B., & Khorshidvand, B. (2023). A new integrated approach based on base-criterion and utility additive methods and its application to supplier selection problem. *Expert Systems with Applications, 221*, 119740. https://doi.org/10.1016/j.eswa.2023.119740.

Bisht, G., & Pal, A. K. (2023). Functional dependency-based group decision-making with incomplete information under social media influence: An application to automobile. *Journal of Intelligent & Fuzzy Systems, 45*, 12341–12363. https://doi.org/10.3233/JIFS-232608.

Bisht, K., & Kumar, A. (2022). Stock portfolio selection hybridizing fuzzy base-criterion method and evidence theory in triangular fuzzy environment. *Operations Research Forum, 3*, 53. https://doi.org/10.1007/s43069-022-00167-3.

Bonab, S. R., Yousefi, S., Tosarkani, B. M., & Ghoushchi, S. J. (2023). A decision-making framework for blockchain platform evaluation in spherical fuzzy environment. *Expert Syst Appl, 231*, 120833. https://doi.org/10.1016/j.eswa.2023.120833.

Debalki, Y. A., Hou, J., Adane, B. Y., Mawutor, V. G., & Dang, H. (2024). A distributed relay selection using a fuzzy-BCM based decision making strategy for multi-hop data dissemination in VANETs. *Wireless Networks, 30*, 2873–2894. https://doi.org/10.1007/s11276-024-03705-5.

Gabriel Rasoanaivo, R., Yazdani, M., Zaraté, P., & Fateh, A. (2024). Combined compromise for ideal solution (CoCoFISo): A multi-criteria decision-making based on the CoCoSo method algorithm. *Expert Syst Appl, 251*, 124079. https://doi.org/10.1016/j.eswa.2024.124079.

Hajiaghaei-Keshteli, M., Cenk, Z., Erdebilli, B., Selim Özdemir, Y., & Gholian-Jouybari, F. (2023). Pythagorean fuzzy TOPSIS method for green supplier selection in the food industry. *Expert Syst Appl, 224*, 120036. https://doi.org/10.1016/j.eswa.2023.120036.

Haseli, G., & Jafarzadeh Ghoushchi, S. (2022). Extended base-criterion method based on the spherical fuzzy sets to evaluate waste management. *Soft Computing, 26*, 9979–9992. https://doi.org/10.1007/s00500-022-07366-4.

Haseli, G., Nazarian-Jashnabadi, J., Shirazi, B., Hajiaghaei-Keshteli, M., & Moslem, S. (2024). Sustainable strategies based on the social responsibility of the beverage industry companies for the circular supply chain. *Engineering Applications of Artificial Intelligence, 133*, 108253. https://doi.org/10.1016/j.engappai.2024.108253.

Haseli, G., Rahnamay Bonab, S., Hajiaghaei-Keshteli, M., Jafarzadeh Ghoushchi, S., & Deveci, M. (2024). Fuzzy ZE-numbers framework in group decision-making using the BCM and CoCoSo to address sustainable urban transportation. *Information Sciences (New York), 653*, 119809. https://doi.org/10.1016/j.ins.2023.119809.

Haseli, G., & Sheikh, R. (2022). Base Criterion Method (BCM) (pp. 17–38). Springer. https://doi.org/10.1007/978-981-16-7414-3_2

Haseli, G., Sheikh, R., & Sana, S. S. (2020). Base-criterion on multi-criteria decision-making method and its applications. *International Journal of Management Science and Engineering Management, 15*, 79–88. https://doi.org/10.1080/17509653.2019.1633964.

Haseli, G., Sheikh, R., & Sana, S. S. (2020). Extension of base-criterion method based on fuzzy set theory. *International Journal of Applied and Computational Mathematics, 6*, 54. https://doi.org/10.1007/s40819-020-00807-4.

Haseli, G., Yaran Ögel, İ., Ecer, F., & Hajiaghaei-Keshteli, M. (2023). Luxury in female technology (FemTech): Selection of smart jewelry for women through BCM-MARCOS group decision-making framework with fuzzy ZE-numbers. *Technological Forecasting and Social Change, 196*, 122870. https://doi.org/10.1016/j.techfore.2023.122870.

Imran, S. M., Rameshan, N., Anand, M. C. J., Martin, N., Tiwari, M., & Mohan, V. (2024). Fuzzy decision-making on strategies for maximizing the utility of electric vehicles. In *2024 IEEE Third International Conference on Power Electronics, Intelligent Control and Energy Systems (ICPEICES)* (pp. 347–352). IEEE. https://doi.org/10.1109/ICPEICES62430.2024.10719078

Liu, X., Tan, Y., Dong, J., Wu, J., Wang, X., & Sun, Z. (2025). Assessing habitat selection parameters of Arabica coffee using BWM and BCM methods based on GIS. *Scientific Reports, 15*, 8. https://doi.org/10.1038/s41598-024-84073-0.

Narang, M., Joshi, M. C., Bisht, K., & Pal, A. (2022). Stock portfolio selection using a new decision-making approach based on the integration of fuzzy CoCoSo with Heronian mean operator. *Decision Making: Applications in Management and Engineering, 5*, 90–112. https://doi.org/10.31181/dmame0310022022n.

Narang, M., Joshi, M. C., & Pal, A. K. (2021). A hybrid fuzzy COPRAS-base-criterion method for multi-criteria decision making. *Soft Computing, 25*, 8391–8399. https://doi.org/10.1007/s00500-021-05762-w.

Narang, M., Joshi, M. C., & Pal, A. K. (2022). A hesitant fuzzy multiplicative base-criterion multi-criteria group decision making method. *Informatica, 46*. https://doi.org/10.31449/inf.v46i2.3452.

Narayanan, U., & Paul, V. (2023). Twin chain: A blockchain-based federated learning intrusion detection system using optimized backpropagation-based neural network for edge-assisted IoT networks. https://doi.org/10.21203/rs.3.rs-3214924/v1

Phulara, S., Kumar, A., Narang, M., & Bisht, K. (2024). A novel hybrid grey-BCM approach in multi-criteria decision making: An application in OTT platform. *Journal of Decision Analytics and Intelligent Computing, 4*, 1–15. https://doi.org/10.31181/jdaic10016012024p.

Rezaei, J. (2015). Best-worst multi-criteria decision-making method. *Omega (Westport), 53*, 49–57. https://doi.org/10.1016/j.omega.2014.11.009.

Saaty, T. L. (2013). Analytic hierarchy process. In *Encyclopedia of Operations Research and Management Science*. Boston, MA: Springer US, 52–64. https://doi.org/10.1007/978-1-4419-1153-7_31.

Sun, L., Yu, C., Li, J., Yuan, Q., & Zhao, S. (2025). A two-stage decision model for sustainable-resilient supplier selection and order allocation under uncertain environment. *Kybernetes, 54*, 4078–4113. https://doi.org/10.1108/K-11-2023-2347.

Wu, Y., Liu, P., & Li, Y. (2024). An integrated QFD and FMEA method under the co-opetitional relationship for product upgrading. *Information Sciences (N Y), 667*, 120505. https://doi.org/10.1016/j.ins.2024.120505.

Wu, Y., Liu, P., & Li, Y. (2026). An improved QFD model with the integration of BCM and CoCoSo method under the trust network. *International Journal of Information Technology & Decision Making*. https://doi.org/10.1142/s0219622026500458.

Zafaranlouei, N., Ghoushchi, S. J., & Haseli, G. (2023). Assessment of sustainable waste management alternatives using the extensions of the base criterion method and combined compromise solution based on the fuzzy Z-numbers. *Environmental Science and Pollution Research, 30*, 62121–62136. https://doi.org/10.1007/s11356-023-26380-z.

Chapter 27

Stratified BCM: stratified base criterion method for multi-attribute decision-making

Javad Nazarian-Jashnabadi[1] and Samuel Yousefi[2]

[1]*Department of Management, Faculty of Economic, Management and Social Science, Shiraz University, Shiraz, Iran,* [2]*Department of Mechanical and Manufacturing Engineering, Ontario Tech University, Oshawa, ON, Canada*

27.1 Introduction

Making scientific and logical decisions in multidimensional problems in various fields is necessary. In such circumstances, the use of multi-criteria decision-making (MCDM) approaches has gained a special place as an effective tool for evaluating and comparing alternatives based on diverse criteria (Emovon & Oghenenyerovwho, 2020). In recent decades, several methods have been developed to respond to the preferences and priorities of decision-makers (DMs) (Kizielewicz et al., 2024). Each of these methods uses a distinct approach to weigh the criteria. As the weighting approach affects the accuracy and correctness of the results and consequently the ranking process, a comprehensive understanding of the nature of the problem and its dimensions is required (Demir et al., 2024). On the other hand, as the inputs of these MCDM methods are experts' opinions, the accuracy, efficiency, and consistency of judgments significantly influence the validity of the findings. Some weighting MCDM methods are based on pairwise comparisons, including the analytical hierarchy process (AHP) (Saaty, 1977), the best–worst method (BWM) (Rezaei, 2015), and, more recently, the base criterion method (BCM) (Haseli et al., 2020a).

One of the constant challenges in weighting methods is the high number of pairwise comparisons and the resulting inconsistency ratio. In the evolution of these methods, efforts have been made to reduce the cognitive burden on experts by minimizing the number of required pairwise comparisons, while simultaneously enhancing the internal consistency of judgments. The AHP represents the first major advancement in this direction. Employing a hierarchical structure and pairwise comparison matrices enabled the systematic weighting of criteria. However, one of its weaknesses is the need for a large number of pairwise comparisons, as n criteria $\frac{n(n-1)}{2}$ comparisons are required (Haseli & Sheikh, 2022). This not only makes it difficult to obtain expert opinions but also increases the likelihood of inconsistency. In AHP, the inconsistency ratio is calculated after the pairwise comparison matrix is completed. If the ratio exceeds the acceptable threshold, the expert judgments must be revised, and the analysis repeated.

The BWM simplifies the comparison process by relying on two reference criteria, including the best criterion and the worst criterion. Therefore, BWM requires $2n - 3$ pairwise comparisons, which represents a significant reduction compared to AHP. This reduction not only decreases the cognitive burden on evaluators but also tends to improve the consistency of judgments. Similar to AHP, the inconsistency ratio in BWM is calculated after implementing the model. If the inconsistency exceeds the acceptable threshold, the process of gathering expert input must be repeated, and the model reanalyzed. To minimize the mental effort required by experts, the BCM was introduced, which requires $n - 1$ pairwise comparisons. A key advantage of BCM lies in its ability to assess inconsistency before solving the model, during the data collection stage (Haseli et al., 2020b). This pre-analysis validation can ensure the full consistency of the pairwise comparisons before model execution. This, in turn, eliminates the need for repeated analyses due to inconsistency. Compared to AHP and BWM, which assess consistency post-solution, BCM enhances efficiency by controlling input quality from the outset.

Encyclopedia of Multi-Attribute Decision-Making (MADM). DOI: https://doi.org/10.1016/B978-0-443-33275-3.00008-7

However, an increasingly critical consideration in decision analysis is the recognition of dynamic environmental conditions. In many real-world situations, the assumption of stability does not hold, as factors such as economic fluctuations, technological advancements, and shifts in stakeholder preferences or needs continuously alter data, priorities, and even the fundamental objectives of decision-making (Moreno-Solaz et al., 2023). Relying solely on methods developed within a static framework, without accounting for future developments, can result in unstable or suboptimal decisions. Accordingly, considering the dynamic decision environment and adapting analytical methodologies to reflect possible future scenarios has become a strategic necessity in MCDM problems. Accurate and realistic assessment of complex problems requires designing and implementing models that account for a range of possible scenarios. Thus, incorporating scenario-based analysis is not merely optional; it is a fundamental requirement for ensuring robust and informed decisions (Torkayesh et al., 2021).

This chapter introduces the stratified base criterion method (SBCM) as a novel technique for evaluating and ranking alternatives under complex and dynamic conditions. SBCM is designed for decision-making problems involving multiple criteria influenced by changing scenarios. The method integrates two advanced approaches, including the BCM and stratified multi-criteria decision-making (SMCDM), which was introduced by Asadabadi (2018). This integration enables the weighting of criteria under uncertainty while accounting for different future scenarios. In SBCM, the weight of each criterion is determined separately within each scenario, and the overall optimal weight is then calculated by considering the probability of occurrence of each scenario. This stratified approach provides a more realistic and flexible representation of uncertain environments. SBCM addresses limitations in existing MCDM methods, particularly their inability to manage dynamic environmental conditions and predict future scenarios. Many decision-making problems are highly complex and uncertain, often requiring evaluation under potential long-term changes. By incorporating scenario-based analysis, SBCM enhances the reliability and accuracy of evaluating alternatives compared to traditional methods. These capabilities make SBCM a practical and effective tool for selecting the most suitable alternatives in complex, dynamic decision-making contexts.

The remainder of this chapter is structured as follows. Section 2 presents a comprehensive literature review of relevant studies. Section 3 details the methodology of the SBCM. Then, a numerical example is solved in Section 4 to demonstrate the application of the proposed method. Finally, Section 5 concludes the chapter with key findings and implications.

27.2 Literature review

Extensive research has focused on the methodological extensions of MCDM techniques to enhance their applicability and performance. These extensions aim to address limitations in traditional models by incorporating factors, such as uncertainty and dynamic environments (Chowdhury & Paul, 2020; Demir et al., 2024; Sotoudeh-Anvari, 2022). This section first reviews the studies related to the BCM and examines the applications of this method. In the following, the combination of the stratified approach with various MCDM methods is studied.

27.2.1 Existing research on the base criterion method

Given the complexity and uncertainties of decision-making problems, organizations and researchers need methods that reduce the computational burden while maintaining accuracy, efficiency, and flexibility. BCM, which was first introduced by Haseli et al. (2020a), has managed to gain a prominent position among MCDM methods due to its reliance on minimal pairwise comparisons between the "base" and "other criteria" and achieving the lowest inconsistency rate among the weights. The simple structure, reduced number of pairwise comparisons, and high level of consistency of the results are among the main advantages that have encouraged researchers to develop and combine BCM with other approaches.

The BCM method has been applied across diverse fields such as sustainable transportation, waste management, and financial and environmental decision-making, demonstrating significant topical and methodological diversity. Haseli, Bonab, et al. (2024); Haseli, Nazarian-Jashnabadi, et al. (2024) utilized BCM to evaluate sustainable urban transportation options, providing an effective framework for sustainable decision-making. Narang et al. (2022) employed hesitant fuzzy BCM, enhancing optimal vehicle selection under uncertainty. In waste management, Haseli and Jafarzadeh Ghoushchi (2022) applied BCM for landfill site selection, while Zafaranlouei et al. (2023) explored sustainable waste management in Iran using economic, social, and environmental criteria. Bisht and Pal (2023) used BCM to rank vehicles in the electronics industry, and Liu et al. (2025) applied it to select Arabica coffee habitats, highlighting BCM's utility in environmental decisions. Narang et al. (2021) used BCM for stock selection under uncertainty, demonstrating its effectiveness in financial decision-making.

BCM has been integrated with various methods to enhance its accuracy and efficiency in MCDM. Haseli, Bonab, et al. (2024); Haseli, Nazarian-Jashnabadi, et al. (2024) combined BCM with combined compromise abbreviations expanded solution (CoCoSo), improving sustainable urban transportation evaluation by reducing computational complexity and enhancing precision. Narang et al. (2022) integrated BCM with hesitant fuzzy sets, strengthening group decision-making under uncertainty. Haseli and Sheikh (2022) used spherical fuzzy sets with BCM, increasing decision accuracy in waste management under ambiguous conditions. Bisht and Pal (2023) combined BCM with decision-making trial and evaluation laboratory (DEMATEL), VlseKriterijumska Optimizacija I Kompromisno Resenje (VIKOR), and Heron averaging, modeling social and functional dependencies in vehicle ranking. Narang et al. (2021) integrated BCM with fuzzy complex proportional assessment, enhancing financial decision-making in high-risk environments. These methodological integrations highlight BCM's adaptability to diverse and complex decision-making challenges. Table 27.1 summarizes the studies related to the BCM field.

TABLE 27.1 Studies on the extensions and applications of the base criterion method (BCM).

Author(s)	Methodology	Fuzzy approach	Application area
Wu et al. (2026)	BCM-CoCoSo	-	Quality function deployment
Liu et al. (2025)	BWM–BCM	-	Habitat selection
Haseli, Bonab, et al. (2024)	BCM–CoCoSo	ZE fuzzy Number	Urban transportation
Haseli, Nazarian-Jashnabadi, et al. (2024)	BCM–MABAC[a]	Fuzzy Z-extended numbers	Circular supply chain management and the beverage industry
Wu et al. (2024)	BCM–CoCoSo–TODIM[a]	Interval-valued intuitionistic fuzzy set	Customer satisfaction and product upgrading
Sun et al. (2025)	BCM–TODIM U-NSGA-III[a] algorithm-TOPSIS[a]	Single-valued neutrosophic	Sustainable-resilient supplier selection
Debalki et al. (2024)	BCM	Original fuzzy set	Traffic flow and speed variations
Phulara et al. (2024)	Gray BCM	-	Over-the-top platforms
Imran et al. (2024)	BCM	Trapezoidal fuzzy numbers	Utility of electric vehicles
Zafaranlouei et al. (2023)	BCM–CoCoSo	Fuzzy Z-numbers	Waste management
Haseli et al. (2023)	BCM–MARCOS[a] group decision-making	Fuzzy ZE-numbers	Smart jewelry selection
Ayough et al. (2023)	BCM-utility additive	-	Supplier selection
Bisht and Pal (2023)	DEMATEL–BCM–VIKOR	-	Electronics industry
Haseli and Sheikh (2022)	BCM	-	Staff selection-product development and transportation mode
Haseli and Sheikh (2022)	BCM	Spherical fuzzy	Landfill site selection
Narang et al. (2022)	BCM	Hesitant fuzzy	Transportation mode and vehicle selection
Bisht and Kumar (2022)	BCM–LSTM[a]	Original fuzzy set	Stock selection
Narang et al. (2021)	BCM–COPRAS	Triangular fuzzy numbers	Stock portfolio selection

[a] *MABAC: Multiattributive border approximation area comparison, TODIM: Técnica Ordinal da informação multicritério, U-NSGA: Nondominated sorting genetic algorithm III, MARCOS: Measurement alternatives and ranking according to compromise solution, LSTM: Long-short-term memory.*

27.2.2 Stratified frameworks in multicriteria decision-making

A review of previous research related to SMCDM shows that the use of mixed MCDM methods with stratified is increasing (Ecer & Torkayesh, 2022). Most of these studies have been conducted by combining stratified and BWM. Torkayesh et al. (2021) and Moreno-Solaz et al. (2023) used the stratified BWM (SBWM) method independently in their research. The combination of this method with other decision-making methods is also observed in some studies. Asadabadi et al. (2023) combined SBWM and technique for order preference by similarity to ideal solution, Konurhan et al. (2023) combined SBWM and geographic information system (GIS), Torkayesh and Simic (2022) used SBWM with CoCoSo and weighted aggregated sum product assessment (WASPAS), and finally Li et al. (2025) combined GIS and SBWM.

From the perspective of the application area, there is considerable diversity in the studies. Asadabadi (2018) and Asadabadi et al. (2023) have addressed the issue of supplier selection with an emphasis on environmental sustainability. Torkayesh et al. (2021) and Torkayesh and Simic (2022) conducted research on urban waste management, focusing on plastic waste recycling and its impact on urban health. Moreno-Solaz et al. (2023) have also addressed the optimal selection of waste collection trucks. Konurhan et al. (2023) applied decision-making methods to assess landslide risks, while Li et al. (2025) used similar techniques to determine service areas for robotaxi deployment. Table 27.2 provides a summary of the existing studies in this field.

27.3 Methodology

BCM, like AHP and BWM, is a method based on pairwise comparisons. Two very important concepts in conducting pairwise comparisons are the strength and direction of comparisons (Haseli et al., 2020a). These comparisons should be made without any inconsistency in their strength and direction. Inconsistency in the direction of comparisons occurs when the relative importance in pairwise comparisons is applied oppositely to another criterion. Besides, inconsistency in strength means that the DM does not evaluate the pairwise comparisons accurately.

The primary advantage of BCM over AHP and BWM methods is its ability to enhance the consistency ratio (CR) in comparisons. In the AHP, inconsistencies can arise in both the direction and strength of pairwise comparisons (Harker, 1987). In contrast, the BWM minimizes issues with directional inconsistencies by using two fundamental criteria—designating one as the best and the other as the worst. However, it still experiences inconsistencies in the strength of comparisons (Tavana et al., 2024). To resolve the inconsistency issue, we need to first reduce the number of pairwise comparisons required. Secondly, we should establish a framework to manage the inputs for these comparisons. This approach will enable the BCM to effectively handle inconsistencies in both strength and direction.

TABLE 27.2 Summary of recent applications of stratified multicriteria decision-making methods.

Author(s)	Methodology	Fuzzy approach	Application area
Asadabadi (2018)	SMCDM	–	Supplier selection
Torkayesh et al. (2021)	SBWM	–	Sustainable waste management
Moreno-Solaz et al. (2023)	SBWM	–	Sustainable selection of waste collection trucks
Asadabadi et al. (2023)	SBWM–TOPSIS	–	Supplier selection to support environmental sustainability
Konurhan et al. (2023)	GIS-SBWM	–	Landslide susceptibility assessment
Torkayesh and Simic (2022)	Hierarchical SBWM, CoCoSo, and WASPAS	–	Healthcare plastic waste recycling facility location
Li et al. (2025)	GIS–SBWM	–	Service area identification for Robotaxi deployment

To solve the inconsistency problem, firstly, the number of required pairwise comparisons must be reduced, and secondly, a framework for controlling the inputs of pairwise comparisons must be defined. In this way, the BCM method can deal with strength and direction inconsistencies. First, the number of pairwise comparisons in this method is $n - 1$, which is significantly reduced compared to the AHP and BWM methods. Also, this method uses a framework for controlling the inputs of pairwise comparisons, which is explained below.

Suppose there are n criteria, and the relative importance of each criterion to the other criteria is to be determined. The pairwise comparison matrix will be like Eq. (27.1).

$$A = \begin{bmatrix} a_{11} & a_{12} & \cdots & a_{1n} \\ a_{21} & a_{22} & \cdots & a_{2n} \\ \vdots & \vdots & \ddots & \vdots \\ a_{m1} & a_{m2} & \cdots & a_{mn} \end{bmatrix} \tag{27.1}$$

In this matrix, a_{ij} represents the relative importance of criterion i relative to criterion j, which is represented using a numerical scale from 1/9 to 9. Similarly, a_{ji} represents the relative importance of the criterion j relative to the criterion i, and $a_{ij} = 1 / a_{ji}$. If there is equal importance between the criteria i and j, $a_{ij} = 1$. In BCM, two types of pairwise comparisons are defined as follows:

(1) Base comparisons: The comparison a_{ij} is defined as a base comparison if i is the base criterion.
(2) Final comparisons: The comparison a_{ij} is defined as a final comparison if i and j are not base criteria.

First, the DM specifies the values of the base comparisons. Final comparisons are a subset of the base comparisons. Therefore, without performing final comparisons, we can obtain the weight values of the criteria. It is recommended to perform final comparisons to complete the matrix of pairwise comparisons and also to determine the relative importance of a pairwise comparison between all criteria. For this purpose, we use Eq. (27.2) so that the comparisons made are fully consistent in terms of direction and strength.

$$a_{Base,i} \times a_{ij} = a_{Base,j} \tag{27.2}$$

The assignment of values to pairwise comparisons by the DM should be done in such a way that the final values of the pairwise comparison are in the numerical range of 1/9 to 9. According to Eq. (27.2), the final comparison a_{ij} is obtained by dividing the base comparison $a_{Base,j}$ by $a_{Base,i}$. Since the numerical value of the comparisons must be in the range of 1/9 to 9, the DM must consider (27.3) when assigning values to the base comparisons.

$$a_{Base,i} \times a_{ij} = a_{Base,j};\ a_{ij} = \frac{a_{Base,j}}{a_{Base,i}}$$

and

$$\frac{1}{9} \leq \frac{a_{Base,j}}{a_{Base,i}} \leq 9 \ or\ \frac{1}{9} \leq a_{ij} \leq \quad 9,\ \forall j = 2,\ \ldots, n,\ \forall i = 1,\ \ldots, j-1 \tag{27.3}$$

Therefore, in BCM, an attempt is made to improve the inconsistency by controlling the inputs. Using (27.3) in performing the pairwise comparisons results in full consistency in the direction and strength of the comparisons. The following nine steps detail the implementation of BCM (see Fig. 27.1).

Step 1: Describing the decision-making problem

The first step is to define a problem that has multiple criteria to evaluate, several alternatives to select, and different scenarios that affect the importance of the criteria. The relative importance of the criteria may change in different scenarios. Making decisions regardless of these differences can lead to inaccurate outcomes. This method makes the final analysis more accurate, valid, and proportional to the realities of the problem, especially when changing scenarios play a significant role in decision-making.

Step 2: Selecting experts for the study

For the proper implementation of SBCM, it is necessary to select the appropriate experts. Experts should possess specialized knowledge, practical experience, and a comprehensive understanding of the various aspects of the problem. Careful selection of experts helps ensure the quality of the input data and the validity of the results. The criteria for selecting experts usually include relevant scientific and professional background, experience in decision-making, and the ability to evaluate criteria and alternatives. To ensure a diverse range of perspectives and minimize bias, efforts are made to select a mix of experts from various backgrounds, such as academic, industrial, and executive fields. The number of

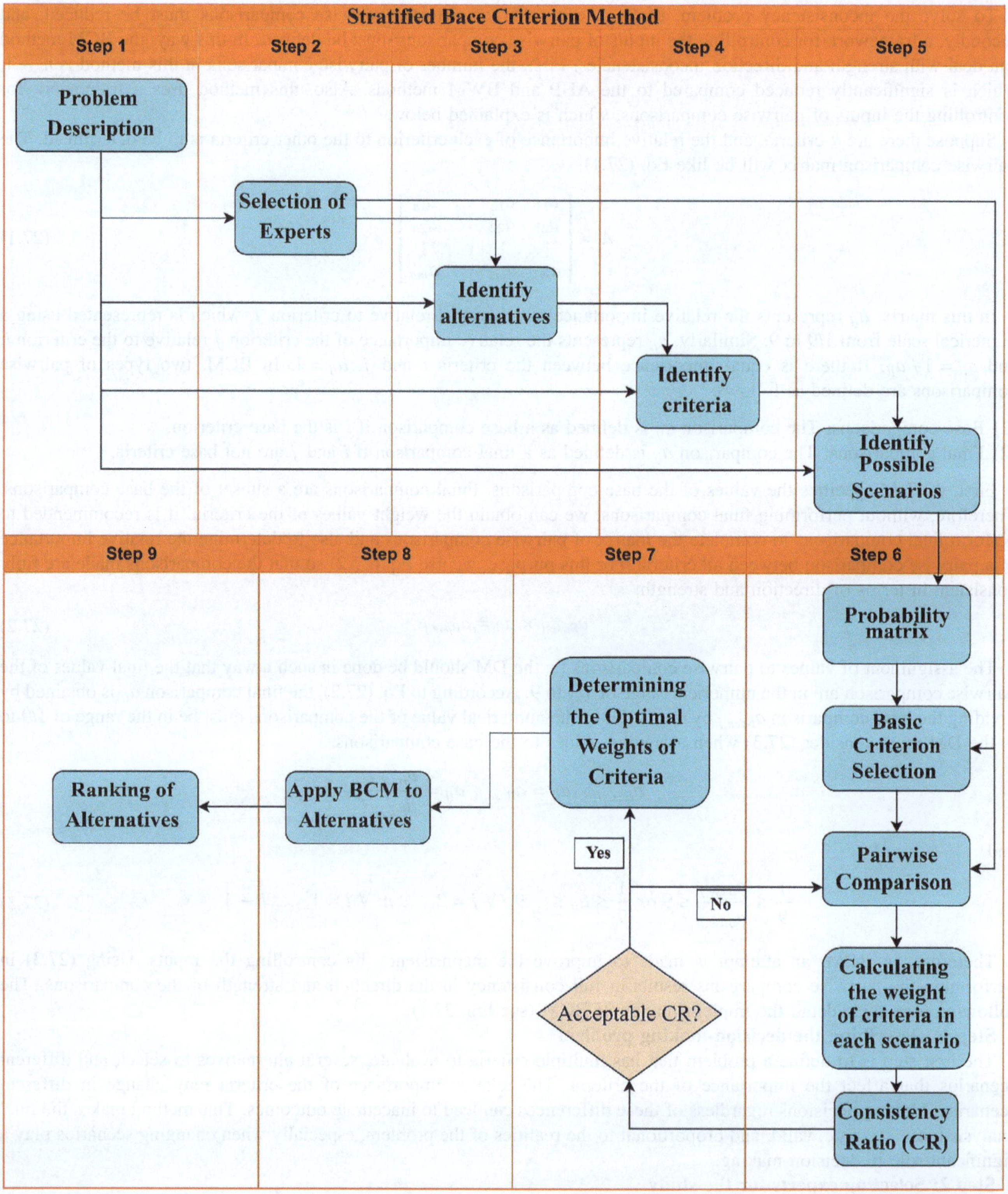

FIGURE 27.1 The proposed framework of the stratified base criterion method.

experts chosen should be sufficient to guarantee the reliability of the data while avoiding unnecessary complexity in the analysis.

Step 3: Specifying the list of alternatives

A set of alternatives $\{A_1, A_2, \ldots A_m\}$ that should be evaluated and compared is identified. The selection of alternatives should encompass all reasonable, realistic, and relevant solutions to the problem. Within the SBCM framework, it is crucial to focus on the diversity of these alternatives, as they may perform differently under varying scenarios. Therefore, it is essential to ensure that the chosen alternatives are not only comparable but also resilient to environmental changes or different conditions. A clear and comprehensive definition of the alternatives provides a solid foundation for more accurate evaluations and more reliable decision-making in subsequent steps.

Step 4: Identifying the set of criteria

The next step is to identify a set of criteria $\{C_1, C_2, \ldots C_n\}$ against which alternatives will be evaluated and compared. Criteria should be identified by reviewing the theoretical literature, conducting an expert survey, or performing an exploratory analysis to ensure that all important aspects of the problem are covered. The selected criteria should have characteristics such as comprehensiveness, lack of overlap, direct relevance to the decision-making goal, and measurability. It is also essential to consider whether the importance of these criteria may change in different scenarios. One of the goals of SBCM is to address variations in the significance of criteria across different data layers or decision conditions. The proper and accurate selection of criteria is crucial for the accuracy of the final results and directly impacts the validity of the decision-making model. If the criteria are identified incompletely or incorrectly, the results of the analysis may not accurately reflect the true realities of the problem.

Step 5: Exploring possible scenarios

A set of different scenarios $\{S_1, S_2, \ldots S_k\}$ that can affect the importance or performance of the decision-making criteria should be identified. These scenarios illustrate various conditions or environments that may develop over time or due to different circumstances, leading to changes in the prioritization of criteria. The purpose of this step is to properly consider the dynamic dimensions of the problem in the decision-making process. In this regard, scenarios should be determined based on a study of the problem environment, an analysis of key uncertainties, and an identification of the drivers of change. Each scenario should have specific characteristics that can explain potential changes in the importance of the criteria or behavior of the alternatives. Accurate and comprehensive identification of the scenarios will enable the SBCM to inform decisions by taking into account possible differences in future optimizations, thereby increasing the credibility of the results.

Step 6: Probability of occurrence and criteria evaluation

(i) Constructing probability matrix

In this step, according to the defined scenarios, a matrix of probabilities (P) is formed like Eq. (27.4). This matrix represents the probability of each scenario occurring. These probabilities indicate the relative weight of each scenario, enabling an accurate analysis of its impact on the final weight of the criteria.

$$P = [P_{s1} \quad P_{s2} \quad \cdots \quad P_{sk}] \tag{27.4}$$

(ii) Selecting basic criterion

A base criterion (C_{Base}) is selected in each scenario. This step plays an important role in determining the final results of decision-making and helps to obtain the weight of each criterion based on comparison with the base criterion.

(iii) Comparing the base criterion to others in each scenario

In each scenario, the base criterion is compared with the other criteria. In this step, $n-1$ comparisons should be performed. (27.5) shows the base comparison vector.

$$a_{Base,j} = (a_{Base,1}, \ a_{Base,2}, \ \ldots, \ a_{Base,n}) \tag{27.5}$$

These comparisons will be shown with a numerical scale of 1/9 to 9 based on Table 27.3. If the C_{Base} is better than jth criterion, we use the scale of 1 to 9, and if jth criterion is better than the C_{Base}; we use the scale of 1/9 to 1.

(iv) Calculating the weight of the criteria in each scenario

According to the pairwise comparisons made, the weight of the criteria in each scenario is obtained. For this purpose, for all j, the maximum absolute difference between $\frac{w_{Base}}{w_j}$ and $a_{Base,j}$ is minimized. Since the weight of the criteria is nonnegative and aggregate, the problem can be expressed in Eq. (27.6).

TABLE 27.3 Comparison scale.

Scale		Description
1	1	Equal importance
1/2	2	Between equal and moderate
1/3	3	Moderately more important than
1/4	4	Between moderate and strong
1/5	5	Strongly more important than
1/6	6	Between strong and very strong
1/7	7	Very strongly more important than
1/8	8	Between very strong and absolute
1/9	9	Absolutely more important than

$$\begin{aligned} & Min \ \max \left| \frac{w_{Base}}{w_j} - a_{Base,j} \right| \\ & S.\,t. \\ & \textstyle\sum_{j=1}^{n} \omega_j = 1 \\ & \omega_j \geq 0 \ \text{for all } j \end{aligned} \tag{27.6}$$

Considering the deviations leading to the inconsistency, Eq. (27.6) can be written in the form of Eq. (27.7). Eq. (27.8) represents the linear transformation of Eq. (27.7).

$$\begin{aligned} & Min \ \xi \\ & S.\,t. \\ & \left| \frac{w_{Base}}{w_j} - a_{Base,j} \right| \leq \xi \\ & \textstyle\sum_{j=1}^{n} \omega_j = 1 \\ & \omega_j \geq 0 \ \text{for all } j \end{aligned} \tag{27.7}$$

$$\begin{aligned} & Min \ \xi \\ & S.\,t. \\ & \left| w_{Base} - w_j \times a_{Base,j} \right| \leq \xi \\ & \textstyle\sum_{j=1}^{n} \omega_j = 1 \\ & \omega_j \geq 0 \ \text{for all } j \end{aligned} \tag{27.8}$$

The model mentioned in Eq. (27.8) is solved in each scenario, and the weights of the criteria are obtained in each scenario. Therefore, the aforementioned model is solved k times, and the output of this stage is expressed in the matrix form of Eq. (27.9).

$$W_C = \begin{array}{c} \\ C_1 \\ C_2 \\ \vdots \\ C_n \end{array} \begin{array}{c} S_1 \quad S_2 \quad \ldots \quad S_k \\ \begin{bmatrix} w_{11} & w_{12} & \ldots & w_{1k} \\ w_{21} & w_{22} & \ldots & w_{2k} \\ \vdots & \vdots & \ddots & \vdots \\ w_{n1} & w_{n2} & \ldots & w_{nk} \end{bmatrix} \end{array} \tag{27.9}$$

(v) Calculating CR

The CR is a metric used to evaluate the consistency of pairwise comparison judgments in a given scenario. This rate is calculated separately for each scenario and ensures that the weighting results are reasonably valid. The CR calculation is based on (27.10), and if its value is high, there is a need to revise the judgments (Rezaei, 2015). According to (27.3) and controlling the inputs of pairwise comparisons in BCM, the value of ξ will be zero. So, according to (27.10), all pairwise comparisons are fully consistent (Haseli et al., 2020a, 2020b).

$$Consistency\ ratio\ (CR) = \frac{\xi}{Consistency\ index} \tag{27.10}$$

Step 7: Determining the optimal weights of criteria

To determine the final optimal weights of the criteria, the scenario probability matrix P (Eq. (27.4)) is multiplied by the criteria weight matrix W (Eq. (27.9)). The output of this step is the final vector of criteria weights, which is represented by W_C^{Final} ((27.11)).

$$W_C^{Final} = [W_C]_{n\times k} \cdot [P]_{k\times 1}^T = \left[w_{C1}^{Final} \quad w_{C2}^{Final} \quad \ldots \quad w_{Cn}^{Final} \right]_{n\times 1} \tag{27.11}$$

Step 8: Applying BCM to alternatives

In this step, to determine which alternative is more suitable for each of the selected criteria, a weighting process is performed. In each criterion, the weight of the alternatives is calculated using the BCM and the alternative weight matrix (W_A) is formed according to Eq. (27.12). Therefore, this step should be done n times to accurately compare alternatives based on each criterion.

$$W_A = \begin{array}{c} \\ A_1 \\ A_2 \\ \vdots \\ A_m \end{array} \begin{array}{c} C_1 \quad C_2 \quad \ldots \quad C_n \\ \begin{bmatrix} w_{11} & w_{12} & \ldots & w_{1n} \\ w_{21} & w_{22} & \ldots & w_{2n} \\ \vdots & \vdots & \ddots & \vdots \\ w_{n1} & w_{n2} & \ldots & w_{mn} \end{bmatrix} \end{array} \tag{27.12}$$

Step 9: Ranking of alternatives

To determine the final ranking of the alternatives, the alternative weight matrix W_A (Eq. (27.12)) is multiplied by the optimal criteria weight matrix W_C^{Final} ((27.11)). The output of this step is the final ranking of the alternatives, which is represented by W_A^{Final} (Eq. (27.13)).

$$W_A^{Final} = [W_A]_{m\times n} \cdot [W_C^{Final}]_{n\times 1} \tag{27.13}$$

27.4 Numerical example

In today's business environment, organizations are compelled to utilize business intelligence (BI) tools to enhance performance and gain a competitive edge. Selecting the right BI tool requires a thorough evaluation of the available options based on key criteria that reflect the technical, operational, and strategic capabilities of each choice. However, the significance and priority of these criteria can vary, influenced by environmental conditions, organizational objectives, and strategic changes. Therefore, analyzing the chosen options should be conducted within the context of different organizational scenarios. In this example, six main alternatives for implementing BI have been examined, which include: using power BI software (A1), implementation of Tableau (A2), internal BI system development (A3), leveraging Google data studio (A4), purchasing hybrid BI and AI-ready platforms (A5), and creating a custom cloud BI platform (A6). These alternatives, along with a brief explanation of each, are listed in Table 27.4. To evaluate these alternatives, seven key criteria, including quick access to data (C1), innovative use of BI (C2), analytical power and algorithms (C3), data security

TABLE 27.4 The list of alternatives for implementing business intelligence (BI).

Symb-ol	Alternative	Definition	Reference
A1	Using power BI software	Microsoft's analytical and visual tool for analyzing data and creating interactive dashboards and reports; a simple and cost-effective solution for monitoring performance.	(Belghith et al., 2024)
A2	Implementation of Tableau	An advanced platform for data analysis and visual reporting with powerful integration capabilities; suitable for complex analyses and more interaction with data.	(Dewi et al., 2024)
A3	Internal BI system development	Developing a BI system in-house, tailored to specific needs, is very flexible but time-consuming and more expensive.	(Ahmad et al., 2020)
A4	Leveraging Google data studio	A free tool for creating simple reports and dashboards that easily connect to data sources; suitable for small and medium-sized businesses.	(Iskandar et al., 2025)
A5	Purchasing hybrid BI and AI-ready platforms	Purchase platforms with advanced analytical capabilities and artificial intelligence algorithms for deep analysis and forecasting future trends.	(Guldogan et al., 2024)
A6	Creating a custom cloud BI platform	Design a custom cloud BI platform with the benefits of scalability and access from anywhere; suitable for large organizations with complex needs.	(Bhatia et al., 2025)

TABLE 27.5 The list of criteria for evaluating alternatives.

Symb-ol	Criteria	Definition	Reference
C1	Quick access to data	The organization's ability to easily and immediately access the data needed for decision-making.	(Al-Sai et al., 2023)
C2	Innovative use of BI	Creative use of data and analytical tools to improve processes.	(Ahmad et al., 2020)
C3	Analytical power and algorithms	The ability to process data and provide accurate analyses and predict trends.	(Cho et al., 2021)
C4	Data security and access control	The organization's ability to protect sensitive data and manage access to it.	(Antoniolli et al., 2022)
C5	Information retention and stability	The organization's ability to maintain reliable and always available data.	(Bukhari et al., 2024)
C6	Real-time decision-making capability	The ability to make quick decisions based on up-to-date and real-time data.	(Jahantigh et al., 2019)
C7	Automated decision-making and dashboards	Automatic generation of reports and dashboards to support management decisions.	(Parra et al., 2022)

and access control (C4), information retention and stability (C5), real-time decision-making capability (C6), and automated decision-making and dashboards (C7), are considered (see Table 27.5).

The ranking process is based on the variability of the importance of the criteria in three distinct scenarios (see Table 27.6). These scenarios are the "Operational productivity scenario" (S1) that focuses on optimizing internal processes

TABLE 27.6 Description of the defined scenarios.

Symbol	Scenario	Description
S1	Operational productivity scenario	This scenario focuses on increasing the speed, accuracy, and efficiency of the organization's internal processes by using smart tools to improve day-to-day performance.
S2	Innovation and marketing scenario	This scenario focuses on the creative use of data and analytical tools to develop new products, attract customers, and enhance a competitive position in the market.
S3	Organizational sustainability scenario	This scenario focuses on information protection, enhancing data security, sustaining technological infrastructure, and supporting long-term and sustainable growth of the organization.

and increasing efficiency, the "Innovation and marketing scenario" (S2) that considers the development of new markets and products, and the "Organizational sustainability scenario" (S3) that emphasizes maintaining security, information durability, and long-term growth. In each scenario, the weight of the criteria is changed by the environmental and strategic priorities, and finally, the sum of the calculated scores is the basis for ranking the alternatives. The necessity of this ranking is that selection without considering environmental changes and the relative importance of criteria can lead to incorrect decisions and impose heavy costs on the organization. By adopting a scenario-based approach and a correct understanding of the changing priorities, DMs will be able to choose the tool that is most compatible with the current and future requirements of the organization and help achieve its strategic goals.

The model was developed in Eq. (27.14) to weigh the criteria in Scenario 1. In this model, C3 was used as the base criterion for pairwise comparison between criteria. Eq. (27.15) shows the model for Scenario 2. In this scenario, C4 is selected as the base criterion. In Scenario 3, the DM also chose C4 as the base criterion, with its model represented in Eq. (27.16). Furthermore, the error rate for these models is zero ($\xi = 0$), indicating complete consistency.

$$
\begin{aligned}
& Min\ \xi \\
& S.t. \\
& |(\omega_3) - (\omega_1 \times 0.5)| \le \xi \\
& |(\omega_3) - (\omega_2 \times 2)| \le \xi \\
& |(\omega_3) - (\omega_4 \times 3)| \le \xi \\
& |(\omega_3) - (\omega_5 \times 5)| \le \xi \\
& |(\omega_3) - (\omega_6 \times 1)| \le \xi \\
& |(\omega_3) - (\omega_7 \times 4)| \le \xi \\
& \textstyle\sum_{j=1}^{n} \omega_j = 1 \\
& \omega_j \ge 0 \text{ for all } j
\end{aligned}
\tag{27.14}
$$

$$
\begin{aligned}
& Min\ \xi \\
& S.t. \\
& |(\omega_4) - (\omega_1 \times 0.25)| \le \xi \\
& |(\omega_4) - (\omega_2 \times 0.143)| \le \xi \\
& |(\omega_4) - (\omega_3 \times 0.17)| \le \xi \\
& |(\omega_4) - (\omega_5 \times 0.5)| \le \xi \\
& |(\omega_4) - (\omega_6 \times 0.2)| \le \xi \\
& |(\omega_4) - (\omega_7 \times 0.33)| \le \xi \\
& \textstyle\sum_{j=1}^{n} \omega_j = 1 \\
& \omega_j \ge 0 \text{ for all } j
\end{aligned}
\tag{27.15}
$$

$$
\begin{aligned}
& Min\ \xi \\
& S.\,t. \\
& |(\omega_4) - (\omega_1 \times 3)| \le \xi \\
& |(\omega_4) - (\omega_2 \times 5)| \le \xi \\
& |(\omega_4) - (\omega_3 \times 4)| \le \xi \\
& |(\omega_4) - (\omega_5 \times 2)| \le \xi \\
& |(\omega_4) - (\omega_6 \times 5)| \le \xi \\
& |(\omega_4) - (\omega_7 \times 6)| \le \xi \\
& \Sigma_{j=1}^{n} \omega_j = 1 \\
& \omega_j \ge 0 \text{ for all } j
\end{aligned} \tag{27.16}
$$

The weight of the criteria in each scenario is given in Table 27.7. The obtained weights, multiplied by the probability matrix of occurrence of each scenario, created the optimal weight of the criteria (see Table 27.8). For example, in Table 27.8, the weight of criterion C1 (0.246) is obtained according to (27.17):

$$
[0.38\ \ 0.142\ \ 0.126] \times \begin{bmatrix} 0.45 \\ 0.35 \\ 0.2 \end{bmatrix} = 0.246 \tag{27.17}
$$

TABLE 27.7 The weight of the criteria under different scenarios.

Scenario		S1	S2	S3
Probability of occurrence		0.45	0.35	0.20
C1	Quick access to data	0.380	0.142	0.126
C2	Innovative use of BI	0.094	0.251	0.075
C3	Analytical power and algorithms	0.189	0.211	0.095
C4	Data security and access control	0.063	0.035	0.377
C5	Information retention and stability	0.038	0.072	0.188
C6	Real-time decision-making capability	0.189	0.179	0.076
C7	Automated decision-making and dashboards	0.047	0.110	0.063

TABLE 27.8 The calculated final weight of the criteria.

Criteria	Final weight
C1	0.246
C2	0.145
C3	0.178
C4	0.116
C5	0.079
C6	0.163
C7	0.073

Since the number of criteria in this example is 7, the process of weighting alternatives has been performed 7 times. Equations (27.18) to (27.24) show the models for weighting alternatives in the first to seventh criteria, respectively. It should be noted that the error rate in these models is zero ($\xi = 0$), indicating perfect consistency.

$$\begin{aligned} &Min\ \xi \\ &S.\ t. \\ &\quad |(\omega_3) - (\omega_1 \times 0.2)| \le \xi \\ &\quad |(\omega_3) - (\omega_2 \times 0.33)| \le \xi \\ &\quad |(\omega_3) - (\omega_4 \times 0.25)| \le \xi \\ &\quad |(\omega_3) - (\omega_5 \times 2)| \le \xi \\ &\quad |(\omega_3) - (\omega_6 \times 0.5)| \le \xi \\ &\quad \textstyle\sum_{j=1}^{n} \omega_j = 1 \\ &\quad \omega_j \ge 0 \text{ for all } j \end{aligned} \tag{27.18}$$

$$\begin{aligned} &Min\ \xi \\ &S.\ t. \\ &\quad |(\omega_2) - (\omega_1 \times 4)| \le \xi \\ &\quad |(\omega_2) - (\omega_3 \times 2)| \le \xi \\ &\quad |(\omega_2) - (\omega_4 \times 6)| \le \xi \\ &\quad |(\omega_2) - (\omega_5 \times 3)| \le \xi \\ &\quad |(\omega_2) - (\omega_6 \times 5)| \le \xi \\ &\quad \textstyle\sum_{j=1}^{n} \omega_j = 1 \\ &\quad \omega_j \ge 0 \text{ for all } j \end{aligned} \tag{27.19}$$

$$\begin{aligned} &Min\ \xi \\ &S.\ t. \\ &\quad |(\omega_4) - (\omega_1 \times 0.25)| \le \xi \\ &\quad |(\omega_4) - (\omega_2 \times 0.17)| \le \xi \\ &\quad |(\omega_4) - (\omega_3 \times 0.33)| \le \xi \\ &\quad |(\omega_4) - (\omega_5 \times 0.2)| \le \xi \\ &\quad |(\omega_4) - (\omega_6 \times 0.5)| \le \xi \\ &\quad \textstyle\sum_{j=1}^{n} \omega_j = 1 \\ &\quad \omega_j \ge 0 \text{ for all } j \end{aligned} \tag{27.20}$$

$$\begin{aligned} &Min\ \xi \\ &S.\ t. \\ &\quad |(\omega_6) - (\omega_1 \times 4)| \le \xi \\ &\quad |(\omega_6) - (\omega_2 \times 3)| \le \xi \\ &\quad |(\omega_6) - (\omega_3 \times 0.5)| \le \xi \\ &\quad |(\omega_6) - (\omega_4 \times 5)| \le \xi \\ &\quad |(\omega_6) - (\omega_5 \times 2)| \le \xi \\ &\quad \textstyle\sum_{j=1}^{n} \omega_j = 1 \\ &\quad \omega_j \ge 0 \text{ for all } j \end{aligned} \tag{27.21}$$

$$
\begin{aligned}
& Min\ \xi \\
& S.\ t. \\
& |(\omega_6) - (\omega_1 \times 2)| \le \xi \\
& |(\omega_6) - (\omega_2 \times 2)| \le \xi \\
& |(\omega_6) - (\omega_3 \times 0.33)| \le \xi \\
& |(\omega_6) - (\omega_4 \times 3)| \le \xi \\
& |(\omega_6) - (\omega_5 \times 0.5)| \le \xi \\
& \textstyle\sum_{j=1}^{n} \omega_j = 1 \\
& \omega_j \ge 0 \text{ for all } j
\end{aligned}
\tag{27.22}
$$

$$
\begin{aligned}
& Min\ \xi \\
& S.\ t. \\
& |(\omega_4) - (\omega_1 \times 3)| \le \xi \\
& |(\omega_4) - (\omega_2 \times 2)| \le \xi \\
& |(\omega_4) - (\omega_3 \times 9)| \le \xi \\
& |(\omega_4) - (\omega_5 \times 6)| \le \xi \\
& |(\omega_4) - (\omega_6 \times 8)| \le \xi \\
& \textstyle\sum_{j=1}^{n} \omega_j = 1 \\
& \omega_j \ge 0 \text{ for all } j
\end{aligned}
\tag{27.23}
$$

$$
\begin{aligned}
& Min\ \xi \\
& S.\ t. \\
& |(\omega_3) - (\omega_1 \times 0.125)| \le \xi \\
& |(\omega_3) - (\omega_2 \times 0.11)| \le \xi \\
& |(\omega_3) - (\omega_4 \times 0.142)| \le \xi \\
& |(\omega_3) - (\omega_5 \times 0.167)| \le \xi \\
& |(\omega_3) - (\omega_6 \times 0.5)| \le \xi \\
& \textstyle\sum_{j=1}^{n} \omega_j = 1 \\
& \omega_j \ge 0 \text{ for all } j
\end{aligned}
\tag{27.24}
$$

The results of the models are presented in Table 27.9. For instance, the values in column C1 were derived from solving Model 18. Likewise, the data in columns C2 to C7 were obtained by solving Models 19 through 24, respectively. It is important to note that for all models, the value of ξ was 0, indicating complete consistency.

TABLE 27.9 The calculated score for the alternatives considering each criterion.

Criteria Alternatives	C1	C2	C3	C4	C5	C6	C7
A1	0.320	0.102	0.191	0.058	0.068	0.149	0.242
A2	0.195	0.408	0.281	0.078	0.068	0.223	0.274
A3	0.065	0.204	0.145	0.467	0.412	0.05	0.030
A4	0.257	0.068	0.048	0.047	0.045	0.447	0.213
A5	0.034	0.136	0.239	0.117	0.272	0.075	0.181
A6	0.129	0.082	0.096	0.233	0.135	0.056	0.060

TABLE 27.10 The calculated final score of the alternatives.

Alternatives	A1	A2	A3	A4	A5	A6
Final weight	0.181	0.228	0.169	0.179	0.131	0.112

The weights obtained in Table 27.9 are multiplied by the optimal weight of the criteria (Table 27.8) to obtain the final weight of the alternatives. The final weights of the alternatives will be obtained with $\xi = 0$ as shown in Table 27.10. For example, in Table 27.10, the weight of alternative A1 (0.181) is calculated according to (27.25):

$$[0.320\ 0.102\ 0.191\ 0.058\ 0.068\ 0.149\ 0.242] \times \begin{bmatrix} 0.246 \\ 0.145 \\ 0.178 \\ 0.116 \\ 0.079 \\ 0.163 \\ 0.073 \end{bmatrix} = 0.181 \tag{27.25}$$

In this example, considering the dynamic conditions and complex decision-making environment, the weights of the criteria in the three main scenarios were obtained separately using the BCM method. In the operational productivity scenario (S1), the focus was on increasing the speed, accuracy, and efficiency of the organization's internal processes through the use of intelligent tools, with quick access to data (C1) receiving the highest weight, as agility and access to information at the right time are the keys to improving daily performance. In the innovation and marketing scenario (S2), the organization seeks to creatively use data and analytical tools to develop new products, attract customers, and improve its competitive position in the market. In this scenario, innovative use of BI (C2) was identified as the most important criterion, as analytical creativity plays a pivotal role in creating competitive differentiation. In the third scenario, organizational sustainability (S3), the focus is on protecting information, improving data security, maintaining technology infrastructure, and supporting the organization's long-term growth. In this situation, data security and access control (C4) received the highest weight, because protecting information assets and creating a secure infrastructure is a prerequisite for achieving long-term sustainability.

Based on the probability of each scenario occurring, the final optimal weights of the criteria were obtained, showing that C1, C3, and C6 were ranked 1 to 3, respectively. Then, the weight of each alternative in each criterion was obtained. Thus, A1 in the first criterion, A2 in the second, third, and seventh criteria, A3 in the fourth and fifth criteria, and A4 in the sixth criterion obtained the highest weight. By multiplying the final weights of the criteria by the weights of the alternatives, the optimal weights of the alternatives were determined, indicating their ranks. Implementation of Tableau (A2), power BI software (A1), and Google data studio (A4) were ranked first to third, respectively.

27.5 Conclusion

In this chapter, after reviewing previous studies and providing an introduction to the common challenges in ranking alternatives, the SBCM has been developed and discussed. This method, specifically applied in dynamic environmental conditions, works based on the ranking of several different criteria, the importance of each of which varies in different conditions. In this framework, the weight of each criterion is calculated separately for each scenario, as various scenarios influence the criteria. Then, by multiplying the matrix of the obtained weights by the probability of each scenario occurring, the optimal weight of each criterion is obtained. Based on these optimal weights, the alternatives are evaluated and ranked. To demonstrate its applicability, the SBCM method was applied to a numerical example, and its results have been discussed. This example illustrates how SBCM can be utilized in complex and dynamic environments, facilitating decision-making. SBCM can provide reliable results against uncertainties and environmental changes by using dynamic weighting. These features make SBCM an efficient tool for decision-making in changing situations.

One important application of this method in future research is analyzing decisions in uncertain and complex conditions, particularly in the fields of sustainable development and organizational strategic planning. One potential improvement for this method is the integration of fuzzy logic to enhance the accuracy of criterion weighting. Utilizing fuzzy systems enables the development of models that offer greater flexibility, especially when precise and definitive information is lacking.

References

Ahmad, S., Miskon, S., Alabdan, R., & Tlili, I. (2020). Towards sustainable textile and apparel industry: Exploring the role of business intelligence systems in the era of industry 4.0. *Sustainability, 12*(7), 2632. https://doi.org/10.3390/su12072632.

Al-Sai, Z. A., Husin, M. H., Syed-Mohamad, S. M., Abdullah, R., Zitar, R. A., Abualigah, L., & Gandomi, A. H. (2023). Big data maturity assessment models: a systematic literature review. *Big Data and Cognitive Computing, 7*(1), 2. https://doi.org/10.3390/bdcc7010002.

Antoniolli, A. F., Naspolini, H. F., De Abreu, J. F., & Rüther, R. (2022). Development of technical and statistical algorithm using Business Intelligence tools for energy yield assessment of large rooftop photovoltaic system ensembles. *Sustainable Energy Technologies and Assessments, 49*, 101686. https://doi.org/10.1016/j.seta.2021.101686.

Asadabadi, M. R. (2018). The stratified multi-criteria decision-making method. *Knowledge-Based Systems, 162*, 115–123.

Ayough, Ashkan, Shargh, Setareh Boshrouei, & Khorshidvand, Behrooz (2023). A new integrated approach based on base-criterion and utility additive methods and its application to supplier selection problem. *Expert Systems with Applications, 221*, 119740. 10.1016/j.eswa.2023.119740.

Asadabadi, M. R., Ahmadi, H. B., Gupta, H., & Liou, J. J. (2023). Supplier selection to support environmental sustainability: The stratified BWM TOPSIS method. *Annals of Operations Research, 322*(1), 321–344.

Belghith, M., Ammar, H. B., Elloumi, A., & Hachicha, W. (2024). A new rolling forecasting framework using Microsoft Power BI for data visualization: A case study in a pharmaceutical industry. *Annales Pharmaceutiques Françaises, 82*(3), 493–506. https://doi.org/10.1016/j.pharma.2023.10.013.

Bhatia, R., Sharma, A., & Sharma, D. (2025). Embracing the synergy of cloud computing and business intelligence. *Smart Systems: Engineering and Managing Information for Future Success: Navigating the Landscape of Intelligent Technologies,* 191–214. https://doi.org/10.1007/978-3-031-76152-2_12.

Bisht, G., & Pal, A. K. (2023). Functional dependency-based group decision-making with incomplete information under social media influence: An application to automobile. *Journal of Intelligent & Fuzzy Systems, 45*(6), 12341–12363.

Bisht, K., & Kumar, A. (2022). Stock portfolio selection hybridizing fuzzy base-criterion method and evidence theory in triangular fuzzy environment. In *Operations Research Forum, Vol. 3*, Cham: Springer International Publishing, 53 No. 4.

Bukhari, S. M. S., Zafar, M. H., Abou Houran, M., Moosavi, S. K. R., Mansoor, M., Muaaz, M., & Sanfilippo, F. (2024). Secure and privacy-preserving intrusion detection in wireless sensor networks: Federated learning with SCNN-Bi-LSTM for enhanced reliability. *Ad Hoc Networks, 155*, 103407. https://doi.org/10.1016/j.adhoc.2024.103407.

Cho, V., Roll, L. C., Wu, C. H., & Tang, V. (2021). Changing digital age in the wake of COVID-19: How does humility impact on virtual leaderless teams? *Journal of Global Information Management (JGIM), 30*(4), 1–23. https://doi.org/10.4018/JGIM.290831.

Chowdhury, P., & Paul, S. K. (2020). Applications of MCDM methods in research on corporate sustainability: A systematic literature review. *Management of Environmental Quality: An International Journal, 31*(2), 385–405.

Debalki, Y. A., Hou, J., Adane, B. Y., Mawutor, V. G., & Dang, H. (2024). A distributed relay selection using a fuzzy-BCM based decision making strategy for multi-hop data dissemination in VANETs. *Wireless Networks, 30*(4), 2873–2894.

Demir, G., Chatterjee, P., & Pamucar, D. (2024). Sensitivity analysis in multi-criteria decision making: A state-of-the-art research perspective using bibliometric analysis. *Expert Systems with Applications, 237*, 121660.

Dewi, N. L. P. T. K., Nilawati, N. K. U., & Anandita, I. B. G. (2024). Visual analysis of marketplace sales data for strategic decision-making using tableau. *TECHNOVATE: Journal of Information Technology and Strategic Innovation Management, 1*(3), 156–169. https://doi.org/10.52432/technovate.1.3.2024.156-169.

Ecer, F., & Torkayesh, A. E. (2022). A stratified fuzzy decision-making approach for sustainable circular supplier selection. *IEEE Transactions on Engineering Management, 71*, 1130–1144.

Emovon, I., & Oghenenyerovwho, O. S. (2020). Application of MCDM method in material selection for optimal design: A review. *Results in Materials, 7*, 100115. https://doi.org/10.1016/j.rinma.2020.100115.

Guldogan, N., Taskin, F., Icten, G. E., Yilmaz, E., Turk, E. B., Erdemli, S., & Aribal, E. (2024). Artificial intelligence in BI-RADS categorization of breast lesions on ultrasound: can we omit excessive follow-ups and biopsies? *Academic Radiology, 31*(6), 2194–2202. https://doi.org/10.1016/j.acra.2023.11.031.

Harker, P. T. (1987). Incomplete pairwise comparisons in the analytic hierarchy process. *Mathematical Modelling, 9*(11), 837–848.

Haseli, G., Bonab, S. R., Hajiaghaei-Keshteli, M., Ghoushchi, S. J., & Deveci, M. (2024). Fuzzy ZE-numbers framework in group decision-making using the BCM and CoCoSo to address sustainable urban transportation. *Information Sciences, 653*, 119809.

Haseli, G., Nazarian-Jashnabadi, J., Shirazi, B., Hajiaghaei-Keshteli, M., & Moslem, S. (2024). Sustainable strategies based on the social responsibility of the beverage industry companies for the circular supply chain. *Engineering Applications of Artificial Intelligence, 133*, 108253.

Haseli, G., & Jafarzadeh Ghoushchi, S. (2022). Extended base-criterion method based on the spherical fuzzy sets to evaluate waste management. *Soft Computing, 26*(19), 9979–9992.

Haseli, G., & Sheikh, R. (2022). Base criterion method (BCM). In *Multiple criteria decision making: Techniques, analysis and applications*. Singapore: Springer Nature Singapore, 17–38.

Haseli, G., Sheikh, R., & Sana, S. S. (2020a). Base-criterion on multi-criteria decision-making method and its applications. *International Journal of Management Science and Engineering Management, 15*(2), 79–88.

Haseli, G., Sheikh, R., & Sana, S. S. (2020b). Extension of base-criterion method based on fuzzy set theory. *International Journal of Applied and Computational Mathematics, 6*(2), 54.

Haseli, G., Ögel, İ. Y., Ecer, F., & Hajiaghaei-Keshteli, M. (2023). Luxury in female technology (FemTech): Selection of smart jewelry for women through BCM-MARCOS group decision-making framework with fuzzy ZE-numbers. *Technological Forecasting and Social Change, 196*, 122870.

Imran, S.M., Rameshan, N., Anand, M.C. J., Martin, N., Tiwari, M., & Mohan, V. (2024). Fuzzy decision-making on strategies for maximizing the utility of electric vehicles. In *2024 IEEE Third International Conference on Power Electronics, Intelligent Control and Energy Systems (ICPEICES)* (pp. 347-352). IEEE.

Iskandar, I., Maulidiawati, C., Zuliyanto, M., & Arifin, M. (2025). Implementasi bussines intelegent Menggunakan software Google Data Studio (Looker Studio). *JATI (Jurnal Mahasiswa Teknik Informatika), 9*(1), 1417–1422.

Jahantigh, F. F., Habibi, A., & Sarafrazi, A. (2019). A conceptual framework for business intelligence critical success factors. *International Journal of Business Information Systems, 30*(1), 109–123. https://doi.org/10.1504/IJBIS.2019.097058.

Kizielewicz, B., Tomczyk, T., Gandor, M., & Sałabun, W. (2024). Subjective weight determination methods in multi-criteria decision-making: a systematic review. *Procedia Computer Science, 246*, 5396–5407.

Konurhan, Z., Yucesan, M., & Gul, M. (2023). Integrating stratified best–worst method and GIS for landslide susceptibility assessment: a case study in Erzurum province (Turkey). *Environmental Science and Pollution Research, 30*(53), 113978–114000.

Li, Y., Tsang, Y. P., Lee, C. K. M., Zhang, Q., & Chen, Z. S. (2025). Service area identification for robotaxi deployment: A GIS-based spatio-temporal multi-criteria decision support framework. *Transport Policy, 171*, 497–512.

Liu, X., Tan, Y., Dong, J., Wu, J., Wang, X., & Sun, Z. (2025). Assessing habitat selection parameters of Arabica coffee using BWM and BCM methods based on GIS. *Scientific Reports, 15*(1), 8.

Moreno-Solaz, H., Artacho-Ramírez, M.Á., Aragonés-Beltrán, P., & Cloquell-Ballester, V. A. (2023). Sustainable selection of waste collection trucks considering feasible future scenarios by applying the stratified best and worst method. *Heliyon, 9*(4), e15481. https://doi.org/10.1016/j.heliyon.2023.e15481.

Narang, M., Joshi, M. C., & Pal, A. K. (2021). A hybrid fuzzy COPRAS-base-criterion method for multi-criteria decision making. *Soft Computing, 25*, 8391–8399.

Narang, M., Joshi, M. C., & Pal, A. K. (2022). A hesitant fuzzy multiplicative base-criterion multi-criteria group decision making method. *Informatica, 46*(2). https://doi.org/10.31449/inf.v46i2.3452.

Parra, X., Tort-Martorell, X., Alvarez-Gomez, F., & Ruiz-Viñals, C. (2022). Chronological evolution of the information-driven decision-making process (1950–2020). *Journal of the Knowledge Economy*, 1–32. https://doi.org/10.1007/s13132-022-00917-y.

Phulara, S., Kumar, A., Narang, M., & Bisht, K. (2024). A novel hybrid grey-BCM approach in multi-criteria decision making: An application in OTT platform. *Journal of Decision Analytics and Intelligent Computing, 4*(1), 1–15.

Rezaei, J. (2015). Best-worst multi-criteria decision-making method. *Omega, 53*, 49–57.

Saaty, T. L. (1977). A scaling method for priorities in hierarchical structures. *Journal of Mathematical Psychology, 15*(3), 234–281. https://doi.org/10.1016/0022-2496(77)90033-5.

Sotoudeh-Anvari, A. (2022). The applications of MCDM methods in COVID-19 pandemic: A state of the art review. *Applied Soft Computing, 126*, 109238.

Sun, L., Yu, C., Li, J., Yuan, Q., & Zhao, S. (2025). A two-stage decision model for sustainable-resilient supplier selection and order allocation under uncertain environment. *Kybernetes, 54*(8), 4078–4113. https://doi.org/10.1108/K-11-2023-2347.

Tavana, M., Sorooshian, S., Rezaei, H., & Mina, H. (2024). A novel fuzzy scenario-based stochastic general best-worst method. *Expert Systems with Applications, 252*, 124246.

Torkayesh, A. E., Malmir, B., & Asadabadi, M. R. (2021). Sustainable waste disposal technology selection: The stratified best-worst multi-criteria decision-making method. *Waste Management, 122*, 100–112.

Torkayesh, A. E., & Simic, V. (2022). Stratified hybrid decision model with constrained attributes: Recycling facility location for urban healthcare plastic waste. *Sustainable cities and society, 77*, 103543.

Wu, Y., Liu, P., & Li, Y. (2024). An integrated QFD and FMEA method under the co-opetitional relationship for product upgrading. *Information Sciences, 667*, 120505.

Wu, Yifan, Liu, Peide, & Li, Ying (2026). An improved QFD model with the integration of BCM and CoCoSo method under the trust network. *International Journal of Information Technology & Decision Making*. 10.1142/s0219622026500458.

Zafaranlouei, N., Ghoushchi, S. J., & Haseli, G. (2023). Assessment of sustainable waste management alternatives using the extensions of the base criterion method and combined compromise solution based on the fuzzy Z-numbers. *Environmental Science and Pollution Research, 30*(22), 62121–62136.

Chapter 28

BCM tradeoff (BCT): Base criterion tradeoff for multi-attribute decision-making

Javad Nazarian-Jashnabadi[1] and Erfan Babaee Tirkolaee[2]
[1]*Department of Management, Faculty of Economic, Management and Social Science, Shiraz University, Shiraz, Iran,* [2]*Department of Industrial Engineering, Istinye University, Istanbul, Türkiye*

28.1 Introduction

In situations where problems have become complex and multidimensional, the use of scientific decision-making approaches becomes doubly important. These approaches are used in diverse fields such as management, economics, and engineering. In such situations, multicriteria decision-making (MCDM) and its sub-branch, multi-attribute decision-making (MADM), are effective tools for weighting criteria and evaluating options based on various criteria (Zhang et al., 2026). Since the accuracy, efficiency, and consistency of expert judgments play a fundamental role in the validity of the results, and many of these methods are based on pairwise comparisons, choosing an appropriate analytical method becomes very important. Techniques such as the analytic hierarchy process (AHP) (Saaty, 1977), the best–worst method (BWM) (Rezaei, 2015), and the base criterion method (BCM) (Haseli & Sheikh, 2022) weight criteria in the decision-making process. Using an approach appropriate to the nature of the problem prevents semantic ambiguity in the data and also ensures the scientific validity of the analyses and conclusions, and indicates the researcher's deep understanding of the dimensions of the problem (Kumar, 2025).

One of the fundamental challenges in weighting methods is the high number of pairwise comparisons and the resulting inconsistency ratio, because increasing the number of comparisons increases the likelihood of inconsistency in the results. The AHP method, as one of the first weighting techniques, enables the weighting process by using a hierarchical structure and a pairwise comparison matrix, but for n criteria, it requires $[n(n-1)]/2$ comparisons, which is difficult for decision-makers to perform and therefore increases the likelihood of inconsistency (Badi et al., 2023). In this method, the inconsistency ratio is calculated only after the model is analyzed, and in the event of inconsistency, it is necessary to repeat the process of collecting opinions and solving the model

In order to improve the inconsistency ratio and reduce the decision-making pressure, the BWM method was introduced, which reduces the number of comparisons to $2n-3$ by selecting two reference criteria, "best" and "worst", and comparing "bes" with other criteria and other criteria with "worst" (Rezaei, 2015). However, in this method, the inconsistency ratio is also calculated based on the model output, and if inconsistency is observed between pairwise comparisons, it is necessary to repeat the decision-making process. With the introduction of the BCM, the number of pairwise comparisons was reduced to $n-1$, and the inconsistency ratio reached zero. This method achieves full consistency by simultaneously collecting judgments and controlling model inputs (Haseli & Sheikh, 2022). This approach prevents subsequent inconsistencies and eliminates the need to repeat the analysis. For this reason, BCM has become an efficient and reliable tool for MCDM in complex environments compared to AHP and BWM (Haseli et al., 2020b).

The tradeoff method has significant key advantages that make it a valuable option in criteria weighting. This method focuses on the foundations of the multi-attribute value theory (MAVT) and also pays attention to the range of attribute changes in the weighting process (Raiffa & Keeney, 1975). Therefore, it is efficient in situations where the difference between alternatives is small. Furthermore, a clearer assessment of the decision-maker's preferences increases

Encyclopedia of Multi-Attribute Decision-Making (MADM). DOI: https://doi.org/10.1016/B978-0-443-33275-3.00085-3

cognitive accuracy and reduces ambiguities. Recent developments in the field of methodology have also shown that when faced with problems that are accompanied by features such as uncertainty, conflict of interests, or interdependence of criteria, combining methods can improve decision-making effectiveness (Liang et al., 2022). Such conditions highlight the need for approaches that, while having a precise and systematic structure, also have sufficient cognitive flexibility to adapt to real complexities.

Despite the significant advantages of BCM and tradeoff, a hybrid approach can take advantage of their strengths to solve more complex problems. In this framework, the BCM approach reduces the cognitive burden of decision-makers by reducing the number of comparisons and ensuring full consistency, while the tradeoff approach, by focusing on the range of attribute changes and utilizing the principles of MAVT, allows for more nuanced analysis and more accurate extraction of preferences. The synergy of these capabilities has led to the formation of the hybrid base criterion tradeoff (BCT) method.

The rest of this chapter is organized as follows: Section 2 reviews the previous studies. First, the studies conducted on the BCM are reviewed, and then the studies conducted on the tradeoff method are analyzed. Section 3 describes the research methodology, including the steps of implementing the BCT method. Section 4 provides a numerical example to evaluate the effectiveness of the model, and Section 5 presents the conclusions.

28.2 Literature review

In recent years, the BCM and its developments have attracted the attention of the scientific community because it is an efficient approach for weighting criteria and making decisions in complex environments. This method is based on pairwise comparisons, but unlike AHP and BWM, which have a large number of pairwise comparisons, the number of pairwise comparisons in the BCM is minimized, and the consistency of the comparisons is also guaranteed. A growing body of literature has extended BCM to fuzzy (Debalki et al., 2024), spherical fuzzy (Haseli & Ghoushchi, 2022), hesitant fuzzy (Narang et al., 2022), gray (Phulara et al., 2024), and neutrosophic (Sun et al., 2024) environments to handle uncertainty, vagueness, and complexity in real-world decision problems. These methodological advancements have been applied across a wide range of domains, including supply chain management, sustainable development, smart technologies, portfolio optimization, transportation, and energy systems.

Bisht & Pal (2023) emphasized the importance of attribute interdependencies and expert relationships by integrating fuzzy BCM with Vlse Kriterijumsk Optimizacija Kompromisno Resenje (VIKOR) and under the influence of social media, while Bisht & Kumar (2022) developed a hybrid framework for stock portfolio selection by unifying fuzzy BCM and evidence theory. Similarly, Debalki et al. (2024) employed fuzzy BCM for relay selection in vehicular ad-hoc networks, highlighting its role in enhancing dissemination efficiency. In sustainable urban transportation, Haseli, Bonab, et al. (2024) combined fuzzy Z-Extended (ZE) numbers, BCM, and constrained combined compromise solution (CoCoSo) to evaluate alternatives for the transportation crisis. These studies demonstrate the adaptability of BCM in dynamic, information-intensive, and large-scale decision-making environments.

An important area of research is the extension of BCM to fuzzy and uncertain environments. Various studies have extended the method with spherical fuzzy sets, linguistic variables, gray systems, and hybrid approaches such as complex proportional assessment (COPRAS) to better model qualitative judgments and situations with uncertainty (Haseli & Ghoushchi, 2022; Haseli et al., 2020b; Narang et al., 2021; Narang et al., 2022; Phulara et al., 2024). Also, several studies have used BCM in the field of sustainability, circular economy and social responsibility, combining it with methods such as multiattributive border approximation area comparison (), CoCoSo, Tomada de Decisão Interativa e Multicritério (TODIM), quality function deployment (QFD), and failure mode and effects analysis (FMEA) to support supplier selection, supply chain strategy design, and product promotion (Haseli, Sheikh, et al., 2024; Sun et al., 2024; Wu et al., 2024; Zafaranlouei et al., 2023). In addition, BCM has been applied in the field of emerging technologies, agriculture, and cybersecurity, and integrated with tools such as measurement alternatives and ranking according to compromise solution (MARCOS), geographic information systems (GIS), and blockchain (Haseli et al., 2023; Imran et al., 2024; Liu et al., 2025; Narayanan & Paul, 2023). These studies demonstrate the flexibility and broad applicability of BCM in complex decision-making and dynamic environments.

Finally, foundational studies have established BCM's theoretical basis. Haseli & Sheikh (2022) provided a systematic explanation of BCM, highlighting its efficiency and consistency compared to AHP and BWM. These contributions, alongside empirical applications across different domains, confirm BCM's growing importance as a robust and flexible tool for MCDM in both certain and uncertain environments. Table 28.1 presents a summary of studies related to BCM.

The study of tradeoffs in MCDM and MADM has been an important part of decision analysis for decades. Raiffa & Keeney (1975) established one of the first theoretical foundations in the field by formalizing the role of preferences and

TABLE 28.1 Summary of studies on the BCM.

Author and year	Research objective	Fuzzy approach	Methodology	Research area/case study
Wu et al. (2026)	Improvement of the Quality Function Deployment (QFD) model	—	CoCoSo	Production of the computer Numerical Control (CNC) machine
Abdollahi et al. (2026)	Evaluation of sustainable strategies for blockchain	Fuzzy ZE-numbers	DNMA	Solar energy supply chain
Liu et al. (2025)	Assess habitat suitability for Arabica coffee using GIS and MCDM.	—	BWM – BCM	Sustainable agricultural land-use planning
Phulara et al. (2024)	Extend BCM to a gray environment for decision-making under uncertainty.	—	Gray BCM	MCDM under uncertainty/ over-the-top platforms – India
Debalki et al. (2024)	Propose a fuzzy-BCM-based relay selection strategy to enhance data dissemination efficiency.	Original fuzzy set	BCM	Traffic flow
Haseli, Bonab, et al. (2024)	Develop a framework for sustainable urban transportation planning.	Fuzzy ZE-numbers	BCM, CoCoSo	Sustainable urban transportation
Haseli, Nazarian-Jashnabadi, et al. (2024)	Evaluate effective factors and propose sustainable solutions for waste management.	Fuzzy ZE-numbers	BCM, mMABAC	Circular supply chain management/beverage industry
Sun et al. (2024)	Develop a two-stage model for sustainable–resilient supplier selection.	Single-Valued neutrosophic	BCM – TODIM Unified Non-dominated Sorting Genetic Algorithm III (U-NSGA-III*)– TOPSIS*	Supplier selection and procurement optimization
Wu et al. (2024)	Integrate QFD and FMEA for product upgrading, considering customer satisfaction and risk.	Interval-Valued Intuitionistic Fuzzy Set (IVIFS)	BCM – CoCoSo – TODIM	Product improvement and risk management
Imran et al. (2024)	Propose strategies to maximize the utility of electric vehicles.	Trapezoidal fuzzy numbers	BCM	Strategic planning and environmental sustainability
Zafaranlouei et al. (2023)	Rank sustainable waste management alternatives.	Fuzzy Z-number	BCM, CoCoSo	Sustainable waste management
Narayanan and Paul (2023)	Enhance intrusion detection in IoT using blockchain-based federated learning.	—	BCM – neural networks	Security and privacy in IoT environments
Bisht and Pal (2023)	Develop a model that captures attribute dependencies and incorporates social media influence on alternative ranking.	—	Decision-Making Trial and Evaluation Laboratory (DEMATEL) – BCM – VIKOR	MCDM model development/ electronics industry
Haseli et al. (2023)	Select the best smart jewelry for women.	Fuzzy ZE-numbers	BCM, MARCOS	Female technology– smart jewelry

(*Continued*)

TABLE 28.1 (Continued)

Author and year	Research objective	Fuzzy approach	Methodology	Research area/case study
Haseli and Sheikh (2022)	Explain the BCM for obtaining optimal criteria weights with fewer pairwise comparisons.	—	BCM	MCDM model development
Narang et al. (2022)	Propose a hesitant fuzzy multiplicative BCM for group decision-making.	Hesitant fuzzy	BCM	Transportation mode selection, car selection
Bisht and Kumar (2022)	Create an MCDM framework to assist novice investors in stock selection.	Original fuzzy Set	BCM – Long Short-Term Memory (LSTM)*	Portfolio selection
Haseli and Ghoushchi (2022)	Extend BCM using spherical fuzzy sets for uncertain and ambiguous environments.	Spherical fuzzy	BCM	Waste management (location selection in Tabriz)
Narang et al. (2021)	Develop a fuzzy approach for stock portfolio selection under uncertainty.	Triangular fuzzy numbers	BCM – cCOPRAS	Financial decision-making under uncertainty
Haseli et al. (2020b)	Extend BCM to uncertain circumstances.	Original fuzzy Set	BCM	Decision-making under uncertainty

value tradeoffs, providing the basis for MAVT. Building on this work, subsequent research has explored both theoretical refinements and practical methods for extracting and applying tradeoffs in a variety of contexts. These studies have addressed topics such as behavioral complexities in weight extraction (Weber & Borcherding, 1993), comparing alternative weighting methods (Borcherding et al., 1991), developing flexible frameworks such as flexible and interactive tradeoff (de Almeida et al., 2016, 2021), investigating behavioral biases such as loss aversion (Bleichrodt & Pinto, 2002), and identifying common mistakes in value extraction (Keeney, 2002). New hybrid and fuzzy approaches have also been proposed for prioritization and decision-making in complex environments (Jaini & Utyuzhnikov, 2017a, 2017b; Jankowski et al., 2019; Liang et al., 2022). The details of these studies are fully presented in Table 28.2.

28.3 Methodology

In this section, the BCT method, a significant new development in the BCM framework, is introduced. Since the BCM, similar to AHP, analytic network process (Saaty, 1996), and BWM, is based on pairwise comparisons, the concept of inconsistency of pairwise comparisons in this method is also important. Two types of inconsistency in comparisons are inconsistency in direction and inconsistency in the strength of pairwise comparisons. Inconsistency in direction occurs when the relative importance of criteria is incorrectly reversed, such as when C1 is more important than C2, and C2 is more important than C3, but C3 is incorrectly considered more important than C1. For example, if C1 is more important than C2 and C2 is more important than C3, we expect C1 to be more important than C3, and if this is not the case, then inconsistency in direction has occurred. Inconsistency in strength occurs when the decision-maker inaccurately assigns numerical values to the importance of criteria, leading to errors in the expected proportional relationships. For example, if the relative importance of C1 to C2 is 2 (on a scale of 1 to 9) and the importance of C2 to C3 is 1, then the relative importance of C1 to C3 should be 2. Therefore, the decision-maker should ensure consistency in the numerical values assigned to the relative importance of criteria. Otherwise, inconsistency in strength occurs (Haseli & Sheikh, 2022).

In the AHP and BWM methods, the consistency ratio is calculated after solving the model using the outputs. If this ratio exceeds the threshold, the decision-maker must reconsider the pairwise comparisons and repeat the solution process (Rezaei, 2015; Saaty, 1977; Chakraborty et al., 2024). BCM significantly reduces the number of pairwise comparisons and provides a framework where model inputs are controlled, so it prevents inconsistencies in the comparisons. As a result of the controlled framework in BCM, the inconsistency ratio is always zero, ensuring full consistency in pairwise comparisons. The inconsistency control framework in this method is explained below.

28.3.1 Base criterion method framework for consistency control

Suppose there are n criteria whose relative importance needs to be evaluated. The pairwise comparison matrix is defined as shown in Eq. (28.1):

$$A = \begin{bmatrix} a_{11} & a_{12} & \cdots & a_{1n} \\ a_{21} & a_{22} & \cdots & a_{2n} \\ \vdots & \vdots & \ddots & \vdots \\ a_{m1} & a_{m2} & \cdots & a_{mn} \end{bmatrix}, \tag{28.1}$$

where a_{ij} represents the relative importance of criterion i compared with criterion j, measured on a numerical scale from 1/9 to 9. A reciprocal relation holds such that $a_{ij} = 1 / a_{ji}$. If the two criteria are of equal importance, then $a_{ij} = 1$.

In BCM, two types of comparisons are distinguished. a_{ij} is a "Base Comparison" when criterion i is selected as the base, and a_{ij} is a "Final Comparison" when neither i nor j is the base criterion (Haseli & Sheikh, 2022). The decision-maker first provides values for the base comparisons. Since the final comparisons can be derived from these, specifying them explicitly is not necessary for estimating weights. (28.2) guarantees both directional and proportional consistency. To preserve validity, the decision-maker must assign base comparison values so that all derived final comparisons fall within the scale of 1/9 to 9.

$$a_{Base,i} \times a_{ij} = a_{Base,j} \tag{28.2}$$

The final comparison a_{ij} is calculated as expressed in (28.3). Accordingly, BCM focuses on minimizing inconsistency by constraining the input values. Enforcing (28.3) ensures full consistency in both the direction and strength of the pairwise comparisons (Haseli et al., 2020a):

$$a_{Base,i} \times a_{ij} = a_{Base,j};\ a_{ij} = \frac{a_{Base,j}}{a_{Base,i}},$$

TABLE 28.2 Summary of studies on the tradeoff method.

Author and year	Research objective	Fuzzy approach	Methodology	Research area/case study
Liang et al. (2022)	To develop the best-worst tradeoff method (BWTO), combining the strengths of BWM and the tradeoff methods while addressing consistency and attribute range issues.	—	BWM + tradeoff	General MADM applications
Kheybari (2021)	To adjust tradeoffs in MCDM by introducing upper and lower expectation levels.	—	Expectation levels approach in MCDM	Cellphone selection case study
de Almeida et al. (2021)	Enhance the FITradeoff method by combining holistic and decomposition paradigms.	—	FITradeoff method	General MCDM applications
Jankowski et al. (2019)	Apply a multiple criteria tradeoff approach to spatial alternative screening.	—	MCDM + GIS	Spatial decision-making
Jaini and Utyuzhnikov (2017a)	Present fuzzy tradeoff ranking method	Triangular fuzzy numbers	Fuzzy Tradeoff, fuzzy TOPSIS, fuzzy VIKOR	Fuzzy MCDM problems
Jaini and Utyuzhnikov (2017b)	Develop a tradeoff ranking method to automatically rank Pareto solutions.	—	Tradeoff ranking method in MCDM; directed search domain algorithm	Pareto frontier analysis
de Almeida et al. (2016)	Propose the FITradeoff method to reduce decision-maker effort in eliciting criteria weights.	—	FITradeoff method	Supplier selection
Bleichrodt and Pinto (2002)	Examine loss aversion and scale compatibility in tradeoffs.	—	Experimental study; utility measurement	Medical decision-making
Keeney (2002)	Identify common mistakes in making value tradeoffs.	—	Prescriptive analysis	General MCDM applications
Weber and Borcherding (1993)	Review behavioral influences on weight judgments in MADM.	—	Literature review	General MADM applications
Borcherding et al. (1991)	Compare four weighting methods for multi-attribute utility measurement	—	Ratio method, swing weighting, tradeoff method, pricing out method	Nuclear waste repository site evaluation
Raiffa and Keeney (1975)	Present theory and procedures for decision analysis with multiple conflicting objectives.	—	MAVT; tradeoff methods	Various applied contexts

and

$$\frac{1}{9} \le \frac{a_{Base,j}}{a_{Base,i}} \le 9 \; or \; \frac{1}{9} \le a_{ij} \le 9, \;\; \forall\, j = 2, \;\; \ldots, \; n, \;\; \forall\, i = 1, \;\; \ldots, j - 1 \tag{28.3}$$

28.3.2 Steps of implementing the base criterion tradeoff method

To implement the BCT method, several steps must be taken. First, the alternatives and attributes are determined by the decision-maker. Then, a value function is determined for each attribute. Next, one of the attributes is selected as the base criterion, and pairwise comparisons of the other attributes with the base criterion are performed. Finally, the optimal weights of the attributes are obtained using a mathematical model. The steps of implementing this method are explained in detail.

Step 1. Alternatives and attributes determination.

In the first step, the alternatives and attributes of the problem must be identified. This step can be done by consulting experts or past studies on the problem under consideration. After determining the alternatives and attributes, primary data that shows the performance of each alternative in different attributes must be collected.

Step 2. Value function determination.

For each of the attributes of the problem, a value function is determined. There are various methods available in the literature to determine the value function (Dyer & Sarin, 1979; Greco et al., 2016; Raiffa & Keeney, 1975). Here, the method presented by Raiffa and Keeney (1975) is used, which is the mid-value splitting technique.

- First, the lowest attribute level (x_0) is set to 0, and the highest attribute level (x_1) is set to 1.
- Next, the midpoint of the interval [x_0, x_1] is calculated and denoted as $x_{0.5}$, with an assigned value of 0.5.
- Then, the midpoint of [x_0, $x_{0.5}$] is obtained, denoted as $x_{0.25}$, and assigned the value 0.25.
- Similarly, the midpoint of [$x_{0.5}$, x_1] is determined, denoted as $x_{0.75}$, and assigned the value 0.75.
- To verify the consistency of the decision-maker's preferences, it must be checked whether $x_{0.5}$ truly lies between $x_{0.25}$ and $x_{0.75}$; if not, adjustments should be made.
- Finally, using the five reference points—(x_0, 0), ($x_{0.25}$, 0.25), ($x_{0.5}$, 0.5), ($x_{0.75}$, 0.75), and (x_1, 1)—the value function for the attribute can be constructed. This function serves as a key foundation for further decision-making analysis.

Step 3. Base criterion identification.

In this step, the decision-maker selects one attribute as the base criterion (C_{Base}). Any attribute can be chosen as the base, and it does not necessarily have to be the most important or the best attribute. Hence, this step is entirely based on the decision-maker's preference.

Step 4. Compare the base criterion to others tradeoffs.

In this step, the base criterion C_{Base} is compared with other criteria. For this purpose, several auxiliary hypothetical consequences are created. If, for a given comparison between C_{Base} and another attribute C_k ($k \neq Base$), the base criterion is more important than the criterion k from the decision-maker's perspective, the two consequences are defined as follows:

- In the first consequence $x^{Base,k}$, the performance level of the base criterion C_{Base} is yet to be defined, while all other attributes are fixed at their minimum level $v_j(\underline{x}_j) = 0$.
- In the second consequence x^k, the kth attribute (C_k) is set to its maximum level $v_k(\overline{x}_k) = 1$, with all remaining attributes kept at their minimum level $v_j(\underline{x}_j) = 0$.

Similarly, if, for a given comparison between C_{Base} and another attribute C_k ($k \neq Base$), the criterion k is more important than the base criterion from the decision-maker's perspective, the two consequences are defined as follows:

- The first consequence ($x^{k,Base}$) corresponds to the situation where the level of C_k remains unspecified, while all other attributes are fixed at their minimum values ($v_j(\underline{x}_j) = 0$).
- The second consequence (x^{Base}) represents the case in which the base criterion C_{Base} is assigned the maximum value ($v_{Base}(\overline{x}_{Base}) = 1$), whereas all remaining attributes are set to their minimum values ($v_j(\underline{x}_j) = 0$).

The decision-maker is then asked to determine the level of performance C_{Base} at the consequence $x^{Base,k}$, and the level of performance C_k at the consequence $x^{k,Base}$, such that $x^{Base,k} \sim x^k$ and $x^{k,Base} \sim x^{Base}$; where ~ indicates indifference between the two consequences. Using the aggregate value function, this level corresponds to the ratio between the weights w_k and w_{Base}. The results of these comparisons are represented as a base comparison vector $a_{Base,j}$ using (28.4):

$$a_{Base,j} = (a_{Base,1}, \; a_{Base,2}, \; \ldots, \; a_{Base,n}) \tag{28.4}$$

Step 5. Find the optimal weights.

After the base comparisons are performed and the base comparison vector $a_{Base,k}$ is formed, an optimization model is created according to Model (5) that obtains the attribute weight vector:

$$\begin{aligned} &\min \max_j \{ \left| W_j a_{Base,j} - W_{Base} \right|, \left| W_{Base} a_{Base,j} - W_j \right| \} \\ &W_1 + W_2 + \ldots + W_n = 1, \\ &W_j \geq 0, \; j = 1, \; 2, \; \ldots, n \end{aligned} \tag{28.5}$$

The Model (28.5) can be rewritten as the Model (28.6):

$$\begin{aligned} &\min \; \xi \\ &\text{subject to} \left| W_j a_{Base,j} - W_{Base} \right| \leq \xi, \;\text{if } C_{Base} \text{ is more important than } C_j, \\ &\left| W_{Base} a_{Base,j} - W_j \right| \leq \xi, \;\text{if } C_{Base} \text{ is less important than } C_j, \\ &W_1 + W_2 + \ldots + W_n = 1, \\ &W_j \geq 0, \;\; j = 1, \; 2, \; \ldots, \; n \end{aligned} \tag{28.6}$$

28.4 Numerical example

Due to the growing demand for energy and the need to transition from fossil fuels to renewable energy sources, selecting the right location for solar power plant construction has become a strategic and multicriteria decision. Each potential site has its own characteristics, advantages, and limitations that can affect the success of the project. In this regard, seven alternatives, including desert areas, semi-agricultural land, abandoned industrial zones, city peripheries, unused government land, foothill areas, and coastal plains, are considered as potential alternatives. Each of these options is evaluated based on a set of key attributes so that the best location can be selected.

The attributes considered include "Solar Irradiance (C1)" (to measure energy generation capacity), "Land Cost (C2)" (to assess the feasibility of the project), "Transmission Line Capacity (C3)" (to facilitate technical feasibility and reduce the need for additional investment), "Distance to Nearest Road (C4)" (to facilitate transportation and logistics), "Employment Potential (C5)" (to enhance local socioeconomic impacts), "Government Incentives (C6)" (to facilitate implementation and increase economic efficiency), and "Population Density (C7)" (to understand are social challenges, land acquisition costs, and the level of social resistance).

The main challenge in this problem is the conflict between the attributes. For example, areas with high radiation (such as deserts) may have high transportation and accessibility costs, while areas close to the transmission network or roads may have higher land costs or higher population density. On the other hand, government support policies and job creation capacity can influence the final choice. In this regard, the purpose of this example is to rank alternatives based on attributes. Based on step 1 of the BCT method, the alternatives and attributes of the problem were identified and are listed in Tables 28.3 and 28.4, respectively.

In the second step of implementing the BCT method, it is necessary to determine a value function for each of the attributes. This is done using the mid-value splitting technique and is shown in Table 28.5.

According to step 3, the decision-maker selected the third attribute, "Transmission Line Capacity", as the base criterion. In step 4, the decision-maker compares the base criterion with the others. The decision-maker believes that the base criterion is less important than the first criterion and more important than the other criteria; therefore, the second two consequences stated in step 4 are used to compare the base criterion with the first criterion, while the first two consequences of step 4 are used to compare the base criterion with the other criteria. In this step, the following consequences are created:

$$x^{1,3} \sim x^3 \leftrightarrow (x^1, \; 60000, \; 5, \; 15, \; 1, \; 1, \; 800) \sim (2.5, \; 60000, \; 150, \; 15, \; 1, \; 1, \; 800),$$

$$x^{3,2} \sim x^2 \leftrightarrow (2.5, \; 60000, \; x^{3,2}, \; 15, \; 1, \; 1, \; 800) \sim (2.5, \; 10000, \; 5, \; 15, \; 1, \; 1, \; 800),$$

$$x^{3,4} \sim x^4 \leftrightarrow (2.5, \; 60000, \; x^{3,4}, \; 15, \; 1, \; 1, \; 800) \sim (2.5, \; 60000, \; 5, \; 0.5, \; 1, \; 1, \; 800),$$

$$x^{3,5} \sim x^5 \leftrightarrow (2.5, \; 60000, \; x^{3,5}, \; 15, \; 1, \; 1, \; 800) \sim (2.5, \; 60000, \; 5, \; 15, \; 10, \; 1, \; 800),$$

$$x^{3,6} \sim x^6 \leftrightarrow (2.5, \; 60000, \; x^{3,6}, \; 15, \; 1, \; 1, \; 800) \sim (2.5, \; 60000, \; 5, \; 15, \; 1, \; 10, \; 800),$$

TABLE 28.3 Available alternatives for solar site selection.

Code	Alternatives	Description
A1	Desert area	High solar radiation, cheap land, limited road access, very low population density, high capacity of job creation, and limited to the construction period.
A2	Semi-agricultural land	Proper radiation, moderate land cost, good road access, and relatively close transmission capacity, but there is a possibility of social resistance.
A3	Abandoned industrial zone	Cheap and ready land, excellent road and transmission network access, a high surrounding population, and often more government incentives for the revitalization of industrial areas.
A4	Urban fringe	Proximity to the power grid and road, relatively high land cost, medium to high population density, high local employment, and modest incentives.
A5	Unused government land	Very low or free land costs, relatively decent access, high government incentives, low population density, and good opportunity for job creation.
A6	Foothill area	Moderate to good radiation, cheap land, more difficult road access, energy transition requiring additional investment, and low population density.
A7	Coastal plain	Suitable radiation, semi-expensive land (dependent on tourism and agriculture), moisture and corrosion of challenging equipment, good transportation access, and high employment opportunities.

TABLE 28.4 Evaluation attributes for solar site selection.

Code	Attribute	Explain	Type
C1	Solar irradiance (kWh/m²/day)	Represents the average daily solar radiation received per square meter, calculated on an annual basis, and used to estimate potential energy generation.	Beneficial
C2	Land cost (€/ha)	Denotes the acquisition cost of land for project development.	Nonbeneficial
C3	Transmission line capacity (MW)	Reflects the capacity of the nearest transmission line to carry generated electricity without requiring additional infrastructure investment.	Beneficial
C4	Distance to nearest road (km)	Assesses site accessibility by measuring the distance to the nearest road, influencing material transport, equipment delivery, and overall logistics.	Nonbeneficial
C5	Employment potential (score 1–10)	Indicates the employment opportunities created during construction, operation, and administration, taking into account regional labor demand and unemployment rates.	Beneficial
C6	Government incentives (score 1–10)	Captures the level of policy incentives such as subsidies, tax benefits, priority grid access, and expedited approval processes.	Beneficial
C7	Population density (persons/km²)	Refers to the area's population density, which can raise land costs, lead to social resistance, and complicate project execution due to possible resettlements.	Nonbeneficial

$$x^{3,7} \sim x^7 \leftrightarrow (2.5,\ 60000,\ x^{3,7},\ 15,\ 1,\ 1,\ 800) \sim (2.5,\ 60000,\ 5,\ 15,\ 1,\ 1,\ 25).$$

The decision-maker evaluated the consequences and proposed the following values:

$$(x^1,\ x^{3,2},\ x^{3,3},\ x^{3,4},\ x^{3,5},\ x^{3,6},\ x^{3,7}) = (4.75,\ 130,\ 150,\ 90,\ 78,\ 110,\ 75).$$

TABLE 28.5 The mid-value points for alternatives.

Code	Min (0%)	25%	50%	75%	Max (100%)
C1	2.50	3.25	4.00	4.75	5.50
C2	60,000	47,500	35,000	22,500	10,000
C3	5.00	41.25	77.50	113.75	150
C4	15.00	11.375	7.750	4.125	0.50
C5	1	3.25	5.50	7.75	10
C6	1	3.25	5.50	7.75	10
C7	800	606.25	412.50	218.75	25

The values determined by the decision-maker are normalized according to the attribute value function. It should be noted that the first attribute value function should be used for the first value, and the base criterion value function should be used for the remaining values. After normalization, the base comparison vector $a_{Base,k}$ was obtained as follows:

$$a_{Base,k} = (0.750,\ 0.862,\ 0.586,\ 0.503,\ 0.724,\ 0.483).$$

In the last step, the mathematical model of the problem was created to determine the optimal weight of the attributes as follows:

$$\begin{aligned}
&\min \xi \\
&\text{subject to} |1.33W_3 - W_1| \le \xi, \\
&|1.16W_2 - W_3| \le \xi, \\
&|1.7W_4 - W_3| \le \xi, \\
&|1.98W_5 - W_3| \le \xi, \\
&|1.38W_6 - W_3| \le \xi, \\
&|2.07W_7 - W_3| \le \xi, \\
&W_1 + W_2 + W_3 + W_4 + W_5 + W_6 + W_7 = 1, \\
&W_j \ge 0,\ \ j = 1,\ 2,\ \ldots,\ 7.
\end{aligned}$$

Solving this model, the value of ξ was obtained as zero, which, as mentioned in Section 3.1, is fully consistent. The weight of each attribute was also obtained by solving the model as follows:

$$w = (0.243,\ 0.157,\ 0.182,\ 0.107,\ 0.092,\ 0.131,\ 0.088)$$

In the next step, the decision-maker evaluated each alternative. To do this, the decision-maker assigned a value to the alternatives in each attribute, considering the minimum and maximum values of each attribute. Table 28.6 reports the evaluation of alternatives based on the attributes.

Finally, the evaluation values of the alternatives were normalized by the value functions associated with each attribute. The normalized values were then multiplied by the attribute weights to obtain the aggregate score of each alternative. Table 28.7 presents the results of this step and the final ranking of the alternatives. For example, the calculations related to normalizing the values of Alternative A1 in Table 28.7 are as follows:

$$C1 \rightarrow \frac{x_{11} - \min_{C1}}{\max_{C1} - \min_{C1}} = \frac{5.25 - 2.5}{5.5 - 2.5} = 0.917$$

$$C2 \rightarrow \frac{x_{12} - \min_{C2}}{\max_{C2} - \min_{C2}} = \frac{12000 - 60000}{10000 - 60000} = 0.960$$

TABLE 28.6 Evaluation of alternatives based on the attributes.

	C1	C2	C3	C4	C5	C6	C7
A1	5.25	12,000	45	13.75	3.85	6	30
A2	5	35,000	115	4.25	6	6.25	220
A3	3.75	12,500	145	1	9.5	9	750
A4	3.65	55,000	140	1	9.75	6	600
A5	4.45	13,000	120	4.5	8	9.25	35
A6	4.5	24,000	42	12	3.5	3.5	220
A7	4.75	45,000	117	1	8	5.75	420
Max	5.5	10,000	150	0.5	10	10	25
Min	2.5	60,000	5	15	1	1	800

TABLE 28.7 Final ranking of the alternatives.

	C1	C2	C3	C4	C5	C6	C7	Score	Ranking
A1	0.917	0.960	0.276	0.086	0.317	0.556	0.994	0.622	5
A2	0.833	0.500	0.759	0.741	0.556	0.583	0.748	0.692	3
A3	0.417	0.950	0.966	0.966	0.944	0.889	0.065	0.738	2
A4	0.383	0.100	0.931	0.966	0.972	0.556	0.258	0.567	6
A5	0.650	0.940	0.793	0.724	0.778	0.917	0.987	0.806	1
A6	0.667	0.720	0.255	0.207	0.278	0.278	0.748	0.471	7
A7	0.750	0.300	0.772	0.966	0.778	0.528	0.490	0.657	4

$$C3 \rightarrow \frac{x_{13} - \min_{C3}}{\max_{C3} - \min_{C3}} = \frac{45 - 5}{150 - 5} = 0.276$$

$$C4 \rightarrow \frac{x_{14} - \min_{C4}}{\max_{C4} - \min_{C4}} = \frac{13.75 - 15}{0.5 - 15} = 0.086$$

$$C5 \rightarrow \frac{x_{15} - \min_{C5}}{\max_{C5} - \min_{C5}} = \frac{3.85 - 1}{10 - 1} = 0.317$$

$$C6 \rightarrow \frac{x_{16} - \min_{C6}}{\max_{C6} - \min_{C6}} = \frac{6 - 1}{10 - 1} = 0.556$$

$$C7 \rightarrow \frac{x_{17} - \min_{C7}}{\max_{C7} - \min_{C7}} = \frac{30 - 800}{25 - 800} = 0.994$$

Also, the score of Alternative A1 in Table 28.7 is calculated by multiplying the above values by the weight of the attributes as follows:

$$[0.917\ 0.960\ 0.276\ 0.086\ 0.317\ 0.556\ 0.994] \times \begin{bmatrix} 0.243 \\ 0.157 \\ 0.182 \\ 0.107 \\ 0.092 \\ 0.131 \\ 0.088 \end{bmatrix} = 0.622$$

Based on the ranking results, Alternative A5 (government unused land) ranked first with the highest score (0.806). This location emerged as the most suitable choice due to its almost free land cost, relatively good accessibility, strong governmental incentives, and low population density, which together make it ideal for large-scale solar power projects. Alternative A3 (abandoned industrial zone) came in second with a score of 0.738. This Alternative has significant advantages due to its low land cost, good access to roads and the electricity grid, and the availability of government support for the regeneration of brownfields. However, the relatively high population density around it could create social and environmental challenges.

In third place, Alternative A2 (semi-agricultural land) scored 0.692, offering adequate solar irradiance, moderate land cost, and good transportation access. Despite its technical feasibility, the risk of social resistance due to the land's agricultural use slightly reduced its rank. Alternative A7 (coastal plain) ranked fourth with a score of 0.657, benefiting from strong accessibility and high employment potential, though challenges such as equipment corrosion caused by humidity and relatively higher land costs limited its attractiveness.

Alternative A1 (desert area), with a score of 0.622, ranked fifth. While it offers excellent solar irradiance and cheap land, limited transportation access restricts its long-term socioeconomic value. Alternative A4 (urban fringe), with a score of 0.567, ranked sixth. Despite strong access to power grids and transportation and high potential for local employment, high land costs and population density reduce its overall feasibility. Finally, Alternative A6 (foothill areas), with the lowest score (0.471), ranked last due to its difficult road access and additional investment needs for energy transmission, despite offering relatively affordable land and acceptable irradiance.

28.5 Conclusion

This chapter describes BCT, which is a designed and novel method in the field of MADM. By using BCM and Tradeoff methods simultaneously, BCT has been able to integrate the key advantages of both approaches and overcome their shortcomings and limitations. This approach reduces the number of pairwise comparisons and makes the weighting of criteria more realistic and more sensitive to environmental changes, because the actual range of changes in the criteria is taken into account in this process.

Due to the advantages of the BCT method in dynamic, complex, and ambiguous environments, it has become an unmatched and valuable tool that is widely used in solving real problems. In such environments, an appropriate decision-making tool should be both simple and efficient and should be able to accurately capture the subjective preferences of decision-makers and allow for analysis of their compatibility. BCT is also highly flexible, easy to learn, and provides reliable performance under uncertain and dynamic conditions. These features make it particularly effective in situations where the alternatives are very similar or where small differences between criteria are important, making it a desirable approach for prospective research designed in unstable environments.

To investigate the practical application of the BCT method, a case study was conducted on the selection of the optimal location for the construction of a solar power plant. In this assessment, seven main criteria including "Solar Irradiance (C1)," "Land Cost (C2)," "Transmission Line Capacity (C3)," "Distance to Nearest Road (C4)," "Employment Potential (C5)," "Government Incentives (C6)" and "Population Density (C7)" were selected as decision-making criteria. After weighting these criteria using the BCT method, seven alternatives, including desert areas, semi-agricultural lands, abandoned industrial zones, urban fringes, unused government land, foothill areas, and coastal plains, were analyzed and ranked.

Based on the results, the highest-scoring alternative, A5 (unused government land), was identified as the most suitable option for building a solar power plant. A combination of features, such as almost zero land costs, easy access, strong government incentives, and low population density, makes this location ideal for large projects. The second alternative,

A3 (abandoned industrial zone), came in second place due to its low land costs, excellent access to road networks and power lines, and government support for the revitalization of industrial areas, although the high population density around it can create social and environmental challenges. Third place went to A2 (semi-agricultural land), which has significant technical advantages with good sunlight and good access, but the possibility of social resistance due to agricultural land use has reduced its score.

The analysis of the alternatives, considering seven key criteria, showed that the selection of the optimal location is a complex and multicriteria process, each option has different advantages and limitations, and decision-making is not possible based on superficial observation alone. The BCT method, with its ability to accurately weight the criteria, reduces the cognitive complexity of decision-makers and provides simultaneous analysis of feature matching. Thus, this method provides a very effective tool for strategic and forward-looking decision-making in unstable environments.

References

Abdollahi, S., Ghoushchi, S. J., & Haseli, G. (2026). Evaluation of sustainable strategies for implementing blockchain technology in the solar energy supply chain under fuzzy ZE-numbers. *Applied Soft Computing, 189*, 114522. https://doi.org/10.1016/j.asoc.2025.114522.

Badi, I., Pamučar, D., Stević, Ž., & Muhammad, L. J. (2023). Wind farm site selection using BWM-AHP-MARCOS method: A case study of Libya. *Scientific African, 19*, e01511.

Bisht, G., & Pal, A. K. (2023). Functional dependency-based group decision-making with incomplete information under social media influence: An application to automobile. *Journal of Intelligent & Fuzzy Systems, 45*(6), 12341–12363.

Bisht, K., & Kumar, A. (2022). Stock portfolio selection hybridizing fuzzy base-criterion method and evidence theory in triangular fuzzy environment. In *Operations research forum*. Cham: Springer International Publishing, 53 (Vols. 3, 4).

Bleichrodt, H., & Pinto, J. L. (2002). Loss aversion and scale compatibility in two-attribute trade-offs. *Journal of Mathematical Psychology, 46*(3), 315–337.

Borcherding, K., Eppel, T., & Von Winterfeldt, D. (1991). Comparison of weighting judgments in multiattribute utility measurement. *Management Science, 37*(12), 1603–1619.

Chakraborty, S., & Saha, A. K. (2024). Selection of forklift unit for transport handling using integrated mcdm under neutrosophic environment. *Facta Universitatis, Series: Mechanical Engineering,* 235. https://doi.org/10.22190/fume220620039c.

de Almeida, A. T., de Almeida, J. A., Costa, A. P. C. S., & de Almeida-Filho, A. T. (2016). A new method for elicitation of criteria weights in additive models: Flexible and interactive tradeoff. *European Journal of Operational Research, 250*(1), 179–191.

de Almeida, A. T., Frej, E. A., & Roselli, L. R. P. (2021). Combining holistic and decomposition paradigms in preference modeling with the flexibility of FITradeoff. *Central European Journal of Operations Research, 29*(1), 7–47.

Debalki, Y. A., Hou, J., Adane, B. Y., Mawutor, V. G., & Dang, H. (2024). A distributed relay selection using a fuzzy-BCM based decision making strategy for multi-hop data dissemination in VANETs. *Wireless Networks, 30*(4), 2873–2894.

Dyer, J. S., & Sarin, R. K. (1979). Measurable multiattribute value functions. *Operations Research, 27*(4), 810–822.

Greco, S., Figueira, J., & Ehrgott, M. (2016). *Multiple criteria decision analysis*. springer (Vol. 37).

Haseli, G., & Ghoushchi, S. J. (2022). Extended base-criterion method based on the spherical fuzzy sets to evaluate waste management. *Soft Computing, 26*(19), 9979–9992.

Haseli, G., & Sheikh, R. (2022). Base criterion method (BCM). In *Multiple criteria decision making: Techniques, Analysis and Applications*. Springer Nature Singapore, 17–38.

Haseli, G., Bonab, S. R., Hajiaghaei-Keshteli, M., Ghoushchi, S. J., & Deveci, M. (2024). Fuzzy ZE-numbers framework in group decision-making using the BCM and CoCoSo to address sustainable urban transportation. *Information Sciences, 653*, 119809.

Haseli, G., Nazarian-Jashnabadi, J., Shirazi, B., Hajiaghaei-Keshteli, M., & Moslem, S. (2024). Sustainable strategies based on the social responsibility of the beverage industry companies for the circular supply chain. *Engineering Applications of Artificial Intelligence, 133*, 108253.

Haseli, G., Ögel, İ. Y., Ecer, F., & Hajiaghaei-Keshteli, M. (2023). Luxury in female technology (FemTech): Selection of smart jewelry for women through BCM-MARCOS group decision-making framework with fuzzy ZE-numbers. *Technological Forecasting and Social Change, 196*, 122870.

Haseli, G., Sheikh, R., & Sana, S. S. (2020a). Base-criterion on multi-criteria decision-making method and its applications. *International journal of management science and engineering management, 15*(2), 79–88.

Haseli, G., Sheikh, R., & Sana, S. S. (2020b). Extension of base-criterion method based on fuzzy set theory. *International Journal of Applied and Computational Mathematics, 6*(2), 54.

Imran, S. M., Rameshan, N., Anand, M. C. J., Martin, N., Tiwari, M., & Mohan, V. (2024). Fuzzy decision-making on strategies for maximizing the utility of electric vehicles. In *2024 IEEE Third International Conference on Power Electronics, Intelligent Control and Energy Systems (ICPEICES)*. IEEE, 347–352.

Jaini, N. I., & Utyuzhnikov, S. V. (2017a). A fuzzy trade-off ranking method for multi-criteria decision-making. *Axioms, 7*(1), 1.

Jaini, N., & Utyuzhnikov, S. (2017b). Trade-off ranking method for multi-criteria decision analysis. *Journal of Multi-Criteria Decision Analysis, 24*(3-4), 121–132.

Jankowski, P., Lotov, A. V., & Gusev, D. (2019). Application of a multiple criteria trade-off approach to spatial decision making. In *Spatial multicriteria decision making and analysis*. Routledge, 127–148.

Keeney, R. L. (2002). Common mistakes in making value trade-offs. *Operations Research, 50*(6), 935–945.
Kheybari, S. (2021). Adjusting trade-offs in multi-criteria decision-making problems. *International Journal of Information Technology & Decision Making, 20*(05), 1499–1517.
Kumar, R. (2025). A comprehensive review of MCDM methods, applications, and emerging trends. *Decision Making Advances, 3*(1), 185–199.
Liang, F., Brunelli, M., & Rezaei, J. (2022). Best-worst tradeoff method. *Information Sciences, 610*, 957–976.
Liu, X., Tan, Y., Dong, J., Wu, J., Wang, X., & Sun, Z. (2025). Assessing habitat selection parameters of Arabica coffee using BWM and BCM methods based on GIS. *Scientific Reports, 15*(1), 8.
Narang, M., Joshi, M. C., & Pal, A. K. (2021). A hybrid fuzzy COPRAS-base-criterion method for multi-criteria decision making. *Soft Computing, 25*, 8391–8399.
Narang, M., Joshi, M. C., & Pal, A. K. (2022). A hesitant fuzzy multiplicative Base-criterion multi-criteria group decision making method. *Informatica, 46*(2).
Narayanan, U., & Paul, V. (2023). Twin chain: A Blockchain based Federated Learning Intrusion Detection System using Optimized Backpropagation based Neural Network for Edge Assisted IoT Networks. https://doi.org/10.21203/rs.3.rs-3214924/v1.
Phulara, S., Kumar, A., Narang, M., & Bisht, K. (2024). A novel hybrid grey-BCM approach in multi-criteria decision making: An application in OTT platform. *Journal of Decision Analytics and Intelligent Computing, 4*(1), 1–15.
Raiffa, H., & Keeney, R. L. (1975). Decision analysis with multiple conflicting objectives, preferences and value tradeoffs. In *IIASA Working Paper*. IIASA, Laxenburg, Austria: WP-75-053.
Rezaei, J. (2015). Best-worst multi-criteria decision-making method. *Omega, 53*, 49–57.
Saaty, T. L. (1977). A scaling method for priorities in hierarchical structures. *Journal of mathematical psychology, 15*(3), 234–281. https://doi.org/10.1016/0022-2496(77)90033-5.
Saaty, T. L. (1996). *Decisions with the analytic network process (ANP)*. (USA), ISAHP: University of Pittsburgh, 96.
Sun, L., Yu, C., Li, J., Yuan, Q., & Zhao, S. (2024). A two-stage decision model for sustainable-resilient supplier selection and order allocation under uncertain environment. *Kybernetes*.
Weber, M., & Borcherding, K. (1993). Behavioral influences on weight judgments in multiattribute decision making. *European Journal of Operational Research, 67*(1), 1–12.
Wu, Y., Liu, P., & Li, Y. (2024). An integrated QFD and FMEA method under the co-opetitional relationship for product upgrading. *Information Sciences, 667*, 120505.
Wu, Y., Liu, P., & Li, Y. (2026). An improved QFD model with the integration of BCM and CoCoSo method under the trust network. *International Journal of Information Technology & Decision Making*. https://doi.org/10.1142/s0219622026500458.
Zafaranlouei, N., Ghoushchi, S. J., & Haseli, G. (2023). Assessment of sustainable waste management alternatives using the extensions of the base criterion method and combined compromise solution based on the fuzzy Z-numbers. *Environmental Science and Pollution Research, 30*(22), 62121–62136.
Zhang, Y., Kong, M., Wang, W. Z., Deveci, M., Bilican, M. S., & Delen, D. (2026). A multi-criteria decision-making framework for metaverse adoption: Evidence from higher education systems. *Expert Systems with Applications, 296*, 129132.

Chapter 29

Nonadditive BCM: Nonadditive base-criterion method for multi-attribute decision-making

Javad Nazarian-Jashnabadi[1], Tahereh Sepahi[2], and Dragan Pamucar[3,4,5]

[1]*Department of Management, Faculty of Economic, Management and Social Science, Shiraz University, Shiraz, Iran,* [2]*Department of Management, Faculty of Management and Accounting, Shahid Beheshti University, Tehran, Iran,* [3]*Department of Operations Research and Statistics, Faculty of Organizational Sciences, University of Belgrade, Belgrade, Serbia,* [4]*Faculty of Engineering, Dogus University, Umraniye, Istanbul, Türkiye,* [5]*UNEC Applied Artificial Intelligence Research Center, Azerbaijan State University of Economics, (UNEC), Baku, Azerbaijan*

29.1 Introduction

The use of scientific decision-making is crucial when faced with complex and multidimensional problems. This decision-making approach is used in various fields, including management, economics, and environmental science. In such situations, the use of multi-attribute decision-making (MADM) approaches is an efficient tool for weighting criteria (Işık et al., 2025). Over time, various methods have been developed to respond to the preferences and priorities of decision makers, each utilizing different but approved computational methods in specific situations and addressing different weighting criteria (Haseli, Ranjbarzadeh, et al., 2023; Stević et al., 2017). Choosing an appropriate analytical method, in addition to ensuring the accuracy and correctness of the results, also indicates the researcher's deep understanding of the dimensions of the problem. Since these methods are based on human judgments and expert opinions, the accuracy, efficiency, and consistency of these judgments play a decisive role in the validity of the results (Demir et al., 2024; Nazarian-Jashnabadi et al., 2023). Some of these methods are based on pairwise comparisons to determine the weight of the criteria, including the analytic hierarchy process (AHP) (Saaty, 1977), the best–worst method (BWM) (Rezaei, 2015), and the base criterion method (BCM) (Haseli & Sheikh, 2022; Haseli et al., 2020a).

The large number of pairwise comparisons and the resulting inconsistency ratio are fundamental challenges in weighting methods. Reducing the number of comparisons increases the consistency of judgments and reduces the inconsistency ratio. The AHP method, which is one of the first weighting methods, can be used to build the weighting process using a hierarchical structure and a pairwise comparison matrix. However, for n criteria, it requires $(n(n-1))/2$ comparisons (Saaty, 2013), which makes it difficult for decision makers to give their opinions and consequently increases the possibility of inconsistency in the results. In the AHP method, the inconsistency ratio is calculated after the model analysis, and to the extent permitted, it is necessary to repeat the opinion-taking and model-solving.

In order to reduce the need for expert opinion and improve the inconsistency ratio, BWM was introduced. In this method, by selecting two reference criteria, the "Best" and the "Worst", by decision makers and comparing the "Best" to others and other criteria to the "Worst", the number of comparisons was reduced to $2n-3$ (Rezaei, 2015). However, BWM still calculates the inconsistency ratio after solving the model, and in case of inconsistency, there is a need to repeat the process. A profound change in this field was introduced with the introduction of BCM. In this method, only $n-1$ pairwise comparisons are needed (Haseli & Sheikh, 2022). More importantly, the inconsistency ratio in BCM is calculated before the model analysis and at the same stage as collecting judgments. This approach prevents the occurrence of subsequent inconsistencies and eliminates the need to repeat the analysis. In other words, by controlling the model inputs, BCM ensures the consistency of judgments before performing the final analysis, which, unlike AHP and BWM, prevents repeated consultation.

Encyclopedia of Multi-Attribute Decision-Making (MADM). DOI: https://doi.org/10.1016/B978-0-443-33275-3.00028-2

However, a significant limitation remains in all the original and extended versions of BCM; they all inherently assume that the criteria are independent and additive. This assumption is often violated in real-world decision-making problems where the criteria are interdependent. This interdependence may be in the form of synergy or redundancy. Considering these two cases and the possibility of zero dependency, there are three possible states between the criteria: synergy, redundancy, or independence. Two or more criteria are synergic (redundant) when their joint weights are greater (less) than the sum of the weights of those criteria (Angilella et al., 2004). For example, Carlsson and Fullér took a constant value (positive or negative) to express the interdependence of the criteria (Carlsson & Fullér, 1995). These interactions necessitate the consideration of nonadditive calculations in decision-making.

The nonadditive BCM described in this chapter offers a new approach for removing the limitations of previous versions of BCM. This method systematically models the interactions of the criteria in the BCM framework by utilizing the Choquet integral and the 2-additive fuzzy measures. Nonadditive BCM calculates the individual importance of each criterion and degrees of couple interaction and evaluates the performance of the alternatives through nonlinear integration. This approach, while maintaining key BCM benefits, such as reducing the number of couples comparisons, full compatibility with preferences, and the stability of the results, eliminates the fundamental limitations of previous methods in ignoring criterion interactions.

The remainder of this chapter is organized as follows. Section 29.2 offers an extensive review of the existing literature. Section 29.3 elaborates on the nonadditive BCM methodology. Section 29.4 illustrates the proposed approach through a numerical case study. Lastly, Section 29.5 summarizes the chapter's main contributions and discusses their implications.

29.2 Literature review

Given the uncertainties in decision-making problems, organizations and researchers are looking for methods that reduce the computational burden while maintaining accuracy, efficiency, and flexibility. Initially proposed by Haseli et al. (2020a), BCM has gained prominence among MADM methods because it requires fewer pairwise comparisons than conventional methods while achieving the lowest inconsistency ratio in weighting. The simple structure, reduced number of comparisons, and high level of consistency of results are among the main advantages of this method, which have encouraged researchers to develop and integrate BCM with other methods.

A review of the literature shows that the BCM has been used in a wide range of scientific and applied fields and has grown significantly in terms of subject and methodological diversity. One of the most significant aspects of this growth is the combination of BCM with various fuzzy methods to increase accuracy, adaptability, and flexibility under uncertainty. Some of these studies have developed this decision-making method by combining fuzzy ZE number (Haseli, Bonab, et al., 2024; Haseli, Nazarian-Jashnabadi, et al., 2024; Haseli, Ögel, et al., 2023) and some by combining fuzzy Z numbers (Zafaranlouei et al., 2023) with BCM. Other fuzzy methods, including spherical fuzzy (Haseli & Jafarzadeh Ghoushchi, 2022), hesitant fuzzy (Narang et al., 2022), interval-valued intuitionistic fuzzy set (Wu et al., 2024), and single-valued neutrosophic (Sun et al., 2024), have also effectively contributed to the development and enhancement of the capabilities of BCM under uncertainty. Trapezoidal fuzzy numbers (Imran et al., 2024; Narang et al., 2021) and original fuzzy set (Bisht & Kumar, 2022; Debalki et al., 2024) methods have also been used by various researchers to improve and develop the BCM.

This method has been used in most cases not independently, but in combination with other MADM methods. This indicates the high flexibility and compatibility of BCM with combined approaches. The combination of BCM with constrained combined compromise solution (CoCoSo) has been used in several studies and is considered one of the most common combinations in the literature (Haseli, Bonab, et al., 2024; Wu et al., 2024; Zafaranlouei et al., 2023). The combination of BCM with Técnica Ordinal Da Informação Multicritério (TODIM) was also observed in two studies (Sun et al., 2024; Wu et al., 2024). The combination of BCM with measurement alternatives and ranking according to compromise solution (MARCOS) has also been used in the context of group decision-making (Haseli, Ögel, et al., 2023). In some other studies, BCM has been combined as a weighting tool with methods based on final rankings, such as multiattributive border approximation area comparison (MABAC) (Haseli, Nazarian-Jashnabadi, et al., 2024) and complex proportional assessment (COPRAS) (Narang et al., 2021). BCM has also been used in combination with causal analyzes such as decision-making trial and evaluation laboratory (DEMATEL) and Vlse Kriterijumsk Optimizacija Kompromisno Resenje (VIKOR) rankings (Bisht & Pal, 2023). This shows that BCM can be well integrated with a diverse range of decision-making methods.

The application of the BCM method in various studies demonstrates its high subject diversity and generalizability in various real-world contexts. In the field of sustainable and circular supply chain management, this method has been applied to supplier selection and e-waste management in the automotive and beverage industries (Haseli, Nazarian-Jashnabadi, et al., 2024; Sun et al., 2024; Zafaranlouei et al., 2023). In transportation planning and traffic flow, papers focusing on

Mexico City and traffic issues have been presented (Debalki et al., 2024; Haseli, Bonab, et al., 2024; Narang et al., 2022). In the field of financial decision-making and investment portfolio selection, BCM has been used for complex analyses in stock selection (Bisht & Kumar, 2022; Narang et al., 2021). Also, in the field of environmental sustainability and agricultural planning, this method has been used in the selection of environmental sites and the development of clean transportation such as electric vehicles (Imran et al., 2024; Liu et al., 2025; Haseli & Jafarzadeh Ghoushchi, 2022). In addition, in the areas of decision-making model development, the use of BCM with hybrid approaches such as neural networks, gray method, and federated learning is also seen (Bisht & Pal, 2023; Narayanan & Paul, 2023; Phulara et al., 2024). This variety of topics and applications indicates that the BCM method has gained a significant position in solving real and interdisciplinary problems, in addition to its development in theoretical areas. Table 29.1 shows the research literature related to the BCM.

The nonadditive approach has increasingly been recognized in recent years as an alternative to traditional MADM methods, primarily because, unlike classical models, it accounts for interactions and interdependencies among criteria. This unique capability has led to its integration with various techniques such as the Choquet integral, DEMATEL, AHP, technique for order preference by similarity to ideal solution (TOPSIS), and the BWM in decision-making problems. For example, sustainable development in Taiwan's aquatic processing industry was assessed using AHP and triangular fuzzy numbers (Chiou et al., 2005), and in the field of carbon technologies, TOPSIS was combined with the Choquet integral and fuzzy measures to evaluate carbon capture, utilization and storage (CCUS) sustainability (He et al., 2024).

In contexts where criterion interaction plays a more prominent role, tools such as DEMATEL have been employed alongside fuzzy measures to analyze feature interdependencies (Guan et al., 2024). A combination of nonadditive gray relational analysis with DEMATEL and genetic algorithms has also been used for pattern classification (Jiang et al., 2021). In more complex decision scenarios such as supplier selection, techniques including interpretive structural modeling (ISM), fuzzy AHP, and triangular fuzzy numbers have been utilized (Yang et al., 2008). Additionally, the nonadditive BWM has been applied to electric vehicle selection (Liang et al., 2023), while healthcare decision support has leveraged the Choquet integral with expert-based evaluations (Anzilli & Giove, 2020). Table 29.2 summarizes the literature about the nonadditive approach in MADM methods.

29.3 Methodology

In this section, nonadditive BCM, which is a new version of the BCM, is presented to determine the relative importance of criteria by considering possible interactions and dependencies between them. This method attempts to provide more accurate and realistic weighting by understanding the relationships between criteria.

BCM is a method based on pairwise comparisons. In methods that rely on pairwise comparisons, such as AHP, analytical network process (ANP), BWM, and BCM, the issue of inconsistency in pairwise comparisons is important. Two types of inconsistency may occur: inconsistency in the direction and inconsistency in the strength of comparisons. Inconsistency in direction means that the relative importance in pairwise comparisons is applied inversely to another criterion. For example, if there are three criteria C1, C2, and C3, and the relative importance of C1 is greater than C2 and the relative importance of C2 is greater than C3, then the relative importance of C1 must also be greater than C3; otherwise, the pairwise comparisons have inconsistency in direction.

Inconsistency in strength also occurs when the decision maker is not careful enough in making pairwise comparisons. For example, if the relative importance of C1 to C2 is 4 on a 1 to 9 scale and the relative importance of C2 to C3 is 1, then the relative importance of C1 to C3 should be 4. If the decision maker does not pay attention to this and assigns a number other than 4 to the relative importance of C1 to C3, an inconsistency in strength occurs.

The AHP method suffers from both types of inconsistency. In this method, the inconsistency ratio is calculated at the last stage, and if it exceeds the threshold, the decision maker must be referred back to reconsider the pairwise comparisons (Saaty, 1977). With the introduction of the BWM method, the problem of inconsistency in the direction of comparisons was solved, because in this method, all comparisons are made with two criteria, the "Best" and the "Worst" (Rezaei, 2015), but the inconsistency in the strength of the pairwise comparisons still remains.

The main advantage of the BCM method over the AHP and ANP methods is that it overcomes the problem of inconsistency in the direction and strength of pairwise comparisons. On the one hand, this method significantly reduces the number of pairwise comparisons, and on the other hand, it controls inconsistency by providing a framework for controlling the inputs. This method ensures that pairwise comparisons are made with full consistency from the beginning, so the inconsistency ratio is zero, and the decision maker does not need to reconsider making pairwise comparisons. The aforementioned framework is described below.

TABLE 29.1 Research literature in base criterion method.

Author & year	Fuzzy approach	Methodology	Research area	Application context/case study
Abdollahi et al. (2026)	Fuzzy ZE number	BCM – DNMAa	Blockchain technology	Solar energy supply chain
Solieman and Duleba (2026)	Fuzzy ZE number	BCM	Urban transportation	Shared mobility
Haseli, Bonab, et al. (2024)	Fuzzy ZE number	BCM – CoCoSo	Sustainable urban transportation	Mexico city's urban transport
Haseli, Nazarian-Jashnabadi, et al. (2024)	Fuzzy ZE number	BCM – MABAC	Circular supply chain management	Beverage industry
Haseli, Ögel, et al. (2023)	Fuzzy ZE number	BCM – MARCOS	Smart jewelry selection	Jewelry industry
Zafaranlouei et al. (2023)	Fuzzy Z numbers	BCM – CoCoSo	Electronic waste management	Mobile, communication equipment
Haseli and Jafarzadeh Ghoushchi (2022)	Spherical fuzzy	BCM	Waste management under uncertainty	Waste disposal location—Iran
Narang et al. (2022)	Hesitant fuzzy	BCM	Multicriteria group decision-making	Transportation mode and car selection
Wu et al. (2024)	IVIFS	BCM – CoCoSo – TODIM	Product upgrading under competitive collaboration	-
Sun et al. (2024)	Single-valued neutrosophic	BCM – TODIM U-NSGA-III[a] algorithm – TOPSIS[a]	Sustainable-resilient supplier selection	Automotive manufacturing industry
Imran et al. (2024)	Trapezoidal fuzzy numbers	BCM	Strategic planning and environmental sustainability	Electric vehicle industry
Narang et al. (2021)	Triangular fuzzy numbers	BCM – COPRAS	Financial decision-making under uncertainty	Stock portfolio selection
Haseli et al. (2020b)	Original fuzzy set	BCM	Decision-making under uncertainty	-
Debalki et al. (2024)	Original fuzzy set	BCM	Traffic flow	-
Bisht and Kumar (2022)	Original fuzzy set	BCM – LSTM[a]	Portfolio selection	Investment in the national stock exchange of India
Wu et al., (2026)	-	BCM – CoCoSo	Quality function deployment	Productions of the computer numerical control machine
Liu et al. (2025)	-	BWM – BCM	Sustainable agricultural land-use planning	Habitat selection
Phulara et al. (2024)	-	Gray BCM	MCDM[a] under uncertainty using gray system theory	Over-the-top platforms—India
Ayough et al. (2023)		BCM – utility additive	Proposing a new integrated approach	Supplier selection
Bisht and Pal (2023)	-	DEMATEL – BCM – VIKOR	MCDM model development	Electronics industry
Narayanan and Paul, 2023	-	BCM – neural networks –	Security and privacy in internet of things environments	-
Haseli and Sheikh (2022)	-	BCM	MCDM model development	-

[a] *DNMA: Double Normalization-based Multiple Aggregation; NSGA: Nondominated sorting genetic algorithm; TOPSIS: Technique for order preference by similarity to ideal solution; LSTM: Neural network with long-short-term memory; MCDM: Multicriteria decision-making; CoCoSo: Constrained combined compromise solution; DEMATEL: Decision-making trial and evaluation laboratory; BCM: Base criterion method; VIKOR: Vlse Kriterijumsk Optimizacija Kompromisno Resenje; BWM: Best–worst method; MARCOS: Measurement alternatives and ranking according to compromise solution; MABAC: Multiattributive border approximation area comparison.*

TABLE 29.2 Research literature in the nonadditive approach.

Author and year	Fuzzy approach	Methodology	Research area	Application context/case study
Guan et al. (2024)	2-additive fuzzy measures	DEMATEL	Feature interaction analysis in MCDM	–
Chiou et al. (2005)	Nonadditive fuzzy integral with triangular fuzzy numbers	Factor analysis + AHP + fuzzy integral aggregation	Sustainable development evaluation	Aquatic product processing industry—Taiwan
He et al. (2024)	2-additive fuzzy measure	Choquet integral-based MCDM; TOPSIS	Sustainability assessment of CCUS technologies	Carbon capture utilization, and storage systems
Yang et al. (2008)	Triangular fuzzy numbers	ISM, fuzzy AHP, nonadditive fuzzy integral	Vendor selection under uncertainty	–
Angilella et al. (2016)	Nonadditive fuzzy measures	NAROR[a]	Urban and territorial planning	–
Jiang et al. (2021)	Nonadditive fuzzy measures	Nonadditive GRA[a] + DEMATEL + genetic algorithm	Pattern classification	–
Liang et al. (2023)	–	Nonadditive BWM With Choquet integral	MCDM model development	Battery-powered electric vehicle selection
Anzilli and Giove (2020)	–	Choquet integral, MCDM, expert-based evaluation, error estimation	Healthcare decision support	Cardiovascular risk diagnosis model

[a] *NAROR: Nonadditive robust ordinal regression; GRA: Gray relational analysis; ISM: Interpretive structural modeling; DEMATEL: Decision-making trial and evaluation laboratory; BWM: Best–worst method; MCDM: Multi-criteria decision-making; TOPSIS: Technique for order preference by similarity to ideal solution; AHP: Analytic hierarchy process.*

Assume there are n criteria for which relative importance needs to be assessed. The corresponding pairwise comparison matrix is structured as shown in Eq. 29.1:

$$A = \begin{bmatrix} a_{11} & a_{12} & \cdots & a_{1n} \\ a_{21} & a_{22} & \cdots & a_{2n} \\ \vdots & \vdots & \ddots & \vdots \\ a_{m1} & a_{m2} & \cdots & a_{mn} \end{bmatrix} \tag{29.1}$$

Here, each element a_{ij} denotes the relative importance of criterion i compared to criterion j, expressed on a numerical scale ranging from 1/9 to 9. Accordingly, the reciprocal relation $a_{ij} = 1 / a_{ji}$ holds. If both criteria are considered equally important, then $a_{ij} = 1$. In BCM, two types of pairwise comparisons are defined (Haseli & Sheikh, 2022).

Base comparisons: a_{ij} is classified as a base comparison when i is the base criterion.
Final comparisons: a_{ij} is a final comparison when neither i nor j is the base criterion.

The decision maker/expert initially assigns values to the base comparisons. Since final comparisons can be derived from base comparisons, determining them is not strictly necessary for weight estimation. Eq. 29.2 ensures that the comparisons are directionally and proportionally consistent:

$$a_{Base,i} \times a_{ij} = a_{Base,j} \tag{29.2}$$

To maintain consistency and validity, the decision maker/expert must assign base comparison values such that the resulting final comparisons remain within the allowed scale of 1/9 to 9. According to (29.3), the final comparison a_{ij} is computed as:

$$\frac{1}{9} \le \frac{a_{Base,j}}{a_{Base,i}} \le 9 \;\; or \;\; \frac{1}{9} \le a_{ij} \le 9, \;\; \forall\, j = 2, \ldots, n, \; \forall\, i = 1, \ldots, j - 1 \tag{29.3}$$

Thus BCM emphasizes reducing inconsistency by regulating input values. Enforcing (29.3) during the comparison process ensures full consistency in both the direction and strength of the pairwise comparisons (Haseli et al., 2020a).
The steps for implementing nonadditive BCM are described as follows.

29.3.1 Determining a set of criteria

In the first step, the decision maker/expert defines a set of decision criteria $C = \{c_j, \;\; j = 1, 2, \ldots, n\}$. These criteria should be selected in such a way that, in addition, to their independent impact on the problem, they also allow for the analysis of interactions and mutual effects between them.

29.3.2 Choosing a base criterion and performing pairwise comparisons

The decision maker/expert selects a criterion as the base criterion (C_{Base}). All pairwise comparisons are then made only between this base criterion and the other criteria. To make these comparisons, a numerical scale from 1.9 to 9 based on Table 29.3 is used to measure the strength or weakness of each criterion compared to the base criterion. The results of these comparisons are recorded in the form of a base comparison vector based on (29.4).

$$a_{Base,j} = (a_{Base,1}, \; a_{Base,2}, \; \ldots, \; a_{Base,n}) \tag{29.4}$$

29.3.3 Evaluation of criteria interactions

After performing the base comparisons, the decision maker/expert evaluates the interactions among the criteria. This evaluation leads to the formation of a symmetric interaction matrix $D = (t_{ij})_{n\times n}$ *and* $t_{ij} = t_{ji}, \quad i \ne j, \, i, j = 1, 2, \ldots, n$ based on Eq. 29.5.

$$D = \begin{array}{c} \\ c_1 \\ c_2 \\ \vdots \\ c_n \end{array} \begin{array}{c} \begin{array}{cccc} c_1 & c_2 & \cdots & c_n \end{array} \\ \begin{bmatrix} / & t_{12} & \cdots & t_{1n} \\ t_{21} & / & \cdots & t_{2n} \\ \vdots & \vdots & \ddots & \vdots \\ t_{1n} & t_{2n} & \cdots & / \end{bmatrix} \end{array} \tag{29.5}$$

Where $t_{ij} \in \{+, \;\; -, \;\; \Delta, \text{ u'} \}, \quad i \ne j, \, i, j = 1, 2, \ldots, n$. In this matrix, "+" denotes a positive interaction between two criteria, "–" indicates a negative interaction, "Δ" shows that the criteria are independent with no interaction, and "u" means that the decision maker is unable to specify the nature of the relationship between the two criteria (Liang et al., 2023).

TABLE 29.3 Numerical scale.

Scale		Description
1	1	Equal importance
1/2	2	Between equal and moderate
1/3	3	Moderately more important than
1/4	4	Between moderate and strong
1/5	5	Strongly more important than
1/6	6	Between strong and very strong
1/7	7	Very strongly more important than
1/8	8	Between very strong and absolute
1/9	9	Absolutely more important than

29.3.4 Determining the relative importance of each criterion

In this step, the degree of interaction between the criteria is determined based on Eq. 29.6 and according to the matrix obtained from the previous step. Since $I_{ij} = I_{ji},\ i \neq j,\ i, j = 1, 2, \ldots, n$, only I_{ij}, $\quad i < j; i, j = 1, 2, \ldots, n$ is considered.

$$\begin{cases} I_{ij} > 0, & if \quad t_{ij} = +; \\ I_{ij} < 0, & if \quad t_{ij} = -; \\ I_{ij} = 0, & if \quad t_{ij} = \Delta; \\ I_{ij} \in [-1, 1], & if \quad t_{ij} = \mathrm{u}'; \end{cases} \tag{29.6}$$

The criteria interaction I_{ij} is equivalent to the Mobius representation m_{ij} (Angilella et al., 2004):

$$I_{ij} = m_{ij},\ i \neq j,\ i, j = 1, 2, \ldots, n \tag{29.7}$$

I_j indicates the relative importance of the c_j, which is obtained according to (29.8)ed on the value of the Shapley value (Shapley, 1953) for the 2-additive fuzzy measure.

$$I_j = m_j + \sum\nolimits_{c_i \in C\{c_j\}} \frac{m_{ij}}{2},\ j = 1, 2, \ldots, n \tag{29.8}$$

29.3.5 Formulation of the mathematical model

In this step, the mathematical model of the problem is formulated. According to the (29.9) the maximum absolute difference between pairwise comparisons and their associated weight ratios for all j is minimized.

$$\begin{aligned} &\min \max_j \left| \frac{\mathrm{I}_{Base}}{\mathrm{I}_j} - a_{Base,j} \right| \\ &\text{subject to} \\ &\begin{cases} m(\theta) = 0;\ \sum_{c_j \in C} m_j + \sum_{c_i, c_j \in C} m_{ij} = 1; \\ m_j + \sum_{c_i \in T} m_{ij} \geq 0,\ i, j = 1, 2, \ldots, n \text{ and } T \subseteq C\{c_j\},\ \mathrm{T} \neq \theta; \\ \mathrm{I}_{ij} = m_{ij},\ i \neq j; \\ \mathrm{I}_j = m_j + \sum_{c_i \in C\{c_j\}} \frac{m_{ij}}{2},\ i \neq j; \\ \mathrm{I}_{ij} > 0,\ if\ t_{ij} = +, i < j; \\ \mathrm{I}_{ij} < 0,\ if\ t_{ij} = -, i < j; \\ \mathrm{I}_{ij} = 0,\ if\ t_{ij} = \Delta,\ i < j; \\ \mathrm{I}_{ij} \in [-1, 1],\ if\ t_{ij} = u',\ i < j; \end{cases} \end{aligned} \tag{29.9}$$

Model (9) can be written in the form of model (10).

$$\begin{aligned}
&\min\ \xi \\
&\text{subject to} \\
&m(\Theta) = 0;\ \Sigma_{c_j \in C} m_j + \Sigma_{c_i, c_j \in C} m_{ij} = 1; \\
&m_j + \Sigma_{c_i \in T} m_{ij} \ge 0,\ \ i, j = 1, 2, \ldots, n \ \text{ and } \ T \subseteq C\{c_j\},\ T \ne \Theta; \\
&\mathrm{I}_{ij} = m_{ij},\ \ i \ne j; \\
&\mathrm{I}_j = m_j + \Sigma_{c_i \in C\{c_j\}} \frac{m_{ij}}{2},\ i \ne j; \\
&\left| \frac{\mathrm{I}_{Base}}{\mathrm{I}_j} - a_{Base,j} \right| \le \xi; \\
&\mathrm{I}_{ij} > 0,\ \ \text{if } \ t_{ij} = +, i < j; \\
&\mathrm{I}_{ij} < 0,\ \ \text{if } \ t_{ij} = -, i < j; \\
&\mathrm{I}_{ij} = 0,\ \ \text{if } \ t_{ij} = \Delta,\ i < j; \\
&\mathrm{I}_{ij} \in [-1, 1],\ \ \text{if } \ t_{ij} = \mathrm{u}',\ i < j;
\end{aligned} \tag{29.10}$$

Model (10) involves nonlinear constraints, which pose challenges for solution using conventional methods. It can yield either a single optimal solution or multiple optimal solutions. To address these problems, model (10) can be equivalently transferred into a linear model (11).

$$\begin{aligned}
&\min\ \xi \\
&\text{subject to} \\
&m(\Theta) = 0;\ \Sigma_{c_j \in C} m_j + \Sigma_{c_i, c_j \in C} m_{ij} = 1; \\
&m_j + \Sigma_{c_i \in T} m_{ij} \ge 0,\ \ i, j = 1, 2, \ldots, n \ \text{ and } \ \mathrm{T} \subseteq \mathrm{C}\{c_j\},\ \mathrm{T} \ne \Theta; \\
&\mathrm{I}_{ij} = m_{ij},\ \ i \ne j,\ \ i, j = 1, 2, \ldots, n; \\
&\mathrm{I}_j = m_j + \Sigma_{c_i \in C\{c_j\}} \frac{m_{ij}}{2},\ i \ne j; \\
&\mathrm{I}_{Base} - a_{Base,j}\mathrm{I}_j \le \xi;\ \ \mathrm{I}_{Base} - a_{Base,j}\mathrm{I}_j \ge -\xi; \\
&\mathrm{I}_{ij} > 0,\ \ \textit{if } \ t_{ij} = +, i < j; \\
&\mathrm{I}_{ij} < 0,\ \ \textit{if } \ t_{ij} = -, i < j; \\
&\mathrm{I}_{ij} = 0,\ \ \textit{if } \ t_{ij} = \Delta,\ i < j; \\
&\mathrm{I}_{ij} \in [-1, 1],\ \ \textit{if } \ t_{ij} = \mathrm{u}',\ i < j;
\end{aligned} \tag{29.11}$$

29.3.6 Performance analysis of alternatives based on the criteria

The decision maker/expert evaluates the alternatives and assigns each alternative a score in each criterion. If the set of alternatives is represented by $A = \{a_p, p = 1,2,\ldots,q\}$ and the set of criteria by $C = \{c_j, j = 1,2,\ldots,n\}$, the score of the alternative a_p in criterion c_j is expressed as $g_j(a_p)$. Given that the criteria of the problem may have different scales, normalization is usually performed. Eq. 29.12 is used to normalize the scores of the alternatives (Liang et al., 2023).

$$v(g_j(a_p)) = \begin{cases} \dfrac{g_j(a_p) - l_j}{h_j - l_j}, & \textit{if } \ c_j \ \text{ is a benefit criterion;} \\[2ex] \dfrac{h_j - g_j(a_p)}{h_j - l_j}, & \textit{if } \ c_j \ \text{ is a cost criterion;} \end{cases} \tag{29.12}$$

Where $v(g_j(a_p))$ is the normalized value of $g_j(a_p)$, so $v(g_j(a_p)) \in [0,1]$. It should be noted that h_j and l_j denote the maximum and minimum scores that can be assigned to an alternative in in criterion c_j, respectively. This range is determined by the decision maker/expert.

29.3.7 Final ranking of the alternatives

In the last step, it is necessary to calculate the final score of each alternative in order to rank the alternatives. Eq. 29.13 describes the method of calculating the final score of each alternative, in which the Choquet integral is used. The better-performing alternative a_p will have a higher $C_\mu(a_p)$ and will have a higher rank.

$$C_\mu(a_p) = \sum_{c_j \in C} m_j v(g_j(a_p)) + \sum_{c_i, c_j \in C} m_{ij} \min\{v(g_i(a_p)), v(g_j(a_p))\} \tag{29.13}$$

29.4 Numerical example: ranking of technology-based solutions in the healthcare system

With the rapid growth of new technologies such as artificial intelligence, blockchain, the internet of things (IoT), and big data, health systems are faced with new opportunities to improve service quality, increase productivity, and reduce costs. However, the high diversity of existing solutions and the complexity of choosing the most appropriate option according to technical, economic, social, and legal conditions have made decision-making difficult for policymakers and health managers. In this regard, the use of MADM methods can help identify, evaluate, and prioritize innovative alternatives in the health sector. In this example, seven technological solutions are examined as alternatives, which are listed in Table 29.4.

The criteria selected in this example cover key and influential dimensions in evaluating and prioritizing technology-based solutions in the field of digital health. "Technology maturity and feasibility" indicates the degree of readiness and feasibility of implementing the technology in real conditions. "Stakeholder Acceptance" reflects the level of support and satisfaction of end users, physicians, and related organizations. "Data Security and Privacy Compliance" expresses the importance of complying with regulations and protecting sensitive patient information. "Impact on Access and Equity" examines whether the technology increases equity in access to health services. "Implementation Cost" indicates the financial burden required to implement the technology. "Scalability and Flexibility" indicates the capacity of the technology to be expanded and adapted to different conditions. Finally, "Effectiveness in Clinical Outcomes" assesses the extent to which the technology has an impact on improving patient health. The purpose of selecting these criteria is to provide a comprehensive view for making decisions regarding the selection of technological alternatives in the health system. Table 29.5 displays the aforementioned criteria along with a brief explanation of each.

TABLE 29.4 Different identified alternatives.

Code	Alternative title	Advantages	Disadvantages
A1	Intelligent diagnostic assistant	Improves diagnostic accuracy; reduces human error; speeds up decision-making	High implementation cost; potential for bias in training data
A2	Secure blockchain health record system	Enhances data security and privacy; ensures tamper-proof records	Scalability issues; complex integration with existing systems
A3	Virtual care delivery platform	Increases healthcare accessibility; reduces travel time and cost	Limited in-person interaction; requires stable internet
A4	Smart patient monitoring via internet of things	Enables real-time monitoring; early detection of anomalies	Data privacy concerns; device interoperability challenges
A5	centralized health information hub	Facilitates data sharing; supports coordinated care	Risk of data breaches; complex to manage large-scale data
A6	Digital health education app	Empowers patients; improves health literacy	May not be effective for all demographics; content quality varies
A7	Big data fraud detection engine	Detects anomalies quickly; reduces financial loss	High data requirements; false positives may occur

TABLE 29.5 Different identified criteria.

Code	Criteria title	Brief description
C1	Technology maturity and feasibility	The level of technological advancement and the practicality of implementing the solution.
C2	Stakeholder acceptance	The degree of acceptance and support from key stakeholders, including patients, healthcare providers, and policymakers.
C3	Data security and privacy compliance	The extent to which the solution complies with data protection standards and safeguards patient privacy.
C4	Impact on access and equity	The solution's contribution to improving access to healthcare services and reducing health disparities.
C5	Implementation cost	The total cost of deploying, maintaining, and training users on the technology.
C6	Scalability and flexibility	The ability of the solution to adapt to different contexts and expand across various levels of the health system.
C7	Effectiveness in clinical outcomes	The measurable impact of the solution on enhancing patient health and clinical performance.

TABLE 29.6 Base comparisons.

Criteria	C1	C2	C3	C4	C6	C7
Base criterion (C5)	1/7	1/4	1/8	1/5	1/2	1/9

The decision maker/expert has selected the "Implementation Cost (C5)" as the base criterion. Table 29.6 shows the comparison of this criterion with the other criteria based on the numerical scale expressed in Table 29.3.

The matrix of interactions between criteria was determined by the decision maker/expert.

$$D = \begin{array}{c} \\ c_1 \\ c_2 \\ c_3 \\ c_4 \\ c_5 \\ c_6 \\ c_7 \end{array} \begin{array}{c} \begin{array}{ccccccc} c_1 & c_2 & c_3 & c_4 & c_5 & c_6 & c_7 \end{array} \\ \begin{bmatrix} / & + & u' & + & u' & + & u' \\ + & / & + & u' & \Delta & + & + \\ u' & + & / & + & u' & \Delta & + \\ + & u' & + & / & u' & + & + \\ u' & \Delta & u' & u' & / & u' & + \\ + & + & \Delta & + & u' & / & + \\ u' & + & + & + & + & + & / \end{bmatrix} \end{array} \tag{29.14}$$

For example, some of the interactions in this matrix are described. In the positive interaction between C1 & C2 (t_{12}), stakeholder acceptance is more likely to occur when the technology is mature enough and feasible to implement. In the interaction between C2 & C5 (t_{25}), user acceptance is not necessarily dependent on cost; some inexpensive solutions may not be acceptable. In the interaction between C3 & C6 (t_{36}), security requirements may be designed independently of the scalability of the solution. In the positive interaction between C4 & C7 (t_{47}), improvements in equitable access to health services lead to overall improvements in clinical outcomes.

According to the nonadditive BCM steps, the (29.15) represents the mathematical model of the problem:

$$\begin{aligned}
&\min \quad \xi \\
&\text{subject to} \\
&m(\theta) = 0; \Sigma_{c_j \in C}\, m_j + \Sigma_{c_i, c_j \in C}\, m_{ij} = 1; \\
&m_j + \Sigma_{c_i \in T}\, m_{ij} \geq 0,\ \ i, j = 1,2,\ldots,7 \text{ and } T \subseteq C\{c_j\},\ T \neq \theta; \\
&I_{ij} = m_{ij},\ i \neq j; \\
&I_j = m_j + \Sigma_{c_i \in C\{c_j\}} \frac{m_{ij}}{2},\ i \neq j; \\
&I_5 - 0.142 I_1 \leq \xi;\ I_5 - 0.142 I_1 \geq -\xi; \\
&I_5 - 0.25 I_2 \leq \xi;\ I_5 - 0.25 I_2 \geq -\xi; \\
&I_5 - 0.125 I_3 \leq \xi;\ I_5 - 0.125 I_3 \geq -\xi; \\
&I_5 - 0.2 I_4 \leq \xi;\ I_5 - 0.2 I_4 \geq -\xi; \\
&I_5 - 0.5 I_6 \leq \xi;\ I_5 - 0.5 I_6 \geq -\xi; \\
&I_1 - 0.111 I_7 \leq \xi;\ I_1 - 0.111 I_7 \geq -\xi; \\
&I_{12} > 0;\ I_{13} \in [-1, 1];\ I_{14} > 0;\ I_{15} \in [-1, 1]; I_{16} > 0;\ I_{17} \in [-1,1]; \\
&I_{23} > 0;\ I_{24} \in [-1,1];\ I_{25} = 0; I_{26} > 0;\ I_{27} > 0; \\
&I_{34} > 0;\ I_{35} \in [-1,1];\ I_{36} = 0;\ I_{37} > 0; \\
&I_{45} \in [-1, 1];\ I_{46} > 0;\ I_{47} > 0; \\
&I_{56} \in [-1,1];\ I_{57} > 0; \\
&I_{67} > 0;
\end{aligned} \tag{29.15}$$

Solving this model, we have $\xi^* = 0$, which indicates full consistency of pairwise comparisons and $I_1 = 0.196,\ I_2 = 0.11,\ I_3 = 0.22,\ I_4 = 0.14,\ I_5 = 0.028,\ I_6 = 0.056,\ I_7 = 0.25; I_{12} = 0.0001,\ I_{13} = 0,\ I_{14} = 0.006,\ I_{15} = 0.016,\ I_{16} = 0.003,\ I_{17} = 0,\ I_{23} = 0.009,\ I_{24} = 0,\ I_{25} = 0,\ I_{26} = 0.004,\ I_{27} = 0.013,\ I_{34} = 0.008,\ I_{35} = 0.01,\ I_{36} = 0,\ I_{37} = 0.015,\ I_{45} = 0.011,\ I_{46} = 0.002,\ I_{47} = 0.014,\ I_{56} = 0,\ I_{57} = 0.017,\ I_{67} = 0.019; m_1 = 0.183,\ m_2 = 0.097,\ m_3 = 0.199,\ m_4 = 0.12,\ m_5 = 0.001,\ m_6 = 0.042,\ m_7 = 0.211.$

The decision maker/expert has evaluated each of the alternatives in the specified criteria, and Table 29.7 has been prepared. It should be noted that the minimum and maximum values of the criteria have also been specified by the decision maker/expert in this table.

In the following, the final score of each alternative is calculated according to Eq. 29.13 and displayed in Table 29.8. The ranking of alternatives is also expressed based on two additive and nonadditive approaches.

TABLE 29.7 Performance of alternatives in each criterion.

	C1	C2	C3	C4	C5	C6	C7
A1	7	6	6	5	4	6	9
A2	6	5	9	4	3	6	6
A3	8	8	5	9	7	7	7
A4	7	6	7	6	5	8	8
A5	6	7	6	5	6	9	7
A6	8	9	4	8	9	7	5
A7	5	4	8	3	6	6	6
hj	10	10	10	10	10	10	10
lj	2	2	2	2	2	2	2

TABLE 29.8 Final ranking of the alternatives.

	$V(g_1(a_p))$	$V(g_2(a_p))$	$V(g_3(a_p))$	$V(g_4(a_p))$	$V(g_5(a_p))$	$V(g_6(a_p))$	$V(g_7(a_p))$	Additive value function	Rank	Choquet integral	Rank
A1	0.625	0.5	0.5	0.375	0.25	0.5	0.875	0.59375	3	0.62675	3
A2	0.5	0.375	0.875	0.25	0.125	0.5	0.5	0.52325	6	0.544375	6
A3	0.75	0.75	0.375	0.875	0.625	0.625	0.625	0.64325	1	0.714125	1
A4	0.625	0.5	0.625	0.5	0.375	0.75	0.75	0.625	2	0.685875	2
A5	0.5	0.625	0.5	0.375	0.5	0.875	0.625	0.5485	5	0.6125	4
A6	0.75	0.875	0.25	0.75	0.875	0.625	0.375	0.5565	4	0.62675	5
A7	0.375	0.25	0.75	0.125	0.5	0.5	0.5	0.4505	7	0.544375	7

Based on the nonadditive BCM methodology, virtual care delivery platform (A3, 0.714125) ranked first. Although this solution faces challenges such as reduced face-to-face interaction between patient and doctor and dependence on stable communication infrastructure, it has achieved the highest score due to its critical role in increasing access to healthcare services, reducing healthcare costs, and facilitating service delivery in underserved areas. Smart patient monitoring via IoT (A4, 0.685875) ranked second. Despite concerns about data privacy and technical challenges related to device synchronization, this alternative has been ranked second due to its importance in real-time monitoring of patients' conditions and improving treatment effectiveness. Intelligent diagnostic assistant (A1, 0.62675) ranked third. Although high implementation costs and the possibility of bias in training data are among the challenges of this solution, it was evaluated in third place due to its impact on improving diagnostic accuracy, reducing human errors, and accelerating treatment decisions.

Continuing the ranking, centralized health information hub (A5, 0.6125) came in fourth place; this alternative facilitates the transfer of information between healthcare centers, although it faces challenges in the field of data management and security on a large-scale. Digital health education app (A6, 0.598625) came in fifth place, developed to improve health literacy and empower patients, but its limited effectiveness in some demographic groups and the quality of content variation can prevent the integrated use of this tool. In sixth place, secure blockchain health record system (A2, 0.544375) is located, which, although it helps increase transparency and trust by providing a secure platform for storing and sharing healthcare information, faces limitations due to technical challenges in scalability and integration with existing systems. Finally, big data fraud detection engine (A7, 0.483125) was recognized as the last place. Although this solution performs well in detecting financial fraud and optimizing regulatory processes, the high need for large amounts of data affects its operational efficiency.

29.5 Conclusion

The purpose of this chapter is to introduce the nonadditive BCM method as an advanced approach to solving MADM problems with dependencies between criteria. By utilizing BCM and using the Choquet integral to model the interactions of criteria through 2-additive fuzzy measures, this method overcomes the fundamental shortcoming of previous methods—namely, ignoring the dependent relationships between criteria. Among the key advantages of nonadditive BCM are the need for minimal pairwise comparisons, full consistency, and identification of interactions between criteria. This method has diverse applications in situations where the criteria are inherently related to each other.

To examine nonadditive BCM in practice, a case study, "Ranking Technology-Based Solutions in the Health System," was conducted. In this regard, seven key criteria were identified that were technology-driven factors in the health system. The optimal weight of the criteria was calculated, and the ranking of alternatives was obtained by scoring them on each criterion. The virtual care delivery platform (A3, 0.714125) holds the highest priority, followed by smart patient monitoring via IoT (A4, 0.685875), and intelligent diagnostic assistant (A1, 0.62675) in third place. Next are the centralized health information hub (A5, 0.6125) and digital health education app (A6, 0.598625) in fourth and fifth positions, respectively. The secure blockchain health record system (A2, 0.544375) ranks sixth, while the big data fraud detection engine (A7, 0.483125) holds the lowest rank among the alternatives.

The findings of this case study showed that the nonadditive BCM was able to reveal meaningful differences between alternatives with close scores and provide accurate performance in conditions where the criteria are intertwined. Finally, the results showed that the final ranking of the nonadditive BCM method differs from the additive value function ranking. This difference is because the dependence of the criteria is taken into account in the calculations. Given the importance of ranking and the reason for the existence of ranking, which shows the priority of alternatives well, it is necessary to use nonadditive BCM in problems with dependent criteria. As a new and flexible approach, nonadditive BCM has great potential for use in diverse fields. The application of this method can lead to increased accuracy of analyses and provide more effective support for decision-making processes in complex environments by more accurately representing the fundamental interactions between criteria.

References

Abdollahi, S., Ghoushchi, S. J., & Haseli, G. (2026). Evaluation of sustainable strategies for implementing blockchain technology in the solar energy supply chain under fuzzy ZE-numbers. *Applied Soft Computing, 189*, 114522. https://doi.org/10.1016/j.asoc.2025.114522.

Angilella, S., Greco, S., Lamantia, F., & Matarazzo, B. (2004). Assessing non-additive utility for multicriteria decision aid. *European Journal of Operational Research, 158*(3), 734–744.

Angilella, S., Bottero, M., Corrente, S., Ferretti, V., Greco, S., & Lami, I. M. (2016). Nonadditive robust ordinal regression for urban and territorial planning: An application for siting an urban waste landfill. *Annals of Operations Research, 245*(1), 427–456.

Anzilli, L., & Giove, S. (2020). Multi-criteria and medical diagnosis for application to health insurance systems: a general approach through non-additive measures. *Decisions in Economics and Finance, 43*(2), 559–582.

Ayough, A., Shargh, S. B., & Khorshidvand, B. (2023). A new integrated approach based on base-criterion and utility additive methods and its application to supplier selection problem. *Expert Systems with Applications, 221*, 119740. https://doi.org/10.1016/j.eswa.2023.119740.

Bisht, G., & Pal, A. K. (2023). Functional dependency-based group decision-making with incomplete information under social media influence: An application to automobile. *Journal of Intelligent & Fuzzy Systems, 45*(6), 12341–12363.

Bisht, K., & Kumar, A. (2022). Stock portfolio selection hybridizing fuzzy base-criterion method and evidence theory in triangular fuzzy environment. In *Operations research forum*. Cham: Springer International Publishing, 53 Vol. 3.

Carlsson, C., & Fullér, R. (1995). Multiple criteria decision making: The case for interdependence. *Computers & Operations Research, 22*(3), 251–260.

Chiou, H. K., Tzeng, G. H., & Cheng, D. C. (2005). Evaluating sustainable fishing development strategies using fuzzy MCDM approach. *Omega, 33*(3), 223–234.

Debalki, Y. A., Hou, J., Adane, B. Y., Mawutor, V. G., & Dang, H. (2024). A distributed relay selection using a fuzzy-BCM based decision making strategy for multi-hop data dissemination in VANETs. *Wireless Networks, 30*(4), 2873–2894.

Demir, G., Chatterjee, P., & Pamucar, D. (2024). Sensitivity analysis in multi-criteria decision making: A state-of-the-art research perspective using bibliometric analysis. *Expert Systems with Applications, 237*, 121660.

Guan, X., Guo, K., & Tian, H. (2024). Efficient identification technique for 2-additive fuzzy measures with consideration of objective relationships among features. *International Journal of Machine Learning and Cybernetics, 15*(11), 5217–5237.

Haseli, G., & Jafarzadeh Ghoushchi, S. (2022). Extended base-criterion method based on the spherical fuzzy sets to evaluate waste management. *Soft Computing, 26*(19), 9979–9992.

Haseli, G., Bonab, S. R., Hajiaghaei-Keshteli, M., Ghoushchi, S. J., & Deveci, M. (2024). Fuzzy ZE-numbers framework in group decision-making using the BCM and CoCoSo to address sustainable urban transportation. *Information Sciences, 653*, 119809.

Haseli, G., Nazarian-Jashnabadi, J., Shirazi, B., Hajiaghaei-Keshteli, M., & Moslem, S. (2024). Sustainable strategies based on the social responsibility of the beverage industry companies for the circular supply chain. *Engineering Applications of Artificial Intelligence, 133*, 108253.

Haseli, G., Ögel, İ. Y., Ecer, F., & Hajiaghaei-Keshteli, M. (2023). Luxury in female technology (FemTech): Selection of smart jewelry for women through BCM-MARCOS group decision-making framework with fuzzy ZE-numbers. *Technological Forecasting and Social Change, 196*, 122870.

Haseli, G., Ranjbarzadeh, R., Hajiaghaei-Keshteli, M., Ghoushchi, S. J., Hasani, A., Deveci, M., & Ding, W. (2023). HECON: Weight assessment of the product loyalty criteria considering the customer decision's halo effect using the convolutional neural networks. *Information Sciences, 623*, 184–205.

Haseli, G., & Sheikh, R. (2022). Base criterion method (BCM). In *Multiple criteria decision making: Techniques,*. Singapore: Springer Nature Singapore, 17–38 analysis and applications.

Haseli, G., Sheikh, R., & Sana, S. S. (2020a). Base-criterion on multi-criteria decision-making method and its applications. *International Journal of Management Science and Engineering Management, 15*(2), 79–88.

Haseli, G., Sheikh, R., & Sana, S. S. (2020b). Extension of base-criterion method based on fuzzy set theory. *International Journal of Applied and Computational Mathematics, 6*(2), 54.

He, Q., Ren, X., Li, W., Dong, L., & Hu, X. (2024). Sustainability prioritization of CCUS systems with consideration of criteria interaction: A fuzzy multi-criteria decision-making framework based on 2-additive fuzzy measure and Choquet integral method. *Environment, Development and Sustainability*, 1–25.

Imran, S.M., Rameshan, N., Anand, M.C. J., Martin, N., Tiwari, M., & Mohan, V. (2024). Fuzzy decision-making on strategies for maximizing the utility of electric vehicles. In 2024 IEEE Third International Conference on Power Electronics, Intelligent Control and Energy Systems (ICPEICES) (pp. 347–352). IEEE.

Işık, Ö., Shabir, M., Demir, G., Puska, A., & Pamucar, D. (2025). A hybrid framework for assessing Pakistani commercial bank performance using multi-criteria decision-making. *Financial Innovation, 11*(1), 38.

Jiang, P., Wang, W., Hu, Y. C., Chiu, Y. J., & Tsao, S. J. (2021). Pattern classification using tolerance rough sets based on non-additive grey relational analysis and DEMATEL. *Grey Systems: Theory and Application, 11*(1), 166–182.

Liang, Y., Ju, Y., Tu, Y., & Rezaei, J. (2023). Nonadditive best-worst method: Incorporating criteria interaction using the Choquet integral. *Journal of the Operational Research Society, 74*(6), 1495–1506.

Liu, X., Tan, Y., Dong, J., Wu, J., Wang, X., & Sun, Z. (2025). Assessing habitat selection parameters of Arabica coffee using BWM and BCM methods based on GIS. *Scientific Reports, 15*(1), 8.

Narang, M., Joshi, M. C., & Pal, A. K. (2021). A hybrid fuzzy COPRAS-base-criterion method for multi-criteria decision making. *Soft Computing, 25*, 8391–8399.

Narang, M., Joshi, M. C., & Pal, A. K. (2022). A hesitant fuzzy multiplicative Base-criterion multi-criteria group decision making method. *Informatica, 46*(2).

Narayanan, U., & Paul, V. (2023). Twin chain: A blockchain based federated learning intrusion detection system using optimized backpropagation based neural network for edge assisted IoT networks. https://doi.org/10.21203/rs.3.rs-3214924/v1

Nazarian-Jashnabadi, J., Bonab, S. R., Haseli, G., Tomaskova, H., & Hajiaghaei-Keshteli, M. (2023). A dynamic expert system to increase patient satisfaction with an integrated approach of system dynamics, ISM, and ANP methods. *Expert Systems with Applications, 234*, 121010.

Phulara, S., Kumar, A., Narang, M., & Bisht, K. (2024). A novel hybrid grey-BCM approach in multi-criteria decision making: An application in OTT platform. *Journal of Decision Analytics and Intelligent Computing, 4*(1), 1–15.

Rezaei, J. (2015). Best-worst multi-criteria decision-making method. *Omega, 53*, 49–57.

Saaty, T. L. (1977). A scaling method for priorities in hierarchical structures. *Journal of Mathematical Psychology, 15*(3), 234–281. https://doi.org/10.1016/0022-2496(77)90033-5.

Saaty, T. L. (2013). Analytic hierarchy process. In *Encyclopedia of operations research and management science*. Boston, MA: Springer, 52–64.

Shapley, L. S. (1953). A value for n-person games. In H. W. Kuhn, & A. W. Tucker (Eds.). *Contributions to the theory of Games II* (pp. 307–317). *Princeton University Press*.

Solieman, H., & Duleba, S. (2026). *Reliable Decision-Making for Sustainable Transportation*. Elsevier, 169–201. https://doi.org/10.1016/b978-0-443-33740-6.00007-4.

Stević, Ž., Pamučar, D., Vasiljević, M., Stojić, G., & Korica, S. (2017). Novel integrated multi-criteria model for supplier selection: Case study construction company. *Symmetry, 9*(11), 279.

Sun, L., Yu, C., Li, J., Yuan, Q., & Zhao, S. (2024). A two-stage decision model for sustainable-resilient supplier selection and order allocation under uncertain environment. *Kybernetes*.

Wu, Y., Liu, P., & Li, Y. (2024). An integrated QFD and FMEA method under the co-opetitional relationship for product upgrading. *Information Sciences, 667*, 120505.

Wu, Y., Liu, P., & Li, Y. (2026). An improved QFD model with the integration of BCM and CoCoSo method under the trust network. *International Journal of Information Technology & Decision Making*. https://doi.org/10.1142/s0219622026500458.

Yang, J. L., Chiu, H. N., Tzeng, G. H., & Yeh, R. H. (2008). Vendor selection by integrated fuzzy MCDM techniques with independent and interdependent relationships. *Information Sciences, 178*(21), 4166–4183.

Zafaranlouei, N., Ghoushchi, S. J., & Haseli, G. (2023). Assessment of sustainable waste management alternatives using the extensions of the base criterion method and combined compromise solution based on the fuzzy Z-numbers. *Environmental Science and Pollution Research, 30*(22), 62121–62136.

Chapter 30

BRAW: Block-wise rating of attribute weights for multi-attribute decision-making

Amir H. Malekijoo[1] and Reyhane Malekijoo[2]
[1]*Information Sciences and Technology, George Mason University, Fairfax County, VA, United States,* [2]*Department of Physics and Energy Engineering, AmirKabir University of Technology, Tehran, Iran*

30.1 Introduction

Determining the relative importance of criteria is a central step in multiple attribute decision-making because criterion weights directly influence how alternatives are evaluated, aggregated, and ranked (Hatefi, 2024). Many traditional weighting techniques rely on extensive pairwise comparisons, direct numerical assessments, or subjective priority ratings, all of which can impose a significant cognitive load on decision makers (Kizielewicz et al., 2024). As the number of criteria increases, these methods often become difficult to implement, and they may produce inconsistent judgments (Tavana et al., 2023). At the same time, real-world decision environments frequently involve uncertain preferences, small performance differences, and incomplete information (Olschewski et al., 2024). These conditions create additional challenges for deriving stable and meaningful weights through classical approaches.

The block-wise rating of attribute weights method (BRAW) was introduced to address these limitations by redesigning how preference information is elicited and transformed into criterion weights (Hatefi, 2021). Instead of comparing full sets of criteria or large matrices of alternatives, BRAW uses compact two-by-two blocks that include two criteria and two alternatives in each comparison. This design reduces complexity and allows decision makers to express simple qualitative judgments such as preference, indifference, or varying degrees of intensity (Chen et al., 2022). BRAW also incorporates the concept of an indifference threshold that filters out negligible performance differences and prevents small fluctuations from influencing the resulting weights. Through a structured examination of these blocks, the method generates linear preference relations that reflect both the comparative behavior of decision makers and the underlying performance contrasts across criteria (Hatefi, 2021).

Beyond simplifying judgments, BRAW integrates subjective and objective components within a goal programming framework. Judged blocks impose behavioral constraints, while an objective target vector derived from an independent method, such as indifference threshold-based attribute ratio analysis, guides the search for balanced and consistent weights. This combination makes the method robust against inconsistencies, reduces the need for exhaustive comparisons, and retains theoretical discipline in its mathematical formulation. As a result, BRAW provides a practical, flexible, and analytically grounded procedure that is suitable for complex decision problems where traditional weighting methods struggle to capture nuanced preferences or maintain consistency. Through these features, BRAW has become an appealing alternative for researchers and practitioners who seek efficient and cognitively manageable techniques for deriving attribute weights.

To structure the chapter, the next section presents a focused literature review of weighting techniques in multiple attribute decision-making and highlights the theoretical and practical motivations for using the BRAW method. The methodological section then provides a detailed explanation of the block construction process, the role of indifference thresholds, the formation of linear constraints, and the optimization model used to derive the final weights. Two numerical examples follow to illustrate the mechanics of BRAW under different decision environments, including both sustainable

Encyclopedia of Multi-Attribute Decision-Making (MADM). DOI: https://doi.org/10.1016/B978-0-443-33275-3.00078-6

supply chain evaluation and renewable energy project prioritization. The chapter concludes with a summary of insights regarding the strengths, limitations, and practical considerations associated with applying the BRAW method in real decision settings.

30.2 Literature review

Recent studies in multiple attribute decision-making emphasize the need for weighting methods that can handle complex, vague, or uncertain evaluations while remaining computationally efficient. Classical subjective techniques such as direct rating, step-wise weight assessment ratio analysis, and belief-based best-worse method rely entirely on decision makers' judgments, which can be burdensome when the number of criteria increases (Hatefi, 2021). Objective techniques such as entropy, CCSD, and SECA avoid elicitation but may fail to reflect true preference structures because they depend solely on data dispersion. Integrated methods attempt to combine the strengths of both groups. For example, Chen et al. (2022) incorporated Fermatean fuzzy linguistic sets with the constrained combined compromise solution approach to produce flexible risk assessments under ambiguity, and used an extended version of BRAW to determine criteria weights within their occupational health and safety risk model. Their findings showed that block-wise elicitation reduces inconsistency and offers higher discriminability when dealing with imprecise expert input.

Among integrated techniques, the BRAW method has gained attention for its cognitively simple yet analytically strong structure (Hatefi, 2021). Unlike methods such as rank order centroid (ROC) or the Improved ROC model, which approximate weights based on rank positions and may lose preference intensity information, BRAW captures the trade-offs between criteria by using two-by-two blocks that require minimal judgment effort. This design reduces the number of comparisons, minimizes inconsistency, and allows the integration of subjective constraints with an objective target vector through goal programming.

30.3 Methods and materials

The BRAW method is an optimization-based procedure for deriving criterion weights in multi-attribute decision-making. The method constructs linear constraints from the decision maker's local judgments over small two-by-two sub-matrices known as blocks. These constraints form a convex feasible region, referred to as the weight space, from which the final weights are obtained (Hatefi, 2021).

Let the decision matrix be $D_{m\times n}$. For every pair of alternatives A_u and A_v with $u < v$, and every pair of criteria C_s and C_t with $s < t$, a two-by-two block is constructed as follows:

$$\begin{array}{lccc} & & C_s & C_t \\ Block_{uvst}: & A_u & (d_{us} & d_{ut}), \\ & A_v & (d_{vs} & d_{vt}) \end{array} \quad u,\ v = 1,\ \ldots,\ \ m\ |u < v,\quad s,\ t = 1, \ldots, n|\ s < t. \tag{30.1}$$

This block contains the non-normalized scores for the selected alternatives and criteria. A normalized version is then computed using the standard normalization functions.

For each normalized block with entries r_{us}, r_{vs}, and r_{vt}, the significant subtraction for criterion C_s is defined as follows:

$$\Delta_{uvs} = \begin{cases} (r_{us} - r_{vs}) - \pi_s^N & if\ \pi_s^N < (r_{us} - r_{vs}) \\ (r_{us} - r_{vs}) + \pi_s^N & if\ \pi_s^N < (r_{vs} - r_{us}), \\ 0 & if\ \pi_s^N \geq |\ r_{us} - r_{vs}\ | \end{cases} \quad \forall\ block \in B, \tag{30.2}$$

where π_s^N is the normalized indifference threshold for criterion C_s. A similar expression holds for Δ_{uvt}.

Using these values, the level of significant contrast between the two criteria in the block is obtained as follows:

$$\mu_{uvst} = -\frac{\Delta_{uvt}}{\Delta_{uvs}}, \quad \forall\ block \in B, \tag{30.3}$$

Assuming an additive value function, if the decision maker prefers A_u over A_v in the block, then:

$$r_{us} w_s + r_{ut} w_t > r_{vs} w_s + r_{vt} w_t \tag{30.4}$$

To incorporate indifference thresholds, the subtraction terms are replaced with the significant subtraction values, leading to the following:

$$\Delta_{uvs}\ w_s > -\Delta_{uvt}\ w_t \tag{30.5}$$

When preferences are expressed using the degree of preference scale, the constraint becomes:

$$\begin{cases} \frac{w_s}{w_t} > \mu_{uvst} + \varphi\theta \; if \, (A_u \gg A_u, \, \Delta_{uvs} > 0) or \, (A_u \ll A_u, \, \Delta_{uvs} < 0) \\ \frac{w_s}{w_t} < \mu_{uvst} - \varphi\theta \; if \, (A_u \gg A_u, \, \Delta_{uvs} < 0) or \, (A_u \ll A_u, \, \Delta_{uvs} > 0), \\ \frac{w_s}{w_t} = \mu_{uvst} \qquad if \, (A_u \equiv A_v) \end{cases} \quad \forall \, block \in B, \tag{30.6}$$

To convert these relationships into linear constraints, a small positive number ε is introduced, resulting in:

$$\begin{cases} w_s - (\mu_{uvst} + \varphi\theta) \quad if \, (A_u \gg A_u, \, \Delta_{uvs} > 0) or \, (A_u \ll A_u, \, \Delta_{uvs} < 0) \\ w_s - (\mu_{uvst} - \varphi\theta) \quad if \, (A_u \gg A_u, \, \Delta_{uvs} < 0) or \, (A_u \ll A_u, \, \Delta_{uvs} > 0), \\ w_s - \quad \mu_{uvst} w_t = 0 \;\; if \, (A_u \equiv A_v) \end{cases} \quad \forall \, block \in B, \tag{30.7}$$

These constraints define the feasible weight space before optimization (Hatefi, 2021).

To derive a unique weight vector, the optimization model minimizes the sum of deviation variables introduced to absorb inconsistencies. The objective function is as follows:

$$Min \; Z = \sum_{j=1}^{n} (\sigma_j + \sigma_j') \tag{30.8}$$

Subject to constraints:

$$\begin{cases} w_s - (\mu_{uvst} + \varphi\theta) w_t + \alpha_{uvst} \geq \varepsilon \\ w_s - (\mu_{uvst} - \varphi\theta) w_t - \beta_{uvst} \leq -\varepsilon, \\ w_s - \mu_{uvst} w_t + \gamma_{uvst} - \gamma'_{uvst} = 0 \end{cases} \quad \forall \, block \in B,$$

$$w_j + \sigma_j + \sigma_j' = \delta_j, \quad j = 1, 2, \ldots, n,$$

$$\sum_{j=1}^{n} w_j = 1, \tag{30.9}$$

Solving this linear optimization model produces a weight vector that is fully consistent with the decision maker's blockwise judgments and the additive value structure.

30.4 Numerical example 1

The numerical example begins with the construction of the decision matrix containing the performance of five logistics providers across five criteria. These criteria include reliability, cost, digital tracking, sustainability, and flexibility. The values show clear variation among providers. For instance, DHL offers the highest reliability at 98, while DB Schenker records the highest shipment cost at 140. This matrix forms the foundation for all subsequent steps in the BRAW method (see Table 30.1).

The next step applies normalization to convert all entries into comparable unit-free values. Benefit criteria such as reliability and tracking are normalized by dividing by the maximum observed value. The cost criterion is normalized using

TABLE 30.1 Decision matrix D.

Provider	Reliability (%)	Cost (€/shipment)	Digital tracking	Sustainability	Flexibility
DHL	98.0	120.0	9.2	85.0	8.5
FedEx	95.0	135.0	8.8	78.0	7.9
UPS	97.0	128.0	9.0	82.0	8.2
DB Schenker	93.0	140.0	7.5	88.0	8.8
Kuehne + Nagel	96.0	132.0	8.5	90.0	9.0

the decreasing function that assigns higher normalized scores to lower costs. This produces the normalized matrix shown below, which indicates strong performance for DHL and Kuehne + Nagel and weaker tracking performance for DB Schenker (see Table 30.2).

The BRAW method proceeds by calculating the indifference threshold for each criterion. Each threshold represents the minimum difference required for the decision maker to perceive one provider as distinctly better. The threshold is computed as 10% of the value range for each criterion. The normalized threshold value π_j^N is equal to 0.1 for all criteria (see Table 30.3).

After introducing thresholds, the method constructs 100 possible blocks formed by pairing two alternatives and two criteria at a time. Using the significant subtraction rule, only blocks with meaningful contrast are retained. Out of 100 potential blocks, only four survive the screening process. These blocks contain the highest discriminative information needed to infer weights (see Table 30.4).

TABLE 30.2 Normalized matrix R.

Provider	Reliability	Cost	Digital tracking	Sustainability	Flexibility
DHL	1.0000	1.00	1.0000	0.9444	0.9444
FedEx	0.9694	0.25	0.9565	0.8667	0.8778
UPS	0.9898	0.60	0.9783	0.9111	0.9111
DB Schenker	0.9490	0.00	0.8152	0.9778	0.9778
Kuehne + Nagel	0.9796	0.40	0.9239	1.0000	1.0000

TABLE 30.3 Indifference thresholds.

Criterion	π_j (raw)	π_j^N
Reliability	0.50	0.1
Cost	2.00	0.1
Digital tracking	0.17	0.1
Sustainability	1.20	0.1
Flexibility	0.11	0.1

TABLE 30.4 Screened blocks.

Block description	Δ_{uvs}	Δ_{uvt}	μ
FedEx vs DB Schenker, cost vs sustainability	0.1500	-0.0111	0.0741
FedEx vs DB Schenker, cost vs flexibility	0.1500	0.0000	0.0000
FedEx vs DB Schenker, tracking vs sustainability	0.0413	-0.0111	0.2690
FedEx vs DB Schenker, tracking vs flexibility	0.0413	0.0000	0.0000

The remaining blocks are then evaluated by the decision maker. For each block, the decision maker judges whether one alternative is clearly better or whether the two appear indifferent. These judgments directly determine the form of the linear constraints that will be later used to infer criterion weights. The next table shows the judgments collected for the four screened blocks (see Table 30.5).

Using these judgments, the method generates five linear constraints, along with the nonnegativity and sum to one condition, and forms a linear program. Solving this program produces the inferred weights. Due to the small number of effective blocks, the inferred weights differ sharply from the true weights. The cost criterion receives an extremely high inferred weight of 0.9919, while the other criteria receive weights close to zero (see Table 30.6).

Finally, the inferred weights are multiplied by the normalized matrix to compute the multi-attribute additive value (MAV) score for each provider. These scores generate the final ranking shown below. DHL achieves the top position with a score of 0.9997. UPS and Kuehne + Nagel follow, while FedEx and DB Schenker obtain lower scores due to weaker cost performance (see Table 30.7).

TABLE 30.5 Decision maker judgments.

Block	μ	Δ_{uvs}	Judgment
Cost vs sustainability	0.074	0.150	$A_u >> A_v$
Cost vs flexibility	0.000	0.150	$A_u >> A_v$
Tracking vs sustainability	0.269	0.041	$A_u = A_v$
Tracking vs flexibility	0.000	0.041	$A_u >> A_v$

TABLE 30.6 Inferred weights.

Criterion	True weight	BRAW weight	Abs error
Reliability	0.30	0.0010	0.2990
Cost	0.20	0.9919	0.7919
Digital tracking	0.18	0.0013	0.1787
Sustainability	0.22	0.0048	0.2152
Flexibility	0.10	0.0010	0.0990

TABLE 30.7 Final ranking using multi-attribute additive value (MAV).

Provider	MAV score
DHL	0.9997
UPS	0.6027
Kuehne + Nagel	0.4047
FedEx	0.2552
DB Schenker	0.0077

To demonstrate the mechanics of the BRAW method, one complete block is manually calculated from start to finish. The selected block compares FedEx (A2) and Kuehne +Nagel (A5) under the criteria cost (C2) and flexibility (C5). This block is chosen because it survives the significant contrast screening and therefore contributes to the weight inference process.

The calculation begins by extracting the raw values from the decision matrix. FedEx has a shipment cost of 135 and a flexibility score of 7.9, while Kuehne + Nagel has a shipment cost of 132 and a flexibility score of 9.0. These values form the starting point for normalization.

$$dus = 135,\ dvs = 132,\ dut = 7.9,\ dvt = 9.0$$

Next, normalization is applied. Since cost is a cost criterion, its normalized score is computed. The Flexibility criterion is a benefit measure and is normalized by dividing by its maximum observed value. Using these formulas, FedEx obtains normalized scores $r_{us} = 0.25$ and $r_{ut} = 0.8778$, while Kuehne + Nagel obtains $r_{vs} = 0.40$ and $r_{vt} = 1.0$.

$$r_{us} = 0.2500,\ r_{vs} = 0.4000,\ r_{ut} = 0.8778,\ r_{vt} = 1.00$$

The next step computes the indifference thresholds. For both cost and flexibility, the normalized indifference threshold π^N is equal to 0.1. These thresholds determine whether the difference between the two alternatives is large enough to be meaningful in the decision maker's eyes. Using these thresholds, the significant subtraction rule is applied. For the cost criterion, the normalized difference is –0.15, which exceeds the threshold magnitude. Therefore, the adjusted difference becomes –0.05. For flexibility, the normalized difference is –0.1222, and after subtracting the threshold in the appropriate direction, the adjusted contrast becomes –0.0222. Since both Δ_{uvs} and Δ_{uvt} are nonzero, the block survives the screening phase.

$$\Delta_{uvs} = -0.0500,\ \Delta_{uvt} = -0.0222$$

Substituting the values above results in $\mu = 0.4440$. This parameter plays a central role in translating the block into a linear constraint for the weighting model.

$$\mu_{uvst} = 0.4440$$

The decision maker's judgment is now simulated using the known true weights. The MAV score for each alternative is computed as the weighted sum of normalized values under the two criteria. FedEx obtains a score of 0.1378 while Kuehne + Nagel obtains 0.1800. Since the score of Kuehne + Nagel is larger by more than the tolerance margin, the decision maker judges that alternative v dominates u under this block, meaning FedEx is inferior to Kuehne + Nagel ($A_u \ll A_v$).

$$MAV\ FedEx = 0.1378,\ MAV\ KN = 0.1800$$

Judgment: $A_u \ll A_v$

This judgment determines the form of the linear constraint for the weight estimation model. Because the judgment is $A_u \ll A_v$ and the significant difference in the first criterion (cost) is negative, the appropriate constraint becomes

$$w_s \le (\mu + \phi\theta)\ w_t - \varepsilon$$

where $\varphi = 0.15$, $\theta = 2$, and $\varepsilon = 0.001$. Substituting values yields a constraint of the form

$$w_2 \le 0.744\ w_5 - 0.001$$

Finally, once the full linear programming (LP) is solved globally using all surviving constraints, the MAV scores are recomputed for FedEx and Kuehne + Nagel using the inferred BRAW weights. The final scores confirm that Kuehne + Nagel ranks above FedEx, with values 0.4047 and 0.2552, respectively.

$$\text{FedEx} = 0.2552,\ \text{Kuehne + Nagel} = 0.4047$$

This completes the full chain of calculations for one illustrative block of the BRAW method. It shows clearly how raw values enter the process, how they are normalized and screened, how judgments translate into constraints, and how these constraints influence the final weight and ranking outcome.

30.5 Numerical example 2

The second numerical example focuses on the selection of a sustainable third-party logistics provider using nine environmental and operational criteria. The evaluation involves five green logistics companies that differ significantly in

TABLE 30.8 Decision matrix D (5×9).

Provider	Reliability (%)	Cost (€/ton)	Carbon emission (kg CO_2e)	Renewable energy (%)	Digital tracking	Reverse logistics	Circular compliance	Green certification	Flexibility score
DHL green	98.5	285.0	42.0	88.0	9.4	8.8	9.1	9.5	8.7
Maersk eco	96.0	310.0	58.0	72.0	8.6	7.9	8.0	8.0	8.3
Kuehne + Nagel NetZero	97.8	295.0	38.0	95.0	9.6	9.3	9.5	9.8	9.1
DB Schenker green	94.0	320.0	65.0	68.0	7.8	8.5	7.7	7.5	8.0
UPS carbon neutral	97.0	278.0	45.0	85.0	9.0	8.7	8.8	9.0	8.9

reliability, logistics cost, carbon performance, energy profile, digital capability, circular practices, green certification, and flexibility. The decision matrix below summarizes the raw performance data and forms the foundation for all subsequent calculations in the BRAW method (see Table 30.8).

The next stage converts the raw data into dimensionless values using benefit and cost normalization formulas. Benefit criteria are normalized by dividing each value by the maximum observed value, while cost criteria use an inverse transformation to reward lower values. The resulting normalized matrix preserves the relative strengths of the providers. Kuehne + Nagel NetZero obtains the highest values in most sustainability-related criteria, while DB Schenker green receives the weakest scores in carbon emissions and certification (see Table 30.9).

The BRAW method then computes the indifference thresholds for each criterion at 10% of its observed range. These thresholds are necessary to determine whether the contrast between two alternatives is meaningful. Because the ranges differ across reliability, energy usage, emissions, or certification score, the resulting raw thresholds also vary, but the normalized thresholds for all criteria converge to 0.1 due to the scaling process (see Table 30.10).

After defining the thresholds, the method constructs all 360 possible two-by-two blocks of alternatives and criteria. Only four blocks survive the significant contrast screening process, which means that the majority of interactions do not produce strong enough differences once the threshold is applied. With only four meaningful blocks, the model generates five linear constraints for the weighting step. However, the constraint system becomes infeasible when solved simultaneously, mainly because the limited number of surviving blocks produces conflicting directional information for the weights (see Table 30.11).

TABLE 30.9 Normalized matrix R.

Provider	Relia.	Cost	Carbon	Renew.	DigTrack	Reverse	Circular	Cert	Flex
DHL	1.0000	0.8333	0.8519	0.9263	0.9792	0.9462	0.9579	0.9694	0.9560
Maersk	0.9746	0.2381	0.2593	0.7579	0.8958	0.8495	0.8421	0.8163	0.9121
Kuehne + Nagel	0.9929	0.5952	1.0000	1.0000	1.0000	1.0000	1.0000	1.0000	1.0000
DB Schenker	0.9543	0.0000	0.0000	0.7158	0.8125	0.9140	0.8105	0.7653	0.8791
UPS	0.9848	1.0000	0.7407	0.8947	0.9375	0.9355	0.9263	0.9184	0.9780

TABLE 30.10 Indifference thresholds.

Criterion	Range	π_j	π_j^N
Reliability	4.5	0.45	0.1
Logistics cost	42.0	4.20	0.1
Carbon emission	27.0	2.70	0.1
Renewable energy	27.0	2.70	0.1
Digital tracking	1.8	0.18	0.1
Reverse logistics	1.4	0.14	0.1
Circular compliance	1.8	0.18	0.1
Green certification	2.3	0.23	0.1
Flexibility	1.1	0.11	0.1

TABLE 30.11 Summary of block screening and model feasibility.

Item	Value
Total possible blocks	360
Surviving blocks	4
Constraints formed	5
LP status	Infeasible

TABLE 30.12 Inferred vs true weights.

Criterion	True weight	BRAW weight	Abs error
Reliability	0.16	0.9817	0.8217
Logistics cost	0.12	0.0010	0.1190
Carbon emission	0.18	0.0060	0.1740
Renewable energy	0.14	0.0063	0.1337
Digital tracking	0.09	0.0010	0.0890
Reverse logistics	0.07	0.0010	0.0690
Circular compliance	0.09	0.0010	0.0890
Green certification	0.08	0.0010	0.0790
Flexibility	0.07	0.0010	0.0690

Even though the LP system is infeasible, the implementation still reports the inferred weights obtained from the closest feasible projection used for analysis. The estimated weights diverge noticeably from the true weights. Delivery reliability receives an excessively large inferred weight, while all other criteria collapse to values near zero. This outcome reflects the structural limitation caused by too few screened blocks, which prevents the method from recovering meaningful trade-off information across criteria (see Table 30.12).

The mean absolute error for numerical example 2 is 0.1826, indicating that the reconstructed weights deviate substantially from the intended weighting structure. The example demonstrates the sensitivity of BRAW to the number of surviving blocks and the richness of contrast information available in the normalized matrix. In sustainable logistics evaluation, where criteria tend to move together due to similar green initiatives, high correlations may reduce the number of strong discriminations and thus limit the accuracy of the weight extraction method.

This illustrative block examines the contrast between Kuehne + Nagel NetZero and UPS carbon neutral under the criteria carbon emission (C3) and renewable energy usage (C4). The raw performance values show that Kuehne + Nagel achieves a lower carbon footprint at 38.0 and higher renewable energy usage at 95.0, while UPS records 45.0 and 85.0, respectively. After normalization, Kuehne + Nagel attains perfect scores on both criteria, whereas UPS receives 0.7407 for carbon emissions and 0.8947 for renewable energy usage. These normalized differences exceed the indifference threshold and therefore produce significant contrasts of $\Delta_{uvs} = 0.1593$ and $\Delta_{uvt} = 0.0053$ (see Table 30.13).

Using the BRAW formula, the contrast ratio becomes $\mu = -0.0330$. The MAV values computed with the true weights indicate that Kuehne + Nagel clearly dominates UPS, producing the judgment $A_u >> A_v$. This judgment generates the linear constraint $w_3 \geq 0.267 \cdot w_4 + 0.001$, which becomes one of the valid constraints fed into the BRAW weight inference model. All steps strictly follow the procedure described by Hatefi (2021).

TABLE 30.13 Detailed computation for one block (Kuehne + Nagel NetZero vs UPS carbon neutral).

Step	Calculation	Result
Raw values	Kuehne + Nagel: C3 = 38.0, C4 = 95.0	
UPS: C3 = 45.0, C4 = 85.0	—	
Normalized r_{us}	38.0 normalized on C3 range	1.0000
Normalized r_{vs}	45.0 normalized on C3 range	0.7407
Normalized r_{ut}	95.0 normalized on C4 range	1.0000
Normalized r_{vt}	85.0 normalized on C4 range	0.8947
Significant diff Δ_{uvs}	$1.0000\text{-}0.7407\text{-}\pi^N = 0.1593$	0.1593
Significant diff Δ_{uvt}	$1.0000\text{-}0.8947\text{-}\pi^N = 0.0053$	0.0053
Contrast ratio μ	$-\Delta_{uvt}/\Delta_{uvs}$	−0.0330
MAV (true weights)	KN = 0.3200, UPS = 0.2586	KN > UPS
Judgment	Based on MAV	$A_u >> A_v$
LP constraint	$w_3 \geq (\mu + \varphi\theta)\ w4 + \varepsilon$	$w_3 \geq 0.267 \cdot w_4 + 0.001$

30.6 Conclusion

The BRAW method offers a practical and analytically disciplined framework for extracting criterion weights in situations where traditional weighting techniques may become cognitively demanding or inconsistent. By decomposing the decision environment into two-by-two blocks, BRAW reduces judgment complexity and preserves the structure of the decision maker's preferences, even when performance differences are small or uncertain. The integration of indifference thresholds ensures that only meaningful contrasts influence the inferred weights, while the optimization model provides a transparent mechanism for resolving inconsistencies and balancing subjective and objective information.

The numerical examples demonstrate that the performance of BRAW depends on the richness of contrast information available in the decision matrix and the number of screened blocks that survive the threshold filtering process. When the matrix contains strong discriminative signals, BRAW can successfully recover stable and interpretable weight structures. When contrasts are limited, the resulting weight space may become narrow or infeasible, which highlights the importance of data diversity and criterion heterogeneity in practical applications. Taken together, these findings show that BRAW is a valuable and flexible tool for researchers and practitioners who require a simple, preference-based, and mathematically grounded method for weighting criteria in multi-attribute decision-making contexts.

References

Chen, Q.-Y., Liu, H.-C., Wang, J.-H., & Shi, H. (2022). New model for occupational health and safety risk assessment based on Fermatean fuzzy linguistic sets and CoCoSo approach. *Applied Soft Computing, 126*, 109262.

Hatefi, M. A. (2021). BRAW: Block-wise rating the attribute weights in MADM. *Computers & Industrial Engineering, 156*, 107274.

Hatefi, M. A. (2024). A new method for weighting decision making attributes: An application in high-tech selection in oil and gas industry. *Soft Computing-A Fusion of Foundations, Methodologies & Applications, 28*(1).

Kizielewicz, B., Tomczyk, T., Gandor, M., & Sałabun, W. (2024). Subjective weight determination methods in multi-criteria decision-making: A systematic review. *Procedia Computer Science, 246*, 5396–5407.

Olschewski, S., Luckman, A., Mason, A., Ludvig, E. A., & Konstantinidis, E. (2024). The future of decisions from experience: Connecting real-world decision problems to cognitive processes. *Perspectives on Psychological Science, 19*(1), 82–102.

Tavana, M., Soltanifar, M., & Santos-Arteaga, F. J. (2023). Analytical hierarchy process: Revolution and evolution. *Annals of Operations Research, 326*(2), 879–907.

Chapter 31

CIMAS: Criteria importance assessment for multi-attribute decision-making

Galip Cihan Yalçın[1] and Karahan Kara[1,2]

[1]*Department of Business, Faculty of Economics and Administrative Sciences, OSTIM Technical University, Ankara, Türkiye,* [2]*Department of Data Science and Analytics, Faculty of Economics and Administrative Sciences, İzmir Katip Çelebi University, İzmir, Türkiye*

31.1 Introduction

In contemporary decision-making environments, organizations are increasingly confronted with complex problems that require the evaluation and prioritization of multiple, often conflicting, criteria. Multi-attribute decision-making (MADM) approaches have emerged as essential tools for addressing such challenges, offering systematic frameworks for informed and robust decision-making. Among these approaches, the criteria importance assessment (CIMAS) method, initially introduced by Bošković et al. (2025), has gained significant attention due to its ability to determine criterion weights through linear normalization and max–min distance calculations, while ensuring robustness and reliability via the reliability index (RI). CIMAS has demonstrated versatility in various decision contexts, including supplier selection, innovation capacity evaluation, risk prioritization, financial performance assessment, and healthcare system optimization.

The CIMAS method is frequently integrated with other MADM techniques to enhance decision support frameworks. For example, its combination with the criteria importance through intercriteria correlation method enables the derivation of hybrid criterion weights that integrate both subjective expert judgments and objective intercriteria correlations (Bošković et al., 2025; Liu & Lai, 2025). Similarly, hybridizations with methods such as AROMAN, weighted aggregated sum product assessment, logarithmic decomposition of criteria importance - ranking based on distance and range (LODECI-RADAR), alternative ranking technique based on adaptive standardized intervals (ARTASI), weighted integrated sum product (WISP), complex proportional assessment, and alternative ranking using two-step logarithmic normalization (ARLON) have been employed across diverse domains, including green port operations (Yalçın, 2025), e-commerce platform evaluation (Biswas et al., 2025), blockchain platform selection (Kara, Yalçın, Simic, et al., 2024), authentication system assessment (Yalçın et al., 2025), human resource management in power enterprises (Sun, 2025), and energy performance certificate platform analysis (Shakeel et al., 2025). These integrations enable a comprehensive evaluation framework by combining subjective assessments, objective data, and advanced ranking mechanisms to ensure reliable and actionable results.

Moreover, fuzzy set extensions of CIMAS (such as fermatean fuzzy, interval-valued spherical fuzzy, intuitionistic fuzzy, picture fuzzy, and rungs fuzzy sets) have been widely adopted to address uncertainty and imprecision in expert judgments, further enhancing the robustness and applicability of hybrid MADM frameworks (Kara, Yalçın, Çetinkaya, et al., 2024; Xiang & Zhang, 2025). The recent literature highlights the growing prevalence and versatility of ranking methods such as ARLON, alternative ranking order method accounting for two-step normalization (AROMAN), and ARTASI, which have been successfully employed to rank alternatives in complex decision-making scenarios, ranging from supplier selection and technology adoption to digital platform evaluation (Aytekin & Korucuk, 2024; Bouraima et al., 2024; Kara, Yalçın, Kaygısız et al., 2024; Švadlenka et al., 2024).

The remainder of this paper is organized as follows: Section 31.2 provides a detailed description of the CIMAS method; Section 31.3 and Section 31.4 present the application of the CIMAS framework through numerical examples; and Section 31.5 concludes the study with key findings, managerial implications, and directions for future research.

Encyclopedia of Multi-Attribute Decision-Making (MADM). DOI: https://doi.org/10.1016/B978-0-443-33275-3.00009-9

31.2 Methodology

The CIMAS criterion weighting method determines criterion weights based on linear normalization and max–min values (Bošković et al., 2025). In addition, it incorporates the calculation of the RI to verify the consistency and robustness of the obtained criterion weights. The CIMAS method is structured into seven sequential steps, outlined as follows:

Step 1: In the first phase of the CIMAS method, the criteria assessment decision matrix ($X = [X_{kj}]_{LN}$) is constructed, as expressed in (31.1). This matrix represents the evaluations of each criterion (C_j) with respect to each expert (E_k) (experts evaluate the criteria on a 1–10 scale). Each element of the matrix (X_{kj}) corresponds to the value of the *j–th* criterion under the *k–th* expert. The structure of the decision matrix consists of *N* criteria and *K* experts, necessitating a clear definition of both the set of criteria $C = \{C_1, C_2, \ldots, C_j, \ldots, C_N\}$ $(j = 1, 2, \ldots, N)$ and the set of experts $E = \{E_1, E_2, \ldots, E_k, \ldots, E_M\}$ $(k = 1, 2, \ldots, L)$ within the decision-making framework:

$$X = \begin{bmatrix} X_{11} & \cdots & X_{1j} & \cdots & X_{1N} \\ \vdots & \cdots & \vdots & \cdots & \vdots \\ X_{k1} & \cdots & X_{kj} & \cdots & X_{kN} \\ \vdots & \cdots & \vdots & \cdots & \vdots \\ X_{L1} & \cdots & X_{Lj} & \cdots & X_{LN} \end{bmatrix}; \ (k = 1, 2, \ldots, L; \ j = 1, 2, \ldots, N). \tag{31.1}$$

Step 2: In the second stage of the CIMAS method, the elements of the criteria assessment decision matrix are subjected to linear normalization procedures. The application of the linear normalization yields the normalized matrix ($Z = [Z_{kj}]_{LN}$) presented in (31.2):

$$Z_{kj} = \frac{X_{kj}}{\sum_{k=1}^{L} X_{kj}}; \ (k = 1, 2, \ldots, L; \ j = 1, 2, \ldots, N). \tag{31.2}$$

Step 3: In the third stage of the CIMAS method, the normalized matrix is integrated with the expert weight vector $w = \{w_1, w_2, \ldots, w_k, \ldots, w_L\}$ $(k = 1, 2, \ldots, L)$ through a multiplicative operation, as formulated in (31.3). This procedure generates the weighted normalized matrix ($D = [D_{kj}]_{LN}$), in which the relative importance of each expert is systematically embedded into the evaluation process:

$$D_{kj} = w_k * Z_{kj}; \ (k = 1, 2, \ldots, L; \ j = 1, 2, \ldots, N). \tag{31.3}$$

herein, $\sum_{k=1}^{L} w_k = 1$.

Step 4: In the fourth step of the CIMAS method, the weighted normalized matrix is employed to calculate the maximum value vector ($M^{\max} = [M_j^{\max}]_N$) and the minimum value vector ($M^{\min} = [M_j^{\min}]_N$), as expressed in Eqs. (31.4) and (31.5), respectively:

$$M_j^{\max} = \max_k D_{kj}; \ (k = 1, 2, \ldots, L; \ j = 1, 2, \ldots, N). \tag{31.4}$$

$$M_j^{\min} = \min_k D_{kj}; \ (k = 1, 2, \ldots, L; \ j = 1, 2, \ldots, N). \tag{31.5}$$

Step 5: In the fifth step of the CIMAS method, the distance vector ($M = [M_j]_N$) between the maximum value vector and the minimum value vector is determined using (31.6).

$$M_j = M_j^{\max} - M_j^{\min}; \ (j = 1, 2, \ldots, N). \tag{31.6}$$

Step 6: In the sixth step of the CIMAS method, the elements of the distance vector are subjected to linear normalization procedures. The application of the linear normalization yields the criteria weight vector ($R = [R_j]_N$) presented in (31.7):

$$R_j = \frac{M_j}{\sum_{j=1}^{N} M_j}; \ (j = 1, 2, \ldots, N). \tag{31.7}$$

Step 7: In the seventh (Checking) step of the CIMAS method, each expert re-evaluates the criteria in percentage terms (experts evaluate the criteria on a 1–100 scale), ensuring that the total of all assigned values equals 100. This is the second decision matrix ($Y = [Y_{kj}]_{LN}$) as stated (31.8). Based on these assessments, the second round of criterion weighting is calculated. The criterion weight matrix for this round is derived using the arithmetic average of expert evaluations using (31.9), thus the arithmetic mean vector ($T = [T_j]_N$) is obtained. Subsequently, the reliability index (*RI*) matrix is computed by applying (31.10). To ensure the consistency of the criterion weights, the calculated *RI* value must be less than 0.1.

When this condition is satisfied, the criterion weights are considered consistent, and the procedure proceeds to the subsequent step. However, if the RI value exceeds 0.1, the weighting process is deemed inconsistent, necessitating a repetition of the criterion weighting stage:

$$Y = \begin{bmatrix} Y_{11} & \cdots & Y_{1j} & \cdots & Y_{1N} \\ \vdots & \cdots & \vdots & \cdots & \vdots \\ Y_{k1} & \cdots & Y_{kj} & \cdots & Y_{kN} \\ \vdots & \cdots & \vdots & \cdots & \vdots \\ Y_{L1} & \cdots & Y_{Lj} & \cdots & Y_{LN} \end{bmatrix}; \ (k = 1,\ 2,\ \ldots,\ L;\ j = 1,\ 2,\ \ldots,\ N). \tag{31.8}$$

$$T_j = \frac{\sum_{k=1}^{L} Y_{kj}}{L}; \ (k = 1,\ 2,\ \ldots,\ L;\ j = 1,\ 2,\ \ldots,\ N). \tag{31.9}$$

$$RI = \frac{\sum_{j=1}^{N} |R_j * 100 - T_j|}{100}; \ (k = 1,\ 2,\ \ldots,\ L;\ j = 1,\ 2,\ \ldots,\ N). \tag{31.10}$$

The algorithm of the CIMAS method is presented in Table 31.1.

TABLE 31.1 The algorithm illustrates the steps of the criteria importance assessment (CIMAS) criteria weighting method.

Algorithm:	**The purpose of this algorithm is to present the procedural steps of the CIMAS method.**	
Input	A set of experts: $E = \{E_1,\ E_2,\ \ldots,\ E_k,\ \ldots,\ E_L\}\ (k = 1, 2,\ \ldots,\ L)$, A set of criteria: $C = \{C_1,\ C_2,\ \ldots,\ C_j,\ \ldots,\ C_N\}\ (j = 1, 2,\ \ldots,\ N)$, A expert weigh vector: $w = \{w_1,\ w_2,\ \ldots,\ w_k,\ \ldots,\ w_L\}\ (k = 1, 2,\ \ldots,\ L)$.	
Step-1:	Construct the criteria assessment matrix ($X = [X_{kj}]_{LN}$) as (31.1) ($X_{kj} \in [1, 10]$).	$X = \begin{bmatrix} X_{11} & \cdots & X_{1j} & \cdots & X_{1N} \\ \vdots & \cdots & \vdots & \cdots & \vdots \\ X_{k1} & \cdots & X_{kj} & \cdots & X_{kN} \\ \vdots & \cdots & \vdots & \cdots & \vdots \\ X_{L1} & \cdots & X_{Lj} & \cdots & X_{LN} \end{bmatrix}$
Step-2:	Calculate the normalized matrix ($Z = [Z_{kj}]_{LN}$) by employing (31.2).	$Z_{kj} = \frac{X_{kj}}{\sum_{k=1}^{L} X_{kj}}$
Step-3:	Calculate the weighted normalized matrix ($D = [D_{kj}]_{LN}$) by employing (31.3).	$D_{kj} = w_k * Z_{kj}$
Step-4:	Calculate the maximum value vector ($M^{max} = [M_j^{max}]_N$) and the minimum value vector ($M^{min} = [M_j^{min}]_N$) by employing Eqs. (31.4) and (31.5).	$M_j^{max} = \max_k D_{kj}$ $M_j^{min} = \min_k D_{kj}$
Step-5:	Calculate the distance vector ($M = [M_j]_N$) by employing (31.6).	$M_j = M_j^{max} - M_j^{min}$
Step-6:	Determine the criteria weight vector ($R = [R_j]_N$) by employing (31.7).	$R_j = \frac{M_j}{\sum_{j=1}^{N} M_j}$
Step-7:	Construct the re-evaluation matrix ($Y = [Y_{kj}]_{LN}$) as (31.8) ($Y_{kj} \in [1, 100]$) *and* $\left(\sum_{j=1}^{N} Y_{kj} = 100\right)$ and calculate the arithmetic mean vector ($T = [T_j]_N$) and compute the RI value.	$Y = \begin{bmatrix} Y_{11} & \cdots & Y_{1j} & \cdots & Y_{1N} \\ \vdots & \cdots & \vdots & \cdots & \vdots \\ Y_{k1} & \cdots & Y_{kj} & \cdots & Y_{kN} \\ \vdots & \cdots & \vdots & \cdots & \vdots \\ Y_{L1} & \cdots & Y_{Lj} & \cdots & Y_{LN} \end{bmatrix}$ $T_j = \frac{\sum_{k=1}^{L} Y_{kj}}{L}$ $RI = \frac{\sum_{j=1}^{N} \mid R_j * 100 - T_j \mid}{100}$
Output	A criteria weight vector: R= $\{R_1,\ R_2,\ \ldots,\ R_j,\ \ldots,\ R_N\}\ (j = 1, 2,\ \ldots,\ N)$.	

31.3 Numerical example 1

For *numerical example 1*, the essential inputs required to implement the CIMAS algorithm, as presented in Table 31.1, consist of a set of experts $E = \{E_1, E_2, E_3, E_4\}$ $(i = 1, 2, 3, 4)$, a set of criteria $C = \{C_1, C_2, C_3\}$ $(j = 1, 2, 3)$, and a experts weight vector $w = \{0.20, 0.30, 0.40, 0.10\}$. Based on these inputs, the procedural steps of the CIMAS method were systematically executed in the following order:

Step 1: The criteria assessment matrix $(X = [X_{kj}]_{LN})$ for *numerical example 1* is presented in Table 31.2:

Step 2: The normalized matrix $(Z = [Z_{kj}]_{LN})$ derived from (31.2), is provided in Table 31.3.

Step 3: By employing (31.5), the normalized matrix was multiplied by their respective experts' weights to obtain the weighted normalized matrix $(D = [D_{kj}]_{LN})$, presented in Table 31.4.

Step 4: The maximum value vector $(M^{\max} = [M_j^{\max}]_N)$ and the minimum value vector $(M^{\min} = [M_j^{\min}]_N)$ were calculated by employing Eqs. (31.4) and (31.5), respectively. It is also shown in Table 31.4.

Step 5: The distance vector $(M = [M_j]_N)$ was computed by employing (31.6). It is also presented in Table 31.4.

Step 6: The criteria weight vector $(R = [R_j]_N)$ was computed by employing (31.7). It is presented in Table 31.5.

TABLE 31.2 The criteria assessment matrix.

X_{kj}	C_1	C_2	C_3
E_1	7	7	7
E_2	7	6	7
E_3	8	7	6
E_4	8	8	7

TABLE 31.3 The normalized matrix.

Z_{kj}	C_1	C_2	C_3
E_1	0.2333	0.2500	0.2593
E_2	0.2333	0.2143	0.2593
E_3	0.2667	0.2500	0.2222
E_4	0.2667	0.2857	0.2593

TABLE 31.4 The weighted normalized matrix, the maximum-minimum value vectors, and the distance vector.

D_{kj}	C_1	C_2	C_3
E_1	0.0467	0.0500	0.0519
E_2	0.0700	0.0643	0.0778
E_3	0.1067	0.1000	0.0889
E_4	0.0267	0.0286	0.0259
M_j^{max}	0.1067	0.1000	0.0889
M_j^{min}	0.0267	0.0286	0.0259
M_j	0.0800	0.0714	0.0630

TABLE 31.5 The criteria weight vector.

	C_1	C_2	C_3
R_j	0.3731	0.3332	0.2937
Rank	1	2	3

TABLE 31.6 The second criteria assessment matrix, the arithmetic mean vector, and the reliability index value.

Y_{kj}	C_1	C_2	C_3
E_1	34	33	33
E_2	35	30	35
E_3	36	34	30
E_4	35	35	30
T_j	35	33	32
RI	0.0526		

TABLE 31.7 The criteria assessment matrix.

X_{kj}	C_1	C_2	C_3	C_4	C_5	C_6	C_7
E_1	7	7	8	7	7	7	8
E_2	7	6	8	8	8	7	7
E_3	8	7	7	7	7	6	7
E_4	8	8	8	8	7	7	8
E_5	7	7	7	7	8	7	8
E_6	6	8	7	7	7	6	7
E_7	8	6	8	7	6	8	9
E_8	7	6	8	8	7	8	7

Step 7: The re-evaluation matrix ($Y = [Y_{kj}]_{LN}$) was determined by experts and shown in Table 31.6. The arithmetic mean vector ($T = [T_j]_N$) was calculated by (31.9), then RI value was calculated by employing (31.10) and shown in Table 31.6.

31.4 Numerical example 2

For *numerical example 2*, the essential inputs required to implement the CIMAS algorithm, as presented in Table 31.1, consist of a set of experts $E = \{E_1, E_2, E_3, E_4, E_5, E_6, E_7, E_8\} (i = 1, 2, \ldots, 8)$, a set of criteria $C = \{C_1, C_2, C_3, C_4, C_5, C_6, C_7\} (j = 1, 2, \ldots, 7)$, and a experts weight vector $w = \{0.125, 0.125, 0.125, 0.125, 0.125, 0.125, 0.125\}$. Based on these inputs, the procedural steps of the CIMAS method were systematically executed in the following order:

Step 1: The criteria assessment matrix ($X = [X_{kj}]_{LN}$) for *numerical example 2* is presented in Table 31.7:

Step 2: The normalized matrix ($Z = [Z_{kj}]_{LN}$) derived from (31.2), is provided in Table 31.8.

Step 3: By using (31.5), the normalized matrix was multiplied by their respective experts' weights to obtain the weighted normalized matrix ($D = [D_{kj}]_{LN}$), presented in Table 31.9.

Step 4: The maximum value vector ($M^{\max} = [M_j^{\max}]_N$) and the minimum value vector ($M^{\min} = [M_j^{\min}]_N$) were calculated by employing Eqs. (31.4) and (31.5), respectively. It is also shown in Table 31.9.

Step 5: The distance vector ($M = [M_j]_N$) was computed by employing (31.6). It is also presented in Table 31.9.

Step 6: The criteria weight vector ($R = [R_j]_N$) was computed by employing (31.7). It is presented in Table 31.10.

Step 7: The re-evaluation matrix ($Y = [Y_{kj}]_{LN}$) was determined by experts and shown in Table 31.11. The arithmetic mean vector ($T = [T_j]_N$) was calculated by (31.9), then RI value was calculated by employing (31.10) and shown in Table 31.11.

TABLE 31.8 The normalized matrix.

Z_{ij}^{1st}	C_1	C_2	C_3	C_4	C_5	C_6	C_7
E_1	0.1207	0.1273	0.1311	0.1186	0.1228	0.1250	0.1311
E_2	0.1207	0.1091	0.1311	0.1356	0.1404	0.1250	0.1148
E_3	0.1379	0.1273	0.1148	0.1186	0.1228	0.1071	0.1148
E_4	0.1379	0.1455	0.1311	0.1356	0.1228	0.1250	0.1311
E_5	0.1207	0.1273	0.1148	0.1186	0.1404	0.1250	0.1311
E_6	0.1034	0.1455	0.1148	0.1186	0.1228	0.1071	0.1148
E_7	0.1379	0.1091	0.1311	0.1186	0.1053	0.1429	0.1475
E_8	0.1207	0.1091	0.1311	0.1356	0.1228	0.1429	0.1148

TABLE 31.9 The weighted normalized matrix, the maximum-minimum value vectors, and the distance vector.

D_{kj}	C_1	C_2	C_3	C_4	C_5	C_6	C_7
E_1	0.0151	0.0159	0.0164	0.0148	0.0154	0.0156	0.0164
E_2	0.0151	0.0136	0.0164	0.0169	0.0175	0.0156	0.0143
E_3	0.0172	0.0159	0.0143	0.0148	0.0154	0.0134	0.0143
E_4	0.0172	0.0182	0.0164	0.0169	0.0154	0.0156	0.0164
E_5	0.0151	0.0159	0.0143	0.0148	0.0175	0.0156	0.0164
E_6	0.0129	0.0182	0.0143	0.0148	0.0154	0.0134	0.0143
E_7	0.0172	0.0136	0.0164	0.0148	0.0132	0.0179	0.0184
E_8	0.0151	0.0136	0.0164	0.0169	0.0154	0.0179	0.0143
M_j^{max}	0.0172	0.0182	0.0164	0.0169	0.0175	0.0179	0.0184
M_j^{min}	0.0129	0.0136	0.0143	0.0148	0.0132	0.0134	0.0143
M_j	0.0043	0.0045	0.0020	0.0021	0.0044	0.0045	0.0041

TABLE 31.10 The criteria weight vector.

	C_1	C_2	C_3	C_4	C_5	C_6	C_7
R_j	0.1660	0.1750	0.0789	0.0816	0.1689	0.1719	0.1578
Rank	4	1	7	6	3	2	5

TABLE 31.11 The second criteria assessment matrix, the arithmetic mean vector, and reliability index value.

Y_{kj}	C_1	C_2	C_3	C_4	C_5	C_6	C_7
E_1	14	19	11	9	18	17	12
E_2	14	19	10	10	16	17	14
E_3	16	19	9	11	18	16	11
E_4	16	16	10	9	18	16	15
E_5	14	19	9	9	18	17	14
E_6	14	16	12	12	16	16	14
E_7	16	18	10	10	15	17	14
E_8	13	20	9	10	18	18	14
T_j	14.625	18.25	10	10	17.125	16.75	13.5
RI	0.0963						

31.5 Conclusion

This paper has presented a detailed exposition of the CIMAS criteria weighting method and demonstrated its practical application through two numerical examples. The study highlights several strengths of the CIMAS method. Notably, CIMAS provides a systematic and transparent procedure for determining criterion weights by combining linear normalization and max–min distance calculations. The inclusion of the RI further enhances the robustness of the weighting process, offering a quantitative measure of confidence in the derived weights. This feature distinguishes CIMAS from many traditional weighting methods, as it allows decision-makers to assess the stability and consistency of the assigned weights, particularly in complex MADM contexts.

Despite these advantages, the CIMAS method also exhibits certain limitations. Its reliance on accurate input data and expert judgments may introduce subjectivity, particularly when the criteria set is extensive or the expertise of evaluators varies. Additionally, while RI provides a measure of reliability, it does not fully address all forms of uncertainty inherent in linguistic or imprecise evaluations, suggesting potential benefits from integrating fuzzy or hybrid fuzzy extensions in future applications.

Based on the findings and insights from the current study, several recommendations for future research can be proposed. First, further investigations could explore the integration of CIMAS with advanced fuzzy sets, such as intuitionistic, interval-valued, or rungs fuzzy sets, to better handle uncertainty and imprecision in criteria weighting. Second, hybridization with alternative ranking methods could be examined to develop comprehensive decision support systems for a wider range of practical problems. Finally, comparative studies across different industries and decision contexts would help to further validate the robustness, generalizability, and practical applicability of the CIMAS methodology.

In conclusion, CIMAS offers a reliable and structured framework for criteria weighing in MADM problems, combining methodological rigor with practical flexibility. While some limitations remain, the method's strengths, particularly the use of the RI value for weight validation, make it a valuable tool for researchers and practitioners, and future enhancements hold promise for even broader application in complex decision-making scenarios.

References

Aytekin, A., & Korucuk, S. (2024). Assessing the innovation capacity of manufacturing firms in Ordu Province: A multi-criteria evaluation using CIMAS. *Journal of Intelligent Management Decision, 3*(4), 224–230. https://doi.org/10.56578/jimd030403.

Biswas, S., Biswas, B., & Mitra, K. (2025). A novel group decision making model to compare online shopping platforms. *Spectrum of Decision Making and Applications, 2*(1), 1–27. https://doi.org/10.31181/sdmap2120259.

Bošković, S., Jovčić, S., Simic, V., Švadlenka, L., Dobrodolac, M., & Bacanin, N. (2025). A new criteria importance assessment (Cimas) method in multi-criteria group decision-making: Criteria evaluation for supplier selection. *Facta Universitatis, Series: Mechanical Engineering, 23*(2), 335–349. https://doi.org/10.22190/FUME230730050B.

Bouraima, M. B., Jovčić, S., Švadlenka, L., Simic, V., Badi, I., & Maraka, N. D. (2024). An integrated multi-criteria approach to formulate and assess healthcare referral system strategies in developing countries. *Healthcare analytics, 5100*, 315. https://doi.org/10.1016/j.health.2024.100315.

Kara, K., Yalçın, G. C., Çetinkaya, A., Simic, V., & Pamucar, D. (2024). A single-valued neutrosophic CIMAS-CRITIC-RBNAR decision support model for the financial performance analysis: A study of technology companies. *Socio-economic Planning Sciences, 92*, 101851. https://doi.org/10.1016/j.seps.2024.101851.

Kara, K., Yalçın, G. C., Kaygısız, E. G., Simic, V., Örnek, A.Ş., & Pamucar, D. (2024). A picture fuzzy CIMAS-ARTASI model for website performance analysis in human resource management. *Applied Soft Computing, 162*. https://doi.org/10.1016/j.asoc.2024.111826.

Kara, K., Yalçın, G. C., Simic, V., Korkuç, Ç., Çiçek, İ., Afacan, E., & Pamucar, D. (2024). An interval-valued spherical fuzzy CIMAS-WISP group decision-analytic model for blockchain platform selection in digital projects. *Applied Soft Computing, 162*, 111810. https://doi.org/10.1016/j.asoc.2024.111810.

Liu, W., & Lai, X. (2025). Integrating decision tools for efficient operations management through innovative approaches. *Scientific Reports, 15*(1), 16187. https://doi.org/10.1038/s41598-025-99022-8.

Shakeel, H. M., Farid, H. M. A., Iram, S., Hill, R., & Simic, V. (2025). Multi-stage decision support system for evaluating visual energy performance certificate platforms. *Sustainable Energy, Grids and Networks*101767. https://doi.org/10.1016/j.segan.2025.101767.

Sun, Q. (2025). Performance evaluation of human resource management in power enterprises using multi-criteria decision-making methodology and treesoft set. *Neutrosophic Sets and Systems, 82*, 321–334. https://digitalrepository.unm.edu/cgi/viewcontent.cgi?article=3158&context=nss_journal.

Švadlenka, L., Bajec, P., Pivtorak, H., Bošković, S., Jovčić, S., & Dobrodolac, M. (2024). Risk prioritization from the crowd-shipping provider's perspective using the CIMAS method. *Spectrum of Engineering and Management Sciences, 2*(1), 234–246. https://doi.org/10.31181/sems21202430s.

Xiang, Z., & Zhang, X. (2025). An integrated decision support system for supplier selection and performance evaluation in global supply chains. *Applied Soft Computing*113325. https://doi.org/10.1016/j.asoc.2025.113325.

Yalçın, G. C. (2025). Development of a fuzzy-based decision support system for sustainable tractor selection in green ports. *Facta Universitatis, Series: Mechanical Engineering*. https://doi.org/10.22190/FUME250610029Y.

Yalçın, G. C., Kara, K., Edinsel, S., Kaygısız, E. G., Simic, V., & Pamucar, D. (2025). Authentication system selection for performance appraisal in human resource management using an intuitionistic fuzzy CIMAS-ARLON model. *Applied Soft Computing, 171*, 112786. https://doi.org/10.1016/j.asoc.2025.112786.

Chapter 32

MEREC: Method based on the removal effects of criteria for multi-attribute decision-making

Mehdi Keshavarz-Ghorabaee
Department of Management, Faculty of Humanities (Azadshahr Branch), Gonbad Kavous University, Gonbad Kavous, Iran

32.1 Introduction

One of the main issues in multicriteria decision-making (MCDM) is determining the weights of evaluation criteria. Practical decisions involve trade-offs among alternative performance scores as well as the relative influence of each criterion. For instance, when rating suppliers, companies tend to prioritize price and quality targets over delivery schedules or environmental practices (Raveena & Umamaheswari, 2025; Xiang & Zhang, 2025). As these weights directly affect outcomes in their ordinal scale, correct weight specification is an essential factor for the effectiveness of MCDM. The process requires great care because of the multiplicative effect of small weight adjustments on the final decision, especially when comparing complex alternatives and many conflicting criteria (Ayan et al., 2023; Singh & Pant, 2021).

Various methods have been developed to determine criterion weights, which can be categorized into three major classes: subjective, objective, and hybrid methods. Subjective methods apply human knowledge in a model or analysis and combine opinions formed by specialists, feedback from stakeholders, or systematic methodological processes such as the analytic hierarchy process and Delphi technique. While useful for recording contextual knowledge, these techniques are limited by their consistency and potential biases, particularly when there are many considerations or conflicting expert opinions (Akbas & Akin, 2025; Kašpar et al., 2025). On the other hand, objective methods compute weights by using equations based on the decision matrix and are thus free from human subjectivity. These methods search for statistical patterns in the data set (variance, spreading, and interdependence of the criteria) to determine the weights. Common objective methods such as the entropy method, criteria importance through intercriteria correlation (CRITIC), and standard deviation (SD) can be found in the literature. They work based on the essential assumption that more varied or differentiation-capable criteria among the alternatives bear more valuable information and should therefore receive higher weights. For instance, a criterion that varies very little from alternative to alternative would provide little aid in distinguishing between alternatives and would be given lower weight in the analysis (Das & Behera, 2024; Mukhametzyanov, 2021; Zardari et al., 2014; Zavadskas & Podvezko, 2016).

The majority of classical objective methods suffer from the same drawback: they assume that all criteria always exist and function in the model. In the process, they pay no attention to the impact (positive or negative) of individual criteria on the final decision. They are based on internal properties (such as, the SD of criterion values or the correlation of a criterion's values with other criteria), not on the effect of a criterion on the performance of the aggregated decision criteria of the alternatives. From an application viewpoint, however, this perspective can be too rigid and cannot fully describe the dynamic trade-off relationships among the factors. The method based on the removal effects of criteria (MEREC) method introduces a completely new perspective, interesting from the criteria weighting point of view. Instead of studying the degree of variation or correlation between criteria, MEREC utilizes an exclusion-oriented logic, which means it examines the question: What is the influence of a criterion's absence on the preference ordering of alternatives? In other words, rather than directly analyzing a criterion's value, MEREC aims to assess its contribution by observing what happens when it is removed from the decision model. This provides a more relevance-based measure of importance; when omitting a criterion severely affects the evaluation result, the criterion is considered necessary for the integrity of the decision process (Keshavarz-Ghorabaee, Amiri, et al., 2021; Makki & Abdulaal, 2023; Mohamed et al., 2024; Saidin et al., 2023).

Encyclopedia of Multi-Attribute Decision-Making (MADM). DOI: https://doi.org/10.1016/B978-0-443-33275-3.00024-5

This deletion approach is intuitive and informative. It makes sense in system design and evaluation: the importance of a component is often measured by the extent to which the system changes when the component is removed. In MCDM, this notion is implemented by calculating the total performance of each alternative for all criteria and then again for all criteria except one at a time. The magnitude of the variation between these two sets of results can be used as a quantitative measure of the criterion's influence. The deviations are then combined for each criterion, and the final weights are normalized to be comparable. MEREC's approach offers multiple benefits. Having "everything in the box" permits the analyst to move beyond statistical features of the data and to concentrate on how each criterion actually supports the decision-making endpoint. This makes the resulting weights more interpretable and the process more transparent. In addition, the MEREC concept is especially suitable for automatic or algorithm-based domains, such as decision support systems or AI-based evaluation tools, where subjective input may be missing, not wanted, or difficult to justify (Kamari et al., 2025; Keshavarz-Ghorabaee, 2021; Narang et al., 2023).

A further strength of MEREC is that it can be used flexibly with many MCDM methods. It is mainly designed for criterion weight calculation but can also work in combination with other evaluation methods, making it applicable to many different decision problems. This makes MEREC a suitable objective weighting approach in composite decision-making systems. In addition, MEREC has practical utility in cases where "what-if" analysis is critical. For intricate projects, stakeholders often demand to know the impact of omitting certain criteria (because of, for instance, no data availability, unspecified goals, or measurement uncertainty). This issue is inherently accounted for in MEREC, as it measures how a decision conclusion changes when a criterion is discarded. This sensitivity awareness enhances the resilience of decisions and enables adaptive modeling, which proves particularly useful in uncertain or dynamic settings. While conceptually clear and providing several practical benefits, MEREC is slightly more computationally demanding than straightforward objective approaches such as entropy or SD. It has a computational load that increases with the number of criteria because it needs to re-evaluate the decision problem for each criterion's removal. Yet, for typical modern computational tasks that are relatively inexpensive, the added cost is well worth it in exchange for more insight and better decision support.

The MEREC method offers a powerful and innovative approach that has been applied to several real-world problems, including evaluating airport service quality (Sarıgül et al., 2023), material selection (Kumar et al., 2025), measuring innovation performance (Ecer & Aycin, 2022), supplier evaluation (Eydi & GholamAzad, 2025), assessing groundwater quality (Das & Das, 2023), sustainable resources management (Mondal et al., 2024), and prioritizing strategic objectives (Abdelaal et al., 2024). Its theoretical basis guarantees that criterion weights represent not only the characteristics of the data but also their real impact on decision results.

The remainder of this chapter consists of a few sections. First, the method section describes the MEREC procedure in a step-by-step format to illustrate how the importance of criteria is evaluated based on their deletion effects. This is followed by two examples: a small one demonstrating the underlying principles, and a real-world case showing its practical application. The chapter also includes a comparative analysis between MEREC and other objective weighting methods, which illustrates the consistency and usefulness of the proposed method.

32.2 Methodology

MEREC is a quantification technique for weight evaluation in decision-making processes with multiple criteria. Unlike subjective weighting methods, which require expert opinion for calculating weights, MEREC derives weights completely from data. Thus the influence of each criterion on the performance of alternatives can be evaluated. The greater a criterion's impact when discarded, the larger its weight value. The following steps explain the procedure:

Step 1: Construct the decision matrix

Let us assume a decision-making problem with nnn alternatives and mmm criteria. The initial step is to form the decision matrix $X = [x_{ij}]$, where x_{ij} represents the performance value of the i th alternative under the j th criterion. All performance values must be positive ($x_{ij} > 0$). If the matrix includes negative values, they should be transformed into positive values using a suitable normalization method.

$$X = \begin{bmatrix} x_{11} & x_{12} & \cdots & x_{1j} & \cdots & x_{1m} \\ x_{21} & x_{22} & \cdots & x_{2j} & \cdots & x_{2m} \\ \vdots & \vdots & \ddots & \vdots & \ddots & \vdots \\ x_{i1} & x_{i2} & \cdots & x_{ij} & \cdots & x_{im} \\ \vdots & \vdots & \cdots & \vdots & \cdots & \vdots \\ x_{n1} & x_{n2} & \cdots & x_{nj} & \cdots & x_{nm} \end{bmatrix} \tag{32.1}$$

Step 2: Normalize the decision matrix

To allow for comparison across different criteria scales, the decision matrix must be normalized. MEREC uses a linear normalization technique that transforms all criteria into a minimization form.

Let n_{ij}^{x} be the normalized value for element x_{ij} . If B denotes the set of beneficial criteria (where higher values are preferred), and H the set of nonbeneficial criteria (where lower values are preferred), normalization is carried out as follows:

$$n_{ij}^{x} = \begin{cases} \dfrac{\min\limits_{k} x_{kj}}{x_{ij}} \; if\ j \in B \\ \dfrac{x_{ij}}{\max\limits_{k} x_{kj}} \; if\ j \in H \end{cases} \tag{32.2}$$

This approach ensures that all criteria behave consistently as cost type (i.e., smaller values are better).

Step 3: Calculate the overall performance of alternatives

In this step, the performance of each alternative is calculated using a nonlinear logarithmic measure that incorporates equal weights for all criteria. This function is designed to reflect the relative desirability of each alternative, with lower normalized values resulting in better performance.

$$S_i = \ln\left(1 + \left(\frac{1}{m}\sum_{j} |\ln(n_{ij}^{x})|\right)\right) \tag{32.3}$$

Step 4: Calculate the performance of alternatives by removing each criterion

Next, to evaluate the effect of each criterion, the performance of alternatives is recalculated while individually omitting each criterion. For each alternative i and each criterion j, a new performance score S_{ij}' is computed as:

$$S_{ij}' = \ln\left(1 + \left(\frac{1}{m}\sum_{k,\ k\neq j} |\ln(n_{ik}^{x})|\right)\right) \tag{32.4}$$

This process produces m distinct sets of performance scores, one for each criterion removed.

Step 5: Compute the summation of absolute deviations

To measure the effect of removing each criterion, the absolute deviation between the full-performance scores S_i and the scores with the j-th criterion removed S_{ij}' is computed. The total deviation for criterion j, denoted by E_j , is given as:

$$E_j = \sum_{i} |S_{ij}' - S_i| \tag{32.5}$$

A greater deviation indicates that removing the criterion significantly alters the performance scores, implying higher importance.

Step 6: Determine the final weights of the criteria

Finally, the objective weight w_j of each criterion is determined by normalizing the removal effects E_j The final weights are calculated as:

$$w_j = \frac{E_j}{\sum_k E_k} \tag{32.6}$$

This ensures that the weights reflect the relative contribution of each criterion to the overall evaluation process.

32.3 Numerical example 1

To illustrate how the MEREC method works and how it operates, a MCDM problem is provided in this section. This small example is chosen to focus on the basic computational properties of the model and to help understand how we can determine a criterion's importance based on its removal effect.

This hypothetical problem includes four alternatives (A_1 to A_4) and four criteria (C_1 to C_4). Among these criteria, one criterion (C_3) is of the cost-type (nonbeneficial), where lower values are preferred, while the remaining three criteria are benefit type (beneficial), where higher values are desirable.

An important feature of the MEREC method is that it evaluates the sensitivity of the overall performance of alternatives to the removal of each criterion. Therefore, in this example, the values of criterion C_4 are deliberately kept constant across all alternatives. This design choice helps demonstrate how the method treats uninformative or invariant criteria, highlighting one of MEREC's distinctive capabilities.

Step 1: Constructing the decision matrix

The initial decision matrix, containing the raw performance values of the alternatives across the four criteria, is shown in Table 32.1.

Step 2: Normalizing the decision matrix

In the MEREC method, all criteria are normalized and transformed into a cost-type form using Eq. (32.2). This means that, after normalization, smaller values are always better, regardless of the original type of the criterion. This transformation ensures uniformity and enables consistent aggregation.

As seen in Table 32.2, after normalization, all values lie between 0 and 1, and the logic of "the lower, the better" applies to all criteria. Also, due to the constant values in C_4, the normalized values in that column are equal across all alternatives, reinforcing that this criterion holds no discriminative power in this case.

Step 3: Calculating the overall performance of alternatives

The initial performance score of each alternative is computed using the full set of normalized criteria and Eq. (32.3). The computation is based on an aggregated score. The results are presented in Table 32.3.

Step 4: Calculating the performance of alternatives by removing each criterion

Next, using Eq. (32.4) the performance of each alternative is recalculated multiple times, each time removing one of the criteria as shown in Table 32.4. These recalculated scores are denoted as S'_{ij}, where i is the alternative and j is the omitted criterion. This process reveals how sensitive the overall performance is to each criterion's presence.

These values highlight how much each criterion contributes to the overall performance of alternatives. For instance, removing C_1 leads to a large drop in performance for A_2 and A_3, suggesting that this criterion plays a critical role.

Step 5: Computing the summation of absolute deviations

The absolute deviation between the original and removed-criterion scores is computed for each alternative and criterion. The sum of deviations across all alternatives gives the overall removal effect (total deviation) E_j for each criterion (as shown in Table 32.5).

TABLE 32.1 Initial decision matrix (example 1).

	C_1 (B)	C_2 (B)	C_3 (H)	C_4 (B)
A_1	10	1.3	1500	3
A_2	120	1.1	1100	3
A_3	50	1.2	800	3
A_4	5	1.4	500	3

TABLE 32.2 Normalized decision matrix (example 1).

	C_1	C_2	C_3	C_4
A_1	0.5	0.846	1	1
A_2	0.042	1	0.733	1
A_3	0.1	0.917	0.533	1
A_4	1	0.786	0.333	1

TABLE 32.3 Initial performance scores of alternatives (example 1).

	S_i
A_1	0.195
A_2	0.627
A_3	0.562
A_4	0.289

TABLE 32.4 Performance scores with criterion removal (example 1).

	S'_{i1}	S'_{i2}	S'_{i3}	S'_{i4}
A_1	0.041	0.160	0.195	0.195
A_2	0.075	0.627	0.585	0.627
A_3	0.165	0.550	0.468	0.562
A_4	0.289	0.243	0.059	0.289

TABLE 32.5 Absolute deviations and removal effects for each criterion (example 1).

	$\lvert S'_{i1} - S_i \rvert$	$\lvert S'_{i2} - S_i \rvert$	$\lvert S'_{i3} - S_i \rvert$	$\lvert S'_{i4} - S_i \rvert$
A_1	0.154	0.035	0	0
A_2	0.552	0	0.042	0
A_3	0.398	0.012	0.094	0
A_4	0	0.046	0.230	0
E_j	1.104	0.094	0.367	0

As seen, the removal of C_1 results in the largest total deviation, confirming its significant influence. In contrast, C_4 shows no deviation, validating that a nonvarying criterion has no impact on the outcome.

Step 6: Determining the final weights of the criteria

Finally, the weights of criteria are calculated by normalizing the overall removal effects E_j as shown in Table 32.6. The idea is that criteria causing greater disruptions to performance scores upon removal are deemed more important.

The results clearly demonstrate the core concept of the MEREC method: criterion C_1, with the highest influence on the ranking, receives the highest weight, while criterion C_4, having no variation or influence, receives a zero weight.

32.4 Numerical example 2

In this section, we demonstrate the practical usefulness of the MEREC approach in a real-world decision-making context. Specifically, this example focuses on determining the importance of various decision criteria in the selection process of

TABLE 32.6 Final weights of criteria (example 1).

	C_1	C_2	C_3	C_4
w_j	0.706	0.060	0.234	0

TABLE 32.7 Decision matrix of flexible manufacturing system selection problem.

	Reduction in labor cost	Reduction in work-in-process	Reduction in setup cost	Increase in market responsiveness	Improvement in quality	Capital and maintenance cost	Floor space used
	C_1 (*B*)	C_2 (*B*)	C_3 (*B*)	C_4 (*B*)	C_5 (*B*)	C_6 (*H*)	C_7 (*H*)
A_1	30	23	5	0.745	0.745	1500	5000
A_2	18	13	15	0.745	0.745	1300	6000
A_3	15	12	10	0.5	0.5	950	7000
A_4	25	20	13	0.745	0.745	1200	4000
A_5	14	18	14	0.255	0.745	950	3500
A_6	17	15	9	0.745	0.5	1250	5250
A_7	23	18	20	0.5	0.745	1100	3000
A_8	16	8	14	0.255	0.5	1500	3000

flexible manufacturing systems (FMSs), which represent a strategic and high-investment area in manufacturing industries. It is essential to emphasize that the MEREC method in this context is applied not for ranking the alternatives, but rather to determine the objective weights of criteria based on the variations in alternative performances.

A FMS integrates computer numerical control (CNC) machines, industrial robots, automated transport systems, and centralized computer control to create a versatile and adaptive production system. The "flexibility" of such systems refers to their ability to handle different types of products and quickly adjust production volumes and sequences in response to dynamic market demands. FMSs offer several strategic advantages, including reductions in labor and setup costs, lower work-in-process inventory, enhanced product quality, quicker market responsiveness, and optimal use of floor space.

Given the complexity and capital intensity involved in FMS implementation, selecting the most suitable system configuration requires a careful evaluation of multiple criteria. In the widely cited study by Karsak & Kuzgunkaya (2002), eight alternative FMS designs were evaluated based on seven critical criteria that influence the system's overall effectiveness. These criteria are:

C_1: Reduction in labor cost-Beneficial
C_2: Reduction in work-in-process-Beneficial
C_3: Reduction in setup cost-Beneficial
C_4: Increase in market responsiveness—Beneficial
C_5: Improvement in quality-Beneficial
C_6: Capital and maintenance cost-Nonbeneficial
C_7: Floor space used-Nonbeneficial

To begin the MEREC analysis, the decision matrix, shown in Table 32.7, is first normalized, converting all criteria into a comparable scale. Beneficial criteria are normalized such that higher values are preferable, while nonbeneficial criteria are normalized to reflect preference for lower values. The results are presented in Table 32.8.

Next, the MEREC methodology is applied to calculate the overall performance of each alternative with and without each criterion, and determine how much each criterion influences the decision outcome. The results are presented in Table 32.9. Based on the total deviations caused by omitting each criterion, the final weights are derived.

The total deviations resulting from criterion removal are calculated and used to compute the final criterion weights. The deviations and derived weights are shown in Table 32.10.

As shown, C_3 (setup cost reduction), C_4 (market responsiveness), and C_2 (work-in-process reduction) receive the highest weights, highlighting their significance in FMS evaluation.

32.5 Comparative analysis

To test the robustness, consistency, and practical reliability of the MEREC method's weights, a comparison has been performed with three other most commonly used objective weighting methods in MCDM: CRITIC, entropy, and SD. These were chosen both for their common use and theoretical virtues, but also because they, like MEREC, depend on the information content and variation in the decision matrix rather than on subjective judgments.

TABLE 32.8 Normalized decision matrix (example 2).

	C_1	C_2	C_3	C_4	C_5	C_6	C_7
A_1	0.467	0.348	1.000	0.342	0.671	1.000	0.714
A_2	0.778	0.615	0.333	0.342	0.671	0.867	0.857
A_3	0.933	0.667	0.500	0.510	1.000	0.633	1.000
A_4	0.560	0.400	0.385	0.342	0.671	0.800	0.571
A_5	1.000	0.444	0.357	1.000	0.671	0.633	0.500
A_6	0.824	0.533	0.556	0.342	1.000	0.833	0.750
A_7	0.609	0.444	0.250	0.510	0.671	0.733	0.429
A_8	0.875	1.000	0.357	1.000	1.000	1.000	0.429

TABLE 32.9 Overall performance scores and performance scores with criteria removal.

	S_i	S'_{i1}	S'_{i2}	S'_{i3}	S'_{i4}	S'_{i5}	S'_{i6}	S'_{i7}
A_1	0.417	0.343	0.313	0.417	0.311	0.379	0.417	0.385
A_2	0.415	0.391	0.368	0.306	0.309	0.377	0.402	0.401
A_3	0.284	0.276	0.239	0.206	0.209	0.284	0.233	0.284
A_4	0.514	0.463	0.433	0.429	0.418	0.479	0.495	0.465
A_5	0.395	0.395	0.314	0.290	0.395	0.356	0.350	0.326
A_6	0.352	0.332	0.287	0.291	0.238	0.352	0.333	0.323
A_7	0.533	0.490	0.462	0.409	0.474	0.499	0.506	0.459
A_8	0.252	0.238	0.252	0.131	0.252	0.252	0.252	0.154

TABLE 32.10 Total deviations and derived weights.

	C_1	C_2	C_3	C_4	C_5	C_6	C_7
E_j	0.234	0.495	0.682	0.556	0.184	0.173	0.367
w_j	0.087	0.184	0.254	0.207	0.069	0.064	0.136

TABLE 32.11 The comparison results.

	MEREC	CRITIC	Entropy	SD
w_1	0.087	0.116	0.121	0.130
w_2	0.184	0.116	0.149	0.144
w_3	0.254	0.165	0.213	0.155
w_4	0.207	0.227	0.256	0.201
w_5	0.069	0.087	0.060	0.117
w_6	0.064	0.122	0.050	0.099
w_7	0.136	0.168	0.150	0.153
r	—	0.664	0.897	0.77

To make a fair and appropriate comparison, the initial decision matrix should be normalized by linear normalization, transforming all criteria into nondimensional values on the same scale. This normalization ensures that all methods evaluate under common conditions and that the intrinsic differences between the criteria are maintained on a standard basis. After normalization, the three methods were individually used to calculate the weights of the criteria, generating three separate weight vectors.

Weights in the CRITIC method are determined by considering both the SD of each criterion (as a measure of contrast intensity) and the conflict (or correlation) between criteria. It assigns higher weights to criteria with higher variability and lower correlation with other criteria. The entropy method measures the degree of disorder or uncertainty in the performance information of each criterion. More discriminative power is assigned to selection criteria with higher weights. The SD method, the most rudimentary of all, simply evaluates the spread or dispersion of values for each factor and assumes that factors that vary more are also more important for discriminating among alternatives.

After deriving the weights from each method, the results were compared with those obtained from the MEREC approach as shown in Table 32.11. To measure the level of agreement and consistency across the different sets of weights, the correlation coefficient (r) was calculated between MEREC and each of the other three techniques. This statistic evaluates the degree to which two variables are related. The resulting correlation coefficients were all found to be above 0.6, which indicates a moderate to strong positive relationship between the results produced by MEREC and the other considered methods.

The degree of reliability of the MEREC method indicates that, despite its formulation being different from all other methods (which are statistical formulas for weight determination), the approach appears to provide suitable weight selection from a performance reduction perspective. In this sense, the results confirm the validity and usefulness of MEREC as a tool for handling real-world MCDM problems, particularly when an objective, data-driven weighting scheme is required.

This analysis shows how MEREC can be potentially useful in practice for eliciting objective and variation-sensitive decisional weights for decision problem criteria. The model yields not only interpretable weights but also demonstrates strong consistency with traditional approaches, which enhances its credibility and utility in MCDM.

32.6 Conclusions

The novel MEREC approach constitutes a major development in methods for objective weighting in MCDM. With the introduction of a removal-based evaluation process, MEREC is a more context-dependent and consequence-oriented method for assessing the importance of criteria. Unlike classical objective approaches based only on internal data variability or intercriteria correlation, MEREC evaluates the contribution of each criterion to the final results of alternatives by measuring the effect of its removal. This paradigm change allows weighting criteria not solely based on statistical aspects but on the practical importance of the criteria in decisions. In this chapter, the MEREC technique has been explained and examined. The first example, applied to a small-scale problem, allowed us to confirm the basic computational mechanism and showed how MEREC can distinguish between influential and noninfluential criteria. The second example used a real project application for FMS selection, demonstrating MEREC's capability to handle complex decisions. Importantly, comparisons with the CRITIC, entropy, and SD methods resulted in strong correlations, supporting the method's validity and robustness. This comes at the cost of increased computational demand (since each criterion is recalculated upon removal), which is hardly noticeable in practice today due to modern computer performance. One of the most interesting features of MEREC is its capability to be combined with a broad range of different MCDM ranking methods. It can complement other MCDM methods as a weighting methodology. The exclusion-based logical structure also makes it well suited for "what-if" analysis and supporting resilient decision-making, especially in uncertain or changing environments.

There are several future research directions to consider moving forward. One significant direction is generalizing MEREC for fuzzy environments where input data and criteria values are imprecise, vague, or linguistically expressed. Developing fuzzy versions could make the proposed method more capable of dealing with uncertainty, which would make it more applicable in risk analysis, policy planning, and human-centered evaluation. Moreover, comprehensibility in cases of vague or insufficient information complexity could be improved by using gray systems theory or rough set theory. Another potential research direction is applying MEREC in different and cross-disciplinary fields. Although its utility has been demonstrated in manufacturing system selection, MEREC can be easily employed for sustainability assessment, healthcare prioritization, supply chain design, financial portfolio optimization, smart city planning, educational performance evaluation, etc. Furthermore, incorporating MEREC into automatic decision support systems and AI-based assessment schemes could guarantee that large-scale or even immediate decisions preserve objectivity and repeatability. In such systems, subjective input is sometimes infeasible or problematic, making objective, interpretable weighting strategies such as MEREC increasingly critical.

References

Abdelaal, R. M. S., Makki, A. A., Al-Madi, E. M., & Qhadi, A. M. (2024). Prioritizing strategic objectives and projects in higher education institutions: A new hybrid fuzzy MEREC-G-TOPSIS approach. *IEEE Access, 12*, 89735–89753. https://doi.org/10.1109/ACCESS.2024.3419701.

Akbas, M., & Akin, F. D. (2025). A comparative weighting analysis using AHP and CRITIC for recycled pavement material selection: A case study from Istanbul. *Results in Engineering, 27*, 106837. https://doi.org/10.1016/j.rineng.2025.106837.

Ayan, B., Abacıoğlu, S., & Basilio, M. P. (2023). A comprehensive review of the novel weighting methods for multi-criteria decision-making. *Information, 14*, 285.

Das, C. R., & Das, S. (2023). Acceptability of MEREC criteria compared to existing weighted WQI models to assess coastal groundwater quality in eastern India. *Journal of Coastal Conservation, 27*, 44. https://doi.org/10.1007/s11852-023-00975-7.

Das, U., & Behera, B. (2024). Geospatial assessment of ecological vulnerability of fragile Eastern Duars Forest integrating GIS-based AHP, CRITIC and AHP-TOPSIS models. *Geomatics, Natural Hazards and Risk, 15*, 2330529.

Ecer, F., & Aycin, E. (2022). Novel comprehensive MEREC weighting-based score aggregation model for measuring innovation performance: The case of G7 countries. *Informatica, 34*, 53–83. https://doi.org/10.15388/22-infor494.

Eydi, A., & GholamAzad, M. (2025). Proposing a new integrated MEREC-NDEA algorithm for assessing and selecting the optimal sustainable suppliers: A case study. *International Transactions in Operational Research*, n/a. https://doi.org/10.1111/itor.13586.

Kamari, M. S. M., Rodzi, Z. M., & Kamis, N. H. (2025). Pythagorean neutrosophic method based on the removal effects of criteria (PNMEREC): An innovative approach for establishing objective weights in multi-criteria decision-making challenges. *Malaysian Journal of Fundamental and Applied Sciences, 21*, 1678–1696.

Karsak, E. E., & Kuzgunkaya, O. (2002). A fuzzy multiple objective programming approach for the selection of a flexible manufacturing system. *International Journal of Production Economics, 79*, 101–111.

Kašpar, J., Badr, S., Tahri, M., Maanan, M., Tahri, H., Mohammadi, Z., Novotný, M., & Yousfi, N. (2025). A new automatic AHP tool to assess the forest vulnerability to wind damage. *Ecological Indicators, 178*, 113607. https://doi.org/10.1016/j.ecolind.2025.113607.

Keshavarz-Ghorabaee, M. (2021). Assessment of distribution center locations using a multi-expert subjective–objective decision-making approach. *Scientific Reports, 11*, 19461. https://doi.org/10.1038/s41598-021-98698-y.

Keshavarz-Ghorabaee, M., Amiri, M., Zavadskas, E. K., Turskis, Z., & Antucheviciene, J. (2021). Determination of objective weights using a new method based on the removal effects of criteria (MEREC). *Symmetry, 13*, 525. https://doi.org/10.3390/sym13040525.

Kumar, S., Ahijith Kumar, P. V., Bharati, K., Patnaik, L., Ranjan Maity, S., & Łepicka, M. (2025). Coating material selection for bulk metal forming dies: A MEREC-integrated approach with multiple MCDM methods. *International Journal on Interactive Design and Manufacturing (IJIDeM), 19*, 4055–4070. https://doi.org/10.1007/s12008-024-01983-z.

Makki, A. A., & Abdulaal, R. M. S. (2023). A hybrid MCDM approach based on fuzzy MEREC-G and Fuzzy RATMI. *Mathematics, 11*, 3773.

Mohamed, M., Salam, A., Ye, J., & Yong, R. (2024). Single-valued neutrosophic MCDM approaches integrated with MEREC and RAM for the selection of UAVs in forest fire detection and management. *Neutrosophic Systems with Applications, 19*, 1–14.

Mondal, M. K., Mahapatra, B. S., Bera, M. B., & Mahapatra, G. S. (2024). Sustainable forest resources management model through Pythagorean fuzzy MEREC–MARCOS approach. *Environment, Development and Sustainability*. https://doi.org/10.1007/s10668-024-05164-6.

Mukhametzyanov, I. (2021). Specific character of objective methods for determining weights of criteria in MCDM problems: Entropy, CRITIC and SD. *Decision Making: Applications in Management and Engineering, 4*, 76–105.

Narang, M., Kumar, A., & Dhawan, R. (2023). A fuzzy extension of MEREC method using parabolic measure and its applications. *Journal of Decision Analytics and Intelligent Computing, 3*, 33–46.

Raveena, R., & Umamaheswari, S. (2025). Integrated MCDM framework for sustainable pharmacy supplier selection using pioneering criteria with fuzzy TOPSIS SVR and GRA. *Scientific Reports, 15*, 19144. https://doi.org/10.1038/s41598-025-02975-z.

Saidin, M. S., Lee, L. S., Marjugi, S. M., Ahmad, M. Z., & Seow, H.-V. (2023). Fuzzy method based on the removal effects of criteria (MEREC) for determining objective weights in multi-criteria decision-making problems. *Mathematics, 11*, 1544.

Sarıgül, S. S., Ünlü, M., & Yaşar, E. (2023). A new MCDM approach in evaluating airport service quality: MEREC-based MARCOS and CoCoSo methods. *Uluslararası Yönetim Akademisi Dergisi, 6*, 90–108.

Singh, M., & Pant, M. (2021). A review of selected weighing methods in MCDM with a case study. *International Journal of System Assurance Engineering and Management, 12*, 126–144. https://doi.org/10.1007/s13198-020-01033-3.

Xiang, Z., & Zhang, X. (2025). An integrated decision support system for supplier selection and performance evaluation in global supply chains. *Applied Soft Computing, 180*, 113325. https://doi.org/10.1016/j.asoc.2025.113325.

Zardari, N. H., Ahmed, K., Shirazi, S. M., & Yusop, Z. B. (2014). *Weighting methods and their effects on multi-criteria decision making model outcomes in water resources management*. New York: Springer.

Zavadskas, E. K., & Podvezko, V. (2016). Integrated determination of objective criteria weights in MCDM. *International Journal of Information Technology & Decision Making, 15*, 267–283.

Chapter 33

LMAW: Logarithm methodology of additive weights for multi-attribute decision-making

Gülay Demir[1], **Dragan Pamučar**[2,3], **and Vladimir Simic**[4,5]

[1]*High School of Health Vocational Services, Sivas Cumhuriyet University, Sivas, Türkiye,* [2]*Department of Operations Research and Statistics, University of Belgrade, Belgrade, Serbia,* [3]*UNEC Applied Artificial Intelligence Research Center, Azerbaijan State University of Economics (UNEC), Baku, Azerbaijan,* [4]*Faculty of Transport and Traffic Engineering, University of Belgrade, Belgrade, Serbia,* [5]*Faculty of Engineering, Dogus University, Istanbul, Türkiye*

33.1 Introduction

Multicriteria decision-making (MCDM) problems consist of complex processes that assume great importance in many sectors, such as the field of business, engineering, or public administration, as they involve finding the most suitable solution within a set of multiple, often conflicting, criteria. This activity encompasses the joint assessment of many different criteria with different levels of priority, adding more complexity to the decision. Logarithm methodology of additive weights (LMAW), a technique designed to address such difficulties, represents a new approach in the MCDM area that can handle both qualitative and quantitative information, being distinguished for its robustness, particularly in large-sized sets, as well as its ability to tackle complex decision situations. Its fundamental process basically entails determining the criteria's weight while accounting for the alternatives' distances from the reference point (Pamučar et al., 2021).

To this end, the LMAW brings forth a twofold innovative approach. Firstly, the LMAW utilizes logarithmic functions in processing initial decision data. By so doing, the logarithmic functions accomplish two different tasks. They standardize different criteria into a uniform scale, which is dimensionless. This helps in ease any negative effects associated with different assessment parameters. Consequently, more effective comparisons emerge. Secondly, the LMAW incorporates the use of the Bonferroni aggregator. This is a sophisticated operator that goes further than merely adding weighted scores. Rather, this operator assesses the geometric mean of criterion interactions, taking into consideration the comparison of every criterion with all other participants. At this juncture, the overpowering effect of a criterion, as well as the joint interactions of all assessment variables, is well considered. This assists in comprehensively synthesizing diversity and any conflicting views associated with different experts, as presented by multiple assessment variables, within a uniform group decision-making mathematical model.

The importance of LMAW is most clearly shown through its built-in and robust resistance to the "rank reversal" phenomenon, a well-documented weakness whereby merely adding or removing a suboptimal alternative may generate illogical changes to the already established order of the existing choices. Specifically, the use of a logarithmic normalization scale with a Bonferroni-based aggregation formula in LMAW mathematically incorporates every effort to prevent such illogicalities. By focusing its assessment process on the absolute, comparative measures of the alternatives with respect to their determined basic structural framework, as opposed to concrete, process-centered yardsticks, LMAW is guaranteed to retain its starting, revised order of the remaining alternatives. Such is not only a process-oriented strength but greatly adds to the methodological integrity of its outcome, as well as its applicability within dynamic decision support technology, strategic planning, and other applications that would necessitate the integrity of the decision-support framework itself.

Encyclopedia of Multi-Attribute Decision-Making (MADM). DOI: https://doi.org/10.1016/B978-0-443-33275-3.00044-0

TABLE 33.1 Comparing the analytic hierarchy process (AHP) and technique for order preference by similarity to ideal solution (TOPSIS) with the logarithm methodology of additive weights method.

Feature/comparison criteria	LMAW method	AHP method	TOPSIS method
Weight determination	Objective/integrated: uses logarithmic deviation for weight calculation, often from the decision matrix itself, reducing direct subjectivity.	Subjective: consistency problems may arise because it mainly relies on pairwise comparison matrices from expert judgment.	External: weights are determined separately and subjectively, then imported into the model.
Normalization and value aggregation	Logarithmic and Bonferroni: this method uses the Bonferroni operator and log-based normalization for interactive, nonlinear aggregation.	Eigenvector and linear: uses eigenvector derivation for weights and linear additive aggregation for final scores.	Vector and linear: it makes use of vector normalization alongside linear weighted aggregation, with roots in the Euclidean distance.
Rank reversal problem	High resistance: because it is anchored in logarithmic relative distances, it is structurally designed to reduce rank reversal.	Highly sensitive: known to be susceptible to rank reversal with the addition or removal of alternatives.	Sensitivity: the rankings may change with changes in the list of alternatives, because of re-scaling of distances with respect to ideal solutions.
Handling uncertainty and expert diversity	Integrated harmonization: divergent expert opinions are naturally balanced and synthesized by the Bonferroni aggregator to produce a coherent group outcome.	Prior consistency check: needs consistency validation but finds it difficult to combine very different points of view artificially.	Limitations: typically supports one set of weights and requires prior aggregation of experts' judgments.
Core philosophy	Mathematical stability and robust synthesis: achieves reliable, stable rankings through objective mathematical principles and interactive criteria synthesis.	Consistency in subjective judgments: structures complex decisions-based on decomposed pairwise comparisons.	Geometric proximity to the ideal: this approach finds the solution alternative that is closest to the ideal solution while being farthest from the negative perfect solution.

Source: Created by the authors.

For a better understanding of the innovative nature of LMAW, a comparative analysis of LMAW with two of the first MCDM methods, analytic hierarchy process and technique for order preference by similarity to ideal solution (TOPSIS), is given in Table 33.1.

As shown in Table 33.1, the novelty of LMAW lies in its paradigm shift, which changes from subjective weight assessment with linear distance mechanics, such that the method incorporates a comprehensive approach that utilizes logarithmic math with interactive aggregation. This helps LMAW move beyond being a mathematical calculation method, as this new paradigm better owns LMAW the capabilities that enhance decision-making with fixed result integrity that completely incorporates group intelligence, thus being a marked improvement over existing notions necessary for applications that hugely depend on high reliability within dynamic settings.

The remaining portions of this literature review will clarify the theoretical background and procedure involved in the LMAW method. These novelties achieved in the LMAW method, as found in existing literature (Božanić et al., 2022; Pamučar et al., 2021; Radovanović et al., 2024), can thus be enumerated as: being a maximally stable, consistent methodology for MCDM, having the ability to overcome the reversal of rankings whereby adding or removing elements wouldn't alter the rankings, allowing more flexibility within the decision-making environment for the decision maker, assisting in arriving at objective, consistent, and sound decisions through a straightforward, practical, and applicable mathematical formula, allowing experts' views that don't correspond with group decisions, which would then align with the Bonferroni formula. Thus, as established, LMAW presents a marked innovation as well as a useful alternative within the existing frameworks established within the realm of MCDM.

Lastly, this chapter on LMAW is outlined as follows: Section 33.2 assigns space for a literature review on the integration of the method with fuzzy logic, as well as the hybrid models that this method belongs to. It is further segmented into a segment that explains the methodology behind the method. Case studies, further subdivided into simple and complex, come next within Section 33.4. Concluding statements, as well as recommendations, follow within Section 33.5.

33.2 Literature review

The LMAW methodological approach is being widely adopted in different scientific areas, often supported by extensive methodological improvements, as its fuzzy expansions, applications, and hybrid models will be reviewed in this section, based on the literature that currently prevails.

33.2.1 Fuzzy and uncertainty-based extensions

The most important strength of the LMAW method is its flexibility in dealing with uncertain situations. Being modified with triangular fuzzy numbers, as identified in (Božanić et al., 2022; Nayeb-Pashaei et al., 2025), LMAW was used in strategic decisions, such as the landing point of military logistics. The Z-numbers-based hybrid model (Puška et al., 2022) minimized uncertainty by integrating the confidence ratings of expert opinions in green supplier selection in agriculture. Fuzzy rough sets (Puška et al., 2024) have transformed subjective assessments into mathematical objectivity in tractor selection and (Puška et al., 2023) in green supplier selection in agricultural enterprises. Z Extension-LMAW (ZE-LMAW) was used to assess climate change resilient land-use transportation projects that received green funding (Haseli et al., 2024). In particular, fuzzy LMAW (F-LMAW) (Darıcı et al., 2025) has gained flexibility in postearthquake critical infrastructure prioritization by analyzing gray swan scenarios.

33.2.2 Sectoral application diversity

Finance and banking: Pakistani commercial banks: the hybrid model of F-LBWA, F-LMAW, and measurement alternatives and ranking according to compromise solution (MARCOS) produced consistent results in evaluating bank performance under conflicting financial criteria (profitability, risk, sustainability) (Işık et al., 2025).

Logistics and transportation: autonomous buses: an evaluation of 20 autonomous buses with 33 sustainability criteria using F-LMAW and fuzzy Dombi Bonferroni identified Proterra catalyst as the most sustainable alternative (Görçün et al., 2025). Domino accidents: weighting 16 criteria with LMAW for accident analysis in the chemical industry highlighted the critical criteria of "applicability" and "accuracy" (Gholamizadeh et al., 2024).

Environment and energy management: ecotourism potential: F-LMAW produced a high accuracy outcome in land suitability assessment in Sivas, Turkey, with 24 variables (Karakuş, 2024). Solar power plant site selection: F-LMAW with Z-numbers found that solar intensity was the most important factor in Mersin (Ünsal et al., 2024). Ecological compensation: coupling of LMAW with MARCOS, bipolar trapezoidal neurotopic clusters gave satisfactory agreement of watershed restoration schemes in Anhui province, China (Zhang & Wang, 2025).

Social policy and governance: sustainable development goals (SDGs): prioritization of SDG carried out through F-LMAW in the Dominican Republic, reported "Decent Work and Economic Growth" as the most important objective (Fernández-Portillo et al., 2024). Open government data: LMAW–logarithmic percentage change-driven objective weighing–Bayesian hybrid approach pinpointed "Air quality" along with "procurement" as important key performance measures in the G20 nations (Demir et al., 2023).

33.2.3 Hybrid models and stability improvements

LMAW's robustness was improved through the development of synergistic models with other MCDM tools: weighting hybrids: F-LMAW + full consistency method + gray evaluation based on distance from Average Solution (G-EDAS) (Radovanović et al., 2024) improved the weighting of the criteria with the Bonferroni adder for drone choice. Ranking hybrids: Z-Number F-LMAW + Fuzzy compromise ranking of alternatives from distance to ideal solution (Puška et al., 2022) and fuzzy rough LMAW + multi-attributive border approximation area comparison (Puška et al., 2023) were invariant to uncertainty in supplier ordering. Dynamic cenario analysis: F-LMAW + fuzzy decision-making trial and evaluation laboratory (Darıcı et al., 2024) analyzed the effects of artificial intelligence on job creation in the framework of "post-Luddism."

33.2.4 Methodological validation and limitations

Evidence from existing literature shows that LMAW has been validated through three consistency tests: sensitivity analysis (ranking robustness for ±50% changes in criterion weights, (Božanić et al., 2022)); comparative analysis (Spearman correlation value of >0.90 with other MCDM models such as TOPSIS, VlseKriterijumska Optimizacija I Kompromisno Resenje, complex proportional assessment); simulation-based validation (Monte Carlo simulation for statistical verification of solutions, (Tešić et al., 2024)).

Limitations include computational complexity (especially in hybrid models) and the need for parameter optimization. While maintaining its fundamental methodological robustness, LMAW has undergone significant evolution in uncertainty management with its fuzzy, Z-number, and rough set extensions, as well as in industrial applications with hybrid models. Ranking stability, especially in dynamic decision environments, makes it an indispensable tool in the MCDM literature.

33.3 Methodology

Criteria are prioritized by the experts in the group according to the value from the established linguistic scale. Scale: absolutely high (AH = 5), very high (VH = 4.5), high (H = 4), medium high (MH = 3.5), equal (E = 3), medium (M = 2.5), low (L = 2), very low (VL = 1.5), and absolutely low (AL = 1). The method of prioritizing entails assigning a higher value from the linguistic scale to the criteria of more importance and a lower value to the criteria of lesser significance.

Step 1: Determining the ultimate antiideal point (γ_{AIP})

The absolute antiideal point should be less than the least value in the priority vector, and it is calculated using the priority vector's minimum values. The value of $\gamma_{AIP} = \gamma^e_{\min}/s$ may be defined as $\gamma^e_{\min} = \{\gamma^e_{C_1}, \gamma^e_{C_2}, ..., \gamma^e_{C_n}\}$, and "$s$" is a number larger than the base of the logarithm (A). s = 3 if we consider ln to be a logarithmic function.

Step 2: The relationship between the members of the priority vector and the absolute antiideal point (γ_{AIP}) is ascertained by using Eq. (33.1).

$$\eta^e_{C_t} = \frac{\gamma^e_{C_t}}{\gamma_{AIP}} \tag{33.1}$$

Thus, we obtain relation vector $R^e = \{\eta^e_{C_1}, \eta^e_{C_2}, ..., \eta^e_{C_n}\}$, where R^e displays the relation vector of the expert, and $\eta^e_{C_t}$ displays the relation vector's value that is produced by using Eq. (33.1)

Step 3: Locating the vector of weight coefficients (w_j)

The values of the weight coefficients of the criterion for the experts are found by using Eq. (33.2).

$$w^e_j = \frac{\log_A(\eta^e_{C_t})}{\log_A\left(\Pi^n_{t=1}\eta^e_{C_t}\right)} \tag{33.2}$$

where the elements of the relation vector R^e are shown by $\eta^e_{C_t}$. These weight coefficient values satisfy the requirement $\sum^n_{j=1} w^e_j = 1$. The aggregated vector of weight coefficients $w_j = (w_1, w_2, ..., w_n)^T$, is obtained by using the Bonferroni aggregator as in Eq. (33.3).

$$w_j = \left(\frac{1}{k(k-1)}\sum_{x=1}^{k}(w_j^{(x)})^p \cdot \sum_{y=1,\ (x\neq y)}^{k}(w_j^{(y)})^q\right)^{\frac{1}{p+q}} \tag{33.3}$$

where w^e_j shows the weight coefficients derived from the assessments of the e-th expert $1 \le e \le k$, and $p, q \ge 0$ show the stabilizing settings of the Bonferroni aggregator.

33.4 Case study

In this section, the process steps of the LMAW method are shown in detail with numerical examples using the simple case and complex case designed as hypothetical scenarios.

33.4.1 Numerical example 1

33.4.1.1 Logistics performance measurement

In example 1, a hypothetical scenario, a logistics management team aims to identify which criteria are most important in the decision-making process for operational improvement efforts. To do this, four experts from various fields assessed five criteria commonly used in logistics performance measurement.

Criteria: C1 on-time delivery rate (%) (benefit), C2 cost per shipment (USD) (cost), C3 damage rate (%) (cost), C4 IT integration score (1–10) (benefit), C5 flexibility and adaptability score (benefit).

Purpose: Using the LMAW technique, identify which criteria are most prioritized in the logistics management decision-making process.

The experts rated the importance of the factors on a scale of 1 (absolutely low) to 5 (absolutely high). Table 33.2 shows information on the expert group.

Four priority vectors were established since four specialists conducted the assessment:

$$P^1 = \{AH,\ M,\ E,\ E,\ H\}$$

$$P^2 = \{AH,\ M,\ M,\ L,\ MH\}$$

$$P^3 = \{AH,\ L,\ M,\ L,\ E\}$$

$$P^4 = \{VH,\ VL,\ H,\ VL,\ VH\}$$

Step 1: The absolute antiideal point's value is arbitrary $\gamma_{AIP} = 0{,}5$.

Step 2: The connection between the absolute antiideal point and the priority vector's components $\gamma_{AIP} = 0.5$, is found by applying Eq. (33.1) to the data from the expert priority vectors and $\gamma_{AIP} = 0.5$. The connections between the vector of priorities components and the anti ideal point are shown in the section that follows:

$$R^1 = \{10,\ 5,\ 6,\ 6,\ 8\}$$

$$R^2 = \{10,\ 5,\ 5,\ 4,\ 7\}$$

$$R^3 = \{10,\ 4,\ 5,\ 4,\ 6\}$$

$$R^4 = \{9,\ \ 3,\ \ 8,\ \ 3,\ \ 9\}$$

The following is how to apply Eq. (33.1) to find the members of the vector R^1.

$$\eta^1_{C_1} = \frac{5}{0.5} = 10,\quad \eta^1_{C_2} = \frac{2.5}{0.5} = 5,\quad \eta^1_{C_3} = \frac{3}{0.5} = 6,\quad \eta^1_{C_4} = \frac{3}{0.5} = 6,\quad \eta^1_{C_5} = \frac{4.5}{0.5} = 9$$

The remaining vectors R^2, R^3 and R^4 are produced similarly.

$$w^1_j = \{0.2405,\ 0.1681,\ 0.1871,\ 0.1871,\ 0.2172\}$$

$$w^2_j = \{0.2601,\ 0.1818,\ 0.1818,\ 0.1566,\ 0.2198\}$$

$$w^3_j = \{0.2716,\ 0.1637,\ 0.1899,\ 0.1635,\ 0.2114\}$$

TABLE 33.2 Expert profiles.

Expert	Role/area of expertise	Focus
E1	Logistics operations manager	Delivery time and process efficiency
E2	Finance manager	Cost control and damage-related losses
E3	Customer experience manager	Customer satisfaction and damage rate
E4	IT integration leader	System integration and data sharing

$$w_j^4 = \{0.2534,\ 0.1267,\ 0.2398,\ 0.1267,\ 0.2534\}$$

Applying Eq. (33.2) yields the elements of the first expert's vector w_j^1.

$$w_1^1 = \frac{\ln(10)}{\ln(10.5.6.6.8)} = 0.2405,\quad w_2^1 = \frac{\ln(5)}{\ln(10.5.6.6.8)} = 0.1681,\quad w_3^1 = \frac{\ln(6)}{\ln(10.5.6.6.8)} = 0.1871,$$
$$w_4^1 = \frac{\ln(6)}{\ln(10.5.6.6.8)} = 0.1871,\quad w_5^1 = \frac{\ln(8)}{\ln(10.5.6.6.8)} = 0.2172$$

The acquired weight coefficient values that were found satisfy the requirement that $\Sigma_{j=1}^5 w_j^1 = 1$. $(0.2405 + 0.1681 + 0.1871 + 0.1871 + 0.2172 = 1)$. Similar methods are used to derive the members of the remaining vectors, w_j^2, w_j^3, and w_j^4.

The aggregated vector of the weight coefficients is obtained by applying Eq. (33.3).

$$w_j = (0.2563,\ 0.1596,\ 0.1992,\ 0.1580,\ 0.2252)^T$$

The weight coefficient $w_1 = 0.2563$ is calculated by averaging the values $w_j^e\ (1 \le e \le 4)$ for each expert, that is, $w_j^1 = 0.2405,\ w_j^2 = 0.2601,\ w_j^3 = 0.2716$ and $w_j^4 = 0.2534$. We get the averaged value by using Eq. (33.3):

$$w_1 = (0.2405,\ 0.2601,\ 0.2716,\ 0.2534)^{p=q=1}$$
$$= \left\{\frac{1}{4(4-1)}(0.2405^1(0.2601^1 + 0.2716^1 + 0.2534^1) + \ldots,\ 0.2534^1(0.2405^1 + 0.2601^1 + 0.2716^1))\right\}^{\frac{1}{1+1}} = 0.2563$$

Similar procedures are used to acquire the remaining weight coefficient vector values. The weight coefficients for $\Sigma_{j=1}^5 w_j = 1$ are normalized.

$$w_1 = \frac{0.2563}{0.2563 + 0.1596 + 0.1992 + 0.1580 + 0.2252} = 0.2567$$

Similar methods are used to produce the remaining normalized weight coefficient values, which are displayed in Fig. 33.1.

In Fig. 33.1, on-time delivery rate =0.2567 has the highest weight. This shows that on-time delivery is the most critical factor in the operational improvement process. In other words, the most important determinant of logistics performance is the delivery of shipments to customers at the scheduled time. Flexibility and adaptability score =0.2256 comes second. This demonstrates that the system's ability to quickly adapt to changing conditions (demand fluctuations, route changes, urgent orders, etc.) provides a significant competitive advantage. Damage rate =0.1995 is of medium importance. Reducing the damage rate directly impacts customer satisfaction and cost control. Cost per shipment =0.1599 and IT integration Score =0.1583 are the criteria with the lowest weights, close to each other. The outcome of this analysis

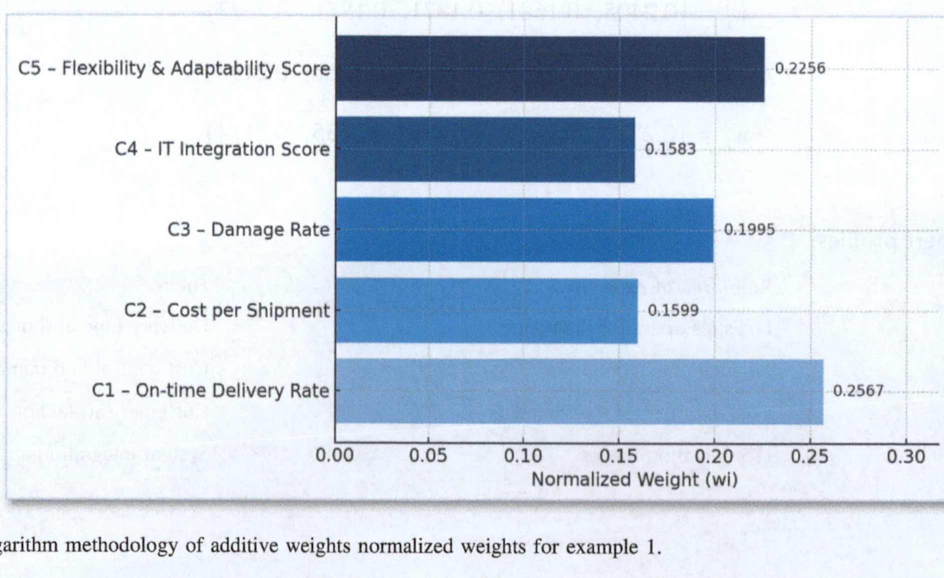

FIGURE 33.1 Logarithm methodology of additive weights normalized weights for example 1.

indicates that, for improvement, cost and digital integration are of primary importance, but their priorities stand relatively low. From the LMAW outcome, the strategy that focuses on speed and flexibility (C1 & C5) will generate the highest returns. While cost and digitalization are important, customer experience and process reliability should be prioritized.

33.4.2 Numerical example 2

33.4.2.1 Smart city project investment prioritization

A municipality wants to determine the areas to invest in smart city projects within the next 5 years. Five different experts (urban planner [E1], environmental engineer [E2], transportation expert [E3], data analyst [E4], and public representative [E5]) evaluate based on seven criteria.

Criteria: C1 traffic flow improvement (max), C2 air quality impact (max), C3 energy efficiency (max), C4 implementation cost (min), C5 public acceptance (max), C6 data integration capability (max), C7 long-term maintenance needs (min).

Purpose: To determine which criteria are more prioritized in municipal investments using the LMAW method.

The experts' assessment is provided in Table 33.3.

The elements of the experts' priority vector are displayed in Table 33.3. The relationship obtained with γ_{AIP} = 0,5 is given in Table 33.4.

Then, using Eq. (33.2), the criteria weight coefficient vector for each expert is obtained and is given in Table 33.5.

Eq. (33.3) yields the criterion weights, which are listed in Table 33.6.

The weight coefficients for $\sum_{j=1}^{7} w_j = 1$ are derived as normalized values.

$$w_1 = \frac{0.1536}{0.1536 + 0.1515 + 0.1545 + 0.1205 + 0.1490 + 0.1468 + 0.1232} = 0.1527$$

TABLE 33.3 Hypothetical expert evaluation matrix.

Criterion/expert	E1	E2	E3	E4	E5
C1	4.5 (very high [VH])	3.5 (medium high [MH])	5 (absolutely high [AH])	3 (equal [E])	3.5 (medium high [MH])
C2	3.5 (MH)	5 (AH)	3 (E)	3.5 (MH)	4 (high [H])
C3	4 (H)	4.5 (VH)	3.5 (MH)	4 (H)	3.5 (MH)
C4	2 (low [L])	2.5 (medium [M])	2.5 (M)	3 (E)	2.5 (M)
C5	3 (E)	3.5 (MH)	3 (E)	4 (H)	5 (AH)
C6	3 (E)	2.5 (M)	4 (H)	4.5 (VH)	4 (H)
C7	2.5 (M)	3 (E)	2 (L)	2.5 (M)	3 (E)

TABLE 33.4 The antiideal point and the priority vector's relationship.

	C1	C2	C3	C4	C5	C6	C7
E1	9	7	8	4	6	6	5
E2	7	10	9	5	7	5	6
E3	10	6	7	5	6	8	4
E4	6	7	8	6	8	9	5
E5	7	8	7	5	10	8	6

TABLE 33.5 Weights for each expert's criteria.

	C1	C2	C3	C4	C5	C6	C7	Total
w_j^1	0.1716	0.1520	0.1624	0.1083	0.1400	0.1400	0.1257	1.0000
w_j^2	0.1452	0.1718	0.1639	0.1201	0.1452	0.1201	0.1337	1.0000
w_j^3	0.1784	0.1388	0.1508	0.1247	0.1388	0.1611	0.1074	1.0000
w_j^4	0.1328	0.1442	0.1541	0.1328	0.1541	0.1628	0.1193	1.0000
w_j^5	0.1415	0.1512	0.1415	0.1170	0.1674	0.1512	0.1303	1.0000

TABLE 33.6 Criterion weight values.

	C1	C2	C3	C4	C5	C6	C7
w_j	0.1536	0.1515	0.1545	0.1205	0.1490	0.1468	0.1232

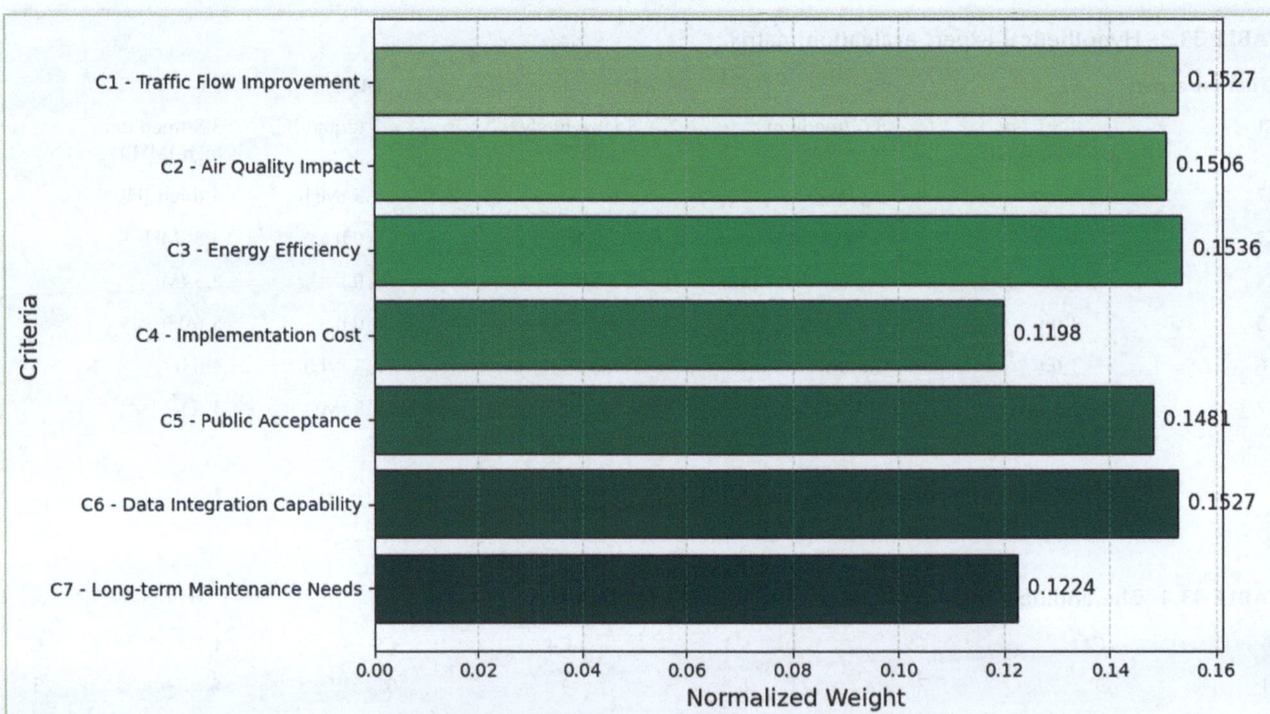

FIGURE 33.2 Logarithm methodology of additive weights normalized weights for example 2.

Fig. 33.2 shows the residual values of the normalized weight coefficients.

According to Fig. 33.2, the highest weight: energy efficiency =0.1536 → energy efficiency is the top priority criterion in municipal investments. The second highest weight: traffic flow improvement =0.1527 and data integration capability =0.1527 → traffic flow and data integration are also important criteria. Medium-level criteria: air quality impact =0.1506 and public acceptance =0.1481 → environmental impact and public acceptance should be considered, but are slightly less important than the others. Low-priority criteria: implementation cost =0.1198 and long-term maintenance needs =0.1224 → cost and maintenance requirements are lower priorities than other criteria; cost advantages can be considered when making decisions.

33.5 Conclusion and future work

The LMAW is a stable and reliable method that makes a significant contribution to the field of MCDM. This section summarizes the key features, strengths, and potential future research areas of the LMAW method. LMAW's main strength is its use of logarithmic functions in determining criteria weights, thus grounding subjective expert opinions in an objective and consistent mathematical foundation. By virtue of its ability to evade the rank reversal phenomenon, this method is unique. This property of the method ensures that the existing alternatives' ranking is unaltered with the addition or deletion of a new alternative from the list, thus greatly increasing its credibility. Example 1 (logistic service): time (26%) reliability as well as flexibility (23%) feature prominently in improvement, though cost considerations (16%) rate low. Example 2 (smart city): of the seven considerations, energy efficiency (15.4%), traffic management (15.3%), and data integration (15.3%) feature high, though cost (12%) rates low. In both instances, LMAW ensured that its weightage was well balanced, and this remained unaltered with the size of the dataset. Despite being flexible, with the capability of processing both numerical and nonnumerical datasets side by side, the method's applications in different sectors have been quite successful.

According to a literature review, various types of LMAW models have been developed that incorporate diverse theories of uncertainty, such as fuzzy sets, Z-numbers, and rough sets. These different models of LMAW further improve its existing abilities in decision-making with regard to uncertainties, as well as help it cope with the complexities involved in real-life situations. Also, its application in different areas such as finance, logistics, environmental management, and social policies, testifies that this method was applicable in a number of different tasks. Moreover, hybrid models were developed that combined this method with other models of multiple attribute decision-making, such as evaluation based on distance from average solution (EDAS), and MARCOS.

LMAW provides vast prospective areas for further studies, which may further develop the method on theoretical as well as practical fronts: Integration of the LMAW method with interval-valued numbers, intuitionistic fuzzy sets, neutrosophic sets, or any other new theories of uncertainty may further enhance its applications in more complex and uncertain environments. Integration of the LMAW method with machine learning algorithms or artificial intelligence may provide vast prospective areas, such as automatically processing large amounts of data, which may further optimize decision-making. Integration of the LMAW method with hybrid models may provide vast prospective areas, mostly in prediction, classification, or optimization. Integration of real-time dynamic decision models with LMAW may further provide fast decision-making solutions in constantly varying conditions. This will provide vast beneficial applications, mostly in, but not restricted to, supply chain management, smart city models, or decision support in natural disasters. Applying the LMAW method in more real applications, mostly in healthcare, energy, manufacturering, and service industry models, will further provide vast prospective areas of testing its applicational correctness in real decision environments. Applying the method will provide vast knowledge on its correctness, strengths, and weaknesses. Writing friendly computer-based soft tools or libraries in LMAW will further provide vast prospective applications, mostly in assisting decision-makers. This will further enhance its applications and adoption. More comprehensive comparative studies of the LMAW method with other recently developed MCDM models, such as combined compromise abbreviations expanded solution, EDAS, and weighted aggregated sum product assessment, will further enhance its applicational correctness, strengths, and advantages.

LMAW is a marked improvement in the area of MCDM. Its strong mathematical background, capacity for processing uncertainties, as well as sequence stability, confirm its potency in solving intricate decision issues. Future studies will broaden the applicability of LMAW, ensuring its continuous contributions to decision-making research.

References

Božanić, D., Pamučar, D., Milić, A., Marinković, D., & Komazec, N. (2022). Modification of the logarithm methodology of additive weights (LMAW) by a triangular fuzzy number and its application in multi-criteria decision making. *Axioms, 11*(3), 89. https://doi.org/10.3390/axioms11030089.

Darıcı, S., Demir, G., Bilgili, F. F., & Pamučar, D. (2025). Hunting swans: Looking to the future through fuzzy LMAW analysis of a gray swan scenario. *Environment, Development and Sustainability,* 1–34. https://doi.org/10.1007/s10668-025-06559-9.

Darıcı, S., Riaz, M., Demir, G., Tamer Gencer, Z., & Pamučar, D. (2024). How will i break AI? Post-luddism in the ai age: Fuzzy MCDM synergy. *Technological Forecasting and Social Change, 202*, 123327. https://doi.org/10.1016/j.techfore.2024.123327.

Demir, G., Riaz, M., & Almalki, Y. (2023). Multi-criteria decision making in evaluation of open government data indicators: An application in G20 countries. *AIMS Mathematics, 8*(8), 18408–18434. https://doi.org/10.3934/math.2023936.

Fernández-Portillo, L. A., Demir, G., Sianes, A., et al. (2024). Setting a shared development agenda: Prioritizing the sustainable development goals in the dominican republic with fuzzy-LMAW. *Scientific Reports, 14*, 12146. https://doi.org/10.1038/s41598-024-62790-w.

Gholamizadeh, K., Moslem, S., Zarei, E., & Esztergar-Kiss, D. (2024). Influential criteria in domino accident analysis: An evaluation using the logarithm methodology of additive weights. *Journal of Loss Prevention in the Process Industries, 92*, 105436. https://doi.org/10.1016/j.jlp.2024.105436.

Görçün, Ö. F., Özçalıcı, M., Gurler, H. E., Pamučar, D., & Simic, V. (2025). Promoting sustainable urban mobility: An integrated fuzzy decision-making model for assessing autonomous bus alternatives. *Engineering Applications of Artificial Intelligence, 156*, 111034. https://doi.org/10.1016/j.engappai.2025.111034.

Haseli, G., Deveci, M., Isik, M., Gokasar, I., Pamucar, D., & Hajiaghaei-Keshteli, M. (2024). Providing climate change resilient land-use transport projects with green finance using Z extended numbers based decision-making model. *Expert Systems with Applications, 243*, 122858. https://doi.org/10.1016/j.eswa.2023.122858.

Işık, Ö., Shabir, M., Demir, G., Puska, A., & Pamučar, D. (2025). A hybrid framework for assessing Pakistani commercial bank performance using multi-criteria decision-making. *Financial Innovation, 11*(1), 38. https://doi.org/10.1186/s40854-024-00613-5.

Karakuş, C. B. (2024). Assessment of ecotourism potentiality based on GIS-based fuzzy logarithm methodology of additive weights (F-LMAW) method for sustainable natural resource management. *Environment, Development and Sustainability, 26*(10), 27001–27055. https://doi.org/10.1007/s10668-024-05032-3.

Nayeb-Pashaei, K., Vahabzadeh, S., Hosseinian-Far, A., & Ghoushchi, S. J. (2025). Sustainable urban transportation: Key criteria for a greener future. *Spectrum of Operational Research, 3*(1), 103–127. https://doi.org/10.31181/sor31202634.

Pamučar, D., Žižović, M., Biswas, S., & Božanić, D. (2021). A new logarithm methodology of additive weights (LMAW) for multi-criteria decision-making: application in logistics. *Facta Universitatis Series: Mechanical Engineering, 19*(3), 361–380. https://doi.org/10.22190/FUME210214031P.

Puška, A., Božanić, D., Nedeljković, M., & Janošević, M. (2022). Green supplier selection in an uncertain environment in agriculture using a hybrid MCDM model: Z-numbers–fuzzy LMAW–fuzzy CRADIS model. *Axioms, 11*(9), 427. https://doi.org/10.3390/axioms11090427.

Puška, A., Štilić, A., Nedeljković, M., Božanić, D., & Biswas, S. (2023). Integrating fuzzy rough sets with LMAW and MABAC for green supplier selection in agribusiness. *Axioms, 12*(8), 746. https://doi.org/10.3390/axioms12080746.

Puška, A., Štilić, A., Nedeljković, M., et al. (2024). Application of fuzzy-rough approach in tractor selection. *Journal of Computational and Cognitive Engineering, 3*(4), 434–446. https://doi.org/10.56578/jcce030405.

Radovanović, M., Petrovski, A., Cirkin, E., Behlić, A., Jokić, Ž., Chemezov, D., Hashimov, E. G., Bouraima, M. B., & Jana, C. (2024). Application of the new hybrid model LMAW-G-EDAS multi-criteria decision-making when choosing an assault rifle for the needs of the army. *Journal of Decision Analytics and Intelligent Computing, 4*(1), 16–31. https://doi.org/10.31181/jdaic10021012024r.

Tešić, D. Z., Božanić, D. I., & Puška, A. (2024). Application for the selection of a location for crossing a water obstacle by fording in a defense operation. *Military Technical Courier, 72*(3), 1120–1146. https://scindeks.ceon.rs/Issue.aspx?issue=18246.

Ünsal, Ö., Demir, G., Karakuş, C. B., & Pamučar, D. (2024). Application of Z-number-based fuzzy MCDM in solar power plant location selection problem in spatial planning. *Energy Reports, 12*, 4034–4054. https://doi.org/10.1016/j.egyr.2024.09.055.

Zhang, S., & Wang, Y. (2025). An analysis of bipolar trapezoidal neutrosophic sets (BTNSs) for examining the income-increasing and poverty-reduction effects of ecological compensation in the huai river basin of anhui province: A comprehensive study. *Neutrosophic Sets and Systems, 81*, 638–654.

Chapter 34

IROC: improved rank order centroid method for multi-attribute decision-making

Neda Mansouri and Mahmoud Tajik
School of Industrial Engineering, Iran University of Science and Technology, Tehran, Iran

34.1 Introduction

In contemporary operational and strategic contexts, decision-makers (DMs) are frequently confronted with intricate problems characterized by conflicting objectives and numerous alternative courses of action, necessitating rigorous mechanisms to identify the optimal choice (Greco et al., 2002). Modern decision-making contexts are inherently complex, frequently demanding the simultaneous evaluation of numerous possible paths against a diverse array of performance metrics, which complicates the clear identification of the optimal action. Furthermore, the used criteria for evaluation often conflict (e.g., maximizing performance on one factor may inevitably lead to a reduction in performance on another). The constant challenge of evaluating, prioritizing, and selecting among alternatives has underscored the growing importance of using rational, transparent, and structured methodologies in decision support. Consequently, a structured methodology is essential to aid DMs in navigating these compromises, leading to the widespread application of multi-criteria decision-making MCDM) methods across various fields (Roszkowska, 2013).

The existing studies offer a comprehensive overview of MCDM techniques, each exhibiting comparative advantages dictated by the unique constraints of the problem. In general, these techniques are broadly divided into two interdependent categories: (i) weighting methods, which determine the relative importance of criteria, and (ii) outranking methods, which prioritize the alternatives. In terms of methodological orientation, weighting methods are delineated into three principal categories: subjective, objective, and integrated methods (Roszkowska, 2013). Subjective methods rely on the modeling of DM preferences, such as the analytic hierarchy process (AHP) (Saaty, 1987), the best worst method (BWM) (Rezaei, 2015), and step-wise weight assessment ratio analysis (SWARA) (Keršuliene et al., 2010). In contrast, objective methods derive weights from the statistical properties of the data, with prominent instances, including the entropy method (Shannon, 1948), criteria importance through intercriteria correlation (CRITIC) method (Diakoulaki et al., 1995), and criterion impact loss (CILOS) method (Zavadskas & Podvezko, 2016). Due to limitations and issues of using the subjective methods and objective methods separately, the third category, integrated methods, synthesizes these methods to harness both expert judgment and data structure, like factor relationship (Ginevičius, 2011) and the AHP–CILOS method (Tajik et al., 2023). Subsequently, outranking methods, such as technique for order preference by similarity to ideal solution method (Lai et al., 1994), Vlsekriterijumska Optimizacija I Kompromisno Resenje method (Opricovic, 1998), and measurement alternatives and ranking according to compromise solution method (Stević et al., 2020), aggregate the weighted scores to establish a definitive preference order among the various alternatives. Therefore, this thorough classification establishes the methodological boundaries and provides the necessary context for introducing the weighting methods in this chapter.

This chapter specifically emphasizes the perspective of Barron and Barrett, who argued that subjective approaches for deriving precise weights from DMs are inherently prone to severe methodological limitations (Barron & Barrett, 1996). The main challenge in establishing reliable criteria weights is that subjective methods used to obtain precise weights from DMs often possess significant methodological limitations (Hatefi, 2023). The subjective methods argue that the resulting outcomes are highly sensitive to the specific procedure used for weight assessment, highlighting the absence of a generalized consensus on which method produces the most valid or reliable weights. This instability becomes increasingly important in multicriteria

Encyclopedia of Multi-Attribute Decision-Making (MADM). DOI: https://doi.org/10.1016/B978-0-443-33275-3.00032-4

group decision-making (MCGDM) contexts, which have received substantial scholarly attention recently. This increased focus highlights the complexity of collective evaluations and the challenge of aggregating the various preferences of multiple DMs into a solid and defensible consensus (Diao et al., 2022).

Among the existing subjective weighting methods, rank order centroid (ROC), developed by Barron and Barrett (1996), has been applied in different decision-making problems. Following that, to overcome the issues and problems of the ROC method, including ordinary averaging, the improved rank order centroid (IROC), developed by Hatefi (2023), has been utilized. Given the extensive and growing adoption of the IROC method across diverse MCDM problems, the primary objective of this chapter is to describe the underlying theory and foundational steps of this specific weighting technique.

The rest of the chapter is structured as follows: Section 34.2 examines the existing literature on two types of weighting methods: subjective weighting methods and objective weighting methods. The IROC methodology is described in Section 34.3, which outlines the theoretical principles and procedural steps of the IROC method. Sections 34.4, 34.5 represent the implementation of the IROC method through two distinct numerical examples. The chapter concludes with Section 34.6, summarizing the key insights and offering recommendations for further study.

34.2 Literature review

In this section, the literature review on the weighting methods is categorized into two groups: objective weighting methods and subjective weighting methods.

7In terms of objective methods, Yoon (1980) developed Shannon's entropy method to calculate objective weights from the data itself, thereby eliminating the potential bias associated with subjective methods (e.g., expert surveys). Furthermore, this method assigns higher weights to criteria that perform a better job of differentiating between the available options. Diakoulaki et al. (1995) proposed an objective weighting method, known as the CRITIC method, to identify the information sources conveyed by different criteria in MCDM problems. Zavadskas and Podvezko (2016) introduced the CILOS method, an objective weighting approach that measures the relative impact loss experienced by an alternative's criterion when another criterion is selected as the best. Keshavarz-Ghorabaee et al. (2021) developed an objective weighting method known as the method based on the removal effects of criteria (MEREC). Moreover, the MEREC method utilizes a novel approach to determine the weights of criteria by assessing the impact of each criterion's removal on the performance of alternatives. Ecer and Pamucar (2022) introduced an objective weighting method called the logarithmic percentage change-driven objective weighting (LOPCOW). The LOPCOW method offers several advantages, including the ability to eliminate disparities caused by data size, produce more rational weightings, and incorporate both positive and negative data into the weighting process.

Regarding the topic of subjective methods, Linstone and Turoff (1975) developed a subjective weighting method, known as the Delphi method, which relies on a panel of experts. The purpose of the Delphi method is to achieve a convergence of opinion on a complex real-world issue. Saaty (1987) introduced the AHP method to assess the subjective weights of criteria, taking into account their independence using a comparison matrix. Following that, Saaty (2004) proposed a subjective weighting method, named analytic network process, which incorporates both individual and group decisions, maintaining the independence of the criteria from the alternatives while also addressing the interdependence and feedback within the entire decision structure. To extend the subjective weighting methods, Rezaei (2015) developed the BWM to evaluate and rank potential facility locations within the proposed multiobjective mathematical model for a humanitarian supply chain network. In addition, Pamučar et al. (2018) developed the full consistency method to address MCDM problems, highlighting its novel approach to determining criteria weights.

34.3 Methodology

The IROC method seeks to improve the ROC formula by addressing ordinary averaging and enhancing the weighting method's performance. In doing so, the IROC method uses different coefficients instead of equal coefficients in the process of the weighting method. To determine the coefficients of the IROC method, two approaches have been utilized: (i) extraction of coefficients based on the DM's perspectives (i.e., subjective approach) and (ii) extraction of default coefficients (i.e., objective approach) (Hatefi, 2023). Owing to the IROC method, default coefficients are estimated by considering a set of systematic simulation experiments using the MCDM problem. To accomplish that, the multi-attribute additive value (MAV) function is employed to compute the utility of alternatives (Danielson & Ekenberg, 2017).

The systematic simulations are applied with respect to two types of weights: true weights, which serve as the reference weights from an underlying random distribution, and weights obtained by the IROC method. After that, two efficiency measures, including hit ratio (*HR*) and rank order correlation (*RC*), were used to contribute to determining the default coefficients. The *HR* assesses how often a method (i.e., the IROC method) identifies the same best alternative as the true weights. The *HR* ranges from 0 to 1, where a value of 1 indicates that the best alternative in the two rank orders remains same throughout the entire simulation run. Furthermore, the *RC* shows how similar the rank structures of alternatives are based on true weights and the method used. The values of the *RC* range from −1 to 1, with a value of 1 indicating perfect correspondence between the two rank orders (Winkler & Hays, 1975). To implement the IROC method, the following algorithm should be performed (Hatefi, 2023).

ALGORITHM 34.1 The determination of IROC coefficients and IROC weights

Step 1. Let us set $\pi = 1$, $\gamma = 0$, and $\theta = 0$ to initiate the determination of the IROC coefficients process.

Where π represents the total number of simulation runs, γ indicates the total number of simulation runs in case the method and true weights select the same alternative as the best one. Furthermore, θ is related to the pairwise preference violations between the rank structures of the alternatives by the method and by the true weights.

Step 2. Conduct a normalized random MCDM matrix N using the random performance scores a_{ij} from an independent uniform distribution on the interval (0,1).

$$N = \begin{bmatrix} a_{11}^{norm} & \cdots & a_{1j}^{norm} & \cdots & a_{1n}^{norm} \\ \vdots & \ddots & \vdots & \ddots & \vdots \\ a_{i1}^{norm} & \cdots & a_{ij}^{norm} & \cdots & a_{in}^{norm} \\ \vdots & \ddots & \vdots & \ddots & \vdots \\ a_{m1}^{norm} & \cdots & a_{mj}^{norm} & \cdots & a_{mn}^{norm} \end{bmatrix}_{m \times n} ; \quad i = 1, 2, \ldots, m, \; j = 1, 2, \ldots, n \tag{34.1}$$

Where a_{ij}^{norm} represents the normalized performance score of alternative i for criterion j, which can be determined as shown in Eq. (34.2).

$$a_{ij}^{norm} = \frac{a_{ij} - a_j^{min}}{a_j^{max} - a_j^{min}} \tag{34.2}$$

According to Eq. (34.2), a_j^{min} and a_j^{max} indicate the minimum and maximum scores for criterion j.

Step 3. Determine the criteria true weights considering the following three substeps:

Step 3.1. Produce (n - 1) random numbers using an independent uniform distribution on (0, 1).

Step 3.2. Sort the generated random numbers (see Step 3.1) in ascending order as $u_1, u_2, \ldots, u_{n-1}$, and then compute the difference between adjacent numbers in sequence $1 > u_{n-1} \geq u_{n-2} \geq \ldots \geq u_1 > 0$ based on $(1 - u_{n-1})$, $(u_{n-1} - u_{n-2})$, $(u_1 - 0)$.

Step 3.3. Sort the differences (see Step 3.2) in descending order to determine the true weights, distributed on the weight space.

Step 4. Calculate the criteria weights using the IROC method using Eq. (34.3):

$$\begin{pmatrix} w_1 \\ w_2 \\ \vdots \\ w_n \end{pmatrix} = \varphi_{1n} \begin{pmatrix} 1 \\ 0 \\ \vdots \\ 0 \end{pmatrix} + \varphi_{2n} \begin{pmatrix} 1/2 \\ 1/2 \\ 0 \\ \vdots \\ 0 \end{pmatrix} + \ldots + \varphi_{nn} \begin{pmatrix} 1/n \\ 1/n \\ \vdots \\ 1/n \end{pmatrix} = \sum_{r=j}^{n} \left(\frac{\varphi_{rn}}{r} \right) \tag{34.3}$$

Where $\left\{(1, 0, \ldots, 0), \left(\frac{1}{2}, \frac{1}{2}, 0, \ldots, 0\right), \ldots, \left(\frac{1}{n}, \frac{1}{n}, \ldots, \frac{1}{n}\right)\right\}$ represents vertex methods in the weight space, $(w_1, w_2, \ldots, w_n)$ indicates the criteria weights and φ_{rn} is the weighted averaging coefficient.

Step 5. Determining the MAV for each alternative based on the true weights of criteria and the IROC weights of criteria, owing to Eq. (34.4).

$$MAV_i = \sum_{j=1}^{n} a_{ij}^{norm} w_j \tag{34.4}$$

According to Eq. (34.4), the alternative with the largest MAV is the best, and so on.

Step 6. Updating the γ and θ values with respect to the following two substeps:

Step 6.1. Set $\gamma = \gamma + 1$ when the MAV function selects the same alternative as the best based on true weights and IROC weights of the criteria.

Step 6.2. Set $\theta = \theta + 1$ when there is any violation between the overall rank of alternatives based on true weights and IROC weights of the criteria.

Step 7. Go to step 8 if $\pi = T$; otherwise, set $\pi = \pi + 1$ and go to step 2.

Step 8. Compute the overall value of the *HR* and *RC* using Eqs. (34.5) and (34.6).

$$HR = \frac{\gamma}{\pi} \tag{34.5}$$

$$RC = 1 - \left(\frac{2\theta}{m\pi} \right) \tag{34.6}$$

TABLE 34.1 The default coefficients for the vertex methods in the weight space.

	Number of criteria													
	2	**3**	**4**	**5**	**6**	**7**	**8**	**9**	**10**	**11**	**12**	**13**	**14**	**15**
Default coefficients	0.5115	0.3241	0.2323	0.1791	0.1448	0.1213	0.1027	0.0900	0.0791	0.0710	0.0644	0.0583	0.0532	0.0491
	0.4885	0.3552	0.2688	0.2131	0.1738	0.1463	0.1257	0.1102	0.0974	0.0868	0.0785	0.0714	0.0651	0.0607
		0.3205	0.2629	0.2171	0.1819	0.1557	0.1358	0.1194	0.1060	0.0954	0.0864	0.0785	0.0723	0.0669
			0.2358	0.2041	0.1781	0.1556	0.1371	0.1220	0.1089	0.0988	0.0905	0.0826	0.0761	0.0704
				0.1863	0.1673	0.1494	0.1340	0.1210	0.1098	0.1002	0.0911	0.0845	0.0782	0.0726
					0.1539	0.1406	0.1283	0.1176	0.1078	0.0991	0.0912	0.0843	0.0789	0.0737
						0.1308	0.1216	0.1121	0.1040	0.0968	0.0897	0.0840	0.0786	0.0735
							0.1145	0.1065	0.1001	0.0937	0.0880	0.0821	0.0770	0.0730
								0.1010	0.0957	0.0898	0.0850	0.0800	0.0754	0.0716
									0.0907	0.0859	0.0818	0.0776	0.0731	0.0696
										0.0821	0.0781	0.0748	0.0714	0.0678
											0.0749	0.0719	0.0689	0.0659
												0.0695	0.0668	0.0636
													0.0644	0.0615
														0.0595

TABLE 34.2 The weights of the criteria using the improved rank order centroid method.

	Number of criteria													
	2	3	4	5	6	7	8	9	10	11	12	13	14	15
Weights of criteria	0.7500	0.6111	0.5208	0.4567	0.4083	0.3704	0.3397	0.3143	0.2929	0.2745	0.2586	0.2446	0.2323	0.2212
	0.2500	0.2778	0.2708	0.2567	0.2417	0.2276	0.2147	0.2032	0.1929	0.1836	0.1753	0.1677	0.1608	0.1545
		0.1111	0.1458	0.1567	0.1583	0.1561	0.1522	0.1477	0.1429	0.1382	0.1336	0.1292	0.1251	0.1212
			0.0625	0.0900	0.1028	0.1085	0.1106	0.1106	0.1096	0.1079	0.1058	0.1036	0.1013	0.0990
				0.0400	0.0611	0.0728	0.0793	0.0828	0.0846	0.0851	0.0850	0.0844	0.0834	0.0823
					0.0278	0.0442	0.0543	0.0606	0.0646	0.0670	0.0683	0.0690	0.0692	0.0690
						0.0204	0.0335	0.0421	0.0479	0.0518	0.0544	0.0562	0.0573	0.0579
							0.0156	0.0262	0.0336	0.0388	0.0425	0.0452	0.0471	0.0484
								0.0123	0.0211	0.0275	0.0321	0.0356	0.0381	0.0400
									0.0100	0.0174	0.0229	0.0270	0.0302	0.0326
										0.0083	0.0145	0.0193	0.0230	0.0260
											0.0069	0.0123	0.0165	0.0199
												0.0059	0.0106	0.0143
													0.0051	0.0092
														0.0044

To extract IROC coefficients and IROC weights, the simulation process is conducted 1500 times with five rounds using four levels of alternatives (i.e., m = 3, 5, 7, and 10) and 24 levels of criteria (i.e., n = 2, 3, …, 25), leading to the generation of 96 combination terms. After that, the average *HR* and *RC* of the five rounds are computed, and the correlation between these two indicators is determined, representing a high value. Due to the high correlation between these two indicators (i.e., *HR* and *RC*), *HR* is only considered to contribute to the extraction of IROC coefficients. Furthermore, the geometric mean is applied to combinations with the same number of criteria. Following that, each geometric mean is divided by the sum of the geometric means to determine the normalized coefficients. Finally, the IROC coefficients for n = 2 to n = 15 are shown in Table 34.1.

Subsequently, the IROC weights for n = 2 to n = 15 are calculated using step 4 of algorithm 1 and are demonstrated in Table 34.2.

After identifying the IROC coefficients and IROC weights, the following algorithm is proposed for MCGDM problems.

ALGORITHM 34.2 Incorporating the IROC method in the MCGDM problems

Step 1. Identify a panel of subject matter experts $E(k = 1, 2, \ldots, E)$ who understand the problem and have the skills to make informed judgments.

Step 2. Conduct a criteria breakdown structure (CBS), as shown in Fig. 34.1, including $P(\nu = 1, 2, \ldots, P)$ parent boxes of the criteria using a Delphi method or superior documents/approvals. Furthermore, each parent box includes some subcriteria.

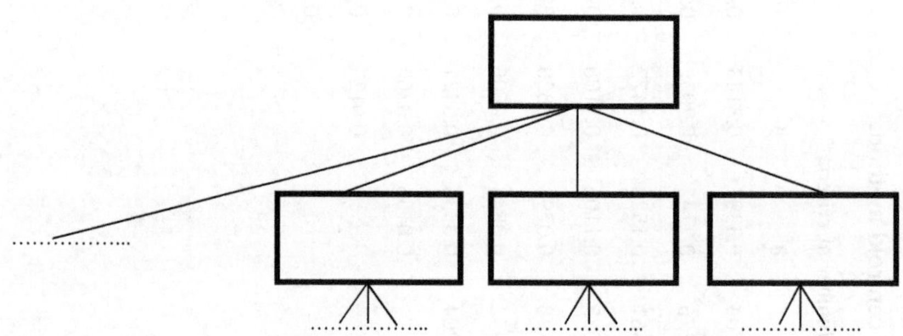

FIGURE 34.1 The schematic of criteria breakdown structure.

Step 3. Determine the rank of the criterion j (i.e., $r_{kj};\ j(j = 1, 2, \ldots, n)$) in parent box ν of the CBS based on the *kth* expert's preferences.

Step 4. Assess the level of agreement among the panelists by using Kendall's coefficient of concordance, which ranges from 0 (i.e., no agreement) to 1 (i.e., complete agreement) (Kendall & Gibbons, 1990). To calculate the Kendall's coefficient, Eqs. (34.7–34.9) should be performed.

$$R_j = \sum_{k=1}^{E} r_{kj},\ j = 1, 2, \ldots, n \tag{34.7}$$

$$\overline{R} = \frac{\sum_{j=1}^{n} R_j}{n} \tag{34.8}$$

$$T = 12\frac{\sum_{j=1}^{n}\left(R_j - \overline{R}\right)^2}{E^2(n^3 - n)} \tag{34.9}$$

Where R_j is the total rank of criterion j, $\overline{R}$ represents the mean of the total rank of each criterion, and T indicates Kendall's coefficient. To gain a deeper understanding of Kendall's coefficient, Table 34.3 is provided.

Step 5. Go to the next step when the consensus in the ranks is in strong, very strong, and complete statuses (i.e., exceeds 0.3); otherwise, revise the individual ranks by the experts.

Step 6. Compute the criteria weights using the IROC method.

Step 7. Go to the next step when $\nu = P$; otherwise, $\nu = \nu + 1$ and go to step 3.

TABLE 34.3 Interpretation of the Kendall's coefficient.

T	Consensus in ranks
[0, 0.1)	Very weak
[0.1, 0.3)	Weak
[0.3, 0.5)	Fair
[0.5, 0.7)	Strong
[0.7, 0.9)	Very strong
[0.9, 1)	Completer

Step 8. Determine the final weights of criteria at the lowest level of CBS using the simple product formula (SPA) (i.e., multiplying the weight of each criterion by its sequential parent's weights in the CBS).

To clearly illustrate the steps outlined by the IROC method, its flowchart procedure is presented in Fig. 34.2.

34.4 Numerical example 1

To determine the weights of the three main criteria using the IROC method, including C_1, C_2, and C_3, five experts (i.e., E_1, E_2, E_3, E_4, and E_5) are selected to prioritize them based on their preferences using the SWARA method. Furthermore, each main criterion contains four subcriteria, and their weights should be determined. In this context, the set of main criteria and their subcriteria is displayed in Table 34.4.

According to Table 34.4, the schematic of CSB considering numerical example 1 is constructed, which is shown in Fig. 34.3.

After that, the rank of the criteria in the first parent box of the CBS based on the expert's preferences using the SWARA method is determined as shown in Table 34.5.

To determine the level of agreement among the panelists using Kendall's coefficient of concordance, the total rank of each main criterion, the mean of the total rank of each main criterion, and Kendall's coefficient are computed using Eqs. (34.10–34.12).

$$\begin{cases} R_1 = 2 + 1 + 2 + 2 + 1 = 8 \\ R_2 = 1 + 2 + 1 + 1 + 2 = 7 \\ R_3 = 3 + 3 + 3 + 3 + 3 = 15 \end{cases} \tag{34.10}$$

$$\overline{R} = \frac{8 + 7 + 15}{3} = 10 \tag{34.11}$$

$$T = 12\frac{(8 - 10)^2 + (7 - 10)^2 + (15 - 10)^2}{5^2(3^3 - 3)} = 0.76 \tag{34.12}$$

According to Eq. (34.12), criterion C_2 has gained the first rank, while criterion C_1 and C_3 are placed in the second and third ranks of the main criteria, respectively. Furthermore, the Kendall's coefficient indicates a strong consensus in rankings. Thus, the criteria weights derived from the IROC method can be effectively applied in decision-making problems. Additionally, the rank of the subcriteria in the second parent box of the CBS based on the expert's preferences using the SWARA method is indicated in Tables 34.6–34.8.

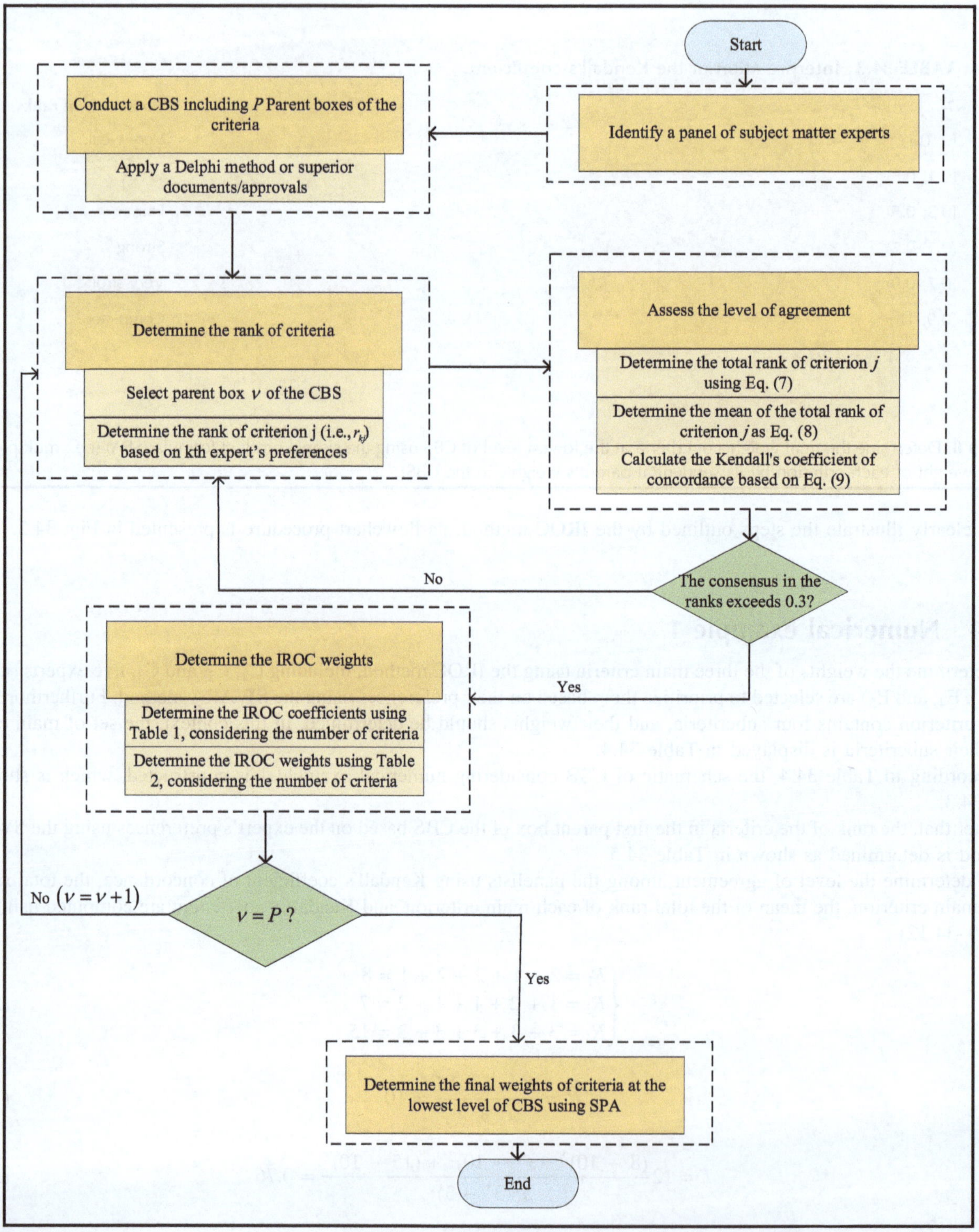

FIGURE 34.2 The procedure of the improved rank order centroid (IROC) method.

TABLE 34.4 The set of main criteria and their subcriteria.

Main criteria	Subcriteria
C_1	C_{11}
	C_{12}
	C_{13}
	C_{14}
C_2	C_{21}
	C_{22}
	C_{23}
	C_{24}
C_3	C_{31}
	C_{32}
	C_{33}
	C_{34}

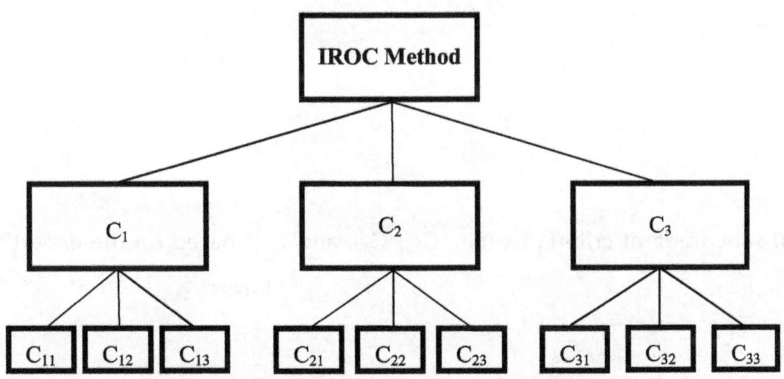

FIGURE 34.3 The schematic of the criteria breakdown structure based on numerical example 1.

TABLE 34.5 The rank of the main criteria based on the expert's preferences.

Main criteria	Expert				
	E_1	E_2	E_3	E_4	E_5
C_1	2	1	2	2	1
C_2	1	2	1	1	2
C_3	3	3	3	3	3

TABLE 34.6 The rank of subcriteria of criteria C_1 (i.e., C_{11}, C_{12}, and C_{13}) based on the expert's preferences.

Criteria	Expert				
	E_1	E_2	E_3	E_4	E_5
C_{11}	2	1	1	2	1
C_{12}	1	2	2	3	2
C_{13}	4	4	3	1	3
C_{14}	3	3	4	4	4

TABLE 34.7 The rank of subcriteria of criteria C_2 (i.e., C_{21}, C_{22}, and C_{23}) based on the expert's preferences.

Criteria	Expert				
	E_1	E_2	E_3	E_4	E_5
C_{21}	3	2	3	4	3
C_{22}	1	1	2	2	1
C_{23}	4	4	4	3	4
C_{24}	2	3	1	1	2

TABLE 34.8 The rank of subcriteria of criteria C_3 (i.e., C_{31}, C_{32}, and C_{33}) based on the expert's preferences.

Criteria	Expert				
	E_1	E_2	E_3	E_4	E_5
C_{31}	2	3	2	2	2
C_{32}	4	4	3	3	4
C_{33}	1	1	1	1	1
C_{34}	3	2	4	4	3

Eventually, the total rank of each subcriterion, the mean of the total rank of each subcriterion, and Kendall's coefficient are determined based on Eqs. (34.13–34.17).

$$\begin{cases} R_{11} = 2 + 1 + 1 + 2 + 1 = 7 \\ R_{12} = 1 + 2 + 2 + 3 + 2 = 10 \\ R_{13} = 4 + 4 + 3 + 1 + 3 = 15 \\ R_{14} = 3 + 3 + 4 + 4 + 4 = 18 \end{cases} \tag{34.13}$$

$$\begin{cases} R_{21} = 3 + 2 + 3 + 4 + 3 = 15 \\ R_{22} = 1 + 1 + 2 + 2 + 1 = 7 \\ R_{23} = 4 + 4 + 4 + 3 + 4 = 19 \\ R_{24} = 2 + 3 + 1 + 1 + 2 = 9 \end{cases} \tag{34.14}$$

$$\begin{cases} R_{31} = 2 + 3 + 2 + 2 + 2 = 11 \\ R_{32} = 4 + 4 + 3 + 3 + 4 = 18 \\ R_{33} = 1 + 1 + 1 + 1 + 1 = 5 \\ R_{34} = 3 + 2 + 4 + 4 + 3 = 16 \end{cases} \tag{34.15}$$

$$\begin{cases} (C_{11}, C_{12}, C_{13}): \ \overline{R} = \frac{7+10+15+8}{4} = 12.5 \\ (C_{21}, C_{22}, C_{23}): \ \overline{R} = \frac{15+7+19+9}{4} = 12.5 \\ (C_{31}, C_{32}, C_{33}): \ \overline{R} = \frac{11+18+5+16}{4} = 12.5 \end{cases} \tag{34.16}$$

$$\begin{cases} (C_{11}, C_{12}, C_{13}): \ T = 12\frac{(7-12.5)^2+(10-12.5)^2+(15-12.5)^2+(18-12.5)^2}{5^2(4^3-4)} = 0.584 \\ (C_{21}, C_{22}, C_{23}): \ T = 12\frac{(15-12.5)^2+(7-12.5)^2+(19-12.5)^2+(9-12.5)^2}{5^2(4^3-4)} = 0.728 \\ (C_{31}, C_{32}, C_{33}): \ T = 12\frac{(11-12.5)^2+(18-12.5)^2+(5-12.5)^2+(16-12.5)^2}{5^2(4^3-4)} = 0.808 \end{cases} \tag{34.17}$$

According to Eq. (34.13), criterion C_{11} is placed in the first rank, while criterion C_{14} is known as the last rank of the subcriteria of main criterion C_1. In addition, criterion C_{22} is the most important criterion, while criterion C_{23} has gained the minimum priority among the subcriteria of main criterion C_2 based on Eq. (34.14). Subsequently, C_{33} is placed in the first rank of alternatives among the subcriteria of main criterion C_3, and C_{32} is regarded as the least important criterion among them. Furthermore, Kendall's coefficient indicates a strong consensus in the rankings of subcriteria, considering the three main criteria (i.e., C_1, C_2, and C_3). Therefore, the subcriteria weights obtained from the IROC method can be effectively utilized in decision-making problems.

After determining the rank of main criteria and subcriteria with a strong consensus in the rankings, the IROC method is used to estimate the weights of main criteria and subcriteria. In this regard, the weights of the main criteria and subcriteria, considering Table 34.4, are represented in Table 34.9.

TABLE 34.9 The weights of criteria and subcriteria using the improved rank order centroid method.

Main criteria	Weight	Subcriteria	Weight
C_1	0.2845	C_{11}	0.5134
		C_{12}	0.281
		C_{13}	0.1466
		C_{14}	0.059
C_2	0.6086	C_{21}	0.1466
		C_{22}	0.5134
		C_{23}	0.059
		C_{24}	0.281
C_3	0.1069	C_{31}	0.281
		C_{32}	0.059
		C_{33}	0.5134
		C_{34}	0.1466

TABLE 34.10 The final weight of subcriteria using the improved rank order centroid method.

Subcriteria	Final weight
C_{11}	0.2845 × 0.5134 = 0.1460
C_{12}	0.2845 × 0.2810 = 0.0799
C_{13}	0.2845 × 0.1466 = 0.0417
C_{14}	0.2845 × 0.0590 = 0.0167
C_{21}	0.6086 × 0.1466 = 0.0892
C_{22}	0.6086 × 0.5134 = 0.3124
C_{23}	0.6086 × 0.0590 = 0.0359
C_{24}	0.6086 × 0.2810 = 0.1710
C_{31}	0.1069 × 0.2810 = 0.0300
C_{32}	0.1069 × 0.0590 = 0.0063
C_{33}	0.1069 × 0.5134 = 0.0548
C_{34}	0.1069 × 0.1466 = 0.0156

TABLE 34.11 The rank of the main criteria based on the expert's preferences.

Main criteria	Expert			
	E_1	E_2	E_3	E_4
Geochemical	1	2	1	1
Geological	2	1	3	2
Faults	3	4	2	4
Alteration	4	3	4	3
Geophysical	5	5	5	5

Eventually, the final weights of criteria at the lowest level of CBS using the SPA method are calculated as follows. Table 34.10.

34.5 Numerical example 2

The DM aims to evaluate the significance of five main criteria: (i) geochemical, (ii) geological, (iii) faults, (iv) alteration, and (v) geophysical in mineral prospectivity mapping. Furthermore, the geochemical criterion includes four subcriteria (i.e., 1.62–2.66, 0.95–1.62, 0.53–0.95, 0.14–0.53, 3.71-0.14), the criterion geological consists of two subcriteria (i.e., andesite and mucovite–chlorite), the fault criterion incorporates five subcriteria (i.e., 2.39–2.86, 1.69–2.39, 0.79–1.69, 0.14–0.79, and 0–0.14) into the decision-making problem, the criterion alteration has five subcriteria (i.e., argillic, phyllic, Fe-oxides, silicic, and propylitic), and the geophysical criterion contains five subcriteria (i.e., 39,270.11–39,527.56,

TABLE 34.12 The rank of the subcriteria based on the expert's preferences.

Geochemical	E_1	Geological	E_1	Faults	E_1	Alteration	E_1	Geophysical	E_1
1.62–2.66	1	Muscovite–chlorite	2	2.39–2.86	1	Fe-oxides	3	39,917.01–39,944.75	1
0.95–1.62	2	Andesite	1	1.69–2.39	2	Silicic	4	39,838.23–39,917.01	2
0.53–0.95	3			0.79–1.69	3	Phyllic	2	39,600.44–39,838.23	3
0.14–0.53	4			0.14–0.79	4	Argillic	1	39,527.56–39,600.44	4
3.71–0.14	5			0–0.14	5	Prophylitic	5	39,270.11–39,527.56	5

TABLE 34.13 The final weights of the main criteria and the subcriteria using the improved rank order centroid method.

Main criteria	Weight	Subcriteria	Weight	Final weight
Geochemical	0.4464	1.62–2.66	0.4464	0.1993
		0.95–1.62	0.2673	0.1193
		0.53–0.95	0.1607	0.0717
		0.14–0.53	0.0883	0.0394
		3.71–0.14	0.0373	0.0167
Geological	0.2673	Muscovite–chlorite	0.2443	0.0653
		Andesite	0.7557	0.2020
Faults	0.1607	2.39–2.86	0.4464	0.0717
		1.69–2.39	0.2673	0.0430
		0.79–1.69	0.1607	0.0258
		0.14–0.79	0.0883	0.0142
		0–0.14	0.0373	0.0060
Alteration	0.0883	Fe-oxides	0.0373	0.0033
		Silicic	0.1607	0.0142
		Phyllic	0.0883	0.0078
		Argillic	0.2673	0.0236
		Prophylitic	0.4464	0.0394
Geophysical	0.0373	39,917.01–39,944.75	0.4464	0.0167
		39,838.23–39,917.01	0.2673	0.0100
		39,600.44–39,838.23	0.1607	0.0060
		39,527.56–39,600.44	0.0883	0.0033
		39,270.11–39,527.56	0.0373	0.0014

39,527.56–39,600.44, 39,600.44–39,838.23, 39,838.23–399,917.01, and 39,917.01–39,944.75) (Panahi et al., 2017). The weights of the main criteria and subcriteria were determined using the AHP method in the original paper; therefore, they are ranked based on their final weights. To utilize the extension of the proposed decision-making problem in the IROC method, another set of experts, including three experts, is invited, and their preferences related to the main criteria are incorporated into the proposed problem.

To implement the IROC method, the rank of the main criteria and subcriteria in the first and second parent boxes of the CBS based on the expert's preferences using the SWARA method is determined as follows (Tables 34.11 and 34.12).

To calculate the level of agreement using the Kendall's coefficient of concordance, the values of R, $\overline{R}$, and T are computed using (34.18).

$$\begin{cases} R_1 = 5 \\ R_2 = 8 \\ R_3 = 13 \\ R_4 = 14 \\ R_5 = 20 \end{cases}, \quad \overline{R} = 13.75,\ T = 0.9332 \tag{34.18}$$

Owing to (34.18), geochemical is placed in the first rank, while geophysical is known as the least important main criterion among the main criteria. Furthermore, Kendall's coefficient shows a complete consensus in rankings. As a result, the main criteria weights derived from the IROC method can be applied in decision-making scenarios. Due to one expert's preference regarding the proposed subcriteria in the second parent box of the CBS, the rank of these subcriteria is used to determine their final weights. Finally, the final weights of the main criteria as well as subcriteria at the lowest level of CBS using the SPA method are computed as shown in Table 34.13.

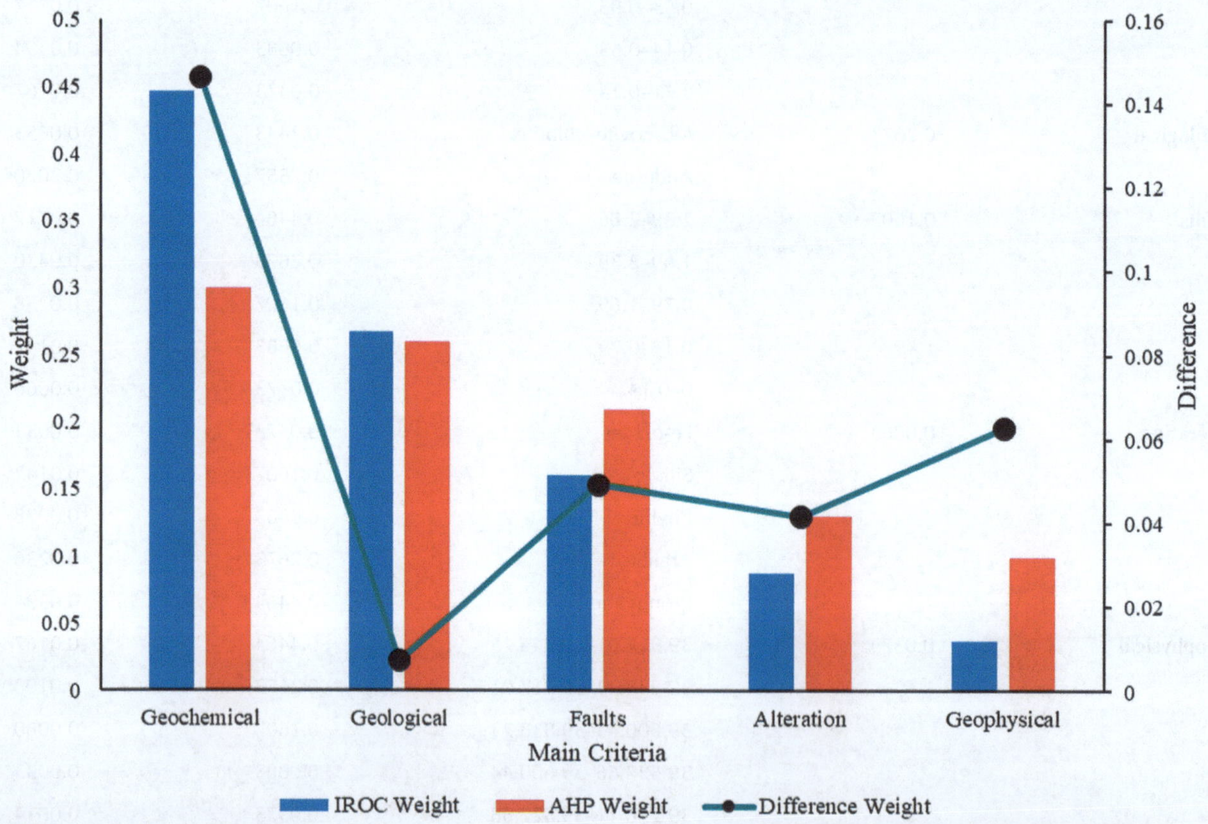

FIGURE 34.4 Comparison of improved rank order centroid (IROC) weights and analytic hierarchy process (AHP) weights for main criteria.

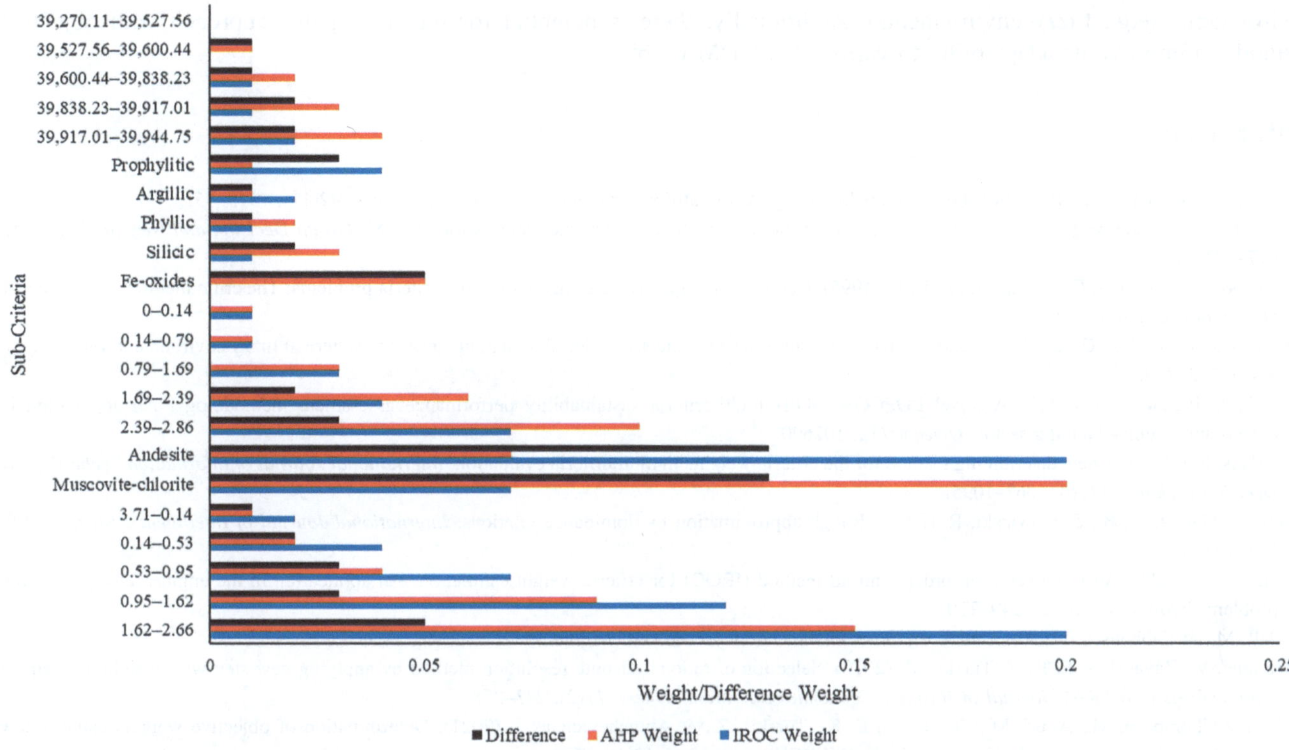

FIGURE 34.5 Comparison of improved rank order centroid (IROC) weights and analytic hierarchy process (AHP) weights for subcriteria.

34.5.1 Comparative analysis

To evaluate the suitability of the IROC method for different problems, its preferences should be compared with those of other weighting methods. This section compares the IROC method with the AHP method by Panahi et al. (2017) with respect to the proposed numerical example 2 in the previous section. In this regard, the IROC weights and AHP weights, as well as the difference between these two weights for the main criteria, are shown in Fig. 34.4.

According to Fig. 34.4, the maximum difference in weight relates to the geochemical criterion (i.e., by 0.1464), while the minimum difference is linked to the geological criterion (i.e., by 0.0073). Following that, the comparison of IROC weights and AHP weights for subcriteria is represented in Fig. 34.5.

Fig. 34.5 demonstrates that the maximum difference in weights corresponds to the muscovite–chlorite and andesite criteria extracted from the main geological criterion, with a value of 0.13. Furthermore, the minimum difference in weights relates to three subcriteria of the fault's main criterion, including "0–0.014," "0.14–0.79," and "0.79–1.69," with a value of 0.

34.6 Conclusions

In complex decision-making problems, the subjective weighting methods for extracting the exact weights require reliable information from DMs. When DMs cannot provide reliable information, approximate weighting methods are used. Among the existing approximate weighting methods, the IROC method has been utilized due to its performance and applicability in various problems. This chapter presents the IROC method as a structured and practical approach to determine the subjective weights of criteria based on the rankings provided by DMs. To implement the IROC method, two algorithms were executed. In the first algorithm, a simulation was conducted 1500 times to determine the coefficients and weights for the criteria. Following this, the application of the IROC method within the framework of MCGDM was explained in the second algorithm. The step-by-step computational process of the IROC method was demonstrated through two numerical examples. Future research could investigate dynamic extensions of the IROC method in uncertain environments (e.g., fuzzy environments). Additionally, there is potential for integrating this approach with objective methods to improve its adaptability to various MCGDM problems.

References

Barron, F. H., & Barrett, B. E. (1996). Decision quality using ranked attribute weights. *Management Science, 42*(11), 1515–1523.

Danielson, M., & Ekenberg, L. (2017). A robustness study of state-of-the-art surrogate weights for MCDM. *Group Decision and Negotiation, 26*(4), 677–691.

Diakoulaki, D., Mavrotas, G., & Papayannakis, L. (1995). Determining objective weights in multiple criteria problems: The critic method. *Computers & Operations Research, 22*(7), 763–770.

Diao, F., Cai, Q., & Wei, G. (2022). Taxonomy method for multiple attribute group decision making under the spherical fuzzy environment. *Informatica, 33*(4), 713–729.

Ecer, F., & Pamucar, D. (2022). A novel LOPCOW-DOBI multi-criteria sustainability performance assessment methodology: An application in developing country banking sector. *Omega, 112*, 102690.

Ginevičius, R. (2011). A new determining method for the criteria weights in multicriteria evaluation. *International Journal of Information Technology & Decision Making, 10*(06), 1067–1095.

Greco, S., Matarazzo, B., & Slowinski, R. (2002). Rough approximation by dominance relations. *International Journal of Intelligent Systems, 17*(2), 153–171.

Hatefi, M. A. (2023). An improved rank order centroid method (IROC) for criteria weight estimation: An application in the engine/vehicle selection problem. *Informatica, 34*(2), 249–270.

Kendall, M., & Gibbons, J. (1990). *Rank correlation method.* London: Edward Arnold.

Keršuliene, V., Zavadskas, E. K., & Turskis, Z. (2010). Selection of rational dispute resolution method by applying new step-wise weight assessment ratio analysis (SWARA). *Journal of Business Economics and Management, 11*(2), 243–258.

Keshavarz-Ghorabaee, M., Amiri, M., Zavadskas, E. K., Turskis, Z., & Antucheviciene, J. (2021). Determination of objective weights using a new method based on the removal effects of criteria (MEREC). *Symmetry, 13*(4), 525.

Lai, Y. J., Liu, T. Y., & Hwang, C. L. (1994). Topsis for MODM. *European Journal of Operational Research, 76*(3), 486–500.

Linstone, H. A., & Turoff, M. (Vol. Eds.), (1975). *The Delphi method: Vol. 1975*, (pp. 3–12). Reading, MA: Addison-Wesley.

Opricovic, S. (1998). Multicriteria optimization of civil engineering systems. *Faculty of Civil Engineering, 2*(1), 5–21 Belgrade.

Pamučar, D., Stević, Ž., & Sremac, S. (2018). A new model for determining weight coefficients of criteria in mcdm models: Full consistency method (fucom). *Symmetry, 10*(9), 393.

Panahi, S., Khakzad, A., & Afzal, P. (2017). Application of stepwise weight assessment ratio analysis (SWARA) for copper prospectivity mapping in the Anarak region, central Iran. *Arabian Journal of Geosciences, 10*(22), 484.

Rezaei, J. (2015). Best-worst multi-criteria decision-making method. *Omega, 53*, 49–57.

Roszkowska, E. (2013). Rank ordering criteria weighting methods–a comparative overview. *Optimum. Studia Ekonomiczne, 5*(65), 14–33.

Saaty, R. W. (1987). The analytic hierarchy process—what it is and how it is used. *Mathematical Modelling, 9*(3-5), 161–176.

Saaty, T. L. (2004). Decision making—the analytic hierarchy and network processes (AHP/ANP). *Journal of Systems Science and Systems Engineering, 13*(1), 1–35.

Shannon, C. E. (1948). A mathematical theory of communication. *The Bell System Technical Journal, 27*(3), 379–423.

Stević, Ž., Pamučar, D., Puška, A., & Chatterjee, P. (2020). Sustainable supplier selection in healthcare industries using a new MCDM method: Measurement of alternatives and ranking according to COmpromise solution (MARCOS). *Computers & Industrial Engineering, 140*, 106231.

Tajik, M., Makui, A., & Tosarkani, B. M. (2023). Sustainable cathode material selection in lithium-ion batteries using a novel hybrid multi-criteria decision-making. *Journal of Energy Storage, 66*, 107089.

Winkler, R. L., & Hays, W. L. (1975). *Statistics: Probability, inference, and decision*. New York: Holt, Rinehart and Winston, 471–536.

Yoon, K. (1980). Systems selection by multiple attribute decision making. Kansas State University.

Zavadskas, E. K., & Podvezko, V. (2016). Integrated determination of objective criteria weights in MCDM. *International Journal of Information Technology & Decision Making, 15*(2), 267–283.

Chapter 35

SWM: Surrogate weighting method for multi-attribute decision-making

Moein Khazaei[1], Elham Elmi[2], Maryam Mehrparvar[3], and Zahra Mohemmi[4]
[1]*School of Engineering and Sciences, Tecnologico de Monterrey, Monterrey, Mexico,* [2]*Department of Industrial management, Islamic Azad University Science and Research Branch, Tehran, Iran,* [3]*Department of mathematics, Bozorgmehr University of Qaenat, Qaen, Iran,* [4]*College of Business, Government and Law, Flinders University, Adelaide, SA, Australia*

35.1 Introduction

In many multicriteria decision-making problems, the assignment of criteria weights plays a central role in representing the decision makers value system (Bonakdari et al., 2026; Thakkar, 2021). Weighting defines the relative importance of each criterion and directly influences the outcome of both additive and outranking models (Foukolaei et al., 2024; Khazaei et al., 2023). However, in real decision settings, decision makers often face substantial difficulty when asked to provide exact numerical weights (Moslem, 2024). Limited cognitive capacity, uncertainty, incomplete information, and the sensitive nature of weight disclosure frequently prevent them from expressing precise quantitative preferences. As a result, the need for methods that incorporate partial or ordinal information has become increasingly important in modern decision analysis (Mahmoudi & Javed, 2023).

Surrogate weighting methods offer a practical solution to this challenge by generating approximate numerical weights based on the decision makers ranking of criteria rather than on explicit numerical judgments (Burk & Nehring, 2023). These procedures start from the simple ordinal information that a decision maker can reliably provide, such as C1 being more important than C2 and C2 being more important than C3. From this ranking, the methods compute a set of weights that respect this order and can be used directly in multicriteria aggregation models (ahin, 2021). This approach minimizes cognitive burden, avoids forcing artificial precision on the decision maker, and maintains consistency with the preference structure expressed through ranks.

Several surrogate weighting procedures have been proposed in the literature, each using a different mathematical logic to translate ordinal importance into normalized weight vectors (Paradowski et al., 2021). Common procedures include equal weights (EW), rank sum (RS),Rank Reciprocal (RR), and rank order centroid (ROC) (Liu et al., 2020). Although simple, these transformations provide meaningful approximations of the true weights and enable decision makers to proceed with the analysis even when precise numerical information is unavailable. These procedures have been widely used in additive value models, where their statistical behavior and decision quality have been extensively studied through simulation and robustness analyses.

The Surrogate weighting Method gains particular relevance in outranking approaches such as preference ranking organization method for enrichment evaluation (PROMETHEE), where weights reflect only the relative importance of criteria and do not carry compensatory meaning. In these noncompensatory models, rank-based weights provide a natural and ethically acceptable alternative for situations in which expressing exact numerical preferences is difficult or undesirable. Recent experimental studies show that surrogate weights can produce stable and reliable PROMETHEE recommendations, especially when using the ROC procedure. This reinforces the value of surrogate weighting as a practical and theoretically grounded approach for preference modeling in complex decision environments.

The remainder of this chapter is structured to guide the reader from conceptual foundations to practical application. Following the introduction, the literature review examines the development, justification, and empirical use of surrogate weighting methods across diverse decision-making contexts. The methods section formalizes the mathematical structure of the four surrogate weighting procedures and explains how ordinal information is transformed into normalized weights. Numerical example 1 then demonstrates these methods in a compact 5-criterion supplier selection problem, while numerical

Encyclopedia of Multi-Attribute Decision-Making (MADM). DOI: https://doi.org/10.1016/B978-0-443-33275-3.00068-3

example 2 extends the analysis to an 8-criterion sustainability-oriented evaluation with hidden true weights and a full PROMETHEE II ranking. The chapter concludes by comparing the performance of the different surrogate weighting rules and summarizing key insights regarding their reliability, advantages, and suitability for complex decision environments.

35.2 Literature review

Surrogate weighting methods have become an important stream in multicriteria decision-making due to the difficulty decision makers often face when providing precise numerical weights. Many real decision environments involve incomplete, imprecise, or purely ordinal information, making rank-based weight estimation a practical alternative to complex elicitation protocols. Early work examining robustness and assumptions of surrogate weighting procedures provided the foundation for modern applications. Danielson & Ekenberg (2017) conducted a comprehensive simulation study on state-of-the-art surrogate weighting approaches and demonstrated how methods such as RS, RR, and ROC behave under uncertainty. Their results highlighted the sensitivity of additive models to poorly elicited weights, while also confirming that surrogate weights offer a realistic and statistically defensible substitute when exact preference information is unavailable.

The application of surrogate weights has expanded significantly across diverse decision domains. Makan & Fadili (2021) used surrogate weights in combination with PROMETHEE to assess the sustainability of healthcare waste treatment systems, converting expert-provided ordinal rankings into usable quantitative weights through an RS function. Their work illustrates the practical value of surrogate weights in real-world contexts where experts can reliably express the importance order of criteria but cannot justify precise numerical values. Beyond environmental and healthcare applications, recent studies have emphasized the need to systematically evaluate and select appropriate surrogate weighting methods. Hatefi et al. (2023) proposed a structured framework for comparing SWMs based on theoretical attributes and operational requirements, offering a guideline for selecting the most suitable method for project portfolio decisions in the petroleum sector. Their results reinforce the idea that different contexts demand different surrogate weighting logics, and no single technique universally dominates across all problem types.

More recent advances extend surrogate weighting ideas to models that integrate additional ordinal or ratio-based information. Chergui and Jimnez-Martn, n.d analyzed the performance of corporate social responsibility (CSR) and full consistency method (FUCOM), two rank-based weighting approaches that incorporate semantic scales or ratio intensities between consecutive criteria. Using Monte Carlo simulations, they found that CSR outperforms FUCOM across multiple problem sizes, thereby strengthening the evidence that surrogate weights remain reliable even when criteria relationships become more complex. Surrogate weighting ideas have also been embedded in geographic information system based hazard mapping and digital technology prioritization studies, often through ROC-based transformations that convert rank orderings into centroid-based weights for PROMETHEE or weighted overlay models (Martins et al., 2025).

35.3 Methods and materials

In a multicriteria decision structure, the weight vector represents the relative importance of the evaluation criteria (Khazaei et al., 2025). This vector must satisfy two basic conditions: each individual weight must be equal to or greater than zero, and the sum of all weights must equal 1. Let the weight vector be W=[w_1, w_2,..., w_n] for n criteria. If the criteria are ranked according to their importance, such that the criterion with rank i is denoted by r_i, then ordinal information is expressed as:

$$w_{r^1} \geq w_{r^1} \geq \ldots \geq w_{r^n} \geq 0 \tag{35.1}$$

This ranking provides the foundation for generating numerical surrogate weights within a normalized interval of (0,1).

Surrogate weighting methods translate this ordinal preference information into numerical values that satisfy the standard requirements of a weight system (Lolli et al., 2019). Several transformations are available for converting a ranking into a set of usable weights, each applying a different logic for distributing importance across criteria. These procedures include EW, RS, RR, and ROC. These methods assume that the ranking of criteria reflects the decision-makers preference and that no further numerical judgments are required (Chergui and Jimnez-Martn, n.d; Hatefi, 2022; Lolli et al., 2019).

35.3.1 Equal weights

The EW procedure assumes that all criteria carry the same importance. The weight allocation is therefore (Chatterjee & Chakraborty, 2024):

$$w_i\,(EW) = \frac{1}{n}, \quad i = 1, \ \ldots, \ n \tag{35.2}$$

This approach is appropriate when no additional information about the relative importance of criteria is available.

35.3.2 Rank sum

The RS method allocates greater weight to higher-ranked criteria based on the inverse of their rank order. The normalized weight is obtained using (Dombi & Jns, 2024):

$$w_i(RS) = \frac{2(n+1-i)}{n(n+1)}, \quad i = 1, \ldots, n \tag{35.3}$$

This procedure ensures that higher-ranked criteria receive proportionally larger weights.

35.3.3 Rank reciprocal

The RR method assigns importance according to the reciprocal of the rank position. After normalization, the weight for each criterion is (Hatefi, 2022):

$$w_i(RR) = \frac{1/i}{\sum_{j=1}^{n}(1/j)}, \quad i = 1, \ldots, n \tag{35.4}$$

This rule gives substantially higher importance to the top-ranked criteria compared with lower-ranked ones.

35.3.4 Rank order centroid

The ROC method calculates weights using the centroid of the feasible weight region defined by the ordinal ranking. The ROC weight formula is (Ahn, 2011):

$$w_i(ROC) = \frac{1}{n}\sum_{j=i}^{n}\frac{1}{j}, \quad i = 1, \ldots, n \tag{35.5}$$

ROC weights decline smoothly from the most important criterion to the least important and often provide a realistic approximation of true underlying preferences.

35.4 Numerical example 1

The first numerical example focuses on a green supplier selection problem involving 5 evaluation criteria ranked by the decision maker in terms of importance (Gholian-Jouybari et al., 2024). The core challenge is that the decision maker cannot provide exact numerical weights, only an ordinal ranking of the criteria. The task is therefore to convert this limited preference information into usable quantitative weights through four surrogate weighting procedures, namely EW, RS, rank reciprocal, and ROC. These weights are then applied within the PROMETHEE II multicriteria outranking method to evaluate and compare suppliers. The problem demonstrates how surrogate weights can support transparent and consistent decision-making when cognitive limitations or uncertainty prevent the specification of precise numerical importance values.

This numerical example demonstrates how surrogate weighting procedures convert ordinal information into numerical weights for PROMETHEE II. The decision maker provides only the ranking of the criteria, and the goal is to generate four different weight vectors using EW, RS, rank reciprocal, and ROC. Each method includes a short explanation followed by a table summarizing the results. The process begins by identifying the criteria and assigning ordinal ranks to reflect their relative importance. A lower rank number means higher importance. In this example, quality is considered the most important criterion and receives rank 1, while CO emissions is the least important and receive rank 5. These rankings guide all subsequent surrogate weight calculations (see Table 35.1).

The rank information above forms the basis for all surrogate weighting techniques. Each procedure interprets these ranks differently, leading to distinct numerical weight patterns.

The EW method assigns the same degree of importance to every criterion. This approach is often used when no additional preference information is available or when the decision maker wishes to avoid subjective emphasis. Although simple, EW provides a useful benchmark for comparing more sophisticated rules (see Table 35.2).

The equal distribution leads to a flat profile where each criterion influences the PROMETHEE evaluation to the same degree. This makes EW easy to apply, but it does not reflect the actual ranking provided by the decision maker. The RS method incorporates the ordinal importance into the calculation by assigning more weight to higher-ranked criteria. The logic behind this method is straightforward: the more important a criterion is, the higher the quantity (n+1rank) assigned to it. After summing all quantities, each one is normalized to create the weight vector (see Table 35.3).

TABLE 35.1 Criteria and ranks.

Criterion	Rank
Quality score	1
Delivery reliability	2
Cost (lower better)	3
Recyclability	4
CO_2 emissions (lower better)	5

TABLE 35.2 Equal weights (EW).

Criterion	Rank	EW weight
Cost	3	0.2
Quality	1	0.2
Delivery reliability	2	0.2
CO_2 emissions	5	0.2
Recyclability	4	0.2

TABLE 35.3 Rank sum (RS) weights.

Criterion	Rank	n + 1-rank	RS weight
Cost	3	3	0.2
Quality	1	5	0.3333
Delivery reliability	2	4	0.2667
CO_2 emissions	5	1	0.0667
Recyclability	4	2	0.1333

RS produces a sharper contrast among criteria compared with EW. Quality receives the highest weight given its rank, while CO emissions, ranked last, receives the smallest weight.

The Rank reciprocal method further emphasizes the importance of higher-ranked criteria by using reciprocal values. Since 1 divided by 1 equals 1 and 1 divided by 5 equals 0.2, this method creates greater differentiation between early and late ranks. After computing reciprocals, all values are normalized to ensure that their sum equals 1 (see Table 35.4).

RR places very strong emphasis on the top-ranked criterion. As a result, quality receives approximately 0.438, making it almost four times more influential than CO emissions.

The ROC method calculates weights by averaging reciprocal values from the assigned rank down to the last rank. This method provides smoother weight decreases compared with the rank reciprocal rule and has been widely used due to its balanced and intuitive structure (see Table 35.5).

TABLE 35.4 Rank reciprocal weights RR).

Criterion	Rank	1 divided by rank	Sum of reciprocals = 2.2833	RR weight
Cost	3	0.3333	2.2833	0.146
Quality	1	1	2.2833	0.438
Delivery reliability	2	0.5	2.2833	0.219
CO_2 emissions	5	0.2	2.2833	0.0876
Recyclability	4	0.25	2.2833	0.1095

TABLE 35.5 Rank order centroid (ROC) weights.

Criterion	Rank	Sum of reciprocals from rank to n	ROC weight
Cost	3	0.7833	0.1567
Quality	1	2.2833	0.4567
Delivery reliability	2	1.2833	0.2567
CO_2 emissions	5	0.2	0.04
Recyclability	4	0.45	0.09

The ROC method generates weights that reflect the rank information while maintaining reasonable proportional differences. Quality remains the dominant criterion, followed by delivery reliability, while CO emissions retain the lowest weight.

This section demonstrates the full calculation for a single criterion and a single pairwise comparison between two suppliers. The goal is to show how one element contributes to the overall preference index in PROMETHEE II. To keep the example clear, we focus on the quality score criterion when comparing Supplier A against Supplier B.

The chosen criterion is quality score, which is measured on a scale from 1 to 10. According to the decision maker, this criterion has rank 1, meaning it is the most important among all five criteria. The performance values for the two suppliers are shown below.

Selected criterion	*Quality score (1 to 10)*
Criterion index	*j=1*
Rank	*r=1*
Supplier A value	*9.2*
Supplier B value	*8.8*

The following steps compute the ROC weight for this criterion, normalize the performances, apply the preference function, and determine the contribution to the pairwise preference index.

The ROC method uses the average of the reciprocal values from the assigned rank to the total number of criteria. Since this criterion has rank 1, the calculation includes all reciprocal values from 1 to 5.

The reciprocals for k=1 to 5 are:

1 divided by 1=1.0000
1 divided by 2=0.5000
1 divided by 3=0.3333
1 divided by 4=0.2500
1 divided by 5=0.2000

The sum of these values equals 2.283333. Dividing this sum by 5 gives the ROC weight.

Sum of reciprocals	*2.283333*
Number of criteria	*5*
ROC weight	*0.456667*

The ROC weight for the quality score criterion is therefore 0.456667.

Quality is a benefit criterion, meaning higher values are better. For benefit criteria, normalization is done by dividing each raw value by the maximum value in the column.

The raw quality scores are:

Supplier A: 9.2
Supplier B: 8.8
Supplier C: 9.5
Supplier D: 8.5

The maximum value is 9.5. The normalized values for A and B are computed as follows:

Supplier	**Raw value**	**Normalized value**
A	*9.2*	*0.9684*
B	*8.8*	*0.9263*

PROMETHEE uses a preference function to convert the difference in normalized performances into a preference degree. In this example, the linear preference function without thresholds is used.

The difference is:

$$d = 0.9684 - 0.9263 = 0.0421$$

Since the difference is positive, the preference function returns the same value. Thus, P(d) equals 0.0421.

Difference d	*0.0421*
P(d)	*0.0421*

The contribution of this criterion to the overall preference index (A, B) is computed by multiplying the ROC weight by the value of the preference function.

ROC weight for criterion	*0.456667*
P(d)	*0.0421*
Contribution to (A,B)	*0.019228*

The quality score criterion, ranked first in importance, receives a ROC weight of 0.456667. Supplier A has a higher quality score than Supplier B, which, after normalization, results in a positive difference of 0.0421. The linear preference function, therefore, returns 0.0421. Multiplying this value by the weight produces a contribution of 0.019228 to the preference index (A, B).

This single value represents one component of the total preference between Supplier A and Supplier B. The full PROMETHEE II evaluation repeats this calculation for every criterion and every pair of suppliers, and then aggregates all contributions to derive the positive, negative, and net flows.

35.5 Numerical example 2

The second numerical example considers a more complex sustainability-oriented supplier evaluation problem involving 8 criteria that capture economic, environmental, and social dimensions (Ghaedi et al., 2024; Ramezani et al., 2024). In this setting, the decision maker again provides only ordinal importance rankings, while the true numerical weights remain unknown. The objective is to investigate how surrogate weighting methods approximate these hidden true weights and how closely they reflect the underlying preference structure. After deriving surrogate weights using EW, RS, RR, and ROC methods, the example applies PROMETHEE II with ROC weights to assess 5 suppliers based on a fully normalized performance matrix. This extended scenario demonstrates the behavior of surrogate weighting methods in higher-dimensional decision spaces and highlights their ability to handle incomplete preference information in complex multicriteria sustainability evaluations.

This numerical example illustrates the behavior of surrogate weighting methods when the decision problem involves 8 sustainability-related criteria and hidden true weights. The decision maker provides only ordinal information in the form of a ranking of criteria. Surrogate weighting procedures are then used to approximate the unknown true weights. After that, PROMETHEE II with ROC weights is applied to rank 5 suppliers based on a normalized performance matrix.

The decision problem concerns green supplier evaluation with 8 criteria that capture economic, environmental, and social aspects. Product quality (defect rate) is considered the most important criterion with rank 1, while social responsibility and labor practices are considered the least important with rank 8. The full list of criteria and ranks is shown below (see Table 35.6).

This ranking reflects the decision makers value system. Economic and operational issues, such as quality, delivery, and cost, are given higher priority, while environmental and social aspects still matter but are assigned lower ranks.

Given that there are 8 criteria, each surrogate weighting method transforms the rank information into quantitative weights. EW simply divides the importance equally among all criteria. RS uses a linear function of the reversed rank. Rank reciprocal uses RR to emphasize top positions. ROC uses averaged reciprocals and usually produces smoother geometric decay in weights.

For this numerical example, hidden true weights are defined (for simulation and error comparison), and the surrogate methods are evaluated against them. The EW method sets each weight equal to 1 divided by 8, which equals 0.1250. The RS method uses the formula weight i=(9 minus rank i) divided by 36. The Rank reciprocal method uses weight i=(1 divided by rank i) divided by the sum of 1 divided by rank j overall criteria. Finally, the ROC method uses weight i=(1 divided by 8) multiplied by the sum of 1 divided by k for k from rank i to 8 (see Table 35.7).

The last column reports the absolute error between the ROC weights and the hidden true weights for each criterion. To summarize the performance of the surrogate methods, the mean absolute error across all 8 criteria is computed. EW shows the largest average error at 0.0738, which confirms that it does not represent the decision makers preference structure very well. Rank reciprocal and RS perform better, with mean absolute errors around 0.0369 and 0.0228, respectively. ROC achieves a mean absolute error of about 0.0274, which in this experiment is the closest to the hidden true weights among the tested methods.

After determining the ROC weights, the next step is to apply PROMETHEE II to rank 5 suppliers. First, all criteria are normalized so that higher values indicate better performance. For benefit criteria, the normalization is usually done by dividing by the maximum value. For cost criteria (lower better), a common transformation is to invert or rescale the values so that lower raw values correspond to higher normalized scores. The resulting normalized performance matrix is shown in Table 35.3 (Table 35.8).

PROMETHEE II uses pairwise comparisons of suppliers for each criterion. For each pair (A, B) and each criterion, the difference in normalized performance is computed. The linear preference function P(d)=max(0, d) is applied, meaning that only positive differences generate a positive preference. These partial preferences are then multiplied by the corresponding

TABLE 35.6 Criteria and ordinal ranks.

Criterion	Description	Rank
C1	Purchase cost (€/unit), lower is better	3
C2	Product quality (defect rate %), lower is better	1
C3	On-time delivery reliability (%), higher is better	2
C4	CO_2 emissions (kg CO_2e per unit), lower is better	6
C5	Water usage (liters per unit), lower is better	5
C6	Recyclability rate (%), higher is better	7
C7	Supplier environmental certification (score 0 to 100), higher is better	4
C8	Social responsibility and labor practices (score 0 to 100), higher is better	8

TABLE 35.7 True and surrogate weights for 8 Criteria.

Criterion	Rank	True weight	EW	RS	RR	ROC	Error ROC
Purchase cost (€/unit)	3	0.20	0.1250	0.1667	0.1226	0.1522	0.0478
Product quality (defect rate %)	1	0.25	0.1250	0.2222	0.3679	0.3397	0.0897
On-time delivery reliability (%)	2	0.22	0.1250	0.1944	0.1840	0.2147	0.0053
CO_2 emissions (kg CO_2e per unit)	6	0.08	0.1250	0.0833	0.0613	0.0543	0.0257
Water usage (liters per unit)	5	0.07	0.1250	0.1111	0.0736	0.0793	0.0093
Recyclability rate (%)	7	0.06	0.1250	0.0556	0.0526	0.0335	0.0265
Supplier environmental certification (0 to 100)	4	0.10	0.1250	0.1389	0.0920	0.1106	0.0106
Social responsibility and labor practices (0 to 100)	8	0.02	0.1250	0.0278	0.0460	0.0156	0.0044

TABLE 35.8 Normalized performance matrix (higher is better for all criteria).

Supplier	C1	C2	C3	C4	C5	C6	C7	C8
A	0.667	0.778	0.980	0.750	0.800	0.926	0.939	0.924
B	0.278	0.333	0.959	0.400	0.350	0.863	0.898	0.978
C	1.000	1.000	1.000	1.000	1.000	1.000	1.000	0.957
D	0.000	0.000	0.939	0.000	0.000	0.789	0.816	0.848
E	0.556	0.667	0.969	0.650	0.650	0.947	0.918	1.000

ROC weights and summed across all 8 criteria, producing the aggregated preference index (A, B) for each ordered pair of suppliers. From the full preference matrix, PROMETHEE II computes the leaving flow, entering flow, and net flow for each supplier.

The net flow for each supplier is defined as the leaving flow minus the entering flow. A higher net flow indicates a better overall position according to the weighted outranking structure. The resulting net flows and final ranking for the 5 suppliers are shown below (Table 35.9).

Supplier C clearly dominates the other suppliers with the highest net flow, reflecting its strong performance across almost all criteria. Supplier A is the second best, followed by Supplier E. Suppliers B and D have negative net flows, indicating that they are outranked more often than they outrank others under this weight structure. This example shows how surrogate weighting, combined with PROMETHEE II, can handle complex multicriteria evaluations when only ordinal information about criterion importance is available.

Detailed calculation for one element

Comparison: Supplier C versus Supplier D

Criterion: Product quality (defect rate percent), rank 1

This trace shows how a single criterion contributes to the PROMETHEE preference index when using ROC weights. The selected criterion is product quality, measured as defect rate percent, where a lower value indicates better quality. The two suppliers being compared are Supplier C, which has a defect rate of 0.6%, and Supplier D, which has a defect rate of 1.5%. Since the decision maker ranked this criterion as the most important among the 8 criteria, it receives the first rank r=1 in the surrogate weighting process.

TABLE 35.9 Preference ranking organization method for enrichment evaluation II net flows and ranking (using rank order centroid weights).

Rank	Supplier	Net Flow φ
1	C	0.3817
2	A	0.1694
3	E	0.0763
4	B	-0.1744
5	D	-0.4530

Criterion information

Item	*Value*
Criterion	*Product quality (defect rate percent)*
Type	*Cost type, lower is better*
Rank r	*1*
Supplier C raw value	*0.6%*
Supplier D raw value	*1.5%*

This table captures all necessary inputs before calculating the ROC weight, normalization, and preference value.

Since the criterion has rank r=1 and the total number of criteria is n=8, the ROC weight is computed using the sum of reciprocals from 1 to 8. The reciprocals are 1, 0.5, 0.3333, 0.25, 0.2, 0.1667, 0.142857, and 0.125. Their sum equals 2.717857. Dividing this value by 8 gives the final ROC weight for this criterion.

Calculation step	*Value*
Reciprocals 1 to 8	*1, 0.5, 0.3333, 0.25, 0.2, 0.1667, 0.142857, 0.125*
Sum of reciprocals	*2.717857*
ROC weight w	*2.717857 divided by 8=0.339732*

Because product quality is the top-ranked criterion, its ROC weight is the highest among all criteria.

For cost type criteria, lower raw values must receive higher normalized scores. In this case, Supplier C has the lowest defect rate and therefore receives a normalized value of 1. Supplier D has the highest defect rate and receives a normalized value of 0.

Supplier	*Raw value*	*Normalized score*
C	*0.6%*	*1.0000*
D	*1.5%*	*0.0000*

This transformation ensures that normalization aligns with the direction of preference.

The preference difference is computed as the normalized score of Supplier C minus the normalized score of Supplier D. This difference equals 1. Since the linear PROMETHEE preference function P(d) equals max(0, d), the preference value is also 1.

Difference d	*1.0000-0.0000=1.0000*
Preference P(d)	*max(0, 1.0000)=1.0000*

This means Supplier C is fully preferred over Supplier D with respect to this criterion.

The contribution of this element to the aggregated preference index is obtained by multiplying the ROC weight by the preference value. The calculation is straightforward: 0.339732 multiplied by 1.0000 equals 0.339732. This value is added to in the PROMETHEE II scoring.

ROC weight w	*0.339732*
Preference P(d)	*1.0000*
Contribution to	*0.339732*

This is one of the 8 contributions included when comparing Supplier C with Supplier D across all criteria.

35.6 Conclusion

The results of this study demonstrate that surrogate weighting offers a credible and effective framework for situations where decision makers can rank criteria but cannot specify exact numerical weights. The numerical experiments show that SWM methods generate consistent weight distributions aligned with the intended preference structure, allowing analysts to proceed with multicriteria evaluation without relying on complex elicitation procedures. Among the tested techniques, the ROC method provides the strongest balance between accuracy, interpretability, and stability, making it particularly suitable for real-world applications that require transparency and low cognitive burden.

When integrated with PROMETHEE II, surrogate weights produce clear and reliable preference rankings across suppliers, even in decision settings involving environmental, economic, and social criteria. The examples confirm that rank-based weights maintain coherence in noncompensatory models and replicate decision maker intentions without forcing artificial precision. Overall, surrogate weighting procedures offer an accessible and theoretically grounded approach for complex evaluations, especially in contexts where information is incomplete or expert judgments are inherently qualitative.

References

ahin, M. (2021). A comprehensive analysis of weighting and multicriteria methods in the context of sustainable energy. *International Journal of Environmental Science and Technology, 18*(6), 1591–1616.

Ahn, B. S. (2011). Compatible weighting method with rank order centroid: Maximum entropy ordered weighted averaging approach. *European Journal of Operational Research, 212*(3), 552–559. https://doi.org/10.1016/j.ejor.2011.02.017.

Bonakdari, H., Khazaei, M., Gholian-Jouybari, F., & Hajiaghaei-Keshteli, M. (2026). Sustainable wastewater-to-hydrogen systems in Canada: A scenario-based decision support analysis. *Renewable Energy, 256*, 124308. https://doi.org/10.1016/j.renene.2025.124308.

Burk, R. C., & Nehring, R. M. (2023). An empirical comparison of rank-based surrogate weights in additive multiattribute decision analysis. *Decision Analysis, 20*(1), 55–72.

Chatterjee, S., & Chakraborty, S. (2024). A study on the effects of objective weighting methods on TOPSIS-based parametric optimization of non-traditional machining processes. *Decision Analytics Journal, 11*, 100451. https://doi.org/10.1016/j.dajour.2024.100451.

Chergui, Z., & Jimnez-Martn, A. (2024). On ordinal information-based weighting methods and comparison analyses. *Information, 15*(9), 527. https://doi.org/10.3390/info15090527

Danielson, M., & Ekenberg, L. (2017). A robustness study of state-of-the-art surrogate weights for MCDM. *Group Decision and Negotiation, 26*(4), 677–691. https://doi.org/10.1007/s10726-016-9494-6.

Dombi, J., & Jns, T. (2024). Learning the weights using attribute order information for multi-criteria decision making tasks. *OPSEARCH, 61*(4), 2379–2409. https://doi.org/10.1007/s12597-024-00779-9.

Foukolaei, P. Z., Asari, F. A., Khazaei, M., Gholian-Jouybari, F., & Hajiaghaei-Keshteli, M. (2024). From responsible sourcing of wastes to sustainable energy consumption in the blue hydrogen supply chain: Case of nearshoring in Nuevo Leon. *International Journal of Hydrogen Energy, 77*, 1387–1400.

Ghaedi, M., Foukolaei, P. Z., Asari, F. A., Khazaei, M., Gholian-Jouybari, F., & Hajiaghaei-Keshteli, M. (2024). Pricing electricity from blue hydrogen to mitigate the energy rebound effect: A case study in agriculture and livestock. *International Journal of Hydrogen Energy, 84*, 993–1003.

Gholian-Jouybari, F., et al. (2024). Developing environmental, social and governance (ESG) strategies on evaluation of municipal waste disposal centers: A case of Mexico. *Chemosphere, 364*, 142961.

Hatefi, M. A. (2022). An improved rank order centroid method (IROC) for criteria weight estimation: An application in the engine/vehicle selection problem. *Informatica, 34*(2), 249–270. https://doi.org/10.15388/23-INFOR507.

Hatefi, M. A., Razavi, S. A., & Abiri, V. (2023). A novel multi-attribute model to select appropriate weighting method in decision making, an empirical application in petroleum industry. *Group Decision and Negotiation, 32*(6), 1351–1390. https://doi.org/10.1007/s10726-023-09846-w.

Khazaei, M., Gholian-Jouybari, F., Ramezani, M., & Hajiaghaei-Keshteli, M. (2025). Environmental, social, and governance enablers of the hydrogen supply chain: Application of community operational research using STRIDES framework. *Journal of Environmental Management, 389*, 126092.

Khazaei, M., Hajiaghaei-Keshteli, M., Rajabzadeh Ghatari, A., Ramezani, M., Fooladvand, A., & Azar, A. (2023). A multi-criteria supplier evaluation and selection model without reducing the level of optimality. *Soft Computing, 27*(22), 17175–17188.

Liu, D., Li, T., & Liang, D. (2020). An integrated approach towards modeling ranked weights. *Computers & Industrial Engineering, 147*, 106629. https://doi.org/10.1016/j.cie.2020.106629.

Lolli, F., et al. (2019). On the elicitation of criteria weights in PROMETHEE-based ranking methods for a mobile application. *Expert Systems with Applications, 120*, 217–227. https://doi.org/10.1016/j.eswa.2018.11.030.

Mahmoudi, A., & Javed, S. A. (2023). Uncertainty analysis in group decisions through interval ordinal priority approach. *Group Decision and Negotiation, 32*(4), 807–833.

Makan, A., & Fadili, A. (2021). Sustainability assessment of healthcare waste treatment systems using surrogate weights and PROMETHEE method. *Waste Management & Research, 39*(1), 73–82. https://doi.org/10.1177/0734242X20947162.

Martins, C. L., dos Santos-Neto, J. B. S., Frej, E. A., da Silva, L. B. L., & de Almeida, A. T. (2025). A GIS-based multicriteria decision support system for natural gas distribution planning. *Discover Applied Sciences, 7*(7), 701. https://doi.org/10.1007/s42452-025-06549-6.

Moslem, S. (2024). A novel parsimonious spherical fuzzy analytic hierarchy process for sustainable urban transport solutions. *Engineering Applications of Artificial Intelligence, 128*, 107447.

Paradowski, B., Shekhovtsov, A., Bczkiewicz, A., Kizielewicz, B., & Saabun, W. (2021). Similarity analysis of methods for objective determination of weights in multi-criteria decision support systems. *Symmetry, 13*(10), 1874.

Ramezani, M., Khazaei, M., Gholian-Jouybari, F., Sandoval-Correa, A., Bonakdari, H., & Hajiaghaei-Keshteli, M. (2024). Turquoise hydrogen and waste optimization: A Bi-objective closed-loop and sustainable supply chain model for a case in Mexico. *Renewable and Sustainable Energy Reviews, 195*, 114329.

Thakkar, J. J. (2021). *Multi-criteria decision making*. Springer.

Chapter 36

LOPCOW: Logarithmic percentage change-driven objective weighting for multi-attribute decision-making

Fatih Ecer
Sub-Department of Operations Research, Faculty of Economics and Administrative Sciences, Afyon Kocatepe University, Afyonkarahisar, Turkey

36.1 Introduction

In solving multiple criteria decision-making (MCDM) problems, it is rare for the criteria considered to have equal decisive levels. In this vein, subjective judgments from experts would be utilized to determine the criterion weights. However, some methods ensure objective weighting regarding the values of the alternatives concerning the criteria, thus considering the data structure of the decision matrix. Logarithmic percentage change-driven objective weighting (LOPCOW) provides objective weighting by taking into consideration the variability of the criteria (Aytekin et al., 2024).

Ecer and Pamucar (2022) developed LOPCOW, a technique that measures the importance of each criterion with a logarithm-based function and variability distribution measure. Unlike entropy and method-based on the removal effects of criteria (MEREC) approaches, which operate logarithmic functions to estimate criterion weights, the LOPCOW method differentiates itself by efficiently directing positive and negative raw data, creating more reasonable and balanced weight values (Brainy et al., 2024). Moreover, using logarithmic operators, the method can significantly reduce the impact of extreme values in the weight determination phase (Cheng et al., 2024). Thus, it targets eliminating the limitations of well-known weighting methods, such as criteria importance through intercriteria correlation (CRITIC) and entropy. LOPCOW aims to overcome the disadvantages arising from data size and to fairly include positive and negative data in the weighting phase (Guo et al., 2024). The instability in other objective weighting methods can be minimized with LOPCOW. This will result in more reliable and logical criterion weights for the target audience, so the results can always be trusted. The method reduces the number of calculation steps, provides operational convenience, and produces satisfactory results. In other words, LOPCOW processes are extremely clear and understandable, which is a paramount superiority this method offers. Besides, it has the potential to recognize negative values in raw data and, unlike many methods, can perform analyses with negative data. The criterion's cost-benefit basis is considered in the analysis process, minimizing its impact on the results (Ji et al., 2025; Jiang et al., 2024). Moreover, the technique yields robust results and excellent stability (Nila & Roy, 2023).

The remainder of the chapter is organized as follows. Section 36.2 reviews the research using the LOPCOW method. Section 36.3 is methodology. Sections 36.4 and 36.5 provide numerical examples on LOPCOW. The last section is the conclusion.

36.2 Literature review

To date, many authors from various fields have used the LOPCOW method to obtain objective weights. Ecer et al. (2025) evaluated the sustainable aviation fuel suppliers for airways using an interval-valued fuzzy neutrosophic LOPCOW-measurement alternatives and ranking according to the compromise solution (MARCOS) approach. The interval-valued fuzzy neutrosophic LOPCOW model is developed to calculate criteria weights. Ecer, Ögel, et al. (2023) introduced an integrated q-rung orthopair fuzzy model including LOPCOW and VlseKriterijumska Optimizacija I Kompromisno Resenje multicriteria methods. To evaluate agricultural unmanned aerial vehicles selection criteria under fuzzy

Encyclopedia of Multi-Attribute Decision-Making (MADM). DOI: https://doi.org/10.1016/B978-0-443-33275-3.00012-9

environments, they proposed the q-rung orthopair fuzzy LOPCOW methodology. Ulutaş et al. (2024) evaluated third-party logistics service providers using a novel MCDM methodology, named integrated grey LOPCOW-preference selection index-MACONT. In their study, the grey LOPCOW framework was developed for the first time to ascertain the weights of third-party logistics service provider selection criteria. Ecer, Küçükönder, et al. (2023) aimed to analyze the sustainability performance of micro-mobility alternatives in transportation. To this aim, the authors offered an interval-valued fuzzy neutrosophic LOPCOW and combined compromise solution (CoCoSo) model. To obtain the criteria weight under uncertainty, they performed an interval-valued fuzzy neutrosophic LOPCOW approach. Nila and Roy (2023) offered a fuzzy LOPCOW-full consistency method (FUCOM)-Dombi Bonferroni model to assess third-party logistics providers. In their work, a fuzzy LOPCOW approach is developed and applied to drive the criteria weights of the criteria. Simic et al. (2023) extended the LOPCOW method with neutrosophic information and applied it to prioritize the criteria of material handling technologies. Ulutaş et al. (2023) employed the LOPCOW method to ascertain the importance weights of the selection criteria in their research on the selection of natural fibers for building insulation.

Korucuk et al. (2024) suggested an interval-valued fermatean fuzzy MCDM methodology based on LOPCOW and ranking of alternatives through functional mapping of criterion subintervals into a single interval. The interval-valued fermatean fuzzy LOPCOW approach was employed to decide the warehouse site selection criteria weights. Rong, Yu, Liu, Simic, Pamucar et al. (2024); Rong, Yu, Liu, Simic, and Garg (2024) introduced an integrated LOPCOW and additive ratio assessment (ARAS) methodology with interval-valued fermatean fuzzy sets to evaluate risk factors for R&D projects. To extract the criteria weights, they utilized the interval-valued fermatean fuzzy LOPCOW model. Biswas et al. (2022) aimed to compare the stock performances of some companies at the Bombay Stock Exchange. They used a LOPCOW-evaluation based on the distance from average solution (EDAS) model for analysis, whereas the LOPCOW method was applied to ascertain the criteria weights. Niu et al. (2022) proposed a fermatean cubic fuzzy LOPCOW-EDAS framework to help choose the most appropriate railway service center. For the first time, they developed the fermatean cubic fuzzy LOPCOW model to determine the significance of the evaluation factors. Guo et al. (2024) aimed to introduce the LOPCOW method-based multi-objective optimization by ratio analysis –density-based spatial clustering of applications with noise methodology with machine learning optimization for transport safety action planning. Sumrit and Keeratibhubordee (2025) proposed an MCDM model under a fuzzy environment using LOPCOW, the analytic hierarchy process, and ARAS methods. Fuzzy LOPCOW is conducted to obtain risk factor weights for reverse logistics in the waste plastic recycling sector.

Aytekin et al. (2024) intended to identify blockchain application obstacles; thus, they developed a bipolar neutrosophic sets-based MCDM approach. They put forward a bipolar neutrosophic LOPCOW methodology to ascertain the weights of blockchain application obstacles. Cheng et al. (2024) aimed to introduce an R-numbers-based LOPCOW-CRADIS approach to evaluate battery logistics path alternatives for clean energy car firms. The Rough-LOPCOW methodology was performed to compute the weight coefficient values of the selection criteria. Abacıoğlu et al. (2025) proposed a comprehensive MCDM model to analyze universities' sustainability performance. In this context, they determined the importance of the weights of sustainability criteria with LOPCOW and MEREC and reached the sustainability ranking of universities using their results. Işık et al. (2024) analyzed cities' competitive levels using an integrated framework that included LOPCOW, CRITIC, and Aczel–Alsina weighted assessment (ALWAS). To this aim, they constructed a LOPCOW-CRITIC weighting model to achieve a reliable prioritization of evaluation indicators. Jiang et al. (2024) proposed an intuitionistic fuzzy LOPCOW-stepwise weight assessment ratio analysis (SWARA)-evaluation based on relative utility and nonlinear standardization (ERUNS) methodology to evaluate food supply chain performance. intuitionistic fuzzy (IF)-LOPCOW and IF-SWARA approaches are offered to ascertain the criteria weights in their research. Rong and Yu, 2024 combined LOPCOW and MARCOS methods as well as generalized Dombi operators to solve the emergency logistics supplier selection problem with q-rung picture fuzzy information. They utilized the q-rung picture fuzzy LOPCOW approach to obtain the weights of assessment drivers. Rong, Yu, Liu, Simic, Pamucar et al. (2024); Rong, Yu, Liu, Simic, and Garg (2024) incorporated interval-valued q-rung orthopair fuzzy sets, LOPCOW, FUCOM, and weighted aggregated sum product assessment to assess risk. Dhruva et al. (2024) introduced a decision tool, incorporating LOPCOW and CoCoSo methods with fermatean fuzzy sets to evaluate cloud suppliers for health centers. The other papers that applied LOPCOW for their analyses are presented in Table 36.1.

36.3 Methodology

LOPCOW offers unique solutions to objective weighting in multicriteria problems and has high potential for implementation in all scientific areas. In summary, LOPCOW provides the following superiorities (Ecer & Pamucar, 2022).

TABLE 36.1 The studies employed the logarithmic percentage change-driven objective weighting (LOPCOW) method.

Author(s)	Aim	Approach	Fuzzy (F)/ Crisp (C)
Sharma et al. (2025)	To concentrate on supplier selection and order allocation	The LOPCOW-DOBI integration and possibilistic multiobjective programming approach	F
Wang and Ren (2025)	To carry out sustainable urban planning	*q*-rung fuzzy LOPCOW-ERUNS and machine learning	F
Shah et al. (2025)	To evaluate employee performance	LOPCOW-MARCOS	C
Dhruva et al. (2025)	To select waste treatment approaches	*q*-rung orthopair fuzzy LOPCOW-COPRAS	F
Xiang and Zhang (2025)	To rank suppliers	*q*-rung orthopair fuzzy LOPCOW-ERUNS	F
Ji et al. (2025)	To evaluate smart technologies	*q*-rung orthopair fuzzy LOPCOW-WASPAS	F
Kiracı (2025)	To rank airlines in terms of their performance	LOPCOW-TOPSIS	C
Balo et al. (2025)	To evaluate natural stones	With a new integrated MCDM model consisting of LOPCOW-CRITIC-LODECI-AROMAN-M	C
Zhang (2025)	To rank text analysis alternatives	Picture fuzzy LOPCOW-ERUNS	F
Belgin et al. (2025)	To select the best technology transfer office	Fuzzy LOPCOW-entropy-VIKOR	F
Zhu and Ding (2025)	To evaluate urban development choices	T-spherical Fuzzy LOPCOW-CRADIS	F
Worku (2025)	To select the most prominent material	LOPCOW-entropy-CRITIC- SVP-MEREC	C
Yasin et al. (2025)	To evaluate solid waste management alternatives	*q*-rung orthopair fuzzy LOPCOW-Choquet integral	F
Aşan et al. (2025)	To assess the project management performance of regional development agencies	LOPCOW-MABAC	C
Brainy et al. (2024)	To evaluate hydrogen storage alternatives for mobility applications	Bipolar linear diophantine fuzzy LOOCOW-MACONT-MARCOS-ELECTRE III	F
Riaz et al. (2024)	To develop innovative solutions for healthcare supply chains	Circular intuitionistic fuzzy LOPCOW-AROMAN	F
Çelebi Demirarslan et al. (2024)	To rank the countries regarding the quality of life index	LOPCOW-MEREC-MPSI-MAIRCA	C
Sanyal et al. (2024)	To evaluate organic foods	Intuitionistic fuzzy LOPCOW-FUCOM-EDAS	F
Demir et al. (2023)	To evaluate open government data indicators	LOPCOW-LMAW-WASPAS	C

- LOPCOW serves as a more equitable approach to distributing criteria weights.
- It allows analyses with negative data.
- It minimizes the effect of data scale via logarithmic transformations, reducing the impact of outliers.
- It can cope with real-world problems that have many criteria and alternatives.

- It uses logarithmic percentage changes to handle data, allowing small changes to be detected. Thereby, a more precise and prominent weight diversity, even if the absolute differences in the data are minor.

On the other hand, LOPCOW has some disadvantages. It ignores human judgment, preferences, or strategic priorities. Thus it cannot be suitable for contexts where decision-makers' judgments and expertise are crucial. Moreover, the results might not accurately reflect reality if the data are biased or limited. Unlike subjective weighting MCDM techniques, which rely on human reasoning, LOPCOW is a purely mathematical approach.

The steps of LOPCOW are as follows (Ecer & Pamucar, 2022).

Step 1. Construct an initial decision matrix (*IM*) for a decision-making problem that has *s* alternatives and *n* criteria.

$$IM = \begin{bmatrix} x_{11} & \cdots & x_{1j} & \cdots & x_{1n} \\ \vdots & \vdots & \vdots & \ddots & \vdots \\ x_{m1} & \cdots & x_{mj} & \cdots & x_{mn} \end{bmatrix}$$

Step 2. Normalize the *IM*. The linear max-min normalization technique is utilized to get the normalized values of initial decision matrix elements.

$$z_{ij} = \frac{x_{\max} - x_{ij}}{x_{\max} - x_{\min}}, \quad \text{if } j \text{ is a non} - \text{benefit criterion} \tag{36.1}$$

$$z_{ij} = \frac{x_{ij} - x_{\min}}{x_{\max} - x_{\min}}, \quad \text{if } j \text{ is a benefit criterion} \tag{36.2}$$

Step 3. Compute the percentage values (PV). The mean square value of each criterion as a percentage of its standard deviation is computed to the extent to which it eliminates the difference (gap) because of the size of the data.

$$PV_{ij} = \left| \ln\left(\frac{\sqrt{\frac{\sum_{i=1}^{m} z_{ij}^2}{s}}}{\sigma} \right). 100 \right| \tag{36.3}$$

where σ represents the standard deviation.

Step 4. Compute the objective weights. Finally, each objective weight is calculated via Eq. (36.4).

$$w_j = \frac{PV_{ij}}{\sum_{i=1}^{n} PV_{ij}} \tag{36.4}$$

Eq. (36.4) guarantees the condition that the sum of the weight values is 1 ($\sum_{i=1}^{n} w_j = 1$).

36.4 Numerical example 1

The economic freedom index measures how countries' institutions and policies allow individuals to make economic choices. The index comprises five subindices: size of government (C1), legal system and property rights with gender adjustment (C2), access to sound money (C3), international trade freedom (C4), and regulation (C5). The index, which takes a value between 1 and 10, indicates that economic freedom increases as it approaches 10 (Gwartney et al., 2024). For this example, the LOPCOW method is utilized to calculate the weights of those criteria (subindices). Table 36.2 presents the actual data gathered from the Fraser Institute-economic freedom dataset. This table is also the *IM* used for analysis.

Using Eq. (36.2), the normalized values are calculated, shown in Table 36.3.

For example, C1 is normalized as follows:

$$z_{C1} = \frac{6.44 - 4.97}{7.35 - 4.97} = 0.616$$

Afterward, Eq. (36.3) computes the PV value, whereas Eq. (36.4) calculates objective weights. Table 36.4 depicts those values.

The PV of C1 is calculated as follows:

$$z_{C1} = \left| \ln\left(\frac{0.5224}{0.3286} \right). 100 \right| = 46.3674$$

TABLE 36.2 Initial decision matrix.

	Size of government (C1)	Legal system & property rights with gender adjustment (C2)	Sound money (C3)	Freedom to trade internationally (C4)	Regulation (C5)
Canada (A1)	6.44	8.30	8.55	8.53	8.14
France (A2)	4.97	7.49	8.78	8.94	7.29
Germany (A3)	5.78	8.15	8.60	8.73	7.75
Italy (A4)	5.30	6.60	8.44	8.97	6.79
Japan (A5)	5.85	7.70	9.55	8.50	7.93
United Kingdom (A6)	6.18	8.01	8.71	8.75	7.75
United States (A7)	7.35	7.78	8.53	8.11	8.66

Source: Fraser Institute-economic freedom dataset (https://efotw.org/economic-freedom/dataset?geozone=world&page=dataset&min-year=2&max-year=0&filter=0).

TABLE 36.3 Normalized decision matrix.

	C1	C2	C3	C4	C5
A1	0.616	1.000	0.106	0.482	0.721
A2	0.000	0.525	0.312	0.965	0.266
A3	0.338	0.914	0.146	0.712	0.513
A4	0.138	0.000	0.000	1.000	0.000
A5	0.370	0.648	1.000	0.444	0.608
A6	0.510	0.829	0.247	0.736	0.511
A7	1.000	0.696	0.087	0.000	1.000

As shown in Table 36.4, criterion C2 (legal system and property rights with gender adjustment) is the most significant factor in deciding the economic freedom of G7 countries, followed by C4 (international trade freedom), C5 (regulation), C1 (government size), and C3 (sound money).

For example, the weight value of C1 is computed as follows:

$$w_{C1} = \frac{46.3674}{277.2465} = 0.1672$$

Fig. 36.1 demonstrates the objective weight values of the criteria.

36.5 Numerical example 2

The second example aims to find the priorities (weights) of the criteria used to evaluate 10 stocks in a sector using the LOPCOW method. Thus the following criteria are determined based on the literature survey.

C1-Average stock return

C2-Return on net worth

C3-Earnings per share

TABLE 36.4 Weight values of the criteria.

	C1	C2	C3	C4	C5
Standard deviation	0.3286	0.3326	0.3377	0.3463	0.3197
Square mean	0.5224	0.7273	0.4137	0.6979	0.5958
PV	46.367	78.2502	20.3074	70.0779	62.2434
Weight	0.1672	0.2822	0.0732	0.2528	0.2245

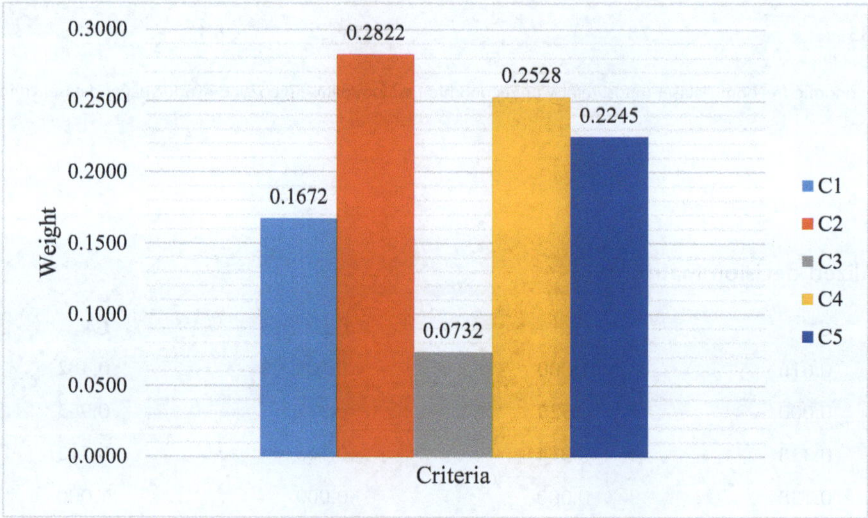

FIGURE 36.1 The objective weights obtained by logarithmic percentage change-driven objective weighting.

C4-P/B
C5-Turnover
C6-Shares traded
C7-Yield
C8-Alpha
C9-Beta
Table 36.5 presents evaluations of alternatives regarding the criteria.
Table 36.6 depicts the normalized decision matrix.
For example, C1 is normalized as follows:

$$z_{C1} = \frac{-0.015 - (-0.0625)}{0.0298 - (-0.0625)} = 0.516$$

Table 36.7 showcases the results.
The PV of C1 is calculated as follows:

$$z_{C1} = \left| \ln\left(\frac{0.6763}{0.3051}\right).\ 100 \right| = 79.5776$$

TABLE 36.5 Initial decision matrix.

	C1 Max	C2 Max	C3 Max	C4 Max	C5 Max	C6 Max	C7 Max	C8 Max	C9 Min
A1	-0.015	8.201	0.291	6.471	4.711	10440	0.001	0.581	1.171
A2	0.001	29.681	68.561	31.611	835.181	12596	0.641	0.361	0.571
A3	0.030	14.001	47.351	3.221	33.031	28530	0.691	-0.019	1.451
A4	-0.038	36.691	11.221	16.481	34.741	50472	1.751	0.241	0.811
A5	0.002	19.731	5.931	12.561	0.031	3100	0.711	0.901	0.311
A6	0.022	83.381	27.631	52.601	181.111	10621	1.231	0.301	0.601
A7	0.013	23.101	10.051	6.721	176.991	59506	1.741	-0.039	0.651
A8	-0.063	24.851	4.521	8.461	0.461	2497	0.271	0.271	0.591
A9	-0.020	20.041	19.651	3.071	2.111	6179	0.681	1.061	0.811
A10	0.006	28.731	6.361	14.251	27.461	7987	1.381	0.351	0.491

TABLE 36.6 Normalized decision matrix.

	C1	C2	C3	C4	C5	C6	C7	C8	C9
A1	0.516	0.000	0.000	0.069	0.006	0.139	0.000	0.564	0.246
A2	0.691	0.286	1.000	0.576	1.000	0.177	0.366	0.364	0.772
A3	1.000	0.077	0.689	0.003	0.040	0.457	0.394	0.018	0.000
A4	0.270	0.379	0.160	0.271	0.042	0.842	1.000	0.255	0.561
A5	0.703	0.153	0.083	0.192	0.000	0.011	0.406	0.855	1.000
A6	0.910	1.000	0.400	1.000	0.217	0.143	0.703	0.309	0.746
A7	0.821	0.198	0.143	0.074	0.212	1.000	0.994	0.000	0.702
A8	0.000	0.221	0.062	0.109	0.001	0.000	0.154	0.282	0.754
A9	0.460	0.157	0.284	0.000	0.002	0.065	0.389	1.000	0.561
A10	0.740	0.273	0.089	0.226	0.033	0.096	0.789	0.355	0.842

TABLE 36.7 Weight values of the criteria.

	C1	C2	C3	C4	C5	C6	C7	C8	C9
Standard deviation	0.3051	0.2766	0.3221	0.3128	0.3083	0.3565	0.3391	0.3242	0.2960
Square mean	0.6763	0.3798	0.4220	0.3892	0.3311	0.4474	0.6110	0.5046	0.6792
PV	79.577	31.696	27.002	21.853	7.1227	22.7109	58.873	44.235	83.043
Weight	0.2116	0.0843	0.0718	0.0581	0.0189	0.0604	0.1565	0.1176	0.2208

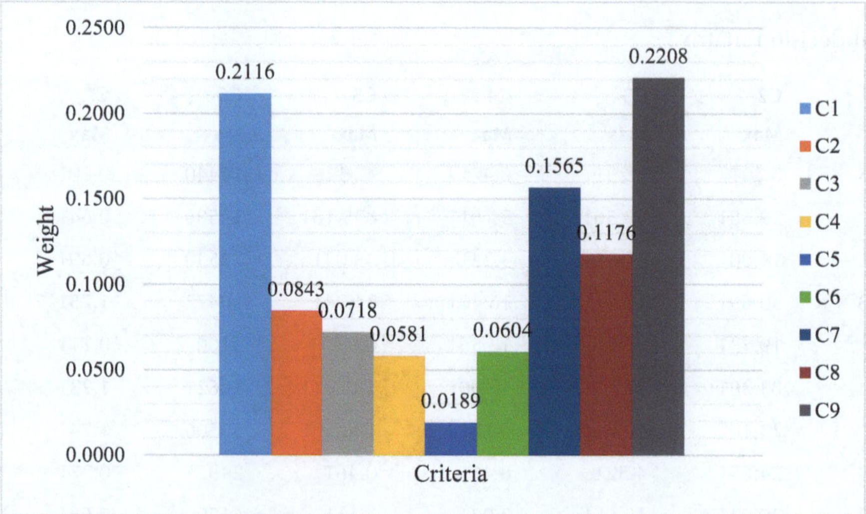

FIGURE 36.2 The objective weights found by logarithmic percentage change-driven objective weighting.

The weight value of C1 is computed as follows:

$$w_{C1} = \frac{79.5776}{376.1154} = 0.2116$$

Based on Table 36.7, the most critical criteria for the findings are C9, C1, C7, and C8. Fig. 36.2 illustrates the calculated weights.

36.6 Conclusion

Determining criterion weights is one of the most crucial stages of MCDM analysis, as weights play a significant role in ranking alternatives. Recently proposed LOPCOW is an objective MCDM method designed to determine criterion weights. With its advantages, including ease of calculation, understandability, and the ability to analyze data with negative values, LOPCOW has been successfully utilized by many researchers across various fields in a relatively short time. During this process, its uncertain extensions have also been proposed in the literature and have been used successfully to cope with uncertainty.

The purpose of this chapter is to introduce the LOPCOW method, provide information about its mathematical structure, discuss studies conducted using it, and illustrate the steps of the method with two examples. In the first example, LOPCOW is used to determine the importance levels of five factors affecting the economic freedoms of G7 countries. Findings indicate that the legal system and property rights, along with gender adjustment, are the most significant factors in deciding economic freedom. In the second example, the importance levels of nine criteria affecting the performance of 10 stocks are investigated. The results show that the beta value is the most crucial factor.

LOPCOW, which is still in its infancy, has great potential for the future. LOPCOW can be applied in all scientific fields, ranging from health to engineering, agriculture to management, and transportation to energy. Additionally, various extensions of fuzzy and rough sets can be developed and utilized to address uncertainty.

References

Abacıoğlu, S., Ayan, B., & Pamucar, D. (2025). The race to sustainability: decoding green university rankings through a comparative analysis (2018–2022). *Innovative Higher Education, 50*(1), 241–275.

Aşan, H., Arsu, T., & Ayçin, E. Proje yönetimi açısından bölgesel kalkınma ajanslarının performanslarının LOPCOW ve MABAC yöntemleri ile değerlendirilmesi. *Afyon Kocatepe Üniversitesi İktisadi ve İdari Bilimler Fakültesi Dergisi, 27*(Özel Sayı), 185-197.

Aytekin, A., Bozkurt, E., Orakçı, E., Uysal, M., Simic, V., Korucuk, S., & Pamucar, D. (2024). A bipolar neutrosophic combined compromise solution-based hybrid model for identifying blockchain application barriers and benchmarking consensus algorithms. *Engineering Applications of Artificial Intelligence, 133*, 108343.

Balo, F., Ulutaş, A., Stević, Ž., Boydak, H., & Zavadskas, E. K. (2025). Hybrid Revit and a new MCDM approach of energy effective nursing-home designed by natural stone and green insulation materials. *Journal of Civil Engineering and Management, 31*(4), 317–336.

Belgin, Ö., Avşar, B. A., & Çekiciler, C. (2025). Evaluating the performance of transfer offices using MCDM approaches. *Journal of the Knowledge Economy,* 1–28.

Biswas, S., Bandyopadhyay, G., Pamucar, D., & Joshi, N. (2022). A multi-criteria based stock selection framework in emerging market. *Operational Research in Engineering Sciences: Theory and Applications, 5*(3), 153–193.

Brainy, J. R. V. J., Narayanamoorthy, S., Pragathi, S., Salahshour, S., Ahmadian, A., & Kang, D. (2024). A sophisticated decision paradigm for the assessment of hydrogen storage technologies for mobility applications. *Journal of Energy Storage, 92*, 112207.

Çelebi Demirarslan, P., Sönmez Çakır, F., & Akansel, I. (2024). Ranking the quality of life indexes by years in Asian countries using multi-criteria decision making methods. *Asia-Pacific Journal of Regional Science, 8*(3), 911–942.

Cheng, R., Fan, J., Wu, M., & Seiti, H. (2024). A large-scale multi-attribute group decision making method with R-numbers and its application to hydrogen fuel cell logistics path selection. *Complex & Intelligent Systems, 10*(4), 5213–5260.

Demir, G., Riaz, M., & Almalki, Y. (2023). Multi-criteria decision making in evaluation of open government data indicators: An application in G20 countries. *Aims Mathematics, 8*(8), 18408–18434.

Dhruva, S., Krishankumar, R., Ravichandran, K. S., Kaklauskas, A., Zavadskas, E. K., & Gupta, P. (2025). Selection of waste treatment methods for food sources: An integrated decision model using q-rung fuzzy data, LOPCOW, and COPRAS techniques. *Clean Technologies and Environmental Policy,* 1–25.

Dhruva, S., Krishankumar, R., Zavadskas, E. K., Ravichandran, K. S., & Gandomi, A. H. (2024). Selection of suitable cloud vendors for health centre: A personalized decision framework with fermatean fuzzy set, LOPCOW, and CoCoSo. *Informatica, 35*(1), 65–98.

Ecer, F., & Pamucar, D. (2022). A novel LOPCOW-DOBI multi-criteria sustainability performance assessment methodology: An application in developing country banking sector. *Omega, 112*, 102690.

Ecer, F., Küçükönder, H., Kaya, S. K., & Görçün, Ö. F. (2023). Sustainability performance analysis of micro-mobility solutions in urban transportation with a novel IVFNN-Delphi-LOPCOW-CoCoSo framework. *Transportation Research Part A: Policy and Practice, 172*, 103667.

Ecer, F., Ögel, İ. Y., Krishankumar, R., & Tirkolaee, E. B. (2023). The q-rung fuzzy LOPCOW-VIKOR model to assess the role of unmanned aerial vehicles for precision agriculture realization in the Agri-Food 4.0 era. *Artificial Intelligence Review, 56*(11), 13373–13406.

Ecer, F., Tanrıverdi, G., Yaşar, M., & Görçün, Ö. F. (2025). Sustainable aviation fuel supplier evaluation for airlines through LOPCOW and MARCOS approaches with interval-valued fuzzy neutrosophic information. *Journal of Air Transport Management, 123*, 102705.

Guo, Z., Liu, J., Liu, X., Meng, Z., Pu, M., Wu, H., ... Chen, F. (2024). An integrated MCDM model with enhanced decision support in transport safety using machine learning optimization. *Knowledge-Based Systems, 301*, 112286.

Gwartney, J., Lawson, R., & Murphy, R. (2024). Economic freedom of the world: 2024 annual report. Fraser Institute.

Işık, Ö., Shabir, M., & Moslem, S. (2024). A hybrid MCDM framework for assessing urban competitiveness: A case study of European cities. *Socio-Economic Planning Sciences, 96*, 102109.

Ji, L., Zhang, D., Wang, Z., Liu, M., Sun, M., Zhang, H., ... Anjum, M. (2025). Paradigm shift in implementing smart technologies for machinery optimisation in manufacturing using decision support system. *Alexandria Engineering Journal, 114*, 526–542.

Jiang, Q., Wang, H., & Tang, L. (2024). Robust fuzzy decision support framework for comprehensive evaluating of food supply chain performance. *IEEE Access.*

Kiracı, K. (2025). An integrated MCDM approach to evaluating global and regional airline performance. *Transport Economics and Management.*

Korucuk, S., Aytekin, A., Görçün, Ö., Simic, V., & Görçün, Ö. F. (2024). Warehouse site selection for humanitarian relief organizations using an interval-valued fermatean fuzzy LOPCOW-RAFSI model. *Computers & Industrial Engineering, 192*, 110160.

Nila, B., & Roy, J. (2023). A new hybrid MCDM framework for third-party logistics provider selection under sustainability perspectives. *Expert Systems with Applications, 234*, 121009.

Niu, W., Rong, Y., Yu, L., & Huang, L. (2022). A novel hybrid group decision making approach based on EDAS and regret theory under a fermatean cubic fuzzy environment. *Mathematics, 10*(17), 3116.

Riaz, M., Qamar, F., Tariq, S., & Alsager, K. (2024). AI-driven LOPCOW-AROMAN framework and topological data analysis using circular intuitionistic fuzzy information: Healthcare supply chain innovation. *Mathematics, 12*(22), 3593.

Rong, Y., & Yu, L. (2024). An extended MARCOS approach and generalized Dombi aggregation operators-based group decision making for emergency logistics suppliers selection utilizing q-rung picture fuzzy information. *Granular Computing, 9*(1), 22.

Rong, Y., Yu, L., Liu, Y., Simic, V., & Garg, H. (2024). The FMEA model based on LOPCOW-ARAS methods with interval-valued Fermatean fuzzy information for risk assessment of R&D projects in industrial robot offline programming systems. *Computational and Applied Mathematics, 43*(1), 25.

Rong, Y., Yu, L., Liu, Y., Simic, V., Pamucar, D., & Garg, H. (2024). A novel failure mode and effect analysis model based on extended interval-valued q-rung orthopair fuzzy approach for risk analysis. *Engineering Applications of Artificial Intelligence, 136*, 108892.

Sanyal, A., Biswas, S., & Sur, S. (2024). An integrated full consistent LOPCOW-EDAS framework for modelling consumer decision making for organic food selection. *Yugoslav Journal of Operations Research,* 22.

Shah, A. K., Shukla, A., & Rao, P. K. (2025). Evaluating employee performance in the Indian manufacturing sectors: Identifying critical success factors. *International Journal of Organizational Analysis*.

Sharma, P., Nila, B., Pamucar, D., & Roy, J. (2025). Integrating LOPCOW-DOBI method and possibilistic programming for two-stage decision making in resilient food supply chain network. *Journal of Industrial Information Integration,* 100847.

Simic, V., Dabic-Miletic, S., Tirkolaee, E. B., Stević, Ž., Ala, A., & Amirteimoori, A. (2023). Neutrosophic LOPCOW-ARAS model for prioritizing industry 4.0-based material handling technologies in smart and sustainable warehouse management systems. *Applied Soft Computing, 143*, 110400.

Sumrit, D., & Keeratibhubordee, J. (2025). Risk assessment framework for reverse logistics in waste plastic recycle industry: A hybrid approach incorporating FMEA decision model with AHP-LOPCOW-ARAS under Trapezoidal fuzzy set. *Decision Making: Applications in Management and Engineering,* 42–81.

Ulutaş, A., Balo, F., & Topal, A. (2023). Identifying the most efficient natural fibre for common commercial building insulation materials with an integrated PSI, MEREC, LOPCOW and MCRAT model. *Polymers, 15*(6), 1500.

Ulutaş, A., Topal, A., Görçün, Ö. F., & Ecer, F. (2024). Evaluation of third-party logistics service providers for car manufacturing firms using a novel integrated grey LOPCOW-PSI-MACONT model. *Expert Systems with Applications, 241*, 122680.

Wang, Z., & Ren, F. (2025). Developing a decision support system for sustainable urban planning using machine learning-based scenario modeling. *Scientific Reports, 15*(1), 13210.

Worku, T. T. (2025). Formwork material selection and optimization by a comprehensive integrated subjective–objective criteria weighting MCDM model. *Discover Materials, 5*(1), 2.

Xiang, Z., & Zhang, X. (2025). An integrated decision support system for supplier selection and performance evaluation in global supply chains. *Applied Soft Computing,* 113325.

Yasin, Y., Riaz, M., & Alsager, K. (2025). Synergy of machine learning and the Einstein Choquet integral with LOPCOW and fuzzy measures for sustainable solid waste management. *AIMS Mathematics, 10*(1), 460–498.

Zhang, D. (2025). Applying multi-criteria decision making to text analysis for optimizing engineering knowledge management. *Alexandria Engineering Journal, 117*, 648–661.

Zhu, W., & Ding, Y. (2025). Integrating decision tools for environmental impact reduction in sustainable urban planning. *IEEE Access*.

Chapter 37

WENSLO: Weights by envelope and slope for multi-attribute decision-making

Gülay Demir
High School of Health Vocational Services, Sivas Cumhuriyet University, Sivas, Türkiye

37.1 Introduction

In multicriteria decision-making (MCDM) methodologies, determining criterion weights constitutes the most critical and sensitive stage of the process. Criterion weights quantitatively reflect the relative importance of each criterion in the overall performance score of an alternative (Haseli et al., 2024). Numerous studies in the literature have clearly demonstrated that the final ranking results are highly sensitive to even small changes in criterion weights (Mukhametzyanov & Pamučar, 2018). This requires that the weighting process properly represent the preference values, context of the problem, and conflict/congruence values among the choice variables. These erroneous values lead to incorrect identification of better alternatives, resource allocation, which ultimately significantly affects the dependability and validity level of the decision mechanism. Therefore, identification of values on a criterion requires intensive technical work, but moreover, is an imperative within the realms of ethics and methodology. The dependability and precision level within the processes of multiple criteria decision-making are significantly dependent upon unbiased and precise calculation values on the criteria weights (Haseli et al., 2023; Singh & Pant, 2021). Traditional methods, with respect to this, rely on subjective estimates given by decision-makers, similar to analytic hierarchy process and analytic network process, while other processes entail systematic errors that are affected by differences in C/B normalization values. This is a problem that could greatly affect dependability within results, especially within processes like sensitive financial risk assessment.

Thus, can one calculate the weights of criteria using an objective method that is completely independent of human subjective judgment and is solely on the basis of the internal structure of the information? Although there exist objective approaches within the literature to cover this issue, it is paramount to validate the effectiveness of these approaches within distinct domains of applications. Regarding this issue, within the context, the weights by envelope and slope (WENSLO) approach introduced by Pamučar et al. (2023) obtains an unbiased measure by considering solely the geometric slope value of any decision matrix. The WENSLO approach is centered on two elementary geometric notions within the normalized decision matrix: "envelope" and "slope." The envelope part captures the holistic decomposition structure of the information contained within the total Euclidean distance value of the whole dataset, while the slope part captures information about trends and orientation contained within the sum value of the criterion mode. The idea is to put more emphasis on those factors that have high values in both parts: envelope and slope.

The most significant advantage of this approach is that weighting can be performed regardless of the cost or benefit characteristics of the criteria (Biswas et al., 2025). Unlike existing methods, criterion trends do not affect the calculation process, and weight values cannot be manipulated by the subjective opinions of decision makers, making them reliable and unbiased. The position of the WENSLO method in the objective weighting literature and its comparison with the entropy and criteria importance through intercriteria correlation methods, which are traditional weighting methods, are presented in Table 37.1.

The main aim of this research work is to offer a comprehensive insight into the theoretical background of the WENSLO method, its implementation procedure, and its objective superiority over two selected conventional approaches. To this end, the following research objectives were identified: to explain how the concepts of envelope and slope, which form the mathematical basis of the WENSLO method, reflect the internal variability and trend of the criteria and to demonstrate the contribution of this geometric structure to objective weighting. To demonstrate the effectiveness and practical applicability of the method through two different

Encyclopedia of Multi-Attribute Decision-Making (MADM). DOI: https://doi.org/10.1016/B978-0-443-33275-3.00061-0

TABLE 37.1 Comparison of the weights by envelope and slope (WENSLO) method with the entropy and criteria importance through intercriteria correlation (CRITIC) methods.

Comparison criteria	WENSLO method	Entropy method	CRITIC method
Basic philosophy	Geometric data decomposition	Information theory (uncertainty measurement)	Correlation and variability
Weighting mechanism	The ratio of the envelope and slope components.	Variability (distribution) of the values in the criterion.	The product of the standard deviation and the correlation between criteria.
Measured data characteristics	Two geometric properties: variability (envelope) and trend (slope).	Variability only (data distribution)	Variability (standard deviation) and conflict between criteria (correlation).
Main advantage	It eliminates decision-maker subjectivity; it utilizes both the variability and trend of the data simultaneously.	Mathematically robust; measures the uncertainty of the data.	Takes into account the conflict between criteria (correlation).
Limitations (WENSLO's advantage)	This is a relatively new method; it involves complex geometric calculations.	Excessive sensitivity to normalization method: according to Mukhametzyanov (2021), the results of the entropy method can vary significantly depending on the normalization technique used (max–min, sum, etc.). WENSLO, on the other hand, is less sensitive to such sensitivities due to its geometric structure.	Interpreting correlation: a high correlation may mean that the criteria convey similar information, but it does not necessarily mean that a criterion is less important.

case studies: the operational performance measurement of regional distribution centers and the assessment of countries' sustainable development performance.

In addition to presenting the theoretical foundation of the WENSLO method, this section empirically demonstrates its effectiveness through two different case studies. The results strongly demonstrate the potential of the WENSLO method to solve various MCDM problems that aim to minimize decision-maker subjectivity by relying solely on attribute data in determining criteria parameters. The WENSLO chapter structure is as follows: Section 37.2 includes a literature review introducing the integration of the method with fuzzy logic and the hybrid models it is applied to. This is followed by a section explaining the methodology of the method. Case studies, characterized as simple and complex cases, are included in section 37.4. Section 37.5 includes the conclusion and recommendations for future work.

37.2 Literature review

This section systematically discusses the methodological development, fuzzy logic extensions, and varied application domains of the WENSLO approach. It is a new MCDM method; thus, for understanding the potential and contribution of the method, one needs to read the literature extensively on its direct applications as well as its hybrids.

In their seminal work, Pamučar et al. (2024) presented the WENSLO method to the media. To ensure objectivity in criterion weighting, this paper provided a systematic method that integrated the "envelope and slope" concepts. The Aczel–Alsina weighted assessment (ALWAS) was first applied to measuring the relative green growth performance of countries. The sensitivity of the WENSLO method to environmental indicators had been successfully proven by the findings in this study, providing strong support for its theoretical basis and practical value. This pioneer study served as a direction for further research.

The WENSLO method has been extended by fusing it with some other fuzzy set theories in order to solve decision-making problems under uncertainty. Applying the WENSLO method to neutrosophic expert assessment and criterion weight computation was also demonstrated by the use of type-2 neutrosophic numbers in the model WENSLO-Alternative

Ranking using two-step Logarithmic Normalization (ARLON) (Kara et al., 2024). The network security analysis has recorded a Trapezoidal Fuzzy Neutrosophic numbers (TFNNs)-supported variant (Zhang Li, 2025). Fuzzy WENSLO and its extensions are also successfully applied in applications such as environmental/landscape assessments based on type-1 triangular neutrosophic number monovalent (mono-) by Liang (2025) and occupational safety and risk assessments by Demir et al. (2025) Moreover, WENSLO-type integrated weighting structures have been integrated with other advanced methods, such as picture fuzzy and q-rung orthopair sets (Kara et al., 2025; Peng et al., 2025). Under the appropriately selected type of fuzzy, these articles show that our WENSLO approach is an efficient tool in dealing with uncertain scenarios; they make note and notice, such as considering concatenation operators and computational time.

This WENSLO approach is commonly employed in the literature for hybrid models with various types of sorting approaches, as essentially it is a weighting method. WENSLO-Alternative Ranking Technique based on Adaptive Standardised Intervals (ARTASI) pair has also been frequently used for determining objective weights, and alternative ordering of airport efficiency studies (Pamučar et al., 2025). It has also been applied as a weighting technique or method for the consistency of results in comparing with ALWAS in green growth performance measurement (Pamučar et al., 2024) and other Multi Criteria Decision Making (MCDM) methods such as Compromise Ranking of Alternatives from Distance to Ideal Solution (CRADIS), Proximity Indexed Value (PIV), Multi-Attributive Border Approximation Area Comparison (MABAC), and Technique for Order of Preference by Similarity to Ideal Solution (TOPSIS) and measurement alternatives and ranking according to compromise solution (Pamučar et al., 2025; Trung et al., 2025).

The WENSLO method with the emergence of a variety of decision problems, the WENSLO method and its extensions have become popular recently.

A summary of commonalities across studies is as follows:

A systematic and accurate ranking could also be developed within a research study wherein both WENSLO-ARTASI and Monte Carlo simulation were applied to assess the quality of auditing firms. It has been revealed that training duration and the number of audits carried out have obtained maximum weightage (Kaya et al., 2025). The efficiency of airports has already shown that WENSLO can provide multiple sets of priority values for multiple criterion groups, namely star level-dependent sets (Pamučar et al., 2025). The importance of green growth evaluation has already revealed that environmental factors like CO_2 emissions and water saving capacity have acquired relatively higher values than other economic and social factors (Pamučar et al., 2024). Green growth evaluation studies, such as electric vehicle choice identification (Trung et al., 2025), internet of things platform assessment (Peng et al., 2025), and material choice identification, have already supported WENSLO to offer systematic and reliable outcomes like other objective weighting approaches. Studies related to both network security investigation (Zhang & Li, 2025) and identification of occupational safety strategies within industry and manufacturing (Demir et al., 2025) have already produced successful results using fuzzy approaches relevant to WENSLO. Similar studies related to subjective processes like logo choice identification within artificial intelligence approaches (Kara et al., 2024, 2025) have already achieved satisfactory outcomes.

37.3 Methodology

Let there be a decision matrix consisting of m alternatives and n criteria (Pamučar et al., 2024):

Step 1. Creating the decision matrix

In the first step, the initial decision matrix $\mathfrak{R}(A, C)_{mxn}$ is constructed as in Eq. (37.1):

$$\mathfrak{R}(A, C) = [\zeta_{ij}]_{mxn} = \begin{bmatrix} A/C & C_1 & C_2 & \cdots & C_j \\ target & \text{max/min} & \text{max/min} & \cdots & \text{max/min} \\ & & \zeta_{12} & \cdots & \zeta_{1j} \\ A_1 & \zeta_{11} & & & \\ A_2 & \zeta_{21} & \zeta_{22} & \cdots & \zeta_{2j} \\ \vdots & \vdots & \vdots & \ddots & \vdots \\ A_i & \zeta_{i1} & & & \\ & & \zeta_{i2} & \cdots & \zeta_{mn} \end{bmatrix} \tag{37.1}$$

where $A1, A2, \ldots, Am$ represent alternatives and m represents the number of alternatives. $C1, C2, \ldots, Cn$ represent criteria, and n represents the number of criteria. The max/min target relates to the direction of each criterion. If the criterion aims to achieve the maximum value, the benefit-based environment applies. If the criterion aims to achieve the minimum value, the cost-based environment also applies. ζij represents the value of the i-th alternative in the matrix with respect to the j-th criterion.

Step 2. Normalizing the decision matrix

Each criterion is represented in the decision matrix with different units of measurement. To compare criteria and perform mathematical operations, a dimensionless decision matrix is created through the normalization process. The normalization process is applied to the elements of the matrix $\Re(A, C)$. In this context, linear normalization is applied in (37.2) below.

$$z_{ij} = \frac{\zeta_{ij}}{\sum_{i=1}^{m} \zeta_{ij}} \quad \forall j \in [1, 2, \ldots, n] \tag{37.2}$$

Thus, a normalized decision matrix is created as Eq. (37.3).

$$Z(A, C) = [z_{ij}]_{mxn} = \begin{bmatrix} z_{11} & \cdots & z_{1j} \\ \cdots & \ddots & \cdots \\ z_{i1} & \cdots & z_{mn} \end{bmatrix} \tag{37.3}$$

where z_{ij} lies in the value range $0 < z_{ij} < 1$.

Step 3. Calculating class interval

The final ranking of alternatives according to a given set of criteria is determined by the influence of each criterion on the ranking. This influence is called criterion weights in decision theory. Defining these weights in a nonsubjective manner is considered an important task. The vector space of the normalized decision matrix is shown by Eq. (37.4).

$$\begin{bmatrix} A \\ A_1 \\ A_2 \\ \vdots \\ A_i \end{bmatrix} = \left(\begin{bmatrix} C_1 \\ z_{11} \\ z_{21} \\ \vdots \\ z_{i1} \end{bmatrix}, \begin{bmatrix} C_2 \\ z_{12} \\ z_{22} \\ \vdots \\ z_{i2} \end{bmatrix}, \cdots, \begin{bmatrix} C_j \\ z_{1j} \\ z_{2j} \\ \vdots \\ z_{ij} \end{bmatrix} \right) \tag{37.4}$$

In terms of Sturges' rule, the dimension of the j-th criterion class interval Δz_j is computed according to (37.5).

$$\Delta z_j = \frac{\underbrace{\max}_{i=1,2,\ldots,m} z_{ij} - \underbrace{\min}_{i=1,2,\ldots,m} z_{ij}}{1 + 3.322 * \log(m)} \quad \forall j \in [1, 2, \ldots, n] \tag{37.5}$$

Step 4. Calculating the criterion slope

The slope of the criterion is computed according to (37.6):

$$\tan \varphi_j = \frac{\sum_{i=1}^{m} z_{ij}}{(m-1) \cdot \Delta z_j} \quad \forall j \in [1, 2, \ldots, n] \tag{37.6}$$

Step 5. Determining the envelope

The sum of the partial Euclidean distance between two successive normalized values of the j-th criterion that is equal to the total Euclidean distance between the first and last normalized values, and is defined according to (37.7):

$$E_j = \sum_{i=1}^{m-1} \sqrt{(z_i + 1, j - z_i, j)^2 + \Delta z_j^2} \quad \forall j \in [1, 2, \ldots, n] \tag{37.7}$$

The envelope of the criterion can be considered to represent the total Euclidean distance. The shape of the envelope resembles a zig-zag line, indicating its values.

Step 6. Calculating the envelope-slope ratio

The ratio of the total Euclidean distance to the slope of the criterion is calculated as a numerical value by (37.8).

$$q_j = \frac{E_j}{\tan \varphi_j} \quad \forall j \in [1, 2, \ldots, n] \tag{37.8}$$

Step 7. Calculating weights

The weight of the criterion is computed according to (37.9).

$$w_j = \frac{q_j}{\sum_{j=1}^{n} q_j} \quad \forall j \in [1, 2, \ldots, n] \tag{37.9}$$

37.4 Case study

In this section, the process steps of the ARTASI method are shown in detail with numerical examples using the simple case and complex case designed as hypothetical scenarios.

37.4.1 Numerical example 1 (simple case)

In logistics and supply chain management, the operational performance of distribution centers plays a direct and decisive role in a company's overall efficiency, cost structure, and customer satisfaction. This study aims to evaluate the performance of five different regional distribution centers (north region (A1), east region (A2), west region (A3), south region (A4), and central/urban distribution center (A5)) of a logistics company. At the same time, it aims to objectively reveal on which critical indicators performance improvement efforts should be focused. The criteria used in the evaluation and the relevant explanations are detailed in Table 37.2.

The initial decision matrix consisting of five distribution regions and six criteria is given in Table 37.3.

The normalized decision matrix is obtained using (37.2) and given in Table 37.4.

The calculation of the normalized value of the C1 criterion for the A1 alternative is shown as an example.

$$z_{A1-C1} = \frac{31582,68}{56510,97} = 0,5589$$

A similar process is repeated for all elements of the matrix. Class ranges are obtained using (37.5) and given in Table 37.5.

The calculation of the value of the C1 criterion in Table 37.4 is presented as an example.

$$\Delta z_{C1} = \frac{0,5589 - 0,0299}{1 + 3,322.\log(5)} = 0,1592$$

Then, slope ($\tan \varphi_j$) values are calculated using (37.6) and given in Table 37.6.

TABLE 37.2 Information on evaluation criteria.

Criteria	Code	Explanation
Monthly shipment volume (units)	C1	Total number of shipments leaving the center during the month
Number of active customers (units)	C2	Number of monthly active corporate/end-user customers connected to the center
Number of delayed shipments (units)	C3	Number of shipments not delivered on the scheduled monthly delivery date
Damage rate (ratio, 0–1)	C4	Rate of damaged incoming/outgoing packages among monthly shipments
Average delivery time (days)	C5	Average number of full days between departure from the center and final delivery
Vehicle/fleet size used (units)	C6	Number of delivery vehicles actively used for that month

TABLE 37.3 Initial decision matrix.

	C1	C2	C3	C4	C5	C6
A1	31582,68	757	1870	0,044	10,4	25
A2	1691,34	63	4468	0,071	3,2	30
A3	11426,32	364	1355	0,039	5,7	20
A4	9820,34	16144	883	0,057	3,4	30
A5	1990,29	73	2543	0,076	3,2	50
Total	56510,97	17401	11119	0,287	25,9	155

TABLE 37.4 Normalized decision matrix.

	C1	C2	C3	C4	C5	C6
A1	0,5589	0,0435	0,1682	0,1533	0,4015	0,1613
A2	0,0299	0,0036	0,4018	0,2474	0,1236	0,1935
A3	0,2022	0,0209	0,1219	0,1359	0,2201	0,1290
A4	0,1738	0,9278	0,0794	0,1986	0,1313	0,1935
A5	0,0352	0,0042	0,2287	0,2648	0,1236	0,3226
min	0,0299	0,0036	0,0794	0,1359	0,1236	0,1290
max	0,5589	0,9278	0,4018	0,2648	0,4015	0,3226

TABLE 37.5 Class ranges of criteria.

	C1	C2	C3	C4	C5	C6
Δz_j	0,1592	0,2782	0,0971	0,0388	0,0837	0,0583

TABLE 37.6 Slope values of the criteria.

	C1	C2	C3	C4	C5	C6
$tan\varphi_j$	1,5701	0,8987	2,5758	6,4419	2,9875	4,2909

The calculation of the value of the C1 criterion in Table 37.5 is presented as an example.

$$\tan \varphi_{C1} = \frac{0,5589 + 0,0299 + 0,2022 + 0,1738 + 0,0352}{(5-1).\ 0,1592} = 1,5701$$

Then, the envelope (E_j) values are calculated using (37.7) and given in Table 37.7.
The calculation of the value of the C1 criterion in Table 37.6 is presented as an example.

$$E_{C1} = \sqrt{(0,0299 - 0,5589)^2 + (0,2022 - 0,0299)^2 + (0,1738 - 0,2022)^2 + (0,0352 - 0,1738)^2 + 0,1592^2}$$
$$= 0,5957$$

Then, the envelope-slope ratio (q_j) values are calculated using (37.8) and given in Table 37.8.
The calculation of the C1 criterion value in Table 37.7 is presented as an example.

$$q_{C1} = \frac{0,5957}{1,5701} = 0,3794$$

Finally, the weights (w_j) of the criteria are calculated using Eq. (37.9) and shown in Table 37.9.
The calculation of the value of the C1 criterion in Table 37.9 is presented as an example.

$$w_{C1} = \frac{0,3794}{2.1858} = 0,1736$$

TABLE 37.7 Envelope values of criteria.

	C1	C2	C3	C4	C5	C6
E_j	0,5957	1,3246	0,4080	0,1764	0,3187	0,1715

TABLE 37.8 Envelope-slope ratio values.

	C1	C2	C3	C4	C5	C6	Total
q_j	0,3794	1,4740	0,1584	0,0274	0,1067	0,0400	2,1858

TABLE 37.9 Weight values of the criteria.

	C1	C2	C3	C4	C5	C6	Total
w_j	0,1736	0,6743	0,0725	0,0125	0,0488	0,0183	1,0000

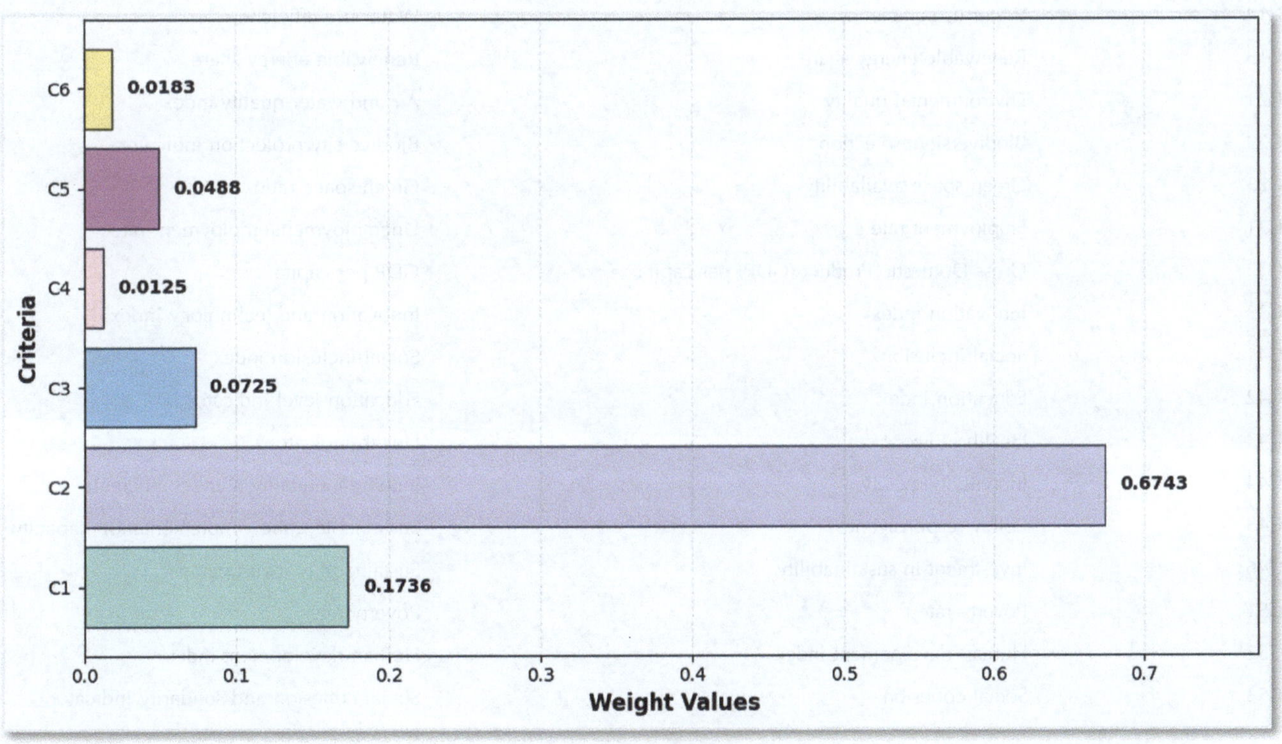

FIGURE 37.1 Weights by envelope and slope method weights for example 1.

The criterion weight values obtained are given in Fig. 37.1.

According to the weight distribution presented in Fig. 37.1, the C2 (number of customers) criterion stands out as the most determining factor in the performance evaluation process, with an absolute weight ratio of 67.43%. This result shows that there is a significantly different value regarding customer portfolio sizes between these two distribution centers, and this factor is playing a very crucial role in determining their final performance. The C1 (shipment volume) factor comes second with a weight percentage value of 17.36%. This result shows that business size and volume are very crucial factors in determining their level of performance, but they are less important when compared to the determinant of customer numbers. The relatively low value regarding the percentage share of other factors to the total weight percentage indicates that this business entity is very concerned about strategic factors like market share sizes and customer portfolio differences during its overall business performance measurement.

37.4.2 Numerical example 2 (complex case)

An international development agency wants to analyze and compare the sustainable development performance achieved by developed countries. The agency also wants to make a comprehensive assessment study to identify the domains where developed countries have scope for improvement. As part of this background, a performance assessment is to be carried out on a total of 20 subindicators pertaining to environment, economy, and social domains. The same is given in Table 37.10.

The primary objective of this research work is to quantitatively determine priority areas that are vital to environmental sustainability, economic equality, and social welfare. Another objective is to formulate recommendations on strategic

TABLE 37.10 Information on evaluation criteria.

Code	Criterion name	Description
C11	Energy productivity	Energy efficiency and resource use
C12	Material productivity	Material/raw material use efficiency
C13	CO_2 emissions per capita	Per capita carbon emissions
C14	Water use efficiency	Water use efficiency
C15	Renewable energy share	Renewable energy share
C21	Environmental quality	Air and water quality index
C22	Biodiversity protection	Biodiversity protection indicator
C23	Green space availability	Green space ratio
C31	Employment rate	Unemployment/employment rate
C32	Gross Domestic Product (GDP) per capita	GDP per capita
C33	Innovation index	Innovation and technology index
C41	Social inclusion	Social inclusion index
C42	Education index	Education level indicator
C43	Health index	Health indicator
C44	Income inequality	Income inequality (Gini coefficient)
C45	Policy responsiveness	Sustainable policy implementation capacity
C46	Investment in sustainability	Sustainability investments
C51	Poverty rate	Poverty rate
C52	Human development index	Human development index
C53	Social cohesion	Social cohesion and solidarity indicator

priorities and allocation using this research. As part of this research, a comparison between these seven developed nations (A1, A2, A3, A4, A5, A6, A7) will be performed according to the values shown in Table 37.11 and objective weighting results concerning the criterion values vital to this research.

The findings obtained by performing the process steps applied for example 1 are given in Table 37.12.

The criterion weight values obtained are given in Fig. 37.2.

The weightage distribution shown in Fig. 37.2 uncovers very interesting results about how much each criterion is to be valued. The result of this analysis has indicated that C11 (energy efficiency 0.2939) and C25 (green area accessibility 0.2604) have higher values on the weightage scale, respectively. As per this research observation, energy efficiency and green area accessibility can play a very important role within this evaluation model. Investment in sustainability (C46 = 0.0811) and Employment Rate (C31 = 0.0771) can both be termed as Medium-High on this priority list. These two measurement perspectives may not actually play very vital roles within this model, but are extremely important and hold tremendous value within this gigantic decision. C15 (renewable energy share 0.0466), C24 (biodiversity conservation 0.0481), and C43 (health index 0.0448) have medium value on this priority list. These results show tremendous promise within this final decision outcome. However, within this model calculation, C32 (GDP per capita 0.0013) and C52 (Human Development Index 0.0003) both show very low values. This implies that this criterion possesses a very marginal role within this theoretical paradigm. This result shows that this sustainability evaluation model is more concerned about the environment. As a matter of fact, almost two very important sustainability criteria are covered within this environmental paradigm. The sensitivity to this economic perspective within this paradigm implies that this sustainability policy is developed on these lines because sustainability is our objective, rather than any GDP advertisement. The second paradigm within social aspects implies that this perspective only takes into account this crucial employment rate value on this priority list. Therefore, on this theoretical paradigm basis, recommendations can be developed so that such sustainability policies can traditionally embrace these two paradigms.

TABLE 37.11 Environmental and resource efficiency of countries.

Country	C11	C12	C13	C14	C15	C21	C22	C23	C31	C32
A1	610,50	5600,00	8,10	16,80	70,00	80,20	6,10	12,00	17,50	85,00
A2	270,00	12500,00	3,50	12,00	25,00	53,00	44,00	1,00	18,00	80,00
A3	600,00	14500,00	3,50	17,00	45,00	47,00	46,00	1,50	29,00	98,00
A4	290,00	15500,00	2,50	19,50	42,00	39,00	54,00	1,10	58,00	97,00
A5	1050,00	12800,00	3,20	7,00	20,00	68,00	25,00	1,50	25,00	82,00
A6	310,00	17500,00	2,40	14,00	44,00	64,00	30,00	1,50	9,00	99,00
A7	4300,00	9500,00	6,50	8,50	20,00	74,00	21,00	2,40	39,00	99,00
Country	C33	C41	C42	C43	C44	C45	C46	C51	C52	C53
A1	86,00	13,00	0,50	4,00	12,00	1,20	9,00	145,00	67,00	1,55
A2	82,00	13,00	0,55	2,00	13,00	2,40	46,00	127,00	62,00	1,90
A3	98,00	14,00	0,60	3,50	20,00	1,70	46,00	125,00	65,00	1,65
A4	95,00	10,00	0,45	3,00	20,00	3,10	6,00	102,00	64,00	1,35
A5	80,00	10,00	0,45	2,60	14,00	1,25	9,00	112,00	60,00	1,40
A6	97,00	12,00	0,50	1,80	12,00	2,10	42,00	135,00	64,00	1,80
A7	76,00	9,00	0,40	0,35	11,00	2,80	20,00	148,00	66,00	1,80

TABLE 37.12 Weights by envelope and slope values for the criteria.

	C11	C12	C13	C14	C15	C21	C22	C23	C31	C32
Δz_j	0,1424	0,0356	0,0504	0,0346	0,0494	0,0254	0,0556	0,1376	0,0658	0,0078
$tan\varphi_j$	1,1700	4,6873	3,3064	4,8126	3,3759	6,5490	2,9953	1,2115	2,5318	21,3750
E_j	1,3520	0,3746	0,5337	0,4534	0,6188	0,2642	0,5670	1,2406	0,7680	0,1084
q_j	1,1555	0,0799	0,1614	0,0942	0,1833	0,0403	0,1893	1,0241	0,3033	0,0051
w_j	0,2939	0,0203	0,0410	0,0240	0,0466	0,0103	0,0481	0,2604	0,0771	0,0013
	C33	C41	C42	C43	C44	C45	C46	C51	C52	C53
Δz_j	0,0094	0,0162	0,0152	0,0556	0,0232	0,0343	0,0590	0,0135	0,0041	0,0126
$tan\varphi_j$	17,7103	10,2800	10,9463	2,9990	7,1918	4,8595	2,8238	12,3327	40,6124	13,2106
E_j	0,1407	0,1747	0,1571	0,5278	0,2395	0,5091	0,9004	0,1335	0,0501	0,1505
q_j	0,0079	0,0170	0,0144	0,1760	0,0333	0,1048	0,3188	0,0108	0,0012	0,0114
w_j	0,0020	0,0043	0,0036	0,0448	0,0085	0,0266	0,0811	0,0028	0,0003	0,0029

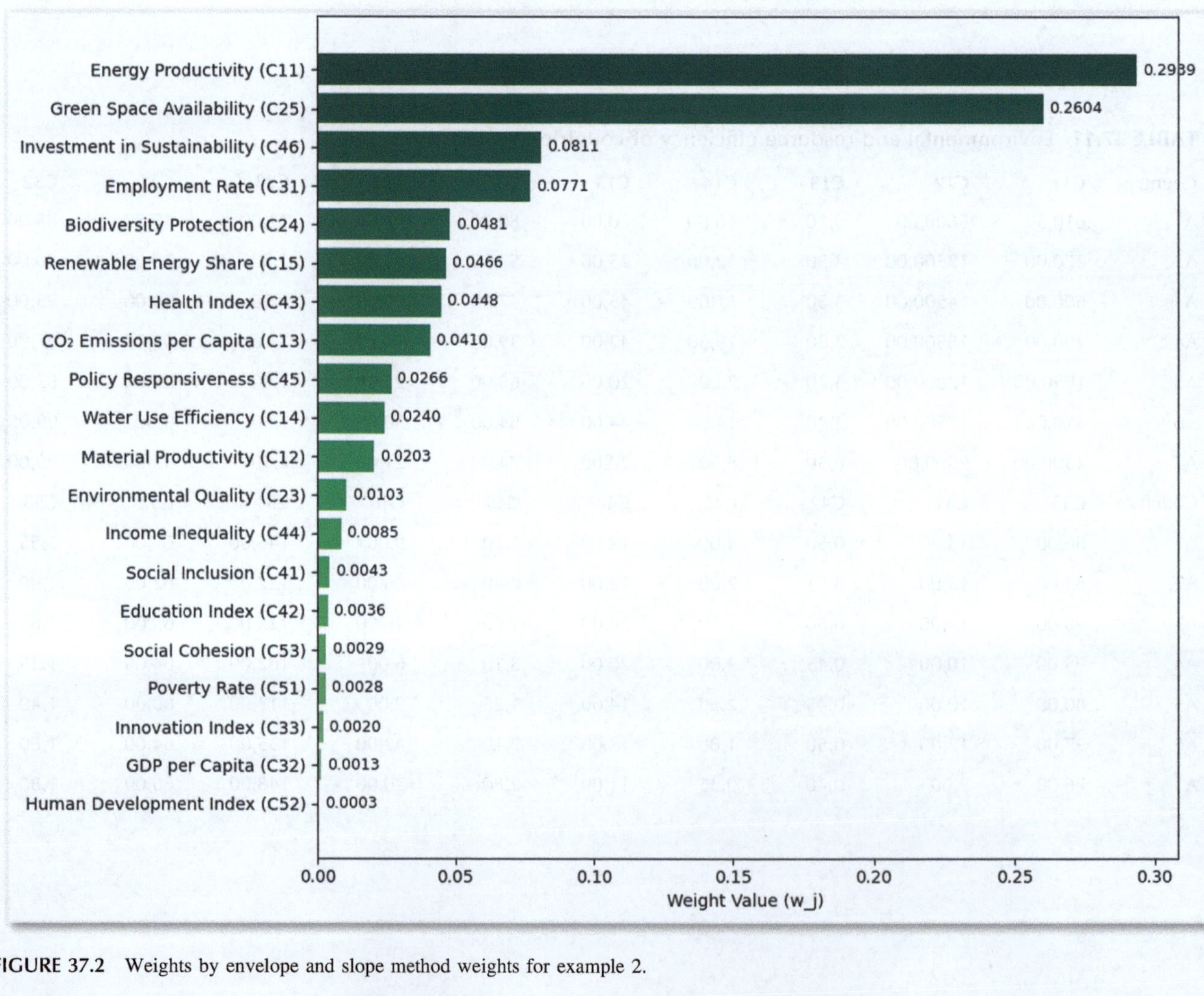

FIGURE 37.2 Weights by envelope and slope method weights for example 2.

The prominence of energy efficiency in this model indicates how important it is to boost funding and policies related to energy efficiency. Emphasis on promoting industrial efficiency projects, enforcing energy efficiency standards, and promoting energy management systems is required.

The fact that the priority level is very high concerning accessibility to green spaces and conserving biodiversity indicates that these issues should receive priority attention within the context of urban planning and environmental policies. It is imperative to increase green space per citizen, design ecological corridors, and employ approaches to urban planning that involve factors related to biodiversity.

The medium–high level of importance attributed to sustainability investments and the rate of employment indicates that synergy can exist between these two factors. Employee training programs and schemes to offer incentives should be developed to increase job opportunities within green economy niches such as renewable energy, the circular economy, and energy efficiency.

That social indicators receive smaller weights within the new approach does not necessarily imply that this policy dimension can and should be disregarded. A decrease in income inequality, social inclusion, and educational opportunities can and should remain on the policy agenda within sustainable development processes.

The results highlighted above can be mapped using a colored policy priority map according to their importance, which is shown in Fig. 37.3.

The color-coded policy priority map shown in Fig. 37.3 is a representation of the priorities concerning the criteria identified. The areas that are colored using shades of red represent the criteria that receive priority, while those colored using shades of green represent those that receive low priority. The results obtained from the analysis show that energy efficiency (C11), accessibility to green spaces (C25), and sustainability funding (C46) have higher priorities.

These results suggest that environment-related variables and long-term initiatives have a very significant role to play within sustainable development policy. Energy efficiency (29.39%) and green space accessibility (26.04%) account for a significant portion of the total weight, while sustainable investments (8.11%) are also at the medium-high priority level.

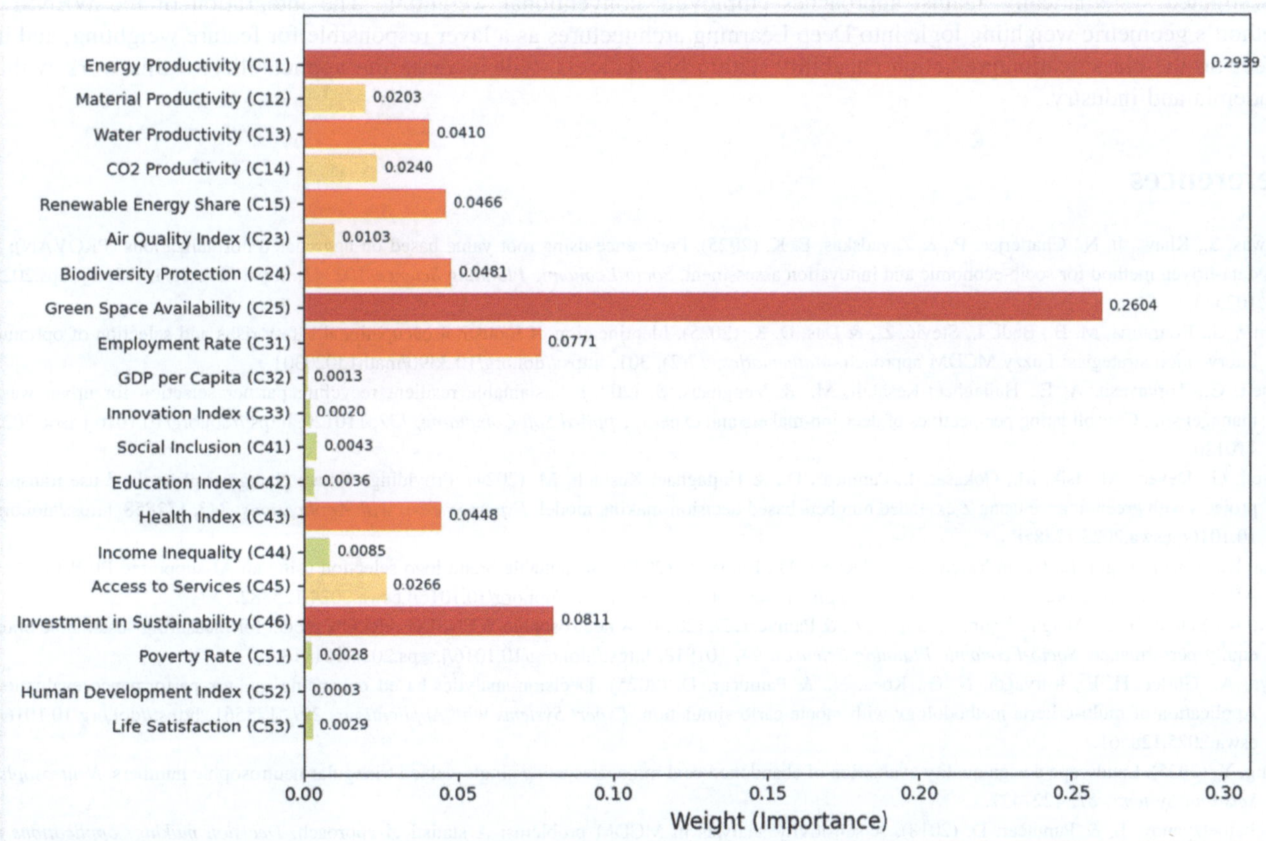

FIGURE 37.3 Policy priority map.

In light of these results, policymakers' resource allocation strategies, energy efficiency improvement projects, and technological innovations, development of urban green infrastructure, increasing accessibility, sustainability-oriented investment programs, and incentive mechanisms.

37.5 Conclusion and future work

In this section, the WENSLO method, developed to overcome the subjectivity problem in determining criteria weights in MCDM problems, is examined in detail through its theoretical foundation and two different case studies. The second difference is that, unlike other subjective weighting approaches, WENSLO uses only the geometric structure of the data because this is the main reason we embarked on this study. From the above analyses, it is shown that, with two geometric variables (envelope and slope) involved simultaneously when assigning weights to criteria, WENSLO provides an absolutely independent method concerning the judgment of the decision-maker when it comes to assigning weights to a decision. This methodological approach has already been proven to work successfully on other case studies, such as calculating the operative capability of regional distribution centers, and it has been successfully implemented to evaluate how countries perform on sustainable development. The outcome shows that WENSLO provides a completely new perspective to the method literature on objective weighting, and it has a great ability to avoid subjective judgment.

Despite the above strengths, there are some drawbacks to WENSLO. These can serve as guidelines for future studies: the geometric nature underlying this method may entail higher computing costs than other linear approaches, particularly when dealing with very large data sets. WENSLO is inherently a weighting approach and requires integration with a hybrid approach such as WENSLO-ARTASI or WENSLO-Ranking of Alternatives with Weights of Criterion (RAWEC) to arrive at a final ranking. Although the efficiency of WENSLO has been proven using crisp data within this study, the fuzzy extensions of WENSLO need to be employed for direct implementation on uncertain domains like type-2 neutral.

Despite these constraints, some unique research avenues can and should be pursued: to make the WENSLO method more relevant to big problems, there is a need to improve the efficiency of this method by utilizing parallel processors or quantum optimization algorithms. The resistance to reversals in WENSLO method-based hybrid approaches has to be investigated systematically against approaches employing conventional weighting. The integration of the WENSLO method's geometric weighting logic into Deep Learning architectures as a layer responsible for feature weighting, and its effect on the classification/prediction capability within big datasets, will increase the applicability of this work within academia and industry.

References

Biswas, S., Khawash, N., Chatterjee, P., & Zavadskas, E. K. (2025). Preference using root value based on aggregated normalizations (PROVAN): A data-driven method for socio-economic and innovation assessment. *Socio-Economic Planning Sciences*102343. https://doi.org/10.1016/j.seps.2025.102343.

Demir, G., Bouraima, M. B., Badi, I., Stević, Ž., & Das, D. K. (2025). Identification of Industrial occupational safety risks and selection of optimum intervention strategies: Fuzzy MCDM approach. *Mathematics, 13*(2), 301. https://doi.org/10.3390/math13020301.

Haseli, G., Torkayesh, A. E., Hajiaghaei-Keshteli, M., & Venghaus, S. (2023). Sustainable resilient recycling partner selection for urban waste management: Consolidating perspectives of decision-makers and experts. *Applied Soft Computing, 137*, 110120. https://doi.org/10.1016/j.asoc.2023.110120.

Haseli, G., Deveci, M., Isik, M., Gokasar, I., Pamučar, D., & Hajiaghaei-Keshteli, M. (2024). Providing climate change resilient land-use transport projects with green finance using Z extended numbers based decision-making model. *Expert Systems with Applications, 243*, 122858. https://doi.org/10.1016/j.eswa.2023.122858.

Kara, K., Akagün Ergin, E., Cihan Yalçın, G., ... Deveci, M., Kadry, S. (2025). Sustainable brand logo selection using an AI-supported PF-WENSLO-ARLON hybrid method. *Expert Systems with Applications, 260*, 125382. https://doi.org/10.1016/j.eswa.2024.125382.

Kara, K., Yalçın, G. C., Akagün Ergin, E., Simic, V., & Pamučar, D. (2024). A neutrosophic WENSLO-ARLON model for measuring sustainable brand equity performance. *Socio-Economic Planning Sciences, 94*, 101918. https://doi.org/10.1016/j.seps.2024.101918.

Kaya, A., Gürler, H. E., Karyağdı, N. G., Koca, N., & Pamučar, D. (2025). Decision-analytics-based enhancing auditor performance evaluation: Application of multi-criteria methodology with monte carlo simulation. *Expert Systems with Applications, 291*, 128561. https://doi.org/10.1016/j.eswa.2025.128561.

Liang, Y. (2025). Landscape design quality evaluation of abandoned coal mine sites using single-valued triangular neutrosophic numbers. *Neutrosophic Sets and Systems, 81*, 422–437.

Mukhametzyanov, I., & Pamučar, D. (2018). A sensitivity analysis in MCDM problems: A statistical approach. *Decision making: applications in management and engineering, 1*(2), 51–80. https://doi.org/10.31181/dmame1802050m.

Mukhametzyanov, I. (2021). Specific character of objective methods for determining weights of criteria in MCDM problems: Entropy, CRITIC, and SD. *Decision Making: Applications in Management and Engineering, 4*(2), 76–105. https://doi.org/10.31181/dmame210402076i.

Pamučar, D., Ecer, F., Gligoric, Z., Gligoric, M., & Deveci, M. (2024). A Novel WENSLO and ALWAS multicriteria methodology and its application to green growth performance evaluation. *IEEE Transactions on Engineering Management, 71*, 9510–9525. https://doi.org/10.1109/TEM.2023.3321697.

Pamučar, D., Özçalıcı, M., & Gürler, H. E. (2025). Evaluation of the efficiency of world airports using WENSLO-ARTASI and monte-carlo simulation. *Journal of Air Transport Management, 124*, 102749. https://doi.org/10.1016/j.jairtraman.2025.102749.

Peng, X., Yu, L., & Wu, X. (2025). q-Rung orthopair fuzzy multi-criteria decision-making method for Internet of things platforms selection. *Engineering Applications of Artificial Intelligence, 148*, 110336. https://doi.org/10.1016/j.engappai.2025.110336.

Singh, M., & Pant, M. (2021). A review of selected weighing methods in MCDM with a case study. *International Journal of System Assurance Engineering and Management, 12*(1), 126–144. https://doi.org/10.1007/s13198-020-01033-3.

Trung, D. D., Ersoy, N., Mai, N. T., & Thinh, H. X. (2025). Applying MCDM methods for electric vehicle selection: A comparative study between CRADIS and PIV methods. *Journal of Applied Engineering Science, 23*(2), 345–358. https://doi.org/10.5937/jaes0-56793.

Zhang, M., & Li, L. (2025). Balancing Usability and protection: A decision-making approach to computer network security evaluation using the neutrosophic fuzzy dombi operator. *Neutrosophic Sets and Systems, 83*, 659–675.

Chapter 38

COBRAC: Comparisons between ranked criteria for multi-attribute decision-making

Dragan Pamucar[1,2,3], Sanjib Biswas[4], and Aparajita Sanyal[4]
[1]*Department of Operations Research and Statistics, Faculty of Organizational Sciences, University of Belgrade, Belgrade, Serbia,* [2]*UNEC Applied Artificial Intelligence Research Center, Azerbaijan State University of Economics (UNEC), Baku, Azerbaijan,* [3]*Faculty of Engineering, Dogus University, Istanbul, Türkiye,* [4]*Amity Business School, Amity University Kolkata, Kolkata, West Bengal, India*

38.1 Introduction

In the rapidly evolving technological landscape, effective decision-making is crucial for corporate success. Nevertheless, intricate circumstances and impediments frequently surpass human analytical capacities. Consequently, innovative solutions are needed to enhance decision-making processes, enabling individuals and organizations to make informed, comprehensive, and deliberate judgments in this rapidly changing environment (Giang & Thinh, 2025). Multicriteria decision-making (MCDM) techniques facilitate complex judgments in uncertain contexts involving diverse stakeholders. MCDM methodologies are very adaptable and efficient in addressing diverse practical challenges, having been effectively used across several domains. One of the essential features of MCDM methods involves allocating weights to choice factors based on their perceived importance or analytical evaluation. Objective weighting methodologies employ information-theoretic concepts, whereas subjective weighting techniques emphasize expert opinions, preferences, or perceptions to influence the weighting process (Chakraborty et al., 2023; Kizielewicz et al., 2024; Więckowski et al., 2023).

Subjective weighing, originating from direct rating, point allocation, and fundamental pairwise comparison models, has progressed as it acknowledges that objective approaches frequently overlook context-specific information, stakeholder values, and qualitative nuances. Subjective weighting techniques enhance decision-making clarity and stakeholder approval by enabling experts to evaluate and assign weights to criteria. This method facilitates more nuanced assessments in particular contexts, rendering it essential in a rapidly changing business landscape. Integrating expert knowledge with sophisticated analytical approaches, subjective weighting methods are crucial for modern decision-making tools, facilitating more precise, efficient, and accurate resolutions to complicated issues and varied challenges (Kizielewicz et al., 2024).

Initially, techniques such as the analytic hierarchy process (AHP) (Saaty, 1980) were employed to determine relative weights. The decision-making trial and evaluation laboratory (DEMATEL) (Gabus & Fontela, 1972) was another contemporary method that has been widely used in determining the interrelationships among criteria and their weights. However, as the domain of MCDM evolved, issues such as cognitive overload, inconsistency, and subjective complexity emerged. Techniques such as the stepwise weight assessment ratio analysis (SWARA) (Keršuliene et al., 2010), best–worst method (BWM) (Rezaei, 2015), full consistency method (FUCOM) (Pamučar et al., 2018), level based weight assessment (LBWA) (Žižović & Pamucar, 2019), along with contemporary methodologies such as pivot pairwise relative criteria importance assessment (Stanujkic et al., 2021), and soft-clusters rectangles (Zakeri et al., 2025) have been formulated to tackle these challenges. The recent decade has witnessed a marked acceleration in the theoretical advancement and practical application of these methods, driven by digital transformation, increased group decision-making contexts, and the need for the systematic utilization of expert knowledge while maintaining cognitive manageability and methodological accuracy.

The comparisons between ranked criteria (COBRAC) approach was developed (Pamucar et al., 2024) to overcome the shortcomings of conventional MCDM methods, particularly in complex scenarios such as selecting big data platforms for

Encyclopedia of Multi-Attribute Decision-Making (MADM). DOI: https://doi.org/10.1016/B978-0-443-33275-3.00096-8

large enterprises. Traditional approaches need long pairwise evaluations, demonstrate inconsistency, and impose cognitive strain. COBRAC offers a mathematically coherent and cognitively efficient approach for establishing criterion weights amidst multiple diverse criteria, while also addressing the challenges of subjectivity and inconsistency inherent in conventional pairwise comparison techniques, such as AHP or BWM. Nonetheless, these procedures often require extensive pairwise comparison matrices, which can impair efficiency as the number of criteria increases, thereby increasing the likelihood of inconsistency, inducing respondent fatigue, and undermining the reliability of expert assessments. In practical situations, specialists may only evaluate connections among closely related criteria, rendering remote comparisons more prone to mistakes. Studies indicate that human assessors face difficulties in consistently conducting paired evaluations across numerous criteria, a limitation rooted in cognitive psychology (Miller, 1956).

The COBRAC method offers several advantages.

- The significant benefit of using the COBRAC method is the number of pairwise comparisons. The COBRAC method utilizes (n - 1) number of localized sequential pairwise comparisons, which is much lower than AHP [n(n - 1)/2], BWM (2n - 3), and DEMATEL [n(n - 1)]. This helps in understanding each criterion's contributions locally and globally through a smaller number of pairwise comparisons.
- The COBRAC approach is an innovative methodology that facilitates pairwise comparisons across sequentially rated criteria, hence alleviating cognitive burden on professionals. This renders the approach feasible even when several elements are considered, a prevalent challenge in contemporary technology selection or risk assessment scenarios.
- COBRAC's mathematical architecture guarantees transitivity and consistency in the weight coefficient set, alleviating prevalent issues such as inconsistency and rank reversal. It precisely reflects systematic, gradual evaluations by experts based on increasingly important criteria. COBRAC has considerable resilience across several domains, integrating both subjective expert assessments and objective data for criteria weighting.
- It integrates effortlessly into group decision-making frameworks such as the Delphi method and is resistant to rank reversal problems.
- The algorithm of the COBRAC is easy to use and explain. It helps the decision-makers to formulate the COBRAC based models for various types of problems. COBRAC's computational algorithm enables researchers to quickly manage and analyze extensive datasets with a large number of respondents.

The methodology combines computational efficiency, objectivity, and intuitive transparency, making it suitable for practical use in domains characterized by complexity, uncertainty, and other evaluative factors that hinder traditional MCDM methods. Table 38.1 outlines the differences between COBRAC and various other methods briefly.

This chapter aims to demonstrate the applications of the COBRAC method in two contemporary research problems related to consumer behavior regarding green products. This study examines the COBRAC method in two distinct yet thematically linked case studies: "Green Pressure and Eco-Friendly Consumer Behavior" and "Greenwashing Perceptions and Corporate Accountability." Customers in developed nations primarily valued ecologically sustainable products more (Bekk et al., 2016). As a result, a large number of business units have initiated special attention towards sustainable approaches (Jayaraman et al., 2023). This depicts the picture of firms' constant pressure to portray their green image. On the other hand, this creates pressure among customers, also influenced by societal factors, to demonstrate their green buying intentions. The firms take the path of greenwashing (GW) by making false green claims due to a lack of authentic effort. The present work aims to understand consumer behavior from a sustainability perspective. In recent days, publicity terms such as "green", "eco", or "sustainable" have been buzzing. As a result, sustainability has become a corporate priority for industries, rather than a commercial choice (Ghosh, 2019). The business units practice greening for several reasons, including law enforcement, strategic benefits, senior leadership programs, green pressure (GP) (Sanyal & Sur, 2023), and stakeholder pressure (Chen, 2008; Singh et al., 2022). At the same time, we posit that due to heightened ecological awareness among stakeholders, many sectors have incorporated green products into their product ranges as substitutes for other "non-green" products (Gelderman et al., 2021). This contributes to the development of "greenwash" (Delmas & Burbano, 2011), a process that misleadingly presents customers with false green claims (Tarabieh, 2021). In this context, the present study has considered two case studies: one on GP and another on GW.

The COBRAC technique provides insights into consumer behavior about green products by evaluating and prioritizing aspects that affect purchasing decisions. The method's mathematical rigor underpins evidence-based approaches to sustainable consumption, linking psychological motivations to market behaviors in the green goods sector, thereby enhancing the understanding of consumer decision-making in eco-conscious markets.

The remaining part of this chapter is organized as follows. Section 38.2 outlines the applications of the COBRAC method in various research problems. Section 38.3 elucidates the procedural steps of the COBRAC method. Section 38.4 describes the first case study. It states the research problem and discusses the data collection process. Then, it

TABLE 38.1 Comparison of the comparisons between ranked criteria (COBRAC) method with other models.

Method	No. of comparisons	Computational complexity	Initial ordering	Consistency check	Intercriteria causal modeling	No. of criteria
Analytic hierarchy process	[n(n - 1)/2]	High	No	Consistency ratio	No	Low
Best–worst method	(2n - 3)	High	Yes (best/worst)	Optimization	No	Moderate
Full consistency method	(n - 1)	Moderate to low	Yes	Yes	No	High
Stepwise weight assessment ratio analysis	(n - 1)	Low	Yes	No	No	High
Pivot pairwise relative criteria importance assessment	(n - 1)	Low	Yes	No	No	High
Decision-making trial and evaluation laboratory	n(n - 1)	High	No	NA	Yes	Low
COBRAC	(n - 1)	Low	Yes	Yes	No	High

("n" is the number of criteria).

demonstrates the application of the COBRAC method. Finally, it provides an insightful discussion on the results. Similarly, Section 38.5 provides details about the second case study and illustrates the application of the COBRAC method. Section 38.6 reports the validation of the COBRAC results. Section 38.7 concludes the chapter and highlights some potential future research agendas.

38.2 Literature review

This section presents a brief overview of the research contributions that used the COBRAC method. There has not been extensive research work utilizing the COBRAC method. The developers (Pamucar et al., 2024) proposed a hybrid COBRAC-alternative ranking technique based on adaptive standardized intervals (ARTASI) model for selecting big data platforms within specified intervals. This methodology simplifies complexity, removes subjective bias, and prioritizes the significance of criteria. It preserves ranking consistency and computing efficiency, in contrast to conventional MCDM approaches. COBRAC's partnership with ARTASI enhances decision sensitivity to defined indicators, making it a flexible instrument for technology adoption decisions in rapidly evolving digital landscapes. Extending the conventional COBRAC method, the study by Biswas et al. (2024) introduced a p, q-quasirung orthopair fuzzy framework for evaluating technology adoption within the sugarcane supply chain, emphasizing the variables that propel digital transformation in agricultural environments. The model addresses linguistic ambiguity, but its subjectivity remains due to the parameter settings. The COBRAC method ensures robustness through a criterion-ordering approach, facilitating explicit prioritization that is independent of membership attributes. Incorporating COBRAC into fuzzy systems helps diminish parameter sensitivity, yielding dependable evaluations of technology adoption variables.

In a recent study (Dağıstanlı, 2025), the author exemplified one of the initial direct implementations of COBRAC, coupled with p, q-quasirung orthopair fuzzy logic, to evaluate the stages of military cyber operations. It illustrates COBRAC's capacity to manage hierarchical and intricate strategic contexts by integrating ranking transparency with a nuanced approach to uncertainty. The efficacy of COBRAC is evident in maintaining operational priorities that are coherent, comprehensible, and adaptable in response to rapidly changing defensive environments. In contrast to exclusively fuzzy or weight-based models, COBRAC maintains methodological clarity in evaluating interconnected cyber processes, hence affirming its appropriateness for defense strategy. The research provides robust confirmation of the significance of COBRAC in critical, uncertainty-laden decision-making contexts.

Scholars (Özçalıcı et al., 2025) employed data-driven decision analysis in textile manufacturing, concentrating on cost allocation, process mapping, and efficiency enhancement. It offers insights into industrial digitization; yet, it is predominantly quantitative and overlooks qualitative trade-offs. COBRAC could enhance the study by selecting cost factors according to managerial preferences. The method emphasizes ordinal evaluations, taking into account intangible factors such as sustainability and digital readiness, leading to more thorough assessments of industrial performance. Biswas et al. (2025) examined the incorporation of quantum cryptography within digital supply chains through a q-rung orthopair fuzzy framework. It assesses security, cost, governance, and technological limitations. The model's focus on fuzzy aggregation may conceal the significance of barriers. The COBRAC methodology has the potential to enhance this strategy by optimizing barrier prioritization with minimal computing effort. Integrating COBRAC with sophisticated fuzzy models may enhance management clarity and help digital supply chains overcome significant challenges.

The literature review highlights the following observations.

- The use of the COBRAC method still needs to be explored in diverse fields. For example, areas such as agriculture, sustainable development, consumer psychology, quality management, behavioral sciences, and technology management, among others, still require exploration of the COBRAC method.
- There is a limited number of extensions of the COBRAC method using fuzzy and rough sets.

38.3 Methodology

This section outlines the procedural steps of the COBRAC method (Pamucar et al., 2024) applied in the case studies described in this chapter.

38.3.1 Notations

$C_{(j)}$ denotes the criteria or variables whose weights are to be computed ($j = 1, 2, .., n$)

$E_{(k)}$ represents the kth respondent ($k = 1, 2, \ldots, m$)

φ_{jk} is the rating of the jth criterion or variable by the kth respondent

ω_k is the priority weight of the kth respondent
ζ_j is the aggregated weighted rating (AWR) of the jth criterion or variable

Step 1. Identify the variables or criteria in the context of the research problem.
Step 2. Selection of the respondents.
Step 3. Determine the weights of the respondents.
The weights are determined based on the education and experience of the respondents as suggested by various scholars (Bošković et al., 2025; Kara et al., 2024). The weights of the respondents are determined through the following sequential steps.
Step 3(a). Determine the weights of the respondents based on their education level.

$$\omega_k^{Edu} = \frac{\gamma_k^{Edu}}{\sum_{k=1}^{m} \gamma_k^{Edu}} \tag{38.1}$$

γ_k^{Edu} is the rating score value based on education level (1: undergraduate, 2: postgraduate, 3: Ph.D).
Step 3(b). Determine the weights of the respondents based on their experience.

$$\omega_k^{Exp} = \frac{\gamma_k^{Exp}}{\sum_{k=1}^{m} \gamma_k^{Exp}} \tag{38.2}$$

γ_k^{Exp} = Score value based on experience level.
Step 3(c). Determine the final weights of the respondents.
The final weights of the respondents are obtained by aggregating the values from the previous steps using the Heron mean, as follows.

$$\psi_k = \lambda\left(\omega_k^{Edu}\omega_k^{Exp}\right)^{1/2} + (1-\lambda)\left(\frac{\omega_k^{Edu} + \omega_k^{Exp}}{2}\right) \tag{38.3}$$

$$\omega_k = \frac{\psi_k}{\sum_{k=1}^{m} \psi_k} \tag{38.4}$$

Here, $\lambda \in [0, 1]$ is a scalar coefficient, used to examine the sensitivity of the model to decision-makers' experience and education levels. For the initial case, we set $\lambda = 0.5$.
Step 4. Obtain the AWR of the criteria.
The AWR values are obtained by aggregating the weighted rating scores (WRSs) of the criteria by all respondents.

$$\zeta_j = \sum_{k=1}^{m} \alpha_{jk} \tag{38.5}$$

$$\alpha_{jk} = \varphi_{jk}\omega_k \tag{38.6}$$

Step 5. Apply the steps of the conventional COBRAC method to determine the weight values of the criteria or variables and rank them.
Step 5 (a). Ranking of the criteria or variables.
First, we sort the criteria or variables in descending order and rank them. The most significant criterion or variable is ranked first, and subsequently, all others are ranked. The most significant criterion is the one that influences the decision-making more than others. Thus at this step, the relative importances of all criteria are evaluated. In this problem, the criterion or variable that has the highest AWR value is ranked first. In general, it is expressed as $C_{j(1)} > C_{j(2)} > \ldots > C_{j(r)}$, where, $r \in [1, n]$ is the rank of the criteria. Example,
Let us assume that there are four criteria. The criterion C_3 is the most important, followed by C_2, C_1 and C_4. Then the order of importance will be $C_{3(1)} > C_{2(2)} > C_{1(3)} > C_{4(4)}$. The values in the bracket indicate the rank of the corresponding criterion.
Step 5 (b). Pairwise comparison of the criteria.
At this stage, we form several sequential pairs starting from the most significant one till the least significant criterion. Within each pair, the corresponding criteria are compared according to their share of contributions.
In the previous example, C_3 and C_2 form a local pair. Suppose the score values of C_3 and C_2 are 0.8 and 0.7, respectively. Then, the relative contribution of C_3, i.e., the preference value of C_3 compared to C_2 is $\frac{0.8}{0.8+0.7} = 0.5333$,

i.e., 53.33%. Therefore the contribution or preference value of C_2 is $1 - 0.5333 = 0.4667$, i.e., 46.67%. A similar calculation is done for each of the other local pairs, i.e., (C_2, C_1) and (C_1, C_4). Thus the COBRAC method requires $(n - 1) = (4 - 1) = 3$ comparisons.

Extending the concept, in general, $\xi_{1,2}$, …, $\xi_{n-1,n}$ denote the preference values ($\xi \in [0, 1]$) assigned to the first and second ranked criteria, to the second-to-last and last ranked criteria.

Step 5 (c). Calculation of the weights of the criteria or variables.

The COBRAC method conducts $(n - 1)$ number of pairwise comparisons for n variables. To check the full consistency in the weight calculations, the following $(n - 1)$ number of relationships are formulated given as below.

$$\begin{aligned} &w_1: w_2 = \xi_{1,2}: (1 - \xi_{1,2}); \\ &\ldots \\ &w_{n-1}: w_n = \xi_{n-1,n}: (1 - \xi_{n-1,n}) \end{aligned} \tag{38.7}$$

The COBRAC method satisfies the condition of transitivity. Accordingly, from Eq. 38.7, we can derive the following equation (Eq. 38.8) under full consistency.

$$\frac{w_{n-1}}{w_n} - \frac{\xi_{n-1,n}}{(1 - \xi_{n-1,n})} = 0 \tag{38.8}$$

However, in real life, deviations from consistency are inevitable. The objective is to minimize such deviations. In other words,

$$\left| \frac{w_{n-1}}{w_n} - \frac{\xi_{n-1,n}}{(1 - \xi_{n-1,n})} \right| \leq 0; \; j = 1, 2 \ldots n \tag{38.9}$$

(38.9) can be transformed into the objective function, set as follows:

$$\begin{aligned} &\min_j \max \left\{ \left| \frac{w_{n-1}}{w_n} - \frac{\xi_{n-1,n}}{(1 - \xi_{n-1,n})} \right| \right\} \\ &s.\,t. \\ &\textstyle\sum_{j=1}^{n} w_j = 1; \; w_j \geq 0 \; \forall \, j \end{aligned} \tag{38.10}$$

Accordingly, a mixed integer nonlinear programming (MINLP) model is formulated as follows to calculate the weights of the criteria or variables.

$$\begin{aligned} &Min \chi \\ &s.\,t. \\ &\left| \frac{w_{n-1}}{w_n} - \frac{\xi_{n-1,n}}{(1 - \xi_{n-1,n})} \right| \leq \chi, \; \forall \, j \\ &\textstyle\sum_{j=1}^{n} w_j = 1; \; w_j \geq 0 \; \forall \, j \end{aligned} \tag{38.11}$$

38.4 Numerical example 1

38.4.1 Case study 1: antecedents of green pressure

This study explores various factors of GP, which a consumer faces to prove individual to "act environmentally friendly." This pressure is generated from various stakeholders to buy different green products. This aligns with the perceived behavioral control of the theory of planned behavior (TPB) (Ajzen, 1991). This pressure is generated by society or community, the reference group, and the government, which customers adopt to demonstrate their transparency in environmental and social issues (Singh et al., 2022). This is consistent with recent empirical evidence demonstrating that GP triggers customers to adopt sustainable consumption patterns (Sanyal & Sur, 2023). Consumers' buying behavior is influenced by various social, cultural, personal, and psychological factors. In the marketing aspect, and based on social influence theory (Gong et al., 2023), socialization is the process that teaches people to behave in a manner accepted by society (Schiffman et al., 2013). This societal teaching encourages customers to adopt an eco-friendly approach. We aim to prioritize the antecedents of the GP. The antecedents (listed in Table 38.2) are identified through a literature review.

TABLE 38.2 Description of the antecedents of green pressure (GP).

S/L	Description of the variables	References
GP1	There are government regulations and initiatives for reducing environmental impact.	Jyothi and Mohan (2025), Gu (2024)
GP2	My family, friends, and neighbors have started using eco-friendly food items.	Zhuang et al. (2021), Islam et al. (2024), Barbu et al. (2022)
GP3	Eco-friendly promotions and campaigns motivate me to buy green products.	Sharma et al. (2023), Ogunmola and Kumar (2024), Ngo et al. (2025)
GP4	Everyone around me talks about green food items.	Zhuang et al. (2021), Islam et al. (2024)
GP5	I give value to environmentally friendly behaviors in daily life.	Zhuang et al. (2021), Mustafa et al. (2022), Barbu et al. (2022)
GP6	I believe that the use of green products helps to protect the environment.	Jyothi and Mohan (2025), Zhuang et al. (2021), Ngo et al. (2025)

They are grounded in the theoretical foundations of the TPB (Ajzen, 1991) and the value-belief-norm (VBN) Theory (Stern et al., 1999).

38.4.2 Data collection

This research was conducted in urban areas. The respondents were selected conveniently through the snowball sampling method. Initially, we approached 30 such respondents. However, after scrutinizing the missing value, 25 was considered. To maintain heterogeneity in the respondent profile, we have ultimately selected 20 individuals. These respondents have substantial experience in using green products and possess in-depth knowledge about them. Table 38.3 presents a summary of the profiles of the 20 respondents.

The experience encompasses the number of years they have been using green products and their level of knowledge about these items. We considered the respondents who have at least 3 years of experience with frequent use of green products (medium: 3 to 5 years; high: 5 to 8 years; very high: more than 8 years). The categorization of the respondents in terms of their use of green products satisfies the credibility requirement of TÜV rheinland green product mark criteria[1] and also found in the literature (Cam, 2023; Zhuang et al., 2021). The responses were collected using a 5-point Likert scale (1: strongly disagree, 5: strongly agree). The responses were collected both offline and through telephonic conversations.

38.4.3 Analysis and results

This section provides the results of the data analysis. First, we determine the weights of the respondents. As previously discussed, the weights of the respondents are calculated based on their experience and educational level. Eqs. 38.1–38.3 are applied to determine the weights. Table 38.14 (Appendix A) exhibits the details of the calculation of respondents' weights. As previously stated, λ is considered to be 0.5 for the initial condition, giving equal priority to education and experience.

The respondents' ratings of the antecedents of GP (i.e., GP1, GP2, ..., GP6) are made using a 5-point Likert scale, as shown in Table 38.4. Then, we obtain the WRS values for each GP (Table 38.5). To this end, the rating of each GP is multiplied by the corresponding respondent's weight. For example, the WRS values for GP1 are calculated as follows.

$$\alpha_{11} = \varphi_{11}\omega_1 = 4 \times 0.064 = 0.256; \alpha_{12} = \varphi_{12}\omega_2 = 1 \times 0.052 = 0.052$$
$$\alpha_{18} = \varphi_{18}\omega_8 = 3 \times 0.0648 = 0.1944$$

1. tuev-rheinland-green-product-mark-writing-instruments-and-cosmetic-pens-criteria-catalog-enPDF (www.tuv.com).

TABLE 38.3 Summary of respondents' profile.

Respondent ID	Current industry	Gender	Experience	Education	Occupation
1	Healthcare	Female	Very high	PG	Private sector employee
2	Healthcare	Female	High	PG	Public sector employee
3	Retail	Male	Very high	PG	Private sector employee
4	Retail	Male	High	PG	Private sector employee
5	Automobile	Female	High	PG	Public sector employee
6	Hospitality and tourism	Male	Very high	PhD	Private sector employee
7	Real estate	Male	Medium	UG	Private sector employee
8	Marketing and advertising	Male	High	PhD	Private sector employee
9	Transportation and logistics	Female	Medium	PhD	Private sector employee
10	Real estate	Male	Very high	UG	Self-employed
11	General insurance	Male	Very high	UG	Self-employed
12	Non-governmental organization (NGO)	Female	High	UG	Self-employed
13	Real estate	Male	Very high	UG	Private sector employee
14	Media and entertainment	Male	Medium	PG	Private sector employee
15	Professional services	Male	High	PhD	Private sector employee
16	Telecommunications	Male	Medium	PG	Private sector employee
17	IT	Female	High	UG	Private sector employee
18	Agriculture	Female	Very high	UG	Public sector employee
19	Professional services	Male	Medium	PG	Private sector employee
20	Finance	Male	High	PG	Private sector employee

Now, we proceed to obtain the AWR of the criteria (Eq. 38.5). The AWR values are obtained by aggregating the WRSs of the criteria by all respondents. For example,

$$\zeta_1 = \sum_{k=1}^{20} \alpha_{jk} = \alpha_{11} + \alpha_{12} + \ldots + \alpha_{18} + \ldots + \alpha_{1(20)} = 0.256 + 0.052 + \ldots + 0.194 + \ldots + 0.156 = 3.0235$$

$$\zeta_2 = 3.4116;\ \zeta_3 = 3.4393;\ \zeta_4 = 3.1075;\ \zeta_5 = 4.0493;\ \zeta_6 = 3.6549$$

Next, we apply the steps of the conventional COBRAC method to determine the weight values of the GP antecedents and rank them. To this end, first, we sort the GPs based on their AWR values. In this example, GP5 is identified as the most significant antecedent based on the AWR value ($\zeta = 4.0493$). Then, we conduct pairwise comparisons and assign preference values to each antecedent. For example,

$$\xi_{5,6} = \frac{\zeta_5}{\zeta_5 + \zeta_6} = \frac{4.0493}{4.0493 + 3.6549} = 0.5256$$

$$\Rightarrow 1 - \xi_{5,6} = 1 - 0.5256 = 0.4744$$

Therefore the assigned value to GP5 is $\frac{\xi_{5,6}}{1 - \xi_{5,6}} = \frac{0.5256}{0.4744} = 1.1079$

Similarly,

$$\xi_{6,3} = \frac{\zeta_6}{\zeta_6 + \zeta_3} = \frac{3.6549}{3.6549 + 3.4393} = 0.5152$$

$$\Rightarrow 1 - \xi_{6,3} = 1 - 0.5152 = 0.4848$$

Hence, the assigned value to GP6 is $\frac{\xi_{6,3}}{1 - \xi_{6,3}} = \frac{0.5152}{0.4848} = 1.0627$

TABLE 38.4 Rating of the antecedents of green pressure (GP).

Resp. weight	**0.0640**	**0.0520**	**0.0640**	**0.0520**	**0.0520**	**0.0781**	**0.0260**	**0.0648**	**0.0494**	**0.0477**
Respondent/ antecedent	**1**	**2**	**3**	**4**	**5**	**6**	**7**	**8**	**9**	**10**
GP1	4	1	1	3	1	3	5	3	5	3
GP2	3	1	5	2	2	3	5	5	3	5
GP3	4	1	2	1	5	3	4	3	3	4
GP4	1	1	4	1	4	3	4	3	3	3
GP5	4	5	1	4	4	5	1	5	5	5
GP6	3	5	1	4	4	5	5	3	3	3
Resp. weight	**0.0477**	**0.0375**	**0.0477**	**0.0383**	**0.0648**	**0.0383**	**0.0375**	**0.0477**	**0.0383**	**0.0520**
Respondent/ antecedent	**11**	**12**	**13**	**14**	**15**	**16**	**17**	**18**	**19**	**20**
GP1	4	1	3	5	3	3	3	5	3	3
GP2	4	1	2	5	3	5	5	4	2	4
GP3	5	5	3	4	3	5	5	5	2	4
GP4	5	1	4	5	3	4	5	5	3	2
GP5	5	3	2	5	5	5	4	5	2	4
GP6	2	3	4	3	5	3	4	5	3	5

TABLE 38.5 Weighted rating scores of the antecedents.

Respondent/ antecedent	**1**	**2**	**3**	**4**	**5**	**6**	**7**	**8**	**9**	**10**
GP1	0.2559	0.0520	0.0640	0.1561	0.0520	0.2342	0.1301	0.1944	0.2469	0.1432
GP2	0.1919	0.0520	0.3199	0.1041	0.1041	0.2342	0.1301	0.3240	0.1481	0.2386
GP3	0.2559	0.0520	0.1279	0.0520	0.2602	0.2342	0.1041	0.1944	0.1481	0.1909
GP4	0.0640	0.0520	0.2559	0.0520	0.2081	0.2342	0.1041	0.1944	0.1481	0.1432
GP5	0.2559	0.2602	0.0640	0.2081	0.2081	0.3903	0.0260	0.3240	0.2469	0.2386
GP6	0.1919	0.2602	0.0640	0.2081	0.2081	0.3903	0.1301	0.1944	0.1481	0.1432
Respondent/ antecedent	**11**	**12**	**13**	**14**	**15**	**16**	**17**	**18**	**19**	**20**
GP1	0.1909	0.0375	0.1432	0.1916	0.1944	0.1150	0.1125	0.2386	0.1150	0.1561
GP2	0.1909	0.0375	0.0955	0.1916	0.1944	0.1916	0.1875	0.1909	0.0766	0.2081
GP3	0.2386	0.1875	0.1432	0.1533	0.1944	0.1916	0.1875	0.2386	0.0766	0.2081
GP4	0.2386	0.0375	0.1909	0.1916	0.1944	0.1533	0.1875	0.2386	0.1150	0.1041
GP5	0.2386	0.1125	0.0955	0.1916	0.3240	0.1916	0.1500	0.2386	0.0766	0.2081
GP6	0.0955	0.1125	0.1909	0.1150	0.3240	0.1150	0.1500	0.2386	0.1150	0.2602

TABLE 38.6 Calculation of weights of green pressure (GP) antecedents and their ranking.

GP antecedent	Score	ξ	1-ξ	$\xi/(1-\xi)$	w	Rank
GP5	4.0493	0.5256	0.4744	1.1079	0.1958	1
GP6	3.6549	0.5152	0.4848	1.0627	0.1767	2
GP3	3.4393	0.5020	0.4980	1.0081	0.1663	3
GP2	3.4116	0.5233	0.4767	1.0979	0.1649	4
GP4	3.1075	0.5069	0.4931	1.0278	0.1502	5
GP1	3.0235				0.1462	6
		χ	0.0000	Sum	1.0000	

This way, we assign preference values to all antecedents. As per Eq. 38.8, for achieving full consistency (ideal case), $\frac{w_5}{w_6} - 1.1079 = 0$; $\frac{w_6}{w_3} - 1.0627 = 0$ and so on. Realistically, we formulate the final model (using Eqs. 38.9–38.11) to determine the weights of the GP antecedents as follows.

$$\begin{aligned}
&Min\chi\\
&s.\ t.\\
&\left|\frac{w_5}{w_6} - 1.1079\right| \le \chi;\ \left|\frac{w_6}{w_3} - 1.0627\right| \le \chi;\ \left|\frac{w_3}{w_2} - 1.0081\right| \le \chi;\\
&\left|\frac{w_2}{w_4} - 1.0979\right| \le \chi;\ \left|\frac{w_4}{w_1} - 1.0278\right| \le \chi;\\
&\textstyle\sum_{j=1}^{6} w_j = 1;\ \ w_j \ge 0\ \forall\ j
\end{aligned} \tag{38.12}$$

It is noteworthy to mention that in this example ($n = 6$), COBRAC requires $n - 1 = 5$ local pairwise comparisons, which is lower than AHP (no. of comparisons =15), and BWM (no. of comparisons =11). We solve the model ((38.12)) using Lingo (version 21) software and obtain the values of the objective function and weights of the antecedents (given in Table 38.6). It is observed that $\chi = 0.0000$, indicating the robustness of the model and very low deviation from complete consistency.

38.4.4 Discussion

The research indicates that inherent human values and a self-driven commitment to sustainability primarily drive the adoption of environmentally friendly items. This aligns with the VBN framework, which posits that individual norms and values influence pro-environmental behaviors. Initiatives aimed at fostering positive environmental values at the individual level are more successful in influencing green purchasing decisions than external incentives or legislation. The second most notable statement, "I believe that the utilization of eco-friendly products contributes to environmental preservation," underscores the importance of outcome expectancies and ecological effectiveness. Additional variables encompass ecologically sustainable promotions, social activities, peer influences, and governmental regulations and policy measures. The results indicate that internalized values and perceived environmental effect, shaped by social context and promotional activities, are the principal determinants of green consumer behavior, offering critical insights for policymakers and marketers aiming to improve sustainable product uptake.

The findings reveal significant research implications.

- There is a need to prioritize internal value-driven activities, since personal sustainability valuation is the most substantial environmental pressure. Fostering a corporate culture of environmental stewardship, staff education, and value-centric marketing may enhance consumer engagement, with messaging that highlights authentic environmental concern proving more successful than just regulatory compliance.
- Social influence, encompassing peer and community endorsements, is essential for fostering sustainable habits. Employing community-driven efforts, social validation, and oral advocacy may improve public discourse and promote

ecologically friendly options. Dynamic, environmentally aware societies can enhance collective efficacy, encouraging sustainable consumption.

- To augment environmental consciousness, technical interventions such as eco-labeling, data transparency, and green product certification are requisite. Technological solutions such as mobile apps, advanced product tracking, and incentives for environmentally sustainable behaviors are advantageous. Tailored promotional initiatives utilizing digital platforms can efficiently encourage environmentally sustainable purchasing.

38.5 Numerical example 2

38.5.1 Case study 2: consumers' perceptions about green washing

The second case study examines consumer insights into corporate GW—the practice of firms making misleading environmental claims—and its impact on trust and corporate social responsibility (CSR) standards. GW is the act of misleading customers by providing deceptive information about products, which involves the seller's insincere and misleading environmental claims to avoid negative feedback (Tarabieh, 2021). Regulatory and customer pressure stimulate firms to adopt green practices and enhance their green innovation presentation (Qi et al., 2021). In these circumstances, the companies started to make exaggerated green claims (Yang et al., 2021), which creates ambiguity in customers' minds. However, there are also some contradictory views, which suggest that the high cost of green products can deter customer demand for green innovations (Huang et al., 2016). These inconsistent outputs suggest a lack of attention in this area. Table 38.7 outlines consumers' perceptions of the GW practices of corporations.

38.5.2 Data collection

The selection of respondents and calculations of their weights are explained in the previous case study. The details of data collection are also elaborated earlier.

TABLE 38.7 Consumers' perceptions about greenwashing (GW) practices in the corporates.

S/L	Description of the variables	References
GW1	Most companies mislead consumers with misleading claims about the environmental features of their products.	Hill et al. (2025), Spaniol et al. (2024)
GW2	Most companies mislead with visuals or graphics about the environmental features of their products.	Fella and Bausa (2024), Hill et al. (2025)
GW3	Most companies provide vague or seemingly unprovable environmental claims for their products.	Spaniol et al. (2024), Lublóy et al. (2025)
GW4	Most companies overstate or exaggerate the environmental features of their products.	Hill et al. (2025), Adamkiewicz et al. (2022)
GW5	Most companies omit or conceal crucial information about the actual environmental impacts of their products.	Hill et al. (2025), Spaniol et al. (2024)
GW6	The companies claim to be greener than they actually are.	Hill et al. (2025), Spaniol et al. (2024)
GW7	The company provides a false eco-label or certificate.	Hill et al. (2025), United Nation[a]
GW8	The company keeps the price higher to support its false claim.	Lublóy et al. (2025), Spaniol et al. (2024)
GW9	The companies exhibit corporate hypocrisy by engaging in decoupling talk but failing to take corresponding actions.	Bothello et al. (2023), Chen et al. (2025)
GW10	The company undertakes this initiative to meet its corporate social responsibility (CSR) standards.	Bothello et al. (2023)

[a] *https://www.un.org/en/climatechange/science/climate-issues/greenwashing (Last accessed on July 30, 2025).*

TABLE 38.8 Rating of the greenwashing (GW) variables.

Exp. weight	**0.0640**	**0.0520**	**0.0640**	**0.0520**	**0.0520**	**0.0781**	**0.0260**	**0.0648**	**0.0494**	**0.0477**
Experts/variables	**1**	**2**	**3**	**4**	**5**	**6**	**7**	**8**	**9**	**10**
GW1	3	3	3	5	3	1	4	3	3	3
GW2	4	5	3	4	4	3	4	3	2	4
GW3	5	4	3	4	4	4	3	4	2	4
GW4	4	4	3	4	4	4	4	2	2	4
GW5	4	4	3	5	4	4	4	4	2	4
GW6	4	3	3	5	3	2	2	3	2	3
GW7	4	3	3	3	4	4	3	3	3	5
GW8	4	4	3	4	4	2	2	3	3	3
GW9	4	4	3	5	4	2	4	2	2	5
GW10	4	4	3	5	4	4	4	2	1	4
Exp. weight	**0.0477**	**0.0375**	**0.0477**	**0.0383**	**0.0648**	**0.0383**	**0.0375**	**0.0477**	**0.0383**	**0.0520**
Experts/variables	**11**	**12**	**13**	**14**	**15**	**16**	**17**	**18**	**19**	**20**
GW1	5	4	4	5	3	5	3	2	5	3
GW2	4	2	4	5	4	5	4	2	5	3
GW3	4	2	2	5	2	5	4	1	5	4
GW4	4	3	4	3	4	5	4	2	5	5
GW5	4	3	4	3	4	5	3	1	5	2
GW6	4	2	3	4	5	3	3	2	1	3
GW7	3	2	2	2	4	3	3	3	5	3
GW8	3	3	2	2	2	4	4	2	5	3
GW9	3	3	5	5	4	5	3	3	5	3
GW10	3	4	5	3	4	4	3	3	5	4

38.5.3 Analysis and results

Likewise, in the previous case study, we first determine the weights of the experts based on their experience and educational level using Eqs. 38.1–38.3 (Table A1). As previously stated, λ is considered to be 0.5 for the initial condition, giving equal priority to education and experience. Table 38.8 presents the ratings of the perception variables, along with the weights assigned by the experts. Then, we obtain the WRS values for each GW (Table 38.9).

Now, we proceed to obtain the AWR of the variables (Eq. 38.5). The AWR values are reported in Table 38.10.

Next, we apply the steps of the conventional COBRAC method to determine the weight values of the GW variables and rank them. To this end, first, we sort the GWs based on their AWR values. In this example, GW4 is identified as the most significant antecedent based on the AWR value (ζ = 3.6651). Then, we conduct pairwise comparisons and assign preference values to each GW. Realistically, we formulate the final model (using Eqs. 38.9–38.11) to determine the weights of the GP antecedents as follows.

TABLE 38.9 Weighted rating scores of the greenwashing (GW) variables.

Experts/variables	1	2	3	4	5	6	7	8	9	10
GW1	0.1919	0.1561	0.1919	0.2602	0.1561	0.0781	0.1041	0.1944	0.1481	0.1432
GW2	0.2559	0.2602	0.1919	0.2081	0.2081	0.2342	0.1041	0.1944	0.0988	0.1909
GW3	0.3199	0.2081	0.1919	0.2081	0.2081	0.3122	0.0781	0.2592	0.0988	0.1909
GW4	0.2559	0.2081	0.1919	0.2081	0.2081	0.3122	0.1041	0.1296	0.0988	0.1909
GW5	0.2559	0.2081	0.1919	0.2602	0.2081	0.3122	0.1041	0.2592	0.0988	0.1909
GW6	0.2559	0.1561	0.1919	0.2602	0.1561	0.1561	0.0520	0.1944	0.0988	0.1432
GW7	0.2559	0.1561	0.1919	0.1561	0.2081	0.3122	0.0781	0.1944	0.1481	0.2386
GW8	0.2559	0.2081	0.1919	0.2081	0.2081	0.1561	0.0520	0.1944	0.1481	0.1432
GW9	0.2559	0.2081	0.1919	0.2602	0.2081	0.1561	0.1041	0.1296	0.0988	0.2386
GW10	0.2559	0.2081	0.1919	0.2602	0.2081	0.3122	0.1041	0.1296	0.0494	0.1909
Experts/variables	**11**	**12**	**13**	**14**	**15**	**16**	**17**	**18**	**19**	**20**
GW1	0.2386	0.1500	0.1909	0.1916	0.1944	0.1916	0.1125	0.0955	0.1916	0.1561
GW2	0.1909	0.0750	0.1909	0.1916	0.2592	0.1916	0.1500	0.0955	0.1916	0.1561
GW3	0.1909	0.0750	0.0955	0.1916	0.1296	0.1916	0.1500	0.0477	0.1916	0.2081
GW4	0.1909	0.1125	0.1909	0.1150	0.2592	0.1916	0.1500	0.0955	0.1916	0.2602
GW5	0.1909	0.1125	0.1909	0.1150	0.2592	0.1916	0.1125	0.0477	0.1916	0.1041
GW6	0.1909	0.0750	0.1432	0.1533	0.3240	0.1150	0.1125	0.0955	0.0383	0.1561
GW7	0.1432	0.0750	0.0955	0.0766	0.2592	0.1150	0.1125	0.1432	0.1916	0.1561
GW8	0.1432	0.1125	0.0955	0.0766	0.1296	0.1533	0.1500	0.0955	0.1916	0.1561
GW9	0.1432	0.1125	0.2386	0.1916	0.2592	0.1916	0.1125	0.1432	0.1916	0.1561
GW10	0.1432	0.1500	0.2386	0.1150	0.2592	0.1533	0.1125	0.1432	0.1916	0.2081

$$
\begin{aligned}
&Min\chi\\
&s.\,t.\\
&\left|\frac{w_4}{w_2}-1.0072\right|\le\chi;\ \left|\frac{w_2}{w_{10}}-1.0038\right|\le\chi;\ \left|\frac{w_{10}}{w_5}-1.0055\right|\le\chi;\\
&\left|\frac{w_5}{w_9}-1.0039\right|\le\chi;\ \left|\frac{w_9}{w_3}-1.0126\right|\le\chi;\ \left|\frac{w_3}{w_1}-1.0630\right|\le\chi;\\
&\left|\frac{w_1}{w_7}-1.0089\right|\le\chi;\ \left|\frac{w_7}{w_8}-1.0774\right|\le\chi;\ \left|\frac{w_8}{w_6}-1.0005\right|\le\chi;\\
&\textstyle\sum_{j=1}^{10}w_j=1;\ w_j\ge 0\ \forall\, j
\end{aligned}
\tag{38.13}
$$

It is noteworthy to mention that in this example ($n = 10$), COBRAC requires $n - 1 = 9$ local pairwise comparisons, which is lower than AHP (no. of comparisons =45), and BWM (no. of comparisons =17). We solve the model ((38.13)) using Lingo (version 21) software and obtain the values of the objective function and weights of the GW variables (given in Table 38.11). It is observed that $\chi = 0.0000$, indicating the robustness of the model and very low deviation from complete consistency.

TABLE 38.10 Calculated aggregated weighted rating (AWR) values of the greenwashing (GW) variables.

Variable	AWR	Variable	AWR
GW1	3.3369	GW6	3.0684
GW2	3.6389	GW7	3.3074
GW3	3.5470	GW8	3.0699
GW4	3.6651	GW9	3.5915
GW5	3.6054	GW10	3.6251

TABLE 38.11 Calculation of weights of greenwashing (GW) variables and their ranking.

Variable	Score	ξ	1-ξ	ξ/(1 - ξ)	w	Rank
GW4	3.6651	0.5018	0.4982	1.0072	0.1064	1
GW2	3.6389	0.5010	0.4990	1.0038	0.1056	2
GW10	3.6251	0.5014	0.4986	1.0055	0.1052	3
GW5	3.6054	0.5010	0.4990	1.0039	0.1046	4
GW9	3.5915	0.5031	0.4969	1.0126	0.1042	5
GW3	3.5470	0.5153	0.4847	1.0630	0.1029	6
GW1	3.3369	0.5022	0.4978	1.0089	0.0968	7
GW7	3.3074	0.5186	0.4814	1.0774	0.0960	8
GW8	3.0699	0.5001	0.4999	1.0005	0.0891	9
GW6	3.0684				0.0890	10
		χ	0.0000	Sum	1.0000	

38.5.4 Discussion

The study reveals significant instances of GW, primarily highlighting firms' exaggeration of their products' environmental qualities to appeal to eco-conscious consumers. This undermines market integrity and consumer confidence, distorting customer perceptions and hindering the distinction of eco-friendly products. The second most significant aspect, misleading visual or graphic assertions, illustrates the growing complexity of marketing techniques, wherein visual elements are employed to create an environmentally friendly image that lacks considerable evidence. The tendency of companies to obscure or omit critical environmental information, combined with the rise of vague and unsubstantiated claims, significantly exacerbates GW, underscoring the importance of transparency and consistency in environmental reporting. Subordinate factors, such as misleading eco-labels, price manipulations, and insincere CSR programs, reveal the intrinsic dishonesty of corporations and the disparity between their words and actions. The results indicate the necessity for enhanced regulatory scrutiny of environmental marketing and augmented consumer education to verify the authenticity of sustainability claims and protect the integrity of green markets.

The study indicates that GW is a widespread concern in corporate sustainability discourse, characterized by exaggerated assertions and misleading visual depictions, which are the most frequent occurrences. This highlights the need for rigorous methodologies to detect and quantify GW strategies in promotional content. Advanced research instruments, including linguistic analysis, semiotics, and machine learning algorithms, are essential for the automatic detection of GW. The psychological and behavioral impacts of GW must be examined across various consumer groups, highlighting how inflated claims and concealed information erode trust and hinder genuine environmental engagement. Cross-cultural and cross-industry comparative investigations can elucidate more successful tactics and enable tailored regulatory and instructional approaches. The efficacy of certification systems and eco-labeling is vital, as deceptive labels can compromise environmental accountability. Longitudinal case studies and content audits are required to examine the discrepancy between policy and actual practices.

TABLE 38.12 Spearman's rank correlation test (comparison of multicriteria decision-making methods used in case study 2).

Method	Level based weight assessment	Full consistency method	Stepwise weight assessment ratio analysis	DIBR-II	CIMAS
Comparisons between ranked criteria	1.000	1.000	0.919	0.988	0.952

(All values are significant at the 0.05 level, two-tailed).

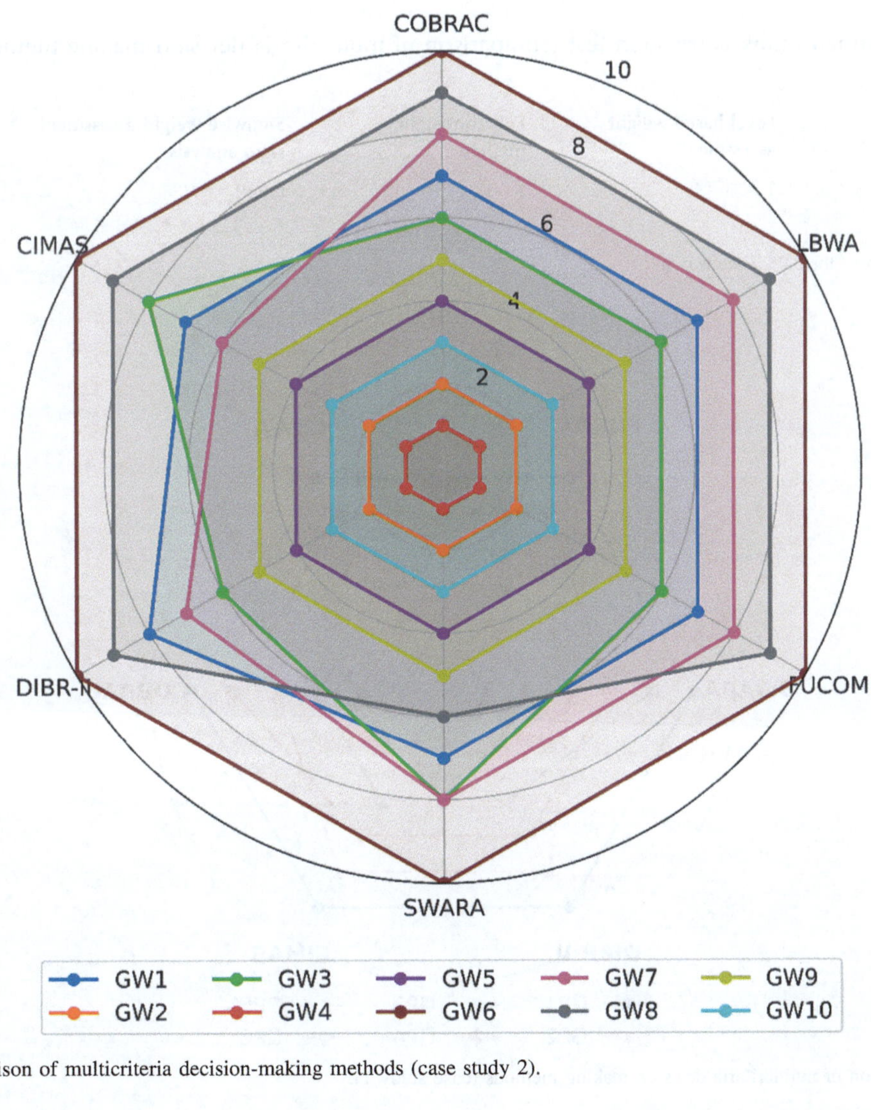

FIGURE 38.1 Comparison of multicriteria decision-making methods (case study 2).

38.6 Validation

The stability and reliability of MCDM model results are influenced by several external conditions, including variations in parameter values, aggregation coefficients, mathematical formulations, experts' weights, and their preferences (Biswas et al., 2025a). Thus the current research offers a two-step validation procedure.

Step 1. Comparative analysis of the results of the present MCDM method (i.e., COBRAC) with those of other established models (recommended in past studies, such as Biswas et al., 2025b; Tufan & Ulutaş, 2026) to ascertain its reliability and generalizability.

Step 2. Conduct a sensitivity analysis to examine the effect of variations in an external condition on the outcome of the COBRAC method (Biswas et al., 2025; Sanyal et al., 2025).

At step 1, we compare the results of the COBRAC method with those of other models, such as LBWA, FUCOM, SWARA, defining interrelationships between ranked criteria II (DIBR-II), and criteria importance assessment (CIMAS). We compute Spearman's rank correlation coefficients and examine the significance (Table 38.12). We observe that all these methods exhibit a statistically significant high association with the COBRAC method, indicating the reliability of the ranking of GWs.

The validity of the COBRAC method for equitable decision-making is affirmed in Fig. 38.1, as it reduces bias and prioritizes method sensitivity. Comparison research confirms its reliability, especially in multidisciplinary situations where equity and transparency in ranking obstacles are crucial academic issues.

TABLE 38.13 Spearman's rank correlation test (comparison of multicriteria decision-making methods used in case study 1).

Method	Level based weight assessment	Full consistency method	Stepwise weight assessment ratio analysis	DIBR-II	CIMAS
Comparisons between ranked criteria	1.000	1.000	0.829	0.943	0.943

(All values are significant at the 0.05 level, two-tailed).

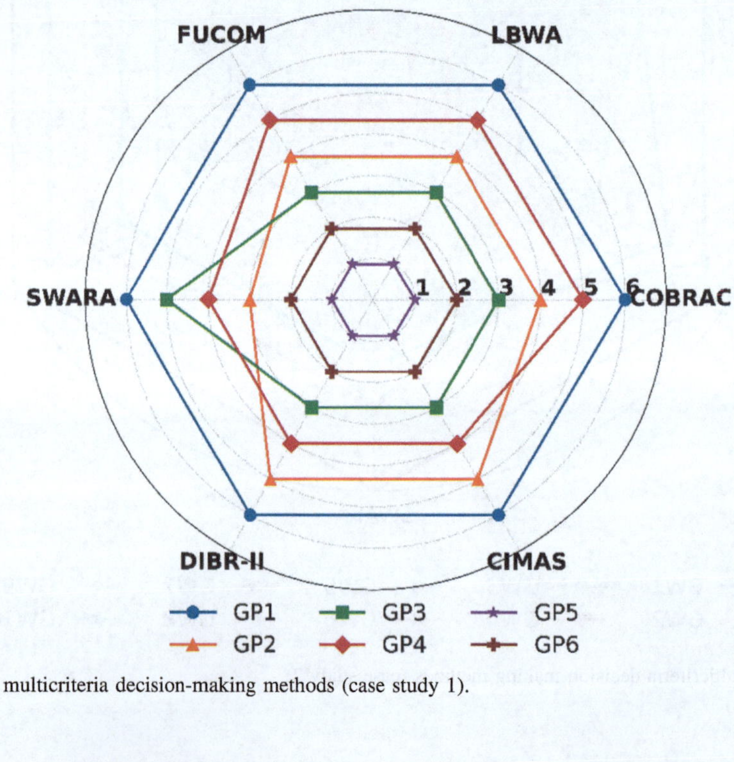

FIGURE 38.2 Comparison of multicriteria decision-making methods (case study 1).

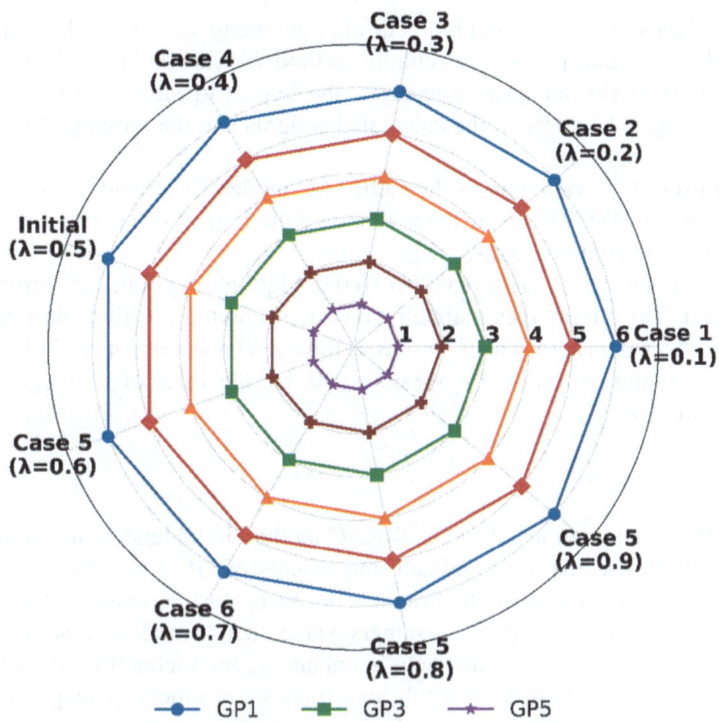

FIGURE 38.3 Effect of variations in experts' weights on the ranking of green pressures (GPs) (case study 1).

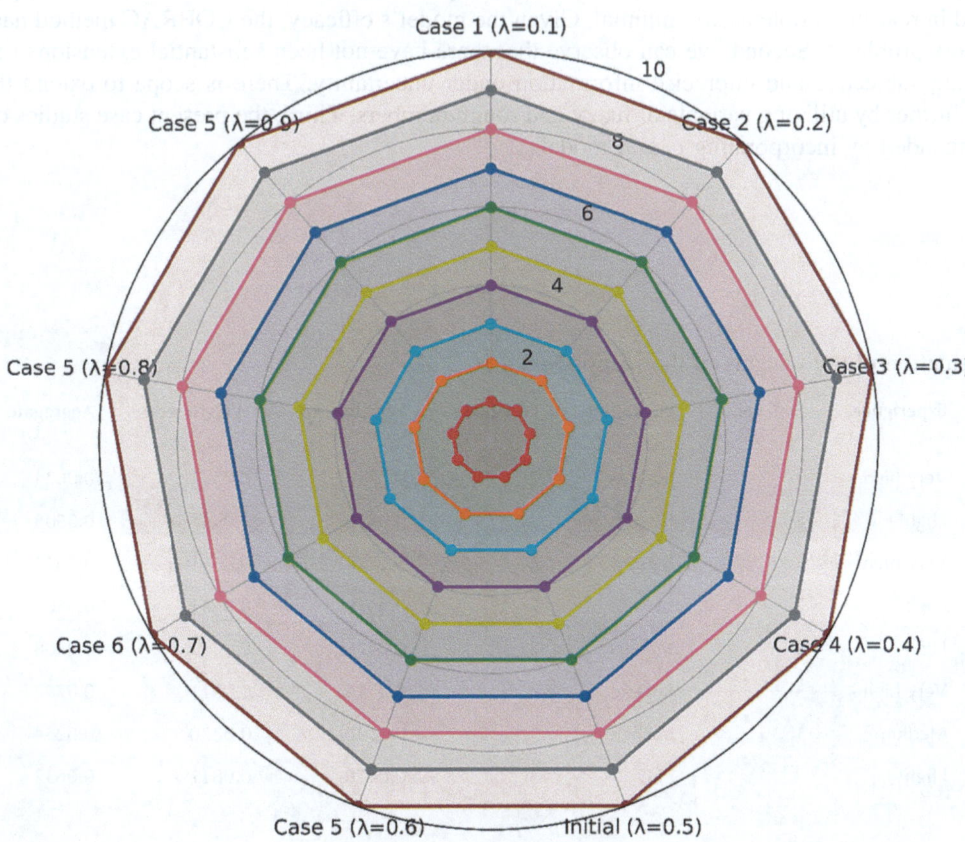

FIGURE 38.4 Effect of variations in experts' weights on the ranking of greenwashings (GWs) (case study 2).

Similarly, we observe statistically significant and high correlation among various methods in Case 1 (Table 38.13). We thus conclude that the COBRAC method provides a reliable method for calculating weights and ranking (Fig. 38.2).

We proceed to conduct the sensitivity analysis to examine the impact of variations in the experts' weights (through varying the values of λ in the range 0.1 to 0.9) on the calculated weights and the ranking of GPs in Case 1 (Fig. 38.3) and GWs in Case 2 (Fig. 38.4).

The sensitivity analysis and stability evaluation of the COBRAC model, illustrated in Figs. 38.3 and 38.4, demonstrate its robustness and reliability for MCDM. The radar maps illustrate the impact of altering the aggregate parameter on the ranking positions of weight and preference groups.

The graphs illustrate rank variations as λ varies from 0.1 to 0.9, highlighting both "sensitive" and "insensitive" criteria or alternatives inside the model. The alternatives maintain consistent ranking positions despite fluctuations in λ. Options that consistently maintain their ranking across all λ values exhibit decision resilience, indicating the robustness of the model irrespective of experts' weights. Additionally, we observed that the value of χ is negligible ($\approx$ 0.0000), suggesting the efficacy of the COBRAC model.

38.7 Conclusion

The current research demonstrates applications of the COBRAC method in understanding consumer behavior. In the first case study, the COBRAC method discerns the dominant antecedents of GP. Over the years, consumers have become increasingly concerned about using environmentally friendly products. In this context, the COBRAC method offers a robust and focused approach to identifying how consumers value their moral obligations towards the environment. Environment-friendly promotions and awareness also help in enhancing the inclination toward using green products. The second case study focuses on the other part of the story. It investigates consumers' perceptions of GW practices followed in the organizations. Consumers opine that companies often overstate their green practices and mislead others through their campaigns. Green practices are merely followed to comply with CSR obligations. In both case studies, the COBRAC model shows significant reliability and stability in results, reflecting its efficacy.

However, the present work can be extended in several ways. First, we have noticed that the applications of the COBRAC method in real-life problems are minimal. Given the model's efficacy, the COBRAC method has high potential for solving complex problems. Second, we can observe that there have not been substantial extensions of the COBRAC model incorporating subjective and imprecise information under uncertainty. There is scope to extend the fundamental COBRAC model further by utilizing variants of fuzzy and rough numbers. Third, the present case studies could be further elaborated and expanded by incorporating causal models.

Appendix A

TABLE A1 Calculation of the weights of the respondents.

Respondent ID	Experience	Exp_code	Education	Edu_code	Weight_exp	Weight_edu	Aggregate	Final weight
1	Very high	3	Masters	2	0.0714	0.0541	0.0624	0.0640
2	High	2	Masters	2	0.0476	0.0541	0.0508	0.0520
3	Very high	3	Masters	2	0.0714	0.0541	0.0624	0.0640
4	High	2	Masters	2	0.0476	0.0541	0.0508	0.0520
5	High	2	Masters	2	0.0476	0.0541	0.0508	0.0520
6	Very high	3	PhD	3	0.0714	0.0811	0.0762	0.0781
7	Medium	1	Bachelors	1	0.0238	0.0270	0.0254	0.0260
8	High	2	PhD	3	0.0476	0.0811	0.0632	0.0648

(Continued)

TABLE A1 (Continued)

Respondent ID	Experience	Exp_code	Education	Edu_code	Weight_exp	Weight_edu	Aggregate	Final weight
9	Medium	1	PhD	3	0.0238	0.0811	0.0482	0.0494
10	Very high	3	Bachelors	1	0.0714	0.0270	0.0466	0.0477
11	Very high	3	Bachelors	1	0.0714	0.0270	0.0466	0.0477
12	High	2	Bachelors	1	0.0476	0.0270	0.0366	0.0375
13	Very high	3	Bachelors	1	0.0714	0.0270	0.0466	0.0477
14	Medium	1	Masters	2	0.0238	0.0541	0.0374	0.0383
15	High	2	PhD	3	0.0476	0.0811	0.0632	0.0648
16	Medium	1	Masters	2	0.0238	0.0541	0.0374	0.0383
17	High	2	Bachelors	1	0.0476	0.0270	0.0366	0.0375
18	Very high	3	Bachelors	1	0.0714	0.0270	0.0466	0.0477
19	Medium	1	Masters	2	0.0238	0.0541	0.0374	0.0383
20	High	2	Masters	2	0.0476	0.0541	0.0508	0.0520

References

Adamkiewicz, J., Kochańska, E., Adamkiewicz, I., & Łukasik, R. M. (2022). Greenwashing and sustainable fashion industry. *Current Opinion in Green and Sustainable Chemistry, 38*, 100710. https://doi.org/10.1016/j.cogsc.2022.100710.

Ajzen, I. (1991). The theory of planned behavior. *Organizational Behavior and Human Decision Processes, 50*(2), 179–211. https://doi.org/10.1016/0749-5978(91)90020-T.

Barbu, A., Catană, A., Deselnicu, D. C., Cioca, L. I., & Ioanid, A. (2022). Factors influencing consumer behavior toward green products: A systematic literature review. *International Journal of Environmental Research and Public Health, 19*(24), 16568. https://doi.org/10.3390/ijerph192416568.

Bekk, M., Spörrle, M., Hedjasie, R., & Kerschreiter, R. (2016). Greening the competitive advantage: antecedents and consequences of green brand equity. *Quality & Quantity*, 50(4), 1727–1746.

Biswas, S., Bhattacharjee, S., Biswas, B., Mitra, K., & Khawas, N. (2025a). An expert opinion-based soft computing framework for comparing nanotechnologies used in agriculture. *Spectrum of Operational Research,* 1–39. https://doi.org/10.31181/sor4156.

Biswas, S., Sanyal, A., & Pamucar, D. (2025b). Students' perceptions about the webinars: An intuitionistic fuzzy force field analysis. *Spectrum of Operational Research, 2*(1), 113–133. https://doi.org/10.31181/sor21202513.

Biswas, S., Mitra, K., & Biswas, B. (2025). Barriers to adapt quantum cryptography technology in digital supply chains: A q-rung Orthopair fuzzy model. *Yugoslav Journal of Operations Research*. https://doi.org/10.2298/YJOR240819019B.

Biswas, S., Pamucar, D., & Simic, V. (2024). Technology adaptation in sugarcane supply chain based on a novel p, q quasirung orthopair fuzzy decision making framework. *Scientific Reports, 14*(1), 26486. https://doi.org/10.1038/s41598-024-75528-5.

Bothello, J., Ioannou, I., Porumb, V. A., & Zengin-Karaibrahimoglu, Y. (2023). CSR decoupling within business groups and the risk of perceived greenwashing. *Strategic Management Journal, 44*(13), 3217–3251. https://doi.org/10.1002/smj.3532.

Bošković, S., Jovčić, S., Simic, V., Švadlenka, L., Dobrodolac, M., & Bacanin, N. (2025). A new criteria importance assessment (Cimas) method in multi-criteria group decision-making: Criteria evaluation for supplier selection. *Facta Universitatis, Series: Mechanical Engineering, 23*(2), 335–349. https://doi.org/10.22190/FUME230730050B.

Cam, L. N. T. (2023). A rising trend in eco-friendly products: A health-conscious approach to green buying. *Heliyon, 9*(9), e19845. https://doi.org/10.1016/j.heliyon.2023.e19845.

Chakraborty, S., Raut, R. D., Rofin, T. M., & Chakraborty, S. (2023). A comprehensive and systematic review of multi-criteria decision-making methods and applications in healthcare. *Healthcare Analytics, 4*, 100232. https://doi.org/10.1016/j.health.2023.100232.

Chen, X., Ji, F., Kong, D., & Tan, Z. (2025). Fintech development and corporate hypocrisy: Evidence from social responsibility decoupling. *Finance Research Letters*, 107603. https://doi.org/10.1016/j.frl.2025.107603.

Chen, Y. S. (2008). The driver of green innovation and green image–green core competence. *Journal of Business Ethics, 81*(3), 531–543. https://doi.org/10.1007/s10551-007-9522-1.

Dağıstanlı, H. A. (2025). Analysis of the stages of military cyber operations using the COBRAC method and p, q quasirung orthopair fuzzy decision making framework. *Journal of Operations Intelligence, 3*(1), 338–348. https://doi.org/10.31181/jopi31202550.

Delmas, M. A., & Burbano, V. C. (2011). The drivers of greenwashing. *California Management Review, 54*(1), 64–87. https://doi.org/10.1525/cmr.2011.54.1.64.

Fella, S., & Bausa, E. (2024). Green or greenwashed? Examining consumers' ability to identify greenwashing. *Journal of Environmental Psychology, 95*, 102281. https://doi.org/10.1016/j.jenvp.2024.102281.

Gabus, A., & Fontela, E. J. B. G. R. C. (1972). World problems, an invitation to further thought within the framework of DEMATEL. *Battelle Geneva Research Center, Geneva, Switzerland, 1*(8), 12–14.

Gelderman, C. J., Schijns, J., Lambrechts, W., & Vijgen, S. (2021). Green marketing as an environmental practice: The impact on green satisfaction and green loyalty in a business-to-business context. *Business strategy and the environment, 30*(4), 2061–2076. https://doi.org/10.1002/bse.2732.

Ghosh, M. (2019). Determinants of green procurement implementation and its impact on firm performance. *Journal of Manufacturing Technology Management, 30*(2), 462–482. https://doi.org/10.1108/JMTM-062018-0168.

Giang, N. T., & Thinh, H. X. (2025). Comparing subjective weighting methods in multi-criteria decision-making: An application to electric bicycle ranking. *Engineering, Technology & Applied Science Research, 15*(2), 21963–21969. https://doi.org/10.48084/etasr.10444.

Gong, M., Bao, X., & Wagner, C. (2023). Why viewers send paid gifts: The role of social influence on massively multiplayer online games live streaming. *Information Processing & Management, 60*(4), 103371. https://doi.org/10.1016/j.ipm.2023.103371.

Gu, W. (2024). Research on strategy optimization of sustainable development towards green consumption of eco-friendly materials. *Journal of King Saud University-Science, 36*(6), 103190. https://doi.org/10.1016/j.jksus.2024.103190.

Hill, S., Nemes, N., Montgomery, A. W., Scanlan, S., McNally, B., Tubiello, F., ... Kaupa, C. (2025). Testing the greenwashing assessment framework. *Ecology & Society, 30*(2), 31. https://doi.org/10.5751/ES-16106-300231.

Huang, X. X., Hu, Z. P., Liu, C. S., Yu, D. J., & Yu, L. F. (2016). The relationships between regulatory and customer pressure, green organizational responses, and green innovation performance. *Journal of Cleaner Production, 112*, 3423–3433. https://doi.org/10.1016/j.jclepro.2015.10.106.

Islam, J. U., Thomas, G., & Albishri, N. A. (2024). From status to sustainability: How social influence and sustainability consciousness drive green purchase intentions in luxury restaurants. *Acta Psychologica, 251*, 104595. https://doi.org/10.1016/j.actpsy.2024.104595.

Jayaraman, K., Jayashree, S., & Dorasamy, M. (2023). The effects of green innovations in organizations: Influence of stakeholders. *Sustainability, 15*(2), 1133. https://doi.org/10.3390/su15021133.

Jyothi, M., & Mohan, P. V. K. (2025). Green consumerism among gen-Z in tier-II Indian cities: A case based exploration of emerging urban markets. *International Journal of Research and Innovation in Social Science, 9*(7), 1885–1900. https://doi.org/10.47772/IJRISS.2025.907000156.

Kara, K., Yalçın, G. C., Simic, V., Baysal, Z., & Pamucar, D. (2024). The alternative ranking using two-step logarithmic normalization method for benchmarking the supply chain performance of countries. *Socio-economic Planning Sciences, 92*, 101822. https://doi.org/10.1016/j.seps.2024.101822.

Keršuliene, V., Zavadskas, E. K., & Turskis, Z. (2010). Selection of rational dispute resolution method by applying new step-wise weight assessment ratio analysis (SWARA). *Journal of Business Economics and Management, 11*(2), 243–258. https://doi.org/10.3846/jbem.2010.12.

Kizielewicz, B., Tomczyk, T., Gandor, M., & Sałabun, W. (2024). Subjective weight determination methods in multi-criteria decision-making: A systematic review. *Procedia Computer Science, 246*, 5396–5407. https://doi.org/10.1016/j.procs.2024.09.673.

Lublóy, Á., Keresztúri, J. L., & Berlinger, E. (2025). Quantifying firm-level greenwashing: A systematic literature review. *Journal of Environmental Management, 373*, 123399. https://doi.org/10.1016/j.jenvman.2024.123399.

Miller, G. A. (1956). The magical number seven, plus or minus two: Some limits on our capacity for processing information. *Psychological Review, 63*(2), 81.

Mustafa, S., Hao, T., Jamil, K., Qiao, Y., & Nawaz, M. (2022). Role of eco-friendly products in the revival of developing countries' economies and achieving a sustainable green economy. *Frontiers in Environmental Science, 10*, 955245. https://doi.org/10.3389/fenvs.2022.955245.

Ngo, Q. H., Nguyen, T. D., & Phan, N. B. (2025). Exploring green purchasing intentions and behaviours among vietnamese generation Z: A perspective from the theory of planned behaviour. *PLoS One, 20*(5), e0323879. https://doi.org/10.1371/journal.pone.0323879.

Ogunmola, G. A., & Kumar, V. (2024). A strategic model for attracting and retaining environmentally conscious customers in E-retail. *International Journal of Information Management Data Insights, 4*(2), 100274. https://doi.org/10.1016/j.jjimei.2024.100274.

Özçalıcı, M., Gürler, H. E., Kaya, A., Pamucar, D., Karyağdı, N. G., & Ciğer, A. (2025). Strategic cost allocation with value stream costing: Data-driven decision analysis in textile manufacturing. *Journal of Industrial Information Integration*, 100906. https://doi.org/10.1016/j.jii.2025.100906.

Pamucar, D., Simic, V., Görçün, Ö. F., & Küçükönder, H. (2024). Selection of the best big data platform using COBRAC-ARTASI methodology with adaptive standardized intervals. *Expert Systems with Applications, 239*, 122312. https://doi.org/10.1016/j.eswa.2023.122312.

Pamučar, D., Stević, Ž., & Sremac, S. (2018). A new model for determining weight coefficients of criteria in mcdm models: Full consistency method (fucom). *Symmetry, 10*(9), 393. https://doi.org/10.3390/sym10090393.

Qi, G., Jia, Y., & Zou, H. (2021). Is institutional pressure the mother of green innovation? Examining the moderating effect of absorptive capacity. *Journal of Cleaner Production, 278*, 123957. https://doi.org/10.1016/j.jclepro.2020.123957.

Rezaei, J. (2015). Best-worst multi-criteria decision-making method. *Omega, 53*, 49–57. https://doi.org/10.1016/j.omega.2014.11.009.

Saaty, T. L. (1980). *The analytic hierarchy process: planning, priority setting, resource allocation*. New York, NY: McGraw-Hill.

Sanyal, A., Biswas, S., & Sur, S. (2025). An integrated full consistent LOPCOW-EDAS framework for modelling consumer decision making for organic food selection. *Yugoslav Journal of Operations Research, 35*(2), 331–364. https://doi.org/10.2298/YJOR240315022S.

Sanyal, A., & Sur, S. (2023). Appraising the impact of green knowledge and green pressure on MSMEs' sustainable competitive advantage: A conceptual framework with special reference to 7Ps. *Third Concept-An International Journal of Idea, 36*(432), 158–163.

Schiffman, L., O'Cass, A., Paladino, A., & Carlson, J. (2013). *Consumer behaviour.* Pearson Higher Education AU.

Sharma, K., Aswal, C., & Paul, J. (2023). Factors affecting green purchase behavior: A systematic literature review. *Business Strategy and the Environment, 32*(4), 2078–2092. https://doi.org/10.1002/bse.3237.

Singh, S. K., Del Giudice, M., Chiappetta Jabbour, C. J., Latan, H., & Sohal, A. S. (2022). Stakeholder pressure, green innovation, and performance in small and medium-sized enterprises: The role of green dynamic capabilities. *Business Strategy and the Environment, 31*(1), 500–514. https://doi.org/10.1002/bse.2906.

Spaniol, M. J., Danilova-Jensen, E., Nielsen, M., Rosdahl, C. G., & Schmidt, C. J. (2024). Defining greenwashing: a concept analysis. *Sustainability, 16*(20), 9055.

Stanujkic, D., Karabasevic, D., Popovic, G., & Sava, C. (2021). Simplified pivot pairwise relative criteria importance assessment (PIPRECIA-S) method. *Romanian Journal of Economic Forecasting, 24*(4), 141–154.

Stern, P. C., Dietz, T., Abel, T., Guagnano, G. A., & Kalof, L. (1999). A value-belief-norm theory of support for social movements: The case of environmentalism. *Human Ecology Review, 6*(2), 81–97. https://www.jstor.org/stable/24707060.

Tarabieh, S. M. Z. A. (2021). The impact of greenwash practices over green purchase intention: The mediating effects of green confusion, green perceived risk, and green trust. *Management Science Letters, 11*(2), 451–464. https://doi.org/10.5267/j.msl.2020.9.022.

Tufan, D., & Ulutaş, A. (2026). Supplier selection in the food sector: An Integrated approach using LODECI and CORASO methods. *Spectrum of Decision Making and Applications, 3*(1), 40–51. https://doi.org/10.31181/sdmap31202631.

Więckowski, J., Sałabun, W., Kizielewicz, B., Bączkiewicz, A., Shekhovtsov, A., Paradowski, B., & Wątróbski, J. (2023). Recent advances in multi-criteria decision analysis: A comprehensive review of applications and trends. *International Journal of Knowledge-based and Intelligent Engineering Systems, 27*(4), 367–393. https://doi.org/10.3233/KES-230487.

Yang, S. P., Chang, S. C., Liang, T. C., Situmorang, R. O. P., & Hussain, M. (2021). Consumer confusion and green consumption intentions from the perspective of food-related lifestyles on organic infant milk formulas. *Sustainability, 13*(4), 1606. https://doi.org/10.3390/su13041606.

Zakeri, S., Konstantas, D., Chatterjee, P., & Zavadskas, E. K. (2025). Soft cluster-rectangle method for eliciting criteria weights in multi-criteria decision-making. *Scientific Reports, 15*(1), 284. https://doi.org/10.1038/s41598-024-81027-4.

Zhuang, W., Luo, X., & Riaz, M. U. (2021). On the factors influencing green purchase intention: A meta-analysis approach. *Frontiers in Psychology, 12*, 644020. https://doi.org/10.3389/fpsyg.2021.644020.

Žižović, M., & Pamucar, D. (2019). New model for determining criteria weights: Level based weight assessment (LBWA) model. *Decision Making: Applications in Management and Engineering, 2*(2), 126–137. https://doi.org/10.31181/dmame1902102z.

Further reading

Feghali, K., Najem, R., & Metcalfe, B. D. (2025). Greenwashing in the era of sustainability: A systematic literature review. *Corporate Governance and Sustainability Review, 9*(1), 18–31. https://doi.org/10.22495/cgsrv9i1p2.

Chapter 39

SiWeC: simple weight calculation for multi-attribute decision-making

Adis Puška[1], Anđelka Štilić[2], and Darko Božanić[3]

[1]*Department of Public Safety, Government of the Brcko District of BiH, Brčko, Bosnia and Herzegovina,* [2]*The College of Tourism, Academy of Applied Studies Belgrade, Belgrade, Serbia,* [3]*Military Academy, University of Defence in Belgrade, Belgrade, Serbia*

39.1 Introduction

When making decisions, the decision maker (DM) faces various challenges in the decision-making process. Some decisions are simple, made daily, often intuitively, and do not require a scientific approach (Kamarul Zaman et al., 2025). In addition to these, the DM must also handle more complex decisions that involve strategic choices impacted by uncertainty and risk (Phulara et al., 2024). Therefore, the DM must approach these decisions carefully, considering multiple factors that influence the outcome (Trung and Truong, 2025). Based on these decisions, decision theory has evolved as an interdisciplinary scientific field that explores models, methods, and procedures for making informed decisions (Komatina, 2025). With the advancement of decision theory, new methods and approaches have emerged to aid in making the best possible decisions (Stević et al., 2024).

To make the right decision, it is essential to consider all possibilities (Khan et al., 2024). Therefore, when making decisions, it is determined what an alternative must fulfill to be chosen as a decision (Malenovic-Nikolic et al., 2025). Fulfillment of requirements is achieved by defining specific criteria that this alternative must meet (Durmuş, 2025). However, if an alternative best satisfies all requirements, the decision-making process becomes easier, and complex calculations or decision-making methods are not necessary (Chakraborty & Saha, 2024). In practice, it is often the case that no single alternative has the best indicator across all criteria, leading to conflicts in decision-making (Bouraima et al., 2024). These conflicts occur because not all criteria can be satisfied simultaneously (Madić et al., 2024). To address this, multicriteria decision-making (MCDM) was developed. This approach involves making decisions based on multiple criteria (Lukić, 2024). The first step in the MCDM process is to determine the importance of each criterion for the DM (Aytekin & Korucuk, 2024). In practice, there are two main approaches to assessing criterion importance: subjective and objective approaches. The subjective approach actively involves DMs, as they determine the importance of the criteria (Çalikoğlu & Łuczak, 2024). The objective approach is passive or does not involve DMs at all. Passive involvement occurs when evaluating alternatives using these criteria, thereby determining the importance of each criterion based on the evaluations. When the importance of criteria is determined without involving decision-makers, it is done using the existing values of alternatives for specific criteria (Saeed et al., 2024). These values are obtained by quantitatively measuring the characteristics of the alternatives (Radović et al., 2024).

This research focuses on a subjective approach to determining the importance of criteria weights. In this approach, the DM must determine the importance of each criterion based on their own opinion. To make this decision easier for DMs, various methods have been developed for the subjective determination of criterion weights. One of the methods introduced in this chapter is the simple weight calculation (SiWeC) method. The basis for calculating the importance of criteria in this method is the ratings provided by the DM. The steps of the SiWeC method then determine the importance of the criteria in the form of criterion weights. This method was first practically applied by the authors Puška, Nedeljković, Pamučar, et al. (2024) to assess the importance of criteria for selling agricultural products. This chapter aims to present the steps of the SiWeC method and explain how this method is applied to determine criterion weights using practical examples.

Encyclopedia of Multi-Attribute Decision-Making (MADM). DOI: https://doi.org/10.1016/B978-0-443-33275-3.00088-9

39.2 Review of the literature

The SiWeC method is a relatively new approach for determining criterion weights, although it has been used in various studies to date. Its development began with Puška, Nedeljković, Pamučar, et al. (2024), who outlined the method's steps and were the first to apply it practically. They used the SiWeC method in both crisp and fuzzy forms to assess the importance of sales channels. El-Jaberi et al. (2024) further advanced this method by developing a fuzzy-rough approach for determining criterion weights. They evaluated the importance of the criteria through projects involving renewable energy options. Puška, Božanić, et al. (2025) used the same approach to evaluate the importance of criteria when selecting a small electric tractor. Wang et al. (2025), on the other hand, determined criterion weights in the context of solar energy combined with cogeneration technology using neutrosophic Z-numbers.

Successful applications of this method in agriculture and agro-technology are evident in the following works. Puška, Nedeljković, Božanić, et al. (2024) used this method to evaluate the importance of weight in selecting drones for agricultural production, using a fuzzy approach. A similar example was provided by Boz (2025) to assess the significance of criteria in choosing agricultural drones using p, q-quasirung orthopair fuzzy sets. Puška, Štilić, et al. (2025) applied a fuzzy method to determine the importance of criteria in selecting agricultural applications for small farmers.

This method has also been applied to problems in transportation and logistics. Kabakuş and Kaya (2025) used the SiWeC method in fuzzy form to assess the importance of criteria for reducing the loss of human lives in traffic accidents. Cao et al. (2025) used the SiWeC method to determine the importance of criteria in identifying digital twin technologies, using a spherical fuzzy approach. Yalçın, Gürdal Limon, et al. (2025), Yalçın, Kara, et al. (2025) applied interval-valued fermatean fuzzy and SiWeC methods to evaluate the importance of criteria related to transportation performance in G-7 countries. Kaya (2025) used the fuzzy logarithm methodology of additive weights in addition to this approach to assess criteria importance in urban mobility. Kaya and Kabakuş (2025) used the fuzzy SiWeC method to identify criteria significance concerning research on the relationship between logistics centers and heavy vehicle accidents.

When examining problems in the education sector, this method was applied in the following studies. Liu (2025) used the SuperHyperSoft set approach to determine the weights of criteria in an example measuring the efficiency of English language teaching at a university using the SiWeC method. A similar study was conducted by Wang (2025), who used the TreeSoft and SiWeC methods to assess the importance of criteria in evaluating the quality of English language teaching at a university. Zhang (2025) used the HyperSoft set to determine the significance of criteria weights in the study of journalism and communication at universities. Puška and Puška (2024) used the fuzzy SiWeC method to evaluate the importance of criteria in selecting digital online learning platforms. Zhao (2025) used fermatean neutrosophic fuzzy sets to determine the weights of criteria in the study of ideological and political education in higher education institutions.

In infrastructure and technology research, the SiWeC method was used in several studies. Gao and Qian (2025) used this method with trapezoidal fuzzy neutrosophic sets to determine criteria weights in the cost-risk assessment of municipal water and sewage network projects. Duc Trung et al. (2025) used it to evaluate the importance of criteria in material selection. Şimşek et al. (2025) applied it to assess the importance of criteria in solar power plant project selection. Katrancı et al. (2025) used this method to identify critical criteria in solid waste disposal issues.

In applications related to selecting socio-economic and financial applications, this method has been used in the following studies. Yalçın, Gürdal Limon, et al. (2025), Yalçın, Kara, et al. (2025) applied intuitionistic fuzzy sets to assess the importance of traffic policy strategies using the SiWeC method. Çizmecioğlu et al. (2025) used p,q-quasirung orthopair fuzzy numbers to determine the importance of criteria in competitive intelligence for website assessment. Puška, Bosna, et al. (2025) used a fuzzy version of this method to identify key criteria for youth housing. Akgül (2025) used this approach to determine the criteria affecting the financial performance of insurance companies.

39.3 Methodology

The SiWeC method belongs to the subjective group of methods for determining the importance of criteria. In this method, DMs determine the importance of individual criteria. They determine, in their opinion, the importance of an individual criterion for the final decision. When evaluating criteria, DMs do not have to take any actions, such as ranking or comparing criteria with each other, nor do they have to make a comparison with the first or last criterion. They only need to provide an assessment of the criterion's importance. The steps of the SiWeC method, as defined by the authors Puška, Nedeljković, Pamučar, et al. (2024), are as follows:

Step 1. Determining the importance of the criteria by DMs. In this step, DMs evaluate each criterion using assessments that indicate its importance to them. These assessments typically range from one to five or from one to seven, but other scales can also be used as long as a minimum and maximum are defined. If a criterion is more important to the DM, they assign it a higher score; if it is less important, they assign it a lower score.

Step 2. Formation of the decision matrix. This matrix is formed based on the DM ratings. The rows in this matrix represent the DMs, while the columns represent the criteria.

$$A = \begin{matrix} DM_1 \\ DM_2 \\ \vdots \\ DM_m \end{matrix} \begin{bmatrix} x_{11} & x_{12} & \dots & x_{1n} \\ x_{21} & x_{22} & \dots & x_{2n} \\ \vdots & \vdots & \ddots & \vdots \\ x_{m1} & x_{m2} & \cdots & x_{mn} \end{bmatrix} \quad (39.1)$$

Where x_{ij} are the ratings of individual criteria.

Step 3. Normalization of the initial decision matrix. This method uses a different type of normalization than other ranking methods. The key feature of this normalization is that all ratings are considered together and divided by the highest rating value.

$$n_{ij} = \frac{x_{ij}}{x_{ij\ \max}} \quad (39.2)$$

When x_{ijmax} is the maximum rating by all DMs.

Step 4. Calculating the standard deviation for DM ratings ($st.\ dev_j$). The goal of calculating the standard deviation is to measure how spread out an individual DM's ratings are. If the ratings are not very varied and there is not much difference among them, the importance of that DM will be lower because its standard deviation will be smaller, and vice versa. This way, the standard deviation helps determine the DM's contribution to the final criterion weight. If a DM's ratings have a smaller standard deviation, they will have less influence on the final criterion weight, and vice versa. Using the standard deviation effectively guides the DM to prioritize specific criteria, giving their ratings more influence on the final weights of the criteria.

Step 5. Calculating normalized ratings using standard deviation. In this step, the normalized criterion values are weighted by the corresponding standard deviation values for individual DMs' ratings.

$$v_{ij} = n_{ij} \times st.\ dev_j \quad (39.3)$$

Step 6. Calculation of the aggregate value of individual criteria. Here, the weighted scores for each criterion are summed.

$$s_j = \sum_{j=1}^{n} v_j \quad (39.4)$$

Step 7. Calculation of criteria weights. In this step, the individual values s_j are divided by the aggregate value s_j. Applying this step, the sum of all criterion weights equals one.

$$w_j = \frac{s_j}{\sum_{j=1}^{n} s_j} \quad (39.5)$$

39.4 Numerical example 1

The growing global demand for electricity influences how this energy is produced. Electricity can be generated through various methods (Idris & Razak, 2025). The main division of electricity production is between fossil fuels and renewable energy sources. Producing electricity from fossil fuels has a negative environmental impact (Nurgaliuly & Smagulova, 2025), primarily through the release of greenhouse gases, air pollution, and a drop in natural resources (Duong et al., 2025). Recently, renewable energy sources have gained priority in electricity generation.

The choice of an appropriate renewable energy source for electricity generation depends on many factors. To determine which sustainable energy sources produce the best results and should be preferred, it is first necessary to evaluate the importance of different criteria. Based on this, this practical example focuses on assessing the importance of economic criteria for selecting alternatives for producing energy from sustainable sources. Four criteria have been defined for this purpose, as follows:

- Investment costs (C1) refer to the initial funds required to start using a particular alternative for electricity generation.
- Return on investment (C2) shows the relationship between time and income generation, indicating how long it takes for invested funds to be returned.

- Cost of produced electricity (C3) indicates the price of generating electricity from these sources.
- The uncertainty of project income (C4) indicates the risk and unpredictability related to implementing different alternatives for renewable electricity production.

Expert opinion will be used to evaluate the importance of these selected criteria. Employees of the Brčko District Government were selected as experts because this research focused on identifying the most suitable renewable energy alternatives for this local community. To qualify as experts, they needed at least five years of relevant experience with these alternatives. Accordingly, five experts were selected, and they rated these criteria on a scale of 1 to 9 (Table 39.1).

After the experts assessed the importance of the criteria, the importance is determined using the SiWeC method. The evaluation by experts is the first step of this method, after which these evaluations are collected and a decision matrix is formed (see Table 39.1). The third step involves normalizing the elements of the decision matrix. In this step, the highest score among all expert evaluations for each criterion is identified. In this example, the highest score is nine. Then, all values in the decision matrix are divided by this score.

In the example of Expert 1 and criteria C1 and C3, this is calculated as follows:

$$n_{11} = \frac{7}{9} = 0.78, \quad n_{13} = \frac{5}{9} = 0.56$$

Applying this method to calculate normalized data results in a normalized decision matrix (see Table 39.2). Using the normalized data, the next step involves calculating the standard deviation of the expert ratings. In this case, Expert 1 has the highest standard deviation (SD = 0.128) because his ratings deviate the most from the average. Expert 5 has the lowest standard deviation (SD = 0.056). Based on these standard deviation values, Expert 1's ratings will exert the greatest influence on the criteria weights, while Expert 5's ratings will have the least influence.

The next step is to multiply the normalized values by the standard deviation values. In the same example, this is done as follows:

$$v_{11} = 0.778 \times 0.128 = 0.100; v_{13} = 0.556 \times 0.128 = 0.071$$

TABLE 39.1 Evaluation of the criteria significance.

	C1	C2	C3	C4
Expert 1	7	7	5	5
Expert 2	8	9	7	7
Expert 3	9	8	9	7
Expert 4	6	6	5	4
Expert 5	7	8	7	7

TABLE 39.2 Normalized decision matrix and standard deviation.

	C1	C2	C3	C4	*st. dev$_j$*
Expert 1	0.778	0.778	0.556	0.556	0.128
Expert 2	0.889	1.000	0.778	0.778	0.106
Expert 3	1.000	0.889	1.000	0.778	0.106
Expert 4	0.667	0.667	0.556	0.444	0.106
Expert 5	0.778	0.889	0.778	0.778	0.056

TABLE 39.3 Weighted normalized decision matrix and criterion weights.

	C1	C2	C3	C4	
Expert 1	0.100	0.100	0.071	0.071	
Expert 2	0.095	0.106	0.083	0.083	
Expert 3	0.106	0.095	0.106	0.083	
Expert 4	0.071	0.071	0.059	0.047	
Expert 5	0.043	0.049	0.043	0.043	$\Sigma_{j=1}^{n} s_j$
s_j	0.415	0.421	0.363	0.327	1.526
w_j	0.272	0.276	0.238	0.214	

By applying this procedure, the normalized data values are weighted using the standard deviation (see Table 39.3). The final steps of the SiWeC method involve calculating the summary values for each criterion and determining the weights of each criterion. When calculating the summary values, all the values for a single criterion are summed. In the example of criterion C1, this is calculated as follows:

$$s_1 = 0.100 + 0.095 + 0.106 + 0.071 + 0.043 = 0.415$$

By applying this method, the summary value for all criteria is calculated, followed by the summary value for the values ($\Sigma_{j=1}^{n} s_j$). This summary value is formed by adding up all the individual summary values for each criterion. Finally, the individual aggregate values of the criteria are divided by this aggregate value, and the final value of the criterion weights is obtained. In the example of criterion C1, this is calculated as follows:

$$w_1 = \frac{0.415}{1.526} = 0.272$$

The results from the expert ratings and the steps of the SiWeC method showed that the most important criterion, C2, is followed by criterion C1, while criterion C4 is the least important. Based on these results, it can be concluded that the experts are primarily focused on the return on investment for these sustainable electricity generation alternatives.

39.5 Numerical example 2

The share of urban logistics is increasing as more consumers shop online and require delivery services. To reduce the environmental impact of traditional city vehicles, alternative options are being explored, especially electric vehicles (EVs). Using EVs for urban deliveries is environmentally friendly because they emit no CO_2 or greenhouse gases, which are known to harm the ozone layer and contribute to climate change (Srdelić, 2024). These vehicles operate with electric motors powered by batteries, which are recharged at charging stations.

This example demonstrates the criteria selection process for purchasing EVs for urban distribution at the **city express** (CE) company. To address this, the CE company hired six DMs who are employees of the organization. To qualify as a DM, an employee needed to be directly involved in urban logistics and have knowledge about EVs. The criteria were evaluated based on ratings from 1 to 9 given by the DMs. The following criteria were used for the evaluation process:

- Price (C1), which indicates the monetary value of the vehicle available on the market.
- Acceleration (C2) indicates the time for which the vehicle can reach a speed from 0 to 100 km/h.
- Range (C3) shows the potential distance an EV can cover with a full 100% battery.
- Engine power (C4) indicates the vehicle's engine power in kilowatts.
- Battery capacity (C5) indicates the battery's capacity in kilowatts.
- Charge time (C6) indicates how long it takes to charge an empty battery to 100%.
- Vehicle consumption (C7) indicates the energy used by EVs per kilometer.
- Max. payload (C8) indicates the maximum load capacity of these vehicles in kilograms.
- Cargo volume (C9) indicates the maximum cargo capacity in liters.

After the ratings from the DMs were collected, a decision matrix was created to display the criteria ratings by the DMs (Table 39.4).

The next step in calculating the weight of criteria using the SiWeC method is to normalize the decision matrix. As in the previous case, since the highest score is 9, all values in the decision matrix are divided by 9 (see Table 39.5). After that,

TABLE 39.4 Decision matrix.

	C1	C2	C3	C4	C5	C6	C7	C8	C9
DM 1	8	8	9	8	8	8	8	8	9
DM 2	7	6	9	6	5	8	8	8	9
DM 3	8	8	9	8	9	7	7	8	9
DM 4	8	7	9	9	9	8	7	8	8
DM 5	9	5	6	6	8	8	7	6	6
DM 6	9	6	7	7	7	6	5	6	7

TABLE 39.5 Normalized decision matrix and standard deviation values.

	C1	C2	C3	C4	C5	C6	C7	C8	C9	St. dev.
DM 1	0.889	0.889	1.000	0.889	0.889	0.889	0.889	0.889	1.000	0.049
DM 2	0.778	0.667	1.000	0.667	0.556	0.889	0.889	0.889	1.000	0.157
DM 3	0.889	0.889	1.000	0.889	1.000	0.778	0.778	0.889	1.000	0.087
DM 4	0.889	0.778	1.000	1.000	1.000	0.889	0.778	0.889	0.889	0.087
DM 5	1.000	0.556	0.667	0.667	0.889	0.889	0.778	0.667	0.667	0.145
DM 6	1.000	0.667	0.778	0.778	0.778	0.667	0.556	0.667	0.778	0.124

TABLE 39.6 Weighted decision matrix and results of the simple weight calculation method.

	C1	C2	C3	C4	C5	C6	C7	C8	C9
DM 1	0.044	0.044	0.049	0.044	0.044	0.044	0.044	0.044	0.049
DM 2	0.122	0.105	0.157	0.105	0.087	0.140	0.140	0.140	0.157
DM 3	0.077	0.077	0.087	0.077	0.087	0.068	0.068	0.077	0.087
DM 4	0.077	0.068	0.087	0.087	0.087	0.077	0.068	0.077	0.077
DM 5	0.145	0.080	0.096	0.096	0.129	0.129	0.112	0.096	0.096
DM 6	0.124	0.083	0.097	0.097	0.097	0.083	0.069	0.083	0.097
s_j	0.589	0.456	0.573	0.505	0.530	0.539	0.500	0.517	0.563
w_j	0.123	0.096	0.120	0.106	0.111	0.113	0.105	0.108	0.118

the standard deviation of the DM scores is calculated (see Table 39.5). Based on the standard deviation, it can be concluded that the scores given by DM 2 will have the greatest impact on the weight of the criteria, while those given by DM 1 will have the least impact.

The next step in the SiWeC method is weighting, where the normalized data are multiplied by the standard deviation values for each DM. Then, the sum of the individual criteria values and the final weights of the criteria are calculated (see Table 39.6). Based on the results of the SiWeC method and the DM scores, criterion C1 has the greatest importance, followed by criterion C3, while criterion C2 has the least importance. These results indicate that for the DM to deliver EVs effectively, they must be well priced and capable of traveling many kilometers on a single charge.

39.6 Conclusions

This chapter aims to present the SiWeC method, one of the newer approaches. Its function is to define or calculate the weighting coefficients of criteria in the group decision-making process. This method is subjective, where the importance of the criteria is determined based on the ratings of DMs, that is, experts. The SiWeC method has several unique features that set it apart from other similar methods. First, experts are responsible for assessing the criteria or defining their importance. Since the method normalizes experts' opinions, different scales can be used to determine the importance of criteria, depending on the specifics of the problem. Another key feature is that the importance of experts is determined based on their opinions. For this, the standard deviation is calculated, where a higher value indicates greater importance of the expert, and vice versa. Another distinctive aspect is the similarity of the method to ranking methods for alternatives, as the normalized values are ultimately weighted by the standard deviation.

These specific features demonstrate that the SiWeC method has distinct steps that distinguish it from others. The method is simple to apply and provides direct access to the criterion weight coefficients. The calculation involves seven straightforward steps. This method has been used in various forms in previous studies, with various variants developed. Therefore, its use is recommended in future research whenever it is necessary to determine criterion weight coefficients in MCDM problems. Based on the examples provided, the clear benefits of the SiWeC method are evident and highlighted as follows:

- The importance of the criteria for this method is assessed simply: DMs only need to rate each criterion.
- The ratings provided by DMs do not need to be whole numbers; decimals are acceptable as long as they fall within the specified rating interval, which can vary significantly.
- The steps of the SiWeC method are simple to follow. There are no complicated mathematical expressions and calculations.
- The criterion weights produced by this method mirror the initial ratings of the DMs.
- The ratings of DMs are more valuable, and their influence on the final value of the criterion weights varies depending on their dispersion. Therefore, DMs need to demonstrate critical thinking when making assessments.

In addition to its advantages, this method also has some disadvantages. When assessing criteria of equal importance, the DMs tend to give similar ratings, which have little impact on the final weight of the criteria. The importance of the DMs' ratings depends more on their dispersion than on their expertise. Therefore, future research could modify this method by allowing DMs to give different ratings. Additionally, different operators could be used to determine the weights, and further steps could be added to tailor the method to the DMs' specific needs.

References

Akgül, Y. (2025). A novel MCDM framework for evaluating corporate financial performance: Evidence from the Turkish insurance sector. *Journal of Operational and Strategic Analytics, 3*(2), 65–79. https://doi.org/10.56578/josa030201.

Aytekin, A., & Korucuk, S. (2024). Assessing the innovation capacity of manufacturing firms in ordu province: A multi-criteria evaluation using CIMAS. *Journal of Intelligent Management Decision, 3*(4), 224–230. https://doi.org/10.56578/jimd030403.

Bouraima, M. B., Jovčić, S., Dobrodolac, M., Pamucar, D., Badi, I., & Maraka, N. D. (2024). Sustainable healthcare system devolution strategy selection using the AROMAN MCDM approach. *Spectrum of Decision Making and Applications, 1*(1), 46–63. https://doi.org/10.31181/sdmap1120243.

Boz, E. (2025). Evaluation for the selection of agricultural spraying drones using p, q-Quasirung orthopair fuzzy logic and multi-criteria methods. *Scientific Reports, 15*(1), 27606. https://doi.org/10.1038/s41598-025-11656-w.

Çalikoğlu, C., & Łuczak, A. (2024). Multidimensional assessment of SDI and HDI using TOPSIS and bilinear ordering. *International Journal of Economic Sciences, 13*(2), 116–128. https://doi.org/10.52950/ES.2024.13.2.007.

Cao, J., Spulbar, C., Eti, S., Horobet, A., Yüksel, S., & Dinçer, H. (2025). Innovative approaches to green digital twin technologies of sustainable smart cities using a novel hybrid decision-making system. *Journal of Innovation & Knowledge, 10*(1), 100651. https://doi.org/10.1016/j.jik.2025.100651.

Chakraborty, S., & Saha, A. (2024). Selection of forklift unit for transport handling using integrated MCDM under neutrosophic environment. *Facta Universitatis, Series: Mechanical Engineering, 22*(2), 235–256. https://doi.org/10.22190/FUME220620039C.

Çizmecioğlu, S., Çalık, A., & Tirkolaee, E. B. (2025). An integrated p,q-quasirung orthopair fuzzy decision-making approach for strategic selection of competitive intelligence platforms. *Engineering Applications of Artificial Intelligence, 158*, 111498. https://doi.org/10.1016/j.engappai.2025.111498.

Duc Trung, D., Dung, H. T., Bao, N. C., & Van Duc, D. (2025). A novel approach for determining criteria weights: Application in ranking materials for mechanical manufacturing processes. *Manufacturing Review, 12*, 16. https://doi.org/10.1051/mfreview/2025014.

Duong, T. T. T., Long, T. H., Anh, D. P., Dai, N. M. T., Ngan, D. N. K., & Xuan, N. T. T. (2025). The impact of education on energy poverty: Empirical evidence from Vietnam. *ECONOMICS - Innovative and Economics Research Journal, 13*(2), 265–281. https://doi.org/10.2478/eoik-2025-0043.

Durmuş, Z. (2025). Assessment of renewable energy performance in Turkey using a novel integrated MSD-CRITIC-RAWEC model. *Journal of Operational and Strategic Analytics, 3*(1), 49–64. https://doi.org/10.56578/josa030105.

El-Jaberi, I. K. A., Stojanović, I., Puška, A., Ljepava, N., & Prodanović, R. (2024). Selection of renewable energy projects from the investor's Point of View based on the fuzzy–rough approach and the Bonferroni mean operator. *Sustainability, 16*(22), 9929. https://doi.org/10.3390/su16229929.

Gao, H., & Qian, K. (2025). Risk assessment of municipal water supply and drainage project costs using neutrosophic numbers. *Neutrosophic Sets and Systems, 81*(1), 712–728.

Idris, A., & Razak, R. A. (2025). Energy transition, green growth and emission on economic growth using spline approach: Evidence from Asia-Pasific countries. *ECONOMICS - Innovative and Economics Research Journal, 13*(2), 139–159. https://doi.org/10.2478/eoik-2025-0034.

Kabakuş, N., & Kaya, Ö. (2025). A new data-driven model for vehicle and pedestrian safety: Statistical approach based on spatial decision-making. *International Journal of Injury Control and Safety Promotion*. https://doi.org/10.1080/17457300.2025.2537683 online first.

Kamarul Zaman, M. M., Rodzi, Z. M., Andu, Y., Shafie, N. A., Sanusi, Z. M., Ghazali, A. W., & Mahyideen, J. M. (2025). Adaptive utility ranking algorithm for evaluating blockchain-enabled microfinance in emerging - A new MCDM perspective. *International Journal of Economic Sciences, 14*(1), 123–146. https://doi.org/10.31181/ijes1412025182.

Katrancı, A., Kundakcı, N., & Arman, K. (2025). Fuzzy SIWEC and fuzzy RAWEC methods for sustainable waste disposal technology selection. *Spectrum of Operational Research, 3*(1), 87–102. https://doi.org/10.31181/sor31202633.

Kaya, Ö. (2025). Designing green and safe micro mobility routes: An advanced geo-analytic decision system based approach to sustainable urban infrastructure. *Engineering Science and Technology an International Journal, 64*, 102027. https://doi.org/10.1016/j.jestch.2025.102027.

Kaya, Ö., & Kabakuş, N. (2025). A data-driven spatial decision framework for assessing the relationship between logistics activities and heavy vehicle accident risks. *Research in Transportation Business & Management, 62*, 101440. https://doi.org/10.1016/j.rtbm.2025.101440.

Khan, A. A., Mashat, D. S., & Dong, K. (2024). Evaluating sustainable urban development strategies through spherical CRITIC-WASPAS analysis. *Journal of Urban Development and Management, 3*(1), 1–17. https://doi.org/10.56578/judm030101.

Komatina, N. (2025). A novel BWM-RADAR approach for multi-attribute selection of equipment in the automotive industry. *Spectrum of Mechanical Engineering and Operational Research, 2*(1), 104–120. https://doi.org/10.31181/smeor21202531.

Liu, J. (2025). Application of the SuperHyperSoft set for comprehensive teaching quality analysis in college english translation courses for enhanced learning results. *Neutrosophic Sets and Systems, 82*(1), 443–457.

Lukić, R. (2024). Evaluation of trade performance dynamics in Serbia using ARAT and rough MABAC methods. *Oeconomica Jadertina, 14*(2), 34–44. https://doi.org/10.15291/oec.4559.

Madić, M., Petrović, G., Petković, D., & Janković, P. (2024). Traditional and integrated MCDM approaches for assessment and ranking of laser cutting conditions. *Spectrum of Mechanical Engineering and Operational Research, 1*(1), 250–257. https://doi.org/10.31181/smeor11202422.

Malenovic-Nikolic, J., Zlatkovic, B., & Milosevic, L. (2025). Education indicators and decision analytics: A basis for using renewable energy sources and knowledge management. *Journal of Decision Analytics and Intelligent Computing, 5*(1), 148–158. https://doi.org/10.31181/jdaic10013072025m.

Nurgaliuly, A., & Smagulova, S. (2025). Economic assessment of energy security of the regions of Kazakhstan. *ECONOMICS - Innovative and Economics Research Journal, 13*(2), 223–243. https://doi.org/10.2478/eoik-2025-0038.

Phulara, S., Kumar, A., Narang, M., & Bisht, K. (2024). A novel hybrid grey-BCM approach in multi-criteria decision making: An application in OTT platform. *Journal of Decision Analytics and Intelligent Computing, 4*(1), 1–15. https://doi.org/10.31181/jdaic10016012024p.

Puška, A., Bosna, J., & Božanić, D. (2025). Evaluation of the housing aggregation model for young people in urban areas. *Journal of Urban Development and Management, 4*(1), 58–70. https://doi.org/10.56578/judm040105.

Puška, A., Božanić, D., Štilić, A., Nedeljković, M., & Khalilzadeh, M. (2025). Application of fuzzy-rough methodology to the selection of electric tractors for small farms in Semberija. *Journal of Fuzzy Extension and Applications, 6*(4), 651–668. https://doi.org/10.22105/jfea.2025.482890.1663.

Puška, A., Nedeljković, M., Božanić, D., Štilić, A., & Muhsen, Y. R. (2024). Evaluation of agricultural drones based on the COmpromise Ranking from Alternative SOlutions (CORASO) methodology. *Engineering Review, 44*(4), 77–90. https://doi.org/10.30765/er.2653.

Puška, A., Nedeljković, M., Pamučar, D., Božanić, D., & Simić, V. (2024). Application of the new simple weight calculation (SIWEC) method in the case study in the sales channels of agricultural products. *MethodsX, 13*, 102930. https://doi.org/10.1016/j.mex.2024.102930.

Puška, A., Štilić, A., Nedeljković, M., Božanić, D., & Pamucar, D. (2025). Evaluation of mobile applications for small farms using fuzzy methods. *International Journal of Research in Industrial Engineering, 14*(3), 426–444. https://doi.org/10.22105/riej.2025.491961.1503.

Puška, E., & Puška, A. (2024). The application of fuzzy multi-criteria methods for the selection of digital platforms for the improvement of the learning process at universities in the Brčko District of BiH. *Education Science and Management, 2*(4), 230–240. https://doi.org/10.56578/esm020404.

Radović, M., Stević, Ž., Mijić, D., Govedarica-lučić, A., Bodiroga, R., & Vico, G. (2024). Evaluation of criteria in fruit production using the interval fuzzy rough PIPRECIA method. *Journal of Operational and Strategic Analytics, 2*(4), 266–274. https://doi.org/10.56578/josa020405.

Saeed, M., Basit Ali, M., Rahman, A., & Yasir Hayat Malik, M. (2024). A multi-attribute decision making context for supply chain management using possibility single-valued neutrosophic soft settings. *Yugoslav Journal of Operations Research, 34*(4), 825–847. https://doi.org/10.2298/YJOR240315033S.

Şimşek, E., Eti, S., Yüksel, S., & Dinçer, H. (2025). Evaluation of purchasing process in solar energy investment projects via SIWEC methodology. *Spectrum of Operational Research, 3*(1), 81–86. https://doi.org/10.31181/sor31202636.

Srdelić, L. (2024). Transition risks of climate change: An analysis of greenhouse gas emissions in Croatia and the Euro Area. *Oeconomica Jadertina, 14*(1), 74–90. https://doi.org/10.15291/oec.4433.

Stević, Ž., Baydaş, M., Kavacık, M., Ayhan, E., & Marinković, D. (2024). Selection of data conversion technique via sensitivity-performance matching: Ranking of small e-vans with PROBID method. *Facta Universitatis, Series: Mechanical Engineering, 22*(4), 643–671. https://doi.org/10.22190/FUME240305023S.

Trung, D., Truong, N., Duc, D., & Bao, N. (2025). Data normalization in RAWEC method: Limitations and remedies. *Yugoslav Journal of Operations Research, 35*(3), 467–482. https://doi.org/10.2298/YJOR240315020T.

Wang, W., Nie, C., Li, K., & Man, J. (2025). Neutrosophic Z-number and hypersoft for integrated energy supply system performance inference of solar energy and cogenerations. *Neutrosophic Sets and Systems, 82*(1), 17–31.

Wang, Y. (2025). Comprehensive analysis of application of multi-criteria decision-making methods with treesoft set for teaching quality improvement of college english learning process. *Neutrosophic Sets and Systems, 82*(1), 562–577.

Yalçın, G. C., Gürdal Limon, E., Kara, K., Limon, O., Gürol, P., Deveci, M., Demirayak, Ö., & Tomášková, H. (2025). A hybrid decision support system for transport policy selection: A case study on Russia's Northern Sea route in Artic region. *Socio-economic Planning Sciences, 98*, 102171. https://doi.org/10.1016/j.seps.2025.102171.

Yalçın, G. C., Kara, K., Özekenci, E. K., Simic, V., & Pamucar, D. (2025). Green maritime transport performance analysis of G-7 countries using an interval-valued Fermatean fuzzy ARLON-based decision model. *Applied Soft Computing, 184*, 113677. https://doi.org/10.1016/j.asoc.2025.113677.

Zhang, X. (2025). Assessing teaching effectiveness in journalism and communication: A data-driven perspective using HyperSoft set. *Neutrosophic Sets and Systems, 83*(1), 65–86. https://doi.org/10.5281/zenodo.15122528.

Zhao, W. (2025). Analysis factors of ideological and political education in colleges and universities in the new media era under the Fermatean neutrosophic sets. *Neutrosophic Sets and Systems, 83*(1), 96–108. https://doi.org/10.5281/zenodo.15122565.

Section 2

Extensions for the MADM methods

Chapter 40

Parsimonious: a concept for multi-attribute decision-making

Sarbast Moslem[1,2], Tapan Senapati[3], and Szabolcs Duleba[4,5]

[1]*Department of Civil, Structural and Environmental Engineering, Trinity College Dublin, Dublin, Ireland,* [2]*Civil Engineering Department, Faculty of Engineering and Natural Sciences, Istinye University, Istanbul, Turkey,* [3]*Saveetha School of Engineering, Saveetha Institute of Medical and Technical Sciences, Chennai, Tamil Nadu, India,* [4]*Department of Transport Technology and Economics, Faculty of Transportation and Vehicle Engineering, Budapest University of Technology and Economics, Budapest, Hungary,* [5]*Institute of Mathematics and Informatics, University of Nyíregyháza, Nyíregyháza, Hungary*

40.1 Introduction

Assessing intricate, real-world issues with the help of decision-making models grows more complex, this occurs in all areas, from ecological concerns to corporate administration. Assessing these involved issues requires considering multiple criteria and alternatives related to the issue, and this increases the effort of assessment and lengthens the time spent when employing conventional multicriteria decision-making (MCDM) models (Butturi et al., 2025; Moslem, 2025). For example, both analytic hierarchy process (AHP) (Saaty, 1977) and best-worst method (BWM) (Rezaei, 2015) necessitate substantial time and effort to assess the pairwise comparison matrices, which not only encumbers evaluators but also amplifies the inconsistency issue in assessments. In this research, the parsimonious preference information has been introduced to considerably reduce the effort and time consumed throughout the assessment process. As an illustration, we present the primary steps of integrating parsimonious preference information with AHP.

Recent studies demonstrate both methodological innovations and diverse applications, establishing parsimony as a cornerstone of next-generation decision-support systems. Kabirifar et al. (2023) designed a cybernetic MCDM framework with the parsimonious preference information to assess the implementation of the Circular Economy in waste disposal. Their research shows how parsimony aids in managing intricacy in evaluating construction and demolition waste strategies. By merging parsimony into a cybernetic control loop, the authors diminish redundancy in evaluations while enhancing adaptability to evolving sustainability objectives.

Methodological advancements are further illustrated by Moslem (2023), who presented a concise BWM with the parsimonious preference information for assessing travel mode preference. Unlike conventional BWM, which could still necessitate many comparisons, the parsimonious preference information utilizes reference points to reduce elicitation needs. Significantly, Moslem demonstrates that parsimony boosts participant involvement and coherence, which are frequently vulnerabilities in survey-based choice processes. This study supports the concept that parsimony can improve methodological dependability and practical applicability. Fattoruso et al. (2022) suggested a dynamic, concise AHP model. Their strategy recognizes that choices within industrial systems evolve over time and must incorporate historical plus recent data. The parsimonious preference information here acts as a filter, permitting decision-makers to concentrate on crucial reference comparisons while securing adaptability. The public sector has also seen benefits from simple and efficient innovations. Duleba (2022) introduced a multilevel Parsimonious analytic hierarchy process (P-AHP) method for transport development, showing how using fewer elements in layers can make the evaluation process easier for decision-makers while keeping the structure of decisions clear and organized. Júnior et al. (2023) used P-AHP in public governance to assess leadership within organizations. Both studies show that using simpler methods can help more people get involved in decision-making, especially when many stakeholders are involved, and complexity might otherwise reduce trust in the process. Butturi et al. (2025) compared different simple methods to set up a supply chain observatory, showing how simplicity helps compare different factors across various areas. In manufacturing, Fattoruso et al. (2024) combined simple

Encyclopedia of Multi-Attribute Decision-Making (MADM). DOI: https://doi.org/10.1016/B978-0-443-33275-3.00041-5

AHP with clustering methods to solve issues with production mistakes, showing how simplicity and data-based methods can work well together. Meanwhile, Moslem (2024) used P-AHP in a more complex setting, called spherical fuzzy, for sustainable urban transport, dealing with uncertain situations while keeping the process of entering preferences simple and clear.

Tourism and environmental uses show how widely this method can be applied. Jamal Mahdi and Esztergár-Kiss (2024) used P-AHP to help people make decisions when choosing where to travel. Carlucci et al. (2021) used P-AHP for protecting whales and dolphins, showing how it can help with managing nature. Wu (2023) created a new system called parsimoniously interactive multiple attribute rating to categorize things in big industries, making it easier to manage large decisions. Al-lami and Török (2025) used P-AHP to check how sustainable public transport is, linking city planning with environmental studies. A common idea in all these studies is that keeping things simple helps keep the order of choices clear and consistent. They often use formulas to make sure the rankings stay the same. This feature helps avoid a common problem in AHP where rankings can change unexpectedly. It also makes it easier for people to make decisions because they don't have to work too hard. Combining this method with fuzzy logic, grouping similar things, or using models that change over time makes it more flexible for tricky or changing situations. All these studies show that keeping things simple isn't just a small change from older methods—it's a big shift in how we think about making decisions with many factors.

In this work, the main steps of integrating the parsimonious preference information with AHP, which is the most popular and applied MCDM method.

40.2 Methodology

The assessment of intricate real-world challenges through the application of decision-making frameworks becomes increasingly convoluted; this phenomenon is pervasive across various domains, ranging from ecological concerns to industrial administration. For instance, AHP requires substantial time and resources to assess the pairwise comparison matrices, which not only imposes a burden on evaluators but also exacerbates the issue of inconsistency within the evaluations. In this research, the introduction of parsimonious preference information is proposed to markedly reduce both the effort and the time expended during the evaluative process. To illustrate this, we delineate the primary steps involved in the integration of parsimonious preference information with AHP.

MCDM methods provide systematic procedures for structuring and solving decision problems involving multiple, often conflicting, criteria. The general process typically involves five main steps, which are shown in Fig. 40.1.

A recurring challenge in MCDM is cognitive burden: many methods require a large number of preference inputs, which can be impractical in real applications. For this reason, methodological innovations increasingly aim to reduce the number

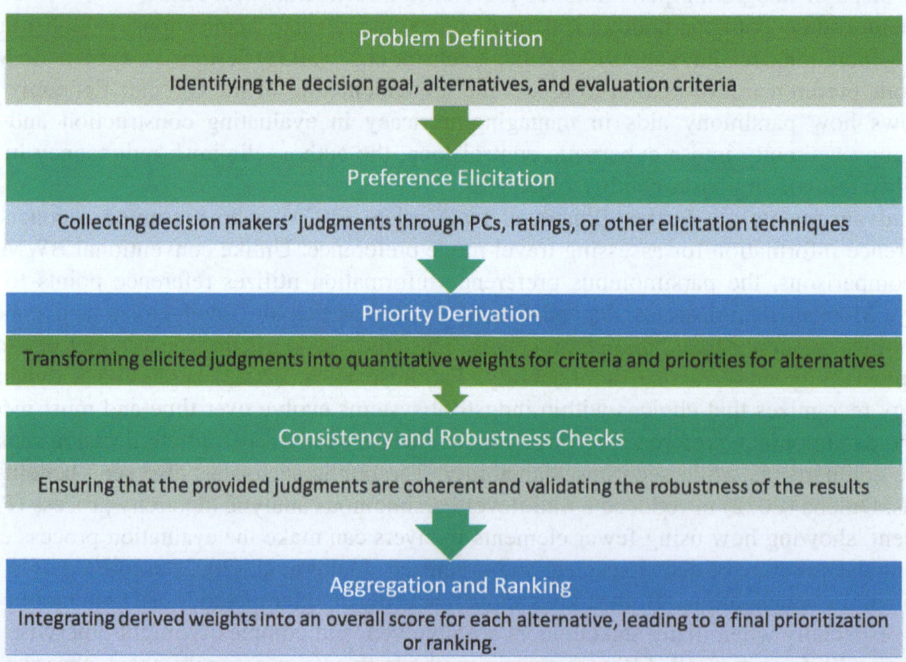

FIGURE 40.1 General framework of multicriteria decision-making models.

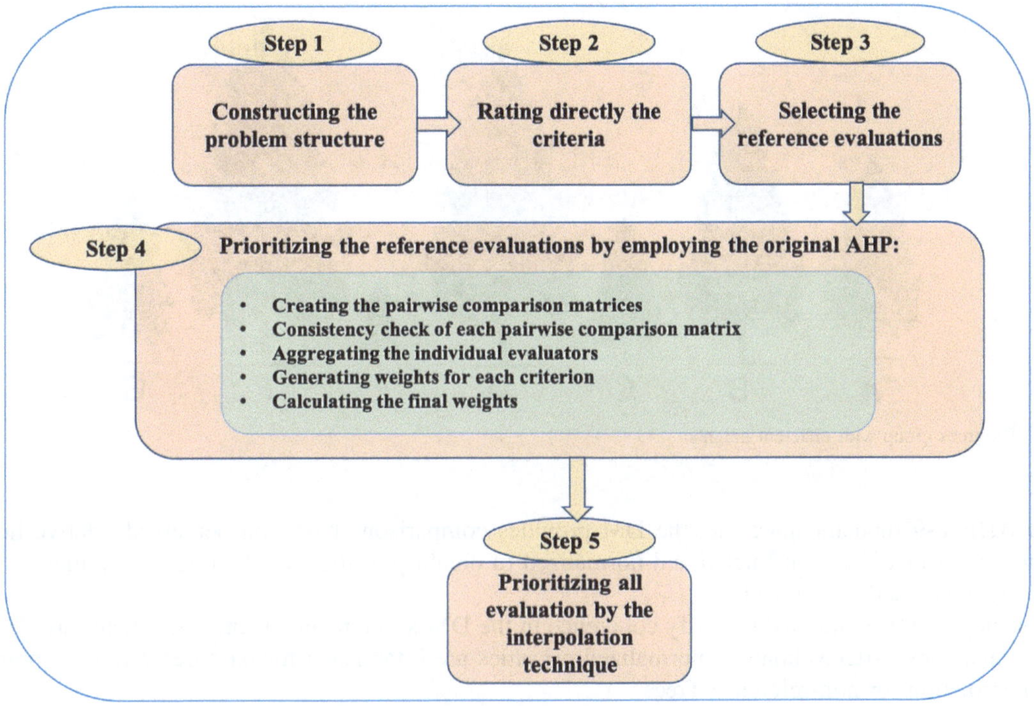

FIGURE 40.2 The main steps of the parsimonious analytic hierarchy process.

of required pairwise comparisons (PCs) while maintaining accuracy and reliability. Here, the parsimonious preference information could play a critical role in reducing the PCs numbers, which significantly decreases the effort and minimizes the evaluation time. The methodology details of the parsimonious AHP are presented in Moslem (2024), and the methodology details of the parsimonious BWM are presented in Moslem (2023).

The main steps of conducting parsimonious AHP are shown in Fig. 40.2.

The main advantages of adopting the parsimonious preference information with MCDM models are saving the time and effort significantly when the problems involve a high number of criteria, which is the general case for most real-world complex problems. It simply minimizes the evaluation process and improves judgment consistency, also more reliable. However, the advantages can be represented by oversimplifying the complex problems, and it may reduce the model's discrimination power.

40.3 Illustrative example (1)

To demonstrate the application of the proposed parsimonious AHP procedure, let us consider a simple problem: estimating the relative height of seven trees (labeled A–G) (see Fig. 40.3). The evaluator is asked to provide a subjective numerical assessment of the height of each tree, normalized with respect to Tree E, which is set as the reference with a value equal to 1. The decision maker (DM) or evaluator supplies the following initial ratings:

Tree E = 1, Tree C = 1.5, Tree G = 2, Tree A = 2.5, Tree B = 3, Tree D = 4, Tree F = 5

Step 1. Direct ratings

The evaluator or DM expresses the relative heights on a common scale, effectively providing initial subjective estimates. This step avoids an exhaustive set of PCs among all trees (21 comparisons).

Step 2. Selection of reference points

From the given ratings, a small subset of trees is chosen to represent the range of performance. Suppose the evaluator selects Trees E (lowest, value = 1), B (midpoint, value = 3), and F (highest, value = 5) as reference points.

Step 3. PCs on references

The DM now performs PCs only among the reference trees. For example:

- E vs B
- E vs F
- B vs F

FIGURE 40.3 The trees group with different heights.

Using the AHP 1–9 fundamental scale, the DM provides comparisons based on perceived relative heights. A local pairwise comparison matrix is constructed and normalized to obtain priorities for the reference points.

Step 4. Consistency and adjustment

The consistency ratio is computed to verify coherence in the DM's judgments. If inconsistencies are detected, the DM can adjust comparisons. After validation, normalized priorities are established for the three reference points.

Step 5. Interpolation for non-reference Trees

The normalized values of Trees C, G, A, and D (nonreference trees) are interpolated using the derived priorities of E, B, and F. For instance, since Tree A (2.5) lies between E (1) and B (3), its final priority is adjusted through linear interpolation to ensure consistency with the pairwise comparisons of the references.

The mathematical model is as follows:

Let us donate: $s(n_m(a))$ the normalized evaluation score of the factor m with respect to alternative a, which is calculated from the interpolation of the values adopted by the reference BWM in the steps 3 and 4,

$s(\gamma_{mr})$ is the normalized BWM score of $r + 1$ reference factor computed from the PC,
γ_{mr} is a direct evaluation of s reference factor by the evaluators,
γ_{mr+1} direct evaluation of the $r + 1$ reference element by the evaluators,
$dc_m(a)$ direct corresponding rating provided by the evaluator to alternative a.

For each $dcm(a) \in [\gamma_{mr}, \gamma_{mr+1}]$, the following value has to be provided, which avoids the rank reversal issue:

$$s(n_m(a)) = s(\gamma_{mr}) + \frac{s(\gamma_{ms+1}) - u(\gamma_{mr})}{\gamma_{mr+1} - \gamma_{mr}}(dc_m(a) - \gamma_{mr}) \tag{40.1}$$

Instead of asking the DM to provide 21 PCs (the full AHP requirement for seven elements), the proposed procedure requires:

- Seven direct ratings (initial height estimates), and
- Three PCs (only among the reference points).

This results in a total of 10 preference inputs, a drastic reduction compared to the classical approach, while ensuring more reliable and cognitively manageable judgments.

Here is a computational example of the illustrative case. Since the evaluator and analyst have agreed to use three reference trees (A, E, F), we need to build the pairwise comparison matrix with Saaty's 1–9 scale. Here's how we can present it step by step in academic style:

Step 1. Selection of reference alternatives

The evaluator selects Tree E (value = 1), Tree A (value = 2.5), and Tree F (value = 5) as reference alternatives. These span the spectrum from the smallest to the tallest tree.

Thus, the reference set is as follows:

$$\Gamma = \{E = 1, |A = 2.5, |F = 5\}$$

Step 2. PCs

The evaluator compares the three reference trees using Saaty's fundamental 1–9 scale. The judgments are based on perceived relative heights:

- A vs E: Since Tree A (2.5) is approximately 2.5 times taller than Tree E (1), the evaluator assigns a preference of three (moderate importance).
- F vs E: Since Tree F (5) is five times taller than Tree E (1), the evaluator assigns a preference of five (strong importance).
- F vs A: Tree F (5) is twice as tall as Tree A (2.5), so the evaluator assigns a preference of two (slight to moderate importance).

Step 3. Pairwise comparison matrix

The corresponding AHP matrix is presented in Table 40.1.

Step 4. Normalization and priority vector

To derive priorities, the matrix is normalized column-wise, and the row averages are computed (classical eigenvector approximation) (Table 40.2).

Step 5. Interpolation of nonreference alternatives

We now have the normalized priority weights of the three reference trees and their associated original height values. The other trees must be mapped into this scale of normalized priorities using linear interpolation between adjacent reference points.

Step 5.1. Define reference segments

- Segment 1: from E = 1 (priority 0.110) to A = 2.5 (priority 0.309)
- Segment 2: from A = 2.5 (priority 0.309) to F = 5 (priority 0.581)

Step 5.2. Interpolation formula

For a tree with value xxx lying between two reference points (x_1, w_1) and (x_2, w_2), the interpolated priority is:

$$w(x) = w_1 + \frac{(x - x_1)}{(x_2 - x_1)} \cdot (w_2 - w_1)$$

Step 5.3. Interpolated priorities

TABLE 40.1 The corresponding analytic hierarchy process matrix.

Reference trees	E (1)	A (2.5)	F (5)
E (1)	1	1/3	1/5
A (2.5)	3	1	1/2
F (5)	5	2	1

TABLE 40.2 The normalized pairwise comparison matrix.

Reference trees	E (9)	A (3.33)	F (1.70)	w	Associated original height values
E (1)	0.111	0.100	0.118	0.110	1
A (2.5)	0.333	0.300	0.294	0.309	2.5
F (5)	0.556	0.600	0.588	0.581	5

TABLE 40.3 The final normalized priority.

Tree	Height value	Normalized priority	Rank
E	1.0	0.110	1
C	1.5	0.176	2
G	2.0	0.243	3
A	2.5	0.309	4
B	3.0	0.363	5
D	4.0	0.472	6
F	5.0	0.581	7

- C = 1.5 (between E = 1 and A = 2.5)

$$w(C) = 0.110 + ((1.5 - 1)/(2.5 - 1)) * (0.309 - 0.110) = 0.110 + (0.5/1.5) * 0.199 = 0.110 + 0.066 = 0.176$$

- G = 2 (between E = 1 and A = 2.5)

$$w(G) = 0.110 + ((2 - 1)/1.5) * 0.199 = 0.110 + (1/1.5) * 0.199 = 0.110 + 0.133 = 0.243$$

B = 3 (between A = 2.5 and F = 5)

$$w(B) = 0.309 + ((3 - 2.5)/2.5) * (0.581 - 0.309) = 0.363$$

- D = 4 (between A = 2.5 and F = 5)

$$w(D) = 0.309 + ((4 - 2.5)/2.5) * 0.272 = 0.472$$

Step 6. Final priority vector for all trees (Table 40.3)

This procedure shows how only a few PCs (among reference points) can generate a full priority scale for all alternatives, reducing the cognitive effort compared to traditional AHP.

40.4 Illustrative example (2)

The second example will be about integrating the parsimonious preference information with BWM, the main steps of the model is similar to the previous example, however, after selecting the reference criteria, we should evaluate them by using BWM, and this is applicable for all other MCDM methods. Moslem (2023) applied BWM with parsimonious preference information, and will present the main steps in detail as it is shown in Fig. 40.4.

We will present the results of the Tree example,

Step 1. Identify the criteria (alternatives here are the seven trees)

The evaluator needs to prioritize the trees by their height.

Step 2. Determine the best and worst alternatives

Best (tallest): F (5)

Worst (shortest): E (1)

Step 3. Compare the best alternative against all others

The evaluator expresses preferences using Saaty's 1–9 scale. For simplicity, let's assume the following judgments (closer heights → smaller value, larger difference → larger value):

- F vs E=9
- F vs C=8
- F vs G=7
- F vs A=6

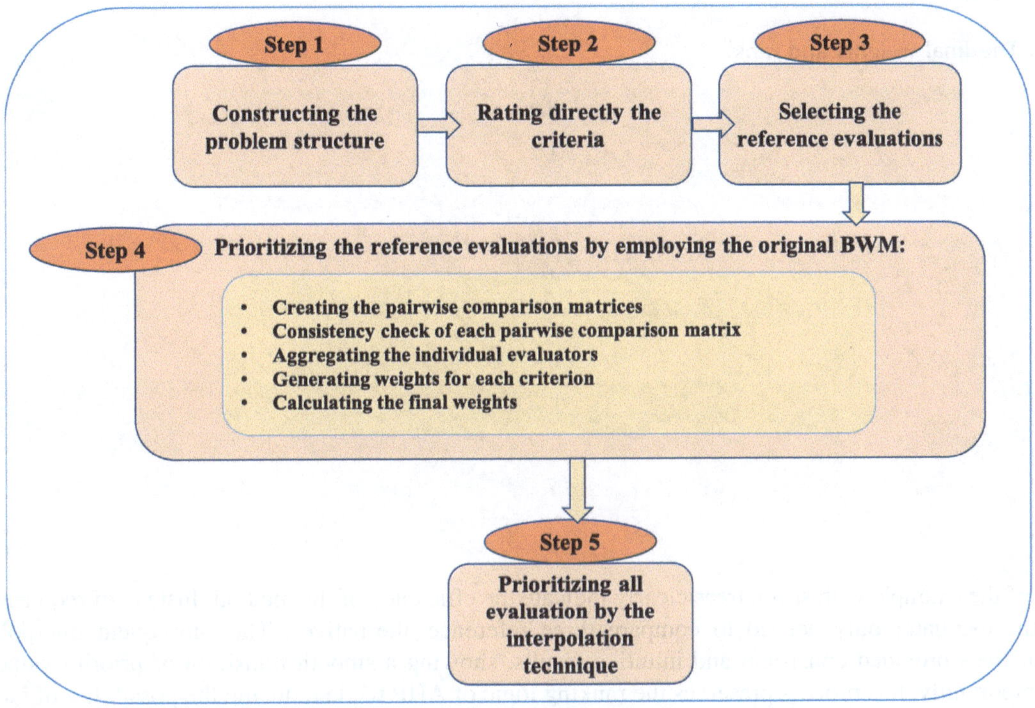

FIGURE 40.4 The main steps of the parsimonious best–worst method.

- F vs B=5
- F vs D=3
- F vs F=1

So, the best-to-others vector = [9, 8, 7, 6, 5, 3, 1].

Step 4. Compare all others against the worst alternative

Now, each tree is compared with E (the worst):

- E vs E=1
- C vs E=2
- G vs E=3
- A vs E=4
- B vs E=5
- D vs E=7
- F vs E=9

So, the others-to-worst vector = [1, 2, 3, 4, 5, 7, 9].

Step 5. Compute the optimal weights

The BWM model minimizes the maximum absolute difference between the weight ratios and the comparison values. Table 40.4

40.5 Discussion and conclusion

The illustrative example demonstrates how the proposed reduction approach in AHP substantially decreases the cognitive effort required from the DM while maintaining reliable prioritization. Traditionally, the AHP process obliges the evaluator to conduct all PCs among the set of alternatives, which quickly becomes burdensome as the number of options increases. In contrast, our methodology relies on selecting a few reference alternatives and interpolating the evaluations of the remaining options. This not only simplifies the elicitation process but also enhances the transparency of the prioritization since the reference points are carefully chosen in collaboration with the DM and represent meaningful benchmarks.

TABLE 40.4 The final weights and rank.

Tree	Rank	Weight
F	1	0.3830
D	2	0.1950
B	3	0.1277
A	4	0.1043
G	5	0.0836
C	6	0.0638
E	7	0.0426

The results of the example with seven trees clearly indicate the efficiency of the method. Instead of requiring 21 PCs for the full set, the evaluator only needed to compare three reference alternatives. The subsequent interpolation of the remaining four trees provided consistent and intuitive results, showing a smooth transition of priority values across the alternatives. Importantly, this process preserves the ranking logic of AHP while reducing the possibility of inconsistencies that often arise from excessive pairwise judgments. When compared with alternative approaches, such as clustering techniques or the BWM, the proposed framework offers additional advantages. Unlike clustering, it avoids group comparisons that may confuse DMs. Compared with BWM, it covers the full spectrum of performances rather than just extremes, while also requiring fewer judgments in cases with many alternatives. Overall, the approach represents a significant improvement to AHP by balancing cognitive feasibility with methodological rigor, ensuring DMs provide preference information that is both reliable and manageable.

References

Al-lami, A., & Török, Á. (2025). Assessing sustainability indicators of public transportation using PAHP. *Sustainable Futures, 9*, 100500.

Butturi, M. A., Lolli, F., & Gamberini, R. (2025). Set up a supply chain observatory through the comparison of multi-criteria parsimonious methods. *Benchmarking: An International Journal, 32*(11), 1–27.

Carlucci, R., Cipriano, G., Fattoruso, G., Oliveri, M. G., Ricci, P., & Squillante, M. (2021). Parsimonious AHP applied to the conservation of cetaceans: a case study in the gulf of taranto. In *2021 International Workshop on Metrology for the Sea; Learning to Measure Sea Health Parameters (MetroSea)*. IEEE, 1–5 October.

Duleba, S. (2022). Introduction and comparative analysis of the multi-level parsimonious AHP methodology in a public transport development decision problem. *Journal of the Operational Research Society, 73*(2), 230–243.

Fattoruso, G., Barbati, M., & Ishizaka, A. (2024). An AHP parsimonious based approach to handle manufacturing errors in production processes. *Production Planning & Control, 35*(16), 2370–2399.

Fattoruso, G., Scognamiglio, S., & Violi, A. (2022). A new dynamic and perspective parsimonious AHP model for improving industrial frameworks. *Mathematics, 10*(17), 3138.

Jamal Mahdi, A., & Esztergár-Kiss, D. (2024). Prioritizing influential factors on tourist decision-making for choosing destinations using parsimonious analytical hierarchy process (PAHP). *Tourism Planning & Development, 21*(3), 330–353.

Júnior, E. L. P., Morreira, M.Â. L., Gomes, C. F. S., dos Santos, M., de Araújo Costa, A. P., Chagas, S. D. S. S., ... Kojima, E. H. (2023). Governance applicable to public organizations: an analysis based on the multicriteria method (MCDM) Parsimonious AHP (PAHP) under the perspective of the leadership mechanism in the light of the Union Court of Audits (TCU). *Procedia Computer Science, 221*, 697–704.

Kabirifar, K., Ashour, M., Yazdani, M., Mahdiyar, A., & Malekjafarian, M. (2023). Cybernetic-parsimonious MCDM modeling with application to the adoption of Circular Economy in waste management. *Applied Soft Computing, 139*, 110186.

Moslem, S. (2023). A novel parsimonious best worst method for evaluating travel mode choice. *IEEE Access, 11*, 16768–16773.

Moslem, S. (2024). A novel parsimonious spherical fuzzy analytic hierarchy process for sustainable urban transport solutions. *Engineering Applications of Artificial Intelligence, 128*, 107447.

Moslem, S. (2025). Evaluation of public bus transportation systems for sustainable cities using a parsimonious grey multi-criteria decision-making model. *Sustainable Futures, 10*, 101363.

Rezaei, J. (2015). Best-worst multi-criteria decision-making method. *Omega, 53*, 49–57.

Saaty, T. L. (1977). A scaling method for priorities in hierarchical structures. *Journal of Mathematical Psychology, 15*(3), 234–281.

Wu, J. Z. (2023). Parsimoniously interactive multiple attribute rating (PIMAR) and its applications to large-scale inventory classification in the context of Industry 3.5. *Computers & Industrial Engineering, 184*, 109546.

Chapter 41

K-means: Algorithm for multi-attribute decision-making

Mahsa Valipour
Concordia Institute for Information Systems Engineering, Concordia University, Montréal, QC, Canada

41.1 Introduction

In an era characterized by vast and rapidly growing data, the ability to identify meaningful patterns and structure within large datasets has become a foundational pillar of intelligent decision-making and analytics. Across diverse fields, including industrial engineering and logistics, healthcare, finance, and environmental management, decision-makers (DMs) and data scientists face the challenge of transforming raw, multidimensional data into interpretable and actionable insights (Ikotun et al., 2023). Clustering methods, widely recognized as a central component of unsupervised learning, play an important role in this process by organizing data into groups (or clusters) such that observations within the same cluster share high similarity, while those in different clusters exhibit dissimilarity (Biswas et al., 2023). Among the various clustering techniques proposed in the literature, the K-means algorithm is considered one of the most extensively utilized and computationally efficient approaches for partitioning large and complex datasets into internally homogeneous groups according to defined similarity or distance measures (Heidari et al., 2024).

Over the past few decades, clustering has become an integral analytical tool in data-driven decision-making, exploratory data analysis, and pattern recognition. Various clustering techniques, such as partition-based methods (e.g., K-means and K-medoids), hierarchical clustering (e.g., Chameleon, clustering using representatives (CURE), and balanced iterative reducing and clustering using hierarchies (BIRCH)), density-based methods (e.g., density-based spatial clustering of applications with noise (DBSCAN) and hierarchical DBSCAN (HDBSCAN)), grid-based methods (e.g., statistical information grid (STING) and spatio-temporal DBSCAN (STDBSCAN)), and model-based methods (e.g., hidden Markov models and gaussian mixture model (GMM)) have been developed to address different problem characteristics and data distributions (Oyewole & Thopil, 2023; Yin et al., 2024). Each approach is characterized by unique assumptions regarding data structure, distance metrics, and cluster formation criteria. Among them, K-means represents the class of partitioning-based clustering algorithms, which aim to divide data into a predetermined number of clusters by minimizing intra-cluster variance (MacQueen, 1967). The algorithm iteratively assigns each data point to the nearest cluster centroid and recalculates the centroids. Through this process, it converges toward a configuration that minimizes the total within-cluster sum of squares (WCSS). The simplicity of this iterative refinement process, coupled with its efficiency in handling large-scale and high-dimensional data, has made K-means a widely adopted approach in modern data analysis and machine learning applications (Ezugwu et al., 2020; Ismkhan, 2018).

Moreover, its capability to partition a set of alternatives into homogeneous groups based on multiple evaluation criteria makes it particularly suitable for multicriteria decision-making (MCDM). In MCDM contexts, alternatives are commonly described by several quantitative attributes, and K-means offers a systematic mechanism for uncovering structures within these multidimensional datasets. By minimizing intra-cluster variability, the algorithm identifies groups of alternatives that exhibit similar performance patterns across attributes. This clustering facilitates comparative assessment, prioritization, and the identification of dominant, critical, or underperforming groups of alternatives. Furthermore, the method's interpretability and computational efficiency make it well aligned with large-scale MCDM problems, where DMs must analyze high-dimensional information and extract meaningful insights to inform strategic, operational, or policy-oriented decisions.

Encyclopedia of Multi-Attribute Decision-Making (MADM). DOI: https://doi.org/10.1016/B978-0-443-33275-3.00030-0

Despite its advantages, the K-means method relies on several critical assumptions that influence its performance and applicability. Specifically, it presumes spherical cluster shapes, uniform cluster sizes, and the use of Euclidean distance as a similarity metric. These assumptions make K-means well-suited for linearly separable datasets but less effective for complex or irregular cluster structures with outliers (Ikotun et al., 2023). To address such limitations, numerous extensions and hybrid approaches have been developed, such as K-medoids (Park & Jun, 2009), fuzzy K-means or fuzzy C-means (Bezdek et al., 1984), and kernel K-means (Couto, 2005), each designed to enhance robustness against noise, handle overlapping clusters, or adapt to nonlinear data distributions. Furthermore, advanced variants integrate K-means with optimization (Qi et al., 2016; Xiong et al., 2016), metaheuristics (Ikotun et al., 2021; Lam et al., 2013), and machine learning paradigms, such as genetic algorithms (Zeebaree et al., 2017) and deep learning (Huang et al., 2021), to improve initialization sensitivity, convergence speed, and clustering accuracy. Given its versatility and broad adoption, K-means has been applied in a wide range of real-world problems that demand efficient data partitioning and pattern recognition. Widely recognized applications include customer segmentation in marketing analytics, anomaly detection, decision-making, healthcare diagnostics, and medical imaging (Ikotun et al., 2023; Rezaee et al., 2018).

Considering the fundamental importance and broad applicability of the K-means algorithm, this chapter aims to provide a comprehensive overview of its theoretical foundation, mathematical formulation, and computational steps. Readers will gain an understanding of how the algorithm partitions data based on distance metrics. The remainder of the chapter is organized as follows: Section 41.2 presents a review of major extensions of the K-means algorithm, including early research and modified models. Section 41.3 outlines the step-by-step implementation of the K-means methodology. Sections 41.4, 41.5, and 41.6 illustrate its application in small-scale, large-scale, and real-world applications, respectively. Finally, Section 41.7 concludes the chapter by summarizing key insights and offering recommendations for further study.

41.2 Literature review

Clustering is one of the most fundamental tasks in unsupervised learning, data mining, and pattern recognition. Among the diverse clustering algorithms proposed in the literature, the K-means algorithm, introduced by MacQueen (1967) and subsequently formalized by Lloyd (1982), remains one of the most established and widely applied techniques. This algorithm partitions a dataset into k nonoverlapping clusters such that each observation belongs to the cluster with the nearest mean, which serves as a centroid. The objective is to minimize the WCSS, or equivalently, the intra-cluster variations. Early research primarily focused on enhancing the initialization strategy and convergence behavior of the algorithm. Arthur and Vassilvitskii (2006) proposed K-means++, a probabilistic seeding technique that selects initial centroids based on their distance from existing ones to improve clustering quality and stability. Pelleg and Moore (2000) introduced X-means as an adaptive extension of K-means that can automatically determine the optimal number of clusters using criteria such as the Bayesian information criterion. In another study, Hamerly and Elkan (2003) proposed Gaussian-means (G-means), which uses statistical tests to refine the number of clusters dynamically. These early contributions established the groundwork for algorithmic self-adaptation and automated model selection within the K-means framework.

The K-means algorithm has undergone significant methodological evolution to overcome its intrinsic limitations related to initialization sensitivity, cluster shape assumptions, and computational scalability. Consequently, a diverse spectrum of enhanced variants has emerged, each tailored to address specific data characteristics, optimization challenges, or computational environments. According to Ikotun et al. (2023), these variants can be systematically classified into two principal categories: (i) algorithm design variants and (ii) algorithm implementation variants. The first group covers modifications that alter the algorithm's internal architecture, mathematical formulation, or parameterization to improve clustering quality and robustness. Within this category, several studies have focused on input modification, including advanced data preprocessing techniques to handle outliers, noise, missing values, and high-dimensional or categorical datasets. Other works emphasize the automatic specification of k, where several techniques and information-theoretic criteria are employed to determine the optimal number of clusters without prior user input. Furthermore, improved centroid initialization methods, such as those based on principal component analysis and heuristics, have been proposed to reduce sensitivity to initial seed selection and enhance convergence stability. Regarding process enhancements, research has explored data-object assignment process modifications by integrating alternative distance metrics to achieve more accurate partitioning. Additionally, iteration reduction strategies have been developed to minimize computational overhead. From an output perspective, recent studies have sought to extend K-means' applicability beyond spherical cluster assumptions by enabling the detection of arbitrarily shaped clusters and by introducing fuzzy, rough, and overlapping clustering formulations that better capture uncertainty and data ambiguity. The last category within the algorithm design variants concentrates on reformulating the core conceptual structure of the standard K-means algorithm to enhance its computational efficiency and reduce overall complexity. The second major category, algorithm implementation variants, refers to advancements that adapt K-means to evolving computational infrastructures and large-scale data processing environments without any change to the algorithm structure. This includes: (i) parallel and distributed implementations that leverage multicore processors to reduce runtime, (ii) MapReduce-based frameworks, which enable scalable clustering in big data ecosystems, (iii) quantum-based K-means, which exploits quantum computing principles to enhance the precision of the results and the convergence rate of the clustering process, and (iv) hybrid frameworks which integrate K-means with other machine learning techniques to enhance its efficiency and scalability. For more comprehensive details on these variants and their methodological advancements, readers are referred to Ikotun et al. (2023) and Ferraro (2024).

In addition to these technical advancements, numerous studies have examined the integration of various K-means variants with MCDM techniques to leverage the strengths of clustering in enhancing decision-making processes. This integration enables clustering results to be evaluated and prioritized based on multiple conflicting criteria, while facilitating more informed and objective decision-making in complex problem domains. For instance, Eghtesadifard et al. (2020) proposed a hybrid framework to identify optimal municipal solid waste landfill sites. The approach integrated decision-making trial and evaluation laboratory and the analytic network process to weight environmental, economic, social, geographical, technical, and legal criteria, which were refined through fuzzy logic analysis. The feasible locations were subsequently clustered using the K-means algorithm, and the most suitable landfill sites were prioritized using MCDM methods (i.e., multiobjective optimization by ratio analysis [MOORA], weighted aggregated sum product assessment, and complex proportional assessment [COPRAS]). Valipour et al. (2022) proposed a methodology for risk assessment, where potential risks were clustered using fuzzy C-means. In the second phase, risks within the critical cluster are prioritized using a hybrid MCDM approach combining the fuzzy best-worst method and combined compromise solution to guide corrective and preventive actions. Yilmaz et al. (2023) integrated K-means++ clustering and MCDM methods to identify and rank optimal locations for energy storage systems (ESS). They applied K-means++ and the elbow method to geographic data from wind power plants to generate potential ESS sites, which are then evaluated using technique for order preference by similarity to ideal solution, additive ratio assessment, evaluation based on distance from average solution, and MOORA, with the BORDA approach consolidating the rankings. Most recently, Al Awadh and Mallick (2024) developed a transparent decision-making framework for landfill site selection by integrating fuzzy analytic hierarchy process (AHP), geographic information system, K-means clustering, and explainable AI. They used fuzzy AHP to weight geophysical, geoecological, and socio-economic criteria, while K-means and self-organizing maps classified the suitability index map into distinct zones. Khan et al. (2025) proposed an integrated optimization framework that combines the AHP and K-means to enhance the classification and evaluation of ultrasonic biodiesel yield performance. AHP is employed to weight and prioritize key operating parameters, such as molar ratio, temperature, reaction time, frequency, and hydrogen supply. These weighted parameters then guide the K-means clustering process to provide priority-based grouping and identification of optimal operating conditions for maximum biodiesel yield. Sevgi and Figen (2025) employed K-means clustering to group 38 Organisation for Economic Co-operation and Development (OECD) memeber countries based on renewable energy performance indicators. To further evaluate and rank the countries within each cluster, the criteria importance through intercriteria correlation method was used to determine the weights of the criteria, and the COPRAS method was employed for ranking countries within each cluster.

41.3 Methodology

The K-Means clustering algorithm is one of the most widely used partitioning techniques in unsupervised learning. It aims to group a given dataset into predefined k clusters, where each cluster represents a group of data points sharing similar characteristics. The algorithm minimizes the distance between objects within the same cluster and their corresponding centroid, while maximizing the separation between objects belonging to different clusters. Given a set of observations (x_1, x_2, …, x_n), where each observation is a d-dimensional real vector, K-means clustering partitions the n observations into k ($\leq n$) sets $S = \{S_1, S_2, \ldots, S_k\}$ to minimize the WCSS. The mathematical formulation of the algorithm's objective function is given in Eq. (41.1).

$$\operatorname{argmin}_s \sum_{i=1}^{k} \sum_{x \in S_i} \| x - \mu_i \|^2 = \operatorname{argmin}_s \sum_{i=1}^{k} | S_i | \operatorname{Var} S_i \tag{41.1}$$

Where, μ_i denotes the centroid of cluster S_i and $|S_i|$ represents the number of data points assigned to cluster i. The general workflow of K-means consists of four main stages: initialization, assignment, centroid update, and convergence. These stages are described in detail below.

41.3.1 Initialization

The first step in K-Means is to determine the number k. This value can be specified by the user based on prior knowledge, or it can be estimated using methods such as the elbow method. Once k is defined, the algorithm initializes k centroids that represent the initial cluster centers. These centroids can be chosen randomly from the dataset or by using more advanced initialization techniques such as K-Means++, which improves clustering performance and convergence by spreading the initial centroids more effectively across the data space.

41.3.2 Assignment step

After initialization, each data point in the dataset is assigned to the nearest cluster centroid. The proximity between a data point and a centroid is usually measured using the Euclidean distance. Mathematically, the assignment step can be expressed as (41.2).

$$S_i^{(t)} = \{x_j: \|x_j - \mu_i^{(t)}\|^2 \leq \|x_j - \mu_l^{(t)}\|^2, \ \forall\, l = 1, 2, \ \ldots, k\} \tag{41.2}$$

41.3.3 Centroid update step

Once all data points have been assigned to their respective clusters, the centroids are recalculated to represent the mean position of all the points within each cluster. The new centroid for cluster i is obtained using Eq. (41.3).

$$\mu_i^{(t+1)} = \frac{1}{|S_i^{(t)}|} \sum_{x_j \in S_i^{(t)}} x_j \tag{41.3}$$

Here, $| S_i^{(t)} |$ denotes the number of data points assigned to cluster i. This step ensures that the centroid moves towards the geometric center of its cluster, reflecting the updated structure of the data.

41.3.4 Repeat

The algorithm iterates between the assignment and centroid update steps until a convergence condition is satisfied. Convergence is typically achieved when the assignments no longer change between iterations, or the algorithm reaches a maximum number of iterations.

41.4 Numerical example 1

To illustrate the K-Means clustering process, consider a simple two-dimensional dataset consisting of six observations. The goal is to partition these observations into two clusters ($k = 2$). Table 41.1 presents the initial dataset with two features, X and Y.

At the beginning of the algorithm (initialization step), two points are selected randomly as the initial centroids: $S_1 = (1,1)$ and $S_2 = (5,7)$. The Euclidean distance is then used to measure the similarity between each point and each centroid, calculated as Eq. (41.4). Table 41.2 summarizes the computed distances and the initial cluster assignment.

$$d = \sqrt{(x_i - x_c)^2 + (y_i - y_c)^2} \tag{41.4}$$

Based on the minimum distance, points A and B are assigned to cluster 1, while points C, D, E, and F are assigned to cluster 2. New centroids are then calculated as the mean of all points in each cluster, as given in Eq. (41.5).

$$S_j = \left(\frac{1}{n_j} \sum_{i=1}^{n_j} x_i, \frac{1}{n_j} \sum_{i=1}^{n_j} y_i \right) \tag{41.5}$$

TABLE 41.1 Input dataset.

Point	*X*	*Y*
A	1.0	1.0
B	1.5	2.0
C	2.5	4.5
D	5.0	7.0
E	3.5	5.0
F	4.5	5.0

TABLE 41.2 Distance of each point to the centroids (iteration 1).

Point	Distance to S_1 (1,1)	Distance to S_2 (5,7)	Assigned cluster
A (1,1)	0.00	7.21	1
B (1.5,2)	1.12	6.10	1
C (3,4)	3.81	3.20	2
D (5,7)	7.21	0.00	2
E (3.5,5)	5.00	2.50	2
F (4.5,5)	5.32	2.24	2

TABLE 41.3 Distance of each point to the new centroids (iteration 2).

Point	Distance to S_1(1.25,1.5)	Distance to S_2 (3.88,5.38)	Assigned cluster
A (1,1)	0.53	5.38	1
B (1.5,2)	0.53	4.63	1
C (3,4)	3.08	1.66	2
D (5,7)	7.01	2.00	2
E (3.5,5)	3.72	0.51	2
F (4.5,5)	3.95	0.47	2

Thus, $S_1 = (1.25,1.5)$ and $S_2 = (3.88,5.38)$. Using the updated centroids, distances are recalculated, and points are reassigned as shown in Table 41.3.

After this iteration, cluster 1 contains points A and B, while cluster 2 includes points C, D, E, and F. Since no changes occur in cluster membership, the algorithm has converged. Fig. 41.1 shows a visual representation of the final clusters obtained from the K-means algorithm for the example dataset.

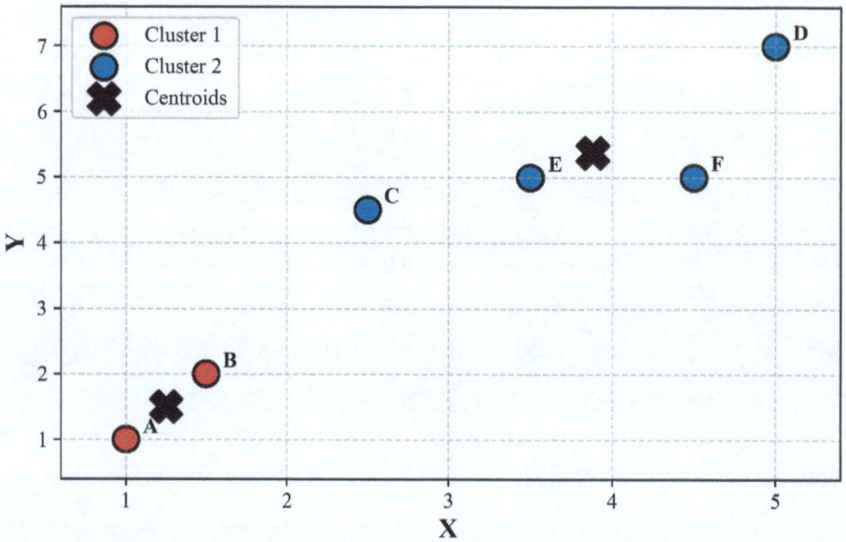

FIGURE 41.1 K-means cluster visualization.

41.5 Numerical example 2

To illustrate the application of K-means clustering on a large-scale dataset, a synthetic dataset is generated and analyzed. The dataset consists of 100,000 observations, each characterized by five features, and is created using the make blobs function from the scikit-learn library. The objective is to partition the data into five distinct clusters. In this example, the k-means++ initialization method is employed to enhance convergence efficiency and ensure that the initial centroids are well-distributed across the feature space. This initialization strategy reduces the likelihood of poor local minima and accelerates the convergence of the algorithm, particularly in large-scale datasets. Following initialization, each observation is iteratively assigned to the nearest centroid based on Euclidean distance, and the centroids are recalculated as the mean of all points assigned to the corresponding cluster. This process continues until convergence, defined as a state where the centroids no longer shift significantly between iterations. The scaled cluster centroids obtained are as follows:

$$S_1 = (-0.4683, \quad -1.0221, \quad 0.8768, \quad 0.8344, \quad 1.4606)$$

$$S_2 = (-1.0286, \quad 1.1582, \quad 0.7280, \quad -1.1991, \quad -0.7411)$$

$$S_3 = (0.4355, \quad 1.1177, \quad 0.3360, \quad 0.8321, \quad -0.8482)$$

$$S_4 = (-0.3640, \quad -0.4357, \quad -0.5042, \quad -0.0635, \quad -0.2772)$$

$$S_5 = (1.4316, \quad -0.8251, \quad -1.4433, \quad -0.3963, \quad 0.4077)$$

The resulting clusters can be further visualized in two or three dimensions to assess the separation and structure of the data and provide an intuitive understanding of how the K-means algorithm partitions large-scale datasets (See Fig. 41.2).

41.6 Numerical example 3

In a case study, adopted from Valipour et al. (2022), a total of 62 risks associated with health, safety, and environmental issues in a manufacturing company are analyzed. Each risk is quantified using five key features of severity (S), occurrence (O), detection (D), time (T), and cost (C). These features represent the potential impact, likelihood, detectability, duration, and financial consequences of each risk. Table 41.4 presents the normalized values of these factors for all risks in the dataset. To extract meaningful patterns and identify clusters of similar risks, the K-means clustering algorithm is applied. In this example, the aim is to group the 62 risks into four clusters, allowing for the identification of the most critical group based on the combination of risk factors. This clustering helps DMs prioritize risk mitigation efforts by focusing on the group of risks that poses the highest potential impact.

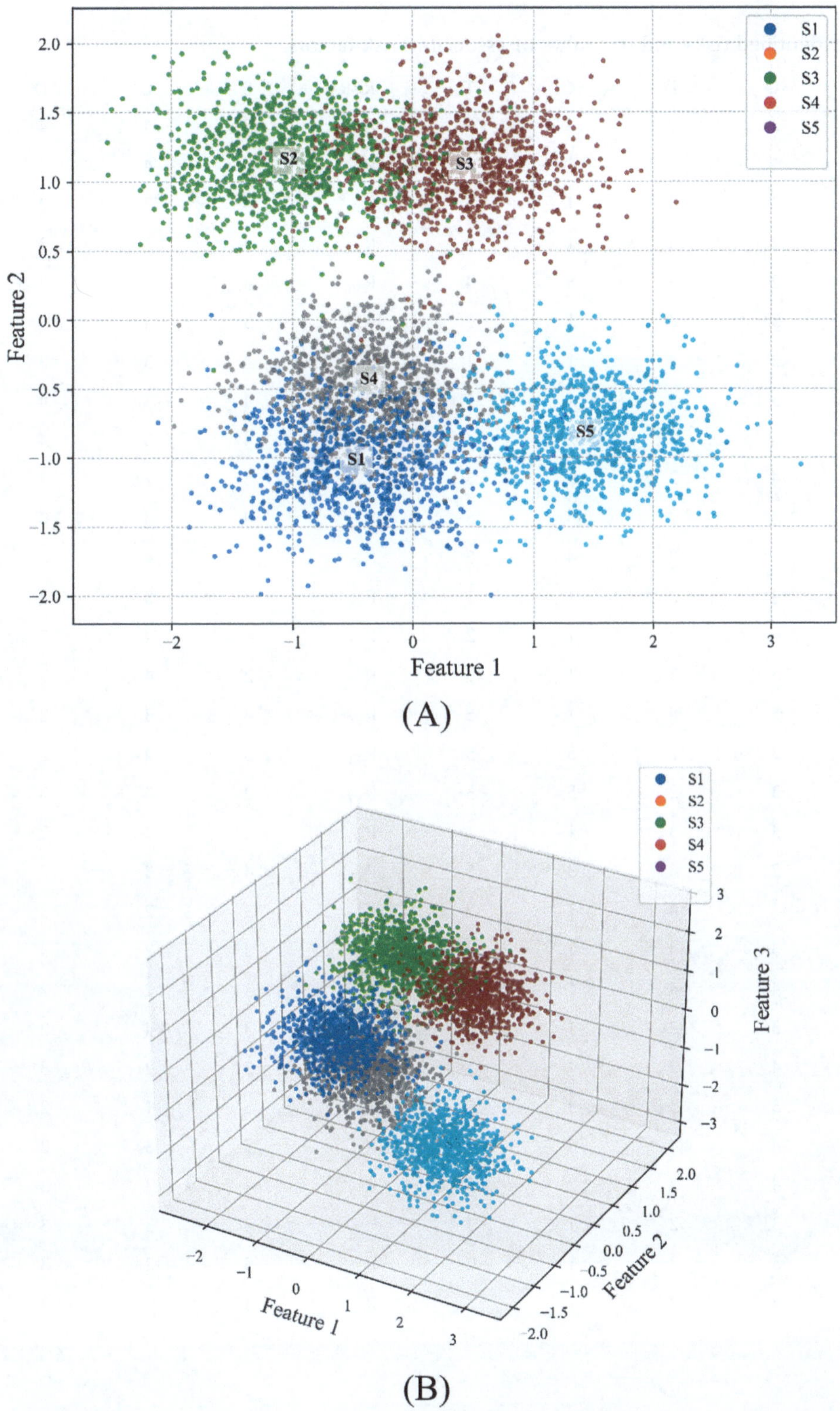

FIGURE 41.2 K-means clustering: (A) 2D visualization for the first two features and (B) 3D visualization for the first three features.

TABLE 41.4 The identified risks and the value of associated risk factors.

Risk	S	O	D	C	T	Risk	S	O	D	C	T
R_{01}	4	3	2	4	3	R_{32}	3	3	4	1	3
R_{02}	5	3	2	1	1	R_{33}	3	4	4	1	2
R_{03}	5	3	3	1	1	R_{34}	4	2	2	1	3
R_{04}	4	2	3	1	2	R_{35}	4	2	3	1	3
R_{05}	4	2	2	5	4	R_{36}	3	3	4	1	3
R_{06}	4	3	2	1	2	R_{37}	3	4	3	1	2
R_{07}	5	2	4	1	1	R_{38}	4	3	2	4	3
R_{08}	4	3	4	1	1	R_{39}	4	3	4	1	2
R_{09}	4	4	3	2	4	R_{40}	4	5	4	1	2
R_{10}	4	4	2	5	5	R_{41}	5	2	2	5	4
R_{11}	4	3	2	3	5	R_{42}	4	3	3	1	2
R_{12}	4	3	2	4	5	R_{43}	2	4	2	1	2
R_{13}	3	4	2	1	1	R_{44}	2	5	3	1	1
R_{14}	3	4	2	1	2	R_{45}	4	4	2	1	2
R_{15}	3	3	3	1	3	R_{46}	2	4	3	1	1
R_{16}	4	5	4	1	5	R_{47}	4	3	2	2	4
R_{17}	4	3	2	5	5	R_{48}	3	4	2	1	3
R_{18}	4	3	2	5	5	R_{49}	2	4	3	1	1
R_{19}	3	3	3	1	1	R_{50}	4	3	2	5	4
R_{20}	4	2	3	3	5	R_{51}	4	3	2	3	5
R_{21}	2	4	4	1	2	R_{52}	3	2	3	1	3
R_{22}	2	3	3	1	3	R_{53}	3	2	4	1	3
R_{23}	2	4	4	1	1	R_{54}	3	2	2	4	5
R_{24}	4	3	2	1	3	R_{55}	3	4	2	1	3
R_{25}	3	4	3	1	1	R_{56}	5	2	3	2	4
R_{26}	4	3	3	3	5	R_{57}	5	1	2	1	2
R_{27}	2	4	4	5	5	R_{58}	5	3	2	1	3
R_{28}	4	4	3	2	5	R_{59}	4	3	3	1	2
R_{29}	4	3	2	1	3	R_{60}	4	3	3	4	3
R_{30}	3	3	3	1	2	R_{61}	5	2	3	2	3
R_{31}	3	4	2	1	3	R_{62}	3	2	3	4	5

K-means algorithm resulted in four clusters with S_1 = (4.3529, 2.5294, 2.5882, 1.1176, 2.3529), S_2 = (2.8333, 3.6667, 3.1250, 1.0000, 2.0000), S_3 = (3.6000, 4.0000, 3.4000, 2.6000, 5.0000), S_4 = (3.9375. 2.7500, 2.1875, 4.0625, 4.3750). Table 41.5 also shows the assignment of each risk to its corresponding cluster.

TABLE 41.5 k-means clustering results.

Risk	Cluster	Risk	Cluster	Risk	Cluster	Risk	Cluster
R_{01}	4	R_{17}	4	R_{33}	2	R_{49}	2
R_{02}	1	R_{18}	4	R_{34}	1	R_{50}	4
R_{03}	1	R_{19}	2	R_{35}	1	R_{51}	4
R_{04}	1	R_{20}	4	R_{36}	2	R_{52}	1
R_{05}	4	R_{21}	2	R_{37}	2	R_{53}	2
R_{06}	1	R_{22}	2	R_{38}	4	R_{54}	4
R_{07}	1	R_{23}	2	R_{39}	2	R_{55}	2
R_{08}	2	R_{24}	1	R_{40}	2	R_{56}	1
R_{09}	3	R_{25}	2	R_{41}	4	R_{57}	1
R_{10}	4	R_{26}	3	R_{42}	1	R_{58}	1
R_{11}	4	R_{27}	3	R_{43}	2	R_{59}	1
R_{12}	4	R_{28}	3	R_{44}	2	R_{60}	4
R_{13}	2	R_{29}	1	R_{45}	1	R_{61}	1
R_{14}	2	R_{30}	2	R_{46}	2	R_{62}	4
R_{15}	2	R_{31}	2	R_{47}	4		
R_{16}	3	R_{32}	2	R_{48}	2		

41.7 Conclusions

This chapter introduced the K-means clustering algorithm as a simple and practical approach for partitioning datasets across various domains. The step-by-step computational process was demonstrated through numerical examples to highlight its applicability to different scenarios. While the algorithm is widely used due to its simplicity, it faces inherent limitations, including sensitivity to initialization, convergence to local optima, and challenges with mixed data types. Numerous variants and improvements have been developed to address these issues, including hybrid approaches, kernel-based implementations, parallel and MapReduce frameworks for big data, and combinations with metaheuristic algorithms. Overall, the chapter emphasized K-means' usefulness in uncovering patterns, supporting data-driven decision-making, and facilitating exploratory data analysis. Future research could focus on further improving its robustness and scalability, exploring hybridizations with swarm intelligence and metaheuristic methods, and investigating its integration with MCDM frameworks to enhance decision-making in complex and uncertain environments. Moreover, studying its performance in large-scale, heterogeneous, or high-dimensional datasets can provide valuable insights for both researchers and practitioners seeking advanced clustering solutions.

References

Al Awadh, M., & Mallick, J. (2024). A decision-making framework for landfill site selection in Saudi Arabia using explainable artificial intelligence and multi-criteria analysis. *Environmental Technology & Innovation, 33*, 103464.

Arthur, D., & Vassilvitskii, S. (2006). *k-means++: The advantages of careful seeding*. Stanford.

Bezdek, J. C., Ehrlich, R., & Full, W. (1984). FCM: The fuzzy c-means clustering algorithm. *Computers & Geosciences, 10*(2-3), 191–203.

Biswas, T. K., Giri, K., & Roy, S. (2023). ECKM: An improved K-means clustering based on computational geometry. *Expert Systems with Applications, 212*, 118862.

Couto, J. (2005). Kernel k-means for categorical data. In *International symposium on intelligent data analysis*. Berlin, Heidelberg: Springer Berlin Heidelberg, 46–56.

Eghtesadifard, M., Afkhami, P., & Bazyar, A. (2020). An integrated approach to the selection of municipal solid waste landfills through GIS, K-means and multi-criteria decision analysis. *Environmental Research, 185*, 109348.

Ezugwu, A. E. S., Agbaje, M. B., Aljojo, N., Els, R., Chiroma, H., & Abd Elaziz, M. (2020). A comparative performance study of hybrid firefly algorithms for automatic data clustering. *IEEE Access, 8*, 121089–121118.

Ferraro, M. B. (2024). Fuzzy k-means: History and applications. *Econometrics and Statistics, 30*, 110–123.

Hamerly, G., & Elkan, C. (2003). Learning the k in k-means. *Advances in Neural Information Processing Systems, 16*.

Heidari, J., Daneshpour, N., & Zangeneh, A. (2024). A novel K-means and K-medoids algorithms for clustering non-spherical-shape clusters non-sensitive to outliers. *Pattern Recognition, 155*, 110639.

Huang, S., Kang, Z., Xu, Z., & Liu, Q. (2021). Robust deep k-means: An effective and simple method for data clustering. *Pattern Recognition, 117*, 107996.

Ikotun, A. M., Almutari, M. S., & Ezugwu, A. E. (2021). K-means-based nature-inspired metaheuristic algorithms for automatic data clustering problems: Recent advances and future directions. *Applied Sciences, 11*(23), 11246.

Ikotun, A. M., Ezugwu, A. E., Abualigah, L., Abuhaija, B., & Heming, J. (2023). K-means clustering algorithms: A comprehensive review, variants analysis, and advances in the era of big data. *Information Sciences, 622*, 178–210.

Ismkhan, H. (2018). Ik-means−+: An iterative clustering algorithm based on an enhanced version of the k-means. *Pattern Recognition, 79*, 402–413.

Khan, O., Khan, M. Z., Alsaduni, I., Parvez, M., Alwetaishi, M., & Keçebaş, A. (2025). Advanced multi-criteria optimization for sustainable biofuels: AHP-guided k-means clustering approach. *Energy, 335*, 138297.

Lam, Y. K., Tsang, P. W. M., & Leung, C. S. (2013). PSO-based K-Means clustering with enhanced cluster matching for gene expression data. *Neural Computing and Applications, 22*(7), 1349–1355.

Lloyd, S. (1982). Least squares quantization in PCM. *IEEE Transactions on Information Theory, 28*(2), 129–137.

MacQueen, J. (1967). Multivariate observations. In *Proceedings of the 5th Berkeley Symposium on Mathematical Statisticsand Probability* (pp. 281–297).

Oyewole, G. J., & Thopil, G. A. (2023). Data clustering: Application and trends. *Artificial Intelligence Review, 56*(7), 6439–6475.

Park, H. S., & Jun, C. H. (2009). A simple and fast algorithm for K-medoids clustering. *Expert Systems with Applications, 36*(2), 3336–3341.

Pelleg, D., & Moore, A. W. (2000). X-means: Extending k-means with efficient estimation of the number of clusters. In Icml (pp. 727–734).

Qi, J., Yu, Y., Wang, L., & Liu, J. (2016). K*-means: An effective and efficient k-means clustering algorithm. In *2016 IEEE International Conferences on Big Data and Cloud Computing (BDCloud), Social Computing and Networking (SocialCom), Sustainable Computing and Communications (SustainCom)* (pp. 242–249). IEEE.

Rezaee, M. J., Jozmaleki, M., & Valipour, M. (2018). Integrating dynamic fuzzy C-means, data envelopment analysis and artificial neural network to online prediction performance of companies in stock exchange. *Physica A: Statistical Mechanics and its Applications, 489*, 78–93.

Sevgi, E., & Figen, A. Z. (2025). Determination of renewable energy growth using cluster analysis and multi-criteria decision-making methods. *Applied Sciences, 15*(3), 1575.

Valipour, M., Yousefi, S., Jahangoshai Rezaee, M., & Saberi, M. (2022). A clustering-based approach for prioritizing health, safety and environment risks integrating fuzzy C-means and hybrid decision-making methods. *Stochastic Environmental Research and Risk Assessment, 36*(3), 919–938.

Xiong, C., Hua, Z., Lv, K., & Li, X. (2016). An improved k-means text clustering algorithm by optimizing initial cluster centers. In *2016 7th International Conference on Cloud Computing and Big Data* (CCBD) (pp. 265–268). IEEE.

Yilmaz, I., Adem, A., & Dağdeviren, M. (2023). A machine learning-integrated multi-criteria decision-making approach based on consensus for selection of energy storage locations. *Journal of Energy Storage, 69*, 107941.

Yin, H., Aryani, A., Petrie, S., Nambissan, A., Astudillo, A., & Cao, S. (2024). A rapid review of clustering algorithms. arXiv preprint arXiv:2401.07389.

Zeebaree, D. Q., Haron, H., Abdulazeez, A. M., & Zeebaree, S. R. (2017). Combination of K-means clustering with genetic algorithm: A review. *International Journal of Applied Engineering Research, 12*(24), 14238–14245.

Chapter 42

OWA: The ordered weighted averaging for multi-attribute decision-making

Mahmoud Tajik
School of Industrial Engineering, Iran University of Science and Technology, Tehran, Iran

42.1 Introduction

Decision-making is an integral part of human activity, encompassing choices ranging from daily personal preferences to complex strategic decisions in business, engineering, and public policy (Hastie & Dawes, 2010). In many real-world scenarios, decision-makers are confronted with multiple attributes that must be considered simultaneously (Ferla et al., 2024). This complexity necessitates systematic methodologies for evaluating options, leading to the development of Multi-attributes decision-making (MADM) techniques (Zayat et al., 2023). The origins of the MADM date to the mid-20th century, building on advances in utility theory and decision analysis. Foundational works include "Decisions with Multiple Objectives" by Keeney & Raiffa (1976) and the development of the analytic hierarchy process by Saaty (1980). Over several decades, MADM has developed by incorporating theoretical and methodological advances from economics, psychology, mathematics, and computer science (Chaube et al., 2024). MADM involves evaluating a finite set of alternatives, each characterized by specific attributes. The objective is to rank, select, and classify these alternatives according to defined decision-making preferences. The process of MADM includes six stages: (i) Problem definition includes clearly stating the decision context and objectives, (ii) Identification of alternatives using listing the possible courses of action, (iii) Attributes selection consists of determining the attributes relevant to the decision, (iv) Measurement of performance includes quantifying how each alternative performs on each criterion, (v) Attributes weighting, namely assigning weights to reflect the relative importance of each criterion, and (vi) Aggregation and ranking based on combining the information to evaluate and rank the alternatives (Belton & Stewart, 2012).

MADM, sometimes referred to as multicriteria decision-making (MCDM), is a branch of operations research and management science that deals with evaluating, prioritizing, and selecting alternatives when multiple and conflicting attributes are involved (Zavadskas et al., 2020). Unlike single-criterion decision-making, MADM provides structured frameworks that enable decision-makers to incorporate their preferences and trade-offs among diverse attributes explicitly (Chaube et al., 2024). MADM methodologies contribute to four sections: (i) Clarify objectives and structure complex problems, (ii) Systematically compare alternatives across diverse attributes, (iii) Incorporate both quantitative and qualitative information, (iv) Make the trade-off process explicit and transparent, and (v) Enhance consistency and rationality in decision-making (Bemthuis, 2025). MADM methods are broadly classified into two categories, noncompensatory and compensatory methods (Xu, 2015). Noncompensatory approaches do not permit such trade-offs, and in compensatory approaches, poor performance in one criterion can be offset by better performance in another. Application areas of the MADM techniques have found widespread application in various fields, including (i) Engineering design and selection (e.g., material, process, and supplier selection), (ii) Environmental management (e.g., site selection and policy evaluation), (iii) Healthcare (e.g., treatment selection and technology assessment), (iv) Transportation planning, and (v) Business and finance (e.g., investment appraisal and project prioritization) (Prince et al., 2012).

Although MADM methods offer significant benefits, these approaches encounter several notable challenges, including (i) Selecting and measuring attributes, which can be challenging, especially when it comes to identifying appropriate and measurable standards, (ii) Weight assignment, namely eliciting accurate weights that reflect true preferences, is often challenging, (iii) Handling uncertainty since real-world data and preferences are rarely precise; robust methods must accommodate uncertainty and vagueness, (iv) Group decision-making involves combining the preferences of multiple

Encyclopedia of Multi-Attribute Decision-Making (MADM). DOI: https://doi.org/10.1016/B978-0-443-33275-3.00095-6

stakeholders, which adds complexity to the process (Triantaphyllou, 2000). To address these issues, researchers have developed extensions of MADM methods, such as fuzzy MADM methods and stochastic methods, to address imprecision and uncertainty in decision processes (Zadeh, 1965; Zimmermann, 2011). Furthermore, the field of MADM is continually evolving by incorporating advancements in computational intelligence, artificial intelligence, and big data analytics (Ma & Li, 2024). Hybrid approaches that combine various MADM methods or integrate MADM with optimization algorithms, such as genetic algorithms and neural networks, are becoming increasingly popular (Mardani et al., 2015). In addition, the increasing availability of large and complex datasets has led to the development of data-driven decision support systems that utilize MADM frameworks (Bousdekis et al., 2021).

Navigating complex decisions is a common challenge, whether it involves selecting the best product, developing sustainable policies, or evaluating competing projects. Often, these decisions must consider multiple factors (e.g., cost and risk) that may pull in different directions (Sriram et al., 2022). This is where MADM plays a role, providing structured tools to evaluate various attributes and facilitate coherent, defensible decisions (Yager, 2002). One particularly intriguing tool in this category is the ordered weighted averaging (OWA) method. In traditional MADM methods, aggregation operators (e.g., arithmetic mean and weighted sum) simply combine the performance of alternatives on different attributes based on fixed weights, which may not reflect the real-world decision context (Malczewski et al., 2003). In general, decision problems involve situations where the importance attached to attributes can depend on the order in which they are performed (Bohra & Anvari-Moghaddam, 2022). The OWA method allows decision-makers to model various aggregation attitudes, ranging from minimum (i.e., AND) to maximum (i.e., OR), as well as any compromise between them. Moreover, the OWA method enables explicit encoding of the decision maker's (DM's) optimism or pessimism by adjusting the OWA weights, a feature not available with traditional additive models. It is particularly beneficial in complex decision-making environments where robustness, fairness, and risk attitude must be considered in the aggregation process (Amin & Hajjami, 2016).

The applications of OWA have been utilized in various fields, including engineering, finance, urban planning, environmental management, and even group decision-making, where achieving consensus is challenging (Ghasemkhani et al., 2020; Mianabadi et al., 2014). However, this flexibility comes with some subtle pitfalls, such as the selection of subjective weights, computational complexity, and the difficulty of making the results easily interpretable for all stakeholders (Ahn & Yager, 2014). To address these challenges, aggregating attribute functions is essential for developing comprehensive decision functions applicable across various fields (Liu, 2008). A key factor in determining the structure of aggregation functions is the relationship among the involved attributes. At one extreme, every attribute should be fully met. In contrast, there are situations where fulfilling any of the attributes is acceptable. Owing to these two cases, "and" and "or" operators can be used to combine the attribute functions (Shao et al., 2020). In this context, the OWA operator, developed by Yager (1988), offers an aggregation method that falls between these two scenarios. The combination of "and" and "or" operators is known as the "orand" operator. Additionally, the "orness" is introduced, referring to the "and-like" or "or-like" aggregation results of an OWA operator. Thus, the operator exists between two extremes, including (i) 1, representing "and-like," and (ii) 0, representing "or-like." The former refers to the situation where all attributes are met.

The remainder of the chapter is structured as follows: Section 2 provides a comprehensive review of the OWA operator and its extensions, along with its applications in various fields. Section 3 outlines the step-by-step implementation of the OWA methodology. Sections 4 and 5 demonstrate its application in small-scale and large-scale MCDM problems, respectively. Finally, Section 6 concludes the chapter by summarizing the key insights and offering recommendations for further study.

42.2 Literature review

The review of existing research on the OWA operator can be divided into four main subsections: (i) The various extensions of the OWA operator, (ii) The determination approaches of OWA operator weights, (iii) The development of the OWA operator under uncertain conditions, and (iv) The applications of the OWA operator.

42.2.1 The extensions of the ordered weighted averaging operator

Yager (1996) investigated maximizing an OWA aggregation for a group of related variables under a set of linear inequalities. The study models this problem as an integer linear programming problem. In addition, the research describes a procedure for evaluating linguistically quantified propositions owing to OWA operators. Mitchell & Schaefer (2000) proposed an induced OWA operator, which allows each input argument a_i to have associated N priority values α_{ip}, $p \in \{1, 2, \ldots, N\}$. Xu & Da (2003) developed the induced ordered weighted geometric averaging and generalized induced ordered weighted geometric averaging operators as the new aggregators and evaluated their desirable properties. Liu & Chen (2004) proposed the parametric geometric ordered weighted averaging (PGOWA) operator and parametric maximum entropy ordered weighted averaging operator, considering the properties of the OWA operator weights. The study also assesses the properties of the PGOWA operator and the consistency of the orness level, along with the aggregation value for any arbitrary aggregated elements using PGOWA weights. Merigó & Gil-Lafuente (2009) introduced the induced generalized ordered weighted averaging operator that provides a wide range of aggregation operators, including all the particular cases of the induced ordered weighted averaging (IOWA) and the generalized ordered weighted averaging (GOWA) operator, the induced ordered weighted geometric operator, and the induced ordered weighted quadratic averaging operator.

After that, Merigo & Casanovas (2010a) developed various generalizations of the hybrid averaging operator. The proposed operator includes the aggregation of weighted averages and OWA operators. They utilized generalized and quasiarithmetic means, fuzzy numbers, and order-inducing variables during the reordering step of the aggregation process. The proposed procedure has been used in fuzzy linear programming problems to find the optimal solutions. Merigo & Casanovas (2010b) utilized a new aggregation model, named induced heavy ordered weighted averaging distance (IHOWAD), that employs induced and heavy aggregation operators in distance measures, such as the Hamming distance. The proposed method was generalized using generalized and quasiarithmetic means, resulting in the induced generalized heavy ordered weighted averaging distanceoperator and the quasi-IHOWAD operator.

Following that, Liu (2011) investigated how to determine the suitable OWA operators, which is a crucial step for all applications involving these operators. The study summarizes various methods for determining OWA operators, categorized into five classifications: (i) Optimization attributes methods, (ii) Sample learning methods, (iii) Function-based methods, (iv) Argument-dependent methods, and (v) Preference methods. The research examines the relationships between methods within the same category, as well as the connections between different categories. It discusses a uniform framework for evaluating the various OWA determination methods. Additionally, it outlines some extensions, identifies notable problems, and suggests future research directions.

42.2.2 The determination approaches of ordered weighted averaging operator weights

Xu (2005) devised a practical method to determine OWA weights, which alleviates the influence of unfair arguments on decision results by assigning these arguments small values. After that, Amin & Emrouznejad (2006) expanded the min-max disparity to determine the weights of the OWA operator using linear programming. The proposed method employs a min-max disparity approach between distinct pairs of weights, utilizing duality in linear programming to demonstrate the feasibility of the extended OWA operator weights model. Llamazares (2007) examined how to determine the weights of the OWA operators using a majority rule approach, particularly in situations where individuals do not provide graded pairwise preferences. Additionally, given the diverse range of OWA operators available, the study proposes a model aimed at selecting the most suitable OWA operators for specific applications.

42.2.3 The development of the ordered weighted averaging operator under uncertain conditions

Xu (2007) devised a method for comparing two intuitionistic fuzzy values and then developed various practical methods, including the intuitionistic fuzzy OWA operator, for aggregating these values. Merigó (2010) devised the fuzzy ordered weighted averaging (FOWA) operator to aggregate information with probabilities, leading to the immediate probability fuzzy ordered weighted averaging (IPFOWA) operator in decision problems. To evaluate the applicability and flexibility of the proposed approach, it was used in a decision-making problem considering the selection of strategies. Merigo & Casanovas (2010c) developed the fuzzy generalized ordered weighted averaging (FGOWA) operator as an extension of the GOWA operator. The FGOWA operator addresses uncertain situations in which information is represented by fuzzy numbers and is applied in strategic decision-making contexts. The FGOWA encompasses a variety of mean operators, including the fuzzy average, the FOWA, and the fuzzy generalized mean. Additionally, the study presents a generalization that employs quasiarithmetic means, which is known as the quasi-FOWA operator.

After that, Merigo & Casanovas (2011) explored various fuzzy aggregation operators to aggregate information, considering all possible scenarios in the analysis. The study introduces new types of fuzzy induced aggregation operators, including the belief structure fuzzy induced ordered weighted averaging and the belief structure fuzzy induced hybrid averaging operator, and their principal properties are examined. Finally, the proposed method is applied to a financial decision-making problem involving the selection of financial strategies.

42.2.4 Applications of the ordered weighted averaging operator

Yager (1997) devised an analytic formulation using the OWA operator for the leximin method. Furthermore, the proposed method has been integrated into mixed integer programming techniques to identify optimal solutions. Ogryczak & Śliwiński (2003) studied solution procedures for linear programs with the OWA objective functions. Wang et al. (2007) proposed an approach for aggregating preference rankings using the OWA operator weights. This method determines the weights for different ranking positions based on the DM's level of optimism, represented by an "orness" degree. In addition, by adjusting the DM's level of optimism, ties can be avoided, and a winner can be selected. Merigo & Gil-Lafuente (2011) assessed the human resources selection using the OWA operator. Following that, Alajlan et al. (2013) employed the OWA operator to aggregate the set of support vector machine mean shift maps. Bazi et al. (2014) utilized IOWA operators within a framework to estimate water chlorophyll concentrations from remote sensing data. Firstly, their study constructs an ensemble of Gaussian process regression estimators modeled with different covariance functions.

Kasperski & Zieliński (2015) discussed the role of the OWA operator as part of a category of combinatorial optimization problems that involve uncertain costs. They applied the traditional robust approach (e.g., min-max strategy), using the OWA operator to generalize these combinatorial optimization problems. They presented new findings that include both positive and negative results in this area. Moradi et al. (2015) used the OWA operator to evaluate the impact of optimism on seismic vulnerability assessment. In addition, they compared their results with those obtained from granular computing and intuitionistic fuzzy models, revealing a similarity of 91% and 89%, respectively. Oukil & Govindaluri (2017) incorporated the OWA operators into the data envelopment analysis to rank the players. Martínez-García et al., 2019 described how the weighted ordered weighted averaging (WOWA) operator can be employed to infer user preferences for various concepts by utilizing the structure of the ontology alongside some partial preference information. Khakzad (2020) developed a new algorithm using the OWA operator to select the most preferred alternative for sediment management in dam reservoirs. The proposed approach aims to meet various technical and executive requirements, economic factors, social welfare considerations, and environmental impacts, taking into account different levels of orness. Additionally, the study suggests analytical forms of the OWA operator weighting functions, each possessing the characteristics of rank-based weights and a consistent level of orness, regardless of the number of objectives involved. Maldonado et al. (2023) introduced an innovative adaptive loss function to improve deep learning performance in classification tasks. The employed function utilizes the OWA operator and integrates it with an adaptive gradient-based learning scheme. Additionally, it has been shown that hyperparameters related to the OWA operators significantly influence performance, and a default configuration is used to achieve good results across various experimental settings.

42.3 Methodology

The OWA method offers a parameterized family of aggregation operators that have been utilized in various applications (Yager, 1988). In the OWA method, a decision matrix is created based on the information provided by the decision-maker in (42.1).

$$D = \begin{bmatrix} x_{11} & \cdots & x_{1j} & \cdots & x_{1n} \\ \vdots & \ddots & \vdots & \ddots & \vdots \\ x_{i1} & \cdots & x_{ij} & \cdots & x_{in} \\ \vdots & \ddots & \vdots & \ddots & \vdots \\ x_{m1} & \cdots & x_{mj} & \cdots & x_{mn} \end{bmatrix}; \; i = 1,\ 2,\ \ldots,m,\ j = 1,\ 2,\ \ldots,n \tag{42.1}$$

Where x_{ij} is the element of the decision matrix for the ith alternative and jth attribute. Furthermore, the decision-maker provides the weights of attributes as $\overrightarrow{W} = [w_1, w_2, \ldots, w_n]$. Regarding the decision matrix and attributes' weights, to perform the OWA method, the following steps should be followed.

Step 1. Normalizing the decision matrix.

To normalize the decision matrix, the min-max normalization type is used, as defined in Eqs. (42.2) and (42.3).

$$x'_{ij} = \frac{x_{ij} - \min\limits_i(x_{ij})}{\max\limits_i(x_{ij}) - \min\limits_i(x_{ij})}; \; i = 1,\ 2,\ \ldots,m;\ j = 1,\ 2,\ \ldots,n \tag{42.2}$$

$$x'_{ij} = \frac{\max\limits_i(x_{ij}) - x_{ij}}{\max\limits_i(x_{ij}) - \min\limits_i(x_{ij})}; \; i = 1,\ 2,\ \ldots,m;\ j = 1,\ 2,\ \ldots,n \tag{42.3}$$

In this context, x'_{ij} represents the element of the normalized decision matrix N for the ith alternative and jth attribute. Eqs. (42.2) and (42.3) are utilized to normalize the elements of the decision matrix for positive and negative attributes, respectively.

Step 2. Calculating the orness measure.

The orness measure evaluates the degree of permissible compensation among the values combined, as calculated in Step 4. To determine the orness measure, taking into account the weights assigned $\overrightarrow{W} = [w_1, w_2, ..., w_n]$ to the combined values, Eq. (42.4) is utilized.

$$Orness(W) = \frac{1}{n-1} \sum_{j=1}^{n} (n-j) w_j \tag{42.4}$$

According to Eq. (42.4), $Orness(W)$ denotes the orness measure of vector W, n represents the number of aggregated values, and w_j indicates the weight assigned to the jth ordered value, arranged from largest to smallest. A higher orness value indicates a more OR-like aggregation, whereas a lower value suggests a more AND-like aggregation. In simpler terms, a value of 1 signifies a pure OR operation (i.e., the maximum of the inputs is chosen), while a value of 0 indicates a pure AND operation (i.e., the minimum of the inputs is chosen). Furthermore, the value between 0 and 1 shows the different degrees of orness, with higher values indicating a strong tendency towards OR-like behavior.

Step 3. Reordering the normalized decision matrix.

After normalizing the decision matrix, the reordered normalized decision matrix is constructed using (42.5).

$$U\begin{bmatrix} x'_{11} & \cdots & x'_{1j} & \cdots & x'_{in} \\ \vdots & \ddots & \vdots & \ddots & \vdots \\ x'_{i1} & \cdots & x'_{ij} & \cdots & x'_{in} \\ \vdots & \ddots & \vdots & \ddots & \vdots \\ x'_{m1} & \cdots & x'_{mj} & \cdots & x'_{mn} \end{bmatrix}_{m\times n} = \begin{bmatrix} b_{11} & \cdots & b_{1j} & \cdots & b_{in} \\ \vdots & \ddots & \vdots & \ddots & \vdots \\ b_{i1} & \cdots & b_{ij} & \cdots & b_{in} \\ \vdots & \ddots & \vdots & \ddots & \vdots \\ b_{m1} & \cdots & b_{mj} & \cdots & b_{mn} \end{bmatrix}; \ i = 1, 2, \ldots, m, \ j = 1, 2, \ldots, n \tag{42.5}$$

Considering (42.5), $U[X']$ shows the ordered normalized decision matrix and b_{ij} indicates the jth largest of $\left(x'_{i1}, x'_{i2}, \ldots, x'_{ij}, \ldots, x'_{in}\right)$.

Step 4. Determining the OWA operator value.

An OWA operator value of dimension n is a function $F: R^n \rightarrow R$ that has an associated n vector $\overrightarrow{W} = [w_1, w_2, ..., w_n]$ such that $w_j \in [0, 1]$ and $\sum_{j=1}^{n} w_j = 1$ is defined as (42.6).

$$F_i\left(x'_{i1}, x'_{i2}, \ldots, x'_{ij}, \ldots, x'_{in}\right) = \sum_{j=1}^{n} w_j b_{ij} \tag{42.6}$$

Step 5. Ranking the alternatives.

The alternatives are ranked in descending order based on their significance values derived from the OWA operator; therefore, the alternative with the highest final value receives the top rank.

To clearly illustrate the steps outlined by the OWA method, its flowchart procedure is presented in Fig. 42.1. This visual representation effectively captures the essence of the method, guiding you through its details with clarity and precision.

42.4 Numerical example 1

The decision-maker needs to choose one option from three alternatives: A_1, A_2, and A_3. Additionally, the decision-maker has identified several important attributes, including C_1, C_2, C_3, and C_4, that will play a role in the decision-making process. After converting qualitative attributes into quantitative ones, the resulting decision matrix is presented in Eq. (42.7).

$$D = \begin{bmatrix} 500 & 20 & 12 & 8 \\ 600 & 30 & 10 & 7 \\ 550 & 25 & 14 & 9 \end{bmatrix} \tag{42.7}$$

Where the weight vector W is $W = [0.4, 0.3, 0.2, 0.1]$, attributes C_1 and C_4 are positive, and C_2 and C_3 are negative.

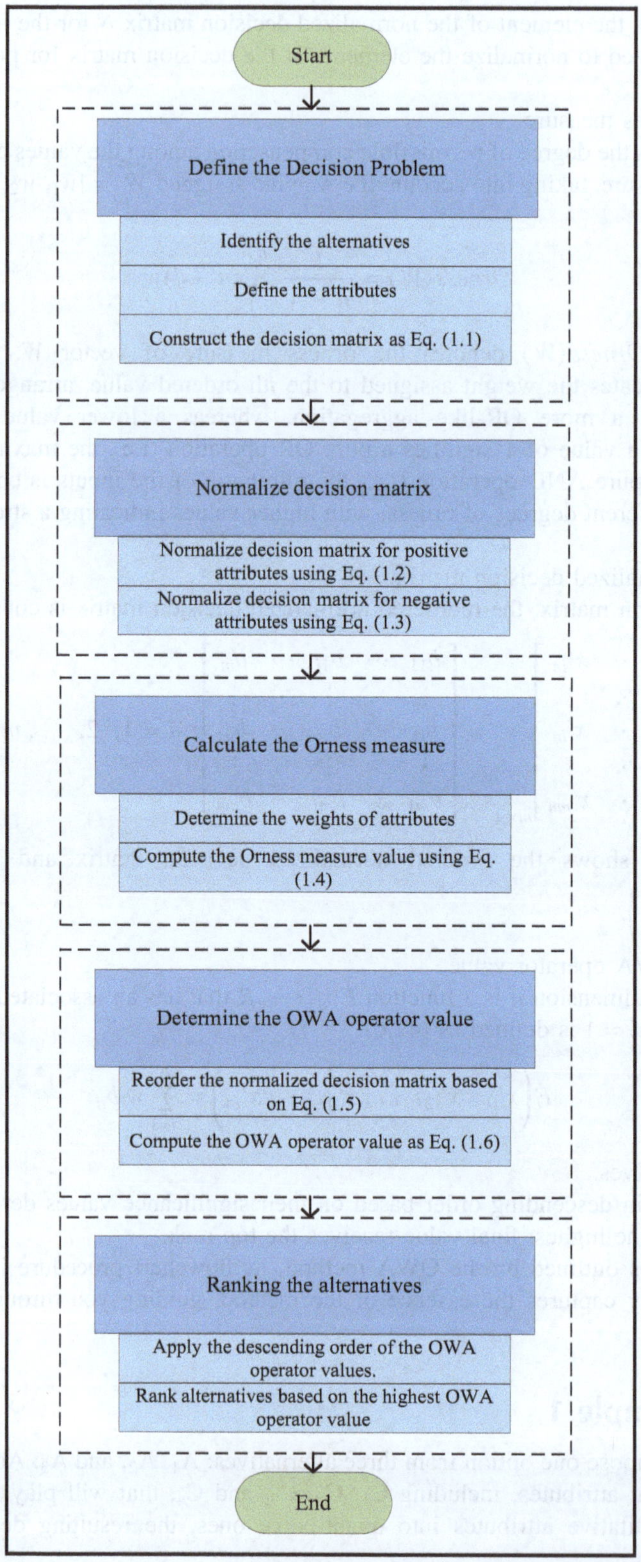

FIGURE 42.1 The flowchart procedure of the ordered weighted averaging (OWA) method.

Step 1. Normalizing the decision matrix.

The normalized values of the decision matrix is stated in Eq. (42.8).

$$N = \begin{bmatrix} 0 & 1 & 0.5 & 0.5 \\ 1 & 0 & 1 & 0 \\ 0.5 & 0.5 & 0 & 1 \end{bmatrix} \quad (42.8)$$

The detailed computations for determining the normalized values of the decision matrix are provided in Eqs. (42.9) to (42.11).

$$A_1: \left\{ x'_{11} = \frac{500-500}{600-500} = 0;\ x'_{12} = \frac{30-20}{30-20} = 1;\ x'_{13} = \frac{14-12}{14-10} = 0.5;\ x'_{14} = \frac{8-7}{9-7} = 0.5 \right. \quad (42.9)$$

$$A_2: \left\{ x'_{21} = \frac{600-500}{600-500} = 1;\ x'_{22} = \frac{30-30}{30-20} = 0;\ x'_{23} = \frac{14-10}{14-10} = 1;\ x'_{24} = \frac{7-7}{9-7} = 0 \right. \quad (42.10)$$

$$A_3: \left\{ x'_{31} = \frac{550-500}{600-500} = 0.5;\ x'_{32} = \frac{30-25}{30-20} = 0.5;\ x'_{33} = \frac{14-14}{14-10} = 0;\ x'_{34} = \frac{9-7}{9-7} = 1 \right. \quad (42.11)$$

Step 2. Calculating the orness measure.

The orness value of the proposed weight vector is determined according to Eq. (42.12).

$$Orness(W) = \frac{1}{4-1}[[(4-1)*0.4] + [(4-2)*0.3] + [(4-3)*0.2] + [(4-4)*0.1]] = 0.66 \quad (42.12)$$

The orness value indicates a comparatively strong tendency towards OR-like behavior in the proposed decision problem.

Step 3. Reordering the normalized decision matrix.

The reordered normalized decision matrix is represented in Eq. (42.13).

$$U \begin{bmatrix} 0 & 1 & 0.5 & 0.5 \\ 1 & 0 & 1 & 0 \\ 0.5 & 0.5 & 0 & 1 \end{bmatrix} = \begin{bmatrix} 1 & 0.5 & 0.5 & 0 \\ 1 & 1 & 0 & 0 \\ 1 & 0.5 & 0.5 & 0 \end{bmatrix} \quad (42.13)$$

Step 4. Determining the OWA operator value.

The OWA operator values of alternatives are computed as in Eqs. (42.14) to (42.16).

$$F_1(1, 0.5, 0.5, 0) = (1*0.4) + (0.5*0.3) + (0.5*0.2) + (0*0.1) = 0.65 \quad (42.14)$$

$$F_2(1, 1, 0, 0) = (1*0.4) + (1*0.3) + (0*0.2) + (0*0.1) = 0.7 \quad (42.15)$$

$$F_3(1, 0.5, 0.5, 0) = (1*0.4) + (0.5*0.3) + (0.5*0.2) + (0*0.1) = 0.65 \quad (42.16)$$

Step 5. Ranking the alternatives.

Based on the values of the OWA operator, the second alternative is the best option, and the first and third alternatives have the same utility.

42.5 Numerical example 2

The decision-maker wants to select one cathode from six alternatives: LCO ($LiCoO_2$), LNO ($LiNiO_2$), NCA (Li [$Ni_{0.8}$ $Co_{0.15}$ $Al_{0.05}$] O_2), NMC (Li [$Ni_{0.33}$ $Mn_{0.33}$ $Co_{0.33}$] O_2), LMO ($LiMn_2O_4$), and LFP ($LiFePO_4$). Furthermore, the expert incorporates attributes, such as C_1: cell voltage, C_2: energy density, C_3: power, C_4: safety, C_5: lifetime, C_6: cost, C_7: toxic components, C_8: discharge capacity, and C_9: stability into the decision-making process (Tajik et al., 2023). After transforming qualitative attributes into quantitative ones, the resulting decision matrix is indicated in Eq. (42.17).

$$D = \begin{bmatrix} 3.9 & 150 & 7 & 3 & 3 & 1 & 3 & 274 & 5 \\ 3.6 & 150 & 5 & 5 & 5 & 7 & 3 & 275 & 1 \\ 3.65 & 130 & 7 & 5 & 7 & 5 & 1 & 279 & 5 \\ 4 & 170 & 5 & 5 & 5 & 5 & 1 & 280 & 7 \\ 4 & 120 & 7 & 7 & 5 & 7 & 7 & 148 & 7 \\ 3.3 & 130 & 7 & 9 & 7 & 7 & 7 & 170 & 9 \end{bmatrix} \quad (42.17)$$

Where the weight vector W is $W = [0.11, 0.19, 0.1, 0.04, 0.06, 0.29, 0.04, 0.12, 0.05]$, and all attributes are positive. According to the OWA method, the first step is to determine the normalized values of the decision matrix. To normalize the initial decision matrix, Eqs. (42.2) and (42.3) are utilized, resulting in the normalized decision matrix as stated in Eq. (42.18).

$$N = \begin{bmatrix} 0.86 & 0.4 & 0 & 0 & 0 & 0 & 0.33 & 0.95 & 0.5 \\ 0.43 & 0.4 & 1 & 0.33 & 0.5 & 1 & 0.33 & 0.96 & 0 \\ 0.5 & 0.8 & 0 & 0.33 & 1 & 0.66 & 0 & 0.99 & 0.5 \\ 1 & 0 & 1 & 0.33 & 0.5 & 0.66 & 0 & 1 & 0.75 \\ 1 & 1 & 0 & 0.66 & 0.5 & 1 & 1 & 0 & 0.75 \\ 0 & 0.8 & 0 & 1 & 1 & 1 & 1 & 0.16 & 1 \end{bmatrix} \tag{42.18}$$

After normalizing the decision matrix, the orness measure value is calculated using the weight vector W in accordance with Eq. (42.4), as outlined in Eq. (42.19). The orness value reflects a moderate tendency toward both AND-like and OR-like behavior in the proposed decision problem.

$$Orness(W) = \frac{1}{9-1}\begin{bmatrix} [(9-1)*0.11] + [(9-2)*0.19] + [(9-3)*0.1]+ \\ [(9-4)*0.04] + [(9-5)*0.06] + [(9-6)*0.29]+ \\ [(9-7)*0.04] + [(9-8)*0.12] + [(9-9)*0.05] \end{bmatrix} = 0.54 \tag{42.19}$$

Following the determination of the tendency of the decision- maker based on the calculated orness measure value, the reordered normalized decision matrix is determined using (42.5) as represented in Eq. (42.20).

$$UN = \begin{bmatrix} 0.95 & 0.86 & 0.5 & 0.4 & 0.33 & 0 & 0 & 0 & 0 \\ 1 & 1 & 0.96 & 0.5 & 0.43 & 0.4 & 0.33 & 0.33 & 0 \\ 1 & 0.99 & 0.8 & 0.66 & 0.5 & 0.5 & 0.33 & 0 & 0 \\ 1 & 1 & 1 & 0.75 & 0.66 & 0.5 & 0.33 & 0 & 0 \\ 1 & 1 & 1 & 1 & 0.75 & 0.66 & 0.5 & 0 & 0 \\ 1 & 1 & 1 & 1 & 1 & 0.8 & 0.16 & 0 & 0 \end{bmatrix} \tag{42.20}$$

To rank the cathode materials using the OWA method, the OWA operator value is calculated using (42.6). The OWA operator values for all alternatives are presented as follows:

LCO	LNO	NCA	NMC	LMO	LFP
0.3537	0.6106	0.5927	0.6278	0.6964	0.7384

TABLE 42.1 The weights assigned to each attribute for each scenario.

Scenario	Weights of attributes								
	C_1	C_2	C_3	C_4	C_5	C_6	C_7	C_8	C_9
S_1	1	0	0	0	0	0	0	0	0
S_2	0	0	0	0	0	0	0	1	0
S_3	0	0	0	0	0	0	1	0	0
S_4	0	0	0	0	0	1	0	0	0
S_5	0	0	0	0	1	0	0	0	0
S_6	0	0	0	1	0	0	0	0	0
S_7	0	0	1	0	0	0	0	0	0
S_8	0	1	0	0	0	0	0	0	0
S_9	0.11	0.11	0.11	0.11	0.11	0.11	0.11	0.11	0.11

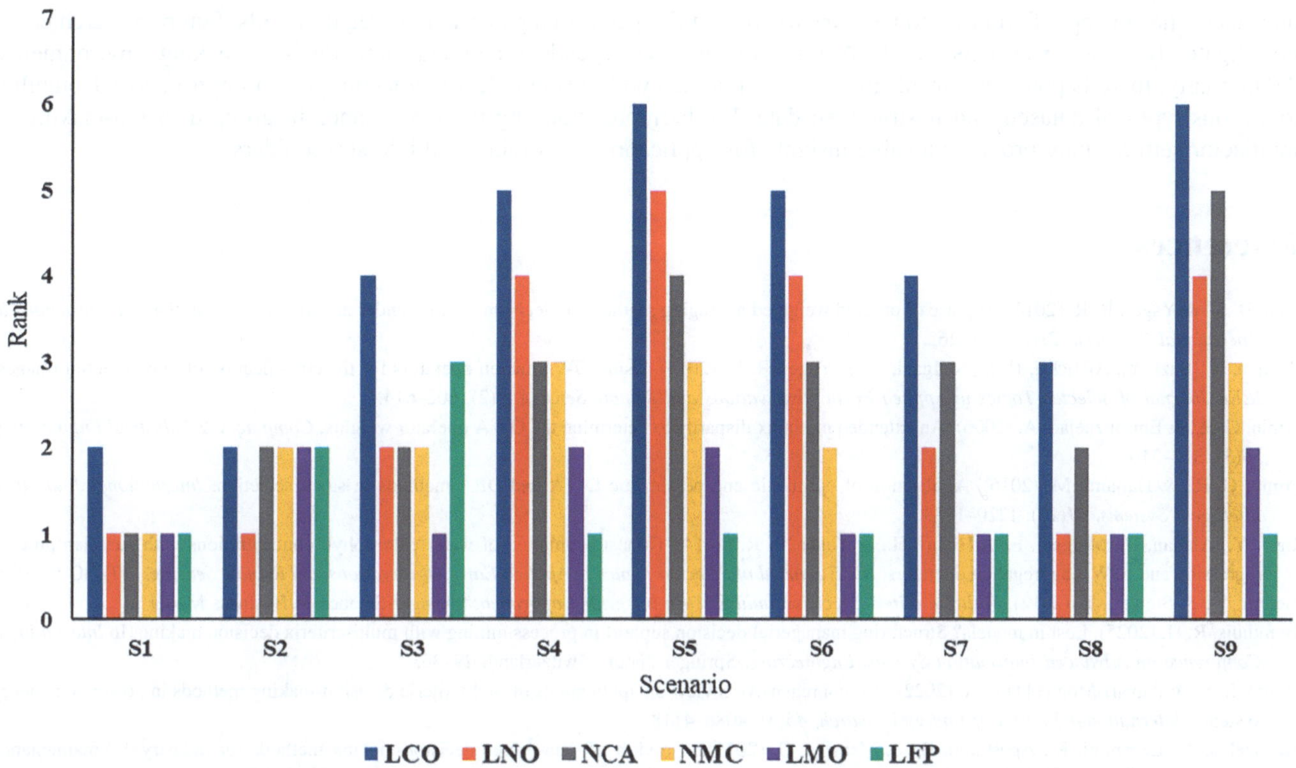

FIGURE 42.2 The rank of cathode materials based on each scenario.

According to the values of the OWA operator, the LFP is the best alternative with a score of 0.7384. Following this, the LMO ranks second with a score of 0.6964, while the LCO ranks last with a score of 0.3537.

In the context of the orness measure, the OWA method is assessed by varying the weights of the attributes across nine different scenarios. This approach allows for an examination of how changes in attributes' weights affect the final ranking of cathode materials through a series of variations. Following this framework, a sensitivity analysis is applied to assess the impact of various weight assignments on the ranking of cathode materials. Table 42.1 presents the weights assigned to each criterion for each scenario, while Fig. 42.2 illustrates the changes in rank points for clarity.

According to Fig. 42.2, four cathode materials (i.e., LNO, NCA, NMC, and LFP) have achieved the best ranking, while LCO is the worst considering scenario 1. Following scenario 2, LNO is known as the worst cathode material, while other cathode materials are the best option. In scenarios 3, 4, 7, and 8, the ranking of alternatives becomes more distinct. Ultimately, the cathode materials have achieved a unique rank in scenario 5. Furthermore, the cathode LFP has gained the best rank when the weights assigned to the attributes are equal, while the LCO cathode is known as the worst one.

42.6 Conclusions

MADM is crucial for tackling complex decisions that involve multiple, frequently conflicting attributes. Traditional aggregation operators in MADM methods, such as the arithmetic mean or weighted sum, utilize fixed weights that may not adequately represent the actual decision context or attitudes like optimism or pessimism. To alleviate this issue, one of the powerful aggegation operator, known as the OWA operator, has been used as a MADM method, which provides a more flexible approach by allowing the importance of attributes to depend on their ordered performance and by adjusting weights to model a range of aggregation attitudes, from pessimistic (i.e., minimum/AND) to optimistic (i.e., maximum/OR), and any compromise in between. This superiority enables explicit representation of risk attitudes and generalizes classical aggregation operators, making the OWA operator valuable in diverse fields such as engineering, finance, and group decision-making. However, OWA operators' strengths come with challenges, including subjective weight selection, computational complexity, and interpretability issues. To overcome these challenges, it is essential to combine attribute functions to develop comprehensive decision functions applicable across different fields. Furthermore, the OWA operator lies between the extremes of "and" (i.e., all attributes must be met) and "or" (i.e., any attribute is sufficient), and introduces the concept of "orness" to measure where on this spectrum a particular aggregation falls. Future research could investigate dynamic extensions of OWA operator in time-dependent and real-time decision-making environments. Additionally, there is potential for integrating this approach with machine learning techniques to improve its adaptability to various types of datasets and unstructured data. Furthermore, studying its performance in group decision-making or multiactor settings may provide valuable insights for applications involving multiple stakeholders.

References

Ahn, B. S., & Yager, R. R. (2014). The use of ordered weighted averaging method for decision making under uncertainty. *International Transactions in Operational Research, 21*(2), 247–262.

Alajlan, N., Bazi, Y., AlHichri, H. S., Melgani, F., & Yager, R. R. (2013). Using OWA fusion operators for the classification of hyperspectral images. *IEEE Journal of Selected Topics in Applied Earth Observations and Remote Sensing, 6*(2), 602–614.

Amin, G. R., & Emrouznejad, A. (2006). An extended minimax disparity to determine the OWA operator weights. *Computers & Industrial Engineering, 50*(3), 312–316.

Amin, G. R., & Hajjami, M. (2016). Application of optimistic and pessimistic OWA and DEA methods in stock selection. *International Journal of Intelligent Systems, 31*(12), 1220–1233.

Bazi, Y., Alajlan, N., Melgani, F., AlHichri, H., & Yager, R. R. (2014). Robust estimation of water chlorophyll concentrations with gaussian process regression and IOWA aggregation operators. *IEEE Journal of Selected Topics in Applied Earth Observations and Remote Sensing, 7*(7), 3019–3028.

Belton, V., & Stewart, T. (2012). *Multiple criteria decision analysis: An integrated approach*. Springer Science & Business Media.

Bemthuis, R. H. (2025). Lost in models? Structuring managerial decision support in process mining with multi-criteria decision making. In *International Conference on Advanced Information Systems Engineering*. Springer Nature Switzerland, 29–36.

Bohra, S. S., & Anvari-Moghaddam, A. (2022). A comprehensive review on applications of multicriteria decision-making methods in power and energy systems. *International Journal of Energy Research, 46*(4), 4088–4118.

Bousdekis, A., Lepenioti, K., Apostolou, D., & Mentzas, G. (2021). A review of data-driven decision-making methods for industry 4.0 maintenance applications. *Electronics, 10*(7), 828.

Chaube, S., Pant, S., Kumar, A., Uniyal, S., Singh, M. K., Kotecha, K., & Kumar, A. (2024). An overview of multi-criteria decision analysis and the applications of AHP and TOPSIS methods. *International Journal of Mathematical, Engineering and Management Sciences, 9*(3), 581.

Ferla, G., Mura, B., Falasco, S., Caputo, P., & Matarazzo, A. (2024). Multi-Criteria Decision Analysis (MCDA) for sustainability assessment in food sector. A systematic literature review on methods, indicators and tools. *Science of the Total Environment, 946*, 174235.

Ghasemkhani, N., Vayghan, S. S., Abdollahi, A., Pradhan, B., & Alamri, A. (2020). Urban development modeling using integrated fuzzy systems, ordered weighted averaging (OWA), and geospatial techniques. *Sustainability, 12*(3), 809.

Hastie, R., & Dawes, R.M. (2010). Rational choice in an uncertain world: The psychology of judgment and decision making.

Kasperski, A., & Zieliński, P. (2015). Combinatorial optimization problems with uncertain costs and the OWA criterion. *Theoretical Computer Science, 565*, 102–112.

Keeney, R. L., & Raiffa, H. (1976). *Decisions with multiple objectives: Preferences and value tradeoffs*. Wiley.

Khakzad, H. (2020). OWA operators with different Orness levels for sediment management alternative selection problem. *Water Supply, 20*(1), 173–185.

Llamazares, B. (2007). Choosing OWA operator weights in the field of Social Choice. *Information Sciences, 177*(21), 4745–4756.

Liu, X. (2008). A general model of parameterized OWA aggregation with given orness level. *International Journal of Approximate Reasoning, 48*(2), 598–627.

Liu, X. (2011). A review of the OWA determination methods: Classification and some extensions. *Recent developments in the Ordered Weighted Averaging Operators: Theory and Practice*, 49–90.

Liu, X., & Chen, L. (2004). On the properties of parametric geometric OWA operator. *International Journal of Approximate Reasoning, 35*(2), 163–178.

Ma, Q., & Li, H. (2024). A decision support system for supplier quality evaluation based on MCDM-aggregation and machine learning. *Expert Systems with Applications, 242*, 122746.

Malczewski, J., Chapman, T., Flegel, C., Walters, D., Shrubsole, D., & Healy, M. A. (2003). GIS–multicriteria evaluation with ordered weighted averaging (OWA): Case study of developing watershed management strategies. *Environment and Planning A, 35*(10), 1769–1784.

Maldonado, S., Vairetti, C., Jara, K., Carrasco, M., & López, J. (2023). OWAdapt: An adaptive loss function for deep learning using OWA operators. *Knowledge-based systems, 280*, 111022.

Mardani, A., Jusoh, A., Nor, K. M., Khalifah, Z., Zakwan, N., & Valipour, A. (2015). Multiple criteria decision-making techniques and their applications–A review of the literature from 2000 to 2014. *Economic Research-Ekonomska Istraživanja, 28*(1), 516–571.

Martínez-García, M., Valls, A., & Moreno, A. (2019). Inferring preferences in ontology-based recommender systems using WOWA. *Journal of Intelligent Information Systems, 52*(2), 393–423.

Merigó, J. M. (2010). Fuzzy decision making with immediate probabilities. *Computers & Industrial Engineering, 58*(4), 651–657.

Merigo, J. M., & Casanovas, M. (2010a). Fuzzy generalized hybrid aggregation operators and its application in fuzzy decision making. *International Journal of Fuzzy Systems, 12*(1).

Merigo, J. M., & Casanovas, M. (2010c). The fuzzy generalized OWA operator and its application in strategic decision making. *Cybernetics and systems: An international journal, 41*(5), 359–370.

Merigo, J. M., & Casanovas, M. (2010b). Induced and heavy aggregation operators with distance measures. *Journal of Systems Engineering and Electronics, 21*(3), 431–439.

Merigo, J. M., & Casanovas, M. (2011). Decision making with Dempster-Shafer theory using fuzzy induced aggregation operators. In *Recent developments in the ordered weighted averaging operators: Theory and practice*. Springer, 209–228.

Merigó, J. M., & Gil-Lafuente, A. M. (2009). The induced generalized OWA operator. *Information Sciences, 179*(6), 729–741.

Merigo, J. M., & Gil-Lafuente, A. M. (2011). Decision-making in sport management based on the OWA operator. *Expert Systems with Applications, 38*(8), 10408–10413.

Mianabadi, H., Sheikhmohammady, M., Mostert, E., & Van de Giesen, N. (2014). Application of the ordered weighted averaging (OWA) method to the Caspian Sea conflict. *Stochastic Environmental Research and Risk Assessment, 28*(6), 1359–1372.

Mitchell, H. B., & Schaefer, P. A. (2000). Multiple priorities in an induced ordered weighted averaging operator. *International Journal of Intelligent Systems, 15*(4), 317–327.

Moradi, M., Delavar, M. R., & Moshiri, B. (2015). A GIS-based multi-criteria decision-making approach for seismic vulnerability assessment using quantifier-guided OWA operator: A case study of Tehran, Iran. *Annals of GIS, 21*(3), 209–222.

Ogryczak, W., & Śliwiński, T. (2003). On solving linear programs with the ordered weighted averaging objective. *European Journal of Operational Research, 148*(1), 80–91.

Oukil, A., & Govindaluri, S. M. (2017). A systematic approach for ranking football players within an integrated DEA-OWA framework. *Managerial and Decision Economics, 38*(8), 1125–1136.

Prince, A. Amalin, Jose, Iven, & Agrawal, V. P. (2012). A new optimal design and analysis method based on MADM for MEMS products development. *The International Journal of Advanced Manufacturing Technology, 63*(9-12), 851–861. https://doi.org/10.1007/s00170-012-3969-7.

Saaty, T. L. (1980). *The analytic hierarchy process*. McGraw-Hill.

Shao, M., Han, Z., Sun, J., Xiao, C., Zhang, S., & Zhao, Y. (2020). A review of multi-criteria decision making applications for renewable energy site selection. *Renewable Energy, 157*, 377–403.

Sriram, S., Ramachandran, M., Chinnasamy, S., & Mathivanan, G. (2022). A review on multi-criteria decision-making and its application. *REST Journal on Emerging trends in Modelling and Manufacturing, 7*(4), 101–107.

Tajik, M., Makui, A., & Tosarkani, B. M. (2023). Sustainable cathode material selection in lithium-ion batteries using a novel hybrid multi-criteria decision-making. *Journal of Energy Storage, 66*, 107089.

Triantaphyllou, E. (2000). A sensitivity analysis approach for MCDM methods. In *In Multi-criteria decision making methods: A comparative study*. Springer US, 131–175.

Wang, Y. M., Luo, Y., & Hua, Z. (2007). Aggregating preference rankings using OWA operator weights. *Information Sciences, 177*(16), 3356–3363.

Xu, Z. (2005). An overview of methods for determining OWA weights. *International Journal of Intelligent Systems, 20*(8), 843–865.

Xu, Z. (2007). Intuitionistic fuzzy aggregation operators. *IEEE Transactions on Fuzzy Systems, 15*(6), 1179–1187.

Xu, Z., & Da, Q. L. (2003). An overview of operators for aggregating information. *International Journal of Intelligent Systems, 18*(9), 953–969.

Xu, Z. (2015). *Uncertain multi-attribute decision making: Methods and applications*. Springer.

Yager, R. R. (1996). Constrained OWA aggregation. *Fuzzy Sets and Systems, 81*(1), 89–101.

Yager, R. R. (1997). On the analytic representation of the Leximin ordering and its application to flexible constraint propagation. *European Journal of Operational Research, 102*(1), 176–192.

Yager, R. R. (1988). On ordered weighted averaging aggregation operators in multicriteria decisionmaking. *IEEE Transactions on Systems, Man, and Cybernetics, 18*(1), 183–190.

Yager, R. R. (2002). On ordered weighted averaging aggregation operators in multicriteria decisionmaking. *IEEE Transactions on Systems, Man, and Cybernetics, 18*(1), 183–190.

Zadeh, L. A. (1965). Fuzzy sets. *Information and Control, 8*(3), 338–353.

Zavadskas, E. K., Pamučar, D., Stević, Ž., & Mardani, A. (2020). Multi-criteria decision-making techniques for improvement sustainability engineering processes. *Symmetry, 12*(6), 986.

Zayat, W., Kilic, H. S., Yalcin, A. S., Zaim, S., & Delen, D. (2023). Application of MADM methods in Industry 4.0: A literature review. *Computers & Industrial Engineering, 177*, 109075.

Zimmermann, H. J. (2011). *Fuzzy set theory—and its applications*. Springer Science & Business Media.

Merigó, J. M., & Casanovas, M. (2010b). Induced and heavy aggregation operators with distance measures. *Journal of Systems Engineering and Electronics*, *21*(3), 431–439.

Merigó, J. M., & Casanovas, M. (2011). Decision making with Dempster-Shafer theory using fuzzy induced aggregation operators. In *Recent developments in the ordered weighted averaging operators: Theory and practice* (pp. 209–228). Springer.

Merigó, J. M., & Gil-Lafuente, A. M. (2009). The induced generalized OWA operator. *Information Sciences*, *179*(6), 729–741.

Merigó, J. M., & Gil-Lafuente, A. M. (2011). Decision making in sport management based on the OWA operator. *Expert Systems with Applications*, *38*(8), 10408–10413.

Mirzabadi, H., Sheikh-Mohammady, M., Monfared, S., Van de Giesen, N. (2014). Application of the ordered weighted averaging (OWA) method to the Caspian sea conflict. *Stochastic Environmental Research and Risk Assessment*, *28*(6), 1359–1372.

Mitchell, H. B., & Schaefer, P. A. (2000). Multiple priorities in an induced ordered weighted averaging operator. *International Journal of Intelligent Systems*, *15*(4), 317–327.

Moradi, M., Delavar, M. R., & Moshiri, B. (2015). A GIS-based multi-criteria decision-making approach to seismic vulnerability assessment using quantifier-guided OWA operator: A case study of Tehran, Iran. *Annals of GIS*, *21*(3), 209–222.

Ogryczak, W., & Śliwiński, T. (2003). On solving linear programs with the ordered weighted averaging objective. *European Journal of Operational Research*, *148*(1), 80–91.

Oukil, A., & Govindaluri, S. M. (2017). A systematic approach for ranking football players within an integrated DEA-OWA framework. *Managerial and Decision Economics*, *38*(8), 1125–1136.

Prince, A. Amalin, Jose, Byron, & Agarwal, V. P. (2012). A new optimal design and analysis model based on MADM for MEMS products development. *The International Journal of Advanced Manufacturing Technology*, *63*(9–12), 831–858. https://doi.org/10.1007/s00170-012-3969-7.

Saaty, T. L. (1980). *The analytic hierarchy process*. McGraw-Hill.

Shao, M., Han, Z., Sun, J., Xiao, C., Zhang, S., & Zhao, Y. (2020). A review of multi-criteria decision making applications for renewable energy site selection. *Renewable Energy*, *157*, 377–403.

Sitaram, S., Ramachandran, M., Chinnasamy, S., & Mathivanan, G. (2022). A review on multi-criteria decision-making and its application. *REST Journal on Emerging trends in Modelling and Manufacturing*, *7*(1), 101–107.

Tozluk, M., Mahmut, A., & Tezerkan, B. M. (2023). Sustainable cathode material selection in lithium-ion batteries using a novel hybrid multi-criteria decision making. *Journal of Energy Storage*, 68, 107680.

Triantaphyllou, E. (2000). A sensitivity analysis approach for MCDM methods. In *Multi-criteria decision making methods: A comparative study*. Springer US. 131–175.

Wang, Y. M., Luo, Y., & Hua, Z. (2007). Aggregating preference rankings using OWA operator weights. *Information Sciences*, *177*(16), 3356–3363.

Xu, Z. (2005). An overview of methods for determining OWA weights. *International Journal of Intelligent Systems*, *20*(8), 843–865.

Xu, Z. (2007). Intuitionistic fuzzy aggregation operators. *IEEE Transactions on Fuzzy Systems*, *15*(6), 1179–1187.

Xu, Z., & Da, Q. L. (2003). An overview of operators for aggregating information. *International Journal of Intelligent Systems*, *18*(9), 953–969.

Xu, Z. (2015). *Uncertain multi-attribute decision making: Methods and applications*. Springer.

Yager, R. R. (1993). Families of OWA operators. *Fuzzy Sets and Systems*, *59*(2), 125–148.

Yager, R. R. (1997). On the analytic representation of the Leximin ordering and its application to flexible constraint propagation. *European Journal of Operational Research*, *102*(1), 176–192.

Yager, R. R. (1988). On ordered weighted averaging aggregation operators in multicriteria decisionmaking. *IEEE Transactions on Systems, Man, and Cybernetics*, *18*(1), 183–190.

Yager, R. R. (2002). On ordered weighted averaging aggregation operators in multicriteria decisionmaking. *IEEE Transactions on Systems, Man, and Cybernetics*, *18*(1), 183–190.

Zadeh, L. A. (1965). Fuzzy sets. *Information and Control*, *8*(3), 338–353.

Zavadskas, E. K., Pamučar, D., Stević, Ž., & Mardani, A. (2020). Multi-criteria decision-making techniques for improvement sustainability engineering processes. *Symmetry*, *12*(6), 986.

Zayat, W., Kilic, H. S., Yalcin, A. S., Zaim, S., & Delen, D. (2023). Application of MADM methods in Industry 4.0: A literature review. *Computers & Industrial Engineering*, *177*, 109075.

Zimmermann, H. J. (2011). *Fuzzy set theory—and its applications*. Springer Science & Business Media.

Chapter 43

FCM: Fuzzy cognitive map for multi-attribute decision-making

Samuel Yousefi
Department of Mechanical and Manufacturing Engineering, Ontario Tech University, Oshawa, ON, Canada

43.1 Introduction

In real-world situations, decision-making typically occurs within complex systems where many components are interconnected. These components do not function in isolation; instead, they affect each other through various relationships. Ignoring the system perspective may lead to unreliable decisions, as it fails to consider how changes in one component impact others (Bakhtavar et al., 2021). To avoid generating unexpected and unreliable outcomes, decision-makers (DMs) must consider the system as a whole. System modeling provides tools to monitor, analyze, and simulate system behavior. These tools allow DMs to assess the current state of the system, observe interactions over time, and test different scenarios before making decisions. Understanding the system in this way improves decision quality and accuracy in environments influenced by multiple factors (Abbaspour Onari et al., 2021b; Papageorgiou & Kontogianni, 2012).

With a focus on multicriteria decision-making (MCDM), several methods, such as the analytic network process (ANP) and the decision-making trial and evaluation laboratory (DEMATEL), have been developed to incorporate interactions among criteria. For example, ANP captures interdependencies through pairwise comparisons and supermatrix calculations (Jharkharia & Shankar, 2007). DEMATEL identifies causal relationships (CRs) among factors and quantifies the strength of these influences, which visualizes interaction structures (Jassbi et al., 2011). Among other existing approaches, structural equation modeling (SEM) uses statistical models to examine relationships between variables. Another technique, interpretive structural modeling (ISM), captures hierarchical relationships and identifies which system elements demonstrate greater influence, though it is limited in representing the strength or dynamics of interactions (Rezaee & Yousefi, 2018). Despite their benefits, ANP and SEM often require large datasets and cannot effectively represent diverse CRs (Yousefi & Tosarkani, 2025). ISM cannot quantify the degree of influence or model feedback loops, while DEMATEL involves a time-consuming and subjective process for setting parameters, such as threshold values and weights of criteria (Li & Tzeng, 2009; Si et al., 2018). These methods also rely heavily on experts' judgment, which can be biased or incomplete. Consequently, DMs may struggle to fully understand system behavior, particularly under conditions of uncertainty.

To address these shortcomings, systems analytics techniques, such as fuzzy cognitive maps (FCMs), can be employed to model relationships among components and analyze them in uncertain environments. FCMs have been introduced as a flexible and adaptive modeling technique capable of incorporating both qualitative and quantitative knowledge while capturing complex system dynamics (Bakhtavar et al., 2021). FCMs were developed by Kosko (1986) based on Tolman's (1948) cognitive maps and Zadeh's (1965) fuzzy logic theory. In FCMs, system elements are represented as concepts connected by weighted causal links that indicate both the direction and strength of influence. Weights can range within [-1,1] or [0,1] or use linguistic terms, allowing the model to capture uncertainty and support subjective decision-making (Groumpos & Gkountroumani, 2014; Salmeron et al., 2019). FCMs enable DMs to explore how changes in one concept propagate throughout the system to effectively capture dynamic system behavior.

FCMs offer several advantages over conventional modeling approaches, making them highly suitable for complex systems analysis. They require less experimental data than dynamic systems modeling, which reduces the risk of unreliable variables and information (Özesmi & Özesmi, 2004; Papageorgiou et al., 2004). Compared to SEM, FCMs provide better parameter estimation and solution convergence when data are limited, and they effectively model systems

Encyclopedia of Multi-Attribute Decision-Making (MADM). DOI: https://doi.org/10.1016/B978-0-443-33275-3.00018-X

with feedback loops (Rezaee & Yousefi, 2018). Unlike MCDM methods and ISM, FCMs can incorporate an unlimited number of variables with CRs (Yousefi & Tosarkani, 2022). Their learning algorithms, such as Hebbian-based and population-based methods, allow the system to refine its causal structure over time and, consequently, reduce reliance on biased expert judgments (Bakhtavar et al., 2021). FCMs are also flexible in handling incomplete information, which is common in real-world problems (Abbaspour Onari et al., 2021b). Furthermore, they support scenario analysis, which enables DMs to test changes and evaluate their effects on the overall system before implementing decisions. This capability is particularly useful in dynamic and uncertain environments. Although FCM model was not originally designed as direct decision-making tools, its modeling capability and solution procedure have attracted researchers and practitioners across multiple domains, supply chain management (Dolatabad et al., 2022; Hosseini Dolatabad et al., 2023), sustainable development (Ameli et al., 2023; Chen et al., 2024), digital transformation (Erkan et al., 2024), risk management (Liu et al., 2025; Soner, 2025), disaster management (Al-Manji et al., 2021; Drakaki & Tzionas, 2021), policy design (Targetti et al., 2021), and energy management (Zare et al., 2022).

Due to the growing applicability of FCM and their extensions, this chapter explains how FCM works and encourages critical thinking about when and how to use it effectively. The fundamental concepts of FCM and the main computational steps for constructing and analyzing models are explained. Readers are introduced to various variants of the FCM developed from different systems modeling perspectives and uncertainty theories. These improvements make FCM more effective in dealing with vague and incomplete information and enhance its applicability for diverse problems. The features of various FCM learning algorithms that improve model accuracy and facilitate the application of scenario-making techniques are discussed. Specifically, the use of these learning algorithms and scenario-making techniques is emphasized for addressing MCDM problems from two perspectives: (i) defining the weights of decision criteria and (ii) prioritizing alternatives while considering CRs. The combination of theoretical concepts of FCM and practical MCDM examples in this chapter improves academic understanding and provides managerial and practical implications for DMs and practitioners.

The remainder of this chapter is structured as follows. Section 43.2 presents a review of applications of FCM and its extended versions in the literature. Section 43.3 provides a step-by-step guide for implementing the FCM model and its learning algorithm. Section 43.4 illustrates the use of FCM for determining the weights of decision criteria, which serve as inputs to an outranking method. This section also discusses a conceptual framework for ranking alternatives and compares its performance with traditional outranking-based MCDM techniques. Section 43.5 concludes the chapter by summarizing key insights.

43.2 Literature review

Since the introduction of FCMs, many researchers have sought to modify the basic concepts of FCMs or extend their applications to various fields. Over the past decade, there has been a significant focus on developing advanced versions of conventional FCM models. These efforts aim to incorporate new perspectives into FCM modeling or to propose innovative learning algorithms for training FCMs. Considering the structure of conventional FCMs, different versions have been presented in the literature. These advancements can be categorized into three main types: time-based, decision-based, and uncertainty-based FCMs. Depending on the data type and the nature of the problem, an appropriate FCM technique and corresponding learning algorithm can be selected for implementation.

In the category of time-based FCMs, the modeling process takes time effects into account. This area of research was developed by Park and Kim (1995), who introduced fuzzy time cognitive maps. This approach incorporates the concept of time into the relationships between nodes in FCMs in order to allow for the modeling of time delays between nodes and the analysis of system statuses over time. In this type of FCM model, each arc has a weight determined by experts, as well as a time lag weight assigned using fuzzy linguistic values. Subsequently, Zhong et al. (2008) presented Temporal FCMs as an extension of conventional FCMs, further integrating time concepts into system modeling. They aimed to enhance fuzzy time cognitive maps by proposing a comprehensive set of time-related features, which included dynamic inputs and both short- and long-term effects. In recent years, FCMs have also been increasingly utilized for modeling and forecasting time series (Feng et al., 2021; Papageorgiou & Poczęta, 2017; Yang et al., 2024).

In the realm of decision-based FCMs, these techniques were initially developed to address decision-making problems. In practice, activities can be influenced by prior stages, making it essential to consider the relationships among these stages when seeking solutions. In this context, Rezaee et al. (2017) conducted a study on assessing complex systems with multiple stages. They introduced multistage FCMs, which take a multistage perspective to account for the interactions among different stages within a system, alongside the existing relationships among concepts within each stage. This type of FCM consists of conventional FCMs that are interconnected as subsystems or stages. The multistage FCM technique has been widely applied in evaluating risks associated with production and logistics processes (Mashhadi Keshtiban et al., 2022; Yousefi et al., 2020). Another variant of FCM was developed by Bakhtavar and Yousefi (2018). They developed multiobjective FCMs that operate within a broader context than conventional FCMs, which allows for the consideration of multiple objectives during the analysis and decision-making process. These multiobjective FCMs incorporate two types of concepts: conventional concepts and target concepts, with CRs established among all concepts. Building upon this foundation, a scenario-based FCM was introduced by Maden and Yücenur (2024) to investigate the effects of changes in specific characteristics on other related ones.

Considering the uncertainty inherent in FCM modeling, various theories such as intuitionistic fuzzy sets, gray theory, and Z-numbers have been adopted to enhance the applicability of FCM models for addressing real-world problems. Fuzzy gray cognitive maps were introduced to manage environments characterized by ambiguity (gray meanings) and to tackle a wide array of issues, particularly in uncertain situations, where data may be incomplete or limited (Salmeron, 2010). Salmeron and Papageorgiou (2012) improved the construction process of fuzzy gray cognitive maps by incorporating an intensity value to better capture the fluctuations of the gray causal impacts. In another study, Salmeron and Gutierrez (2012) integrated these maps into a reliability analysis of a transformer's active section with the aim of enhancing knowledge-based modeling, evaluation, and decision-making. Furthermore, Chen et al. (2021) introduced dynamic extensions of fuzzy gray cognitive maps. Another extension, known as rough FCMs, was presented to manage the diversity of relationships and dynamic dependencies among measures. This approach also represents the state values of concepts and the degrees of uncertain CRs using rough set theory (Chunying et al., 2011). In real-world scenarios, the concepts being studied may exhibit various CRs with differing properties that conventional FCMs cannot adequately handle. Given the significance of a higher level of uncertainty in analyzing system behavior, Z-number FCMs were developed as an extended version of FCM based on Zadeh's (2011) concept of Z-numbers. These maps can account for the reliability of uncertain data collected during the modeling process and consequently result in more realistic conclusions (Xue et al., 2025; Yousefi & Tosarkani, 2024).

Some decision-based FCMs have been extended using theories that account for uncertainty. For instance, a multistage FCM model has been enhanced utilizing Z-number and gray theories. Abbaspour Onari et al. (2021b) proposed a multistage FCM model combined with Z-number theory to address both uncertainty and reliability concerning various risk factors and the weights of CRs. They introduced an innovative learning approach for these maps, which combines particle swarm optimization with an S-shaped transfer function to address a decision-making problem under uncertainty. In another study, Abdollahzadeh and Hayati (2023) developed a multistage fuzzy gray cognitive map to evaluate operating room failures. They incorporated data obtained from failure mode and effects analysis as input, along with the CRs identified by a team of medical experts.

43.3 Fuzzy cognitive map methodology

43.3.1 Fuzzy cognitive map components

An FCM model consists of concept nodes and their CRs. As shown in Fig. 43.1, nodes and CRs between every two nodes are signified by concepts (C_i) and arcs, respectively. The characteristics of a system (e.g., attributes, variables, and states) can be represented by the nodes. A weight ($Wij, i, j = 1, ..., n$) is allocated to each CR between C_i and C_j. The type of a CR can be positive, negative, or neutral (Papageorgiou et al., 2006; Schneider et al., 1998). The FCM model is also capable of capturing recurrent CRs and loop-based CRs. In recurrent CRs, two conventional FCM concepts influence each other directly. The loop-based CRs allow a concept's influence to spread through other concepts and eventually return to the original concept. The FCM concepts can also be considered as the conventional and target concepts (Bakhtavar & Yousefi, 2018). The target concepts serve as evaluation nodes that enable the assessment of how variations in the conventional concept values affect the achievement of the system's goals. For example, C6 and C7 are identified as target concepts because they are directly and indirectly influenced by other conventional concepts, and they do not have any outgoing arcs.

43.3.2 Fuzzy cognitive map modeling process

The FCM technique is implemented in four main steps (see Fig. 43.2): (i) identifying FCM's concepts, (ii) developing the causal-based model, (iii) scenario-making process, and (iv) learning process (Yousefi & Tosarkani, 2025).

Step 1. Recognizing FCM's concepts: Firstly, the concept nodes that describe the system's attributes or the variables for the problem under study are identified through a comprehensive literature survey or expert(s) opinions (Rezaee et al., 2017). In addition to defining the conventional concepts, DMs may also designate certain measures as target concepts.

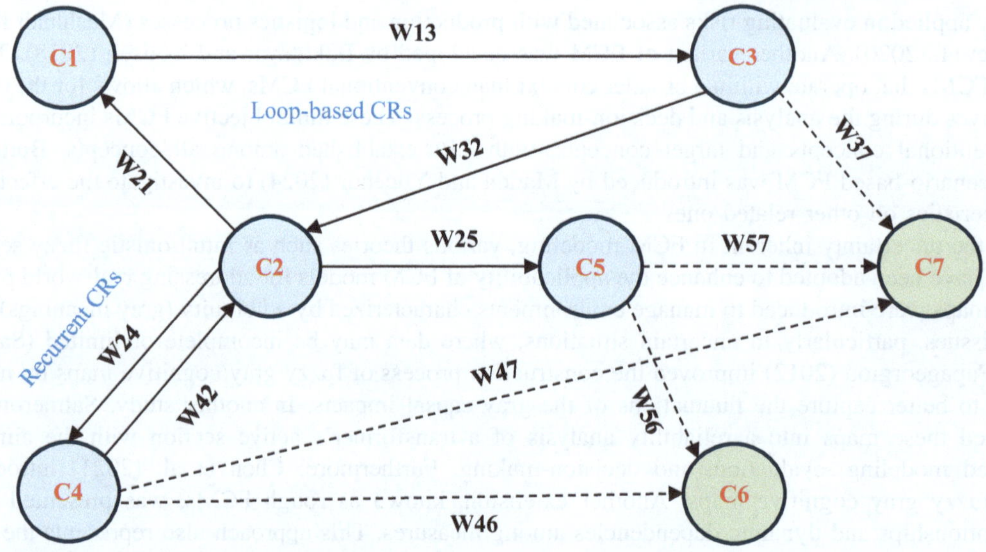

FIGURE 43.1 An fuzzy cognitive map model considering its components.

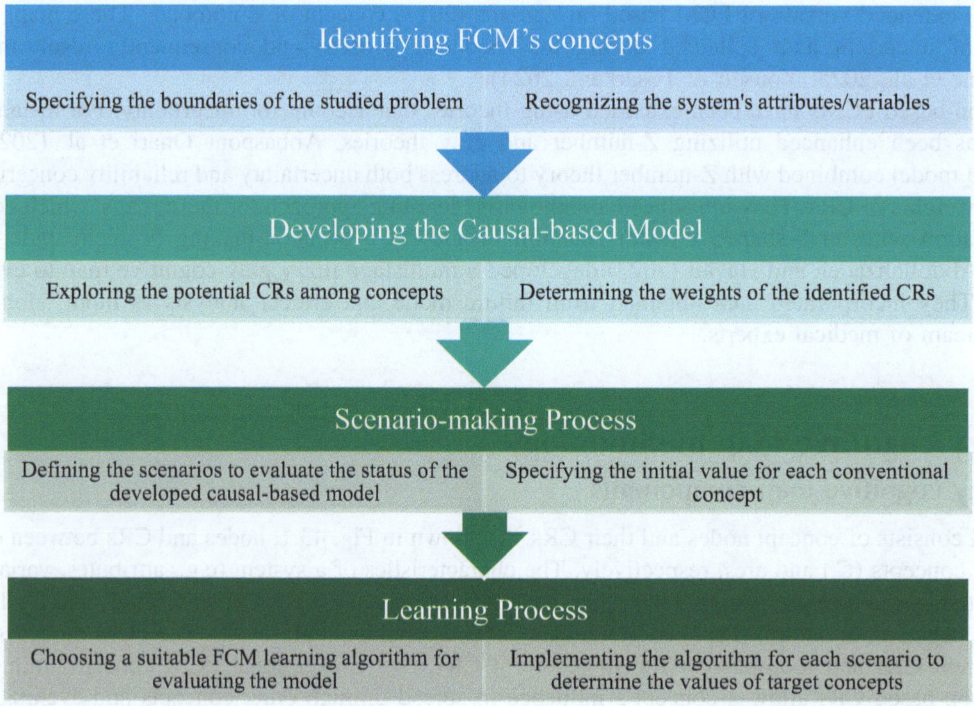

FIGURE 43.2 A step-by-step procedure for the fuzzy cognitive map (FCM) modeling.

These target concepts enable DMs to assess the state of the system as the FCM learning algorithm is executed for each scenario defined during the modeling process.

Step 2. Developing the causal-based model: Secondly, the potential CRs among the concepts recognized in the first step are examined and assigned weights using one of the available construction approaches, either semiautomatic or automatic. The semiautomatic approach relies on experts' judgments to determine the causality weights. In this case, experts determine the weight of each CR using values typically within the ranges [0,1] or [-1,1] (Bakhtavar et al., 2021). However, these expert-based assessments inherently involve uncertainty due to subjective and imprecise evaluations. To address this, uncertainty-based theories can be incorporated to represent the initial weights of CRs. In contrast, in the automatic construction, DMs aim to determine the weights of CRs using historical data or a literature survey (Schneider et al., 1998).

To derive these weights, Eqs. (43.1) and (43.2) can be applied to compute the strength of the direct and inverse CRs between any two given concept nodes, respectively.

$$d_r = |x_1(v_r) - x_2(v_r)| \tag{43.1}$$

$$d_r = |x_1(v_r) - (1 - x_2(v_r))| \tag{43.2}$$

Where d_r shows the distance between the two r elements, and $x_1(v_r)$ and $x_2(v_r)$ indicate the membership degrees of r in the vectors associated with the first and second concepts (i.e., C_1 and C_2). After calculating d_r for all elements, $AD = \frac{\sum_{r=1}^{m} |d_r|}{m}$ is used to calculate the mean distance between two vectors, where m reflects the number of elements. To specify the weight of potential CR, the similarity between two specific vectors is calculated through $S = 1 - AD$.

Step 3. Scenario-making process: Thirdly, multiple scenarios are developed based on the characteristics of the problem under study to investigate the behavior of the causal-based FCM model. For each scenario, a value (e.g., 1) is assigned to the conventional concept(s) in order to monitor how these changes propagate and influence the target concepts. Typically, these scenarios serve as inputs to the FCM learning algorithms. Moreover, scenario development can be used to evaluate the FCM models' performance by examining the behavior of target concepts under complex and dynamic conditions. By considering five conventional concepts and two target concepts, the following scenario can be developed: [$C_1 = 1$, $C_2 = 0$, $C_3 = 0$, $C_4 = 0$, $C_5 = 0$, C_6 (target concept), C_7 (target concept)]. This scenario aims to investigate the effect of changing the value of C_1 from 0 to 1 on the target concepts (i.e., C_6 and C_7) as well as on other related concepts. In some cases, when initial values for the FCM concepts are available, applying an FCM learning algorithm without scenario-making can produce updated values for all concepts and lead the system toward a stable state.

Step 4. Learning process: Lastly, an appropriate learning algorithm is selected and applied to the designed scenarios. The primary inputs to the FCM learning algorithm include the initial weight matrix of the CRs and the concept values, which are specified during the scenario-making process. FCM learning algorithms, classified as either supervised or unsupervised, are generally grouped into four categories: Hebbian-based algorithms, population-based algorithms, hybrid algorithms, and others (Salmeron et al., 2019). The first category includes algorithms derived from Hebbian learning rules, such as the differential Hebbian learning algorithm (Dickerson & Kosko, 1994) and the nonlinear Hebbian learning (NHL) algorithm (Papageorgiou et al., 2003). The second category, population-based learning algorithms, operates on sets of candidate solutions or agents, each representing a possible solution. Their main objective is to reduce or eliminate reliance on experts' judgments when defining the initial weight matrix (Amirkhani et al., 2017). Examples include particle swarm optimization (Hoorfar, 2007), genetic algorithms (Mateou et al., 2005), differential evolution (DE) (Juszczuk & Froelich, 2009), multiobjective evolutionary algorithms (Chi & Liu, 2015), and asexual reproduction optimization and its variants (Salmeron et al., 2019). The third category consists of hybrid algorithms, which combine the advantages of Hebbian-based and population-based approaches. By integrating historical data with expert knowledge, hybrid algorithms (e.g., NHL-DE) enhance the weight adjustment process (Papageorgiou & Groumpos, 2005). Finally, the literature includes additional algorithms that do not fall directly into the above categories, such as the delta rule learning algorithm (Rezaee et al., 2017).

The FCM learning algorithm enables DMs to determine the updated values of the target concepts for each designed scenario while reducing their dependence on subjective or biased judgments (Yousefi & Tosarkani, 2024). After selecting and executing a learning algorithm, Eq. (43.3) is used to iteratively update the values of the concepts until the developed model reaches a stable state (Papageorgiou et al., 2006). In this equation, $A_i^{(k)}$ and $A_j^{(k)}$ denote the values of C_i and C_j in iterations k, respectively, while $A_i^{(k+1)}$ indicates the updated value of C_i at iteration $k+1$. The function $f(x)$ is a transformation function (e.g., sigmoid function) that ensures the updated concept values remain within the predefined range by normalizing the results of the matrix operations. This function supports the training process by stabilizing the propagation and adjustment of concept values.

$$A_i^{(k+1)} = f\left(A_i^{(k)} + \sum_{j \neq i, j=1}^{n} A_j^{(k)}.W_{ji}\right) \tag{43.3}$$

43.4 Application of fuzzy cognitive map for solving multicriteria decision-making problems

The FCM modeling process can be applied to address MCDM problems across a wide range of fields. This technique supports both the determination of decision-criteria weights and the prioritization of alternatives while considering CRs. The following sections outline the procedure that DMs should follow to employ FCM as both a weighting method and an outranking MCDM technique.

43.4.1 Specifying weights of criteria

The FCM technique can be applied to specify the weights of evaluation or decision criteria when CRs exist among them. The procedure consists of three steps, described as follows:

Step 1. Identify the decision criteria.

DMs begin by identifying the set of criteria that are inherently interrelated, treating each criterion as an FCM concept. For example, in the supplier evaluation and selection problem, the price of a product is often causally linked to its quality. Therefore, it is essential to consider these CRs when determining the weights of criteria. The list of criteria can be derived from literature and experts' opinions.

Step 2. Explore potential CRs among the criteria.

DMs then identify the potential CRs among the criteria and determine their type (i.e., direct or inverse). Then, the weights of these CRs must be assigned using one of the FCM construction approaches. Since DMs often deal with new decision-making contexts and may have diverse preferences, the semiautomatic approach is commonly preferred as it allows experts' judgments to be incorporated when developing the causal-based model.

Step 3. Update the causal-based model components to specify the weights of criteria.

At this stage, DMs generate scenarios and implement the FCM learning algorithm without including target concepts in the learning process. Specifically, if there are n criteria, n scenarios are created, each designed to evaluate the importance of one criterion. In each scenario, one criterion is activated by assigning a value of 1 to its corresponding concept node, while all other nodes are set to 0. An FCM learning algorithm is then applied, and the updated value of the activated concept is interpreted as its importance in the decision problem. Because the number of concepts is often small in such MCDM problems, a hybrid learning algorithm can be beneficial to avoid identical or overly similar output values, as it leverages the strengths of multiple learning techniques. This procedure is repeated for all n criteria. The resulting values are then normalized to obtain the final criterion weights, which ensures that their sum equals one. These weights can subsequently be embedded into an outranking MCDM method to rank the alternatives.

43.4.2 Prioritizing alternatives

The FCM approach can also be used to rank alternatives directly by incorporating the CRs among the decision criteria. To do so, DMs should follow the three main steps outlined below.

Step 1. Develop the decision matrix.

DMs first identify the decision criteria and the alternatives under evaluation. Similar to other MCDM methods, the performance values of each option with respect to each criterion must be specified. In the FCM modeling process, the identified criteria serve as FCM concept nodes, while the number of alternatives corresponds to the number of scenarios that will be developed in Step 3.

Step 2. Explore potential CRs among the criteria.

DMs examine the existing CRs among the criteria and determine their weights using the automatic FCM construction approach. Because the values of all criteria for each alternative are available in the decision matrix, these values can be used directly to apply Eqs. (43.1) and (43.2), depending on the type of CR. If a CR exists between two criteria, two vectors are constructed, each containing several elements, as there are alternatives. Using the similarity measure $S = 1 - AD$, the similarity between the two vectors is calculated, which corresponds to the weight of the existing CR between those criteria.

Step 3. Rank the alternatives using the target concept.

In this step, a measurement node (i.e., hypothetical target concept) is added to the FCM model developed in Step 2. The values of the decision criteria, propagated through the CRs, are transmitted to the measurement node using Eq. (43.3). The updated value of the measurement node is then interpreted as the score of the corresponding alternative. To evaluate alternatives, a separate scenario is created for each one. Since the values of FCM concepts range from 0 to 1, the concept values related to decision criteria for each scenario are derived by normalizing the corresponding values in the decision matrix. The target concept is initially set to zero, and after applying the FCM learning algorithm, the updated value of the target concept becomes the score of that alternative. For example, in a supplier selection problem, DMs may introduce a new node called "supplier score" into the FCM model. The learning algorithm is then executed for each alternative individually, which produces a score for each supplier. Finally, alternatives are ranked according to these scores.

43.4.3 Example

In this section, the FCM technique is applied to support supply chain transformation toward smart systems through blockchain technology adoption. One of the key challenges in this process is selecting a blockchain platform that best fits the organization's requirements. Multiple platforms, such as Hyperledger, Quorum, and R3 Corda, offer smart contract capabilities and features relevant to supply chain management. Since each platform has distinct characteristics, DMs must identify an appropriate set of evaluation criteria and determine which platform provides the most suitable option for adoption within the supply chain network. To demonstrate the applicability of the FCM technique for this decision-making problem, an illustrative example is considered involving seven blockchain platform alternatives and 10 evaluation criteria. After identifying the criteria, which serve as FCM concepts within the causal-based model, seven scenarios are developed to evaluate the platforms: R3 Corda, Quorum, Hyperledger, BigChainDB, Chain, Symbiont, and Stratis.

Fig. 43.3 presents the CRs among the 10 evaluation criteria (C1 to C10) and their associated weights, adopted from Yousefi and Tosarkani (2024). The criteria include scalability (C1), reliability (C2), security (C3), portability (C4), consensus support (C5), performance efficiency (C6), interoperability (C7), implementation costs (C8), experience and image (C9), and maintainability and operability (C10). In addition to these conventional FCM concepts, a hypothetical target concept may be added to the initial FCM model to measure the overall performance of each platform while accounting for the CRs among criteria. Depending on the DMs' decision strategies, one of the existing criteria without outgoing arcs can also be designated as the target node. Since C6 and C8 are influenced by most of the other criteria and do not have any outgoing arcs, they can be considered as the potential target concepts. In this study, C8 is considered the measurement node.

After constructing the FCM model, the scenario-making technique is applied to evaluate the suitability of each platform based on the identified criteria. For this purpose, one scenario is constructed for each alternative. In each scenario, the values of 10 concepts corresponding to the evaluation criteria are set using aggregated experts' judgments (see Table 43.1) or values extracted from literature.

The NHL-DE algorithm is employed to run the defined scenarios, as it considers the strengths of both Hebbian and population-based learning approaches to offer solutions with enhanced separability. Unlike purely Hebbian algorithms, the NHL-DE integrates DE to overcome the nonconvergence issues typically associated with NHL. As a result, the updated concept values become more distinguishable, which enhances the reliability of the overall decision-making process

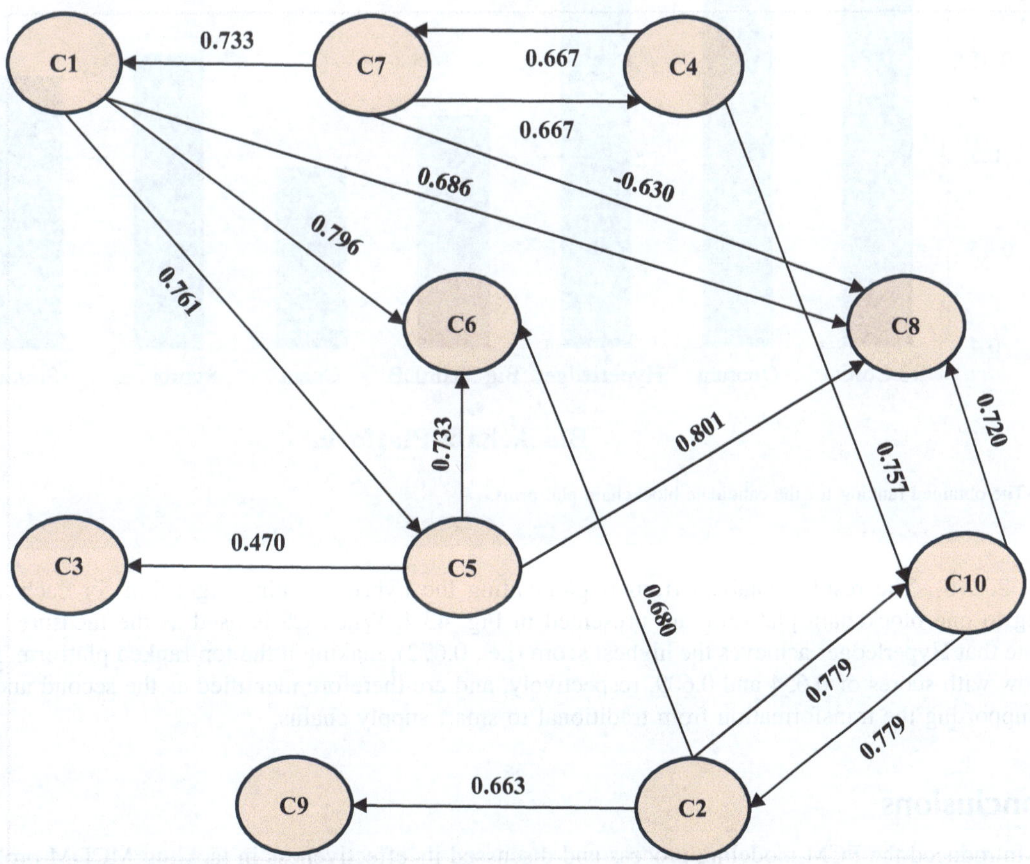

FIGURE 43.3 The causal-based model developed for the blockchain platform selection problem.

TABLE 43.1 The values of the evaluation criteria.

Platform	Criterion									
	C1	C2	C3	C4	C5	C6	C7	C8	C9	C10
R3 Corda	0.73	0.69	0.84	0.34	0.72	0.69	0.69	0.44	0.69	0.45
Quorum	0.57	0.46	0.84	0.69	0.2	0.72	0.44	0.09	0.2	0.57
Hyperledger	0.84	0.74	0.84	0.69	0.69	0.69	0.57	0.69	0.84	0.69
BigChainDB	0.23	0.49	0.69	0.08	0.09	0.33	0.61	0.09	0.23	0.46
Chain	0.20	0.44	0.69	0.09	0.20	0.08	0.46	0.07	0.20	0.20
Symbiont	0.23	0.69	0.84	0.57	0.34	0.09	0.44	0.46	0.08	0.44
Stratis	0.46	0.44	0.73	0.34	0.08	0.21	0.49	0.20	0.20	0.44

Source: Adopted from Yousefi, S., & Tosarkani, B. M. (2024). A decision support framework for best-fitting blockchain platform selection in sustainable supply chains under uncertainty. *Computers & Industrial Engineering, 197*, 110577.

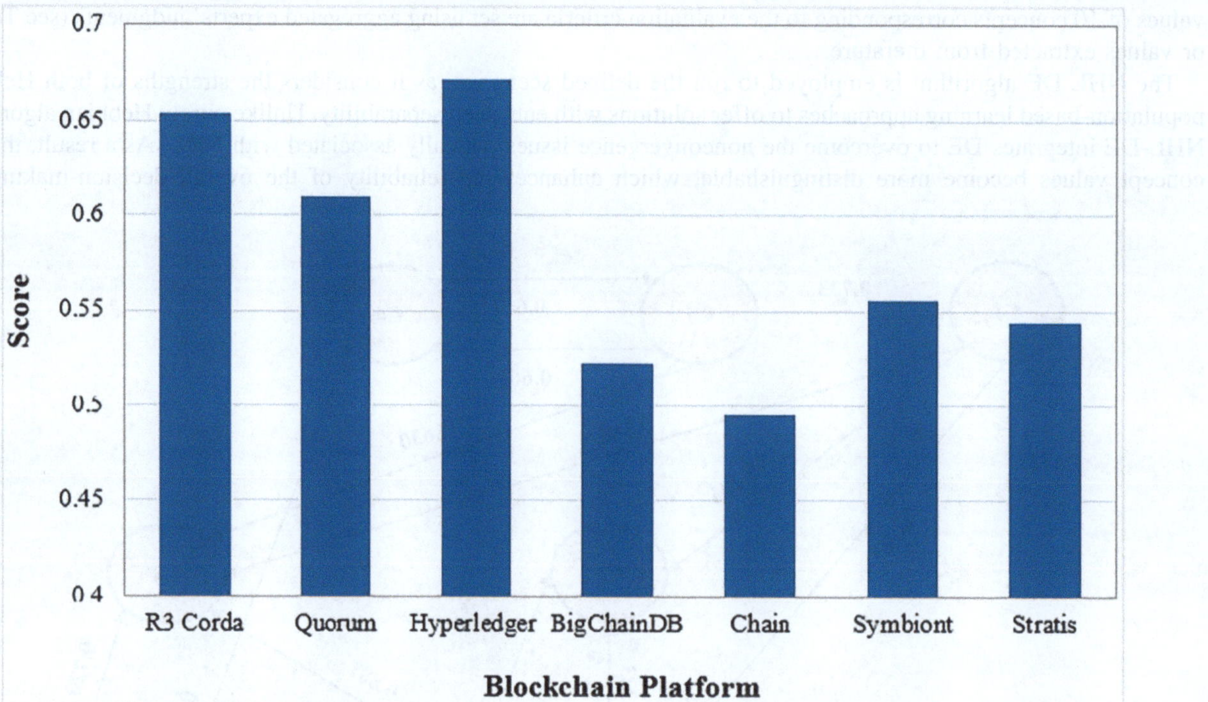

FIGURE 43.4 The obtained ranking for the candidate blockchain platforms.

(Onari et al., 2021b). The results obtained from implementing the hybrid learning algorithm for each scenario, each corresponding to one blockchain platform, are presented in Fig. 43.4. When C8 is used as the measurement node, the results indicate that Hyperledger achieves the highest score (i.e., 0.672), making it the top-ranked platform. R3 Corda and Quorum follow with scores of 0.654 and 0.609, respectively, and are therefore identified as the second and third-ranked options for supporting the transformation from traditional to smart supply chains.

43.5 Conclusions

This chapter introduced the FCM modeling process and discussed its effectiveness in tackling MCDM problems. Unlike many traditional MCDM methods, FCM provides a more comprehensive and systematic approach by modeling the complex CRs that often exist among decision criteria and other system attributes. While some methods assume that criteria are independent, FCM allows for the representation of various types of CRs, including recurrent and looped interactions. This capability enables DMs to accurately reflect the dynamics of real-world decision environments. The chapter outlines two main applications of FCM within the MCDM framework: (i) determining the weights of decision criteria and (ii) ranking the alternatives. Each application is explained with a detailed, step-by-step implementation procedure. The weighting application allows DMs to derive importance for criteria based on their interactions rather than relying solely on subjective numerical assignments. Conversely, the outranking application enables the evaluation of alternatives by considering both their performance scores and the CRs among the criteria. To illustrate the practical application of FCM in a modern decision-making context, a numerical example related to the adoption of blockchain in supply chains has been analyzed. Overall, this chapter demonstrates that FCM provides a robust, flexible, and insightful framework for addressing complex MCDM problems, which makes it an effective tool for DMs across various fields, especially those undergoing rapid technological and structural changes.

References

Abbaspour Onari, M., Yousefi, S., & Jahangoshai Rezaee, M. (2021b). Risk assessment in discrete production processes considering uncertainty and reliability: Z-number multi-stage fuzzy cognitive map with fuzzy learning algorithm. *Artificial Intelligence Review, 54*(2), 1349–1383.

Abdollahzadeh, S., & Hayati, J. (2023). Development of a multi-stage fuzzy cognitive map for an uncertainty environment: Methods and introduction. *Neural Computing and Applications, 35*(6), 4499–4517.

Al-Manji, S., Lovett, J., & Mitchell, G. (2021). Factors affecting disaster resilience in Oman: Integrating stakeholder analysis and fuzzy cognitive mapping. *Risk, Hazards & Crisis in Public Policy, 12*(1), 29–50.

Ameli, M., Esfandabadi, Z. S., Sadeghi, S., Ranjbari, M., & Zanetti, M. C. (2023). COVID-19 and sustainable development goals (SDGs): Scenario analysis through fuzzy cognitive map modeling. *Gondwana Research, 114*, 138–155.

Amirkhani, A., Papageorgiou, E. I., Mohseni, A., & Mosavi, M. R. (2017). A review of fuzzy cognitive maps in medicine: Taxonomy, methods, and applications. *Computer Methods and Programs in Biomedicine, 142*, 129–145.

Bakhtavar, E., & Yousefi, S. (2018). Assessment of workplace accident risks in underground collieries by integrating a multi-goal cause-and-effect analysis method with MCDM sensitivity analysis. *Stochastic Environmental Research and Risk Assessment, 32*(12), 3317–3332.

Bakhtavar, E., Valipour, M., Yousefi, S., Sadiq, R., & Hewage, K. (2021). Fuzzy cognitive maps in systems risk analysis: A comprehensive review. *Complex & Intelligent Systems, 7*(2), 621–637.

Chen, H., Cheng, S., Qin, Y., Xu, W., & Liu, Y. (2024). Sustainability evaluation of urban large-scale infrastructure construction based on dynamic fuzzy cognitive map. *Journal of Cleaner Production, 449*, 141774.

Chen, J., Gao, X., Rong, J., & Gao, X. (2021). The dynamic extensions of fuzzy grey cognitive maps. *IEEE Access, 9*, 98665–98678.

Chi, Y., & Liu, J. (2015). Learning of fuzzy cognitive maps with varying densities using a multiobjective evolutionary algorithm. *IEEE Transactions on Fuzzy Systems, 24*(1), 71–81.

Chunying, Z., Lu, L., Dong, O., & Ruitao, L. (2011). Research of rough cognitive map model. In *International conference on electronic commerce, web application, and communication*. Berlin Heidelberg: Springer, 224–229.

Dickerson, J. A., & Kosko, B. (1994). Virtual worlds as fuzzy cognitive maps. *Presence: Teleoperators & Virtual Environments, 3*(2), 173–189.

Dolatabad, A. H., Mahdiraji, H. A., Babgohari, A. Z., Garza-Reyes, J. A., & Ai, A. (2022). Analyzing the key performance indicators of circular supply chains by hybrid fuzzy cognitive mapping and Fuzzy DEMATEL: Evidence from healthcare sector. *Environment, Development and Sustainability*, 1–27.

Drakaki, M., & Tzionas, P. (2021). Investigating the impact of site management on distress in refugee sites using fuzzy cognitive maps. *International Journal of Disaster Risk Reduction, 60*, 102282.

Erkan, E. F., Uygun, Ö., & Demir, H.İ. (2024). Assessing digital transformation using fuzzy cognitive mapping supported by artificial intelligence techniques. *Applied Soft Computing, 166*, 112199.

Feng, G., Zhang, L., Yang, J., & Lu, W. (2021). Long-term prediction of time series using fuzzy cognitive maps. *Engineering Applications of Artificial Intelligence, 102*, 104274.

Groumpos, P., & Gkountroumani, V. (2014). A new control strategy for modeling wind energy systems using fuzzy cognitive maps. *Journal of Energy and Power Engineering, 8*(11).

Hoorfar, A. (2007). Evolutionary programming in electromagnetic optimization: A review. *IEEE Transactions on Antennas and Propagation, 55*(3), 523–537.

Hosseini Dolatabad, A., Heidary Dahooie, J., Antucheviciene, J., Azari, M., & Razavi Hajiagha, S. H. (2023). Supplier selection in the industry 4.0 era by using a fuzzy cognitive map and hesitant fuzzy linguistic VIKOR methodology. *Environmental Science and Pollution Research, 30*(18), 52923–52942.

Jassbi, J., Mohamadnejad, F., & Nasrollahzadeh, H. (2011). A fuzzy DEMATEL framework for modeling cause and effect relationships of strategy map. *Expert Systems with Applications, 38*(5), 5967–5973.

Jharkharia, S., & Shankar, R. (2007). Selection of logistics service provider: An analytic network process (ANP) approach. *Omega, 35*(3), 274–289.

Juszczuk, P., & Froelich, W. (2009). Learning fuzzy cognitive maps using a differential evolution algorithm. *Polish Journal of Environmental Studies, 12*(3B), 108–112.

Kosko, B. (1986). Fuzzy cognitive maps. *International journal of man-machine studies, 24*(1), 65–75.

Li, C. W., & Tzeng, G. H. (2009). Identification of a threshold value for the DEMATEL method using the maximum mean de-entropy algorithm to find critical services provided by a semiconductor intellectual property mall. *Expert Systems with Applications, 36*(6), 9891–9898.

Liu, P., Dong, X., & Wang, P. (2025). An enhanced fuzzy cognitive map for human risk assessment in maritime transportation: Integrating causal mining and expert elicitation. *Advanced Engineering Informatics, 68*, 103624.

Maden, A., & Yücenur, G. N. (2024). Evaluation of sustainable metaverse characteristics using scenario-based fuzzy cognitive map. *Computers in Human Behavior, 152*, 108090.

Mashhadi Keshtiban, P., Onari, M. A., Shokri, K., & Jahangoshai Rezaee, M. (2022). Enhancing risk assessment of manufacturing production process integrating failure modes and sequential fuzzy cognitive map. *Quality Engineering, 34*(2), 191–204.

Mateou, N. H., Moiseos, M., & Andreou, A. S. (2005). Multi-objective evolutionary fuzzy cognitive maps for decision support. *In 2005 IEEE Congress on Evolutionary Computation, 1*, 824–830 IEEE.

Özesmi, U., & Özesmi, S. L. (2004). Ecological models based on people's knowledge: A multi-step fuzzy cognitive mapping approach. *Ecological Modelling, 176*(1-2), 43–64.

Papageorgiou, E., & Kontogianni, A. (2012). Using fuzzy cognitive mapping in environmental decision making and management: A methodological primer and an application. *International Perspectives on Global Environmental Change, 21*, 427–450.

Papageorgiou, E., Stylios, C., & Groumpos, P. (2003). Fuzzy cognitive map learning based on nonlinear Hebbian rule. In *Australasian joint conference on artificial intelligence*. Berlin Heidelberg: Springer, 256–268.

Papageorgiou, E. I., & Groumpos, P. P. (2005). A new hybrid method using evolutionary algorithms to train fuzzy cognitive maps. *Applied Soft Computing, 5*(4), 409–431.

Papageorgiou, E. I., & Poczęta, K. (2017). A two-stage model for time series prediction based on fuzzy cognitive maps and neural networks. *Neurocomputing, 232*, 113–121.

Papageorgiou, E. I., Stylios, C. D., & Groumpos, P. P. (2004). Active Hebbian learning algorithm to train fuzzy cognitive maps. *International Journal of Approximate Reasoning, 37*(3), 219–249.

Papageorgiou, E. I., Stylios, C., & Groumpos, P. P. (2006). Unsupervised learning techniques for fine-tuning fuzzy cognitive map causal links. *International Journal of Human-Computer Studies, 64*(8), 727–743.

Park, K. S., & Kim, S. H. (1995). Fuzzy cognitive maps considering time relationships. *International Journal of Human-Computer Studies, 42*(2), 157–168.

Rezaee, M. J., & Yousefi, S. (2018). An intelligent decision making approach for identifying and analyzing airport risks. *Journal of Air Transport Management, 68*, 14–27.

Rezaee, M. J., Yousefi, & Babaei, M. (2017). Multi-stage cognitive map for failures assessment of production processes: An extension in structure and algorithm. *Neurocomputing, 232*, 69–82.

Salmeron, J. L. (2010). Modelling grey uncertainty with fuzzy grey cognitive maps. *Expert Systems with Applications, 37*(12), 7581–7588.

Salmeron, J. L., & Gutierrez, E. (2012). Fuzzy grey cognitive maps in reliability engineering. *Applied Soft Computing, 12*(12), 3818–3824.

Salmeron, J. L., & Papageorgiou, E. I. (2012). A fuzzy grey cognitive maps-based decision support system for radiotherapy treatment planning. *Knowledge-Based Systems, 30*, 151–160.

Salmeron, J. L., Mansouri, T., Moghadam, M. R. S., & Mardani, A. (2019). Learning fuzzy cognitive maps with modified asexual reproduction optimisation algorithm. *Knowledge-Based Systems, 163*, 723–735.

Schneider, M., Shnaider, E., Kandel, A., & Chew, G. (1998). Automatic construction of FCMs. *Fuzzy sets and systems, 93*(2), 161–172.

Si, S. L., You, X. Y., Liu, H. C., & Zhang, P. (2018). DEMATEL technique: A systematic review of the state-of-the-art literature on methodologies and applications. *Mathematical Problems in Engineering*. https://doi.org/10.1155/2018/3696457.

Soner, O. (2025). Modeling and analyzing cybersecurity risk propagation in ports using fuzzy cognitive maps: System sensitivity to key threat factors. *Ocean & Coastal Management, 270*, 107857.

Targetti, S., Schaller, L. L., & Kantelhardt, J. (2021). A fuzzy cognitive mapping approach for the assessment of public-goods governance in agricultural landscapes. *Land Use Policy, 107*, 103972.

Tolman, E. C. (1948). Cognitive maps in rats and men. *Psychological Review, 55*(4), 189.

Xue, W., Lin, Z., Su, W., & Zhang, C. (2025). Z-number fuzzy cognitive maps for environmental pollution efficiency evaluation based on a bargaining game. *Journal of the Operational Research Society*, 1–21.

Yang, B., Hong, S., Wang, H., & Zhao, D. (2024). Complex dynamic slow independent symbol aggregation approximation for multimodal temporal fuzzy cognitive map. *IEEE Transactions on Industrial Informatics*.

Yousefi, S., & Tosarkani, B. M. (2022). An analytical approach for evaluating the impact of blockchain technology on sustainable supply chain performance. *International Journal of Production Economics, 246*, 108429.

Yousefi, S., & Tosarkani, B. M. (2024). A decision support framework for best-fitting blockchain platform selection in sustainable supply chains under uncertainty. *Computers & Industrial Engineering, 197*, 110577.

Yousefi, S., & Tosarkani, B. M. (2025). Unlocking blockchain's potential for supply chain transformation: A robust system analysis for enhanced strategic performance. *Technological Forecasting and Social Change, 218*, 124216.

Yousefi, S., Jahangoshai Rezaee, M., & Moradi, A. (2020). Causal effect analysis of logistics processes risks in manufacturing industries using sequential multi-stage fuzzy cognitive map: A case study. *International Journal of Computer Integrated Manufacturing, 33*(10-11), 1055–1075.

Zadeh, L. A. (1965). Fuzzy sets. *Information and Control, 8*(3), 338–353.

Zadeh, L. A. (2011). A note on Z-numbers. *Information Sciences, 181*(14), 2923–2932.

Zare, S. G., Alipour, M., Hafezi, M., Stewart, R. A., & Rahman, A. (2022). Examining wind energy deployment pathways in complex macro-economic and political settings using a fuzzy cognitive map-based method. *Energy, 238*, 121673.

Zhong, H., Miao, C., Shen, Z., & Feng, Y. (2008). Temporal fuzzy cognitive maps. In *2008 IEEE International Conference on Fuzzy Systems (IEEE World Congress on Computational Intelligence)*. IEEE, 1831–1840.

Section 3

Ranking methods

Chapter 44

LINMAP: Linear programming technique for multidimensional analysis of preference for multi-attribute decision-making

Shiji Zhang, Shitao Zhang, and Xiaodi Liu

School of Microelectronics and Data Science, Anhui University of Technology, Ma'anshan, Anhui, P.R. China

44.1 Introduction

Multi-attribute decision-making (MADM) is a crucial area in decision science, offering structured methods to evaluate and choose alternatives based on diverse and conflicting criteria (Zanakis et al., 1998). It is extensively employed in addressing complex issues within production, management, economics, and other fields (Basirat et al., 2025; Bilgen et al., 2025; Lo et al., 2025). Over the past six decades, researchers have developed a broad array of techniques for addressing MADM problems (Alinezhad & Khalili, 2019; Herrera-Viedma et al., 2020; Nwokoro & Ejegwa, 2025). Among them, the linear programming technique for multidimensional analysis of preference (LINMAP), an approach for handling MADM problems, was first proposed by Srinivasan & Shocker (1973). Compared to traditional MADM methods, LINMAP reduces the subjectivity of decision results by using individuals' pairwise judgments of alternatives to objectively determine attribute weights and ideal points.

However, classic LINMAP only handles MADM problems with crisp numbers. To address this, Li and Yang (2004) introduced a fuzzy LINMAP approach tailored for multi-attribute group decision-making (MAGDM) within fuzzy environments, whereas Li and Sun (2007) outlined a fuzzy LINMAP method to tackle MAGDM challenges that involve issues characterized by linguistic variables and incomplete information. Sadi-Nezhad and Akhtari (2008) further developed a possibilistic linear programming model, using triangular fuzzy numbers to represent linguistic preferences, and discussed MAGDM under linguistic environments within the LINMAP framework. Wang and Liu (2013) extended the LINMAP to solve MAGDM problems in interval-valued intuitionistic fuzzy environments, using interval-valued intuitionistic fuzzy numbers to represent decision matrices. Liu et al. (2015) integrated the LINMAP and technique for order preference by similarity to ideal solution (TOPSIS) methods to propose a new approach, which considers positive and negative ideal points to redefine consistency and inconsistency, and thus addresses the limitations of both original approaches. Liu et al. (2016) further extended LINMAP to handle MAGDM under linguistic hesitant fuzzy environments. Zhang et al. (2016) proposed a regret theory-based LINMAP method, developing a group consistency index and a group inconsistency index based on perceived utility values. Considering that individuals may provide evaluations in different forms based on attribute characteristics, some scholars have extended LINMAP to handle decision matrices with heterogeneous information (Wan et al., 2025; Zou et al., 2022).

LINMAP method and its extensions have been widely applied across various fields. These methodologies are employed in the military sector to address the air-fighter selection dilemma (Li, 2008), within the economic domain to tackle the problem of supplier selection (Qin et al., 2017; Song et al., 2018; Wan & Li, 2013), and are further applied in contexts such as incentive selection (Rubiano-Moreno et al., 2022) and risk assessment (Tang et al., 2025).

Encyclopedia of Multi-Attribute Decision-Making (MADM). DOI: https://doi.org/10.1016/B978-0-443-33275-3.00074-9

44.2 Main methodology

In this section, we will introduce the classic LINMAP method in detail.

Define $A = \{a_1, a_2, \ldots, a_m\}$ as a set of m alternatives and let $G = \{g_1, g_2, \ldots, g_n\}$ be the set of n attributes. $W = \{w_1, w_2, \ldots, w_n\}$ is a vector of weights with n elements, where w_j is the weight of criterion g_j. The specific decision-making steps are as follows:

Step 1: Collect preference information from individuals, including the initial decision matrix $B = (b_{ij})_{m\times n}$ and pairwise judgments set $P = \{(k, l)|a_k R a_l,\ a_k,\ a_l \in A\}$ provided by individuals. P contains preference judgments between some alternatives of set A, where $a_k R a_l$ indicates that the individual considers alternative a_k to be preferred to or indifferent to alternative a_l. The set P includes all pairwise preference information and has two key properties:

(1) Pairwise judgments may lack transitivity. For example, if an individual believes alternative a_k is preferred to a_l and a_l is preferred to a_o, they might also believe a_o is preferred to a_k.

(2) No contradictory preferences are allowed. For instance, if an individual states a_k is preferred to a_l, they cannot simultaneously claim a_l is preferred to a_k.

Due to property (1), an individual can provide at most $2n(n-1)$ pairwise judgments. Although some pairwise judgments may be absent, the method retains its applicability. The accuracy of the estimated parameters is enhanced with the provision of additional pairwise judgments.

Step 2: A general normalization method (Trung, 2022) is applied to the initial decision matrix $B = (b_{ij})_{m\times n}$ to obtain the normalized decision matrix $X = (x_{ij})_{m\times n}$.

Step 3: Define inconsistency and consistency indicators. Let the ideal point $X^+ = (x_1^*, x_2^*, \ldots, x_n^*)$ represent the set of evaluations most preferred by the individual after normalization. The weighted squared Euclidean distance between alternative a_i and X^+ is:

$$s_i = \sum_{j=1}^{n} w_j \left(x_{ij} - x_j^* \right)^2 \tag{44.1}$$

Based on the pairwise judgment (k, l), the inconsistency indicator between two alternatives is defined as:

$$(s_l, s_k)^- = \max\{0, s_k - s_l\} \tag{44.2}$$

Similarly, the consistency indicator between two alternatives is:

$$(s_l, s_k)^+ = \max\{0, s_l - s_k\} \tag{44.3}$$

Step 4: Construct the optimization model (M - 1):

$$Min \sum_{(k,l)\in P} (s_l, s_k)^-$$

$$\begin{cases} \sum_{(k,l)\in P} (s_l, s_k)^+ - \sum_{(k,l)\in P} (s_l, s_k)^- \geq h & (a) \\ \sum_{j=1}^{n} w_j = 1 & (b) \\ w_j \geq \varepsilon,\ j = 1, 2, \ldots, n & (c) \end{cases}$$

From Eq. (44.1-44.3), using the positive ideal point and attribute weights, we can estimate the weighted Euclidean distances s_k and s_l of alternatives a_k and a_l from the ideal point. By comparing the sizes of s_k and s_l, the dominance relationship between alternatives a_k and a_l can be determined. The inconsistency indicator $(s_k, s_l)^-$ reflects the deviation between this dominance relationship and the individual's pairwise judgment (k, l). When $(s_k, s_l)^- = 0$, it indicates that the dominance relationship between alternatives a_k and a_l does not violate the preference judgment (k, l); a larger $(s_k, s_l)^-$ shows greater deviation. Thus, minimizing the overall inconsistency indicator ensures that the calculated dominance relationship aligns with individual preferences. The consistency indicator C measures how well the calculated dominance relationship matches all individual preferences. Constraint (a) ensures consistency dominates inconsistency, with h controlling the degree of dominance. Constraints (b) and (c) regulate weight normalization and minimum values.

Step 5: Using the calculated attribute weights $\{w_1, w_2, \ldots, w_n\}$ and ideal point X^+ obtained from step 4, we calculate the weighted squared Euclidean distance s_i, $i = 1, \ldots, m$. By means of the weighted Euclidean distance to the ideal point, all alternatives in set A are ranked.

Remark 1. Srinivasan and Shocker developed a linearization method to convert the aforementioned model (M - 1) into a linear programming model, introducing intermediate variables:

$z_{kl} = (s_l, s_k)^-, \forall (k, l) \in P$ and $v_j = w_j x_j^*, \ \forall j = 1, 2, \ldots, n$

Due to the nonlinearity of variable z_{kl} and constraint (a), we consider the following linearization process. When aiming to minimize the overall inconsistency indicator, (44.2) can be simplified to:

$z_{kl} \ge 0$ and $z_{kl} \ge s_k - s_l$

Combining this with Eq. (44.1), the above inequality can be broken down into

$$\sum_{j=1}^{n}\left[w_j\left(x_{lj}^2 - x_{kj}^2\right)\right] - 2\sum_{j=1}^{n}\left[v_j(x_{lj} - x_{kj})\right] + z_{kl} \ge 0,\ z_{kl} \ge 0,\ \forall (k, l) \in Q$$

Similarly, based on Eq. (44.2) and Eq. (44.3), constraint (a) can be rewritten as:

$$\max\{0,\ s_l - s_k\} - \max\{0,\ s_k - s_l\} \ge h$$

In fact, the two maximum functions cancel each other out, simplifying to:

$$s_l - s_k \ge h$$

By expanding s_l and s_k, the inequality can be rewritten as:

$$\sum_{j=1}^{n} w_j\left(x_{lj} - x_j^*\right)^2 - \sum_{j=1}^{n} w_j\left(x_{kj} - x_j^*\right)^2 \ge h$$

The squared terms involving the ideal point cancel each other out, ultimately leading to:

$$\sum_{j=1}^{n}\left[w_j \sum_{(k,l)\in P}\left(x_{lj}^2 - x_{kj}^2\right)\right] - 2\sum_{j=1}^{n}\left[w_j x_j^* \sum_{(k,l)\in P}(x_{lj} - x_{kj})\right] \ge h$$

Therefore, the resulting linearized model (M - 2) can be written as:

$$Min \sum_{(k,l)\in P} z_{kl}$$

$$\begin{cases} \sum_{j=1}^{n}\left[w_j\left(x_{lj}^2 - x_{kj}^2\right)\right] - 2\sum_{j=1}^{n}\left[v_j(x_{lj} - x_{kj})\right] + z_{kl} \ge 0,\ z_{kl} \ge 0,\ \forall (k, l) \in Q & (d) \\ \sum_{j=1}^{n}\left[w_j \sum_{(k,l)\in P}\left(x_{lj}^2 - x_{kj}^2\right)\right] - 2\sum_{j=1}^{n}\left[v_j \sum_{(k,l)\in P}(x_{lj} - x_{kj})\right] \ge h & (e) \\ \sum_{j=1}^{n} w_j = 1 & (f) \\ w_j \ge \varepsilon,\ j = 1, 2, \ldots, n & (g) \end{cases}$$

Constraint (d) is a newly added constraint, derived by linearly transforming (44.2). Constraint (e) is the linearized version of constraint (a) in model (M - 1).

44.3 Illustrative example

44.3.1 Example 1

This section provides a simple numerical example to validate the classic LINMAP method. Assume a set of alternatives $A = \{a_1, a_2, \ldots, a_6\}$ and a set of attributes $G = \{g_1, g_2, \ldots, g_3\}$. The evaluation values of each alternative under each attribute form a decision matrix $X = (x_{ij})_{6\times3}$. To simplify the problem, we assume all elements in the decision matrix are values between 0 and 1, which allows us to skip the normalization process. The specific decision matrix is shown in Table 44.1. Additionally, the individual provides a pairwise judgment set as follows:

$$P = \{(1, 2), (2, 3), (2, 4), (2, 5), (3, 1), (3, 5), (3, 6), (4, 1), (4, 3), (4, 5), (4, 6), (5, 1), (6, 1), (6, 2)\}$$

Set parameters $h = 0.2$ and $\varepsilon = 0.05$. Based on model (M - 2), the following linear programming model is constructed:

$$Min z_{12} + z_{23} + z_{24} + z_{25} + z_{31} + z_{35} + z_{36} + z_{41} + z_{43} + z_{45} + z_{46} + z_{51} + z_{61} + z_{62}$$

TABLE 44.1 Decision matrix of six alternatives.

	Attribute 1	Attribute 2	Attribute 3
a_1	0	0.5	0.1
a_2	0.5	0.4	0.5
a_3	0	0.2	0.3
a_4	0.1	0.3	0.4
a_5	0.4	0.1	0
a_6	0.2	0.1	0.2

$$\left\{\begin{array}{lr}
0.25w_1 - 0.09w_2 + 0.24w_3 - v_1 + 0.2v_2 - 0.8v_3 + z_{12} \geq 0 & (1) \\
-0.25w_1 - 0.12w_2 - 0.16w_3 + v_1 + 0.4v_2 + 0.4v_3 + z_{23} \geq 0 & (2) \\
-0.24w_1 - 0.07w_2 - 0.09w_3 + 0.8v_1 + 0.2v_2 + 0.2v_3 + z_{24} \geq 0 & (3) \\
-0.09w1 - 0.15w_2 - 0.25w_3 + 0.2v_1 + 0.6v_2 + v3 + z_{25} \geq 0 & (4) \\
0.21w_2 - 0.08w_3 - 0.6v_2 + 0.4v_3 + z_{31} \geq 0 & (5) \\
0.16w_1 - 0.03w_2 - 0.09w_3 - 0.8v_1 + 0.2v_2 + 0.6v_3 + z_{35} \geq 0 & (6) \\
0.04w_1 - 0.03w_2 - 0.05w_3 - 0.4v_1 + 0.2v_2 + 0.2v_3 + z_{36} \geq 0 & (7) \\
-0.01w_1 + 0.16w_2 - 0.15w_3 + 0.2v_1 - 0.4v_2 + 0.6v_3 + z_{41} \geq 0 & (8) \\
-0.01w_1 - 0.05w_2 - 0.07w_3 + 0.2v_1 + 0.2v_2 + 0.2v_3 + z_{43} \geq 0 & (9) \\
0.15w_1 - 0.08w_2 - 0.16w_3 - 0.6v_1 + 0.4v_2 + 0.8v_3 + z_{45} \geq 0 & (10) \\
0.03w_1 - 0.08w_2 - 0.12w_3 - 0.2v_1 + 0.4v_2 + 0.4v_3 + z_{46} \geq 0 & (11) \\
-0.16w_1 + 0.24w_2 + 0.01w_3 + 0.8v_1 - 0.8v_2 - 0.2v_3 + z_{51} \geq 0 & (12) \\
-0.04w_1 + 0.24w_2 - 0.03w_3 + 0.4v_1 - 0.8v_2 + 0.2v_3 + z_{61} \geq 0 & (13) \\
0.21w_1 + 0.15w_2 + 0.21w_3 - 0.6v_1 - 0.6v_2 - 0.6v_3 + z_{62} \geq 0 & (14) \\
0.04w_1 + 0.3w_2 - 0.79w_3 - 0.4v_2 + 3.4v_3 \geq 0.2 & (15) \\
w_1 + w_2 + w_3 = 1 & (16) \\
\&w_j \geq 0.05, \ \forall j = 1, 2, 3 & \&(17) \\
\&z_{12}, z_{23}, z_{24}, z_{25}, z_{31}, z_{35}, z_{36}, z_{41}, z_{43}, z_{45}, z_{46}, z_{51}, z_{61}, z_{62} \geq 0, \ \forall\ (k,\ l) \in P & \&(18)
\end{array}\right.$$

Here, constraints (1)–(14) and constraint (18) correspond to constraint (d) in model (M - 2), while constraints (15)–(17) correspond to constraints (e)–(g), respectively.

Solving the above linear programming model using LINGO or MATLAB®, the results are as follows:

$w_1 = 0.0500, \quad w_2 = 0.3335, \quad w_3 = 0.6165$ and $v_1 = 0.0408, \quad v_2 = 0.0928, \quad v_3 = 0.1830$

Since $x_j^* = v_j/w_j$, it can be known that the ideal point $X^+ = (0.8167, \quad 0.2784, \quad 0.2968)$. The objective function value under the optimal solution is 0.041, indicating that some pairwise judgments do not meet consistency under the solved attribute weights and the ideal point.

Substituting the solved attribute weights and ideal point into Eq. (44.1), the weighted squared Euclidean distances between each alternative and the ideal point X^+ are calculated as:

$$s_1 = 0.0736, \quad s_2 = 0.0354, \quad s_3 = 0.0354, \quad s_4 = 0.0324, \quad s_5 = 0.0736, \quad s_6 = 0.0354$$

Comparing these values, the alternatives' ranking from best to worst is $s_4 \succ s_2 = s_3 = s_6 \succ s_1 = s_5$.

44.3.2 Example 2

Assume a set of alternatives $A = \{a_1, \ a_2, \ \dots, a_8\}$ and a set of attributes $G = \{g_1, \ g_2, \ \dots, g_4\}$. The evaluation values of each alternative under each attribute form a decision matrix $X = (x_{ij})_{8\times4}$. The specific decision matrix is shown in

TABLE 44.2 Decision matrix of eight alternatives.

	Attribute 1	Attribute 2	Attribute 3	Attribute 4
a_1	0.81	0.98	0.52	0.97
a_2	0.58	0.71	0.1	0.65
a_3	0.18	0.5	0.82	0.8
a_4	0.24	0.47	0.82	0.45
a_5	0.89	0.06	0.72	0.43
a_6	0.03	0.68	0.15	0.83
a_7	0.49	0.04	0.66	0.08
a_8	0.17	0.07	0.52	0.13

Table 44.2. Additionally, the individual provides a pairwise judgment set as follows:

$$P = \{(1, 2), (2, 3), (2, 4), (2, 5), (3, 1), (3, 5), (3, 6), (4, 1), (4, 3), (4, 5), (4, 6), (5, 1), (6, 1), (6, 2)\}$$

Set parameters $h = 0.2$ and $\varepsilon = 0.05$. Based on model (M - 2), we constructed the linear programming model, and the results are as follows:

$w_1 = 0.0500$, $w_2 = 0.6611$, $w_3 = 0.2389$, $w_3 = 0.0500$ and $v_1 = 0.0378$, $v_2 = 0.2152$, $v_3 = 0.0639$, $v_4 = 0.0487$

Since $x_j^* = v_j/w_j$, it can be known that the ideal point $X^+ = (0.7568, 0.3256, 0.2675, 0.9735)$. The objective function value under the optimal solution is 0.2129, indicating that some pairwise judgments do not meet consistency under the solved attribute weights and the ideal point.

Substituting the solved attribute weights and ideal point into Eq. (44.1), the weighted squared Euclidean distances between each alternative and the ideal point X^+ are calculated as:

$$s_1 = 0.2985,\quad s_2 = 0.1112,\quad s_3 = 0.1112,\quad s_4 = 0.1138,\quad s_5 = 0.1112,\quad s_6 = 0.1138,\quad s_7 = 0.1342,\quad s_8 = 0.1112$$

Comparing these values, the alternatives' ranking from best to worst is $s_1 \succ s_7 \succ s_4 = s_6 \succ s_2 = s_3 = s_5 = s_8$.

44.4 Comparative analysis

We chose some representative MADM ranking methods for comparison and summarized their characteristics in Table 44.3. TOPSIS is widely used for ranking or sorting problems (Hwang & Yoon, 1981). It uses positive and negative ideal points to the advantage of the relationship between alternatives and only asks decision-makers to input the attribute weights. Therefore, the method is easy to understand. The MACBETH method drives the decision-making process by interactive learning with individuals about evaluation tasks (Bana e Costa et al., 2012). It doesn't need a decision matrix. Instead, it requires individuals to provide pairwise comparisons of all alternatives under each attribute using a linguistic scale. Comparative judgments about attribute importance are invoked to determine the attribute weights. Vlse Kriterijumsk Optimizacija Kompromisno Resenje (VIKOR) characterizes the compromise psychology of individuals (Opricovic & Tzeng, 2004). It combines utility theory and regret theory, and uses the link between alternatives and the ideal solution to identify the best compromise alternatives. This method also requires input of attribute weights, and individuals have to provide the best values and the worst values of all criterion functions. The TODIM method (Gomes & Lima, 1992) is similar to the VIKOR method. It incorporates individuals' decision-making behaviors, such as judging gains and losses based on reference points and being more sensitive to losses, into the decision-making model. The difference is that this method does not introduce ideal solutions. Instead, it derives the overall dominance degrees through the relative dominance relationships among alternatives.

TABLE 44.3 Comparison between existing multi-attribute decision-making ranking methods and linear programming technique for multidimensional analysis of preference (LINMAP).

Method	Information form	Attribute weight	Nature	Key feature
TOPSIS	Decision matrix	Objective	Cause and effect	Low cognitive effort
MACBETH	Pairwise comparison	Subjective	Optimization	Interactive
VIKOR	Decision matrix	Objective	Cause and effect	CPB
TODIM	Decision matrix	Objective	Cause and effect	CPB
LINMAP	Decision matrix	Subjective	Optimization	Linear programming technique

CPB: Considering psychological behavior of individuals; TOPSIS: Technique for order preference by similarity to ideal solution; MACBETH: Measuring attractiveness by a category-based evaluation technique; VIKOR: Vlse Kriterijumsk Optimizacija Kompromisno Resenje; TODIM: An acronym in Portuguese for interactive and multicriteria decision-making.

44.5 Conclusion

LINMAP method develops a linear programming model to ascertain appropriate attribute weights and establishes a positive ideal point through the utilization of pairwise judgments furnished by individuals, thereby presenting an objective mechanism for the determination of decision parameters. It possesses the following advantages:

(1) It fully considers individuals' bounded rationality and remains effective even without requiring all pairwise judgments.
(2) Compared to TOPSIS, LINMAP incorporates individual preferences to objectively determine attribute weights. This not only reduces subjective influence but also ensures that the ranking results better reflect individual preferences.
(3) The method exhibits considerable extensibility, allowing for its expansion to tackle group decision-making challenges, and potentially integrates consensus-building along with social network analysis.
(4) The extended LINMAP can also be applied to solve decision-making problems in fuzzy and uncertain environments.

Nevertheless, in comparison to alternative decision-making approaches, it presents certain limitations. For instance, the establishment of thresholds lacks a well-defined theoretical foundation. Furthermore, the efficacy of the method is substantially diminished when the quantity of pairwise evaluations is limited.

References

Alinezhad, A., & Khalili, J. (2019). *New methods and applications in multiple attribute decision making (MADM)*. Cham: Springer, 199–203.

Bana e Costa, C. A., De Corte, J.-M., & Vansnick, J.-C. (2012). MACBETH. *International Journal of Information Technology & Decision Making, 11*(2), 359–387.

Basirat, S., Raoufi, S., Bazmandeh, D., Khamoushi, S., & Entezami, M. (2025). Ranking of AI-based criteria in health tourism using fuzzy SWARA method. *Computer and Decision Making: An International Journal, 2*, 530–545.

Bilgen, M. K., Guneri, B., & Baldıran, S. (2025). Integrated fermatean fuzzy SWARA and Q-ROF-EDAS methodology for supplier evaluation in the shipyard industry. *Journal of Intelligent Decision Making and Granular Computing, 1*(1), 48–75.

Gomes, L. F. A. M., & Lima, M. M. P. P. (1992). TODIM: Basics and application to multicriteria ranking of projects with environmental impacts. *Foundations of Computing and Decision Sciences, 16*(4), 113–127.

Herrera-Viedma, E., Palomares, I., Li, C. C., Cabrerizo, F. J., Dong, Y., Chiclana, F., & Herrera, F. (2020). Revisiting fuzzy and linguistic decision making: Scenarios and challenges for making wiser decisions in a better way. *IEEE Transactions on Systems, Man, and Cybernetics: Systems, 51*(1), 191–208.

Hwang, C.-L., & Yoon, K. (1981). *Multiple attribute decision making: Methods and applications a state-of-the-art survey*. New York: Springer-Verlag.

Li, D. F. (2008). Extension of the LINMAP for multiattribute decision making under Atanassov's intuitionistic fuzzy environment. *Fuzzy Optimization and Decision Making, 7*, 17–34.

Li, D. F., & Sun, T. (2007). Fuzzy LINMAP method for multiattribute group decision making with linguistic variables and incomplete information. *International Journal of Uncertainty, Fuzziness and Knowledge-Based Systems, 15*(02), 153–173.

Li, D. F., & Yang, J. B. (2004). Fuzzy linear programming technique for multiattribute group decision making in fuzzy environments. *Information Sciences, 158*, 263–275.

Liu, X., Zhu, J., Zhang, S., Hao, J., & Liu, G. (2015). Integrating LINMAP and TOPSIS methods for hesitant fuzzy multiple attribute decision making. *Journal of Intelligent & Fuzzy Systems, 28*(1), 257–269.

Liu, Y. Z., Fan, Z. P., & Gao, G. X. (2016). An extended LINMAP method for MAGDM under linguistic hesitant fuzzy environment. *Journal of Intelligent & Fuzzy Systems, 30*(5), 2689–2703.

Lo, H. W., Chen, W. Y., & Lin, S. W. (2025). Using Bayesian BWM to analyze elevator performance requirements for collaborative product innovation design. *Journal of Intelligent Decision Making and Information Science, 2*, 218–232.

Nwokoro, C. O., & Ejegwa, P. A. (2025). A decade of picture fuzzy sets in multi-criteria decision-making: A comprehensive review of trends, gaps, and future directions. *Knowledge and Decision Systems with Applications, 1*, 145–164.

Opricovic, S., & Tzeng, G. H. (2004). Compromise solution by MCDM methods: A comparative analysis of VIKOR and TOPSIS. *European Journal of Operational Research, 156*(2), 445–455.

Qin, J., Liu, X., & Pedrycz, W. (2017). A multiple attribute interval type-2 fuzzy group decision making and its application to supplier selection with extended LINMAP method. *Soft Computing, 21*, 3207–3226.

Rubiano-Moreno, J., Nucamendi-Guillén, S., Cordero-Franco, A., & Rodríguez-Magaña, A. (2022). An improved LINMAP for multicriteria decision: designing customized incentive portfolios in an organization. *Operational Research, 22*(4), 3489–3520.

Sadi-Nezhad, S., & Akhtari, P. (2008). Possibilistic programming approach for fuzzy multidimensional analysis of preference in group decision making. *Applied Soft Computing, 8*(4), 1703–1711.

Song, W., Zhu, J., Zhang, S., & Liu, X. (2018). A multi-stage uncertain risk decision-making method with reference point based on extended LINMAP method. *Journal of Intelligent & Fuzzy Systems, 35*(1), 1133–1146.

Srinivasan, V., & Shocker, A. D. (1973). Linear programming techniques for multidimensional analysis of preferences. *Psychometrika, 38*(3), 337–369.

Tang, G., Fu, R., Seiti, H., Chiclana, F., & Liu, P. (2025). A novel bi-objective R-mathematical programming method for risk group decision making. *Information Fusion, 118*, 102902.

Trung, D. D. (2022). Development of data normalization methods for multi-criteria decision making: Applying for MARCOS method. *Manufacturing Review, 9*, 22.

Wan, S. P., & Li, D. F. (2013). Fuzzy LINMAP approach to heterogeneous MADM considering comparisons of alternatives with hesitation degrees. *Omega, 41*(6), 925–940.

Wan, S. P., Gao, Y., & Dong, J. Y. (2025). A novel three-way heterogeneous multi-attribute group decision method based on LINMAP for college teacher introduction. *Applied Intelligence, 55*(7), 600.

Wang, W., & Liu, X. (2013). An extended LINMAP method for multi-attribute group decision making under interval-valued intuitionistic fuzzy environment. *Procedia Computer Science, 17*, 490–497.

Zanakis, S. H., Solomon, A., Wishart, N., & Dublish, S. (1998). Multi-attribute decision making: A simulation comparison of select methods. *European Journal of Operational Research, 107*(3), 507–529.

Zhang, S., Zhu, J., Liu, X., & Chen, Y. (2016). Regret theory-based group decision-making with multidimensional preference and incomplete weight information. *Information Fusion, 31*, 1–13.

Zou, W. C., Wan, S. P., & Chen, S. M. (2022). A fairness-concern-based LINMAP method for heterogeneous multi-criteria group decision making with hesitant fuzzy linguistic truth degrees. *Information Sciences, 612*, 1206–1225.

Chapter 45

TOPSIS: Technique for order preference by similarity to ideal solution for multi-attribute decision-making

Mostafa Hajiaghaei-Keshteli
School of Engineering and Science, Tecnologico de Monterrey, Monterrey, Mexico

45.1 Introduction

Multicriteria decision-making (MCDM) involves making decisions with manifold objectives that can also conflict (Habenicht et al., 2002). A MCDM method involves assessing and ranking alternatives based on a predetermined strategy. MCDM methods can be utilized to select a preferred alternative, rank alternatives, and classify alternatives based on their characteristics. For most real-life problems, there is no “ideal“ alternative that meets all objectives. In MCDM, finding a “good“ compromise is the most important step.

The last few decades have seen several researchers either developing some novel MCDM method or applying some existing MCDM method to real-life problems (Velasquez & Hester, 2013). A growing number of problems in real-life have been evaluated using MCDM in recent years, including supplier, site, project, and technology selection, supply chain, waste, environmental, performance, healthcare, and risk management. In recent years, managers in the public and private sectors have increasingly adopted MCDM methods as part of decision-making processes that incorporate sustainable development goals (SDGs), sustainability, psychological factors, and other multidimensional criteria.

Among the listed MCDM techniques, the technique of order preference similarity to the ideal solution (TOPSIS), Hwang and Yoon (1981) and Yoon and Hwang (1995), is one of the basic and well-known methods that is very popular and widely applied. A lot of attention has been given to it by managers as well as researchers in the MCDM field. The main purpose of this algorithm is to find the ideal solution, as well as the anti-ideal solution, and compare how close they are to each other, as its name suggests.

TOPSIS has been successfully utilized in various cases due to its mathematical foundation, ease of applicability, and simplicity (Behzadian et al., 2012). Although TOPSIS is widely used and easy to use, some criticism has resulted in the development of new versions of the technique. As an instance, Deng et al. (2000) proposed one of the earliest modified versions of TOPSIS that received attention from other researchers. Instead of using weighted decision matrices, they propose using weighted Euclidean distances. Some of the well-known examples of modified TOPSIS are Wang and He (2007), Huang et al. (2009), Wang (2009), Li and Ye (2014), dos Santos et al. (2019), Kutlu Gündoğdu & Kahraman (2019). Analytic hierarchy process (AHP), VlseKriterijumska Optimizacija I Kompromisno Resenje, elimination and choice expressing the reality (ELECTRE), and preference ranking organization method for enrichment evaluation are also compared with TOPSIS in most studies.

Section 45.2 reviews some main and recent works that used TOPSIS as their method in different areas of application. The detailed explanation of the considered method in this chapter is explained in section 45.3. Also, some numerical examples are discussed in section 45.4. Finally, we conclude and detail possible future directions in section 45.5.

45.2 Literature review

45.2.1 Technology selection

Sánchez-Lozano et al. (2015) evaluated five training aircraft for the Spanish Air Force Academy using 12 technical and performance-related criteria. A hybrid fuzzy AHP and fuzzy TOPSIS methodology was adopted to handle the complexity

Encyclopedia of Multi-Attribute Decision-Making (MADM). DOI: https://doi.org/10.1016/B978-0-443-33275-3.00090-7

and fuzziness of expert evaluations. The results showed that Pilatus PC-21 (A1) was the best-performing aircraft, while PZL-130 Orlik (A3) ranked lowest. By analyzing price, process analysis, and analytics capabilities, Doğan et al. (2020) selected the most appropriate process mining technology. They selected technologies that enable organizations to efficiently use event log data to enhance their IT systems. Abdelhafeez et al. (2024) stressed the importance of systematically assessing blockchain technology strategies to align them with organizational goals and make them effective. Among the 10 critical evaluation criteria are technological capability, security, privacy, regulatory compliance, and strategic impact. Using fuzzy set theory and the TOPSIS method, the research provides a structured decision-support tool that ranks blockchain strategies under uncertainty.

45.2.2 Supplier selection and supply chain management

Rehman and Ali (2021) used fuzzy TOPSIS to evaluate routes for crude oil import via the China–Pakistan Economic Corridor (CPEC). Based on their analysis, Myanmar's route is the most favorable option, followed by the main CPEC route. Optimal route selection under complex geopolitical and economic constraints is achieved through fuzzy decision-making models. Using the Pythagorean fuzzy TOPSIS, Hajiaghaei-Keshteli et al. (2023) proposed a method for selecting green suppliers for food packaging. The method was developed by reviewing literature and seeking expert opinions, and then ranking five alternative suppliers. Providing a structured and scalable model for evaluating green suppliers under uncertainty is the main contribution of this work to sustainable procurement. In addition to food, their methodology can be applied to the textile and automotive industries. Sithi et al. (2025) presented a structured TOPSIS approach for sustainable supplier selection in the textile industry. Fifteen key criteria were identified to evaluate suppliers across sustainable pillars. By ranking suppliers objectively, the proposed framework helps procurement managers, especially in emerging markets like Bangladesh, align their purchasing decisions with broader sustainability goals.

45.2.3 Energy management

Bilgili et al. (2022) evaluated renewable energy options in Turkey by comparing seven options using 25 evaluation criteria. Solar energy was identified as the most promising energy source by applying intuitionistic fuzzy TOPSIS. Their methodology effectively incorporates both uncertainty and hesitancy. A data-driven strategy for sustainable energy planning in emerging economies is presented in the study. By combining modified Delphi, AHP, and grey-TOPSIS (G-TOPSIS), Irfan et al. (2022) explored barriers to biomass energy development in India. In total, 24 barriers were identified, focusing on implementation and infrastructure challenges. A comprehensive model for prioritizing obstacles to renewable energy deployment under uncertain conditions is provided by the study, which identifies "Technological and Infrastructural" issues as the most significant barriers to biomass energy adoption. Amiri et al. (2024) evaluated renewable energy sources (RES) in Saudi Arabia by combining AHP and TOPSIS methods. RES experts from academia and industry assessed solar, wind, biomass options, as well as their combinations, in terms of cost-effectiveness, intermittency, and social acceptance. Based on the analysis, solar energy was identified as the most cost-effective alternative, followed closely by hybrid solar-wind and solar-geothermal technologies. By aligning RES investments with national sustainability goals, policymakers are able to prioritize RES investments. Tabrizi et al. (2025) first utilized TOPSIS to evaluate and rank the G7 countries based on their transition toward renewable energy. For assessment of environmental and energy performance, five composite indicators were calculated based on primary data, such as power generation, CO_2 emissions, and renewable energy investment. Europe, particularly the United Kingdom, performed better in integrating renewable energy, while Canada ranked last.

45.2.4 Healthcare

Alkan and Kahraman (2021) studied and evaluated strategies of government for managing pandemic situation utilizing fuzzy TOPSIS q-rung orthopairs. According to the evaluation, mandatory quarantine and strict isolation were the most effective public health measures. In designing resilient and effective health policy during pandemics, this model allows for expert input and handles uncertainty. An integrated healthcare system was proposed by Erdebilli et al. (2024), emphasizing the critical role of resource allocation and quality care delivery as key elements. A holistic approach was taken to evaluate hospital performance using TOPSIS and data envelopment analysis. Similarly, using a hybrid approach, Melo et al. (2024) introduced an approach for assessing the quality of healthcare services provided in a Brazilian university hospital. The Kano model and TOPSIS are integrated under fuzzy Theory to capture both subjective perceptions and objective prioritization of service attributes. According to TOPSIS, pharmacy and laboratory exams were rated excellent, while physical environment and outpatient care were rated good. Using the method, hospital managers can make informed quality improvement decisions based on practical feasibility.

45.2.5 Risk assessment

Yazdi et al. (2018) combined fuzzy AHP and fuzzy TOPSIS to assess the risk associated with hydrocarbon storage tanks in fire and explosion scenarios. The hybrid approach was applied to identify and prioritize basic risk events based on expert judgments and fuzzy linguistic terms. Based on a drift diffusion model and TOPSIS, Yu and Liu (2025) developed a dynamic method for measuring financial risks in international engineering projects. Their approach captures how mental states evolve as decision-makers evaluate risk. Under varying expert perceptions, the method provides a nuanced ranking of potential partners based on benefit- and cost-based financial indicators. They demonstrated the impact of dynamic psychological assessments on partner rankings in a real international project.

45.2.6 Site/project selection

Wu et al. (2018) developed a fuzzy TOPSIS model to support group decision-making in restaurant selection. Their framework evaluates five restaurant options using four key criteria. In their study, they demonstrated that their proposed method is robust and flexible. Two problems were addressed by Yoon and Kim (2017) by selecting an energy generation station site among six European ones, and evaluating 10 investment portfolios according to return and risk. Gains and losses are incorporated into the decision-making framework of the study according to behavioral economic principles. The behavioral TOPSIS model proposes a capable way to account for psychological factors in MCDM. Based on TOPSIS and generalized hesitant fuzzy numbers, Keikha (2022) developed a decision-making model for project selection. Their approach allows expert opinions to be expressed more expressively and flexibly by incorporating hesitant fuzzy elements. In complex scenarios involving ambiguity and incomplete information, the study enhances project evaluation precision.

Pourmehdi et al. (2021) proposed a hybrid model utilizing fuzzy TOPSIS to evaluate and select collection centers in a reverse steel supply chain. The model considers both sustainability performance and operational risk factors. A real-life case study shows that combining MCDM and risk assessment leads to more reliable selection outcomes. Final rankings are significantly affected by weight assignment methods and sustainability dimensions, according to sensitivity analyses.

45.2.7 Performance evaluation

Tlig and Rebai (2017) focused on the service quality evaluation in five airports using an intuitionistic fuzzy-valued TOPSIS approach. Their method accounts for the hesitation margin in expert evaluations, making it especially suitable for performance appraisal in uncertain environments. Hatami-Marbini & Kangi (2017) also proposed a fuzzy TOPSIS to evaluate the financial performance of seven automotive companies based on eight financial criteria. According to the study, fuzzy multimodel analysis is capable of providing a nuanced and comprehensive assessment of the financial health of a corporation. Goyal et al. (2021) proposed a hybrid model of fuzzy AHP and TOPSIS to study barriers to adopting sustainable production and consumption. Their approach integrates subjective and objective criteria to rank key deterrents and prioritize interventions based on government-related, financial, and managerial factors. Policymakers and businesses can use the research to encourage sustainable practices.

de Lima Silva et al. (2023) evaluated the economic freedom of 180 countries over four years using 12 criteria, applying a preference disaggregation method based on TOPSIS. Their model provided a ranking between 0 and 100 for each country, enabling systematic and consistent classification. The main contribution of their work was the ability to handle large-scale problems utilizing a refined version of the TOPSIS method. Corrente and Tasiou (2023) conducted a performance evaluation of some banks in the UK in 2020, using a hybrid TOPSIS approach. Their method iteratively ranks banks while aligning multiple performance indicators onto a unified scale. By incorporating uncertainty and preference heterogeneity in decision-making, this study provides a robust framework for analyzing financial performance.

45.3 Technique for order preference by similarity to ideal solution methodology

Basically, TOPSIS evaluates and ranks a finite number of alternatives according on their closeness to an ideal solution through quantitative and qualitative criteria. The optimal alternative is the closest to the positive ideal solution (PIS) and the furthest from the negative ideal solution (NIS). PIS represents the hypothetical alternative with the best values for all criteria, whereas NIS represents the worst alternative. Due to TOPSIS's ability to balance conflicting criteria, it is particularly suitable for MCDM in energy, supply chain, healthcare, and sustainability. Based on Euclidean distances from the ideal and negative solutions, it calculates a relative closeness coefficient based on a best-to-worst ranking (Qin et al., 2008).

According to TOPSIS, alternatives need not be fully independent or consistent in the decision matrix, unlike some other MCDM methods. Further, recent studies have integrated TOPSIS with fuzzy logic, entropy, and AHP to manage uncertainty and improve robustness in complex decision environments. As a result, TOPSIS remains a widely adopted, transparent, and computationally efficient method in a wide range of applications.

45.3.1 The main steps of technique for order preference by similarity to ideal solution

Step1. Analyzing MCDM problems and selecting alternatives and criteria

First, select alternatives, criteria, and subcriteria. For the concerned MCDM problem, a detailed literature review is required, which is finalized by consulting experts and decision makers.

Step 2. Formulation of the MCDM problem

Considering the output of t Step 1 as the alternatives and criteria, they are analyzed and integrated with expert and decision-making opinions. A decision matrix is used to maintain the extracted information. Suppose the following notations:

$\{A_1, A_2, \ldots, A_m\}$: *m* alternatives

$\{C_1, C_2, \ldots, C_n\}$: *n* criteria

$\{w_1, w_2, \ldots, w_n\}$: a weight vector $w_j \in [0, 1]$ for $j = 1, 2, \ldots, n$, and $\sum_j = 1^n\ w_j = 1$.

$A = [a_{ij}]_m \times_n$: the decision matrix, where a_{ij} is a crisp number and the extracted information of A_i for the C_j.

Step 3. Normalization

Various normalization methods are used in the literature. To normalize the decision matrix, $\mathbf{A} = [a_{ij}]_m \times_n$, it can be done by to following equation to reach $\mathbf{R} = [r_{ij}]_m \times_n$:

$$r_{ij} = a_{ij} / \sqrt{(\textstyle\sum_i = 1^m a_{ij}^2)},\ \text{for } j = 1,\ 2,\ \ldots, n.$$

Step 4. Calculating the weighted normalized matrix

To reach $\mathbf{V} = [v_{ij}]$, as the weighted normalized decision matrix, we multiply weight of each criterion to the corresponding value in the normalized matrix **R**, obtained in Step 3, as follows to reach $V = [v_{ij}]$:

$$v_{ij} = w_j \times r_{ij},\ \text{ for all } i = 1,\ 2,\ \ldots, m \text{ and } j = 1,\ 2,\ \ldots,\ n$$

Step 5. Calculating PIS (V^+) and NIS (V^-)

$$V^+ = \left[\left(\max v_{ij},\ \text{for } j \text{ in } J \right), \left(\min v_{ij},\ \text{for } j \text{ in } J' \right),\ \text{for } i = 1,\ 2, \ldots, m \right] = \{v_1^+,\ v_2^+, \ldots, v_n^+\}$$

and

$$V^- = \left[\left(\min v_{ij},\ \text{for } j \text{ in } J \right), \left(\max v_{ij},\ \text{for } j \text{ in } J' \right),\ \text{for } i = 1,\ 2, \ldots, m \right] = \{v_1^-,\ v_2^-, \ldots, v_n^-\}$$

(V^+) and (V^-) are the best and least favorable choices, respectively. *J* and *J′* are also the benefit and cost type criteria sets, respectively.

Step 6. Evaluating the values of separation measures

We evaluate the values of separation measures using Euclidean distance in this step. The separation values D_i^+ and D_i^- for the i-th alternative from V^+ and V^-, respectively:

$$S_i^+ = \sqrt{\left[\sum \left(v_{ij} - v_j^+ \right)^2 \right]}\ \text{for } j = 1 \text{ to } n,\ i = 1,\ 2,\ \ldots,\ m$$

$$S_i^- = \sqrt{\left[\sum (v_{ij} - v_j^-)^2 \right]}\ \text{for } j = 1 \text{ to } n,\ i = 1,\ 2,\ \ldots, m$$

Step 7. Evaluating the relative closeness coefficient

To evaluate the relative closeness coefficient $C_i \in [0, 1]$ for the i-th alternative, we benefit the following equation, and then rank all the alternatives as per their C_i values in descending order.

$$C_i = S_i^- / (S_i^+ + S_i^-) \text{ for } i = 1, 2, \ldots, m$$

45.4 Numerical example

45.4.1 Numerical example #1

Earlier in this chapter, we discussed the site selection problem as a famous and extensively studied problem in operations research and management. Suppose a company tries to select the best site out of five alternatives to locate a recycling center, taking three factors into consideration: investment costs, social impacts, and environmental impacts. As shown in Table 45.1, the first one is quantitative with deterministic values that need to be minimized, while the other two are qualitative and rated from 1 (worst) to 7 (best), which need to be maximized (Fig. 45.1).

First, we calculate the vector normalized decision matrix in Table 45.2 using the TOPSIS steps explained in the previous section. By multiplying the weights associated with each criterion, we get the weighted normalized decision matrix. (Table 45.3)

Below is the calculation of positive and negative ideal solutions. Table 45.4 shows the ideal and anti-ideal solutions.

TABLE 45.1 The initial data and values of the problem.

	Investment costs (million $)	Social impact (1–7)	Environmental impact (1–7)
Weights	0.5	0.2	0.3
Site 1	10	3	1
Site 2	9	4	6
Site 3	11	5	8
Site 4	8	7	3
Site 5	7	6	5

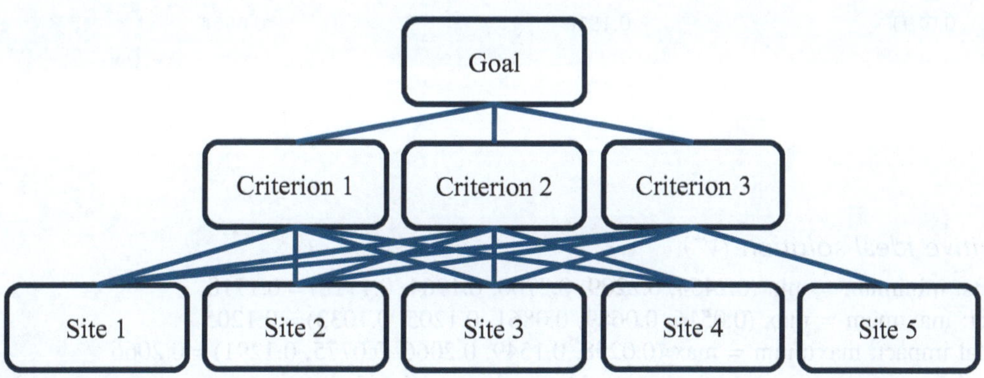

FIGURE 45.1 The hierarchical structure of the problem.

TABLE 45.2 The matrix of normalized decisions.

	Investment costs	Social impact	Environmental impact
Site 1	0.4909	0.2582	0.0861
Site 2	0.4418	0.3443	0.5164
Site 3	0.5400	0.4303	0.6885
Site 4	0.3927	0.6025	0.2582
Site 5	0.3436	0.5164	0.4303

TABLE 45.3 The matrix of normalized weighted decisions.

	Investment costs	Social impact	Environmental impact
Site 1	0.2454	0.0516	0.0258
Site 2	0.2209	0.0689	0.1549
Site 3	0.2700	0.0861	0.2066
Site 4	0.1964	0.1205	0.0775
Site 5	0.1718	0.1033	0.1291

TABLE 45.4 Final ranking of the site location problem.

	S_i^+ (distance to ideal)	S_i^- (distance to antiideal)	C_i (relative closeness)	Ranking
Site 1	0.2070	0.0245	0.1060	5
Site 2	0.0880	0.1392	0.6127	3
Site 3	0.1040	0.1840	0.6388	2
Site 4	0.1314	0.1133	0.4629	4
Site 5	0.0793	0.1516	0.6564	1

45.4.1.1 Positive ideal solution (V^+)

Investment costs: minimum = min (0.2454, 0.2209, 0.2700, 0.1964, 0.1718) = 0.1718

Social impact: maximum = max (0.0516, 0.0689, 0.0861, 0.1205, 0.1033) = 0.1205

Environmental impact: maximum = max (0.0258, 0.1549, 0.2066, 0.0775, 0.1291) = 0.2066

45.4.1.2 Negative ideal solution (V^-)

Investment costs: maximum = max (0.2454, 0.2209, 0.2700, 0.1964, 0.1718) = 0.2700

Social impact: minimum = min (0.0516, 0.0689, 0.0861, 0.1205, 0.1033) = 0.0516

Environmental impact: minimum = min (0.0258, 0.1549, 0.2066, 0.0775, 0.1291) = 0.0258

In Table 45.4, we determine how close each alternative is to the ideal and anti-ideal solution and their distances from them. Table 45.5 is represented graphically in Fig. 45.2 and the best site concluded by this method is Site 5.

TABLE 45.5 The Criteria.

Criterion	Type	SDG alignment	Description
C1. Capital cost (USD million)	Cost (minimize)	SDG 9 (infrastructure)	Initial investment required to construct and commission the project.
C2. Net present value (NPV, USD million)	Benefit (maximize)	SDG 8 (economic growth)	Long-term profitability and return on investment.
C3. Job creation potential	Benefit (maximize)	SDG 1 & 8 (no poverty, economic growth)	Number of direct and indirect jobs created.
C4. Carbon emission reduction (tons CO_2/year)	Benefit (maximize)	SDG 13 (climate action)	Annual reduction of CO_2 emissions compared to conventional sources.
C5. Land use impact (hectares)	Cost (minimize)	SDG 15 (life on land)	Total land area required, including negative ecological effects.
C6. Community acceptance index (1–10)	Benefit (maximize)	SDG 11 (sustainable communities)	A score based on local surveys, reflecting public support and acceptance.
C7. Energy accessibility impact score (1–10)	Benefit (maximize)	SDG 7 (affordable & clean energy)	Contribution to increasing access to clean, reliable energy in remote/underserved areas.

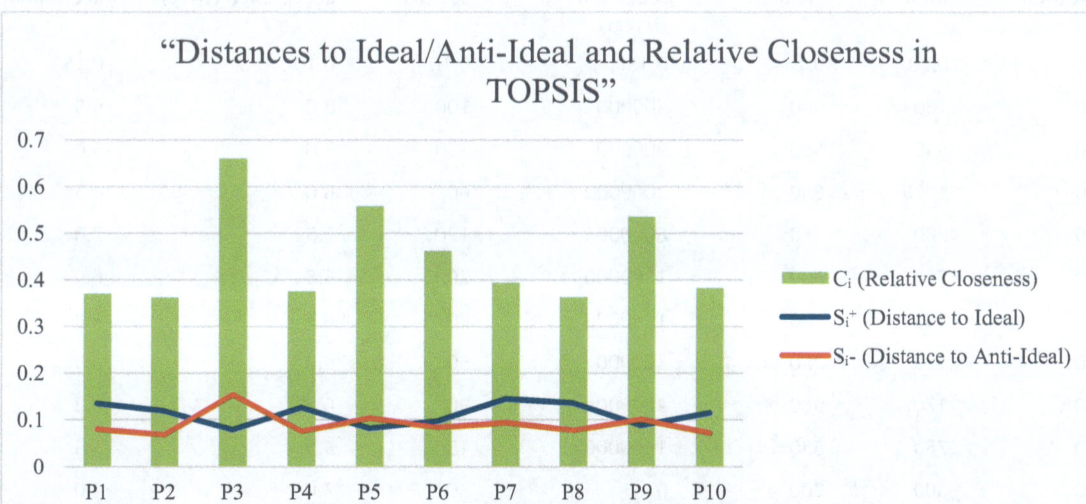

FIGURE 45.2 The final ranking of the site location problem with corresponding.

45.4.2 Numerical example #2

This example comes closer to real-world applications and has a larger number of criteria and alternatives. We want to rank and select the most suitable energy/power project for national investment and implementation, based on multiple criteria reflecting sustainability, economic viability, and societal impact, in alignment with the SDGs. Tables 45.5 and 45.6 show the defined criteria and alternatives.

TABLE 45.6 The alternatives: the list of energy and power projects.

Project code	Description
P1	Large-scale solar PV plant (utility-scale, desert region)
P2	Offshore wind farm (50 turbines in coastal area)
P3	Small modular nuclear reactor (SMR)
P4	Biomass plant using agricultural waste
P5	Hydropower plant (dam-based, mountain region)
P6	Geothermal power plant (rural high-temperature zone)
P7	Urban rooftop solar program (distributed generation)
P8	Waste-to-energy incineration facility
P9	Green hydrogen production facility (electrolysis-based)
P10	Battery storage mega-project (paired with renewables)

TABLE 45.7 The initial data and values of the problem.

	C1. Capital cost (M$)	C2. NPV (M$)	C3. Job creation	C4. CO_2 reduction (t/year)	C5. Land use (ha)	C6. Community acceptance (1–10)	C7. Energy accessibility (1–10)
W	0.15	0.20	0.15	0.15	0.10	0.10	0.15
P1	150	180	300	500000	100	8.0	6.5
P2	320	350	500	900000	250	7.0	5.0
P3	700	1000	800	2000000	60	6.0	4.5
P4	220	200	450	600000	120	7.5	7.0
P5	500	700	600	1500000	200	6.5	6.0
P6	400	500	350	1000000	80	8.5	6.8
P7	100	120	250	300000	50	9.0	8.5
P8	180	170	380	400000	90	6.5	6.2
P9	600	750	550	1300000	150	5.5	5.5
P10	350	300	200	0	30	7.0	4.0

The initial decision matrix for the 10 energy and power projects, containing values for all 7 criteria, is shown in Table 45.7.

Tables 45.8 and 45.9 show the normalized and weighted normalized decision matrices based on TOPSIS steps explained in section 45.2.

Now, we PIS and NIS, considering for benefit criteria, PIS = maximum value and NIS = minimum value, and also for cost criteria, such as capital cost and land use, PIS = minimum value and NIS = maximum value, as shown in Table 45.10.

As shown in Table 45.11, the Euclidean distances between each alternative and V^+ and V^- are calculated. Then we calculate the relative closeness (C_i) to the ideal solution.

TABLE 45.8 The matrix of normalized decisions.

	Capital cost (M$)	NPV (M$)	Job creation	CO_2 reduction (t/year)	Land use (ha)	Community acceptance (1–10)	Energy accessibility (1–10)
P1	0.1187	0.1110	0.2016	0.1535	0.2419	0.3501	0.3354
P2	0.2531	0.2158	0.3360	0.2763	0.6047	0.3063	0.2580
P3	0.5537	0.6165	0.5376	0.6140	0.1451	0.2626	0.2322
P4	0.1740	0.1233	0.3024	0.1842	0.2903	0.3282	0.3612
P5	0.3955	0.4316	0.4032	0.4605	0.4838	0.2844	0.3096
P6	0.3164	0.3083	0.2352	0.3070	0.1935	0.3719	0.3508
P7	0.0791	0.0740	0.1680	0.0921	0.1209	0.3938	0.4385
P8	0.1424	0.1048	0.2554	0.1228	0.2177	0.2844	0.3199
P9	0.4746	0.4624	0.3696	0.3991	0.3628	0.2407	0.2838
P10	0.2769	0.1850	0.1344	0.0000	0.0726	0.3063	0.2064

TABLE 45.9 The matrix of weighted normalized decisions.

	Capital cost (M$)	NPV (M$)	Job creation	CO_2 reduction (t/year)	Land use (ha)	Community acceptance (1–10)	Energy accessibility (1–10)
P1	0.0178	0.0222	0.0302	0.0230	0.0242	0.0350	0.0503
P2	0.0380	0.0432	0.0504	0.0414	0.0605	0.0306	0.0387
P3	0.0831	0.1233	0.0806	0.0921	0.0145	0.0263	0.0348
P4	0.0261	0.0247	0.0454	0.0276	0.0290	0.0328	0.0542
P5	0.0593	0.0863	0.0605	0.0691	0.0484	0.0284	0.0464
P6	0.0475	0.0617	0.0353	0.0461	0.0194	0.0372	0.0526
P7	0.0119	0.0148	0.0252	0.0138	0.0121	0.0394	0.0658
P8	0.0214	0.0210	0.0383	0.0184	0.0218	0.0284	0.0480
P9	0.0712	0.0925	0.0554	0.0599	0.0363	0.0241	0.0426
P10	0.0415	0.0370	0.0202	0.0000	0.0073	0.0306	0.0310

TABLE 45.10 The weighted normalized decision matrix.

	Capital cost (M$)	NPV (M$)	Job creation	CO_2 reduction (t/year)	Land use (ha)	Community acceptance (1–10)	Energy accessibility (1–10)
Positive ideal (V^+)	0.0119	0.1233	0.0806	0.0921	0.0073	0.0394	0.0658
Negative ideal (V^-)	0.0831	0.0148	0.0202	0.0000	0.0605	0.0241	0.0310

TABLE 45.11 Final ranking of the site location problem.

	S_i^+ (distance to ideal)	S_i^- (distance to antiideal)	C_i (relative closeness)	Ranking
P1	0.1346	0.0794	0.3711	8
P2	0.1193	0.0680	0.3629	10
P3	0.0791	0.1539	0.6606	1
P4	0.1264	0.0760	0.3753	7
P5	0.0821	0.1037	0.5582	2
P6	0.0978	0.0840	0.4621	4
P7	0.1449	0.0942	0.3941	5
P8	0.1358	0.0775	0.3633	9
P9	0.0881	0.1013	0.5349	3
P10	0.1152	0.0714	0.3824	6

According to Table 45.11 and the same information shown in a Fig. 45.2, P3, small modular nuclear, has the best trade-off across all SDG-aligned criteria, despite high cost; its performance in emissions reduction, job creation, and NPV dominates.

45.5 Conclusion

Our main objective in this chapter was to explain the origin, methodology, and applications of TOPSIS, as one of the main methods of the MCDM. Various modifications and experiments could be carried out based on the original version. The method was also studied practically to help researchers wishing to put it into practice. A wide range of applications have been successfully employed with TOPSIS, and the number of applications is increasing at an increasing rate, demonstrating the potential of this method.

TOPSIS offers several advantages that explain its wide adoption in engineering and managerial decision problems. Its logic is intuitive, and the method is computationally efficient, transparent, and scalable to many alternatives and criteria. It can accommodate both quantitative and qualitative criteria after normalization, and it does not require strict consistency in judgments. Moreover, the method is flexible and has been successfully extended with fuzzy, hesitant, and probabilistic frameworks to manage uncertainty.

Despite its strengths, TOPSIS has limitations that motivate continued methodological development. Results can be sensitive to the chosen normalization technique and to the criteria weights. Also, the common Euclidean distance measure may not reflect real decision-maker perception in all contexts, and rank reversal can occur when alternatives are added or removed.

This method has also been proven to be one of the best and most applicable methods not only in engineering, but also in managerial areas. Future researchers may extend TOPSIS toward dynamic and real-time decision environments by integrating machine learning, deep learning, and reinforcement learning. Also, uncertainty through fuzzy, rough, probabilistic, and evidential TOPSIS, as well as on explainable and transparent weighting schemes, can be considered. In terms of applications, TOPSIS can play a stronger role in sustainability rating, circular-economy design, healthcare, resource allocation, smart-city and mobility planning, resilient supply chain and humanitarian logistics, renewable and hydrogen or recent energy portfolio selection, fintech credit and risk scoring, and cybersecurity prioritization.

References

Abdelhafeez, A., Shreyas, J., & Udayaprasad, P. K. (2024). A fuzzy TOPSIS method for assessment blockchain technology strategies. *Information Sciences with Applications, 1*, 1–9.

Alkan, N., & Kahraman, C. (2021). Evaluation of government strategies against COVID-19 pandemic using q-rung orthopair fuzzy TOPSIS method. *Applied Soft Computing, 110*, 107653.

Amiri, A. A., Wahid, M. N., Al-Buraiki, A. S., & Al-Sharafi, A. (2024). A strategic multi-criteria decision-making framework for renewable energy source selection in Saudi Arabia using AHP-TOPSIS. *Renewable Energy, 236*, 121523.

Behzadian, M., Otaghsara, S. K., Yazdani, M., & Ignatius, J. (2012). A state-of-the-art survey of TOPSIS applications. *Expert Systems with Applications, 39*(17), 13051–13069.

Bilgili, F., Zaralı, F., Ilgün, M. F., Dumrul, C., & Dumrul, Y. (2022). The evaluation of renewable energy alternatives for sustainable development in Turkey using intuitionistic fuzzy-TOPSIS method. *Renewable Energy, 189*, 1443–1458.

Corrente, S., & Tasiou, M. (2023). A robust TOPSIS method for decision-making problems with hierarchical and non-monotonic criteria. *Expert Systems with Applications, 214*, 119045.

de Lima Silva, D. F., Ferreira, L., & de Almeida Filho, A. T. (2023). Preference disaggregation on TOPSIS for sorting applied to an economic freedom assessment. *Expert Systems with Applications, 215*, 119341.

Deng, H., Yeh, C. H., & Willis, R. J. (2000). Inter-company comparison using modified TOPSIS with objective weights. *Computers & Operations Research, 27*(10), 963–973.

Doğan, O., Deveci, M., Canıtez, F., & Kahraman, C. (2020). A corridor selection for locating autonomous vehicles using an interval-valued intuitionistic fuzzy AHP and TOPSIS method. *Soft Computing, 24*, 8937–8953.

dos Santos, B. M., Godoy, L. P., & Campos, L. M. (2019). Performance evaluation of green suppliers using entropy-TOPSIS-F. *Journal of Cleaner Production, 207*, 498–509.

Erdebilli, B., Sicakyuz, C., & Yilmaz, İ. (2024). An integrated multiple-criteria decision-making and data envelopment analysis framework for efficiency assessment in sustainable healthcare systems. *Healthcare Analytics, 5*, 100327.

Goyal, S., Garg, D., & Luthra, S. (2021). Sustainable production and consumption: analysing barriers and solutions for maintaining green tomorrow by using fuzzy-AHP–fuzzy-TOPSIS hybrid framework. *Environment, Development and Sustainability, 23*, 16934–16980.

Habenicht, W., Scheubrein, B., & Scheubrein, R. (2002). Multiple-criteria decision making. In *Optimization and Operations Research, Vol. 4*, Oxford, UK: EOLSS Publishers, 257–279. Retrieved from https://www.eolss.net/Sample-Chapters/C02/E6-05-06-05.pdf.

Hajiaghaei-Keshteli, M., Cenk, Z., Erdebilli, B., Özdemir, Y. S., & Gholian-Jouybari, F. (2023). Pythagorean fuzzy TOPSIS method for green supplier selection in the food industry. *Expert Systems with Applications, 224*, 120036.

Hatami-Marbini, A., & Kangi, F. (2017). An extension of fuzzy TOPSIS for a group decision making with an application to Tehran Stock Exchange. *Applied Soft Computing, 52*, 1084–1097.

Huang, J.W., Wang, X.X., & Zhou, Y.H. (2009, September). Multi-objective decision optimization of construction schedule based on improved TOPSIS. In IEEE International Conference on Management and Service Science (MASS'09) (pp. 1–4).

Hwang, C.-L., & Yoon, K. (1981). Methods for multiple attribute decision making. In C.-L. Hwang, & K. Yoon (Eds.). *Multiple attribute decision making: Methods and applications – A state-of-the-art survey* (pp. 58–191). Springer.

Irfan, M., Elavarasan, R. M., Ahmad, M., Mohsin, M., Dagar, V., & Hao, Y. (2022). Prioritizing and overcoming biomass energy barriers: Application of AHP and G-TOPSIS approaches. *Technological Forecasting and Social Change, 177*, 121524.

Keikha, A. (2022). Generalized hesitant fuzzy numbers and their application in solving MADM problems based on TOPSIS method. *Soft Computing, 26*, 4673–4683.

Kutlu Gündoğdu, F., & Kahraman, C. (2019). Spherical fuzzy sets and spherical fuzzy TOPSIS method. *Journal of Intelligent & Fuzzy Systems, 36*(1), 337–352.

Li, C., & Ye, C.. (2014). Comprehensive evaluation of the operating performance for commercial banks in China based on improved TOPSIS. In Proceedings of the International Conference on Global Economy, Commerce and Service Science (GECSS'14) (Vol. 78, pp. 17–21).

Melo, F. J. C. D., Albuquerque, A. P. G. D., Xavier, L. D. A., & Medeiros, D. D. D. (2024). Evaluation of quality in health services: The customer satisfaction as an input for fuzzy topsis. *International Journal of Services and Operations Management, 49*(1), 21–41.

Pourmehdi, M., Paydar, M. M., & Asadi-Gangraj, E. (2021). Reaching sustainability through collection center selection considering risk: Using the integration of Fuzzy ANP-TOPSIS and FMEA. *Soft Computing, 25*, 10885–10899.

Qin, X., Huang, G., Chakma, A., Nie, X., & Lin, Q. (2008). A MCDM-based expert system for climate-change impact assessment and adaptation planning: A case study for the Georgia Basin, Canada. *Expert Systems with Applications, 34*(3), 2164–2179.

Rehman, O. U., & Ali, Y. (2021). Optimality study of China's crude oil imports through China–Pakistan economic corridor using fuzzy TOPSIS and cost–benefit analysis. *Transportation Research Part E: Logistics and Transportation Review, 148*, 102246.

Sánchez-Lozano, J., Serna, J., & Dolón-Payán, A. (2015). Evaluating military training aircrafts through the combination of multi-criteria decision making processes with fuzzy logic: A case study in the Spanish Air Force Academy. *Aerospace Science and Technology, 42*, 58–65.

Sithi, S. S., Ara, M., Dhrubo, A. T., Rony, A. H., & Shabur, M. A. (2025). Sustainable supplier selection in the textile industry using triple bottom line and SWARA-TOPSIS approaches. *Discover Sustainability, 6*(1), 1–23.

Tabrizi, A., Yousefi, H., Abdoos, M., & Ghasempour, R. (2025). Evaluating renewable energy adoption in G7 countries: A TOPSIS-based multi-criteria decision analysis. *Discover Energy, 5*(1), 2.

Tlig, H., & Rebai, A. (2017). A TOPSIS method based on intuitionistic fuzzy values: A case study of North African airports. *Management Science Letters, 7*(7), 351–358.

Velasquez, M., & Hester, P. T. (2013). An analysis of multi-criteria decision making methods. *International Journal of Operations Research, 10*(2), 56–66.

Wang, X. (2009). Comprehensive evaluation on e-commerce website applying improved TOPSIS method. In IEEE International Conference on Electronic Commerce and Business Intelligence (ECBI) (pp. 91–94).

Wang, Y., & He, Z. (2007). Optimal multi-response problems on the improved TOPSIS method. In IEEE International Conference on Wireless Communications, Networking and Mobile Computing (WiCom) (pp. 5092–5094).

Wu, T., Liu, X., & Liu, F. (2018). An interval type-2 fuzzy TOPSIS model for large-scale group decision-making problems with social network information. *Information Sciences, 432*, 392–410.

Yazdi, M., Korhan, O., & Daneshvar, S. (2018). Application of fuzzy fault tree analysis based on modified fuzzy AHP and fuzzy TOPSIS for fire and explosion in the process industry. *International Journal of Occupational Safety and Ergonomics, 26*, 319–335.

Yoon, K. P., & Hwang, C.-L. (1995). *Multiple attribute decision making: An introduction*. Sage Publications Vol. 104.

Yoon, K. P., & Kim, W. K. (2017). The behavioral TOPSIS. *Expert Systems with Applications, 89*, 266–272.

Yu, W., & Liu, X. (2025). Dynamic financial risk assessment with TOPSIS and drift diffusion models for partner selection of international engineering projects. *Expert Systems with Applications*126654.

Wang, X. (2009). Comprehensive evaluation on e-commerce website applying improved TOPSIS method. In IEEE International Conference on Electronic Commerce and Business Intelligence (ECBI) (pp. 91–94).
Wang, Y., & He, Z. (2008). Optimal multi-response problems of the improved TOPSIS method. In 4th International Conference on Wireless Communications, Networking and Mobile Computing (WiCom) (pp. 5092–5094).
Wu, T., Liu, X., & Liu, F. (2018). An interval type-2 fuzzy TOPSIS model for large scale group decision making problems with social network information. *Information Sciences, 432*, 392–410.
Yazdi, M., Korhan, O., & Daneshvar, S. (2018). Application of fuzzy fault tree analysis based on modified fuzzy AHP and fuzzy TOPSIS for fire and explosion in the process industry. *International Journal of Occupational Safety and Ergonomics, 26*, 319–335.
Yoon, K. P., & Hwang, C.-L. (1995). *Multiple attribute decision making: An introduction*. Sage Publications, Vol. 104.
Yoon, K. P., & Kim, W. K. (2017). The behavioral TOPSIS. *Expert Systems with Applications, 89*, 266–272.
Yu, W., & Liu, X. (2023). Dynamic financial risk assessment with TOPSIS and their diffusion models for partner selection of international engineering projects. *Expert Systems with Applications*, 12665.

Chapter 46

VIKOR: VlseKriterijumska Optimizacija I Kompromisno Resenje for multi-attribute decision-making

Mahmoud Tajik[1] and Samuel Yousefi[2]
[1]*School of Industrial Engineering, Iran University of Science and Technology, Tehran, Iran,* [2]*Department of Mechanical and Manufacturing Engineering, Ontario Tech University, Oshawa, ON, Canada*

46.1 Introduction

In an increasingly complex and data-driven world, decision-makers (DMs) across various domains, from management to engineering, are often faced with problems that involve evaluating multiple criteria. These types of problems, known as multiple-criteria decision-making (MCDM) problems, arise when alternatives must be assessed and ranked based on different dimensions that do not necessarily align. As DMs handle tasks, such as evaluating, prioritizing, or selecting among alternatives, the need for rational, transparent, and structured decision-making tools has become increasingly important. MCDM methods have been developed to help DMs identify compromise solutions that account for trade-offs among competing objectives. These methods typically involve defining relevant criteria, assigning weights to reflect their relative importance, and ranking feasible alternatives accordingly. The growing complexity and diversity of decision environments have led to the widespread adoption of MCDM approaches in both academic research and industrial applications (Basílio et al., 2022; Sahoo & Goswami, 2023).

Over the past decades, a wide variety of MCDM methods have been proposed, each offering distinct strengths and assumptions to support decision-making under various conditions. A commonly used classification divides these methods into two broad categories: weighting methods and outranking (or aggregation-based) methods. Weighting methods, such as the analytic hierarchy process (AHP) (Saaty, 1987), best–worst method (BWM) (Rezaei, 2015), and entropy-based approaches, are used to determine the importance (i.e., weights) of criteria, often based on expert judgment or objective data. These weights are then applied in outranking or aggregation techniques such as the technique for order preference by similarity to ideal solution (TOPSIS) (Lai et al., 1994), ELimination Et Choix Traduisant La REalité (ELECTRE) (Roy, 1968), and Vlsekriterijumska Optimizacija I Kompromisno Resenje (VIKOR) (Opricovic, 1998), which are used to rank alternatives based on the weighted evaluations. Understanding this classification allows DMs to choose methods suited to the problem context and the available information to ensure a structured and reliable evaluation of alternatives.

Among these, the VIKOR method and its extended versions have gained significant recognition. The VIKOR method is particularly valuable for discrete decision-making problems involving noncommensurable and conflicting criteria, where the goal is to identify a compromise solution rather than a strictly optimal one (Opricovic & Tzeng, 2004; Opricovic & Tzeng, 2007). Unlike other distance-based methods like TOPSIS, VIKOR is rooted in compromise programming, aiming to find a feasible solution that is closest to the ideal. This focus on compromise makes VIKOR especially suitable for MCDM problems involving conflicting criteria and multiple stakeholders. Assuming that each alternative is evaluated according to each criterion, the compromise ranking can be performed by comparing the measure of closeness to the ideal alternative (Gul et al., 2016). Given its effectiveness in dealing with MCDM problems, VIKOR has been extended over time to address various forms of uncertainty and ambiguity, including the integration with fuzzy logic and hybrid models (Gul et al., 2016; Yazdani & Graeml, 2014). Demonstrating its adaptability and relevance in both theoretical and applied contexts, VIKOR has been applied to diverse decision problems, such as supplier evaluation and selection

Encyclopedia of Multi-Attribute Decision-Making (MADM). DOI: https://doi.org/10.1016/B978-0-443-33275-3.00006-3

(Alora & Gupta, 2024), industrial robot selection (Naz et al., 2024), evaluation of renewable energy sources (Çelikbilek, 2025), selection of smart vehicle transportation systems (Khan et al., 2024), risk prioritization (Chen & Shen, 2024), and selection of healthcare waste treatment technologies (Gao et al., 2024).

Due to the diverse real-world applications of VIKOR and its extensions, this chapter seeks to offer a clear and structured introduction to this method by outlining its theoretical foundation and computational steps. Readers will be guided through the practical implementation of the method in both small- and large-scale decision problems, gaining insight into how VIKOR can be applied to assess alternatives across diverse domains. In addition, the chapter explores major extensions of the method, including fuzzy and hybrid variants, which enhance its flexibility in complex and uncertain decision environments. By combining theoretical explanation with practical illustrations, this chapter aims to support both academic understanding and professional application of the VIKOR method. The overall goal is not only to explain how the method works but also to encourage critical thinking about its use in real-world decision-making contexts.

The remainder of the chapter is organized as follows: Section 46.2 presents a review of VIKOR applications and its major extensions, including fuzzy and hybrid models. Section 46.3 outlines the step-by-step implementation of the VIKOR methodology. Sections 46.4 and 46.5 illustrate its application in small-scale and large-scale MCDM problems, respectively. Section 46.6 discusses the comparative analysis between the VIKOR method and other MCDM methods (i.e., TOPSIS, a combined compromise solution [CoCoSo], and measurement alternatives and ranking according to compromise solution [MARCOS] methods). Finally, Section 46.7 concludes the chapter by summarizing key insights and offering recommendations for further study.

46.2 Literature review

This section presents a comprehensive review of the literature on the VIKOR method and its extended versions, with a particular focus on their application to real-world MCDM problems. The discussion emphasizes studies that utilize VIKOR independently, in hybrid frameworks, or with methodological modifications aimed at enhancing its capacity to manage conflicting criteria and uncertainty. A structured overview is provided to illustrate how these extensions have been applied across various domains, highlighting key trends, methodological innovations, and areas where VIKOR has shown notable effectiveness. Several review studies have critically analyzed methodological advancements and categorized the diverse applications of VIKOR. For instance, Gul et al. (2016) conducted a state-of-the-art review that classified, analyzed, and interpreted research on VIKOR, with particular attention to its extensions in fuzzy environments. Mardani et al. (2016) presented a systematic review of VIKOR applications in fields such as sustainability and renewable energy. More recently, Yu & Ye (2025) introduced a comprehensive main path analysis framework to uncover the intellectual structure of the VIKOR literature, identifying key developments and influential contributions that have shaped the evolution of the method.

Since the initial introduction of the VIKOR method, numerous applications and extensions have emerged across a wide range of decision-making problems. Focusing on individual applications, Gao et al. (2019) applied the VIKOR method to address material selection challenges in the context of concrete bridge repair projects, using target-based criteria for ranking alternatives. Balasundaram et al. (2023) employed VIKOR to identify the most suitable phase change material for thermal energy storage in a solar dryer system. In another study, Jing et al. (2019) utilized an improved version of the VIKOR method to select the most appropriate lean management tool, based on an analysis of a yogurt production line. Similarly, Zheng & Wang (2020) applied the VIKOR method to evaluate and rank renewable energy system schemes for tourist resorts, supporting the selection of optimal solutions in sustainable energy planning.

The extended versions of the VIKOR method under uncertainty have garnered considerable attention from researchers in recent years. For instance, Njock et al. (2022) developed a VIKOR-based model within the framework of fuzzy set theory to evaluate contamination risks associated with clusters of wastewater treatment plants. Krishankumar et al. (2020) introduced an extension of the VIKOR method by incorporating intuitionistic fuzzy sets, which account for both membership and nonmembership degrees, to address personnel selection problems. To integrate information reliability, Shen & Wang (2018) extended the VIKOR method to operate in a Z-information environment for selecting regional circular economy development plans. In a related development, Garg, & Das, Maiti, et al. (2020) proposed a novel risk prioritization model, granulized Z-VIKOR, by combining Z-numbers, rough numbers, and probabilistic distance measures. Recognizing that the original defining function of VIKOR does not satisfy the axioms of a dissimilarity measure, Khan et al. (2022) introduced a new dissimilarity measure and refined the method accordingly for Pythagorean fuzzy sets. Similarly, Mousavi et al. (2021) proposed a risk-based fuzzy VIKOR methodology using the R-numbers approach to consistently model and analyze risk in new product development projects under uncertainty. To further address ambiguous and imprecise data in MCDM problems, Mishra et al. (2022) modified the VIKOR method using fermatean hesitant fuzzy sets, enhancing its capacity to handle higher levels of fuzziness and hesitation in expert evaluations.

Focusing on hybrid approaches, the VIKOR method has been widely integrated with other MCDM weighting techniques to support the determination of criteria weights. Among the existing methods, the AHP and BWM have been commonly combined with VIKOR to enhance decision-making robustness. For instance, Ikram et al. (2020) employed the AHP to prioritize main criteria and subcriteria, followed by the application of fuzzy VIKOR to rank management standards within integrated management systems. La Fata et al. (2021) also utilized a hybrid AHP-VIKOR approach to overcome limitations of the traditional risk matrix in prioritizing occupational risks within a Sicilian manufacturing company. Abdul et al. (2022) integrated AHP with VIKOR to prioritize the most relevant renewable energy sources for electricity generation in developing countries, considering six main criteria (i.e., social, economic, energy quality, political, technical, and environmental) as well as 16 subcriteria. In another study, İç et al. (2022) developed an AHP-modified VIKOR framework to create a flexible structure capable of periodically monitoring the financial performance of companies in the wholesale and retail sectors.

The integration of the BWM with the VIKOR method has primarily focused on addressing VIKOR's inherent limitation in determining the weights of criteria. In this context, several studies have proposed hybrid approaches to enhance the robustness and applicability of the VIKOR method. For example, Rafieyan et al. (2020) developed a combined BWM-VIKOR framework to prioritize tasks in managing user requests for cloud resources and to optimize their allocation. Similarly, Kumar et al. (2020) applied a hybrid BWM-VIKOR methodology to determine the weights of performance criteria and rank green airports accordingly. Garg & Sharma (2020) adopted this hybrid approach to establish an evaluation system for selecting sustainable outsourcing partners in the electronics industry, specifically from a supply chain perspective. More recently, Saner et al. (2022) proposed a Bayesian BWM integrated with the VIKOR method to assess hospital disaster preparedness, considering six main criteria and 34 subcriteria, thereby offering a more comprehensive and probabilistically grounded weighting mechanism.

In addition to AHP and BWM, several other weighting MCDM methods have also been employed to complement the VIKOR method in various studies. For instance, Ong et al. (2021) proposed a hybrid approach combining the full consistency method (FUCOM) with VIKOR. The FUCOM-VIKOR approach was used to determine the intensity of importance for each criterion and subsequently rank alternatives in a multiobjective decision-making problem related to recycling cleaning solutions in the rubber glove manufacturing process. Li et al. (2022) integrated the criteria importance through intercriteria correlation (CRITIC) method with VIKOR to address pipeline risk assessment. The CRITIC method was applied to capture internal correlations and inconsistencies among risk factors and assign appropriate weights to the indices, while the VIKOR method was used to evaluate and rank the risk levels of different pipeline sections in an MCDM framework. Similarly, Saraji et al. (2023) introduced a novel Fermatean-CRITIC-VIKOR approach to explore the challenges associated with adopting renewable energy technologies in rural areas. In their model, Fermatean-CRITIC was employed to determine the significance of the challenges, followed by the application of Fermatean-VIKOR to rank four district government offices based on the weighted challenges.

46.3 Methodology

The VIKOR technique is one of the compensatory methods that discovers the closest alternative to the ideal solution. This technique primarily focuses on ranking alternatives and selecting one that possesses conflicting attributes. Ultimately, it provides a compromise solution that aids the DM in reaching a final decision (Opricovic, 1998). In the VIKOR method, a decision matrix is constructed based on the information provided by the DM in (46.1).

$$D = \begin{bmatrix} x_{11} & \cdots & x_{1j} & \cdots & x_{1n} \\ \vdots & \ddots & \vdots & \ddots & \vdots \\ x_{i1} & \cdots & x_{ij} & \cdots & x_{in} \\ \vdots & \ddots & \vdots & \ddots & \vdots \\ x_{m1} & \cdots & x_{mj} & \cdots & x_{mn} \end{bmatrix}_{m\times n} ; \quad i = 1,\ 2,\ \ldots,m,\quad j = 1,\ 2,\ \ldots,n \tag{46.1}$$

Where x_{ij} denotes the element of the decision matrix for the ith alternative and jth attribute. Furthermore, the DM provides the attribute weights as $\overrightarrow{W} = [w_1, w_2, \ldots, w_n]$. Owing to the decision matrix and attribute weights, to implement the VIKOR method, the following steps should be performed. The VIKOR method uses the Lp-metric method to find the closest alternative to the ideal solution with respect to (46.2).

$$L_i^p = \left\{ \sum_{j=1}^{n} \left[\frac{w_j \left(f_j^* - f_{ij} \right)}{\left(f_j^* - f_j^- \right)} \right]^p \right\}^{1/p}; \quad i = 1,\ 2,\ \dots,\ m;\ 1 \le p \le \infty \tag{46.2}$$

In this context, p represents the parameter that specifies the Lp family, and w_j denotes the criteria associated with attribute j. In addition, f_{ij} indicates the value of the ith alternative in the jth attribute, f_j^* and f_j^- are the best and worst of f_{ij}, respectively, which can be determined using Eqs. (46.3) and (46.4).

Step 1. Determination of f_j^* and f_j^-

To apply the Lp family method to the VIKOR method, the best and worst values of f_{ij} are calculated using Eqs. (46.3) and (46.4).

$$\begin{cases} f_j^* = \max\limits_i \left(f_{ij} \right) \\ f_j^- = \min\limits_i \left(f_{ij} \right) \end{cases} \tag{46.3}$$

$$\begin{cases} f_j^* = \min\limits_i \left(f_{ij} \right) \\ f_j^- = \max\limits_i \left(f_{ij} \right) \end{cases} \tag{46.4}$$

Where Eq. (46.3) determines the best and worst value of f_{ij} for positive attributes, and Eq. (46.4) computes the best and worst value of f_{ij} for negative attributes.

Step 2. The calculation of S and R indexes

Considering the various values of the p parameter in the Lp family, L_i^1 is known as S_i, and L_i^∞ is introduced by R_i in the VIKOR method. To determine the S_i and R_i, Eqs. (46.5) and (46.6) are used.

$$S_i = \sum_{j=1}^{n} w_j \frac{\left(f_j^* - f_{ij} \right)}{\left(f_j^* - f_j^- \right)}; \quad i = 1,\ 2,\ \dots,\ m \tag{46.5}$$

$$R_i = \max_j \left[w_j \frac{\left(f_j^* - f_{ij} \right)}{\left(f_j^* - f_j^- \right)} \right]; \quad i = 1,\ 2,\ \dots,\ m; \quad j = 1,\ 2,\ \dots,\ n \tag{46.6}$$

[

Step 3. The computation of the VIKOR index

The VIKOR index is calculated for each alternative using Eqs. (46.7) and (46.8).

$$Q_i = \nu \left[\frac{(S_i - S^*)}{(S^- - S^*)} \right] + (1 - \nu) \left[\frac{(R_i - R^*)}{(R^- - R^*)} \right] \tag{46.7}$$

$$S^* = \min_i (S_i)\ ; \quad S^- = \max_i (S_i)\ ; \quad R^* = \min_i (R_i)\ ; \quad R^- = \max_i (R_i) \tag{46.8}$$

Step 4. Ranking the alternatives

In this step, alternatives are ranked in descending order based on their values of S, R, and Q. The alternative with the lowest values in these attributes is considered the best alternative.

To clearly illustrate the steps outlined by the VIKOR method, its flowchart procedure is presented in Fig. 46.1.

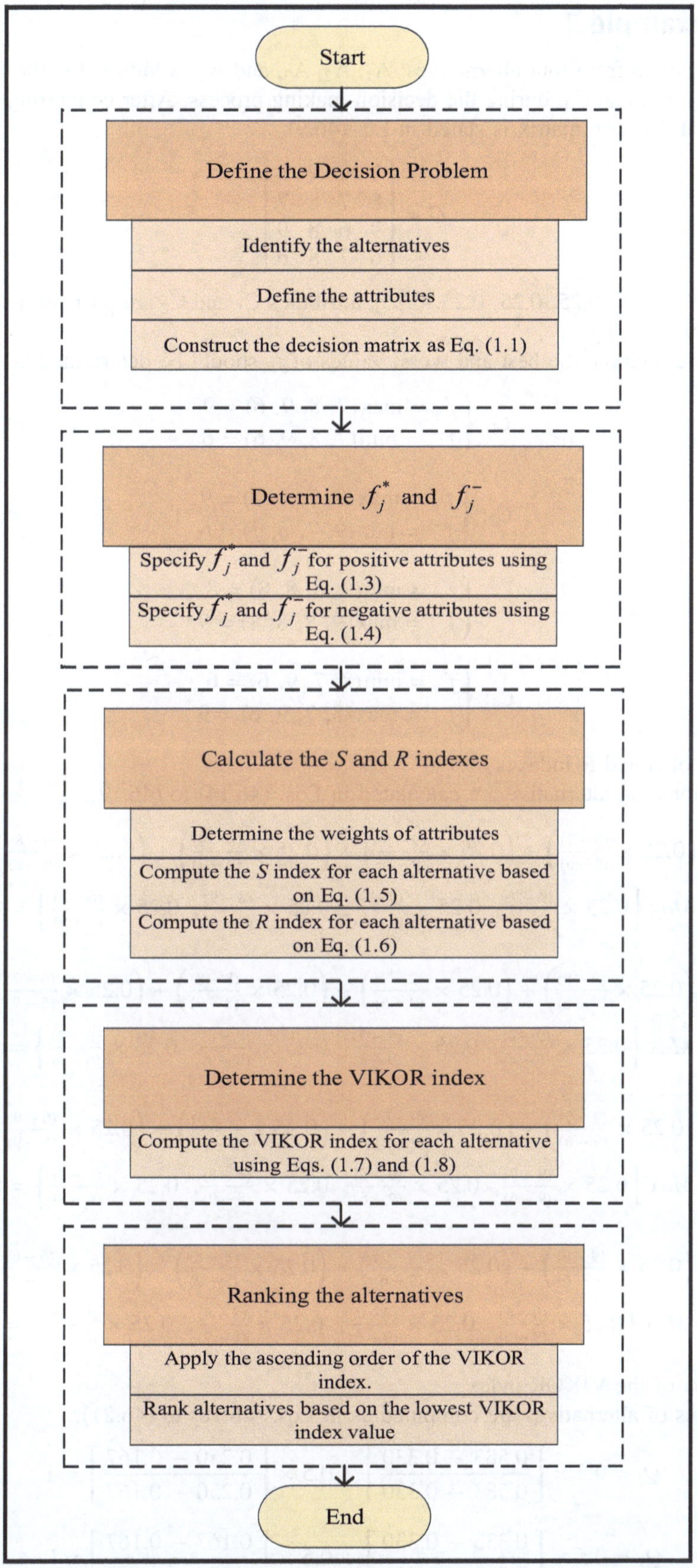

FIGURE 46.1 The procedure of the Vlsekriterijumska Optimizacija I Kompromisno Resenje (VIKOR) method.

46.4 Numerical example 1

The DM must choose one option from four alternatives: A_1, A_2, A_3, and A_4. Additionally, the DM considers several key attributes, including C_1, C_2, C_3, and C_4, during the decision-making process. After converting qualitative attributes into quantitative ones, the initial decision matrix is stated in Eq. (46.9).

$$D = \begin{bmatrix} 7 & 9 & 9 & 8 \\ 8 & 7 & 8 & 7 \\ 9 & 6 & 8 & 9 \\ 6 & 7 & 8 & 6 \end{bmatrix} \tag{46.9}$$

Where the weight vector W is $W = [0.25, 0.25, 0.25, 0.25]$, attributes C_1 and C_2 are positive, and C_3 and C_4 are negative.

Step 1. Determination of f_j^* and f_j^-

To perform the Lp-metric method, the best and worst values of f_{ij} should be determined as follows.

$$C_1: \begin{cases} f_* = \max(7, 8, 9, 6) = 9 \\ f^- = \min(7, 8, 9, 6) = 6 \end{cases} \tag{46.10}$$

$$C_2: \begin{cases} f_* = \max(9, 7, 6, 7) = 9 \\ f^- = \min(9, 7, 6, 7) = 6 \end{cases} \tag{46.11}$$

$$C_3: \begin{cases} f_* = \min(9, 8, 8, 8) = 8 \\ f^- = \max(9, 8, 8, 8) = 9 \end{cases} \tag{46.12}$$

$$C_4: \begin{cases} f_* = \min(8, 7, 9, 6) = 6 \\ f^- = \max(8, 7, 9, 6) = 9 \end{cases} \tag{46.13}$$

Step 2. The calculation of S and R indexes

The values of S and R for each alternative are calculated in Eqs. (46.14) to (46.17).

$$A_1: \begin{cases} S_1 = \left(0.25 \times \frac{(9-7)}{(9-6)}\right) + \left(0.25 \times \frac{(9-9)}{(9-6)}\right) + \left(0.25 \times \frac{(8-9)}{(8-9)}\right) + \left(0.25 \times \frac{(6-8)}{(6-9)}\right) = 0.583 \\ R_1 = Max\left\{0.25 \times \frac{(9-7)}{(9-6)},\ 0.25 \times \frac{(9-9)}{(9-6)},\ 0.25 \times \frac{(8-9)}{(8-9)},\ 0.25 \times \frac{(6-8)}{(6-9)}\right\} = 0.250 \end{cases} \tag{46.14}$$

$$A_2: \begin{cases} S_2 = \left(0.25 \times \frac{(9-8)}{(9-6)}\right) + \left(0.25 \times \frac{(9-7)}{(9-6)}\right) + \left(0.25 \times \frac{(8-8)}{(8-9)}\right) + \left(0.25 \times \frac{(6-7)}{(6-9)}\right) = 0.333 \\ R_2 = Max\left\{0.25 \times \frac{(9-8)}{(9-6)},\ 0.25 \times \frac{(9-7)}{(9-6)},\ 0.25 \times \frac{(8-8)}{(8-9)},\ 0.25 \times \frac{(6-7)}{(6-9)}\right\} = 0.167 \end{cases} \tag{46.15}$$

$$A_3: \begin{cases} S_3 = \left(0.25 \times \frac{(9-9)}{(9-6)}\right) + \left(0.25 \times \frac{(9-6)}{(9-6)}\right) + \left(0.25 \times \frac{(8-8)}{(8-9)}\right) + \left(0.25 \times \frac{(6-9)}{(6-9)}\right) = 0.500 \\ R_3 = Max\left\{0.25 \times \frac{(9-9)}{(9-6)},\ 0.25 \times \frac{(9-6)}{(9-6)},\ 0.25 \times \frac{(8-8)}{(8-9)},\ 0.25 \times \frac{(6-9)}{(6-9)}\right\} = 0.250 \end{cases} \tag{46.16}$$

$$A_4: \begin{cases} S_4 = \left(0.25 \times \frac{(9-6)}{(9-6)}\right) + \left(0.25 \times \frac{(9-7)}{(9-6)}\right) + \left(0.25 \times \frac{(8-8)}{(8-9)}\right) + \left(0.25 \times \frac{(6-6)}{(6-9)}\right) = 0.417 \\ R_4 = Max\left\{0.25 \times \frac{(9-6)}{(9-6)},\ 0.25 \times \frac{(9-7)}{(9-6)},\ 0.25 \times \frac{(8-8)}{(8-9)},\ 0.25 \times \frac{(6-6)}{(6-9)}\right\} = 0.250 \end{cases} \tag{46.17}$$

Step 3. The computation of the VIKOR index

The VIKOR index values of alternatives are computed as in Eqs. (46.18) to (46.21).

$$Q_1 = 0.5 \times \left[\frac{0.583 - 0.330}{0.583 - 0.330}\right] + 0.5 \times \left[\frac{0.250 - 0.167}{0.250 - 0.167}\right] = 1 \tag{46.18}$$

$$Q_2 = 0.5 \times \left[\frac{0.333 - 0.330}{0.583 - 0.330}\right] + 0.5 \times \left[\frac{0.167 - 0.167}{0.250 - 0.167}\right] = 0 \tag{46.19}$$

$$Q_3 = 0.5 \times \left[\frac{0.500 - 0.330}{0.583 - 0.330}\right] + 0.5 \times \left[\frac{0.250 - 0.167}{0.250 - 0.167}\right] = 0.834 \quad (46.20)$$

$$Q_4 = 0.5 \times \left[\frac{0.417 - 0.330}{0.583 - 0.330}\right] + 0.5 \times \left[\frac{0.250 - 0.167}{0.250 - 0.167}\right] = 0.668 \quad (46.21)$$

Step 4. Ranking the alternatives

Since alternative A_2 has the lowest values for S, R, and Q indices among the alternatives, it is selected as the best choice. After determining the rank of alternative A_2, it is found that alternatives A_1, A_3, and A_4 have equal R values. However, alternative A_4 receives the second rank because it has the lowest S value and VIKOR index among the alternatives.

46.5 Numerical example 2

The expert aims to select the best piston material for an internal combustion engine from eight options: A_1: aluminum 2618-T61, A_2: aluminum 4032-T6, A_3: aluminum A360.0-F, A_4: aluminum 6061-T6, A_5: grey cast iron, A_6: AISI 8660 steel, A_7: AISI 4140 steel, and A_8: ductile iron grade 65–45-12. In addition, the expert incorporates significant attributes, including C_1: density, C_2: Knoop hardness, C_3: yield strength, C_4: modulus of elasticity, C5: specific heat capacity, C_6: material cost, C_7: machinability, and C_8: fatigue strength, into the decision-making process (Chatterjee & Chakraborty, 2022). After converting qualitative attributes into quantitative ones, the initial decision matrix is represented in Eq. (46.22).

$$D = \begin{bmatrix} 2.76 & 144 & 372 & 74.5 & 0.875 & 2.072 & 9 & 90 \\ 2.68 & 150 & 317 & 78.6 & 0.85 & 2.128 & 7 & 110 \\ 2.68 & 97 & 165 & 71 & 0.963 & 1.064 & 5 & 150 \\ 2.7 & 120 & 276 & 68.9 & 0.896 & 1.904 & 9 & 95 \\ 7.15 & 271 & 310 & 200 & 0.49 & 1.428 & 3 & 119 \\ 7.85 & 220 & 1551 & 205 & 0.475 & 0.854 & 5 & 335 \\ 7.85 & 369 & 1050 & 205 & 0.561 & 0.532 & 5 & 590 \\ 7.15 & 195 & 310 & 168 & 0.49 & 1.54 & 5 & 193 \end{bmatrix} \quad (46.22)$$

Where the weight vector W is $W = [0.0287, 0.100, 0.3362, 0.1255, 0.0474, 0.0202, 0.0636, 0.2784]$, the C_6 attribute is negative, and other attributes are positive. To initiate the VIKOR method, the best and worst of all alternatives in each attribute are determined using Eqs. (46.3) and (46.4), and represented in (46.23).

$$\begin{aligned} f_*&: \; f_1^* = 7.78, \; f_2^* = 369, \; f_3^* = 1551, \; f_4^* = 205, \; f_5^* = 0.963, \; f_6^* = 0.532, \; f_7^* = 9, \; f_8^* = 590 \\ f^-&: \; f_1^- = 2.68, \; f_2^- = 97, \; f_3^- = 165, \; f_4^- = 68.9, \; f_5^- = 0.475, \; f_6^- = 2.128, \; f_7^- = 3, \; f_8^- = 90 \end{aligned} \quad (46.23)$$

After determining values f_j^* and f_j^-, the values of S and R for each alternative are calculated using Eqs. (46.5) and (46.6) as follows.

$$S: \; S_1 = 0.824, \; S_2 = 0.845, \; S_3 = 0.883, \; S_4 = 0.854, \; S_5 = 0.729, \; S_6 = 0.291, \; S_7 = 0.203, \; S_8 = 0.725 \quad (46.24)$$

$$R: \; R_1 = 0.286, \; R_2 = 0.299, \; R_3 = 0.336, \; R_4 = 0.309, \; R_5 = 0.301, \; R_6 = 0.142, \; R_7 = 0.122, \; R_8 = 0.301 \quad (46.25)$$

Subsequently, the VIKOR index is computed for each alternative according to Eqs. (46.7) and (46.8), as expressed in (46.26), which aids in ranking the alternatives.

$$Q: \; Q_1 = 0.84, \; Q_2 = 0.886, \; Q_3 = 1, \; Q_4 = 0.916, \; Q_5 = 0.805, \; Q_6 = 0.111, \; Q_7 = 0, \; Q_8 = 802 \quad (46.26)$$

Since alternative A_7 has the minimum values for S, R, and Q indices among the alternatives, it is selected as the best choice. After determining the rank of alternative A_7, alternative A_6 is referred to as the second alternative due to having the lowest values of S, R, and Q among the alternatives.

46.6 Sensitivity and comparative analyses

This section conducts sensitivity and comparative analyses in two subsections, utilizing the dataset from numerical example 2. The first subsection evaluates the sustainability and robustness of the VIKOR method by examining changes in the criteria weights. Following this, a comparative analysis is performed to assess the ranking of alternatives using the VIKOR method alongside several popular MCDM methods, including TOPSIS, CoCoSo, and MARCOS.

46.6.1 Sensitivity analysis

To evaluate the sustainability and robustness of the VIKOR method, the results of its implementation are analyzed by varying the weights of the criteria across four distinct scenarios. In doing so, the most significant attribute (i.e., C_3), based on the initial weights of the attributes, is selected, which states scenario 1 of the proposed approach. In this process, 0.014 is subtracted from the C_3 weight in scenario 2, 0.028 in scenario 3, and 0.042 in scenario 4. These amounts are then distributed equally among the weights of the other attributes. This approach provides a valuable opportunity to explore how adjustments in attributes' weights can positively impact the final ranking of alternatives through a range of variations. Table 46.1 vividly illustrates the shifts in rank points, offering clarity and insight into the various defined scenarios.

In both scenarios 1 and 2, the rankings of the alternatives remain consistent, illustrating a stable preference among the alternatives available. This indicates that the impacts of the attributes used for evaluation hold steady and do not lead to any shifts in judgment. However, in scenarios 3 and 4, there is a noticeable change in the rankings (i.e., one shift change), particularly impacting the positions of alternatives A_1 and A_2. This alteration suggests that, under the conditions of these scenarios, the factors influencing decision-making have shifted, due to changes in evaluation attributes. Namely, the ranking of alternatives remains unchanged until the weight of attribute C_3 exceeds 0.3222. However, if the weight of attribute C_3 is lower than 0.3222, the ranks of alternatives A_1 and A_2 will change.

46.6.2 Comparative analysis

To assess the suitability of the VIKOR method for various problems, its rankings and preferences should be compared with those of other MCDM methods. This section compares the VIKOR method with a popular set of MCDM methods, including (i) TOPSIS developed by Lai et al. (1994), (ii) CoCoSo developed by Yazdani et al. (2019), and (iii) MARCOS developed by Stević et al. (2020), using the correlation coefficient indicator. The final ranking results of these three methods are shown in Fig. 46.2.

Even though the overall consistency is high, alternatives A_2 and A_4 are particularly notable due to their stable rankings across the four different MCDM methods. Fig. 46.2 illustrates that the VIKOR method has the strongest correlation, with a value of 1, to both the TOPSIS and MARCOS methods. This is because it generates a ranking of alternatives similar to the TOPSIS method and MARCOS method. Additionally, among the comparative analyses conducted, the CoCoSo method also provides a ranking of alternatives that closely resembles that of the VIKOR method, except for the rankings of

TABLE 46.1 The rank of alternatives based on different scenarios.

Alternative	Scenario			
	Scenario 1	Scenario 2	Scenario 3	Scenario 4
A_1	5	5	6	6
A_2	6	6	5	5
A_3	8	8	8	8
A_4	7	7	7	7
A_5	4	4	4	4
A_6	2	2	2	2
A_7	1	1	1	1
A_8	3	3	3	3

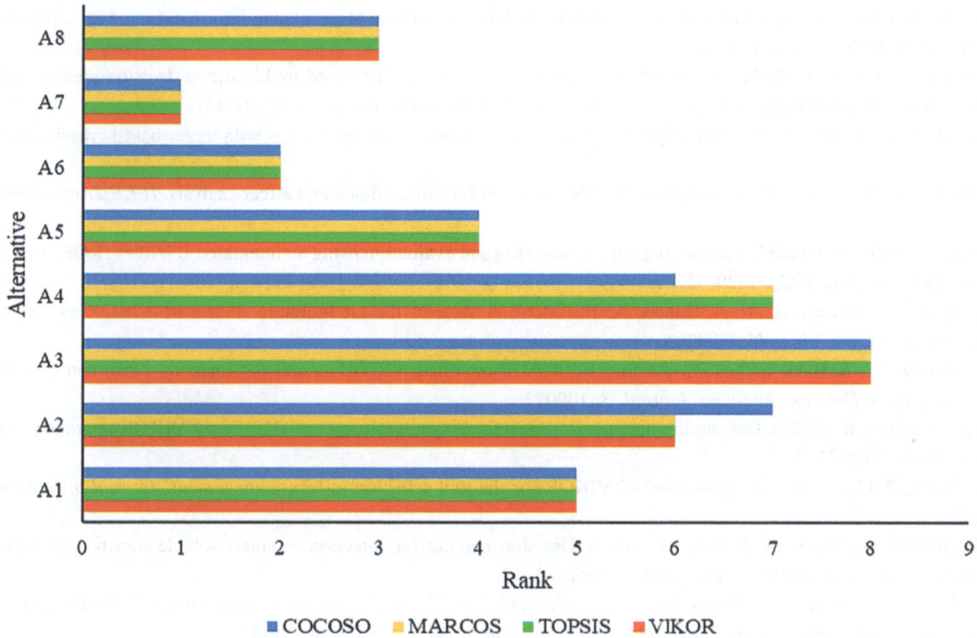

FIGURE 46.2 The comparative analysis results.

alternatives A_2 and A_4. As a result, the correlation between the VIKOR and CoCoSo methods is lower than that between the VIKOR–TOPSIS and VIKOR–MARCOS methods.

46.7 Conclusions

This chapter introduced the VIKOR method as a practical and structured approach for solving MCDM problems involving multiple conflicting criteria. By focusing on compromise solutions, the method supports balanced evaluations when trade-offs are required. The step-by-step computational process of the VIKOR method has been demonstrated through numerical examples, highlighting its applicability to both simple and complex scenarios. The flexibility of VIKOR in handling different types of criteria and its compatibility with various weighting techniques make it a robust decision support tool. Overall, this chapter has emphasized the usefulness of the studied outranking MCDM method in supporting consistent and effective decision-making in diverse real-world contexts. Future research could explore dynamic extensions of VIKOR for time-dependent or real-time decision environments. There is also potential in integrating this method with data-driven techniques to enhance its adaptability to large-scale or unstructured data. Moreover, investigating its performance in group decision-making or multiactor settings may offer valuable insights for multistakeholder applications.

References

Abdul, D., Wenqi, J., & Tanveer, A. (2022). Prioritization of renewable energy source for electricity generation through AHP-VIKOR integrated methodology. *Renewable Energy, 184*, 1018–1032.

Alora, A., & Gupta, H. (2024). Supplier selection among manufacturing companies based on their MSME partners' supply chain finance adoption capability using BWM and VIKOR. *Journal of Business & Industrial Marketing, 39*(6), 1337–1351.

Balasundaram, P., Baranidharan, B., & Sivaram, N. M. (2023). A VIKOR based selection of phase change material for thermal energy storage in solar dryer system. *Materials Today: Proceedings, 90*, 245–249.

Basílio, M. P., Pereira, V., Costa, H. G., Santos, M., & Ghosh, A. (2022). A systematic review of the applications of multi-criteria decision aid methods (1977–2022). *Electronics, 11*(11), 1720.

Çelikbilek, Y. (2025). Evaluation of the renewable energy sources with an integrated neutrosophic DEMATEL-ANP-VIKOR approach. *Environmental Progress & Sustainable Energy, 44*(3), e14589.

Chatterjee, S., & Chakraborty, S. (2022). A multi-attributive ideal-real comparative analysis-based approach for piston material selection. *Opsearch, 59*(1), 207–228.

Chen, M. R., & Shen, K. W. (2024). Risk prioritization by Z-VIKOR method under incomplete reliable information and its application in CCUS project site selection. *Applied Soft Computing, 154*, 111357.

Gao, F., Han, M., Wang, S., & Gao, J. (2024). A novel Fermatean fuzzy BWM-VIKOR based multi-criteria decision-making approach for selecting health care waste treatment technology. *Engineering Applications of Artificial Intelligence, 127*, 107451.

Gao, Z., Liang, R. Y., & Xuan, T. (2019). VIKOR method for ranking concrete bridge repair projects with target-based criteria. *Results in Engineering, 3*, 100018.

Garg, A., Das, S., Maiti, J., & Pal, S. K. (2020). Granulized Z-VIKOR model for failure mode and effect analysis. *IEEE Transactions on Fuzzy Systems, 30*(2), 297–309.

Garg, C. P., & Sharma, A. (2020). Sustainable outsourcing partner selection and evaluation using an integrated BWM–VIKOR framework. *Environment, Development and Sustainability, 22*(2), 1529–1557.

Gul, M., Celik, E., Aydin, N., Gumus, A. T., & Guneri, A. F. (2016). A state of the art literature review of VIKOR and its fuzzy extensions on applications. *Applied Soft Computing, 46*, 60–89.

İç, Y. T., Çelik, B., Kavak, S., & Baki, B. (2022). An integrated AHP-modified VIKOR model for financial performance modeling in retail and wholesale trade companies. *Decision Analytics Journal, 3*, 100077.

Ikram, M., Zhang, Q., & Sroufe, R. (2020). Developing integrated management systems using an AHP-Fuzzy VIKOR approach. *Business Strategy and the Environment, 29*(6), 2265–2283.

Jing, S., Niu, Z., & Chang, P. C. (2019). The application of VIKOR for the tool selection in lean management. *Journal of Intelligent Manufacturing, 30*(8), 2901–2912.

Khan, H. U., Ali, F., Sohail, M., Nazir, S., & Arif, M. (2024). Decision making for selection of smart vehicle transportation system using VIKOR approach. *International Journal of Data Science and Analytics*, 1–15.

Khan, M. J., Ali, M. I., Kumam, P., Kumam, W., Aslam, M., & Alcantud, J. C. R. (2022). Improved generalized dissimilarity measure-based VIKOR method for Pythagorean fuzzy sets. *International Journal of Intelligent Systems, 37*(3), 1807–1845.

Krishankumar, R., Premaladha, J., Ravichandran, K. S., Sekar, K. R., Manikandan, R., & Gao, X. Z. (2020). A novel extension to VIKOR method under intuitionistic fuzzy context for solving personnel selection problem. *Soft Computing, 24*(2), 1063–1081.

Kumar, A., Aswin, A., & Gupta, H. (2020). Evaluating green performance of the airports using hybrid BWM and VIKOR methodology. *Tourism Management, 76*, 103941.

La Fata, C. M., Giallanza, A., Micale, R., & La Scalia, G. (2021). Ranking of occupational health and safety risks by a multi-criteria perspective: Inclusion of human factors and application of VIKOR. *Safety Science, 138*, 105234.

Lai, Y. J., Liu, T. Y., & Hwang, C. L. (1994). Topsis for MODM. *European Journal of Operational Research, 76*(3), 486–500.

Li, X., Han, Z., Yazdi, M., & Chen, G. (2022). A CRITIC-VIKOR based robust approach to support risk management of subsea pipelines. *Applied Ocean Research, 124*, 103187.

Mardani, A., Zavadskas, E. K., Govindan, K., Amat Senin, A., & Jusoh, A. (2016). VIKOR technique: A systematic review of the state of the art literature on methodologies and applications. *Sustainability, 8*(1), 37.

Mishra, A. R., Chen, S. M., & Rani, P. (2022). Multiattribute decision making based on Fermatean hesitant fuzzy sets and modified VIKOR method. *Information Sciences, 607*, 1532–1549.

Mousavi, S. A., Seiti, H., Hafezalkotob, A., Asian, S., & Mobarra, R. (2021). Application of risk-based fuzzy decision support systems in new product development: An R-VIKOR approach. *Applied Soft Computing, 109*, 107456.

Naz, S., ul Hassan, M. M., Mehmood, A., Espitia, G. P., & Butt, S. A. (2024). Enhancing industrial robot selection through a hybrid novel approach: Integrating CRITIC-VIKOR method with probabilistic uncertain linguistic q-rung orthopair fuzzy. *Artificial Intelligence Review, 58*(2), 59.

Njock, P. G. A., Shen, S. L., Zhou, A., & Lin, S. S. (2022). A VIKOR-based approach to evaluate river contamination risks caused by wastewater treatment plant discharges. *Water Research, 226*, 119288.

Ong, M. C., Leong, Y. T., Wan, Y. K., & Chew, I. M. L. (2021). Multi-objective optimization of integrated water system by FUCOM-VIKOR approach. *Process Integration and Optimization for Sustainability, 5*(1), 43–62.

Opricovic, S. (1998). Multicriteria optimization of civil engineering systems. *Faculty of Civil Engineering, Belgrade, 2*(1), 5–21.

Opricovic, S., & Tzeng, G. H. (2004). Compromise solution by MCDM methods: A comparative analysis of VIKOR and TOPSIS. *European Journal of Operational Research, 156*(2), 445–455.

Opricovic, S., & Tzeng, G. H. (2007). Extended VIKOR method in comparison with outranking methods. *European Journal of Operational Research, 178*(2), 514–529.

Rafieyan, E., Khorsand, R., & Ramezanpour, M. (2020). An adaptive scheduling approach based on integrated best-worst and VIKOR for cloud computing. *Computers & Industrial Engineering, 140*, 106272.

Rezaei, J. (2015). Best-worst multi-criteria decision-making method. *Omega, 53*, 49–57.

Roy, B. (1968). Classement et choix en présence de points de vue multiples. *Revue française d'informatique et de recherche opérationnelle, 2*(8), 57–75.

Saaty, R. W. (1987). The analytic hierarchy process—What it is and how it is used. *Mathematical Modelling, 9*(3-5), 161–176.

Sahoo, S. K., & Goswami, S. S. (2023). A comprehensive review of multiple criteria decision-making (MCDM) methods: Advancements, applications, and future directions. *Decision Making Advances, 1*(1), 25–48.

Saner, H. S., Yucesan, M., & Gul, M. (2022). A Bayesian BWM and VIKOR-based model for assessing hospital preparedness in the face of disasters. *Natural Hazards, 111*(2), 1603–1635.

Saraji, M. K., Aliasgari, E., & Streimikiene, D. (2023). Assessment of the challenges to renewable energy technologies adoption in rural areas: A Fermatean CRITIC-VIKOR approach. *Technological Forecasting and Social Change, 189*, 122399.

Shen, K. W., & Wang, J. Q. (2018). Z-VIKOR method based on a new comprehensive weighted distance measure of Z-number and its application. *IEEE Transactions on Fuzzy Systems, 26*(6), 3232–3245.

Stević, Ž., Pamučar, D., Puška, A., & Chatterjee, P. (2020). Sustainable supplier selection in healthcare industries using a new MCDM method: Measurement of alternatives and ranking according to COmpromise solution (MARCOS). *Computers & Industrial Engineering, 140*, 106231.

Yazdani, M., & Graeml, F. R. (2014). VIKOR and its applications: A state-of-the-art survey. *International Journal of Strategic Decision Sciences (IJSDS), 5*(2), 56–83.

Yazdani, M., Zarate, P., Kazimieras Zavadskas, E., & Turskis, Z. (2019). A combined compromise solution (CoCoSo) method for multi-criteria decision-making problems. *Management Decision, 57*(9), 2501–2519.

Yu, D., & Ye, T. (2025). Uncovering the academic evolution of VIKOR method: A comprehensive main path analysis. *Journal of the Operational Research Society, 76*(2), 393–409.

Zheng, G., & Wang, X. (2020). The comprehensive evaluation of renewable energy system schemes in tourist resorts based on VIKOR method. *Energy, 193*, 116676.

Saraji, M. K., Aliasgari, E., & Streimikiene, D. (2023). Assessment of the challenges to renewable energy technologies adoption in rural areas: A Fermatean CRITIC-VIKOR approach. *Technological Forecasting and Social Change, 189*, 122399.

Shen, K.-W., & Wang, J.-Q. (2018). Z-VIKOR method based on a new comprehensive weighted distance measure of Z-number and its application. *IEEE Transactions on Fuzzy Systems, 26*(6), 3232–3245.

Stević, Ž., Pamučar, D., Puška, A., & Chatterjee, P. (2020). Sustainable supplier selection in healthcare industries using a new MCDM method: Measurement of alternatives and ranking according to COmpromise solution (MARCOS). *Computers & Industrial Engineering, 140*, 106231.

Yazdani, M., & Graeml, F. R. (2014). VIKOR and its applications: A state-of-the-art survey. *International Journal of Strategic Decision Sciences (IJSDS), 5*(2), 56–83.

Yazdani, M., Zarate, P., Kazimieras Zavadskas, E., & Turskis, Z. (2019). A combined compromise solution (CoCoSo) method for multi-criteria decision-making problems. *Management Decision, 57*(9), 2501–2519.

Yu, D., & Ye, T. (2023). Uncovering the academic evolution of VIKOR method: A comprehensive main path analysis. *Journal of the Operational Research Society, 74*(1), [illegible].

Zhang, C., & Wang, X. (2020). The comprehensive evaluation of renewable energy system schemes in tourist resorts based on VIKOR method. *Energy*, [illegible].

Chapter 47

MOORA: Multiobjective optimization on the basis of ratio analysis for multi-attribute decision-making

Hossein Reyhani Yamchi[1] and Shabnam Rahnamay Bonab[2]
[1]*La Trobe Business School, La Trobe University, Melbourne, VIC, Australia,* [2]*Department of Management, Monash University, Melbourne, VIC, Australia*

47.1 Introduction

Effective decision-making is a basic psychological and managerial skill, affecting not only everyday choices but also strategic outcomes in organizations. The complexity of modern environments demands models that allow for multiple, sometimes conflicting, goals (Haseli et al., 2023a; Moslem et al., 2024). Multicriteria decision-making (MCDM) addresses this need by supplying a methodological framework that evaluates options on many dimensions simultaneously (Haseli & Sheikh, 2022). Unlike naive or intuitive models, MCDM is cognitively demanding and minimizes errors arising from heuristics or short-term emotional choices (Ashofteh & Dougaheh, 2024; Haseli et al., 2023b). It also provides a way of managing conflicting stakeholder interests in group decision-making processes by introducing weighted priorities and explicit criteria. The process typically involves the identification of pertinent options, establishing evaluative criteria, deciding the importance of each criterion, and consolidating the views of the people concerned with the decision (Haseli et al., 2023a; Soni et al., 2022). In this way, MCDM supports the development of decisions that are both analytically sound and in line with long-term strategic goals (Haseli et al., 2025; Mahmudah et al., 2024).

The multiobjective optimization on the basis of ratio analysis (MOORA) method, one of the recognized techniques in MCDM, was introduced by Brauers and Zavadskas (2006). This method is considered a multicriteria decision-making technique for ranking options and is used to solve complex decision-making problems in various fields (Jafarzadeh Ghoushchi et al., 2022). The MOORA method has gained significant interest from researchers and decision-makers across management, logistics, and engineering because of its straightforwardness, clarity, and substantial effectiveness (Brauers & Zavadskas, 2009). This method has several advantages, including its understandable and straightforward numerical calculations that do not require the use of complex software and are therefore very practical in practice (Soni et al., 2022).

Other outstanding features of this method include its high flexibility and adaptability, which allow it to be combined with other decision-making methods and even fuzzy environments (Shahzadi et al., 2022). This approach enables decision-makers to handle uncertainty in decision-making scenarios effectively. Additionally, the MOORA method is applicable to group decision-making, providing outcomes that are both consistent and dependable (Rajput et al., 2024). Due to these advantages, the MOORA method has become one of the popular tools among decision-makers and researchers, especially in cases where they are looking for a simple, yet accurate and effective method for analyzing and selecting the best options (Akkaya et al., 2015).

47.2 Literature review

Table 47.1 below presents a review of various studies that have employed the MOORA method to address decision-making and optimization challenges across diverse domains. These studies showcase the adaptability and robustness of

Encyclopedia of Multi-Attribute Decision-Making (MADM). DOI: https://doi.org/10.1016/B978-0-443-33275-3.00094-4

TABLE 47.1 Studies using MOORA method.

Author(s)	Research objective	methodology
Brauers and Zavadskas (2009)	Demonstrate MOORA's robustness in multiobjective optimization for the facilities sector	MOORA
Gadakh et al. (2013)	Optimize welding parameters and validate MOORA's applicability	MOORA
Chakraborty (2011)	Assist manufacturing decision-making by applying MOORA for optimizing process and technology selection	MOORA
Moslem and Çelikbilek (2020)	Improve the quality of public transportation services	AHP-MOORA
Shahzadi et al. (2022)	Select an adaptive intelligent manufacturing system	Fermatean fuzzy MOORA
Mavi et al. (2017)	Evaluate and rank sustainable third-party reverse logistics providers	SWARA-MOORA
Arabsheybani et al. (2018)	Evaluate supplier performance and mitigate risks	Fuzzy MOORA-FMEA
Akkaya et al. (2015)	Assist industrial engineering students in choosing their future career sectors	Fuzzy AHP-fuzzy MOORA
Luviano Cruz et al. (2018)	Integrate MOORA with Pythagorean fuzzy sets for decision-making	Pythagorean fuzzy MOORA
Chakraborty et al. (2023)	Review MOORA applications across industries and propose future research directions	MOORA
Rajput et al. (2024)	Rank epoxy composites with Kota stone dust selection	AHP-MOORA
Kumar Sahu et al. (2014)	Develop a multicriteria model for benchmarking supply chain performance	MOORA
Dabbagh and Yousefi (2019)	Prioritize OHS risks for more accurate risk assessment	MOORA-FMEA-FCM
Rane et al. (2021)	Determine the optimal fleet purchase	MOORA
Gupta et al. (2022)	Evaluate the usability of mHealth applications designed for patients with type 2 diabetes mellitus	Fuzzy CODAS-Fuzzy AHP–Fuzzy MOORA
Mitra (2022)	Apply MOORA method for fabric selection based on multicriteria decision-making analysis	MOORA
Gorener et al. (2013)	Apply MOORA method for material selection, ensuring robustness against weighting and normalization method	MOORA
Rizk-Allah et al. (2020)	Apply MOORA for decision-making in engineering designs	MOORA

MOORA in addressing multiobjective problems, from manufacturing process optimization to public transport service quality improvement and material selection. The table highlights the research focus and methodologies used in each study, providing a comprehensive look at how MOORA is applied in different contexts.

47.3 Methodology

This section provides a comprehensive step-by-step explanation of the MOORA method, with each stage supported by corresponding mathematical equations to ensure clarity and facilitate understanding of the computational procedure.

Step 1: Creation of the decision matrix

The initial stage of the MOORA method involves constructing the decision matrix. This matrix consists of criteria as columns and alternatives as rows, where each cell contains the score of a specific alternative connecting a particular criterion. The elements of the decision matrix are symbolized x_{ij}.

$$X = \begin{bmatrix} r_{11} & \cdots & r_{1n} \\ \vdots & \ddots & \vdots \\ r_{m1} & \cdots & r_{mn} \end{bmatrix}_{m*n} ; \; i = 1, \ldots, m; \quad j = 1, \ldots, n \tag{47.1}$$

In the decision matrix represented by (47.1), r_{ij} indicates the value corresponding to the *ith* alternative and the *jth* attribute. The decision-maker assigns weights to the attributes, denoted as $\{w_1 . w_2 . \ldots . w_n\}$, with the condition that the weights are normalized such that $\sum_{j=1}^{n} W_j = 1$.

Step 2: Creation of normalized decision matrix

In this step, it should be determined whether the criterion is positive or negative.

Normalization is a customary procedure in MCDM methodologies. At this point, utilizing the (47.2) delineated below, the decision matrix is normalized.

$$r^*_{ij} = \frac{r_{ij}}{\sqrt{\sum_{i=1}^{m} r_{ij}^2}}; \; j = 1, \ldots, n \tag{47.2}$$

Thus, r^*_{ij} represents the normalized value of the decision matrix element for the *ith* alternative under the *jth* attribute.

Step 3: The weighted normalized decision matrix

In this step, the values from the normalized decision matrix are multiplied by the respective criterion weights to produce the weighted decision matrix, as shown in Eq. (47.3):

$$v_{ij} = r^*_{ij} . \, w_j; \tag{47.3}$$

where w_j denotes the weight of the criterion j, v_{ij} is the weighted normalized value for the i alternative with respect to criterion j, and r^*_{ij} is the normalized value.

Step 4: The assessment values

Considering the attribute weights $\{w_1 . w_2 . \ldots . w_n\}$, the evaluation scores for each alternative are calculated using (47.4).

$$y_j = \sum_{j \in B} v_{ij} - \sum_{j \in C} v_{ij}; \; i = 1, \ldots, m \tag{47.4}$$

- v_{ij} is the weighted normalized value from the previous step.
- y_j is the overall performance value of alternative i.
- B is the set of indices for benefit criteria.
- C is the set of indices for cost criteria.

Step 5: The final ranking of the alternative

Following the previous step, the maximum y_j values for each *ith* alternative are identified. These values are then arranged in descending order, with the most significant value receiving the highest rank.

47.4 Case study 1

In this section, two case studies are presented to examine the application of the MOORA method. Also, complete, step-by-step explanations are provided for a better understanding and further learning of the method.

Suppose a student wants to buy a laptop to carry out his research activities. After initial research, he has considered four alternatives for purchase. The student seeks to evaluate and compare these four laptop models based on three main criteria: battery life (hours of operation), memory, and price (Table 47.2).

In the first step, the decision matrix is constructed based on the alternatives and criteria, as shown in (47.1). In this matrix, the columns represent the evaluation criteria, and the rows correspond to the available alternatives (Table 47.3).

During the second step, the decision matrix undergoes normalization according to (47.2). The normalized matrix obtained is presented in Table 47.4.

In the third step, the normalized matrix is multiplied by the criteria weights provided in Table 47.2, according to Eq. (47.3). The resulting weighted normalized decision matrix is shown in Table 47.5.

TABLE 47.2 The information related to the criteria.

Criteria	Type	Symbol	Weight
Battery life (hours of operation)	Positive	(C_1)	0.38
Memory	Positive	(C_2)	0.46
Price	Negative	(C_3)	0.16

TABLE 47.3 The initial decision matrix.

Alternative/criteria	C_1	C_2	C_3
A1	6	6	5
A2	8	5	7
A3	4	7	5
A4	7	6	8

TABLE 47.4 The normalized decision matrix.

Alternative/criteria	C_1	C_2	C_3
A1	0.467	0.497	0.392
A2	0.623	0.414	0.548
A3	0.311	0.579	0.392
A4	0.545	0.497	0.627

TABLE 47.5 The weighted normalized decision matrix.

Alternatives/criteria	C_1	C_2	C_3
A1	0.1775	0.2286	0.0627
A2	0.2367	0.1904	0.0877
A3	0.1182	0.2663	0.0627
A4	0.2071	0.2286	0.1003

TABLE 47.6 The ranking of alternatives.

Alternatives	y_j
A1	0.3434
A2	0.3394
A3	0.3218
A4	0.3354

Step-by-Step calculation:
A1:

- C1: 0.467 × 0.38 = 0.17750.467\times 0.38 = 0.17750.467 × 0.38 = 0.1775
- C2: 0.497 × 0.46 = 0.22860.497\times 0.46 = 0.22860.497 × 0.46 = 0.2286
- C3: 0.392 × 0.16 = 0.06270.392\times 0.16 = 0.06270.392 × 0.16 = 0.0627

A2:

- C1: 0.623 × 0.38 = 0.23670.623\times 0.38 = 0.23670.623 × 0.38 = 0.2367
- C2: 0.414 × 0.46 = 0.19040.414\times 0.46 = 0.19040.414 × 0.46 = 0.1904
- C3: 0.548 × 0.16 = 0.08770.548\times 0.16 = 0.08770.548 × 0.16 = 0.0877

In the fourth step, the reference point value for each alternative is calculated using (47.4). This involves calculating the difference between the total of positive (benefit) criteria and the total of negative (cost) criteria for each alternative. We should take into account the type of each criterion, whether it is a *benefit* (positive) or a *cost* (negative) criterion. For this problem, the "price" criterion is considered a negative (cost) criterion, while the other two criteria are positive (benefit) criteria.

A1:

$$y_{A1} = (0.1775 + 0.2286) - 0.0627 = 0.4061 - 0.0627 = 0.3434$$

Finally, in the last step, the alternatives are ranked based on their reference point values. The alternatives are sorted in descending order of their scores. As shown in Table 47.6, Alternative 1 ranks first with the highest reference value of 0.3434. Alternatives 2 and 4 follow in second and third place with values of 0.3394 and 0.3354, respectively, while Alternative 3, with the lowest value, ranks last.

47.5 Case study 2

To better explain and demonstrate the application of the MOORA method, a more complex case study has been considered. This helps assess the effectiveness of the MOORA method in dealing with real-world problems.

Assume the goal is to assess the obstacles hindering the implementation of the circular economy within healthcare waste management. In this case, 12 barriers have been identified and are presented in Table 47.7. These barriers will be evaluated based on three criteria: severity (C_1), likelihood of occurrence (C_2), and detectability (C_3).

The assessment is carried out by three decision-makers. First, a decision matrix is created using (47.1), based on the values (1–10) provided by each decision-maker for each barrier. Since there are three decision-makers, three separate decision matrices are formed. The final decision matrix is derived by averaging the scores provided by all three decision-makers. This is shown in Table 47.8.

Next, the normalized decision matrix is created using (47.2) to scale the values. Following this, the weighted normalized decision matrix is generated by applying Eq. (47.3), using the following weights assigned to each criterion:

- Severity (C_1): 0.3
- Likelihood of occurrence (C_{12}): 0.4
- Detectability (C_3): 0.3

TABLE 47.7 Barriers.

Barriers	Symbol
Lack of legal support	B_1
Financial resource shortage	B_2
Lack of incentives	B_3
Technical complexity	B_4
Managerial issues	B_5
Lack of inter-organizational collaboration	B_6
Resistance to change	B_7
Insufficient infrastructure	B_8
Lack of standardization	B_9
Agency and ownership issues	B_{10}
Absence of a uniform regulatory framework	B_{11}
Lack of sufficient motivation	B_{12}

TABLE 47.8 The initial decision matrix.

Barrier	C_1	C_2	C_3
B_1	5	6.67	6
B_2	6	7	7
B_3	5.33	5	7
B_4	7.67	6.67	7.67
B_5	7	6.67	6
B_6	6	6.33	7
B_7	7.67	7	6
B_8	7	7.67	6
B_9	6	5.67	8
B_{10}	5	7	6.67
B_{11}	7	6	5.33
B_{12}	7	7.67	6.67

These weights represent the relative significance of each criterion. The weighted matrix is presented in Table 47.9.

In the next step, we calculate y_j based on the nature of each criterion. In this problem, severity and likelihood of occurrence are considered benefit criteria (the higher the value, the more critical the barrier). At the same time, detectability is a cost criterion (a higher detectability means it is easier to identify and manage, so it's less problematic).

TABLE 47.9 The normalized and weighted decision matrix.

The normalized decision matrix				The weighted normalized decision matrix			
Barrier	C_1	C_2	C_3	**Barrier**	C_1	C_2	C_3
B_1	0.2236	0.2893	0.2604	B_1	0.0559	0.1041	0.1015
B_2	0.2683	0.3037	0.3037	B_2	0.0671	0.1093	0.1185
B_3	0.2385	0.2170	0.3037	B_3	0.0596	0.0781	0.1185
B_4	0.3429	0.2893	0.3327	B_4	0.0857	0.1041	0.1297
B_5	0.3130	0.2893	0.2604	B_5	0.0783	0.1041	0.1015
B_6	0.2683	0.2748	0.3037	B_6	0.0671	0.0989	0.1185
B_7	0.3429	0.3037	0.2604	B_7	0.0857	0.1093	0.1015
B_8	0.3130	0.3327	0.2604	B_8	0.0783	0.1198	0.1015
B_9	0.2683	0.2459	0.3471	B_9	0.0671	0.0885	0.1354
B_{10}	0.2236	0.3037	0.2893	B_{10}	0.0559	0.1093	0.1128
B_{11}	0.3130	0.2604	0.2314	B_{11}	0.0783	0.0937	0.0903
B_{12}	0.3130	0.3327	0.2893	B_{12}	0.0783	0.1198	0.1128

TABLE 47.10 The ranking of barriers.

Barrier	y_j
B_1	0.0585
B_2	0.0579
B_3	0.0192
B_4	0.0601
B_5	0.0809
B_6	0.0475
B_7	0.0935
B_8	0.0966
B_9	0.0202
B_{10}	0.0524
B_{11}	0.0817

Using (47.4), we compute y_j values, the assessment value for each barrier. Barriers are then ranked in descending order according to their y_j values, where a higher value indicates a more significant barrier (Table 47.10).

As shown in Fig. 47.1, barriers 8 and 7 rank the highest with y_j values of 0.0966 and 0.0935, respectively, indicating they are the most critical. In contrast, barrier 3, with a y_j value of 0.0192, is ranked lowest, suggesting it is the least concerning among the listed barriers.

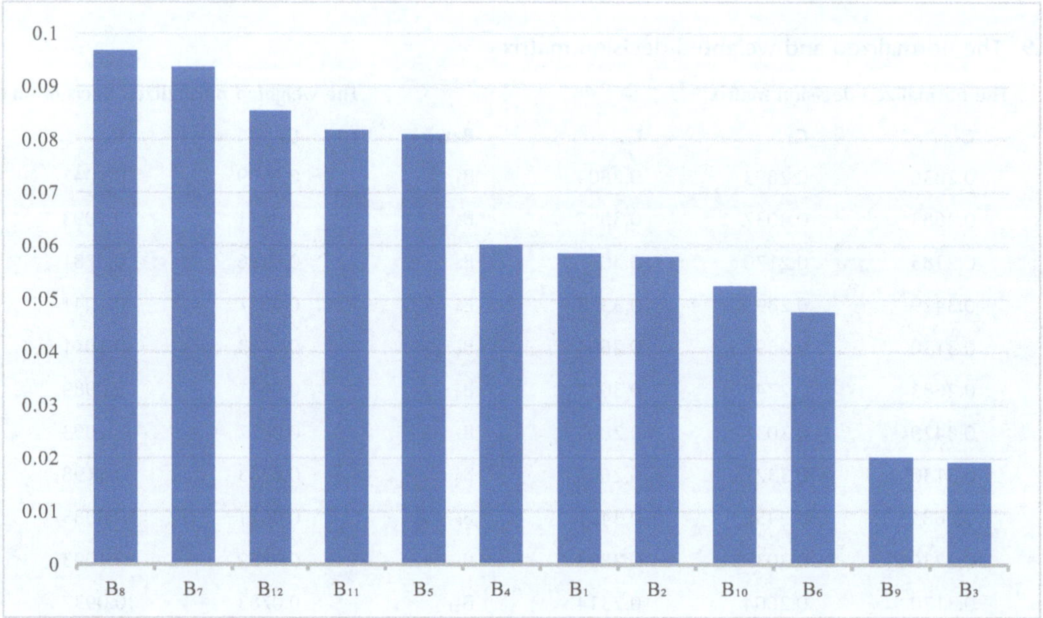

FIGURE 47.1 The ranking of barriers.

47.6 Conclusion

This chapter offers an in-depth overview of the MOORA method, a widely applied multicriteria decision-making technique used for ranking alternatives across diverse disciplines. It starts with an introduction to the MOORA approach, followed by a review of relevant studies that have employed this method. Subsequently, a detailed explanation of the MOORA process is provided. To illustrate its practical utility, two case studies are included, highlighting the method's adaptability while shedding light on its advantages and potential limitations. Overall, this chapter aims to deliver a comprehensive understanding of the MOORA method and its capability to tackle complex decision-making challenges in various domains.

Despite the efficiency and simplicity of the MOORA method in solving MCDM problems, this method also has limitations that should be considered by researchers and users. First, the results of the MOORA method are strongly influenced by the selection of criteria and their weighting. If the weights are not determined correctly based on real conditions, the results may not fully reflect the reality of the problem. Second, this method assumes that the criteria are independent of each other, while in many real problems, there are mutual relationships and correlations between the criteria. Given these limitations, several directions for future research can be suggested. First, developing hybrid models that combine MOORA with approaches such as fuzzy, gray, or artificial intelligence-based methods can help increase accuracy and flexibility. Second, examining how to consider the dependence between criteria and using techniques such as analytic network process can improve the applicability of this method.

References

Akkaya, G., Turanoğlu, B., & Öztaş, S. (2015). An integrated fuzzy AHP and fuzzy MOORA approach to the problem of industrial engineering sector choosing. *Expert Systems with Applications, 42*(24), 9565–9573. https://doi.org/10.1016/j.eswa.2015.07.061.

Arabsheybani, A., Paydar, M. M., & Safaei, A. S. (2018). An integrated fuzzy MOORA method and FMEA technique for sustainable supplier selection considering quantity discounts and supplier's risk. *Journal of Cleaner Production, 190*, 577–591. https://doi.org/10.1016/j.jclepro.2018.04.167.

Ashofteh, P. S., & Dougaheh, M. P. (2024). Ranking the optimal combination of low-impact urban development systems under climate change with the TODIM multi-criteria decision-making method. *Journal of Cleaner Production, 434*, 140108.

Brauers, W. K. M., & Zavadskas, E. K. (2009). Robustness of the multi-objective MOORA method with a test for the facilities sector. *Technological and Economic Development of Economy, 15*(2), 352–375. https://doi.org/10.3846/1392-8619.2009.15.352-375.

Brauers, W. K., & Zavadskas, E. K. (2006). The MOORA method and its application to privatization in a transition economy. *Control and Cybernetics, 35*(2), 445–469.

Chakraborty, S. (2011). Applications of the MOORA method for decision making in manufacturing environment. *International Journal of Advanced Manufacturing Technology, 54*(9–12), 1155–1166. https://doi.org/10.1007/s00170-010-2972-0.

Chakraborty, S., Datta, H. N., Kalita, K., & Chakraborty, S. (2023). A narrative review of multi-objective optimization on the basis of ratio analysis (MOORA) method in decision making. *Opsearch, 60*(4), 1844–1887. https://doi.org/10.1007/s12597-023-00676-7.

Dabbagh, R., & Yousefi, S. (2019). A hybrid decision-making approach based on FCM and MOORA for occupational health and safety risk analysis. *Journal of Safety Research, 71*, 111–123. https://doi.org/10.1016/j.jsr.2019.09.021.

Gadakh, V. S., Shinde, V. B., & Khemnar, N. S. (2013). Optimization of welding process parameters using MOORA method. *International Journal of Advanced Manufacturing Technology, 69*(9–12), 2031–2039. https://doi.org/10.1007/s00170-013-5188-2.

Gorener, A., Dincer, H., & Hacioglu, Ü. (2013). Application of multi-objective optimization on the basis of ratio analysis (MOORA) method for bank branch location selection. *International Journal of Finance & Banking Studies, 2*(2), 41–52. https://doi.org/10.20525/ijfbs.v2i2.145.

Gupta, K., Roy, S., Poonia, R. C., Kumar, R., Nayak, S. R., Altameem, A., & Saudagar, A. K. J. (2022). Multi-Criteria Usability evaluation of mHealth applications on Type 2 diabetes mellitus using two Hybrid MCDM Models: CODAS-FAHP and MOORA-FAHP. *Applied Sciences, 12*(9), 4156. https://doi.org/10.3390/app12094156.

Haseli, G., & Sheikh, R. (2022). Base criterion method (BCM). In *Multiple criteria decision making: Techniques, analysis and applications*. Singapore: Springer Nature Singapore, 17–38.

Haseli, G., Ranjbarzadeh, R., Hajiaghaei-Keshteli, M., Jafarzadeh Ghoushchi, S., Hasani, A., Deveci, M., & Ding, W. (2023a). HECON: Weight assessment of the product loyalty criteria considering the customer decision's halo effect using the convolutional neural networks. *Information Sciences, 623*, 184–205. https://doi.org/10.1016/j.ins.2022.12.027.

Haseli, G., Torkayesh, A. E., Hajiaghaei-Keshteli, M., & Venghaus, S. (2023a). Sustainable resilient recycling partner selection for urban waste management: Consolidating perspectives of decision-makers and experts. *Applied Soft Computing, 137*, 110120. https://doi.org/10.1016/j.asoc.2023.110120.

Haseli, G., Yaran Ögel, İ., Ecer, F., & Hajiaghaei-Keshteli, M. (2023b). Luxury in female technology (FemTech): Selection of smart jewelry for women through BCM-MARCOS group decision-making framework with fuzzy ZE-numbers. *Technological Forecasting and Social Change, 196*, 122870. 10.1016/j.techfore.2023.122870.

Haseli, G., Yazdani, M., Shaayesteh, M. T., & Hajiaghaei-Keshteli, M. (2025). Logistic hub location problem under fuzzy Extended Z-numbers to consider the uncertainty and reliable group decision-making. *Applied Soft Computing, 171*, 112751. https://doi.org/10.1016/j.asoc.2025.112751.

Jafarzadeh Ghoushchi, S., Memarpour Ghiaci, A., Rahnamay Bonab, S., & Ranjbarzadeh, R. (2022). Barriers to circular economy implementation in designing of sustainable medical waste management systems using a new extended decision-making and FMEA models. *Environmental Science and Pollution Research International, 29*(53), 79735–79753. https://doi.org/10.1007/s11356-022-19018-z.

Kumar Sahu, A., Datta, S., & Sankar Mahapatra, S. (2014). Supply chain performance benchmarking using grey-MOORA approach: An empirical research. *Grey Systems, 4*(1), 24–55. https://doi.org/10.1108/GS-07-2013-0011.

Luviano Cruz, D., Alvarado-Iniesta, A., Rodríguez-Picón, L. A., Pérez-Domínguez, L., Xu, Z., & Domingo, R. (2018). MOORA under pythagorean fuzzy set for multiple criteria decision making. *Complexity (New York, N.Y.), 2018*, 1–10. https://doi.org/10.1155/2018/2602376.

Mahmudah, R. S., Putri, D. I., Abdullah, A. G., Shafii, M. A., Hakim, D. L., & Setiadipura, T. (2024). Developing a multi-criteria decision-making model for nuclear power plant location selection using fuzzy analytic hierarchy process and fuzzy VIKOR methods focused on socio-economic factors. *Cleaner Engineering and Technology, 19*, 100737.

Mavi, R. K., Goh, M., & Zarbakhshnia, N. (2017). Sustainable third-party reverse logistic provider selection with fuzzy SWARA and fuzzy MOORA in plastic industry. *International Journal of Advanced Manufacturing Technology, 91*(5–8), 2401–2418. https://doi.org/10.1007/s00170-016-9880-x.

Mitra, A. (2022). Application of multi-objective optimization on the basis of ratio analysis (MOORA) for selection of cotton fabrics for optimal thermal comfort. *Research Journal of Textile and Apparel, 26*(2), 187–203. https://doi.org/10.1108/RJTA-02-2021-0021.

Moslem, S., & Çelikbilek, Y. (2020). An integrated grey AHP-MOORA model for ameliorating public transport service quality. *European Transport Research Review, 12*(1), 1–13. https://doi.org/10.1186/s12544-020-00455-1.

Moslem, S., Gündoğdu, F. K., Saylam, S., & Pilla, F. (2024). A hybrid decomposed fuzzy multi-criteria decision-making model for optimizing parcel lockers location in the last-mile delivery landscape. *Applied Soft Computing, 154*, 111321.

Rajput, V., Soni, R., Jha, A., & Agrawal, A. (2024). Ranking of epoxy/Kota stone dust composite by MCDM approach using hybrid AHP-MOORA methods. *MATEC Web of Conferences, 393*, 1006. https://doi.org/10.1051/matecconf/202439301006.

Rane, S. B., Potdar, P. R., & Rane, S. (2021). Data-driven fleet management using MOORA: a perspective of risk management. *Journal of Modelling in Management, 16*(1), 310–338. https://doi.org/10.1108/JM2-03-2019-0069.

Rizk-Allah, R. M., Hassanien, A. E., & Slowik, A. (2020). Multi-objective orthogonal opposition-based crow search algorithm for large-scale multi-objective optimization. *Neural Computing & Applications, 32*(17), 13715–13746. https://doi.org/10.1007/s00521-020-04779-w.

Shahzadi, G., Luqman, A., Ali Al-Shamiri, M. M., & Pamučar, D. (2022). The extended MOORA method based on fermatean fuzzy information. *Mathematical Problems in Engineering, 2022*, 1–15. https://doi.org/10.1155/2022/7595872.

Soni, A., Das, P. K., & Sarma, M. (2022). Application of MOORA method for parametric optimization of manufacturing process of floor tiles using waste plastics. *Process Integration and Optimization for Sustainability, 6*(1), 113–123. https://doi.org/10.1007/s41660-021-00205-3.

Chapter 48

MULTIMOORA: Multiobjective optimization by ratio analysis plus full multiplicative form for multi-attribute decision-making

Maryam Eghbalizarch[1] and Nazanin Ghaemi-Zadeh[2]

[1]*Department of Industrial and Systems Engineering, Southern Polytechnic College of Engineering and Engineering Technology, Kennesaw State University, Marietta, GA, United States,* [2]*Department of Industrial Engineering, Faculty of Engineering, Sharif University of Technology, Tehran, Iran*

48.1 Introduction

In real-world decision-making, individuals and organizations often face the challenge of selecting the best alternative from a set of options based on multiple—and sometimes conflicting—criteria. Multicriteria decision-making (MCDM) methods provide a structured approach to address such problems, enabling more informed, consistent, and transparent decisions. These methods are particularly valuable in fields such as engineering, healthcare, management, and economics, where trade-offs between competing objectives must be carefully evaluated. Among the more advanced MCDM techniques, the multiobjective optimization by ratio analysis plus the full multiplicative form (MULTIMOORA) method has gained significant attention. Originally introduced in 2006 as the multiobjective optimization on the basis of ratio analysis (MOORA) method by Brauers and Zavadskas, it combined the ratio system and the reference point approach to support multicriteria assessment. To enhance its robustness, the authors extended MOORA in 2010 by introducing the MULTIMOORA method, which incorporated the full multiplicative form and applied dominance theory to consolidate the results of all three subordinate methods into a final ranking (Brauers & Zavadskas, 2010).

This tri-method structure—merging ratio analysis, reference point evaluation, and multiplicative aggregation—offers a more comprehensive and reliable decision-making framework, as each method compensates for the limitations of the others. Specifically, the ratio system is a fully compensatory model, the reference point approach is noncompensatory, and the full multiplicative form is incompletely compensatory; therefore, integrating their outcomes mitigates individual weaknesses and enhances overall robustness (Hafezalkotob et al., 2019). As Brauers & Zavadskas (2012) noted, "use of two different methods of multiobjective optimization is more robust than the use of a single method; the use of three methods is more robust than the use of two, and so on," thereby supporting the claim that MULTIMOORA is more robust than MOORA. By combining these complementary approaches, MULTIMOORA effectively captures performance differences among alternatives, leading to more consistent and accurate outcomes. Additionally, the method is computationally efficient, adaptable to uncertainty (including fuzzy environments), and applicable across a wide range of domains (Hafezalkotob et al., 2019). The ratio system applies an arithmetic weighted aggregation and is suitable for problems with independent criteria, where each criterion contributes separately to the final evaluation. The reference point approach, based on the min–max metric, adopts a conservative strategy that favors alternatives with consistently acceptable performance across all criteria (Hafezalkotob et al., 2019). In contrast, the full multiplicative form uses a geometric aggregation operator, making it especially effective in scenarios with interdependent criteria, where a poor value in one criterion can significantly influence the overall result (Hafezalkotob et al., 2019).

To consolidate the rankings from these three methods, dominance theory is typically used, as suggested in the original MULTIMOORA framework. This aggregation process ensures that the final decision reflects a comprehensive and robust

Encyclopedia of Multi-Attribute Decision-Making (MADM). DOI: https://doi.org/10.1016/B978-0-443-33275-3.00005-1

evaluation. Due to its simplicity and capacity to handle uncertainty, MULTIMOORA continues to gain popularity in both academic research and real-world decision-making applications.

48.2 Literature review

MULTIMOORA has been extensively applied and enhanced in recent years across a wide range of domains, benefiting from its flexibility, robustness, and ability to integrate with other techniques. This section classifies the related literature into two main categories: (1) applications across various sectors, and (2) methodological extensions under uncertainty.

48.2.1 Applications of MULTIMOORA in various domains

The MULTIMOORA method has extensive use in diverse sectors. One of its key application areas is sustainable energy and environmental management. For instance, Zhang et al. (2025) applied an extended MULTIMOORA approach to select optimal locations for photovoltaic waste recycling centers, ensuring sustainability in renewable energy infrastructure. Similarly, Chen et al. (2024) proposed a two-stage framework integrating Geographic Information Systems (GIS) and MULTIMOORA under a Pythagorean triangular fuzzy environment for offshore wind-to-hydrogen project site selection. The method has also been employed to assess barriers to renewable energy adoption (Asante et al., 2020). In supply chain and logistics, Vaezi et al. (2024) developed a hybrid best–worst method (BWM)–MULTIMOORA and bi-objective programming approach for sustainable supplier selection and order allocation, highlighting its effectiveness in green supply chain management. Additionally, Sarabi & Darestani (2021) utilized fuzzy MULTIMOORA to select logistics service providers, demonstrating its applicability in enhancing operational efficiency. Urban planning and mobility represent another significant area where MULTIMOORA has been applied. Yucesan et al. (2024) evaluated the sustainability of urban mobility in Asian cities using an integrated interval type-2 fuzzy BWM–MULTIMOORA approach. Lin et al. (2020) employed a picture fuzzy MULTIMOORA model for selecting car-sharing station sites, while Rahimi et al. (2020) combined fuzzy group BWM, MULTIMOORA, and GIS for sustainable landfill site selection. The healthcare sector has also benefited from MULTIMOORA's decision-making capabilities. Liang et al. (2022) introduced a medical triangular fuzzy MULTIMOORA approach to evaluate healthcare delivery quality in Ghana. In biomedical engineering, Hafezalkotob & Hafezalkotob (2015) applied MULTIMOORA for material selection in medical applications, ensuring optimal performance under stringent requirements. Additionally, Eghbalizarch et al. (2018) successfully utilized MULTIMOORA for pharmacological therapy selection in type 2 diabetes treatment, further showing its performance in clinical decision-making. Another critical application is in risk assessment and failure mode analysis. Yu et al. (2023) proposed a rough cloud model-based MULTIMOORA method for failure mode and effects analysis in mooring systems, enhancing safety in maritime operations. Chen et al. (2020) extended MULTIMOORA with the Choquet integral for risk prioritization, while Liu et al. (2022) used an evidential MULTIMOORA approach to assess disaster risk reduction strategies. Emerging technologies, particularly artificial intelligence (AI) and blockchain, have also seen the integration of MULTIMOORA. Siddiqui & Haroon (2023) developed an MCDM fuzzy comprehensive evaluation model combining MULTIMOORA to evaluate blockchain adoption factors. Zhang et al. (2024) incorporated MULTIMOORA into an AI-driven group consensus model for crop disease detection, showcasing its adaptability in smart agriculture.

48.2.2 Extensions and hybridizations of MULTIMOORA

To address uncertainty and improve decision-making accuracy, researchers have extended MULTIMOORA using various fuzzy and hybrid techniques. Pythagorean fuzzy sets have been widely integrated, as seen in Zhou et al. (2024) and Rani & Mishra (2021), to handle imprecise data in offshore wind power station selection and electric vehicle charging station evaluation, respectively. Interval type-2 fuzzy sets (Qin & Ma, 2022; Yucesan et al., 2024) and hesitant fuzzy linguistic term sets (Liao et al., 2019) have also been employed to enhance robustness in linguistic decision-making. Hybrid models combining MULTIMOORA with other MCDM techniques have further expanded its applicability. The integration of BWM with MULTIMOORA (Shang et al., 2022; Vaezi et al., 2024) has improved criteria weighting in supplier selection. The step-wise weight assessment aatio analysis method has been coupled with MULTIMOORA for community-based tourism development (He et al., 2021), while the decision-making trial and evaluation laboratory has been used to refine quality function deployment (Chen et al., 2021). Future research can investigate dynamic decision-making, interpretability, and integration with AI to enhance the method's applicability.

48.3 Methodology

This section presents a detailed overview of the methodology. It begins with an introduction to the MULTIMOORA framework in Section 3.1, where the key ranking techniques—ratio system, reference point approach, and full multiplicative form—are discussed. Section 3.2 then focuses on the ranking aggregation tools employed to synthesize the results obtained from these three methods into a unified decision. Although the sections are presented sequentially, each technique operates independently and does not rely on the outcomes of the others. This structure highlights the methodological modularity of MULTIMOORA while offering a comprehensive and robust approach to decision-making.

48.3.1 MULTIMOORA framework

MULTIMOORA employs vector normalization to generate comparable ratings and incorporates three subordinate ranking techniques: the ratio system, the reference point approach, and the full multiplicative form. While each of these methods has its advantages, they also come with limitations. To mitigate these drawbacks, MULTIMOORA integrates multiple approaches. This section provides an overview of these three ranking methods to enhance comprehension of the MULTIMOORA framework. The flowchart of this method is shown in Fig. 48.1. The initial step in any MCDM problem involves constructing a decision matrix and a weight vector. For MULTIMOORA, the decision matrix is formed by evaluating m alternative solutions against n criteria, where each element x_{ij} represents the performance rating of the i-th alternative (A_i) with respect to the j-th criterion (c_j). The set of alternatives is defined as $A_i = \{A_1, A_2, A_3, \ldots, A_m\}$, and the set of criteria is given by $c_j = \{c_1, c_2, c_3, \ldots, c_n\}$. The matrix is structured as follows (Hafezalkotob & Hafezalkotob, 2017):

$$X = \begin{bmatrix} x_{11} & \cdots & x_{1j} & \cdots & x_{1n} \\ \vdots & \vdots & \vdots & \vdots & \vdots \\ x_{i1} & \cdots & x_{ij} & \cdots & x_{in} \\ \vdots & \vdots & \vdots & \vdots & \vdots \\ x_{m1} & \cdots & x_{mj} & \cdots & x_{mn} \end{bmatrix} \quad (48.1)$$

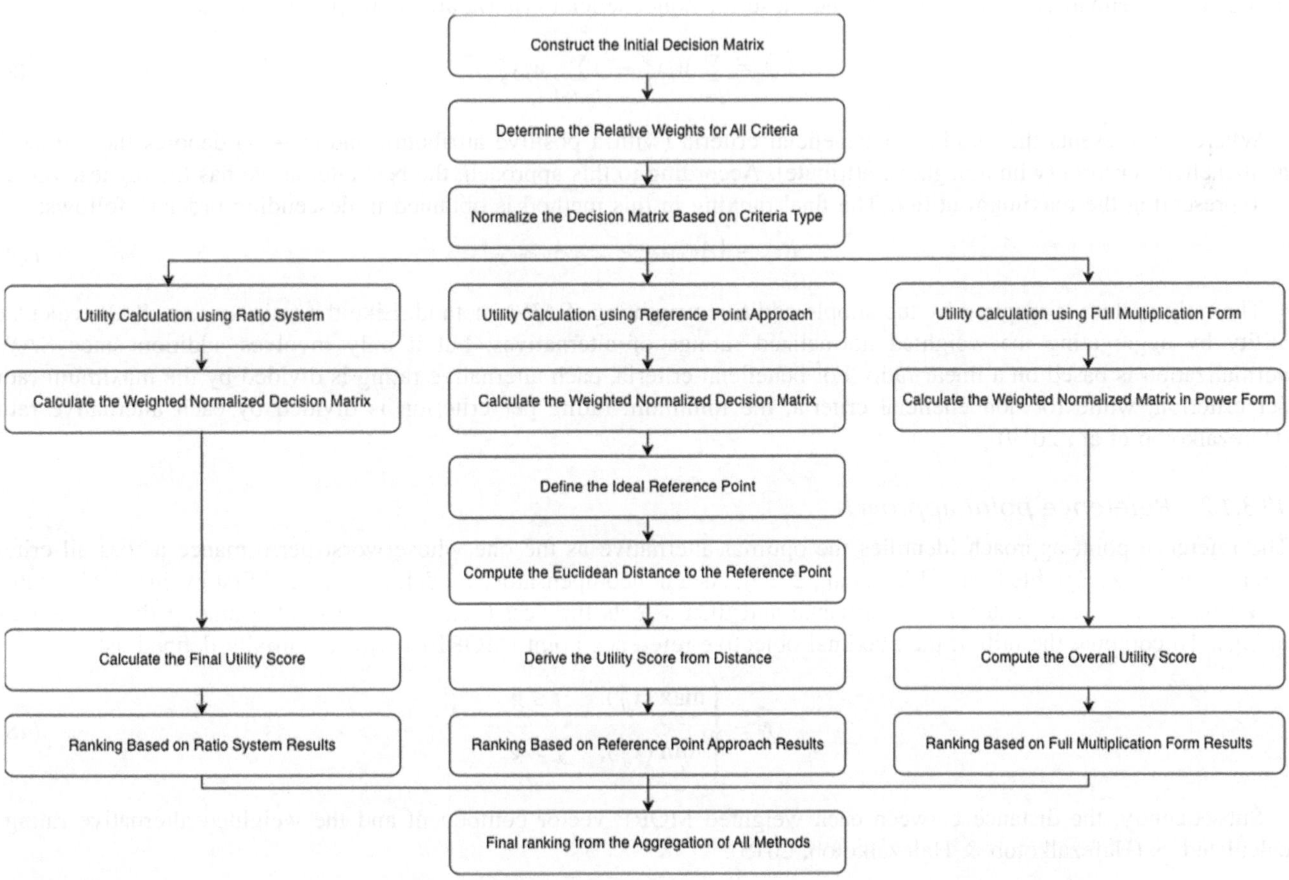

FIGURE 48.1 Flowchart of the MULTIMOORA method.

Here, each row corresponds to an alternative, and each column represents a criterion. The weight vector $W = \{w_1, w_2, w_3, \ldots, w_n\}$ assigns relative importance to each criterion in the evaluation process. Since the ratings of alternatives across various criteria in the problem may have different scales, it is necessary to normalize the ratings before applying them in an MCDM model (Ghaemi-Zadeh & Eghbalizarch, 2024).

Various normalization techniques have been used in MCDM approaches. According to Brauers et al. (2008), the vector normalization method is considered the most reliable option for use in MULTIMOORA. The vector normalization method is defined as follows (Brauers & Zavadskas, 2006; Nijkamp & Delft, 1977):

$$x_{ij}^* = \frac{x_{ij}}{\sqrt{\sum_{i=1}^{m} (x_{ij})^2}} \tag{48.2}$$

The ratio system, a fully compensatory model, is effective for problems involving "independent" criteria. In contrast, the full multiplicative form, an incompletely compensatory model, is more suitable when "dependent" criteria are present. The reference point approach, as a noncompensatory model, offers a more "conservative" alternative compared to the other two methods. While both the ratio system and full multiplicative form allow for offsetting weak performance on one criterion with stronger performance on others (though to varying degrees), the reference point approach does not permit such compensation. Since real-world problems may contain both "dependent" and "independent" criteria, MULTIMOORA combines these three methods to leverage their individual strengths and produce a more robust final result (Brauers & Zavadskas, 2012). In the following discussion, the derivation of the three subordinate ranking methods is explained as follows:

48.3.1.1 Ratio system

The ratio system, which utilizes the arithmetic weighted aggregation operator, is a fully compensatory model. This means that low normalized values of an alternative can be completely offset by equally large values. In other words, an alternative with poor performance in some criteria but good performance in others can be replaced by an alternative with moderate performance across all criteria. To calculate the utility in the ratio system method, the weighted normalized ratings for beneficial criteria are added, and those for nonbeneficial criteria are subtracted as follows:

$$y_i = \sum_{j=1}^{g} w_j x_{ij}^* - \sum_{j=g+1}^{n} w_j x_{ij}^* \tag{48.3}$$

Where g represents the number of beneficial criteria (with a positive attribute), and $(n - g)$ denotes the number of nonbeneficial criteria (with a negative attribute). According to this approach, the best alternative has the highest value of y_i, representing the maximum utility. The final ranking in this method is obtained in descending order as follows:

$$R_{RS} = \{A_{i|\max_i y_i} > \ldots > A_{i|\min_i y_i}\} \tag{48.4}$$

The ratio system is inspired by the simple additive weighting (SAW) method. Like the ratio system, SAW calculates utility by aggregating the weighted normalized ratings of alternatives, but it only involves addition since SAW's normalization is based on a linear ratio. For beneficial criteria, each alternative rating is divided by the maximum rating per criterion, while for nonbeneficial criteria, the minimum rating per criterion is divided by each alternative rating (Hafezalkotob et al., 2019).

48.3.1.2 Reference point approach

The reference point approach identifies the optimal alternative as the one whose worst performance across all criteria remains within acceptable limits (Liao et al., 2019). As a noncompensatory model, this method first evaluates alternatives based on their weakest criterion performance and then selects the best (i.e., minimum) value among these worst-case ratings. To compute the utility, the maximal objective reference point (MORP) vector is initially defined as:

$$r_j = \begin{cases} \max_i (x_{ij}^*), & j \le g \\ \min_i (x_{ij}^*), & j > g \end{cases} \tag{48.5}$$

Subsequently, the distance between each weighted MORP vector component and the weighted alternative rating is calculated as (Hafezalkotob & Hafezalkotob, 2015):

$$d_{ij} = |w_j r_j - w_j x_{ij}^*| \tag{48.6}$$

The utility in the reference point approach is derived by maximizing this distance:

$$z_i = \max_j d_{ij} \tag{48.7}$$

The optimal alternative corresponds to the minimum utility value z_i, with rankings determined in ascending order:

$$R_{RPA} = \{A_{i|\min_i z_i} \succ \ldots \succ A_{i|\max_i z_i}\} \tag{48.8}$$

The classical reference point approach focuses solely on the MORP vector, disregarding the aspiration objective reference point (AORP) vector. However, Eghbalizarch et al. (2018) proposed an Extended reference point approach that incorporates the AORP vector to enhance discrimination among alternatives.

48.3.1.3 Full multiplicative form

The full multiplicative form is an incompletely compensatory model that employs a geometric weighted aggregation operator. Unlike fully compensatory methods, small normalized values in an alternative cannot be entirely offset by larger values in other criteria. Consequently, an alternative with moderate but balanced performance may be preferred over one exhibiting both exceptionally high and low values across different criteria (Liao et al., 2019). The utility in full multiplicative form is calculated by dividing the product of weighted normalized ratings for beneficial criteria by the product of weighted normalized ratings for nonbeneficial criteria (Hafezalkotob & Hafezalkotob, 2016):

$$u_i = \prod_{j=1}^{g} (x_{ij}^*)^{w_j} / \prod_{j=g+1}^{n} (x_{ij}^*)^{w_j} \tag{48.9}$$

Since multiplying normalized ratings by weights yields the same outcome as an unweighted model, weights must be incorporated as exponents in the utility equation. The optimal alternative corresponds to the maximum utility u_i, with rankings determined in descending order:

$$R_{FMF} = \{A_{i|\max_i u_i} \succ \ldots \succ A_{i|\min_i u_i}\} \tag{48.10}$$

A similar multiplicative aggregation principle is applied in other MCDM techniques, such as weighted aggregated sum product assessment (WASPAS), where the second term of its utility index resembles a full multiplicative form. However, WASPAS employs a linear ratio normalization based on the maximum and minimum values of alternative ratings, distinguishing it from the full multiplicative form's geometric approach (Hafezalkotob et al., 2019).

48.3.2 Ranking aggregation tools

Once the subordinate rankings are obtained, they need to be combined to derive the final ranking of alternatives. As noted by Brauers & Zavadskas (2012), merging multiple subordinate rankings can lead to a comprehensive ranking list that is more reliable than any single individual ranking. This section focuses on a review of some tools available for ranking aggregation. These aggregation methods fall into four main categories as classified by Hafezalkotob et al. (2019): dominance-based approaches (such as the original dominance theory and dominance-directed graph), mathematical operators (including arithmetic and geometric means, Borda rule, enhanced Borda rule, and the rank position method), MCDM techniques (like the organísation, rangement et Synthèse de données relationnelles method and technique of precise order preference), and optimization-based models (e.g., nonlinear optimization). While dominance theory has historically been the most frequently applied, recent developments have favored more advanced tools due to their superior performance, scalability, and ability to incorporate additional information. Among these, the improved Borda rule (IBR) is particularly noteworthy, as it uniquely incorporates both subordinate rankings and utility values, leading to a more informative and discriminative final ranking (Hafezalkotob et al., 2019). The section continues by elaborating on the principles behind some ranking aggregation techniques used in the MULTIMOORA approach.

48.3.2.1 Dominance theory

Dominance theory was initially applied in the original MULTIMOORA method. It is built upon several foundational concepts, including types of dominance (absolute and partial dominance), equability (absolute and partial equality, as well as circular reasoning-based equality), and the principle of transitivity (Brauers & Zavadskas, 2012). Despite its foundational role, dominance theory presents several limitations (Hafezalkotob et al., 2019): (1) determining the ranking of alternatives is challenging due to the lack of automation in the process; (2) it relies solely on ordinal data, ignoring the relative significance of alternatives; and (3) circular reasoning can occur, resulting in indistinguishable rankings that reduce the method's effectiveness. A concise overview of dominance theory is provided by Brauers & Zavadskas (2010, 2012):

- Absolute dominance refers to a scenario where one alternative ranks higher than all others across all evaluation methods. This dominance is represented by uniform top ranks, such as (1-1-1).
- General dominance applies when an alternative outperforms others in two out of three methods, illustrated by cases like (d-a-a) dominating (c-b-b), (a-d-a) dominating (b-c-b), or (a-a-d) dominating (b-b-c). In such cases, the property of transitivity fully applies—meaning if alternative a dominates b, and b dominates c, then a also dominates c.
- Overall dominance is when an alternative, such as (a-a-a), clearly outperforms another like (b-b-b), establishing a complete superiority.
- Equability occurs when alternatives have equal rankings. Absolute equability is shown as (e-e-e), indicating full equality, whereas partial equability appears when two out of three ranks are equal, such as in (5-e-7) versus (6-e-3).
- Circular reasoning arises when rankings contradict transitive logic. For instance, alternative A (11-20-14) generally dominates B (14-16-15), B dominates C (15-19-12), but paradoxically, C dominates A—resulting in an unresolved loop and identical ranks for all three alternatives.

These drawbacks have led researchers to explore more advanced ranking aggregation methods that address such inconsistencies and enhance robustness in final decision-making.

48.3.2.2 Rank position method

This ranking aggregation technique, also known as the reciprocal rank method, evaluates the rank position of each alternative based on the outcomes from all subordinate ranking methods (Altuntas et al., 2015). The rank position method calculates a score for each alternative, denoted as $RPM\,(A_i)$, which is then used to determine the final ranking. The score is computed using the following formula (Altuntas et al., 2015):

$$RPM\,(A_i) = \left(\frac{1}{\left(\frac{1}{r(y_i)}\right) + \left(\frac{1}{r(z_i)}\right) + \left(\frac{1}{r(u_i)}\right)} \right) \tag{48.11}$$

Where $r(y_i)$, $r(z_i)$, and $r(u_i)$ represent the ranks assigned to the alternative A_i by the ratio system, reference point approach, and full multiplicative form, respectively. According to this method, the most preferred alternative is the one with the lowest $RPM\,(A_i)$ value.

48.3.2.3 Borda rules

The Borda Rule, also known as Borda count, is a straightforward yet efficient method commonly used in single-winner voting systems, where the number of votes matches the number of available alternatives (Altuntas et al., 2015). In this method, if there are t alternatives, the top-ranked alternative receives t points, the second-ranked gets $(t-1)$ points, and so on. The final Borda score is obtained by summing the scores assigned by all subordinate ranking methods. The alternative with the highest total Borda score is considered the best. The IBR builds upon the traditional Borda count (Wu et al., 2018), but with a key enhancement: it incorporates both cardinal values (utilities) and ordinal values (rankings) from the MULTIMOORA subordinate methods. This integration gives IBR an advantage over the dominance theory by utilizing more detailed information. To apply the IBR, the utility values from each subordinate method—ratio system, reference point, and full multiplicative form—are first normalized using vector normalization, resulting in y_i, z_i, and u_i. The assessment score for each alternative, denoted as $IMB\,(A_i)$, is calculated using the following formula (Wu et al., 2018):

$$IMB\,(A_i) = \left(y_i^* \times \frac{m - r(y_i) + 1}{m(m+1)/2} \right) - \left(z_i^* \times \frac{r(z_i)}{m(m+1)/2} \right) + \left(u_i^* \times \frac{m - r(u_i) + 1}{m(m+1)/2} \right) \tag{48.12}$$

Where $r(y_i)$, $r(z_i)$, and $r(u_i)$ are the rankings of the ratio system, reference point approach, and full multiplicative form, respectively, and m is the total number of alternatives. According to this method, the best alternative is the one with the highest $IMB\,(A_i)$ score.

Remark. Dominance theory involves complex pairwise comparisons and can suffer from circular reasoning, making it less practical—especially as the number of criteria and alternatives increases. It relies heavily on manual processing, which can be overwhelming for decision-makers. In contrast, the IBR is automated, does not require manual comparisons, and is free from such complications.

48.3.2.4 Optimization model

An alternative approach for deriving the final ranking in the MULTIMOORA method involves formulating an optimization model. The underlying principle of this model is to determine a final ranking that minimizes the total deviation from the three subordinate rankings. In other words, it seeks a solution that is as close as possible to the results of the ratio system, reference point approach, and full multiplicative form (Chen et al., 2018). The objective of the model is to minimize the sum of absolute differences between the final rank R_i and the subordinate ranks $r(y_i)$, $r(z_i)$, and $r(u_i)$ for all alternatives $i = 1,\ 2,\ \ldots, m$, as expressed below:

$$\min\left(\sum_{i=1}^{m} |R_i - r(y_i)| + \sum_{i=1}^{m} |R_i - r(z_i)| + \sum_{i=1}^{m} |R_i - r(u_i)|\right)$$

Subject to:

$$R_i = R_k,\quad i, k = 1,\ 2,\ \ldots,\ m,\quad i \neq k,$$

$$R_i > R_k,\ \text{if } r(y_i) > r(y_k),\quad r(z_i) > r(z_k),\ \text{and } r(u_i) > r(u_k),$$

$$R_i \leq R_k,\ \text{if } r(y_i) \leq r(y_k),\quad r(z_i) \leq r(z_k),\ \text{and } r(u_i) \leq r(u_k),$$

$$1 \leq R_i \leq m,\quad i = 1,\ 2,\ \ldots,\ m \tag{48.13}$$

This formulation results in a nonlinear programming model, which requires mathematical computation for solution. More detailed explanations and solution techniques for this model can be found in Chen et al. (2018) study.

48.4 Numerical example 1: laptop selection (simple real case)

This case study, originally developed by Aytaç Adalı & Tuş Işık (2017), addresses the problem of selecting the most suitable laptop for use in the administrative offices of a supermarket chain. The purchasing department, composed of three decision-makers, is tasked with evaluating various laptop options and determining the most appropriate choice that meets multiple technical and financial requirements. This problem is well-suited for an MCDM framework, particularly due to the presence of several conflicting evaluation criteria. To simplify the example and make it more suitable for the initial stages of the learning process, some alternatives and criteria have been intentionally omitted. To solve this problem, the MULTIMOORA method is applied. This approach, known for its robust and transparent structure, integrates three decision-making techniques: the ratio system, the reference point approach, and the full multiplicative form. These methods work together to evaluate and rank alternatives based on both beneficial and nonbeneficial criteria. In this case, six laptop alternatives, labeled A_1 to A_6, are considered. Each laptop is evaluated based on six criteria: processor speed (GHz), storage capacity (GB), RAM (GB), brand reliability (on a scale from 1 to 10), weight (in kg), and cost (in Turkish Lira). Among these, the first four criteria are beneficial, meaning that higher values are preferred, while the last two—weight and cost—are nonbeneficial, where lower values are considered more desirable. The final weights of the criteria derived from the analytic hierarchy process method are represented in Table 48.1. The decision matrix, which includes the performance values of all six alternatives across the six criteria, is shown in Table 48.2. This matrix serves as the basis for applying the MULTIMOORA method to rank the alternatives and identify the most suitable laptop for the organization's needs.

TABLE 48.1 The weights of the criteria.

w_j	w_1	w_2	w_3	w_4	w_5	w_6
	0.4641	0.0391	0.0547	0.1188	0.2406	0.0828

TABLE 48.2 Decision matrix.

Alternatives	C_1^+	C_2^+	C_3^+	C_4^+	C_5^-	C_6^-
A_1	3.50	1256.00	16.00	8.00	2.82	4100.00
A_2	3.10	1000.00	8.00	5.00	3.08	3800.00
A_3	3.60	2000.00	16.00	5.00	2.90	4000.00
A_4	3.00	1000.00	8.00	5.00	2.60	3500.00
A_5	3.30	1008.00	12.00	8.00	2.30	3800.00
A_6	3.60	1000.00	16.00	5.00	2.80	4000.00

TABLE 48.3 Normalized decision matrix.

Alternatives	C_1^+	C_2^+	C_3^+	C_4^+	C_5^-	C_6^-
A_1	0.4255	0.4055	0.4961	0.5298	0.4170	0.4323
A_2	0.3768	0.3229	0.2481	0.3311	0.4554	0.4007
A_3	0.4376	0.6457	0.4961	0.3311	0.4288	0.4218
A_4	0.3647	0.3229	0.2481	0.3311	0.3844	0.3691
A_5	0.4012	0.3254	0.3721	0.5298	0.3401	0.4007
A_6	0.4376	0.3229	0.4961	0.3311	0.4140	0.4218

To apply the ratio system method, the decision matrix is first normalized using vector normalization (Table 48.3). For example, to normalize the value for alternative A_1 under all criteria, the values are divided by the square root of the sum of squares of all values in each criterion. The resulting normalized value for A_1 under each criterion is calculated as follows:

$$x_{11}^* = \frac{3.50}{\sqrt{(3.50)^2 + (3.10)^2 + (3.60)^2 + (3.00)^2 + (3.30)^2 + (3.60)^2}} = 0.4255$$

$$x_{12}^* = \frac{1256.00}{\sqrt{(1256.00)^2 + (1000.00)^2 + (2000.00)^2 + (1000.00)^2 + (1008.00)^2 + (1000.00)^2}} = 0.4055$$

$$x_{13}^* = \frac{16.00}{\sqrt{(16.00)^2 + (8.00)^2 + (16.00)^2 + (8.00)^2 + (12.00)^2 + (16.00)^2}} = 0.4961$$

$$x_{14}^* = \frac{8.00}{\sqrt{(8.00)^2 + (5.00)^2 + (5.00)^2 + (5.00)^2 + (8.00)^2 + (5.00)^2}} = 0.5298$$

$$x_{15}^* = \frac{2.82}{\sqrt{(2.82)^2 + (3.08)^2 + (2.90)^2 + (2.60)^2 + (2.30)^2 + (2.80)^2}} = 0.4170$$

$$x_{16}^* = \frac{4100.00}{\sqrt{(4100.00)^2 + (3800.00)^2 + (4000.00)^2 + (3500.00)^2 + (3800.00)^2 + (4000.00)^2}} = 0.4323$$

This process is repeated for all alternatives and criteria to generate the normalized decision matrix.

Each normalized value is then multiplied by its respective weight, resulting in a weighted normalized decision matrix (Table 48.4). For example, the weighted normalized value for alternative A_1 under all criteria is calculated by multiplying

TABLE 48.4 Weighted normalized decision matrix.

Alternatives	C_1^+	C_2^+	C_3^+	C_4^+	C_5^-	C_6^-
A_1	0.1974	0.0158	0.0271	0.0629	0.1003	0.0358
A_2	0.1749	0.0126	0.0136	0.0393	0.1096	0.0332
A_3	0.2031	0.0252	0.0271	0.0393	0.1032	0.0349
A_4	0.1692	0.0126	0.0136	0.0393	0.0925	0.0306
A_5	0.1862	0.0127	0.0203	0.0629	0.0818	0.0332
A_6	0.2031	0.0126	0.0271	0.0393	0.0996	0.0349

TABLE 48.5 Overall performance of alternatives in the ratio system.

Alternatives	$\Sigma_{j=1}^{g} w_j x_{ij}^*$	$\Sigma_{j=g+1}^{n} w_j x_{ij}^*$	y_i	Ranking
A_1	0.3033	0.1361	0.1672	1
A_2	0.2404	0.1428	0.0976	6
A_3	0.2948	0.1381	0.1567	3
A_4	0.2347	0.1231	0.1117	5
A_5	0.2821	0.1150	0.1671	2
A_6	0.2822	0.1346	0.1476	4

the normalized values by the weight vector $w = (0.4641,\ 0.0391,\ 0.0547,\ 0.1188,\ 0.2406,\ 0.0828)$. Below is the step-by-step calculation:

Weighted value for A1 under C1 → $w_1 x_{11}^* = 0.4641 \times 0.4255 = 0.1974$
Weighted value for A1 under C2 → $w_2 x_{12}^* = 0.0391 \times 0.4055 = 0.0158$
Weighted value for A1 under C3 → $w_3 x_{13}^* = 0.0547 \times 0.4961 = 0.0271$
Weighted value for A1 under C4 → $w_4 x_{14}^* = 0.1188 \times 0.5298 = 0.0629$
Weighted value for A1 under C5 → $w_5 x_{15}^* = 0.2406 \times 0.4170 = 0.1003$
Weighted value for A1 under C6 → $w_6 x_{16}^* = 0.0828 \times 0.4323 = 0.0358$

This calculation is repeated for all alternatives and criteria.

The overall performance score of each alternative is calculated by summing the weighted normalized values corresponding to beneficial criteria and subtracting the sum of the weighted normalized values for nonbeneficial criteria (Table 48.5). For example, for alternative A_1, the sum for the beneficial criteria is:

$$0.1974 + 0.0158 + 0.0271 + 0.0629 = 0.3033$$

And the sum for nonbeneficial criteria is:

$$0.1003 + 0.0358 = 0.1361$$

Thus, the overall performance score for A_1 is:

$$y_i = 0.3033 - 0.1361 = 0.1672$$

This calculation is repeated for all alternatives, and the alternative with the highest score is ranked as the best. According to the results, alternative A_1 achieves the highest score and is therefore ranked first under the ratio system.

In the next stage, the reference point approach is applied to the normalized decision matrix. A reference point is constructed using the best performance values across all criteria. For beneficial criteria (C_1 to C_4), the maximum normalized value among alternatives is chosen, and for nonbeneficial criteria (C_5 and C_6), the minimum value is selected. The reference point values for this case are:

$$r_j = (0.4376,\ 0.6457,\ 0.4961,\ 0.5298,\ 0.3401,\ 0.3691)$$

The Chebyshev metric is used to compute the maximum deviation of each alternative from the ideal reference point. For each alternative, z_i is calculated as follows:

$$z_i = \max_j d_{ij} = \max_j \{ |w_j r_j - w_j x_{ij}^*| \} = \max_j \{ w_j .\ |r_j - x_{ij}^*| \}$$

Where x_{ij}^* is the normalized value of the alternative A_i for criterion j, and w_j is the weight of criterion j. The details of the calculation for A_1 are represented as:

$$z_1 = \max \left\{ \begin{array}{l} |0.4641 \times (0.4376 - 0.4255)|, \\ |0.0391 \times (0.6457 - 0.4055)|, \\ |0.0547 \times (0.4961 - 0.4961)|, \\ |0.1188 \times (0.5298 - 0.5298)|, \\ |0.2406 \times (0.3401 - 0.4170)|, \\ |0.0828 \times (0.3691 - 0.4323)| \end{array} \right\} = \max\ \{0.0056,\ 0.0094,\ 0.0000,\ 0.0000,\ 0.0185,\ 0.0052\} = 0.0185$$

The alternatives are then ranked based on their z_i values, with smaller deviations indicating better performance. According to this method, alternative A_5 achieves the best ranking, exhibiting the least deviation from the reference point. The results of the reference point approach are summarized in Table 48.6.

Finally, the full multiplicative form is used to assess each alternative's overall utility. In this step, the normalized decision matrix is used. The utility score of each alternative is calculated by taking the product of the values of all beneficial criteria raised to their respective weights, divided by the product of the values of all nonbeneficial criteria raised to their respective weights. Higher utility scores indicate better performance. For example, the calculation for alternative A_1 is:

$$u_1 = \frac{(0.4255)^{0.4641} \times (0.4055)^{0.0391} \times (0.4961)^{0.0547} \times (0.5298)^{0.1188}}{(0.4170)^{0.2406} \times (0.4323)^{0.0828}} = \frac{0.5795}{0.7558} = 0.7667$$

According to this method, alternative A_5 achieves the highest utility score and secures the top rank, as shown in Table 48.7.

The final aggregated rankings of alternatives in MULTIMOORA are determined using dominance theory, which evaluates each alternative's relative performance across the three methods. Absolute Dominance occurs when an alternative consistently outperforms all others across all methods. In this case, alternative A_3, with identical ranks (3–3–3) across all submethods, exhibits absolute dominance relative to alternatives ranked lower overall. The other alternatives demonstrate general dominance, where they outperform others in two out of three methods but not consistently across all.

TABLE 48.6 Distance from the reference points and overall performance of alternatives in the reference point approach.

Alternatives	C_1^+	C_2^+	C_3^+	C_4^+	C_5^-	C_6^-	z_i	Ranking
A_1	0.0056	0.0094	0.0000	0.0000	0.0185	0.0052	0.0185	2
A_2	0.0282	0.0126	0.0136	0.0236	0.0278	0.0026	0.0282	5
A_3	0.0000	0.0000	0.0000	0.0236	0.0213	0.0044	0.0236	3
A_4	0.0338	0.0126	0.0136	0.0236	0.0107	0.0000	0.0338	6
A_5	0.0169	0.0125	0.0068	0.0000	0.0000	0.0026	0.0169	1
A_6	0.0000	0.0126	0.0000	0.0236	0.0178	0.0044	0.0236	3
r_j	0.4376	0.6457	0.4961	0.5298	0.3401	0.3691	-	-

TABLE 48.7 Overall performance of alternatives in the full multiplicative form.

Alternatives	$\Pi_{j=1}^{g} (x_{ij}^{*})^{w_j}$	$\Pi_{j=g+1}^{n} (x_{ij}^{*})^{w_j}$	u_i	Ranking
A_1	0.5795	0.7558	0.7667	2
A_2	0.4943	0.7672	0.6443	6
A_3	0.5654	0.7594	0.7446	3
A_4	0.4869	0.7316	0.6655	5
A_5	0.5503	0.7151	0.7695	1
A_6	0.5503	0.7530	0.7308	4

TABLE 48.8 Final aggregated ranking of the MULTIMOORA method based on the dominance theory.

Alternatives	Ratio system	Reference point approach	Full multiplicative form	Dominance theory
A_1	1	2	2	**2**
A_2	6	5	6	**6**
A_3	3	3	3	**3**
A_4	5	6	5	**5**
A_5	2	1	1	**1**
A_6	4	3	4	**4**

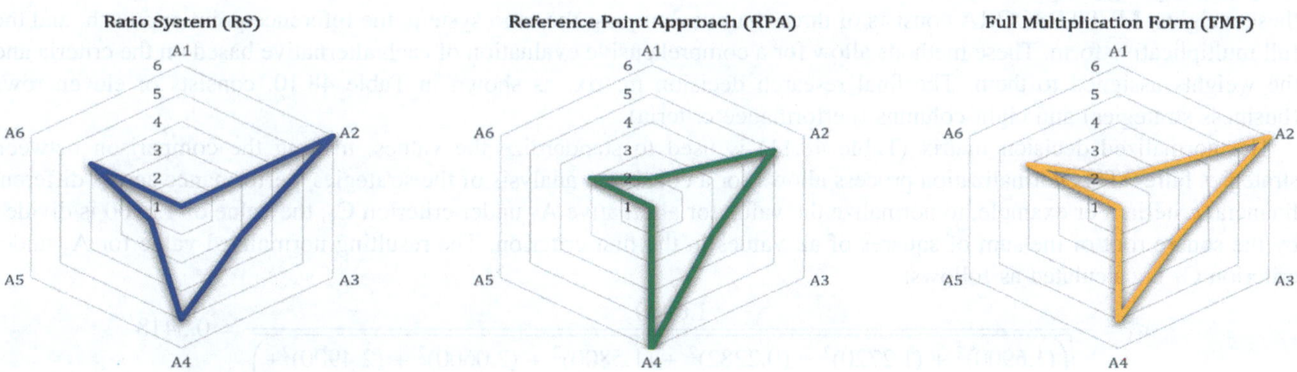

FIGURE 48.2 Subrankings of the MULTIMOORA method.

For example, A_5 ranks (2–1–1), dominating most alternatives and thus is assigned a final aggregated rank of 1, while A_1, with ranks (1–2–2), performs well in two methods and is assigned a final rank of 2. Similarly, the remaining alternatives are ranked based on their relative performance across methods. The final aggregated rankings are shown in Table 48.8, and Fig. 48.2 illustrates the rankings of the alternatives in each segment of the MULTIMOORA method. This case study demonstrates the practical application of MULTIMOORA in a real-world engineering and procurement context, and the consistent rankings across all three techniques highlight the robustness of the method and its ability to support reliable and well-informed MCDM.

48.5 Numerical example 2: evaluation of business strategies (complex real case)

This case study, designed by Ghaemi-Zadeh & Eghbalizarch (2024), evaluates business strategies of four different types of corporations based on their financial performance and the behavior of investors, loan-holders, and stockholders. The business strategies being analyzed are defenders, analyzers, reactors, and prospectors, with each strategy being evaluated at three levels: low, medium, and high. These strategies represent different approaches to competition within a business environment, as classified by Miles & Snow (1978). The defenders strategy focuses on maintaining a stable position within a mature market, offering a limited range of products and emphasizing operational efficiency. Analyzers adopt a balanced approach, innovating slowly while protecting their established markets. Reactors, on the other hand, lack a clear and consistent strategy and only react to external pressures and changes, rather than proactively shaping their market positions. The prospectors strategy is characterized by innovation, actively seeking new products and markets to fuel growth. The goal of this case study is to identify which business strategy yields the highest returns and is the most effective in maximizing benefits for all stakeholders. To achieve this, the authors employ an MCDM approach, integrating two powerful methods: the distance correlation-based criteria importance through intercriteria correlation (D-CRITIC) weighting method and the MULTIMOORA ranking method. These techniques help evaluate the business strategies by assessing the companies' financial performance using multiple criteria.

The first step in this evaluation process involves defining the alternatives (the business strategies) and the criteria by which they will be assessed. The financial performance criteria chosen for this analysis include current ratio, which measures the company's ability to cover its short-term liabilities with its short-term assets; inventory turnover ratio, which shows how efficiently a company is managing its inventory and selling products; liability ratio, which indicates the proportion of the company's assets financed by debt, reflecting its financial risk; earnings per share, which reflects the earnings attributable to each share of stock, a key metric for stockholders; return on sales, indicating the company's profitability in relation to its sales; return on assets, which measures how effectively a company is using its assets to generate profits; share price to earnings ratio, which provides insight into the company's stock valuation relative to its earnings; and sales growth ratio, which indicates the company's success in increasing its sales over time. These eight criteria are essential for assessing a company's overall financial health and the potential success of its business strategy. Once the alternatives and criteria are established, a decision matrix is created, where the financial data of each company is placed under the corresponding business strategy. The decision matrix reflects the performance of each strategy across all selected criteria. The next step is to determine the importance of each criterion in the decision-making process, for which the D-CRITIC method is applied. This method uses standard deviation to measure the variation within each criterion and distance correlation to account for the interdependence of variables. By examining the variability and correlation of each criterion, the D-CRITIC method assigns weights to the criteria based on their relative importance, as represented in Table 48.9.

After assigning weights to the criteria, the MULTIMOORA method is used to rank the business strategies based on these weights. MULTIMOORA consists of three main techniques: the ratio system, the reference point approach, and the full multiplicative form. These methods allow for a comprehensive evaluation of each alternative based on the criteria and the weights assigned to them. The final research decision matrix, as shown in Table 48.10, consists of eleven rows (business strategies) and eight columns (performance criteria).

The normalized decision matrix (Table 48.11) is used to standardize the values, making the comparison between strategies fairer. This normalization process allows for a consistent analysis of the strategies' performance across different financial criteria. For example, to normalize the value for alternative A_1 under criterion C_1, the value of 1.6900 is divided by the square root of the sum of squares of all values in the first criterion. The resulting normalized value for A_1 under criterion C_1 is calculated as follows:

$$x_{11}^{*} = \frac{1.6900}{\sqrt{\begin{pmatrix}(1.6900)^2 + (1.2720)^2 + (0.2282)^2 + (1.5800)^2 + (2.0600)^2 + (2.4900)^2 + \\ (1.5200)^2 + (1.4800)^2 + (1.4600)^2 + (0.2600)^2 + (0.5300)^2\end{pmatrix}}} = 0.3418$$

This process is repeated for all alternatives and criteria to generate the normalized decision matrix.

TABLE 48.9 The weights of the criteria.

w_j	w_1	w_2	w_3	w_4	w_5	w_6	w_7	w_8
	0.0948	0.2526	0.1292	0.0776	0.1204	0.0291	0.1487	0.1476

TABLE 48.10 Decision matrix.

Alternatives	C_1^+	C_2^+	C_3^-	C_4^+	C_5^+	C_6^+	C_7^-	C_8^+
A_1	1.6900	13.5300	0.3900	218.00	1.8600	8.1100	29.5000	0.0500
A_2	1.2720	32.9600	0.2699	352.00	22.9556	18.5326	10.0100	0.5200
A_3	0.2282	3.35000	0.7172	1039.00	16.4527	9.3153	7.3700	0.2200
A_4	1.5800	141.920	0.3581	2085.00	42.4652	35.0527	6.2254	0.5200
A_5	2.0600	219.360	0.2600	6448.00	59.9400	61.5000	5.6200	0.7300
A_6	2.4900	137.790	0.3700	1482.67	39.8300	31.5500	5.7600	0.8500
A_7	1.5200	252.170	0.5200	2557.00	29.5600	14.9500	13.2000	0.1400
A_8	1.4800	207.210	0.5900	2473.33	35.8500	20.7100	6.7400	0.4100
A_9	1.4600	147.420	0.7000	465.00	3.6099	5.1944	30.2151	-0.010
A_{10}	0.2600	0.1400	0.8600	724.00	76.8700	4.5400	19.3785	0.7913
A_{11}	0.5300	55.1600	0.8000	-126.00	-13.2729	-9.6383	-9.0159	1.5300

TABLE 48.11 Normalized decision matrix.

Alternatives	C_1^+	C_2^+	C_3^-	C_4^+	C_5^+	C_6^+	C_7^-	C_8^+
A_1	0.3418	0.0289	0.2067	0.0275	0.0147	0.0950	0.5659	0.0224
A_2	0.2573	0.0703	0.1430	0.0444	0.1812	0.2170	0.1920	0.2325
A_3	0.0462	0.0071	0.3801	0.1311	0.1299	0.1091	0.1414	0.0984
A_4	0.3196	0.3027	0.1898	0.2631	0.3353	0.4104	0.1194	0.2325
A_5	0.4166	0.4679	0.1378	0.8138	0.4733	0.7200	0.1078	0.3264
A_6	0.5036	0.2939	0.1961	0.1871	0.3145	0.3694	0.1105	0.3801
A_7	0.3074	0.5378	0.2756	0.3227	0.2334	0.1750	0.2532	0.0626
A_8	0.2993	0.4419	0.3127	0.3121	0.2831	0.2425	0.1293	0.1833
A_9	0.2953	0.3144	0.3710	0.0587	0.0285	0.0608	0.5796	-0.0045
A_{10}	0.0526	0.0003	0.4558	0.0914	0.6069	0.0532	0.3717	0.3538
A_{11}	0.1072	0.1176	0.4240	-0.0159	-0.1048	-0.1128	-0.1729	0.6841

Next, the ratio system method and the reference point method are applied to the normalized decision matrix to evaluate the overall performance of the alternatives. These techniques are summarized in Tables 48.12 and 48.13, showing how each strategy ranks based on different aspects of the decision-making process. In the full multiplicative form, Table 48.14 presents the results based on this final method, which evaluates the overall utility of each alternative. The ratio system evaluates each alternative by summing the weighted beneficial criteria and subtracting the weighted nonbeneficial criteria. For A_1, the calculation is:

$$y_1 = \begin{pmatrix} (0.0948 \times 0.3418)+ \\ (0.2526 \times 0.0289)+ \\ (0.0776 \times 0.0275)+ \\ (0.1204 \times 0.0147)+ \\ (0.0291 \times 0.0950)+ \\ (0.1476 \times 0.0224) \end{pmatrix} - \begin{pmatrix} (0.1292 \times 0.2067)+ \\ (0.1487 \times 0.5659) \end{pmatrix} = (0.0497 - 0.1108) = -0.0612$$

TABLE 48.12 Overall performance of alternatives in the ratio system.

Alternatives	$\Sigma_{j=1}^{g} w_j x_{ij}^*$	$\Sigma_{j=g+1}^{n} w_j x_{ij}^*$	y_i	Ranking
A_1	0.0497	0.1108	-0.0612	11
A_2	0.1080	0.0470	0.0610	7
A_3	0.0497	0.0701	-0.0205	10
A_4	0.2138	0.0423	0.1715	4
A_5	0.3469	0.0338	0.3131	1
A_6	0.2412	0.0418	0.1994	2
A_7	0.2325	0.0733	0.1592	5
A_8	0.2324	0.0596	0.1728	3
A_9	0.1165	0.1341	-0.0176	9
A_{10}	0.1390	0.1142	0.0248	8
A_{11}	0.1237	0.0291	0.0946	6

TABLE 48.13 Distance from the reference points and overall performance of alternatives in the reference point method.

Alternatives	C_1^+	C_2^+	C_3^-	C_4^+	C_5^+	C_6^+	C_7^-	C_8^+	z_i	Ranking
A_1	0.015	0.129	0.009	0.061	0.071	0.018	0.110	0.098	0.129	9
A_2	0.023	0.118	0.001	0.060	0.051	0.015	0.054	0.067	0.118	8
A_3	0.043	0.134	0.031	0.053	0.057	0.018	0.047	0.086	0.134	10
A_4	0.017	0.059	0.007	0.043	0.033	0.009	0.043	0.067	0.067	3
A_5	0.008	0.018	0.000	0.000	0.016	0.000	0.042	0.053	0.053	1
A_6	0.000	0.062	0.008	0.049	0.035	0.010	0.042	0.045	0.062	2
A_7	0.019	0.000	0.018	0.038	0.045	0.016	0.063	0.092	0.092	5
A_8	0.019	0.024	0.023	0.039	0.039	0.014	0.045	0.074	0.074	4
A_9	0.020	0.056	0.030	0.059	0.070	0.019	0.112	0.102	0.112	7
A_{10}	0.043	0.136	0.041	0.056	0.000	0.019	0.081	0.049	0.136	11
A_{11}	0.038	0.106	0.037	0.064	0.086	0.024	0.000	0.000	0.106	6

Thus, A_1 obtains a negative performance score under the ratio system, ranked 11th in Table 48.12. In the reference point approach, the best performance values across all criteria are chosen as the reference point vector:

$r_j = (0.5036,\ 0.5378,\ 0.1378,\ 0.8138,\ 0.6069,\ 0.7200,\ -0.1729,\ 0.6841)$

The Chebyshev metric is applied to measure the weighted distance of each alternative from this reference. For A_1:

$$z_1 = \max\left\{\begin{array}{l} |0.0948 \times (+0.5036 - 0.3418)|, \\ |0.2526 \times (+0.5378 - 0.0289)|, \\ |0.1292 \times (+0.1378 - 0.2067)|, \\ |0.0776 \times (+0.8138 - 0.0275)|, \\ |0.1204 \times (+0.6069 - 0.0147)|, \\ |0.0291 \times (+0.7200 - 0.0950)|, \\ |0.1487 \times (-0.1729 - 0.5659)|, \\ |0.1476 \times (+0.6841 - 0.0224)| \end{array}\right\} = \max\{0.0153,\ 0.1285,\ 0.0089,\ 0.0610,\ 0.0713,\ 0.0182,\ 0.1099,\ 0.0977\} = 0.1285$$

TABLE 48.14 Overall performance of alternatives in the full multiplicative form.

Alternatives	$\Pi_{j=1}^{g}(x_{ij}^{*})^{w_j}$	$\Pi_{j=g+1}^{n}(x_{ij}^{*})^{w_j}$	u_i	Ranking
A_1	0.0895	0.7495	0.1194	10
A_2	0.2217	0.6085	0.3643	6
A_3	0.0954	0.6598	0.1446	9
A_4	0.4121	0.5882	0.7007	3
A_5	0.5737	0.5558	1.0321	1
A_6	0.4424	0.5839	0.7578	2
A_7	0.3712	0.6902	0.5378	5
A_8	0.4255	0.6348	0.6703	4
A_9	0.1444	0.8112	0.1780	8
A_{10}	0.0600	0.7798	0.0769	11
A_{11}	0.2311	0.6894	0.3352	7

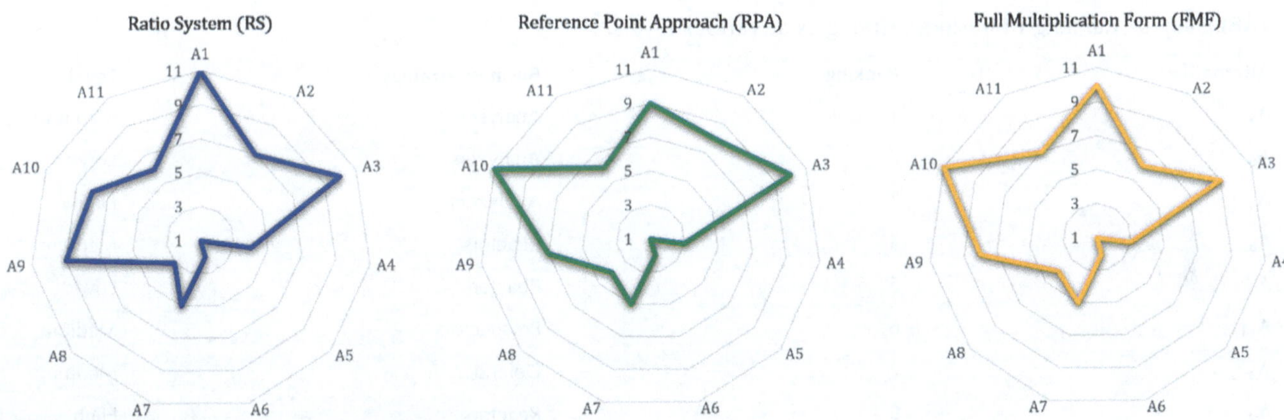

FIGURE 48.3 Subrankings of the MULTIMOORA method.

Therefore, A_1's deviation from the reference point is 0.1285, ranking it ninth in Table 48.13. The full multiplicative form computes the ratio of the product of beneficial criteria to the product of nonbeneficial criteria; each raised to their respective weights. The details of the calculations for A_1 are shown as follows:

$$u_1 = \frac{(0.3418)^{0.0948} \times (0.0289)^{0.2526} \times (0.0275)^{0.0776} \times (0.0147)^{0.1204} \times (0.0950)^{0.0291} \times (0.0224)^{0.1476}}{(0.2067)^{0.1292} \times (0.5659)^{0.1487}} = \frac{0.0895}{0.7495}$$

$$= 0.1194$$

Hence, A_1 achieves a utility score of 0.1194, placing it 10th overall in Table 48.14.

Fig. 48.3 demonstrates the ranking of the assumed alternatives in each segment of the MULTIMOORA method.

Ultimately, the rankings from all three methods are aggregated using dominance theory to obtain a final ranking, as shown in Table 48.15. The dominance theory approach helps synthesize the results from each method, leading to a clear ranking of the strategies based on their overall performance. The business strategy rankings at various levels (low, medium, and high) are summarized in Table 48.16, providing insights into which strategies are most effective depending on their strategic positioning. For instance, analyzers consistently perform well at all levels, while prospectors rank poorly

TABLE 48.15 Final aggregated ranking of the MULTIMOORA method based on the dominance theory.

Alternatives	Ratio system	Reference point approach	Full multiplication form	Dominance theory
A_1	11	9	10	**9**
A_2	7	8	6	**7**
A_3	10	10	9	**10**
A_4	4	3	3	**3**
A_5	1	1	1	**1**
A_6	2	2	2	**2**
A_7	5	5	5	**5**
A_8	3	4	4	**4**
A_9	9	7	8	**8**
A_{10}	8	11	11	**11**
A_{11}	6	6	7	**6**

TABLE 48.16 Ranking of business strategies at various levels.

Alternatives	Ranking	Business strategy	Level
A_5	1	Analyzers	Medium
A_6	2	Analyzers	Low
A_4	3	Analyzers	High
A_8	4	Reactors	Medium
A_7	5	Reactors	Low
A_{11}	6	Prospectors	Medium
A_2	7	Defenders	Medium
A_9	8	Reactors	High
A_1	9	Defenders	High
A_3	10	Defenders	Low
A_{10}	11	Prospectors	Low

across the board. This study provides a comprehensive, data-driven evaluation of business strategies, offering valuable insights for decision-makers to select the optimal strategy based on financial performance and stakeholder needs.

Based on dominance theory, each alternative can be classified according to its ranking pattern. Alternatives A_5 (1–1–1), A_6 (2–2–2), and A_7 (5–5–5) demonstrate absolute dominance, since they hold identical ranks across all three methods. Alternatives A_3 (10–10–9), A_4 (4–3–3), A_8 (3–4–4), A_{10} (8–11–11), and A_{11} (6–6–7) exhibit general dominance, as they outperform weaker strategies in at least two out of three methods. In contrast, A_1 (11–9–10), A_2 (7–8–6), and A_9 (9–7–8) show no dominance, with mixed or unstable performance across the three evaluation approaches. When comparing these nondominant strategies directly, a clearer hierarchy emerges. Between A_1, A_2, and A_9, alternative A_2 (7–8–6) dominates both A_1 and A_9, since it consistently performs better in two methods. A_9 (9–7–8) performs moderately, ranking above A_1 but below A_2. A_1 (11–9–10) is the weakest of the three, as it lags behind in nearly all evaluations.

48.6 Conclusions

MULTIMOORA is a powerful MCDM method that integrates three subordinate ranking techniques—ratio system, reference point approach, and full multiplicative form—to provide a comprehensive decision-making framework. It has gained widespread attention due to its ability to handle complex problems involving multiple alternatives and criteria. MULTIMOORA's key strengths include its higher accuracy in decision-making by integrating multiple decision outcomes, its capability to tackle complex problems, and its relatively fast computation speed. Despite these advantages, MULTIMOORA faces several challenges. The method's reliance on various normalization techniques, ranking aggregation tools, and criteria weighting methods can increase computational cost, particularly when the decision-making process involves uncertainty or complex data structures like fuzzy sets. Future research should explore ways to optimize the method's computational efficiency. This could include developing more efficient algorithms or integrating MULTIMOORA with other models, such as artificial neural networks or risk management techniques. Moreover, incorporating uncertainty theories, such as fuzzy logic and neutrosophic sets, could enhance its robustness and applicability in uncertain environments. Another challenge lies in group decision-making. In real-world scenarios, decision-makers often possess different levels of expertise, and their subjective judgments can influence the outcome. Future studies should investigate multilevel group decision-making models, where a senior decision-maker holds more influence, or cooperative and noncooperative decision-making structures. This would improve MULTIMOORA's adaptability in organizational settings. Additionally, the integration of ranking aggregation tools could help improve the decision-making process by combining results from multiple ranking systems.

References

Altuntas, S., Dereli, T., & Kemal Yılmaz, M. (2015). Evaluation of excavator technologies: Application of data fusion-based MULTIMOORA methods. *Journal of Civil Engineering and Management, 21*(8), 977–997.

Asante, D., He, Z., Adjei, N. O., & Asante, B. (2020). Exploring the barriers to renewable energy adoption utilising the MULTIMOORA- EDAS method. *Energy Policy, 142*, 111479.

Aytaç Adalı, E., & Tuş Işık, A. (2017). The multi-objective decision-making methods based on MULTIMOORA and MOOSRA for the laptop selection problem. *Journal of Industrial Engineering International, 13*(2), 229–237.

Brauers, W., & Zavadskas, E. (2006). The MOORA method and its application to privatization in a transition economy. *Control Cybern, 35*(2), 445–469.

Brauers, W. K. M., & Zavadskas, E. K. (2010). Project management by MULTIMOORA as an instrument for transition economies. *Technological and Economic Development of Economy, 16*(1), 5–24.

Brauers, W. K. M., & Zavadskas, E. K. (2012). Robustness of MULTIMOORA: A method for multi-objective optimization. *Informatica, 23*(1), 1–25.

Brauers, W. K. M., Zavadskas, E. K., Peldschus, F., & Turskis, Z. (2008). Multi-objective decision-making for road design. *Transport, 23*(3), 183–193.

Chen, W., Jiang, X., Huang, N., Huang, Y., Yong, X., & Xu, C. (2024). A two-stage framework for site selection of deep-sea offshore wind-to-hydrogen projects based on GIS - MULTIMOORA method under Pythagorean triangular fuzzy environment. *Ocean Engineering, 313*, 119416.

Chen, X., Zhao, L., & Liang, H. (2018). A novel multi-attribute group decision-making method based on the MULTIMOORA with linguistic evaluations. *Soft Computing, 22*(16), 5347–5361.

Chen, Y., Ran, Y., Huang, G., Xiao, L., & Zhang, G. (2021). A new integrated MCDM approach for improving QFD based on DEMATEL and extended MULTIMOORA under uncertainty environment. *Applied Soft Computing, 105*, 107222.

Chen, Y., Ran, Y., Wang, Z., Li, X., Yang, X., & Zhang, G. (2020). An extended MULTIMOORA method based on OWGA operator and Choquet integral for risk prioritization identification of failure modes. *Engineering Applications of Artificial Intelligence, 91*, 103605.

Eghbalizarch, M., Tavakkoli-Moghaddam, R., Esfahanian, F., Sepehri, M. M., & Azaron, A. (2018). Pharmacological therapy selection of type 2 diabetes based on the SWARA and modified MULTIMOORA methods under a fuzzy environment. *Artificial Intelligence in Medicine, 87*, 20–33.

Ghaemi-Zadeh, N., & Eghbalizarch, M. (2024). Evaluation of business strategies based on the financial performance of the corporation and investors' behavior using D-CRITIC and fuzzy MULTIMOORA techniques: A real case study. *Expert Systems with Applications, 247*, 123183.

Hafezalkotob, A., & Hafezalkotob, A. (2015). Comprehensive MULTIMOORA method with target-based attributes and integrated significant coefficients for materials selection in biomedical applications. *Materials Design, 87*, 949–959.

Hafezalkotob, A., & Hafezalkotob, A. (2016). Extended MULTIMOORA method based on Shannon entropy weight for materials selection. *Journal of Industrial Engineering International, 12*(1), 1–13.

Hafezalkotob, A., & Hafezalkotob, A. (2017). Interval MULTIMOORA method with target values of attributes based on interval distance and preference degree: Biomaterials selection. *Journal of Industrial Engineering International, 13*(2), 181–198.

Hafezalkotob, A., Hafezalkotob, A., Liao, H., & Herrera, F. (2019). An overview of MULTIMOORA for multi-criteria decision-making: Theory, developments, applications, and challenges. *Information Fusion, 51*, 145–177.

He, J., Huang, Z., Mishra, A. R., & Alrasheedi, M. (2021). Developing a new framework for conceptualizing the emerging sustainable community-based tourism using an extended interval-valued Pythagorean fuzzy SWARA-MULTIMOORA. *Technological Forecasting and Social Change, 171*, 120955.

Liang, D., Linda, B. E., Wang, M., & Xu, Z. (2022). Hospital health-care delivery quality evaluation in Ghana: An integrated medical triangular fuzzy MULTIMOORA approach. *Information Sciences, 605*, 99–118.
Liao, H., Qin, R., Gao, C., Wu, X., Hafezalkotob, A., & Herrera, F. (2019). Score-HeDLiSF: A score function of hesitant fuzzy linguistic term set based on hesitant degrees and linguistic scale functions: An application to unbalanced hesitant fuzzy linguistic MULTIMOORA. *Information Fusion, 48*, 39–54.
Lin, M., Huang, C., & Xu, Z. (2020). MULTIMOORA based MCDM model for site selection of car sharing station under picture fuzzy environment. *Sustainable Cities and Society, 53*, 101873.
Liu, R., Fei, L., & Mi, J. (2022). An evidential MULTIMOORA approach to assessing disaster risk reduction education strategies under a heterogeneous linguistic environment. *International Journal of Disaster Risk Reduction, 78*, 103114.
Miles, R. E., & Snow, C. C. (1978). Organizational strategy, structure and process. *The Academy of Management Review, 3*(3), 546–562.
Nijkamp, P., & Van Delft, A. (1977). Multi-criteria analysis and regional decision-making. *Springer Science Business Media, 8*.
Qin, J., & Ma, X. (2022). An IT2FS-PT 3 based emergency response plan evaluation with MULTIMOORA method in group decision making. *Applied Soft Computing, 122*, 108812.
Rahimi, S., Hafezalkotob, A., Monavari, S. M., Hafezalkotob, A., & Rahimi, R. (2020). Sustainable landfill site selection for municipal solid waste based on a hybrid decision-making approach: Fuzzy group BWM-MULTIMOORA-GIS. *Journal of Cleaner Production, 248*, 119186.
Rani, P., & Mishra, A. R. (2021). Fermatean fuzzy Einstein a1ggregation operators-based MULTIMOORA method for electric vehicle charging station selection. *Expert Systems with Applications, 182*, 115267.
Sarabi, E. P., & Darestani, S. A. (2021). Developing a decision support system for logistics service provider selection employing fuzzy MULTIMOORA BWM in mining equipment manufacturing. *Applied Soft Computing, 98*, 106849.
Shang, Z., Yang, X., Barnes, D., & Wu, C. (2022). Supplier selection in sustainable supply chains: Using the integrated BWM, fuzzy Shannon entropy, and fuzzy MULTIMOORA methods. *Expert Systems with Applications, 195*, 116567.
Siddiqui, Z. A., & Haroon, M. (2023). Research on significant factors affecting adoption of blockchain technology for enterprise distributed applications based on integrated MCDM FCEM-MULTIMOORA-FG method. *Engineering Applications of Artificial Intelligence, 118*, 105699.
Vaezi, A., Rabbani, E., & Yazdian, S. A. (2024). Blockchain-integrated sustainable supplier selection and order allocation: A hybrid BWM-MULTIMOORA and bi-objective programming approach. *Journal of Cleaner Production, 444*, 141216.
Wu, X., Liao, H., Xu, Z., Hafezalkotob, A., & Herrera, F. (2018). Probabilistic linguistic MULTIMOORA: A multicriteria decision making method based on the probabilistic linguistic expectation function and the improved borda rule. *IEEE Transactions on Fuzzy Systems, 26*(6), 3688–3702.
Yu, J., Zeng, Q., Yu, Y., Wu, S., Ding, H., Ma, W., Gao, H., & Yang, J. (2023). Failure mode and effects analysis based on rough cloud model and MULTIMOORA method: Application to single-point mooring system. *Applied Soft Computing, 132*, 109841.
Yucesan, M., Özkan, B., Mete, S., Gul, M., & Özceylan, E. (2024). Evaluating sustainability of urban mobility of Asian cities: An integrated approach of interval type-2 fuzzy best-worst method and MULTIMOORA. *Engineering Applications of Artificial Intelligence, 127*, 107266.
Zhang, C., Wang, B., Li, W., & Li, D. (2024). Incorporating artificial intelligence in detecting crop diseases: Agricultural decision-making based on group consensus model with MULTIMOORA and evidence theory. *Crop Protection, 179*, 106632.
Zhang, X., Li, J., & Wang, N. (2025). Sustainable location selection for photovoltaic waste recycling centers: An extended MULTIMOORA approach. *Sustainable Cities and Society, 124*, 106316.
Zhou, Q., Ye, C., & Geng, X. (2024). A decision framework of offshore wind power station site selection using a MULTIMOORA method under pythagorean hesitant fuzzy environment. *Ocean Engineering, 291*, 116416.

Chapter 49

SAW: Simple additive weighting for multi-attribute decision-making

Saeed Sadeghi Darvazeh, Farzaneh MansooriMooseloo, and Andrés Esteban Acero-López
School of Engineering and Sciences, Tecnológico de Monterrey, Monterrey, Mexico

49.1 Introduction

Decision-making is a core cognitive process that has shaped human progress from early civilization to the modern era (Farooq, 2025). As the complexity of contemporary decision environments increases, driven by globalization, digital transformation, and the proliferation of available alternatives, traditional intuitive approaches are often insufficient for producing consistent and rational outcomes (Akram et al., 2024). To address these challenges, structured decision support systems, particularly those grounded in multi-attribute decision-making (MADM) methodologies, have gained widespread adoption across academic and industrial domains (Sahoo et al., 2025).

MADM techniques provide formal frameworks for evaluating and ranking alternatives in situations where multiple, often conflicting, criteria must be considered (Momena et al., 2024). These methods draw on interdisciplinary foundations in operations research, systems engineering, management science, and behavioral decision theory, making them essential tools in sectors ranging from supply chain management to healthcare and public policy (Kumar & Pamucar, 2025). Among the various MADM techniques, the simple additive weighting (SAW) method stands out due to its simplicity, interpretability, and computational efficiency (Kaliszewski & Podkopaev, 2016).

SAW is particularly well-suited for decision contexts where transparency and ease of implementation are crucial. Unlike more sophisticated approaches such as technique for order of preference by similarity to ideal solution (TOPSIS), VlseKriterijumska Optimizacija i Kompromisno Resenje (VIKOR), Elimination et Choix Traduisant la Realité (ELECTRE), complex proportional assessment, preference ranking organization method for enrichment evaluations (PROMETHEE), the SAW method relies on linear aggregation, allowing decision-makers to intuitively assign weights and directly compute scores for alternatives (Radulescu & Radulescu, 2024). This accessibility has led to its widespread adoption, particularly in resource-constrained environments or among users unfamiliar with complex mathematical modeling.

Over the past two decades, SAW has been applied extensively across a broad range of domains, including supplier selection (Sahu et al., 2023; Suryadi et al., 2025), employee performance evaluation (Mehdi et al., 2024), renewable energy planning (Lotfipour & Mohtavipour, 2024), and transportation systems (Aziz et al., 2020). Fig. 49.1 presents a treemap illustrating the top application fields of the SAW method based on publication frequency. The most significant portion of SAW-related research belongs to the field of engineering electrical and electronic, with 5089 publications, indicating its dominant role in supporting decision-making in technical and engineering systems. This is followed by environmental sciences, with 1849 publications, reflecting the method's growing importance in evaluating sustainability, environmental impact, and policy alternatives. The third most frequent field is computer science information systems, with 1306 publications, highlighting SAW's relevance in areas such as data analysis, information system optimization, and intelligent decision support systems. These top three fields demonstrate the widespread adoption of SAW in both technical and interdisciplinary research domains.

Fig. 49.2 illustrates the annual number of publications related to the SAW from 2005 to 2025. The data reveal a strong upward trend in the use of SAW across academic literature. In 2005, there were 1073 publications, and this number steadily increased over the years, reaching a peak of 5075 in 2024. This growth reflects nearly a fivefold increase in the number of publications over the two-decade period. A particularly sharp rise is observed between 2019 and 2021, where

Encyclopedia of Multi-Attribute Decision-Making (MADM). DOI: https://doi.org/10.1016/B978-0-443-33275-3.00016-6

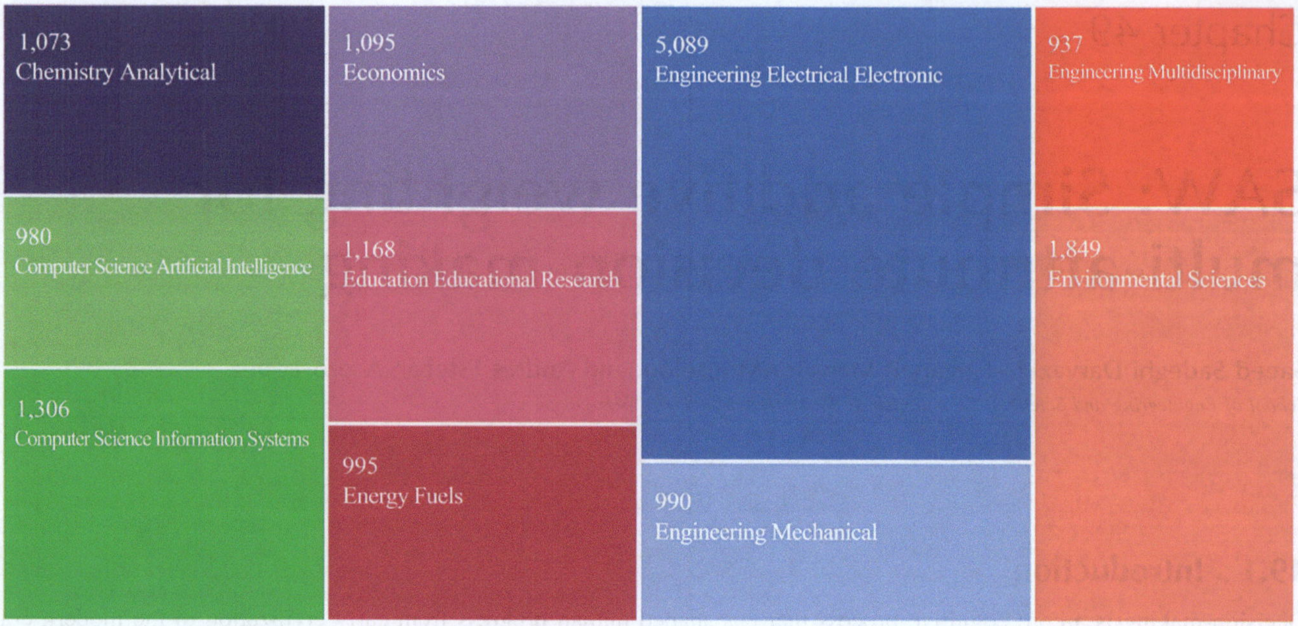

FIGURE 49.1 Top 10 application fields of the simple additive weighting method.

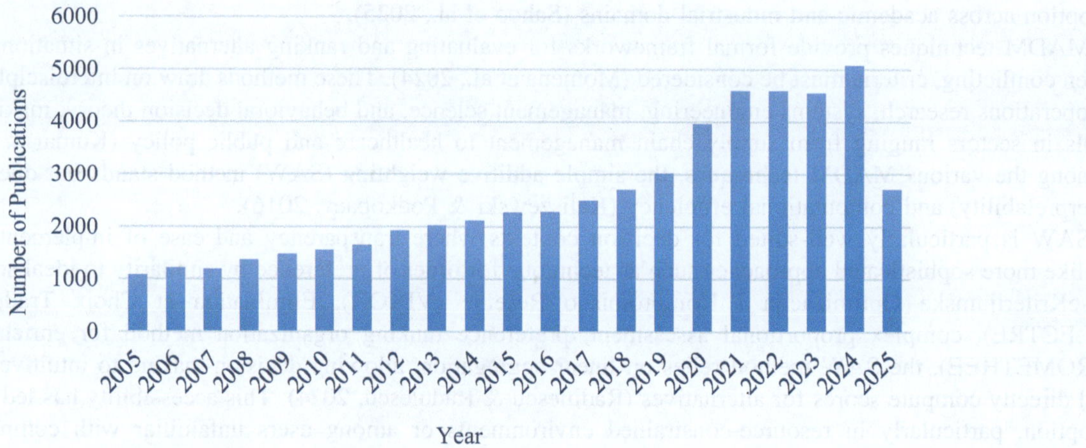

FIGURE 49.2 Number of publications in simple additive weighting applications.

publications increased from 3017 to 4592, indicating a growing interest in decision-making tools such as SAW, possibly driven by global challenges that require structured evaluation approaches. Although the projection for 2025 (2715) appears lower, this may be due to partial data availability for the current year. Overall, the chart underscores the expanding relevance and application of the SAW method in research.

This paper revisits the SAW method from both theoretical and applied perspectives. Following a comprehensive literature review of its applications, the paper details the underlying methodology and presents three illustrative components: (1) a didactic example on car selection, designed as an educational tool for students and practitioners; (2) a real-world case study on supplier selection for Iran's largest e-retailer, demonstrating the method's scalability and practical relevance; and (3) a sensitivity analysis and comparative evaluation with TOPSIS, aimed at highlighting key methodological nuances and the influence of model choice on decision-making outcomes. This study contributes to the MADM body of knowledge by:

- Offering a comprehensive review of SAW applications, thereby illuminating its broad relevance and contextual adaptability;
- Providing a step-by-step methodological guide tailored to both academic and professional audiences;
- Presenting a practitioner-oriented case study that demonstrates the practical implementation of SAW in high-stakes decision environments.

Through these contributions, the paper aims to reaffirm the relevance of the SAW method while equipping decision-makers with practical insights for its effective application in both academic and operational contexts.

The paper is organized as follows: Section 49.2 reviews recent literature on SAW applications, highlighting its development and scope; Section 49.3 explains the steps of the SAW method; Section 49.4 is divided into two subsections, Subsection 49.4.1 presents a simple car selection example to illustrate the technique for teaching purposes, and subsection 4.2 demonstrates SAW's application in a real supplier selection case for Iran's largest e-retailer. Finally, Section 49.5 presents the conclusion, summarizing the findings and suggesting directions for future research.

49.2 Literature review

Reviewing the literature has shown that SAW, as one of the widely used MADM methods in ranking alternatives, has been employed in a variety of fields. In the following subsections, a comprehensive literature review of SAW applications is provided.

49.2.1 Bibliometric analysis

To provide a bibliometric overview of SAW applications, we searched the terms "simple additive weighting" or "SAW" or "weighted sum method" in the web of science database. The search was limited to research articles published between 2005 and 2025. Only English-language journal articles were considered to ensure academic rigor.

Fig. 49.3 highlights the top 10 scholars who have most frequently applied the SAW method in their research. Leading the list is Fu Y.Q., with 141 publications, primarily focused on leveraging SAW for ranking alternatives across various domains. Close behind are Wang W. and Wang Y., with 130 and 125 publications respectively, indicating their significant contributions to advancing the method's application in MADM contexts.

Fig. 49.4 presents the top five journals that have published the highest number of research articles involving the SAW method. PLOS ONE leads with 473 publications, underscoring its strong focus on interdisciplinary research and its relevance to decision-making and operations research. Following closely are the *IEEE transactions on ultrasonics, ferroelectrics, and frequency control* with 281 articles and *scientific reports* with 256, reflecting SAW's broad applicability and growing recognition across diverse scientific and engineering disciplines.

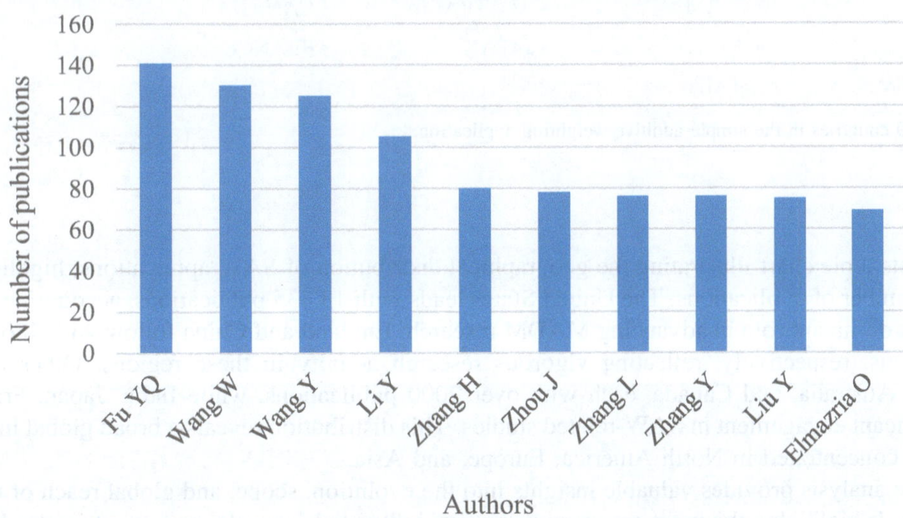

FIGURE 49.3 Top 10 scholars in the simple additive weighting application.

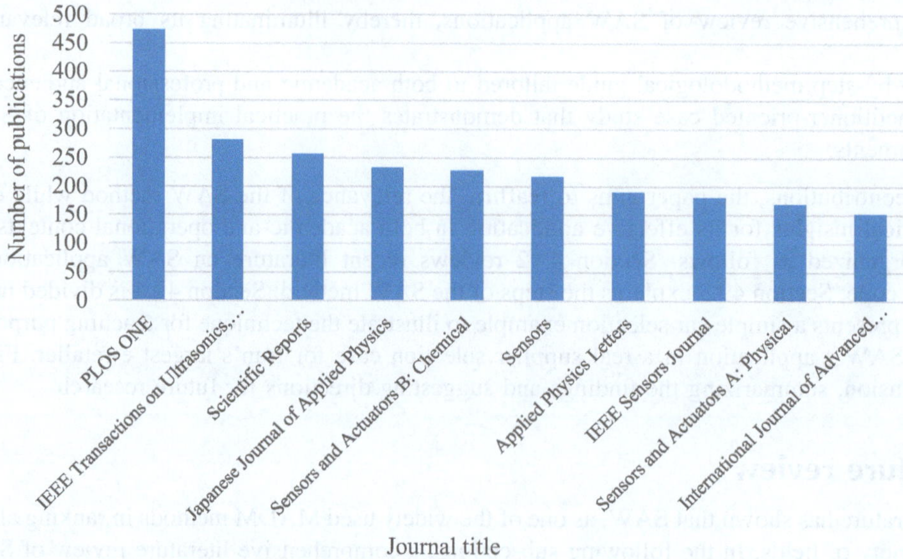

FIGURE 49.4 Top 10 journals in the simple additive weighting application.

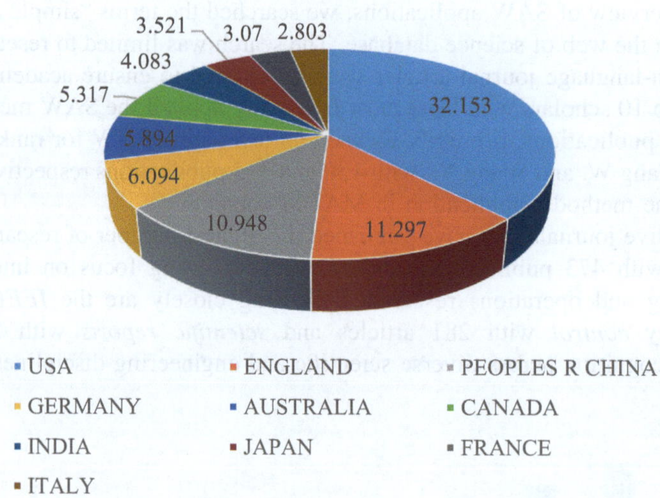

FIGURE 49.5 Top 10 countries in the simple additive weighting application.

Fig. 49.5 presents a pie chart illustrating the geographical distribution of SAW applications, highlighting the countries with the highest number of publications. The United States leads with 13,835 publications, accounting for over 32% of the total, indicating its dominant role in advancing MADM research. England and China follow with 4861 (11.3%) and 4711 (10.9%) publications, respectively, reflecting vigorous research activity in these regions. Other notable contributors include Germany, Australia, and Canada, each with over 2000 publications, while India, Japan, France, and Italy also demonstrate significant engagement in SAW-related studies. This distribution reveals a broad global interest in SAW, with regional strengths concentrated in North America, Europe, and Asia.

The bibliometric analysis provides valuable insights into the evolution, scope, and global reach of the SAW method in academic research. It highlights the most active contributors, influential journals, and countries leading in SAW-related publications, reflecting the method's widespread adoption across disciplines and geographies. These patterns underscore the method's relevance in addressing complex decision-making problems. Building on this quantitative perspective, the following section presents a qualitative analysis to explore the methodological depth and practical applications of SAW in greater detail.

49.2.2 Qualitative analysis

While bibliometric data offers an overview of publication patterns and contributors, a qualitative analysis provides a deeper understanding of how SAW has been applied across various domains and in combination with other methods. The SAW method is one of the most widely used techniques in MADM, valued for its straightforward and intuitive approach. It functions by normalizing data, assigning weights to each criterion based on its importance, and then summing the weighted scores to rank the available alternatives. Due to its simplicity and transparency, SAW has become a popular tool for solving real-world decision-making problems across diverse fields, including logistics, energy, healthcare, education, and supplier evaluation. Its capacity to handle complex decisions involving multiple, sometimes conflicting, criteria makes it particularly practical for real-life situations. In the following sections, we examine the application of SAW in various sectors and highlight key studies that demonstrate its practical relevance and impact.

Table 49.1 summarizes some studies in the SAW application domain (e.g., supply chain, energy, healthcare, environment, manufacturing), integrated techniques (e.g., fuzzy logic, analytic hierarchy process [AHP], VIKOR, TOPSIS), and decision-making contexts (e.g., supplier selection, location analysis, policy evaluation).

The SAW method has been successfully applied across a broad spectrum of real-world domains, reflecting its flexibility in addressing MADM problems. In healthcare, SAW has been used to rank reform priorities, select treatment options, and manage patient-centered care under uncertainty. Environmental and urban planning studies employed SAW for landfill site selection, groundwater potential mapping, air quality monitoring, and subsidence risk evaluation. Industrial and engineering applications include optimizing facility locations, selecting manufacturing equipment, improving electrochemical machining parameters, and refining orthotic designs. In information and communication technologies, SAW has assisted with route selection in logistics, network optimization in wireless systems, and cache placement in networking. Additionally, agriculture, food science, and tourism sectors have adopted SAW for tasks such as banana ripening optimization, DNA extraction comparison, gluten-free bread evaluation, and destination management. These varied applications demonstrate SAW's capacity to structure complex decisions across both technical and social contexts.

While SAW's simplicity makes it attractive, many researchers have extended its capabilities by integrating it with other techniques. Fuzzy logic is one of the most prevalent enhancements, used to handle vagueness and imprecise input data, especially in group decision-making and socio-environmental assessments. Examples include the use of interval type-2 fuzzy sets and oriented fuzzy numbers to preserve uncertainty during evaluation. AHP is another frequently paired method, often used to determine criteria weights before applying SAW. This is evident in studies dealing with healthcare reforms and landfill site selection. Other hybridizations involve data envelopment analysis for benchmarking, Shannon entropy and criteria importance through intercriteria correlation (CRITIC) for objective weight determination, and genetic algorithms or artificial neural networks for optimization tasks. These combinations enhance SAW's robustness, enabling more accurate and context-sensitive decision support.

The literature shows that SAW remains a relevant and adaptable method in MCDM, especially when complemented by other techniques to manage complexity, uncertainty, or large-scale datasets. Compared to other MCDM methods like TOPSIS or best–worst method (BWM), SAW is often preferred for its computational efficiency and interpretability, making it especially suitable in time-sensitive or resource-constrained decision environments. However, studies also highlight SAW's limitations, particularly its sensitivity to criteria weighting and data normalization. By integrating SAW with fuzzy sets, entropy-based weighting, or advanced optimization algorithms, many researchers have successfully overcome these challenges, thus reaffirming SAW's utility in both standalone and hybrid forms. The reviewed applications suggest that SAW will continue to play a significant role in structured decision-making across a broad array of disciplines.

49.3 Methodology

This section outlines the methodological approach used in this study. We adopt the SAW technique, one of the oldest, most intuitive, and widely applied MADM methods. Originating from classical utility theory, SAW is grounded in the concept of additive utility, where overall preference is assumed to be the sum of performance scores across multiple criteria. Its theoretical foundation and operational simplicity have made it a preferred tool in fields such as supply chain optimization, project selection, environmental assessment, and resource allocation.

TABLE 49.1 A summary of prominent studies in simple additive weighting applications.

Authors	Application	Methodology	Key contributions/findings
Chou et al. (2008)	Facility location/supply chain management	Fuzzy SAW + group decision-making	Introduced a fuzzy SAW model for facility location selection using both objective and subjective criteria in a group decision-making context. The model integrated fuzzy sets, factor rating systems, and SAW, and was demonstrated through a numerical example.
Abolhalaj et al. (2012).	Healthcare financial reform (Iran)	SAW + analytic hierarchy process (AHP)	Used SAW and AHP to rank the strengths of Iran's health financial reform. SAW effectively identified managerial support as the most impactful factor. Suggested that further research should identify reform weaknesses.
Shakouri et al. (2014)	Energy (nuclear vs fossil power)	SAW + data envelopment analysis (DEA)	Applied SAW and DEA to compare fossil-fuel and nuclear power plants. Results showed fossil fuel with carbon capture and storage slightly outperformed nuclear. Demonstrated the complementarity of SAW with DEA in energy evaluation.
	Wireless networks	Generalized SAW +game theory	Proposed a novel game-theoretic model using generalized SAW for network selection in heterogeneous wireless networks. The model incorporated user preferences and achieved high network utility.
Chen (2014)	Healthcare decision-making/group MCDM	SAW with type-2 fuzzy sets	Developed an interactive SAW method based on interval type-2 fuzzy sets and signed distances to address incomplete preference information in patient-centered care decisions.
Kek et al. (2018).	Food science/DNA extraction	SAW	Compared DNA extraction methods for honey samples. SAW was used to rank four techniques based on DNA quality, purity, and processing time. The DNeasy method ranked highest.
Abrams et al. (2018).	Environmental science/ groundwater potential	SAW + AHP + Probability frequency ratio	Used SAW alongside AHP and PFR to map groundwater potential in the UAE and Oman using geographic Information Systemand remote sensing. The SAW-based model showed high accuracy when validated with real groundwater data.
Niroomand et al. (2019)	Facility location/industrial planning	Hybrid SAW (interval data + constraints)	Proposed a hybrid SAW approach formulated as a mixed-integer linear model to solve a constrained facility location problem under uncertainty. Demonstrated in Iran's glass industry.
Aziz et al. (2020)	Traffic management/ tourism	SAW + genetic algorithm	Combined SAW with a genetic algorithm to optimize route planning for tourists in congested areas. SAW was used for weighting factors like distance and attraction density.
Piasecki et al. (2019)	Negotiation/decision support	Fuzzy SAW (oriented fuzzy numbers)	Introduced an oriented fuzzy SAW method that avoids defuzzification. Applied to negotiation scoring, retaining more uncertainty information in rankings.
	Real estate/sustainability	SAW versus TOPSIS	Compared SAW and TOPSIS in evaluating real estate project sustainability. Found significant ranking differences; SAW was less sensitive to data variations, making it more stable for specific assessment contexts.

(Continued)

TABLE 49.1 (Continued)

Authors	Application	Methodology	Key contributions/findings
	Agriculture/production optimization	SAW	Used SAW to optimize banana ripening process parameters based on temperature, gas concentration, and duration. Found the most cost-efficient combination yielding quality results and reduced losses.
	Food science	SAW in sensory evaluation	Used SAW to evaluate sensory and physical qualities of gluten-free bread with psyllium powder; optimal ratio improved texture and consumer satisfaction.
Quek et al. (2021).	Food science/DNA extraction	SAW	Used SAW to evaluate five DNA extraction methods for edible bird's nest identification. The hybrid Qiagen method was most cost-effective, while Qiagen alone was most efficient based on DNA quality, purity, and amplifiability.
Khan et al. (2021)	Cryptography/ cybersecurity	SAW + entropy weighting	Developed a combined SAW and entropy weighting method to select optimal substitution boxes (S-boxes) for encryption. Identified the most secure and nonlinear S-box configuration to enhance cryptographic resistance.
Karabulut et al. (2022)	Urban planning/waste management	SAW + AHP + GIS	Applied AHP and SAW integrated with GIS for landfill site selection in a fast-growing Turkish metropolitan area. Produced suitability maps and identified the best candidate sites based on multicriteria evaluation.
Singh et al. (2022).	Materials science/ biocomposites	SAW + entropy	Used entropy-weighted SAW to rank biocomposites filled with varying wood waste content. Identified 2.5 wt.% as the optimal composition, balancing strength and wear properties. Validated results against other MCDM methods.
Yamagishi et al. (2023).	Tourism/island management	Fuzzy SAW + fuzzy BWM	Combined fuzzy SAW with fuzzy best–worst method (BWM) to evaluate destination management in the Philippine islands. Provided a composite performance index aligned with the tourist area life cycle model.
Aliyeva et al. (2023).	Investment decision-making	Fuzzy SAW +group MCDM	Developed a fuzzy SAW model for group decision-making in capital investment (car fleet purchase). Demonstrated effectiveness in handling subjective preferences and ranking viable investment alternatives.
Palaniswamy et al. (2025).	Electrochemical micromachining	SAW + CRITIC +artificial neural networks	Combined SAW with criteria importance through intercriteria correlation (CRITIC) and ANN to optimize performance; identified key process parameters for maximizing and minimizing overcut.
Manafiazar et al. (2024).	Environmental engineering (subsidence)	AI-enhanced	Developed AI-driven SAWF to map subsidence vulnerability in Tehran plain, improving predictive accuracy via and ANN models.
Siolemba Patiro et al. (2024).	Ecotourism impact assessment	SAW with socio-theoretical frameworks	Assessed residents' preferences on ecotourism impacts at Mount Rinjani using SAW, with economic impact ranked highest; integrated social representation and identity theories.

(Continued)

TABLE 49.1 (Continued)

Authors	Application	Methodology	Key contributions/findings
Migo-Sumagang et al. (2024)	Process systems engineering	BWM + SAW for selection problems	Demonstrated how BWM coupled with SAW improves decision-making in selecting chemical reactors, waste management methods, and 3D printers in process engineering.
Om et al. (2025)	Medical engineering (orthotics)	SAW + regression modeling	Applied SAW and simulation to optimize the structure of printed orthopedic orthosis, enhancing strength, comfort, and material efficiency.
Restrepo-Tamayo et al. (2025)	Software development productivity	SAW for gamification factors	Explored the relationship between gamification elements and social/human factors affecting software team productivity using SAW-based analysis.
Soltani et al. (2025).	Networking (cache placement)	SAW + Shannon entropy	Proposed strategy using SAW and entropy methods to improve cache hit rate and reduce delivery time in named data networks.

Compared to other MCDM techniques, such as TOPSIS or ELECTRE (ELimination Et Choix Traduisant la REalité, i.e., Elimination and Choice Expressing Reality) , SAW is favored for its ease of understanding, practical applicability, and low computational complexity. While techniques such as VIKOR and TOPSIS require the calculation of distances to ideal solutions, SAW relies solely on basic algebraic operations, normalization, weighting, and aggregation, which makes it highly efficient, especially for large-scale problems. Moreover, its transparency enables decision-makers to easily trace and justify their results, thereby enhancing stakeholder confidence in the decision-making process. SAW is particularly useful in situations where simplicity, speed, and clarity are crucial. It is easy to implement in spreadsheet software and can be taught and applied even by those without advanced mathematical or programming skills. These characteristics make it an ideal choice for both educational purposes and practical decision-making scenarios.

The following steps describe the SAW procedure in detail:

Step 1. Construct the decision matrix

Let there be m alternatives and n criteria. The decision matrix is formed as Eq. 49.1:

$$D = [x_{ij}], \quad i = 1, 2, \ldots, m; j = 1, 2, \ldots, n \tag{49.1}$$

Where x_{ij} represents the performance score of the i-th alternative to the j-th criterion.

Step 2. Normalize the decision matrix

To ensure comparability among criteria with different units or scales, the decision matrix is normalized. For benefit criteria, the normalization is as in Eq. 49.2:

$$r_{ij} = \frac{x_{ij}}{\max_i x_{ij}} \tag{49.2}$$

For cost criteria, where lower values are preferable, the formula becomes Eq. 49.3:

$$r_{ij} = \frac{\min_i x_{ij}}{x_{ij}} \tag{49.3}$$

This results in a normalized matrix $R = [r_{ij}]$, where all values fall within the range [0, 1].

Step 3. Assign weights to criteria

Each criterion j is assigned a nonnegative weight w_j, such that Eq. 49.4:

$$\sum_{j=1}^{n} w_j = 1 \text{and} w_j \geq 0 \tag{49.4}$$

Weights can be derived from expert judgment, stakeholder surveys using techniques such as AHP, BWM, or base criterion method (BCM), or objective techniques like entropy or CRITIC methods, depending on the decision context.

Step 4. Calculate the weighted scores

Each normalized value is multiplied by its respective weight as in Eq. 49.5:

$$v_{ij} = w_j \cdot r_{ij} \tag{49.5}$$

The overall score for each alternative i is then obtained by summing its weighted values across all criteria (Eq. 49.6):

$$S_i = \sum_{j=1}^{n} v_{ij} \tag{49.6}$$

49.4 Simple additive weighting applications

This section illustrates the practical application of the SAW method in real-world decision-making scenarios. To demonstrate its functionality, Subsection 49.4.1 presents a basic example in which an individual is planning to purchase a car and must choose among four alternatives based on five evaluation criteria. Subsection 49.4.2 presents a more advanced case study, in which a major e-retailer company ranks its 100 dairy food suppliers using the SAW method.

49.4.1 A case study on car selection using the simple additive weighting

Selecting the most suitable car requires a systematic evaluation of multiple conflicting criteria. This case study applies the SAW method to identify the best alternative among four popular car models. The decision problem is structured using five criteria, encompassing both cost and benefit attributes.

Problem definition:

The objective is to select the most preferred vehicle among the following four alternatives:

- A1: Toyota Corolla
- A2: Honda Civic
- A3: Mazda 3
- A4: Hyundai Elantra

The evaluation is based on five key criteria:

- C1: price (USD)—*cost criterion*
- C2: fuel efficiency (km/l)—*benefit criterion*
- C3: safety rating (scale 1–5)—*benefit criterion*
- C4: maintenance cost (USD/year)—*cost criterion*
- C5: comfort (scale 1–10)—*benefit criterion*

Fig. 49.6 illustrates the hierarchical structure of the decision problem, depicting the goal, criteria, and alternatives.

Step 1. Construct the decision matrix

The initial decision matrix is constructed using available specifications and expert input for each alternative across the five criteria. The raw data are presented in Table 49.2. Note that C1 and C4 are cost criteria (lower values are preferable); C2, C3, and C5 are benefit criteria (higher values are better).

Step 2. Normalize the decision matrix

Normalization is necessary to transform data measured in different units into a comparable scale, typically ranging from 0 to 1. The normalized value of x_{ij} is computed following the rules in Eqs. 49.2 and 49.3. For instance, the r_{11} and r_{45} are obtained as follows:

$$r_{11}\text{: } \textit{cost criterion} \rightarrow r_{11} = \frac{\min\limits_i x_{i1}}{x_{11}} = \frac{21000}{22000} \approx 0.9545 \approx 0.955$$

$$r_{45}\text{: } \textit{benefit criterion} \rightarrow r_{45} = \frac{x_{45}}{\max\limits_i x_{i5}} = \frac{7}{8.5} \approx 0.8235 \approx 0.824$$

The normalized values of the remaining cells in the normalized matrix are calculated in the same manner and presented in Table 49.3.

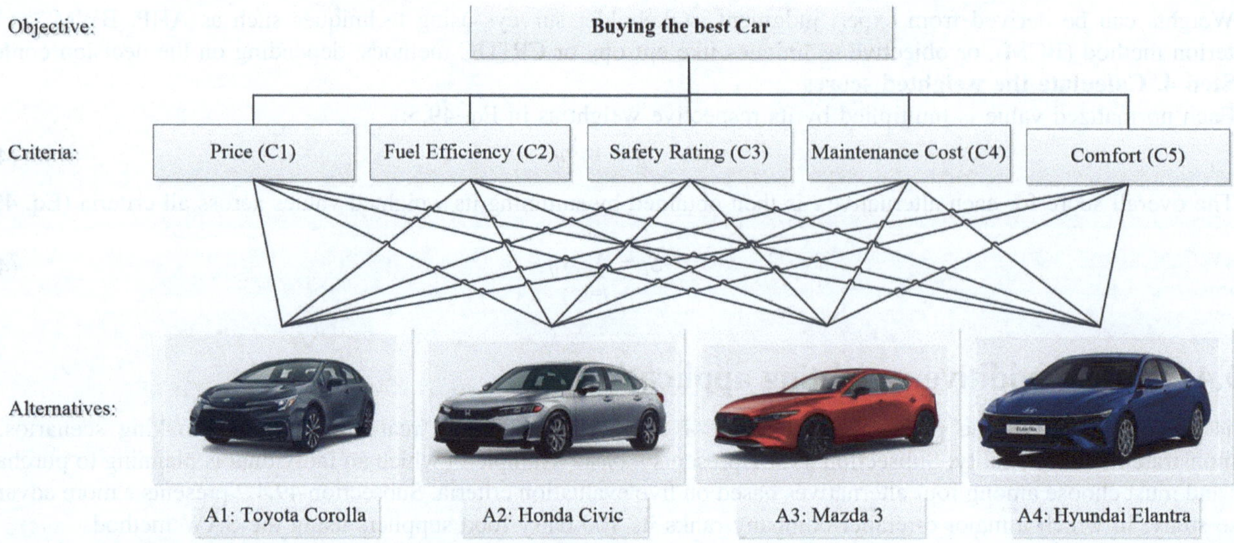

FIGURE 49.6 Hierarchical structure of the problem: selecting the best car.

TABLE 49.2 Initial decision matrix.

	C_1^- Price	C_2^+ Fuel efficiency	C_3^+ Safety rating	C_4^- Maintenance cost	C_5^+ Comfort
A1: Corolla	22,000	17	4.5	700	7.5
A2: Civic	23,500	16.5	4.7	750	8
A3: Mazda 3	24,000	15.5	4.8	720	8.5
A4: Elantra	21,000	16.8	4.6	680	7

TABLE 49.3 Normalized decision matrix.

	Price	Fuel efficiency	Safety rating	Maintenance cost	Comfort
A1: Corolla	0.955	1	0.938	0.971	0.882
A2: Civic	0.894	0.971	0.979	0.907	0.941
A3: Mazda 3	0.875	0.912	1	0.944	1
A4: Elantra	1	0.988	0.958	1	0.824

Step 3. Assign criteria weights

The importance of each criterion is represented by a normalized weight, determined based on expert judgment or weighting techniques such as the BWM. In this case, the following weights are assumed:

- w_1 (price): 0.25
- w_2 (fuel efficiency): 0.20
- w_3 (safety rating): 0.20
- w_4 (maintenance cost): 0.15
- w_5 (comfort): 0.20

These weights reflect the relative importance of each criterion from the decision-maker's perspective and sum to 1, satisfying normalization conditions.

Step 4. Compute the weighted scores

Each normalized value is multiplied by its corresponding weight (Eq. 49.5). The total score for each alternative is calculated by summing the weighted values across all criteria (Eq. 49.6). The final scores and rankings are shown in Table 49.4. For instance, the v_{11} and S_1 are obtained as follows:

$$v_{11} = w_1 \cdot r_{11} = 0,\, 25 \times 0.955 \approx 0.2387 \approx 0.239$$

$$S_1 = \sum_{j=1}^{n} v_{1j} = 0.239 + 0.2 + 0.188 + 0.146 + 0.176 = 0.949$$

Based on the total scores, the Hyundai Elantra (A4) ranks highest among the alternatives, making it the most preferred option under the specified criteria and weightings. The SAW method offers a straightforward, transparent, and computationally efficient approach to evaluating multiple alternatives in a multicriteria setting. Its interpretability makes it especially valuable for decision-makers seeking clarity and ease of implementation.

49.4.1.1 Sensitivity analysis

To assess the robustness of the SAW method, a sensitivity analysis was conducted by varying the weight of the most influential criterion from 0.1 to 0.9 (Fig. 49.7). The results show that Mazda 3 (A3) emerges as the top-ranked alternative only when the weight of price is very low (≤0.15), indicating that A3 performs best when cost is not heavily prioritized. As the weight of price increases beyond 0.15, the ranking of the alternatives remains stable across the rest of the weight range. In all scenarios where price weight is greater than 0.15, the Hyundai Elantra (A4) consistently holds the highest score and remains the most preferred alternative. These findings demonstrate the stability and reliability of the SAW method, suggesting that small or even moderate changes in weight assignment for the most important criterion do not significantly alter the outcome, indicating that the decision model is robust and the selected alternative is not overly sensitive to subjective weighting assumptions.

49.4.2 A case study on supplier selection using the simple additive weighting

In today's competitive and sustainability-focused market, selecting suppliers based solely on traditional cost and quality metrics is no longer sufficient. For an e-retailer company specializing in dairy products, it is essential to evaluate suppliers based on a comprehensive set of sustainability-oriented criteria. This study employs the SAW method to rank and select

TABLE 49.4 Weighted scores and final ranking.

	Price	Fuel efficiency	Safety rating	Maintenance cost	Comfo-rt	Total score	Rank
A1:Corolla	0.239	0.2	0.188	0.146	0.176	0.949	2
A2: Civic	0.224	0.194	0.196	0.136	0.188	0.938	3
A3: Mazda 3	0.219	0.182	0.2	0.141	0.2	0.942	4
A4: Elantra	0.25	0.198	0.192	0.15	0.165	0.955	1

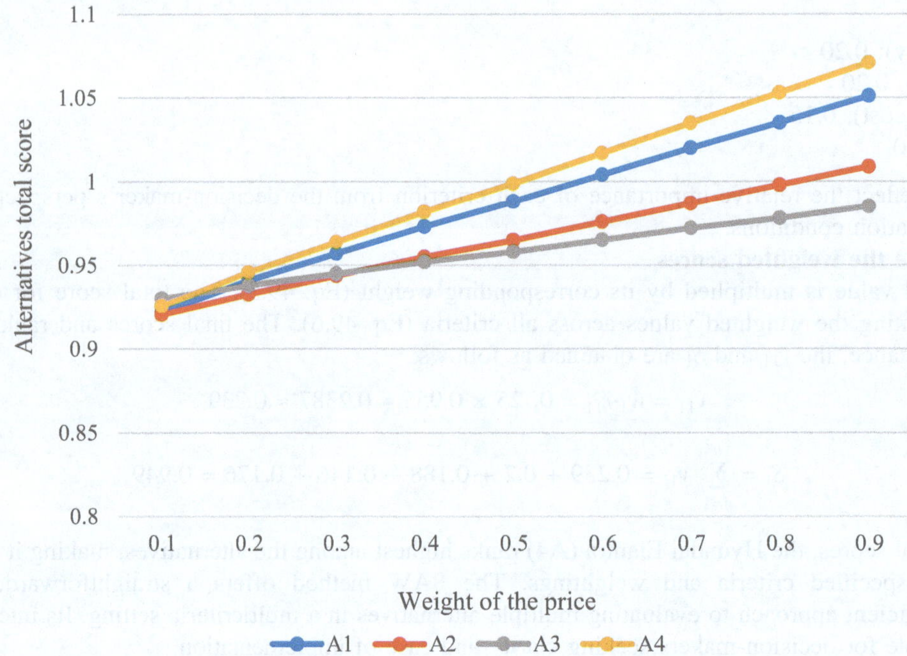

FIGURE 49.7 Sensitivity analysis based on the most important criterion.

25 dairy food suppliers, taking into account a range of environmental, social, and performance-based factors. The criteria used for the evaluation process are as follows:

- C1: price
- C2: delivery reliability
- C3: product quality
- C4: ease of handling defective products
- C5: social responsibility and responsiveness
- C6: use of green raw materials
- C7: implementation of green technologies
- C8: avoidance of harmful animal drugs
- C9: use of eco-Friendly packaging

These criteria reflect a balanced approach to evaluating supplier performance across economic, operational, ethical, and environmental dimensions. The next step involves constructing the decision matrix.

Step 1. Construct the decision matrix

The decision matrix is built using expert evaluations and available data for each of the 25 suppliers across the nine criteria. Among these, C1 (price) is the only cost criterion (lower values are preferable), while C2 through C9 are benefit criteria (higher values are preferable). The raw scores from supplier assessments are presented in Table 49.5, forming the initial decision matrix.

Step 2. Normalize the decision matrix

Normalization is carried out to convert all criteria values to a comparable scale, typically ranging from 0 to 1. The normalized value of x_{ij} is computed following the rules in Eqs. 49.2 and 49.3. For instance, the r_{11} and r_{45} are obtained as follows:

$$r_{11}\text{: } \textit{cost criterion} \rightarrow r_{11} = \frac{\min\limits_{i} x_{i1}}{x_{11}} = \frac{0.81}{1.06} \approx 0.764 \approx 0.76$$

TABLE 49.5 Initial decision matrix.

Supplier	C_1^-	C_2^+	C_3^+	C_4^+	C_5^+	C_6^+	C_7^+	C_8^+	C_9^+
S1	1.06	3	7	4	9	3	5	3	7
S2	1.47	5	9	7	2	4	9	2	9
S3	1.31	5	2	4	7	8	3	1	4
S4	1.22	2	8	4	2	6	6	4	6
S5	0.91	2	2	4	8	7	9	8	5
S6	0.91	2	5	8	9	9	1	9	7
S7	0.84	9	8	1	8	8	3	1	8
S8	1.41	3	3	1	5	7	9	7	9
S9	1.22	8	2	1	7	7	8	5	3
S10	1.30	8	6	3	1	3	5	3	1
S11	0.81	5	7	7	9	3	7	1	4
S12	1.48	4	5	7	7	4	7	3	6
S13	1.38	2	9	5	6	4	7	9	7
S14	0.95	1	1	9	9	4	9	3	7
S15	0.93	6	8	9	5	1	3	8	6
S16	0.93	8	9	4	1	1	4	7	2
S17	1.01	3	1	5	1	8	1	1	2
S18	1.17	2	6	7	5	1	1	3	2
S19	1.10	5	6	7	4	7	8	1	6
S20	1.00	8	5	4	2	6	6	1	9
S21	1.23	6	3	4	4	3	3	3	4
S22	0.90	7	4	9	1	8	7	2	8
S23	1.00	1	9	9	2	7	3	7	9
S24	1.06	4	1	2	1	5	5	7	9
S25	1.12	9	3	3	3	4	8	6	8

$$r_{45}: \textit{benefit criterion} \rightarrow r_{45} = \frac{x_{45}}{\max_i x_{i5}} = \frac{2}{9} \approx 0.222 \approx 0.22$$

The normalized values of the remaining cells in the normalized matrix are calculated in the same manner and presented in Table 49.6.

Step 3. Assign criteria weights

Each criterion is assigned a normalized weight to reflect its relative importance in the supplier selection process. These weights can be derived through expert judgment or formal weighting techniques. In this study, the weights are determined by experts familiar with sustainable supply chain management and dairy product standards using the BCM. Table 49.7 indicates the weights of the criteria. Table 49.8 represents the weighted sum matrix.

Step 4. Compute the weighted scores

TABLE 49.6 Normalized decision matrix.

Supplier	C1	C2	C3	C4	C5	C6	C7	C8	C9
S1	**0.76**	0.33	0.78	0.44	1.00	0.33	0.56	0.33	0.78
S2	0.55	0.56	1.00	0.78	0.22	0.44	1.00	0.22	1.00
S3	0.62	0.56	0.22	0.44	0.78	0.89	0.33	0.11	0.44
S4	0.66	0.22	0.89	0.44	**0.22**	0.67	0.67	0.44	0.67
S5	0.89	0.22	0.22	0.44	0.89	0.78	1.00	0.89	0.56
S6	0.89	0.22	0.56	0.89	1.00	1.00	0.11	1.00	0.78
S7	0.96	1.00	0.89	0.11	0.89	0.89	0.33	0.11	0.89
S8	0.57	0.33	0.33	0.11	0.56	0.78	1.00	0.78	1.00
S9	0.66	0.89	0.22	0.11	0.78	0.78	0.89	0.56	0.33
S10	0.62	0.89	0.67	0.33	0.11	0.33	0.56	0.33	0.11
S11	1.00	0.56	0.78	0.78	1.00	0.33	0.78	0.11	0.44
S12	0.55	0.44	0.56	0.78	0.78	0.44	0.78	0.33	0.67
S13	0.59	0.22	1.00	0.56	0.67	0.44	0.78	1.00	0.78
S14	0.85	0.11	0.11	1.00	1.00	0.44	1.00	0.33	0.78
S15	0.87	0.67	0.89	1.00	0.56	0.11	0.33	0.89	0.67
S16	0.87	0.89	1.00	0.44	0.11	0.11	0.44	0.78	0.22
S17	0.80	0.33	0.11	0.56	0.11	0.89	0.11	0.11	0.22
S18	0.69	0.22	0.67	0.78	0.56	0.11	0.11	0.33	0.22
S19	0.74	0.56	0.67	0.78	0.44	0.78	0.89	0.11	0.67
S20	0.81	0.89	0.56	0.44	0.22	0.67	0.67	0.11	1.00
S21	0.66	0.67	0.33	0.44	0.44	0.33	0.33	0.33	0.44
S22	0.90	0.78	0.44	1.00	0.11	0.89	0.78	0.22	0.89
S23	0.81	0.11	1.00	1.00	0.22	0.78	0.33	0.78	1.00
S24	0.76	0.44	0.11	0.22	0.11	0.56	0.56	0.78	1.00
S25	0.72	1.00	0.33	0.33	0.33	0.44	0.89	0.67	0.89

TABLE 49.7 Weights of the criteria.

Criteria	C1	C2	C3	C4	C5	C6	C7	C8	C9
Weight	0.10	0.10	0.15	0.10	0.10	0.10	0.10	0.15	0.10

Each normalized value is multiplied by its respective weight to compute a weighted score for each criterion per supplier. The total score for each supplier is obtained by summing these weighted scores across all nine criteria. The final rankings of the 25 suppliers, based on total scores, are presented in Table 49.8.

TABLE 49.8 Weighted scores and final ranking.

Supplier	C1	C2	C3	C4	C5	C6	C7	C8	C9	Total score	Rank
S1	0.076	0.033	0.117	0.044	0.1	0.033	0.056	0.0495	0.078	0.5865	13
S2	0.055	0.056	0.15	0.078	0.022	0.044	0.1	0.033	0.1	0.638	7
S3	0.062	0.056	0.033	0.044	0.078	0.089	0.033	0.0165	0.044	0.4555	21
S4	0.066	0.022	0.1335	0.044	0.022	0.067	0.067	0.066	0.067	0.5545	19
S5	0.089	0.022	0.033	0.044	0.089	0.078	0.1	0.1335	0.056	0.6445	6
S6	0.089	0.022	0.084	0.089	0.1	0.1	0.011	0.15	0.078	0.723	1
S7	0.096	0.1	0.1335	0.011	0.089	0.089	0.033	0.0165	0.089	0.657	5
S8	0.057	0.033	0.0495	0.011	0.056	0.078	0.1	0.117	0.1	0.6015	12
S9	0.066	0.089	0.033	0.011	0.078	0.078	0.089	0.084	0.033	0.561	18
S10	0.062	0.089	0.1005	0.033	0.011	0.033	0.056	0.0495	0.011	0.445	22
S11	0.1	0.056	0.117	0.078	0.1	0.033	0.078	0.0165	0.044	0.6225	9
S12	0.055	0.044	0.084	0.078	0.078	0.044	0.078	0.0495	0.067	0.5775	15
S13	0.059	0.022	0.15	0.056	0.067	0.044	0.078	0.15	0.078	0.704	2
S14	0.085	0.011	0.0165	0.1	0.1	0.044	0.1	0.0495	0.078	0.584	14
S15	0.087	0.067	0.1335	0.1	0.056	0.011	0.033	0.1335	0.067	0.688	4
S16	0.087	0.089	0.15	0.044	0.011	0.011	0.044	0.117	0.022	0.575	16
S17	0.08	0.033	0.0165	0.056	0.011	0.089	0.011	0.0165	0.022	0.335	25
S18	0.069	0.022	0.1005	0.078	0.056	0.011	0.011	0.0495	0.022	0.419	24
S19	0.074	0.056	0.1005	0.078	0.044	0.078	0.089	0.0165	0.067	0.603	11
S20	0.081	0.089	0.084	0.044	0.022	0.067	0.067	0.0165	0.1	0.5705	17
S21	0.066	0.067	0.0495	0.044	0.044	0.033	0.033	0.0495	0.044	0.43	23
S22	0.09	0.078	0.066	0.1	0.011	0.089	0.078	0.033	0.089	0.634	8
S23	0.081	0.011	0.15	0.1	0.022	0.078	0.033	0.117	0.1	0.692	3
S24	0.076	0.044	0.0165	0.022	0.011	0.056	0.056	0.117	0.1	0.4985	20
S25	0.072	0.1	0.0495	0.033	0.033	0.044	0.089	0.1005	0.089	0.61	10

The SAW method offers a transparent, efficient, and easily interpretable approach for MADM. It is particularly useful in supplier selection scenarios where sustainability, ethical sourcing, and performance need to be balanced objectively. This approach enables decision-makers to identify the supplier that best aligns with the e-retailer's strategic goals and sustainability values.

49.4.2.1 Sensitivity analysis

To evaluate the robustness of the SAW method, a sensitivity analysis was carried out by varying the weight of the most influential environmental criterion, avoidance of harmful animal drugs (C8), from 0.05 to 0.25. As shown in Fig. 49.8, supplier S6 consistently holds the top rank across all weight scenarios, indicating strong performance in both environmental and overall evaluation criteria. Although slight shifts in rankings are observed among other top suppliers (such as S13 and S23), the overall preference order remains relatively stable. Supplier S23, for instance, slightly improves

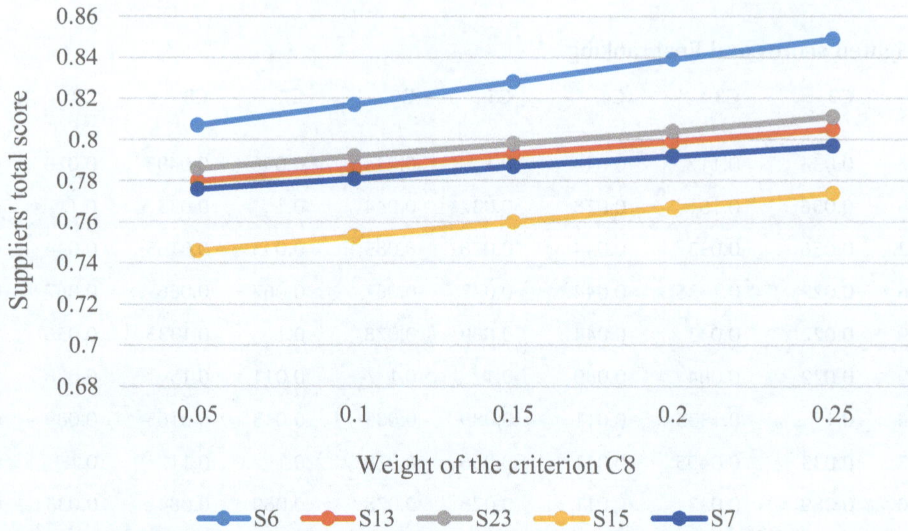

FIGURE 49.8 Sensitivity analysis based on the most important criterion.

its position as the weight of C8 increases, suggesting that it performs well in this specific criterion. Conversely, suppliers like S7 and S11 show minimal change in score, indicating a more balanced but less responsive profile to C8 weighting. These findings affirm the robustness of the SAW model in this supplier selection context and indicate that moderate changes in the importance of the most important criterion do not significantly disrupt the overall rankings, reinforcing the reliability of the decision-making process.

49.5 Conclusion and future research directions

This study explored the application and versatility of the SAW method within the context of MADM. A bibliometric analysis of research conducted from 2005 to 2025 revealed the sustained academic and practical relevance of SAW across various domains, including supply chain management, healthcare, environmental engineering, and food science. The method continues to be widely used due to its transparency, ease of implementation, and ability to handle both qualitative and quantitative data.

To illustrate its practical value, we presented two examples, a basic car selection case for didactic purposes and a real-world supplier evaluation scenario related to Iran's largest e-retailer. These cases demonstrated SAW's simplicity and effectiveness in delivering structured, interpretable results with minimal computational burden.

Compared to more complex MCDM techniques such as TOPSIS, VIKOR, and PROMETHEE, SAW provides a user-friendly approach that remains accessible to decision-makers with limited technical resources. While advanced methods offer deeper analytical capabilities, they often require more effort in terms of modeling, computation, and interpretation. SAW's straightforward logic and explainability make it particularly suitable for early-stage decision support, rapid screening, and participatory decision environments.

Future research can benefit from integrating SAW into hybrid frameworks, combining it with optimization models, fuzzy logic, or AI-based algorithms. Notably, SAW can serve as a preprocessing tool in large-scale optimization projects. For example, in renewable energy applications such as designing hydrogen supply chains, SAW can be used to determine suitable locations for supply centers, refinery centers, storage centers, and distribution centers. By eliminating less desirable locations based on expert judgments and multicriteria evaluations, SAW can significantly reduce the number of indices in the optimization phase, thus decreasing computational complexity.

References

Abolhalaj, M., Marnani, A. B., Bastani, P., Ramezanian, M., & Jafari, J. (2012). Ranking the strengths of Iranian health new financial management reform with approach of experts' attitude, group hierarchical analysis and simple additive weighted model. *HealthMED, 6*(8), 2871–2877.

Abrams, W., Ghoneim, E., Shew, R., LaMaskin, T., Al-Bloushi, K., Hussein, S., & El-Baz, F. (2018). Delineation of groundwater potential (GWP) in the northern United Arab Emirates and Oman using geospatial technologies in conjunction with simple additive weight (SAW), analytical hierarchy process (AHP), and probabilistic frequency ratio (PFR) techniques. *Journal of Arid Environments, 157*, 77–96.

Akram, M., Sultan, M., & Deveci, M. (2024). An integrated multi-polar fuzzy N-soft preference ranking organization method for enrichment of evaluations of the digitization of global economy. *Artificial Intelligence Review, 57*(3), 74.

Aliyeva, K., Aliyeva, A., Aliyev, R., & Özdeşer, M. (2023). Application of fuzzy simple additive weighting method in group decision-making for capital investment. *Axioms, 12*(8), 797.

Aziz, A., Nasution, S. M., & Setianingsih, C. (2020). Analysis simple additive weighting and genetic algorithm for traffic management system. *International Journal of Integrated Engineering, 12*(7), 104–112.

Chen, T. Y. (2014). An interactive signed distance approach for multiple criteria group decision-making based on simple additive weighting method with incomplete preference information defined by interval type-2 fuzzy sets. *International Journal of Information Technology & Decision Making, 13*(05), 979–1012.

Chou, S. Y., Chang, Y. H., & Shen, C. Y. (2008). A fuzzy simple additive weighting system under group decision-making for facility location selection with objective/subjective attributes. *European Journal of Operational Research, 189*(1), 132–145.

Farooq, B. (2025). Exploring social dynamics: An introduction to social science. *Pakistan Journal of Health Solutions, 3*(01), 20–26.

Kaliszewski, I., & Podkopaev, D. (2016). Simple additive weighting—A metamodel for multiple criteria decision analysis methods. *Expert Systems with Applications, 54*, 155–161.

Karabulut, A.İ., Yazici-Karabulut, B., Derin, P., Yesilnacar, M. I., & Cullu, M. A. (2022). Landfill siting for municipal solid waste using remote sensing and geographic information system integrated analytic hierarchy process and simple additive weighting methods from the point of view of a fast-growing metropolitan area in GAP area of Turkey. *Environmental Science and Pollution Research, 29*(3), 4044–4061.

Kek, S. P., Chin, N. L., Tan, S. W., Yusof, Y. A., & Chua, L. S. (2018). Comparison of DNA extraction methods for entomological origin identification of honey using simple additive weighting method. *International Journal of Food Science and Technology, 53*(11), 2490–2499.

Khan, M., Haj Ismail, A. A. K., Ishaque, I., & Hussain, I. (2021). New combination of simple additive and entropy weighting criteria for the selection of best substitution box. *Journal of Intelligent & Fuzzy Systems, 41*(1), 2325–2338.

Kumar, R., & Pamucar, D. (2025). A comprehensive and systematic review of multi-criteria decision-making (MCDM) methods to solve decision-making problems: Two decades from 2004 to 2024. *Spectrum of Decision Making and Applications, 2*(1), 178–197.

Lotfipour, A., & Mohtavipour, S. S. (2024). A multi-criteria decision-making model to determine the optimal share of variable renewable energy sources in a wholesale electricity market. *Sustainable Energy, Grids and Networks, 39*, 101408.

Manafiazar, A., Khamehchiyan, M., Nadiri, A. A., & Sharifikia, M. (2024). Learning simple additive weighting parameters for subsidence vulnerability indices in Tehran plain (Iran) by artificial intelligence methods. *European Journal of Environmental and Civil Engineering, 28*(1), 108–127.

Mehdi, K. G., Abdolghani, R., Maghsoud, A., Zavadskas, E. K., & Antuchevičienė, J. (2024). Multi-criteria personnel evaluation and selection using an objective pairwise adjusted ratio analysis (OPARA). *Economic computation and economic cybernetics studies and research, 58*(2), 23–45.

Migo-Sumagang, M. V., Aviso, K. B., & Tan, R. R. (2024). Best–worst method and simple additive weighting for selection problems in process systems engineering. *Process Integration and Optimization for Sustainability, 8*(4), 1309–1316.

Momena, A. F., Gazi, K. H., Rahaman, M., Sobczak, A., Salahshour, S., Mondal, S. P., & Ghosh, A. (2024). Ranking and challenges of supply chain companies using mcdm methodology. *Logistics, 8*(3), 87.

Niroomand, S., Mosallaeipour, S., & Mahmoodirad, A. (2019). A hybrid simple additive weighting approach for constrained multicriteria facilities location problem of glass production industries under uncertainty. *IEEE Transactions on Engineering Management, 67*(3), 846–854.

Om, M. S., Yang, W. C., Choe, C. M., Kim, U. H., Ri, W. S., & Sok, S. H. (2025). A reasonable approach to determine structural dimension of FDM fabricated orthopedic orthosis using finite element simulation and simple additive weighting method. *Proceedings of the Institution of Mechanical Engineers, Part C: Journal of Mechanical Engineering Science, 239*(4), 1212–1226.

Palaniswamy, V., Peyyala, A., Paramasivam, P., & Veeranjaneyulu, I. (2025). Performance analysis of electrochemical micromachining using simple additive weighting, criteria importance through intercriteria correlation, and artificial neural network methods. *Chemical Industry and Chemical Engineering Quarterly, 31*(2), 123–130.

Piasecki, K., Roszkowska, E., & Łyczkowska-Hanćkowiak, A. (2019). Simple additive weighting method equipped with fuzzy ranking of evaluated alternatives. *Symmetry, 11*(4), 482.

Quek, M. C., Chin, N. L., & Tan, S. W. (2021). Optimum DNA extraction methods for edible bird's nest identification using simple additive weighting technique. *Foods, 10*(5), 1086.

Radulescu, C. Z., & Radulescu, M. (2024). A hybrid group multi-criteria approach based on SAW, TOPSIS, VIKOR, and COPRAS methods for complex IoT selection problems. *Electronics, 13*(4), 789.

Restrepo-Tamayo, L. M., Gasca-Hurtado, G. P., Machuca-Villegas, L., & Morillo-Puente, S. (2025). Relationship between gamification elements and social and human factors using the simple additive weighting method. *PLoS One, 20*(4), e0320419.

Sahoo, S. K., Pamucar, D., & Goswami, S. S. (2025). A review of multi-criteria decision-making (MCDM) applications to solve energy management problems from 2010-2025: Current state and future research. *Spectrum of Decision Making and Applications, 2*(1), 219–241.

Sahu, A. K., Sharma, M., Raut, R. D., Sahu, A. K., Sahu, N. K., Antony, J., & Tortorella, G. L. (2023). Decision-making framework for supplier selection using an integrated MCDM approach in a lean-agile-resilient-green environment: Evidence from Indian automotive sector. *The TQM Journal, 35*(4), 964–1006.

Shakouri, H., Nabaee, M., & Aliakbarisani, S. (2014). A quantitative discussion on the assessment of power supply technologies: DEA (data envelopment analysis) and SAW (simple additive weighting) as complementary methods for the "grammar. *Energy, 64*, 640–647.

Singh, T., Pattnaik, P., Kumar, S. R., Fekete, G., Dogossy, G., & Lendvai, L. (2022). Optimization on physicomechanical and wear properties of wood waste filled poly (lactic acid) biocomposites using integrated entropy-simple additive weighting approach. *South African Journal of Chemical Engineering, 41*, 193–202.

Siolemba Patiro, S. P., Hendarto, K. A., Parmono, V. R., Wibowo, L. R., Suka, A. P., Abdurakhman, A., & Yatma, T. D. N. (2024). Analyzing residents' preferences to ecotourism impacts using simple additive weighting: The case of Mount Rinjani National Park, Indonesia. *Forest Science and Technology, 20*(1), 25–37.

Soltani, M., Barekatain, B., Hendessi, F., & Beheshti, Z. (2025). PSSN: a novel cache placement method based on adapted Shannon entropy and simple additive weighting method in named data networking. *Knowledge and Information Systems, 67*(2), 1507–1540.

Suryadi, A., Muiz, A. A., & Hidayat, A. A. (2025). Implementation of a decision support system for selecting the best supplier using the SAW method. *bit-Tech, 7*(3), 928–935.

Yamagishi, K., Gantalao, C., Tiu, A. M., Tanaid, R. A., Medalla, M. E., Abellana, D. P., & Ocampo, L. (2023). Evaluating the destination management performance of small islands with the fuzzy best-worst method and fuzzy simple additive weighting. *Current Issues in Tourism, 26*(8), 1224–1253.

Chapter 50

MAUT: Multi-attribute utility theory method for multi-attribute decision-making

Moein Khazaei[1], Ashkan Hafezalkotob[2], and Reza Kia[3]
[1]*School of Engineering and Sciences, Tecnologico de Monterrey, Monterrey, Mexico,* [2]*Department of Management and Marketing, La Trobe University, Melbourne, VIC, Australia,* [3]*Department of Operations Management and Business Statistics, Sultan Qaboos University, Muscat, Oman*

50.1 Introduction

Decision-making in complex environments often involves evaluating multiple, sometimes conflicting, criteria (Khazaei et al., 2023). Multi-attribute utility theory (MAUT) provides a robust and structured framework for such evaluations, enabling decision-makers to articulate preferences across diverse attributes and integrate them into a coherent model (Hou, 2025). Unlike simpler decision tools that rely on ad hoc weighting or qualitative rankings, MAUT is rooted in a rigorous axiomatic foundation, offering consistency, transparency, and rationality in multicriteria analysis (Brunner & Starkl, 2004). It is especially useful in contexts where trade-offs must be made between attributes like cost, risk, performance, and sustainability (Foukolaei et al., 2024).

MAUT distinguishes itself by allowing both value functions (used under certainty) and utility functions (used under risk) to represent a decision maker's preferences (Durbach & Stewart, 2012). These functions enable the transformation of qualitative judgments into quantitative scores that reflect the strength or intensity of preferences (Hou, 2025). Through this mathematical representation, MAUT supports more informed and analytically sound decisions, particularly in environments where uncertainty or complexity makes intuitive reasoning inadequate (Peters et al., 2024). The theory also accommodates both additive and multiplicative models, depending on whether the decision-making context involves independent or interdependent criteria (Khazaei, Gholian-Jouybari, Dolatabadi, et al., 2025).

One of the key strengths of MAUT is its flexibility across application domains. It has been employed in fields such as environmental planning, healthcare prioritization, infrastructure investment, military logistics, and corporate strategy (Kim & Song, 2009). In public sector settings, it helps policymakers balance social, economic, and environmental considerations. In business, it assists executives in choosing between investment projects, suppliers, or new markets (Özomay, 2023). Its ability to handle both deterministic and probabilistic scenarios make it a powerful tool for both strategic and operational decision-making (Khazaei, Gholian-Jouybari, Ramezani, et al., 2025).

Despite its theoretical rigor, MAUT also faces practical challenges, particularly in assessing the underlying preference functions (Mohd Zain et al., 2025). These assessments can be demanding, requiring structured interviews, trade-off analyses, or indirect elicitation techniques. Nevertheless, when carefully applied, MAUT yields models that reflect the true preferences of decision-makers and are capable of supporting defensible, reproducible, and accountable decisions. Furthermore, many widely used decision-making tools, can be viewed as special cases or approximations of MAUT under certain assumptions (Passos Neto et al., 2023).

In this chapter, we aim to present a clear and practical exposition of the MAUT method. We begin by outlining the theoretical foundations of preference functions under both certainty and risk, then explore the decomposition of utility functions into additive and multiplicative forms. Following this conceptual overview, we provide two detailed numerical examples that demonstrate how MAUT can be applied in real-world decision contexts. These examples will illustrate both the logic of the method and the computational steps involved in constructing and applying a multi-attribute utility function.

Encyclopedia of Multi-Attribute Decision-Making (MADM). DOI: https://doi.org/10.1016/B978-0-443-33275-3.00069-5

The remainder of this chapter is organized as follows. While Section 50.2 provides a literature review, Section 50.3 presents the step-by-step methodology of the MAUT method, including normalization, utility score computation, and ranking. Sections 50.4 and 50.5 provide two detailed numerical examples: the first focuses on selecting an optimal wind turbine technology, and the second addresses site selection for an organic waste recycling facility. Each example includes structured decision matrices and corresponding weighted evaluations. Section 50.6 concludes the chapter by summarizing key insights, discussing the method's limitations, and offering directions for future research and applications.

50.2 Literature review

MAUT, a foundational approach in multicriteria decision-making (MCDM), has been widely applied across diverse fields for solving complex problems involving competing criteria. In diplomatic human resource decisions, Taufik et al. (2021) applied MAUT to support the Indonesian Ministry of Foreign Affairs in objectively selecting representatives, achieving a high 94% accuracy in aligning candidates with defined criteria. Similarly, MAUT was used by Kim and Song (2009) to evaluate dismantling scenarios for Korea Research Reactor-1, where its integration helped quantify diverse impacts such as worker exposure and cost in decommissioning. Özomay (2023) further demonstrated MAUT's adaptability in sustainable textile engineering by selecting optimal natural dye recipes for Alanya silk, considering environmental friendliness and colorfastness.

Recent research has extended MAUT by integrating it with fuzzy logic, Delphi methods, entropy weighting, and other MCDM techniques to handle uncertainty and group decision-making more effectively. Çetinkaya et al. (2023) proposed an entropy-weighted MAUT-GIS hybrid framework to identify optimal COVID-19 mass vaccination sites in Turkey, incorporating spatial and nonspatial data. In the tourism sector, Genç et al. (2024) used a Gray MAUT method alongside Gray analytic hierarchy process and Gray Multi-Objective Optimization on the basis of Ratio Analysis (MOORA) to evaluate hotel staff performance based on detailed personal and professional criteria. Kang et al. (2022) combined intuitionistic fuzzy numbers, the best–worst method, and MAUT to prioritize medical service robots during the pandemic, addressing vague human judgments and conducting sensitivity analyses. Alhamad and Al-Mandil (2024) introduced a hybrid model with the fuzzy analytic hierarchy process to guide R&D investments in the mining sector, emphasizing the method's effectiveness in mitigating managerial bias through data-driven rankings.

Beyond applications, methodological developments have enhanced MAUT's theoretical depth. Bedford and Cooke (1999) proposed a new preference modeling framework that weakens strict independence assumptions by using indifference curves, making MAUT more practical for real-world analysis. Matarazzo (1991) introduced the new model, which blends compensatory principles from MAUT with dominance structures from outranking methods like elimination and choice translating reality, offering a balanced approach in multicriteria evaluations. Jiménez et al. (2013) addressed the imprecision of preferences through fuzzy MAUT, introducing dominance intensity measures based on trapezoidal fuzzy weights and linear programming. Kong and Wu (2023) developed the new model, combining probabilistic linguistic terms with utility theory to manage complex, uncertain datasets, particularly in group decision-making scenarios. Additional studies, such as Majumdar et al. (2019) on software release timing.

50.3 Methodology

The MAUT is a structured approach used in MCDM problems, particularly when both qualitative and quantitative criteria must be considered. As a compensatory method, MAUT allows trade-offs among criteria, meaning that poor performance in one attribute can be compensated by better performance in another. This flexibility makes it especially suitable for complex evaluations where diverse and sometimes conflicting objectives exist.

The process begins by constructing a decision matrix, where each row represents an alternative and each column corresponds to a decision criterion. The elements of the matrix reflect the performance levels of alternatives with respect to each criterion, as shown in (50.1). To incorporate the decision maker's preferences, a weight is assigned to each criterion, representing its relative importance in the overall evaluation.

$$X = \begin{bmatrix} r_{11} & \cdots & r_{1j} & \cdots & r_{1n} \\ \vdots & \ddots & \vdots & \ddots & \vdots \\ r_{i1} & \cdots & r_{ij} & \cdots & r_{in} \\ \vdots & \ddots & \vdots & \ddots & \vdots \\ r_{m1} & \cdots & r_{mk} & \cdots & r_{mn} \end{bmatrix}_{m\times n} ; \; i = 1, \; \ldots, \; m, \quad j = 1, \; \ldots, \; n \tag{50.1}$$

Next, normalization is applied to the matrix to bring all values onto a comparable scale. This step is performed differently for benefit-type and cost-type criteria. Following normalization, marginal utility scores are calculated to reflect the utility derived from each attribute level. Finally, the overall utility score for each alternative is obtained by aggregating the weighted marginal utilities. The alternatives are then ranked based on these final utility scores, and the one with the highest score is selected as the most preferred option.

To ensure comparability among criteria with different units and scales, the next step in the MAUT method involves normalizing the decision matrix. This normalization process depends on the nature of each criterion. For benefit-type attributes, where higher values are preferred (such as efficiency or capacity), the normalization is conducted using (50.2). This transformation adjusts the values within each criterion to a scale between 0 and 1, preserving the relative performance of each alternative.

$$r_{ij}^{*} = \frac{r_{ij} - \min(r_{ij})}{\max(r_{ij}) - \min(r_{ij})}; \; i = 1, \ldots, m, \quad j = 1, \ldots, n \tag{50.2}$$

$$r_{ij}^{*} = 1 + \left(\frac{r_{ij} - \min(r_{ij})}{\max(r_{ij}) - \min(r_{ij})}\right); \; i = 1, \ldots, m, \quad j = 1, \ldots, n \tag{50.3}$$

In contrast, for cost-type attributes, where lower values indicate better performance (such as cost or risk), normalization is performed using (50.3). This approach inversely scales the values, ensuring that the most favorable (i.e., lowest) raw data corresponds to the highest normalized value. Through this two-fold normalization approach, all criteria (regardless of directionality) are converted into a common scale, allowing them to be meaningfully aggregated in subsequent steps of the MAUT process.

Once the decision matrix has been normalized, the next step is to determine the marginal utility score for each alternative with respect to each criterion. This transformation is carried out using (50.4), which applies a nonlinear utility function to reflect the decision maker's perceived value of performance levels. The function enhances differentiation between alternatives, especially when attribute values are close to the extremes of the scale.

$$u_{ij} = \frac{e^{(r_{ij}^{*})^{2}} - 1}{1.71}; \; i = 1, \ldots, m, \quad j = 1, \ldots, n \tag{50.4}$$

After computing the marginal utility scores, the overall utility score for each alternative is calculated through a weighted aggregation process. As shown in (50.5), the marginal utility scores for each alternative are multiplied by their corresponding criterion weights and then summed. This results in a single composite score that reflects both the performance of the alternative and the importance of each criterion in the decision context.

$$U_i = \sum_{j=1}^{n} u_{ij}.\, w_j; \; i = 1, \ldots, m \tag{50.5}$$

In the final step, all alternatives are ranked based on their overall utility scores in descending order. The alternative with the highest utility score is considered the most desirable choice according to the preferences and priorities established by the decision maker. This ranking provides a rational and transparent basis for selecting the best option among multiple competing alternatives.

50.4 Numerical example 1

In recent years, the increasing demand for clean energy and the global push toward decarbonization have intensified (Hasanzadeh et al., 2025) the need to identify the most suitable technologies for wind energy generation (Gholian-Jouybari et al., 2024). Decision-makers often face the challenge of choosing among various wind turbine technologies, each with different economic, technical, environmental, and integration characteristics (Foukolaei et al., 2024). In this example, five widely recognized wind energy technologies (including onshore and offshore variants) are evaluated using the MAUT method. The objective is to support a structured and transparent selection process that accounts for key decision criteria such as levelized cost of energy (LCOE), capacity factor, installation and maintenance complexity, environmental impact, and scalability for grid integration. This case demonstrates how MAUT can assist policymakers, utility companies, and energy planners in systematically identifying the most balanced and context-appropriate wind energy solution.

To illustrate the MAUT method, a decision-making problem is defined involving the selection of the most suitable wind energy technology from five available options. The technologies considered include onshore horizontal-axis wind turbines (HAWT) (T1), offshore fixed-bottom turbines (T2), floating offshore turbines (T3), vertical-axis wind turbines (T4), and small-scale distributed wind systems (T5).

Five decision criteria are used to evaluate these alternatives: LCOE (C1), capacity factor (C2), installation and maintenance complexity (C3), environmental impact (C4), and scalability and grid integration potential (C5). Table 50.1 summarizes the relative importance weights assigned to each criterion based on expert judgment.

The performance values of each technology across these five criteria are presented in Table 50.2. These values form the basis of the decision matrix, which will be used in subsequent steps of the MAUT process.

Fig. 50.1 illustrates the final utility scores of five wind energy technologies as evaluated using the MAUT method. Among the alternatives, offshore fixed-bottom wind turbines received the highest score, indicating their superior performance across the weighted criteria. This suggests a balanced trade-off between high-capacity factor, strong scalability potential, and acceptable levels of environmental impact and installation complexity.

Conversely, onshore HAWT scored the lowest, suggesting that although they typically offer lower costs, they may be less favorable in other evaluated dimensions such as capacity factor or grid integration. Small-scale distributed wind systems and vertical-axis wind turbines performed moderately well, showing strong acceptance in specific areas but lacking a consistently dominant profile.

For C1 (LCOE), which is a cost-type criterion, the original value for T2 is 0.085, the minimum is 0.045, and the maximum is 0.120. Applying the cost-type normalization formula:

$$r^*_{T2,C1} = 1 + \frac{0.085 - 0.045}{0.120 - 0.045} = 1 + \frac{0.04}{0.075} = 1.5333$$

This results in a normalized cost value of 1.5333 for T2 under C1.

TABLE 50.1 Criteria and their assigned weights.

Criterion	Code	Weight (wj)
Levelized cost of energy (USD/kWh)	C1	0.20
Capacity factor (%)	C2	0.15
Installation and maintenance complexity	C3	0.30
Environmental impact	C4	0.10
Scalability and grid integration potential	C5	0.25

TABLE 50.2 Decision matrix for wind power technology alternatives.

Technology	C1	C2	C3	C4	C5
T1: Onshore HAWT	0.045	37	4	5	8
T2: Offshore fixed-bottom	0.085	48	7	4	9
T3: Floating offshore	0.110	52	8	6	7
T4: Vertical-axis wind turbine	0.065	28	3	3	5
T5: Small-scale distributed wind	0.120	25	2	2	4

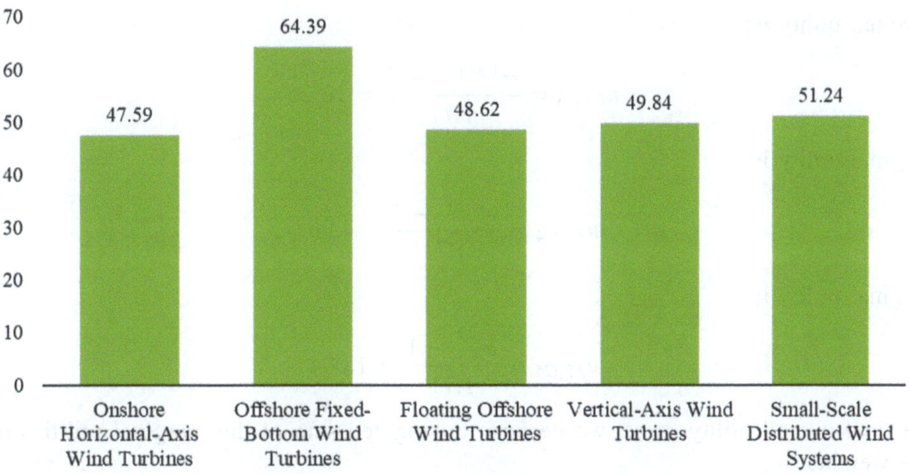

FIGURE 50.1 Final utility scores of wind energy technology alternatives based on multi-attribute utility theory.

For C2 (capacity factor), which is a benefit-type criterion, the original value for T2 is 48, the minimum is 25, and the maximum is 52. Using the benefit-type normalization formula:

$$r^*_{T2,C2} = \frac{48 - 25}{52 - 25} = \frac{23}{27} = 0.8519$$

Thus, the normalized benefit score for T2 under C2 is 0.8519.

For C3 (installation and maintenance complexity), another cost-type criterion, the original value is 7, the minimum is 2, and the maximum is 8. We normalize as follows:

$$r^*_{T2,C3} = 1 + \frac{7 - 2}{8 - 2} = 1 + \frac{5}{6} = 1.8333$$

This yields a normalized score of 1.8333 for T2 under C3.

For C4 (environmental impact), also a cost-type criterion, the original value is 4, the minimum is 2, and the maximum is 6. Applying the cost-type formula:

$$r^*_{T2,C4} = 1 + \frac{4 - 2}{6 - 2} = 1 + \frac{2}{4} = 1.5$$

The resulting normalized score for T2 under C4 is 1.5.

For C5 (scalability and grid integration), a benefit-type criterion, the original value is 9, with a minimum of 4 and maximum of 9. Using the benefit normalization formula:

$$r^*_{T2,C2} = \frac{9 - 4}{9 - 4} = \frac{5}{5} = 1$$

The normalized benefit score for T2 under C5 is 1.0.

Next, we calculate the marginal utility of each normalized value using the exponential utility function defined as:

$$u_{ij} = \frac{e^{(rij^*)^2} - 1}{1.71}$$

For C1, the marginal utility is:

$$u_{T2,C1} = \frac{e^{(1.5333)^2} - 1}{1.71} = \frac{e^{2.351} - 1}{1.71} \approx \frac{10.49 - 1}{1.71} = 5.55$$

For C2, the marginal utility is:

$$u_{T2,C2} = \frac{e^{(0.8519)^2} - 1}{1.71} = 0.623$$

For C3, the marginal utility is:

$$u_{T2,C3} = \frac{e^{(1.8333)^2} - 1}{1.71} = 16.26$$

For C4, the marginal utility is:

$$u_{T2,C4} = \frac{e^{(1.5)^2} - 1}{1.71} = 4.96$$

For C5, the marginal utility is:

$$u_{T2,C5} = \frac{e^{(1)^2} - 1}{1.71} = 1.004$$

To calculate the final overall utility score, we perform a weighted sum of the marginal utilities using the following formula. Given the weights:

$$C1 = 0.20, \quad C2 = 0.15, \quad C3 = 0.30, \quad C4 = 0.10, \quad C5 = 0.25$$

We compute the final utility for T2 as:

$$U_{T2} = (0.20)(5.55) + (0.15)(0.623) + (0.30)(16.26) + (0.10)(4.96) + (0.25)(1.004) = 6.828$$

So, the raw aggregated utility score for T2 is 6.828.
If needed, this score can be rescaled to a 0–100 scale using:

$$U_{T2'} = \frac{6.828 - 2.90}{9.0 - 2.90} \times 100 = 64.39$$

Thus, the normalized utility score of offshore fixed-bottom wind turbine (T2) is approximately 64.39 out of 100.

Fig. 50.2 presents a radar chart showing the normalized performance profiles of five wind power technologies across the five selected criteria. Each colored line represents a technology's performance relative to others in terms of LCOE, capacity factor, environmental impact, installation and maintenance complexity, and scalability. The chart visually emphasizes the trade-offs among technologies: for example, offshore fixed-bottom and floating offshore technologies score higher in capacity factor and scalability, while onshore and small-scale systems perform better in terms of environmental impact and cost.

This visual comparison highlights the multidimensional nature of the decision problem. While no single technology dominates across all criteria, the radar chart helps identify relative strengths and weaknesses. For instance, the small-scale

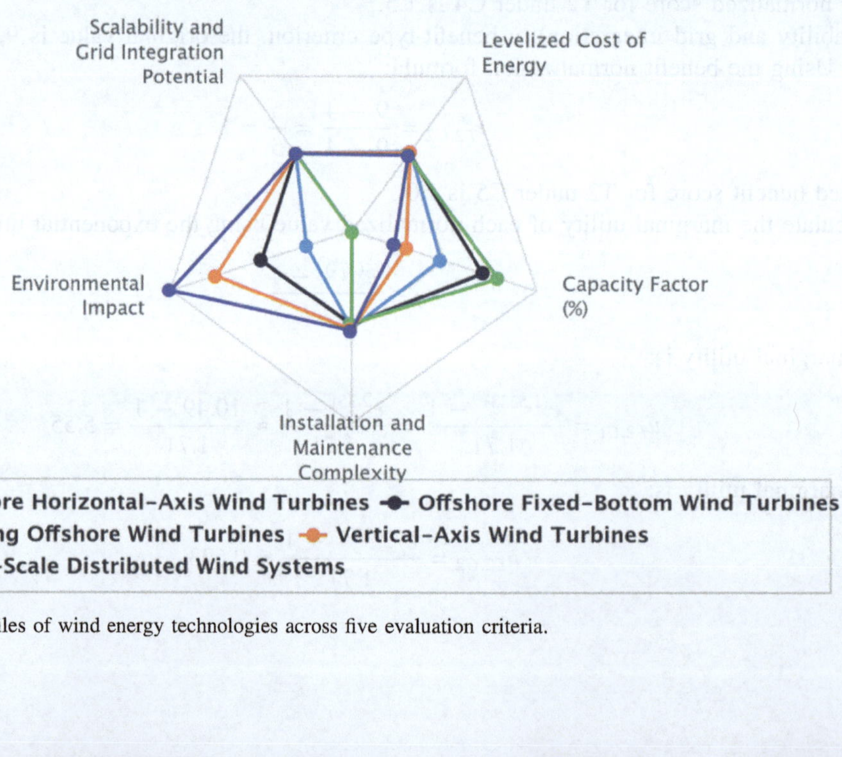

FIGURE 50.2 Performance profiles of wind energy technologies across five evaluation criteria.

distributed wind systems offer lower complexity and environmental impact, whereas the offshore fixed-bottom system shows superior performance in scalability and output efficiency.

Fig. 50.3 displays the stability intervals for each criterion's weight, indicating how much the weights can vary without affecting the identity of the top-ranked alternative. The blue bars represent the allowable ranges (min–max) within which the weights can change, and the black dots show the current assigned weights. The widest interval is observed for scalability and grid integration potential, which can vary from 0% to 100% without altering the top choice, suggesting this criterion is strongly aligned with the best-performing alternative.

On the other hand, environmental impact and capacity factor have narrower stability intervals, indicating that small deviations in their weights could potentially shift the final ranking. This sensitivity analysis provides valuable insights for decision-makers by identifying which criteria are more critical and should be carefully validated. It also confirms the robustness of the current ranking, particularly under flexible changes in economic and technical priorities.

Fig. 50.4 illustrates how the final scores of each wind energy technology evolve as the relative weight of the capacity factor (%) criterion changes from 0% to 100%. The current assigned weight (15%) is indicated by the dashed vertical line. As the weight of capacity factor increases, floating offshore wind turbines and offshore fixed-bottom wind turbines show noticeable gains in their scores, indicating their strong performance under this criterion.

In contrast, small-scale distributed wind systems and vertical-axis wind turbines experience declining scores as more emphasis is placed on capacity factor. This analysis reveals that the capacity factor is a strategic criterion that can shift the

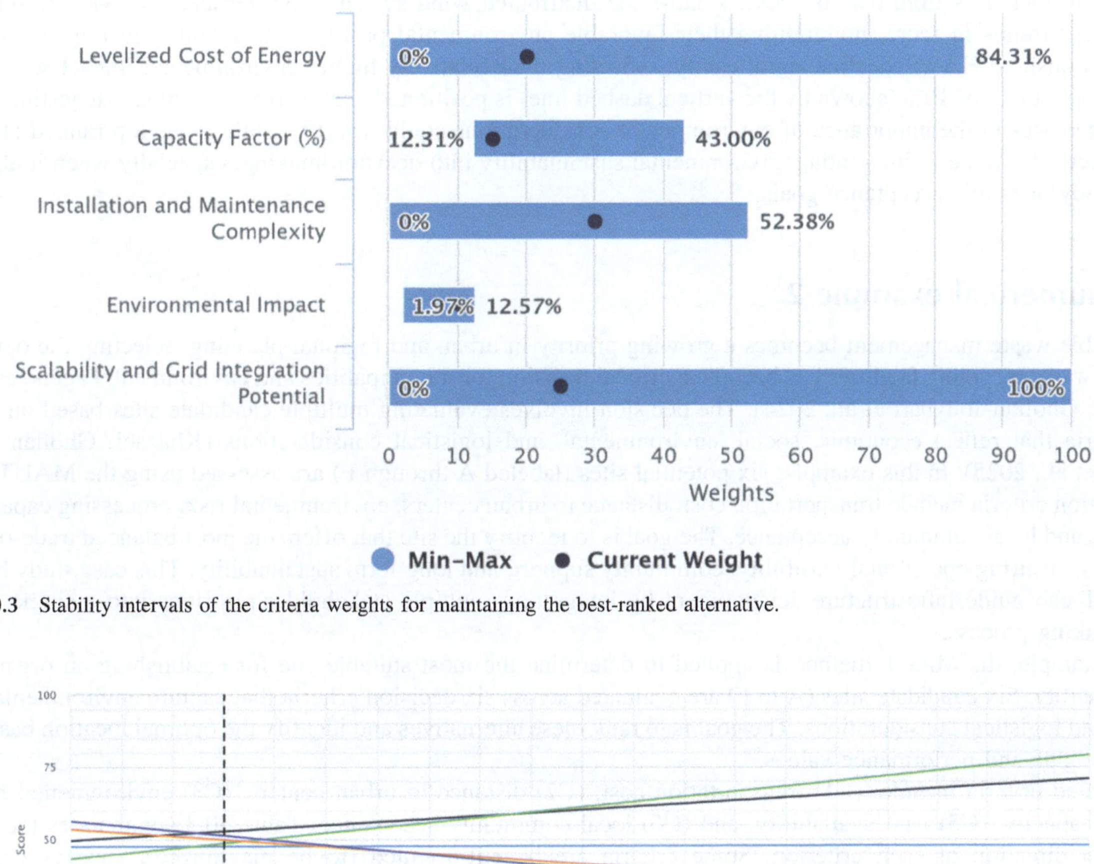

FIGURE 50.3 Stability intervals of the criteria weights for maintaining the best-ranked alternative.

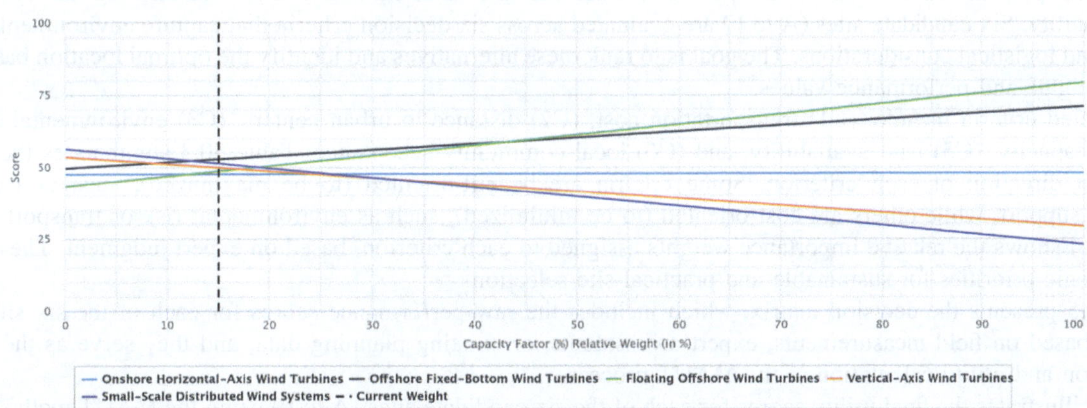

FIGURE 50.4 Scores evolution of wind energy technologies with respect to changes in capacity factor weight.

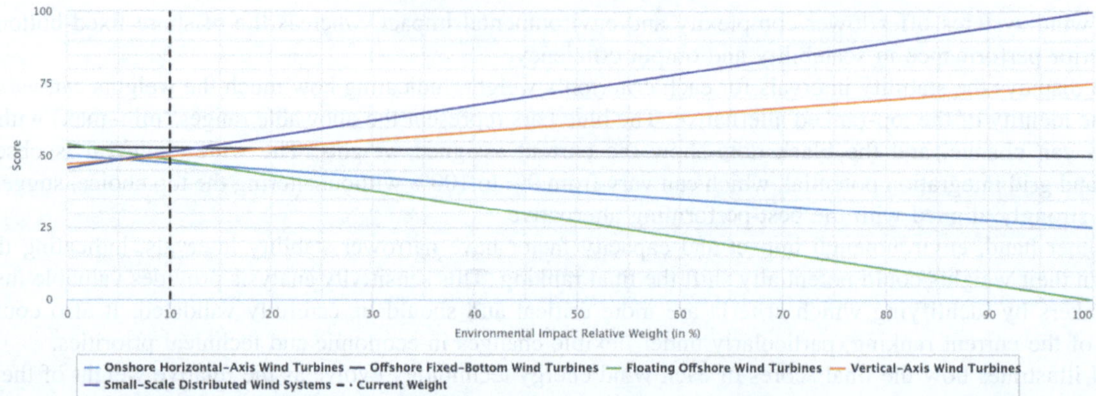

FIGURE 50.5 Scores evolution of wind energy technologies with respect to changes in environmental impact weight.

ranking in favor of offshore technologies. The chart is useful for understanding how sensitive the final decision is to the prioritization of energy output efficiency in the model.

Fig. 50.5 displays the sensitivity of alternative scores to variations in the weight of the environmental impact criterion. As the weight increases from 0% to 100%, small-scale distributed wind systems and vertical-axis wind turbines show strong upward trends in score, highlighting their favorable environmental profiles. Meanwhile, floating offshore wind turbines and onshore HAWT decline significantly, reflecting their relatively higher environmental impact scores.

The current weight of 10% (shown by the vertical dashed line) is positioned near a crossover zone, suggesting that even moderate increases in the importance of environmental considerations could lead to a shift in the top-ranked alternative. This reinforces the value of integrating environmental sustainability into decision-making, especially when it aligns with broader policy or public acceptance goals.

50.5 Numerical example 2

As sustainable waste management becomes a growing priority in urban and regional planning, selecting the optimal site for organic waste recycling facilities has become a critical decision for municipalities and environmental agencies (Ghaedi et al., 2024; Gholian-Jouybari et al., 2024). The decision involves evaluating multiple candidate sites based on a diverse set of criteria that reflect economic, social, environmental, and logistical considerations (Khazaei, Gholian-Jouybari, Ramezani, et al., 2025). In this example, six potential sites (labeled A through F) are assessed using the MAUT method. Key evaluation criteria include transportation cost, distance to urban centers, environmental risk, processing capacity, land availability, and local community acceptance. The goal is to identify the site that offers the most balanced trade-off among these factors, ensuring operational feasibility, community support, and long-term sustainability. This case study highlights how MAUT can guide infrastructure development by integrating multiple stakeholder priorities into a single, coherent decision-making process.

In this example, the MAUT method is applied to determine the most suitable site for establishing an organic waste recycling facility. Six candidate sites (A to F) are evaluated across six decision criteria that capture environmental, social, technical, and logistical considerations. The goal is to rank these alternatives and identify the optimal location based on the assigned weights and performance values.

The selected criteria include: (C1) transportation cost, (C2) distance to urban centers, (C3) environmental risk, (C4) processing capacity, (C5) land availability, and (C6) local community acceptance. Table 50.3 summarizes the type and optimization direction of each criterion. Some criteria are benefit-oriented (to be maximized), such as capacity or community support, while others are cost-oriented (to be minimized), such as environmental risk or transport cost.

Table 50.4 shows the relative importance weights assigned to each criterion, based on expert judgment. These weights reflect strategic priorities for sustainable and practical site selection.

Table 50.5 presents the decision matrix, which includes the raw performance scores for each of the six sites. These values are based on field measurements, expert assessments, or existing planning data, and they serve as the input for normalization and utility calculation in the MAUT process.

Fig. 50.6 illustrates the final utility scores for each of the six candidate sites (A to F) using the MAUT method. Among them, Site E ranks the highest with a utility score of 73.80, followed closely by Site C with 66.99. These two alternatives

TABLE 50.3 Description and optimization direction of the evaluation criteria.

Criterion	Type	Goal	Rationale
C1: Transportation cost	Quantitative	Minimize	Lower cost improves economic feasibility
C2: Distance to urban centers	Quantitative	Minimize	Shorter distance reduces emissions and transport effort
C3: Environmental risk	Qualitative (scaled)	Minimize	Lower risk ensures environmental safety and regulatory compliance
C4: Processing capacity	Quantitative	Maximize	Higher capacity improves processing efficiency and future scalability
C5: Land availability	Quantitative	Maximize	Greater land area allows for infrastructure development and expansion
C6: Community acceptance	Qualitative (scaled)	Maximize	Higher acceptance reduces social resistance and accelerates implementation

TABLE 50.4 Assigned weights for the evaluation criteria.

Criterion	Weight (wj)
C1	0.10
C2	0.12
C3	0.23
C4	0.18
C5	0.17
C6	0.20
Total	1.00

TABLE 50.5 Decision matrix for site selection alternatives.

Site	C1	C2	C3	C4	C5	C6
A	12.5	18	6	85	7.0	5
B	9.0	35	9	60	3.5	3
C	15.0	10	3	100	5.0	9
D	7.5	42	8	55	8.5	4
E	13.0	15	2	110	6.0	8
F	11.0	25	5	75	4.0	6

significantly outperform the rest in terms of their overall performance across all weighted criteria, indicating strong suitability in terms of processing capacity, land availability, and community acceptance.

On the other hand, Site B registers the lowest score (24.00), suggesting it is the least favorable option due to high environmental risk, low community acceptance, and limited land area. Sites A, D, and F occupy intermediate positions,

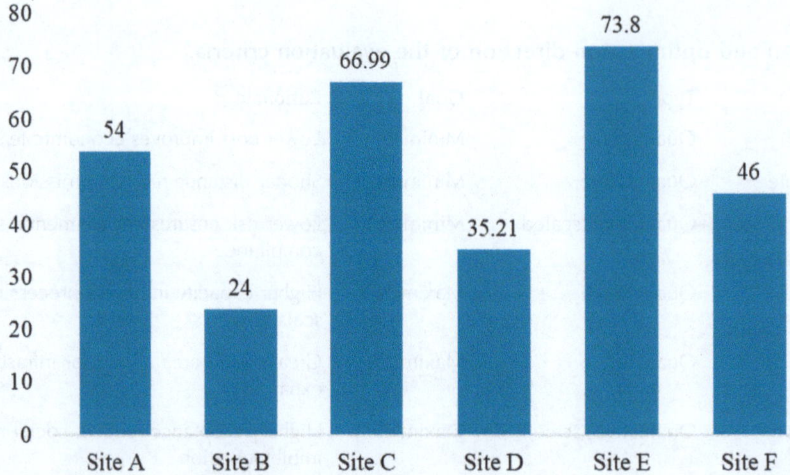

FIGURE 50.6 Final utility scores of the candidate sites for organic waste recycling.

with scores of 54.00, 35.21, and 46.00, respectively. This distribution confirms that the MAUT method effectively differentiates between alternatives by incorporating multiple criteria and providing a rational basis for prioritizing investment in the most suitable location.

In details for Site E as an example, first, the raw data are taken from the decision matrix as:

$$C1 = 13.0, \quad C2 = 15, \quad C3 = 2, \quad C4 = 110, \quad C5 = 6.0, \quad C6 = 8C$$

Then, the normalized value for C1 (transportation cost, a cost criterion) is calculated using (50.3) as:

$$r_{E1}^{*} = 1 + \frac{13.0 - 7.5}{15.0 - 7.5} = 1.733$$

Next, the normalized value for C2 (distance, a cost criterion) is calculated using (50.3) as:

$$r_{E2}^{*} = 1 + \frac{15 - 10}{42 - 10} = 1.156$$

The normalized value for C3 (environmental risk, a cost criterion) is calculated using (50.3) as:

$$r_{E3}^{*} = 1 + \frac{2 - 2}{9 - 2} = 1.0$$

The normalized value for C4 (processing capacity, a benefit criterion) is calculated using (50.2) as:

$$r_{E4}^{*} = \frac{110 - 55}{110 - 55} = 1.0$$

The normalized value for C5 (land availability, a benefit criterion) is calculated using (50.2) as:

$$r_{E5}^{*} = \frac{6.0 - 3.5}{8.5 - 3.5} = 0.500$$

The normalized value for C6 (community acceptance, a benefit criterion) is calculated using (50.2) as:

$$r_{E5}^{*} = \frac{8 - 3}{9 - 3} = 0.833$$

After normalization, the marginal utility for C1 is calculated using (50.4) as:

$$u_{E1}^{*} = \frac{e^{(1.733)^2} - 1}{1.71} = \frac{e^{3.002} - 1}{1.71} = \frac{20.10 - 1}{1.71} = 11.17$$

Similarly, the marginal utility for C2 is calculated using (50.4) as:

$$u_{E2}^{*} = \frac{e^{(1.156)^2} - 1}{1.71} = 1.64$$

The marginal utility for C3 is calculated as:

$$u_{E1}^{*} = \frac{e^{(1.000)^2} - 1}{1.71} = 1.00$$

For C5, the marginal utility is calculated as:

$$u_{E1}^{*} = \frac{e^{(0.5)^2} - 1}{1.71} = 0.166$$

For C6, the marginal utility is calculated as:

$$u_{E1}^{*} = \frac{e^{(0.833)^2} - 1}{1.71} = 0.584$$

Then, each marginal utility is multiplied by its weight and summed as:

$$U_E = 0.738$$

Finally, for better comparison, the score is rescaled to a 0–100 range by multiplying by 100, resulting in:

$$U_E^{final} = 0.780 \times 100 = 73.80,$$

which is the final MAUT score for Site E.

50.6 Conclusion

The MAUT method provides a structured and robust approach for addressing complex decision-making problems involving multiple, and often conflicting, evaluation criteria. By transforming diverse qualitative and quantitative attributes into a common utility scale, MAUT facilitates rational comparisons across alternatives. Its compensatory nature allows trade-offs between attributes, making it especially suitable for real-world applications where ideal solutions are rarely attainable. The method's clarity in assigning weights and calculating utility scores ensures transparency and reproducibility in decision outcomes.

Through the systematic steps of normalizing decision matrices, computing marginal utilities, and aggregating weighted scores, MAUT enables decision-makers to identify the most preferable option based on both expert knowledge and stakeholder priorities. Its flexibility in handling different data types and the ability to accommodate varying preference structures make it widely applicable across domains such as energy planning, site selection, transportation, and strategic policy design.

The MAUT method also presents certain limitations. One key constraint is its reliance on predefined utility functions, which may not always capture the nonlinear preferences of decision-makers. Additionally, the assumption of independence among criteria can be overly simplistic in real-world cases where criteria may be interdependent. Furthermore, the method is sensitive to the accuracy of assigned weights, making expert judgment a critical but sometimes subjective component of the process.

To overcome these limitations and expand the applicability of MAUT, future research could focus on hybridizing MAUT with other decision-support methods, such as fuzzy logic or stochastic modeling, to handle uncertainty and vagueness in input data. Moreover, dynamic versions of MAUT could be developed to account for time-dependent preferences or evolving criteria weights. Integration with AI-powered tools could also automate parts of the normalization and utility estimation process, making the approach more scalable and user-friendly in real-time decision-making environments.

References

Alhamad, H. E., & Al-Mandil, S. M. (2024). From intuition to optimization: A hybrid FAHP-MAUT model for informed R&D investment decision in mining. *Mining, Metallurgy & Exploration, 41*(5), 2457–2478.

Bedford, T., & Cooke, R. (1999). A new generic model for applying MAUT. *European Journal of Operational Research, 118*(3), 589–604.

Brunner, N., & Starkl, M. (2004). Decision aid systems for evaluating sustainability: A critical survey. *Environmental Impact Assessment Review, 24*(4), 441–469.

Çetinkaya, C., Erbaş, M., Kabak, M., & Özceylan, E. (2023). A mass vaccination site selection problem: An application of GIS and entropy-based MAUT approach. *Socio-economic Planning Sciences, 85*, 101376.

Durbach, I. N., & Stewart, T. J. (2012). A comparison of simplified value function approaches for treating uncertainty in multi-criteria decision analysis. *Omega, 40*(4), 456–464.

Foukolaei, P. Z., Asari, F. A., Khazaei, M., Gholian-Jouybari, F., & Hajiaghaei-Keshteli, M. (2024). From responsible sourcing of wastes to sustainable energy consumption in the blue hydrogen supply chain: Case of nearshoring in Nuevo Leon. *International Journal of Hydrogen Energy, 77*, 1387–1400.

Genç, E., Keleş, M. K., & Özdağoğlu, A. (2024). A hybrid MCDM model for personnel selection based on a novel Gray AHP, Gray MOORA and Gray MAUT methods in terms of business management: An application in the tourism sector. *Journal of Decision Analytics and Intelligent Computing, 4*(1), 263–284.

Ghaedi, M., Foukolaei, P. Z., Asari, F. A., Khazaei, M., Gholian-Jouybari, F., & Hajiaghaei-Keshteli, M. (2024). Pricing electricity from blue hydrogen to mitigate the energy rebound effect: A case study in agriculture and livestock. *International Journal of Hydrogen Energy, 84*, 993–1003.

Gholian-Jouybari, F., Khazaei, M., Saen, R. F., Kia, R., Bonakdari, H., Hajiaghaei-Keshteli, M., & Ramezani, M. (2024). Developing environmental, social and governance (ESG) strategies on evaluation of municipal waste disposal centers: A case of Mexico. *Chemosphere, 364*, 142961.

Hasanzadeh, H., Mohammadi, S., Shafii, M. B., & Daneshvar, M. (2025). Designing and constructing a solar thermal water desalination system: Evaluating the role of thermoelectric in enhancing evaporation and condensation process. *Next Energy, 9*, 100388.

Hou, H. (2025). Utility theory application in decision-making behavior for energy use and management: A systematic review. *Energies, 18*(8), 2125.

Jiménez, A., Suárez-Figueroa, M. C., Mateos, A., Gómez-Pérez, A., & Fernández-López, M. (2013). A MAUT approach for reusing domain ontologies on the basis of the NeOn methodology. *International Journal of Information Technology & Decision Making, 12*(5), 945–968.

Kang, D., Devi, S. A., Felix, A., Narayanamoorthy, S., Kalaiselvan, S., Balaenu, D., & Ahmadian, A. (2022). Intuitionistic fuzzy MAUT-BW Delphi method for medication service robot selection during COVID-19. *Operations Research Perspectives, 9*, 100258.

Khazaei, M., Gholian-Jouybari, F., Dolatabadi, M. D., Alamdari, A. P., Eskandari, H., & Hajiaghaei-Keshteli, M. (2025). Renewable energy portfolio in Mexico for Industry 5.0 and SDGs: Hydrogen, wind, or solar? *Renewable and Sustainable Energy Reviews, 213*, 115420.

Khazaei, M., Gholian-Jouybari, F., Ramezani, M., & Hajiaghaei-Keshteli, M. (2025). Environmental, social, and governance enablers of the hydrogen supply chain: Application of community operational research using STRIDES framework. *Journal of Environmental Management, 389*, 126092.

Khazaei, M., Hajiaghaei-Keshteli, M., Rajabzadeh Ghatari, A., Ramezani, M., Fooladvand, A., & Azar, A. (2023). A multi-criteria supplier evaluation and selection model without reducing the level of optimality. *Soft Computing, 27*(22), 17175–17188.

Kim, S.-K., & Song, O. (2009). A MAUT approach for selecting a dismantling scenario for the thermal column in KRR-1. *Annals of Nuclear Energy, 36*(2), 145–150.

Kong, Q., & Wu, L. (2023). Combinatorial design of the MAUT and PAMSSEM II methods for multiple attributes group decision making with probabilistic linguistic information. *Soft Computing, 27*(4), 2093–2108.

Majumdar, R., Kapur, P., & Khatri, S. K. (2019). Assessing software upgradation attributes and optimal release planning using DEMATEL and MAUT. *International Journal of Industrial and Systems Engineering, 31*(1), 70–94.

Matarazzo, B. (1991). MAPPAC as a compromise between outranking methods and MAUT. *European Journal of Operational Research, 54*(1), 48–65.

Mohd Zain, F. A., Wan Abdullah, W. A., Muhamad Nasir, M. N., & Hassan, M. F. (2025). Development of a comprehensive sustainability performance index for takaful operators: Integrating Maqasid Al-Shariah and stakeholder perspectives. *International Journal of Islamic and Middle Eastern Finance and Management, 18*(3), 628–648.

Özomay, M. (2023). Sustainable and environmental dyeing with maut method comparative selection of the dyeing recipe. *Sustainability, 15*(3), 2738.

Passos Neto, G. D. M., Alencar, L. H., & Valdes-Vasquez, R. (2023). Multiple-criteria methods for assessing social sustainability in the built environment: A systematic review. *Sustainability, 15*(23), 16231.

Peters, S., Tönsfeuerborn, M., & von Nitzsch, R. (2024). Integrating uncertainties in a multi-criteria decision analysis with the ENTSCHEIDUNGSNAVI. *Mathematics, 12*(11), 1746.

Taufik, I., Alam, C., Mustofa, Z., Rusdiana, A., & Uriawan, W. (2021). Implementation of multi-attribute utility theory (MAUT) method for selecting diplomats. *IOP Conference Series: Materials Science and Engineering*.

Chapter 51

MPSI: Modified preference selection index for multi-attribute decision-making

Gülay Demir
High School of Health Vocational Services, Sivas Cumhuriyet University, Sivas, Türkiye

51.1 Introduction

The relevance and importance of using multicriteria decision-making (MCDM) techniques include their capacity to handle complexities present within decision-making processes that incorporate multiple goals, criteria, and decision-makers (Hasan et al., 2022). The use of MCDM ensures that there is a systematic and organized approach to decision-making, which enables decision-makers to break down a complex situation into a list of criteria to compare different options and make informed decisions that are governed by specific rules (Haseli et al., 2023; Li et al., 2020). The majority of decisions that arise are normally associated with multiple goals that need to be handled simultaneously (Ferla et al., 2024; Haseli et al., 2024).

Despite this, the dependability and correctness of the results obtained by MCDM processes are significantly affected by the objective and efficient calculation of criterion weights. The conventional MCDM approaches, specifically those using the subjective judgment of the decision-maker to identify criterion weights (like analytic hierarchy process and best–worst method), jeopardize the dependability and replicability of results. This immediately affects the efficiency of the decision-supporting process and its relevance to resolve conflicts arising among experts on matters pertaining to priority (Demir & Moslem, 2024).

Therefore, can there be a method that is capable of carrying out both criteria weighting and alternative ranking processes very efficiently without any involvement of subjective judgment on the part of the decision-maker? In this scenario, the preference selection index (PSI) method developed by Maniya and Bhatt within the literature in 2010 provides a remedy to this issue by not requiring any priority among the criteria and finding out the overall preference value of attributes by using statistical ideas. PSI is particularly useful when there is a conflict in determining the relative importance of criteria. It eliminates the need for decision-makers to make pairwise comparisons or check consistency, thus increasing the efficiency of the decision-making process (Sutrisno & Kumar, 2022, p. 321).

The modified preference selection index (MPSI) method, based on the traditional PSI method, was introduced to the literature by Gligorić and colleagues in 2022. MPSI offers a minimal yet effective modification by eliminating a specific computational step in the original methodology (Gligorić et al., 2022, p. 2). This minimal change increases the final values of the weight coefficients and brings these values closer to those obtained with other objective weighting methods, such as ENTROPY, method based on the removal effects of criteria (MEREC), and criteria importance through intercriteria correlation (CRITIC), thus improving the reliability and consistency of the weights.

The primary motivation for this section is to examine in detail the methodological superiority of the MPSI method and its good performance compared to other traditional models, as evidenced by the high average Spearman rank correlation coefficient (Gligorić et al., 2022, p. 16). The primary reason for choosing MPSI is that it is implemented initially to prevent unbalanced weights resulting from any biases stemming from decision-makers' personal perspectives, automatically set for each criterion, and is based on objectivity. To better illustrate these advantages of MPSI, a comparison of it with other basic objective weighting methods is presented in Table 51.1.

Accordingly, the following research objectives were determined for this section: to methodologically analyze the minimal step by which the MPSI method differs from the original PSI method and the impact of this change on the reliability of the weighting coefficients. To empirically demonstrate the applicability and effectiveness of the method

Encyclopedia of Multi-Attribute Decision-Making (MADM). DOI: https://doi.org/10.1016/B978-0-443-33275-3.00057-9

TABLE 51.1 Comparison of the modified preference selection index (MPSI) method with other basic objective weighting methods.

Comparison criteria	MPSI method	ENTROPY method	CRITIC method	MEREC method
Basic philosophy	Preference selection index (PSI)	Information theory (uncertainty measurement)	Correlation and variability	Criterion performance loss
Weighting mechanism	Overall preference value of criteria (statistical concept)	Variability (distribution) of values in the criterion.	The product of the standard deviation and the correlation between criteria.	Measuring the impact of removing a criterion on alternatives.
Output type	Both weight and ranking (integrated method)	Weight only (weighting method)	Weighting only (weighting method)	Weighting only (weighting method)
Computational efficiency	High (faster than PSI with minimal modification)	Medium (includes logarithmic calculations)	Medium (requires correlation matrix calculation)	Low (each criterion must be removed and recalculated individually)
Main advantage	Provides fast and integrated decision-making, free from subjectivity; does not require pairwise comparisons.	Mathematically robust; measures uncertainty.	Accounts for conflict (correlation) between criteria.	Measures the importance of a criterion based on its direct impact on the performance of alternatives.
Limitations	A minimal modification to the original PSI.	Extremely sensitive to normalization method; focuses only on variability.	Interpreting the correlation between criteria is complex.	Computation time is long; may be inefficient with large data sets.

through two different case studies: prioritizing operational improvement criteria in logistics management and evaluating the criteria affecting the determination of renewable energy types.

This section examines in detail the methodological superiority of the MPSI method and its high consistency with other objective methods, presenting the applicability of this fast, efficient, and subjective method to the MCDM literature. The MPSI chapter structure is as follows: Section 51.2 includes a literature review introducing the integration of the method with fuzzy logic and the hybrid models it is applied to. This is followed by a section explaining the methodology of the method. Case studies, characterized as simple and complex cases, are included in Section 51.4. Section 51.5 includes the conclusion and recommendations for future work.

51.2 Literature review

This section provides a comprehensive review of the literature on applications of MPSI method and hybrid approaches, which is very important to understand its methodological contributions.

The MPSI method has a very flexible structure because it can be combined with different fuzzy set theories. For instance, Yalçın et al. (2025) introduced a new method, which is a combination of MPSI and continuous Pythagorean fuzzy sets to evaluate the operational performance of port authorities. In this chapter, expert weights were determined based on parameters such as risk propensity and expertise level. Babaçoğlu et al. (2025) performed MPSI-based parameter weighting using interval-valued global fuzzy sets within the scope of a sustainable digital transformation maturity assessment of universities. In another important study, Kara et al. (2024) used MPSI in a hybrid model with the two-stage logarithmic normalization alternative ranking using two-step logarithmic normalization (ARLON) method to measure the supply chain performance of 72 countries.

The MPSI method has also been effectively applied to complex decision problems in engineering and energy. Zhou et al. (2025) combined MPSI with Sobol global sensitivity analysis and hybrid surrogate models for a multiobjective optimization problem in automobile seat design. This approach significantly reduced the complexity of weight calculations. Wittig Vianna et al. (2025) used the MPSI-Combined compromise abbreviations expanded solution hybrid model in a comparative analysis of renewable energy transition efforts in Organisation for Economic Co-operation and Development (OECD) countries. Özekenci (2025) evaluated the environmental performance of Asia-Pacific countries by integrating the extended alternative ranking order method accounting two-step normalization method with MPSI-based criterion weights. Socio-economic performance analyses also hold an important place among the application areas of the method. Çelebi Demirarslan et al. (2024) compared MPSI with other objective weighting methods, such as MEREC and logarithmic percentage change-driven objective weighing in the problem of ranking Asian countries according to quality of life indicators. The study results revealed that MPSI produces the most consistent results, especially for problems with a large number of alternatives. Unlike the traditional PSI method, MPSI has been proven to produce stable weight values even for high-dimensional matrices containing more than 20 alternatives.

MPSI-based hybrid models have been validated through sensitivity analyses and real-world case studies. Babaçoğlu et al. (2025) and Özekenci (2025) conducted sensitivity analyses, while Zhang et al. (2022) conducted real-world case studies. The above studies have shown that the method is reliable and can be applied to industrial decision support systems. From the literature, there is sufficient proof of compatibility between MPSI method and fuzzy logic, multicriteria optimization, and its wide applicability to socio-economic disciplines.

51.3 Methodology

The MPSI objective criterion weighting method is an improved version of the PSI method developed by Maniya and Bhatt (2010). This improved version was introduced to the literature by Gligorić et al. (2022) in their study on the underground mine support system selection problem.

The basic steps of the MPSI method are as follows (Gligorić et al., 2022):

Step 1. Construct initial decision matrix

The decision matrix with alternatives A = {A_1, A_2, ..., A_m} and criteria $C = \{C_1, C_2, ..., C_n\}$ is shown by Eq. (51.1).

$$[x_{ij}]_{m*n} = \begin{bmatrix} x_{11} & x_{12} & \cdots & x_{1n} \\ x_{21} & x_{22} & \cdots & x_{2n} \\ \vdots & \vdots & \ddots & \vdots \\ x_{m1} & x_{m2} & \cdots & x_{mn} \end{bmatrix} \tag{51.1}$$

where x_{ij} is the performance of alternative i under criterion j.

Step 2. Normalize the matrix

Apply linear normalization for beneficial (maximize) and nonbeneficial (minimize) criteria. Eq. (51.2) is used for normalization of beneficial criteria, and Eq. (51.3) is used for nonbeneficial criteria.

$$r_{ij} = \frac{x_{ij}}{\max(x_{ij})} \tag{51.2}$$

$$r_{ij} = \frac{\min(x_{ij})}{x_{ij}} \tag{51.3}$$

Resulting in a normalized matrix $R = [r_{ij}]_{mxn}$

Step 3. Calculate mean value per criterion

The average of the normalized values for criterion j is calculated by Eq. (51.4).

$$v_j = \frac{1}{m}\sum_{i=1}^{m} r_{ij} \tag{51.4}$$

Step 4. Compute preference variation

Determination of the variance for criterion j is obtained by Eq. (51.5).

$$\rho_j = \sum_{i=1}^{m} (r_{ij} - v_j)^2 \tag{51.5}$$

Step 5. Derive criteria weights

Eq. (51.6) is used to normalize preference variations.

$$w_j = \frac{\rho_j}{\sum_{j=1}^{n} \rho_j} \tag{51.6}$$

Higher ρ_j = higher weight, indicating greater criterion discriminability.

51.4 Case study

In this section, the process steps of the MPSI method are shown in detail with numerical examples using the simple case and complex case designed as hypothetical scenarios.

51.4.1 Numerical example 1

A logistics management team conducts a multicriteria analysis to determine which criteria are of the highest importance in operational improvement efforts. Four different improvement strategies will be evaluated in light of five key performance criteria, and critical priorities will be identified using a scientific methodology. The criteria used in the evaluation and their related explanations are detailed in Table 51.2.

The criteria affecting the recovery strategies that make up the decision matrix are given in Table 51.2. In light of this information, the initial decision matrix is given in Table 51.3.

The normalized decision matrix obtained using Eq. (51.2) and Eq. (51.3) is given in Table 51.4.

Calculation of normalized values for criteria C2 and C3 for alternative S1 is shown as an example.

$$r_{C2} = \frac{18}{24} = 0{,}7500, \quad r_{C3} = \frac{85}{92} = 0{,}9239$$

The criteria mean calculated using Eq. (51.4) are given in Table 51.5.

The calculation of the average value of the C1 criterion is shown in Table 51.4.

$$v_{C1} = \frac{1{,}0000 + 0{,}6250 + 0{,}7692 + 0{,}6944}{4} = 0{,}7722$$

The preference variation calculated using Eq. (51.5) is given in Table 51.6.

The calculation of the preference variation value for the C1 criterion is shown in Table 51.5.

$$\rho_{C1} = (1{,}0000 - 0{,}7722)^2 + (0{,}6250 - 0{,}7722)^2 + (0{,}7692 - 0{,}7722)^2 + (0{,}6944 - 0{,}7722)^2 = 0{,}0796$$

TABLE 51.2 Information on evaluation criteria.

Criterion name/code	Optimization direction	Description
Cost (₺) C1	Min	This represents the total expenses incurred in operational processes. The goal is to minimize this criterion, which directly impacts business profitability. It includes transportation, storage, labor, and general administrative costs.
Delivery time (hours) C2	Min	It represents the total time required to deliver an order to the customer. It is a critical indicator of supply chain performance and is directly related to customer satisfaction and operational efficiency.
Capacity utilization rate (%) C3	Max	It indicates the efficient use of existing resources (warehouse space, vehicle capacity, and workforce). Optimization is crucial for minimizing idle capacity and maximizing resource efficiency.
Error rate (%) C4	Min	It reflects the rate of error operations in operational processes. It encompasses quality problems such as incorrect deliveries, damaged products, and incomplete shipments. It directly impacts customer satisfaction and operational costs.
Operational efficiency (1–10) C5	Max	It is a composite indicator that measures the integrated performance of all operational processes. It evaluates the level of resource utilization efficiency, process flow optimization, and overall operational excellence.

TABLE 51.3 Initial decision matrix.

Strategy	C1	C2	C3	C4	C5
S1	500	24	85	8	7
S2	800	18	92	5	9
S3	650	30	78	12	6
S4	720	22	90	6	8

TABLE 51.4 Normalized decision matrix.

Strategy	C1	C2	C3 max	C4	C5 max
S1	1,0000	0,7500	0,9239	0,6250	0,7778
S2	0,6250	1,0000	1,0000	1,0000	1,0000
S3	0,7692	0,6000	0,8478	0,4167	0,6667
S4	0,6944	0,8182	0,9783	0,8333	0,8889

TABLE 51.5 Criteria means.

	C1	C2	C3 max	C4	C5 max
v_j	0,7722	0,7920	0,9375	0,7188	0,8333

TABLE 51.6 Preference variations.

	C1	C2	C3 max	C4	C5 max
p_j	0,0796	0,0826	0,0138	0,1923	0,0617

TABLE 51.7 Criterion weights.

	C1	C2	C3 max	C4	C5 max
w_j	0,1852	0,1920	0,0321	0,4472	0,1436

The criterion weights calculated using Eq. (51.6) are given in Table 51.7.

The calculation of the weight of criterion C1 is shown in Table 67.

$$w_{C1} = \frac{0{,}0796}{0{,}0796 + 0{,}0826 + 0{,}0138 + 0{,}1923 + 0{,}0617} = 0{,}1852$$

The obtained criteria weight values are given in Fig. 51.1.

Fig. 51.1 provides valuable insights into the logistics team's operational priorities: the significant weighting of error rate (44.72%) demonstrates that the team embraces the "zero defect" principle as a core operational philosophy. This approach prioritizes strategic values such as long-term customer loyalty and brand reputation. The balanced distribution between cost (18.52%) and delivery time (19.20%) demonstrates that the team aims for the optimal balance, rather than falling into the "either fast or cheap" dilemma. This reflects the need to meet customer expectations in terms of both economic and time sensitivity. The moderate weighting of operational efficiency (14.36%) suggests that this criterion is viewed as a consequence of success in other criteria rather than a key performance indicator. The relatively low weighting of the capacity utilization rate (3.21%) suggests that the team considers short-term operational excellence and long-term capacity planning separately. This situation can be interpreted as either that existing operational resources are deemed sufficient or that capacity optimization is considered as a more strategic planning issue.

This weight distribution reveals that the team adopts a customer-focused and quality-centered operational model, but also manages cost and time efficiency in a balanced manner.

51.4.2 Numerical example 2

Renewable energy sources play an essential role in the sustainability of modern energy systems. The environmental damage caused by fossil fuels, energy security concerns, and climate change risks have made renewable energy

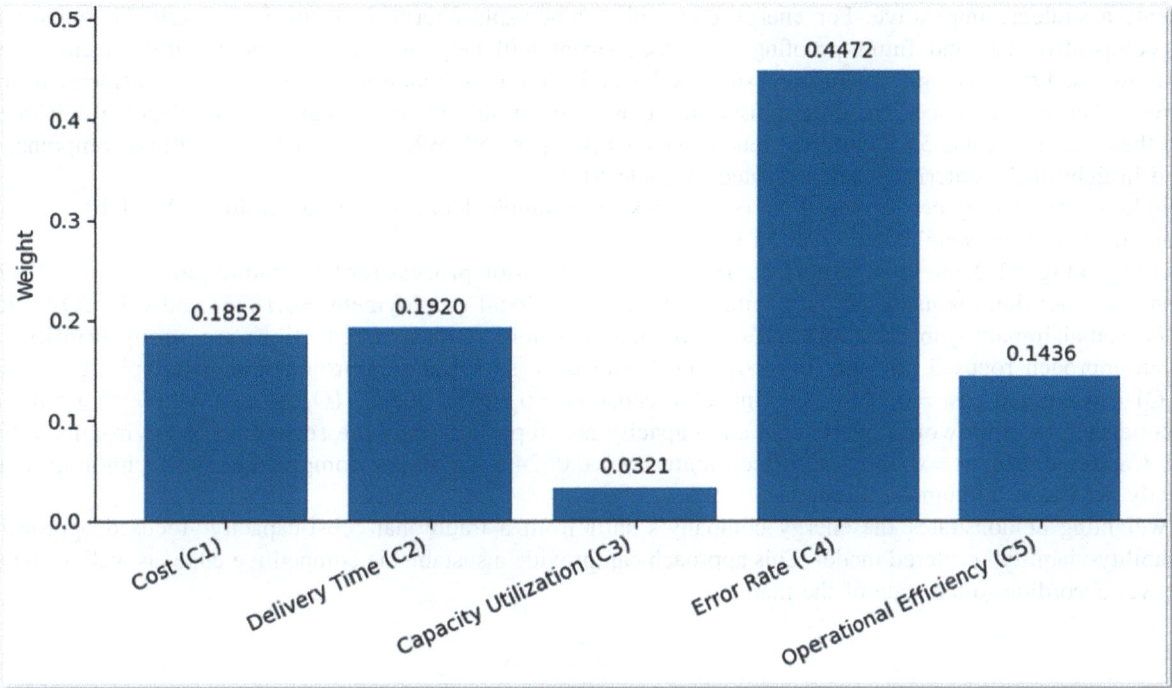

FIGURE 51.1 Modified preference selection index weights for example 1.

TABLE 51.8 Information on assessment criteria.

Criteria/code	Description	Optimization direction	Evaluation criteria
Investment cost (million $) (C1)	Total installation and commissioning costs	Min	Equipment, construction, engineering, and licensing costs
Operation and maintenance cost (M$/year) (C2)	Annual operational expenses	Min	Personnel, maintenance, spare parts, and insurance costs
Carbon emission reduction (tons of CO_2) (C3)	Annual carbon emission reduction potential	Max	Prevention of fossil fuel-related emissions
Energy production capacity (MW) (C4)	Maximum installed power capacity	Max	Nominal electricity generation capacity
Technological maturity (1–10) (C5)	Technology readiness level	Max	TRL level, reliability, and predictability
Land use requirement (hectares) (C6)	Total required physical space	Min	Land required for production facilities and infrastructure
Local employment impact (persons) (C7)	Direct and indirect employment potential	Max	Employment during construction and operation
Government incentive eligibility (1–10) (C8)	Legal compliance and incentive eligibility	Max	Yatırım indirimi, alım garantisi, vergi avantajı

investments a strategic imperative. For energy companies, renewable energy investments are critical for sustainable growth, competitiveness, and future-proofing. This assessment will help the company both fulfill its environmental responsibilities and ensure long-term financial success. Diversification into renewable energy is now considered a strategic imperative rather than a choice. The criteria used in the assessment and related explanations are detailed in Table 51.8.

Using the criteria in Table 51.8, different renewable energy types (A1, A2, A3, A4, A5, A6) will be comprehensively evaluated in light of the criteria values presented in Table 51.9.

The findings obtained by performing the process steps for Example 1 in order are given in Table 51.10.

The obtained criterion weights are given in Fig. 51.2.

According to Fig. 51.2, the most important criterion in the decision process for C6 (land requirement = 0.2232) was the extent to which land is used, or "site suitability." For C7 (local employment = 0.1873) and C3 (CO_2 reduction = 0.1657), social impact (job creation) and environmental benefit (emission reduction) are strong priorities. This reflects an approach focused not only on economic but also on social and environmental sustainability. Economic criteria C1 (investment cost = 0.1114), C4 (installed capacity = 0.1061), and C2 (O&M cost = 0.0978) are important but "secondary." In other words, while cost and capacity are important, they are secondary to environmental/social benefits. C8 (regulation fit = 0.0561), C5 (tech maturity = 0.0524), regulatory compliance, and technology maturity are already seen as minimum requirements.

This weighting demonstrates the energy company's shift from a traditional "cost-capacity"-focused approach to a "sustainability-viability"-centered model. This approach can provide a sustainable competitive edge, as well as the ability to maneuver according to the state of the market.

TABLE 51.9 Initial decision matrix.

Alternative	C1	C2	C3	C4	C5	C6	C7	C8
A1 (solar energy systems)	120	2,5	50,000	80	9	200	200	8
A2 (wind energy systems)	180	3,0	80,000	100	8	300	150	7
A3 (biomass)	90	4,0	30,000	50	7	150	250	6
A4 (geothermal)	150	3,5	40,000	60	8	100	100	9
A5 (wave/tidal)	200	4,5	20,000	40	5	50	50	5
A6 (hydroelectric power plants)	100	2,0	60,000	70	7	250	120	7

TABLE 51.10 Modified preference selection index values of the criteria.

	C1	C2	C3	C4	C5	C6	C7	C8
v_j	0,7000	0,6638	0,5833	0,6667	0,8148	0,4083	0,5800	0,7778
p_j	0,2450	0,2151	0,3646	0,2333	0,1152	0,4910	0,4120	0,1235
w_j	0,1114	0,0978	0,1657	0,1061	0,0524	0,2232	0,1873	0,0561

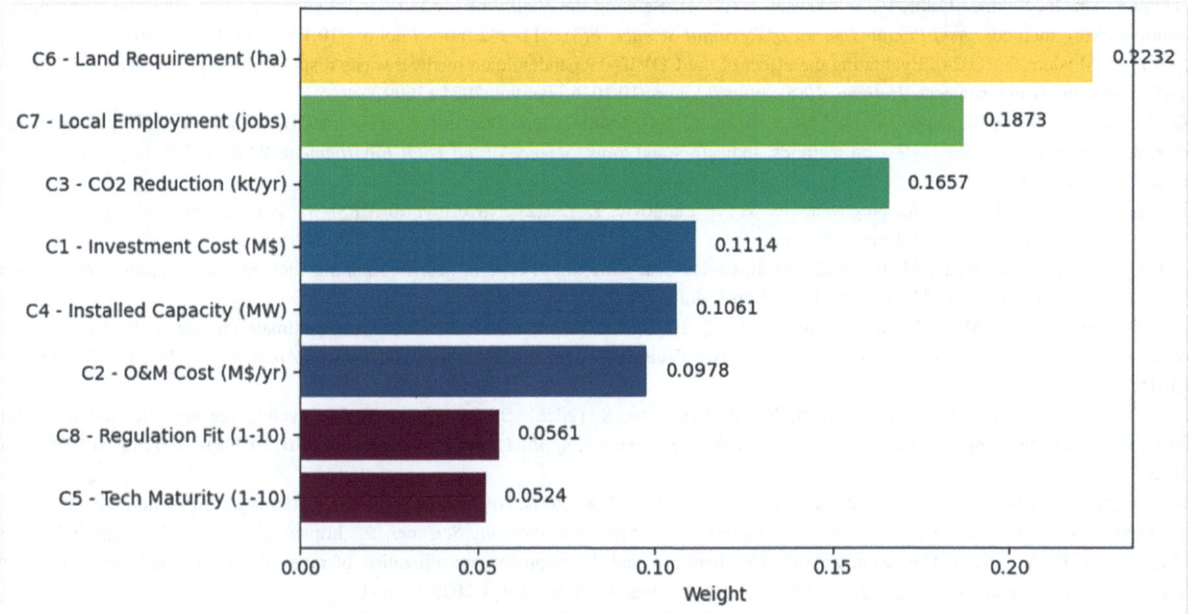

FIGURE 51.2 Modified preference selection index method weights for example 2.

51.5 Conclusion and future work

This concluding section assessed the superiority in methodology and applicability to practical applications of the MPSI method developed to objectively assign weights to criteria in MCDM problems. The main objective of this research work is to offer an objective, fast, and efficient weight assignment solution that completely avoids any biases associated with human judgment-based weight assignment approaches. The two examples have empirically shown how MPSI assigns unbiased weights to criteria on the basis of data distribution. More specifically, due to its automatic assignment of higher priority to crucial criteria such as "Error Rate" with priority C4, 44.72% within the "Logistics Management" example and to "Land Use" with priority C6, 22.32% within the "Renewable Energy" example, there is strong evidence to prove how this method successfully discovers hidden priorities within a decision-making approach automatically without any human assistance. Moreover, because this method optimizes the processing to take less computing time to solve matrices consisting of 4–6 alternatives and 5–8 criteria within both examples, it indicates how this method is very much practically applicable to small to medium-scale problems.

However, there are some disadvantages to the MPSI method. These can serve as guidelines for future work: currently, the method is formulated using crisp information, and hence its incorporation with fuzzy logic or interval information is necessary if it is to be useful in a decision environment where uncertainty is involved. For complex matrices with more than 50 alternatives and/or more than 15 criteria, computation time can increase.

Considering these constraints, there exist several distinct research avenues that could be pursued: to make the method more scalable, parallel computing approaches or hybrid approaches such as MPSI + CRITIC can be developed to attain algorithmic optimization. To enhance the dependability level of this approach, reliability should actually be calculated by specifying worst/best scenario definitions on values of criteria. Research on the validation of MPSI with applications in real-life domains, such as health care (optimization of resources within hospitals) or supply chain management (selection of suppliers), and implementation within industrial decision support systems should receive increased emphasis from both academia and industry.

References

Babaçoğlu, S., Yalçın, G. C., Kara, K., Polat, M., & Pamucar, D. (2025). Promoting benchmarking and best practices in education: An interval-valued spherical fuzzy model for assessing sustainable digital transformation maturity. *Technology in Society*, (81), 102850. https://doi.org/10.1016/j.techsoc.2025.102850.

Çelebi Demirarslan, P., Sönmez Çakır, F., & Akansel, I. (2024). Ranking the quality of life indexes by years in Asian countries using multi-criteria decision-making methods. *Asia Pacific Journal of Regional Science, 8*(3), 911–942. https://doi.org/10.1007/s41685-024-00350-w.

Demir, A. T., & Moslem, S. (2024). Evaluating the effect of the COVID-19 pandemic on medical waste disposal using preference selection index with CRADIS in a fuzzy environment. *Heliyon, 10*(5). https://doi.org/10.1016/j.heliyon.2024.e26997.

Ferla, G., Mura, B., Falasco, S., Caputo, P., & Matarazzo, A. (2024). Multi-Criteria Decision Analysis (MCDA) for sustainability assessment in food sector. A systematic literature review on methods, indicators and tools. *Science of the Total Environment, 946*, 174235. https://doi.org/10.1016/j.scitotenv.2024.174235.

Gligorić, M., Gligorić, Z., Lutovac, S., Negovanović, M., & Langović, Z. (2022). Novel hybrid MPSI–MARA decision-making model for support system selection in an underground mine. *Systems, 10*(6), 248. https://doi.org/10.3390/systems10060248.

Hasan, M. G., Ashraf, Z., & Khan, M. F. (2022). Multi-choice best-worst multi-criteria decision-making method and its applications. *International Journal of Intelligent Systems, 37*(2), 1129–1156. https://doi.org/10.1002/int.22663.

Haseli, G., Deveci, M., Isik, M., Gokasar, I., Pamučar, D., & Hajiaghaei-Keshteli, M. (2024). Providing climate change resilient land-use transport projects with green finance using Z extended numbers based decision-making model. *Expert Systems with Applications, 243*, 122858. https://doi.org/10.1016/j.eswa.2023.122858.

Haseli, G., Torkayesh, A. E., Hajiaghaei-Keshteli, M., & Venghaus, S. (2023). Sustainable resilient recycling partner selection for urban waste management: Consolidating perspectives of decision-makers and experts. *Applied Soft Computing, 137*, 110120. https://doi.org/10.1016/j.asoc.2023.110120.

Kara, K., Yalçın, G. C., Simic, V., Baysal, Z., & Pamučar, D. (2024). The alternative ranking uses a two-step logarithmic normalization method for benchmarking the supply chain performance of countries. *Socio Economic Planning Sciences, 92*. https://doi.org/10.1016/j.seps.2024.101822.

Li, T., Li, A., & Guo, X. (2020). The sustainable development-oriented development and utilization of renewable energy industry-A comprehensive analysis of MCDM methods. *Energy, 212*, 118694. https://doi.org/10.1016/j.energy.2020.118694.

Maniya, K., & Bhatt, M. G. (2010). A selection of material using a novel type decision-making method: Preference selection index method. *Materials & Design, 31*(4), 1785–1789. https://doi.org/10.1016/j.matdes.2009.11.020.

Özekenci, E. K. (2025). A hybrid MPSI-extended AROMAN decision-making model for assessing green logistics performance: The case of Asia-Pacific countries. *Logforum, 21*(1), 87–105. https://doi.org/10.17270/J.LOG.001154.

Sutrisno, A., & Kumar, V. (2022). Supply chain sustainability risk decision support model using integrated Preference Selection Index (PSI) method and prospect theory. *Journal of Advances in Management Research, 19*(2), 316–346.

Wittig Vianna, V., dos Santos, M., Francisco Simões Gomes, C., & Lauro, A. (2025). Application of the MPSI-CoCoSo method to rank OECD member countries towards the energy transition. *Computational Economics*. https://doi.org/10.1007/s10614-025-10963-8.

Yalçın, G. C., Kara, K., Gürol, P., Simic, V., & Pamučar, D. (2025). Enhancing operational efficiency and promoting best practices in the maritime industry: A decision support model for port authority performance evaluation. *Research in Transportation Business and Management, 62*, 101450. https://doi.org/10.1016/j.rtbm.2025.101450.

Zhang, X., Wang, D., Kong, D., Zhang, Z., & He, Y. (2022). The anti-fatigue, lightweight design of the heavy tractor frame is based on a modified decision method. *Structural and Multidisciplinary Optimization, 65*(10), 280. https://doi.org/10.1007/s00158-022-03385-9.

Zhou, X., Gao, T., & Long, J. (2025). Lightweight optimization design for the automotive front seat frame based on comprehensive Sobol global sensitivity analysis. *Proceedings of the Institution of Mechanical Engineers, Part C: Journal of Mechanical Engineering Science, 239*(18), 7321–7340. https://doi.org/10.1177/09544062251352410.

Chapter 52

OCRA: Operational competitiveness ratings assessment for multi-attribute decision-making

Yu Chen[1], Weizhong Wang[1], Shuping Cheng[2], and Muhammet Deveci[3]

[1]*School of Economics and Management, Anhui Normal University, Wuhu, Anhui Province, P.R. China,* [2]*School of Business Administration, Chaohu University, Hefei, Anhui Province, P.R.China,* [3]*Department of Industrial Engineering, Turkish Naval Academy, National Defence University, Istanbul, Türkiye*

52.1 Introduction

The operational competitiveness rating assessment (OCRA) was initially introduced by Parkan (1994) as a tool for operational performance measurement. Subsequent studies, particularly those examining the intersection of operational evaluation and multi-attribute decision-making (MADM), have confirmed the methodological equivalence between the two domains (Parkan & Wu, 1997). From a methodological perspective, the OCRA approach combines a straightforward average weighting technique with a max-min normalization process, providing a clear and computationally efficient solution for addressing MADM problems. It was specifically developed to address several inherent limitations of traditional techniques, such as data envelopment analysis (DEA), including the reliance on frontier construction, computational complexity, local comparison scope, sensitivity imbalance, vulnerability to outliers, and inability to incorporate managerial priorities and technological constraints. The OCRA method seeks to leverage the strengths of MADM techniques while addressing the limitations of traditional performance evaluation models. It possesses several distinctive advantages: (i) it employs ratio-based calculations and max-min normalization, which simplify the computational process and facilitate rapid implementation across diverse decision scenarios; (ii) the method's algorithmic transparency and structural simplicity enhance user comprehension and promote practical usability; (iii) it exhibits balanced sensitivity to variations across different criteria, ensuring robustness and stability in both homogeneous and heterogeneous decision environments; (iv) the method allows for the incorporation of criteria weights and decision-maker preferences, offering flexibility to align evaluations with strategic objectives or decision-maker opinions. Due to these features, the OCRA method has been widely applied across various fields, such as demolition waste transportation (Elshaboury & Marzouk, 2020), thermal barrier-coated diesel engine (Erdoğan et al., 2020), and temporary waste treatment facilities (Thakur, 2022), etc.

The remainder of the paper is organized as follows: the second section of the paper contains a literature review on the OCRA method; in the third section, the methodology to be used is presented; the application of the proposed methodology is presented in Section 52.4 through a simple numerical example, and further validated in Section 52.5 using a more complex case study; ultimately, the conclusion is given.

52.2 Literature review

The OCRA method, first introduced by Parkan (1994), was proposed to gauge the performance of a group of operating entities called production units, and was further improved by Parkan and Wu (1997). In recent years, OCRA has been expanded to various ambiguous contexts for addressing complex problems. For example, Parkan et al. (1997) applied the OCRA to rank the relative operational performance of the application software development in terms of a large bank in Hong Kong. Parkan and Wu (1999) adopted the OCRA method to select the most suitable robust. Agrell and Martin West (2001)

Encyclopedia of Multi-Attribute Decision-Making (MADM). DOI: https://doi.org/10.1016/B978-0-443-33275-3.00010-5

adopted the OCRA method to assess the performance development of a decision-making unit. Chatterjee and Chakraborty (2012) adopted the OCRA method to solve the material selection challenges in the engineering design process. Roman-Liu et al. (2013) analyzed the convergence of the OCRA method and the upper limb risk assessment to assess the risks of developing musculoskeletal disorders at 18 respective task workstations. Madić et al. (2015) discussed the OCRA method for solving nonconventional matching process selection problems. Mohammed et al. (2021) presented the OCRA approach to rank the suppliers of scrap metal for a steel manufacturing company.

In addition, due to the simplicity and flexibility in generating reliable ranking outcomes, the OCRA method has been widely applied in fuzzy environments to address real-world and practical decision-making problems. Stanujkic et al. (2017) extended the OCRA method using interval grey numbers to assess the linear performance grades for both benefit and cost criteria. Ulutaş (2019) proposed a hybrid model integrating the analytic hierarchy process (AHP) with the OCRA models under triangular fuzzy numbers to select five fabric suppliers for the Turkish textile industry. Ulutaş et al. (2020) extended the OCRA method with the grey numbers to evaluate and select employees for specific work positions in a textile factory. A hesitant fuzzy AHP and OCRA method were developed by Candan (2020) to prioritize the efficiency and performance of economic research in 15 organisation for economic co-operation and development (OECD) member countries between 2010 and 2017. Thakur (2022) constructed a novel grey-AHP-OCRA method for prioritizing and selecting the optimal location for temporary healthcare waste treatment facilities. In Ref (Mishra et al., 2023), the authors developed an integrated intuitionistic fuzzy closeness coefficient-based OCRA method to analyze and determine the most suitable and sustainable urban transportation. Madhavi et al. (2023) developed a hybrid grey pivot pairwise relative criteria importance assessment (PIPRECIA) and grey OCRA methods to rank sensor nodes and dynamically isolate the least cooperative nodes from the routing path. Rani et al. (2023) applied the interval-valued Pythagorean fuzzy OCRA method to assess and prioritize the Metaverse integration options of the sharing economy in the transportation sector.

52.3 Methodology

The OCRA model is a typical MADM method used to rank a set of alternatives. The implementation process of the OCRA model consists of the following key steps:

Step 1. Establish an initial decision matrix.

To solve the MADM problem, we assume that $A_i = \{A_1, A_2, \cdots, A_m\}$ is the set of alternatives and $C_j = \{C_1, C_2, \cdots, C_n\}$ represents a set of evaluation criteria. The corresponding decision matrix is given by $Y = (y_{ij})_{m\times n}$ defined as follows:

$$Y = \begin{bmatrix} y_{11} & y_{12} & \cdots & y_{1n} \\ y_{21} & y_{22} & \cdots & y_{2n} \\ \vdots & \vdots & \ddots & \vdots \\ y_{m1} & y_{m2} & \cdots & y_{mn} \end{bmatrix}, \tag{52.1}$$

where y_{ij} denotes the evaluation information of the alternative A_i with respect to the criterion C_j. Depending on the characteristics of the problem, y_{ij} can be expressed in the form of fuzzy numbers, linguistic models, and precise numerical values.

Step 2. Compute the performance rating for benefit criteria.

For benefit criteria, the performance rating is computed as follows:

$$P_i = \sum_{j\in s_b} \varpi_j \left(\frac{y_{ij} - \min_j y_{ij}}{\max_j y_{ij} - \min_j y_{ij}} \right), \; i = 1, 2, \cdots, m. \tag{52.2}$$

where ϖ_j is the weight of the criteria C_j. It can be acquired by using subjective or objective methods, depending on the characteristics of the problem.

Step 3. Find the linear performance rating for the benefit criteria.

For benefit criteria, the linear performance rating is obtained as follows:

$$\overline{P}_i = P_i - \min_i P_i, \; i = 1, 2, \cdots, m. \tag{52.3}$$

Step 4. Get the performance rating for cost criteria.

For cost criteria, the performance rating is estimated as follows:

$$Q_i = \sum_{j\in s_n} \varpi_j \left(\frac{\max y_{ij} - y_{ij}}{\max_j y_{ij} - \min_j y_{ij}} \right), \; i = 1, 2, \cdots, m. \tag{52.4}$$

Step 5. Calculate the linear performance rating for cost criteria.

For cost criteria, the linear performance rating is calculated as follows:

$$\overline{Q}_i = Q_i - \min_i Q_i,\ i = 1, 2, \cdots, m. \tag{52.5}$$

Step 6. Determine the total performance rating.

The total performance rating of each alternative is determined as follows:

$$O_i = (\overline{P}_i + \overline{Q}_i) - \min_i (\overline{P}_i + \overline{Q}_i),\ i = 1, 2, \cdots, m. \tag{52.6}$$

Step 7. Rank the alternatives.

The OCRA method prioritizes the alternatives based on the value of the total performance rating (Q_i). The alternatives are prioritized with decreasing degrees of the total performance rating (Q_i). The alternative with the highest value of total performance rating (Q_i) is the optimal alternative.

52.4 Numerical example 1

This section provides a simple numerical example to illustrate the application of the OCRA method in selecting an optimal commuting mode for daily urban travel. In modern cities, individuals often need to choose between several transportation options. The decision-making process is further complicated by various factors, including traffic congestion, environmental awareness, urban planning policies, and individual lifestyle preferences. With the increasing emphasis on sustainability, personal time efficiency, and environmental responsibility, choosing a suitable commuting mode has become a critical task for urban residents. This selection process is inherently a MADM problem, as individuals take into account multiple criteria such as travel time, cost, comfort, schedule reliability, and ecological considerations. By applying the OCRA framework, this example aims to demonstrate how the method provides a structured, transparent, and robust approach for resolving real-world MADM problems in the context of urban transportation planning.

In this example, 4 commuting modes are considered, namely: subway (A_1), private car (A_2), shared bike (A_3), and ride-hailing service (A_4). These commuting modes are assessed based on 6 evaluation criteria, which include 2 benefit type criteria (C_1, C_2) and three cost type criteria (C_3, C_4, C_5), as shown below: comfort level (C_1), environmental friendliness (C_2), daily travel cost (C_3), average travel time (C_4), and walking distance to assess point (C_5). Then, the decision-making process is subsequently carried out using the OCRA method, as outlined below.

Step 1. Establish an initial decision matrix.

In this step, the positive integers {1, 2, 3, 4, 5, 6, 7} are utilized to symbolize the evaluation information. Subsequently, experts are invited to assess each commuting mode based on each criterion, with the comprehensive evaluation details displayed in Table 52.1.

Step 2. Compute the performance rating for benefit criteria.

Let the weight of five criteria be $\varpi_1 = 0.20$, $\varpi_2 = 0.15$, $\varpi_3 = 0.30$, $\varpi_4 = 0.25$, and $\varpi_5 = 0.10$. As represented in Table 52.1, the criteria C_1 and C_2 are the beneficial criteria. Based on these values, the performance rating for benefit

TABLE 52.1 The detailed evaluation information of each commuting mode.

	C_1	C_2	C_3	C_4	C_5
A_1	4	6	3	4	5
A_2	7	2	7	6	1
A_3	3	7	2	5	6
A_4	6	4	6	3	2

criteria can be computed by using Eq. (52.2). For instance, the performance rating of the alternative A_1 can be obtained by using Eq. (52.7). The performance rating for benefit criteria is displayed in Table 52.2.

$$P_1 = \varpi_1\left(\frac{y_{11} - \min_j y_{1j}}{\max_j y_{1j} - \min_j y_{1j}}\right) + \varpi_2\left(\frac{y_{12} - \min_j y_{1j}}{\max_j y_{1j} - \min_j y_{1j}}\right)$$
$$= 0.2 \times \left(\frac{4-3}{7-3}\right) + 0.15 \times \left(\frac{6-2}{7-2}\right) = 0.17 \tag{52.7}$$

Step 3. Find the linear performance rating for the benefit criteria.

The linear performance rating for benefit criteria can be calculated by using Eq. (52.3). For instance, the linear performance rating of an alternative A_1 can be estimated by using Eq. (52.8), and the linear performance rating for the benefit criteria is exhibited in Table 52.3.

$$\overline{P}_1 = P_1 - \min_i P_i = 0.17 - 0.15 = 0.020 \tag{52.8}$$

Step 4. Get the performance rating for cost criteria.

As represented in Table 52.1, the criteria C_3, C_4, and C_5 are cost criteria. Based on these values, the performance rating for cost criteria can be obtained by using Eq. (52.4). For instance, the performance of an alternative A_1 can be calculated with the help of Eq. (52.9), and the performance rating for cost criteria is displayed in Table 52.4.

$$Q_1 = \varpi_3\left(\frac{\max y_{1j} - y_{13}}{\max_j y_{1j} - \min_j y_{1j}}\right) + \varpi_4\left(\frac{\max y_{1j} - y_{14}}{\max_j y_{1j} - \min_j y_{1j}}\right) + \varpi_5\left(\frac{\max y_{1j} - y_{15}}{\max_j y_{1j} - \min_j y_{1j}}\right)$$
$$= 0.3 \times \left(\frac{7-3}{7-2}\right) + 0.25 \times \left(\frac{6-4}{6-3}\right) + 0.1 \times \left(\frac{6-5}{6-1}\right) = 0.427 \tag{52.9}$$

TABLE 52.2 The performance rating for benefit criteria.

	A_1	A_2	A_3	A_4
P_i	0.170	0.200	0.150	0.210

TABLE 52.3 The linear performance rating for benefit criteria.

	A_1	A_2	A_3	A_4
$\overline{P}_i$	0.020	0.050	0.000	0.060

TABLE 52.4 The performance rating for cost criteria.

	A_1	A_2	A_3	A_4
Q_i	0.427	0.100	0.383	0.390

TABLE 52.5 The linear performance rating for cost criteria.

	A_1	A_2	A_3	A_4
$\overline{Q}_i$	0.327	0.000	0.283	0.290

TABLE 52.6 The total performance rating.

	A_1	A_2	A_3	A_4
O_i	0.297	0.000	0.233	0.300
Rank	4	1	3	2

Step 5. Calculate the linear performance rating for cost criteria.

The linear performance rating for cost criteria can be obtained by using Eq. (52.5). For instance, the linear performance rating of an alternative A_1 can be acquired by using Eq. (52.10), and the linear performance for cost criteria is depicted in Table 52.5.

$$\overline{Q}_1 = Q_1 - \min_i Q_i = 0.43 - 0.1 = 0.327 \tag{52.10}$$

Step 6. Determine the total performance rating.

Based on the results shown in Tables 52.3 and 52.5, the total performance rating of each alternative can be derived by referring to Eq. (52.6). For instance, the total performance rating of an alternative A_1 can be determined by using Eq. (52.11), and the total performance rating is exhibited in Table 52.6.

$$O_1 = (\overline{P}_1 + \overline{Q}_1) - \min_i(\overline{P}_i + \overline{Q}_i) = 0.297 \tag{52.11}$$

Step 7. Rank the alternatives.

Hence, the ranking order of commuting modes is $A_4 \succ A_1 \succ A_3 \succ A_2$, indicating that the ride-hailing service (A_4) is identified as the most preferred commuting mode.

52.5 Numerical example 2

To illustrate the practical relevance of the OCRA method in solving real-world decision-making problems, this study presents a comprehensive case involving the selection of renewable energy suppliers. In modern industrial contexts, green energy suppliers are fundamental components of sustainable production systems, yet their contribution to enterprise decarbonization and operational reliability may vary substantially depending on their capabilities, technologies, and service attributes. In light of the increasing urgency for low-carbon transformation, the task of identifying an optimal clean energy provider has become both strategically significant and analytically complex. This complexity stems from the rapid expansion and diversification of renewable energy technologies, including solar panels, wind turbines, and integrated hybrid systems, along with the emergence of numerous competing suppliers. Each supplier presents unique business models, technical skills, and environmental credentials. To support experts in managing such complexity, this study employs the OCRA method to systematically evaluate the performance of multiple suppliers across a broad range of technical, economic, and sustainability factors. Therefore, this section proposes an IVSF-OCRA method to evaluate the criteria and the performance of a renewable energy supplier.

As previously discussed, the identification and prioritization of evaluation criteria for each renewable energy supplier are critical steps in implementing sustainable and resilient energy strategies within the manufacturing sector. In this illustrative example, 8 different renewable energy suppliers are selected for analysis. Specifically, the selected suppliers include:

- Huaneng green power (A_1): A new energy enterprise specializing in wind and solar power generation. It has a wide market presence and industry influence across multiple provinces and regions in China.

- Sunshine energy group (A_2): A multinational enterprise group specializing in distributed solar energy solutions and customized photovoltaic services. It offers a full range of services from design, installation, financing, and maintenance to ongoing support for solar energy projects.
- Envision energy (A_3): A global leader in smart wind turbines and green energy systems, leveraging advanced digital capabilities to drive the global energy transition.
- China three gorges new energy (A_4): A state-backed developer that leverages the hydropower expertise of its parent company, China Three Gorges Corporation, to expand into large-scale wind and solar projects.
- Goldwind supply chain division (A_5): A vertically integrated wind turbine manufacturer that offers comprehensive and efficient delivery and operation solutions, including project planning, design, engineering, construction, installation, and maintenance services.
- SPIC (State power investment corporation)-clean energy division (A_6): A comprehensive clean energy provider under a major state-owned utility, with expertise in solar, wind, and grid integration.
- GCL new energy holding (A_7): A solar-focused enterprise engaged in the investment, construction, and operation of solar power plants, with a global presence and a diversified portfolio in renewable energy solutions.
- LONGi green energy (A_8): The world's largest solar module supplier, offering cost-effective photovoltaic solutions to global markets through continuous innovation and sustainable development.

Then, we identified 10 criteria for selecting renewable energy suppliers in the context of low-carbon manufacturing. These include:

- Unit electricity price (C_1): It represents the supplier's quoted price per kilowatt-hour of electricity. Lower unit electricity costs imply better cost-efficiency and improved economic performance for the manufacturing enterprise. It directly affects the enterprise's operational costs and competitiveness in energy-intensive production environments.
- Service response time (C_2): It measures the average time required by the supplier to respond to equipment faults, outages, or service requests. Faster response times indicate a more proactive and customer-oriented service system, which is essential for minimizing production downtime and ensuring energy continuity in industrial operations.
- Geographic proximity (C_3): It captures the physical distance between the renewable energy supplier's main generation facility and the manufacturing plant. Shorter geographic distances typically result in lower transmission losses and reduced infrastructure dependency, contributing to both cost savings and improved supply reliability.
- Annual supply capability (C_4): It reflects the supplier's capability to deliver a consistent and sufficient amount of renewable electricity on an annual basis. A higher annual supply capability indicates stronger scalability and reliability, ensuring that the supplier can meet long-term energy demands, particularly during peak operational periods.
- Technological maturity (C_5): It assesses the level of advancement and integration in the supplier's renewable energy technologies, including solar, wind, biomass, and energy storage systems. Higher technological maturity implies better operational efficiency, lower risk of system failure, and alignment with modern energy infrastructure standards.
- Green certification level (C_6): It measures the extent to which the supplier's energy products have been verified and certified by recognized environmental or governmental bodies. A higher certification level assures compliance with environmental regulations and enhances the environmental credibility of the manufacturing firm in the supply chain.
- Contract flexibility (C_7): This reflects the supplier's willingness and capacity to offer adaptable contract terms, such as pricing mechanisms, load adjustment clauses, and duration renegotiation. Greater flexibility enables manufacturers to better cope with demand fluctuations, price volatility, and market changes.
- Transparency of sustainability strategy (C_8): It evaluates the extent to which the supplier publicly discloses its sustainability goals, environmental performance, and carbon reduction initiatives. Higher transparency fosters better alignment with the manufacturer's environmental, social, and governance strategies and contributes to reputational synergy.
- Past cooperation satisfaction (C_9): It is based on previous client evaluations, survey results, or historical cooperation records. It provides insight into the supplier's reliability, communication effectiveness, and ability to meet contractual obligations, serving as a proxy for long-term relationship quality and trustworthiness.
- Risk management capability (C_{10}): It assesses the supplier's ability to foresee, prevent, and manage potential risks associated with renewable energy provision, including market price volatility, regulatory shifts, extreme weather events, and grid instability. A higher score in this dimension ensures greater energy security and supply resilience for the manufacturer.

In this numerical example, four experts participate in the decision-making process, and the OCRA method is employed to determine the overall ranking of the alternatives. The criteria and corresponding alternatives are illustrated in Fig. 52.1.

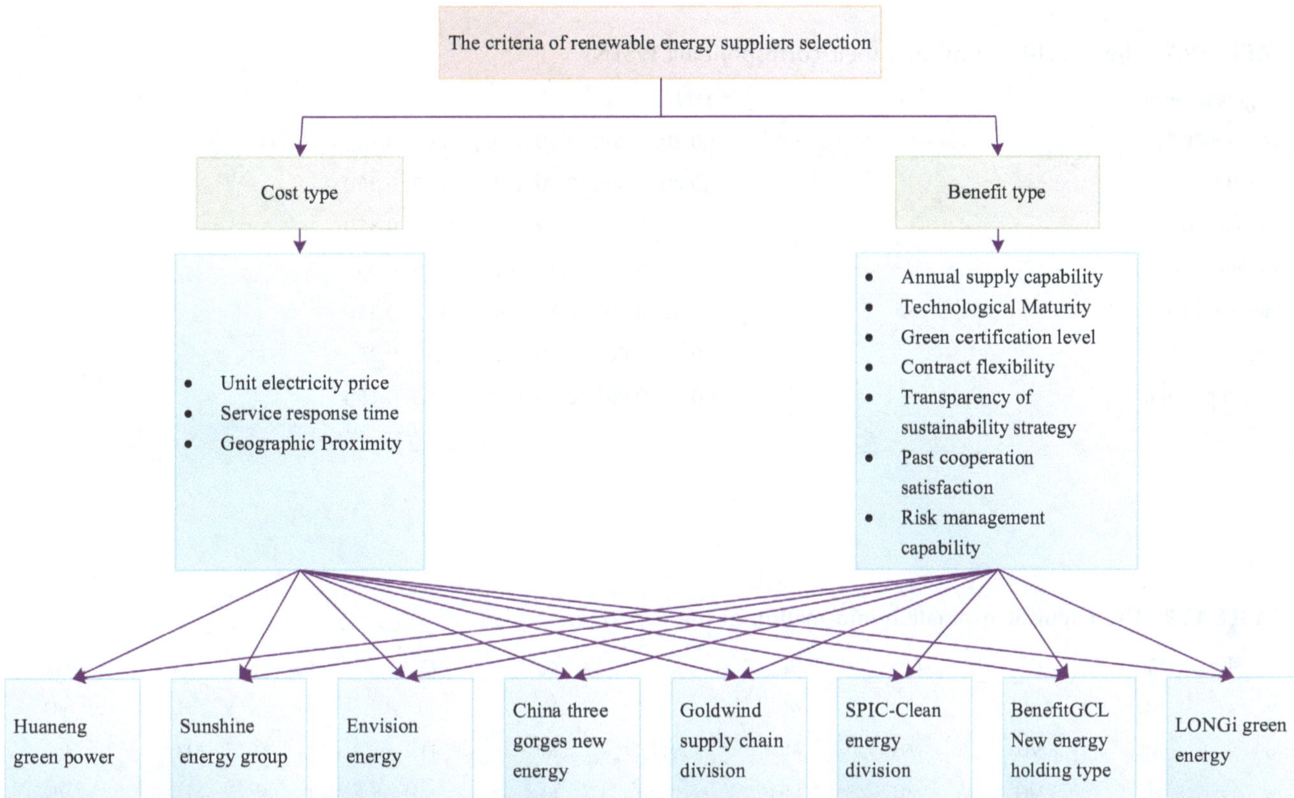

FIGURE 52.1 The criteria of renewable energy suppliers selection.

Step 1. Establish an initial decision matrix.

In this step, four experts are invited to evaluate the alternatives using linguistic terms, as defined in Table 52.7. These linguistic assessments are subsequently converted into interval-valued spherical fuzzy numbers (IVSFNs) based on the linguistic scale in Table 52.7. The evaluation information from four experts is displayed in Tables 52.8–52.11.

Step 2. Fusion individual performance.

Let the experts' weights be $w_1 = 0.25$, $w_2 = 0.30$, $w_3 = 0.20$, and $w_4 = 0.25$. We use the interval-valued spherical fuzzy weighted arithmetic (IVSFWA) operator to integrate the individual evaluating matrix by Eq. (52.12). The group evaluating matrix is represented in Table 52.12.

$$\mathrm{IVSFWA}_w(S_1, S_2, \cdots, S_n) = \left\langle \begin{array}{c} \left[\sqrt{1 - \Pi_{t=1}^{q}\left(1-(P_k^L)^2\right)^{w_t}}, \sqrt{1 - \Pi_{t=1}^{q}\left(1-(P_k^U)^2\right)^{w_t}}\right], \\ \left[\Pi_{t=1}^{q}(N_k^L)^{w_t}, \Pi_{t=1}^{q}(N_k^U)^{w_t}\right], \left[\Pi_{t=1}^{q}(I_k^L)^{w_t}, \Pi_{t=1}^{q}(I_k^U)^{w_t}\right] \end{array} \right\rangle \tag{52.12}$$

Based on the group preference matrix, the value of the score function can be calculated by using Eq. (52.13). The score function value matrix is shown in Table 52.13.

$$Score(S) = \frac{1}{3}\left[(P_S^L)^2 + (P_S^U)^2 - (N_S^L)^2 - (N_S^U)^2 - (I_S^L)^2 - (I_S^U)^2\right] \tag{52.13}$$

Step 3. Compute the performance rating for benefit criteria.

Let the weights of 10 criteria be $\varpi_1 = 0.10$, $\varpi_2 = 0.08$, $\varpi_3 = 0.10$, $\varpi_4 = 0.12$, $\varpi_5 = 0.10$, $\varpi_6 = 0.08$, $\varpi_7 = 0.10$, $\varpi_8 = 0.10$, $\varpi_9 = 0.10$, and $\varpi_{10} = 0.12$. Criteria C_1, C_2, and C_3 are the beneficial criteria. Then, the performance rating for benefit criteria is obtained by referring to Eq. (52.2) and displayed in Table 52.14.

Step 4. Find the linear performance rating for the benefit criteria.

The linear performance rating for benefit criteria can be computed by using Eq. (52.3) and represented in Table 52.15.

TABLE 52.7 The linguistic terms and their corresponding IVSFNs.

Linguistic term	TFNs
Very low (VL)	([0.10, 0.20], [0.80, 0.90], [0.05, 0.15])
Low (L)	([0.20, 0.30], [0.70, 0.80], [0.15, 0.25])
Medium low (ML)	([0.30, 0.40], [0.60, 0.70], [0.20, 0.35])
Medium (M)	([0.45, 0.55], [0.40, 0.50], [0.35, 0.45])
Medium high (MH)	([0.60, 0.70], [0.30, 0.40], [0.25, 0.35])
High (H)	([0.70, 0.80], [0.20, 0.30], [0.15, 0.25])
Very high (VH)	([0.80, 0.90], [0.10, 0.20], [0.05, 0.15])

TABLE 52.8 The linguistic evaluation information of the expert e_1.

	C_1	C_2	C_3	C_4	C_5	C_6	C_7	C_8	C_9	C_{10}
A_1	ML	VL	M	M	VH	VH	VL	ML	H	VH
A_2	ML	VL	MH	ML	VH	ML	H	M	M	L
A_3	H	VH	ML	MH	L	M	MH	L	L	VL
A_4	MH	ML	ML	H	ML	ML	MH	M	MH	H
A_5	MH	ML	ML	L	VL	L	L	VL	VL	VH
A_6	VL	H	L	ML	ML	VL	VH	VH	VH	VL
A_7	VL	L	ML	VL	VH	H	M	VH	MH	L
A_8	M	MH	VH	VH	L	VL	H	H	VL	H

TABLE 52.9 The linguistic evaluation information of the expert e_2.

	C_1	C_2	C_3	C_4	C_5	C_6	C_7	C_8	C_9	C_{10}
A_1	MH	VL	VH	VH	H	VH	ML	VL	ML	M
A_2	L	MH	L	VL	L	ML	ML	MH	VL	VH
A_3	VH	L	ML	ML	M	ML	ML	ML	H	ML
A_4	L	M	H	M	M	ML	ML	VL	VH	VL
A_5	VL	M	L	ML	L	ML	MH	VH	VL	M
A_6	VH	L	ML	L	VH	ML	MH	H	MH	ML
A_7	MH	L	VL	ML	VH	H	ML	MH	ML	H
A_8	ML	M	ML	L	VH	H	M	ML	VH	M

TABLE 52.10 The linguistic evaluation information of the expert e_3.

	C_1	C_2	C_3	C_4	C_5	C_6	C_7	C_8	C_9	C_{10}
A_1	MH	MH	VH	VH	L	ML	M	ML	L	ML
A_2	L	MH	ML	M	H	H	L	VH	ML	M
A_3	ML	MH	L	VL	ML	VL	L	H	ML	M
A_4	VL	VL	L	MH	ML	ML	VL	M	L	H
A_5	ML	MH	ML	H	L	H	VL	VH	VL	M
A_6	VL	M	ML	VH	L	VL	VH	VL	VL	H
A_7	VL	MH	H	VH	MH	ML	VH	H	M	VH
A_8	VH	VL	M	VL	L	VH	ML	H	VL	VL

TABLE 52.11 The linguistic evaluation information of the expert e_4.

	C_1	C_2	C_3	C_4	C_5	C_6	C_7	C_8	C_9	C_{10}
A_1	VL	VH	M	H	H	VH	L	L	L	H
A_2	H	H	H	VH	MH	ML	VH	ML	L	VH
A_3	ML	M	L	VL	L	MH	M	L	ML	M
A_4	VH	VH	VL	H	MH	VH	H	MH	ML	VH
A_5	L	H	L	VH	VH	L	L	VL	VH	H
A_6	VL	ML	MH	L	MH	VH	MH	L	M	MH
A_7	VH	L	H	H	M	MH	H	VL	MH	ML
A_8	MH	VH	VL	VL	VH	L	ML	VL	VL	VH

TABLE 52.12 The group preference matrix.

	C_1	C_2
A_1	([0.470, 0.569], [0.456, 0.563], [0.158,0.283])	([0.544, 0.660], [0.391, 0.525], [0.069, 0.178])
A_2	([0.437, 0.541], [0.492, 0.605],[0.161, 0.272])	([0.571, 0.673], [0.346, 0.456], [0.147, 0.260])
A_3	([0.635, 0.752], [0.266, 0.389], [0.123, 0.250])	([0.582, 0.698], [0.316, 0.438], [0.156, 0.273])
A_4	([0.563, 0.680], [0.358, 0.487], [0.104, 0.216])	([0.543, 0.661], [0.360, 0.486], [0.127, 0.258])
A_5	([0.366, 0.461], [0.572, 0.679], [0.130, 0.250])	([0.543, 0.647], [0.351, 0.458], [0.230, 0.347])
A_6	([0.519, 0.640], [0.429, 0.573], [0.050, 0.150])	([0.470, 0.574], [0.440, 0.551], [0.191, 0.306])
A_7	([0.571, 0.686], [0.354, 0.484], [0.081, 0.193])	([0.339, 0.435], [0.591, 0.696],[0.166, 0.267])
A_8	([0.575, 0.689], [0.319, 0.436], [0.184, 0.315])	([0.595, 0.709], [0.302, 0.423], [0.134, 0.258])

(Continued)

TABLE 52.12 (Continued)

	C_3	**C_4**
A_1	([0.681, 0.797], [0.200, 0.316], [0.132, 0.260])	([0.722, 0.832], [0.168, 0.278],[0.107, 0.224])
A_2	([0.517, 0.621], [0.402, 0.513], [0.181, 0.291])	([0.528, 0.647], [0.385, 0.516],[0.104, 0.231])
A_3	([0.260, 0.359], [0.643, 0.743], [0.176, 0.301])	([0.367, 0.461], [0.574, 0.681], [0.113, 0.239])
A_4	([0.459, 0.562], [0.478, 0.594], [0.122, 0.239])	([0.624, 0.728], [0.267, 0.370], [0.214, 0.319])
A_5	([0.251, 0.350], [0.653, 0.753], [0.171, 0.291])	([0.590, 0.708], [0.320, 0.447], [0.124, 0.243])
A_6	([0.394, 0.493], [0.524, 0.629], [0.197, 0.322])	([0.471, 0.590], [0.456, 0.586], [0.129, 0.246])
A_7	([0.530, 0.635], [0.399, 0.516], [0.116, 0.233])	([0.576, 0.691], [0.342, 0.469], [0.100, 0.220])
A_8	([0.531, 0.650], [0.380, 0.509], [0.112, 0.241])	([0.488, 0.608], [0.457, 0.596], [0.070, 0.175])
	C_5	**C_6**
A_1	([0.685, 0.794], [0.216, 0.330], [0.114, 0.220])	([0.753, 0.863], [0.143, 0.257], [0.066, 0.178])
A_2	([0.634, 0.747], [0.271, 0.391], [0.130, 0.239])	([0.435, 0.539], [0.482, 0.591], [0.189, 0.327])
A_3	([0.319, 0.416], [0.574, 0.676], [0.205, 0.319])	([0.424, 0.523], [0.483, 0.588], [0.184, 0.315])
A_4	([0.446, 0.547], [0.447, 0.550], [0.250, 0.377])	([0.528, 0.649], [0.383, 0.512], [0.141, 0.283])
A_5	([0.493, 0.614], [0.445, 0.583], [0.087, 0.194])	([0.409, 0.512], [0.520, 0.632], [0.164, 0.277])
A_6	([0.602, 0.719], [0.304, 0.429], [0.132, 0.254])	([0.500, 0.620], [0.436, 0.573], [0.076, 0.193])
A_7	([0.712, 0.824], [0.176, 0.289], [0.112, 0.234])	([0.628, 0.731], [0.276, 0.382], [0.181, 0.291])
A_8	([0.664, 0.785], [0.240, 0.373], [0.082, 0.189])	([0.585, 0.700], [0.337, 0.465], [0.091, 0.199])
	C_7	**C_8**
A_1	([0.287, 0.382], [0.618, 0.721], [0.147, 0.274])	([0.233, 0.329], [0.680, 0.780], [0.123, 0.250])
A_2	([0.607, 0.724], [0.300, 0.425], [0.124, 0.243])	([0.585, 0.698], [0.308, 0.423], [0.186, 0.315])
A_3	([0.430, 0.530], [0.470, 0.575], [0.230, 0.348])	([0.409, 0.512], [0.520, 0.632],[0.164, 0.277])
A_4	([0.516, 0.620], [0.406, 0.518], [0.149, 0.272])	([0.441, 0.539], [0.458, 0.564], [0.179, 0.304])
A_5	([0.380, 0.476], [0.558, 0.665], [0.140, 0.250])	([0.635, 0.757], [0.283, 0.424], [0.050, 0.150])
A_6	([0.711, 0.820], [0.183, 0.293],[0.121, 0.239])	([0.612, 0.727], [0.304, 0.432], [0.091, 0.199])
A_7	([0.606, 0.720], [0.288, 0.405], [0.162, 0.289])	([0.640, 0.751], [0.269,0.389], [0.101, 0.214])
A_8	([0.493, 0.598], [0.404, 0.512], [0.220, 0.347])	([0.533, 0.638], [0.393, 0.509], [0.124, 0.243])
	C_9	**C_{10}**
A_1	([0.440, 0.544], [0.489, 0.601],[0.164, 0.277])	([0.632, 0.746], [0.258, 0.374], [0.156, 0.281])
A_2	([0.291, 0.385], [0.614, 0.717], [0.141, 0.266])	([0.679, 0.797], [0.215, 0.340], [0.097, 0.212])
A_3	([0.474, 0.579], [0.448, 0.561], [0.171, 0.291])	([0.352, 0.449], [0.537, 0.641], [0.182, 0.317])
A_4	([0.602, 0.719], [0.304, 0.429], [0.132, 0.254])	([0.655, 0.767], [0.255, 0.377], [0.082, 0.189])
A_5	([0.481, 0.600], [0.476, 0.618], [0.050, 0.150])	([0.645, 0.757], [0.238, 0.350], [0.174, 0.295])
A_6	([0.601, 0.715], [0.298, 0.418], [0.132, 0.255])	([0.492, 0.594], [0.435, 0.547], [0.141, 0.265])
A_7	([0.507, 0.608], [0.391, 0.495], [0.250, 0.368])	([0.597, 0.712], [0.313, 0.437], [0.129, 0.246])
A_8	([0.519, 0.640], [0.429, 0.573], [0.050, 0.150])	([0.624, 0.738], [0.273, 0.394], [0.118, 0.237])

TABLE 52.13 The score function value matrix.

	C_1	C_2	C_3	C_4	C_5	C_6	C_7	C_8	C_9	C_{10}
A_1	-0.028	0.089	0.291	0.349	0.294	0.396	-0.257	-0.329	-0.071	0.215
A_2	-0.075	0.121	0.037	0.073	0.220	-0.082	0.183	0.141	-0.250	0.293
A_3	0.223	0.145	-0.297	-0.172	-0.218	-0.086	-0.087	-0.115	-0.023	-0.169
A_4	0.119	0.094	-0.042	0.188	-0.070	0.064	0.040	-0.056	0.174	0.256
A_5	-0.174	0.069	-0.307	0.158	0.012	-0.115	-0.155	0.230	-0.014	0.231
A_6	0.047	-0.026	-0.138	-0.020	0.174	0.024	0.329	0.192	0.175	0.005
A_7	0.131	-0.209	0.064	0.138	0.335	0.196	0.176	0.231	0.010	0.166
A_8	0.127	0.167	0.077	0.003	0.273	0.152	0.002	0.068	0.047	0.211

TABLE 52.14 The performance rating for benefit criteria.

	A_1	A_2	A_3	A_4	A_5	A_6	A_7	A_8
P_i	0.200	0.153	0.177	0.183	0.059	0.123	0.139	0.220

TABLE 52.15 The linear performance rating for benefit criteria.

	A_1	A_2	A_3	A_4	A_5	A_6	A_7	A_8
$\overline{P}_i$	0.141	0.093	0.118	0.123	0.000	0.064	0.080	0.161

TABLE 52.16 The performance rating for cost criteria.

	A_1	A_2	A_3	A_4	A_5	A_6	A_7	A_8
P_i	0.286	0.300	0.595	0.273	0.326	0.254	0.178	0.266

Step 5. Get the performance rating for cost criteria.

Criteria C_4, C_5, C_6, C_7, C_8, C_9, and C_{10} are cost criteria. The performance rating for cost criteria is calculated by using Eq. (52.4) and shown in Table 52.16.

Step 6. Calculate the linear performance rating for cost criteria.

The linear performance rating for cost criteria can be calculated by using Eq. (52.5) and displayed in Table 52.17.

TABLE 52.17 The linear performance rating for benefit criteria.

	A_1	A_2	A_3	A_4	A_5	A_6	A_7	A_8
$\overline{Q}_i$	0.141	0.093	0.118	0.123	0.000	0.064	0.080	0.161

TABLE 52.18 The total performance rating.

	A_1	A_2	A_3	A_4	A_5	A_6	A_7	A_8
O_i	0.169	0.136	0.455	0.139	0.068	0.060	0.000	0.169
Rank	3	8	1	4	2	5	6	7

Step 7. Determine the total performance rating.

Based on the outcomes shown in Tables 52.15 and 52.17, the total performance rating of each alternative can be obtained by adopting Eq. (52.6) and is shown in Table 52.18.

Step 8. Rank the alternatives.

Hence, the prioritization of alternatives for renewable energy suppliers is $A_3 \succ A_8 \succ A_1 \succ A_4 \succ A_2 \succ A_5 \succ A_6 \succ A_7$, and Envision energy ($A_3$) is the best renewable energy supplier.

52.6 Conclusions

In this chapter, we presented the OCRA method, a typical technique in the domain of MADM. We began by outlining its background and key characteristics of the OCRA approach. Subsequently, a comprehensive review of existing literature was conducted to highlight the methodological advancements and wide-ranging applications of the OCRA method across different decision-making contexts. To facilitate a clear understanding of the method's logic, a simple numerical example related to urban commuting options was introduced, accompanied by a step-by-step interpretation of the main computational procedures. Building on this foundation, a more complex numerical example involving the selection of renewable energy suppliers was provided to demonstrate the practical applicability of the OCRA method in solving real-world MADM problems. In this context, we further introduced the IVSF-OCRA method to enhance decision-making support in renewable energy supplier evaluation within the manufacturing sector.

Reference

Agrell, P. J., & Martin West, B. (2001). A caveat on the measurement of productive efficiency. *International Journal of Production Economics, 69*(1), 1–14.

Candan, G. (2020). Efficiency and performance analysis of economics research using hesitant fuzzy AHP and OCRA methods. *Scientometrics, 124*(3), 2645–2659.

Chatterjee, P., & Chakraborty, S. (2012). Material selection using preferential ranking methods. *Materials & Design, 35*, 384–393.

Elshaboury, N., & Marzouk, M. (2020). Optimizing construction and demolition waste transportation for sustainable construction projects. *Engineering, Construction and Architectural Management, 28*(9), 2411–2425.

Erdoğan, S., Aydın, S., Balki, M. K., & Sayin, C. (2020). Operational evaluation of thermal barrier coated diesel engine fueled with biodiesel/diesel blend by using MCDM method base on engine performance, emission and combustion characteristics. *Renewable Energy, 151*, 698–706.

Madhavi, S., Praveen, R., Jagadish Kumar, N., & Udhaya Sankar, S. M. (2023). Hybrid grey PIPRECIA and grey OCRA method-based dynamic multi-criteria decision-making model for mitigating non-cooperating node attacks in WSNs. *Peer-to-Peer Networking and Applications, 16*(5), 2607–2629.

Madić, M., Petković, D., & Radovanović, M. (2015). Selection of non-conventional machining processes using the OCRA method. *Serbian Journal of Management, 10*(1), 61–73.
Mishra, A. R., Rani, P., Cavallaro, F., Hezam, I. M., & Lakshmi, J. (2023). An integrated intuitionistic fuzzy closeness coefficient-based OCRA method for sustainable urban transportation options selection. *Axioms, 12*(2), 144.
Mohammed, A., Yazdani, M., Oukil, A., & Santibanez Gonzalez, E. D. R. (2021). A Hybrid MCDM approach towards resilient sourcing. *Sustainability, 13*(5), 2695.
Parkan, C. (1994). Operational competitiveness ratings of production units. *Managerial Decision Economics, 15*(3), 201–221.
Parkan, C., Lam, K., & Hang, G. (1997). Operational competitiveness analysis on software development. *Journal of the Operational Research Society, 48*(9), 892–905.
Parkan, C., & Wu, M.-L. (1999). Decision-making and performance measurement models with applications to robot selection. *Computers & Industrial Engineering, 36*(3), 503–523.
Parkan, C., & Wu, M. L. (1997). On the equivalence of operational performance measurement and multiple attribute decision making. *International Journal of Production Research, 35*(11), 2963–2988.
Rani, P., Alrasheedi, A. F., Mishra, A. R., & Cavallaro, F. (2023). Interval-valued pythagorean fuzzy operational competitiveness rating model for assessing the metaverse integration options of sharing economy in transportation sector. *Applied Soft Computing, 148*, 110806.
Roman-Liu, D., Groborz, A., & Tokarski, T. (2013). Comparison of risk assessment procedures used in OCRA and ULRA methods. *Ergonomics, 56*(10), 1584–1598.
Stanujkic, D., Zavadskas, E. K., Liu, S., Karabasevic, D., & Popovic, G. (2017). Improved OCRA method based on the use of interval grey numbers. *Journal of Grey System, 29*(4), 49–60.
Thakur, D. V. (2022). Locating temporary waste treatment facilities in the cities to handle the explosive growth of HCWs during pandemics: A novel Grey-AHP-OCRA hybrid approach. *Sustainable Cities and Society, 82*, 103907.
Ulutaş, A. (2019). Supplier selection by using a fuzzy integrated model for a textile company. *Engineering Economics, 30*(5), 579–590.
Ulutaş, A., Popovic, G., Stanujkic, D., Karabasevic, D., Zavadskas, E. K., & Turskis, Z. (2020). A new hybrid MCDM Model for personnel selection based on a novel grey PIPRECIA and grey OCRA methods. *Mathematics, 8*(10), 1698.

Chapter 53

EATWIOS: Efficiency analysis technique with input and output satisficing for multi-attribute decision-making

Ömer Faruk Görçün, and Cem Niyazi Durmuş
Department of Business Administration, Faculty of Economic, Administration, and Social Sciences, Kadir Has University, Istanbul, Türkiye

53.1 Introduction

Efficiency analysis technique with output satisficing (EATWOS) was first developed by Peters and Zelewski (2006) and introduced to the literature. It stands out as a performance/effectiveness analysis approach that aims to provide appropriate, satisfactory, and balanced solutions, especially in multicriteria decision-making (MCDM) processes. Unlike traditional and classical decision-making tools, this method offers satisfactory alternative solutions to decision-makers instead of producing optimal results, allowing decision-makers to make the most appropriate and satisfactory choices depending on the criteria prioritized. While classical and traditional decision-making frameworks mainly aim to achieve the ideal solution, the EATWOS appraises the performance of decision units based on their distance from the average solution, thus making it possible to obtain more feasible results. This procedure, which is used to analyze the operational, financial, and sustainability performance and efficiency of businesses and organizations, helps to address and evaluate input and output factors in a balanced way, providing a flexible framework for measuring performance, effectiveness, and efficiency in relative terms.

The development of the EATWOS method stemmed from the need to fill a critical gap in the literature, especially in MCDM and efficiency and performance analysis. Traditional methods, such as data envelopment analysis (DEA), operational competition rating analysis (OCRA), and stochastic bounds analysis, are frequently preferred to measure the efficiency of decision units. In contrast, because these procedures operate under specific assumptions, they do not always entirely reflect real-world uncertainties, multidimensional performance criteria, and their interactions. The EATWOS method offers a broader perspective, especially overcoming the constraints imposed by DEA. While deterministic models such as DEA identify the limits of efficiency based on specific mathematical assumptions, the EATWOS method provides a more flexible evaluation by considering the distances of the alternatives to the mean solution. In this aspect, EATWOS is a decision-making tool that can offer satisfactory solutions in different scenarios rather than just identifying the best options.

The EATWOS approach provides critically essential and practical contributions and advantages for decision-makers in decision-making processes. Due to its flexible structure, input and output satisfaction-based activity analysis can be easily integrated with different weighting approaches, such as criteria importance through intercriteria correlation (CRITIC) (Diakoulaki et al., 1992), entropy (Shannon & Weaver, 1949), logarithmic percentage change-driven objective weighting (LOPCOW) (Ecer & Pamucar, 2022), and method based on the removal effects of criteria (Keshavarz et al., 2021). The fact that this method can be integrated with different weighting approaches shows that it is not only intuitive but also built on a strong foundation in terms of mathematical application. This procedure, which is used in many different fields such as urban transportation, energy, logistics, and athlete selection in the literature, produces reasonable solutions to decision-making problems encountered in different industries while providing a comprehensive and multidimensional approach to operational efficiency and measuring performances in different contexts, while at the same time providing the opportunity

Encyclopedia of Multi-Attribute Decision-Making (MADM). DOI: https://doi.org/10.1016/B978-0-443-33275-3.00025-7

to improve and develop strategies regarding the resource use of enterprises, institutions and organizations, and organizational structures of different natures.

EATWOS has several advantages over DEA and OCRA methods. While DEA measures the efficiency of decision units with linear programming methods, EATWOS can evaluate alternatives without needing any linear programming model. It reduces the technique's computational complexity and gives decision-makers faster results (Görçün, 2019b). Besides, while the DEA generally works on analytical models that minimize inputs or maximize outputs, the EATWOS method offers a more extensive assessment by ensuring that inputs and outputs are balanced. Similarly, the OCRA method concentrates on sorting decision units using weighted coefficients. In contrast, the EATWOS method evaluates the performance of decision units relative to the distance to the average solution (Özbek, 2018). For this reason, the EATWOS method is more effective, especially in situations involving uncertainty or scenarios where decision units need to produce satisfactory solutions instead of the absolute best solution.

Studies conducted in recent years show that the EATWOS method is used effectively in various sectors. For example, Yüksekyıldız (2021) revealed that the EATWOS method offers a more flexible and practical approach than DEA when analyzing the efficiency of container ports in Turkey. Similarly, in a study conducted by Alnıpak (2022), the operational efficiency of the ports operated by the Republic of Turkey State Railways (TCDD) was examined, and more reliable and detailed results were obtained by integrating the EATWOS method with the CRITIC method. In the study, correlation analysis was applied to analyze the relationship between the operational efficiency and profitability of the ports, and the results showed that the efficiency scores obtained by the EATWOS method were positively related to profitability.

The EATWIOS method, which emerged as an improved version of EATWOS, offers a more advanced framework, especially in logistics efficiency and efficiency analysis. In a study conducted by Altintaş (2022), the EATWIOS method was used while analyzing the logistics performance efficiency of G7 countries, and it was determined that this method provides more detailed and reliable results compared to traditional MCDM techniques. One of the key differentiators of EATWIOS is that the inputs and outputs are not only weighted but also handled together with satisfactory solutions. This allows the method to be used more effectively, especially in multivariate and dynamic logistics and supply chain management.

The EATWOS method provides a flexible, practical, and reliable MCDM and performance analysis technique. This framework, which offers a broader perspective by handling the classical optimization methods' restrictions, is a powerful tool, especially in increasing the efficiency of operational processes and optimizing resource utilization. It has less computational complexity and produces satisfactory solutions compared to commonly used techniques such as DEA and OCRA is one of the most critical factors that make the method preferred in decision-making. In this context, EATWOS and EATWIOS methods continue to be an important area of research in terms of both academic and practical applications.

53.2 Research background

EATWOS and EATWIOS frameworks are MCDM approaches from performance, efficiency, and effectiveness analyses of decision alternatives and units considered in a decision-making problem. These two procedures can produce balanced and reasonable solutions by overcoming traditional methods' structural issues and limitations. When the evolution of the relevant literature from early studies to the present day is examined, these approaches have increased flexibility, accuracy, and reliability in decision-making processes (Alnıpak, 2022). Peters and Zelewski introduced the EATWOS approach and then used it to address complex decision-making problems faced in different industries and generate solutions.

In general, when the studies in the literature are evaluated, it is seen that this performance analysis method is applied to solve complex decision problems that arise in many different fields, from sports to production industries. However, it is seen that researchers use this framework to evaluate the relative performance of the decision units included in the evaluation process, which is different from the ranking techniques, and to determine the alternative with the highest efficiency, efficiency, or performance among them. In addition, since the weighting values of the factors and criteria affecting the decision-making process in real-life problems will differ, most authors preferred to integrate a weighting technique with the EATWOS method in their studies. Table 53.1 exhibits detailed information about the studies using EATWOS or EATWIOS methods in the literature.

When the studies in Table 53.1 are examined, it is observed that EATWOS and EATWIOS methods have shown significant and critical evolution in the literature and important developments related to these methods. In early studies, researchers used these performance and efficiency analysis methods mainly to analyze enterprises' financial performance and evaluate their efficiency. By applying these methods, sector-based evaluations such as individual and corporate finance analysis, gold mining, and performance analysis of nongovernmental organizations were carried out. The studies

TABLE 53.1 The preceding studies regarding EATWOS and EATWIOS.

Author/year	Subject	Methodology			The number of			CI[1]	Robustness		
		Weighting	Ranking	Fuzzy sets	I	O	Alt		SA[2]	RRT[3]	CA[4]
Alnıpak (2022)	Port operational efficiency	CRITIC	EATWOS	-	3	2	7	UC	-	-	-
Altintaş (2022)	Logistics performances of the G7 countries	Entropy	EATWIOS	-	3	3	7	UC	-	-	✓
Arslan and Arslan (2022)	Thermal energy storage	-	EATWOS	-	5	5	10	UC	-	-	-
Arslan and Arslan (2024)	Geothermal-driven integrated power	-	EATWOS	-	6	2	24	UC	✓	-	✓
Arslan et al. (2019)	Organic rankine cycle (ORC)-binary geothermal power plant	-	EATWOS	-	3	2	31	UC	✓	-	✓
Arslan, Arslan, et al. (2023)	Domestic thermal energy storage	-	EATWOS	-	-	-	66	UC	-	-	-
Arslan, Ergenekon Arslan, et al. (2023)	New geothermal district heating system	-	EATWOS	-	-	-	111	UC	-	-	-
Arslan et al. (2024)	Geothermal district heating system	-	EATWOS	-	-	-	95	UC	-	-	-
Aytekin et al. (2022)	Global innovation efficiency assessment	-	DEA, EATWIOS	-	5	2	32	LS	-	-	-
Bansal et al. (2014)	Evaluation of vendors' ranking	AHP	EATWOS	-	2	3	12	UC	-	-	-
Bayar (2024)	Productivity analysis of ship recycling facilities	Entropy	EATWIOS	-	2	2	8	R	-	-	-
Çaloğlu and Tozan (2022)	Electric vehicles performance	CRITIC	EATWIOS	-	7	4	11	UC	-	-	-
Çanakçıoğlu (2019)	Financial performance of cement firms	Entropy	EATWIOS	-	4	4	15	UC	-	-	-
Çilek and Karavardar (2023)	Efficiency analysis of Turkish public banks	Entropy	EATWIOS	-	3	3	3	EO	-	-	-
Doğan (2020)	R&D efficiency of Turkey and EU countries	Entropy	EATWOS	-	2	3	27	LS	-	-	-
Görçün (2019a)	Logistics and transportation performances	Entropy	EATWOS	-	10	8	7	R	-	-	-
Görçün (2021)	Productivity analysis of Black Sea container ports	Entropy	EATWOS	-	9	4	9	IMO	-	-	-
Görçün (2021)	Efficiency analysis of container seaports	Entropy	OCRA and EATWOS		9	4	9	EO	-	-	-

(*Continued*)

TABLE 53.1 (Continued)

Author/year	Subject	Methodology			The number of			CI[1]	Robustness		
		Weighting	Ranking	Fuzzy sets	I	O	Alt		SA[2]	RRT[3]	CA[4]
Görçün et al. (2022)	Impacts of public expenditures on innovation	Entropy and CRITIC	EATWOS	-	7	8	8	OECD	✓	-	✓
Görçün et al. (2022)	Performance of global retail supply chains	SWARA	EATWIOS	Classical fuzzy sets (CFS)	8	3	12	EO	✓	✓	✓
Ilıkkan et al. (2021)	Efficiency analysis of Turkseker firms	CRITIC	EATWIOS	-	4	2	24	UC	-	-	-
Keskin and Delice (2023)	Effectiveness of countries in combating pandemics	SWARA and CRITIC	OCRA and EATWOS	CFS	9	5	9	OECD	-	-	✓
Kundakcı (2019)	Supplier evaluation	-	EATWOS	-	1	2	6	UC	-	-	-
Orakçı (2024)	Efficiency of countries in the logistics performance	-	OCRA and EATWOS and REF-III	-	4	3	31	UC	-	-	-
Özbek (2015a)	Efficiency of nongovernmental organizations	-	OCRA and EATWOS	-	2	2	5	UC	-	-	-
Özbek (2015b)	Private pension companies in Turkey	-	EATWOS	-	3	2	19	LS	-	-	-
Özbek (2015c)	Efficiency analysis of the Turkish Red Crescent	-	OCRA and EATWOS	-	2	2	3	LS	-	-	-
Özbek (2016)	Efficiency analysis of gold mining companies	-	EATWOS	-	2	1	6	UC	-	-	-
Özbek (2018)	Efficiency analysis in charity organizations	-	DEA and EATWOS	-	2	3	9	UC	-	-	-
Özdağoğlu (2018)	Evaluation of Borsa Istanbul stock exchange (BIST) industry companies	Gray entropy	EATWIOS	-	4	2	152	UC	-	-	-
Uludağ and Şahin (2023)	Productivity in health tourism	Entropy	EATWIOS	-	4	2	12	TÜİK	-	-	-
Uludağ (2020)	The productivity of selected airports	Entropy	EATWOS	-	4	2	18	UC	-	-	-
Yüksekyıldız (2021)	Productivity analysis of Turkey container ports	Entropy	EATWOS	-	4	1	21	UC	-	-	-
Zolfani et al. (2023)	Efficiency analysis of container shipping companies	Entropy	EATWOS	T2NFN	12	9	12	Delphi	✓	✓	✓

AHP: analytical hierarchy process, DEA: data envelopment analysis, Cr: criteria, DM: decision maker, Alt: alternative, CI: approach for identifying the criteria set, SA: sensitivity analysis, RRT: rank reversal problem, CA: comparative analysis, T2NFN: type-2 neutrosophic fuzzy sets, CFS: classical fuzzy set, CRITIC: criteria importance through in-tercriteria correlation, SWARA: stepwise weight assessment ratio analysis, EATWOS: output satisfaction-based activity analysis, EATWIOS: input and output satisfaction-based activity analysis, DEA: data envelopment analysis, OCRA: operational competition rating analysis.

during this period focused on developing these performance analysis methods as an alternative to traditional MCDM methods.

In the following period, EATWOS and EATWIOS started to be used from a broader perspective and in the field. They were applied to address decision-making problems encountered in many industries and to develop solutions. By applying these approaches, studies such as the operational efficiency of ports in Turkey, the logistics performance of G7 countries, and the profitability and operational efficiency analysis of TCDD ports have been carried out in the field of port efficiency and logistics performance. In energy and sustainability analysis, decision-making problems encountered for thermal energy storage systems, geothermal energy projects, and integrated power systems were tried to be solved. In this period, the applicability of these performance and effectiveness analysis methods in different sectors has increased, and versatile usage areas have been created.

In addition to the financial and logistics industries, EATWOS and EATWIOS methods are used effectively and successfully in healthcare, tourism, and public services. Studies such as efficiency analysis in health tourism and the effectiveness of countries in the fight against the pandemic have allowed these methods to be integrated into public policies and the service sector. Studies such as global innovation effectiveness assessment in production and technology and financial performance analysis of cement companies in Turkey show that the methods can also be used in the industrial and manufacturing sectors.

When the main trends in the literature are examined, it is seen that EATWOS and EATWIOS methods differ from traditional MCDM approaches and offer a more flexible structure. These methods have been developed as an alternative to DEA and OCRA, integrated with weighting techniques, and spread to a much wider range of applications. Its use has increased with weighting methods such as CRITIC, entropy, and stepwise weight assessment ratio analysis (SWARA), thus making decision processes more precise and reliable. Initially used in financial analysis, the methods have spread to logistics, energy, and sustainability. In recent years, studies on artificial intelligence (AI) and its integration with data-driven models have revealed new research areas that envisage the integration of these methods into decision-support systems. In the future, it is expected that EATWOS and EATWIOS methods will be more integrated with data-driven decision mechanisms and used more effectively in automation-supported systems.

53.3 Methodology

This chapter examines and illustrates the implementation steps and evaluates the basic algorithm of the EATWOS approach. Below is the basic algorithm of the method, which consists of six implementation steps (Peters & Zelewski, 2007).

Step 1. Determination of decision-making units (DMUs): in this step, alternatives such as companies, projects, system designs, etc., whose performance or efficiency will be analyzed, are determined. The most critical thing to consider here is that DMUs are comparable.

Step 2. Selection of input and output factors: researchers identify sources directly affecting alternatives' effectiveness, performance, or efficiency in this process. These resources refer to inputs such as the number of employees added to the system, investments, machinery, and equipment purchased for the outputs planned to be obtained. In the same process, output factors such as production amount, energy efficiency, number of customers served, profit, and turnover to be used to define efficiency or performance are also determined. Input and output criteria should be expressed in quantitative measurements.

Step 3. Normalization of input and output data: the input and output values are normalized in the range of 0–1 to make them comparable. The method of normalizing by the maximum value is used for the output. In this step, with the help of Eqs. (53.1) and (53.2), all elements of the decision matrices are normalized, and normalized matrices are created.

$$s_{ij} = \frac{x_{ij}}{\sqrt{\sum_{i=1}^{m} x_{ij}^2}}; \forall j \tag{53.1}$$

$$r_{ij} = \frac{y_{ij}}{\sqrt{\sum_{i=1}^{m} y_{ij}^2}}; \forall j \tag{53.2}$$

Step 4. Calculation of the input and output distances: there are two applications for determining distance measurements for input and output factors. For input factors, the smallest value of each column of the input matrix is determined first. Then, with the help of Eq. (53.3), distance dimensions are determined for the input factors.

$$ip_k = 1 - (s_{ik} - s_k^*); \quad \forall j = 1, \ldots, J \tag{53.3}$$

Here, s_k^* can be identified as $s_k^* = \min\{\overrightarrow{r_j}\};\ \forall j = 1, 2, \ldots, 1;\ \forall k = 1, 2, \ldots, K$

The output distance dimensions are calculated using Eq. (53.4) for the outputs.

$$op_k = 1 - \left(r_j^* - r_{ij}\right);\ \forall i = 1, \ldots, I;\ \forall j = 1, \ldots, J \tag{53.4}$$

Here, r_j^* can be identified as $r_{ij} = \max\{\overrightarrow{s_j}\};\ \forall j = 1, 2, \ldots, 1;\ \forall k = 1, 2, \ldots, J$

Step 5. Weighting of distance measures: in the seventh step, using the entropy method, the factor weights determined in the first four steps and the distance dimension values obtained in the sixth step are multiplied separately, and the distance dimensions are weighted. In this step, Eqs. (53.5) and (53.6) are used.

$$ip_{ja} = ip_k \,.\, w_{ij}^+ \tag{53.5}$$

$$op_{ka} = op_k \,.\, w_{ij}^- \tag{53.6}$$

Step 6. Calculation of performance/efficiency values: first, the weighted distance measures of the input and output factors for each decision alternative are collected separately, and the efficiency value is calculated by dividing the weighted distance measure obtained for the input factor of each decision alternative by the sum of the distance measures for the outputs calculated for the same alternative. For calculating the performance coefficients of each alternative, Eq. (53.7) is employed.

$$F_i = \frac{\sum_{j=1}^{J} ip_{ja}}{\sum_{k=1}^{K} op_{ka}} \tag{53.7}$$

If the F_i value for a decision alternative is high, the performance and efficiency level of the alternative are high. If it is low, the alternative in question has relatively low performance. As a result, decision alternatives can be ranked according to their efficiency scores.

53.4 A numerical illustration

This section shows the application of the EATWOS approach, whose mathematical operations and application steps were given in the previous section, to address the decision problem related to selecting an independent audit firm and to obtain reasonable and rational solutions and the results obtained in this context.

For businesses in different industries, especially large-scale companies, choosing companies from which they will receive independent audit services is a critical and complex decision-making problem regarding having more solid and reliable information about their financial structure and ensuring the trust of external stakeholders, including investors. Selecting a suitable and trustworthy independent audit firm, especially for large-scale enterprises, ensures the reliability of financial audit reports, assisting decision-makers in making strategic decisions more efficiently while enabling shareholders and external stakeholders to make more informed decisions about the business. In addition, each independent audit firm can be advantageous and powerful when considering different aspects, and choosing the appropriate firm can be difficult when considering complex and contradictory criteria. In this context, selecting an independent audit firm with a decision-making procedure that allows robust, reliable, and multidimensional analyses allows the results to be more reliable.

The EATWOS approach stands out as an effective and successful evaluation and decision-making tool for comparative analysis of the performance and efficiency of independent audit firms, and to determine the company with the highest performance. This procedure allows independent audit firms to be evaluated according to factors such as the number of auditors, training period, audit revenues, customer portfolio, and service diversity. This approach provides an analytical and systematic framework for determining the alternatives with the highest performance and selecting the most suitable audit firm for businesses by analyzing input and output factors separately.

Step 1. In this study, the criteria and data used in the survey conducted by Akçakanat (2021), in which the selection of four sizeable independent audit firms was examined with the help of the multiattributive ideal-real comparative analysis method, were used directly. While the criterion weights were determined by the entropy method, the performance of the four sizeable independent audit firms was evaluated by the EATWOS method.

Step 2. The author used the following criteria in his study. In this study, in consultation with experts in the independent auditing and accounting sector, it was determined which of these criteria are input and which are output factors. Table 53.2 illustrates these factors.

TABLE 53.2 The input and output factors for evaluating independent auditing firms.

Input factors	
Certified public accountant (CPA) responsible auditor – I1	It refers to the number of specialists employed in the firm to be able to carry out audit services. More experts contribute to better service delivery, which is also a cost factor.
Training duration – I2	It refers to the training period to increase auditors' professional knowledge and competencies. Although this period provides more qualified service, it is an investment cost.
Output factors	
Independent audit services revenue – O1	The revenues obtained from the independent audit services offered by the company are an output that shows the performance and effectiveness of the company.
Other audit and assurance service revenues – O2	Revenues obtained from additional services other than independent audits are an output that measures the company's service diversity and success.
Revenues from nonaudited services – O3	The income earned by the company from nonaudit services, such as consultancy and financial consultancy, is considered an output that shows the success of its fields of activity.
Number of public interest organization – O4	The number of large-scale companies audited by independent audit firms is an output factor that shows the effectiveness and reliability of the firm in the market.

TABLE 53.3 The initial decision input and output matrices.

	Inputs		Outputs			
	I1	I2	O1	O2	O3	O4
PWC	20.4	769.8	97.708	2.919	29.475	369
E&Y	18.2	1026	64.278	2.579	13.248	272.4
KPMG	18.8	699.3	81.941	11.375	45.551	282.8
Deloitte	21.25	805	84.888	1.137	43.745	170.5

Then, the companies whose performances will be analyzed in the study were determined. Accordingly, four international independent audit firms PricewaterhouseCoopers (PWC), Ernst & Young (E&Y), Klynveld Peat Marwick Goerdeler (KPMG), and Deloitte), defined as the big four, have been chosen as alternatives. Considering the input and output factors, the values in the transparency reports published by these companies were taken, the averages from 2015 to 2019 were taken, and the decision matrix was created as follows. (Table 53.3).

Step 3. In this step, the elements in the matrices are normalized using Eqs. (53.1) and (53.2). Table 53.4 shows the normalized input and output matrices.

For example, the value of the element s_{PwC-I1} in the first cell of the input matrix is calculated with the help of Eq. (53.1), and the value of the first element of the output matrix, r_{PwC-O1}, is calculated using Eq. (53.2) as follows.

$$s_{PwC-I1} = \frac{20.4}{\sqrt{20.40^2 + 18.20^2 + 18.80^2 + 21.25^2}} = \frac{20.4}{39.40} = 0.5178$$

$$r_{PwC-O1} = \frac{2.919}{\sqrt{2.919^2 + 2.579^2 + 11.375^2 + 1.137^2}} = \frac{2.919}{166.13} = 0.5881$$

TABLE 53.4 The normalized decision input and output matrices.

	Inputs		Outputs			
	I1	I2	O1	O2	O3	O4
PWC	0.5178	0.4615	0.5881	0.2417	0.4155	0.6529
E&Y	0.4619	0.6151	0.3869	0.2135	0.1867	0.4820
KPMG	0.4772	0.4192	0.4932	0.9419	0.6421	0.5004
Deloitte	0.5393	0.4826	0.5110	0.0941	0.6166	0.3017

TABLE 53.5 The input and output distance matrices.

	Inputs		Outputs			
	I1	I2	O1	O2	O3	O4
PWC	1.0558	1.0423	1.0000	0.2998	0.7734	1.0000
E&Y	1.0000	1.1959	0.7988	0.2717	0.5447	0.8291
KPMG	1.0152	1.0000	0.9051	1.0000	1.0000	0.8475
Deloitte	1.0774	1.0634	0.9228	0.1523	0.9745	0.6488

Step 4. Two applications were carried out to determine distance measurements for entry and exit factors. For input factors, the minimum value of each column of the input matrix is determined first. Then, with the help of Eq. (53.3), the distance dimensions were determined for the input factors. Calculations were made using Eq. (53.4) for the dimensions of the output distance. Table 53.5 exhibits the distance measures for inputs and outputs.

For example, with the help of Eq. (53.3) for ip_{PwC-I1} and Eq. (53.4) for op_{PwC-I1}, the calculations were made as follows.

$$ip_{PwC-I1} = 1 - (0.5178 - 0.4772) = 1.0558$$

$$op_{PwC-I1} = 1 - (0.5881 - 0.5881) = 1.0000$$

Step 5. Using the entropy method, the factor weights determined in the first four steps and the distance dimension values obtained in the fourth step were multiplied separately, and the distance dimensions were weighted. For this, Eqs. (53.5) and (53.6) were used. Table 53.6 shows the weighted values obtained.

For example, weighted matrix element values were determined as follows by using equality 5 for ip^w_{PwC-I1} and equality 6 for op^w_{PwC-O1}.

$$ip^w_{PwC-I1} = 1.0558x0.1540 = 0.1621$$

$$op^w_{PwC-O1} = 1.000x0.022 = 0.0223$$

Step 6. Finally, the performance values of the alternatives were computed with the help of Eq. (53.7). The obtained values and conclusions are demonstrated in Table 53.7.

As an example, the input and output values and performance values of the alternatives were calculated using equality 7 as shown below.

$$F_{PwC} = \frac{0.1621 + 0.8822}{0.0223 + 0.2171 + 0.1409 + 0.0714} = 0.4325$$

TABLE 53.6 The weighted input and output distance matrices.

	Inputs		Outputs			
	I1	I2	O1	O2	O3	O4
PWC	0.1621	0.8822	0.0223	0.2171	0.1409	0.0714
E&Y	0.1535	1.0122	0.0179	0.1967	0.0992	0.0592
KPMG	0.1559	0.8465	0.0202	0.7241	0.1822	0.0605
Deloitte	0.1654	0.9001	0.0206	0.1103	0.1775	0.0463

TABLE 53.7 The conclusions and ranking of the alternatives.

	Input	Output	Performance values	Ranking
PWC	1.0443	0.4517	0.4325	2
E&Y	1.1658	0.3730	0.3199	4
KPMG	1.0023	0.9870	0.9847	1
Deloitte	1.0655	0.3547	0.3329	3

As shown in Table 53.7, the independent audit firm with the highest performance/effectiveness was determined as KPMG, while the others were ranked as PWC > Deloitte > E&Y with different performance scores.

53.5 Robustness and validity check

A comprehensive robustness test has been conducted to demonstrate the validity and reliability of the performance and efficacy analysis method proposed in this section. First, the weights of each input and output factor were reduced, starting with the most important one in its group. For this, by following the algorithm introduced by Görçün et al. (2021), the weight of the factor considered in each scenario was reduced by 10% at an increasing level, and the weight coefficient of the factor was continued until it was zero. Suppose the factor under consideration is the input factor. In that case, the output factors are kept constant; if the output factor is the input factor, the input factors are kept constant.

In contrast, the criterion's weight, which is the input or output factor, is reduced, and the resulting difference value is added equally to the others, thus providing the condition that the sum of the factors is equal to one. According to the new weight values obtained, the calculations performed to rank the alternatives according to their performance were repeated. Thus, 60 scenarios were created (Fig. 53.1).

In the second stage, it was observed that some minor changes occurred in ranking the alternatives according to their performance because of the inclusion of the criterion weights obtained with the help of three different weighting techniques in the analysis. When the LOPCOW method was applied, PWC and KPMG were mutually replaced, while no change was found in the ranking performance of the others. In the second stage, the literature's most used weight methods were applied, and the criterion weight values obtained were applied to the EATWOS method. The results obtained are shown in Fig. 53.2.

As shown in Fig. 53.2, KPMG, the most suitable alternative, and PWC, which has the second-best performance, were replaced only according to the results of the LOPCOW method, while the ranking result of the options remained the same in all other methods. In the next stage, the EATWOS method's results were compared with those obtained by applying the OCRA approach. Fig. 53.3 shows the results of the comparison between the two methods.

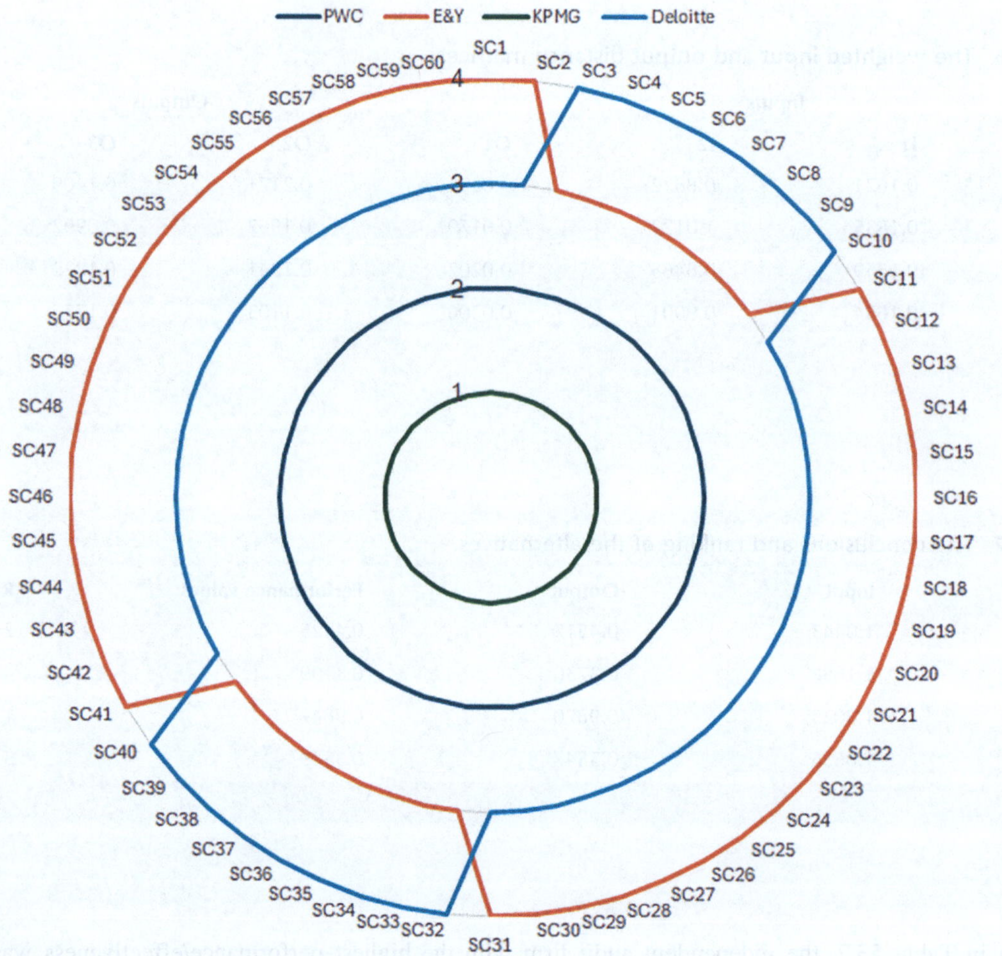

FIGURE 53.1 Re-ranking the alternatives for 70 scenarios.

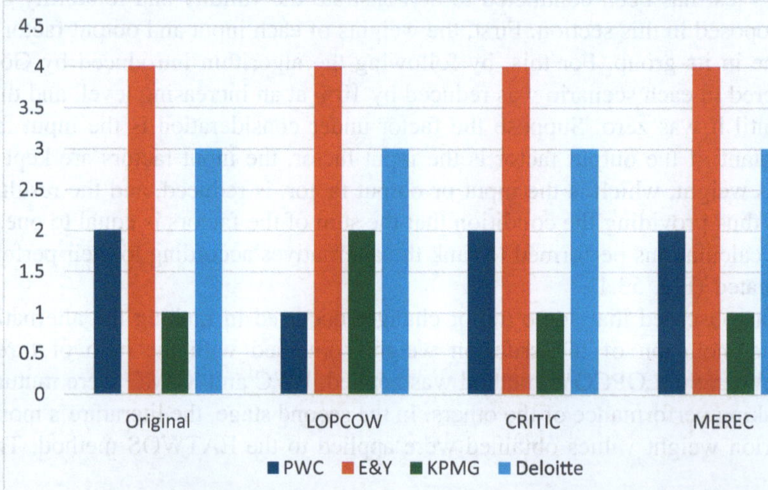

FIGURE 53.2 Comparative result of the comparative analysis.

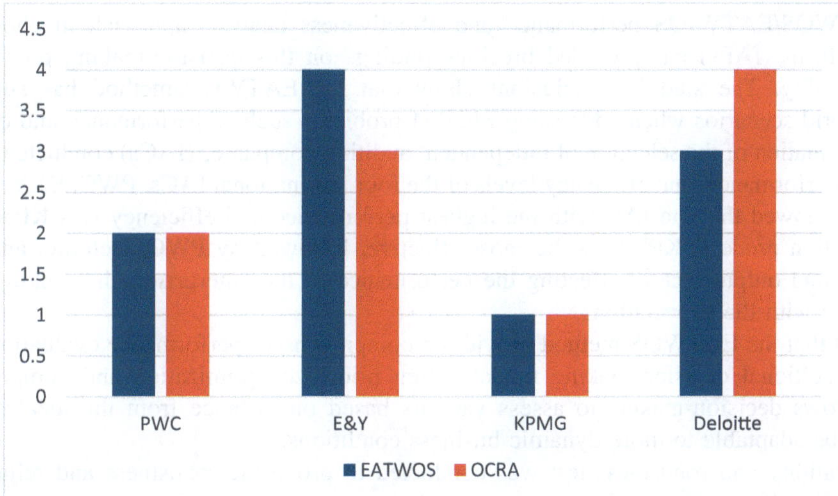

FIGURE 53.3 Comparative analysis result between evaluation based on distance from average solution (EATWOS) and operational competition rating analysis (OCRA).

TABLE 53.8 The conclusions of the rank reversal test.

	Input
Original	KPMG > PWC > Deloitte > E&Y
Scenario-1	KPMG > PWC > Deloitte
Scenario-2	KPMG > PWC
Scenario-3	KPMG

Results close to the previous analysis were also obtained at this stage. While the positions of KPMG and PWC alternatives in the ranking were the same in both methods, the other two options were mutually replaced. Finally, the resistance of the EATWOS method to the sequence flipping problem was tested; for this, the calculations were renewed by removing the last order in each scenario, and the new ranking results acquired were compared with the previous ones. Table 53.8 shows the results obtained regarding the durability of the proposed model.

When the results were examined, there was no change in the ranking performance of the alternatives in all scenarios. It shows that the proposed model mainly resists the rank reversal problem. In general, the robust test results prove that the EATWOS method and the results obtained by applying this method are consistent, robust, and reliable.

53.6 Results and discussion

A comprehensive robustness test has been conducted to demonstrate the validity and reliability of the performance and efficacy analysis method proposed in this section. First, the weights of each input and output factor were reduced, starting with the most important one in its group. For this, by following the algorithm introduced by Görçün et al. (2021), the weight of the factor considered in each scenario was reduced by 10% at an increasing level, and the weight coefficient of the factor was continued until it was zero. Suppose the factor under consideration is the input factor. In that case, the output factors are kept constant; if the output factor is the input factor, the input factors are kept constant.

Applying the EATWOS/EATWIOS performance and effectiveness analysis approach in choosing and evaluating independent auditing firms (IAFs) has provided precious findings on this decision-making procedure's effectiveness, reliability, and practicality. The study's conclusions show that the EATWOS method has superior flexibility and adaptability to real-world scenarios when addressing MCDM problems such as performance and effectiveness analysis.

The comparative evaluation of the selection of independent auditing companies (IACs) conducted in this study revealed that the effectiveness, performance, and efficiency levels of the four international IACs, PWC, E&Y, KPMG, and Deloitte, differed. The findings showed that the IAC with the highest performance and efficiency was KPMG. Among the IACs included in the evaluation process, KPMG is the most effective, followed by PWC, Deloitte, and E&Y, respectively. Considering the input and output factors affecting the performance of the enterprises, the ranking results obtained are rational and compatible with the expectations.

The findings exhibit that the EATWOS method provides a comprehensive performance evaluation by balancing inputs and outputs. While traditional decision-making models often prioritize optimization and compromise flexibility, the EATWOS method allows decision-makers to assess variants based on distance from the ideal solution. This feature enables the results to be adaptable to more dynamic business conditions.

A comprehensive validity and robustness test was conducted to prove the robustness and reliability of the findings obtained in the study. The effect of gradually reducing the relative weight values of input and output factors on ranking is examined. Despite potentially extraordinary changes in weight distributions, the order of alternatives has remained essentially consistent, proving that the EATWOS model remains robust and consistent against sensitivity changes.

In addition, the EATWOS method was compared with other MCDM techniques, such as operational competitive assessment analysis (OCRA), and the consistency of the resulting sequencing supported the validity of the proposed approach. The small and insignificant differences observed in the ranking are due to methodological differences, especially regarding how inputs and outputs are normalized and weighted.

Various scenarios were created to test the resistance of the EATWOS method to the sequence reversal problem, and the calculations were repeated in each scenario. The conclusions showed that the suggested model is highly resistant to the rank reversal problem. Overall, the robust test results have proven that the EATWOS method and the results obtained using this method are consistent, robust, and reliable.

This study reinforces the increasing importance of the EATWOS/EATWIOS procedure in MCDM applications. Thanks to its ability to integrate with various weighting approaches such as CRITIC, entropy, and SWARA, this methodology provides a comprehensive tool for evaluating decision alternatives in decision-making problems encountered in different industries. The results and findings show that the EATWOS method is beneficial in areas that require sensitive assessments, such as financial services, logistics, and sustainability studies.

In addition, it is emphasized that EATWOS has the potential to improve decision-making capabilities further by integrating AI, deep learning, and machine learning models. Future research may develop integrated procedures that assemble data-driven analytics with MCDM approaches, thereby improving prediction accuracy and decision consistency.

The results from this study confirm that the EATWOS method effectively evaluates performance within a structured decision-making framework. The framework has exhibited strong reliability, robustness, and adaptability when assessing the efficiency of independent audit firms. Given these advantages, EATWOS/EATWIOS methods can be a valuable decision-support tool in various industries. Future studies should focus on extending this methodology to other complex decision environments and improving analytical accuracy through AI-powered improvements.

53.7 Conclusions and future research direction

This review examines the historical development of the EATWOS/EATWIOS approach and its application as a performance/effectiveness analysis framework. The findings show that EATWOS and its improved version of EATWIOS offer a more flexible, dynamic, and effective alternative to traditional evaluation methods such as DEA and OCRA. These frameworks enable decision-makers to perform more extensive performance appraisals, offering advantages such as dynamic weighting, sensitivity to data changes, and adaptability to complex decision-making environments.

The study results reveal that EATWOS/EATWIOS methods offer satisfactory solutions instead of the absolute best solution compared to strict optimization models and thus better adapt to real-world conditions. In addition, the fact that it can be integrated with weighting techniques such as CRITIC, entropy, SWARA, and LOPCOW increases the analytical power of the method, contributing to more reliable decisions. Applications in various sectors show that the technique can be successfully used in logistics, financial auditing, port efficiency, health, and sustainability. In addition, the model has undergone comparative tests with rank reversal, sensitivity analysis, and other methods, and its reliability has been proven.

The investigation has some constraints. Primarily, the method's accuracy depends on the quality and completeness of the input-output data used. Incomplete or biased data can adversely affect the accuracy of the decisions obtained. In addition, although EATWOS/EATWIOS reduces some computational difficulties, it may require high computational costs in large-scale decision problems involving many criteria and alternatives. Although it is advantageous to integrate the method with different weighting techniques, a specific subjective approach is required to choose which method to use, which can affect the final ranking. Furthermore, although the technique has been widely applied in the logistics, finance, and energy sectors, more empirical testing is needed in public policy decisions, healthcare management, and digital transformation.

Future research should address these restrictions and make the method more effective. Improving decision accuracy by combining EATWOS/EATWIOS with AI-based predictive analytics can help make the technique more intelligent and autonomous. Developing software tools by integrating them with decision-support systems will provide practitioners with ease of use. Besides, studies can be conducted on how the method can be applied in new areas, such as blockchain technology, thoughtful city planning, and green supply chain management.

The impact of subjective elements can be reduced by developing new models to make weighting mechanisms more objective. The strengths and weaknesses of the method can be examined in more detail by conducting comparative studies with alternative MCDM methods. Integration with fuzzy logic-based methods, such as neutrosophic or T-spherical fuzzy sets, can improve the ability to handle uncertainties.

As a result, this chapter reveals that the EATWOS method effectively evaluates performance within a structured decision-making framework. This method has demonstrated strong reliability, robustness, and adaptability when assessing the efficiency of independent audit firms. Given these advantages, EATWOS/EATWIOS methods can be a valuable decision-support tool in various industries. Future studies should focus on extending this method to more complex decision environments and improving analytical accuracy through AI-powered improvements.

References

Akçakanat, Ö. (2021). Dört büyük bağımsız denetim firmasının MAIRCA yöntemi ile karşılaştırılması *Muhasebe Ve Denetime Bakış 21*(64), 123–146.

Alnıpak, S. (2022). Liman operasyonel verimliliğinin Karlılık İle İlişkisi: TCDD Limanları Üzerine Bir Araştırma. *Maliye Finans Yazıları 118*. https://doi.org/10.33203/mfy.1150928.

Altintaş, F. F. (2022). G7 ülkelerinin lojistik etkinlik ve verimlilik performanslarının değerlendirilmesi. *Verimlilik Dergisi, 1*. https://doi.org/10.51551/verimlilik.734258.

Arslan, A. E., Arslan, O., & Genc, M. S. (2024). Hybrid modelling for the multi-criteria decision making of energy systems: An application for geothermal district heating system. *Energy, 286*. https://doi.org/10.1016/j.energy.2023.129590.

Arslan, O., & Arslan, A. E. (2022). Performance evaluation and multi-criteria decision analysis of thermal energy storage integrated geothermal district heating system. *Process Safety and Environmental Protection, 167*. https://doi.org/10.1016/j.psep.2022.08.073.

Arslan, O., & Arslan, A. E. (2024). Multi-criteria optimization of a new geothermal driven integrated power and hydrogen production system via a new Index: Economic sustainability (EcoSI). *Fuel, 358*. https://doi.org/10.1016/j.fuel.2023.130160.

Arslan, O., Arslan, A. E., & Kurtbas, I. (2023). Exergoeconomic and exergoenvironmental based multi-criteria optimization of a new geothermal district heating system integrated with thermal energy storage driven heat pump. *Journal of Building Engineering, 73*. https://doi.org/10.1016/j.jobe.2023.106733.

Arslan, O., Ergenekon Arslan, A., & Eddine Boukelia, T. (2023). Modelling and optimization of domestic thermal energy storage based heat pump system for geothermal district heating. *Energy and Buildings, 282*. https://doi.org/10.1016/j.enbuild.2023.112792.

Arslan, O., Ergenekon Arslan, A., & Şentürk Acar, M. (2019). o-TİPİ ORC-BINARY JEOTERMAL GÜÇ SANTRALI OPTİMİZASYONU: EATWOS ANALİZİ. *Bilecik Şeyh Edebali Üniversitesi Fen Bilimleri Dergisi, 6*. https://doi.org/10.35193/bseufbd.601745.

Aytekin, A., Ecer, F., Korucuk, S., & Karamaşa, Ç. (2022). Global innovation efficiency assessment of EU member and candidate countries via DEA-EATWIOS multi-criteria methodology. *Technology in Society, 68*, 101896. https://doi.org/10.1016/J.TECHSOC.2022.101896.

Bansal, A., Kr. Singh, R., Issar, S., & Varkey, J. (2014). Evaluation of vendors ranking by EATWOS approach. *Journal of Advances in Management Research, 11*(3). https://doi.org/10.1108/JAMR-02-2014-0009.

Bayar, S. (2024). Aliağa bölgesi gemi söküm tesislerinin verimlilik analizi. *Black Sea Journal of Engineering and Science, 7*(4), 705–716.

Çaloğlu, B. E., & Tozan, H. (2022). Elektrikli Araçlarin Performanslarının CRITIC-EATWIOS ile Değerlendirilmesi. *Düzce Üniversitesi. Bilim ve Teknoloji Dergisi, 10*(4).

Çanakçıoğlu, M. (2019). Borsa İstanbul'da İşlem Gören Çimento Firmalarının Entropi-Eatwios Bütünleşik Yaklaşımı İle Finansal Performanslarının Değerlendirmesi. *Yaşar Üniversitesi E-Dergisi, 14*(56), 407–421.

Çilek, A., & Karavardar, A. (2023). Hibrit Entropi ve EATWIOS teknikleri ile Türk kamu bankalarının verimlilik analizi. *Business & Management Studies: An International Journal, 11*(1). https://doi.org/10.15295/bmij.v11i1.2185.

Doğan, H. (2020). Türkiye ve AB Ülkelerinin AR-GE Verimliliklerinin Entropi-EATWOS Yöntemleri ile Karşılaştırılması *Karadeniz Sosyal Bilimler Dergisi*. https://doi.org/10.38155/ksbd.792763.

Diakoulaki, D., Mavrotas, G., & Papayannakis, L. (1992). A multicriteria approach for evaluating the performance of industrial firms. *Omega, 20*(4), 467–474. https://doi.org/10.1016/0305-0483(92)90021-x.

Ecer, F., & Pamucar, D. (2022). A novel LOPCOW-DOBI multi-criteria sustainability performance assessment methodology: An application in developing country banking sector. Omega, 112, 102690. https://doi.org/10.1016/j.omega.2022.102690

Görçün, Ö. F. (2019a). Entegre Entropi ve Eatwos Yöntemleri Kullanilarak Karadeniz Konteyner Limanlarinin Verimlilik Analizi. *Eskişehir Osmangazi Üniversitesi İktisadi ve İdari Bilimler Dergisi, 14*(3), 811–830.

Görçün, Ö. F. (2019b). Orta Asya Türk Cumhuriyetlerinin Lojistik ve Taşimacilik Performanslari ve Verimliliklerinin Analizi için Hibrid bir Çok Kriterli Karar Verme Modeli. *MANAS Sosyal Araştırmalar Dergisi, 8*(3), 2775–2798.

Görçün, Ö. F. (2021). Efficiency analysis of black sea container seaports: Application of an integrated MCDM approach. *Maritime Policy and Management, 48*(5), 672–699. https://doi.org/10.1080/03088839.2020.1783467.

Görçün, Ö. F., Küçükönder, H., & Çanakçıoğlu, M. (2022). Araştirma geliştirme harcamalarinin G-7 ülkelerinin gelişmişlik düzeyine etkilerinin incelenmesi: yeni bir karar modeli. *Mali Çözüm, 32*(172), 133–169.

Görçün, Ö. F., Senthil, S., & Küçükönder, H. (2021). Evaluation of tanker vehicle selection using a novel hybrid fuzzy MCDM technique. *Decision Making: Applications in Management and Engineering, 4*(2), 140–162. https://doi.org/10.31181/dmame210402140g.

Görçün, Ö. F., Zolfani, S. H., & Çanakçıoğlu, M. (2022). Analysis of efficiency and performance of global retail supply chains using integrated fuzzy SWARA and fuzzy EATWOS methods. *Operations Management Research*. https://doi.org/10.1007/s12063-022-00261-z.

Ilıkkan, Ö. M., Soyu, E., Bağcı, H., & Demirtaş, C. (2021). Türkşeker firmalarinda CRITIC ve EATWIOS yöntemiyle verimlilik analizi. *Nevşehir Hacı Bektaş Veli Üniversitesi SBE Dergisi, 11*(1). https://doi.org/10.30783/nevsosbilen.877622.

Keshavarz-Ghorabaee, M., Amiri, M., Zavadskas, E. K., Turskis, Z., & Antucheviciene, J. (2021). Determination of objective weights using a new method based on the removal effects of criteria (MEREC). Symmetry, 13(4), 525. https://doi.org/10.3390/sym13040525

Keskin, Z. B., & Delice, E. K. (2023). Determining the effectiveness of countries in combating pandemics: COVID-19 case. *RAIRO - Operations Research, 57*(4). https://doi.org/10.1051/ro/2023077.

Kundakcı, N. (2019). A comparative analyze based on EATWOS and OCRA methods for supplier evaluation. *Alphanumeric Journal, 7*(1), 103–112.

Orakçı, E. (2024). EATWOS, OCRA ve REF III Teknikleriyle Ülkelerin Lojistik Performans İndeksine Dayalı Etkinliklerinin İncelenmesi. *İktisadi İdari ve Siyasal Araştırmalar Dergisi, 9*(25), 590–611. https://doi.org/10.25204/iktisad.1486017.

Özbek, A. (2015a). Analysis of private pension companies in Turkey by EATWOS. *European Journal of Business and Management, 7*(26), 31–43.

Özbek, A. (2015b). Efficiency analysis of non-governmental organizations based in Turkey. *International Business Research, 8*(9). https://doi.org/10.5539/ibr.v8n9p95.

Özbek, A. (2015c). Efficiency analysis of the Turkish Red Crescent between 2012 and 2014. *International Journal of Economics and Finance, 7*(9). https://doi.org/10.5539/ijef.v7n9p322.

Özbek, A. (2016). Efficiency analysis of gold mining companies through financial statements. *International Journal of Academic Research in Business and Social Sciences, 6*(10). https://doi.org/10.6007/ijarbss/v6-i10/2357.

Özbek, A. (2018). Çok Ölçütlü Karar Verme Yöntemleriyle Hayırsever Kuruluşlarında Verimlilik Analizi. *Anadolu Üniversitesi Sosyal Bilimler Dergisi, 18*(2). https://doi.org/10.18037/ausbd.552414.

Özdağoğlu, A. (2018). BİST sınai işletmelerinin GRİ ENTROPİ-EATWIOS bütünleşik yaklaşımı ile performans değerlendirmesi. *Dokuz Eylül Üniversitesi İşletme Fakültesi Dergisi, 19*(2). https://doi.org/10.24889/ifede.415061.

Peters, M., & Zelewski, S. (2006). Efficiency analysis under consideration of satisficing levels for output quantities. *Seventeenth Annual Conference of POMS*, 1–19.

Peters, M. L., & Zelewski, S. (2007). Effizienz-analyse mit EATWOS. *Controlling, 19*(2). https://doi.org/10.15358/0935-0381-2007-2-75.

Shannon, C. E., & Weaver, W. (1949). The mathematical theory of communication. University of Illinois Press.

Uludağ, A. S. (2020). Measuring the productivity of selected airports in Turkey. *Transportation Research Part E: Logistics and Transportation Review, 141*. https://doi.org/10.1016/j.tre.2020.102020.

Uludağ, A. S., & Şahin, E. (2023). Verimlilik analizlerinde tatmin seviyesi tayin edilmemiş EATWIOS mu? OCRA mı?: Sağlık turizmi üzerine bir araştırma. *Verimlilik Dergisi, 57*(2). https://doi.org/10.51551/verimlilik.1155635.

Yüksekyıldız, E. (2021). Entropi ve EATWOS Yöntemleri ile Türkiye Konteyner Limanlarının Verimlilik Analizi. *Verimlilik Dergisi, 2*. https://doi.org/10.51551/verimlilik.660708.

Zolfani, S. H., Faruk Görçün, Ö., Çanakçıoğlu, M., & Tirkolaee, E. B. (2023). Efficiency analysis technique with input and output satisficing approach based on type-2 neutrosophic fuzzy sets: A case study of container shipping companies. *Expert Systems with Applications, 218*. https://doi.org/10.1016/j.eswa.2023.119596.

Chapter 54

ARAS: Additive ratio assessment for multi-attribute decision-making

Nikola Petrović[1], Nikola Komatina[2], Dragan Marinković[3,4,5], and Željko Stević[6,7]
[1]*Faculty of Mechanical Engineering, University of Niš, Niš, Serbia,* [2]*Faculty of Engineering, University of Kragujevac, Kragujevac, Serbia,* [3]*Department of Structural Analysis, Technical University of Berlin, Berlin, Germany,* [4]*Institute of Mechanical Science, Vilnius Gediminas Technical University, Vilnius, Lithuania,* [5]*University College, Korea University, Seongbuk-gu, Seoul, Republic of Korea,* [6]*Faculty of Transport and Traffic Engineering, University of East Sarajevo, Doboj, Bosnia and Herzegovina,* [7]*Department of Mobile Machinery and Railway Transport, Faculty of Transport Engineering, Vilnius Gediminas Technical University, Vilnius, Lithuania*

54.1 Introduction

Multicriteria decision-making (MCDM) methods are widely applied across various domains of human activity to support decision-making processes in complex situations that involve multiple, often conflicting, criteria (Damjanović et al., 2022; Kutut et al., 2013; Pramanik et al., 2021). In an MCDM problem, each alternative is described by a set of criteria, which may be either qualitative or quantitative, and which may differ in terms of measurement scales and directions of optimization (Petrović, Jovanović, Marković, et al., 2025; Zavadskas et al., 2017). Consequently, normalization of criteria values is necessary to ensure mutual comparability (Petrović, Jovanović, Petrović, et al., 2025; Stević et al., 2024).

Unlike the single-criterion approach, which attempts to consolidate all aspects of a problem into a single aggregated measure, the multicriteria approach enables the simultaneous analysis of several conflicting objectives. This makes it particularly suitable for complex real-world scenarios that require the integration of multiple perspectives. Within the MCDM framework, the primary task of the decision-maker is to evaluate the final set of alternatives in order to identify the optimal solution, rank the available options, classify them, or assess the extent to which specific criteria are met (Đalić et al., 2021; Petrović, Marković, et al., 2024).

Among the many MCDM methods developed, the additive ratio assessment (ARAS) method, first introduced in the paper (Zavadskas & Turskis, 2010), offers a systematic approach for evaluating alternatives. This method enables the calculation of the utility of each alternative based on the relative ratios of the criteria values and their associated weights. The core principle of the ARAS method is to assess the composite relative efficiency of each alternative by comparing it to a predefined ideal solution (Zavadskas, Sušinskas, et al., 2012). In doing so, the method integrates all criteria into a single utility function, thus providing clarity and transparency in the decision-making process and facilitating the identification of the most favorable option.

Despite the existence of numerous MCDM techniques, differences in weight application, optimal solution selection, objective scaling, and incorporation of additional parameters often lead to variations in results for the same decision problem, known as the inconsistent ranking problem (Dehshiri & Firoozabadi, 2023). Nevertheless, the ARAS method, as a quantitative approach, provides a structured and transparent decision-making framework, with clearly defined criteria and interrelationships. It enables the ranking of alternatives based on their proximity to the ideal solution, offering a logical basis for decision-making in complex scenarios.

Evaluating the effectiveness of individual MCDM methods in solving complex problems is inherently challenging (Simić et al., 2023). In the ARAS method, the utility value—representing the overall efficiency of a specific alternative—is directly dependent on the relative importance and quantitative values of the analyzed criteria. Based on the derived utility function, a priority list of alternatives can be established, thereby allowing systematic comparison and ranking. The degree of utility is determined through comparison with the optimal (ideal) solution, offering a benchmark to identify potential improvements for specific alternatives (Tupenaite et al., 2010; Zavadskas, Vainiūnas, et al., 2012).

Encyclopedia of Multi-Attribute Decision-Making (MADM). DOI: https://doi.org/10.1016/B978-0-443-33275-3.00037-3

MCDM combines both deductive and inductive reasoning and is often applied to domains characterized by imprecision or incomplete data (Nedeljković et al., 2021; Zavadskas et al., 2015). In this context, fuzzy multicriteria decision-making (FMCDM) is particularly useful for modeling complex situations with inherent uncertainty (Radović et al., 2018; Shariati et al., 2014; Tadić et al., 2025). Unlike traditional optimization and statistical approaches, which assume a single, well-defined objective, modern engineering and management problems typically involve multiple conflicting goals, diverse stakeholder preferences, and complex evaluation processes. The use of fuzzy data enhances the applicability of the model in real-world contexts, particularly when reliable and accurate data—especially qualitative indicators—are not available (Liao et al., 2019; Sudžum et al., 2024; Zamani et al., 2014).

The main advantages of MCDM methods include their capacity to manage complex decision-making processes, integrate both qualitative and quantitative indicators, increase the transparency of decisions, encourage active stakeholder participation, and support the use of flexible and scientifically grounded procedures. Fuzzy logic further extends this flexibility, especially in analyzing problems involving imprecise or uncertain data.

The ARAS method is particularly appropriate in cases where:

- All criteria are quantitative.
- The aim is to aggregate benefits and compare them to an ideal solution.
- A transparent and straightforward approach is needed.
- There is no requirement for explicit modeling of conflict or uncertainty.

Key advantages of the ARAS method include:

- Simplicity and visual clarity of all steps.
- Logical and easily interpretable decision processes.
- Rapid evaluation of "what-if" scenarios, as changes in weight coefficients lead to immediate changes in ranking outcomes.

However, ARAS may not be suitable in situations where:

- Criteria exhibit significant conflict-methods.
- There is high uncertainty or fuzziness-fuzzy-based methods should be considered.
- No quantitative data is available-in such cases.

To demonstrate the practical application of the ARAS method, two real-world case studies are presented. The first involves the multicriteria ranking of handling equipment in the design of a container terminal, evaluating four alternatives across six criteria. The second case involves a multicriteria analysis of seven logistics companies, assessed against seven criteria by five experts. This analysis aims to identify the most efficient logistics company and provide a comprehensive evaluation of fleet performance.

54.2 Fundamental bibliometric analysis

By using relative utility measures, the ARAS method simplifies complex decision tasks and enables the selection of the most favorable option relative to an ideal reference. Owing to its ease of implementation and interpretability, ARAS has attracted significant scholarly attention. Between 2010 and July 2025, over 450 academic contributions addressed or applied the method. Moreover, it has undergone substantial expansion in both theoretical scope and practical relevance.

Based on the analyzed papers, the ARAS method has been applied across a range of domains, reflecting its flexibility and suitability for various MCDM scenarios (Fig. 54.1) (Web of Science, n.d):

- Period 2010–15: The number of papers was low and variable, ranging from 1 to 5 papers per year, without a clear trend.
- Period 2016–18: There is a slight increase from 9 papers in 2016, a drop to 5 in 2017, and a re-growth to 8 in 2018.
- Period 2019–24: A significant and constant growth is observed, indicating an increase in scientific papers or production activity, with 42 papers in 2024 (the largest number so far).
- Year 2025 (by July): By the middle of the year, 19 papers have already been recorded, indicating that by the end of the year, last year's maximum could be reached or exceeded if the trend continues.

The Fig. 54.1 clearly shows the trend of exponential growth in the number of papers since 2019, which may indicate:

- Increased productivity or investments in the chapter,
- Strengthening of institutions or teams behind the papers,

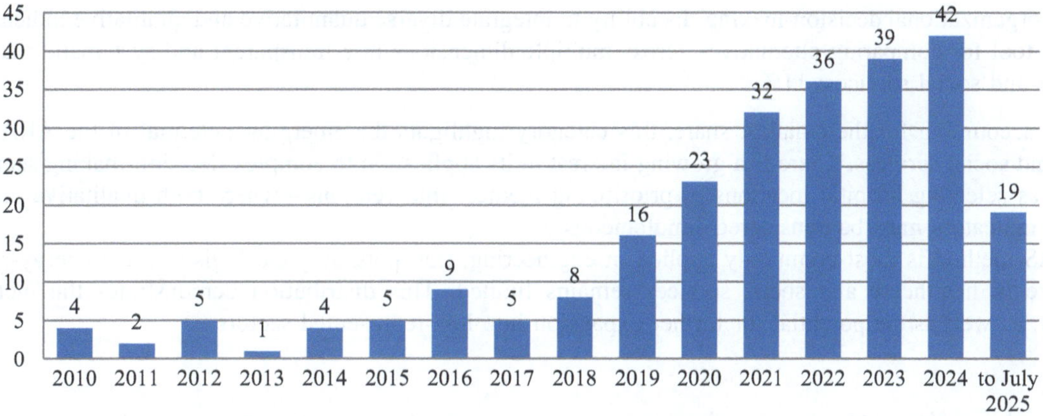

FIGURE 54.1 Number of papers applying the additive ratio assessment method by year.
Authors' calculation.

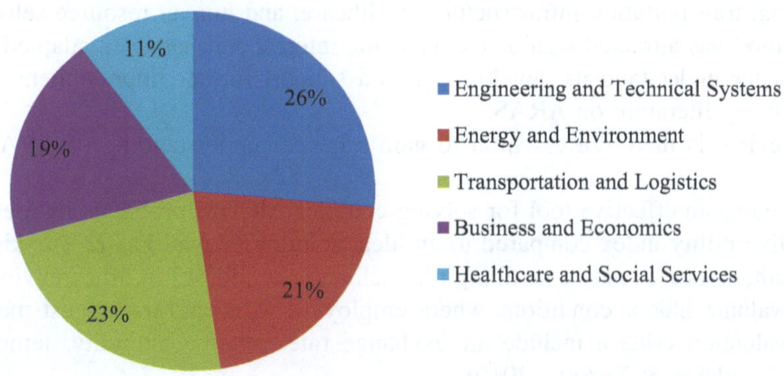

FIGURE 54.2 Percentage of papers by field where the additive ratio assessment method was used.
Authors' calculation.

- Greater visibility and engagement in the scientific community.

The next Fig. 54.2 shows the percentage of academic papers in each field where the ARAS method has been used (Web of Science, n.d).

The data are presented in the form of a pie chart and reveal the following distribution:

- Engineering and technical systems: 26%
  This field demonstrates the highest frequency of ARAS method application, indicating its strong relevance for technical and engineering decision-making processes. The method's ability to handle quantitative data and rank alternatives makes it a natural fit for engineering design and evaluation tasks.
- Transportation and logistics: 23%
  The significant use of the method in this field highlights its suitability for evaluating and optimizing complex logistics systems and transportation processes. ARAS has been used in route selection, supplier evaluation, and transport mode decisions. In these cases, its simplicity and ease of computation provide practical benefits for real-world logistics and supply chain management applications.
- Energy and environment: 21%
  The ARAS method is frequently employed in assessing sustainability, energy efficiency, and environmental impact. A significant number of studies utilize ARAS in energy planning, sustainable energy source selection, and environmental impact assessments.
- Business and economics: 19%
  The ARAS method is employed to facilitate strategic planning, optimize resource allocation, and evaluate investment options. Within this domain, it is particularly useful for financial performance assessment, project prioritization, and

long-term organizational decision-making. Its ability to integrate diverse quantitative and qualitative indicators makes it a valuable tool for comparing alternatives across multiple dimensions in a transparent and systematic manner.

- Healthcare and social services: 11%

Although accounting for the smallest share, this category highlights the emerging potential of the ARAS method in healthcare and social services. There is a growing interest in its application to complex decision-making scenarios in this field—such as selecting hospital locations or prioritizing medical interventions—where both qualitative judgments and quantitative indicators must be considered simultaneously.

The ARAS method is most commonly applied in engineering, transportation and logistics, and energy-related fields, while its use in healthcare and social services remains limited. This distribution demonstrates the method's broad applicability, as well as the potential for further expansion into less-represented sectors.

54.3 Review literature

The ARAS method continues to gain recognition across diverse domains due to its adaptability, simplicity, and capacity to integrate criteria. Its applicability extends well beyond organizational decision-making, as demonstrated by a growing body of literature covering fields such as engineering, environmental management, cultural heritage preservation, sustainable energy planning, transportation infrastructure, healthcare, and human resource selection.

To date, the ARAS method has attracted significant academic interest and has been adapted for various data contexts and practical fields. To better understand its development and support further improvement, this chapter of the paper systematically reviews existing literature on ARAS.

A thorough literature review is therefore essential to gain a deeper understanding of ARAS and support its further advancement.

The method is recognized as an effective tool for solving complex MCDM problems by identifying the most suitable alternative through a relative utility index compared to an ideal solution (Zavadskas & Turskis, 2010). To illustrate the application of this new method, a case study examining microclimatic conditions in office environments is presented. The goal of this study is to evaluate indoor conditions where employees work and to suggest measures for improving the working environment. Evaluation criteria include air exchange rate, relative humidity, temperature, illumination, air velocity, and dew point (Zavadskas & Turskis, 2010).

Initial validation of the ARAS methodology is demonstrated through its application to selecting the best foundation system for a building located on terrain with groundwater presence (Zavadskas et al., 2010). The decision-making framework incorporates a broad set of criteria, including construction cost, installation time, decision complexity, specific advantages and disadvantages of each solution, maintainability and transferability of the foundation type, and prior experience with similar engineering projects. In this context, ARAS demonstrates its utility as a decision-support tool, with potential extensions to other construction-related evaluations, including technology selection and investment planning (Zavadskas et al., 2010).

The method has also shown substantial value in environmental and agricultural applications. Recognizing that greenhouse gases such as nitrous oxide (N_2O), methane (CH_4), and carbon dioxide (CO_2) are major contributors to climate change (Petrović, Bojović, et al., 2023), the paper (Balezentiene & Kusta, 2012) explores sustainable fertilization strategies in Lithuanian grasslands treated with various mineral fertilizers by the ARAS method. By balancing environmental impact and biomass productivity, the study identifies optimal fertilizer treatments, thereby supporting data-driven sustainability practices in agriculture (Balezentiene & Kusta, 2012).

The ARAS method has also been effectively adapted for use in cultural heritage management and urban planning. Governments increasingly seek to develop methodologies that aid in the preservation and prioritization of immovable cultural assets. In this vein, the study (Kutut et al., 2013) employs the ARAS method to prioritize the reconstruction of historically significant buildings in Vilnius. A set of indicators—encompassing historical, archeological, architectural, economic, and social dimensions—is used to formulate a structured algorithm for prioritization. The model offers a transparent and systematic foundation for decision-making, balancing cultural importance with urban development priorities (Kutut et al., 2013).

In the field of sustainable architecture, the method has been used to improve the assessment of green building performance. Paper (Medineckiene et al., 2015) introduces a new MCDM approach for selecting sustainability indicators by combining the Swedish Miljöbyggnad certification system with additional criteria from the LEED framework. Weights are assigned using analytic hierarchy process (AHP) with both the traditional Saaty scale and an alternative scale, while

ARAS is employed for ranking. This hybrid model not only ensures methodological rigor but also aligns with internationally recognized sustainability standards (Medineckiene et al., 2015).

Corporate sustainability strategies have also benefited from the ARAS methodology. In the context of corporate social responsibility (CSR), the paper (Karabašević et al., 2016) proposes a model that integrates stepwise weight assessment ratio analysis (SWARA) for weighting stakeholder-relevant criteria with ARAS for ranking company performance. Validated through real-world application, the model demonstrates the effectiveness of MCDM tools in evaluating CSR initiatives and supporting strategic decision-making aligned with stakeholder expectations (Karabašević et al., 2016).

In energy policy and planning, ARAS has proven instrumental in evaluating sustainable energy technologies. Study (Ghenai et al., 2020) offers a comprehensive hybrid model combining SWARA and ARAS to assess renewable energy options—specifically wind power, solar energy, and two types of fuel cells—based on five primary dimensions of sustainability and fourteen subcriteria. Expert evaluations guide the decision process, and results identify onshore wind energy as the most favorable technology, underscoring the model's suitability for long-term energy strategy development (Ghenai et al., 2020).

Similarly, paper (Balki et al., 2020) explores optimizing internal combustion engine parameters under evolving environmental regulations. In response to stricter emission standards and decreasing use of high-emission diesel engines (Nikolić et al., 2025), the study examines spark ignition engines operating on pure ethanol and methanol. Using a SWARA-ARAS approach to analyze 729 experimental configurations, methanol is found to perform best under specific conditions. The findings support the role of FMCDM models in guiding technical decisions for cleaner fuel alternatives (Balki et al., 2020). The method's scalability and robustness are further exemplified in the context of transport infrastructure planning. Selecting high-speed rail (HSR) corridors involves balancing spatial, economic, and social considerations (Nikolić et al., 2025).

Study (Petrović, Jovanović, Marinković, et al., 2025) presents a geographic information system (GIS)-based MCDM framework integrating fuzzy AHP for weighting and ARAS for evaluation, applied to twenty candidate HSR routes across Turkey. The analysis reveals potential travel time reductions of up to 46%, demonstrating the model's utility in guiding strategic transport investments (Eren et al., 2021).

In academic personnel selection, where human capital significantly influences institutional performance, the study (Gottwald & Jovčić, 2022) applies a hybrid entropy-ARAS model to select a PhD candidate at the University of Pardubice. The entropy method is employed for objective criterion weighting, followed by ARAS-based ranking of candidates. Results are presented both graphically and descriptively, illustrating the framework's practical value in structured academic hiring processes (Gottwald & Jovčić, 2022).

Traditional risk assessment methods are frequently limited by subjective bias, data uncertainty, and rigid weighting schemes. To address these shortcomings, the study (Soltani & Aliabadi, 2023) proposes a fuzzy MCDM model that integrates SWARA and ARAS to evaluate occupational hazards in firefighting, based on the Fine–Kinney risk criteria. The approach enhances objectivity and precision in risk prioritization under high-stakes conditions (Soltani & Aliabadi, 2023).

In agriculture, increasing global food demands have heightened interest in sustainable farming methods. Study (Yücenur & Maden, 2024) employs a combined entropy-ARAS approach to determine the optimal locations for geothermal-powered hydroponic greenhouses in Turkey. Considering factors like infrastructure, sustainability potential, and geothermal resource availability, Denizli Province stands out as the top choice. The findings offer strategic insights for eco-friendly agricultural development (Yücenur & Maden, 2024).

The importance of location selection is equally clear in urban logistics, where rapid e-commerce growth and supply chain complexity require optimal warehouse placement. Study (Kozoderović et al., 2025) uses a hybrid SWARA-ARAS model to evaluate five urban locations in Belgrade across eight criteria, identifying Batajnica as the most suitable site because of its operational efficiency, cost benefits, and accessibility (Kozoderović et al., 2025).

Finally, in the increasingly climate-impacted domain of water resource management, a study (Dehkordi et al., 2025) develops an integrated fuzzy Shannon entropy-ARAS framework to evaluate drought scenarios in Iran's Chaharmahal and Bakhtiari provinces. Incorporating expert judgment, the model provides a rigorous and adaptable method for ranking and selecting drought mitigation strategies under uncertainty (Dehkordi et al., 2025).

In today's dynamic economic environment—characterized by rapid technological advancements, shifting market conditions, and evolving societal demands—decision-making processes in economics have become increasingly complex. The selection of the most suitable alternative to maximize profit and resource efficiency often requires the incorporation of both quantitative and qualitative factors, particularly under uncertainty and subjectivity. In this regard, FMCDM methods provide a robust framework, as they can accommodate imprecise and linguistic evaluations commonly found in human judgment (Jovanović et al., 2023).

The enhanced version of the ARAS method, known as additive ratio assessment with fuzzy numbers (ARAS-F), has proven its practical applicability under such uncertain conditions through the use of triangular fuzzy numbers. For example, its application in selecting the optimal location for a logistics center among several alternatives demonstrates its capacity to support complex spatial decisions (Turskis & Zavadskas, 2010a). In this case, four main criteria were considered: investment cost, operational duration, future expansion potential, and market proximity. Within the ARAS-F framework, the overall utility of each alternative is computed based on the weighted contributions of all criteria, while performance is benchmarked against an ideal solution. This comparative structure enables systematic ranking and identifies areas for improvement (Turskis & Zavadskas, 2010a).

Beyond logistical planning, FMCDM models are increasingly applied in human resource decision-making, particularly in the selection of candidates for strategic roles, such as architects or financial executives. These decisions frequently involve subjective factors like creativity, leadership, and personality traits. Fuzzy set theory provides a suitable approach to modeling such ambiguity. In this context, the paper (Keršulienė & Turskis, 2011) introduces an integrated FMCDM model that combines ARAS-F with the SWARA method for determining criterion weights. The model effectively incorporates both linguistic and numerical evaluations from multiple decision-makers via fuzzy linguistic aggregation. A case study on architect selection confirms the method's reliability and practical relevance in real-world decision-making (Keršulienė & Turskis, 2011).

A similar methodology has been applied to the high-stakes selection of a chief accounting officer (CAO)—a role critical for ensuring financial transparency and compliance. Paper (Keršulienė & Turskis, 2014) addresses this issue by presenting a comprehensive fuzzy MCDM framework that integrates fuzzy information fusion, ARAS-F, the fuzzy weighted product model, and the AHP method. It offers a structured approach for handling personnel decisions that involve multiple performance dimensions and high degrees of subjectivity (Keršulienė & Turskis, 2014).

Further reinforcing the applicability of ARAS-F and related methods, the paper (Yapici Pehlivan et al., 2018) investigates strategic distribution channel selection in the context of globalization and technological disruption. Although traditional and fuzzy MCDM approaches have been widely used, integrated frameworks remain underutilized. To address this gap, a hybrid FMCDM model is proposed, incorporating FAHP for criterion weighting and employing WASPAS-F, EDAS-F, and ARAS-F for ranking strategic alternatives. By accommodating uncertainty through linguistic evaluation, the model identifies managerial and financial factors as most influential. Consistent results across all methods confirm the robustness and practical value of this integrated approach in strategic decision-making under dynamic and uncertain conditions (Yapici Pehlivan et al., 2018).

Finally, study (Mistarihi et al., 2025) contributes to the discourse on sustainable energy planning, focusing on the United Arab Emirates' efforts to advance green energy solutions. Also, the same study proposes a robust evaluation model that integrates multiple methods—the complex proportional assessment (COPRAS), Fuzzy COPRAS, ARAS, and Fuzzy ARAS—to assess renewable energy alternatives. Solar and wind energy emerged as top priorities, with the hybrid FCOPRAS—ARAS-F approach delivering the most consistent rankings (Mistarihi et al., 2025).

Additionally, the improved ARAS method has been applied to the supplier selection process, aiming to identify the vendor that best meets stakeholder requirements (Turskis & Zavadskas, 2010b). The selection and weighting of criteria were aligned with stakeholder goals and priorities. To address this problem, an advanced version of the ARAS method, incorporating gray values—ARAS-G—was utilized. The proposed model provides a robust analytical foundation for decision-making in areas such as sustainable development, environmental impact assessment, and the selection of technologies, structural systems, and investment alternatives (Turskis & Zavadskas, 2010b).

The energy sector—particularly within the European Union (EU)—represents a critical arena where the complexity of policy objectives, ranging from greenhouse gas emissions reduction (Petrović et al., 2020) to the promotion of renewable energy, necessitates the application of advanced decision-support methodologies. In response to this challenge, the paper (Baležentis & Streimikiene, 2017) investigates the use of MCDM techniques to evaluate and rank energy development scenarios. By employing a combination of weighted aggregated sum product assessment (WASPAS), ARAS, and technique for order preference by similarity to ideal solution (TOPSIS) methods, along with sensitivity analysis to examine the influence of criterion weight variation, the study demonstrates the significant impact of model architecture on scenario outcomes (Baležentis & Streimikiene, 2017).

In parallel with the global emphasis on decarbonization and energy security, hydrogen production from renewable sources is gaining momentum as a cornerstone of sustainable energy strategies. Addressing this imperative, the study (Almutairi et al., 2021) conducts a detailed assessment of 15 cities in Iran's Fars province to identify the most suitable locations for renewable hydrogen production. The study employs a comprehensive suite of MCDM methods—ARAS, simple additive weighting (SAW), combinative distance-based assessment (CODAS), and TOPSIS—to evaluate cities based on criteria such as solar and wind energy potential, topographical suitability, infrastructure readiness, disaster risk, and labor availability. The analysis concludes with the identification of Izadkhast as the most favorable location, offering a replicable and transparent framework for strategic planning in emerging hydrogen economies (Almutairi et al., 2021).

Extending the discourse on sustainable infrastructure planning, the paper (Rekik et al., 2025) introduces an integrated framework for wind farm site selection in Tunisia, combining GIS-based spatial analysis with FAHP and six distinct MCDM methods, among which ARAS and COPRAS feature prominently. The proposed approach highlights the critical role of integrated, multimethod evaluation frameworks in advancing renewable energy deployment while balancing ecological sensitivity and socio-economic equity (Rekik et al., 2025).

Financial performance is a key indicator of an organization's fiscal stability and its ability to meet debt obligations, making it essential in credit evaluation processes. To support objective and accurate assessment, the paper (Heidary Dahooie et al., 2019) proposes a model that integrates the correlation coefficient and standard deviation (CCSD) weighting method with a hybrid fuzzy C-means and additive ratio assessment (FCM-ARAS) approach. The model is applied to 58 Iranian manufacturing firms seeking bank loans, using eight financial criteria such as the debt ratio, equity-to-assets ratio, and return on assets (ROA). While CCSD guarantees objectivity in weighting, the FCM-ARAS method allows for clustering and ranking of firms, providing valuable insights for financial decision-making (Heidary Dahooie et al., 2019).

The management of end-of-life vehicles (ELVs) has become a pressing environmental issue, with recycling processes playing a central role in achieving environmental and economic sustainability. In this context, study (Karagöz et al., 2021) applied an extended version of the ARAS method within an interval type-2 fuzzy environment to determine the optimal location for an ELV recycling center in Istanbul—the Turkish city with the highest number of registered vehicles. The results confirmed the reliability and practical value of the proposed approach over traditional MCDM techniques (Karagöz et al., 2021).

The ARAS method, known for its efficiency in handling complex decision-making problems by evaluating alternatives relative to an ideal solution, has faced challenges related to attribute interdependence and sensitivity to scaling. To enhance its robustness, scientific paper (Wang et al., 2024) introduces a novel T-spherical fuzzy environment, incorporating new cross-entropy and aggregation operators to improve adaptability and accuracy. A group decision-making model was developed and validated through a case study on sustainable supplier selection for power battery echelon utilization in 5 G base stations, confirming its effectiveness (Wang et al., 2024).

In the domain of transport safety, the study (Xie & Chen, 2024) presents a hybrid model (meethod based on the removal effects of criteria [MEREC]–ARAS–quantile-based k-means clustering [QBKM]) combining removal effects of criteria MEREC, ARAS, and QBKM to assess road safety performance. By enhancing clustering stability and integrating multicriteria evaluation, the model identifies regional disparities and supports evidence-based policymaking for improved safety outcomes (Xie & Chen, 2024).

Similarly, addressing environmental challenges in freight transport, the study (Görçün et al., 2024) proposes a multilayered framework integrating neutrosophic Delphi, MGqNS-based SWARA, and ARAS methods to evaluate the sustainability of transportation modes. Results highlight "cargo security" and "accident rates" as key decision criteria, with maritime transport emerging as the most sustainable mode. These findings offer strategic insights for developing eco-efficient logistics networks (Görçün et al., 2024).

Further advancing methodological understanding, the paper (Aleksic et al., 2019) offers a comprehensive review of the ARAS framework, analyzing at least 95 academic contributions between 2010 and 2020. The review encompasses bibliometric trends, theoretical enhancements—including the integration of uncertainty and hybrid data—and practical applications. It also identifies current limitations and future directions for improving the robustness and applicability of the ARAS method (Liu & Xu, 2021).

In recent years, the increasing complexity of decision-making environments—driven by technological progress, globalization, regulatory requirements, and sustainability goals—has required the development and use of robust MCDM frameworks. In various fields like human resource management, sustainable construction, corporate responsibility, energy policy, and distribution strategies, the ARAS method, especially its fuzzy and hybrid versions, has been key in supporting rational, transparent, and flexible decision-making under uncertainty. Overall, these studies highlight the flexibility and effectiveness of ARAS and fuzzy ARAS methods in solving complex, multidimensional decision problems across many sectors. By combining qualitative and quantitative data, including expert judgment and hybrid modeling techniques, these approaches offer valuable decision-support tools that can improve strategic planning, operational efficiency, and sustainable development.

54.4 Conceptual framework of the additive ratio assessment method

The classic ARAS method is relatively simple and intuitive, and is often used in engineering management, logistics, economics, and other fields where a choice between multiple options is required based on multiple criteria.

The advantages of the ARAS method are its simplicity to implement and understand. It shows a clear relative relationship between the alternatives and the ideal solution and is easily combined with other MCDM methods.

The ARAS method is based on the idea of additive optimality: the best alternative is the one that has the highest overall utility when all criteria values are added together, taking into account their weights. The essence of the method can be represented through the following characteristics:

1. Additive nature of decision-making. The basis of the method is an additive approach to decision-making: the total utility of the alternative is obtained collectively, by adding the values of all criteria, taking into account the relative importance (weight) of each criterion. This is analogous to economic rationality—the more benefits (or the fewer costs), the better the solution. This is in contrast to methods that use ratios or distances (e.g., TOPSIS (Aleksic et al., 2019)), because ARAS uses absolute utility values, which allows direct comparison between alternatives.
2. Introduction of an ideal (optimal) alternative. One of the key philosophical bases of the method is defining the ideal solution. The ideal alternative does not necessarily appear in reality—it is hypothetical and represents a "perfect" combination of values of all criteria. This serves as a fixed point of comparison—each realistic alternative is measured against the ideal.
3. Normalization as an expression of relative value. Normalization of criterion values has a double role:
   - Eliminates differences in measurement units, which allows, for example, liters, kilometers, and euros to add up.
   - Converts values into relative shares, which reflect the contribution of an individual criterion to the total value through a proportion.
4. This highlights the relative effectiveness of each alternative in the context of the total available value for that criterion.
5. Inclusion of criteria weights—the role of preferences. The method uses the weight coefficients of the criteria to reflect the decision maker's preferences. This introduces a subjective component: the importance of each criterion determines how much it contributes to the final score. This is important because different situations may have different priorities: cost may be more important in one decision, while reliability is key in another.
6. The utility coefficient is a measure of relative dominance. The utility coefficient $Q_i = S_i/S_0$ shows how close each alternative is to the ideal. If $Q_i = 1$, the alternative is identical to the ideal. If it is close to zero, then the alternative is bad. This is essentially a relative ranking, but derived from absolute aggregate values, which are conceptually clearer to many decision makers.
7. Compromising character. The method allows for a compromise solution: no single alternative has to dominate in all criteria, but it can have the best overall performance. This means that the alternative is not required to be the best in every criterion, but to create a balanced result that leads to high utility overall.

Compared to other methods, ARAS is similar to the SAW method (Tupenaite et al., 2010), but differs in that it introduces normalization and an ideal solution, thus adding a layer of interpretation (Table 54.1). ARAS is an upgrade of the SAW method and is more suitable when comparison with the "best possible solution" is important. ARAS is more suitable when it is necessary to quantify the closeness to the ideal in absolute values, while TOPSIS is better for scenarios with clearly defined boundaries (ideal and antiideal) (Petrović, Mihajlović, et al., 2023). VlseKriterijumska Optimizacija I Kompromisno Resenje is more suitable for conflict situations where you have to balance between criteria, while ARAS is better for evaluating the overall performance compared to the ideal (Opricovic, 2009). AHP is better in situations where there is no numerical data, while ARAS is better for pure quantitative decisions with clearly defined criteria (Komatina et al., 2022; Petrović, Jovanović, et al., 2023).

TABLE 54.1 Comparison of additive ratio assessment (ARAS) with popular methods.

Method	Basis	Utility type	The essence of the comparison
ARAS	Additive sum	Absolute	Relationship to the ideal aggregate value
TOPSIS	Geometric distance	Relative	Distance from ideal and antiideal solutions
SAW	Additive sum	Absolute	Direct addition without normalization
VIKOR	Compromise and balance	Relative	Proximity to ideal + regret measure
AHP	Hierarchy and comparison	Relative	Matrix comparison of criteria and decisions

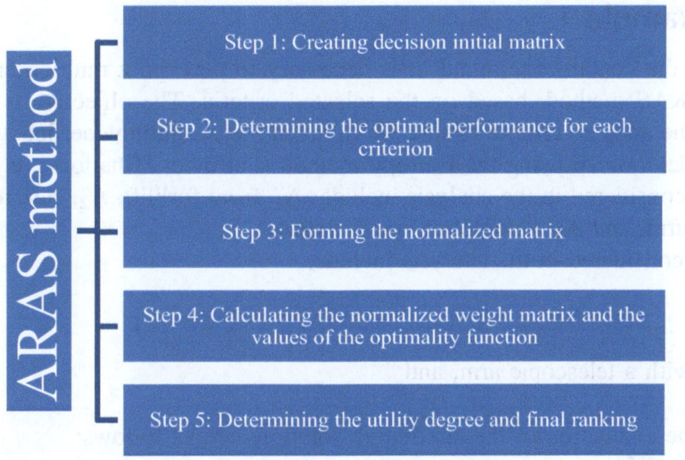

FIGURE 54.3 Basic steps of the additive ratio assessment (ARAS) method.

The procedure for solving a multicriteria decision-making problem (Fig. 54.3) using the classical ARAS method can be systematically defined through the following steps (Zavadskas & Turskis, 2010):

Step 1. Construction of the decision matrix based on the complete set of considered alternatives and the defined or adopted criteria.

Step 2. Determination of the optimal performance for each criterion. In this step, the decision-maker defines the optimal value for each criterion. If the decision-maker does not express specific preferences, the optimal performance can be determined according to predefined rules or standard procedures:

$$x_{0j} = \begin{cases} \max\limits_{i} x_{ij}; & j \in \Omega_{\max} \\ \min\limits_{i} x_{ij}; & j \in \Omega_{\min} \end{cases} \tag{54.1}$$

In this context, x_{0j} denotes the optimal performance of the *j*-th criterion, where $\Omega_{\max}$ represents the set of benefit criteria, and $\Omega_{\min}$ represents the set of cost criteria.

Step 3. Calculation of the normalized decision matrix. The normalized matrix is obtained by transforming the initial decision matrix in accordance with the type of each criterion and can be calculated as follows:

$$r_{ij} = \begin{cases} \dfrac{x_{ij}}{\sum_{i=0}^{m} x_{ij}}; & j \in \Omega_{\max} \\ \dfrac{1/x_{ij}}{\sum_{i=0}^{m} 1/x_{ij}}; & j \in \Omega_{\min} \end{cases} \tag{54.2}$$

criteria, $i = 0, 1, \ldots, m$.

Step 4. Determination of the overall performance for each alternative. The overall performance of a given alternative is calculated by aggregating the weighted normalized values of all criteria, as defined by the following expression:

$$S_i = \sum_{j=1}^{n} w_j r_{ij} \tag{54.3}$$

In this expression, S_i denotes the total (aggregated) performance of the i-th alternative, where $i = 0, 1, \ldots, m$.

Step 5. Calculation of the degree of utility for each alternative. The degree of utility is determined by comparing the total performance of each alternative to that of the optimal alternative, as expressed by the following formula:

$$Q_i = \frac{S_i}{S_0} \tag{54.4}$$

In this formula, Q_i represents the degree of utility of the *i*-th alternative, S_0 is the overall performance index of the optimal alternative, and $i = 1, 2, \ldots, m$.

The relative efficiency of the alternatives is determined based on the degree of utility values, expressed through the Q_i ratios, which range between 0 and 1. After calculating the degree of utility, the alternative with the highest Q_i value is considered the most preferred option.

54.5 Numerical example 1

During the design phase of the container terminal, it is necessary to perform a multicriteria ranking of the alternatives (manipulators) using the ARAS method, based on the selected criteria. The objective is to identify the most suitable alternative that aligns with the adopted criteria (Table 54.2), given the weighting coefficients [0.153, 0.083, 0.100, 0.230, 0.213, 0.220], which were determined using the Entropy method (Petrović, Mihajlović, et al., 2023).

The alternative solutions considered in the analysis include: A_1: front forklift, A_2: side forklift truck, A_3: front forklift equipped with a telescopic arm, and A_4: side portal manipulator.

The alternative solutions considered in the analysis include:

A_1: front forklift,
A_2: side forklift,
A_3: front forklift equipped with a telescopic arm, and
A_4: side portal manipulator.
The criteria considered in the evaluation of the alternative solutions are as follows:
f_1: cost of handling equipment [\$],
f_2: performance [t/h],
f_3: travel distance [m],
f_4: storage area [m^2],
f_5: degree of warehouse area utilization, and
f_6: degree of warehouse volume utilization.

Since the decision-maker does not have his preferences, in the first step, the determination of the extreme performances (Table 54.3), that is, the minimum and maximum values of the criterion A_0, is carried out according to Eq. (54.1):

In Step 3, the normalized decision matrix (Table 54.4) is constructed in accordance with Eq. (54.2). For example, the normalized value r_{11} of a cost-oriented (minimization) criterion is calculated as follows:

$$r_{11} = \frac{1/x_{11}}{\sum_{i=0}^{4} 1/x_{i1}} = \frac{\frac{1}{310000}}{\frac{1}{310000} + \frac{1}{310000} + \frac{1}{380000} + \frac{1}{420000} + \frac{1}{580000}} = 0.2446$$

Meanwhile, the normalized value r_{21} of a benefit-oriented (maximization) criterion is calculated as follows:

$$r_{21} = \frac{x_{21}}{\sum_{i=0}^{4} x_{i1}} = \frac{10}{16 + 10 + 15 + 16 + 14} = 0.1408$$

In the fourth step, the overall performance of each alternative is determined. For example, the value of S_1, calculated according to Eq. (54.3), is shown in Table 54.5:

$$S_1 = \sum_{j=1}^{6} w_1 r_{1j} = 0.153 \cdot 0.2446 + 0.083 \cdot 0.1408 + 0.100 \cdot 0.1414 + 0.230 \cdot 0.1216 + 0.213 \cdot 0.1129 + 0.220 \cdot 0.1119$$

$$S_1 = 0.0374 + 0.0117 + 0.0142 + 0.0280 + 0.0241 + 0.0246$$

TABLE 54.2 Initial decision matrix.

Optimization direction	f_1	f_2	f_3	f_4	f_5	f_6
	min	max	min	min	max	max
A_1	310000	10	444	23300	0.72	0.239
A_2	380000	15	322	10300	1.38	0.457
A_3	420000	16	316	15800	1.14	0.379
A_4	580000	14	270	19000	1.57	0.530

TABLE 54.3 Decision matrix with weight coefficients and optimal performance.

Optimization direction	f_1	f_2	f_3	f_4	f_5	f_6
	min	max	min	min	max	max
Weight coefficients	0.153	0.083	0.100	0.230	0.213	0.220
A_0	310000	16	270	10300	1.57	0.530
A_1	310000	10	444	23300	0.72	0.239
A_2	380000	15	322	10300	1.38	0.457
A_3	420000	16	316	15800	1.14	0.379
A_4	580000	14	270	19000	1.57	0.530

TABLE 54.4 Normalized decision matrix.

Optimization direction	f_1	f_2	f_3	f_4	f_5	f_6
	min	max	min	min	max	max
Weight coefficients	0.153	0.083	0.100	0.230	0.213	0.220
A_0	0.2446	0.2909	0.2325	0.2750	0.2461	0.2482
A_1	0.2446	0.1408	0.1414	0.1216	0.1129	0.1119
A_2	0.1995	0.2113	0.1950	0.2750	0.2163	0.2141
A_3	0.1805	0.2254	0.1987	0.1793	0.1787	0.1775
A_4	0.1307	0.1972	0.2325	0.1491	0.2461	0.2482

TABLE 54.5 Weighted-normalized decision-making matrix and solution results.

	f_1	f_2	f_3	f_4	f_5	f_6	S_i	Q_i	Rank
A_0	0.0374	0.0242	0.0233	0.0633	0.0525	0.0546	0.2554	1.0000	
A_1	0.0374	0.0117	0.0142	0.0280	0.0241	0.0246	0.1400	0.5483	4
A_2	0.0305	0.0176	0.0195	0.0633	0.0461	0.0471	0.2242	0.8779	1
A_3	0.0276	0.0188	0.0199	0.0413	0.0381	0.0391	0.1847	0.7234	3
A_4	0.0200	0.0164	0.0233	0.0343	0.0525	0.0546	0.2012	0.7877	2

$$S_1 = 0.1400$$

In the final step, the utility degree Q_i for each alternative can be calculated. For instance, the utility degree Q_1 for alternative A_1, determined according to Eq. (54.4), can be calculated as follows:

$$Q_1 = \frac{S_1}{S_0} = \frac{0.1400}{0.2554} = 0.5483$$

The value of Q_i in this context represents the overall evaluation of each alternative with respect to the defined criteria, taking into account both the positive and negative aspects of each option. A higher Q_i value indicates that the alternative is more aligned with the decision-making objectives, that is, it demonstrates better overall performance across all considered criteria. Based on the obtained Q_i values, all alternatives are then ranked in descending order: $A_2 > A_4 > A_3 > A_1$ (Table 54.5), where the alternative with the highest Q_i is evaluated as the most optimal choice—A_2 ($Q_2 = 0.8779$) representing the side forklift. This approach enables more objective and rational decision-making, particularly in complex situations involving multiple conflicting criteria.

54.6 Numerical example 2

In order to identify the most efficient logistics company and conduct a comprehensive evaluation of fleet performance, a multicriteria decision analysis using the ARAS method is required. The analysis includes seven logistics companies, denoted as $A_i = (A_1, A_2,..., A_7)$, which are evaluated according to seven relevant criteria $C_j = (C_1, C_2,..., C_7)$. These criteria, presented in Table 54.6, encompass key operational aspects that enable a comprehensive and balanced assessment of the economic, operational, and environmental performance of the vehicle fleet.

The criteria have been carefully selected to ensure representativeness and objectivity in the evaluation. Each criterion in Table 54.6 includes a detailed explanation of its significance and role in the logistics context, as well as the corresponding unit of measurement and type (maximization or minimization criterion), in accordance with the nature of the assessed characteristics. Economic criteria focus on cost efficiency and profitability; operational criteria emphasize reliability, availability, and resource utilization, while environmental criteria reflect alignment with modern sustainability requirements and environmental protection standards.

The data utilized for determining the weighting coefficients and ranking the alternatives of the criteria were obtained via online questionnaires. The study involved five experts—decision makers (DM1-DM5), whose individual responses are detailed in Table 54.7.

To establish the relative importance of the criteria, expert judgments were collected using a structured nine-point linguistic scale:

1. Extremely low (AL),
2. Very low (VL),
3. Low (L),
4. Medium-low (ML),
5. Medium (M),
6. Medium-high (MH),
7. High (H),
8. Very high (VH), and
9. Absolutely high (AH).

TABLE 54.6 The selected and used criteria.

	Criteria	Explanation of criteria	Unit	Type
C_1	Fleet size	Number of company-operated vehicles	Number	Min
C_2	Cost of fuel consumption	Annual fuel expenses for transportation	EUR/year	Min
C_3	Vehicle operating hours	The time a fleet vehicle was in use	h/year	Min
C_4	Total mileage	Total annual mileage of all vehicles	km/year	Max
C_5	Volume of cargo transported	Annual volume of cargo carried by vehicles	t/year	Max
C_6	Vehicle utilization rate	Efficiency of load capacity usage during transportation	%	Max
C_7	CO_2 emissions per ton-km	Carbon dioxide emitted per transported ton per km	kg CO_2/tkm	Min

TABLE 54.7 Expert evaluation of criteria importance.

		C_1	C_2	C_3	C_4	C_5	C_6	C_7
A_1	DM1	H	VH	ML	M	MH	M	MH
	DM2	MH	M	M	MH	VH	MH	ML
	DM3	VH	MH	MH	ML	M	M	M
	DM4	EH	H	VH	M	MH	VH	MH
	DM5	H	MH	M	MH	VH	MH	ML
A_2	DM1	VH	MH	M	MH	VH	MH	M
	DM2	M	ML	L	ML	M	MH	L
	DM3	MH	M	M	MH	H	VH	ML
	DM4	H	M	ML	MH	MH	VH	L
	DM5	VH	MH	MH	VH	VH	H	M
A_3	DM1	MH	ML	MH	VH	MH	VH	L
	DM2	ML	L	M	MH	M	MH	M
	DM3	M	L	ML	ML	M	VH	ML
	DM4	VH	MH	MH	M	VH	H	MH
	DM5	MH	M	ML	M	MH	VH	MH
A_4	DM1	M	L	M	MH	MH	VH	ML
	DM2	L	VL	MH	VH	VH	MH	L
	DM3	ML	L	MH	VH	MH	M	MH
	DM4	H	MH	M	MH	M	ML	VH
	DM5	VH	M	MH	MH	H	VH	MH
A_5	DM1	ML	L	M	MH	M	ML	M
	DM2	VL	L	ML	M	L	ML	ML
	DM3	L	VL	ML	ML	VL	L	M
	DM4	MH	ML	M	VH	M	ML	VH
	DM5	VH	MH	H	H	MH	M	H
A_6	DM1	L	L	MH	VH	MH	M	M
	DM2	MH	ML	M	MH	ML	L	ML
	DM3	M	L	MH	MH	M	ML	M
	DM4	ML	VL	VH	H	VH	MH	ML
	DM5	L	VL	H	VH	M	ML	M
A_7	DM1	L	L	VH	H	MH	ML	L
	DM2	ML	L	MH	VH	M	L	ML
	DM3	VL	EL	H	H	MH	L	L
	DM4	ML	ML	MH	VH	ML	VL	M
	DM5	VL	VL	VH	H	VH	M	MH

A survey was conducted to gather expert opinions regarding the significance of each criterion. The experts provided linguistic evaluations for all criteria and alternatives, based on the linguistic descriptors.

These qualitative assessments were subsequently transformed into precise numerical values. The resulting crisp scores were then aggregated to form consolidated judgments. Tables 54.8 and 54.9 present the linguistic assessments and the corresponding crisp values.

The decision matrix is obtained by calculating the arithmetic mean of the evaluations provided by the experts (decision-makers) for each alternative A_i and each criterion C_j. For instance, for alternative A_1 and criterion C_1 (highlighted in Bold in Table 54.8), the element x_{11} would be as shown in Table 54.9:

$$x_{11} = \frac{\sum C_{1n}}{n} = \frac{8+6+7+9+8}{5} = 7.60$$

The weight coefficients were derived from the decision matrix (Table 54.9) using the FANMA method (Petrović, Jovanović, et al., 2024), resulting in the following values: [0.1571, 0.1172, 0.1336, 0.2090, 0.1098, 0.1358, and 0.1374].

In the first step, the decision matrix is constructed, followed by determining the extreme performances—that is, the maximum and minimum values of the criteria for the reference alternative A0 —calculated according to Eq. (54.1).

In the following step, the normalized decision matrix is constructed (Table 54.10) according to Eq. (54.2). For example, the normalized value r_{11} of the criterion with a minimization orientation is:

$$r_{11} = \frac{1/x_{11}}{\sum_{i=1}^{7} 1/x_{i1}} = \frac{\frac{1}{7.60}}{\frac{1}{3.00}+\frac{1}{7.60}+\frac{1}{6.60}+\frac{1}{5.60}+\frac{1}{5.40}+\frac{1}{4.40}+\frac{1}{4.20}+\frac{1}{3.00}} = 0.0740$$

while the normalized value r_{41} of the criterion with a maximization orientation is:

$$r_{41} = \frac{x_{41}}{\sum_{i=1}^{7} x_{i1}} = \frac{5.20}{7.60+5.20+5.80+5.40+6.40+6.00+6.80+7.60} = 0.1024$$

In the fourth step, the overall performance for each alternative is determined. For example, the overall performance value S_1, calculated according to Eq. (54.3), is shown in Table 54.11:

$$S_1 = \sum_{j=1}^{7} w_1 r_{1j} = 0.1571\cdot0.0740 + 0.1172\cdot0.0693 + 0.1336\cdot0.1239 + 0.2090\cdot0.1024 + 0.1098\cdot0.1325 + 0.1358\cdot0.1312$$
$$+ 0.1374\cdot0.1157$$

$$S_1 = 0.0116 + 0.0081 + 0.0166 + 0.0214 + 0.0145 + 0.0178 + 0.0159$$

$$S_1 = 0.1060$$

At the final stage of the procedure, the utility degree Q_i is calculated for each alternative. For alternative A_1, the utility degree Q_1, determined according to Eq. (54.4), can be calculated as follows:

$$Q_1 = \frac{S_1}{S_0} = \frac{0.1060}{0.1570} = 0.6749$$

The ranking of alternatives indicates the relative efficiency of each in comparison to the ideal solution (A_0), which has the highest overall evaluation value $S_i = 0.1570$ and serves as the reference point with a utility degree $Q_i = 1.0000$. The best-ranked alternative, A_7, with value $Q_7 = 0.8685$, occupies the first position as it shows the greatest similarity to the ideal solution. Following it are alternatives A_6 with $Q_6 = 0.7962$, and A_2 with $Q_2 = 0.7830$, which take second and third places respectively due to their high and balanced criterion values. Alternatives A_4 with $Q_4 = 0.7672$, and A_3 with $Q_3 = 0.7638$, are positioned fourth and fifth because of slightly lower scores. Although competitive, alternative A_5 ranks sixth with $Q_5 = 0.7149$, while A_1 is ranked lowest with $Q_1 = 0.6749$, indicating its greatest deviation from the ideal value. This distribution demonstrates how even small differences in values can impact the final ranking, and the method enables precise identification of the best alternatives according to the specified criteria.

The application of the ARAS method not only allows for determining the relative efficiency of each logistics company under consideration but also facilitates their ranking based on the achieved overall utility values: $A_7 > A_6 > A_2 > A_4 > A_3 > A_5 > A_1$. This method is characterized by transparency, simplicity, and the ability to incorporate criteria of varying types and importance. The result of this analysis is a ranking list of logistics companies that can serve as

TABLE 54.8 Expert evaluation of the relative importance of decision-making criteria.

		C_1	C_2	C_3	C_4	C_5	C_6	C_7
A_1	DM1	**8**	7	4	5	6	5	6
	DM2	**6**	5	5	6	7	6	4
	DM3	**7**	6	6	4	5	5	5
	DM4	**9**	8	7	5	6	7	6
	DM5	**8**	6	5	6	7	6	4
A_2	DM1	7	6	5	6	7	6	5
	DM2	5	4	3	4	5	6	3
	DM3	6	5	5	6	8	7	4
	DM4	8	5	4	6	6	7	3
	DM5	7	6	6	7	7	8	5
A_3	DM1	6	4	6	7	6	7	3
	DM2	4	3	5	6	5	6	5
	DM3	5	3	4	4	5	7	4
	DM4	7	6	6	5	7	8	6
	DM5	6	5	4	5	6	7	6
A_4	DM1	5	3	5	6	6	7	4
	DM2	3	2	6	7	7	6	3
	DM3	4	3	6	7	6	5	6
	DM4	8	6	5	6	5	4	7
	DM5	7	5	6	6	8	7	6
A_5	DM1	4	3	5	6	5	4	5
	DM2	2	3	4	5	3	4	4
	DM3	3	2	4	4	2	3	5
	DM4	6	4	5	7	5	4	7
	DM5	7	6	8	8	6	5	8
A_6	DM1	3	3	6	7	6	5	5
	DM2	6	4	5	6	4	3	4
	DM3	5	3	6	6	5	4	5
	DM4	4	2	7	8	7	6	4
	DM5	3	2	8	7	5	4	5
A_7	DM1	3	3	7	8	6	4	3
	DM2	4	3	6	7	5	3	4
	DM3	2	1	8	8	6	3	3
	DM4	4	4	6	7	4	2	5
	DM5	2	2	7	8	7	5	6

TABLE 54.9 Decision matrix and maximum and minimum values of the criteria.

Logistics company	Criteria						
	C_1	C_2	C_3	C_4	C_5	C_6	C_7
Optimization direction	min	min	min	max	max	max	min
Weight of criteria—w	0.1571	0.1172	0.1336	0.2090	0.1098	0.1358	0.1374
Optimal value—A_0	3	2.6	4.6	7.6	6.6	7	4
A_1	7.60	6.40	5.40	5.20	6.20	5.80	5.00
A_2	6.60	5.20	4.60	5.80	6.60	6.80	4.00
A_3	5.60	4.20	5.00	5.40	5.80	7.00	4.80
A_4	5.40	3.80	5.60	6.40	6.40	5.80	5.20
A_5	4.40	3.60	5.20	6.00	4.20	4.00	5.80
A_6	4.20	2.80	6.40	6.80	5.40	4.40	4.60
A_7	3.00	2.60	6.80	7.60	5.60	3.40	4.20

TABLE 54.10 Normalized decision matrix.

Optimization direction	x_1	x_2	x_3	x_4	x_5	x_6	x_7
	min	**min**	**min**	**max**	**max**	**max**	**min**
Weight of criteria—w	0.1571	0.1172	0.1336	0.2090	0.1098	0.1358	0.1374
A_0	0.1874	0.1706	0.1455	0.1496	0.1410	0.1584	0.1446
A_1	0.0740	0.0693	0.1239	0.1024	0.1325	0.1312	0.1157
A_2	0.0852	0.0853	0.1455	0.1142	0.1410	0.1538	0.1446
A_3	0.1004	0.1056	0.1339	0.1063	0.1239	0.1584	0.1205
A_4	0.1041	0.1168	0.1195	0.1260	0.1368	0.1312	0.1113
A_5	0.1278	0.1232	0.1287	0.1181	0.0897	0.0905	0.0997
A_6	0.1338	0.1585	0.1046	0.1339	0.1154	0.0995	0.1258
A_7	0.1874	0.1706	0.0984	0.1496	0.1197	0.0769	0.1377

TABLE 54.11 Weighted-normalized decision-making matrix and solution results.

	x_1	x_2	x_3	x_4	x_5	x_6	x_7	S_i	Q_i	Rank
A_0	0.0294	0.0200	0.0194	0.0313	0.0155	0.0215	0.0199	0.1570	1.0000	
A_1	0.0116	0.0081	0.0166	0.0214	0.0145	0.0178	0.0159	0.1060	0.6749	7
A_2	0.0134	0.0100	0.0194	0.0239	0.0155	0.0209	0.0199	0.1229	0.7830	3
A_3	0.0158	0.0124	0.0179	0.0222	0.0136	0.0215	0.0166	0.1199	0.7638	5
A_4	0.0164	0.0137	0.0160	0.0263	0.0150	0.0178	0.0153	0.1205	0.7672	4
A_5	0.0201	0.0144	0.0172	0.0247	0.0099	0.0123	0.0137	0.1123	0.7149	6
A_6	0.0210	0.0186	0.0140	0.0280	0.0127	0.0135	0.0173	0.1250	0.7962	2
A_7	0.0294	0.0200	0.0131	0.0313	0.0131	0.0104	0.0189	0.1364	0.8685	1

a basis for strategic decision-making, improvement of internal processes, or the selection of an optimal logistics partner within the supply chain.

54.7 Conclusions

This chapter provides a thorough overview of the ARAS method application conducted from 2010 to July 2025. It focuses on its theoretical development, expanding application areas, and future research directions. According to key findings from bibliometric analysis, scholarly interest in the ARAS method has shown a steady increase, especially after 2019.

In practice, ARAS has been applied in five main areas: Engineering and Technical Systems, Transportation and Logistics, Energy and Environment, Business and Economics, and Healthcare and Social Services. The chapter outputs are thematically diverse, covering many journals and subject areas; however, there is a noticeable concentration in journals related to engineering and technical systems. This demonstrates the method's broad utility and operational flexibility.

After reviewing the method's fundamental principles, theoretical progress, and practical applications, several challenges are identified. These primarily relate to group decision-making processes, data organization, and decision timing. Theoretically, the ARAS method has significantly improved through integration with alternative ranking techniques, interdisciplinary tools, and adaptation to various data environments. These advancements have enhanced its robustness, versatility, and practical usability.

Future research should address key gaps such as building consensus, understanding decision-makers' risk preferences, improving data processing, managing multiperiod decision scenarios, and developing quick-response strategies. These issues are expected to guide future studies and further advance the ARAS methodology.

References

Aleksic, A., Runic Ristic, M., Komatina, N., & Tadic, D. (2019). Advanced risk assessment in reverse supply chain processes: A case study in Republic of Serbia. *Advances in Production Engineering & Management, 14*(4), 421–434. https://doi.org/10.14743/apem2019.4.338.

Almutairi, K., Mostafaeipour, A., Jahanshahi, E., Jooyandeh, E., Himri, Y., Jahangiri, M., Issakhov, A., Chowdhury, S., Hosseini Dehshiri, S. J., Hosseini Dehshiri, S. S., & Techato, K. (2021). Ranking locations for hydrogen production using hybrid wind-Solar: A case study. *Sustainability, 13*(8), 4524. https://doi.org/10.3390/su13084524.

Balezentiene, L., & Kusta, K. (2012). Reducing greenhouse gas emissions in grassland ecosystems of the central lithuania: Multi-criteria evaluation on a basis of the ARAS method. *The Scientific World Journal,* 11. https://doi.org/10.1100/2012/908384.

Baležentis, T., & Streimikiene, D. (2017). Multi-criteria ranking of energy generation scenarios with Monte Carlo simulation. *Applied Energy, 185*(1), 862–871. https://doi.org/10.1016/j.apenergy.2016.10.085.

Balki, M. K., Sinan Erdoğan, S., Aydın, S., & Sayin, C. (2020). The optimization of engine operating parameters via SWARA and ARAS hybrid method in a small SI engine using alternative fuels. *Journal of Cleaner Production, 258*, 120685. https://doi.org/10.1016/j.jclepro.2020.120685.

Đalić, I., Stević, Ž., Ateljević, J., Turskis, Z., Zavadskas, E., & Mardani, A. (2021). A novel integrated MCDM-SWOT-TOWS model for the strategic decision analysis in transportation company. *Facta Universitatis, Series: Mechanical Engineering, 19*(3), 401–422. https://doi.org/10.22190/FUME201125032D.

Damjanović, M., Stević, Ž., Stanimirović, D., Tanackov, I., & Marinković, D. (2022). Impact of the number of vehicles on traffic safety: Multiphase modeling. *Facta Universitatis, Series: Mechanical Engineering, 20*(1), 177–197. https://doi.org/10.22190/FUME220215012D.

Dehkordi, M. F., Hatefi, S. M., & Tamošaitienė, J. (2025). An integrated fuzzy shannon entropy and fuzzy ARAS model using risk indicators for water resources management under uncertainty. *Sustainability, 17*(11), 5108. https://doi.org/10.3390/su17115108.

Dehshiri, S. S. H., & Firoozabadi, B. (2023). Comparison, evaluation and prioritization of solar photovoltaic tracking systems using multi criteria decision making methods. *Sustainable Energy Technologies and Assessments, 55*. https://doi.org/10.1016/j.seta.2022.102989.

Eren, Ö., Mehmet, E., Cihan, C., & Mehmet, K. (2021). Analysis of potential high-speed rail routes: A case of gis-based multicriteria evaluation in Turkey. *Journal of Urban Planning and Development, 147*(2). https://doi.org/10.1061/(ASCE)UP.1943-5444.0000674.

Ghenai, C., Albawab, M., & Bettayeb, M. (2020). Sustainability indicators for renewable energy systems using multi-criteria decision-making model and extended SWARA/ARAS hybrid method. *Renewable Energy, 146*, 580–597. https://doi.org/10.1016/j.renene.2019.06.157.

Gottwald, D., & Jovčić, S. (2022). Multi-criteria decision-making approach in personnel selection problem – a case study at the university of pardubice. *Economic computation and economic cybernetics studies and research, 56*, 149–164. https://doi.org/10.24818/18423264/56.2.22.10.

Görçün, Ö. F., Tirkolaee, E. B., Aytekin, A., & Korucuk, S. (2024). Sustainability performance assessment of freight transportation modes using an integrated decision-making framework based on m-generalized q-neutrosophic sets. *Artificial Intelligence Review, 57*(121). https://doi.org/10.1007/s10462-024-10751-0.

Heidary Dahooie, J., Zavadskas, E. K., Vanaki, A. S., Firoozfar, H. R., Lari, M., & Turskis, Z. (2019). A new evaluation model for corporate financial performance using integrated CCSD and FCM-ARAS approach. *Economic Research, 32*(1), 1088–1113. https://doi.org/10.1080/1331677X.2019.1613250.

Jovanović, S., Zavadskas, E. K., Stević, Ž., Marinković, M., Alrasheedi, A. F., & Badi, I. (2023). An intelligent fuzzy MCDM model based on D and Z numbers for paver selection: IMF D-SWARA—fuzzy ARAS-Z model. *Axioms, 12*(6), 573. https://doi.org/10.3390/axioms12060573.

Karabašević, D., Paunkovic, J., & Stanujkić, D. (2016). Ranking of companies according to the indicators of corporate social responsibility based on SWARA and ARAS methods. *Serbian Journal of Management, 11*(1), 43–53. https://doi.org/10.5937/sjm11-7877.

Karagöz, S., Deveci, M., Simic, V., & Aydin, N. (2021). Interval type-2 fuzzy ARAS method for recycling facility location problems. *Applied Soft Computing, 102*, 107107. https://doi.org/10.1016/j.asoc.2021.107107.

Keršulienė, V., & Turskis, Z. (2011). Integrated fuzzy multiple criteria decision making model for architect selection. *Technological and Economic Development of Economy, 17*(4), 645–666. https://doi.org/10.3846/20294913.2011.635718.

Keršulienė, V., & Turskis, Z. (2014). A hybrid linguistic fuzzy multiple criteria group selection of a chief accounting officer. *Journal of Business Economics and Management, 15*(2), 232–252. https://doi.org/10.3846/16111699.2014.903201.

Komatina, N., Tadić, D., Aleksić, A., & Jovanović, A. D. (2022). The assessment and selection of suppliers using AHP and MABAC with type-2 fuzzy numbers in automotive industry. *Proceedings of the Institution of Mechanical Engineers, Part O: Journal of Risk and Reliability, 237*(4), 836–852. https://doi.org/10.1177/1748006X221095359.

Kozoderović, J., Pajić, V., & Andrejić, M. (2025). A multi-criteria analysis for e-commerce warehouse location selection using SWARA and ARAS methods. *Journal of Engineering, Management and Systems Engineering, 4*(2), 122–132. https://doi.org/10.56578/jemse040204.

Kutut, V., Zavadskas, E. K., & Lazauskas, M. (2013). Assessment of priority options for preservation of historic city centre buildings using MCDM (ARAS). *Procedia Engineering, 57*, 657–661. https://doi.org/10.1016/j.proeng.2013.04.083.

Liao, H., Wen, Z., & Liu, L. (2019). Integrating BWM and ARAS under hesitant linguistic environment for digital supply chain finance supplier section. *Technological and Economic Development of Economy, 25*(6), 1188–1212. https://doi.org/10.3846/tede.2019.10716.

Liu, N., & Xu, Z. (2021). An overview of ARAS method: Theory development, application extension, and future challenge. *International Journal of Intelligent Systems, 36*, 3524–3565. https://doi.org/10.1002/int.22425.

Medineckiene, M., Zavadskas, E. K., Björk, F., & Turskis, Z. (2015). Multi-criteria decision-making system for sustainable building assessment/certification. *Archives of Civil and Mechanical Engineering, 15*(1), 11–18. https://doi.org/10.1016/j.acme.2014.09.001.

Mistarihi, M. Z., Magableh, G. M., & Dalu, S. A. (2025). Evaluation of potential sustainable green energy sources for United Arab Emirates. *Results in Engineering, 26*, 104527. https://doi.org/10.1016/j.rineng.2025.104527.

Nedeljković, M., Puška, A., Doljanica, S., Virijević Jovanović, S., Brzaković, P., Stević, Ž., & Marinković, D. (2021). Evaluation of rapeseed varieties using novel integrated fuzzy PIPRECIA - Fuzzy MABAC model. *PLoS One, 16*(2), e0246857. https://doi.org/10.1371/journal.pone.0246857.

Nikolić, B., Marković, S., Petrović, N., Marinković, D., & Jovanović, V. (2025). Biodiesel and feedstocks-possibilities and characteristics: A review. *Thermal Science,* 58. https://doi.org/10.2298/TSCI250205058N -58.

Opricovic, S. (2009). A compromise solution in water resources planning. *Water Resource Manage, 23*, 1549–1561. https://doi.org/10.1007/s11269-008-9340-y.

Petrović, N., Bojović, N., Marinković, D., Jovanović, V., & Milanović, S. (2023). A two-phase model for the evaluation of urbanization impacts on carbon dioxide emissions from transport in the European Union. *Tehnički vjesnik, 30*(2), 514–520. https://doi.org/10.17559/TV-20221018103946.

Petrović, N., Mihajlović, J., Jovanović, V., Ćirić, D., & Živojinović, T. (2023). Evaluating annual operation performance of Serbian railway system by using multiple criteria decision-making technique. *Acta Polytechnica Hungarica, 20*(1), 157–168. https://doi.org/10.12700/APH.20.1.2023.20.11.

Petrović, N., Jovanović, V., Petrović, M., Nikolić, B., & Pavlović, J. (2023). Evaluating the operation performance of the Serbian transport freight system by using multiple criteria decision-making technique. *Engineering TODAY, 1*(4). https://doi.org/10.5937/engtoday2204033P.

Petrović, N., Bojović, N., Petrović, M., & Jovanović, V. (2020). A study of the environmental kuznets curve for transport greenhouse gas emissions in the European union. *Facta Universitatis, Series: Mechanical Engineering, 18*(3), 513–524. https://doi.org/10.22190/FUME171212010P.

Petrović, N., Jovanović, V., Petrović, M., Nikolić, B., & Mihajlović, J. (2025). Comparative investigation of normalization techniques and their influence on MCDM ranking – a case study. *Spectrum of Mechanical Engineering and Operational Research, 2*(1), 172–190. https://doi.org/10.31181/smeor21202542.

Petrović, N., Jovanović, V., Marković, S., Marinković, D., & Nikolić, B. (2025). Multi-criteria decision-making approach for choising e-bus for urban public transport in the city of Niš *Acta Technica Jaurinensis, 18*(1), 1–8. https://doi.org/10.14513/actatechjaur.00758.

Petrović, N., Jovanović, V., Marinković, D., Marković, S., & Nikolić, B. (2025). Measuring the efficiency of rail freight transport - A case study. *Acta Polytechnica Hungarica, 22*(4). https://doi.org/10.12700/APH.22.4.2025.4.8.

Petrović, N., Jovanović, V., Marković, S., Marinković, D., & Petrović, M. (2024). Multicriteria sustainability assessment of transport modes: A European Union case study for 2020. *Journal of Green Economy and Low-Carbon Development, 3*(1), 36–44. https://doi.org/10.56578/jgelcd030104.

Petrović, N., Marković, S., Nikolić, B., Jovanović, V., & Petrović, M. (2024). Evaluating alternative propulsion systems for urban public transport in Niš: A multicriteria decision-making approach. *Journal of Engineering, Management and Systems Engineering, 3*(2), 72–81. https://doi.org/10.56578/jemse030202.

Pramanik, P. K. D., Biswas, S., Pal, S., Marinković, D., & Choudhury, P. (2021). A comparative analysis of multi-criteria decision-making methods for resource selection in mobile crowd computing. *Symmetry, 13*(9), 1713. https://doi.org/10.3390/sym13091713.

Radović, D., Stević, Ž., Pamučar, D., Zavadskas, E. K., Badi, I., Antuchevičiene, J., & Turskis, Z. (2018). Measuring performance in transportation companies in developing countries: A novel rough ARAS model. *Symmetry, 10*(10), 434. https://doi.org/10.3390/sym10100434.

Rekik, S., Khabbouchi, I., & El Alimi, S. (2025). A spatial analysis for optimal wind site selection from a sustainable supply-chain-management perspective. *Sustainability, 17*(4), 1571. https://doi.org/10.3390/su17041571.

Shariati, S., Yazdani-Chamzini, A., Armin Salsani, A., & Tamošaitienė, J. (2014). Proposing a new model for waste dump site selection: Case study of ayerma phosphate mine. *Economics of Engineering Decisions, 25*(4), 410–419. https://doi.org/10.5755/j01.ee.25.4.6262.

Simić, V., Dabić-Miletić, S., Tirkolaee, E. B., Stević, Ž., Ala, A., & Amirteimoori, A. (2023). Neutrosophic LOPCOW-ARAS model for prioritizing industry 4.0-based material handling technologies in smart and sustainable warehouse management systems. *Applied Soft Computing, 143*, 110400. https://doi.org/10.1016/j.asoc.2023.110400.

Soltani, E., & Aliabadi, M. M. (2023). Risk assessment of firefighting job using hybrid SWARA-ARAS methods in fuzzy environment. *Heliyon, 9*(11), e22230. https://doi.org/10.1016/j.heliyon.2023.e22230.

Stević, Ž., Baydaş, M., Kavacık, M., Ayhan, E., & Marinković, D. (2024). Selection of data conversion technique via sensitivity-performance matching: Ranking of small e-vans with probid method. *Facta Universitatis, Series: Mechanical Engineering,* 643–671. https://doi.org/10.22190/FUME240305023S.

Sudžum, R., Nestić, S., Komatina, N., & Kraišnik, M. (2024). An intuitionistic fuzzy multi-criteria approach for prioritizing failures that cause overproduction: A case study in process manufacturing. *Axioms, 13*(6), 357. https://doi.org/10.3390/axioms13060357.

Tadić, D., Lukić, J., Komatina, N., Marinković, D., & Pamučar, D. (2025). A fuzzy decision-making approach to electric vehicle evaluation and ranking. *Tehnički vjesnik, 32*(3), 1066–1075. https://doi.org/10.17559/TV-20250223002410.

Tupenaite, L., Zavadskas, E. K., Kaklauskas, A., Turskis, Z., & Seniut, M. (2010). Multiple criteria assessment of alternatives for built and human environment renovation. *Journal of Civil Engineering and Management, 16*(2), 257–266. https://doi.org/10.3846/jcem.2010.30.

Turskis, Z., & Zavadskas, E. K. (2010a). A new fuzzy additive ratio assessment method (ARAS-F). case study: The analysis of fuzzy multiple criteria in order to select the logistic centers location. *Transport, 25*(4), 423–432. https://doi.org/10.3846/transport.2010.52.

Turskis, Z., & Zavadskas, E. K. (2010b). A novel method for multiple criteria analysis: Grey additive ratio assessment (ARAS-G) method. *Informatica, 21*(4), 597–610. https://doi.org/10.15388/Informatica.2010.307.

Wang, H., Xu, T., Feng, L., & Ullah, K. (2024). An improved ARAS approach with T-spherical fuzzy information and its application in multi-attribute group decision-making. *International Journal of Fuzzy Systems, 26*, 2132–2156. https://doi.org/10.1007/s40815-024-01718-y.

Web of Science, https://www.webofscience.com/wos/alldb/basic-search.

Xie, Z., & Chen, F. (2024). Auditing road safety achievement using MEREC–ARAS–QBKM model: An empirical study for APEC member economies. *Scientific Reports, 14*, 23049. https://doi.org/10.1038/s41598-024-73069-5.

Yapici Pehlivan, N., Şahin, A., Zavadskas, E. K., & Turskis, Z. (2018). A comparative study of integrated FMCDM methods for evaluation of organizational strategy development. *Journal of Business Economics and Management, 19*(2), 360–381. https://doi.org/10.3846/jbem.2018.5683.

Yücenur, G. N., & Maden, A. (2024). Sequential MCDM methods for site selection of hydroponic geothermal greenhouse: ENTROPY and ARAS. *Renewable Energy, 226*, 120361. https://doi.org/10.1016/j.renene.2024.120361.

Zamani, M., Rabbani, A., Yazdani-Chamzini, A., & Turskis, Z. (2014). An integrated model for extending brand based on fuzzy ARAS and ANP methods. *Journal of Business Economics and Management, 15*(3), 403–423. https://doi.org/10.3846/16111699.2014.923929.

Zavadskas, E. K., Antucheviciene, J., Kalibatas, D., & Kalibatiene, D. (2017). Achieving nearly zero-energy buildings by applying multi-attribute assessment. *Energy and Buildings, 143*, 162–172. https://doi.org/10.1016/j.enbuild.2017.03.037.

Zavadskas, E. K., Sušinskas, S., Daniūnas, A., Turskis, Z., & Sivilevičius, H. (2012). Multiple criteria selection of pile-column construction technology. *Journal of Civil Engineering and Management, 18*(6), 834–842. https://doi.org/10.3846/13923730.2012.744537.

Zavadskas, E. K., & Turskis, Z. (2010). A new additive ratio assessment (ARAS) method in multicriteria decision-making. *Technological and Economic Development of Economy, 16*(2), 159–172. https://doi.org/10.3846/tede.2010.10.

Zavadskas, E. K., Turskis, Z., & Bagočius, V. (2015). Multi-criteria selection of a deep-water port in the Eastern Baltic Sea. *Applied Soft Computing, 26*, 180–192. https://doi.org/10.1016/j.asoc.2014.09.019.

Zavadskas, E. K., Turskis, Z., & Vilutiene, T. (2010). Multiple criteria analysis of foundation instalment alternatives by applying additive ratio assessment (ARAS) method. *Archives of Civil and Mechanical Engineering, 10*(3), 123–141. https://doi.org/10.1016/S1644-9665(12)60141-1.

Zavadskas, E. K., Vainiūnas, P., Turskis, Z., & Tamošaitienė, J. (2012). Multiple criteria decision support system for assessment of projects managers in construction. *International Journal of Information Technology & Decision Making, 11*(2), 501–520. https://doi.org/10.1142/S0219622012400135.

Chapter 55

TODIM: Tomada de decisão interativa multicriterio method for multi-attribute decision-making

Babek Erdebilli[1,2], and Yavuz Selim Özdemir[3]

[1]*Department of Industrial Engineering, Ankara Yıldırım Beyazıt University, Ankara, Turkiye,* [2]*School of Business, Worcester Polytechnic Institute, Worcester, MA, United States,* [3]*Department of Industrial Engineering, Ankara Bilim University, Ankara, Turkiye*

55.1 Introduction

Today, higher education institutions are increasingly dependent on digital technology that supports learning and training processes. In particular, with the growth of online learning spaces, universities are obligated to make strategic decisions when selecting digital course sites. The choice of a suitable site requires a wide-ranging consideration of different facets, covering not only technology functionality but equally technology-supported student experience, teaching performance, cost-effectiveness, and information protection. Among these decision-making activities, it is crucial for decision-makers to strike a rational balance among multidimensional and often conflicting criteria.

At this point, multicriteria decision-making (MCDM) methods serve as a powerful tool in solving complex selection problems by providing decision-makers with a systematic and analytical framework (Ayyildiz & Taskin Gumus, 2020). Classical MCDM techniques generally base their work on finding out the weight of each criterion and comparing alternatives with respect to these criteria. Yet, most methods are incapable of modeling behavioral elements, such as decision-makers' risk perception and asymmetric loss and gain attitudes, directly. Nevertheless, it is human nature that cognitive biases like these affect decision procedures.

The interactive and multicriteria decision-making (TODIM) method, developed by Brazilian researchers Gomes and Lima, stands out as a behaviorally based MCDM approach that can model the decision-maker's sensitivity to gains and losses (Gomes & Lima, 1991). TODIM is based on prospect theory, developed by Kahneman and Tversky (Tversky & Kahneman, 1992). According to this theory, individuals evaluate relative gains and losses about their current situation rather than absolute outcomes when making decisions, and losses weigh more heavily psychologically than gains. By incorporating this behavioral reality into its decision-making model, TODIM differentiates itself from classical MCDM techniques (Ding et al., 2023).

TODIM aims to determine the "dominance" relationships between alternatives in multicriteria decision-making problems (Ji et al., 2018). At its core, the method normalizes the performance difference between two alternatives for each criterion according to a specific reference criterion weight and determines the gain–loss situation. Suppose the compared alternative performs better than the reference alternative in a criterion. In that case, this difference is evaluated as a positive gain, and a benefit value based on the square root function is calculated. In the opposite case, that is, if the alternative's performance is low, this difference is perceived as a loss, and a penalty coefficient modulated by the θ parameter affects (Tian et al., 2021).

The θ parameter represents the psychological impact of losses on the decision-maker. When the θ value is small, losses are punished much more severely; when it is high, the weight difference between gains and losses decreases (Zhao et al., 2022). This feature is one of TODIM's strongest points because it provides flexibility in modeling the behavior of decision-makers with different risk profiles.

Encyclopedia of Multi-Attribute Decision-Making (MADM). DOI: https://doi.org/10.1016/B978-0-443-33275-3.00013-0

In TODIM, the "dominance values" obtained from intercriterion comparisons are summed to calculate the total dominance score (ξi) for each alternative. These scores are normalized to get the final ranking. The method can be applied to both qualitative and quantitative data because it preserves the binary comparison logic. Additionally, it can be integrated with other methods, such as the analytic hierarchy process (AHP), in the weight determination process (Hanine et al., 2016).

The primary motivation for selecting the TODIM method in this study is the need to consider not only technical criteria but also decision-makers' risk perception when choosing a digital course platform for the university (Wu et al., 2011). For example, a platform that performs poorly in the "Security Level" criterion may be penalized heavily at low θ values, even if it is advantageous in terms of cost. This is particularly important in higher education environments, where information security risks are critical.

The importance of TODIM can be summarized under three main points. First, the inclusion of the behavioral dimension. While many other AHP methods treat gains and losses equally, TODIM performs an asymmetric evaluation in line with human psychology. Second, sensitivity analysis capability. By systematically adjusting the θ parameter, it is possible to see how ranking results change under different risk scenarios. This is a key advantage for testing the robustness of the decision. Finally, application flexibility. TODIM is suitable for evaluating options with complex features, such as software platforms, as it can work with both quantitative and qualitative criteria. With these features, TODIM is a powerful tool that enables data-driven and realistic decision-making in multistakeholder environments with high risk sensitivity, such as universities.

The second section of the study reviews related literature, and the third section provides a detailed explanation of the steps of the TODIM method. The fourth section applies the technique, and the fifth section conducts a sensitivity analysis. The sixth and final section presents the results and discusses future research.

55.2 Literature review

MCDM methods are widely used, especially in complex and multidimensional decision problems. Among these methods, classical techniques such as AHP, technique for order of preference by similarity to ideal solution, VIseKriterijumska Optimizacija I Kompromisno Resenje, and elimination and choice translating reality occupy a prominent place in the literature, but approaches that take human psychology and behavioral factors into account are gaining importance. The TODIM method is recognized as a significant innovation in the field of Behavioral MCDM.

By integrating the fundamental assumptions of prospect theory into the decision model, TODIM distinguishes itself from classical methods through its asymmetric sensitivity mechanism to losses. This feature more realistically reflects the nature of decisions made under risk and uncertainty (Yang et al., 2011). For example, the TODIM method is used in investment decisions in the energy sector and has demonstrated that the method's sensitivity analysis improved decision quality (Wu et al., 2018).

MCDM approaches are increasingly being used in the evaluation of educational technologies. Digital learning platforms could be evaluated by using technical specifications, user-friendly interfaces, support services, cost, and security (Liu et al., 2022). The literature shows that methods that model decision-makers' diverse priorities and risk perceptions enable them to make more informed choices (Tosun & Akyüz, 2015).

Expert assessments in the real world are rarely precise numbers; they often contain fuzzy, hesitant, or probabilistic expressions. As a result, extensions such as fuzzy-TODIM, hesitant fuzzy-TODIM, probabilistic hesitant fuzzy-TODIM, and interval-valued hesitant fuzzy-TODIM have been extensively developed in the TODIM literature (Ji et al., 2020; Tian et al., 2021). These studies enhance the modeling of uncertainty, allowing for a more nuanced representation of expert opinions, and have been applied in areas such as supplier selection, emergency decision-making, and environmental assessments.

In situations requiring more comprehensive uncertainty representation, neutrosophic and picture fuzzy set theories have been combined with TODIM (Wei, 2018). These approaches have been particularly used for sustainable energy choices and collective expert decisions by modeling positive/negative/neutral opinions, as well as truth, uncertainty, and decision components (Tian & Peng, 2020). Neutrosophic-TODIM studies have expanded the flexibility of the method and its areas of application (Ji et al., 2018).

In the literature, recent studies show that the TODIM method is a suitable and effective tool, both theoretically and practically (Wu et al., 2024). For decision problems where multidimensional and behavioral factors, such as the selection of educational technology, are critical. This study aims to fill this gap and demonstrate the applicability of TODIM in the selection of digital platforms in universities with a concrete example. TODIM is a method that has been used in the literature for a long time. In general, TODIM is used as a hybrid form with different weighting approaches and/or fuzzy logic approaches. A brief literature review is given in Table 55.1.

TABLE 55.1 Interactive and multicriteria decision-making (TODIM) literature.

Authors and Year	Title of the study	Methodlogy	Application domain
Autran Monteiro Gomes and Duncan Rangel (2009)	An application of the TODIM method to the multicriteria rental evaluation of residential properties	TODIM	Rental evaluation of residential properties
Gomes et al. (2009)	Multicriteria analysis of natural gas destination in Brazil: an application of the TODIM method	TODIM	Analysis of natural gas destination
Tseng et al. (2014)	Using TODIM to evaluate green supply chain practices under uncertainty	TODIM	Green supply chain
Li et al. (2015)	An intuitionistic fuzzy-TODIM method to solve the distributor evaluation and selection problem	Intuitionistic fuzzy-TODIM	Distributor evaluation and selection problem
Sang and Liu (2016)	An interval type-2 fuzzy sets-based TODIM method and its application to green supplier selection	Interval type-2 fuzzy TODIM	Green supplier selection
Qin et al. (2017)	An extended TODIM multicriteria group decision-making method for green supplier selection in an interval type-2 fuzzy environment	Type-2 fuzzy TODIM, group decision-making	Green supplier selection
Hu et al. (2018)	A novel TODIM method-based three-way decision model for medical treatment selection	TODIM method-based three-way decision model	Medical Treatment Selection
Ji et al. (2018)	A projection-based TODIM method under multivalued neutrosophic environments and its application in personnel selection	TODIM under multivalued neutrosophic environments	Personnel selection
Yuan et al. (2019)	Investment risk assessment of coal-fired power plants in countries along the Belt and Road initiative based on ANP-entropy-TODIM method	ANP-entropy-TODIM	Risk assessment of coal-fired power plants
Liang et al. (2019)	Pythagorean fuzzy VIKOR approaches based on TODIM for evaluating internet banking website quality of the Ghanaian banking industry	Pythagorean fuzzy VIKOR–TODIM	Evaluating internet banking website quality
Tian and Peng (2020)	An integrated picture fuzzy ANP–TODIM multicriteria decision-making approach for tourism attraction recommendation	Picture fuzzy ANP–TODIM	Tourism attraction recommendation
Liu et al. (2020)	Supplier selection in the nuclear power industry with an integrated ANP–TODIM method under z-number circumstances	ANP–TODIM	Supplier selection in the nuclear power industry
Zhang et al. (2022)	Product selection based on sentiment analysis of online reviews: an intuitionistic fuzzy TODIM method	Fuzzy TODIM	Product selection
Seker and Kahraman (2022)	A Pythagorean cubic fuzzy methodology based on TOPSIS and TODIM methods and its application to the software selection problem	Pythagorean cubic fuzzy TOPSIS–TODIM	Software selection problem
Ding et al. (2023)	A decision framework for cultural and creative products based on the IF-TODIM method and group consensus reaching model	IF-TODIM	A decision framework for cultural and creative products
Chawla et al. (2024)	A fuzzy Pythagorean TODIM method for sustainable ABC analysis in inventory management	Fuzzy Pythagorean TODIM	ABC analysis in inventory management

55.3 Methodology

Using the residual value function, the TODIM method's primary goal is to quantify the degree of dominance of each alternative in relation to the others (Gomes & Lima, 1991). A value function, whose shape is identical to that of the gain and loss function in the expectation theory, is employed in the procedure to accomplish this goal. This function allows for the simultaneous expression of the concepts of gain and loss. Using the residual value function, the TODIM method's primary goal is to quantify each alternative's degree of dominance in relation to the others (Wei et al., 2015). A value function, whose shape is identical to that of the gain and loss function in the expectation theory, is employed in the procedure to accomplish this goal. This function allows for the simultaneous expression of the concepts of gain and loss (Autran Monteiro Gomes & Duncan Rangel, 2009). The steps of the method are detailed below.

Notations

mn	number of alternatives where $j = 1, \ldots, n$
n	number of criteria where $j = 1, \ldots, n$
x_{ij}	performance score of alternative i for criterion j
w_j	weight of jth criteria
r_{ij}	normalization result
w_{ref}	reference criterion weight
w_{jr}	relative weight of jth criteria
θ	loss aversion parameter

Step 1. Creating a decision matrix
Based on the data, both the benefit and cost criteria sets are determined. Then, the initial decision matrix is generated and given in (55.1).

$$X = [x_{ij}]m*n, \quad (i = 1, 2, \ldots, m), \ (j = 1, 2, \ldots, n) \tag{55.1}$$

Step 2. Normalization
Linear normalization is used to normalize the decision matrix. For the benefit and cost criterion, normalization procedures are carried out independently, as shown in Eqs. (55.2) and (55.3), respectively:

$$r_{ij} = \frac{x_{ij} - \min(x_{ij})}{\max(x_{ij}) - \min(x_{ij})}, \quad \forall (i, j) \tag{55.2}$$

$$r_{ij} = \frac{\max(x_{ij}) - x_{ij}}{\max(x_{ij}) - \min(x_{ij})}, \quad \forall (i, j) \tag{55.3}$$

Step 3. Determining criterion weights
Here, the criteria weights are determined as given in Eq. (55.4). The decision-maker may use different MCDM techniques like AHP, ENTROPI, or criteria importance through intercriteria correlation.

$$\sum\nolimits_{j=1}^{n} w_j = 1 \ and \ w_j \geq 0 \tag{55.4}$$

Step 4. Determining the reference weight
In this study, the reference weight was determined as given in Eq. (55.5).

$$w_{ref} = \max(w_j) \tag{55.5}$$

Step 5. Relative weight calculation
Relative weights are calculated as given in Eq. (55.6).

$$w_{jr} = \frac{w_j}{w_{ref}} \tag{55.6}$$

Step 6. Dominance component

Calculation of the dominance component is given in Eq. (55.7)

$$\phi_c(A_i, A_j) = \begin{cases} \sqrt{\dfrac{w_{cr}(r_{ic} - r_{jc})}{\sum_{c=1}^{n} w_{cr}}} & if\ r_{ic} - r_{jc} > 0 \\ -\dfrac{1}{\theta}\sqrt{\dfrac{(\sum_{c=1}^{n} w_{cr})(r_{ic} - r_{jc})}{w_{cr}}} & if\ r_{ic} - r_{jc} < 0 \\ 0 & if\ r_{ic} - r_{jc} = 0 \end{cases} \tag{55.7}$$

Step 7. Dominance score

Calculation of the dominance score is given in Eq. (55.8)

$$\delta(A_i, A_j) = \sum_{j=1}^{n} \varphi_c(A_i, A_j), \quad \forall\ (i, j) \tag{55.8}$$

Step 8. Normalization of partial dominance

In the final step, normalization of partial dominance scores is calculated and given in Eq. (55.9). Ranking of alternatives based on their overall normalized dominance scores.

$$\xi_i = \frac{\sum_{j=1}^{m} \delta(A_i, A_j) - \min \sum_{j=1}^{m} \delta(A_i, A_j)}{\max \sum_{j=1}^{m} \delta(A_i, A_j) - \min \sum_{j=1}^{m} \delta(A_i, A_j)} \tag{55.9}$$

One of the most significant advantages of the TODIM method in this study is its ability to evaluate gains and losses separately. In traditional methods, the performance of each alternative is typically calculated within the framework of a linear utility function, which cannot adequately model decision-makers' varying sensitivity levels to potential risks (Ulu & Şahin, 2021). TODIM, however, makes the decision process more realistic by calculating a nonlinear positive benefit in gain situations and a negative benefit scaled by the θ coefficient in loss situations (Nie et al., 2019). This feature is particularly critical in organizations that serve the public interest, such as universities, when high-cost and long-term investments are involved.

Another advantage is TODIM's dominance approach, which is based on pairwise comparisons (Zhang et al., 2022). Comparing both alternatives in terms of all criteria reveals the degree of superiority of each alternative over the others, rather than just individual scores. This approach makes it easier to see which platform stands out in which criteria, especially when the differences between alternatives are not very clear.

55.4 Numerical example

This section presents an application study on the selection of a distance learning platform for a university using the TODIM method. Four alternative platforms were evaluated in the decision-making process based on the criteria of ease of use, technical support quality, cost, and security level (Ozkan & Koseler, 2009). First, the criterion weights were determined, and then the dominance scores of each alternative were calculated using the TODIM method. Additionally, a sensitivity analysis was conducted by examining scenarios where the θ parameter took different values. This revealed how the rankings of the alternatives changed based on risk perception and assessed the flexibility of the decision-making process. Decision-makers are evaluating four different alternatives based on the following criteria:

C_1 – ease of use (benefit type)
C_2 – technical support quality (benefit type)
C_3 – cost (cost type)
C_4 – security level (benefit type)

In this step, there are four different alternatives A_1: EduMax, A_2: LearnPro, A_3: SmartStudy, and A_4: ClassTech. The decision matrix shows the evaluation scores of four alternatives in terms of four different criteria in the process of selecting a distance learning platform: ease of use, technical support quality, cost, and security level. Decision-makers have evaluated each alternative on a scale of 1–10 (a lower score in the cost criterion indicates a lower cost). The evaluation table is given in Table 55.2.

The normalized decision matrix is created to make criteria with different scales comparable, and is given in Table 55.3. In benefit criteria, each value is normalized by dividing it by the maximum value of that criterion. For the cost criteria, an

TABLE 55.2 Initial values.

	C_1	C_2	C_3	C_4
A_1	8	7	6	9
A_2	6	9	5	8
A_3	7	8	7	7
A_4	9	6	8	6

TABLE 55.3 Normalized values.

	C_1	C_2	C_3	C_4
A_1	0,6667	0,3333	0,6667	1,0000
A_2	0,0000	1,0000	1,0000	0,6667
A_3	0,3333	0,6667	0,3333	0,3333
A_4	1,0000	0,0000	0,0000	0,0000

TABLE 55.4 Dominance.

	A_1	A_2	A_3	A_4
A_1	0,0000	0,1268	1,2671	1,5292
A_2	−0,1268	0,0000	1,1434	1,4747
A_3	−1,2671	−1,1434	0,0000	0,9273
A_4	−1,5292	−1,4747	−0,9273	0,0000

inverse transformation is performed using the minimum value as a reference. All criteria are converted to a range between 0 and 1 and made suitable for the weighting stage. The normalization process eliminates biases arising from the measurement units of the criteria and enables accurate comparisons in TODIM analysis.

The weights have been determined by the decision-makers (to total 1): $w1 = 0{,}30$, $w2 = 0{,}25$, $w3 = 0{,}20$, $w4 = 0{,}25$. The dominance table reveals the criteria-based superiority or weakness of each alternative relative to the others, and is given in Table 55.4. In the TODIM method, this calculation is performed using normalized decision matrix values, criterion weights, and the θ parameter. Positive values indicate that the alternative in the row is superior to the alternative in the column, while negative values indicate that it is at a disadvantage. This stage models the psychological foundations of the decision-making process, taking into account different levels of sensitivity to gains and losses. Thus, the decision-maker's perception of risk is reflected in the process.

The total dominance score table shows the sum of each alternative's dominance values relative to the others. These scores indicate the performance of alternatives in the TODIM method. Positive total scores indicate that the alternative is competitive, while negative scores indicate that it is weak in terms of competitiveness. The scores are normalized to determine the final

TABLE 55.5 Results.

	Total score	Normalized score	Rank
A_1	2,9231	1,0000	1
A_2	2,4914	0,9370	2
A_3	−1,4832	0,3572	3
A_4	−3,9313	0,0000	4

preference ranking. Thus, the combination of criterion weights, the θ parameter, and pairwise comparison results objectively determines which alternative is the most suitable option. The values are given in Table 55.5.

One of the most important contributions of this study is that the analyses conducted using the TODIM method add a behavioral dimension to the university's decision-making process. The selection of a distance learning platform is a problem that involves not only technical criteria but also many other factors, such as user satisfaction, security concerns, and long-term sustainability. The behavioral flexibility provided by TODIM enables decision-makers to evaluate factors based on their risk perceptions (Tang et al., 2024).

Another contribution is the ability to perform sensitivity analysis. Suppose that the ranking obtained under a single θ value changes significantly under different parameters. In that case, this indicates the sensitivity of the decision and points to the need for additional steps, such as gathering more information or reevaluating the criteria. In this way, TODIM not only reveals "which alternative to choose" but also "how reliable the decision is."

55.5 Comparative analysis

In this section, a comparative sensitivity analysis is presented for the example given in Section 55.4. In general, sensitivity analysis in MCDM techniques involves systematically examining how decision outcomes change across different parameter values and assumptions. It investigates how slight variations in criteria weights, parameters, or alternative values used in decision models affect the final ranking and decision. This analysis enables decision-makers to assess the model's robustness and comprehend the reliability of the results. Especially with complex and multidimensional problems, sensitivity analysis becomes a vital part of the decision-making process.

The TODIM method is an MCDM approach that models decision-makers' asymmetric attitudes toward gains and losses based on the Expectation Theory. One of the distinctive features of TODIM is the θ parameter, which determines the weight of losses. This parameter reflects the decision-maker's sensitivity to losses, that is, their perception of risk. High sensitivity to losses means that the decision-maker is more affected by negative outcomes; conversely, in the case of low sensitivity, losses are evaluated as less severe. Therefore, the θ value is a critical parameter that provides behavioral flexibility to the TODIM model and directly affects ranking results.

The primary objective of sensitivity analysis in the TODIM method is to examine how the model's outputs change when the θ parameter takes different values. It is an essential tool for understanding the performance of alternatives under different risk scenarios. For example, when the θ value is kept low (e.g., 0.25 or 0.5), losses are penalized more heavily in the model. This represents a more cautious approach to potential risks. Conversely, when θ is high (e.g., 1), the differences between gains and losses are evaluated more evenly, and the decision-maker is less averse to risk. Thus, sensitivity analysis removes the decision process from being tied to a single set of parameters and reveals how different alternatives are ranked according to the decision-maker's risk tolerance.

Here, the sensitivity analysis of the TODIM method provides decision-makers with the opportunity to reevaluate their decisions under different conditions. Hence, if the ranking is highly sensitive to changes in θ, measures such as gathering additional information or re-evaluating criterion weights may be considered during the decision-making process. On the other hand, if the ranking remains generally stable as a result of the sensitivity analysis, this is a positive indicator of the consistency and reliability of the decisions made by decision-makers.

Sensitivity analysis in the TODIM method is not only a mathematical requirement but also a fundamental element of a holistic evaluation process that takes into account the psychological and behavioral aspects of the decision-maker

TABLE 55.6 Sensitivity.

	$\theta = 0{,}25$		$\theta = 0{,}5$		$\theta = 0{,}75$		$\theta = 1{,}0$	
	δ(Ai,Aj)	Normal	δ(Ai,Aj)	Normal	δ(Ai,Aj)	Normal	δ(Ai,Aj)	Normal
A1	−4,0404	1,0000	0,6019	1,0000	2,1494	1,0000	2,9231	1,0000
A2	−6,2713	0,8817	−0,4295	0,9050	1,5177	0,9229	2,4914	0,9370
A3	−14,4773	0,4468	−5,8145	0,4091	−2,9270	0,3801	−1,4832	0,3572
A4	−22,9066	0,0000	−10,2564	0,0000	−6,0396	0,0000	−3,9313	0,0000

(Liu et al., 2020). This analysis not only ensures that the decision-making process is more transparent, flexible, and reliable, but also enables the performance of alternatives to be understood based on the risk perceptions of different stakeholders. Thus, TODIM provides more suitable and comprehensive solutions to complex decision-making problems in real-life situations. The results are given in Table 55.6.

The sensitivity analysis conducted in the study revealed the depth provided by the TODIM method in the decision-making process. Since the θ parameter determines the weight given to losses by the decision-maker, the rankings obtained under different θ values showed the effect of risk perception on the alternatives.

Low θ value (0,25): The impact of losses has increased significantly. Platforms that are disadvantageous in terms of cost and security criteria have experienced ranking losses. This situation is suitable for scenarios where there is a high tendency to avoid risk. It is a scenario where relatively safer, but perhaps more expensive or technically limited platforms are more likely to be preferred.

Medium θ values (0,50 and 0,75): The balance between gains and losses has become more equitable, and the magnitude of changes in rankings has decreased. These scenarios reflect a balanced risk approach, ensuring that platforms deemed most suitable in terms of both technical performance and cost-security balance remain at the top of the rankings.

High θ value (1): Losses have reached nearly the same level as gains. The ranking has become relatively stable. This reflects a decision-maker's approach that does not avoid risk and prioritizes potential gains.

The analysis results show that the ranking is quite sensitive to changes in θ in some cases, but certain alternatives manage to remain at the top of the list in every scenario. Such platforms can be considered reliable choices even under different risk perceptions. This situation offers decision-makers the opportunity to identify alternatives that will provide consistent results not only under a specific set of parameters but also across a wide range of risks.

55.6 Conclusions

This study addressed the issue of choosing a distance learning platform for a university using the TODIM method, one of the MCDM approaches. The main goal was to develop a practical and reliable decision support process that considers the behavioral attitudes of decision-makers when evaluating alternatives across different criteria. The evaluations focused on four key criteria: usability, technical support quality, cost, and security level. Based on these criteria, four different platforms were compared.

In summary, this study has demonstrated that the TODIM method is an appropriate tool for ranking decision-making problems involving multidimensional and behavioral factors, such as selecting a distance-learning platform. It also demonstrates that the method provides a robust analytical framework for testing the consistency and flexibility of decisions. Using sensitivity analysis based on the θ parameter, it was determined which alternatives emerged in different risk scenarios. This provided a strategic perspective to the university's decision-making process. TODIM's ability to model gain–loss balance, conduct dominance analysis through pairwise comparisons, and provide parametric flexibility makes it a valuable tool both academically and practically.

The TODIM method can also be adapted to decision problems at different scales. The findings obtained in the selection of the university's distance learning platform are a concrete demonstration of the advantages offered by this method, contributing to decision-makers making more reliable, balanced, and behaviorally consistent decisions.

The results of this study show that TODIM is a suitable tool for decision problems in the field of educational technology. In future studies, a larger set of criteria and a greater number of alternatives can be used to generalize the model. Additionally, studies can be conducted to dynamically determine the θ parameter based on the decision-maker profile. This would enable a more accurate modeling of the method's sensitivity.

Furthermore, integrating TODIM with techniques such as fuzzy logic, gray theory, or entropy-based criterion weighting will further enhance its decision-making capacity under uncertainty. Especially considering the rapid changes in user expectations and market conditions in educational technologies, such hybrid approaches will provide a strategic advantage.

References

Autran Monteiro Gomes, L. F., & Duncan Rangel, L. A. (2009). An application of the TODIM method to the multicriteria rental evaluation of residential properties. *European Journal of Operational Research, 193*(1). https://doi.org/10.1016/j.ejor.2007.10.046.

Ayyildiz, E., & Taskin Gumus, A. (2020). A novel spherical fuzzy AHP-integrated spherical WASPAS methodology for petrol station location selection problem: A real case study for İstanbul. *Environmental Science and Pollution Research.* https://doi.org/10.1007/s11356-020-09640-0.

Chawla, V. K., Itika, I., Singh, P., & Singh, S. (2024). A fuzzy Pythagorean TODIM method for sustainable ABC analysis in inventory management. *Journal of Future Sustainability, 4*(2). https://doi.org/10.5267/j.jfs.2024.5.003.

Ding, N., Yu, S. H., Chu, J. J., Chen, C., & Shu, X. Y. (2023). A decision framework for cultural and creative products based on IF-TODIM method and group consensus reaching model. *Advanced Engineering Informatics, 55.* https://doi.org/10.1016/j.aei.2023.101891.

Gomes, L. F.a M., & Lima, M. M. P. P. (1991). Todim: Basic and application to multicriteria ranking of projects with environmental impacts. *Foundations of Computing and Decision Sciences, 16*(4).

Gomes, L. F. A. M., Rangel, L. A. D., & Maranhão, F. J. C. (2009). Multicriteria analysis of natural gas destination in Brazil: An application of the TODIM method. *Mathematical and Computer Modelling, 50*(1–2). https://doi.org/10.1016/j.mcm.2009.02.013.

Hanine, M., Boutkhoum, O., Tikniouine, A., & Agouti, T. (2016). Comparison of fuzzy AHP and fuzzy TODIM methods for landfill location selection. *SpringerPlus, 5*(1). https://doi.org/10.1186/s40064-016-2131-7.

Hu, J., Yang, Y., & Chen, X. (2018). A novel TODIM method-based three-way decision model for medical treatment selection. *International Journal of Fuzzy Systems, 20*(4). https://doi.org/10.1007/s40815-017-0320-3.

Ji, P., Zhang, H.yu, & Wang, J.qiang (2018). A projection-based TODIM method under multi-valued neutrosophic environments and its application in personnel selection. *Neural Computing and Applications, 29*(1). https://doi.org/10.1007/s00521-016-2436-z.

Ji, X., Yu, L., & Fu, J. (2020). Evaluating personal default risk in P2P lending platform: Based on dual hesitant pythagorean fuzzy TODIM approach. *Mathematics, 8*(1). https://doi.org/10.3390/MATH8010008.

Li, M., Wu, C., Zhang, L., & You, L. N. (2015). An intuitionistic fuzzy-todim method to solve distributor evaluation and selection problem. *International Journal of Simulation Modelling, 14*(3). https://doi.org/10.2507/IJSIMM14(3)CO12.

Liang, D., Zhang, Y., Xu, Z., & Jamaldeen, A. (2019). Pythagorean fuzzy VIKOR approaches based on TODIM for evaluating internet banking website quality of Ghanaian banking industry. *Applied Soft Computing Journal, 78.* https://doi.org/10.1016/j.asoc.2019.03.006.

Liu, Y., Bao, T., Zhao, D., Sang, H., & Fu, B. (2022). Evaluation of student-perceived service quality in higher education for sustainable development: A fuzzy TODIM-ERA method. *Sustainability (Switzerland), 14*(8). https://doi.org/10.3390/su14084761.

Liu, Y. H., Peng, H. M., Wang, T. L., Wang, X. K., & Wang, J. Q. (2020). Supplier selection in the nuclear power industry with an integrated anp-todim method under z-number circumstances. *Symmetry, 12*(8). https://doi.org/10.3390/sym12081357.

Nie, S., Liao, H., Wu, X., & Xu, Z. (2019). Green supplier selection with a continuous interval-valued linguistic todim method. *IEEE Access, 7.* https://doi.org/10.1109/ACCESS.2019.2937994.

Ozkan, S., & Koseler, R. (2009). Multi-dimensional students' evaluation of e-learning systems in the higher education context: An empirical investigation. *Computers and Education, 53*(4). https://doi.org/10.1016/j.compedu.2009.06.011.

Qin, J., Liu, X., & Pedrycz, W. (2017). An extended TODIM multi-criteria group decision making method for green supplier selection in interval type-2 fuzzy environment. *European Journal of Operational Research, 258*(2). https://doi.org/10.1016/j.ejor.2016.09.059.

Sang, X., & Liu, X. (2016). An interval type-2 fuzzy sets-based TODIM method and its application to green supplier selection. *Journal of the Operational Research Society, 67*(5). https://doi.org/10.1057/jors.2015.86.

Seker, S., & Kahraman, C. (2022). A Pythagorean cubic fuzzy methodology based on TOPSIS and TODIM methods and its application to software selection problem. *Soft Computing, 26*(5). https://doi.org/10.1007/s00500-021-06469-8.

Tang, J., Liu, X., & Wang, W. (2024). Consensus-based generalized TODIM approach for occupational health and safety risk analysis with opinion interactions. *Applied Soft Computing, 150.* https://doi.org/10.1016/j.asoc.2023.111093.

Tian, C., & Peng, J. J. (2020). An integrated picture fuzzy anp-todim multi-criteria decision-making approach for tourism attraction recommendation. *Technological and Economic Development of Economy, 26*(2). https://doi.org/10.3846/tede.2019.11412.

Tian, X., Niu, M., Zhang, W., Li, L., & Herrera-Viedma, E. (2021). A novel todim based on prospect theory to select green supplier with Q-rung orthopair fuzzy set. *Technological and Economic Development of Economy, 27*(2). https://doi.org/10.3846/tede.2020.12736.

Tosun, Ö., & Akyüz, G. (2015). A Fuzzy TODIM Approach for the Supplier Selection Problem. *International Journal of Computational Intelligence Systems, 8*(2). https://doi.org/10.1080/18756891.2015.1001954.

Tseng, M. L., Lin, Y. H., Tan, K., Chen, R. H., & Chen, Y. H. (2014). Using TODIM to evaluate green supply chain practices under uncertainty. *Applied Mathematical Modelling, 38*(11–12). https://doi.org/10.1016/j.apm.2013.11.018.

Tversky, A., & Kahneman, D. (1992). Advances in prospect theory: Cumulative representation of uncertainty. *Journal of Risk and Uncertainty, 5*(4). https://doi.org/10.1007/BF00122574.

Ulu, M., & Şahin, H. (2021). An integrated approach for fire extinguishers selection with DEMATEL and TODIM methods. *Business & Management Studies: An International Journal, 9*(4). https://doi.org/10.15295/bmij.v9i4.1928.

Wei, C., Ren, Z., & Rodríguez, R. M. (2015). A hesitant fuzzy linguistic TODIM method based on a score function. *International Journal of Computational Intelligence Systems, 8*(4). https://doi.org/10.1080/18756891.2015.1046329.

Wei, G. (2018). TODIM Method for picture fuzzy multiple attribute decision making. *Informatica (Netherlands), 29*(3). https://doi.org/10.15388/Informatica.2018.181.

Wu, H. Y., Lin, Y. K., & Chang, C. H. (2011). Performance evaluation of extension education centers in universities based on the balanced scorecard. *Evaluation and Program Planning*. https://doi.org/10.1016/j.evalprogplan.2010.06.001.

Wu, X., Zhu, Z., Chen, G., Pedrycz, W., Liu, L., & Aggarwal, M. (2024). Generalized TODIM method based on symmetric intuitionistic fuzzy Jensen–Shannon divergence. *Expert Systems with Applications, 237*. https://doi.org/10.1016/j.eswa.2023.121554.

Wu, Y., Wang, J., Hu, Y., Ke, Y., & Li, L. (2018). An extended TODIM-PROMETHEE method for waste-to-energy plant site selection based on sustainability perspective. *Energy, 156*. https://doi.org/10.1016/j.energy.2018.05.087.

Yang, J. B., Xu, D. L., Xie, X., & Maddulapalli, A. K. (2011). Multicriteria evidential reasoning decision modelling and analysisprioritizing voices of customer. *Journal of the Operational Research Society, 62*(9). https://doi.org/10.1057/jors.2010.118.

Yuan, J., Li, X., Xu, C., Zhao, C., & Liu, Y. (2019). Investment risk assessment of coal-fired power plants in countries along the Belt and Road initiative based on ANP-Entropy-TODIM method. *Energy, 176*. https://doi.org/10.1016/j.energy.2019.04.038.

Zhang, Z., Guo, J., Zhang, H., Zhou, L., & Wang, M. (2022). Product selection based on sentiment analysis of online reviews: An intuitionistic fuzzy TODIM method. *Complex and Intelligent Systems, 8*(4). https://doi.org/10.1007/s40747-022-00678-w.

Zhao, M., Gao, H., Wei, G., Wei, C., & Guo, Y. (2022). Model for network security service provider selection with probabilistic uncertain linguistic todim method based on prospec t theory. *Technological and Economic Development of Economy, 28*(3). https://doi.org/10.3846/tede.2022.16483.

Chapter 56

COPRAS: Complex proportional assessment method for multi-attribute decision-making

Luis Martínez[1], Rosa M. Rodríguez[1], Álvaro Labella[1], and Diego García-Zamora[2]
[1]*Department of Computer Sciences, University of Jaén, Jaén, Spain,* [2]*Department of Mathematics, University of Jaén, Jaén, Spain*

56.1 Introduction

The complex proportional assessment (COPRAS) method was originally proposed by Zavadskas, Kaklauskas, and Sarka in 1994 in a local Lithuanian journal (Zavadskas et al., 1994); thus its visibility was limited due to the language. In 2007, researchers Zagorskas, Burinskiene, Zavadskas, and Turskis published another scientific article, in which they further detailed the COPRAS method in English (Zagorskas et al., 2007). From then on, the COPRAS method started to gain significant attention in the field of multicriteria decision-making (MCDM) due to its simplicity and ability to handle both beneficial and cost criteria to assess the alternatives. It was extended to deal with fuzzy information (Kazimieras Zavadskas and Antucheviciene, 2007) and later on it has been used with other fuzzy extensions. Further, it has been widely applied to different areas such as sustainability (Basaran and C¸akir, 2021; Kumari and Mishra, 2020; Rahim et al., 2024), healthcare (Chaurasiya and Jain, 2022; Zheng et al., 2018), or strategic planning (Das Adhikary et al., 2014; Akram et al., 2023; Goran et al., 2018).

This chapter makes a deep revision of the COPRAS method, which considers its extensions and real-world applications. Afterwards, it explains its methodology together with a short comparison with other MCDM methods. Finally, two case studies are introduced to show the performance of COPRAS.

56.2 Literature review

Over the last decade, the COPRAS method has been extensively applied and extended to address different forms of uncertainty and imprecision in expert evaluations and a wide range of decision-making problems. This section provides a structured synthesis of COPRAS-related research published in peer-reviewed journals indexed in the Journal Citation Report. To compile the literature for this review, a customized query was conducted using the Web of Science database. The search targeted publications containing the term "COPRAS" in the title to ensure that the method constituted the central focus of the study. To identify fuzzy extensions of COPRAS, the keyword "fuzzy" was additionally searched within the abstract and author keywords. Furthermore, the terms "application," "case study," and "real-world" were included in the abstract and keyword fields to capture research that apply the COPRAS method to practical decision-making problems. From these results, a total of 163 articles were found. After that, a selection process was carried out to discard nonrelevant proposals. The contributions that were written in a language other than English or were not published in peer-reviewed, indexed journals were excluded. In addition, we also discarded those contributions that developed proposals that combine the COPRAS method with other MCDM approaches. The number of papers that passed this filter was 57. These 57 articles have been analyzed and classified into two main categories based on their primary contribution (some of them may be included in both):

- Methodological extensions of COPRAS
- Real-world applications

This classification serves as the basis for the sections that follow, where each category is discussed in further detail.

Encyclopedia of Multi-Attribute Decision-Making (MADM). DOI: https://doi.org/10.1016/B978-0-443-33275-3.00003-8

56.2.1 Methodological extensions of complex proportional assessment

This section briefly describes the extensions of COPRAS through several environments according to the uncertainty modeling.

56.2.1.1 Type-1 and type-2 fuzzy sets

Various fuzzy extensions of the COPRAS method with type-1 fuzzy sets and type-2 fuzzy sets have been proposed to offer a more flexible framework for modeling ambiguity in human assessments.

The first fuzzy adaptation of COPRAS was proposed by Kazimieras Zavadskas and Antucheviciene, 2007, who introduced the use of triangular fuzzy numbers triangular fuzzy numbers (TFNs) to model uncertainty in evaluations. In this extension, crisp values were replaced by TFNs. This representation enables the model to incorporate the inherent vagueness of the preferences provided by experts by linguistic term sets. Although the method preserves the overall structure of classical COPRAS, all calculations were adapted to fuzzy arithmetic, and a defuzzification step was added to produce a final crisp ranking of alternatives. Building on this direction, Keshavarz Ghorabaee et al (Keshavarz Ghorabaee et al., 2014) extended the method further into the realm of interval Type-2 fuzzy sets (Zadeh, 1975). Their proposal adapts the COPRAS method for MCDM scenarios under high uncertainty. A centroid-based ranking approach is introduced to compare interval Type-2 fuzzy numbers, which is then integrated into the COPRAS steps—from aggregation of expert evaluations and normalization to the computation of utility degrees—offering a complete and structured framework suitable for imprecise and complex group decision problems.

56.2.1.2 Hesitant environment

The hesitant fuzzy environment (Rodrıguez et al., 2014; Torra, 2010) has emerged as a powerful framework for modeling situations in which experts express uncertainty through multiple potential values rather than a single assessment. To address this, several extensions of the COPRAS method have been proposed.

One of the earliest works focuses on hesitant fuzzy linguistic environments, where expert judgments are expressed using sets of linguistic labels rather than numeric values (Zheng et al., 2018). proposed an adaptation of COPRAS to this setting by constructing a decision matrix with hesitant fuzzy linguistic elements and redefining aggregation, normalization, and comparison steps to handle sets of qualitative terms (Mishra et al., 2019). Further advanced the modeling of complex hesitancy by integrating the Shapley value into a hesitant fuzzy set environment. Their Shapley-COPRAS model accounts for interdependencies among criteria, an aspect neglected in traditional additive weighting schemes. To support this integration, the authors developed entropy and divergence measures specifically tailored to hesitant fuzzy sets, enabling a more nuanced computation of criteria weights under interactive influence. The psychological dimension of decision-making is explored by , (Peter Darko & Liang, 2020), who combine hesitant fuzzy information with cumulative prospect theory (Fennema & Wakker, 1997). This hybrid model incorporates behavioral insights into how gains and losses are perceived relative to a reference point. Additionally, they introduced a novel distance measure for hesitant fuzzy sets, enhancing the aggregation and ranking stages. Recent efforts have expanded the hesitant paradigm to other fuzzy extensions, such as the notion of probabilistic hesitant fuzzy sets (Krishankumar et al., 2021;Xu & Zhou, 2017), or hesitant fuzzy soft sets (Peng & Dai, 2017).

56.2.1.3 Intuitionistic environment

To better capture the duality and hesitation present in human judgments, intuitionistic fuzzy sets (IFSs) (Atanassov, 1999) offer a richer framework than traditional fuzzy sets. IFSs characterize each element by a degree of membership, a degree of nonmembership, and a hesitation margin. This enhanced expressiveness has motivated the development of several COPRAS extensions.

One of the earliest formulations was introduced by Hossein et al. (2013), who proposed the COPRAS-IVIF method based on interval-valued intuitionistic fuzzy sets (IVIFs). This extension models uncertainty in both the ratings of alternatives and the criteria weights using intervals for membership and nonmembership degrees. Subsequent work focused on refining weight determination mechanisms within the IFS context. In (Kumari & Mishra, 2020), the authors present IF-COPRAS, a model that introduces parametric divergence and entropy measures, rooted in information theory, to compute objective weights. Similarly, (Thakur et al., 2021. propose a novel entropy function specifically designed to quantify the inherent uncertainty in IFS representations, which is then integrated into a modified COPRAS algorithm. Other researchers have explored more sophisticated extensions of the IFS framework, using possibility intuitionistic fuzzy soft sets (Garg & Arora, 2020), complex intuitionistic fuzzy soft sets (Rajareega & Vimala, 2021), or interval Type-2 fuzzy sets (Nafteh & Shahrokhi, 2023).

56.2.1.4 Neutrosophic environment

Neutrosophic sets (Smarandache, 1999) offer an expanded framework for modeling uncertainty, incorporating not only degrees of truth and falsity, as in IFSs, but also an explicit degree of indeterminacy. As a result, several researchers have extended the COPRAS method into neutrosophic environments.

One of the earliest contributions is the work by Kumari and Mishra, 2020, who proposed the COPRAS method based on single-valued neutrosophic (COPRAS-SVNS) sets. Their model introduces a three-phase process: (i) crisp expert evaluations are translated into SVNS through a neutrosophication step using linguistic variables; (ii) decision evaluation is carried out using neutrosophic arithmetic operations; and (iii) a de-neutrosophication procedure is applied using a newly defined score function to rank alternatives. Further advancing the integration of qualitative and quantitative information. Wei et al. (2021) introduced a COPRAS model under the framework of single-valued neutrosophic 2-tuple linguistic sets. This hybrid representation combines the interpretability of the linguistic 2-tuple model (Mart´ınez et al., 2015) with the flexibility of neutrosophic logic. Building on this foundation, Garg (2019) developed a more expressive model by combining neutrosophic and probabilistic-linguistic elements into the possibility linguistic single-valued neutrosophic set.

56.2.1.5 Spherical environment

Spherical fuzzy sets (Ashraf et al., 2019) represent an evolution in uncertainty modeling by simultaneously capturing membership, nonmembership, and hesitancy degrees, all constrained within a spherical boundary condition. In recent years, several extensions of the COPRAS method have been developed to operate within the spherical fuzzy environment and its variants.

A foundational contribution is the work by Omerali & Kaya (2021), which introduces a five-step framework involving the computation of weighted decision matrices, relative significance, and utility values. The same authors also proposed an interval-valued version of this model (IVSF-COPRAS) (Omerali & Kaya, 2022), who introduced the SF-COPRAS method, an adaptation of classical COPRAS using spherical fuzzy numbers. Further refinement of the model is presented in the T-spherical fuzzy COPRAS method developed by Fan, Han, et al. (2022). In this model, each component of the spherical fuzzy set—membership, nonmembership, and hesitancy is raised to a power q, yielding greater flexibility in representing uncertainty. In addition, several hybrid approaches combine spherical fuzzy models with linguistic frameworks (Akram et al., 2023; Naz et al., 2023). More advanced formulations have also been explored, introducing, for instance, complex spherical fuzzy sets (Ebru et al., 2023).

56.2.1.5.1 q-Rung environment

The q-rung orthopair fuzzy set (q-ROFS) framework (Yager & Smarandache, 2017)has emerged as a powerful generalization of intuitionistic and pythagorean fuzzy sets, offering enhanced flexibility for modeling uncertainty and hesitation in decision-making. Several recent studies have proposed COPRAS-based decision models within this framework and its extensions.

Ahemad et al. (2023) introduced a novel extension of the COPRAS method using interval-valued q-rung orthopair fuzzy sets IVq-ROFSs). The authors define new score and accuracy functions tailored to IVq-ROFSs and incorporate an entropy-based weighting scheme to compute objective importance for each criterion. Zhang et al. (2023) further enrich the modeling capacity by integrating the preference selection index method with COPRAS under an interval-valued q-ROFS environment. Finally, (Mishra et al., 2024) present a COPRAS-based decision framework that incorporates similarity measures specifically designed for q-ROF sets.

56.2.1.6 Other approaches

Beyond the previous environments, several authors have explored more specialized or emerging frameworks to further extend the applicability of the COPRAS method. While fewer, these studies highlight the flexibility of COPRAS in accommodating diverse mathematical representations of uncertainty and expert knowledge.

For instance, Zavadskas et al. (2008) developed COPRAS-G, an extension based on grey systems theory. The method integrates optimistic and pessimistic bounds into the COPRAS framework through customized normalization and weighting procedures. Similarly, Roy et al. (2019) propose a version of COPRAS based on interval rough numbers, while (Fan, Cheng, et al., 2022) introduce R-COPRAS, which makes use of R-sets, a generalization of rough sets.

Other contributions introduce probabilistic or stochastic elements. Ayrim et al. (2018) propose Stochastic COPRAS COPRAS-S), incorporating random variables into the evaluation process. Likewise, Ramana et al. (2022) present the nonlinear Variance-COPRAS method, which integrates a variance-based objective weighting scheme into an interactive COPRAS structure capable of handling nonlinear fuzzy data. A number of studies extend COPRAS to alternative fuzzy set theories. Lu et al., 2021 adapt the method to the picture fuzzy set environment (Cuong, 2014). Mishra et al. (2022) introduce propose interval-valued hesitant Fermatean fuzzy sets- COPRAS (IVHFF-COPRAS), which employs IVHFF, which employs interval-valued hesitant Fermatean fuzzy sets (Senapati & Yager, 2020). In a related line, Akram et al. (2022) propose with novel Hamy mean aggregation operators that model inter-attribute relationships during the evaluation process. Finally, Sagiroglu et al. (2024) Introduce DF-COPRAS, which incorporates decomposed fuzzy sets (Cebi et al., 2023).

56.2.2 Real-world applications

In addition to the methodological developments, the COPRAS method has been widely applied to tackle complex real-world decision-making problems. In what follows, we highlight a selection of studies in which COPRAS has been employed as a central instrument for supporting meaningful decisions.

A broad set of applications can be found in productive sectors such as business, manufacturing, and construction. In business environments, COPRAS has been used to evaluate service quality (Mishra et al., 2019), support product life-cycle management system selection (Omerali and Kaya, 2021), and analyze trade efficiency (Lali´c et al., 2021). In the manufacturing sector, its use spans material selection (Ghose et al., 2023; Kang et al., 2023), system performance (Jain and Chand, 2021; Makhesana, 2015), and energy efficiency (Ullah et al., 2022), helping to identify optimal solutions under technical, economic, and environmental constraints. Similarly, in construction-related decisions, COPRAS has provided systematic and transparent evaluations for sustainable building practices (Raudeliuniene et al., 2025), building information modelling (BIM) implementation (Ullah et al., 2022), infrastructure resilience (Yazdani et al., 2011), project manager selection (Zavadskas et al., 2008), and rural regeneration strategies (Kazimieras Zavadskas & Antucheviciene, 2007).

Another key application area is infrastructure and energy planning. COPRAS has been used to evaluate energy infrastructure projects, such as hydropower plants and coal-fired thermal power stations, contributing robust prioritization under uncertainty (Akram et al., 2023; Das Adhikary et al., 2014). The method also supports decision-making in the renewable energy transition, offering structured assessment frameworks for both energy source selection and storage technology evaluation (Guan et al., 2023; Yontar, 2023). Strategic infrastructure decisions, such as the placement of electric vehicle charging stations, have similarly benefited from COPRAS-based ranking approaches (Mishra et al., 2024). In land consolidation planning, COPRAS has helped to identify the most balanced and beneficial regional projects (Goran et al., 2018).

Supply chain management is another domain where COPRAS has seen widespread adoption, particularly for supplier selection problems. As environmental sustainability becomes increasingly relevant, COPRAS has facilitated green supplier evaluations, integrating ecological, regulatory, and performance-related criteria (Basaran & C¸akir, 2021;Kumari & Mishra, 2020; Rahim et al., 2024).

The method also supports innovation and strategic decisions within the context of Industry 4.0. For example, it has been employed to assess whether to internally develop or externally acquire technologies within the transfer of technology domain (O¨merali & Kaya, 2020).

In public service and policy domains, COPRAS has enabled more transparent and evidence-based decisions. In healthcare, it has helped assess disease severity (Zheng et al., 2018) and prioritize technologies for medical waste treatment (Chaurasiya & Jain, 2022). In the education sector, it has been applied to evaluate the quality of e-learning platforms (Garg et al., 2018), while in logistics, it has supported the assessment of national logistics performance (Mercang¨oz et al., 2020). The method has also been used in the waste management domain to rank sustainable alternatives (Naz et al., 2023), and in the context of disaster management to evaluate nongovernmental organizations' collaboration effectiveness (Sagiroglu et al., 2024).

Emerging application areas further showcase the method's versatility. In the mining sector, COPRAS has supported safety risk evaluations in smart mining projects (Fan, Cheng, et al., 2022), while in sustainable building renovation, it has been combined with emotion recognition technologies to include occupants' well-being in modernization planning (Velykorusova et al., 2023). In tourism, the method has been used to rank hotels based on diverse criteria relevant to user satisfaction (Roy et al., 2019), and in artificial intelligence, it has helped in feature selection for multilabel text classification problems (Mohanrasu et al., 2024).

56.3 Methodology

The COPRAS method is based on the principle of proportionality: the relative significance of each alternative is evaluated by taking into account both the positive (benefit) and negative (cost) criteria (Zagorskas et al., 2007). The method begins by normalizing the decision matrix and weighting the criteria according to their relative importance. It then calculates the weighted sums of beneficial and nonbeneficial criteria for each alternative. The overall significance of each alternative is computed by combining these two components proportionally, with higher beneficial scores and lower cost scores leading to a better ranking. Finally, a utility degree is derived by comparing each alternative's relative significance to the best-performing option. COPRAS is appreciated for its simplicity, transparency, and the interpretability of its results, making it particularly useful in decision problems where clarity and justification of the ranking are essential. Below, we detail a formal, step-by-step explanation of the COPRAS method.

Let us consider the MCDM problem consisting of evaluating the alternatives $\{A_1, \ldots, A_m\}$ under the criteria $\{C_1, \ldots, C_n\}$. Denote the performance matrix as:

$$X = (x_{ij}), \quad i = 1, \ldots, m, \quad j = 1, \ldots, n,$$

where x_{ij} represents the performance of alternative A_i under criterion C_j. The steps of the method are as follows:

1. To normalize the decision matrix. Normalize each element x_{ij} as follows:

$$r_{ij} = \frac{x_{ij}}{\sum_{i=1}^{m} x_{ij}}, \quad i = 1, \ldots, m, \quad j = 1, \ldots, n.$$

2. To compute the weighted normalized matrix. Let w_j be the weight of criterion C_j, with $\sum_{j=1}^{n} w_j = 1$. The weighted normalized value is:

$$q_{ij} = w_j \cdot r_{ij}, \quad i = 1, \ldots, m, \quad j = 1, \ldots, n.$$

3. To compute the sums of weighted beneficial and nonbeneficial criteria. Separate the criteria into beneficial J^+ and nonbeneficial J^-. Then compute:

$$S_i^+ = \sum_{j \in J^+} q_{ij}, \quad S_i^- = \sum_{j \in J^-} q_{ij}, \quad i = 1, \ldots, m.$$

4. To compute the relative significance. The relative significance of alternative A_i is given by:

$$Q_i = S_i^+ + \frac{\sum_{k=1}^{m} S_k^-}{S_i^- \sum_{k=1}^{m} \frac{1}{S_k^-}}.$$

   Note that one of the major strengths of this method lies in its ability to handle both beneficial (maximizing) and nonbeneficial (minimizing) criteria separately. This separation allows experts to model real-world problems more accurately, especially when trade-offs between gains and costs must be explicitly considered. Additionally, the proportional nature of the method ensures that the contribution of each criterion to the final ranking is easy to trace, offering good interpretability of results—something crucial in contexts where justification of decisions is important. Let us provide some advantages and shortcomings of COPRAS regarding other classical MCDM methods.

5. To obtain the utility degree. The utility degree (in percentage) is calculated as:

$$N_i = \frac{Q_i}{\max(Q_i)} \cdot 100.$$

Note that one of the major strengths of this method lies in its ability to handle both beneficial (maximizing) and nonbeneficial (minimizing) criteria separately. This separation allows experts to model real-world problems more accurately, especially when trade-offs between gains and costs must be explicitly considered. Additionally, the proportional nature of the method ensures that the contribution of each criterion to the final ranking is easy to trace, offering good interpretability of results, something crucial in contexts where justification of decisions is important. Let us provide some advantages and shortcomings of COPRAS regarding other classical MCDM methods.

In comparison to technique for ordering preferences by similarity to ideal solution (TOPSIS) (Opricovic and Tzeng, 2004), COPRAS does not rely on the concept of an ideal and anti-ideal solution, nor on geometric distance. While

TOPSIS evaluates alternatives based on their relative closeness to ideal points, COPRAS aggregates weighted normalized scores and considers the ratio of cost-type criteria to their minimum. This can be advantageous when experts prefer a purely additive and proportional method rather than one based on Euclidean geometry.

Compared to VlseKriterijumska Optimizacija I Kompromisno Resenje (VIKOR) (Opricovic & Tzeng, 2004), which introduces a compromise ranking based on regret and utility measures, COPRAS is simpler and avoids the use of nonlinear aggregations or additional preference parameters (such as the weight for the "majority rule" in VIKOR). COPRAS also tends to provide a full ranking of alternatives with clearly defined utility degrees, making it suitable for applications where ranking stability and explainability are important.

Unlike Elimination and choice translating reality (ELECTRE) methods (Roy, 1991), which are based on outranking relationships and require complex concordance and discordance indices, COPRAS operates with normalized values and simple arithmetic operations. While ELECTRE is more appropriate for situations involving high uncertainty or qualitative judgments, COPRAS is preferred in more structured, quantitative decision environments.

One limitation of COPRAS is its sensitivity to the normalization method used, particularly in the presence of outliers or noncommensurable criteria. Moreover, since it does not explicitly model uncertainty or imprecision (as fuzzy extensions of MCDM methods do), its classical form may be less suitable for problems with vague or imprecise data, though fuzzy and interval-valued extensions of COPRAS have been proposed in the literature to address this issue.

56.4 Numerical example 1: basic application of complex proportional assessment

In this section, we demonstrate the COPRAS method with a decision-making problem involving 5 alternatives (A_1 to A_5) and 4 criteria (C_1 to C_4). Criteria C_1, C_2, and C_3 are beneficial (to be maximized), while C_4 is nonbeneficial (to be minimized). The decision matrix $X = (x_{ij})$ represents the performance of each alternative with respect to the criteria. The corresponding weights w_j for each criterion are also given.

$$X = \begin{pmatrix} 80 & 90 & 70 & 60 \\ 85 & 75 & 65 & 55 \\ 78 & 82 & 80 & 50 \\ 92 & 88 & 75 & 58 \\ 76 & 80 & 85 & 52 \end{pmatrix}, \quad w = (0.25 \;\; 0.30 \;\; 0.20 \;\; 0.25).$$

Below, we exemplify all the steps of the method.

1. To normalize the decision matrix. Each element x_{ij} is normalized by dividing by the column sum:

$$r_{ij} = \frac{x_{ij}}{\sum_{i=1}^{m} x_{ij}}$$

where $m = 5$ is the number of alternatives. First, we compute column sums:

$$\sum_{i=1}^{m} x_{i1} = 411, \quad \sum_{i=1}^{m} x_{i2} = 415, \quad \sum_{i=1}^{m} x_{i3} = 375, \quad \sum_{i=1}^{m} x_{i4} = 275.$$

Then we normalize:

$$R = \begin{pmatrix} 0.1946 & 0.2169 & 0.1867 & 0.2182 \\ 0.2068 & 0.1807 & 0.1733 & 0.2000 \\ 0.1997 & 0.1976 & 0.2133 & 0.1818 \\ 0.2238 & 0.2120 & 0.2000 & 0.2109 \\ 0.1849 & 0.1928 & 0.2267 & 0.1891 \end{pmatrix}$$

2. To compute the weighted normalized matrix. We multiply each normalized element by the corresponding weight:

$$q_{ij} = w_j \cdot r_{ij}$$

$$Q = \begin{pmatrix} 0.0487 & 0.0650 & 0.0373 & 0.0545 \\ 0.0517 & 0.0542 & 0.0347 & 0.0500 \\ 0.0474 & 0.0593 & 0.0427 & 0.0455 \\ 0.0559 & 0.0636 & 0.0400 & 0.0527 \\ 0.0462 & 0.0578 & 0.0453 & 0.0473 \end{pmatrix}$$

3. To compute the sums of weighted beneficial and nonbeneficial Criteria.
We define:

$$S_i^+ = \sum_{\text{beneficial}j} q_{ij}, \quad S_i^- = \sum_{\text{non-beneficial}j} q_{ij}$$

In our case, C_1, C_2, and C_3 are beneficial; C_4 is nonbeneficial. Hence:

$$S_1^+ = 0.0487 + 0.0650 + 0.0373 = 0.1511, \quad S_1^- = 0.0545$$
$$S_2^+ = 0.0517 + 0.0542 + 0.0347 = 0.1406, \quad S_2^- = 0.0500$$
$$S_3^+ = 0.0474 + 0.0593 + 0.0427 = 0.1494, \quad S_3^- = 0.0455$$
$$S_4^+ = 0.0559 + 0.0636 + 0.0400 = 0.1595, \quad S_4^- = 0.0527$$
$$S_5^+ = 0.0462 + 0.0578 + 0.0453 = 0.1494, \quad S_5^- = 0.0473$$

4. To compute the relative significance. First, we compute the sum and the sum of the inverses of the values S_i^-:

$$\sum_{k=1}^{m} S_k^- = 0.25, \quad \sum_{k=1}^{m} 1/S_k^- \approx 100.45$$

Then, the relative significance is given by:

$$Q_i = S_i^+ + \frac{\sum_{k=1}^{m} S_k^-}{S_i^- \sum_{k=1}^{m} 1/S_k^-}$$

Applying this:

$$Q_1 = 0.1511 + \frac{1}{0.0545} \cdot \frac{0.25}{100.45} \approx 0.1966$$
$$Q_2 = 0.1406 + \frac{1}{0.0500} \cdot \frac{0.25}{100.45} \approx 0.1904$$
$$Q_3 = 0.1494 + \frac{1}{0.0455} \cdot \frac{0.25}{100.45} = 0.2041$$
$$Q_4 = 0.1595 + \frac{1}{0.0527} \cdot \frac{0.25}{100.45} \approx 0.2068$$
$$Q_5 = 0.1494 + \frac{1}{0.0473} \cdot \frac{0.25}{100.45} \approx 0.2020$$

To obtain the utility degree. The utility degree expresses the relative quality of each alternative compared to the best one:

$$N_i = \frac{Q_i}{\max Q_i} \cdot 100$$

The best score is:

$$\max_{i=1,\ldots,5} Q_i = Q_4 = 0.2068$$

Utility degrees:

$$N_1 \approx \frac{0.1966}{0.2068} \cdot 100 \approx 95.1\%$$
$$N_2 \approx \frac{0.1904}{0.2068} \cdot 100 \approx 92.1\%$$
$$N_3 \approx \frac{0.2041}{0.2068} \cdot 100 \approx 98.7\%$$
$$N_4 = 100.0\%$$
$$N_5 \approx \frac{0.2020}{0.2068} \cdot 100 \approx 97.7\%$$

Based on the utility degrees, the final ranking from best to worst is:

$$A_4 \succ A_3 \succ A_5 \succ A_1 \succ A_2$$

56.5 Numerical example 2: group application of complex proportional assessment

A manufacturer company wants to select the best supplier from a set of seven alternatives,

$$\{A_1, A_2, A_3, A_4, A_5, A_6, A_7\}$$

which are assessed by means of 6 criteria, $\{C_1$: quality, C_2: ecological design, C_3: pollution, C_4: management system, C_5: use of green technology, C_6: supply consumption$\}$. The company director has chosen a set of four experts,

$$\{e_1, e_2, e_3, e_4\},$$

to handle the selection of the most suitable green supplier. In this problem, Criteria 1 and 2 are cost criteria; the remaining are benefit criteria. The criteria weights are the following ones, $\{w_1: 0.15, w_2: 0.20, w_3: 0.10, w_4: 0.20, w_5: 0.20, w_6: 0.15\}$. The decision matrices provided by the experts are:

$$X_1 = \begin{pmatrix} 72 & 82 & 58 & 76 & 84 & 38 \\ 66 & 86 & 54 & 71 & 79 & 34 \\ 82 & 74 & 63 & 89 & 87 & 43 \\ 74 & 92 & 71 & 86 & 80 & 40 \\ 59 & 69 & 49 & 62 & 75 & 34 \\ 67 & 79 & 60 & 71 & 80 & 35 \\ 83 & 89 & 66 & 89 & 89 & 37 \end{pmatrix}, \quad X_2 = \begin{pmatrix} 71 & 81 & 61 & 74 & 86 & 41 \\ 64 & 84 & 56 & 69 & 81 & 36 \\ 79 & 76 & 66 & 91 & 89 & 41 \\ 76 & 89 & 69 & 84 & 83 & 38 \\ 61 & 71 & 51 & 59 & 77 & 32 \\ 69 & 77 & 63 & 73 & 78 & 37 \\ 81 & 87 & 69 & 87 & 92 & 39 \end{pmatrix},$$

$$X_3 = \begin{pmatrix} 68 & 79 & 62 & 77 & 87 & 42 \\ 67 & 83 & 57 & 72 & 82 & 36 \\ 78 & 76 & 67 & 92 & 88 & 41 \\ 76 & 91 & 68 & 86 & 81 & 38 \\ 59 & 69 & 51 & 61 & 75 & 33 \\ 68 & 77 & 63 & 71 & 78 & 36 \\ 81 & 88 & 67 & 88 & 90 & 39 \end{pmatrix}, \quad X_4 = \begin{pmatrix} 69 & 78 & 59 & 73 & 83 & 39 \\ 63 & 87 & 53 & 68 & 78 & 34 \\ 81 & 74 & 64 & 88 & 88 & 43 \\ 74 & 88 & 72 & 84 & 84 & 40 \\ 61 & 71 & 49 & 58 & 77 & 33 \\ 68 & 79 & 62 & 73 & 80 & 36 \\ 83 & 88 & 70 & 88 & 93 & 37 \end{pmatrix}.$$

1. To aggregate the individual decision matrices. The arithmetic mean is used to obtain a collective decision matrix.

$$X = \begin{pmatrix} 70 & 80 & 60 & 75 & 85 & 40 \\ 65 & 85 & 55 & 70 & 80 & 35 \\ 80 & 75 & 65 & 90 & 88 & 42 \\ 75 & 90 & 70 & 85 & 82 & 39 \\ 60 & 70 & 50 & 60 & 76 & 33 \\ 68 & 78 & 62 & 72 & 79 & 36 \\ 82 & 88 & 68 & 88 & 91 & 38 \end{pmatrix}$$

2. To compute the weighted normalized matrix.

$$Q = \begin{pmatrix} 0.021 & 0.028 & 0.014 & 0.028 & 0.029 & 0.023 \\ 0.02 & 0.03 & 0.013 & 0.026 & 0.028 & 0.02 \\ 0.024 & 0.027 & 0.015 & 0.033 & 0.03 & 0.024 \\ 0.022 & 0.032 & 0.016 & 0.031 & 0.028 & 0.022 \\ 0.018 & 0.025 & 0.012 & 0.022 & 0.026 & 0.019 \\ 0.02 & 0.028 & 0.014 & 0.027 & 0.027 & 0.021 \\ 0.025 & 0.031 & 0.016 & 0.033 & 0.031 & 0.022 \end{pmatrix}$$

3. To compute the sums of weighted beneficial and nonbeneficial criteria.

$$S^+ = (0.106,\ 0.103,\ 0.114,\ 0.114,\ 0.091,\ 0.102,\ 0.12)$$
$$S^- = (0.037,\ 0.033,\ 0.039,\ 0.039,\ 0.03,\ 0.035,\ 0.037)$$

From these values, we infer that

$$\Sigma_{k=1}^{m} S_k^- = 0.25,$$
$$\Sigma_{k=1}^{m} 1/S_k^- = 197.413,$$
$$\frac{\Sigma_{k=1}^{m} S_k^-}{\Sigma_{k=1}^{m} 1/S_k^-} = 0.013.$$

4. To compute the relative significance.

$$(0.1407,\ 0.1417,\ 0.1465,\ 0.1469,\ 0.1327,\ 0.1381,\ 0.1534)$$

5. To obtain the utility degree.

$$(91.76,\ 92.35,\ 95.53,\ 95.76,\ 86.51,\ 90.00,\ 100.00)$$

Based on the utility degrees, the final ranking is:

$$A_7 \succ A_4 \succ A_3 \succ A_2 \succ A_1 \succ A_6 \succ A_5.$$

56.6 Conclusions

This chapter has provided a structured overview of the COPRAS method, focusing on its methodological developments and practical applications in MCDM. Based on a literature review, we classified COPRAS-related research into two main areas: methodological extensions and real-world applications.

The methodological analysis revealed the adaptability of COPRAS to various uncertainty modeling frameworks, such as fuzzy sets, hesitant fuzzy sets, etc. These extensions enhance the method's ability to manage imprecise, subjective, and group-based evaluations. The review also highlighted recent hybrid models that integrate COPRAS with other decision-making tools to tackle complex and domain-specific problems.

Two numerical case studies illustrated both individual and group decision-making contexts. The examples highlighted COPRAS's strengths: conceptual simplicity, proportional logic, ability to distinguish between beneficial and cost criteria, and ease of interpretation. A comparison with other MCDM techniques, including TOPSIS, VIKOR, and ELECTRE, emphasized COPRAS's transparency and full ranking output, but noting limitations such as sensitivity to normalization and the absence of intrinsic uncertainty modeling in its classical form.

In conclusion, COPRAS is a robust and evolving tool in decision analysis, with a broad range of applications across sectors. Future research may explore its integration with intelligent systems, big data environments, and consensus-building frameworks.

References

Das Adhikary, D., et al. (2014). Multi criteria FMECA for coal-fired thermal power plants using COPRAS-G. *International Journal of Quality & Reliability Management, 31*(5), 601–614.

Ahemad, F., et al. (2023). Multi-attribute group decision-making for solid waste management using interval-valued q-rung orthopair fuzzy COPRAS. *RAIRO-Operations Research, 57*(3), 1239–1265.

Akram, M., et al. (2023). Assessment of hydropower plants in Pakistan: Muirhead mean-based 2-tuple linguistic t-spherical fuzzy model combining SWARA with COPRAS. *In: Arabian Journal for Science and Engineering, 48*(5), 5859–5888.

Akram, M., Ramzan, N., & Feng, F. (2022). Extending COPRAS method with linguistic Fermatean fuzzy sets and Hamy mean operators. *Journal of Mathematics, 2022*(1), 8239263.

Ashraf, S., et al. (2019). Spherical fuzzy sets and its representation of spherical fuzzy t-norms and t-conorms. *Journal of Intelligent & Fuzzy Systems, 36*(6), 6089–6102.

Atanassov, K. T. (1999). Intuitionistic fuzzy sets. In *Intuitionistic fuzzy sets: theory and applications*. Springer, 1–137.

Ayrim, Y., Didem Atalay, K., & Can, G. F. (2018). A new stochastic MCDM approach based on COPRAS. *International Journal of Information Technology & Decision Making, 17*(03), 857–882.

Basaran, B., & C¸akir, S.¨leyman (2021). Evaluation of food safety and halal criteria in supplier selection: An application in food sector with fuzzy COPRAS method. *International food research journal, 28*(3), 576–585.

Bausys, R., Zavadskas, E. K., & Kaklauskas, A.¯ras (2015). Application of neutrosophic set to multicriteria decision making by COPRAS. *Infinite Study*.

Cebi, S., Gu¨ndo˘gdu, F. K., & Kahraman, C. (2023). Consideration of reciprocal judgments through decomposed fuzzy analytical hierarchy process: a case study in the pharmaceutical industry. *Applied Soft Computing, 134*, 110000.

Chaurasiya, R., & Jain, D. (2022). Pythagorean fuzzy entropy measurebased complex proportional assessment technique for solving multi-criteria healthcare waste treatment problem. *Granular computing, 7*(4), 917–930.

Cuong, B. (2014). Picture fuzzy sets. *Journal of computer science and cybernetics, 30*(4), 409.

Ebru, A.˘gdu, et al. (2023). A novel entropy measure with its application to the COPRAS method in complex spherical fuzzy environment. *Informatica, 34*(4), 679–711.

Fan, J., Han, D., & Wu, M. (2022). T-spherical fuzzy COPRAS method for multi-criteria decision-making problem. *Journal of Intelligent & Fuzzy Systems, 43*(3), 2789–2801.

Fan, J., Cheng, R., & Wu, M. (2022). R-set COPRAS (R-COPRAS) methods-based multi-attribute decision-making with RBM and RGBM operators: a case study of smart mine project safety assessment. *IEEE Access, 10*, 43481–43500.

Fennema, H., & Wakker, P. (1997). Original and cumulative prospect theory: A discussion of empirical differences. *Journal of Behavioral Decision Making, 10*(1), 53–64.

Garg, H. (2019). Algorithms for possibility linguistic single-valued neutrosophic decision-making based on COPRAS and aggregation operators with new information measures. *Measurement, 138*, 278–290.

Garg, H., & Arora, R. (2020). Algorithms Based on COPRAS and Aggregation Operators with New Information Measures for Possibility Intuitionistic Fuzzy Soft Decision-Making. *Mathematical Problems in Engineering 2020, 1*, 1563768.

Garg, R., Kumar, R., & Garg, S. (2018). MADM-based parametric selection and ranking of E-learning websites using fuzzy COPRAS. *IEEE Transactions on Education, 62*(1), 11–18.

Ghose, D., et al. (2023). Optimal material for solar electric vehicle application using an integrated Fuzzy-COPRAS model. *Energy sources, part A: Recovery, utilization, and environmental effects, 45*(2), 3859–3878.

Goran, M.´c, et al. (2018). Application of COPRAS method for land consolidation projects ranking. *Archives for Technical Sciences, 1*(19), 35–44.

Guan, Y., et al. (2023). Evaluating batteries for renewable energy storage: A hybrid MCDM framework based on combined objective weights and uncertainty-preserved COPRAS. *Journal of Renewable and Sustainable Energy, 15*(4).

Hossein, S., Hajiagha, R., Hashemi, S. S., & Kazimieras Zavadskas, E. (2013). A complex proportional assessment method for group decision making in an interval-valued intuitionistic fuzzy environment. *Technological and Economic Development of Economy, 19*(1), 22–37.

Jain, V., & Chand, M. (2021). Decision making in FMS by COPRAS approach. *International Journal of Business Performance Management, 22*(1), 75–92.

Kang, D., et al. (2023). A novel MCDM approach to selecting a biodegradable dynamic plastic product: a probabilistic hesitant fuzzy set-based COPRAS method. *Journal of Environmental Management, 340*, 117967.

Kazimieras Zavadskas, E., & Antucheviciene, J. (2007). Multiple criteria evaluation of rural building's regeneration alternatives. *Building and Environment, 42*(1), 436–451.

Keshavarz Ghorabaee, M., et al. (2014). Multiple criteria group decision-making for supplier selection based on COPRAS method with interval type-2 fuzzy sets. *The International Journal of Advanced Manufacturing Technology, 75*(5), 1115–1130.

Krishankumar, R., et al. (2021). An integrated decision-making COPRAS approach to probabilistic hesitant fuzzy set information. *Complex & Intelligent Systems, 7*(5), 2281–2298.

Kumari, R., & Mishra, A. R. (2020). Multi-criteria COPRAS method based on parametric measures for intuitionistic fuzzy sets: application of green supplier selection. *Iranian journal of science and technology, Transactions of Electrical Engineering, 44*(4), 1645–1662.

Lali´c, S., Jovici´c, Z.˘eljana, & Lukic, R. (2021). Application of the COPRAS Method in the evaluation of trade efficiency in Serbia. *Emc Review-Economy And Market Communication Review, 22*(2), 497–509.

Lu, J., et al. (2021). COPRAS method for multiple attribute group decision making under picture fuzzy environment and their application to green supplier selection. *Technological and economic development of economy, 27*(2), 369–385.

Makhesana, M. A. (2015). Application of improved complex proportional assessment (COPRAS) method for rapid prototyping system selection. *Rapid Prototyping Journal, 21*(6), 671–674.

Mart´ınez, L., Rodriguez, R. M., & Herrera, F. (2015). 2-tuple linguistic model. In *The 2-tuple Linguistic Model: Computing with Words in Decision Making*. Springer, 23–42.

Mercang¨oz, B. A., Yıldırım, B. F., & Yıldırım, S. K. (2020). Time period based COPRAS-G method: application on the Logistics Performance Index. *LogForum, 16*(2), 239–250.

Mishra, A. R., et al. (2024). Multi-criteria decision analysis model using the q-rung orthopair fuzzy similarity measures and the COPRAS method for electric vehicle charging station site selection. *Granular Computing, 9*(1), 23.

Mishra, A. R., Liu, P., & Rani, P. (2022). COPRAS method based on interval-valued hesitant Fermatean fuzzy sets and its application in selecting desalination technology. *Applied soft computing, 119*, 108570.

Mishra, A. R., Rani, P., & Pardasani, K. R. (2019). Multiplecriteria decision-making for service quality selection based on Shapley COPRAS method under hesitant fuzzy sets. *Granular Computing, 4*(3), 435–449.

Mohanrasu, S. S., Janani, K., & Rakkiyappan, R. (2024). A COPRAS-based approach to multi-label feature selection for text classification. *Mathematics and Computers in Simulation, 222*, 3–23.

Nafteh, M. A., & Shahrokhi, M. (2023). Improving the COPRAS Multicriteria Group Decision-Making Method for Selecting a Sustainable Supplier Using Intuitionistic and Fuzzy Type 2 Sets. *Jordan Journal of Mechanical & Industrial Engineering, 17*(2).

Naz, S., Akram, M., & Muzammal, M. (2023). Group decision-making based on 2-tuple linguistic T-spherical fuzzy COPRAS method. *Soft Computing, 27*(6), 2873–2902.

Omerali, M., & Kaya, T. (2021). Product lifecycle management application selection framework based on interval-valued spherical fuzzy COPRAS. *Journal of Intelligent & Fuzzy Systems, 42*(1), 425–438.

Omerali, M., & Kaya, T. (2022). Augmented reality application selection framework using spherical fuzzy COPRAS multi criteria decision making. *Cogent Engineering, 9*(1), 2020610.

Opricovic, S., & Tzeng, G.-H. (2004). Compromise solution by MCDM methods: A comparative analysis of VIKOR and TOPSIS. *European Journal of Operational Research, 156*(2), 445–455.

O¨merali, M., & Kaya, T. (2020). Should firms investigating in IOT domain buy or implement in their Industry 4.0 initiatives? An application of Type-2 Fuzzy COPRAS. *Journal of Intelligent & Fuzzy Systems, 39*(5), 6539–6552.

Peng, X., & Dai, J. (2017). Hesitant fuzzy soft decision making methods based on WASPAS, MABAC and COPRAS with combined weights. *Journal of Intelligent & Fuzzy Systems, 33*(2), 1313–1325.

Peter Darko, A., & Liang, D. (2020). An extended COPRAS method for multiattribute group decision making based on dual hesitant fuzzy Maclaurin symmetric mean. *International Journal of Intelligent Systems, 35*(6), 1021–1068.

Rahim, M., et al. (2024). Improved COPRAS method with unknown weights under p, q-quasirung orthopair fuzzy environment: Application to green supplier selection. *IEEE Access, 12*, 69783–69795.

Rajareega, S., & Vimala, J. (2021). Operations on complex intuitionistic fuzzy soft lattice ordered group and CIFS-COPRAS method for equipment selection process. *Journal of Intelligent & Fuzzy Systems, 41*(5), 5709–5718.

Ramana, K. N. S. V., et al. (2022). An integrated variance-COPRAS approach with nonlinear fuzzy data for ranking barriers affecting sustainable operations. *Sustainability, 14*(3), 1093.

Raudeliuniene, J., et al. (2025). Application of Multi-Criteria Decision-Making Approach COPRAS for Developing Sustainable Building Practices in the European Region. *Sustainability, 17*(8), 3740.

Rodrıguez, R. M., et al. (2014). Hesitant fuzzy sets: state of the art and future directions. *International journal of intelligent systems, 29*(6), 495–524.

Roy, B. (1991). The outranking approach and the foundations of ELECTRE methods. *Theory and Decision, 31*(1), 49–73.

Roy, J., et al. (2019). An extended COPRAS model for multi-criteria decisionmaking problems and its application in web-based hotel evaluation and selection. *Economic research-Ekonomska istrazivanja, 32*(1), 219–253.

Sagiroglu, A., Demir, M. C., & Taskin, A. (2024). Assessing collaboration performance of NGOs by a decomposed Fuzzy approach utilizing AHP and COPRAS methods: Turkiye case. *International Journal of Disaster Risk Reduction, 111*, 104744.

Senapati, T., & Yager, R. R. (2020). Fermatean fuzzy sets. *Journal of ambient intelligence and humanized computing, 11*(2), 663–674.

Smarandache, F. (1999). A unifying field in Logics: Neutrosophic Logic. In *Philosophy*. American Research Press, 1–141.

Subba, R. (2022). and Shabbiruddin. "Optimum harnessing of solar energy with proper selection of phase changing material using integrated fuzzy-COPRAS Model. *International Journal of Management Science and Engineering Management, 17*(4), 269–278.

Thakur, P., et al. (2021). A new entropy measurement for the analysis of uncertain data in MCDA problems using intuitionistic fuzzy sets and COPRAS method. *Axioms, 10*(4), 335.

Torra, V. (2010). Hesitant fuzzy sets. *International journal of intelligent systems, 25*(6), 529–539.

Ullah, K., et al. (2022). Readiness assessment for BIM-based building permit processes using Fuzzy-COPRAS. *Journal of Civil Engineering and Management, 28*(8), 620–633.

Velykorusova, A., et al. (2023). Intelligent multi-criteria decision support for renovation solutions for a building based on emotion recognition by applying the COPRAS method and BIM integration. *Applied Sciences, 13*(9), 5453.

Wei, G., et al. (2021). An extended COPRAS model for multiple attribute group decision making based on single-valued neutrosophic 2-tuple linguistic environment. *Technological and Economic Development of Economy, 27*(2), 353–368.

Xu, Z., & Zhou, W. (2017). Consensus building with a group of decision makers under the hesitant probabilistic fuzzy environment. *Fuzzy Optimization and Decision Making, 16*(4), 481–503.

Yager, R. R., & Smarandache, F. (2017). q-Rung Orthopair Fuzzy Sets. *Neutrosophic Sets and Systems, 17*, 28–35.

Yazdani, M., Alidoosti, A., & Kazimieras Zavadskas, E. (2011). Risk analysis of critical infrastructures using fuzzy COPRAS. *Economic research-Ekonomska istraˇzivanja, 24*(4), 27–40.

Yontar, E. (2023). Selection of suitable renewable energy sources for Turkey: SEM–COPRAS method integrated solution. *International Journal of Environmental Science and Technology, 20*(6), 6131–6146.

Zadeh, L. A. (1975). The concept of a linguistic variable and its application to approximate reasoning—I. *Information Sciences, 8*(3), 199–249.

Zagorskas, J., et al. (2007). Urbanistic assessment of city compactness on the basis of GIS applying the COPRAS method. *Ekologija, 53*, 55–63.

Zavadskas, E., Kaklauskas, A., & Sarka, V. (1994). The new method of multicriteria complex proportional assessment of projects. *Technological and Economic Development of Economy, 1*(3), 131–139 ISSN: 2029-4913.

Zavadskas, E. K., et al. (2008). Multicriteria selection of project managers by applying grey criteria. *Technological and economic development of economy, 14*(4), 462–477.

Zhang, X., Dai, L., & Wan, B. (2023). NA operator-based intervalvalued q-rung orthopair fuzzy PSI-COPRAS group decision-making method. *International Journal of Fuzzy Systems, 25*(1), 198–221.

Zheng, Y., et al. (2018). Severity assessment of chronic obstructive pulmonary disease based on hesitant fuzzy linguistic COPRAS method. *Applied Soft Computing, 69*, 60–71.

Chapter 57

EDAS: Evaluation based on distance from average solution for multi-attribute decision-making

Mehdi Keshavarz-Ghorabaee
Department of Management, Faculty of Humanities (Azadshahr Branch), Gonbad Kavous University, Gonbad Kavous, Iran

57.1 Introduction

It has become quite a complex affair to make decisions in today's complex world. Whether in public policy, business, engineering, medicine, or urban design, decision-makers often have to address multiple, competing objectives at the same time. Situations like these require a strategy to select the most appropriate solution out of many possible solutions. Multicriteria decision-making (MCDM), an important subfield of decision science, developed as a response to this very problem. It also provides systematic approaches for performance evaluation and ranking of alternatives, which are usually measured by multiple criteria, many of which are frequently conflicting (Basílio et al., 2022; Villalba et al., 2024; Yalcin et al., 2022).

Simple additive weighting (SAW), technique for order preference by similarity to ideal solution (TOPSIS), VlseKriterijumska Optimizacija I Kompromisno Resenje (VIKOR), weighted aggregated sum product assessment (WASPAS), and complex proportional assessment (COPRAS), etc., have been developed over the years. They all provide different views on how to deal with criterion trade-offs and interpret the relative performance of the alternatives (Cai et al., 2024; Chakraborty et al., 2024; Pandey et al., 2023). Techniques like SAW, WASPAS, and COPRAS do not depend on an external reference to evaluate the data. Instead, a weighted sum or ratio of objectives is calculated over all objectives. Subsequently, the results are sorted according to the aggregated scores. These methods are versatile for various problems in the sense that they are simple and computationally efficient. Yet, as they have no exact point of reference for judging performance, interpretation may be lacking. Conversely, methods like VIKOR and TOPSIS add an explicit reference point within their evaluation model. Typically, these are the ideal solution and the anti-ideal solution. The ideal solution is the artificial alternative with the best value observed for each criterion, and the anti-ideal solution is the artificial alternative with the worst value observed for each criterion. Decisions are made by comparing the alternatives to these two benchmarks. The rationale of these approaches is based on the Utopian–Dystopian paradigm, where an alternative is better the closer it is to the ideal and the further it is from the anti-ideal. Although useful for an easier grasp of desirability, this idea is not perfect. Extremal values may be problematic to the extent that they are sensitive to outlying scenarios and may not reflect realistic expectations in a decision context with uncertainty or variability (Chang, 2010; Opricovic & Tzeng, 2004; Podvezko, 2011).

Evaluation based on distance from average solution (EDAS) by Keshavarz Ghorabaee et al. (2015) proposes a reference-based approach, where the alternatives are judged with respect to an average, rather than ideal or antiideal alternatives. It was applied to compensate for the deficiencies of the classic methods and to offer a much more stable and representative reference point—the mean value. The central concept of EDAS is a very intuitive one. Picture the following: you want to go from city A to city B. At the outset, when you are getting further away from the start, you feel more distant from the end. When you reach the halfway mark, though, you start to get the sense that you are getting closer to the home stretch. The midway point at which the direction of the progress changes this breakpoint serves as a metaphor for the average solution in EDAS.

Encyclopedia of Multi-Attribute Decision-Making (MADM). DOI: https://doi.org/10.1016/B978-0-443-33275-3.00101-9

In the EDAS methodology, every alternative is objectively appraised by considering and systematically measuring the positive and negative deviations that its values produce with respect to the average (or mean) value of each criterion, considering all of the alternatives. This average provides a frame of reference, offering a reasonable and consistent point of comparison. Positive distance from average (PDA) represents the degree to which an alternative is superior to the average in a particular criterion. In particular, for benefit-type attributes (where higher scores are considered better), PDA measures the extent to which an alternative is above average, and in so doing, its relative level of advantage or superiority. In the cost-based criteria, where low values are preferable, using PDA indicates how much below the average the performance is (better than average performance). On the other hand, negative distance from average (NDA) describes underperformance compared to the average. For benefit criteria, NDA represents by how much an alternative lags behind the mean and indicates a loss in performance. For cost criteria, NDA shows how much a candidate is greater than the average, which in this case means a higher and thus less desirable cost. Since EDAS reflects PDA and NDA for each criterion, it guarantees that the advantages and disadvantages of every alternative will clearly be taken into account in the decision process. This combined measure supports balanced and nuanced evaluations of the performance of each alternative and can be used to reach more informed, transparent, and justified selections in complex multicriteria settings (Ayan & Abacıoğlu, 2022; Ilieva et al., 2018; Keshavarz Ghorabaee et al., 2016).

EDAS has some advantages compared to the traditional MCDM methods. Contrary to ideal-based methods with best and worst observed values that may be extreme or outliers, the EDAS method has the mean as a point of reference. This results in more reliable and lifelike assessments. The average is an intuitive concept and easier to communicate to stakeholders than the distance from an ideal solution that may be difficult to articulate. EDAS overcomes the simplification of nonreferential techniques and the complexity of extreme-value approaches. By comparing alternatives against the average, EDAS also offers a rational and achievable reference. It also facilitates the handling of benefit and cost criteria as well as data in different scales using a simple normalization process. Through the use of both positive and negative deviations from the ideal, EDAS provides more fine-grained discrimination between alternatives and helps decision-makers more effectively rank the decision alternatives (Feng et al., 2018; Han & Wei, 2020; Kacprzak, 2024).

One of the distinguishing features of EDAS is its flexibility of interpretation. The average solution can be conceived as a group or societal norm, and the distance from it can be used to reflect whether or not one is at an advantage or disadvantage within different contexts. This interpretation is especially relevant when participatory decision-making methods are adopted, and the stakeholders might disagree on what constitutes "ideal" behavior. In addition, since EDAS does not take into account subjective parameters and ideal values, it can help in more objective and reasonable decision-making. It places importance on equity in evaluation by weighting all alternatives according to the same benchmark and providing decision-makers with insight as to where each alternative sits relative to a common standard. EDAS has been successfully applied in a variety of domains, including robot selection (Rashid et al., 2021), material selection (Dhanalakshmi et al., 2022), evaluation of renewable energy resources (Yazdani et al., 2020), flood susceptibility modeling (Mitra & Das, 2023), hospital selection (Kutlu Gündoğdu et al., 2018), and supply chain management (Liu et al., 2022). Its capacity for delivering accurate and well-considered advice is particularly valuable when perfect benchmarks are not precisely or simply defined.

The rest of this chapter is organized as follows: first, the EDAS technique is presented in detail through numerous steps. Two numerical examples, including a small-scale example and a real-life case study, are presented to vigorously illustrate and validate the practical utilization and applicability of the method. The chapter closes with a summary and outlook for future research and applications.

57.2 Methodology

The EDAS approach is one of the newly emerging methods with increasing popularity in the family of MCDM methods. Originally proposed by Keshavarz Ghorabaee et al. (2015), the EDAS technique was first proposed to be used for inventory classification, but it has been used in many other MCDM problems (Torkayesh et al., 2023). The theoretical foundation of EDAS is based on comparing alternatives with an "average solution" without using reference points such as ideal or antiideal points. Thus, EDAS is particularly useful for problems where a decision-maker favors a reference that is based on the true data distribution.

Step 1: Construction of the decision matrix

Suppose that we have n alternatives and m criteria, and the weight of each criterion (w_j, $j \in \{1,2,\ldots,m\}$) is known. Accordingly, the decision matrix is defined as follows:

$$X = \begin{bmatrix} x_{11} & x_{12} & \cdots & x_{1j} & \cdots & x_{1m} \\ x_{21} & x_{22} & \cdots & x_{2j} & \cdots & x_{2m} \\ \vdots & \vdots & \ddots & \vdots & \ddots & \vdots \\ x_{i1} & x_{i2} & \cdots & x_{ij} & \cdots & x_{im} \\ \vdots & \vdots & \ddots & \vdots & \ddots & \vdots \\ x_{n1} & x_{n2} & \cdots & x_{nj} & \cdots & x_{nm} \end{bmatrix} \tag{57.1}$$

Where x_{ij} represents the performance value of alternative A_i with respect to criterion C_j.

In EDAS, alternatives are evaluated based on their positive and negative distances from the average solution. The more an alternative exceeds the average in benefit-type criteria (and stays below the average in cost-type criteria), the more desirable it is considered. The overall procedure of EDAS can be broken down into six well-defined steps:

Step 2: Calculation of the elements of the average solution

Before assessing the performance of alternatives, EDAS computes an average reference point for each criterion across all alternatives. This reference point acts as a benchmark to evaluate how each alternative deviates from the average as follows:

$$\mathscr{G}_j = \frac{\sum_{i=1}^{n} x_{ij}}{n} \tag{57.2}$$

Where $\mathscr{G}_j$ is the average value of criterion j.

Step 3: Determination of positive and negative distances

The core evaluation mechanism in EDAS lies in computing two types of deviations from the average value for each criterion: positive distance and negative distance. The idea is that alternatives should ideally have a higher-than-average value for benefit criteria and a lower-than-average value for cost criteria. Accordingly, the distance formulas are as follows:

$$\mathscr{P}_{ij}^{d} = \begin{cases} \dfrac{\max(0, x_{ij} - \mathscr{G}_j)}{\mathscr{G}_j} & if\ j \in B \\ \dfrac{\max(0, \mathscr{G}_j - x_{ij})}{\mathscr{G}_j} & if\ j \in C \end{cases} \tag{57.3}$$

$$\mathscr{N}_{ij}^{d} = \begin{cases} \dfrac{\max(0, \mathscr{G}_j - x_{ij})}{\mathscr{G}_j} & if\ j \in B \\ \dfrac{\max(0, x_{ij} - \mathscr{G}_j)}{\mathscr{G}_j} & if\ j \in C \end{cases} \tag{57.4}$$

Where B and C denote the sets of benefit and cost criteria, respectively.

This formulation ensures that both positive and negative deviations are nonnegative and comparable across criteria with different scales.

Step 4: Computation of weighted summation of distances

To incorporate the relative importance of criteria, EDAS employs a weighted aggregation of the previously computed distances. The contribution of each criterion to the overall performance of an alternative is weighted based on predefined criterion weights as follows:

$$\mathscr{P}_i^{w} = \sum_{j=1}^{m} w_j \mathscr{P}_{ij}^{d} \tag{57.5}$$

$$\mathscr{N}_i^{w} = \sum_{j=1}^{m} w_j \mathscr{N}_{ij}^{d} \tag{57.6}$$

Where $\mathscr{P}_i^{w}$ and $\mathscr{N}_i^{w}$ are the total positive and negative distances of alternative i. This step transforms disaggregated deviation information into a summary performance profile for each alternative, reflecting both positive contributions and negative penalties.

Step 5: Normalization of the weighted summation values

As the aggregated distances may vary significantly in scale, normalization is performed to make them comparable across alternatives as follows:

$$\mathscr{P}_i^n = \frac{\mathscr{P}_i^w}{\max_k \mathscr{P}_k^w} \tag{57.7}$$

$$\mathscr{N}_i^n = 1 - \frac{\mathscr{N}_i^w}{\max_k \mathscr{N}_k^w} \tag{57.8}$$

Here, the positive distances are normalized by the maximum observed positive value, and negative distances are normalized in an inverse manner so that lower original negative values yield higher normalized values. This formulation aligns with the logic that better alternatives should have higher normalized scores.

Step 6: Calculation of the appraisal score

To arrive at a final composite score for each alternative, EDAS computes the mean of the normalized positive and negative distances as follows:

$$\mathscr{S}_i = \frac{1}{2}(\mathscr{P}_i^n + \mathscr{N}_i^n) \tag{57.9}$$

The resulting value, $\mathscr{S}_i$, is the appraisal score of alternative i, which reflects its desirability in a balanced manner, accounting for both favorable and unfavorable deviations from the average solution.

Step 7: Ranking the alternatives

Finally, the alternatives are ranked based on their appraisal scores $\mathscr{S}_i$ in descending order. A higher score indicates a more desirable alternative.

57.3 Numerical example 1

In this section, a numerical example is provided to show the step-by-step computational procedure of the EDAS method. For clarity of explanation and ease of comprehension, a small-scale illustrative example is presented. This example has four alternatives and three criteria. Of these criteria, two are of the benefit type (to be maximized), while one is of the cost type (to be minimized).

The decision matrix is intentionally designed so that the best and worst alternatives can be identified at a glance. This helps better understand and validate the final ranking results obtained through the EDAS method.

Step 1: Constructing the decision matrix

The decision matrix, as shown in Table 57.1, includes the performance values of four alternatives (A_1 to A_4) with respect to three criteria (C_1 to C_3). The types of criteria are as follows:

- C_1: Benefit
- C_2: Cost
- C_3: Benefit

TABLE 57.1 Decision matrix (example 1).

Alternative	C_1 (Benefit)	C_2 (Cost)	C_3 (Benefit)
A_1	2	43	1200
A_2	9	21	3800
A_3	5	32	1800
A_4	3	38	2700

The weights assigned to the criteria are:

- $w_1 = 0.3$, $w_2 = 0.3$, $w_3 = 0.4$

From visual inspection of the matrix, it is evident that Alternative A_2 is the most favorable, while Alternative A_1 appears to be the least desirable.

Step 2: Computing the elements of the average solution

The average (mean) value of each criterion is computed across all alternatives using Eq. (57.2). This average solution acts as a reference point for calculating the distances (Table 57.2).

Step 3: Calculating positive and negative distances

Using Eqs. (57.3) and (57.4) provided in the EDAS methodology, the positive distance ($\mathscr{P}_{ij}^d$) and negative distance ($\mathscr{N}_{ij}^d$) of each alternative from the average solution are calculated based on whether the criterion is to be maximized or minimized (Table 57.3).

A higher value of positive deviation and a lower value of negative deviation indicate a more desirable alternative. As seen in the table, A_2 exhibits the highest positive distances and zero negative distances, while A_1 shows the opposite behavior.

Step 4: Computing the weighted summation of distances

Each alternative's weighted sum of positive and negative distances is calculated using the criterion weights and Eqs. (57.5) and (57.6)(Table 57.4).

Steps 5 to 7: Normalizing the weighted summation values, calculating the scores and ranking the alternatives

To compare the weighted distances, they are first normalized using Eqs. (57.7) and (57.8). Then, the final assessment score ($\mathscr{S}_i$) for each alternative is calculated by averaging the normalized positive and negative distances according to Eq. (57.9) (Table 57.5).

As expected, Alternative A_2 receives the highest score and ranks first, confirming its superiority. Conversely, Alternative A_1, which had the poorest performance across all criteria, is ranked last. This simple example clearly demonstrates how the EDAS method evaluates alternatives based on their distances from the average solution, ensuring a fair and informative assessment.

57.4 Numerical example 2

In this section, a real-world example is used to demonstrate the practicality and performance of the EDAS approach in complex decision-making situations. The example can be found in a study by Ginevičius & Podvezko (2008), which

TABLE 57.2 Elements of the average solution (example 1).

Criterion	C_1 ($\mathscr{G}_1$)	C_2 ($\mathscr{G}_2$)	C_3 ($\mathscr{G}_3$)
Value	4.75	33.5	2375

TABLE 57.3 Positive and negative distances (example 1).

Alternative	$\mathscr{P}_{i1}^d$	$\mathscr{P}_{i2}^d$	$\mathscr{P}_{i3}^d$	$\mathscr{N}_{i1}^d$	$\mathscr{N}_{i2}^d$	$\mathscr{N}_{i3}^d$
A_1	0	0	0	0.578	0.283	0.494
A_2	0.894	0.373	0.6	0	0	0
A_3	0.052	0.044	0	0	0	0.242
A_4	0	0	0.136	0.368	0.134	0

TABLE 57.4 Weighted aggregated distances (example 1).

Alternative	$\mathcal{P}_i^w$	$\mathcal{N}_i^w$
A_1	0	0.456
A_2	0.620	0
A_3	0.029	0.096
A_4	0.054	0.150

TABLE 57.5 Normalized scores and rankings (example 1).

Alternative	$\mathcal{P}_i^n$	$\mathcal{N}_i^n$	$\mathcal{S}_i$	Rank
A_1	0	0	0	4
A_2	1	1	1	1
A_3	0.047	0.787	0.417	2
A_4	0.088	0.669	0.378	3

TABLE 57.6 The evaluation criteria (example 2).

Criterion	Description
C_1	Number of departments for servicing individual clients (benefit)
C_2	Waiting time to be attended (cost)
C_3	Number of ATMs (benefit)
C_4	Number of individual clients (benefit)
C_5	Number of online banking clients (benefit)
C_6	Number of issued credit/debit cards (benefit)
C_7	Interest rate for one-year deposit (benefit)
C_8	Mean margin of property loan interest (benefit)
C_9	Cost of preparing loan package (cost)
C_{10}	Cost of changing contract terms (cost)
C_{11}	Possibility to postpone loan repayment (benefit)
C_{12}	Charges on cash payments (cost)
C_{13}	Website quality (benefit)
C_{14}	Long-term debt rating (benefit)
C_{15}	Net bank profit (benefit, made positive if needed)

TABLE 57.7 The decision matrix (example 2).

	C_1	C_2	C_3	C_4	C_5	C_6	C_7	C_8	C_9	C_{10}	C_{11}	C_{12}	C_{13}	C_{14}	C_{15}
w_j	0.0733	0.07	0.0644	0.0633	0.0856	0.0467	0.0822	0.0878	0.0411	0.04	0.0522	0.0511	0.0856	0.0822	0.0744
A_1	78	17	150	500	220	302	5	1	450	450	2	0.5	6	19	52603
A_2	245	9	327	241	833	706	5.5	0.875	300	200	2	1	5	12	33768
A_3	71	38	274	1059	704	1213	4.7	0.8235	450	300	3	0.6667	5	19	221608
A_4	128	21	370	1015	833	1278	4.15	0.875	450	450	2	0.6667	1	22	145268
A_5	52	5	28	89	44	66	6	0	450	200	0.17	1	3	13	51258
A_6	17	10	57	65	60	73	4.65	1	300	200	1	0.5	6	20	16849
A_7	50	3	11	104	20.8	42	5.55	0.4516	100	150	1	0.8	3	13	21783
A_8	20	16	61	40	21.7	28	5.51	0.875	450	200	3	1	4	14	1
A_9	12	1	45	66.3	63	67	5.6	0.778	450	250	0.25	0	2	21	11088
A_{10}	45	1	0	15.4	4	0	6.5	0.113	450	200	1	0.5	3	9	4270

aimed at measuring the reliability of banks for individual clients in a certain European country. With the growing competition in financial markets, the need to evaluate and compare banks' performance while considering a variety of factors has become imperative for society and regulators' interests. The assessment considers 15 individual criteria, covering both quantitative and qualitative elements of reliability, such as infrastructure, customer service efficiency, access, financial transparency, and technology features. A total of 10 commercial banks have been included as alternatives. The multicriteria feature of the problem, considering benefit and cost type indicators, provides a good opportunity to apply the EDAS method because it provides a well-balanced and data-driven assessment, and complex normalization processes or subjective inputs are not required. A description of the evaluation criteria is given in Table 57.6.

Among these, criteria C_2, C_9, and C_{10} are of cost type, meaning lower values are preferred. The remaining criteria are benefit type, where higher values are considered better.

The decision matrix for the 10 banks (Alternatives A_1 to A_{10}) and the 15 criteria is shown in Table 57.7. The weights of the criteria (w_j) are also included in this table.

By following the steps outlined in the methodology section, the EDAS method is applied to the data. After performing all computations, the weighted positive ($\mathscr{P}_i^w$) and weighted negative deviations ($\mathscr{N}_i^w$), as well as their normalized forms ($\mathscr{P}_i^n$ and $\mathscr{N}_i^n$), and the final appraisal scores ($\mathscr{S}_i$) are obtained and shown in Table 57.8.

Based on the final scores $\mathscr{S}_i$, the alternatives are ranked from best to worst, as shown in Table 57.9.

57.5 Comparative analysis

To validate the results and examine the consistency of the EDAS method with other established MCDM approaches, the same decision problem (numerical example 2) was solved using five alternative techniques: SAW, WASPAS, TOPSIS, COPRAS, and VIKOR. The final rankings of the 10 banks obtained from each method are shown in Table 57.9. As can be seen, although there are some slight variations in the rankings, the top-performing banks remain largely consistent across all methods, with Alternatives A_3 and A_4 ranking among the best options in almost all cases. This consistency confirms the robustness of the decision structure and reliability of the underlying data.

More importantly, to quantitatively assess the congruence of EDAS with the other methods, Spearman's rank correlation coefficient (ρ) was calculated between the EDAS rankings and the rankings produced by each of the five comparison methods. All correlation values exceeded 0.83, with the highest being 0.976 for both the COPRAS and TOPSIS methods, as presented in Table 57.9. These high correlation values indicate a strong positive association between the rankings derived from EDAS and those from traditional methods. This implies that EDAS produces results that are not only consistent but also compatible with widely accepted MCDM techniques.

TABLE 57.8 The computed variables of the evaluation based on distance from average solution method.

	$\mathscr{P}_i^w$	$\mathscr{N}_i^w$	$\mathscr{P}_i^n$	$\mathscr{N}_i^n$	$\mathscr{S}_i$	Rank
A_1	0.171	0.114	0.220	0.780	0.500	4
A_2	0.614	0.066	0.786	0.872	0.829	3
A_3	0.779	0.173	0.997	0.665	0.831	2
A_4	0.781	0.169	1.000	0.674	0.837	1
A_5	0.087	0.409	0.111	0.210	0.160	8
A_6	0.141	0.341	0.180	0.341	0.260	5
A_7	0.114	0.372	0.146	0.281	0.213	6
A_8	0.117	0.380	0.150	0.265	0.208	7
A_9	0.107	0.460	0.137	0.110	0.124	9
A_{10}	0.092	0.517	0.118	0.000	0.059	10

TABLE 57.9 The ranking results and comparison.

	EDAS	SAW	WASPAS	COPRAS	TOPSIS	VIKOR
A_1	4	4	4	4	4	3
A_2	3	2	2	3	2	1
A_3	2	1	1	1	3	2
A_4	1	3	3	2	1	4
A_5	8	10	10	8	9	10
A_6	5	5	5	6	5	5
A_7	6	7	6	5	6	8
A_8	7	6	7	7	7	6
A_9	9	8	8	9	8	7
A_{10}	10	9	9	10	10	9
ρ	—	0.915	0.927	0.976	0.976	0.83

EDAS has unique features that are different from conventional approaches. Unlike traditional methodologies, which frequently demand complex data normalization or subjective preference functions, EDAS operates directly with unprocessed data, preserving its integrity and eliminating the possibility of bias. The special power of the method lies in the analysis of the positive and negative deviations from the average values, which leads to a fair and accurate selection among alternatives. Due to its explicit nature, transparent mechanism, objective structure, and consistent correlation with conventional methods, the proposed EDAS has demonstrated its practical efficacy for real multicriteria decision problems. Its balanced perspective is of particular interest in complex situations where trade-offs among various criteria in diverse industries must be considered simultaneously.

57.6 Conclusions

The EDAS method has been proven practical and intuitive in MCDM problems. The difference from approaches based on idealized or extreme reference points is that EDAS considers average performance as the reference, which results in an evaluation that is more stable and practical—an important element when dealing with real problems (where, for instance, ideal values are unknown or, worse yet, misleading due to the presence of imperfect data). The method's distinctive strength lies in its balanced assessment of how alternatives perform relative to the average, examining both superior and inferior deviations. This rigorous assessment guarantees that both advantages and disadvantages are taken into account when determining the final score. This procedure can contribute to the method's validity and helps when results need to be more understandable and acceptable to decision-makers, e.g., in partnerships. The chapter has described EDAS in a structured manner by introducing its theoretical framework and computation processes along with two illustrative numerical examples. The bank reliability example shows the efficiency of EDAS and its applicability to complex, multidimensional decision problems with real data. It is worth mentioning that the proposed approach is in good accordance with other traditional methods, such as SAW, TOPSIS, and VIKOR, which indicates that the model is reasonable and feasible in practical applications. Crucially, EDAS accomplishes this without the need for subjective utility functions or complex normalization steps, ensuring objectivity as well as preserving the structure of the original data.

There are many potential avenues for future investigation of EDAS. One such approach with high potential is to extend EDAS methods by integrating them with fuzzy logic and other advanced tools to directly assess uncertainty, ambiguity, or imprecise data inputs in decision-making—a prevalent situation nowadays in the complex decision landscape. The improved fuzzy EDAS versions may allow decision-makers to express their evaluations in natural linguistic terms or in numerical intervals, which can significantly enhance the flexibility of the method and increase the application of its extensions in different real-world areas such as healthcare systems, smart city development, comprehensive risk evaluation, policy control in environmental terms, and strategic planning of organizations. Moreover, the development of hybrid models that integrate EDAS with state-of-the-art machine learning algorithms, advanced clustering algorithms, or novel metaheuristic optimization methods is a promising avenue. Such integration would substantially increase the computational efficiency, problem-solving ability, and adaptivity of the technique. These versions would be especially useful for solving problems involving huge decision spaces and might lead to more adaptive forms of decision-making in the face of dynamic circumstances. The introduction of advanced EDAS extensions comprises an interesting frontier of MCDM research with great practical implications in various application areas.

References

Ayan, B., & Abacıoğlu, S. (2022). Bibliometric analysis of the MCDM methods in the last decade: WASPAS, MABAC, EDAS, CODAS, COCOSO, and MARCOS. *International Journal of Business and Economic Studies, 4*, 65–85.

Basflio, M. P., Pereira, V., Costa, H. G., Santos, M., & Ghosh, A. (2022). A systematic review of the applications of multi-criteria decision aid methods (1977–2022). *Electronics, 11*, 1720.

Cai, J., Hu, Y., Peng, Y., Guo, F., Xiong, J., & Zhang, R. (2024). A hybrid MCDM approach based on combined weighting method, cloud model and COPRAS for assessing road construction workers' safety climate. *Frontiers in Public Health, Volume 12*, 2024. https://doi.org/10.3389/fpubh.2024.1452964.

Chakraborty, S., Raut, R. D., Rofin, T., & Chakraborty, S. (2024). A narrative literature review on optimization of manufacturing processes using weighted aggregated sum product assessment (WASPAS) method. *OPSEARCH,* 1–25.

Chang, C.-L. (2010). A modified VIKOR method for multiple criteria analysis. *Environmental Monitoring and Assessment, 168*, 339–344. https://doi.org/10.1007/s10661-009-1117-0.

Dhanalakshmi, C. S., Madhu, P., Karthick, A., Mathew, M., & Vignesh Kumar, R. (2022). A comprehensive MCDM-based approach using TOPSIS and EDAS as an auxiliary tool for pyrolysis material selection and its application. *Biomass Conversion and Biorefinery, 12*, 5845–5860. https://doi.org/10.1007/s13399-020-01009-0.

Feng, X., Wei, C., & Liu, Q. (2018). EDAS method for extended hesitant fuzzy linguistic multi-criteria decision making. *International Journal of Fuzzy Systems, 20*, 2470–2483.

Ginevičius, R., & Podvezko, V. (2008). Multicriteria evaluation of Lithuanian banks from the perspective of their reliability for clients. *Journal of business economics and management, 9*, 257–267.

Han, L., & Wei, C. (2020). An extended EDAS method for multicriteria decision-making based on multivalued neutrosophic sets. *Complexity, 2020*, 7578507.

Ilieva, G., Yankova, T., & Klisarova-Belcheva, S. (2018). Decision analysis with classic and fuzzy EDAS modifications. *Computational and Applied Mathematics, 37*, 5650–5680.

Kacprzak, D. (2024). A new extension of the EDAS method in a fuzzy environment for group decision-making. *DECISION, 51*, 263–277. https://doi.org/10.1007/s40622-024-00396-x.

Keshavarz Ghorabaee, M., Zavadskas, E. K., Amiri, M., & Turskis, Z. (2016). Extended EDAS method for fuzzy multi-criteria decision-making: an application to supplier selection. *International Journal of Computers Communications & Control, 11*, 358–371.

Keshavarz Ghorabaee, M., Zavadskas, E. K., Olfat, L., & Turskis, Z. (2015). Multi-criteria inventory classification using a new method of evaluation based on distance from average solution (EDAS). *Informatica, 26*, 435–451. https://doi.org/10.1142/S0219622015500212.

Kutlu Gündoğdu, F., Kahraman, C., & Civan, H. N. (2018). A novel hesitant fuzzy EDAS method and its application to hospital selection. *Journal of Intelligent & Fuzzy Systems, 35*, 6353–6365.

Liu, C., Rani, P., & Pachori, K. (2022). Sustainable circular supplier selection and evaluation in the manufacturing sector using Pythagorean fuzzy EDAS approach. *Journal of Enterprise Information Management, 35*, 1040–1066.

Mitra, R., & Das, J. (2023). A comparative assessment of flood susceptibility modelling of GIS-based TOPSIS, VIKOR, and EDAS techniques in the Sub-Himalayan foothills region of Eastern India. *Environmental Science and Pollution Research, 30*, 16036–16067. https://doi.org/10.1007/s11356-022-23168-5.

Opricovic, S., & Tzeng, G.-H. (2004). Compromise solution by MCDM methods: A comparative analysis of VIKOR and TOPSIS. *European Journal of Operational Research, 156*, 445–455. https://doi.org/10.1016/S0377-2217(03)00020-1.

Pandey, V., Komal, & Dincer, H. (2023). A review on TOPSIS method and its extensions for different applications with recent development. *Soft Computing, 27*, 18011–18039. https://doi.org/10.1007/s00500-023-09011-0.

Podvezko, V. (2011). The comparative analysis of MCDA methods SAW and COPRAS. *Engineering Economics, 22*, 134-146.

Rashid, T., Ali, A., & Chu, Y.-M. (2021). Hybrid BW-EDAS MCDM methodology for optimal industrial robot selection. *Plos one, 16*, e0246738.

Torkayesh, A. E., Deveci, M., Karagoz, S., & Antucheviciene, J. (2023). A state-of-the-art survey of evaluation based on distance from average solution (EDAS): Developments and applications. *Expert systems with applications, 221*, 119724.

Villalba, P., Sánchez-Garrido, A. J., & Yepes, V. (2024). A review of multi-criteria decision-making methods for building assessment, selection, and retrofit. *Journal of Civil Engineering and Management, 30*, 465–480.

Yalcin, A. S., Kilic, H. S., & Delen, D. (2022). The use of multi-criteria decision-making methods in business analytics: A comprehensive literature review. *Technological Forecasting and Social Change, 174*, 121193. https://doi.org/10.1016/j.techfore.2021.121193.

Yazdani, M., Torkayesh, A. E., Santibanez-Gonzalez, E. D., & Otaghsara, S. K. (2020). Evaluation of renewable energy resources using integrated Shannon Entropy—EDAS model. *Sustainable Operations and Computers, 1*, 35–42.

Chapter 58

CODAS: Combinative distance-based assessment for multi-attribute decision-making

Shabnam Rahnamay Bonab[1] and Hossein Reyhani Yamchi[2]

[1]*Department of Management, Monash University, Melbourne, VIC, Australia,* [2]*La Trobe Business School, La Trobe University, Melbourne, VIC, Australia*

58.1 Introduction

Making decisions is an important skill that influences many parts of our lives, from our daily routines to how organisations are managed. The choices we make can affect our personal lives, work, relationships, and even cultural values. Because of this, it's important to use a method that helps guide these decisions in a thoughtful and effective way (Ashofteh & Dougaheh, 2024; Haseli, Ranjbarzadeh, et al., 2023). One useful approach is multicriteria decision-making (MCDM). This method helps people and organisations evaluate different options by looking at several important factors at once, rather than just concentrating on a single aspect (Haseli et al., 2025). This gives a more balanced view and helps avoid missing out on key information (Mahmudah et al., 2024). MCDM also reduces the chances of being influenced by emotions or personal biases, which can often lead to poor decisions. It works especially well in group settings where different opinions need to be considered (Haseli et al., 2020). By clearly defining what matters most and weighing the importance of each factor, MCDM makes the decision-making process more structured, equitable, and easier to comprehend. The process generally includes identifying all possible options, setting the criteria for comparison, deciding how important each criterion is, and considering the views of everyone involved (Haseli, Yaran Ögel, et al., 2023; Moslem et al., 2024).

The combinative distance-based assessment (CODAS) technique is a distance-based assessment method. This technique was first introduced by Keshavarz Ghorabaee et al. (2016). It is one of the MCDM methods, and its purpose is to rank options based on several criteria. The CODAS method determines the desirability of options using two approaches (Mitra, 2024). The first approach calculates the Euclidean distance of the options from the negative ideal, and the second approach calculates the taxicab distance of the options from the negative ideal (Jafarzadeh Ghoushchi et al., 2023).

Among its advantages are the simplicity and transparency of the implementation steps, so that this method is easy to understand and use (Ghorabaee et al., 2017). Also, CODAS can evaluate options based on different criteria and with different weights, allowing decision makers to choose the most accurate options (Kumari & Acherjee, 2022). This method also uses Euclidean and taxi distances to calculate the distance of each option from the positive and negative ideal, which makes decision-making more accurate and closer to real conditions (Keshavarz Ghorabaee et al., 2016). In addition, CODAS does not require complex assumptions and can perform well under conditions of uncertainty. This method is easily combined with other decision-making techniques and has wide application in various industries, including manufacturing, services, investment selection, and business strategies (Farnam et al., 2024; Ghorabaee et al., 2017). Overall, CODAS is a simple, transparent, and efficient method that can help decision makers, especially in complex and multicriteria issues, to select appropriate options based on accurate and comprehensive analysis.

58.2 Literature review

In recent years, the growing complexity of decision-making problems and the uncertain environment have led to the widespread adoption of decision-making methods in critical areas such as energy, transportation, logistics, and

Encyclopedia of Multi-Attribute Decision-Making (MADM). DOI: https://doi.org/10.1016/B978-0-443-33275-3.00080-4

sustainability (Haseli, Torkayesh, et al., 2023). Researchers use MCDM methods for structured and logical evaluation. The CODAS method has attracted the attention of researchers in many fields to assess the weight of criteria due to its high applicability and simple calculations. Researchers have also improved its accuracy and applicability by combining the CODAS method with other decision-making methods such as stepwise weight assessment ratio analysis (SWARA), technique for order preference by similarity to ideal solution (TOPSIS), best–worst method (BWM), and fuzzy logic. As shown in Table 58.1, researchers have benefited from this method in various fields.

TABLE 58.1 Review of articles.

Author(s)	Research objective/focus	Methodology/approach used
Jafarzadeh Ghoushchi et al. (2023)	Assessing and prioritizing clean energy barriers	Spherical fuzzy SWARA–CODAS
Keshavarz Ghorabaee et al. (2017)	Enhancing market segment selection under uncertainty	Fuzzy CODAS
Yeni and Özçelik (2019)	Developing intuitionistic fuzzy CODAS for stable, robust, and efficient decision-making	Intuitionistic fuzzy CODAS
Garg et al. (2023)	Enhancing CODAS using Dombi sine aggregation for robust fuzzy decision-making	Fuzzy CODAS
Simic et al. (2021)	Robust site selection for vehicle shredding facilities	Picture fuzzy CODAS
Peng and Ma (2020)	Developing a Pythagorean fuzzy CODAS algorithm for effective MCDM problem-solving	Pythagorean fuzzy CODAS
Deveci et al. (2020)	Choosing renewable energy options in Turkey	Interval-valued intuitionistic fuzzy CODAS
Biswas et al. (2021)	Ranking smartphone brands in India	Fermatean fuzzy CODAS
Farnam et al. (2024)	Improving CODAS with new weighted distance measures for MCDM	Neutrosophic CODAS
Amusan et al. (2024)	Selecting the best hybrid energy system	CRITIC–CODAS
Ashofteh et al. (2023)	Selecting the best game theory method for water allocation	SWARA–CODAS
Mitra (2024)	Grading and selecting Tossa jute fibers based on multiple properties	TOPSIS–CODAS
Ijadi Maghsoodi et al. (2020)	Optimal site selection of a shopping center in Tehran	BWM–CODAS
Ning et al. (2022)	Solving MADM problems, including enterprise credit risk evaluation	Probabilistic dual hesitant fuzzy CODAS
Baydas et al. (2024)	Comparing economic performances of G-20 countries, focusing on normalization techniques and data types	Fuzzy CODAS
Gupta et al. (2022)	Assessing and ranking mHealth applications for managing type 2 diabetes mellitus	AHP–MOORA–CODAS
Wątróbski et al. (2022)	Evaluating sustainable electricity generation using renewable energy sources	CODAS–COMET
Farid et al. (2023)	Overcoming obstacles in managing sustainable supply chains	Fermatean fuzzy CODAS
Andukuri and Rao (2024)	Evaluating condition monitoring devices for rotating equipment	Fuzzy CODAS
Kavitha et al. (2024)	Extending the CODAS method for multilabel feature selection with improved accuracy	q-rung orthopair hesitant fuzzy CODAS

58.3 Description of combinative distance-based assessment method

This section provides a comprehensive step-by-step explanation of the CODAS method, with each stage supported by corresponding mathematical equations to ensure clarity and facilitate understanding of the computational procedure.

Step 1. Creation of decision matrix

The initial step in this approach involves creating the decision matrix. In the CODAS method, this matrix resembles those used in other techniques like TOPSIS, VlseKriterijumska Optimizacija I Kompromisno Resenje, or ELECTRE, where the columns represent the criteria and the rows correspond to the alternatives under consideration. The decision matrix generally takes the following form:

$$x = [x_{ij}]_{n*m} = \begin{bmatrix} x_{11} & \cdots & x_{1m} \\ \vdots & \ddots & \vdots \\ x_{n1} & \cdots & x_{nm} \end{bmatrix} \tag{58.1}$$

Step 2. The normalized decision matrix

The second step is normalizing the decision matrix. Normalization is performed using the following relations. If the criterion has a positive aspect (benefit), the first relation is used, and if the criterion has a negative aspect (cost), the second relation is used.

$$n_{ij} = \begin{cases} \dfrac{x_{ij}}{\max\limits_i x_{ij}} & \text{if } j \in N_b \\ \dfrac{\min\limits_i x_{ij}}{x_{ij}} & \text{if } j \in N_c \end{cases} \tag{58.2}$$

Step 3. Constructing the weighted normalized decision matrix

In the third step of the CODAS method, the weighted normalized decision matrix is created by multiplying the normalized matrix by the criteria weights. These weights can be derived through various approaches, including the analytic hierarchy process, or more recent techniques like the BWM and SWARA.

Step 4. Determine the ideal and anti-ideal solutions

In this step, the Euclidean distance E_i and taxicab distances T_i must be computed from the negative ideal. These distances are derived from the Eqs. (58.3) and (58.4). In these equations, ns_j represents the negative ideal of the criteria.

$$E_i = \sqrt{\sum_{j=1}^{m} (r_{ij} - ns_j)^2} \tag{58.3}$$

$$T_i = \sum_{j=1}^{m} |r_{ij} - ns_j| \tag{58.4}$$

Step 5. Calculate the relative closeness to the ideal solution

In this step, the relative evaluation matrix should be created using the following equation. In this equation, Ψ represents a threshold function used to determine the equality of the Euclidean distance between two options.

$$h_{ik} = (E_i - E_k) + (\ \Psi(E_i - E_k) * (T_i - T_k)) \tag{58.5}$$

In some cases, the threshold function (Ψ) may simply assign a value of 1 when the distances are equal, and a value less than 1 if the distances are different.

Step 6. The final ranking of the alternative

In this step, by summing the values of h_{ik} for the alternatives, they can be ranked. The higher the value of h_i, the better the rank of the option.

$$h_i = \sum h_{ik} \tag{58.6}$$

58.4 Numerical example 1

In this section, two case studies are presented to examine the application of the CODAS method. Also, complete, step-by-step explanations are provided for a better understanding and further learning of the method.

58.4.1 Ranking robots

In this example, we are aiming to rank five robots based on five criteria: payload capacity (C_1), maximum speed (C_2), repeatability (C_3), memory capacity (C_4), and user accessibility (C_5). This will be done using the CODAS method. Below are the detailed steps, explained and presented with tables for clarity.

The initial step involves constructing a decision matrix according to Eq. 58.1. This matrix displays how each alternative (robot) performs relative to every criterion. Table 58.2 illustrates this decision matrix, with rows corresponding to different robots and columns representing the evaluation criteria. The weights assigned to each criterion have been determined beforehand.

Next, we normalize the decision matrix based on (58.2). In this case, the criterion "maximum speed" is considered a negative criterion (lower values are better), and all other criteria are positive (higher values are better). The normalized decision matrix has been provided in Table 58.3.

Next, the normalized values are multiplied by the respective criterion weights to generate the weighted normalized decision matrix. This step reflects the weighted significance of each criterion for every alternative, as shown in Table 58.4.

Next, we compute the Euclidean and taxicab distances for each robot from the negative ideal solution using Eqs. 58.3 and 58.4. The negative ideal solution represents the option with the lowest values across all criteria. Below is the detailed calculation for robot R1 regarding both the Euclidean and taxicab distances from this negative ideal point (Table 58.5):

Euclidean:

$$\sqrt{\begin{array}{l}\sqrt{(0.173-0.115)^2}+(0.170-0.097)^2+(0.129-0.129)^2+\\+(0.171-0.143)^2+(0.110-0.110)^2\end{array}}=\sqrt{0.00336+0.00533+0+0.000784+0}$$

$$\approx\sqrt{0.00947}\approx 0.\,0973$$

Taxicab:

$$|0.173-0.115|+|0.170-0.097|+0+|0.171-0.143|+0=0.058+0.073+0.028=0.159$$

Using these distances, the relative evaluation matrix is computed for each robot using Eq. 58.5. The H_{ik} value represents the relative performance of each option, combining information from both distance measures.

To increase the sensitivity of the CODAS method and better differentiate between alternatives, we set the threshold parameter $\Psi = 0.8$. This parameter plays a key role in combining the Euclidean and taxicab distances when calculating the final comparative score H_{ik} for each alternative against others. The sum of all H_{ik} values was used to rank each alternative which is shown in table 58.6. The higher the sum, the better the overall performance of the vehicle across all criteria.

Based on the H_i values, we can rank the robots. The robot with the highest H_i value is considered the best option, while the robot with the lowest H_i value is considered the worst. Thus, based on the Table 58.6, robot 4 with the value of 0.1374 is ranked the highest, and robot 3 with the value of 0.0110 is ranked the lowest.

Fig. 58.1

TABLE 58.2 The initial decision matrix.

Criteria	C_1	C_2	C_3	C_4	C_5
Weight	0.23	0.17	0.18	0.20	0.22
R1	6	4	5	6	4
R2	7	6	7	5	8
R3	4	6	7	6	7
R4	8	7	6	7	8
R5	6	7	5	6	7

TABLE 58.3 Normalized decision matrix.

Alt	C_1	C_2	C_3	C_4	C_5
R1	6/8 = 0.75	4/4 = 1.00	5/7 ≈ 0.714	6/7 ≈ 0.857	4/8 = 0.500
R2	7/8 = 0.875	4/6 ≈ 0.667	7/7 = 1.000	5/7 ≈ 0.714	8/8 = 1.000
R3	4/8 = 0.500	4/6 ≈ 0.667	7/7 = 1.000	6/7 ≈ 0.857	7/8 = 0.875
R4	8/8 = 1.000	4/7 ≈ 0.571	6/7 ≈ 0.857	7/7 = 1.000	8/8 = 1.000
R5	6/8 = 0.75	4/7 ≈ 0.571	5/7 ≈ 0.714	6/7 ≈ 0.857	7/8 = 0.875

TABLE 58.4 Weighted normalized decision matrix.

Alt	C_1	C_2	C_3	C_4	C_5
R1	0.173	0.170	0.129	0.171	0.110
R2	0.201	0.113	0.180	0.143	0.220
R3	0.115	0.113	0.180	0.171	0.193
R4	0.230	0.097	0.154	0.200	0.220
R5	0.173	0.097	0.129	0.171	0.193

TABLE 58.5 Euclidean and taxicab distances.

Robot	E_i	T_i
R1	0.0973	0.159
R2	0.1495	0.263
R3	0.1027	0.178
R4	0.1707	0.307
R5	0.1051	0.169

TABLE 58.6 The final ranking.

Robot	H_i	Ranking
R1	0.0145	4
R2	0.0878	2
R3	0.0110	5
R4	0.1374	1
R5	0.0161	3

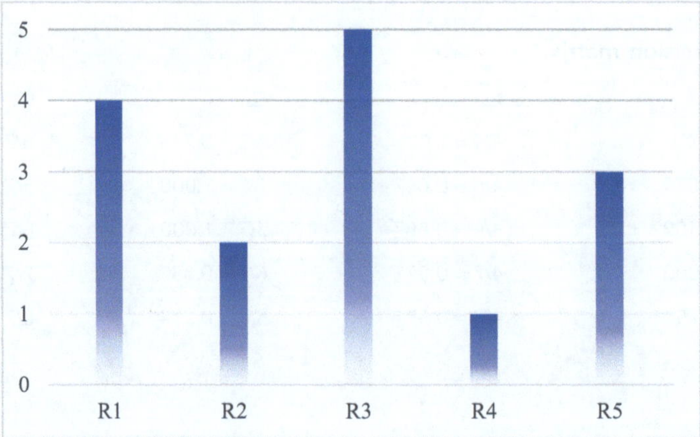

FIGURE 58.1 Ranking of robots.

TABLE 58.7 The alternatives.

No.	Brand name	Country of origin	Symbol
1	Tesla	United States	A1
2	BYD	China	A2
3	Nissan	Japan	A3
4	BMW	Germany	A4
5	Hyundai	South Korea	A5
6	Kia	South Korea	A6
7	Volkswagen (VW)	Germany	A7
8	Lucid Motors	United States	A8
9	Rivian	United States	A9
10	Mercedes-Benz EQ	Germany	A10
11	Audi e-tron	Germany	A11
12	Polestar	Sweden/China	A12
13	Chevrolet (GM)	United States	A13

58.5 Numerical example 2: Evaluating electric vehicles for a corporate fleet

This section explores a more intricate case study to assess the applicability of the CODAS method. The scenario focuses on a large multinational corporation planning to replace its current vehicle fleet with electric vehicles (EVs) to advance its goals of lowering carbon emissions and enhancing environmental sustainability. To facilitate this shift, a team of three principal decision-makers—the Chief Financial Officer, Chief Operations Officer, and Sustainability Manager—works together to evaluate and prioritize various EV alternatives (Table 58.7).

The evaluation process is based on eight criteria: efficiency (C_1), purchase price (C_2), safety (C_3), driving range (C_4), maintenance cost (C_5), charging infrastructure (C_6), environmental impact (C_7), and brand reputation (C_8). These criteria are used to compare several EV models, which are listed in Table 58.8. In the first step of the CODAS method, a decision matrix is constructed using Eq. 58.1. Since three decision-makers are involved, their evaluations are averaged to create an aggregated decision matrix, as presented in Table 58.9. In this matrix, the columns represent the evaluation criteria, while the rows correspond to the EV alternatives under consideration.

In the following step, the combined decision matrix is normalized using (58.2), as shown in Table 58.10. Normalization transforms all criteria values onto a uniform scale, allowing comparison across different units or magnitudes. After completing normalization, each value is multiplied by its respective criterion weight to produce the weighted decision matrix. This weighted matrix is displayed in Table 58.11.

TABLE 58.8 Weights and classification of evaluation criteria.

Criterion (C)	Symbol	Weight	Type
Efficiency	C_1	0.18	Benefit
Purchase price	C_2	0.15	Cost
Safety	C_3	0.14	Benefit
Driving range	C_4	0.16	Benefit
Maintenance cost	C_5	0.10	Cost
Charging infrastructure	C_6	0.08	Benefit
Environmental impact	C_7	0.10	Benefit
Brand reputation	C_8	0.09	Benefit

TABLE 58.9 The aggregated decision matrix.

Alternative	C_1	C_2	C_3	C_4	C_5	C_6	C_7	C_8
A1	9.0	6.33	9.0	9.67	6.33	9.67	9.0	10.0
A2	8.0	8.67	7.33	7.0	5.67	7.0	8.67	7.67
A3	7.0	6.33	7.0	7.0	7.0	7.0	7.0	8.0
A4	9.0	4.0	9.0	7.0	8.0	6.33	7.0	9.0
A5	8.0	6.67	8.0	7.0	6.33	7.0	9.0	8.33
A6	7.0	6.33	8.0	7.0	6.0	7.0	9.0	7.33
A7	7.0	6.67	8.0	7.0	7.0	7.0	7.0	9.0
A8	9.0	3.0	9.0	10.0	8.0	5.0	9.0	8.0
A9	7.0	4.0	9.0	9.0	7.0	5.67	9.0	8.0
A10	9.0	4.33	9.0	7.0	8.0	7.0	9.0	10.0
A11	9.0	4.33	9.0	7.0	8.0	7.0	9.0	10.0
A12	8.0	6.0	7.0	7.0	7.0	7.0	9.0	8.0
A13	7.0	6.67	7.0	7.0	7.0	7.0	7.0	7.0

TABLE 58.10 The normalized decision matrix.

Alt	C1	C2	C3	C4	C5	C6	C7	C8
A1	9.0/9 = 1.00	3.0/6.33 = 0.47	9.0/9 = 1.00	9.67/10 = 0.97	5.0/6.33 = 0.79	9.67/9.67 = 1.00	9.0/9 = 1.00	10/10 = 1.00
A2	8.0/9 = 0.89	3.0/8.67 = 0.35	7.33/9 = 0.81	7.0/10 = 0.70	5.0/5.67 = 0.88	7.0/9.67 = 0.72	8.67/9 = 0.96	7.67/10 = 0.77
A3	7.0/9 = 0.78	3.0/6.33 = 0.47	7.0/9 = 0.78	7.0/10 = 0.70	5.0/7.0 = 0.71	7.0/9.67 = 0.72	7.0/9 = 0.78	8.0/10 = 0.80
A4	9.0/9 = 1.00	3.0/4.0 = 0.75	9.0/9 = 1.00	7.0/10 = 0.70	5.0/8.0 = 0.63	6.33/9.67 = 0.65	7.0/9 = 0.78	9.0/10 = 0.90
A5	8.0/9 = 0.89	3.0/6.67 = 0.45	8.0/9 = 0.89	7.0/10 = 0.70	5.0/6.33 = 0.79	7.0/9.67 = 0.72	9.0/9 = 1.00	8.33/10 = 0.83
A6	7.0/9 = 0.78	3.0/6.33 = 0.47	8.0/9 = 0.89	7.0/10 = 0.70	5.0/6.0 = 0.83	7.0/9.67 = 0.72	9.0/9 = 1.00	7.33/10 = 0.73
A7	7.0/9 = 0.78	3.0/6.67 = 0.45	8.0/9 = 0.89	7.0/10 = 0.70	5.0/7.0 = 0.71	7.0/9.67 = 0.72	7.0/9 = 0.78	9.0/10 = 0.90
A8	9.0/9 = 1.00	3.0/3.0 = 1.00	9.0/9 = 1.00	10/10 = 1.00	5.0/8.0 = 0.63	5.0/9.67 = 0.52	9.0/9 = 1.00	8.0/10 = 0.80
A9	7.0/9 = 0.78	3.0/4.0 = 0.75	9.0/9 = 1.00	9.0/10 = 0.90	5.0/7.0 = 0.71	5.67/9.67 = 0.59	9.0/9 = 1.00	8.0/10 = 0.80
A10	9.0/9 = 1.00	3.0/4.33 = 0.69	9.0/9 = 1.00	7.0/10 = 0.70	5.0/8.0 = 0.63	7.0/9.67 = 0.72	9.0/9 = 1.00	10/10 = 1.00
A11	9.0/9 = 1.00	3.0/4.33 = 0.69	9.0/9 = 1.00	7.0/10 = 0.70	5.0/8.0 = 0.63	7.0/9.67 = 0.72	9.0/9 = 1.00	10/10 = 1.00
A12	8.0/9 = 0.89	3.0/6.0 = 0.50	7.0/9 = 0.78	7.0/10 = 0.70	5.0/7.0 = 0.71	7.0/9.67 = 0.72	9.0/9 = 1.00	8.0/10 = 0.80
A13	7.0/9 = 0.78	3.0/6.67 = 0.45	7.0/9 = 0.78	7.0/10 = 0.70	5.0/7.0 = 0.71	7.0/9.67 = 0.72	7.0/9 = 0.78	7.0/10 = 0.70

TABLE 58.11 The normalized weighted decision matrix.

Alt	C1	C2	C3	C4	C5	C6	C7	C8
A1	0.1800	0.0705	0.1400	0.1552	0.0790	0.0800	0.1000	0.0900
A2	0.1602	0.0525	0.1134	0.1120	0.0880	0.0576	0.0960	0.0693
A3	0.1404	0.0705	0.1092	0.1120	0.0710	0.0576	0.0780	0.0720
A4	0.1800	0.1125	0.1400	0.1120	0.0630	0.0528	0.0780	0.0810
A5	0.1602	0.0675	0.1246	0.1120	0.0790	0.0576	0.1000	0.0749
A6	0.1404	0.0705	0.1246	0.1120	0.0830	0.0576	0.1000	0.0659
A7	0.1404	0.0675	0.1246	0.1120	0.0710	0.0576	0.0780	0.0810
A8	0.1800	0.1500	0.1400	0.1600	0.0630	0.0416	0.1000	0.0720
A9	0.1404	0.1125	0.1400	0.1440	0.0710	0.0472	0.1000	0.0720
A10	0.1800	0.1035	0.1400	0.1120	0.0630	0.0576	0.1000	0.0900
A11	0.1800	0.1035	0.1400	0.1120	0.0630	0.0576	0.1000	0.0900
A12	0.1602	0.0750	0.1092	0.1120	0.0710	0.0576	0.1000	0.0720
A13	0.1404	0.0675	0.1092	0.1120	0.0710	0.0576	0.0780	0.0630

TABLE 58.12 The final ranking.

Alt	E_i	T_i	H_i	Ranking
A1	0.080	0.093	0.1055	6
A2	0.143	0.167	0.0452	10
A3	0.169	0.202	0.1010	8
A4	0.167	0.190	0.1408	5
A5	0.129	0.155	1.0574	1
A6	0.157	0.183	0.5294	2
A7	0.168	0.197	0.0000	12
A8	0.245	0.288	0.0000	12
A9	0.197	0.238	0.2713	4
A10	0.111	0.131	0.4018	3
A11	0.111	0.131	0.1055	6
A12	0.172	0.211	0.0452	10
A13	0.188	0.224	0.1010	8

Subsequently, two distance measures are computed for each alternative to reflect how far each option is from the ideal solution. These are the Euclidean distance (based on Eq. 58.3) and the taxicab distance (based on Eq. 58.4). Using these distances, the H_i is calculated for each vehicle. The H_i value represents the relative performance of each option, combining information from both distance measures.

To increase the sensitivity of the CODAS method and better differentiate between alternatives, we set the threshold parameter $\Psi = 0.8$. This parameter plays a key role in combining the Euclidean and taxicab distances when calculating the final comparative score H_{ik} for each alternative against the others. The sum of all H_{ik} values were used to rank each alternative using (58.6). The higher the sum, the better the overall performance of the vehicle across all criteria (Table 58.12).

Based on table 2, alternative A5 achieved the highest performance score and ranked first, indicating it consistently outperformed other options in both Euclidean and taxicab distances. This was followed by A6 and A10, showing strong all-around performance. Alternatives A7 and A8 received scores of zero, meaning they did not outperform any other alternatives significantly in the comparison. These findings demonstrate the CODAS method's capability to effectively assist in complex MCDM tasks, particularly in the context of adopting sustainable technologies.

58.6 Conclusion

In this chapter, we provide a thorough overview of the CODAS method, a MCDM technique used for ranking alternatives. The method has found extensive application across numerous disciplines. The chapter starts with an introduction to the CODAS approach, followed by a review of relevant studies that have implemented it. A detailed explanation of the method is then offered. To illustrate its practical use and versatility, two case studies are included, showcasing both the strengths and limitations of CODAS. Overall, this chapter aims to deliver a comprehensive understanding of the CODAS method and highlight its capability to solve complex and challenging decision-making problems in various fields.

References

Amusan, O. T., Nwulu, N. I., & Gbadamosi, S. L. (2024). Multi-criteria decision-based hybrid energy selection system using CRITIC weighted CODAS approach. *Scientific African, 26*, e02372. https://doi.org/10.1016/j.sciaf.2024.e02372.

Andukuri, R., & Rao, C. M. (2024). Application of fuzzy CODAS for the optimal selection of condition monitoring equipment in industrial rotating machinery. *Operations Research Forum, 5*(4), 88. https://doi.org/10.1007/s43069-024-00376-y.

Ashofteh, P. S., & Dougaheh, M. P. (2024). Ranking the optimal combination of low-impact urban development systems under climate change with the TODIM multi-criteria decision-making method. *Journal of Cleaner Production, 434*, 140108.

Ashofteh, P.-S., Far, S. M., & Golfam, P. (2023). Application of multi-criteria decision-making of CODAS and SWARA in reservoir optimal operation using marine predator algorithm based on game theory. *Water Resources Management, 37*(11), 4385–4412. https://doi.org/10.1007/s11269-023-03560-7.

Baydas, M., Yilmaz, M., Jovic, Z., Stevic, Z., Özuyar, S. E. G., & Özçil, A. (2024). A comprehensive MCDM assessment for economic data: Success analysis of maximum normalization, CODAS, and fuzzy approaches. *Financial Innovation, 10*(1), 105–129. https://doi.org/10.1186/s40854-023-00588-x.

Biswas, S., Pamucar, D., Kar, S., & Sana, S. S. (2021). A new integrated FUCOM–CODAS framework with fermatean fuzzy information for multi-criteria group decision-making. *Symmetry (Basel), 13*(12), 2430. https://doi.org/10.3390/sym13122430.

Deveci, K., Cin, R., & Kağızman, A. (2020). A modified interval valued intuitionistic fuzzy CODAS method and its application to multi-criteria selection among renewable energy alternatives in Turkey. *Applied Soft Computing, 96*, 106660. https://doi.org/10.1016/j.asoc.2020.106660.

Farid, H. M. A., Bouye, M., Riaz, M., & Jamil, N. (2023). Fermatean fuzzy CODAS approach with topology and its application to sustainable supplier selection. *Symmetry (Basel), 15*(2), 433. https://doi.org/10.3390/sym15020433.

Farnam, M., Shirdel, G. H., & Darehmiraki, M. (2024). An integrated CODAS method and novel surface-based weighted distance measures under neutrosophic environment. *Neutrosophic Sets and Systems, 68*, 198. https://doi.org/10.5281/zenodo.11479254.

Garg, H., Olgun, M., Ünver, M., & Türkarslan, E. (2023). An extension of CODAS method for multi-criteria group decision making with complex intuitionistic fuzzy information via Dombi sine weighted arithmetic aggregation operators. *Granular Computing (Internet), 8*(6), 1467–1480. https://doi.org/10.1007/s41066-023-00383-0.

Ghorabaee, M. K., Amiri, M., Zavadskas, E. K., Hooshmand, R., & Antuchevičienė, J. (2017). Fuzzy extension of the CODAS method for multi-criteria market segment evaluation. *Journal of Business Economics and Management, 18*(1), 1–19.

Gupta, K., Roy, S., Poonia, R. C., Kumar, R., Nayak, S. R., Altameem, A., & Saudagar, A. K. J. (2022). Multi-criteria usability evaluation of mhealth applications on type 2 diabetes mellitus using two hybrid MCDM models: CODAS-FAHP and MOORA-FAHP. *Applied Sciences, 12*(9), 4156. https://doi.org/10.3390/app12094156.

Haseli, G., Ranjbarzadeh, R., Hajiaghaei-Keshteli, M., Jafarzadeh Ghoushchi, S., Hasani, A., Deveci, M., & Ding, W. (2023). HECON: Weight assessment of the product loyalty criteria considering the customer decision's halo effect using the convolutional neural networks. *Information Sciences, 623*, 184–205. https://doi.org/10.1016/j.ins.2022.12.027.

Haseli, G., Sheikh, R., & Sana, S. S. (2020). Base-criterion on multi-criteria decision-making method and its applications. *International Journal of Management Science and Engineering Management, 15*(2), 79–88. https://doi.org/10.1080/17509653.2019.1633964.

Haseli, G., Torkayesh, A. E., Hajiaghaei-Keshteli, M., & Venghaus, S. (2023). Sustainable resilient recycling partner selection for urban waste management: Consolidating perspectives of decision-makers and experts. *Applied Soft Computing, 137*, 110120. https://doi.org/10.1016/j.asoc.2023.110120.

Haseli, G., Yaran Ögel, İ., Ecer, F., & Hajiaghaei-Keshteli, M. (2023). Luxury in female technology (FemTech): Selection of smart jewelry for women through BCM-MARCOS group decision-making framework with fuzzy ZE-numbers. *Technological Forecasting & Social Change, 196*, 122870. https://doi.org/10.1016/j.techfore.2023.122870.

Haseli, G., Yazdani, M., Shaayesteh, M. T., & Hajiaghaei-Keshteli, M. (2025). Logistic hub location problem under fuzzy Extended Z-numbers to consider the uncertainty and reliable group decision-making. *Applied Soft Computing, 171*, 112751. https://doi.org/10.1016/j.asoc.2025.112751.

Ijadi Maghsoodi, A., Rasoulipanah, H., Martínez López, L., Liao, H., & Zavadskas, E. K. (2020). Integrating interval-valued multi-granular 2-tuple linguistic BWM-CODAS approach with target-based attributes: Site selection for a construction project. *Computers & Industrial Engineering, 139*, 106147. https://doi.org/10.1016/j.cie.2019.106147.

Jafarzadeh Ghoushchi, S., Garg, H., Rahnamay Bonab, S., & Rahimi, A. (2023). An integrated SWARA-CODAS decision-making algorithm with spherical fuzzy information for clean energy barriers evaluation. *Expert Systems with Applications, 223*, 119884. https://doi.org/10.1016/j.eswa.2023.119884.

Kavitha, S., Satheeshkumar, J., & Amudha, T. (2024). Multi-label feature selection using q-rung orthopair hesitant fuzzy MCDM approach extended to CODAS. *Mathematics and Computers in Simulation, 222*, 148–173. https://doi.org/10.1016/j.matcom.2023.07.032.

Keshavarz Ghorabaee, M., Amiri, M., Zavadskas, E. K., Hooshmand, R., & Antuchevičienė, J. (2017). Fuzzy extension of the CODAS method for multi-criteria market segment evaluation. *Journal of Business Economics and Management, 18*(1), 1–19. https://doi.org/10.3846/16111699.2016.1278559.

Keshavarz Ghorabaee, M., Zavadskas, E.K., Turskis, Z., & Antuchevičienė, J. (2016). A new combinative distance-based assessment (CODAS) method for multi-criteria decision-making.

Kumari, A., & Acherjee, B. (2022). Selection of non-conventional machining process using CRITIC-CODAS method. *Materials Today: Proceedings, 56*, 66–71. https://doi.org/10.1016/j.matpr.2021.12.152.

Mahmudah, R. S., Putri, D. I., Abdullah, A. G., Shafii, M. A., Hakim, D. L., & Setiadipura, T. (2024). Developing a multi-criteria decision-making model for nuclear power plant location selection using fuzzy analytic hierarchy process and fuzzy VIKOR methods focused on socio-economic factors. *Cleaner Engineering and Technology, 19*, 100737.

Mitra, A. (2024). Combinative distance-based assessment (CODAS) approach of multi-criteria decision-making for grading of Tossa jute fibres. *Research Journal of Textile and Apparel, 28*(3), 458–477. https://doi.org/10.1108/RJTA-05-2022-0054.

Moslem, S., Gündoğdu, F. K., Saylam, S., & Pilla, F. (2024). A hybrid decomposed fuzzy multi-criteria decision-making model for optimizing parcel lockers location in the last-mile delivery landscape. *Applied Soft Computing, 154*, 111321.

Ning, B., Lei, F., & Wei, G. (2022). CODAS method for multi-attribute decision-making based on some novel distance and entropy measures under probabilistic dual hesitant fuzzy sets. *International Journal of Fuzzy Systems, 24*(8), 3626–3649. https://doi.org/10.1007/s40815-022-01350-8.

Peng, X., & Ma, X. (2020). Pythagorean fuzzy multi-criteria decision making method based on CODAS with new score function. *Journal of Intelligent & Fuzzy Systems, 38*(3), 3307–3318. https://doi.org/10.3233/JIFS-190043.

Simic, V., Karagoz, S., Deveci, M., & Aydin, N. (2021). Picture fuzzy extension of the CODAS method for multi-criteria vehicle shredding facility location. *Expert Systems with Applications, 175*, 114644. https://doi.org/10.1016/j.eswa.2021.114644.

Wątróbski, J., Bączkiewicz, A., Król, R., & Sałabun, W. (2022). Green electricity generation assessment using the CODAS-COMET method. *Ecological Indicators, 143*, 109391. https://doi.org/10.1016/j.ecolind.2022.109391.

Yeni, F. B., & Özçelik, G. (2019). Interval-valued atanassov intuitionistic fuzzy CODAS method for multi criteria group decision making problems. *Group Decision and Negotiation, 28*(2), 433–452. https://doi.org/10.1007/s10726-018-9603-9.

Chapter 59

MAIRCA: Multi-attributive ideal-real comparative analysis for multi-attribute decision-making

Amir Hossein Nobil
School of Engineering and Sciences, Tecnolo gico de Monterrey, Mexico

59.1 Introduction

Most of the decision problems in all scientific fields involve multiple criteria and alternatives. This means that to reach a reliable decision, a set of criteria and measurable alternatives should be evaluated (Haseli, Ranjbarzadeh, et al., 2023). In this way, at first, all criteria are assessed to determine the impact of each criterion. Then, all alternatives are evaluated based on the impact of the criteria on each alternative. In this regard, the criteria have a different impact during the alternatives assessments. Some of the criteria express benefits to be maximized (e.g., performance), while others represent cost attributes to be minimized (e.g., expense) (Ecer & Pamucar, 2022; Haseli, Yaran Ögel, et al., 2023). To bring different criteria into a normal form, the multi-attribute decision-making (MADM) procedures use a normalization approach. Therefore, normalization rescales the criterion values so that they become comparable. Additionally, a frequent elicitation tool for comparison is the pairwise comparison. Using this approach, decision-makers express relative preference between two criteria at a time (Haseli, Torkayesh, et al., 2023; Pamučar et al., 2021). This creates a transparent record of judgment that can be converted into numerical weights. These core concepts, alternatives, criteria, benefit-cost direction, normalization, weights, and pairwise judgments form the lingua franca of the MADM analysis.

Multiattributive ideal-real comparative analysis (MAIRCA) is introduced by Pamučar et al. (2014) and occupies a distinctive niche within the MADM methods. In MAIRCA, the reference against which alternatives are evaluated is not an arbitrary external target but a constructed theoretical rating matrix (Ul Haq et al., 2023). Theoretical ratings tp_{ij} are formed by distributing an initial preference mass PA_i across criteria according to criterion weights w_j. By scaling tpij with the normalized observations. The elementwise gap $g_{ij} = tp_{ij} - tr_{ij}$ quantifies the shortfall of alternative i on criterion j, and the aggregate gap provides a single score for ranking alternatives (Pamucar et al., 2022). Smaller Q_i indicates an alternative closer to the theoretical allocation and is therefore preferred. Historically, MAIRCA emerged as a pragmatic response to two common needs in applied decision contexts. First, decision-makers frequently want a single, easily communicable score that expresses how far an option is from meeting a set of prioritized objectives. Second, many problems combine heterogeneous data types and mixed scales, requiring a robust procedure for normalization and aggregation (Chatterjee et al., 2018). MAIRCA satisfies both requirements while preserving clarity about the role of weights and whether criteria are framed as desirable or undesirable. Practically, analysts supply a decision matrix of observed performances, a specification of criterion directions (benefit or cost), and a weight vector. Alternatives with the smallest weighted gap are preferred because they are closest to the ideal in the sense defined by the decision context.

MAIRCA's methodological profile contrasts with several familiar MADM paradigms. Where outranking methods emphasize pairwise dominance relations and thresholds, and methods such as technique for Order preference by similarity to ideal solution compute relative closeness to a positive and negative ideal using Euclidean geometry. MAIRCA centers on the comparative shortfall and its policy interpretation. The numeric output is immediately actionable as an estimate of the improvement required to attain a chosen standard (Pamučar et al., 2017). This feature

Encyclopedia of Multi-Attribute Decision-Making (MADM). DOI: https://doi.org/10.1016/B978-0-443-33275-3.00066-X

makes MAIRCA well-suited to allocation and prioritization tasks in which limited resources must be directed toward closing the most consequential gaps. At the same time, MAIRCA is intentionally transparent and modular. It means that choices about normalization, the construction of the ideal, and weight elicitation are explicit parts of the workflow and, therefore, subject to scrutiny and sensitivity analysis. Subsequently, the MAIRCA strengths are balanced by important caveats. Moreover, MAIRCA does not, by itself, model interactions among criteria. If criteria are causally linked or exhibit feedback, complementary techniques may be necessary to capture system dynamics that a purely comparative metric will miss.

This chapter aims to present MAIRCA in a way that is both rigorous and accessible. After this introduction, the chapter will outline the literature review and methodology steps in detail. Then, two numerical examples are provided in Sections 59.4, 59.5 to illustrate computational nuances and discuss extensions and practical considerations for implementation. Conclusions and the method's role within a broader MADM toolkit are explained in Section 59.6.

59.2 Literature review

Table 59.1 collates twenty representative MAIRCA studies, organized to make their contributions and differences easy to scan. Entries report each paper's authors and year, the methodological variant deployed (crisp, fuzzy, intuitionistic fuzzy, probabilistic, hybrid, etc.), the application domain, and the principal technical contribution. Together, these works illustrate two clear trends: researchers frequently extend MAIRCA to handle uncertainty and to combine its gap-oriented logic with complementary methods for weighting or interaction analysis.

59.3 Methodology

This section presents a clear stepwise formulation of the MAIRCA procedure together with the algebraic relations needed. Therefore, notions are introduced first, and then the algorithmic steps are given with the corresponding formulas. In this regard, m alternatives ($i = 1,2, \ldots, m$) and n criteria ($j = 1,2, \ldots, n$) are identified for each decision problem to solve based on the framework of the MAIRCA. Therefore, the decision (performance) matrix is $X = [x_{ij}]_{m \times n}$, where x_{ij} is the observed performance of alternative A on criterion C_j. Weight vector $w = (w_1, w_2, \ldots, w_n)$ with $w_j \geq 0$ and $\Sigma_{j=1}^{n} w_j = 1$. Direction indicators $d_j \in$ {benefit, cost} for each criterion. Initial preference vector (prior) for alternatives $PA = (PA_1, \ldots, PA_m)$ with $PA_i \geq 0$ and typically $\Sigma_i^m PA_i = 1$. A common default is $PA_i = 1/m$ for all i. Therefore, all subsequent matrices are expressed in terms of these inputs. In this way, the steps of the MAIRCA to solve decision problems are as follows:

Step 1. Construct the theoretical (expected) rating matrix T_p.

MAIRCA begins by distributing the overall alternative prior across criteria according to criterion weights. Define the theoretical rating matrix $Tp = [tp_{ij}]$ by the following:

$$tp_{ij} = PA_i .\ w_j \tag{59.1}$$

Each row i of T_p sums to PA_i; each column j sums to w_j. Intuitively, tp_{ij} is the share of the decision mass that alternative i would receive on criterion j under the prior.

Step 2. Normalize the observed decision matrix to obtain relative performances.

Transform raw scores x_{ij} into dimensionless relative performances $r_{ij} \in [0,1]$ so different measurement units become comparable. Use min–max normalization with direction awareness.

$$r_{ij} \begin{cases} \dfrac{x_{ij} - \min_i x_{ij}}{\max_i x_{ij} - \min_i x_{ij}}, & \text{if } d_j = benefit \\ \dfrac{\max_i x_{ij} - x_{ij}}{\max_i x_{ij} - \min_i x_{ij}}, & \text{if } d_j = benefit \end{cases} \tag{59.2}$$

If $\max_i x_{ij} = \min_i x_{ij}$ (no variation on criterion j), set $r_{ij} = 1$ for all i if that criterion should be neutralized, or set $r_{ij} = 0.5$ and document the choice; be explicit about the convention used.

Step 3. Build the real rating matrix Tr.

Translate normalized performances into the realized distribution of the prior mass across criteria. The standard MAIRCA formulation uses elementwise multiplication of the theoretical matrix by the normalized performance.

$$tr_{ij} = tp_{ij} .\ r_{ij} \tag{59.3}$$

Thus, tr_{ij} represents the realized (actual) portion of alternative i on criterion j relative to the theoretical allocation tp_{ij}.

TABLE 59.1 Studies that have used or expanded on the multiattributive ideal-real comparative analysis method.

Study	Combined methods	Uncertainty	Application
Gigović et al. (2016)	DEMATEL and ANP	-	Ammunition depots sites selection
Pamučar et al.(2017)	DEMATEL and ANP	Interval rough number	Proposing novel approach
Badi and Ballem (2018)	BWMO	Rough number	Pharmaceutical supplying in Libya
Chatterjee et al. (2018)	DEMATEL and ANP	Rough number	Green supply chain
Can and Kıran (2019)	-	-	Health and safety performance evaluation
Boral et al. (2020)	AHP	Fuzzy sets	Failure modes and effects analysis
García Mestanza and Bakhat (2021)	AHP	-	Overtourism assessment in Malaga
Hadian et al. (2022)	-	-	Flood susceptibility evaluation
Ecer (2022)	-	Intuitionistic fuzzy sets	Coronavirus vaccine selection
Pamucar et al. (2022)	FUCOM	-	Serbian railways infrastructure projects
Riahi et al. (2022)	CoCoSo	-	Prospectivity mapping of porphyry Cu
Ul Haq et al. (2023)	-	Interval-valued neutrosophic	Sustainable material selection
Srivastava et al. (2023)	MOORA	-	India's water supply utilities
Qahtan et al. (2023)	-	Fermatean probabilistic hesitant-fuzzy sets	Agriculture-food 4.0 supply chain
Yontar (2023)	ANP	-	Agri-food supply chain
Ozdemir et al. (2023)	MEREC	-	Green deal performance
Abbas et al. (2024)	-	q-rung orthopair fuzzy 2-tuple	Assessing of the lecturers' research capabilitie
Wang et al. (2025)	Entropy	-	Agricultural development
Chen (2025a)	-	Circular intuitionistic fuzzy	Cloud services
Negi et al. (2025)	CRITIC	-	Solar distillation systems
Zorlu et al. (2025)	LBWA	Spherical fuzzy sets	Measuring degradation risk levels
Chen (2025b)	MEREC	T-Spherical fuzzy sets	Urban agriculture
Yang and Liang (2025)	TODIM	Hesitant fuzzy	Social trust networks

Step 4. Compute the gap matrix G.

Measure shortfalls by the elementwise difference between theoretical and realized ratings.

$$g_{ij} = tp_{ij} - tr_{ij} = tp_{ij}(1 - r_{ij}) \tag{59.4}$$

By construction $g_{ij} \geq 0$ when $0 \leq r_{ij} \leq 1$, and it quantifies how much of the expected share of alternative i on criterion j is not realized.

Step 5. Aggregate gaps to obtain alternative scores.

Aggregate each alternative's gaps across criteria to produce a single comparative gap score.

$$Q_i = \sum_{j=1}^{n} g_{ij} = \sum_{j=1}^{n} tp_{ij}(1 - r_{ij}) \tag{59.5}$$

Since $\sum tp_{ij} = PA_i$, typical bounds are $0 \leq Q_i \leq PA_i$. When PA_i are normalized to sum to unity, the Q_i are directly comparable across alternatives. Alternatives are ranked by ascending Q_i. The smaller Q_i indicates a smaller overall shortfall from the theoretical ratings and therefore a better alternative. Optionally define a performance index for easier interpretation as follows:

$$S_i = PA_i - Q_i = \sum_{j=1}^{n} tr_{ij} \tag{59.6}$$

or a normalized closeness score

$$\widetilde{S_i} = \frac{S_i}{\sum_{k=1}^{m} S_k} \tag{59.7}$$

if a probabilistic-like normalization is desirable.

Step 6. Post-processing and decision rules

- Ranking: rank by Q_i (ascending) or by $Si/\widetilde{S_i}$ (descending).
- Ties: break ties using secondary indicators such as (a) the largest single tr_{ij} value, (b) the alternative with superior performance on the highest-weight criterion, or (c) sensitivity analysis outcomes.
- Reporting: present T_p, $R = [r_{ij}]$, Tr, G, and $\{Q_i\}$ so readers can trace how the gap scores arise.

59.4 Numerical example 1

The first numerical example is a simple decision problem on selecting the best location for a new logistics center. Four candidate sites are under consideration. Additionally, the evaluation is based on five criteria. The set of criteria is proximity to major highways (C1), land cost (C2), accessibility to ports/rail terminals (C3), availability of skilled labor (C4), and environmental restrictions (C5). In this way, the C1, C3, and C4 are benefit criteria. Furthermore, the C2 and C5 are the cost criteria. All criteria are considered to select the best location for a new logistics center from the four alternatives A1, A2, A3, and A4. In this regard, according to the first step of the MAIRCA, the theoretical (expected) rating matrix T_p is created based on the decision-maker's judgment. The result for the theoretical (expected) rating matrix T_p is provided in Table 59.2.

All presented values in Table 59.3 are based on the nature of each criterion. In this regard, the C1 and C3 indices are measured in kilometers (km), C2 in USD, C4 in %, and C5 in zones. After conducting the T_p matrix, all elements of the T_p matrix should be normalized based on step 2. The results for the normalized matrix and weight of the criteria are presented in Table 59.3. In this numerical example, the weights of the criteria are considered as [0.25, 0.2, 0.20, 0.20, 0.15]. However, for other decision problems, it can use other criteria weighting methods to find the weight of each criterion. In this regard, some new weighting methods such as the base-criterion method (Haseli & Sheikh, 2022; Haseli et al., 2020), logarithm methodology of additive weights (Pamučar et al., 2021), and logarithmic percentage change-driven objective weighting (Ecer & Pamucar, 2022).

The result of the normalized matrix is used to calculate the real rating matrix Tr. According to Eq. (59.3) in step 3, the real rating matrix Tr values are calculated. For example, the value of A1 in C1 is ((0.25*0.25)*(0.6579)) = 0.0411. All calculated results for the real rating matrix are presented in Table 59.4.

TABLE 59.2 Theoretical (expected) rating matrix T_p.

	C1	C2	C3	C4	C5
A1	2.5	1200000	18	22	1
A2	5	900000	25	28	0
A3	1.2	1500000	12	18	2
A4	3.8	1100000	20	30	0

TABLE 59.3 Normalized matrix and weights of the criteria.

Alt.	C1	C2	C3	C4	C5
w_j	0.25	0.2	0.2	0.2	0.15
A1	0.6579	0.5000	0.5385	0.3333	0.5000
A2	0.0000	1.0000	0.0000	0.8333	1.0000
A3	1.0000	0.0000	1.0000	0.0000	0.0000
A4	0.3158	0.6667	0.3846	1.0000	1.0000

TABLE 59.4 Real rating matrix Tr.

Alt.	C1	C2	C3	C4	C5	S
A1	0.0411	0.0250	0.0269	0.0167	0.0187	0.1285
A2	0.0000	0.0500	0.0000	0.0417	0.0375	0.1292
A3	0.0625	0.0000	0.0500	0.0000	0.0000	0.1125
A4	0.0197	0.0333	0.0192	0.0500	0.0375	0.1598

According to the mentioned steps for the MAIRCA, the gap matrix G, and aggregate gaps should be calculated to find the score of each alternative. The calculated results for each alternative are presented in Table 59.5.

Based on the calculated final result for each alternative, the lowest value is considered the first rank. Therefore, the priority of the alternatives' ranks is A4, A2, A1, and A3.

59.5 Numerical example 2

The second numerical example is a transportation site selection problem. To solve this problem, eight sites are considered. To evaluate each site, seven criteria were identified. The identified criteria are distance to nearest major highway (C1), land acquisition cost (C2), travel time to main distribution hub (C3), share of area with multimodal facilities (C4), skilled labor availability (C5), annual accident incidents per 10,000 shipments (C6), and environmental sensitivity index (C7). In this way, the C1, C2, C3, C6, and C7 are cost criteria. Furthermore, the C4 and C5 are the benefit criteria. All criteria are considered to select the best transportation site among the eight alternatives. In this regard, according to the first step of the MAIRCA, the theoretical (expected) rating matrix T_p is created based on the decision-maker's judgment. The result for the theoretical (expected) rating matrix T_p is provided in Table 59.6.

All presented values in Table 59.6 are based on the nature of each criterion. In this regard, the C1 index is measured in km, C2 in USD, C3 in time, C4 and C5 in %, C6 in number per 10,000, and C7 in environmental sensitivity index.

After conducting the T_p matrix, all elements of the T_p matrix should be normalized based on step 2. The results for the normalized matrix and weight of the criteria are presented in Table 59.7. In this numerical example, the weights of the criteria are considered as [0.18, 0.17, 0.15, 0.15, 0.15, 0.10, 0.10]. However, as mentioned in the first numerical example, it can use other criteria weighting methods to find the weight of each criterion.

The result of the normalized matrix is used to calculate the real rating matrix Tr. According to Eq. (59.3) in step 3, the real rating matrix Tr values are calculated. For example, the value of A1 in C1 is $((0.125*0.18)*(0.9565) = 0.0411$. All calculated results for the real rating matrix are presented in Table 59.8.

According to the mentioned steps for the MAIRCA, the gap matrix G, and aggregate gaps should be calculated to find the score of each alternative. The calculated results for each alternative are presented in Table 59.9.

TABLE 59.5 Score and rank of each alternative.

Alt.	$PA_i - S_i$	Q_i	Rank
A1	0.2500–0.1285	0.1215	3
A2	0.2500–0.1292	0.1208	2
A3	0.2500–0.1125	0.1375	4
A4	0.2500–0.1598	0.0902	1

TABLE 59.6 Theoretical (expected) rating matrix T_p for the transportation site selection problem.

	C1	C2	C3	C4	C5	C6	C7
A1	1.2	45000	25	40	35	1.2	20
A2	6.5	38000	50	20	28	2.0	35
A3	3.0	55000	40	50	42	1.0	15
A4	10.0	30000	80	10	15	3.5	60
A5	0.8	60000	20	35	30	0.8	25
A6	4.2	48000	35	45	40	1.5	30
A7	2.0	70000	30	55	50	0.7	10
A8	8.0	33000	60	15	20	4.0	50

TABLE 59.7 Normalized matrix and weights of the criteria for the transportation site selection problem.

	C1	C2	C3	C4	C5	C6	C7
w_j	0.18	0.17	0.15	0.15	0.15	0.10	0.10
A1	0.9565	0.6250	0.9167	0.6667	0.5714	0.8485	0.8000
A2	0.3804	0.8000	0.5000	0.2222	0.3714	0.6061	0.5000
A3	0.7609	0.3750	0.6667	0.8889	0.7714	0.9091	0.9000
A4	0.0000	1.0000	0.0000	0.0000	0.0000	0.1515	0.0000
A5	1.0000	0.2500	1.0000	0.5556	0.4286	0.9697	0.7000
A6	0.6304	0.5500	0.7500	0.7778	0.7143	0.7576	0.6000
A7	0.8696	0.0000	0.8333	1.0000	1.0000	1.0000	1.0000
A8	0.2174	0.9250	0.3333	0.1111	0.1429	0.0000	0.2000

Based on the calculated final result for each alternative, the lowest value is considered the first rank. Therefore, the priority of the alternatives' ranks is A7, A1, A3, A5, A6, A8, and A4. To better understand the differences between the alternatives, the S_i values of each alternative are presented in Fig. 59.1.

TABLE 59.8 Real rating matrix Tr for the transportation site selection problem.

	C1	C2	C3	C4	C5	C6	C7	S
A1	0.0215	0.0133	0.0172	0.0125	0.0107	0.0106	0.0100	0.0958
A2	0.0086	0.0170	0.0094	0.0042	0.0070	0.0076	0.0063	0.0599
A3	0.0171	0.0080	0.0125	0.0167	0.0145	0.0114	0.0113	0.0913
A4	0.0000	0.2125	0.0000	0.0000	0.0000	0.0121	0.0000	0.0231
A5	0.0225	0.0053	0.0187	0.0104	0.0080	0.0121	0.0087	0.0859
A6	0.0142	0.0117	0.0141	0.0146	0.0134	0.0095	0.0075	0.0849
A7	0.0196	0.0000	0.0156	0.0187	0.0187	0.0125	0.0125	0.0977
A8	0.0049	0.0197	0.0062	0.0021	0.0027	0.0000	0.0025	0.0381

TABLE 59.9 Score and rank of each alternative for the transportation site selection problem.

Alt.	$PA_i - S_i$	Q_i	Rank
A1	0.125–0.0958	0.0292	2
A2	0.125–0.0599	0.0651	6
A3	0.125–0.0913	0.0337	3
A4	0.125–0.0213	0.1019	8
A5	0.125–0.0859	0.0391	4
A6	0.125–0.0849	0.0401	5
A7	0.125–0.0977	0.0273	1
A8	0.125–0.0381	0.0869	7

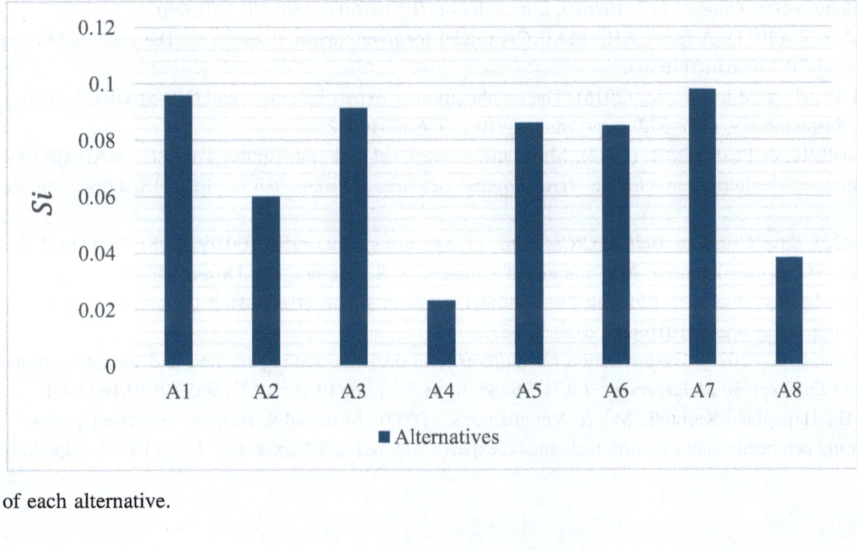

FIGURE 59.1 S_i values of each alternative.

59.6 Conclusions

The results show that the MAIRCA offers a transparent route from raw performance data to a single, easily interpretable ranking. The main advantage of the MAIRCA method is its simplicity. The MAIRCA produces gap scores that are immediately meaningful to stakeholders by separating the *Tp* from the *Tr*. In this chapter, two numerical examples illustrate how the MAIRCA is not only a ranking tool but also a diagnostic instrument for targeted improvement. Practically, MAIRCA scales well across problem sizes and data types. MAIRCA accommodates mixed units through normalization, and it produces outputs that map intuitively to managerial actions. The algebra of the MAIRCA method is linear and tractable, so MAIRCA can be implemented in spreadsheets or modest scripts.

Despite the advantages of the MAIRCA, this method has limitations that users must acknowledge. First, results are sensitive to the specification of weights and the prior preference vector PA. This means that different plausible choices can reorder rankings. Therefore, transparent weight elicitation and routine sensitivity checks are essential. Second, the min–max normalization commonly used in MAIRCA can distort comparisons when the criterion distributions are skewed or when extreme outliers are present. Another limitation of the MAIRCA method is in the modeling assumptions. MAIRCA treats criteria as independent dimensions and aggregates gaps linearly. Therefore, it does not capture causal chains among criteria.

References

Abbas, F., Ali, J., & Mashwani, W. K. (2024). Partitioned Hamy mean aggregation for multi-criteria group decision-making in the MAIRCA framework with *q*-rung orthopair fuzzy 2-tuple linguistic information. *Granular Computing, 9*(3), 62. https://doi.org/10.1007/s41066-024-00483-5.

Badi, I., & Ballem, M. (2018). Supplier Selection using Rough BWM-MAIRCA model: A case study in pharmaceutical supplying in Libya. *Decision Making: Applications in Management and Engineering, 1*(2). https://doi.org/10.31181/dmame1802016b.

Boral, S., Howard, I., Chaturvedi, S. K., McKee, K., & Naikan, V. N. A. (2020). An integrated approach for fuzzy failure modes and effects analysis using fuzzy AHP and fuzzy MAIRCA. *Engineering Failure Analysis, 108*, 104195. https://doi.org/10.1016/j.engfailanal.2019.104195.

Can, G. F., & Kıran, M. B. (2019). Occupational health and safety performance evaluation of countries based on MAIRCA. *International Journal of Intelligent Computing and Cybernetics, 13*(1), 1–24. https://doi.org/10.1108/IJICC-07-2019-0077.

Chatterjee, K., Pamucar, D., & Zavadskas, E. K. (2018). Evaluating the performance of suppliers based on using the R'AMATEL-MAIRCA method for green supply chain implementation in electronics industry. *Journal of Cleaner Production, 184*, 101–129. https://doi.org/10.1016/j.jclepro.2018.02.186.

Chen, T.-Y. (2025a). Enhanced multi-attribute ideal-real comparative analysis with the circular intuitionistic fuzzy framework: Application to hybrid cloud services. *Advanced Engineering Informatics, 65*, 103184. https://doi.org/10.1016/j.aei.2025.103184.

Chen, T.-Y. (2025b). Hybrid T-spherical fuzzy decision analytics methodology: Leveraging lance distance induction. *Engineering Applications of Artificial Intelligence, 144*, 111513. https://doi.org/10.1016/j.engappai.2025.111513.

Ecer, F. (2022). An extended MAIRCA method using intuitionistic fuzzy sets for coronavirus vaccine selection in the age of COVID-19. *Neural Computing and Applications, 34*(7), 5603–5623. https://doi.org/10.1007/s00521-021-06728-7.

Ecer, F., & Pamucar, D. (2022). A novel LOPCOW-DOBI multi-criteria sustainability performance assessment methodology: An application in developing country banking sector. *Omega, 112*, 102690. https://doi.org/10.1016/j.omega.2022.102690.

García Mestanza, J., & Bakhat, R. (2021). A fuzzy AHP-MAIRCA model for overtourism assessment: The case of Malaga Province. *Sustainability, 13*(11), 6394. https://doi.org/10.3390/su13116394.

Gigović, L., Pamučar, D., Bajić, Z., & Milićević, M. (2016). The combination of expert judgment and GIS-MAIRCA analysis for the selection of sites for ammunition depots. *Sustainability, 8*(4), 372. https://doi.org/10.3390/su8040372.

Hadian, S., Shahiri Tabarestani, E., & Pham, Q. B. (2022). Multi attributive ideal-real comparative analysis (MAIRCA) method for evaluating flood susceptibility in a temperate Mediterranean climate. *Hydrological Sciences Journal, 67*(3), 401–418. https://doi.org/10.1080/02626667.2022.2027949.

Haseli, G., & Sheikh, R. (2022). *Base Criterion Method (BCM)* (pp. 17–38). https://doi.org/10.1007/978-981-16-7414-3_2.

Haseli, G., Ranjbarzadeh, R., Hajiaghaei-Keshteli, M., Jafarzadeh Ghoushchi, S., Hasani, A., Deveci, M., & Ding, W. (2023). HECON: Weight assessment of the product loyalty criteria considering the customer decision's halo effect using the convolutional neural networks. *Information Sciences, 623*, 184–205. https://doi.org/10.1016/j.ins.2022.12.027.

Haseli, G., Sheikh, R., & Sana, S. S. (2020). Base-criterion on multi-criteria decision-making method and its applications. *International Journal of Management Science and Engineering Management, 15*(2), 79–88. https://doi.org/10.1080/17509653.2019.1633964.

Haseli, G., Torkayesh, A. E., Hajiaghaei-Keshteli, M., & Venghaus, S. (2023). Sustainable resilient recycling partner selection for urban waste management: Consolidating perspectives of decision-makers and experts. *Applied Soft Computing, 137*, 110120. https://doi.org/10.1016/j.asoc.2023.110120.

Haseli, G., Yaran Ögel, İ., Ecer, F., & Hajiaghaei-Keshteli, M. (2023). Luxury in female technology (FemTech): Selection of smart jewelry for women through BCM-MARCOS group decision-making framework with fuzzy ZE-numbers. *Technological Forecasting and Social Change, 196*. https://doi.org/10.1016/j.techfore.2023.122870.

Negi, A., Ranakoti, L., Singh, V., Bhandari, P., Wang, M., Fekete, G., & Singh, T. (2025). A hybrid CRITIC-MAIRCA framework for optimal phase change material selection in solar distillation systems. *International Journal of Thermofluids, 27*, 101167. https://doi.org/10.1016/j.ijft.2025.101167.

Ozdemir, S., Demirel, N., Zaralı, F., & Çelik, T. (2023). Multi-criteria assessment framework for evaluation of green deal performance. *Environmental Science and Pollution Research, 31*(3), 4686–4704. https://doi.org/10.1007/s11356-023-31370-2.

Pamucar, D., Macura, D., Tavana, M., Božanić, D., & Knežević, N. (2022). An integrated rough group multicriteria decision-making model for the ex-ante prioritization of infrastructure projects: The Serbian Railways case. *Socio-economic Planning Sciences, 79*, 101098. https://doi.org/10.1016/j.seps.2021.101098.

Pamučar, D., Mihajlović, M., Obradović, R., & Atanasković, P. (2017). Novel approach to group multi-criteria decision making based on interval rough numbers: Hybrid DEMATEL-ANP-MAIRCA model. *Expert Systems with Applications, 88*, 58–80. https://doi.org/10.1016/j.eswa.2017.06.037.

Pamučar, D., Vasin, L., & Lukovac, L. (2014). Selection of railway level crossings for investing in security equipment using hybrid DEMATEL-MARICA model. *XVI International Scientific-Expert Conference on Railway*, 89–92.

Pamučar, D., Žižović, M., Biswas, S., & Božanić, D. (2021). A new logarithm methodology of additive weights (LMAW) for multi-criteria decision-making: application in logistics. *Facta Universitatis, Series: Mechanical Engineering, 19*(3), 361. https://doi.org/10.22190/FUME210214031P.

Qahtan, S., Alsattar, H. A., Zaidan, A. A., Deveci, M., Pamucar, D., Delen, D., & Pedrycz, W. (2023). Evaluation of agriculture-food 4.0 supply chain approaches using Fermatean probabilistic hesitant-fuzzy sets based decision making model. *Applied Soft Computing, 138*, 110170. https://doi.org/10.1016/j.asoc.2023.110170.

Riahi, S., Bahroudi, A., Abedi, M., & Aslani, S. (2022). Hybrid outranking of geospatial data: Multi attributive ideal-real comparative analysis and combined compromise solution. *Geochemistry, 82*(3), 125898. https://doi.org/10.1016/j.chemer.2022.125898.

Srivastava, A., Parmar, D., & Pamucar, D. (2023). Comparing multi-criteria models for ranking the performance of India's water supply utilities. *Utilities Policy, 84*, 101652. https://doi.org/10.1016/j.jup.2023.101652.

Ul Haq, R. S., Saeed, M., Mateen, N., Siddiqui, F., & Ahmed, S. (2023). An interval-valued neutrosophic based MAIRCA method for sustainable material selection. *Engineering Applications of Artificial Intelligence, 123*, 106177. https://doi.org/10.1016/j.engappai.2023.106177.

Wang, C.-N., Tran Thi, D.-O., Nhieu, N.-L., & Hsueh, M.-H. (2025). An integrated entropy–MAIRCA approach for multi-dimensional strategic classification of agricultural development in East Africa. *Mathematics, 13*(15), 2465. https://doi.org/10.3390/math13152465.

Yang, W., & Liang, C. (2025). A large-scale consensus decision-making model for non-cooperative behavior based on incomplete probabilistic hesitant fuzzy information in social trust networks. *Information Sciences, 714*, 122196. https://doi.org/10.1016/j.ins.2025.122196.

Yontar, E. (2023). Critical success factor analysis of blockchain technology in agri-food supply chain management: A circular economy perspective. *Journal of Environmental Management, 330*, 117173. https://doi.org/10.1016/j.jenvman.2022.117173.

Zorlu, K., Polat, S., Dede, V., & Yılmaz, A. (2025). Measuring degradation risk levels of resources in sustainable geotourism development: A multi-criteria decision making (MCDM) approach under spherical fuzzy environments. *International Journal of Geoheritage and Parks, 13*(2), 250–273. https://doi.org/10.1016/j.ijgeop.2024.11.011.

Chapter 60

MACBETH: Measuring attractiveness by a categorical-based evaluation technique for multi-attribute decision-making

Moein Khazaei[1], Ashkan Hafezalkotob[2], and Reza Kia[3]

[1]*School of Engineering and Sciences, Tecnologico de Monterrey, Monterrey, Mexico,* [2]*Department of Management and Marketing, La Trobe University, Melbourne, VIC, Australia,* [3]*Department of Operations Management and Business Statistics, Sultan Qaboos University, Muscat, Oman*

60.1 Introduction

Since the emergence of multiple criteria decision-making (MCDM) methods in the late 1950s (Zavadskas & Turskis, 2011), a wide array of models and techniques has been developed to address complex decision problems that require the evaluation of competing factors (Khazaei et al., 2023). As the field has evolved, MCDM approaches have found applications across nearly all scientific domains (Khazaei, Gholian-Jouybari, Ramezani, et al., 2025), driven by advancements in modeling, evaluation theories, and structured methodologies (Taghipour et al., 2024). Among these, the measuring attractiveness by a categorical-based evaluation technique (MACBETH) method, introduced by Bana e Costa and Vansnick (1994) in the early 1990s, represents a notable development.

MACBETH distinguishes itself through a constructivist and human-centric approach that focuses on supporting decision-makers in structuring and evaluating their preferences (Ferreira & Santos, 2021). Unlike traditional methods that rely on quantitative comparisons or complex mathematical assumptions, MACBETH uses a qualitative, interactive procedure in which decision-makers assess the difference in attractiveness between alternatives using a semantic scale (Gokasar et al., 2023). These judgments are then converted into numerical interval scales through linear programming. This method is supported by visual and interactive software (M-MACBETH), which simplifies the modeling process and aids in detecting inconsistencies (Ferreira & Santos, 2021). The ability to incorporate incomplete judgments and transform them into cardinal value functions makes MACBETH particularly appealing in uncertain or data-scarce environments (Bastos et al., 2024).

A key advantage of MACBETH over more established techniques, such as the analytic hierarchy process (AHP), lies in its use of difference-of-attractiveness judgments rather than ratio scales (Tamošiūnas, 2023). This allows the method to capture both positive and negative preferences, enabling the modeling of repulsive or undesirable alternatives, something not possible in AHP. Moreover, MACBETH avoids direct numerical scaling, which can be cognitively demanding for decision-makers, and instead relies on qualitative linguistic categories (Gkouvitsos & Giannikos, 2022). Although the method requires dedicated facilitator support and assumes independence among criteria, enhancements such as integration with the Choquet integral have expanded its analytical capacity, especially in capturing interactions among criteria (Oliveira et al., 2019).

The primary objective of this chapter is to demonstrate the practical application of the MACBETH method in a real-world multicriteria decision-making context. By guiding the reader through a structured evaluation and ranking process, this chapter aims to highlight how MACBETH can effectively convert qualitative expert judgments into quantitative scores to support complex decisions. The approach is particularly useful when preferences are expressed verbally rather than numerically, making it suitable for scenarios where data is limited or subjective assessments are central. Through a step-by-step methodology, the chapter illustrates how MACBETH facilitates transparent, consistent, and rational decision-making in sustainability-focused supplier selection, offering a replicable framework for similar evaluations across various sectors.

Encyclopedia of Multi-Attribute Decision-Making (MADM). DOI: https://doi.org/10.1016/B978-0-443-33275-3.00056-7

To guide readers through the structure of this chapter, the remaining sections are organized as follows. Section 60.2 presents a concise review of the MACBETH method, highlighting its theoretical foundations and recent developments. Section 60.3 explains the methodological steps, including criteria definition, pairwise comparison, and attractiveness scoring. Sections 60.4 and 60.5 provide two detailed numerical examples: the first focuses on sustainable supplier selection for biofuel and low-emission hydrogen production, and the second addresses renewable energy (RE) facility location selection. Each example demonstrates how qualitative judgments are translated into quantitative scores and aggregated to derive rankings. Section 60.6 concludes the chapter by discussing the key findings, limitations of the MACBETH approach, and promising directions for future research and applications.

60.2 Literature review

The MACBETH method was first introduced by Bana e Costa and Vansnick (1994) to provide a user-friendly, interactive framework for constructing cardinal value functions based on qualitative pairwise comparisons of attractiveness. Rather than requiring ratio or interval scale inputs, MACBETH enables decision-makers to express preferences using semantic judgments, which are then converted into numerical scales using a sequence of linear programming models. This structure not only increases accessibility but also reduces cognitive burden on stakeholders. The method was originally designed to support decision-making under uncertainty and has since demonstrated broad applicability in both academic and industrial settings. It maintains coherence with measurement theory while ensuring internal consistency in performance evaluation (Clivillé et al., 2007).

Over the past two decades, MACBETH has undergone significant theoretical and methodological evolution. Ferreira and Santos (2021) conducted a comprehensive bibliometric review of 192 MACBETH-related studies published between 1994 and 2016, highlighting its widespread application in areas such as operations research, industrial engineering, and supply chain management. Many scholars have extended the classical MACBETH framework to address real-world complexities. For example, Dhouib (2014) developed a fuzzy-MACBETH approach that integrates 2-tuple linguistic models for analyzing reverse logistics of automobile tire waste under imprecise conditions. Similarly, Bastos et al. (2023) proposed a hybrid fuzzy-MACBETH model using triangular fuzzy numbers to resolve cardinal inconsistencies in semantic scales. This line of research was further advanced in 2024 when a genetic algorithm was incorporated into fuzzy-MACBETH to generate cardinal scales aligned with decision-makers' initial qualitative assessments (Bastos et al., 2024).

MACBETH's practical impact is evident across various decision-making contexts. In the domain of flexible manufacturing systems, Karande and Chakraborty (2013) applied MACBETH to address investment decisions involving both tangible and intangible criteria, demonstrating its capacity to handle mixed data types. In the area of real-time traffic management, Gokasar et al. (2023) introduced a rough numbers-based MACBETH extension to evaluate connected autonomous vehicle systems under dynamic environmental conditions. Moreover, Kundakcı (2019) integrated MACBETH with the evaluation based on distance from average solution (EDAS) method to assess steam boiler alternatives in textile industries, highlighting its utility in multicriteria evaluations with operational cost implications. Akyüz et al. (2018) utilized MACBETH to rank supplier performance, incorporating both quantitative (e.g., return rate, delivery performance) and qualitative (e.g., ecological awareness, flexibility [F]) criteria.

60.3 Methods and materials

The MACBETH technique enables decision-making based on the comparison of attractiveness differences between alternatives (Bastos et al., 2024). Specifically, decision-makers are required to assess the difference in attractiveness between two elements using qualitative judgments, based on a predefined semantic scale (Akyüz et al., 2018).

These verbal judgments are then translated into numerical values that are consistent with the MACBETH scale (Clivillé et al., 2007). Ultimately, the total score of each alternative, calculated as the sum of its weighted scores across all criteria, represents its overall attractiveness. These scores are computed using dedicated MACBETH software, and the alternatives are subsequently ranked accordingly (Tamošiūnas, 2023). The most appropriate option in a MACBETH analysis is typically a hypothetical alternative that achieves the most preferred utility value across all criteria. The structured overview of the MACBETH method is presented in Fig. 60.1. In the following sections, the steps for weight elicitation and ranking using the MACBETH method are presented in detail (Bastos et al., 2023).

Step 1. Weighting stage

Step 1.1. Criteria definition

The first step involves identifying and clearly defining the evaluation criteria relevant to the decision-making context.

Step 1.2. Definition of the pairwise comparison scale

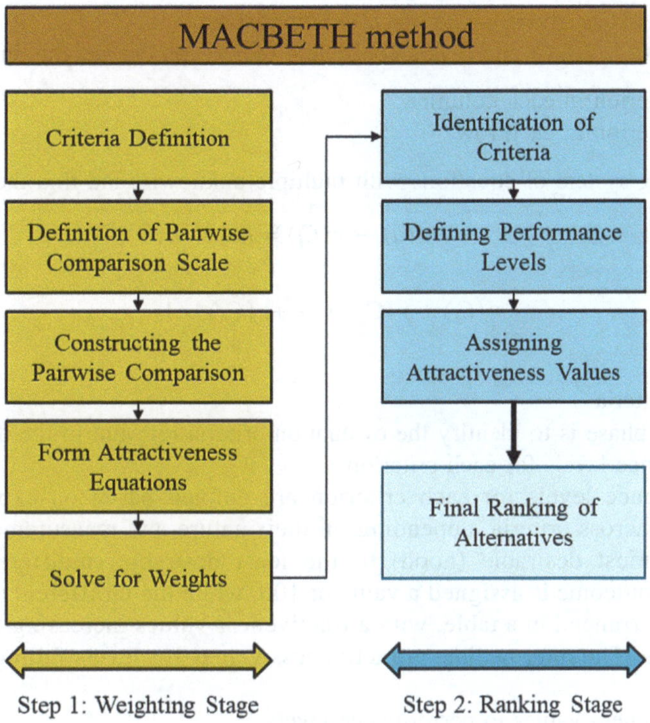

FIGURE 60.1 Structured overview of the MACBETH method.

TABLE 60.1 Semantic scale of attractiveness differences in the MACBETH method.

Semantic judgment	Numerical equivalent	Attractiveness ratio
Indifference between the two alternatives	0	None
One alternative is very weakly more attractive	1	Very weak
One alternative is weakly more attractive	2	Weak
One alternative is moderately more attractive	3	Moderate
One alternative is strongly more attractive	4	Strong
One alternative is very strongly more attractive	5	Very strong
One alternative is extremely more attractive	6	Extreme (complete dominance)

In MACBETH, a fixed verbal scale is used to compare the differences in attractiveness between criteria or alternatives. This predefined semantic scale (as illustrated in Table 60.1) includes categories such as "None," "Very Weak," "Weak," "Moderate," "Strong," "Very Strong," and "Extreme," which are later mapped to a corresponding numerical scale (Ferreira & Santos, 2021).

Step 1.3. Constructing the pairwise comparison table and assessing attractiveness differences.

To construct the pairwise comparison matrix, the evaluation criteria should first be arranged both horizontally (rows) and vertically (columns) in descending order of importance, as determined by expert judgment. Using the semantic scale defined in the previous step, the decision-maker then evaluates the difference in attractiveness between each pair of criteria. In the MACBETH approach, the matrix is symmetric with respect to the diagonal, meaning that the judgments below the main diagonal are reciprocal. Therefore, it is sufficient to conduct pairwise comparisons only for the upper triangular portion of the matrix. An illustrative example is presented below, where criterion 1 is considered the most important, and criterion 3 is the least important.

Step 1.4. Form the equation $v(C_i) - v(C_j) = h\alpha$ for all comparisons:
In the above equation, $h = \{0, 1, \ ..., 6\}$ and α is a coefficient that keeps the weights in the range of 0 to 100.

- $v\ (C_i)$: The value of each criterion in each column
- $v\ (C_j)$: The value of each criterion in each row

Step 1.5. Solve the following system of equations with multiple unknowns and find the weights of the criteria:

$$v(C_i) - v(C_j) = h\alpha \tag{60.1}$$

$$v(C_1) + v(C_2) + \cdots + v(C_n) = 1 \tag{60.2}$$

Step 2. Ranking
Step 2.1. Identification of criteria
The first step in the ranking phase is to identify the evaluation criteria relevant to the decision-making problem.
Step 2.2. Defining performance levels for each criterion
At this stage, the performance levels for each criterion are defined based on expert opinion. The number of performance levels may vary across criteria, depending on their nature and measurement. For each criterion, these levels are ranked from the most desirable (good) to the least desirable (indifferent). The performance level representing the best possible outcome is assigned a value of 100, while the indifferent (or baseline) level is assigned a value of 0. These levels are arranged in a table, with attractiveness values increasing from left to right in rows and from top to bottom in columns. The intermediate attractiveness values for levels falling between these extremes are calculated in the next step.
Step 2.3. Assigning attractiveness values to performance levels
In this step, a pairwise comparison matrix is constructed for each criterion. The decision-maker assesses the difference in attractiveness between the defined performance levels using the MACBETH semantic scale. This comparison enables the calculation of numerical values representing the relative attractiveness of each level, which are then used to derive the final scores.

The same semantic comparison scale is also used in this phase. After completing the pairwise comparisons, a set of linear equations of the form $v(L_i)$ - $v(L_j) = ha$ is constructed for all comparisons. Solving this system of equations allows the determination of the numerical attractiveness value for each performance level. If the decision-maker is unable to express a preference between two performance levels, the symbol P is placed at the intersection of the corresponding cells in the matrix, and no equation is written for that comparison. Where:

- $v(L_i)$ represents the attractiveness value of level i (column),
- $v(L_j)$ represents the attractiveness value of level j (row),

and both values lie within the [0, 100] interval.

In the final step, a decision matrix is constructed using the performance scores for each alternative. Similar to the simple additive weighting (SAW) method, a weighted score is calculated for each alternative (Kaliszewski & Podkopaev, 2016). The alternatives are then ranked in descending order based on their overall scores.

$$v\ (x_i) = \sum_{j=1}^{n} w_j\,(v_j) \tag{60.3}$$

$$v\ (x_i) = \sum_{j=1}^{n} w_j = 1, \quad w_j > 0 \ \ and \begin{cases} v_j\,(x_j^{+}) = 100 \\ v_j\,(x_j^{0}) = 0 \end{cases} \tag{60.4}$$

To conclude this chapter, the MACBETH method provided a systematic and transparent framework for evaluating and ranking alternatives based on expert judgments and verbal comparisons. By translating qualitative assessments into quantitative scores, it ensured that subjectivity was structured and made analytically tractable. The two main stages (criteria weighting and alternative ranking) allowed for a nuanced understanding of both the relative importance of each criterion and the performance levels of various options. This approach not only facilitated decision-making under multiple criteria but also made the underlying preferences and trade-offs explicitly visible, enabling more informed and justifiable conclusions.

60.4 Numerical example 1

To design a supplier evaluation framework aligned with the goals of sustainable hydrogen and biofuel production (Ramezani et al., 2024), a conceptual model was developed and validated through expert consultation. Drawing from a broad body of literature in the areas of green supply chain management, circular economy, and hydrogen infrastructure, an initial list of evaluation criteria was compiled (Foukolaei et al., 2024). A structured questionnaire was distributed to a panel of experts in the fields of waste valorization, clean energy, and industrial procurement (Taghipour et al., 2023).

The selection process involves four potential suppliers, labeled S1 through S4, each of whom is evaluated based on five essential criteria. These criteria are chosen to capture both the technical feasibility and the long-term operational compatibility of the suppliers (Ghaedi et al., 2024). The selected criteria include: distance to the conversion facility (DCF), purity of supplied waste (PSW), monthly supply capacity (MSC), environmental compliance score (ECS), and strategic partnership potential (SPP) (Table 60.2).

Among these criteria, DCF is treated as a nonbeneficial factor, where a shorter distance is preferred due to lower transportation costs and reduced emissions. The remaining four criteria are beneficial, with higher values indicating better performance. The first four criteria (DCF, PSW, MSC, and ECS) are quantitatively measured, while the fifth criterion SPP is qualitative in nature. SPP is assessed through expert judgment and reflects the potential for establishing a long-term collaborative relationship based on trust, previous cooperation, and strategic alignment. These evaluations form the basis for further analysis and ranking of the suppliers using the MACBETH methodology.

To quantify the qualitative values associated with the SPP criterion, semantic judgments were mapped to numerical attractiveness scores using the MACBETH scale. This transformation allows for the consistent integration of both qualitative and quantitative data into the decision matrix. Table 60.3 presents the mapped attractiveness scores for each supplier based on their assessed SPP level. Supplier S2, with a "Very Strong" partnership potential, holds the highest attractiveness score, while supplier S4, rated as "Low", scores considerably lower. These scores reflect the perceived long-term strategic alignment, trust, and collaboration experience with each supplier.

TABLE 60.2 Decision matrix for selecting the optimal waste supplier for biofuel and hydrogen production.

Supplier	DCF (km)	PSW (%)	MSC (tons/month)	ECS (%)	SPP
S1	48	89	135	88	Very low
S2	36	76	120	81	High
S3	62	84	155	60	Average
S4	79	87	125	93	Low

TABLE 60.3 Comparison of attractiveness between reference levels for the strategic partnership potential criterion.

From\To	Excellent (Ex)	Very high (VH)	High (H)	Average (A)	Low (L)	Very low (VL)	None (N)
Excellent (Ex)	No	Very weak	Weak	Moderate	Strong	Very strong	Extreme
Very high (VH)		No	Very weak	Weak	Moderate	Strong	Very strong
High (H)			No	Very weak	Weak	Moderate	Strong
Average (A)				No	Very weak	Weak	Moderate
Low (L)					No	Very weak	Weak
Very low (VL)						No	Very weak
None (N)							No

After defining the four supplier alternatives (S1, S2, S3, and S4) and their performance across the five selected criteria, the next step involves determining the relative importance of each criterion. These criteria include: ECS, MSC, PSW, DCF, and SPP. To derive the weights, a structured pairwise comparison was conducted using qualitative preference judgments between criteria, based on their contribution to the overall goal of sustainable and efficient feedstock procurement.

The criteria were arranged in descending order of perceived importance, beginning with ECS due to its alignment with regulatory and sustainability goals. This was followed by MSC, PSW, DCF, and finally the qualitative criterion SPP. Using a semantic scale ranging from "no difference" to "extreme difference," judgments were made regarding the relative importance of each criterion over the others. Once the consistency of judgments was verified, the weights were calculated accordingly. The final adjusted weight values, reflecting the decision-makers' preferences and ensuring logical consistency, are summarized in Table 60.4. These weights will be used in the aggregation step to evaluate and rank the supplier alternatives.

The final attractiveness scores for each of the four supplier alternatives were calculated by aggregating their performance values across the five evaluation criteria using a weighted sum approach. Table 60.5 presents the normalized performance scores and the overall scores derived from the MACBETH-based procedure. The criteria weights used in the calculation were previously established through pairwise judgments and are shown at the bottom of the table.

Based on the calculated overall attractiveness scores, the ranking of suppliers is determined as follows: S1 > S4 > S3 > S2, with supplier 1 emerging as the most suitable candidate for sourcing waste feedstock in alignment with the objectives of sustainable and reliable hydrogen and biofuel production.

To enhance transparency and provide a better understanding of the MACBETH aggregation process, this section presents a sample calculation of the overall attractiveness score for supplier S1, using the weights and normalized scores provided in Table 60.5.

$$100.00 \times 0.3395 = 33.95$$

$$71.43 \times 0.2429 = 17.36$$

TABLE 60.4 MACBETH is weighing judgments for supplier selection criteria.

From\To	ECS	MSC	PSW	DCF	SPP	All lower
ECS	No	Weak	Moderate	Mod–strg	Mod–strg	Positive
MSC		No	VWeak–Weak	Moderate	Moderate	Positive
PSW			No	Weak–mod	Weak–mod	Positive
DCF				No	Weak–mod	Positive
SPP					No	Positive
All lower						No

TABLE 60.5 MACBETH table of scores for the supplier selection problem.

Supplier	Overall	ECS	MSC	PSW	DCF	SPP
S1	82.17	100.00	71.43	91.67	89.16	16.67
S2	46.99	14.29	14.29	66.67	100.00	66.67
S3	51.01	42.86	100.00	12.50	76.51	50.00
S4	64.94	64.29	52.38	100.00	15.66	33.33
Weights		0.3395	0.2429	0.2065	0.1159	0.0952

$$91.67 \times 0.2065 = 18.93$$

$$89.16 \times 0.1159 = 10.34$$

$$16.67 \times 0.0952 = 1.59$$

Summing the weighted contributions:

$$v(x_{S1}) = 33.95 + 17.36 + 18.93 + 10.34 + 1.59 = 82.17$$

This sample calculation ensures that readers unfamiliar with the MACBETH procedure can clearly see how the weighted scores translate into a final decision metric, strengthening the interpretability and transparency of the method.

60.5 Numerical example 2

In this second case study, a strategic decision is made to select the most suitable site for establishing a RE facility (Khazaei, Gholian-Jouybari, Dolatabadi, et al., 2025). Five potential locations (RE1 to RE5) are evaluated based on five qualitative criteria reflecting technical feasibility (Hasanzadeh et al., 2025), operational performance, and economic concerns (Gholian-Jouybari et al., 2024). These criteria include: F, flow effectiveness (FE), space utilization (SU), safety (S), and investment requirement. Among these, the investment criterion is nonbeneficial (lower levels preferred), while the other four criteria are beneficial (higher levels preferred). The decision matrix for evaluating the five RE locations is shown in Table 60.6.

To maintain consistency across qualitative assessment, a seven-level scale is adopted. For beneficial criteria, the levels are ordered from most to least attractive. For the nonbeneficial criterion (investment), this order is reversed to reflect the preference for lower investment needs. This matrix forms the basis for MACBETH-based qualitative analysis, where each alternative's performance across criteria is converted to numerical attractiveness scores to enable comparison and final ranking.

To determine the ranking of the proposed RE facility locations, the evaluation process begins by entering the alternatives, criteria, performance scale, and associated assessments into the MACBETH framework. The seven-level qualitative performance scale is translated into proportional attractiveness values through consistent pairwise comparisons

TABLE 60.6 Decision matrix for the renewable energy location selection problem.

Alternative	Flexibility	Flow effectiveness	Space utilization	Safety	Investment
RE1	Moderate	Strong	Very strong	Weak	Strong
RE2	Strong	Medium strong	Strong	Weak	Weak
RE3	Very strong	Medium strong	Medium strong	Very weak	Strong
RE4	Moderate	Medium strong	Medium weak	weak	Moderate
RE5	Medium weak	Moderate	Strong	Moderate	MG

TABLE 60.7 Weighting judgments for the renewable energy location selection problem.

Criteria	F	FE	I	S	SU	[all lower]	Current scale
F	no	weak	weak-mod	moderate	mod-strg	positive	36.96
FE		no	weak	weak-mod	weak-mod	positive	27.72
I			no	weak	mod-strg	positive	18.48
S				no	very weak	positive	9.25
SU					no	positive	7.60
[all lower]						no	0.00

using a semantic judgment scale. These pairwise comparisons allow for converting subjective assessments into quantitative scores that reflect the relative attractiveness of each alternative across all criteria (Table 60.7).

To calculate the weights for each criterion, a matrix of pairwise comparisons is developed based on the relative importance of the criteria. The criteria are ordered from most to least important as follows: F, FE, Investment, S, and SU. The semantic evaluations in the matrix are used to derive the final weights. These judgments were transformed via MACBETH's internal linear programming model to derive the final normalized weights (summing to 1.0000):

Criterion	Weight
F	*0.3696*
FE	*0.2772*
I	*0.1848*
S	*0.0925*
SU	*0.0760*

The resulting weight vector is: $w_F = 0.3696$, $w_{FE} = 0.2772$, $w_I = 0.1848$, $w_S = 0.0925$, and $w_{SU} = 0.0760$. These values indicate the dominant importance of F and FE in the decision-making process, with SU receiving the least weight. Each criterion was assessed using a 7-level ordinal scale and qualitative ratings, for example, RE2 were translated into normalized attractiveness scores using MACBETH:

Criterion	RE2 level	Attractiveness score
F	*Strong*	*83.33*
FE	*Medium strong*	*66.67*
I	*Strong*	*83.33*
S	*Weak*	*16.67*
SU	*Weak*	*83.33*

The final MACBETH score for RE2 is calculated using the weighted sum model:

Criterion	Weight	Score	Contribution
F	*0.3696*	*83.33*	*30.79*
FE	*0.2772*	*66.67*	*18.49*
SU	*0.0760*	*83.33*	*6.34*
S	*0.0925*	*16.67*	*1.54*
I	*0.1848*	*83.33*	*15.39*
Total	–	–	*72.55*

In other words:

$$v(x_{RE_2}) = 30.79 + 18.48 + 6.33 + 1.54 + 15.39 = 72.55$$

TABLE 60.8 MACBETH table of scores for the renewable energy location selection problem.

Options	Overall	F	FE	SU	S	I
RE1	53.79	50.00	83.33	100.00	16.67	16.67
RE2	72.55	83.33	66.67	83.33	16.67	83.33
RE3	63.58	100.00	66.67	66.67	0.00	16.67
RE4	50.27	50.00	66.67	33.33	16.67	50.00
RE5	43.29	33.33	50.00	83.33	50.00	33.33
[all upper]	100.00	100.00	100.00	100.00	100.00	100.00
[all lower]	0.00	0.00	0.00	0.00	0.00	0.00
Weights		0.3696	0.2772	0.0760	0.0925	0.1848

Based on the computed MACBETH scores and the previously derived criteria weights, the overall performance scores for the five RE facility location alternatives were calculated using the weighted additive aggregation model. The results are presented in Table 60.8 and have been converted into Table 60.8, showing individual criterion scores as well as overall scores for each alternative.

The ranking of the alternatives based on their overall scores is as follows: RE2 > RE3 > RE1 > RE4 > RE5. This suggests that RE2 is the most attractive renewable energy site location, whereas RE5 is the least preferred. Notably, RE2 achieves high performance across all beneficial criteria and accepts relatively low investment, which aligns with its top ranking. Conversely, RE5 ranks lowest due to poor scores in both F and FE, the two most critical criteria in this decision model.

60.6 Conclusion

The application of the MACBETH method in this chapter demonstrates its practical value for evaluating suppliers in the context of sustainable energy systems. By structuring both quantitative and qualitative criteria into a coherent decision model, MACBETH facilitates balanced, expert-driven evaluations. The results show a clear differentiation among suppliers based on their performance across critical dimensions such as distance, purity, capacity, environmental compliance, and strategic alignment. The method's semantic scale enables the consistent transformation of verbal judgments into actionable rankings, avoiding the need for predefined utility functions. Moreover, the use of pairwise comparisons enhances the transparency of the weighting and scoring processes. Ultimately, this approach supports strategic decision-making for biofuel and hydrogen producers seeking to align operational efficiency with long-term sustainability objectives.

Despite its strengths, the MACBETH method has several limitations. It assumes independence among criteria, which may not always hold in real-world contexts, particularly when interactions exist between economic, environmental, and social factors. The method also requires careful facilitation to ensure consistency in semantic judgments, which can be time-intensive when many alternatives or criteria are involved. Furthermore, while the M-MACBETH software simplifies implementation, large-scale problems may still face computational and interpretive challenges.

Future research can address these limitations by integrating MACBETH with complementary techniques such as fuzzy logic, the Choquet integral, or metaheuristic algorithms to capture interdependencies and imprecision more effectively. Another promising direction is the development of automated or AI-assisted MACBETH systems that can process expert input dynamically, provide real-time consistency feedback, and scale to big-data decision environments. Extending the method to participatory decision-making platforms could also strengthen its role in collaborative and multi-stakeholder contexts such as energy planning, public policy, and sustainable supply chain management.

References

Akyüz, G., Tosun, Ö., & Aka, S. (2018). Multi criteria decision-making approach for evaluation of supplier performance with MACBETH method. *International Journal of Information and Decision Sciences, 10*(3), 249–262.

Bana e Costa, C. A., & Vansnick, J.-C. (1994). MACBETH—An interactive path towards the construction of cardinal value functions. *International Transactions in Operational Research, 1*(4), 489–500.

Bastos, T. R., Longaray, A. A., dos Santos Machado, C. M., Ensslin, L., Ensslin, S. R., & Dutra, A. (2023). Fuzzy-MACBETH hybrid method: Mathematical treatment of a qualitative scale using the fuzzy theory. *International Journal of Computational Intelligence Systems, 16*(1), 21.

Bastos, T. R., Longaray, A. A., dos Santos Machado, C. M., Ensslin, L., Ensslin, S. R., & Dutra, A. (2024). Applying a genetic algorithm to implement the fuzzy-MACBETH method in decision-making processes. *International Journal of Computational Intelligence Systems, 17*(1), 48.

Clivillé, V., Berrah, L., & Mauris, G. (2007). Quantitative expression and aggregation of performance measurements based on the MACBETH multi-criteria method. *International Journal of Production Economics, 105*(1), 171–189.

Dhouib, D. (2014). An extension of MACBETH method for a fuzzy environment to analyze alternatives in reverse logistics for automobile tire wastes. *Omega, 42*(1), 25–32.

Ferreira, F. A., & Santos, S. P. (2021). Two decades on the MACBETH approach: A bibliometric analysis. *Annals of Operations Research, 296*(1), 901–925.

Foukolaei, P. Z., Asari, F. A., Khazaei, M., Gholian-Jouybari, F., & Hajiaghaei-Keshteli, M. (2024). From responsible sourcing of wastes to sustainable energy consumption in the blue hydrogen supply chain: Case of nearshoring in Nuevo Leon. *International Journal of Hydrogen Energy, 77*, 1387–1400.

Ghaedi, M., Foukolaei, P. Z., Asari, F. A., Khazaei, M., Gholian-Jouybari, F., & Hajiaghaei-Keshteli, M. (2024). Pricing electricity from blue hydrogen to mitigate the energy rebound effect: A case study in agriculture and livestock. *International Journal of Hydrogen Energy, 84*, 993–1003.

Gholian-Jouybari, F., Khazaei, M., Saen, R. F., Kia, R., Bonakdari, H., Hajiaghaei-Keshteli, M., & Ramezani, M. (2024). Developing environmental, social and governance (ESG) strategies on evaluation of municipal waste disposal centers: A case of Mexico. *Chemosphere, 364*, 142961.

Gkouvitsos, I., & Giannikos, I. (2022). Using a MACBETH based multicriteria approach for virtual weight restrictions in each stage of a DEA multi-stage ranking process. *Operational Research, 22*(3), 1787–1811.

Gokasar, I., Pamucar, D., Deveci, M., & Ding, W. (2023). A novel rough numbers based extended MACBETH method for the prioritization of the connected autonomous vehicles in real-time traffic management. *Expert Systems with Applications, 211*, 118445.

Hasanzadeh, H., Mohammadi, S., Shafii, M. B., & Daneshvar, M. (2025). Designing and constructing a solar thermal water desalination system: Evaluating the role of thermoelectric in enhancing evaporation and condensation process. *Next Energy, 9*, 100388.

Kaliszewski, I., & Podkopaev, D. (2016). Simple additive weighting—a metamodel for multiple criteria decision analysis methods. *Expert Systems with Applications, 54*, 155–161.

Karande, P., & Chakraborty, S. (2013). Evaluation and selection of flexible manufacturing systems using MACBETH method. *International Journal of Services and Operations Management, 16*(1), 123–144.

Khazaei, M., Gholian-Jouybari, F., Dolatabadi, M. D., Alamdari, A. P., Eskandari, H., & Hajiaghaei-Keshteli, M. (2025). Renewable energy portfolio in Mexico for Industry 5.0 and SDGs: Hydrogen, wind, or solar? *Renewable and Sustainable Energy Reviews, 213*, 115420.

Khazaei, M., Gholian-Jouybari, F., Ramezani, M., & Hajiaghaei-Keshteli, M. (2025). Environmental, social, and governance enablers of the hydrogen supply chain: Application of community operational research using STRIDES framework. *Journal of Environmental Management, 389*, 126092.

Khazaei, M., Hajiaghaei-Keshteli, M., Rajabzadeh Ghatari, A., Ramezani, M., Fooladvand, A., & Azar, A. (2023). A multi-criteria supplier evaluation and selection model without reducing the level of optimality. *Soft Computing, 27*(22), 17175–17188.

Kundakcı, N. (2019). An integrated method using MACBETH and EDAS methods for evaluating steam boiler alternatives. *Journal of Multi-Criteria Decision Analysis, 26*(1-2), 27–34.

Oliveira, M. D., Mataloto, I., & Kanavos, P. (2019). Multi-criteria decision analysis for health technology assessment: Addressing methodological challenges to improve the state of the art. *The European Journal of Health Economics, 20*(6), 891–918.

Ramezani, M., Khazaei, M., Gholian-Jouybari, F., Sandoval-Correa, A., Bonakdari, H., & Hajiaghaei-Keshteli, M. (2024). Turquoise hydrogen and waste optimization: A Bi-objective closed-loop and sustainable supply chain model for a case in Mexico. *Renewable and Sustainable Energy Reviews, 195*, 114329.

Taghipour, A., Foukolaei, P. Z., Ghaedi, M., & Khazaei, M. (2023). Sustainable multi-objective models for waste-to-energy and waste separation site selection. *Sustainability, 15*(22), 15764.

Taghipour, A., Padash, A., Etemadi, V., Khazaei, M., & Ebrahimi, S. (2024). Sustainable and circular hotels and the water–food–energy nexus: Integration of agrivoltaics, hydropower, solar cells, water reservoirs, and green roofs. *Sustainability, 16*(5), 1985.

Tamošiūnas, A. (2023). Selecting rooftop solar photovoltaic modules by measuring their attractiveness by a categorical-based evaluation technique (MACBETH): The case of lithuania. *Energies, 16*(7), 2999.

Zavadskas, E. K., & Turskis, Z. (2011). Multiple criteria decision making (MCDM) methods in economics: An overview. *Technological and economic development of economy, 17*(2), 397–427.

Chapter 61

WSM and WPM: Weighted sum model and weighted product model for multi-attribute decision-making

Goran Petrović[1], Miloš Madić[1], and Dragan Marinković[2,3,4]
[1]*Faculty of Mechanical Engineering, University of Niš, Niš, Serbia,* [2]*Department of Structural Analysis, Technical University Berlin, Berlin, Germany,* [3]*Mechanical Science Institute, Vilnius Gediminas Technical University-VILNIUS TECH, Vilnius, Lithuania,* [4]*University College, Korea University, Seoul, Republic of Korea*

61.1 Introduction

In today's dynamic business and technical environment, decision-making represents one of the most important challenges faced by managers, engineers, and analysts. Multicriteria decision-making (MCDM) supports decision-makers in ranking, comparing, and selecting the most favorable option among multiple possible alternatives. The particular value of these methods lies in their ability to approach problems from multiple perspectives, taking into account both quantitative and qualitative data. In this way, the risk of making subjective and suboptimal decisions is significantly reduced.

Within the framework of MCDM, numerous methods have been developed, differing in their approach, data processing techniques, and procedures for ranking and selecting the optimal alternative. Two of the most well-known and frequently applied methods in this field are the weighted sum model (WSM) and the weighted product model (WPM). Although simple to implement, these methods provide reliable results and are often used in practical situations where speed, application receptivity, and decision-making efficiency are of crucial importance.

WSM and WPM represent fundamental methods for solving MCDM problems involving a finite number of discrete alternatives. Their application enables the rapid ranking and selection of the optimal alternative based on predefined criteria and their corresponding relative significance expressed via weight coefficients. The primary advantage of these methods lies in their simplicity and transparency, making them suitable for a wide range of users.

Although categorized as simpler MCDM methods, WSM and WPM serve as the foundation for the development of more advanced and complex decision-making methods. Their use is particularly appropriate in situations where clearly defined criteria are available, when decisions need to be made within a short time frame, and when the results must be easy to interpret—especially in organizations without specialized analytical teams. By applying the WSM and WPM, it becomes possible to systematize various criteria and quantify their influence on the final decision. In the case of handling uncertain attribute values and difficulties in determining the exact criteria weight values, the use of fuzzy MCDM methodology is recommended (Trifunović et al., 2025; Zulqarnain et al., 2021), while the fuzzy extensions of WSM and WPM have already been introduced (Triantaphyllou & Lin, 1996).

61.2 Literature review

The WSM is one of the simplest methods in MCDM. Its roots can be found in additive utility theory from the 1950s (e.g., Churchman et al., 1954; Fishburn, 1967; MacCrimon, 1968). This method was formally described and applied as a benchmark simple additive weighting/WSM technique in the study of Hwang and Yoon (1981). However, identifying the exact date or author of its first publication is difficult, as the method is highly intuitive and naturally emerged from linear algebra and engineering decision-making practices. The WSM has been applied across various fields, including product selection (Kumar & Parimala, 2020), sustainable urban mobility plans selection (Garcia-Ayllon et al., 2021), procurement

Encyclopedia of Multi-Attribute Decision-Making (MADM). DOI: https://doi.org/10.1016/B978-0-443-33275-3.00091-9

and selection of rail vehicles (Frankowski, 2025), sustainability assessment of urban transportation vehicles (Mitropoulos & Prevedouros, 2016), and identifying suitable locations for electric vehicle charging stations (Gönül et al., 2024).

Following WSM, another fundamental approach within the field of MCDM is the WPM. This method is based on a multiplicative aggregation of alternatives' performance values, where each value is raised to the power of the assigned criteria weight, reflecting its relative importance. Although multiplicative models had previously been applied in fields such as economics and production analysis (Miller & Starr, 1969), WPM was more clearly formalized and integrated into the MCDM context through later works, most notably by Triantaphyllou and Mann (1989) and subsequent methodological reviews. In these studies, WPM was positioned alongside other classical MCDM methods as a valuable alternative to additive models like WSM, particularly in situations where proportional and relative performance comparisons are more appropriate. The WPM has been utilized in various application areas, such as employee performance evaluation (Sinaga & Maulana, 2022), value engineering in construction projects (Ochieng' Wao, 2018), drinking water quality assessment (Chinnasami et al., 2023), best student selection (Murdani et al., 2020), and the selection of quality textile materials (Martunasia et al., 2023).

In addition to the previously described methods (WSM and WPM), one can mention MCDM methods that integrate them by defining an overall optimality criterion, such as weighted aggregated sum product assessment (WASPAS), multiobjective optimization by ratio analysis plus the full multiplicative form, combined compromise solution, and the Simple weighted integrated sum product (WISP) method (Stanujkic, 2023).

In the historical review of the origin and development of the WSM and WPM , an important place is occupied by their evolution into the WASPAS method. The WASPAS method represents a modern extension and unification of the classical WSM and WPM methods. By integrating both additive and multiplicative aggregation principles, WASPAS provides greater flexibility in modeling decision problems. Due to its simplicity, computational efficiency, and improved discriminative capacity, the WASPAS method has gained significant attention in recent years across engineering, logistics, and management decision-making applications. This unified model was originally proposed by Zavadskas et al. (2012). Some applications of the WASPAS method across various fields encompass the assessment of alternative building design solutions (Zavadskas et al., 2013), solving manufacturing decision-making problems (Chakraborty & Zavadskas, 2014), human risk assessment of dams (Bid & Siddique, 2019), university location selection (Miç & Antmen, 2021), and selection of cutting conditions in turning operations (Turudija et al., 2023).

The second interesting integration of WSM and WPM was proposed by Stanujkicć et al. (2021). They presented a new approach named the simple WISP method, which represents a further step in unifying the classical WSM and WPM frameworks. The simple WISP method integrates the additive aggregation logic of WSM with the multiplicative aggregation principles of WPM to create a simple, yet effective, approach for ranking alternatives. The method offers a user-friendly structure that can be applied even by decision-makers with limited expertise in MCDM, making it suitable for a broad range of applications. The Simple WISP method has been applied in various fields, including contractor and industrial robot selection (Stanujkic et al., 2021), the evaluation and selection of personnel (Stanujkic, 2023), pallet truck selection (Ulutaş et al., 2022), telescopic forklift selection (Görçün et al., 2024), and the determination of the optimal separation density in the gravity separation of coal (Soković et al., 2025).

61.3 Methodology

Decision-making problems are characterized by the existence of a predetermined set of possible solutions—alternatives that need to be evaluated considering multiple criteria, each of which has a certain importance in the overall decision. Since decision-making criteria can be both quantitative and qualitative and are frequently mutually conflicting, the process of reaching an optimal decision becomes significantly more complex. The significance of MCDM methods lies in their ability to provide a structured and rational approach to problem analysis, thereby minimizing the risk of making subjective, hasty, and suboptimal decisions.

The structure of any MCDM problem can be defined by constructing a decision matrix (DM) and criteria weights vector, based on which the evaluation of alternatives is performed using an appropriate MCDM method. Formally, the DM is defined as shown in Eq. 61.1.

$$X = \begin{array}{c} \\ A_1 \\ A_2 \\ \vdots \\ A_m \end{array} \begin{array}{c} \begin{array}{cccc} C_1 & C_2 & \cdots & C_n \end{array} \\ \begin{bmatrix} x_{11} & x_{12} & \cdots & x_{1n} \\ x_{21} & x_{22} & \cdots & x_{2n} \\ \vdots & \vdots & \ddots & \vdots \\ x_{m1} & x_{m2} & \cdots & x_{mn} \end{bmatrix} \end{array} \tag{61.1}$$

The DM consists of three basic elements:

- The set of alternatives represents possible (feasible, *a priori* known) solutions to the decision-making problem. Each alternative A_i, $(i = 1 \div m)$ is represented by one row in the DM, where m is the total number of alternatives.
- The set of criteria consists of measurable or descriptive indicators based on which a comparative analysis of alternatives is conducted within the MCDM process. In the DM, each criterion C_j, $(j = 1 \div n)$ is represented by a separate column, where n is the total number of criteria.
- Attributes, or the performances of alternatives with respect to a given criterion, represent the values that quantitatively or qualitatively express the extent to which a particular alternative i meets the requirements of that criterion j. In the DM attribute values are denoted with x_{ij}.

In real MCDM problems, the criteria typically do not have the same level of importance. The weights of criteria (also referred to as coefficients) represent the relative importance that each criterion holds within the overall decision-making process. The weights are commonly expressed in the form of numerical values w_j, $(j = 1 \div n)$, where each w_j represents the importance of the j-th criterion, and n is the total number of criteria. It is necessary to point out that when solving a particular decision-making problem, the sum of all coefficients is equal to 1, and a higher value indicates a greater significance of a given criterion.

MCDM methods enable the objective evaluation of alternatives through two fundamental and interrelated subprocesses: the determination of criteria weights and the ranking of alternatives. Determination of criteria weights is of essential importance, as it reflects the preferences of the decision-maker(s) and enables the quantification of the influence that individual criterion has on the selection of the optimal alternative. Methods for determining the criteria weights can be subjective (based on the expertise of the decision maker), objective (based on statistical data analysis), or combined, depending on the nature of the problem and the availability of data. A common and desirable approach in the process of determining criteria weights is group decision-making, where various aggregation operators can be used to combine the individual preferences, opinions, or judgments of group members into a collective decision (Petrović et al., 2023).

Ranking alternatives is the second, also very important, subprocess. Once the criteria weights have been determined, the process proceeds with the evaluation and ranking of alternatives based on their performance with respect to each individual criterion. The aim of this step is to determine the overall value (score) of each alternative, using the available attribute values and an appropriate method, and to establish a ranking list from the most to the least favorable alternative. Given the nature of the problem considered in this chapter, the following text will provide a methodological presentation of two widely applied methods for ranking alternatives, WSM and WPM.

61.3.1 The weighted sum model

Considering the way an MCDM problem is defined through a DM and a criteria weight vector, the stepwise procedure of the WSM can be summarized as follows (Jahan et al., 2022; Vani & RamaMohanBabu, 2023):

Step 1: Define the DM in the form given by Eq. (61.1), where x_{ij} represents the performance of the i-th alternative with respect to the j-th criterion, m is the number of alternatives, and n is the number of criteria.

Step 2: Determine the normalized DM $\overline{\mathrm{X}}$, where the matrix elements $\overline{x}_{ij}$ are calculated using the following expressions (linear normalization of initial attribute values):

- For maximization criteria:

$$\overline{x}_{ij} = \frac{x_{ij}}{\max\limits_{i} x_{ij}}, \quad i = 1, \; \ldots, \; m \tag{61.2a}$$

- For minimization criteria:

$$\overline{x}_{ij} = \frac{\min\limits_{i} x_{ij}}{x_{ij}}, \quad i = 1, \; \ldots, \; m \tag{61.2b}$$

where $\overline{x}_{ij}$ represents normalized attribute value.

Step 3: Calculation of the optimality criterion for each alternative in the form of a weighted sum of its normalized performance values. The optimality score for each alternative is obtained by multiplying the normalized attribute value of each criterion by its corresponding weight and then summing these products across all criteria. This can be expressed as (Triantaphyllou & Mann, 1989):

$$S_i = \sum_{j=1}^{n} \bar{x}_{ij} \cdot w_j, \quad i = 1, \ \ldots, \ m \tag{61.3}$$

where S_i is the overall score of the i-th alternative and w_j is the weight of the j-th criterion.

Step 4: Selection of the best alternative. The alternative with the highest value of S_i is considered the most preferable alternative (MPA) as follows:

$$MPA^{WSM} = \max_i S_i, \quad i = 1, \ \ldots, \ m \tag{61.4}$$

61.3.2 The weighted product model

The basic steps of WPM are similar to the procedure defined in the case of WSM. The following four steps can be used for the implementation of WPM (Bozorg-Haddad et al., 2021; Jahan et al., 2022):

Step 1: The same as defined in the case of WSM.

Step 2: The same as defined in the case of WSM.

Step 3: Calculation of the optimality criterion for each alternative in the form of a weighted product of its normalized performance values. The optimality score for each alternative is obtained by raising the normalized attribute value of each criterion to the power of its corresponding weight and then multiplying these weighted values across all criteria. This step can be expressed as (Triantaphyllou & Mann, 1989):

$$P_i = \prod_{j=1}^{n} \bar{x}_{ij}^{\,w_j}, \quad i = 1, \ \ldots, \ m \tag{61.5}$$

where P_i is the overall score of the i-th alternative.

Step 4: Selection of the best alternative. The alternative with the highest value of P_i is considered the MPA:

$$MPA^{WPM} = \max_i P_i, \quad i = 1, \ \ldots, \ m \tag{61.6}$$

61.4 Numerical example 1: supplier selection

The first simple numerical example, representing the practical application of the WSM, WPM, and WASPAS methods, is defined based on the case study, *THK linear motion guide supplier selection (THK Co., Ltd., Japan)*, which was presented in the paper by Petrović Sekulic et al. (2018). The case study was conducted in the company "Lagerton" in Serbia, which specializes in the distribution of mechanical components. The aim of the research was to apply a MCDM approach in the process of selecting suppliers for THK linear motion guides, specifically for the components SRS 12 GM UU (linear block) and SRS 12/570–10–10 (guide rail). For the evaluation and selection of suppliers, MCDM methods such as analytic hierarchy process (AHP) and stepwise weight assessment ratio analysis (SWARA) were used as weighting methods, while AHP and technique for order preference by similarity to ideal solution (TOPSIS) were applied for the alternative ranking. These methods enabled the quantification and ranking of suppliers based on different criteria. Four suppliers (SP_1, SP_2, SP_3, and SP_4) were evaluated according to five criteria: product price (C_1), transportation cost (C_2), delivery time (C_3), company rating (C_4), and established cooperation (C_5). The first three criteria represent cost-related factors to be minimized, whereas the last two are benefit-oriented and should be maximized.

The defined MCDM problem is solved by applying the WSM and WPM, following the previously described four-step calculation procedure.

61.4.1 The calculation procedure using the weighted sum model, example 1

Step 1 WSM: The authors of the study Petrović Sekulic et al. (2018), based on interviews with the company's management, defined the DM as presented in Table 61.1. In the last row of the table, the values of the weight coefficient vector, obtained using the AHP method, are shown.

Step 2 WSM: Based on Eqs. (61.2a) and (61.2b), the normalized DM $\overline{\mathrm{X}}$ is obtained as presented in Table 61.2.

Step 3 WSM: The optimality criterion for each alternative is obtained using (61.3) and values are shown in Table 61.3.

TABLE 61.1 Decision matrix X and criteria weights for supplier's performance ratings.

	Criteria				
	C_1 [EUR]	C_2 [EUR]	C_3 [days]	C_4 [-]	C_5 [-]
Alternatives	min	min	min	max	max
SP_1	350	50	15	9	9
SP_2	390	60	15	9	1
SP_3	400	60	15	5	1
SP_4	367	60	7	4	1
w_j	0.298	0.170	0.099	0.032	0.400

TABLE 61.2 Normalized decision matrix $\overline{X}$—example 1.

	Criteria				
	C_1	C_2	C_3	C_4	C_5
Alternatives	min	min	min	max	max
SP_1	$\frac{350}{350} = 1.000$	$\frac{50}{50} = 1.000$	$\frac{7}{15} = 0.467$	$\frac{9}{9} = 1.000$	$\frac{9}{9} = 1.000$
SP_2	$\frac{350}{390} = 0.897$	$\frac{50}{60} = 0.833$	$\frac{7}{15} = 0.467$	$\frac{9}{9} = 1.000$	$\frac{1}{9} = 0.111$
SP_3	$\frac{350}{400} = 0.875$	$\frac{50}{60} = 0.833$	$\frac{7}{15} = 0.467$	$\frac{5}{9} = 0.556$	$\frac{1}{9} = 0.111$
SP_4	$\frac{350}{367} = 0.954$	$\frac{50}{60} = 0.833$	$\frac{7}{7} = 1.000$	$\frac{4}{9} = 0.444$	$\frac{1}{9} = 0.111$

Step 4 WSM: Considering that the ranking of the optimality criteria is in descending order (0.946 > 0.583 > 0.531 > 0.510), according to the WSM, the alternatives are ranked as follows: $SP_1 > SP_4 > SP_2 > SP_3$, i.e., the most preferable alternative (MPA) is alternative SP_1.

61.4.2 The calculation procedure using weighted product method: example 2

Step 3 WPM: The optimality criterion for each alternative is obtained using (61.5) and values are shown in Table 61.3. (Table 61.4)

Step 4 WPM: In the case of the WPM , the descending order of the optimality criteria is (0.927 > 0.386 > 0.361 > 0.352), and the alternatives are ranked in the same order as in the case of the WSM method: $SP_1 > SP_4 > SP_2 > SP_3$. *MPA* is alternative SP_1.

61.5 Numerical example 2: selection of cutting insert

To demonstrate the practical application of the WSM, WPM, and WASPAS method, a second, more complex real-life example, based on the case study described by Madić et al. (2024), is presented. This study addresses the MCDM problem related to the selection of the most suitable cutting insert for medium turning operations. The decision problem considers longitudinal turning of unalloyed structural steel C45E, characterized by a hardness of 190 HB and tensile strength of 650 N/mm². The turning operations are to be performed on Computer Numerical Control (CNC) lathes with motor power up to 25 kW, using a PCLNR 3225 P12 toolholder. Fourteen alternative CNMG (standardized designation/code name) cutting inserts were selected for evaluation. These alternatives were sourced from eight internationally recognized cutting tool manufacturers. The insert alternatives varied in their geometric and technological properties relevant to the specific

TABLE 61.3 The optimality criterion for each alternative S_i.

Alternatives	Criteria					S_i
	C_1 min	C_2 min	C_3 min	C_4 max	C_5 max	
SP_1	1.000·0.298 = 0,298	1.000·0.170 = 0,170	0.467·0.099= 0.046	1.000·0.032 = 0.032	1.000·0.400 = 0.400	**0.946**
SP_2	0.897·0.298 = 0.268	0.833·0.170 = 0.141	0.467·0.099 = 0.046	1.000·0.032 = 0.032	0.111·0.400 = 0.044	**0.531**
SP_3	0.875·0.298 = 0.261	0.833·0.170 = 0.141	0.467·0.099 = 0.046	0.556·0.032 = 0.018	0.111·0.400 = 0.044	**0.510**
SP_4	0.954·0.298 = 0.285	0.833·0.170 = 0.141	1.000·0.099 = 0.099	0.444·0.032 = 0.014	0.111·0.400 = 0.044	**0.583**

TABLE 61.4 The optimality criterion for each alternative P_i.

Alternatives	Criteria					P_i
	C_1 min	C_2 min	C_3 min	C_4 max	C_5 max	
SP_1	$1.000^{0.298} = 1.000$	$1.000^{0.170} = 1.000$	$0.467^{0.099} = 0.927$	$1.000^{0.032} = 1.000$	$1.000^{0.400} = 1.000$	**0.927**
SP_2	$0.897^{0.298} = 0.968$	$0.833^{0.170} = 0.970$	$0.467^{0.099} = 0.927$	$1.000^{0.032} = 1.000$	$0.111^{0.400} = 0.415$	**0.361**
SP_3	$0.875^{0.298} = 0.961$	$0.833^{0.170} = 0.970$	$0.467^{0.099} = 0.927$	$0.556^{0.032} = 0.981$	$0.111^{0.400} = 0.415$	**0.352**
SP_4	$0.954^{0.298} = 0.986$	$0.833^{0.170} = 0.970$	$1.000^{0.099} = 1.000$	$0.444^{0.032} = 0.974$	$0.111^{0.400} = 0.415$	**0.386**

machining conditions. A total of seven criteria were defined to comprehensively evaluate the suitability of each cutting insert. The first criterion was the rake angle, expressed in degrees, which directly affects chip formation and cutting forces. The second criterion was the nose radius, expressed in millimeters, influencing surface finish and cutting tool strength. The feed rate range, expressed in mm/rev, was included as the third criterion, determining the material removal rate (MRR) and surface finish. The fourth criterion was the allowable depth-of-cut range in millimeters, which defines the maximum material thickness removable per pass. Cutting speed range, in m/min, was considered as the fifth criterion, essential for process efficiency and tool life. The sixth criterion was the maximum achievable MRR in cm^3/min, representing the productivity potential of each insert. Finally, the seventh criterion was the market price of each cutting insert in euros. Among these, price was the only minimization criterion, while the remaining six were treated as maximization criteria. To determine the relative importance of the criteria, the AHP method was applied. The consistency of the comparison matrix was verified using a consistency ratio, ensuring reliable weight coefficients. These criteria reflected the decision-makers' priorities, balancing economic and technical aspects of the cutting process. The structured problem definition and well-established evaluation framework enabled a systematic application of multiple MCDM methods in later phases of the study.

In the following text, the defined MCDM problem is solved by applying the WSM and WPM. The results generated by these two methods are separately presented.

61.5.1 The calculation procedure using weighted sum model, example 2

Step 1 WSM: The MCDM model for the selection of a CNMG cutting insert, consisting of the corresponding decision matrix and the criteria weights vector, is presented in Table 61.5. The criteria weights are obtained using the AHP method and are presented in the last row of Table 61.5.

Step 2 WSM: The normalized decision matrix, obtained based on Eqs. (61.2a) and (61.2b), is presented in Table 61.6.

TABLE 61.5 Multi-criteria decision-making model for selection of CNMG cutting insert.

Alternatives (cutting inserts)	Criteria						
	C_1 [°]	C_2 [mm]	C_3 [mm/rev]	C_4 [mm]	C_5 [m/min]	C_6 [cm^3/min]	C_7 [EUR]
	max	max	max	max	max	max	min
A_1	16.0	0.8	0.24	2.90	96.0	493.9	5.00
A_2	16.0	1.2	0.36	2.60	144.0	695.5	5.00
A_3	14.5	0.8	0.18	2.20	144.0	253.8	12.39
A_4	14.5	1.2	0.20	1.80	138.0	289.8	12.39
A_5	11.0	0.8	0.35	5.00	85.0	563.8	15.43
A_6	11.0	1.2	0.42	4.70	85.0	676.5	15.43
A_7	0.0	0.8	0.30	4.60	95.0	701.0	11.06
A_8	6.0	0.8	0.30	4.30	85.0	625.0	11.06
A_9	20.0	0.8	0.39	4.70	85.0	757.0	11.06
A_{10}	12.0	0.8	0.23	2.5	240	588	9.61
A_{11}	15.0	0.8	0.22	4.4	88	816	15.10
A_{12}	28.0	0.8	0.18	8.10	85.0	790.0	11.06
A_{13}	15.0	0.8	0.20	3.20	55.0	605.0	6.50
A_{14}	15.0	1.2	0.40	3.20	110.0	907.0	6.50
w_j	0.048	0.04	0.094	0.134	0.094	0.234	0.357

TABLE 61.6 The normalized decision matrix - selection of CNMG cutting insert.

Alternatives (cutting inserts)	Criteria						
	C_1	C_2	C_3	C_4	C_5	C_6	C_7
	max	max	max	max	max	max	min
A_1	0.571	0.667	0.571	0.358	0.400	0.545	1.000
A_2	0.571	1.000	0.857	0.321	0.600	0.767	1.000
A_3	0.518	0.667	0.429	0.272	0.600	0.280	0.404
A_4	0.518	1.000	0.476	0.222	0.575	0.320	0.404
A_5	0.393	0.667	0.833	0.617	0.354	0.622	0.324
A_6	0.393	1.000	1.000	0.580	0.354	0.746	0.324
A_7	0.000	0.667	0.714	0.568	0.396	0.773	0.452
A_8	0.214	0.667	0.714	0.531	0.354	0.689	0.452
A_9	0.714	0.667	0.929	0.580	0.354	0.835	0.452
A_{10}	0.429	0.667	0.548	0.309	1.000	0.648	0.520
A_{11}	0.536	0.667	0.524	0.543	0.367	0.900	0.331
A_{12}	1.000	0.667	0.429	1.000	0.354	0.871	0.452
A_{13}	0.536	0.667	0.476	0.395	0.229	0.667	0.769
A_{14}	0.536	1.000	0.952	0.395	0.458	1.000	0.769

Step 3 and 4 WSM: The optimality criterion S_i, $(i = 1, \ldots, m)$ for each alternative is obtained using (61.3), and the results are shown in Table 61.7. In the last column of the table, the rankings of alternatives according to WSM ((61.4)), are provided.

61.5.2 The calculation procedure using weighted product model, example 2

Step 3 and 4 WPM: As in the first example, the first two steps of the WPM are the same as those in the WSM and will thus not be presented again. The optimality criterion for each alternative is obtained using (61.5), and the values are presented in Table 61.8. Additionally, the rankings of the alternatives, as determined by the WPM method ((61.6)), are presented in the last column of the table.

61.6 Comparative and sensitivity analysis

61.6.1 The comparative evaluation of the obtained results

A comparative analysis of the results obtained using the considered methods and those reported by Petrović Sekulic et al. (2018) and Madić et al. (2024) is presented in this section. In the case of the first example—supplier selection, the results obtained using different MCDM approaches are given in Table 61.9.

The strong consistency among the results obtained using different MCDM approaches can be attributed to the simplicity of the analyzed problem. A slight deviation was observed only in the case of the hybrid SWARA + TOPSIS approach, as a result of the modified weight coefficients assigned to the criteria.

In the case of the second example, selection of cutting insert, the final rankings of alternatives are obtained using WSM, WSP, and six other methods: additive ratio assessment (ARAS), complex proportional assessment (COPRAS), multiobjective optimization by ratio analysis (MOORA), VlseKriterijumska Optimizacija I Kompromisno Resenje

TABLE 61.7 The optimality criterion according to the WSM method.

Alternatives (cutting inserts)	Criteria							Σ	Rang WSM
	C_1	C_2	C_3	C_4	C_5	C_6	C_7		
	max	max	max	max	max	max	min		
A_1	0.027	0.027	0.053	0.048	0.037	0.127	0.357	0.677	**3**
A_2	0.027	0.040	0.080	0.043	0.056	0.179	0.357	0.783	**1**
A_3	0.025	0.027	0.040	0.036	0.056	0.065	0.144	0.394	**14**
A_4	0.025	0.040	0.045	0.030	0.054	0.075	0.144	0.412	**13**
A_5	0.019	0.027	0.078	0.082	0.033	0.145	0.116	0.500	**12**
A_6	0.019	0.040	0.094	0.077	0.033	0.175	0.116	0.554	**8**
A_7	0.000	0.027	0.067	0.076	0.037	0.181	0.161	0.549	**9**
A_8	0.010	0.027	0.067	0.071	0.033	0.161	0.161	0.531	**11**
A_9	0.034	0.027	0.087	0.077	0.033	0.195	0.161	0.615	**5**
A_{10}	0.021	0.027	0.051	0.041	0.094	0.152	0.186	0.571	**7**
A_{11}	0.026	0.027	0.049	0.073	0.034	0.211	0.118	0.537	**10**
A_{12}	0.048	0.027	0.040	0.134	0.033	0.204	0.161	0.647	**4**
A_{13}	0.026	0.027	0.045	0.053	0.021	0.156	0.275	0.602	**6**
A_{14}	0.026	0.040	0.089	0.053	0.043	0.234	0.275	0.759	**2**

(VIKOR), TOPSIS, and WASPAS. The results revealed noticeable ranking inconsistencies between the methods. (Table 61.10)

The relationships between the final rankings can be evaluated by means of Kendall's tau-b rank correlation coefficients. The corresponding results are provided in Table 61.11.

As can be observed from Tables 61.10 and 61.11, a stronger positive association between the final rankings obtained by the WSM, WPM, and WASPAS ($\lambda = 0.5$) method is evident. This is a direct consequence of the fact that the WASPAS method represents a linear combination of the WSM and WPM. It is also important to highlight the excellent agreement between the WSM and the COPRAS method results, with a Kendall's tau-b value of 0.978. Both WSM and WPM show a relatively lower degree of association with the rankings determined by the ARAS method. It should be noted that the results obtained by the other methods also exhibit somewhat weaker correlations with the ARAS method outcomes—a conclusion similarly reported by Madić et al. (2024).

Despite their reliance on relatively simple calculations, WSM and WPM frequently deliver results comparable in quality to those obtained by more sophisticated MCDM approaches. Therefore, they should be considered in decision-making scenarios characterized by a smaller number of alternatives and criteria, or when simplicity and computational efficiency are prioritized. With this in mind, they can be effectively applied for benchmarking purposes.

It should be noted that in situations where there is substantial ranking inconsistency obtained by different MCDM methods, one should consider performing a sensitivity analysis, applying integrated approaches, or developing a robust decision-making rule for the assessment and ranking of alternatives (Madić et al., 2022).

61.6.2 Sensitivity analysis of final rankings with respect to criteria weight changes

Conducting a sensitivity analysis within MCDM methods represents a crucial step in evaluating the stability and reliability of the obtained ranking of alternatives in relation to changes in criteria weights. Given that the assignment of criteria

TABLE 61.8 The optimality criterion according to the weighted product method.

Alternatives (cutting inserts)	Criteria							Σ	Rank WPM
	C_1	C_2	C_3	C_4	C_5	C_6	C_7		
	max	max	max	max	max	max	min		
A_1	0.974	0.984	0.949	0.872	0.918	0.867	1.000	0.631	**3**
A_2	0.974	1.000	0.986	0.859	0.953	0.940	1.000	0.739	**1**
A_3	0.969	0.984	0.924	0.840	0.953	0.742	0.723	0.379	**13**
A_4	0.969	1.000	0.933	0.818	0.950	0.766	0.723	0.389	**12**
A_5	0.956	0.984	0.983	0.938	0.907	0.895	0.669	0.471	**11**
A_6	0.956	1.000	1.000	0.930	0.907	0.934	0.669	0.504	**9**
A_7	0.000	0.984	0.969	0.927	0.917	0.941	0.753	0.000	**14**
A_8	0.929	0.984	0.969	0.919	0.907	0.917	0.753	0.510	**8**
A_9	0.984	0.984	0.993	0.930	0.907	0.959	0.753	0.586	**5**
A_{10}	0.960	0.984	0.945	0.855	1.000	0.904	0.792	0.546	**7**
A_{11}	0.971	0.984	0.941	0.922	0.910	0.976	0.674	0.496	**10**
A_{12}	1.000	0.984	0.924	1.000	0.907	0.968	0.753	0.601	**4**
A_{13}	0.971	0.984	0.933	0.883	0.871	0.910	0.911	0.568	**6**
A_{14}	0.026	0.040	0.089	0.053	0.043	0.234	0.275	0.759	**2**

TABLE 61.9 A summary of the final rankings of suppliers.

Alternatives	Multicriteria decision-making methods				
	AHP	AHP + TOPSIS	SWARA + TOPSIS	AHP + WSM	AHP + WPM
SP_1	1	1	1	1	1
SP_2	3	3	2	3	3
SP_3	4	4	4	4	4
SP_4	2	2	2	2	2

weights in these methods often involves subjective assessments or relies on uncertain and variable information, it is essential to assess the extent to which such changes may influence the final results (Petrović Madic et al., 2018). Sensitivity analysis enables the identification of criteria whose weight variations can lead to significant shifts in the ranking of alternatives, thus revealing so-called critical criteria. Particularly important is the assessment of solution robustness, i.e., the degree to which rankings remain stable under different weighting scenarios. In this way, greater confidence is ensured in the decision outcomes, especially in situations characterized by uncertainty or differing opinions regarding the relative importance of the criteria. Furthermore, sensitivity analysis provides insights into the behavior of different MCDM methods under changes in criteria weights, enabling the selection of those methods that demonstrate the least sensitivity to such variations. Additionally, by determining stability intervals for criteria weights, it becomes possible

TABLE 61.10 A summary of the final rankings of cutting inserts.

Alternatives	Multicriteria decision-making methods analytic hierarchy process +...							
	WSM	WPM	ARAS	COPRAS	MOORA	VIKOR	TOPSIS	WASPAS $\lambda = 0.5$
A_1	3	3	11	3	5	3	3	3
A_2	1	1	4	1	2	1	2	1
A_3	14	13	14	14	14	14	13	13
A_4	13	12	13	13	13	13	14	12
A_5	12	11	9	12	12	12	12	11
A_6	8	9	5	9	10	10	11	8
A_7	9	14	8	8	8	8	8	14
A_8	11	8	10	11	9	9	9	9
A_9	5	5	3	5	4	7	6	5
A_{10}	7	7	7	7	6	5	7	7
A_{11}	10	10	6	10	11	11	10	10
A_{12}	4	4	2	4	3	6	4	4
A_{13}	6	6	12	6	7	4	5	6
A_{14}	2	2	1	2	1	2	1	2

TABLE 61.11 Kendall's tau-b rank correlation coefficients of cutting insert rankings.

	WSM	WPM	ARAS	COPRAS	MOORA	VIKOR	TOPSIS	WASPAS $\lambda = 0.5$
WSM	1.000	0.846	0.538	0.978	0.846	0.846	0.846	0.868
WPM	0.846	1.000	0.429	0.824	0.780	0.780	0.780	0.978
ARAS	0.538	0.429	1.000	0.516	0.560	0.385	0.429	0.451
COPRAS	0.978	0.824	0.516	1.000	0.868	0.868	0.868	0.846
MOORA	0.846	0.780	0.560	0.868	1.000	0.824	0.868	0.758
VIKOR	0.846	0.780	0.385	0.868	0.824	1.000	0.868	0.758
TOPSIS	0.846	0.780	0.429	0.868	0.868	0.868	1.000	0.758
WASPAS	0.868	0.978	0.451	0.846	0.758	0.758	0.758	1.000

to define domains within which the ranking remains unchanged, facilitating the communication of results and recommendations to decision-makers. This approach reduces the risk of making decisions based on unrepresentative or unstable outcomes. Ultimately, the systematic application of sensitivity analysis enhances the transparency and objectivity of the decision-making process, making it more resilient to subjective influences and methodological weaknesses.

In order to assess the sensitivity of the WSM and WPM to variations in criteria weights, a Monte Carlo simulation encompassing 1000 distinct scenarios was conducted. The simulation experiment was performed for eight MCDM methods: WSM, WPM, ARAS, COPRAS, MOORA, VIKOR, TOPSIS, and WASPAS. The experimental procedure followed the framework defined in Petrović Madic et al. (2018). The values of the criteria weights were randomly

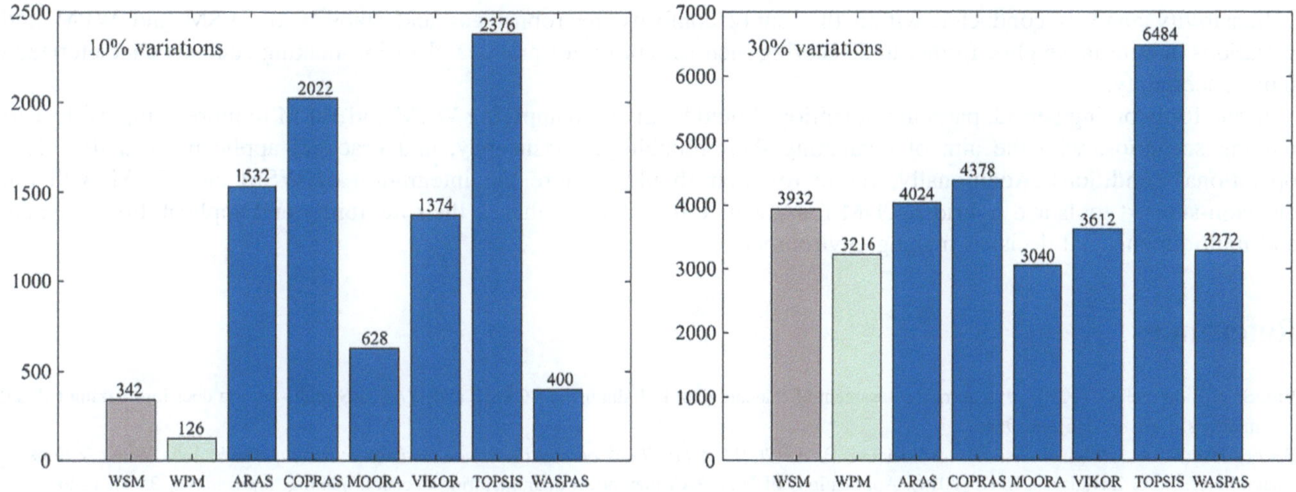

FIGURE 61.1 Changes in ranks relative to the original criteria weights solution.

generated within the defined intervals $[0.9w_j,\ 1.1w_j]$ and $[0.7w_j,\ 1.3w_j]$, where the upper and lower boundaries of each interval were defined as ±10% and ±30% of each original weight w_j. For these two cases, and across the eight MCDM methods, the complete rankings of the alternatives were computed. This procedure was repeated 1000 times with different randomly generated criteria weights. The changes in the ranks of the alternatives relative to the initial solution (obtained using the original criteria weights) were recorded, and the aggregate sums of all ranking changes are presented in Fig. 61.1.

Findings from the Monte Carlo experiment reveal that, under the 10% variation scenario, WPM and WSM exhibit notably lower total rank shifts (126 and 342, respectively), indicating a high degree of robustness to minor perturbations in criteria weights. In contrast, methods such as TOPSIS and COPRAS display significantly greater sensitivity (2376 and 2022, respectively), suggesting that their rankings are more susceptible to small fluctuations in criteria weights.

Under the 30% variation scenario, an overall increase in rank shifts is observed across all methods, which is expected due to the broader perturbation range. TOPSIS shows the highest sensitivity with a total of 6484 rank changes, followed by COPRAS and ARAS with 4378 and 4024, respectively. WPM and WSM maintain lower rank changes (3216 and 3932), reinforcing their comparative stability even under substantial criteria weight variations.

WSM and WPM demonstrate robustness and stability due to their additive and multiplicative aggregation structures, which mitigate the propagation of small criteria weight variations into significant rank changes. This structural simplicity ensures that minor fluctuations in criteria weights do not substantially affect the overall ranking outcomes.

61.7 Conclusions

MCDM constitutes one of the most recognized and extensively utilized domains within decision theory. Fundamentally, MCDM methods offer a systematic and structured approach to addressing decision-making problems characterized by the presence of multiple, often mutually conflicting, criteria and a predefined set of feasible alternatives. Although the procedures for formulating decision rules or aggregate optimality criteria may differ in form and complexity, each incorporates a mathematical framework, whether simple or advanced, designed to assess both the positive and negative implications associated with selecting a particular course of action.

At present, a wide variety of MCDM methods exist, some of which are highly sophisticated and computationally intensive, for instance, analytic network process, PROMETHEE, and ELECTRE. Although these advanced approaches offer powerful modeling capabilities, especially in dealing with complex decision-making environments, they often require considerable computational resources and expert knowledge for proper implementation. On the other hand, simpler methods such as WSM and WPM rely on relatively straightforward arithmetic operations, yet in most cases, they are capable of producing results that are comparable in quality to those obtained by more complex methods. Therefore, these simpler methods remain highly suitable for decision-making problems involving a limited number of alternatives and criteria, or in situations where transparency, computational efficiency, and ease of application are prioritized.

Sensitivity analysis conducted within this study confirms the robustness and stability of WSM and WPM under variations in criteria weights, further underscoring their suitability for practical decision-making contexts characterized by input uncertainty.

In the forthcoming period, particular attention should be given to applying WSM and WPM to more complex decision-making scenarios, with the aim of evaluating their reliability, consistency, and practical applicability under diverse operational conditions. Additionally, future research should explore the integration of WSM and WPM with other decision-support tools and hybrid MCDM frameworks, in order to enhance their flexibility and applicability in dynamic and multidimensional decision-making environments.

References

Bid, S., & Siddique, G. (2019). Human risk assessment of Panchet dam in India using TOPSIS and WASPAS multi-criteria decision-making (MCDM) methods. *Heliyon, 5*(6), e01956.

Bozorg-Haddad, O., Zolghadr-Asli, B., & Loaiciga, H. A. (2021). *A handbook on multi-attribute decision-making methods*. John Wiley & Sons.

Chakraborty, S., & Zavadskas, E. K. (2014). Applications of WASPAS method in manufacturing decision making. *Informatica, 25*(1), 1–20.

Chinnasami, S., RajKumar, S., Ramachandran, M., & Selvam, M. (2023). Evaluation of drinking water quality for salem district using weighted product method. *Materials and its Characterization, 2*(2), 01–09.

Churchman, C. W., Ackoff, R. L., & Smith, E. L. (1954). An approximate measure of value. *Journal of the Operations Research Society of America, 2*(2), 172–187.

Fishburn, P. C. (1967). Additive utilities with incomplete product sets: Applications to priorities and assignments. *Operations Research, 15*(3), 537–542. https://doi.org/10.1287/opre.15.3.537.

Frankowski, M. (2025). Application of multi criteria decision making using weighted sum method in tender procedures for the procurement of rail vehicles with innovative power sources. *Zeszyty Naukowe Politechniki Poznańskiej seria Organizacja i Zarządzanie, 90*, 223–238.

Garcia-Ayllon, S., Hontoria, E., & Munier, N. (2021). The contribution of MCDM to SUMP: The case of Spanish cities during 2006–2021. *International Journal of Environmental Research and Public Health, 19*(1), 294.

Gönül, Ö., Duman, A. C., & Güler, Ö. (2024). A comprehensive framework for electric vehicle charging station siting along highways using weighted sum method. *Renewable and Sustainable Energy Reviews, 199*, 114455.

Görçün, Ö. F., Ulutaş, A., Topal, A., & Ecer, F. (2024). Telescopic forklift selection through a novel interval-valued Fermatean fuzzy PIPRECIA–WISP approach. *Expert Systems with Applications, 255*, 124674.

Hwang, C. L., & Yoon, K. (1981). *Multiple attribute decision making: Methods and applications, a state-of-the-art survey*. Springer-Verlag. https://doi.org/10.1007/978-3-642-48318-9 (Lecture Notes in Economics and Mathematical Systems Vol. 186).

Jahan, F., Soni, M., Wakeel, S., Ahmad, S., & Bingol, S. (2022). Selection of automotive brake material using different MCDM techniques and their comparisons. *Journal of Engineering Science & Technology Review, 15*(1).

Kumar, G., & Parimala, N. (2020). A weighted sum method MCDM approach for recommending product using sentiment analysis. *International Journal of Business Information Systems, 35*(2), 185–203.

MacCrimon, K. R. (1968). Decision making among multiple attribute alternatives: A survey and consolidated approach. *Rand memorandum, RM-4823-ARPA*.

Madić, M., Petrović, G., Petković, D., Antucheviciene, J., & Marinković, D. (2022). Application of a robust decision-making rule for comprehensive assessment of laser cutting conditions and performance. *Machines, 10*(2), 153. https://doi.org/10.3390/machines10020153.

Madić, M., Trifunović, M., & Petrović, G. (2024). Selection of cutting insert for longitudinal turning of unalloyed steel using robust decision making. In Proceedings of the XX International May Conference on Strategic Management – IMCSM24, Bor, Serbia. https://doi.org/10.5937/IMCSM24034M.

Martunasia, A., Putra, T. A., & Mahessya, R. A. (2023). Selection of quality textile materials as a support for supply chain management with the weighted product method. *Journal of Computer Scine and Information Technology,* 107–111.

Miç, P., & Antmen, Z. F. (2021). A decision-making model based on TOPSIS, WASPAS, and MULTIMOORA methods for university location selection problem. *Sage Open, 11*(3) 21582440211040115.

Miller, D. W., & Starr, M. K. (1969). *Executive decisions and operations research*. Englewood Cliffs, NJ: Prentice-Hall.

Mitropoulos, L. K., & Prevedouros, P. D. (2016). Urban transportation vehicle sustainability assessment with a comparative study of weighted sum and fuzzy methods. *Journal of Urban Planning and Development, 142*(4), 04016013.

Murdani, F.A. S., Hutahaean, H.D., Sinaga, S.B., & Denni, M.R. (2020). Implementation of the weighted product method in the best student selection decision making system application. In 1st Unimed International Conference on Economics Education and Social Science (UNICEES), Medan, Indonesia, (October 31, 2018) (pp. 99-104).

Ochieng'Wao, J. (2018). Weighted product method in the value engineering process for construction project. *International Journal of Scientific Research and Management (IJSRM, 6*(12).

Petrović, G. S., Madić, M., & Antucheviciene, J. (2018). An approach for robust decision making rule generation: Solving transport and logistics decision making problems. *Expert Systems with Applications, 106*, 263–276. https://doi.org/10.1016/j.eswa.2018.04.002.

Petrović, G. S., Sekulić, V., Madić, M., & Mihajlović, J. (2018). A study of multicriteria decision making for selecting suppliers of linear motion guide. *Facta Universitatis, Series: Economics and Organization, 15*(2), 97–110. https://doi.org/10.22190/FUEO1802097P.

Petrović, G., Mihajlović, J., Marković, D., Hashemkhani Zolfani, S., & Madić, M. (2023). Comparison of aggregation operators in the group decision-making process: A real case study of location selection problem. *Sustainability, 15*(10), 8229. https://doi.org/10.3390/su15108229.

Sinaga, A., & Maulana, D. (2022). Implementation of weighted product method for evaluating performance of technicians. *International Journal of Modern Education and Computer Science, 11*(4), 30.

Sokolović, J., Stanujkić, D., Štirbanović, Z., & Ilić, I. (2025). Comparative analysis on washability indices of anthracite coal by using MCDM methods. *Physicochemical Problems of Mineral Processing, 61*(1).

Stanujkic, D., Popovic, G., Karabasevic, D., Meidute-Kavaliauskiene, I., & Ulutaş, A. (2021). An integrated simple weighted sum product method—WISP. *IEEE Transactions on Engineering Management, 70*(5), 1933–1944.

Stanujkic, M. (2023). Comparative analysis of MULTIMOORA, WASPAS and WISP methods: The case of candidate selection. *Journal of Process Management and New Technologies, 11*(3-4), 79–88.

Triantaphyllou, E., & Lin, C. T. (1996). Development and evaluation of five fuzzy multiattribute decision-making methods. *International Journal of Approximate Reasoning, 14*(4), 281–310. https://doi.org/10.1016/0888-613X(95)00119-2.

Triantaphyllou, E., & Mann, S. H. (1989). An examination of the effectiveness of multi-dimensional decision-making methods: A decision-making paradox. *Decision Support Systems, 5*(3), 303–312. https://doi.org/10.1016/0167-9236(89)90037-7.

Trifunović, M., Madić, M., Petrović, G., Marinković, D., & Janković, P. (2025). Fuzzy MCDM methodology for analysis of fibre laser cutting process. *Applied Sciences, 15*(13), 7364. https://doi.org/10.3390/app15137364.

Turudija, R., Radović, L., Stanković, A., & Stojković, M. (2023, March). Multi-criteria decision making in turning operations using AHP, TOPSIS and WASPAS methods. In Conference on Information Technology and its Applications (pp. 193–205). Cham: Springer Nature Switzerland.

Ulutaş, A., Stanujkic, D., Karabasevic, D., Popovic, G., & Novaković, S. (2022). Pallet truck selection with MEREC and WISP-S methods. *Strategic Management - International Journal of Strategic Management and Decision Support Systems in Strategic Management, 27*(4).

Vani, K. A., & RamaMohanBabu, K. N. (2023). An intelligent server load balancing based on multi-criteria decision-making in SDN. *International Journal of Electrical and Computer Engineering Systems, 14*(4), 433–442.

Zavadskas, E. K., Antuchevičienė, J., Šaparauskas, J., & Turskis, Z. (2013). MCDM methods WASPAS and MULTIMOORA: Verification of robustness of methods when assessing alternative solutions. *Economic Computation & Economic Cybernetics Studies & Research, 47*(2), 5–20.

Zavadskas, E. K., Turskis, Z., Antuchevičienė, J., & Zakarevičius, A. (2012). Optimization of weighted aggregated sum product assessment. *Elektronika ir Elektrotechnika, 122*(6), 3–6. https://doi.org/10.5755/j01.eee.122.6.1810.

Zulqarnain, R. M., Siddique, I., Ali, R., Pamucar, D., Marinkovic, D., & Bozanic, D. (2021). Robust aggregation operators for intuitionistic fuzzy hypersoft set with their application to solve MCDM problem. *Entropy, 23*(6), 688. https://doi.org/10.3390/e23060688.

Chapter 62

WASPAS: Weighted aggregated sum product assessment for multi-attribute decision-making

Bartosz Paradowski
National Institute of Telecommunications, Warsaw, Poland

62.1 Introduction

The increasing complexity of contemporary decision-making processes necessitates the adoption of analytical frameworks capable of simultaneously considering multiple, often conflicting, criteria while accounting for stakeholder preferences and inherent uncertainties. Multicriteria decision-making (MCDM) has therefore emerged as a cornerstone of modern operations research, offering systematic approaches to support rational evaluation of alternatives across diverse objectives. Over the past five decades, MCDM has experienced remarkable growth, as evidenced by the exponential rise in publications and citations, reflecting its importance in both theoretical advancements and practical applications (Mühlbacher & Kaczynski, 2016; Wieckowski et al., 2023).

The popularity of MCDM methods began to rise significantly during the 1970s and 1980s, coinciding with the development of nowadays popular techniques, such as Saaty's analytic hierarchy process (AHP) (Saaty, 2013), the technique for order preference by similarity to ideal solution (Lai et al., 1994), and a wide range of multiobjective optimization approaches. At the same time, classical models such as the weighted sum model (WSM) (Fishburn et al., 1968) and the weighted product model (WPM) (Fishburn et al., 1968) remained fundamental due to their mathematical elegance and computational efficiency. However, despite their widespread use, both approaches exhibit intrinsic limitations that may compromise decision quality under complex scenarios.

The WSM, one of the earliest MCDM models, aggregates performance scores by linearly combining weighted criteria values. Its intuitive interpretation and computational tractability have contributed to its extensive adoption, particularly in problems where criteria are measured on comparable scales. Nonetheless, WSM suffers from limitations, especially when applied to heterogeneous, multidimensional decision contexts, where normalization procedures become critical. Its purely additive structure also allows for complete compensation among criteria, meaning that poor performance in one dimension can be offset entirely by strong performance in another, potentially obscuring essential trade-offs.

The WPM, in contrast, applies multiplicative aggregation, calculating alternative scores as weighted geometric means of normalized criteria. This structure provides a higher degree of flexibility and mitigates some of the compensation effects inherent to additive models. However, the multiplicative formulation introduces sensitivity to extreme values and may complicate interpretation for decision-makers unfamiliar with nonlinear aggregation. These complementary advantages and disadvantages have motivated the pursuit of hybrid models capable of reconciling their respective strengths.

The weighted aggregated sum product assessment (WASPAS) method was introduced by Zavadskas (1987) as an integrated approach to MCDM, later formalized and further elaborated by Šaparauskas et al. (2011), and systematized in the work of Zavadskas et al. (2012). WASPAS represents a significant methodological advancement by combining the additive WSM and multiplicative WPM into a unified framework via a linear aggregation parameter λ. This hybridization leverages the interpretability and efficiency of WSM with the dimensional adaptability of WPM, while enabling optimization of λ to enhance ranking accuracy.

Encyclopedia of Multi-Attribute Decision-Making (MADM). DOI: https://doi.org/10.1016/B978-0-443-33275-3.00060-9

Since its inception, WASPAS has been applied across a broad range of domains, including manufacturing system evaluation (Chakraborty et al., 2015), sustainable energy planning (Ilbahar et al., 2023), construction management (Badalpur & Nurbakhsh, 2021), healthcare decision-making (Mishra & Rani, 2021), and supply chain optimization (Sharma et al., 2023). Moreover, numerous methodological extensions have been proposed, incorporating fuzzy sets (Kizielewicz & Baczkiewicz, 2021), intuitionistic fuzzy sets (Mishra & Rani, 2018), neutrosophic sets (Kaya et al., 2023), and interval-based approaches (Zavadskas et al., 2014) to address uncertainty and imprecision in real-world data. These developments illustrate the method's adaptability and its alignment with contemporary research trends toward hybrid, flexible, and uncertainty-aware decision-making frameworks.

Against this background, WASPAS stands out as a robust and versatile MCDM tool, striking a balance between mathematical rigor and practical applicability. Its continuing development and widespread adoption underscore its significance within the evolving landscape of decision sciences.

62.2 Literature review

The WASPAS method was originally proposed by Zavadskas (1987) and subsequently refined in later works, most notably by Šaparauskas et al. (2011). A comprehensive formalization of the method and its optimization aspects was later provided by Zavadskas et al. (2012). Since then, WASPAS has become one of the prominent hybrid MCDM techniques, attracting considerable attention in both theoretical research and practical applications.

The popularity of WASPAS has stimulated a growing body of literature focusing on two principal directions: methodological extensions aimed at enhancing the method's flexibility and ability to incorporate uncertainty (Section 62.2.1) and applications across diverse decision-making environments, ranging from engineering design to socio–economic planning (Section 62.2.2). To provide a structured overview, the following sections examine these two dimensions in detail.

62.2.1 Extensions of weighted aggregated sum product assessment

Since its original formulation, the WASPAS method has been the subject of substantial methodological development. These extensions have primarily aimed to enhance its ability to capture uncertainty, imprecision, and vagueness inherent in real-world decision-making environments. Among the earliest and most widely studied directions are fuzzy-based generalizations. Classical fuzzy sets, intuitionistic fuzzy sets, and interval-valued fuzzy models have been incorporated into WASPAS to better represent linguistic judgments and hesitation in expert evaluations. For instance, Stanujkić & Karabašević (2018) introduced an intuitionistic fuzzy WASPAS model that demonstrated their performance in decision contexts characterized by uncertainty and hesitation.

Building on this foundation, more advanced fuzzy paradigms have been adopted. Pythagorean (Mahmood et al., 2025) and spherical fuzzy WASPAS (Cheng, 2025) variants extend the representation of membership and nonmembership degrees. These approaches improve modeling flexibility when decision-makers cannot provide single, crisp judgments. Further generalizations include q-rung orthopair fuzzy WASPAS (Deveci et al., 2022), which relaxes traditional constraints on membership values, often in combination with advanced aggregation operators, thereby offering enhanced modeling power in highly uncertain contexts. Similarly, Fermatean fuzzy WASPAS offers a comprehensive domain relaxing the representation of expert judgments and has been applied in healthcare (Rao & Sujatha, 2023) and waste management domains (Mishra & Rani, 2021), where uncertainty and ambiguity are particularly pronounced.

Beyond fuzzy environments, WASPAS has been extended into neutrosophic domains, where truth, indeterminacy, and falsity are modeled explicitly. Both single-valued (Goyal & Rani, 2024) and type-2 neutrosophic WASPAS (Kaya et al., 2023) frameworks have been shown to perform well in highly uncertain and contradictory environments. Parallel developments include gray WASPAS (Zavadskas et al., 2015), which addresses incomplete information through gray numbers, and probabilistic linguistic WASPAS (Darko & Liang, 2022) variants have also emerged, allowing the incorporation of probability distributions and linguistic term sets to explicitly account for expert confidence levels.

Another line of research has focused on hybridization and weight-determination enhancements. WASPAS has been combined with other MCDM techniques such as AHP (Alam et al., 2018), best–worst method (Balezentis et al., 2021), and stepwise weight assessment ratio analysis (Yücenur & Ipekçi, 2021). These integrations improve weight assignment robustness and enable the method to reflect varying risk attitudes of decision-makers. Finally, the development of computational tools such as the waspasR package and web-based Shiny application (Barbara et al., 2023) has simplified practical adoption of WASPAS and its variants, making them more accessible to researchers and practitioners alike.

62.2.2 Applications of weighted aggregated sum product assessment

The broad adaptability of WASPAS and its extensions has been demonstrated across a wide range of application domains. In manufacturing and industrial engineering, the method has been applied to robot selection (Sampathkumar et al., 2023), evaluation of cutting fluids (Chakraborty & Zavadskas, 2014), and process optimization (Radomska-Zalas, 2023). In the domain of sustainability and renewable energy, WASPAS has been widely utilized for green supplier selection (Xiong et al., 2020), evaluation of renewable energy companies (Erdoğan et al., 2022), and sustainable supply chain management (Pamucar et al., 2022).

Healthcare applications of WASPAS include patient prioritization (Darko & Liang, 2022), evaluation of hospital service quality (Komijan et al., 2024), medical equipment selection (Mazloum et al., 2019), and healthcare waste disposal site identification (Menekse & Akdağ, 2023). In these contexts, uncertainty and imprecision are unavoidable, which explains the frequent reliance on fuzzy and neutrosophic extensions. Similarly, in transportation and logistics, WASPAS has been applied to last-mile delivery optimization (Aktas & Kabak, 2022), mode choice (Simić et al., 2021), and port sustainability evaluations (Kaya et al., 2023).

Further applications extend to information and communication technologies, including keyword extraction (Chen et al., 2025), cloud computing product evaluation (Alam et al., 2018), and infrastructure planning in telecommunications (Mishra et al., 2019). The method has also been adopted in environmental and agricultural domains, water resource management (Foladi et al., 2020), waste management (Mishra & Rani, 2021), and environmental risk assessments (Ebadzadeh et al., 2023). Finally, in finance and business management, WASPAS has been employed for supplier evaluation (Keshavarz-Ghorabaee et al., 2020), contractor selection (Amalia et al., 2024), and corporate sustainability performance measurement (Bathrinath et al., 2022).

Taken together, these applications underscore WASPAS's robustness as a general-purpose MCDM tool. Its adaptability to diverse problem structures, ranging from quantitative industrial data to qualitative expert-driven evaluations, demonstrates the effectiveness of the method and its variants in supporting decision-making under conditions of complexity, uncertainty, and conflicting objectives.

62.3 Methodology

62.3.1 Weighted aggregated sum product assessment

The WASPAS method evaluates decision alternatives through the following steps:

1. Construct a decision matrix of dimension $n \times m$, where n denotes the number of alternatives and \$m\$ the number of evaluation criteria (Eq. 62.1):

$$X = [x_{ij}] = \begin{bmatrix} x_{11} & x_{12} & \cdots & x_{1m} \\ x_{21} & x_{22} & \cdots & x_{2m} \\ \vdots & \vdots & \ddots & \vdots \\ x_{n1} & x_{n2} & \cdots & x_{nm} \end{bmatrix}, \tag{62.1}$$

where x_{ij} represents the performance of alternative i under criterion j.

2. Normalize the decision matrix to eliminate scale effects among criteria by applying linear normalization, for profit-type criteria (Eq. 62.2) or cost-type criteria (62.3):

$$r_{ij} = \frac{x_{ij}}{\max_i x_{ij}}, \quad \text{if the j−th criterion is of the profit type,} \tag{62.2}$$

$$r_{ij} = \frac{\min_i x_{ij}}{x_{ij}}, \quad \text{if the j−th criterion is of the cost type,} \tag{62.3}$$

where r_{ij} denotes the normalized value of alternative i under criterion j.

3. For each alternative i, compute the WSM and the WPM values as:

$$WSM_i = \sum_{j=1}^{m} r_{ij} w_j, \tag{62.4}$$

$$WPM_i = \prod_{j=1}^{m} (r_{ij})^{w_j}, \tag{62.5}$$

where w_j is the weight associated with the j-th criterion.

4. Calculate the total relative performance score Q_i for each alternative i by aggregating the WSM and WPM scores using the aggregation coefficient $\lambda \in [0,1]$:

$$Q_i = \lambda\, WSM_i + (1-\lambda)\, WPM_i = \lambda \sum_{j=1}^{m} r_{ij} w_j + (1-\lambda) \prod_{j=1}^{m} (r_{ij})^{w_j}. \tag{62.6}$$

The coefficient λ controls the balance between additive and multiplicative aggregation. A commonly used value is λ=0.5, which assigns equal importance to both indices.

5. Rank alternatives in descending order of Q_i; the alternative with the highest score is considered the most preferable.

62.3.2 Estimation accuracy and optimization of the aggregation coefficient in weighted aggregated sum product assessment

Zavadskas et al. (2012) proposed an approach to evaluate the accuracy of WASPAS rankings and to determine the optimal value of the aggregation coefficient λ. The accuracy of estimation is quantified through the variance of the aggregated preference value Q_i, expressed as:

$$\sigma^2(Q_i) = \lambda^2 \sigma^2\left(Q_i^{(1)}\right) + (1-\lambda)^2 \sigma^2\left(Q_i^{(2)}\right) \tag{62.7}$$

where $\sigma^2(Q_i^{(1)})$ and $\sigma^2(Q_i^{(2)})$ represent the variances of the WSM- and WPM-based preference estimates, respectively. These are computed as:

$$\sigma^2\left(Q_i^{(1)}\right) = \sum_{j=1}^{n} w_j^2 \sigma^2(r_{ij}) \tag{62.8}$$

$$\sigma^2\left(Q_i^{(2)}\right) = \sum_{j=1}^{n} \left(\frac{\prod_{j=1}^{n} (r_{ij})^{w_j} w_j}{(r_{ij})^{w_j} (r_{ij})^{\left(1-w_j\right)}} \right)^2 \sigma^2(r_{ij}) \tag{62.9}$$

with $\sigma^2(r_{ij})$ denoting the variance of the normalized criterion values.

The variance of normalized criteria is estimated as:

$$\sigma^2(r_{ij}) = \left(\frac{r_{ij} k}{t}\right)^2 \tag{62.10}$$

where k is a coefficient reflecting the uncertainty of the measurement, and t is a distribution-dependent multiplier determined by the confidence level q. For example, when the uncertainty of estimation is approximately 10% of the mean criterion value (k=0.10) and assuming normally distributed errors with confidence q=0.05 (t=2.0), this reduces to:

$$\sigma^2(r_{ij}) = \left(0.05 r_{ij}\right)^2. \tag{62.11}$$

Thus, the variance of WASPAS estimates (Eq. 62.7) depends on the individual variances of the WSM and WPM estimates (Eqs. 62.8–62.9) and on the aggregation coefficient λ. The optimization task consists of determining the value of λ that minimizes $\sigma^2(Q_i)$, thereby ensuring maximum estimation accuracy. The optimal coefficient is obtained by differentiating Eq. 62.7 with respect to λ and setting the derivative equal to zero:

$$2\lambda\sigma^2\left(Q_i^{(1)}\right) - 2\sigma^2\left(Q_i^{(2)}\right) + 2\lambda\sigma^2\left(Q_i^{(2)}\right) = 0,$$

$$\lambda = \frac{\sigma^2\left(Q_i^{(2)}\right)}{\sigma^2\left(Q_i^{(1)}\right) + \sigma^2\left(Q_i^{(2)}\right)}. \tag{62.12}$$

Accordingly, the optimal $\lambda*$ (Eq. 62.12) should be determined individually for each alternative prior to applying the WASPAS aggregation rule (Eq. 62.6). Its value depends on the ratio $\sigma^2(Q_i^{(1)})/\sigma^2(Q_i^{(2)})$, and may therefore vary across different decision-making scenarios.

62.4 Numerical example I

This section introduces a simple theoretical decision-making problem characterized by four alternatives evaluated across four criteria. In this section, only the base method will be presented step by step to provide a clear understanding of how to apply it to decision-making problems without in-depth analysis. The performance values of the alternatives were generated randomly from a uniform distribution over the interval [0,1]. Criterion weights were determined using the entropy method, a widely applied technique in the literature. For the sake of simplicity, all criteria are assumed to be of the profit type, implying that higher values are preferable. The resulting decision matrix is presented in Table 62.1.

The subsequent step involves the computation of the normalized decision matrix. For profit-type criteria, normalization is performed according to Eq. 62.2, while for cost-type criteria, (62.3) is applied. This procedure standardizes the criteria values, ensuring comparability across different scales and preventing disproportionate influence on the final results. The resulting normalized decision matrix is presented in Table 62.2.

In the next step, preference values are computed using the aggregated WASPAS model, which combines the WSM and WPM. The aggregation coefficient λ was varied over the interval [0,1] with an increment of 0.1, yielding eleven sets of preference scores for the considered alternatives (Table 62.3).

For practical applications, it is common in the literature to adopt λ=0.5, which provides a balanced compromise between the additive and multiplicative aggregation schemes. Under this setting, the resulting ranking is: $A_2 \succ A_3 \succ A_1 \succ A_4$, where $\succ$ denotes preference order.

To further illustrate the ranking dynamics, Fig. 62.1 presents the ordering of alternatives as a function of λ. It can be observed that the ranking obtained for λ=0.5 predominates across most cases (7 out of 11 values of λ). Notably, changes in ranking occur for λ>0.6, where A_4 surpasses A_1 and A_3 alternates its position with A_2.

TABLE 62.1 Decision matrix of the theoretical decision-making problem.

A_i	C_1	C_2	C_3	C_4
A_1	0.5077	0.3179	0.3525	0.3422
A_2	0.7798	0.4451	0.6213	0.2583
A_3	0.8716	0.4604	0.8565	0.1488
A_4	0.2234	0.4722	0.7337	0.4555
weights	0.4391	0.0491	0.1977	0.3141
type	*Profit*	*Profit*	*Profit*	*Profit*

TABLE 62.2 Normalized decision matrix of the theoretical decision-making problem.

A_i	C_1	C_2	C_3	C_4
A_1	0.5825	0.6732	0.4116	0.7513
A_2	0.8947	0.9426	0.7254	0.5671
A_3	1.0000	0.9750	1.0000	0.3267
A_4	0.2563	1.0000	0.8566	1.0000

TABLE 62.3 Preference values calculated using weighted aggregated sum product assessment for different values of λ.

A_i	λ=0.0	λ=0.1	λ=0.2	λ=0.3	λ=0.4	λ=0.5	λ=0.6	λ=0.7	λ=0.8	λ=0.9	λ=1.0
A_1	0.5933	0.5946	0.5959	0.5971	0.5984	0.5997	0.6010	0.6023	0.6036	0.6049	0.6062
A_2	0.7457	0.7472	0.7487	0.7502	0.7517	0.7532	0.7547	0.7562	0.7577	0.7592	0.7607
A_3	0.7028	0.7113	0.7197	0.7281	0.7366	0.7450	0.7535	0.7619	0.7704	0.7788	0.7873
A_4	0.5335	0.5446	0.5558	0.5669	0.5781	0.5893	0.6004	0.6116	0.6228	0.6339	0.6451

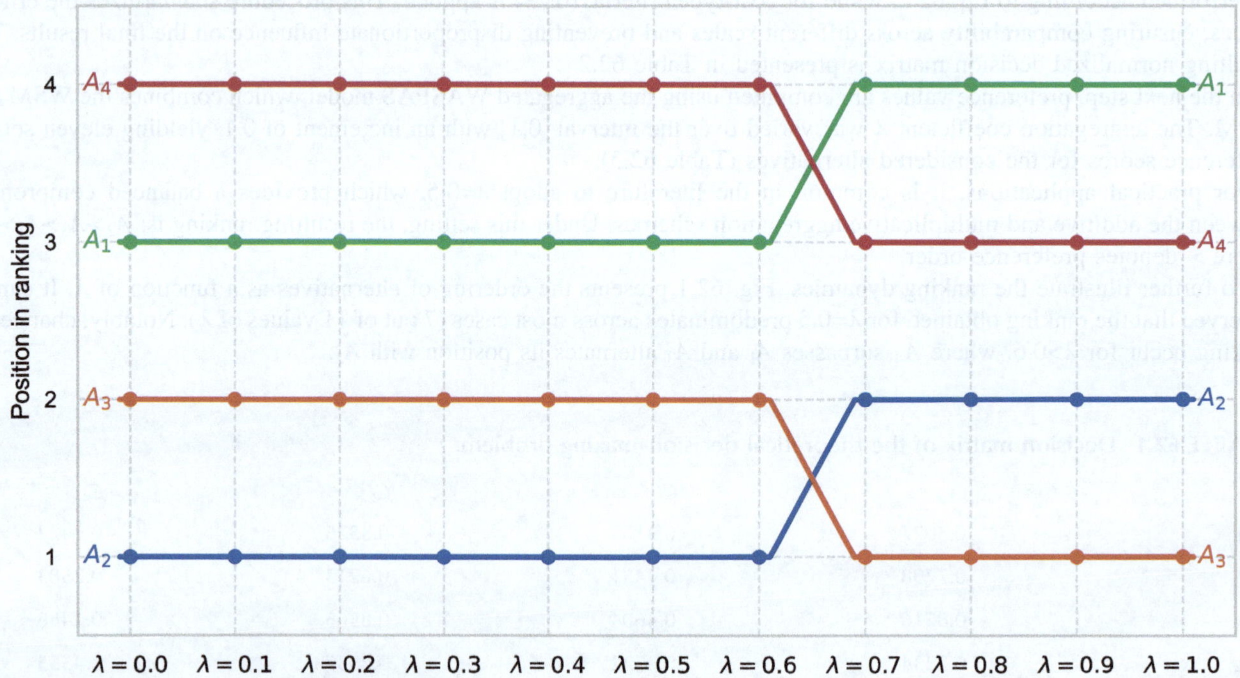

FIGURE 62.1 Ranking dynamics of alternatives across different values of λ for the theoretical decision-making problem.

62.5 Numerical example II

The second numerical example is adapted from the work of Chatterjee and Chakraborty (2016), who investigated the relative performance of grinding wheel abrasive materials. In their study, the authors employed the VlseKriterijumska Optimizacija I Kompromisno Resenje method and obtained the following ranking of alternatives: $A_5 \succ A_3 \succ A_2 \succ A_4 \succ A_6 \succ A_1 \succ A_7 \succ A_8$

The alternatives considered include titanium carbide (A_1), tungsten carbide (A_2), cubic boron nitride (A_3), aluminum oxide (A_4), synthetic polycrystalline diamond (A_5), silicon carbide (A_6), boron carbide (A_7), and yttria-stabilized zirconia (A_8). These materials are characterized using seven evaluation criteria: knoop hardness (KHN, C_1), modulus of elasticity (GPa, C_2), compressive strength (MPa, C_3), shear strength (MPa, C_4), thermal conductivity (W/m·K, C_5), fracture toughness (MPa·m$^{1/2}$, C_6), and material cost (USD/kg, C_7).

The normalized decision matrix for this case study is provided in Table 62.4, together with the corresponding criterion weights and the type of each criterion (profit or cost). The normalization step ensures that criteria with different measurement units and magnitudes exert commensurate influence on the subsequent multicriteria evaluation process. The

TABLE 62.4 Decision matrix of the grinding wheel abrasive materials performance evaluation problem.

A_i	C_1	C_2	C_3	C_4	C_5	C_6	C_7
A_1	0.4000	0.4732	0.5036	0.1613	0.0142	0.4826	0.5556
A_2	0.3000	0.7240	0.7210	0.2824	0.0817	0.3488	0.1667
A_3	0.6250	0.8919	1.0000	0.3268	0.0108	0.5233	0.0116
A_4	0.3750	0.4197	0.5507	0.1875	0.0250	0.4651	0.0658
A_5	1.0000	1.0000	0.9710	1.0000	1.0000	1.0000	0.0077
A_6	0.3188	0.4617	0.6667	0.1024	0.1667	0.3605	1.0000
A_7	0.3500	0.4827	0.2494	0.1280	0.0750	0.2907	0.2000
A_8	0.1500	0.1679	0.2536	0.1323	0.0018	0.9535	0.2222
weights	0.3552	0.0429	0.4356	0.1248	0.01661	0.0001	0.0252
types	*Profit*	*Profit*	*Profit*	*Profit*	*Profit*	*Profit*	*Cost*

TABLE 62.5 Preference values calculated using weighted aggregated sum product assessment for different values of λ.

A_i	λ=0.0	λ=0.1	λ=0.2	λ=0.3	λ=0.4	λ=0.5	λ=0.6	λ=0.7	λ=0.8	λ=0.9	λ=1.0
A_1	0.3792	0.3829	0.3866	0.3903	0.3940	0.3977	0.4014	0.4051	0.4088	0.4125	0.4162
A_2	0.4366	0.4422	0.4478	0.4534	0.4590	0.4646	0.4702	0.4758	0.4814	0.4869	0.4925
A_3	0.6071	0.6201	0.6331	0.6461	0.6591	0.6721	0.6852	0.6982	0.7112	0.7242	0.7372
A_4	0.3737	0.3780	0.3823	0.3866	0.3909	0.3952	0.3995	0.4037	0.4080	0.4123	0.4166
A_5	0.8733	0.8822	0.8912	0.9001	0.9091	0.9180	0.9270	0.9359	0.9449	0.9538	0.9628
A_6	0.3945	0.4015	0.4084	0.4154	0.4224	0.4293	0.4363	0.4433	0.4503	0.4572	0.4642
A_7	0.2594	0.2611	0.2627	0.2644	0.2660	0.2677	0.2693	0.2710	0.2727	0.2743	0.2760
A_8	0.1750	0.1768	0.1786	0.1804	0.1823	0.1841	0.1859	0.1877	0.1896	0.1914	0.1932

weight distribution indicates that compressive strength (C_3) and hardness (C_1) are the dominant performance measures, whereas fracture toughness (C_6) carries negligible influence.

Following the construction of the decision matrix, WASPAS preference values were calculated for different values of the aggregation parameter λ. The results are summarized in Table 62.5, which illustrates how the composite performance score (Q) of each alternative varies across the range $\lambda \in [0,1]$. The analysis reveals that alternatives A_5, A_3, and A_2 consistently outperform the remaining options, while A_7 and A_8 obtain the lowest scores.

For clarity of interpretation, the ranking dynamics are visualized in Fig. 62.2. The figure demonstrates that the ranking of alternatives remains largely stable across the entire range of λ. Only at λ=1.0 do alternatives A_1 and A_4 exchange positions, while the overall order remains unchanged in all other cases. Thus, the WASPAS results yield the following ranking: $A_5 \succ A_3 \succ A_2 \succ A_6 \succ A_1 \succ A_4 \succ A_7 \succ A_8$, which differs slightly from the ordering reported in (Chatterjee & Chakraborty, 2016).

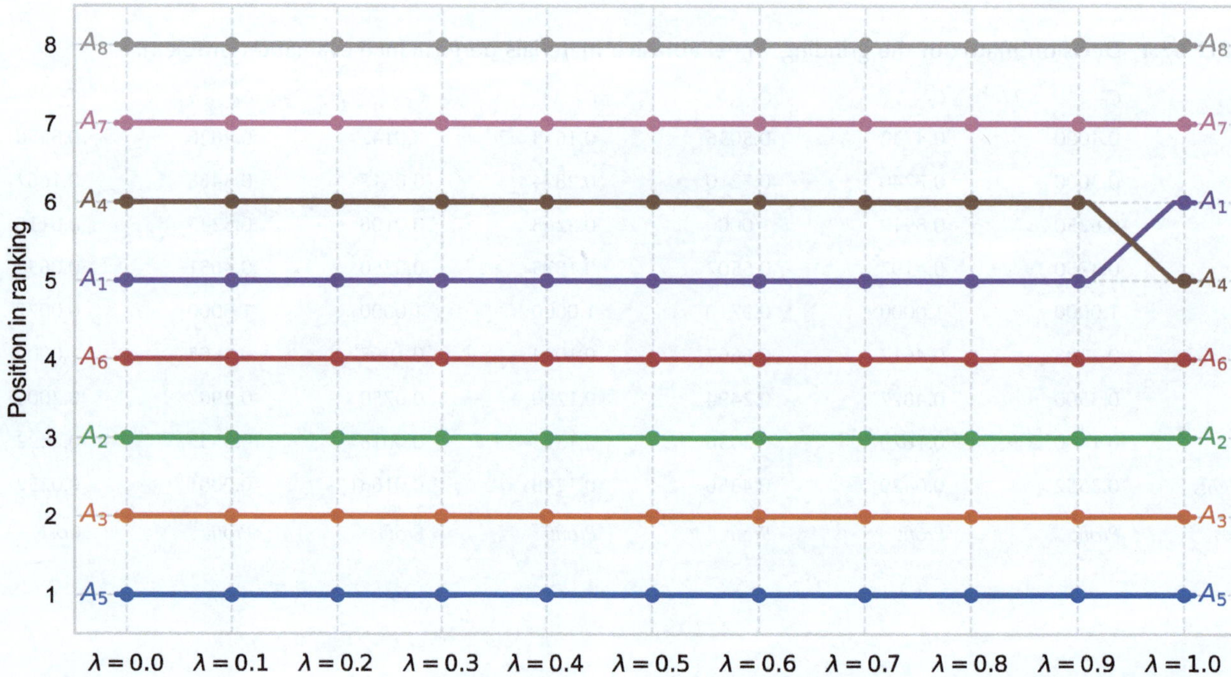

FIGURE 62.2 Ranking dynamics of alternatives across different values of λ using the weighted aggregated sum product assessment method.

TABLE 62.6 Accuracy of estimation (std) depending on λ.

A_i	λ=0.0	λ=0.1	λ=0.2	λ=0.3	λ=0.4	λ=0.5	λ=0.6	λ=0.7	λ=0.8	λ=0.9	λ=1.0
A_1	0.0110	0.0100	0.0092	0.0086	0.0084	0.0086	0.0090	0.0098	0.0108	0.0119	0.0132
A_2	0.0126	0.0115	0.0106	0.0102	0.0101	0.0105	0.0112	0.0123	0.0136	0.0151	0.0167
A_3	0.0175	0.0160	0.0149	0.0143	0.0144	0.0151	0.0163	0.0180	0.0200	0.0222	0.0246
A_4	0.0108	0.0098	0.0091	0.0086	0.0085	0.0088	0.0093	0.0102	0.0112	0.0125	0.0138
A_5	0.0252	0.0229	0.0210	0.0196	0.0189	0.0190	0.0198	0.0213	0.0233	0.0257	0.0284
A_6	0.0114	0.0104	0.0096	0.0093	0.0093	0.0097	0.0105	0.0115	0.0127	0.0142	0.0157
A_7	0.0075	0.0068	0.0062	0.0058	0.0056	0.0056	0.0058	0.0063	0.0069	0.0076	0.0084
A_8	0.0051	0.0046	0.0042	0.0040	0.0039	0.0040	0.0042	0.0046	0.0051	0.0056	0.0062

To further assess the robustness of the WASPAS evaluation, the accuracy of estimation was analyzed by quantifying the standard deviation of preference scores as a function of λ (Eq. 62.7). The computed accuracy measures are presented in Table 62.6, where lower standard deviation values indicate more reliable preference estimation.

The error dynamics are further visualized in Fig. 62.3, which illustrates how the estimation error evolves with λ. As can be observed, the combined use of both WSM and WPM (i.e., λ between 0 and 1) achieves higher ranking accuracy than employing either method independently.

Finally, optimal λ values were determined for each alternative using Eq. 62.12, followed by computation of their corresponding preference values (Q) and confidence intervals at a significance level of q=0.05. The final results are summarized in Table 62.7, which presents the refined WASPAS ranking. These results confirm the superior performance of synthetic polycrystalline diamond (A_5), followed by cubic boron nitride (A_3) and tungsten carbide (A_2).

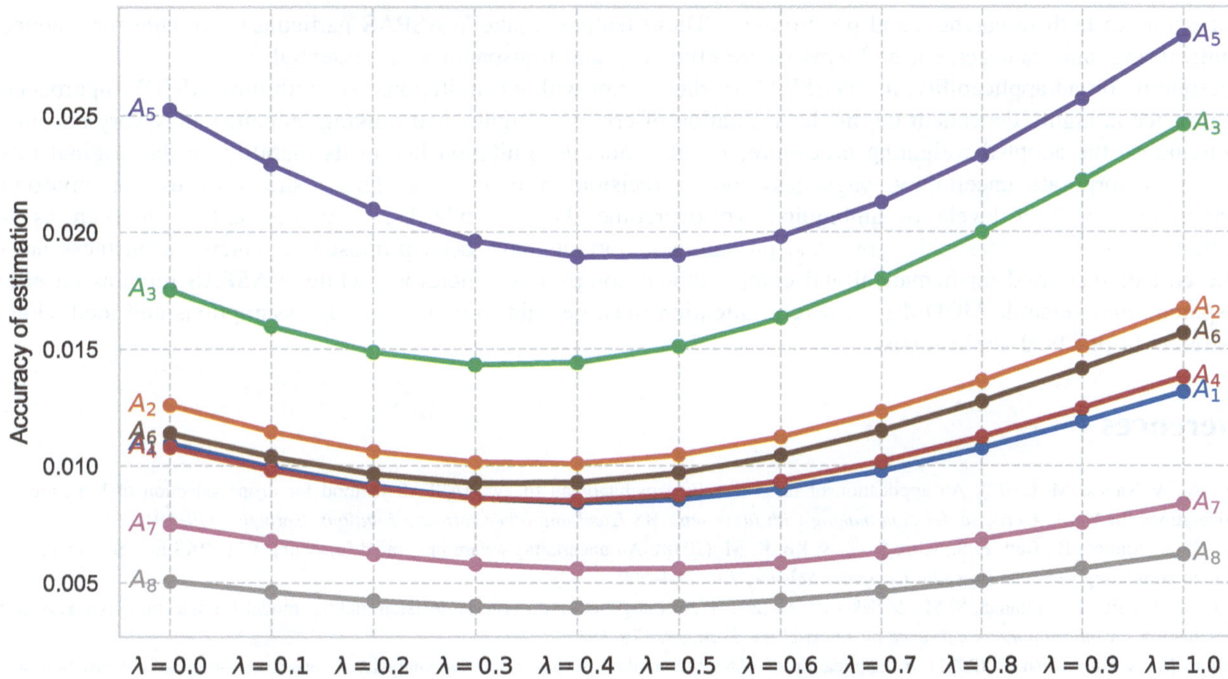

FIGURE 62.3 Dependence of estimation errors on values of λ.

TABLE 62.7 Final preference values based on optimal λ.

A_i	Optimal λ	Q	Confidence interval
A_1	0.4094	0.3943	0.0004
A_2	0.3622	0.4569	0.0005
A_3	0.3372	0.6510	0.0011
A_4	0.3800	0.3900	0.0004
A_5	0.4413	0.9128	0.0021
A_6	0.3459	0.4186	0.0004
A_7	0.4457	0.2668	0.0002
A_8	0.3992	0.1823	0.0001

62.6 Conclusions

The WASPAS method provides a practical balance between additive and multiplicative aggregation techniques, integrating the WSM and WPM through the adjustment parameter λ. This hybridization allows decision-makers to capture the benefits of both approaches: the simplicity and interpretability of WSM, alongside the multiplicative sensitivity of WPM. As a result, WASPAS provides stable and consistent rankings across a wide range of λ values, which enhances the reliability of its outcomes. Furthermore, the ability to optimize λ improves ranking accuracy, enabling the method to adapt flexibly to different decision-making contexts.

In addition to its robustness, WASPAS remains computationally efficient, even when applied to large-scale problems. Its mathematical formulation is straightforward, which facilitates implementation in decision-support systems and makes it accessible to both researchers and practitioners. These features make WASPAS particularly suitable for engineering, manufacturing, and management problems where efficiency and transparency are essential.

Despite its broad applicability, the WASPAS method is not without limitations. As with most MCDM approaches, its performance is highly dependent on the determination of criteria weights, and ranking outcomes may vary considerably depending on the adopted weighting procedure. Another notable limitation lies in its inability, in the original form, to explicitly incorporate uncertainty, vagueness, or imprecision in input data. This restricts its use in environments characterized by high levels of ambiguity. To overcome these drawbacks, numerous extensions-such as fuzzy, intuitionistic fuzzy, neutrosophic, gray, and probabilistic variants-have been proposed, enhancing robustness but often at the cost of increased mathematical and computational complexity. Therefore, while WASPAS remains an efficient, transparent, and versatile MCDM tool, careful attention must be paid to its underlying assumptions and methodological constraints in practical applications.

References

Aktas, A., & Kabak, M. (2022). An application of interval valued pythagorean fuzzy WASPAS method for drone selection to last mile delivery operations. In *Multiple criteria decision making with fuzzy sets: MS Excel and other software solutions*. Springer, 179–191.

Alam, K. A., Ahmed, R., Butt, F. S., Kim, S. G., & Ko, K. M. (2018). An uncertainty-aware integrated fuzzy ahp-WASPAS model to evaluate public cloud computing services. *Procedia Computer Science, 130*, 504–509.

Amalia, C., Ismail, A., Shuhidan, S. M., & Sakamat, N. (2024). An integrated multi criteria decision making model for selection contractor in tender evaluation. In *International conference on smart cities*. Springer, 175–188.

Badalpur, M., & Nurbakhsh, E. (2021). An application of WASPAS method in risk qualitative analysis: A case study of a road construction project in iran. *International Journal of Construction Management, 21*(9), 910–918.

Balezentis, T., Siksnelyte-Butkiene, I., & Streimikiene, D. (2021). Stakeholder involvement for sustainable energy development based on uncertain group decision making: Prioritizing the renewable energy heating technologies and the BWM-WASPAS-in approach. *Sustainable Cities and Society, 73*, 103114.

Barbara, F., dos Santos, M., Silva, A. S., Moreira, M.Â. L., Fávero, L. P., Pereira Junior, E. L., dos Anjos Carvalho, W., Muradas, F. M., de Moura Pereira, D. A., & Portella, A. G. (2023). Interactive internet framework proposal of WASPAS method: A computational contribution for decision-making analysis. *Mathematics, 11*(15), 3375.

Bathrinath, S., Mohan, S., Koppiahraj, K., Bhalaji, R., & Santhi, B. (2022). Analysis of factors affecting sustainable performance in construction sites using fuzzy AHP-WASPAS methods. *Materials Today: Proceedings, 62*, 3118–3121.

Chakraborty, S., & Zavadskas, E. K. (2014). Applications of WASPAS method in manufacturing decision making. *Informatica, 25*(1), 1–20.

Chakraborty, S., Zavadskas, E. K., & Antuchevičienė, J. (2015). Applications of WASPAS method as a multi-criteria decision-making tool.

Chatterjee, P., & Chakraborty, S. (2016). A comparative analysis of vikor method and its variants. *Decision Science Letters, 5*(4), 469–486.

Chen, L. C., Chang, K. H., & Hung, J. F. (2025). WASPAS-based natural language processing method for handling content words extraction and ranking issues: An example of sdgs corpus. *Information, 16*(3), 198.

Cheng, H. (2025). Extension of the WASPAS model for decision-making with spherical fuzzy sets and its application. *International Journal of Fuzzy Systems*, 1–12.

Darko, A. P., & Liang, D. (2022). Probabilistic linguistic WASPAS method for patients' prioritization by developing prioritized maclaurin symmetric mean aggregation operators. *Applied Intelligence, 52*(8), 9537–9555.

Deveci, M., Gokasar, I., Pamucar, D., Coffman, D., & Papadonikolaki, E. (2022). Safe e-scooter operation alternative prioritization using a q-rung orthopair fuzzy einstein based WASPAS approach. *Journal of Cleaner Production, 347*, 131239.

Ebadzadeh, F., Monavari, S. M., Jozi, S. A., Robati, M., & Rahimi, R. (2023). An integrated of fuzzy-WASPAS and E-FMEA methods for environmental risk assessment: A case study of petrochemical industry, Iran. *Environmental Science and Pollution Research, 30*(14), 40315–40326.

Erdoğan, H., Tutcu, B., Talas, H., & Terzioğlu, M. (2022). Performance analysis in renewable energy companies: Application of SWARA and WASPAS methods. *Journal of Sustainable Finance & Investment*, 1–22.

Fishburn, P. C., Murphy, A. H., & Isaacs, H. H. (1968). Sensitivity of decisions to probability estimation errors: A reexamination. *Operations Research, 16*(2), 254–267.

Foladi, M., Mahdavi Najafabadi, R., Rezai, M., & Moslemi, H. (2020). Wetland management strategies with emphasis on water resources using, SWOT and WASPAS models. *Journal of Ecohydrology, 7*(1), 165–182.

Goyal, S., & Rani, P. (2024). Multi-criteria decision-making based on einstein operators, WASPAS method and quadripartitioned single-valued neutrosophic sets. *Granular Computing, 9*(3), 54.

Ilbahar, E., Kahraman, C., & Cebi, S. (2023). Evaluation of sustainable energy planning scenarios with a new approach based on FCM, WASPAS and impact effort matrix: E. ilbahar et al. *Environment, Development and Sustainability, 25*(10), 11931–11955.

Kaya, S. K., Kundu, P., & Görçün, Ö. F. (2023). Evaluation of container port sustainability using WASPAS technique using on type-2 neutrosophic fuzzy numbers. *Marine Pollution Bulletin, 190*, 114849.

Keshavarz-Ghorabaee, M., Amiri, M., Hashemi-Tabatabaei, M., Zavadskas, E. K., & Kaklauskas, A. (2020). A new decision-making approach based on fermatean fuzzy sets and WASPAS for green construction supplier evaluation. *Mathematics, 8*(12), 2202.

Kizielewicz, B., & Baczkiewicz, A. (2021). Comparison of fuzzy TOPSIS, fuzzy VIKOR, fuzzy WASPAS and fuzzy MMOORA methods in the housing selection problem. *Procedia Computer Science, 192*, 4578–4591.

Komijan, A. R., Yazdi, A. K., Tan, Y., Ocampo, L., & Nasrollahpourniazi, F. (2024). Spherical fuzzy multicriteria decision making for evaluating healthcare service quality of hospitals during the global pandemic. *International Journal of Computational Intelligence Systems, 17*(1), 105.

Lai, Y. J., Liu, T. Y., & Hwang, C. L. (1994). Topsis for MODM. *European Journal of Operational Research, 76*(3), 486–500.

Mahmood, T., Emam, W., Ahmmad, J., Iftikhar, M., Rehman, Uu, & Pamucar, D. (2025). Classification of possible solutions regarding business engineering problems by using complex pythagorean fuzzy rough WASPAS approach. *Scientific Reports, 15*(1), 16538.

Mazloum, V.S., Masoudi, A.I., Hajinabi, K., Riahi, L., et al., (2019). Medical equipment replacement planning using the SWOT-ANP-WASPAS hybrid approach.

Menekse, A., & Akdağ, H. C. (2023). Medical waste disposal planning for healthcare units using spherical fuzzy critic-WASPAS. *Applied Soft Computing, 144*, 110480.

Mishra, A. R., & Rani, P. (2018). Interval-valued intuitionistic fuzzy WASPAS method: Application in reservoir flood control management policy. *Group Decision and Negotiation, 27*(6), 1047–1078.

Mishra, A. R., & Rani, P. (2021). Multi-criteria healthcare waste disposal location selection based on fermatean fuzzy WASPAS method. *Complex & Intelligent Systems, 7*(5), 2469–2484.

Mishra, A. R., Singh, R. K., & Motwani, D. (2019). Multi-criteria assessment of cellular mobile telephone service providers using intuitionistic fuzzy WASPAS method with similarity measures. *Granular Computing, 4*(3), 511–529.

Mühlbacher, A. C., & Kaczynski, A. (2016). Making good decisions in healthcare with multi-criteria decision analysis: The use, current research and future development of MCDA. *Applied Health Economics and Health Policy, 14*(1), 29–40.

Pamucar, D., Deveci, M., Gokasar, I., & Popovic, M. (2022). Fuzzy hamacher WASPAS decision-making model for advantage prioritization of sustainable supply chain of electric ferry implementation in public transportation. *Environment, Development and Sustainability, 24*(5), 7138–7177.

Radomska-Zalas, A. (2023). Application of the WASPAS method in a selected technological process. *Procedia Computer Science, 225*, 177–187.

Rao, C. N., & Sujatha, M. (2023). A consensus-based fermatean fuzzy WASPAS methodology for selection of healthcare waste treatment technology selection. *Decision Making: Applications in Management and Engineering, 6*(2), 600–619.

Saaty, T. L. (2013). Analytic hierarchy process. In *Encyclopedia of operations research and management science*. Springer, 52–64.

Sampathkumar, S., Augustin, F., Kaabar, M. K., & Yue, X. G. (2023). An integrated intuitionistic dense fuzzy entropy-COPRAS-WASPAS approach for manufacturing robot selection. *Advances in Mechanical Engineering, 15*(3) 16878132231160265.

Šaparauskas, J., Kazimieras Zavadskas, E., & Turskis, Z. (2011). Selection of facade's alternatives of commercial and public buildings based on multiple criteria. *International Journal of Strategic Property Management, 15*(2), 189–203.

Sharma, H., Sohani, N., & Yadav, A. (2023). A fuzzy SWARA-WASPAS based approach for determining the role of lean practices in enabling the supply chain agility. *International Journal of System Assurance Engineering and Management, 14*(Suppl 1), 492–511.

Simić, V., Lazarević, D., & Dobrodolac, M. (2021). Picture fuzzy WASPAS method for selecting last-mile delivery mode: A case study of belgrade. *European transport research review, 13*(1), 43.

Stanujkić, D., & Karabašević, D. (2018). An extension of the WASPAS method for decision-making problems with intuitionistic fuzzy numbers: A case of website evaluation. *Operational Research in Engineering Sciences: Theory and Applications, 1*(1), 29–39.

Wieckowski, J., Sałabun, W., Kizielewicz, B., Baczkiewicz, A., Shekhovtsov, A., Paradowski, B., & Watróbski, J. (2023). Recent advances in multi-criteria decision analysis: A comprehensive review of applications and trends. *International Journal of Knowledge-based and Intelligent Engineering Systems, 27*(4), 367–393.

Xiong, L., Zhong, S., Liu, S., Zhang, X., & Li, Y. (2020). An approach for resilient-green supplier selection based on WASPAS, BWM, and TOPSIS under intuitionistic fuzzy sets. *Mathematical Problems in Engineering, 2020*(1), 1761893.

Yücenur, G. N., & Ipekçi, A. (2021). SWARA/WASPAS methods for a marine current energy plant location selection problem. *Renewable Energy, 163*, 1287–1298.

Zavadskas, E. K. (1987). *Complex estimation and choice of resource saving decisions in construction*. Vilnius: Mokslas (in Russian).

Zavadskas, E. K., Antucheviciene, J., Hajiagha, S. H. R., & Hashemi, S. S. (2014). Extension of weighted aggregated sum product assessment with interval-valued intuitionistic fuzzy numbers (WASPAS-IVIF). *Applied Soft Computing, 24*, 1013–1021.

Zavadskas, E. K., Turskis, Z., & Antucheviciene, J. (2015). Selecting a contractor by using a novel method for multiple attribute analysis: Weighted aggregated sum product assessment with grey values (WASPAS-G). *Studies in Informatics and Control, 24*(2), 141–150.

Zavadskas, E. K., Turskis, Z., Antucheviciene, J., & Zakarevicius, A. (2012). Optimization of weighted aggregated sum product assessment. *Elektronika ir elektrotechnika, 122*(6), 3–6.

Keshavarz Ghorabaee, M., Amiri, M., Hashemi-Tabatabaei, M., Zavadskas, E. K., & Kaklauskas, A. (2020). A new decision-making approach based on Fermatean fuzzy sets and WASPAS for green construction supplier evaluation. *Mathematics*, *8*(12), 2202.
Keshavarz, B., & Bağrıyanık, A. (2023). Comparison of fuzzy TOPSIS, fuzzy VIKOR, fuzzy WASPAS and fuzzy MMOORA methods in the housing selection problem. *Procedia Computer Science*, *192*, 4578–4591.
Komatina, N., Tadić, D., Aleksić, A., & Jovanović, A. D. (2023). Spherical fuzzy multicriteria decision making for evaluating healthcare service quality of hospitals during the global pandemic. *International Journal of Computational Intelligence Systems*, *16*(1), 105.
Lai, Y. J., Liu, T. Y., & Hwang, C. L. (1994). Topsis for MODM. *European Journal of Operational Research*, *76*(3), 486–500.
Mahmood, T., Ali, W., Ahmmad, J., Abdullah, S., Rehman, U. U., & Pamucar, D. (2025). Classification of possible solutions regarding business engineering problems by using complex pythagorean fuzzy rough WASPAS approach. *Scientific Reports*, *15*(1), 19338.
Mardani, A., Nilashi, M., Zakuan, N., Loganathan, N., Soheilirad, S., Saman, M. Z. M., & Ibrahim, O. (2017). A systematic review and meta-analysis of SWARA and WASPAS methods: Theory and applications with recent fuzzy developments.
Mendoza, A., & Aydın, H. C. (2023). Medical waste disposal planning for healthcare units using spherical fuzzy CRITIC-WASPAS. *Applied Soft Computing*, *144*, 110480.
Mishra, A. R., & Rani, P. (2018). Interval-valued intuitionistic fuzzy WASPAS method: Application in reservoir flood control management policy. *Group Decision and Negotiation*, *27*(6), 1047–1078.
Mishra, A. R., & Rani, P. (2021). Multi-criteria healthcare waste disposal location selection based on Fermatean fuzzy WASPAS method. *Complex & Intelligent Systems*, *7*(5), 2469–2484.
Mishra, A. R., Singh, R. K., & Motwani, D. (2019). Multi-criteria assessment of cellular mobile telephone service providers using intuitionistic fuzzy WASPAS method with similarity measures. *Granular Computing*, *4*(3), 511–529.
Mühlbacher, A. C., & Kaczynski, A. (2016). Making good decisions in healthcare with multi-criteria decision analysis: The use, current research and future development of MCDA. *Applied Health Economics and Health Policy*, *14*(1), 29–40.
Pamučar, D., Yazdani, M., Obradović, R., Kumar, A., & Torres-Jiménez, M. (2020). A novel fuzzy hybrid neutrosophic decision-making approach for the resilient supplier selection problem. *International Journal of Intelligent Systems*, *35*(12), 1934–1986.
Radomska-Zalas, A. (2021). Application of the WASPAS method in a selected technological process. *Procedia Computer Science*, *225*, 177–187.
Rani, P., Mishra, A. R., Deveci, M., & Antucheviciene, J. (2022). New complex proportional assessment approach using Einstein aggregation operators and improved score function for interval-valued Fermatean fuzzy sets. *Computers & Industrial Engineering*, *169*, 108165.
Saaty, T. L. (2013). Analytic hierarchy process. In *Encyclopedia of operations research and management science*. Springer, 52–64.
Sathyakumar, S., Augustin, F., Kaabar, M. K., & Yue, X. G. (2024). An integrated intuitionistic dense fuzzy entropy-COPRAS-WASPAS approach for manufacturing robot selection. *Advances in Mechanical Engineering*, *16*(3), 16878132241240264.
Šiožinytė, E., Antuchevičienė, J., & Kutut, V. (2014). Upgrading the old vernacular building to contemporary norms: Multiple criteria approach. *Journal of Civil Engineering and Management*, *20*(2), 291–298.
Sharma, H., Sohani, N., & Yadav, A. (2024). A fuzzy SWARA–WASPAS based approach for determining the role of lean practices in enabling the supply chain agility. *International Journal of System Assurance Engineering and Management*, *15*(Suppl. 1), 492–511.
Simić, V., Lazarević, D., & Dobrodolac, M. (2021). Picture fuzzy WASPAS method for selecting last-mile delivery mode: A case study of Belgrade. *European Transport Research Review*, *13*(1), 43.
Stanujkić, D., & Karabašević, D. (2018). An extension of the WASPAS method for decision-making problems with intuitionistic fuzzy numbers: A case of website evaluation. *Operational Research in Engineering Sciences: Theory and Applications*, *1*(1), 29–39.
Wątróbski, J., Sałabun, W., Karczmarczyk, A., Bączkiewicz, A., Shekhovtsov, A., Paradowski, B., & Więckowski, J. (2023). Recent advances in multi-criteria decision analysis: A comprehensive review of applications and trends. *International Journal of Knowledge-based and Intelligent Engineering Systems*, *27*(4), 367–394.
Wang, L., Zhong, X., Lin, S., Zhang, Y., & Li, Y. (2020). An approach for resilient-green supplier selection based on WASPAS, BWM, and TOPSIS under intuitionistic fuzzy sets. *Mathematical Problems in Engineering*, *2020*(1), 1761893.
Yücenur, G. N., & İpekçi, A. (2021). SWARA/WASPAS methods for a marine current energy plant location selection problem. *Renewable Energy*, *163*, 1287–1298.
Zavadskas, E. K. (1987). *Complex estimation and choice of resource-saving decisions in construction*. Vilnius: Mokslas (in Russian).
Zavadskas, E. K., Antucheviciene, J., Hajiagha, S. H. R., & Hashemi, S. S. (2014). Extension of weighted aggregated sum product assessment with interval-valued intuitionistic fuzzy numbers (WASPAS-IVIF). *Applied Soft Computing*, *24*, 1013–1021.
Zavadskas, E. K., Turskis, Z., & Antucheviciene, J. (2015). Selecting a contractor by using a novel method for multiple attribute analysis: Weighted aggregated sum product assessment with grey values (WASPAS-G). *Studies in Informatics and Control*, *24*(2), 141–150.
Zavadskas, E. K., Turskis, Z., Antucheviciene, J., & Zakarevicius, A. (2012). Optimization of weighted aggregated sum product assessment. *Elektronika ir Elektrotechnika*, *122*(6), 3–6.

Chapter 63

MABAC: Multi-attributive border approximation area comparison for multi-attribute decision-making

Osamah Albahri[1,2], Ahmed Shihab Albahri[3,4], Abdullah Alamoodi[5,6], and Iman Mohamad Sharaf[7]

[1]*Institute of Innovation, Science and Sustainability, Federation University Australia, Melbourne, VIC, Australia,* [2]*Computer Techniques Engineering Department, Mazaya University College, Nasiriyah, Iraq,* [3]*Technical Engineering College, Imam Jafar Alsadiq University, Baghdad, Iraq,* [4]*University of Information Technology and Communication (IJOITC), Baghdad, Iraq,* [5]*MEU Research Unit, Middle East University, Amman, Jordan,* [6]*META, UPSI, Tanjung Malim, Malaysia,* [7]*Department of Basic Sciences, Higher Technological Institute, Tenth of Ramadan City, Egypt*

63.1 Introduction

Decision-making has always been involved in people's activities, whether in their day-to-day lives or in industrial and social decision-making processes. The complexity of decision-making has grown rapidly in recent decades. It is driven by globalization, fast-paced technological change, and rising competitive pressures. So, many organizations across different sectors now struggle to analyse and prioritize multiple, often conflicting, criteria at the same time. These situations call for multicriteria decision-making (MCDM) methods, which offer a structured and logical way to handle trade-offs among several quantitative and qualitative factors (Chakraborty et al., 2023). Among the many MCDM approaches, the multiattributive border approximation area comparison (MABAC) method has emerged as a powerful tool. Originally proposed by Pamučar and Ćirović to overcome some limitations of earlier models, such as weak responsiveness to changes in input data and difficulty dealing with uncertainty. MABAC provides a more robust framework for complex decision problems (Pamučar & Ćirović, 2015).

MABAC is unlike many conventional MCDM methods that rely solely on the distance to ideal or antiideal solutions. MABAC introduces the concept of a border approximation area (BAA). This boundary divides alternatives into upper and lower regions. So, enabling a more balanced and transparent ranking. Alternatives located in the upper region of the BAA are closer to the optimal solution. Those in the lower region perform relatively poorly. This distinctive representation strengthens MABAC's ability to produce consistent and interpretable results (Liu et al., 2021).

The growing demand for reliable decision support tools has created a strong need for methods that are both computationally simple and theoretically sound. Many widely MCDM techniques can produce unstable results when the input data are inaccurate, biased, or volatile (Sharaf et al., 2024). MABAC addresses this limitation by offering a straightforward mathematical framework and improves computational efficiency and makes practical implementation easier. MABAC flexibility makes it particularly suitable for problems characterized by uncertainty and vagueness, especially those that rely on linguistic assessments or expert judgments (Aljburi et al., 2024).

MABAC has quickly become a recognized and powerful decision-support tool in terms of practical relevance. MABAC has been applied across diverse domains, including healthcare, engineering, transportation, supply chain management, energy planning, and sustainability (Albahri et al., 2023). For example, in healthcare supplier selection (where cost, quality, reliability, responsiveness, and performance must be evaluated simultaneously), MABAC and its extensions combined with fuzzy set theory and its more advanced variants (such as intuitionistic, Pythagorean, neutrosophic, hesitant, spherical, and Fermatean fuzzy sets). MABAC permits researchers to capture the inherent vagueness of qualitative judgments while still producing stable and consistent rankings (Hosseinzadeh Lotfi et al., 2023). These integrations

Encyclopedia of Multi-Attribute Decision-Making (MADM). DOI: https://doi.org/10.1016/B978-0-443-33275-3.00064-6

enhance the flexibility of the MABAC approach and help make it more applicable in ambiguous situations where subjectivity is required.

One of the remarkable benefits of MABAC is that it can categorize alternatives into different performance areas. This feature enables finding not only the most favorable ones, but also the weaker ones that do not pass the border approximation limit. Consequently, MABAC is not only developing a rating but also provides diagnostic information that can be used in benchmarking and to improve performance. Other similar comparative studies also show that MABAC is as stable and reliable in its results as other well-established MCDM methods (technique for order of preference by similarity to ideal solution [TOPSIS], VlseKriterijumska Optimizacija I Kompromisno Resenje [VIKOR], weighted aggregated sum product assessment [WASPAS], and preference ranking organization method for enrichment evaluation [PROMETHEE]), and it can be even more stable and reliable (Jafari & Naghdi Khanachah, 2024). Reliable and adaptive decision-making procedures will also continue to grow in demand as industries and societies become more complex, networked, and data-oriented.

The strength of the MABAC methodology and the widening range of its applications make it a highly promising tool for contemporary decision problems. MABAC integration with fuzzy logic, probabilistic reasoning, and AI also highlights its potential for future research and development (Chatterjee & Chakraborty, 2023). Building on this, the chapter provides a detailed discussion of the MABAC approach, beginning with its theoretical foundations and mathematical formulation, then followed by numerical examples that illustrate its practical use. This chapter reviews advanced fuzzy extensions of MABAC and presents a comparative analysis with other MCDM techniques. In doing so, the chapter aims to enrich the growing body of literature on decision science and demonstrate how MABAC can be applied effectively in complex real-world situations.

The rest of this chapter is organized as follows: Section 2 gives a concise overview of the state of the art on the MABAC method and the integration with other MCDM techniques. Section 3 explains the classical MABAC methodology in detail and covering both its mathematical formulation and step-by-step procedure. Sections 4 and 5 present two numerical energy-related case studies that demonstrate how MABAC can be applied in practice and how it affects the resulting rankings. Finally, Section 6 summarizes the key insights from the chapter, reflects on the main limitations of the MABAC method, and outlines several promising directions for future research.

63.2 Literature review

One of the more recent methods of MCDM is the MABAC method. Pamucar and Cirovic first presented this method in 2015 (Torkayesh et al., 2023). It's considered a ranking method, created to facilitate decision-making in logistics and transportation systems where complex decisions with numerous parameters are prevalent. MABAC, in contrast to conventional approaches such as TOPSIS or VIKOR, places greater emphasis on determining the distance to an optimal or compromise solution (Božanić et al., 2024). Traditional MCDM methods (such as TOPSIS and VIKOR) often have limitations in terms of stability and sensitivity when addressing complex logistics and transportation problems. Pamučar and Ćirović introduced the BAA concept in order to provide more robust comparisons between alternatives, improve discrimination power (so the alternatives don't end up with very close or identical scores), and to ensure that both "better than average" and "worse than average" performances are clearly reflected (Komatina et al., 2023). The BAA is the average of all alternatives and criteria. The deviation of each option from this border area is then measured as a positive or negative deviation. However, if an alternative performs better than the BAA, it receives a positive score; if it performs worse, it receives a negative score (Komatina et al., 2023). MABAC has been extended and adapted, combining it with fuzzy sets, grey numbers, neuromorphic sets, and more to handle uncertainty in decision-making. In addition, it has been implemented in other areas like logistics, supply chains management, project assessment, energy planning, and risk analysis (Verma, 2021). MABAC demonstrates superior ranking discrimination, but certain older approaches (such as TOPSIS) can give very similar scores, so it is hard to distinguish between the alternatives. This issue will be minimized in MABAC because it introduces the BAA that emphasizes differences more explicitly. In addition, it also balances the good and the bad performance; it does not simply measure how close an alternative is to the ideal-like solution, but also considers how far underaverage performance an alternative is, which results in a more balanced assessment (Peng & Dai, 2018). Moreover, MABAC has been demonstrated to present less sensitive rankings to small perturbations in the input data, and thus is more useful in complex and real-world problems. Moreover, MABAC has also been modified to support fuzzy, grey, and neutrosophic logic and, therefore, to process uncertain, unclear, or incomplete data (Liang et al., 2019). It is broadly applicable, as well, having been applied in logistics (Pamučar and Božanić, 2019), transport (Keshavarz-Ghorabaee et al., 2021), supply chain management (Mehdiabadi et al., 2025), risk assessment (Bakhat and Rajaa, 2020), and energy planning (Delice, 2017). There are many different methods that can be combined and integrated with the MABAC method and can be separated into three different categories: (i) The first category is made up of weighting methods. They are applied to ascertain the relative value of every criterion. (ii) The second category is the uncertainty and fuzzy extensions, which are meant to deal with vague, imprecise, or uncertain information in decision-making. (iii) The third one is hybrid approaches, which involve integrating MABAC with other decision-making or optimization techniques to enhance overall ranking outcomes. These categories can be shown in Fig. 63.1.

As shown in Fig. 63.1, weighting methods constitute the first category and are used to assign weights to each criterion before the ranking phase. Some of these methods can be used, such as analytic hierarchy process (AHP) (Sonar & Kulkarni, 2021), fuzzy AHP (FAHP) (Božanić et al., 2018), which manages all the unpredictability in the expert opinion, and best–worst method (BWM), which is particularly effective when the number of comparisons has to be reduced (Luo & Xing, 2019). Others are stepwise weight assessment ratio analysis (SWARA) (Liu et al., 2020), which uses expert-defined weighting; and finally, the entropy method, which uses data dispersion to compute objective weights (Eligüzel & Eligüzel, 2024); and the CRITIC method, which uses contrast intensity and correlation with other criteria.

Many studies have been conducted that integrate the MABAC with many weighted methods:

The study (Sonar & Kulkarni, 2021) proposed an integrated AHP-MABAC approach for electric vehicle (EV) selection, where the AHP method was used for criteria weighting and MABAC for ranking six EVsas alternatives. The study added novelty by applying this hybrid method to the EV domain. However, it considered only a limited number of alternatives (EV), which may limit how its findings can be applied in other areas.

The other study (Komatina et al., 2023) considered the uncertainty in selecting suppliers in the automotive industry, and the authors utilized the type-2 fuzzy sets to manage imprecise information. The research combined both IT2F-AHP and IT2F-MABAC to calculate the weights of the criteria and to rank suppliers, respectively, and generalized the traditional MABAC scheme to the fuzzy scenarios. Additionally, it was tested on real supply chain data, demonstrating its reliability and effectiveness in supporting rational decision-making in supplier selection.

The authors in (Biswas & Das, 2019) presented an integrated fuzzy AHP–MABAC approach for selecting commercial EVs, in which fuzzy AHP was used to determine criterion weights under uncertainty, and MABAC was used to rank the

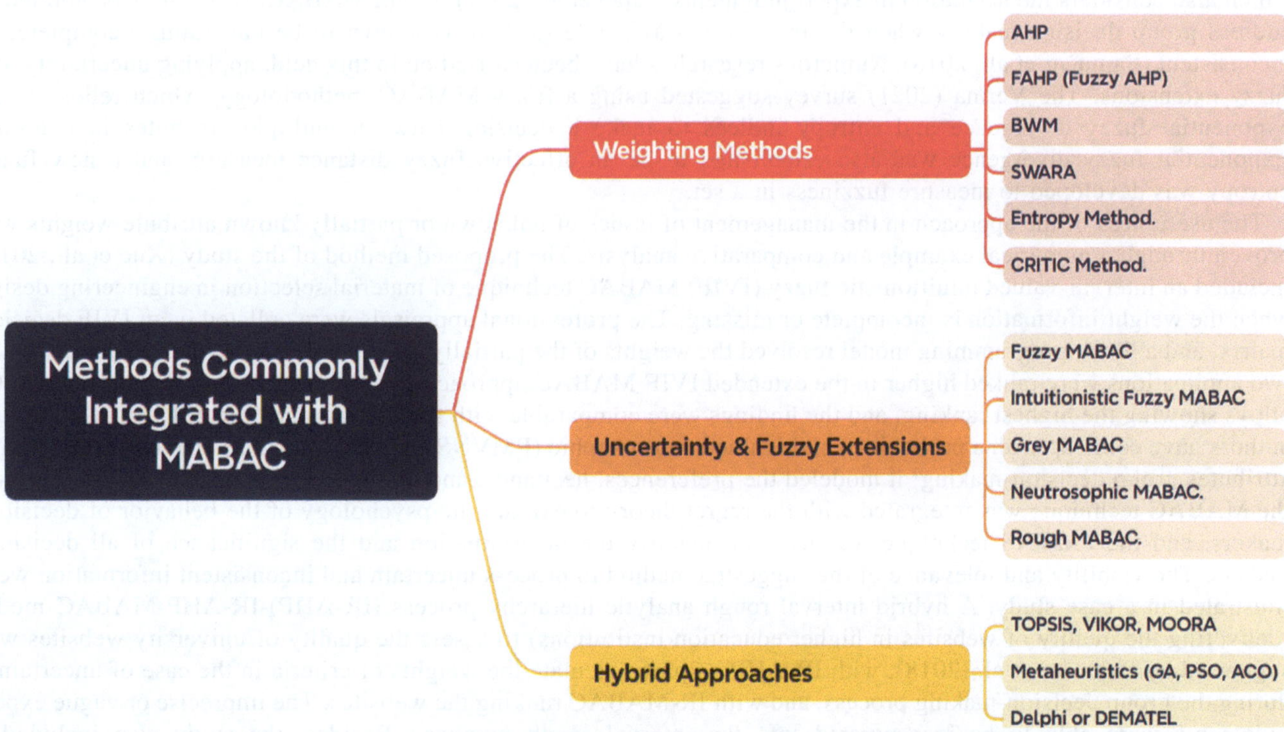

FIGURE 63.1 Methods commonly integrated with multiattributive border approximation area comparison (MABAC).

alternatives. They also considered multiple technical attributes, including fuel economy, base model price, acceleration time, battery range, and top speed. The stability of the rankings was verified through sensitivity analysis.

The other study (Komatina et al., 2023) introduced a hybrid model (named [fuzzy AHP-MABAC]) to rank the alternatives, but to rank the options, fuzzy MABAC was applied, and the criteria weights were determined using fuzzy AHP. It is used to choose the appropriate places to deep wade by tanks in the Serbian army, which proves to be effective in a complicated and uncertain situation of decision-making.

BWM, which is another weighting technique combined with the MABAC technique in the supply chain, is proposed by the study as a hybrid of BWM and MABAC approaches to the task of supplier selection in the supply chain (Muravev & Mijic, 2020). In this case, BWM is used to estimate the criteria weights, and MABAC is used to rank the providers. The stability and applicability of the model were tested with the help of the comparison with the MAIRCA and VIKOR approaches and the sensitivity analysis under 18 scenarios. Further, the reliability of the results was proved by Spearman correlation, which proved that the hybrid approach is effective in making decisions based on multicriteria in complex supply chains.

The presented study (Vesković et al., 2018) suggested a model, that is, the hybrid Delphi-SWARA-MABAC, to test the railway management models in Bosnia and Herzegovina. The ranking of the criteria was done with the Delphi approach, the weights with the SWARA approach, and the most suitable alternative with MABAC. Additive ratio assessment, WASPAS, simple additive weighting (SAW), and evaluation based on distance from average solution sensitivity analysis validated the strength of the results and showed the suitability of the integrated method to the complex transport decision-making.

In the study (Eligüzel & Eligüzel, 2024), the sustainable transportation practices in 25 European Union countries were determined with the help of a combined grey relational analysis (GRA) and entropy-MABAC method. Various aspects of sustainability were measured using 12 criteria; the integration approach gave uniform results, with Sweden and Germany the highest and Poland the lowest. This correlation analysis (0.8218) confirmed the reliability and consensus between these two approaches and proved the usefulness of the approaches in making informed transportation policy and investment decisions.

Uncertainty and fuzzy extensions is the second category, which is concerned with imprecise, vague, or uncertain information in decision-making. Some of the most common strategies are fuzzy MABAC (Verma, 2021), which uses fuzzy numbers to represent the linguistic judgment, for example, high, medium, or intuitionistic fuzzy MABAC, which also considers the hesitation in expert judgments (Zhao et al., 2021); rough MABAC, which may be applied to address group decision-making when the information available to them is known to be uncertain, incomplete, or inconsistent (Pamučar et al., 2018). Numerous researches have been carried on in this field, applying uncertainty and fuzzy extensions. The Verma (2021) survey suggested using a fuzzy MABAC methodology, which relies on the exponential fuzzy divergence and entropy indices to make a decision between multiple attributes in a group. Exponential fuzzy divergence was also established to be an effective fuzzy distance measure, and a new fuzzy entropy was developed to measure fuzziness in a set.

The usefulness of the approach in the management of issues of unknown or partially known attribute weights was proven through a numerical example and comparative analysis. The proposed method of the study (Xue et al., 2016) included an interval-valued intuitionistic fuzzy (IVIF) MABAC technique of material selection in engineering design when the weight information is incomplete or missing. The professional appraisals were collated in an IVIF decision matrix, and a linear programming model resolved the weights of the partially known criteria. Further, materials in the two applications were ranked higher in the extended IVIF-MABAC approach practise with polypropylene and Co-Cr alloys showing the highest ranking, and the findings were comparable with the literature. In Liu & Cheng (2020), the authors have come up with a probability multivalued neutrosophic (PMVNS)-MABAC technique to perform a multi-attributes group decision-making; it modeled the preferences, hesitance, and ambiguity of decision-makers. Further, the MABAC technique was integrated with the regret theory to explain the psychology of the behavior of decision-makers, and the PMVNS technique was used to quantify the determination and the significance of all decision-makers. The viability and relevance of the suggested method to process uncertain and inconsistent information were illustrated in a case study. A hybrid interval rough analytic hierarchy process (IR-AHP)-IR-AHP-MABAC model (delivering the quality of websites in higher education institutions) to assess the quality of university websites was suggested by Pamučar et al. (2018), with IR-AHP helping calculate the weights of criteria in the case of uncertainty during the group decision-making process, and with IR-MABAC ranking the websites. The imprecise or vague expert judgments were able to be incorporated into the interval rough numbers. Besides, the study also included a comparative analysis with traditional AHP, fuzzy AHP, and other MCDM techniques in order to prove the credibility and effectiveness of the approach in generating credible rankings when faced with uncertain information.

The third category, hybrid approaches, combines MABAC with other approaches to improve ranking accuracy and decision quality. These may involve cross-validation of MABAC with other MCDM approaches such as TOPSIS, VIKOR, or Multiobjective optimization by ratio analysis; using it in conjunction with metaheuristic optimization algorithms such as genetic algorithms (GA), particle swarm optimisation (PSO), or ant colony optimisation (ACO) on larger scales; and using it in conjunction with expert-based models such as Delphi or DEMATEL to refine objectives and remove redundancy prior to application of MABAC. The study (Radulescu & Radulescu, 2024) proposed a hybrid group multicriteria approach. This approach combined the BWM weighting method with (SAW, TOPSIS, VIKOR, and COPRAS) methods in order to solve the IoT selection problems. However, the authors first applied it by weighting the criteria using BWM, then evaluated the IoT platforms using four MCDM methods, and finally aggregated the results into a single consolidated solution. The strength of this approach lies in producing a robust, reliable selection by mitigating the limitations of individual methods. Another study (Afrasiabi et al., 2022) proposed a hybrid fuzzy MCDM method to solve sustainable-resilient supplier selection problems.

The method first employs BWM to weight the criteria, then applies a combined GRA and TOPSIS method to evaluate suppliers in a fuzzy environment using triangular fuzzy numbers. This method addressed decision-making uncertainty and ambiguity while providing robust, validated results for sustainable, resilient supplier selection, as demonstrated in a real-life manufacturing case study. Some studies have used hybrid MABAC with optimization algorithms. For instance, the study by Jiang & Ma (2020) proposed an optimum homomorphic wavelet fusion method for medical image fusion, integrating wavelet and logarithmic domains with a hybrid PSO and ACO approach. The method decomposes multimodal medical images into multilevel coefficients, fuses them using pixel-based averaging, and optimizes the fusion with PSO-ACO algorithms. The strength of this method lies in producing high-quality fused images that combine functional and structural data efficiently, and then validating them across multiple medical imaging modalities (MR-PET, MR-SPECT, MR T1-T2, and MR-CT). The author in (Zhang et al., 2025) proposed an improved hybrid ACO and GA for multimap path planning of rescue robots in mine disaster scenarios. It develops a mathematical model based on multiple environmental maps with subjective probabilities. The hybrid ACO-GA algorithm is applied to path optimization and incorporates a grid-based obstacle-avoidance strategy. It has effectively handled complex, uncertain environments, improved convergence speed, and ultimately produced optimized paths to rescue robots across multiple disaster maps.

The discussion and comparison of the MABAC ranking method with other popular MCDM methods, such as AHP, TOPSIS, VIKOR, and COPRAS, are essential. The comparison is based on key features of each technique, including ranking mechanism, sensitivity to weights, handling of uncertainty, computational complexity, and applicability, as seen in Table 63.1. The MABAC ranking method stands out for its high discrimination power and sensitivity, making it effective for distinguishing closely ranked alternatives. However, the tables show that AHP is ideal for hierarchical decision-making problems, while TOPSIS and VIKOR excel at generating compromise solutions. The COPRAS method is more straightforward and focuses on identifying the best alternative, but it has limited sensitivity and lower discrimination among alternatives. Overall, the choice of methods depends on the decision problem's complexity, number of alternatives, and the preference for sensitivity versus simplicity.

The MABAC ranking technique is especially applicable when there are numerous options and competing criteria, as it effectively differentiates between options that share similar ranks and can handle fuzzy or ambiguous information to yield a more realistic choice. Traditional methods may struggle to rank alternatives clearly when there are many options, particularly when the alternatives are highly similar (see Fig. 63.2).

The power of this approach lies in its ability to handle multiple alternatives, address conflicting criteria, and incorporate uncertainty, making it highly versatile across fields such as business, engineering, healthcare, environmental science, and technology. As seen in Fig. 63.2, which shows the application of the MABAC method among different sectors, it can be described as follows:

1. **Engineering and technology**: In this area, MABAC was utilized to solve various selection problems, such as material selection, where the best material is chosen based on mechanical, thermal, and cost criteria. Moreover, it was widely used for supplier selection, ranking suppliers based on quality, price, delivery, and reliability. Furthermore, it was used in project prioritization to select engineering projects with multiple conflicting criteria (Lukić, 2021).
2. **Environmental management**: MABAC was applied to sustainable development areas to rank renewable energy options and environmental policies, and to select optimal recycling and waste treatment methods. Additionally, it was utilized to prioritize water conservation and treatment projects (Torkayesh et al., 2023).

TABLE 63.1 Comparison of MABAC with other popular multicriteria decision-making (MCDM) ranking methods (Hezer et al., 2021; Tien et al., 2022; Torkayesh et al., 2023).

Feature/criteria	MABAC	analytic hierarchy process (AHP)	TOPSIS	VIKOR	COPRAS
Ranking mechanism	Measures the distance from a border approximation area	Pairwise comparison and hierarchical weighting	Distance to ideal and antiideal solution	Compromise ranking using utility and regret measures	Proportional evaluation relative to the best alternative
Consistency of ranking	High; good at differentiating mid-ranked alternatives	Moderate; may struggle with similar scores	Moderate	Moderate	Low; may not distinguish lower-ranked alternatives
Sensitivity to criteria weights	High rankings change noticeably with weight variations	Moderate; hierarchical structure may hide sensitivity	Moderate	Moderate	Low; less reactive to weight changes
Handling uncertainty	Can incorporate fuzzy logic for uncertain data	Fuzzy AHP exists; standard AHP is deterministic	Fuzzy TOPSIS extensions exist	Fuzzy VIKOR extensions exist	Primarily deterministic; fuzzy COPRAS exists
Computational complexity	Moderate to high; distance calculations for all alternatives	Moderate; requires pairwise comparisons and consistency checks	Low; involves normalization and distance calculations	Low; involves normalization and utility/regret calculation	Low; simple proportional calculations
Ease of use	Moderate; requires careful setup of the distance matrix	Moderate; can be time-consuming with many criteria	Easy, straightforward calculations	Easy; similar to TOPSIS, but adds a compromise step	Easy, simple formula-based evaluation
Applicability/ strengths	Effective for large sets of alternatives; distinguishes closely-ranked options.	Suitable for hierarchical decision problems; structured approach	Works well when ideal solutions are known	Best for compromise solutions with conflicting criteria	The main goal is to identify the best alternative.
Weaknesses/ limitations	Computationally intensive; requires precise criteria values	Pairwise comparisons may become inconsistent; limited discrimination	May not clearly separate mid-ranked alternatives	A compromise approach may be less intuitive	Low discrimination among lower-ranked alternatives; less flexible with weight changes
Decision type	Multicriteria ranking	Multicriteria prioritization	Multicriteria ranking	Multicriteria ranking and compromise	Multicriteria evaluation
Integration with other methods	Easily combined with fuzzy MCDM approaches	Compatible with fuzzy logic, ANP, and other hierarchical methods	Fuzzy and hybrid extensions are common	Fuzzy, hybrid, and integrated with AHP/ entropy	Can be combined with fuzzy logic and weight optimization methods

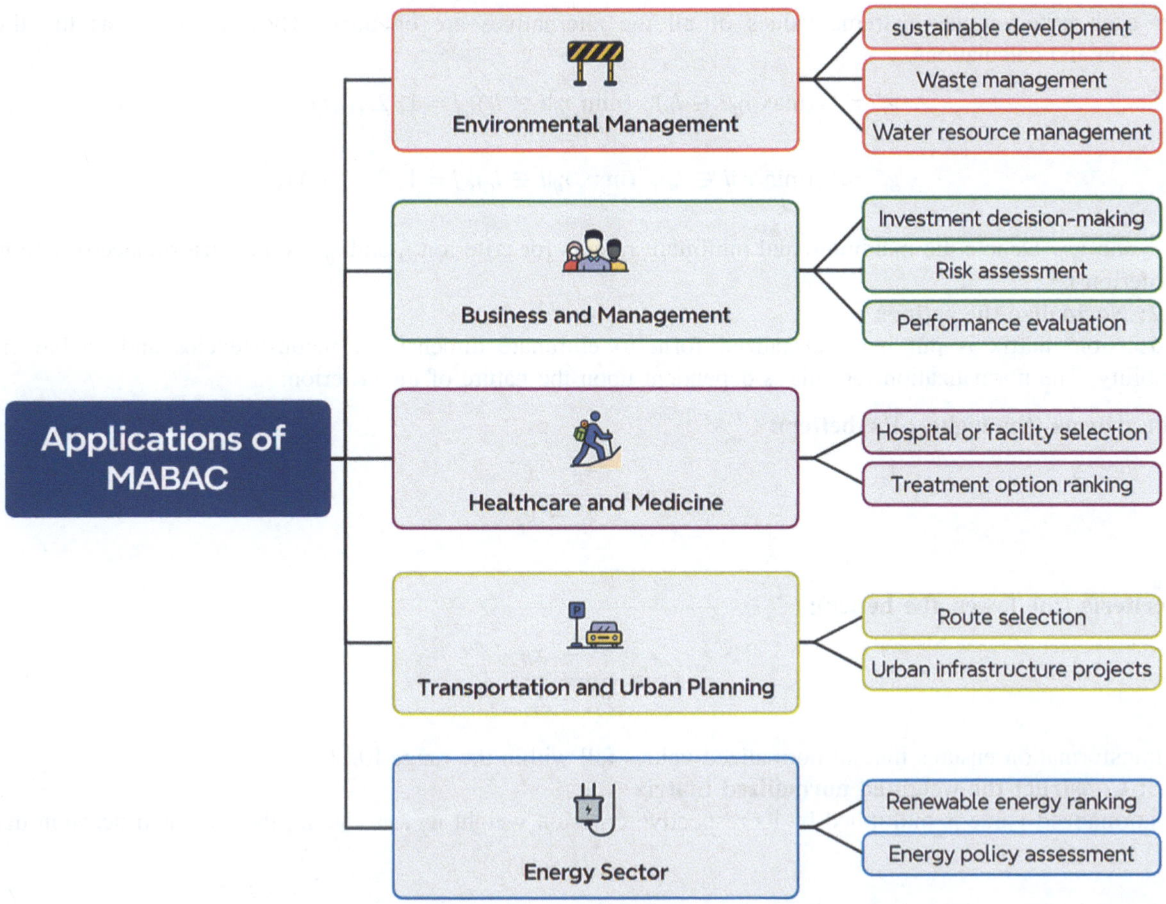

FIGURE 63.2 Application of multiattributive border approximation area comparison (MABAC) in different sectors.

3. **Business and management**: MABAC was applied in this area for selecting the most profitable and sustainable investment alternatives. Moreover, for evaluating operational or financial risks across alternatives. And finally, ranking employees, departments, or branches based on multiple KPIs (Estiri et al., 2021).
4. **Healthcare and medicine**: MABAC was widely applied in hospital or facility selection to select hospitals based on treatment quality, cost, and location. Moreover, in order to choose optimal medical procedures based on effectiveness, cost, and side effects (Seker & Aydin, 2024).
5. **Transportation and urban planning**: MABAC was applied to rank transport routes based on cost, time, and safety. Also, to prioritize infrastructure development projects (Keshavarz-Ghorabaee et al., 2021).
6. **Energy sector**: The MABAC method was applied to evaluate solar, wind, and hydro options based on efficiency, cost, and environmental impact. And for comparing energy policies in terms of sustainability and feasibility (Yalçın et al., 2025).

63.3 Methodology

The MABAC approach (Pamučar & Ćirović, 2015) is a fairly robust MCDM method intended to provide consistent and reasonable rankings of the options. Compared with other distance-based techniques, such as TOPSIS or VIKOR, which take into account closeness to one or more perfect or antioptimal solutions, MABAC considers options based on their distances in the revelation of BAA. The BAA is a theoretical distinction between good and bad solutions and is intended to ensure that alternatives are not compared against an extreme criterion rather than an objective one. The method is a systematic computational process that involves the following steps.

Step 1: Define extreme ratings for each criterion

Under each criterion, the extreme values of all the alternatives are obtained. They are taken as the limits of normalization and calculations.

$$g_i^+ = \{((\max_j r_{ij}|i \in I_b),\ (\min_j r_{ij}|i \in I_c), j = 1, 2, \ldots, m)\}, \tag{63.1}$$

$$g_i^- = \{((\min_j r_{ij}|i \in I_b),\ (\max_j r_{ij}|i \in I_c), j = 1, 2, \ldots, m)\}, \tag{63.2}$$

where g_i^+ and g_i^- Denote the maximum and minimum ratings for criterion j, and r_{ij} is the performance of alternative i under criterion j.

Step 2: Normalize the ratings

The decision matrix is put into normalized form to eliminate dimensional inconsistencies and enable criterion comparability. The normalization formula is dependent upon the nature of the criterion:

- **Benefit criteria (the higher, the better):**

$$r_{ij} = \frac{x_{ij} - g_j^-}{g_j^+ - g_j^-}, \tag{63.3}$$

- **Cost criteria (the lower, the better):**

$$r_{ij} = \frac{g_j^+ - x_{ij}}{g_j^+ - g_j^-}. \tag{63.4}$$

This transformation ensures that all normalized values fall within the range [0,1].

Step 3: Construct the weighted normalized matrix

Each normalized value is multiplied by its respective criterion weight w_j , producing the weighted decision matrix:

$$v_{ij} = w_i \cdot (r_{ij} + 1). \tag{63.5}$$

Step 4: Form the border approximation area matrix

Each criterion BAA is obtained as an arithmetic mean of the weighted normalized scores of the alternatives:

$$g_i = \left(\prod_{j=1}^{m} v_{ij}\right)^{(1/m)} \tag{63.6}$$

where m is the number of alternatives. The vector $g = (g_1, g_2, \ldots, g_n)$ represents the BAA.

Step 5: Construct the difference matrix

The difference matrix is then obtained by subtracting the BAA values from the weighted normalized ratings:

$$q_{ij} = v_{ij} - g_j \tag{63.7}$$

The positive difference measure suggests that the alternative performs better on average (BAA) under the criterion, but the negative difference measure indicates that the alternative performs worse.

Step 6: Calculate the overall performance score

For each alternative, the total difference from the BAA across all criteria is computed:

$$Q_i = \sum_{j=1}^{n} q_{ij} \tag{63.8}$$

Here, Q_i represents the aggregate performance of alternative i. A higher Q_i value implies stronger performance relative to the BAA.

Step 7: Rank the alternatives

Finally, alternatives are ranked based on their total performance scores Q_i . The optimal choice corresponds to the alternative with the maximum positive deviation from the BAA.

The following sections (4 and 5) present the application of the MABAC method through two illustrative numerical examples that demonstrate both complex and straightforward decision-making scenarios. The aim is to show how MABAC handles trade-offs, balances cost and benefit criteria, and highlights the strengths and weaknesses of alternatives in relation to the BAA.

TABLE 63.2 Numerical example 1—MABAC calculation process (raw matrix, normalisation, weighted matrix, border approximation area [BAA], and distances).

Raw matrix (X)					
Alternative	**Cost criterion**	**Benefit criterion**	**Benefit criterion**	**Cost criterion**	**Benefit criterion**
	C1: investment ↓	**C2: efficiency ↑**	**C3: emission reduction ↑**	**C4: maintenance ↓**	**C5: social acceptance ↑**
A1 solar	80	75	3000	5	8
A2 wind	100	82	3500	4	7
A3 biomass	70	65	2500	6	6
A4 hydro	120	88	4000	3	9
Best	70	88	4000	3	9
Worst	120	65	2500	6	6
Normalize matrix					
A1 solar	0.8	0.4348	0.3333	0.3333	0.6667
A2 wind	0.4	0.7391	0.6667	0.6667	0.3333
A3 biomass	1	0	0	0	0
A4 hydro	0	1	1	1	1
Weighted matrix					
Weights	0.2	0.25	0.25	0.15	0.15
A1 solar	0.36	0.3587	0.3333	0.2	0.25
A2 wind	0.28	0.4348	0.4167	0.25	0.2
A3 biomass	0.4	0.25	0.25	0.15	0.15
A4 hydro	0.2	0.5	0.5	0.3	0.3
BAA (G)	0.29966611	0.373660398	0.362989765	0.217793859	0.217793859
Distance of the alternative from the BAA matrix (Q)					
A1 solar	0.0603	-0.0150	-0.0297	-0.0178	0.0322
A2 wind	-0.0197	0.0611	0.0537	0.0322	-0.0178
A3 biomass	0.1003	-0.1237	-0.1130	-0.0678	-0.0678
A4 hydro	-0.0997	0.1263	0.1370	0.0822	0.0822

63.4 Numerical example 1

This example presents a simple case with a small number of criteria and alternatives. It is designed to illustrate the basic computational steps of the MABAC method and to show how it clearly distinguishes between strong and weak alternatives in a straightforward decision context. The full MABAC procedure for example 1 is reported in Table 63.2, and the resulting ranking of the alternatives is summarized in Table 63.3.

TABLE 63.3 Numerical example 1—final MABAC scores (Qi) and ranking of alternatives.

Alternatives	MABAC score (Qi)	Order
A1 solar	0.0301	3
A2 wind	0.1095	2
A3 biomass	-0.2719	4
A4 hydro	0.3281	1

The results show the following ranking of alternatives: A4 hydro (first) > A2 wind (second) > A1 solar (third) > A3 biomass (fourth). Hydro obtains the highest score (0.3281), mainly because it combines high efficiency, maximum CO_2 reduction, and the lowest maintenance cost, which together compensate for its high initial investment. Wind also performs strongly, offering a good balance between efficiency and emissions reduction. Solar is ranked third, largely due to its lower efficiency compared with wind and hydro. Biomass performs the worst (–0.2719), driven by relatively low efficiency (higher maintenance costs) and weaker social acceptance.

This example illustrates how MABAC separates strong and weak options by comparing them to the BAA. Alternatives with positive Qi values lie above the BAA and can be considered relatively strong, whereas those with negative Qi values (such as Biomass) highlight weaknesses. This may require policy interventions or technological improvements. Even with only five criteria in this simple setting, MABAC offers clear insight into trade-offs and supports both ranking and targeted improvement decisions.

63.5 Numerical example 2

The second example extends the analysis to a more complex setting with additional criteria and alternatives. This example better reflect real-world decision-making. It shows how MABAC adapts to higher dimensional problems and how it can be used to rank alternatives and to identify where improvements are needed. The full MABAC procedure is reported in Table 63.4 and the final ranking of the alternatives is summarized in Table 63.5.

The final ranking is A5 geothermal (first) > A6 nuclear SMR (second) > A4 hydro (third) > A2 wind (fourth) > A1 solar (fifth) > A3 biomass (sixth). Geothermal scores the highest, 0.1448, benefiting from high efficiency, strong CO_2 reduction, relatively low land requirements, and excellent reliability. Nuclear SMR ranks second (0.0643) because it delivers outstanding performance in efficiency, CO_2 reduction, and reliability, despite being penalized by high investment and maintenance costs as well as low social acceptance. Hydro remains strong in third place and is offering a good balance between environmental performance and efficiency with only moderate land requirements. Solar and wind occupy middle positions reflecting trade-offs between cost, land use, and performance. Biomass again ranks last, showing consistent underperformance across the main evaluation dimensions.

This example highlighted how expanding the evaluation framework can significantly influence the results. By adding land requirement and reliability as criteria, the preferred option shifts from hydro in the first example to geothermal in second example. MABAC does more than just rank alternatives. It offers diagnostic insight. The relatively high position of nuclear SMR (for instance, points to its strategic potential), even though public acceptance is currently limited. These insights are valuable for policymakers. They reveal the strongest current options and also those that could become attractive through targeted measures such as public awareness campaigns or financial incentives. Overall, second example demonstrates the robustness and flexibility of MABAC in complex decision settings. It is reinforcing its usefulness for sustainability-oriented energy planning.

TABLE 63.4 Numerical example 2,MABAC calculation process (raw matrix, normalisation, weighted matrix, border approximation area [BAA], and distances).

Alternative	C1 investment (↓)	C2 efficiency (↑)	C3 CO_2 red. (↑)	C4 maintenance (↓)	C5 social acceptance (↑)	C6 land req. (↓)	C7 reliability (↑)
Raw matrix (X)							
A1 solar	80	75	3000	5	8	12	30
A2 wind	100	82	3500	4	7	25	40
A3 biomass	70	65	2500	6	6	15	60
A4 hydro	120	88	4000	3	9	30	50
A5 geothermal	90	85	3800	4	8	10	80
A6 nuclear small modular reactors (SMR)	150	92	5000	7	5	8	90
Best	70	92	5000	3	9	8	90
Worst	150	65	2500	7	5	30	30
Normalized (R)							
A1 solar	0.875	0.3704	0.2000	0.5	0.7500	0.818181818	0.0000
A2 wind	0.625	0.6296	0.4000	0.75	0.5000	0.227272727	0.1667
A3 biomass	1	0.0000	0.0000	0.25	0.2500	0.681818182	0.5000
A4 hydro	0.375	0.8519	0.6000	1	1.0000	0	0.3333
A5 geothermal	0.75	0.7407	0.5200	0.75	0.7500	0.909090909	0.8333
A6 nuclear SMR	0	1.0000	1.0000	0	0.0000	1	1.0000
Weighted matrix							
Weights	0.15	0.2	0.2	0.1	0.1	0.1	0.15
A1 solar	0.28125	0.274074074	0.24	0.15	0.175	0.181818182	0.15
A2 wind	0.24375	0.325925926	0.28	0.175	0.15	0.122727273	0.175
A3 biomass	0.3	0.2	0.2	0.125	0.125	0.168181818	0.225
A4 hydro	0.20625	0.37037037	0.32	0.2	0.2	0.1	0.2
A5 geothermal	0.2625	0.348148148	0.304	0.175	0.175	0.190909091	0.275

(Continued)

TABLE 63.4 (Continued)

Alternative	C1 investment (↓)	C2 efficiency (↑)	C3 CO_2 red. (↑)	C4 maintenance (↓)	C5 social acceptance (↑)	C6 land req. (↓)	C7 reliability (↑)
A6 nuclear SMR	0.15	0.4	0.4	0.1	0.1	0.2	0.3
BAA (G)	0.234672476	0.311946078	0.283844491	0.150205059	0.150205059	0.155848397	0.214519098
Distance of the alternative from the BAA matrix (Q)							
A1 solar	0.0466	-0.0379	-0.0438	-0.0002	0.0248	0.0260	-0.0645
A2 wind	0.0091	0.0140	-0.0038	0.0248	-0.0847	-0.0331	-0.0395
A3 biomass	0.0653	-0.1119	-0.0838	-0.0252	-0.1097	0.0123	0.0105
A4 hydro	-0.0284	0.0584	0.0362	0.0498	-0.0347	-0.0558	-0.0145
A5 geothermal	0.0278	0.0362	0.0202	0.0248	-0.0597	0.0351	0.0605
A6 nuclear SMR	-0.0847	0.0881	0.1162	-0.0502	-0.1347	0.0442	0.0855

TABLE 63.5 Numerical example 2—final MABAC scores (Qi) and ranking of alternatives.

Alternatives	MABAC score (Qi)	Order
A1 solar	-0.0491	4
A2 wind	-0.1133	5
A3 biomass	-0.2425	6
A4 hydro	0.0109	3
A5 geothermal	0.1448	1
A6 nuclear SMR	0.0643	2

63.6 Conclusions

This chapter has offered a comprehensive overview of the MABAC method as a flexible and interpretable MCDM technique. We first positioned MABAC within the broader MCDM family, noting how it relates to established methods, such as TOPSIS, VIKOR, COPRAS, and WASPAS. Then outlined its mathematical foundation, including the construction of the normalized decision matrix, the weighted matrix, and the BAA, and the difference matrix, and showed how these elements work together to generate the final ranking of alternatives. A review of the literature showed that MABAC has already been applied across a wide range of fields, often in combination with different weighting procedures and fuzzy extensions.

This chapter applied MABAC to two energy-related case studies. The first is a relatively simple example showed how positive and negative values in the difference matrix indicate the extent to which each alternative performs above or below the BAA on each criterion. The second is a more complex example that introduced additional criteria such as land requirements and reliability, which changed the identity of the top-ranked alternatives and demonstrated how MABAC can clearly reflect tradeoffs between economic, technical, and environmental factors. In both cases, the method provided not only an overall ranking of energy options but also fine-grained insight into the strengths and weaknesses of each alternative across criteria, which is valuable for decision-makers who must justify and communicate their choices.

Despite these advantages, MABAC also has several limitations that should be acknowledged. First, like many MCDM methods, MABAC assumes that the criteria weights are known and reliable. If the weights are poorly elicited, inconsistent, or biased, the resulting rankings may not reflect true preferences. Second, the method typically assumes independence among criteria and an additive preference structure; interactions or synergies between criteria (for example, cost–risk or efficiency–emissions trade-offs) are not explicitly modeled. Third, while the BAA concept enhances interpretability, its geometric meaning and the sign of the difference values may not be immediately intuitive for nonspecialist stakeholders without careful explanation and visualization. Fourth, in high-dimensional problems with many criteria and alternatives, the matrices can become large, increasing computational effort and making it harder to communicate results succinctly. Finally, most published studies—including the examples in this chapter—are based on single-period, static decision contexts; dynamic preferences and time-varying data are not directly captured.

These limitations suggest several directions for future research and methodological enhancement. One avenue is to integrate more advanced weighting and preference-learning techniques (e.g., data-driven or interactive approaches) to reduce reliance on subjective expert judgment. Another is to develop MABAC variants that account for interdependent criteria, perhaps by combining MABAC with network-based or interaction-aware weighting models. Extending MABAC to fuzzy, interval, probabilistic, or rough environments can further improve its ability to handle uncertainty and incomplete information, and some of these directions have already begun to emerge in the literature. In addition, more work is needed on visual analytics and decision dashboards that present BAA and difference-matrix information in a user-friendly way for practitioners. Finally, applying MABAC to larger, real-world case studies and comparing its performance systematically with alternative MCDM methods would strengthen the empirical evidence base for its use.

References

Afrasiabi, A., Tavana, M., & Di Caprio, D. (2022). An extended hybrid fuzzy multi-criteria decision model for sustainable and resilient supplier selection. *Environmental Science and Pollution Research, 29*(25), 37291–37314.

Albahri, O., Alamoodi, A., Deveci, M., Albahri, A., Mahmoud, M. A., Sharaf, I. M., & Coffman, D. M. (2023). Multi-perspective evaluation of integrated active cooling systems using fuzzy decision making model. *Energy Policy, 182*, 113775.

Aljburi, M. T., Albahri, A., Albahri, O., Alamoodi, A., Mohammed, S. M., Deveci, M., & Tomášková, H. (2024). Exploring decision-making techniques for evaluation and benchmarking of energy system integration frameworks for achieving a sustainable energy future. *Energy Strategy Reviews, 51*, 101251.

Bakhat, R., & Rajaa, M. (2020). Risk Assessment of a Wind Turbine Using an AHP-MABAC Approach with Grey System Theory: A Case Study of Morocco. *Mathematical Problems in Engineering, 2020*, 1–22. https://doi.org/10.1155/2020/2496914.

Biswas, T. K., & Das, M. C. (2019). Selection of commercially available electric vehicle using fuzzy AHP-MABAC. *Journal of The Institution of Engineers (India): Series C, 100*(3), 531–537.

Božanić, D., Epler, I., Puška, A., Biswas, S., Marinković, D., & Koprivica, S. (2024). Application of the DIBR II–rough MABAC decision-making model for ranking methods and techniques of lean organization systems management in the process of technical maintenance. *Facta Universitatis, Series: Mechanical Engineering, 22*(1), 101–123.

Božanić, D., Tešić, D., & Milićević, J. (2018). A hybrid fuzzy AHP-MABAC model: Application in the Serbian army—the selection of the location for deep wading as a technique of crossing the river by tanks. *Decision Making: Applications in Management and Engineering, 1*(1), 143–164.

Chakraborty, S., Raut, R. D., Rofin, T., Chatterjee, S., & Chakraborty, S. (2023). A comparative analysis of multi-attributive border approximation area comparison (MABAC) model for healthcare supplier selection in fuzzy environments. *Decision Analytics Journal, 8*, 100290.

Chatterjee, S., & Chakraborty, S. (2023). Optimization of friction stir welding processes using multi-attributive border approximation area comparison (MABAC) method in neutrosophic fuzzy environment. *International Journal on Interactive Design and Manufacturing (IJIDeM, 17*(4), 1979–1994.

Delice, A. P. E. K. (2017). Selection of on-site energy generation technology with a new MCDM approach using MABAC & AHP. *Jaffar Beikzad and Amir Gharifard, 5*, 126.

Eligüzel, İ. M., & Eligüzel, N. (2024). Evaluation of sustainable transportation in 25 European countries using gra and entropy mabac. *Journal of Transportation and Logistics, 9*(2), 245–259.

Estiri, M., Heidary Dahooie, J., Salar Vanaki, A., Banaitis, A., & Binkytė-Vėlienė, A. (2021). A multi-attribute framework for the selection of high-performance work systems: The hybrid DEMATEL-MABAC model. *Economic research-Ekonomska istraživanja, 34*(1), 970–997.

Hezer, S., Gelmez, E., & Özceylan, E. (2021). Comparative analysis of TOPSIS, VIKOR and COPRAS methods for the COVID-19 regional safety assessment. *Journal of infection and public health, 14*(6), 775–786.

Hosseinzadeh Lotfi, F., Allahviranloo, T., Pedrycz, W., Shahriari, M., Sharafi, H., & Razipour GhalehJough, S. (2023). Multi attributive border approximation area comparison (MABAC) in uncertainty environment. In *Fuzzy decision analysis: Multi attribute decision making approach*. Springer, 275–289.

Jafari, M., & Naghdi Khanachah, S. (2024). An integrated multi-attributive border approximation area comparison (MABAC) method for evaluating resilience and knowledge sharing of suppliers in pythagorean fuzzy environment. *Artificial Intelligence Review, 57*(9), 227.

Jiang, Y., & Ma, Y. (2020). Application of hybrid particle swarm and ant colony optimization algorithms to obtain the optimum homomorphic wavelet image fusion. *Annals of Translational Medicine, 8*(22), 1482. https://doi.org/10.21037/atm-20-5997.

Keshavarz-Ghorabaee, M., Amiri, M., Hashemi-Tabatabaei, M., & Ghahremanloo, M. (2021). Sustainable public transportation evaluation using a novel hybrid method based on fuzzy BWM and MABAC. *The Open Transportation Journal, 15*(1).

Komatina, N., Tadić, D., Aleksić, A., & Jovanović, A. D. (2023). The assessment and selection of suppliers using AHP and MABAC with type-2 fuzzy numbers in automotive industry. *Proceedings of the Institution of Mechanical Engineers, Part O: Journal of Risk and Reliability, 237*(4), 836–852.

Liang, R.-x, He, S.-s, Wang, J.-q, Chen, K., & Li, L. (2019). An extended MABAC method for multi-criteria group decision-making problems based on correlative inputs of intuitionistic fuzzy information. *Computational and Applied Mathematics, 38*(3), 112.

Liu, P., & Cheng, S. (2020). An improved MABAC group decision-making method using regret theory and likelihood in probability multi-valued neutrosophic sets. *International Journal of Information Technology & Decision Making, 19*(05), 1353–1387.

Liu, P., Pan, Q., & Xu, H. (2021). Multi-attributive border approximation area comparison (MABAC) method based on normal q-rung orthopair fuzzy environment. *Journal of Intelligent & Fuzzy Systems, 40*(5), 9085–9111.

Liu, R., Hou, L.-X., Liu, H.-C., & Lin, W. (2020). Occupational health and safety risk assessment using an integrated SWARA-MABAC model under bipolar fuzzy environment. *Computational and Applied Mathematics, 39*(4), 276.

Lukić, R. (2021). Application of MABAC method in evaluation of sector efficiency in Serbia. *Revista de management comparat internațional, 22*(3), 400–418.

Luo, S.-z, & Xing, L.-n (2019). A hybrid decision making framework for personnel selection using BWM, MABAC and PROMETHEE. *International Journal of Fuzzy Systems, 21*(8), 2421–2434.

Mehdiabadi, A., Sadeghi, A., Karbassi Yazdi, A., & Tan, Y. (2025). Sustainability service chain capabilities in the oil and gas industry: a fuzzy hybrid approach SWARA-MABAC. *Spectrum of Operational Research,* 2(1), 114–134. https://doi.org/10.31181/sor21202512.

Muravev, D., & Mijic, N. (2020). A novel integrated provider selection multicriteria model: the BWM-MABAC model. *Decision Making: Applications in Management and Engineering, 3*(1), 60–78. https://doi.org/10.31181/dmame2003078m.

Pamučar, D., & Božanić, D. (2019). Selection of a location for the development of multimodal logistics center: Application of single-valued neutrosophic MABAC model. *Operational Research in Engineering Sciences: Theory and Applications, 2*(2). https://doi.org/10.31181/oresta1902039p.

Pamučar, D., & Ćirović, G. (2015). The selection of transport and handling resources in logistics centers using multi-attributive border approximation area comparison (MABAC). *Expert Systems with Applications, 42*(6), 3016–3028.

Pamučar, D., Stević, Ž., & Zavadskas, E. K. (2018). Integration of interval rough AHP and interval rough MABAC methods for evaluating university web pages. *Applied Soft Computing, 67*, 141–163.

Peng, X., & Dai, J. (2018). Approaches to single-valued neutrosophic MADM based on MABAC, TOPSIS and new similarity measure with score function. *Neural Computing and Applications, 29*(10), 939–954.

Radulescu, C. Z., & Radulescu, M. (2024). A hybrid group multi-criteria approach based on SAW, TOPSIS, VIKOR, and COPRAS methods for complex IoT selection problems. *Electronics, 13*(4), 789.

Seker, S., & Aydin, N. (2024). Analyzing barriers and strategies in digital transformation for resilient SC in healthcare using AHP and MABAC under uncertain environment. *Journal of Enterprise Information Management*.

Sharaf, I. M., Albahri, O., Alsalem, M., Alamoodi, A., & Albahri, A. (2024). A novel dual-level multi-source information fusion approach for multicriteria decision making applications. *Applied Intelligence, 54*(22), 11577–11602.

Sonar, H. C., & Kulkarni, S. D. (2021). An integrated AHP-MABAC approach for electric vehicle selection. *Research in Transportation Business & Management, 41*, 100665.

Tien, D. H., Trung, D., & Thien, N. (2022). Comparison of multi-criteria decision making methods using the same data standardization method. *Strojnícky časopis. Journal of Mechanical Engineering, 72*(2), 57–72.

Torkayesh, A. E., Tirkolaee, E. B., Bahrini, A., Pamucar, D., & Khakbaz, A. (2023). A systematic literature review of MABAC method and applications: An outlook for sustainability and circularity. *Informatica, 34*(2), 415–448.

Verma, R. (2021). Fuzzy MABAC method based on new exponential fuzzy information measures. *Soft Computing, 25*(14), 9575–9589.

Vesković, S., Stević, Ž., Stojić, G., Vasiljević, M., & Milinković, S. (2018). Evaluation of the railway management model by using a new integrated model DELPHI-SWARA-MABAC. *Decision Making: Applications in Management and Engineering, 1*(2), 34–50.

Xue, Y.-X., You, J.-X., Lai, X.-D., & Liu, H.-C. (2016). An interval-valued intuitionistic fuzzy MABAC approach for material selection with incomplete weight information. *Applied Soft Computing, 38*, 703–713.

Yalçın, G. C., Edinsel, S., Chatterjee, P., & Zakeri, S. (2025). An interval-valued spherical fuzzy framework for strategic renewable energy selection. *Decision Analytics Journal,* 100625.

Zhang, J., Xu, Z., Liu, H., Zhu, X., & Lan, B. (2025). An improved hybrid ant colony optimization and genetic algorithm for multi-map path planning of rescuing robots in mine disaster scenario. *Machines, 13*(6), 474.

Zhao, M., Wei, G., Chen, X., & Wei, Y. (2021). Intuitionistic fuzzy MABAC method based on cumulative prospect theory for multiple attribute group decision making. *International Journal of Intelligent Systems, 36*(11), 6337–6359.

Chapter 64

SECA: Simultaneous evaluation of criteria and alternatives for multi-attribute decision-making

Mehdi Keshavarz-Ghorabaee
Department of Management, Faculty of Humanities (Azadshahr Branch), Gonbad Kavous University, Gonbad Kavous, Iran

64.1 Introduction

In today's complex decision-making situations, reliance on subjectivity or experience when evaluating multiple alternatives against various, often conflicting criteria is common. Multicriteria decision-making (MCDM) is a powerful decision science technique that deals with these kinds of problems systematically and rationally (Kumar & Pamucar, 2025; Namin et al., 2022; Tighnavard Balasbaneh et al., 2025). One popular way to classify MCDM methods is to distinguish them into two major categories: methods aimed at evaluating and prioritizing alternatives, and those aimed at determining criterion weights. Several classical MCDM techniques, such as simple additive weighting (SAW), technique for order preference by similarity to ideal solution (TOPSIS), complex proportional assessment, and VlseKriterijumska Optimizacija I Kompromisno Resenje (VIKOR), have been developed to prioritize alternatives using known or hypothesized prescribed weights. On the other hand, algorithms such as criteria importance through intercriteria correlation (CRITIC), entropy, and method based on the removal effects of criteria have been introduced to estimate objective criterion weights extracted from intrinsic information in the decision matrix (Fan et al., 2024; Hashemkhani Zolfani, 2024; Radulescu & Radulescu, 2024; Solanki & Agarwal, 2024).

Simultaneous evaluation of criteria and alternatives (SECA) is a modern method in the MCDM family that has an innovative feature: it can calculate both criterion weights and alternative rankings using a decision matrix. This holistic characteristic distinguishes SECA from most classical MCDM techniques, which typically assume preassigned, expert-defined, or subjectively assigned weights. SECA uses a rigorous data-driven multiobjective mathematical programming model where both evaluations and weights are obtained directly from the dataset. This dual functionality of SECA sets it apart from other MCDM methods, providing robust analysis, minimizing subjective judgments, and enabling valid implementation of MCDM models, which contributes to its practical significance in complex decision-making. The main motivation for SECA stems from the observation that in most practical decision-making problems, criterion weights and alternative preferences are inherently related. Frequently, establishing appropriate weights is as important as ranking alternatives. Conventional techniques that separate these two aspects can compromise analysis homogeneity, particularly when subjective weights are applied without considering all statistical or contextual data characteristics. SECA bridges this gap by utilizing decision matrix information to jointly determine both parameter sets, leading to a consistent, fair, and reproducible evaluation process that reflects the problem's specific properties (Keshavarz-Ghorabaee et al., 2018).

SECA is fundamentally based on multiobjective optimization. Instead of finding and assigning weights only as a fixed (and possibly arbitrary) solution, SECA aims at optimizing multiple objectives at the same time. To do so, SECA exploits important statistical features of the decision matrix. Namely, it derives two important sets of parameters: (i) the standard deviation of each criterion, which reflects the level of differences of that criterion's values across all alternatives, and (ii) the correlation coefficients between each pair of criteria, which provide a measure for the similarity of behavior between two criteria. The two variables, degree of variation and degree of redundancy, are used as the core of SECA's weighting mechanism. A large standard deviation means a criterion is capable of distinguishing clearly between alternatives; it is a

Encyclopedia of Multi-Attribute Decision-Making (MADM). DOI: https://doi.org/10.1016/B978-0-443-33275-3.00001-4

more informative criterion. On the other hand, low correlation with other criteria indicates that the criterion supplies exclusive nonredundant information, thus making it more desirable for the decision-making analysis. SECA leverages this logic to prioritize discriminative and distinct criteria such that the weights of individual criteria are more meaningful and balanced (Bazrafshan et al., 2021; Keshavarz-Ghorabaee et al., 2018).

To facilitate this reasoning, SECA develops a multiobjective mathematical programming model. That is, a set of criterion weights is sought to characterize the dispersion and conflict of the criteria, and at the same time, performance scores are obtained for alternatives. In the basic formulation of SECA, a min–max optimization methodology was used to seek a balanced solution that can achieve stable performance across all objectives. Other optimization methods (e.g., the weighted-sum method) have also been used in the literature to solve the problem in other versions of SECA, showing that this framework is also able to address a wide range of computational and decision-making problems. One of the key features of SECA is that it treats weights and scores simultaneously. In traditional MCDM procedures, the alternative assessment is typically carried out after criterion weights have been assigned by subjective decision, expert estimation, or easy-to-use statistical methods. This generic two-step procedure might cause discrepancies, notably when the attributed weights do not match well the distribution or interrelation of the data. SECA seeks to deal with this problem by incorporating weight measurement in the assessment process itself. Thus, we are encouraged by the fact that the inferred weights are contextual and well-posed within the structure of the data, therefore resulting in fairer and more defensible evaluations (Eghbali-Zarch et al., 2023; Keshavarz-Ghorabaee et al., 2019).

From a computational perspective, SECA is not free of complexity, since it involves solving a mathematical programming model. But this extra complication is a legitimate and understandable concession in view of the enormous analytical benefits of the method. SECA removes the separate and possibly inconsistent steps in MCDM algorithms. By operating based on objective data only as opposed to subjective parameters, SECA eliminates much of the bias while dramatically improving the reproducibility of results. Moreover, the fact that SECA incorporates intercriterion correlation explicitly contributes to avoiding overemphasizing interredundant information, which makes the distinction between alternatives more substantive. Another important aspect of SECA is its emphasis on statistical foundations for weight determination. The use of standard deviation ensures that criteria with greater variability and thus greater discriminating power receive more attention in the evaluation process. This renders SECA particularly appealing for problems in which the decision matrix consists of various types of criteria that are measured in different units and ranges (Eghbali-Zarch et al., 2023; Keshavarz-Ghorabaee et al., 2019).

SECA provides a powerful and integrated approach to multicriteria decision-making, and it has been applied to several real-world problems including power distribution feeder identification (Bahrami & Rastegar, 2022), optimal wastewater allocation (Azbari et al., 2021), occupational health and safety risk assessment (Tian et al., 2024), site selection for solar hydrogen production plan (Zhang et al., 2024), food waste management (Antwi et al., 2025), optimization of hybrid machining processes (Das & Chakraborty, 2022), site selection for shared charging and swapping stations (Lu et al., 2022), financial performance evaluation (Balcı, 2024) and sustainable e-waste scenario management (Keshavarz-Ghorabaee et al., 2022).

The rest of the chapter is organized as follows. In the next section, the SECA method is explained in detail, where each computational process that is necessary for determining simultaneously the weights of criteria as well as the rankings of the alternatives is described. Then two numerical examples follow: one is a small demonstration example used to illustrate the application of the method, and the other is a real-world example to reveal the practical employment and robustness of SECA. Finally, the chapter ends with a discussion of the main findings and future avenues of research.

64.2 Methodology

The SECA approach has been developed to better address the problem of weight and performance score concurrent determination in multicriteria decision-making processes. The difference from traditional MCDM methods, where the weights of criteria are generally assumed a priori before the alternatives can be evaluated, is that SECA attempts to find objective weights from the decision matrix itself by capturing both internal and cross-criteria variability. This combination helps to increase the reality and stability of the decision. This process involves the following steps:

Step 1. Construct the decision matrix

Begin with a standard decision matrix $X = [x_{ij}]_{n \times m}$, where:

- x_{ij} is the performance value of alternative A_i on criterion C_j.
- n is the number of alternatives.
- m is the number of criteria.

Assume that all $x_{ij} > 0$, and the weights w_j for the criteria are initially unknown.

Step 2. Normalize the decision matrix

Normalize the decision matrix to obtain $X^N = [x_{ij}^N]_{n\times m}$, ensuring all criteria are comparable:

$$x_{ij}^N = \begin{cases} \dfrac{x_{ij}}{\max\limits_k x_{kj}} & if \quad j \in BC \\ \dfrac{\min\limits_k x_{kj}}{x_{ij}} & if \quad j \in NC \end{cases}, \tag{64.1}$$

where BC and NC denote the sets of beneficial and nonbeneficial criteria, respectively. This step guarantees that all performance scores are scaled between 0 and 1 based on their relative desirability.

Step 3. Calculate within-criterion variation (standard deviation)

For each criterion C_j, compute the standard deviation of its normalized values to reflect within-criterion variation:

$$\sigma_j = StdDev\left(x_{1j}^N,\ x_{2j}^N,\ \ldots,\ x_{nj}^N\right), \tag{64.2}$$

The standard deviation σ_j of this vector is computed to reflect the extent of dispersion in the performance values. A higher standard deviation indicates that the criterion has a greater discriminatory power across alternatives.

Step 4. Calculate between-criterion variation (correlation-based conflict)

To assess how distinct each criterion is compared to others, calculate the total correlation-based conflict π_j using pairwise Pearson correlations:

$$\pi_j = \sum_{l=1}^{m} (1 - r_{jl}), \tag{64.3}$$

where r_{jl} is the Pearson correlation between the normalized vectors of C_j and C_l. Higher π_j implies greater independence or conflict with other criteria.

Step 5. Normalize variation measures

Normalize the values of σ_j and π_j to convert them into reference weights:

$$\sigma_j^N = \frac{\sigma_j}{\sum_{l=1}^m \sigma_l} \tag{64.4}$$

$$\pi_j^N = \frac{\pi_j}{\sum_{l=1}^m \pi_l} \tag{64.5}$$

These normalized values serve as baseline estimates for assigning objective weights to criteria.

Step 6. Formulate the multiobjective optimization model

Develop a nonlinear multiobjective optimization model with the following goals: maximize the overall performance of alternatives, and minimize the deviation of actual weights from the reference weights σ_j^N and π_j^N.

$$\max \quad S_i = \textstyle\sum_{j=1}^m w_j x_{ij}^N, \quad \forall\, i \in \{1,\ 2,\ \ldots,\ n\} \tag{64.6}$$

$$\min \quad \lambda_b = \textstyle\sum_{j=1}^m \left(w_j - \sigma_j^N\right)^2 \tag{64.7}$$

$$\min \quad \lambda_c = \textstyle\sum_{j=1}^m \left(w_j - \pi_j^N\right)^2 \tag{64.8}$$

$$s.\ t.\ \ \textstyle\sum_{j=1}^m w_j = 1 \tag{64.9}$$

$$w_j \le 1, \quad \forall\, j \in \{1,\ 2,\ \ldots,\ m\} \tag{64.10}$$

$$w_j \ge \varepsilon, \quad \forall\, j \in \{1,\ 2,\ \ldots,\ m\} \tag{64.11}$$

Each weight must be greater than a small positive number ε. The suggested value for this parameter is 10^{-3}.

Step 7. Convert the model to a single-objective form

To solve the model efficiently, transform it into a scalar single-objective form using min–max and weighted summation approach:

$$\max \quad Z = \lambda_a - \beta(\lambda_b + \lambda_c) \tag{64.12}$$

$$s.t.\ \lambda_a \le S_i,\quad \forall\, i \in \{1,\ 2,\ \ldots,\ n\} \tag{64.13}$$

$$S_i = \textstyle\sum_{j=1}^{m} w_j x_{ij}^N,\quad \forall\, i \in \{1,\ 2,\ \ldots,\ n\} \tag{64.14}$$

$$\lambda_b = \sum_{j=1}^{m} (w_j - \sigma_j^N)^2 \tag{64.15}$$

$$\lambda_c = \sum_{j=1}^{m} (w_j - \pi_j^N)^2 \tag{64.16}$$

$$\sum_{j=1}^{m} w_j = 1 \tag{64.17}$$

$$w_j \le 1,\quad \forall\, j \in \{1,\ 2,\ \ldots,\ m\} \tag{64.18}$$

$$w_j \ge \varepsilon,\quad \forall\, j \in \{1,\ 2,\ \ldots,\ m\} \tag{64.19}$$

The scalar model aims to maximize the minimum performance across all alternatives while penalizing deviations from objective reference weights. The coefficient β controls the trade-off between performance maximization and consistency with reference weights.

64.3 Numerical example 1

In this part, a simple numerical example is given to make the computational process of the SECA method described above clear. It is worthwhile to mention here that one of the remarkable features of the SECA technique is its capability to determine simultaneously both the weights of the criteria and the performance scores of the alternatives. Accordingly, one does not need to preassign weights to criteria at the beginning of the decision process. This property makes SECA particularly appealing when decision-makers either do not have enough information to form reliable weights, or when they prefer a transparent, data-based weighting scheme.

To ensure the clarity and ease of understanding, the example considered here involves four alternatives (A_1–A_4) and four criteria (C_1–C_4). Among the four criteria, C_1 and C_2 are of benefit type (BC), meaning that higher values are preferred, while C_3 and C_4 are cost criteria (NC), where lower values are more desirable.

Step 1. Constructing the decision matrix

The first phase of the SECA technique is to develop the decision matrix, which is an $n \times m$ matrix that includes the performance score for each criterion for any one of the alternatives. It is also worth mentioning that all elements in the decision matrix should be positive in accordance with the mathematical form of the SECA model. The values for the decision matrix in this example are shown in Table 64.1.

Step 2. Normalizing the decision matrix

In this stage, the decision matrix is normalized according to Eq. (64.1) in the methodology section. Max-normalization is used for benefit criteria, and inverse normalization (min-based) is applied to cost criteria. The resulting matrix after normalization is presented in Table 64.2.

TABLE 64.1 Decision matrix for the illustrative example 1.

	C_1 *(BC)*	C_2 *(BC)*	C_3 *(NC)*	C_4 *(NC)*
A_1	2	21	1300	143
A_2	4	25	1600	121
A_3	3	11	2100	176
A_4	1	17	1900	196

TABLE 64.2 Normalized decision matrix (example 1).

	C_1	C_2	C_3	C_4
A_1	0.5	0.84	1	0.846
A_2	1	1	0.812	1
A_3	0.75	0.44	0.619	0.687
A_4	0.25	0.68	0.684	0.617

TABLE 64.3 Standard deviation (σ_j) and conflict intensity (π_j) of criteria (example 1).

	C_1	C_2	C_3	C_4
σ_j	0.279	0.206	0.145	0.147
π_j	1.946	1.167	1.687	0.817

TABLE 64.4 Normalized standard deviation (σ_j^N) and conflict intensity (π_j^N) (example 1).

	C_1	C_2	C_3	C_4
σ_j^N	0.358	0.265	0.186	0.189
π_j^N	0.346	0.207	0.3	0.145

Steps 3 and 4. Computing the standard deviations and conflict measures

For obtaining scores, the information used in the SECA method is the following two: (1) the standard deviation of the performance of each criterion (reflecting the dispersion of the performance values among alternatives), and (2) the intensity of the conflicts, which is evaluated using the correlation coefficient of each criterion with the rest.

A larger standard deviation denotes more discriminative power of the criterion, and a larger conflict intensity means that a criterion is more independent and less redundant with others. They are calculated and tabulated in Table 64.3 based on Eqs. (64.2) and (64.3).

Step 5. Normalizing σ_j and π_j to obtain reference points

Next, both the standard deviation and conflict intensity values are normalized to derive reference points for each criterion's contribution to the weight determination process. These normalized values are calculated using Eqs. (64.4) and (64.5), as shown in Table 64.4.

Steps 6 and 7. Solving the optimization model

Using the normalized decision matrix and the derived reference values for criteria weights, the SECA model is formulated. As described in the methodology, Model (7) includes a parameter β that balances the reference vectors, and a small parameter ε used to ensure strict ranking. In this example, $\beta = 3$ and $\varepsilon = 0.001$ are applied.

The resulting optimization model is then solved using LINGO software. This yields the final performance scores of each alternative and the computed weights of criteria, which are shown in Tables 64.5 and 64.6, respectively.

TABLE 64.5 Final scores and rankings of alternatives (example 1).

	S_i	Rank
A_1	0.770	2
A_2	0.952	1
A_3	0.629	3
A_4	0.529	4

TABLE 64.6 Weights of the criteria obtained via simultaneous evaluation of criteria and alternatives (example 1).

	w_j
C_1	0.326
C_2	0.246
C_3	0.253
C_4	0.172

As observed in Table 64.5, Alternative A_2 achieves the highest performance score and is ranked first. This is consistent with a visual analysis of the original decision matrix, where A_2 appears to perform well across both benefit and cost criteria. Conversely, Alternative A_4 receives the lowest performance score, indicating it is the least preferred among the four options.

The results in Table 64.6 show that C_1 (benefit criterion) has the highest weight, indicating that it is the most influential criterion in this decision-making problem. On the other hand, C_4 (a cost criterion) received the lowest weight, suggesting its role in discriminating between alternatives is relatively less significant.

64.4 Numerical example 2

To illustrate the effectiveness and reliability of the SECA algorithm, it is applied to the following real-world case in this section. An example is the choice of the correct material for building a cryogenic storage tank intended for the transportation of liquid nitrogen. Such tanks have to meet formidable safety and performance demands, considering the harsh environment in which they usually operate.

This case is adapted from the study by Dehghan-Manshadi et al. (2007), where a set of seven alternative materials was evaluated based on seven technical criteria related to mechanical and thermal properties. The primary objective was to identify a material that ensures both structural integrity and thermal efficiency under cryogenic conditions. The materials must meet several criteria, including high toughness, yield strength, and Young's modulus (which are beneficial attributes), while also maintaining low density, specific heat, thermal expansion coefficient, and thermal conductivity (which are nonbeneficial attributes). These performance attributes are critical to ensure the material is not only strong and stiff but also stable, safe, and efficient in cryogenic environments.

Step 1. Constructing the decision matrix

The criteria used in this decision-making problem are as follows:

C_1: Toughness index (TI) - beneficial

C_2: Yield strength (YS) - beneficial

C_3: Young's modulus (YM) - beneficial

C_4: Density (D) - nonbeneficial

TABLE 64.7 Decision matrix for material selection problem.

	TI	YS	YM	D	TE	TC	SH
A_1	75.5	420	74.2	2.8	21.4	0.37	0.16
A_2	95	91	70	2.68	22.1	0.33	0.16
A_3	770	1365	189	7.9	16.9	0.04	0.08
A_4	187	1120	210	7.9	14.4	0.03	0.08
A_5	179	875	112	4.43	9.4	0.016	0.09
A_6	239	1190	217	8.51	11.5	0.31	0.07
A_7	273	200	112	8.53	19.9	0.29	0.06

TABLE 64.8 Normalized decision matrix (example 2).

	C_1	C_2	C_3	C_4	C_5	C_6	C_7
A_1	0.098	0.308	0.342	0.957	0.439	0.043	0.375
A_2	0.123	0.067	0.323	1.000	0.425	0.048	0.375
A_3	1.000	1.000	0.871	0.339	0.556	0.400	0.750
A_4	0.243	0.821	0.968	0.339	0.653	0.533	0.750
A_5	0.232	0.641	0.516	0.605	1.000	1.000	0.667
A_6	0.310	0.872	1.000	0.315	0.817	0.052	0.857
A_7	0.355	0.147	0.516	0.314	0.472	0.055	1.000

C_5: Thermal expansion coefficient (TE) - nonbeneficial
C_6: Thermal conductivity (TC) - nonbeneficial
C_7: Specific heat (SH) - nonbeneficial

The decision matrix, which includes the performance values of each alternative material with respect to these criteria, is shown in Table 64.7.

Step 2. Normalizing the decision matrix

To standardize the criteria values for comparison, the decision matrix is normalized. The resulting normalized matrix is presented in Table 64.8.

Steps 3 to 5. Computing within and between-criterion variations

As part of the SECA framework, each criterion's discriminatory power and conflict level are evaluated. Standard deviation (σ_j) reflects variability, and conflict intensity (π_j) is derived from correlation among criteria. Their values and normalized versions are provided in Table 64.9.

Steps 6 and 7. Solving the optimization model

The SECA model is now formulated and solved using Model 7, as defined in the methodology section. The parameters are set as $\beta = 3$ and $\varepsilon = 0.001$. Solving this multiobjective model with LINGO yields the performance score for each alternative, which is shown in Table 64.10 along with rankings from other well-known MCDM methods.

The Spearman rank correlation coefficient (ρ) was used to compare SECA results with other methods. All correlation values were greater than 0.90, confirming a high degree of consistency between SECA and traditional MCDM methods.

TABLE 64.9 Standard deviation and conflict intensity for each criterion (example 2).

	C_1	C_2	C_3	C_4	C_5	C_6	C_7
σ_j	0.284	0.347	0.270	0.286	0.200	0.339	0.217
π_j	4.947	3.774	4.267	9.524	4.363	4.613	5.130
σ_j^N	0.146	0.179	0.139	0.147	0.103	0.175	0.112
π_j^N	0.135	0.103	0.117	0.260	0.119	0.126	0.140

TABLE 64.10 Performance scores and ranking comparison of simultaneous evaluation of criteria and alternatives (SECA) and other methods.

		Rank						
	S_i	SECA	SAW	WASPAS	COPRAS	TOPSIS	VIKOR	EDAS
A_1	0.431	5	6	6	6	6	6	6
A_2	0.412	6	7	7	7	7	7	7
A_3	0.664	1	1	1	1	1	2	1
A_4	0.587	3	3	3	3	2	3	2
A_5	0.655	2	2	2	2	3	1	3
A_6	0.575	4	4	4	4	4	4	4
A_7	0.412	6	5	5	5	5	5	5
ρ	—	—	0.937	0.937	0.937	0.901	0.901	0.901

To further validate the credibility of the SECA-generated weights, they were compared with weights obtained from the CRITIC method, an objective technique that also considers intra-criteria variability and intercriteria conflict, similar to SECA. The results are shown in Table 64.11.

The high correlation ($\rho = 0.902$) between SECA and CRITIC weights provides strong evidence of reliability, supporting the objective capability of SECA to accurately reflect the importance of criteria in complex, real-world engineering problems.

64.5 Conclusions

The SECA approach is a novel and remarkable contribution to the multicriteria decision-making literature, since it establishes the criteria weights as well as the ranking of the alternatives simultaneously in a single mathematical model. Unlike other established approaches that rely on either predefined or expert-assigned weights, both elements of SECA are extracted from the inherent structure of the decision matrix. The foundation of SECA is based on its use of statistical characteristics (in particular, standard deviation and correlation-based conflict). A large standard deviation indicates a strong discriminative characteristic, and a minimum correlation with other criteria indicates unique informativeness. These approaches are incorporated in a multiobjective optimization framework to provide more comprehensive decision support. Such a unified method is especially useful in practical situations when the subjective determination of weights is not convenient or reliable due to lack of complete information or expert consensus. The use of SECA in practical problems of

TABLE 64.11 Comparison of simultaneous evaluation of criteria and alternatives (SECA) and criteria importance through intercriteria correlation (CRITIC) weights.

	SECA	CRITIC
w_1	0.128	0.138
w_2	0.119	0.129
w_3	0.130	0.114
w_4	0.236	0.268
w_5	0.118	0.086
w_6	0.124	0.154
w_7	0.146	0.110
ρ	—	0.902

material selection, such as those illustrated in this study, also validates its effectiveness and applicability. In the cited case study, the ranking provided by SECA is in accordance with that of a number of popular MCDM methods (like SAW, VIKOR, and TOPSIS) and objective weighting techniques (like CRITIC), and also shows a strong correlation between them. These results confirm that SECA can make consistent and repeatable decisions without relying on specific weight values. Despite its major strengths, the use of optimization modeling makes SECA typically high in computational complexity. However, this trade-off is acceptable due to the improvements in performance and data-driven accuracy that it provides. Standard software packages like LINGO and MATLAB® can quickly solve the model, making it usable for large-scale decision problems.

Several possible directions for future research are expected to further extend the effectiveness and flexibility of SECA. One important extension is to develop SECA in fuzzy settings. In many real-life problems, ambiguities, inexactness, or linguistic expressions can be appropriately modeled by fuzzy sets. The development of fuzzy-SECA models could allow decision-makers to deal more effectively with fuzziness, e.g., in supply chain, environmental sustainability, strategic planning, etc. Another interesting direction is the extension of SECA to group decision-making processes. In many applications, decisions are made collectively, multiple decision-makers can be involved, and even when a single decision-maker exists, several stakeholders must agree on that decision. However, improving the tool to handle group-based inputs, while keeping it objective and internally consistent, can significantly increase its capability for use in group decision-making settings. In addition, future research could examine industry-sector-specific applications of SECA. Potential applications include energy policy design, healthcare resource planning, urban infrastructure design, transportation and logistics network design, and portfolio allocation.

References

Antwi, C. O., Darko, A. P., Zhang, J., Asamoah, K. O., Affum-Osei, E., & Ren, J. (2025). Enhancing the sustainability of food waste management practices in emerging economies' hospitality industry through SECA multi-criteria group decision-making. *International Journal of Hospitality Management, 130*, 104233.

Azbari, K. E., Ashofteh, P.-S., Golfam, P., & Singh, V. P. (2021). Optimal wastewater allocation with the development of an SECA multi-criteria decision-making method. *Journal of Cleaner Production, 321*, 129041.

Bahrami, S., & Rastegar, M. (2022). Security-based critical power distribution feeder identification: Application of fuzzy BWM-VIKOR and SECA. *International Journal of Electrical Power & Energy Systems, 134*, 107395.

Balcı, N. (2024). Azerbaijan banking sector financial performance evaluation with SECA method. In *Recent Developments in Financial Management and Economics*. IGI Global Scientific Publishing, 146–165.

Bazrafshan, R., Hashemkhani Zolfani, S., & Al-e-hashem, S. M. J. M. (2021). Comparison of the sub-tour elimination methods for the asymmetric traveling salesman problem applying the SECA method. *Axioms, 10*, 19.

Das, P. P., & Chakraborty, S. (2022). Application of simultaneous evaluation of criteria and alternatives (SECA) method for parametric optimization of hybrid machining processes. *International Journal on Interactive Design and Manufacturing (IJIDeM), 16*, 1497–1509.

Dehghan-Manshadi, B., Mahmudi, H., Abedian, A., & Mahmudi, R. (2007). A novel method for materials selection in mechanical design: Combination of non-linear normalization and a modified digital logic method. *Materials & Design, 28*, 8–15. https://doi.org/10.1016/j.matdes.2005.06.023.

Eghbali-Zarch, M., Zeynab Zabihi, S., & Masoud, S. (2023). A novel fuzzy SECA model based on fuzzy standard deviation and correlation coefficients for resilient-sustainable supplier selection. *Expert Systems with Applications, 231*, 120653. https://doi.org/10.1016/j.eswa.2023.120653.

Fan, J., Lei, T., & Wu, M. (2024). MEREC-MABAC method based on cumulative prospect theory for picture fuzzy sets: Applications to wearable health technology devices. *Expert Systems with Applications, 255*, 124749. https://doi.org/10.1016/j.eswa.2024.124749.

Hashemkhani Zolfani, S. (2024). Objective weighting in mcdm: A comparative study of critic, itara, merec, and beyond. *Decision Making and Artificial Intelligence Trends, 1*, 105–120.

Keshavarz-Ghorabaee, M., Amiri, M., Zavadskas, E. K., Turskis, Z., & Antucheviciene, J. (2018). Simultaneous evaluation of criteria and alternatives (SECA) for multi-criteria decision-making. *Informatica, 29*, 265–280.

Keshavarz-Ghorabaee, M., Amiri, M., Zavadskas, E. K., Turskis, Z., & Antucheviciene, J. (2022). A fuzzy simultaneous evaluation of criteria and alternatives (F-SECA) for sustainable E-waste scenario management. *Sustainability, 14*, 10371.

Keshavarz-Ghorabaee, M., Govindan, K., Amiri, M., Zavadskas, E. K., & Antuchevičienė, J. (2019). An integrated type-2 fuzzy decision model based on WASPAS and SECA for evaluation of sustainable manufacturing strategies. *Journal of Environmental Engineering and Landscape Management, 27*, 187–200.

Kumar, R., & Pamucar, D. (2025). A comprehensive and systematic review of multi-criteria decision-making (MCDM) methods to solve decision-making problems: Two decades from 2004 to 2024. *Spectrum of Decision Making and Applications, 2*, 178–197.

Lu, F., Yan, L., & Huang, B. (2022). Site selection for shared charging and swapping stations using the SECA and TRUST methods. *Energy Reports, 8*, 14606–14622.

Namin, F. S., Ghadi, A., & Saki, F. (2022). A literature review of multi criteria decision-making (MCDM) towards mining method selection (MMS). *Resources Policy, 77*, 102676. https://doi.org/10.1016/j.resourpol.2022.102676.

Radulescu, C. Z., & Radulescu, M. (2024). A hybrid group multi-criteria approach based on SAW, TOPSIS, VIKOR, and COPRAS methods for complex IoT selection problems. *Electronics, 13*, 789.

Solanki, V. S., & Agarwal, P. K. (2024). Identification of key performance indicators using hybrid COPRAS-TOPSIS for urban public transit systems by evaluating with AHP and FAHP. *Multimedia Tools and Applications, 83*, 82439–82469. https://doi.org/10.1007/s11042-024-18851-3.

Tian, H., Zhang, S., Garg, H., & Liu, X. (2024). An extended SECA-GDM method considering flexible linguistic scale optimization and its application in occupational health and safety risk assessment. *Alexandria Engineering Journal, 88*, 317–330.

Tighnavard Balasbaneh, A., Aldrovandi, S., & Sher, W. (2025). A systematic review of implementing multi-criteria decision-making (MCDM) approaches for the circular economy and cost assessment. *Sustainability, 17*, 5007.

Zhang, W., Geng, X., Cheng, S., Zhou, Q., & Liu, Y. (2024). Simultaneous evaluation of criteria and alternatives method-based site selection for solar hydrogen production plant in Inner Mongolia, China. *Sustainable Energy Technologies and Assessments, 61*, 103583.

Chapter 65

TAOV: Total area based on orthogonal vectors for multi-attribute decision-making

Seyed Hossein Razavi Hajiagha[1], **Shide Sadat Hashemi**[2], **and Mahsa Pashang**[1]

[1]*Department of Management, Faculty of Management and Financial Sciences, Khatam University, Tehran, Iran,* [2]*Department of Management, Behin Avina co, MST Park, Tehran, Iran*

65.1 Introduction

A decision problem can be described as choosing the best or a good option among a set of alternatives based on a set of given criteria used to assess the quality of other options (Aruldoss et al., 2013; Ehrgott, 2005). Multicriteria decision-making (MCDM) is a scientific field that facilitates the making of such decisions. MCDM methods are categorized into multi-attribute decision-making (MADM) methods, involving the selection of the best one among a prespecified set of alternatives, and multiobjective decision-making, which consists of a design problem with several objectives without a given set of other options (Alinezhad & Khalili, 2019; Gavade, 2014). MADM methods are widely studied and developed by researchers. These methods are commonly applied in different areas. Site selection, meaning to select a location for a business, is one of the widely used areas of MADM (Hashemkhani Zolfani et al., 2022). The MADM method is also commonly used in the context of supplier selection (Chai et al., 2013; Karakoç et al., 2024). Also, there is a wide range of different applications for MADM in other fields, for example, Industry 4.0 (Zayat et al., 2023), sustainable manufacturing management (Pelissari et al., 2022), environmental and water resource planning and management (Zolghadr-Asli et al., 2021), and environmental pollution management (Safarzadeh & Jafari, 2025).

Considering the plurality of MADM methods, several categorizations of these methods have been presented. Carlsson and Fullér classified the methods as outranking, value and utility theory-based, multiple objective programming, and group decision and negotiation theory-based (Carlsson & Fullér, 1996). Later, Dantas Silva et al. (2024) extended this categorization into six main categories:

i. Value measurement-based: approximating alternatives' utility by sum-based or multiplicative-based functions, for example, simple additive weighting (Zionts & Wallenius, 1983), combined compromise solution (Yazdani et al., 2019), weighted aggregated sum product assessment (Zavadskas et al., 2012), and the total area based on orthogonal vectors (TAOV) (Razavi Hajiagha et al., 2018).

ii. Grey system-based: using grey system concepts to rank the alternatives, for example, grey relation analysis (Deng, 1982).

iii. Similarity distance-based: ranking alternatives based on their distance to a reference (ideal, nadir–ideal, or both of them) solution, for example, the technique for order of preference by similarity to ideal solution (TOPSIS) (Hwang & Yoon, 1981), and VlseKriterijumska Optimizacija I Kompromisno Resenje (VIKOR) (Opricovic, 1998).

iv. Outranking-based: using pairwise comparison of alternatives to determine their preferences by assessing the degree of dominance, for example, elimination and choice translating reality (Roy, 1968), and preference ranking organization method for enrichment evaluation (Brans, 1982).

v. Markov chain-based: building a Markov transition decision matrix and ranking alternatives according to the stationary distribution, for example, weighted Markov chain (Wang et al., 2008).

Encyclopedia of Multi-Attribute Decision-Making (MADM). DOI: https://doi.org/10.1016/B978-0-443-33275-3.00051-8

vi. User-centric/MADM hybrid: where MADM methods are combined with user-centric approaches, for example, opportune context-aware network selection (Honarvar et al., 2022).

The current chapter introduces the TAOV method, as mentioned in the value measurement-based approaches. Additive utility functions are a common class of functions used in MADM problems. Keeney (1972) believed that additive utility is the most common type of evaluating multidimensional consequences as simply as possible. The main assumption regarding additive utility is that the desirability of any alternative depends on the marginal probability of each criterion independently and not on their joint likelihood. Usually, the additive utility-based MADM methods like SAW, Kemeny median indicator ranks accordance (Krylovas et al., 2016), analytic hierarchy process (Saaty, 1980), suppose directly or implicitly that attributes are independent or uncorrelated (Alinezhad & Khalili, 2019). Triantaphyllou (2000) also stated that some anomaly in the ranking of alternatives using different MADM methods might be caused by attribute dependence. The main contribution of the TAOV method is to present a technique that guarantees independence of attributes. To this end, the original problem, defined in the initial attribute space, which may be dependent, is first transformed into a general, independent space using an orthogonalization method, such as principal component analysis (PCA). Finally, the alternatives are compared using an aggregation function of orthogonal attributes.

The chapter is organized as follows. A brief review of the applications of the TAOV method is presented in Section 65.2. The TAOV method's methodology is then described in Section 65.3. A set of simple and complex examples is then defined and solved in Sections 65.4 and 65.5, respectively. Finally, the chapter concludes in Section 65.6.

65.2 Literature review

The TAOV was introduced by Razavi Hajiagha et al. (2018). As mentioned in the introduction section, the primary motivation of the method is to address MADM problems where decision-making attributes are correlated and can lead to bias in additive utility functions. In their study, Razavi Hajiagha et al. (2018) described a numerical example and solved it using the TAOV method, and compared the results with several well-known MADM methods, such as SAW, TOPSIS, VIKOR, etc. The technique illustrated a good homogeneity with the compared methods.

Garoosi Mokhtarzadeh et al. (2018) applied the TAOV along with the best–worst method (BMW) (Rezaei, 2015) for attribute weights determination in a technology selection problem.

Peng et al. (2021) extended the TAOV method under q-rung orthopair fuzzy (q-ROF) sets, known as q-ROF-TAOV, and applied the proposed method in a mobile edge caching scheme selection problem. A comparison of the proposed method with a set of various MADM methods developed under the q-ROF environment revealed high agreement between q-ROF-TAOV and other methods. Urošević et al. (2021) proposed two novel MADM methods, known as multiple criteria ranking by alternative trace and the second is ranking alternatives by perimeter similarity, and compared these methods with several well-known MADM methods, including the TAOV, on a mining problem. Their experience showed that the TAOV had acceptable homogeneity with the previous techniques and their proposed methods. Amoozad Mahdiraji et al. (2021) used the TAOV along with the BWM (Rezaei, 2015) to sort the customer clusters in the banking industry.

Ali and Garg (2023) extended and applied the TAOV method under a spherical fuzzy environment with incomplete weights and used the proposed method to assess third-party reverse logistics providers (Aydin and Oruç, 2024). The multi-attribute utility theory was used to derive the weight vector of the attributes, and then the TAOV method was applied to rank the renewable energy resources of Turkey.

Considering the reviewed studies, first, it is evident that the TAOV method is used in different ranking and selection studies. Additionally, various methods, such as BWM or MAUT, are employed to determine the weight vector of the attributes, which is a crucial requirement of the TAOV method. On the other hand, it appears that the TAOV method holds promise for being extended to uncertain conditions where decision-making information is not precisely determined. Finally, the main advantages of the TAOV method are its relative simplicity, which guarantees the independence of attributes, and the absence of limitations on the scale of attributes (Urošević et al., 2021; Youssef & Saleem, 2023).

65.3 Methodology

Suppose there is a multicriteria decision-making problem involving the evaluation of m alternative options, that is, $A_1, A_2, \ldots, A_m$, where the performance of them is evaluated in terms of n criteria, that is, $C_1, C_2, \ldots, C_n$. Also, the criteria weight vector is determined as $W = (w_1, w_2, \ldots, w_n)$ determined by one of the objective or subjective methods. In short, the problem can be represented in the form of a decision matrix as represented in Eq. (65.1).

$$X=\begin{bmatrix} x_{11} & x_{12} & \dots & x_{1n} \\ x_{21} & x_{22} & \dots & x_{2n} \\ \vdots & \vdots & \vdots & \vdots \\ x_{m1} & x_{m2} & \dots & x_{mn} \end{bmatrix} \tag{65.1}$$

where x_{ij} represents the performance score of the ith alternative, A_i, regarding the jth criterion, C_j. The TAOV algorithm proceeds based on the following steps.

Step 1. Decision-matrix normalization. Since the criteria are measured using different scales, the first step is to normalize the criteria to be comparable. For benefit criteria, where a higher value is better, the normalized value is calculated as:

$$n_{ij} = \frac{x_{ij}}{\max\limits_i x_{ij}}, \quad j \in B \tag{65.2}$$

where B represents the subset of benefit criteria. For cost-type criteria, where the smaller value is better, normalization is conducted as:

$$n_{ij} = \frac{\min\limits_i xij}{x_{ij}}, \quad j \in C \tag{65.3}$$

where C represents the subset of cost criteria. Once the normalization step is done, the normalized decision matrix N is obtained:

$$N=\begin{bmatrix} n_{11} & n_{12} & \dots & n_{1n} \\ n_{21} & n_{22} & \dots & n_{2n} \\ \vdots & \vdots & \vdots & \vdots \\ n_{m1} & n_{m2} & \dots & n_{mn} \end{bmatrix} \tag{65.4}$$

Step 2. Forming the weighted normalized decision-matrix. At the next step, the weighted normalized decision matrix, that is, WN, is constructed by multiplying each normalized element n_{ij} by its corresponding criterion weight w_j:

$$WN = \begin{bmatrix} \overline{n}_{11} & \overline{n}_{12} & \cdots & \overline{n}_{1n} \\ \overline{n}_{21} & \overline{n}_{22} & \cdots & \overline{n}_{2n} \\ \vdots & \vdots & \vdots & \vdots \\ \overline{n}_{m1} & \overline{n}_{m2} & \cdots & \overline{n}_{mn} \end{bmatrix} \tag{65.5}$$

Step 3. Independentizing decision-matrix criteria. A critical consideration of additive value measurement-based methods is to ensure the independence of decision-making criteria. At the third step of the TAOV method, the vectors of the weighted normalized matrix, WN, are independentized. In other words, for any two columns $\overline{n}_k = (\overline{n}_{1k}, \overline{n}_{2k}, \dots, \overline{n}_{mk})$ and $\overline{n}_l = (\overline{n}_{1l}, \overline{n}_{2l}, \dots, \overline{n}_{ml})$ for the WN matrix, it is necessary to ensure that the elements are uncorrelated. Since the TAOV method operates on orthogonal vectors, the next step transforms the current criterion vectors $C_1, C_2, \dots, C_n$, into a set of orthogonal vectors $Y_1, Y_2, \dots, Y_n$. To achieve this aim, the PCA is applied to the WN matrix. PCA identifies linear combinations of correlated criterion vectors, known as principal components (PC), which are mutually independent. Each principal component y_j is expressed as a linear combination of the weighted normalized vectors:

$$Y = WN \times A^T$$

where A contains the coefficients determined by PCA for transforming correlated criteria into independent components (Sanguansat, 2012). PCA can be performed using standard software packages such as SPSS. After applying PCA, the score of each alternative A_i on the jth principal component, denoted by y_{ij} is calculated as:

$$y_{ij} = a_{j1}\overline{n}_{i1} + a_{j2}\overline{n}_{i2} + \dots + a_{jn}\overline{n}_{in}$$

This transformation produces an orthogonal set of performance measures for each alternative, eliminating redundancy caused by correlated criteria. The matrix of transformed scores can be written as:

$$Y = \begin{bmatrix} y_{11} & y_{12} & \cdots & y_{1n} \\ y_{21} & y_{22} & \cdots & y_{2n} \\ \vdots & \vdots & \vdots & \vdots \\ y_{m1} & y_{m2} & \cdots & y_{mn} \end{bmatrix} \tag{65.6}$$

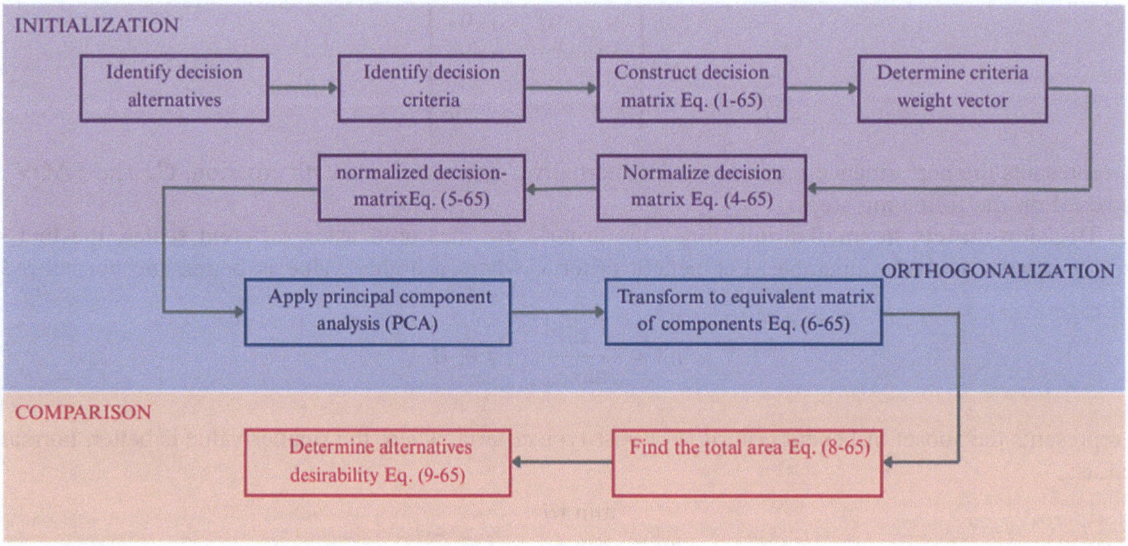

FIGURE 65.1 Total area based on orthogonal vectors algorithm.

This matrix serves as the basis for the subsequent steps in the TAOV method, where the PC are used to assess and rank the alternatives.

Step 4. Calculation of distances between components. Since the principal component matrix Y consists of mutually orthogonal columns, the difference between alternatives across criteria can be quantified using Euclidean distances. For an alternative A_i, the Euclidean distance between any two orthogonal components y_k and y_l can be calculated using the Pythagorean theorem as:

$$d^i_{k,l} = \sqrt{y_{ik}^2 + y_{il}^2} \tag{65.7}$$

Step 5. Computation of the total area for each alternative. The total area for each alternative is then obtained by summing the Euclidean distances between all consecutive components:

$$TA_i = \sum_{j=1}^{n-1} d^i_{j,j+1} \tag{65.8}$$

This measure provides an aggregated representation of the alternative's performance across all criteria. Finally, alternatives can be ranked based on their total area values. To express the results in a normalized desirability scale, the normalized total area (NTA) is defined as:

$$NTA_i = \frac{TA_i}{\sum_{k=1}^{m} TA_k} \tag{65.9}$$

where NTA_i represents the NTA for the alternative A_i. The alternatives are ranked in descending order of NTA values. The TAOV methodology is summarized in Fig. 65.1

65.4 Numerical example 1

Contracts play a vital role in projects, and therefore, maintenance contractor selection is a crucial step in the completion of any project (Fawzy et al., 2024). Different methods are proposed for contractor selection. This is a multicriteria problem, since it is not limited to the bid price only (Zavadskas & Vilutiene, 2006). A large body of research and studies has been devoted to proposing multicriteria methods for the maintenance contractor selection problem (Dissanayake et al., 2025; Fawzy et al., 2024; Zubair et al., 2024).

The current example pertains to the selection of a maintenance contractor by a steel manufacturing company. This company is one of the largest and longest-standing active steel companies in the Middle East. The company considered five alternative contractors for evaluation and then planned to select the most favorable one.

To assess the contractor's capability, the procurement unit of the company defined four different criteria as follows: (i) service cost (1000$) (Enshassi et al., 2013; Zavadskas & Vilutiene, 2006), (ii) field experience (years) (Naji et al., 2022; Zubair & Zhang, 2022), (iii) emergency response time (hours) (de Araújo et al., 2017; Araujo et al., 2018), and (iv) qualifications and licenses (Tan et al., 2014; Tayeh et al., 2017). The qualifications and licenses are evaluated by a team of experts from the procurement department, who inquire about the available permits and then appraise them using the scale represented in Table 65.1.

The decision matrix for the problem, which evaluates candidate contractors based on the mentioned criteria, is presented in Table 65.2. The criteria weights are obtained based on the decision-maker's opinion as $w = (w_1, w_2, w_3, w_4) = (0.3, 0.3, 0.2, 0.2)$.

First, the normalized decision matrix is obtained by applying Eqs. (65.2) and (65.3) to the data presented in Table 65.2. The first criterion (service cost) is of the cost type, where a smaller value indicates better performance. Therefore, Eq. (65.3) is applied as follows:

$$n_{ij} = \frac{\min_i xij}{x_{ij}} = \frac{Min\{180,\ 160,\ 200,\ 150,\ 170\}}{180} = \frac{150}{180} = 0.833$$

Similarly, for benefit-type criteria, such as "Field experience," normalization is performed using Eq. (65.2): {{{Table 65.3}}}

$$n_{ij} = \frac{x_{ij}}{\max_i x_{ij}} = \frac{12}{Min\{12,\ 9,\ 7,\ 10,\ 8\}} = \frac{12}{12} = 1.000$$

TABLE 65.1 Competency of qualifications and licenses.

Competency	Value
Very poor (unacceptable)	1
Poor	2
Medium	3
Good	4
Very good	5

TABLE 65.2 Maintenance contractor selection matrix for the steel company.

Contractor	Service cost	Field experience	Emergency response time	Qualifications and licenses
A	180	12	8.5	4
B	160	9	7	3
C	200	7	11	3
D	150	10	4	5
E	170	8	10	4

TABLE 65.3 Normalized decision matrix.

Contractor	Service cost	Field experience	Emergency response time	Qualifications and licenses
A	0.833	1.000	0.471	0.800
B	0.938	0.750	0.571	0.600
C	0.750	0.583	0.364	0.600
D	1.000	0.833	1.000	1.000
E	0.882	0.667	0.400	0.800

TABLE 65.4 Weighed normalized decision matrix.

Contractor	Service cost	Field experience	Emergency response time	Qualifications and licenses
A	0.250	0.300	0.094	0.160
B	0.281	0.225	0.114	0.120
C	0.225	0.175	0.073	0.120
D	0.300	0.250	0.200	0.200
E	0.265	0.200	0.080	0.160

Then, the weighted normalized decision matrix is obtained by multiplying each normalized value $\overline{n}_{ij}$ by its corresponding criterion weight w_j according to Eq. (65.5). For example, for the first row and the "Service cost" column:

$$WN_{ij} = \overline{n}_{11} \times w_j = 0.833 \times 0.3 = 0.250$$

The resulting weighted normalized matrix is illustrated in Table 65.4

To orthogonalize the criteria vector, the PC are extracted by using the MINITAB software based on the correlation matrix of the weighted normalized matrix. Therefore, the principal component vectors, that is, the eigenvalues of the correlation matrix of the standardized weighted normalized matrix are extracted as follows:

Variable	PC1	PC2	PC3	PC4
Service cost	0.525	0.384	-0.497	0.574
Field experience	0.369	-0.866	-0.333	-0.047
Emergency response time	0.557	0.304	-0.066	-0.770
Qualifications and licenses	0.527	-0.097	0.799	0.275

For instance, applying the first PCs coefficients on the weighted normalized matrix elements of the A contractor, the following value is obtained:

$$0.525 \times (-0.493) + 0.369 \times (1.456) + 0.557 \times (-0.351) + 0.527 \times (0.239) = 0.208$$

where, the numbers in parentheses are obtained by standardizing the weighted normalized matrix by subtracting the mean of each criterion from the considered observation and then dividing it by the criterion's standard deviation. The resulting components are illustrated in Table 65.5.

TABLE 65.5 Principal component matrix.

Contractor	PC1	PC2	PC3	PC4
A	0.208	-1.581	-0.025	-0.015
B	-0.208	0.423	-1.026	0.052
C	-2.068	0.328	0.344	-0.401
D	2.511	0.496	0.277	-0.222
E	-0.443	0.334	0.431	0.586

TABLE 65.6 The final ranking of alternatives.

Contractor	d_{12}	d_{23}	d_{34}	Total area	Normalized total area	Rank
A	1.594	1.581	0.029	3.204	0.225	2
B	0.471	1.110	1.028	2.609	0.183	4
C	2.094	0.476	0.529	3.099	0.218	3
D	2.560	0.568	0.354	3.482	0.245	1
E	0.555	0.545	0.727	1.828	0.129	5

For each alternative, the Pythagorean distance between components is computed using Eq. (65.7) and the corresponding total area is calculated by Eq. (65.8). Considering the alternative A,

$$d_{12} = \sqrt{0.208^2 + (-1.581)^2} = 1.594$$

$$d_{23} = \sqrt{(-1.581)^2 + (-0.025)^2} = 1.581$$

$$d_{34} = \sqrt{(-0.025)^2 + (-0.015)^2} = 0.029$$

Finally, the total area alternative A is calculated as:

$$1.594 + 1.581 + 0.029 = 3.204$$

The alternatives are ranked based on NTA using Eq. (65.9). The results are summarized in Table 65.6. Finally, the NTA values are computed using Eq. (65.9):

$$NTA_i = \frac{TA_i}{\sum_{k=1}^{m} TA_k} = \frac{3.204}{14.22134} = 0.225$$

65.5 Numerical example 2

Material selection is a prominent and well-established area of multicriteria decision-making in the construction industry. Bajwa et al. (2025) reviewed about 60 papers between 2010 and 2023 in this field. This decision has a great impact on product development and design (Kumar & Jagadish, 2014). Inappropriate selection of materials negatively affects producer and customer expectations (Hassan et al., 2024). There are numerous projects and products that have failed due to inappropriate material selection. Mukhopadhyay (2018) introduced material selection as one of the main causes of failure in construction projects.

The importance of material selection in construction projects directly affects the technical, energy productivity, life cycle costs, and environmental sustainability of constructs (Ashby, 2011). As mentioned above, the nature of this decision is inherently based on multiple criteria since engineers and decision-makers are forced to balance different and sometimes conflicting factors, like mechanical properties, cost, availability, ease of use, adaptation to climate conditions, environmental effects, safety requirements, etc. (Moussavi Nadoushani & Akbarnezhad, 2015). This complexity increases when projects are defined in turbulent environments, have time constraints, or have high sustainability requirements.

Carelessness or simplicity in the selection of materials can have significant consequences, from increased maintenance and repair costs to reduced useful life of the structure, structural damage, and even risks to user safety (Shi et al., 2013). Additionally, unsuitable materials may not comply with building codes or environmental standards, which can lead to project halts, legal fines, or a reduction in the economic value of the structure. As a result, the selection of materials as a strategic decision in project management should be made using scientific approaches and MCDM tools to achieve maximum compatibility with the project's functional, economic, and environmental objectives while reducing risks (San Cristóbal, 2011).

The problem examined in this section concerns the construction of a two-story building in a hot and dry climate in Iran. Design engineers are seeking to select the best type of material for the exterior wall, considering functional, economic, environmental, and implementation considerations. The engineering team, consisting of three expert engineers, identified seven types of materials for selection:

A1: Cement-coated compressed brick;
A2: Gypsum-cement-coated clay block;
A3: Autoclaved aerated concrete block;
A4: 3D sandwich panels;
A5: Lightweight concrete prefabricated wall;
A6: Drywall with an internal thermal insulation system;
A7: Insulated concrete forms (ICF).

Reviewing the literature and according to previous experience, the team determined eight criteria to evaluate the materials as follows:

C1: Initial cost (Ashby, 2011);
C2: Heat transfer coefficient (U-value) (Road, Housing & Urban Development Research Center, 2025);
C3: Construction speed (design engineers);
C4: Seismic performance (Moussavi Nadoushani & Akbarnezhad, 2015);
C5: Durability (Ashby, 2011);
C6: Environmental impact;
C7: Availability (design engineers);
C8: Sound insulation.

The initial cost of materials (C1) is inquired by the procurement unit of the project. C2, C5, C6, and C8 criteria are also experimentally evaluated by the technical unit of the project using different tests. Other criteria, including C3, C4, and C9, are evaluated individually by design engineers using a 9-point scale as follows:

1 dislike extremely
2 dislike very much
3 dislike moderately
4 dislike slightly
5 neither like nor dislike
6 like slightly
7 like moderately
8 like very much
9 like extremely

The criteria weights are determined in a focus group between engineers as W = (0.124, 0.131, 0.125, 0.125, 0.124, 0.124, 0.124, 0.124). (Table 65.7)

These matrices are aggregated by taking the geometric mean of individual matrices, as shown in Table 65.8.

Applying the TAOV method to the above decision matrix, the results are demonstrated in Table 65.9. According to the results, the ICF material is selected.

TABLE 65.7 Individual decision matrices of engineers.

First engineer	C1	C2	C3	C4	C5	C6	C7	C8
A1	611	1.9	3	3	7	280	9	50
A2	556	1.4	4	4	6	260	8	48
A3	778	0.35	6	6	6	180	6	42
A4	944	0.25	9	7	7	210	5	40
A5	833	0.6	8	7	8	230	6	47
A6	722	0.3	8	5	5	190	8	46
A7	1000	0.28	7	8	9	240	4	52
Second engineer	C1	C2	C3	C4	C5	C6	C7	C8
A1	611	1.9	3	4	7	280	9	50
A2	556	1.4	5	4	6	260	8	48
A3	778	0.35	6	5	6	180	7	42
A4	944	0.25	8	7	7	210	6	40
A5	833	0.6	8	6	8	230	6	47
A6	722	0.3	7	5	5	190	8	46
A7	1000	0.28	7	9	9	240	5	52
Third engineer	C1	C2	C3	C4	C5	C6	C7	C8
A1	611	1.9	2	3	7	280	8	50
A2	556	1.4	4	5	6	260	8	48
A3	778	0.35	5	6	6	180	6	42
A4	944	0.25	9	8	7	210	5	40
A5	833	0.6	8	6	8	230	6	47
A6	722	0.3	8	4	5	190	9	46
A7	1000	0.28	6	8	9	240	4	52

TABLE 65.8 Aggregated decision matrix.

	C1	C2	C3	C4	C5	C6	C7	C8
A1	611	1.90	2.62	3.30	7.00	280	8.65	50
A2	556	1.40	4.31	4.31	6.00	260	8.00	48
A3	778	0.35	5.65	5.65	6.00	180	6.32	42
A4	944	0.25	8.65	7.32	7.00	210	5.31	40
A5	833	0.60	8.00	6.32	8.00	230	6.00	47
A6	722	0.30	7.65	4.64	5.00	190	8.32	46
A7	1000	0.28	6.65	8.32	9.00	240	4.31	52

TABLE 65.9 The total area based on orthogonal vectors method, results in the material selection problem.

	Total area	Normalized total area	Rank
A1	5.881	0.158	2
A2	4.180	0.112	6
A3	5.286	0.142	5
A4	5.298	0.142	4
A5	3.750	0.101	7
A6	5.814	0.156	3
A7	7.000	0.188	1

65.6 Conclusion

Decision-making is an ever-growing field both in theoretical and practical dimensions. MADM methods are proposed to deal with the complex and multi-attribute nature of real-world decision-making problems. As mentioned in the introduction of the current chapter, a great number of methods have been developed for solving the MADM problems. One of the first and most widely used categories of multicriteria decision-making methods is scoring methods based on additive functions, assuming independence of the indicators.

In the current chapter, the TAOV method is introduced as a novel method of handling attributes' interrelationship. After formalizing a multi-attribute decision problem, the TAOV method proceeds by independentizing the attributes using the PC method. Since PCA ensures the criteria independence, the total area of each alternative is then computed by summing the distances between its orthogonal components, and these areas are used to compare and rank the results. Two numerical examples are also solved using the TAOV method. To check the ability of the technique in identifying the ideal alternative, a hypothetical ideal alternative is added to the first example with a vector of (140, 13, 3, 5). Running the TAOV method with the considered attributes' weights, the hypothetical vector is determined as the best alternative.

Razavi Hajiagha et al. (2018) examined the TAOV method's performance regarding the features of a prominent decision-making technique introduced by Saaty and Ergu (2015). Previous studies, as mentioned in the literature review section, illustrated a good consistency of the TAOV method with other MADM techniques. Therefore, the method illustrated a good capability in recognizing the best alternative, and it also has satisfactory consistency with previous well-known methods. As a clue for future studies, extending the TAOV method under different uncertainty environments can be considered. While the method has been extended under q-ROF sets and a spherical fuzzy environment, other types of uncertainty can be considered for developing the method. Also, its application can be extended using different attribute weighting methods. Comparison of the TAOV application in large-scale problems with previous well-known methods can also be considered for future studies.

References

Ali, J., & Garg, H. (2023). On spherical fuzzy distance measure and TAOV method for decision-making problems with incomplete weight information. *Engineering Applications of Artificial Intelligence, 119*, 105726.

Alinezhad, A., & Khalili, J. (2019). *New methods and applications in multiple attribute decision making (MADM)*. Cham: Springer.

Amoozad Mahdiraji, H., Tavana, M., Mahdiani, P., & Abbasi Kamardi, A. (2021). A multi-attribute data mining model for rule extraction and service operations benchmarking. *Benchmarking: An International Journal, 29*(2), 456–495.

Araujo, M., Alencar, L., & Mota, C. (2018). Decision criteria for contractor selection in construction industry: A literature review. In *2018 IEEE International Conference on Industrial Engineering and Engineering Management (IEEM)*. Bangkok, Thailand: IEEE, 637–640.

de Araújo, M., Alencar, L., & de Miranda Mota, C. (2017). Project procurement management: A structured literature review. *International Journal of Project Management, 35*(3), 353–377.

Aruldoss, M., Lakshmi, T., & Venkatesan, V. (2013). A survey on multi criteria decision making methods. *American Journal of Information Systems, 1*(1), 31–43.

Ashby, M. (2011). *Materials selection in mechanical design*. Burlington, MA: Elsevier.

Aydin, B., & Oruç, O. (2024). Determining the most useful renewable energy alternative for Turkey by combining MAUT and TAOV methods. *International Journal of Energy Studies, 9*(2), 291–308.

Bajwa, A., Siriwardana, C., Shahzad, W., & Naeem, M. (2025). Material selection in the construction industry: A systematic literature. *Environment Systems and Decisions, 45*, 1–22.

Brans, J. (1982). L'ingénierie de la décision: Élaboration d'instruments d'aide à la décision. In *La méthode PROMETHEE*. Quebec: Presses de l'Université Laval.

Carlsson, C., & Fullér, R. (1996). Fuzzy multiple criteria decision making: Recent developments. *Fuzzy Sets and Systems, 78*(2), 139–153.

Chai, J., Liu, J., & Ngai, E. (2013). Application of decision-making techniques in supplier selection: A systematic review of literature. *Expert Systems with Applications, 40*(10), 3872–3885.

Dantas Silva, F., Lima, M., Corujo, D., Venâncio Neto, A., & Esposito, F. (2024). A comprehensive step-wise survey of multiple attribute decision-making mobility approaches. *IEEE Access, 12*, 108616–108656.

Deng, J. (1982). Control problems of grey systems. *Systems & control letters, 1*(5), 288–294.

Dissanayake, N., Xia, B., Skitmore, M., Trigunarsyh, B., & Menadue, V. (2025). Developing a generic fuzzy multi-attribute analysis model for EPC contractor selection. *Built Environment Project and Asset Management*. https://doi.org/10.1108/BEPAM-11-2024-0257.

Ehrgott, M. (2005). *Multicriteria optimization*. Berlin, Heidelberg: Springer.

Enshassi, A., Mohamed, S., & Modough, Z. (2013). Contractors' selection criteria: Opinions of palestinian construction professionals. *International Journal of Construction Management, 13*(1), 19–37.

Fawzy, M., Elsharkawy, A., Khalifa, Y., & Hassan, A. (2024). Contractor selection by using multi-criteria decision-making for Egyptian road maintenance. *International Journal of System Assurance Engineering and Management, 15*, 2351–2365.

Garoosi Mokhtarzadeh, N., Amoozad Mahdiraji, H., Beheshti, M., & Zavadskas, E. (2018). A novel hybrid approach for technology selection in the information technology industry. *Technologies, 6*(1), 34.

Gavade, R. (2014). Multi-criteria decision making: An overview of. *International Journal of Computer Science and Information Technology, 5*(4), 5643–5646.

Hashemkhani Zolfani, S., Hasheminasab, H., Ebadi Torkayesh, A., Zavadskas, E., & Derakhti, A. (2022). A literature review of MADM applications for site selection problems—One decade review from 2011 to 2020. *International Journal of Information Technology & Decision Making, 21*(1), 7–57.

Hassan, R., Arfeen, Z., Azam, M., Akhtar, Z., Siddique, A., & Rashid, M. (2024). Determination of the best materials for development and designing product using a multi-criteria decision-making. *Railway Sciences, 3*(5), 541–557.

Honarvar, R., Zolghadrasli, A., & Monemi, M. (2022). Context-oriented performance evaluation of network selection algorithms in 5G heterogeneous networks. *Journal of Network and Computer Applications, 202*, 103358.

Hwang, C., & Yoon, K. (1981). *Multiple attribute decision making: Methods and applications*. New York: Springer-Verlag.

Karakoç, Ö., Memiş, S., & Sennaroglu, B. (2024). A review of sustainable supplier selection with decision-making methods from 2018 to 2022. *Sustainability, 16*(1), 125. https://doi.org/10.3390/su16010125.

Keeney, R. (1972). Utility functions for multiattributed consequences. *Management science, 18*(5), 276–287.

Krylovas, A., Zavadskas, E., & Kosareva, N. (2016). Multiple criteria decision-making KEMIRA-M method for solution of location alternatives. *Economic Research, 29*(1), 50.

Kumar, R., & Jagadish, A. (2014). Selection of material for optimal design using multi-criteria decision making. *Procedia Materials Science, 6*, 590–596.

Moussavi Nadoushani, Z., & Akbarnezhad, A. (2015). Effects of structural system on the life cycle carbon footprint of buildings. *Energy and Buildings, 102*, 337–346.

Mukhopadhyay, G. (2018). Construction failures due to improper materials, manufacturing, and design. In A. Makhlouf, & M. Aliiofkhazraei (Eds.). *Handbook of materials failure analysis with case studies from the construction industries* (pp. 59–81). Elsevier.

Naji, K., Gunduz, M., & Falamarzi, M. (2022). Assessment of construction project contractor selection success factors considering their interconnections. *KSCE Journal of Civil Engineering, 26*, 3677–3690.

Opricovic, S. (1998). Multicriteria optimization of civil engineering systems. *Faculty of Civil Engineering*, 5–21 2.1.

Pelissari, R., Khan, S., & Ben-Amor, S. (2022). Application of multi-criteria decision-making methods in sustainable manufacturing management: A systematic literature review and analysis of the prospects. *International Journal of Information Technology & Decision Making, 21*(2), 493–515.

Peng, X., Huang, H., & Luo, Z. (2021). q-Rung orthopair fuzzy decision-making framework for integrating mobile edge caching scheme preferences. *International Journal of Intelligent Systems, 31*, 2229–2266.

Razavi Hajiagha, S., Amoozad Mahdiraji, H., & Hashemi, S. (2018). Total area based on orthogonal vectors (TAOV) as a novel method of multi-criteria decision aid. *Technological and Economic Development of Economy, 24*(4), 1679–1694.

Rezaei, J. (2015). Best-worst multi-criteria decision-making method. *Omega, 53*, 49–57.

Road, Housing & Urban Development Research Center. (2025). Iran's National Building Regulations: Topic Nineteen: Energy Saving. Tehran, Iran: Islamic Republic of Iran Ministry of Roads & Urban Development.

Roy, B. (1968). Classement et choix en présence de points de vue multiples (la méthode ELECTRE). *La Revue d'Informatique et de Recherche Opérationelle, 8*, 57–75.

Saaty, T. (1980). *The analytic hierarchy process*. McGraw-Hill.

Saaty, T., & Ergu, D. (2015). When is a decision-making method trustworthy? Criteria for evaluating multi-criteria decision-making methods. *International Journal of Information Technology & Decision Making, 14*(6), 1171–1187.

Safarzadeh, S., & Jafari, H. (2025). On the application of multi-criteria decision-making methods in environmental pollution management: A comprehensive systematic review. *Environment, Development and Sustainability*. https://doi.org/10.1007/s10668-025-06041-6.

San Cristóbal, J. (2011). Multi-criteria decision-making in the selection of a renewable energy project in spain: The Vikor method. *Renewable Energy, 36*(2), 498–502.

Sanguansat, P. (2012). *Principal component analysis multidisciplinary applications*. IntechOpen.

Shi, Q., Zuo, J., Huang, R., Huang, J., & Pullen, S. (2013). Identifying the critical factors for green construction – an empirical study in China. *Habitat International, 40*, 1–8.

Tan, Y., Shen, L., Langston, C., & Yam, M. (2014). Critical success factors for building maintenance business: A Hong Kong case study. *Facilities, 32*(5-6), 208–225.

Tayeh, B., Al-Hallaq, K., Yusuf, M., & Sabha, F. (2017). Effects of construction phase errors on maintenance of school buildings in Gaza strip. *International Journal of Management, Information Technology and Engineering, 5*(1), 21–34.

Triantaphyllou, E. (2000). *Multi-criteria decision making methods a comparative study*. Boston: Springer.

Urošević, K., Gligorić, Z., Miljanović, I., Belji, C., & Gligori, M. (2021). Novel methods in multiple criteria decision-making. *Process (MCRAT and RAPS)—Application in the Mining Industry. Mathematics, 9*(16), 1980.

Wang, Y., Yuan, J., Zhou, Y., & Zhang, P. (2008). Vertical handover decision in an enhanced media independent handover framework. In *IEEE Wireless Communications and Networking Conference*. Las Vegas: IEEE, 2693–2698.

Yazdani, M., Zarate, P., Zavadskas, E., & Turskis, Z. (2019). A combined compromise solution (CoCoSo) method for multi-criteria decision-making problems. *Management Decision, 57*(9), 2501–2519.

Youssef, A., & Saleem, K. (2023). A hybrid MCDM approach for evaluating web-based e-learning platforms. *IEEE Access, 11*, 72436–72447.

Zavadskas, E., Turskis, Z., Antucheviciene, J., & Zakarevicius, A. (2012). Optimization of weighted aggregated sum product assessment. *Elektronika ir Elektrotechnika, 6*, 3–6.

Zavadskas, E., & Vilutiene, T. (2006). A multiple criteria evaluation of multi-family apartment block's maintenance contractors: I—Model for maintenance contractor evaluation and the determination of its selection criteria. *Building and Environment, 41*(5), 621–632.

Zayat, W., Kilic, H., Yalcin, A., Zaim, S., & Delen, D. (2023). Application of MADM methods in Industry 4.0: A literature review. *Computers & Industrial Engineering, 177*, 109075.

Zionts, S., & Wallenius, J. (1983). A method for identifying redundant constraints and extraneous variables in linear programming. redundancy in mathematical programming. In *Lecture notes in economics and mathematical systems*. Berlin, Heidelberg: Springer, 28–35.

Zolghadr-Asli, B., Bozorg-Haddad, O., Enayati, M., & Chu, X. (2021). A review of 20-year applications of multi-attribute decision-making in environmental and water resources planning and management. *Environment, Development and Sustainability, 23*, 14379–14404.

Zubair, M., Farid, O., Hassan, M., Aziz, T., & Ud-Din, S. (2024). Framework for strategic selection of maintenance contractors. *Sustainability, 16*(6), 2488.

Zubair, M., & Zhang, X. (2022). Investigation and improvements of the existing best-Value selection criteria for elevator maintenance contractors. *Journal of Management Engineering, 38*(1) 04021083.

Chapter 66

CoCoSo: Combined compromise solution for multi-attribute decision-making

Morteza Yazdani[1], Amir Mehdiabadi[2], and Homa Molavi[3]
[1]*European University of Madrid, Villaviciosa de odon Campus, Madrid, Spain,* [2]*Department of Industrial Management, Islamic Azad University, Semnan, Iran,* [3]*School of Business, Operations and Strategy, University of Greenwich, London, United Kingdom*

66.1 Introduction multiple criteria decision-making

The growth of multiple criteria decision-making (MCDM) techniques development over the last 20 years has accelerated, and researchers have been competing to deliver precise and qualified algorithms for different applications. Feedback from the academic society also indicates the necessity of new techniques and the lack of diverse algorithms in the MCDM domain. The advantage of proposing a novel algorithm that supports decision-makers in complex conditions and facilitates a smooth decision-making process is clear to most researchers in this sector. Confidential results and the degree of accuracy in MCDM tools are an inevitable matter, and the researcher's effort is to reach secure solutions that are affordable for senior or executive managers. It might be mentioned that wrong or incorrect solutions can demonstrate negative consequences in any project, and this directly influences economic or beneficial goals. The development of complex proportional ratio analysis assessment (COPRAS), designed by Zolfani et al. (2011), marked the beginning of a long journey. The main features of COPRAS are its stability with respect to data and the variation method. Consequently, several other methods, such as evaluation based on distance from average solution (EDAS), combinative distance-based assessment, best–worst method (BWM), MABAC, measurement alternatives and ranking according to compromise solution, and combined compromise solution (CoCoSo) were developed by other groups of experts. It is worth noting that each method's application will be demonstrated within a distinct concept, dimension, and parameters, which will evidently produce a different result from other studies.

Historically, MCDM methods were designed to aid policy and decision-makers in specific circumstances where there is complexity and conflict of objectives. Each method contains a unique algorithm that needs a matrix of alternatives and criteria and a mixture of several mathematical disciplines. By this matrix and logical mathematical relations, the algorithm will be able to produce a ranking of the alternatives or the criteria weights. The MCDM method begins with a primal matrix composed of alternatives, decision criteria, and importance (weights) of the criteria. At the end, alternative scores will be computed, and we will have their rankings. As mentioned in different resources, various methods reflect different algorithms that make them unique in action. In 2019, a group of researchers in France and Lithuania presented a novel method that handles a combination of tools, such as different weighting methods and aggregation. This method is named the combined compromise solution, the acronym of CoCoSo (Yazdani et al., 2019). The idea behind CoCoSo is to deliver an optimal solution when decision-makers are unable to find a compromised agreement between all presented parties (Yazdani et al., 2024). Decision-makers who use CoCoSo can rely on uncertain decision-making problems. Moreover, the ranking results provided by CoCoSo may not change considerably with the changing of the weight of decision attributes. In other words, the algorithm is less sensitive to the criteria weight replacement and consequently, alternative ranking alters slightly (Ecer et al., 2025). CoCoSo reflects an innovative MCDM strategy that produces the alternative ranking score precisely using three different strategies that compose compromise aggregation functions. The CoCoSo technique combines simple additive weighting (SAW) with exponentially weighted product models to identify the optimal alternative, and this benefit of CoCoSo has priority over methods such as technique for order of preference by similarity to the ideal solution (TOPSIS) and VlseKriterijumska Optimizacija I Kompromisno Resenje (Ferdous et al., 2025).

Encyclopedia of Multi-Attribute Decision-Making (MADM). DOI: https://doi.org/10.1016/B978-0-443-33275-3.00054-3

Sriariyanun et al. (2025) stated that CoCoSo brings a platform for decision-makers to handle the difficulties of multiobjective optimization, and its transparent and structured algorithm empowers stakeholders to make well-informed decisions based on logical interplay between various decision objectives. Haseli et al. (2024) proposed a novel fuzzy extension of CoCoSo, where they developed a program for a sustainable urban transport system. The research explains that CoCoSo is a decision-making tool that combines multiplicative exponential weighting, SAW, and weighted aggregated sum product assessment (WASPAS) tools.

This chapter introduces the CoCoSo method with several examples in a simple way as a reference, and practitioners and academic centers will be able to utilize it widely. The following section provides a brief literature review of the method and its application. Then, several examples and analyses to implement CoCoSo will be developed. At the end conclusion and some practical implications are provided.

66.2 Combined compromise solution method application

66.2.1 Method background

Since its introduction by Yazdani et al in 2018, the CoCoSo method has garnered over 975 citations, reflecting its growing impact and recognition in the field. As decision-making environments often involve uncertainty, vagueness, or imprecise data, following this, other researchers have extended the CoCoSo model into fuzzy, interval, and rough set frameworks to handle such uncertainty better.

In their 2019 article, Yazdani et al. extend the traditional CoCoSo method by integrating grey numbers, resulting in a new method called CoCoSo-G. This extension is aimed at improving supplier selection in construction management by addressing the inherent uncertainty and imprecision in supplier performance evaluations. Grey numbers, typically represented as grey intervals, allow experts to express uncertain or imprecise evaluations. For instance, if an expert is unsure about a supplier's exact performance on a given criterion, they can provide a grey interval like [3, 5], indicating that the supplier's performance is within that range. To calculate the weights of the evaluation criteria, the authors employ two methods: decision-making trial and evaluation laboratory (DEMATEL) and BWM. DEMATEL is used to identify the best and worst criteria by understanding the relationships between different criteria and their influence on supplier selection. Following this, BWM is applied to rank the criteria based on expert evaluations, converting qualitative judgments into quantitative weights using linear programming. This combined approach ensures that the weights reflect both the relationships between criteria and their relative importance. Once the criteria weights are established, CoCoSo-G is used to rank suppliers based on their grey evaluations, calculating an overall score by combining the weighted performance data. This approach helps select the supplier whose performance is closest to the ideal solution, considering the uncertainty in expert assessments. The study compares the results of CoCoSo-G with the COPRAS method and finds that CoCoSo-G delivers more reliable outcomes by effectively handling uncertainties and combining weights. Ultimately, CoCoSo-G enhances the original CoCoSo method by applying grey numbers to model uncertainty, providing a more robust decision-making framework for complex supplier selection scenarios (Yazdani et al., 2019). Table 66.1 presents the varipus applications of the CoCoSo method found in the literature.

66.2.2 Classification of combined compromise solution applications

Since its introduction (Yazdani et al., 2018), the CoCoSo method has gained substantial traction in the field of MCDM. Recognized for its integrative approach, CoCoSo merges the strengths of various classical MCDM techniques into a single, cohesive framework. Its relatively simple algorithm and ease of implementation have made it an attractive tool for researchers and practitioners across diverse sectors (Torkayesh, Ecer, et al., 2021). CoCoSo has garnered significant attention within the decision-making community, receiving numerous citations in the research literature. It has been widely applied across various sectors, including supplier selection (Parsa Rad et al., 2024; Razzaq et al., 2024; Yazdani et al., 2019), waste management (Adar et al., 2022; Wang et al., 2010; Yazdani et al., 2025), transport (Bouraima et al., 2023), cement transportation network (Rashidian et al., 2024), logistics (Ulutaş et al., 2020; Zhang & Wei, 2023), healthcare sectors (Torkayesh, Ecer, et al., 2021), circular economy (Cui et al., 2021; Khan & Haleem, 2021), spray painting robot selection (Kumar et al., 2022), 5 G industry evaluation (Peng & Zhang, & Luo, 2020), industry 4.0 (Choudhary & Mishra, 2022), blockchain platform evaluation (Lai et al., 2022), environmental impacts (Banihashemi et al., 2021), energy planning (Nguyen & Chaysiri, 2025), to name a few.

These studies have demonstrated the versatility and adaptability of CoCoSo in addressing complex decision-making scenarios. For example, Rasoanaivo et al. (2024) explored an enhanced variant of CoCoSo—namely, the CoCoFISo method—within the context of a university campus case study. Their research benchmarked CoCoFISo against other

TABLE 66.1 Combined compromise solution (CoCoSo) method survey and summary.

Authors	Methods	Fuzzy sets	Fuzzy numbers	Case study
Erceg et al. (2019)	Full consistency method (FUCOM) and CoCoSo	-	-	Building materials industry
Peng and Smarandache (2020)	Neutrosophic soft CoCoSo	NSS	SVNN	Rare earth industry
Ecer and Pamucar (2020)	F-BWM and uzzy CoCoSo with Bonferroni (CoCoSo'B)	TFNs	TFNs	Home appliance industry
Lahane and Kant (2021)	PF-CoCoSo and PF-AHP	PFS	Pythagorean fuzzy numbers	Manufacturing
Torkayesh, Pamucar, et al. (2021)	CoCoSo	-	-	OECD
Demir et al. (2022)	Fuzzy-FUCOM and fuzzy-CoCoSo	Linguistic assessment fuzzy sets	TFNs	Urban planning
Pamucar and Görçün (2022)	Fuzzy LBWA and fuzzy CoCoSo'B	TFNs	FTN	Maritime industry
Xu et al. (2022)	DEMATEL and CoCoSo	SFSs	Fuzzy Z-numbers	Accommodation servicequality
Ghoushchi et al. (2022)	SWARA and CoCoSo	SPSs	-	Wind turbine failure modes
Karami et al. (2023)	IVF-SWARA and IVF-CoCoSo	IVFNs	IVFNs	Construction projects
Haseli et al. (2023)	BWM and CoCoSo	TFNs	Fuzzy ZE-numbers	Recycling partner selection
Zafaranlouei et al. (2023)	BCM and CoCoSo	TFNs	Fuzzy Z-numbers	Waste management
Ogundoyin and Kamil (2023)	Fuzzy-BWM, fuzzy-LBWA, V-fuzzy-CoCoSo-LD	-	-	Fog computing services
Yang and Li (2024)	CoCoSo	TFNSs	TFNN	Higher education institutions
Rasoanaivo et al. (2024)	CoCoFISo, PROMETHEE, WSM, TOPSIS	-	-	Higher education institutions
Dhruva et al. (2024)	LOPCOW and CoCoSo	IFS and FFS	Fermatean fuzzy number	Healthcare industry
Yazdani et al. (2025)	AHP and CoCoSo	IFSs	Fuzzy extended Z-numbers	Waste management
Xiao and Zhang (2025)	PF-CoCoSo and TOPSIS-CoCoSo	TFNs	TFNNs	Physical education teaching

prominent MCDM methods, such as the preference ranking organization method for enrichment evaluations (PROMETHEE), the weighted sum method, and the TOPSIS. The findings revealed that CoCoSo effectively handles *multidimensional evaluation problems*, while CoCoFISo further addresses some of the methodological limitations inherent in the original CoCoSo model, offering more stable and reliable outcomes (Rasoanaivo et al., 2024).

Wang et al. (2024) utilized the CoCoSo method within a Pythagorean fuzzy environment to assess design attributes (DAs) of mobile medical applications. The study integrated CoCoSo with quality function deployment (QFD), a customer-oriented design methodology that translates customer requirements (CRs) into product or service DAs. Traditional QFD methods often struggle with accurately evaluating the strength of relationships between CRs and DAs, as well as the interdependencies among DAs. To overcome these limitations, Wang et al. proposed an improved QFD framework that incorporates CoCoSo-based ranking under Pythagorean fuzzy logic. This hybrid model provided more *nuanced evaluations and improved decision support under uncertainty* (Wang et al., 2024).

66.3 Combined compromise solution method

The CoCoSo method is able to obtain the ranking of alternatives using the steps below, after obtaining the weights of the criteria:

Step 1. Determine the performance matrix containing the alternatives and the various criteria, including their optimization direction. Formula (66.1) shows this matrix.

$$x_{ij} = \begin{bmatrix} x_{11} & x_{12} & \cdots & x_{1n} \\ x_{21} & x_{22} & \cdots & x_{2n} \\ \cdots & \cdots & \cdots & \cdots \\ x_{m1} & x_{m2} & \cdots & x_{mn} \end{bmatrix}; \ i = 1,\ 2,\ \ldots,\ m;\ j = 1,\ 2,\ \ldots,\ n \tag{66.1}$$

Step 2. Normalize the performance matrix, distinguishing between criteria to be maximized and those to be minimized. Formulas (66.2) and (66.3) give us this new normalization of the matrix.

$$r_{ij} = \frac{x_{ij} - \min_i x_{ij}}{\max_i x_{ij} - \min_i x_{ij}}; \text{ benefit criteria;} \tag{66.2}$$

$$r_{ij} = \frac{\max_i x_{ij} - x_{ij}}{\max_i x_{ij} - \min_i x_{ij}}; \text{ cost criteria} \tag{66.3}$$

Step 3. Carry out a sequential comparability of the weights by calculating the two magnitudes S_i and P_i according to formulas (66.4) and (66.5).

$$S_i = \sum_{j=1}^{n} (w_j r_{ij}) \tag{66.4}$$

$$P_i = \sum_{j=1}^{n} (r_{ij})^{w_j} \tag{66.5}$$

Step 4. Find the three aggregation strategies k_{ia}, k_{ib} and k_{ic} according to formulas (66.6)–(66.8)

$$k_{ia} = \frac{P_i + S_i}{\sum_{i=1}^{m} (P_i + S_i)} \tag{66.6}$$

$$k_{ib} = \frac{S_i}{\min_i S_i} + \frac{P_i}{\min_i P_i} \tag{66.7}$$

$$k_{ic} = \frac{\lambda(S_i) + (1 - \lambda)(P_i)}{(\lambda \max_i S_i + (1 - \lambda)\max_i P_i)}; 0 \le \lambda \le 1 \tag{66.8}$$

Step 5. Extract the ranks of the alternatives according to the value of k_i obtained by formula (66.9).

$$k_i = (k_{ia} k_{ib} k_{ic})^{\frac{1}{3}} + \frac{1}{3}(k_{ia} + k_{ib} + k_{ic}) \tag{66.9}$$

66.4 Implementation and examples

This section presents two examples of the implementation of the CoCoSo method in two subcategories.

66.4.1 Problem of vehicle selection

Suppose that TRT, a transport company, planned to renew its business strategy by buying new and high-tech vehicles. After searching the market and studying different brands, several options were proposed by the manager of the section. They supposed four types of cars, like FIAT, Renault, Peugeot, and VW. To compare these models, the manager employed these variables (criteria): price, technology level, and guarantee. Therefore, a questionnaire was designed, and the manager responded to it regarding the information of each vehicle and contacting relevant concessionaires. It should be mentioned that only the responsible manager participated in the evaluation process and conducted a single decision-making process. The process of computation with CoCoSo starts with an initial decision (evaluation) matrix where the alternatives are rated under the selected criteria. The proposed case includes C1–C4 (number of criteria) while alternatives are named A1–A4. Among our three criteria, price is a cost-type criterion. while the two others are considered benefit criteria. Therefore, C1 is a cost-based attribute, and C2–C4 are placed as benefits. The evaluation matrix obtained by the questionnaire (a scale of 1–10) is seen in Table 66.2 (formula (66.1)). Following the CoCoSo algorithm, this latter matrix should be normalized using formulas (66.2) and (66.3). For the price, we use formula (66.3), and for the benefit, formula (66.2) must be used. In this case, the weight of each criterion is 0.3, 0.25, 0.4, and 0.05, respectively.

In the next step, data normalization is performed based on formulas (66.2) and (66.3). C1 is a cost criterion, so C1 column for alternatives is maximum 8 and minimum 6. C2 to C4 are also benefits (we use formula (66.2)). Table 66.3 indicates the normalized matrix.

In the next step, according to formula (66.4), we obtain (Table 66.4):

In the continuation, we calculate the power weighted normalized matrix and consequently the values of S_i *(formula* (66.4)) *and* P_i *(formula* (66.5)):

S_i (sum of normalized weighted scores) is obtained by this order:

- FIAT: $0.3+0+0+0=0.3$

TABLE 66.2 The initial evaluation matrix.

Alternative	C_1 (cost)	C_2(benefit)	C_3(benefit)	C_4(benefit)
FIAT	6	5	5	4
Renault	7	6	6	7
Peugeot	7	7	6	5
VW	8	8	7	7

TABLE 66.3 Normalization matrix.

Alternative	C_1	C_2	C_3	C_4
FIAT	$(8-6)/(8-6)=1$	$(5-5)/(8-5)=0$	$(5-5)/(7-5)=0$	$(4-4)/(7-4)=0$
Renault	$(8-7)/(8-6)=0.5$	$(6-5)/(8-5)\approx 0.33$	$(6-5)/(7-5)=0.5$	$(7-4)/(7-4)=1$
Peugeot	$(8-7)/(8-6)=0.5$	$(7-5)/(8-5)\approx 0.67$	$(6-5)/(7-5)=0.5$	$(5-4)/(7-4)\approx 0.33$
VW	$(8-8)/(8-6)=0$	$(8-5)/(8-5)=1$	$(7-5)/(7-5)=1$	$(7-4)/(7-4)=1$

TABLE 66.4 Weighted normalized matrix.

Alternative	C_1	C_2	C_3	C_4
FIAT	$0.3 \times 1 = 0.3$	$0.25 \times 0 = 0$	$0.4 \times 0 = 0$	$0.05 \times 0 = 0$
Renault	$0.3 \times 0.5 = 0.15$	$0.25 \times 0.33 \approx 0.0825$	$0.4 \times 0.5 = 0.2$	$0.05 \times 1 = 0.05$
Peugeot	$0.3 \times 0.5 = 0.15$	$0.25 \times 0.67 \approx 0.1675$	$0.4 \times 0.5 = 0.2$	$0.05 \times 0.33 \approx 0.0165$
VW	$0.3 \times 0 = 0$	$0.25 \times 1 = 0.25$	$0.4 \times 1 = 0.4$	$0.05 \times 1 = 0.05$

- Renault: $0.15 + 0.0825 + 0.2 + 0.05 = 0.4825$
- Peugeot: $0.15 + 0.1675 + 0.2 + 0.0165 \approx 0.534$
- VW: $0 + 0.25 + 0.4 + 0.05 = 0.7$

$\Sigma S_i = 0.3 + 0.4825 + 0.534 + 0.7 = 2.0165$

Then the P_i (sum of weighted product normalized matrix) values are as seen below:

FIAT:
$P1 = (1.0)^{0.3} + (0.0)^{0.25} + (0.0)^{0.4} + (0.0)^{0.05}$

- Note: Replace 0.00.0 with $\epsilon = 10^{-6}$ to avoid division by zero:

$P1 = (1.0)^{0.3} + (10^{-6})^{0.25} + (10^{-6})^{0.4} + (10^{-6})^{0.05}$

$P1 = 1.0 + 0.001 + 0.001 + 0.999 \approx 1.0$

Renault:
$P2 = (0.5)^{0.3} + (0.33)^{0.25} + (0.5)^{0.4} + (1.0)^{0.05}$

$P2 = 0.812 + 0.760 + 0.758 + 1.0 \approx 3.330$

Peugeot:
$P3 = (0.5)^{0.3} + (0.67)^{0.25} + (0.5)^{0.4} + (0.33)^{0.05}$

$P3 = 0.812 + 0.904 + 0.758 + 0.887 \approx 3.361$

VW:
$P4 = (0.0)^{0.3} + (1.0)^{0.25} + (1.0)^{0.4} + (1.0)^{0.05}$

- Replace 0.00.0 with $\epsilon\epsilon$:

$P4 = (10^{-6})^{0.3} + (1.0)^{0.25} + (1.0)^{0.4} + (1.0)^{0.05}$

$P4 = 0.001 + 1.0 + 1.0 + 1.0 \approx 3.001$

Final P_i matrix (Table 66.5):

Thereafter, from the previous formulas, we compute the total value of $S_i + P_i = 12.7055$

In the next step, we calculate the aggregation strategies using formulas (66.6)–(66.8)

k_{ia}:

- FIAT: $1.3 / 12.7055 \approx 0.102$
- Renault: $3.8115 / 12.7055 \approx 0.300$
- Peugeot: $3.894 / 12.7055 \approx 0.307$
- VW: $3.7 / 12.7055 \approx 0.291$

k_{ib}:

- FIAT: $0.3 / 0.3 + 1.0 / 1.0 = 2.0$
- Renault: $0.4825 / 0.3 + 3.329 / 1.0 \approx 4.608$
- Peugeot: $0.534 / 0.3 + 3.360 / 1.0 \approx 5.140$
- VW: $0.7 / 0.3 + 3.0 / 1.0 \approx 5.333$

$k_{ic}(\lambda = 0.5)$:

- FIAT: $0.65 / 2.03 \approx 0.320$
- Renault: $1.906 / 2.03 \approx 0.939$
- Peugeot: $1.947 / 2.03 \approx 0.959$

TABLE 66.5 Final P_i matrix.

Alternative	Calculated P_i
FIAT	1
Renault	3.33
Peugeot	3.361
VW	3.001

TABLE 66.6 Final ranking score.

Alternative	k_i	Rank
VW	**3.361**	**1**
Peugeot	3.336	2
Renault	3.079	3
FIAT	1.212	4

- VW: 1.85 / 2.03 ≈ 0.911

According to Table 66.6, the final ranking score (k_i) (formula (66.9)) is produced:

As Table 66.6 reflects, VW is selected as the best alternative, which has the highest k_i score.

66.4.2 Sustainable supplier selection problem

TRT company, as mentioned before, is expanding its strategic operations horizon and wants to evaluate the current group of suppliers based on sustainable variables. At this moment, TRT is working with eight suppliers with different profiles, and they come from various countries. The idea is to perform an assessment platform to measure the practical performance of each supplier, compare them, and release a list of the best to worst suppliers. To measure such performance, we developed an initial matrix to show the comparison of the suppliers as seen in the table below. Seven criteria, named as *financial stability, price, quality, social responsibility, environmental certification, carbon footprint standards, and employee protection*, are under evaluation. All suppliers are evaluated with a scale of 1–10, where 1 is the worst score and 10 is the best score. This process is handled by a group of experts who have known the suppliers for years and have worked with them constantly. Each of the four experts delivered their opinions, and the CoCoSo method will produce the supplier scores and rankings. Among the criteria, only price takes the cost orientation. Experts decided the weight of each criterion should be as (W1 to W7): 0.08; 0.17; 0.25; 0.15; 0.1; 0.2, and 0.05.

First, it is necessary to combine the opinions of the four experts (Table 66.7) and convert them into an initial matrix. For this matter, the arithmetic mean is used:

We combine the four decision matrices from the experts using the **arithmetic mean, using formula** (66.10):

$$X_{ij} = \frac{x_{ij}^{(1)} + x_{ij}^{(2)} + x_{ij}^{(3)} + x_{ij}^{(4)}}{4} \tag{66.10}$$

The average decision matrix is observed in Table 66.8:

The next step is normalization of the decision matrix (Table 66.9):

The next step is to determine the weighted normalized matrix (Table 66.10), using formula (66.4).

Then, the next step is to calculate the S_i *and* P_i (Tables 66.11 and 66.12) values.

TABLE 66.7 Supplier performance comparison from the four experts.

Supplier	C_1	C_2	C_3	C_4	C_5	C_6	C_7
Expert 1 ($x_{ij}^{(1)}$)							
S1	2	3	5	4	4	4	5
S2	3	4	6	3	5	7	5
S3	6	6	7	3	5	5	4
S4	5	5	8	6	5	5	6
S5	7	7	5	6	7	8	6
S6	4	6	8	8	7	3	6
S7	4	5	6	6	6	4	7
S8	8	5	6	5	3	5	4
Expert 2 ($x_{ij}^{(2)}$)							
Supplier	C_1	C_2	C_3	C_4	C_5	C_6	C_7
S1	5	4	4	6	6	4	5
S2	5	4	5	3	5	7	5
S3	6	5	7	2	5	5	6
S4	5	5	6	6	4	4	4
S5	7	3	5	6	7	6	8
S6	2	6	3	5	7	3	6
S7	4	5	6	6	6	7	3
S8	7	7	5	1	4	5	4
Expert 3 ($x_{ij}^{(3)}$)							
Supplier	C_1	C_2	C_3	C_4	C_5	C_6	C_7
S1	3	4	2	6	5	4	4
S2	5	4	5	1	5	7	5
S3	6	5	7	2	4	5	6
S4	5	5	6	5	3	5	4
S5	6	3	4	6	7	6	6
S6	7	6	3	5	7	3	6
S7	5	5	3	8	6	3	3
S8	8	7	4	6	3	5	6
Expert 4 ($x_{ij}^{(4)}$)							
Supplier	C_1	C_2	C_3	C_4	C_5	C_6	C_7
S1	1	4	5	2	4	3	8
S2	5	6	8	6	5	5	5
S3	8	5	7	8	6	5	6
S4	5	4	3	5	6	3	6

(Continued)

TABLE 66.7 (Continued)

Expert 1 ($x_{ij}^{(1)}$)							
Supplier	C_1	C_2	C_3	C_4	C_5	C_6	C_7
S5	6	3	3	5	5	5	6
S6	5	7	3	4	5	7	5
S7	5	5	5	7	6	3	3
S8	4	6	4	6	3	5	3

TABLE 66.8 Average opinion of experts (initial decision matrix).

Supplier	C1 (benefit)	C2 (cost)	C3 (benefit)	C4 (benefit)	C5 (benefit)	C6 (benefit)	C7 (benefit)
S1	2.75	3.75	4	4.5	4.75	3.75	5.5
S2	4.5	4.5	6	3.25	5	6.5	5
S3	6.5	5.5	7	3.75	5	5	5.5
S4	5	4.75	5.75	5.5	4.5	4.25	5
S5	6.5	4	4.25	5.75	6.5	6.25	6.5
S6	4.5	6.25	4.25	5.5	6.5	4	5.75
S7	4.5	5	5	6.75	6	4.25	4
S8	6.75	5.75	4.75	4.5	3.25	5	4.25

TABLE 66.9 Normalization matrix.

Supplier	C1	C2	C3	C4	C5	C6	C7
S1	0	1	0	0.3571	0.4615	0	0.6
S2	0.4375	0.7	0.6667	0	0.5385	1	0.4
S3	0.9375	0.3	1	0.1429	0.5385	0.4545	0.6
S4	0.5625	0.6	0.5833	0.6429	0.3846	0.1818	0.4
S5	0.9375	0.9	0.0833	0.7143	1	0.9091	1
S6	0.4375	0	0.0833	0.6429	1	0.0909	0.7
S7	0.4375	0.5	0.3333	1	0.8462	0.1818	0
S8	1	0.2	0.25	0.3571	0	0.4545	0.1

TABLE 66.10 Weighted normalized matrix.

Supplier	C1	C2	C3	C4	C5	C6	C7
S1	0	0.17	0	0.0536	0.0462	0	0.03
S2	0.035	0.119	0.1667	0	0.0538	0.2	0.02
S3	0.075	0.051	0.25	0.0214	0.0538	0.0909	0.03
S4	0.045	0.102	0.1458	0.0964	0.0385	0.0364	0.02
S5	0.075	0.153	0.0208	0.1071	0.1	0.1818	0.05
S6	0.035	0	0.0208	0.0964	0.1	0.0182	0.035
S7	0.035	0.085	0.0833	0.15	0.0846	0.0364	0
S8	0.08	0.034	0.0625	0.0536	0	0.0909	0.005

TABLE 66.11 Weighted sum.

• *Supplier*	• S_i
S1	0.2997
S2	0.5945
S3	0.5722
S4	0.4841
S5	0.6878
S6	0.3054
S7	0.4743
S8	0.326

TABLE 66.12 Weighted product.

Supplier	P_i
S1	3.7573
S2	5.676
S3	6.3255
S4	6.2568
S5	6.4463
S6	5.0105
S7	5.2792
S8	5.07

The next step is to find the three aggregation strategies (Table 66.13) and finally the ranking score of each supplier as seen in Table 66.14:

Based on the previous table results, the ranking of suppliers is listed below:

S5 > S3 > S2 > S4 > S7 > S8 > S6 > S1.

66.4.2.1 Comparison with other multiple attribute decision-making methods

We have conducted a comparison of the CoCoSo with other methods such as MABAC, WASPAS, and EDAS. The results are presented in Table 66.15. Some key notes about Table 66.15:

- Supplier S5 ranks first in all methods, indicating consistency of results.
- There is a slight difference in the ranking of S3 and S7 between methods (especially in MABAC).
- All methods identified S1 as the weakest supplier.
- In addition, we computed the rank correlation (Spearman's coefficient), which is seen in Table 66.16. Surprisingly, all the correlations are higher than 80% of similarity, which is a high percentage. The highest agreement is released

TABLE 66.13 Aggregation strategies.

Supplier	k_{ia}	k_{ib}	k_{ic}	
S1	0.0853	2	with λ = 0.5	0.5687
S2	0.1318	3.4942		0.8789
S3	0.145	3.5926		0.9669
S4	0.1417	3.2804		0.9449
S5	0.15	4.0104		1
S6	0.1118	2.3526		0.7452
S7	0.121	2.9876		0.8065
S8	0.1134	2.437		0.7564

TABLE 66.14 Final ranking score.

Supplier	k_i	Rank
S1	1.3441	**8**
S2	2.2414	**3**
S3	2.3638	**2**
S4	2.2158	**4**
S5	2.5643	**1**
S6	1.6507	**7**
S7	1.968	**5**
S8	1.6958	**6**

TABLE 66.15 Multiple attribute decision-making ranking comparison.

Supplier	CoCoSo	MABAC	WASPAS	EDAS
S1	**8**	8	8	8
S2	**3**	3	3	3
S3	**2**	5	4	4
S4	**4**	6	5	5
S5	**1**	**1**	**1**	**1**
S6	**7**	7	7	7
S7	**5**	4	6	6
S8	**6**	2	2	2

TABLE 66.16 Spearman ranking correlation.

Methods	**CoCoSo**	**MABAC**	**WASPAS**	**EDAS**
CoCoSo	1	0.9	0.95	0.93
MABAC	0.9	1	0.88	0.85
WASPAS	0.95	0.88	1	0.98
EDAS	0.93	0.85	0.98	1

between WASPAS versus EDAS, with 98%, and the lowest agreement is demonstrated between MABAC versus EDAS (0.85) due to MABAC's border approximation approach.

Spearman's correlation coefficient (ρ) is calculated with the following formula (66.11):

$$\rho = 1 - \frac{6\sum d_i^2}{n\,(n^2 - 1)} \tag{66.11}$$

where d_i is the difference in ranks for each supplier in the two methods. n number of suppliers. Calculated values:

- CoCoSo vs MABAC: $\rho = 0.90$
- CoCoSo vs WASPAS: $\rho = 0.95$
- CoCoSo vs EDAS: $\rho = 0.93$
- WASPAS vs EDAS: $\rho = 0.98$ (Highest agreement)
- MABAC vs EDAS: $\rho = 0.85$ (Least agreement)

66.4.2.2 *Results accuracy by sensitivity analysis*

To evaluate the robustness of the results, we conduct a random sensitivity analysis across weight replacement. Table 66.17 indicates the 20 tests and weights assigned for each of them. We applied the CoCoSo algorithm (like previous steps) and developed the ranking matrix for sensitivity tests. After generating the ranking scores by CoCoSo, which are seen in Table 66.17, the results denote several items. S1 is consistently the worst supplier in almost all experiments, while S5

TABLE 66.17 Twenty random weight replacement tests.

	W1	W2	W3	W4	W5	W6	W7
T1	0.17	0.08	0.25	0.15	0.1	0.2	0.05
T2	0.05	0.17	0.08	0.25	0.15	0.1	0.2
T3	0.05	0.2	0.17	0.08	0.25	0.15	0.1
T4	0.05	0.2	0.1	0.17	0.08	0.25	0.15
T5	0.05	0.2	0.1	0.15	0.17	0.08	0.25
T6	0.05	0.2	0.1	0.15	0.25	0.17	0.08
T7	0.05	0.2	0.1	0.15	0.25	0.08	0.17
T8	0.25	0.17	0.08	0.15	0.1	0.2	0.05
T9	0.25	0.17	0.15	0.08	0.1	0.2	0.05
T10	0.25	0.17	0.15	0.1	0.08	0.2	0.05
T11	0.25	0.17	0.15	0.1	0.2	0.08	0.05
T12	0.25	0.17	0.15	0.1	0.2	0.05	0.08
T13	0.25	0.17	0.15	0.1	0.2	0.08	0.05
T14	0.1	0.08	0.17	0.25	0.15	0.2	0.05
T15	0.1	0.08	0.17	0.25	0.15	0.05	0.2
T16	0.1	0.08	0.17	0.05	0.2	0.25	0.15
T17	0.1	0.08	0.17	0.05	0.2	0.15	0.25
T18	0.1	0.15	0.17	0.2	0.05	0.08	0.25
T19	0.1	0.25	0.17	0.15	0.08	0.2	0.05
T20	0.1	0.25	0.17	0.08	0.15	0.2	0.05

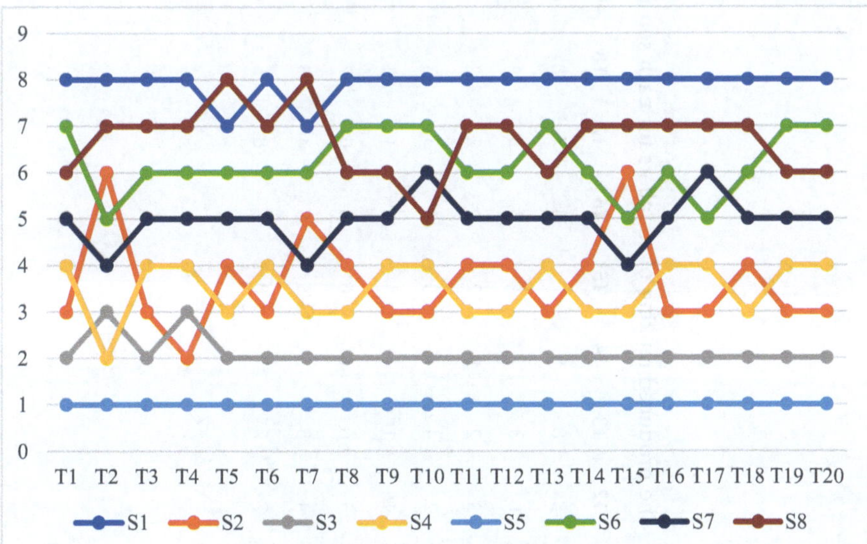

FIGURE 66.1 The ranking distribution transparency for the random test.

TABLE 66.18 The produced ranking of suppliers for each sensitivity analysis test.

	T1	T2	T3	T4	T5	T6	T7	T8	T9	T10	T11	T12	T13	T14	T15	T16	T17	T18	T19	T20	Org.
S1	8	8	8	8	7	8	7	8	8	8	8	8	8	8	8	8	8	8	8	8	8
S2	3	6	3	2	4	3	5	4	3	3	4	4	3	4	6	3	3	4	3	3	3
S3	2	3	2	3	2	2	2	2	2	2	2	2	2	2	2	2	2	2	2	2	2
S4	4	2	4	4	3	4	3	3	4	4	3	3	4	3	3	4	4	3	4	4	4
S5	1	1	1	1	1	1	1	1	1	1	1	1	1	1	1	1	1	1	1	1	1
S6	7	5	6	6	6	6	6	7	7	7	6	6	7	6	5	6	5	6	7	7	7
S7	5	4	5	5	5	5	4	5	5	6	5	5	5	5	4	5	6	5	5	5	5
S8	6	7	7	7	8	7	8	6	6	5	7	7	6	7	7	7	7	7	6	6	6

maintains the best supplier in all 20 random tests. The same condition is observed for S3 as the second-best supplier in 90% of the tests. Confidentially and based on the sensitivity analysis, we guarantee that our results are stable in any change in weight replacement and do not show any special sensitivity to weight modification. Fig. 66.1 exhibits the visual distribution of rankings (Table 66.18) for effective comprehension. In this figure, the horizontal axis shows the different sensitivity tests, while the vertical axis reveals the supplier ranking level. As seen, S5 maintains the first ranking in all tests.

66.5 Conclusion

The advancement of decision-making methods in applications and real-world problems demonstrates a supportive function to fulfill management commitment. The role of multicriteria decision-making MCDM methods became more prominent when the first tools, like the analytical hierarchy process, TOPSIS, PROMETHEE, and other tools, were being implemented in different research projects. The growing trend of MCDM utilization was studied in many research articles, projects, conferences, and books. This chapter is dedicated to step-by-step recognition and introduction of the CoCoSo method. In this chapter, an attempt has been made to synthesize CoCoSo in a way that is easier to facilitate its application and operations for all the researchers, students, and public readers who want to obtain general information about it. It starts with a thorough literature exploration and CoCoSo application classification, and then the mathematical algorithm is presented. Two empirical examples are explained to demonstrate the user-friendliness and utility of the method. In each example, depending on the problem dimension, exhaustive computation is detailed, and readers can seek any specific mathematical operations. We use Excel software as well to indicate how it can aid in finding a solution in case of a larger matrix. In a second example, an already defined decision problem about energy source selection is proposed. Solution and comparisons are provided for an effective understanding and learning process. Authors hope this will help the MCDM community encounter such models as reliable in their complex and multilevel decision or evaluation problems where a high quantity of alternatives should be compared and finally sorted under respective decision criteria.

References

Adar, E., Delice, E. K., & Adar, T. (2022). Prioritizing of industrial wastewater management processes using an integrated AHP–CoCoSo model: Comparative and sensitivity analyses. *International Journal of Environmental Science and Technology, 19*(6), 4691–4712.

Banihashemi, S. A., Khalilzadeh, M., Zavadskas, E. K., & Antucheviciene, J. (2021). Investigating the environmental impacts of construction projects in time-cost trade-off project scheduling problems with CoCoSo multi-criteria decision-making method. *Sustainability, 13*(19), 10922.

Bouraima, M. B., Qiu, Y., Stević, Ž., & Simić, V. (2023). Assessment of alternative railway systems for sustainable transportation using an integrated IRN SWARA and IRN CoCoSo model. *Socio-Economic Planning Sciences, 86*, 101475.

Choudhary, V., & Mishra, A. (2022). Analyzing the critical success enablers of industry 4.0 using hybrid fuzzy AHP–CoCoSo method. *Journal of Industrial Integration and Management, 7*(04), 493–514.

Cui, Y., Liu, W., Rani, P., & Alrasheedi, M. (2021). Internet of Things (IoT) adoption barriers for the circular economy using Pythagorean fuzzy SWARA-CoCoSo decision-making approach in the manufacturing sector. *Technological Forecasting and Social Change, 171*, 120951.

Demir, G., Damjanović, M., Matović, B., & Vujadinović, R. (2022). Toward sustainable urban mobility by using fuzzy-FUCOM and fuzzy-CoCoSo methods: The case of the SUMP podgorica. *Sustainability, 14*(9), 4972.

Dhruva, S., Krishankumar, R., Zavadskas, E. K., Ravichandran, K. S., & Gandomi, A. H. (2024). Selection of suitable cloud vendors for health centre: A personalized decision framework with fermatean fuzzy set. *LOPCOW, and CoCoSo. Informatica, 35*(1), 65–98.

Ecer, F., & Pamucar, D. (2020). Sustainable supplier selection: A novel integrated fuzzy best worst method (F-BWM) and fuzzy CoCoSo with Bonferroni (CoCoSo'B) multi-criteria model. *Journal of cleaner production, 266*, 121981.

Ecer, F., Saha, A., Dinçer, H., & Yüksel, S. (2025). Evaluating energy management investments for sustainable transition of smart cities through a new intuitionistic fuzzy consensus-based CoCoSo methodology. *Renewable Energy,* 122655.

Erceg, Ž., Starčević, V., Pamučar, D., Mitrović, G., Stević, Ž., & Žikić, S. (2019). A new model for stock management in order to rationalize costs: ABC-FUCOM-interval rough CoCoSo model. *Symmetry, 11*(12), 1527.

Ferdous, O., Yousefi, S., & Tosarkani, B. M. (2025). A multi-disruption risk analysis system for sustainable supply chain resilience. *International Journal of Disaster Risk Reduction, 116*, 105136.

Ghoushchi, S. J., Jalalat, S. M., Bonab, S. R., Ghiaci, A. M., Haseli, G., & Tomaskova, H. (2022). Evaluation of wind turbine failure modes using the developed SWARA-CoCoSo methods based on the spherical fuzzy environment. *IEEE Access, 10*, 86750–86764.

Haseli, G., Torkayesh, A. E., Hajiaghaei-Keshteli, M., & Venghaus, S. (2023). Sustainable resilient recycling partner selection for urban waste management: Consolidating perspectives of decision-makers and experts. *Applied Soft Computing, 137*, 110120.

Haseli, G., Bonab, S. R., Hajiaghaei-Keshteli, M., Ghoushchi, S. J., & Deveci, M. (2024). Fuzzy ZE-numbers framework in group decision-making using the BCM and CoCoSo to address sustainable urban transportation. *Information sciences, 653*, 119809.

Karami, S., Mousavi, S. M., & Antucheviciene, J. (2023). Enhancing contractor selection process by a new interval-valued fuzzy decision-making model based on SWARA and cocoso methods. *Axioms, 12*(8), 729.

Khan, S., & Haleem, A. (2021). Investigation of circular economy practices in the context of emerging economies: A CoCoSo approach. *International Journal of Sustainable Engineering, 14*(3), 357–367.

Kumar, V., Kalita, K., Chatterjee, P., Zavadskas, E. K., & Chakraborty, S. (2022). A SWARA-CoCoSo-based approach for spray painting robot selection. *Informatica, 33*(1), 35–54.

Lahane, S., & Kant, R. (2021). A hybrid Pythagorean fuzzy AHP–CoCoSo framework to rank the performance outcomes of circular supply chain due to adoption of its enablers. *Waste Management, 130*, 48–60.

Lai, H., Liao, H., Long, Y., & Zavadskas, E. K. (2022). A hesitant Fermatean fuzzy CoCoSo method for group decision-making and an application to blockchain platform evaluation. *International Journal of Fuzzy Systems, 24*(6), 2643–2661.

Nguyen, V. T., & Chaysiri, R. (2025). CRITIC-CoCoSo Model application in hybrid solar-wind energy plant location selection problem: A case study in vietnam. *Energy Engineering, 122*(2).

Ogundoyin, S. O., & Kamil, I. A. (2023). An integrated fuzzy-BWM, fuzzy-LBWA and V-fuzzy-CoCoSo-LD model for gateway selection in fog-bolstered Internet of things. *Applied Soft Computing, 143*, 110393.

Pamucar, D., & Görçün, Ö. F. (2022). Evaluation of the European container ports using a new hybrid fuzzy LBWA-CoCoSo'B techniques. *Expert systems with applications, 203*, 117463.

Peng, X., & Smarandache, F. (2020). A decision-making framework for China's rare earth industry security evaluation by neutrosophic soft CoCoSo method. *Journal of Intelligent & Fuzzy Systems, 39*(5), 7571–7585.

Peng, X., Zhang, X., & Luo, Z. (2020). Pythagorean fuzzy MCDM method based on CoCoSo and CRITIC with score function for 5G industry evaluation. *Artificial Intelligence Review, 53*(5), 3813–3847.

Parsa Rad, A., Khalilzadeh, M., Banihashemi, S. A., Božanić, D., Milić, A., & Ćirović, G. (2024). Supplier selection in downstream oil and gas and petrochemicals with the fuzzy BWM and gray CoCoSo methods considering sustainability criteria and uncertainty conditions. *Sustainability, 16*(2), 880.

Rashidian, F., Eydi, A., & Roghanian, E. (2024). Reliable and green road-rail routing using a hybrid procedure of DANP, COCOSO, and FMEA criticality methods: A case study of cement transportation network in Iran. *Journal of cleaner production, 447*, 141250.

Rasoanaivo, R. G., Yazdani, M., Zaraté, P., & Fateh, A. (2024). Combined compromise for ideal solution (CoCoFISo): A multi-criteria decision-making based on the CoCoSo method algorithm. *Expert systems with applications, 251*, 124079.

Razzaq, A., Riaz, M., & Aslam, M. (2024). Efficient picture fuzzy soft CRITIC-CoCoSo framework for supplier selection under uncertainties in Industry 4.0. *AIMS Mathematics, 9*(1), 665–701.

Sriariyanun, M., Uthirapathi, E., Rajamohan, S., Paramasivam, B., Tawai, A., & Thirugnanasambandam, A. (2025). An integrated biorefinery of wood apple kernel for bio-oil and bio-diesel production: Optimization of engine attributes using taguchi, RSM, and CRITIC-COCOSO hybrid techniques. *International Journal of Environmental Research, 19*(3), 1–23.

Torkayesh, A. E., Ecer, F., Pamucar, D., & Karamaşa, Ç. (2021). Comparative assessment of social sustainability performance: Integrated data-driven weighting system and CoCoSo model. *Sustainable Cities and Society, 71*, 102975.

Torkayesh, A. E., Pamucar, D., Ecer, F., & Chatterjee, P. (2021). An integrated BWM-LBWA-CoCoSo framework for evaluation of healthcare sectors in Eastern Europe. *Socio-Economic Planning Sciences, 78*, 101052.

Ulutaş, A., Karakuş, C. B., & Topal, A. (2020). Location selection for logistics center with fuzzy SWARA and CoCoSo methods. *Journal of Intelligent & Fuzzy Systems, 38*(4), 4693–4709.

Wang, H., Zhang, F., & Ullah, K. (2010). Waste clothing recycling channel selection using a CoCoSo-D method based on sine trigonometric interaction operational laws with Pythagorean fuzzy information. *Energies, 15*(6).

Wang, J., Yu, L., & Rong, Y. (2024). A new CoCoSo ranking-based QFD approach in pythagorean fuzzy environment and its application on evaluating design attributes of mobile medical app. *Journal of Intelligent & Fuzzy Systems, 46*(2), 3677–3700.

Xiao, J., & Zhang, Y. (2025). Enhanced TOPSIS-CoCoSo framework for multi-attribute decision-making with triangular fuzzy neutrosophic sets:"Effect evaluation of intelligent technology empowering physical education teaching" case. *Soft Computing*, 1–15.

Xu, X.-G., Zhang, L., Mao, L.-X., & Li, K. (2022). New approach for quality function deployment using an extended CoCoSo method with spherical fuzzy sets. *Systems, 10*(6), 253.

Yang, L., & Li, Q. (2024). CoCoSo framework for multi-attribute decision-making with triangular fuzzy neutrosophic sets:"Innovation and entrepreneurship" evaluation case. *International Journal of Knowledge-Based and Intelligent Engineering Systems, 28*(2), 263–277.

Yazdani, M., Zarate, P., Kazimieras Zavadskas, E., & Turskis, Z. (2018). A combined compromise solution (CoCoSo) method for multi-criteria decision-making problems. *Management Decision, 57*(9), 2501–2519.

Yazdani, M., Wen, Z., Liao, H., Banaitis, A., & Turskis, Z. (2019). A grey combined compromise solution (CoCoSo-G) method for supplier selection in construction management. *Journal of Civil Engineering and Management, 25*(8), 858–874.

Yazdani, M., Ariza-Montes, A., Arjona-Fuentes, J. M., & Radic, A. (2024). Cruise hotel sustainable supplier management using a grey-based decision support framework. *Journal of Travel & Tourism Marketing, 41*(4), 538–558.

Yazdani, M., Ye, C., Shaayesteh, M. T., & Zaraté, P. (2025). Decision support system for waste management: Fuzzy group AHP-CoCoSo. *International Journal of Production Management and Engineering, 13*(1), 77–92.

Zafaranlouei, N., Ghoushchi, S. J., & Haseli, G. (2023). Assessment of sustainable waste management alternatives using the extensions of the base criterion method and combined compromise solution based on the fuzzy Z-numbers. *Environmental Science and Pollution Research, 30*(22), 62121–62136.

Zhang, H., & Wei, G. (2023). Location selection of electric vehicles charging stations by using the spherical fuzzy CPT–CoCoSo and D-CRITIC method. *Computational and Applied Mathematics, 42*(1), 60.

Zolfani, S. H., Rezaeiniya, N., Zavadskas, E. K., & Turskis, Z. (2011). Forest roads locating based on AHP and COPRAS-G methods: An empirical study based on Iran. *Ekonomie, 4*, 6–21.

Chapter 67

CoCoFISo: Combined compromise for ideal solution for multi-attribute decision-making

Morteza Yazdani[1], **Mahsa Pishdar**[2], **and Homa Molavi**[3]

[1]*European University of Madrid, Villaviciosa de odon campus, Madrid, Spain,* [2]*Management and Accounting Faculty, College of Farabi, University of Tehran, Qom, Iran,* [3]*University of Greenwich, School of Business, Operations & Strategy, London, United Kingdom*

67.1 Introduction and literature review

Multiple criteria decision-making (MCDM) offers a range of algorithms and frameworks to solve decision problems involving multiple criteria and alternatives. MCDM methods assign weights to both criteria and alternatives to support evaluation, sorting, classification, and ranking tasks (Haseli et al., 2024a). Over the past 30 years, tools like analytic hierarchy process, elimination and choice translating reality, preference ranking organization method for enrichment evaluation, and newer methods such as the best–worst method (BWM) have enhanced the field. Some methods, like BWM, step-wise weight assessment ratio analysis, and criteria importance through intercriteria correlation, focus on criteria weighting, while others—such as technique for order of preference by similarity to ideal solution (TOPSIS), VlseKriterijumska Optimizacija I Kompromisno Resenje, complex proportional assessment, and combined compromise solution (CoCoSo)—rank alternatives. CoCoSo, for instance, integrates additive and multiplicative approaches to produce a complete ranking, offering flexibility and adaptability to complex decision-making environments (Rasoanaivo et al., 2024; Sisto et al., 2022; Torkayesh et al., 2022). The combined compromise for ideal solution (CoCoFIso) method was developed as an improvement over CoCoSo, addressing its limitations in handling complex criterion relationships. By introducing advanced normalization and more flexible weighting schemes, CoCoFIso enhances decision-making accuracy (Rasoanaivo et al., 2024).

Rasoanaivo (2025) applied CoCoFISo method within a decision support framework to evaluate the equitable distribution of educational resources in Madagascar's high schools. Recognizing the critical impact of resource allocation on student enrollment and success, the study assessed 23 Regional Directorates of National Education (DRENs) using a multicriteria decision support system (MADREN) that integrated nine indicators covering material resources, human resources, and student outcomes. The centroid method was used to weight the criteria, while CoCoFISo was employed to rank the DRENs across rural, urban, and hybrid contextual models. CoCoFISo played a critical role in objectively synthesizing complex and diverse criteria to produce actionable insights, thus supporting more equitable and strategic policy decisions. This application underscores CoCoFISo's broader value as a robust multicriteria decision-making tool capable of guiding resource allocation and performance evaluation in public sector planning and beyond (Rasoanaivo, 2025).

Tsirimbelona and Rasoanaivo developed the Compromise Solver, an open-access decision support system that operationalizes the CoCoFISo method for solving a wide range of MCDM problems. The Compromise Solver software automates the process of consistent and robust rankings, allowing users to define decision problems, input criteria and alternatives, assign weights, and obtain clear, ranked outcomes. Notably, the tool is designed to be user-friendly and accessible even to nonspecialists, making it particularly valuable for decision-makers in fields requiring transparent and reliable evaluations. This work not only exemplifies the practical utility of CoCoFISo but also extends its accessibility,

Encyclopedia of Multi-Attribute Decision-Making (MADM). DOI: https://doi.org/10.1016/B978-0-443-33275-3.00026-9

reinforcing its relevance as a flexible and effective tool for multicriteria analysis across diverse domains (Tsirimbelona & Rasoanaivo, 2025).

Esfandiari (2025) introduced a novel application of the CoCoFISo method to enhance data quality in social networks by identifying influential nodes. As the volume and complexity of social network data continue to grow, eliminating irrelevant information has become essential for optimizing data-driven methodologies. Traditional approaches to detecting influential nodes—such as manual combinations of structural graph properties or conventional MCDM techniques—have often lacked the accuracy and resolution needed for complex networks. To address this gap, Esfandiari employed the CoCoFISo method to optimally combine five complementary graph structural features, including k-shell and PageRank, enabling a more precise ranking of nodes based on their potential for information dissemination. The findings show that the proposed approach significantly outperforms 12 state-of-the-art methods, including HCURank and HGSM, with improvements in accuracy, correlation, computational efficiency, and resolution. By introducing CoCoFISo for the optimal integration of features in key node identification, Esfandiari establishes it as a powerful and versatile decision-making tool in network analysis (Esfandiari, 2025).

Nirinarivelo and Rasoanaivo (2024) applied the CoCoFISo method, alongside the multicriteria mean weight approach, to evaluate and rank Madagascar's regions based on employment-related criteria. In their study, CoCoFISo was used as a decision-making tool to calculate the relative importance of multiple socio-economic indicators and generate a comparative ranking of regions in terms of employment potential. This application demonstrates the effectiveness of CoCoFISo in regional socio-economic evaluation, offering policymakers a strategic tool for identifying development priorities and allocating resources more efficiently. Moreover, the results provide practical guidance for the working-age population by highlighting regions with higher employment opportunities, thereby supporting informed decisions about long-term settlement and career planning (Nirinarivelo & Rasoanaivo, 2024).

67.1.1 Extensions of combined compromise for ideal solution

In a recent study, Sen and Toksoy (2024) extended the CoCoFISo method and developed a new approach called CoCoFISo-G. Their research focused on addressing the green supplier selection problem within the cosmetics industry, particularly in sourcing perfume bottles. Recognizing that supplier selection is a complex MCDM problem, especially when considering environmental and social sustainability factors, they proposed CoCoFISo-G to improve decision quality under uncertainty. The CoCoFISo-G method builds on the original CoCoFISo by incorporating gray numbers, allowing for better handling of uncertainty and imprecision in expert evaluations. By integrating gray system theory into CoCoFISo, the CoCoFISo-G method enables a more robust and flexible framework for sustainable supplier evaluation. This extension significantly improves the applicability of the method in real-world, ambiguous decision environments like those found in the green supply chain management of the cosmetics sector (Sen & Toksoy, 2024).

The picture fuzzy combined compromise for ideal solution (PF-CoCoFISo) method, introduced by Chang (2025), represents a significant advancement of the original CoCoFISo model by integrating picture fuzzy sets (PFSs) to address complex decision-making in uncertain environments—specifically, in the domain of digital media and intangible heritage digitalization. PF-CoCoFISo enhances the CoCoFISO framework by using picture fuzzy logic, which allows for a more nuanced representation of *uncertainty*. Unlike traditional fuzzy sets or even intuitionistic fuzzy sets, PFSs include three degrees of assessment: membership, nonmembership, and neutral (hesitation). This added dimension provides a more flexible and accurate modeling of expert opinions, especially in scenarios where evaluators may feel partially informed or indecisive. In Chang's study, PF-CoCoFISo was applied to the strategic selection of digitalization methods for preserving intangible cultural heritage, such as languages, artistic expressions, and traditions. The method was used to evaluate various digital archiving strategies across conflicting criteria such as technological adaptability, preservation standards, accessibility, cultural authenticity, data security, and sustainability. By using PFSs within the CoCoFISo structure, the PF-CoCoFISo approach enables better handling of vagueness and ambiguity, leading to more reliable and balanced decisions. In summary, PF-CoCoFISo extends CoCoFISo by incorporating picture fuzzy logic to handle higher degrees of uncertainty and hesitation in expert evaluations, making it particularly effective for digital transformation decisions in culturally and technologically volatile environments (Chang, 2025). Fig. 67.1 shows the different discussions about the improved version of the CoCoSo method.

67.2 Combined compromise for ideal solution method

The idea of CoCoFISo lies in two parts of the previously developed algorithm. On one side, when a criterion shows the same value for all the alternatives, this causes some problems in computing the normalization process, and another one is

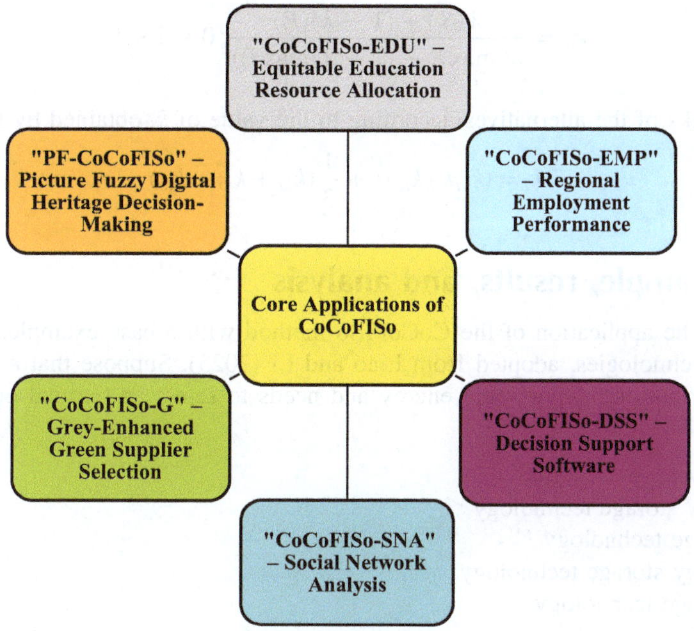

FIGURE 67.1 Core applications of the combined compromise for ideal solution (CoCoFISo) method based on the current literature.

when an alternative has the worst value in all the criteria. The latter issue produces errors in the aggregation step of the CoCoSo method. Such issues are easier to resolve in the initial screening of the decision matrix when we face a small or medium-sized matrix, however, if the decision matrix is composed of a higher volume of alternatives, finding the alternatives' ranking will be complicated. Therefore the new method algorithm with modification is able to obtain the ranking of alternatives using the steps below:

Step 1. Composing a matrix of alternatives and criteria, including their optimization direction. Formula 1 shows this matrix:

$$x_{ij} = \begin{bmatrix} x_{11} & x_{12} & \dots & x_{1n} \\ x_{21} & x_{22} & \dots & x_{2n} \\ \dots & \dots & \dots & \dots \\ x_{m1} & x_{m2} & \dots & x_{mn} \end{bmatrix};\ i = 1,\ 2,\ \dots,\ m;\ j = 1,\ 2,\ \dots,\ n \tag{67.1}$$

Step 2. Normalizing the performance matrix using formula 2, where r_{ij} is the normalized value of x_{ij}:

$$r_{ij} = \frac{x_{ij}}{\sqrt{\sum_{i=1}^{m} (x_{ij})^2}} \tag{67.2}$$

Step 3. Determining the weighted product and power-weighted matrices by calculating the two magnitudes S_i and P_i:

$$S_i = \sum_{j=1}^{n} (w_j r_{ij}) \tag{67.3}$$

$$P_i = \sum_{j=1}^{n} (r_{ij})^{w_j} \tag{67.4}$$

Step 4. Finding the three aggregated matrices using k_{ia}, k_{ib}, and k_{ic}:

$$k_{ia} = \frac{P_i + S_i}{\sum_{i=1}^{m} (P_i + S_i)} \tag{67.5}$$

$$k_{ib} = \left(\frac{S_i + P_i}{1 + \frac{S_i}{1+S_i} + \frac{P_i}{1+P_i}} \right) \tag{67.6}$$

$$k_{ic} = \frac{\lambda(S_i) + (1 - \lambda)(P_i)}{(\lambda \max_i S_i + (1 - \lambda)\max_i P_i)}; 0 \le \lambda \le 1. \quad (67.7)$$

Step 5. Producing the ranks of the alternatives according to the value of k_i obtained by formula 8.

$$k_i = (k_{ia}k_{ib}k_{ic})^{\frac{1}{3}} + \frac{1}{3}(k_{ia} + k_{ib} + k_{ic}) \quad (67.8)$$

67.3 Numerical example, results, and analysis

In this section, we explore the application of the CoCoFISo method with a case example. The case is about choosing renewable energy storage technologies, adopted from Liao and Li (2025). Suppose that a company needs to solve the problem of unbalanced distribution of renewable energy and needs to select an optimal option from the following six alternatives:

- A1: pumped storage technology
- A2: compressed air energy storage technology
- A3: flywheel energy storage technology
- A4: superconducting energy storage technology
- A5: hydrogen energy storage technology
- A6: battery storage technology.

While they considered eleven evaluation variables (criteria): C1: health and safety; C2: lifetime; C3 (job creation); C4 (environment impact); C5 (response time); C6 (energy density); C7 (social acceptance); C8 (power cost); C9 (self-discharge losses); C10 (energy cost); C11 (round-trip efficiency). It should be noticed that C4, C8, C10, C9, and C5 are cost criteria, and the rest of them are beneficial. The weights of the criteria are: 0.11, 0.05, 0.08, 0.1, 0.15, 0.13, 0.08, 0.07, 0.12, 0.085, 0.025.

67.3.1 Computation

When the decision matrix (Table 67.1) is provided, the next step is to determine the normalized matrix. As shown in Eq. 67.2, to normalize the matrix, square each number in a column, sum them, and take the square root of the sum. Then, divide each column entry by this value and place the result in the normalized table. The normalized performance matrix by using Eq. 67.2 is determined in Table 67.2.

☞ When using Excel, assume your decision matrix's first column is located in cells **A2:A6**. To normalize the data, enter the formula = A2/(SUM(($A$2:$A$6)^2)^0.5) in the first cell of the normalized decision matrix and then drag it down for the remaining rows.

- Absolute references (A$2:A$6) ensure the scores mentioned in the first column remain fixed when copying the formula to other cells of the first column.
- Drag the formula to the right and complete the other columns of the normalized matrix.

TABLE 67.1 Decision matrix.

Energy sources	C1	C2	C3	C4	C5	C6	C7	C8	C9	C10	C11
A1	2	3	5	4	4	4	5	7	3	4	5
A2	3	4	6	3	5	7	5	1	4	5	3
A3	6	6	7	3	5	5	4	1	2	6	7
A4	5	5	8	6	5	5	6	4	2	6	7
A5	7	7	5	6	7	8	6	5	5	7	6
A6	4	6	8	8	7	3	6	2	3	3	4

TABLE 67.2 Normalized decision matrix.

	C1	C2	C3	C4	C5	C6	C7	C8	C9	C10	C11
A1	0.17	0.23	0.31	0.31	0.29	0.29	0.38	0.71	0.37	0.31	0.37
A2	0.25	0.31	0.37	0.23	0.36	0.51	0.38	0.10	0.49	0.38	0.22
A3	0.51	0.46	0.43	0.23	0.36	0.36	0.30	0.10	0.24	0.46	0.52
A4	0.42	0.38	0.49	0.46	0.36	0.36	0.45	0.41	0.24	0.46	0.52
A5	0.59	0.54	0.31	0.46	0.51	0.58	0.45	0.51	0.61	0.54	0.44
A6	0.34	0.46	0.49	0.61	0.51	0.22	0.45	0.20	0.37	0.23	0.29

TABLE 67.3 Values of S_i, P_i.

	S_i	P_i
A_1	0.33	9.9
A_2	0.35	9.95
A_3	0.35	9.95
A_4	0.4	10.11
A_5	0.52	10.35
A_6	0.39	10.04

When the normalized matrix is determined, the weighted product and power-weighted matrices should be calculated using Eqs. 67.3 and 67.4. To determine S_i, each row's elements should be multiplied by their respective weights, followed by a row-wise summation (see the values of S_i in Table 67.3).

☞If the Excel is used to calculate the S_i values, the formula of "=SUMPRODUCT(A1:K1, $A$7:$K$7)" can be applied. Assuming the first row of the normalized matrix is in Row 1 (A1:K1), and the weights are in Row 7 (A7:K7).

- SUMPRODUCT multiplies each corresponding element in the two arrays (normalized values and weights) and sums the results.
- Absolute references ($A$7:$K$7) ensure the weights remain fixed when copying the formula to other cells.

However, to calculate P_i, first raise each element in the row to the power of its corresponding weight, then perform a row-wise summation of these values (see the values of P_i also in Table 67.3).

☞To calculate P_i in Excel, the following formula can be used as "=SUM(A1:K1^($A$7:$K$7))." Assuming the first row of the normalized matrix is in Row 1 (A1:K1), and the weights are in Row 7 (A7:K7).

By determination of S_i and P_i values, the values of K_{ia}, K_{ib}, and K_{ic} should be derived from Eqs. 67.5–67.7. To calculate K_{ia}, first, we find the sum of all P_i and S_i values. Then divide each alternative's $(P_i + S_i)$ by this total sum. However, to determine K_{ib}, first divide each alternative's S by $(1 + S)$. Repeat the same operation for P. Then add 1 to this value to form the denominator. Finally, divide the alternative's $(P_i + S_i)$ sum by this resulting denominator. Determine the λ (lambda) value based on research background or expert opinion. λ is considered equal to 0.5 in this study. To determine K_{ic}, identify which alternatives contain the maximum S and P values. Multiply this maximum by λ and $(1 - \lambda)$ respectively, then sum the results to form the denominator for K_{ic} calculation. For each alternative, multiply its S by λ and its P by $(1 - \lambda)$, sum these products, then divide by the denominator obtained earlier.

Finally, the alternatives are ranked based on the K_i values computed using Eq. 67.8, and results are shown in Table 67.4. To determine K_i, multiply all previous K_{ia}, K_{ib}, and K_{ic} values of the alternatives together and take the cube root (raise to

TABLE 67.4 *kia*, k_{ib}, k_{ic} and final ranks of alternatives.

	K_{ia}	K_{ib}	K_{ic}	K_i	Rank
A1	0.163	4.75	0.941	2.85	6
A2	0.164	4.75	0.948	2.86	5
A3	0.164	4.75	0.948	2.86	4
A4	0.168	4.79	0.967	2.89	2
A5	0.173	4.82	1	2.94	1
A6	0.167	4.77	0.96	2.88	3

the power 1/3). Then we calculate the arithmetic mean of the *K* values and sum these two quantities for each alternative. The alternative with the highest sum reflects the best alternative.

☞ Use formula as "=PRODUCT($A15:$C15)^(1/3)+(1/3)*(SUM($A15:$C15))" to determine K_i, considering that K_{ia}, K_{ib}, and K_{ic} are in cells of (A15:C15).

☞ For ranking the K_i, we could use the formula of "=RANK.EQ(G5, $G$5:$G$10, 0)" considering that the K_i of the alternatives are in the cells of G5:G10. In this way, the formula gives the rank of the first alternative. To determine the rank of the others, we just drag till the position of the last alternative.

As is depicted in Table 67.4, alternative 5 (hydrogen energy storage) has obtained the first rank, while it shows that alternative 1, as "Pumped storage technology," is the least important option among other alternatives.

67.3.2 Sensitivity analysis

In this section, we propose random tests to check the accuracy of the results achieved by CoCoFISo. The sensitivity analysis for weight replacement is performed to see how the alternative ranking would react. We have produced different sets of weights which are shown in Table 67.5, and consequently, the relevant ranking system of alternatives is indicated in Table 67.6.

It is obvious that the ranking of the alternatives is not sensitive not only to the weights of the criteria but also to the initial decision-making matrix that is determined based on the experts' opinions. Considering the last weighting system, if the score of A5 regarding C_1 and C_2 becomes 3, its ranking among all would become 2.

67.3.3 Combined compromise for ideal solution method versus technique for order preference by similarity to ideal solution method

The technique for order preference by similarity to ideal solution (TOPSIS) (Behzadian et al., 2012) is another multi-attribute decision-making method that ranks alternatives based on their closeness to an ideal solution and their distance from a negative-ideal solution. TOPSIS assumes that the best alternative should be closest to the "ideal best" solution (hypothetical alternative with the best values across all criteria). Also, it should be farthest from the "ideal worst" solution (hypothetical alternative with the worst values across all criteria). This is carried out using "Euclidean distance" calculations in a normalized decision space. To determine the ranks of the alternatives with TOPSIS, the following steps should be taken, given the previous decision matrix as Table 67.1 introduced.

Step 2. Normalize the decision matrix using Eq. 67.2. The normalized matrix would be the same as demonstrated in Table 67.2. Example for C_1 (health and safety) computation:

$$\text{Sum of squares} = 2^2 + 3^2 + 6^2 + 5^2 + 7^2 + 4^2 = 4 + 9 + 36 + 25 + 49 + 16 = 139$$

$$r_{11} = 2/(139)\text{^}0.5 = 0.169$$

Step 3. Apply weights to the normalized matrix. To do so, we multiply normalized values by criteria weights:

$$v_{ij} = w_j \times r_{ij} \tag{67.9}$$

TABLE 67.5 17 different sets of criteria weights.

	T1	T2	T3	T4	T5	T6	T7	T8	T9	T10	T11	T12	T13	T14	T15	T16	T17
C1	0.110	0.142	0.158	0.008	0.130	0.090	0.110	0.010	0.030	0.130	0.100	0.140	0.010	0.090	0.100	0.120	0.160
C2	0.050	0.190	0.026	0.156	0.160	0.150	0.130	0.020	0.060	0.190	0.040	0.090	0.020	0.140	0.060	0.120	0.070
C3	0.080	0.100	0.071	0.060	0.160	0.160	0.030	0.150	0.080	0.020	0.050	0.080	0.070	0.130	0.120	0.040	0.070
C4	0.100	0.162	0.065	0.003	0.080	0.110	0.100	0.070	0.120	0.220	0.140	0.010	0.120	0.050	0.090	0.030	0.190
C5	0.150	0.087	0.038	0.054	0.050	0.010	0.120	0.090	0.110	0.030	0.050	0.040	0.130	0.140	0.050	0.070	0.010
C6	0.130	0.001	0.129	0.144	0.150	0.050	0.070	0.080	0.120	0.220	0.060	0.140	0.080	0.100	0.080	0.020	0.010
C7	0.080	0.072	0.012	0.104	0.100	0.120	0.030	0.140	0.130	0.030	0.110	0.120	0.130	0.140	0.050	0.010	0.070
C8	0.070	0.008	0.130	0.157	0.020	0.250	0.140	0.170	0.100	0.040	0.060	0.120	0.090	0.030	0.200	0.150	0.020
C9	0.120	0.129	0.146	0.164	0.030	0.040	0.080	0.080	0.120	0.010	0.130	0.070	0.070	0.070	0.050	0.220	0.160
C10	0.085	0.097	0.144	0.074	0.040	0.010	0.060	0.180	0.100	0.050	0.150	0.070	0.150	0.100	0.170	0.080	0.130
C11	0.025	0.012	0.081	0.076	0.080	0.010	0.130	0.010	0.030	0.060	0.110	0.120	0.130	0.010	0.030	0.140	0.110
SUM	1	1	1	1	1	1	1	1	1	1	1	1	1	1	1	1	1

TABLE 67.6 The ranks of alternatives based on different ways of the weighting system.

	T1	T2	T3	T4	T5	T6	T7	T8	T9	T10	T11	T12	T13	T14	T15	T16	T17
A1	6	6	4	3	6	4	4	3	4	6	5	5	4	6	3	4	6
A2	5	5	6	5	5	6	6	5	5	5	6	6	6	5	6	6	5
A3	4	4	3	6	3	5	5	6	6	4	4	3	5	4	5	5	4
A4	2	3	2	2	2	2	2	2	2	2	2	2	2	2	2	2	2
A5	1	1	1	1	1	1	1	1	1	1	1	1	1	1	1	1	1
A6	3	2	5	4	4	3	3	4	3	3	3	4	3	3	4	3	3

TABLE 67.7 Weighted normalized matrix by use of the TOPSIS method.

	C1	C2	C3	C4	C5	C6	C7	C8	C9	C10	C11
A1	0.019	0.012	0.024	0.031	0.043	0.037	0.033	0.049	0.060	0.035	0.010
A2	0.028	0.016	0.029	0.023	0.053	0.065	0.033	0.007	0.080	0.043	0.006
A3	0.056	0.024	0.034	0.023	0.053	0.046	0.026	0.007	0.040	0.052	0.014
A4	0.047	0.020	0.038	0.046	0.053	0.046	0.039	0.028	0.040	0.052	0.014
A5	0.065	0.028	0.024	0.046	0.075	0.074	0.039	0.035	0.100	0.061	0.012
A6	0.037	0.024	0.038	0.062	0.075	0.028	0.039	0.014	0.060	0.026	0.008

Example for A1-C1:

$$v_{11} = 0.11 \times 0.169 \approx 0.019$$

☞ Considering that the first cell of the normalized decision matrix, which has been determined through the previous technique, is provided in an Excel file and in cell A1, and the relevant weight is in cell A7, use the formula "=A1*A$7" to determine the first cell of the weighted normalized matrix. Drag to complete the matrix. You could determine the result of the calculation as a weighted normalized matrix in an Excel file and in cells A9:K14. A complete normalized matrix is determined in Table 67.7.

Step 4: Determine ideal (A*) and antiideal (A^-) solutions.

Benefit criteria (C1, C2, C3, C6, C7, C11): higher is better → $A^* = \max(v_{ij}),\ A^-(\text{Anti} - \text{Ideal}) = \min(v_{ij})$

Cost criteria (C4, C5, C8, C9, C10): lower is better → $A^* = \min(v_{ij}),\ A^-(\text{Anti} - \text{Ideal}) = \max(v_{ij})$

☞ Determine the nature of each criterion by the symbols of (+) if it is a benefit and (-) if it is a cost for instance, in an Excel file and in cells of A15:K15, use the formula:

"=IF(A15="(+)" MAX(A9:A14), MIN(A9:A14))."

Considering that the first column of the weighted normalized matrix is Excel file and in A9:A14. Repeat this procedure for other columns of the matrix too. By considering the nature of each criterion and the values of the weighted normalized matrix, A* and A^- would become:

Ideal solution (A^*):

$$[0.0651 \quad 0.0283 \quad 0.0384 \quad 0.0231 \quad 0.0426 \quad 0.0738 \quad 0.0392 \quad 0.007 \quad 0.04 \quad 0.026 \quad 0.0143]$$

Antiideal solution (A^-):

$$[0.0186 \quad 0.0121 \quad 0.024 \quad 0.0615 \quad 0.0745 \quad 0.0277 \quad 0.0261 \quad 0.049 \quad 0.1 \quad 0.0607 \quad 0.0061]$$

Step 5. Calculate separation measures (S_i^* *and* S_i^-)

In this step, we calculate the distance of each alternative from its positive and negative ideal solutions based on the following equations.

$$S_i^* = \sqrt{\sum_{j=1}^{n} (v_{ij} - A_j^*)^2} \quad (67.10)$$

$$S_i^- = \sqrt{\sum_{j=1}^{n} (v_{ij} - A_j^-)^2} \quad (67.11)$$

☞ Use the formula of "=SQRT(SUM((A9:K9 - $A$16:$K$16)^2))" in Excel to determine S^*_1, considering that the row of A1 is the first attribute in an Excel file and in cells A9:K9, and the values of A^* are in an Excel file and in cells A16:K16. Determine values of other S*s similarly.

- You could calculate the S_1^- in a similar way. Just consider the values of A^- in an Excel file and in cells of A17:K17 in the formula above. Do the same to determine all the S_i^-.
- Fix the cells related to A^* as shown in the formula by use of the $ symbol. In this way, you would be able to drag down the formula and obtain the relevant values for another:
- Press ctrl+shift+enter (array formula).

We can check in Table 67.8 below the values of S_i^* *and* S_i^- for attributes.

Step 6. Compute closeness relevancy (CL_i)

The closeness index represents the score of each alternative and is calculated based on the following formula. The closer this index is to 1, the more superior the alternative is. The ranking system is shown in Table 67.9 and compared with the

TABLE 67.8 S_i^* *and* S_i^- **for attributes.**

Alternatives	S_i^*	S_i^-
A1	0.0593	0.0381
A2	0.0562	0.0349
A3	0.0447	0.0486
A4	0.0338	0.0585
A5	0.0312	0.0684
A6	0.0519	0.0374

TABLE 67.9 Relative closeness (C_i^*) for each alternative.

Alternative	C_i^*
A5	0.687
A4	0.634
A3	0.521
A6	0.419
A1	0.391
A2	0.383

TABLE 67.10 Comparison of the TOPSIS method ranking to combined compromised for ideal solution (CoCoFISo).

Alternative	TOPSIS ranking	CoCoFISo ranking
A5	1	A5
A4	2	A4
A3	3	A6
A6	4	A3
A1	5	A2
A2	6	A1

results of the CoCoFISo method. Relative closeness (C_i^*) for each alternative is shown in Table 67.9.

$$CL_i^* = \frac{S_i^-}{(S_i^- + S_i^*)} \tag{67.12}$$

Each alternative that receives the highest value of "Relative Closeness" is selected as the best alternative among all. Other alternatives are ranked similarly, as shown in Table 67.10.

- A5 ranks highest due to strong performance on high-weight criteria like response time [C5] and energy density [C6]. The same result is observed by the use of the CoCOFISo method. Therefore, both methods agree that A5 is the best, as it dominates in high-weight criteria (e.g., response time [C5], energy density [C6]) while managing costs effectively.
- A4 follows closely, balancing job creation [C3] and low self-discharge losses [C9]. Again, the result is the same as the result of the CoCOFISo method.
- A2 is ranked as the least important due to poor scores on power cost [C8] and round-trip efficiency [C11]. However, by the use of the CoCoFISo method, A1 reflects the lowest rank.
- About A3 versus A6 (which are ranked by swapping third and fourth place). It should be noticed that TOPSIS favors A3 due to strong performance on benefit criteria (e.g., health and safety [C1] and job creation [C3]), while CoCoFISo prioritizes A6 because of its balanced compromise between benefit and cost criteria (e.g., high job creation [C3] but lower energy cost [C10]). CoCoFISo's aggregation methods (e.g., arithmetic, geometric, harmonic means) amplify A6's middle-ground performance.

However, paying attention to A1 versus A2 (swapping 5 and 6 rankings) makes it evident that TOPSIS penalizes A2 more heavily for extreme weaknesses (e.g., worst power cost [C8] and round-trip efficiency [C11]). While CoCoFISo tolerates A2's poor scores if it performs slightly better on some criteria (e.g., job creation [C3]), as CoCoFISo considers multiple aggregation perspectives. Here, we develop several key considerations:

- TOPSIS measures Euclidean distance to ideal/antiideal solutions and is sensitive to extreme values. However, CoCoFISo combines three aggregation strategies (sum, minimum, and maximum) to find a compromise solution, less sensitive to outliers and more forgiving of partial weaknesses.
- TOPSIS strictly separates cost (minimize) and benefit (maximize) criteria, while CoCoFISo's hybrid approach may balance trade-offs differently, allowing alternatives with mixed performance to rise.

67.4 Conclusion and recommendation

Haseli et al. (2023) in their work stand on the applicability and reliability of the CoCoSo method. The focus on the main algorithm allowed decision-making experts to extend CoCoSo and apply this method in different fields of knowledge. The combined compromise for an ideal solution contains an improved format of the classic CoCoSo algorithm in normalization and ranking aggregation. This chapter proposed a new window for an effective and simple explanation of the CoCoFISo method using several examples and analysis. We extracted an example from a study on energy source technology selection and implemented the method. Our detailed computation can assist graduate and undergraduate students in comprehending the step-by-step formulation. After several sensitivity tests for the criteria weight replacement were conducted, and the results were produced. The contribution of the CoCoSo method and its improvement with a high percentage showed that the results are not affected by the weight replacement. In addition, we compared the results of the CoCoFISo with the TOPSIS method (which is a distance-based method), and we are not surprised that it still keeps the same ranking in the first and second best alternatives. All cases indicated a strong capacity and application of the CoCoFIso in multiple attribute decision-making problems.

As the original CoCoSo method was applied in diverse applications aiding managers and practitioners in their research projects, such as supply chain (Ortíz-Barrios et al., 2023), or in agricultural development (Fernández-Portillo et al., 2023), the improved method is becoming popular based on feedback and reaction in academic communities (Rasoanaivo, 2025). The authors of this chapter suggest investigating the wide range of CoCoFISo extensions in fuzzy or probabilistic approaches to reduce uncertainty in decision-making environments. Another idea can be a comparison of the CoCoSo and CoCoFISo in different scenarios and dimensions in various projects, such as supply chain, food security, public and sustainable systems, energy sector, etc.

References

Behzadian, M., Otaghsara, S. K., Yazdani, M., & Ignatius, J. (2012). A state-of the-art survey of TOPSIS applications. *Expert Systems with Applications, 39*(17), 13051–13069.

Chang, H. (2025). Decision algorithm for digital media and intangible-heritage digitalization using picture fuzzy combined compromise for ideal solution in uncertain environments. *Symmetry, 17*(3), 443.

Esfandiari, S. (2025). Enhancing data quality by identifying influential nodes: Integrating complementary features with CoCoFISo. *Companion Proceedings of the ACM on Web Conference 2025.*

Fernández-Portillo, L. A., Yazdani, M., Estepa-Mohedano, L., & Sisto, R. (2023). Prioritisation of strategies for the adoption of organic agriculture using BWM and fuzzy CoCoSo. *Soft Computing,* 1–32.

Haseli, G., Bonab, S. R., Hajiaghaei-Keshteli, M., Ghoushchi, S. J., & Deveci, M. (2024a). Fuzzy ZE-numbers framework in group decision-making using the BCM and CoCoSo to address sustainable urban transportation. *Information Sciences, 653*, 119809.

Haseli, G., Torkayesh, A. E., Hajiaghaei-Keshteli, M., & Venghaus, S. (2023). Sustainable resilient recycling partner selection for urban waste management: Consolidating perspectives of decision-makers and experts. *Applied Soft Computing, 137*, 110120. https://doi.org/10.1016/j.asoc.2023.110120.

Liao, H., & Li, X. (2025). A multi-criterion decision making method for renewable energy storage technology selection with incomplete evaluation information. *Technological Forecasting and Social Change, 215*, 124116.

Nirinarivelo, H., & Rasoanaivo, R. G. (2024). Multi-criteria evaluation of Madagascar's regions in the context of employment using the CoCoFISo method. *Spectrum of Decision Making and Applications, 2*(1), 135–156.

Ortíz-Barrios, M.A., Madrid-Sierra, S.L., Petrillo, A., & Quezada, L.E. (2023). A novel approach integrating IF-AHP, IF-DEMATEL and CoCoSo methods for sustainability management in food digital manufacturing supply chain systems. Journal of Enterprise Information Management.

Rasoanaivo, R. G. (2025). Decision support system using centroidous and CoCoFISo methods for analyzing resource availability in high schools. *Journal of Operations Intelligence, 3*(1), 197–226.

Rasoanaivo, R. G., Yazdani, M., Zaraté, P., & Fateh, A. (2024). Combined compromise for ideal solution (CoCoFISo): A multi-criteria decision-making based on the CoCoSo method algorithm. *Expert Systems with Applications, 251*, 124079.

Sen, H., & Toksoy, M. S. (2024). Green supplier selection with CoCoFISo-G. *The Eurasia Proceedings of Science Technology Engineering and Mathematics, 32*, 257–265.

Sisto, R., Fernández-Portillo, L. A., Yazdani, M., Estepa-Mohedano, L., & Torkayesh, A. E. (2022). Strategic planning of rural areas: Integrating participatory backcasting and multiple criteria decision analysis tools. *Socio-Economic Planning Sciences, 82*, 101248.

Torkayesh, A. E., Yazdani, M., & Ribeiro-Soriano, D. (2022). Analysis of industry 4.0 implementation in mobility sector: An integrated approach based on QFD, BWM, and stratified combined compromise solution under fuzzy environment. *Journal of Industrial Information Integration, 30*, 100406.

Tsirimbelona, J.N., & Rasoanaivo, R.G. (2025). Compromise Solver, an open access software for implementing the CoCoFISo method to solve any type of multi-criteria problem.

Chapter 68

Simple WISP: Simple weighted sum product for ideal solution for multi-attribute decision-making

Alptekin Ulutaş[1], Ayşe Topal[2], and Ali Aygün Yürüyen[3]

[1]*Department of International Trade and Logistics, Faculty of Economics and Administrative Sciences, Inonu University, Malatya, Turkiye,* [2]*Department of Business Administration, Faculty of Economics and Administrative Sciences, Nigde Omer Halisdemir University, Nigde, Turkiye,* [3]*Department of Transportation Services, Ardahan University, Göle, Ardahan, Turkey*

68.1 Introduction

There are various alternatives that have different characteristics in decision problems. It is difficult to choose the optimal one among them as there are many factors to consider. Therefore, an analytical approach is needed to compare these alternatives effectively and choose one alternative over others (Singh & Malik, 2014). multicriteria decision-making (MCDM) methods are useful tools to identify the best alternative in decision problems when there are many alternatives and conflicting criteria (Stević et al., 2020). MCDM methods are commonly used to solve complicated decision problems encountered in real life (Emovon & Oghenenyerovwho, 2020). The most popular MCDM methods are the technique for order of preference by similarity to ideal solution (TOPSIS) (Hwang, 1981), VlseKriterijumska Optimizacija I Kompromisno Resenje (VIKOR) (Opricovic, 1998), additive ratio assessment (ARAS) (Zavadskas & Turskis, 2010), multiobjective optimization by ratio analysis plus the full multiplicative form (MULTIMOORA) (Brauers & Zavadskas, 2010), weighted aggregated sum product assessment (WASPAS) (Zavadskas et al., 2012), and combined compromise solution (CoCoSo) (Stanujkić, Karabašević, et al., 2021; Yazdani et al., 2019). Although these methods are all MCDM methods, they differ in terms of normalization. TOPSIS uses a vector-based normalization process and the distance to ideal and antiideal solutions in Euclidean space. VIKOR uses the Minkovsky metric to measure distance and a unique normalization method. Simple additive weighting utilizes the sum of weighted and normalized performance criteria (Stanujkić, 2023).

Stanujkić, Popovic, et al. (2021) merged a few MCDM methods, which are the ARAS, WASPAS, CoCoSo, and MULTIMOORA methods, to develop a new technique, the simple weighted sum product (WISP) method. It utilizes the max normalization, which differs from other techniques and merges the weighted sum (WS) and weighted product (WP). This method uses a maximum value-based normalization process and does not differentiate between benefit and cost criteria (Stanujkić, 2023). It is easy to use for individuals who are not familiar with MCDM methods, as the calculation is easy to comprehend and adhere to (Ulutaş, Stanujkic, et al., 2022).

There are several studies in the literature using the WISP method. Stanujkić, Popovic, et al. (2021) analyzed the contractor and industrial robot alternatives. Karabašević et al. (2022) created the fuzzy version of the method. Stanujkic et al. (2022) developed the neutrosophic extension of WISP. Ulutaş, Topal, et al. (2022) evaluated the sustainable suppliers. Zavadskas et al. (2022) used square root and sum normalization in WISP analysis. Kirmizi et al. (2023) integrated the WISP, TOPSIS, and linear programming to choose the best design used in the drainage systems of ships. Stanujkic et al. (2023) compared investment projects. Diniz et al. (2024) used the WISP to select an airline. Rani, Mishra, et al. (2024) selected a location for a wind farm. Rani, Pamucar, et al. (2024) extended the WISP with interval-valued Pythagorean fuzzy to evaluate Industry 4.0 systems. Bulut (2025) assessed the capacity of the provincial health sector in

Encyclopedia of Multi-Attribute Decision-Making (MADM). DOI: https://doi.org/10.1016/B978-0-443-33275-3.00062-2

Turkey using the WISP. Mishra et al. (2025) developed a single-valued neutrosophic extension of the WISP to compare energy storage alternatives.

The main objective of this chapter is to present that the simple WISP approach can be used to solve both simple and complex decision problems. In the following part, the chapter methodology is explained. In the application 1 section, a simple decision problem with a small number of criteria and options is solved with the WISP. In application 2 section, a decision-making problem with a complex decision problem is solved with the WISP. The results are presented in detail, and ideas for future research are offered in conclusion.

68.2 Methodology

The steps of the simple WISP method are explained below according to Stanujkić, Popovic, et al. (2021):

Step 1. The decision matrix (D) is created based on the collected data.

$$D = [d_{ij}]_{m \times n} \tag{68.1}$$

d_{ij} represents the performance level or score of the alternative numbered i regarding the criteria j; m represents the total number of alternatives; and n represents the number of criteria.

Step 2. The decision matrix (D) containing m alternatives and n criteria is normalized by applying Eq. (68.2).

$$t_{ij} = \frac{d_{ij}}{d_j^{\max}} \tag{68.2}$$

t_{ij} represents a unit-independent value showing the normalized evaluation of the alternative numbered i according to the criteria j.

Step 3. The four utility function values are calculated as specified in Eqs (68.3)–(68.6).

$$\mathrm{v}_i^{wsd} = \sum_{j \in \Omega_{\max}} t_{ij} w_j - \sum_{j \in \Omega_{\min}} t_{ij} w_j \tag{68.3}$$

$$\mathrm{v}_i^{wpd} = \prod_{j \in \Omega_{\max}} t_{ij} w_j - \prod_{j \in \Omega_{\min}} t_{ij} w_j \tag{68.4}$$

$$\mathrm{v}_i^{wsr} = \frac{\sum_{j \in \Omega_{\max}} t_{ij} w_j}{\sum_{j \in \Omega_{\min}} t_{ij} w_j} \tag{68.5}$$

$$\mathrm{v}_i^{wpr} = \frac{\prod_{j \in \Omega_{\max}} t_{ij} w_j}{\prod_{j \in \Omega_{\min}} t_{ij} w_j} \tag{68.6}$$

v_i^{wsd} and v_i^{wpd} indicate the difference between the impact of beneficial and unbeneficial criteria on the final utility of alternative i obtained based on the WS and WP models, respectively. Likewise, v_i^{wsr} and v_i^{wpr} indicate the ratio between the impact of beneficial and nonbeneficial criteria on the final utility of alternative i obtained based on the WS and WP models, respectively.

Step 4. The four utility function values are calculated again as specified in Eqs (68.7)–(68.10).

$$\overline{\mathrm{v}}_i^{wsd} = \frac{1 + \mathrm{v}_i^{wsd}}{(1 + \mathrm{v}_{maxi}^{wsd})} \tag{68.7}$$

$$\overline{\mathrm{v}}_i^{wpd} = \frac{1 + \mathrm{v}_i^{wpd}}{\left(1 + \mathrm{v}_{maxi}^{wpd}\right)} \tag{68.8}$$

$$\overline{\mathrm{v}}_i^{wsr} = \frac{1 + \mathrm{v}_i^{wsr}}{(1 + \mathrm{v}_{maxi}^{wsr})} \tag{68.9}$$

$$\overline{\mathrm{v}}_i^{wpr} = \frac{1 + \mathrm{v}_i^{wpr}}{\left(1 + \mathrm{v}_{maxi}^{wpr}\right)} \tag{68.10}$$

$\overline{v}_i^{wsd}$, $\overline{v}_i^{wpd}$, $\overline{v}_i^{wsr}$ and $\overline{v}_i^{wpr}$ denote the normalized values of v_i^{wsd}, v_i^{wpd}, v_i^{wsr} , and v_i^{wpr}. The values of v_i^{wsd} and v_i^{wsr} can be negative, zero, or positive. Therefore, before calculating the total benefit level of each alternative, it must be converted to the range [0, 1] by applying Eqs. (68.7) and (68.11).

Step 5. The total benefit level v_i for all alternatives is calculated by applying Eq. (68.11).

$$v_i = \frac{1}{4}\left(\overline{v}_i^{wsd} + \overline{v}_i^{wpd} + \overline{v}_i^{wsr} + \overline{v}_i^{wpr}\right) \tag{68.11}$$

Step 6. The alternatives are ranked in decreasing order according to the benefit values obtained, and the alternative with the highest benefit value is evaluated as the most preferable option.

68.3 Numerical examples

In this chapter, two separate applications were carried out to demonstrate the applicability of the simple WISP method.

68.3.1 Numerical example 1

In the chapter, the decision matrix was derived using the Monte Carlo simulation technique. The criteria were determined using the equal weighting approach. While the C1 and C2 criteria in the matrix are beneficial criteria, the C3 and C4 criteria represent nonbeneficial criteria. Table 68.1 contains the data on the decision matrix used in the analysis.

All values in the decision matrix were normalized according to Eq. (68.2), and the normalized decision matrix is given in Table 68.2. How to calculate an element of a matrix t_{ij} is explained below.

$$t_{11} = \frac{26}{66} = 0.3939$$

Weighted criteria weights were calculated by multiplying the normalized values by the criteria weights. The calculated values are shown in Table 68.3. The mathematical calculation procedures are given below.

$$t_{11}^{*} = 0.3939 \times 0.25 = 0.0985$$

The methods described in Eqs (68.3)–(68.6) were applied to calculate the benefit scores. The calculated values are shown in Table 68.4. The mathematical operations of the calculations are shown below.

$$v_1^{wsd} = 0.\ 2020 - 0.\ 3748 = -0.\ 1728$$

$$v_1^{wpd} = 0.\ 0102 - 0.\ 0351 = -0.\ 0249$$

$$v_1^{wsr} = \frac{0.\ 2020}{0.\ 3748} = 0.\ 5390$$

TABLE 68.1 Decision matrix.

w_j	0.25	0.25	0.25	0.25
Criteria direction	Beneficial	Beneficial	Nonbeneficial	Nonbeneficial
	C1	C2	C3	C4
Alt1	26	36	29	65
Alt2	40	19	5	84
Alt3	44	56	40	23
Alt4	66	87	35	66
Alt5	51	18	9	75

TABLE 68.2 Normalized decision matrix.

	C1	C2	C3	C4
Alt1	0.3939	0.4138	0.7250	0.7738
Alt2	0.6061	0.2184	0.1250	1
Alt3	0.6667	0.6437	1	0.2738
Alt4	1	1	0.8750	0.7857
Alt5	0.7727	0.2069	0.2250	0.8929

TABLE 68.3 Weighted normalized decision matrix.

	C1	C2	C3	C4
Alt1	0.0985	0.1035	0.1813	0.1935
Alt2	0.1515	0.0546	0.0313	0.2500
Alt3	0.1667	0.1609	0.2500	0.0685
Alt4	0.2500	0.2500	0.2188	0.1964
Alt5	0.1932	0.0517	0.0563	0.2232

TABLE 68.4 Utility function values.

	v_i^{wsd}	v_i^{wpd}	v_i^{wsr}	v_i^{wpr}
Alt1	-0.1728	-0.0249	0.5390	0.2906
Alt2	-0.0752	0.0004	0.7327	1.0571
Alt3	0.0091	0.0097	1.0286	1.5662
Alt4	0.0848	0.0195	1.2042	1.4544
Alt5	-0.0346	-0.0026	0.8762	0.7949

$$v_1^{\text{wpr}} = \frac{0.\ 0102}{0.\ 0351} = 0.\ 2906$$

Four basic financial performance scores were obtained through Eqs (68.7)–(68.10). The overall performance evaluation was carried out according to Eq. (68.11), and the relevant analysis results are presented in Table 68.5. The mathematical operations of the calculations are shown below.

$$\overline{v}_1^{\text{wsd}} = \frac{1 + (-0.\ 1728)}{1 + 0.\ 0848} = 0.\ 7625$$

TABLE 68.5 Weighted sum product method performance values and rankings.

	$\overline{v}_i^{wsd}$	$\overline{v}_i^{wpd}$	$\overline{v}_i^{wsr}$	$\overline{v}_i^{wpr}$	v_i	Rank
Alt1	0.7625	0.9564	0.6982	0.5029	0.7300	5
Alt2	0.8525	0.9813	0.7861	0.8016	0.8554	3
Alt3	0.9302	0.9904	0.9203	1	0.9602	2
Alt4	1	1	1	0.9564	0.9891	1
Alt5	0.8899	0.9783	0.8512	0.6994	0.8547	4

$$\overline{v}_1^{wpd} = \frac{1 + (-0.\ 0249)}{1 + 0.\ 0195} = 0.\ 9564$$

$$\overline{v}_1^{wsr} = \frac{1 + 0.\ 5390}{1 + 1.\ 2042} = 0.\ 6982$$

$$\overline{v}_1^{wpr} = \frac{1 + 0.\ 2906}{1 + 1.\ 5662} = 0.\ 5029$$

$$v_1 = \frac{0.\ 7625 + 0.\ 9564 + 0.\ 6982 + 0.\ 5029}{4} = 0.\ 7300$$

According to the analysis findings regarding the simple WISP method shown in Table 68.5, the relative superiority order of the alternatives is as follows: Alt4 > Alt3 > Alt2 > Alt5 > Alt1.

68.3.2 Numerical example 2

The decision matrices used in the chapter were created by the Monte Carlo simulation method by considering four expert opinions. The initial decision matrix to be used in the final analysis was created by calculating the arithmetic means of the decision matrices created based on different expert opinions. Criteria weights were determined by an equal weighting approach. In the evaluation phase, 10 alternatives were analyzed based on seven different criteria. While the first three criteria in the matrix (C1, C2, and C3) are beneficial criteria, the last four criteria (C4, C5, C6, and C7) represent nonbeneficial criteria. Individual decision matrices of expert opinions are given in Table 68.6 (DM1), Table 68.7 (DM2), Table 68.8 (DM3) and Table 68.9 (DM4), respectively. Information on the initial decision matrix created by taking the arithmetic average of these matrices is given in Table 68.10.

$$d_{11} = \frac{670 + 348 + 314 + 154}{4} = 371.5$$

All values in the decision matrix were normalized according to Eq. (68.2); the resulting normalized decision matrix is given in Table 68.11. How to calculate an element of the matrix t_{ij} is explained below.

$$t_{11} = \frac{371.5}{786,\ 75} = 0.4722$$

Weighted criteria weights were calculated by multiplying the normalized values by the criteria weights. The calculated values are shown in Table 68.12. The mathematical calculation procedures are given below.

$$t_{11}^* = 0.4722 \times 0.1429 = 0.0675$$

The methods described in Eqs (68.3)–(68.6) were applied to calculate the benefit scores. The calculated values are shown in Table 68.13. The mathematical operations of the calculations are shown below.

$$v_1^{wsd} = 0.\ 3100 - 0.\ 3821 = -0.\ 0721$$

TABLE 68.6 Decision matrix of DM1.

w_j	0.1429	0.1429	0.1429	0.1429	0.1429	0.1429	0.1429
Criteria direction	**Beneficial**	**Beneficial**	**Beneficial**	**Nonbeneficial**	**Nonbeneficial**	**Nonbeneficial**	**Nonbeneficial**
	C1	**C2**	**C3**	**C4**	**C5**	**C6**	**C7**
Alt1	670	319	906	29	717	419	451
Alt2	786	296	649	658	30	669	900
Alt3	58	117	364	417	867	482	60
Alt4	562	326	127	623	73	704	317
Alt5	444	40	613	737	582	604	176
Alt6	735	717	49	565	969	900	76
Alt7	788	843	608	932	378	525	104
Alt8	65	612	315	158	402	584	712
Alt9	893	956	111	476	136	536	679
Alt10	443	228	13	688	233	442	585

TABLE 68.7 Decision matrix of DM2.

w_j	0.1429	0.1429	0.1429	0.1429	0.1429	0.1429	0.1429
	C1	**C2**	**C3**	**C4**	**C5**	**C6**	**C7**
Alt1	348	483	859	761	835	43	43
Alt2	963	696	425	897	236	305	206
Alt3	129	52	785	75	894	383	10
Alt4	948	537	778	266	954	782	922
Alt5	377	550	174	291	632	901	925
Alt6	172	928	514	129	770	309	19
Alt7	21	2	433	674	274	36	570
Alt8	618	606	762	487	266	766	496
Alt9	157	24	966	430	379	404	629
Alt10	719	720	132	308	277	666	931

$$v_1^{wpd} = 0.000961 - \left(5.7246E - 05\right) = 0.0009$$

$$v_1^{wsr} = \frac{0.3100}{0.3821} = 0.8113$$

TABLE 68.8 Decision matrix of DM3.

w_j	0.1429	0.1429	0.1429	0.1429	0.1429	0.1429	0.1429
	C1	C2	C3	C4	C5	C6	C7
Alt1	314	735	409	257	883	258	393
Alt2	555	275	459	257	370	756	646
Alt3	208	332	948	530	310	91	769
Alt4	613	457	514	119	619	195	619
Alt5	77	965	828	658	558	918	151
Alt6	449	645	725	448	526	759	469
Alt7	857	501	680	340	122	844	446
Alt8	342	852	926	482	889	746	124
Alt9	416	544	662	531	898	873	341
Alt10	336	874	908	148	371	549	827

TABLE 68.9 Decision matrix of DM4.

w_j	0.1429	0.1429	0.1429	0.1429	0.1429	0.1429	0.1429
	C1	C2	C3	C4	C5	C6	C7
Alt1	154	721	779	999	390	68	926
Alt2	843	334	504	217	522	832	822
Alt3	980	595	720	222	800	518	973
Alt4	267	571	434	289	862	403	742
Alt5	909	799	459	918	136	89	43
Alt6	356	949	885	715	449	724	345
Alt7	792	671	617	415	534	838	273
Alt8	180	328	745	355	152	634	701
Alt9	913	354	990	423	724	277	464
Alt10	877	262	739	538	469	654	602

$$v_1^{wpr} = \frac{0.000961}{(5.7246E-05)} = 16.7823$$

Four basic financial performance scores were obtained through Eqs (68.7)–(68.10). The overall performance evaluation was carried out according to Eq. (68.11), and the relevant analysis results are presented in Table 68.14. The mathematical operations of the calculations are shown below.

$$\overline{v}_1^{wsd} = \frac{1 + (-0.0721)}{1 + (-0.6600)} = 0.9935$$

TABLE 68.10 Initial decision matrix.

w_j	0.1429	0.1429	0.1429	0.1429	0.1429	0.1429	0.1429
	C1	C2	C3	C4	C5	C6	C7
Alt1	371.5	564.5	738.25	511.5	706.25	197	453.25
Alt2	786.75	400.25	509.25	507.25	289.5	640.5	643.5
Alt3	343.75	274	704.25	311	717.75	368.5	453
Alt4	597.5	472.75	463.25	324.25	627	521	650
Alt5	451.75	588.5	518.5	651	477	628	323.75
Alt6	428	809.75	543.25	464.25	678.5	673	227.25
Alt7	614.5	504.25	584.5	590.25	327	560.75	348.25
Alt8	301.25	599.5	687	370.5	427.25	682.5	508.25
Alt9	594.75	469.5	682.25	465	534.25	522.5	528.25
Alt10	593.75	521	448	420.5	337.5	577.75	736.25

TABLE 68.11 Normalized decision matrix.

	C1	C2	C3	C4	C5	C6	C7
Alt1	0.4722	0.6971	1	0.7857	0.9840	0.2886	0.6156
Alt2	1	0.4943	0.6898	0.7792	0.4033	0.9385	0.8740
Alt3	0.4369	0.3384	0.9539	0.4777	1	0.5399	0.6153
Alt4	0.7595	0.5838	0.6275	0.4981	0.8736	0.7634	0.8829
Alt5	0.5742	0.7268	0.7023	1	0.6646	0.9201	0.4397
Alt6	0.5440	1	0.7359	0.7131	0.9453	0.9861	0.3087
Alt7	0.7811	0.6227	0.7917	0.9067	0.4556	0.8216	0.4730
Alt8	0.3829	0.7404	0.9306	0.5691	0.5953	1	0.6903
Alt9	0.7560	0.5798	0.9241	0.7143	0.7443	0.7656	0.7175
Alt10	0.7547	0.6434	0.6068	0.6459	0.4702	0.8465	1

$$\overline{v}_1^{wpd} = \frac{1 + 0.0009}{1 + 0.0011} = 0.9998$$

$$\overline{v}_1^{wsr} = \frac{1 + 0.8113}{1 + 0.8262} = 0.9918$$

$$\overline{v}_1^{wpr} = \frac{1 + 16.7823}{1 + 16.7823} = 1$$

TABLE 68.12 Weighted normalized decision matrix.

	C1	C2	C3	C4	C5	C6	C7
Alt1	0.0675	0.0996	0.1429	0.1123	0.1406	0.0412	0.0880
Alt2	0.1429	0.0706	0.0986	0.1113	0.0576	0.1341	0.1249
Alt3	0.0624	0.0484	0.1363	0.0683	0.1429	0.0772	0.0879
Alt4	0.1085	0.0834	0.0897	0.0712	0.1248	0.1091	0.1262
Alt5	0.0821	0.1039	0.1004	0.1429	0.0950	0.1315	0.0628
Alt6	0.0777	0.1429	0.1052	0.1019	0.1351	0.1409	0.0441
Alt7	0.1116	0.0890	0.1131	0.1296	0.0651	0.1174	0.0676
Alt8	0.0547	0.1058	0.1330	0.0813	0.0851	0.1429	0.0986
Alt9	0.1080	0.0829	0.1321	0.1021	0.1064	0.1094	0.1025
Alt10	0.1078	0.0919	0.0867	0.0923	0.0672	0.1210	0.1429

TABLE 68.13 Utility function values.

	v_i^{wsd}	v_i^{wpd}	v_i^{wsr}	v_i^{wpr}
Alt1	-0.0721	0.0009	0.8113	16.7823
Alt2	-0.1158	0.0009	0.7294	9.2641
Alt3	-0.1292	0.0003	0.6567	6.2154
Alt4	-0.1497	0.0007	0.6529	6.6345
Alt5	-0.1458	0.0007	0.6627	7.6393
Alt6	-0.0962	0.0011	0.7720	13.6549
Alt7	-0.0660	0.0011	0.8262	16.7771
Alt8	-0.1144	0.0007	0.7195	7.8958
Alt9	-0.0974	0.0011	0.7683	9.7090
Alt10	-0.1370	0.0008	0.6764	8.0088

$$v_1 = \frac{0.9935 + 0.9998 + 0.9918 + 1}{4} = 0.9963$$

According to the analysis findings regarding the simple WISP method shown in Table 68.14, the relative superiority order of the alternatives is as follows: Alt7 > Alt1 > Alt6 > Alt9 > Alt2 > Alt8 > Alt10 > Alt5 > Alt3 = Alt4.

TABLE 68.14 Weighted sum product method performance values and rankings.

	$\overline{v}_i^{wsd}$	$\overline{v}_i^{wpd}$	$\overline{v}_i^{wsr}$	$\overline{v}_i^{wpr}$	v_i	Rank
Alt1	0.9935	0.9998	0.9918	1	0.9963	2
Alt2	0.9467	0.9998	0.9470	0.5772	0.8677	5
Alt3	0.9323	0.9992	0.9072	0.4058	0.8111	9
Alt4	0.9104	0.9996	0.9051	0.4293	0.8111	9
Alt5	0.9146	0.9996	0.9105	0.4858	0.8276	8
Alt6	0.9677	1	0.9703	0.8241	0.9405	3
Alt7	1	1	1	0.9997	0.9999	1
Alt8	0.9482	0.9996	0.9416	0.5003	0.8474	6
Alt9	0.9664	1	0.9683	0.6022	0.8842	4
Alt10	0.9240	0.9997	0.9180	0.5066	0.8371	7

68.4 Conclusion

In today's complex and multidimensional decision-making environments, MCDM methods are an important tool for solving problems encountered in various fields. Numerous different methods have been developed and published in the literature to meet the needs of decision-makers. These methods incorporate various mathematical and analytical approaches to contribute to the decision-making process. Some of these methods are based on hybrid models that use the well-established and widely used techniques of WS and WP in combination or in comparison. Methods that integrate these two approaches offer the opportunity to implement both criteria weighting and alternative evaluation with greater flexibility and complexity. The continued use of established approaches such as WS and WP in various forms demonstrates the soundness of their theoretical foundations and their practical success. The simple WISP method is an MCDM method that integrates WS and WP.

In this chapter, two numerical examples were solved to present the usability of the simple WISP method. The first one is a basic example that explains the process in a simple decision problem. The second one is a complicated example as it involves several decision-makers, criteria, and alternatives. It shows how effective WISP is in group decision-making.

Alternatives are ordered as Alt4 > Alt3 > Alt2 > Alt5 > Alt1 in the first example. This shows that the simple WISP method can effectively outline the difference between alternatives and rank them easily in basic decision problems. The second example shows that alternatives are ordered as Alt7 > Alt1 > Alt6 > Alt9 > Alt2 > Alt8 > Alt10 > Alt5 > Alt3 = Alt4. It can be concluded that the simple WISP can present the difference between alternatives in a meaningful way when there are a lot of complicated criteria to consider.

The simple WISP method can be applied to solve decision problems successfully in various areas such as sustainability, energy, operations, logistics, manufacturing, and so on. As it has a flexible process, it can be used in either basic decision matrices or extended ones, such as fuzzy, gray, and rough. It can also be integrated with other MCDM methods to make a comprehensive decision model or be used as a method in comparative analyses.

References

Brauers, W. K. M., & Zavadskas, E. K. (2010). Project management by MULTIMOORA as an instrument for transition economies. *Technological and Economic Development of Economy, 16*(1), 5–24. https://doi.org/10.3846/tede.2010.01.

Bulut, T. (2025). Evaluation of Turkish health system capacity at provincial level by WISP method based on weighting methods. *Journal of Productivity, 59*(1), 143–166. https://doi.org/10.51551/verimlilik.1549245.

Diniz, B. P., de Moura Pereira, D. A., dos Santos, M., Moreira, M.Â. L., de Moraes, A. B., Pereira, F. R. R., de Oliveira Costa, D., Araújo, G. N., & Neto, J. C. (2024). New approach to choosing an aircraft carrier for Brazil from the AHP and WISP multicriteria decision methods. *Procedia Computer Science, 242*, 544–551. https://doi.org/10.1016/j.procs.2024.08.102.

Emovon, I., & Oghenenyerovwho, O. S. (2020). Application of MCDM method in material selection for optimal design: A review. *Results in Materials, 7*, 100115. https://doi.org/10.1016/j.rinma.2020.100115.

Hwang, C. L. (1981). *Multiple attribute decision making: Methods and applications*. Boca Raton: CRC Press.

Karabašević, D., Ulutaş, A., Stanujkić, D., Saračević, M., & Popović, G. (2022). A new fuzzy extension of the simple WISP method. *Axioms, 11*(7), 332. https://doi.org/10.3390/axioms11070332.

Kirmizi, M., Karakas, S., & Uçar, H. (2023). Selecting the optimal naval ship drainage system design alternative based on integer linear programming, TOPSIS, and simple WISP methods. *Journal of Ship Production and Design, 39*(02), 63–74. https://doi.org/10.5957/JSPD.01220003.

Mishra, A. R., Pamucar, D., Rani, P., & Hezam, I. M. (2025). Single-valued neutrosophic distance measure-based MEREC-RANCOM-WISP for solving sustainable energy storage technology problem. *Cognitive Computation, 17*(2), 87. https://doi.org/10.1007/s12559-025-10437-x.

Rani, P., Mishra, A. R., Cavallaro, F., & Alrasheedi, A. F. (2024). Location selection for offshore wind power station using interval-valued intuitionistic fuzzy distance measure-RANCOM-WISP method. *Scientific Reports, 14*(1), 4706. https://doi.org/10.1038/s41598-024-54929-6.

Rani, P., Pamucar, D., Mishra, A. R., Hezam, I. M., Ali, J., & Ahammad, S. H. (2024). An integrated interval-valued Pythagorean fuzzy WISP approach for industry 4.0 technology assessment and digital transformation. *Annals of Operations Research, 342*(2), 1235–1274. https://doi.org/10.1007/s10479-023-05355-w.

Singh, A., & Malik, S. K. (2014). Major MCDM techniques and their application-a review. *IOSR Journal of Engineering, 4*(5), 15–25.

Stanujkić, M. (2023). Comparative analysis of MULTIMOORA, WASPAS and WISP methods: The case of candidate selection. *Journal of Process Management and New Technologies, 11*(3-4), 79–88. https://doi.org/10.5937/jpmnt11-47703.

Stanujkic, D., Fedajev, A., & Santos, M. (2023). Investment projects evaluation in a fuzzy environment using the simplified WISP method. *Serbian Journal of Management, 18*(2), 225–235. https://doi.org/10.5937/sjm18-44522.

Stanujkic, D., Karabasevic, D., Popovic, G., Smarandache, F., Stanimirović, P. S., Saračević, M., & Katsikis, V. N. (2022). A single valued neutrosophic extension of the simple WISP method. *Informatica, 33*(3), 635–651. https://doi.org/10.15388/22-INFOR483.

Stanujkić, D., Karabašević, D., Popović, G., Zavadskas, E. K., Saračević, M., Stanimirović, P. S., Ulutaş, A., Katsikis, V., & Meidute-Kavaliauskiene, I. (2021). Comparative analysis of the simple WISP and some prominent MCDM methods: A Python approach. *Axioms, 10*(4), 347. https://doi.org/10.3390/axioms10040347.

Stanujkić, D., Popovic, G., Karabasevic, D., Meidute-Kavaliauskiene, I., & Ulutaş, A. (2021). An integrated simple weighted sum product method—WISP. *IEEE Transactions on Engineering Management, 70*(5), 1933–1944. https://doi.org/10.1109/TEM.2021.3075783.

Stević, Ž., Pamučar, D., Puška, A., & Chatterjee, P. (2020). Sustainable supplier selection in healthcare industries using a new MCDM method: Measurement of alternatives and ranking according to COmpromise solution (MARCOS). *Computers & Industrial Engineering, 140*, 106231. https://doi.org/10.1016/j.cie.2019.106231.

Opricovic, S. (1998). *Multicriteria optimization of civil engineering systems*. PhD Thesis, Faculty of Civil Engineering, University of Belgrade, Belgrad, Serbia.

Ulutaş, A., Stanujkic, D., Karabasevic, D., Popovic, G., & Novaković, S. (2022). Pallet truck selection with MEREC and WISP-S methods. *Strategic Management-International Journal of Strategic Management and Decision Support Systems in Strategic Management, 27*(4). https://doi.org/10.5937/StraMan2200013U%20.

Ulutaş, A., Topal, A., Pamučar, D., Stević, Ž., Karabašević, D., & Popović, G. (2022). A new integrated multi-criteria decision-making model for sustainable supplier selection based on a novel grey WISP and grey BWM methods. *Sustainability, 14*(24), 16921. https://doi.org/10.3390/su142416921.

Yazdani, M., Wen, Z., Liao, H., Banaitis, A., & Turskis, Z. (2019). A grey combined compromise solution (CoCoSo-G) method for supplier selection in construction management. *Journal of Civil Engineering and Management, 25*(8), 858–874. https://doi.org/10.3846/jcem.2019.11309.

Zavadskas, E. K., Stanujkic, D., Karabasevic, D., & Turskis, Z. (2022). Analysis of the simple WISP method results using different normalization procedures. *Studies in Informatics and Control, 31*(1), 5–12. https://doi.org/10.24846/v31i1y202201.

Zavadskas, E. K., & Turskis, Z. (2010). A new additive ratio assessment (ARAS) method in multicriteria decision-making. *Technological and Economic Development of Economy, 16*(2), 159–172. https://doi.org/10.3846/tede.2010.10.

Zavadskas, E. K., Turskis, Z., Antucheviciene, J., & Zakarevicius, A. (2012). Optimization of weighted aggregated sum product assessment. *Elektronika ir elektrotechnika, 122*(6), 3–6. https://doi.org/10.5755/j01.eee.122.6.1810.

Chapter 69

SD–MCRAT: Standard deviation–multiple criteria ranking by alternative trace for multi-attribute decision-making

Osman Yakıt[1], Nazlı Ersoy[2], Mustafa Kocaoğlu[3], and Mustafa Kavacık[3]
[1]*Akdeniz University, Antalya, Türkiye,* [2]*Osmaniye Korkut Ata University, Osmaniye, Türkiye,* [3]*Necmettin Erbakan University, Konya, Türkiye*

69.1 Introduction

In engineering applications, the material selection process holds critical importance, as it directly affects a product's performance, longevity, and expense of a product. Selecting appropriate materials is important to ensure the product's functionality, productivity, and long-term usability (Trung et al., 2024). The development and use of a materials selection process, based on decision theory and information processing principles, is critical at the design stage of a new material (Omosa et al., 2024).

Multi-criteria decision-making (MCDM) techniques are gaining attention in the field of material selection technology in an attempt to avoid poor choices made and to provide the same, rational, and reproducible methodology that is applied to engineering (Hosouli et al., 2023). MCDM is a widely accepted technique applied in various fields to facilitate decision-making whenever multiple and sometimes conflicting criteria need to be considered. Unlike conventional methods, which aim only at one factor, MCDM evaluates alternatives on the basis of different criteria and their significance, supports decision-makers (DMs) to set preferences among alternatives, and makes the best decisions (Zakeri et al., 2025). MCDM is a discipline within the field of operations research, which deals with solving problems that are characterized by multicriteria, frequently contradictory (Tavana et al., 2024). In MCDM, a DM chooses from a finite number of alternatives after comparing these alternatives in terms of multiple criteria (Wan et al., 2021).

MCDM methods provide structured and rational methods of incorporating the varying importance of the criteria in decision-making across alternatives, and have been widely applied in optimization of supply chain (Wang et al., 2024), energy planning (Akpahou et al., 2024), resource allocation in health care (Yang et al., 2022), sustainable development evaluations (Seker, 2025), etc. The MCDM methods have been increasing gradually over recent decades (Cinelli et al., 2022; Madanchian & Taherdoost, 2025; Taherdoost & Madanchian, 2023), and it is expected that at least 200 different MCDM methods have been presented in the published literature (Baydaş et al., 2023; Danesh et al., 2017).

Among the methods in this classification, the standard deviation (SD) method (Diakoulaki et al., 1995) has been widely applied in MCDM studies, particularly for addressing complex and uncertain problems such as those encountered in material selection (Jahan et al., 2012), financial performance analysis (Baydaş & Pamučar, 2022), and sustainability development assessment (Deepa et al., 2019). The multiple criteria ranking by alternative trace (MCRAT) method, introduced by Urošević et al. (2021), is a more recent development. This approach uses the concept of perimeter similarity for ranking the alternatives. The technique, although being fairly novel, has become highly recommended among researchers taking about different subjects (Ersoy et al., 2026; Son et al., 2025; Stević et al., 2024; Shaaban et al., 2025; Van Dua, 2024).

In this study, material selection was carried out for two distinct engineering applications using an MCDM approach. In the first scenario, material selection was performed for gear manufacturing, while in the second scenario, it was conducted for bearings production. In both applications, the most suitable material was identified using the SD–MCRAT model. The contributions of this paper are: (i) The usage of the MCDM method for two different engineering cases of material

Encyclopedia of Multi-Attribute Decision-Making (MADM). DOI: https://doi.org/10.1016/B978-0-443-33275-3.00099-3

selection has integrated a systematic and unbiased manner of decision-making about different alternatives. (ii) A thorough evaluation of different methods for criteria weighting and ranking has established new trends in the efficiency and reputation of these techniques. (iii) The new application of the SD–MCRAT model, applied in a material selection problem, for the first time in the literature, has increased its practical application and suggests a new methodological framework.

The rest of this study is structured as follows: Section 69.2 reviews the literature on material selection problems and the application of MCDM methods to these problems. Section 69.3 provides the theoretical foundations and detailed steps of the SD and MCRAT methods employed in the study. Section 69.4 provides the application of the SD–MCRAT approach to material selection within the scope of two distinct engineering scenarios. In Section 69.5, the obtained results are evaluated through a comparative analysis. Finally, Section 69.6 outlines the main results of the research.

69.2 Literature review

Selection of material is a basic step in design and manufacturing which affect the product performance, cost, and sustainability. The application of MCDM in various material selection problems has been documented by various authors. For instance, (Trung et al., 2024) applied the entropy-(combined compromise solution) model to select the appropriate material for piston and cylinder systems of heavy-duty mechanical and hydraulic systems, and performed a comprehensive sensitivity analysis to prove that the results stand up strongly (Anojkumar et al., 2014) applied four fuzzy analytic hierarchy process-based MCDM methods to select pipe materials for the sugar industry and found VlseKriterijumska Optimizacija I Kompromisno Resenje to be the most effective in ranking stainless steel alternatives across seven criteria (Rathod and Kanzaria, 2011) developed a hybrid analytic hierarchy process–entropy–technique for order of preference by similarity to ideal solution (TOPSIS) approach for selecting optimal phase change materials based on combined subjective and objective criteria weights (Mousavi-Nasab and Sotoudeh-Anvari, 2017) applied an integrated MCDM framework combining complex proportional assessment and TOPSIS for general material selection problems, supported by a review of over 100 studies (Van Dua et al., 2024) integrated five objective weighting methods with three MCDM techniques to evaluate material selection across three industrial cases, concluding that the Magnitude of the Area for the Ranking of Alternatives (MARA), Root Assessment Method (RAM), and proximity indexed value (PIV) exhibit different suitability depending on the application, with logarithmic percentage change-driven objective weighting (LOPCOW) and entropy producing notably contrasting weight patterns.

Hosouli et al. (2023) applied a graph theory and matrix approach-based MCDM method to select optimal materials for high-temperature thermochemical energy storage in industrial waste heat recovery, identifying the best candidate for use in a steelworks operating above 500°C (Chatterjee and Chakraborty, 2021) employed decision-making trial and evaluation laboratory to analyze interrelationships among selection criteria and applied a novel MCDM method to rank mechanical component materials, validating the results through Spearman's rank correlation (Maity et al., 2023) applied MCDM techniques to evaluate and rank five common materials for flying robot wing structures, considering mechanical and vibration resistance properties, to guide optimal material selection in drone design (Kumar et al., 2025) applied four MCDM methods combined with method based on the removal effects of criteria to select optimal coating materials for sheet metal forming, confirming the robustness of TOPSIS rankings through multistep sensitivity analysis (Omosa et al., 2024) used entropy based grey relation analysis and TOPSIS methods to evaluate and rank eight shape memory polymer matrix materials based on nine criteria, identifying thermoplastic polyurethane as the optimal choice (Alinezhad and Khalili, 2024) discussed the integration of MCDM and data envelopment analysis methods for material selection and efficiency evaluation, highlighting their complementary strengths through automotive parts manufacturing case studies (Şahin, 2024) proposed an ensemble MCDM approach that incorporates four weighting methods and five ranking techniques for material selection, applying it to various problems and demonstrating that the combination of methods yields more reliable results.

69.3 Methodology

This section provides detailed explanations of the methods employed in the study. Accordingly, the mathematical formulations of the SD method, used for criteria weighting, are presented first, followed by the MCRAT method, which is utilized for evaluating the alternatives.

69.3.1 Standard deviation method

This method (Diakoulaki et al., 1995) places low importance on criteria showing little variation across the alternatives, similar to the entropy approach (Jahan et al., 2012). The steps of the method are as follows (Baydaş & Pamučar, 2022; Diakoulaki et al., 1995).

Step 1. The decision matrix is normalized.

$$F_{ij} = \frac{f_{ij} - \min_{i\in m f_{ij}}}{\max_{i\in m f_{ij}} - \min_{i\in m f_{ij}}} \text{ (for benefit)} \tag{69.1}$$

$$F_{ij} = \frac{\max_{i\in m f_{ij}} - f_{ij}}{\max_{i\in m f_{ij}} - \min_{i\in m f_{ij}}} \text{ (for cost)} \tag{69.2}$$

Step 2. The SD of each ranking is calculated.

$$\sigma_j = \sqrt{\frac{\sum_{i=1}^{m} (F_{ij} - \overline{F_j})^2}{m}} \; j \in \{1,\ 2,\ \ldots,\ n\} \tag{69.3}$$

Step 3. The criteria weights are calculated.

$$w_j = \frac{\sigma_j}{\sum_{k=1}^{m} \sigma_k} \tag{69.4}$$

69.3.2 Multiple criteria ranking by alternative trace method

The MCRAT method, developed by Urošević et al. (2021), which utilizes the principle of environmental similarity in the ranking of alternatives, is outlined in the stages below (Urošević et al., 2021).

Step 1. Normalizing input data: first, the decision matrix is normalized.

$$r_{ij} = \frac{x_{ij}}{\max_i(x_{ij})}, \quad \forall_i \in [1,\ 2,\ \ldots,\ m] \wedge j \in S_{\max} \textit{ (for maximum or benefit)} \tag{69.5}$$

$$r'_{ij} = \frac{\min_i(x_{ij})}{x_{ij}}, \quad \forall_i \in [1,\ 2,\ \ldots,\ m] \wedge j \in S_{\min} \textit{ (for minimum or cost)} \tag{69.6}$$

Here, $S_{\max}$ represents a set of criteria that must be maximized, and $S_{\min}$ represents a set of criteria that must be minimized, and as a result of the relevant normalization process, a normalized decision matrix is obtained in the form of $R = [r_{ij}]_{mxn}$.

Step 2. Weighting of normalized data: in this step, the weighted matrix is generated.

$$u_{ij} = w_j r_{ij}, \quad \forall_i \in [1,\ 2,\ \ldots,\ m], \quad \forall_j \in [1,\ 2,\ \ldots,\ n] \tag{69.7}$$

The weighted matrix here is of the form $U = [u_{ij}]_{mxn}$.

Step 3. Determination of optimum alternative: each element of the optimum alternative is determined according to (69.8), and the optimum alternative is represented by the set in (69.9):

$$q_j = (\max\ (u_{ij}) | 1 \le j \le n), \; \forall_i \in [1, 2, \ldots, m] \tag{69.8}$$

$$Q = \{q_1,\ q_2,\ \ldots,\ q_j\}, \quad j = 1,\ 2,\ \ldots,\ n \tag{69.9}$$

Step 4. Disintegration of the optimum alternative: the optimum alternative is decomposed into two distinct components.

$$Q = Q^{\max} \cup Q^{\min} \tag{69.10}$$

k is the number of criteria to be maximized, and $h=n-k$ represents the number of criteria to be minimized. Therefore, the optimum alternative is specified as:

$$Q = \{q_1,\ q_2,\ \ldots,\ q_k\} \cup \{q_1, q_2, \ldots, q_h\}, \; k + h = j \tag{69.11}$$

Step 5. Disintegration of the alternative: each alternative is disintegrated using a logic similar to that in the fourth step:

$$U_i = U_i^{\max} \cup U_i^{\min}, \quad \forall_i \in [1,\ 2,\ \ldots,\ m] \tag{69.12}$$

$$U_i = \{u_{i1},\ u_{i2},\ \dots,\ u_{ik}\} \cup \{u_{i1},\ u_{i2},\ \dots,\ u_{ih}\}, \quad \forall_i \in [1,\ 2,\ \dots,\ m] \tag{69.13}$$

Step 6. Calculating component magnitude: the magnitude of each component of the optimum alternative is calculated using Eqs. (69.14) and (69.15).

$$Q_k = \sqrt{q_1^2 + q_2^2 + ..+q_k^2} \tag{69.14}$$

$$Q_h = \sqrt{q_1^2 + q_2^2 + ..+q_h^2} \tag{69.15}$$

For each alternative the same approach is utilized.

$$U_{ik} = \sqrt{u_{i1}^2 + u_{i2}^2+\dots+u_{ik}^2}, \quad \forall_i \in [1,\ 2,\ \dots,\ m] \tag{69.16}$$

$$U_{ih} = \sqrt{u_{i1}^2 + u_{i2}^2+\dots+u_{ih}^2}, \quad \forall_i \in [1,\ 2,\ \dots,\ m] \tag{69.17}$$

Step 6.1. Finding rankings according to MCRAT: the following substeps are performed.
Step 6.1.1. The F matrix consisting of the optimum alternative components is created.

$$F = \begin{bmatrix} Q_k & 0 \\ 0 & Q_h \end{bmatrix} \tag{69.18}$$

Step 6.1.2. In addition, G_i matrix consisting of alternative components is created.

$$G_i = \begin{bmatrix} U_{ik} & 0 \\ 0 & U_{ih} \end{bmatrix}, \quad \forall_i \in [1,\ 2,\ \dots,\ m] \tag{69.19}$$

Step 6.1.3. The matrix T_i, which is the product of matrices F and G_i, is obtained.

$$T_i = F\ x\ G_i = \begin{bmatrix} t_{11;i} & 0 \\ 0 & t_{22;i} \end{bmatrix}, \quad \forall_i \in [1,\ 2,\ \dots,\ m] \tag{69.20}$$

Step 6.1.4. And thus, the trace of the T matrix becomes:

$$tr\,(T_i) = t_{11;i} + t_{22;i}, \quad \forall_i \in [1,\ 2,\ \dots,\ m] \tag{69.21}$$

Ranking of the alternatives is performed based on the descending values (T_i).

69.3.3 The Spearman rank correlation coefficient

The Spearman rank correlation coefficient is employed to quantify the observed similarity in scores produced by MCDM methods, and is computed as follows (Chatterjee & Chakraborty, 2014):

$$r_s = 1 - 6\frac{\sum_{i=1}^{m} D_i^2}{m\,(m^2 - 1)} \tag{69.22}$$

69.4 Numerical example 1

This section will focus on the selection of various materials used in the production of gear components. All data used in this example are hypothetically generated, and the criteria are symbolized as C1–C6, respectively. All these criteria belong to type B. Table 69.1 shows the material types used in the production of gears.

First, (69.1) is used for normalization, and the obtained results are presented in Table 69.2. For the A1 row and the C1 column; $\frac{255-210}{425-210} = 0.209$.

SD of each ranking is calculated using (69.3), and finally, criteria weights are determined using Eq. (69.4). All results are presented in Table 69.3.

According to the weights obtained through the SD method, criterion C4 (18.32%) has the highest impact, while C1 (15.67%) has the lowest weight. This distribution indicates a reasonable balance among the criteria and highlights that C4 plays a more prominent role in the decision-making process.

TABLE 69.1 Alternative materials for producing a gear component.

	C1	C2	C3	C4	C5	C6
A1	255	58.2	92.1	41	39	46
A2	228	69	36.5	40	15	16
A3	240	42.1	71.4	25	47	41
A4	210	75.3	63.8	30	34	32
A5	315	35.6	40.2	29	45	33
A6	425	26.1	78.4	26	26	13

TABLE 69.2 Normalization decision matrix.

	C1	C2	C3	C4	C5	C6
A1	0.209	0.652	1.000	1.000	0.750	1.000
A2	0.084	0.872	0.000	0.938	0.000	0.091
A3	0.140	0.325	0.628	0.000	1.000	0.848
A4	0.000	1.000	0.491	0.313	0.594	0.576
A5	0.488	0.193	0.067	0.250	0.938	0.606
A6	1.000	0.000	0.754	0.063	0.344	0.000

TABLE 69.3 Standard deviation values and the corresponding criteria weights.

	C1	C2	C3	C4	C5	C6
σ	0.373	0.396	0.392	0.436	0.380	0.401
$\sum\sigma$	2.377	2.377	2.377	2.377	2.377	2.377
w_j	0.1567	0.1668	0.1649	0.1832	0.1598	0.1686

To apply the MCRAT method, normalization was first performed using (69.5). The weighted decision matrix was then constructed using (69.7) and all decimal places of the weights given in Table 69.3 (see Table 69.4). The optimum alternative and its disintegration were determined considering Eqs. 69.8–69.11 as shown in Table 69.5.

Table 69.6, prepared by considering Eqs. 69.12 and 69.13 illustrate the decomposition of each alternative to reach the optimum solution.

In the subsequent stage of the selection process, the magnitudes of the optimum and other components were calculated considering Eqs. (69.14–69.17), and the results obtained are presented in Table 69.7.

As a result of the evaluation conducted using the MCRAT method, alternative A1 was recognized as the optimum material, having the highest T_i value (0.14864), while A6, with the lowest T_i value, ranked last. The ranking of the T_i values aligns with the projection traces, indicating consistency in the results and clearly demonstrating the superiority of A1 over the other alternatives. The overall ranking is as follows: A1 > A3 > A4> A5 > A2 > A6.

TABLE 69.4 Normalized and weighted decision matrix.

	Normalized decision matrix						Weighted decision matrix					
	C1	C2	C3	C4	C5	C6	C1	C2	C3	C4	C5	C6
A1	0.600	0.773	1	1	0.830	1	0.094	0.129	0.165	0.183	0.133	0.169
A2	0.536	0.916	0.396	0.976	0.319	0.348	0.084	0.153	0.065	0.179	0.051	0.059
A3	0.565	0.559	0.775	0.610	1	0.891	0.088	0.093	0.128	0.112	0.160	0.150
A4	0.494	1	0.693	0.732	0.723	0.696	0.077	0.167	0.114	0.134	0.116	0.117
A5	0.741	0.473	0.436	0.707	0.957	0.717	0.116	0.079	0.072	0.130	0.153	0.121
A6	1	0.347	0.851	0.634	0.553	0.283	0.157	0.058	0.140	0.116	0.088	0.048

TABLE 69.5 Optimum/disintegration of the optimum alternative.

	C1	C2	C3	C4	C5	C6
Optimum alternative	Max	Max	Max	Max	Max	Max
	q1	*q2*	*q3*	*q4*	*q5*	*q6*
Q	0.1567	0.1668	0.1649	0.1832	0.1598	0.1686
Disintegration of the optimum alternative						
Q^{max}	0.1567	0.1668	0.1649	0.1832	0.1598	0.1686
Q^{min}	-	-	-	-	-	-

TABLE 69.6 Disintegration of alternatives.

	C1	C2	C3	C4	C5	C6
	u1	*u2*	*u3*	*u4*	*u5*	*u6*
A1 U^{max}	0.094	0.129	0.165	0.183	0.133	0.169
A1 U^{min}	—	—	—	—	—	—
A2 U^{max}	0.084	0.153	0.065	0.179	0.051	0.059
A2 U^{min}	—	—	—	—	—	—
A3 U^{max}	0.088	0.093	0.128	0.112	0.160	0.150
A3 U^{min}	—	—	—	—	—	—
A4 U^{max}	0.077	0.167	0.114	0.134	0.116	0.117
A4 U^{min}	—	—	—	—	—	—
A5 U^{max}	0.116	0.079	0.072	0.130	0.153	0.121
A5 U^{min}	—	—	—	—	—	—
A6 U^{max}	0.157	0.058	0.140	0.116	0.088	0.048
A6 U^{min}	—	—	—	—	—	—

TABLE 69.7 Magnitude of optimum alternative and alternatives.

	Max	Min	Trace	Value	Rank
	Qk	*Qh*			
Q	**0,4088**	—			
Alternative	υ_{ik}	υ_{ih}			
A1	0.36362	—	$tr(T_1)$	0.14864	1
A2	0.26960	—	$tr(T_2)$	0.11020	5
A3	0.30574	—	$tr(T_3)$	0.12498	2
A4	0.30324	—	$tr(T_4)$	0.12395	3
A5	0.28237	—	$tr(T_5)$	0.11542	4
A6	0.26679	—	$tr(T_6)$	0.10906	6

69.5 Numerical example 2

In this section, the selection of seven commonly used materials in bearing manufacturing is aimed. All data used in this example are hypothetically generated. Seven alternatives and eight criteria were used to characterize each material. Among the eight evaluation criteria used in this study, only C6 and C8 are considered cost-oriented, all remaining criteria are defined as benefit-oriented. Table 69.8 shows the decision matrix.

First, Eqs. (69.1–69.4) were utilized to determine the criteria weights using the SD method, and the results are summarized in Table 69.9.

According to the weights obtained using the SD method, criteria C5 (14.30%) and C3 (14.05%) are the most influential, while C7 (11.16%) holds the least importance. Using the criteria weights from Table 69.9, the seven alternatives were ranked with the MCRAT method, and the results are also summarized in Table 69.10.

According to the results in Table 69.10, alternative A3 was recognized as the optimal material with the highest T_i value of 0.1179. Alternatives A2 (T_i= 0.1169) and A1 (T_i= 0.1142) ranked second and third, respectively, standing out as other strong candidates. These three alternatives are more advantageous compared to the others in terms of decision criteria. On the other hand, alternatives A4, A5, A6, and A7 received lower T_i values and occupied the lower ranks. In particular, A4 (T_i= 0.1051) was evaluated as the material with the poorest performance. These results indicate that A3 is the most balanced and preferable option in the MCDM process.

69.6 Comparative analysis

Validation of the ranking results generated from a particular MCDM model is an important test (Biswas et al., 2024). The legitimacy and reliability of the presented results by the proposed technique are examined in this section through comparison with the results obtained from other algorithms.

In each case, the performance of the SD–MCRAT model will be compared to MCRAT results produced using entropy, WENSLO, symmetry point of criterion (SPC), and LOPCOW weighting techniques. Finally, the MCRAT results will be validated by comparing them with the results obtained from SD-based simple additive weighting (SAW), weighted aggregated sum product assessment (WASPAS), TOPSIS, compromise ranking of alternatives from distance to ideal solution (CRADIS), and PIV methods. The reason for choosing these methods is their practical applicability and ease of mechanization.

Firstly, the proposed model will be evaluated according to the Spearman rank correlation test with the results obtained with various weighting techniques and ranking methods. Finally, the stability of the resulting rankings will be examined through the R-score method. To objectively evaluate these combinations, stability is expressed as the ratio of the highest to the lowest score and is called R-score, with low R-score values corresponding to higher stability (Zavadskas & Podvezko, 2016).

TABLE 69.8 Materials for bearing manufacturing.

Material	C1	C2	C3	C4	C5	C6	C7	C8
A1	2.73	72.5	185	102	955	89	120	22.3
A2	2.69	72.8	197	120	958	83	95	20.1
A3	2.84	71.3	208	131	960	76	78	23
A4	2.77	72.6	135	97	875	95	98	21.5
A5	3.15	72.9	128	128	845	92	82	24.2
A6	2.93	71.8	108	138	868	88	72	19.4
A7	2.87	71.9	112	108	885	78	85	20.9

TABLE 69.9 Final criteria weights (example 2).

C1	C2	C3	C4	C5	C6	C7	C8
0.1120	0.1245	0.1405	0.1273	0.1430	0.1248	0.1116	0.1163
11.20%	12.45%	14.05%	12.73%	14.30%	12.48%	11.16%	11.63%

TABLE 69.10 Magnitude of optimum alternative and alternatives.

	Max	Min	Trace	Value	Rank
	Qk	Qh			
Q	0.3113	0.1706			
Alternative	υ_{ik}	υ_{ih}			
A1	0.0891	0.0251	$tr(T_1)$	0.1142	3
A2	0.0895	0.0273	$tr(T_2)$	0.1169	2
A3	0.0908	0.0271	$tr(T_3)$	0.1179	1
A4	0.0804	0.0247	$tr(T_4)$	0.1051	7
A5	0.0830	0.0237	$tr(T_5)$	0.1067	6
A6	0.0816	0.0270	$tr(T_6)$	0.1086	4
A7	0.0792	0.0277	$tr(T_7)$	0.1070	5

69.6.1 Comparative analysis for numerical example 1

In this section, the correlation between the SD–MCRAT model and rankings obtained using other criteria, weighting, and ranking techniques is first examined. The results are presented in Table 69.11. Subsequently, the R-score values of the SD method and four other weighting techniques are provided in Table 69.12.

TABLE 69.11 Spearman's coefficient between the MCRAT method based on various techniques (example 1).

MCRAT					
	Standard deviation (SD)	**Entropy**	**WENSLO**	**SPC**	**LOPCOW**
SD		0.911	0.992	0.939	0.891
Entropy			0.858	0.995	0.985
WENSLO				0.894	0.839
SPC					0.988
SD–MCRAT	SD–SAW	SD–WASPAS	SD–TOPSIS	SD–CRADIS	SD–PIV
	0.9636	0.9494	0.9480	0.9857	0.9429

TABLE 69.12 R-score ratios across different weighting techniques (example 1).

	Standard deviation (SD)	**Entropy**	**WENSLO**	**SPC**	**LOPCOW**
C1	0.15669	0.10288	0.16379	0.14557	0.07512
C2	0.16678	0.20257	0.15479	0.19079	0.17613
C3	0.16485	0.16414	0.16569	0.15314	0.20410
C4	0.18322	0.06290	0.20398	0.10358	0.09750
C5	0.15985	0.18676	0.16224	0.18067	0.23909
C6	0.16861	0.28075	0.14952	0.22626	0.20807
$R_{score} = \frac{w_{max}}{w_{min}}$	1.16928	4.46332	1.36429	2.18444	3.18287

Tables 69.1 and 69.11 evaluates the consistency of the MCRAT method's results obtained using different criteria weighting techniques and ranking approaches through the Spearman correlation coefficient. In the first part, it is observed that the MCRAT results exhibit high correlations with various weighting methods such as SD, entropy, WENSLO, SPC, and LOPCOW (e.g., SD–WENSLO: 0.992 and entropy-SPC: 0.995), indicating that the ranking outcomes are largely similar and that MCRAT produces stable results even when the weighting technique varies. In the second part, the correlation between MCRAT and different ranking methods such as SAW, WASPAS, TOPSIS, CRADIS, and PIV is consistently found to be high; this demonstrates that MCRAT aligns well with various ranking approaches and stands out as a reliable method for alternative rankings.

As shown in Table 69.12, the ranking stability of different weighting techniques was compared using R-score ratios, with the SD method achieving the highest stability by exhibiting the lowest R-score value of 1.16928. This indicates that the SD method produces consistent and balanced results when determining criteria weights, leading to more reliable and robust ranking performance. The WENSLO (1. 36429) method also demonstrated a relatively low R-score value, offering more stable and dependable rankings compared to other techniques. In contrast, the entropy (4.46332) and LOPCOW (3.18287) methods yielded higher R-score values, indicating less stable results.

69.6.2 Comparative analysis for numerical example 2

In this section, a correlation analysis was performed between the rankings obtained using the SD–MCRAT model and the rankings obtained from other criteria weighting and ranking methods. The results are presented in Table 69.13. Additionally, the R-score values for the SD method and five other weighting methods are provided in Table 69.14.

TABLE 69.13 Spearman's coefficient between MCRAT methods based on various techniques (example 2).

MCRAT					
	Standard deviation (SD)	**Entropy**	**WENSLO**	**SPC**	**LOPCOW**
SD		0.912	0.881	0.926	0.877
Entropy			0.991	0.998	0.624
WENSLO				0.992	0.573
SPC					0.649
SD–MCRAT	SD–SAW	SD–WASPAS	SD–TOPSIS	SD–CRADIS	SD–PIV
	0.9494	0.9591	0.9798	0.9901	0.7500

TABLE 69.14 R-score ratios across different weighting techniques (example 2).

	Standard deviation (SD)	**Entropy**	**WENSLO**	**SPC**	**LOPCOW**
C1	0.11204	0.02028	0.04430	0.06169	0.08984
C2	0.12445	0.00048	0.00224	0.00957	0.17099
C3	0.14050	0.52741	0.36436	0.34450	0.10533
C4	0.12735	0.12512	0.14425	0.14914	0.14688
C5	0.14304	0.02076	0.03081	0.06251	0.09981
C6	0.12476	0.04846	0.07184	0.09087	0.12244
C7	0.11157	0.21557	0.26968	0.20008	0.09882
C8	0.11629	0.04192	0.07251	0.08163	0.16589
$R_{score} = \frac{w_{max}}{w_{min}}$	1.28204	1098.95463	162.41501	36.00008	1.90341

Table 69.13 reveals the similarity of the MCRAT method's results obtained based on different criteria weighting techniques and ranking methods through the Spearman correlation coefficient. In the first part, high correlations are observed among the SD, entropy, WENSLO, and SPC methods (e.g., WENSLO–SPC: 0.992; entropy–WENSLO: 0.991), indicating that these weighting techniques yield largely consistent results in MCRAT rankings. However, LOPCOW shows notably lower correlations with entropy (0.624) and WENSLO (0.573), suggesting that this method can produce rankings that differ more significantly from the others. In the second part of the table, the alignment of MCRAT with various ranking methods is assessed, showing especially high correlations with SAW, WASPAS, TOPSIS, and CRADIS, whereas a lower correlation is found with PIV (0.7500). Overall, this table demonstrates that the MCRAT method delivers highly consistent and stable results across different weighting and ranking approaches.

Table 69.14 shows the stability of different weighting techniques at the criterion level using R-score ratios. Here, the SD method again shows the highest stability with the lowest overall R-score value of 1.28204. Other methods, particularly entropy (1098.95463), WENSLO (162.41501), and SPC (36.00008), show extremely high R-score values, indicating significant fluctuations and instability in the criterion weighting results. Although the LOPCOW method has a slightly higher R-score (1.90341) than SD, it still demonstrates relatively stable performance. These findings clearly demonstrate that the SD method is more appropriate for obtaining reliable and consistent results in decision-making processes.

69.7 Conclusions

The primary goal of this study is to address complex material selection problems by employing the SD–MCRAT model. To validate its relevance and performance, the proposed approach was implemented in two example engineering scenarios: selecting optimal materials for gear and bearing production.

In the first case, involving six alternative materials and six mechanical criteria, the results indicated that C4 had the highest impact on the decision-making process. Among the alternatives, A1 emerged as the most suitable material, demonstrating the best performance across the weighted criteria. In the second case, which considered seven materials evaluated by eight technical criteria, C5 was the most critical criterion. The material A3 ranked highest, followed by A2 and A1, showing a balanced performance and suitability for bearing manufacturing.

To test the viability of the suggested approach, comprehensive comparative analyses with all objective weighting methods (entropy, WENSLO, SPC, LOPCOW) and ranking procedures (SAW, WASPAS, TOPSIS, CRADIS, PIV) were performed. The SD–MCRAT results were highly different with those from other methods, as indicated by the Spearman's rho. In addition, the R-scores reflected that the SD method enabled the most stable and most reliable weighting results, regardless of the example case studies, and surpassed other methods in ranking stability.

The results demonstrate that the SD–MCRAT model not only performs effectively and accurately but also provides consistent and reliable decisions, especially in complex engineering problems such as material selection with multiple conflicting criteria, when all criteria are considered benefit criteria. This combined model provides a useful tool for engineers and DMs seeking to increase material selection precision and confidence in multicriteria environments.

References

Akpahou, R., Mensah, L. D., Quansah, D. A., & Kemausuor, F. (2024). Long-term energy demand modeling and optimal evaluation of solutions to renewable energy deployment barriers in Benin: A LEAP-MCDM approach. *Energy Reports, 12*, 1888–1904. https://doi.org/10.1016/j.egyr.2024.07.055.

Alinezhad, A., & Khalili, J. (2024). MCDM, DEA, and their relationship in materials selection. In *Decision-making models and applications in manufacturing environments*. New York: Apple Academic Press, 1–45. https://doi.org/10.1201/9781003394723-1.

Anojkumar, L., Ilangkumaran, M., & Sasirekha, V. (2014). Comparative analysis of MCDM methods for pipe material selection in sugar industry. *Expert Systems with Applications, 41*, 2964–2980. https://doi.org/10.1016/j.eswa.2013.10.028.

Baydaş, M., Eren, T., Stević, Ž., Starčević, V., & Parlakkaya, R. (2023). Proposal for an objective binary benchmarking framework that validates each other for comparing MCDM methods through data analytics. *PeerJ Computer Science, 9*, e1350. https://doi.org/10.7717/peerj-cs.1350.

Baydaş, M., & Pamučar, D. (2022). Determining objective characteristics of MCDM methods under uncertainty: An exploration study with financial data. *Mathematics, 10*, 1115. https://doi.org/10.3390/math10071115.

Biswas, S., Pamucar, D., Dawn, S., & Simic, V. (2024). Evaluation based on relative utility and nonlinear standardization (ERUNS) method for comparing firm performance in energy sector. *Decision Making Advances, 2*, 1–21. https://doi.org/10.31181/dma21202419.

Chatterjee, P., & Chakraborty, S. (2014). Investigating the effect of normalization norms in flexible manufacturing sytem se-lection using multi - criteria decision - making methods. *Journal of Engineering Science and Technology Review, 7*, 141–150. https://doi.org/10.25103/jestr.073.23.

Chatterjee, S., & Chakraborty, S. (2021). Material selection of a mechanical component based on criteria relationship evaluation and MCDM approach. *Materials Today: Proceedings, 44*, 1621–1626. https://doi.org/10.1016/j.matpr.2020.11.817.

Cinelli, M., Kadziński, M., Miebs, G., Gonzalez, M., & Słowiński, R. (2022). Recommending multiple criteria decision analysis methods with a new taxonomy-based decision support system. *European Journal of Operational Research, 302*, 633–651. https://doi.org/10.1016/j.ejor.2022.01.011.

Danesh, D., Ryan, M. J., & Abbasi, A. (2017). A systematic comparison of multi-criteria decision making methods for the improvement of project portfolio management in complex organisations. *International Journal of Management and Decision Making, 16*(1). https://doi.org/10.1504/IJMDM.2017.10005690.

Deepa, N., Ganesan, K., Srinivasan, K., & Chang, C.-Y. (2019). Realizing sustainable development via modified integrated weighting MCDM model for ranking agrarian dataset. *Sustainability, 11*, 6060. https://doi.org/10.3390/su11216060.

Diakoulaki, D., Mavrotas, G., & Papayannakis, L. (1995). Determining objective weights in multiple criteria problems: The critic method. *Computers & Operations Research, 22*, 763–770. https://doi.org/10.1016/0305-0548(94)00059-H.

Ersoy, N., Özçalıcı, M., & Trung, D. D. (2026). A hybrid MCDM approach for SDGs assessment of EU countries. *Spectrum of Decision Making and Applications, 3*, 164–186. https://doi.org/10.31181/sdmap31202637.

Hosouli, S., Elvins, J., Searle, J., Boudjabeur, S., Bowyer, J., & Jewell, E. (2023). A multi-criteria decision making (MCDM) methodology for high temperature thermochemical storage material selection using graph theory and matrix approach. *Materials & Design, 227*, 111685. https://doi.org/10.1016/j.matdes.2023.111685.

Jahan, A., Mustapha, F., Sapuan, S. M., Ismail, M. Y., & Bahraminasab, M. (2012). A framework for weighting of criteria in ranking stage of material selection process. *The International Journal of Advanced Manufacturing Technology, 58*, 411–420. https://doi.org/10.1007/s00170-011-3366-7.

Kumar, S., Ahijith Kumar, P. V., Bharati, K., Patnaik, L., Ranjan Maity, S., & Łepicka, M. (2025). Coating material selection for bulk metal forming dies: A MEREC-integrated approach with multiple MCDM methods. *International Journal on Interactive Design and Manufacturing (IJIDeM, 19*, 4055–4070. https://doi.org/10.1007/s12008-024-01983-z.

Madanchian, M., & Taherdoost, H. (2025). Applications of multi-criteria decision making in information systems for strategic and operational decisions. *Computers, 14*, 208. https://doi.org/10.3390/computers14060208.

Maity, R., Mishra, R., Kumar Pattnaik, P., & Pandey, A. (2023). Selection of sustainable material for the construction of UAV aerodynamic wing using MCDM technique. *Mater Today Proc*. https://doi.org/10.1016/j.matpr.2023.12.025.

Mousavi-Nasab, S. H., & Sotoudeh-Anvari, A. (2017). A comprehensive MCDM-based approach using TOPSIS, COPRAS and DEA as an auxiliary tool for material selection problems. *Materials & Design, 121*, 237–253. https://doi.org/10.1016/j.matdes.2017.02.041.

Omosa, G. B., Mwema, F. M., Akinlabi, E. T., Jen, T. C., & Mutua, J. M. (2024). Matrix-phase material selection for shape memory polymer composites: A comparative analysis of multi-criteria decision-making. *Polymer Engineering and Science, 64*, 3363–3378. https://doi.org/10.1002/pen.26775.

Rathod, M. K., & Kanzaria, H. V. (2011). A methodological concept for phase change material selection based on multiple criteria decision analysis with and without fuzzy environment. *Materials & Design, 32*, 3578–3585. https://doi.org/10.1016/j.matdes.2011.02.040.

Şahin, M. (2024). Ensemble multi-attribute decision-making for material selection problems. *Soft Comput, 28*, 5437–5460. https://doi.org/10.1007/s00500-023-09296-1.

Seker, S. (2025). Evaluation of agile attributes for low-cost carriers to achieve sustainable development using an integrated MCDM approach. *Management Decision, 63*, 1229–1261. https://doi.org/10.1108/MD-10-2023-1896.

Shaaban, M. S., El-Sherif, A. M., Hammam, A. A., Attaalfadeel, H. M., & Mesalam, I. Y. (2025). Petroleum well site selection using MCRAT integrated with rough set theory. *European Journal of Pure and Applied Mathematics, 18*, 6049. https://doi.org/10.29020/nybg.ejpam.v18i2.6049.

Son, N. H., Thao, D. X., & Thien, N. V. (2025). Development of alternative data normalization methods for the MCRAT method in multi-criteria decision-making. *EUREKA: Physics and Engineering,* 132–140. https://doi.org/10.21303/2461-4262.2025.003391.

Stević, Ž., Ersoy, N., Başar, E. E., & Baydaş, M. (2024). Addressing the global logistics performance index rankings with methodological insights and an innovative decision support framework. *Applied Sciences, 14*, 10334. https://doi.org/10.3390/app142210334.

Taherdoost, H., & Madanchian, M. (2023). Multi-criteria decision making (MCDM) Methods and Concepts. *Encyclopedia, 3*, 77–87. https://doi.org/10.3390/encyclopedia3010006.

Tavana, M., Sorooshian, S., Rezaei, H., & Mina, H. (2024). A novel fuzzy scenario-based stochastic general best-worst method. *Expert Syst Appl, 252*, 124246. https://doi.org/10.1016/j.eswa.2024.124246.

Trung, D. D., Ersoy, N., & Uyen, V. T. (2024). Cylinder and piston: Material selection in the design phase. *Journal of Applied Engineering Science, 22*, 789–803. https://doi.org/10.5937/jaes0-52884.

Urošević, K., Gligorić, Z., Miljanović, I., Beljić, Č., & Gligorić, M. (2021). Novel methods in multiple criteria decision-making process (MCRAT and RAPS)—Application in the mining industry. *Mathematics, 9*, 1980. https://doi.org/10.3390/math9161980.

Van Dua, T. (2024). Development of the PSI-RAPS-MCRAT method: A hybrid model. *EUREKA: Physics and Engineering,* 141–151. https://doi.org/10.21303/2461-4262.2025.003404.

Van Dua, T., Van Duc, D., Bao, N. C., & Trung, D. D. (2024). Integration of objective weighting methods for criteria and MCDM methods: Application in material selection. *EUREKA: Physics and Engineering,* 131–148. https://doi.org/10.21303/2461-4262.2024.003171.

Wan, S., Dong, J., & Chen, S.-M. (2021). Fuzzy best-worst method based on generalized interval-valued trapezoidal fuzzy numbers for multi-criteria decision-making. *Information Sciences (N Y), 573*, 493–518. https://doi.org/10.1016/j.ins.2021.03.038.

Wang, M., Ji, L., Xie, Y., & Huang, G. (2024). Regional bioethanol supply chain optimization with the integration of GIS-MCDM method and quantile-based scenario analysis. *Journal of Environmental Management, 351*, 119883. https://doi.org/10.1016/j.jenvman.2023.119883.

Yang, C. H., Hsu, W., & Wu, Y. L. (2022). A hybrid multiple-criteria decision portfolio with the resource constraints model of a smart healthcare management system for public medical centers. *Socio-economic Planning Sciences, 80*, 101073. https://doi.org/10.1016/j.seps.2021.101073.

Zakeri, S., Konstantas, D., Chatterjee, P., & Zavadskas, E. K. (2025). Soft cluster-rectangle method for eliciting criteria weights in multi-criteria decision-making. *Scientific Reports, 15*, 284. https://doi.org/10.1038/s41598-024-81027-4.

Zavadskas, E. K., & Podvezko, V. (2016). Integrated determination of objective criteria weights in MCDM. *International Journal of Information Technology & Decision Making, 15*(02), 267–283. https://doi.org/10.1142/S0219622016500036.

Chapter 70

MACONT: Mixed aggregation by comprehensive normalization technique for multi-attribute decision-making

Ali Sibevei[1], and Fatemeh Mirsaeedi[2]
[1]*University of Torbat Heydarieh, Torbat Heydarieh, Iran,* [2]*Department of Industrial Engineering, University of Tehran, Tehran, Iran*

70.1 Introduction

Decision-making is an analytical procedure aimed at selecting the most suitable alternative from several options to accomplish a particular objective (Wen et al., 2020). This activity is widely used in organizational settings, where managers regularly face decisions involving various and often conflicting criteria (Llanes & Benítez, 2021). A typical challenge in decision-making processes lies in selecting the most appropriate alternative from a set of options, considering multiple and often conflicting evaluation criteria. Therefore the application of multicriteria decision-making (MCDM) techniques has become increasingly prevalent across various decision-making environments (Sibevei & Roozkhosh, 2024). However, with more than 200 MCDM techniques currently available, the resulting rankings of alternatives can differ substantially depending on the method employed, which in turn complicates the task of selecting the most appropriate decision-making approach (Do et al., 2024). Since no single MCDM method is universally accepted as the best, recent developments in the field have concentrated on expanding the applicability of existing techniques and introducing new methods that are simpler to apply (Trung et al., 2024).

The core procedure in most MCDM methods revolves around two fundamental components: normalization and aggregation (Sen et al., 2024). The mixed aggregation by comprehensive normalization technique (MACONT) method has introduced innovative enhancements specifically in these two critical areas (Wen et al., 2020). It was proposed by Wen et al. (2020) as a recently developed tool within the MCDM framework, designed to combine and evaluate multiple criteria throughout the decision-making process (Sen et al., 2024). This approach accommodates both noncompensatory and compensatory perspectives in evaluating alternatives (Simic et al., 2023). To fully understand the MACONT method, it is essential to explore these two aspects in greater depth.

In MCDM, normalization methods and mixed aggregation procedures offer significant benefits by facilitating fair comparisons among criteria and assigning weights based on their relative importance. They also allow decision-makers to articulate their preferences and priorities (Sen et al., 2024; Wen et al., 2020). Normalization serves to convert diverse data scales into a comparable format (Do et al., 2024). Most multiple attribute decision-making (MADM) methods transform attribute values into nondimensional quantities, and this must be done using appropriate normalization strategies. Consequently, decisions will be based on more consistent and reliable data, aiding more effective management in strategizing and directing organizational efforts

Literature reviews indicate that even within a single MADM method, the use of different normalization procedures can yield significantly different results when identifying the optimal alternative. Although various MCDM methods incorporate distinct normalization techniques, not all of these approaches are equally appropriate or effective (Simanavičienė et al., 2022; Trung et al., 2024). Many MCDM methods include at least one data normalization method by default (Trung et al., 2024). However, relying on just one normalization method can reduce the accuracy of the results and consequently weaken the quality of decision-making (Ali et al., 2025). So, some integrate more than one. For instance, the ranking of alternatives with weights of criterion method incorporates two data normalization methods (Puška et al., 2024), and the combined compromise solution integrates two (Yazdani et al., 2019). The integration of multiple data normalization techniques within an MCDM

Encyclopedia of Multi-Attribute Decision-Making (MADM). DOI: https://doi.org/10.1016/B978-0-443-33275-3.00042-7

framework captures a more comprehensive representation of the original data, minimizes evaluation distortions, and ultimately improves the reliability of the final decision outcomes (Trung et al., 2024).

There are numerous normalization techniques, twelve common methods used in MCDM include linear normalization (N1), Weitendorf normalization (N2), vector normalization (N3), z-score normalization (N4), enhanced accuracy normalization (N5), sum linear normalization (N6), logarithmic normalization (N7), max linear normalization (N8), min linear normalization (N9), Jüttler-Körth normalization (N10), Peldschus normalization (N11), and stop normalization (N12) (Do & Nguyen, 2023). To address this, Wen et al. (2020) introduced a comprehensive normalization approach that integrates three different normalization techniques to capture more realistic and representative information (Ali et al., 2025). The key advantage of the MACONT model lies in its structural design, which facilitates the generation of more robust and reliable results. Unlike traditional MCDM methods, which are highly sensitive to the choice of normalization techniques, MACONT addresses this limitation by incorporating three distinct normalization approaches.

As mentioned earlier, MACONT combines three linear normalization techniques to process performance values (Amiri et al., 2025). Furthermore, to obtain the overall measure used for comparing the alternatives, an appropriate aggregation method is employed to integrate the normalized performance scores while accounting for the relative importance of each criterion. Among the commonly used methods are the arithmetic weighted average and the geometric weighted average operators (Chakraborty et al., 2024).

In summary, MACONT demonstrates several notable advantages: (1) it integrates three linear normalization techniques according to the types of criteria to reduce biases arising from single normalization methods; (2) it evaluates both good and bad performances of an alternative against others using only one reference alternative, ensuring simplicity and persuasiveness; (3) it employs two hybrid aggregation operators to provide robust outcomes from both compensatory and noncompensatory perspectives; and (4) it incorporates adjustable parameters, enhancing applicability and allowing experts to adapt parameter values to real-world decision-making contexts, thereby ensuring logical and reliable results (Wen et al., 2020). Despite its advantages, the MACONT method also has limitations. First, its reliance on three linear normalization techniques makes it sensitive to data distributions, and in some cases, problematic results may arise when zero values are present, indicating that additional normalization strategies may be required (Nguyen, 2023). Second, the classical MACONT formulation only handles crisp values and does not address uncertainty, vagueness, or linguistic information, which has led researchers to propose fuzzy, neutrosophic, and interval extensions (e.g., Mishra et al., 2025). The next section presents a brief review of the literature on the theory and practical applications of the MACONT method.

70.2 Literature Review

Since its introduction by Wen et al. (2020) for evaluating and ranking alternatives in a sustainable third-party reverse logistics context, the MACONT method has gained considerable scholarly attention. Numerous studies have explored both its applications and methodological advancements. This section reviews several recent studies that have applied the MACONT method. Most of these studies have focused on the classical (crisp) version of MACONT.

Wen and Liao (2021) introduced a quantifier-based extension of the MACONT method and applied it to the selection of a retirement service organization. Aksakal et al. (2022) integrated MACONT with the fuzzy best–worst method and criteria importance through intercriteria correlation (CRITIC) to choose thermal insulation materials. Sen et al. (2024) used MACONT for decision-making in laser metal-polymer welding. Simic et al. (2023) developed the two-stage 2 neutrosophic number cross-entropy-based optimization model-MACONT model, and used it in the management of end-of-life tires. Brainy et al. (2024) prioritized storage systems by integrating three MADM models (MACONT, measurement alternatives, and ranking according to compromise solution, and elimination et choix traduisant la réalité III) with bipolar linear diophantine fuzzy set. Mishra et al. (2025) introduce a hybrid multicriteria evaluation method, namely Pythagorean fuzzy (PF)-modified symmetry point of criterion (SPC), relative closeness coefficient, and MACONT, and employed the proposed ranking approach for evaluating digital transformation challenges in the sustainable financial services. Yalçın et al. (2025), by introducing the PF-SPC-MACONT hybrid model, investigated the process of selecting an infrastructure as a service cloud provider for a logistics company. Amiri et al. (2025), by using a CRITIC-MACONT framework, ranked the countries based on their COVID-19 performance. Ulutaş et al. (2024) evaluated third-party logistics service providers for car manufacturing firms using a novel integrated gray logarithmic percentage change-driven objective weights, preference selection index, and MACONT model. Ecer et al. (2025) proposed a FR- defining interrelationships between ranked criteria-MACONT framework and applied it to a real-world case study involving selecting optimal electric vehicle charging stations locations across seven alternative districts in Izmir, Turkey. Chen and Liu (2025), interval neutrosophic numbers-MACONT framework with interval neutrosophic multiple-attribute group decision-making and enhanced services performance evaluation.

70.3 Methodology

As stated earlier, Wen et al. (2020) introduced the MACONT approach, which considers a synthetic normalization model and two mixed aggregation operators to get credible results. The classical MACONT approach generally follows a structured sequence of steps, which includes (Chakraborty et al., 2024; Mishra et al., 2025):

(1) Constructing the initial matrix
(2) Normalizing the initial decision matrix by three techniques
(3) Aggregating three normalized performance values
(4) Computing two mixed aggregation scores and
(5) Calculating the final score of each alternative (Chakraborty et al., 2024; Mishra et al., 2025; Wen & Liao, 2021)

70.3.1 The initial decision matrix is constructed

Initially, in an MCDM problem, it is necessary to define a set of alternatives (*a*1, *a*2,…, *ai*,…, *am*) and evaluation criteria (*c*1, *c*2,…, *cj*,…, *cn*). One or more experts are then consulted to assess the performance of each alternative with respect to the specified criteria. Based on the experts' input, a decision matrix is constructed. If multiple experts are involved, their evaluations can be aggregated by applying appropriate weighting to generate a unified decision matrix as illustrated below (Wen et al., 2020):

$$\begin{bmatrix} x_{11} & x_{12} & \cdots & x_{1j} & \cdots & x_{1n} \\ x_{21} & x_{22} & \cdots & x_{23} & \cdots & x_{2n} \\ \vdots & \vdots & \ddots & \vdots & \ddots & \vdots \\ x_{i1} & x_{i2} & \cdots & x_{ij} & \cdots & x_{in} \\ \vdots & \vdots & \ddots & \vdots & \ddots & \vdots \\ x_{m1} & x_{m2} & \cdots & x_{mj} & \cdots & x_{mn} \end{bmatrix}$$

where x_{ij} is the performance value of the *ith* alternative under the *jth* criterion, and i = 1, 2,…, m, j = 1, 2,…, n.

70.3.2 Three different normalization techniques are applied to the decision matrix

Subsequently, the decision matrix constructed in step 1 is normalized using three distinct normalization techniques as follows:

1.1. Linear sum-based normalization
For benefit criteria:

$$\hat{x}_{ij}^{1} = \frac{x_{ij}}{\sum_{i=1}^{m} x_{ij}} \text{For cost criteria:} \tag{70.1}$$

$$\hat{x}_{ij}^{1} = \frac{\frac{1}{x_{ij}}}{\sum_{i=1}^{m} \frac{1}{x_{ij}}}$$

1.2. Linear ratio-based normalization
For benefit criteria:

$$\hat{x}_{ij}^{2} = \frac{x_{ij}}{\max\limits_{i} x_{ij}} \text{For cost criteria:} \tag{70.2}$$

$$\hat{x}_{ij}^{2} = \frac{\min\limits_{i} x_{ij}}{x_{ij}}$$

1.3. Linear max-min normalization

For benefit criteria:

$$\hat{x}_{ij}^{3} = \frac{x_{ij} - \min_i x_{ij}}{\max_i x_{ij} - \min_i x_{ij}} \quad \text{For cost criteria:} \tag{70.3}$$

$$\hat{x}_{ij}^{3} = \frac{\max_i x_{ij} - x_{ij}}{\min_i x_{ij} - \max_i x_{ij}}$$

70.3.3 Normalized performance values are aggregated

Once the three types of normalized performance values for the alternatives across the criteria are obtained, two balance parameters, λ and μ, are introduced to enhance the flexibility of the decision-making process. These parameters are used to integrate the normalized values, as described in the following equation (Eq. 70.1):

$$\hat{x}_{ij} = \lambda\hat{x}_{ij}^{1} + \mu\hat{x}_{ij}^{2} + (1 - \lambda - \mu)\hat{x}_{ij}^{3} \tag{70.4}$$

Where $0 \leq \lambda, \mu \leq 1$, and the values of these two balancing parameters are determined by experts. When experts focus more on the overall performance of each alternative among all options, a larger value of λ value is chosen; Conversely, when the emphasis is placed on the best-performing alternatives, a larger μ value is chosen. If the experts emphasize a large gap between alternatives, that is, they highlight the best performance of alternatives but do not ignore the worst performance of alternatives, then λ and μ are assigned smaller values.

70.3.4 Two mixed aggregation scores are calculated

Considering the distance between each alternative and the virtual reference alternative ($\bar{x}_j$), two subordinate comprehensive scores of each alternative, $S_1(a_i)$ and $S_2(a_i)$, are determined employing the following two mixed aggregation operators (Wen et al., 2020).

One of the aggregation operators represents a hybrid of the arithmetic weighted aggregation and geometric weighted aggregation techniques, while the other combines the evaluation of both the best and worst performance of alternatives under criteria (Wen & Liao, 2021):

$$S_1(a_i) = \delta\frac{\rho_i}{\sqrt{\sum_{i=1}^{m}(\rho_i)^2}} + (1 - \delta)\frac{\varphi_i}{\sqrt{\sum_{i=1}^{m}(\varphi_i)^2}}, \quad \text{i} = 1,\ 2,\ \ldots,\ \text{m} \tag{70.5}$$

$$S_2(a_i) = \vartheta\max_j(w_j(\hat{x}_{ij} - \bar{x}_j)) + (1 - \vartheta)\min_j(w_j(\hat{x}_{ij} - \bar{x}_j)), \quad \text{i} = 1,\ 2,\ \ldots,\ \text{m} \tag{70.6}$$

Where:

$$\rho_i = \sum_{j=1}^{n} w_j(\hat{x}_{ij} - \bar{x}_j),$$

$$\varphi_i = \frac{\Pi_{\gamma}^{n}(\bar{x}_j - \hat{x}_{ij})^{w_j}}{\Pi_{\eta}^{n}(\hat{x}_{ij} - \bar{x}_j)^{w_j}}, \quad \text{for } i = 1,\ 2,\ \ldots,\ m.$$

$w_j(j = 1,2,\ \ldots,n)$ represent the weights of criteria determined by experts, and $\sum_{j=1}^{n} w_j = 1$.

For each criterion, a virtual reference alternative ($\bar{x}_j$(j = 1, 2,…, n) of alternatives on each criterion) is created that represents the average performance of the alternatives. The concept of a virtual reference alternative is introduced to mitigate cognitive bias (Simic et al., 2023). Thus both the advantages and disadvantages of an alternative compared to other alternatives are evaluated simultaneously (Yürüyen & Altay, 2025).

Here, $\gamma\ (\gamma = 1, 2,\ \ldots,\ n)$ denotes the subset of criteria that satisfy $\hat{x}_{ij} < \bar{x}_j$, and $\eta\ (\eta = 1, 2,\ \ldots,\ n)$ represents the part of criteria that satisfy $\hat{x}_{ij} \geq \bar{x}_j$. The δ and ϑ $0 \leq \delta, \vartheta \leq 1$ parameters are set according to expert judgment. A higher δ indicates that experts emphasize the overall performance of alternatives, whereas a lower δ reflects focus on individual performances. Similarly, a higher ϑ corresponds to emphasizing the best-performing alternatives, while a lower ϑ corresponds to giving more weight to the worst-performing alternatives (Amiri et al., 2025; Wen et al., 2020). It must be noted that the two mixed aggregation operators are respectively inspired by the weighted aggregated sum product assessment and multiplicative multiobjective optimization by ratio analysis method (Wen & Liao, 2021).

70.3.5 Final score of each alternative is calculated

Next, the overall comprehensive score $S(a_i)$ of each alternative is determined according to (70.7) (Wen & Liao, 2021). The alternatives can then be ranked in descending order based on these scores. The alternative achieving the highest comprehensive score is identified as the optimal choice.

$$S(a_i) = \frac{1}{2}\left(S_1(a_i) + \frac{S_2(a_i)}{\sqrt{\sum_{i=1}^{m}(S_2(a_i))^2}}\right), \quad i = 1, 2, \ldots, m \tag{70.7}$$

To better understand the steps of the methodology, a diagram is presented below (Fig. 70.1).

70.4 Examples

The following sections present two numerical examples to illustrate the application of the MACONT method. The first example involves a simplified case designed to enhance conceptual understanding, while the second features a more complex scenario, incorporating sensitivity analysis on key parameters to further clarify the method's behavior.

70.4.1 Numerical example 1

In recent years, resilience has emerged as a critical strategy to mitigate the adverse effects of low-probability but high-impact disruptions in supply chains. Achieving supply chain resilience requires organizations to systematically identify and address the barriers that hinder its development (Sibevei & Roozkhosh, 2024).

Among the supply chains with direct implications for human life, the blood supply chain holds particular importance due to its sensitivity and critical role in healthcare systems. In their research, Sibevei and Roozkhosh (2024) identified and ranked the primary barriers affecting the resilience of this chain, along with the key evaluation criteria. In this section, the MACONT method is employed to analyze and rank these barriers. Given the extensive number of alternatives (27) in the original study, a subset has been selected.

The criteria considered in this example represent the most crucial components of the blood supply chain that may be impacted by the identified barriers. Tables 70.1 and 70.2 present the selected criteria along with their assigned weights, as determined by expert consensus, and list the barriers (alternatives) used in the analysis.

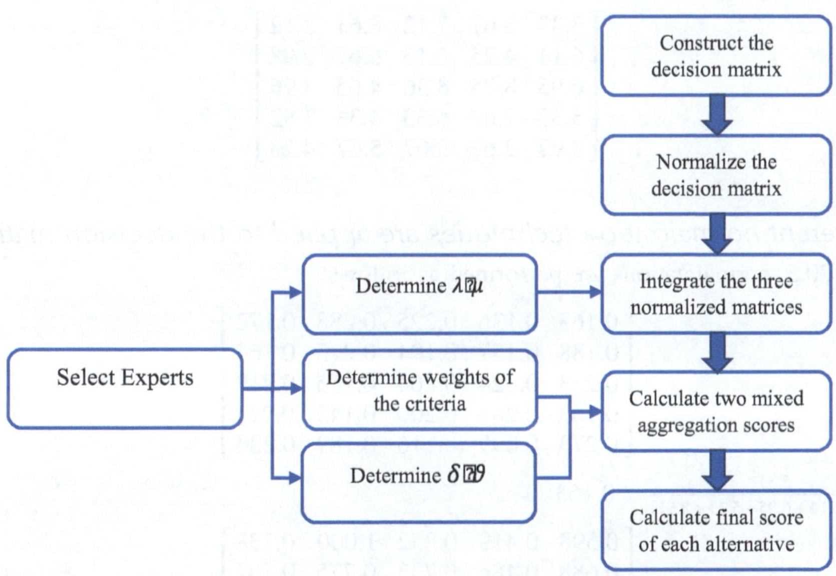

FIGURE 70.1 Steps of the mixed aggregation by comprehensive normalization technique methodology.

TABLE 70.1 Criteria and weights of example 1.

C1	C2	C3	C4	C5
Max	Max	Max	Max	Max
Blood donation	Equipment supply	Internal SC	Blood reception	External environment
0.31	0.31	0.17	0.11	0.1

TABLE 70.2 Barriers of blood supply chain resilience.

NO	Barriers
a1	Weakness in the distribution and blood supply
a2	Lack of full establishment of blood consumption management system in the hospital
a3	Exhausted equipment
a4	Lack of sufficient backup equipment
a5	Inadequate blood donation sites in terms of population or risk

70.4.1.1 The initial decision matrix is constructed

Based on the opinions of experts and the collected data, the decision-making matrix has been constructed as follows:

$$\begin{bmatrix} 5.33 & 3.67 & 7.12 & 8.61 & 3.12 \\ 6.14 & 4.25 & 6.13 & 6.67 & 2.98 \\ 6.95 & 8.75 & 8.36 & 4.65 & 3.96 \\ 5.33 & 7.67 & 6.33 & 4.33 & 3.82 \\ 8.92 & 2.67 & 3.67 & 5.67 & 4.23 \end{bmatrix}$$

70.4.1.2 Three different normalization techniques are applied to the decision matrix

Using Equations 70.1–70.3, normalizations are performed as follows:

$$\begin{bmatrix} 0.163 & 0.136 & 0.225 & 0.288 & 0.172 \\ 0.188 & 0.157 & 0.194 & 0.223 & 0.165 \\ 0.213 & 0.324 & 0.264 & 0.155 & 0.219 \\ 0.163 & 0.284 & 0.200 & 0.145 & 0.211 \\ 0.273 & 0.099 & 0.116 & 0.189 & 0.234 \end{bmatrix}$$

For example: $\frac{5.33}{(5.33+6.14+6.95+5.33+8.92)} = 0.163$

$$\begin{bmatrix} 0.598 & 0.419 & 0.852 & 1.000 & 0.738 \\ 0.688 & 0.486 & 0.733 & 0.775 & 0.704 \\ 0.779 & 1.000 & 1.000 & 0.540 & 0.936 \\ 0.598 & 0.877 & 0.757 & 0.503 & 0.903 \\ 1.000 & 0.305 & 0.439 & 0.659 & 1.000 \end{bmatrix}$$

For example: $\frac{5.33}{8.92} = 0.598$

$$\begin{bmatrix} 0.000 & 0.164 & 0.736 & 1.000 & 0.112 \\ 0.226 & 0.260 & 0.525 & 0.547 & 0.000 \\ 0.451 & 1.000 & 1.000 & 0.075 & 0.784 \\ 0.000 & 0.822 & 0.567 & 0.000 & 0.672 \\ 1.000 & 0.000 & 0.000 & 0.313 & 1.000 \end{bmatrix}$$

For example: $\frac{5.33 - 5.33}{8.92 - 5.33} = 0.000$

70.4.1.3 Normalized performance values are integrated

The normalized values are integrated using Eq. (70.4). In this example, the λ and μ parameters are set to 0.4 and 0.3, respectively.

$$\begin{bmatrix} 0.245 & 0.230 & 0.566 & 0.715 & 0.324 \\ 0.349 & 0.287 & 0.455 & 0.486 & 0.277 \\ 0.454 & 0.730 & 0.706 & 0.247 & 0.604 \\ 0.245 & 0.623 & 0.477 & 0.209 & 0.557 \\ 0.709 & 0.131 & 0.178 & 0.367 & 0.693 \end{bmatrix}$$

For example: $\hat{x}_{11} = 0.4 \times 0.163 + 0.3 \times 0.598 + 0.3 \times 0 = 0.245$

70.4.1.4 Two mixed aggregation scores are calculated

$S_1(a_i)$ and $S_2(a_i)$ are calculated using (70.5) and (70.6). δ and ϑ are set to 0.5. The results are summarized in Table 70.3. $\bar{x}_j$ (j = 1, 2,…, 5) are 0.400, 0.400, 0.477, 0.405, 0.491, and 0.372, respectively.

For example: $\bar{x}_1 = (0.245 + 0.349 + 0.454 + 0.245 + 0.709)/5 = 0.400$

For example:

$$\rho_1 = 0.31 \times (0.245 - 0.4) + 0.31 \times (0.230 - 0.4) + 0.17 \times (0.566 - 0.477) + 0.11 \times (0.715 - 0.405) + 0.1 \times (0.324 - 0.491) = -0.0685$$

$$\varphi_1 = \frac{(0.4 - 0.245)^{0.31} \times (0.23 - 0.4)^{0.31} \times (0.324 - 0.491)^{0.1}}{(0.566 - 0.477)^{0.17} \times (0.715 - 0.405)^{0.11}} = \frac{0.2716}{0.5837} = 0.4653$$

$$S_1(a_1) = 0.5 \times \frac{-0.685}{\sqrt{0.0327}} + 0.5 \times \frac{0.4653}{\sqrt{31.81}} = -0.1480$$

$$S_2(a_1) = 0.5 \times \max(-0.48, -0.053, 0.015, 0.034, -0.017) + 0.5 \times \min(-0.48, -0.053, 0.015, 0.034, -0.017) = -0.0094$$

TABLE 70.3 The results of $S_1(a_i)$ and $S_2(a_i)$.

Barriers	ρ_i	φ_i	$S_1(a_i)$	$S_2(a_i)$
a1	-0.0685	0.4653	-0.1480	-0.0094
a2	-0.0671	0.1192	-0.1749	-0.0131
a3	0.1517	4.5524	0.8228	0.0424
a4	0.0061	3.2329	0.3034	0.0104
a5	-0.0222	0.6374	-0.0049	0.0062

70.4.1.5 The final score of each alternative is calculated

The final score $S(a_i)$ of each alternative is computed using (70.7), and the resulting ranking of the barriers is listed (Table 70.4).

For example: $S(a_1) = \frac{1}{2}\left(-0.1480 + \frac{-0.0094}{\sqrt{(-0.0094^2 + -0.0131^2 + 0.0424^2 + 0.0104^2 + 0.0062^2)}}\right) = -0.1736$

70.4.2 Numerical example 2

One of the critical responsibilities of supply managers across industries is to ensure the procurement of appropriate quantities of materials at the optimal price and timing. Achieving this objective largely depends on the selection of suitable suppliers (Nguyen et al., 2024). It is a topic extensively addressed in the literature through the identification of diverse evaluation criteria.

In this example, the ranking of 9 suppliers in an automobile manufacturing supply chain, taking into account some of the most important criteria, is done. The criteria specified by a group of experts, along with their weights, are listed below. Max/min of each criterion is also determined (Table 70.5 and Table 70.6).

70.4.2.1 Initial decision matrix is constructed

Based on the opinions of experts and the collected data, the 8×7 decision-making matrix has been compiled as follows:

$$\begin{bmatrix} 4.50 & 3.80 & 4.23 & 3.88 & 4.58 & 4.12 & 3.72 \\ 4.12 & 4.20 & 3.87 & 3.78 & 4.03 & 3.61 & 3.48 \\ 3.94 & 4.48 & 4.13 & 4.21 & 4.24 & 3.88 & 3.57 \\ 4.73 & 3.42 & 3.83 & 3.49 & 4.52 & 4.39 & 3.88 \\ 4.21 & 4.08 & 3.61 & 3.63 & 3.87 & 3.72 & 3.58 \\ 4.01 & 4.32 & 4.31 & 4.10 & 4.12 & 4.01 & 3.79 \\ 3.62 & 4.41 & 4.04 & 4.29 & 3.68 & 3.49 & 3.87 \\ 4.30 & 3.95 & 4.13 & 3.88 & 4.19 & 3.91 & 4.12 \end{bmatrix}$$

70.4.2.2 Three different normalization techniques are applied to the decision matrix

Using equations 70.1–70.3, normalizations are performed as follows:

$$\begin{bmatrix} 0.1346 & 0.1334 & 0.1184 & 0.1241 & 0.1378 & 0.1323 & 0.1240 \\ 0.1232 & 0.1207 & 0.1294 & 0.1209 & 0.1213 & 0.1160 & 0.1160 \\ 0.1179 & 0.1131 & 0.1213 & 0.1347 & 0.1276 & 0.1246 & 0.1190 \\ 0.1415 & 0.1482 & 0.1308 & 0.1116 & 0.1360 & 0.1410 & 0.1293 \\ 0.1259 & 0.1242 & 0.1387 & 0.1161 & 0.1165 & 0.1195 & 0.1193 \\ 0.1200 & 0.1173 & 0.1162 & 0.1312 & 0.1240 & 0.1288 & 0.1263 \\ 0.1083 & 0.1149 & 0.1240 & 0.1372 & 0.1107 & 0.1121 & 0.1290 \\ 0.1286 & 0.1283 & 0.1213 & 0.1241 & 0.1261 & 0.1256 & 0.1373 \end{bmatrix}$$

TABLE 70.4 The results of $S(a_i)$.

Barrie-rs	$S(a_i)$	Rank
a1	-0.1736	4
a2	-0.2272	5
a3	0.8628	1
a4	0.2630	2
a5	0.0635	3

TABLE 70.5 Criteria and weights of example 2.

C1	C2	C3	C4	C5	C6	C7
Max	Min	Min	Max	Max	Max	Max
Quality	Price	Lead time	Flexibility	Technical capability	Reputation	Sustainability
0.25	0.15	0.15	0.10	0.15	0.10	0.10

TABLE 70.6 Suppliers of the automobile supply chain.

a1	a2	a3	a4	a5	a6	a7	a8
Supplier 1	Supplier 2	Supplier 3	Supplier 4	Supplier 5	Supplier 6	Supplier 7	Supplier 8

$$\begin{bmatrix} 0.9514 & 0.9000 & 0.8534 & 0.9044 & 1.0000 & 0.9385 & 0.9029 \\ 0.8710 & 0.8143 & 0.9328 & 0.8811 & 0.8799 & 0.8223 & 0.8447 \\ 0.8330 & 0.7634 & 0.8741 & 0.9814 & 0.9258 & 0.8838 & 0.8665 \\ 1.0000 & 1.0000 & 0.9426 & 0.8135 & 0.9869 & 1.0000 & 0.9417 \\ 0.8901 & 0.8382 & 1.0000 & 0.8462 & 0.8450 & 0.8474 & 0.8689 \\ 0.8478 & 0.7917 & 0.8376 & 0.9557 & 0.8996 & 0.9134 & 0.9199 \\ 0.7653 & 0.7755 & 0.8936 & 1.0000 & 0.8035 & 0.7950 & 0.9393 \\ 0.9091 & 0.8658 & 0.8741 & 0.9044 & 0.9148 & 0.8907 & 1.0000 \end{bmatrix}$$

$$\begin{bmatrix} 0.7928 & 0.6415 & 0.1143 & 0.4875 & 1.0000 & 0.7000 & 0.3750 \\ 0.4505 & 0.2642 & 0.6286 & 0.3625 & 0.3889 & 0.1333 & 0.0000 \\ 0.2883 & 0.0000 & 0.2571 & 0.9000 & 0.6222 & 0.4333 & 0.1406 \\ 1.0000 & 1.0000 & 0.6857 & 0.0000 & 0.9333 & 1.0000 & 0.6250 \\ 0.5315 & 0.3774 & 1.0000 & 0.1750 & 0.2111 & 0.2556 & 0.1563 \\ 0.3514 & 0.1509 & 0.0000 & 0.7625 & 0.4889 & 0.5778 & 0.4844 \\ 0.0000 & 0.0660 & 0.3857 & 1.0000 & 0.0000 & 0.0000 & 0.6094 \\ 0.6126 & 0.5000 & 0.2571 & 0.4875 & 0.5667 & 0.4667 & 1.0000 \end{bmatrix}$$

70.4.2.3 Normalized performance values are integrated

The normalized values are integrated using formula 4. In this example, the λ and μ are 0.5 and 0.2, respectively.

$$\begin{bmatrix} 0.4954 & 0.4391 & 0.2642 & 0.3892 & 0.5689 & 0.4639 & 0.3551 \\ 0.3710 & 0.3024 & 0.4398 & 0.3454 & 0.3533 & 0.2624 & 0.2269 \\ 0.3120 & 0.2092 & 0.3126 & 0.5336 & 0.4356 & 0.3691 & 0.2750 \\ 0.5707 & 0.5741 & 0.4596 & 0.2185 & 0.5454 & 0.5705 & 0.4405 \\ 0.4004 & 0.3430 & 0.5694 & 0.2798 & 0.2906 & 0.3059 & 0.2803 \\ 0.3349 & 0.2623 & 0.2256 & 0.4855 & 0.3886 & 0.4204 & 0.3924 \\ 0.2072 & 0.2324 & 0.3564 & 0.5686 & 0.2161 & 0.2151 & 0.4352 \\ 0.4299 & 0.3873 & 0.3126 & 0.3892 & 0.4160 & 0.3809 & 0.5686 \end{bmatrix}$$

70.4.2.4 Two mixed aggregation scores are calculated

$S_1(a_i)$c and $S_2(a_i)$ are calculated using formulas 5 and 6. δ and ϑ are 0.3 and 0.7, respectively. The results are listed in Table 70.7. $\overline{x}_j$ (j = 1, 2,…, 7) are 0.39, 0.344, 0.368, 0.402, 0.374, and 0.372, respectively.

TABLE 70.7 The results of $S_1(a_i)$ and $S_2(a_i)$.

Barriers	ρ_i	φ_i	$S_1(a_i)$	$S_2(a_i)$
a1	0.0563	1.26163	0.2165	0.0138
a2	-0.0386	0.10783	-0.0557	0.0032
a3	-0.0398	0.23734	-0.0453	0.0032
a4	0.1233	4.74578	0.6629	0.0261
a5	-0.0120	0.47746	0.0250	0.0162
a6	-0.0341	0.33270	-0.0266	-0.0005
a7	-0.0847	0.24392	-0.1216	-0.0020
a8	0.0296	5.42138	0.5671	0.0113

TABLE 70.8 The results of $S(a_i)$.

Barriers	$S(a_i)$	Rank
a1	0.3001	3
a2	0.0174	6
a3	0.0221	5
a4	0.6955	1
a5	0.2381	4
a6	-0.0201	7
a7	-0.0888	8
a8	0.4412	2

TABLE 70.9 Sensitivity analysis of δ and ϑ.

	Main scenario	Scenario 1	Scenario 2	Scenario 3
	$\delta = 0.3, \vartheta = 0.7$	$\delta = 0.2, \vartheta = 0.8$	$\delta = 0.1, \vartheta = 0.9$	$\delta = 0.4, \vartheta = 0.6$
a1	0.3001	0.2960	0.2876	0.2886
a2	0.0174	0.0468	0.0686	-0.0267
a3	0.0221	0.0616	0.0901	-0.0379
a4	0.6955	0.6818	0.6665	0.6910
a5	0.2381	0.2464	0.2505	0.2131
a6	-0.0201	0.0257	0.0586	-0.0877
a7	-0.0888	0.0112	0.0829	-0.2355
a8	0.4412	0.4655	0.4889	0.4088

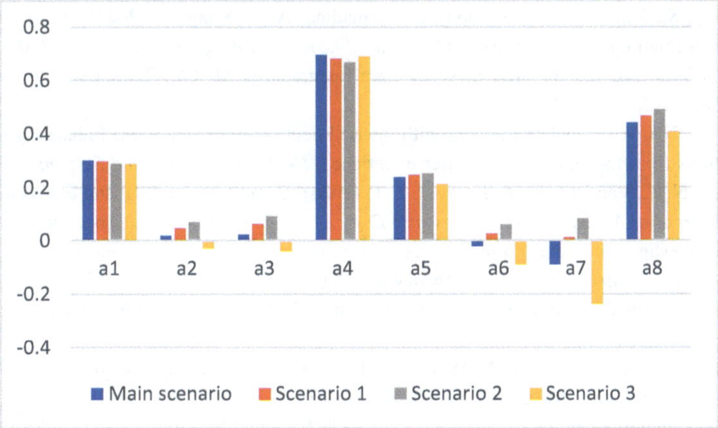

FIGURE 70.2 Sensitivity analysis of δ and ϑ.

70.4.2.5 Final score of each alternative is calculated

The final score $S(a_i)$ of each alternative is computed using (70.7) and the ranking of the barriers is listed (Table 70.8).

To better examine and analyze the status of the rankings after changing the parameters, the δ and ϑ parameters were changed. As is clear, rankings one to four did not change after changing these parameters, and the changes in subsequent rankings are also insignificant (Table 70.9 and Fig. 70.2).

The last part of this chapter summarizes what has been said and also provides suggestions for future research.

70.5 Conclusion

This chapter presented the MACONT method as a novel and integrated approach within the field of MCDM. By focusing on the two fundamental elements of normalization and aggregation, MACONT addresses key limitations found in many traditional MCDM techniques. Through the use of three distinct linear normalization strategies and their weighted integration, the method ensures greater flexibility and realism in representing performance values. Furthermore, by incorporating both compensatory and noncompensatory mixed aggregation operators, it offers a more balanced and comprehensive evaluation of alternatives.

The two numerical case studies focused on blood supply chain resilience and supplier selection in the automotive industry, demonstrated the practical applicability and robustness of the MACONT approach. The results confirmed its capacity to handle complex decision environments with multiple and often conflicting criteria. Additionally, the stability of rankings under various parameter settings highlighted the method's reliability and adaptability, reinforcing its potential for real-world managerial applications.

Future research can explore several directions to further develop the MACONT methodology. First, as stated in the literature, although work has been done on combining this method with fuzzy approaches, this area needs further investigation and development, and may enhance its ability to manage uncertainty and subjective judgments better. Second, developing automated or AI-based mechanisms for tuning the method's balance parameters could increase efficiency and reduce reliance on expert input. Third, since this method emphasizes normalization techniques, it is useful to consider other normalization combinations and examine their effectiveness in the MACONT method. Finally, comparative empirical studies across diverse industries and decision contexts would provide broader validation and help refine the method for domain-specific adaptations.

References

Aksakal, B., Ulutaş, A., Balo, F., & Karabasevic, D. (2022). A new hybrid MCDM model for insulation material evaluation for healthier environment. *Buildings, 12*(5), 655.

Ali, T., Aghaloo, K., Nahian, A. J., Chiu, Y. R., & Ahmad, M. (2025). Exploring the best hybrid energy system for the off-grid rural energy scheme in Bangladesh using a comprehensive decision framework. *Energy Sources, Part A: Recovery, Utilization, and Environmental Effects, 47*(2), 1887975.

Amiri, A. S., Babaei, A., & Khedmati, M. (2025). Country-level assessment of COVID-19 performance: A cluster-based MACONT-CRITIC analysis. *Applied Soft Computing, 171*, 112762.

Brainy, J. R. V. J., Narayanamoorthy, S., Pragathi, S., Salahshour, S., Ahmadian, A., & Kang, D. (2024). A sophisticated decision paradigm for the assessment of hydrogen storage technologies for mobility applications. *Journal of Energy Storage, 92*, 112207.

Chakraborty, S., Raut, R. D., Rofin, T. M., & Chakraborty, S. (2024). An integrated G-MACONT approach for healthcare supplier selection. *Grey Systems: Theory and Application, 14*(2), 318–336.

Chen, J., & Liu, X. (2025). Integrated INN-MACONT framework with interval neutrosophic MAGDM: Enhancing services performance evaluation in library and information institutions from the perspective of user experience. *Neutrosophic Sets and Systems, 77*(1), 28.

Do, D. T., Dudić, B., Ašonja, A., Bao, N. C., Van Duc, D., & Thuy, D. T. T. (2024). Comparison of SRP and FUCA methods in selecting industrial tools and equipment. *International Journal of Advanced Technology and Engineering Exploration, 11*(116), 1066.

Do, D. T., & Nguyen, N. T. (2023). Investigation of the appropriate data normalization method for combination with preference selection index method in MCDM. *Operational Research in Engineering Sciences: Theory and Applications, 6*(1).

Llanes, R. P., & Benítez, N. G. (2021). Original research article comparison and selection of artificial intelligence technology in pre-dicting milk yield. *Journal of Autonomous Intelligence, 4*(2).

Mishra, A. R., Rani, P., Alrasheedi, A. F., & Alshamrani, A. M. (2025). Evaluating the challenges of digital transformation in sustainable financial services using an integrated pythagorean fuzzy MACONT model. *Kybernetes*.

Nguyen, A. T. (2023). Expanding the data normalization strategy to the MACONT method for multi-criteria decision making. *Engineering, Technology & Applied Science Research, 13*(2), 10489–10495.

Nguyen, T., Amin, S. H., & Shah, B. (2024). A perspective on supplier selection and order allocation: Literature review. *Administrative Sciences, 14*(9), 206.

Puška, A., Štilić, A., Pamučar, D., Božanić, D., & Nedeljković, M. (2024). Introducing a novel multi-criteria ranking of alternatives with weights of criterion (RAWEC) model. *MethodsX, 12*, 102628.

Sen, A., Banerjee, N., Samanta, A., Roy, N., Pramanik, D., Biswas, S., & Biswas, R. (2024). Multi-criteria decision-making for laser metal-polymer welding: A MACONT approach. In *International conference on mechanical engineering*. Singapore: Springer Nature Singapore, 565–579.

Sibevei, A., & Roozkhosh, P. (2024). Prioritizing barriers to resilience in blood supply chains: An integrated multi-criteria decision-making approach. In *Operations Research Forum, Vol. 5*, Cham: Springer International Publishing, 44 No. 2.

Simanavičienė, R., Jakučionytė, V., & Deltuvienė, D. (2022). Sensitivity study of TOPSIS and COPRAS methods with respect to normalization techniques.

Simic, V., Dabic-Miletic, S., Tirkolaee, E. B., Stević, Ž., Deveci, M., & Senapati, T. (2023). Neutrosophic CEBOM-MACONT model for sustainable management of end-of-life tires. *Applied Soft Computing, 143*, 110399.

Trung, D. D., Truong, N. X., Duc, D. V., & Bao, N. C. (2024). Data normalization in RAWEC method: Limitations and remedies. *Yugoslav Journal of Operations Research,* (00), 20 -20.

Ulutaş, A., Topal, A., Görçün, Ö. F., & Ecer, F. (2024). Evaluation of third-party logistics service providers for car manufacturing firms using a novel integrated grey LOPCOW-PSI-MACONT model. *Expert Systems with Applications, 241*, 122680.

Wen, Z., & Liao, H. (2021). Pension service institution selection by a personalized quantifier-based MACONT method. *International Journal of Strategic Property Management, 25*(6), 446–458.

Wen, Z., Liao, H., & Zavadskas, E. K. (2020). MACONT: Mixed aggregation by comprehensive normalization technique for multi-criteria analysis. *Informatica, 31*(4), 857–880.

Yalçın, G. C., Kara, K., Saygıner, C., Simic, V., & Pamucar, D. (2025). Selecting cloud providers of infrastructure as a service: A picture fuzzy symmetry point of criterion-based expert-driven model. *Engineering Applications of Artificial Intelligence, 157*, 111132.

Yazdani, M., Zarate, P., Kazimieras Zavadskas, E., & Turskis, Z. (2019). A combined compromise solution (CoCoSo) method for multi-criteria decision-making problems. *Management Decision, 57*(9), 2501–2519. https://doi.org/10.1108/md-05-2017-0458.

Yürüyen, A. A., & Altay, H. (2025). Evaluating the logistics performance of one belt one road project countries with multi criteria decision making methods. *Journal of Mehmet Akif Ersoy University Economics and Administrative Sciences Faculty, 12*(2), 750–774.

Chapter 71

OPTBIAS: Ordering preference targeting at bi-ideal average solutions for multi-attribute decision-making

Fatemeh Mirsaeedi[1] **and Ali Sibevei**[2]
[1]*School of Industrial Engineering, College of Engineering, University of Tehran, Tehran, Iran,* [2]*University of Torbat Heydarieh, Torbat Heydarieh, Iran*

71.1 Introduction

Decision-making is a core cognitive activity that involves selecting the most appropriate option from a set of feasible alternatives based on available information. It serves as a foundational mechanism in problem-solving across disciplines and is essential for achieving effective outcomes. In organizational contexts, timely and accurate decision-making supports strategic planning, resource optimization, and operational agility. Conversely, poor decisions can lead to inefficiencies and adverse consequences (Amor et al., 2023; Nain et al., 2023).

When decisions must be evaluated against multiple, often conflicting criteria—both qualitative and quantitative—the process is referred to as multicriteria decision-making (MCDM). MCDM is widely applied in fields such as engineering, economics, environmental management, and healthcare, where trade-offs between competing objectives are common. The complexity of MCDM arises from the presence of conflicting goals, diverse stakeholder preferences, and varying degrees of uncertainty (Khan et al., 2023). To address these challenges, a range of mathematical techniques has been developed to support decision-makers in identifying compromise solutions that balance competing priorities (Velasquez & Hester, 2013).

In the context of multiobjective optimization problems, decision-makers often generate a set of Pareto-optimal solutions, each representing a different trade-off among objectives (Wang, Parhi, et al., 2020). Although these solutions are mathematically nondominated and equivalent in terms of optimality (Luna et al., 2021), selecting a preferred solution from this set remains a decision-making challenge (Lemos et al., 2018). Comparative studies, such as that by Wang and Rangaiah (2017), have demonstrated the importance of simplicity and computational efficiency in MCDM methods, particularly in practical applications involving multiple objectives (Lin et al., 2021).

Effective MCDM methods are expected to satisfy key properties such as weight sensitivity and ordering consistency. Weight sensitivity ensures that the relative importance of criteria—whether derived from subjective preferences or objective data—is accurately reflected in the ranking of alternatives. Ordering consistency refers to the stability of rankings when equivalent evaluation indices are used, such as net return versus economic potential or exergy efficiency versus exergy destruction (Meramo-Hurtado & Gonz´alez-Delgado, 2021; Pamucar & Cirovic, 2015).

Among the established MCDM techniques, the technique for order preference by similarity to ideal solution (TOPSIS) is widely adopted due to its conceptual clarity and ease of implementation (Singh & Meena, 2020). TOPSIS ranks alternatives based on their Euclidean distances to positive-ideal and negative-ideal reference points. Its strengths include interpretability, spreadsheet-friendly computation, and scalability to high-dimensional problems (Hwang & Yoon, 1981; Shih et al., 2007; Velasquez & Hester, 2013).

However, TOPSIS also faces several limitations:

It does not account for correlations among attributes, leading to potential redundancy.

Weight assignment can be complex and uncertain.

Alternatives may simultaneously be close to both ideal points.

Encyclopedia of Multi-Attribute Decision-Making (MADM). DOI: https://doi.org/10.1016/B978-0-443-33275-3.00038-5

It struggles with imprecise or vague data.

Rankings may change when criteria or alternatives are added or removed (rank reversal).

It lacks mechanisms to incorporate weight-based prioritization in distance calculations (Çelikbilek & Tüysüz, 2020; Li et al., 2011; Xu et al., 2015).

To overcome these limitations, numerous variants of TOPSIS have been proposed (Ghorabaee et al., 2016; Liu et al., 2019; Madanchian & Taherdoost, 2023; Wang et al., 2021; Wang, Wen, et al., 2020; Xu et al., 2021). Despite these efforts, few methods have simultaneously achieved simplicity, weight sensitivity, and ordering consistency—particularly under transformations of equivalent indices (Dai et al., 2023).

In response, Dai et al. (2023) introduced the ordering preference targeting at bi-ideal average solutions (OPTBIAS) method. Building on the preference ranking on the basis of ideal-average distance (PROBID) framework, OPTBIAS constructs bi-positive and bi-negative ideal points by aggregating the top and bottom thirds of the solution set, and incorporates the average (A) solution as an additional reference. The method evaluates alternatives based on their relative distances to these reference points, weighted by their importance. This approach enhances ranking consistency while maintaining computational efficiency, making OPTBIAS a valuable addition to the MCDM toolkit.

The remainder of this chapter is organized as follows:

Section 71.2 outlines the procedural steps of OPTBIAS.

Section 71.3 presents a numerical example in a healthcare supply chain context.

Section 71.4 extends the method to a more complex scenario.

Section 71.5 provides a comparative analysis with other MCDM methods.

Section 71.6 concludes with key insights and future directions.

71.2 Methodology

The OPTBIAS method provides a structured approach for ranking Pareto-optimal solutions in multiobjective decision-making contexts. Its design addresses common limitations found in traditional MCDM techniques, such as sensitivity to index transformations and inconsistencies in solution ordering. To ensure a balanced and interpretable ranking, OPTBIAS incorporates three reference constructs:

Bi-positive ideal solution: derived from the top third of the Pareto-optimal set

Bi-negative ideal solution: derived from the bottom third of the Pareto-optimal set

A solution: representing the central tendency across all objectives

These reference points are considered simultaneously, and their relative importance is integrated into the evaluation process. By doing so, OPTBIAS enhances ranking consistency while maintaining computational simplicity. The procedural framework of OPTBIAS is outlined in Fig. 71.1 and consists of the following steps:

Step 1. Begin by formulating the initial objective matrix $\boldsymbol{F}$, also referred to as the decision matrix, where each element f_{ij} represents the value of the jth objective (or criterion) for the ith alternative (or solution). To standardize the scale of evaluation across different objectives, the matrix is normalized using the vector normalization method. The resulting

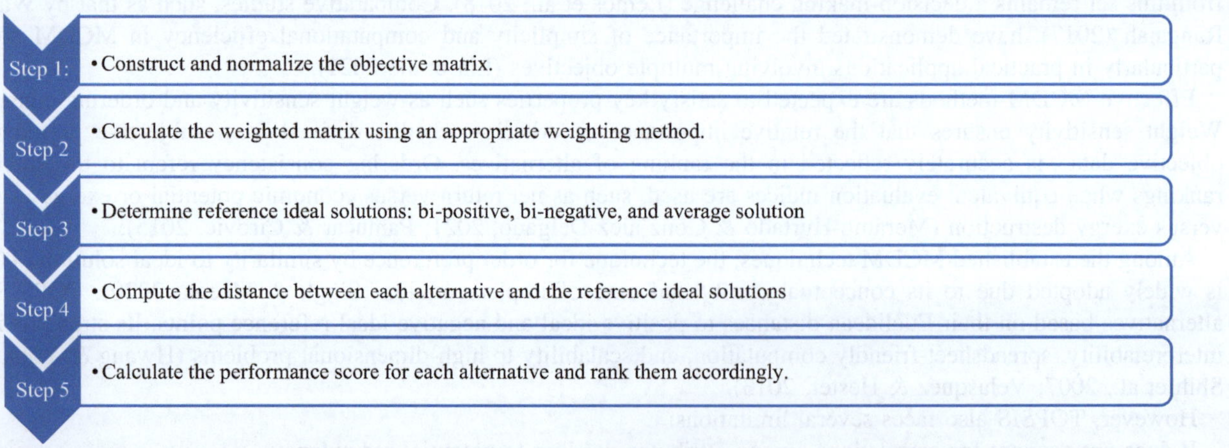

FIGURE 71.1 Steps of the OPTBIAS method.

matrix, denoted as ***NF***, comprises normalized entries nf_{ij}, which are obtained according to Eq. (71.1) and further elaborated through Eqs. (71.2) and (71.3).

$$F = [f_{ij}]_{n*m} = \begin{bmatrix} f_{11} & f_{12} & \cdots & f_{1m} \\ f_{21} & f_{22} & \cdots & f_{2m} \\ \vdots & \vdots & \cdots & \vdots \\ f_{n1} & f_{n2} & \cdots & f_{nm} \end{bmatrix} \quad (71.1)$$

$$\mathrm{NF} = [nf_{ij}]_{n*m} = \begin{bmatrix} nf_{11} & nf_{12} & \cdots & nf_{1m} \\ nf_{21} & nf_{22} & \cdots & nf_{2m} \\ \vdots & \vdots & \cdots & \vdots \\ nf_{n1} & nf_{n2} & \cdots & nf_{nm} \end{bmatrix} \quad (71.2)$$

$$nf_{ij} = \frac{f_{ij}}{\sqrt{\sum_{k=1}^{n} f_{kj}^2}} \quad (71.3)$$

Step 2. Construct the weighted normalized objective matrix **V** by multiplying each column of the normalized matrix **NF** by its corresponding objective weight coefficient w_m. This operation accounts for the relative importance of each objective and results in a matrix **V** as defined in Eq. (71.4).

$$\mathrm{V} = [v_{ij}]_{n*m} = \begin{bmatrix} v_{11} & v_{12} & \cdots & v_{1m} \\ v_{21} & v_{22} & \cdots & v_{2m} \\ \vdots & \vdots & \cdots & \vdots \\ v_{n1} & v_{n2} & \cdots & v_{nm} \end{bmatrix} = \begin{bmatrix} w_1.\ nf_{11} & w_2.\ nf_{12} & \cdots & w_m.\ nf_{1m} \\ w_1.\ nf_{21} & w_2.\ nf_{22} & \cdots & w_m.\ nf_{2m} \\ \vdots & \vdots & \cdots & \vdots \\ w_1.\ nf_{n1} & w_2.\ nf_{n2} & \cdots & w_m.\ nf_{nm} \end{bmatrix} \quad (71.4)$$

Step 3. Inspired by the proven efficacy of PROBID and its refined variant sPROBID (Wang et al., 2021), OPTBIAS establishes its reference framework using an expanded set of ideal points. This includes the most favorable (bi-positive) and least favorable (bi-negative) solutions, derived from the top third and bottom third of the ranked Pareto-optimal solutions, respectively, in conjunction with the A solution.

$$RA_{(p)} = \left\{ \left(MAx(v_j,\ p) | j \in J \right), \left(Min(v_j,\ p) | j \in J' \right) \right\} = \{v_{(p)1},\ v_{(p)2},\ \ldots,\ v_{(p)m}\},\ \ p \in \{1,\ 2,\ \ldots,\ n\} \quad (71.5)$$

$$PI_{(k)} = \begin{cases} RA_{(p)|p=1} & k = 1 \\ \sum_{p=2}^{n/3} \frac{RA(p)}{p} & k = 2 \end{cases} \quad (71.6)$$

$$NI_{(k)} = \begin{cases} RA_{(p)|p=n} & k = 1 \\ \sum_{p=n+1-\left(\frac{n}{3}\right)}^{n-1} \frac{RA_{(p)}}{n-p+1} & k = 2 \end{cases} \quad (71.7)$$

$$\mathrm{k} = \begin{cases} 1 & n > 6 \\ 1,\ 2 & n \geq 6 \end{cases} \quad (71.8)$$

$$\overline{A} = [\overline{v}_j]_m = [\overline{v}_1\ \overline{v}_1\ \overline{v}_1 \cdots \overline{v}_j \cdots \overline{v}_m] = \left[\frac{\sum_{i=1}^{n} v_{(i)1}}{n}\ \ \frac{\sum_{i=1}^{n} v_{(i)2}}{n}\ \ \cdots \frac{\sum_{i=1}^{n} v_{(i)j}}{n}\ \ \cdots\ \ \frac{\sum_{i=1}^{n} v_{(i)m}}{n} \right] \quad (71.9)$$

Each reference point $RA_{(p)}$ represents a composite of the pth best value for every objective. Specifically:

$RA_{(1)}$ is formed by selecting the maximum value for benefit-type objectives and the minimum value for cost-type objectives—this constitutes the most "positive" ideal solution.

Successive reference points $RA_{(2)}$, $RA_{(3)}$, …, $RA_{(n)}$ follow the same logic, encapsulating decreasing preference rankings.

Conversely, the least preferred solution $RA_{(n)}$ represents the most "negative" ideal solution.

Objective sets are categorized as:

J: Benefit-type objectives (to be maximized)

J': Cost-type objectives (to be minimized)

For each objective j, the functions Max (v_j,p) and Min(v_j,p) denote the pth largest and smallest values in the weighted normalized dataset, respectively.

Equations (71.5)–(71.8) formalize the construction of bi-positive and bi-negative solutions:

Bi-positive ideal (PI) solutions include both the top-ranked individual values and the aggregated values from the top third of each objective's ranking.

Bi-negative ideal (NI) solutions similarly incorporate the lowest-performing individual values and aggregates from the bottom third.

A computational adjustment applies when n < 6, where the top and bottom third only yield one representative point each, thereby simplifying calculations while maximizing reference point significance.

Finally, the A solution is calculated as the arithmetic mean of each objective across all Pareto-optimal solutions, as defined in Eq. (71.9).

Step 4. For each Pareto-optimal solution, compute the Euclidean distances to the following reference points:

PI solutions

NI solutions

A solution

These are denoted respectively by the distance matrices **SP**, **SN**, and **SA**, each capturing the distance from individual solutions to their corresponding bi-ideal references.

$$\mathrm{SP} = [SP_i]_n = \begin{bmatrix} SP_1 \\ SP_2 \\ \vdots \\ SP_n \end{bmatrix}, \quad SP_i = \begin{cases} \sum_{k=1}^{2} \sqrt{\sum_{j=1}^{m} (v_{ij} - PI_{(k)j})^2} & \mathrm{n} \geq 6 \\ \sqrt{\sum_{j=1}^{m} (v_{ij} - PI_{(1)j})^2} & n < 6 \end{cases} \tag{71.10}$$

$$\mathrm{SN} = [SN_i]_n = \begin{bmatrix} SN_1 \\ SN_2 \\ \vdots \\ SN_n \end{bmatrix}, \quad SN_i = \begin{cases} \sum_{k=1}^{2} \sqrt{\sum_{j=1}^{m} (v_{ij} - NI_{(k)j})^2} & \mathrm{n} \geq 6 \\ \sqrt{\sum_{j=1}^{m} (v_{ij} - NI_{(1)j})^2} & n < 6 \end{cases} \tag{71.11}$$

$$\mathrm{SA} = [SA_i]_n = \begin{bmatrix} SA_1 \\ SA_2 \\ \vdots \\ SA_n \end{bmatrix} = \begin{bmatrix} \sqrt{\sum_{j=1}^{m} (v_{1j} - \overline{v_j})^2} \\ \sqrt{\sum_{j=1}^{m} (v_{2j} - \overline{v_j})^2} \\ \vdots \\ \sqrt{\sum_{j=1}^{m} (v_{nj} - \overline{v_j})^2} \end{bmatrix} \tag{71.12}$$

Compared with the **PROBID** approach, which requires calculating distances to all individual ideal and average points, OPTBIAS simplifies this process by aggregating rankings:

The top third and bottom third ranked points are merged into second bi-positive and second bi-negative solutions.

Only five distances are necessary: two for the PI solutions (PI_1 and PI_2), two for the NI solutions (NI_1 and NI_2), and one for the A solution.

Step 5. Once all distances are computed, the **performance score matrix (P)** is derived using the ratio R_i of a solution's proximity to the positive and NI solutions, adjusted for the A solution:

The **ratio** R_i reflects the relative closeness of solution i to the bi-positive versus bi-negative references.

A power function is applied to **amplify the influence** of bi-ideal distances, ensuring their dominance in the ranking process.

A reduction coefficient of $\frac{1}{2n}$ is introduced to **moderate** the effect of the A solution distance.

Higher $R_i \rightarrow$ solution is closer to the positive ideal, yielding a **higher** performance score P_i

Lower $R_i \rightarrow$ solution is closer to the negative ideal, resulting in a **lower** P_i. The solution with the maximum P_i is recommended as the optimal choice.

The calculations pertaining to R and P are outlined in Eqs. 71.13 and 71.14.

$$P = [P_i]_n = \begin{bmatrix} P_1 \\ P_2 \\ \vdots \\ P_n \end{bmatrix} = \begin{bmatrix} \exp\left(\frac{R_1}{3}\right) + \frac{SA_1}{2n} \\ \exp\left(\frac{R_2}{3}\right) + \frac{SA_2}{2n} \\ \vdots \\ \exp\left(\frac{R_n}{3}\right) + \frac{SA_n}{2n} \end{bmatrix} \tag{71.13}$$

$$R = [R_i]_n = \begin{bmatrix} R_1 \\ R_2 \\ \vdots \\ R_n \end{bmatrix} = \begin{bmatrix} \frac{SN_1}{SP_1} \\ \frac{SN_2}{SP_2} \\ \vdots \\ \frac{SN_n}{SP_n} \end{bmatrix} \tag{71.14}$$

71.3 Numerical example 1

Healthcare decision-making is widely acknowledged as a complex and multidimensional process, shaped by a diverse set of factors including medical requirements, technological advancements, social dynamics, ethical considerations, economic constraints, and environmental conditions. This complexity is further amplified by the presence of multiple, often conflicting objectives and the involvement of various stakeholders with differing priorities and expectations. To navigate these intricacies, a range of MCDM techniques has been employed, offering structured frameworks that support transparent, consistent, and timely decision-making across healthcare systems (Chakraborty et al., 2023).

The COVID-19 pandemic placed unprecedented strain on global healthcare infrastructures, particularly in terms of supply chain resilience. The surge in demand for medical supplies and essential goods revealed critical vulnerabilities in procurement, distribution, and inventory management. In this context, Islam et al. (2022) conducted a comprehensive study to identify and analyze the operational challenges faced by suppliers during the pandemic. Their research emphasized the strategic role of Industry 4.0 technologies in mitigating disruptions and enhancing supply chain responsiveness.

Through a structured evaluation, the study identified seven key criteria and eleven distinct challenges influencing supply chain performance among healthcare retailers. The relative importance of these criteria was assessed using the analytic hierarchy process, with detailed weightings and rankings presented in Table 71.1. Among the findings, the equilibrium between supply and demand emerged as the most influential factor, underscoring its central role in maintaining service effectiveness under crisis conditions.

To streamline the analysis and enhance model tractability, this section employs a simplified approach by focusing on the five most influential attributes (P1 to P5), which collectively account for the majority of the decision-making impact. To ensure methodological particularity, the weights of these selected attributes are normalized to sum to unity, as detailed in Table 71.2.

TABLE 71.1 Ranking of attributes based on weightage.

Attribute (criteria)	Weight	Rank
Balance in supply and demand (P1)	0.275286	1
Safety of employees (P2)	0.265144	2
Distribution & transportation capability (P4)	0.164123	3
Trust between retailer and consumer (P3)	0.099406	4
Shortage of manpower (P5)	0.095395	5
Consumer behavior (P6)	0.058545	6
Capacity constraints (P7)	0.042104	7

TABLE 71.2 Normalized weights of selected attributes for simplified model.

Attribute (criteria)	Normalized weight
Balance in supply and demand (P1)	0.3104
Safety of employees (P2)	0.2990
Distribution & transportation capability (P4)	0.1852
Trust between retailer and consumer (P3)	0.1124
Shortage of manpower (P5)	0.0930

TABLE 71.3 Ranking of challenges affecting supply chain.

Challenge	Description	Simplified example
Maintenance of an appropriate balance among supply and demand (C8)	Imbalance of supply and demand requires adaptive retail chain strategies	*
Lack of viability (C10)	Lack of feasible planning tools for long-term supply chain disruptions	*
Absence of government funding (C2)	Lack of government funding and the need for collaborative contracts	*
Lack of access (C11)	Absence of structured operational approaches to safe goods transportation	*
Absence of confidence (C3)	Absence of trust across supply chain participants, requiring blockchain for accountability	*
Scarcity of workforce (C6)	Workforce shortage driven by job insecurity and infection risk	
Lack of security and safety (C5)	Inadequate safety measures and policies for workers during crises	
Deficiency of surplus medical amenities (C9)	Limited access to medical infrastructure and barriers to technology adoption	
Consumer attitude (C7)	Unpredictable shifts in consumer behavior during emergencies	
Absence of supply chain flexibility (C1)	High cost of enhancing adaptability under uncertainty	
Communication problems (C4)	Communication gaps between authorities and industry, demanding IoT-based solutions	

Similarly, of the eleven challenges identified by Islam et al. (2022), the top five in terms of priority scores have been selected for inclusion in the simplified model (see Table 71.3). These challenges are:

Maintenance of an appropriate balance between supply and demand
Lack of viability
Absence of government funding
Limited access
Absence of confidence

This reduction in complexity facilitates focused analysis on the most critical supply chain challenges encountered during the pandemic, without compromising the analytical integrity essential for sound decision-making.

Step 1. Construct and normalize the objective matrix

The simplified model, integrating the normalized key attributes and selected high-priority challenges, is subjected to evaluation using the OPTBIAS method. This approach strikes a balance between analytical depth and computational efficiency, making it particularly well-suited for preliminary decision-making processes or scenarios characterized by constrained data availability. The decision matrix for this analysis is presented in Table 71.4.

Step 2. Calculate the weighted matrix using an appropriate weighting method

Following normalization and weighting, the weighted normalized decision matrix is summarized in Table 71.5.

Step 3. Determine reference ideal solutions

Now, let us proceed to the next step. Since the number of Pareto-optimal solutions in this case is less than six, the parameter k is set to 1, as defined by the OPTBIAS framework. This simplifies the construction of reference points: instead of averaging over the top and bottom thirds of the ranked solutions, the bi-positive and bi-NI solutions are directly derived from the first and last reference points.

Given that all objectives in this case are challenge-type (i.e., cost-type or negatively oriented), the bi-positive ideal solution corresponds to the alternative with the lowest value across all objectives, while the bi-negative ideal solution corresponds to the one with the highest value. This aligns with the OPTBIAS framework, which adapts its reference construction based on the nature of the objectives. For example, $RA_{(1)}$ is composed of the best value of each objective

TABLE 71.4 Initial and normalized decision matrix (simplified).

Challenges	Initial					Normalized				
	P1	P2	P3	P4	P5	P1	P2	P3	P4	P5
Absence of government funding (C2)	1	2	2	4	2	0.14	0.34	0.49	0.23	0.5
Absence of confidence (C3)	3	3	5	4	1	0.42	0.51	0.49	0.58	0.25
Maintenance of an appropriate balance among supply and demand (C8)	4	1	4	3	1	0.55	0.17	0.37	0.46	0.25
Lack of viability (C10)	5	2	5	1	1	0.69	0.34	0.12	0.58	0.25
Lack of access (C11)	1	4	2	5	3	0.14	0.69	0.61	0.23	0.75

TABLE 71.5 Weighted normalized decision matrix (simplified).

Challenges	P1	P2	P3	P4	P5
C2	0.04	0.1	0.09	0.03	0.05
C3	0.13	0.15	0.09	0.07	0.02
C8	0.17	0.05	0.07	0.05	0.02
C10	0.22	0.1	0.02	0.07	0.02
C11	0.04	0.21	0.11	0.03	0.07

TABLE 71.6 Reference ideal solutions (simplified).

Reference ideal solutions	P1	P2	P3	P4	P5
PI	0.04	0.05	0.02	0.03	0.02
NI	0.22	0.21	0.11	0.07	0.07
$\overline{A}$	0.12	0.122	0.076	0.05	0.036

TABLE 71.7 Distance between each alternative and the reference ideal solutions (simplified).

Challenges	SA	SN	SP
C2	0.09	0.22	0.09
C3	0.04	0.12	0.16
C8	0.09	0.18	0.14
C10	0.12	0.15	0.19
C11	0.13	0.18	0.19

among all the Pareto-optimal solutions—that is, the minimum value for each cost-type objective. This point represents the first-ranked ideal solution, commonly referred to as the most "positive" ideal solution. Correspondingly, $RA_{(n)}$ captures the worst value of each objective—namely, the maximum values for cost-type objectives—and represents the most "negative" ideal solution.

Therefore, in this case:

$$\text{The bi} - \text{positive ideal solution is defined as } PI_{(1)} = RA_{(1)}$$

$$\text{Thebi} - \text{negativeidealsolutionis defined as } NI_{(1)} = RA_{(n)}$$

In addition to these two extremes, the A solution is calculated by taking the arithmetic mean of each objective across all Pareto-optimal alternatives. This average point serves as a neutral reference, capturing the central tendency of the solution space and complementing the ideal extremes used in bias analysis. Table 71.6 shows reference ideal solutions.

Step 4. Compute the distance between each alternative and the reference ideal solutions

Based on Eqs. (71.10), (71.11), and (71.12), the Euclidean distances were calculated for each Pareto-optimal solution relative to three reference points: the positive ideal solution (PI), the negative ideal solution (NI), and the A solution. These distances are represented by the matrices SP, SN, and SA, respectively. SP reflects the distance to the most favorable (bi-positive) ideal solution, SN captures the distance to the least favorable (bi-negative) ideal solution, and SA indicates the distance to the A solution, which represents the central tendency of the solution space. The results of these calculations are presented in Table 71.7.

Step 5. Calculate the performance score for each alternative and rank them accordingly

Based on Eqs. (71.13) and (71.14), the resulting prioritization of challenges, derived from this analysis, is reported in Table 71.8.

71.3.1 Absence of government funding (C2)

The absence of government funding emerged as the most critical constraint, receiving the highest performance score ($P = 2.26$) and a notable signal-to-noise (SN/SP) ratio of 2.44. During the COVID-19 pandemic, numerous commercial entities endeavored to independently fulfill urgent public needs; however, the lack of coordinated fiscal backing rendered producers financially vulnerable. The pandemic highlighted systemic risks, exemplified by the collapse of several medical

TABLE 71.8 Challenges ranking (simplified).

Challenges	R = SN/SP	P	Rank
C2	2.44	2.26	1
C3	0.75	1.29	5
C8	1.29	1.55	2
C10	0.79	1.31	4
C11	0.95	1.39	3

institutions facing unpredictable demand patterns. Ostrom et al. (2010) argued that well-designed capital structures and targeted incentive mechanisms are pivotal in mitigating such vulnerabilities. This constraint underscores the indispensable role of institutional support in ensuring the continuity, stability, and resilience of retail supply chains during crises and other systemic shocks.

71.3.2 Maintenance of an appropriate balance among supply and demand (C8)

The pandemic severely disrupted conventional supply-demand equilibria, marked by a surge in consumer demand for essential goods, which outstripped available inventories. This imbalance, reflected by a performance score of 1.55, was further aggravated by limited operational flexibility and suboptimal demand forecasting capabilities. Chen et al. (2008) noted that insufficient awareness and sluggish responsiveness within supply chain teams contributed significantly to order fulfillment failures. Retailers were frequently unprepared for rapid shifts in consumer behavior, resulting in stockouts, service delays, and customer dissatisfaction. This constraint highlights the critical necessity for agile inventory management strategies and real-time, data-driven demand sensing mechanisms that can sustain operational balance amid volatile and uncertain market conditions.

71.3.3 Lack of access (C11)

Access constraints, primarily driven by lockdown measures and transportation disruptions, ranked third in severity with a performance score of 1.39. Although government restrictions were effective in mitigating viral transmission, they inadvertently obstructed the flow of essential goods within fragmented logistics networks. Retailers and manufacturers faced considerable challenges navigating these disruptions, leading to significant delays in deliveries and production bottlenecks. The severity of this constraint underscores its strong linkage to national policy environments and the preparedness of infrastructure systems. Proactive investments in decentralized distribution networks and the development of contingency routing strategies are essential for enhancing supply chain robustness and ensuring uninterrupted supply continuity in future emergency scenarios.

71.3.4 Lack of viability (C10)

Viability, encompassing an enterprise's resilience, flexibility, and renewability, is a core dimension of sustainable supply chains. Scoring 1.31 on the performance scale, this constraint reflects the economic fragility faced by many retail operations during the pandemic. Challenges such as declining foot traffic, escalating compliance costs, and shifting consumer priorities rendered numerous conventional business models unviable. As Islam et al. (2022) emphasize, viability extends beyond mere survival; it demands the capacity for continuous adaptation, innovation, and value delivery amid dynamic and uncertain environments. Addressing viability issues necessitates structural transformation, accelerated digital adoption, and enhanced financial agility to support long-term sustainability.

71.3.5 Absence of confidence (C3)

Although rated lowest in terms of immediate impact (P = 1.29,$P = 1.29$), the absence of consumer and stakeholder confidence poses a significant strategic risk with far-reaching implications. Trust erosion—amplified by widespread misinformation, transparency deficits, and health safety concerns—undermined critical consumer-retailer relationships throughout the pandemic. To restore credibility, retailers adopted "no-touch" delivery systems alongside digital verification mechanisms. Soderberg and Bengtsson (2010) indicate that emerging technologies such as blockchain and e-commerce monitoring can enhance traceability and reinforce trustworthiness. While this constraint may exert less immediate operational disruption, rebuilding and maintaining confidence is crucial for preserving brand integrity and fostering customer loyalty in the evolving postpandemic economic landscape.

The prioritization of these five constraints provides a nuanced understanding of vulnerabilities within retail supply chains exposed by the COVID-19 crisis. Among them, financial support (C2) and supply-demand balance (C8) stand out as predominant operational challenges, whereas access (C11), viability (C10), and confidence (C3) represent critical structural and relational resilience factors. Effectively addressing these multidimensional challenges requires a comprehensive and integrated approach that combines policy reform, technological innovation, and organizational flexibility to develop robust, adaptive, and future-ready supply chains.

71.4 Numerical example 2

The complete model employs all seven attributes and all eleven challenges as detailed in Tables 71.1 and 71.3. By including the full dataset, the model aims to capture the complexity and interdependencies of supply chain challenges resulting from COVID-19 disruptions more thoroughly.

This comprehensive approach is particularly valuable for policymakers and supply chain managers who require a deep understanding of the intricate dynamics and relative importance of all factors involved. The decision-making process uses the original weights without normalization, ensuring that all factors are represented according to their reported significance in the foundational research.

Step 1. Construct and normalize the objective matrix

Using the OPTBIAS method, the full model results in a detailed prioritization that supports strategic planning and robust supply chain risk management. Decision matrix follows as Table 71.9.

Step 2. Calculate the weighted matrix using an appropriate weighting method

After normalization and weighting, the weighted normalized decision matrix is according to Table 71.10.

Step 3. Determine reference ideal solutions

TABLE 71.9 Initial and normalized decision matrix.

Challenges	Initial							Normalized						
	P1	P2	P3	P4	P5	P6	P7	P1	P2	P3	P4	P5	P6	P7
C1	5	4	2	5	3	3	1	0.37	0.35	0.16	0.42	0.32	0.3	0.1
C2	1	2	2	4	2	4	3	0.07	0.18	0.16	0.34	0.21	0.4	0.3
C3	3	3	5	4	1	3	1	0.22	0.26	0.4	0.34	0.11	0.3	0.1
C4	4	5	5	3	5	3	2	0.29	0.44	0.4	0.25	0.53	0.3	0.2
C5	4	3	5	3	3	3	4	0.29	0.26	0.4	0.25	0.32	0.3	0.4
C6	5	2	4	2	4	1	5	0.37	0.18	0.32	0.17	0.43	0.1	0.5
C7	5	4	3	5	2	1	3	0.37	0.35	0.24	0.42	0.21	0.1	0.3
C8	4	1	4	3	1	3	4	0.29	0.09	0.32	0.25	0.11	0.3	0.4
C9	5	5	1	1	3	5	4	0.37	0.44	0.08	0.08	0.32	0.51	0.4
C10	5	2	5	1	1	1	1	0.37	0.18	0.4	0.08	0.11	0.1	0.1
C11	1	4	2	5	3	3	2	0.07	0.35	0.16	0.42	0.32	0.3	0.2

TABLE 71.10 Weighted normalized decision matrix.

Challenges	P1	P2	P3	P4	P5	P6	P7
C1	0.101	0.093	0.016	0.07	0.03	0.018	0.004
C2	0.02	0.047	0.016	0.056	0.02	0.023	0.012
C3	0.061	0.07	0.04	0.056	0.01	0.018	0.004
C4	0.081	0.117	0.04	0.042	0.051	0.018	0.008
C5	0.081	0.07	0.04	0.042	0.03	0.018	0.017
C6	0.101	0.047	0.032	0.028	0.041	0.006	0.021
C7	0.101	0.093	0.024	0.07	0.02	0.006	0.012
C8	0.081	0.023	0.032	0.042	0.01	0.018	0.017
C9	0.101	0.117	0.008	0.014	0.03	0.029	0.017
C10	0.101	0.047	0.04	0.014	0.01	0.006	0.004
C11	0.02	0.093	0.016	0.07	0.03	0.018	0.008

Since the number of Pareto-optimal solutions in this case is 11, which satisfies the condition $n \geq 6$, the parameter k is set to 2 according to Eq. (71.8). This affects the construction of the bi-positive and bi-NI solutions, which are now computed using aggregated values from the top and bottom thirds of the ranked Pareto-optimal set.

According to (71.5), each reference point $RA_{(P)}$ is constructed by selecting the maximum value for benefit-type objectives (set J) and the minimum value for cost-type objectives (set J′) from the p-th ranked solution. In this case, since all objectives are cost-type, $RA_{(P)}$ consists of the minimum values for each objective in the p-th solution.

The bi-positive ideal solution $PI_{(2)}$, as defined in Eq. (71.6), is calculated by averaging the reference points from the top third of the ranked solutions. Given that n = 11, the top third includes solutions ranked from p = 2 to p = 3 (since 11/3 ≈ 3.67, rounded down to 3). Therefore:

$$PI_{(2)} = (RA_{(2)} + RA_{(3)})/2 \tag{71.15}$$

Similarly, the bi-negative ideal solution $NI_{(2)}$, as defined in Eq. (71.7), is calculated by averaging the reference points from the bottom third of the ranked solutions. This includes solutions ranked from p = 9 to p = 10 (since $n + 1 - n/3 = 11 + 1 - 3.67 \approx 8.33$, rounded up to 9). Therefore:

$$NI_{(2)} = (RA_{(9)} + RA_{(10)})/2$$

The A solution $\overline{A}$, as defined in Eq. (71.9), is computed by taking the arithmetic mean of each objective across all 11 Pareto-optimal solutions. Table 71.11 shows reference ideal solutions.

Step 4. Compute the distance between each alternative and the reference ideal solutions

In this step, Euclidean distances are calculated for each Pareto-optimal solution with respect to three reference points: the *PI* solutions, the *NI* solutions, and the *A* solution. These distances are organized into three matrices— *SP*, *SN*, and *SA* —each representing the proximity of individual solutions to their corresponding bi-ideal references.

Since the number of Pareto-optimal solutions is 11 (i.e., $n \geq 6$), the OPTBIAS framework uses both the first and second bi-ideal solutions in the calculations. Specifically, *SP* includes distances to $PI_{(1)}$ and $PI_{(2)}$, *SN* includes distances to $NI_{(1)}$ and $NI_{(2)}$, and *SA* includes distances to the A solution $\overline{A}$. This results in a total of five reference-based distances per solution. The results of these distance calculations are presented in Table 71.12.

Step 5. Calculate the performance score for each alternative and rank them accordingly

Once the Euclidean distances are calculated, the performance score matrix (P) is derived using the ratio *R*, which compares each solution's closeness to the positive and negative ideal points. A power function amplifies the influence of ideal distances, while a reduction factor adjusts for the A solution. Higher *R* values lead to higher performance scores *P*, indicating better solutions. The final results of this step are shown in Table 71.13.

TABLE 71.11 Reference ideal solutions.

Reference ideal solutions	P1	P2	P3	P4	P5	P6	P7
$PI_{(1)}$	0.02	0.023	0.008	0.014	0.01	0.006	0.004
$NI_{(1)}$	0.101	0.117	0.04	0.07	0.051	0.029	0.021
$PI_{(2)}$	0.0405	0.047	0.016	0.021	0.01	0.006	0.004
$NI_{(2)}$	0.101	0.105	0.04	0.07	0.051	0.0205	0.021
$\overline{A}$	0.077	0.074	0.028	0.046	0.026	0.016	0.011

TABLE 71.12 Distance between each alternative and the reference ideal solutions.

Challenges	SA	SN	SP
C1	0.04	0.08	0.22
C2	0.06	0.22	0.11
C3	0.03	0.15	0.14
C4	0.05	0.08	0.23
C5	0.02	0.12	0.15
C6	0.04	0.15	0.17
C7	0.04	0.09	0.21
C8	0.06	0.22	0.13
C9	0.07	0.14	0.23
C10	0.05	0.2	0.15
C11	0.06	0.18	0.17

TABLE 71.13 Challenges ranking.

Challenges	R = SN/SP	P	Rank
C1	0.36	1.13	9
C2	2	1.95	1
C3	1.07	1.43	4
C4	0.35	1.13	9
C5	0.8	1.31	6
C6	0.88	1.34	5
C7	0.43	1.16	8
C8	1.69	1.76	2
C9	0.61	1.23	7
C10	1.33	1.56	3
C11	1.06	1.43	4

This evaluation presents a refined prioritization of eleven critical challenges affecting retail supply chains, particularly in the context of systemic disruptions such as the COVID-19 pandemic. Using the OPTBIAS approach, each challenge is assessed. The final Ranking ensures that challenges with equal performance scores share the same rank, while subsequent ranks continue sequentially without gaps.

71.4.1 Absence of government funding (C2)

This challenge remains the most critical, achieving the highest performance score (P = 1.95 $P = 1.95$). It accentuates the vital role of public sector financial support in stabilizing retail supply chains during crises. The absence of such backing leads to liquidity constraints, diminished operational capacity, and threatens the long-term sustainability of retailers.

71.4.2 Maintenance of an appropriate balance among supply and demand (C8)

The second-highest ranked challenge (P = 1.76) reflects the volatility in consumer demand and supply chain responsiveness. Disruptions in inventory flow and forecasting accuracy led to mismatches that strained logistics and customer satisfaction. This underscores the need for dynamic demand sensing and agile inventory management.

71.4.3 Lack of viability (C10)

Scoring 1.56, this challenge emphasizes the imperative to reimagine supply chains for economic sustainability, adaptability, and resilience. Addressing viability involves diversification, digital transformation, and strategic partnerships aimed at equipping supply chains to withstand future shocks.

71.4.4 Absence of confidence (C3) and lack of access (C11)

Both challenges scored 1.43, indicating their shared strategic importance. Confidence erosion—due to misinformation, health concerns, and inconsistent service—undermined consumer trust. Simultaneously, restricted access to goods and services, especially in lockdown scenarios, disrupted retail continuity. Addressing these requires transparent communication and decentralized distribution models.

71.4.5 Scarcity of workforce (C6)

Labor shortages, driven by health risks and mobility restrictions, impaired supply chain operations. The score of 1.34 suggests that workforce resilience—through automation, remote enablement, and flexible staffing—is essential for future-proofing retail logistics.

71.4.6 Lack of security and safety (C5)

This challenge (P = 1.31) reflects vulnerabilities in both physical and digital domains. Ensuring employee safety and cybersecurity is vital for operational integrity, especially in high-risk environments.

71.4.7 Deficiency of surplus medical amenities (C9)

With a performance score of 1.23 and ranked seventh, this challenge reflects the critical shortfall of excess medical supplies needed to meet sudden and unpredictable surges in demand during crisis situations. The deficiency of surplus medical amenities limits the capacity of healthcare and retail supply chains to respond effectively in emergencies. This highlights the necessity for strategic stockpiling, enhanced demand forecasting, and improved inventory management to build robust buffers that ensure supply continuity in times of acute need.

71.4.8 Consumer attitude (C7)

Unpredictable consumer behavior, including panic buying and shifting preferences, complicated demand forecasting. Retailers must invest in behavioral analytics and personalized engagement strategies to better anticipate and respond to consumer trends.

71.4.9 Absence of supply chain flexibility (C1) and communication problems (C4)

Both challenges share a performance score of 1.13 and are jointly ranked ninth. The absence of supply chain flexibility points to the inflexibility and rigidity within supply chain systems, hindering their ability to rapidly adjust to changing conditions and disruptions. Concurrently, communication problems denote fragmented or ineffective information exchange and coordination among supply chain actors, which exacerbate delays and reduce the effectiveness of crisis response. Addressing these intertwined issues requires investing in scalable, adaptable supply chain architectures alongside robust and transparent communication frameworks that facilitate real-time collaboration and decision-making during emergencies.

The updated ranking provides a more accurate and equitable prioritization of retail supply chain challenges. It reveals that while financial and operational constraints dominate the top ranks, behavioral and infrastructural issues remain critical to long-term resilience. Retailers and policymakers must adopt a holistic approach—combining financial support, technological innovation, and strategic agility—to build robust, adaptive supply chains capable of withstanding future disruptions.

71.5 Comparative analysis of ordering preference targeting at bi-ideal average solutions applications

This section presents a structured evaluation of the OPTBIAS method through its application in two distinct decision-making models. The first model adopts a simplified framework, incorporating a reduced set of criteria and challenges to facilitate rapid assessment and operational responsiveness. The second model expands the scope to include a comprehensive array of challenges and full performance metrics, enabling a more strategic and systemic analysis. Together, these models illustrate the adaptability and analytical depth of OPTBIAS in prioritizing supply chain vulnerabilities under varying decision contexts.

71.5.1 Methodological overview of ordering preference targeting at bi-ideal average solutions

OPTBIAS is a multicriteria decision-making (MCDM) technique designed to rank alternatives based on their relative proximity to both positive and NI solutions. This dual-referencing mechanism enables a balanced evaluation that accounts for both desirable and undesirable performance thresholds. The method is particularly suited to environments characterized by uncertainty, trade-offs, and multidimensional evaluation criteria—conditions commonly encountered in supply chain disruption analysis.

Key strengths of the OPTBIAS method include:

Bi-ideal referencing: Each alternative is evaluated against both optimal and worst-case benchmarks, resulting in a more balanced and realistic prioritization.

Robustness in multicriteria contexts: The method effectively handles conflicting criteria, capturing strategic, operational, and behavioral dimensions.

Equitable ranking: Alternatives with similar performance profiles are treated fairly, minimizing artificial gaps in prioritization.

Scalability: OPTBIAS is applicable to both small-scale and large-scale decision matrices, making it suitable for diverse analytical scopes.

Sensitivity to performance d: The method highlights not only top-performing options but also those approaching critical thresholds, supporting risk identification and mitigation.

Despite its advantages, OPTBIAS presents certain limitations:

Computational complexity: The procedure involves normalization, distance calculation, and aggregation, which may be resource-intensive for large datasets.

Normalization dependency: The accuracy of results is sensitive to the scaling method used; inconsistent normalization can distort proximity scores.

Interpretability challenges: The bi-ideal framework may be less intuitive for nonspecialist stakeholders, requiring clear explanation and visualization.

Weight sensitivity: Rankings may shift significantly with changes in criteria weights, necessitating sensitivity analysis to ensure robustness.

These methodological characteristics provide the foundation for evaluating OPTBIAS across models of differing scope and complexity.

71.5.2 Application across simplified and comprehensive models

To assess the practical utility of OPTBIAS, two models were constructed:

The simplified model included five key criteria and five high-priority challenges, selected to streamline analysis and support rapid decision-making.

The comprehensive model incorporated all eleven challenges identified in the literature, along with the full set of evaluation metrics, offering a broader perspective on systemic vulnerabilities.

TABLE 71.14 Comparative analysis of challenge rankings across two models.

Challenge	Simplified model rank	Comprehensive model rank	Interpretation
Absence of government funding	1	1	Institutional support is consistently the top priority across all contexts.
Balance in supply and demand	2	2	Demand volatility and supply constraints are persistent strategic concerns.
Lack of viability	3	3	Structural resilience is essential in both localized and systemic evaluations.
Absence of confidence	4	4	Trust and perception remain key behavioral factors regardless of model scope.
Lack of access	4	4	Accessibility challenges are equally significant across operational levels.

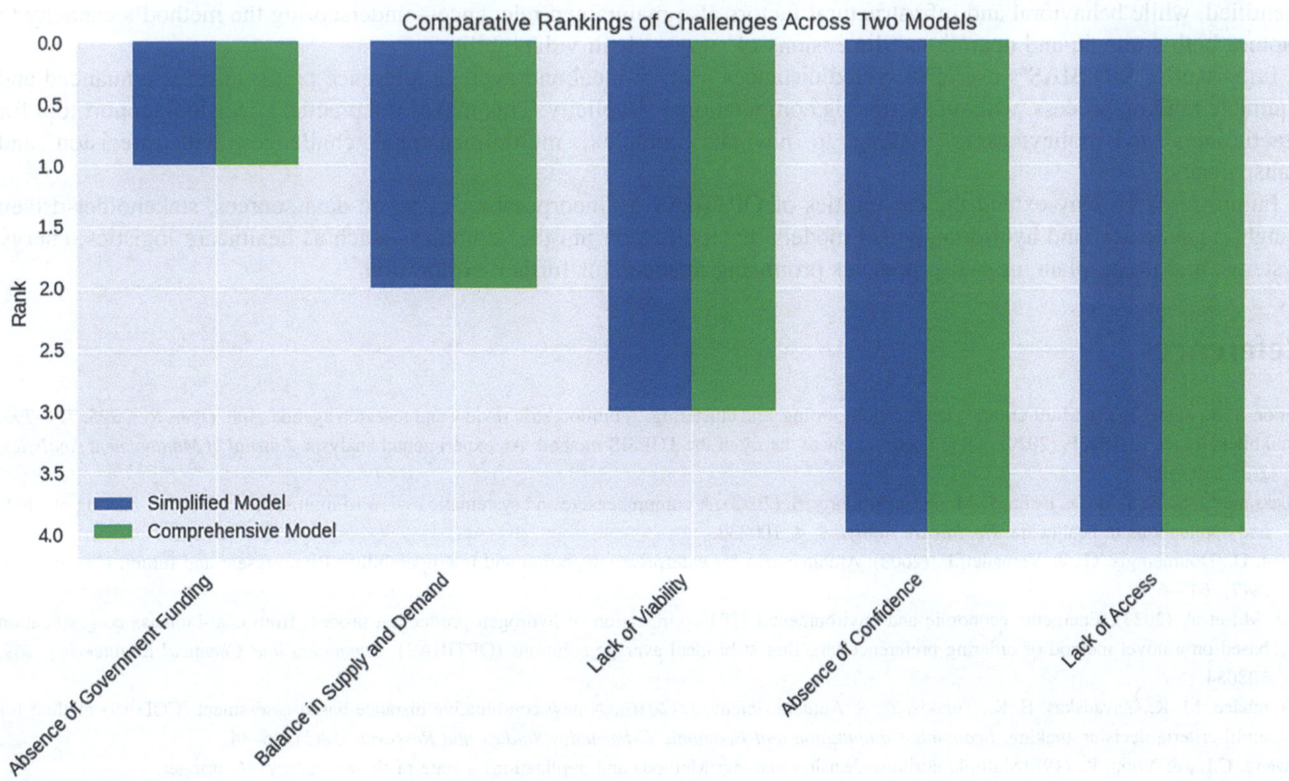

FIGURE 71.2 Comparative rankings across two models.

Although the models differed in scale, several challenges appeared in both, allowing for direct comparison. As shown in Table 71.14 and Fig. 71.2, the rankings of shared challenges remained consistent across both models, underscoring the reliability and stability of the OPTBIAS method.

These findings yield several insights:

Ranking stability: The consistent prioritization of shared challenges confirms the methodological reliability of OPTBIAS across varying decision environments.

Strategic alignment: High-priority issues such as funding, supply-demand balance, and viability were consistently ranked at the top, reinforcing their systemic importance.

Behavioral and infrastructural relevance: Mid-ranked challenges like confidence and access maintained their significance, highlighting their relevance in both tactical and strategic planning.

Model depth versus result integrity: Despite the simplified model's reduced input scope, OPTBIAS preserved the relative importance of key challenges, demonstrating its robustness and adaptability.

In summary, the comparative application of OPTBIAS across two models illustrates its effectiveness in both focused and comprehensive decision-making contexts. The method's ability to maintain ranking consistency, accommodate multiple criteria, and reflect nuanced trade-offs positions it as a valuable tool for prioritizing supply chain challenges under uncertainty.

71.6 Conclusions

This chapter has examined the OPTBIAS method as a structured and adaptable approach to multicriteria decision-making, particularly in the context of supply chain disruption. Building upon the foundational PROBID framework, OPTBIAS introduces a significant advancement by integrating three reference constructs—the bi-positive ideal, bi-negative ideal, and A solution—into a unified ranking mechanism. This structure enables a more balanced and sensitive evaluation of Pareto-optimal solutions, addressing persistent challenges such as ordering inconsistency and computational inefficiency.

Through its application in both simplified and comprehensive decision models, OPTBIAS demonstrated notable strengths in scalability, consistency, and analytical clarity. Despite variations in model complexity, the ranking of key challenges remained stable, validating the method's ability to preserve decision integrity across diverse analytical settings. High-priority concerns such as lack of government funding, supply-demand imbalance, and viability were consistently identified, while behavioral and infrastructural factors also maintained relevance—underscoring the method's capacity to capture both strategic and operational dimensions of supply chain vulnerability.

Importantly, OPTBIAS's use of weighted distances from bi-ideal and average reference points ensures a nuanced and equitable ranking process, without sacrificing computational simplicity. This makes it a practical decision-support tool for practitioners and policymakers seeking to navigate complex, multidimensional challenges with precision and transparency.

Future research may extend the capabilities of OPTBIAS by incorporating dynamic data sources, stakeholder-driven weighting schemes, and hybrid analytical models. Its application in other domains—such as healthcare logistics, energy systems, and urban planning—also presents promising avenues for further exploration.

References

Amor, S. B., et al. (2023). Multi-criteria classification, sorting, and clustering: A bibliometric review and research agenda. *Ann. Oper. Res. 325*, 771–793.

Çelikbilek, Y., & Tüysüz, F. (2020). An in-depth review of theory of the TOPSIS method: An experimental analysis. *Journal of Management Analytics, 7*(2), 281–300.

Chakraborty, S., Raut, R. D., Rofin, T. M., & Chakraborty, S. (2023). A comprehensive and systematic review of multi-criteria decision-making methods and applications in healthcare. *Healthcare Analytics, 4*, 100232.

Chen, D., Doumeingts, G., & Vernadat, F. (2008). Architectures for enterprise integration and interoperability: Past, present and future. *Comput. Ind. 59*(7), 647–659.

Dai, M., et al. (2023). Energetic, economic and environmental (3E) optimization of hydrogen production process from coal-biomass co-gasification based on a novel method of ordering preference targeting at bi-ideal average solutions (OPTBIAS). *Computers and Chemical Engineering, 169*, 108084.

Ghorabaee, M. K., Zavadskas, E. K., Turskis, Z., & Antucheviciene, J. (2016). A new combinative distance-based assessment (CODAS) method for multi-criteria decision-making. *Economic Computation and Economic Cybernetics Studies and Research, 50*(3), 25–44.

Hwang, C.L., & Yoon, K. (1981Multiple attribute decision making: Methods and applications a state-of-the-art survey186Springer.

Islam, S. U., et al. (2022). Assessment of challenges and problems in supply chain among retailers during COVID-19 epidemic through AHP-TOPSIS hybrid MCDM technique. *Internet of Things and Cyber-Physical Systems, 2*, 180–193.

Khan, S. A., et al. (2023). A hybrid multicriteria decision-making approach to evaluate interrelationships and impacts of supply chain performance factors on pharmaceutical industry. *Journal of Multi-Criteria Decision Analysis, 30*, 62–90.

Lemos, L. P., Lima, E. L., & Pinto, J. C. (2018). New decision making criterion for multiobjective optimization problems. *Industrial & Engineering Chemistry Research, 57*(3), 1014–1025.

Li, X., Liu, Z., & Peng, Q. (2011). Improved algorithm of TOPSIS model and its application in river health assessment (Chinese). *Advanced Engineering Sciences, 43*(2), 14–20.

Lin, J., et al. (2021). Relative optimization potential: A novel perspective to address trade-off challenges in urban energy system planning. *Applied Energy, 304*, 117741.

Liu, D., et al. (2019). A resilience evaluation method for a combined regional agricultural water and soil resource system based on weighted mahalanobis distance and a gray-TOPSIS model. *Journal of Cleaner Production, 229*, 667–679.

Luna, R., L´opez, F., & P´erez-Correa, J. R. (2021). Design of optimal wine distillation recipes using multi-criteria decision-making techniques. *Computers & Chemical Engineering, 145*, 107194.

Madanchian, M., & Taherdoost, H. (2023). A comprehensive guide to the TOPSIS method for multi-criteria decision making. *Sustainable Social Development, 1*(1), 1–6.

Meramo-Hurtado, S. I., & Gonz´alez-Delgado, A. D. (2021). Process synthesis, analysis, and optimization methodologies toward chemical process sustainability. *Industrial & Engineering Chemistry Research. 60*(11), 4193–4217.

Nain, A., Jain, D., & Trivedi, A. (2023). Multi-criteria decision-making methods: Application in humanitarian operations. *Benchmarking: An International Journal*. https://doi.org/10.1108/BIJ-11-2022-0673.

Ostrom, A. L., Bitner, M. J., Brown, S. W., et al. (2010). Moving forward and making a difference: Research priorities for the science of service. *Journal of Service Research, 13*(1), 4–36.

Pamucar, D., & Cirovic, G. (2015). The selection of transport and handling resources in logistics centers using multi-attributive border approximation area comparison (MABAC). *Expert Syst. Appl. 42*(6), 3016–3028.

Shih, H. S., Shyur, H. J., & Lee, E. S. (2007). An extension of TOPSIS for group decision making. *Mathematical and Computer Modelling, 45*(7-8), 801–813.

Singh, P., Meena, N. K., et al. (2020). Multi-criteria decision making monarch butterfly optimization for optimal distributed energy resources mix in distribution networks. *Applied Energy, 278*, 115723.

Soderberg, L., & Bengtsson, L. (2010). Supply chain management maturity and performance in SMEs. *Operations Management Research, 3*(1/2), 90–97.

Velasquez, M., & Hester, P. T. (2013). An analysis of multi-criteria decision making methods. *International Journal of Operations Research, 10*(2), 56–66.

Wang, Y., Wen, Z., & Li, H. (2020). Symbiotic technology assessment in iron and steel industry based on entropy TOPSIS methodJournal of Cleaner Production. J. Clean. Prod, 260120900.

Wang, Z., & Rangaiah, G. P. (2017). Application and analysis of methods for selecting an optimal solution from the Pareto-optimal front obtained by multiobjective optimization. *Industrial & Engineering Chemistry Research, 56*(2), 560–574.

Wang, Z., Parhi, S. S., Rangaiah, G. P., & Jana, A. K. (2020). Analysis of weighting and selection methods for Pareto-optimal solutions of multiobjective optimization in chemical engineering applications. *Industrial & Engineering Chemistry Research, 59*(33), 14850–14867.

Wang, Z., Rangaiah, G. P., & Wang, X. (2021). Preference ranking on the basis of ideal-average distance method for multi-criteria decision-making. *Industrial & Engineering Chemistry Research, 60*(30), 11216–11230.

Xu, Q., Zhang, Y. B., & Lv, X. G. (2015). Improved TOPSIS model and its application in the evaluation of NCAA basketball coaches. *Modern Applied Science, 9*(2), 259.

Xu, X., Zhang, Z., Long, T., Sun, S., & Gao, J. (2021). Mega-city region sustainability assessment and obstacles identification with GIS–entropy–TOPSIS model: A case in Yangtze River Delta urban agglomeration Journal of Cleaner Production .J. Clean. Prod, 294126147.

Chapter 72

MARCOS: Measurement alternatives and ranking according to compromise solution for multi-attribute decision-making

Željko Stević[1,2], Eldina Huskanović[1], Edmundas Kazimieras Zavadskas[3], and Dragan Marinković[4,5,6]
[1]*Faculty of Transport and Traffic Engineering, University of East Sarajevo, Doboj, Bosnia and Herzegovina,* [2]*Department of Mobile Machinery and Railway Transport, Faculty of Transport Engineering, Vilnius Gediminas Technical University, Vilnius, Lithuania,* [3]*Department of Construction Management and Real Estate, Vilnius Gediminas Technical University, Vilnius, Lithuania,* [4]*Department of Structural Analysis, Faculty of Mechanical and Transport Systems, TU Berlin, Berlin, Germany,* [5]*Institute of Mechanical Science, Vilnius Gediminas Technical University, Vilnius, Lithuania,* [6]*University College, Korea University, Seoul, Republic of Korea*

72.1 Introduction

One of the more recent and increasingly popular multicriteria decision-making (MCDM) methods is the measurement of alternatives and ranking according to compromise solution (MARCOS) method, developed by Stević and collaborators in 2020. This method is based on evaluating the performance of each alternative relative to the ideal and antiideal solution, allowing for the creation of a compromise solution that best satisfies the defined criteria. A key feature of the MARCOS method is the introduction of a utility ratio between each alternative and reference values, which contributes to a more accurate and stable ranking (Stević et al., 2020). Decision-making in contemporary conditions is becoming increasingly complex due to the growing volume of available information, rising competition, and complex economic, technical, environmental, and social factors. In such an environment, traditional decision-making methods, based on a single criterion or solely on experience, are no longer sufficient. For this reason, MCDM methods have been developed. These methods enable the analysis of multiple alternatives based on a larger number of criteria, taking into account preferences and weighting coefficients. The MARCOS method was developed as a response to the shortcomings of existing MCDM methods, particularly regarding ranking stability and sensitivity to changes in weighting coefficients. The authors aimed to create a methodology that would be intuitive for practitioners while remaining sufficiently precise and reliable for research purposes. The MARCOS method is a flexible and simple method that can also be integrated with other methods, such as Entropy, AHP, BWM, SWARA, CRITIC, etc.

The aim of the paper is to define the significance and growing popularity of the MARCOS method, achieved over a relatively short period of its application. Additionally, the algorithm of this method is presented, and its application is explained through two numerical examples. Furthermore, a literature review is provided to illustrate how researchers have applied the MARCOS method in various contexts and how it can be integrated with other MCDM methods. Some of the fields in which the MARCOS method has already found application include logistics, supply chains, engineering, sustainable development, economics, etc. The aim of this section is to present the MARCOS method in detail, its mathematical steps, advantages and limitations, and to demonstrate its practical application through two specific examples of MCDM. Due to its simple structure and ease of result interpretation, the MARCOS method is suitable not only for researchers and the academic community but also for practitioners in the real sector. Its application in business, public institutions, and strategic planning contributes to better decision-making and risk reduction. Based on the above, the MARCOS method represents a significant contribution to the field of MCDM, and an efficient tool for solving complex problems.

Encyclopedia of Multi-Attribute Decision-Making (MADM). DOI: https://doi.org/10.1016/B978-0-443-33275-3.00034-8

72.2 Literature review

The MARCOS method was first applied in the selection of suppliers in the healthcare sector, after which the trend of applying the MARCOS method in healthcare continued. In this study, Ecer & Pamucar (2021) ranked ten insurance companies according to seven defined criteria, and the results were validated using other methods. This study highlights the need for modern tools in the evaluation of insurance companies and offers an innovative solution applicable beyond the healthcare sector. Study Khosravi et al. (2022), using the FUCOM–MARCOS model, suggests that the private structure in Iranian hospitals is the most efficient, while the budgetary structure is the least efficient. Additionally, gradual changes and attention to the accessibility of healthcare services are proposed. Paper Alrasheedi et al. (2024) presents a combination of mathematical methods and fuzzy logic for a more accurate assessment. The presented FF-modified SPC-RS-MARCOS model was used for selecting sustainable suppliers in the healthcare supply chain. Apart from these examples, the MARCOS method in healthcare was also used for locating a disinfection facility for hazardous waste. A three-phase RF-RFE-ITARA-MARCOS model was developed under uncertain conditions, such as the COVID-19 pandemic. This model was used in a real case in Istanbul, where one of five locations was selected for the disinfection facility (Simic et al., 2023). To ensure successful transplantation surgeries, it is important to thoroughly select the appropriate supplier of medical devices. In the paper Salimian et al. (2022), the E-VIKOR-MARCOS model with fuzzy logic was developed to better manage uncertainties in real decision-making conditions. Economic, social, and environmental criteria were used to evaluate four offered alternatives. The evaluation showed that the surgical instrument supplier was the most suitable.

Among all the areas where the MARCOS method has been applied, it can be said that its most extensive application is in the logistics and transportation sector. In the paper Stević et al. (2023), the FUCOM–MARCOS model was applied to determine the best distribution channel for the company Bingo d.o.o. Out of six criteria, cost proved to be the most important factor, while the breadth of the product range had the least significance. Using the MARCOS method, various distribution models were ranked, with the manufacturer–retailer–customer model being the best choice. The MARCOS method can also be combined with multiple methods simultaneously. For example, when combined with DEA and CRITIC methods, it contributed to the ranking of vehicles by efficiency over a five-year period for a municipal company in Doboj. This model can be used in countries aiming to utilize green fund opportunities and improve their fleet (Huskanović et al., 2024). Study Tešić et al. (2023) develops a model for selecting dump trucks for military engineering units using fuzzy LMAW for determining criteria weights and a modified MARCOS method for ranking alternatives. Data were collected from experts, and the sensitivity of the model to weight changes was analyzed. Results showed that the model is stable but sensitive to weight variations, which requires careful determination by professionals. Paper Wang & Dang (2024) develops an innovative method combining fuzzy logic and MCDM methods (FAHP and FMARCOS) for accurate ranking and selection of the best logistics provider. The focus is on technological, environmental, and social factors related to new industrial technologies. The method was tested in a manufacturing company and proved to be stable and reliable through additional analyses.

Although the results are limited in their applicability to other sectors, the framework offers a strong decision-making tool in the digitized business world and opens the door for further research and application in different industries. In the study by Tešić et al. (2022), the proposed DIBR–FMARCOS model effectively assists in selecting the best location for deploying a heavy mechanized bridge (TMM-3). The DIBR method simplifies the determination of criterion importance, while Fuzzy MARCOS accurately ranks options despite unclear data. This approach could be further improved with a more detailed definition of the criteria and the integration of new decision-making techniques. Study Görçün & İyigün (2025) uses a hybrid MCDM approach combining Picture Fuzzy CRITIC and the MARCOS method. Picture Fuzzy CRITIC helps determine the importance of criteria when data is vague or subjective, while MARCOS ranks alternatives based on their distance from the ideal solution. Applying these methods, it was found that trailer load capacity is the most important criterion for heavy transport. The HeavyHaul semitrailer A4) was identified as the best option due to its traction power and stability. This serves as a guide for decision-makers in selecting trailers for project logistics and heavy transport using a hybrid decision-making procedure. Study Miškić et al. (2023) develops a special model for European Union countries that includes an analysis of the impact of changes in the importance of these factors on final results. Using the MEREC method, new criterion weights were determined, and the MARCOS method was applied to rank EU member states. Germany held the best position. It was shown that the ranking significantly changes with changes in factor weights, emphasizing the need to tailor the evaluation to each country's specific needs. Paper Xu et al. (2023) developed a new fuzzy model, TrIT2F PIPRECIA–MARCOS, for evaluating and ranking road infrastructure and assessing traffic flow efficiency and exploitation indicators. Results demonstrated model stability and enabled identification of the best segment for traffic management. In the field of energy and sustainability, the MARCOS method has been frequently used. In the paper, Gong et al. (2021), developed a combined decision-making framework that includes various factors such as the network, source, consumption, social impacts, and risks. Testing shows that this approach is stable and applicable in practice. Furthermore, a hybrid interval rough Dombi MARCOS model was applied for selecting the best alternative regarding the conversion of the natural gas network to hydrogen (Iordache et al., 2022). Study Younis et al. (2025) presents the MARCOS model in combination with Pythagorean indeterminate fuzzy sets. The industry and manufacturing sectors also offer a wide scope for applying the MARCOS method in all their subsystems. To achieve the desired stability and productivity to meet customer demands, it is important to choose the best supplier in the heavy industry. In a study, Chakraborty et al. (2020) used the MARCOS method to rank iron and steel suppliers. A similar application of the MARCOS method can be seen in the paper Badi & Pamucar (2020), which ranks suppliers of a company in Libya. The Grey-MARCOS model identified the best supplier among six alternatives. Electric vehicles represent an alternative that reduces pollution and environmental harm. Therefore in the study by Wang et al. (2023), the MARCOS method was used to analyze which electric vehicle has the best indicators for urban logistics. In addition to all these areas, MCDM methods, with an emphasis on the MARCOS method, have also found their application in tourism. The MARCOS method was applied to rank alternative tourist locations that make up a travel package for Bali (Sarja et al., 2021). Furthermore, the IT sector and software engineering have recognized the importance of the MARCOS method. In a study by Puška et al. (2020), the best-rated project management software by project users in the United Arab Emirates was investigated. The research was conducted in the UAE, and the MARCOS method was used to evaluate software programs. A very complex approach to improving the quality of e-services of airlines can be seen in the paper Bakır & Atalık (2021), where, for the first time, the F-AHP-F-MARCOS model is used. This study covered 13 criteria and, for the first time, analyzed e-services of Turkish airlines.

The literature review indicates that the MARCOS method has been applied across a variety of industries, including healthcare, logistics, transportation, energy, manufacturing, tourism, and information technology. Its adaptability, especially when combined with other MCDM techniques and fuzzy logic, allows for decision-making that is precise, reliable, and stable even in complex or uncertain situations. Studies highlight that the MARCOS method effectively addresses practical challenges such as supplier selection, resource allocation, infrastructure assessment, and strategic planning, while also providing a solid foundation for academic research through detailed ranking and sensitivity analyses. Overall, MARCOS is a flexible and powerful tool that delivers value to both practitioners and researchers, and holds significant potential for applications in emerging and interdisciplinary fields.

72.3 Algorithm of the measurement of alternatives and ranking according to compromise solution method

The MARCOS method is one of the favorite tools of many researchers for solving MCDM problems, which has been confirmed with many applications in various areas. This method calculates utility functions based on defining the level of closeness or distance between ideal and antiideal variants, and their compromise solution. The MARCOS method is elaborated within the equations represented below, Puška et al. (2021); Ulutaş et al. (2020).

Step 1. Development of the initial decision matrix with multiple criteria (n) and variants (m).

Step 2. In this step, the user should perform extension of the initial matrix with the ideal (AI) and antiideal (AAI) solutions.

$$X = \begin{array}{c} \\ AAI \\ A_1 \\ A_2 \\ \cdots \\ A_m \\ AI \end{array} \begin{array}{c} \begin{array}{cccc} C_1 & C_2 & \ldots & C_n \end{array} \\ \begin{bmatrix} x_{aa1} & x_{aa2} & \cdots & x_{aan} \\ x_{11} & x_{12} & \cdots & x_{1n} \\ x_{21} & x_{22} & \cdots & x_{2n} \\ \cdots & \cdots & \cdots & \cdots \\ x_{m1} & x_{22} & \cdots & x_{mn} \\ x_{ai1} & x_{ai2} & \cdots & x_{ain} \end{bmatrix} \end{array} \quad (72.1)$$

The AAI is the worst value among the considered variants, depending on the type of criteria, while the AI is the best value, and it has been defined using the Eqs. (72.2–72.3):

$$AAI = \min_j x_{ij} \text{ if } j \in \text{B and } \max_j x_{ij} \text{ if } j \in \text{C} \quad (72.2)$$

$$AI = \max_j x_{ij} \text{ if } j \in \text{B and } \min_j x_{ij} \text{ if } j \in \text{C} \quad (72.3)$$

The benefit set of criteria is marked with B, while the cost is marked with C.

Step 3. Calculate normalized matrix N by applying the following expressions:

$$n_{ij} = \frac{x_{ai}}{x_{ij}} \text{ if } \in \text{Cj} \tag{72.4}$$

$$n_{ij} = \frac{x_{ij}}{x_{ai}} \text{ if j} \in \text{B} \tag{72.5}$$

Step 4. Determination of the weighted matrix $V = [v_{ij}]$ mxn, where the previous matrix needs to be weighed with the criteria weights:

$$v_{ij} = n_{ij} \times w_j \tag{72.6}$$

Step 5. Perform the procedure of calculation of the utility degree of the variant K_i, which has been related to AAI and AI.

$$K_I^- = \frac{S_i}{S_{aai}} \tag{72.7}$$

$$K_I^+ = \frac{S_i}{S_{ai}} \tag{72.8}$$

Where S_i (i=1,2,…,m) is the sum of the elements of the weighted matrix V:

$$S_i = \sum_{i=1}^{n} v_{ij} \tag{72.9}$$

Step 6. Computation of the utility function of the alternative $f(K_i)$, which is a compromise of the observed variant in relation to the AI and AAI solution.

$$f(K_i) = \frac{K_i^+ + K_i^-}{1 + \frac{1-f(K_i^+)}{f(K_i^+)} + \frac{1-f(K_i^-)}{f(K_i^-)}} \tag{72.10}$$

Where $f(K_I^-)$ is the utility function relative to the AAI solution, and $f(K_i^+)$ is the utility function relative to the AI solution:

$$f(K_I^-) = \frac{K_i^+}{K_i^+ + K_i^-} \tag{72.11}$$

$$f(K_I^+) = \frac{K_i^-}{K_i^+ + K_i^-} \tag{72.12}$$

Step 7. Perform rank of variants according to their values.

Some of the main advantages of the MARCOS method in MCDM are:

- Simplicity and clarity—The MARCOS method follows a clear and logical step-by-step procedure that is easy to understand and apply.
- Consideration of ideal and antiideal solutions—The method simultaneously uses both the ideal (best possible) and antiideal (worst possible) solutions for a more precise ranking of alternatives.
- Flexibility—It is possible to use different types of criteria (qualitative and quantitative) and various methods for determining the weights of the criteria.
- Precise ranking—It enables precise ranking of all alternatives relative to a compromise solution, which is useful when making decisions among multiple competing options.
- Robustness—It provides reliable results and stability even in situations involving uncertainty and data ambiguity.
- Compatibility with other MCDM methods—It can be combined with other multicriteria methods or used as part of more complex decision-making systems.
- Suitability for real-world problems—It is widely applicable in diverse fields such as healthcare, logistics, management, technology, and transportation.

The limitations of the MARCOS method are primarily linked to the quality of input data, since the reliability of the results is largely determined by the accuracy and credibility of the available information. Nonetheless, it should be emphasized that this constitutes a common methodological constraint inherent to many MCDM approaches.

72.4 Numerical example 1

In the company "XYZ," there are four active vehicles (V1, V2, V3, V4) representing the alternatives. Five criteria—C1: fuel costs, C2: regular maintenance costs, C3: extraordinary maintenance costs, C4: total number of all minor accidents or damages, C5: number of operating hours—have been defined to calculate the efficiency of the vehicles. The weighting coefficients of the criteria were calculated using the CRITIC method (Durmus, 2025; Stević et al., 2024), while the ranking of the vehicles was performed using the MARCOS method.

Step 1. The initial matrix (X) is shown in Table 72.1.

Step 2. The extended initial matrix is presented in Table 72.2.

Step 3. The components of the normalized matrix are presented in Table 72.3.

$$n_{ij} = \frac{x_{ai}}{x_{ij}}; x_{21} = \frac{25490}{41300} = 0.617$$

$$n_{ij} = \frac{x_{ij}}{x_{ai}}; n_{15} = \frac{4000}{4300} = 0.930$$

The next procedure represents computation of the weighted normalized matrix, which has been calculated by multiplying the whole normalized matrix by the criteria weights (w1 = 0.172, w2 = 0.171, w3 = 0.136, w4 = 0.185, w5 = 0.335) obtained by the CRITIC method (Table 72.4).

$$v_{ij} = n_{ij} \times w_j; v_{11} = 0.557 \times 0.172 = 0.096$$

By applying the rest of the steps results of the MARCOS method were obtained, as shown in Table 72.5.

$$K_I^- = \frac{S_i}{S_{aai}}; S_i = \sum_{i=1}^{n} v_{ij}; S_1 = 0.096 + 0.165 + 0.071 + 0.062 + 0.312 = 0.706$$

$$K_1^- = \frac{S_1}{S_{aai}} = \frac{0.706}{0.483} = 1.462$$

$$K_I^+ = \frac{S_i}{S_{ai}}; K_1^+ = \frac{S_1}{S_{ai}} = \frac{0.706}{1.000} = 0.706$$

$$f(K_I^-) = \frac{K_i^+}{K_i^+ + K_i^-}; f(K_1^-) = \frac{K_1^+}{K_1^+ + K_1^-} = \frac{0.706}{0.706 + 1.462} = 0.325$$

$$f(K_I^+) = \frac{K_i^-}{K_i^+ + K_i^-}; f(K_1^+) = \frac{K_1^-}{K_1^+ + K_1^-} = \frac{1.462}{0.706 + 1.462} = 0.675$$

TABLE 72.1 Initial matrix for defining the efficiency of the vehicles.

	C1	C2	C3	C4	C5
V1	45,800	880	1900	3	4000
V2	41,300	920	1850	2	3500
V3	25,490	850	990	1	2200
V4	31,200	920	2000	2	4300
V5	30,000	1500	2100	2	2100

TABLE 72.2 Decision matrix after extension of AI and AAI.

	C1	C2	C3	C4	C5
AAI	45,800	1500	2100	3	2100
V1	45,800	880	1900	3	4000
V2	41,300	920	1850	2	3500
V3	25,490	850	990	1	2200
V4	31,200	920	2000	2	4300
V5	30,000	1500	2100	2	2100
AI	25,490	850	990	1	4300

TABLE 72.3 Normalized matrix.

	C1	C2	C3	C4	C5
AAI	0.557	0.567	0.471	0.333	0.488
V1	0.557	0.966	0.521	0.333	0.930
V2	0.617	0.924	0.535	0.500	0.814
V3	1.000	1.000	1.000	1.000	0.512
V4	0.817	0.924	0.495	0.500	1.000
V5	0.850	0.567	0.471	0.500	0.488
AI	1.000	1.000	1.000	1.000	1.000

TABLE 72.4 Weighted normalized matrix.

	C1	C2	C3	C4	C5
AAI	0.096	0.097	0.064	0.062	0.164
V1	0.096	0.165	0.071	0.062	0.312
V2	0.106	0.158	0.073	0.093	0.273
V3	0.172	0.171	0.136	0.185	0.172
V4	0.141	0.158	0.067	0.093	0.335
V5	0.147	0.097	0.064	0.093	0.164
AI	0.172	0.171	0.136	0.185	0.335

TABLE 72.5 Results of the efficiency of the vehicles.

	Ki-	Ki+	fK-	fK+	Ki	Rank
V1	1.462	0.706	0.325	0.675	0.610	3
V2	1.456	0.703	0.325	0.675	0.607	4
V3	1.733	0.836	0.325	0.675	0.723	1
V4	1.646	0.794	0.325	0.675	0.686	2
V5	1.169	0.564	0.325	0.675	0.487	5

$$f(K_i) = \frac{K_i^+ + K_i^-}{1 + \frac{1-f(K_i^+)}{f(K_i^+)} + \frac{1-f(K_i^-)}{f(K_i^-)}};$$

$$f(K_1) = \frac{K_1^+ + K_1^-}{1 + \frac{1-f(K_1^+)}{f(K_1^+)} + \frac{1-f(K_1^-)}{f(K_1^-)}} = \frac{1.462 + 0.706}{1 + \frac{1-0.675}{0.675} + \frac{1-0.325}{0.325}} = 0.610$$

The results obtained, which are presented in Table 72.5, show that Vehicle 3 has the highest efficiency, and Vehicle 5 has the lowest.

72.5 Numerical example 2

Managers of a company evaluated twelve potential locations for the installation of parcel lockers (L1, L2, L3, L4, L5, L6, L7, L8, L9, L10, L11, L12) based on seven defined criteria (C1, C2, C3, C4, C5, C6, C7) using the following ratings: Very Poor – 1, Poor – 2, Fairly Poor – 3, Fairly Good – 4, Good – 5, Very Good – 6, Excellent – 7. The weighting coefficients of the criteria were calculated using the FUCOM method (Alossta et al., 2024), while the ranking of alternatives was performed using the MARCOS method. The criteria are: C1 – Availability, C2 – Accessibility, C3 – Location rental costs, C4 – Parcel locker maintenance costs, C5 – Safety and security, C6 – Pedestrian traffic density, C7 – Frequency of customer delivery requests.

Step 1. The initial matrix (X) is shown in Table 72.6.

The extended initial matrix is presented in Table 72.7.

The elements of the normalized matrix are shown in Table 72.8.

The next procedure represents computation of the weighted normalized matrix, which has been calculated by multiplying the whole normalized matrix and the criteria weights (w1 = 0.271, w2 = 0.159, w3 = 0.135, w4 = 0.077, w5 = 0.108, w6 = 0.068, w7 = 0.181) obtained by the FUCOM method (Table 72.9).

By applying the rest of the steps, the results of the MARCOS method were obtained, as shown in Table 72.10.

According to the results presented in Table 72.10, it can be concluded that Location L5 represents the best location for installing a parcel locker. This is followed by Locations L8 and L1, and then Location L4. The least suitable location for the installation of a parcel locker is Location L11.

72.6 Comparative analysis

This section presents a comparison of the results obtained using the MARCOS method of Example 2 with the results achieved by other MCDM methods. In this case, a comparative analysis was conducted using the ARAS, MABAC, SAW, WASPAS, and COCOSO methods. The results of the comparative analysis are shown in Fig. 72.1.

The results of the comparative analysis show that the results obtained using the MARCOS method are stable, that is, there are no changes in the ranking of alternatives when other MCDM methods are applied. Minor changes occurred with the MABAC and COCOSO methods.

TABLE 72.6 Initial matrix for evaluation locations.

	C1	C2	C3	C4	C5	C6	C7
L1	7	7	5	5	7	7	7
L2	5	5	5	5	7	2	5
L3	7	6	5	4	6	7	6
L4	7	7	5	6	7	7	5
L5	7	7	5	6	7	7	7
L6	6	6	5	5	6	6	6
L7	5	5	5	5	6	5	5
L8	7	7	5	5	7	7	7
L9	7	7	1	5	6	7	7
L10	7	6	1	5	6	7	7
L11	6	5	1	5	5	6	6
L12	7	7	1	5	5	3	5

TABLE 72.7 Extended initial matrix for evaluation locations.

	C1	C2	C3	C4	C5	C6	C7
AAI	5.00	5.00	1.00	4.00	5.00	2.00	5.00
L1	7	7	5	5	7	7	7
L2	5	5	5	5	7	2	5
L3	7	6	5	4	6	7	6
L4	7	7	5	6	7	7	5
L5	7	7	5	6	7	7	7
L6	6	6	5	5	6	6	6
L7	5	5	5	5	6	5	5
L8	7	7	5	5	7	7	7
L9	7	7	1	5	6	7	7
L10	7	6	1	5	6	7	7
L11	6	5	1	5	5	6	6
L12	7	7	1	5	5	3	5
AI	7.00	7.00	5.00	6.00	7.00	7.00	7.00

TABLE 72.8 Normalized matrix.

	C1	C2	C3	C4	C5	C6	C7
AAI	0.714	0.714	0.200	0.667	0.714	0.286	0.714
L1	1.000	1.000	1.000	0.833	1.000	1.000	1.000
L2	0.714	0.714	1.000	0.833	1.000	0.286	0.714
L3	1.000	0.857	1.000	0.667	0.857	1.000	0.857
L4	1.000	1.000	1.000	1.000	1.000	1.000	0.714
L5	1.000	1.000	1.000	1.000	1.000	1.000	1.000
L6	0.857	0.857	1.000	0.833	0.857	0.857	0.857
L7	0.714	0.714	1.000	0.833	0.857	0.714	0.714
L8	1.000	1.000	1.000	0.833	1.000	1.000	1.000
L9	1.000	1.000	0.200	0.833	0.857	1.000	1.000
L10	1.000	0.857	0.200	0.833	0.857	1.000	1.000
L11	0.857	0.714	0.200	0.833	0.714	0.857	0.857
L12	1.000	1.000	0.200	0.833	0.714	0.429	0.714
AI	1.000	1.000	1.000	1.000	1.000	1.000	1.000

TABLE 72.9 Weighted normalized matrix.

	C1	C2	C3	C4	C5	C6	C7
AAI	0.194	0.114	0.027	0.052	0.077	0.019	0.129
L1	0.271	0.159	0.135	0.065	0.108	0.068	0.181
L2	0.194	0.114	0.135	0.065	0.108	0.019	0.129
L3	0.271	0.137	0.135	0.052	0.093	0.068	0.155
L4	0.271	0.159	0.135	0.077	0.108	0.068	0.129
L5	0.271	0.159	0.135	0.077	0.108	0.068	0.181
L6	0.232	0.137	0.135	0.065	0.093	0.058	0.155
L7	0.194	0.114	0.135	0.065	0.093	0.048	0.129
L8	0.271	0.159	0.135	0.065	0.108	0.068	0.181
L9	0.271	0.159	0.027	0.065	0.093	0.068	0.181
L10	0.271	0.137	0.027	0.065	0.093	0.068	0.181
L11	0.232	0.114	0.027	0.065	0.077	0.058	0.155
L12	0.271	0.159	0.027	0.065	0.077	0.029	0.129
AI	0.271	0.159	0.135	0.077	0.108	0.068	0.181

TABLE 72.10 Results of the evaluation of potential locations.

	Ki-	Ki+	fK-	fK+	Ki	Rank
AAI	1.613	0.987	0.380	0.620	0.801	2
L1	1.249	0.764	0.380	0.620	0.620	10
L2	1.487	0.910	0.380	0.620	0.739	5
L3	1.550	0.948	0.380	0.620	0.770	4
L4	1.634	1.000	0.380	0.620	0.812	1
L5	1.429	0.875	0.380	0.620	0.710	6
L6	1.271	0.778	0.380	0.620	0.631	9
L7	1.613	0.987	0.380	0.620	0.801	2
L8	1.411	0.863	0.380	0.620	0.701	7
L9	1.374	0.840	0.380	0620	0.682	8
L10	1.190	0.728	0.380	0.620	0.591	12
L11	1.238	0.757	0.380	0.620	0.615	11

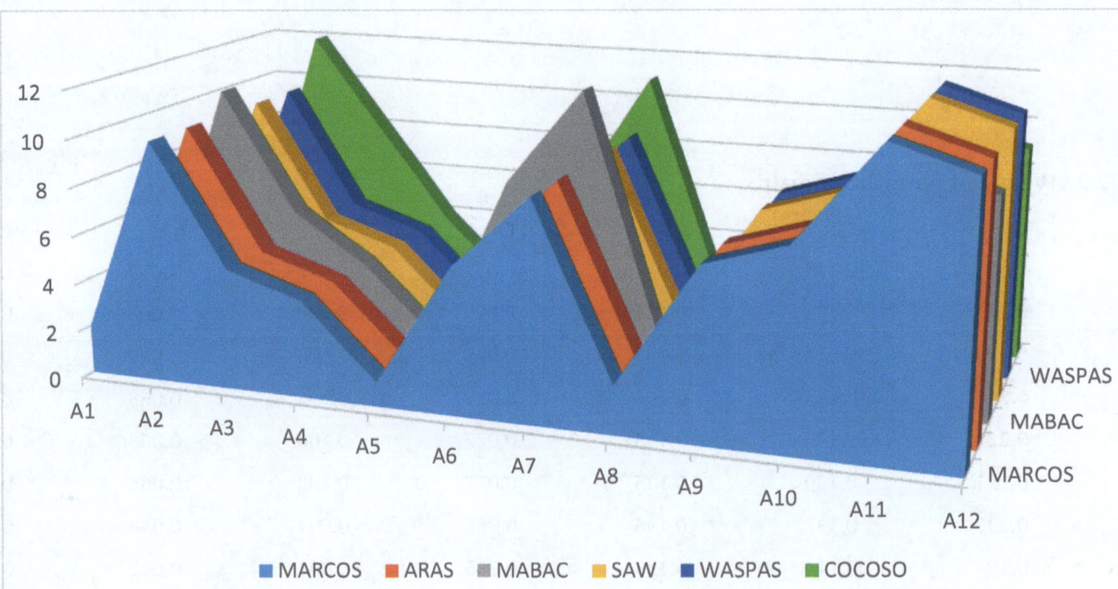

FIGURE 72.1 Results of the comparative analysis.

72.7 Conclusion

In modern decision-making conditions, where we are faced with a large number of alternatives and complex criteria, MCDM methods represent an indispensable tool for achieving optimal and rational solutions. Among contemporary MCDM methods, the MARCOS method has stood out as an efficient and flexible model that enables decision-making aligned with a compromise solution, taking into account both ideal and antiideal alternatives. Through the theoretical framework and literature analysis, the wide applicability of the MARCOS method has been confirmed in fields such as logistics, transportation, healthcare, energy, industry, tourism, and the IT sector. Its ability to be integrated with other methods, such as CRITIC, FUCOM, AHP, DEA, and fuzzy logic, further enhances its analytical potential and applicability in various conditions. The practical application of the MARCOS method in this paper encompassed two cases: the selection of the most efficient vehicle in a fleet and the identification of the optimal location for installing a parcel locker. In both cases, the MARCOS method enabled a clear and precise ranking of alternatives, and the obtained results were validated through a comparative analysis with other MCDM methods, indicating the stability and reliability of this method. Due to its simplicity and transparency, the MARCOS method is recommended for widespread use in making both strategic and operational decisions. The MARCOS method not only represents a significant contribution to the theory and practice of MCDM but also opens up opportunities for further development, adaptation, and expansion in accordance with the requirements of future decision-making challenges.

Acknowledgment

The paper is a part of the research conducted within the project No. 19.032/961-55/24, titled "Development of a location model for the installation of parcel lockers as an important factor in the sustainability of city logistics," supported by the Ministry of Scientific and Technological Development and Higher Education of the Republic of Srpska.

References

Alossta, A., Eltariki, I., Elmansouri, O., & Badi, I. (2024). Optimizing construction and demolition waste management strategies in Libya: a FUCOM-EDAS multi-criteria decision-making approach. *Journal of Green Economy and Low-Carbon Development, 3*(4), 258–272. https://doi.org/10.56578/jgelcd030405.

Alrasheedi, A. F., Rani, P., Mishra, A. R., Alshamrani, A. M., & Cavallaro, F. (2024). Fermatean fuzzy distance and Sugeno–Weber operators-based SPC-MARCOS approach for sustainable supplier evaluation in the healthcare supply chain. *Scientific Reports, 14*(1), 27373. https://doi.org/10.1038/s41598-024-78284-8.

Badi, I., & Pamucar, D. (2020). Supplier selection for steelmaking company by using combined Grey-MARCOS methods. *Decision Making: Applications in Management and Engineering, 3*(2), 37–48. https://doi.org/10.31181/dmame2003037b.

Bakır, M., & Atalık, Ö. (2021). Application of fuzzy AHP and fuzzy MARCOS approach for the evaluation of e-service quality in the airline industry. *Decision Making: Applications in Management and Engineering, 4*(1), 127–152. https://doi.org/10.31181/dmame2104127b.

Chakraborty, S., Chattopadhyay, R., & Chakraborty, S. (2020). An integrated D-MARCOS method for supplier selection in an iron and steel industry. *Decision Making: Applications in Management and Engineering, 3*(2), 49–69. https://doi.org/10.31181/dmame2003049c.

Durmus, Z. (2025). Assessment of renewable energy performance in Turkey using a novel integrated MSD-CRITIC-RAWEC model. Journal of Operations Strategy and Analysis, *3*(1), 49–64. https://doi.org/10.56578/josa030105.

Ecer, F., & Pamucar, D. (2021). MARCOS technique under intuitionistic fuzzy environment for determining the COVID-19 pandemic performance of insurance companies in terms of healthcare services. *Applied Soft Computing, 104*, 107199. https://doi.org/10.1016/j.asoc.2021.107199.

Gong, X., Yang, M., & Du, P. (2021). Renewable energy accommodation potential evaluation of distribution network: a hybrid decision-making framework under interval type-2 fuzzy environment. *Journal of Cleaner Production, 286*, 124918. https://doi.org/10.1016/j.jclepro.2020.124918.

Görçün, Ö. F., & İyigün, I. (2025). Evaluation of the selection of low-bed trailers in the transportation of oversized and overweight cargo: a hybrid picture fuzzy critic-marcos model. *Journal of Soft Computing and Decision Analytics, 3*(1), 72–91. https://doi.org/10.31181/jscda31202556.

Huskanović, E., Bjelić, D., & Novarlić, B. (2024). Optimising the efficiency of municipal utility vehicle fleets using DEA-CRITIC-MARCOS: A sustainable waste management approach. Journal of Intelligent Management Decision, *3*, 139–149. https://doi.org/10.56578/jimd030301.

Iordache, M., Pamucar, D., Deveci, M., Chisalita, D., Wu, Q., & Iordache, I. (2022). Prioritizing the alternatives of the natural gas grid conversion to hydrogen using a hybrid interval rough based Dombi MARCOS model. *International Journal of Hydrogen Energy, 47*(19), 10665–10688. https://doi.org/10.1016/j.ijhydene.2022.01.130.

Khosravi, M., Haqbin, A., Zare, Z., & Shojaei, P. (2022). Selecting the most suitable organizational structure for hospitals: an integrated fuzzy FUCOM-MARCOS method. *Cost Effectiveness and Resource Allocation, 20*(1), 29. https://doi.org/10.1186/s12962-022-00362-3.

Miškić, S., Stević, Ž., Tadić, S., Alkhayyat, A., & Krstić, M. (2023). Assessment of the LPI of the EU countries using MCDM model with an emphasis on the importance of criteria. *World Review of Intermodal Transportation Research, 11*(3), 258–279. https://doi.org/10.1504/WRITR.2023.132501.

Puška, A., Stević, Ž., & Stojanović, I. (2021). Selection of sustainable suppliers using the fuzzy MARCOS method. *Current Chinese Science, 1*(2), 218–229. https://doi.org/10.2174/2210298101999201109214028.

Puška, A., Stojanović, I., Maksimović, A., & Osmanović, N. (2020). Project management software evaluation by using the measurement of alternatives and ranking according to compromise solution (MARCOS) method. *Operational Research in Engineering Sciences: Theory and Applications, 3*(1), 89–102. https://doi.org/10.31181/oresta2001089p.

Salimian, S., Mousavi, S. M., & Antucheviciene, J. (2022). An interval-valued intuitionistic fuzzy model based on extended VIKOR and MARCOS for sustainable supplier selection in organ transplantation networks for healthcare devices. *Sustainability, 14*(7), 3795. https://doi.org/10.3390/su14073795.

Sarja, N. K. P. G., Candiasa, I. M., & Aryanto, K. Y. E. (2021). Decision support system for tour package recommendation in bali using BWM-MARCOS method. *Jurnal Ilmiah Merpati (Menara Penelitian Akademika Teknologi Informasi), 9*(2), 143–152. https://doi.org/10.24843/JIM.2021.V09.I02.P05.

Simic, V., Ebadi Torkayesh, A., & Ijadi Maghsoodi, A. (2023). Locating a disinfection facility for hazardous healthcare waste in the COVID-19 era: a novel approach based on Fermatean fuzzy ITARA-MARCOS and random forest recursive feature elimination algorithm. *Annals of Operations Research, 328*(1), 1105–1150. https://doi.org/10.1007/s10479-022-04822-0.

Stević, Ž., Mujaković, N., Goli, A., & Moslem, S. (2023). Selection of logistics distribution channels for final product delivery: FUCOM-MARCOS model. *Journal of Intelligent Management and Decision.* 2(4), 172–178. https://doi.org/10.56578/jimd020402.

Stević, Ž., Pamučar, D., Puška, A., & Chatterjee, P. (2020). Sustainable supplier selection in healthcare industries using a new MCDM method: measurement of alternatives and ranking according to COmpromise solution (MARCOS). *Computers & Industrial Engineering, 140*, 106231. https://doi.org/10.1016/j.cie.2019.106231.

Stević, Ž., Baydaş, M., Kavacık, M., Ayhan, E., & Marinković, D. (2024). Selection of data conversion technique via sensitivity-performance matching: ranking of small e-vans with probid method. *Facta Universitatis, Series: Mechanical Engineering, 22*(4), 643–671. https://doi.org/10.22190/FUME240305023S.

Tešić, D., Božanić, D., Pamučar, D., & Din, J. (2022). DIBR -fuzzy MARCOS model for selecting a location for a heavy mechanized bridge. *Vojnotehnički Glasnik, 70*(2), 314–339. https://doi.org/10.5937/vojtehg70-35944.

Tešić, D., Božanić, D., Puška, A., Milić, A., & Marinković, D. (2023). Development of the MCDM fuzzy LMAW-grey MARCOS model for selection of a dump truck. *Reports in Mechanical Engineering, 4*(1), 1–17. https://doi.org/10.31181/rme20008012023t.

Ulutaş, A., Karabasevic, D., Popovic, G., Stanujkic, D., Nguyen, P. T., & Karaköy, Ç. (2020). Development of a novel integrated CCSD-ITARA-MARCOS decision-making approach for stackers selection in a logistics system. *Mathematics, 8*(10), 1672. https://doi.org/10.3390/math8101672.

Wang, C. N., & Dang, T. T. (2024). Third-party logistics provider selection in the industry 4.0 era by using a fuzzy AHP and fuzzy MARCOS methodology. *IEEE Access*. https://doi.org/10.1109/ACCESS.2024.3392892.

Wang, N., Xu, Y., Puška, A., Stević, Ž., & Alrasheedi, A. F. (2023). Multi-criteria selection of electric delivery vehicles using fuzzy–rough methods. *Sustainability, 15*(21), 15541. https://doi.org/10.3390/su152115541.

Xu, W., Das, D. K., Stević, Ž., Subotić, M., Alrasheedi, A. F., & Sun, S. (2023). Trapezoidal interval type-2 fuzzy PIPRECIA-MARCOS model for management efficiency of traffic flow on observed road sections. *Mathematics, 11*(12), 2652. https://doi.org/10.3390/math11122652.

Younis, M., Ashraf, S., Abdullah, S., Shahid, T., & KC, G. (2025). Strategic MARCOS model for optimizing renewable energy investments under pythagorean hesitant fuzzy assessments. *Advances in Fuzzy Systems, 2025*(1), 6193403. https://doi.org/10.1155/adfs/6193403.

Chapter 73

DNMA: Double normalization-based multiple aggregation for multi-attribute decision-making

Xingli Wu and Huchang Liao
Business School, Sichuan University, Chengdu, Sichuan Province, P.R. China

73.1 Introduction

Given the inherent complexity of practical decision-making problems, addressing them with a single criterion is often impractical. These problems involve multiple, frequently conflicting features, goals, or criteria (hereinafter referred to as "attributes"), making it difficult to achieve an optimal solution simultaneously (Yalcin et al., 2022). Multi-attribute decision-making (MADM) aims to model and simplify these complexities by balancing different attributes to select, rank, or classify alternatives within a limited set. MADM can be mainly divided into three types: utility/value-based methods, outranking methods, and decision rule-based methods. Utility/value-based methods, such as SMART (simple multi-attribute rating technique), TOPSIS (technique for order preference by similarity to ideal solution), VIKOR (multi-criteria optimization with compromise solution), MULTIMOORA (multiplicative multi-objective optimization by ratio analysis), are especially popular because of their simplicity, ease of understanding, and effectiveness in ranking alternatives, making them the most common MADM approaches in real-world applications. The core idea is that each attribute has an associated utility function, usually normalized into a single attribute scale. These utilities are then combined across all attributes for each alternative using an aggregation operator, enabling straightforward ranking based on the preference order indicated by these overall utilities.

The fundamental differences among existing utility/value-based MADM approaches mainly lie in the normalization techniques and the aggregation operators (Wu & Liao, 2019). Common normalization methods include linear and vector normalization (Jahan & Edwards, 2015), while aggregation operators primarily consist of the weighted average operator, the weighted geometric operator, and the weighted min-max operator. The SMART method (Edwards & Barron, 1994) uses the weighted average operator alongside linear normalization. The MULTIMOORA method (Brauers & Zavadskas, 2010) employs three aggregation operators with vector normalization for comprehensive evaluations and incorporates dominance theory to combine these subordinate aggregation results. The TOPSIS method (Chen & Hwang, 1992), which relies on vector normalization and the weighted average operator, identifies the best alternative by measuring distances to both positive and negative ideal solutions. The VIKOR method (Opricovic, 1998), based on linear normalization, uses both the weighted average operator and the weighted min-max operator, with the overall utility of each alternative being an integration of utilities from the two operators. In summary, most utility/value-based MADM approaches are limited to a single normalization technique, making their decision outcomes susceptible to inappropriate normalization. Additionally, although methods like VIKOR and MULTIMOORA use multiple aggregation operators for thorough evaluations, effectively combining these results into a single ranking of alternatives remains a significant research challenge.

To address the challenges mentioned above, Liao & Wu (2020) proposed a double normalization-based multiple aggregation (DNMA) method. This approach combines two normalization techniques (linear normalization and vector normalization) with three types of aggregation operators (the weighted average operator, the weighted geometric operator, and the weighted max operator). Linear normalization effectively handles dimensionality issues in MADM by preserving the relative proportional relationships of attribute performance values within their respective ranges; however, it has

Encyclopedia of Multi-Attribute Decision-Making (MADM). DOI: https://doi.org/10.1016/B978-0-443-33275-3.00079-8

difficulty accurately representing the actual differences between alternatives. In contrast, vector normalization precisely captures variability among alternatives. The DNMA method develops the first two aggregation models, known as the complete compensatory model (CCM) and the uncompensatory model (UCM), by pairing linear normalization with the weighted average operator and the weighted max operator, respectively. This pairing maintains the proportional characteristics of the original data while satisfying the computational requirements for ideal solution distance metrics. The CCM embodies a full compensation mechanism, allowing poor performance in one attribute to be fully offset by good performance in others. The UCM, based on the "shortest plank" principle, concentrates solely on the worst performance across all attributes for each alternative. The third aggregation model, the incomplete compensatory model (ICM), combines vector normalization with the weighted geometric operator. This combination ensures the nonnegativity requirement imposed by the geometric operator on normalization values and capitalizes on the benefits of vector normalization. The ICM models risk-averse decision-making behavior by permitting partial compensation among attributes. The integration of CCM, UCM, and ICM leverages the strengths of different normalization techniques and aggregation operators, creating a comprehensive attribute trade-off system that covers various compensation scenarios in MADM. During the result integration phase, the DNMA method uses a weighted Euclidean distance operator to combine the subordinate utilities and rankings from the three aggregation models, establishing overall utilities and rankings for the alternatives. This paper aims to review the progress of the DNMA method's research and reformulate the DNMA framework with a focus on precise attribute values to improve both understanding and practical application of this method.

The rest of this paper is organized as follows: Section 73.2 reviews the extensions and applications of the DNMA method. Section 73.3 introduces the framework of the DNMA method. Section 73.4 presents a simple numerical example. Section 73.5 conducts a complex case study. Conclusions are pointed out in Section 73.6.

73.2 Literature review

73.2.1 Studies on the extension of the double normalization-based multiple aggregation method

The DNMA method was first proposed by Liao & Wu (2020). Wu et al. (2023) further developed a large-scale group DNMA framework incorporating a consensus-reaching process. Wu & Liao (2019) compared the DNMA method with TOPSIS, VIKOR, and MULTIMOORA across three dimensions: normalization, attribute aggregation, and result integration, demonstrating DNMA's advantages in solving MADM problems. Inspired by the DNMA method, scholars have increasingly recognized the limitations of single normalization methods in MADM and begun adopting hybrid normalization methods combining linear and vector normalization (Deb et al., 2022; Esangbedo & Wei, 2023; Gopisetty & Sama, 2025; Saha, Simic, et al., 2022; Tong & Wang, 2023). In attribute aggregation, scholars have focused on compensation effects among attributes, constructing various aggregation models to capture different compensation relationships. Representative studies include the mixed aggregation by comprehensive normalization technique, a method using compensatory and noncompensatory aggregation operators (Wen et al., 2020); the score-based double normalized measurement alternatives and ranking according to the compromise solution, a method integrating CCM and ICM (Saha, Simic, et al., 2022); and the extension of the measurement alternatives and ranking according to the compromise solution method using the CCM, UCM, and ICM (Ivanović et al., 2022). The integration mechanism for the results obtained by the three subordinate aggregation models of the DNMA method has also attracted scholars' attention. For instance, Kumar & Kumar (2024) pointed out the limitations of the combined compromise solution (CoCoSo) method that only employed utilities from three aggregation models while ignoring ranking information, and introduced the DNMA's integration operator into the CoCoSo framework, enhancing the reliability of decision outcomes.

To address qualitative attributes in MADM problems, where attributes' performance often relies on subjective assessments by experts or decision-makers, researchers have extended the DNMA method to address various types of evaluation information. Key extensions include: the probabilistic linguistic term set-based DNMA method (Liao & Wu, 2020), the hesitant fuzzy set-based DNMA method (Liao et al., 2019), the q-rung orthopair fuzzy set-based DNMA method (Liao et al., 2020; Saha, Mishra, et al., 2022; Yang et al., 2023), the intuitionistic fuzzy set-based DNMA method (Hezam et al., 2022; Wang & Rani, 2022), the interval-valued intuitionistic fuzzy set-based DNMA method (Al-Barakati & Rani, 2024), the linguistic D number-based DNMA method (Lai & Liao, 2021), the Pythagorean fuzzy set-based DNMA method (Song et al., 2023; Zhang et al., 2020), the interval-valued Pythagorean fuzzy set-based DNMA method (Rahimi et al., 2022), the type-2 Pythagorean fuzzy set-based DNMA method (Mourad et al., 2025), the Fermatean fuzzy set-based DNMA method (Hezam et al., 2023), the interval-valued Fermatean fuzzy set-based DNMA method (Mishra, Rani, Deveci, et al., 2023), the single-valued neutrosophic set-based DNMA method (Mishra, Rani, Saha, et al., 2023), the

Z-number-based DNMA method (Lai et al., 2020; Liao et al., 2024), and the trapezium cloud model-based DNMA method (Weng et al., 2025).

73.2.2 Studies on the applications of the double normalization-based multiple aggregation method

The DNMA method has been successfully applied in multiple fields. In macroeconomic analysis, Ecer & Zolfani (2022) utilized this method to evaluate the level of economic freedom in The Organization of the Petroleum Exporting Countries (OPEC), while Lukic (2024) systematically analyzed the dynamic performance of the Serbian economy from 2013 to 2022. In the energy and environmental sector, Önden et al. (2024) applied it to the siting of offshore wind farms for meeting energy demand in Turkish railway transportation, and Weng et al. (2025) innovatively used it for the selection of phase change materials. In industrial engineering and safety management, Moslem et al. (2025) assessed various accident analysis and investigation methods through the DNMA method, particularly validating its superiority in managing domino accident scenarios in process industries; Yousefi et al. (2023) applied it to enterprise production scheduling. In supply chain management, Durán et al. (2024) used this method to rank and prioritize key factors influencing the adoption of blockchain technology, while Wang & Rani (2022) successfully applied it to risk assessment for supply chain sustainability. In healthcare, Liu et al. (2023) built an evaluation and recommendation system for psychologists based on data from haodf.com, Liao et al. (2019) extended its use to optimize lung cancer screening programs, and Al-Barakati & Rani (2024) applied it to optimize medical waste treatment processes. In textile engineering, Acar et al. (2024) used the DNMA method for structural optimization of denim fabrics containing recycled cotton.

73.3 Methodology

Consider an MADM problem involving m alternatives (denoted as $A = \{a_1, a_2, \ldots, a_m\}$), each evaluated through n attributes (denoted as $C = \{c_1, c_2, \ldots, c_n\}$). The specific performance values (denoted as g_{ij}, $\forall\, i \in \{1, 2, \ldots, m\}, j \in \{1, 2, \ldots, n\}$) of all alternatives across these attributes are known, and each attribute has a preset target value (denoted as g_j^*, $\forall\, j \in \{1, 2, \ldots, n\}$) representing the desired level of performance by the decision-maker. Specifically, for benefit-oriented attributes, the target value can be set to $g_j^* = \max_i g_{ij}$; whereas for cost-oriented attributes, it can be set to $g_j^* = \min_i g_{ij}$. The target value may also represent an intermediate value or fall within a specific range of the attribute. The weight for each attribute (denoted as w_j, $\forall\, j \in \{1, 2, \ldots, n\}$) is known or can be determined through appropriate methods, such as the analytic hierarchical process and the best-worst method.

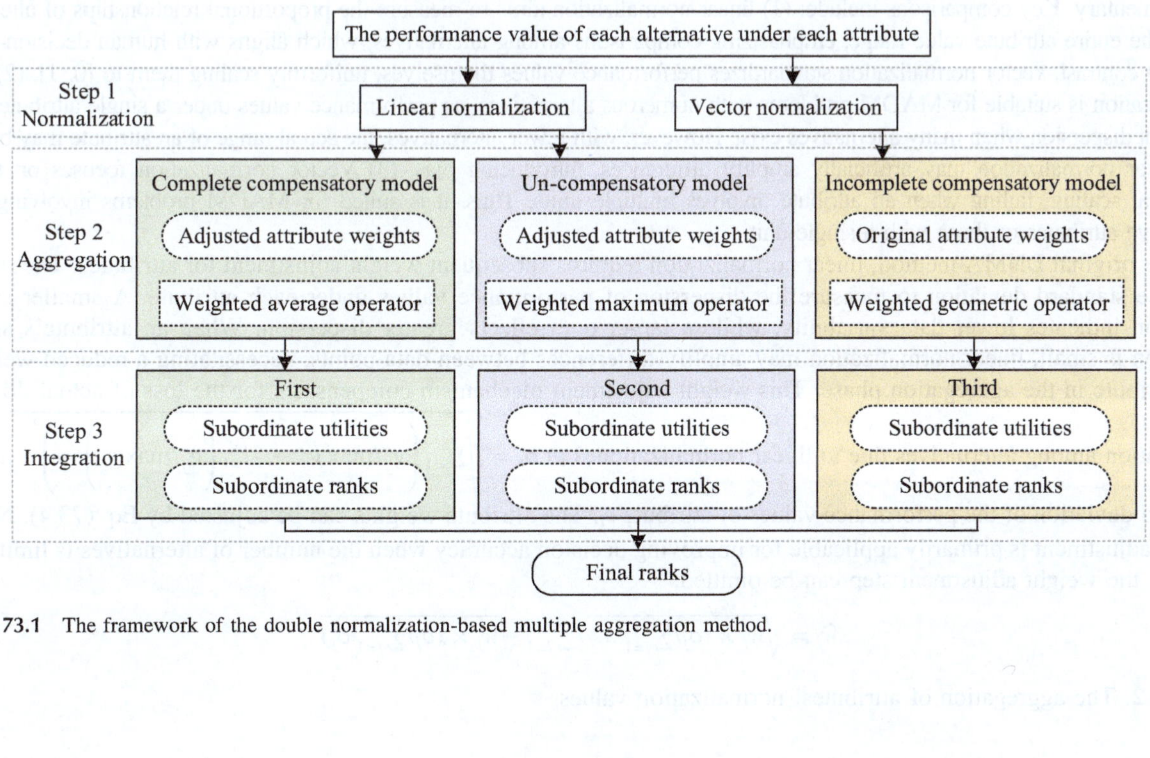

FIGURE 73.1 The framework of the double normalization-based multiple aggregation method.

The solution process of the DNMA method is illustrated in Fig. 73.1. The specific steps are as follows. Firstly, the performance values of attributes are normalized using linear normalization and vector normalization, respectively, to ensure they are mapped to [0, 1]. Subsequently, the subordinate utilities and ranks for each alternative are calculated based on the three aggregation models (CCM, UCM, and ICM), respectively. Finally, the subordinate utilities and ranks are integrated to obtain the overall utilities and rankings of the alternatives.

Step 1. The normalization of attributes' performance values

In the DNMA method, the linear normalization and vector normalization techniques are formulated in Eqs. (73.1) and (73.2), respectively. It is crucial to preprocess the performance values to guarantee their nonnegativity before applying vector normalization. The normalization values derived from both techniques are constrained within [0, 1]. Attributes subjected to linear normalization frequently converge to the boundary values of this interval (*i.e.* 0 or 1, or both); conversely, attributes processed through vector normalization may not reach these boundary values. To ensure consistency across diverse attribute dimensions, an additional normalization step, outlined in Eq. (73.3), can be implemented. This step normalizes the maximum normalization value under each attribute to 1 by dividing the normalization values of each attribute by their respective maxima.

$$N_{ij}^{\text{lin}} = 1 - \frac{\left|g_{ij} - g_j^*\right|}{\max\left\{\max_i g_{ij},\, g_j^*\right\} - \min\left\{\min_i g_{ij},\, g_j^*\right\}} \tag{73.1}$$

$$N_{ij}^{\text{vec}} = 1 - \frac{\left|g_{ij} - g_j^*\right|}{\sqrt{\sum_{i=1}^{m}(g_{ij})^2 + (g_j^*)^2}} \tag{73.2}$$

$$\begin{cases} \widetilde{N}_{ij}^{\text{lin}} = N_{ij}^{\text{lin}} / \max_i N_{ij}^{\text{lin}} \\ \widetilde{N}_{ij}^{\text{vec}} = N_{ij}^{\text{vec}} / \max_i N_{ij}^{\text{vec}} \end{cases} \tag{73.3}$$

Vector normalization maintains the original data distribution but disregards the effect of attribute unit scales on the results, whereas linear normalization eliminates unit-induced biases but does not preserve the original distribution. These two methods are complementary. Key comparisons include: (1) linear normalization aims to measure the proportional relationships of alternatives across the entire attribute value range, emphasizing comparisons among alternatives, which aligns with human decision-making logic. In contrast, vector normalization standardizes performance values themselves, uniformly scaling them to [0, 1]. (2) Linear normalization is suitable for MADM problems with numerous alternatives, as performance values under a single attribute exhibit sufficient dispersion when many alternatives exist. However, with fewer alternatives, the actual range of an attribute may be small, and linear normalization may artificially amplify differences, introducing bias. (3) Vector normalization focuses on uniform numerical scaling, failing when an attribute involves multiple units. Thus, it is suited for MADM problems involving purely qualitative attributes or those with a single unit.

In the original DNMA method, linear normalization requires subsequent weight adjustment for attributes. The rationale is to use standard deviation to measure the dispersion of performance values under each attribute. A smaller standard deviation indicates lower data variability, while a larger one reflects greater dispersion. When an attribute's standard deviation is small, linear normalization may amplify differences between data points, necessitating a reduced weight for that attribute in the aggregation phase. This weight adjustment mechanism compensates for the loss of actual difference information among alternatives due to linear normalization. Let $\sigma_j = \sqrt{\sum_{i=1}^{m}\left(g_{ij}/\max_i g_{ij} - \sum_{i=1}^{m}\left(g_{ij}/\max_i g_{ij}\right)/m\right)^2/m}$ be the standard deviation of the performance values of attribute c_j. The attribute weights can be adjusted by Eq. (73.4). Notably, weight adjustment is primarily applicable for improving decision accuracy when the number of alternatives is limited. For brevity, the weight adjustment step can be omitted.

$$\widetilde{w}_j = \sqrt{w_j \times \left(\sigma_j / \sum_{j=1}^{n}\sigma_j\right)} \Big/ \sum_{j=1}^{n}\sqrt{w_j \times \left(\sigma_j / \sum_{j=1}^{n}\sigma_j\right)} \tag{73.4}$$

Step 2. The aggregation of attributes' normalization values

The three aggregation models utilized in the DNMA method are the CCM (Eq. (73.5)), UCM (Eq. (73.6)), and ICM (Eq. (73.7)), respectively. The CCM employs a weighted average operator to calculate the complete compensatory utility $\mathrm{CCM}(a_i)\in[0,1]$ of each alternative, where a higher value indicates superior overall performance, leading to the complete compensatory ranking $R_{\mathrm{CCM}} = \{r_{\mathrm{CCM}}(a_1), r_{\mathrm{CCM}}(a_2), \ldots, r_{\mathrm{CCM}}(a_m)\}$; the UCM uses the maximum operator to obtain the uncompensatory utility $\mathrm{UCM}(a_i) \in [0, 1]$ of each alternative, with a lower value reflecting weaker shortcoming effects (*i.e.* better performance), resulting in the uncompensatory ranking $R_{\mathrm{UCM}} = \{r_{\mathrm{UCM}}(a_1), r_{\mathrm{UCM}}(a_2), \ldots, r_{\mathrm{UCM}}(a_m)\}$; the ICM applies the weighted geometric operator to compute the incomplete compensatory utility $\mathrm{ICM}(a_i) \in [0, 1]$, where a higher value signifies better balance, yielding the incomplete compensatory ranking $R_{\mathrm{ICM}} = \{r_{\mathrm{ICM}}(a_1), r_{\mathrm{ICM}}(a_2), \ldots, r_{\mathrm{ICM}}(a_m)\}$.

$$\mathrm{CCM}(a_i) = \sum_{j=1}^{n} \widetilde{w}_j \widetilde{N}_{ij}^{\mathrm{lin}} \tag{73.5}$$

$$\mathrm{UCM}(a_i) = \max_j \widetilde{w}_j \left(1 - \widetilde{N}_{ij}^{\mathrm{lin}}\right) \tag{73.6}$$

$$\mathrm{ICM}(a_i) = \prod_j \left(\widetilde{N}_{ij}^{\mathrm{vec}}\right)^{w_j} \tag{73.7}$$

The CCM represents a complete compensatory mechanism, allowing superior performance values to compensate for inferior ones to an equal extent. The UCM uses a noncompensatory mechanism that solely focuses on the worst performance among all attributes. The ICM applies an incomplete compensatory mechanism, allowing superior performance values to compensate for inferior ones to a certain degree. Complete compensatory and incomplete compensatory mechanisms permit very poor attribute performance in selected alternatives, whereas the noncompensatory mechanism ignores compensatory effects among attributes and imposes heavy penalties on extreme performance. The complete compensation, noncompensation, and incomplete compensation correspond to decision-makers' preferences for risk neutrality (tolerant of extreme attribute performance), complete risk aversion (averse to extreme attribute performance), and partial risk aversion (preference for moderate alternatives), respectively (Wu & Liao, 2023). In practice, decision-makers often focus on the worst attribute while allowing a certain degree of compensation among attributes. Therefore, the comprehensive application of these three aggregation models can enhance flexibility in addressing actual compensation requirements.

Step 3. The integration of subordinate utilities and rankings

The DNMA method integrates subordinate utilities and rankings from three aggregation models using the weighted Euclidean distance operator in Eq. (73.8) to derive comprehensive utilities and final rankings of alternatives. Utilities accurately reflect quantitative differences among alternatives while rankings capture their dominance relationships. Sole reliance on utilities makes results overly sensitive to the weight settings of aggregation models, whereas depending exclusively on rankings fails to reflect actual performance gaps. DNMA therefore combines both subordinate utilities and rankings, ensuring both robustness against weight variations and accurate representation of performance differences.

$$\begin{aligned} DN(a_i) = {} & \gamma_{\mathrm{CCM}} \sqrt{\varphi\left(\mathrm{CCM}(a_i)/\max_i \mathrm{CCM}(a_i)\right)^2 + (1-\varphi)\left(\frac{m - r_{\mathrm{CCM}}(a_i) + 1}{m}\right)^2} \\ & - \gamma_{\mathrm{UCM}} \sqrt{\varphi\left(\mathrm{UCM}(a_i)/\max_i \mathrm{UCM}(a_i)\right)^2 + (1-\varphi)\left(\frac{r_{\mathrm{UCM}}(a_i)}{m}\right)^2} \\ & + \gamma_{\mathrm{ICM}} \sqrt{\varphi\left(\mathrm{ICM}(a_i)/\max_i \mathrm{ICM}(a_i)\right)^2 + (1-\varphi)\left(\frac{m - r_{\mathrm{ICM}}(a_i) + 1}{m}\right)^2} \end{aligned} \tag{73.8}$$

The overall utility of alternative a_i is denoted as $DN(a_i)$, with a larger overall utility indicating a superior alternative. The weight coefficient φ reflects the relative importance between utilities and rankings for integration, typically set at $\varphi = 0.5$. The weight coefficients γ_{CCM}, γ_{UCM}, and γ_{ICM} represent the relative importance of three aggregation models, respectively, and their sum is 1. The weights of the three aggregation models can be determined based on decision-makers' risk attitudes. Risk-neutral decision-makers focusing on overall performance should assign higher weights to the CCM; risk-averse ones should emphasize the UCM; while those valuing both performance and risk mitigation should prioritize the ICM. Additionally, the weighting should consider the relative importance of normalization methods. When linear normalization is more applicable, both CCM and UCM should receive higher weights; otherwise, greater weight goes to the ICM. Overall, the weights of the three aggregation models should be determined by considering both normalization techniques and decision-makers' risk attitudes.

73.4 Numerical example 1: supplier selection

In this section, we address a supplier selection problem, aiming to determine the optimal supplier from five alternatives for the automotive manufacturing industry. The evaluation process is based on four key attributes: "operating cost" (a cost-oriented attribute, where lower values are preferred, reflecting the direct impact of the suppliers' annual operating expenses on procurement economy), "consumer satisfaction" (a benefit-oriented attribute, where higher values are preferred, quantifying supplier service quality and potential for sustainable cooperation), "delivery lead time" (a target-oriented attribute with an optimal target value being 7 days, measuring supply chain response efficiency and the risk of production plan disruptions due to deviations from this target), and "market share growth rate" (a benefit-oriented attribute, where higher values are preferred, indicating the suppliers' market competitiveness and long-term cooperation value). The performance values of each alternative under these attributes are presented in Table 73.1.

The target values of the four attributes are 52, 94, 7, and 21, respectively. First, the performance values of attributes are normalized through linear normalization (Eq. (73.1)) and vector normalization (Eq. (73.2)), with results shown in Tables 73.2 and 73.3, respectively. In this numerical example, since the maximum normalization values under each attribute have reached 1, the normalization results adjusted by Eq. (73.3) remain identical to the initial normalization values. Additionally, the weight adjustment step is not considered here.

Assuming the decision-maker assigns weights of 0.35, 0.25, 0.2, and 0.2 to the four attributes, respectively. We calculate the subordinate utilities of each alternative based on the three aggregation models (Eqs. (73.5)-(73.7)), respectively, and determine the corresponding rankings of the alternatives accordingly. The specific calculation results are detailed in Table 73.4. Finally, we assign equal weights to the three aggregation models. The weight adjustment step is omitted here. Based on Eq. (73.8), the three subordinate utilities and rankings are integrated to obtain the overall utilities for the five alternatives, which are 0.56, 0.15, 0.13, 0.33, and 0.43, respectively. Consequently, the optimal supplier is the first one.

73.5 Numerical example 2: electric vehicle recommendation

A consumer in China is looking to purchase an electric vehicle (EV) within a price range of ¥100,000 to ¥200,000. The market offers 42 EV (EV1—EV42) series as potential options. Each series is evaluated based on the following attributes: (1) price (c_1, ¥, the average selling price of vehicles, lower = better), (2) max power (c_2, kW, performance capability, higher = better acceleration), (3) pure electric range (c_3, km, distance per full charge, longer = better), (4) fast charging time (c_4, h, time to charge 10% –80%, shorter = better), (5) dimensions (c_5, mm, vehicle size, length + width + height, higher = better, (6) space (c_6, 5-star scale, consumer feedback), (7) driving experience (c_7, 5-star scale, consumer

TABLE 73.1 The performance values of the suppliers under different attributes.

Supplier	Operational cost ($\times 10^4$ CNY)	Consumer satisfaction (%)	Delivery lead time (days)	Market share growth rate (%)
a_1	58	81	8	18
a_2	67	72	10	20
a_3	88	94	7	18
a_4	52	88	4	11
a_5	71	79	7	21

TABLE 73.2 The linear normalization values of attributes.

Alternative	Operational cost	Consumer satisfaction	Delivery lead time	Market share growth rate
a_1	0.83	0.41	0.83	0.70
a_2	0.58	0.00	0.50	0.90
a_3	0.00	1.00	1.00	0.70
a_4	1.00	0.73	0.50	0.00
a_5	0.47	0.32	1.00	1.00

TABLE 73.3 The vector normalization values of attributes.

Alternative	Operational cost	Consumer satisfaction	Delivery lead time	Market share growth rate
a_1	0.96	0.94	0.94	0.93
a_2	0.91	0.89	0.83	0.98
a_3	0.78	1.00	1.00	0.93
a_4	1.00	0.97	0.83	0.78
a_5	0.88	0.93	1.00	1.00

TABLE 73.4 The utilities and rankings of the suppliers.

Alternative	CCM		UCM		ICM	
	Utility	Rank	Utility	Rank	Utility	Rank
a_1	0.70	1	0.15	1	0.95	1
a_2	0.48	5	0.25	4	0.90	5
a_3	0.59	4	0.35	5	0.90	4
a_4	0.63	3	0.20	3	0.91	3
a_5	0.64	2	0.18	2	0.94	2

feedback), (8) exterior design (c_8, 5-star scale, consumer feedback), (9) interior design (c_9, 5-star scale, consumer feedback), (10) cost performance (c_{10}, 5-star scale, consumer feedback), (11) intelligence (c_{11}, 5-star scale, consumer feedback), and (12) number of reviews (c_{12}, 5-star scale, higher = more trusted). Data was collected in March 2025 from

TABLE 73.5 The utilities and rankings of electric vehicles (EVs).

	CCM		UCM		ICM		Overall	
	Utility	Rank	Utility	Rank	Utility	Rank	Utility	Rank
EV1	0.69	10	0.02	2	0.96	3	0.44	2
EV2	0.61	22	0.02	37	0.92	26	0.15	32
EV3	0.66	13	0.02	3	0.94	7	0.40	4
EV4	0.69	9	0.02	1	0.95	4	0.45	1
EV5	0.61	20	0.02	29	0.92	28	0.18	27
EV6	0.65	17	0.02	21	0.96	2	0.32	13
EV7	0.68	11	0.02	8	0.97	1	0.39	5
EV8	0.58	28	0.02	8	0.93	15	0.26	19
EV9	0.47	40	0.02	26	0.91	37	0.10	36
EV10	0.53	36	0.02	30	0.93	22	0.13	33
EV11	0.79	1	0.02	34	0.94	9	0.33	12
EV12	0.69	8	0.02	5	0.94	10	0.38	7
EV13	0.69	7	0.02	11	0.95	5	0.39	6
EV14	0.59	26	0.02	14	0.92	30	0.21	24
EV15	0.66	14	0.02	18	0.93	17	0.28	14
EV16	0.73	4	0.02	25	0.93	11	0.33	11
EV17	0.70	5	0.02	17	0.93	12	0.35	9
EV18	0.56	30	0.02	12	0.92	29	0.20	26
EV19	0.59	25	0.02	4	0.93	18	0.28	15
EV20	0.54	34	0.02	10	0.93	20	0.22	22
EV21	0.74	3	0.02	7	0.94	6	0.42	3
EV22	0.70	6	0.02	16	0.93	13	0.34	10
EV23	0.65	18	0.02	13	0.93	21	0.27	16
EV24	0.59	24	0.02	22	0.93	24	0.21	25
EV25	0.65	16	0.02	23	0.93	16	0.26	17
EV26	0.25	42	0.02	37	0.90	41	-0.02	42
EV27	0.52	37	0.02	27	0.91	34	0.12	35
EV28	0.54	35	0.02	28	0.91	36	0.12	34
EV29	0.67	12	0.02	33	0.92	27	0.21	23
EV30	0.49	39	0.02	37	0.91	35	0.06	40
EV31	0.62	19	0.02	20	0.93	23	0.23	21
EV32	0.55	32	0.02	19	0.92	32	0.17	29
EV33	0.58	29	0.02	15	0.93	14	0.24	20

(Continued)

TABLE 73.5 (Continued)

	CCM		UCM		ICM		Overall	
	Utility	Rank	Utility	Rank	Utility	Rank	Utility	Rank
EV34	0.59	27	0.02	6	0.93	19	0.26	18
EV35	0.77	2	0.02	24	0.94	8	0.37	8
EV36	0.55	33	0.02	37	0.91	40	0.08	38
EV37	0.60	23	0.02	32	0.92	33	0.15	31
EV38	0.55	31	0.02	36	0.91	39	0.09	37
EV39	0.61	21	0.02	31	0.92	31	0.16	30
EV40	0.50	38	0.02	35	0.91	38	0.07	39
EV41	0.66	15	0.02	37	0.93	25	0.18	28
EV42	0.25	41	0.02	37	0.90	42	-0.02	41

autohome.com. For consumer feedback, the star rating is calculated as the average star rating given by consumers for each attribute, with higher ratings being preferred. The performance values of the 42 EVs under the 12 attributes are shown in Table A1 in the appendix. The serial numbers of EVs are assigned based on their sales volume within six months, in descending order.

Due to space constraints, this paper does not present the linear and vector normalization results of attribute performance values. The consumer assigns equal weight to all attributes and to the three aggregation models. Table 73.5 presents the subordinate utilities and their rankings for the EVs, calculated by the three aggregation models, respectively. It also displays the overall utilities and final ranking of EVs, obtained by integrating the subordinate utilities and rankings based on Eq. (73.7). Note that although the table shows only two decimal places, the ranking of EVs according to CCM, UCM, and ICM is based on their actual values, not the rounded ones. The results indicate that the top five EVs are EV4, EV1, EV21, EV3, and EV7, respectively, and these EVs can be recommended to the consumer.

73.6 Conclusions

This paper reviewed the research progress of the DNMA method, which has been successfully extended to various linguistic information environments and widely applied across multiple domains. It also outlined the framework of DNMA in precise information contexts, with three core processes: normalization, attribute aggregation, and result integration. The applicability of the DNMA method in MADM problems was verified through two numerical examples: supplier selection (small-scale) and EV recommendation (large-scale).

The DNMA method offers notable advantages: (1) methodological flexibility: allowing for adjustable weight coefficients among different aggregation models based on specific decision goals, constraints, and decision-makers' risk tolerance. (2) Result reliability: complementary dual normalization strategies (linear and vector normalization) effectively reduce information loss, while the synergetic use of three aggregation models (CCM, UCM, and ICM) ensures a balanced evaluation between overall and extreme performance. (3) Operational simplicity: the computation is concise and efficient, with the integration process directly generating a complete ranking set of alternatives.

Appendix

TABLE A1 The performance values of the electric vehicles (EVs) under different attributes.

	c_1	c_2	c_3	c_4	c_5	c_6	c_7	c_8	c_9	c_{10}	c_{11}	c_{12}
EV1	12.78	150.00	478.00	0.50	2648.33	4.72	4.74	4.88	4.53	4.78	4.84	1501.00
EV2	10.33	94.00	381.00	0.50	2605.00	4.77	4.68	4.91	4.65	4.75	4.79	301.00
EV3	15.88	153.33	548.33	0.50	2778.33	4.86	4.71	4.78	4.49	4.85	4.78	587.00
EV4	12.58	160.00	494.00	0.33	2728.67	4.91	4.62	4.72	4.75	4.76	4.57	716.00
EV5	13.78	153.33	571.67	0.43	2707.00	4.30	4.63	4.83	4.37	4.79	4.76	82.00
EV6	10.88	98.00	438.00	0.46	2540.00	4.71	4.69	4.84	4.62	4.73	4.81	1781.00
EV7	13.68	100.00	456.00	0.50	2715.67	4.70	4.67	4.86	4.52	4.83	4.78	1991.00
EV8	11.38	100.00	462.00	0.57	2685.00	4.86	4.57	4.72	4.54	4.76	4.50	500.00
EV9	13.29	100.00	485.00	0.50	2756.00	4.61	4.48	4.52	4.25	4.61	4.13	93.00
EV10	12.79	125.00	451.00	0.75	2535.67	4.67	4.80	4.87	4.34	4.77	4.52	596.00
EV11	14.99	290.00	627.50	0.42	2791.33	4.98	4.79	4.87	4.85	4.81	4.85	47.00
EV12	15.48	158.33	603.33	0.30	2715.00	4.84	4.71	4.80	4.62	4.75	4.68	332.00
EV13	18.78	241.33	658.33	0.33	2774.33	4.89	4.70	4.51	4.55	4.89	4.91	479.00
EV14	12.48	135.00	441.00	0.50	2677.00	4.66	4.78	4.91	4.63	4.68	4.09	199.00
EV15	14.58	165.00	583.00	0.45	2680.00	4.83	4.84	4.84	4.40	4.74	4.80	169.00
EV16	14.83	240.00	619.50	0.33	2743.33	4.77	4.62	4.95	4.66	4.83	4.39	104.00
EV17	14.39	190.00	563.33	0.33	2758.67	4.88	4.68	4.85	4.76	4.85	4.33	184.00
EV18	11.08	119.57	429.57	0.50	2552.00	4.60	4.64	4.90	4.57	4.59	4.64	229.00
EV19	18.17	155.63	529.25	0.67	2701.33	4.79	4.75	4.90	4.52	4.75	4.64	502.00
EV20	18.68	173.75	551.00	0.67	2691.00	4.75	4.76	4.86	4.33	4.60	4.20	513.00
EV21	17.08	285.00	604.00	0.29	2798.33	4.62	4.83	4.85	4.64	4.71	4.56	309.00
EV22	11.68	150.00	510.00	0.33	2771.67	4.95	4.68	4.85	4.64	4.74	4.45	186.00
EV23	17.09	174.00	554.00	0.47	2826.00	4.92	4.73	4.80	4.61	4.68	4.43	227.00
EV24	17.40	246.00	510.40	0.50	2619.33	4.41	4.78	4.84	4.80	4.50	4.51	155.00
EV25	12.88	150.00	550.00	0.33	2676.33	4.64	4.69	4.87	4.55	4.55	4.73	143.00
EV26	19.99	190.00	480.00	0.53	2700.67	4.86	3.86	4.43	3.86	3.43	3.71	7.00
EV27	18.95	190.00	582.50	0.68	2693.00	4.72	4.79	4.75	4.60	4.62	3.91	92.00

EV28	15.43	116.67	440.00	0.50	2692.00	4.47	4.75	4.69	4.60	4.78	4.54	83.00
EV29	10.73	120.00	476.00	0.37	2702.33	4.94	4.74	4.82	4.80	4.76	4.56	50.00
EV30	10.88	70.00	405.00	0.50	2516.67	4.58	4.60	4.71	4.45	4.69	4.57	154.00
EV31	12.84	158.75	502.50	0.42	2739.67	4.96	4.41	4.75	4.36	4.77	4.70	158.00
EV32	10.48	100.00	431.43	0.52	2599.00	4.88	4.57	4.63	4.73	4.55	4.73	166.00
EV33	13.33	168.00	447.00	0.43	2546.33	4.63	4.71	4.85	4.40	4.72	4.69	305.00
EV34	15.53	147.86	538.57	0.49	2757.33	4.79	4.72	4.67	4.44	4.76	4.32	331.00
EV35	17.89	236.00	694.00	0.25	2750.67	4.58	4.87	4.94	4.87	4.87	4.62	113.00
EV36	12.93	100.00	441.00	0.77	2648.33	4.72	4.79	4.85	4.46	4.89	4.82	87.00
EV37	14.47	140.00	553.33	0.50	2744.00	4.75	4.74	4.82	4.38	4.69	4.38	61.00
EV38	15.93	110.00	479.20	0.50	2663.33	4.69	4.85	4.92	4.42	4.73	4.27	26.00
EV39	19.53	160.00	606.00	0.45	2735.00	4.66	4.72	4.86	4.55	4.58	4.62	65.00
EV40	19.43	152.50	601.25	0.53	2733.33	4.70	4.67	4.61	4.33	4.36	4.36	33.00
EV41	19.99	273.20	607.60	0.50	2815.67	4.76	4.65	4.87	4.78	4.57	4.24	46.00
EV42	16.20	140.00	619.00	0.75	2643.67	3.40	4.10	4.50	4.50	3.60	3.50	10.00

References

Acar, E., Tama Birkocak, D., Özdağoğlu, A., Ünal, Z., Özdemir, G., & Josè Abreu, M. (2024). Prioritizing sustainable denim fabric through integrated decision-making framework. *Materials, 17*(13), 3291.

Al-Barakati, A., & Rani, P. (2024). Assessment of healthcare waste treatment methods using an interval-valued intuitionistic fuzzy double normalization-based multiple aggregation approach. *Environment, Development and Sustainability, 26*(8), 19397–19424.

Brauers, W. K. M., & Zavadskas, E. K. (2010). Project management by MULTIMOORA as an instrument for transition economies. *Technological and Economic Development of Economy, 16*(1), 5–24.

Chen, S. J., & Hwang, C. L. (1992). *Fuzzy multiple attribute decision making*. Berlin: Springer.

Deb, P. P., Bhattacharya, D., Chatterjee, I., Saha, A., Mishra, A. R., & Ahammad, S. H. (2022). A decision-making model with intuitionistic fuzzy information for selection of enterprise resource planning systems. *IEEE Transactions on Engineering Management, 71*, 4820–4834.

Durán, C., Yazdi, A. K., Derpich, I., & Tan, Y. (2024). Leveraging blockchain for maritime port supply chain management through multicriteria decision making. *Mathematics, 12*(10), 1511.

Ecer, F., & Zolfani, S. H. (2022). Evaluating economic freedom via a multi-criteria MEREC-DNMA model-based composite system: Case of OPEC countries. *Technological and Economic Development of Economy, 28*(4), 1158–1181.

Edwards, W., & Barron, F. H. (1994). SMARTS and SMARTER: Improved simple methods for multiattribute utility measurement. *Organizational Behavior and Human Decision Processes, 60*(3), 306–325.

Esangbedo, M. O., & Wei, J. (2023). Grey hybrid normalization with period based entropy weighting and relational analysis for cities rankings. *Scientific Reports, 13*(1), 13797.

Gopisetty, Y. B., & Sama, H. R. (2025). An integrated MCDM approach using double normalization: Introducing the DN-WENSLO and DN-RPEM methods for socio-economic performance evaluation. *Journal of the Operational Research Society,* 1–27.

Hezam, I. M., Mishra, A. R., Rani, P., & Alshamrani, A. (2023). Assessing the barriers of digitally sustainable transportation system for persons with disabilities using Fermatean fuzzy double normalization-based multiple aggregation method. *Applied Soft Computing, 133*, 109910.

Hezam, I. M., Mishra, A. R., Rani, P., Cavallaro, F., Saha, A., Ali, J., Strielkowski, W., & Štreimikienė, D. (2022). A hybrid intuitionistic fuzzy-MEREC-RS-DNMA method for assessing the alternative fuel vehicles with sustainability perspectives. *Sustainability, 14*(9), 5463.

Ivanović, B., Saha, A., Stević, Ž., Puška, A., & Zavadskas, E. K. (2022). Selection of truck mixer concrete pump using novel MEREC DNMARCOS model. *Archives of Civil and Mechanical Engineering, 22*(4), 173.

Jahan, A., & Edwards, K. L. (2015). A state-of-the-art survey on the influence of normalization techniques in ranking: Improving the materials selection process in engineering design. *Materials & Design, 65*, 335–342 (1980-2015).

Kumar, R., & Kumar, S. (2024). An extended combined compromise solution framework based on novel intuitionistic fuzzy distance measure and score function with applications in sustainable biomass crop selection. *Expert Systems with Applications, 239*, 122345.

Lai, H., & Liao, H. C. (2021). A multi-criteria decision making method based on DNMA and CRITIC with linguistic D numbers for blockchain platform evaluation. *Engineering Applications of Artificial Intelligence, 101*, 104200.

Lai, H., Liao, H. C., Šaparauskas, J., Banaitis, A., Ferreira, F. A., & Al-Barakati, A. (2020). Sustainable cloud service provider development by a Z-number-based DNMA method with Gini-coefficient-based weight determination. *Sustainability, 12*(8), 3410.

Liao, H. C., & Wu, X. L. (2020). DNMA: A double normalization-based multiple aggregation method for multi-expert multi-criteria decision making. *Omega, 94*, 102058.

Liao, H. C., Long, Y. L., Tang, M., Streimikiene, D., & Lev, B. (2019). Early lung cancer screening using double normalization-based multi-aggregation (DNMA) and Delphi methods with hesitant fuzzy information. *Computers & Industrial Engineering, 136*, 453–463.

Liao, H. C., Xiao, Y., Wu, X. L., & Bausys, R. (2024). Z-DNMASort: A double normalization-based multiple aggregation sorting method with Z-numbers for multi-criterion sorting problems. *Information Sciences, 653*, 119782.

Liao, H., Xue, J., Mehrbakhsh, N., Wu, X. L., & Jurgita, A. (2020). Partner selection for automobile manufacturing enterprises with a q-rung orthopair fuzzy double normalization-based multi-aggregation method. *Transformations in Business & Economics, 19*(2A), 338–368.

Liu, F., Liao, H. C., & Al-Barakati, A. (2023). Physician selection based on user-generated content considering interactive criteria and risk preferences of patients. *Omega, 115*, 102784.

Lukic, R. (2024). Research of the dynamics of the economic performance of the Serbian economy based on LMAW-DNMA methods. *Journal of Economics, 9*(2), 15–29.

Mishra, A. R., Rani, P., Deveci, M., Gokasar, I., Pamucar, D., & Govindan, K. (2023). Interval-valued Fermatean fuzzy heronian mean operator-based decision-making method for urban climate change policy for transportation activities. *Engineering Applications of Artificial Intelligence, 124*, 106603.

Mishra, A. R., Rani, P., Saha, A., Hezam, I. M., Cavallaro, F., & Chakrabortty, R. K. (2023). An extended DNMA-based multi-criteria decision-making method and its application in the assessment of sustainable location for a lithium-ion batteries' manufacturing plant. *Heliyon, 9*(3).

Moslem, S., Gholamizadeh, K., Zarei, E., Pasman, H. J., Martinez-Pastor, B., & Pilla, F. (2025). A comparative assessment of domino accident analysis methods in process industries using LMAW and DNMA techniques. *Reliability Engineering & System Safety, 260*, 110981.

Mourad, N., Zaidan, A. A., Alsattar, H. A., Qahtan, S., Zaidan, B. B., Deveci, M., Pamucar, D., & Pedrycz, W. (2025). Dynamic localization based-utility decision approach under type-2 pythagorean fuzzy set for developing internet of modular self-reconfiguration robot things. *Engineering Applications of Artificial Intelligence, 139*, 109671.

Önden, İ., Kara, K., Yalçın, G. C., Deveci, M., Önden, A., & Eker, M. (2024). Strategic location analysis for offshore wind farms to sustainably fulfill railway energy demand in Turkey. *Journal of Cleaner Production, 434*, 140142.

Opricovic, S. (1998). Multicriteria optimization of civil engineering systems. Belgrade: PhD Thesis, Faculty of Civil Engineering.

Rahimi, M., Kumar, P., Moazzamigodarzi, M., & Mishra, A. R. (2022). Digital transformation challenges in sustainable financial service systems using novel interval-valued Pythagorean fuzzy double normalization-based multiple aggregation approach. *Environment, Development and Sustainability*. https://doi.org/10.1007/s10668-022-02719-3.

Saha, A., Mishra, A. R., Rani, P., Hezam, I. M., & Cavallaro, F. (2022). A q-rung orthopair fuzzy FUCOM double normalization-based multi-aggregation method for healthcare waste treatment method selection. *Sustainability, 14*(7), 4171.

Saha, A., Simic, V., Senapati, T., Dabic-Miletic, S., & Ala, A. (2022). A dual hesitant fuzzy sets-based methodology for advantage prioritization of zero-emission last-mile delivery solutions for sustainable city logistics. *IEEE Transactions on Fuzzy Systems, 31*(2), 407–420.

Song, Z., Mishra, A. R., & Saeidi, S. P. (2023). Technological capabilities in the era of the digital economy for integration into cyber-physical systems and the IoT using decision-making approach. *Journal of Innovation & Knowledge, 8*(2), 100356.

Tong, X., & Wang, Z. J. (2023). New additive-consistency-driven methods for deriving two types of normalized utility vectors from additive reciprocal preference relations. *Journal of the Operational Research Society, 74*(6), 1475–1494.

Wang, L., & Rani, P. (2022). Sustainable supply chains under risk in the manufacturing firms: An extended double normalization-based multiple aggregation approach under an intuitionistic fuzzy environment. *Journal of Enterprise Information Management, 35*(4/5), 1067–1099.

Wen, Z., Liao, H., & Zavadskas, E. K. (2020). MACONT: Mixed aggregation by comprehensive normalization technique for multi-criteria analysis. *Informatica, 31*(4), 857–880.

Weng, L., Lin, J., Xu, Z. S., & Lu, J. (2025). The trapezium cloud-based method with heterogeneous information for selecting phase change materials in the latent heat energy storage system. *Journal of Energy Storage, 123*, 116649.

Wu, X. L., & Liao, H. C. (2019). Comparison analysis between DNMA method and other MCDM methods. *ICSES Transaction on Neural and Fuzzy Computing, 2*(1), 4–10.

Wu, X. L., & Liao, H. C. (2023). A compensatory value function for modeling risk tolerance and criteria interactions in preference disaggregation. *Omega, 117*, 102836.

Wu, X. L., Nie, S., Liao, H. C., & Gupta, P. (2023). A large-scale group decision making method with a consensus reaching process under cognitive linguistic environment. *International Transactions in Operational Research, 30*(3), 1340–1365.

Yalcin, A. S., Kilic, H. S., & Delen, D. (2022). The use of multi-criteria decision-making methods in business analytics: A comprehensive literature review. *Technological Forecasting and Social Change, 174*, 121193.

Yang, L., Zou, H. B., Shang, C., Ye, X. M., & Rani, P. (2023). Adoption of information and digital technologies for sustainable smart manufacturing systems for industry 4.0 in small, medium, and micro enterprises (SMMEs). *Technological Forecasting and Social Change, 188*, 122308.

Yousefi, S., Baqeri, M., Tosarkani, B. M., Amin, S. H., & Zolfagharinia, H. (2023). A decision support framework for sustainable production planning of paper recycling systems. *Computers & Industrial Engineering, 183*, 109500.

Zhang, H. R., Liao, H. C., Wu, X. L., Zavadskas, E. K., & Al-Barakati, A. (2020). Internet financial investment product selection with pythagorean fuzzy DNMA method. *Engineering Economics, 31*(1), 61–71.

Chapter 74

TRUST: A multinormalization multidistance assessment for multi-attribute decision-making

Muhammet Deveci[1], Mehtap Isik[2], Şeyma Duymaz[1], and Bartu Güneri[1]

[1]*Department of Industrial Engineering, Turkish Naval Academy, National Defence University, Istanbul, Türkiye,* [2]*Department of International Trade, Bogazici University, Bebek, Istanbul, Türkiye*

74.1 Introduction

In recent decades, Türkiye has faced the dual challenge of meeting its growing energy demand while aligning with global sustainability goals. As a rapidly developing economy with increasing urbanization and industrial activity, the country remains heavily dependent on energy imports, currently meeting around 70% of its energy needs from abroad, which exposes it to economic risks and undermines energy security (IEA, n.d.; World Bank, 2025).

Türkiye possesses a wide range of renewable energy resources, including high solar potential in Central and Southeastern Anatolia, robust wind corridors along the Aegean and Marmara coasts, considerable hydropower capacity in the Eastern Black Sea, and rich geothermal reserves in Western Anatolia. In order to utilize this potential, the government has introduced various policy instruments such as Renewable Energy Resource Areas (YEKA), feed-in tariffs, and local content requirements aimed at accelerating renewable energy adoption (TSKB, 2025).

In parallel, decentralized energy systems and smart grid technologies have begun to emerge, particularly in regions where centralized infrastructure is less feasible (Ministry of Energy and Natural Resources of Türkiye, 2024). While these developments promise greater energy resilience and accessibility, challenges exist. These include high capital costs, intermittency issues, potential public opposition to infrastructure projects, and uneven regional development outcomes (Erat et al., 2021; Ministry of Energy and Natural Resources of Türkiye, 2024).

To ensure reliability during peak periods and transitional phases, natural gas continues to play a strategic, although controversial, role in Türkiye's energy mix (Gürsan and de Gooyert, 2021). Additionally, the scale and complexity of new energy projects necessitate innovative financing models, including public–private partnerships (PPPs), which are increasingly employed in initiatives like clustered green energy investment zones (Presidency of Strategy and Budget, 2023).

This chapter investigates the complex decision-making process surrounding energy investment prioritization in Türkiye's sustainable energy transition. A multidimensional analytical framework is adopted, integrating environmental, economic, social, and technical criteria. Given competing objectives such as emission reduction, affordability, equity, and grid stability, multicriteria decision-making (MCDM) methods provide a structured and transparent approach to evaluating alternatives.

This chapter applies the TRUST method (a multinormalization multidistance assessment) to rank four representative renewable energy strategies in Türkiye: (1) a balanced renewable energy mix; (2) decentralized systems with smart grids; (3) renewables combined with natural gas; and (4) hybrid green energy zones supported by PPPs. These are evaluated against 13 criteria grouped under four strategic pillars: environmental sustainability, economic efficiency, social and regional development, and technical and operational feasibility. The aim is to inform more holistic and evidence-based energy policy decisions in Türkiye.

Encyclopedia of Multi-Attribute Decision-Making (MADM). DOI: https://doi.org/10.1016/B978-0-443-33275-3.00089-0

The remainder of the chapter is structured as follows: Section 74.2 presents the literature review, which forms the basis for the selection of both the set of alternatives and the evaluation criteria. Section 74.3 outlines the work methodology and provides a detailed explanation of the TRUST method. In Section 74.4, the TRUST model is applied to the case of Türkiye to address the decision-making problem related to energy investment strategies. Section 74.5 presents the results of the sensitivity analysis. Finally, Section 74.6 concludes the chapter by offering policy recommendations derived from the findings.

74.2 Literature review

Türkiye's energy transition has become a focus of policies related to technological innovation and investment strategy, with growing emphasis on sustainability, energy security, and economic resilience. Recent studies emphasize the multidimensional nature of this transformation. Acar et al. (2023) offer a comprehensive assessment of the economic, environmental, and social implications of transforming Türkiye's power system by 2030. Their findings highlight the potential of renewable energy to reduce emissions while stimulating job creation, especially in underdeveloped regions. Complementarily, Aktemur (2017) and Gürsan and de Gooyert (2021) concentrate on the role of natural gas in the transition. While Aktemur (2017) presents natural gas as the backbone of Türkiye's current system, Gürsan and de Gooyert (2021) question its role as a transition fuel, warning of long-term path dependencies that could hinder decarbonization.

Technological and institutional readiness remain central themes. Gulaydin and Mourshed (2025) explore Türkiye's net-zero roadmap, identifying both the country's renewable potential and barriers to scaling solar and wind technologies. Melikoglu and Aslan (2025) propose green hydrogen blending into natural gas as a viable mid-term option aligned with emission reduction goals. Karipoğlu and Denizli (2025) contribute to the discussions on decentralization through the concept of "renewable energy islands," arguing for regional energy hubs based on local resource profiles.

Naimoglu and Akal (2023) show a positive relationship between energy efficiency, renewable deployment, and environmental outcomes. Especially from an environmental point of view, smart grids are critical to managing intermittency and improving system efficiency under certain circumstances. Keskin (2021) provides an overview of Türkiye's current grid and digital transformation prospects, while Oral et al. (2022) present case studies illustrating the emissions-reduction potential of smart grids when combined with behavioral change and effective governance.

Public engagement also plays a significant role. Acikgoz and Yorulmaz (2024) explore the attitudes of Türkiye's younger generation, revealing that their support for renewables is driven by environmental awareness, perceived control, and trust in institutions. Calikoglu and Koksal (2022) focus on green electricity certification, finding that trust and transparency are key to consumer demand for guarantees of origin.

Financial feasibility remains a core challenge. Erden Topal and Gursoy Haksevenler (2025) emphasize institutional barriers faced by renewable energy entrepreneurs, while Balcilar et al. (2023) show that PPPs can enhance energy efficiency if properly managed. Cedrick and Long (2017) and Durna et al. (2024) further support PPPs as effective mechanisms for mobilizing capital and managing risk, contingent on strong legal frameworks and stakeholder cooperation.

Altogether, the literature underlines the complexity of Türkiye's energy transformation and the importance of adopting a multicriteria, integrative approach to prioritize sustainable energy investment strategies.

From a methodological standpoint, Akusta et al. (2025) apply a fuzzy analytical hierarchy process (AHP) approach to identify investment barriers, highlighting financial risk, policy uncertainty, and technological complexity as critical challenges. Dumrul et al. (2024) utilize an intuitionistic fuzzy evaluation based on distance from average solution method to evaluate renewable alternatives, emphasizing the need to manage uncertainty in expert assessments. Their results reinforce the viability of solar and wind investments in Türkiye. Ozsoy et al. (2024) compare Türkiye's energy preferences with those of European countries, showing that while environmental concerns dominate EU priorities, Türkiye focuses more on economic and operational feasibility. Aksoy (2019) offers an integrated model that considers both regional resource diversity and socio-economic conditions, supporting geographically tailored investment strategies. These studies justify the use of a robust, multicriteria framework like TRUST in evaluating Türkiye's energy transformation pathways.

74.3 Methodology

The utilization of MCDM methodologies and techniques is imperative in the resolution of intricate problems. This section will discuss a ranking method known as TRUST.

The TRUST method was proposed in a contribution by Torkayesh and Deveci (2021) as a method that aims to address the shortcomings that arise when normalization techniques are used alone in MCDM methods by combining different normalization and distance measures. The approach is centered on the evaluation and subsequent ranking of alternatives. In the present work, a constraint-based normalization formula is proposed. The constraint-based normalization technique is intended to enhance the reliability of the normalization process by considering the nature of the criteria, real-life preferences, and standards. The technique under discussion is a hybrid approach that incorporates four distinct normalization techniques.

The remaining three normalization techniques comprise linear ratio-based, linear sum-based, linear maximum minimum, and logarithmic normalization. In the final stage, the results obtained from each of these techniques are combined using a balancing parameter to obtain a collective normalized decision matrix. Subsequently, the constraint-based normalized matrix and the hybrid normalized matrix are combined to produce the constrained normalized decision matrix.

The TRUST method is an analytical framework that utilizes four distinct distance measures, namely, Euclidean, Manhattan, Lorentz, and Pearson, to ascertain the distances of alternatives from the negative-ideal solution. The application of these four distance measures enables the calculation of the final performance scores of alternatives according to the specified criteria via a combined scoring function. The algorithm of the proposed TRUST method is presented in detail below.

Step 1. The initial decision matrix is structured in accordance with Eq. (74.1). In this matrix, x_{ij} represents the initial performance score of each alternative with respect to each criterion.

$$X = [x_{ij}]_{n\times m} = [x_{11}\ x_{12} \quad \cdots \quad x_{1m}\ x_{21} \quad \vdots \quad x_{n1}\ x_{22} \quad \vdots \quad x_{n2} \quad \cdots \quad x_{2m} \quad \vdots \quad \vdots \quad \cdots \quad x_{nm}] \tag{74.1}$$

Step 2. The TRUST method employs four distinct normalization techniques to transform the initial decision matrix into a normalized decision matrix.

Step 2.1. The calculation of the normalized values of the initial decision matrix is undertaken by way of the linear ratio approach, as follows Eqs. (74.2) and (74.3)(Keshavarz Ghorabaee et al., 2016).

$$x_{ij}^{a} = \frac{x_{ij}}{x_{ij}} \quad \text{If } j \in B \tag{74.2}$$

$$x_{ij}^{a} = \frac{x_{ij}}{x_{ij}} \quad \text{If } j \in C \tag{74.3}$$

where x_{ij}^{a} represents an element of normalized decision matrix according to normalization type-1.

Step 2.2. Normalization type-2 utilizes a linear sum-based technique to normalize initial decision matrix elements, as in Eqs. (74.4) and (74.5) (Wen et al., 2020).

$$x_{ij}^{b} = \frac{x_{ij}}{\sum_{i=1}^{m} x_{ij}} \quad \text{If } j \in B \tag{74.4}$$

$$x_{ij}^{b} = \frac{\frac{1}{x_{ij}}}{\sum_{i=1}^{m} \frac{1}{x_{ij}}} \quad \text{If } j \in C \tag{74.5}$$

where x_{ij}^{b} represents an element of normalized decision matrix according to normalization type-2.

Step 2.3. Normalization type-3 utilizes the linear max–min technique to normalize initial decision matrix elements, as in Eqs. (74.6) and (74.7) (Yazdani et al., 2019).

$$x_{ij}^{c} = \frac{(x_{ij} - x_{ij})}{(x_{ij} - x_{ij})} \quad \text{If } j \in B \tag{74.6}$$

$$x_{ij}^{c} = \frac{(x_{ij} - x_{ij})}{(x_{ij} - x_{ij})} \quad \text{If } j \in C \tag{74.7}$$

where x_{ij}^{c} represents an element of normalized decision matrix according to normalization type-3.

Step 2.4. Normalization type-4 utilizes logarithmic technique to normalize initial decision matrix elements, as in Eq. (74.8) (Zolfani et al., 2020).

$$x_{ij}^{d} = \frac{\log(x_{ij})}{\log\left(\prod_{i=1}^{m} x_{ij}\right)} \tag{74.8}$$

where x_{ij}^d represents an element of normalized decision matrix according to normalization type-4.

Step 2.5. All normalized decision matrices are aggregated using four parameters α_i in order to construct an aggregated normalized decision matrix, as in Eq. (74.9).

$$h_{ij} = \alpha_1 x_{ij}^a + \alpha_2 x_{ij}^b + \alpha_3 x_{ij}^c + \alpha_4 x_{ij}^d \tag{74.9}$$

where the sum of all α_i values must be equal to one as follows in Eq. (74.10).

$$\alpha_1 + \alpha_2 + \alpha_3 + \alpha_4 = 1 \tag{74.10}$$

Step 3. Preliminary data regarding limited attributes is used to create an initial decision matrix, which is then referred to as the "satisfaction level" (Abdelli et al., 2019, 2020). The matrix is derived according to the specified constraint values of the criteria, and each element is represented by f_{ij}. The following section delineates the steps of the constraint-based normalization technique.

Based on experts' opinions or real data in the matrix X, $x_j^{\min} = Min\,(x_{ij})$ and $x_j^{\max} = MAX\,(x_{ij})$ represents minimum and maximum values.

Step 3.1. Constraint values for each criterion can be determined by decision-makers based on their experience or technical features of each criterion. Constraint value is represented as an interval number as $[LB_j, UB_j]$ where LB_j denotes lower bound of constraint value of criterion j and UB_j represents upper bound of constraint value of criterion j. Assigned constraint values must be within $x_j^{\min}$ and $x_j^{\max}$ values. Mathematically, constraint values should hold Eq. (74.11).

$$Co_j = [LB_j, UB_j] \subseteq [x_j^{\min}, x_j^{\max}] \tag{74.11}$$

Step 3.2. Satisfaction degree of initial decision matrix is calculated based on constraint values. A secondary version of initial decision matrix is considered as F, where f_{ij} represents degree of constraint satisfaction of alternative i with respect to constrained value of criterion j. Elements of matrix F can be determined as follows.

For a benefit criterion as shown in Eqs. (74.12)–(74.14):

$$f_{ij} = 1, \text{ if } x_{ij} \in [LB_j, UB_j] \tag{74.12}$$

$$f_{ij} = 1 - \frac{LB_j - x_{ij}}{Max\,(LB_j - x_j^{\min},\ x_j^{\max} - UB_j) + 1}, \text{ if } x_{ij} \in [x_j^{\min}, LB_j] \tag{74.13}$$

$$f_{ij} = 1 - \frac{1 - UB_j + x_{ij}}{Max\,(LB_j - x_j^{\min},\ x_j^{\max} - UB_j) + 1}, \text{ if } x_{ij} \in [UB_j, x_j^{\max}] \tag{74.14}$$

For a cost criterion as shown in Eqs. (74.15)–(74.17):

$$f_{ij} = \frac{1}{Max\,(LB_j - x_j^{\min},\ x_j^{\max} - UB_j) + 1}, \text{ if } x_{ij} \in [LB_j, UB_j] \tag{74.15}$$

$$f_{ij} = \frac{LB_j - x_{ij}}{Max\,(LB_j - x_j^{\min},\ x_j^{\max} - UB_j)}, \text{ if } x_{ij} \in [x_j^{\min}, LB_j] \tag{74.16}$$

$$f_{ij} = \frac{x_{ij} - UB_j}{Max\,(LB_j - x_j^{\min},\ x_j^{\max} - UB_j)}, \text{ if } x_{ij} \in [UB_j, x_j^{\max}] \tag{74.17}$$

Step 4. Aggregated normalized decision matrix and matrix related to satisfaction degree of constraint, calculated in step 2, are used to generate constrained aggregated normalized decision matrix. Elements constrained aggregated normalized decision matrix, $Y = [y_{ij}]_{n*m}$, are shown by y_{ij}, as shown in Eq. (74.18).

$$y_{ij} = f_{ij}\ h_{ij} \tag{74.18}$$

Step 5. Constrained aggregated normalized decision matrix is multiplied by weight vector of involved criteria to generate a weight-constrained aggregated normalized matrix, $G = [g_{ij}]_{n*m}$, as follows in Eq. (74.19).

$$g_{ij} = y_{ij}\ w_j \tag{74.19}$$

where g_{ij} represents elements of weighted matrix and w_j represents weight of a criterion j.

Step 6. Negative-ideal solution of weighted matrix G is determined according to Eq. (74.20).

$$\eta_j = g_{ij} \tag{74.20}$$

where η_j denotes negative-ideal solution of criterion j.

Step 7. TRUST applies a two-stage operation to calculate distances of alternatives from the negative-ideal solution.

Step 7.1. In stage 1, Euclidean and Manhattan distance measures are used as follows in Eqs. (74.21) and (74.22).

$$E_i = \sqrt{\sum_{i=1}^{m} (g_{ij} - \eta_j)^2} \tag{74.21}$$

$$T_i = \sum_{i=1}^{m} |g_{ij} - \eta_j| \tag{74.22}$$

Step 7.2. In stage 2, Lorentzian distance measure (Cha, 2008) and Pearson distance measure (Cha, 2008) are used to calculate distances of alternatives from the negative-ideal solution as follows in Eqs. (74.23) and (74.24).

$$L_i = \sum_{i=1}^{m} 1 + |g_{ij} - \eta_j| \tag{74.23}$$

$$P_i = \sum_{i=1}^{m} \frac{(g_{ij} - \eta_j)^2}{\eta_j} \tag{74.24}$$

Step 8. According to distance measures, two relative distance assessment matrices are constructed as $ET = [\theta_{ij}]_{n*n}$ and $LP = [\varphi_{ij}]_{n*n}$, respectively, as shown in Eqs. (74.25) and (74.26).

$$\theta_{ik} = (E_i - E_k) + ((E_i - E_k)*(T_i - T_k)) \tag{74.25}$$

$$\varphi_{ik} = (L_i - L_k) + ((L_i - L_k)*(P_i - P_k)) \tag{74.26}$$

where $k \in \{1, 2, \ldots, n\}$.

Step 9. A combined score for each alternative, Ω_i, is calculated as follows in Eq. (74.27).

$$\Omega_i = \beta \sum_{k=1}^{n} \theta_{ik} + (1 - \beta) \sum_{k=1}^{n} \varphi_{ik} \tag{74.27}$$

where β represents a parameter that is used to calculate a combined distance assessment score using two relative distance assessment matrices. β is a nonnegative parameter smaller than 1, which usually takes a value of 0.5 in decision-making problems. Alternatives are ranked based on their combined distance assessment score, Ω_i, in a decreasing order such that an alternative with the highest Ω_i value is considered as the best alternative.

74.4 Case study

74.4.1 Numerical example 1: case of Türkiye energy investment decision

In light of the dynamics that are discussed in the introduction section, Türkiye has initiated various policy approaches reflecting these alternatives. This chapter formulates the problem of analyzing energy investment strategies through a multidimensional lens, incorporating environmental, economic, social, and technical considerations. Specifically, four comprehensive policy alternatives are constructed, each representing current and emerging energy investment directions in Türkiye. These alternatives are evaluated using a set of 13 criteria, grouped under four principal dimensions: environmental sustainability, economic efficiency, social and regional development, and technical and operational feasibility. The criteria have been identified based on literature reviews and expert consultation, comprising four main categories and 13 specific subcriteria.

The evaluation criteria and attributes are reported in Fig. 74.1. Decision-makers will assess four alternatives based on their performance with respect to the established decision criteria.

74.4.1.1 Definition of alternatives

A_1: Balanced renewable mix: Türkiye has a strong capacity to deploy solar, wind, hydro, and geothermal in regions where each source has the highest potential. Türkiye already implements a de facto version of this strategy under its regional planning and energy zoning model (YEKA). This alternative reflects current policy momentum. Karapınar solar power plant in Konya, Bergama and Soma wind power projects in the Aegean region, Zile Geothermal Project in Tokat, Deriner and Yusufeli Dams in Eastern Black sea are some example projects.

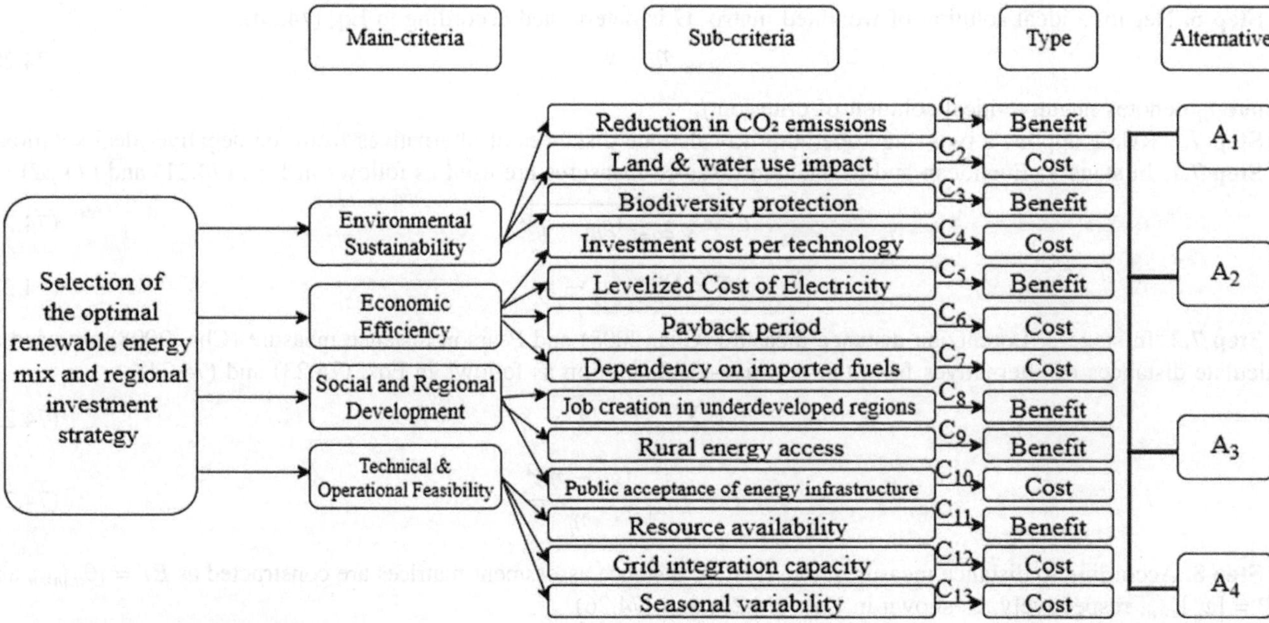

FIGURE 74.1 The decision hierarchy of the problem.

***A_2*:** Decentralized systems + smart grids: This alternative represents the projects that promote rooftop solar, microgrids, and distributed energy systems with grid digitalization. These projects are being increasingly relevant for Türkiye's goals to electrify rural regions and enhance energy equity, especially in provinces with weaker grid infrastructure. Rooftop solar in Gaziantep Organized Industrial Zone, Bozcaada Island (Çanakkale) Pilot Project. EU-Türkiye smart grid demonstrations with TÜBİTAK funds are some examples.

***A_2*:** *Renewables + natural gas as backup*: This alternative includes the projects that combine renewables with natural gas power plants for grid stability and dispatchable energy. While natural gas is seen as a transition fuel, Türkiye's import dependency makes this strategy sensitive to geopolitical shocks. However, it is still widely practiced for reliability. Ambarlı natural gas combined cycle plant with wind integration in Istanbul and Silivri underground natural gas storage with solar projects are some projects alive.

***A_4*:** Hybrid public–private green energy zones: Projects under this alternative create designated areas where renewables, storage, green industry, and local manufacturing are colocated and cofinanced by public and private stakeholders. Türkiye's YEKA and Green Organized Industrial Zone (OIZ) programs are converging toward this model. The EU green deal and carbon border adjustment mechanism push Turkish industry to adopt such integrated decarbonization strategies. Karapınar YEKA solar with local manufacturing zone in Konya and organized industrial zones-based green transition clusters in Denizli and Bursa are some examples.

74.4.1.2 Definition of criteria

1. Environmental sustainability criteria:
   - ***C_1*:** Reduction in CO_2 emissions (benefit): measures how much the alternative helps cut greenhouse gas emissions.
   - ***C_2*:** Land and water use impact (cost): assesses the environmental burden on ecosystems and natural resources.
   - ***C_3*:** Biodiversity protection (benefit): evaluates the extent to which the alternative avoids harming local flora and fauna.
2. Economic efficiency criteria:
   - ***C_4*:** Investment cost per technology (cost): reflects the initial capital required to implement the energy system.
   - ***C_5*:** Levelized cost of electricity (benefit): indicates the average cost per unit of electricity over the system's lifetime.
   - ***C_6*:** Payback period (cost): shows how long it takes to recover the investment.
   - ***C_7*:** Dependency on imported fuels (cost): measures vulnerability to external energy sources and price volatility.
3. Social and regional development criteria:
   - ***C_8*:** Job creation in underdeveloped regions (benefit): captures employment opportunities in less-developed areas.
   - ***C_9*:** Rural energy access (benefit): assesses the potential to expand electricity services to rural communities.
   - ***C_{10}*:** Public acceptance of energy infrastructure (cost): reflects possible social resistance or support for projects.

4. Technical and operational feasibility criteria:

***C_{11}*:** Resource availability (benefit): examines the local abundance and reliability of energy resources.

***C_{12}*:** Grid integration capacity (cost): measures the technical ease and cost of incorporating the system into the existing grid.

***C_{13}*:** Seasonal variability (cost): considers performance fluctuations due to seasonal resource changes.

74.4.1.3 Multinormalization multidistance assessment method application

This section presents the results of the TRUST method applied in the chapter. A questionnaire was prepared to evaluate the proposed alternatives based on the defined criteria. Each alternative was scored by experts according to the criteria. The questionnaires were sent to four experts, and the evaluation results were subsequently collected.

Accordingly, four experts were involved in this work to evaluate the four different alternatives based on all previously defined criteria. To determine the weight coefficients of the criteria, the Shannon entropy method was applied using the initial decision matrix. The aggregated initial decision matrix, as shown in Eq. (74.1), based on the opinions of the four experts, is represented in Table 74.1.

Based on the information in Table 74.1, Shannon's entropy determined the weight coefficients as follows.

$C_1 = 0.0456$, $C_2 = 0.0723$, $C_3 = 0.0618$, $C_4 = 0.0897$, $C_5 = 0.0812$, $C_6 = 0.\ 0945$, $C_7 = 0.0694$, $C_8 = 0.0789$, $C_9 = 0.0631$, $C_{10} = 0.0876$, $C_{11} = 0.1024$, $C_{12} = 0.0483$ and $C_{13} = 0.1052$.

The initial step following the formation of the decision matrix is the application of type-1 normalization, as given in Eqs. (74.2) and (74.3). For the purpose previously outlined, it is first necessary to establish the minimum and maximum values for alternative performances for each criterion. Using minimum and maximum values and based on nature of criteria, normalized decision matrix for type-1 technique is reported in Table 74.2.

In the second step, the normalization of type-2 is applied to normalize the aggregated initial decision matrix according to Eqs. (74.4) and (74.5). Table 74.3 presents the normalized type-2 matrix.

The max–min normalization process (type-3 normalization) is performed according to Eqs. (74.6) and (74.7) with the objective of generating a normalized decision matrix, as presented in Table 74.4.

Finally, type-4 form of normalization (logarithmic normalization) is employed, as shown in Eq. (74.8), to derive a normalized decision matrix, as provided in Table 74.5.

TABLE 74.1 Aggregated initial decision matrix.

	C_1	C_2	C_3	C_4	C_5	C_6	C_7	C_8	C_9	C_{10}	C_{11}	C_{12}	C_{13}
A_1	6.5	4.5	7.25	4.5	7.75	4	4.25	6.25	4.75	4.5	6.5	4.25	4.25
A_2	8	4.25	7.25	5.5	7.25	4.75	4.75	7.5	6.75	3.75	6.25	4.75	4.75
A_3	6.5	4.5	7	3.75	7	5.25	5	6.75	5	4.25	6.75	4.5	5
A_4	6.25	3.5	6.75	3.5	6.5	3.75	4	6.25	4.75	3.75	5.75	3.75	3.5

TABLE 74.2 Normalization type-1.

	C_1	C_2	C_3	C_4	C_5	C_6	C_7	C_8	C_9	C_{10}	C_{11}	C_{12}	C_{13}
A_1	0.813	0.778	1.000	0.778	1.000	0.938	0.941	0.833	0.704	0.833	0.963	0.882	0.824
A_2	1.000	0.824	1.000	0.636	0.935	0.789	0.842	1.000	1.000	1.000	0.926	0.789	0.737
A_3	0.813	0.778	0.966	0.933	0.903	0.714	0.800	0.900	0.741	0.882	1.000	0.833	0.700
A_4	0.781	1.000	0.931	1.000	0.839	1.000	1.000	0.833	0.704	1.000	0.852	1.000	1.000

TABLE 74.3 Normalization type-2.

	C_1	C_2	C_3	C_4	C_5	C_6	C_7	C_8	C_9	C_{10}	C_{11}	C_{12}	C_{13}
A_1	0.239	0.230	0.257	0.232	0.272	0.272	0.263	0.234	0.224	0.224	0.257	0.252	0.253
A_2	0.294	0.229	0.257	0.178	0.254	0.225	0.231	0.280	0.318	0.258	0.248	0.218	0.214
A_3	0.239	0.219	0.248	0.261	0.246	0.208	0.222	0.252	0.235	0.237	0.267	0.230	0.206
A_4	0.229	0.335	0.239	0.352	0.228	0.342	0.331	0.234	0.224	0.326	0.228	0.333	0.345

TABLE 74.4 Normalization type-3.

	C_1	C_2	C_3	C_4	C_5	C_6	C_7	C_8	C_9	C_{10}	C_{11}	C_{12}	C_{13}
A_1	0.143	0.000	1.000	0.500	1.000	0.833	0.750	0.000	0.000	0.000	0.750	0.500	0.500
A_2	1.000	0.250	1.000	0.000	0.600	0.333	0.250	1.000	1.000	1.000	0.500	0.000	0.167
A_3	0.143	0.000	0.500	0.875	0.400	0.000	0.000	0.400	0.125	0.333	1.000	0.250	0.000
A_4	0.000	1.000	0.000	1.000	0.000	1.000	1.000	0.000	0.000	1.000	0.000	1.000	1.000

TABLE 74.5 Normalization type-4.

	C_1	C_2	C_3	C_4	C_5	C_6	C_7	C_8	C_9	C_{10}	C_{11}	C_{12}	C_{13}
A_1	0.245	0.264	0.253	0.260	0.261	0.234	0.241	0.241	0.235	0.269	0.254	0.248	0.247
A_2	0.272	0.253	0.253	0.295	0.252	0.263	0.260	0.265	0.288	0.236	0.249	0.267	0.266
A_3	0.245	0.264	0.249	0.229	0.248	0.280	0.268	0.252	0.243	0.259	0.259	0.258	0.274
A_4	0.239	0.219	0.244	0.217	0.239	0.223	0.231	0.241	0.235	0.236	0.238	0.227	0.214

TABLE 74.6 Aggregated normalized decision matrix.

	C_1	C_2	C_3	C_4	C_5	C_6	C_7	C_8	C_9	C_{10}	C_{11}	C_{12}	C_{13}
A_1	0.360	0.318	0.628	0.443	0.633	0.569	0.549	0.327	0.291	0.332	0.556	0.471	0.456
A_2	0.641	0.389	0.628	0.277	0.511	0.403	0.396	0.636	0.651	0.623	0.481	0.319	0.346
A_3	0.360	0.315	0.491	0.575	0.449	0.301	0.323	0.451	0.336	0.428	0.632	0.393	0.295
A_4	0.312	0.639	0.354	0.642	0.326	0.641	0.640	0.327	0.291	0.641	0.329	0.640	0.640

The integration of the four normalization techniques is achieved through the utilization of Eq. (74.9). In this scenario, the α_i values are allocated uniformly across all techniques. In summary, $\alpha_1 = 0.25$. $\alpha_2 = 0.25$. $\alpha_3 = 0.25$. and $\alpha_4 = 0.25$, their sum is equal to 1 as shown in Eq. (74.10). Consequently, the resulting aggregated normalized decision matrix is presented in Table 74.6.

Eq. (74.9) utilizes assigned α values to calculate h_{ij} values, for instance:

$$h_{11} = 0.25(0.813) + 0.25(0.239) + 0.25(0.143) + 0.25(0.245)$$

$$h_{11} = 0.360$$

Step 3 initiates the procedure for the constraint-based normalization. In the initial process, experts are tasked with determining constraint interval values. To this end, they assign LB_j and UB_j values for each criterion. These values are determined based on the experts' expertise, historical data, or real-life standards, as given in Eq. (74.11) (see Table 74.7).

According to the constraint values in Table 74.7, as well as nature of criteria satisfaction degree of initial decision matrix is determined using Eqs. (74.12)–(74.14) for benefit criteria and Eqs. (74.15)–(74.17) for cost criteria. The initial decision matrix's satisfaction degree is presented in Table 74.8.

Satisfaction degree is calculated for f_{54} as follows. As C_5 is a benefit criterion, then $f_{54} = 1$ since the performance score of alternative A_4 is within constraint value of C_5. Now, let us consider another example where the performance score is not completely within constraint value. Performance of A_4 against C_5 is not within constraint value. Therefore the satisfaction degree is calculated as:

$$f_{54} = 1 - \frac{6.75 - 6.5}{Max(6.75 - 6.5, 7.75 - 7.75) + 1} = 0.800$$

The calculation of the final aggregated normalized decision matrix (G) is based on two significant matrices. Aggregated normalized decision matrix and satisfaction degree matrix are integrated using Eq. (74.18). Table 74.9 provides an overview of the elements of the constrained aggregated normalized decision matrix (Y).

Weight coefficients obtained from Shannon's entropy method are used to generate weighted decision matrix based on Eq. (74.19). Table 74.10 presents the weighted constrained aggregated normalized decision matrix.

The negative-ideal solution for each criterion is derived according to Eq. (74.20). As presented in Table 74.10, these values are incorporated into the decision matrix.

According to two-stage distance assessment process Eqs. (74.21) and (74.22) are used to determine θ_{ik} values in Eq. (74.25). Similarly, Eqs. (74.23) and (74.24) are used to determine φ_{ik} values in Eq. (74.26). The outcomes of the distance measures are documented in Table 74.11.

Using θ_{ik} and φ_{ik} values final score of alternatives Ω_i is calculated considering $\beta = 0.5$. According to Table 74.11, A_2 is selected as the most suitable alternative. The following presentation offers a simplified overview of the calculation process employed to determine the final score for the alternative's operations associated with A_2.

TABLE 74.8 Satisfaction degree values.

	C_1	C_2	C_3	C_4	C_5	C_6	C_7	C_8	C_9	C_{10}	C_{11}	C_{12}	C_{13}
A_1	1.000	1.000	1.000	1.000	1.000	1.000	1.000	0.800	0.800	1.000	1.000	1.000	1.000
A_2	1.000	1.000	1.000	1.000	1.000	1.000	1.000	1.000	1.000	1.000	1.000	1.000	1.000
A_3	1.000	1.000	1.000	1.000	1.000	1.000	1.000	1.000	1.000	1.000	1.000	1.000	1.000
A_4	1.000	0.400	1.000	1.000	0.800	0.800	1.000	0.800	0.800	1.000	0.800	1.000	0.667

TABLE 74.7 Constraint values of the criteria.

	C_1	C_2	C_3	C_4	C_5	C_6	C_7	C_8	C_9	C_{10}	C_{11}	C_{12}	C_{13}
LB_j	min	min	min	min	6,75	4	min	6,5	5	min	6	min	4
UB_j	max	4,25	7,25	max	max	max	max	max	max	max	max	max	max

TABLE 74.9 Constrained aggregated normalized decision matrix.

	C_1	C_2	C_3	C_4	C_5	C_6	C_7	C_8	C_9	C_{10}	C_{11}	C_{12}	C_{13}
A_1	0.360	0.318	0.628	0.443	0.633	0.569	0.549	0.262	0.232	0.332	0.556	0.471	0.456
A_2	0.641	0.389	0.628	0.277	0.511	0.403	0.396	0.636	0.651	0.623	0.481	0.319	0.346
A_3	0.360	0.315	0.491	0.575	0.449	0.301	0.323	0.451	0.336	0.428	0.632	0.393	0.295
A_4	0.312	0.255	0.354	0.642	0.261	0.513	0.640	0.262	0.232	0.641	0.263	0.640	0.426

TABLE 74.10 Weighted constrained aggregated normalized decision matrix.

	C_1	C_2	C_3	C_4	C_5	C_6	C_7	C_8	C_9	C_{10}	C_{11}	C_{12}	C_{13}
A_1	0.016	0.023	0.039	0.040	0.051	0.054	0.038	0.021	0.015	0.029	0.057	0.023	0.048
A_2	0.029	0.028	0.039	0.025	0.041	0.038	0.027	0.050	0.041	0.055	0.049	0.015	0.036
A_3	0.016	0.023	0.030	0.052	0.036	0.028	0.022	0.036	0.021	0.037	0.065	0.019	0.031
A_4	0.014	0.018	0.022	0.058	0.021	0.048	0.044	0.021	0.015	0.056	0.027	0.031	0.045

TABLE 74.11 Results of TRUST approach.

	E_i	T_i	L_i	P_i	$\sum_{k=1}^{n}\theta_{ik}$	$\sum_{k=1}^{n}\varphi_{ik}$	Ω_i	**Rank**
A_1	0.060	0.164	0.070	0.146	0.009	0.021	0.015	2
A_2	0.062	0.186	0.080	0.189	0.019	0.061	0.040	1
A_3	0.053	0.128	0.055	0.114	-0.018	-0.039	-0.029	4
A_4	0.056	0.131	0.056	0.126	-0.007	-0.034	-0.021	3

To calculate θ_{ik} value for alternative A_2:

$$E_2 = \sqrt{0.0002 + 0.0001 + 0.0003 + 0.0004 + 0.0001 + 0.0009 + 0.0007 + 0.0007 + 0.0005} = 0.0623$$

$$T_2 = 0.0150 + 0.0097 + 0.0169 + 0.0203 + 0.0097 + 0.0051 + 0.0296 + 0.0264 + 0.0256 + 0.0222 + 0.0053 = 0.1857$$

$$\sum_{k=1}^{n} \theta_{2k} = 0.0026 + 0 + 0.0098 + 0.0068 = 0.0192$$

And to calculate φ_{ik} value for alternative A_2:

$$L_2 = 0.0065 + 0.0042 + 0.0073 + 0.0087 + 0.0042 + 0.0022 + 0.0127 + 0.0113 + 0.0110 + 0.0096 + 0.0023 = 0.0798$$

$$P_2 = 0.0158 + 0.0050 + 0.0131 + 0.0194 + 0.0033 + 0.0012 + 0.0423 + 0.0477 + 0.0225 + 0.0183 + 0.0009 = 0.1895$$

$$\sum_{k=1}^{n} \varphi_{2k} = 0.0098 + 0 + 0.0267 + 0.0250 = 0.0615$$

74.5 Sensitivity analysis

The objective of conducting a sensitivity analysis is to ascertain the impact of the parameters of the approach on its ultimate scores and the resulting ranking order. For the purpose of analysis, three distinct tests are conducted on α and β values.

As previously mentioned, the TRUST initiative aspires to furnish a comprehensive normalization procedure, with the objective of mitigating the subjectivity inherent in employing a solitary normalization technique. α is the most critical parameter in the normalization part that is used to integrate normalized values from four different techniques. In order to observe the impact of changes in the score of the alternatives and their subsequent rankings, a series of scenarios has been defined. As illustrated in Table 74.12, the α scenarios and their associated results are presented. The results in Table 74.12 show that different values of α do not significantly affect the ranking, with only one scenario where alternative A_2 is ranked second while alternative A_4 is ranked first. In all the remaining scenarios, alternative A_2 was selected as the best alternative. However, when other alternative rankings are examined, it is seen that the order of the alternatives has changed in some scenarios.

While the primary objective of this work is to address a selection problem, the most significant goal is to determine the optimal ranking of alternatives in sorting problems. In such cases, the α values can play a pivotal role. Therefore experts or decision-makers must determine α values based on the nature of their respective data problems and their individual preferences.

β is a nonnegative parameter that ranges from 0 to 1. This parameter is used to determine the final score of the alternatives, as shown in Eq. (74.27). β is a parameter that must be determined in order to ascertain the proportion of the final score that should be attributed to Euclidean and Manhattan distance measures, as well as Lorentzian and Pearson

TABLE 74.12 Impacts of α on score and ranking order.

α_1	α_2	α_3	α_4	Ω_i				Rank			
				A_1	A_2	A_3	A_4	A_1	A_2	A_3	A_4
0.25	0.25	0.25	0.25	0.015	0.040	-0029	-0.0.21	2	1	4	3
1	0	0	0	0.019	0.051	0.016	-0.075	2	1	3	4
0	1	0	0	-0.003	0.000	-0.008	0.010	3	2	4	1
0	0	0	1	0.012	0.035	0.031	-0.070	3	1	2	4
0.33	0.33	0.34	0	0.018	0.041	-0.046	-0.005	2	1	4	3
0.1	0.2	0.5	0.2	0.025	0.058	-0.057	0.008	2	1	4	3
0.5	0.1	0.1	0.3	0.014	0.044	0.000	-0.052	2	1	3	4
0.2	0.1	0.1	0.6	0.013	0.040	0.003	-0.050	2	1	3	4
0.3	0	0	0.7	0.017	0.042	0.025	-0.075	3	1	2	4
0.1	0.7	0.1	0.1	0.004	0.015	-0.017	-0.002	2	1	4	3
0	0	0.5	0.5	0.029	0.071	-0.048	-0.004	2	1	4	3
0	0.5	0	0.5	0.006	0.019	0.010	-0.033	3	1	2	4
0.5	0.5	0	0	0.007	0.025	0.004	-0.034	2	1	3	4
0.5	0	0.5	0	0.029	0.065	-0.060	-0.012	2	1	4	3

distance measures. Typically, β is regarded as 0.5 to ensure an equilibrium between the scores of these distance measures. However, decision-makers and experts may opt for different values of β due to the nature of the problem. To observe the impact of varying β values (ranging from 0 to 1) on the outcomes of the TRUST approach, eleven distinct scenarios are generated. Table 74.13 presents that there are significant changes in the final score of alternatives as β value is changed; however, there are no changes on ranking order of the alternatives.

74.5.1 Numerical example 2: a simple case

In this section, the solution will be realized based on six criteria and four alternatives. For clarity, the criteria and alternatives are not defined. Criteria C_1, C_3 and C_5 relate to benefit types, while criteria C_2, C_4, and C_6 relate to cost types. Table 74.14 presents the evaluations of four experts on the six criteria in relation to the alternatives, as given in Eq. (74.1).

Based on the information in Table 74.14, AHP determined the weight coefficients as follows:

$C_1 = 0.173$, $C_2 = 0.\ 092$, $C_3 = 0.\ 208$, $C_4 = 0.\ 141$, $C_5 = 0.\ 276$ and $C_6 = 0.\ 110$.

Based on the nature of the criteria and the minimum and maximum values, the normalized decision matrix for the type-1 technique is reported in Table 74.15. The application of type-1 normalization was facilitated by Eqs. (74.2) and (74.3).

The application of type-2 normalization to normalize the initial aggregated decision matrix is presented in Table 74.16. The application of type-2 normalization was facilitated by Eqs. (74.4) and (74.5).

The results after max–min normalization (type-3 normalization) are presented in Table 74.17. As given in Table 74.17, Eqs. (74.6) and (74.7) were utilized during the normalization type-3 stage.

Table 74.18 presents the results obtained by using type-4 normalization (logarithmic normalization) to obtain a normalized decision matrix. Eq. (74.8) was used during the process of type-4 normalization.

For the integration of the four normalization techniques, α_i values were distributed equally to all techniques, and the resulting combined normalized decision matrix is presented in Table 74.19. The values presented in Table 74.19 have been

TABLE 74.14 Aggregated initial decision matrix.

	C_1	C_2	C_3	C_4	C_5	C_6
A_1	5	3.25	6.25	4	6	4.5
A_2	6	5	6	5.25	6	4.5
A_3	4.5	3.25	5	4.25	5.5	5
A_4	5.25	4	5.25	4	5.75	4.25

TABLE 74.13 Impacts of β on score and ranking order.

β		0	0.1	0.2	0.3	0.4	0.5	0.6	0.7	0.8	0.9	1
A_1	Rank	2	2	2	2	2	2	2	2	2	2	2
	Ω_1	0.021	0.020	0.019	0.017	0.016	0.015	0.014	0.012	0.011	0.010	0.009
A_2	Rank	1	1	1	1	1	1	1	1	1	1	1
	Ω_2	0.061	0.057	0.053	0.049	0.045	0.040	0.036	0.032	0.028	0.023	0.0019
A_3	Rank	4	4	4	4	4	4	4	4	4	4	4
	Ω_3	-0.039	-0.037	-0.035	-0.033	-0.031	-0.029	-0.027	-0.024	-0.022	-0.020	-0.018
A_4	Rank	3	3	3	3	3	3	3	3	3	3	3
	Ω_4	-0.034	-0.032	-0.029	-0.026	-0.023	-0.021	-0.018	-0.015	-0.012	-0.010	-0.007

TABLE 74.15 Normalization type-1.

	C_1	C_2	C_3	C_4	C_5	C_6
A_1	0.833	1.000	1.000	1.000	1.000	0.944
A_2	1.000	0.650	0.960	0.762	1.000	0.944
A_3	0.750	1.000	0.800	0.941	0.917	0.850
A_4	0.875	0.813	0.840	1.000	0.958	1.000

TABLE 74.16 Normalization type-2.

	C_1	C_2	C_3	C_4	C_5	C_6
A_1	0.241	0.289	0.278	0.270	0.258	0.253
A_2	0.289	0.188	0.267	0.206	0.258	0.249
A_3	0.217	0.289	0.222	0.254	0.237	0.230
A_4	0.253	0.304	0.233	0.334	0.247	0.324

TABLE 74.17 Normalization type-3.

	C_1	C_2	C_3	C_4	C_5	C_6
A_1	0.333	1.000	1.000	1.000	1.000	0.667
A_2	1.000	0.000	0.800	0.000	1.000	0.667
A_3	0.000	1.000	0.000	0.800	0.000	0.000
A_4	0.500	0.571	0.200	1.000	0.500	1.000

TABLE 74.18 Normalization type-4.

	C_1	C_2	C_3	C_4	C_5	C_6
A_1	0.245	0.220	0.266	0.236	0.255	0.248
A_2	0.273	0.301	0.260	0.282	0.255	0.248
A_3	0.229	0.220	0.234	0.246	0.242	0.265
A_4	0.253	0.259	0.241	0.236	0.249	0.239

TABLE 74.19 Aggregated normalized decision matrix.

	C_1	C_2	C_3	C_4	C_5	C_6
A_1	0.413	0.627	0.636	0.626	0.628	0.528
A_2	0.641	0.285	0.572	0.312	0.628	0.527
A_3	0.299	0.627	0.314	0.560	0.349	0.336
A_4	0.470	0.487	0.378	0.643	0.489	0.641

TABLE 74.20 Constraint values of the criteria.

	C_1	C_2	C_3	C_4	C_5	C_6
LB_j	min	min	min	min	5.75	4.25
UB_j	max	4.25	6	max	max	max

TABLE 74.21 Satisfaction degree values.

	C_1	C_2	C_3	C_4	C_5	C_6
A_1	1,000	1,000	1,200	1,000	1,000	1,250
A_2	1,000	1,429	1,000	1,000	1,000	1,000
A_3	1,000	1,000	1,000	1,000	0,800	1,000
A_4	1,000	1,000	1,000	1,000	1,000	1,000

derived through the application of Eqs. (74.9) and (74.10). In this scenario, the a values are equally distributed among all techniques, in other words, $\alpha_1 = 0.25$, $\alpha_2 = 0.25$, $\alpha_3 = 0.25$ and $\alpha_4 = 0.25$ also their sum is equal to 1.

In the first process of starting the constraint-based normalization procedure, experts are tasked with determining the constraint interval values. For this purpose, they determine the values LB_j and UB_j for each criterion. Table 74.20 reports the values determined, as shown in Eq. (74.11).

The degree of satisfaction of the initial decision matrix created according to the nature of the criteria (benefit-type criteria and cost-type criteria) is presented in Table 74.21. Eqs. (74.12)–(74.14) were utilized to calculate the benefit-type criteria, while Eqs. (74.15)–(74.17) were employed to calculate the cost-type criteria.

The calculation of the final aggregated normalized decision matrix G is based on two significant matrices. The following section provides a synopsis of the elements of the constrained aggregated normalized decision matrix (see Table 74.22), as given in Eq. (74.18).

The weighting coefficients obtained from the AHP are used to create a weighted decision matrix. Table 74.23 presents the weighted constrained combined normalized decision matrix, as shown in Eq. (74.19).

The negative-ideal solution for each criterion is derived according to Eq. (74.20). As given in Table 74.23, these values are incorporated into the decision matrix.

TABLE 74.22 Constrained aggregated normalized decision matrix.

	C_1	C_2	C_3	C_4	C_5	C_6
A_1	0.413	0.627	0.763	0.626	0.628	0.660
A_2	0.641	0.407	0.572	0.312	0.628	0.527
A_3	0.299	0.627	0.314	0.560	0.279	0.336
A_4	0.470	0.487	0.378	0.643	0.489	0.641

TABLE 74.23 Weighted constrained aggregated normalized decision matrix.

	C_1	C_2	C_3	C_4	C_5	C_6
A_1	0.071	0.058	0.159	0.088	0.173	0.073
A_2	0.111	0.037	0.119	0.044	0.173	0.058
A_3	0.052	0.058	0.065	0.079	0.077	0.037
A_4	0.081	0.045	0.079	0.091	0.135	0.070

TABLE 74.24 Results of TRUST approach.

	E_i	T_i	L_i	P_i	$\sum_{k=1}^{n}\theta_{ik}$	$\sum_{k=1}^{n}\varphi_{ik}$	Ω_i	Rank
A_1	0.148	0.310	0.130	0.352	0.227	0.237	0.015	2
A_2	0.126	0.230	0.096	0.243	0.122	0.076	0.040	1
A_3	0.040	0.055	0.024	0.039	-0.193	-0.182	-0.029	4
A_4	0.088	0.188	0.080	0.144	-0.036	0.008	-0.021	3

It is evident that the two-stage distance assessment process, Eqs. (74.21) and (74.22) are utilized in order to determine θ_{ik} values in Eq. (74.25). Similarly, Eqs. (74.23) and (74.24) are employed to determine φ_{ik} values in Eq. (74.26). The outcomes of the distance measures are reported in Table 74.24.

Using θ_{ik} and φ_{ik} values final score of alternatives Ω_i is calculated considering $\beta = 0.5$. According to Table 74.24, A_2 is selected as the most suitable alternative.

74.6 Conclusion

Türkiye possesses significant renewable energy potential in solar, wind, hydropower, and geothermal resources. Moreover, the country's rapid pace of technological diffusion has facilitated the deployment of smart grid systems, particularly in regions where centralized energy infrastructure is less feasible. However, the integration of these renewable sources presents complexities in many respects. Transitioning from the existing energy supply system to a more sustainable and diversified model remains a critical and demanding task. In this context, the strategic use of existing energy sources such as natural gas, especially to meet peak demand, continues to serve as a transitional solution. From a financial perspective, the development of new energy projects often necessitates partnerships between the public and private sectors.

The objective of this work is to develop an innovative decision-making methodology to address complex problems such as the one defined in the case of Türkiye. This work tests the new decision-making approach, TRUST, which is a pioneering contribution to the literature on MCDM to solve the case problem. TRUST employs a multinormalization procedure that integrates various normalization techniques and constraint-based attributes, offering a unique and innovative approach to decision-making in this field. TRUST proposed to utilize a multidistance framework by applying four well-known distance measure formulas, including Euclidean, Manhattan, Lorentzian, and Pearson measures, to determine an aggregated score based on the performance of alternatives against several criteria.

The application of the TRUST method reveals a clear prioritization among the proposed energy investment strategies for Türkiye. The top-ranked alternative, decentralized systems and smart grids (A_2), reflects the growing recognition of the importance of localized, flexible, and resilient energy solutions. This alternative offers advantages in reducing transmission losses, enhancing energy access in remote areas, and supporting the integration of variable renewable sources, especially critical in regions where centralized infrastructure is insufficient or costly to expand.

Balanced mix of renewables (A_1) ranks second, indicating strong support for a diversified portfolio that capitalizes on Türkiye's regional resource strengths in solar, wind, hydro, and geothermal energy. This strategy enhances energy security while contributing to emissions reduction, though it may require substantial investment in grid modernization and balancing mechanisms.

Hybrid public–private green energy zones (A_4) is placed third, highlighting the potential of innovative financing and institutional collaboration. However, its relatively lower score may reflect uncertainties around regulatory frameworks, risk-sharing mechanisms, and regional equity.

Renewables combined with natural gas as backup (A_3), the lowest-ranked option, suggests that while natural gas remains a strategic component of Türkiye's current energy landscape, its long-term role is increasingly viewed as less sustainable. This finding aligns with concerns about carbon lock-in and the need to avoid overreliance on transitional fossil fuels.

Overall, the ranking implies a strategic shift toward decentralized and renewable-heavy systems, with policy and investment efforts increasingly favoring environmentally and technically forward-looking approaches.

Despite the proposal of a new procedure by TRUST to address complex, real-life challenges, the efficacy of this approach remains to be evaluated. The potential for enhancement of this construct through the application of diverse theoretical frameworks and experimental conditions is a promising avenue for future work. A potential future direction for each innovative MCDM method is to be applied in different problems and fields. The resolution of complex problems with uncertain information is contingent upon the enhancement of trust through the utilization of uncertain models. Such models encompass a range of approaches, including fuzzy sets, triangular fuzzy numbers, hesitant fuzzy logic, intuitionistic fuzzy logic, and picture fuzzy logic. Additionally, neutrosophic numbers, encompassing single-valued, interval-valued, and other extensions, serve as a means to address the ambiguity inherent in information. The application of rough set theory and grey interval numbers further complicates the landscape, underscoring the need for comprehensive and multifaceted solutions to address the intricacies of decision-making under uncertainty. Another significant enhancement for the TRUST can be achieved through the integration of Bonferroni functions, Dombi aggregators, weighted and geometric power Heronian functions, and numerous other functions. These additions have the potential to enhance the reliability of mathematical operations within the TRUST framework.

References

Abdelli, A., Hammal, Y., & Mokdad, L. (2019, June). ISOCOV: A new MCDM method to handle value constraints in web service selection. In 2019 IEEE Symposium on Computers and Communications (ISCC) (pp. 1022–1027). IEEE.

Abdelli, A., Mokdad, L., & Hammal, Y. (2020). Dealing with value constraints in decision making using MCDM methods. *Journal of Computational Science, 44*, 101154.

Acar, S., Kat, B., Rogner, M., Saygin, D., Taranto, Y., & Yeldan, A. E. (2023). Transforming Türkiye's power system: An assessment of economic, social, and external impacts of an energy transition by 2030. *Cleaner Energy Systems, 4*, 100064.

Acikgoz, F., & Yorulmaz, O. (2024). Renewable energy adoption among Türkiye's future generation: What influences their intentions? *Energy for Sustainable Development, 80*, 101467.

Aksoy, A. (2019). Integrated model for renewable energy planning in Turkey. *International journal of green energy, 16*(1), 34–48.

Aktemur, C. (2017). An overview of natural gas as an energy source for various purposes. *International Journal of Engineering Technologies IJET, 3*(3), 91–104 Renewables in Türkiye.

Akusta, E., Ari, A., & Cergibozan, R. (2025). Barriers to renewable energy investments in Turkiye: A fuzzy AHP approach. *Renewable Energy, 240*, 122161.

Balcilar, M., Uzuner, G., Nwani, C., & Bekun, F. V. (2023). Boosting energy efficiency in Turkey: The role of public–private partnership investment. *Sustainability, 15*(3), 2273.

Calikoglu, U., & Koksal, M. A. (2022). Green electricity and renewable energy guarantees of origin demand analysis for Türkiye. *Energy Policy, 170*, 113229.

Cedrick, B. Z. E., & Long, P. W. (2017). Investment motivation in renewable energy: A PPP approach. *Energy Procedia, 115*, 229–238.

Cha, S. H. (2008). Taxonomy of nominal type histogram distance measures. *City, 1*(2), 1.

Dumrul, C., Bilgili, F., Zarali, F., Dumrul, Y., & Kiliçarslan, Z. (2024). The evaluation of renewable energy alternatives in Turkey using intuitionistic-fuzzy EDAS methodology. *Environmental Science and Pollution Research, 31*(10), 15503–15524.

Durna, E., Özorhon, B., & Caglayan, S. (2024). Identifying critical success factors of public private partnership projects in Türkiye. *Sakarya University Journal of Science, 28*(1), 30–50.

Erat, S., Telli, A., Ozkendir, O. M., & Demir, B. (2021). Turkey's energy transition from fossil-based to renewable up to 2030: Milestones, challenges and opportunities. *Clean Technologies and Environmental Policy, 23*(2), 401–412.

Erden Topal, Y., & Gursoy Haksevenler, B. H. (2025). Challenges and opportunities for renewable energy entrepreneurs in turkiye: The case of solar energy. *Energy Entrepreneurship, Sustainability, Innovation and Financing: Practical Applications and Future Directions*, 153–173.

Gulaydin, O., & Mourshed, M. (2025). Net-zero Turkey: Renewable energy potential and implementation challenges. *Energy for Sustainable Development*, 87.

Gürsan, C., & de Gooyert, V. (2021). The systemic impact of a transition fuel: Does natural gas help or hinder the energy transition? *Renewable and Sustainable Energy Reviews, 138*, 110552.

International Energy Agency. (n.d.). Energy system of Turkey. Retrieved July 24, 2025. https://www.iea.org/countries/turkiye.

Karipoğlu, F., & Denizli, O. (2025). Towards renewable energy islands in Türkiye: Potential and challenges. *Renewable and Sustainable Energy Reviews, 211*, 115324.

Keshavarz Ghorabaee, M., Zavadskas, E. K., Turskis, Z., & Antucheviciene, J. (2016). A new combinative distance-based assessment (CODAS) method for multi-criteria decision-making. *Economic Computation & Economic Cybernetics Studies & Research, 50*(3).

Keskin, M. (2021). Smart grids and Turkey: An overview of the current power system and smart grid development.

Melikoglu, M., & Aslan, F. B. (2025). Green hydrogen blending in natural gas: A global review and a local analysis on Türkiye based on greenhouse gas emission reduction targets. *International Journal of Hydrogen Energy, 97*, 150–159.

Ministry of Energy and Natural Resources of Türkiye. (2024). *Türkiye* - renewable energy integration (REI) investment plan. https://enerji.gov.tr/Media/Dizin/BHIM/tr/Duyurular/CIFRE26J2024FINAL_202406271608.docx.

Naimoglu, M., & Akal, M. (2023). The relationship between energy technology, energy efficiency, renewable energy, and the environment in Türkiye. *Journal of Cleaner Production, 418*, 138144.

Oral, H. V., Saygın, H., Mera-Paz, J. A., & Colmenares-Quintero, R. F. (2022). Smart grids to lower energy usage and carbon emissions: Case study examples from Colombia and Turkey. In *The Palgrave encyclopedia of urban and regional futures*. Cham: Springer International Publishing, 1–17.

Ozsoy, F. N., Ecemiş, O., & Özpolat, A. (2024). Renewable energy preferences of european countries and türkiye: Use of multi-criteria decision making. *Smart Grids and Sustainable Energy, 9*(1), 22.

Presidency of Strategy and Budget. (2023). *Twelfth Development Plan (2024-2028)*. https://www.sbb.gov.tr/wp-content/uploads/2025/03/Twelfth-Development-Plan_2024-2028.pdf.

Torkayesh, A. E., & Deveci, M. (2021). A mulTi-noRmalization mUlti-distance aSsessmenT (TRUST) approach for locating a battery swapping station for electric scooters. *Sustainable cities and society, 74*, 103243.

TSKB. (2025). *Energy Outlook 2023*. https://www.tskb.com.tr/uploads/file/energy-outlook-2023-final.pdf.

Wen, Z., Liao, H., & Zavadskas, E. K. (2020). MACONT: Mixed aggregation by comprehensive normalization technique for multi-criteria analysis. *Informatica, 31*(4), 857–880.

World Bank. (April, 2025). *Türkiye Overview*. Retrieved July 24, 2025. https://www.worldbank.org/en/country/turkey/overview.

Yazdani, M., Zarate, P., Zavadskas, E. K., & Turskis, Z. (2019). A combined compromise solution (CoCoSo) method for multi-criteria decision-making problems. *Management Decision*.

Zolfani, S., Yazdani, M., Pamucar, D., & Zarate, P. (2020). A VIKOR and TOPSIS focused reanalysis of the MADM methods based on logarithmic normalization. arXiv preprint arXiv:2006.08150.

Chapter 75

AROMAN: Alternative ranking order method accounting for two-step normalization for multi-attribute decision-making

Karahan Kara[1,2] and Galip Cihan Yalçın[2]

[1]*Department of Data Science and Analytics, Faculty of Economics and Administrative Sciences, İzmir Katip Çelebi University, İzmir, Türkiye,*
[2]*Department of Business, Faculty of Economics and Administrative Sciences, OSTIM Technical University, Ankara, Türkiye*

75.1 Introduction

The alternative ranking order method accounting for two-step normalization (AROMAN) was introduced by Bošković et al. (2023) as a novel multi-attribute decision-making approach. The distinctiveness of AROMAN lies in its simultaneous application of linear and vector normalization techniques, enabling precise ranking of alternatives. The method further differentiates between cost-based and benefit-based criteria by calculating separate scores for each type and aggregating them proportionally based on the number of cost-based criteria. This dual-normalization approach also allows for parameter-based aggregation calculations, facilitating comprehensive sensitivity analyses.

The AROMAN method has recently been applied across a wide range of decision-making contexts, often in combination with various weighting techniques and fuzzy set extensions. For instance, Bošković et al. (2023) validated AROMAN for electric vehicle selection, while Čubranić-Dobrodolac et al. (2023) integrated it with decision-making trial and evaluation laboratory and Fuller's pairwise comparisons for professional driver selection, enhancing the method with a novel parameter-based algorithm. Nikolić et al. (2023) applied an Interval Type-2 fuzzy AROMAN framework supported by full consistency method-based weighting to optimize rural postal networks, offering policymakers a structured decision-making tool.

Further applications include Pishahang et al. (2023), who employed AROMAN to rank wildfire risks in Arizona counties, demonstrating its robustness and adaptability for disaster risk assessment. Kara, Yalçın, Simic, Yıldırım, et al. (2024) integrated spherical fuzzy sets with AROMAN to evaluate the sustainable performance of water and energy production plants, while Anjum et al. (2024) applied a pythagorean fuzzy criteria importance through intercriteria correlation-AROMAN model to assess metaverse integration strategies in intelligent transportation systems. Other notable studies include Hu et al. (2024) for city selection in sports events, Bošković et al. (2024) for sustainable propulsion technology selection in commercial vehicles, Kara, Yalçın, Simic, Erbay, et al. (2024) for fish cage selection, Olteanu et al. (2024) for environmental, social, and governence (ESG) investment evaluation, Bouraima et al. (2024) for health sector strategy prioritization, Kara, Yalçın, Acar, et al. (2024) for sustainable competitiveness assessment, Yalçın et al. (2023) for EcoPort performance evaluation, Kara, Yalçın, Acar, et al. (2024), Kara, Yalçın, Simic, Erbay, et al. (2024), Kara, Yalçın, Simic, Yıldırım, et al. (2024) for vehicle routing software selection, Önden et al. (2024) for software development strategies, and Rani et al. (2025) for solar panel selection. Durdu (2025) introduces the AROMAN method as an innovative decision-making tool for evaluating and ranking firm financial performance, offering an alternative framework for robust and systematic performance assessment. Collectively, these studies illustrate AROMAN's versatility and robustness across diverse domains and decision-making contexts.

Encyclopedia of Multi-Attribute Decision-Making (MADM). DOI: https://doi.org/10.1016/B978-0-443-33275-3.00022-1

This chapter is organized into five sections. Section 75.2 presents a detailed explanation of the AROMAN method. Sections 75.3, 75.4 demonstrate the application of AROMAN through two numerical examples. Finally, Section 75.5 concludes the study with insights into the method's effectiveness and applicability.

75.2 Methodology

The AROMAN alternative ranking method is an approach based on two normalization procedures and the separate aggregation of cost-based and benefit-based criteria (Bošković et al., 2023). The method is implemented in six fundamental steps, which are as follows:

Step 1. In the first step of the AROMAN method, the initial matrix ($X = [X_{ij}]_{MN}$) is constructed ((75.1)). In this matrix, values corresponding to each alternative (A_i) are assigned with respect to each criterion (C_j). Each element (X_{ij}) in the initial matrix represents the value of the ith alternative with respect to the jth criterion. The initial matrix consists of M alternatives and N criteria. Within this matrix, both the set of criteria $C = \{C_1, C_2, \ldots, C_j, \ldots, C_N\}$ $(j = 1, 2, \ldots, N)$ and the set of alternatives $A = \{A_1, A_2, \ldots, A_i, \ldots, A_M\}$ $(i = 1, 2, \ldots, M)$ must be defined:

$$X = \begin{bmatrix} X_{11} \cdots X_{1j} \cdots X_{1N} \\ \vdots \cdots \vdots \cdots \vdots \\ X_{i1} \cdots X_{ij} \ldots X_{iN} \\ \vdots \cdots \vdots \cdots \vdots \\ X_{M1} \cdots X_{Mj} \ldots X_{MN} \end{bmatrix}; (i = 1, 2, \ldots, M; j = 1, 2, \ldots, N). \quad (75.1)$$

Step 2. In the second step of the AROMAN method, the values in the initial matrix are subjected to two distinct normalization processes. The first normalization is linear normalization, while the second is vector normalization. The main rationale for employing two different normalization techniques in this method is to enhance the robustness of the normalization process. The linear normalized matrix ($Z^L = [Z_{ij}^L]_{MN}$) is computed using (75.2), whereas the vector normalized matrix ($Z^V = [Z_{ij}^V]_{MN}$) is obtained using (75.3). While Bošković et al. (2023) applied a single normalization procedure simultaneously to both cost-based and benefit-based criteria, Kara, Yalçın, Acar, et al. (2024), Kara, Yalçın, Simic, Erbay, et al. (2024), Kara, Yalçın, Simic, Yıldırım, et al. (2024) performed separate normalization processes for cost-based and benefit-based criteria. Given the necessity of differentiating the normalization procedure according to the type of criterion, the equations proposed by Kara, Yalçın, Acar, et al. (2024), Kara, Yalçın, Simic, Erbay, et al. (2024), Kara, Yalçın, Simic, Yıldırım, et al. (2024) were adopted in this study:

$$Z_{ij}^L = \begin{cases} \dfrac{X_{ij} - \min\limits_j X_{ij}}{\max\limits_j X_{ij} - \min\limits_j X_{ij}} \text{ for } j \in C^+ \\ \dfrac{\max\limits_j X_{ij} - X_{ij}}{\max\limits_j X_{ij} - \min\limits_j X_{ij}} \text{ for } j \in C^- \end{cases}; (i = 1, 2, \ldots, M; j = 1, 2, \ldots, N). \quad (75.2)$$

$$Z_{ij}^V = \begin{cases} \dfrac{X_{ij}}{\sqrt{\sum_{i=1}^{M}(X_{ij})^2}} \text{ for } j \in C^+ \\ 1 - \dfrac{X_{ij}}{\sqrt{\sum_{i=1}^{M}(X_{ij})^2}} \text{ for } j \in C^- \end{cases}; (i = 1, 2, \ldots, M; j = 1, 2, \ldots, N). \quad (75.3)$$

Step 3. In the third step of the AROMAN method, the linear normalized matrix and the vector normalized matrix obtained in *Step 2* are aggregated based on the arithmetic mean. In this aggregation process, the parameter α is employed. This parameter represents the contribution level of the linearly normalized matrix, whereas $1 - \alpha$ denotes the contribution level of the vector normalized matrix. The aggregated normalized matrix ($Z = [Z_{ij}]_{MN}$) is calculated using (75.4). Typically, the value of α is set to 0.5, thereby ensuring that both normalization procedures contribute equally to the aggregated normalization matrix:

$$Z_{ij} = \frac{\alpha(Z_{ij}^L) + (1 - \alpha)(Z_{ij}^V)}{2}; (i = 1, 2, \ldots, M; j = 1, 2, \ldots, N; \alpha \in [0, 1]). \quad (75.4)$$

Step 4. In the fourth step of the AROMAN method, the normalized matrix is multiplied ((75.5)) by the criterion weight vector $w = \{w_1, w_2, \ldots, w_j, \ldots, w_N\}$ $(j = 1, 2, \ldots, N)$ to obtain the weighted normalized matrix ($D = [D_{ij}]_{MN}$). In this way, by incorporating the criterion weights, weighted values are derived from both cost-based and benefit-based criteria:

TABLE 75.1 The algorithm illustrates the steps of the AROMAN alternative ranking method.

Algorithm:	**The purpose of this algorithm is to present the procedural steps of the AROMAN method.**	
Input	A set of criteria: $C = \{C_1, C_2, \ldots, C_j, \ldots, C_N\}$ $(j = 1, 2, \ldots, N)$, A set of alternatives: $A = \{A_1, A_2, \ldots, A_i, \ldots, A_M\}$ $(i = 1, 2, \ldots, M)$, A criteria weight vector: $w = \{w_1, w_2, \ldots, w_j, \ldots, w_N\}$ $(j = 1, 2, \ldots, N)$.	
Step-1:	Construct the initial matrix ($X = [X_{ij}]_{MN}$) as (75.1)	$X_{ij} = \begin{bmatrix} X_{11}\cdots X_{1j}\cdots X_{1N} \\ \vdots\cdots\vdots\cdots\vdots \\ X_{i1}\cdots X_{ij}\ldots X_{iN} \\ \vdots\cdots\vdots\cdots\vdots \\ X_{M1}\cdots X_{Mj}\ldots X_{MN} \end{bmatrix}$
Step-2:	Calculate the linear normalized matrix ($Z^L = [Z^L_{ij}]_{MN}$) and vector normalized matrix ($Z^V = [Z^V_{ij}]_{MN}$) by employing (75.2) and (75.3).	$Z^L_{ij} = \begin{cases} \frac{X_{ij} - \min_j X_{ij}}{\max_j X_{ij} - \min_j X_{ij}} \text{ for } j \in C^+ \\ \frac{\max_j X_{ij} - X_{ij}}{\max_j X_{ij} - \min_j X_{ij}} \text{ for } j \in C^- \end{cases}$ Z^V_{ij} $Z^V_{ij} = \begin{cases} \frac{X_{ij}}{\sqrt{\Sigma_{i=1}^M (X_{ij})^2}} \text{ for } j \in C^+ \\ 1 - \frac{X_{ij}}{\sqrt{\Sigma_{i=1}^M (X_{ij})^2}} \text{ for } j \in C^- \end{cases}$
Step-3:	Calculate the aggregated normalized matrix ($Z = [Z_{ij}]_{MN}$) by employing (75.4).	$Z_{ij} = \frac{\alpha(Z^L_{ij}) + (1-\alpha)(Z^V_{ij})}{2}$
Step-4:	Calculate the weighted normalized matrix ($D = [D_{ij}]_{MN}$) by employing (75.5).	$D_{ij} = w_j * Z_{ij}$
Step-5:	Calculate the cost-based sum vector ($R^- = [R^-_i]_M$) and benefit-based sum vector ($R^+ = [R^+_i]_M$) by employing (75.6), (75.7).	$R^-_i = \Sigma_{j=1}^N D_{ij}$ *for* $j \in C^-$ $R^+_i = \Sigma_{j=1}^N D_{ij}$ for $j \in C^+$
Step-6:	Determine the ranking score vector ($R = [R_i]_M$) by employing (75.8).	$R_i = (R^-_i)^{\beta} + (R^+_i)^{(1-\beta)}$
Output	A ranking score vector: $R = \{R_1, R_2, \ldots, R_i, \ldots, R_M\}$ $(i = 1, 2, \ldots, M)$.	

$$D_{ij} = w_j * Z_{ij}; \ (i = 1, 2, \ldots, M; \ j = 1, 2, \ldots, N). \tag{75.5}$$

herein, $\Sigma_{j=1}^N w_j = 1$.

Step 5. In the fifth step of the AROMAN method, for each alternative (A_i) in the weighted normalized matrix, the values corresponding to cost-based criteria ((75.6)) and those corresponding to benefit-based criteria ((75.7)) are summed separately. This process yields the cost-based sum vector ($R^- = [R^-_i]_M$) and the benefit-based sum vector ($R^+ = [R^+_i]_M$). The former represents the total value of the ith alternative with respect to cost-based criteria, while the latter represents the total value of the ith alternative with respect to benefit-based criteria:

$$R^-_i = \sum_{j=1}^{N} D_{ij} \text{ for } j \in C^-; \ (i = 1, 2, \ldots, M; \ j = 1, 2, \ldots, N). \tag{75.6}$$

$$R^+_i = \sum_{j=1}^{N} D_{ij} \text{ for } j \in C^+; \ (i = 1, 2, \ldots, M; \ j = 1, 2, \ldots, N). \tag{75.7}$$

Step 6. In the sixth step of the AROMAN method, (75.8) is employed to determine the ranking score vector of the alternatives. Here, the parameter β denotes the ratio of the number of cost-based criteria to the total number of criteria. Within the ranking score vector ($R = [R_i]_M$), the alternative with the highest value is identified as the best alternative, whereas the alternative with the lowest value is defined as the worst alternative.

$$R_i = (R_i^-)^{\beta} + (R_i^+)^{(1-\beta)}; (i = 1,\ 2,\ \ldots,\ M;\ j = 1,\ 2,\ \ldots,\ N). \tag{75.8}$$

The algorithm of the AROMAN method is presented in Table 75.1.

75.3 Numerical example 1

For numerical example 1, the inputs required to run the AROMAN algorithm, as shown in Table 75.1, are provided below: A set of alternatives $C = \{C_1,\ C_2,\ C_3\}(j = 1, 2, 3)$, a set of criteria $A = \{A_1,\ A_2,\ A_3,\ A_4\}$ $(i = 1, 2, 3, 4)$ and a criteria weight vector: $w = \{0.30, 0.40, 0.30\}$. The procedural steps of the AROMAN method were executed in the following sequence:

Step 1. The initial matrix ($X = [X_{ij}]_{MN}$) for *numerical example 1* is presented in Table 75.2.

Step 2. The linear normalization matrix ($Z^L = [Z_{ij}^L]_{MN}$) was obtained using (75.2), and the vector normalization matrix ($Z^V = [Z_{ij}^V]_{MN}$) was obtained using (75.3); these are presented in Tables 75.3, 75.4, respectively.

TABLE 75.2 The initial matrix.

X_{ij}	C_1	C_2	C_3
A_1	1200	800	12
A_2	1100	700	15
A_3	1250	700	11
A_4	1000	750	16

TABLE 75.3 The linear normalization matrix.

Z_{ij}^L	C_1	C_2	C_3
A_1	0.8000	1.0000	0.8000
A_2	0.4000	0.0000	0.2000
A_3	1.0000	0.0000	1.0000
A_4	0.0000	0.5000	0.0000

TABLE 75.4 The vector normalization matrix.

Z_{ij}^V	C_1	C_2	C_3
A_1	0.5256	0.5415	0.5606
A_2	0.4818	0.4738	0.4508
A_3	0.5475	0.4738	0.5973
A_4	0.4380	0.5077	0.4142

Example:. The calculation for Z_{11}^L is as follows: $Z_{11}^L = \frac{(1200-1000)}{1250-1000} = 0.8000$ and the calculation for Z_{11}^V is as follows: $Z_{11}^V = \frac{1200}{\sqrt{((1200)^2+(1100)^2+(1250)^2+(1000)^2)}} = 0.5256$.

Step 3. By applying (75.4), the linear and vector normalized matrices were aggregated ($\alpha = 0.5$) to produce the aggregated normalized matrix ($Z = [Z_{ij}]_{MN}$), as shown in Table 75.5.

Example:. The calculation for Z_{11} is as follows: $Z_{11} = \frac{0.5(0.8000)+(1-0.5)(0.5256)}{2} = 0.3314$.

Step 4. Using (75.5), the aggregated normalized values were weighted by the corresponding criterion weights to produce the weighted normalized matrix ($D = [D_{ij}]_{MN}$), as shown in Table 75.6.

Example:. The calculation for D_{11} is as follows: $D_{11} = 0.30*0.3314 = 0.0994$.

Step 5. The cost-based sum vector was calculated using (75.6), and the benefit-based sum vector was calculated using (75.7); these vectors are presented in Table 75.7.

Example:. The calculation for R_1^- is as follows: $R_1^- = 0.1020 = 0.1020$ and the calculation for R_1^+ is as follows: $R_1^+ = 0.0994 + 0.1542 = 0.2536$.

Step 6. To determine the ranking score vector and the rankings of the alternatives, (75.8) was applied. Given that one of the three total criteria is cost-based, the parameter β was assigned a value of $\left(\beta = \frac{1}{3} = 0.3333\right)$. The resulting ranking score vector ($R = [R_i]_M$) is shown in Table 75.7.

Example:. The calculation for R_1 is as follows: $R_1 = (0.1020)^{0.3333} + (0.2536)^{(1-0.3333)} = 0.8679$.

TABLE 75.5 The aggregated normalized matrix.

Z_{ij}	C_1	C_2	C_3
A_1	0.3314	0.3854	0.3402
A_2	0.2205	0.1185	0.1627
A_3	0.3869	0.1185	0.3993
A_4	0.1095	0.2519	0.1035

TABLE 75.6 The weighted normalized matrix.

D_{ij}	C_1	C_2	C_3
A_1	0.0994	0.1542	0.1020
A_2	0.0661	0.0474	0.0488
A_3	0.1161	0.0474	0.1198
A_4	0.0329	0.1008	0.0311

TABLE 75.7 The cost-based sum and benefit-based sum vectors.

	R_i^-	R_i^+	R_i	Rank
A_1	0.1020	0.2536	0.8679	1
A_2	0.0488	0.1135	0.5999	3
A_3	0.1198	0.1634	0.7919	2
A_4	0.0311	0.1336	0.5757	4

TABLE 75.8 The initial matrix.

X_{ij}	C_1	C_2	C_3	C_4	C_5	C_6
A_1	1200	800	10	0.8	12	50
A_2	1100	700	3	0.6	15	58
A_3	1250	700	5	0.7	11	56
A_4	1000	750	6	0.4	16	60
A_5	900	850	8	0.3	7	52
A_6	1150	850	2	0.5	13	54

75.4 Numerical example 2

For Numerical example 2, the inputs required to run the AROMAN algorithm, as shown in Table 75.1, are provided below: a set of alternatives $C = \{C_1, C_2, C_3, C_4, C_5, C_6\}$ $(j = 1, 2, \ldots, 6)$, a set of criteria $A = \{A_1, A_2, A_3, A_4, A_5, A_6\}$ $(i = 1, 2, \ldots, 6)$, and a criteria weight vector: $w = \{0.15, 0.25, 0.10, 0.05, 0.25, 0.20\}$. The procedural steps of the AROMAN method were executed in the following sequence:

Step 1. The initial matrix ($X = [X_{ij}]_{MN}$) for *numerical example 2* is presented in Table 75.8.

Step 2. The linear normalization matrix ($Z^L = [Z_{ij}^L]_{MN}$) and the vector normalization matrix ($Z^V = [Z_{ij}^V]_{MN}$) are presented in Tables 75.9, 75.10, respectively.

Example:. The calculation for Z_{11}^L is as follows: $Z_{11}^L = \frac{(1200-900)}{1250-900} = 0.8571$ and the calculation for Z_{11}^V is as follows: $Z_{11}^V = \frac{1200}{\sqrt{((1200)^2+(1100)^2+(1250)^2+(1000)^2+(900)^2+(1150)^2)}} = 0.4428.$

Step 3. The normalized matrix ($Z = [Z_{ij}]_{MN}$) is shown in Table 75.11 ($\alpha = 0.5$).

Example:. The calculation for Z_{11} is as follows: $Z_{11} = \frac{0.5(0.8571)+(1-0.5)(0.4428)}{2} = 0.3250.$

Step 4. The weighted normalized matrix ($D = [D_{ij}]_{MN}$) is shown in Table 75.12.

Example:. The calculation for D_{11} is as follows: $D_{11} = 0.15*0.3250 = 0.0487$.

Step 5. The cost-based sum vector and the benefit-based sum vector are presented in Table 75.13.

Example:. The calculation for R_1^- is as follows: $R_1^- = 0.0661 + 0.0815 = 0.1476$ and the calculation for R_1^+ is as follows: $R_1^+ = 0.0487 + 0.0679 + 0.0412 + 0.0196 = 0.1775$.

TABLE 75.9 The linear normalization matrix.

z_{ij}^L	C_1	C_2	C_3	C_4	C_5	C_6
A_1	0.8571	0.6667	1.0000	1.0000	0.4444	1.0000
A_2	0.5714	0.0000	0.1250	0.6000	0.1111	0.2000
A_3	1.0000	0.0000	0.3750	0.8000	0.5556	0.4000
A_4	0.2857	0.3333	0.5000	0.2000	0.0000	0.0000
A_5	0.0000	1.0000	0.7500	0.0000	1.0000	0.8000
A_6	0.7143	1.0000	0.0000	0.4000	0.3333	0.6000

TABLE 75.10 The vector normalization matrix.

z_{ij}^V	C_1	C_2	C_3	C_4	C_5	C_6
A_1	0.4428	0.4200	0.6482	0.5671	0.6135	0.6296
A_2	0.4059	0.3675	0.1945	0.4253	0.5169	0.5703
A_3	0.4612	0.3675	0.3241	0.4962	0.6457	0.5851
A_4	0.3690	0.3938	0.3889	0.2836	0.4847	0.5555
A_5	0.3321	0.4463	0.5186	0.2127	0.7745	0.6148
A_6	0.4243	0.4463	0.1296	0.3544	0.5813	0.5999

TABLE 75.11 The aggregated normalized matrix.

z_{ij}	C_1	C_2	C_3	C_4	C_5	C_6
A_1	0.3250	0.2717	0.4121	0.3918	0.2645	0.4074
A_2	0.2443	0.0919	0.0799	0.2563	0.1570	0.1926
A_3	0.3653	0.0919	0.1748	0.3241	0.3003	0.2463
A_4	0.1637	0.1818	0.2222	0.1209	0.1212	0.1389
A_5	0.0830	0.3616	0.3171	0.0532	0.4436	0.3537
A_6	0.2847	0.3616	0.0324	0.1886	0.2287	0.3000

Step 6. Given that two of the four total criteria are cost-based, the parameter β was assigned a value of $\left(\beta = \frac{2}{6} = 0.3333\right)$. The resulting ranking score vector ($R = [R_i]_M$) is shown in Table 75.13.

Example:. The calculation for R_1 is as follows: $R_1 = (0.1476)^{0.3333} + (0.1775)^{(1-0.3333)} = 0.8443$.

TABLE 75.12 The weighted normalized matrix.

D_{ij}	C_1	C_2	C_3	C_4	C_5	C_6
A_1	0.0487	0.0679	0.0412	0.0196	0.0661	0.0815
A_2	0.0366	0.0230	0.0080	0.0128	0.0392	0.0385
A_3	0.0548	0.0230	0.0175	0.0162	0.0751	0.0493
A_4	0.0246	0.0454	0.0222	0.0060	0.0303	0.0278
A_5	0.0125	0.0904	0.0317	0.0027	0.1109	0.0707
A_6	0.0427	0.0904	0.0032	0.0094	0.0572	0.0600

TABLE 75.13 The cost-based sum and benefit-based sum vectors.

	R_i^-	R_i^+	R_i	Rank
A_1	0.1476	0.1775	0.8443	1
A_2	0.0778	0.0804	0.6132	5
A_3	0.1243	0.1114	0.7307	4
A_4	0.0581	0.0983	0.6002	6
A_5	0.1816	0.1372	0.8324	2
A_6	0.1172	0.1458	0.7663	3

75.5 Conclusion

This chapter has provided a comprehensive explanation of the AROMAN method and demonstrated its practical application through two numerical examples. The analysis highlights several strengths of the AROMAN method. Notably, its simultaneous use of linear and vector normalization ensures more precise and reliable ranking results. The separate treatment of cost-based and benefit-based criteria, followed by aggregation, enhances the method's flexibility and adaptability to different decision-making scenarios. Furthermore, the incorporation of a parameter-based aggregation process facilitates sensitivity analyses, allowing decision-makers to assess the robustness of the results effectively.

Despite these advantages, certain limitations exist. The method's computational complexity may increase with the number of alternatives and criteria, potentially requiring advanced computational resources for large-scale applications. Additionally, the reliance on expert judgment for criteria weighting may introduce subjectivity, which could affect the final rankings if not carefully managed.

For future research, the AROMAN method could be extended in several directions. Integration with other fuzzy or probabilistic frameworks may improve its handling of uncertainty and imprecision. Applications across diverse domains, including sustainability, logistics, and technology adoption, can further validate its versatility. Moreover, developing software tools or algorithms to automate the AROMAN procedure could enhance its accessibility and efficiency for both researchers and practitioners. Overall, the AROMAN method represents a robust and adaptable multicriteria decision-making tool, offering significant potential for refinement and broader application in complex decision-making environments.

References

Anjum, M., Simic, V., Min, H., & Kraiem, N. (2024). Transformative pathways to metaverse integration in intelligent transportation systems using pythagorean fuzzy CRITIC-AROMAN method. *IEEE Access*. https://doi.org/10.1109/ACCESS.2024.3449417.

Bošković, S., Švadlenka, L., Jovčić, S., Dobrodolac, M., Simić, V., & Bacanin, N. (2023). An alternative ranking order method accounting for two-step normalization (AROMAN)—A case study of the electric vehicle selection problem. *IEEE Access, 11*, 39496–39507. https://doi.org/10.1109/ACCESS.2023.3265818.

Bošković, S., Švadlenka, L., Jovčić, S., Simic, V., Dobrodolac, M., & Elomiya, A. (2024). Sustainable propulsion technology selection in penultimate mile delivery using the FullEX-AROMAN method. *Socio-economic Planning Sciences, 95*, 102013. https://doi.org/10.1016/j.seps.2024.102013.

Bouraima, M. B., Jovčić, S., Dobrodolac, M., Pamucar, D., Badi, I., & Maraka, N. D. (2024). Sustainable healthcare system devolution strategy selection using the AROMAN MCDM approach. *Spectrum of Decision Making and Applications, 1*(1), 46–63. https://doi.org/10.31181/sdmap1120243.

Čubranić-Dobrodolac, M., Jovčić, S., Bošković, S., & Babić, D. (2023). A decision-making model for professional drivers selection: A hybridized fuzzy–AROMAN–Fuller approach. *Mathematics, 11*(13), 2831. https://doi.org/10.3390/math11132831.

Durdu, D. (2025). Evaluating financial performance with SPC-LOPCOW-AROMAN hybrid methodology: A case study for firms listed in BIST sustainability index. *Knowledge and Decision Systems with Applications, 1*, 92–111. https://doi.org/10.59543/kadsa.v1i.13879.

Hu, L., Yu, Q., Jana, C., Simic, V., & Bin-Mohsin, B. (2024). An intuitionistic fuzzy SWARA-AROMAN decision-making framework for sports event management. *IEEE Access, 12*, 57711–57726. https://doi.org/10.1109/ACCESS.2024.3377099.

Kara, K., Yalçın, G. C., Acar, A. Z., Simic, V., Konya, S., & Pamucar, D. (2024). The MEREC-AROMAN method for determining sustainable competitiveness levels: A case study for Turkey. *Socio-economic Planning Sciences, 91*, 101762. https://doi.org/10.1016/j.seps.2023.101762.

Kara, K., Yalçın, G. C., Simic, V., Erbay, M., & Pamucar, D. (2024). A type-2 neutrosophic entropy-based group decision analytics model for sustainable aquaculture engineering. *Engineering Applications of Artificial Intelligence, 134*, 108615. https://doi.org/10.1016/j.engappai.2024.108615.

Kara, K., Yalçın, G. C., Simic, V., Yıldırım, A. T., Pamucar, D., & Siarry, P. (2024). A spherical fuzzy-based DIBR II-AROMAN model for sustainability performance benchmarking of wind energy power plants. *Expert Systems with Applications, 253*, 124300. https://doi.org/10.1016/j.eswa.2024.124300.

Nikolić, I., Milutinović, J., Božanić, D., & Dobrodolac, M. (2023). Using an interval type-2 fuzzy AROMAN decision-making method to improve the sustainability of the postal network in rural areas. *Mathematics, 11*(14), 3105. https://doi.org/10.3390/math11143105.

Olteanu, A. L., Ionaşcu, A. E., Cosma, S., Barbu, C. A., Popa, A., Cioroiu, C. G., & Goswami, S. S. (2024). Prioritizing the European investment sectors based on different economic, social, and governance factors using a fuzzy-MEREC-AROMAN decision-making model. *Sustainability, 16*(17), 7790. https://doi.org/10.3390/su16177790.

Önden, A., Kara, K., Önden, İ., Yalçın, G. C., Simic, V., & Pamucar, D. (2024). Exploring the adoption of the metaverse and chat generative pre-trained transformer: A single-valued neutrosophic Dombi Bonferroni-based method for the selection of software development strategies. *Engineering Applications of Artificial Intelligence, 133*, 108378. https://doi.org/10.1016/j.engappai.2024.108378.

Pishahang, M., Jovcic, S., Hashemkhani Zolfani, S., Simic, V., & Görçün, Ö. F. (2023). MCDM-based wildfire risk assessment: A case study on the state of Arizona. *Fire, 6*(12), 449. https://doi.org/10.3390/fire6120449.

Rani, P., Mishra, A. R., Pamucar, D., Alshamrani, A. M., Alrasheedi, A. F., & Simic, V. (2025). Decision-making-based solar panel selection: Sugeno-weber operators and fermatean fuzzy distance measure with AROMAN methodology. *Cognitive Computation, 17*(3), 102. https://doi.org/10.1007/s12559-025-10456-8.

Yalçın, G. C., Kara, K., Toygar, A., Simic, V., Pamucar, D., & Köleoğlu, N. (2023). An intuitionistic fuzzy-based model for performance evaluation of EcoPorts. *Engineering Applications of Artificial Intelligence, 126*, 107192. https://doi.org/10.1016/j.engappai.2023.107192.

Chapter 76

CRADIS: Compromise ranking of alternatives from distance to ideal solution for multi-attribute decision-making

Qiaohong Zheng, Chong Gao, and Haifeng Wang
Department of Economics and Management, North China Electric Power University, Baoding, Hebei, P.R. China

76.1 Introduction

Compromise ranking of alternatives from distance to ideal solution (CRADIS) was first introduced by Puska, Stevic, et al. (2022) to address the multi-attribute decision-making (MADM) problem. It is a utility theory-based method, which prioritizes the alternatives based on their distance to ideal and anti-ideal solutions. CRADIS is a method of using existing and modified steps of existing MADM methods, such as additive ratio assessment (ARAS), measurement of alternatives and ranking according to compromise solution (MARCOS), and technique for order performance by similarity to ideal solution (TOPSIS) methods. This method aims to take advantage of the existing MADM methods while minimizing their disadvantages. CRADIS possesses several distinctive features: (i) it considers the nature of criteria, an important aspect for ranking; (ii) it attempts to choose a solution that is neither too optimistic nor too pessimistic, which reflects a human-like decision strategy; (iii) it can be modified by integrating with various normalization techniques and different distance measures. These enable CRADIS to produce ranking results in a straightforward, practical, functional, and robust manner. Therefore it is extensively utilized in various fields, such as risk analysis (Han et al., 2025), investment analysis (Aytekin et al., 2025), waste management (Chatterjee & Seikh, 2024), supply chain management (Puska, Bozanic, et al., 2022), etc.

The remainder organizational structure of the paper is presented as follows. Section 76.2 reviews the literature on CRADIS. Section 76.3 shows the relative concepts of CRADIS and its steps. Sections 76.4 and 76.5, respectively, present a simple and complex numerical example to show their application. Section 76.6 compares CRADIS to the existing utility value-based MADM methods. Section 76.7 introduces the conclusion and future research directions.

76.2 Literature review

CRADIS, first introduced by Puska, Stevic, et al. (2022), is employed in the selection of healthcare waste incinerators. Recently, CRADIS has been expanded to various fuzzy contexts for addressing complex problems. Puska, Nedeljkovic, et al. (2022) extended the CRADIS approach to the triangular fuzzy numbers (TFNs) to assess the market of pear varieties in Serbia. Krishankumar and Ecer (2023) extended CRADIS to q-rung orthopair fuzzy (q-ROF) information to select IoT service providers for sustainable transport. Wang et al. (2024) enhanced the CRADIS approach under the interval-valued spherical fuzzy (IVSF) environment to assess occupational hazard. Ashraf et al. (2024) improved the CRADIS approach to optimize radioactive waste reduction through transmutations in the context of disc spherical fuzzy (DSF) information. Krishankumar and Ecer (2024) introduced an improved CRADIS method with the double hierarchy hesitant fuzzy linguistic term set (DHHFLTS) to select the electric vehicle charging location. Fetanat and Tayebi (2024) introduced an enhanced CRADIS with single-valued neutrosophic sets (SVNSs) to prioritize hydrogen technologies for decarbonization in the oil refining industry. Rani et al. (2025) extended the CRADIS to the picture fuzzy set (PFS) context and illustrated its reliability by a case study of selecting blockchain technology platforms in logistics firms. Cheng et al. (2024) enhanced the CRADIS method under the R-numbers environment to solve the hydrogen fuel cell logistics path selection problems. These extensions enable CRADIS to address complex and uncertain MADM problems.

Encyclopedia of Multi-Attribute Decision-Making (MADM). DOI: https://doi.org/10.1016/B978-0-443-33275-3.00063-4

In addition, due to the simplicity and flexibility of the CRADIS method in deriving reliable ranking results, numerous studies have utilized existing CRADIS approaches, including both the original and enhanced versions, to address real-world and practical problems. Krishankumar, Ecer, et al. (2024) proposed a CRADIS method considering experts' personal choices under the DHHFLTS environment for selecting cloud vendors for medical centers. Aytekin et al. (2024) utilized the q-ROF-based CRADIS to identify the best transportation demand management strategy. Krishankumar, Dhruva, et al. (2024) combined the DHHFLTS-based CRADIS approach with the Copeland strategy to rank the blockchain service providers for data management within the internet of medical things. Shamsi et al. (2025) utilized CRADIS, MARCOS, combined compromise solution (COCOSO), combinative distance-based assessment (CODAS), VIse kriterijumska optimizacija I kompromisno resenje (VIKOR), TOPSIS, etc., to rank the technology for mining overburden waste utilization using green & climate-smart mining. Wang et al. (2025) utilized IVSF-based CRADIS to evaluate the quality of the massive open online courses. Krishankumar et al. (2025) utilized q-ROF-based CRADIS to prioritize the solar panel types.

76.3 Methodology

The CRADIS method is a typical MADM method for ranking alternatives. The steps for implementing the CRADIS method are introduced as follows:

Step 1. Forming an initial decision matrix.

For a MADM problem with n criteria $c_j (j = 1, 2, \ldots, n)$ and m alternatives $a_i (i = 1, 2, \ldots, m)$. The decision matrix $X = (x_{ij})_{m \times n}$ is defined as follows.

$$X = \begin{bmatrix} x_{11} & x_{12} & \cdots & x_{1n} \\ x_{21} & x_{22} & \cdots & x_{2n} \\ \vdots & \vdots & \ddots & \vdots \\ x_{m1} & x_{m2} & \cdots & x_{mn} \end{bmatrix} \tag{76.1}$$

where x_{ij} is the evaluation information of the alternative a_i under the criterion c_j. x_{ij} can be expressed in the form of fuzzy numbers, linguistic models, and precise numerical values, depending on the nature of the problem.

Step 2. Normalization of the decision matrix.

Considering the nature of the criteria, the decision matrix can be normalized by using the following expressions:

$$n_{ij} = \begin{cases} \dfrac{x_{ij}}{x_{j\,\max}}, & if\ j \in J' \\ \dfrac{x_{j\,\min}}{x_{ij}}, & if\ j \in J'' \end{cases} \tag{76.2}$$

where J' indicates the subset of criteria to be the benefit type, and J'' is the subset of criteria to be the cost type. It is worth noting that there are numerous normalization approaches, such as min-max normalization, vector normalization, sum normalization, z-score normalization, etc. A normalization method can be selected based on the specific characteristics of the problem.

Step 3. Deriving weighted decision-making matrices.

The weighted decision matrix is derived by applying the corresponding weights to the normalized decision matrix, as shown in the following expression:

$$v_{ij} = n_{ij} w_j \tag{76.3}$$

where w_j represents the weight of the criterion c_j. It can be obtained by using subjective or objective methods, depending on the characteristics of the problem.

Step 4. Determining the ideal and anti-ideal solution.

The ideal solution is determined by identifying the largest value v_{ij} in the weighted decision matrix, while the anti-ideal solution is determined by identifying the smallest value v_{ij} in the weighted decision matrix.

$$\tilde{v}_j^+ = \max_i v_{ij} \tag{76.4}$$

$$\tilde{v}_j^- = \min_i v_{ij} \tag{76.5}$$

Step 5. Deriving the deviation from the ideal and anti-ideal solution.

The deviation of each element in the weighted decision-making matrices from the ideal solution is determined by subtracting it from the ideal solution $\tilde{v}_j^+$, while the deviation from the anti-ideal solution is obtained by subtracting it from the anti-ideal solution $\tilde{v}_j^-$.

$$d_{ij}^+ = \tilde{v}_j^+ - v_{ij} \tag{76.6}$$

$$d_{ij}^- = v_{ij} - \tilde{v}_j^- \tag{76.7}$$

Step 6. Calculation of the deviation of each alternative.

The positive and negative deviations of each alternative can be derived by using the following forms.

$$s_i^+ = \sum_{j=1}^{n} d_{ij}^+ \tag{76.8}$$

$$s_i^- = \sum_{j=1}^{n} d_{ij}^- \tag{76.9}$$

Step 7. Calculation of the utility function for each alternative.

The negative and positive utility functions of each alternative are determined based on its deviation from the optimal alternative.

$$K_i^+ = \frac{s_0^+}{s_i^+} \tag{76.10}$$

$$K_i^- = \frac{s_i^-}{s_0^-} \tag{76.11}$$

where s_0^+ and s_0^- indicate the optimal alternative with the smallest and largest deviation degrees, respectively.

Step 8. Ranking the alternatives.

The CRADIS method prioritizes the alternatives based on the average value of their negative and positive utility, which is shown in the following form.

$$Rd_i = \frac{K_i^+ + K_i^-}{2} \tag{76.12}$$

Where, the higher the value of Rd_i, the higher the prioritization of the alternative a_i.

76.4 Numerical example 1

In this section, a simple numerical example is introduced to show the application of the CRADIS method. In practice, users are faced with a vast array of movies available across various streaming platforms for users to watch, especially due to the rapid development of digital technology. Movie recommendation plays a critical role in helping users select movies that are in line with their preferences.

Movie recommendation is inherently a multi-attribute problem, as users often consider multiple criteria such as director popularity, acting performance, plot quality, thematic appeal, etc. To this end, the movie recommendation task can be considered as an MADM problem.

In this example, eight movies were selected from the highest-grossing films in North America in 2023, namely Barbie (a_1), Guardians of the Galaxy Vol. 3 (a_2), Oppenheimer (a_3), The Little Mermaid (a_4), Wonka (a_5), and Sound of Freedom (a_6). Each movie is evaluated based on six criteria, namely director popularity (c_1), acting performance (c_2), plot quality (c_3), thematic appeal (c_4), visual effect (c_5), and influence of production company (c_6). Then, the CRADIS can be conducted as follows.

Step 1. Forming an initial decision matrix.

In this step, the positive integers $\{1, 2, 3, 4, 5, 6, 7\}$ are utilized to represent the evaluation information. Then, experts are invited to evaluate each movie under each criterion, and the detailed evaluation information is shown in Table 76.1.

Step 2. Normalization of the decision matrix.

As shown in Table 76.1, all the criteria are benefit-type. Then, the maximum evaluation value under each criterion is identified. Based on these values, the decision matrix can be normalized by referring to Eq. (76.2). For instance, the

TABLE 76.1 The detailed evaluation information of each movie.

	c_1	c_2	c_3	c_4	c_5	c_6
a_1	6	4	6	6	5	5
a_2	6	5	5	5	6	6
a_3	6	6	6	6	4	5
a_4	5	5	5	5	4	6
a_5	4	4	6	4	5	5
a_6	3	4	4	3	3	4

TABLE 76.2 The normalized decision matrix.

	c_1	c_2	c_3	c_4	c_5	c_6
a_1	1.00	0.67	1.00	1.00	0.83	0.83
a_2	1.00	0.83	0.83	0.83	1.00	1.00
a_3	1.00	1.00	1.00	1.00	0.67	0.83
a_4	0.83	0.83	0.83	0.83	0.67	1.00
a_5	0.67	0.67	1.00	0.67	0.83	0.83
a_6	0.50	0.67	0.67	0.50	0.50	0.67

maximum evaluation value under the criterion c_1 is $x_{1\max} = 6$. Then, the normalized evaluation value of the alternative a_5 with respect to the criterion c_1 can be derived by using Eq. (76.13). The normalized decision matrix is shown in Table 76.2.

$$n_{51} = \frac{x_{51}}{x_{1\max}} = \frac{4}{6} = 0.67 \tag{76.13}$$

Step 3. Deriving weighted decision-making matrices.

Let the weight of six criteria be $w_1 = 0.25,\ w_2 = 0.20,\ w_3 = 0.20,\ w_4 = 0.15, w_5 = 0.10$, and $w_6 = 0.10$. According to Eq. (76.3), the weighted decision matrix can be derived. For instance, the weight of the criterion c_1 is $w_1 = 0.25$. The weighted evaluation value of the alternative a_5 with respect to the criterion c_1 can be derived by using (76.14). The weighted decision matrix is shown in Table 76.3.

$$v_{51} = n_{51} \times w_1 = 0.67 \times 0.25 = 0.17 \tag{76.14}$$

Step 4. Determining the ideal and anti-ideal solution.

According to Eqs. (76.4) and (76.5), the ideal solution and anti-ideal solution can be identified, which are shown in Table 76.4.

Step 5. Deriving the deviation from the ideal and anti-ideal solution.

The deviation of each element from the ideal and anti-ideal solution can be derived by using Eqs. (76.6) and (76.7). For instance, the deviation of the element v_{51} from the ideal and anti-ideal solution with respect to the criterion c_1 can be derived by using Eqs. (76.15) and (76.16). The deviation of each element from the ideal solution is shown in Table 76.5, while the deviation from the anti-ideal solution is shown in Table 76.6.

$$d_{51}^{+} = v_1^{+} - v_{51} = 0.25 - 0.17 = 0.08 \tag{76.15}$$

$$d_{51}^{-} = v_{51} - v_1^{-} = 0.17 - 0.13 = 0.04 \tag{76.16}$$

TABLE 76.3 The weighted decision matrix.

Alternative	c_1	c_2	c_3	c_4	c_5	c_6
a_1	0.25	0.13	0.20	0.15	0.08	0.08
a_2	0.25	0.17	0.17	0.13	0.10	0.10
a_3	0.25	0.20	0.20	0.15	0.07	0.08
a_4	0.21	0.17	0.17	0.13	0.07	0.10
a_5	0.17	0.13	0.20	0.10	0.08	0.08
a_6	0.13	0.13	0.13	0.08	0.05	0.07

TABLE 76.4 The ideal and anti-ideal solution.

Alternative	c_1	c_2	c_3	c_4	c_5	c_6
$\tilde{v}_j^+$	0.25	0.20	0.20	0.15	0.10	0.10
$\tilde{v}_j^-$	0.13	0.13	0.13	0.08	0.05	0.07

TABLE 76.5 The deviation of each element from the ideal solution.

	c_1	c_2	c_3	c_4	c_5	c_6
a_1	0.00	0.07	0.00	0.00	0.02	0.02
a_2	0.00	0.03	0.03	0.03	0.00	0.00
a_3	0.00	0.00	0.00	0.00	0.03	0.02
a_4	0.04	0.03	0.03	0.03	0.03	0.00
a_5	0.08	0.07	0.00	0.05	0.02	0.02
a_6	0.13	0.07	0.07	0.08	0.05	0.03

Step 6. Calculation of the deviation of each alternative.

The positive and negative deviations of each alternative can be derived by using Eqs. (76.8) and (76.9). The results are shown in Table 76.7.

Step 7. Calculation of the utility function for each alternative.

The negative and positive utility functions of each alternative can be derived by using Eqs. (76.10) and (76.11). For instance, as shown in Table 76.7, parameters s_0^+ and s_0^- can be identified as 0.05 and 0.37. Then, the negative and positive utility of the alternative a_5 can be calculated by using Eqs. (76.17) and (76.18). The positive and negative utility functions of each alternative are shown in Table 76.8.

$$K_5^+ = \frac{s_0^+}{s_5^+} = \frac{0.05}{0.23} = 0.21 \tag{76.17}$$

$$K_5^- = \frac{s_5^-}{s_0^-} = \frac{0.18}{0.37} = 0.50 \tag{76.18}$$

TABLE 76.6 The deviation of each element from the anti-ideal solution.

	c_1	c_2	c_3	c_4	c_5	c_6
a_1	0.13	0.00	0.07	0.08	0.03	0.02
a_2	0.13	0.03	0.03	0.05	0.05	0.03
a_3	0.13	0.07	0.07	0.08	0.02	0.02
a_4	0.08	0.03	0.03	0.05	0.02	0.03
a_5	0.04	0.00	0.07	0.03	0.03	0.02
a_6	0.00	0.00	0.00	0.00	0.00	0.00

TABLE 76.7 The positive and negative deviations of each alternative.

	a_1	a_2	a_3	a_4	a_5	a_6
s_i^+	0.10	0.09	0.05	0.17	0.23	0.42
s_i^-	0.32	0.33	0.37	0.25	0.18	0.00

TABLE 76.8 The positive and negative utility of each alternative.

	a_1	a_2	a_3	a_4	a_5	a_6
K_i^+	0.50	0.55	1.00	0.30	0.21	0.12
K_i^-	0.86	0.89	1.00	0.68	0.50	0.00

TABLE 76.9 The average utility and ranking of each alternative.

	a_1	a_2	a_3	a_4	a_5	a_6
Rd_i	0.68	0.72	1.00	0.49	0.36	0.06
Ranking	3	2	1	4	6	8

Step 8. Ranking the alternatives.

Based on the results shown in Table 76.8, the average value of each alternative's negative and positive utility can be derived by referring to Eq. (76.12), and accordingly, the ranking of each alternative can be determined. The results are shown in Table 76.9.

76.5 Numerical example 2

To better demonstrate the practical applicability of CRADIS in a real-world decision-making context, a complex numerical example of car selection is introduced. In practice, the car purchasing process represents a complex and highly relevant decision problem. On the one hand, the rapid evolution of automotive technologies and the growing number of models available in the market have significantly increased the complexity of car selection. On the other hand, car purchasing decisions are often shaped by multiple decision-makers, such as spouses, family members, professional advisors, etc., whose demands, preferences, knowledge, and experience may be diverse. Especially, some decision-makers may emphasize economic considerations, such as purchase price and fuel efficiency, while others may prioritize safety performance, comfort, or brand prestige.

Car selection involves evaluating a set of alternatives with respect to numerous criteria. These criteria may include both subjective perceptions (e.g., brand prestige and driving experience) and objective measures (e.g., fuel efficiency and safety ratings), increasing the complexity of the decision process. In addition, market uncertainty, rapidly shifting technology trends (e.g., electric vs. internal combustion engines), and policy factors (e.g., environmental regulations and tax incentives) result in dynamism and ambiguity in the decision process.

As introduced above, the car selection problem can be modeled as an MADM problem. In this illustrative example, 10 popular new energy vehicles in China, priced between 150,000 and 250,000 RMB, are selected for analysis. These include BYD Qin PLUS DM-I (a_1), BYD Song PLUS DM-I (a_2), BYD Dolphin (a_3), BYD Seagull (a_4), Tesla Model 3 (a_5), Tesla Model Y (a_6), GAC Aion S (a_7), GAC Aion Y (a_8), Geely Emgrand EV (a_9), and Changan UNI-K PHEV (a_{10}). Each car is evaluated with respect to eight attributes, namely purchase price (c_1), energy consumption per 100 kilometers (c_2), maintenance cost (c_3), powertrain performance (c_4), safety rating (c_5), comfort level (c_6), brand reputation (c_7), and battery durability (c_8). In this case, three experts are involved in the decision process, and the CRADIS method is applied to derive the comprehensive ranking of the alternatives.

Step 1. Forming an initial decision matrix.

In this step, three experts are invited to evaluate eight new energy vehicles by linguistic terms, which are shown in Table 76.10. Then, the linguistic evaluation information can be transferred to the corresponding TFNs according to Table 76.10. The linguistic evaluation information of three experts is shown in Tables 76.11-76.13.

Step 2. Normalization of the decision matrix.

First, it can be noticed that the criteria c_1, c_2, and c_3 are the cost type, and the criteria c_4, c_5, c_6, c_7, and c_8 are the benefit type. Then, the minimum evaluation value $x_{j\,\min}$ and the maximum evaluation value $x_{j\,\max}$ under each criterion are identified. Then, based on the min-max normalization approach and the distance measure of TFNs introduced by Wang et al. (2018), the evaluation information can be normalized, which is shown in (76.19). For instance, the normalized decision matrix of e^1 is shown in Table 76.14. Similarly, the normalized decision matrix of e^2 and e^3 can be obtained,

$$n_{ij} = \begin{cases} \dfrac{d(x_{ij}, x_{j\,\min})}{d(x_{j\,\min}, x_{j\,\max})}, & if\ j \in J' \\ 1 - \dfrac{d(x_{ij}, x_{j\,\min})}{d(x_{j\,\min}, x_{j\,\max})}, & if\ j \in J'' \end{cases} \tag{76.19}$$

where J' indicates the subset of criteria to be the benefit type, and J'' is the subset of criteria to be the cost type.

TABLE 76.10 The linguistic terms and their corresponding triangular fuzzy numbers (TFNs).

Linguistic term	TFNs
Very low (VL)	(0.0, 0.0, 0.1)
Low (L)	(0.0, 0.1, 0.3)
Medium low (ML)	(0.1, 0.3, 0.5)
Medium (M)	(0.3, 0.5, 0.7)
Medium high (MH)	(0.5, 0.7, 0.9)
High (H)	(0.7, 0.9, 1.0)
Very high (VH)	(0.9, 1.0, 1.0)

TABLE 76.11 The linguistic evaluation information of expert e^1.

	c_1	c_2	c_3	c_4	c_5	c_6	c_7	c_8
a_1	L	L	L	M	M	M	H	H
a_2	ML	M	ML	M	MH	MH	H	H
a_3	VL	VL	L	ML	ML	ML	MH	MH
a_4	VL	VL	VL	L	L	L	M	M
a_5	VH	ML	VH	VH	H	M	VH	VH
a_6	H	MH	VH	VH	VH	H	VH	VH
a_7	ML	M	M	M	M	M	MH	MH
a_8	L	MH	ML	ML	ML	MH	M	MH
a_9	L	MH	ML	L	ML	ML	ML	M
a_{10}	MH	VH	H	H	H	VH	M	H

TABLE 76.12 The linguistic evaluation information of expert e^2.

	c_1	c_2	c_3	c_4	c_5	c_6	c_7	c_8
a_1	ML	L	L	M	MH	M	MH	H
a_2	MH	ML	ML	MH	H	H	H	MH
a_3	VL	VL	VL	ML	M	ML	MH	MH
a_4	VL	VL	VL	L	ML	L	M	M
a_5	H	MH	M	VH	H	MH	VH	H
a_6	H	H	H	H	VH	H	VH	VH
a_7	ML	M	ML	M	M	M	M	M
a_8	ML	ML	ML	ML	ML	MH	ML	ML
a_9	ML	M	ML	L	ML	ML	ML	ML
a_{10}	MH	VH	MH	H	H	VH	M	M

Let the experts' weights be $\omega_1 = 0.3$, $\omega_2 = 0.4$, $\omega_3 = 0.3$. Based on the normalized decision matrix of each expert, the collective normalized decision matrix can be obtained based on the weighted averaging operator, which is shown in Table 76.15.

Step 3. Deriving weighted decision-making matrices.

Let the weight of the eight criteria be $w_1 = 0.15$, $w_2 = 0.15$, $w_3 = 0.10$, $w_4 = 0.15$, $w_5 = 0.15$, $w_6 = 0.10$, $w_7 = 0.10$, and $w_8 = 0.10$. According to Eq. (76.3), the weighted decision matrix can be derived, which is shown in Table 76.16.

Step 4. Determining the ideal and anti-ideal solution.

According to Eqs. (76.4) and (76.5), the ideal solution and anti-ideal solution can be identified, which are shown in Table 76.17.

Step 5. Deriving the deviation from the ideal and anti-ideal solution.

The deviation of each element from the ideal and anti-ideal solution can be derived by using Eqs. (76.6) and (76.7). The deviation of each element from the ideal solution is shown in Table 76.18, while the deviation from the anti-ideal solution is shown in Table 76.19.

TABLE 76.13 The linguistic evaluation information of expert e^3.

	c_1	c_2	c_3	c_4	c_5	c_6	c_7	c_8
a_1	ML	L	ML	M	MH	M	H	MH
a_2	M	M	ML	MH	H	H	H	MH
a_3	VL	VL	VL	ML	M	ML	MH	M
a_4	VL	VL	VL	L	L	L	M	ML
a_5	H	M	MH	VH	VH	MH	VH	H
a_6	VH	MH	H	H	VH	H	VH	VH
a_7	ML	ML	M	M	M	M	M	M
a_8	L	ML	ML	ML	M	M	M	M
a_9	L	MH	ML	L	ML	ML	ML	ML
a_{10}	MH	VH	H	H	H	VH	MH	MH

TABLE 76.14 The normalized decision matrix of the expert e^1.

	c_1	c_2	c_3	c_4	c_5	c_6	c_7	c_8
a_1	0.86	0.86	0.86	0.44	0.44	0.44	0.84	0.77
a_2	0.68	0.48	0.68	0.44	0.68	0.68	0.84	0.77
a_3	1.00	1.00	0.86	0.21	0.21	0.21	0.59	0.41
a_4	1.00	1.00	1.00	0.00	0.00	0.00	0.29	0.00
a_5	0.00	0.68	0.00	1.00	0.88	0.44	1.00	1.00
a_6	0.10	0.27	0.00	1.00	1.00	0.88	1.00	1.00
a_7	0.68	0.48	0.48	0.44	0.44	0.44	0.59	0.41
a_8	0.86	0.27	0.68	0.21	0.21	0.68	0.29	0.41
a_9	0.86	0.27	0.68	0.00	0.21	0.21	0.00	0.00
a_{10}	0.27	0.00	0.10	0.88	0.88	1.00	0.29	0.77

TABLE 76.15 The collective normalized decision matrix.

	c_1	c_2	c_3	c_4	c_5	c_6	c_7	c_8
a_1	0.72	0.86	0.79	0.44	0.57	0.44	0.74	0.74
a_2	0.43	0.56	0.66	0.61	0.80	0.82	0.84	0.64
a_3	1.00	1.00	0.96	0.21	0.31	0.21	0.59	0.45
a_4	1.00	1.00	1.00	0.00	0.00	0.00	0.29	0.12
a_5	0.03	0.46	0.23	1.00	0.90	0.61	1.00	0.89
a_6	0.03	0.21	0.00	0.91	1.00	0.88	1.00	1.00
a_7	0.67	0.54	0.53	0.44	0.38	0.44	0.38	0.33
a_8	0.78	0.56	0.66	0.21	0.19	0.61	0.18	0.21
a_9	0.78	0.36	0.66	0.00	0.12	0.21	0.00	0.00
a_{10}	0.24	0.00	0.11	0.88	0.86	1.00	0.38	0.52

TABLE 76.16 The weighted decision matrix.

	c_1	c_2	c_3	c_4	c_5	c_6	c_7	c_8
a_1	0.11	0.13	0.08	0.07	0.09	0.04	0.07	0.07
a_2	0.06	0.08	0.07	0.09	0.12	0.08	0.08	0.06
a_3	0.15	0.15	0.10	0.03	0.05	0.02	0.06	0.04
a_4	0.15	0.15	0.10	0.00	0.00	0.00	0.03	0.01
a_5	0.00	0.07	0.02	0.15	0.13	0.06	0.10	0.09
a_6	0.00	0.03	0.00	0.14	0.15	0.09	0.10	0.10
a_7	0.10	0.08	0.05	0.07	0.06	0.04	0.04	0.03
a_8	0.12	0.08	0.07	0.03	0.03	0.06	0.02	0.02
a_9	0.12	0.05	0.07	0.00	0.02	0.02	0.00	0.00
a_{10}	0.04	0.00	0.01	0.13	0.13	0.10	0.04	0.05

TABLE 76.17 The ideal and anti-ideal solution.

	c_1	c_2	c_3	c_4	c_5	c_6	c_7	c_8
$\tilde{v}_j^+$	0.15	0.15	0.10	0.15	0.15	0.10	0.10	0.10
$\tilde{v}_j^-$	0.00	0.00	0.00	0.00	0.00	0.00	0.00	0.00

TABLE 76.18 The deviation of each element from the ideal solution.

	c_1	c_2	c_3	c_4	c_5	c_6	c_7	c_8
a_1	0.04	0.02	0.02	0.08	0.06	0.11	0.08	0.08
a_2	0.09	0.07	0.03	0.06	0.03	0.07	0.07	0.09
a_3	0.00	0.00	0.00	0.12	0.10	0.13	0.09	0.11
a_4	0.00	0.00	0.00	0.15	0.15	0.15	0.12	0.14
a_5	0.15	0.08	0.08	0.00	0.02	0.09	0.05	0.06
a_6	0.15	0.12	0.10	0.01	0.00	0.06	0.05	0.05
a_7	0.05	0.07	0.05	0.08	0.09	0.11	0.11	0.12
a_8	0.03	0.07	0.03	0.12	0.12	0.09	0.13	0.13
a_9	0.03	0.10	0.03	0.15	0.13	0.13	0.15	0.15
a_{10}	0.11	0.15	0.09	0.02	0.02	0.05	0.11	0.10

TABLE 76.19 The deviation of each element from the anti-ideal solution.

	c_1	c_2	c_3	c_4	c_5	c_6	c_7	c_8
a_1	0.11	0.13	0.08	0.07	0.09	0.04	0.07	0.07
a_2	0.06	0.08	0.07	0.09	0.12	0.08	0.08	0.06
a_3	0.15	0.15	0.10	0.03	0.05	0.02	0.06	0.04
a_4	0.15	0.15	0.10	0.00	0.00	0.00	0.03	0.01
a_5	0.00	0.07	0.02	0.15	0.13	0.06	0.10	0.09
a_6	0.00	0.03	0.00	0.14	0.15	0.09	0.10	0.10
a_7	0.10	0.08	0.05	0.07	0.06	0.04	0.04	0.03
a_8	0.12	0.08	0.07	0.03	0.03	0.06	0.02	0.02
a_9	0.12	0.05	0.07	0.00	0.02	0.02	0.00	0.00
a_{10}	0.04	0.00	0.01	0.13	0.13	0.10	0.04	0.05

TABLE 76.20 The positive and negative deviations of each alternative.

	a_1	a_2	a_3	a_4	a_5	a_6	a_7	a_8	a_9	a_{10}
s_i^+	0.49	0.49	0.55	0.71	0.52	0.54	0.68	0.72	0.87	0.65
s_i^-	0.66	0.66	0.60	0.44	0.63	0.61	0.47	0.43	0.28	0.50

TABLE 76.21 The positive and negative utility of each alternative.

	a_1	a_2	a_3	a_4	a_5	a_6	a_7	a_8	a_9	a_{10}
K_i^+	1.00	0.99	0.89	0.69	0.94	0.91	0.72	0.68	0.56	0.75
K_i^-	1.00	0.99	0.90	0.67	0.95	0.92	0.72	0.65	0.42	0.75

Step 6. Calculation of the deviation of each alternative.

The positive and negative deviations of each alternative can be derived by using Eqs. (76.8) and (76.9). The results are shown in Table 76.20.

Step 7. Calculation of the utility function for each alternative.

The negative and positive utility functions of each alternative can be derived by using Eqs. (76.10) and (76.11). The positive and negative utility of each alternative is shown in Table 76.21.

Step 8. Ranking the alternatives.

Based on the results shown in Table 76.21, the average value of each alternative's negative and positive utility can be derived by referring to Eq. (76.12), and the ranking of each alternative can be determined. The results are shown in Table 76.22.

According to the results shown in Table 76.22, BYD Qin PLUS DM-I (a_1) is the best choice with respect to the given evaluation criteria.

TABLE 76.22 The average utility and ranking of each alternative.

	a_1	a_2	a_3	a_4	a_5	a_6	a_7	a_8	a_9	a_{10}
Rd_i	1.00	0.99	0.90	0.68	0.95	0.91	0.72	0.66	0.49	0.75
Ranking	1	2	5	8	3	4	7	9	10	6

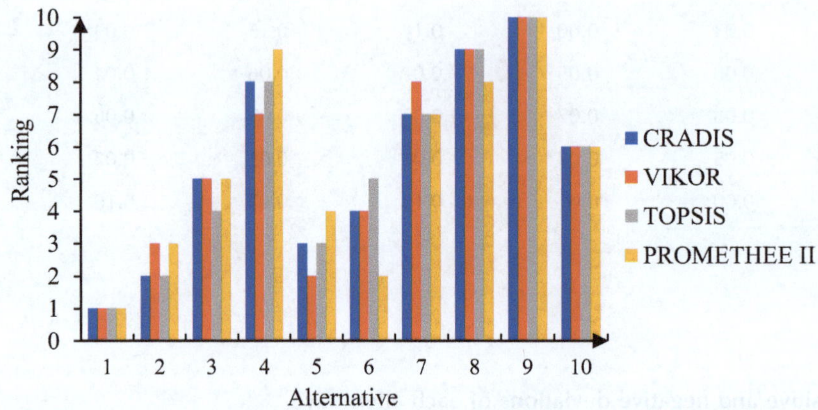

FIGURE 76.1 The ranking results obtained by different methods.

76.6 Comparative analysis

This section conducts a comparison analysis to show the efficiency of the CRADIS. VIKOR, TOPSIS, and preference ranking organization method for enrichment evaluation II (PROMETHEE II) are utilized to analyze the case shown in Section 76.5. The ranking results obtained by these methods are shown in Fig. 76.1.

As shown in Fig. 76.1, the ranking results of most alternatives determined by the CRADIS method are the same as those determined by VIKOR, TOPSIS, and PROMETHEE II. This indicates that the proposed method is highly homogeneous with the other three methods. Especially, the ranking of alternatives a_1, a_9, and a_{10} obtained by the four methods is the same. This indicates that the CRADIS method is a reliable technique to address the MADM problems. However, the ranking results of several alternatives determined by the four methods are different. These differences are further analyzed based on comparative analyses.

First, the ranking results derived by the CRADIS and VIKOR methods are compared. The ranking results of a_2, a_4, a_5, and a_7 derived by these two methods are different, which results from their distinct methodological foundations. In detail, the CRADIS method derives the ranking results based on the distances between the alternatives and the positive and negative ideal solutions, leading to more stable ranking results by mitigating the impact of extreme attribute values on the final ranking. In contrast, VIKOR derives the ranking results based on maximizing group utility and minimizing individual regret, thereby highlighting alternatives with significant differences in performance. Therefore, CRADIS is more suitable for handling the MADM problems where attribute values vary greatly but have no clear preference, whereas VIKOR is more appropriate for scenarios involving group negotiation and conflicts.

Second, the ranking results derived from the CRADIS and TOPSIS methods are compared. The ranking results of a_3 and a_6 derived by these two methods are different. Although these two methods are constructed based on the distances between the alternatives and the positive and negative ideal solutions. However, CRADIS focuses on the relative balance between an alternative's distances to the ideal and anti-ideal solutions, while TOPSIS ranks alternatives based on a closeness coefficient derived from absolute distances. Additionally, the CRADIS method offers greater flexibility by allowing any type of normalization without its effects being diminished, unlike TOPSIS, which prescribes specific normalization.

Lastly, the ranking results derived by the CRADIS and PROMETHEE II methods are compared. The ranking results of a_2, a_4, a_5, a_6, and a_8 derived by these two methods are different. The difference can be attributed to the fact that they are two different types of MADM methods. CRADIS is a typical utility values-based MADM technique, which ranks alternatives based on the distances between the alternatives and the positive and negative ideal solutions. PROMETHEE II is a typical outranking-based MCDM technique, which ranks alternatives based on their pairwise comparisons. Therefore CRADIS can derive robust ranking results in a simple way, while PROMETHEE can capture complex preferences and provide detailed rankings.

76.7 Conclusions

In this chapter, we have presented the CRADIS, a typical MADM method. First, the background and key features of the CRADIS method are introduced in detail. Second, a review of the literature on the extensions of CRADIS and its diverse applications is provided. Third, the step-by-step procedure of applying the CRADIS methodology is outlined. Next, a simple numerical example involving the movie recommendation is used to illustrate the application of CRADIS, with a detailed explanation of the main equation to facilitate understanding. Following this, a more complex numerical example related to the car selection is introduced to demonstrate the method's applicability in addressing intricate MADM problems. Finally, a comparative analysis is conducted to highlight the strengths and limitations of the CRADIS approach. Research indicates that the CRADIS method can be further improved in several key areas. First, the CRADIS method overlooks experts' psychological characteristics, which may significantly influence the prioritization results. It is of great significance to combine it with the behavioral decision-making models. Second, the original CRADIS assumes predefined attribute weights, which are usually unknown in practice. Therefore incorporating subjective and/or objective weighting techniques is essential to improve the reliability of weight determination. Finally, as a utility-based method, CRADIS has certain limitations in terms of robustness. To address this, it would be valuable to integrate CRADIS with other MADM approaches to enhance both the robustness and interpretability of the decision-making process.

References

Ashraf, S., Iqbal, W., Hameed, M. S., Simic, V., & Bacanin, N. (2024). An enhanced CRADIS decision model for optimizing radioactive waste reduction through transmutations based on Disc Spherical Fuzzy information. *Applied Soft Computing, 167*.

Aytekin, A., Korucuk, S., & Gorcun, O. F. (2024). Determining the factors affecting transportation demand management and selecting the best strategy: A case study. *Transport Policy, 146*, 150–166.

Aytekin, A., Kucuk, H. O., Aytekin, M., Simic, V., & Pamucar, D. (2025). Evaluation of international market entry strategies for mineral oil companies using a neutrosophic SWARA-CRADIS methodology. *Applied Soft Computing, 174*.

Chatterjee, P., & Seikh, M. R. (2024). Evaluating municipal solid waste management with a confidence level-based decision-making approach in q-rung orthopair picture fuzzy environment. *Journal of Industrial Information Integration, 42*.

Cheng, R., Fan, J. P., Wu, M. Q., & Seiti, H. (2024). A large-scale multi-attribute group decision-making method with R-numbers and its application to hydrogen fuel cell logistics path selection. *Complex & Intelligent Systems, 10*, 5213–5260.

Fetanat, A., & Tayebi, M. (2024). Sustainability and reliability-based hydrogen technologies prioritization for decarbonization in the oil refining industry: A decision support system under single-valued neutrosophic set. *International Journal of Hydrogen Energy, 52*, 765–786.

Han, X., Cao, Y., Yu, G., Han, Q., & Wang, W. (2025). An integrated fine-kinney framework based on a T-spherical Fuzzy CPT-CRADIS model for estimating occupational risk in the coal mine industry. *International Journal of Fuzzy Systems*.

Krishankumar, R., Dhruva, S., Ravichandran, K. S., & Kar, S. (2024). Selection of a viable blockchain service provider for data management within the internet of medical things: An MCDM approach to Indian healthcare. *Information Sciences, 657*.

Krishankumar, R., Ecer, F., Yilmaz, M. K., & Deveci, M. (2024). Selection of cloud vendors for medical centers using personalized ranking with evidence-based fuzzy decision-making algorithm. *IEEE Transactions on Engineering Management, 71*, 10040–10053.

Krishankumar, R., Dincer, H., Yuksel, S., Zavadskas, E. K., & Ravichandran, K. S. (2025). A decision system with choice-based ranking and orthopair fuzzy data for prioritization of solar panels to facilitate solar energy. *Annals of Operations Research*.

Krishankumar, R., & Ecer, F. (2023). Selection of IoT service provider for sustainable transport using q-rung orthopair fuzzy CRADIS and unknown weights. *Applied Soft Computing, 132*.

Krishankumar, R., & Ecer, F. (2024). A multi-criteria framework for electric vehicle charging location selection using double hierarchy preferences and unknown weights. *Engineering Applications of Artificial Intelligence, 133*.

Puska, A., Bozanic, D., Nedeljkovic, M., & Janosevic, M. (2022). Green supplier selection in an uncertain environment in agriculture using a hybrid MCDM Model: Z-numbers-fuzzy LMAW-fuzzy CRADIS model. *Axioms, 11*.

Puska, A., Nedeljkovic, M., Prodanovic, R., Vladisavljevic, R., & Suzic, R. (2022). Market assessment of pear varieties in serbia using fuzzy CRADIS and CRITIC methods. *Agriculture-Basel, 12*.

Puska, A., Stevic, Z., & Pamucar, D. (2022). Evaluation and selection of healthcare waste incinerators using extended sustainability criteria and multi-criteria analysis methods. *Environment Development and Sustainability, 24*, 11195–11225.

Rani, P., Mishra, A. R., Alshamrani, A. M., Alrasheedi, A. F., & Tirkolaee, E. B. (2025). Picture fuzzy compromise ranking of alternatives using distance-to-ideal-solution approach for selecting blockchain technology platforms in logistics firms. *Engineering Applications of Artificial Intelligence, 142*.

Shamsi, M., Zakerinejad, M., & Zareifard, M. R. (2025). Optimal, reliable, and sustainable technology selection for mining overburden waste utilization using green & climate-smart mining (GCSM): A hybrid fuzzy multi-criteria decision-making tool. *Journal of Environmental Chemical Engineering, 13*.

Wang, W. Z., Chen, Y., Yang, Z. Y., Hu, Y., Deveci, M., & Tomásková, H. (2025). The quality appraisal of massive open online courses using decision support model. *Complex & Intelligent Systems, 11*.

Wang, W. Z., Liu, X. W., & Qin, Y. (2018). A fuzzy fine-kinney-based risk evaluation approach with extended MULTIMOORA method based on choquet integral. *Computers & Industrial Engineering, 125*, 111–123.

Wang, Y., Wang, W. Z., Deveci, M., & Yu, X. Y. (2024). An integrated interval-valued spherical fuzzy Choquet integral based decision making model for prioritizing risk in fine-kinney. *Engineering Applications of Artificial Intelligence, 127*, 107437.

Chapter 77

ADAM: the axial-distance-based aggregated measurement method for multi-attribute decision-making

Jing Tang[1,2], Weizhong Wang[3], and Muhammet Deveci[4]

[1]*School of Digital Commerce and Trade, Zhejiang Polytechnic University of Mechanical and Electrical Engineering, Hangzhou, Zhejiang, P.R. China,* [2]*School of Economics and Management, Southeast University, Nanjing, Jiangsu, P.R. China,* [3]*School of Economics and Management, Anhui Normal University, Wuhu, Anhui, P.R. China,* [4]*Department of Industrial Engineering, Turkish Naval Academy, National Defence University, Istanbul, Türkiye*

77.1 Introduction

Recent advances in multi-attribute decision-making (MADM) have explored diverse approaches for handling complex decision environments in fields, such as infrastructure planning, sustainable development, and healthcare system evaluation (Badi et al., 2025; Demir & Ulusoy, 2024; Demir, 2025; Gökalp et al., 2025). These studies have highlighted the importance of robust aggregation mechanisms and ranking stability under varying criteria weights. The axial-distance-based aggregated measurement (ADAM) method was first introduced by Krstić et al. (2023) as a new geometric MADM method. Rather than computing a simple distance to an ideal point, the ADAM method constructs a complex polyhedron in 3D space for each alternative. The vertices of this polyhedron are defined by the origin, a set of attribute-specific reference points on a 2D plane, and a corresponding set of weighted reference points that add a third dimension. The volume of this polyhedron is then used as the aggregated score for the alternative. This formulation ensures that each attribute's contribution is accounted for independently along its axis.

The ADAM method possesses several distinctive features: (i) its calculation is based on a novel geometric construction using axial projections, where the volume of a constructed polyhedron serves as the aggregated performance score; (ii) its ranking stability under weight perturbations has been demonstrated compared to traditional MADM methods; (iii) it follows a straightforward computational process that does not require the determination of an ideal solution, simplifying its application. Due to its stability and clear methodology, the ADAM framework has been utilized in fields such as supply chain management, sustainable development for site selection, and public transportation system evaluation (Krstić et al., 2024; Krstić et al., 2025; Tadić et al., 2025).

The rest of this chapter is organized as follows. Section 2 reviews the literature on ADAM and its applications. Section 3 details the concepts and steps of the ADAM method. Sections 4 and 5, respectively, present a simple and a complex numerical example to demonstrate its application. Section 6 compares ADAM to existing MADM methods. Finally, Section 7 concludes this chapter.

77.2 Literature review

Beyond traditional distance-based methods, many recent MADM studies have emphasized geometric or volume-based perspectives to capture the multidimensional structure of alternatives (Goutam et al., 2022; Munir et al., 2021; Wang & Liu, 2025). The ADAM method was first introduced by Krstić et al. (2023) as a novel geometric MADM technique rather than a traditional distance-based method. ADAM constructs for each alternative a complex polyhedron—whose vertices are the origin, attribute-specific reference points, and corresponding weighted reference points—and uses the volume of this polyhedron as the aggregated performance score. In their foundational study, the authors validated ADAM against methods, such as Technique for Order of Preference by Similarity to Ideal Solution (TOPSIS) and Višekriterijumska

Encyclopedia of Multi-Attribute Decision-Making (MADM). DOI: https://doi.org/10.1016/B978-0-443-33275-3.00049-X

Optimizacija I Kompromisno Rešenje (VIKOR), and demonstrated that its resulting ranking exhibits significantly lower variation than those methods under comparative analysis. Since it was proposed, the ADAM framework has been methodologically extended to operate within uncertain environments. For instance, Tadić et al. (2025) extended the method by integrating triangular fuzzy numbers (TFNs) to create the F-ADAM model, designed for planning and managing the intermodal routes. Similarly, Krstić & Tadić (2023) proposed an integrated framework that combines TFNs with the ADAM method to enhance the selection process of cold chain logistics service providers, addressing the inherent uncertainties in subjective judgments and the decision process.

In addition to its methodological evolution, the ADAM method has been utilized by several researchers to address various complex, real-world problems. In agriculture and circular economy studies, Agnusdei et al. (2023) combined ADAM with methods, such as SWOT analysis and the analytic network process, to assess digitalization strategies and support sustainable development. For tourism and infrastructure projects, ADAM has been combined with objective and subjective weighting approaches, such as the preference selection index and the pivot pairwise relative criteria importance assessment to select optimal accommodation types (Popović et al., 2024). Furthermore, Krstić et al. (2024) integrated ADAM with Delphi, the analytic hierarchy process, and the best–worst method to evaluate Industry 4.0 technologies and rank suppliers in risk management for circular supply chains and smart manufacturing. Kovač et al. (2023) developed a robust methodology for designing and evaluating sustainable city logistics concepts based on city-dry port micro-consolidation centers, using ADAM to rank different infrastructure configurations for the city network of Belgrade. These studies show that ADAM, frequently used in combination with various weight determination techniques, provides a structured and flexible approach for complex decision-making across diverse application fields.

77.3 Methodology

The ADAM method involves a systematic, step-by-step process to rank alternatives. Its core concept is to represent each alternative as a polyhedron in a geometric space and to use the polyhedron's volume as the alternative's aggregated performance score. The steps are as follows:

Step 1. Construct the initial decision matrix

For a MADM problem with n attributes $c_j (j = 1, 2, \ldots, n)$ and m alternatives $a_i (i = 1, 2, \ldots, m)$, the first step is to establish the initial decision matrix $E = (e_{ij})_{m \times n}$.

$$E = \begin{bmatrix} e_{11} & e_{12} & \cdots & e_{1n} \\ e_{21} & e_{22} & \cdots & e_{2n} \\ \vdots & \vdots & \ddots & \vdots \\ e_{m1} & e_{m2} & \cdots & e_{mn} \end{bmatrix} \tag{77.1}$$

where e_{ij} is the evaluation of the alternative a_i under attribute c_j.

Step 2. Sort attributes by importance

The columns of the initial decision matrix $E = (e_{ij})_{m \times n}$ are rearranged in descending order of their corresponding attribute weights w_j, while the order of alternatives remains unchanged. The resulting sorted decision matrix is denoted as $S = (s_{ij})_{m \times n}$. Hereafter, w_j denotes the weight of the j-th attribute after sorting.

$$S = \begin{bmatrix} s_{11} & s_{12} & \cdots & s_{1n} \\ s_{21} & s_{22} & \cdots & s_{2n} \\ \vdots & \vdots & \ddots & \vdots \\ s_{m1} & s_{m2} & \cdots & s_{mn} \end{bmatrix} \tag{77.2}$$

Step 3. Normalize the sorted evaluations

Transform each s_{ij} into a normalized score n_{ij} so that benefit attributes scale positively and cost attributes scale inversely, that is,

$$n_{ij} = \begin{cases} \dfrac{s_{ij}}{\max\limits_i s_{ij}}, & if\ j \in B \\ \dfrac{\min\limits_i s_{ij}}{s_{ij}}, & if\ j \in C \end{cases} \tag{77.3}$$

where n_{ij} is the normalized evaluation, B is the set of benefit attributes, and C is the set of cost attributes.

Step 4. Determine polyhedron vertices

For each normalized value n_{ij}, compute two points in 3D space, which are the reference point $R_{ij} = (x_{ij}, y_{ij}, 0)$ and the weighted reference point $P_{ij} = (x_{ij}, y_{ij}, z_{ij})$.

$$x_{ij} = n_{ij} \times \sin \alpha_j, \ \forall j = 1, \cdots, n; \ \forall i = 1, \cdots, m \tag{77.4}$$

$$y_{ij} = n_{ij} \times \cos \alpha_j, \ \forall j = 1, \cdots, n; \ \forall i = 1, \cdots, m \tag{77.5}$$

$$z_{ij} = \begin{cases} 0, \ for \ R_{ij} \\ w_j, \ for \ P_{ij} \end{cases}, \ \forall j = 1, \cdots, n; \ \forall i = 1, \cdots, m \tag{77.6}$$

where the coordinates (x_{ij}, y_{ij}) locate the attribute axis direction (via an angle α_j) and z_{ij} corresponds to the weight w_j.

$$\alpha_j = (j-1)\frac{90^\circ}{n-1}, \ \forall j = 1, \cdots, n \tag{77.7}$$

Step 5. Compute the polyhedron volume

Each alternative a_i defines a complex polyhedron formed by connecting the origin O, its sequence of reference points R_{ij}, and weighted points P_{ij}. Decompose this shape into a series of pyramids between consecutive attribute axes. The volume V_i^C equals the sum of the volumes of the pyramids of which it is composed using the following equation:

$$V_i^C = \sum_{k=1}^{n-1} V_{ik}, \ \forall i = 1, \cdots, m \tag{77.8}$$

where V_{ik} is the volume of the pyramid obtained by applying the following equation:

$$V_{ik} = \frac{1}{3} B_{ik} \times h_{ik}, \ \forall k = 1, \cdots, n-1 \tag{77.9}$$

where B_{ik} is the area of the base of the pyramid defined by the reference and weighted reference points of two consecutive attributes and is obtained by applying the following equation:

$$B_{ik} = c_k \times \ell_{ik} + \frac{\ell_{ik} \times (b_k - c_k)}{2} \tag{77.10}$$

where ℓ_{ik} is the Euclidean distance between the reference points of two consecutive attributes,

$$\ell_{ik} = \sqrt{(x_{i,k+1} - x_{ik})^2 + (y_{i,k+1} - y_{ik})^2} \tag{77.11}$$

b_k and c_k are the z-coordinates of the weighted reference points P_{ik},$P_{i,k+1}$ respectively.

$$b_k = z_{ik} \tag{77.12}$$

$$c_k = z_{i,k+1} \tag{77.13}$$

h_{ik} is the height of the pyramid from the defined base to the top of the pyramid located in the coordinate origin (O)and is obtained by applying the following equation:

$$h_{ik} = \frac{2\sqrt{\sigma_{ik}(\sigma_{ik} - \ell_{ik})(\sigma_{ik} - d_{ik})(\sigma_{ik} - r_{ik})}}{\ell_{ik}} \tag{77.14}$$

where σ_{ik} is the semiperimeter of the triangle defined by the x and y coordinates of two consecutive attributes and the coordinate origin and is obtained as follows:

$$\sigma_{ik} = \frac{\ell_{ik} + d_{ik} + r_{ik}}{2} \tag{77.15}$$

where d_{ik} and r_{ik} are the Euclidean distances of the reference points of two consecutive attributes from the coordinate origin and are obtained as follows:

$$d_{ik} = \sqrt{x_{ik}^2 + y_{ik}^2} \tag{77.16}$$

$$r_{ik} = \sqrt{x_{i,k+1}^2 + y_{i,k+1}^2} \tag{77.17}$$

Step 6. Rank alternatives

Rank the alternatives according to the decreasing values of the volumes of complex polyhedra V_i^C ($\forall$ $i = 1, \cdots m$). The best alternative is the one with the highest volume.

77.4 Numerical example 1

In this section, a simple numerical example is presented to demonstrate the application of the ADAM method. In today's saturated market, selecting a new smartphone can be a challenging task for consumers. Numerous brands offer products with varying advantages and disadvantages, making it difficult to determine the most suitable alternative. This is a typical MADM problem, as the consumer must consider multiple attributes simultaneously when making a purchase decision, such as performance, camera quality, battery life, and price.

In this example, four smartphone brands are selected from the current market, namely Apple (a_1), Samsung (a_2), Huawei (a_3), and Xiaomi (a_4). Each brand is evaluated based on four attributes: performance (c_1), camera quality (c_2), battery life (c_3), and price (c_4). The ADAM method can then be conducted as follows.

Step 1. Construct the initial decision matrix

In this step, the positive integers {1, 2, 3, 4, 5, 6, 7, 8, 9, 10} are utilized to represent the evaluation information. Then, a decision maker is invited to evaluate each brand under each attribute, and the detailed evaluation information$E = (e_{ij})_{m\times n}$ is shown in Table 77.1.

Step 2. Sort attributes by importance

Let the weight of four attributes be $w_1 = 0.35,\ w_2 = 0.2,\ w_3 = 0.2,\ w_4 = 0.25$. The initial decision matrix $E = (e_{ij})_{m\times n}$ is transformed into the sorted matrix $S = (s_{ij})_{m\times n}$ by rearranging its columns in descending order of their respective weights w_j.

Step 3. Normalize the sorted evaluations

Based on Eq. (77.3), transform each s_{ij} into a normalized score n_{ij}. Among them, $c_1,\ c_2,\ c_3$ are benefit attributes. c_4 is the cost attribute. The normalized evaluation information is shown in Table 77.2.

Step 4. Determine polyhedron vertices

Compute the reference point $R_{ij} = (x_{ij},\ y_{ij},\ 0)$ and the weighted reference point $P_{ij} = (x_{ij},\ y_{ij},\ z_{ij})$ according to Eqs. (77.4)–(77.6). The angle α_j is calculated using (77.7). These coordinates are presented in Tables. 77.3 and 77.4, respectively.

TABLE 77.1 The initial evaluation information of each brand.

	c_1	c_2	c_3	c_4
a_1	8	8	7	8
a_2	7	6	8	6
a_3	6	7	8	8
a_4	6	5	7	5

TABLE 77.2 The normalized evaluation information of each brand.

	n_{i1}	n_{i2}	n_{i3}	n_{i4}
a_1	1	0.625	1	0.875
a_2	0.875	0.8333	0.75	1
a_3	0.75	0.625	0.875	1
a_4	0.75	1	0.625	0.875

TABLE 77.3 Coordinates of the reference points.

	R_{i1}	R_{i2}	R_{i3}	R_{i4}
a_1	(0, 1, 0)	(0.313, 0.541, 0)	(0.866, 0.5, 0)	(0.875, 0, 0)
a_2	(0, 0.875, 0)	(0.417, 0.722, 0)	(0.65, 0.375, 0)	(1, 0, 0)
a_3	(0, 0.75, 0)	(0.313, 0.541, 0)	(0.758, 0.438, 0)	(1, 0, 0)
a_4	(0, 0.75, 0)	(0.5, 0.866, 0)	(0.541, 0.313, 0)	(0.875, 0, 0)

TABLE 77.4 Coordinates of the weighted reference points.

	P_{i1}	P_{i2}	P_{i3}	P_{i4}
a_1	(0, 1, 0.35)	(0.313, 0.541, 0.25)	(0.866, 0.5, 0.20)	(0.875, 0, 0.20)
a_2	(0, 0.875, 0.35)	(0.417, 0.722, 0.25)	(0.65, 0.375, 0.20)	(1, 0, 0.20)
a_3	(0, 0.75, 0.35)	(0.313, 0.541, 0.25)	(0.758, 0.438, 0.20)	(1, 0, 0.20)
a_4	(0, 0.75, 0.35)	(0.5, 0.866, 0.25)	(0.541, 0.313, 0.20)	(0.875, 0, 0.20)

TABLE 77.5 The ranking results of smartphone brands.

Alternatives	Volume	Rank
a_1	0.084	2
a_2	0.085	1
a_3	0.073	4
a_4	0.079	3

Step 5. Compute the polyhedron volume

The volume V_i^C equals the sum of the volumes of the pyramids according to Eqs. (77.8)–(77.17). The volume is shown in Table 77.5.

Step 6. Rank alternatives

The ranking principle is that a larger polyhedral volume signifies a more preferable alternative. Rank the alternatives according to the decreasing values of the volumes of complex polyhedra. The ranking results are shown in Table 77.5. The complete ranking order is $a_2 \succ a_1 \succ a_4 \succ a_3$.

77.5 Numerical example 2

To better demonstrate the practical applicability of the ADAM method in a real-world decision-making context, a complex numerical example of evaluating supply chain sustainability innovation is introduced. In practice, assessing and improving sustainability within a supply chain represents a critical, complex decision problem for modern enterprises. On the one hand, growing pressure from consumers, investors, and regulatory bodies has made supply chain sustainability a key factor for competitive advantage and corporate reputation. On the other hand, such evaluations are often shaped by multiple experts, such as managers from procurement, environmental compliance, and operations, whose priorities and knowledge may differ significantly. Evaluating supply chain sustainability innovation involves assessing a set of alternatives (e.g., suppliers) against numerous attributes spanning multiple dimensions, including economic, environmental, social, and institutional factors. These attributes can include both objective measures (e.g., R&D investment, carbon emissions) and subjective judgments (e.g., corporate image, partner collaboration), which increases the complexity of the decision process.

As introduced above, this evaluation can be modeled as a MADM problem. In this illustrative example, a global electronics firm aims to evaluate seven suppliers. The seven suppliers are Innovatec Inc. (a_1), Green-Metal Corp. (a_2), Eco-Components Ltd. (a_3), Sustaina-Circuits (a_4), Future-Fab Co. (a_5), Nexus Parts (a_6), and Vertex Assemblies (a_7). Each supplier is evaluated against eight key performance attributes derived from the four dimensions of sustainability innovation, namely R&D Investment in Green Tech (c_1), Production Cost Reduction (c_2), Green Product Design (c_3), Carbon Emission Reduction (c_4), Employee Health and Safety(c_5), Corporate Social Responsibility Image (c_6), Collaboration with Green Partners (c_7), Regulatory Compliance (c_8). In this case, three experts are involved in the decision process, and the ADAM method is applied to derive the comprehensive ranking of the alternatives.

Step 1. Construct the initial decision matrix

For the evaluation process, three experts $D = \{d^1, d^2, d^3\}$ are engaged to assess seven suppliers. The experts utilized a set of linguistic terms, and the conversion of these terms into their corresponding numerical values on a nine-point scale is defined in Table 77.6 (Krstić et al., 2023). The linguistic evaluation information of three experts is shown in Tables 77.7–77.9.

Once the linguistic evaluations from the three experts are converted into their numerical equivalents using the nine-point scale, the next step is to aggregate these individual assessments into a collective evaluation matrix. This integration is performed by calculating the weighted average of the experts' evaluations for each attribute. Let the experts' weights be $\omega_1 = 0.25$, $\omega_2 = 0.4$, $\omega_3 = 0.35$. The collective evaluation matrix is shown in Table 77.10.

Step 2. Sort attributes by importance

Let the weight of eight attributes be $w_1 = 0.15$, $w_2 = 0.1$, $w_3 = 0.2$, $w_4 = 0.05$, $w_5 = 0.1$, $w_6 = 0.2$, $w_7 = 0.1$, and $w_8 = 0.1$. Rearrange the columns of the collective evaluation matrix in descending order of the corresponding attribute weights w_j, producing a sorted matrix $S = (s_{ij})_{m\times n}$. The attribute order after sorting is (c_3, c_6, c_1, c_2, c_5, c_7, c_8, c_4), the sorted evaluation matrix is shown in Table 77.11.

Step 3. Normalize the sorted evaluations

Based on Eq. (77.3), transform each s_{ij} into a normalized score n_{ij}. These eight attributes are all benefit attributes. The normalized evaluation information is shown in Table 77.12.

Step 4. Determine polyhedron vertices

Compute the reference point $R_{ij} = (x_{ij}, y_{ij}, 0)$ and the weighted reference point$P_{ij} = (x_{ij}, y_{ij}, z_{ij})$ according to Eqs. (77.4)–(77.6). The angle α_j is calculated using (77.7). These coordinates are presented in Tables 77.13 and 77.14, respectively.

TABLE 77.6 Evaluation scale

Linguistic Evaluation	Abbreviation	Numerical Value
None	N	1
Very low	VL	2
Low	L	3
Fairly low	FL	4
Medium	M	5
Fairly high	FH	6
High	H	7
Very high	VH	8
Extremely high	EH	9

Source: (adapted from Krstić et al. (2023), Table 77.1, licensed under CC BY 4.0).

TABLE 77.7 The linguistic evaluation information of expert d^1.

	c_1	c_2	c_3	c_4	c_5	c_6	c_7	c_8
a_1	EH	FH	VH	H	H	FH	H	VH
a_2	M	H	FH	VH	H	H	M	EH
a_3	H	FH	EH	H	VH	H	FH	VH
a_4	VH	H	VH	H	H	VH	VH	H
a_5	VH	VH	H	FH	FH	M	M	H
a_6	L	M	L	FL	H	L	L	M
a_7	FL	H	M	M	VH	FH	FL	H

TABLE 77.8 The linguistic evaluation information of expert d^2.

	c_1	c_2	c_3	c_4	c_5	c_6	c_7	c_8
a_1	H	M	H	FH	VH	H	M	EH
a_2	FL	EH	M	H	H	FH	FH	EH
a_3	M	H	H	FH	EH	H	H	VH
a_4	FH	FH	H	M	H	FH	M	VH
a_5	H	H	FH	L	M	L	FL	H
a_6	VL	VH	L	M	H	M	FH	H
a_7	L	VH	FL	FH	VH	H	H	EH

TABLE 77.9 The linguistic evaluation information of expert d^3.

	c_1	c_2	c_3	c_4	c_5	c_6	c_7	c_8
a_1	H	M	H	H	VH	VH	H	H
a_2	M	H	FH	VH	H	H	VH	VH
a_3	H	FH	VH	H	VH	EH	VH	H
a_4	VH	H	VH	VH	H	EH	EH	H
a_5	H	FH	H	M	FH	M	L	FH
a_6	L	M	L	L	M	L	L	M
a_7	FL	H	M	FH	H	H	M	VH

Step 5. Compute the polyhedron volume

The volume V_i^C equals the sum of the volumes of the pyramids according to Eqs. (77.8)–(77.17). The volume is represented in Table 77.15. To aid in visualization, Fig 77.1 shows the geometric representation of the complex polyhedron for alternative a_1.

TABLE 77.10 The collective evaluation matrix.

	c_1	c_2	c_3	c_4	c_5	c_6	c_7	c_8
a_1	7.5	5.25	7.25	6.6	7.75	7.1	6.2	8.05
a_2	4.6	7.8	5.6	7.6	7	6.6	6.45	8.65
a_3	6.2	6.4	7.85	6.6	8.4	7.7	7.1	7.65
a_4	7.2	6.6	7.6	6.55	7	7.55	7.15	7.4
a_5	7.25	6.9	6.6	4.45	5.6	4.2	3.9	6.65
a_6	2.6	6.2	3	4.05	6.3	3.8	4.2	5.8
a_7	3.6	7.4	4.6	5.75	7.65	6.75	5.55	8.15

TABLE 77.11 The sorted evaluation matrix.

	s_{i1}	s_{i2}	s_{i3}	s_{i4}	s_{i5}	s_{i6}	s_{i7}	s_{i8}
a_1	7.25	7.1	7.5	5.25	7.75	6.2	8.05	6.6
a_2	5.6	6.6	4.6	7.8	7	6.45	8.65	7.6
a_3	7.85	7.7	6.2	6.4	8.4	7.1	7.65	6.6
a_4	7.6	7.55	7.2	6.6	7	7.15	7.4	6.55
a_5	6.6	4.2	7.25	6.9	5.6	3.9	6.65	4.45
a_6	3	3.8	2.6	6.2	6.3	4.2	5.8	4.05
a_7	4.6	6.75	3.6	7.4	7.65	5.55	8.15	5.75

TABLE 77.12 The normalized evaluation matrix.

	n_{i1}	n_{i2}	n_{i3}	n_{i4}	n_{i5}	n_{i6}	n_{i7}	n_{i8}
a_1	0.924	0.922	1	0.673	0.923	0.867	0.931	0.868
a_2	0.713	0.857	0.613	1	0.833	0.902	1	1
a_3	1	1	0.827	0.821	1	0.993	0.884	0.868
a_4	0.968	0.981	0.96	0.846	0.833	1	0.855	0.862
a_5	0.841	0.545	0.967	0.885	0.667	0.545	0.769	0.586
a_6	0.382	0.494	0.347	0.795	0.75	0.587	0.671	0.533
a_7	0.586	0.877	0.48	0.949	0.911	0.776	0.942	0.757

TABLE 77.13 Coordinates of the reference points.

	R_{i1}	R_{i2}	R_{i3}	R_{i4}	R_{i5}	R_{i6}	R_{i7}	R_{i8}
a_1	(0, 0.924, 0)	(0.205, 0.899, 0)	(0.434, 0.901, 0)	(0.42, 0.5262, 0)	(0.721, 0.575, 0)	(0.781, 0.376, 0)	(0.907, 0.207, 0)	(0.868, 0, 0)
a_2	(0, 0.713, 0)	(0.191, 0.836, 0)	(0.266, 0.553, 0)	(0.624, 0.782, 0)	(0.652, 0.52, 0)	(0.813, 0.392, 0)	(0.975, 0.223, 0)	(1, 0, 0)
a_3	(0, 1, 0)	(0.223, 0.9745, 0)	(0.359, 0.745, 0)	(0.512, 0.642, 0)	(0.782, 0.624, 0)	(0.895, 0.431, 0)	(0.862, 0.197, 0)	(0.868, 0, 0)
a_4	(0, 0.968, 0)	(0.218, 0.956, 0)	(0.417, 0.865, 0)	(0.528, 0.662, 0)	(0.652, 0.52, 0)	(0.901, 0.434, 0)	(0.834, 0.190, 0)	(0.862, 0, 0)
a_5	(0, 0.841, 0)	(0.121, 0.532, 0)	(0.42, 0.871, 0)	(0.552, 0.692, 0)	(0.521, 0.416, 0)	(0.492, 0.237, 0)	(0.75, 0.171, 0)	(0.586, 0, 0)
a_6	(0, 0.382, 0)	(0.11, 0.481, 0)	(0.151, 0.312, 0)	(0.496, 0.622, 0)	(0.586, 0.468, 0)	(0.529, 0.255, 0)	(0.654, 0.149, 0)	(0.533, 0, 0)
a_7	(0, 0.586, 0)	(0.195, 0.855, 0)	(0.208, 0.433, 0)	(0.592, 0.742, 0)	(0.712, 0.568, 0)	(0.699, 0.337, 0)	(0.919, 0.21, 0)	(0.757, 0, 0)

TABLE 77.14 Coordinates of the weighted reference points.

	P_{i1}	P_{i2}	P_{i3}	P_{i4}	P_{i5}	P_{i6}	P_{i7}	P_{i8}
a_1	(0, 0.924, 0.2)	(0.205, 0.899, 0.2)	(0.434, 0.901, 0.15)	(0.42, 0.5262, 0.1)	(0.721, 0.575, 0.1)	(0.781, 0.376, 0.1)	(0.907, 0.207, 0.1)	(0.868, 0, 0.05)
a_2	(0, 0.713, 0.2)	(0.191, 0.836, 0.2)	(0.266, 0.553, 0.15)	(0.624, 0.782, 0.1)	(0.652, 0.52, 0.1)	(0.813, 0.392, 0.1)	(0.975, 0.223, 0.1)	(1, 0, 0.05)
a_3	(0, 1, 0.2)	(0.223, 0.9745, 0.2)	(0.359, 0.745, 0.15)	(0.512, 0.642, 0.1)	(0.782, 0.624, 0.1)	(0.895, 0.431, 0.1)	(0.862, 0.197, 0.1)	(0.868, 0, 0.05)
a_4	(0, 0.968, 0.2)	(0.218, 0.956, 0.2)	(0.417, 0.865, 0.15)	(0.528, 0.662, 0.1)	(0.652, 0.52, 0.1)	(0.901, 0.434, 0.1)	(0.834, 0.190, 0.1)	(0.862, 0, 0.05)
a_5	(0, 0.841, 0.2)	(0.121, 0.532, 0.2)	(0.42, 0.871, 0.15)	(0.552, 0.692, 0.1)	(0.521, 0.416, 0.1)	(0.492, 0.237, 0.1)	(0.75, 0.171, 0.1)	(0.586, 0, 0.05)
a_6	(0, 0.382, 0.2)	(0.11, 0.481, 0.2)	(0.151, 0.312, 0.15)	(0.496, 0.622, 0.1)	(0.586, 0.468, 0.1)	(0.529, 0.255, 0.1)	(0.654, 0.149, 0.1)	(0.533, 0, 0.05)
a_7	(0, 0.586, 0.2)	(0.195, 0.855, 0.2)	(0.208, 0.433, 0.15)	(0.592, 0.742, 0.1)	(0.712, 0.568, 0.1)	(0.699, 0.337, 0.1)	(0.919, 0.21, 0.1)	(0.757, 0, 0.05)

TABLE 77.15 The ranking results of seven suppliers.

Alternatives	Volume	Rank
a_1	0.052	3
a_2	0.046	4
a_3	0.056	1
a_4	0.055	2
a_5	0.034	6
a_6	0.020	7
a_7	0.038	5

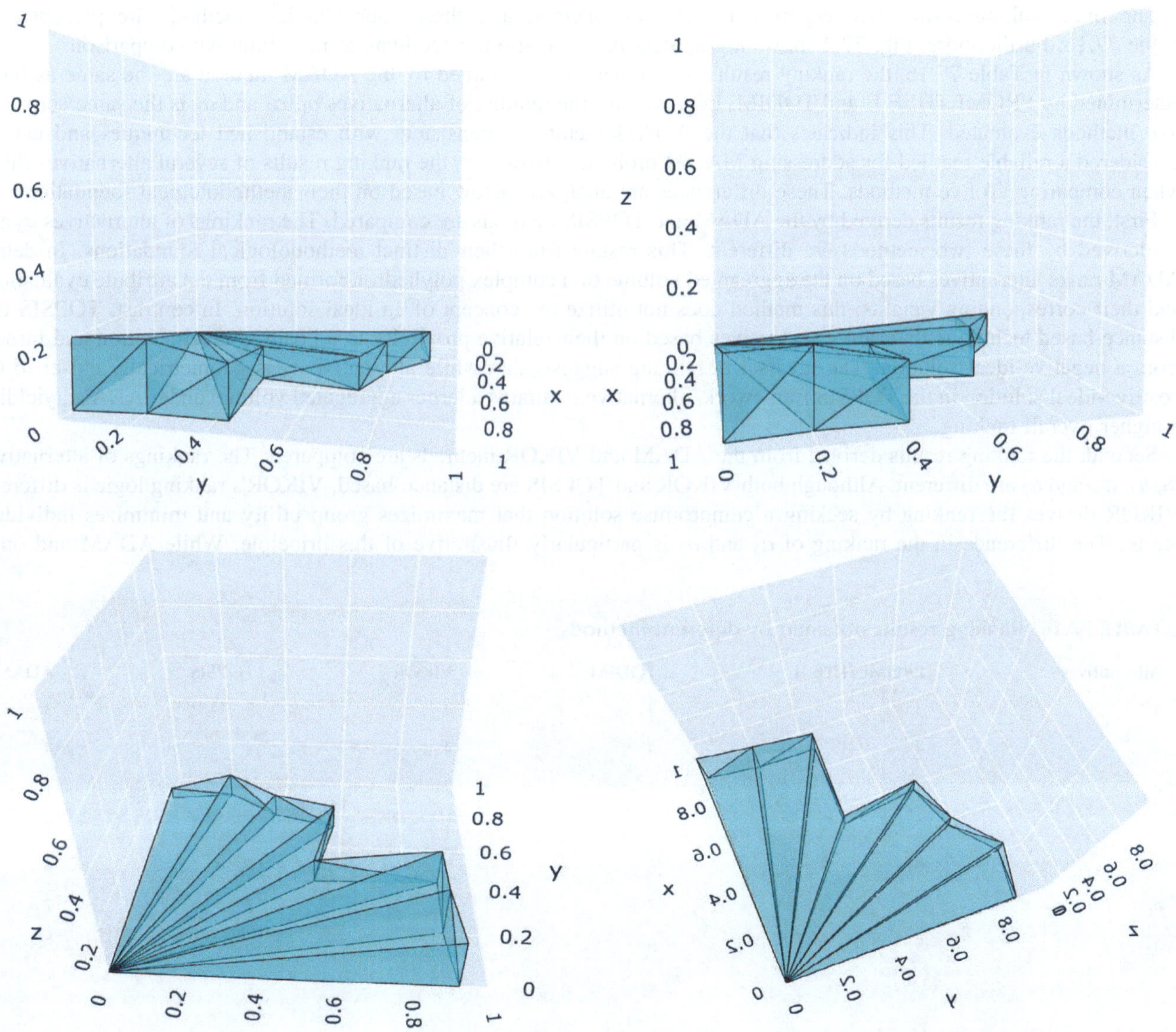

FIGURE 77.1 The polyhedra for the alternative a_1.

Step 6. Rank alternatives

The final step in the ADAM method is to rank the alternatives based on the calculated volumes V_i^C. The alternatives are ranked in descending order according to the volumes of the complex polyhedra. The calculations for ranking the alternatives based on polyhedral volumes are performed using the software, http://adam-mcdm.com/ (accessed on 18 September 2025). The detailed volume calculations and the resultant ranking for each alternative are presented in Table 77.15.

Based on the ADAM method analysis, the top-ranked supplier is Eco-Components Ltd. (a_3), which achieved the highest volume of 0.056. The complete ranking order for all evaluated alternatives is derived as follows: $a_3 \succ a_4 \succ a_1 \succ a_2 \succ a_7 \succ a_5 \succ a_6$.

77.6 Comparative analysis

This section presents a comparative analysis to compare the ranking results obtained byseveral MADM methods, including ADAM, preference ranking organization method for enrichment evaluation II (PROMETHEE II) (Goswami, 2020; Zhang et al., 2019), TODIM (Tomada de Decisão Interativa Multicritério, Portuguese for interactive and multicriteria decision-making) (He et al., 2022; Hong et al., 2021), VIKOR (Qin et al., 2015), and TOPSIS (Lei et al., 2020). These methods are applied to the numerical example 2 described in Section 5.

The final ranking results derived from the ADAM method and these four classical methods are presented in Table 77.16. Furthermore, Fig. 77.2 shows a graphical representation to facilitate a more intuitive comparison.

As shown in Table 77.16, the ranking results of alternatives determined by the ADAM method are the same as those determined by PROMETHEE II and TODIM. In particular, the ranking of alternatives a_1, a_2 and a_6 is the same across all five methods evaluated. This indicates that the ADAM method is consistent with established techniques and can be considered a reliable method for addressing MADM problems. However, the ranking results of several alternatives differ when comparing all five methods. These differences are analyzed below based on their methodological foundations.

First, the ranking results derived by the ADAM and TOPSIS methods are compared. The rankings of alternatives a_3 and a_4 derived by these two methods are different. This results from their distinct methodological foundations. In detail, ADAM ranks alternatives based on the aggregated volume of a complex polyhedron formed from the attribute evaluations and their corresponding weights; this method does not utilize the concept of an ideal solution. In contrast, TOPSIS is a distance-based technique that ranks alternatives based on their relative proximity to a positive-ideal solution and farness from a negative-ideal solution. The reversal in ranking suggests that while alternative a_4 is geometrically closer to the positive-ideal solution in the TOPSIS framework, alternative a_3 attains a larger aggregated volume under ADAM, yielding a higher overall ranking.

Second, the ranking results derived from the ADAM and VIKOR methods are compared. The rankings of alternatives a_3, a_4, a_5, and a_7 are different. Although both VIKOR and TOPSIS are distance-based, VIKOR's ranking logic is different. VIKOR derives the ranking by seeking a compromise solution that maximizes group utility and minimizes individual regret. The difference in the ranking of a_5 and a_7 is particularly illustrative of this principle. While ADAM and other

TABLE 77.16 Ranking results obtained by different methods.

Alternatives	PROMETHEE II	TODIM	VIKOR	TOPSIS	ADAM
a_1	3	3	3	3	3
a_2	4	4	4	4	4
a_3	1	1	2	2	1
a_4	2	2	1	1	2
a_5	6	6	5	6	6
a_6	7	7	7	7	7
a_7	5	5	6	5	5

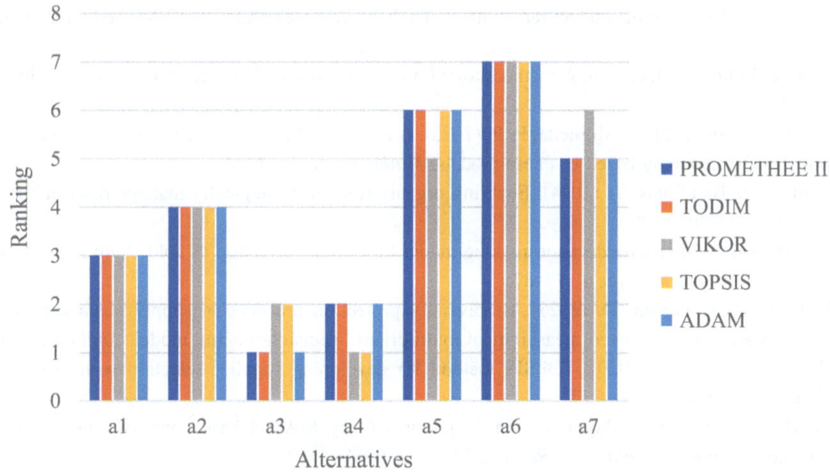

FIGURE 77.2 The ranking results obtained by different methods.

methods rank a_7 higher, VIKOR prefers a_5. This can be attributed to VIKOR's emphasis on minimizing individual regret; alternative a_5 has a better performance on its single worst attribute compared to a_7, making it a more acceptable compromise solution under VIKOR's framework.

Lastly, the ranking results derived by the ADAM and PROMETHEE II methods are the same, despite their fundamentally different mechanisms. PROMETHEE II is an outranking method based on net-flow scores from pairwise comparisons, while ADAM relies on a geometric volume calculation. Their agreement suggests that, for this decision context, the pairwise preference structure captured by PROMETHEE II corresponds closely to the geometric distinctions identified by ADAM—further validating the ranking results.

77.7 Conclusions

In this chapter, we have presented the ADAM method, a recent approach in the field of MADM. First, the theoretical background and core principles of ADAM are introduced, with emphasis on its geometric foundation based on the construction and volume calculation of complex polyhedra. Second, a review of relevant literature is provided. Third, the steps of the ADAM method are described in detail. A simple illustrative example is then presented to demonstrate the calculation process of ADAM. Subsequently, a more comprehensive evaluation involving seven suppliers is conducted to demonstrate the method's applicability to practical decision-making scenarios. Finally, a comparative analysis with other MADM methods is carried out to assess the performance characteristics and advantages of the ADAM method.

References

Agnusdei, L., Krstić, M., Palmi, P., & Miglietta, P. P. (2023). Digitalization as driver to achieve circularity in the agroindustry: A SWOT-ANP-ADAM approach. *Science of the Total Environment, 882*, 163441.

Badi, I., Bouraima, M. B., & Zonon, B. I. P. (2025). A multi-criteria decision-making model for prioritizing the causes of inflation in libya using the best-worst method and analytic hierarchy process. *Knowledge and Decision Systems with Applications, 1*, 165–176.

Demir, G. (2025). Fuzzy multi-criteria decision-making based security management: Risk assessment and countermeasure selection in smart cities. *Knowledge and Decision Systems with Applications, 1*, 70–91.

Demir, G., & Ulusoy, E. I. (2024). Wind power plant location selection with fuzzy logic and multi-criteria decision-making methods. *Computer and Decision Making: An International Journal, 1*, 211–234.

Gökalp, Y., Eti, S., Yüksel, S., & Dinçer, H. (2025). Towards sustainable healthcare: A fuzzy multi-criteria framework for green hospital investments. *Computer and Decision Making: An International Journal, 2*, 419–424.

Goswami, S. S. (2020). Outranking methods: PROMETHEE I and PROMETHEE II. *Foundations of Management, 12*, 93–110.

Goutam, S., Unnikrishnan, S., Karandikar, A., & Goutam, A. (2022). Algorithm for vertical handover decision using geometric mean and MADM techniques. *International Journal of Information Technology, 14*, 2691–2699.

He, S., Wang, Y., Peng, J., & Wang, J. (2022). Risk ranking of wind turbine systems through an improved FMEA based on probabilistic linguistic information and the TODIM method. *Journal of the Operational Research Society, 73*, 467–480.

Hong, X., Bai, X., & Song, Y. (2021). Selection of product recycling channels based on extended TODIM method. *Expert Systems with Applications, 168*, 114295.

Kovač, M., Tadić, S., Krstić, M., & Veljović, M. (2023). A methodology for planning city logistics concepts based on city-dry port micro-consolidation centres. *Mathematics, 11*, 3347.

Krstić, M., Agnusdei, G. P., Tadić, S., Kovač, M., & Miglietta, P. P. (2023). A novel axial-distance-based aggregated measurement (ADAM) method for the evaluation of agri-food circular-economy-based business models. *Mathematics, 11*, 1334.

Krstić, M., Agnusdei, L., Palmi, P., & Baležentis, T. (2024). Enabling organizations to strategically manage risks in circular supply chains. *Business Strategy and the Environment, 33*, 5996–6009.

Krstić, M., & Tadić, S. (2023). Hybrid multi-criteria decision-making model for optimal selection of cold chain logistics service providers. *Journal of Organizations, Technology and Entrepreneurship, 1*, 77–87.

Krstić, M., Tadić, S., Miglietta, P. P., & Porrini, D. (2025). Biodiversity protection practices in supply chain management: A novel hybrid grey best–worst method/axial distance-based aggregated measurement multi-criteria decision-making model. *Applied Sciences, 15*, 1354.

Lei, F., Wei, G., Gao, H., Wu, J., & Wei, C. (2020). TOPSIS method for developing supplier selection with probabilistic linguistic information. *International Journal of Fuzzy Systems, 22*, 749–759.

Munir, M., Mahmood, T., & Hussain, A. (2021). Algorithm for T-spherical fuzzy MADM based on associated immediate probability interactive geometric aggregation operators. *Artificial Intelligence Review, 54*, 6033–6061.

Popović, G., Mirčetić, V., & Karabašević, D. (2024). Selection of tourism accommodation facilities for development: An ADAM-based approach. *Quaestus, 24*, 133–149.

Qin, J., Liu, X., & Pedrycz, W. (2015). An extended VIKOR method based on prospect theory for multiple attribute decision making under interval type-2 fuzzy environment. *Knowledge-Based Systems, 86*, 116–130.

Tadić, S., Mićić, B., & Krstić, M. (2025). Evaluating sustainable intermodal transport routes: A hybrid fuzzy delphi-factor relationship (FARE)-axial distance based aggregated measurement (ADAM) model. *Sustainability, 17*, 6071.

Wang, H., & Liu, J. (2025). Some spherical uncertain linguistic aggregation operators and their application in multi-attribute decision-making. *Journal of Intelligent Decision Making and Granular Computing, 1*, 106–126.

Zhang, H. J., Zhou, Y., & Gan, Q. H. (2019). An extended PROMETHEE-II-based risk prioritization method for equipment failures in the geothermal power plant. *International Journal of Fuzzy Systems, 21*, 2490–2509.

Chapter 78

OPLO-POCOD: Opportunity losses-based polar coordinate distance for multi-attribute decision-making

Reza Sheikh and Soheila Senfi
Faculty of Industrial Management and Administration, Shahrood University of Technology, Shahrood, Iran

78.1 Introduction

The scarcity of money, time, and productive capacity, coupled with the central role of opportunity cost as the linchpin of economic reasoning, presents a fundamental challenge: every choice entails a foregone alternative, the value of which constitutes the opportunity cost. Scholars, however, diverge in their conceptual framing, debating whether this cost reflects the value of the best foregone alternative or the willingness to pay required to obtain a chosen alternative. These definitional nuances have significant implications for measurement, analysis, and policy (Fleckenstein et al., 2025). The discussion integrates insights from consumer psychology, noting that considering all available alternatives can complicate decision-making and influence satisfaction, yet the optimization logic remains paramount: individuals and organizations strive to select the best feasible alternative given information and constraints, producing trade-offs that illuminate opportunity costs (Kraszkiewicz, 2024).

Given the variety of definitions in the literature, many studies adopt the value of the best foregone alternative as the standard conception while recognizing value-based perspectives as well, aiming to provide a clear, practical foundation for applying the concept in theory and practice, with implications for personal decision-making and policy design (Breser, 2024). The introduction emphasizes that opportunity cost guides everyday decisions from budgeting and time management to broader policy choices and that a robust consideration of foregone opportunities can lead to more informed judgments, sharper analysis, and better decision-making in an ever-changing environment. It underscores the importance of explicitly stating the adopted conception of opportunity cost to ensure comparability and transparency, and it highlights how measurement choices influence conclusions and policy recommendations (Haghpour et al., 2022).

By weaving theoretical foundations with empirical and behavioral insights, the chapter offers a framework that accommodates both conventional economic reasoning and contemporary perspectives from psychology and behavioral economics, enabling readers to think critically about what is gained and what is forgone in any decision, and to communicate trade-offs effectively to stakeholders (O'Mahony, 2021). The practical relevance extends across personal finance, labor and time allocation, corporate strategy, and public policy, where opportunity costs shape budgets, capital allocation, opportunity-set evaluation, and program design (Suardana, 2025). The two-page narrative thus prepares readers for a structured exploration of concepts, methods, and applications: conceptual definitions, measurement challenges, methodological approaches to identifying and quantifying foregone opportunities, empirical illustrations across domains, and extensions that address behavioral deviations, dynamic settings, and context-specific adaptations (Sudirjo et al., 2024).

In summary, this integrated introduction establishes a rigorous yet accessible foundation that bridges microeconomic theory with real-world decision-making. It equips researchers, practitioners, and students with a coherent framework for reasoning about opportunity costs, conducting transparent analyses, and articulating trade-offs. This approach enhances accountability, understanding, and principled decision-making in environments defined by scarcity (Dwyer, 2025). The subsequent segments of this chapter are organized as follows: Section 78.2 delivers the literature review; Section 78.3 discusses the methodology; Section 78.4 presents numerical example 1, which centers on choosing a material for the brake

Encyclopedia of Multi-Attribute Decision-Making (MADM). DOI: https://doi.org/10.1016/B978-0-443-33275-3.00077-4

booster valve body in the vehicle; Section 78.5 provides numerical example 2, which addresses the assessment and prioritization of mutual funds; Section 78.6 outlines the validity check of the innovative method; and lastly, Section 78.7 wraps up with a concise summary of the findings and their implications.

78.2 Literature review

78.2.1 The concept of opportunity cost and opportunity losses

In managerial decision-making, opportunity cost represents the implicit cost of allocating scarce resources to a chosen project at the expense of the next-best alternative (Buchanan, 1987). This lost value can be analyzed from two complementary viewpoints: value-based (opportunity cost as the foregone benefits), which asks what the next-best alternative would be worth in terms of satisfaction, utility, or payoff, and price-based (opportunity cost as the implicit cost of resources), which highlights the resources time, money, inputs spent on the chosen alternative and their potential uses elsewhere (O'Mahony, 2021; Stone, 2015). These viewpoints are not merely labels; they can yield different numerical assessments of cost, such as when the market price of an alternative is X but a consumer would be willing to pay Y to obtain it, causing the opportunity cost to vary depending on whether we measure it by X or by Y. Consequently, definitions of opportunity cost can influence analysis, interpretation, and policy implications (Seele et al., 2021; Smith, 2004).

Opportunity losses (OPL) extend the concept by focusing on what is lost beyond direct expenditures, encompassing not only the explicit costs of a chosen path but also foregone opportunities that could have produced greater welfare under alternative scenarios. In decision-making under uncertainty, OPL are tied to the risk-adjusted value of forgone alternatives and the potential regret associated with choices that turn out unfavorably (Araf et al., 2025). The concept is central to both economics and management practice. Managers use OPL to evaluate decisions and strive to minimize potential foregone benefits, recognizing that the nature of OPL varies across contexts, manufacturing, service, transportation, and beyond (Mooney et al., 1996). In manufacturing, for example, OPL may include halted production, lost income, inventory shortages, unfulfilled orders, and diminished staff morale. To quantify and manage these intangible risks, businesses employ methods such as lost profit analysis, information asset value analysis, business process analysis, labor cost analysis, stock market reaction analysis, and other risk-management tools. These approaches help estimate potential losses and inform strategic choices (Roffia et al., 2025).

78.2.2 Understanding distance: concepts and measurement

In applied contexts, distance is interpreted within specific spatial-temporal frames. The polar coordinate system serves as a practical two-dimensional parameterization where a point is specified by the radius r and angle θ relative to the origin. Converting to Cartesian coordinates for tabulation or visualization uses $x = r\cos(\theta)$ and $y = r\sin(\theta)$ (Eiter & Mannila, 1997; Liu et al., 2025).

78.2.3 Polar coordinates distance

For plotting and visualization, Cartesian coordinates provide a point as (x, y) in the plane (and $[x, y, z]$ in space), representing offsets along the axes. Polar coordinates describe the same point with (r, θ), where r is the distance from the origin, and θ is the angle from the horizontal axis measured counterclockwise. The two representations are linked in the accompanying figures (Fig. 78.1; Fig. 78.2).

On a polar grid, every vector is represented by its magnitude r and its direction θ, with $\theta \in [0, 2\pi)$ and $r \geq 0$, which together cover the entire plane. The grid enhances intuition about angular separation between vectors. In the exemplar, points (4, 105 degrees) and (3, 225 degrees) are plotted on the grid (Fig. 78.3). The corresponding polar axes are shown in Fig. 78.4 (x-axis: radius; y-axis: angle), and the intervector angle is indicated in Fig. 78.5.

On a polar grid, the angle between two vectors is obtained by taking the absolute difference of their polar angles: $\Delta\theta = |225 \text{ degrees} - 105 \text{ degrees}| = 120$ degrees. This angular gap is indicated in Fig. 78.6, where the two points are plotted on the grid.

In Fig. 78.7, the gap between the first and second points is shown as the distance between two radial lines from the pole to (4, 105 degrees) and to (3, 225 degrees), highlighting the angular separation on the polar plot.

The cosine rule (law of cosines) says that for any triangle:

$$a^2 = b^2 + c^2 - 2bc\cos A, \tag{78.1}$$

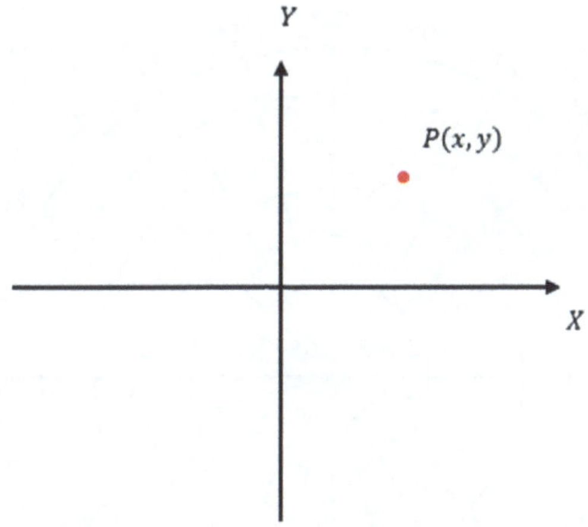

FIGURE 78.1 A point in Cartesian coordinates.

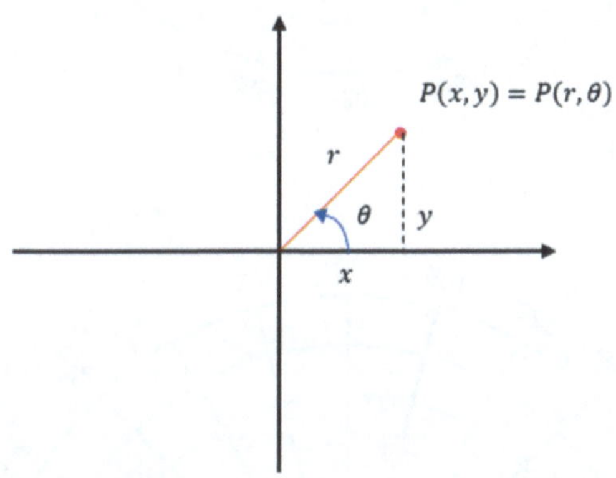

FIGURE 78.2 A point in polar coordinates.

This helps solve triangle problems. In our polar-grid setup, take the two known sides as b = 4 and c = 3, with the angle between them given by the difference of their polar angles (105 degrees and 225 degrees). The side a, which is the distance between the two polar points, can be found by plugging into the formula.

$$a^2 = 4^2 + 3^2 - 2(4)(3)cos120^\circ$$

$$a^2 = 16 - 9 - \left(24 * -\frac{1}{2}\right)$$

$$a^2 = 25 - (-12) = 37$$

$$a = \sqrt{37}.$$

Let two polar coordinates be ($r1$, $\theta 1$) and ($r2$, $\theta 2$), where $r1$ and $r2$ are the known radii. The angular separation between the corresponding radii is $\Delta\theta = \theta 2 - \theta 1$. Using the law of cosines with sides $r1$, $r2$, and included angle $\Delta\theta$, the opposite side length can be determined.

$$a^2 = b^2 + c^2 - 2bc \cos A,$$

In place of an unnamed side, we employ d to signify the separation between the two known sides, following the conventions established in Eqs. 78.2 and 78.3.

$$d^2 = r_1{}^2 + r_2{}^2 - 2r_1r_2cos(\theta_2 - \theta_1), \tag{78.2}$$

$$d = \sqrt{r_1{}^2 + r_2{}^2 - 2r_1r_2cos(\theta_2 - \theta_1)}, \tag{78.3}$$

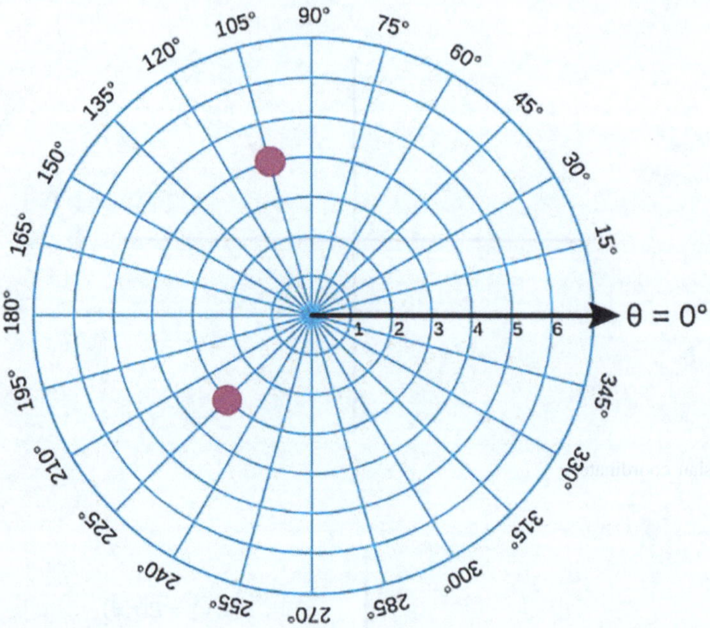

FIGURE 78.3 Two points shown on the grid.

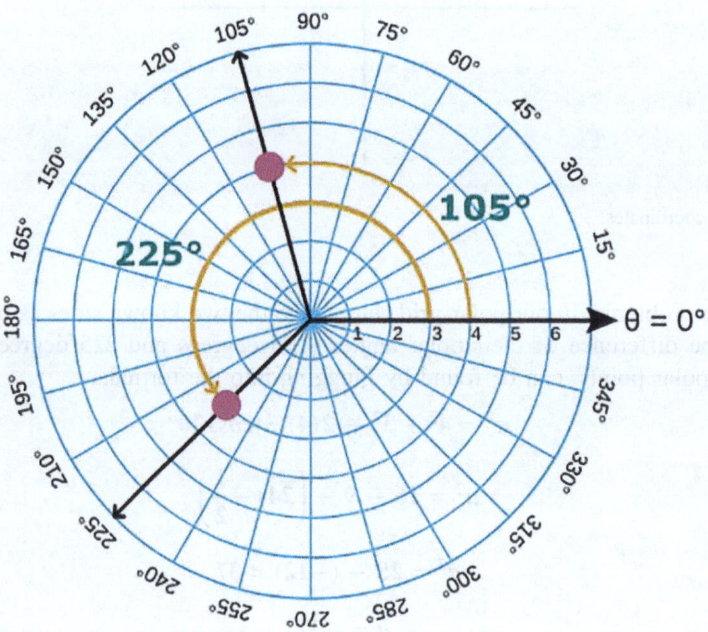

FIGURE 78.4 Angle between a point and the origin.

78.2.4 Cosine similarity

From a geometric viewpoint, two nonzero vectors are compared by the angle between them, computed via the dot product:

$$\cos(\theta) = (a \cdot b)/(\|a\|\ \|b\|).$$

This matches the form presented as (78.4) in the literature (Nugraheni & Sari, 2022; Ye, 2011).

$$\mathbf{A.}\ B = \|A\|\,\|B\|\cos\theta, \tag{78.4}$$

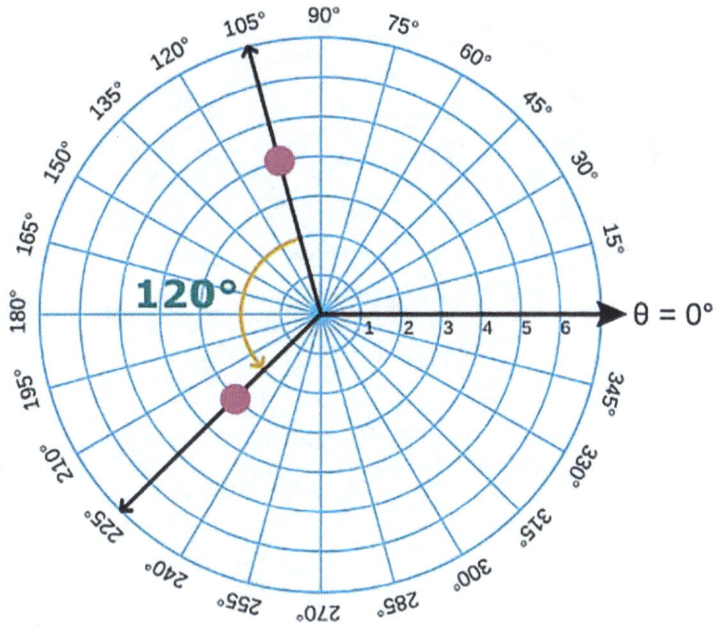

FIGURE 78.5 Angle between two grid points.

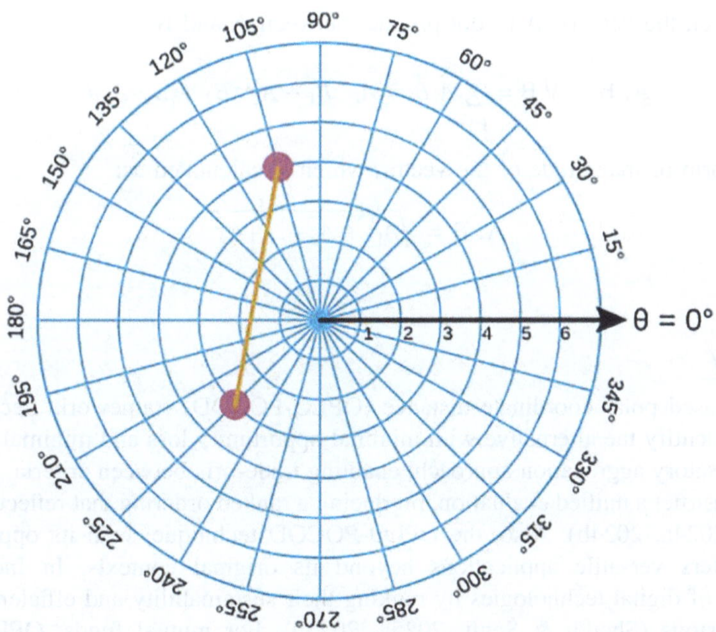

FIGURE 78.6 Distance between two grid points.

The similarity between vectors A and B is quantified by the cosine of the angle between them, cos(θ), obtained from their inner product and their norms (as given by Eq. 78.5). Specifically, cos(θ) is computed from the dot product ⟨A, B⟩ and the magnitudes ||A|| and ||B||, via the standard relation cos(θ) = ⟨A, B⟩ / (||A|| ||B||).

$$\textbf{\textit{Cosine}}\ \textit{similarity} = S_C(\boldsymbol{A},\ \boldsymbol{B}) := \cos(\theta) = \frac{\boldsymbol{A}.\ \boldsymbol{B}}{\|\boldsymbol{A}\|\ \ \|\boldsymbol{B}\|} = \frac{\sum_{i=1}^{n} A_i B_i}{\sqrt{\sum_{i=1}^{n} A_i^2}\ \sqrt{\sum_{i=1}^{n} B_i^2}}, \tag{78.5}$$

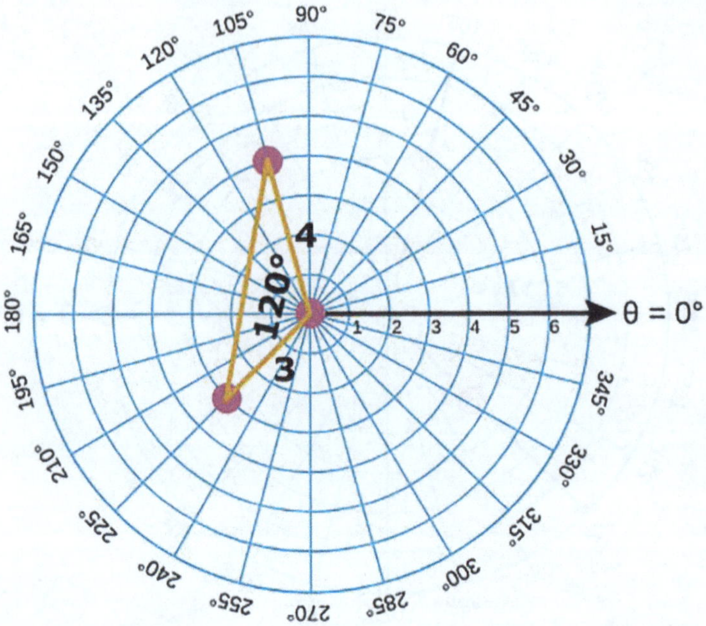

FIGURE 78.7 Geometric interpretation of the distance.

Where θ is the angle between the vectors, A.B, dot product between A and B.

$$A.\ B = A^T B = \sum_{i=1}^{n} A_i B_i = A_1 \quad B_1 + A_2 \quad B_2 + \ldots + A_n \ B_n,$$

||A|| represents the L2 norm or magnitude of the vector, which is calculated as:

$$A.\ B = \sqrt{A_1^2 + A_2^2 + \ldots + A_n^2}$$

78.3 Methodology

In the opportunity-losses-based polar coordinate distance (OPLO-POCOD) framework, decision choices are evaluated across multiple criteria to identify the alternative with minimal opportunity loss and minimal distance in the polar space. The method uses a compensatory aggregation approach, enabling trade-offs between criteria. Qualitative and quantitative factors are quantified to construct a unified evaluation, producing a ranked ordering that reflects the best overall balance of criteria (Sheikh & Senfi, 2024a, 2024b). Also, the OPLO-POCOD technique, with its opportunity-losses–based polar coordinate framework, offers versatile applications beyond its original contexts. In Industry 4.0, it can support prioritization and selection of digital technologies by ranking their sustainability and efficiency impacts, guiding capital allocation and policy decisions (Sheikh & Senfi, 2025a, 2025b). For mutual funds, OPLO-POCOD enables robust evaluation and classification of investment alternatives by balancing trade-offs among risk, return, liquidity, and fees, even when data are uncertain or imprecise (Sheikh & Senfi, 2024a, 2024b).

In customer analytics, the method can classify customers into promoters, passives, and detractors, and rank service improvements by measuring OPL across multiple satisfaction dimensions (Sheikh & Senfi, 2023). Within service organizations, OPLO-POCOD can assess and benchmark performance across operational dimensions (e.g., reliability, responsiveness, empathy, assurance, tangibles) to identify high-impact improvement areas (Sheikh et al., 2024). Finally, for quality-of-life research, the approach can integrate diverse indicators, such as economic, health, education, and environmental factors, into a coherent ranking that highlights policy levers with the greatest potential to reduce OPL and enhance overall well-being. Across these domains, the method's compensatory aggregation and polar-distance perspective help reconcile conflicting criteria, support transparent decision-making, and provide actionable insights for managers and policymakers (Sheikh & Senfi, 2025a, 2025b).

78.3.1 The executive steps of the opportunity losses-based polar coordinate distance method are as follows

Step 1. Initialization of the decision matrix.

Construct the initial decision matrix, containing m alternatives evaluated against n criteria, with entries a_{ij} (forming A ∈ ℝ^{$m \times n$}). This matrix is assembled from the information supplied by the decision-maker, as described by Eq. (78.6).

$$A = \begin{bmatrix} a_{11} & \cdots & a_{1j} & \cdots & a_{1n} \\ \vdots & \ddots & \vdots & \ddots & \vdots \\ a_{i1} & \cdots & a_{ij} & \cdots & a_{in} \\ \vdots & \ddots & \vdots & \ddots & \vdots \\ a_{m1} & \cdots & a_{mj} & \cdots & a_{mn} \end{bmatrix}_{m \times n}, \quad i = 1 \quad to\ m;\ j = 1 \quad to\ n. \tag{78.6}$$

The decision matrix comprises elements x_{ij}, where i indexes alternatives and j indexes criteria.

Across survey research, multiple rating scales have been proposed to capture subjective judgments. The Likert scale, introduced by Likert in 1932, is arguably the most common instrument for assessing attitudes. Users respond on a five- or seven-point scale, with each alternative assigned a numerical value to quantify the attitude under study (Table 78.1) (Ponsiglione et al., 2022).

Step 2. Formation of the normalized decision matrix.

If the units of measurement for the criteria are not the same, the normalized matrix (9) is constructed based on linear normalization, as illustrated in Eqs. (78.7) and (78.8).

$$n_{ij} = \frac{x_{ij}}{\sum_{i=1}^{m} x_{ij}} \text{For profit nature} \tag{78.7}$$

$$n_{ij} = \frac{1/x_{ij}}{\sum_{i=1}^{m} 1/x_{ij}} \text{For cost nature} \tag{78.8}$$

$$X = \begin{bmatrix} x_{11} & \cdots & x_{1j} & \cdots & x_{1n} \\ \vdots & \ddots & \vdots & \ddots & \vdots \\ x_{i1} & \cdots & x_{ij} & \cdots & x_{in} \\ \vdots & \ddots & \vdots & \ddots & \vdots \\ x_{m1} & \cdots & x_{mj} & \cdots & x_{mn} \end{bmatrix}_{m x n}, \quad i = 1 \quad to\ m; j = 1 \quad to\ n. \tag{78.9}$$

Step 3. Constitution of the opportunity losses matrix.

For every criterion state, determine the regret by taking the difference between the state's payoff and the extremal payoff (the maximum in gain scenarios or the minimum in cost scenarios). The resulting matrix summarizes the foregone opportunities for all alternatives and criteria.

$$\textit{Opportunity Loss} = \textit{best value for each action} - \quad \textit{value course of action}. \tag{78.10}$$

$$\begin{array}{c} \\ X = \\ \\ \text{Best value} \end{array} \begin{array}{c} \begin{matrix} & c_1 & & c_j & & c_n \end{matrix} \\ \begin{bmatrix} x_{11} & \cdots & x_{1j} & \cdots & x_{1n} \\ \vdots & \ddots & \vdots & \ddots & \vdots \\ x_{i1} & \cdots & x_{ij} & \cdots & x_{in} \\ \vdots & \ddots & \vdots & \ddots & \vdots \\ x_{m1} & \cdots & x_{mj} & \cdots & x_{mn} \end{bmatrix}_{m x n} \\ \begin{matrix} & x_{i1}^* & & x_{ij}^* & & x_{in}^* \end{matrix} \end{array}, \quad i = 1\ to\ m\ ;\ j = 1\ to\ n.$$

TABLE 78.1 Seven-point scale-based assessment of attitudes.

Poor	Fairly weak	Medium	Fairly good	Good	Very good	Excellent
1	2	3	4	5	6	7

For each state, define x_{best} as the minimum value when the criterion is negative, and as the maximum value when the criterion is positive.

$$X = \begin{bmatrix} x_{11}-x_1^* & \cdots & x_{1j}-x_j^* & \cdots & x_{1n}-x_n^* \\ \vdots & \ddots & \vdots & \ddots & \vdots \\ x_{i1}-x_1^* & \cdots & x_{ij}-x_j^* & \cdots & x_{in}-x_n^* \\ \vdots & \ddots & \vdots & \ddots & \vdots \\ x_{m1}-x_1^* & \cdots & x_{mj}-x_j^* & \cdots & x_{mn}-x_n^* \end{bmatrix}_{m\times n} \begin{matrix} \\ \\ ,\quad i = 1\ to\ m; \quad j = 1\ to\ n. \end{matrix}$$

(columns c_1, c_j, c_n)

$$Opportunity\ losses = |x_{ij} - x_{best}|\ for \quad \forall \quad x_{ij}\ i = 1 \quad to\ m; j = 1 \quad to\ n. \tag{78.13}$$

Following Eqs. 78.9 and 78.13, the OPL matrix is constructed in accordance with Eq. 78.11. This formulation yields a matrix that encapsulates the foregone benefits across alternatives, as dictated by the relationships specified in these equations.

$$\text{OPL} = \begin{bmatrix} opl_{11} & \cdots & opl_{1j} & \cdots & opl_{1n} \\ \vdots & \ddots & \vdots & \ddots & \vdots \\ opl_{i1} & \cdots & opl_{ij} & \cdots & opl_{in} \\ \vdots & \ddots & \vdots & \ddots & \vdots \\ opl_{m1} & \cdots & opl_{mj} & \cdots & opl_{mn} \end{bmatrix}_{m\times n} ,\quad i = 1\ to\ m;\ j = 1\ to\ n.$$

(columns c_1, c_j, c_n)

Step 4. At this stage, the X_{pair}, an ordered pair matrix, is constructed. Each ordered pair comprises the component x_{ij} (as defined in Eq. 78.11) and the corresponding opl_{ij} (as given in Eq. 78.13). This pairing captures both the performance score and the foregone-value information for every alternative–criterion entry.

$$Xpair_{ij} = (x_{ij}, \quad OPL_{ij}), \quad i = 1 \quad to\ m; j = 1 \quad to\ n. \tag{78.15}$$

$$X_{pair} = \begin{bmatrix} (x_{11}, opl_{11}) & \ldots & (x_{1j}, opl_{1j}) & \ldots & (x_{1n}, opl_{1n}) \\ \vdots & \ddots & \vdots & \ddots & \vdots \\ (x_{i1}, opl_{i1}) & \ldots & (x_{ij}, opl_{ij}) & \ldots & (x_{in}, opl_{in}) \\ \vdots & \ddots & \vdots & \ddots & \vdots \\ (x_{m1}, opl_{m1}) & \ldots & (x_{mj}, opl_{mj}) & \ldots & (x_{mn}, opl_{mn}) \end{bmatrix}_{m\times n}, \tag{78.16}$$

$$i = 1 to\ m; j = 1 to\ n.$$

Step 5. Compute the distance matrix expressed in polar coordinates.

In this stage, the distance from each evaluated point to the optimal reference for its criterion is determined. Specifically, each point is given by (x_{ij}, opl_{ij}), and the corresponding benchmark point for the same criterion is (x_{best}, $opl_{x_{best}}$). By definition, the reference opportunity loss satisfies $opl_{x_{best}} = 0$, and the polar-distance to this best point is computed accordingly.

Eq. 78.14 provides the distance between these two points.

$$d_{ij} = \sqrt{A_{ij}^2 + B_{ij}^2 - 2A_{ij}B_{ij}\cos(\theta_2 - \theta_1)}, \tag{78.17}$$

Which $A = (xij, plij)$ and $B = (xbest, oplxbest)$ and $(A, \theta 1)$ and $(B, \theta 2)$.

$$\mathbf{A.\ B} = \|A\| \quad \|B\| \cos\theta$$

$$\cos(\theta_2 - \theta_1) = \frac{\text{A. B}}{\|\text{A}\| \quad \|\text{B}\|} = \frac{\sum_{i=1}^{n} A_i B_i}{\sqrt{\sum_{i=1}^{n} A_i^2}\sqrt{\sum_{i=1}^{n} B_i^2}}$$

The cosine similarity from Eq. 78.5 yields the angular difference between vectors, whose cosine is used. In line with Eq. 78.18, the distance matrix D is assembled accordingly.

$$D = \begin{bmatrix} d_{11} & \dots & d_{1j} & \dots & d_{1n} \\ \vdots & \ddots & \vdots & \ddots & \vdots \\ d_{i1} & \dots & d_{ij} & \dots & d_{in} \\ \vdots & \ddots & \vdots & \ddots & \vdots \\ d_{m1} & \dots & d_{mj} & \dots & d_{mn} \end{bmatrix}_{m \times n}, \quad i = 1 \quad to\ m;\ j = 1 \quad to\ n. \tag{78.18}$$

Step 6. Construction of the weighted distance matrix.

Given that the criteria carry different magnitudes, appropriate weights are assigned to each criterion. Consequently, the weighted distance matrix D_w (as in Eq. 78.20) is derived from Eq. 78.19.

$$\overline{d}_{ij} = w_j * d_{ij} \tag{78.19}$$

$$D_w = \begin{bmatrix} \overline{d}_{11} & \dots & \overline{d}_{1j} & \dots & \overline{d}_{1n} \\ \vdots & \ddots & \vdots & \ddots & \vdots \\ \overline{d}_{i1} & \dots & \overline{d}_{ij} & \dots & \overline{d}_{in} \\ \vdots & \ddots & \vdots & \ddots & \vdots \\ \overline{d}_{m1} & \dots & \overline{d}_{mj} & \dots & \overline{d}_{mn} \end{bmatrix}_{m \times n}, \quad i = 1 \quad to\ m; j = 1 \quad to\ n. \tag{78.20}$$

Step 7. Calculate the total distance.

During this step, the aggregate distance for every alternative (row) is calculated according to the formula shown thereafter:

$$S_i = \sum_{j=1}^{n} \overline{d}_{ij}, \quad i = 1 \quad to\ m. \tag{78.21}$$

$$S_T = \sum_{i=1}^{m} S_i \tag{78.22}$$

Here, S_T is the total distance.

Step 8. For each alternative, compute the opportunity loss and the corresponding percentage of opportunity achieved with the equation below.

$$Degree\ opportunity\ loss\,(DOL_i) = \frac{S_i}{S_T}, \tag{78.23}$$

Here, $\sum_{i=1}^{m} DOL_i = 1$.

$$Percentage\ of\ opportunity\ achievement\,(POA_i) = 1 - DOL_i. \tag{78.24}$$

The DOL_i metric is confined to the interval [0, 1], where values nearer to 0 indicate fewer opportunities for the top-ranked alternative, and values nearer to 1 signify greater opportunities for the lowest-ranked alternative. In discussing the POA_i value, it is important to note that numbers close to zero reflect a reduced level of opportunity realization for that particular alternative (the eventual bottom rank), while values close to one indicate enhanced opportunity realization (the top rank). The methodology offers several advantages. First, by incorporating OPL, it provides a more comprehensive evaluation of alternatives, accounting for potential benefits foregone when choosing one alternative over another. Second, the polar-coordinate representation of pairwise distances among alternatives offers an intuitive understanding of their relative positions. Third, the framework enables a thorough assessment across multiple criteria, capturing the complexity inherent in real-world decision problems. Fourth, OPLO-POCOD introduces distinctive features, notably transforming OPL into polar distances, thus presenting a novel perspective on decision-making. Finally, the approach aims to minimize OPL, modeling the decision-maker's preferences to support more informed and effective choices. In summary, the OPLO-POCOD technique yields meaningful advantages and adds value to the suite of multicriteria decision-making methods.

78.3.2 Schematic diagram

Fig. 78.8 shows the schematic of the OPLO-POCOD method for determining alternative priorities.

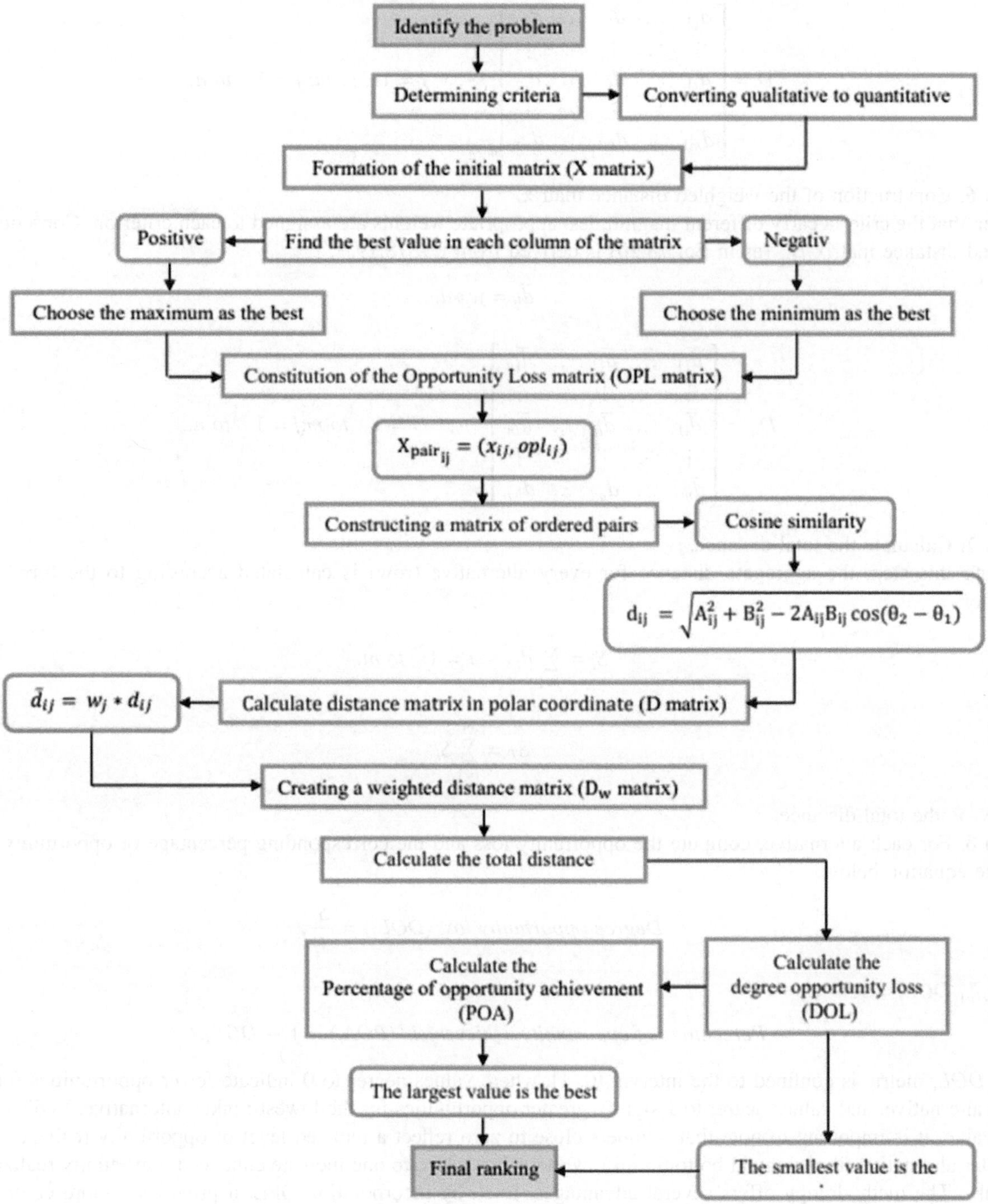

FIGURE 78.8 A schematic overview of the ordered steps underpinning the proposed methodology.

78.4 Material selection for the brake booster valve body in an automotive application

To demonstrate the OPLO-POCOD framework, we employ an exemplar within this segment. The task of selecting valve-body materials for booster-system failures in automotive contexts serves as a pertinent test case for the proposed methodology, aligning with the analysis conducted in Moradian's work. This particular problem has also been addressed through a variety of MADM approaches. To apply the authors' approach to the material-selection problem, the following sequence of steps is recommended:

Step 1. Formation of the preliminary decision matrix. Based on the compiled data, the initial decision matrix is constructed, comprising four evaluation criteria across 16 alternatives, as indicated in Table 78.2.

In this set of criteria, C1 and C2 are positive criteria, while C3 and C4 are negative criteria. Specifically, C1 represents tensile strength (maximum - positive), C2 represents material deviation temperature (maximum - positive), C3 represents material density (minimum - negative), and C4 represents product cost (minimum - negative). The overall interpretation is that higher values of C1 and C2 are favorable, whereas lower values of C3 and C4 are favorable.

The weights of the criteria were determined based on pairwise comparisons by experts and are shown in the last row of Table 78.2.

Step 2. Construction of the best value matrix. In this stage, the optimal value for each column of Table 78.3 is determined. As illustrated in Table 78.3, the best value for criteria C3 and C4 is the minimum entry in their respective columns, whereas for the remaining criteria, it is the maximum entry.

Step 3. Forming the OPL matrix. According to relations 2–6, the OPL matrices are formed as shown in Table 78.4.

Step 4. Forming the ordered pair matrix. Based on relations 12 and 13, the ordered-pair matrices of the alternatives are formed (Table 78.5).

Step 5. Creating the distance matrix in polar space. According to relations 7–10, the distance matrix is computed as shown in Table 78.6.

Step 6. Creating the weighted distance matrix. Using the expert-provided weights, the weighted distance matrix is computed as shown in Table 78.7.

TABLE 78.2 Initial decision matrix.

Room no.	C1	C2	C3	C4
	Max	Max	Min	Min
A1	**80***[a]	80	1.37	1
A2	185	222	1.66	1.5
A3	36	53	0.9	1.6
A4	110	150	1.1	2.3
Weight	0.5405	0.1802	0.0688	0.2015

[a] *Value* =80.*

TABLE 78.3 Best value matrix.

Room no.	C1	C2	C3	C4
	Max	Max	Min	Min
Best value	185.00*[a]	222.00	0.90	1.00

[a] *Best value* =185.*

TABLE 78.4 Opportunity losses matrix of the alternatives.

Room no.	C1	C2	C3	C4
A1	**105.00***[a]	142.00	0.47	0.00
A2	0.00	0.00	0.76	0.50
A3	149.00	169.00	0.00	0.60
A4	75.00	72.00	0.20	1.30

[a] *OPL*=|80 − 185| = 105.*

TABLE 78.5 Pairwise comparison matrix of the alternatives.

Room no.	C1	C2	C3	C4
	Max	Max	Min	Min
A1	**(80,105)*[a]**	(80,142)	(1.37,0.47)	(1,0)
A2	(185,0)	(222,0)	(1.66,0.76)	(1.5,0.5)
A3	(36,149)	(53,169)	(0.9,0)	(1.6,0.6)
A4	(110,75)	(150,72)	(1.1,0.2)	(2.3,1.3)

[a] *A = (80, 105); B = (185, 0).*

TABLE 78.6 Distance matrix of each alternative from the best value.

Room no.	C1	C2	C3	C4
A1	**148.49*[a]**	200.82	0.66	0.00
A2	0.00	0.00	1.07	0.71
A3	210.72	239.00	0.00	0.85
A4	106.07	101.82	0.28	1.84

[a] *IIAII = 132; IIBII = 185; IIAII IIBII = 24,420.70; A.B = 14,800; cosθ = 14,800 / (24,420.7) = 0.6060; d* = 148.49.*

TABLE 78.7 Weighted distance matrix.

Room No.	C1	C2	C3	C4
A1	**80.26*[a]**	36.19	0.05	0.00
A2	0.00	0.00	0.07	0.14
A3	113.89	43.07	0.00	0.17
A4	57.33	18.35	0.02	0.37

[a] $\bar{d}^* = 80.26$.

Step 7. Computing the total distance and degree of opportunity losses (DOL) and the percentage of opportunity achieved (POA). Following relations 13–16, the values of OPL and opportunity gained are obtained as shown in Table 78.8.

Step 8. Ranking the alternatives. Based on the DOL and POA values, the alternatives are ranked as shown in Table 78.9.

Total Distance, DOL, and POA for each alternative (A1 to A4) have been computed. For each alternative, DOL indicates the share of the total OPL attributed to that alternative, and POA is its complement (the opportunity gained); the values in Table 78.8 show that A2 has a very small DOL (0.000619) and an almost complete POA (0.999381), indicating the highest share of opportunity gained and consequently relatively good performance. A1, A4, and A3 have progressively higher DOL values, reflecting more opportunity losses relative to the total, with A3 having the highest DOL (0.449066) and the lowest POA (0.550934). In general, the smaller the DOL, the better the alternative performs relative to the whole set, and the higher the POA. Ranking of the alternatives based on DOL and POA has been performed, and because the relationship between DOL and POA is inverse, typically alternatives with lower DOL and higher POA appear higher in the ranking; Table 78.9 shows that A2 is the best alternative with rank 1 (lowest DOL and highest POA), A4 ranks second, A1 ranks third, and A3 ranks fourth, the worst among these criteria. If the goal is optimization, usually alternatives with low DOL and high POA are preferred; in this set, A2 is the best alternative, and A3 has the poorest performance.

TABLE 78.8 Opportunity losses degree and percentage of opportunity gained for the alternatives.

Room no.	DOL	POA
A1	0.332925*[a]	0.667075*[b]
A2	0.000619	0.999381
A3	0.449066	0.550934
A4	0.217391	0.782609

[a] $Si^* = 80.26 + 36.19 + 0.05 + 0 = 116.49$, $ST^* = 349.91$, $DOL^* = 116.49 / 349.91 = 0.332925$.
[b] $POA^* = 1 - 0.332925 = 0.667075$.

TABLE 78.9 Ranking of the alternatives.

Room no.	Rank
A1	3
A2	1
A3	4
A4	2

78.5 Numerical example 2: evaluation and prioritization of mutual funds

Mutual funds have a long history, beginning in 1882 with the emergence of the first investment company by William O. and continuing with the establishment of the modern mutual fund in Boston in 1924. Iran follows this pattern: mutual funds trace back to 2004–2005 (1383) with the approval of the regulations for providing advisory services and portfolio management and the regulations for establishing a mutual investment portfolio, leading to the formation of both pooled and dedicated mutual portfolios. After the securities market law was enacted in November 2005 (1394), the first mutual fund started operating in March 2007 (1387). The early pioneers, Pooya, Bank Saderat, Hafez, Khabgaran Saam, Pishtez, and Bank Melli, launched mutual funds officially and via public subscriptions; within five years, the number of mutual funds grew to 87 by the end of 2012 (1391). Today, in 1402, there are 428 active mutual funds in the capital market. For this study, equity funds were selected from the broader set of active mutual funds to assess performance, with 107 active equity funds listed on the Tehran Stock Exchange, available as either exchange-traded funds (ETFs) or mutual funds that rely on creation and redemption mechanisms. In creation-and-redemption mutual funds, investors are issued units upon inquiry, and upon payment and transactions in ETFs, the mutual fund units are redeemed, similar to trading shares on the stock market. Using data from the Iran Financial Information Processing Center (FIPiran) and applying filters for mutual fund size and 1-, 2-, and 3-year performance, 20 equity mutual funds with the largest assets and strongest performance were selected. The chosen mutual funds include Aseman armani saham, Bazar omid afarin, Firozeh movafaghiat, Hamyan sepehr, Hasti bakhsh agah, Moshtarek agah, Moshtarek arzesh kavan ayande, Moshtarek Bank khavarmiane, Moshtarek kargozari Bank meli iran, Moshtarek omid toseh, Moshtarek pishro, Moshtarek pishtaz, Moshtarek yekom aban, Moshtarek yekom exir farabi, Ofoghe melat, Sahami sepand karizma, Sarv sodmand modaberan, Sepehr aval bazar, Tejarat shakhesi kardan, and Toseh atlas mofid. These equity funds offer alternative choices prioritized according to predefined criteria. The evaluation framework combines two categories of criteria, qualitative and quantitative, with quantitative measures comprising "Mutual Fund Characteristics" and "Mutual Fund Performance Evaluation Criteria," and a qualitative measure capturing the "Personality Characteristics of the Mutual Fund Manager," which are quantified on a Likert scale; numerous subcriteria accompany each main criterion as detailed in Table 78.10.

Implementation of the OPLO-POCOD technique

Step 1. Forming the initial decision matrix. Based on the data obtained for the considered mutual funds, the initial decision matrix is constructed according to Table 78.11.

TABLE 78.10 Criteria and subcriteria for evaluating the performance of mutual funds.

Criteria	C1			C2		C3						
	Features of mutual fund			**Personality characteristics of the mutual fund managers**		**Criteria for evaluating the performance of the mutual fund**						
Subcriteria	SC1	SC2	SC3	SC4	SC5	SC6	SC7	SC8	SC9	SC10	SC11	SC12
	Mutual fund size	Life cycle	Degree of diversity of the portfolio	Average managers' literacy	Managers' performance	Beta coefficient	Jensen's alpha index	Annual return	Sharpe ratio	Sortino ratio	Treynor ratio	M2 ratio
The nature of the subcriteria	Positive maximum	Positive maximum	Positive maximum	Positive maximum	Positive maximum	Positive maximum	Positive maximum	Positive maximum	Positive maximum	Positive maximum	Positive maximum	Positive maximum

TABLE 78.11 Initial decision matrix.

The nature of the subcriteria	+	+	+	+	+	+	+	+	+	+	+	+
subcriteria	**SC1**	**SC2**	**SC3**	**SC4**	**SC5**	**SC6**	**SC7**	**SC8**	**SC9**	**SC10**	**SC11**	**SC12**
A1	2517586747127	16.666667	110	5.3	5	0.77	29.8	58.8	0.41	0.65	0.53	0.99
A2	2563450617565	16.666667	55	3.7	4	0.89	10.82	41.82	0.23	0.38	0.27	0.65
A3	2205263995208	16.668333	110	3.7	3	0.99	15.08	48.08	0.26	0.38	0.3	0.48
A4	4017049966738	16.666667	94	4.8	4	1.02	16.58	49.58	0.27	0.45	0.31	0.76
A5	9860020533520	16.666667	109	4	5	0.9	19.78	51.78	0.33	0.97	0.37	0.84
A6	3028782903895	16.666667	142	4	1	1.24	-1.91	35.09	0.14	0.22	0.14	0.35
A7	5933164640040	16.485	42	5.3	5	0.98	19.16	51.16	0.29	0.47	0.34	0.52
A8	7486951933077	16.603333	112	5	4	0.93	19.23	51.23	0.31	0.49	0.36	0.52
A9	1773243155638	16.666667	150	4.7	5	0.85	31.3	62.3	0.46	0.85	0.52	1.08
A10	4166591326633	16.666667	175	2.7	4	0.98	9.06	42.06	0.24	0.41	0.24	0.42
A11	6281662878022	16.666667	165	1.7	3	0.81	6.01	36.01	0.2	0.3	0.22	0.36
A12	10191492328668	16.666667	119	2.3	4	0.94	9.63	41.63	0.24	0.46	0.25	0.66
A13	10408189307434	16.666667	107	1.7	3	1.15	18.82	53.82	0.31	0.56	0.31	0.54
A14	23230485566433	46.311667	178	5.3	5	0.88	17.15	48.15	0.33	0.66	0.34	0.8
A15	17859556054519	40.251667	142	2.7	4	0.94	16.26	48.26	0.31	0.61	0.32	0.79
A16	2521726598465	46.29	178	4.8	3	1.03	21.32	55.32	0.35	0.62	0.36	0.56
A17	2859712921289	42.835	159	2	1	0.94	10.67	42.67	0.24	0.37	0.26	0.43
A18	2286149895813	32.986667	98	2.3	3	1.2	9.94	45.94	0.23	0.42	0.23	0.68
A19	12601761721265	30.798333	86	1.3	5	0.87	15.16	45.16	0.27	0.42	0.31	0.45
A20	3584326079395	33.476667	101	4	4	1.08	16.42	50.42	0.3	0.51	0.3	0.51

TABLE 78.12 Best value matrix.

subcriteria	SC1	SC2	SC3	SC4	SC5	SC6	SC7	SC8	SC9	SC10	SC11	SC12
Best value	23230-48556-6433	46.31	178.00	5.30	5.00	1.24	31.30	62.30	0.46	0.97	0.53	1.08

TABLE 78.13 Opportunity losses matrix of mutual funds.

	SC1	SC2	SC3	SC4	SC5	SC6	SC7	SC8	SC9	SC10	SC11	SC12
A1	20712898819306	29.645	68	0	0	0.47	1.5	3.5	0.05	0.32	0	0.09
A2	20667034948868	29.645	123	1.6	1	0.35	20.48	20.48	0.23	0.59	0.25	0.43
A3	21025221571225	29.64333	68	1.6	2	0.25	16.22	14.22	0.2	0.59	0.22	0.6
A4	19213435599695	29.645	84	0.5	1	0.22	14.72	12.72	0.19	0.52	0.22	0.32
A5	13370465032913	29.645	69	1.3	0	0.34	11.52	10.52	0.13	0.00	0.16	0.24
A6	20201702662538	29.645	36	1.3	4	0	33.21	27.21	0.32	0.75	0.39	0.73
A7	17297320926393	29.82667	136	0	0	0.26	12.14	11.14	0.17	0.50	0.19	0.56
A8	15743533633356	29.70833	66	0.3	1	0.31	12.07	11.07	0.15	0.48	0.17	0.56
A9	21457242410795	29.645	28	0.6	0	0.39	0	0	0	0.12	0.01	0
A10	19063894239800	29.645	3	2.6	1	0.26	22.24	20.24	0.22	0.56	0.29	0.66
A11	16948822688411	29.645	13	3.6	2	0.43	25.29	26.29	0.26	0.67	0.31	0.72
A12	13038993237765	29.645	59	3	1	0.3	21.67	20.67	0.22	0.51	0.28	0.42
A13	12822296258999	29.645	71	3.6	2	0.09	12.48	8.48	0.15	0.41	0.22	0.54
A14	0	0	0	0	0	0.36	14.15	14.15	0.13	0.31	0.19	0.28
A15	5370929511914	6.06	36	2.6	1	0.3	15.04	14.04	0.15	0.36	0.21	0.29
A16	20708758967968	0.021667	0	0.5	2	0.21	9.98	6.98	0.11	0.35	0.17	0.52
A17	20370772645144	3.476667	19	3.3	4	0.3	20.63	19.63	0.22	0.60	0.27	0.65
A18	20944335670620	13.325	80	3	2	0.04	21.36	16.36	0.23	0.55	0.3	0.4
A19	10628723845168	15.51333	92	4	0	0.37	16.14	17.14	0.19	0.55	0.22	0.63
A20	19646159487038	12.835	77	1.3	1	0.16	14.88	11.88	0.16	0.46	0.23	0.57

TABLE 78.14 Matrix of ordered pairs of alternatives.

	Mutual fund size	Life cycle	Degree of diversity of the portfolio	Average managers' literacy	Managers' performance
A1	(2517586747126.5,20712898819306)	(16.67,29.642)	(110,68)	(5.3,0)	(5,0)
A2	(2563450617564.5,20667034948868)	(16.666667,29.645)	(55,123)	(3.7,1.6)	(4,1)
A3	(2205263995207.5,21025221571225)	(16.668333,29.643334)	(110,68)	(3.7,1.6)	(3,2)
A4	(4017049966737.5,19213435599695)	(16.666667,29.645)	(94,84)	(4.8,0.5)	(4,1)
A5	(9860020533520,13370465032912.5)	(16.666667,29.645)	(109,69)	(4,1.3)	(5,0)
A6	(3028782903894.5,20201702662538)	(16.666667,29.645)	(142,36)	(4,1.3)	(1,4)
A7	(5933164640040,17297320926392.5)	(16.485,29.826667)	(42,136)	(5.3,0)	(5,0)
A8	(7486951933077,15743533633355.5)	(16.603333,29.708334)	(112,66)	(5,0.3)	(4,1)
A9	(1773243155638,21457242410794.5)	(16.666667,29.645)	(150,28)	(4.7,0.6)	(5,0)
A10	(4166591326632.5,19063894239800)	(16.666667,29.645)	(175,3)	(2.7,2.6)	(4,1)
A11	(6281662878021.5,16948822688411)	(16.666667,29.645)	(165,13)	(1.7,3.6)	(3,2)
A12	(10191492328668,13038993237764.5)	(16.666667,29.645)	(119,59)	(2.3,3)	(4,1)
A13	(10408189307434,12822296258998.5)	(16.666667,29.645)	(107,71)	(1.7,3.6)	(3,2)
A14	(23230485566432.5,0)	(46.311667,0)	(178,0)	(5.3,0)	(5,0)
A15	(17859556054518.5,5370929511914)	(40.251667,6.06)	(142,36)	(2.7,2.6)	(4,1)
A16	(2521726598464.5,20708758967968)	(46.29,0.021667)	(178,0)	(4.8,0.5)	(3,2)
A17	(2859712921289,20370772645143.5)	(42.835,3.476667)	(159,19)	(2,3.3)	(1,4)
A18	(2286149895812.5,20944335670620)	(32.986667,13.325)	(98,80)	(2.3,3)	(3,2)
A19	(12601761721265,10628723845167.5)	(30.798333,15.513334)	(86,92)	(1.3,4)	(5,0)
A20	(3584326079395,19646159487037.5)	(33.476667,12.835)	(101,77)	(4,1.3)	(4,1)

	Beta coefficient	Jensen's alpha index	Annual return	Sharpe ratio	Sortino ratio	Treynor ratio	M2 ratio
A1	(0.77,0.47)	(29.8,1.5)	(58.8,3.5)	(0.41,0.05)	(0.65,0.32)	(0.53,0)	(0.99,0.01)
A2	(0.89,0.35)	(10.82,20.48)	(41.82,20.48)	(0.23,0.23)	(0.38,0.59)	(0.27,0.25)	(0.65,0.43)
A3	(0.99,0.25)	(15.08,16.22)	(48.08,14.22)	(0.26,0.2)	(0.38,0.59)	(0.3,0.22)	(0.48,0.6)
A4	(1.02,0.22)	(16.58,14.72)	(49.58,12.72)	(0.27,0.19)	(0.45,0.52)	(0.31,0.22)	(0.76,0.32)
A5	(0.9,0.34)	(19.78,11.52)	(51.78,10.52)	(0.33,0.13)	(0.97,0)	(0.37,0.16)	(0.84,0.24)
A6	(1.24,0)	(-1.91,33.21)	(35.09,27.21)	(0.14,0.32)	(0.22,0.75)	(0.14,0.39)	(0.35,0.73)
A7	(0.98,0.26)	(19.16,12.14)	(51.16,11.14)	(0.29,0.17)	(0.47,0.5)	(0.34,0.19)	(0.52,0.56)
A8	(0.93,0.31)	(19.23,12.07)	(51.23,11.07)	(0.31,0.15)	(0.49,0.48)	(0.36,0.17)	(0.52,0.56)
A9	(0.85,0.39)	(31.3,0)	(62.3,0)	(0.46,0)	(0.85,0.12)	(0.52,0.01)	(1.08,0)
A10	(0.98,0.26)	(9.06,22.24)	(42.06,20.24)	(0.24,0.22)	(0.41,0.56)	(0.24,0.29)	(0.42,0.66)
A11	(0.81,0.43)	(6.01,25.29)	(36.01,26.29)	(0.2,0.26)	(0.3,0.67)	(0.22,0.31)	(0.36,0.72)
A12	(0.94,0.3)	(9.63,21.67)	(41.63,20.67)	(0.24,0.22)	(0.46,0.51)	(0.25,0.28)	(0.66,0.42)
A13	(1.15,0.09)	(18.82,12.48)	(53.82,8.48)	(0.31,0.15)	(0.56,0.41)	(0.31,0.22)	(0.54,0.54)
A14	(0.88,0.36)	(17.15,14.15)	(48.15,14.15)	(0.33,0.13)	(0.66,0.31)	(0.34,0.19)	(0.8,0.28)
A15	(0.94,0.3)	(16.26,15.04)	(48.26,14.04)	(0.31,0.15)	(0.61,0.36)	(0.32,0.21)	(0.79,0.29)
A16	(1.03,0.21)	(21.32,9.98)	(55.32,6.98)	(0.35,0.11)	(0.62,0.35)	(0.36,0.17)	(0.56,0.52)
A17	(0.94,0.3)	(10.67,20.63)	(42.67,19.63)	(0.24,0.22)	(0.37,0.6)	(0.26,0.27)	(0.43,0.65)
A18	(1.2,0.04)	(9.94,21.36)	(45.94,16.36)	(0.23,0.23)	(0.42,0.55)	(0.23,0.3)	(0.68,0.4)
A19	(0.87,0.37)	(15.16,16.14)	(45.16,17.14)	(0.27,0.19)	(0.42,0.55)	(0.31,0.22)	(0.45,0.63)
A20	(1.08,0.16)	(16.42,14.88)	(50.42,11.88)	(0.3,0.16)	(0.51,0.46)	(0.3,0.23)	(0.51,0.57)

TABLE 78.15 Distance matrix.

	SC1	SC2	SC3	SC4	SC5	SC6	SC7	SC8	SC9	SC10	SC11	SC12	Distance
A1	2930	41.920	96.167	0.000	0.000	0.665	2.121	4.950	0.071	0.453	0.000	0.127	3076.47
A2	2920	41.924	173.948	2.263	1.414	0.495	28.963	28.963	0.325	0.834	0.361	0.608	3200.10
A3	2970	41.922	96.167	2.263	2.828	0.354	22.939	20.110	0.283	0.834	0.318	0.849	3158.87
A4	2720	41.924	118.794	0.707	1.414	0.311	20.817	17.989	0.269	0.735	0.311	0.453	2923.72
A5	1890	41.924	97.581	1.838	0.000	0.481	16.292	14.878	0.184	0.000	0.226	0.339	2063.74
A6	2860	41.924	50.912	1.838	5.657	0.000	46.966	38.481	0.453	1.061	0.552	1.032	3048.88
A7	2450	42.181	192.333	0.000	0.000	0.368	17.169	15.754	0.240	0.707	0.269	0.792	2719.81
A8	2230	42.014	93.338	0.424	1.414	0.438	17.070	15.655	0.212	0.679	0.240	0.792	2402.28
A9	3030	41.924	39.598	0.849	0.000	0.552	0.000	0.000	0.000	0.170	0.014	0.000	3113.11
A10	2700	41.924	4.243	3.677	1.414	0.368	31.452	28.624	0.311	0.792	0.410	0.933	2814.15
A11	2400	41.924	18.385	5.091	2.828	0.608	35.765	37.180	0.368	0.948	0.438	1.018	2544.55
A12	1840	41.924	83.439	4.243	1.414	0.424	30.646	29.232	0.311	0.721	0.396	0.594	2033.34
A13	1810	41.924	100.409	5.091	2.828	0.127	17.649	11.993	0.212	0.580	0.311	0.764	1991.89
A14	0	0.000	0.000	0.000	0.000	0.509	20.011	20.011	0.184	0.438	0.269	0.396	41.82
A15	760	8.570	50.912	3.677	1.414	0.424	21.270	19.856	0.212	0.509	0.297	0.410	867.55
A16	2930	0.031	0.000	0.707	2.828	0.297	14.114	9.871	0.156	0.495	0.240	0.735	2959.47
A17	2880	4.917	26.870	4.667	5.657	0.424	29.175	27.761	0.311	0.849	0.382	0.919	2981.93
A18	2960	18.844	113.137	4.243	2.828	0.057	30.208	23.137	0.325	0.778	0.424	0.566	3154.55
A19	1500	21.939	130.108	5.657	0.000	0.523	22.825	24.240	0.269	0.778	0.311	0.891	1707.54
A20	2780	18.151	108.894	1.838	1.414	0.226	21.044	16.801	0.226	0.651	0.325	0.806	2950.38

TABLE 78.16 Total distance for each alternative.

Alternative	**A1**	**A2**	**A3**	**A4**	**A5**	**A6**	**A7**	**A8**	**A9**	**A10**
Distance	3076.47	3200.10	3158.87	2923.72	2063.74	3048.88	2719.81	2402.28	3113.11	2814.15
Alternative	A11	A12	A13	A14	A15	A16	A17	A18	A19	A20
Distance	2544.55	2033.34	1991.89	41.82	867.55	2959.47	2981.93	3154.55	1707.54	2950.38

TABLE 78.17 Degree of opportunity losses and percentage of opportunity gained.

Mutual fund	DOL	POA	Mutual fund	DOL	POA
A1	0.061833	0.938167	A11	0.051142	0.948858
A2	0.064318	0.935682	A12	0.040868	0.959132
A3	0.06349	0.93651	A13	0.040035	0.959965
A4	0.058763	0.941237	A14	0.000841	0.999159
A5	0.041479	0.958521	A15	0.017437	0.982563
A6	0.061279	0.938721	A16	0.059482	0.940518
A7	0.054665	0.945335	A17	0.059933	0.940067
A8	0.048283	0.951717	A18	0.063403	0.936597
A9	0.06257	0.93743	A19	0.03432	0.96568
A10	0.056561	0.943439	A20	0.059299	0.940701

TABLE 78.18 Ranking of mutual funds.

Alternative	Rank	Alternative	Rank
A1	16	**A11**	8
A2	20	**A12**	5
A3	19	**A13**	4
A4	11	**A14**	1
A5	6	**A15**	2
A6	15	**A16**	13
A7	9	**A17**	14
A8	7	**A18**	18
A9	17	**A19**	3
A10	10	**A20**	12

Step 2. Finding the best value for each criterion based on the nature of the criteria and subcriteria. Since all criteria and subcriteria in this study are of a positive nature, the best value for each subcriterion is the maximum value in its corresponding column. The best values are shown in Table 78.12.

Step 3. Forming the OPL Matrix. Given relations 2 to 5, the OPL matrices are formed as shown in Table 78.13.

Step 4. Forming the ordered pair matrix. Based on relation 6, the ordered pair matrices are formed as in Table 78.14.

Step 5. Creating the distance matrix in the polar space. According to relations 7 to 10, the distance from the best value is computed as in Table 78.15.

Step 6. Forming the weighted distance matrix. In this example, the weights of all criteria are taken as equal to 1. Therefore, the weighted distance matrix is the same as Table 78.15.

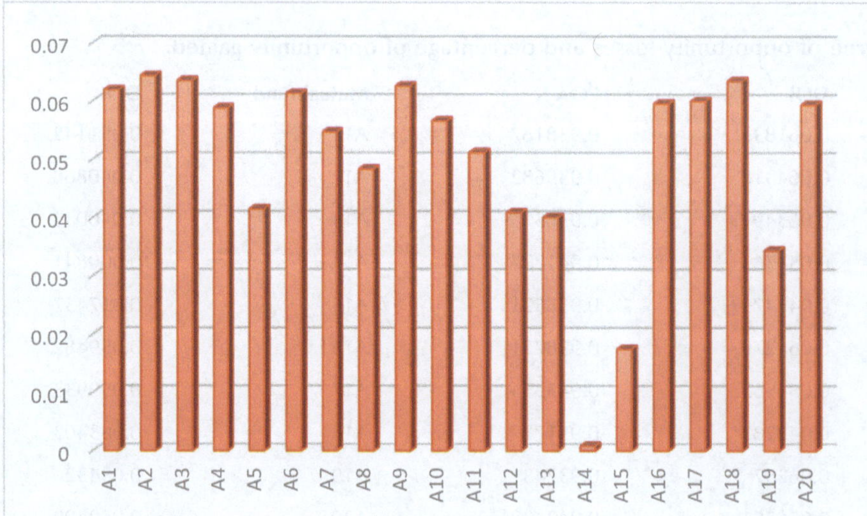

DIAGRAM 78.1 Comparison of mutual funds based on opportunity losses.

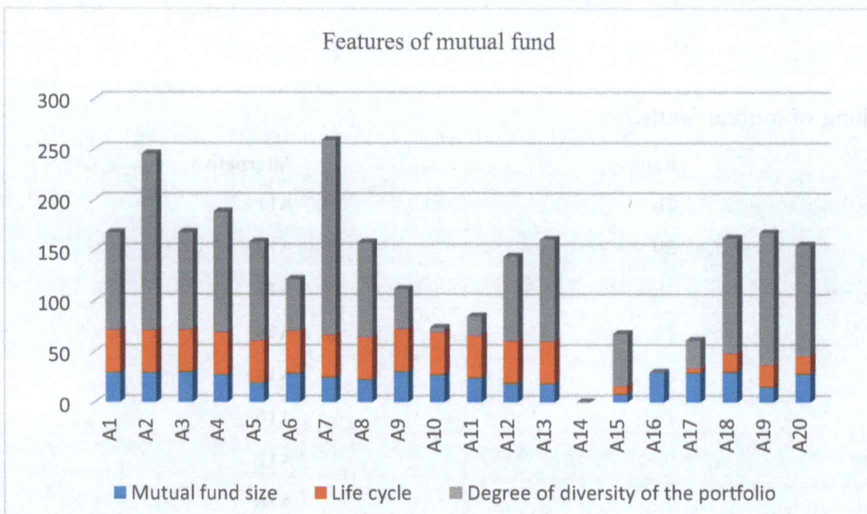

DIAGRAM 78.2 Comparison of mutual funds based on the distance from the best value in the mutual fund characteristics criterion.

Step 7. Computing the total distance and the sum of distances. The total distance for each alternative, based on each subcriterion, is obtained by summing the values of each row in the distance matrix from the previous step. The results are shown in Table 78.16. The total distances sum to 49,754.15.

Step 8. Computing the DOL and the POA. Based on relations 13 to 15, by dividing the total distance values by the sum of distances on a row-by-row basis, the OPL values for the alternatives are obtained. Finally, according to relation 16, the opportunities gained by the alternatives are calculated. The DOL and POA results are presented in Table 78.17.

Step 9. Ranking the alternatives. Row interpretation shows the ranking of the alternatives. Considering the DOL and POA values, the mutual funds are ranked as shown in Table 78.18.

Here is a precise English translation of your text, preserving the structure and specific references to the charts and subcriteria:

According to Diagram 78.1, mutual fund 14 has the lowest OPL, which makes it the most favorable investment alternative. Also, mutual fund 2 has the highest OPL and is placed at the lowest priority for investment.

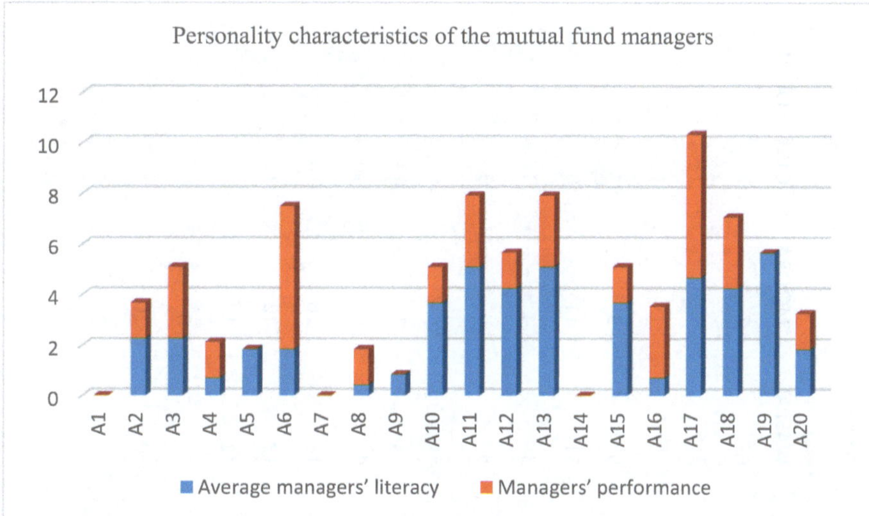

DIAGRAM 78.3 Comparison of mutual funds based on the distance from the best value in the mutual fund manager's personality criterion.

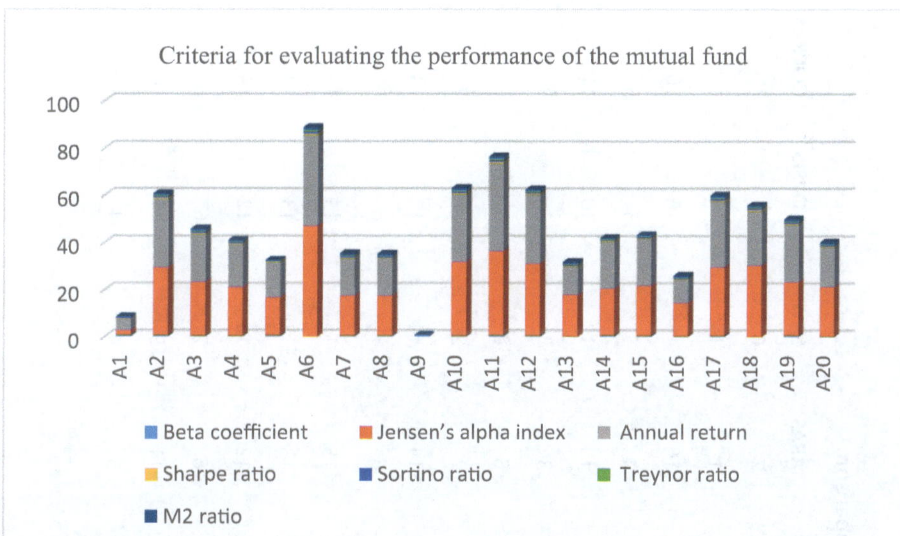

DIAGRAM 78.4 Comparison of mutual funds based on the distance from the best value in the mutual fund performance evaluation criteria.

Although, from a general interpretation, mutual fund 14 has the least OPL and is comparatively of higher priority than the others, in the detailed view and based on the distance values shown in Diagrams 78.2–78.4, only in the subcriteria SC1, SC2, SC3, SC4, and SC5 does the OPL equal zero. Therefore, to achieve 100% efficiency and attain the absolute best state (total OPL equal to zero), the managers of this mutual fund should model themselves on the following subcriteria: SC6 from mutual fund 6; SC7, SC8, SC9, and SC12 from mutual fund 9; SC10 from mutual fund 5; and SC11 from mutual fund 1, and work to improve the mutual fund's weaknesses so that the distance from the best value for each criterion becomes zero.

78.6 Validity check of the innovative method

The proposed approach was validated by benchmarking it against various MADM methods. The case study, drawn from Moradian et al. (2019), examines material selection for the break booster valve body in a vehicle and was re-evaluated by Abdulaal and Bafail (2022) using several MADM techniques. Applying OPLO-POCOD to this same

TABLE 78.19 MADM method-based ranking comparison.

No.	RAMS	RATMI	MCRAT	RAPS	ARAS	SAW	TOPSIS	COPRAS	VIKOR	WASPAS	MOORA	OPLO-POCOD
A1	7	7	7	7	7	6	7	7	7	6	7	7
A2	1	1	1	1	1	1	1	1	1	1	1	1
A3	16	16	15	16	16	16	16	16	15	15	15	15
A4	5	5	5	5	4	5	5	5	5	5	5	4
A5	12	12	10	12	10	12	10	11	11	11	11	8
A6	3	3	3	3	3	3	3	3	3	3	4	3
A7	8	8	8	8	8	8	8	8	8	8	8	9
A8	2	2	2	2	2	2	2	2	2	2	2	2
A9	14	14	14	14	14	14	14	14	14	14	14	14
A10	10	9	9	11	9	11	9	9	9	9	9	10
A11	15	15	16	15	15	15	15	15	16	16	16	16
A12	13	13	13	13	13	13	13	12	12	13	12	11
A13	9	11	12	9	12	10	12	13	13	12	13	13
A14	6	6	6	6	6	7	6	6	6	7	6	6
A15	11	10	11	10	11	9	11	10	10	10	10	12
A16	4	4	4	4	5	4	4	4	4	4	3	5

TABLE 78.20 Comparative correlation of rankings: OPLO-POCOD and other MADM methods.

	r_s											
	RAMS	**RATMI**	**MCRAT**	**RAPS**	**ARAS**	**SAW**	**TOPSIS**	**COPRAS**	**VIKOR**	**WASPAS**	**MOORA**	**OPLO-POCOD**
RAMS	1											
RATMI	0.991	1										
MCRAT	0.976	0.988	1									
RAPS	0.997	0.988	0.971	1								
ARAS	0.976	0.988	0.994	0.971	1							
SAW	0.988	0.988	0.971	0.994	0.971	1						
TOPSIS	0.979	0.991	0.997	0.974	0.997	0.974	1					
COPRAS	0.971	0.991	0.991	0.968	0.991	0.974	0.994	1				
VIKOR	0.968	0.988	0.994	0.965	0.988	0.971	0.991	0.997	1			
WASPAS	0.976	0.991	0.994	0.974	0.988	0.982	0.991	0.991	0.994	1		
MOORA	0.965	0.985	0.991	0.962	0.982	0.968	0.988	0.994	0.997	0.991	1	
OPLO-POCOD	0.938	0.950	0.979	0.932	0.979	0.932	0.976	0.971	0.974	0.965	0.968	1

example yielded results that were compared to those from the other methods. Table 78.19 presents the rankings across methods.

To assess concordance among methods, we applied the Spearman rank correlation to derive ρ values. Table 78.20 summarizes how closely the novel approach agrees with the remaining MADM methods in this instance. Since ρ is appropriate for ranked data, values above 0.8 reflect a very strong relationship. The table shows that every ρ surpasses 0.8, reinforcing the validity of the OPLO-POCOD results.

Table 78.20 demonstrates that the OPLO-POCOD method attains the smallest correlation (approximately 93.2%) with the RAPS and SAW techniques, while exhibiting correlations above 95% with the remaining comparison methods. Collectively, these results indicate that the proposed framework consistently preserves the ordinal ranking of alternatives and effectively differentiates among alternatives.

78.7 Conclusion

Recent years have witnessed a surge in the deployment of MADM across diverse real-world contexts, accompanied by substantial advancements in the development and refinement of numerous MADM methodologies. In this work, we introduce the OPLO-POCOD framework as an innovative contribution to the MADM literature, which synergistically integrates the concept of OPL with a polar-coordinate distance metric to assess and rank alternatives. The method starts from a heterogeneous decision matrix that includes quantitative and qualitative criteria, from which a Best-value matrix is constructed, and OPL values are extracted to obtain an ordered-pair representation for each alternative. Using a weighted polar distance metric, the total distance, DOL, and POA are computed. This approach enables compensatory aggregation across criteria and guides the decision-making process toward minimal DOL and maximal POA.

Numerical studies, including the mutual funds case, show that OPLO-POCOD demonstrates high efficiency and consistency relative to classical MADM methods, with strong ordinal correlations with established methods such as technique for order preference by similarity to ideal solution, complex proportional assessment, additive ratio assessment, and MCRAT. Specifically, Spearman correlations are above 0.9, and overall correlations exceed 98.5%, indicating robustness and reliability of the framework. Practically, this method provides a clear visual representation of foregone opportunities, clarifies trade-offs, and offers scalability to diverse domains, enabling decision-makers to make decisions based on precise and traceable analyses. Limitations of the current study and directions for future work include broader assessments in dynamic environments, the development of user-friendly software tools to implement OPLO-POCOD, and deeper sensitivity analyses to evaluate stability under substantial data changes.

78.7.1 The advantages of the opportunity losses-based polar coordinate distance method

The OPLO-POCOD approach advances MADM analysis by fusing the concept of OPL with a polar-coordinate representation, offering a fresh lens for evaluating alternatives. This combination produces a more cohesive and interpretable assessment framework, capturing a dimension of cost that many traditional MADM methods overlook. Consequently, decision-makers are better equipped to compare and discriminate among alternatives. The adoption of polar coordinates enhances visualization and comprehension, with shorter radial distances signaling smaller OPL and thus facilitating intuitive ranking and selection. Additionally, the method's unique features, not typically found in other MADM approaches, offer a new perspective that can lead to more accurate and effective outcomes. Consequently, by combining the consideration of OPL with distance-based ranking in a polar space, OPLO-POCOD enhances the discrimination among alternatives and supports more robust decision-making across varied domains.

78.7.2 Future research directions

Possible directions for future research discussed in this chapter include validating and applying the OPLO-POCOD framework to real-world decision problems across a range of industries to evaluate its practicality, reliability, and performance in operational settings. Additional benchmarking against MADM methods beyond the eleven studied could further substantiate its advantages and robustness. A sensitivity analysis could explore how changes in criterion weights and values influence final rankings, highlighting the method's stability under different decision scenarios. Extending the framework to dynamic decision-making would require a structure that can handle time-varying criteria and alternatives, with rankings updated as new information becomes available. Incorporating uncertainty and risk through extensions such as fuzzy logic, Monte Carlo simulation, or Bayesian inference would provide a more comprehensive view of potential outcomes and associated risks. Finally, developing user-friendly software tools that implement OPLO-POCOD and offer intuitive interfaces for entering criteria, computing OPL, and generating final rankings would enhance practicality and broad accessibility. On weighting, emerging techniques like the base criterion method (BCM) could be employed; BCM, introduced by Haseli et al. in Haseli et al. (2020) and further discussed by Haseli and Sheikh in Haseli and Sheikh (2022), utilizes a two-stage pairwise comparison approach to derive weights by separating base and final comparisons.

References

Abdulaal, R. M., & Bafail, O. A. (2022). Two new approaches (RAMS-RATMI) in multi-criteria decision-making tactics. *Journal of Mathematics, 2022*(1), 6725318.

Araf, M. S. I., Hoque, S. F., Chowdhury, M. A., Rahman, M., & Alam, M. Z. (2025). Can artificial intelligence (AI) based pricing achieve sustainability? A systematic review from business, customer & policymaking perspectives. *A Systematic Review from Business, Customer & Policymaking Perspectives.*.

Breser, E.S. (2024). Dupes versus original luxury products: the impact of product similarity and opportunity costs on consumers' purchase behaviors and perceptions (Master's thesis, Universidade Catolica Portuguesa (Portugal)).

Buchanan, J. M. (1987). The constitution of economic policy. *Science (New York, N.Y.), 236*(4807), 1433–1436.

Dwyer, L. (2025). Cost-benefit analysis. In *Encyclopedia of tourism*. Cham: Springer Nature Switzerland, 217–218.

Eiter, T., & Mannila, H. (1997). Distance measures for point sets and their computation. *Acta Informatica, 34*(2), 109–133.

Fleckenstein, D., Klein, R., Klein, V., & Steinhardt, C. (2025). On the concept of opportunity cost in integrated demand management and vehicle routing. *Transportation Science, 59*(1), 125–142.

Haghpour, B., Sahabeh, E., & Halvari, H. (2022). Opportunity cost in consumer behavior: Definitions, operationalizations, and ambiguities. *International Journal of Consumer Studies, 46*(5), 1942–1959.

Haseli, G., & Sheikh, R. (2022). Base criterion method (BCM). In *Multiple criteria decision making: Techniques, analysis and applications*. Singapore: Springer Nature Singapore, 17–38.

Haseli, G., Sheikh, R., & Sana, S. S. (2020). Extension of base-criterion method based on fuzzy set theory. *International Journal of Applied and Computational Mathematics, 6*(2), 54.

Kraszkiewicz, A. (2024). Opportunity Cost (Cost of Lost Profits) as an Element of Decision-Making Analysis. In Farm Machinery and Processes Management in Sustainable Agriculture: XII International Scientific Symposium 2024 (Vol. 609, p. 229). Springer Nature.

Liu, Z., Zhu, S., Senapati, T., Deveci, M., Pamucar, D., & Yager, R. R. (2025). New distance measures of complex Fermatean fuzzy sets with applications in decision making and clustering problems. *Information Sciences, 686*, 121310.

Mooney, J. G., Gurbaxani, V., & Kraemer, K. L. (1996). A process oriented framework for assessing the business value of information technology. *ACM SIGMIS Database: The DATABASE for Advances in Information Systems, 27*(2), 68–81.

Moradian, M., Modanloo, V., & Aghaiee, S. (2019). Comparative analysis of multi criteria decision making techniques for material selection of brake booster valve body. *Journal of traffic and transportation engineering (English edition), 6*(5), 526–534.

Nugraheni, M., & Sari, I.P. (2022). A case-based reasoning for detection coronavirus (Covid-19) using cosine similarity. In Conference on Broad Exposure to Science and Technology 2021 (BEST 2021) (pp. 178-183). Atlantis Press.

O'Mahony, T. (2021). Cost-Benefit Analysis and the environment: The time horizon is of the essence. *Environmental Impact Assessment Review, 89*, 106587.

Ponsiglione, A. M., Amato, F., Cozzolino, S., Russo, G., Romano, M., & Improta, G. (2022). A hybrid analytic hierarchy process and likert scale approach for the quality assessment of medical education programs. *Mathematics, 10*(9), 1426.

Roffia, P., Henschel, T., & Getzin, F. (2025). Nice to value. Unraveling the nexus between management accounting use and financial performance: A quantitative study of SMEs. *Journal of the International Council for Small Business, 6*(1), 48–54.

Seele, P., Dierksmeier, C., Hofstetter, R., & Schultz, M. D. (2021). Mapping the ethicality of algorithmic pricing: A review of dynamic and personalized pricing. *Journal of Business Ethics*, 697–719.

Sheikh, R., & Senfi, S. (2023). Rapid assessment of customers and their classification with the OPportunity LOsess Based POlar COordinate Distance Sort (OPLO-POCOD SORT) and Net Promoter Score (NPS). *Journal of Business Management Perspective, 22*(55), 82–112.

Sheikh, R., & Senfi, S. (2024a). A novel opportunity losses-based polar coordinate distance (OPLO-POCOD) approach to multiple criteria decision-making. *Journal of Mathematics, 2024*(1), 8845886.

Sheikh, R., & Senfi, S. (2024b). Evaluation and ranking of stock funds using opportunity losses-based polar coordinate distance (OPLO-POCOD) technique. *Journal of Industrial Management Perspective, 14*(3), 117–140.

Sheikh, R., & Senfi, S. (2025a). *Evaluation and classification of the quality of life using a new technique: Opportunity losses-based PolarCoordinate DistanceSort(OPLO-POCOD-SORT.* Total Quality Management & Business Excellence. (In press.

Sheikh, R., & Senfi, S. (2025b). Evaluation of sustainable performance of industry 4.0 technologies using a novel fuzzy OPLO-POCOD method. *Applied Computational Intelligence and Soft Computing, 2025*(1), 5821453.

Sheikh, R., Senfi, S., & Hashemi Moghadam, S. (2024). The opportunity losses-based polar coordinate distance technique (OPLO-POCOD) and the SERVQUAL model; A Novel Tool for Analyzing and Evaluating the Performance of Service Organizations: A Case Study (Five-Star Hotels in Mashhad). 10th International Conference on Industrial Engineering and Systems, Mashhad. https://civilica.com/doc/2119454

Smith, G. S. (2004). Assessment strategies: What is being measured in student course evaluations? *Accounting Education, 13*(1), 3–28.

Stone, D. F. (2015). Clarifying (opportunity) costs. *The American Economist, 60*(1), 20–25.

Suardana, I. G. P. (2025). The evolution of consumer behavior in the age of information: An analytical review. *Vifada Management and Digital Business, 2*(1), 1–16.

Sudirjo, F., Ausat, A. M. A., Suherlan, S., & Azzaakiyyah, H. K. (2024). Understanding psychological dynamics in consumer decision-making processes in the digital marketing era: A review. *Jurnal Penelitian Inovatif, 4*(2), 635–644.

Ye, J. (2011). Cosine similarity measures for intuitionistic fuzzy sets and their applications. *Mathematical and Computer Modelling, 53*(1-2), 91–97.

Chapter 79

ARLON: Alternative ranking using two-step logarithmic normalization for multi-attribute decision-making

Karahan Kara[1,2] and Galip Cihan Yalçın[2]

[1]*Department of Data Science and Analytics, Faculty of Economics and Administrative Sciences, İzmir Katip Çelebi University, İzmir, Türkiye,*
[2]*Department of Business, Faculty of Economics and Administrative Sciences, OSTIM Technical University, Ankara, Türkiye*

79.1 Introduction

Logarithmic normalization-based alternative ranking using the two-step logarithmic normalization (ARLON) method was developed by Kara et al. (2024a) to enhance the reliability of alternative ranking results. The ARLON method improves the normalization process by employing and aggregating two distinct logarithmic normalization operations. Additionally, criteria are defined as cost-based or benefit-based, with each group internally weighted and summed, and the final alternative ranking calculated based on the ratio of benefit-based criteria to total criteria, aiming to maximize overall benefit. The primary objective of this research is to present the application steps of the ARLON method and demonstrate its practicality through a numerical example.

Recent literature shows that ARLON has been integrated with various decision-making approaches across multiple domains. For instance, Kara et al. (2024a) introduced a hybrid framework combining the modified preference selection index (MPSI) method for criterion weighting with ARLON to evaluate supply chain performance across 72 countries. Similarly, Kara et al. (2024b) developed a type-2 neutrosophic numbers (T2NN)-weights by envelope and slope (WENSLO)-ARLON hybrid system to rank sustainable brand equity in the cosmetics sector. Kara et al. (2024c) proposed an single-valued neutrosophic (SVN)-Dombi Bonferroni-ARLON hybrid model for finished vehicle logistics provider selection. Other studies include Kahreman (2024), who combined ARLON with logarithmic percentage change-driven objective weighing to evaluate G8 countries' governance and economic performance, and Yuan (2025), who applied ARLON with neutrosophic sets and the Hammer Operator to rank product quality monitoring systems in machining lines. Further applications of ARLON include evaluations in the economic and insurance sectors (Kahreman and Taşcı, 2025), commercial banks (Demirhan et al., 2025), Recycling 4.0 alternatives (Shamsi et al., 2025), mechanical component springs (Qu et al., 2025), AI-generated sustainable logos (Kara et al., 2025), authentication systems (Yalçın et al., 2025a), green maritime transport (Yalçın et al., 2025b), Arctic transport policy selection (Yalçın et al., 2025c), bicycle pooling locations (Yalçın et al., 2025d), green energy storage investments (Liu et al., 2025), and multicriteria decision-making with Laguerre polynomials (Süzülmüş, 2025). These studies demonstrate that ARLON can be effectively integrated with various methods such as MPSI, WENSLO, SVN, stepwise weight assessment ratio analysis, simple weight calculation (SIWEC), criteria importance assessment (CIMAS), skewness impact through distributional evaluation (SITDE), logarithmic decomposition of criteria importance (LODECI), and analytic hierarchy process (AHP) for robust decision-making across different application domains.

The growing prevalence of ARLON in recent literature highlights its versatility and effectiveness for alternative ranking in complex multi-attribute decision-making (MADM) problems. This chapter is organized as follows: Section 79.2 provides a detailed explanation of the ARLON method; Sections 79.3 and 79.4 demonstrate its application through two numerical examples; and Section 79.5 concludes the study with insights into the method's effectiveness and practical applicability.

Encyclopedia of Multi-Attribute Decision-Making (MADM). DOI: https://doi.org/10.1016/B978-0-443-33275-3.00015-4

79.2 Methodology

The ARLON method is a decision-making approach that relies on dual logarithmic normalization procedures and treats cost-based and benefit-based criteria separately during the aggregation process (Kara et al., 2024a, 2024b, 2024c). The procedure is carried out through six essential steps, outlined as follows:

Step 1. In the first step of the alternative ranking order method accounting for two-step normalization method, the initial decision matrix ($X = [X_{ij}]_{MN}$) is established ((79.1)). In this matrix, the performance values of each alternative (A_i) are recorded with respect to the corresponding criteria (C_j). Specifically, each element (X_{ij}) of the matrix denotes the value of the ith alternative with respect to the jth criterion. The matrix is composed of M alternatives and N criteria. Accordingly, both the set of criteria $C = \{C_1, C_2, \ldots, C_j, \ldots, C_N\}$ $(j = 1,2, \ldots, N)$ and the set of alternatives $A = \{A_1, A_2, \ldots, A_i, \ldots, A_M\}$ $(i = 1,2, \ldots, M)$ must be clearly defined within this structure:

$$X = \begin{bmatrix} X_{11} & \cdots & X_{1j} & \cdots & X_{1N} \\ \vdots & \cdots & \vdots & \cdots & \vdots \\ X_{i1} & \cdots & X_{1j} & \cdots & X_{iN} \\ \vdots & \cdots & \vdots & \cdots & \vdots \\ X_{M1} & \cdots & X_{Mj} & \cdots & X_{MN} \end{bmatrix}; \; (i = 1,\ 2,\ \ldots,\ M;\ j = 1,\ 2,\ \ldots,\ N) \quad (79.1)$$

Step 2. In the second stage of the ARLON method, the elements of the initial decision matrix undergo two separate logarithmic normalization procedures. Specifically, first logarithmic normalization (Zavadskas & Turskis, 2008) is applied as the first procedure, followed by second logarithmic normalization (Jahan & Edwards, 2015) as the second. The use of these two levels of normalization techniques is intended to strengthen the reliability and consistency of the normalization process. The first logarithmic normalization ($Z^{1^{st}} = [Z_{ij}^{1^{st}}]_{MN}$) results in the matrix expressed in (79.2), while the second logarithmic normalization ($Z^{2^{nd}} = [Z_{ij}^{2^{nd}}]_{MN}$) produces the matrix presented in (79.3):

$$Z_{ij}^{1^{st}} = \begin{cases} \dfrac{\ln(X_{ij})}{\ln(\prod_{i=1}^{M} X_{ij})} & \text{for } j \in C^{+} \\ \dfrac{1 - \frac{\ln(X_{ij})}{\ln(\prod_{i=1}^{M} X_{ij})}}{M-1} & \text{for } j \in C^{-} \end{cases}; \; (i = 1,\ 2,\ \ldots,\ M;\ j = 1,\ 2,\ \ldots,\ N) \quad (79.2)$$

$$Z_{ij}^{2^{nd}} = \begin{cases} \dfrac{\log_2(X_{ij})}{\sum_{i=1}^{M}(\log_2(X_{ij}))} & \text{for } j \in C^{+} \\ 1 - \dfrac{\log_2(X_{ij})}{\sum_{i=1}^{M}(\log_2(X_{ij}))} & \text{for } j \in C^{-} \end{cases}; \; (i = 1,\ 2,\ \ldots,\ M;\ j = 1,\ 2,\ \ldots,\ N) \quad (79.3)$$

Step 3. In the third phase of the ARLON approach, the matrices obtained from the first and second logarithmic normalization in Step 2 are combined through an aggregation process based on the Heron mean. This integration employs the parameter α, which specifies the weight assigned to the arithmetic mean results, while $1 - \alpha$ reflects the weight associated with the geometric mean results. The aggregated normalized matrix ($Z = [Z_{ij}]_{MN}$) is then derived using (79.4). In most applications, α is set to 0.5, thereby assigning equal importance to both mean techniques in the construction of the aggregated matrix:

$$Z_{ij} = \left((1-\alpha)\sqrt{(Z_{ij}^{1^{st}})(Z_{ij}^{2^{nd}})}\right) + \left((\alpha)\frac{(Z_{ij}^{1^{st}} + Z_{ij}^{2^{nd}})}{2}\right); \; (i = 1,\ 2,\ \ldots,\ M;\ j = 1,\ 2,\ \ldots,\ N;\ \alpha \in [0,\ 1]) \quad (79.4)$$

Step 4. In the fourth stage of the ARLON method, the aggregated normalized matrix is combined with the criterion weight vector $w = \{w_1, w_2, \ldots, w_j, \ldots, w_N\}$ $(j = 1,2, \ldots, N)$ through multiplication, as expressed in (79.5). This operation yields the weighted normalized matrix ($D = [D_{ij}]_{MN}$), where the influence of each criterion is explicitly incorporated:

$$D_{ij} = w_j * Z_{ij}; \; (i = 1,\ 2,\ \ldots,\ M;\ j = 1,\ 2,\ \ldots,\ N) \quad (79.5)$$

herein, $\sum_{j=1}^{N} w_j = 1$.

Step 5. In the fifth step of the ARLON method, the values of each alternative within the weighted normalized matrix are aggregated separately for cost-based and benefit-based criteria. Specifically, the summation of cost-based criteria is performed using (79.6), while the summation of benefit-based criteria is carried out using (79.7). This procedure produces two distinct vectors: the cost-based sum vector ($R^{-} = [R_i^{-}]_M$) and the benefit-based sum vector ($R^{+} = [R_i^{+}]_M$). The cost-based sum vector reflects the overall performance of the ith alternative with respect to cost-related criteria,

TABLE 79.1 **The algorithm illustrates the steps of the ARLON alternative ranking method.**

Algorithm:	**The purpose of this algorithm is to present the procedural steps of the ARLON method.**	
Input	A set of criteria: $C = \{C_1, C_2, \ldots, C_j, \ldots, C_N\}$ $(j = 1, 2, \ldots, N)$, A set of alternatives: $A = \{A_1, A_2, \ldots, A_i, \ldots, A_M\}$ $(i = 1, 2, \ldots, M)$, A criteria weigh vector: $w = \{w_1, w_2, \ldots, w_j, \ldots, w_N\}$ $(j = 1, 2, \ldots, N)$.	
Step-1:	Construct the initial matrix ($X = [X_{ij}]_{MN}$) as (79.1)	$X_{ij} = \begin{bmatrix} X_{11} & \cdots & X_{1j} & \cdots & X_{1N} \\ \vdots & \cdots & \vdots & \cdots & \vdots \\ X_{i1} & \cdots & X_{1j} & \cdots & X_{iN} \\ \vdots & \cdots & \vdots & \cdots & \vdots \\ X_{M1} & \cdots & X_{Mj} & \cdots & X_{MN} \end{bmatrix}$
Step-2:	Calculate the first logarithmic normalized matrix ($Z^{1^{st}} = [Z_{ij}^{1^{st}}]_{MN}$) and second logarithmic normalized matrix ($Z^{2^{nd}} = [Z_{ij}^{2^{nd}}]_{MN}$) by employing Eq. (79.2) and Eq. (79.3).	$Z_{ij}^{1^{st}} = \begin{cases} \frac{\ln(X_{ij})}{\ln(\prod_{i=1}^{M} X_{ij})} \text{ for } j \in C^+ \\ \frac{1 - \frac{\ln(X_{ij})}{\ln(\prod_{i=1}^{M} X_{ij})}}{M-1} \text{ for } j \in C^- \end{cases}$ $Z_{ij}^{2^{nd}} = \begin{cases} \frac{\log_2(X_{ij})}{\sum_{i=1}^{M}(\log_2(X_{ij}))} \text{ for } j \in C^+ \\ 1 - \frac{\log_2(X_{ij})}{\sum_{i=1}^{M}(\log_2(X_{ij}))} \text{ for } j \in C^- \end{cases}$
Step-3:	Calculate the aggregated normalized matrix ($Z = [Z_{ij}]_{MN}$) by employing Heron mean as stated in (79.4) ($\alpha \in [0,1]$).	$Z_{ij} = ((1-\alpha)\sqrt{(Z_{ij}^{1^{st}})(Z_{ij}^{2^{nd}})}) + \left((\alpha)\frac{(Z_{ij}^{1^{st}} + Z_{ij}^{2^{nd}})}{2}\right)$
Step-4:	Calculate the weighted normalized matrix ($D = [D_{ij}]_{MN}$) by employing (79.5).	$D_{ij} = w_j * Z_{ij}$
Step-5:	Calculate the cost-based sum vector ($R^- = [R_i^-]_M$) and benefit-based sum vector ($R^+ = [R_i^+]_M$) by employing Eq. (79.6) and Eq. (79.7).	$R_i^- = \sum_{j=1}^{N} D_{ij}$ for $j \in C^-$ $R_i^+ = \sum_{j=1}^{N} D_{ij}$ for $j \in C^+$
Step-6:	Determine the ranking score vector ($R = [R_i]_M$) by employing (79.8) ($\beta \in [0,1]$).	$R_i = (R_i^-)^{(1-\beta)} + (R_i^+)^{(\beta)}$
Output	A ranking score vector: $R = \{R_1, R_2, \ldots, R_i, \ldots, R_M\}$ $(i = 1, 2, \ldots, M)$.	

whereas the benefit-based sum vector captures the cumulative performance of the ith alternative with respect to benefit-related criteria.

$$R_i^- = \sum_{j=1}^{N} D_{ij} \text{ for } j \in C^-; (i = 1, 2, \ldots, M; j = 1, 2, \ldots, N) \tag{79.6}$$

$$R_i^+ = \sum_{j=1}^{N} D_{ij} \text{ for } j \in C^+; (i = 1, 2, \ldots, M; j = 1, 2, \ldots, N) \tag{79.7}$$

Step 6. In the sixth step of the ARLON method, (79.8) is applied to compute the ranking score vector of the alternatives. In this formulation, the parameter β represents the proportion of benefit-based criteria relative to the total number of criteria. Based on the ranking score vector ($R = [R_i]_M$), the alternative with the highest score is designated as the most preferred option, while the alternative with the lowest score is identified as the least preferred option:

$$R_i = (R_i^-)^{(1-\beta)} + (R_i^+)^{(\beta)}; (i = 1, 2, \ldots, M) \tag{79.8}$$

The algorithm of the ARLON method is presented in Table 79.1.

79.3 Numerical example 1

For numerical example 1, the necessary inputs to implement the ARLON algorithm, as outlined in Table 79.1, are defined as follows: a set of alternatives $A = \{A_1, A_2, A_3, A_4\} (i = 1,2,3,4)$, a set of criteria $C = \{C_1, C_2, C_3\} (j = 1,2,3)$, (The third criterion is a cost-based criterion.) and a criterion weight vector $w = \{0.30,0.40,0.30\}$. Using these inputs, the procedural steps of the ARLON method were carried out in the following sequence:

Step 1. The initial matrix ($X = [X_{ij}]_{MN}$) for *numerical example 1* is presented in Table 79.2:

Step 2. The first logarithmic normalization matrix ($Z^{1^{st}} = [Z_{ij}^{1^{st}}]_{MN}$), calculated using (79.2), is presented in Table 79.3, while the second logarithmic normalization matrix ($Z^{2^{nd}} = [Z_{ij}^{2^{nd}}]_{MN}$), derived from (79.3), is provided in Table 79.4.

Example: The calculation for $Z_{11}^{1^{st}}$ is as follows: $Z_{11}^{1^{st}} = \frac{\ln(1200)}{\ln(1200 * 1100 * 1250 * 1000)} = 0.25203$ and the calculation for $Z_{11}^{2^{nd}}$ is as follows: $Z_{11}^{2^{nd}} = \frac{\log_2(1200)}{\log_2(1200) + \log_2(1100) + \log_2(1250) + \log_2(1000)} = 0.25203$.

Step 3. Using Heron mean as stated in (79.4), the first and second logarithmic normalized matrices were combined ($\alpha = 0.5$) to generate the aggregated normalized matrix ($Z = [Z_{ij}]_{MN}$), which is presented in Table 79.5.

Example: The calculation for Z_{11} is as follows: $Z_{11} = ((1 - 0.5)\sqrt{(0.25203)(0.25203)}) + \left((0.5)\frac{(0.25203 + 0.25203)}{2}\right) = 0.25203$.

TABLE 79.2 The initial matrix.

X_{ij}	C_1	C_2	C_3
A_1	1200	800	12
A_2	1100	700	15
A_3	1250	700	11
A_4	1000	750	16

TABLE 79.3 The first logarithmic normalization matrix.

$Z_{ij}^{1^{st}}$	C_1	C_2	C_3
A_1	0.25203	0.25314	0.25341
A_2	0.24894	0.24808	0.24623
A_3	0.25348	0.24808	0.25621
A_4	0.24555	0.25070	0.24415

TABLE 79.4 The second logarithmic normalization matrix.

$Z_{ij}^{2^{nd}}$	C_1	C_2	C_3
A_1	0.25203	0.25314	0.76022
A_2	0.24894	0.24808	0.73869
A_3	0.25348	0.24808	0.76862
A_4	0.24555	0.25070	0.73246

TABLE 79.5 The aggregated normalized matrix.

Z_{ij}	C_1	C_2	C_3
A_1	0.25203	0.25314	0.47287
A_2	0.24894	0.24808	0.45947
A_3	0.25348	0.24808	0.47809
A_4	0.24555	0.25070	0.45560

TABLE 79.6 The weighted normalized matrix.

D_{ij}	C_1	C_2	C_3
A_1	0.07561	0.10126	0.14186
A_2	0.07468	0.09923	0.13784
A_3	0.07604	0.09923	0.14343
A_4	0.07366	0.10028	0.13668

TABLE 79.7 The cost-based sum and benefit-based sum vectors.

	R_i^+	R_i^-	R_i	**Rank**
A_1	0.17686	0.14186	0.8366	2
A_2	0.17391	0.13784	0.8281	3
A_3	0.17528	0.14343	0.8366	1
A_4	0.17394	0.13668	0.8267	4

Step 4. Applying (79.5), the aggregated normalized values were multiplied by their respective criterion weights to obtain the weighted normalized matrix ($D = [D_{ij}]_{MN}$), presented in Table 79.6.

Example: The calculation for D_{11} is as follows: $D_{11} = 0.30 \times 0.25203 = 0.07561$.

Step 5. The cost-based sum vector and the benefit-based sum vector were computed using Eq. (79.6) and Eq. (79.7), respectively, and are presented in Table 79.7.

Example: The calculation for R_1^- is as follows: $R_1^- = 0.14186 = 0.14186$ and the calculation for R_1^+ is as follows: $R_1^+ = 0.07561 + 0.10126 = 0.17686$.

Step 6. (79.8) was applied to determine the ranking score vector and the corresponding rankings of the alternatives. Considering that two of the three total criteria are benefit-based, the parameter β was assigned a value of $\left(\beta = \frac{2}{3} = 0.6666\right)$. The resulting ranking score vector ($R = [R_i]_M$) is presented in Table 79.7.

Example: The calculation for R_1 is as follows: $R_1 = (0.17686)^{0.6666} + (0.14186)^{(1-0.6666)} = 0.8679$.

79.4 Numerical example 2

For numerical example 2, the necessary inputs to implement the ARLON algorithm, as outlined in Table 79.1, are defined as follows: a set of alternatives $A = \{A_1, A_2, A_3, A_4, A_5, A_6, A_7, A_8\}(i = 1,2, \ldots,8)$, a set of criteria $C = \{C_1, C_2, C_3, C_4, C_5, C_6, C_7\}(j = 1,2, \ldots,7)$, (The sixth and seventh criteria are cost-based criteria.) and a criterion weight vector $w = \{0.15,0.12,0.18,0.15,0.16,0.11,0.13\}$. Using these inputs, the procedural steps of the ARLON method were carried out in the following sequence:

Step 1. The initial matrix ($X = [X_{ij}]_{MN}$) for *numerical example 2* is presented in Table 79.8:

Step 2. The first logarithmic normalization matrix ($Z^{1^{st}} = [Z_{ij}^{1^{st}}]_{MN}$) and the second logarithmic normalization matrix ($Z^{2^{nd}} = [Z_{ij}^{2^{nd}}]_{MN}$) are presented in Tables 79.9 and 79.10, respectively.

Example: The calculation for $Z_{11}^{1^{st}}$ is as follows: $Z_{11}^{1^{st}} = \frac{\ln(650)}{\ln(650 * 720 * 700 * 685 * 725 * 690 * 715 * 730)} = 0.12355$ and the calculation for $Z_{11}^{2^{nd}}$ is as follows: $Z_{11}^{2^{nd}} = \frac{\log_2(650)}{\log_2(650)+\log_2(720)+\log_2(700)+\log_2(685)+\log_2(725)+\log_2(690)+\log_2(715)+\log_2(730)} = 0.12355.$

Step 3. The normalized matrix ($Z = [Z_{ij}]_{MN}$) is shown in Table 79.11 ($\alpha = 0.5$).

Example: The calculation for Z_{11} is as follows: $Z_{11} =((1 - 0.5)\sqrt{(0.12355)(0.12355)}) + \left((0.5)\frac{(0.12355+0.12355)}{2}\right) = 0.12355.$

TABLE 79.8 The initial matrix.

X_{ij}	C_1	C_2	C_3	C_4	C_5	C_6	C_7
A_1	650	7000	16	47	50.2	24	50
A_2	720	6000	11	49	50.8	29	58
A_3	700	6500	15	49	51.1	28	56
A_4	685	7500	18	55	48.8	31	60
A_5	725	7650	18	48	49.7	26	62
A_6	690	6850	14	51	48.5	33	54
A_7	715	7150	12	50	50.5	36	58
A_8	730	7250	14	52	50.4	39	54

TABLE 79.9 The first logarithmic normalization matrix.

$Z_{ij}^{1^{st}}$	C_1	C_2	C_3	C_4	C_5	C_6	C_7
A_1	0.12355	0.12506	0.12943	0.12298	0.12513	0.12623	0.12553
A_2	0.12550	0.12289	0.11193	0.12431	0.12551	0.12525	0.12487
A_3	0.12496	0.12402	0.12641	0.12431	0.12570	0.12543	0.12503
A_4	0.12455	0.12604	0.13492	0.12800	0.12423	0.12490	0.12472
A_5	0.12563	0.12632	0.13492	0.12365	0.12481	0.12582	0.12458
A_6	0.12469	0.12476	0.12319	0.12559	0.12403	0.12457	0.12519
A_7	0.12537	0.12536	0.11600	0.12496	0.12532	0.12411	0.12487
A_8	0.12576	0.12556	0.12319	0.12621	0.12526	0.12370	0.12519

TABLE 79.10 The second logarithmic normalization matrix.

Z_{ij}^{2nd}	C_1	C_2	C_3	C_4	C_5	C_6	C_7
A_1	0.12355	0.12506	0.12943	0.12298	0.12513	0.88364	0.87873
A_2	0.12550	0.12289	0.11193	0.12431	0.12551	0.87672	0.87412
A_3	0.12496	0.12402	0.12641	0.12431	0.12570	0.87800	0.87521
A_4	0.12455	0.12604	0.13492	0.12800	0.12423	0.87427	0.87307
A_5	0.12563	0.12632	0.13492	0.12365	0.12481	0.88071	0.87206
A_6	0.12469	0.12476	0.12319	0.12559	0.12403	0.87198	0.87634
A_7	0.12537	0.12536	0.11600	0.12496	0.12532	0.86880	0.87412
A_8	0.12576	0.12556	0.12319	0.12621	0.12526	0.86587	0.87634

TABLE 79.11 The aggregated normalized matrix.

Z_{ij}	C_1	C_2	C_3	C_4	C_5	C_6	C_7
A_1	0.12355	0.12506	0.12943	0.12298	0.12513	0.41946	0.41713
A_2	0.12550	0.12289	0.11193	0.12431	0.12551	0.41617	0.41494
A_3	0.12496	0.12402	0.12641	0.12431	0.12570	0.41678	0.41546
A_4	0.12455	0.12604	0.13492	0.12800	0.12423	0.41501	0.41445
A_5	0.12563	0.12632	0.13492	0.12365	0.12481	0.41807	0.41396
A_6	0.12469	0.12476	0.12319	0.12559	0.12403	0.41393	0.41600
A_7	0.12537	0.12536	0.11600	0.12496	0.12532	0.41242	0.41494
A_8	0.12576	0.12556	0.12319	0.12621	0.12526	0.41102	0.41600

TABLE 79.12 The weighted normalized matrix.

D_{ij}	C_1	C_2	C_3	C_4	C_5	C_6	C_7
A_1	0.01853	0.01501	0.02330	0.01845	0.02002	0.04614	0.05423
A_2	0.01882	0.01475	0.02015	0.01865	0.02008	0.04578	0.05394
A_3	0.01874	0.01488	0.02275	0.01865	0.02011	0.04585	0.05401
A_4	0.01868	0.01512	0.02429	0.01920	0.01988	0.04565	0.05388
A_5	0.01884	0.01516	0.02429	0.01855	0.01997	0.04599	0.05382
A_6	0.01870	0.01497	0.02217	0.01884	0.01985	0.04553	0.05408
A_7	0.01880	0.01504	0.02088	0.01874	0.02005	0.04537	0.05394
A_8	0.01886	0.01507	0.02217	0.01893	0.02004	0.04521	0.05408

TABLE 79.13 The cost-based sum and benefit-based sum vectors.

	R_i^-	R_i^+	R_i	Rank
A_1	0.10037	0.09530	0.7050	3
A_2	0.09972	0.09245	0.7001	8
A_3	0.09986	0.09514	0.7041	4
A_4	0.09953	0.09717	0.7064	1
A_5	0.09980	0.09681	0.7063	2
A_6	0.09961	0.09453	0.7028	6
A_7	0.09931	0.09352	0.7010	7
A_8	0.09929	0.09508	0.7031	5

Step 4. The weighted normalized matrix ($D = [D_{ij}]_{MN}$) is shown in Table 79.12.

Example: The calculation for D_{11} is as follows: $D_{11} = 0.15 \times 0.12355 = 0.01853$.

Step 5. The cost-based sum vector and the benefit-based sum vector are presented in Table 79.13.

Example: The calculation for R_1^- is as follows: $R_1^- = 0.04614 + 0.05423 = 0.10037$ and the calculation for R_1^+ is as follows: $R_1^+ = 0.01853 + 0.01501 + 0.02330 + 0.01845 + 0.02002 = 0.09530$.

Step 6. Given that five of the seven total criteria are benefit-based, the parameter β was assigned a value of $\left(\beta = \frac{5}{7} = 0.7142\right)$. The resulting ranking score vector ($R = [R_i]_M$) is shown in Table 79.13.

Example: The calculation for R_1 is as follows: $R_1 = (0.09530)^{0.7142} + (0.10037)^{(1-0.7142)} = 0.7050$.

79.5 Conclusion

This chapter presented the ARLON method and demonstrated its application through two numerical examples. The study highlights several key strengths of the ARLON approach. Firstly, the dual logarithmic normalization process enhances the robustness of the alternative ranking by mitigating the influence of extreme values and ensuring more balanced comparisons among criteria. Secondly, the method's ability to handle both cost-based and benefit-based criteria independently before aggregation allows for a flexible and comprehensive evaluation framework. Thirdly, ARLON can be effectively integrated with various weighting methods and hybrid decision-making models, making it suitable for a wide range of MADM problems across diverse application domains.

Despite these advantages, certain limitations should be considered. The method requires careful selection of normalization parameters, and its reliance on logarithmic transformations may introduce complexity for datasets containing negative or zero values. Additionally, while ARLON provides reliable alternative rankings, it does not inherently account for the uncertainty or vagueness in expert judgments, which may require integration with fuzzy, neutrosophic, or probabilistic approaches for more nuanced decision-making.

For future research, several directions are recommended. First, extending ARLON to handle uncertain, imprecise, or dynamic data using fuzzy sets, neutrosophic sets, or probabilistic models could further enhance its applicability. Second, comparative studies with other advanced MADM methods can provide additional insights into the relative performance and robustness of ARLON. Third, applying ARLON in larger-scale, real-world decision-making scenarios across different industries can validate its practical effectiveness and uncover further methodological improvements. Overall, the ARLON method presents a versatile and reliable tool for alternative ranking in MADM, and its integration with other advanced techniques holds promising potential for future research.

References

Demirhan, A., Ulutaş, A., & Pala, O. (2025). BİST'te İşlem Gören Seçili Ticari Bankaların LODECI ve ARLON Yöntemleriyle Performansının Değerlendirilmesi. *İzmir İktisat Dergisi, 40*(3), 918–941. https://doi.org/10.24988/ije.1595885.

Jahan, A., & Edwards, K. L. (2015). A state-of-the-art survey on the influence of normalization techniques in ranking: Improving the materials selection process in engineering design. *Materials & Design (1980-2015), 65*, 335–342. https://doi.org/10.1016/j.matdes.2014.09.022.

Kahreman, Y. (2024). Toplumsal mutluluğun kaynağı ekonomik performans mı? Yönetişim performansı mı? *Nevşehir Hacı Bektaş Veli Üniversitesi SBE Dergisi, 14*(3), 1620–1644. https://doi.org/10.30783/nevsosbilen.1511390.

Kahreman, Y., & Taşcı, M. Z. (2025). Makroekonomik ve Sigortacılık Performanslarının Karşılaştırmalı Analizi: OECD Ülkeleri Üzerine SPC–SWARA Temelli ARLON Modeliyle Çok Kriterli Bir Yaklaşım. *Scientific Journal of Finance and Financial Law Studies, 5*(1), 61–77. https://dergipark.org.tr/en/pub/sjffls/issue/90208/1683776.

Kara, K., Ergin, E. A., Yalçın, G. C., Çelik, T., Deveci, M., & Kadry, S. (2025). Sustainable brand logo selection using an AI-supported PF-WENSLO-ARLON hybrid method. *Expert Systems with Applications, 260*, 125382. https://doi.org/10.1016/j.eswa.2024.125382.

Kara, K., Yalçın, G. C., Simic, V., Baysal, Z., & Pamucar, D. (2024a). The alternative ranking using two-step logarithmic normalization method for benchmarking the supply chain performance of countries. *Socio-economic planning sciences, 92*, 101822. https://doi.org/10.1016/j.seps.2024.101822.

Kara, K., Yalçın, G. C., Ergin, E. A., Simic, V., & Pamucar, D. (2024b). A neutrosophic WENSLO-ARLON model for measuring sustainable brand equity performance. *Socio-economic Planning Sciences, 94*, 101918. https://doi.org/10.1016/j.seps.2024.101918.

Kara, K., Yalcin, G. C., Gurol, P., Simic, V., & Pamucar, D. (2024c). Enhancing decision support system for finished vehicle logistics service provider selection through a single-valued neutrosophic Dombi bonferroni-based model. *Engineering Applications of Artificial Intelligence, 138*, 109441. https://doi.org/10.1016/j.engappai.2024.109441.

Liu, P., Eti, S., Dinçer, H., Yüksel, S., Ergün, E., & Özdemir, S. (2025). Zero-shot learning and pythagorean fuzzy decision-making modeling for prioritizing green energy storage investment criteria in Scandinavian countries. *Journal of Energy Storage, 129*, 117326. https://doi.org/10.1016/j.est.2025.117326.

Qu, H., Duan, C., & Yu, J. (2025). Effective approach to shock absorption performance evaluation of mechanical component springs using the single valued trapezoidal neutrosophic numbers for structural stability. *Neutrosophic Sets and Systems, 81*, 560–574. https://digitalrepository.unm.edu/nss_journal/vol81/iss1/34/.

Shamsi, M., Zakerinejad, M., & Zareifard, M. R. (2025). Waste to emerging and sustainable wealth: An integrated Mining 4.0-Recycling 4.0-Decision Making 4.0 framework overcoming greener red mud recycling technologies promotion. *Environmental Technology & Innovation*104440. https://doi.org/10.1016/j.eti.2025.104440.

Süzülmüş, S. (2025). Laguerre polinomlari Yardimiyla Çok Kriterli Karar Verme Yöntemi Geliştirilmesi. *Dokuz Eylül Üniversitesi İşletme. Fakültesi Dergisi, 26*(1), 198–226. https://dergipark.org.tr/en/pub/ifede/issue/92630/1645218.

Yalçın, G. C., Kara, K., Edinsel, S., Kaygısız, E. G., Simic, V., & Pamucar, D. (2025a). Authentication system selection for performance appraisal in human resource management using an intuitionistic fuzzy CIMAS-ARLON model. *Applied Soft Computing, 171*, 112786. https://doi.org/10.1016/j.asoc.2025.112786.

Yalçın, G. C., Kara, K., Özekenci, E. K., Simic, V., & Pamucar, D. (2025b). Green maritime transport performance analysis of G-7 countries using an interval-valued Fermatean fuzzy ARLON-based decision model. *Applied Soft Computing*113677. https://doi.org/10.1016/j.asoc.2025.113677.

Yalçın, G. C., Limon, E. G., Kara, K., Limon, O., Gürol, P., Deveci, M., ... Tomášková, H. (2025c). A hybrid decision support system for transport policy selection: A case study on Russia's Northern Sea route in Artic region. *Socio-economic Planning Sciences, 98*, 102171. https://doi.org/10.1016/j.seps.2025.102171.

Yalçın, G. C., Gürol, P., & Kara, K. (2025d). Developing a GIS-supported SVN-WENSLO-ARLON hybrid method for bicycle pooling location selection: A case study in Turkey. In *Intelligent Urban Mobility*. Academic Press, 103–148. https://doi.org/10.1016/B978-0-443-34160-1.00014-6.

Yuan, S. (2025). Neutrosophic hammer operator for assessment of product processing quality monitoring system in a machining line. *Neutrosophic Sets and Systems, 83*, 625–640. https://digitalrepository.unm.edu/nss_journal/vol83/iss1/36.

Zavadskas, E. K., & Turskis, Z. (2008). A new logarithmic normalization method in games theory. *Informatica, 19*(2), 303–314. https://doi.org/10.3233/INF-2008-19(2)09.

Chapter 80

ARWEN: Alternatives ranking with elected nominee for multi-attribute decision-making

Shervin Zakeri[1], Dimitri Konstantas[1], and Prasenjit Chatterjee[2]

[1]*Geneva School of Economics and Management, University of Geneva, Geneva, Switzerland,* [2]*Department of Mechanical Engineering, MCKV Institute of Engineering, Howrah, West Bengal, India*

80.1 Introduction

Decision-making rarely unfolds along a single dimension. Economic, social, environmental, or technical contexts typically require evaluating numerous criteria that may conflict in both magnitude and direction. To address such complexity, multicriteria decision-making (MCDM) methods were developed to structure problems, quantify preferences, and rank alternatives based on weighted assessments. Classic methods like analytic hierarchy process (AHP) (Saaty, 1980), technique for order preference by similarity to ideal solution (TOPSIS) (Hwang & Yoon, 1981), VlseKriterijumska Optimizacija I Kompromisno Resenje (VIKOR) (Opricovic & Tzeng, 2004), ELimination Et Choix Traduisant la REalité (ELECTRE) (Roy, 1991), and preference ranking organization method for enrichment evaluations (PROMETHEE) (Brans & Vincke, 1985) have become staples of operations research and policy analysis. Yet, despite decades of refinement, they still exhibit recurring challenges: excessive reliance on normalization, rank reversals when options change, sensitivity to weighting procedures, and difficulties in interpretation for nonspecialists. These methodological fragilities undermine confidence in the reproducibility and fairness of results, especially in sustainability, engineering, and governance applications where decisions have tangible ethical and financial consequences. The persistence of these limitations motivated the formulation of alternatives ranking with elected nominee (ARWEN), a framework that redefines the reference structure of ranking by grounding evaluation in an elected nominee (EN) rather than in abstract idealized points. By adopting this perspective, ARWEN reclaims interpretability and stability, ensuring that the ranking process corresponds to an intuitive notion of "closeness" to an explicit, context-anchored benchmark.

80.1.1 Foundations of multicriteria decision-making

The mathematical underpinnings of MCDM derive from multi-attribute utility theory, operations research, and systems engineering. In general form, a decision problem can be expressed as a matrix:

$$D = [x_{ij}], \quad i = \{1, \ldots, m\};\ j = \{1, \ldots, n\}; \tag{80.1}$$

where m represents alternatives and n represents criteria. Each element $x_{(ij)}$ denotes the performance of alternative i-th under j-th criterion. Weights w_j reflect the relative importance of each criterion, typically normalized such that $\sum w_j = 1$.

The central objective of any MCDM method is to identify a preference order $R = \{A_1 \succ A_2 \succ \ldots \succ A\square\}$ that reflects both performance and criterion significance. Achieving this apparently simple goal demands addressing several mathematical and epistemological questions:

1. **Commensurability**—How to compare criteria expressed in different units?
2. **Normalization**—Which transformation preserves meaning without distortion?
3. **Aggregation**—How to combine weighted performances into a scalar or geometric indicator?
4. **Consistency**—How stable is the ranking under parameter or data variation?

Encyclopedia of Multi-Attribute Decision-Making (MADM). DOI: https://doi.org/10.1016/B978-0-443-33275-3.00023-3

80.1.2 Classical approaches

TOPSIS remains one of the most influential distance-based methods. It calculates each alternative's Euclidean distance from an ideal (best) and antiideal (worst) solution, ranking by relative closeness to the ideal. VIKOR introduces a compromise metric balancing group utility and individual regret, producing a utility index S_i and a regret index R_i. Outranking methods such as ELECTRE and PROMETHEE rely on pairwise dominance relations, while utility-based methods like AHP and multi-attribute utility theory (MAUT) (Keeney and Raiffa, 2014) convert preferences into cardinal scales. Although these approaches differ algorithmically, they share dependence on normalization, weighted aggregation, and reference constructs that are often abstract rather than data-anchored. These assumptions introduce interpretive ambiguity and potential instability (Belton & Gear, 1983; Opricovic & Tzeng, 2004).

80.1.3 Evolution and recent directions

The 21st century brought a proliferation of hybrid and metaheuristic MCDM models: entropy-based objective weighting, criteria importance through intercriteria correlation (CRITIC), best–worst method (BWM), and vital-immaterial-mediocre (VIMM); fuzzy and gray extensions; and analytic-geometry-based methods like ranking based on optimal points (Zakeri et al., 2022) and simple ranking process (Zakeri et al., 2023a). While these methods aimed to overcome traditional limitations, they often introduced new layers of complexity. Normalization remained an unavoidable preprocessing step, and interpretability suffered as algorithms became increasingly opaque. Amid this landscape, ARWEN emerged to restore conceptual simplicity and cognitive alignment without sacrificing analytical rigor.

80.1.4 Theoretical limitations of existing methods

Several systematic studies [9–13] have documented inconsistencies across MCDM methods when applied to identical datasets (Zakeri et al., 2023a; Zakeri et al., 2023b). Triantaphyllou and Mann (1989) and Zanakis et al., (1998) identified rank reversals, weight sensitivity, and scaling effects as recurrent sources of contradiction. Four interrelated factors explain these phenomena:

1. Most MCDM methods transform raw data to a common scale (e.g., min–max, vector, linear) to ensure unit-free comparison. Yet normalization can distort proportional relationships, exaggerate small differences, or compress large ones.
2. Different methods aggregate or scale data through divergent functional forms, distance, ratio, or outranking, which may yield incompatible rankings for the same problem.
3. Subjective weighting (AHP, BWM) introduces human bias, while objective weighting (entropy, CRITIC) may neglect contextual significance.
4. Ideal or antiideal points are often theoretical constructs not represented within the dataset, obscuring the semantic meaning of "closeness."

These challenges highlight a structural weakness in traditional MCDM approaches, where reliance on artificial normalization and abstract reference points separates the mathematical results from the decision-maker's (DM's) intuitive understanding. Recognizing this limitation led to the development of the ARWEN framework.

80.1.5 Conceptual motivation for alternatives ranking with elected nominee

The principal innovation of ARWEN lies in redefining how *reference* is conceptualized in decision analysis. Instead of comparing alternatives to an artificial ideal, ARWEN introduces the notion of an EN, a benchmark chosen directly from existing data or explicitly specified by the DM. This reframing shifts the evaluative perspective from abstraction to contextual realism. When EN is data-driven, it corresponds to the best observed performance in each criterion; when it is DM-defined, it represents an aspirational profile reflecting policy goals, market expectations, or sustainability thresholds. In both cases, EN anchors the analysis within the domain of meaningful values, preserving interpretability.

The second motivation concerns scale independence. Because ARWEN operates directly on unnormalized data, proportional relationships remain intact, ensuring that rankings are invariant to unit transformations. This property is particularly vital for multidomain evaluations where each dimension may have a different magnitude but equal strategic importance. ARWEN emphasizes semantic transparency. Distance from the EN has an immediate, intuitive meaning: it measures how far an alternative's performance deviates from a target profile. This clarity stands in contrast to the composite indices of traditional MCDM, whose internal scaling often obscures interpretation.

80.1.6 Structure of the paper

The remainder of this paper is organized as follows: Section 80.2 describes the ARWEN framework, including its conceptual foundation, mathematical formulation, and operational logic. Section 80.3 presents a numerical example involving the cloud-provider selection problem, outlining the criteria, alternatives, and construction of the evaluation matrix. Section 80.4 reports the main results and discussion, interpreting ARWEN's outputs in relation to decision-making insights. Section 80.5 provides a comparative analysis with established MCDM methods, supported by a rank concordance assessment. Section 80.6 offers a detailed sensitivity analysis, incorporating both one-at-a-time and Monte Carlo-based global evaluations, as well as the identification of threshold conditions for criterion dominance. Section 80.7 discusses the theoretical and practical implications of ARWEN, focusing on its interpretability, robustness, and computational efficiency. Finally, Section 80.8 concludes the study by summarizing key findings, outlining methodological contributions, and suggesting avenues for future research.

80.2 Alternatives ranking with elected nominee framework

80.2.1 Core principles

ARWEN is a distance-based, normalization-free ranking framework organized around a proximity coefficient G_i that measures how close each alternative A_i is to the EN. The model supports four principal variants, including ARWEN I to IV and one bounded form (E-ARWEN). Each variant corresponds to a particular information condition regarding weights and nominee specification (see Table 80.1).

80.2.2 Operational logic

ARWEN method follows a structured sequence of steps to evaluate and rank alternatives. First, all criteria are converted into a benefit form to ensure consistent interpretation. Depending on the decision context, the nominee is then determined either from the observed maximum values or defined externally by the DM. For each criterion, the deviation $\Delta_{ij} = |x_{ij} - n_n|$ is computed, where n_j represents the nominee value. If weights are applied, each deviation is multiplied by its corresponding weight w_j. The resulting total deviation vector forms the basis of the distance measure that defines G_i. The alternatives are then ranked in decreasing order of G_i, where a higher G_i indicates greater proximity to the nominee.

80.2.3 Alternatives ranking with elected nominee algorithm

ARWEN method provides a flexible decision-making framework that adapts to the amount of information available to DMs. It consists of four variants named ARWEN I, ARWEN II, ARWEN III, and ARWEN IV, each designed to function under different levels of information availability. In ARWEN, EN represents a reference alternative, either selected directly from the decision matrix or defined by the DMs based on their expectations. Except in specific cases, this nominee does not possess an independent existence but serves as a benchmark for comparison. Alternatives are ranked according to

TABLE 80.1 Variants of the alternatives ranking with elected nominee (ARWEN) method with corresponding information conditions.

Variant	Nominee	Weighting	Input requirement
I	Data-driven	None	Raw performance matrix
II	DM-defined	None	Target profile only
III	Data-driven	Weighted	External weight vector
IV	DM-defined	Weighted	Full information
E-ARWEN	Positive and negative nominees	Weighted/ unweighted	Bounded evaluation

their degree of similarity to this EN, where higher similarity values indicate better performance. The algorithm's core principle is expressed through Eq. (80.2).

$$\Gamma_i = (2n) - \left(\sum_{j=1}^{n} w_j (\max_i r_{ij} \cdot (r_{ij})^{-1}) \right), \quad i = \{1, \ldots, m\}, \quad j = \{1, \ldots, n\}; \tag{80.2}$$

80.2.3.1 Alternatives ranking with elected nominee forms

ARWEN operates under four hypothetical conditions depending on the DMs' knowledge of the criteria:

1. Criteria unidentified for DMs
This category includes ARWEN I and ARWEN II.
- ARWEN I: Applied when all criteria are *beneficial*, meaning higher values indicate better performance.
- ARWEN II: Used when the criteria set contains both *benefit* and *cost* criteria.

2. Criteria identified for DMs
This group includes ARWEN III and ARWEN IV, which differ based on the DMs' access to information:
- ARWEN III: DMs have partial or imperfect knowledge about the criteria.
- ARWEN IV: DMs possess complete and perfect information about all criteria.

The methodological steps for each form are described below.

80.2.3.2 Alternatives ranking with elected nominee procedures

ARWEN method is divided into two main groups based on whether the criteria are known or unknown to the DMs.

1. Criteria unidentified
In real-world situations, DMs often make choices without complete or accurate information. ARWEN handles this uncertainty through two extensions, ARWEN I and ARWEN II, which aim to minimize the differences between the alternatives and the EN.

a) *ARWEN I Steps:*

Step 1: Construct the decision matrix $D = [x_{ij}]$, where i denotes criteria and j denotes alternatives (Eq. 80.3).

$$X_{ij} = r_{ij}; \tag{80.3}$$

Step 2: Identify the EN based on the largest value of each criterion (Eq. 80.4).

$$A_i^+ = \{\max_{\leq j \leq n} r_{ij}\}, \quad i = \{1, \ldots, m\}; \tag{80.4}$$

Step 3: Transform the matrix using Eq. (80.5) to express all alternatives relative to the nominee.

$$v_{ij} = \max_i r_{ij} \cdot (r_{ij})^{-1}, \quad 1 \leq v_{ij}^+ \leq 2; \tag{80.5}$$

Step 4: Calculate the proximity coefficient for each alternative (Eq. 80.6), representing its similarity to the nominee.

$$\Gamma_i = (2n) - \left(\sum_{j=1}^{n} v_{ij} \right); \tag{80.6}$$

Step 5: Rank the alternatives in descending order of their proximity coefficients.

b) *ARWEN II Steps:*

ARWEN II extends ARWEN I to include both benefit and cost criteria. The only distinction lies in the matrix transformation step:

Step 1: Convert the decision matrix into a benefit matrix using Eqs. (80.7) and (80.8) for cost criteria.

$$p_{ij} = r_{ij}^- \cdot \left(\sum_{i=1}^{m} r_{ij}^- \right)^{-1}; \tag{80.7}$$

$$r_{ij}^+ = (1 - p_{ij}); \tag{80.8}$$

Step 2: Repeat the subsequent steps of ARWEN I.

2. Criteria identified and known

ARWEN III and IV are applied when DMs can recognize the criteria but differ in the extent of available information.

c) ***ARWEN III Steps:***

Step 1: Construct the decision matrix $D = [x_{ij}]$, with criteria weights w_i determined by the DMs.
Step 2: Transform the matrix into its benefit form (Eqs. 80.7 and 80.8).
Step 3: Determine the weighted EN (Eq. 80.5).
Step 4: Compute the weighted proximity coefficient (Eq. 80.9).

$$\Gamma_i^* = (2n) - \left(\sum_{j=1}^{n} \langle \max_i r_{ij}/r_{ij} \rangle w_j \right) \tag{80.9}$$

Step 5: Rank alternatives based on the highest proximity values.

d) ***ARWEN IV Steps:***

When DMs have complete knowledge of all alternatives and criteria, ARWEN IV allows them to define an *ideal nominee* that embodies their expectations or organizational strategy.
Step 1: Construct the decision matrix following ARWEN III Step 1.
Step 2: Define an EN based on DMs' expectations, where all criteria are optimal (Eq. 80.10).

$$\forall\, C_n^* \in C_j^* \rightarrow \quad C_n^* \geq C_n, \quad C_j = \{C_1, C_2, \cdots, C_n\} \tag{80.10}$$

Step 3: Transform the matrix into a benefit matrix (Eqs. 80.7 and 80.8).
Step 4: Rank the alternatives according to the largest proximity coefficient (Eq. 80.8).

80.2.4 Bounded evaluation and percent convergence coefficient

In E-ARWEN (see Eq. 80.11), evaluation occurs within a bounded range defined by positive and negative nominees (N^+ and N^-). The percent convergence coefficient (PCC) expresses how near an alternative is to N^+ relative to the total spread between N^+ and N^-:

$$PCC_i = \frac{\sum_j w_j (x_{ij} - N_j^-)}{\sum_j w_j (N_j^+ - N_j^-)} \times 100; \tag{80.11}$$

This ratio produces results in [0%, 100%], facilitating intuitive interpretation: 100 % = fully converged to N^+, 0% = identical to N^-. The PCC provides bounded comparability across datasets and enables threshold-based evaluation in sustainability and risk contexts.

80.2.5 Properties of alternatives ranking with elected nominee

ARWEN method exhibits several desirable properties that enhance its reliability and interpretability in decision-making. It is normalization-free, as it operates directly on the original data and produces results that remain unchanged under linear scaling. The method is semantically transparent, meaning that the distance from the EN carries a clear and intuitive interpretation. ARWEN is also flexible, allowing the inclusion or exclusion of weights without altering its structural framework. Moreover, it is scale-independent, ensuring that the ranking of alternatives remains consistent across decision matrices of different sizes. ARWEN is rank-stable, since the addition or removal of dominated alternatives does not affect the ranking order.

80.2.6 Comparative theoretical evaluation

The theoretical distinctiveness of ARWEN emerges when contrasted with conventional MCDM techniques that rely on dual-reference or compromise constructs. While TOPSIS and VIKOR measure how close each alternative is to an idealized extreme, ARWEN evaluates proximity to a tangible reference known as EN. This fundamental distinction has significant implications for both interpretability and robustness.

80.2.6.1 Reference construction

In the TOPSIS method, ideal and antiideal solutions are synthesized from best and worst normalized criterion scores, producing composite profiles that may not correspond to any feasible alternative. VIKOR's compromise solution likewise derives from these artificial boundaries. ARWEN dispenses with such abstractions: its EN is either observed directly from data or explicitly articulated by the DM, ensuring empirical or normative validity.

80.2.6.2 Normalization independence

Because ARWEN does not normalize, the metric of closeness remains invariant to units and linear transformations. If the unit of a criterion changes, for example, from USD to EUR, all deviations scale proportionally, ensuring that the ranking of alternatives remains unchanged. This independence from preprocessing functions eliminates one of the primary causes of rank inconsistency identified by Triantaphyllou and Mann (1989) and Zanakis et al. (1998).

80.2.6.3 Weight integration and flexibility

ARWEN considers weighting as an optional input instead of a built-in part of its framework. Weights can be obtained through any preferred method, whether subjective methods such as AHP, BWM, and VIMM, or objective ones such as entropy, CRITIC, and information values connected to the equilibrium points. These weights are applied multiplicatively to the criterion deviations. Since the aggregation process is linear, any change in ranking remains both interpretable and proportional to the variation in weights.

80.2.6.4 Bounded evaluation and interpretation

E-ARWEN's bounded logic transforms the abstract notion of "optimality" into a tangible measure of *acceptability*. By referencing both N^+ and N^-, it captures the intuitive notion of performance within an interval of desirability. A PCC of 80%, for example, indicates that an alternative achieves 80% of the desirable range between worst and best. Such expressiveness enhances communication between technical analysts and decision stakeholders.

80.2.6.5 Rank consistency and cognitive interpretability

Rank reversals in traditional methods often result from the redefinition of ideal or average reference points when new alternatives are added. ARWEN's EN is invariant unless the DM explicitly redefines it or a new extreme emerges in data. Hence, any rank change reflects genuine contextual evolution, not algorithmic instability. This transparency aligns ARWEN with psychological theories of reference-dependent utility, wherein individuals evaluate outcomes relative to aspirational or status-quo baselines. The comparative summary of some of the MCDM methods is shown in Table 80.2.

80.3 Numerical example—cloud provider selection problem

Obxerver Tech needs a primary cloud provider for its AI-driven environmental, social, and governance (ESG) and planetary health analytics platform. The choice must balance operating cost with technical performance, regulatory posture, sustainability commitments, AI/ML capability, and ecosystem fit for partner integrations. Five leading providers are considered as alternatives, evaluated on six criteria scored on a common 1–10 scale (higher = better).

TABLE 80.2 Comparative summary of multicriteria decision-making methods.

Feature	TOPSIS	VIKOR	EDAS	ARWEN I-IV	E-ARWEN
Normalization	Required	Required	Required	Not required	Not required
Dual reference	Yes	Yes	Average	Single nominee	Dual nominees
Weight flexibility	Moderate	High	Moderate	Very high	Very high
Rank stability	Sensitive	Sensitive	Moderate	High	High
Interpretability	Moderate	Moderate	Moderate	High	Very high

Alternatives: A1: AWS • A2: Microsoft Azure • A3: Google Cloud • A4: IBM Cloud • A5: Oracle Cloud
Criteria (all beneficial on a 1–10 scale) (see Table 80.3).
C1: Cost efficiency (price/performance and discounts; higher = cheaper for the same workload)
C2: Performance and scalability (latency, throughput, global regions, autoscaling robustness)
C3: Compliance and certifications (breadth/depth of industry and regional attestations)
C4: Sustainability and renewables (data-center efficiency, clean-energy matching, reporting)
C5: AI/ML service maturity (breadth, depth, and operational readiness of AI stack)
C6: Integration and ecosystem (marketplace, partner tooling, SDKs, connectors)
Weights: $w = [C1: \ 0.20, C2: \ 0.18, C3: \ 0.17, C4: \ 0.15, C5: \ 0.17, C6: \ 0.13]$

80.4 Results and discussion

80.4.1 Results

Applying the ARWEN algorithm to the defined decision matrix produced the results summarized in Table 80.2. Using Eq. (80.2), the similarity scores (Γ_i) were calculated for each alternative. Here, $n = 6$ corresponds to the number of criteria, and $\max_i r_{ij}$ represents the best value for each criterion, serving as the EN. Each alternative's relative distance from this nominee was determined by computing the weighted ratio $\max_i r_{ij}/r_{ij}$, and the resulting values were aggregated to form S_i. The final ARWEN scores were then obtained as $\Gamma_i = 12 - S_i$.

As shown in Table 80.4, AWS (A_1) achieved the highest similarity score (10.9812), indicating the closest alignment with the EN and thus representing the most balanced option across all evaluated criteria. Google Cloud (A_3) ranked a close second, differing only marginally in its overall performance. Microsoft Azure (A_2) followed in third place, while Oracle Cloud (A_5) and IBM Cloud (A_4) showed notably lower alignment scores, primarily due to weaker performance in cost efficiency and AI service maturity. ARWEN results confirm that AWS provides the most favorable trade-off among cost, technical capacity, sustainability, and AI readiness for the intended application. The small gap between AWS and Google Cloud also suggests a competitive balance at the top tier of providers, reflecting the robustness of the ARWEN framework in differentiating high-performing alternatives with nuanced precision.

80.5 Comparative analysis

To evaluate the robustness and consistency of the ARWEN algorithm, the same decision matrix was analyzed using three widely recognized MCDM methods including, TOPSIS, VIKOR, and weighted aggregated sum product assessment (WASPAS). Each method was applied under the same criteria, weights, and normalization conditions used in the ARWEN evaluation. The purpose of this comparison is to assess whether ARWEN produces consistent rankings relative to established methods and to identify its distinctive advantages in sensitivity, interpretability, and discriminatory power.

TABLE 80.3 Cloud systems evaluation decision matrix, where (scores 1–10; higher = better).

Cloud provider	C1	C2	C3	C4	C5	C6
A1	7	9	9	8	9	9
A2	6	8	9	8	9	9
A3	7	9	8	9	9	8
A4	5	7	8	7	6	7
A5	6	7	8	6	6	7

TABLE 80.4 Results and ranking of the alternatives ranking with elected nominee method.

Cloud provider	S_i	$\Gamma_i = 12 - S_i$	Rank
A1	1.0188	10.9812	1
A2	1.0213	10.9787	2
A3	1.0839	10.9161	3
A4	1.296	10.704	4
A5	1.328	10.672	5

TABLE 80.5 TOPSIS results.

Cloud provider	C_i^*	Rank
A1	0.924	1
A2	0.913	2
A3	0.872	3
A4	0.741	4
A5	0.713	5

TABLE 80.6 VIKOR results.

Cloud provider	Q_i	Rank
A1	0	1
A2	0.028	2
A3	0.061	3
A4	0.321	4
A5	0.358	5

80.5.1 Comparison with results of TOPSIS method

TOPSIS determines the best alternative as the one with the shortest distance to the positive ideal solution and the farthest distance from the negative ideal solution. After normalization and applying the weight vector, the relative closeness coefficients (C_i^*) were computed as follows (see Table 80.5).

The ranking order derived from TOPSIS, AWS > GCP > Azure > Oracle > IBM, mirrors the one produced by ARWEN, confirming consistency in the selection outcome.

80.5.2 Comparison with results of VIKOR method

VIKOR method focuses on ranking and selecting from a set of alternatives with conflicting criteria by introducing a multicriteria measure of compromise. Using the same normalized decision matrix, the compromise ranking values (Q_i) were obtained (see Table 80.6).

VIKOR results are fully aligned with ARWEN, confirming AWS as the best alternative and IBM as the least favorable. The small difference between AWS and GCP highlights their competitive performance.

80.5.3 Comparison with results of WASPAS method

WASPAS combines the weighted sum model and weighted product model for more stable rankings. The aggregated performance index (Q_i) for each alternative was computed as given in Table 80.7. WASPAS results also replicate the ranking pattern observed in ARWEN, TOPSIS, and VIKOR.

80.5.4 Similarity coefficients analysis

To further evaluate the consistency between ARWEN and the three comparative MCDM methods (TOPSIS, VIKOR, and WASPAS), a similarity analysis was conducted using two statistical measures: Spearman's rank correlation coefficient (ρ) and Kendall's tau (τ). These coefficients quantify the degree of agreement between the ranking sequences produced by different methods, ranging from −1 (complete disagreement) to +1 (perfect concordance). The ranking orders obtained were identical across all methods. AWS (A_1) ranked first, followed by Google Cloud (A_3), Azure (A_2), Oracle (A_5), and IBM (A_4), suggesting strong concordance. The similarity coefficients were computed based on rank positions rather than raw scores, ensuring comparability across methods with differing mathematical formulations (see Table 80.8).

Both coefficients confirm a complete alignment ($\rho = 1.000$, $\tau = 1.000$) among all methods. This outcome indicates that the ARWEN framework not only produces consistent rankings with established MCDM techniques but also demonstrates strong ranking stability and methodological reliability. Such perfect concordance reinforces the robustness of the ARWEN algorithm as a valid decision-making tool. Unlike methods that depend heavily on normalization procedures (*e.g.*, TOPSIS) or compromise parameters (*e.g.*, VIKOR), ARWEN achieves identical outcomes through a more direct

TABLE 80.7 WASPAS results.

Cloud provider	Q_i	Rank
A1	0.944	1
A2	0.933	2
A3	0.902	3
A4	0.781	4
A5	0.753	5

TABLE 80.8 Comparisons between alternatives ranking with elected nominee (ARWEN) and the considered multicriteria decision-making (MCDM) methods.

Method	Spearman's ρ	Kendall's τ	Interpretation
ARWEN vs TOPSIS	1	1	Perfect similarity
ARWEN vs VIKOR	1	1	Perfect similarity
ARWEN vs WASPAS	1	1	Perfect similarity
TOPSIS vs VIKOR	1	1	Perfect similarity
TOPSIS vs WASPAS	1	1	Perfect similarity
VIKOR vs WASPAS	1	1	Perfect similarity

similarity-based computation. This structural simplicity improves transparency, interpretability, and replicability, which are essential qualities in real-world decision contexts involving technology selection, sustainability evaluation, and policy prioritization. The similarity coefficient analysis demonstrates that ARWEN maintains full coherence with conventional MCDM methods while offering a more intuitive and computationally efficient framework for multicriteria evaluation.

80.6 Sensitivity analysis

A sensitivity analysis was conducted to assess the robustness of the ARWEN results against variations in the criteria weights. Because ARWEN relies on a linear weighted structure, expressed as in Eq. (80.2), it allows direct examination of how changes in the weighting scheme influence the ranking outcome. Both local (one-at-a-time) and global (Monte Carlo) sensitivity analyzes were performed to evaluate ranking stability and the influence of each criterion on the final decision.

80.6.1 Local sensitivity (±20%)

Each criterion's weight was individually perturbed by ±20%, while the remaining weights were proportionally adjusted to maintain a total sum of one. The results are summarized in Table 80.9, showing that AWS (A_1) consistently remained the top-ranked alternative across all scenarios. The ranking order was unchanged: $A_1 > A_3 > A_2 > A_5 > A_4$, confirming that moderate changes in weights do not affect the outcome.

This confirms that ARWEN results are locally stable, as no single-criterion fluctuation within ±20% changes the final ranking.

80.6.2 Global sensitivity (Monte Carlo simulation)

A global sensitivity test was performed using 20,000 random weight vectors sampled from a Dirichlet (1, …, 1) distribution to uniformly explore the weight space. For each configuration, ARWEN scores were recalculated, and the top-ranked alternative was recorded.

As displayed in Fig. 80.1, AWS (A_1) maintained dominance, ranking first in approximately 74.9% of all simulations, while Google Cloud (A_3) ranked first in 25.1%. Azure, IBM, and Oracle never achieved first place under any weight configuration (see Table 80.10).

These findings highlight the global robustness of the ARWEN decision: AWS's leadership persists across the vast majority of possible weighting combinations, with only minor sensitivity to extreme redistributions of weights.

80.6.3 Critical weight thresholds

A threshold analysis was conducted to determine which single criterion could most significantly alter the decision outcome. Each criterion's weight was gradually increased from 0.01 to 0.95, redistributing the remaining weight evenly among the others. The objective was to identify the minimum single-criterion weight required to dethrone AWS as the top-ranked alternative (see Table 80.11).

Only C_4 (sustainability) was capable of overturning the ranking when its weight exceeded approximately 0.287 (28.7%). Beyond this threshold, Google Cloud (A_3) surpassed AWS (A_1) as the preferred alternative, as illustrated in Fig. 80.2.

TABLE 80.9 One-at-a-time (±20%) sensitivity results.

Scenario	Top-ranked alternative	Ranking order
C_1 ±20%	AWS (A_1)	$A_1 > A_3 > A_2 > A_5 > A_4$
C_2 ±20%	AWS (A_1)	$A_1 > A_3 > A_2 > A_5 > A_4$
C_3 ±20%	AWS (A_1)	$A_1 > A_3 > A_2 > A_5 > A_4$
C_4 ±20%	AWS (A_1)	$A_1 > A_3 > A_2 > A_5 > A_4$
C_5 ±20%	AWS (A_1)	$A_1 > A_3 > A_2 > A_5 > A_4$
C_6 ±20%	AWS (A_1)	$A_1 > A_3 > A_2 > A_5 > A_4$

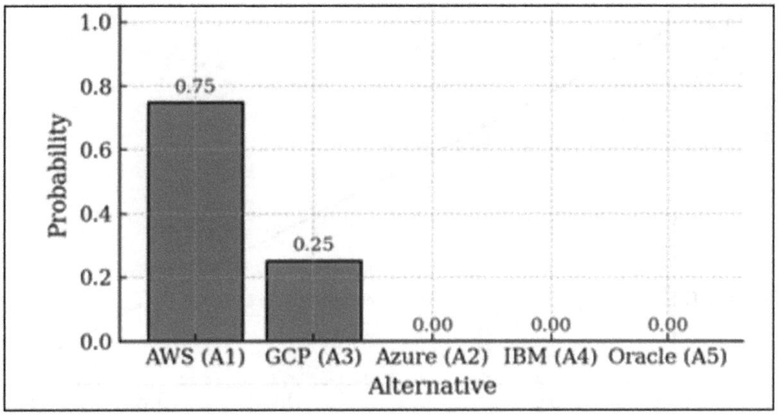

FIGURE 80.1 Probability of ranking first under random weights (alternatives ranking with elected nominee global sensitivity).

TABLE 80.10 Probabilities of top-ranked alternatives under random weight distribution.

Cloud provider	Probability of ranking first
A1	0.749
A2	0.251
A3	0
A4	0
A5	0

TABLE 80.11 Minimum criterion weight required to alter the top-ranked alternative.

Criteria	Minimum $w_{\mathscr{K}}$ to dethrone AWS
C_1 (cost-efficiency)	> 0.95
C_2 (performance and scalability)	> 0.95
C_3 (compliance and certifications)	> 0.95
C_4 (sustainability)	0.287
C_5 (AI/ML service maturity)	> 0.95
C_6 (ecosystem integration)	> 0.95

This indicates that the choice between AWS and GCP becomes sensitive only when sustainability is given an exceptionally high level of importance, which is a reasonable condition for organizations guided by ESG principles. The combined local and global sensitivity results demonstrate that the ARWEN algorithm exhibits high robustness and interpretability. AWS remains the preferred alternative in nearly all reasonable weighting configurations, and only extreme prioritization of sustainability shifts the ranking. Monte Carlo results confirm that the stability of ARWEN does not depend on any specific weight distribution and is instead an inherent feature of the structural design. ARWEN provides a stable, transparent, and reliable decision-making framework, capable of maintaining consistency across broad variations in preference structures. Its interpretability and resilience make it particularly suitable for sustainability-oriented evaluations and high-stakes technology selection scenarios.

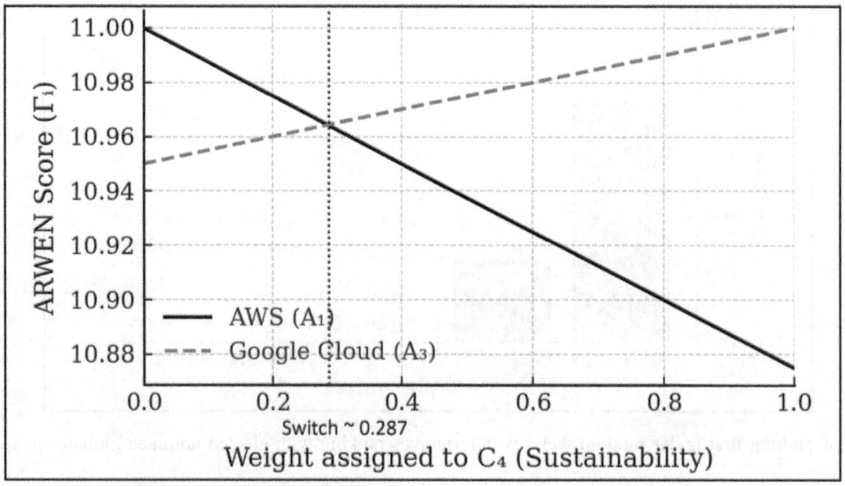

FIGURE 80.2 Critical weight threshold analysis for C_4 (sustainability).

80.6.4 Comparative ranking behavior

The comparative stability of ARWEN was empirically assessed in earlier studies (Zakeri et al., 2023b; Zakeri et al., 2024), where it was applied alongside TOPSIS and VIKOR across multiple industrial decision problems. Results revealed nearly identical ranking orders in consistent datasets but markedly reduced volatility under normalization shifts. Rank correlation between ARWEN and normalized models remained high (>0.9), confirming methodological coherence. However, ARWEN uniquely avoided reversal effects when the number of alternatives changed, demonstrating **context-dependent stability**.

This behavior occurs because the reference point in ARWEN, known as the nominee, remains unchanged unless it is explicitly modified through new data extremes or by a DM's input. As a result, ARWEN is able to distinguish between genuine contextual changes, such as variations in data or preferences, and artificial instabilities that stem from mathematical artifacts.

80.6.5 Weight variation sensitivity

Sensitivity analysis involves perturbing the weight vector by ±10% and ±25%. Traditional MCDM methods exhibit nonlinear rank shifts due to normalization interplay, but ARWEN's additive aggregation ensures linear and interpretable adjustments. If a criterion's importance increases by 10%, its deviation contribution grows proportionally. This proportional sensitivity allows DMs to trace rank variation directly to altered preferences rather than hidden normalization interactions.

ARWEN IV and E-ARWEN thereby offer **transparent elasticity**, where rank movements reflect rational preference recalibration.

80.6.6 Normalization and transformation sensitivity

Normalization-free computation is one of ARWEN's defining strengths. Tests using linear, vector, and min–max normalization on the same dataset yield identical orderings in ARWEN, while significant divergence occurs in TOPSIS or VIKOR. Because ARWEN compares deviations directly on the data's original scale, its internal logic is immune to transformation distortions, thereby ensuring **cross-unit robustness**—a rare property in distance-based MCDM methods (Zakeri et al., 2023b).

80.6.7 Scale sensitivity and rank reversal

ARWEN's design ensures that rank stability is unaffected by decision matrix size. When additional dominated alternatives are added or redundant criteria are removed, the rank order among dominant alternatives remains identical. This property stems from the **fixed reference architecture**: the EN defines a stable geometric and semantic center independent of sample composition.

Empirical experiments further confirm that ARWEN's correlation with the DM's intuitive preferences remains high even in small-scale problems (3×3 matrices) where most geometric methods exhibit instability (Zakeri et al., 2023b).

80.6.8 Interpretability and cognitive validity

Beyond numerical robustness, ARWEN provides cognitive interpretability aligned with behavioral decision theory. Individuals commonly judge performance relative to an aspiration level or status quo rather than to an abstract ideal. *EN* formalizes this intuition mathematically. Each alternative's distance conveys psychological meaning: *how far* an option is from a target the DM actually values. This alignment with cognitive patterns enhances the legitimacy of ARWEN outcomes in participatory or policy-oriented decision environments. It converts complex quantitative output into a communicable narrative: "Alternative A_1 meets 92% of our target performance," which is more intuitively graspable than an abstract composite index.

80.6.9 Comparison with other distance-based methods

This section presents a comparative evaluation of the ARWEN algorithm against several well-established distance-based MCDM methods, including TOPSIS, VIKOR, combinative distance-based assessment (CODAS), and measurement of alternatives and ranking according to compromise solution (MARCOS). The purpose of this comparison is to highlight ARWEN's conceptual and computational advantages in terms of interpretability, robustness, and transparency, while maintaining simplicity and consistency in ranking outcomes. Conventional distance-based methods typically rely on the notion of an *ideal* and *antiideal* solution, measuring the Euclidean or compromise distance between each alternative and these reference points. Although these methods have proven effective in many decision-making contexts, they are often constrained by well-documented limitations, including sensitivity to normalization, dependence on measurement units, and the occurrence of rank reversal.

In contrast, the ARWEN framework eliminates the need for normalization or unit conversion by directly using proportional similarity to a *single EN* (or to *dual nominees* in its extended E-ARWEN version). This structure not only simplifies computation but also enhances interpretability by expressing results as relative similarity measures rather than abstract distances.

Table 80.12 compares the ARWEN algorithm (and its extended version, E-ARWEN) with several well-known distance-based MCDM approaches. ARWEN eliminates normalization requirements and unit sensitivity while maintaining full linearity in weight dependence, resulting in minimal rank reversal and high interpretability.

The comparison highlights the methodological clarity of ARWEN and its capacity to deliver consistent and explainable results without depending on normalization procedures or complex distance formulations. The use of an EN as a reference point makes ARWEN inherently more intuitive and robust than traditional methods, positioning it as a significant advancement in similarity-based decision-making frameworks.

80.7 Theoretical and practical implications

The conceptual developments introduced in ARWEN have significant implications for decision theory and applied analytics. Theoretically, the method redefines proximity and reference as flexible constructs that can be chosen rather than treated as fixed mathematical ideals, creating a balance between descriptive realism and prescriptive precision. In practical application, its normalization-free structure simplifies computation and reduces the likelihood of data distortion during

TABLE 80.12 Comparative characteristics of alternatives ranking with elected nominee (ARWEN) and other distance-based multicriteria decision-making (MCDM) methods.

Property	TOPSIS	VIKOR	CODAS	MARCOS	ARWEN (I-IV)	E-ARWEN
Reference type	Ideal/antiideal	Compromise	Average/border	Hybrid	Single nominee	Dual nominees
Normalization	Required	Required	Required	Required	Not required	Not required
Sensitivity to units	High	High	Moderate	High	None	None
Weight dependence	Nonlinear	Nonlinear	Moderate	Moderate	Linear and transparent	Linear and transparent
Rank reversal	Frequent	Possible	Moderate	Moderate	Minimal	Minimal
Interpretability	Medium	Medium	Low	Low	High	High

preprocessing. Its bounded form (E-ARWEN) extends beyond pure ranking to evaluative benchmarking, applicable to sustainability scoring, risk assessment, and organizational performance tracking. Because PCC values map directly onto percentage ranges, DMs can set thresholds (e.g., PCC ≥ 70% denotes acceptable compliance).

80.8 Conclusions

This work reorients distance-based MCDM around an *EN*, yielding a normalization-free, scale-independent proximity model with clear semantics and linear, transparent weight effects. We presented ARWEN I-IV and the bounded E-ARWEN form, established their properties, and contrasted them theoretically with TOPSIS, VIKOR, CODAS, and MARCOS. Empirically, ARWEN reproduced benchmark rankings with perfect rank similarity ($\rho = 1.0$, $\tau = 1.0$), remained locally stable under ±20% weight shifts, and exhibited global robustness in Monte Carlo analysis (top-rank share ≈ 0.75 for the leading alternative). The top-ranked alternative changed only when sustainability was given a very high weight of about 0.287, offering valuable insight into the preference conditions that can influence the decision outcome. The extended version, E-ARWEN, enhances this analysis by providing bounded, percentage-based measures that improve clarity in compliance and risk evaluation. ARWEN's transparency and unit invariance reduce preprocessing choices that typically drive instability. The nominee concept also aligns with reference-dependent cognition, improving stakeholder communication in practice. The case study is single-domain and uses crisp scores; broader testing across domains, fuzzy/gray data, group decision-making, and dynamic nominees are warranted. Future research should (*i*) integrate objective/subjective hybrid weighting with uncertainty, (*ii*) examine computational scaling on very large matrices, (*iii*) operationalize PCC thresholds for regulation/ESG audits, and (*iv*) release open tools for reproducibility.

References

Belton, V., & Gear, T. (1983). On a shortcoming of Saaty's method of analytic hierarchies. *Omega, 11*(3), 228–230. http://dx.doi.org/10.1016/0305-0483(83)90047-6.

Brans, J.-P., & Vincke, P. (1985). A preference ranking organization method: The PROMETHEE method. *Management science, 31*(6), 647–656.

Hwang, C.-L., & Yoon, K. (1981). *Multiple attribute decision making: Methods and applications*. Springer.

Keeney, R. L., & Raiffa, H. (2014). *Decisions with multiple objectives: Preferences and value tradeoffs*. Wiley. https://doi.org/10.1017/CBO9781139174084.

Opricovic, S., & Tzeng, G.-H. (2004). Compromise solution by MCDM methods: A comparative analysis of VIKOR and TOPSIS. *European Journal of Operational Research, 156*(2), 445–455.

Roy, B. (1991). The outranking approach and the foundations of ELECTRE methods. *Theory and Decision, 31*(1), 49–73.

Saaty, T. L. (1980). *The analytic hierarchy process*. McGraw-Hill.

Triantaphyllou, E., & Mann, S. H. (1989). An examination of the effectiveness of multi-dimensional decision-making methods: A decision-making paradox. *Decision Support Systems, 5*(3), 303–312. https://doi.org/10.1016/0167-9236(89)90037-7.

Zakeri, S., Chatterjee, P., Cheikhrouhou, N., & Konstantas, D. (2022). Ranking based on optimal points and win-loss-draw multi-criteria decision-making with application to supplier evaluation problem. *Expert Systems With Applications, 191*, 116258. https://doi.org/10.1016/j.eswa.2021.116258.

Zakeri, S., Chatterjee, P., Konstantas, D., & Ecer, F. (2023a). A decision analysis model for material selection using simple ranking process. *Scientific Reports, 13*(1), 8631. https://doi.org/10.1038/s41598-023-35405-z.

Zakeri, S., Chatterjee, P., Konstantas, D., & Farr, A. S. (2023b). Introducing alternatives ranking with elected nominee (ARWEN) method: A case study of supplier selection. *Decision Analytics Journal, 29*(3), 1080–1126. https://doi.org/10.3846/tede.2023.18789.

Zakeri, Shervin, Konstantas, Dimitri, Sorooshian, Shahryar, & Chatterjee, Prasenjit (2024). A novel ML-MCDM-based decision support system for evaluating autonomous vehicle integration scenarios in Geneva's public transportation. *Artificial Intelligence Review, 57*(11). 10.1007/s10462-024-10917-w.

Zanakis, S. H., Solomon, A., Wishart, N., & Dublish, S. (1998). Multi-attribute decision making: A simulation comparison of select methods. *European Journal of Operational Research, 107*(3), 507–529. https://doi.org/10.1016/S0377-2217(97)00147-1.

Chapter 81

RAM: Root assessment method for multi-attribute decision-making

Alireza Sotoudeh-Anvari

Department of Industrial Engineering, Science and Research Branch, Islamic Azad University, Tehran, Iran

81.1 Introduction

The nature of the encyclopedia reasonably requires that the reader be familiar with basic aspects of multiple criteria decision-making (MCDM) theory, such as ranking methods, weighting methods, compensatory methods, outranking methods, normalization techniques, aggregation functions, and possible pitfalls in the existing methods. Interested readers are referred to Sotoudeh-Anvari (2022) and Sotoudeh-Anvari (2023) and references therein for the concepts and methods.

81.1.1 Background

It is well-known among researchers that management is synonymous with decision-making. MCDM (also known as multi-attribute decision-making [MADM]), as a very popular branch of management science, is one of the most applicable tools to deal with multidimensional decision-making problems. So far, a large number of MCDM methods have been introduced, and it is expected that this trend will continue. Each MCDM method has its own strategy to rank the alternatives, and none of these methods can be considered the best, but they may be more suitable for a given problem (Sotoudeh-Anvari, 2022). On the one hand, the key controversial issue is that different MCDM methods may produce different ranking results of alternatives (Zanakis et al., 1998). The reasons for this discrepancy are challenging and multifactorial, which can restrict the utilization of MCDM methods in practice, as discussed in the literature (see e.g., Sotoudeh-Anvari, 2023). For example, ensemble MCDM combines the ranking results derived from various MCDM methods to enhance the decision-making robustness and mitigate their individual disadvantages (Zaidan et al., 2024). On the other hand, MCDM theory suffers from some limitations that have plagued it for a long time. For example, nearly all existing MCDM methods are prone to the serious problem of rank reversal, where the ranking order of alternatives may be reversed after deleting or adding another alternative (see e.g., Dehshiri & Firoozabadi, 2023). Rank reversal can call into question the applicability and readability of MCDM methods. Because of such concerns, the literature review shows that practitioners prefer to use simple and transparent MCDM methods.

In fact, it is vital to understand the theoretical basis of an MCDM method to avoid potential pitfalls and to understand why an MCDM method produced a particular outcome (Mela et al., 2012). However, none of the existing MCDM methods is perfect (at least so far as we are aware). For example, as the most well-known MCDM methods, the analytic hierarchy process (AHP) and techniques for order preference by similarity to an ideal solution (TOPSIS) suffer from serious problems (see e.g., Abootalebi et al., 2019; Munier et al., 2021; Opricovic & Tzeng, 2004; Sotoudeh-Anvari, 2023). vlsekriterijumska optimizacija i kompromisno resenje (VIKOR) is another popular MCDM method where the ranking result is performed by integrating two subordinate rankings (group utility measure and regret measure). However, the ranking order derived from VIKOR may not be a complete ranking of alternatives. Moreover, the results obtained by VIKOR may turn out to be opposite when giving a perturbation of its additional parameter, that is υ. For another example, multiobjective optimization by ratio analysis plus the full multiplicative form (MULTIMOORA) and combined compromise solution (CoCoSo) are relatively new and two of the most popular MCDM methods in literature. MULTIMOORA has three subordinate rankings, and they should be aggregated to derive the final result. But it is not a trivial task and may severely affect the rankings. Also very recently, Rasoanaivo et al. (2024) revealed the drawback of CoCoSo

Encyclopedia of Multi-Attribute Decision-Making (MADM). DOI: https://doi.org/10.1016/B978-0-443-33275-3.00047-6

and suggested an improved version of it. For further details, readers are referred to Chang (2010), Lin et al. (2021), Sotoudeh-Anvari (2023), and references therein. This means that there is a need to develop new, reliable, straightforward, and computationally efficient MCDM methods that can better tackle complex real-world problems.

81.1.2 Root assessment method as a new multiple criteria decision-making method

As a very young MCDM method that appeared in October 2023, the root assessment method (RAM) is motivated by diverse problems encountered in the MCDM literature. Classical RAM performs linear sum normalization to make the values comparable and uses only one aggregation function to rank the alternatives based on a radical expression whose radicand is the sum of benefit criteria and whose index is the sum of cost criteria of an alternative. As a compensatory method, RAM allows for trade-offs between evaluation criteria. Nevertheless, the philosophy of RAM, which distinguishes this method from existing MCDM techniques, is that RAM severely penalizes the alternative that has poor performance regarding benefit criteria. More precisely, the poor performance with respect to benefit criteria cannot be compensated by the same degree of large scores with respect to cost criteria. This is because (as mentioned) RAM uses an aggregating function based on a radical expression, and the compensation degree between the radicand and index is different.

On the other hand, like some existing MCDM methods, such as complex proportional assessment (COPRAS), MULTIMOORA, and multiobjective optimization on the basis of simple ratio analysis (MOOSRA), RAM uses the sums of weighted normalized values for benefit criteria (S_{+i}) and cost criteria (S_{-i}) to obtain aggregated indexes to evaluate the alternatives. The important point is that, using a new aggregating function, RAM can overcome some of the limitations of the aforementioned MCDM methods. For example, MOOSRA used a simple ratio, that is $y_i = \frac{S_{+i}}{S_{-i}}$ to derive the overall score of the alternative i. But in some cases, when all criteria are benefit type (see e.g., numerical example 1 of the current chapter), the denominator of y_i becomes zero. Fortunately, RAM does not face this limitation.

To sum up the above discussions, RAM has key advantages as follows.

- RAM provides a unique compensation degree between benefit and cost criteria, which is rare in the previous methods.
- Implementing the RAM procedure is straightforward and requires no interaction by the DM after constructing the decision matrix.
- In contrast to some existing methods, such as the weighted aggregated sum product assessment method (WASPAS), the ranking result derived from RAM is not affected by any parameter.
- In contrast to some MCDM methods, such as VIKOR, RAM uses only one aggregating function based on a radical expression to rank the alternatives.
- Unlike some previous MCDM methods, such as preference ranking organization method for enrichment evaluation II and CoCoSo, RAM has no peculiar behavior so far (see e.g., Mela et al., 2012; Rasoanaivo et al., 2024).
- Contrary to AHP, no special software is necessary to execute RAM.
- RAM allows for a complete ranking of available alternatives.
- Unlike the outranking methods, such as elimination et choice translating reality (ELECTRE), there is no restriction on the number of alternatives ranked by RAM.
- RAM has the advantage of preventing rank reversal in some case studies, whereas VIKOR is subject to this problem in the same cases (please see numerical example 1 of the current paper).

Through comparing with many MCDM methods, it is demonstrated that RAM can achieve comparable results with some other methods or better results in terms of simplicity as well as sensitivity. Very recently, Więckowski et al. (2025) compared the performance of RAM, COPRAS, TOPSIS, and measurement alternatives and ranking according to compromise solution and pointed out that RAM consistently exhibited the highest level of stability, and its robustness stems from the unique aggregation function.

81.2 Literature review

RAM, as an emerging MCDM method, has received wide attention owing to the benefits it brings compared to the existing methods. In this section, a brief literature review on RAM is provided.

Dudic et al. (2024) conducted an interesting study to identify the appropriate normalization techniques in RAM using 13 normalization techniques. Hezam et al. (2024) integrated RAM with spherical fuzzy sets to select the best electricity production technology in Egypt toward sustainability. Trung et al. (2024) used RAM to optimize the selection of fertilizer types and mushroom plant care mixtures. Mohamed et al. (2024) integrated the method based on the removal effects of criteria and RAM under a single-valued neutrosophic environment to assess the efficiency of unmanned aerial vehicles in fire forest management. Thinh (2024) employed three MCDM methods, including simple additive weighting (SAW), RAM, and proximity indexed value (PIV), to evaluate material choices for screw shaft, gearbox casing, and gear wheel. Dudić et al. (2024) used RAM to assess lecturers based on student evaluations. Alrashdi et al. (2025) extended RAM under a single-valued neutrosophic set to rank alternative vehicle technologies. Trung et al. (2025) developed R-RAM, combining the strengths of R and RAM methods, and evaluated the performance of R-RAM in four case studies, including ranking metal cutting experiments, electric bicycles, automotive protective materials, and 3D printers. Li and Chen (2025) combined indifference threshold-based attribute ratio analysis and RAM under probabilistic simplified neutrosophic set to rank the alternatives of multilingual higher education internationalization. Biswas et al. (2025) extended RAM with multiple normalizations and developed a hybrid modified preference selection index (PSI)-RAM for a decision-making model to compare online shopping platforms. Thanh et al. (2025) studied the application of RAM for battery electric vehicles. Mai (2025) combined PSI with faire un choix adequat, RAM, and PIV and used these frameworks to rank Vietnamese cities based on digital transformation efforts. Xing et al. (2025) integrated RAM with plithogenic sets to evaluate super high-rise concrete structures. Komasi et al. (2024) utilized a modified alternative ranking order method accounting for two-step normalization in conjunction with RAM to prioritize nine countries based on eight economic development indicators. Yang et al. (2025) extended RAM under

interval valued neutrosophic environment to evaluate computer network security as multiple-criteria group decision-making (MCGDM). Sotoudeh-Anvari (2025) extended RAM with single-valued trapezoidal neutrosophic numbers. Linh et al. (2025) used four MCDM methods, including RAM, SAW, TOPSIS, and PIV, to analyze sustainable energy development. Rong et al. (2024) and Haseli et al. (2024) evaluated the performance of RAM under various fuzzy environments by comparing with state-of-the-art methods.

Other applications of RAM can be found in Van Dua et al. (2024), Salem et al. (2024), Setiawansyah (2024), Elsayed (2024), Yalçın et al. (2025), Yang (2025), Giang and Thinh (2025), Więckowski et al. (2025), Hien et al. (2025) and Wang et al. (2025).

Vietnam has topped the chart for the most published RAM papers, and the most frequent countries where RAM has been used are Egypt, United Arab Emirates, China, Saudi Arabia, Norway, Serbia, Chile, India, Mexico, Slovakia, Turkey, and Poland. It is worth mentioning that RAM can be executed using the functionality in the *pymcdm* package (Shekhovtsov et al., 2025).

81.3 Steps of root assessment method

A typical MCDM method seeks to rank a finite number of alternatives with respect to a finite number of conflicting criteria. Mathematically, DM rates the performance value of m alternatives ($A_i\,(i = 1, 2, .., m)$) with respect to n evaluation criteria ($C_j\,(j = 1, 2, .., n)$) to construct the decision matrix (Model 1). Let w_j be the weight of criterion j, and the condition $\sum_{j=1}^{n} w_j = 1,\ w_j > 0$ is met.

$$
\begin{array}{c} \\ \\ D = \end{array}
\begin{array}{c c}
 & \begin{array}{ccc} C_1 & C_2 & C_n \end{array} \\
\begin{array}{c} A_1 \\ A_2 \\ \vdots \\ A_m \end{array} &
\begin{bmatrix} x_{11} & x_{12} & \cdots & x_{1n} \\ x_{21} & x_{21} & \cdots & x_{1n} \\ \vdots & \vdots & & \vdots \\ x_{m1} & x_{m2} & \cdots & x_{mn} \end{bmatrix}
\end{array}
\quad W = [w_1,\ w_2,\ \ldots,\ w_n] \tag{81.1}
$$

The steps of classical RAM are as follows (Sotoudeh-Anvari, 2023):

Step 1. Decision matrix (Model 1) is normalized using Model (2) as follows:

$$r_{ij} = \frac{x_{ij}}{\sum_{i=1}^{m} x_{ij}},\ j = 1,\ 2,\ ..,\ n \tag{81.2}$$

Step 2. The weighted normalized decision matrix is calculated using Model (3):

$$y_{ij} = r_{ij} w_j \tag{81.3}$$

Step 3. The sum of weighted normalized score of benefit criteria, as well as the sum of weighted normalized score of cost criteria of alternative i are calculated by Model (4) as follows:

$$S_{+i} = \sum_{j=1}^{n} y_{+ij}$$
$$S_{-i} = \sum_{j=1}^{n} y_{-ij} \tag{81.4}$$

Step 4. Overall score of alternative i is calculated using Model (5) as follows:

$$RI_i = \sqrt[2+S_{-i}]{2 + S_{+i}} \tag{81.5}$$

Step 5. The ranking of alternatives can be obtained based on RI_i.
The greater the RI_i is, the higher the rank of alternative i is.

81.4 Numerical example 1

Consider the following numerical example borrowed from Yang and Wu (2020), where five alternatives are evaluated regarding four benefit criteria, and the weights of the criteria are the same. The decision matrix can be found in Table 81.1.

Now, the alternatives are evaluated and ranked using RAM. First, the decision matrix (Table 81.1) is normalized by using Model (2). Normalization of the decision matrix is necessary to deal with different types of criteria. Next, the weighted normalized decision matrix is calculated by multiplying the weights of criteria ($w_1 = w_2 = w_3 = w_4 = 0.25$) with the normalized decision matrix (see Table 81.2).

After that, Model (4) is used to calculate S_{+i} and S_{-i}. For example, we have the following for alternative 1:

$$S_{+1} = 0.1005 + 0.1111 + 0.0429 + 0.0052 = 0.2597$$
$$S_{-1} = 0$$

Finally, Model (5) is used to obtain the overall score of each alternative. The results are listed in Table 81.3. More formally, when RAM is used to rank the alternatives, we get the ranking result as 5-1-2–3-4. The results obtained by RAM are provided in Table 81.3.

If we apply TOPSIS to this case study, the ranking of choices is derived as 5-1-2–3-4. We can notice this result is exactly the same as that of RAM. It is clear that MOOSRA fails to rank the alternatives.

According to Table 81.3, A_4 is the worst among the five alternatives, and we can drop this choice from the set of alternatives. Now, we consider four alternatives together and obtain a new ranking for them by RAM as 5-1-2–3. Clearly, the rank reversal problem does not occur in RAM. After the elimination of A_4, the ranking order obtained by TOPSIS is also 5-1-2–3, namely, there is no change in the result, and hence, there is no rank reversal in TOPSIS. Now, VIKOR is used to rank the aforementioned alternatives. According to the VIKOR result, the preference order of choices is obtained as 5-1-4-2-3. When A_3 is eliminated from the original set, we get 5-4-1–2, and one can notice the ranking order between A_4 and A_1 is reversed. Simply speaking, VIKOR suffers from rank reversal in this case. Nevertheless, if we apply R-VIKOR introduced by Yang and Wu (2020) for this example, we have the ranking sequence as 5-1-4-2-3. After the deletion of A_3, the ranking order remains unchanged as 5-1-4-2. Consequently, R-VIKOR is immune to rank reversal in

TABLE 81.1 Decision matrix of example 1.

Alternatives	Criteria			
	$C_1(+)$	$C_2(+)$	$C_3(+)$	$C_4(+)$
A_1	78	56	34	6
A_2	4	45	3	97
A_3	18	2	50	63
A_4	9	14	11	92
A_5	85	9	100	29

TABLE 81.2 Weighted normalized decision matrix of example 1.

Alternatives	Criteria			
	$C_1(+)$	$C_2(+)$	$C_3(+)$	$C_4(+)$
A_1	0.1005	0.1111	0.0429	0.0052
A_2	0.0051	0.0892	0.0037	0.0844
A_3	0.0231	0.0039	0.0631	0.05487
A_4	0.0115	0.0277	0.0138	0.0801
A_5	0.1095	0.01785	0.1262	0.02526

TABLE 81.3 The ranking obtained using root assessment method (example 1).

Alternatives	S_{+i}	S_{-i}	$\sqrt[2+S_{-i}]{2+S_{+i}}$	Normalization results of RI_i	Rank
A_1	0.259782	0	1.503257	0.8703	2
A_2	0.182723	0	1.477404	0.3426	3
A_3	0.145173	0	1.464641	0.0821	4
A_4	0.133404	0	1.460618	0	5
A_5	0.278917	0	1.509608	1	1

TABLE 81.4 Ranking result using RAM, TOPSIS, VIKOR, and R-VIKOR (example 1).

Priority of alternatives	TOPSIS	VIKOR	R-VIKOR	RAM
1	A_5	A_5	A_5	A_5
2	A_1	A_1	A_1	A_1
3	A_2	A_4	A_4	A_2
4	A_3	A_2	A_2	A_3
5	A_4	A_3	A_3	A_4

this case, whereas this paradox occurs in VIKOR. The ranking order of alternatives obtained by the aforementioned MCDM methods can be found in Table 81.4.

The results presented in Table 81.4 indicate that the first two alternatives identified by all MCDM methods are exactly the same. To compare the ranking performances of RAM and R-VIKOR, although Spearman's rank correlation coefficient (SRCC) is obtained as 0.7, the weighted similarity (WS) coefficient is computed as 0.901, which indicates a strong correlation between results derived using these methods (see e.g., Kizielewicz et al.,2024). In this case, clearly, the WS coefficient can measure the similarity of rankings more persuasively (closer to human thinking) than SRCC.

81.5 Numerical example 2

81.5.1 Background

With the increase in industrialization and urbanization, the world stands on the precipice of an energy crisis. For example, owing to the improvement of living standards, the energy consumption of buildings comprises around 40% of the world's total energy use (Xin et al., 2024). Nevertheless, according to the World Health Organization (WHO), around 10% of the world's population (675 million people) suffers from the lack of access to electricity, and 2.3 billion people rely on non-clean fuels for cooking (Alegre-Bravo & Anderson, 2023; Yang et al., 2024). Unfortunately, the use of such fuels can exacerbate the indoor air pollution, causing 3.2 million deaths, including 237,000 children under 5 years old in 2020 (Feng et al., 2025). Although the rapid progress of renewable energy technologies has brought a glimmer of hope for a sustainable energy transition, challenges remain. For example, Taiwan imports around 98% of its energy supply from the Middle East, and most of its energy demand is made up of fossil fuel sources (Bergero et al., 2021). Bui et al. (2024) pointed out that the energy system of Taiwan must be improved, otherwise an energy crisis in this country is inevitable. In order to overcome the serious challenges of energy security and the reduction of greenhouse gas emissions, expanding the utilization of renewable energy resources has become a key energy policy for Taiwan. Fortunately, Taiwan enjoys different resources of renewable energy, offering an opportunity for a sustainable alleviation of the energy crisis (Chung et al., 2024). The current numerical example uses RAM to rank the priority of renewable energy resources in this country.

81.5.2 Case study

Please consider the following real case taken from Lee and Chang (2018), where five types of renewable energy resources in Taiwan, namely solar(A_1), wind(A_2), hydro(A_3), biomass(A_4), and geothermal(A_5) are assessed on the basis of ten criteria. Following Lee and Chang (2018), Shannon's entropy was used to obtain the weights of the criteria. The decision matrix on Taiwan's renewable energy resources is provided in Table 81.5. In Table 81.5, the sign (+) and sign (-) denote the benefit and cost criteria, respectively.

First, we apply RAM to the data of Example 2. The results provided in Table 81.6 shows A_3 and A_5 are ranked first and last, respectively. We can notice from Table 81.4 that A_3 has excellent performance in terms of benefit criteria and also performs very well under cost criteria. As mentioned, RAM permits trade-offs between benefit criteria. Hence, the relatively poor performance of A_3 under C_5 can be compensated for by its excellent performance in C_4. Also, according to RAM, compensation between the cost criteria can exist. We can see that the excellent performance of A_3 under C_2 can counterbalance its very poor performance in C_8. Similarly, the poor performance of A_1 under C_5 can be compensated for by its excellent performance in C_9. In contrast, A_5 performs very poorly regarding both benefit and cost criteria. It should be noted that although the performance ofA_5 is not the worst under some important criteria, such as C_9, its total performance is very poor. Also, we can see from Table 81.5, A_4 and A_5 take the last two positions, and the overall scores of them are very close to each other. Finally, RAM ranked A_1 2nd, which was predictable because it performs very well with respect to benefit criteria and relatively well under cost criteria.

TABLE 81.5 The decision matrix for renewable energy sources selection.

Alternatives	Weight	Criteria									
		$C_1(-)$	$C_2(-)$	$C_3(-)$	$C_4(+)$	$C_5(+)$	$C_6(+)$	$C_7(-)$	$C_8(-)$	$C_9(+)$	$C_{10}(+)$
		0.026	**0.154**	**0.089**	**0.199**	**0.115**	**0.039**	**0.080**	**0.123**	**0.172**	**0.003**
A_1		4550	30	6.74	20	15	5	85	150	0.87	4.76
A_2		3005	60.86	2.4	35	27	4	26	200	0.17	4.51
A_3		2040	14.85	1.7	90	25	5	26	500	0.27	4.19
A_4		3370	99.4	3.25	25.3	54	3	45	222	0.21	3.78
A_5		3920	112.6	4.93	11.4	71.7	2	50	100	0.25	4.11

TABLE 81.6 Priority of choices by root assessment method (example 2).

Alternatives	S_{+i}	S_{-i}	$RI_i = \sqrt[2+S_{-i}]{2 + S_{+i}}$	*Normalization results of* RI_i	*Rank*
A_1	0. 12633	0.09998	1.432239	0.5424	2
A_2	0. 07981	0. 07653	1.422824	0.2023	3
A_3	0. 15057	0. 08056	1.444904	1	1
A_4	0. 08703	0. 10876	1.417504	0.0102	4
A_5	0. 08425	0. 10614	1.417221	0	5

TABLE 81.7 Priority of choices by diverse multiple criteria decision-making methods (example 2).

Priority of alternatives	TOPSIS	WSM	ELECTRE	WASPAS	VIKOR	RAM
1	A_3	A_3	A_3	A_3	A_3	A_3
2	A_1	A_1	A_1	A_1	A_2	A_1
3	A_2	A_2	A_2	A_2	A_1	A_2
4	A_5	A_5	A_5	A_4	A_4	A_4
5	A_4	A_4	A_4	A_5	A_5	A_5

In order to further verify the reliability of RAM, we compare the ranking order derived by RAM with other MCDM methods, such as the weighted sum model (WSM), TOPSIS, VIKOR, ELECTRE, and WASPAS. The ranking results derived by RAM and the tested methods are presented in Table 81.7.

From Table 81.7, it can be seen that RAM and all other methods ranked A_3, A_1 andA_2 in the top three positions (VIKOR ranked A_2 and A_1 2nd and 3rd, respectively). More precisely, A_3 is the first choice according to all MCDM methods, and all methods ranked A_1 2nd except VIKOR. Also, based on RAM and any other MCDM method, A_4 and A_5 are ranked in the last two positions. In fact, the RI_i listed in Table 81.6 shows that the scores of A_5 and A_4 are very close to each other. Also, we can see from the above results that RAM and WASPAS derived the same ranking of options.

We are going to evaluate the derived results by the SRCC and WS coefficient. According to Table 81.7, RAM, VIKOR, TOPSIS, WSM, and ELECTRE agree on the ranking of three of the five choices. Statistically speaking, SRCC between RAM and VIKOR, between RAM and WSM, between RAM and TOPSIS, and between RAM and ELECTRE are also computed as 0.9. However, the WS coefficient for comparing RAM and VIKOR is computed as 0.854, whereas for RAM and TOPSIS, RAM and WSM, and RAM and ELECTRE, the value of the WS coefficient is 0.971.

Of course, the differences at the top of the ranked list are more significant than the bottom, and one can notice that the WS coefficient can be better suited than SRCC for comparing the similarity of results in this case. Again, it is worth mentioning that since RAM and ELECTRE have different backgrounds (RAM is a partially compensatory method, while ELECTRE is a noncompensatory method), such comparisons should be cautiously interpreted. A visual comparison of results is shown in Fig. 81.1. It can be observed from Fig. 81.1 that there are slight discrepancies among intermediate rankings obtained by different MCDM methods.

It is important to recall that in many situations, a decision is not made by one DM only. In fact, MCDM can be enriched with MCGDM to integrate the individual opinions into group decisions. Fortunately, RAM has been efficiently extended to tackle an MCGDM (see e.g., Yang et al., 2025), and modified RAM can be easily applied to the above case in a group decision-making environment.

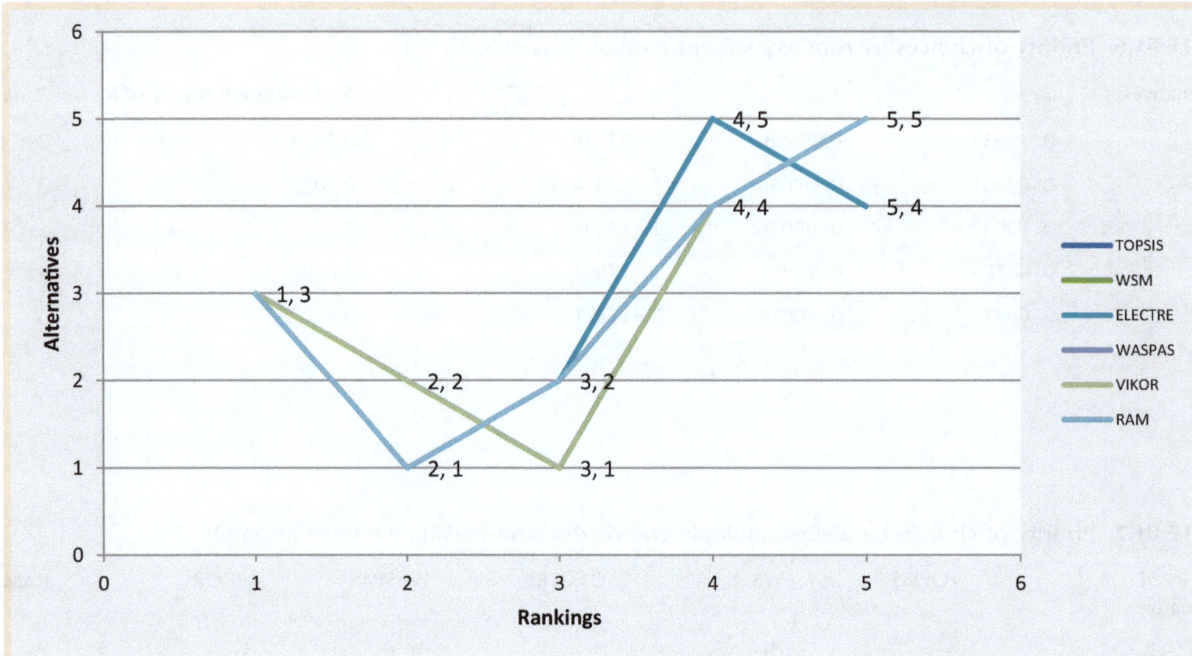

FIGURE 81.1 Comparison of ranking positions for example 2.

81.6 Conclusion

RAM, which first appeared in October 2023, is unique in the way it approaches an MCDM problem. The RAM algorithm is intuitively appealing, easy to implement, and requires no parameter tuning. RAM prevents the "black box" phenomenon encountered in some MCDM methods, produces interpretable results, and obtains comparable results with classical and state-of-the-art MCDM methods. Fortunately, RAM overcame some of the limitations of traditional MCDM methods. The fast-growing applications of RAM are clear through this literature review. Like any new MCDM method, RAM is in its infancy; further verifications are necessary, and much remains to be learned.

Some directions for future research are summarized as follows. While nonmonotonic criteria are extensively used in real-world problems, the work considering nonmonotonic criteria in RAM is rare (see e.g., Corrente & Tasiou, 2023). Also, studying how various normalization techniques may affect the rank reversal in RAM is another interesting research topic. Another future research includes extending RAM under Fermatean fuzzy Z-numbers (see e.g., Sari, 2024) and Z^E-numbers (see e.g., Haseli et al., 2025) to handle the high levels of uncertainty. From the perspective of application scenarios, the use of RAM in the field of energy poverty evaluation (see e.g., Hasheminasab et al., 2023) can be interesting for future work. While approximately 50% of buildings' energy consumption is consumed by heating, ventilating, and air-conditioning (HVAC) systems, 40% of this energy may be saved using energy-efficient systems. Developing an MCDM framework based on RAM to evaluate and rank the most suitable HVAC systems (see e.g., Bac et al., 2021), considering sustainability criteria, particularly those related to energy efficiency, is of practical significance.

Acknowledgments

The author would like to thank DAMANDEH Company as an international and leading company in the HVAC industry[1] (Electromotors, Residential ventilators, Industrial fans, Car-parks and Tunnel ventilation, and Home appliances), for its support during this research, and also Dr. Iman Abshang (Director of human capital/ DAMANDEH Company) for helpful discussions on issues.

1. https://www.damandeh.com/

References

Abootalebi, S., Hadi-Vencheh, A., & Jamshidi, A. (2019). Ranking the alternatives with a modified TOPSIS method in multiple attribute decision making problems. *IEEE Transactions on Engineering Management, 69*(5), 1800–1805.

Alegre-Bravo, A., & Anderson, C. L. (2023). Exploring the influence of multidimensional variables on access to electricity in rural areas of the Global South. *Applied Energy, 333*, 120509.

Alrashdi, I., Ali, A. M., Sallam, K. M., & Abdel-Basset, M. (2025). Intelligent decision support framework for assessment of alternative vehicle technologies in transportation system: A sustainable approach toward environmental remedy. *Sustainable Futures,* 100472.

Bac, U., Alaloosi, K. A. M. S., & Turhan, C. (2021). A comprehensive evaluation of the most suitable HVAC system for an industrial building by using a hybrid building energy simulation and multi criteria decision making framework. *Journal of Building Engineering, 37*, 102153.

Bergero, C., Binsted, M., Chao, C. W., Chou, K. T., Wu, C. C., Wei, Y., & McJeon, H. C. (2021). An integrated assessment of a low coal low nuclear future energy system for Taiwan. *Energy and Climate Change, 2*, 100022.

Biswas, S., Biswas, B., & Mitra, K. (2025). A novel group decision making model to compare online shopping platforms. *Spectrum of Decision Making and Applications, 2*(1), 1–27.

Bui, T. D., Kumpimpa, T., Lin, C. W. R., Lim, M. K., & Tseng, M. L. (2024). Assessing energy resilience under uncertainty in Taiwan: System response ability and energy sufficiency. *Energy Strategy Reviews, 53*, 101403.

Chang, C. L. (2010). A modified VIKOR method for multiple criteria analysis. *Environmental Monitoring and Assessment, 168*, 339–344.

Chung, Y. C., Kunene, N., & Chang, H. H. (2024). Renewable energy certificates and firm value: Empirical evidence in Taiwan. *Energy Policy, 184*, 113870.

Corrente, S., & Tasiou, M. (2023). A robust TOPSIS method for decision making problems with hierarchical and non-monotonic criteria. *Expert Systems with Applications, 214*, 119045.

Dehshiri, S. S. H., & Firoozabadi, B. (2023). A new multi-criteria decision making approach based on wins in league to avoid rank reversal: A case study on prioritizing environmental deterioration strategies in arid urban areas. *Journal of Cleaner Production, 383*, 135438.

Van Dua, T., Trung, D. D., Giang, N. T. P., & Van Duc, D. (2024). Comparison of two methods: RAM and AROMAN. In *International conference on sustainability and emerging technologies for smart manufacturing*. Singapore: Springer Nature Singapore, 727–735.

Dudic, B., Nguyen, N. T., & Ašonja, A. (2024). Data normalization for root assessment methodology. *International Journal of Industrial Engineering and Management, 15*(2), 156–168.

Dudić, B., Van Duc, D., Son, N. H., & Mittelman, A. (2024). Building a ranking system for lecturers based on student evaluations in teaching a specific course: A Case Study at a University in Vietnam. *International Journal of Cognitive Research in Science, Engineering and Education, 12*(2), 335–350.

Elsayed, A. (2024). TrS-RAM: Leveraging novel MCDM techniques for evaluating sustainability of fuel cell vehicles based on tree soft technique. *HyperSoft Set Methods in Engineering, 1*, 46–58.

Feng, Y., Han, Y., Hu, S., & Pan, Y. (2025). Alleviating energy poverty globally: Does digital government matter? *Energy Economics,* 108272.

Giang, N. T., & Thinh, H. X. (2025). Comparing subjective weighting methods in multi-criteria decision-making: An application to electric bicycle ranking. *Engineering, Technology & Applied Science Research, 15*(2), 21963–21969.

Haseli, G., Nazarian-Jashnabadi, J., Shirazi, B., Hajiaghaei-Keshteli, M., & Moslem, S. (2024). Sustainable strategies based on the social responsibility of the beverage industry companies for the circular supply chain. *Engineering Applications of Artificial Intelligence, 133*, 108253.

Haseli, G., Yazdani, M., Shaayesteh, M. T., & Hajiaghaei-Keshteli, M. (2025). Logistic hub location problem under fuzzy extended Z-numbers to consider the uncertainty and reliable group decision-making. *Applied Soft Computing, 171*, 112751.

Hasheminasab, H., Streimikiene, D., & Pishahang, M. (2023). A novel energy poverty evaluation: Study of the European Union countries. *Energy, 264*, 126157.

Hezam, I. M., Ali, A. M., Sallam, K., Hameed, I. A., Foul, A., & Abdel-Basset, M. (2024). An extension of root assessment method (RAM) under spherical fuzzy framework for optimal selection of electricity production technologies toward sustainability: A case study. *International Journal of Energy Research, 2024*(1), 7985867.

Hien, N. T. T., Quynh, P. H., & Minh, V. Q. (2025). A comparative analysis of multi-criteria decision-making methods. *Engineering, Technology & Applied Science Research, 15*(5), 26369–26375.

Kizielewicz, B., Shekhovtsov, A., Więckowski, J., Wątróbski, J., & Sałabun, W. (2024). Intelligent characteristic objects method (INCOME): A data knowledge-based multi-criteria decision analysis. *Artificial Intelligence Review, 57*(10), 266.

Komasi, H., Nemati, A., Zolfani, S. H., Williams, N. L., & Šaparauskas, J. (2024). Comparative analysis of economic development indicators among South American countries based on a novel MCDM model. *Journal of Competitiveness, 16*(3), 97–121.

Lee, H. C., & Chang, C. T. (2018). Comparative analysis of MCDM methods for ranking renewable energy sources in Taiwan. *Renewable and sustainable energy reviews, 92*, 883–896.

Li, Q., & Chen, W. (2025). Clear approach to education quality evaluation of multilingual higher education internationalization under probabilistic simplified neutrosophic sets for academic improvement. *Neutrosophic Sets and Systems, 81*, 526–539.

Lin, M., Chen, Z., Xu, Z., Gou, X., & Herrera, F. (2021). Score function based on concentration degree for probabilistic linguistic term sets: An application to TOPSIS and VIKOR. *Information Sciences, 551*, 270–290.

Linh, N. T. D., Son, N. H., & Thao, D. X. (2025). Evaluating the impact of weighting methods on the stability of scores for alternatives in multi-criteria decision-making problems. *Engineering, Technology & Applied Science Research, 15*(1), 19998–20004.

Mai, N. T. (2025). Hybrid multi-criteria decision making methods: Combination of preference selection index method with faire un choix adèquat, root assessment method, and proximity indexed value. *Engineering, Technology & Applied Science Research, 15*(1), 19086–19090.

Mela, K., Tiainen, T., & Heinisuo, M. (2012). Comparative study of multiple criteria decision making methods for building design. *Advanced Engineering Informatics, 26*(4), 716–726.

Mohamed, M., Salam, A., Ye, J., & Yong, R. (2024). Single-valued neutrosophic MCDM approaches integrated with MEREC and RAM for the selection of UAVs in forest fire detection and management. *Neutrosophic Systems with Applications, 19*, 1–14.

Munier, N., Hontoria, E., Munier, N., & Hontoria, E. (2021). Shortcomings of the AHP method. *Uses and Limitations of the AHP Method: A Non-mathematical and Rational Analysis,* 41–90.

Opricovic, S., & Tzeng, G. H. (2004). Compromise solution by MCDM methods: A comparative analysis of VIKOR and TOPSIS. *European Journal of Operational Research, 156*(2), 445–455.

Rasoanaivo, R. G., Yazdani, M., Zaraté, P., & Fateh, A. (2024). Combined compromise for ideal solution (CoCoFISo): A multi-criteria decision-making based on the CoCoSo method algorithm. *Expert Systems with Applications, 251*, 124079.

Rong, Y., Yu, L., Liu, Y., Simic, V., & Pamucar, D. (2024). A pharmaceutical cold-chain logistics service quality model using a q-rung orthopair fuzzy framework with distance measure. *Engineering Applications of Artificial Intelligence, 136*, 109019.

Sari, I. U. (2024). Fermatean fuzzy Z-analytic hierarchy process: An application to third party logistics providers. *Engineering Applications of Artificial Intelligence, 133*, 108327.

Setiawansyah, S. (2024). Integration of root assessment method and entropy weighting in determining business location selection. *Journal of Artificial Intelligence and Technology Information, 2*(4), 209–221.

Shekhovtsov, A., Kizielewicz, B., & Sałabun, W. (2025). Version [1.3]-[pymcdm–The universal library for solving multi-criteria decision-making problems]. *SoftwareX*, 102051.

Sotoudeh-Anvari, A. (2022). The applications of MCDM methods in COVID-19 pandemic: A state of the art review. *Applied Soft Computing, 126*, 109238.

Sotoudeh-Anvari, A. (2023). Root assessment method (RAM): A novel multi-criteria decision making method and its applications in sustainability challenges. *Journal of Cleaner Production, 423*, 138695.

Sotoudeh-Anvari, A. (2025). Root assessment method (RAM) under neutrosophic environment. In *Neutrosophic paradigms: Advancements in decision making and statistical analysis: Neutrosophic principles for handling uncertainty*. Cham: Springer Nature Switzerland, 123–138.

Thanh, P. V., Van Duc, D., Khoa, H. X., & Van Dua, T. (2025). Integrating the root assessment method with subjective weighting methods for battery electric vehicle selection. *Engineering, Technology & Applied Science Research, 15*(2), 21526–21531.

Thinh, H. X. (2024). The use of saw, ram and piv decision methods in determining the optimal choice of materials for the manufacture of screw gearbox acceleration boxes. *International Journal of Mechanical Engineering and Robotics Research, 13*(3), 338–347.

Trung, D. D., Duc, D. V., Bao, N. C., Son, N. H., Thuy, D. T. T., & Nga, N. T. T. (2025). R-RAM: A novel hybrid model for option ranking. *Yugoslav Journal of Operations Research,* (00), 9 -9.

Trung, D. D., Duc, D. V., Bao, N. C., & Thuy, D. T. T. (2024). Using the root assessment method to choose the optimal solution for mushroom cultivation. *Yugoslav Journal of Operations Research,* (00), 7 -7.

Wang, J., Darwis, D., Gunawan, R.D., & Ariany, F. (2025). Optimizing E-commerce platform selection using root assessment method and MEREC weighting.

Więckowski, J., Hernes, M., & Sałabun, W. (2025). Comparison of multi-criteria decision analysis methods under comprehensive sensitivity analysis. *IEEE Access*.

Xin, X., Zhang, Z., Zhou, Y., Liu, Y., Wang, D., & Nan, S. (2024). A comprehensive review of predictive control strategies in heating, ventilation, and air-conditioning (HVAC): Model-free VS model. *Journal of Building Engineering,* 110013.

Xing, K., Wang, X., & Chen, P. (2025). Robust seismic performance evaluation of super high-rise concrete structures using MCDM and plithogenic-RAM approach. *Neutrosophic Sets and Systems, 80*, 229–246.

Yalçın, G. C., Kara, K., & Özyürek, H. (2025). Evaluating financial performance of companies in the borsa istanbul sustainability index using the CRITIC-MABAC method. *Spectrum of Operational Research, 2*(1), 323–346.

Yang, L., Niu, J., & Li, J. (2025). Interval-valued neutrosophic sets-based IVNS-RAM method for enhanced security evaluation in computer networks. *Neutrosophic Sets and Systems, 77*, 479–491.

Yang, W., & Wu, Y. (2020). A new improvement method to avoid rank reversal in VIKOR. *IEEE Access, 8*, 21261–21271.

Yang, X. (2025). Advanced combined multi-criteria decision-making methodology with indetermsoft set for comprehensive analysis of blended physical education teaching in colleges framework. *Neutrosophic Sets and Systems, 82*, 515–529.

Yang, Y., Jiang, M., Li, X., & Chen, Y. (2024). Energy poverty and household development resilience: Household level evidence from China. *Energy, 309*, 133003.

Zaidan, B. B., Ibrahim, H. A., Mourad, N., Zaidan, A. A., Pilehkouhic, H., Qahtan, S., & Delen, D. (2024). An in-depth analysis of ensemble multi-criteria decision making: A comprehensive guide to terminology, design, applications, evaluations, and future prospects. *Applied Soft Computing, 167*, 112267.

Zanakis, S. H., Solomon, A., Wishart, N., & Dublish, S. (1998). Multi-attribute decision making: A simulation comparison of select methods. *European Journal of Operational Research, 107*(3), 507–529.

Chapter 82

RANCOM: Ranking comparison for multi-attribute decision-making

Wojciech Sałabun[1,2] and Andrii Shekhovtsov[1,2]
[1]*National Institute of Telecommunications, Warsaw, Poland,* [2]*West Pomeranian University of Technology in Szczecin, Szczecin, Poland*

82.1 Introduction

Multicriteria decision analysis (MCDA) provides tools and techniques to support decisions in the presence of multiple, often conflicting criteria (Sun, 2024). One of the fundamental components of MCDA methods is the determination of the weights of the criteria, as they quantify the relative importance of the criteria within the decision-making process. Because the weighting stage often relies on expert knowledge, subjective weighting methods are essential in practical applications in engineering, management, economics, public policy, and related fields (Więckowski et al., 2023a). However, subjective assessments are frequently influenced by cognitive limitations, uncertainty, and inconsistency, especially as the number of criteria grows or when experts must operate with incomplete information (Roszkowska & Wachowicz, 2021).

Historically, structured subjective weighting procedures have undergone substantial development. The introduction of Saaty's analytic hierarchy process (AHP) in the early 1980s formalized expert judgment through pairwise comparison matrices and consistency assessment (Tavana et al., 2023). Subsequent methods extended this concept by introducing direct scoring schemes, point-allocation strategies, and trade-off mechanisms to improve expressiveness and practical applicability (Moslem et al., 2023). More recent approaches, such as the best–worst method (BWM), further streamlined the elicitation process by reducing the number of required comparisons while preserving methodological soundness (Liang et al., 2020). Despite these advances, traditional approaches still rely on precise preference judgments and often assume a high degree of internal consistency, assumptions that are difficult to satisfy in real-world decision environments, particularly when experts face uncertainty, limited information, or cognitive constraints (Funk et al., 2020). This highlights the need for methods capable of accommodating imprecision and hesitation while maintaining practical usability and robustness in various decision-making situations.

To address these limitations, the ranking comparison (RANCOM) method introduces a ranking-based approach to subjective weighting in MCDA. Instead of relying on precise numerical judgments, RANCOM operates on simplified pairwise relations derived from expert-provided rankings. The method also employs a reduced judgment scale and allows ties between criteria, reflecting situations where experts consider certain criteria to be of comparable importance. This design reduces cognitive burden, increases tolerance to hesitation and imprecision, and improves robustness to inconsistency, particularly when the number of criteria increases, conditions under which classical methods such as AHP often exhibit reduced stability (Więckowski et al., 2023b).

The procedure begins by constructing a matrix of ranking comparison (MAC) based on the pairwise relations implied by the expert rankings. A normalization process is then applied to obtain the final weights of the criteria. Experimental studies indicate that RANCOM produces repeatable, reliable, and stable weight vectors, achieving high agreement with established methods while demonstrating greater resilience to expert errors and inconsistencies. As a result, RANCOM offers a practical and cognitively efficient alternative for subjective weighting in complex decision environments.

This chapter provides a comprehensive and structured overview of the RANCOM method by clarifying its theoretical foundations, presenting the complete computational procedure, and demonstrating its practical relevance. A simple numerical example is included to illustrate the core mechanism and transparency of the approach, followed by a more complex decision scenario that demonstrates scalability to higher-dimensional problems. Furthermore, a comparative

Encyclopedia of Multi-Attribute Decision-Making (MADM). DOI: https://doi.org/10.1016/B978-0-443-33275-3.00017-8

analysis highlights the strengths and limitations of the method in relation to classical subjective weighting techniques, with particular emphasis on cognitive simplicity and robustness to inconsistency.

The remainder of this chapter is organized as follows. Section 82.2 presents a review of the literature on the applications of the RANCOM method and the main directions of its development. Section 82.3 describes the RANCOM method, introduces the required notation, and details the computational procedure. Section 82.4 presents a simple numerical example illustrating the basic implementation of the method, while Section 82.5 extends the analysis to a more complex decision scenario to demonstrate its scalability and practical applicability. Section 82.6 provides a comparative and sensitivity analysis. Finally, Section 82.7 concludes the chapter and suggests directions for future research.

82.2 Literature review

The RANCOM method has appeared in recent years as a robust alternative to classical subjective weighting procedures in MCDA. Its initial formulation introduced a ranking-comparison mechanism designed to reduce cognitive burden and mitigate inconsistency in expert judgments, showing superior stability over AHP in problems involving five or more criteria (Więckowski et al., 2023b). Following its introduction, research attention has increasingly focused on methodological refinement and extension of the approach. A significant development is the fuzzy extension of RANCOM, in which triangular fuzzy numbers were incorporated to better capture uncertainty in expert assessments while maintaining computational simplicity and outperforming fuzzy AHP in ambiguous environments (Więckowski and Kizielewicz, 2025). Further advances are reflected in the RANCOM-ST variant, where statistical thresholds derived from Monte Carlo simulations are used to adjust subjective assessments and reduce expert bias, improving stability, particularly in small-scale decision settings (Shkurina, 2025).

Other methodological developments include the introduction of the weights similarity coefficient to systematically evaluate the closeness of weight vectors generated by different subjective weighting techniques and to compare the reliability of RANCOM against established methods (Shekhovtsov & Dobryakova, 2023). Adaptive and group-decision versions have also been proposed, extending the method to large expert panels and enabling the aggregation of diverse judgments while maintaining robustness (Więckowski and Kizielewicz, 2025). Sensitivity studies have also highlighted the resilience of RANCOM to perturbations in input data and the importance of criteria, positioning it favorably among subjective weighting approaches in terms of stability and reliability (Więckowski and Sałabun, 2023; Więckowski et al., 2023c). In parallel to theoretical advances, the method has been implemented in the open-source pymcdm library, ensuring accessibility for practitioners and researchers and facilitating integration with other MCDA techniques (Kizielewicz and Shekhovtsov, 2023; Shekhovtsov and Kizielewicz, 2025).

In parallel with methodological advancements, a burgeoning body of research highlights RANCOM's practical use in various fields. Early studies illustrated its effectiveness in consumer-oriented decision support, such as laptop selection using RANCOM combined with Stable Preference Ordering Towards Ideal Solution (SPOTIS) and Reference Ideal Method (RIM) (Shekhovtsov & Dobryakova, 2023). Subsequent work applied RANCOM to energy and environmental sustainability, including offshore wind power station location analysis under intuitionistic fuzzy conditions with interval values (Rani et al., 2024) and comparative evaluation of renewable-energy MCDA techniques such as complex proportional assessment, preference ranking organization method for enrichment evaluation II, and evaluation based on distance from average solution (Więckowski et al., 2024a). Hybrid approaches have used RANCOM in conjunction with Expected Solution Point SPOTIS (ESP-SPOTIS) for personalized electric-vehicle selection (Więckowski et al., 2024b) and in comprehensive sustainability ranking models (Więckowski et al., 2023c). Extensions into neutrosophic, q-rung orthopair fuzzy, and picture fuzzy environments demonstrate its flexibility in complex decision spaces (Arunodaya et al., 2024; Rani et al., 2025a, 2025b). Applications in organizational and industrial settings include sustainable human-resource management (Rani et al., 2025b), evaluation of logistics barriers 4.0 using fuzzy polytopic RANCOM (Korucuk & Aytekin, 2024), decision-support frameworks for small- and medium-sized enterprises (SMEs) (Mishra et al., 2024), and risk assessment in digital-transformation programs (Rani et al., 2025a). Finally, comparative studies employing weighted similarity metrics have further confirmed the reliability of RANCOM in generating stable weights in a range of aggregation models (Shekhovtsov, 2023).

In general, the literature demonstrates that RANCOM has evolved from a simple ranking-based weighting approach to a versatile methodological platform with strong theoretical foundations, numerous uncertainty-aware variants, and growing adoption in practical MCDA applications. The recent surge in research activity and diverse application contexts highlights its relevance as a cognitively efficient, error-resilient, and flexible tool for subjective weighting in decision-making environments.

82.3 Methodology

The RANCOM method determines subjective importance weights of criteria based solely on the ordinal preference information provided by the decision-maker. Unlike classical ratio-based pairwise comparison approaches, this method relies on simple preference ordering and allows ties, operating on a reduced conceptual scale that requires only basic preference statements rather than precise intensity judgments (Więckowski et al., 2023b). This limited comparison vocabulary reduces the cognitive burden on the expert and increases the resilience to inconsistency.

Let $C = \{c_1, c_2, \ldots, c_n\}$ denote the set of criteria. In the standard use of the method, the decision-maker provides a ranking of criteria, where $c_i \succ c_j$ indicates that the criterion c_i is preferred over c_j, and $c_i \sim c_j$ denotes the same importance (a tie). If the expert cannot provide a complete ranking, RANCOM can alternatively accommodate direct pairwise judgments between all criteria using the same reduced preference scale. Based on the ordinal information supplied, the MAC $A = [a_{ij}]$ is constructed by assigning:

$$a_{ij} = \begin{cases} 1, & \text{if} c_i \succ c_j, \\ 0.5, & \text{if} c_i \sim c_j \text{or} i = j, \\ 0, & \text{if} c_i \prec c_j. \end{cases} \tag{82.1}$$

The importance score of the criterion c_i is then calculated as the sum of its comparison values:

$$SCW_i = \sum_{j=1}^{n} a_{ij}. \tag{82.2}$$

To obtain the normalized importance weights $\mathbf{w} = (w_1, \ldots, w_n)$, each score is divided by the total score sum:

$$w_i = \frac{SCW_i}{\sum_{k=1}^{n} SCW_k}, \quad i=1, \ldots, n, \tag{82.3}$$

ensuring $w_i \geq 0$ and $\sum_{i=1}^{n} w_i = 1$.

The fixed scale $\{1, 0.5, 0\}$ reflects a reduced linguistic judgment domain corresponding to three basic preference states: preferred, equal, and less preferred. Such a simplified comparison space supports intuitive reasoning and eliminates the need for ratio-scale assessments typically required in classical methods such as AHP. The method preserves monotonicity, meaning that a criterion positioned higher in the preference structure always receives a weight greater than a criterion positioned lower. Due to the ordinal nature of the input, RANCOM avoids ratio-scale inconsistencies and is resilient to minor judgment conflicts. The resulting weights are transparent and easy to interpret, making the method particularly suitable for decision scenarios where eliciting precise quantitative preference intensities is impractical.

The computational complexity of the method is $O(n^2)$ due to the construction of the comparison matrix, followed by $O(n)$ for score aggregation and normalization. This ensures that RANCOM remains efficient for decision problems involving both small and moderately large sets of criteria. For group decision-making, individual MAC matrices provided by experts can be aggregated using arithmetic averaging (Więckowski and Kizielewicz, 2025):

$$A = \frac{1}{m} \sum_{k=1}^{m} A^{(k)}, \tag{82.4}$$

followed by the same scoring and normalization procedure. The above formulation corresponds to the case of equal expert weights (for m experts). In situations where experts are assigned different importance levels, the aggregation should be performed using their respective importance:

$$A = \sum_{k=1}^{m} \omega_k A^{(k)}, \quad \sum_{k=1}^{m} \omega_k = 1, \quad \omega_k \geq 0, \tag{82.5}$$

where ω_k denotes the importance assigned to expert k. This aggregation mechanism enables the inclusion of multiple expert opinions while preserving the ordinal character of the input and maintaining methodological transparency.

82.4 Numerical example 1

Consider a weighting task with five criteria $C = \{c_1, \ldots, c_5\}$ in which a single expert provides the following ranking with ties:

$$c_2 \succ c_3 \succ (c_1 \sim c_4) \succ c_5.$$

Following the RANCOM procedure described in Section 82.3, the ranking is converted into pairwise relations to construct the MAC $A = [a_{ij}]$ according to the assignment rule (1).

Using the order of rows/columns (c_1, c_2, c_3, c_4, c_5), the MAC is constructed as:

$$A = \begin{bmatrix} 0.5 & 0 & 0 & 0.5 & 1 \\ 1 & 0.5 & 1 & 1 & 1 \\ 1 & 0 & 0.5 & 1 & 1 \\ 0.5 & 0 & 0 & 0.5 & 1 \\ 0 & 0 & 0 & 0 & 0.5 \end{bmatrix}.$$

For each criterion, the importance score SCW_i is computed using Eq. (82.2):

$$SCW_i = \sum_{j=1}^{5} a_{ij},$$

yielding the scores

$$(SCW_1, \ldots, SCW_5) = (2.0,\ 4.5,\ 3.5,\ 2.0,\ 0.5), \quad \sum_{i=1}^{5} SCW_i = 12.5.$$

The normalized importance weights are then obtained using Eq. (82.3):

$$w_i = \frac{SCW_i}{\sum_{k=1}^{5} SCW_k}, \quad i = 1, \ldots, 5,$$

resulting in the final weight vector

$$\mathbf{w} = (0.16,\ 0.36,\ 0.28,\ 0.16,\ 0.04).$$

Table 82.1 summarizes the importance scores and normalized weights for all criteria.

The resulting weights align with the expert's ranking: the criterion c_2 receives the highest weight (0.36), followed by c_3 (0.28), the tied pair c_1 and c_4 (0.16 each), and finally c_5 (0.04). This shows that RANCOM preserves the ordinal preference structure, while transforming it into a normalized weight vector using only simple preference statements, without requiring intensity assessments.

82.5 Numerical example 2

We consider a group decision-making scenario with 10 criteria $C = \{c_1, \ldots, c_{10}\}$ and 3 experts ($m = 3$). Each expert provides an ordinal ranking with ties, ordering the criteria from the most important to the least important. The individual rankings are as follows:

$$\begin{aligned} &\text{Expert1: } c_2 \succ c_3 \succ (c_1 \sim c_4) \succ c_5 \succ (c_6 \sim c_7) \succ c_8 \succ c_9 \succ c_{10}, \\ &\text{Expert2: } c_3 \succ c_2 \succ c_5 \succ (c_1 \sim c_6) \succ c_4 \succ c_7 \succ (c_8 \sim c_9) \succ c_{10}, \\ &\text{Expert3: } (c_2 \sim c_5) \succ c_3 \succ c_1 \succ (c_4 \sim c_6) \succ c_7 \succ c_8 \succ c_9 \succ c_{10}. \end{aligned}$$

TABLE 82.1 Importance scores and normalized weights.

Criterion	c_1	c_2	c_3	c_4	c_5	Sum
SCW_i	2.00	4.50	3.50	2.00	0.50	12.50
w_i	0.16	0.36	0.28	0.16	0.04	1.00

Following the RANCOM procedure described in Section 82.3, each expert's ranking is transformed into a MAC $A^{(k)} = [a_{ij}^{(k)}]$ using the assignment rule (1). For expert k, the matrix elements are determined as:

$$a_{ij}^{(k)} = \begin{cases} 1, & \text{if} c_i \succ c_j, \\ 0.5, & \text{if} c_i \sim c_j \text{or} i = j, \\ 0, & \text{if} c_i \prec c_j. \end{cases}$$

Since we have three experts with equal importance, the group MAC is obtained by arithmetic averaging according to Eq. (82.4):

$$A = \frac{1}{3} \sum_{k=1}^{3} A^{(k)}.$$

For each expert k and each criterion c_i, the individual importance score $SCW_i^{(k)}$ is computed using Eq. (82.2):

$$SCW_i^{(k)} = \sum_{j=1}^{10} a_{ij}^{(k)}.$$

The aggregated importance score SCW_i is then obtained by averaging the individual scores across all experts:

$$SCW_i = \sum_{j=1}^{10} a_{ij} = \frac{1}{3} \sum_{k=1}^{3} SCW_i^{(k)}.$$

The normalized importance weights are computed using Eq. (82.3):

$$w_i = \frac{SCW_i}{\sum_{r=1}^{10} SCW_r}, \quad i=1, \ldots, 10.$$

Table 82.2 presents the importance scores provided by each expert, the aggregated scores, and the final normalized weights for all criteria. For readability, the individual 10 × 10 MAC matrices are omitted, as they can be reconstructed directly from the rankings using the assignment rule.

The resulting weights reflect the consensus among the three experts. The criterion c_2 receives the highest weight (0.180), closely followed by c_3 (0.170) and c_5 (0.147). The criteria c_1, c_4, and c_6 occupy the middle range with weights between 0.100 and 0.130, while the criteria c_7 through c_{10} receive progressively lower weights, with c_{10} assigned the

TABLE 82.2 Individual and aggregated importance scores with normalized weights.

Criterion	$SCW_i^{(1)}$	$SCW_i^{(2)}$	$SCW_i^{(3)}$	SCW_i	w_i
c_1	7.00	6.00	6.50	6.500	0.130
c_2	9.50	8.50	9.00	9.000	0.180
c_3	8.50	9.50	7.50	8.500	0.170
c_4	7.00	4.50	5.00	5.500	0.110
c_5	5.50	7.50	9.00	7.333	0.147
c_6	4.00	6.00	5.00	5.000	0.100
c_7	4.00	3.50	3.50	3.667	0.073
c_8	2.50	2.00	2.50	2.333	0.047
c_9	1.50	2.00	1.50	1.667	0.033
c_{10}	0.50	0.50	0.50	0.500	0.010
Sum	50.00	50.00	50.00	50.000	1.000

smallest weight (0.010). This distribution demonstrates how RANCOM aggregates individual expert preferences into a coherent group weight vector while preserving the overall ordinal structure and accommodating ties in the rankings.

This example illustrates the scalability of RANCOM to larger sets of criteria and its practical applicability in group decision-making contexts. Despite differences in individual expert rankings and the presence of multiple ties, the method produces a transparent and interpretable group weight vector without requiring ratio-scale judgments or explicit consistency checks. In the RANCOM method, the full pairwise preference structure is employed most often, resulting in computational complexity $O(n^2)$, as this approach preserves the entire relational structure of preferences, including ties. If the task were reduced solely to determining a linear order of criteria, it could be transformed into a classical sorting problem with $O(n \log n)$ complexity (e.g., merge sort or quicksort). However, RANCOM intentionally relies on pairwise preference information rather than enforcing a strict total order, thereby naturally accommodating equal preferences and retaining richer ordinal information from decision-makers.

82.6 Comparative analysis

One of the fundamental advantages of RANCOM lies in its deliberate reduction of the comparison scale to three basic preference states: preferred, equal, and less preferred. This design choice addresses a well-documented limitation in human judgment: the difficulty of maintaining consistent evaluations across fine-grained numerical scales. Classical methods such as AHP employ a nine-point scale (ranging from 1 to 9) to capture varying intensities of preference. Although theoretically richer, such scales impose a substantial cognitive burden on decision-makers, who often struggle to distinguish reliably between adjacent scale values or to maintain consistency across multiple comparisons. Empirical evidence from psychology and decision theory suggests that humans have a limited capacity for processing and maintaining multilevel distinctions, particularly when the number of criteria increases. Decision-makers frequently lose track of the scale's meaning, leading to inconsistent judgments and decreased reliability of the elicited preferences. In practical settings, experts rarely possess the precision required to meaningfully differentiate between, for instance, a preference intensity of five versus six on the AHP scale. This cognitive overload results in increased error rates and decreased confidence in the resulting weights.

RANCOM circumvents these difficulties by restricting the input vocabulary to a minimal but sufficient set of relations. The three-value scale aligns with the natural capacity for ordinal reasoning, enabling decision-makers to express their preferences without requiring quantitative precision. This simplification not only reduces the time and effort needed for the elicitation but also enhances the transparency and interpretability of the process. The resulting weights remain grounded in a clear and intuitive input structure, which is particularly valuable in group decision-making contexts where consensus and communication are essential.

An important feature of the RANCOM method is its flexibility in the manner of eliciting input data from the decision-maker. Regardless of the chosen form of elicitation, all approaches lead to the construction of the MAC, while preserving the fundamental principle of asking only about dominance relations, rather than about the strength or intensity of preference. The decision-maker may provide a complete ranking of criteria in which all criteria are ordered from most important to least important, with ties allowed for criteria of equal importance. Alternatively, it is possible to use a partially ordered set of criteria, which can then be refined through an interactive sorting algorithm that asks the decision-maker about dominance relations for selected pairs of criteria until a complete ordering is obtained. In cases where the decision-maker is unable or unwilling to provide a complete ranking, the method also accommodates partial pairwise comparisons, in which the expert evaluates only selected pairs of criteria according to preference relations. Finally, it is possible to generate a complete comparison matrix by systematically asking questions about every possible pair of criteria, which for n criteria requires $n(n-1)/2$ dominance assessments. Regardless of the chosen path for preference elicitation, the key difference compared to methods such as AHP remains the fact that the decision-maker is asked only to state which criterion is more important (or whether they are equivalent), without the need to quantify by how much one criterion exceeds another. This difference is fundamental in reducing the cognitive burden and increasing the reliability of the judgments obtained.

A key advantage of RANCOM is its natural tolerance to inconsistency in judgment. While classical pairwise-comparison approaches such as AHP require global transitivity and enforce consistency checks, often rejecting expert input through mechanisms like the consistency ratio and forcing iterative revisions, RANCOM accepts minor contradictions as inherent to real decision contexts. This flexibility is particularly important when many criteria are considered or when information is uncertain, aligning RANCOM with modern views on bounded rationality. Empirical results show that RANCOM maintains coherent and stable weight structures even in the presence of expert errors, outperforming AHP for problems with five or more criteria (Więckowski et al., 2023b). Moreover, similar to the local consistency evaluation based on triads in the matrix of expert judgements extension of characteristic objects method (Sałabun and Shekhovtsov, 2021), RANCOM allows one to assess the coherence of triads without imposing strict transitivity, and recent advances such as RANCOM-ST further strengthen robustness by integrating statistical thresholds (Shkurina, 2025).

The performance of RANCOM improves relative to that of classical methods as the number of criteria increases. For decision problems involving five or fewer criteria, ratio-based methods such as AHP can still be manageable, and the additional precision they offer may be beneficial. However, when dealing with 10 or more criteria, the cognitive load imposed by AHP becomes prohibitive. The number of pairwise comparisons grows quadratically with the number of criteria, and maintaining consistency across all judgments becomes increasingly difficult for human decision-makers. RANCOM addresses this challenge by converting a complete ranking into a comparison matrix. This transformation requires the expert to provide only one ranking statement rather than separate ratio judgments $n(n-1)/2$. For 10 criteria, this translates to one ranking input versus 45 pairwise comparisons in the classical approach. Reduction in required input alleviates cognitive fatigue and increases the likelihood that the expert can provide reliable and thoughtful preferences. Moreover, the ordinal nature of the input ensures that minor ranking errors propagate gracefully through the computation, resulting in only modest changes to the final weights.

AHP offers detailed ratio-based comparisons but becomes cognitively demanding and sensitive to inconsistency in large-scale problems. The nine-point scale, while theoretically expressive, often exceeds the practical judgment capacity of experts, leading to arbitrary or inconsistent input. BWM reduces the number of comparisons by focusing on best and worst criteria, but still relies on precise numerical judgments, which may be difficult for non-experts or in situations where preference intensities are uncertain. RANCOM differentiates itself by requiring only simple rankings with ties, significantly reducing cognitive load while providing results comparable to those of classical methods. Studies comparing RANCOM with AHP and BWM consistently indicate that RANCOM produces competitive or superior stability and repeatability, especially when expert uncertainty is high, and the complexity of decisions increases (Shekhovtsov & Dobryakova, 2023; Więckowski et al., 2023b).

RANCOM offers a number of benefits that make it particularly suitable for practical decision-making contexts. The method imposes a low cognitive burden due to simplified elicitation based on rankings rather than numerical judgments. It demonstrates strong robustness to expert errors, uncertainty, and minor inconsistencies in preferences. The scoring mechanism is interpretable, and the computational procedure is transparent, making it easy to communicate to stakeholders. The method naturally supports ties and hesitation in expert judgments, reflecting realistic decision-making behavior. Empirical evidence shows superior consistency and stability for decision problems involving five or more criteria, and the method scales efficiently to a large set of criteria without a proportional increase in cognitive load.

However, some limitations should be acknowledged. RANCOM provides limited resolution in weight differentiation compared to fine-grained ratio scales, which may be restrictive when precise trade-offs between criteria are known and can be reliably quantified. The method is less informative in scenarios where experts possess detailed quantitative knowledge about preference intensities and are capable of maintaining consistency across complex ratio judgments. Large expert groups may require aggregation strategies, although this limitation is addressed by extensions such as group RANCOM (Więckowski and Kizielewicz, 2025). The ordinal nature of the input precludes capturing nonlinear or disproportionate preference intensities that may exist in certain decision contexts.

82.7 Conclusions

This chapter presented the RANCOM method as a cognitively efficient and robust approach to deriving subjective weights in multicriteria decision analysis. By relying on ordinal preferences with ties, RANCOM eliminates the need for ratio-based judgments and consistency checks, allowing decision-makers to express preferences naturally. The method's fundamental principle, asking only about dominance relations rather than preference intensities, addresses well-documented limitations in human judgment capacity and significantly reduces cognitive burden, particularly for problems involving many criteria.

The numerical examples and comparative analysis confirmed that RANCOM exhibits strong resistance to inconsistency and expert error, outperforming classical approaches such as AHP in scenarios with many criteria or uncertain expert input. Its methodological transparency, computational simplicity, and flexibility in accommodating various input formats contribute to its practical applicability in different decision contexts. The method represents a pragmatic compromise between simplicity and expressiveness, prioritizing reliability and usability over theoretical precision, making it particularly suitable for complex decision contexts, group settings, and situations where expert uncertainty is present.

Future research directions include improving weight differentiation resolution through adaptive elicitation strategies that selectively request more detailed comparisons for closely ranked criteria, extending the method to more sophisticated group decision-making mechanisms for heterogeneous expert panels, and integrating statistical calibration procedures such as RANCOM-ST to further mitigate systematic biases. Additionally, incorporating RANCOM into hybrid MCDA pipelines with learning-based and probabilistic components, as well as expanding software implementations and conducting comprehensive benchmarking studies, will facilitate broader adoption in real-world decision systems. The continued evolution of RANCOM demonstrates that methodological simplicity and practical robustness can coexist with effective decision support.

References

Funk, P., et al. (2020). Individual inconsistency and aggregate rationality: Overcoming inconsistencies in expert judgment at the technical frontier. *Technological Forecasting and Social Change, 155*, 119984.

Kizielewicz, B., Shekhovtsov, A., & Sałabun, W. (2023). pymcdm - The universal library for solving multi-criteria decision-making problems. *SoftwareX, 22*, 101368. https://doi.org/10.1016/j.softx.2023.101368.

Korucuk, S., & Aytekin, A. (2024). A field study examining barriers to logistics 4.0 using polytopic fuzzy RANCOM. *Journal of Process Management and New Technologies, 12*, 90–100. https://doi.org/10.5937/jpmnt12-54800.

Liang, F., Brunelli, M., & Rezaei, J. (2020). Consistency issues in the best worst method: Mea-surements and thresholds. *In: Omega, 96*, 102175.

Mishra, A. R., et al. (2024). Evaluation and prioritization of sustainable enterprise resource planning in SMEs using q-rung orthopair fuzzy rough set-based decision support model. *IEEE Transactions on Fuzzy Systems, 32*(5), 3260–3273. https://doi.org/10.1109/TFUZZ.2024.3374799.

Moslem, S., et al. (2023). A systematic review of analytic hierarchy process applications to solve trans-portation problems: From 2003 to 2022. *IEEE Access, 11*, 11973–11990.

Rani, P., et al. (2024). Location selection for offshore wind power station using interval-valued in-tuitionistic fuzzy distance measure-RANCOM-WISP method. *Scientific Reports, 14*(1), 4706. https://doi.org/10.1038/s41598-024-54929-6.

Rani, J. P., et al. (2025a). Digital transformation project risks assessment using hybrid picture fuzzy distance measure-based additive ratio assessment method. *Scientific Reports, 15*(1), 3286. https://doi.org/10.1038/s41598-025-86598-4.

Rani, P., et al. (2025b). New distance measure-based RANCOM-AROMAN approach for evaluating sustainable human resource management factors in the manufacturing firms. *Operational Re-search, 25*(2), 41.. https://doi.org/10.1007/s12351-025-00916-2.

Roszkowska, E., & Wachowicz, T. (2021). Towards cognitive decision support: A model of be-havioural assessment of multi-criteria methods. *Control and Cybernetics, 50*(1), 145–168.

Sałabun, W., Shekhovtsov, A., & Kizielewicz, B. (2021). A new consistency coefficient in the multi-criteria decision analysis domain. In *International conference on computational science*. Springer, 715–727.

Shekhovtsov, A. (2023). Evaluating the performance of subjective weighting methods for multi-criteria decision-making using a novel weights similarity coefficient. *Procedia Computer Science, 225*, 4785–4794. https://doi.org/10.1016/j.procs.2023.10.478.

Shekhovtsov, A., & Dobryakova, L. (2023). Comparison of multi-criteria decision methods for customer-centered decision making: A practical study case. *Procedia Computer Science, 225*, 4824–4835. https://doi.org/10.1016/j.procs.2023.10.482.

Shekhovtsov, A., Kizielewicz, B., & Sałabun, W. (2025). Version [1.3J-[pymcdm-the universal library for solving multi-criteria decision-making problems]. *SoftwareX, 30*, 102051. https://doi.org/10.1016/j.softx.2025.102051.

Shkurina, A. (2025). An adaptive RANCOM-ST method for bias reduction using statistical thresholds. In *International conference on computational science*. Springer, 281–295. https://doi.org/10.1007/978-3-031-97567-7_22.

Sun, P. (2024). MABAC-based evaluation of multimedia technology application effect in film and television post-production. *International Journal of Knowledge-Based and Intelligent Engineering Systems, 28*(1), 59–72. eprint: https://doi.org/10.3233/KES-230074, https://journals.sagepub.com/doi/pdf/10.3233/KES-230074, https://journals.sagepub.com/doi/abs/10.3233/KES-230074.

Tavana, M., Soltanifar, M., & Santos-Arteaga, F. J. (2023). Analytical hierarchy process: Revolution and evolution. *In: Annals of operations research, 326*(2), 879–907.

Więckowski, J., Kizielewicz, B., & Sałabun, W. (2025). A new approach to large-scale multi-criteria group decision-making based on the RANCOM method. In *International conference on computational science*. Springer, 250–264. https://doi.org/10.1007/978-3-031-97567-7_20.

Więckowski, J., et al. (2023a). Recent advances in multi-criteria decision analysis: A comprehensive review of applications and trends. *International Journal of Knowledge-Based and Intelligent Engineering Systems, 27*(4), 367–393. eprint: https://doi.org/10.3233/KES-230487, https://journals.sagepub.com/doi/pdf/10.3233/KES-230487, https://journals.sagepub.com/doi/abs/10.3233/KES-230487.

Więckowski, J., et al. (2023b). RANCOM: A novel approach to identifying criteria relevance based on inaccuracy expert judgments. *Engineering Applications of Artificial Intelligence, 122*, 106114.. https://doi.org/10.1016/j.engappai.2023.106114.

Więckowski, J., et al. (2023c). "Complex sensitivity analysis in MCDA: An application to the selection of an electric car. *Journal of Cleaner Production, 390*, 136051. https://doi.org/10.1016/j.jclepro.2023.136051.

Więckowski, J., et al. (2024a). Application of COPRAS, PROMETHEE, and EDAS methods in sustain-able energy development: A comparative study case. *Procedia Computer Science, 246*, 5428–5438. https://doi.org/10.1016/j.procs.2024.09.680.

Więckowski, J., et al. (2024b). Adaptive multi-criteria decision making for electric vehicles: A hybrid approach based on RANCOM and ESP-SPOTIS. *Artificial Intelligence Review, 57*(10), 270.. https://doi.org/10.1007/s10462-024-10901-4.

Więckowski, J., Kizielewicz, B., & Sałabun, W. (2025). Fuzzy RANCOM: A novel approach for modeling uncertainty in decision-making processes. *Information Sciences, 694*, 121716. https://doi.org/10.1016/j.ins.2024.121716.

Więckowski, J., & Sałabun, W. (2023). Sensitivity analysis approaches in multi-criteria decision analysis: A systematic review. *In: Applied Soft Computing, 148*, 110915. https://doi.org/10.1016/j.asoc.2023.110915.

Więckowski, J., et al. (2024b). Adaptive multi-criteria decision making for electric vehicles: A hybrid approach based on RANCOM and ESP-SPOTIS. *Artificial Intelligence Review, 57*(10), 270. https://doi.org/10.1007/s10462-024-10901-4.

Więckowski, J., Kizielewicz, B., & Sałabun, W. (2024). Fuzzy RANCOM: A novel approach for modeling uncertainty in decision-making processes. *Information Sciences*, [illegible]. https://doi.org/10.1016/j.ins.2024.[illegible].

Więckowski, J., & Sałabun, W. (2023). Sensitivity analysis approaches in multi-criteria decision analysis: A systematic review. *Applied Soft Computing, 148*, 110915. https://doi.org/10.1016/j.asoc.2023.110915.

Chapter 83

RAWEC: Ranking of alternatives with weights of criterion for multi-attribute decision-making

Golman Rahmanifar[1], Mostafa Mohammadi[2], Mostafa Hajiaghaei-Keshteli[3], Gaetano Fusco[4], and Chiara Colombaroni[4]

[1]*Department of Industrial Engineering & Innovation Sciences, Eindhoven University of Technology, Eindhoven, North Brabant, Netherlands,* [2]*Department of Industrial Economics and Technology Management, Norwegian University of Science and Technology, Trondheim, Trøndelag, Norway,* [3]*School of Science and Engineering, Tecnologico de Monterrey, Monterrey, Mexico,* [4]*Department of Civil, Constructional and Environmental Engineering, Sapienza University of Rome, Rome, Italy*

83.1 Introduction to multiple-criteria decision-making

Real-world decisions in logistics, energy planning, healthcare, public policy, and manufacturing rarely hinge on a single objective; they require careful trade-offs among economic, technical, environmental, and social criteria, often under uncertainty and stakeholder disagreement (Greco et al., 2016; Ishizaka & Nemery, 2013). Multiple-criteria decision-making (MCDM) also called multiple-criteria decision analysis (MCDA) offers a family of models and procedures to structure such problems, elicit preferences, and rank or select alternatives (Hwang & Yoon, 1981; Triantaphyllou, 2000). In a typical study, the analyst first structures the problem by defining the decision context, stakeholders, and feasible alternatives $A_1, \ldots, A_m$; then models the criteria $C_1, \ldots, C_n$ and their scales (benefit vs cost; quantitative vs qualitative); next captures preferences through the elicitation of importance weights and, where appropriate, value or utility functions or indifference and preference thresholds (Keeney & Raiffa, 1993); subsequently synthesizes performances and preferences to deliver a ranking, a choice, or a sorting/classification outcome (Triantaphyllou, 2000); and finally examines robustness through sensitivity and uncertainty analyses while cross-checking against alternative MCDM methods (Greco et al., 2016; Ishizaka & Nemery, 2013).

MCDM methods fall into several broad families that differ in both preference representation and the rules used for aggregating across criteria. Value- and utility-based models multi-attribute utility theory (MAUT)/multi-attribute value theory (MAVT)) quantify preferences with value or utility functions and typically aggregate additively or multiplicatively (Keeney & Raiffa, 1993). Hierarchical ratio-scale models, such as the analytic hierarchy process (AHP) and analytic network process, derive priority weights from pairwise comparisons within a hierarchy or network and then combine local priorities into global scores (Saaty, 1980). Outranking approaches, including elimination and choice translating reality (ELECTRE) and preference ranking organization method for enrichment evaluation (PROMETHEE), construct preference relations using concordance–discordance logic, allowing incomparabilities and partial orders that are meaningful in contentious, multistakeholder settings (Roy, 1996). Distance-to-ideal and compromise models, exemplified by technique for order preference by similarity to ideal solution (TOPSIS) and VlseKriterijumska Optimizacija I Kompromisno Resenje (VIKOR), assess each alternative by its closeness to an ideal point and remoteness from an antiideal configuration (Hwang & Yoon, 1981; Triantaphyllou, 2000). Beyond these, reference-based disaggregation, such as the Additive Utilities (UTA) family, objective weighting schemes such as entropy and criteria importance through intercriteria correlation (CRITIC), and numerous hybrids extend the toolkit to address data- or context-specific needs (Greco et al., 2016; Ishizaka & Nemery, 2013).

Encyclopedia of Multi-Attribute Decision-Making (MADM). DOI: https://doi.org/10.1016/B978-0-443-33275-3.00048-8

Because criteria are heterogeneous, normalization maps raw scores to comparable scales. Linear max–min rescaling, vector normalization, and double normalization are common choices, selected with an eye to interpretability, scale properties, and method compatibility. Weights can be elicited subjectively through methods such as direct rating, swing weighting, or AHP; derived objectively from data dispersion using entropy or CRITIC; or combined to balance expertise with evidence. The elicitation route should be transparent about underlying value judgments, responsive to data quality, and aligned with stakeholder needs (Ishizaka & Nemery, 2013; Triantaphyllou, 2000).

Modern MCDM increasingly incorporates uncertainty and group decision-making. Probabilistic representations and a variety of fuzzy extensions (including intuitionistic, hesitant, and neutrosophic variants) support imprecision in both performances and preferences, while group settings motivate procedures for aggregating judgments, reconciling disagreements, and documenting consensus or conflict (Greco et al., 2016; Ishizaka & Nemery, 2013). Robustness is typically explored through local and global sensitivity analyses, scenario analysis, and method cross-validation; in health technology assessment, for example, good-practice recommendations emphasize explicit problem structuring, transparent criteria definitions, and systematic sensitivity checks (Thokala et al., 2016).

Within the distance-to-ideal stream, recent work introduced the ranking of alternatives with weights of criterion (RAWEC) model, designed to retain conceptual clarity while reducing computational overhead. By pairing double normalization with a compact deviation-based index, RAWEC aims to preserve validity and interpretability while streamlining the number of procedural steps. The remainder of this chapter positions RAWEC in relation to established methods, details its mathematical foundations, and illustrates its use with a worked example and application scenarios (Puška et al., 2024).

83.2 Methodology

Building on the conceptual discussion in the previous sections, this section develops the RAWEC model in a more formal way. We first offer an overview that highlights the main ideas of the method and its four-step workflow from raw data to a final ranking. We then introduce the mathematical notation and normalization schemes in detail, leading to the deviation-based index Q_i that underpins the ranking of alternatives. This structure is intended to keep the link between the intuitive description and the underlying formulas transparent, and to facilitate implementation in practical decision studies.

83.2.1 Overview of the ranking of alternatives with weights of criterion method

The RAWEC is a recent MCDM procedure designed to streamline the path from raw performance data to a final ranking while remaining compatible with standard practices such as explicit weighting and normalization (Puška et al., 2024). RAWEC handles both benefit criteria, where higher values are preferable, and cost criteria, where lower values are preferable, and it does so by employing a two-track normalization that produces parallel "benefit" and "cost" views of the same decision matrix. The key idea is to evaluate each alternative's closeness to an ideal benchmark in the benefit-normalized space while simultaneously evaluating its remoteness from a worst-case benchmark in the cost-normalized space, and then to combine these insights through a compact index.

Let $X = [x_{ij}]$ denote the initial decision matrix with m alternatives $A_1, \ldots, A_m$ and n criteria $C_1, \ldots, C_n$, and let $w_1, \ldots, w_n$ be nonnegative criterion weights summing to one. RAWEC begins by creating two normalized matrices in [0,1]. The first converts all criteria into a benefit perspective so that larger normalized values are favorable. For a benefit criterion C_j, the transformation is $n_{ij} = x_{ij}/\max_i\{x_{ij}\}$; for a cost criterion, the transformation is $n_{ij} = \min_i\{x_{ij}\}/x_{ij}$. This yields $N = [n_{ij}]$, where the best observed performance under each criterion is scaled to 1 , and other performances are expressed proportionally. In parallel, RAWEC constructs a second matrix that reflects a cost perspective so that larger normalized values correspond to less favorable outcomes from a "cost" vantage. For a benefit criterion C_j, this mapping is $n'_{ij} = \min_i\{x_{ij}\}/x_{ij}$; for a cost criterion, it is $n'_{ij} = x_{ij}/\max_i\{x_{ij}\}$. This yields $N' = [n'_{ij}]$, again within [0,1], but now aligned with a complementary antiideal interpretation.

Rather than weighting first and then computing ideal or antiideal distances separately, RAWEC folds these operations together by measuring weighted deviations from the top value 1 in each normalized matrix. For each alternative A_i, the deviation under the benefit-normalized view is

$$v_i = \sum_{j=1}^{n} w_j(1 - n_{ij}),$$

so smaller v_i means A_i is closer to the benefit-side ideal across criteria once weights are considered. Symmetrically, the deviation under the cost-normalized view is

$$v'_i = \sum_{j=1}^{n} w_j(1 - n'_{ij}),$$

which decreases as A_i moves away from the antiideal cost-side. The method then synthesizes these two pieces of information into a single score

$$Q_i = \frac{v'_i - v_i}{v'_i + v_i},$$

which lies in $[-1,1]$ and increases with desirability. Alternatives with larger Q_i are preferred, and the complete ranking follows by sorting Q_i in descending order (Puška et al., 2024).

An appealing feature of RAWEC is that it remains agnostic about how the weights w_j are obtained: expert-based procedures (e.g., direct rating, swing weighting, or AHP), data-driven schemes (e.g., entropy or CRITIC), or hybrid approaches can all be used prior to the RAWEC aggregation without modifying the core mechanics. Conceptually, the method leverages a transparent "double look" at the same evidence—benefit-oriented and cost-oriented—so that the final score reflects both closeness to the ideal and distance from the antiideal without introducing additional constructs or thresholds. In practice, this yields a concise four-step workflow from raw data to ranking: build the decision matrix, apply the dual normalizations, compute the two weighted deviations, and evaluate the Q_i index. The compressed pipeline reduces intermediate objects and calculations relative to many distance-to-ideal procedures, while retaining interpretability at each stage (Puška et al., 2024).

Empirical validations reported for the original formulation show that RAWEC typically delivers rankings that are strongly aligned with widely used comparators such as simple additive weighting (SAW), TOPSIS, additive ratio assessment (ARAS), and weighted aggregated sum product assessment (WASPAS), with differences primarily attributable to the choice of normalization and distance constructs; importantly, RAWEC achieves this agreement with fewer computational steps and a single closed-form index for interpretation (Puška et al., 2024). This blend of parsimony and fidelity makes it particularly attractive in applications where traceability and speed are essential, and where analysts may wish to compare results seamlessly against other MCDM baselines without retooling the entire pipeline.

83.2.2 Mathematical details and notation

Let $A = \{A_1, \ldots, A_m\}$ denote the set of alternatives and $C = \{C_1, \ldots, C_n\}$ the set of evaluation criteria. Performances are collected in the decision matrix $X = [x_{ij}] \in \mathbb{R}^{m\times n}$, where x_{ij} is the observed (or assessed) performance of alternative A_i on criterion C_j. Each criterion is designated either as a benefit (larger is better) or a cost (smaller is better), and each criterion receives a nonnegative importance weight w_j with $\sum_{j=1}^{n} w_j = 1$. In applications, the weights can be obtained by expert-based or data-driven procedures; RAWEC itself is agnostic about the elicitation step and only requires a normalized vector $\mathbf{w} = (w_1, \ldots, w_n)$ as input (Puška et al., 2024).

RAWEC builds two normalized views of X on the unit interval $[0,1]$ and then measures weighted deviations from the top value 1 in each view. The first view, $N = [n_{ij}]$, converts all criteria to a benefit perspective so that larger values are more desirable. For a benefit criterion C_j, the mapping is $n_{ij} = x_{ij}/\max_i\{x_{ij}\}$, while for a cost criterion it is $n_{ij} = \min_i\{x_{ij}\}/x_{ij}$. The result satisfies $0 \le n_{ij} \le 1$ provided the denominators are strictly positive, and it sets the column-wise best observed performance to 1. In parallel, a complementary cost-oriented view $N' = [n'_{ij}]$ is formed. For a benefit criterion C_j, this mapping is $n'_{ij} = \min_i\{x_{ij}\}/x_{ij}$, while for a cost criterion it is $n'_{ij} = x_{ij}/\max_i\{x_{ij}\}$, again yielding values in $[0,1]$ with column-wise extremes mapped to 1 but now aligned with an antiideal interpretation (Puška et al., 2024). These monotone, ratio-based normalizations are standard in distance-to-ideal procedures and preserve the order of performances within each criterion (Triantaphyllou, 2000).

Given (N, N') and $\mathbf{w}$, RAWEC folds weighting and distance assessment into a single deviation computation per view. For each alternative A_i, the deviation from the benefit-side ideal is

$$v_i = \sum_{j=1}^{n} w_j(1 - n_{ij}),$$

which decreases as the alternative approaches the ideal value 1 across criteria after weighting. Symmetrically, the deviation from the cost-side antiideal is

$$v'_i = \sum_{j=1}^{n} w_j(1 - n'_{ij}),$$

which decreases as the alternative moves away from the antiideal. RAWEC synthesizes these quantities into a closed-form index

$$Q_i = \frac{v'_i - v_i}{v'_i + v_i},$$

which lies in $[-1,1]$ whenever $v'_i + v_i > 0$; larger Q_i indicates a more desirable alternative, and ranking follows by sorting Q_i in descending order (Puška et al., 2024). The denominator is strictly positive except in degenerate cases where all criteria are constant across alternatives (so that $n_{ij} = n'_{ij} = 1$ for every (i, j)), in which case it is natural to set $Q_i = 0$ by continuity and treat all alternatives as tied.

The inputs required by RAWEC are the decision matrix with clearly declared benefit and cost directions for each criterion, together with a nonnegative weight vector normalized to sum to one. The columnwise extrema used in the two normalizations must be strictly positive; if a column can take zero or negative values, a monotone shift should be applied prior to scaling so that the minimum and maximum are positive and ratios are well defined. When a column has no dispersion, meaning its minimum equals its maximum, the criterion carries no discriminative power and can be retained with all normalized entries set to one in both views without affecting the index, or removed with weights renormalized across the remaining criteria. Missing entries should be imputed before normalization or, if imputation is undesirable, the affected criterion can be excluded for all alternatives and the weights renormalized. All computations are carried out in full precision, with rounding deferred to presentation; ties arise naturally when alternatives share identical deviations.

Several properties follow from the construction. First, RAWEC is scale-invariant to positive multiplicative (ratio-scale) rescalings applied per criterion before normalization, because the min–max ratios defining N and N' cancel such scalings at the column level; it is not, however, invariant to arbitrary additive shifts. Second, RAWEC is weakly monotone with respect to each criterion: improving x_{ij} on a benefit criterion (or decreasing it on a cost criterion), holding all other entries and weights fixed, cannot worsen Q_i because n_{ij} increases and n'_{ij} decreases in a way that reduces v_i relative to v'_i. Third, the method's sensitivity to weights is explicit: if the analyst increases w_j for a criterion on which A_i is closer to its ideal in N than to its antiideal in N', then Q_i tends to increase; conversely, emphasizing criteria where A_i performs relatively poorly tends to decrease Q_i. These directional effects make weight-driven sensitivity analysis straightforward to interpret (Puška et al., 2024; Triantaphyllou, 2000).

83.3 Numerical example 1: simple ranking of alternatives with weights of criterion application

To illustrate RAWEC in practice, consider the selection of a logistics facility among three alternatives A_1, A_2, A_3 evaluated on four criteria $C_1, \ldots, C_4$. Let C_1 and C_4 be benefits (larger is better) and C_2 and C_3 be costs (smaller is better). Suppose the weight vector is $\mathbf{w}=(0.25,0.20,0.30,0.25)$, reflecting the relative importance of capacity, acquisition cost, access, and readiness, respectively. The initial decision matrix $X = [x_{ij}]$ is shown below (areas in acres, costs in thousands of dollars, distances in kilometers, and a readiness score on a 1–10 scale):

$X =$

	C_1 (benefit)	C_2 (cost)	C_3 (cost)	C_4 (benefit)
A_1	15	400	25	5
A_2	20	350	40	8
A_3	10	300	20	6

Following RAWEC, two normalized views are created (Puška et al., 2024). In the benefit-oriented view $N = [n_{ij}]$, each column is scaled so that higher numbers are more desirable. For a benefit criterion, $n_{ij} = x_{ij}/\max_i x_{ij}$; for a cost criterion, $n_{ij} = \min_i x_{ij}/x_{ij}$. With $\max C_1=20$ and $\max C_4=8$ for the benefit criteria, and $\min C_2=300$ and $\min C_3=20$ for the cost criteria, the resulting matrix is

$N =$

	C_1	C_2	C_3	C_4
A_1	0.750	0.750	0.800	0.625
A_2	1.000	0.857	0.500	1.000
A_3	0.500	1.000	1.000	0.750

In the complementary cost-oriented view $N' = [n'_{ij}]$, each column is scaled so that larger values reflect less favorable (cost-side) outcomes. For a benefit criterion, $n'_{ij} = \min_i x_{ij}/x_{ij}$; for a cost criterion, $n'_{ij} = x_{ij}/\max_i x_{ij}$. Using $\min C_1=10$ and $\min C_4=5$ for the benefits, and $\max C_2=400$ and $\max C_3=40$ for the costs, we obtain

$$N' = \begin{array}{c|cccc} & C_1 & C_2 & C_3 & C_4 \\ A_1 & 0.667 & 1.000 & 0.625 & 1.000 \\ A_2 & 0.500 & 0.875 & 1.000 & 0.625 \\ A_3 & 1.000 & 0.750 & 0.500 & 0.833 \end{array}$$

RAWEC merges weighting and distance assessment by computing, for each alternative, the weighted deviations from the top value 1 in both views (Puška et al., 2024; Triantaphyllou, 2000). For transparency, consider A_1: under the benefit normalization, v_1=0.25(1 − 0.750) + 0.20(1 − 0.750) + 0.30(1 − 0.800) + 0.25(1 − 0.625)=0.26625. Under the cost normalization, v'_1=0.25(1 − 0.667) + 0.20(1 − 1.000) + 0.30(1 − 0.625) + 0.25(1 − 1.000)=0.195833 .... All other values are computed analogously from N' and $\mathbf{w}$. Carrying this out yields v_2=0.178571, v_3=0.1875, and v'_2=0.24375, v'_3=0.241667.

RAWEC then synthesizes these two pieces into a single score

$$Q_i = \frac{v_i' - v_i}{v_i' + v_i},$$

which lies in [−1,1] provided $v'_i + v_i > 0$ (Puška et al., 2024). Substituting the values above, one obtains

$$Q_1 = -0.1524, \quad Q_2 = 0.1543, \quad Q_3 = 0.1262,$$

where the values are rounded at four decimals from full-precision calculations. The ranking is therefore $A_2 \succ A_3 \succ A_1$. Interpreting the numbers, A_2 enjoys the largest capacity and the highest readiness score while keeping acquisition cost moderate; A_3 benefits from the lowest costs and shortest distance but is penalized by limited capacity and a middling readiness score; A_1 lags on readiness and cost simultaneously, giving it the lowest index. Because Q_i is constructed from deviations in both normalized views, this ordering jointly reflects closeness to the ideal in the benefit space and distance from the antiideal in the cost space without the need to compute those reference points explicitly or to introduce additional thresholds (Puška et al., 2024).

This toy problem also illustrates two practical aspects. First, changes in $\mathbf{w}$ translate transparently into changes in Q_i because the deviations are linear in the weights; for instance, increasing w_1 (capacity) would further boost A_2 relative to A_3 due to A_2 's advantage on C_1. Second, recomputation is lightweight: updating column extrema, the normalized matrices, and the (v_i, v'_i, Q_i) triplets is $O(mn)$, which supports interactive what-if analysis during stakeholder workshops and facilitates side-by-side comparisons with alternative MCDM baselines (Puška et al., 2024).

83.4 Numerical example 2: complex group decision case

This second example illustrates the application of RAWEC in a more complex, group decision-making context with more than six alternatives and criteria, in line with the chapter guidelines. We consider the selection of a location for a regional agricultural distribution center. Three decision-makers (DMs) jointly evaluate seven candidate sites on seven criteria that mix cost, accessibility, environmental, and social dimensions.

83.4.1 Problem description and criteria

The set of alternatives is $A = \{A_1, \ldots, A_7\}$, representing candidate sites in the region. The criteria are: C_1—land acquisition cost (k$/ha, cost), C_2—distance to main producers (km, cost), C_3—distance to main urban market (km, cost), C_4—transport access score (1–10, higher = better, benefit), C_5—environmental risk index (1–10, higher = worse, cost), C_6—expansion potential (1–10, higher = better, benefit), and C_7—local employment support index (1–10, higher = better, benefit). Table 83.1 shows the initial decision matrix $X = [x_{ij}]$. Costs are given in thousands of dollars per hectare, distances in kilometers, and scores on a 1–10 scale.

83.4.2 Group weighting of criteria

Three DMs provide their own importance weights over the seven criteria, each weight vector normalized to sum to one. DM1 (more cost-oriented) uses $w^{(1)}$=(0.20, 0.15, 0.15, 0.15, 0.10, 0.15, 0.10); DM2 (emphasizes accessibility and expansion) uses $w^{(2)}$=(0.15, 0.10, 0.10, 0.20, 0.10, 0.20, 0.15); and DM3 (emphasizes environmental and social criteria) uses $w^{(3)}$=(0.10, 0.10, 0.10, 0.15, 0.15, 0.20, 0.20).

To obtain a collective group weighting, a simple arithmetic mean is used, that is $w = \frac{1}{3}(w^{(1)} + w^{(2)} + w^{(3)})$, which yields the aggregated weight vector $w \approx$ (0.150, 0.117, 0.117, 0.167, 0.117, 0.183, 0.150), normalized to sum to one. In this

TABLE 83.1 Decision matrix X (seven alternatives, seven criteria).

Alt.	C_1	C_2	C_3	C_4	C_5	C_6	C_7
A_1	35	25	40	7	6	7	6
A_2	30	30	35	8	5	8	7
A_3	28	20	50	6	4	9	8
A_4	40	18	45	9	7	6	5
A_5	32	22	38	7	3	7	9
A_6	27	28	42	5	4	8	7
A_7	33	24	36	8	5	6	8

TABLE 83.2 Benefit-oriented normalized matrix N.

Alt.	C_1	C_2	C_3	C_4	C_5	C_6	C_7
A_1	0.771	0.720	0.875	0.778	0.500	0.778	0.667
A_2	0.900	0.600	1.000	0.889	0.600	0.889	0.778
A_3	0.964	0.900	0.700	0.667	0.750	1.000	0.889
A_4	0.675	1.000	0.778	1.000	0.429	0.667	0.556
A_5	0.844	0.818	0.921	0.778	1.000	0.778	1.000
A_6	1.000	0.643	0.833	0.556	0.750	0.889	0.778
A_7	0.818	0.750	0.972	0.889	0.600	0.667	0.889

configuration, expansion potential (C_6) and land cost (C_1) are the most influential criteria, followed by transport access (C_4) and local employment support (C_7).

83.4.3 Application of the ranking of alternatives with weights of criterion method

We now apply the RAWEC procedure using the group weight vector w and the cost/benefit pattern specified above.

83.4.3.1 Dual normalization

First, columnwise minima and maxima are computed for each criterion:

$$\min C=(27,\ 18,\ 35,\ 5,\ 3,\ 6,\ 5),\ \max C=(40,\ 30,\ 50,\ 9,\ 7,\ 9,\ 9).$$

The benefit-oriented view $N = [n_{ij}]$ is obtained as $n_{ij} = x_{ij}/\max_i x_{ij}$ for benefit criteria C_j, and $n_{ij} = \min_i x_{ij}/x_{ij}$ for cost criteria C_j. Table 83.2 reports the resulting normalized matrix (rounded to three decimals).

The cost-oriented view $N' = [n'_{ij}]$ is defined symmetrically as $n'_{ij} = \min_i x_{ij}/x_{ij}$ for benefit criteria C_j, and $n'_{ij} = x_{ij}/\max_i x_{ij}$ for cost criteria C_j. Table 83.3 shows the corresponding normalized matrix N' (rounded to three decimals).

TABLE 83.3 Cost-oriented normalized matrix N'.

Alt.	C_1	C_2	C_3	C_4	C_5	C_6	C_7
A_1	0.875	0.833	0.800	0.714	0.857	0.857	0.833
A_2	0.750	1.000	0.700	0.625	0.714	0.750	0.714
A_3	0.700	0.667	1.000	0.833	0.571	0.667	0.625
A_4	1.000	0.600	0.900	0.556	1.000	1.000	1.000
A_5	0.800	0.733	0.760	0.714	0.429	0.857	0.556
A_6	0.675	0.933	0.840	1.000	0.571	0.750	0.714
A_7	0.825	0.800	0.720	0.625	0.714	1.000	0.625

TABLE 83.4 Deviations and ranking of alternatives with weights of criterion index Q_i.

Alt.	v_i	v'_i	Q_i
A_1	0.2676	0.1770	− 0.2039
A_2	0.1806	0.2570	0.1748
A_3	0.1534	0.2790	0.2905
A_4	0.2691	0.1324	− 0.3405
A_5	0.1316	0.2963	0.3847
A_6	0.2181	0.2139	− 0.0097
A_7	0.2026	0.2343	0.0725

83.4.3.2 Deviations and ranking of alternatives with weights of criterion index

For each alternative A_i, RAWEC computes the deviation from the benefit-side ideal in N, $v_i = \sum_{j=1}^{7} w_j(1 - n_{ij})$, and the deviation from the cost-side antiideal in N', $v'_i = \sum_{j=1}^{7} w_j(1 - n'_{ij})$. The RAWEC index is then defined as

$$Q_i = \frac{v_i' - v_i}{v_i' + v_i},$$

which lies in $[-1,1]$ whenever $v'_i + v_i > 0$. Using the group weight vector w, we obtain the values in Table 83.4 (rounded to four decimals).

Ranking the alternatives in descending order of Q_i gives $A_5 \succ A_3 \succ A_2 \succ A_7 \succ A_6 \succ A_1 \succ A_4$.

83.5 Comparative analysis: advantages and limitations of ranking of alternatives with weights of criterion

In line with the comparative-analysis role of this section, we now examine the RAWEC method in terms of its main strengths and weaknesses. Earlier sections have positioned RAWEC within the distance-to-ideal family and illustrated its mechanics through numerical examples; here, the focus shifts to a critical assessment of how the method behaves relative to well-known MCDM approaches such as SAW, TOPSIS, VIKOR, and outranking procedures. The aim is to provide decision analysts with a clear view of when RAWEC is an appropriate choice and when alternative methods may be more suitable.

83.5.1 Advantages of the ranking of alternatives with weights of criterion method

RAWEC was explicitly designed to preserve the conceptual clarity of distance-to-ideal reasoning while reducing procedural complexity. Its most salient advantages concern its computational parsimony, interpretability, and compatibility with existing weighting practices.

First, RAWEC has a compact four-step structure: construction of the decision matrix, dual benefit-cost normalization, computation of the two weighted deviations, and evaluation of a single index Q_i. Unlike methods such as TOPSIS or VIKOR, RAWEC does not require explicit construction of ideal and antiideal points or separate distance measures. This lowers computational overhead and simplifies implementation while retaining the basic ideal/antiideal logic.

Second, the dual normalization provides a rich yet transparent view of performance. By building two normalized matrices—one from a benefit perspective and one from a cost perspective—RAWEC simultaneously captures closeness to the ideal and remoteness from the antiideal without introducing additional parameters or thresholds. This "double look" at the same evidence clarifies how benefit and cost aspects jointly affect the ranking and can be presented in straightforward tabular form.

Third, RAWEC synthesizes information into a single symmetric index $Q_i \in [-1,1]$. Alternatives with larger Q_i are preferred, and the bounded, symmetric scale supports intuitive interpretation: values close to 1 indicate strong overall performance, values near 0 indicate balanced or middling performance, and negative values reflect alternatives that are closer to the cost-side antiideal than to the benefit-side ideal. This compact representation is easier to communicate than multicomponent measures.

Fourth, the method is neutral with respect to weight elicitation. Any normalized weight vector can be used, whether obtained from subjective schemes (such as direct rating, swing weighting, or AHP), objective schemes (such as entropy or CRITIC), or hybrid procedures. RAWEC's aggregation mechanism remains unchanged, which allows practitioners to integrate the method into existing organizational or sector-specific weighting protocols without reworking the core algorithm.

Finally, empirical evidence suggests strong alignment with established methods. The original formulation of RAWEC reports that its rankings are typically highly correlated with those obtained from SAW, TOPSIS, ARAS, and WASPAS, with differences largely attributable to normalization and distance choices rather than to contradictory preference modeling (Puška et al., 2024). This makes RAWEC attractive both as a lean alternative and as a robustness check alongside more elaborate distance-based methods.

83.5.2 Limitations and when other methods may be preferable

Alongside these advantages, RAWEC exhibits limitations that should be recognized to avoid inappropriate use. These limitations arise primarily from its compensatory nature, its normalization strategy, and the absence of explicit mechanisms for modeling uncertainty or incomparability.

First, RAWEC is fully compensatory: weak performance on one criterion can be offset by strong performance on others. In decision contexts where certain criteria are critical, so that very low scores should disqualify an alternative regardless of its strengths elsewhere, this property may be undesirable. Outranking methods such as ELECTRE and PROMETHEE, which can incorporate veto thresholds and model incomparabilities, are better suited to such noncompensatory preference structures (Roy, 1996).

Second, RAWEC relies on ratio-based normalization using columnwise minima and maxima. This makes the method sensitive to outliers or noisy extreme values, because the best and worst observed performances determine the scaling for each criterion. If the extrema are unrepresentative, normalized scores may overstate or understate differences between alternatives. In practice, careful preprocessing—such as checking data quality, trimming extreme observations, or exploring robust variants of normalization is recommended before applying RAWEC.

Third, the normalization formulas require strictly positive denominators. When a criterion can take zero or negative values, the data must be shifted or transformed to ensure positive minima and maxima before computing ratios. Although these transformations can be monotone and therefore preserve the ordering within each criterion, they introduce additional modeling choices that must be justified and documented, especially in sensitive decision contexts.

Fourth, RAWEC in its basic form does not model uncertainty or fuzziness. Performances and weights are treated as precise quantities. While RAWEC can in principle be embedded within fuzzy, probabilistic, or interval-valued frameworks, such extensions go beyond the core method. In problems where deep uncertainty, imprecise judgments, or group aggregation are central, approaches explicitly tailored to those features may be more appropriate.

Finally, RAWEC always produces a complete ranking of alternatives. It does not natively represent indifference ranges, preference thresholds, or incomparabilities. In controversial or multistakeholder settings where it is important to acknowledge that some alternatives cannot be cleanly ranked without additional value judgments, outranking-based or interactive MCDA procedures may offer a more nuanced representation of the decision situation as suggested by Haseli et al., (2020, 2023).

83.5.3 When to use ranking of alternatives with weights of criterion versus other multiple-criteria decision-making methods

The advantages and limitations outlined above indicate that RAWEC is particularly appealing in situations where the decision-maker seeks to minimize computational complexity without sacrificing methodological transparency. Because it merges dual normalization with deviation computation into a single four-step pipeline, it offers a leaner path from raw data to ranking than methods such as TOPSIS, VIKOR, or PROMETHEE, which typically require the separate construction of ideal and antiideal reference points or additional preference structures. The single scalar index Q_i produced by RAWEC provides an immediate sense of each alternative's desirability by balancing closeness to the benefit-oriented ideal with remoteness from the cost-oriented antiideal, enabling straightforward interpretation even for audiences unfamiliar with MCDM theory (Puška et al., 2024).

Furthermore, the method accommodates both objective data, such as distances, costs, and physical capacities, and subjective data, such as expert opinions or assessments of intangible attributes, without altering its computational framework. This makes RAWEC suitable for applications ranging from logistics and facility location to supplier evaluation and project selection, provided that a fully compensatory aggregation is acceptable.

There are, however, contexts where other MCDM methods may be more appropriate. When the decision process requires advanced features such as pairwise comparisons, as in the AHP (Saaty, 1980), or outranking relations that can represent incomparability and veto conditions, as in ELECTRE and PROMETHEE (Roy, 1996), RAWEC's compensatory structure may not capture the necessary preference logic. Likewise, if the problem involves complex nonlinear value functions, fuzzy or other uncertainty modeling frameworks, or if there is a need for built-in mechanisms to manage group consensus or iterative adjustment of weights, then more elaborate approaches may be preferable.

Because the deviation terms are linear in the weights, sensitivity analysis with respect to weight changes is straightforward: small perturbations of the weight vector lead to gradual, predictable changes in the values of Q_i, as illustrated in the numerical examples presented earlier in the chapter. Overall, the choice between RAWEC and alternative MCDM methods should be guided by the interplay between the problem's complexity, the decision-maker's informational and procedural requirements, and the desired balance between computational efficiency, transparency, and richness of preference modeling.

83.5.4 Application areas and use cases of ranking of alternatives with weights of criterion

The conceptual structure of RAWEC, with its dual normalization and single deviation-based index, lends itself to decision contexts where clarity, computational efficiency, and comparability with other distance-to-ideal methods are paramount. Because the method does not require explicit construction of ideal and antiideal points beyond the columnwise extrema already implicit in the normalizations, it avoids intermediate calculations that can obscure the link between raw data and final scores. This makes it a strong candidate in operational settings where DMs expect to see, in a single table, both the original measurements and the normalized performances that drive the ranking (Puška et al., 2024).

One natural area of application is facility location selection, where alternatives must be judged on a mix of cost and benefit attributes, often measured in different units. RAWEC can accommodate purely quantitative data (e.g., distances, capacities, costs) as well as qualitative or expert-scored indicators (e.g., environmental impact, strategic fit), provided these are placed on a consistent numerical scale before normalization. In such problems, the simplicity of RAWEC's four-step process supports transparent communication of results to nontechnical stakeholders while still aligning closely with the outputs of established methods like TOPSIS or SAW. This makes it particularly valuable in public-sector site selection exercises, where transparency and reproducibility are essential (Triantaphyllou, 2000).

Supplier and partner evaluation is another context where RAWEC's strengths are evident. Here, benefit criteria might include quality ratings, on-time delivery rates, and innovation capacity, while cost criteria might include unit price and lead time. The method's linear response to weight adjustments allows procurement teams to explore trade-offs interactively, understanding exactly how emphasizing one dimension changes the ordering of suppliers. Similar logic applies in project or investment appraisal, where projects may be compared on returns, risks, timelines, and strategic alignment.

In manufacturing and production planning, RAWEC can be used to choose among process improvements, technology upgrades, or production line configurations. The ability to combine objective data (e.g., throughput, defect rate) with subjective assessments (e.g., maintainability, worker satisfaction) without altering the aggregation mechanics is a practical advantage in cross-functional teams. The method is equally applicable in infrastructure planning for energy and transport, where alternatives differ on capital cost, operating efficiency, environmental performance, and resilience, and where stakeholders may require rapid recalculation as assumptions change.

When deciding between RAWEC and other MCDM methods, the trade-offs center on procedural complexity, interpretability, and the handling of ideal/antiideal constructs. Compared to SAW, RAWEC incorporates an explicit deviation framework that balances closeness to the ideal with remoteness from the antiideal in one index, which can better reflect cases where an alternative is strong in some dimensions but weak in others. Compared to TOPSIS or VIKOR, RAWEC avoids vector normalization and the separate computation of reference points, reducing the number of intermediate matrices while still producing rankings that empirical studies show to be highly correlated with those methods (Puška et al., 2024). For outranking approaches such as ELECTRE or PROMETHEE (Roy, 1996), RAWEC offers a simpler numeric pathway when a complete ranking is desired without indifference or incomparability relations.

In summary, RAWEC is best suited to decision problems where the analyst seeks a balance between methodological rigor and computational economy, where inputs are a mix of cost and benefit criteria across diverse scales, and where the audience values a direct link from original data to final ranking. Its design makes it an attractive first-choice method in many applied MCDM settings, and an effective companion or validation tool alongside more elaborate procedures.

83.6 Conclusion

The RAWEC method offers a concise yet robust approach for multicriteria ranking of alternatives that integrates seamlessly into the broader family of distance-to-ideal procedures. Its four-step structure—comprising the creation of the decision matrix, dual normalization to produce benefit and cost views, computation of deviations from the weighted ideal and antiideal, and synthesis into a single Q_i index—strikes an effective balance between simplicity and analytical rigor. By transforming both benefit and cost criteria into normalized forms before aggregation, RAWEC ensures that all decision dimensions are properly represented on a common scale, preserving the comparability of heterogeneous attributes.

From the standpoint of practical takeaways, RAWEC demonstrates that fewer procedural steps need not imply weaker results. Empirical validations have shown that its rankings align closely with those from established methods such as SAW, TOPSIS, and VIKOR, even though its computations are simpler and require fewer intermediate constructs (Puška et al., 2024). Its flexibility allows the analyst to adopt any suitable weighting procedure—expert-based, data-driven, or hybrid—without modification to the aggregation mechanics, and its design naturally accommodates both quantitative and qualitative data. This combination of parsimony, adaptability, and broad applicability makes RAWEC a reliable tool for diverse decision contexts, from supply-chain management and facility location selection to project evaluation and policy analysis. By enabling DMs to move efficiently from raw, heterogeneous information to a transparent and interpretable ranking, RAWEC contributes a pragmatic and methodologically sound option to the MCDM toolkit.

References

Greco, S., Figueira, J., & Ehrgott, M. (2016). *Multiple criteria decision analysis*. Springer Volume 37.

Haseli, G., Ranjbarzadeh, R., Hajiaghaei-Keshteli, M., Ghoushchi, S. J., Hasani, A., Deveci, M., & Ding, W. (2023). Hecon: Weight assessment of the product loyalty criteria considering the customer decision's halo effect using the convolutional neural networks. *Information Sciences, 623*, 184–205.

Haseli, G., Sheikh, R., & Sana, S.S. (2020). Base-criterion on multi-criteria decision-making method and its applications. International journal of management science and engineering management, 15, 79–88.

Hwang, C.-L., & Yoon, K. (1981). *Multiple attribute decision making: Methods and applications*. Berlin: Springer. http://10.1007/978-3-642-48318-9.

Ishizaka, A., & Nemery, P. (2013). *Multi-criteria decision analysis: Methods and software*. Chichester: Wiley. http://10.1002/9781118644898.

Keeney, R. L., & Raiffa, H. (1993). *Decisions with multiple objectives: Preferences and value tradeoffs*. Cambridge: Cambridge University Press.

Puška, A., Štilic′, A., Pamučar, D., Božanic′, D., & Nedeljkovic′, M. (2024). Introducing a novel multi-criteria ranking of alternatives with weights of criterion (rawec) model. *MethodsX, 12*, 102628. https://doi.org/10.1016/j.mex.2024.102628.

Roy, B. (1996). *Multicriteria methodology for decision aiding*. New York: Springer. http://10.1007/978-1-4757-2500-1.

Saaty, T. L. (1980). *The analytic hierarchy process: Planning, priority setting, resource allocation*. New York: McGraw-Hill.

Thokala, P., Devlin, N., Marsh, K., Baltussen, R., Boysen, M., Kalo, Z., Longrenn, T., Mussen, F., Peacock, S., Watkins, J., & Ijzerman, M. (2016). Multiple criteria decision analysis for health care decision making—An introduction: Report 1 of the ispor mcda emerging good practices task force. *Value in Health, 19*, 1–13. https://doi.org/10.1016/j.jval.2015.12.007.

Triantaphyllou, E. (2000). *Multi-criteria decision making methods: A comparative study*. Boston, MA: Springer. http://10.1007/978-1-4757-3157-6 Volume 44 of Applied Optimization.

Chapter 84

ERUNS: Evaluation based on relative utility and nonlinear standardization for multi-attribute decision-making

Sanjib Biswas[1], Prasenjit Chatterjee[2], and Dragan Pamucar[3,4,5]

[1]*Amity Business School, Amity University Kolkata, Kolkata, West Bengal, India,* [2]*Department of Mechanical Engineering, MCKV Institute of Engineering, Howrah, West Bengal, India,* [3]*Faculty of Organizational Sciences, University of Belgrade, Belgrade, Serbia,* [4]*UNEC Applied Artificial Intelligence Research Center, Azerbaijan State University of Economics (UNEC), Baku, Azerbaijan,* [5]*Faculty of Engineering, Dogus University, Istanbul, Türkiye*

84.1 Introduction

Decision-making in complex environments often involves assessing several criteria that can conflict with one another, where decision-makers must weigh alternatives based on both qualitative and quantitative criteria. To effectively manage these challenges, the field of multicriteria decision-making (MCDM) has been developed to rank, select, and prioritize options, aiding in better decision-making (Zavadskas et al., 2014). Within MCDM, ranking methods play a vital role. MCDM ranking methods provide a prioritized list of alternatives, rather than simply classifying them. MCDM ranking methods have gained popularity because they help decision-makers structure the ordering of options when faced with multiple and often conflicting criteria. These methods are appreciated for their straightforwardness, ease of understanding, and ability to consider both the positive and negative aspects of alternatives simultaneously. Classic methods, such as simple additive weighting (SAW) (Harsanyi, 1955), technique for order preference by similarity to ideal solution (TOPSIS) (Hwang & Yoon, 1981), visekriterijumska optimizacija i kompromisno resenje (Opricovic & Tzeng, 2004), preference ranking organization method for enrichment evaluation (PROMETHEE) (Brans & Vincke, 1985), and elimination et choice translating reality (Roy, 1968) have laid the groundwork. Over the years, newer methods, such as complex proportional assessment (Zavadskas et al., 1994), additive ratio assessment (Zavadskas & Turskis, 2010), multi-attributive border approximation area comparison (MABAC) (Pamučar & Ćirović, 2015), evaluation based on distance from average solution (Ghorabaee et al., 2015), combinative distance-based assessment (Ghorabaee et al., 2016), MARCOS (Stević et al., 2020), and compromise ranking of alternatives from distance to ideal solution (Puška et al., 2021) emerged. In recent years, the scope of ranking methods has further expanded through the integration of fuzzy sets, gray systems, rough sets, and artificial intelligence techniques, enabling better handling of uncertainty, vagueness, and large-scale data. Hybrid and advanced approaches provide greater flexibility for decision-making across diverse domains (Kumar, 2025).

Although the existing ranking methods have made important contributions, they still have some methodological limitations. In MCDM problems, criteria are usually expressed on different scales, which requires standardizing the data before combining it. However, linear and other standard normalization methods often fail to maintain the actual performance differences among alternatives (Mukhametzyanov & Pamucar, 2024). Another challenge is the rank-reversal phenomenon, where adding or removing alternatives can change the ranking of those that remain. The choice of weighting methods, whether subjective or objective, can significantly impact the results, and sensitivity to parameters remains a significant issue. The reasons for rank reversal are also often linked to how information is processed in ranking models. Specifically, distance and similarity measures can be susceptible to even small changes in criteria values. Normalization techniques also add to the rank reversal problem (Shyur & Shih, 2024). When normalization is used, the proportional

Encyclopedia of Multi-Attribute Decision-Making (MADM). DOI: https://doi.org/10.1016/B978-0-443-33275-3.00100-7

differences among the alternatives can be distorted, which in turn affects the relative positioning of the alternatives in the ranking. This problem becomes more important when reference points are involved. The identification of ideal and antiideal solutions depends on the selected normalization and includes a degree of subjectivity. The interaction between these two factors often alters the distances or similarities among alternatives, resulting in changes to their ranking order. Additionally, many traditional models struggle with zero, negative, or uncertain data, which are becoming more common in today's decision-making situations. MCDM results are often susceptible to criteria weights or combinations of parameters, which raises concerns about their reliability. These limitations underscore the need for innovative MCDM methods that can deliver consistent, reliable, and flexible performance across diverse decision-making environments.

In response to these limitations, new methods are being proposed to enhance normalization flexibility, reduce sensitivity to parameter or data changes, and prevent rank reversal. One such method is evaluation based on relative utility and nonlinear standardization (ERUNS). This method combines interval-based nonlinear standardization with a softmax-based utility framework. This combination provides more robust, interpretable, and stable rankings. Biswas et al. (2024) introduced ERUNS to overcome the shortcomings of conventional normalization techniques, which often distort performance differences among alternatives. ERUNS employs a nonlinear interval standardization technique, enabling decision-makers to map values from the decision matrix into a flexible interval [α, β]. This ensures a proportional distribution and gives greater control over the transformation process. After standardization, ERUNS applies a softmax utility formulation. Positive and negative utility degrees are calculated in relation to ideal and antiideal solutions. These are then combined into appraisal scores using a modulation parameter (δ) that balances their influence. This method keeps ERUNS free from rank reversal, maintains stability in sensitivity analysis, and can highlight subtle differences among alternatives. Several studies have shown that ERUNS is practically applicable in various decision-making contexts. Yalçın et al. (2025) developed a decision support system to assess the performance of social movements using a hybrid model. This model combined type-2 neutrosophic numbers, Schweizer–Sklar aggregation, symmetry point of criterion (SPC) weighting, and ERUNS for ranking. A case study in Türkiye showed that the "early retirement scheme victims" movement was the most effective, demonstrating model effectiveness, consistency, and the ability to change subjective assessments into precise, data-driven evaluations. Zhang (2025) introduced a decision-making framework for selecting the most suitable text analysis tools in engineering knowledge management within Industry 4.0. This framework used LOPCOW for objective weighting, ERUNS for ranking, and picture fuzzy sets to account for uncertainty in expert judgments. A case study evaluating five text analysis tools found semantic search and knowledge graph to be the most suitable alternatives. Babaçoğlu et al. (2025) proposed a decision support system (DSS) to evaluate the maturity of sustainable digital transformation in universities using a hybrid model. This model combined interval-valued spherical fuzzy sets, a modified preference selection index (MPSI), and ERUNS to weight criteria and rank universities based on expert evaluations and strategy documents. A case study of eight Turkish universities indicated that strategic innovation was the most important factor. Sensitivity and comparative analyses confirmed the approach's robustness and consistency. Xiang and Zhang (2025) designed an integrated DSS for evaluating global supply chain performance. The DSS employed criteria importance assessment for subjectively weighting criteria, logarithmic percentage change-driven objective weighting (LOPCOW) for objective weighting, and ERUNS with q-rung fuzzy sets (q-RFSs) for supplier ranking. A case study showed that the system effectively managed uncertainty, improved accuracy, and exceeded traditional methods in decision-making and operational efficiency. Wang and Ren (2025) developed a DSS for sustainable urban planning. This system combines machine learning-based feature selection with fuzzy MCDM. It uses random forest recursive feature elimination for criterion selection and LOPCOW for weighting. The ERUNS method, utilizing q-RFSs, ranks urban development strategies. A case study identified green urbanization as the best choice, showing the DSS's capability to support data-driven and sustainable urban planning decisions. Biswas et al. (2025) developed an MCDM framework to compare renewable energy sources in India. It integrated an extended technology-organization-environment approach with expert opinions. The study introduced a fair aggregation operator for p, q-quasirung orthopair fuzzy sets (p, q-QOFS), MPSI with nonlinear standardization for criterion weighting, and an extended ERUNS method employing p, q-QOFS weighted fair aggregation. A case study identified solar cells and waste-to-energy as the top renewable energy sources.

The ongoing research demonstrates the application of the ERUNS method in two real-life case studies based on objective information. The current study aims to evaluate the corporate social responsibility (CSR) performance of the firms listed on the BSE 100 ESG index. Additionally, the second case study aims to evaluate their valuations. The rest of this chapter is organized as follows. Section 84.2 elaborates on the procedural steps of the suggested framework. It outlines the steps of the ERUNS method in the context of the present research. Section 84.3 describes the first case study. It demonstrates data collection and illustrates the application of the ERUNS method. It reports key findings obtained by using the ERUNS method. Additionally, it validates the result and presents the outcome of the sensitivity analysis. Section 84.4 deals with the second case study in a similar manner. Section 84.5 presents a brief discussion of key findings, highlighting the advantages and limitations of the method. Additionally, it sheds light on research implications and highlights some future scopes for further extensions. Finally, Section 84.6 concludes the chapter.

84.2 Methodology

This section outlines the steps taken to implement the proposed methodology in the context of the research problems.

Step 1. Formation of the initial decision matrix (IDM).

The IDM consists of $i = 1, 2, ..., m$ alternative options and $j = 1, 2, ..., n$ indicators as criteria. Suppose P_{ij} is the performance value of the ith alternative subject to the impact of the jth criterion.

Step 2. Determine the criteria weights.

The criteria weights are determined using the procedural steps of the SPC method (Gligorić et al., 2023). The SPC method has been applied to several research problems from diverse domains (e.g., Ali, 2024; Alrasheedi et al., 2024; Biswas et al., 2023).

Step 3. Evaluate the performance of the firms applying the steps of the ERUNS method (Biswas et al., 2024).

Step 3a. Standardization of the IDM.

The standardization is done by mapping the elements of the IDM to a specified range or interval denoted as $[\alpha, \beta]$ where α is the lower limit, and β is the upper limit of the interval. The determination of the interval's boundary values relies on the decision-makers within the problem's context. The ERUNS technique offers a significant benefit by providing decision-makers the freedom to significantly differentiate the performance values of options based on the specific challenge at hand. For instance, when the issue involves several criteria and alternatives with closely clustered performance values in the decision matrix, a broad interval is used to illustrate the impact of the criteria on the alternatives.

The standardization is done through two stages.

1. Mapping to the interval $[\alpha, \beta]$

   The mapping of the elements of the IDM to the specified interval is done by using Eq. 19 as follows:

$$\varphi_{ij} = \left(\frac{P_j^{\min}}{P_{ij}}\right)^3 \beta + \frac{\alpha}{P_j^{\min}} \tag{84.1}$$

2. Formation of the standardized decision matrix (SDM) considering the criteria types

   Suppose, $\Psi = (\psi_{ij})_{m\times n}$ is the SDM. The elements are derived as follows:

$$\psi_{ij} = \begin{cases} -\varphi_{ij} + \max\limits_{1\le i\le m}\left(\varphi_{ij}\right) + \min\limits_{1\le i\le m}\left(\varphi_{ij}\right); & j \in B \\ \varphi_{ij}; \; j \in NB \end{cases} \tag{84.2}$$

Here, B denotes the beneficial or max type criteria while NB is an indication of nonbeneficial or min type criteria.

Step 3b. Obtain the weighted values of the elements of the SDM.

The weighted SDM is derived by calculating the weighted values of the SDM elements using the softmax function as follows. The application of the softmax function offers multiple benefits, including i) the enhancement of distinctions between advantageous and disadvantageous effects, facilitating effective alternative classification; ii) the provision of a smooth and differentiable classification; iii) its capacity to manage extensive decision matrices.

Suppose, $\Upsilon = (\gamma_{ij})_{m\times n}$ is the weighted version of the SDM. Then, the elements are computed as follows:

$$\gamma_{ij} = \frac{\exp\left(f(\psi_{ij})/g\right)w_j}{\sum_{j=1}^{n}\exp\left(f(\psi_{ij})/g\right)w_j} \tag{84.3}$$

Here,

$$f(\psi_{ij}) = \frac{\psi_{ij}}{\sum_{j=1}^{n}\psi_{ij}} \tag{84.4}$$

The weight of the jth criterion is denoted by w_j, while the modulation parameter $g > 0$ is used to examine the sensitivity of the model.

Step 3c. Obtain utility degrees subject to the ideal and antiideal references.

With respect to the ideal reference as follows:

$$\mho_i^+ = \frac{\prod_{j=1}^{n}\left(\psi_{ij}\right)^{\gamma_{ij}}}{\sum_{j=1}^{n}\gamma_j^+} \tag{84.5}$$

With respect to the antiideal reference as follows:

$$\mho_i^- = \frac{\sum_{j=1}^{n}\gamma_j^-}{\prod_{j=1}^{n}(\psi_{ij})^{\gamma^{ij}}} + \max_{1\le i\le m}\left(\frac{\sum_{j=1}^{n}\gamma_j^-}{\prod_{j=1}^{n}(\psi_{ij})^{\gamma^{ij}}}\right) + \min_{1\le i\le m}\left(\frac{\sum_{j=1}^{n}\gamma_j^-}{\prod_{j=1}^{n}(\psi_{ij})^{\gamma^{ij}}}\right) \tag{84.6}$$

Where $\gamma_j^+ = \max_{1\le i\le m}(\psi_{ij}\cdot w_j)$ and $\gamma_j^- = \min_{1\le i\le m}(\psi_{ij}\cdot w_j)$ $(i = 1, 2... m;\ j = 1, 2... n)$.

Step 3d. Derive the utility function values (UFV) with respect to the ideal and antiideal references.

With respect to the ideal reference as follows:

$$f(\mho_i^+) = \frac{\mho_i^+}{\mho_i^+ + \mho_i^-} \tag{84.7}$$

With respect to the counter-ideal reference as follows:

$$f(\mho_i^-) = \frac{\mho_i^-}{\mho_i^+ + \mho_i^-} \tag{84.8}$$

It is worth noting that UFVs are additive in nature.

Step 3e. Compute the final assessment score (FAS) values and rank the alternatives.

The FAS values are computed using Eq. 84.9.

$$\Im_i = (\mho_i^+ + \mho_i^-)\frac{(1+f(\mho_i^+))^{\tau}(1+f(\mho_i^-))^{1-\tau} - (1-f(\mho_i^+))^{\tau}(1-f(\mho_i^-))^{1-\tau}}{(1+f(\mho_i^+))^{\tau}(1+f(\mho_i^-))^{1-\tau} + (1-f(\mho_i^+))^{\tau}(1-f(\mho_i^-))^{1-\tau}} \tag{84.9}$$

The final aggregation parameter $\tau \in [0, 1]$ is used to determine the effect of UFV on the outcome. The developers suggested $\tau = 0.5$ to obtain the FAS values.

Ranking rule: The higher the value for FAS, the better the alternative.

84.3 Numerical example 1

84.3.1 Case study 1: corporate social responsibility performance of firms

The CSR has a significant impact on firm performance (Costa & Menichini, 2013; Gharbi & Jarboui, 2024). CSR performance is crucial for assessing how corporations incorporate sustainability into their operational and social structures (Biswas et al., 2024). This case study examines CSR expenditures on employee welfare, training, social and community initiatives, and utility expenses, such as power, fuel, and water. Employee welfare and training are acknowledged as strategic tools for enhancing employee engagement, skill development, and retention.

Assessing CSR performance involves examining various spending categories, including employee welfare, social and community expenditures, and utility costs. Expenditures connected to social and community efforts, including philanthropy, education, healthcare, and rural development, are the basis of external CSR projects. This enables firms to comprehend the integration of sustainability and value development. Strategic CSR investments in social activities are correlated with corporate reputation, customer loyalty, and sustained financial success (Audi & Yu, 2024; Kaimal & Uzma, 2024).

Investment in employee wellness and training enhances engagement, skill development, and retention, hence influencing organizational culture and productivity. Research indicates that CSR involvement fosters interpersonal skills and collaboration, leading to increased morale and motivation (Ampong, 2024; Gandasari et al., 2024; Onkila & Sarna, 2022).

The inclusion of energy, fuel, and water costs in CSR evaluations reflects a nuanced recognition of the environmental operational expenditures incurred by companies. Energy efficiency and sustainable resource use have become essential metrics for environmental management and financial governance. Water intensity metrics are increasingly vital performance indicators, augmenting conventional CSR expenditure reporting to foster transparency and comparability across organizations (Wang & Zheng, & Zhang, 2025). Research reveals that whereas CSR investments promote environmental innovation and sustainability, financial advantages may manifest in the long term rather than providing immediate returns (Chaudhuri et al., 2023). Consequently, firms must establish comprehensive and cohesive CSR frameworks that align social responsibility with their strategic commercial goals and environmental responsibilities.

In a nutshell, evaluating CSR effectiveness through the analysis of financial allocations toward employee welfare, social activities, and sustainability-related operational expenses offers a holistic perspective on corporate responsibility. Organizations that proactively allocate resources to these domains are more likely to realize social impact, improve employee engagement, and pursue sustainable growth in alignment with evolving global expectations.

Research indicates that CSR investment may yield long-term financial benefits, rendering comprehensive CSR frameworks indispensable (Barman & Mahakud, 2024). These frameworks must reconcile social responsibility with corporate profitability, enhance transparency, and standardize the reporting of expenditure categories to bolster accountability and stakeholder trust. Hence, actual utilization of CSR funds is an indicator of trust and accountability (Adib et al., 2021). In view of the above discussions, the current study considers four indicators to measure CSR performance (Table 84.1).

84.3.2 Data collection

The current research considers the financial year 2024–2025 as the study period. The data was collected from the CMIE Prowess database. We consider the leading companies listed on the BSE 100 ESG index in India. Considering the data availability, among the top 20 companies, we could list nine firms (Table 84.2).

Accordingly, the IDM is formulated to assess the CSR performance of the selected firms for FY 2024-25 (Table 84.3).

84.3.3 Analysis and results

This section demonstrates step-by-step application of the suggested methodology to evaluate the CSR performance of the firms. First, we formulate the IDM (Table 84.3). Then, we proceed to determine the weights of the criteria CS1, CS2, CS3, and CS4. In this case, $m = 9$ and $n = 4$. The criteria weights are obtained by applying the steps of the SPC method (Gligorić et al., 2023). The steps of the SPC method are described in Appendix A. To this end, first, we obtain the symmetry points for each criterion. The symmetry points are given as: $M_1 = 0.750$; $M_2 = 448.38$; $M_3 = 331.3$ and $M_4 = 3589.635$.

Then, we calculate the absolute distances (Eq. A2) to formulate the matrix of absolute distances around the symmetry points (Table 84.4). Now, we utilize Eq. (A.4) to obtain the moduli of the symmetry values and apply Eq. (A.5) to get the modulus of the symmetry criterion. Finally, we utilize Eq. (A.6) to calculate criteria weights (Table 84.5).

We utilize the calculated criteria weights to evaluate firms' CSR performances, following the steps of the ERUNS method (Biswas et al., 2024).

TABLE 84.1 List of indicators measuring corporate social responsibility (CSR) performance.

S/L	Description	UOM	Goal
CS1	CSR utilization rate*	Times	Max
CS2	Staff welfare and training expenses	Rs. Crore	Max
CS3	Social and community expenses	Rs. Crore	Max
CS4	Power, fuel and water charges	Rs. Crore	Min
*Total amount spent/Scheduled expenditure			

TABLE 84.2 List of firms under comparison.

Sl.No	Company Name
F1	Adani Power Ltd.
F2	Bharat Electronics Ltd.
F3	Hindustan Aeronautics Ltd.
F4	I T C Ltd.
F5	Infosys Ltd.
F6	Mahindra & Mahindra Ltd.
F7	Maruti Suzuki India Ltd.
F8	N T P C Ltd.
F9	Tata Steel Ltd.

TABLE 84.3 Initial decision matrix to evaluate the corporate social responsibility performance.

Indicators/Firms	CS1	CS2	CS3	CS4
F1	0.7588	60.0600	187.0400	362.0100
F2	0.3560	158.9700	77.9900	67.8600
F3	1.1442	186.9300	158.3800	211.5200
F4	1.0017	301.5900	461.5000	942.4700
F5	0.9748	378.0000	540.0000	196.0000
F6	1.0009	391.0200	152.3600	432.3900
F7	0.9663	490.5000	158.5000	749.7000
F8	0.9475	809.5500	295.2900	1108.2400
F9	1.0078	836.7000	584.6100	7111.4100

First, we standardize IDM (Step 3a). Following the developers of the method, we set $\alpha = 1$ and $\beta = 9$ for the initial case. Applying Eq. 84.1, we map the elements of IDM (given in Table 84.3) to the interval [1, 9]. It is noteworthy to mention that in this case, CS1, CS2, and CS3 are beneficial type criteria, while CS4 is a nonbeneficial one. We utilize Eq. 84.2 to complete the standardization of IDM. Examples of calculations are given below. Tables 84.6 and 84.7 represent the intermediate and final SDM, respectively.

$$\varphi_{11} = \left(\frac{P_1^{min}}{P_{11}}\right)^3 \beta + \frac{\alpha}{P_1^{min}}$$

$$\alpha = 1; \beta = 9;$$

$$P_1^{min} = Min(P_{11}, P_{21}, \ldots ,P_{91}) = Min(0.7588, 0.3560, ..,1.0078) = 0.3560$$

$$Thus,\ \varphi_{11} = \left(\frac{P_1^{min}}{P_{11}}\right)^3 \beta + \frac{\alpha}{P_1^{min}} = \left(\frac{0.3560}{0.7588}\right)^3 \times 9 + \frac{1}{0.3560} = 3.7385$$

$$\text{Similarly, } \varphi_{14} = \left(\frac{P_4^{min}}{P_{14}}\right)^3 \beta + \frac{\alpha}{P_4^{min}} = \left(\frac{67.86}{362.01}\right)^3 \times 9 + \frac{1}{67.86} = 0.0740$$

TABLE 84.4 Absolute distance matrix (corporate social responsibility performance).

Criteria/Firms	CS1	CS2	CS3	CS4
F1	0.0087	388.3200	144.2600	3227.6250
F2	0.3941	289.4100	253.3100	3521.7750
F3	0.3941	261.4500	172.9200	3378.1150
F4	0.2517	146.7900	130.2000	2647.1650
F5	0.2247	70.3800	208.7000	3393.6350
F6	0.2508	57.3600	178.9400	3157.2450
F7	0.2162	42.1200	172.8000	2839.9350
F8	0.1974	361.1700	36.0100	2481.3950
F9	0.2577	388.3200	253.3100	3521.7750
Average	0.2439	222.8133	172.2722	3129.8517

TABLE 84.5 Moduli of the symmetry matrix, modulus of the symmetry criterion, and criteria weights.

Criteria/Firms	CS1	CS2	CS3	CS4
F1	0.3215	3.7098	0.9210	8.6458
F2	0.6853	1.4016	2.2089	46.1222
F3	0.2132	1.1920	1.0877	14.7970
F4	0.2435	0.7388	0.3733	3.3209
F5	0.2502	0.5895	0.3190	15.9686
F6	0.2437	0.5698	1.1307	7.2385
F7	0.2524	0.4543	1.0869	4.1748
F8	0.2575	0.2752	0.5834	2.8242
F9	0.2420	0.2663	0.2947	0.4401
ξ	0.3010	1.0219	0.8895	11.5036
Weight	0.0219	0.0745	0.0649	0.8387

Hence, we obtain

$\psi_{11} = -\varphi_{11} + \max_{1 \le i \le 9}(\varphi_{i1}) + \min_{1 \le i \le 9}(\varphi_{i1}) = -3.7385 + 11.8093 + 3.0803 = 11.1510$*(CS1 is beneficial type)*

$\psi_{41} = \varphi_{41} = 0.0740$(CS1 is a nonbeneficial type)

Now, we use the softmax function to derive the weighted values of the elements of SDM (Table 84.8). We use the calculated criteria weights (Table 84.5) and apply Eqs. 84.3 and 84.4.

Example of calculation

$$f(\psi_{11}) = \frac{\psi_{11}}{\sum_{j=1}^{4} \psi_{1j}} = \frac{11.1510}{11.1510 + 0.0200 + 8.3817 + 0.0740} = 0.5682$$

TABLE 84.6 Formulation of a standardized decision matrix (Intermediate stage).

Criteria/Firms	CS1	CS2	CS3	CS4
F1	3.7385	9.0167	0.6653	0.0740
F2	11.8093	0.5020	9.0128	9.0147
F3	3.0803	0.3152	1.0875	0.3119
F4	3.2131	0.0877	0.0563	0.0181
F5	3.2475	0.0528	0.0399	0.3883
F6	3.2142	0.0493	1.2199	0.0495
F7	3.2592	0.0332	1.0850	0.0214
F8	3.2866	0.0203	0.1786	0.0168
F9	3.2059	0.0200	0.0342	0.0147
Max	11.8093	9.0167	9.0128	9.0147
Min	3.0803	0.0200	0.0342	0.0147
Max+min	14.8895	9.0366	9.0470	9.0295

TABLE 84.7 Formulation of the final standardized decision matrix.

Criteria/Firms	CS1	CS2	CS3	CS4	Sum
F1	11.1510	0.0200	8.3817	0.0740	19.6267
F2	3.0803	8.5346	0.0342	9.0147	20.6638
F3	11.8093	8.7215	7.9596	0.3119	28.8022
F4	11.6764	8.9489	8.9908	0.0181	29.6342
F5	11.6420	8.9839	9.0071	0.3883	30.0213
F6	11.6754	8.9874	7.8271	0.0495	28.5393
F7	11.6303	9.0035	7.9620	0.0214	28.6172
F8	11.6030	9.0163	8.8684	0.0168	29.5044
F9	11.6837	9.0167	9.0128	0.0147	29.7279

$$\gamma_{11} = \frac{\exp(f(\psi_{11})/g)w_1}{\sum_{j=1}^{4}\exp(f(\psi_{1j})/g)w_j}$$
$$= \frac{\exp(f(\psi_{11})/g)w_1}{\exp(f(\psi_{11})/g)w_1+\exp(f(\psi_{12})/g)w_2+\exp(f(\psi_{13})/g)w_3+\exp(f(\psi_{14})/g)w_4}$$
$$= \frac{\exp(0.5682/1)\times 0.0219}{\exp(0.5682/1)\times 0.0219+\exp(0.0010/1)\times 0.0745+\exp(0.4271/1)\times 0.0649+\exp(0.0038/1)\times 0.8387}$$
$$= \frac{0.0387}{0.0387+0.0746+0.0994+0.8419} = 0.0367$$

We assume g =1 for the initial case (Biswas et al., 2024). Next, we proceed to obtain utility degrees subject to the ideal and antiideal references.

TABLE 84.8 Weighted standardized decision matrix.

Criteria/Firms	CS1	CS2	CS3	CS4
F1	0.0367	0.0707	0.0943	0.7983
F2	0.0170	0.0750	0.0433	0.8647
F3	0.0310	0.0945	0.0801	0.7944
F4	0.0307	0.0950	0.0828	0.7914
F5	0.0302	0.0939	0.0818	0.7940
F6	0.0312	0.0963	0.0804	0.7922
F7	0.0311	0.0963	0.0808	0.7918
F8	0.0307	0.0954	0.0826	0.7914
F9	0.0307	0.0952	0.0828	0.7914

The ideal and antiideal references are given by the following:

$$\gamma_1^+ = \max_{1\le i\le 9}(\psi_{i1}\cdot w_1) = \max\{(11.1510 \times 0.0219), (3.0803 \times 0.0219), \ldots, (11.6837 \times 0.0219)\} = 0.2592$$

$$\gamma_2^+ = 0.6718;\ \gamma_3^+ = 0.5845;\ \gamma_4^+ = 7.5606$$

Similarly, $\gamma_1^- = 0.0676$; $\gamma_2^- = 0.0015$; $\gamma_3^- = 0.0022$; $\gamma_4^- = 0.0124$

Then, we obtain the utility degrees with respect to the ideal and antiideal references utilizing Eqs. 84.5 and 84.6. Example of calculation,

$$\mho_1^+ = \frac{\prod_{j=1}^4 (\psi_{1j})^{\gamma_{1j}}}{\sum_{j=1}^4 \gamma_j^+} = \frac{(\psi_{11})^{\gamma_{11}} \times (\psi_{12})^{\gamma_{12}} \times (\psi_{13})^{\gamma_{13}} \times (\psi_{14})^{\gamma_{14}}}{\gamma_1^+ + \gamma_2^+ + \gamma_3^+ + \gamma_4^+}$$

$$= \frac{(11.1510)^{0.0367} \times (0.02)^{0.0707} \times (8.3817)^{0.0943} \times (0.0740)^{0.7983}}{0.2592 + 0.6718 + 0.5845 + 7.5606} = 0.0140$$

With respect to the antiideal reference:

$$\mho_1^- = -\frac{\sum_{j=1}^4 \gamma_j^-}{\prod_{j=1}^4 (\psi_{1j})^{\gamma_{1j}}} + \max_{1\le i\le 9}\left(\frac{\sum_{j=1}^4 \gamma_j^-}{\prod_{j=1}^4 (\psi_{ij})^{\gamma_{ij}}}\right) + \min_{1\le i\le 9}\left(\frac{\sum_{j=1}^4 \gamma_j^-}{\prod_{j=1}^4 (\psi_{ij})^{\gamma_{ij}}}\right)$$

$$= -\frac{\sum_{j=1}^4 \gamma_j^-}{\prod_{j=1}^4 (\psi_{1j})^{\gamma_{1j}}}$$

$$+ \max_{1\le i\le 9}\left\{\left(\frac{\sum_{j=1}^4 \gamma_j^-}{\prod_{j=1}^4 (\psi_{1j})^{\gamma_{1j}}}\right), \left(\frac{\sum_{j=1}^4 \gamma_j^-}{\prod_{j=1}^4 (\psi_{2j})^{\gamma_{2j}}}\right), \left(\frac{\sum_{j=1}^4 \gamma_j^-}{\prod_{j=1}^4 (\psi_{3j})^{\gamma_{3j}}}\right), \ldots, \left(\frac{\sum_{j=1}^4 \gamma_j^-}{\prod_{j=1}^4 (\psi_{9j})^{\gamma_{9j}}}\right)\right\}$$

$$+ \min_{1\le i\le 9}\left\{\left(\frac{\sum_{j=1}^4 \gamma_j^-}{\prod_{j=1}^4 (\psi_{1j})^{\gamma_{1j}}}\right), \left(\frac{\sum_{j=1}^4 \gamma_j^-}{\prod_{j=1}^4 (\psi_{2j})^{\gamma_{2j}}}\right), \left(\frac{\sum_{j=1}^4 \gamma_j^-}{\prod_{j=1}^4 (\psi_{3j})^{\gamma_{3j}}}\right), \ldots, \left(\frac{\sum_{j=1}^4 \gamma_j^-}{\prod_{j=1}^4 (\psi_{9j})^{\gamma_{9j}}}\right)\right\}$$

$$\frac{\sum_{j=1}^4 \gamma_j^-}{\prod_{j=1}^4 (\psi_{1j})^{\gamma_{1j}}} = \frac{\gamma_1^- + \gamma_2^- + \gamma_3^- + \gamma_4^-}{(\psi_{11})^{\gamma_{11}} \times (\psi_{12})^{\gamma_{12}} \times (\psi_{13})^{\gamma_{13}} \times (\psi_{14})^{\gamma_{14}}}$$

$$= \frac{0.0676 + 0.0015 + 0.0022 + 0.0124}{(11.1510)^{0.0367} \times (0.02)^{0.0707} \times (8.3817)^{0.0943} \times (0.0740)^{0.7983}} = 0.6605$$

$$\mho_1^- = -0.6605 + \max\{0.6605, 0.0121, \ldots 1.4763\} + \min\{0.6605, 0.0121, \ldots 1.4763\} = 0.8279$$

Now, we derive the UFV with respect to the ideal and antiideal references and compute the FAS values of the alternatives utilizing Eqs. 84.7–84.9. We set τ=0.5 for the initial case (Biswas et al., 2024). Table 84.9 presents the calculated values of utility degrees, UFVs, and FAS for the alternatives, along with their ranking.

TABLE 84.9 Calculation of final assessment score and ranking of alternatives (corporate social responsibility performance).

Values/Firms	$\mho_i^+$	$\mho_i^-$	$f(\mho_i^+)$	$f(\mho_i^-)$	$\Im_i$	Rank
F1	0.0140	0.8279	0.0166	0.9834	0.7029	5
F2	0.7630	1.4763	0.3407	0.6593	1.1593	1
F3	0.0683	1.3534	0.0480	0.9520	1.0518	3
F4	0.0073	0.2312	0.0307	0.9693	0.1870	7
F5	0.0824	1.3764	0.0565	0.9435	1.0540	2
F6	0.0160	0.9135	0.0173	0.9827	0.7734	4
F7	0.0083	0.3750	0.0216	0.9784	0.3122	6
F8	0.0069	0.1550	0.0427	0.9573	0.1218	8
F9	0.0062	0.0121	0.3407	0.6593	0.0095	9

TABLE 84.10 Spearman's rank correlation test (corporate social responsibility ranking).

Method	SAW	PIV	MABAC	CoCoSo	RAM
ERUNS	0.933	0.950	0.933	0.983	0.933

All coefficients are significant at the 0.05 level, two-tailed.

Example,

$$f(\mho_1^+) = \frac{\mho_1^+}{\mho_1^+ + \mho_1^-} = \frac{0.0140}{0.0140 + 0.8279} = 0.0166$$

$$f(\mho_1^-) = \frac{\mho_1^-}{\mho_1^+ + \mho_1^-} = \frac{0.8279}{0.0140 + 0.8279} = 0.9834$$

$$\Im_1 = (\mho_1^+ + \mho_1^-)\frac{(1 + f(\mho_1^+))^{\tau}(1 + f(\mho_1^-))^{1-\tau} - (1 - f(\mho_1^+))^{\tau}(1 - f(\mho_1^-))^{1-\tau}}{(1 + f(\mho_1^+))^{\tau}(1 + f(\mho_1^-))^{1-\tau} + (1 - f(\mho_1^+))^{\tau}(1 - f(\mho_1^-))^{1-\tau}}$$

$$= (0.0140 + 0.8279)\frac{\{(1 + 0.0166)^{0.5}(1 + 0.9834)^{1-0.5}\} - \{(1 - 0.0166)^{0.5}(1 - 0.9834)^{1-0.5}\}}{\{(1 + 0.0166)^{0.5}(1 + 0.9834)^{1-0.5}\} + \{(1 - 0.0166)^{0.5}(1 - 0.9834)^{1-0.5}\}} = 0.7029$$

84.3.4 Validation

Evaluating alternatives using various MCDM methods and comparing them is crucial to ensure the reliability and credibility of the results. Diverse MCDM strategies employ varying procedures, which may result in inconsistencies in rankings or decision outcomes (Kolour et al., 2026). A comparative analysis guarantees uniformity among methodologies, mitigates biases, and offers an extensive comprehension of the decision-making issue (Komatina et al., 2026). This methodology fosters openness and trust in complex decision-making scenarios that involve multiple criteria (Biswas & Pamucar, 2023). This study ranks firms based on their CSR methods using several methods, including ERUNS. Then, it conducts a Spearman's rank correlation test among them (Table 84.10). We find that various methods maintain statistically significant high rank correlations with ERUNS, suggesting the reliability of the outcome of the latter.

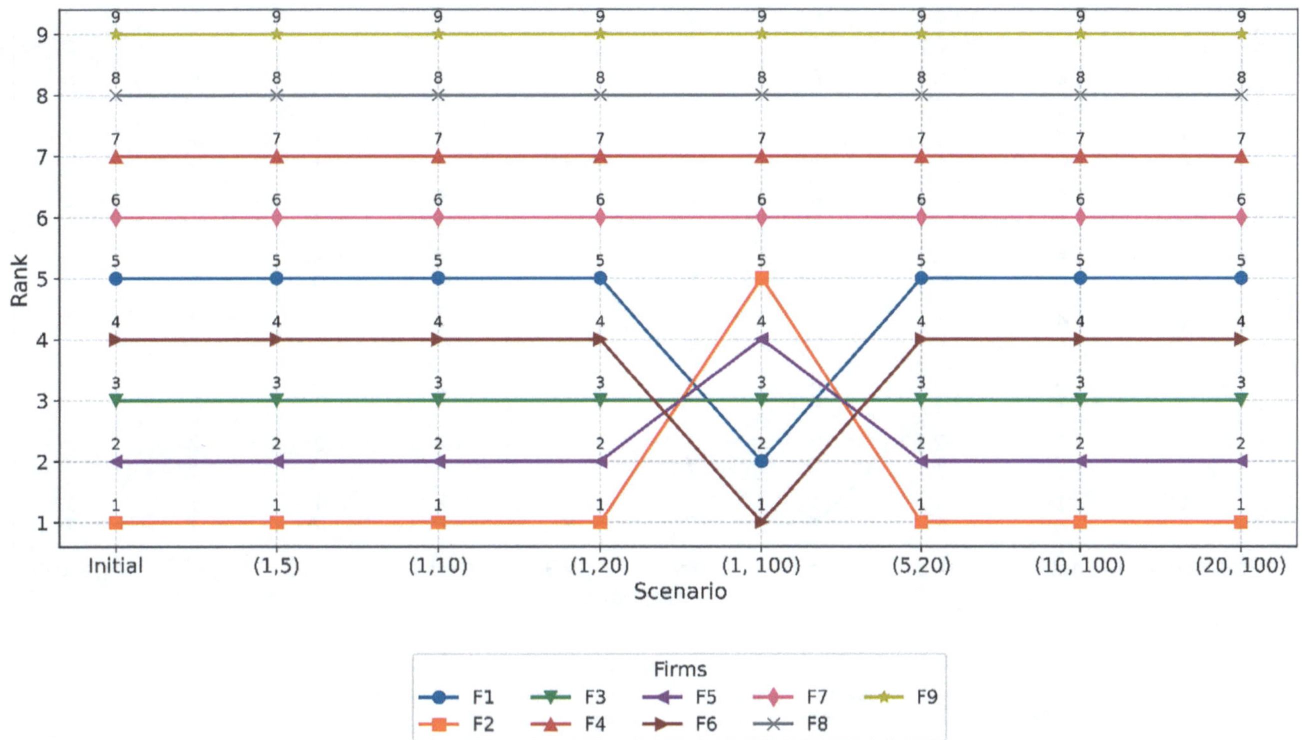

FIGURE 84.1 Effect of variations in the interval selection on the corporate social responsibility-based ranking of alternatives.

84.3.5 Sensitivity analysis

Sensitivity analysis in MCDM assesses the dependability of decision outcomes in relation to variations in input data. It analyzes critical elements influencing judgments and assesses whether minor alterations result in significant changes in outcomes. This strategy validates the efficacy of the selected method and bolsters confidence in the decision-making process. Sensitivity analysis elucidates uncertainty, alleviates decision bias, and helps stakeholders make informed and resilient decisions (Katrancı et al., 2026; Li et al., 2026; Sanyal et al., 2025). In our study, several parameters are considered, including α, β, g, and τ. We therefore vary the initial values of these parameters and examine their impacts on CSR performance ranking (see Figs. 84.1–84.3) and FAS values (see Fig. 84.4–84.6).

The study indicates (see Fig. 84.1) that the CSR-based ranking of firms remains largely stable over various interval selections (F3, F4, F5, F7, F8, and F9), with the majority of possibilities preserving consistent ranks. Nevertheless, some variations are noted for F1, F2, and F6, especially in the (1,100) area. The stability of the decision model is demonstrated by the reversal of ranks in subsequent situations. The ranking approach is dependable for managerial decision-making; yet, boundary restrictions may influence marginal instances. The sensitivity analysis in Fig. 84.2 demonstrates that CSR-based rankings exhibit stability despite parameter adjustments, with little difference between F2 and F3, signifying localized sensitivity for tightly ranked choices. Furthermore, rankings restore stability, demonstrating consistency across a broader range of parameters. This consistency validates the authenticity of the CSR-based evaluation technique for management and policy decisions, while underscoring the necessity for sensitivity analyses for companies with marginal scores.

The sensitivity study shown in Fig. 84.3 indicates that CSR-based rankings remain predominantly stable despite fluctuations in the τ parameter. Most firms uphold stable viewpoints, signifying methodological consistency. Only F3 and F5 exhibit minor changes, suggesting that only analogous companies demonstrate sensitivity to fluctuations in τ. These findings confirm the dependability of CSR-based evaluations and underscore the necessity for meticulous evaluation of marginally competitive options.

Fig. 84.4 shows the impact of interval selection on the CSR performance ratings of options. While most firms have consistent results, certain ones, such as F4 and F7, demonstrate heightened sensitivity. Fig. 84.5 shows a consistent rising trend in ratings for each firm as g increases, reflecting scale and comparative rankings across scenarios. Fig. 84.6 shows

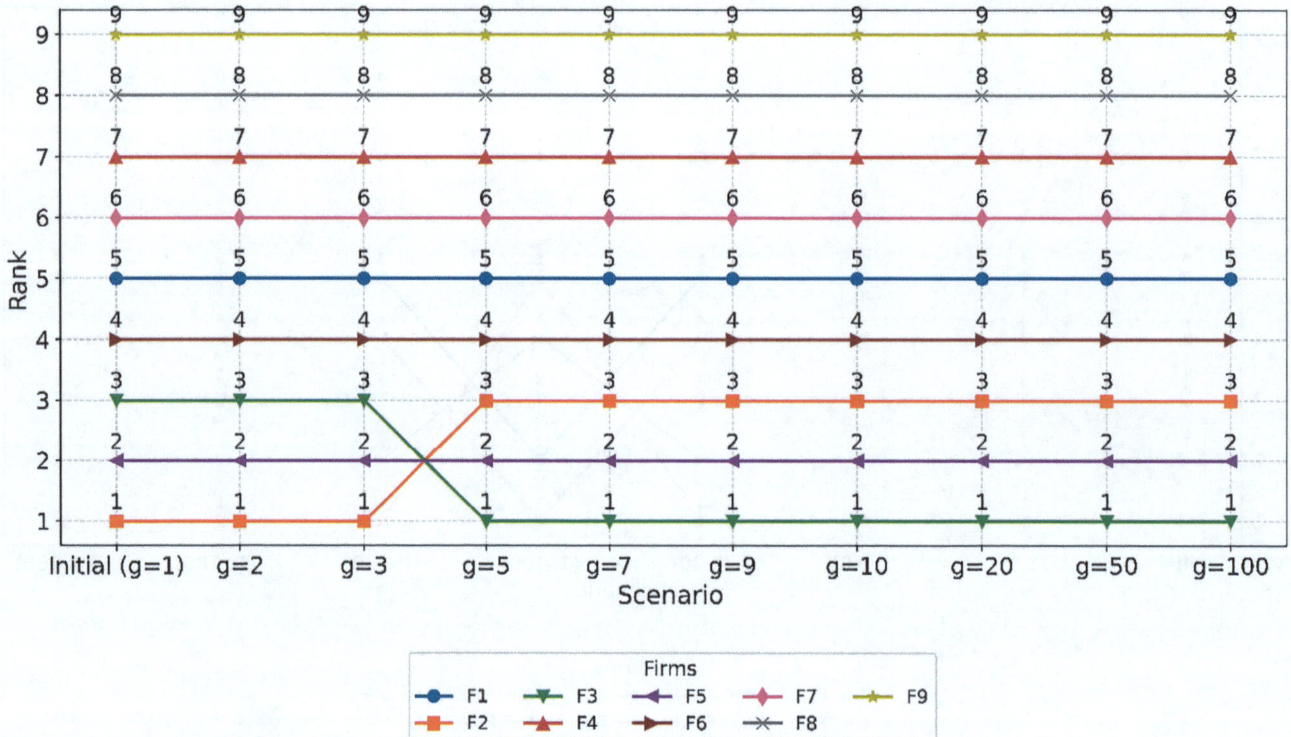

FIGURE 84.2 Effect of variations in g values on the corporate social responsibility-based ranking of alternatives.

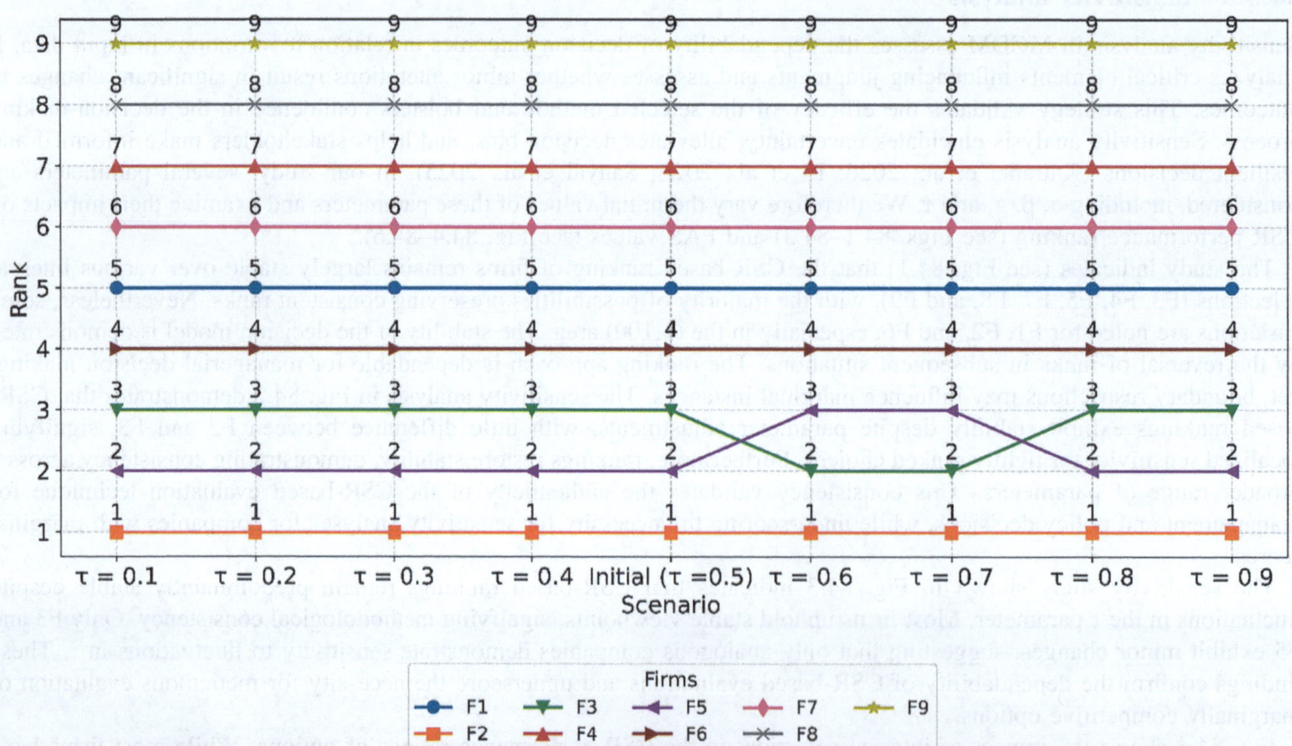

FIGURE 84.3 Effect of variations in τ values on the corporate social responsibility-based ranking of alternatives.

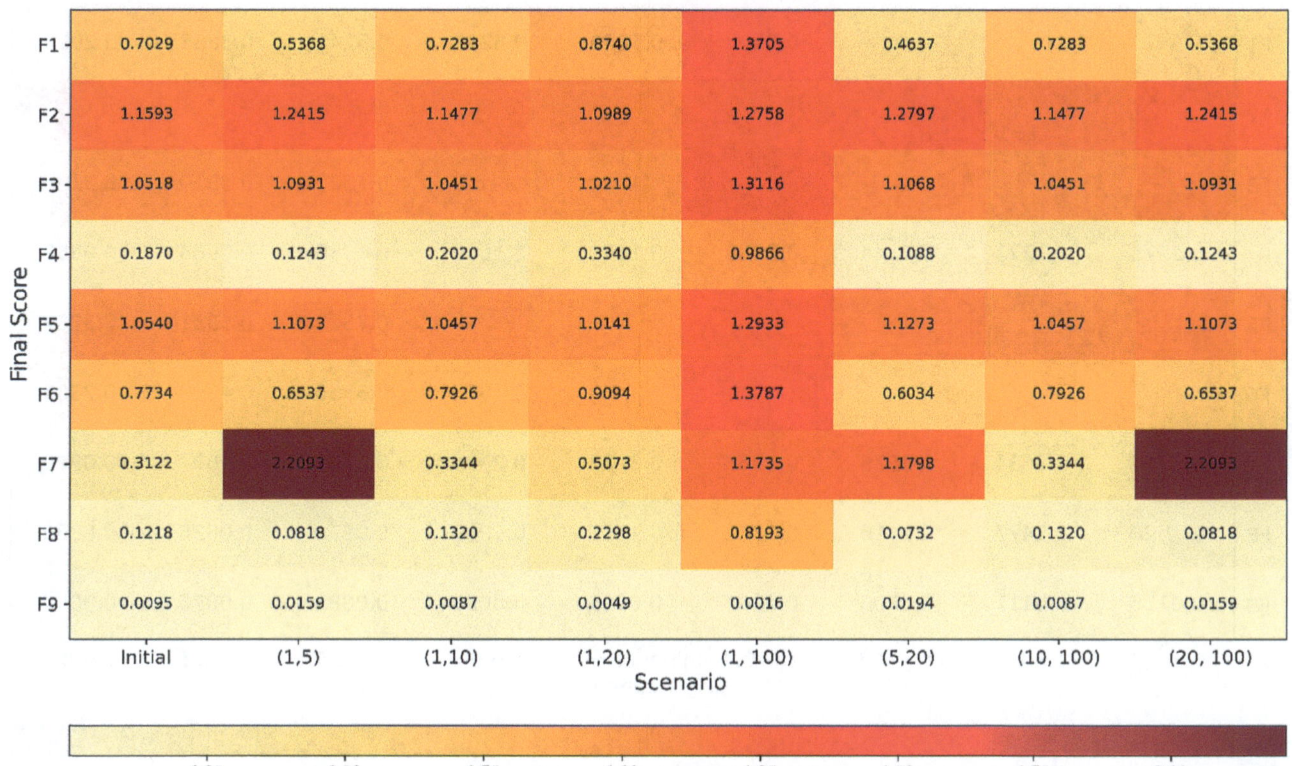

FIGURE 84.4 Effect of variations in the interval selection on the corporate social responsibility performance scores of alternatives.

FIGURE 84.5 Effect of variations in g values on the corporate social responsibility performance scores of alternatives.

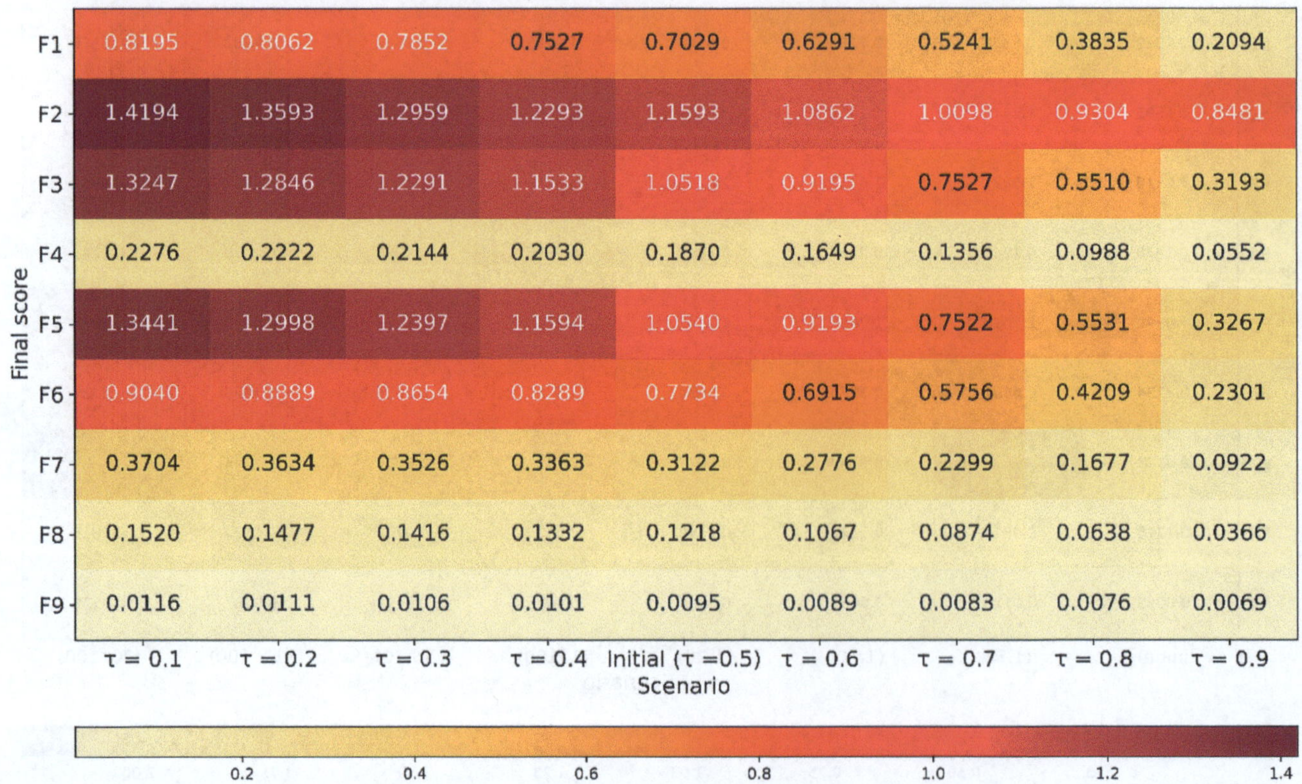

FIGURE 84.6 Effect of variations in τ values on the corporate social responsibility performance scores of alternatives.

that an escalation in τ values reduces performance scores and increases variability, signifying the model's vulnerability to risk tolerance in CSR assessment.

84.4 Numerical example 2

84.4.1 Case study

Valuation indicators are crucial for stakeholders, including investors, management, regulators, and analysts, as they provide a comprehensive and quantifiable assessment of a company's financial position and market standing. The indicators encompass market capitalization (MC), enterprise value (EV), return on net worth (RONW), return on capital employed (ROCE), return on total assets (ROTA), price-earnings (P/E) ratio, price-book (P/B) ratio, and total turnover (TT), reflecting profitability, growth potential, asset efficiency, and market expectations (Baydaş & Elma, 2021). Investors may utilize these indicators to make educated investment choices, whilst management may employ them to guide strategic decisions on capital investment, finance, and performance improvement. These indicators enhance openness and accountability, hence strengthening corporate governance and increasing investor confidence. Consequently, thorough evaluation of robust valuation measures is crucial for both academic research and practical financial analysis, offering extensive insights that enhance market efficiency and corporate success.

MC signifies a company's stock value; however, its limitations include the exclusion of debt and cash balances (Bui et al., 2023), resulting in a preference for EV as a more comprehensive measure of a firm's worth. Researchers demonstrate that EV-based multiples, such as EV/Sales and EV/earnings before interest, taxes, depreciation, and amortization (EBITDA), enhance comparability across firms and industries (Rodríguez-Valencia et al., 2023). RONW is a key metric that measures a company's profitability by reflecting the earnings generated from shareholders' investments. It assists investors and management in measuring a company's financial effectiveness, comparing its performance with that of competitors, and evaluating the capital efficiency of equity owners. A heightened RONW signifies enhanced profitability and financial stability (Baydaş & Pamučar, 2022).

ROCE serves as a metric of enduring success, with higher ROCE values associated with greater growth potential and increased investor confidence (Tripathi et al., 2022). ROTA is a crucial indicator for assessing a company's profitability and for comparing enterprises within the same sector. It offers insights into operational performance and capital efficiency; a higher ROTA signifies superior asset management and enhanced revenue generation, reflecting more value and operational efficiency (Kara et al., 2024)

Market-based valuation multiples, including P/E and P/B ratios, are crucial in modern corporate valuation research. The P/B ratio reflects investors' willingness to pay for a company's book value, especially in industries with significant asset holdings. Nonetheless, its interpretability is hindered in firms that possess significant intangible assets or have a negative book value (Biswas et al., 2022).

TT, a metric of company scale and market participation, augments value assessments by illustrating operational scope and revenue-generating capacity. Recent empirical research reveals a nuanced relationship between high turnover and favorable financial performance; yet, excessive human turnover may signify instability that negatively impacts corporate valuation. Consequently, stakeholders are increasingly using turnover indicators in conjunction with value ratios for a comprehensive assessment of companies (Pamucar & Biswas, 2023).

Recent advancements in company valuation incorporate environmental, social, and governance (ESG) factors with traditional financial metrics, suggesting that sustainable corporate practices enhance firm worth and mitigate risk profiles. The integration of ESG data with financial indicators, such as ROCE and market multiples, provides a holistic approach that aligns with investors' preferences for responsible investing.

From a methodological perspective, MCDM has been notably applied in evaluating firm values. For instance, PROMETHEE (Baydaş & Elma, 2021), method based on the removal effects of criteria-reference based normalization alternative ranking (Kara et al., 2024), and fuzzy analytic hierarchy process (FAHP)-TOPSIS (Baydaş & Pamučar, 2022) have been applied. The current research aims to assess the firms (listed on the BSE 100 ESG index, as shown in Table 84.2) based on eight valuation indicators outlined in Table 84.11.

84.4.2 Data collection

The data collection is explained in detail in Section 84.4.2. Table 84.12 presents the IDM for evaluating the firms based on valuation indicators.

84.4.3 Analysis and results

Likewise, in the previous case study, we also follow a similar step-by-step approach to evaluate the firms ($m = 9$) based on valuation indicators or criteria ($n = 8$). It is noteworthy to mention that in this case study, all criteria are beneficial types. We first calculate the weights of the criteria utilizing the SPC method (Table 84.13).

TABLE 84.11 List of indicators measuring firm valuation.

S/L	Indicator	UOM	Goal
V1	Market capitalization (MC)	Rs. Cr	Max
V2	Enterprise value (EV)	Rs. Cr	Max
V3	Return on net worth (RONW)	%	Max
V4	Return on capital employed (ROCE)	%	Max
V5	Return on total assets (ROTA)	%	Max
V6	Price to earnings (P/E)	Times	Max
V7	Price to book value (P/B)	Times	Max
V8	Total turnover (TT)	Lacs	Max

Description of the indicators: MC: Total value of the outstanding shares of the company, indicating overall market valuation; EV: The "takeover price" encompassing the market cap, debt, and cash; RONW: Net profit generated from shareholders' equity, indicating the efficiency of the firms in utilizing shareholders' funds; ROCE: Generated earnings before interest and tax (EBIT) using both debt and equity capital, reflecting company's ability to yield profits and enhance shareholders' value; ROTA: Profit generated by utilizing the resources, reflecting the ability to optimize the value of the assets; Investors' willingness to invest in the firm given its earnings, indicating company's earnings prospect; P/B: Market value of the firm to its book value per share, indicating the intrinsic valuation of the companies; TT: Total monetary value of all completed trades in a day for a specific stock, indicating the liquidity.

TABLE 84.12 Initial decision matrix to evaluate the firm's valuation.

Indicators/Firms	V1	V2	V3	V4	V5	V6	V7	V8
F1	196433.90	232200.85	20.60	11.32	9.24	123.25	4.99	4261.72
F2	220258.26	210922.19	28.07	27.98	11.46	44.89	12.53	6394.42
F3	279377.41	241601.15	22.06	21.79	7.29	44.22	9.05	6999.07
F4	512828.63	478978.22	27.77	27.68	22.54	26.24	7.29	3848.03
F5	652332.32	625275.32	29.91	28.68	20.61	26.55	8.18	6786.68
F6	331568.31	243426.32	22.74	22.02	13.99	28.10	5.61	2554.88
F7	362259.36	359244.86	16.66	16.63	12.48	25.58	4.01	3753.28
F8	346801.26	452768.77	11.22	5.10	3.97	23.85	2.23	2124.60
F9	192558.47	249719.16	9.09	6.50	4.67	19.70	1.31	2090.62

TABLE 84.13 Calculated criteria weights (Firm valuation).

Criteria	V1	V2	V3	V4	V5	V6	V7	V8
Weight	0.0983	0.0912	0.0668	0.1193	0.1191	0.2719	0.1412	0.0924

TABLE 84.14 Formulation of the final standardized decision matrix (Firm valuation).

Criteria/Firms	V1	V2	V3	V4	V5	V6	V7	V8
F1	0.7537	2.5999	8.5894	8.4237	8.5872	9.0508	9.6108	8.1779
F2	3.2179	0.3455	9.0570	9.1922	8.9269	8.3269	9.7634	8.9258
F3	6.2847	3.3570	8.7330	9.1313	7.8475	8.2917	9.7463	9.0005
F4	8.7550	8.5769	9.0470	9.1904	9.2519	5.2791	9.7214	7.7970
F5	9.0000	9.0000	9.1100	9.1961	9.2367	5.4109	9.7367	8.9772
F6	7.4687	3.4907	8.7878	9.1349	9.0954	5.9864	9.6590	4.3091
F7	7.8798	7.5239	7.9008	8.9871	9.0114	4.9766	9.4599	7.6850
F8	7.6909	8.4356	4.5768	0.2467	0.3011	4.0156	7.9492	0.6653
F9	0.2315	3.9223	0.3626	4.8995	3.7719	0.0875	0.7736	0.2403

Then, we follow the procedural steps of the ERUNS method to evaluate the firms based on the valuation indicators. Table 84.14 exhibits the final SDM, obtained using the interval (1, 9).

Then, we proceed to obtain the weighted SDM utilizing the calculated weights and applying Eqs. 84.3 and 84.4 (Table 84.15).

Next, we proceed to obtain the FAS values and rank the firms utilizing Eqs. 84.5–84.9 (Table 84.16).

TABLE 84.15 Weighted standardized decision matrix (Firm valuation).

Criteria/Firms	V1	V2	V3	V4	V5	V6	V7	V8
F1	0.0870	0.0835	0.0680	0.1211	0.1213	0.2792	0.1465	0.0934
F2	0.0911	0.0804	0.0684	0.1225	0.1217	0.2751	0.1464	0.0944
F3	0.0956	0.0847	0.0675	0.1214	0.1187	0.2731	0.1451	0.0938
F4	0.0994	0.0920	0.0678	0.1214	0.1213	0.2612	0.1448	0.0921
F5	0.0995	0.0923	0.0676	0.1210	0.1208	0.2612	0.1443	0.0934
F6	0.0987	0.0855	0.0686	0.1232	0.1229	0.2661	0.1472	0.0878
F7	0.0988	0.0912	0.0671	0.1220	0.1218	0.2610	0.1455	0.0926
F8	0.1086	0.1030	0.0673	0.1058	0.1058	0.2695	0.1571	0.0829
F9	0.0886	0.1064	0.0607	0.1490	0.1374	0.2425	0.1321	0.0833

Assuming $g = 1$.

TABLE 84.16 Calculation of final assessment score and ranking of alternatives (Firm valuation).

Values/Firms	$\mho_i^+$	$\mho_i^-$	$f(\mho_i^+)$	$f(\mho_i^-)$	$\mathfrak{I}_i$	Rank
F1	0.7017	0.4237	0.6235	0.3765	0.5745	6
F2	0.6811	0.4223	0.6173	0.3827	0.5621	7
F3	0.8477	0.4316	0.6626	0.3374	0.6633	3
F4	0.8501	0.4318	0.6632	0.3368	0.6648	2
F5	0.8735	0.4328	0.6687	0.3313	0.6793	1
F6	0.7552	0.4269	0.6389	0.3611	0.6068	5
F7	0.8023	0.4295	0.6513	0.3487	0.6355	4
F8	0.2775	0.3527	0.4403	0.5597	0.3166	8
F9	0.0752	0.0373	0.6687	0.3313	0.0585	9

Assuming $\tau = 0.5$.

TABLE 84.17 Spearman's rank correlation test (Firm valuation).

Method	SAW	PIV	MABAC	CoCoSo	RAM
ERUNS	0.959	0.933	0.950	0.917	0.959

All coefficients are significant at the 0.05 level, two-tailed.

84.4.4 Validation

Similar to the previous case study, we compare the results of several other MCDM models with those of the ERUNS and conduct Spearman's rank correlation test (Table 84.17). We find that the methods are highly consistent, and the correlation coefficients are statistically significant.

84.4.5 Sensitivity analysis

The sensitivity analysis is performed similarly by varying the values of α, β, g, and τ. Figs. 84.7–84.9 show the effects of the parameter changes on the firm rankings, while Figs. 84.10–84.12 show the impact on the FAS values.

We notice that irrespective of changes in the parameter (g and τ) and interval limits (α and β), there has not been any variation in the overall positioning of the firms based on their valuations. It suggests that firms behave similarly in terms of their values, even as the underlying conditions change. Hence, the performance-based ranking of the firms based on the valuation indicators shows comprehensive stability.

The sensitivity analysis indicates that the valuation scores of alternatives remain robust, although they exhibit fluctuations in response to alterations in parameters. Fig. 84.10 shows robust consistency in firm evaluation ratings, with negligible fluctuations attributed to variations in parameter configurations. Companies F3, F4, and F5 consistently achieve high rankings, indicating strong performance. Despite significant parameter alterations, score variations remain negligible, demonstrating the ranking mechanism's insensitivity toward top firms. F8 and F9 consistently occupy the lowest positions, signifying persistent underperformance. This consistency validates the reliability and usefulness of ERUNS in corporate evaluation.

The variations in the parameter g (see Fig. 84.11) indicate considerable stability and minimal fluctuation in firm evaluation ratings. As g escalates from 1 to 100, fluctuations in scores are incremental and do not influence business ranking. Leading enterprises achieve elevated ratings, whilst underachievers continuously occupy the lowest ranks. This insensitivity confirms the reliability and credibility of the evaluation methodology.

The sensitivity analysis (see Fig. 84.12) indicates that as the parameter τ increases from 0.1 to 0.9, assessment scores for all enterprises improve, while the relative ranking remains unchanged. High-performing enterprises (F3, F4, F5) typically get superior results, whilst underperforming corporations (F8, F9) occupy the lowest positions. The resilience of the

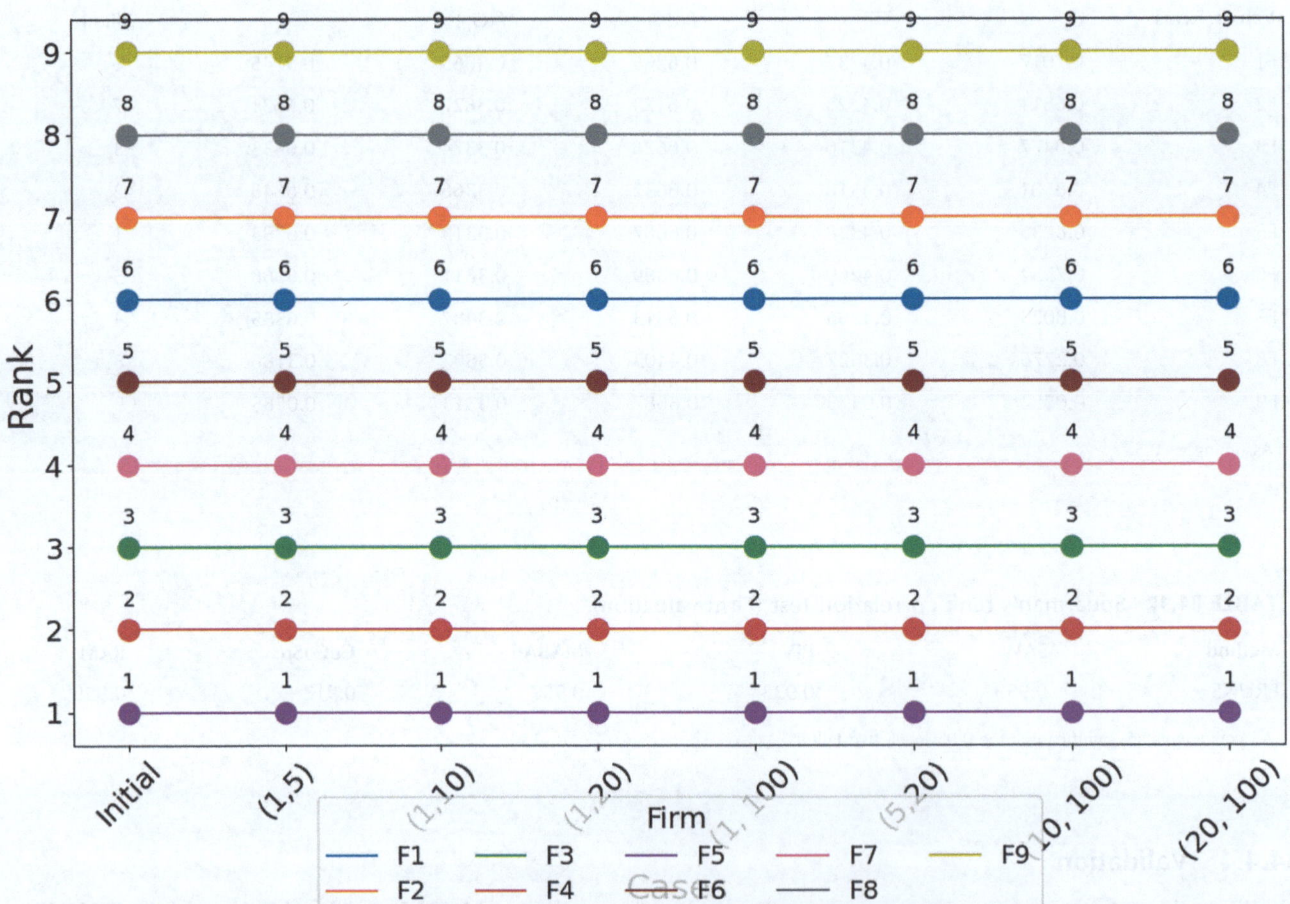

FIGURE 84.7 Effect of variations in the interval selection on the valuation-based ranking of alternatives.

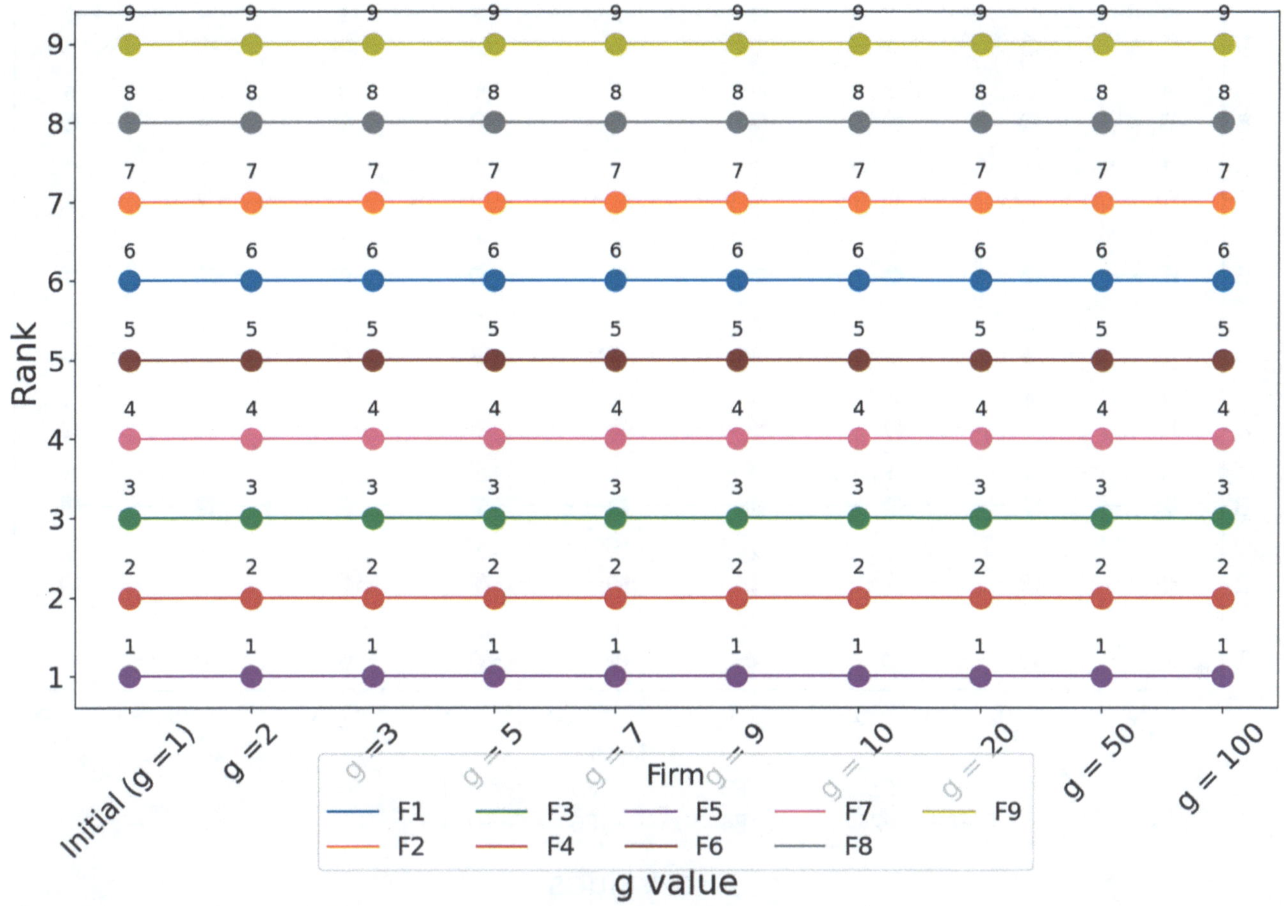

FIGURE 84.8 Effect of variations in g values on the valuation-based ranking of alternatives.

decision model to parameter variations and its persistent stability in company rankings affirm its efficacy and reliability in competitive business evaluations.

Overall, these findings confirm the model's reliability and highlight the nuanced impact of parameter selection on rankings.

84.5 Discussion

The research introduces the SPC-ERUNS technique, an advanced MCDM approach that evaluates company performance using CSR and firm value indicators. The findings indicate that Bharat Electronics Ltd. (F2), Infosys Ltd. (F5), and Hindustan Aeronautics Ltd. (F3) excel in CSR execution, social spending, and sustainable resource management. Tata Steel Ltd. (F9) and NTPC Ltd. (F8) hold lower positions, signifying rather subpar CSR outcomes.

The valuation analysis by SPC-ERUNS reveals that MC, EV, and profitability ratios have a substantial impact on appraisal ratings. Infosys Ltd. (F5) secured first place, followed by ITC Ltd. (F4) and Hindustan Aeronautics Ltd. (F3), underscoring a persistent relationship between enduring financial stability and corporate market success. The methodology's thorough analysis of valuation metrics enables a balanced alignment between market forces and shareholder expectations.

The sensitivity analysis conducted on critical parameters, including the upper and lower limits of the interval used in standardization of the IDM, gradient parameters g, and threshold τ, illustrates the intrinsic robustness of SPC-ERUNS. The final evaluation scores and rankings exhibit stability despite changes in parameters, indicating insensitivity to modifications of subjective thresholds and scale adjustments. This resilience is crucial in practical choice analysis contexts marked by parameter uncertainty.

The strong positive Spearman's rank correlation coefficients (sometimes surpassing 0.9) between the SPC-ERUNS ranks and traditional MCDM methods validate its accuracy and reliability. SPC-ERUNS utilizes enhanced uncertain

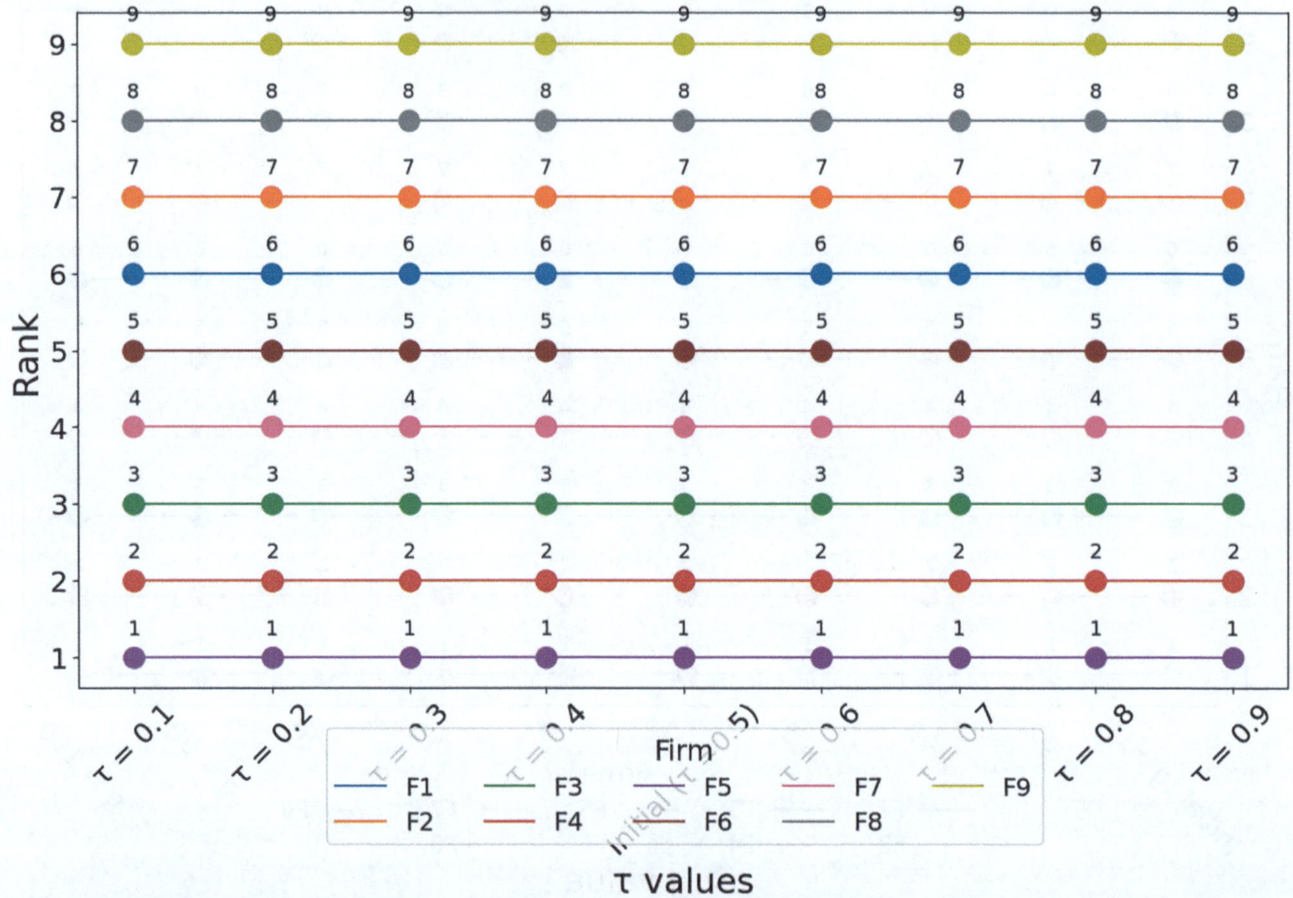

FIGURE 84.9 Effect of variations in τ values on the valuation-based ranking of alternatives.

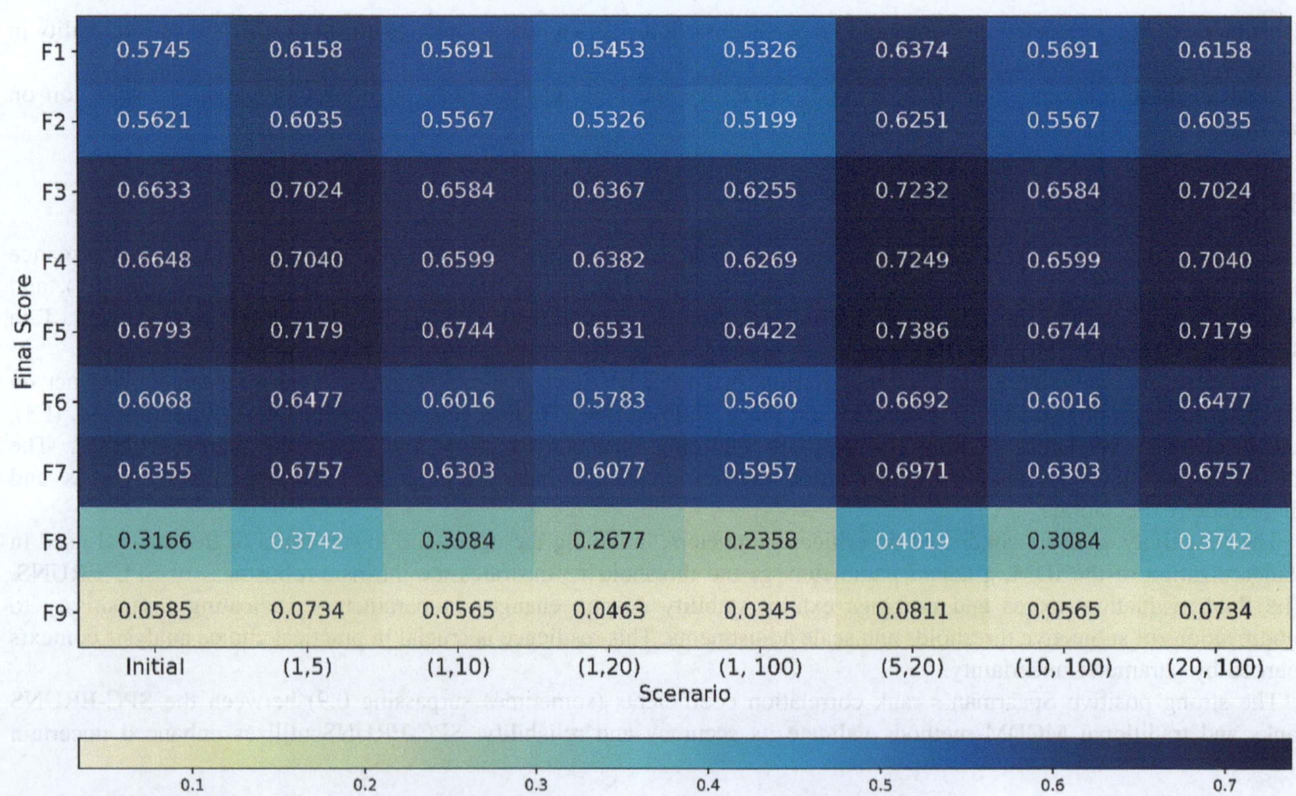

FIGURE 84.10 Effect of variations in the interval selection on the valuation scores of alternatives.

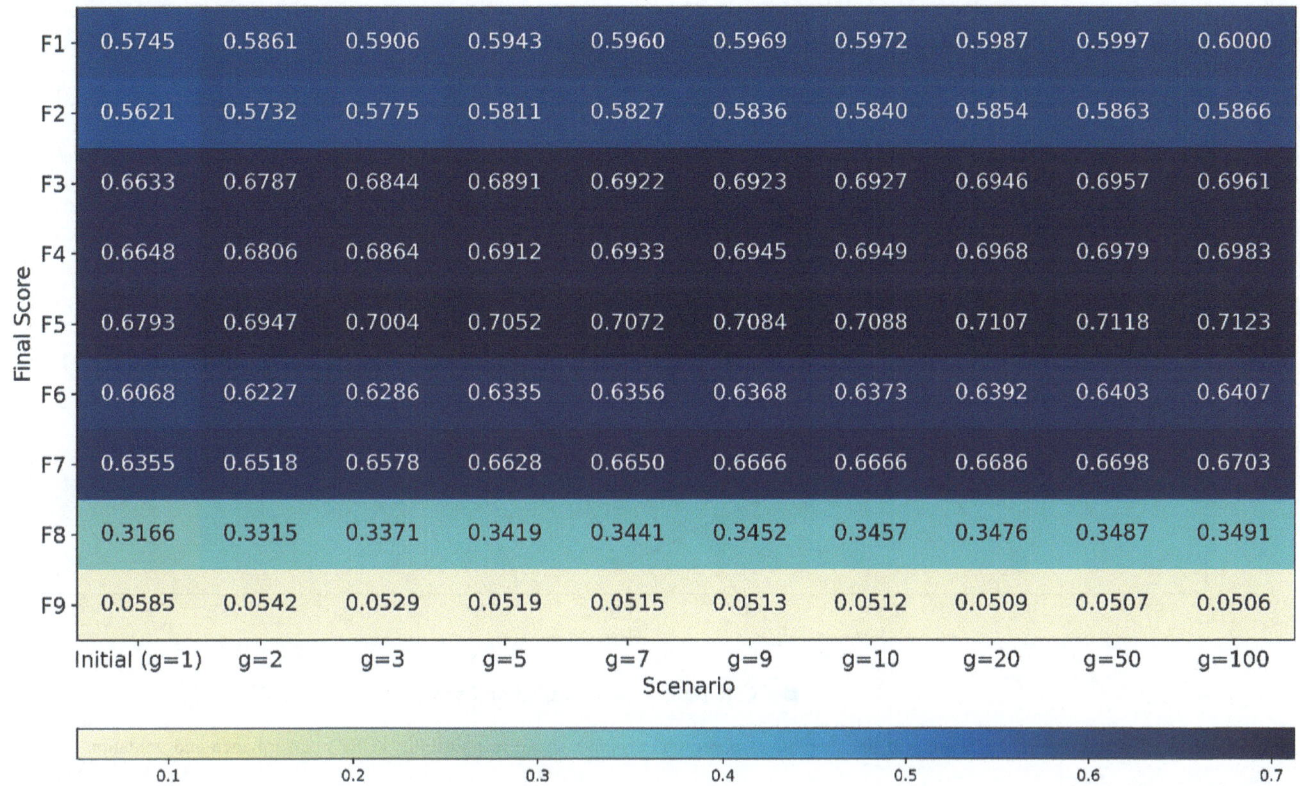

FIGURE 84.11 Effect of variations in g values on the valuation scores of alternatives.

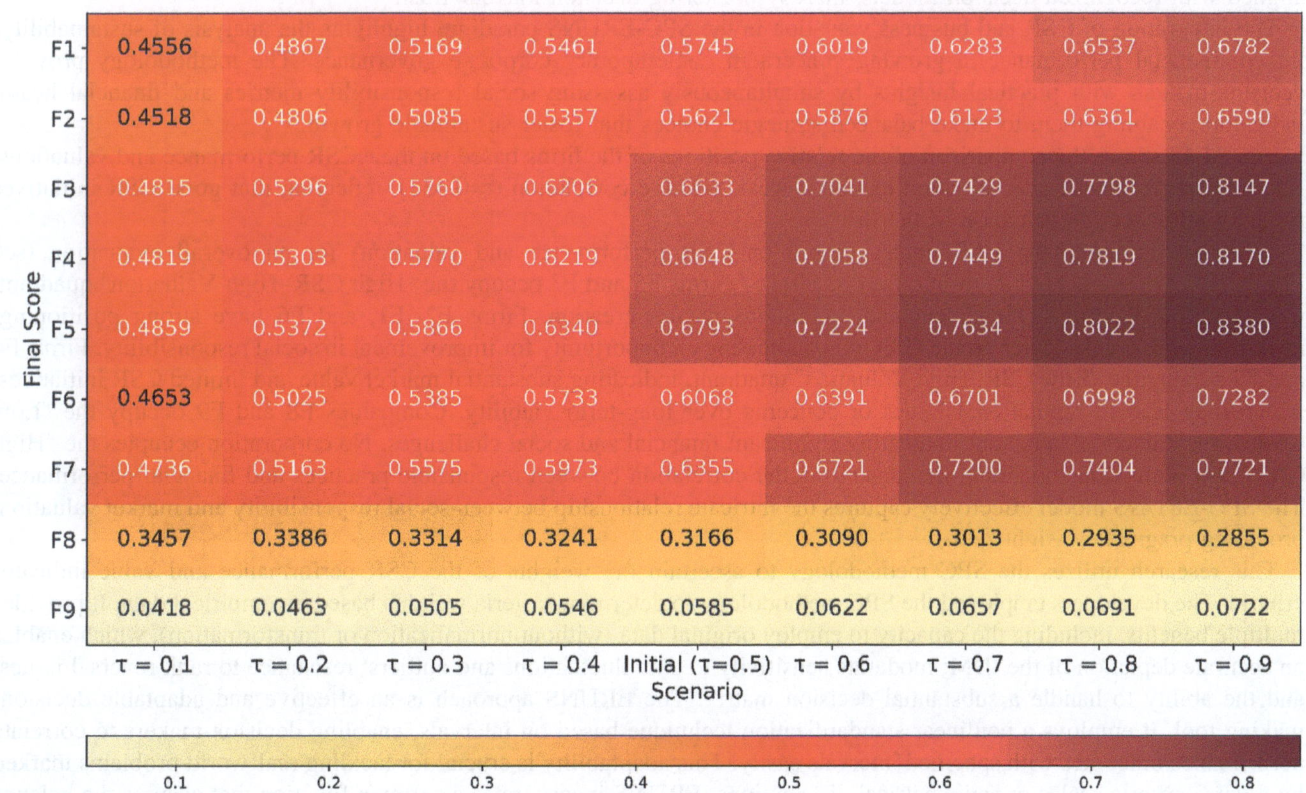

FIGURE 84.12 Effect of variations in τ values on the valuation scores of alternatives.

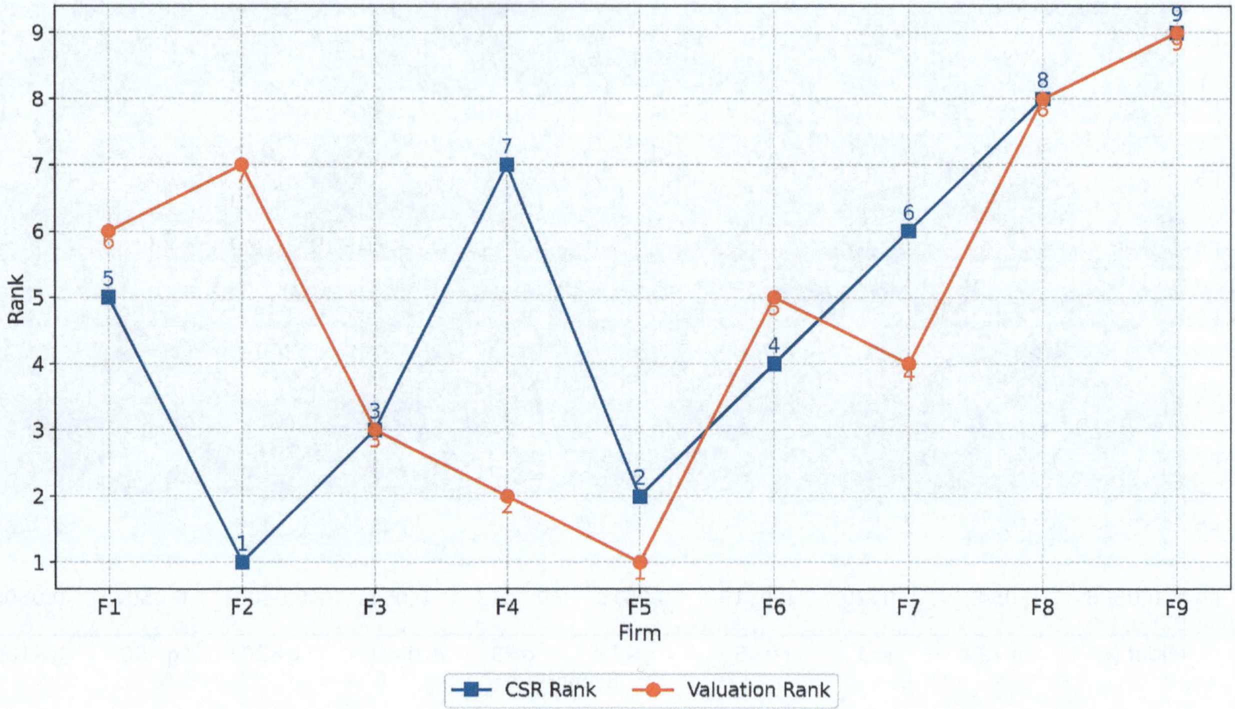

FIGURE 84.13 Comparison of the ranking of the alternatives based on corporate social responsibility (CSR) performance and valuation.

linguistic scales and optimized membership functions for superior discrimination, yielding rankings that are statistically aligned with recognized decision models, thereby bolstering decision-makers' trust.

The integration of CSR and business valuation in the SPC-ERUNS paradigm highlights the analysis of sustainability-linked financial performance, a growing concern in contemporary corporate governance. The methodology provides decision-makers with practical insights by simultaneously assessing social responsibility metrics and financial health indicators, enabling them to make balanced strategic choices that foster sustainable growth.

Fig. 84.13 shows the comparison of the relative positions of the firms based on their CSR performance and valuations. The CSR performance and valuation exhibit a weak positive correlation ($r=0.433$), reflecting that good CSR initiatives partially influence the valuation of the firms.

When we combine the FAS values (based on CSR performance and valuation) for an overall evaluation (see Fig. 84.14), we segmented them into four quadrants. Firms F5 and F3 occupy the "High CSR–High Valuation" quadrant, indicating outstanding achievement and continuous wealth creation. Firms F2, F1, and F6 have strong positioning; nevertheless, F2 ranks lower on the CSR axis, indicating an opportunity for improvement in social responsibility. Firms F4 and F7 occupy the "Low CSR–High Valuation" quadrant, indicating substantial market value and limited CSR initiatives, which may lead to reputational issues or concerns over long-term viability. Companies F8 and F9 occupy the "Low CSR–Low Valuation" quadrant, indicating significant financial and social challenges. No corporation occupies the "High CSR–Low Valuation" quadrant, demonstrating the correlation between responsible practices and financial performance. The SPC-ERUNS model effectively captures the intricate relationship between social responsibility and market valuation, providing pragmatic insights.

This research utilizes the SPC methodology to ascertain the weights of the CSR performance and value indicator criteria. The developers employed the SPC methodology to determine criteria weights based on empirical data. It provides multiple benefits, including the capacity to employ original data (without normalization or transformation), which enables an accurate depiction of the IDM; moderate sensitivity to data fluctuations and outliers; resistance to rank reversal issues; and the ability to handle a substantial decision matrix. The ERUNS approach is an effective and adaptable decision-making tool. It employs a nonlinear standardization technique based on intervals, enabling decision-makers to correlate performance outcomes with specified intervals easily. This adaptability is crucial for tackling real-world problems marked by diverse criteria scales or asymmetrical distributions. ERUNS incorporates a softmax function that ensures the balance of the utility of the criteria. It operates effectively with decision matrices that include zero and negative values, and it

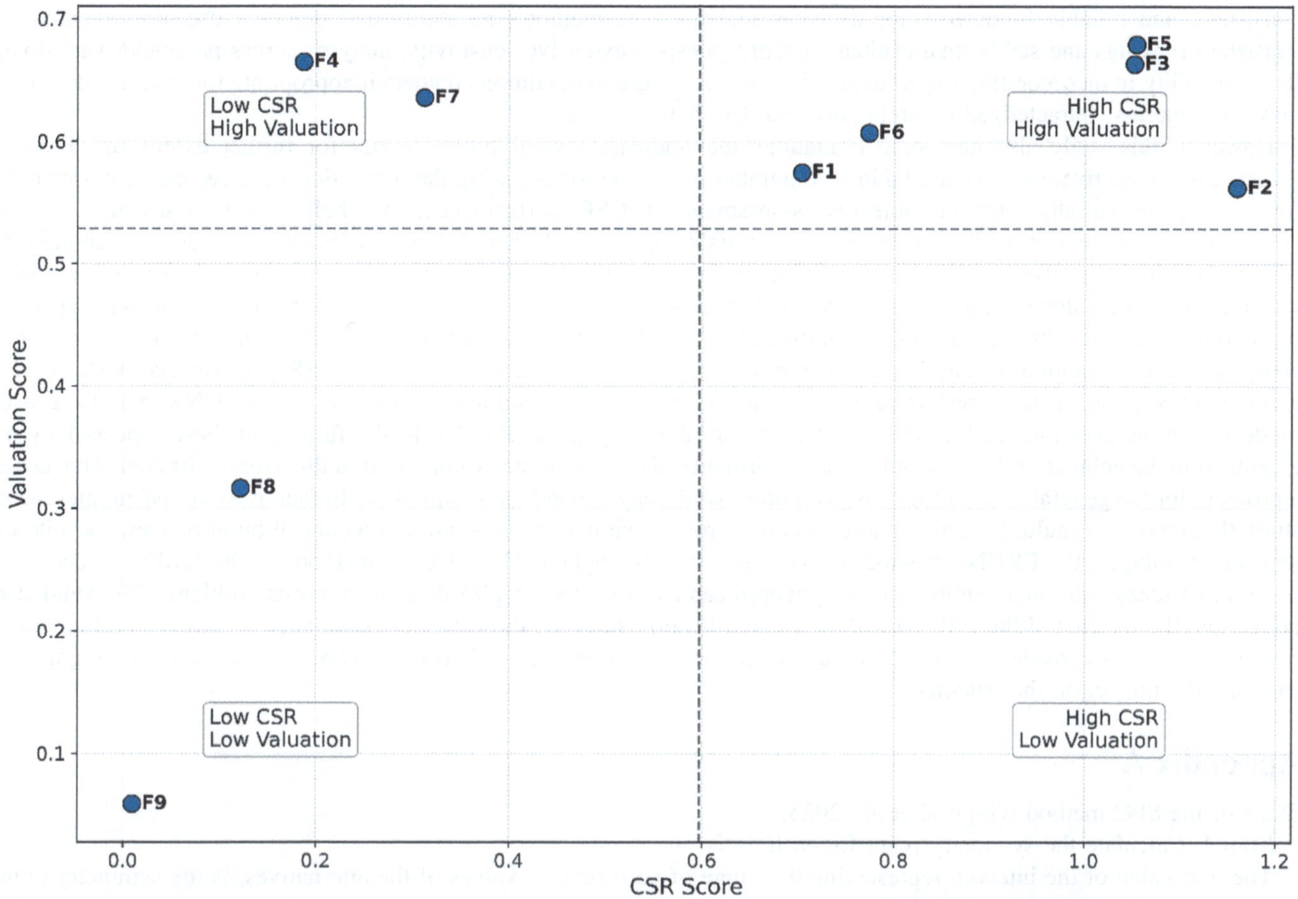

FIGURE 84.14 Combined performance of the firms.

proficiently manages several criteria and options. By employing ERUNS, decision-makers may establish interval limitations based on the prevailing conditions. This makes it a more efficient, versatile, and advantageous alternative to traditional MCDM methods.

The current study offers several implications for managerial decision-making, societal impacts, and policy formulations. The SPC-ERUNS methodology is a reliable assessment framework that enables decision-makers to evaluate organizations holistically, aligning CSR performance with financial valuation. It enhances openness and objectivity in company evaluation, aiding strategic planning and stakeholder communication. The emphasis on CSR indicators promotes accountability and sustainability, urging corporations to adopt socially responsible activities that benefit communities and the environment. This method helps investors and public stakeholders make informed decisions that promote ethical company practices, thereby enhancing corporate citizenship and social equity. SPC-ERUNS advances MCDM literature by integrating uncertain linguistic scales and advanced normalization and aggregation techniques, thereby tackling data ambiguity and uncertainties in expert assessments. It assists regulators and policymakers in methodically evaluating company sustainability disclosures and financial stability, enabling the formulation of governance frameworks and incentive programs to promote responsible business behavior. It provides empirical evidence for governmental measures aimed at enhancing CSR compliance and financial transparency in the corporate sector.

84.6 Conclusion

The present chapter presents demonstrations of the efficient application of the ERUNS method in evaluating firm performance based on their CSR activities and valuations. A group of nine leading firms listed on the BSE 100 ESG index in India is the subject of MCDM-based comparison. We observe that the SPC-ERUNS methodology offers a stable, consistent, and reliable framework for decision analysis. The method's reliability and practical use are validated by consistent rankings and stable final evaluation scores, despite extensive sensitivity analyses across parameter variations. Its adaptability in incorporating expert evaluations under uncertain conditions renders it appropriate for intricate decision-making scenarios characterized by ambiguity and data heterogeneity.

However, this study also has some limitations that indicate several future scopes for further extensions. From a theoretical perspective, we have used a limited number of criteria for assessing the firms. For instance, we have used only four indicating variables for an objective assessment of CSR performance. We believe this assessment is not comprehensive, though it exhibits a scientific and reliable approach. Hence, future studies may consider a large number of criteria (with subjective and objective information) to assess the CSR performance. Further, the evaluation of company valuation has been done using nine indicators. Future work may also indicate various financial indicators, such as profitability and efficiency measures, liquidity aspects, and Tobin's Q, Altman Z, and Ohlson's O indicators for a comprehensive evaluation. It may be fascinating to explore the interrelationship among CSR performance, ESG scores, green practices, and financial performance, using not only ranking methodologies (such as SPC-ERUNS) but also causal models, such as decision-making trial and evaluation laboratory (DEMATEL). In the future, all these aspects may be examined in the context of their overall stock performance. The sample size (nine) used in this work is limited. This poses a problem for the generalization of the results. Future work may expand the sample size. In fact, it would be an interesting study that considers multiple sectors and conducts a cross-sectional analysis. From a technical point of view, despite its several advantages, the ERUNS method has not been widely applied. The ERUNS method can be further extended to incorporate fuzzy and rough numbers, making it applicable to various complex decision analysis problems. We could also notice that the weights of the CSR indicators are significantly skewed (showing an overreliance on power and fuel cost). Future studies may consider various other methods for criteria weighting, such as LOPCOW, to determine the weights and examine the impact on the outcome.

Appendix A

Steps of the SPC method (Gligorić et al., 2023)

Step 1. Calculate the symmetry point for each criterion.

The mid-value of the interval, representing the range of performance values of the alternatives, is the symmetry point for each criterion, obtained as follows:

$$M_j = \frac{Min\,(P_{ij}) + Max\,(P_{ij})}{2};\ \forall\, j \in [1, n],\ i \in [1, m] \tag{A.1}$$

Step 2. Derive the absolute distances of the alternatives with respect to the corresponding symmetry points.

The absolute distances are obtained by using Eq. A.2 as follows:

$$D_{ij} = \left| P_{ij} - M_j \right| \tag{A.2}$$

Accordingly, the absolute distance matrix is formulated as follows:

$$D = \begin{pmatrix} D_{11} & \cdots & D_{1n} \\ \vdots & \ddots & \vdots \\ D_{m1} & \cdots & D_{mn} \end{pmatrix}_{m \times n} \tag{A.3}$$

Step 3. Obtain the moduli of the symmetry values

The values of the elements of the moduli of the symmetry matrix are obtained as follows:

$$\zeta_{ij} = \frac{\left(\frac{1}{m}\sum_{i=1}^{m} D_{ij}\right)}{P_{ij}};\ j = 1,\ 2,\ \ldots,\ n \tag{A.4}$$

Step 4. Obtain the modulus of the symmetry criterion.

The modulus of the symmetry criterion is a new row vector, whose elements are obtained as follows:

$$\xi_j = \frac{\sum_{i=1}^{m} \zeta_{ij}}{m};\ j = 1,\ 2, \ldots,\ n \tag{A.5}$$

Step 5. Compute the weights of the criteria.

The criteria weights are computed as follows:

$$w_j = \frac{\xi_j}{\sum_{j=1}^{n} \xi_j} \left(w_j > 0; \ \sum w_j = 1 \right) \tag{A.6}$$

References

Adib, M., Zhang, X., AA Zaid, M., & Sahyouni, A. (2021). Management control system for corporate social responsibility implementation–a stakeholder perspective. *Corporate Governance: The International Journal of Business in Society, 21*(3), 410–432. https://doi.org/10.1108/CG-06-2020-0247.

Ali, J. (2024). Spherical fuzzy symmetric point criterion-based approach using Aczel–Alsina prioritization: Application to sustainable supplier selection. *Granular Computing, 9*(2), 33. https://doi.org/10.1007/s41066-024-00449-7.

Alrasheedi, A. F., Rani, P., Mishra, A. R., Alshamrani, A. M., & Cavallaro, F. (2024). Fermatean fuzzy distance and sugeno–weber operators-based SPC-MARCOS approach for sustainable supplier evaluation in the healthcare supply chain. *Scientific Reports, 14*(1), 27373. https://doi.org/10.1038/s41598-024-78284-8.

Ampong, I. (2024). Assessing the effect of employee welfare and compensation on organizational performance: A case of Sahel Sahara Bank Ghana limited. *Cogent Business & Management, 11*(1), 2315690. https://doi.org/10.1080/23311975.2024.2315690.

Audi, M., & Yu, H. (2024). Strategic value creation through corporate social responsibility adoption for sustainable financial performance. *Journal of Policy Options, 7*(4), 14–21.

Babaçoğlu, S., Yalçın, G. C., Kara, K., Turen, U., Simic, V., Polat, M., & Pamucar, D. (2025). Promoting benchmarking and best practices in education: An interval-valued spherical fuzzy model for assessing sustainable digital transformation maturity. *Technology in Society, 81*, 102850.

Barman, S., & Mahakud, J. (2024). Corporate social responsibility and financial performance: Do group affiliation and mandatory corporate social responsibility norms matter? *IIMB Management Review, 36*(3), 256–268. https://doi.org/10.1016/j.iimb.2024.06.003.

Baydaş, M., & Elma, O. E. (2021). An objectıve criteria proposal for the comparison of MCDM and weighting methods in financial performance measurement: An application in Borsa Istanbul. *Decision Making: Applications in Management and Engineering, 4*(2), 257–279. https://doi.org/10.31181/dmame210402257b.

Baydaş, M., & Pamučar, D. (2022). Determining objective characteristics of MCDM methods under uncertainty: An exploration study with financial data. *Mathematics, 10*(7), 1115. https://doi.org/10.3390/math10071115.

Biswas, S., Bandyopadhyay, G., Pamucar, D., & Joshi, N. (2022). A multi-criteria based stock selection framework in emerging market. *Operational Research in Engineering Sciences: Theory and Applications, 5*(3), 153–193. https://doi.org/10.31181/oresta161122121b.

Biswas, S., Demir, G., & Chatterjee, P. (2025). A novel P, Q-Quasirung Orthopair Fuzzy Group Decision-Making Framework for selection of Renewable Energy sources. In Optimization in Sustainable Energy: Methods and Applications (pp. 27-67). https://doi.org/10.1002/9781394242139.ch2

Biswas, S., Božanić, D., Pamučar, D., & Marinković, D. (2023). A spherical fuzzy based decision making framework with Einstein aggregation for comparing preparedness of SMES in quality 4.0. *Facta Universitatis, Series: Mechanical Engineering, 21*(3), 453–478. https://doi.org/10.22190/FUME230831037B.

Biswas, S., Joshi, N., & Kar, S. (2024). A novel computational framework for comparing CSR performance: Evidence from India. *International journal of supply and operations management, 11*(1), 19–42. https://doi.org/10.22034/ijsom.2023.110009.2816.

Biswas, S., & Pamucar, D. (2023). A modified EDAS model for comparison of mobile wallet service providers in India. *Financial innovation, 9*(1), 41. https://doi.org/10.1186/s40854-022-00443-5.

Biswas, S., Pamucar, D., Dawn, S., & Simic, V. (2024). Evaluation based on relative utility and nonlinear standardization (ERUNS) method for comparing firm performance in energy sector. *Decision Making Advances, 2*(1), 1–21. https://doi.org/10.31181/dma21202419.

Brans, J. P., & Vincke, P. (1985). A preference ranking organisation method: The PROMETHEE method. *Management Science, 31*(6), 647–656.

Bui, T. N., Nguyen, X. H., & Pham, K. T. (2023). The effect of capital structure on firm value: A study of companies listed on the Vietnamese stock market. *International Journal of Financial Studies, 11*(3), 100. https://doi.org/10.3390/ijfs11030100.

Chaudhuri, T., Mitra, S., Guha, B., Biswas, S., & Kumar, P. (2023). CSR contributions for environmental sustainability: A comparison of private banks in emerging market. *Decision Making: Applications in Management and Engineering, 6*(2), 747–771. https://doi.org/10.31181/dmame622023852.

Costa, R., & Menichini, T. (2013). A multidimensional approach for CSR assessment: The importance of the stakeholder perception. *Expert systems with applications, 40*(1), 150–161. https://doi.org/10.1016/j.eswa.2012.07.028.

Gandasari, D., Tjahjana, D., Dwidienawati, D., & Ichsan, M. (2024). How to attract talents? The role of CSR, employer brand, benefits and career development. *Cogent Business & Management, 11*(1), 2323774. https://doi.org/10.1080/23311975.2024.2323774.

Gharbi, M., & Jarboui, A. (2024). The impact of corporate social responsibility on firm financial performance: Does corporate governance matter? *International Journal of Law and Management, 66*(6), 681–693. https://doi.org/10.1108/IJLMA-09-2023-0203.

Ghorabaee, M. K., Zavadskas, E. K., Olfat, L., & Turskis, Z. (2015). Multi-criteria inventory classification using a new method of evaluation based on distance from average solution (EDAS). *Informatica, 26*(3), 435–451.

Ghorabaee, M. K., Zavadskas, E. K., Turskis, Z., & Antucheviciene, J. (2016). A new combinative distance-based assessment (CODAS) method for multi-criteria decision-making. *Economic Computation and Economic Cybernetics Studies and Research, 50*(3), 25–44. https://EconPapers.repec.org/RePEc:cys:ecocyb:v:50:y:2016:i:3:p:25-44.

Gligorić, Z., Gligorić, M., Miljanović, I., Lutovac, S., & Milutinović, A. (2023). Assessing criteria weights by the symmetry point of criterion (novel SPC Method)–Application in the efficiency evaluation of the mineral deposit multi-criteria partitioning algorithm. *CMES-Computer Modeling in Engineering & Sciences, 136*(1), 955–979. https://doi.org/10.32604/cmes.2023.025021.

Harsanyi, J. C. (1955). Cardinal welfare, individualistic ethics, and interpersonal comparisons of utility. *Journal of Political Economy, 63*(4), 309–321.

Hwang, C. L., & Yoon, K. (1981). *Multiple attribute decision making: Methods and applications*. Springer.

Kaimal, A., & Uzma, S. H. (2024). Corporate social responsibility expenditure and financial performance: The moderating role of family ownership. *Corporate Governance: The International Journal of Business in Society, 24*(1), 101–118. https://doi.org/10.1108/CG-03-2022-0128.

Kara, K., Özyürek, H., Yalçın, G. C., & Burgaz, N. (2024). Enhancing financial performance evaluation: The MEREC-RBNAR hybrid method for sustainability-indexed companies. *Journal of Soft Computing and Decision Analytics, 2*(1), 236–257. https://doi.org/10.31181/jscda21202444.

Katrancı, A., Kundakcı, N., & Arman, K. (2026). Fuzzy SIWEC and Fuzzy RAWEC methods for sustainable waste disposal technology selection. *Spectrum of Operational Research, 3*(1), 87–102. https://doi.org/10.31181/sor31202633.

Kolour, H. R., Momayezi, V., & Momayezi, F. (2026). Enhancing supplier selection in public manufacturing: A hybrid multi-criteria decision-making approach. *Spectrum of Decision Making and Applications, 3*(1), 1–20. https://doi.org/10.31181/sdmap31202629.

Kumar, R. (2025). A comprehensive review of MCDM methods, applications, and emerging trends. *Decision Making Advances, 3*(1), 185–199.

Komatina, N., Marinkovic, D., & Babič, M. (2026). Fundamental characteristics and applicability of the RADAR method: Proof of ranking consistency. *Spectrum of Operational Research, 3*(1), 63–80. https://doi.org/10.31181/sor31202635.

Li, D., Wan, G., & Rong, Y. (2026). An enhanced spherical cubic fuzzy WASPAS method and its application for the assessment of service quality of crowdsourcing logistics platform. *Spectrum of Decision Making and Applications, 3*(1), 100–123. https://doi.org/10.31181/sdmap31202641.

Mukhametzyanov, I., & Pamucar, D. (2024). "Thin" structure of relations in MCDM Models: Equivalence of the MABAC, TOPSIS(L1) and RS methods to the weighted sum method. *Decision Making: Applications in Management and Engineering, 7*(2), 418–442.

Onkila, T., & Sarna, B. (2022). A systematic literature review on employee relations with CSR: State of art and future research agenda. *Corporate Social Responsibility and Environmental Management, 29*(2), 435–447. https://doi.org/10.1002/csr.2210.

Opricovic, S., & Tzeng, G. H. (2004). Compromise solution by MCDM methods: A comparative analysis of VIKOR and TOPSIS. *European Journal of Operational Research, 156*(2), 445–455.

Pamucar, D., & Biswas, S. (2023). A novel hybrid decision making framework for comparing market performance of metaverse crypto assets. *Decision Making Advances, 1*(1), 49–62. https://doi.org/10.31181/dma1120238.

Pamučar, D., & Ćirović, G. (2015). The selection of transport and handling resources in logistics centers using multi-attributive border approximation area comparison (MABAC). *Expert Systems with Applications, 42*(6), 3016–3028. https://doi.org/10.1016/j.eswa.2014.11.057.

Puška, A., Stević, Ž., & Pamučar, D. (2021). Evaluation and selection of healthcare waste incinerators using extended sustainability criteria and multi-criteria analysis methods. *Environment Development and Sustainability, 24*(9), 11195–11225. https://doi.org/10.1007/s10668-021-01902-2.

Rodríguez-Valencia, L., Lamothe-Fernández, P., & Alaminos, D. (2023). The market value of SMEs: a comparative study between private and listed firms in alternative stock markets. *Annals of Finance, 19*(1), 95–117. https://doi.org/10.1007/s10436-022-00420-z.

Roy, B. (1968). Classement et choix en présence de points de vue multiples, Revue française d'informatique et de recherche opérationnelle. 2(8), 57–75.

Sanyal, A., Biswas, S., & Sur, S. (2025). An integrated full consistent LOPCOW-EDAS framework for modelling consumer decision making for organic food selection. *Yugoslav Journal of Operations Research, 35*(2), 331–364. https://doi.org/10.2298/YJOR240315022S.

Shyur, H., & Shih, H. (2024). Resolving rank reversal in TOPSIS: A comprehensive analysis of distance metrics and normalization methods. *Informatica*, 1–22. https://doi.org/10.15388/24-infor576.

Tripathi, M., Kashiramka, S., & Jain, P. K. (2022). Has EVA evolved to outperform conventional earnings measures in determining firm's value? A case of Indian consumer firms. *Asia-Pacific Journal of Accounting & Economics, 29*(2), 487–501. https://doi.org/10.1080/16081625.2019.1584760.

Stević, Ž., Pamučar, D., Puška, A., & Chatterjee, P. (2020). Sustainable supplier selection in healthcare industries using a new MCDM method: Measurement Alternatives and Ranking according to COmpromise Solution (MARCOS). *Computers & Industrial Engineering, 140*, 106231.

Wang, Z., & Ren, F. (2025). Developing a decision support system for sustainable urban planning using machine learning-based scenario modeling. *Scientific Reports, 15*(1). https://doi.org/10.1038/s41598-025-90057-5.

Wang, M., Zheng, L., & Zhang, Y. (2025). Dried out and priced up: Physical water risk, CSR strategies, and the cost of equity. *Water, 17*(13), 1881. https://doi.org/10.3390/w17131881.

Xiang, Z., & Zhang, X. (2025). An integrated decision support system for supplier selection and performance evaluation in global supply chains. *Applied Soft Computing*113325. https://doi.org/10.1016/j.asoc.2025.113325.

Yalçın, G. C., Kara, K., Işık, G., Simic, V., & Pamucar, D. (2025). Development of a decision support system for performance measurement of social movements. *Cognitive Computation, 17*(1). https://doi.org/10.1007/s12559-024-10385-y.

Zavadskas, E. K., Kaklauskas, A., & Sarka, V. (1994). The new method of multicriteria complex proportional assessment of projects. *Technological and Economic Development of Economy, 1*(3), 131–139.

Zavadskas, E. K., & Turskis, Z. (2010). A new additive ratio assessment (ARAS) method in multicriteria decision making. *Technological and Economic Development of Economy, 16*(2), 159–172. https://doi.org/10.3846/tede.2010.10.

Zavadskas, E. K., Turskis, Z., & Kildienė, S. (2014). State of art surveys of overviews on MCDM/MADM methods. *Technological and Economic Development of Economy, 20*(1), 165–179. https://doi.org/10.3846/20294913.2014.892037.

Zhang, D. (2025). Applying multi-criteria decision-making to text analysis for optimizing engineering knowledge management. *Alexandria Engineering Journal, 117*, 648–661. https://doi.org/10.1016/j.aej.2025.01.028.

Further reading

Torkayesh, A. E., & Deveci, M. (2021). A mulTi-noRmalization mUlti-distance aSsessmenT (TRUST) approach for locating a battery swapping station for electric scooters. *Sustainable Cities and Society, 74*, 103243.

Chapter 85

FUCA: Faire un choix adéquat for multi-attribute decision-making

Mahmut Baydaş[1], Željko Stević[2,3], Enes Emre Başar[4], and Bengü Tosun[5]

[1]*Faculty of Applied Sciences, Necmettin Erbakan University, Konya, Türkiye,* [2]*Department of Mobile Machinery and Railway Transport, Faculty of Transport Engineering, Vilnius Gediminas Technical University, Vilnius, Lithuania,* [3]*Faculty of Transport and Traffic Engineering, University of East Sarajevo, Doboj, Bosnia and Herzegovina,* [4]*Faculty of Economics and Administrative Sciences, Faculty of Economics and Administrative Sciences, Anadolu University, Eskisehir, Türkiye,* [5]*Department of Economics, Istanbul Nişantaşı University, İstanbul, Türkiye*

85.1 Introduction

Multicriteria decision-making (MCDM) methods are analytical tools that enable ranking, selecting, or classifying different alternatives. In today's complex decision-making environments, considering multiple criteria simultaneously in many areas is becoming necessary, as single-dimensional assessments are no longer sufficient. In today's world, where artificial intelligence, machine learning, big data, and digitalization are rapidly developing and gaining multifaceted dimensions, MCDM methods offer decision-makers useful analysis opportunities, undeniably improving decision quality significantly compared to alternatives at both the micro and macro levels.

However, a significant area of debate in the literature is which MCDM method to use for which problem. Today, more than 200 methods have been defined, and these are generally classified as utility-based, distance-based, outranking, and mixed methods (Stević, Baydaş, et al., 2024). Various criteria have been considered in method selection: sensitivity analysis, rank reversal problems, correlation with external factors, consistency of model equations, and the level of compensatory power of the methods (Stević, Ersoy, et al., 2024). However, one of the least discussed topics among these criteria has been compensatory power. A compensatory power means that a low value on one criterion in a decision matrix can be compensated for by a high value on another criterion. This meaning seems to evoke a negative connotation (de França Dantas Daher & de Almeida, 2013). The calculation method used for classical (especially performance-oriented) rankings is actually a simple weighted aggregation method, the most classic example of which is the SAW method in the literature. Therefore, in this calculation method, it is often the case that a few high-scoring criteria dominate others. In other words, the current aggregation method has a higher compensability. For example, an alternative A1 that lacks sufficient scores on "Criteria-1" and "Criteria-2" can focus on high performance on relatively easier criteria like "Criteria-3." Thus, A1, which scores low on one or two criteria, compensates by scoring higher than average on another criterion and outperforms its competitors. In this context, "outranking," "utility," and "distance-based" approaches may have a lower or milder compensatory effect compared to classical aggregation methods. In fact, the extent to which one criterion can compensate for others directly impacts the fairness and reliability of the decision. Therefore, addressing the compensatory dimension with more comprehensive and stimulating analyses is an imperative for researchers.

An in-depth examination of MCDM methods in terms of compensatory power is rare. Compensatory power plays a critical role, especially in personnel selection: when a subjective criterion (e.g., interview score) surpasses three objective criteria (exam performance), meritocracy and fairness can be severely compromised. This not only distorts the results but also raises serious doubts about the system's reliability. This study demonstrates how such a risk can occur with simple examples and highlights the potential solutions of low-compensatory methods. In particular, a comparison of 14 different MCDM methods using sensitivity analysis demonstrates the stability and reliability of the Faire Un Choix Adéquat (FUCA)/make an adequate choice method.

It has been emphasized in many studies that the FUCA method performs very well in correlation-based sensitivity analyses, that is, by not disrupting the relationship with the external factor and maintaining stability. The FUCA method

Encyclopedia of Multi-Attribute Decision-Making (MADM). DOI: https://doi.org/10.1016/B978-0-443-33275-3.00083-X

stands out with its ranking-based structure and extremely simple formula. By considering an alternative's rank on each criterion, FUCA prevents any single criterion from suppressing others thanks to its low compensatory natüre (Baydaş et al., 2023). This prevents subjective criteria, such as interviews in personnel selection, from overshadowing other objective performance and thus compromising the integrity of the system. Similar to other outranking methods, FUCA maintains the superiority of numerical majority criteria to a certain extent and stands out with its ease of calculation, practicality, and consistent results. Therefore, the FUCA method is considered a method that deserves greater attention in both academic literature and applied decision-making problems.

The remainder of the study is structured as follows: first, MCDM methods and the issue of compensatory performance are discussed in the literature. The methodology section then describes the dataset, criteria, weighting scenarios, and the 14 methods compared. The findings are then discussed, detailing how FUCA stands out from other methods in terms of stability, robustness, and reliability. The final section evaluates the results and offers policy recommendations to support the principles of fairness and merit in personnel selection.

85.2 Literature review

MCDM methods have been extensively applied in diverse fields since the 1960s. In the literature, these methods are generally categorized as utility-based, distance-based, outranking, and hybrid approaches. MCDM methods offer decision-makers a multicriteria evaluation opportunity for ranking, selection, and classification problems, and the fact that over 200 methods have been identified demonstrates that method selection itself is a decision-making problem. While the number of MCDM methods has exceeded 200, there is no consensus on the criteria for selecting the most appropriate MCDM method to provide the best alternative, making the task even more difficult. This is because an objective evaluation method for selection remains a controversial issue (Danesh et al., 2017). Each MCDM method has different algorithms, and the rankings produced by MCDM methods exhibit a characteristic distribution. This further exacerbates the problem of which method should be used, and the fact that there is no single MCDM method that can handle all decision-making problems (Cinelli et al., 2022). Evaluation criteria for MCDM method selection include the axiomatic nature of the methods' computational algorithms, advanced mathematical capabilities, sensitivity analyses to weight coefficients, sensitivity to correlation with external factors, rank reversal, and computational cost (Cinelli et al., 2022; Emamat et al., 2022). In the current environment, where there is no consensus-based objective MCDM selection framework, decision-makers may mistakenly conclude that MCDM methods that produce similar rankings are equivalent. The difficulty in comparing MCDM methods stems from the uncertainty surrounding the best consensus approach (Stanujkic et al., 2013).

At this point, the aspects of the compensatory nature of some MCDM methods that undermine fairness necessitate the consideration of this criterion. We would like to highlight the “compensatory” aspect of MCDM methods. In this context, MCDM methods can be classified as compensatory, partially compensatory, and noncompensatory. MCDM methods that utilize the grand total “utility theory” are argued to be more compensatory than methods based on the “outranking” school (Ziemba, 2019). Clearly, a compensatory effect means that a low value on one criterion in a decision matrix can be compensated for by a high value on another. This connotation evokes a negative connotation. Methods based on aggregation over alternatives demonstrate the existence of compensatory effects in the process. Additive methods can actually move undesirable or unacceptable alternatives higher in the rankings (de França Dantas Daher & de Almeida, 2013). This is precisely why a few high-scoring criteria dominate others. This calculation system clearly has a higher compensability. In this sense, FUCA can be considered a softer compensatory method.

The FUCA method, introduced in recent stages of the literature, is attracting attention due to its simple ranking-based structure and ease of calculation. FUCA ranks alternatives for each criterion and reaches a final decision based on the weighted average rank values. Thanks to this structure, it has lower compensatory power compared to classical aggregation methods; that is, high performance in a single criterion cannot easily override low performance in other criteria. FUCA is used in various fields in the literature; however, it is noteworthy that systematic comparisons in terms of compensatory power are limited (Baydaş et al., 2024). While the compensatory power dimension has often been overlooked in the MCDM literature, it plays a critical role, particularly in areas where merit and fairness are paramount, such as personnel selection. Existing studies have not sufficiently addressed the risk of subjective criteria overriding objective criteria in personnel selection. In this context, there is a need to raise awareness that less compensatory methods (e.g., outranking approaches like FUCA or ELimination Et Choix Traduisant la REalité [ELECTRE]) can produce more reliable and fair results in personnel selection (Banihabib et al., 2017).

85.3 Materials and methods

This section provides detailed descriptions of the methods used in the study. The FUCA method, used in the evaluation of alternatives, is presented first. Because the other methods are numerous (14), they are only briefly mentioned.

First, the mathematical formulation of the FUCA method, the main methodology of the study, is presented, followed by a list of other MCDM methods used for comparison. The study considers a scenario with 4 criteria and 10 alternatives for personnel selection. Three of these criteria represent objective exam scores, while one represents a more subjective criterion, such as a jury/commission evaluation. Because the criteria scores are evaluated on the same scale, ranging from 0 to 100, no normalization was applied. The primary objective of the study is to compare the compensatory nature of the classical weighted aggregation method SAW, commonly used in daily life, with FUCA and 13 other MCDM methods, and to illuminate the impact of this on merit and fairness.

Fig. 85.1 below shows the flow diagram of the study.

85.3.1 Faire un choix adéquat/make an adequate choice methods

The FUCA method is a ranking-based MCDM method that produces robust results with relatively simple steps (Baydaş & Pamučar, 2022; Do, 2022; Dudić et al., 2024; Thinh & Mai, 2023; Wang et al., 2024):

Step 1. Alternatives are ranked for each criterion. The ranking is performed so that the best value is 1 and the worst value is m (number of alternatives).

Step 2. The score value (vi) for each alternative is calculated by summing the products of the ranking values and the criterion weights. A weighted summation for each optimal solution i is computed as:

$$v_i = \sum_{j=1}^{n} (r_{ij} \times w_j) \tag{85.1}$$

85.3.2 Other multicriteria decision-making methods

For comparison, 13 other methods commonly used in the literature were included in the analysis. These MCDM methods are: SAW, technique for order preference by similarity to ideal solution (TOPSIS), VlseKriterijumska Optimizacija I Kompromisno Resenje (VIKOR), combinative distance-based assessment (CODAS), complex proportional assessment (COPRAS), ELECTRE-III, linear programming technique for multidimensional analysis of preference (LINMAP), Multi-Attributive Border Approximation area Comparison (MABAC), multiobjective optimization by ratio analysis (MOORA), multiplicative exponential weighting (MEW), Net Flow Method (NFM), preference ranking on the basis of ideal-average distance (PROBID), and Simpler Preference Ranking on the Basis of Ideal-Average Distance (s-PROBID) (Deveci et al., 2022; Peci et al., 2025; Petrović et al., 2023; Wang & Rangaiah, 2017; Wang et al., 2020; Wang et al., 2021). Note that these methods cover all combinations of utility, distance-based, outranking, addition, multiplication, and hybrid methods. We used all variations in this study to make a fair comparison.

85.4 Application

The study employs two hypothetical scenarios: a simple one and a complex one. Both relate to personnel selection. The first scenario will demonstrate the equally weighted FUCA method for clarity. The calculation steps will be presented sequentially. The second, complex hypothetical personnel selection scenario, includes 10 alternatives and 8criteria.

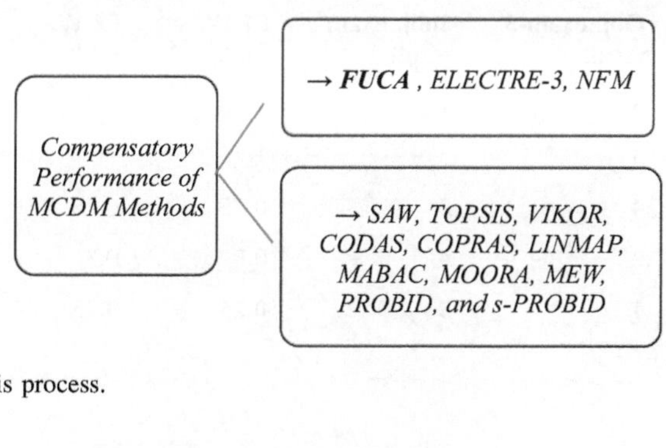

FIGURE 85.1 The diagram of the analysis process.

This realistic yet scenario-based application aims to demonstrate the impact of compensatory factors on rankings in personnel selection. A decision matrix was prepared consisting of six alternative candidates and four criteria. Three of the criteria represent objective exam scores, while one represents a subjective jury evaluation. The fact that the directive hypothetically prioritizes objective criteria can be inferred from both the number of criteria and the weighting coefficients assigned.

85.4.1 Case scenario-1 (numerical example-simple)

In this first table (decision matrix), the alternatives (candidates): A1, A2, A3, …, A5, and criteria (exam types): C1 = objective exam-1, C2 = objective exam-2, C3 = objective exam-3, C4 = subjective exam (interview/judge). Scores out of 100 are assigned for each candidate. This table serves as the raw data (decision matrix) to be used in MCDM methods.

Table 85.1 is the first decision matrix showing the scores received by personnel candidates, that is, the raw scores before weighting. Table 85.2 below shows the rankings achieved by the candidates for each criterion. It can be seen more clearly below, together with the weighting results in the calculation.

Alternative A5, with the lowest value in the ranking, came first. Note that the final result for A5 is (1 x 0.25) + (1 x 0.25) + (1 x 0.25) + (5 x 0.25) = 2. Here, the weight coefficient for each criterion is 0.25 because it is equal. The final score of other alternatives is calculated with the same logic.

Table 85.2 clearly demonstrates, as do the analysis findings that will be discussed later, that the race is essentially between candidates A1 and A5. Note that A1 is the best candidate (i.e., the first) in the subjective criteria, while it ranks last in the objective criteria. A5, on the other hand, is the best candidate (i.e., the strongest candidate) in the objective criteria, but it scores low in the subjective criteria. This dramatically demonstrates that, based on the MCDM method, compensatory power will determine which of these two candidates will take the lead in the future.

We now examine the findings of the case scenarios, considering each weight scenario individually.

TABLE 85.1 Initial decision matrix showing the scores received by personnel candidates.

	Objective exam-1 result	Objective exam-2 result	Objective exam-3 result	Subjective exam result
A1	70	70	70	100
A2	75	70	80	70
A3	80	75	70	70
A4	85	75	80	45
A5	100	100	100	20

TABLE 85.2 The rankings achieved by the candidates according to each criterion.

	Obj. exam-1 result	Obj. exam-2 result	Obj. exam-3 result	Subj. exam result	F1 W. rank	F2 W. rank	F3 W. rank	F4 W. rank	Final rank
A1	5	5	5	1	1.25	1.25	1.25	0.25	4
A2	4	4	3	3	1	1	0.75	0.75	3.5
A3	3	3	4	2	0.75	0.75	1	0.5	3
A4	2	2	2	4	0.5	0.5	0.5	1	2.5
A5	**1**	**1**	**1**	**5**	**0.25**	**0.25**	**0.25**	**1.25**	**2**

85.4.2 Case scenario-2 (numerical example-2)

In this different scenario, we're using a decision matrix with 10 alternatives and 8 criteria for personnel selection. Our goal is to identify and select the best candidate personnel. Two of the eight exams are subjective (interviews or jury members' subjective evaluations), and the remaining six are objective (written exams the candidate has previously taken). C1: objective exam-1, C2: objective exam-2, C3: objective exam-3, C4: subjective exam, C5: objective exam-5, C6: objective exam-6, C7: objective exam-7, C8: subjective exam-2. The Table 85.3 below shows the candidates' scores in the first decision matrix for this scenario. The weight coefficient will be evaluated equally (Table 85.4).

Alternative A5, with the lowest value in the ranking, came first. Note that the final result for A5 is 0.125 x 4 + 0.75 x 2 = 8 x 0.25 = 2.25. Here, the weight coefficient for each criterion is 0.125 because it is equal. The final score of other alternatives is calculated with the same logic.

85.4.3 Comparative analysis

As mentioned in the literature section, a critical issue for MCDM methods is how they compare to other methods. Sensitivity analysis is one such approach. If a method's rankings are too flexible and variable with respect to weighting coefficients, meaning it changes the ranking too much, this indicates that the method is too sensitive. This also implies that the methods are not good because they lack robustness. And the opposite is true. A good method is one with low sensitivity. Now, based on the results obtained above and the weighting coefficients, we present a simple sensitivity analysis comparing the FUCA method with 14 other MCDM methods, along with the nuanced aspect of compensatory performance. As mentioned in the literature, compensatory performance means obtaining high scores on one criterion to compensate for low scores on other criteria. Some MCDM methods do not allow for this, and "outranking schools" methods, including FUCA, are among them.

85.4.3.1 Weight-1 scenario

In the weight-1 scenario, the weight coefficients for each criterion (C1, C2, C3, C4, ...) are determined as follows, as can be seen in Table 85.5 below: C1: 0.15, C2: 0.05, C3: 0.15, C4: 0.15, C5: 0.15, C6: 0.05, C7: 0.15, and C8: 0.15.

There are two reasons why we focus solely on A1 and A5 in these rankings. First, this fierce competition is between A1 and A5. In fact, all 14 MCDM methods ranked either A1 or A5 first. The other candidates had no claim to first place. Second, the outcome of the competition between A1 and A5 is critical for understanding the concept of "compensation" along with sensitivity, as will be explained later.

For Table 85.5, it can be clearly said that the method choice under these weightings determines the outcome. While full compensators make a decision based on two criteria, superiority/ranking-based procedures maintain the majority rule. If the goal of merit is to "limit the dominance of a single or two criteria," the ELECTRE-III/FUCA/VIKOR-Q/NFM families are compatible with this normative goal.

TABLE 85.3 Initial decision matrix showing the scores received by personnel candidates.

	C1	C2	C3	C4	C5	C6	C7	C8
A1	70	70	70	100	52	52	52	75
A2	75	70	80	70	56	52	60	52
A3	80	75	70	70	60	56	52	52
A4	85	75	80	45	63	56	60	33
A5	100	100	100	20	75	75	75	15
A6	85	83	80	35	63	62	60	26
A7	86	90	82	15	64	67	61	11
A8	85	85	85	3	63	63	63	2
A9	88	80	80	2	66	60	60	1
A10	82	96	83	2	61	72	62	1

TABLE 85.4 The rankings achieved by the candidates according to each criterion.

	F1 rank	F2 rank	F3 rank	F4 rank	F5 rank	F6 rank	F7 rank	F8 rank	F1 W. rank	F2 W. rank	F3 W. rank	F4 W. rank	F5 W. rank	F6 W. rank	F7 W. rank	F8 W. rank	Final rank
A1	10	10	10	1	10	10	10	1	1.25	1.25	1.25	0.125	1.25	1.25	1.25	0.125	7.75
A2	9	9	8	3	9	9	8	3	1.125	1.125	1	0.375	1.125	1.125	1	0.375	7.25
A3	8	8	9	2	8	8	9	2	1	1	1.125	0.25	1	1	1.125	0.25	6.75
A4	6	7	7	4	6	7	7	4	0.75	0.875	0.875	0.5	0.75	0.875	0.875	0.5	6
A5	**1**	**1**	**1**	**6**	**1**	**1**	**1**	**6**	**0.125**	**0.125**	**0.125**	**0.75**	**0.125**	**0.125**	**0.125**	**0.75**	**2.25**
A6	5	5	6	5	5	5	6	5	0.625	0.625	0.75	0.625	0.625	0.625	0.75	0.625	5.25
A7	3	3	4	7	3	3	4	7	0.375	0.375	0.5	0.875	0.375	0.375	0.5	0.875	4.25
A8	4	4	2	8	4	4	2	8	0.5	0.5	0.25	1	0.5	0.5	0.25	1	4.5
A9	2	6	5	10	2	6	5	10	0.25	0.75	0.625	1.25	0.25	0.75	0.625	1.25	5.75
A1-0	7	2	3	9	7	2	3	9	0.875	0.25	0.375	1.125	0.875	0.25	0.375	1.125	5.25

TABLE 85.5 Ranking results produced by multicriteria decision-making methods according to the weight-1 scenario.

	CODAS	COPRAS	ELECTRE-3	FUCA	LINMAP	MABAC	MEW	MOORA	NFM	PROBID	SAW	s_PROBID	TOPSIS	VIKOR-Q
A1	1	1	5	**10**	1	1	1	1	4	1	1	1	1	**10**
A5	4	2	1	**1**	6	2	6	2	1	7	2	6	5	**1**

85.4.3.2 Weight-2 scenario

We continue the sensitivity analysis of these scenarios and change the weight coefficients: weight-2 coefficients are as follows. (C1, C2, C3, …) coefficients are 0.11, 0.14, 0.11, 0.14, 0.11, 0.13, 0.12, 0.14, respectively. As can be seen in Table 85.6 below, the results have not changed much.

Sensitivity analysis shows that, with reasonable changes in weights, the decision divergence persists: compensatory methods lead A1. Compensatory methods (FUCA, ELECTRE-III, NFM, VIKOR-Q) currently maintain the lead of A5.

85.4.3.3 Weight-3 scenario

This time, we're changing the criterion weights radically. We're significantly increasing the weight of criterion C4 and C8, favoring criterion c4 and c8. Weight-3 coefficients are as follows: (C1, C2, C3, …) coefficients are 0.08, 0.12, 0.08, 0.24, 0.07, 0.10, 0.07, 0.24. respectively. The results are interesting, as can be seen in Table 85.7 below.

Highly compensating methods (SAW, TOPSIS, CODAS, COPRAS, LINMAP, MABAC, MEW, MOORA, PROBID, s_PROBID) continue to assign A1 first. Interestingly, VIKOR-Q now also ranks A1 as the best choice. FUCA, ELECTRE-III, and NFM still rank A5 1 and are determined to do so. VIKOR-Q appears to heavily penalize the "worst criterion." When C4 and C8 = 48%, A5 rank at C8 and C4 = 10th results in a significant penalty, leading to a shift toward A1. SAW/TOPSIS and similar methods are highly compensating. When C4 and C8 are given such a high weight, A1 100 points suppress its total/benefit/distance score.

Even if you almost halve the weights in favor of C4 and C8, the method choice determines two-criterion dominance: full compensators push A1 ahead, while FUCA/ELECTRE-III/NFM doesn't allow two criteria to overturn the system and keeps A5 in the lead. This proves that the problem isn't so much the "weight" as the methodology.

85.4.3.4 Weight-4 scenario

This time, we reverse the weighting coefficients and significantly reduce the weight of the subjective criteria C4 and C8. Another interesting result emerged: almost all MCDM methods reverse the axis and rank A5 first, not A1. With a slight difference: only PROBID, which had placed A1 first all along and consistently chose A1 again this time, is interesting, as can be seen in Table 85.8 below. The weighting coefficients for (C1, C2, C3,…) are 0.24, 0.11, 0.24, 0.08, 0.08, 0.1, 0.08, 0.07, respectively.

As seen in Table 85.8, when the weighting axis shifts in favor of the objectives (C1 and C3 are dominant), A5, the absolute leader in three objectives, dominates in almost all methods. PROBID's persistence is likely based on two technical features: a full compensatory and/or ideal-point-close type of summation/ratio structure; in C4 and C8, A1 100 creates a proportional advantage, reversing the result even at low weights.

Considering the three weighting regimes together, it can be argued that method selection is more decisive than weight adjustment. High compensators: when C4 and C8 are prominent, A1 is prominent, while when it is lowered, A5 is prominent. Outranking/rank-based (FUCA, ELECTRE-III, NFM): weights protect A5 even at both extremes, structurally limiting "single criterion dominance." If the fairness/merit objective is to prevent a single criterion from overturning the system, the FUCA/ELECTRE-III/NFM framework aligns with the normative objective.

85.5 Discussion and results

We obtained striking findings across the various MCDM scenarios we used to determine compensatory power. Fourteen different MCDM methods were applied in the study, focusing on the comparison of candidates A1 and A5, where competition is particularly intense. As the weighting coefficients were adjusted, the rankings of both the first and second-place candidates shifted in all methods except PROBID. Furthermore, in methods other than FUCA, the position of the first-place candidate and the rankings of A1 and A5 constantly changed depending on the weightings. In contrast, FUCA demonstrated remarkable stability in every scenario, always ranking A5 first and A1 tenth. This finding demonstrates that FUCA's low compensatory power eliminates the ranking fluctuations seen in other methods, providing a more robust and reliable preference structure.

This study demonstrates that MCDM methods can produce dramatically different results depending on the level of compensatory power. Although the criteria used in the scenario under consideration (three objective, one subjective) remained constant, the best and worst candidates were observed to be reversed depending on the chosen method. Highly compensatory methods allowed a high score on a single criterion (subjective evaluation) to dominate the entire system, highlighting A1 as the best candidate. In contrast, outranking methods that limit compensatory power, such as FUCA, ranked the same candidate worst (10th) in every scenario, leaving A5, which has an absolute advantage in objective exams, in the lead under all circumstances. This situation highlights a gap rarely encountered in the literature: "The

TABLE 85.6 Ranking results produced by multicriteria decision-makingmethods according to the weight-2 scenario.

	CODAS	COPRAS	ELECTRE-3	FUCA	LINMAP	MABAC	MEW	MOORA	NFM	PROBID	SAW	s_PROBID	TOPSIS	VIKOR-Q
A1	1	1	5	**10**	1	1	1	1	4	1	1	1	1	**10**
A5	4	2	1	**1**	6	2	6	2	1	7	2	6	5	**1**

TABLE 85.7 Ranking results produced by multicriteria decision-makingmethods according to the weight-3 scenario.

	CODAS	COPRAS	ELECTRE-3	FUCA	LINMAP	MABAC	MEW	MOORA	NFM	PROBID	SAW	s_PROBID	TOPSIS	*VIKOR-Q*
A1	1	1	5	**10**	1	1	1	1	4	1	1	1	1	*1*
A5	4	2	1	**1**	6	2	6	2	1	7	2	6	5	*4*

TABLE 85.8 Ranking results produced by multicriteria decision-making methods according to the weight-4 scenario.

	CODAS	COPRAS	ELECTRE-3	FUCA	LINMAP	MABAC	MEW	MOORA	NFM	*PROBID*	SAW	s_PROBID	TOPSIS	VIKOR-Q
A1	2	5	8	**10**	6	6	5	5	6	*1*	5	3	2	**10**
A5	1	1	1	**1**	1	1	1	1	1	2	1	1	1	**1**

reversal of first and last ranks" demonstrates the sensitivity of the method to the level of compensatory power. While MCDM methods are normally thought to largely converge on results, this example demonstrates that the choice of method can be decisive in discussions of fairness and merit.

Under four different weighting scenarios, the FUCA method consistently ranked A5 first and A1 last. This remarkable stability, unlike the volatile results of compensatory methods, consistently favors merit. ELECTRE-III and NFM also ranked A5 above A1 in every case but failed to stabilize A1's position. This finding demonstrates that FUCA is the method that systematically rejects "single-criterion dominance" and stabilizes the fairest ranking.

These findings point to two critical conclusions:

1. The choice of the MCDM method is not a purely technical choice, but a normative one. The compensatory nature of the method used directly affects whether the principles of merit and fairness are upheld.
2. The FUCA method stands out as one of the most reliable methods, especially in areas requiring high precision, such as personnel selection, with its low compensatory nature, simple calculation steps, and exceptional stability.

   This analysis demonstrates that choices made without considering the compensatory nature of MCDM methods can lead to fairness and transparency shortcomings, such as the elimination of qualified candidates and the promotion of weaker candidates. The stability provided by FUCA stands out with its structure, which leaves no room for deception in personnel selection, limits the dominance of subjective criteria, and prioritizes merit.

   The study's findings demonstrate that ignoring compensatory power in MCDM methods can pose critical risks, both methodologically and practically. If compensatory power is not given due importance and sensitivity analysis is not conducted, the seemingly best alternative may be overlooked, often being the weakest. This situation constitutes a "tragic point of deception" for methodologists, as the findings demonstrate that the choice of method is a more decisive factor than weighting coefficients. In practice, this error has far more serious consequences. In objective personnel selection, the least successful candidate can be promoted to first place based solely on a subjective assessment, while the most objectively successful candidate can be eliminated under the pressure of a single criterion. This can undermine merit and lead institutions to hire the least qualified individuals. Such an outcome directly undermines not only individual but also institutional productivity and the perception of social justice. Therefore, it is imperative that compensatory power be systematically addressed as a methodological parameter in MCDM research. Our study demonstrates that FUCA, thanks to its high stability and low compensatory nature, can eliminate such manipulations. In this context, it is clear that outranking methods should be preferred, especially in decision problems where merit, fairness, and reliability are highly sensitive.

85.6 Conclusion

This study has highlighted the critical importance of the compensatory aspect of MCDM methods. Especially in processes sensitive to merit and fairness, such as personnel selection, the use of a single criterion to dominate the others can lead to serious drawbacks. As the analyses demonstrate, the subjective interview score, when combined with traditional methods with high compensatory power, can lead to the elimination of the strongest candidate and the selection of the weakest.

Sensitivity analyses conducted under four different weighting scenarios showed that most MCDM methods alter the ranking results, rendering the decision unstable. However, the FUCA method demonstrated exceptional stability and reliability; in every scenario, it objectively ranked the strong candidate A5 first and the weak candidate A1 last. This finding demonstrates that FUCA, thanks to its low compensatory power, offers a merit-based, fair, and manipulation-proof decision-making mechanism.

The FUCA method has been found to be quite successful in previous studies in correlation with an exogenous factor, rank reversal, standard deviation, and intensive sensitivity analyses. This study adds a new dimension and highlights a distinct advantage of FUCA from a compensatory perspective.

Consequently, ignoring compensatory performance is both methodologically misleading and can lead to unfair results in practical applications. Therefore, researchers should consider not only technical suitability but also the level of compensatory performance when selecting an MCDM method. The study's findings suggest that the FUCA method should be considered a strong alternative to the classical SAW method and other compensatory approaches, particularly in critical decision problems such as personnel selection.

References

Banihabib, M. E., Hashemi-Madani, F. S., & Forghani, A. (2017). Comparison of compensatory and non-compensatory multi criteria decision making models in water resources strategic management. *Water Resources Management, 31*(12), 3745–3759. https://doi.org/10.1007/s11269-017-1702-x.

Baydaş, M., Elma, O. E., & Stević, Ž. (2024). Proposal of an innovative MCDA evaluation methodology: Knowledge discovery through rank reversal, standard deviation, and relationship with stock return. *Financial Innovation, 10*(1), 4. https://doi.org/10.1186/s40854-023-00526-x.

Baydaş, M., Eren, T., Stević, Ž., Starčević, V., & Parlakkaya, R. (2023). Proposal for an objective binary benchmarking framework that validates each other for comparing MCDM methods through data analytics. *PeerJ Computer Science, 9*, e1350. https://doi.org/10.7717/peerj-cs.1350.

Baydaş, M., & Pamučar, D. (2022). Determining objective characteristics of MCDM methods under uncertainty: An exploration study with financial data. *Mathematics, 10*(7), 1115. https://doi.org/10.3390/math10071115.

Cinelli, M., Kadziński, M., Miebs, G., Gonzalez, M., & Słowiński, R. (2022). Recommending multiple criteria decision analysis methods with a new taxonomy-based decision support system. *European Journal of Operational Research, 302*(2), 633–651. https://doi.org/10.1016/j.ejor.2022.01.011.

Danesh, D., Ryan, M. J., & Abbasi, A. (2017). A systematic comparison of multi-criteria decision making methods for the improvement of project portfolio management in complex organisations. *International Journal of Management and Decision Making, 16*(3), 280–320. https://doi.org/10.1504/IJMDM.2017.085638.

de França Dantas Daher, S., & de Almeida, A. T. (2013). Minimizing the compensatory effect of MCDM group decision additive aggregation using the veto concept. In *International conference on evolutionary multi-criterion optimization*. Berlin: Springer, 500–512 https://doi.org/10.1007/978-3-642-37140-0_38.

Deveci, M., Mishra, A. R., Gokasar, I., Rani, P., Pamucar, D., & Özcan, E. (2022). A decision support system for assessing and prioritizing sustainable urban transportation in metaverse. *IEEE Trans Fuzzy Syst, 31*(2), 475–484. https://doi.org/10.1109/TFUZZ.2022.3190613.

Do, D. T. (2022). Application of FUCA method for multi-criteria decision making in mechanical machining processes. *Operational Research in Engineering Sciences: Theory and Applications, 5*(3), 131–152. https://doi.org/10.31181/oresta051022061d.

Dudić, B., Van Duc, D., Son, N. H., & Ašonja, A. (2024). Comparison of MCDM methods effectiveness in the selection of plastic injection molding machines. *Teknomekanik, 7*(1), 1–19. https://doi.org/10.24036/teknomekanik.v7i1.29272.

Emamat, M. S. M. M., Mota, C. M. D. M., Mehregan, M. R., Sadeghi Moghadam, M. R., & Nemery, P. (2022). Using ELECTRE-TRI and FlowSort methods in a stock portfolio selection context. *Financial Innovation, 8*(1), 11. https://doi.org/10.1186/s40854-021-00318-1.

Peci, A., Puška, A., Marinković, D., & Nedeljković, M. (2025). Evaluation of tractors based on sustainability criteria using multi-criteria decision-making methods. *Engineering Review, 45*(1), 0. https://doi.org/10.30765/er.2706.

Petrović, N., Živanović, T., & Mihajlović, J. (2023). Evaluating the annual operational efficiency of passenger and freight road transport in Serbia through entropy and TOPSIS methods. *Journal of Engineering Management and Systems Engineering, 2*(4), 204–211. https://doi.org/10.56578/jemse020402.

Stanujkic, D., Dordevic, B., & Dordevic, M. (2013). Comparative analysis of some prominent MCDM methods: A case of ranking Serbian banks. *Serbian Journal of Management, 8*(2), 213–241. https://doi.org/10.5937/sjm8-3774.

Stević, Ž., Baydaş, M., Kavacık, M., Ayhan, E., & Marinković, D. (2024). Selection of data conversion technique via sensitivity-performance matching: ranking of small e-vans with PROBID method. *Facta Universitatis, Series: Mechanical Engineering*, 643–671. https://doi.org/10.22190/FUME240305023S.

Stević, Ž., Ersoy, N., Başar, E. E., & Baydaş, M. (2024). Addressing the global logistics performance index rankings with methodological insights and an innovative decision support framework. *Applied Sciences, 14*(22), 10334. https://doi.org/10.3390/app142210334.

Thinh, H. X., & Mai, N. T. (2023). Comparison of two methods in multi-criteria decision-making: application in transmission rod material selection. *EUREKA: Physics and Engineering,* (6), 59–68. https://doi.org/10.21303/2461-4262.2023.003046.

Wang, Z., Nabavi, S. R., & Rangaiah, G. P. (2024). Multi-criteria decision making in chemical and process engineering: Methods, progress, and potential. *Processes, 12*(11), 2532. https://doi.org/10.3390/pr12112532.

Wang, Z., Parhi, S. S., Rangaiah, G. P., & Jana, A. K. (2020). Analysis of weighting and selection methods for pareto-optimal solutions of multiobjective optimization in chemical engineering applications. *Industrial & Engineering Chemistry Research, 59*(33), 14850–14867. https://doi.org/10.1021/acs.iecr.0c00969.

Wang, Z., & Rangaiah, G. P. (2017). Application and analysis of methods for selecting an optimal solution from the Pareto-optimal front obtained by multiobjective optimization. *Industrial & Engineering Chemistry Research, 56*(2), 560–574. https://doi.org/10.1021/acs.iecr.6b03453.

Wang, Z, Rangaiah, G. P., & Wang, X (2021). Preference ranking on the basis of ideal-average distance method for multi-criteria decision-making. *Ind Eng Chem Res, 60*(30), 11216–11230. https://doi.org/10.1021/acs.iecr.1c01413.

Ziemba, P. (2019). Towards strong sustainability management – A generalized PROSA method. *Sustainability, 11*(6), 1555. https://doi.org/10.3390/su11061555.

Chapter 86

COBRA: Comprehensive distance-based ranking for multi-attribute decision-making

Ali Aygün Yürüyen[1], Alptekin Ulutaş[2], and Ayşe Topal[3]

[1]*Department of Transportation Services, Ardahan University, Göle, Ardahan, Turkiye,* [2]*Department of International Trade and Logistics, Faculty of Economics and Administrative Sciences, Inonu University, Malatya, Turkiye,* [3]*Department of Business Administration, Faculty of Business and Economics Sciences, Nigde Omer Halisdemir University, Nigde, Turkiye*

86.1 Introduction

Assessing alternatives and determining the most appropriate option requires a complex evaluation process involving a large number of criteria, often conflicting with each other. This makes the decision-making process difficult and causes intuitive approaches to be inadequate. However, such problems can be overcome by integrating systematic and numerical-based decision models into the decision process. At this point, multicriteria decision-making (MCDM) methods are among the effective tools widely adopted in the literature because they allow multidimensional and multicriteria decision problems to be handled analytically (Popović et al., 2022).

The comprehensive distance-based ranking for multi-attribute decision-making (COBRA) method is a distance-based MCDM method that evaluates alternatives. Among the distance-based MCDM methods developed, prominent methods include technique for ordering preferences by similarity to ideal solution, weighted aggregated sum product assessment, VlseKriterijumska Optimizacija I Kompromisno Resenje evaluation based on distance from average solution, Comprehensive Distance-based Ranking (CODAS), multiobjective optimization on the basis of ratio analysis, and measurement of alternatives and ranking according to co mpromise solution. The common denominator of these methods is that the approach taken as a basis for ranking the alternatives is based on the relative distances of each alternative to a specific reference alternative (such as ideal, antiideal, or average solutions). In other words, the basic principle in the decision-making process is to evaluate the performance of the alternatives based on their distances to various reference points (Krstić et al., 2022a).

The structural feature of the COBRA method allows the decision-making process to be completed with less computational load and a simple sequence of operations. In particular, its application without requiring complex algorithmic structures or a large number of decision-maker inputs is an element that increases the usability of the method in practice. One of the main advantages of this method is that it simplifies the decision process as much as possible, allowing the decision maker to reach effective results with less effort and information. In this context, COBRA allows direct solutions to be obtained by processing the criteria weights and alternative performances after the creation of the decision matrix. With this advantage that reduces complexity, it has become one of the preferred methods, especially in cases where there are time and resource constraints. These qualities of the method enable it to present a balanced approach that combines simplicity and analytical precision in solving multicriteria problems (Krstić et al., 2022a).

Another advantage of the COBRA method compared to the distance-based methods described is that it offers a comprehensive evaluation approach. This method performs an analysis over comprehensive distances, considering not only the positive ideal and negative ideal solutions but also the average solution when ranking the alternatives. In contrast, the distance-based methods generally use at most two reference solutions. Furthermore, the COBRA method increases the reliability of the results by using both Euclidean distance and taxicab distance in distance calculations. Using different

Encyclopedia of Multi-Attribute Decision-Making (MADM). DOI: https://doi.org/10.1016/B978-0-443-33275-3.00097-X

distance measurements increases the accuracy and reliability of the decision-making process by providing a more precise differentiation between alternatives with close values (Krstić et al., 2022a).

In addition, the COBRA method also points to a fundamental limitation that brings with it a significant complexity in terms of structure. The method is not limited to only three basic reference solutions; it also requires the calculation of four different types of distances: distance to the positive ideal solution, distance to the negative ideal solution, positive deviation from the average solution, and negative deviation from the average solution. These distance types are determined based on combinations of two separate distance measurement techniques, necessitating the acquisition of comprehensive distance values that include all these components in a holistic manner. Although this multidimensional structure increases the analytical power of the method, it also requires more processing power and high resources, especially in terms of time, to achieve final results (Krstić et al., 2022b; Tadić et al., 2024).

COBRA has been used in the literature to solve decision problems in different fields. Katrancı et al. (2025) analyzed the financial performance of companies using the indifference threshold-based attribute ratio analysis (ITARA) and COBRA. Krstić et al. (2022a) utilized the best–worst method (BWM) and COBRA to examine the usability of Industry 4.0 applications in reverse logistics. Popović et al. (2022) assessed e-commerce strategies with the Method based on the removal effects of criteria (MEREC) and COBRA. Verma et al. (2023) used BWM Improved and COBRA methods in evaluating cybersecurity platforms for the energy sector. Asker (2024) analyzed the financial performance of airlines with the MEREC and COBRA methods. Tadić et al. (2023) determined smart material handling solutions for city logistics systems using fuzzy analytic hierarchy process and fuzzy comprehensive distance-based ranking methods. Zorlu et al. (2024) used a hybrid MCDM model including the step-wise weight assessment ratio analysis (SWARA) and COBRA to assess geosites. Tadić et al. (2024) used fuzzy Delphi-based fuzzy factor relationship (Fuzzy D-FARE) and COBRA methods to evaluate strategies to overcome obstacles in drone use. Mirčetić et al. (2024) integrated Criteria Importance Through Intercriteria Correlation (CRITIC), Simplified Pivot Pairwise Relative Criteria Importance Assessment (PIPRECIA-S), and COBRA methods in the innovative human resources management selection problem. Sandra et al. (2025) used the integrated complex cubic t-spherical fuzzy, simultaneous evaluation of criteria and alternatives, and COBRA methods for the selection of sustainable fracture techniques in hot dry rock geothermal systems. Rani et al. (2025) used standard deviation (SD), SWARA, and Pythagorean fuzzy COBRA methods to evaluate Industry 4.0 strategies. Mim et al. (2025) used the Decision-Making Trial and Evaluation Laboratory (DEMATEL) and COBRA methods to determine the effects of ChatGPT on student learning. Ahmadi Pargo and Hashemkhani Zolfani (2025) used the gray ITARA and COBRA method for hardware selection. Alshamrani et al. (2025) used picture fuzzy SD, ranking comparison, and the COBRA method in the evaluation of software tools.

The main purpose of this chapter is to demonstrate the applicability of the COBRA method to both low and high complexity decision-making problems. In the following section, the methodological framework of the chapter is presented, and the theoretical foundations of the COBRA method are explained in detail. In the following application 1 section, a relatively simple decision problem is considered, and the basic operation process of the COBRA method is exemplified. In the application 2 section, a more complex decision problem with a large number of criteria and alternatives is analyzed. In this context, the performance of the method against increasing problem complexity is evaluated. Finally, in the conclusion section, the findings are discussed in detail, and various suggestions are presented for future research in which the COBRA method will be applied.

86.2 Methodology

The steps to be followed for the implementation of the COBRA method created by Krstić et al. (2022a), which ranks the alternatives based on distance, are listed below (Krstić et al., 2022a):

Step 1. Decision matrix $\boldsymbol{F}$ is developed based on the obtained data with Eq. 86.1.

$$F = [f_{ij}]_{m \times n} \tag{86.1}$$

Here, f_{ij} represents the performance level or score of the alternative numbered i regarding the criteria j; m represents the total number of alternatives; and n represents the number of criteria.

Step 2. The values in the decision matrix are subjected to the normalization process based on Eq. (86.2).

$$\alpha_{ij} = \frac{f_{ij}}{\max f_{ij}} \tag{86.2}$$

Step 3. The data in the normalized decision matrix are weighted by Eq. (86.3) by taking into account the criteria weights.

$$\Delta_{w=[w_j \times \alpha_{ij}]} \tag{86.3}$$

Step 4. For each of the criteria functions, the positive ideal solution (PIS_j) is calculated using Eq. (86.4) for beneficial (B) criteria and Eq. (86.5) for nonbeneficial (NB) criteria. For each of the criteria functions, the negative ideal solution (NIS_j) is calculated using Eq. (86.6) for B criteria and Eq. (86.7) for NB criteria. The average solution (AS_j) is calculated using Eq. (86.8).

$$PIS_j = \max_i (w_j \times \alpha_{ij}), \quad \forall j = 1, \ldots, m \; j \in J^B \tag{86.4}$$

$$PIS_j = \min_i (w_j \times \alpha_{ij}), \quad \forall j = 1, \ldots, m \; j \in J^{NB} \tag{86.5}$$

$$NIS_j = \min_i (w_j \times \alpha_{ij}), \quad \forall j = 1, \ldots, m \; j \in J^B \tag{86.6}$$

$$NIS_j = \max_i (w_j \times \alpha_{ij}), \quad \forall j = 1, \ldots, m \; j \in J^{NB} \tag{86.7}$$

$$AS_j = \frac{\Sigma_i^n 1 (w_j \times \alpha_{ij})}{n}, \quad \forall j = 1, \ldots, m \; j \in J^B, \;\; J^{NB} \tag{86.8}$$

Step 5. The distances from the positive ideal solution ($d(PIS_j)$) and the negative ideal solution ($d(NIS_j)$) are calculated. In addition, the distances from the positive average solution ($d(AS_j^+)$) and the negative average solution ($d(AS_j^-)$) are obtained within the framework of the following equations.

$$d(S_j) = dE(S_j) + \sigma \times dE(S_j) \times dT(S_j), \; \forall j = 1, \ldots, m \tag{86.9}$$

S_j in Eq. (86.9) represents any solution (PIS_j, NIS_j veya AS_j), and σ is the correction coefficient calculated by Eq. (86.10).

$$\sigma = \max_i dE(S_j)_i - \min_i dE(S_j)_i \tag{86.10}$$

$dE(S_j)$ and $dT(S_j)$ are the Euclidean and Taxi distances for the positive ideal solution obtained as follows, respectively.

$$dE(PIS_j)_i = \sqrt{\sum_{j=1}^{m} (PIS_j - w_j \times \alpha_{ij})^2}, \quad \forall i = 1, \ldots, n, \quad \forall j = 1, \ldots, m \tag{86.11}$$

$$dT(PIS_j)_i = \sum_{j=1}^{m} |PIS_j - w_j \times \alpha_{ij}| \tag{86.12}$$

Distances to the negative ideal solution are determined using different distance measurement methods. In this context, the Euclidean distance is calculated with Eq. (86.13) and the Taxi distance is calculated with Eq. (86.14).

$$dE(NIS_j)_i = \sqrt{\sum_{j=1}^{m} (NIS_j - w_j \times \alpha_{ij})^2} \tag{86.13}$$

$$dT(NIS_j)_i = \sum_{j=1}^{m} |NIS_j - w_j \times \alpha_{ij}| \tag{86.14}$$

Positive distances from the mean solution are obtained by Eqs. (86.15) and (86.16):

$$dE(AS_j)_i^+ = \sqrt{\sum_{j=1}^{m} T^+ (AS_j - w_j \times \alpha_{ij})^2} \tag{86.15}$$

$$dE(AS_j)_i^+ = \sum_{j=1}^{m} T^+ |AS_j - w_j \times \alpha_{ij}| \tag{86.16}$$

$$T^+ = \begin{cases} 1, & eğer \; \& \; AS_j < w_j \times \alpha_{ij} \\ 0, & eğer \; \& \; AS_j > w_j \times \alpha_{ij} \end{cases} \tag{86.17}$$

Negative distances from the mean solution are obtained by Eqs. (86.18) and (86.19):

$$dE\,(AS_j)_i^- = \sqrt{\sum_{j=1}^{m} T^-(AS_j - w_j \times \alpha_{ij})^2} \tag{86.18}$$

$$dE\,(AS_j)_i^- = \sum_{j=1}^{m} T^- \,|AS_j - w_j \times \alpha_{ij}| \tag{86.19}$$

$$T^- = \begin{cases} 1, & eğer\ \&\ AS_j > w_j \times \alpha_{ij} \\ 0, & eğer\ \&\ AS_j < w_j \times \alpha_{ij} \end{cases} \tag{86.20}$$

Step 6. The comprehensive distance values (dC_i) calculated based on Eq. (86.21) reflect the overall performance of each alternative. These values are ranked in ascending order to determine the preference order of the alternatives.

$$dC_i = \frac{d\,(PIS_j)_i - d\,(NIS_j)_i - d\,(AS_j)_i^+ + d\,(AS_j)_i^-}{4} \quad \forall 1 = 1,\ \ldots, n \tag{86.21}$$

86.3 Numerical examples

In this chapter, two separate applications were carried out to demonstrate the applicability of the COBRA method.

86.3.1 Numerical example 1

The first application includes a simple and explanatory problem scenario that allows understanding the basic operating principles of the method. In the chapter, the decision matrix was derived using the Monte Carlo simulation technique. The criteria weights (w_j) were determined using the equal weighting approach. While the CR1 and CR2 criteria in the matrix are B criteria, the CR3, CR4, and CR5 criteria represent NB criteria. Table 86.1 contains the data regarding the decision matrix used in the analysis.

All values in the decision matrix were normalized according to Eq. (86.2) and it is given in Table 86.2. How to calculate an element of the matrix α_{ij} is explained below:

$$\alpha_{11} = \frac{64}{98} = 0.6531$$

Weights were applied to the values on the normalized matrix via Eq. (86.3), and the weighted normalized decision matrix resulting from this process is shown in Table 86.3. How to calculate an element of the matrix Δ_w is explained below:

$$\Delta_{11} = 0.20 \times 0.6531 = 0.1306$$

TABLE 86.1 Decision matrix.

w_j	0.20	0.20	0.20	0.20	0.20
Criteria direction	**B**	**B**	**NB**	**NB**	**NB**
	CR1	**C2**	**CR3**	**CR4**	**CR5**
Alt1	64	68	71	97	18
Alt2	98	63	41	68	60
Alt3	27	73	88	58	51
Alt4	5	88	33	48	79

TABLE 86.2 Normalized decision matrix.

	CR1	C2	CR3	CR4	CR5
Alt1	0.6531	0.7727	0.8068	1	0.2278
Alt2	1	0.7159	0.4659	0.7010	0.7595
Alt3	0.2755	0.8295	1	0.5979	0.6456
Alt4	0.0510	1	0.3750	0.4948	1

TABLE 86.3 Weighted normalized decision natrix.

	CR1	C2	CR3	CR4	CR5
Alt1	0.1306	0.1545	0.1614	0.2000	0.0456
Alt2	0.2000	0.1432	0.0932	0.1402	0.1519
Alt3	0.0551	0.1659	0.2000	0.1196	0.1291
Alt4	0.0102	0.2000	0.0750	0.0990	0.2000
PIS	0.2000	0.2000	0.0750	0.0990	0.0456
NIS	0.0102	0.1432	0.2000	0.2000	0.2000
AS	0.0990	0.1659	0.1324	0.1397	0.1317

TABLE 86.4 COBRA method ranking results.

	$d\,(PIS)$	$d\,(NIS)$	$d\,(AS)^+$	$d\,(AS)^-$	dC	Rank
Alt1	0.1622	0.2072	0.0743	0.0874	-0.0080	2
Alt2	0.1320	0.2414	0.1034	0.0455	-0.0418	1
Alt3	0.2227	0.1213	0.0678	0.0486	0.0206	3
Alt4	0.2545	0.1759	0.0766	0.1147	0.0292	4

Based on the Euclidean and Taxi distance approaches, the distances to the positive, negative, and average ideal points were calculated within the scope of the steps defined between Eqs. (86.4) and (86.21) and the final ranking of the alternatives was made according to these distances. The results of the COBRA method are presented in Table 86.4. How to calculate

$d\,(PIS_1)$, $d\,(NIS_1)$, $d\,(AS_1)^+$, $d\,(AS_1)^-$ and dC_1 is explained below:

$$dE\,(PIS_1) = \sqrt{(0.2000-0.1306)^2+(0.2000-0.1545)^2+(0.0750-0.1614)^2+(0.0990-0.2000)^2+(0.0456-0.0456)^2}$$
$$= 0.1567$$

$$dE\,(PIS_2) = \sqrt{(0.2000-0.2000)^2+(0.2000-0.1432)^2+(0.0750-0.0932)^2+(0.0990-0.1402)^2+(0.0456-0.1519)^2}$$
$$= 0.1287$$

$$dE(PIS_3) = \sqrt{(0.2000 - 0.0551)^2 + (0.2000 - 0.1659)^2 + (0.0750 - 0.2000)^2 + (0.0990 - 0.1196)^2 + (0.0456 - 0.1291)^2}$$
$$= 0.2126$$

$$dE(PIS_4) = \sqrt{(0.2000 - 0.0102)^2 + (0.2000 - 0.2000)^2 + (0.0750 - 0.0750)^2 + (0.0990 - 0.0990)^2 + (0.0456 - 0.2000)^2}$$
$$= 0.2447$$

$$dT(PIS_1) = |0.2000 - 0.1306| + |0.2000 - 0.1545| + |0.0750 - 0.1614| + |0.0990 - 0.2000| + |0.0456 - 0.0456|$$
$$= 0.3023$$

$$d(PIS_\sigma) = (0.2447 - 0.1287) = 0.1160$$

$$d(PIS_1) = 0.1567 + (0.1567 \times 0.3023 \times 0.1160) = 0.1622$$

$$dE(NIS_1) = \sqrt{(0.0102 - 0.1306)^2 + (0.1432 - 0.1545)^2 + (0.2000 - 0.1614)^2 + (0.2000 - 0.2000)^2 + (0.2000 - 0.0456)^2}$$
$$= 0.1999$$

$$dE(NIS_2) = \sqrt{(0.0102 - 0.2000)^2 + (0.1432 - 0.1432)^2 + (0.2000 - 0.0932)^2 + (0.2000 - 0.1402)^2 + (0.2000 - 0.1519)^2}$$
$$= 0.2309$$

$$dE(NIS_3) = \sqrt{(0.0102 - 0.0551)^2 + (0.1432 - 0.1659)^2 + (0.2000 - 0.2000)^2 + (0.2000 - 0.1196)^2 + (0.2000 - 0.1291)^2}$$
$$= 0.1184$$

$$dE(NIS_4) = \sqrt{(0.0102 - 0.0102)^2 + (0.1432 - 0.2000)^2 + (0.2000 - 0.0750)^2 + (0.2000 - 0.0990)^2 + (0.2000 - 0.2000)^2}$$
$$= 0.1705$$

$$dT(NIS_1) = |0.0102 - 0.1306| + |0.1432 - 0.1545| + |0.2000 - 0.1614| + |0.2000 - 0.2000| + |0.2000 - 0.0456|$$
$$= 0.3248$$

$$d(NIS_\sigma) = (0.2309 - 0.1184) = 0.1125$$

$$d(NIS_1) = 0.1999 + (0.1999 \times 0.3248 \times 0.1125) = 0.2072$$

$$d(AS_1)^+ = 0.0743$$

$$d(AS_1)^- = 0.0874$$

$$dC_1 = \frac{0.1622 - 0.2072 - 0.0743 + 0.0874}{4} = -0.0080$$

According to the analysis findings regarding the COBRA method shown in Table 86.4, the relative superiority order of the alternatives is as follows: Alt2 > Alt1 > Alt3 > Alt4.

The COBRA method results for numerical example 1 are presented graphically in Fig. 86.1.

86.3.2 Numerical example 2

The second application focuses on a decision problem with more criteria and alternatives, hence higher complexity. The decision matrix used in the chapter was created by the Monte Carlo simulation method. The criteria weights were determined using the equal weighting approach. In the evaluation phase, ten alternatives were analyzed based on ten different criteria. While the first five criteria in the matrix (CR1, CR2, CR3, CR4, and CR5) are B oriented, the last five criteria (CR6, CR7, CR8, CR9, and CR10) represent NB elements. Table 86.5 contains data on the decision matrix used in the analysis.

The normalization of values in the decision matrix above is done according to Eq. (86.2), and the normalized values are given in Table 86.6. How to calculate an element of the matrix α_{ij} is explained below:

$$\alpha_{11} = \frac{983}{983} = 1$$

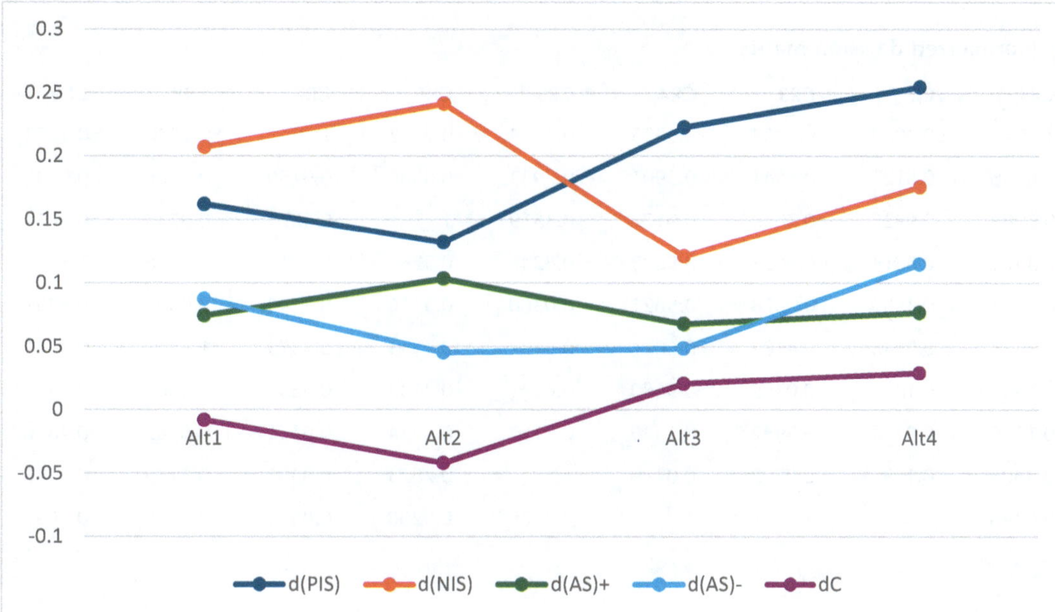

FIGURE 86.1 Data obtained as a result of the COBRA method.

TABLE 86.5 Decision matrix.

w_j	0.10	0.10	0.10	0.10	0.10	0.10	0.10	0.10	0.10	0.10
	B	B	B	B	B	NB	NB	NB	NB	NB
	CR1	C2	CR3	CR4	CR5	CR6	CR7	CR8	CR9	CR10
Alt1	983	392	693	525	269	61	951	194	138	12
Alt2	615	779	624	570	683	856	871	848	792	622
Alt3	687	952	729	886	303	997	525	840	569	747
Alt4	342	826	66	491	710	525	734	238	835	157
Alt5	700	341	83	543	31	530	299	51	689	920
Alt6	942	925	418	581	447	113	511	863	304	538
Alt7	157	133	72	936	546	273	528	7	462	452
Alt8	115	897	565	140	788	481	585	549	404	343
Alt9	374	153	67	26	861	780	797	444	187	294
Alt10	34	959	954	966	233	926	814	194	721	372

Weights were applied to the values on the normalized matrix via Eq. (86.3) and the weighted normalized values are presented in Table 86.7. How to calculate an element of the matrix Δ_w is explained below:

$$\Delta_{11} = 0.1000 \times 1 = 0.1000$$

Based on the Euclidean and Taxi distance approaches, the distances to the positive, negative, and average ideal points were calculated within the scope of the steps defined between Eqs. (86.4) and (86.21), and the final ranking of the

TABLE 86.6 Normalized decision matrix.

	CR1	C2	CR3	CR4	CR5	CR6	CR7	CR8	CR9	CR10
Alt1	1	0.4088	0.7264	0.5435	0.3124	0.0612	1	0.2248	0.1653	0.0130
Alt2	0.6256	0.8123	0.6541	0.5901	0.7933	0.8586	0.9159	0.9826	0.9485	0.6761
Alt3	0.6989	0.9927	0.7642	0.9172	0.3519	1	0.5521	0.9733	0.6814	0.8120
Alt4	0.3479	0.8613	0.0692	0.5083	0.8246	0.5266	0.7718	0.2758	1	0.1707
Alt5	0.7121	0.3556	0.0870	0.5621	0.0360	0.5316	0.3144	0.0591	0.8251	1
Alt6	0.9583	0.9645	0.4382	0.6014	0.5192	0.1133	0.5373	1	0.3641	0.5848
Alt7	0.1597	0.1387	0.0755	0.9689	0.6341	0.2738	0.5552	0.0081	0.5533	0.4913
Alt8	0.1170	0.9353	0.5922	0.1449	0.9152	0.4824	0.6151	0.6362	0.4838	0.3728
Alt9	0.3805	0.1595	0.0702	0.0269	1	0.7823	0.8381	0.5145	0.2240	0.3196
Alt10	0.0346	1	1	1	0.2706	0.9288	0.8559	0.2248	0.8635	0.4043

TABLE 86.7 Weighted normalized decision matrix.

	CR1	C2	CR3	CR4	CR5	CR6	CR7	CR8	CR9	CR10
Alt1	0.1000	0.0409	0.0726	0.0544	0.0312	0.0061	0.1000	0.0225	0.0165	0.0013
Alt2	0.0626	0.0812	0.0654	0.0590	0.0793	0.0859	0.0916	0.0983	0.0949	0.0676
Alt3	0.0699	0.0993	0.0764	0.0917	0.0352	0.1000	0.0552	0.0973	0.0681	0.0812
Alt4	0.0348	0.0861	0.0069	0.0508	0.0825	0.0527	0.0772	0.0276	0.1000	0.0171
Alt5	0.0712	0.0356	0.0087	0.0562	0.0036	0.0532	0.0314	0.0059	0.0825	0.1000
Alt6	0.0958	0.0965	0.0438	0.0601	0.0519	0.0113	0.0537	0.1000	0.0364	0.0585
Alt7	0.0160	0.0139	0.0076	0.0969	0.0634	0.0274	0.0555	0.0008	0.0553	0.0491
Alt8	0.0117	0.0935	0.0592	0.0145	0.0915	0.0482	0.0615	0.0636	0.0484	0.0373
Alt9	0.0381	0.0160	0.0070	0.0027	0.1000	0.0782	0.0838	0.0515	0.0224	0.0320
Alt10	0.0035	0.1000	0.1000	0.1000	0.0271	0.0929	0.0856	0.0225	0.0864	0.0404
PIS	0.1000	0.1000	0.1000	0.1000	0.1000	0.0061	0.0314	0.0008	0.0165	0.0013
NIS	0.0035	0.0139	0.0069	0.0027	0.0036	0.1000	0.1000	0.1000	0.1000	0.1000
AS	0.0503	0.0663	0.0448	0.0586	0.0566	0.0556	0.0696	0.049	0.0611	0.0484

alternatives was made according to these distances. The results of the COBRA method are presented in Table 86.8. How to calculate

$d(PIS_1)c$, $d(NIS_1)$, $d(AS_1)^+$, $d(AS_1)^-$ and dC_1 is explained below:

$$dE(PIS_1) = \sqrt{(0.1000-0.1000)^2+(0.1000-0.0409)^2+\ldots+(0.0165-0.0165)^2+(0.0013-0.0013)^2} = 0.1274$$

$$dT(PIS_1) = |0.1000-0.1000| + |0.1000-0.0409| + \ldots + |0.0165-0.0165| + |0.0013-0.0013| = 0.2911$$

$$d(PIS_\sigma) = (0.2021-0.1274) = 0.0747$$

TABLE 86.8 COBRA method ranking results.

	d (*PIS*)	*d* (*NIS*)	$d(AS)^{+}$	$d(AS)^{-}$	*dC*	Rank
Alt1	0.1302	0.2324	0.0649	0.0952	-0.0180	2
Alt2	0.1948	0.1515	0.0826	0	-0.0098	5
Alt3	0.1895	0.1754	0.0961	0.0259	-0.0140	3
Alt4	0.1732	0.1780	0.0516	0.0571	0.0002	6
Alt5	0.2104	0.1591	0.0598	0.0934	0.0212	9
Alt6	0.1493	0.2033	0.0759	0.0539	-0.0190	1
Alt7	0.1763	0.1918	0.0390	0.0950	0.0101	8
Alt8	0.1659	0.1767	0.0490	0.0627	0.0007	7
Alt9	0.2094	0.1600	0.0512	0.0968	0.0238	10
Alt10	0.1847	0.1967	0.0916	0.0626	-0.0103	4

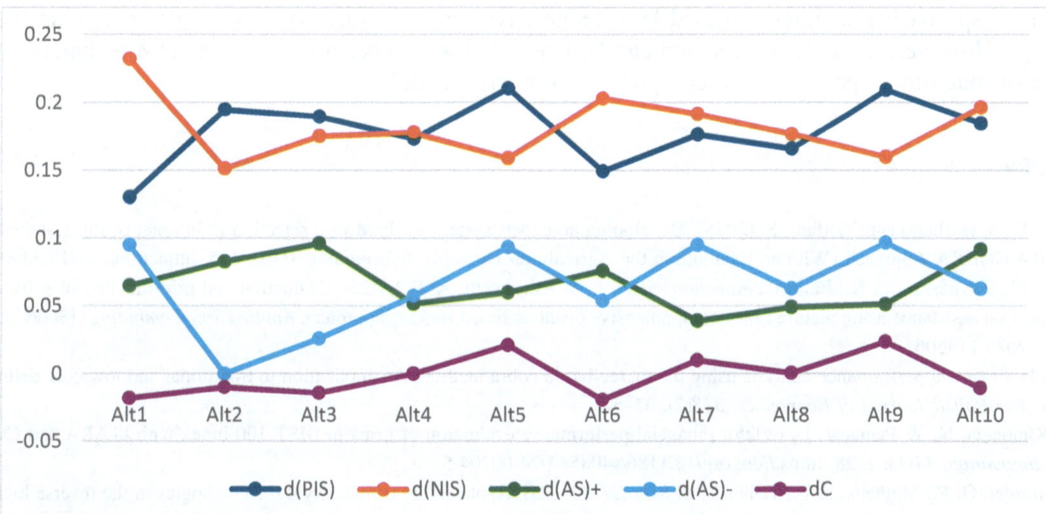

FIGURE 86.2 COBRA method results.

$$d(PIS_1) = 0.1274 + (0.1274 \times 0.2911 \times 0.0747) = 0.1302$$

$$dE(NIS_1) = \sqrt{(0.0035 - 0.1000)^2 + (0.0139 - 0.0409)^2 + \ldots + (0.1000 - 0.0165)^2 + (0.1000 - 0.0013)^2} = 0.2221$$

$$dT(NIS_1) = |0.0035 - 0.1000| + |0.0139 - 0.0409| + \ldots + |0.1000 - 0.0165| + |0.1000 - 0.0013| = 0.6221$$

$$d(NIS_\sigma) = (0.2221 - 0.1473) = 0.0748$$

$$d(NIS_1) = 0.2221 + (0.2221 \times 0.6221 \times 0.0748) = 0.2324$$

$$d(AS_1)^{+} = 0.0650$$

$$d(AS_1)^{-} = 0.0951$$

$$dC_1 = \frac{0.1302 - 0.2324 - 0.0650 + 0.0951}{4} = -0.0180$$

According to the analysis findings regarding the COBRA method shown in Table 86.8, the relative superiority order of the alternatives is as follows: Alt6 > Alt1 > Alt3 > Alt10 >Alt2 > Alt4 > Alt8 > Alt7 > Alt5 > Alt9.

The graphical representation of the COBRA method results for numerical example 2 is included in Fig. 86.2.

86.4 Conclusion

The COBRA method is an analytical technique that offers a model based on the concept of distance within the MCDM approaches. This method evaluates each alternative based on its distance to a specific reference point and ensures that the most appropriate option is determined. The COBRA method provides decision makers with a systematic, comprehensive, and understandable analysis tool, thus simplifying and making the decision-making process reliable.

In this chapter, two separate numerical examples were carried out to demonstrate the applicability of the COBRA method. The first application includes a simple problem scenario that will allow the basic operation of the method to be understood; the second application focuses on a more complex decision problem with more criteria and alternatives. According to the ranking obtained as a result of the first numerical example, the alternatives are listed as follows: Alt2 > Alt1 > Alt3 > Alt4. This result demonstrates the ability of the COBRA method to distinguish and rank alternatives in simple problem scenarios. According to the ranking obtained as a result of the second numerical example, the alternatives are listed as follows: Alt6 > Alt1 > Alt3 > Alt10 > Alt2 > Alt4 > Alt8 > Alt7 > Alt5 > Alt9. This result shows that the COBRA method can be effectively applied to more complex decision problems and can make a meaningful distinction between a large number of criteria and alternatives.

In future studies, the COBRA method can be used as an effective tool in solving any MCDM problems encountered in various disciplines. The flexible structure of the method allows it to be adapted not only to classical decision matrices but also to heuristic approaches or interval-based knowledge environments (such as fuzzy logic, rough set theory, or gray system theory). However, the COBRA method can be integrated with other traditional MCDM techniques, allowing the development of much more powerful and comprehensive hybrid models.

References

Ahmadi Pargo, T., & Hashemkhani Zolfani, S. (2025). Developing an expert system for hardware selection in internet of things-based system design: Grey ITARA-COBRA Approach (With an Example in the Agricultural Domain). *Information, 16*(6), 425. https://doi.org/10.3390/info16060425.

Alshamrani, A. M., Zavadskas, E. K., Rani, P., Antucheviciene, J., & Alrasheedi, A. F. (2025). Evaluation and prioritization of software packages for remote education assistance using picture fuzzy comprehensive distance-based ranking approach. *Applied Soft Computing*113606. https://doi.org/10.1016/j.asoc.2025.113606.

Asker, V. (2024). Financial performance analysis using the merec-based cobra method: An application to traditional and low-cost airlines. *Gospodarka Narodowa. The Polish Journal of Economics, 318*(2), 35–52.

Katrancı, A., Kundakcı, N., & Pamucar, D. (2025). Financial performance evaluation of firms in BIST 100 index with ITARA and COBRA methods. *Financial Innovation, 11*(1), 1–28. https://doi.org/10.1186/s40854-024-00704-5.

Krstić, M., Agnusdei, G. P., Miglietta, P. P., Tadić, S., & Roso, V. (2022a). Applicability of industry 4.0 technologies in the reverse logistics: A circular economy approach based on comprehensive distance based ranking (COBRA) method. *Sustainability, 14*(9), 5632. https://doi.org/10.3390/su14095632.

Krstić, M., Agnusdei, G. P., Miglietta, P. P., & Tadić, S. (2022b). Logistics 4.0 toward circular economy in the agri-food sector. *Sustainable Futures, 4*, 100097. https://doi.org/10.1016/j.sftr.2022.100097.

Mim, J. F., Islam, M. M., & Raza, A. H. (2025). A hybrid MCDM approach for unveiling ChatGPT's effect on students' learning. *Computers and Education: Artificial Intelligence*100457. https://doi.org/10.1016/j.caeai.2025.100457.

Mirčetić, V., Popović, G., Vukotić, S., Mihić, M., Kovačević, I., Đoković, A., & Slavković, M. (2024). Navigating the complexity of HRM practice: A multiple-criteria decision-making framework. *Mathematics, 12*(23), 3769. https://doi.org/10.3390/math12233769.

Popović, G., Pucar, Đ., & Smarandache, F. (2022). MEREC-COBRA approach in e-commerce development strategy selection. *Journal of Process Management and New Technologies, 10*(3-4), 66–74. https://doi.org/10.5937/jpmnt10-41073.

Rani, P., Mishra, A. R., Tirkolaee, E. B., Alshamrani, A. M., & Alrasheedi, A. F. (2025). Pythagorean fuzzy comprehensive distance-based ranking approach for assessing industry 4.0 adoption strategies in the automotive manufacturing sector. *Advanced Engineering Informatics, 65*, 103359. https://doi.org/10.1016/j.aei.2025.103359.

Sandra, M., Narayanamoorthy, S., Almakayeel, N., & Pamucar, D. (2025). A fuzzy multi-criteria decision model for sustainable fracturing technique selection in hot dry rock geothermal systems. *Journal of Cleaner Production, 524*, 146472. https://doi.org/10.1016/j.jclepro.2025.146472.

Tadić, S., Krstić, M., Dabić-Miletić, S., & Božić, M. (2023). Smart material handling solutions for city logistics systems. *Sustainability, 15*(8), 6693. https://doi.org/10.3390/su15086693.

Tadić, S., Krstić, M., & Radovanović, L. (2024). Assessing strategies to overcome barriers for drone usage in last-mile logistics: A novel hybrid fuzzy MCDM model. *Mathematics, 12*(3), 367. https://doi.org/10.3390/math12030367.

Verma, R., Koul, S., & KV, A. (2023). Evaluation and selection of a cybersecurity platform: Case of the power sector in India. *Decision Making: Applications in Management and Engineering, 7*(1), 209–236. https://doi.org/10.31181/dmame712024891.

Zorlu, K., Tuncer, M., & Yılmaz, A. (2024). Assessment of resources for geotourism development: Integrated SWARA-COBRA approach under spherical fuzzy environments. *Geoheritage, 16*(3), 89. https://doi.org/10.1007/s12371-024-00993-3.

Chapter 87

ALWAS: Aczel–Alsina weighted assessment for multi-attribute decision-making

Hande Küçükönder[1] and Ömer Faruk Görçün[2]
[1]*Department of Business, Faculty of Economics and Administrative Sciences, Bartın University, Bartın, Turkey,* [2]*Department of Business Administration, Faculty of Economic, Administration, and Social Sciences, Kadir Has University, Istanbul, Türkiye*

87.1 Introduction

Senior managers in various industries often encounter multidimensional and intricate decision-making issues influenced by contradictory criteria in which nonlinear relationships exist. Solving these decision-making problems in a rational, reliable, and compatible manner with real-life conditions requires the correct modeling and management of uncertainties and ambiguities, as well as decision-maker hesitations, the correct and rational determination of the impact and importance of the criteria affecting the evaluation process, and the logical ordering of alternatives. In this respect, the Aczél–Alsina weighted assessment (ALWAS) procedure is an innovative and reliable ranking method introduced to the literature in recent years. ALWAS is a computational tool capable of nonlinear and flexible information processing, and depending on this ability, it allows for the simulation of decisions with different risk levels. In addition, it makes it possible to process uncertain and ambiguous information in a rational and reliable context. (Deveci et al., 2024; Gokasar et al., 2023; Işık et al., 2024; Pamucar et al., 2024).

In addition, the ability of this mathematical calculation tool to process nonlinear information, as mentioned above, and its ability to simulate decision alternatives at different risk levels are related to its use of Aczel–Alsina norms. Within the framework of these structural features, ALWAS stands out as a flexible and versatile solution method, and it is a straightforward, practical, and easy-to-understand approach compared to traditional and classical decision-making tools (Pamucar et al., 2024). Another essential advantage of this method is its innovative normalization approach while preserving the order of standardized data (Deveci et al., 2024). This normalization procedure eliminates violations of the data range by stabilizing the positions of standardized weight values, regardless of the orientation and characteristics of the criteria. However, it makes it possible to obtain results based on the initial decision matrix, which accurately reflects each criterion's level of impact and importance in the evaluation process. These advantages of the ALWAS method make the application of the technique more transparent, practical, reliable, and robust, and enable the method to give highly rational and real-life results in decision-making processes.

The ALWAS method was first used to evaluate the green growth performance of G7 countries, for which Pamucar et al. (2024) integrated this method with the weights by envelope and slope weighting method. In this study, the authors revealed that environmental criteria are more decisive than economic and social dimensions. These findings show that ALWAS can be used effectively in decision problems that are complex, multidimensional, and work with environmental data.

Additionally, in the study by Gokasar et al. (2023), ALWAS was combined with fuzzy full consistency method (FUCOM) weighting and applied to determine the most suitable alternative in the metaverse integration of autonomous vehicles. This study demonstrates ALWAS's ability to simultaneously evaluate multiple technical, environmental, practical, and financial criteria. Similarly, in the Deveci et al. (2024) study, the ALWAS method, which is integrated with fuzzy ordinal priority approach (OPA) and combined compromise solution models, was used to increase digital carbon footprint awareness and optimize the sustainable mobility performance of cities. This application reinforces the method's advantages in terms of processing ambiguous and incomplete information, simulating different risk scenarios, and reliably ranking alternatives.

Encyclopedia of Multi-Attribute Decision-Making (MADM). DOI: https://doi.org/10.1016/B978-0-443-33275-3.00040-3

Another study by Işık et al. (2024) examined the integration of ALWAS into a hybrid multicriteria decision-making (MCDM) framework with logarithmic percentage change-driven objective weighting and criteria importance through intercriteria correlation (CRITIC) weighting methods. The study focused on the assessment of the competitiveness levels of European cities and revealed the success of ALWAS in the ranking phase. In addition, sensitivity and comparison analyses confirmed the reliability and robustness of the method. These examples show that ALWAS can be adapted to a broader range of applications, not just by itself, but by integrating different weighting methods and sequencing models.

All these studies show that although ALWAS has already been used in a limited number of studies (four primary studies), it may be preferred in many more MCDM applications in the near future, thanks to its innovative approach, nonlinear information processing capability, and flexibility in managing uncertainties.

In addition to these prior applications, the present study extends the use of ALWAS by applying it to a real-world logistics problem. Specifically, a case study is conducted on the selection of reach truck stackers for a medium-sized logistics company in Turkey. This decision-making problem involves multiple economic, technical, and operational criteria, such as purchase price, maintenance costs, maximum payload, maneuverability, and fuel consumption. The criteria and alternatives were identified through consultations with industry experts and validated using technical specifications provided by manufacturers. By focusing on reach truck selection, this study demonstrates the practical applicability of the ALWAS method in warehouse operations, which represent a critical component of modern logistics systems.

The primary aim of this study is to evaluate the effectiveness and robustness of the ALWAS method when applied to a practical MCDM problem in the logistics industry. In this context, the study pursues three main objectives: (i) to demonstrate how ALWAS can be integrated with objective weighting methods such as CRITIC, (ii) to test the ability of the method to handle complex trade-offs among multiple criteria in reach truck selection, and (iii) to assess the sensitivity and reliability of the outcomes under varying conditions. Through these objectives, the study seeks to contribute to the literature by providing empirical evidence of the advantages and potential limitations of ALWAS in real-life decision-making environments.

The main advantages distinguishing the method from traditional methods are that it can be adapted to individual and group decision-making processes, it can sort normalized information without being dependent on data type, and it can simulate different risk levels.

Within the scope of this study, the ALWAS method was integrated with the CRITIC weighting method and applied as a hybrid framework. The proposed framework was applied as a case study to the problem of the selection of reach truck stackers used in logistics enterprises' warehouses. It produced reliable and robust results in the context of the method, the criteria's importance, and the alternatives' ranking. In particular, C12 (total width, mm) was the most effective criterion, while A4 (Cat NSR12N) was the most optimal alternative. The robustness checks prove the reliability and stability of the results of the proposed model.

87.2 Aczel–Alsina weighted assessment approach

This section details the mathematical background of the ALWAS approach. Details for the four stages of the method, which are flexible and extremely easy to apply, are presented below (Işık et al., 2024; Pamucar et al., 2024):

Step 1. Let assume decision problem involves n number of criteria ($C_1, C_2,\ldots, C_n$) and m number of alternatives ($O_1, O_2,\ldots, O_m$), the initial decision matrix can be formed as Eq. (87.1).

$$[\wp_{ij}]_{mxn} = \begin{bmatrix} \wp_{11} & \wp_{12} & \cdots & \wp_{1n} \\ \wp_{21} & \wp_{22} & \cdots & \wp_{2n} \\ \vdots & \vdots & \ddots & \vdots \\ \wp_{m1} & \wp_{m2} & \cdots & \wp_{mn} \end{bmatrix} i = 1, \quad 2, \quad \ldots, \quad m; j = 1, \quad 2, \quad \ldots, \quad n \tag{87.1}$$

Step 2. To standardize the decision matrix, the normalization of the criteria is completed by using the equation presented in Eq. (87.2), the mathematical expansion of which is given in Eq. (87.2), taking into account whether the criteria are elements of the benefit or cost set.

$$\mathfrak{V}_{ij} = \begin{cases} \mathfrak{V}_{ij} = \dfrac{\wp_{ij}}{\wp_j^*}, & j \in Benefit \\ \mathfrak{V}_{ij} = -\dfrac{\wp_{ij}}{\wp_j^*} + \max\limits_{1 \le i \le m}\left(\dfrac{\wp_{ij}}{\wp_j^*}\right) + \min\limits_{1 \le i \le m}\left(\dfrac{\wp_{ij}}{\wp_j^*}\right), & j \in Cost \end{cases} \tag{87.2}$$

$\wp_j^* = \max\limits_{1 \le i \le m}(\wp_{ij})$ in the equation is calculated as.

Step 3. In this step, two different weighted mean values are calculated, based on the Aczél–Alsina functions (Aczél & Alsina, 1982), in which the criterion weights are also considered, to evaluate each decision alternative.

In this context, two different weighted addition tool-based score values are calculated for each alternative: "Aczél–Alsina weighted averaging AAWA ($\mathfrak{A}_i^{(1)\theta}$)" according to Eq. (87.3) and "Aczél–Alsina weighted geometric averaging AAWGA ($\mathfrak{A}_i^{(2)\theta}$)" according to Eq. (87.4).

$$\mathfrak{A}_i^{(1)\theta} = \sum_{j=1}^{n} \mathfrak{V}_{ij} \left(1 - e^{-\left(\sum_{j=1}^{n} \omega_j (-\ln (1 - f(\mathfrak{V}_{ij})))^{\theta} \right)^{1/\theta}} \right) \tag{87.3}$$

$$\mathfrak{A}_i^{(2)\theta} = \sum_{j=1}^{n} \mathfrak{V}_{ij} . e^{-\left(\sum_{j=1}^{n} \omega_j (-\ln (f(\mathfrak{V}_{ij})))^{\theta} \right)^{1/\theta}} \tag{87.4}$$

Here, $\omega_j = (\omega_1, \omega_2, \ldots, \omega_n)$ denotes weight coefficient information for criteria and $f(\mathfrak{V}_{ij}) = \left(\mathfrak{V}_{ij}/\sum_{j=1}^{n} \mathfrak{V}_{ij}\right)$, $\theta \geq 0$.

Step 4. (87.5) is used to integrate the information $\mathfrak{A}_i^{(1)\theta} and \mathfrak{A}_i^{(2)\theta}$ calculated with the help of AAWA and AAWGA functions for each decision alternative and to evaluate the relative suitability of the alternatives. The values calculated according to this function are sorted from largest to smallest, and the most significant value is suggested as the most suitable alternative.

$$\Omega_i = \left(\frac{\mathfrak{A}_i^{(1)\theta} + \mathfrak{A}_i^{(2)\theta}}{1 + \left(\gamma \left(\frac{1 - f(\mathfrak{A}_i^{(1)\theta})}{f(\mathfrak{A}_i^{(1)\theta})} \right)^{\lambda} + (1 - \gamma) \left(\frac{1 - f(\mathfrak{A}_i^{(2)\theta})}{f(\mathfrak{A}_i^{(2)\theta})} \right)^{\lambda} \right)^{1/\lambda}} \right) \tag{87.5}$$

The parameters in the equation are expressed as $\lambda > 0$, $\gamma \geq 0$ and taking the values of these parameters in the initial solution are recommended as $\lambda = 1$, $\gamma = 0.5$, $\theta = 1$ by Pamucar et al. (2024). Besides, it is calculated as $f(\mathfrak{A}_i^{(1)\theta}) = \mathfrak{A}_i^{(1)\theta}/(\mathfrak{A}_i^{(1)\theta} + \mathfrak{A}_i^{(2)\theta}), f(\mathfrak{A}_i^{(2)\theta}) = \mathfrak{A}_i^{(2)\theta}/(\mathfrak{A}_i^{(1)\theta} + \mathfrak{A}_i^{(2)\theta})$.

87.3 Case study

This section illustrates the application of the ALWAS method by considering a case study on reach truck selection. In this context, the criteria and alternatives to the decision problem are presented in Table 87.1. The case study used in this study is based on a decision-making problem encountered in real-life conditions. It is related to the selection of stacking vehicles to be employed by a medium-sized logistics company operating in Turkey to be used in the new warehouse to be established. In this direction, the data set used in the study was obtained from the technical data sheets published by the reach truck stacking vehicle manufacturers regarding their products. The criteria and alternatives used were determined from interviews with experts, and the numerical data to be used in the context of these alternatives and criteria were collected from the technical documents published by the manufacturers on their websites. Before proceeding with the analysis process, these data were verified in meetings with experts.

In this study, the initial decision matrix based on the collected data for the multicriteria decision problem of interest is given in Table 87.2.

Considering the maximization or minimization of the evaluation criteria, the initial decision matrix was normalized with the help of Eq. 87.2, and the results are given in Table 87.3.

For example, the normalized value of $\mathfrak{V}_{11}$ in A1–C1 that is minimum and $\mathfrak{V}_{13}$ in A1–C3 with the maximum direction are computed as follows:

$$\mathfrak{V}_{11} = -\frac{26000}{37000} + \max_{1 \leq i \leq 7} \left(\frac{26000}{37000}, \frac{37000}{37000}, \ldots, \frac{26000}{37000} \right) + \min_{1 \leq i \leq m} \left(\frac{26000}{37000}, \frac{37000}{37000}, \ldots, \frac{26000}{37000} \right) = 0.973$$

$$\mathfrak{V}_{13} = \frac{1250}{1600} = 0.781$$

After obtaining the normalized matrix, according to Eqs. 87.3 and 87.4, it is determined that $\mathfrak{A}_i^{(1)\theta}$ and $\mathfrak{A}_i^{(2)\theta}$ values were calculated, and then the final score values (Ω_i) were calculated, in which the information obtained from these two aggregation strategies were synthesized according to (87.5). Here, criterion weights are based on the individual

TABLE 87.1 Criteria and alternative information of the decision problem.

No.	Criteria	Criteria direction
C1	Purchase price (€)	Min
C2	Average maintenance costs (TL)	Min
C3	Maximum payload (KG)	Max
C4	Brand awareness	Max
C5	Fuel consumption (kW)	Min
C6	Warranty period (working hours)	Max
C7	Movement speed (loaded)	Max
C8	Lifting speed	Max
C9	Spare parts supply	Max
C1-0	Outer turning radius (mm)	Min
C1-1	Lifting height (mm)	Max
C1-2	Overall width (mm)	Min
Alternatives		
No.	**Brands/models**	
A1	Toyota-8FBR13	
A2	Jungheinrich ETV-112	
A3	Mitsubishi FBC15N	
A4	Cat NSR12N	
A5	Komatsu FB14-12	
A6	Hyundai 16B-9	
A7	Manitou ME 315c	

TABLE 87.2 Initial decision matrix.

Criteria	C1	C2	C3	C4	C5	C6	C7	C8	C9	C10	C11	C12
Alt.	**Min**	**Min**	**Max**	**Max**	**Min**	**Max**	**Max**	**Max**	**Max**	**Min**	**Max**	**Min**
A1	26000	900	1250	9.00	4.9	2	9	0.45	8.89	1490	4000	1090
A2	37000	1528	1200	9.00	2.9	2	11	0.43	9.00	1595	5942	1120
A3	25500	700	1500	7.17	6.8	2	18	0.53	6.75	1790	3320	0.947
A4	29000	750	1200	8.69	2.2	2	7	0.30	8.18	1665	5400	0.610
A5	25600	650	1350	9.00	4.5	3	15	1.22	8.79	1750	3000	1110
A6	25000	800	1600	8.07	4.7	2	16	0.41	7.76	1710	3325	1074
A7	26000	700	1500	8.15	4	2	9.5	0.22	7.29	1510	3000	990

TABLE 87.3 Normalized decision matrix.

Alt.	C1	C2	C3	C4	C5	C6	C7	C8	C9	C10	C11	C12
A1	0.973	0.836	0.781	1.000	0.603	0.667	0.500	0.369	0.988	1.000	0.673	0.027
A2	0.676	0.425	0.750	1.000	0.897	0.667	0.611	0.352	1.000	0.941	1.000	0.001
A3	0.986	0.967	0.938	0.797	0.324	0.667	1.000	0.434	0.750	0.832	0.559	1.000
A4	0.892	0.935	0.750	0.966	1.000	0.667	0.389	0.246	0.909	0.902	0.909	1.000
A5	0.984	1.000	0.844	1.000	0.662	1.000	0.833	1.000	0.977	0.855	0.505	0.009
A6	1.000	0.902	1.000	0.897	0.632	0.667	0.889	0.336	0.862	0.877	0.560	0.042
A7	0.973	0.967	0.938	0.906	0.735	0.667	0.528	0.180	0.810	0.989	0.505	0.117

TABLE 87.4 The criteria weights.

Criteria	C1	C2	C3	C4	C5	C6
Weights	0.077	0.073	0.091	0.078	0.075	0.071
Criteria	C7	C8	C9	C10	C11	C12
Weights	0.081	0.065	0.082	0.094	0.098	0.115

TABLE 87.5 Score values and ranking results of alternatives according to the ALWAS method.

Alternative	A1	A2	A3	A4	A5	A6	A7
$\mathfrak{A}_i^{(1)\theta}$	0.6917	0.6911	0.7870	0.8162	0.7729	0.7101	0.6860
$\mathfrak{A}_i^{(2)\theta}$	0.5063	0.3210	0.7463	0.7661	0.5048	0.5443	0.5673
Ω_i	0.5847	0.4383	0.7661	0.7904	0.6107	0.6163	0.6210
Rank	6	7	2	1	5	4	3

preferences of the decision-makers, using objective weighting techniques Logarithmic Percentage Change-driven Objective Weighting (LOPCOW), ENTROPY, LOgarithmic DEcomposition Of Criteria Importance (LODECI), Symmetry-based Proximity to the Ideal Solution (SPC), Criteria importance through inter criteria correlation (CRITIC), …, etc.) or subjective weighting techniques (step-wise weight assessment ratio analysis, best–worst method, analytic hierarchy process, FUCOM, … etc), as well as different weight estimations can be found by choosing mixed approaches using both. In the present study, the CRITIC (Diakoulaki et al., 1995) method was used as an objective weighting approach to determine the criterion weights, and the weight information for each criterion was calculated as shown in Table 87.4. For detailed information on the application of the CRITIC method, the study of Diakoulaki et al. (1995) can be examined.

The values of $\mathfrak{A}_i^{(1)\theta}$, $\mathfrak{A}_i^{(2)\theta}$, and Ω_i computed for each alternative by using the criteria weights given in Table 87.4 are presented in Table 87.5. In this phase, the parameter values regarding functions in computations are taken as $\lambda = 1$, $\gamma = 0.5$, $\theta = 1$.

The values are calculated respectively for A1 alternatives demonstrated in Table 87.5 by taking as $\lambda = 1,\ \gamma = 0.5,\ \theta = 1$ as follows:

$$\mathfrak{A}_i^{(1)\theta=1} = 8.417 * \left(1 - e^{-\left(\sum_{j=1}^{12} 0.077\left(-\ln\left(1-\left(\frac{0.973}{8.417}\right)\right)\right)^1 + 0.073\left(-\ln\left(1-\left(\frac{0.836}{8.417}\right)\right)\right)^1 + \ldots + 0.115\left(-\ln\left(1-\left(\frac{0.027}{8.417}\right)\right)\right)^1 \right)^{\frac{1}{1}}} \right)$$

$$= 0.6917$$

$$\mathfrak{A}_i^{(2)\theta=1} = 8.417 * \left(e^{-\left(\sum_{j=1}^{12} 0.077\left(-\ln\left(\left(\frac{0.973}{8.417}\right)\right)\right)^1 + 0.073\left(-\ln\left(\left(\frac{0.836}{8.417}\right)\right)\right)^1 + \ldots + 0.115\left(-\ln\left(\left(\frac{0.027}{8.417}\right)\right)\right)^1 \right)^{\frac{1}{1}}} \right) = 0.5063$$

$$\Omega_{A1} = \left(\frac{0.6917 + 0.5063}{1 + \left(0.5\left(\frac{1-\left(\frac{0.6917}{0.6917+0.5063}\right)}{0.5774} \right)^1 + (1-0.5)\left(\frac{1-\left(\frac{0.5063}{0.6917+0.5063}\right)}{0.4226} \right)^1 \right)^{1/1}} \right) = 0.5847$$

According to the results presented in Table 87.5, the alternatives were ranked considering the calculated final score values (Ω_i) A4 > A3 > A7 > A6 > A5 > A 1 > A2.

87.4 Robustness and validity check

In the systematic solution of a complex multidimensional decision problem, analyzing the robustness and reliability of the method represents a critical stage of the decision-making process (Więckowski & Sałabun, 2023). However, different subjective preferences may come to the fore when determining the weight levels of the selection criteria according to the decision makers' risk perception and behavioral tendencies or when choosing the optimum value of the model parameter. In this context, it is essential for the rationality and quality of the decision to evaluate the results that arise according to the changing conditions in different decision-making scenarios with a holistic understanding. In this context, in this part of the study, the sensitivity analysis is divided into three parts. First, the calculated weight information for all criteria was considered, and based on the algorithm proposed by Görçün et al. (2021), the weight of each criterion was recalculated with an ongoing reduction of 10% and its multiples, keeping the others constant. Accordingly, 120 test scenarios were designed that included different combinations of all criteria by changing the importance weights. Fig. 87.1 shows the change in the rankings of the alternatives in each scenario.

When the rankings given in Fig. 87.1 are examined, it is seen that the A4 alternative, which ranked first in the initial solution, continued to maintain its ranking in 87.5% of the scenarios. In contrast, in other scenarios, it was affected by the decrease in the weight information of the C1, C2, and C9 criteria at different proportional levels. As a result, it dropped one place and took second place. The second A3 alternative, on the other hand, maintained its ranking in 86.7% of the scenarios and was affected by the varying importance weights of the C1, C2, C9, and C10 criteria in the other scenarios. When the rankings for the different decision alternatives were examined, all other options except A5 and A6 maintained their first rankings on average in more than 80% of the scenarios. As a result, all other options were jointly affected by the change in the importance weight of the C1 purchase price criterion, and it was observed that possible decreases in the weight of this criterion may cause differences in preference rankings.

Secondly, in the sensitivity analysis, the θ, λ, and γ parameters of the method were adapted to various decision-making scenarios by taking into account the definition ranges, and the effects of the alternatives on their rankings were examined. In this context, 50 test cases were created for the θ parameter, and the value of the parameter was increased by one consecutively in each scenario. Accordingly, Fig. 87.2 shows the ranking

When the ranking results in Fig. 87.2 are examined, it is seen that the A4 alternative continued to maintain its position in the first place for the values defined in the range $\theta \in [1, 5]$, while the score value decreased for the $\theta \in [5, 20]$ values and left its place in the first place to the A3 alternative. Alternatives A2, A6, and A7 remained steadfast in their initial order in the face of increasing values of the θ parameter and did not exhibit any changes. Therefore, it can be said that the stability of these alternatives is strengthened in the face of increasing values of the θ parameter. On the other hand, the A1

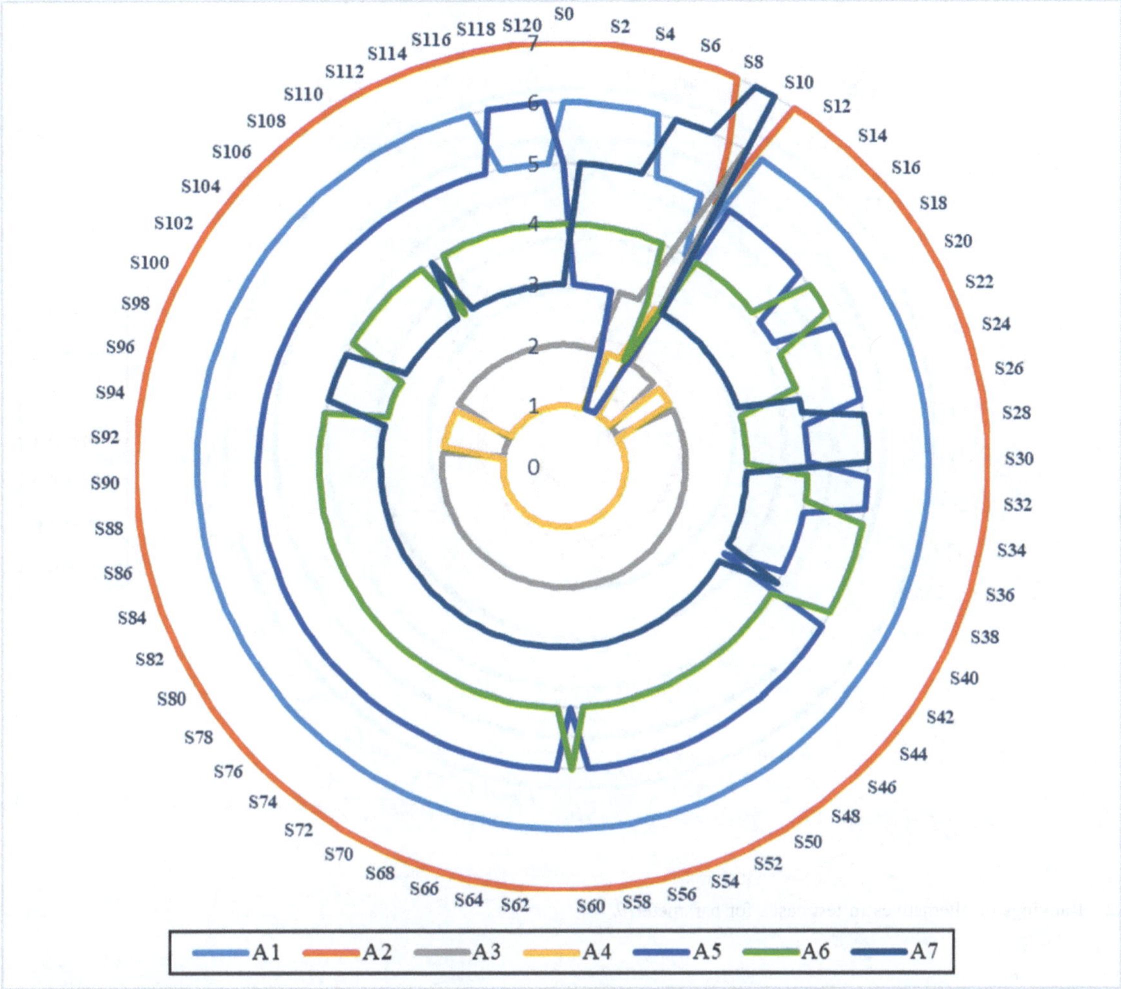

FIGURE 87.1 Ranking of alternatives according to scenarios involving the change of criterion weight information.

and A5 alternatives have changed their order in all scenarios and have become the most sensitive alternative among the alternatives. Another parameter of the model, λ, was defined as $\lambda = 1$ in the first solution. In the trials in which the value of this parameter was changed by adding $\lambda = 2, 3, \ldots, 50$, the alternatives were listed as in Fig. 87.3.

According to the ranking results in Fig. 87.3, only the order of the A1 and A5 alternatives was displaced for the values of this parameter between $\lambda \in [8, 50]$, and the stability of the first rankings continued for the rest. Finally, the ranking results obtained in the scenarios created for the γ parameter of the model are given in Table 87.6.

According to Table 87.6, for $\gamma \in [0, 1]$, the sort order of the first place A4 and the second row A3 alternative remained the same, while the rest showed some ranking differences in the face of increasing or decreasing values of the parameter.

Finally, in the sensitivity analysis, the reliability of the ranking results provided by the ALWAS method for the alternatives was evaluated by comparing them with weighted aggregated sum product assessment (WASPAS)(Zavadskas et al., 2012), ranking of alternatives with weights of criterion (RAWEC) (Puška et al., 2024), complex proportional assessment (COPRAS) (Zavadskas et al., 2009), and additive ratio assessmen (ARAS) (Zavadskas et al., 2010) methods. In Fig. 87.4, the ranking results obtained according to the methods at this stage are presented.

According to the ALWAS method, the A4 alternative was the first choice in the initial solution. According to Fig. 87.4, as a result of applying all procedures, it continued its position in the first place. Apart from this, another alternative that maintained its position was the A3 in second place. Although slight differences were observed in the rankings of other alternatives according to the methods, it can be said that the rankings were consistent. As a result, it can be concluded that the findings of the comprehensive sensitivity analysis are consistent with each other. From this point of view, it can be concluded that the ALWAS method is a robust, powerful, and flexible evaluation tool.

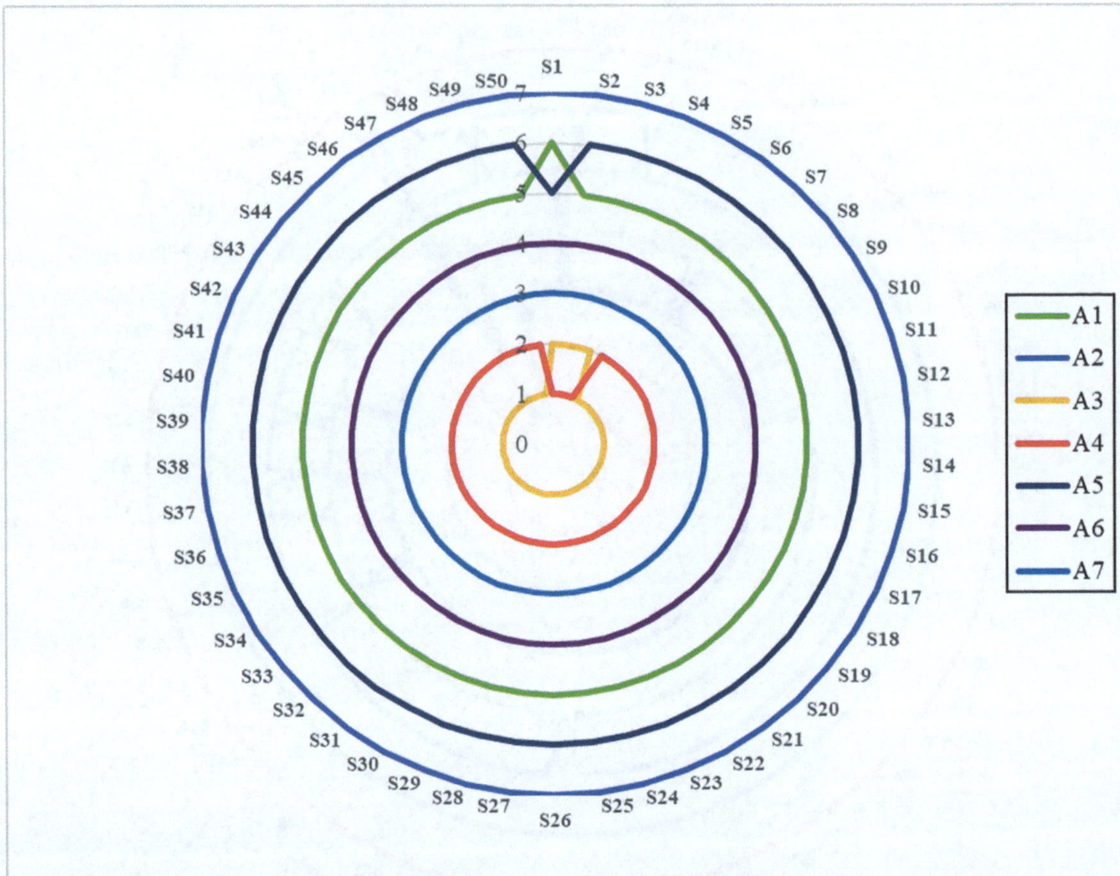

FIGURE 87.2 Rankings of alternatives in test cases for parameter θ.

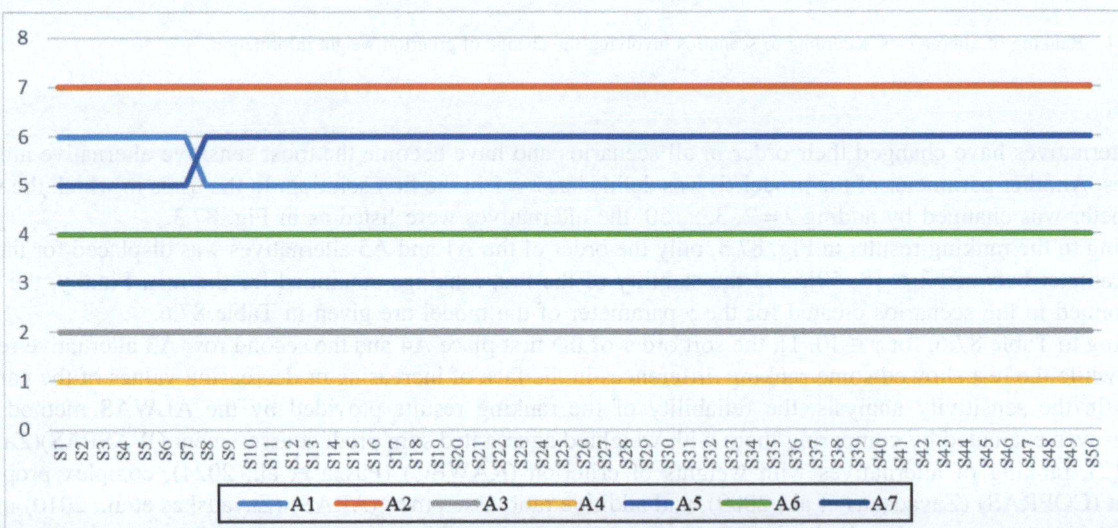

FIGURE 87.3 Results of reordering alternatives based on λ varying according to scenarios.

87.5 Results and discussion

The empirical results of the proposed hybrid ALWAS–CRITIC framework provide valuable insights into the decision-making process for reach truck selection in the logistics sector. Based on the criteria weights obtained through the CRITIC

TABLE 87.6 Ranking results obtained in scenarios created for γ parameter.

Alt.	$\gamma = 0.1$	$\gamma = 0.2$	$\gamma = 0.3$	$\gamma = 0.4$	$\gamma = 0.5$ (original model)	$\gamma = 0.6$	$\gamma = 0.7$	$\gamma = 0.8$	$\gamma = 0.9$	$\gamma = 1$
A1	5	6	6	6	6	6	6	6	6	5
A2	7	7	7	7	7	7	7	7	7	6
A3	2	2	2	2	2	2	2	2	2	2
A4	1	1	1	1	1	1	1	1	1	1
A5	6	5	5	5	5	3	3	3	3	3
A6	4	4	4	4	4	5	4	4	4	4
A7	3	3	3	3	3	4	5	5	5	7

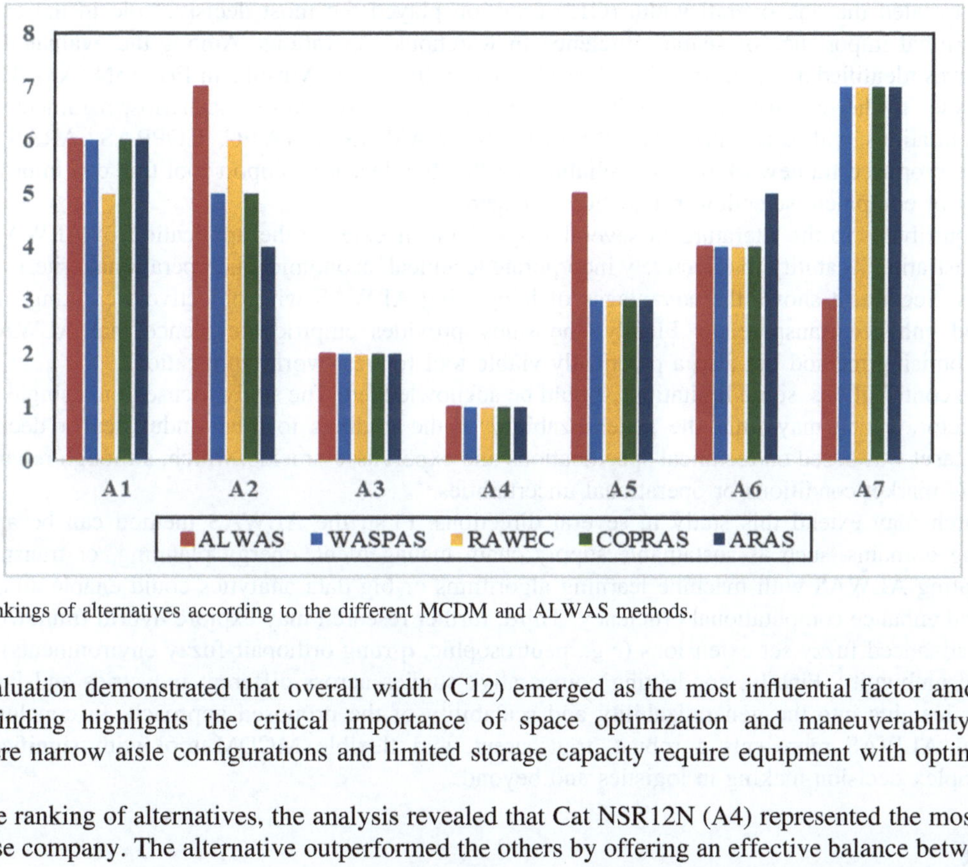

FIGURE 87.4 Rankings of alternatives according to the different MCDM and ALWAS methods.

method, the evaluation demonstrated that overall width (C12) emerged as the most influential factor among all decision criteria. This finding highlights the critical importance of space optimization and maneuverability in warehouse operations, where narrow aisle configurations and limited storage capacity require equipment with optimal dimensional characteristics.

Regarding the ranking of alternatives, the analysis revealed that Cat NSR12N (A4) represented the most suitable reach truck for the case company. The alternative outperformed the others by offering an effective balance between cost-related and technical attributes, thereby meeting operational efficiency requirements. The subsequent ranking order was determined as A4 > A3 > A7 > A6 > A5 > A1 > A2, where A3 (Mitsubishi FBC15N) and A7 (Manitou ME 315c) closely followed the optimal solution. The relatively lower performance of A1 (Toyota-8FBR13) and A2 (Jungheinrich ETV-112) indicates that, despite strong brand awareness, these models were disadvantaged by certain cost and dimensional factors.

The robustness and validity analyses confirmed the reliability of the obtained results. Sensitivity tests on the criteria weights indicated that the top-ranked alternative (A4) consistently preserved its position under 87.5% of the scenarios, while A3 maintained its second-place ranking in 86.7% of the cases. Although slight variations were observed in the middle-ranked alternatives, the stability of the two leading options underlines the resilience of the model. Similarly, the parameter sensitivity analysis for θ, λ, and γ demonstrated that the ranking of A4 and A3 remained robust across different configurations, reinforcing the method's adaptability to changes in risk perception and decision-maker preferences.

Furthermore, comparative analyses with alternative MCDM approaches—such as WASPAS, RAWEC, COPRAS, and ARAS—produced consistent outcomes. Despite minor variations in the rankings of lower-ranked alternatives, the leading positions of A4 and A3 were preserved across all methods, verifying the robustness and generalizability of the ALWAS approach. This consistency across methods emphasizes that the proposed framework offers a powerful, flexible, and reliable decision-support tool for addressing multidimensional problems in logistics operations.

From a managerial perspective, the findings suggest that logistics enterprises can significantly improve decision quality by adopting advanced MCDM approaches such as ALWAS. In particular, the integration of objective weighting methods with ALWAS enables decision-makers to mitigate subjectivity while capturing the complexity of real-world trade-offs. By applying such methodologies, companies can ensure that their equipment selection processes align with both operational requirements and long-term efficiency goals.

87.6 Conclusions and future research direction

This study proposed and applied a hybrid decision-making framework that integrates the ALWAS method with the CRITIC weighting technique to address a real-world logistics problem. The empirical analysis, conducted on the selection of reach truck stackers for a medium-sized logistics enterprise in Turkey, demonstrated the effectiveness, robustness, and practical value of the ALWAS approach in handling multidimensional decision problems.

The results revealed that the overall width (C12) criterion played the most decisive role in the evaluation process, reflecting the critical importance of spatial efficiency in warehouse operations. Among the evaluated alternatives, Cat NSR12N (A4) was identified as the most suitable reach truck, followed by Mitsubishi FBC15N (A3). The robustness and sensitivity analyses further confirmed the stability of the rankings across various scenarios, parameter adjustments, and comparative validations with alternative MCDM methods (WASPAS, RAWEC, COPRAS, ARAS). These findings indicate that the proposed framework offers a reliable and flexible decision-support tool that can improve the rationality and consistency of equipment selection in logistics management.

The study contributes to the literature in several ways. First, it extends the application of ALWAS to the logistics industry, demonstrating its ability to effectively incorporate technical, economic, and operational criteria into the decision-making process. Second, it shows the advantages of integrating ALWAS with objective weighting methods to reduce subjectivity and enhance transparency. Finally, the study provides empirical evidence that ALWAS is not only a theoretically promising method but also a practically viable tool for real-world applications.

Despite these contributions, some limitations should be acknowledged. The study focused on a single case study within the logistics sector, which may limit the generalizability of the findings to other industries or decision contexts. In addition, the dataset was based on technical specifications and expert assessments, which, although reliable, may not fully capture dynamic market conditions or operational uncertainties.

Future research may extend this study in several directions. First, the ALWAS method can be applied to broader decision-making domains, such as sustainable supply chain management, energy planning, or transportation systems. Second, integrating ALWAS with machine learning algorithms or big data analytics could enable automated parameter optimization and enhance computational efficiency. Third, further research may explore hybrid frameworks that combine ALWAS with advanced fuzzy set extensions (e.g., neutrosophic, q-rung orthopair fuzzy environments) to better address uncertainty and ambiguity. Finally, conducting comparative studies across different industries and larger datasets will provide deeper insights into the generalizability and scalability of the proposed approach. In conclusion, the findings underscore that ALWAS represents a robust, transparent, and flexible MCDM tool with significant potential for supporting complex decision-making in logistics and beyond.

References

Aczél, J., & Alsina, C. (1982). Characterizations of some classes of quasilinear functions with applications to triangular norms and to synthesizing judgements. *Aequationes Mathematicae, 25*(1). https://doi.org/10.1007/BF02189626.

Deveci, M., Gokasar, I., Pamucar, D., Zaidan, A. A., Wei, W., & Pedrycz, W. (2024). Advantage prioritization of digital carbon footprint awareness in optimized urban mobility using fuzzy Aczél Alsina based decision making. *Applied Soft Computing, 151*. https://doi.org/10.1016/j.asoc.2023.111136.

Diakoulaki, D., Mavrotas, G., & Papayannakis, L. (1995). Determining objective weights in multiple criteria problems: The critic method. *Computers and Operations Research, 22*(7). https://doi.org/10.1016/0305-0548(94)00059-H.

Gokasar, I., Pamucar, D., Deveci, M., Gupta, B. B., Martinez, L., & Castillo, O. (2023). Metaverse integration alternatives of connected autonomous vehicles with self-powered sensors using fuzzy decision making model. *Information Sciences, 642*. https://doi.org/10.1016/j.ins.2023.119192.

Görçün, Ö. F., Senthil, S., & Küçükönder, H. (2021). Evaluation of tanker vehicle selection using a novel hybrid fuzzy MCDM technique. *Decision Making: Applications in Management and Engineering, 4*(2), 140–162. https://doi.org/10.31181/dmame210402140g.

Işık, Ö., Shabir, M., & Moslem, S. (2024). A hybrid MCDM framework for assessing urban competitiveness: A case study of European cities. *Socio-economic Planning Sciences, 96*, 102109. https://doi.org/10.1016/j.seps.2024.102109.

Pamucar, D., Ecer, F., Gligorić, Z., Gligorić, M., & Deveci, M. (2024). A novel WENSLO and ALWAS multicriteria methodology and its application to green growth performance evaluation. *IEEE Transactions on Engineering Management, 71*, 9510–9525. https://doi.org/10.1109/TEM.2023.3321697.

Puška, A., Štilić, A., Pamučar, D., Božanić, D., & Nedeljković, M. (2024). Introducing a novel multi-criteria ranking of alternatives with weights of criterion (RAWEC) model. *In MethodsX, 12*. https://doi.org/10.1016/j.mex.2024.102628.

Więckowski, J., & Sałabun, W. (2023). Sensitivity analysis approaches in multi-criteria decision analysis: A systematic review. *In Applied Soft Computing, 148*. https://doi.org/10.1016/j.asoc.2023.110915.

Zavadskas, E. K., Kaklauskas, A., & Vilutiene, T. (2009). Multicriteria evaluation of apartment blocks maintenance contractors: Lithuanian case study. *International Journal of Strategic Property Management, 13*(4). https://doi.org/10.3846/1648-715X.2009.13.319-338.

Zavadskas, E. K., Turskis, Z., Antucheviciene, J., & Zakarevicius, A. (2012). Optimization of weighted aggregated sum product assessmet. *Elektronika Ir Elektrotechnika, 122*(6), 3–6.

Zavadskas, E. K., Turskis, Z., & Vilutiene, T. (2010). Multiple criteria analysis of foundation instalment alternatives by applying additive ratio assessment (ARAS) method. *Archives of Civil and Mechanical Engineering, 10*(3), 123–141.

Chapter 88

RADAR: Ranking based on distance and range for multi-attribute decision-making

Nikola Komatina[1], Dragan Marinković[2,3,4], and Nikola Petrović[5]

[1]*Faculty of Engineering, University of Kragujevac, Kragujevac, Serbia,* [2]*Faculty of Mechanical Engineering and Transport Systems, TU Berlin, Berlin, Germany,* [3]*Mechanical Science Institute, Vilnius Gediminas Technical University-VILNIUS TECH, Vilnius, Lithuania,* [4]*University College, Korea University, Seoul, Korea,* [5]*Faculty of Mechanical Engineering, University of Niš, Niš, Serbia*

88.1 Introduction

Multicriteria decision-making methods can be characterized as a methodological framework designed to support the decision-making process in a mathematically grounded manner. A specific subset of these methods comprises multi-attribute decision-making (MADM) approaches, which are applied to discrete decision problems. Generally speaking, such problems involve a predefined set of feasible alternatives. In other words, the goal is to rank the available alternatives from the most to the least preferred. Additionally, MADM methods can be used for the selection of the best alternative or for classifying alternatives into predefined categories. The resolution of these problems is based on evaluating or comparing alternatives across multiple criteria or attributes. There is also a group of MADM methods specifically developed for determining the relative importance or weight of the evaluation criteria.

This chapter focuses on a method primarily intended for ranking a given set of alternatives based on a predefined set of attributes, the ranking based on distance and range (RADAR) method. Although a large number of MADM methods have been developed and extensively discussed in the literature with various, and in some cases similar, mathematical foundations—none can be considered universally perfect or applicable to every decision-making problem. Each method, including RADAR, has its own advantages and limitations.

Many commonly used MADM ranking methods tend to evaluate alternatives based strictly on their absolute performance with respect to each criterion. In certain decision contexts, such an approach may lead to misleading conclusions. For instance, an alternative that performs exceptionally well on a single, highly weighted criterion, but poorly on several less important ones—may still attain a high position in the overall ranking. In contrast, an alternative that performs consistently above average across most criteria, but without extreme values, may be ranked lower. While this type of outcome may be desirable in some cases, it can be problematic in others, particularly in fields such as risk assessment or reliability analysis.

To address this issue, the RADAR method, first published in (Komatina, 2024), was developed with the aim of finding a balance between alternatives that perform strongly on the most important criteria and those that demonstrate consistent performance across a broader set of attributes. In other words, RADAR relies on proportional relationships between alternative values within each criterion, taking into account the range of variation, thereby providing an opportunity for alternatives with stable, well-rounded performance to attain a favorable ranking.

This chapter, which introduces the fundamentals of the RADAR method, is organized into several sections. Following the introduction, Section 88.2 provides a brief literature overview. Section 88.3 outlines the main steps of the proposed methodology. Sections 88.4 and 88.5 are devoted to numerical case studies, while Section 88.6 presents a comparative analysis with other MADM approaches. The chapter concludes with final observations and recommendations.

Encyclopedia of Multi-Attribute Decision-Making (MADM). DOI: https://doi.org/10.1016/B978-0-443-33275-3.00086-5

88.2 Literature review

RADAR, as one of the newer MADM methods, has so far been used in only a few scientific publications to solve decision-making problems and has been cited in several research and review papers. Although it was first introduced in (Komatina, 2024), a detailed presentation of the mathematical foundations and characteristics of the method was provided in (Komatina et al., 2026). The basic method, in combination with the best–worst method (BWM), was applied for equipment selection in the automotive industry (Komatina, 2025a).

So far, it has primarily been used in industrial contexts, most often in combination with failure mode and effect analysis (FMEA). For instance, in the paper where it was first mentioned, it was applied within the FMEA framework (Komatina, 2024) for prioritizing failure modes. To solve a similar problem, it was used in (Komatina et al., 2025), where the method was extended through the use of triangular fuzzy numbers. The same approach for modeling uncertainty, combined with the RADAR method, was also applied in (Komatina, 2025b) for assessing risks in football player transfers. In that study, the analytic hierarchy process was used to determine the weights of the criteria. The fuzzy RADAR method was also used in the study (Karjust et al., 2025), where the authors applied it to prioritize key performance indicators in small and medium-sized enterprises.

In the domain of personnel selection, specifically for choosing members of an FMEA team, it was employed in Komatina & Marinković (2025), where the basic RADAR method was extended by incorporating Pythagorean fuzzy numbers.

As a method used in the literature, it was mentioned in a review paper (Aleksić et al., 2025), while it was also highlighted as a potentially applicable method for solving future research problems in (Abdulvahitoğlu, 2025; Marinato et al., 2025), or listed as one of the approaches used in the literature in (Ecer et al., 2025; Mandal et al., 2025; Petrović, Jovanović et al., 2025; Petrović, Tadić et al., 2025; Sandra et al., 2025; Spasenić et al., 2025; Tadić et al., 2025; Więckowski & Sałabun, 2025). As a control method for determining the robustness of the proposed approach, it was applied in (Runic Ristic et al., 2025).

88.3 Methodology

This section presents the steps of the basic RADAR method. Any additional modification, such as RADAR II (Komatina et al., 2026), can be implemented by adjusting the normalization procedure, the method of weighting the values, the application of different approaches for modeling uncertainty, and so on.

In addition to outlining the steps and presenting them through formulas, a brief explanation and the significance of each step are provided. The explanations are adapted from (Komatina et al., 2026), where readers can find a detailed description and mathematical proof for each step.

The basic RADAR method is implemented through the following steps:

Let there be a defined set of alternatives $\{1, \ldots, i, \ldots, I\}$, which need to be evaluated and ranked according to a set of criteria $\{1, \ldots, j, \ldots, J\}$.

Step 1. Formation of the decision matrix:

$$[M_{ij}]_{I\times J}$$

Step 2. The maximum proportion matrix, α:

$$[\alpha_{ij}]_{I\times J}$$

For the benefit-type of criteria:

$$\alpha_{ij} = \frac{\frac{\max\limits_{i} M_{ij}}{M_{ij}}}{\left(\left(\frac{\max\limits_{i} M_{ij}}{M_{ij}}\right) + \left(\frac{M_{ij}}{\min\limits_{i} M_{ij}}\right)\right)}$$

For the cost-type of criteria:

$$\alpha_{ij} = \frac{\frac{M_{ij}}{\min\limits_{i} M_{ij}}}{\left(\left(\frac{\max\limits_{i} M_{ij}}{M_{ij}}\right) + \left(\frac{M_{ij}}{\min\limits_{i} M_{ij}}\right)\right)}$$

Step 3. The minimum proportion matrix, β:

$$[\beta_{ij}]_{I\times J}$$

For the benefit-type of criteria:

$$\beta_{ij} = \frac{\frac{M_{ij}}{\min\limits_{i} M_{ij}}}{\left(\left(\frac{\max\limits_{i} M_{ij}}{M_{ij}}\right) + \left(\frac{M_{ij}}{\min\limits_{i} M_{ij}}\right)\right)}$$

For the cost-type of criteria:

$$\beta_{ij} = \frac{\frac{\max\limits_{i} M_{ij}}{M_{ij}}}{\left(\left(\frac{\max\limits_{i} M_{ij}}{M_{ij}}\right) + \left(\frac{M_{ij}}{\min\limits_{i} M_{ij}}\right)\right)}$$

From the given information, the following rules can be concluded:

- a_{ij} for a benefit-type criterion is calculated in the same way as β_{ij} for a cost-type criterion. The reverse also holds.
- For every considered i, $i = 1, \ldots I$ evaluated according to any $j = 1, \ldots, J$, the following holds: $a_{ij} + \beta_{ij} = 1$.

Explanation: In the RADAR method, the normalization process is carried out in a dual manner, meaning that a single normalized value is not obtained. Instead, the normalized distance from both the maximum (a_{ij}) and minimum (b_{ij}) values of the alternatives within each criterion is calculated.

Step 4. The empty range matrix:

$$[E_{ij}]_{I\times J}$$

where

$$E_{ij} = |\alpha_{ij} - \beta_{ij}|$$

Explanation: The empty range matrix is the result of subtracting the values of the maximum and minimum proportion matrix. The values of this matrix are always within the range from 0 to 1.

Step 5. The relative relationship matrix:

$$[RR_{ij}]_{I\times J}$$

where:

$$RR_{ij} = \frac{\alpha_{ij}}{\beta_{ij} + E_{ij}}$$

Explanation: The relative relationship matrix, like the empty range matrix, falls within the range from 0 to 1. The importance of this step is to highlight alternatives that are above the relative average with respect to a given criterion, while treating those below the relative average equally. This step favors alternatives that demonstrate stable performance across a greater number of criteria.

Step 6. The weighted relative relationship matrix:

$$[WRR_{ij}]_{I\times J}$$

Where:

$$WRR_{ij} = RR_{ij} \cdot \omega_j$$

Explanation: The weighted relative relationship matrix is the step in which the weights of the considered criteria are taken into account. This adds a second dimension to the ranking of alternatives, amplifying the influence of alternatives that perform above average according to the most important criteria.

Step 7. The aggregated ranking index, RI_i:

$$RI_i = \frac{\min \sum_{j=1}^{J} WRR_i}{\sum_{j=1}^{J} WRR_i}$$

The values of RI_i need to be sorted in a nonincreasing order. The best alternative is the one with the highest RI_i value, which is always 1. The lowest-ranked alternative is the one with the smallest value of this coefficient.

88.4 Numerical example 1

A manufacturing company plans to acquire a new metal-cutting machine to improve the production process. There are a total of four options available on the market, which can be designated as alternatives, i, $i = 1, \ldots I$, where $I = 4$. The considered alternatives are evaluated and analyzed based on three criteria: cutting speed expressed in mm/min ($j = 1$), energy efficiency expressed as the number of meters cut per kWh ($j = 2$), and the machine price expressed in euros ($j = 3$). The first two criteria are benefit-type criteria, while the third is a cost-type criterion. Let the company management consider the criterion weights as $\omega_1 = 0.4$, $\omega_2 = 0.25$, and $\omega_3 = 0.35$. The decision matrix, that is, the input data, is given in Table 88.1.

After the decision matrix, which represents the first step in applying the RADAR method, the second and third steps involve calculating the elements of the maximum and minimum proportion matrices, as shown in Tables 88.2 and 88.3.

An example of calculating a single element of the maximum and minimum proportion matrix:

$$a_{11} = \frac{\frac{1300}{1250}}{\left(\left(\frac{1300}{1250}\right) + \left(\frac{1250}{1100}\right)\right)} = 0.478 \quad \beta_{11} = \frac{\frac{1250}{1100}}{\left(\left(\frac{1300}{1250}\right) + \left(\frac{1250}{1100}\right)\right)} = 0.522$$

In Step 4, the empty range matrix is calculated, as presented in Table 88.4.

TABLE 88.1 Decision matrix.

	$j = 1$	$j = 2$	$j = 3$
$i = 1$	1250	45	85000
$i = 2$	1300	42	89000
$i = 3$	1100	48	79000
$i = 4$	1250	51	88000

TABLE 88.2 Maximum proportion matrix.

	$j = 1$	$j = 2$	$j = 3$
$i = 1$	0.478	0.514	0.507
$i = 2$	0.458	0.548	0.530
$i = 3$	0.542	0.482	0.470
$i = 4$	0.478	0.452	0.524

TABLE 88.3 Minimum proportion matrix.

	$j = 1$	$j = 2$	$j = 3$
$i = 1$	0.522	0.486	0.493
$i = 2$	0.542	0.452	0.470
$i = 3$	0.458	0.518	0.530
$i = 4$	0.522	0.548	0.476

TABLE 88.4 Empty range matrix.

	$j = 1$	$j = 2$	$j = 3$
$i = 1$	0.044	0.028	0.014
$i = 2$	0.083	0.097	0.060
$i = 3$	0.083	0.036	0.060
$i = 4$	0.044	0.097	0.048

An example of calculating the first element of the empty range matrix:

$$E_{11} = |0.478 - 0.522| = 0.044$$

In Steps 5 and 6, the elements of the relative relationship matrix and the weighted relative relationship matrix are calculated, as shown in Tables 88.5 and 88.6.

The following section provides an example of calculating one element of the relative relationship matrix and one element of the weighted relative relationship matrix:

$$RR_{11} = \frac{0.478}{0.522 + 0.044} = 0.844 \quad WRR_{11} = 0.844 \cdot 0.4 = 0.337$$

In Table 88.7, according to Step 7 of the RADAR method application, the aggregated ranking index has been calculated and presented.

The first step in calculating the aggregated ranking index is to sum all WRR_{ij} values of the alternative across all criteria:

$$\sum_{j=1}^{J} WRR_1 = 0.337 + 0.250 + 0.350 = 0.937 \quad \sum_{j=1}^{J} WRR_2 = 0.293 + 0.250 + 0.350 = 0.893$$

$$\sum_{j=1}^{J} WRR_3 = 0.400 + 0.217 + 0.279 = 0.896 \quad \sum_{j=1}^{J} WRR_4 = 0.337 + 0.175 + 0.350 = 0.862$$

Then, the formula from the seventh step is applied:

$$RI_1 = \frac{0.862}{0.937} = 0.920 \quad RI_2 = \frac{0.862}{0.893} = 0.965$$

$$RI_3 = \frac{0.862}{0.896} = 0.962 \quad RI_4 = \frac{0.862}{0.862} = 1.000$$

TABLE 88.5 Relative relationship matrix.

	$j = 1$	$j = 2$	$j = 3$
$i = 1$	0.844	1.000	1.000
$i = 2$	0.733	1.000	1.000
$i = 3$	1.000	0.869	0.798
$i = 4$	0.844	0.700	1.000

TABLE 88.6 Weighted relative relationship matrix.

	$j = 1$	$j = 2$	$j = 3$
$i = 1$	0.337	0.250	0.350
$i = 2$	0.293	0.250	0.350
$i = 3$	0.400	0.217	0.279
$i = 4$	0.337	0.175	0.350

TABLE 88.7 The aggregated ranking index.

	$\sum_{j=1}^{J} WRR_i$	Ranking index	Rank
$i = 1$	0.937	0.920	4
$i = 2$	0.893	0.965	2
$i = 3$	0.896	0.962	3
$i = 4$	0.862	1.000	1

After that, the RI_i values are sorted in descending order to obtain the final ranking of the alternatives.

By applying the RADAR method, it was determined that the machine labeled as alternative $i = 4$ is the most suitable solution. A deeper analysis reveals that this alternative ranks second according to the most important criterion, ranks first according to the second criterion (which is the least important), and ranks second or third according to the third criterion, which is slightly less important than the most important one.

The alternative ranked second is $i = 2$. While it ranks first according to the most important criterion, it ranks last for the other two criteria. Out of the two conditions—extreme values for the most important criterion and stability across all criteria—only the first one is satisfied.

Alternative $i = 3$ is in third place. Although it performs worst with respect to the most important criterion, it performs best on the third criterion, which is only slightly less important than the first. For the second, least important criterion, it ranks second.

The last-ranked alternative is $i = 1$. This alternative is not the best according to any of the criteria. It shares second and third place for the first criterion, ranks third for the second, and second for the third. Therefore, it can be said that this alternative shows stability across two criteria, but it is not particularly strong in any of them to stand out as a leading option.

It should be emphasized that the differences between the values of the alternatives for each considered criterion are relatively small, that is, there is only a slight deviation between their values. Therefore, a sensitivity analysis will be conducted to examine how changes in weights affect the ranking of alternatives.

88.5 Numerical example 2

A company engaged in the sale and distribution of home appliances intends to purchase new delivery vehicles. Based on the company's budget and operational needs, a total of seven vehicle models have been shortlisted, denoted as alternatives, i, $i = 1, \ldots I$, where $I = 7$. The management evaluates the considered alternatives according to seven criteria: vehicle payload expressed in kilograms ($j = 1$), esthetic impression rated on a scale from 1 to 10 (assessed by multiple management members) ($j = 2$), fuel consumption expressed in liters per 100 km ($j = 3$), estimated annual maintenance costs expressed in euros ($j = 4$), volume of cargo space expressed in cubic meters ($j = 5$), driver comfort rated on a scale from 1 to 10 (evaluated by multiple drivers) ($j = 6$), and vehicle price expressed in euros ($j = 7$). The criteria $j = \{1, 2, 5, 6\}$ are benefit-type criteria, while the criteria $j = \{3, 4, 7\}$ are cost-type criteria. Let the company management consider the criterion weights as $\omega_1 = 0.18$, $\omega_2 = 0.07$, $\omega_3 = 0.17$, $\omega_4 = 0.13$, $\omega_5 = 0.12$, $\omega_6 = 0.08$, and $\omega_7 = 0.25$. The decision matrix is given in Table 88.8.

In the second and third steps, the elements of the maximum and minimum proportion matrices are determined (see Tables 88.9 and 88.10).

In fourth step, the empty range matrix is calculated, as presented in Table 88.11.

In Steps 5 and 6, the elements of the relative relationship matrix and the weighted relative relationship matrix are calculated, as shown in Tables 88.12 and 88.13.

In Table 88.14, according to Step 7 of the RADAR method application, the aggregated ranking index has been calculated and presented.

Based on the application of the RADAR method, alternative $i = 6$ was ranked first. It performs best according to the most important criterion $j = 7$, and is also the best with respect to criterion $j = 4$, which ranks fourth in importance. It holds second place for criterion $j = 3$, the third most important one. Although it performs below average for the remaining criteria, two of these four have very low, almost negligible importance.

TABLE 88.8 Decision matrix.

	$j = 1$	$j = 2$	$j = 3$	$j = 4$	$j = 5$	$j = 6$	$j = 7$
$i = 1$	1300	7.67	7.8	950	9	8.33	35000
$i = 2$	1250	7.33	7.4	880	8.5	6.67	32000
$i = 3$	1350	9.00	8.1	1000	10.5	9.33	42000
$i = 4$	1200	5.67	7.1	870	8	5.00	30000
$i = 5$	1320	8.00	7.6	920	9.8	7.00	38000
$i = 6$	1180	6.67	7.3	850	7.5	6.33	29000
$i = 7$	1400	6.67	8.3	1050	11	6.67	40000

TABLE 88.9 Maximum proportion matrix.

	$j = 1$	$j = 2$	$j = 3$	$j = 4$	$j = 5$	$j = 6$	$j = 7$
$i = 1$	0.494	0.465	0.508	0.503	0.505	0.402	0.501
$i = 2$	0.514	0.487	0.482	0.465	0.533	0.512	0.457
$i = 3$	0.475	0.387	0.527	0.528	0.428	0.349	0.592
$i = 4$	0.534	0.613	0.461	0.459	0.563	0.651	0.425
$i = 5$	0.487	0.444	0.495	0.487	0.462	0.488	0.542
$i = 6$	0.543	0.534	0.475	0.447	0.595	0.538	0.408
$i = 7$	0.457	0.534	0.539	0.553	0.405	0.512	0.568

TABLE 88.10 Minimum proportion matrix.

	$j = 1$	$j = 2$	$j = 3$	$j = 4$	$j = 5$	$j = 6$	$j = 7$
$i = 1$	0.506	0.535	0.492	0.497	0.495	0.598	0.499
$i = 2$	0.486	0.513	0.518	0.535	0.467	0.488	0.543
$i = 3$	0.525	0.613	0.473	0.472	0.572	0.651	0.408
$i = 4$	0.466	0.387	0.539	0.541	0.437	0.349	0.575
$i = 5$	0.513	0.556	0.505	0.513	0.538	0.512	0.458
$i = 6$	0.457	0.466	0.525	0.553	0.405	0.462	0.592
$i = 7$	0.543	0.466	0.461	0.447	0.595	0.488	0.432

TABLE 88.11 Empty range matrix.

	$j = 1$	$j = 2$	$j = 3$	$j = 4$	$j = 5$	$j = 6$	$j = 7$
$i = 1$	0.011	0.071	0.016	0.006	0.009	0.196	0.003
$i = 2$	0.028	0.026	0.037	0.071	0.066	0.024	0.087
$i = 3$	0.049	0.227	0.054	0.057	0.144	0.302	0.183
$i = 4$	0.069	0.227	0.078	0.082	0.126	0.302	0.150
$i = 5$	0.027	0.113	0.010	0.027	0.076	0.025	0.085
$i = 6$	0.085	0.068	0.050	0.105	0.189	0.076	0.183
$i = 7$	0.085	0.068	0.078	0.105	0.189	0.024	0.136

TABLE 88.12 Relative relationship matrix.

	$j = 1$	$j = 2$	$j = 3$	$j = 4$	$j = 5$	$j = 6$	$j = 7$
$i = 1$	0.956	0.766	1.000	1.000	1.000	0.506	1.000
$i = 2$	1.000	0.904	0.868	0.766	1.000	1.000	0.725
$i = 3$	0.829	0.460	1.000	1.000	0.598	0.366	1.000
$i = 4$	1.000	1.000	0.747	0.736	1.000	1.000	0.586
$i = 5$	0.901	0.663	0.961	0.902	0.753	0.908	1.000
$i = 6$	1.000	1.000	0.825	0.680	1.000	1.000	0.527
$i = 7$	0.728	1.000	1.000	1.000	0.517	1.000	1.000

TABLE 88.13 Weighted relative relationship matrix.

	$j = 1$	$j = 2$	$j = 3$	$j = 4$	$j = 5$	$j = 6$	$j = 7$
$i = 1$	0.172	0.054	0.170	0.130	0.120	0.041	0.250
$i = 2$	0.180	0.063	0.148	0.100	0.120	0.080	0.181
$i = 3$	0.149	0.032	0.170	0.130	0.072	0.029	0.250
$i = 4$	0.180	0.070	0.127	0.096	0.120	0.080	0.146
$i = 5$	0.162	0.046	0.163	0.117	0.090	0.073	0.250
$i = 6$	0.180	0.070	0.140	0.088	0.120	0.080	0.132
$i = 7$	0.131	0.070	0.170	0.130	0.062	0.080	0.250

TABLE 88.14 The aggregated ranking index.

	$\Sigma_{j=1}^{J} WRR_i$	Ranking index	Rank
$i = 1$	0.936	0.866	7
$i = 2$	0.872	0.930	4
$i = 3$	0.832	0.974	3
$i = 4$	0.819	0.989	2
$i = 5$	0.902	0.898	6
$i = 6$	0.811	1.000	1
$i = 7$	0.893	0.907	5

The second-ranked alternative is $i = 4$. This alternative performs best for criterion $j = 3$ and ranks second for the most important criterion $j = 7$, as well as for the third most important criterion $j = 4$. For the remaining criteria, it ranks either second-to-last or last.

The lowest-ranked alternative is $i = 1$. For as many as five criteria, this alternative does not appear among the top three (i.e., not in the upper half of the ranking). It holds second and third place only for criteria $j = 6$ and $j = 2$, respectively. It is important to note that these two criteria are the least important and have very little influence.

Additional explanation of the obtained ranking in this example, as well as in the numerical example 1, will be provided through a comparative analysis with other MADM methods.

88.6 Comparative and sensitivity analysis

In this section, a comparative analysis was conducted between the results obtained using the RADAR method and those derived from the application of the technique for order of preference by similarity to ideal solution (TOPSIS) (Hwang & Yoon, 1981) and elimination and choice translating reality (ÉLimination Et Choix Traduisant la REalité [ELECTRE]) (Roy, 1968) methods on the same numerical examples.

In addition to being two of the most widely used and well-established MADM methods in the literature, TOPSIS and ELECTRE are based on fundamentally different mathematical principles. The RADAR method combines certain characteristics of TOPSIS, which represents a compensatory type of method, with features of ELECTRE, which belongs to the noncompensatory category. For example, the use of proportional matrices in RADAR aligns with the logic of TOPSIS, as it involves measuring the distance from the best and worst possible solutions. On the other hand, dual normalization, relative dominance of alternatives within each criterion, and the "penalization" of poorly performing alternatives reflect principles found in ELECTRE. For this reason, comparing the results obtained using these three methods on the same numerical examples is particularly insightful.

In addition to the comparative analysis, this section also includes a sensitivity analysis conducted by varying the criteria weights. The comparative analysis is presented in Subsection 88.6.1, while the sensitivity analysis is provided in Subsection 88.6.2.

88.6.1 Comparative analysis

The first comparison of the obtained rankings using the RADAR, TOPSIS, and ELECTRE methods was conducted on numerical example 1. The results obtained by applying these three methods are presented in Table 88.15.

Based on the insights from Table 88.15, it is evident that alternative $i = 4$ is ranked as the best by all three considered methods. This is primarily due to its relatively stable performance across all criteria—it is not ranked last according to any of them.

The most significant difference in this example lies in the ranking of alternatives $i = 1$ and $i = 2$. ELECTRE places them in a tie for second and third place, whereas RADAR and TOPSIS reverse their positions—placing one in second and the other in fourth place. This discrepancy occurs because TOPSIS is a compensatory method, allowing alternative $i = 1$ to be ranked second even though it is not the best in any single criterion.

In contrast, RADAR penalizes alternative $i = 1$ for not being particularly strong in any criterion, especially since it is only tied for second/third place with respect to the most important one. In this case, RADAR favors $i = 2$ because it performs best on the most important criterion, even though it performs worst on the other two. Nevertheless, being the best on the most important criterion was not sufficient for it to achieve the top overall ranking.

Another notable difference in this example is that ELECTRE ranks alternative $i = 3$ last. Apparently, the fact that it performs worst on the most important criterion is considered a significant "penalty" by the ELECTRE method.

Of course, the results should be interpreted with caution, as even small changes in the criterion weights or the decision matrix elements can affect the final ranking. When it comes to numerical example 2, Table 88.16 presents the ranking results obtained by applying the three methods. What follows is an explanation of the results.

As in numerical example 1, in this case as well, one alternative is ranked the best by all three methods ($i = 6$). In fact, this alternative holds the first position for the most important criterion, and ranks first and second in two other important criteria (as explained in Section 88.5). Since all three methods are in agreement on this matter, there is no need for further discussion regarding the position of this alternative.

Significant discrepancies in the results can be observed for several alternatives. First, for alternative $i = 1$, RADAR penalizes it due to its instability. It performs below average in five criteria, which is why it is placed at the very bottom of the ranking. On the other hand, TOPSIS allows for compensation, and good results in the remaining criteria help this

TABLE 88.15 Ranking results for numerical example 1 using RADAR, TOPSIS, and ELECTRE.

	RADAR	TOPSIS	ELECTRE
$i = 1$	4	2	2–3
$i = 2$	2	4	2–3
$i = 3$	3	3	4
$i = 4$	1	1	1

TABLE 88.16 Ranking results for numerical example 2 using RADAR, TOPSIS, and ELECTRE.

	RADAR	TOPSIS	ELECTRE
$i = 1$	7	3	5–6
$i = 2$	4	2	2
$i = 3$	3	4	5–6
$i = 4$	2	6	3–4
$i = 5$	6	5	3–4
$i = 6$	1	1	1
$i = 7$	5	7	7

alternative achieve a better overall rank. Finally, ELECTRE places it around fifth or sixth, as a kind of compromise—acknowledging its strong performance, but mostly in less important criteria.

A major difference is also seen with alternative $i = 4$. RADAR ranks it second, because it is second in the most important criterion and performs well in two other important ones (as also explained in Section 88.5). TOPSIS places it next to last, as it ranks last or second to last in four criteria—one of which is the second most important. ELECTRE recognizes this alternative's dominance, especially in the most important criterion and two others, and thus positions it in the middle of the ranking, around third or fourth place.

Aside from some smaller variations (by one or possibly two positions), there is also a notable discrepancy in the case of alternative $i = 7$. TOPSIS and ELECTRE both place it last, while RADAR ranks it fifth. Although it performs below the relative average in five criteria, it is ranked first in the second most important criterion and in one other. According to RADAR's logic, this was enough to move it from the last to the fifth position.

Thus, it can be concluded that the differences in the mathematical basis and the underlying logic of various MADM methods may lead to different rankings of alternatives. For this reason, a good strategy is to apply multiple methods and seek a compromise solution. Comparative analysis, such as the one presented in this section, enables decision-makers to view the problem from multiple perspectives, allowing them to conduct a better analysis before making a final decision.

88.6.2 Sensitivity analysis

In this subsection, a sensitivity analysis of the obtained solution using the RADAR method was conducted. The aim is to determine how changes in the criteria weights affect potential changes in the ranking of alternatives. Table 88.17 presents numerical example 1 with three new variants of weight values, in which the weight of criterion $j = 1$ is gradually decreased, while the weight of criterion $j = 2$ is increased.

TABLE 88.17 Sensitivity analysis of numerical example 1—gradual decrease of ω_1 and increase of ω_2.

	0.4; 0.25; 0.35	0.35; 0.3; 0.35	0.3; 0.35; 0.35	0.25; 0.4; 0.35
$i = 1$	4	4	4	4
$i = 2$	2	3	3	3
$i = 3$	3	2	2	2
$i = 4$	1	1	1	1

TABLE 88.18 Sensitivity analysis of numerical example 1—gradual decrease of ω_2 and increase of ω_3

	0.25; 0.4; 0.35	0.25; 0.35; 0.4	0.25; 0.3; 0.45	0.25; 0.25; 0.5
$i = 1$	4	4	4	4
$i = 2$	3	3	3	3
$i = 3$	2	2	1	1
$i = 4$	1	1	2	2

Table 88.17 shows that the only change observed across the three newly considered scenarios is the swap between the second and third positions in the ranking. By increasing the value of ω_2 and simultaneously decreasing ω_1, alternative $i = 3$ moved to second place, while $i = 2$ dropped to third. This occurred because alternative $i = 3$ had performed poorly according to the most important criterion, ω_1, but was ranked highly for the other two criteria. As the importance of this criterion decreased, this alternative gained the opportunity to improve its ranking position.

Now, we can focus on the current set of weights (the last scenario): $\omega_1 = 0.25$, $\omega_2 = 0.4$, and $\omega_3 = 0.35$, and gradually decrease the weight of the criterion $i = 2$ while increasing the weight of the criterion $i = 3$ (Table 88.18).

In the first change of criteria weights, there was no alteration in the ranking of alternatives. With the second change, it is observed that the top two alternatives switched places. Alternative $i = 3$ became the top-ranked option because criterion $j = 3$, in which this alternative performs best, became extremely important. Additionally, this alternative ranks second with respect to criterion $j = 2$, which at this point is the second most important criterion. In the final weight adjustment, the ranking remained unchanged, as the first two criteria combined were now equally important as the third criterion, according to which this alternative performs best.

Considering that numerical example 2 has seven criteria, and it is very difficult to closely follow the changes, as was the case with numerical example 1, the sensitivity analysis in this case will be conducted by swapping the weights of the most important and the least important criteria. Thus, $\omega_7 = 0.25$ will now be $\omega_7 = 0.07$, while $\omega_2 = 0.07$ will now be $\omega_2 = 0.25$. The ranking results for these two scenarios are presented in Table 88.19.

Following the aforementioned change in criterion weights, where the most important criterion becomes the least important and vice versa, slight but, in some cases, drastic changes occurred. For alternatives $i = \{1,3,4,7\}$, these changes are reflected in a shift of two positions (either an improvement or a decline). For alternatives $i = 1$ and $i = 7$, these changes were positive, as both alternatives perform better with respect to criterion $j = 2$, which is the most important one in the second scenario.

Furthermore, alternative $i = 3$ jumped from third to first place in the ranking. Simply put, this alternative performs best according to the most important criterion in the second scenario and also ranks highly in three other criteria, including second place with respect to the second most important criterion. In contrast, alternative $i = 4$ dropped from second to fourth place. The main reason lies in the fact that it now ranks last with respect to the most important criterion.

TABLE 88.19 Ranking results after the weight swap between the most and the least important criteria in numerical example 2.

	$\omega_2 = 0.07; \omega_7 = 0.25$	$\omega_2 = 0.25; \omega_7 = 0.07$
$i = 1$	7	5
$i = 2$	4	7
$i = 3$	3	1
$i = 4$	2	4
$i = 5$	6	2
$i = 6$	1	6
$i = 7$	5	3

Alternative $i = 2$ worsened its ranking by three positions, falling from fourth to seventh place. This change occurred because in the first scenario it was ranked third according to the most important criterion, whereas now it is ranked fourth (below the relative average).

Besides these "minor" changes, there were also two drastic shifts in ranking. Alternative $i = 5$ jumped from sixth to second place. In the first scenario, it was fifth with respect to the most important criterion, whereas now it ranks second. Conversely, alternative $i = 6$ significantly dropped in ranking, falling from first to sixth place. This occurred because it was ranked first according to the most important criterion in the first scenario, but now ranks fifth.

88.7 Conclusions

This chapter presented the main characteristics and the application procedure of the RADAR method. The method was illustrated through two numerical examples, and the obtained results were compared with two well-known and reliable methods that are based on different mathematical principles and decision-making logic—TOPSIS and ELECTRE. In addition, a sensitivity analysis of the results was conducted by varying the weights of the criteria.

Through comparison with TOPSIS and ELECTRE, it was shown that these methods were in complete agreement regarding the alternatives that were ranked the highest. However, each method produced slightly different results due to their distinct decision-making logic. In some cases, the results obtained using the RADAR method were more aligned with those from TOPSIS, while in other cases, they were more similar to the results from ELECTRE. As previously mentioned, this is because RADAR combines certain elements of both compensatory and noncompensatory MADM methods. For this reason, in some situations, TOPSIS and ELECTRE may assign the same rank to a particular alternative, while RADAR positions the same alternative noticeably higher or lower in the ranking.

The sensitivity analysis showed that RADAR is responsive to changes in the weights of the criteria, especially in cases where the weights of the most and the least important criteria are swapped. In this way, the method proved to be reliable, as it reacts to changes in the ranking of alternatives in accordance with decision-making logic. Furthermore, it can be said that the method does not automatically favor alternatives with high numerical values, but rather responds dynamically to changes in criterion importance.

The method clearly identifies the weaknesses of alternatives with respect to the most important criteria and does not easily allow for compensation through less important ones. Additionally, it provides an opportunity for alternatives that demonstrate stable performance across multiple, particularly important, criteria to achieve a higher rank.

Based on all the above, it can be concluded that RADAR can serve as a reliable decision-making tool, but care should be taken in choosing the appropriate context for its application. After all, the same holds true for any other MADM method. Ultimately, it is up to the decision-makers to assess which method to use in a given situation or whether to apply multiple methods in order to analyze the problem from different perspectives.

References

Abdulvahitoğlu, A. (2025). A symmetry-based spherical Fuzzy MCDM approach for the strategic assessment of alternative fuels toward sustainable energy policies. *Symmetry, 17*, 1089. https://doi.org/10.3390/sym17071089.

Aleksić, A., Tadić, D., Komatina, N., & Nestić, S. (2025). Failure mode and effects analysis integrated with multi-attribute decision-making methods under uncertainty: A systematic literature review. *Mathematics, 13*, 2216. https://doi.org/10.3390/math13132216.

Ecer, F., Pamucar, D., & Demir, G. (2025). Decision-analytics-based electric vehicle charging station location selection: A cutting-edge fuzzy rough framework. *Energy Reports, 14*, 711–735. https://doi.org/10.1016/j.egyr.2025.06.035.

Hwang, C. L., & Yoon, K. (1981). Methods for multiple attribute decision making. *Multiple attribute decision making: methods and applications a state-of-the-art survey,* 58–191.

Karjust, K., Mehrparvar, M., Kaganski, S., & Raamets, T. (2025). Development of a sustainability-oriented KPI Selection model for manufacturing processes. *Sustainability, 17*, 6374. https://doi.org/10.3390/su17146374.

Komatina, N. (2024). A compromise-based MADM approach for prioritizing failures: Integrating the RADAR method within the FMEA framework. *Jurnal Sistem Dan Manajemen Industri, 8*, 73–88. https://doi.org/10.30656/jsmi.v8i2.9283.

Komatina, N. (2025a). A novel BWM-RADAR approach for multi-attribute selection of equipment in the automotive industry. *Spectrum of Mechanical Engineering and Operational Research, 2*, 104–120. https://doi.org/10.31181/smeor21202531.

Komatina, N. (2025b). Integrating hybrid FAHP–FRADAR approach and the FMEA framework for evidence-informed risk assessment in football player transfers. *Journal of Data Science and Intelligent Systems*. https://doi.org/10.47852/bonviewjdsis52025293.

Komatina, N., & Marinković, D. (2025). Optimization of PFMEA team composition in the automotive industry using the IPF-RADAR approach. *Algorithms, 18*, 342. https://doi.org/10.3390/a18060342.

Komatina, N., Marinković, D., Tadić, D., & Pamučar, D. (2025). Advancing PFMEA decision-making: FRADAR based prioritization of failure modes using AP, RPN, and multi-attribute assessment in the automotive industry. *Tehnički Glasnik/Technical Journal*. 19:accepted for publication. https://doi.org/10.31803/tg-20250221185213.

Komatina, N., Marinkovic, D., & Babič, M. (2026). Fundamental characteristics and applicability of the RADAR method: Proof of ranking consistency. *Spectrum of Operational Research, 3*, 63–80. https://doi.org/10.31181/sor31202635.

Mandal, N., Sarkar, P., & Petrović, N. (2025). Multi-criteria decision-making for ranking renewable energy sources: A case study from the republic of Serbia. *JEMSE, 4*, 109–121. https://doi.org/10.56578/jemse040203.

Marinato, V. H. A., Cazeri, G. T., Moraes, G. H. S. M. D., Zanon, L. G., Sigahi, T. F. A. C., Rampasso, I. S., et al. (2025). Assessing the quality of virtual student internships in Brazilian organizations: Potential and use of fuzzy TOPSIS class. *AppliedMath, 5*, 84. https://doi.org/10.3390/appliedmath5030084.

Petrović, N., Jovanović, V., Petrović, M., Nikolić, B., & Mihajlović, J. (2025). Comparative investigation of normalization techniques and their influence on MCDM ranking – A case study. *Spec Mech Eng Oper Res, 2*, 172–190. https://doi.org/10.31181/smeor21202542.

Petrović, T., Tadić, D., Marinković, D., Đurić, G., & Komatina, N. (2025). Developing a new approach for assessing and improving business excellence: Integrating fuzzy analytic hierarchical process and constraint programming model. *Symmetry, 17*, 607. https://doi.org/10.3390/sym17040607.

Roy, B. (1968). Classement et choix en présence de points de vue multiples. *Revue Française d'informatique et de Recherche Opérationnelle, 2*, 57–75. https://doi.org/10.1051/ro/196802v100571.

Runic Ristic, M., Savic Tot, T., Ristic, I., Tot, V., Radosevic, T., & Marinkovic, D. (2025). Evaluation of leadership styles in multinational corporations using the fuzzy TOPSIS method. *Systems, 13*, 636. https://doi.org/10.3390/systems13080636.

Sandra, M., Narayanamoorthy, S., Suvitha, K., Pamucar, D., & Kang, D. (2025). Optimizing non-invasive remote sensing for geothermal exploration with T-spherical dual hesitant fuzzy decision model. *Facta Universitatis, Series: Mechanical Engineering*. https://doi.org/10.22190/FUME241116016S Online first.

Spasenić, I., Tadić, D., Čabarkapa, M., Marinković, D., & Komatina, N. (2025). Cloud platform selection using extended multi-attribute decision-making methods with interval type-2 fuzzy sets. *Axioms, 14*, 469. https://doi.org/10.3390/axioms14060469.

Tadić, D., Lukić, J., Komatina, N., Marinković, D., & Pamučar, D. (2025). A Fuzzy decision-making approach to electric vehicle evaluation and ranking. *Tehnicki Vjesnik/Technical Gazette, 4*, 1066–1075. https://doi.org/10.17559/TV-20250223002410.

Więckowski, J., & Sałabun, W. (2025). Making more informed decisions in multi-criteria problems under uncertain conditions of criteria weights: Drone selection study case. *Facta Universitatis, Series: Mechanical Engineering*. https://doi.org/10.22190/FUME240930019W Online first.

Chapter 89

OPARA: Objective pairwise adjusted ratio analysis for multi-attribute decision-making

Mehdi Keshavarz-Ghorabaee

Department of Management, Faculty of Humanities (Azadshahr Branch), Gonbad Kavous University, Gonbad Kavous, Iran

89.1 Introduction

In the complex field of decision-making, multicriteria decision-making (MCDM) techniques provide very useful aids to stakeholders for assessing complex alternatives with numerous and sometimes conflicting criteria. Such methods are indeed crucial for situations when, in order to make the best decision, trade-offs need to be considered between aspects related to different dimensions (economic, social, technical, environmental) at the same time. Within the broad class of MCDM methods, one persistent difficulty has been to make effective use of the complete decision matrix in the evaluation process. Many existing techniques assess alternatives according to their individual information or to partially aggregated ones, disregarding valuable interalternative and intercriterion relationships (Kou et al., 2011; Mikhailov, 2003; Taherdoost & Madanchian, 2023; Wang & Triantaphyllou, 2008).

To address this issue, a new method, called objective pairwise adjusted ratio analysis (OPARA), has been proposed. OPARA is based on a comprehensive framework that considers pairwise comparisons among all alternatives for each criterion, which could lead to a more stable outcome and preserve the information in the decision-making process. This approach is intended to better address the shortcomings of traditional methods, and at the same time, to ensure a more open and interpretable decision-making activity based on including the full scope of available data (Keshavarz-Ghorabaee et al., 2024).

Classical MCDM techniques, including simple additive weighting (SAW), weighted aggregated sum product assessment (WASPAS), and complex proportional assessment (COPRAS), aggregate directly the normalized (standardized to unity) and weighted performance scores of the alternatives. These procedures consider but do not take into account the context of the performance of one alternative versus the others in the alternative set. They are computationally simple and practical but may neglect comparative dynamics, which can provide deeper insights into the relative strengths and weaknesses of the alternatives (Cai et al., 2024; Podvezko, 2011; Wang et al., 2016; Zavadskas et al., 2013). On the other hand, techniques like technique for order preference by similarity to ideal solution (TOPSIS), VIseKriterijumska Optimizacija I Kompromisno Resenje (VIKOR), and evaluation based on distance from average solution (EDAS) use reference-point approaches, in which each alternative is evaluated according to its distance from the ideal and nadir solutions. These approaches offer a comparative benchmarking result, comparing alternatives to idealized benchmarks. Although useful, they still do not take the best advantage of the structure of the actual decision matrix, particularly the relations between every pair of alternatives (Çelikbilek & Tüysüz, 2020; Jahan et al., 2011; Khan & Maity, 2017; Özçekiç, 2025).

A common drawback of these methods is that the decision matrix is only partially employed. The majority of techniques utilize only the row-wise data of individual alternatives or the comparisons with artificially created reference points, and so the useful pairwise information encoded in the matrix is largely overlooked. This issue motivated the development of OPARA, which makes it possible to exploit the entire grid through all pairwise comparisons of all pairs of alternatives with respect to all criteria. OPARA is a systematic method that uses the whole decision matrix by comparing all the alternatives against each other for each criterion. Richer information about each alternative's position within the whole decision context can be obtained by ratio-based comparisons in OPARA. The basic insight is that an informative evaluation may not be obtained by evaluating an alternative by itself or with respect to a fixed reference, and that knowing how the alternative performs with respect to the other alternatives can be more effective (Damjanović et al., 2024; Keshavarz-Ghorabaee et al., 2025; Milinković et al., 2025).

Encyclopedia of Multi-Attribute Decision-Making (MADM). DOI: https://doi.org/10.1016/B978-0-443-33275-3.00058-0

For each criterion, the method calculates the pairwise ratio of each alternative to all the remaining ones. The ratios signal how much better or worse one choice is than the rest, reflecting both direct and contextual performance. The outcome is a matrix of pairwise ratios for a detailed view of the decision space. However, unadjusted pairwise ratios can become distorted by particular aspects, for example, the magnitude or the type of each criterion. OPARA mitigates this problem by taking two crucial adjustment factors into account, namely, range-based and linearity-based adjustments. The range of values of each criterion can have a great impact on the calculation of the ratios. The one with a large range can change, for instance, the relative role of the signs inside the pairwise comparisons. To alleviate this, OPARA includes an adjustment parameter where the range is used as a moderating factor, preventing criteria with larger variability from dominating the evaluation. On the other hand, other criteria could be nonlinear. OPARA provides decision-making experts with the ability to include a linearity adjustment parameter to represent their domain knowledge or empirical knowledge that affects the criterion. This parameter allows for a correct interpretation of the pairwise ratios depending on the characteristics of the criterion. Based on the adjustments, OPARA maintains the original data without using any normalization process, which usually results in an unavoidable loss of, or distortion to, the information (Keshavarz-Ghorabaee et al., 2024; Vo, 2024).

There are several advantages to our OPARA approach compared to other MCDM methods. Since all entries of the decision matrix are included and all alternatives are compared to one another, the myopic approach of partial rankings is circumvented, and no information is wasted. Furthermore, OPARA retains interpretable information in the sense that no scale or transformation of the data is needed, as opposed to many other methods. Additionally, the presence of range and linearity adjustments allows OPARA to be adapted to particular decision situations and criterion characteristics. OPARA is inspired by methods such as the analytic hierarchy process, which can consider pairwise comparisons, but instead embeds these principles into an objective framework, without the requirement for judgment matrices. It can be used in research and applied opportunities, especially in areas where the semantics of raw data matter (e.g., for environmental assessment, financial evaluation, or policy analysis).

The remainder of this chapter details the OPARA method, along with two illustrative examples (a simple example and a computer numerical control [CNC] machine selection example taken from an industrial application). A comparison with other MCDM approaches is then made to verify the efficiency of the method. Key thoughts and future directions for research and application are offered at the end of the chapter.

89.2 Methodology

The OPARA method is a new MCDM method where the evaluation and ranking of alternatives based on objective information is enhanced and does not require a normalizing process or subjective judgment. This approach utilizes two specific parameters: range-based and linearity-based, for pairwise comparison in order to provide a more balanced and comprehensive evaluation. The approach includes the following steps:

Step 1. Construct the decision matrix

The first step involves identifying the decision criteria and assigning weights to each criterion based on their relative importance. Then, the set of alternatives to be evaluated is defined, and a decision matrix is constructed. All entries in the decision matrix must be strictly positive. If any values are zero or negative, a transformation technique should be applied to ensure positivity.

Let $X = [x_{ij}]_{n \times m}$ denote the decision matrix, where:

- n is the number of alternatives,
- m is the number of criteria,
- x_{ij} represents the performance value of alternative i with respect to criterion j,
- w_j is the weight of criterion j, with $\sum w_j = 1$.

Step 2. Compute range-based pairwise adjusted ratios (RPAR)

In this step, the relative dominance of alternative k over alternative l is evaluated through range-adjusted ratios, which account for the variability of each criterion across all alternatives.

For each pair (k, l), the RPAR is calculated as:

$$RPAR_{kl} = \sum_{j \in BC} w_j \left(\frac{x_{kj}}{x_{lj}} \right)^{\rho_j} + \sum_{j \in NC} w_j \left(\frac{x_{lj}}{x_{kj}} \right)^{\rho_j}, \quad k,\ l \in \{1,\ 2,\ \ldots,\ n\} \tag{89.1}$$

Here:

- BC and NC denote the sets of benefit and cost criteria, respectively.

- ρ_j is a range-based adjustment parameter for criterion j, computed using:

$$\rho_j = \begin{cases} \dfrac{(\alpha - 1)\max\limits_i x_{ij} + \min\limits_i x_{ij}}{\alpha \max\limits_i x_{ij}} & if \ \dfrac{\max\limits_i x_{ij} - \min\limits_i x_{ij}}{\max\limits_i x_{ij} + \min\limits_i x_{ij}} > \beta \\ 1 & otherwise \end{cases} \tag{89.2}$$

Recommended values for the parameters are $\alpha = 5$ and $\beta = 0.8$. This adjustment moderates the impact of criteria with large ranges, reducing potential dominance over the decision outcome.

Step 3. Compute linearity-based pairwise adjusted ratios (LPAR)

This step adjusts pairwise comparisons based on the linearity or nonlinearity of the criteria's scales. The LPAR between alternatives k and l is calculated as:

$$LPAR_{kl} = \sum_{j \in BC} w_j \left(\frac{x_{kj}}{x_{lj}}\right)^{\tau_j} + \sum_{j \in NC} w_j \left(\frac{x_{lj}}{x_{kj}}\right)^{\tau_j}, \quad k, \ l \in \{1, \ 2, \ \ldots, \ n\} \tag{89.3}$$

Where:

- τ_j is a linearity adjustment parameter set by the decision-maker,

- $\tau_j = 1$ indicates a linear criterion,
- $\tau_j > 1$ amplifies the effect,
- $\tau_j < 1$ diminishes the effect.

This parameter allows customization of the evaluation process according to the intrinsic nature of each criterion.

Step 4. Compute aggregated pairwise adjusted ratios (APAR)

The two types of adjusted ratios (RPAR and LPAR) are then aggregated using a convex combination:

$$APAR_{kl} = \omega RPAR_{kl} + (1 - \omega) LPAR_{kl} \tag{89.4}$$

Where:

- $\omega \in [0, \ 1]$ is the aggregation parameter that balances the influence of range-based and linearity-based adjustments.

Step 5. Compute final scores and ranking

The final score of each alternative i is calculated based on its relative dominance over all other alternatives. The score is defined as:

$$S_i = \frac{1}{n}\left(\sum_{l=1}^{n}\left(\frac{APAR_{il}}{\sum_{k=1}^{n} APAR_{kl}}\right)\right) \tag{89.5}$$

Higher scores indicate better performance. Alternatives are ranked in descending order of their scores.

89.3 Numerical example 1

To illustrate the practical steps and computational procedure of the OPARA method, a simplified MCDM example is presented in this section. This example serves as a basic demonstration of the OPARA methodology and highlights how it can be applied to derive a meaningful ranking of alternatives without the need for data normalization.

The decision problem involves evaluating four alternatives against three criteria. Among these, the first two criteria (C_1) and (C_2) are benefit-type criteria where higher values are preferred, whereas the third criterion (C_3) is a cost-type criterion where lower values are more desirable.

The performance of the alternatives with respect to each criterion, along with their corresponding weights and linearity adjustment parameters, is summarized in Table 89.1.

As stated in the methodology, the OPARA method does not require normalization of the decision matrix. Instead, it applies two types of pairwise comparisons: one based on the range of each criterion (RPAR) and the other based on the assumed linearity or nonlinearity of the criteria (LPAR). These two are then aggregated to calculate the final scores of each alternative. For this example, it is assumed that the following values for the OPARA parameters, as determined by the decision-maker as:

$\alpha = 5$ (range adjustment sensitivity),
$\beta = 0.8$ (threshold for range-based adjustment activation),
$\omega = 0.5$ (equal weighting of RPAR and LPAR in the aggregation step).

TABLE 89.1 Decision matrix with criteria weights and threshold values (example 1).

	C_1 (BC)	C_2 (BC)	C_3 (NC)
w_j	0.25	0.35	0.4
τ_j	1	0.9	1.1
A_1	100	9	1100
A_2	10	7	1400
A_3	120	25	1000
A_4	110	1	1700

TABLE 89.2 Range-based pairwise adjusted ratios values for each pair of alternatives (example 1).

	A_1	A_2	A_3	A_4
A_1	1.000	2.577	0.732	2.915
A_2	0.638	1.000	0.444	2.207
A_3	1.529	3.441	1.000	5.665
A_4	0.588	2.174	0.494	1.000

Using Eq. (89.2) for each criterion, and the values of α and β as defined above, the ρ_j values are computed as follows:

ρ_1=0.817 (benefit criterion),
ρ_2=0.808 (benefit criterion),
ρ_3=1 (cost criterion).

For example,

$$\rho_1 = \frac{(5-1) \times 120 + 10}{5 \times 120} = 0.817$$

These values moderate the influence of criteria with wide ranges and ensure no single criterion dominates the evaluation due to scale alone. Using (89.1) and the calculated ρ_j values, the weighted RPAR values for each pair of alternatives are computed. The RPAR matrix is shown in Table 89.2.
For example,

$$RPAR_{12} = \left(0.25 \times \left(\frac{100}{10}\right)^{0.817}\right) + \left(0.35 \times \left(\frac{9}{7}\right)^{0.808}\right) + \left(0.4 \times \left(\frac{1400}{1100}\right)^{1}\right) = 2.577$$

Diagonal elements are always 1.0, reflecting that each alternative is equally preferable to itself.
Next, (89.3) and the τ_j values are used to reflect the effect of linearity or nonlinearity in each criterion's scale. The computed LPAR values are given in Table 89.3.
For example,

$$LPAR_{23} = \left(0.25 \times \left(\frac{10}{120}\right)^{1}\right) + \left(0.35 \times \left(\frac{7}{25}\right)^{0.9}\right) + \left(0.4 \times \left(\frac{1000}{1400}\right)^{1.1}\right) = 0.408$$

These values reflect how performance differences are scaled based on the assumed behavior (linear or nonlinear) of each criterion.

According to Eq. (89.4) and $\omega = 0.5$, a simple average of the RPAR and LPAR values is computed to obtain the APAR, shown in Table 89.4.

For example,

$$APAR_{34} = 0.5 \times 5.665 + 0.5 \times 7.332 = 6.498$$

The aggregated matrix provides a comprehensive view of each alternative's dominance over others, integrating both range sensitivity and nonlinearity effects.

Using the APAR matrix and Eq. (89.5), the final score of each alternative is computed based on its average relative dominance across all comparisons, as outlined in the OPARA methodology. The results are presented in Table 89.5.

TABLE 89.3 **Linearity-based pairwise adjusted ratios values for each pair of alternatives (example 1).**

	A_1	A_2	A_3	A_4
A_1	1.000	3.460	0.708	3.402
A_2	0.611	1.000	0.408	2.535
A_3	1.622	4.680	1.000	7.332
A_4	0.571	3.134	0.472	1.000

TABLE 89.4 **Aggregated pairwise adjusted ratios values for each pair of alternatives (example 1).**

	A_1	A_2	A_3	A_4
A_1	1.000	3.019	0.720	3.158
A_2	0.625	1.000	0.426	2.371
A_3	1.576	4.060	1.000	6.498
A_4	0.580	2.654	0.483	1.000

TABLE 89.5 **Final scores and ranking of alternatives (example 1).**

	S_i	**Rank**
A_1	0.266	2
A_2	0.151	4
A_3	0.419	1
A_4	0.165	3

For example,

$$S_1 = \frac{1}{4}\left(\frac{1}{3.78} + \frac{3.019}{10.733} + \frac{0.720}{2.629} + \frac{3.158}{13.027}\right) = 0.266$$

As can be observed, alternative A_3 achieves the highest final score, indicating its superior performance across the three criteria when evaluated using the OPARA framework. Alternative A_2, on the other hand, receives the lowest score and is therefore ranked last. The results demonstrate the ability of the OPARA method to distinguish among competing alternatives without requiring normalization or subjective inputs.

89.4 Numerical example 2

In this section, a real application example is provided to illustrate the practical value and efficiency of the OPARA approach. The chosen case concerns the selection of the best CNC machine tool, a very important task in today's competitive manufacturing industry. This example demonstrates how the OPARA method can be used in complex real-world decision-making problems, where various conflicting criteria need to be taken into account.

CNC machines have become essential in the contemporary fabrication and manufacturing industry as a result of their high precision, flexibility, and automation capability. Choosing the suitable CNC machine from the numerous available ones is a fundamental step, and determines directly the production efficiency, the product quality, as well as the operational cost. The investment in CNC machinery is considerable, and therefore, such a decision should be based on objective and truthful information.

Classic techniques like cost-based comparison or subjective assessment by domain experts can have biased and not ideal selection in practice. To alleviate this limitation, MCDM approaches, such as OPARA, provide an attractive alternative; it incorporates quantitative analysis and pairwise performance comparison without the need for normalization and subjective judgment.

This example is taken from the research of Sun (2002) in which the technical efficiency of 21 CNC lathes was assessed with data envelopment analysis. The machines were examined with respect to its cost and specifications. The same data set is used, and the OPARA approach is considered for ranking and selecting the best machine. This evaluation takes into account seven criteria of decision:

CC: Capital cost (NT$) – nonbeneficial criterion
SS: Spindle speed range (rpm) – beneficial
TC: Tool capacity (number of tools) – beneficial
TX: Rapid traverse rate of X-Axis (m/min) – nonbeneficial
TZ: Rapid traverse rate of Z-Axis (m/min) – nonbeneficial
MD: Maximum machining diameter (mm) – beneficial
ML: Maximum machining length (mm) – beneficial

These criteria collectively reflect the economic and technical capabilities of each machine. The decision matrix includes 21 machines (A_1 to A_{21}), whose performances across the seven criteria are listed in Table 89.6 (provided in the original text). The weight vector representing the relative importance of each criterion is as follows: $w_1 = 0.1148$ (CC), $w_2 = 0.1808$ (SS), $w_3 = 0.1884$ (TC), $w_4 = 0.1197$ (TX), $w_5 = 0.1148$ (TZ), $w_6 = 0.1546$ (MD), $w_7 = 0.1268$ (ML). These weights reflect a balanced consideration of both cost and technical performance. To apply the OPARA method, the following parameter values were used: $\alpha = 5$, $\beta = 0.8$, $\omega = 0.5$, $\tau_j = 1$ for all criteria, indicating that each criterion is assumed to have a linear effect. The decision matrix for 21 CNC lathes based on these criteria is presented in Table 89.6.

After computing the adjusted pairwise ratios and aggregating them, the final scores and rankings of all 21 alternatives were obtained. These results are compared with six other well-known MCDM techniques, including SAW, WASPAS, COPRAS, TOPSIS, VIKOR, and EDAS.

To assess the consistency of the OPARA results with other established methods, Spearman's rank correlation coefficient (ρ) was calculated. The results are shown in Table 89.7.

The results obtained through the OPARA method demonstrate a high level of consistency with other well-established MCDM techniques. To quantitatively assess this consistency, Spearman's rank correlation coefficient (ρ) was employed, comparing the OPARA-derived ranking of the 21 CNC machines with those produced by six

TABLE 89.6 Decision matrix for computer numerical control machine tool selection.

	CC	SS	TC	TX	TZ	MD	ML
A_1	1200000	5590	8	24	24	205	350
A_2	1550000	3465	8	20	20	280	520
A_3	1400000	5950	12	15	20	250	469
A_4	1100000	5940	12	12	15	230	600
A_5	1200000	5940	12	12	16	150	330
A_6	1500000	3465	12	6	12	260	420
A_7	2600000	3960	12	12	16	300	625
A_8	1320000	4950	12	24	30	240	340
A_9	1180000	4480	8	24	24	250	330
A_{10}	1550000	3950	12	15	20	280	460
A_{11}	1600000	3450	12	15	20	280	460
A_{12}	1200000	3465	8	20	24	264	400
A_{13}	1350000	2970	8	20	24	264	400
A_{14}	1400000	2970	12	24	30	300	600
A_{15}	1350000	3465	12	30	30	264	350
A_{16}	1450000	2970	12	20	24	300	400
A_{17}	1520000	2475	12	20	24	300	400
A_{18}	1376000	4752	12	20	24	235	350
A_{19}	1440000	4752	12	20	24	235	600
A_{20}	1824000	3790	10	12	20	300	530
A_{21}	1920000	3790	10	12	20	300	1030

alternative methods: SAW, WASPAS, COPRAS, TOPSIS, VIKOR, and EDAS. The Spearman's ρ values between OPARA and each of these methods are remarkably high, with all correlations exceeding 0.86, and several above 0.97.

The result supports a good and statistically significant overlap between OPARA and the other methods that are considered. Such strong convergence indicates that the OPARA approach is not only theoretically well-grounded but also effective in reproducing decision patterns found in other credible approaches. In addition, the high agreement of OPARA results with techniques such as TOPSIS and VIKOR demonstrates OPARA's ability to capture not only the absolute but also the relative performance of alternatives in multicriteria frameworks. The pairwise adjusted ratio approach of OPARA, which considers both range-based and linearity-based adjustments, leads to finer ranking by directly comparing the relative dominance of each alternative over others. The latter treatment leads to rankings that are more consistent with the decision context and decision matrix structure. Furthermore, OPARA does not require normalization of the input data or any subjective mapping of data, and therefore it is very suitable for real-world industrial problems in which the technical attributes are measured in different units and scales. The OPARA approach maintains the original nature and interpretation of the data through direct comparisons and mathematically-based refinements, thereby enhancing the transparency and credibility of decision-making.

TABLE 89.7 The results of objective pairwise adjusted ratio analysis (OPARA) and the other multicriteria decision-making approaches.

	S_i	Rank						
		OPARA	SAW	WASPAS	COPRAS	TOPSIS	VIKOR	EDAS
A_1	0.0435	16	16	17	17	12	18	17
A_2	0.0436	15	19	16	15	15	17	14
A_3	0.0526	4	3	3	4	3	2	3
A_4	0.0587	2	1	1	1	1	1	1
A_5	0.0520	6	5	6	5	5	12	5
A_6	0.0599	1	2	2	2	4	7	4
A_7	0.0523	5	6	5	6	6	6	8
A_8	0.0447	13	12	13	14	14	11	15
A_9	0.0422	18	18	18	19	17	19	19
A_{10}	0.0486	9	8	7	8	9	4	6
A_{11}	0.0474	10	10	10	10	10	9	10
A_{12}	0.0421	19	20	20	18	18	20	18
A_{13}	0.0403	21	21	21	21	20	21	20
A_{14}	0.0452	12	13	12	12	13	15	13
A_{15}	0.0414	20	17	19	20	21	13	21
A_{16}	0.0441	14	14	14	13	16	14	12
A_{17}	0.0429	17	15	15	16	19	16	16
A_{18}	0.0457	11	11	11	11	11	10	11
A_{19}	0.0487	8	7	8	7	7	3	7
A_{20}	0.0489	7	9	9	9	8	8	9
A_{21}	0.0552	3	4	4	3	2	5	2
ρ	—	—	0.971	0.987	0.99	0.97	0.865	0.966

89.5 Conclusions

The introduction of the OPARA method is a remarkable breakthrough in the MCDM research area. Formulated to address the major limitations of traditional methods, OPARA presents a systematic and neutral procedure that corresponds to the intricate interactions between options without the need for data standardization, subjective judgment matrices, or external standards. The basic idea of OPARA is to compare each alternative with the others on each criterion (i.e., make pairwise comparisons) in order to judge their performance. This method is robust in the sense that it uses all of the information in the decision matrix, which may not be the case in any traditional aggregation-based methods, which may even ignore the context-based or relational information. Moreover, the introduction of range-based and linearity-based adjustment factors can provide flexibility for applying criteria with a wide variety of distributions and characteristics. Such adjustments serve to counterbalance any imbalance brought by scale or the nonlinearity of patterns, thus supporting the balance and fairness of the evaluation. To illustrate, in this chapter, two cases were presented: one synthetic and the other a real-world CNC machine tool selection, which show the practical applicability and interpretability of the OPARA method. In the CNC case study with 21 alternatives and seven criteria, for example, OPARA was shown to provide detailed, information-based rankings. A comparison with Spearman's rank correlation coefficient using each of the five most popular MCDM methods (SAW, WASPAS, TOPSIS, VIKOR, and EDAS) revealed that the findings were strongly consistent with these techniques. These results confirm the empirical justification of OPARA and further demonstrate its relevance to high-stakes industrial decision problems.

OPARA can be extended in future research. A promising avenue is the incorporation of fuzzy logic in the OPARA framework to manage uncertainty, vagueness, and subjectiveness in decision criteria, which is a common phenomenon in practical problems such as risk assessment, healthcare planning, and disaster management. A variant of fuzzy-OPARA may use fuzzy pairwise ratios and fuzzy adjustment parameters, which may improve the capacity of the method to deal with ambiguous or linguistic data. Another good line for further research is the application of OPARA to other fields. For example, in the holistic analysis of environmental sustainability, where factors range from ecological to economic to social with different units and scales, the fact that there is no need for data normalization, according to the original scale found in OPARA, affords better data integrity to be preserved. Likewise, in business decision-making (for instance, in financial decisions or in project portfolio selection), where the trade-off between returns, risk, and compliance is considered, the OPARA approach can bring subtle recommendations with its pairwise, criterion-sensitive value assessments. In addition, the creation of hybrid OPARA algorithms that combine OPARA with metaheuristic optimization algorithms, such as genetic algorithms and particle swarm optimization, could increase its applicability to large-scale or dynamic decision problems.

References

Cai, J., Hu, Y., Peng, Y., Guo, F., Xiong, J., & Zhang, R. (2024). A hybrid MCDM approach based on combined weighting method, cloud model and COPRAS for assessing road construction workers' safety climate. *Frontiers in Public Health, 12*, 1452964.

Çelikbilek, Y., & Tüysüz, F. (2020). An in-depth review of theory of the TOPSIS method: An experimental analysis. *Journal of Management Analytics, 7*, 281–300.

Damjanović, S., Katanić, P., Zavadskas, E. K., Stević, Ž., Krsmanović, B., & Djalić, N. (2024). Novel fuzzy MCDM model for comparison of programming languages. *Studies in Informatics and Control, 33*, 5–14.

Jahan, A., Mustapha, F., Ismail, M. Y., Sapuan, S., & Bahraminasab, M. (2011). A comprehensive VIKOR method for material selection. *Materials & Design, 32*, 1215–1221.

Keshavarz-Ghorabaee, M., Mohammadi-Ostadkalayeh, A., Amiri, M., & Antucheviciene, J. (2025). A fuzzy OPARA-based group decision-making approach: Application to sustainable solutions assessment. *Informatica, 36*, 33–63.

Keshavarz-Ghorabaee, M., Rastegar, A., Amiri, M., Zavadskas, E. K., & Antuchevičienė, J. (2024). Multi-Criteria personnel evaluation and selection using an objective pairwise adjusted ratio analysis (OPARA). *Economic Computation and Economic Cybernetics Studies and Research, 58*, 23–45.

Khan, A., & Maity, K. (2017). Application of MCDM-based TOPSIS method for the selection of optimal process parameter in turning of pure titanium. *Benchmarking: An International Journal, 24*, 2009–2021.

Kou, G., Miettinen, K., & Shi, Y. (2011). Multiple criteria decision making: Challenges and advancements. *Journal of Multi-Criteria Decision Analysis, 18*, 1–4. https://doi.org/10.1002/mcda.476.

Mikhailov, L. (2003). Deriving priorities from fuzzy pairwise comparison judgements. *Fuzzy Sets and Systems, 134*, 365–385. https://doi.org/10.1016/S0165-0114(02)00383-4.

Milinković, A., Brkljač, D., Škorić, S., Stević, Ž., Danilevičius, A., & Das, D. K. (2025). Evaluation of potentials for urban planning using the Fuzzy FUCOM-IMF SWARA-fuzzy OPARA model. *Buildings, 15*, 803.

Özçekiç, E. (2025). Electric vehicle charging station positioning problem: Multi-criteria decision making analysis with entropy, CoCoSo and EDAS methods. *Biga İktisadi ve İdari Bilimler Fakültesi Dergisi, 5*, 187–202.

Podvezko, V. (2011). The comparative analysis of MCDA methods SAW and COPRAS. *Engineering Economics, 22*, 134-146.

Sun, S. (2002). Assessing computer numerical control machines using data envelopment analysis. *International Journal of Production Research, 40*, 2011–2039.

Taherdoost, H., & Madanchian, M. (2023). Multi-criteria decision making (MCDM) methods and concepts. *Encyclopedia, 3*, 77–87.

Vo, T. N. U. (2024). Integrating FUCA, SRP, and OPARA methods to assess faculty's scientific research capacity. *Engineering, Technology & Applied Science Research, 14*, 17870–17875.

Wang, P., Zhu, Z., & Wang, Y. (2016). A novel hybrid MCDM model combining the SAW, TOPSIS and GRA methods based on experimental design. *Information sciences, 345*, 27–45.

Wang, X., & Triantaphyllou, E. (2008). Ranking irregularities when evaluating alternatives by using some ELECTRE methods. *Omega, 36*, 45–63. https://doi.org/10.1016/j.omega.2005.12.003.

Zavadskas, E. K., Antucheviciene, J., Saparauskas, J., & Turskis, Z. (2013). MCDM methods WASPAS and MULTIMOORA: Verification of robustness of methods when assessing alternative solutions. *Economic Computation and Economic Cybernetics Studies and Research, 47*, 5–20.

Chapter 90

ARTASI: Alternative ranking technique based on adaptive standardized intervals for multi-attribute decision-making

Gülay Demir
High School of Health Vocational Services, Sivas Cumhuriyet University, Sivas, Türkiye

90.1 Introduction

The complexity of today's world requires decision-makers to assess, at the same time, an ever-increasing number of conflicting criteria, measured in diverse units. This situation highlights the need for sound and consistent decisions to be made through joint evaluation and consensus of groups representing different expertise rather than an individual approach (Haseli et al., 2023, 2024). In this respect, the role of multicriteria decision-making (MCDM) models becomes crucial, as they create a systematic, logical approach in finding the best available choice based on integrated criteria evaluations (Haseli et al., 2020; Taherdoost & Madanchian, 2023). Despite the widely accepted usage of existing models, like technique for order preference by similarity to ideal solution (TOPSIS) and VlseKriterijumska Optimizacija I Kompromisno Resenje (VIKOR), in the research community, they demonstrate some inherent limitations, particularly in dynamic, vague, and massive decision conditions, as highlighted (Ceballos et al., 2016; Opricovic & Tzeng, 2004). The most well-known shortcomings of MCDM models include the so-called rank reversal, the information lost when quantifying the values of the criteria in bounded intervals, as well as the inability to adjust the models in response to the risk attitude of the decision-makers. These weaknesses make the applied model outputs precarious, concerning validity as well as accuracy, potentially giving rise to erroneous decision-making in crucial situations.

Therefore, couldn't decision-making models not be made more flexible, consistent, and more responsive to decision-makers? This gap in the literature constitutes the primary motivation and main research question of this chapter. In this context, this chapter aims to examine the alternative ranking technique based on the adaptive standardized intervals (ARTASI) method, developed as an alternative to the rigid normalization and ranking mechanisms of traditional methods.

The primary objective of this chapter is to demonstrate the theoretical advantages of the ARTASI method by applying it to real-world problems and to analyze the method's performance in different decision-making scenarios. To this end, the following research objectives have been identified: to demonstrate the operation of the ARTASI method practically by explaining the algorithmic steps of the method step-by-step in a medium-scale decision problem, namely, bus company selection. To demonstrate how the method can be applied to a group decision model for a more complex, multicriteria scenario, namely the smart factory location problem. Through these case studies, we demonstrate how ARTASI's theoretical advantages, such as ranking consistency and flexibility, yield practical results and validate the method's effectiveness.

The main contribution of this chapter to the literature is its presentation of a methodology that is both theoretically sound and practically flexible, directly addressing the limitations of existing MCDM methods. To further understand the innovative approach offered by the ARTASI method, a comparison of the method with the two most widely used traditional techniques, TOPSIS and VIKOR, is presented in Table 90.1.

As shown in Table 90.1, unlike traditional methods, the ARTASI method uses a standardization range that adjusts itself according to the structure of the problem, rather than confining the data to a predefined narrow range. Furthermore, thanks to the α and φ parameters, it offers a personalized decision model that can be adjusted to the expectations of decision-

Encyclopedia of Multi-Attribute Decision-Making (MADM). DOI: https://doi.org/10.1016/B978-0-443-33275-3.00102-0

TABLE 90.1 Comparison of the ARTASI method with TOPSIS and VIKOR methods.

Feature/ comparison criteria	ARTASI method	TOPSIS method	VIKOR method
Normalization technique	Adaptive standardization: protects data distribution and minimizes information loss.	Vector normalization: used to calculate the Euclidean distance to ideal and antiideal solutions.	Linear normalization: performs normalization according to ideal and antiideal values.
Ranking reversal problem	High resistance: structurally designed to minimize this problem.	Sensitive: rank reversals are common when the set of alternatives changes.	Partially sensitive: while some control is provided by the compromise parameter (v), the ranking may change.
Decision maker's risk profile	Included in the model (α and φ parameters): the model can be adjusted according to risk attitude.	Not included: performs a mechanical distance calculation.	Partially included (v parameter): adjusts the balance between group benefit and individual regret.
Basic philosophy	Reliability and personalization: producing a reliable ranking that is consistent and responsive to the decision-maker's preferences.	Closeness to ideal: finding the alternative closest to the positive ideal solution and farthest from the negative ideal solution.	Compromise solution: seeks a compromise solution that comes closest to the ideal solution and creates the least "regret."
Solution determination	A single ranking: a single ranking is obtained based on the final utility function.	A single ranking: a single ranking is obtained based on the relative closeness (R) value.	Compromise solution: proposes a set of one or more alternatives determined by two conditions (acceptable advantage and acceptable stability).

Source: Created by the author.

makers with different profiles, such as "guarantor" or "risk taker." In this way, the ARTASI approach, endowed with these characteristics, surpasses the level of a mathematical tool for the classification process, as it includes the human factor involved in the process.

In this section, the theoretical basis of the ARTASI approach, the process of its algorithm, as well as the advantages mentioned in the foregoing, will be described in the context of the case studies introduced. The ARTASI chapter structure is as follows: Section 90.2 includes a literature review introducing the integration of the method with fuzzy logic and the hybrid models it is applied to. This is followed by a section explaining the methodology of the method. Case studies, characterized as simple and complex cases, are included in Section 90.4. Section 90.5 includes the conclusion and recommendations for future work.

90.2 Literature review

The ARTASI method was first introduced in the literature by Pamučar et al. (2024) in a problem involving the selection of the best big data platform. Because of its strong theoretical foundations and usefulness, this relatively new approach has quickly emerged as a leading one in the field of MCDM. There aren't many studies on this approach because it's still relatively new. The fundamental algorithm and its initial application domains are the primary focus of current research. The position of the ARTASI method in the body of existing literature, its notable fuzzy extensions, hybrid models that can be produced with other approaches, and possible interdisciplinary application areas are all methodically examined in this section.

90.2.1 Fuzzy logic integrations

To increase decision-making ability under uncertainty, Table 90.2 shows enhanced ARTASI methods combined with different fuzzy set theories.

These studies in Table 90.2 demonstrate the compatibility of the ARTASI method with different mathematical models and its effective applicability to real-life problems.

TABLE 90.2 Fuzzy set versions of the ARTASI method.

Author/(s)	Fuzzy set type	Hybrid model	Application area
Tatar et al., 2025	Spherical fuzzy	FUCOM-ARTASI	Ergonomic risks in port operations
Dağıstanlı and Temel Gencer (2025)	q-ROFS (q-rung orthopair)	q-ROFS-ARTASI	Forest fire helicopter selection
Chen and Zhang (2025)	Plithogenic set	Plithogenic-ARTASI	Eco-efficiency in petrochemical companies
Kara et al. (2024)	Picture fuzzy	CIMAS-ARTASI	Website performance in human resources management

TABLE 90.3 ARTASI method combined with other multicriteria decision-making techniques.

Author/(s)	Hybrid model	Advantages
Yalçın et al. (2024)	LODECI-ARTASI	Maintaining consistency and stability in the weights of the criteria
Kara et al. (2024)	CIMAS-ARTASI	Using pictorial fuzzy sets to model expert opinions in a flexible and rich way
Demir et al. (2025)	Fuzzy WENSLO-fuzzy ARTASI	Parametric flexibility and adaptability in occupational safety strategies
Çobanoğulları et al. (2026)	Entropy-CRITIC-ARTASI	Objective weighting and data-based stability; minimizing subjective bias

90.2.2 Hybrid models and methodological innovations

The synergies and methodological innovations arising from the integration of the ARTASI method with other MCDM techniques are summarized in Table 90.3.

In addition to demonstrating the adaptable structure of the ARTASI approach, the hybrid studies in Table 90.3 greatly broaden the scope of methodological solutions for challenging decision problems originating from various fields.

90.3 Methodology

Algorithmic steps of the ARTASI method (Pamučar et al., 2024):

Step 1. Creating a standardized decision matrix

Step 1.1. Absolute min/max values

The absolute min $\wp_j^{\min}$ and max $\wp_j^{\max}$ values for each criterion C_j are calculated by Eq. (90.1).

$$\wp_j^{\max} = \max_{1\le i\le m}(\wp_{ij}) + [\max_{1\le i\le m}(\wp_{ij})]^{1/m}, \wp_j^{\min} = \min_{1\le i\le m}(\wp_{ij}) - [\min_{1\le i\le m}(\wp_{ij})]^{1/m} \tag{90.1}$$

where m is the number of alternatives.

Step 1.2. Adaptive standardization

The criteria values are converted to the range $[\psi^{(l)}, \psi^{(u)}]$ defined by the decision maker (e.g., [1, 100]) using Eq. (90.2).

$$\phi_{ij} = \frac{\psi^{(u)} - \psi^{(l)}}{\wp_j^{\max} - \wp_j^{\min}}\wp_{ij} + \frac{\wp_j^{\max}.\ \psi^{(l)} - \wp_j^{\min}.\ \psi^{(u)}}{\wp_j^{\max} - \wp_j^{\min}} \tag{90.2}$$

Step 1.3. Reverse ranking for minimum criteria
Reverse ranking is applied with Eq. (90.3) in the minimum criteria.

$$\zeta_{ij} = -\phi_{ij} + \max_{1 \le i \le m}(\phi_{ij}) + \min_{1 \le i \le m}(\phi_{ij}) \tag{90.3}$$

Step 2. Calculation of utility degrees
Step 2.1. Calculating ideal ($\mathscr{I}^{+}$) and antiideal ($\mathcal{I}^{-}$) utility levels
Utility ratings are obtained using Eqs. (90.4) and (90.5), respectively.

$$\vartheta_{ij}^{+} = \frac{\zeta_{ij}}{\max_{1 \le i \le m}(\zeta_{ij})}.\ w_j.\ \psi^{(u)}\ \vartheta_{ij} = \frac{\min_{1 \le i \le m}(\zeta_{ij})}{\zeta_{ij}}.\ w_j.\ \psi^{(u)} \tag{90.4}$$

$$\vartheta_{ij}^{-} = -\vartheta_{ij} + \max_{1 \le i \le m}(\vartheta_{ij}) + \min_{1 \le i \le m}(\vartheta_{ij}) \tag{90.5}$$

Step 2.2. Calculation of total utility degrees
Total utility degrees are calculated with Eq. (90.6).

$$\mathscr{I}^{+} = \sum_{j=1}^{n} \vartheta_{ij}^{+} \mathscr{I}^{-} = \sum_{j=1}^{n} \vartheta_{ij}^{-} \tag{90.6}$$

Step 3. Obtaining the final ranking

Utility function (Ω_i): flexible combining with α(risk weight) and φ (stabilization parameter) is done with Eq. (90.7).

$$\Omega_i = (\mathscr{I}_i^{+} + \mathscr{I}_i^{-}).\left[\alpha.\left(\frac{\mathscr{I}_i^{+}}{\mathscr{I}_i^{+} + \mathscr{I}_i^{-}}\right)^{\varphi} + (1-\alpha).\left(\frac{\mathscr{I}_i^{-}}{\mathscr{I}_i^{+} + \mathscr{I}_i^{-}}\right)^{\varphi}\right]^{1/\varphi} \tag{90.7}$$

Default values: $\varphi = 1$, $\alpha = 0.5$.

90.4 Case study

In this section, the process steps of the ARTASI method are shown in detail with numerical examples using the simple case and complex case designed as hypothetical scenarios.

90.4.1 Numerical example 1 (simple case)

Example 1. (hypothetical scenario)

A travel company compares six different bus companies (B1, B2, B3, B4, B5, B6) operating the Istanbul-Ankara route within the framework of five criteria for performance evaluation. The criteria used in the evaluation and the relevant explanations are detailed in Table 90.4.

The initial decision matrix consisting of six bus companies and five criteria is given in Table 90.5.

Criterion weights are assumed to be w = [0.25, 0.20, 0.20, 0.15, 0.20].

Step 1. Applying Eq. (90.1), the absolute minimum and maximum values within each criterion are calculated and given in Table 90.6.

The calculation of the absolute minimum and maximum values for criterion C1 is shown.

1. Absolute maximum values (23,6739) for criterion C1 are obtained as follows:

$$\wp_{C1}^{max} = \max_{1 \le i \le 6}(152018221719) + \sqrt[6]{\max_{1 \le i \le 6}(152018221719)} = 23,6739$$

TABLE 90.4 Evaluation criteria and detailed explanations.

Criterion name	Code	Optimization direction	Description
Ticket price (₺)	C1	Min	This is the primary indicator of transportation cost and represents economic accessibility. Lower values reflect cost-effectiveness and market competitiveness for the consumer.
Comfort rating (1–10)	C2	Max	This is an internal service quality indicator that directly impacts the passenger experience. It encompasses a composite assessment of factors such as seat ergonomics, luggage space, air conditioning, and cleanliness.
Travel duration (hours)	C3	Min	This is a fundamental metric of operational efficiency and transportation performance. It is directly related to factors such as traffic conditions, route optimization, and vehicle performance.
Wi-Fi quality (1–5)	C4	Max	This is a digital service quality indicator that meets modern passenger expectations. It includes technical parameters such as uninterrupted connection, bandwidth, and ease of use.
Cancellation policy (1–5)	C5	Max	This is a flexibility indicator directly related to customer satisfaction and risk management. It encompasses factors such as ease of return, refund rate, and procedural simplicity.

TABLE 90.5 Initial decision matrix.

Alternative	C1	C2	C3	C4	C5
B1	15	8,5	5,0	3	2
B2	20	9,2	4,5	4	4
B3	18	7,8	6,0	2	3
B4	22	9,0	4,0	5	5
B5	17	8,0	5,5	3	4
B6	19	8,7	4,8	4	3

TABLE 90.6 Absolute minimum and maximum values.

Criteria	$\wp_j^{max}$	$\wp_j^{min}$
C1	23,6739	10,6475
C2	13,4296	6,3917
C3	23,6739	10,6475
C4	13,4296	6,3917
C5	23,6739	10,6475

2. Absolute minimum values (10,6475) for criterion C1 are obtained as follows:

$$\wp_{C1}^{min} = \min_{1 \le i \le 6} (152018221719) - \sqrt[6]{\min_{1 \le i \le 6} (152018221719)} = 10,\ 6475$$

The remaining values in Table 90.5 were obtained in a similar way. The absolute minimum and maximum values were used to standardize the criteria values in the matrix.

The matching of criterion values in Table 90.6 was converted to the criterion range [1,100]. Standardization of the max criteria is achieved by applying Eq. (90.2), while the standardization of the min type of criteria is performed in two steps. First, by using Eq. (90.3), the values of the min criterion are transformed into a defined criterion interval (in our case, [1,100]). The standardized initial decision matrix is shown in Table 90.7.

The standardization procedure for the element in position B1-C1 is given in Table 90.7. By applying the expression of Eq. (90.2), the transformation to the [1,100] criterion range was performed.

$$\phi_{B1,C1} = \frac{100 - 1}{23,\ 6739 - 13,\ 4296} .\ 15 + \frac{23,\ 6739.1 - 13,\ 4296.100}{23,\ 6739 - 13,\ 4296} = 16,\ 1763$$

Since the C1 criterion belongs to the min criterion group, the transformation was made using Eq. (90.3).

$$\zeta_{B1,C1} = -16,\ 1763 + \max_{1 \le i \le 6} (16,\ 176364,\ 4956.\ ..54,\ 8318) + \min_{1 \le i \le 6} (16,\ 176364,\ 4956.\ ..54,\ 8318) = 83,\ 8234$$

Similarly, the remaining values of the min criteria (C1 and C3) in Table 90.4 are standardized and given in Table 90.8.

Step 2. By applying Eqs. (90.4)–(90.6), the usefulness level of the alternatives is defined according to ideal and nonideal values. The procedure for defining the usefulness level in positions B1-C1 of Tables 90.9 and 90.10 is shown.

TABLE 90.7 Degrees of the usefulness of alternatives to the ideal value.

Alternative	C1	C2	C3	C4	C5
B1	16,1763	50,0431	49,5538	39,6959	21,4643
B2	64,4956	66,3267	38,8114	57,9276	57,9276
B3	45,1679	33,7594	71,0385	21,4643	39,6959
B4	83,8234	61,6743	28,0690	76,1592	76,1592
B5	35,5040	38,4119	60,2961	39,6959	57,9276
B6	54,8318	54,6956	45,2568	57,9276	39,6959

TABLE 90.8 Degrees of usefulness of alternatives to the antiideal value.

Alternative	C1	C2	C3	C4	C5
B1	83,8234	50,0431	49,5538	39,6959	21,4643
B2	35,5040	66,3267	60,2961	57,9276	57,9276
B3	54,8318	33,7594	28,0690	21,4643	39,6959
B4	16,1763	61,6743	71,0385	76,1592	76,1592
B5	64,4956	38,4119	38,8114	39,6959	57,9276
B6	45,1679	54,6956	53,8507	57,9276	39,6959

TABLE 90.9 Aggregated usefulness ratings of alternatives relative to the ideal value.

ϑ_{ij}^{+}	C1	C2	C3	C4	C5	$\mathcal{I}^{+}$
B1	25,0000	15,0899	13,9512	7,8183	5,6367	67,4962
B2	10,5889	20,0000	16,9756	11,4092	15,2122	74,1860
B3	16,3534	10,1797	7,9025	4,2275	10,4245	49,0876
B4	4,8245	18,5971	20,0000	15,0000	20,0000	78,4216
B5	19,2356	11,5826	10,9269	7,8183	15,2122	64,7757
B6	13,4712	16,4928	15,1610	11,4092	10,4245	66,9586

TABLE 90.10 Usefulness ratings of alternatives relative to antiideal value.

ϑ_{ij}^{-}	C1	C2	C3	C4	C5
B1	4,8245	13,4921	11,3287	8,1108	20,0000
B2	11,3905	10,1797	9,3104	5,5581	7,4107
B3	7,3754	20,0000	20,0000	15,0000	10,8144
B4	25,0000	10,9477	7,9025	4,2275	5,6367
B5	6,2703	17,5776	14,4643	8,1108	7,4107
B6	8,9534	12,3445	10,4248	5,5581	10,8144

1. The degree of usefulness of alternative B1 for criterion C1 with respect to the ideal value is defined by Eqs. (90.4), (90.6), and given in Table 90.7.

$$\vartheta_{B1,C1}^{+} = \frac{83,\ 8234}{\max\limits_{1\le i\le 6}(83,\ 8234...45,\ 1679)}.\ 0,\ 25.100 = 25,\ 0000$$

$$\mathcal{I}_1^{+} = 25,\ 0000 + 15,\ 0899 + 13,\ 9512 + 7,\ 8183 + 5,\ 6367 = 67,\ 4962$$

2. Defining the degree of usefulness of alternative B1 for criterion C1 in relation to the antiideal value, Eqs. (90.5), (90.6) and given in Table 90.10.

$$\vartheta_{B1,C1} = \frac{\min\limits_{1\le i\le 6}(83,\ 8234...45,\ 1679)}{83,\ 8234}.\ 0,\ 25.100 = 4,\ 8245$$

Then, using Eq. (90.4), we define the degree of usefulness of alternative B1 for criterion C1 in relation to the antiideal value as given in Table 90.11.

$$\vartheta_{B1,C1}^{-} = -4,\ 8245 + \max\limits_{1\le i\le 6}(4,\ 8245...8,\ 9534) + \min\limits_{1\le i\le 6}(4,\ 8245...8,\ 9534) = 25,\ 0000$$

f

Step 3. Using Eq. (90.7), the final utility functions of the alternatives were calculated and ranked, and given in Table 90.12. The values $\varphi = 1$ and $\alpha = 0.5$ were adopted to calculate the final utility functions.

TABLE 90.11 Aggregated usefulness ratings of alternatives relative to antiideal value.

ϑ_{ij}^{-}	C1	C2	C3	C4	C5	$\mathscr{I}^{-}$
B1	25,0000	16,6876	16,5738	11,1168	5,6367	75,0148
B2	18,4341	20,0000	18,5921	13,6695	18,2260	88,9216
B3	22,4491	10,1797	7,9025	4,2275	14,8223	59,5812
B4	4,8245	19,2321	20,0000	15,0000	20,0000	79,0566
B5	23,5542	12,6021	13,4382	11,1168	18,2260	78,9372
B6	20,8711	17,8352	17,4777	13,6695	14,8223	84,6759

TABLE 90.12 Utility functions and ranking alternatives.

Alternative	$f(\mathscr{I}_i^{+})$	$f(\mathscr{I}_i^{-})$	Ω_i	Rank
B1	0,4736	0,5264	71,2555	5
B2	0,4548	0,5452	81,5538	1
B3	0,4517	0,5483	54,3344	6
B4	0,4980	0,5020	78,7391	2
B5	0,4507	0,5493	71,8564	4
B6	0,4416	0,5584	75,8172	3

The calculation of the final utility function of alternative B1 is given as an example.

$$\Omega_{A1} = (67,4962 + 75,0148).\{0,5.0,4736^{1} + 0,5.0,5264^{1}\}^{1/1} = 71,2555$$

$$f(\mathscr{I}_i^{+}) = \frac{67,4962}{67,4962 + 75,0148} = 0,4736 f(\mathscr{I}_i^{-}) = \frac{75,0148}{67,4962 + 75,0148} = 0,5264$$

The utility functions of the remaining alternatives are defined in a similar way.

Fig. 90.1 graphically presents the utility functions of the alternatives.

According to Fig. 90.1, in order to ensure customer satisfaction and sustainable competition on the Istanbul-Ankara line, B2 and B4 companies set an example in terms of quality, while especially B3 company needs to make improvements.

90.4.2 Numerical example 2 (complex case)

Example 2. (hypothetical scenario)

A logistics company evaluates the installation of a smart factory in six candidate regions (B1–B6) in Europe according to 10 criteria. Information about the criteria is given in Table 90.13.

The group decision matrix created with the opinions of three experts is given in Table 90.14.

The findings obtained by performing the process steps applied for Example 1 are given in Table 90.15.

According to the results of the ARTASI method in Table 90.15, the most suitable region for smart factory installation is B2. Fig. 90.2 shows the utility functions of the alternatives graphically.

This ranking in Fig. 90.2 was supported by the balanced and high performance of cost, environmental impact, energy use, and supply chain criteria.

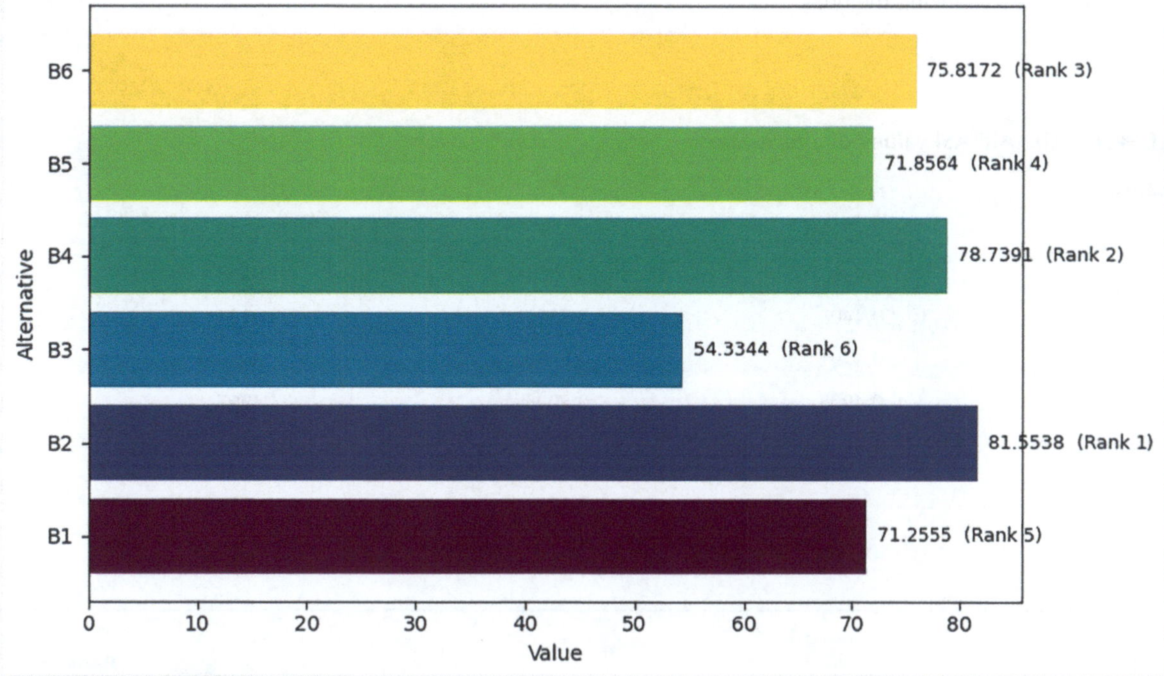

FIGURE 90.1 ARTASI method for example 1.

TABLE 90.13 Information about the criteria.

Criteria	Code	Optimization direction	Weight
Investment cost (€ million)	C1	Min	0.12
Skilled labor (1–10)	C2	Max	0.15
Logistics cost (€/ton)	C3	Min	0.10
Renewable energy rate (%)	C4	Max	0.11
R&D infrastructure (1–10)	C5	Max	0.13
Government incentives (1–5)	C6	Max	0.09
Environmental impact (1–10, 1 = good)	C7	Min	0.08
Supply chain strength (1–10)	C8	Max	0.14
Political stability (1–10)	C9	Max	0.07
Climate resilience (1–10)	C10	Max	0.11

TABLE 90.14 The decision matrix.

Alternative	C1	C2	C3	C4	C5	C6	C7	C8	C9	C10
B1	85	8,2	120	65	7,5	4	3,2	8,1	7,8	8,0
B2	110	9,0	95	80	8,8	3	2,5	9,2	8,5	7,5
B3	95	7,5	110	70	6,5	5	4,0	7,5	6,0	6,5
B4	75	8,8	130	60	9,2	4	3,8	8,8	7,0	8,5
B5	150	8,5	85	90	7,0	2	1,8	9,5	9,0	9,0
B6	100	9,2	100	75	8,5	3	2,2	8,5	8,0	7,0

TABLE 90.15 The ARTASI values of alternatives.

Alternative	$f(\mathscr{I}_i^+)$	$f(\mathscr{I}_i^-)$	Ω_i	Rank
B1	0,4223	0,5777	78,1749	4
B2	0,4497	0,5503	92,0594	1
B3	0,4405	0,5595	59,0184	6
B4	0,4791	0,5209	77,3003	5
B5	0,4905	0,5095	83,3967	3
B6	0,4430	0,5570	87,8101	2

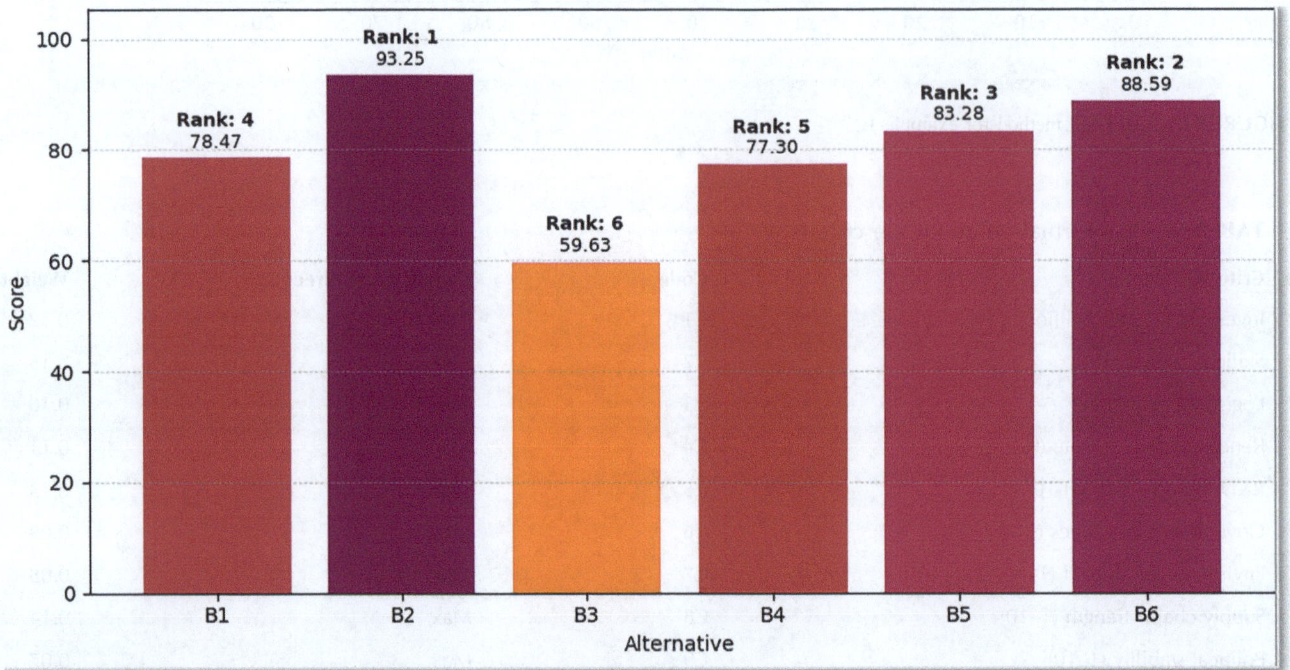

FIGURE 90.2 The result of the ARTASI method for example 2.

90.5 Conclusion and future work

In this section, the proposed ARTASI approach, designed to correct the limitations in the MCDM literature, will be described in detail based on its theory, as well as demonstrated in the form of two separate case examples. In this regard, the emphasis will be upon the limitations in the existing models, as well as the innovative way in which the ARTASI approach resolves them.

Through the analyses and case studies that were performed, it has been made clear that the ARTASI approach offers three key contributions to the body of knowledge in the following manner:

Instead of being constrained to a previously defined range, the values of the criteria are standardized using the decision problem-adaptive standardization in ARTASI, as defined in Eqs. 90.1 and 90.2 below. This reduces the information loss associated with other standardization procedures, where the original data information, in terms of the distribution, remains intact, particularly when the criteria, in this case, price, duration, or the level of comfort, are measured in different units, as in the case of evaluating the bus companies. The unique standardization algorithm, as well as the ultimate use function in the proposed approach, showed excellent resistance to the so-called rank reversal problem, in the case when a new option is added to, or removed from, the set of alternatives. A sufficiently high resistance level allows this approach to demonstrate stable results in dynamic decision conditions. The approach involves the direct integration of the parameters α and φ, which are related to the risk attitude of the decision maker, into the proposed approach (Eq. 90.7). The parameter α determines the levels of closeness to the ideal solution and the distance from the antiideal solution, while the φ parameter determines the stability in the process of aggregating the ratings of the benefits related to various criteria. Based on the parameters, the proposed ARTASI approach can be easily adapted to decision-makers having diverse risk profiles.

The merits of the proposed approach are also demonstrated in this research by considering two separate case studies. The first case study aims to explain, in detail, the operation of the proposed approach in solving a decision-making scenario, like the selection of a bus service. In the second and more complex analysis, the robustness and scalability of the method in industrial decision processes are demonstrated using a ten-criterion group decision model, such as smart factory location selection. Despite the innovations offered by the ARTASI method, the current study has some limitations. These limitations provide a roadmap for future research: the method's adaptive standardization mechanism may require higher computational costs compared to traditional linear normalization methods, especially for very large-scale problems (e.g., hundreds of alternatives and criteria). This cost was not analyzed in the current study. Determining the α and φ parameters by the decision maker requires subjective input. A systematic optimization approach to determine the sensitivity of these parameters to the ranking and their optimal values has not yet been developed. The study was conducted assuming that the criteria values are crisp. While fuzzy set integrations (spherical fuzzy set, q-rung orthopair fuzzy set, picture fuzzy set) mentioned in the literature review are available, the performance of the ARTASI method under uncertainty was not tested in this study.

Considering the current limitations and the potential of the method, the following original directions for future research are suggested: to increase the applicability of ARTASI to large-scale problems, it is recommended that the method's core algorithms be redesigned using GPU-based parallel processors or quantum optimization algorithms (e.g., Grover-based search) and its computational efficiency be experimentally tested. ARTASI should be integrated into the real-time data stream provided by Internet of Things sensor networks and digital twin technologies. This integration will maximize the method's practical value in industrial automation and smart manufacturing systems. A machine learning-based approach (e.g., genetic algorithms or Bayesian optimization) should be developed to determine the optimal values of the parameters α and φ. This will reduce the decision maker's subjective burden and increase the objectivity of the method. Extending the method to relatively understudied interdisciplinary areas, such as climate change-resilient crop selection in agriculture and decision models balancing patient satisfaction and cost-effectiveness in the healthcare sector, is critical to testing the ARTASI method's general validity.

References

Ceballos, B., Lamata, M. T., & Pelta, D. A. (2016). A comparative analysis of multi-criteria decision-making methods. *Progress in Artificial Intelligence, 5*, 315–322. https://doi.org/10.1007/s13748-016-0093-1.

Chen, H., & Zhang, D. (2025). Ecological efficiency evaluation in petrochemical enterprises using plithogenic-ARTASI model. *Neutrosophic Sets and Systems, 80*, 597–608. https://doi.org/10.61387/NSS/XYZ.

Çobanoğulları, G., Daldıran, K., & Daldıran, B. (2026). Analysis of innovation performance of south-eastern European Countries in transition economies: An application of the entropy-based ARTASI method. *Spectrum of Operational Research*, 193–214. https://doi.org/10.31181/sor31202642.

Dağıstanlı, H. A., & Temel Gencer, C. (2025). Evaluation of medium-lift forest fire helicopter using q-rung orthopair fuzzy set-based alternative ranking technique based on adaptive standardized intervals approach. *Engineering Applications of Artificial Intelligence, 148*, 110468. https://doi.org/10.1016/j.engappai.2025.110468.

Demir, G., Bouraima, M. B., Badi, I., Stević, Ž., & Das, D. K. (2025). Identification of industrial occupational safety risks and selection of optimum intervention strategies: Fuzzy MCDM approach. *Mathematics, 13*(2), 301. https://doi.org/10.3390/math13020301.

Haseli, G., Sheikh, R., & Sana, S. S. (2020). Base-criterion on multi-criteria decision-making method and its applications. *International Journal of Management Science and Engineering Management, 15*(2), 79–88. https://doi.org/10.1080/17509653.2019.1633964.

Haseli, G., Ögel, İ. Y., Ecer, F., & Hajiaghaei-Keshteli, M. (2023). Luxury in female technology (FemTech): Selection of smart jewelry for women through BCM-MARCOS group decision-making framework with fuzzy ZE-numbers. *Technological Forecasting and Social Change, 196*, 122870. https://doi.org/10.1016/j.techfore.2023.122870.

Haseli, G., Bonab, S. R., Hajiaghaei-Keshteli, M., Ghoushchi, S. J., & Deveci, M. (2024). Fuzzy ZE-numbers framework in group decision-making using the BCM and CoCoSo to address sustainable urban transportation. *Information Sciences, 653*, 119809. https://doi.org/10.1016/j.ins.2023.119809.

Kara, K., Yalçın, G. C., Kaygısız, E. G., Örnek, A.Ş., & Pamučar, D. (2024). A picture fuzzy CIMAS-ARTASI model for website performance analysis in human resource management. *Applied Soft Computing, 162*, 111826. https://doi.org/10.1016/j.asoc.2024.111826.

Opricovic, S., & Tzeng, G. H. (2004). Compromise solution by MCDM methods: A comparative analysis of VIKOR and TOPSIS. *European journal of operational research, 156*(2), 445–455. https://doi.org/10.1016/S0377-2217(03)00020-1.

Pamučar, D., Simic, V., Görçün, Ö. F., & Küçükönder, H. (2024). Selection of the best big data platform using the COBRAC-ARTASI methodology with adaptive standardized intervals. *Expert Systems with Applications, 239*, 122312. https://doi.org/10.1016/j.eswa.2023.122312.

Taherdoost, H., & Madanchian, M. (2023). Multi-criteria decision making (MCDM) methods and concepts. *Encyclopedia, 3*(1), 77–87. https://doi.org/10.3390/encyclopedia3010006.

Tatar, V., Ayvaz, B., & Pamučar, D. (2025). A quantitative ergonomic risk assessment model of maritime port operations: An integrated spherical fuzzy-FUCOM-ARTASI approach. *Ocean and Coastal Management, 267*, 107710. https://doi.org/10.1016/j.ocecoaman.2025.107710.

Yalçın, G. C., Kara, K., & Senapati, T. (2024). A hybrid spherical fuzzy logarithmic decomposition of criteria importance and an alternative ranking technique based on the Adaptive Standardized Intervals model with application. *Decision Analytics Journal, 11*, 100441. https://doi.org/10.1016/j.dajour.2024.100441.

Chapter 91

RBNAR: Reference-based normalization alternative ranking for multi-attribute decision-making

Karahan Kara[1,2] and Galip Cihan Yalçın[2]
[1]*Department of Data Science and Analytics, Faculty of Economics and Administrative Sciences, İzmir Katip Çelebi University, İzmir, Türkiye,*
[2]*Department of Business, Faculty of Economics and Administrative Sciences, OSTIM Technical University, Ankara, Türkiye*

91.1 Introduction

The reference-based normalization alternative ranking (RBNAR) method, developed by Kara, Yalçın, et al. (2024), is a multi-attribute decision-making (MADM) approach that utilizes normalization procedures based on distances to reference values. Unlike conventional methods that rely on max–min distances, RBNAR determines the optimal ranking of alternatives by measuring their distances to desired reference points. For each criterion, a reference vector is defined, and a two-stage normalization procedure is applied accordingly.

The primary aim of this study is to present the procedural steps of the RBNAR method and demonstrate its application through two numerical examples. Although RBNAR has been applied in literature to various domains, its use remains relatively limited. Kara, Yalçın, et al. (2024) developed a hybrid decision support system to evaluate the financial performance of Borsa Istanbul-listed technology companies, integrating RBNAR for alternative ranking with single-valued neutrosophic (SVN)-criteria importance assessment and criteria importance through intercriteria correlation approaches for criterion weighting. Similarly, Kara, Özyürek, et al. (2024) applied RBNAR to assess financial performance in the sustainability index, incorporating the method based on the removal effects of criteria method for weight determination criterion. Zhang and Li (2025) employed RBNAR in a hospital operations management evaluation framework, integrating plithogenic sets to strengthen the decision-making process. Kara et al. (2025) applied RBNAR to rank companies listed on both the corporate governance and sustainability 25 indices, utilizing interval-valued spherical fuzzy sets for expert-based criterion weighting. Furthermore, Özyürek et al. (2025) demonstrated a robust RBNAR-based financial performance evaluation framework in combination with the fermatean ubic uzzy - simple weight calculation (FCF-SIWEC) method for criteria weighting across multiple years of Borsa Istanbul data.

These studies collectively highlight RBNAR's versatility and effectiveness for alternative ranking in complex MADM problems. The remainder of this chapter is organized as follows: Section 91.2 provides a detailed explanation of the RBNAR method; Sections 91.3, 91.4 present its application through two numerical examples; and Section 91.5 concludes the study with insights into the method's practical applicability and effectiveness.

91.2 Methodology

The RBNAR method constitutes a structured decision-making framework that employs two distinct reference-based normalization procedures (Kara, Özyürek, et al., 2024). The methodology is implemented through five fundamental steps, which are summarized as follows:

Step 1. In the initial stage of the RBNAR method, the decision matrix ($X = [X_{ij}]_{MN}$) is constructed, as expressed in Eq. (91.1). This matrix systematically records the performance scores of each alternative (A_i) relative to the corresponding

Encyclopedia of Multi-Attribute Decision-Making (MADM). DOI: https://doi.org/10.1016/B978-0-443-33275-3.00031-2

criteria (C_j), where each entry represents the evaluation of the ith alternative with respect to the jth criterion. The decision matrix comprises M alternatives and N criteria, necessitating a precise definition of both the alternative set $A = \{A_1, A_2, \ldots, A_i, \ldots, A_M\} (i = 1,2, \ldots, M)$ and the criterion set $C = \{C_1, C_2, \ldots, C_j, \ldots, C_N\} (j = 1,2, \ldots, N)$ within this framework. Additionally, reference values for each criterion are established to serve as benchmarks for normalization and comparison. These reference values are organized in a vector format ($Y = [Y_j]_N$), as illustrated in Eq. (91.2), providing a standardized basis for subsequent analytical steps within the RBNAR methodology:

$$X = \begin{bmatrix} X_{11} \cdots X_{1j} \cdots X_{1N} \\ \vdots \cdots \vdots \cdots \vdots \\ X_{i1} \cdots X_{ij} \ldots X_{iN} \\ \vdots \cdots \vdots \cdots \vdots \\ X_{M1} \cdots X_{Mj} \ldots X_{MN} \end{bmatrix}; (i = 1, 2, \ldots, M; j = 1, 2, \ldots, N). \quad (91.1)$$

$$Y = [Y_1 \cdots Y_j \cdots Y_N]; (j = 1, 2, \ldots, N). \quad (91.2)$$

Step 2. In the second phase of the RBNAR method, the elements of the initial decision matrix are subjected to two distinct reference-based normalization procedures. The first procedure involves the application of Z-score (nonmonotonic) normalization proposed by Shih et al. (2007), while the second procedure employs Aytekin's reference-based normalization approach introduced by Aytekin (2021). The sequential implementation of these two reference-based normalization techniques is designed to enhance the robustness, reliability, and internal consistency of the normalization process. As a result, the Z-score normalization ($Z^{1^{st}} = [Z_{ij}^{1^{st}}]_{MN}$) yields the normalized matrix presented in Eq. (91.3), whereas the application of the Aytekin's reference-based normalization ($Z^{2^{nd}} = [Z_{ij}^{2^{nd}}]_{MN}$) generates the matrix shown in Eq. (91.4):

$$Z_{ij}^{1^{st}} = e^{\left(\frac{(X_{ij}-Y_j)^2}{-2(\sigma_j)^2}\right)}; (i = 1, 2, \ldots, M; j = 1, 2, \ldots, N). \quad (91.3)$$

$$Z_{ij}^{2^{nd}} = 1 - \frac{|X_{ij} - Y_j|}{|Y_j| + 10^{\delta}}; (i = 1, 2, \ldots, M; j = 1, 2, \ldots, N). \quad (91.4)$$

herein, σ_j indicates the standard deviation of the jth criterion and δ is parameter of the Aytekin's reference-based normalization technique $\delta \in [0, \infty]$.

Step 3. In the third stage of the RBNAR method, the normalized matrices obtained from the Z-score normalization and Aytekin's reference-based normalization transformations are integrated through an aggregation procedure utilizing the Heron mean. This process incorporates a weighting parameter, denoted as α, which determines the contribution of the arithmetic mean, while the complementary term $1 - \alpha$ represents the contribution of the geometric mean. The resulting aggregated normalized matrix ($Z = [Z_{ij}]_{MN}$) is formulated as expressed in Eq. (91.5). In practical implementations, α is commonly assigned a value of 0.5, thereby ensuring an equal balance between the arithmetic and geometric mean components in constructing the aggregated representation:

$$Z_{ij} = ((1 - \alpha)\sqrt{(Z_{ij}^{1^{st}})(Z_{ij}^{2^{nd}})}) + \left((\alpha)\frac{(Z_{ij}^{1^{st}} + Z_{ij}^{2^{nd}})}{2}\right); (i = 1, 2, \ldots, M; j = 1, 2, \ldots, N; \alpha \in [0, 1]). \quad (91.5)$$

Step 4. In the fourth phase of the RBNAR methodology, the aggregated normalized matrix is integrated with the vector of criterion weights $w = \{w_1, w_2, \ldots, w_j, \ldots, w_N\} (j = 1,2, \ldots, N)$ through a multiplicative operation, as formulated in Eq. (91.6). This step produces the weighted normalized matrix ($D = [D_{ij}]_{MN}$), in which the relative importance of each criterion is systematically embedded, ensuring that the decision outcomes reflect both the reference-based normalized performance values and the predefined priority structure of the criteria:

$$D_{ij} = w_j * Z_{ij}; (i = 1, 2, \ldots, M; j = 1, 2, \ldots, N). \quad (91.6)$$

herein, $\sum_{j=1}^{N} w_j = 1$.

Step 5. In the fifth stage of the RBNAR method, Eq. (91.7) is utilized to derive the ranking score vector ($R = [R_i]_M$) corresponding to the set of alternatives. This vector provides a quantitative representation of the overall performance of each alternative with respect to all considered criteria. Consequently, the alternative associated with the maximum score is identified as the most favorable option, whereas the one with the minimum score is regarded as the least desirable:

$$R_i = \sum_{j=1}^{N} D_{ij};(i = 1, 2, \ldots, M; j = 1, 2, \ldots, N). \tag{91.7}$$

The algorithm of the RBNAR method is presented in Table 91.1.

91.3 Numerical example 1

For numerical example 1, the required inputs for implementing the RBNAR algorithm are specified in Table 91.1. These include the set of alternatives $A = \{A_1, A_2, A_3, A_4\} (i = 1,2,3,4)$, the set of criteria $C = \{C_1, C_2, C_3\} (j = 1,2,3)$, the reference value vector $Y = \{Y_1, Y_2, Y_3\} (j = 1,2,3)$ (with the third criterion defined as cost-based), and the criterion weight vector $w = \{0.30,0.40,0.30\}$. Based on these inputs, the procedural steps of the RBNAR method were subsequently executed in the following order:

Step 1. The initial matrix ($X = [X_{ij}]_{MN}$) and reference value vector ($Y = [Y_j]_N$) for *numerical example 1* is presented in Table 91.2.

Step 2. The Z-score normalization ($Z^{1^{st}} = [Z_{ij}^{1^{st}}]_{MN}$), calculated using Eq. (91.3), is presented in Table 91.3, while Aytekin's reference-based normalization ($Z^{2^{nd}} = [Z_{ij}^{2^{nd}}]_{MN}$), ($\delta = 6$) derived from Eq. (91.4), is provided in Table 91.4.

Example:. The calculation for $Z_{11}^{1^{st}}$ is as follows: $Z_{11}^{1^{st}} = e^{\left(\frac{(1200-2000)^2}{-2(12291.66667)^2}\right)} = 0.000000000004858222$, and the calculation for $Z_{11}^{2^{nd}}$ is as follows: $Z_{11}^{2^{nd}} = 1 - \frac{|1200 - 2000|}{|2000| + 10^6} = 0.99920159680638700$.

TABLE 91.1 The algorithm illustrates the steps of the RBNAR alternative ranking method.

Algorithm:	The purpose of this algorithm is to present the procedural steps of the RBNAR method.	
Input	A set of criteria: $C = \{C_1, C_2, \ldots, C_j, \ldots, C_N\} (j = 1,2, \ldots, N)$, A set of alternatives: $A = \{A_1, A_2, \ldots, A_i, \ldots, A_M\} (i = 1,2, \ldots, M)$, A reference values vector: $Y = \{Y_1, Y_2, \ldots, Y_j, \ldots, Y_N\} (j = 1,2, \ldots, N)$, A criteria weigh vector: $w = \{w_1, w_2, \ldots, w_j, \ldots, w_N\} (j = 1,2, \ldots, N)$.	
Step-1:	Construct the initial matrix ($X = [X_{ij}]_{MN}$) as Eq. (91.1) and reference values vector ($Y = [Y_j]_N$) as Eq. (91.2)	$X_{ij} = \begin{bmatrix} X_{11} \cdots X_{1j} \cdots X_{1N} \\ \vdots \cdots \vdots \cdots \vdots \\ X_{i1} \cdots X_{ij} \ldots X_{iN} \\ \vdots \cdots \vdots \cdots \vdots \\ X_{M1} \cdots X_{Mj} \ldots X_{MN} \end{bmatrix}$ $Y = [Y_1 \cdots Y_j \cdots Y_N]$
Step-2:	Calculate the Z-score normalization ($Z^{1^{st}} = [Z_{ij}^{1^{st}}]_{MN}$) and Aytekin's reference-based normalization ($Z^{2^{nd}} = [Z_{ij}^{2^{nd}}]_{MN}$) ($\delta > 0$) by employing Eq. (91.3) and Eq. (91.4)	$Z_{ij}^{1^{st}} = e^{\left(\frac{(X_{ij}-Y_j)^2}{-2(\sigma_j)^2}\right)}$ $Z_{ij}^{2^{nd}} = 1 - \frac{\lvert X_{ij} - Y_j \rvert}{\lvert Y_j \rvert + 10^{\delta}}$
Step-3:	Calculate the aggregated normalized matrix ($Z = [Z_{ij}]_{MN}$) by employing Heron mean as stated Eq. (91.5) ($\alpha \in [0,1]$).	$Z_{ij} = ((1 - \alpha)\sqrt{(Z_{ij}^{1^{st}})(Z_{ij}^{2^{nd}})}) + \left((\alpha)\frac{(Z_{ij}^{1^{st}} + Z_{ij}^{2^{nd}})}{2}\right)$
Step-4:	Calculate the weighted normalized matrix ($D = [D_{ij}]_{MN}$) by employing Eq. (91.6).	$D_{ij} = w_j * Z_{ij}$
Step-5:	Determine the ranking score vector ($R = [R_i]_M$) by employing Eq. (91.7).	$R_i = \sum_{j=1}^{N} D_{ij}$
Output	A ranking score vector: $R = \{R_1, R_2, \ldots, R_i, \ldots, R_M\} (i = 1,2, \ldots, M)$.	

TABLE 91.2 The initial matrix.

X_{ij}	C_1	C_2	C_3
A_1	1200	800	12
A_2	1100	700	15
A_3	1250	700	11
A_4	1000	750	16
Y_j	2000	1000	10

TABLE 91.3 The Z-score normalization matrix.

Z_{ij}^{2nd}	C_1	C_2	C_3
A_1	0.000000000004858222	0.000161212478788136	0.702461844555103000
A_2	0.000000000000004801	0.000000002928511780	0.109999857729190000
A_3	0.000000000113887020	0.000000002928511780	0.915494384894197000
A_4	0.000000000000000002	0.000001185933670502	0.041649007613967700

TABLE 91.4 The Aytekin's reference-based normalization matrix.

Z_{ij}^{1st}	C_1	C_2	C_3
A_1	0.99920159680638700	0.99980019980020000	0.99999800002000000
A_2	0.99910179640718600	0.99970029970030000	0.99999500005000000
A_3	0.99925149700598800	0.99970029970030000	0.99999900001000000
A_4	0.99900199600798400	0.99975024975025000	0.99999400005999900

Step 3. By employing the Heron mean, as formulated in Eq. (91.5), the matrices obtained from the Z-score normalization and Aytekin's reference-based normalization procedures were integrated ($\alpha = 0.5$), resulting in the aggregated normalized matrix presented in Table 91.5.

Example:. The calculation for Z_{11} is as follows:

$$Z_{11} = ((1 - 0.5)\sqrt{(0.000000000004858222)(0.99920159680638700)}) + \left((0.5)\frac{(0.000000000004858222 + 0.99920159680638700)}{2}\right).$$

$= 0.2498015$

Step 4. Through the application of Eq. (91.6), the aggregated normalized matrix was integrated with the corresponding criterion weights, thereby generating the weighted normalized matrix ($D = [D_{ij}]_{MN}$) shown in Table 91.6.

Example:. The calculation for D_{11} is as follows: $D_{11} = 0.30 \times 0.2498015 = 0.0749405$.

TABLE 91.5 The aggregated normalized matrix.

Z_{ij}	C_1	C_2	C_3
A_1	0.2498015	0.2563382	0.8446795
A_2	0.2497755	0.2499521	0.4433294
A_3	0.2498182	0.2499521	0.9572805
A_4	0.2497505	0.2504823	0.3624509

TABLE 91.6 The weighted normalized matrix.

D_{ij}	C_1	C_2	C_3
A_1	0.0749405	0.1025353	0.2534039
A_2	0.0749326	0.0999809	0.1329988
A_3	0.0749455	0.0999809	0.2871841
A_4	0.0749251	0.1001929	0.1087353

TABLE 91.7 The ranking score vector.

	R_i	Rank
A_1	0.4309	2
A_2	0.3079	3
A_3	0.4621	1
A_4	0.2839	4

Step 5. By applying Eq. (91.7), the ranking score vector of the alternatives was derived, from which their relative rankings were established. The computed ranking score vector ($R = [R_i]_M$) is reported in Table 91.7.

Example:. The calculation for R_1 is as follows: $R_1 = 0.0749405 + 0.1025353 + 0.2534039 = 0.4309$.

91.4 Numerical example 2

For numerical example 2, the necessary inputs for the implementation of the RBNAR algorithm are defined in Table 91.1. These include the set of alternatives $A = \{A_1, A_2, A_3, A_4, A_5, A_6, A_7, A_8\}(i = 1,2, \ldots,8)$, the set of criteria $C = \{C_1, C_2, C_3, C_4, C_5, C_6, C_7\}(j = 1,2, \ldots,7)$, the reference value vector $Y = \{Y_1, Y_2, Y_3, Y_4, Y_5, Y_6, Y_7\}(j = 1,2, \ldots,7)$ (the sixth and seventh criteria are cost-based criteria.), and the criterion weight vector $w = \{0.15,0.12,0.18,0.15,0.16,0.11,0.13\}$. Based on these inputs, the procedural steps of the RBNAR method were subsequently executed in the following order:

Step 1. The initial matrix ($X = [X_{ij}]_{MN}$) and reference value vector ($Y = [Y_j]_N$) for numerical example 2 is presented in Table 91.8.

Step 2. The Z-score normalization ($Z^{1^{st}} = [Z_{ij}^{1^{st}}]_{MN}$) and Aytekin's reference-based normalization ($Z^{2^{nd}} = [Z_{ij}^{2^{nd}}]_{MN}$) ($\delta = 6$) are presented in Tables 91.9, 91.10, respectively.

Example:. The calculation for $Z_{11}^{1^{st}}$ is as follows: $Z_{11}^{1^{st}} = e^{\left(\frac{(650-750)^2}{-2(706.6964286)^2}\right)} = 0.0008421$, and the calculation for $Z_{11}^{2^{nd}}$ is as follows: $Z_{11}^{2^{nd}} = 1 - \frac{|650-750|}{|750|+10^6} = 0.9999001$.

Step 3. The normalized matrix ($Z = [Z_{ij}]_{MN}$) is shown in Table 91.11 ($\alpha = 0.5$).

Example:. The calculation for Z_{11} is as follows:

$$Z_{11} = ((1-0.5)\sqrt{(0.0008421)(0.9999001)}) + \left((0.5)\frac{(0.0008421+0.9999001)}{2}\right) = 0.2646941.$$

Step 4. The weighted normalized matrix ($D = [D_{ij}]_{MN}$) is shown in Table 91.12.

TABLE 91.8 The initial matrix.

X_{ij}	C_1	C_2	C_3	C_4	C_5	C_6	C_7
A_1	650	7000	16	47	50.2	24	50
A_2	720	6000	11	49	50.8	29	58
A_3	700	6500	15	49	51.1	28	56
A_4	685	7500	18	55	48.8	31	60
A_5	725	7650	18	48	49.7	26	62
A_6	690	6850	14	51	48.5	33	54
A_7	715	7150	12	50	50.5	36	58
A_8	730	7250	14	52	50.4	39	54
Y_j	750	8000	20	60	52	20	50

TABLE 91.9 The Z-score normalization matrix.

$Z_{ij}^{2^{nd}}$	C_1	C_2	C_3	C_4	C_5	C_6	C_7
A_1	0.0008421	0.1779433	0.2918408	0.0000019	0.1546934	0.7318536	1.0000000
A_2	0.5287878	0.0010026	0.0019602	0.0000792	0.4362799	0.2058958	0.1110843
A_3	0.1703481	0.0205652	0.1459791	0.0000792	0.6271450	0.2868777	0.2905224
A_4	0.0502297	0.6494869	0.7349986	0.1421187	0.0027437	0.0943426	0.0322725
A_5	0.6424426	0.8093931	0.7349986	0.0000132	0.0474939	0.4953982	0.0071239
A_6	0.0781854	0.1019759	0.0626006	0.0017972	0.0008620	0.0369812	0.5773154
A_7	0.4201025	0.2872953	0.0072541	0.0004079	0.2736108	0.0067731	0.1110843
A_8	0.7533798	0.3786896	0.0626006	0.0067731	0.2288667	0.0008731	0.5773154

TABLE 91.10 The Aytekin's reference-based normalization matrix.

$Z_{ij}^{1^{st}}$	C_1	C_2	C_3	C_4	C_5	C_6	C_7
A_1	0.9999001	0.9990079	0.9999960	0.9999870	0.9999982	0.9999960	1.0000000
A_2	0.9999700	0.9980159	0.9999910	0.9999890	0.9999988	0.9999910	0.9999920
A_3	0.9999500	0.9985119	0.9999950	0.9999890	0.9999991	0.9999920	0.9999940
A_4	0.9999350	0.9995040	0.9999980	0.9999950	0.9999968	0.9999890	0.9999900
A_5	0.9999750	0.9996528	0.9999980	0.9999880	0.9999977	0.9999940	0.9999880
A_6	0.9999400	0.9988591	0.9999940	0.9999910	0.9999965	0.9999870	0.9999960
A_7	0.9999650	0.9991567	0.9999920	0.9999900	0.9999985	0.9999840	0.9999920
A_8	0.9999800	0.9992560	0.9999940	0.9999920	0.9999984	0.9999810	0.9999960

TABLE 91.11 The aggregated normalized matrix.

Z_{ij}	C_1	C_2	C_3	C_4	C_5	C_6	C_7
A_1	0.2646941	0.5050498	0.5930701	0.2506810	0.4853281	0.8607037	1.0000000
A_2	0.7457730	0.2655708	0.2726248	0.2544673	0.6893269	0.5283494	0.4444149
A_3	0.4989356	0.3264188	0.4775291	0.2544673	0.8027483	0.5895212	0.5921289
A_4	0.3745974	0.8151015	0.8624090	0.4740211	0.2768751	0.4271583	0.3478879
A_5	0.8113620	0.9020148	0.8624090	0.2518141	0.3708382	0.7257696	0.2939794
A_6	0.4093355	0.4347860	0.3907488	0.2716435	0.2648944	0.3553938	0.7742335
A_7	0.6790878	0.5894996	0.2943969	0.2601983	0.5799412	0.2928383	0.4444149
A_8	0.8723229	0.6520607	0.3907488	0.2928405	0.5464162	0.2649876	0.7742335

TABLE 91.12 The weighted normalized matrix.

D_{ij}	C_1	C_2	C_3	C_4	C_5	C_6	C_7
A_1	0.0397041	0.0606060	0.1067526	0.0376022	0.0776525	0.0946774	0.1300000
A_2	0.1118660	0.0318685	0.0490725	0.0381701	0.1102923	0.0581184	0.0577739
A_3	0.0748403	0.0391703	0.0859552	0.0381701	0.1284397	0.0648473	0.0769768
A_4	0.0561896	0.0978122	0.1552336	0.0711032	0.0443000	0.0469874	0.0452254
A_5	0.1217043	0.1082418	0.1552336	0.0377721	0.0593341	0.0798347	0.0382173
A_6	0.0614003	0.0521743	0.0703348	0.0407465	0.0423831	0.0390933	0.1006504
A_7	0.1018632	0.0707400	0.0529914	0.0390297	0.0927906	0.0322122	0.0577739
A_8	0.1308484	0.0782473	0.0703348	0.0439261	0.0874266	0.0291486	0.1006504

TABLE 91.13 The ranking score vector.

	R_i	Rank
A_1	0.5470	2
A_2	0.4572	6
A_3	0.5084	5
A_4	0.5169	4
A_5	0.6003	1
A_6	0.4068	8
A_7	0.4474	7
A_8	0.5406	3

Example:. The calculation for D_{11} is as follows: $D_{11} = 0.15*0.2646941 = 0.0397041$.

Step 5. By applying Eq. (91.7), the ranking score vector of the alternatives was derived, from which their relative rankings were established. The computed ranking score vector ($R = [R_i]_M$) is reported in Table 91.13.

Example:. The calculation for R_1 is as follows: $R_1 = 0.0397041 + 0.0606060 + 0.1067526 + 0.0376022 + 0.0776525 + 0.0946774 + 0.1300000 = 0.5470$.

91.5 Conclusion

This study has presented the RBNAR method as an effective approach for multicriteria decision-making problems, detailing its procedural steps and demonstrating its applicability through two numerical examples. The RBNAR method offers several notable advantages, including its flexibility in handling reference points, the incorporation of reference values to improve ranking precision, and the ability to integrate seamlessly with other criterion weighting approaches, enhancing the robustness of decision-making frameworks. However, certain limitations remain. The selection of appropriate reference values can be subjective and may influence ranking results, and the method's computational complexity increases with the number of alternatives and criteria. Future research may focus on developing systematic approaches for reference value determination, extending RBNAR (Yalçın et al., 2026) to dynamic or fuzzy environments (Li et al., 2025; Wang et al., 2025), and exploring hybridizations with other normalization and weighting techniques (Badi et al., 2025) to further enhance its applicability and reliability across diverse decision-making contexts.

References

Aytekin, A. (2021). Comparative analysis of the normalization techniques in the context of MCDM problems. *Decision Making: Applications in Management and Engineering, 4*(2), 1–25. https://doi.org/10.31181/dmame210402001a.

Badi, I., Bouraima, M. B., & Zonon, B. I. P. (2025). A multi-criteria decision-making model for prioritizing the causes of inflation in libya using the best-worst method and analytic hierarchy process. *Knowledge and Decision Systems with Applications, 1*, 165–176. https://doi.org/10.59543/kadsa.v1i.14259.

Kara, K., Özyürek, H., Yalçın, G. C., & Burgaz, N. (2024). Enhancing financial performance evaluation: The MEREC-RBNAR hybrid method for sustainability-indexed companies. *Journal of Soft Computing and Decision Analytics, 2*(1), 236–257. https://doi.org/10.31181/jscda21202444.

Kara, K., Yalçın, G. C., Çetinkaya, A., Simic, V., & Pamucar, D. (2024). A single-valued neutrosophic CIMAS-CRITIC-RBNAR decision support model for the financial performance analysis: A study of technology companies. *Socio-economic Planning Sciences, 92*, 101851. https://doi.org/10.1016/j.seps.2024.101851.

Kara, K., Yalçın, G. C., & Özyürek, H. (2025). Financial performance evaluation of companies listed in corporate governance and sustainability indices: Application of the IVSF-RBNAR method. *Journal of Data Analytics and Artificial Intelligence Applications, 1*(1), 36–60. https://dergipark.org.tr/en/pub/jdaia/issue/90530/1607081.

Li, Y., Zhu, S., Liao, J., Letchmunan, S., Shi, J., & Liu, Z. (2025). Application of new divergence measure in complex fermatean fuzzy sets for post-flood assessment. *Journal of Intelligent Decision Making and Granular Computing, 1*(1), 127–142. https://doi.org/10.31181/jidmgc1120258.

Özyürek, H., Yalçın, G.C., Kara, K., 2025. Development of the novel FCF-SIWEC-RBNAR hybrid method for financial performance evaluation. Available from: https://www.scitepress.org/Papers/2025/134621/134621.pdf.

Shih, H. S., Shyur, H. J., & Lee, E. S. (2007). An extension of TOPSIS for group decision making. *Mathematical and Computer Modelling, 45*(7-8), 801–813. https://doi.org/10.1016/j.mcm.2006.03.023.

Wang, D., Letchmunan, S., Liao, J., Qiu, H., & Liu, Z. (2025). Construction of new similarity measures for complex pythagorean fuzzy sets and their applications in decision-making problems. *Journal of Intelligent Decision Making and Information Science, 2*, 156–173. https://doi.org/10.59543/jidmis.v2i.11737.

Yalçın, Galip Cihan, Kara, Karahan, Özyürek, Hamide, Simic, Vladimir, & Pamucar, Dragan (2026). Benchmarking the financial performance of initial public offering companies via a Z score normalization-based MPSI-RBNAR hybrid approach. *Financial Innovation, 12*(1). https://doi.org/10.1186/s40854-025-00902-9.

Zhang, M., & Li, Y. (2025). Quality evaluation in hospital operations management using multi-criteria decision-making with plithogenic approach to address uncertainty and enhance decision-making processes. *Neutrosophic Sets and Systems, 80*, 564–575. https://digitalrepository.unm.edu/nss_journal/vol80/iss1/33/.

Chapter 92

CARD: Comprehensive approach based on relative difference for multi-attribute decision-making

Moein Khazaei[1] and Amirhossein Mostofi[2]
[1]*School of Engineering and Sciences, Tecnologico de Monterrey, Monterrey, Mexico,* [2]*Department of Management, Technology and Organization, Auckland University of Technology, New Zealand*

92.1 Introduction

In recent decades, decision-making has become increasingly complex due to the rapid interplay of technological advancements, environmental changes, and evolving socio-economic conditions (Khazaei et al., 2025a). As problems grow more interconnected and involve multiple dimensions, human reasoning alone often falls short in delivering consistently rational and structured evaluations (Khazaei et al., 2025b). To navigate such intricacies, multi-attribute decision-making (MADM) methods have gained traction across various fields (Khazaei et al., 2023). These methods now play a crucial role in areas like supply chain optimization, sustainability planning (Momeni et al., 2021), infrastructure evaluation, and energy system analysis (Francis & Thomas, 2023). By aggregating information from several often conflicting criteria, MADM models help guide decisions in a more systematic way (Pelissari et al., 2021). They not only bring objectivity to the process but also offer structured comparisons that support informed choices across both public and private sectors (Foukolaei et al., 2024).

Even with their popularity, most MADM techniques come with notable limitations. A significant issue is their reliance on absolute differences and normalization procedures to assess performance (Silva et al., 2024). While this seems straightforward, it can create inconsistencies in rankings depending on the normalization method used (He et al., 2021). More importantly, these approaches often fail to account for the proportional significance of criteria across different alternatives. For instance, a five-unit change in cost does not always equate to the same level of impact as a five-unit change in emissions or lead time (Wolde-Rufael & Mulat-Weldemeskel, 2023). These types of misalignments can lead to questionable prioritization. Furthermore, many existing models are limited in scope, typically handling either numerical ratings or pairwise preferences, but not both. This restricts their real-world applicability, where decision inputs are often hybrid in nature, combining quantitative scores with expert opinions (Azimi & Chen, 2025).

To overcome these challenges, this chapter introduces a new framework called the comprehensive approach based on relative difference (CARD) (Seiti et al., 2024). Instead of relying on absolute scales, CARD calculates the performance of each alternative in relation to a central reference point using logarithmic relative differences. This approach removes the need for traditional normalization and ensures that scale-independent comparisons are context-sensitive. Another key strength of CARD lies in its flexible strictness function, which lets decision-makers specify how strictly an option must align with the best or worst performers. Most notably, CARD can handle a mix of numerical data and qualitative preferences within the same decision matrix. This makes it especially valuable for complex situations that don't fit neatly into conventional evaluation frameworks. Overall, CARD contributes not just a new set of formulas but a more adaptive and realistic way to approach multicriteria decision-making.

The remainder of this chapter is organized as follows. Section 92.2 reviews related MADM literature and outlines the motivation for the CARD method. Section 3 presents the methodological framework in detail. Section 4 demonstrates the application of CARD through two numerical examples. Section 5 offers a sensitivity analysis and discussion. Finally, Section 6 concludes with key findings, strengths, limitations, and future research directions.

Encyclopedia of Multi-Attribute Decision-Making (MADM). DOI: https://doi.org/10.1016/B978-0-443-33275-3.00087-7

92.2 Literature review

Over the past decade, the MADM literature has witnessed significant growth, with numerous ranking models emerging (Silva et al., 2024). Despite these advancements, many of these methods still operate within traditional frameworks based on normalization or fixed utility aggregation (Dong et al., 2025). The CARD method was developed in response to two critical shortcomings in existing MADM models. First, it addresses the absence of relative performance modeling by introducing a logarithmic relative difference approach that compares each alternative to a central support point (SP) (Seiti et al., 2024). This SP, calculated as a geometric mean, allows for scale-independent comparisons and ensures that variations in magnitude are evaluated more contextually. This is especially relevant in domains such as environmental planning and risk assessment, where the significance of changes can vary depending on scale and context. Second, CARD introduces a flexible mechanism to unify hybrid evaluation formats, enabling the simultaneous use of direct numerical assessments and pairwise preference judgments. This capability significantly enhances the method's relevance in real-world settings where expert knowledge and incomplete quantitative data often coexist (Seiti et al., 2024).

While past models have advanced MADM methodology in various ways, they continue encountering structural limitations such as sensitivity to normalization, difficulties in compensatory aggregation, and rigid data input assumptions (Sahoo & Goswami, 2023). By contrast, CARD offers a more adaptable and integrated framework. Its SP logic, relative difference modeling, and adjustable closeness function combine to provide a decision-making tool that aligns better with real-world complexity. Whether applied in renewable energy site selection (Hasanzadeh et al., 2025), supplier evaluation for sustainable logistics, or urban planning strategies, CARD delivers both computational strength and practical relevance (Seiti et al., 2024). This positions it as a promising next-generation approach for tackling multidimensional decision challenges with greater nuance and interpretability.

92.3 Methods and materials

This study applies the CARD method to evaluate and prioritize decision alternatives within an MADM context. As a compensatory approach, CARD brings together several foundational elements, including relative difference analysis, SP modeling, and weighted utility-loss calculations, to assess the overall strength of each alternative (Seiti et al., 2024). Unlike many conventional ranking techniques that depend on absolute values or fixed ideal references, CARD adopts a more nuanced structure. It uses logarithmic transformations and geometric means to evaluate performance in a direction-sensitive and scale-independent way.

Step 1. Constructing the decision matrix

The process begins by defining the decision matrix D, where mmm alternatives are evaluated across n criteria. Each element x_{ij} in the matrix represents the performance score of the i alternative on the j criterion. This matrix provides the foundational structure of the problem, where rows correspond to decision alternatives, and columns represent evaluation criteria. Each entry is a direct evaluation, assumed to be beneficial (i.e., higher values indicate better performance), unless specified otherwise (Seiti et al., 2024).

$$D = \begin{bmatrix} x_{11} & \cdots & x_{1j} & \cdots & x_{1m} \\ \vdots & \ddots & \vdots & \ddots & \vdots \\ x_{i1} & \cdots & x_{ij} & \cdots & x_{im} \\ \vdots & \ddots & \vdots & \ddots & \vdots \\ x_{m1} & \cdots & x_{mk} & \cdots & x_{nm} \end{bmatrix}; \; i = 1, \; \ldots, \; n, \quad j = 1, \; \ldots, \; m \tag{92.1}$$

Step 2. Calculating relative performance using logarithmic difference

The relative difference is calculated using a logarithmic transformation to compare each alternative's performance relative to others under each criterion. The average performance of the i alternative with respect to all others under criterion j is computed as (Seiti et al., 2024):

$$P_{ij}^{d} = \frac{1}{m} \sum_{k=1}^{m} \ln\left(\frac{x_{ij}}{x_{kj}}\right) = \ln(x_{ij}) - \frac{1}{m} \sum_{k=1}^{m} \ln(x_{kj}) \tag{92.2}$$

This equation evaluates the average relative performance of alternative i under criterion j by comparing it to every other alternative. The logarithmic form captures the proportional difference rather than the absolute one, ensuring scale-invariance and interpretability. The right-hand side shows that this is equivalent to subtracting the mean of log-values from the log of the specific alternative's score. This value helps determine whether the alternative performs above or below the group's central tendency (geometric mean).

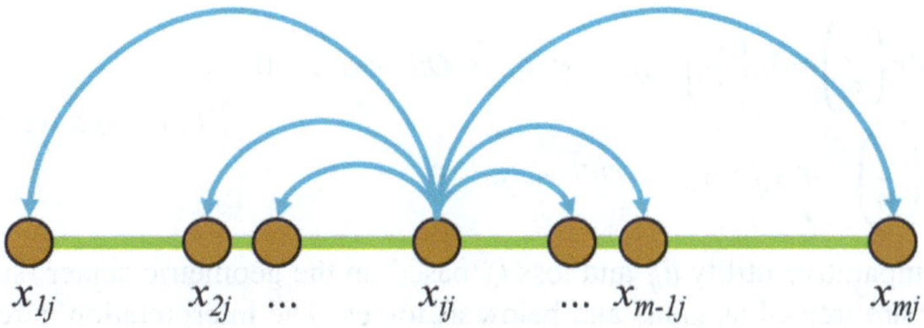

FIGURE 92.1 Relative difference and the concept of support point (Seiti et al., 2024).

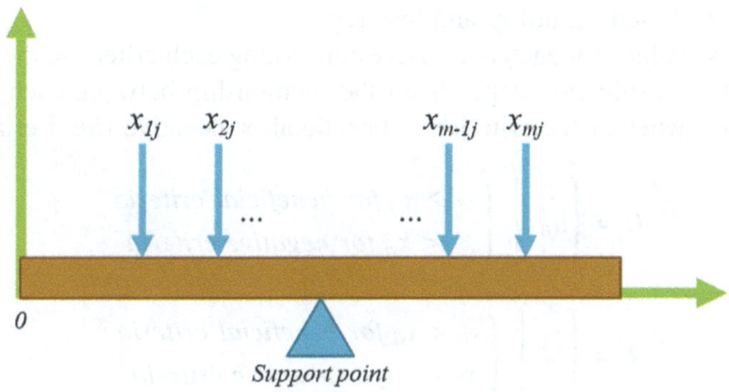

FIGURE 92.2 Support point as the balance of relative performances (Seiti et al., 2024).

Fig. 92.1 illustrates how the performance of a given alternative x_{ij} is compared with all other alternatives under the same criterion j using logarithmic ratios. Each blue arc represents the relative difference between the target alternative and the others. The SP x_{sj}, shown at the center, acts as the equilibrium point or center of gravity of these relative comparisons, where the sum of gains and losses equals zero (Seiti et al., 2024).

Step 3. Identifying the support point using geometric mean

The SP x_{sj} for each criterion j is the unique value at which the sum of all logarithmic relative differences across alternatives is zero. Mathematically, it satisfies the condition (Seiti et al., 2024):

$$\ln\left(\frac{x_{sj}}{x_{1j}}\right) + \ln\left(\frac{x_{sj}}{x_{2j}}\right) + \ldots + \ln\left(\frac{x_{sj}}{x_{mj}}\right) = 0 \rightarrow x_{sj} = \sqrt[m]{\prod_{i=1}^{m} x_{ij}} \tag{92.3}$$

This equation determines the SP x_{sj} as the geometric mean of all evaluations for criterion j. It serves as a balanced benchmark that separates utilities (when $x_{ij} \geq x_{sj}$) from losses (when $x_{ij} < x_{sj}$). Using the geometric mean preserves multiplicative consistency and enables the later use of logarithmic transformations without requiring data normalization.

Fig. 92.2 offers a visual interpretation of the SP concept, positioning it as a central pivot that balances each alternative's perceived utility and loss. The blue arrows indicate the logarithmic distances, reflecting how much an alternative deviates from the support value on a given criterion. When an alternative performs better than the SP, it contributes positively in the form of utility. In contrast, alternatives falling below this benchmark contribute to the loss. Placed at the center of the distribution, the SP represents the equilibrium where the net relative difference is minimized. This centrality gives it a stabilizing role in the evaluation process, helping to maintain consistency across varied performance scales (Seiti et al., 2024).

Step 4. Computing utility and loss relative to the support point

Once the SP x_{sj} for each criterion, the CARD method identifies the utility and loss of each alternative by comparing its score to the SP. The approach differs based on whether the criterion is beneficial (higher values are better) or negative (lower values are better) (Seiti et al., 2024).

$$\begin{cases} u_{ij}^{S} = \ln\left(\frac{x_{ij}}{x_{sj}}\right) \quad \text{if } x_{ij} \geq x_{sj}, \quad \text{Otherwise} \quad 0 \\ l_{ij}^{S} = -\ln\left(\frac{x_{ij}}{x_{sj}}\right) = \ln\left(\frac{x_{sj}}{x_{ij}}\right) \quad \text{if } x_{ij} < x_{sj}, \quad \text{Otherwise} \quad 0 \end{cases} \quad \textit{For Beneficial Criteria} \tag{92.4}$$

$$\begin{cases} u_{ij}^S = -\ln\left(\frac{x_{ij}}{x_{sj}}\right) = \ln\left(\frac{x_{sj}}{x_{ij}}\right) & \textit{if } x_{ij} < x_{sj}, \quad \textit{Otherwise} \quad 0 \\ l_{ij}^S = \ln\left(\frac{x_{ij}}{x_{sj}}\right) & \textit{if } x_{ij} \geq x_{sj}, \quad \textit{Otherwise} \quad 0 \end{cases} \quad \textit{For Negative Criteria} \tag{92.5}$$

These equations define comparative utility u_{ij}^S and loss l_{ij}^S based on the geometric center (support point). For beneficial criteria, values above the SP are treated as gains and below as losses. The interpretation is reversed for negative criteria (e.g., cost or risk). The logarithmic scale ensures proportional sensitivity and eliminates the need for normalization. If an alternative's score equals the SP, utility and loss are zero.

Step 5. Segregating alternatives based on utility and loss regions

After calculating utility and loss values for each alternative concerning each criterion, the other options are grouped into utility (U) and loss (L) sets. The classification depends on the relationship between each alternative's score x_{ij} and the corresponding SP x_{sj}, and also on whether the criterion is beneficial or negative (Seiti et al., 2024).

$$U = \left\{ u_{ij}^S \;\middle|\; \begin{cases} x_{ij} \geq x_{sj} \textit{ for beneficial criteria} \\ x_{ij} < x_{sj} \textit{ for negative criteria} \end{cases} \right. \tag{92.6}$$

$$L = \left\{ l_{ij}^S \;\middle|\; \begin{cases} x_{ij} < x_{sj} \textit{ for beneficial criteria} \\ x_{ij} \geq x_{sj} \textit{ for negative criteria} \end{cases} \right. \tag{92.7}$$

These sets serve as filters to separate performance values into gains and losses, depending on their position relative to the SP. This classification allows the model to handle each performance direction independently, crucial in building the later relative closeness functions.

Step 6. Identifying extremes in utility and loss

Once all utility and loss values are assigned to their respective sets, each set's minimum and maximum values are extracted. These serve as reference points for evaluating how relatively good or bad a specific alternative is compared to others (Seiti et al., 2024).

$$\begin{cases} u_j^{S\,\min} = \min_i(u_{ij}^S) \\ u_j^{S\,\max} = \max_i(u_{ij}^S) \\ l_j^{S\,\min} = \min_i(l_{ij}^S) \\ l_j^{S\,\max} = \max_i(l_{ij}^S) \end{cases} \tag{92.8}$$

These four values are the benchmark extremes for each criterion j. The relative performance of each alternative will later be scaled between these bounds using the weighted closeness coefficients, which account for both strictness preferences and the relative distance of values.

Step 7. Defining subjective weights of criteria

In MADM, decision-makers may assign subjective importance levels to criteria based on their preferences or expert judgment. These weights are defined as (Seiti et al., 2024):

$$W^S = [W_j^S]_{1\times n}\; j = 1, 2, \ldots, n \tag{92.9}$$

This row vector W^S contains the subjective weights assigned to each criterion j. These weights are typically obtained from decision-makers using methods such as analytical hierarchical process, direct rating, or expert elicitation. Each value W_j^S represents the relative importance of criterion j in the overall evaluation process.

Step 8. Calculating support-based dispersion for objective weighting

To complement subjective weights, the CARD method also introduces an objective weighting scheme based on how much variation exists in a criterion relative to its SP. This is measured using a logarithmic deviation-based dispersion metric (Seiti et al., 2024):

$$TD_j = \sqrt[2]{\left(\ln\left(\frac{x_{1j}}{x_{sj}}\right)\right)^2 + \left(\ln\left(\frac{x_{2j}}{x_{sj}}\right)\right)^2 + \ldots + \left(\ln\left(\frac{x_{mj}}{x_{sj}}\right)\right)^2} \tag{92.10}$$

The total deviation TD_j quantifies how much the alternatives deviate from the SP x_{sj} under criterion j. It is analogous to a standard deviation, but instead of using the arithmetic mean and absolute differences, it uses the geometric mean (support point) and logarithmic relative differences. Higher values of TD_j indicate greater discrimination power of that criterion across alternatives, which justifies assigning a higher objective weight.

Step 9. Computing objective weights based on support-point dispersion

After computing the dispersion TD_j for each criterion using Eq. (92.10), the objective weight for each criterion is calculated by normalizing these values across all criteria (Seiti et al., 2024):

$$W_j^o = \frac{TD_j}{\sum_{j=1}^{n} TD_j} \tag{92.11}$$

This equation assigns higher weights to criteria with greater variation in performance across alternatives, meaning they are more influential in distinguishing between options. The sum of all objective weights equals 1. This data-driven weight assignment method ensures that criteria with higher discriminatory power receive more emphasis in the decision process.

Step 10. Aggregating subjective and objective weights

To achieve a balanced and fair weighting structure (Mostofi et al., 2020), the CARD method combines the subjective weight W_j^s and objective weight W_j^o for each criterion into a final aggregated weight W_j, using the geometric mean (Seiti et al., 2024):

$$W_j = \frac{\sqrt{W_j^o . W_j^s}}{\sum_{j=1}^{n} \sqrt{W_j^o . W_j^s}} \tag{92.12}$$

This equation calculates the hybrid weight W_j, considering both the decision-maker's preferences (subjective) and the intrinsic discriminatory power of the criterion (objective). The geometric mean preserves proportionality and avoids dominance by extreme values. The resulting weights W_j are normalized to sum to 1, ensuring compatibility with subsequent weighted aggregation steps.

Step 11. Computing total weighted utility and loss for each alternative

After obtaining the relative utility u_{ij}^r and loss l_{ij}^r values for each alternative and attribute, and calculating the aggregated weights w_j, the total performance of each alternative is computed using a weighted sum (Seiti et al., 2024):

$$\begin{cases} u_i = \sum_{j=1}^{n} w_j . u_{ij}^r \\ l_i = \sum_{j=1}^{n} w_j . l_{ij}^r \end{cases} \tag{92.13}$$

These equations calculate the total weighted utility u_i and total weighted loss l_i for each alternative i. The utility score reflects how close an alternative is to high-performing benchmarks across beneficial criteria, while the loss score penalizes its distance from undesirable (or low-performance) benchmarks.

Step 12. Normalizing the utility and loss values

To ensure that both scores are scaled consistently and comparably across all alternatives, a normalization step is performed using max-normalization (Mazziotta & Pareto, 2022):

$$\begin{cases} u_i^n = \frac{u_i}{\max_i(u_i)} \\ l_i^n = 1 - \frac{l_i}{\max_i(l_i)} \end{cases} \tag{92.14}$$

The normalized utility u_i^n scales each alternative's utility between 0 and 1, where 1 represents the best utility observed. For losses, normalization is reversed such that lower losses yield higher scores. The best-performing alternative (with the lowest total loss) will receive the highest normalized loss score.

Step 13. Calculating the final performance score and ranking

Finally, the overall performance score P_i for each alternative is calculated as the average of its normalized utility and normalized (inverse) loss:

$$P_i = \frac{1}{2}(u_i^n + l_i^n), \quad 0 \le P_i \le 1 \tag{92.15}$$

This equation balances the alternative's utility (strengths) and minimizes losses (weaknesses). The result P_i reflects the overall suitability of each alternative, with higher values indicating better performance. Alternatives can then be ranked in descending order of P_i to support the final decision.

92.4 Numerical example 1

The first numerical example evaluates three potential policy interventions aimed at improving the performance of the biofuel supply chain (Marufuzzaman & Ekşioğlu, 2017). The policies include (A1) subsidies for biofuel producers, (A2) tax exemptions for consumers, and (A3) investment in supply chain infrastructure. The decision-making framework incorporates four criteria: greenhouse gas (GHG) reduction, total implementation cost, improvement of supply chain resilience, and enhancement of feedstock availability (Ghaedi et al., 2024). These criteria encompass beneficial (maximization) and negative (minimization) aspects of sustainability, resilience, and economic feasibility (Table 92.1).

Given the complexity of balancing environmental impact with economic and operational considerations (Gholian-Jouybari et al., 2024), the CARD method offers a robust approach to multicriteria decision-making under uncertainty. Using a strictness ratio of 0.5, the CARD approach facilitates structured comparison of policies by distinguishing performance ranges and applying compound weightings. The unequal weights applied across the criteria reflect their differing priorities, ensuring the final ranking is sensitive to real-world preferences. The results allow policymakers to identify which intervention delivers the most balanced and effective improvement in biofuel supply chain outcomes (Table 92.2).

The decision-making setup for this numerical example involves three alternative policies, A1 (subsidy), A2 (tax exempt), and A3 (infrastructure), evaluated across four criteria (Table 92.2): C1 (GHG reduction, beneficial), C2 (total implementation cost, negative), C3 (supply chain resilience, beneficial), and C4 (feedstock availability, beneficial). The decision matrix (D) contains the performance values for each policy under each criterion.

To demonstrate how values in Table 92.3 are calculated using the CARD method, the policy alternative A1 (subsidy) under criterion C3 (supply chain resilience) is selected as an example. The procedure begins by computing the SP for C3 using the geometric mean of the three alternatives:

$$SP_{C3} = \sqrt[3]{6.5 \times 5.8 \times 7.23} \approx \sqrt[3]{271.323} \approx 6.48$$

Next, the logarithmic relative difference is calculated. Since C3 is a beneficial criterion, the utility is computed for values above the SP, and the loss is computed for values below it. For A1:

$$u_{A1,C3} = \ln\left(\frac{6.5}{6.48}\right) \approx \ln(1.0031) \approx 0.0031$$

TABLE 92.1 Decision criteria and characteristics (Numerical example 1) .

Code	Criterion description	Type	Units
C1	Greenhouse gas reduction	Beneficial	% CO_2 reduction
C2	Total implementation cost	Negative	Million USD
C3	Supply chain resilience improvement	Beneficial	Composite index
C4	Feedstock availability increases	Beneficial	% Increase

TABLE 92.2 Decision matrix for biofuel policy alternatives under multiple criteria.

Policy/criterion	C1	C2	C3	C4
A1 (Subsidy)	18	40	6.5	15
A2 (Tax exempt)	15	30	5.8	12
A3 (Infrastructure)	20	50	7.2	18

TABLE 92.3 Final CARD results for biofuel policy alternatives, including total utility, loss, and normalized scores under equal strictness ($\xi = 0.5$).

Code	u_i	l_i	u_i^n	l_i^n	P_i
A1	0.1325	0.0443	0.1825	0.9388	0.5607
A2	0.2743	0.7256	0.3779	0	0.1889
A3	0.7256	0.2743	1	0.6220	0.8110

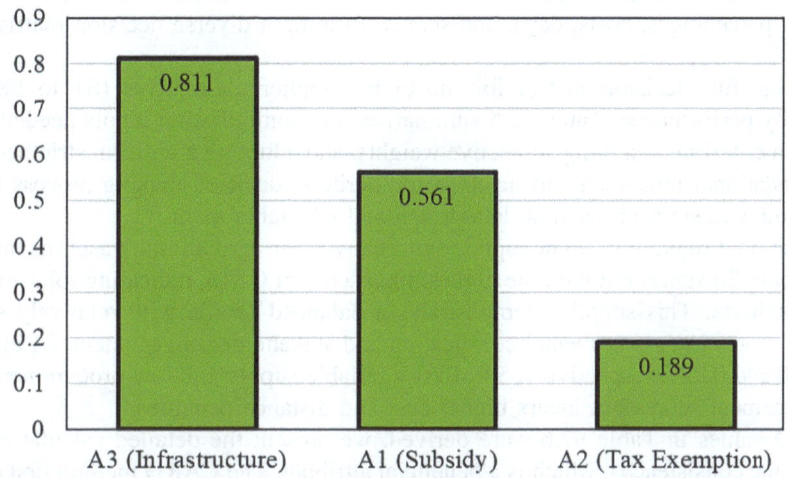

FIGURE 92.3 Comparative performance scores (P_i) of each biofuel policy alternative using the CARD method.

Then, utilities and losses are weighted using the assigned subjective weights (not shown in the snippet), aggregated across criteria, and normalized to obtain the final score. For A1, this process results in:

$$u_i^n = 0.1825, \quad l_i^n = 0.9388, \quad P_1 = \frac{u_i^n}{u_i^n + l_i^n} = \frac{0.1825 + 0.9388}{2} = 0.5607$$

This example illustrates how each value in Table 92.3 is derived using the CARD methodology, ensuring transparency and reproducibility. The results of the CARD method application for the biofuel policy selection problem are summarized in Table 92.3 and visualized in Fig. 92.3. Among the three alternatives, A3 (infrastructure investment) achieved the highest final performance score ($P_i = 0.811$), demonstrating its superiority in utility and acceptable loss levels. This suggests that infrastructure development is the most balanced and robust option in enhancing the biofuel supply chain under the given criteria. A1 ranks second with a moderate score ($P_i = 0.561$), indicating potential effectiveness but lower resilience compared to A3. A2, despite offering a lower cost, scored the lowest ($P_i = 0.189$) due to its limited contribution to resilience and feedstock availability, making it the least favorable among the three policy choices.

The results of numerical example 1 demonstrate the effectiveness of the CARD method in evaluating policy alternatives under a structured multicriteria decision-making framework. Among the three proposed biofuel supply chain policies, A3 consistently outperformed the others, achieving the highest final performance score ($P_i = 0.811$) at the base strictness level ($\xi = 0.5$).

92.5 Numerical example 2

This numerical example addresses the challenge of selecting a sustainable supplier for agricultural waste management by evaluating eight diverse alternatives (Taghipour et al., 2023). These suppliers (S1 to S8) represent a broad spectrum of operational models, including local cooperatives, regional aggregators, certified organic collectors, and municipal recycling programs (Ramezani et al., 2024). The goal is to identify the most appropriate option based on a multicriteria sustainability assessment that captures environmental responsibility, operational efficiency, and long-term viability.

The decision-making process incorporates six evaluation criteria, each with different significance levels. The criteria include beneficial and adverse attributes, such as emission reduction, processing cost, service reliability, and waste recovery rate. Subjective weights are assigned to reflect the decision-makers' priorities, and a strictness coefficient of $\xi = 0.5$ is applied across all criteria to balance conservatism and differentiation in performance assessment. This example illustrates the applicability of the CARD method in complex sustainability decisions that require both structured evaluation and nuanced interpretation.

The sustainable supplier selection problem for agricultural waste management incorporates a set of six carefully chosen criteria that reflect operational performance and sustainability objectives. These criteria are transportation distance (C1), supply volume consistency (C2), environmental certification score (C3), cost per tonne (C4), procurement response time (C5), and stakeholder engagement score (C6). These indicators capture environmental, economic, and social aspects, and include both beneficial (C2, C3, C6) and negative (C1, C4, C5) attributes. Each criterion is measured using appropriate units such as kilometers, percentages, costs, days, and scores, forming a diverse decision matrix suitable for real-world supplier evaluation.

Table 92.4 provides the full decision matrix for the eight supplier alternatives (S1 to S8), reflecting real-world variability in sustainability performance. Table 92.5 summarizes the configuration inputs needed for the CARD method, including classifying each criterion, assigning subjective weights, and adopting a uniform strictness value of $\xi = 0.5$ across all attributes. These foundational inputs support a robust multicriteria decision-making process aimed at identifying the most sustainable agricultural waste supplier in a data-driven and adaptable manner.

Table 92.6 presents the final ranking of eight supplier alternatives for agricultural waste management, evaluated using the CARD method. Supplier S6 stands out with the highest final score of 0.818, indicating robust performance across both beneficial and negative criteria. This supplier demonstrates a balanced profile with relatively short transport distance, moderate cost, and solid scores in environmental certification and stakeholder engagement. S1 and S4 also perform well, with final scores of 0.760 and 0.727, respectively. S1 offers a reliable supply and low procurement delay, while S4 excels in certification and engagement scores but incurs higher cost and distance penalties.

To clarify how CARD values in Table 92.6 were derived, we present the detailed calculation for supplier S1 under criterion C2 (supply volume consistency), which is a beneficial attribute. The CARD method first computes the SP for this criterion using the geometric mean of all suppliers' C2 values:

$$SP_{C2} = \sqrt[8]{90 \times 85 \times 80 \times 95 \times 92 \times 88 \times 89 \times 86} \approx \sqrt[8]{4.97 \times 1015} \approx 87.97$$

Since S1's value (90) is greater than the SP, it gains utility:

$$u_{S1,C2} = \ln\left(\frac{90}{87.97}\right) \approx \ln\,(1.023) \approx 0.0227$$

And:

$$l_{S1,C2} = 0$$

TABLE 92.4 Decision criteria and characteristics (Numerical example 2).

Code	Criterion description	Type	Unit
C1	Transportation distance	Negative	*km*
C2	Supply volume consistency	Beneficial	% Reliability
C3	Environmental certification score	Beneficial	0–100 scale
C4	Cost per ton	Negative	USD/ton
C5	Response time (procurement delay)	Negative	Days
C6	Stakeholder engagement score	Beneficial	0–10 scale

TABLE 92.5 Decision matrix for supplier evaluation.

Supplier/criterion	C1 (*km*)	C2 (%)	C3 (0–100)	C4 ($/ton)	C5 (days)	C6 (0–10)
S1	35	90	70	45	5	7.5
S2	60	85	75	40	7	6.0
S3	20	80	65	48	4	5.5
S4	50	95	90	52	6	8.5
S5	75	92	85	55	9	7.0
S6	25	88	72	42	5	6.5
S7	40	89	80	49	6	7.0
S8	30	86	68	47	3	6.0

TABLE 92.6 Final scores of suppliers based on CARD method ($\xi = 0.5$).

Code	u_i	l_i	u_i^n	l_i^n	P_i
S1	0.302084	0.112635	0.715211	0.805005	0.760108
S2	0.127754	0.504666	0.302468	0.126314	0.214391
S3	0.388322	0.452032	0.919385	0.217436	0.56841
S4	0.422371	0.315575	1	0.453671	0.726836
S5	0.261692	0.577629	0.619579	0	0.309789
S6	0.35379	0.117024	0.837628	0.797406	0.817517
S7	0.160677	0.150298	0.380417	0.739802	0.560109
S8	0.33194	0.285645	0.785896	0.505487	0.645692

If we consider another supplier such as S2 (C2 = 85), which is below the SP:

$$u_{S2,C2} = 0,$$

$$l_{S2,C2} = \ln\left(\frac{87.97}{85}\right) \approx \ln\,(1.035) \approx 0.0344$$

The total utility and loss for S1 are calculated by repeating this process for all six criteria and then applying the subjective weights. The normalized utility and loss are computed by scaling all utility and loss scores across suppliers to a 0–1 range. Finally, S1's performance index is computed as:

$$P_{S1} = \frac{u_i^n}{u_i^n + l_i^n} = \frac{0.7152 + 0.8050}{2} = 0.7601$$

This example illustrates how the CARD method calculates values from raw data to final scores by leveraging geometric means, logarithmic transformation, and structured aggregation.

Fig. 92.4 visually compares the final scores of the suppliers, highlighting the dominance of S6 in the selection process. The figure shows a noticeable performance gap between the top three suppliers (S6, S1, and S4) and the remaining

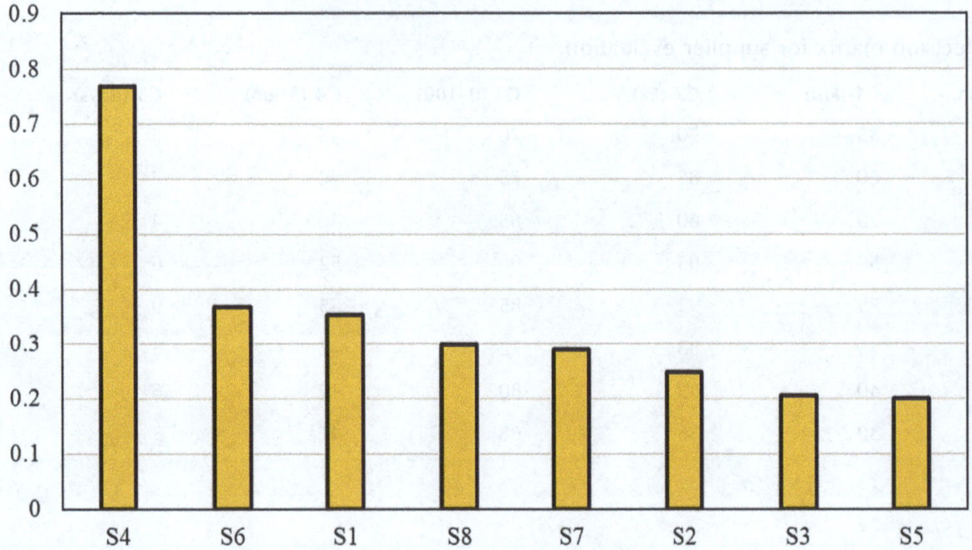

FIGURE 92.4 Final scores of supplier alternatives in sustainable agricultural waste selection.

alternatives. Suppliers like S5 and S3 score below 0.55, mainly due to poor performance on negative criteria such as high cost or longer delivery times. The bar chart effectively communicates the overall trade-offs. It supports decision-makers in identifying the most sustainable and practical supplier for agricultural waste sourcing under the specified decision criteria and strictness level.

The numerical analysis conducted in this section underscores the practical capability of the CARD method in supporting sustainability-driven decision-making for supplier selection in agricultural waste management. The model could rank and differentiate suppliers based on six heterogeneous economic, environmental, and social criteria by applying the method to a diverse set of eight real-world-inspired supplier alternatives. The computed performance scores reflect each supplier's strengths and weaknesses and integrate subjective preferences and relative penalties through a unified strictness setting ($\xi = 0.5$). The results demonstrate that the CARD method balances optimism (utility) and caution (loss) while maintaining interpretability and decision relevance.

92.6 Comparative analysis

For the numerical examples, to evaluate the robustness of the CARD method under varying levels of strictness, a sensitivity analysis was conducted by adjusting the parameter ξ from 0.1 to 0.9. Table 92.7 presents the sensitivity analysis of the CARD method results under varying levels of strictness ($\xi = 0.1$ to 0.9). The utility and loss values for each alternative shift significantly as the strictness increases, particularly affecting A1. At lower strictness ($\xi = 0.1$), A1 achieves a high final score ($P_1 = 0.767$), indicating strong utility with minimal penalization. However, as ξ increases, the method becomes more stringent about deviations, causing A1 score to drop gradually to $P_1 = 0.428$ at $\xi = 0.9$. On the other hand, A2 remains constant across all ξ values due to its consistently high loss and low utility, resulting in a fixed low performance score ($P_2 = 0.189$). A3 maintains its dominance across all scenarios, showing robust performance even under high strictness, highlighting its balanced advantage in both benefit and cost-related criteria.

Fig. 92.5 summarizes the best-performing policy for each strictness level based on the final CARD scores. Across all tested values of strictness ($\xi = 0.1$ to 0.9), A3 remains the top-ranked alternative. Interestingly, its score slightly improves from 0.811 at $\xi = 0.1$ to 0.874 at $\xi = 0.9$, suggesting that A3 benefits from the method's growing emphasis on consistent, superior performance. This consistency reinforces A3's role as the most resilient and effective biofuel policy, capable of withstanding stricter evaluation scenarios without losing its position.

Sensitivity analysis further confirmed the robustness of A3 across a range of strictness values, with its final score steadily improving under more stringent evaluation. In contrast, A2 consistently lagged due to its lower utility and high associated losses. The analysis reveals that A3 strikes the most balanced compromise between reducing emissions, improving resilience, and increasing feedstock availability, even though it incurs the highest cost. Thus, the CARD method supports a comprehensive and nuanced policy evaluation that accounts for subjective preferences and data-driven performance variation across decision scenarios.

TABLE 92.7 Sensitivity analysis of CARD method results across five ξ, showing changes in utility, loss, normalized values, and final performance score for each alternative (numerical example 1).

Alternative	Strictness	u_i	l_i	u_i^n	l_i^n	P_i
A1	0.1	0.404609	0.016566	0.557551	0.977173	0.767362
A2	0.1	0.274309	0.725691	0.377997	0	0.188999
A3	0.1	0.725691	0.274309	1	0.622003	0.811001
A1	0.3	0.214061	0.027224	0.294975	0.962485	0.62873
A2	0.3	0.274309	0.725691	0.377997	0	0.188999
A3	0.3	0.725691	0.274309	1	0.622003	0.811001
A1	0.5	0.1325	0.044341	0.182584	0.938898	0.560741
A2	0.5	0.274309	0.725691	0.377997	0	0.188999
A3	0.5	0.725691	0.274309	1	0.622003	0.811001
A1	0.7	0.084899	0.076342	0.11699	0.8948	0.505895
A2	0.7	0.274309	0.725691	0.377997	0	0.188999
A3	0.7	0.725691	0.274309	1	0.622003	0.811001
A1	0.9	0.053242	0.157568	0.073367	0.782872	0.42812
A2	0.9	0.274309	0.725691	0.377997	0	0.188999
A3	0.9	0.725691	0.274309	1	0.622003	0.811001

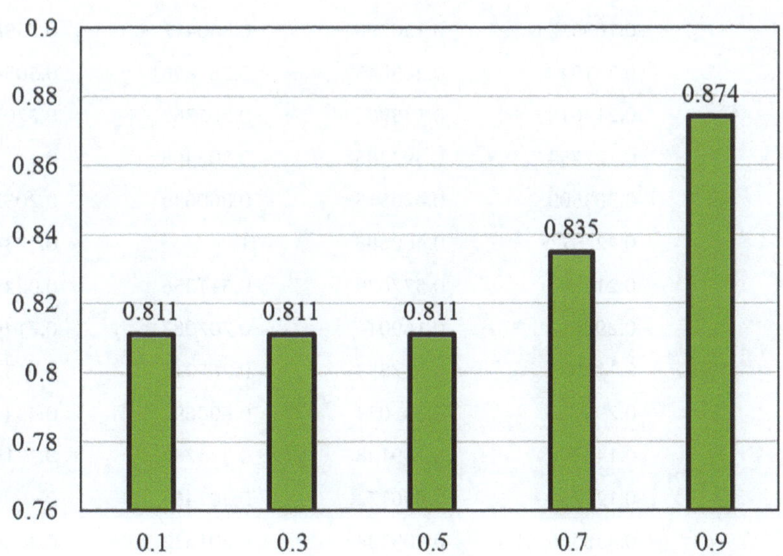

FIGURE 92.5 Best-performing biofuel policy (A3) for each strictness level based on P (numerical example 1).

For the second numerical example, as observed across the scenarios through Table 92.8, supplier S6 consistently maintains a strong position, with P_i remaining above 0.60 in all settings and peaking at 0.91 for $\xi = 0.3$. This highlights its reliability and balanced performance across both beneficial and negative criteria, especially when decision-makers prioritize moderate caution in utility-loss trade-offs.

TABLE 92.8 Sensitivity analysis results of P_i across ξ values (numerical example 2).

Supplier	Strictness	u_i	l_i	u_i^n	l_i^n	P_i
S1	0.1	0.638783	0.066971	1	0.884059	0.942029
S2	0.1	0.127754	0.325866	0.199995	0.435856	0.317926
S3	0.1	0.437619	0.434069	0.685082	0.248534	0.466808
S4	0.1	0.422371	0.178484	0.661212	0.691007	0.676109
S5	0.1	0.37705	0.577629	0.590263	0	0.295131
S6	0.1	0.500017	0.053198	0.782764	0.907903	0.845334
S7	0.1	0.336407	0.064727	0.526637	0.887943	0.70729
S8	0.1	0.427267	0.187612	0.668875	0.675203	0.672039
S1	0.3	0.427459	0.089699	1	0.844711	0.922355
S2	0.3	0.127754	0.417121	0.298867	0.277874	0.288371
S3	0.3	0.413025	0.441193	0.966232	0.2362	0.601216
S4	0.3	0.422371	0.243244	0.988097	0.578892	0.783495
S5	0.3	0.31212	0.577629	0.730174	0	0.365087
S6	0.3	0.413901	0.080573	0.968281	0.86051	0.914396
S7	0.3	0.228851	0.100299	0.535374	0.82636	0.680867
S8	0.3	0.374738	0.237465	0.876663	0.588897	0.73278
S1	0.5	0.302084	0.112635	0.715211	0.805005	0.760108
S2	0.5	0.127754	0.504666	0.302468	0.126314	0.214391
S3	0.5	0.388322	0.452032	0.919385	0.217436	0.56841
S4	0.5	0.422371	0.315575	1	0.453671	0.726836
S5	0.5	0.261692	0.577629	0.619579	0	0.309789
S6	0.5	0.35379	0.117024	0.837628	0.797406	0.817517
S7	0.5	0.160677	0.150298	0.380417	0.739802	0.560109
S8	0.5	0.33194	0.285645	0.785896	0.505487	0.645692
S1	0.7	0.213619	0.13578	0.505762	0.770753	0.638257
S2	0.7	0.127754	0.592286	0.302468	0	0.151234
S3	0.7	0.363509	0.470515	0.860639	0.205595	0.533117
S4	0.7	0.422371	0.400688	1	0.323488	0.661744
S5	0.7	0.21594	0.577629	0.511256	0.024746	0.268001
S6	0.7	0.298653	0.16901	0.707087	0.714648	0.710868
S7	0.7	0.111933	0.227857	0.265011	0.615293	0.440152
S8	0.7	0.295107	0.335054	0.698692	0.434303	0.566498
S1	0.9	0.145206	0.159138	0.343789	0.77141	0.5576
S2	0.9	0.127754	0.696172	0.302468	0	0.151234
S3	0.9	0.338586	0.509134	0.801632	0.268668	0.53515
S4	0.9	0.422371	0.508619	1	0.269406	0.634703
S5	0.9	0.170147	0.577629	0.402838	0.170279	0.286559
S6	0.9	0.240858	0.254045	0.570252	0.635083	0.602668
S7	0.9	0.074667	0.380487	0.176782	0.453458	0.31512
S8	0.9	0.262933	0.39017	0.622516	0.43955	0.531033

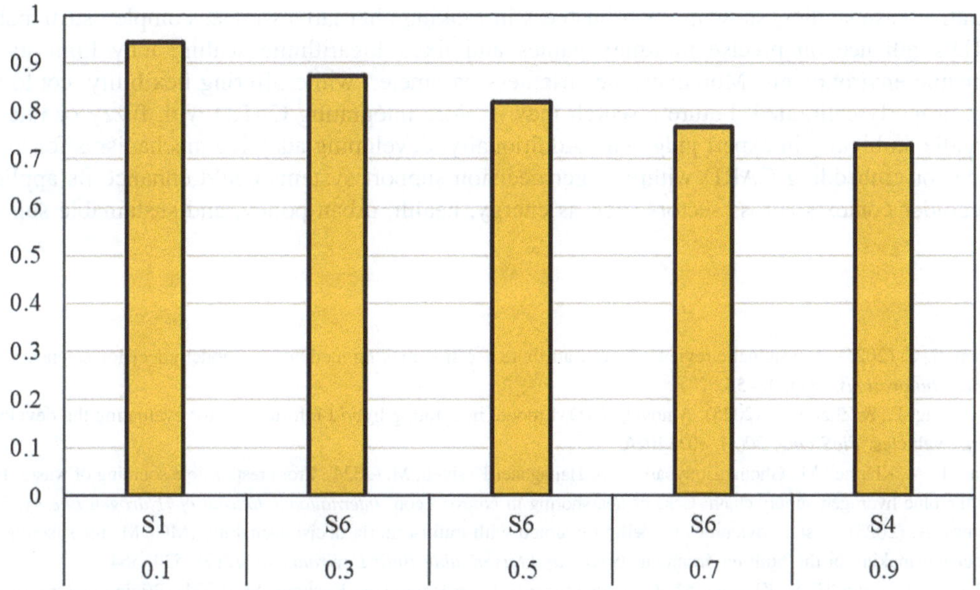

FIGURE 92.6 Variation in P_i of top suppliers across ξ in each scenario (numerical example 2).

In contrast, Suppliers S2 and S5 display significant sensitivity to changes in ξ. Both suppliers start with low performance (e.g., $P_i < 0.32$ for S2 under $\xi = 0.1$) and experience further rank degradation or inconsistency when strictness increases. This instability suggests that their selection is more vulnerable to the decision-maker's risk attitude and may only be acceptable under highly lenient conditions. On the other hand, suppliers like S1 and S4 remain relatively stable across most scenarios. S1's P_i ranges from 0.92 ($\xi = 0.3$) to 0.55 ($\xi = 0.9$), still preserving a competitive ranking among top candidates. S4 also demonstrates resilience with only slight drops in ranking as ξ increases, indicating robust performance when evaluated under both lenient and strict conditions.

The sensitivity results reinforce prioritizing suppliers like S6 and S1, especially under moderate ξ values (0.3–0.5), where utility and loss are fairly balanced. Fig. 92.6 illustrates the decreasing trend of P_i for most suppliers as strictness increases, validating that decision-maker preferences significantly affect supplier selection outcomes. This robustness check ensures that final decisions remain stable under varying risk tolerance levels, making the CARD method flexible and transparent for practical procurement contexts.

92.7 Conclusion

This study introduced the CARD method as a new approach to multi-attribute decision-making. By defining separate utility and loss functions and integrating them into a single performance index, the method captures optimistic and pessimistic outlooks within decision analysis. CARD was applied to two illustrative cases: a traditional supplier selection scenario and a more complex sustainable agricultural waste supplier evaluation. The second case involved mixed beneficial and nonbeneficial criteria and varying levels of decision-maker strictness. The outcomes from both examples showed that CARD handles noncompensatory conditions, asymmetric criteria behavior, and decision flexibility effectively, supporting its potential as a versatile tool in applied decision-making environments.

Among its key strengths, CARD offers high adaptability and intuitive interpretability. The method introduces a strictness parameter that allows decision-makers to adjust sensitivity toward deviations across attributes, offering a tailored approach in evaluating trade-offs. It simultaneously deals with beneficial and detrimental criteria and supports subjective weights without depending on traditional distance-based assumptions. Another advantage lies in the explicit separation and normalization of utility and loss, which brings greater transparency into the scoring logic. CARD's graphical and tabular results enhance its clarity, making it a good fit for sustainability assessments, procurement analysis, and other strategic decision domains.

This chapter introduced the CARD, a novel MADM technique designed to overcome key challenges in conventional decision models such as normalization dependency, lack of scale independence, and limited flexibility in handling hybrid inputs. By leveraging SPs and logarithmic relative differences, CARD offers a unified utility-loss framework that reflects both beneficial and nonbeneficial criteria under varying degrees of decision-maker strictness. The method was validated using two illustrative case studies, showing its robustness in ranking alternatives under complex sustainability scenarios. However, CARD's reliance on precise min-max values and fixed logarithmic scaling may limit its adaptability in uncertain or dynamic environments. Moreover, the strictness parameter, while offering flexibility, could introduce result sensitivity if not properly calibrated. Future research may explore integrating CARD with fuzzy or interval-based data, enabling it to handle ambiguity in expert judgment. Additionally, developing adaptive mechanisms for learning decision-maker preferences or embedding CARD within larger decision-support systems could enhance its applicability in real-time, multistakeholder contexts across sectors such as energy, health, urban policy, and sustainable supply chains.

References

Azimi, S. M., & Chen, S.-C. (2025). A systematic review of multi-attribute decision making methods for modern decision science. *Information Sciences and Technological Innovations, 2*(1), 48–56.

Dong, Y., Wang, D., Zeng, F., & Zhang, Y. (2025). A novel MADM model integrating hybrid information for evaluating the development prospects of urban new energy vehicles. *PloS One, 20*(1), e0314026.

Foukolaei, P. Z., Asari, F. A., Khazaei, M., Gholian-Jouybari, F., & Hajiaghaei-Keshteli, M. (2024). From responsible sourcing of wastes to sustainable energy consumption in the blue hydrogen supply chain: Case of nearshoring in Nuevo Leon. *International Journal of Hydrogen Energy, 77*, 1387–1400.

Francis, A., & Thomas, A. (2023). System dynamics modelling coupled with multi-criteria decision-making (MCDM) for sustainability-related policy analysis and decision-making in the built environment. *Smart and Sustainable Built Environment, 12*(3), 534–564.

Ghaedi, M., Foukolaei, P. Z., Asari, F. A., Khazaei, M., Gholian-Jouybari, F., & Hajiaghaei-Keshteli, M. (2024). Pricing electricity from blue hydrogen to mitigate the energy rebound effect: A case study in agriculture and livestock. *International Journal of Hydrogen Energy, 84*, 993–1003.

Gholian-Jouybari, F., et al. (2024). Developing environmental, social and governance (ESG) strategies on evaluation of municipal waste disposal centers: A case of Mexico. *Chemosphere, 364*, 142961.

Hasanzadeh, H., Mohammadi, S., Shafii, M. B., & Daneshvar, M. (2025). Designing and constructing a solar thermal water desalination system: Evaluating the role of thermoelectric in enhancing evaporation and condensation process. *Next Energy, 9*, 100388.

He, L., Ishibuchi, H., Trivedi, A., Wang, H., Nan, Y., & Srinivasan, D. (2021). A survey of normalization methods in multiobjective evolutionary algorithms. *IEEE Transactions on Evolutionary Computation, 25*(6), 1028–1048.

Khazaei, M., Gholian-Jouybari, F., Dolatabadi, M. D., Alamdari, A. P., Eskandari, H., & Hajiaghaei-Keshteli, M. (2025b). Renewable energy portfolio in Mexico for Industry 5.0 and SDGs: Hydrogen, wind, or solar? *Renewable and Sustainable Energy Reviews, 213*, 115420.

Khazaei, M., Gholian-Jouybari, F., Ramezani, M., & Hajiaghaei-Keshteli, M. (2025a). Environmental, social, and governance enablers of the hydrogen supply chain: Application of community operational research using STRIDES framework. *Journal of Environmental Management, 389*, 126092.

Khazaei, M., Hajiaghaei-Keshteli, M., Rajabzadeh Ghatari, A., Ramezani, M., Fooladvand, A., & Azar, A. (2023). A multi-criteria supplier evaluation and selection model without reducing the level of optimality. *Soft Computing, 27*(22), 17175–17188.

Marufuzzaman, M., & Ekşioğlu, S. D. (2017). Designing a reliable and dynamic multimodal transportation network for biofuel supply chains. *Transportation Science, 51*(2), 494–517.

Mazziotta, M., & Pareto, A. (2022). Normalization methods for spatio-temporal analysis of environmental performance: Revisiting the min–max method. *Environmetrics, 33*(5), e2730.

Momeni, M. A., Kumar, S., Jain, V., Mostofi, A., & Chandra, C. (2021). A perspective on improving the multicriteria decision-making environment. *IEEE Engineering Management Review, 49*(2), 196–203.

Mostofi, A., Kumar, S., Jain, V., Chandra, C., & Momeni, M. A. (2020). The interactive weighting method concerning consistency, inadequacy, complementary and supplementary properties of criteria. *IEEE Transactions on Engineering Management, 69*(5), 2014–2025.

Pelissari, R., Oliveira, M. C., Abackerli, A. J., Ben-Amor, S., & Assumpção, M. R. P. (2021). Techniques to model uncertain input data of multi-criteria decision-making problems: A literature review. *International Transactions in Operational Research, 28*(2), 523–559.

Ramezani, M., Khazaei, M., Gholian-Jouybari, F., Sandoval-Correa, A., Bonakdari, H., & Hajiaghaei-Keshteli, M. (2024). Turquoise hydrogen and waste optimization: A Bi-objective closed-loop and sustainable supply chain model for a case in Mexico. *Renewable and Sustainable Energy Reviews, 195*, 114329.

Sahoo, S. K., & Goswami, S. S. (2023). A comprehensive review of multiple criteria decision-making (MCDM) methods: Advancements, applications, and future directions. *Decision Making Advances, 1*(1), 25–48.

Seiti, H., Boral, S., Hafezalkotob, A., Ben-Amor, S., Hafezalkotob, A., & Makui, A. (2024). CARD: Comprehensive approach based on relative difference for decision-making problems with dual evaluation forms– Application to sustainable renewable energy selection. *Expert Systems with Applications, 255*, 124643.

Silva, F. S. D., Lima, M. P., Corujo, D., Neto, A. J. V., & Esposito, F. (2024). A comprehensive step-wise survey of multiple attribute decision-making mobility approaches. *IEEE Access, 12*, 108616–108656.

Taghipour, A., Foukolaei, P. Z., Ghaedi, M., & Khazaei, M. (2023). Sustainable multi-objective models for waste-to-energy and waste separation site selection. *Sustainability, 15*(22), 15764.

Wolde-Rufael, Y., & Mulat-Weldemeskel, E. (2023). Effectiveness of environmental taxes and environmental stringent policies on CO_2 emissions: The European experience. *Environment, Development and Sustainability, 25*(6), 5211–5239.

Section 4

Outranking methods

Chapter 93

ELECTRE: Elimination and choice expressing reality for multi-attribute decision-making

Babek Erdebilli[1,2] and Yeşim Erdebilli[1]
[1]*Department of Industrial Engineering, Ankara Yıldırım Beyazıt University, Ankara, Turkey,* [2]*School of Business, Worcester Polytechnic Institute, Worcester, MA, United States*

93.1 Introduction

At this stage, multi-criteria decision-making (MCDM) methods provide a robust and systematic framework for addressing complex selection problems, offering decision-makers (DMs) an analytical approach to evaluate alternatives (Ayyildiz & Taskin Gumus, 2020; Haseli & Sheikh, 2022; Haseli et al., 2023; Torkabadi et al., 2025). Traditional MCDM techniques typically focus on determining the weight of each criterion and comparing alternatives based on these weights. However, most of these methods fall short in directly capturing behavioral factors, such as DMs' risk perceptions and asymmetric attitudes toward gains and losses, even though such cognitive biases naturally influence human decision-making processes.

The ELimination Et Choix Traduisant la RÉalité (ELECTRE) method, originally developed by Roy (Benayoun & Billsberry, 2007), is a widely used decision-making approach in operations management for determining preferences and priorities in complex problems. It accommodates both qualitative and quantitative criteria, supporting DMs in diverse problem contexts.

Traditional ELECTRE allows users to work with ordered numerical scales without converting them into obscure rankings, and it incorporates indifference and preference thresholds, which were difficult to define in earlier models, thereby enabling better handling of imprecise or flawed information. The method typically proceeds in two stages: constructing the outranking relations and analyzing these relations (Kahraman et al., 2003).

At its core, the ELECTRE method is grounded in pairwise comparisons of alternatives with respect to each evaluation criterion. Rather than merely producing a complete ranking, ELECTRE seeks to determine the outranking relationships—identifying whether one alternative can be considered sufficiently superior to another, given the decision-maker's preferences and the relative importance of each criterion. This approach allows for situations in which some criteria may strongly support one alternative while others may not, reflecting a more nuanced and realistic decision process compared to purely aggregative models.

Due to its flexibility and adaptability, ELECTRE has gained substantial attention across diverse decision-making domains, including urban and regional planning, environmental management, transportation project evaluation, supply chain optimization, and industrial engineering. Over time, a series of variants—such as ELECTRE I, II, III, IV, and ELECTRE TRI—have been developed, each tailored to specific decision contexts. For example, ELECTRE II is often used for ranking problems with a focus on stability over time, ELECTRE III incorporates fuzzy and imprecise data through pseudo-criteria and indifference thresholds, ELECTRE IV is suited for cases without explicit weighting of criteria, and ELECTRE TRI is designed for sorting alternatives into predefined categories. Although these variants differ in procedural details, such as concordance/discordance threshold definitions, aggregation rules, and treatment of indifference or preference thresholds—they all share a common set of foundational principles relating to outranking relations, concordance/discordance analysis, and exploitation procedures.

Encyclopedia of Multi-Attribute Decision-Making (MADM). DOI: https://doi.org/10.1016/B978-0-443-33275-3.00052-X

93.2 Literature review

The ELECTRE was first developed for real-world trading and financial decision applications (Andriosopoulos et al., 2012; Roy & Bertier, 1973). ELECTRE I, ELECTRE IS, ELECTRE II, and ELECTRE III (Chen, 2016) are just a few of the variations of the methodology that have emerged since its inception, all of which are intended to better suit various decision environments and analytical requirements.

ELECTRE was first created to overcome significant shortcomings of conventional compensatory decision-making models, particularly in situations where trade-offs between criteria are not entirely acceptable, uncertainty is common, or qualitative judgments are crucial. The method is especially well-suited for complex, conflicting, or multidimensional evaluation problems because of its basic noncompensatory logic, which produces a more realistic representation of real-world decision behavior. With the help of numerous academics, the method has been improved and strengthened theoretically over time. Among the most significant are who developed the theoretical underpinnings of outranking approaches, and whose work increased ELECTRE's usefulness in planning, public policy, and spatial analysis contexts. Through their efforts, ELECTRE evolved from a specialized decision-making tool to a widely used framework in a variety of fields, such as supply chain decision-making, engineering, finance, and environmental management.

The first two steps of the ELECTRE method—normalizing the decision matrix and applying weights to criteria—closely resemble the early stages of the technique for order preference by similarity to ideal solution (TOPSIS) method, which is an intriguing methodological observation. However, ELECTRE concentrates on creating and evaluating outranking relations to eliminate less desirable options, whereas TOPSIS moves forward by calculating distances to an ideal solution and an antiideal solution. This distinction highlights ELECTRE's focus on relative dominance as opposed to absolute closeness to an ideal point.

To use ELECTRE, a specific sequence of steps must be followed. Initially, the decision matrix was designed to handle the various measurement units. The normalized criteria are then assigned weights that indicate their relative importance. To determine how much better one option is than the other, a concordance matrix is then created. A discordance matrix is then created. This matrix displays the relative inferiority of each option for each criterion. These matrices establish outranking relations by comparing the concordance and discordance indices to establish thresholds. Ultimately, these outranking results either eliminate some options or rank them, resulting in a full list or a better set of options. Ultimately, these outranking results either eliminate some options or rank them, resulting in a better selection of options or a complete list of all the options.

Through these phases, ELECTRE gives DMs a methodical, transparent, and logically sound tool for handling challenging issues requiring the integration of both quantitative and qualitative assessments.

93.3 Methodology

MCDM techniques are widely used, especially when handling multidimensional and complex decision problems. In the literature, conventional methods like analytic hierarchy process, analytic network process, TOPSIS, VlseKriterijumska Optimizacija I Kompromisno Resenj, and ELECTRE are still widely used. On the other hand, methods that take into account human behavioral dynamics are becoming more and more popular. In this section, the ELECTRE helps DMs navigate challenging issues requiring the integration of both quantitative and qualitative assessments.

Benayoun first presented the ELECTRE method, an MCDM technique, in 1966. To establish a preference structure, it uses pairwise comparisons between alternatives for each evaluation criterion. According to Triantaphyllou (2000), the procedure consists of eight methodical steps. A thorough description of these procedures can be found below:

Notations:

m: number of alternatives where $i = 1, \ldots, m$

n: number of criteria where $j = 1, \ldots, n$

A: decision matrix

X: standard decision matrix

Y: weighted normalized decision matrix

C_{kl}: concordance sets

D_{kl}: discordance sets

F: concordance dominance matrices

G: discordance dominance matrices

E: aggregate dominance matrix

Step 1. Construction of the decision matrix (*A*)

The rows of the decision matrix represent the decision points (alternatives) whose preferences are to be ranked, while the columns contain the evaluation factors (criteria) to be utilized in the decision-making process. The decision matrix (*A*) contains alternatives as rows and evaluation criteria as columns. It shows the initial input from the decision-maker.

Let:

$$A_{ij} = \begin{bmatrix} a_{11} & a_{12}\ldots & a_{1n} \\ a_{21} & a_{22}\ldots & a_{2n} \\ a_{m1} & a_{m2}\ldots & a_{mn} \end{bmatrix}$$

As given below:

m = *number of alternatives (rows) where* $i = 1, \ldots, m$

n = *number of evaluation criteria (columns) where* $j = 1, \ldots, n$

Step 2. Forming standard decision matrix (*X*)

The standard decision matrix (*X*) is applied for all elements.

$$X_{ij} = \begin{bmatrix} x_{11} & x_{12}\ldots & x_{1n} \\ x_{21} & x_{22}\ldots & x_{2n} \\ x_{m1} & x_{m2}\ldots & x_{mn} \end{bmatrix}$$

The criteria are given below in the formula:

For benefit criteria

$$X_{ij} = \frac{a_{ij}}{\sqrt{\sum_{k=1}^{m} a_{kj}^2}} \quad i = 1, \ldots, m \; j = 1, \ldots, n$$

For cost criteria

$$X_{ij} = \frac{1/a_{ij}}{\sqrt{\sum_{k=1}^{m} [1/a_{ij}]^2}} \quad i = 1, \ldots, m \; j = 1, \ldots, n$$

Step 3. Calculation of the weighted normalized decision matrix (*Y*)

First, the weights of the evaluation factors (w_j) are determined, satisfying the condition:

$$\sum_{j=1}^{n} w_j = 1$$

Then, the normalized decision matrix is multiplied by the corresponding weighted (w_j) values to obtain the weighted normalized decision matrix (Y_{ij}).

$$Y_{ij} = w_{ij}x_{ij} \quad i = 1, \ldots, m \; j = 1, \ldots, n$$

$$Y_{ij} = \begin{bmatrix} w_1x_{11} & w_2x_{12}\ldots & w_nx_{1n} \\ w_1x_{21} & w_2x_{22}\ldots & w_nx_{2n} \\ w_1x_{m1} & w_2x_{m2}\ldots & w_nx_{mn} \end{bmatrix}$$

Step 4: The concordance (C_{kl}) and discordance (D_{kl}) sets are determined

The Y_{ij} matrix is used to determine the concordance sets. Decision points are compared with each other in terms of evaluation factors, and sets are determined by the following relationships.

$$C_{kl} = \{j, y_{kj} \geq y_{lj}\}$$

$$D_{kl} = \{j, y_{kj} < y_{lj}\}$$

The formula is essentially based on comparing the magnitudes of the row elements relative to each other. In a MCDM problem, the number of concordance sets is $m \times m - m$.

I. This is because, when forming concordance sets, the indices k and l must satisfy the condition $k \neq l$

II. The number of elements in a concordance set can be at most equal to the number of evaluation factors n.

Step 5: Construction of

- The concordance matrix (C_{kl}) is constructed using the concordance sets. The C_{kl} matrix has dimensions m × m times mm × m and does not take a value when k = l.
- The elements of the C_{kl} matrix are calculated using the relationship given in the formula below.

$$C_{kl} = \sum_{j \in C_{kl}} W_j$$

The elements of the D_{kl} matrix are calculated using the relationship given in the formula below.

$$D_{kl} = \frac{\max_{j \in D_{kl}} |y_{kj} - y_{lj}|}{\max_j |y_{kj} - y_{lj}|}$$

Step 6: Construction of the concordance dominance (*F*) and discordance dominance (*G*) matrices

The concordance dominance (*F*) has dimensions m×m times, and its elements are obtained by comparing the concordance threshold value $\underline{c}$ with the elements of the concordance matrix C_{kl}.

The concordance threshold value $\underline{c}$ is calculated using the formula given below.

$$\underline{c} = \frac{1}{m\,(m - 1)\sum_{k=1}^{m}\sum_{l=1}^{m} c_{kl}}$$

The discordance dominance matrix (*G*) is an m × m matrix constructed in a similar way to the **F** (concordance dominance) matrix, but using discordance values. The disconcordance threshold value $\underline{d}$ is calculated using the formula given below.

$$\underline{d} = \frac{1}{m\,(m - 1)\sum_{k=1}^{m}\sum_{l=1}^{m} d_{kl}}$$

Step 7: Aggregate dominance matrix (*E*)

The elements e_{kl} of the aggregate dominance matrix (*E*) are equal to the product of the corresponding f_{kl} and g_{kl} elements. The *E* matrix is m × m in size, depends on the **C** and **D** matrices, and contains only **1** or **0** values.

Step 8: Final ranking

Alternatives are ranked based on the number of times they dominate others in matrix E.

93.4 Numerical example

For companies looking to stay competitive in fast-paced international markets, supply chain management (SCM) effectiveness has become more and more important. A company's capacity to meet market demands and produce better results is directly impacted by cutting production costs, increasing operational effectiveness, and shortening production cycles. Companies often outsource services, components, and raw materials to outside vendors as they prioritize their core competencies. In this situation, choosing the right supplier guarantees rapid, economical, and high-quality procurement, making supplier selection a strategic MCDM problem. On the other hand, selecting the wrong suppliers can result in significant delays, financial losses, reputational harm, and operational disruptions (Erdebilli et al., 2023; Rouyendegh & Erol, 2012).

SCM seeks to efficiently meet customer needs while reducing costs and optimizing value by coordinating and integrating all business processes, from upstream suppliers to downstream end users. Since its official inception in the 1980s, SCM has developed into a comprehensive management philosophy focused on value creation via process integration, teamwork, and efficient information flow. Since supply chains function in environments marked by uncertainty, competing goals, and complex performance criteria, decision-making is at the core of this philosophy.

Techniques for MCDM are crucial for improving the decisions' consistency, quality, and transparency. MCDM techniques assist in resolving trade-offs, defining priorities, and promoting structured reasoning in challenging SCM-related issues by allowing DMs to concurrently assess options from several angles. Inventory management, logistics planning, transportation optimization, and, most importantly, supplier selection—one of the most important and research-intensive topics within SCM—are all areas where these techniques are particularly useful (Erdebilli & Sıcakyüz, 2024; Pinar et al., 2021; Rouyendegh et al., 2014). SCM practitioners are better able to make evidence-based, well-informed decisions that boost overall competitiveness, strengthen supply chain resilience, and improve operational performance when MCDM tools are integrated.

This section illustrates the application of supplier selection in a company. Supplier selection is a critical challenge, particularly in dynamic markets where C1, C2, C3, and C4 are key factors.

93.4.1 Description of criteria

Quality (C1): This criterion covers factors such as compliance with quality standards, the rate of quality-related rejections, adherence to quality commitments, and the robustness of the supplier's quality management systems.

Cost (C2): This represents the total cost incurred by the company when working with the supplier, including product costs, purchasing expenses, and procurement-related costs.

Delivery time (C3): This criterion reflects the supplier's ability to provide reliable and timely deliveries, their overall service quality, and their flexibility in responding to changing conditions. Delivery reliability directly affects the company's operational performance.

Technical competence and technology (C4): This involve the supplier's capability to address product or equipment failures, provide necessary maintenance, and adapt to current as well as emerging technologies.

In this example, four possible suppliers (alternatives) are subjected to four evaluation criteria. Ranking these suppliers by evaluating each option in light of the chosen criteria is the decision-maker's goal. Each supplier's overall performance score is calculated using the ELECTRE method, which also determines the weights of the criteria based on their relative importance. This procedure offers a clear and methodical way to assess suppliers, enabling the company to find the best choice for its procurement requirements.

A clear and transparent comparison of the options under consideration is made possible by a numerical illustration that shows how the ELECTRE method is applied to produce the final ranking of alternatives. In this instance, a business assesses three possible supplier options. Based on well-established findings in the literature, professional opinions, and pragmatic factors pertinent to supplier performance, the criteria used in the analysis were carefully chosen. The example demonstrates how the ELECTRE methodically reduces the options and finds the best supplier in an organized, evidence-based way by tracking every computational stage, from the creation of the decision matrix to the computation of concordance and discordance indices and, finally, the creation of the outranking relation.

The decision matrix shows the evaluation scores of three alternatives in terms of four different criteria in the process of selecting a distance learning platform: ***quality***, ***cost***, ***delivery time***, and ***technical competence and technology***. The evaluation table is given in Table 93.1.

The relative importance of each criterion is used to determine the weights of the evaluation factors (wj). Criteria with higher strategic or operational significance are guaranteed to have a greater impact on the ultimate decision outcome thanks to this weighting process. The DM can represent the organization's priorities by allocating the proper weights, such as prioritizing timely delivery over technological capability or stressing quality over cost.

$w_1 = 0{,}4$, $w_2 = 0{,}7$, $w_3 = 0{,}8$ and $w_4 = 0{,}1$ The weights have been determined by the decision-makers (to total 1)

$$A = \begin{bmatrix} 170 & 50 & 40 & 80 \\ 70 & 110 & 70 & 30 \\ 80 & 120 & 60 & 110 \end{bmatrix}$$

The standard decision matrix (*X*) is created by compiling the performance values of each supplier against each evaluation criterion. Each row represents a supplier, and each column represents a criterion, forming a clear and organized structure. The matrix entries are based on expert evaluations.

$$X = \begin{bmatrix} 0{,}85 & 0{,}29 & 0{,}40 & 0{,}57 \\ 0{,}35 & 0{,}65 & 0{,}70 & 0{,}22 \\ 0{,}40 & 0{,}70 & 0{,}60 & 0{,}79 \end{bmatrix}$$

TABLE 93.1 Evaluation matrix of alternatives with respect to criteria.

Supplier	C_1	C_2	C_3	C_4
Supplier A	170	50	40	80
Supplier B	70	110	70	30
Supplier C	80	120	60	110

$$X_{11} = \frac{170}{\sqrt[2]{170^2 + 70^2 + 80^2}} = 0,85$$

The normalized decision matrix is scaled by the criterion weights (wj) to form the weighted normalized decision matrix (Y), incorporating both performance scores and the importance of each criterion.

$$Y_{11} = W_1 * X_{11} = 0,4 * 0,85 = 0,34$$

$$Y_{21} = W_1 * X_{21} = 0,4 * 0,35 = 0,14$$

$$Y_{31} = W_1 * X_{31} = 0,4 * 0,4 = 0,16$$

$$Y = \begin{bmatrix} 0,34 & 0,20 & 0,32 & 0,057 \\ 0,14 & 0,46 & 0,56 & 0,022 \\ 0,16 & 0,49 & 0,48 & 0,079 \end{bmatrix}$$

$$Y_{11} = 0,34 > Y_{21} = 0,14$$

$$Y_{12} = 0,20 < Y_{22=}0,46$$

$$Y_{13} = 0,32 < Y_{23=}0,56$$

$$Y_{14} = 0,057 > Y_{24} = 0,022$$

The concordance (C_{kl}) and discordance (D_{kl}) sets represent the criteria on which one alternative is respectively better than or worse than another. These sets form the basis for comparing pairs of alternatives and determining the degree to which one dominates the other within the ELECTRE method.

$$C_{12} = \{1,4\} C_{12} = \{2,3\}$$

$$C_{13} = \{1\} C_{13} = \{2,3,4\}$$

$$C_{21} = \{2,3\} C_{21} = \{1,4\}$$

$$C_{23} = \{3\} C_{23} = \{1,2,4\}$$

$$C_{31} = \{2,3,4\} C_{31} = \{1\}$$

$$C_{32} = \{1,2,4\} C_{32} = \{3\}$$

By integrating the concordance and discordance values across all criteria, the concordance (C) and discordance (D) matrices provide a summary of each alternative's strengths and weaknesses in relation to the others.

$$C = \begin{bmatrix} - & 0,5 & 0,4 \\ 1,5 & & 0,8 \\ 1,6 & 1,2 & - \end{bmatrix}$$

$$Y = \begin{bmatrix} 0,34 & 0,20 & 0,32 & 0,057 \\ 0,14 & 0,46 & 0,56 & 0,022 \\ 0,16 & 0,49 & 0,48 & 0,079 \end{bmatrix}$$

$$j = 2 \rightarrow |y_{12} - y_{22}| = |0,20 - 0,46| = 0,26$$

$$j = 3 \rightarrow |y_{13} - y_{23}| = |0,32 - 0,56| = 0,24$$

$$j = 1 \rightarrow |y_{11} - y_{21}| = |0,34 - 0,14| = 0,2$$

$$j = 2 \rightarrow |y_{12} - y_{22}| = |0,20 - 0,46| = 0,26$$

$$j = 3 \rightarrow |y_{13} - y_{23}| = |0,32 - 0,56| = 0,24$$

$$j = 4 \rightarrow |y_{14} - y_{24}| = |0,057 - 0,022| = 0,035$$

$$D_{12} = \frac{\max \mid 0{,}26{:}\ 0{,}24 \mid}{\max \mid 0{,}2{:}\ 0{,}26.0{,}24{:}\ 0{,}035 \mid} = \frac{0{,}26}{0{,}26} = 1$$

$$D = \begin{bmatrix} - & 1 & 1 \\ 0{,}81 & - & 0{,}72 \\ 0{,}62 & 1 & - \end{bmatrix}$$

$$\underline{c} = \frac{1}{3(3-1)}(0{,}5 + 0{,}4 + 1{,}5 + 0{,}8 + 1{,}6 + 1{,}2) = 6/6 = 1$$

Each pair of alternatives is compared to create the concordance dominance (*F*) and discordance dominance (*G*) matrices, where *F* denotes dominance based on concordance indices and *G* indicates dominance based on discordance indices. The specific calculations are given below.

$$f_{12} \rightarrow 0{,}5 < 1 \rightarrow f_{12} = 0$$

$$f_{13} \rightarrow 0{,}4 < 1 \rightarrow f_{13} = 0$$

$$f_{21} \rightarrow 1{,}5 > 1 \rightarrow f_{21} = 1$$

$$f_{23} \rightarrow 0{,}8 < 1 \rightarrow f_{23} = 0$$

$$f_{31} \rightarrow 1{,}6 > 1 \rightarrow f_{31} = 1$$

$$f_{32} \rightarrow 1{,}2 > 1 \rightarrow f_{32} = 1$$

$$F = \begin{bmatrix} - & 0 & 0 \\ 1 & - & 0 \\ 1 & 1 & - \end{bmatrix}$$

$$\underline{d} = \frac{1}{3(3-1)}(1 + 1 + 0{,}81 + 0{,}72 + 0{,}62 + 1) = 5{,}2/6 = 0{,}86$$

$$g_{12} \rightarrow 1 > 0{,}86 \rightarrow g_{12} = 0$$

$$g_{13} \rightarrow 1 > 0{,}86 \rightarrow g_{13} = 0$$

$$g_{21} \rightarrow 0{,}81 < 0{,}86 \rightarrow g_{21} = 1$$

$$g_{23} \rightarrow 0{,}72 < 0{,}86 \rightarrow g_{23} = 1$$

$$g_{31} \rightarrow 0{,}62 < 0{,}86 \rightarrow g_{31} = 1$$

$$g_{32} \rightarrow 1 > 0{,}86 \rightarrow g_{32} = 0$$

$$g = \begin{bmatrix} - & 0 & 0 \\ 1 & - & 1 \\ 1 & 0 & - \end{bmatrix}$$

$$g = \begin{bmatrix} - & 0 & 0 \\ 1 & - & 0 \\ 1 & 0 & - \end{bmatrix}$$

$$C_1 = (0{,}5 + 0{,}4) - (1{,}5 + 1{,}6) = -2{,}2$$

$$C_2 = (1{,}5 + 0{,}8) - (0{,}5 + 1{,}2) = 0{,}6$$

$$C_3 = (1{,}6 + 1{,}2) - (0{,}4 + 0{,}8) = 1{,}6$$

In matrix *E*, alternatives are ranked according to how frequently they outperform others. The specific computations are given below.

The concordance index is used to make decisions.

$$S_C \rightarrow S_B \rightarrow S_A$$

$$D_1 = (1 + 1)-(0{,}81 + 0{,}62) = 0{,}57$$

$$D_2 = (0{,}81 + 0{,}72)-(1 + 1) = -0{,}47$$

$$D_3 = (0{,}62 + 1)-(1 + 0{,}72) = -0{,}1$$

Decisions are made based on the disconcordance index.

$$S_B \rightarrow S_c \rightarrow C_A$$

The DM determines which outranking indices—concordance, discordance, or an integrated combination of both—should be used to create the outranking relation based on the particular context, structure, and priorities of the decision problem. The concordance index is the main basis for decision-making in many real-world applications. This is due to the fact that it provides a thorough and intuitive assessment of the degree to which one option can be considered at least as good as another based on all of the criteria. The concordance index indicates the general degree of agreement among the criteria by adding together the contributions of all criteria that support the superiority of one alternative over another. It makes a methodical, transparent, and uniform comparison process easier by quantifying the percentage of criteria that support an alternative. As a result, it is frequently preferred in real-world decision support contexts where DMs are looking for a clear and balanced depiction of multicriteria dominance, such as supplier evaluation, project selection, or strategic planning. As a result, the concordance index becomes a crucial tool for determining the best options, emphasizing those that receive broad support across the decision criteria, and directing the creation of trustworthy and convincing preference rankings.

93.5 Conclusion

In this chapter, we examined using the ELECTRE method as a reliable and methodical way to deal with MCDM problems. By comparing options using pairwise concordance and discordance indices, ELECTRE makes it easier for DMs to assess complicated situations involving both quantitative and qualitative criteria. In situations where criteria conflict or trade-offs need to be carefully balanced, the method's structured framework offers a clear way to incorporate multiple criteria at once.

To illustrate ELECTRE's usefulness in real-world decision-making situations like supplier selection, infrastructure project prioritization, and resource allocation, a numerical example was provided. The outcomes of these case studies demonstrated the method's capacity to effectively manage conflicting criteria and its benefit in identifying nondominated alternatives as opposed to imposing a rigorous full ranking of all options. This feature is particularly useful when DMs desire to retain flexibility in their final choices or when there is incomparability.

ELECTRE's relevance in industrial, environmental, and public-sector decision-making applications is further enhanced by its ability to incorporate indifference and preference thresholds, which enables it to accommodate uncertainty, imprecise data, and the varying significance of criteria. Despite these advantages, there are some drawbacks to the approach. There may be some subjectivity involved in choosing suitable thresholds and weights, which could affect the results depending on the decision-maker's assessment. Additionally, the efficiency of concordance and discordance matrices for very large-scale problems may be limited by their computational complexity, which rises with the number of alternatives and criteria. Nevertheless, ELECTRE remains to be a potent and adaptable tool for organized, transparent, and knowledgeable decision-making in complex multicriteria environments with careful implementation and sensitivity analysis.

References

Andriosopoulos, D., Gaganis, C., Pasiouras, F., & Zopounidis, C. (2012). An application of multicriteria decision aid models in the prediction of open market share repurchases. *Omega, 40*, 882–890.

Ayyildiz, E., & Taskin Gumus, A. (2020). A novel spherical fuzzy AHP-integrated spherical WASPAS methodology for petrol station location selection problem: A real case study for İstanbul. *Environmental Science and Pollution Research*. https://doi.org/10.1007/s11356-020-09640-0.

Benayoun, R., & Billsberry, J. (2007). *Experiencing recruitment and selection*. Hoboken, NJ: Wiley &Sons.

Chen, T. Y. (2016). An IVIF-ELECTRE outranking method for multiple criteria decision-making with interval-valued intuitionistic fuzzy sets. *Technological and Economic Development of Economy, 22*, 416–452.

Erdebilli, B., & Sıcakyüz, Ç. (2024). An integrated Q-rung orthopair fuzzy (Q-ROF) for the selection of supply-chain management. *Sustainability, 16*, 4901. https://doi.org/10.3390/su16124901.

Erdebilli, B., Yilmaz, İ., Aksoy, T., Hacıoglu, U., Yüksel, S., & Dinçer, H. (2023). An interval-valued pythagorean fuzzy AHP and COPRAS hybrid methods for the supplier selection problem. *International Journal of Computational Intelligence Systems, 16*, 124.

Haseli, G., & Sheikh, R. (2022). Base criterion method (BCM). In *Multiple criteria decision making: Techniques, Analysis and Applications*. Singapore: Springer Nature Singapore, 17–38.

Haseli, G., Ögel, İ. Y., Ecer, F., & Hajiaghaei-Keshteli, M. (2023). Luxury in female technology (FemTech): Selection of smart jewelry for women through BCM-MARCOS group decision-making framework with fuzzy ZE-numbers. *Technological Forecasting and Social Change, 196*, 122870.

Kahraman, Ç., Ruan, D., & Doğan, I. (2003). Fuzzy group decisionmaking for facility location selection. *Information Sciences, 157*, 135–153.

Pinar, A., Rouyendegh, B. D., & Ozdemir, Y. S. (2021). Q-rung orthopair fuzzy TOPSIS method for green supplier selection problem. *Sustainability, 13*, 985.

Rouyendegh, B. D., Baç, U., & Erkan, T. E. (2014). Sector selection for ERP implementation to achieve most impact on supply chain performance by using AHP-TOPSIS hybrid method. *Tehnicki Vjesnik-Technical Gazette*.

Rouyendegh, B. D., & Erol, S. (2012). Selecting the best project using the fuzzy ELECTRE method. *Mathematical Problems in Engineering,* 1–12.

Roy, B., & Bertier, P. (1973). La methode ELECTRE II:Une methode au media-planning [The ELECTRE II method: A method for media planning]. In M. Ross (Ed.). *Operational research* (pp. 291–302). Amsterdam: North-Holland.

Torkabadi, A., Mamoudan, M. M., Erdebilli, B., & Aghsami, A. (2025). A multi-objective game theory model for sustainable profitability in the tourism supply chain: Integrating human resource management and artificial neural networks. *Systems and Soft Computing*.

Triantaphyllou, E. (2000). *Multi-criteria decision making methods: A comparative study*. Kluwer Academic Publishers.

Chapter 94

ELECTRE II: Extension of the elimination and choice expressing reality for multi-attribute decision-making

Seyed Hossein Razavi Hajiagha[1], Salar Keshavarz Hedayati[2], and Shide Sadat Hashemi[3]
[1]*Department of Management, Faculty of Management and Financial Sciences, Khatam University, Tehran, Iran,* [2]*Department of Management, Faculty of Management and Financial Sciences, Khatam University, Tehran, Iran,* [3]*Department of Management, Behin Avina co, MST Park, Tehran, Iran*

94.1 Introduction

Multi-criteria decision-making (MCDM) methods aim to establish a set of preference relationships among a group of alternatives, based on the evaluation of these alternatives with respect to multiple criteria and their associated weights . A common way to solve this problem is to calculate and assign a number, such as $\vartheta(x)$, to alternative x from a set of alternatives X. Accordingly, alternative x is at least as good as y if and only if $\vartheta(x) \geq \vartheta(y)$. The score $\vartheta(x)$ is actually a function of the scores of alternative x on the different attributes on which the comparison of the alternatives is made (Bouyssou, 2001). This way of dealing with an MCDM problem is classified as value measurement theory, where it is assumed that a value function is presented, and preferences are complete and transitive (Belton & Stewart, 2002) . However, the question is whether such assumptions hold in practice? Consider the following example. Suppose there are three alternatives (a), (b), and (c). If we know that alternative (a) is better than (b) and (c), there may be no need to compare alternatives (b) and (c). In fact, these two alternatives will remain incomparable without disturbing the decision-making process. On the other hand, solving a decision-making problem is a gradual process that involves obtaining new information along the way. Hence, it is of great importance to have concepts that allow us to deal with situations such as the incomparability of alternatives during the decision-making process. These considerations have led to the development of outranking methods (Vincke, 1992). Roy (Roy, 1974) defines a outranking relation as follows:

A outranking relation is a binary relation of the form S defined on a set of alternatives A, such that aSb if, given the information available about the decision maker's preferences and the quality of the alternatives' scores and the nature of the problem, there is sufficient reason to conclude that a is at least as good as b, while there is no conclusive reason to reject this proposition. It is noted that the outranking relation is not a precise mathematical definition but rather a general idea. The main difference between the types of outranking methods available in theoretical foundations also lies in the way this nonmathematical definition is objectified. A family of these methods includes the elimination and choice translating reality (ELECTRE) methods, and here, ELECTRE II is discussed in this chapter.

The remainder of this chapter is organized as follows. A review of ELECTRE II method is presented in the next section. Then the methodology of ELECTRE II is described along with the equations. Finally, two numerical examples are defined and solved in Sections 94.4 and 94.5. In conclusion, the main findings are summarized in Section 94.6.

94.2 Literature review

The concept of outranking methods was first formally and thoroughly presented by Roy (1968) through the ELECTRE method. The methods based on utility functions and calculating scores for each alternative are referred to as the American School of MCDM. The outranking method has been introduced as one of the most widely used and accepted methods in the European School of MCDM (Lootsma 1990). The roots of the ELECTRE method date back to 1965 and to the consulting company "Société d'Économie et de Mathématiques Appliquées" (SEMA). At that time, a research group in

Encyclopedia of Multi-Attribute Decision-Making (MADM). DOI: https://doi.org/10.1016/B978-0-443-33275-3.00072-5

this company was studying a real MCDM problem regarding the development of new activities in companies. To address this problem, a general MCDM method called MARSAN was proposed (Laffy, 1966). When the engineers of the SEMA company applied this method, they encountered many weaknesses and problems. To overcome these problems, the company invited Bernard Roy to collaborate and develop a new method. The ELECTRE method was designed as a method for selecting the best alternative(s) from a given set of alternatives and was later introduced as the ELECTRE I method. The initial idea of this method was first published as a research report in 1966 (Benayoun et al., 1966). However, the method gained popularity when Roy (1968) published it in a paper and provided a complete description of the ELECTRE method and the principles of the outranking approach (Figueira et al., 2005; Roy & Vanderpooten, 1996).

This method has been applied in different fields to select various alternatives for decades (Figueira et al., 2010). For instance, a group of studies used the fuzzy or deterministic ELECTRE method for supplier selection problems (Akram et al., 2021; Sevkli, 2010), Salvador et al. (2024) also reviewed this application and emphasize a hybrid approach for more reliable and robust results. ELECTRE is widely applicable in transportation-related selection problems (Wang & Yeo, 2018), evaluation of production techniques (Wen et al., 2016), project selection (Razi, 2015; Vysochan et al., 2022), etc. Even the sustainable approaches have also been evaluated using the ELECTRE method (Vinodh & Girubha, 2012).

94.3 Methodology

ELECTRE II is an MCDM technique used to rank alternatives under conditions of uncertainty and conflicting criteria (Sarwar et al., 2023). It was the first version of the ELECTRE family of methods designed to deal with ranking problems. ELECTRE II is also the first version to use a technique based on constructing a sequence of embedded ranking relations, which makes the method particularly significant (Roy & Bertier, 1971, 1973). This method is also based on developing nonranking relationships between alternatives (E Souza Rodrigues et al., 2021). Considering two alternatives, A_k and A_l from a set of alternatives, c(A_k, A_l) is defined as the concordance index of A_k over A_i. If $\bar{c}$ is defined as the concordance threshold, then the alternative A_k dominates A_i whenever c(A_k, A_l)≥ $\bar{c}$ and c(A_k, A_l)> c(A_l, A_k). To extract outranking relationships among alternatives with this method, the following steps are taken. Suppose $I^+(A_k, A_l)$, $I^-(A_k, A_l)$, and $I^-(A_k, A_l)$ are the sets of attributes that alternative A_k is strongly preferred, indifferent, or strongly dominated over the alternative A_l, respectively. Also, consider $W^+(A_k, A_l)$, $W^-(A_k, A_l)$, and $W^-(A_k, A_l)$ as the sets of attribute weights in the above three sets, respectively. Then, the concordance index of the two alternatives A_k and A_l is defined as follows.

$$c(A_k, A_l) = \frac{W^+(A_k, \quad A_l) + \quad W^-(A_k, \quad A_l)}{W^+(A_k, \quad A_l) + \quad W^-(A_k, A_l) + \quad w^-(A_k, A_l)} \tag{94.1}$$

The discordance index is defined as follows:

$$d(A_k, A_l) = \frac{\max_{i\in I^-(A_k,A_l)} |X_i(A_k) - X_i(A_l)|}{\max_{i\in I}(X_i(A_K), \quad \theta_i)} \tag{94.2}$$

The parameter θ acts as a threshold set by the decision maker in comparing the compatibility and incompatibility between alternatives (Shumaiza & Al-Kenani, 2019). Both the above concordance and discordance indices take values between zero and one. The ELECTRE II method can be described in the following steps. First, determine the concordance threshold limits c^+ and discordance d^+ for strong preference and c^- and d^- for weak preference, such that $c^+ > c^-$ and $d^+ < d^-$. The steps of ELECTRE II can be summarized in the following three phases (Belton & Stewart, 2002).

Step 1. Determine the descending ranking.

1. Suppose A is the complete set of alternatives.
2. Determine the nondominated set N, which consists of the alternatives that are not strongly dominated by the other alternatives A.
3. Determine the first category of the descending ranking by determining the subset N', which consists of the alternatives that are not weakly dominated by the other alternatives N.
4. Repeat stage 3, considering the alternatives in the subset N' until all alternatives are categorized.

Step 2. Determine the ascending ranking.

1. Suppose that A is the complete set of alternatives.
2. Determine the defeated set Z, which consists of the alternatives that have not strongly dominated any other alternative in A.

3. Determine the first category of the ascending ranking by determining the subset Z', which consists of the alternatives that have not weakly dominated the other alternatives Z.
4. Stage 3 is repeated considering the alternatives in the subset Z' until all alternatives are categorized.

Step 3. Determine the final ranking. Based on the common elements of the descending and ascending rankings, the final ranking of the alternatives can be determined.

The methodology is summarized in Fig. 94.1.

94.4 Numerical example

Due to the intersection of social, economic, and environmental dimensions in transportation systems, this issue has become one of the most important topics (Elyemez et al., 2023). The existence of special economic zones (SEZs) has added to the importance of transportation modes. Thus, according to a 2023 report, about 70% of Iran's transit take place through SEZs, which itself indicates the importance of choosing the best method in these areas . The transportation system is a very complex environment that requires strong decision-making strategies in order to choose the best mode (Kabashkin, 2023). Today, choosing the best transportation methods, whether in urban areas or in SEZs, is not done through traditional modes, but with the help of decision-making modes (Buyukozkan & Mukul, 2019; Elyemez et al., 2023; Kabashkin, 2023).

Consider the decision-making problem of choosing the best transportation mode in a SEZ with a relatively long distance to the sea and the airport. In this problem, four transportation modes, sea (alternative 1), road (alternative 2), air (alternative 3), and rail (alternative 4), are selected as the desired alternatives. According to the literature, among the various criteria for selecting the best transportation mode in the SEZ, four criteria, speed, cost, volume, and infrastructure, have been selected as the most important criteria to compare the alternatives (Button, 2010; Morlok, 2017; Rodrigue et al., 2017). It should be

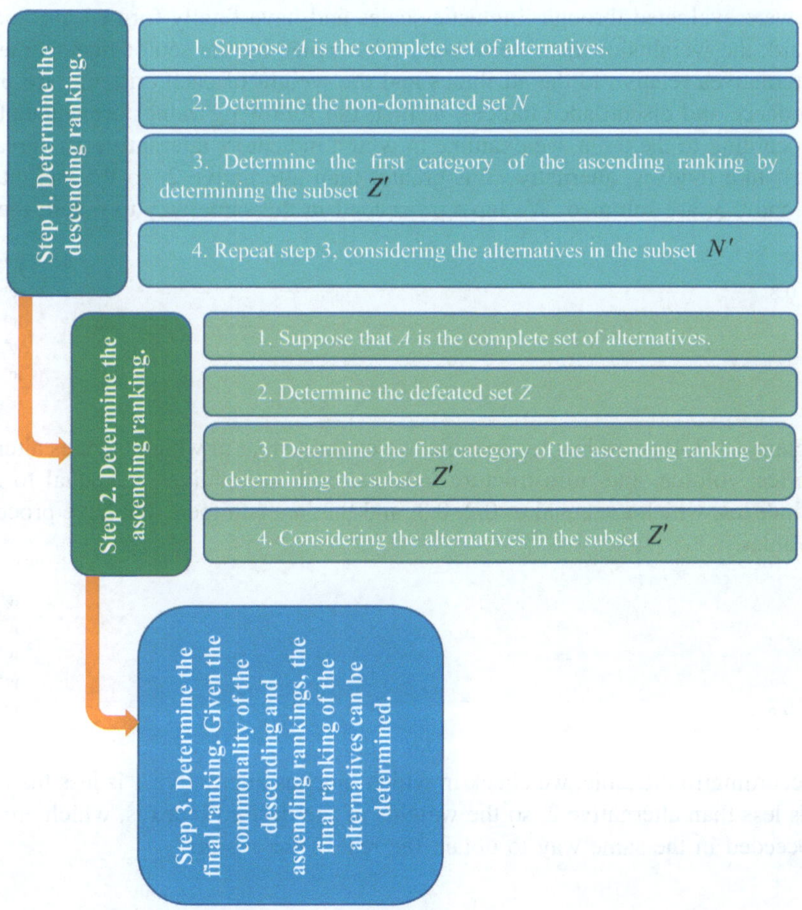

FIGURE 94.1 Summarized proposed methodology diagram.

TABLE 94.1 Decision matrix to choose the best transportation route in a special economic zone.

Index	Speed	Cost	Volume	Infrastructure
Alternative				
Alternative 1	4	2	6	8
Alternative 2	8	9	1	4
Alternative 3	8	2	3	1
Alternative 4	1	2	3	1
Index weight	0.20	0.20	0.30	0.30

noted that the criteria for speed, volume, and infrastructure are considered positive towards the SEZs' goals, and the criterion of cost is considered negative for their purpose.

The key question is how these four modes of transportation are prioritized within the SEZ, based on the criteria of speed, cost, volume, and infrastructure.

For this purpose, the opinions of a panel of experts have been used. The characteristics of these panelists are as follows: These experts hold managerial positions in SEZs, have at least 15 years of employment experience in the SEZs, and have at least a master's degree.

Based on their experience and professional background, they compared the alternatives using four decision-making criteria. These options were evaluated through linguistic scales and have finally formed the final matrix as described in Table 94.1. In this regard, the weights of the criteria were determined by the senior management of the SEZ.

The scores of the alternatives relative to the attributes and the weight of each criterion are presented in Table 94.1.

To obtain the concordance and discordance indices, at first, the following values are calculated:

To obtain $W^+(1,2)$ according to the table, we examine in which indicators alternative 1 is greater than alternative 2. In the volume and infrastructure indexes, alternative 1 is greater than alternative 2, so the weights of the desired indexes, which are equal to 0.3 and 0.3, are summed. We have proceeded in the same way to obtain the rest of the table's cells.

$w^+(1,2) = 0.3 + 0.3 = 0.6$
$w^+(1,3) = 0.3 + 0.3 = 0.6$
$w^+(1,4) = 0.2 + 0.3 + 0.3 = 0.8$
$w^+(2,1) = 0.2 + 0.2 = 0.4$
$w^+(2,3) = 0.2 + 0.3 = 0.5$
$w^+(2,4) = 0.2 + 0.2 + 0.3 = 0.7$
$w^+(3,1) = 0.2$
$w^+(3,2) = 0.3$
$w^+(3,4) = 0.2$
$w^+(4,1) = 0$
$w^+(4,2) = 0.3$
$w^+(4,3) = 0$

As an example, to obtain $w^=(3,4)$ according to the table, we examine that in which indexes alternatives 3 and 4 are equal to each other. In the price, volume, and infrastructure indexes, both alternatives are equal to each other; therefore the weights of the desired indexes, which are equal to 0.2, 0.3, and 0.3, are summed. We have proceeded in the same way to obtain the rest of the values.

$w^=(1,3) = 0$
$w^=(1,3) = 0.2$
$w^=(1,4) = 0.2$
$w^=(2,1) = 0$
$w^=(2,3) = 0.2$
$w^=(2,4) = 0$
$w^=(3,1) = 0.2$
$w^=(3,2) = 0.2$
$w^=(3,4) = 0.2 + 0.3 + 0.3 = 0.8$
$w^=(4,1) = 0.2$
$w^=(4,2) = 0$
$w^=(4,3) = 0.2 + 0.3 + 0.3 = 0.8$

To obtain $w^-(1,2)$ according to the table, we check in which indexes alternative 1 is less than 2. In the speed and price indexes, alternative 1 is less than alternative 2, so the weights of the desired indexes, which are equal to 0.2 and 0.2, are summed. We have proceeded in the same way to obtain the rest of the results.

$w^-(1,2) = 0.4$
$w^-(1,3) = 0.2$
$w^-(1,4) = 0$
$w^-(2,1) = 0.6$
$w^-(2,3) = 0.3$
$w^-(2,4) = 0.3$

$w^-(3,1) = 0.6$ $w^-(3,2) = 0.5$
$w^-(3,4) = 0$ $w^-(4,1) = 0.8$
$w^-(4,2) = 0.7$ $w^-(4,3) = 0.2$

Now, the concordance index can be calculated according to Eq. (94.1). For example, to obtain the concordance index c (A_2, A_1), we first sum the values of $w^+(A_2, A_1)$ and $w^=(A_2, A_1)$, which are 0.4 and 0, respectively, and divide by the sum of $w^+(A_2, A_1)$, $w^=(A_2, A_1)$, and $w^-(A_2, A_1)$, which are 0.4, 0, and 0.6, respectively. The result is 0.4. The remaining coordination indices are calculated in the same way. This index is shown in Table 94.2.

Based on Eq. (94.2), the discordance index for the alternatives is calculated. In this example, the θ_i values are considered equal to one. For instance, the value of the first row and the second column of Table 94.3 is calculated as follows.

$$d(1,2) = \frac{\max(|4-8|, |2-9|)}{\max(4, 2, 6, 8; 1)} = \frac{7}{8} = 0.875$$

Suppose the threshold limits are specified as $c^+ = 0.7$, $c^- = 0.6$, and $d^+ = 0.5$, $d^- = 0.7$. The method for extracting ascending ranking relations is as follows. Given the strong threshold limits, namely$c^+ = 0.7$ and $d^+ = 0.5$, the outranking relations among the alternatives will be as shown in Fig. 94.2.

Accordingly, set N includes alternative 2, which has not been dominated by the other alternatives. In addition, alternative 1 is ranked higher than alternatives 3 and 4 due to its dominance, and alternative 3 has also dominated alternative 4. Hence, the ascending ranking of the alternatives includes alternatives 2, 1, 3, and 4, respectively. In the descending ranking, a similar ranking is obtained. Finally, alternative 2 is ranked first, and alternatives 1, 3, and 4 are ranked next, respectively. As a result, considering the criteria of speed, cost, volume, and infrastructure, the road, sea, air, and rail transportation route alternatives are considered as the best transportation routes, respectively.

As shown in the results, "road transport" emerged as the preferred option, while it is not significantly dominated by any other alternative under the defined thresholds. It consistently achieves priority in both the ascending and descending

TABLE 94.2 Concordance index values.

Alternative / Alternative	Alternative 1	Alternative 2	Alternative 3	Alternative 4
Alternative 1	1	0.6	0.8	1
Alternative 2	0.4	1	0.7	0.7
Alternative 3	0.4	0.5	1	1
Alternative 4	0.2	0.3	0.8	1

TABLE 94.3 Discordance index values.

Alternative / Alternative	Alternative 1	Alternative 2	Alternative 3	Alternative 4
Alternative 1	0	0.875	0.5	0
Alternative 2	0.555	0	0.778	0.778
Alternative 3	0.875	0.875	0	0
Alternative 4	2.33	2.33	2.33	0

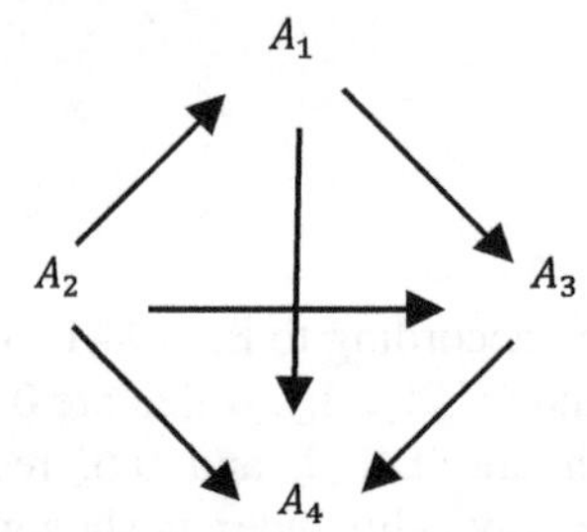

FIGURE 94.2 Strong preference relationships among alternatives.

ranking procedures. Furthermore, "sea transport" is ranked second due to its relative strength over alternatives 3 and 4. Subsequently, "air transport" takes the third position, and "rail transport" stands as the least favorable option.

All in all, this numerical example highlights the strength point of ELECTRE II, which can provide a transparent and systematic framework to prioritize alternatives in a complicated decision-making situation. In fact, this method utilizes the nature of both concordance and discordance indices and threshold parameters, which allows decision-makers to rank the alternatives not only rationally but also make them resilient to conflicts among various criteria. Consequently, the strength of ELECTRE II as a powerful technique for strategic planning and applicability in infrastructure and transportation management is proven again.

94.5 Numerical example 2

A large investment company plans to allocate significant financial resources to one of the instruments available in the financial and insurance markets. The company is looking to select an alternative that can generate an appropriate return while also considering the risks and costs of the investment.

The options under consideration include different types of financial instruments such as government bonds, corporate bonds, stock index funds, real estate investment trusts (REITs), money market instruments, infrastructure project debt, and green bonds. Each of these alternatives has different characteristics in terms of profitability, risk, liquidity, environmental, social, and governance (ESG) compatibility, and management complexity.

Since decision-making in such circumstances is not possible based on only one criterion, the investment company decided to use a MCDM (ELECTRE II method) approach. In this regard, seven main criteria, including expected 1) annual return, 2) volatility (risk), 3) capital lock-up period, 4) liquidity, 5) ESG index, 6) credit quality, and 7) management complexity, were determined to evaluate the options.

To ensure the accuracy and comprehensiveness of the analysis, three senior finance and insurance experts independently assessed the qualitative options. The quantitative criteria (such as return, risk, and capital lock-up period) were based on fixed market data. Then, the decision matrices obtained from the three experts were aggregated to obtain a final matrix that will be the basis for selecting the superior alternative in the rest of the analysis.

94.5.1 Alternatives

A1—Government bonds
A2—High-grade corporate bonds
A3—Equity index funds
A4—Real estate/REITs
A5—Money market instruments
A6—Infrastructure debt
A7—Green bonds

The three experts have determined seven criteria to evaluate the financial instruments as follows:
Criteria and their types:

C1—Expected annual return (%) - benefit - quantitative
C2—Volatility (standard deviation, %) - cost - quantitative
C3—Average term/capital lock-up (years) - cost - quantitative
C4—Liquidity - benefit - qualitative

C5—ESG index/environmental sustainability - benefit - qualitative
C6—Credit quality - benefit - qualitative
C7—Management complexity - cost – qualitative (Table 94.4)

According to Table 94.5, the aggregated matrix is calculated using the geometric mean.
The weights of criteria are defined in the previous decision-making process and are determined as below:

Criteria	C1	C2	C3	C4	C5	C6	C7
Weights	0/2	0/1	0/15	0/11	0/16	0/14	0/14

By applying the ELECTRE II method to the above decision matrix, the results of the concordance and discordance matrixes are shown in Tables 94.6 and 94.7.

TABLE 94.4 Individual decision matrices of experts.

Criteria	C1	C2	C3	C4	C5	C6	C7
Alternatives							
A1	4.0	3.0	5.0	4.0	3.0	5.0	2.0
A2	6.0	5.0	7.0	3.0	3.0	4.0	3.0
A3	9.0	15.0	0.5	5.0	2.0	3.0	4.0
A4	7.0	10.0	8.0	3.0	4.0	3.0	5.0
A5	2.5	1.0	0.1	2.0	3.0	4.0	2.0
A6	7.5	6.0	10.0	4.0	4.0	4.0	3.0
A7	5.5	4.5	5.0	5.0	5.0	3.0	4.0
Criteria	C1	C2	C3	C4	C5	C6	C7
Alternatives							
A1	4.0	3.0	5.0	3.0	4.0	4.0	3.0
A2	6.0	5.0	7.0	4.0	3.0	4.0	3.0
A3	9.0	15.0	0.5	5.0	3.0	3.0	4.0
A4	7.0	10.0	8.0	4.0	4.0	3.0	4.0
A5	2.5	1.0	0.1	3.0	2.0	4.0	3.0
A6	7.5	6.0	10.0	4.0	4.0	3.0	3.0
A7	5.5	4.5	5.0	5.0	5.0	2.0	4.0
Criteria	C1	C2	C3	C4	C5	C6	C7
Alternatives							
A1	4.0	3.0	5.0	4.0	3.0	5.0	2.0
A2	6.0	5.0	7.0	3.0	3.0	5.0	3.0
A3	9.0	15.0	0.5	4.0	2.0	3.0	4.0
A4	7.0	10.0	8.0	3.0	5.0	3.0	4.0
A5	2.5	1.0	0.1	2.0	2.0	5.0	2.0
A6	7.5	6.0	10.0	4.0	4.0	3.0	3.0
A7	5.5	4.5	5.0	5.0	4.0	2.0	4.0

TABLE 94.5 Aggregated decision matrix.

Criteria Alternatives	C1	C2	C3	C4	C5	C6	C7
A1	4.0	3.0	5.0	3.634	3.0	5.0	2.0
A2	6.0	5.0	7.0	3.0	3.0	4.0	3.0
A3	9.0	15.0	0.5	5.0	3.301	2.289	2.0
A4	7.0	10.0	8.0	3.301	2.289	3.0	3.0
A5	2.5	1.0	0.1	5.0	3.0	5.0	1.0
A6	7.5	6.0	10.0	2.289	2.289	3.634	4.0
A7	5.5	4.5	5.0	4.0	5.0	4.0	2.289

TABLE 94.6 Concordance matrix.

	A1	A2	A3	A4	A5	A6	A7
A1	**	0.66	0.38	0.69	0.5	0.65	0.53
A2	0.34	**	0.38	0.69	0.36	0.8	0.34
A3	0.62	0.62	**	0.76	0.47	0.76	0.6
A4	0.31	0.31	0.24	**	0.2	0.56	0.2
A5	0.5	0.64	0.53	0.8	**	0.8	0.64
A6	0.35	0.2	0.24	0.44	0.2	**	0.2
A7	0.47	0.66	0.4	0.8	0.36	0.8	**

TABLE 94.7 Discordance matrix.

	A1	A2	A3	A4	A5	A6	A7
A1	**	1	1	1	1	1	1
A2	0.76619211	**	1	0.49234356	1	0.65257785	1
A3	0.97492897	0.81566288	**	0.35345392	0.87493625	0.50227662	1
A4	0.94784761	1	1	**	1	0.97264941	1
A5	0.39953746	0.6620355	1	0.74344312	**	0.65916955	0.82466795
A6	0.87214303	1	1	1	1	**	1
A7	0.35822435	0.16149428	0.82057261	0.35742001	1	0.47656002	**

The results of the second example showed that "green bonds" (A7) and "equity index funds" (A3) ranked at the highest level. Green bonds are particularly attractive due to their combination of good returns, controlled risk, good credit, and high ESG scores (Khan & Vismara, 2025), while equity index funds maintain their superiority with high returns and very good liquidity. For this reason, these two instruments were identified as equal in the analysis.

In the second step, "corporate bonds" (A2) and "money market instruments" (A5) were ranked, representing two different approaches: A2 with higher returns (Huang & Shi, 2021) but more risk and capital lock-up, and A5 with very low risk (Choudhry et al., 2005) and costs but limited returns. Based on the criteria, neither had a clear advantage over the other and were therefore ranked equal. At the lowest level, "government bonds" (A1), "REITs" (A4) (Van Nieuwerburgh, 2019), and "infrastructure debt" (A6) were ranked. These options failed to achieve sufficient net superiority over the other instruments, either due to lower returns (A1) (Andritzky, 2012) or higher risk and management complexity (A4 and A6).

Overall, ELECTRE II provides a multidimensional picture of the relative performance of the options: the top two options (A7 and A3) as the main choices, the middle two options (A2 and A5) as compromise choices, and the bottom three options (A1, A4, A6) as less attractive. This result suggests that the decision maker can choose between the first- or second-tier options depending on his or her priorities (return vs. risk, or ESG vs. liquidity).

94.6 Conclusion

In this chapter, the ELECTRE II method was introduced and analyzed as one of the most prominent approaches to MCDM. Relying on the concepts of superiority and relative dominance, this method was able to provide a powerful tool for prioritizing and choosing among multiple alternatives in complex situations. Theoretical investigation and then implementation of two numerical examples showed that ELECTRE II is not only able to solve decision-making problems with conflicting criteria and different weights, but also provides the possibility of providing relative rankings of alternatives, which is of great value in many managerial and industrial situations. In fact, this method allows decision-makers to adopt a more comprehensive view based on the multidimensionality of organizational realities, instead of relying solely on classical single-criteria methods.

In particular, in the numerical example presented, it was observed that ELECTRE II was able to clearly identify superiority relationships by calculating the agreement and disagreement indices between alternatives. This process showed that in practice, some alternatives are able to obtain higher rankings due to superior scores in key criteria, while other alternatives, even if they have minor strengths, are relegated to lower rankings due to weaknesses in essential criteria. Such a result highlights the importance of considering the concurrency of criteria and their interaction in decision-making.

From an applied perspective, ELECTRE II can be used in various areas such as supplier selection, investment project evaluation, R&D project ranking, supply chain management, and even more general areas such as public policy and macro strategy evaluation. The ability of this method to adapt to uncertain and multicriteria environments makes it a suitable alternative for organizations that are faced with resource constraints and the need to select the best solutions.

Despite its significant advantages, this method is not without limitations. Among other things, the computational complexity of very large-scale problems and the sensitivity of the results to the weighting of the criteria can be considered. For this reason, future research directions in the field of ELECTRE II can be developed in several directions:

1. Combination with other methods: Integrating ELECTRE II with fuzzy decision-making techniques, Bayesian networks, or data mining methods can enhance its ability to deal with uncertainty and qualitative data.
2. Improving software tools: Designing and developing decision-support systems based on ELECTRE II can facilitate access to this method for managers and decision-makers and make decision-making processes faster and more effective.
3. Empirical validation: Wider use of ELECTRE II in different industries and analysis of real-world results can provide a stronger basis for improving the method and adapting it to the specific needs of organizations.

Overall, ELECTRE II can be considered a valid and efficient tool for decision-making in multicriteria problems that, while having a strong theoretical basis, has a high potential for practical applications. The future of this method depends, above all, on the development of combined and interdisciplinary studies that adapt it to the requirements of more complex and realistic decision-making environments.

Reference

Akram, M., Ilyas, F., & Garg, H. (2021). ELECTRE-II method for group decision-making in Pythagorean fuzzy environment. *Applied Intelligence*.

Andritzky, M. (2012). Government bonds and their investors: What are the facts and do they matter? *International Monetary Fund*.
Belton, V., & Stewart, T. (2002). *Multiple criteria decision analysis: An integrated approach*. Kluwer Academic Publishers.
Benayoun, R., Roy, B., & Sussman, B. (1966). ELECTRE: Une méthode pour guider le choix en présence de points de vue multiples.
Bouyssou, D. (2001). In C. A. Floudas, & P. M. Pardalos (Eds.). *Outranking methodsKluwer Academic Publishers* Presented in.
Button, K. (2010). *Transport economics (3rd ed.)*. Edward Elgar Publishing.
Buyukozkan, G., & Mukul, E. (2019). *Evaluation of smart city logistics solutions with fuzzy MCDM methods. Pamukkale Univ Muh Bilim Derg*.
Choudhry, M., Joannas, D., Pereira, R., & Pienaar, R. (2005). Money market instruments and foreign exchange. In *Capital market instruments: Analysis and valuation*. Palgrave Macmillan UK.
E Souza Rodrigues, B., Martins Floriano, C., Pereira, V., & Costa Roboredo, M. (2021). An algorithm to elicitate ELECTRE II, III and IV parameters. *Data Technologies and Applications, 55*(1), 82–96. https://doi.org/10.1108/DTA-07-2020-0161.
Elyemez, M., Yildiz, K., & Yerlikaya, M. (2023). Novel application of pythagorean fuzzy MCDM in prioritizing transportation alternatives: Insights from Ankara for the ministry of transportation. *Bitlis Eren University Journal of Science*.
Figueira, J., Greco, S., & Ehrgott, M. (2005). *Multiple criteria decision analysis: State of the art surveys*. Springer.
Figueira, J., Greco, S., Roy, B., & Słowiński, R. (2010). *ELECTRE methods: Main features and recent developments*. Springer.
Huang, J., & Shi, Z. (2021). What do we know about corporate bond returns? *Annual Review of Financial Economics*.
Kabashkin, I. (2023). Model of multi criteria decision-making for selection of transportation alternatives on the base of transport needs hierarchy framework and application of petri net. *Sustainability*.
Khan, M., & Vismara, S. (2025). Green bond issuance and corporate environmental and financial performance: A meta-analysis. *International Review of Economics & Finance*.
Laffy, R. (1966). La méthode MARSAN pour la recherche de produits nouveaux. *ESOMAR Congress*.
Lootsma, F. A. (1990). The French and the American school in multi-criteria decision analysis. *RAIRO-operations research, 24*(3), 263–285.
Morlok, E. (2017). *Introduction to transportation engineering and planning*. McGraw-Hill Education.
Van Nieuwerburgh, S. (2019). Why are REITs currently so expensive? *Real Estate Economics*.
Razi, F. (2015). A grey-based fuzzy ELECTRE model for project selection. *Journal of Optimization in Industrial Engineering*.
Rodrigue, J., Comtois, C., & Slack, B. (2017). *The geography of transport systems (4th ed.)*. Routledge.
Roy, B. (1968). Classement et choix en présence de points de vue multiples. *Revue française d'informatique et de recherche opérationnelle, 2*(8), 57–75.
Roy, B. (1974). CRITÈRES MULTIPLES ET MODÉLISATION DES PRÉFÉRENCES (L'apport des relations de surclassement). *Revue d'Economie Politique*.
Roy, B., & Bertier, P. (1971). La methode ELECTRE II: Une method de classement en presence de criteres multiples.
Roy, B., & Bertier, P. (1973). *La methode ELECTRE II—Une application au media planning*. North-Holland Publishing Company.
Roy, B., & Vanderpooten, D. (1996). The European school of MCDA: emergence, basic features and current works. *Journal of Multi-Criteria Decision Analysis*.
Salvador, G., Moura, M., Campos, P., Cardoso, P., Espadinha-Cruz, P., & Godina, R. (2024). ELECTRE applied in supplier selection–a literature review. *Procedia Computer Science*.
Sarwar, M., Gulzar, W., & Ashraf, S. (2023). Improved risk assessment model based on rough integrated clouds and ELECTRE-II method: An application to intelligent manufacturing process. *Granular Computing, 8*(6), 1533–1560. https://doi.org/10.1007/s41066-023-00385-y.
Sevkli, M. (2010). An application of the fuzzy ELECTRE method for supplier selection. *International Journal of Production Research*.
Shumaiza, A., & Al-Kenani, A. (2019). Multiple-attribute decision making ELECTRE II method under bipolar fuzzy model. *Algorithms*. https://doi.org/10.3390/a12110226.
Vincke, P. (1992). *Multicriteria decision-aid*. wiley.
Vinodh, S., & Girubha, R. (2012). *Sustainable concept selection using ELECTRE. Clean Technologies Environmental Policy*.
Vysochan, O., Vysochan, O., Hyk, V., & Boychuk, A. (2022). Multi-criteria evaluation of innovative projects by means of ELECTRE application. *Business: Theory and Practice*.
Wang, Y., & Yeo, G. T. (2018). Intermodal route selection for cargo transportation from Korea to Central Asia by adopting fuzzy Delphi and Fuzzy ELECTRE I methods. *Maritime Policy & Management*.
Wen, Z., Yu, Y., & Yan, J. (2016). Best available techniques assessment for coal gasification to promote cleaner production based on the ELECTRE-II method. *Journal of Cleaner Production*.

Chapter 95

ELECTRE III: Extension of the elimination and choice expressing reality for multi-attribute decision-making

Seyed Hossein Razavi Hajiagha[1], Shide Sadat Hashemi[2], and Salar Keshavarz Hedayati[1]

[1]*Department of Management, Faculty of Management and Financial Sciences, Khatam University, Tehran, Iran,* [2]*Department of Management, Behin Avina co, MST Park, Tehran, Iran*

95.1 Introduction

Multicriteria decision-making encompasses a wide range of methods developed to evaluate alternatives based on multiple criteria. These methods are broadly divided into two main categories: "Compromising" methods, such as technique for order preference by similarity to ideal solution (TOPSIS) and VlseKriterijumska optimizacija I kompromisno resenje (VIKOR), which rely on aggregation of criteria and compensation between them, and "Outranking" methods, such as the elimination and choice translating reality (ELECTRE) family, which operate by pairwise comparisons and the extraction of preference relations (Greco and Figueira, 2016; Roy, 1977). Among outranking methods, ELECTRE III has a special place because, by introducing indifference, preference, and veto thresholds, it allows more realistic modeling of human judgment and is able to simultaneously facilitate the process of ranking alternatives and support sorting and classification in complex problems.

Building on this general classification, it seems more necessary to understand why earlier versions of the ELECTRE family, namely ELECTRE I and ELECTRE II, were insufficient for many real-world applications. Both faced significant challenges in handling realistic and imprecise criteria. With the development of preference relations, methods were proposed to consider indifference thresholds and preference limits. ELECTRE III is a prominent method for multicriteria decision -making (MCDM) (Hashemi et al., 2016; Valipour Malakshah & Amini, 2026). In MCDM, various methods such as measurement alternatives and ranking according to compromise solution (MARCOS), multiattributive ideal -real comparative analysis, VIKOR, and TOPSIS are used for ranking (Valipour Malakshah & Amini, 2026). Among them, ELECTRE III has a more structured way to extract relations between alternatives than the ELECTRE II method. Since many real-world problems involve multicriteria decision-making today, it is natural to face a high degree of uncertainty among them.

In addition to these theoretical advantages, this method also has distinctive features from a practical and operational perspective. One of the most crucial issues in the ELECTRE III method is determining and assigning weights to decision criteria, which is also discussed below. This method allows for analyzing quantitative and qualitative indicators with any level of uncertainty (Mateo, 2012; Del Vasto-Terrientes et al., 2015). However, the most important advantage of this method is the participation of the decision maker in the decision-making process, so that ELECTRE III is considered an interactive method. Other advantages of this method include the definition of indifference thresholds and preferences. This means that if the difference between the performances of two alternatives in a specific situation is less than the previously determined value, the two alternatives would be considered indifferent . The ELECTRE III evaluation process includes determining threshold functions, concordance and discordance indices, extracting nonranking relations, and finally ranking the alternatives.

The remainder of this chapter includes the literature review concentrating on ELECTRE III and its various applications in different fields. Then, the methodology is described for both weight calculation and ELECTRE III itself. To demonstrate

Encyclopedia of Multi-Attribute Decision-Making (MADM). DOI: https://doi.org/10.1016/B978-0-443-33275-3.00055-5

the applicability of this method, we conducted two numerical examples on different scales and fields—one at a basic scale and the other at a significantly larger scale. Finally, the chapter concludes with a summary of the main findings and their implications.

95.2 Literature review

The ELECTRE III method was first proposed by Roy (1978). This method was developed as a ranking method with innovations such as indifference threshold and preference threshold. In this vein, with the increasing number of studies conducted using ELECTRE III, this method has become one of the most established and widely used MCDM methods. Hashemi et al. (2016) introduced ELECTRE III as an extended memberof the ELECTRE family. In their research, they investigated the advantages of ELECTRE III over ELECTRE II and other multicriteria decision analysis methods and described it as suitable for problems under uncertainty, with the possibility of analyzing quantitative and qualitative criteria. Fan et al. (2024) have examined the use of ELECTRE III within a bipolar set using averaging aggregation to improve decision -making in investment for renewable energies. Furthermore, Tamtam & Tourabi (2025) in their research investigated digital supply chain through artificial intelligence using ELECTRE III as an MCDM method.

Ruan et al. (2025) studied ELECTRE III as an extended method based on intuitionisticfuzzy information with interval value. In this chapter, it is stated that the use of evaluation and ranking methods based on decision -making problems is necessary in specific conditions. Accordingly, the ELECTRE III method is proposed as a decision-making method for ranking and selecting the best alternatives. Fernández et al. (2025) conducted a study on the advantages of ELECTRE III as a comprehensive model. Although the model is more advancedand complex, it is necessary to reflect the user preferences accurately. In addition, Chabane et al. (2025) proposed a sustainable multicriteria optimization framework for energy retrofitting in residential buildings in Algeria. In their study, ELECTRE III was applied by weighting environmental, social, and economic criteria. Valipour Malakshah & Amini (2026) applied MCDM methods to evaluate urban intersections in such a way that identifying these critical intersections and removing them from the operational traffic network would be effective. In this chapter, weighting and ranking methods were used, and in the ranking section, one of the methods used was the ELECTRE III method. Taherdoost & Madanchian (2023) reviewed the ELECTRE family comprehensively. In this study, they found that the versatility of the ELECTRE method allows it to be used in a wide range of fields such as engineering, economics, business, environmental management, and many others. Govindan & Jepsen (2016) conducted a comprehensive literature review on ELECTRE and categorized a large number of studies according to applications, fields of problems, and approaches.

Considering the studies and reviews on ELECTRE mentioned above, it can be concluded that this method has significant power and wide application for evaluating and prioritizing decision alternatives in various fields and areas.

95.3 Methodology

This section explains how to use the ELECTRE III method in four steps:

Step 1. Determine the threshold function: Suppose q_j and p_j are the indifference and preference thresholds for the *jth* criterion, respectively. The indifference and preference thresholds indicate the acceptance of a type of uncertainty in the decision -maker's judgment, based on which two alternatives are considered indifferent when the difference in their performance on criterion j is less than a certain value, such that q_j. In fact, q_j can be considered the minimum uncertainty bound in the calculations performed, while p_j represents the maximum allowable error bound. Furthermore, transition from indifference to preference is a gradual matter that occurs with a linear movement from q_j to p_j. Threshold functions are closely related to the idea of a quasicriterion. A criterion such as g_j is a quasicriterion if there are two threshold functions $q(g)$ and $p(g)$ that represent the indifference and preference thresholds, respectively, and for two alternatives A_i and A_j, and $g(A_i)\phi g(A_j)$ shows one of the following three relations between these two alternatives;

1. If $g(A_i)\phi \quad g(A_j) + p(g(A_j))$ then $A_i\ P\ A_j$;
2. If $g(A_j) + q(g(A_j))\pi\ g(A_i) \leq g(A_j) + p(g(A_j))$ then $A_i \quad Q \quad A_j$;
3. If $g(A_j) \leq g(A_i) \leq g(A_i) + q(g(A_j))$ then $A_i\ I\ A_j$;

In these relations, P, Q, and I indicate the strong preference, weak preference, and indifference between alternative A_i and A_j, respectively, and $g(A_i)$ and $g(A_j)$ are the scores of the alternatives A_i and A_j in the *jth* criterion.

To determine the threshold functions, we consider the following:

1. If $g(A_i)\phi \quad g(A_j)$ then $g(A_i) + q(g(A_i))\phi \quad g(A_j) + q(g(A_j))$ and $g(A_i) + p(g(A_i))\phi \quad g(A_j) + p(g(A_j))$

2. For all indicators $p(g) \geq q(g)$

To evaluate $+p(g(A_i))$ and $q(g(A_i))$, the relation presented by Bernard Roy can be used as follows (Skalka et al., 1983):

$$p_j(g_j(A_i)) = \alpha_p + \beta_p g_j(A_i) \tag{95.1}$$

$$q_j(g_j(A_i)) = \alpha_q + \beta_q g_j(A_i) \tag{95.2}$$

Threshold values can be fixed (α fixed and $\beta = 0$) or proportional ($\beta \phi 0$).

Step 2. Index of concordance and discordance: For each pair of alternatives, the index of concordance is defined as follows:

$$C(A_i, A_k) = \frac{1}{W}\sum_{j=1}^{n} w_j.\ c_j(A_i, A_k) \tag{95.3}$$

w_j is the weight of the jth index and $c_j(A_i, A_k)$ is the partial concordance index between alternatives A_i and A_k, and is calculated as follows:

$$C_j(A_i, A_k) = \begin{cases} 1, & g_j(A_i) + q_j \geq g_j(A_k) \\ 0, & g_j(A_i) + q_j \leq g_j(A_k) \\ \frac{(p_j + g_j(A_i) - g_j(A_k))}{(p_j - q_j)} & \text{Otherwise} \end{cases} \tag{95.4}$$

The discordance index of these alternatives is also defined as follows:

$$D_j(A_i, A_k) = \begin{cases} 1, & g_j(A_i) + p_j \geq g_j(A_k) \\ 0, & g_j(A_i) + p_j \leq g_j(A_k) \\ \frac{(g_j(A_k) - g_j(A_i) - p_j)}{(v_j - q_j)} & \text{Otherwise} \end{cases} \tag{95.5}$$

v_j is the veto threshold for the jth index. The veto threshold is the maximum difference value $g_j(A_k) - g_j(A_i)$ beyond which the assumption of A_i prevailing over A_k can be rejected with respect to the relevant index. The veto threshold helps us to prevent an alternative with poor performance in a particular index from being included in the best alternatives category.

Step 3. Extracting outranking relations: The next step involves combining the concordance and discordance indices for each pair of alternatives to extract an index for measuring outranking relations. In fact, a credibility matrix measures the strength of the outranking relation of one alternative over another. The credibility score for each pair of alternatives is defined as follows:

$$S(A_i, A_k) = \begin{cases} C_j(A_i, A_k), & \forall_j\ d_j(A_i, A_k) \leq C(A_i, A_k) \\ C(A_i, A_k), \times \prod_{j \epsilon J(A_i, A_k)} \frac{1 - d_j(A_i, A_k)}{1 - C(A_i, A_k)}, & otherwise \end{cases} \tag{95.6}$$

$J(A_i, A_k)$ is the set of indices for which $d_j(A_i, A_k) \phi C(A_i, A_k)$. The above equations are based on the assumption that if the concordance intensity does not exceed thediscordance, then an adjustment should be made to the concordance index according to the second clause of the equation above.

Step 4. Ranking the alternatives: To obtain a complete ranking of alternatives, the usual ranking method uses a structured approach based on two preliminary rankings: a descending ranking that ranks the alternatives from best to worst and an ascending ranking that ranks the alternatives from worst to best. Finally, the intersection of these two rankings determines the final order of the alternatives. At first, for these preliminary rankings, a factor called λ is defined as follows:

$$\lambda = \begin{cases} \max S(A_i, A_k) \\ (A_i, A_k) \epsilon A \end{cases} \tag{95.7}$$

This factor is actually a parameter used to distinguish preference intensity levels $S(A_i, A_k)$. Now, a new factor is introduced as follows:

$$S(\lambda) = \lambda\alpha + \beta \tag{95.8}$$

Usually, in the equation above, the values of $\beta = 0.3$ and $\alpha = -0.15$ are considered. Then the matrix T is defined as follows:

$$T(A_i, A_k) = \begin{cases} 1, & S(A_i, A_k)\phi \quad \lambda - S(\lambda) \\ 0, & \text{Otherwise} \end{cases} \tag{95.9}$$

The net credibility scoreof each alternative, $Q(A_i)$ is defined as the number of alternatives inferior to A_i minus the number of alternatives dominant to it. In simpler terms, $Q(A_i)$ is the difference between row sum and column sum of matrix T. In descending ranking, the sum of the alternatives with the highest desirability gets higher ranks. After the highest-desirability alternatives are removed, the values of λ and $S(\lambda)$ are calculated again, and the process continues until all alternatives are ranked. The result of the descending ranking is shown as Z_1; the results of ascending ranking, Z_2, are obtained similarly, in which the alternatives with the least preferredare determined first. The final ranking is also based on $Z_1 I Z_2$.

Li and Wang (2007) proposed another method based on three concepts of concordance credibility, discordance credibility, and net credibility for ranking alternatives in ELECTRE III.

1. The degree of concordance validity, which indicates the characteristic of dominance, is equal to:

$$\phi^+(A_i) = \sum_{A_k \in A} S(A_i, A_k) \tag{95.10}$$

2. The degree of discordance, which indicates the characteristic of being dominated, is equal to:

$$\phi^-(A_i) = \sum_{A_k \in A} S(A_k, A_i) \tag{95.11}$$

3. Finally, the net credit score is defined as follows:

$$\phi(A_i) = \phi^+(A_i) - \phi^-(A_i) \tag{95.12}$$

The larger the net credit score, indicates greater desirability of the relevant alternative.

95.3.1 Determining the weights of indicators in the elimination and choice expressing reality III method

One of the most important steps in solving decision -making problems with the ELECTRE III method is determining the weights of the evaluation criteria. Basically, the weights of the indicators in this method reflect the relative interpretation of the criteria. These methods are based on multicriteria decision-making theories for determining preferences among alternatives, mainly on the concept of trade-off rate, in which poor performance in one criterion can be compensated by strong performance in another criterion. Based on these methods, the theoretical foundations for determining criteria weights in ELECTRE III are presented. In this section of the present chapter, we will introduce two widely used methods in this regard.

95.3.1.1 *Simos method*

Simos (1989, 1990) proposed a method for determining the weights of various indicators by the decision maker and expressing these weights in the form of numerical values. The main innovation of this method is that it provides the decision maker with a card for each indicator. The ability to arrange the cards in order of importance and also consider the null cards allows the decision makerto have a better intuitive understanding of this method. Suppose we have a set of n indicators $\{C_1, C_2, \cdots, C_n\}$. The process of this method is as follows:

a. We provide the decision makerwith a set of cards. Each card has the name of an indicator written on it along with some additional information. We will have a set of n cards. These cards should not contain numerical values that could affect the results. We also distribute a set of null cards, the number of which depends on the decision maker's preference.

b. We ask the evaluator to arrange these cards in order of importance (from least to most). In fact, the person in question arranges the indicators in ascending order according to their preference. More than one indicator can be placed in a category. As a result, a complete ranking of n indicators is obtained along with null cards. Suppose the cards are arranged in $\bar{n}$ categories. We indicate the first rank with the number 1, the second rank with 2, etc.

c. It is assumed that the importance levels of two consecutive classes do not differ much from each other. If a larger difference is perceived between the two classes, a greater number of null cards will be placed between the classes. In fact, the absence of null cards means that the difference between two consecutive classes is equal to one. The following example shows how to calculate the weights in this method (see Fig. 95.1).

- **Simos numerical example**

Suppose we aim to determine theweights of a set of 12 indicators. The user has classified the cards associated with indicators with the same weight into six groups. Table 95.1 shows the rankings of these cards, along with the null cards between the classes.

To convert the rankings in the table into weights (1–97), Simos suggests the following steps:

a. Arrange the similar subsets from least to most important, taking into account the null cards.

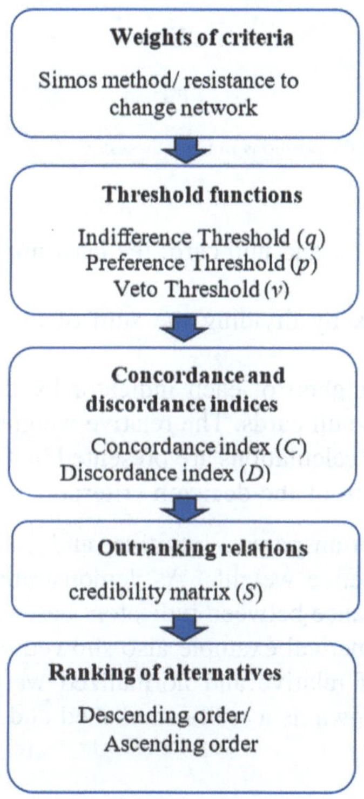

FIGURE 95.1 Methodology diagram.

TABLE 95.1 Card set information.

Number of cards by rank	Similar subcategories	Rank
3	$\{C_3, C_7, C_{12}\}$	1
1	$\{C_4\}$	2
1	null	3
4	$\{C_2, C_6, C_9, C_{10}\}$	4
1	$\{C_5\}$	5
2	$\{C_1, C_8\}$	6
1	$\{C_{11}\}$	7

TABLE 95.2 Converting ranks to weights using the Simos method.

Relative weights	Average weights	Situations	Number of cards	Similar subcategories
$\frac{2}{86} \times 100 \approx 2.326 \rightarrow 2$	$\frac{1+2+3}{3} = 2$	1,2,3	3	$\{C_3, C_7, C_{12}\}$
$\frac{4}{86} \times 100 \approx 4.651 \rightarrow 5$	4	4	1	$\{C_4\}$
.....	.....	(5)	1	null
$\frac{7.5}{86} \times 100 \approx 8.72 \rightarrow 9$	$\frac{6+7+8+9}{4} = 7.5$	6,7,8,9	4	$\{C_2, C_6, C_9, C_{10}\}$
$\frac{10}{86} \times 100 \approx 11.628 \rightarrow 12$	10	10	1	$\{C_5\}$
$\frac{11.5}{86} \times 100 \approx 13.372 \rightarrow 13$	$\frac{11+12}{2} = 11.5$	11,12	2	$\{C_1, C_8\}$
$\frac{13}{86} \times 100 \approx 15.116 \rightarrow 15$	13	13	1	$\{C_{11}\}$
	.....	86*	13	sum

(The asterisk (*) indicates that the sum does not include the positions in parentheses).

b. Assign a position (or rank) to each indicator and null card: the least important card(s) receive position 1, the next card (s) receive position 2, and so on.

c. Obtain the average weights of each rank by dividing the sum of the positions within that rank by the number of indicators (cards) in it.

d. Obtain the unscaled weights (relative weights) of each indicator by dividing the average weight by the sum of all positions, without taking into account the null cards. The relative weights are expressed without decimals and rounded to the nearest integer. The results of these calculations are presented in Table 95.2. The rounded numbers in the column of relative weights indicate the importance of the decision criteria.

In summary, the Simos method enables transparent, intuitive, and consistent weighting by converting the decision maker's qualitative preferences into quantitative weights. As demonstrated in the numerical example, this method can quantitatively represent difference in importance between indicators based only on the order of the cards and the number of empty cards between categories. The numerical example also showed that this method, while preserving the decision maker's intuition, allows the calculation of relative and normalized weights for use in outranking processes such as ELECTRE III. Therefore, this method is known as a well-established and widely used weighting method in the MCDM literature.

95.3.1.2 Resistance -to-change network method

Based on the theory of personal constructs, Rogers & Bruen (1998) proposed the resistance to change network (RCN) as a method for determining the importance weights of decision-making indicators. Accordingly, when two constructs are compared, one of them shows more resistance to change, its importance will also be greater. In this method, two different constructs are evaluated by the individual, and the individual is asked which one they would prefer not to change if they could change either of the two constructs.. If a set of n criteria is under evaluation, the resistance to change network is represented as a matrix $n \times n$. In each cell of this matrix, the following symbols are used to compare the two constructs:

X: When the column element is resistant to change.

Null: The row element is resistant to change.

I: It is not possible to change one without changing the other.

e: Both changes are undesirable.

The score is calculated as the sum of all null cells in the rows and Xs in the index columns, which indicate each element's resistance to change.

- **Resistance -to -change network numerical example**

Consider a set of eight criteria $\{C_1, C_2, \cdots, C_8\}$. The network of resistance to change for these criteria is shown in Table 95.3.

TABLE 95.3 Example resistance to change network.

	C_1	C_2	C_3	C_4	C_5	C_6	C_7	C_8	Score	Weight
C_1	-								7	0.26
C_2	-	-							6	0.22
C_3	-	-	-	X		X	X	X	1	0.04
C_4	-	-	-	-		I		X	3	0.11
C_5	-	-	-	-	-	X		X	1	0.04
C_6	-	-	-	-	-	-		X	3	0.11
C_7	-	-	-	-	-	-	-	X	1	0.04
C_8	-	-	-	-	-	-	-	-	5	0.18

For example, the score for the criterion C_6 in the table above is calculated as follows:

$$3 = 2 + 1 = \text{"Number X in the sixth column + Number of null cells in the sixth row"}$$

Finally, the weight of each criterion is equal to the score of that criterion divided by the sum of all criterion scoresin question. Now consider the following example of solving a decision-making problem with the ELECTRE III method.

95.4 Numerical Example 1

In the first numerical example, a real-world caseis used to select an appropriate waste disposal method for a special economic zone (SEZ). In this case, a waste management facility in a SEZ aims to prioritize four food waste disposal methods and select the most approprite option to reduce the environmental impact. In this vein, these four methods are shown in the following Table 95.4:

Further, based on the opinion of the senior management of the SEZ central organization, several important goals of sustainable development goals have been considered as criteria for evaluating these waste management methods, which are illustrated in Table 95.5:

Furthermore, based on official data and information published in various units of the SEZ central organization, including health, safety and environment (HSE) and waste management, Table 95.6 was constructed:

95.4.1 Determining the weights of the criteria

Since, from the perspective of the senior management of the central organization, these goals are considered equally important in alignment with the sustainability goals of the SEZ, the weight of these criteria has been considered equal.

95.4.2 Determining thresholds (q, p, v)

Indifference (q_j): 10% of the range of each criterion.

Preference (p_j): 30% of the range of each criterion.

Rejection (v_j): 80% of the range of each criterion.

According to the managerial policy, the choice of these values for the thresholds is justified; these values (10%, 30%, 80%) represent a simple, repeatable, and conservative rule, q is small enough to ignore minor differences, p reflects a meaningful preference threshold, and v is sufficiently large so that only very large differences can lead to a veto.

95.4.3 Calculating thresholds

Cost range = $120 - 30 = 90 \rightarrow q = 4.5,\ p = 18,\ v = 72$

GHG range = $600 - 200 = 400 \rightarrow q = 20,\ p = 80,\ v = 320$

Resource range = $60 - 30 = 30 \rightarrow q = 1.5,\ p = 6,\ v = 24$

Local benefit range = $70 - 50 = 20 \rightarrow q = 1,\ p = 4,\ v = 16$

TABLE 95.4 Four waste disposal method.

Waste management method	Code	Description	Source
Composting	A	Composting- Organic waste composting has been widely recommended as an alternative with low greenhouse gas (GHG) impacts and low local impact.	Al-Rumaihi et al. (2020)
Anaerobic digestion	B	Anaerobic digestion with biogas recovery—In many life cycle assessment (LCA), anaerobic digestion with biogas production (as a fossil fuel replacement) shows significant net GHG reductions.	Xiao et al. (2022)
Mechanical–biological treatment (MBT)	C	Material separation/recovery and refuse-derived fuel (RDF) and biogas production—In some studies, MBT has significant environmental benefits when combined with gas recovery and refining.	Beylot et al., 2015
Advanced thermal treatment	D	Advanced thermal technology with energy recovery and emission control—Recent studies, advanced thermal technologies (with energy recovery and pollution control) can have environmental benefits in some scenarios, but depend on the quality of the process and recycling.	Quan et al. (2025)

TABLE 95.5 Criteria for evaluating waste disposal methods.

Criteria	Description	Desirable direction
Cost (USD/per ton of waste)	Cost is important for the implementation of SDG12 and SDG11	Negative
GHG avoided (kg CO_2-eq /per ton of waste)	Greenhouse gas emissions reduction (kg CO_2-eq/ton) related to SDG13 and SDG12	Positive
Recycling rate (%)	Directly linked to SDG12 on waste reduction and the circular economy	Positive
Local environmental benefit index (0–100)	A set of local impacts, such as reduced water/soil/air pollution related to SDG6 and SDG15	Positive

TABLE 95.6 Completed table.

Criteria Alternatives	Cost ($/ton)	GHG avoided (kgCO2-eq/ton)	Resource recovery (%)	Local benefit (0–100)
A (Compost)	30	200	40	70
B (AD)	50	600	50	65
C (MBT)	70	300	60	60
D (ATT)	120	400	30	50

95.4.4 Concordance matrix

$$C = \begin{bmatrix} 1 & 0.5 & 0.5 & 0.75 \\ 0.5 & 1 & 0.75 & 1 \\ 0.5 & 0.25 & 1 & 0.75 \\ 0.25 & 0 & 0.25 & 1 \end{bmatrix}$$

95.4.5 Discordance matrices

1. Cost $D_C = \begin{bmatrix} 0 & 0 & 0 & 0 \\ 0.037 & 0 & 0 & 0 \\ 0.4 & 0.037 & 0 & 0 \\ 1 & 0.96 & 0.59 & 0 \end{bmatrix}$

2. GHG avoided $D_G = \begin{bmatrix} 0 & 1 & 0.08 & 0.5 \\ 0 & 0 & 0 & 0 \\ 0 & 0.91 & 0 & 0.08 \\ 0 & 0.5 & 0 & 0 \end{bmatrix}$

3. Recycling rate $D_R = \begin{bmatrix} 0 & 0.22 & 0.77 & 0 \\ 0 & 0 & 0.22 & 0 \\ 0 & 0 & 0 & 0 \\ 0.22 & 0.77 & 1 & 0 \end{bmatrix}$

4. Local environmental benefit index $D_L = \begin{bmatrix} 0 & 0 & 0 & 0 \\ 0.08 & 0 & 0 & 0 \\ 0.5 & 0.08 & 0 & 0 \\ 1 & 0.91 & 0.5 & 0 \end{bmatrix}$

95.4.6 Credibility matrix (S)

After applying the adjustment formula with inconsistencies, the credibility matrix was obtained:

$$S = \begin{bmatrix} 1.0000 & 0.0000 & 0.2222 & 0.7500 \\ 0.5000 & 1.0000 & 0.7500 & 1.0000 \\ 0.5000 & 0.0278 & 1.0000 & 0.7500 \\ 0.0000 & 0.0000 & 0.0000 & 1.0000 \end{bmatrix}$$

$S(B, D) = 1.000 \rightarrow$ The assertion"B outranks D" has full or very high validity.
$S(A, B) = 0.000 \rightarrow$ That is, after considering the inconsistency (e.g., large GHG or cost difference), the validity of the claim "A ≥ B" becomes zero.

95.4.7 Calculating credit scores

OC = The sum of the credibility values in its row (excluding itself)
OD = The sum of the credibility matrix in its column (excluding itself)
$ON = OD–OC$
Credit scores are displayed in Table 95.7:

95.4.8 Final ranking (based on descending order of ON)

- Rank 1: B—anaerobic digestion (ON =+2.222)
- Rank 2: C—MBT (ON =+0.306)
- Rank 3: A—composting (ON =–0.028)
- Rank 4: D—advanced thermal treatment (ON =–2.500)

95.5 Numerical Example 2

This numerical example examines a larger-scale supplier selection problem for a mining products manufacturer. In this problem, the commercial management of the manufacturing company must prepare a report on the performance of mineral

TABLE 95.7 Credit scores.

Alternative	OC (the sum of the credits it has over others)	OD (the sum of the credibility values assigned by other alternatives)	ON = OD − OC
A	0.9722	1.0000	−0.0277
B	2.2500	0.0277	+2.2222
C	1.2777	0.9722	+0.3055
D	0.0000	2.5000	−2.5000

suppliers and provide their rankings based on reliable and industry-relevant criteria, to support the board members in future strategicdecision-making, particularly regarding raw material procurement. For this purpose, the commercial manager first selected the evaluation criteria based on previous experience and reliable studies, and selected seven criteria illustrated in Table 95.8.

To perform this assessment, we first calculate the weights of the above criteria using the Simos card method. Reasons for choosing the method:

- It is intuitive and easy to justify,
- It is widely used and referenced in the ELECTRE literature (Figueira & Roy, 2002), and
- It is both practical for decision-makers and produces repeatable numerical output (Ashari & Parsaei, 2014)

Using the Simos method: The cards are numbered sequentially; The null cards also receive positions, whereas the criteria do not. The numbers start from 1. With the order and number of nulls above, the resulting positions are as follows:

- G1 (C3): position 1
- G2 (C4): position 2
- G3 (C7): position 3
- nulls (one card between G3 and G4): position 4
- G4 (two criteria: C2 and C6): positions 5 and 6
- nulls (one card between G4 and G5): position 7
- G5 (C1): position 8
- nulls (two cards between G5 and G6): positions 9 and 10
- G6 (C5): position 11

These numbers indicate the "ordinal scale + intervals between groups."

95.5.1 Calculation of the average position for each group (p_i) and the values $u_i = p_i - 1$

For groups containing multiple criteria, the average position is the average of the position numbers of the cards in the same group.

- G1 (C3): $p_1 = 1$
- G2 (C4): $p_2 = 2$
- G3 (C7): $p_3 = 3$
- G4 (C2, C6): $p_4 = (5+6)/2 = 5.5$
- G5 (C1): $p_5 = 8$
- G6 (C5): $p_6 = 11$

$$u_i = p_i - 1$$

- $u_1 = 1 - 1 = 0$
- $u_2 = 2 - 1 = 1$
- $u_3 = 3 - 1 = 2$
- $u_4 = 5.5 - 1 = 4.5$

TABLE 95.8 Vendor selection criteria.

No.	Criteria (code)	Desirable direction	Unit/scale	Scoring method/basis	Reference
1	Price (C1)	negative	Money	Price refers to the amount paid by the buyer to obtain each unit of raw material from a supplier.	Zeng et al. (2021)
2	Transport cost (C2)	negative	(USD/t)	Includes door-to-door transportation costs, loading, freight charges, unloading, insurance, and tolls.	Tahvanainen and Anttila (2011)
3	Logistic risk index (C3)	negative	%	Probability of route disruption (floods, landslides, strikes, blockages)	McKinnon (2014)
4	Supplier reputation (C4)	positive	Composite score 0–100 or rank 1–5	]ncludes: – References/customer reviews – Certifications/standards and quality records (ISO, OHSAS, mining standards) – History of operation (years) and market share – No history of major defects/ complaints or environmental violations "Each componentis scored on a scale of 0–100, and the average is weighted".	Ferreira and Silva (2022)
5	Ore quality/grade (C5)	positive	Unit depending on the ore: e.g., "percent metal" (%) or "grams per ton (g/t)" for precious metals	Central technical criterion in mineral supplier selection: Average grade supplied or average shipments.	Vieira et al. (2012)
6	Delivery reliability/lead time (C6)	positive	Average delivery time (days; lower values are preferred)	Using % on-time deliveries in the last 12 months as the main indicator, as well as average lead time. Data is collected from shipping records/enterprise resource planning (ERP), or supplier inquiries.	Leng et al. (2024)
7	Environmental/ESG and regulatory compliance (C7)	positive	Composite score 0–100 or checklist review (environmental, social, governance)	Including: environmental certificates, operating/release permits, environmental incident history, waste management plan, and tailings management.	Luthra and Govindan, 2017

- $u_5 = 8 - 1 = 7$
- $u_6 = 11 - 1 = 10$

$$\sum u_i = 0 + 1 + 2 + 4.5 + 7 + 10 = 24.5$$

Convert u_6 to normalized weights and assign to criteria:

- G1 (C3): W_G1 = 0/24.5 = 0.0000 → C3 = 0.0000
- G2 (C4): 1/24.5 = 0.0408163265 → C4 = 0.0408
- G3 (C7): 2/24.5 = 0.0816326531 → C7 = 0.0816
- G4 (C2 and C6): 4.5/24.5 = 0.1836734694→ C2 and C6 = 0.0918 (equally distributed between C2 and C6)

- G5 (C1): 7/24.5 = 0.2857142857 → C1 = 0.2857
- G6 (C5): 10/24.5 = 0.4081632653 → C5 = 0.4082

Total weights: 0 + 0.0408 + 0.0816 + 0.0918 + 0.0918 + 0.2857 + 0.4082 ≈ 1.0000. (exact sum =1)

95.5.2 Final weight

The final weight of the criteria is shown in Table 95.9.

95.5.3 Decision matrix and data source

The values of the decision matrix for each supplier were obtained based on actual organizational data or data collection processes according to Table 95.10.

95.5.4 Decision matrix

The decision matrix is presented in Table 95.11.

95.5.5 Setting thresholds

Indifference, preference, and veto thresholds were determined from reliable sources and are presented in Table 95.12.

TABLE 95.9 Final weight.

Criteria (code)	weight
C1—PRICE	0.2857
C2—Transport cost	0.0918
C3—Logistics disruption risk	0.0000
C4—Supplier reputation	0.0408
C5—Ore quality/grade	0.4082
C6—Delivery reliability/lead time	0.0918
C7—ESG and compliance	0.0816

TABLE 95.10 The Data collection method for decision matrix values.

Criteria	How to collect data
Price (C1)	Average prices offered by suppliers in the commercial unit
Transport cost (C2)	Calculation of transportation costs (loading, route, unloading, insurance) by the logistics unit
Logistic risk (C3)	Path risk probability
Supplier reputation (C4)	A combined score of standards, track record, and customer satisfaction based on suppliers records
Ore quality (C5)	Ore grade based on sampling and historical data in the incoming and laboratory quality control unit
Delivery reliability (C6)	On-time delivery percentage of ERP reports
ESG and compliance (C7)	Environmental permits and HSE records checklist score

TABLE 95.11 Decision matrix.

Alternative	C1	C2	C3	C4	C5	C6	C7
1	100	50	2	70	55	90	80
2	110	55	3	60	50	85	75
3	95	60	2	65	60	88	70
4	105	45	4	75	52	87	78
5	120	70	5	50	48	80	72
6	98	52	3	68	57	89	74
7	115	65	4	55	53	82	76
8	102	48	2	72	56	86	79
9	108	50	3	63	54	84	77

TABLE 95.12 Determined Indifference, preference, and rejection thresholds.

Criteria	q	P	v	Direction
C1	5	20	50	min
C2	2	10	30	min
C3	1	5	10	min
C4	1	5	10	max
C5	1	10	20	max
C6	1	5	10	max
C7	1	5	10	max

95.5.6 Concordance matrix

The 9 × 9 concordance matrix is presented in Table 95.13.

95.5.7 Discordance matrix

In this section, the 9 × 9 discordance matrix is presented in Table 95.14.

95.5.8 Credibility matrix

The 9 × 9 credibility matrix is presented in Table 95.15.

95.5.9 Final results

The results obtained from the ELECTRE III analysis are presented in Table 95.16.

TABLE 95.13 Concordance matrix.

C	O1	O2	O3	O4	O5	O6	O7	O8	O9
O1	1	0.51	0.63	0.57	0.44	0.60	0.48	0.58	0.52
O2	0.49	1	0.55	0.50	0.41	0.52	0.45	0.50	0.48
O3	0.37	0.45	1	0.42	0.39	0.50	0.40	0.46	0.43
O4	0.43	0.50	0.58	1	0.46	0.55	0.50	0.57	0.51
O5	0.56	0.59	0.61	0.54	1	0.58	0.53	0.56	0.52
O6	0.40	0.48	0.50	0.45	0.42	1	0.44	0.50	0.46
O7	0.52	0.55	0.57	0.50	0.47	0.56	1	0.53	0.50
O8	0.42	0.50	0.54	0.43	0.44	0.50	0.47	1	0.48
O9	0.48	0.52	0.57	0.49	0.48	0.50	0.50	0.52	1

TABLE 95.14 Discordance matrix.

D	O1	O2	O3	O4	O5	O6	O7	O8	O9
O1	0	0.48	0.40	0.45	0.55	0.42	0.50	0.46	0.44
O2	0.52	0	0.46	0.50	0.57	0.48	0.52	0.50	0.50
O3	0.60	0.54	0	0.55	0.61	0.50	0.60	0.54	0.57
O4	0.55	0.50	0.45	0	0.52	0.48	0.50	0.46	0.49
O5	0.45	0.41	0.39	0.48	0	0.42	0.47	0.44	0.48
O6	0.58	0.52	0.50	0.55	0.58	0	0.56	0.50	0.54
O7	0.50	0.48	0.40	0.50	0.53	0.44	0	0.47	0.50
O8	0.54	0.50	0.46	0.57	0.56	0.50	0.53	0	0.52
O9	0.52	0.50	0.43	0.51	0.52	0.46	0.50	0.48	0

TABLE 95.15 Credibility matrix.

i \ j	O1	O2	O3	O4	O5	O6	O7	O8	O9
O1	1.00	0.51	0.63	0.57	0.35	0.60	0.46	0.58	0.52
O2	0.46	1.00	0.55	0.50	0.29	0.52	0.39	0.50	0.46
O3	0.23	0.37	1.00	0.32	0.24	0.50	0.26	0.39	0.32
O4	0.33	0.50	0.58	1.00	0.40	0.55	0.50	0.57	0.51
O5	0.56	0.59	0.61	0.54	1.00	0.58	0.53	0.56	0.52
O6	0.28	0.44	0.50	0.36	0.30	1.00	0.34	0.50	0.39
O7	0.52	0.55	0.57	0.50	0.41	0.56	1.00	0.53	0.50
O8	0.33	0.50	0.54	0.32	0.34	0.50	0.41	1.00	0.44
O9	0.44	0.52	0.57	0.47	0.44	0.50	0.50	0.52	1.00

TABLE 95.16 Final results.

Alternative	ϕ	rank
O1	0.30	1
O9	0.20	2
O6	0.18	3
O2	0.12	4
O8	0.10	5
O4	0.05	6
O7	-0.05	7
O3	-0.08	8
O5	-0.12	9

95.6 Conclusion

The ELECTRE III method is one of the most advanced and widely usedMCDM methods. Its more significant difference compared to compensatorydecision-making methods is its noncompensatory approach. As a result, this method is particularly suitable for complex and uncertain decision-making problems. ELECTRE III can model various preferences through a set of indifference (q), preference (p), and veto (v) thresholds. Accordingly, this method not only reflects the sensitivity of the criteria to the performance differences, but also combines data variability with the subjective judgments of the decision-makers. This feature makes ELECTRE III one of the most suitable methods for handling imprecise data and expert judgments. This method identifies outranking relations between the options by calculating the concordance matrix, the discordance matrix, the credibility matrix, and the distillation procedure . The relations extracted from ELECTRE III, unlike those extracted from classical methods, are more suitable for real-world decision-making. This makes the output known as a reliable ranking and appropriate to the conditions of decision-makers.

In general, ELECTRE III is considered a suitable method for decision-making at both strategic and operational levels. It is recommended to use this method in issues such as urban management, environmental management and sustainability, transportation, energy management, risk assessment, and risk policy-making, which involve multiple criteria and uncertain data. ELECTRE III requires precise determination of thresholds, weights, and as well asprofessional interpretation of the results, which increases its complexity, but has made it a powerful analytical tool in sensitive and multidimensional problems.

The following are different directions for future research with the EECTRE III method:

1. Integrating ELECTRE III with machine learning. Given the increasing volume of data and the increasing role of data-driven systems in decision-making processes, integrating ELECTRE III with machine learning could significantly improve decision-making under uncertainty. Machine learning can support automatic estimation of criteria weights, prediction of performance values, or clustering of alternatives, thereby improving the consistency and data-driven nature of the ELECTRE III framework.
2. Real-world problems often involve ambiguous, imprecise, or incomplete data. For future research, it could be suggested to focus on developing variants of ELECTRE III based on fuzzy sets, gray systems, probabilistic models, evidence theory, or mixed uncertainty frameworks to better reflect the complexity of real-world decision-making environments.
3. The subjective determination of indifference, preference, and veto thresholds could be one of the major methodological challenges in ELECTRE III. Future studies could propose data-driven, statistical, or optimization-based approaches to reduce subjectivity and improve the repeatability and reliability of threshold determination.
4. With changing technologies and the emergence of new challenges such as sustainability, circular economy strategies, smart cities, renewable energy planning, and cybersecurity issues, it can be inferred that the nature of decision-making has also evolvedsignificantly and broader applications of ELECTRE III can be expected. These applications demonstrate the relevance of this method in complex, multidimensional, and rapidly changing environments.

References

Al-Rumaihi, A., McKay, G., Mackey, H. R., & Al-Ansari, T. (2020). Environmental impact assessment of food waste management using two composting techniques. *Sustainability, 12*(4), 1595.

Ashari, H. E., & Parsaei, M. (2014). Application of the multi-criteria decision method ELECTRE III for the Weapon selection. *Decision Science Letters, 3*(4), 511–522.

Beylot, A., Vaxelaire, S., Zdanevitch, I., Auvinet, N., & Villeneuve, J. (2015). Life cycle assessment of mechanical biological pre-treatment of municipal solid waste: A case study. *Waste Management, 39*, 287–294.

Chabane, N., Mokhtari, A. M., Kacemi, M., Harrat, Z. R., Hilal, N., Ademović, N., & Hadzima-Nyarko, M. (2025). A Sustainable Multi-Criteria Optimization Approach for the Energy Retrofit of Collective Housing in Algeria Using the ELECTRE III Tool. *Sustainability, 17*(10), 4273. https://doi.org/10.3390/su17104273.

Fan, J., Hao, G., & Wu, M. (2024). A Bipolar Complex Fuzzy CRITIC-ELECTRE III Approach Using Einstein Averaging Aggregation Operators for Enhancing Decision Making in Renewable Energy Investments. *International Journal of Fuzzy Systems, 26*(7), 2359–2369. https://doi.org/10.1007/s40815-024-01739-7.

Fernández, E., Figueira, J. R., Navarro, J., Solares, E., & Díaz, R. (2025). Integrating second-order effects in ELECTRE methods with an interval-based approach. *Omega, 137*, 103353. https://doi.org/10.1016/j.omega.2025.103353.

Ferreira, A., & Silva, A.M. (2022). *Supplier selection and procurement in SMEs: Insights from the literature on key criteria and purchasing strategies.*

Figueira, J., & Roy, B. (2002). Determining the weights of criteria in the ELECTRE type methods with a revised Simos' procedure. *European Journal of Operational Research, 139*(2), 317–326.

Govindan, K., & Jepsen, M. B. (2016). ELECTRE: A comprehensive literature review on methodologies and applications. *European Journal of Operational Research, 250*(1), 1–29.

Greco, S., Figueira, J., & Ehrgott, M. (2016). Springer Multiple criteria decision analysisVol. 37.

Hashemi, S. S., Hajiagha, S. H. R., Zavadskas, E. K., & Mahdiraji, H. A. (2016). Multicriteria group decision making with ELECTRE III method based on interval-valued intuitionistic fuzzy information. *Applied Mathematical Modelling, 40*(2), 1554–1564. https://doi.org/10.1016/j.apm.2015.08.011.

Leng, M., Becerril-Arreola, R., Parlar, M., & Ferguson, M. (2024). Disclosing delivery performance information when consumers are sensitive to promised delivery time, delivery reliability, and price. *Manufacturing & Service Operations Management, 26*(5), 1918–1924.

Li, H.-F., & Wang, J.-J. (2007). An improved ranking method for ELECTRE III. In International Conference on Wireless Communications, Networking and Mobile Computing (pp. 6659–6662). IEEE.

Luthra, S., Govindan, K., Kannan, D., Mangla, S. K., & Garg, C. P. (2017). An integrated framework for sustainable supplier selection and evaluation in supply chains. *Journal of Cleaner Production, 140*, 1686–1698.

Mateo, J. R. S. C. (2012). Springer Multi criteria analysis in the renewable energy industryVol. 639.

McKinnon, A. (2014). *Building supply chain resilience: A review of challenges and strategies.*

Quan, C., Ravelomanantsoa, V. S., Olazar, L., Santamaria, L., Lopez, G., Liu, L., & Gao, N. (2025). Thermochemical conversion of waste into energy: A review. *Environmental Chemistry Letters*, 1–26.

Rogers, M., & Bruen, M. (1998). A new system for weighting environmental criteria for use within ELECTRE III. *European Journal of Operational Research, 107*(3), 552–563.

Roy, B. (1977). Partial preference analysis and decision-aid: The fuzzy outranking relation concept. *Conflicting Objectives in Decisions*, 40–75.

Roy, B. (1978). ELECTRE III: Un algorithme de classements fondé sur une repré- sentation floue des préférences en présence de critères multiples. *Cahiers du Centre d'études de recherche operationnelle, 20*, 3–24.

Ruan, C., Gong, S., & Chen, X. (2025). Multi-criteria group decision-making with extended ELECTRE III method and regret theory based on probabilistic interval-valued intuitionistic hesitant fuzzy information. *Complex & Intelligent Systems, 11*(1), 92. https://doi.org/10.1007/s40747-024-01645-3.

Simos, J. (1989). *L'évaluation environnementale: Un processus cognitif négocié.* éditeur non identifié.

Simos, J. (1990). Presses polytechniques et universitaires romandes Lausanne Evaluer l'impact sur l'environnement: Une approche originale par l'analyse multicritère et la négociationVol. 1015.

Skalka, J.M., Bouyssou, D., & Bernabeu, Y.A. (1983). *Electre III et IV: aspects méthologiques et guide d'utilisation.*

Taherdoost, H., & Madanchian, M. (2023). A comprehensive overview of the ELECTRE method in multi-criteria decision-making. *Taherdoost, H., Madanchian, M*, 5–16.

Tahvanainen, T., & Anttila, P. (2011). Supply chain cost analysis of long-distance transportation of energy wood in Finland. *Biomass and Bioenergy, 35*(8), 3360–3375.

Tamtam, F., & Tourabi, A. (2025). Advancing Digital Supply Chains through Generative AI: A Strategic Framework with the ELECTRE III Method. *Complex Systems Informatics and Modeling Quarterly*, (43), 17–33. https://doi.org/10.7250/csimq.2025-43.02.

Valipour Malakshah, M. R., & Amini, Z. (2026). Intersection importance assessment for an operationally resilient urban traffic network: A multi-criteria decision-making-based framework. *Reliability Engineering & System Safety, 266*, 111661. https://doi.org/10.1016/j.ress.2025.111661.

Del Vasto-Terrientes, L., Valls, A., Słowiński, R., & Zielniewicz, P. (2015). ELECTRE-III-H: An outranking-based decision aiding method for hierarchically structured criteria. *Expert Systems with Applications, 42*, 4910–4926. https://doi.org/10.1016/j.eswa.2015.02.016.

Vieira, M. D. M., Goedkoop, M. J., Storm, P., & Huijbregts, M. A. J. (2012). Ore grade decrease as life cycle impact indicator for metal scarcity: the case of copper. *Environmental Science & Technology, 46*(23), 12772–12778.

Xiao, H., Zhang, D., Tang, Z., Li, K., Guo, H., Niu, X., & Yi, L. (2022). Comparative environmental and economic life cycle assessment of dry and wet anaerobic digestion for treating food waste and biogas digestate. *Journal of Cleaner Production, 338*, 130674.

Zeng, L., Liu, S. Q., Kozan, E., Corry, P., & Masoud, M. (2021). A comprehensive interdisciplinary review of mine supply chain management. *Resources Policy, 74*, 102274.

Chapter 96

ELECTRE TRI: elimination and choice expressing reality TRI for multi-attribute decision-making

Babek Erdebilli[1,2] and Gül Uslu[3]

[1]*Department of Industrial Engineering, Ankara Yıldırım Beyazıt University, Ankara, Türkiye,* [2]*School of Business, Worcester Polytechnic Institute, Worcester, MA, United States,* [3]*Department of Occupational Health and Safety, Sinop University, Sinop, Türkiye*

96.1 Introduction

Complex decision-making problems are one of the main challenges faced by decision-makers in different disciplines in today's world (Akmaludin et al., 2024). Uncertainty, multiple evaluation criteria, conflicting stakeholder expectations, and the need to evaluate qualitative and quantitative data together make decision-making processes even more complex. At this point, multiqualitative decision-making methods enable decision-makers to make evaluations in a systematic, consistent, and transparent manner.

Elimination and choice expressing the reality (ELECTRE) employs an outranking approach to assess alternatives, with ELECTRE Triage (or sorting/assignment) (TRI) specifically classifying them into predefined categories (Roy & Bouyssou, 1993).

The ELECTRE family uses an outranking-based approach to compare alternatives, while ELECTRE TRI is tailored for classification tasks, assigning options to predefined categories (Roy & Bouyssou, 1993). It further accommodates both numerical and preference-driven information, including uncertainty and threshold variations, allowing it to capture the nuanced reasoning processes of decision-makers (Roy & Bouyssou, 1993).

In this section, the theoretical foundations, methodological structure, strengths, and effectiveness of the ELECTRE TRI method in different application areas will be discussed; in addition, how more consistent and explanatory results can be achieved in complex decision environments through the method will be detailed. The ultimate goal of the section is to clarify the added value provided by the ELECTRE TRI method in both academic and practical contexts, and to shed light on how it can be used effectively in multiqualitative decision processes (Certa et al., 2017).

Table 96.1 summarizes studies using ELECTRE TRI and its derivatives. When the studies are examined thematically, the method has been applied in different fields such as logistics, energy, credit evaluation, risk analysis, policies, optimization, and social indicators. It is seen that machine learning and hybrid models are integrated into the method in studies after 2020.

In recent years, the ELECTRE TRI method has been widely applied in energy efficiency, renewable energy projects, and the assessment of critical raw material supply risks. Probability ELECTRE-TRI (pELECTRE-TRI) probabilistically addresses uncertainties in criterion values, thresholds, and classification profiles, enabling its application in energy efficiency classification and measuring decision reliability under different scenarios via Monte Carlo simulations (Figueira et al., 2023). Similarly, stochastic multicriteria acceptability analysis (SMAA)-TRI has been used to classify supply risks of critical minerals (e.g., lithium, cobalt, nickel) when parameters are uncertain (García et al., 2025). Furthermore, at the community level, ELECTRE TRI-B has been applied for prioritizing renewable energy projects and resource allocation, combining classification logic with group decision-making processes (Smith & Müller, 2024). Another key development is the creation of open-source Python libraries for pELECTRE-Tri, which enhance reproducibility and transparency in decision-making (Chen et al., 2025).

Encyclopedia of Multi-Attribute Decision-Making (MADM). DOI: https://doi.org/10.1016/B978-0-443-33275-3.00082-8

TABLE 96.1 Literature summary.

Year	Study	Scope	Methodological contribution
2005	Zehra Isik	Facility layout	ELECTRE-TRI applied field study
2009	Yucel & Ulutas	Logistics/site selection	Site selection with Electre
2013	Angilella & Mazzù	subject matter expert (SME) credit assessment	stochastic multicriteria acceptability analysis (SMAA)-TRI + soft criteria integration
2014	Simsek	Energy/wind turbine	Geographic information system + elimination and choice expressing the reality (ELECTRE) III/III classification
2014	Keleş	Technopark selection	Hierarchical analytic hierarchy process (AHP) + ELECTRE III
2018	Demir	Pharmaceutical policies	Stakeholder analysis + ELECTRE III
2019	Demirbas	Financial risk analysis	AHP + ELECTRE TRI + FLOWSORT
2020	Montenegro & Pereira	Parameter optimization	Random forest + genetic algorithm
2021	Şener & Yılmaz	Country welfare level	Entropy-based ELECTRE TRI + K-means
2023	Ribeiro & Mota	Rural cooperatives	Performance classification with ELECTRE TRI
2024	Bouyssou et al.	Electre model theory	ELECTRE TRI-nB axiomatic analysis
2024	Salvador et al.,	Social indicators	ML-based parameter extraction
2025	Rahman and Wong,	Sustainable procurement	Integration of fuzzy weights into the ELECTRE method to enable more reliable green supplier selection under uncertainty.
2025	Prasiwiningrum et al.	Concrete selection	The ELECTRE method as a decision support tool for concrete type selection in building structures.
2025	Martins et al.	Occupational diseases	An ELECTRE TRI–based analytical method to systematically establish causal links in occupational diseases under conditions of uncertainty.

In the coming years, the ELECTRE TRI method is expected to evolve in several directions. Integration with artificial intelligence and machine learning will allow the method to support more adaptive and dynamic decision-making systems (Figueira et al., 2023). Combining ELECTRE TRI with big data and IoT technologies will enable real-time, data-driven decision-making (Chen et al., 2025). Incorporating social and environmental criteria into decision processes will contribute to achieving sustainable development goals (Smith & Müller, 2024). Additionally, the expansion of open-source software tools will improve accessibility, reproducibility, and transparency (García et al., 2025). Finally, hybridization with fuzzy, probabilistic, and Bayesian approaches is expected to increase reliability in areas with high measurement uncertainty.

96.2 History of elimination and choice expressing the reality methods

ELECTRE methods are outranking-based approaches developed to solve multi-attribute decision-making problems. ELECTRE methods have been adapted to different decision problems over time and developed in various versions (Table 96.2).

96.2.1 Elimination and choice expressing the reality TRI method

ELECTRE TRI is a ranking (outranking) method developed for classification purposes in the field of multicriteria decision-making (MCDM). The method aims to assign each alternative to one of the predefined categories. These categories are arranged in a specific order, each representing a certain level of quality or priority. ELECTRE TRI offers

TABLE 96.2 Elimination and choice expressing the reality (ELECTRE) method development process.

ELECTRE version	Period developed	Basic features	Application areas	Featured resources
ELECTRE II	1973	- Alternatives are ranked- includes strong and weak superiority relations- dynamic ranking structure	- Performance evaluation- technology selection	Roy and Bertier (1973)
ELECTRE III	1985	- Includes preference, uncertainty, and veto thresholds- provides decision support under uncertainty- takes fuzziness into account	- Environmental planning- transportation systems	Roy (1985)
ELECTRE IV	1993	- Analysis can be done without specifying criteria weights- weightless superiority analysis	- Social choice problems- prioritization studies	Roy and Bouyssou (1993)
ELECTRE V	1993	- Group decision-making approach- suitable for multiple decision-makers	- Joint investment decisions- strategic planning	Roy and Bouyssou (1993)
ELECTRE TRI	1992	- Alternatives are classified into predefined categories- boundary profiles are used	- Risk classification- credit scoring- waste management	Yu (1992)

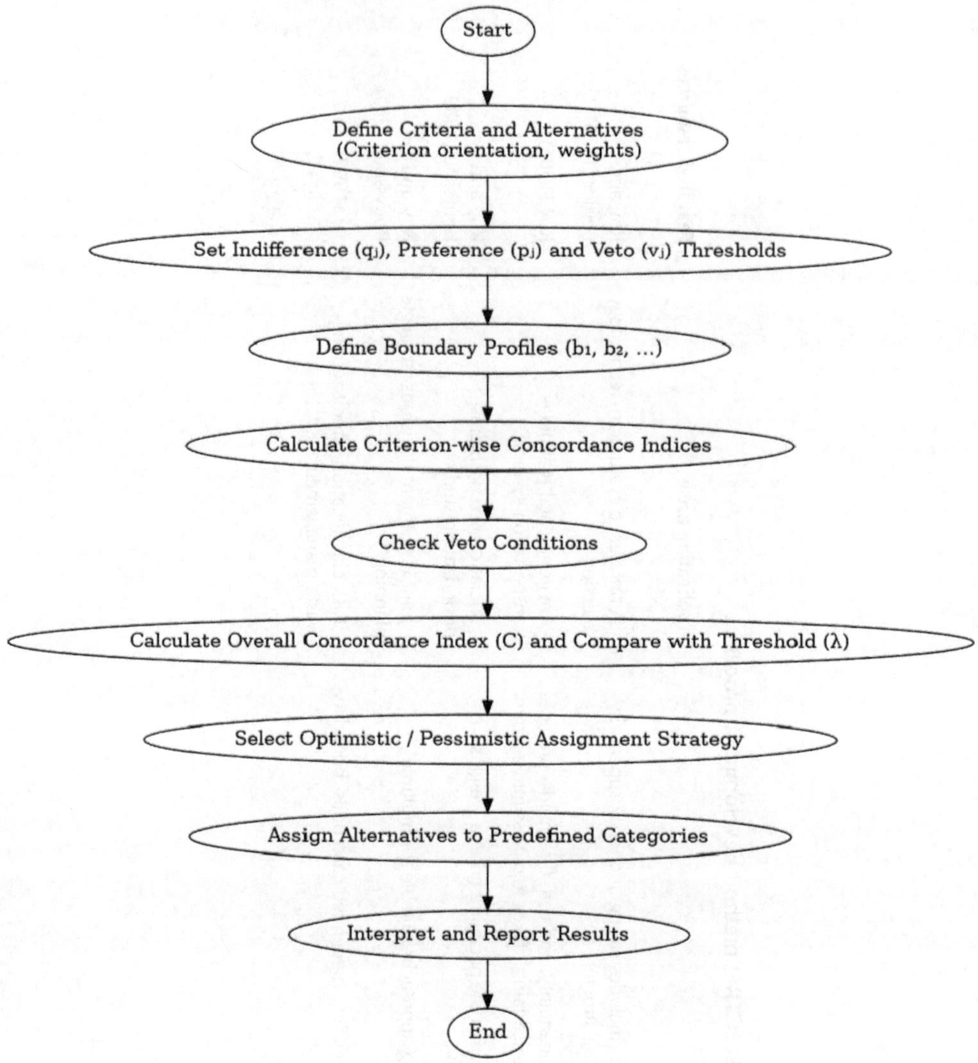

FIGURE 96.1 ELECTRE TRI flow diagram.

flexibility to decision makers, especially in cases of uncertainty, conflicting criteria, and insufficient information (Roy & Bouyssou, 1993).

The implementation process of the ELECTRE TRI method consists of a series of systematic steps. The algorithm flow diagram given in Fig. 96.1 summarizes the process steps followed from the beginning to the end of the method (Doumpos et al., 2009). In the first stage, the criteria, alternatives and their direction and weight values belonging to the decision problem are defined; then indifference (q_j), preference (p_j), and veto (v_j) thresholds are determined. In the next step, criterion-based compliance (concordance) indexes are calculated by creating predefined category boundary profiles, and veto conditions are checked. After comparing the total compliance index with the threshold value (λ), alternatives are assigned to appropriate categories by choosing an optimistic or pessimistic classification strategy. This flow reflects the basic operation logic of the ELECTRE TRI method defined by Roy and Bouyssou (1993) and Yu (1992).

ELECTRE TRI is based on the evaluation of alternatives ($A = \{a_1, \ldots, a_n\}$) according to the criteria set ($G = \{g_1, \ldots, g_m\}$). The direction (maximization/minimization) and weights (w_j) of the criteria are determined and normalized so that $\Sigma w_j = 1$. Boundary profiles between categories ($C_1 \prec C_2 \prec \ldots \prec C_p$) are defined by $b_1, \ldots, b_{p-1}$ (Salvador et al., 2024).

Three threshold values are defined for each criterion:

- Indifference threshold (q_j): The range where the difference is considered insignificant.
- Preference threshold (p_j): The lower limit where a clear superiority is observed.
- Veto threshold (v_j): The limit that invalidates the general superiority if exceeded.

Criterion-based compliance function is defined as $c_j(a,b_h) \in [0,1]$. Total compliance index:

$$C(a, b_h) = \left(\frac{\sum_{j \in J_c(a,b_h)} w_j}{\sum_{j \in J} w_j} \right)$$

Here;

- J: Set of all criteria
- $Jc(a,b_h)$: The set of criteria for which alternative aaa is at least as good as profile bh (compliant)
- w_j: Weight of criterion j

The criterion-based compliance function to measure the superiority of alternative a over profile b_h is defined as follows (Baseer et al., 2023):

$$c_j(a, b_h) = \begin{cases} 1, & \text{if } g_j(a) \geq g_j(b_h) - q_j \\ 0, & \text{if } g_j(a) \leq g_j(b_h) - p_j \\ \frac{g_j(a) - g_j(b_h) + p_j}{p_j - q_j}, & \text{in other cases} \end{cases}$$

This function produces a compliance value in the range of [0, 1] for each criterion.
The total compliance index is calculated as follows (Fontana & Cavalcante, 2013):

$$v_j(a, b_h) = \begin{cases} 1, & \text{if } g_j(b_h) - g_j(a) \geq q_j \\ 0, & \text{otherwise} \end{cases}$$

In some cases, a large difference in one criterion may prevent the overall superiority of the alternative. In this case, the veto function comes into play:

$$v_j(a, b_h) = \begin{cases} 1, & \text{if } g_j(b_h) - g_j(a) \geq v_j \\ 0, & \text{otherwise} \end{cases}$$

If it is for any j criterion, $vj(a, b_h) = 1a > b_h$ *superiority relationship rejected.*
Two conditions must be met for a general outranking relation to be established:

1. The consistency index must be above a certain threshold value (λ):

$$C(a, b_h) \geq \lambda, \quad \lambda \in [0.5, 1]$$

2. No veto should be applied for any criterion: $\forall_j, \ v_j(a, b_h) = 0$

In this case, alternative a is considered superior to the b_h profile. $a > b_h$
Veto condition:

$$V_j(a, b_h) = 1 \text{ if } g_j(b_h) - g_j(a) \geq v_j,$$

Two conditions must be met for the outranking relation a S b_h:

1. $C(a,b_h) \geq \lambda$
2. There should be no veto

Classification process
ELECTRE TRI offers two different strategies for assigning alternatives to categories (Biluca et al., 2020):

- Optimistic: Assignment to the highest suitable category
- Pessimistic: Assignment to the safe lower category

a. Optimistic approach
Aims to assign the alternative to the highest possible category. The smallest h value that satisfies the following condition is found:

$$a > b_{h-1} \Rightarrow a \in C_h$$

b. Pessimistic (cautious) approach
Prioritizes assigning the alternative to a safe lower category. The largest h value that satisfies the following condition is found:

c. $b_h \not\succ a \Rightarrow a \in C_{h+1}$
The use of these two approaches is shaped by the perception of risk and the level of security in the decision-making context.

96.3 Example application: airport location selection in the black sea region—a classification with the elimination and choice expressing the reality TRI method

In this section, four provinces located in the Black Sea region (Sinop, Samsun, Ordu-Giresun, and Trabzon) were evaluated based on their socio-economic and spatial characteristics through a MCDM approach. The method applied assigns each alternative to predefined categories, offering a classification-based decision support structure.

The evaluation was conducted based on the following five criteria:

- Population density
- Tourism potential
- Economic development
- Geographical suitability
- Availability of alternative transportation

Criterion weights were determined with expert judgment, and threshold values were defined in accordance with the methodological requirements. Data were obtained from the Turkish statistical institute and up-to-date reports from regional development agencies.

Three priority categories were constructed for classification purposes:

- C_1: Low priority
- C_2: Medium priority
- C_3: High priority

Two boundary profiles (b_1 and b_2) were used to represent the thresholds between these categories. Each province was compared with these profiles to determine its category assignment.

When the province of Sinop was compared against the upper boundary profile (b_2, representing the C_2/C_3 threshold), it was observed that the values related to population density and tourism potential were significantly lower than the profile values. The differences in these two criteria exceeded the veto thresholds defined in the model. Although Sinop performed relatively well in the other criteria, the presence of two veto conditions prevented it from being assigned to the high-priority category (C_3). As a result, Sinop was classified in the low priority category (C_1).

In the Black Sea region, the provinces of Sinop, Samsun, Ordu-Giresun, and Trabzon are divided into three categories (C_1 low, C_2 medium, C_3 high priority). Criteria: population density, tourism potential, economic development, geographical suitability, and alternative transportation. Weights and threshold values are determined. Data were obtained from Turkish Statistical Institute (TURKSTAT) and local development reports. Calculation example (Sinop vs b_2): population (40 vs 70, difference -30, veto), tourism (45 vs 70, difference -25, veto), although other criteria are positive, it is not assigned to C_3 due to two vetoes. Similarly, all provinces were evaluated, and Samsun and Trabzon were classified as C_3, Ordu-Giresun as C_2, and Sinop as C_1.

1. Alternatives will be classified into three categories: C1 (low priority investment region), C2 (medium priority investment region), and C3 (high priority investment region):
g_1: Population density ⇒ 0.25 ($q = 5$, $p = 10$, $v = 25$)
g_2: Tourism potential ⇒ 0.20 ($q = 5$, $p = 15$, $v = 30$)
g_3: Economic development ⇒ 0.20 ($q = 5$, $p = 10$, $v = 20$)
g_4: Geographical suitability ⇒ 0.15 ($q = 5$, $p = 10$, $v = 25$)
g_5: Alternative transportation opportunities ⇒ 0.20 ($q = 5$, $p = 10$, $v = 20$)
Limit profiles:
b_1: [50, 50, 40, 50, 50]
b_2: [70, 70, 60, 65, 65]

TABLE 96.3 Criteria and weights.

Criterion (g_j)	Description	Direction	Weight	Hesitation q_j	Preference p_j	Veto v_j
g_1	Population density	Max.	0.25	5	10	25
g_2	Tourism potential	Max.	0.20	5	15	30
g_3	Economic development	Max.	0.20	5	10	20
g_4	Geographical suitability	Max.	0.15	5	10	25
g_5	Alternative transportation options	Max.	0.20	5	10	20

2. Criteria and weights are determined (Table 96.3).
Table 96.3 summarizes the criteria, their orientations, relative weights, and the pseudo-criteria thresholds (indifference, preference, and veto) that guided the ELECTRE TRI analysis. Five main criteria were considered: population density (g_1), tourism potential (g_2), economic development (g_3), geographical suitability (g_4), and alternative transportation options (g_5). All criteria were defined with a maximization orientation, meaning that higher values represent more favorable conditions. The assigned weights reflect the relative importance of each factor in the decision-making process. For instance, population density received the highest weight (0.25), emphasizing its critical role in determining regional investment priorities, while geographical suitability had the lowest weight (0.15). Pseudo-criteria thresholds were introduced to better capture the gradual perception of differences among alternatives. The indifference threshold (q) indicates the range within which small differences are treated as negligible, the preference threshold (p) identifies when a significant difference becomes evident, and the veto threshold (v) sets a critical boundary that prevents an alternative from being assigned to a higher category if the gap is too large. For example, in the case of population density, a difference greater than 25 units triggers a veto, which excludes the alternative from being classified in the upper category regardless of its performance in other criteria. This structure allows the method to handle uncertainty in a more realistic way: minor variations are tolerated, medium differences are gradually recognized, and substantial disadvantages act as decisive barriers. Consequently, the ELECTRE TRI approach provides a robust framework for classifying provinces into low, medium, or high investment priority categories.

3. Then the performance of the alternatives is determined (Table 96.4).
As presented in Table 96.4, the performance scores of the provinces vary considerably across the five criteria. Samsun and Trabzon achieve the highest values overall, particularly in population density, tourism, and economic development, while Sinop records the lowest scores except for geographical suitability, where it performs best. Ordu-Giresun generally remains at an intermediate level across most indicators. These variations clearly demonstrate the regional disparities that shape the final categorization in the ELECTRE TRI analysis.

4. Class boundaries are determined (Table 96.5).
Grades: C_1, C_2, C_3
Limit profiles:
b_1: $C_1 \leftrightarrow C_2$ limit
b_2: $C_2 \leftrightarrow C_3$ limit
As shown in Table 96.5, the boundary profiles represent the reference levels that separate the three investment priority categories. The lower profile ($b_1 = [50, 50, 40, 50, 50]$) defines the threshold between C_1 (low priority) and C_2 (medium priority), while the upper profile ($b_2 = [70, 70, 60, 65, 65]$) establishes the minimum performance required to enter C_3 (high priority). Each profile value corresponds to a specific criterion—population density, tourism potential, economic

TABLE 96.4 Performances of the alternatives.

Alternative	g_1	g_2	g_3	g_4	g_5
Sinop	40	45	35	60	55
Samsun	80	75	70	70	85
Ordu-Giresun	65	65	55	50	60
Trabzon	75	85	65	45	70

TABLE 96.5 Class profiles of citeria.

Profile	g_1	g_2	g_3	g_4	g_5
b_1	50	50	40	50	50
b_2	70	70	60	65	65

development, geographical suitability, and alternative transportation options. These benchmarks serve as decision thresholds in the ELECTRE TRI procedure: alternatives are first compared with b_2 to test their eligibility for C_3, and if they fail to outrank it, they are then compared with b_1 to determine whether they belong to C_2 or remain in C_1. This structure ensures that the final categorization reflects not only overall performance but also the critical importance of meeting minimum requirements across all criteria.

5. "a S b_h" decision-making

Each alternative a is first compared with b_2:

If a S b_2 → category C_3

If not, then compared with b_1:

If a S b_1 → category C_2

Otherwise → category C_1

For a S b_h to be true:

The concordance index should be high: a should be better than or similar to b_h.

There should be no veto: b_h should not be much better than a.

6. Comparison – detailed analysis (Table 96.6).

As presented in Table 96.6, the concordance indices and veto conditions between the provinces and the boundary profiles are summarized. Samsun and Trabzon achieved full concordance with both profiles, placing them directly in C_3 (high priority). Ordu-Giresun obtained a concordance index of 0.85 against b_2, which resulted in its classification into C_2 (medium priority). Sinop, on the other hand, showed a very low concordance with b_2 (0.15) and was subject to a veto, preventing its assignment to a higher category. Although it reached 0.75 against b_1, it remained in C_1 (low priority).

Sinop vs. b_2 ($C_2 \leftrightarrow C_3$ boundary)

Is Sinop good enough to enter C_3, the highest class? (Table 96.7).

As shown in Table 96.7, the performance of Sinop was evaluated against the b_2 profile across all criteria. The results indicate that significant gaps in population density (-30) and economic development (-25) triggered veto effects, while tourism potential (-25) showed a clear disadvantage without exceeding the veto threshold. In contrast, the differences in geographical suitability (-5) and alternative transportation (-10) were relatively small and did not lead to veto. Overall, the

TABLE 96.6 Analysis of alternatives.

Alternative	Profile	Concordance index (C)	Veto present
Sinop	b2	0.15	Yes
Sinop	b1	0.75	No
Samsun	b2	1.0	No
Samsun	b1	1.0	No
Ordu-Giresun	b2	0.85	No
Ordu-Giresun	b1	1.0	No
Trabzon	b2	0.85	No
Trabzon	b1	1.0	No

TABLE 96.7 The performance of Sinop was evaluated against.

Criterion	Sinop (a)	b_2 Profile	Difference (a - b_2)	Is the difference small?	Is there a veto?
Population	40	70	−30	✗	✓
Tourism	45	70	−25	✗	✗
Economic level	35	60	−25	✗	✓
Geographical suitability	60	65	-5	✓	✗
Alternative transportation	55	65	−10	✓	✗

table highlights that Sinop could not surpass the b_2 profile due to major weaknesses in key criteria, which prevented its assignment to the highest category (C_3).

Veto limit exceeded in 2 criteria (Ppopulation and economic level) → VETO applied

a S b_2 not provided
Sinop → cannot enter C_3

Sinop vs. b_1 ($C_1 \leftrightarrow C_2$ boundary)
Could Sinop enter C_2? (Table 96.8).

As presented in Table 96.8, the comparison results with the boundary profiles and the final category assignments are summarized. Sinop, due to its very low population and economic performance combined with veto effects, could not surpass either b_2 or b_1 and was classified into C_1 (low priority). Samsun, with consistently high values across all criteria, directly exceeded b_2 and was assigned to C_3 (high priority). Ordu-Giresun failed to pass b_2 but surpassed b_1, placing it in C_2 (medium priority). Finally, Trabzon, supported by strong tourism potential and high population density, successfully outranked b_2 and was allocated to C_3.

As shown in Table 96.9, Sinop's performance was compared with the b_1 profile across all criteria. The results indicate that while Sinop falls below the profile in population (-10), the difference does not trigger a veto. For tourism (-5) and economic development (-5), the gaps are small enough to be considered within the indifference range. On the other hand, Sinop exceeds the profile in geographical suitability (+10) and alternative transportation (+5). Overall, these outcomes

TABLE 96.8 The comparison results with the boundary profiles and the final category.

Province	S b_2?	S b_1?	Assigned class	Description
Sinop	✗	✗	C_1	Very low population and economy → veto
Samsun	✓	-	C_3	High in every criterion, clear passage
Ordu-Giresun	✗	✓	C_2	Medium level performance → middle class
Trabzon	✓	-	C_3	Strong tourism, high population → high

TABLE 96.9 Sinop`s performance.

Criterion	Sinop (a)	b_1 Profile	Difference (a - b_1)	Is the difference small?	Is there a veto?
Population	40	50	-10	✗	✗
Tourism	45	50	-5	✓	✗
Economic level	35	40	-5	✓	✗
Geographical suitability	60	50	+10	✓	✗
Alternative transportation	55	50	+5	✓	✗

reveal that although Sinop demonstrates strengths in certain criteria, it does not consistently surpass the b_1 profile, which justifies its final classification in C_1 (low priority).

Fig. 96.2 illustrates the spatial distribution of the four provinces (Sinop, Samsun, Ordu-Giresun, and Trabzon) within the Black Sea region in relation to the investment priority classification obtained through the ELECTRE TRI analysis. The figure visually associates each province with its assigned category—C_1 (low priority), C_2 (medium priority), or C_3 (high priority)—allowing a clearer understanding of the geographical differentiation.

The graphical representation highlights how Samsun and Trabzon, identified as high-priority provinces (C_3), stand out with stronger demographic, economic, and infrastructural characteristics. Ordu-Giresun appears in the medium category (C_2), reflecting its moderate performance across most criteria. Sinop, located further west, is classified as low priority (C_1), mainly due to its lower scores in population density and economic development, despite relatively favorable geographical suitability.

This visualization not only complements the tabular results but also emphasizes the regional disparities by mapping them spatially. It enables decision-makers to interpret the results more intuitively, as it links numerical outcomes with geographic realities. Moreover, Fig. 96.2 supports the overall conclusion that investment priorities are unevenly distributed across the Black Sea region, shaped by both socio-economic and physical factors.

Axes (criteria): population density, tourism potential, economic development, geographic suitability, alternative transportation.

Color-coded classes (C_1, C_2, C_3): represent decision priority groups from low to high.

Values close to the outside of the circle indicate higher performance in terms of thecriteria.

Green (C_3): high priority provinces (Samsun, Trabzon)

Yellow (C_2): medium priority province (Ordu-Giresun)

Red (C_1): low priority province (Sinop)

Sensitivity analysis results

The application of sensitivity analysis within the ELECTRE TRI framework indicated that the overall classification structure remained largely stable, yet alternatives situated close to the predefined category thresholds were more prone to

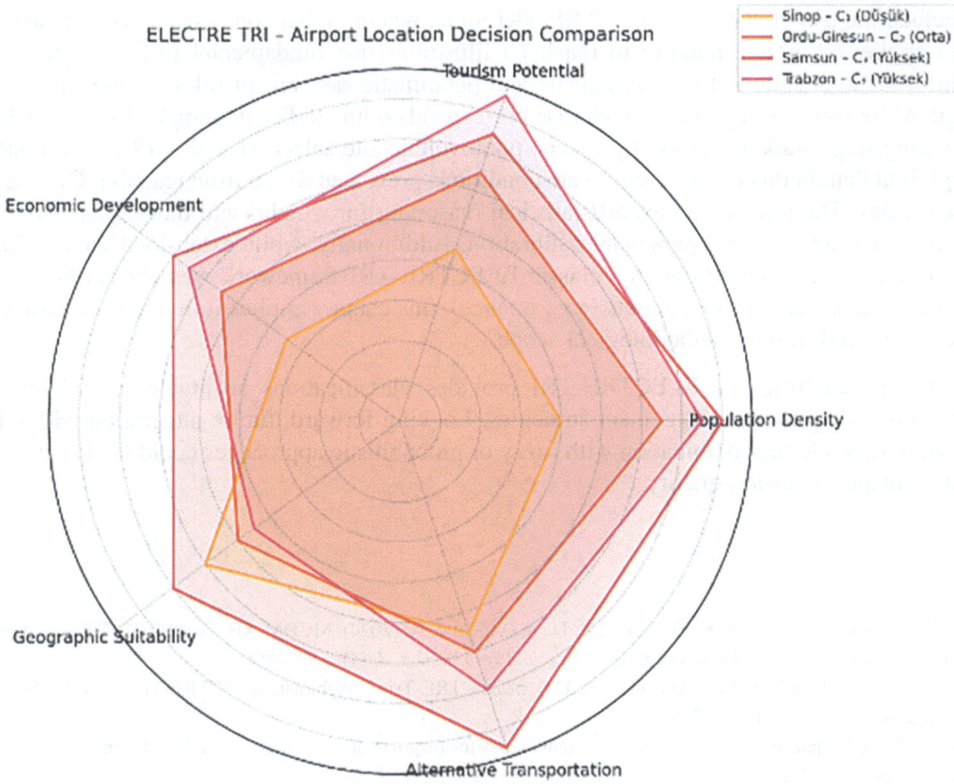

FIGURE 96.2 Performance of criteria used in airport location evaluation.

changes when parameters were adjusted. A ±5% variation in the criteria weights and a ±10% adjustment in the pseudo-criteria thresholds (q, p, v) did not substantially affect the classification of Samsun and Trabzon, which consistently occupied the higher category, thus suggesting robust outcomes for these alternatives. By contrast, Sinop and Ordu-Giresun exhibited shifts between categories under certain parameter settings, underscoring their greater sensitivity. Monte Carlo simulations supported these observations: alternatives that predominantly clustered in a single category can be regarded as reliable, whereas those with frequent shifts across classes should be treated with caution. These findings are consistent with earlier studies emphasizing that small variations in weights or thresholds can significantly influence category assignments in outranking-based approaches (Yu, 1992). Overall, the analysis highlights the critical role of weight and threshold specification, particularly for borderline alternatives, since minor parameter changes may decisively affect their final categorization.

96.4 Conclusion

This section has demonstrated the applicability of the ELECTRE TRI method for classifying provinces in the Black Sea region according to investment priority. The method produces realistic and robust outcomes by assigning alternatives directly into predefined categories and by using pseudo-criteria thresholds (q, p, v), which allow small differences to be neglected, moderate differences to be gradually acknowledged, and major disadvantages to be blocked through veto. Nevertheless, the approach is sensitive to parameter settings (especially thresholds and the cut-off level λ), and the reliance on expert judgment in determining criteria weights introduces a degree of subjectivity. In addition, the logic of vetoes and concordance indices may be relatively difficult for nonexpert stakeholders to interpret. Despite these limitations, ELECTRE TRI offers significant value in MCDM processes, particularly due to its ability to handle uncertainty and ensure that critical weaknesses in key criteria are not overlooked.

In the specific findings of this chapter, Samsun and Trabzon were assigned to C_3, Ordu-Giresun to C_2, and Sinop to C_1, reflecting both parallels and distinctions with previous ELECTRE-TRI and multicriteria location selection studies in the literature.

- Parallelisms include the use of standard ELECTRE-TRI logic, where global concordance is compared with a threshold (λ) unless veto applies—Sinop's inability to reach C_3 illustrates this fundamental rule consistently noted in earlier studies. Similarly, the application of both optimistic and pessimistic assignment rules demonstrates the method's risk-sensitive design. Moreover, the regional airport case corresponds with studies that applied ELECTRE-TRI in transport and spatial planning (e.g., Balkan transport projects, photovoltaic site selection with GIS integration).
- Separations highlight that, in this chapter, strict veto conditions prevented Sinop from reaching C_3, whereas some studies adopt softer veto rules. The reliance on expert/statistical reasoning for weights and thresholds also differs from works using optimization or learning-based parameter calibration. Additionally, while extensions such as ELECTRE TRI-nB offer more flexible boundary definitions, the classic ELECTRE-TRI framework was chosen here. Finally, while the method is often applied to large-scale datasets (e.g., finance), this chapter applies it in a regional context with only four alternatives, reflecting a different methodological scope.

Overall, the findings confirm that ELECTRE-TRI provides classifications adaptable to different risk perceptions through both cautious and optimistic assignment strategies. Looking forward, future integration with GIS can strengthen spatial decision support, while the combination with fuzzy or probabilistic approaches could further improve the modeling of uncertainty and enhance decision quality.

References

Akmaludin, A., Samudi, S., Baidawi, T., Dalis, S., Suriyanto, A. D., & Widianto, K. (2024). MCDM-AHP and ELECTRE collaboration apps for the best vendor selection technique. *Bulletin of Electrical Engineering and Informatics, 13*(4), 2878–2889.

Baseer, M., Ghiaus, C., Viala, R., Gauthier, N., & Daniel, S. (2023). pELECTRE-Tri: Probabilistic ELECTRE-Tri method—Application for the energy renovation of buildings. *Energies, 16*(14), 5296.

Biluca, J., de Aguiar, C. R., & Trojan, F. (2020). Sorting of suitable areas for disposal of construction and demolition waste using GIS and ELECTRE TRI. *Waste Management, 114*, 307–320.

Certa, A., Enea, M., Galante, G. M., & La Fata, C. M. (2017). ELECTRE TRI-based approach to the failure modes classification on the basis of risk parameters: An alternative to the risk priority number. *Computers & Industrial Engineering, 108*, 100–110.

Chen, X., Wang, Y., & Li, J. (2025). Implementation of pELECTRE-Tri in Python for robust decision support systems. *Journal of Decision Analytics, 12*(3), 45–63. https://www.sciencedirect.com/science/article/pii/S2665963825000417.

Doumpos, M., Marinakis, Y., Marinaki, M., & Zopounidis, C. (2009). An evolutionary approach to construction of outranking models for multicriteria classification: The case of the ELECTRE TRI method. *European Journal of Operational Research, 199*(2), 496–505.

Figueira, J., Greco, S., & Ehrgott, M. (2023). Probabilistic ELECTRE TRI approach for energy efficiency classification. *Energies, 16*(14), 5296. https://www.mdpi.com/1996-1073/16/14/5296.

Fontana, M. E., & Cavalcante, C. A. V. (2013). Electre tri method used to storage location assignment into categories. *Pesquisa Operacional, 33*, 283–303.

García, P., López, R., & Martínez, A. (2025). Risk assessment of critical minerals using SMAA-TRI. *Scientific Reports, 15*, 94848. https://www.nature.com/articles/s41598-025-94848-8.

Roy, B. (1985). Méthodologie multicritère d'aide à la décision. *Economica*.

Roy, B., & Bertier, P. (1973). La méthode ELECTRE II: Une méthode de classement en présence de critères multiples. *Note de travail, SEMA*.

Roy, B., & Bouyssou, D. (1993). Aide multicritère à la décision: méthodes et cas. *Economic*.

Salvador, G., Moura, M., Campos, P., Cardoso, P., Espadinha-Cruz, P., & Godina, R. (2024). ELECTRE applied in supplier selection–a literature review. *Procedia Computer Science, 232*, 1759–1768.

Smith, L., & Müller, H. (2024). Application of ELECTRE TRI-B for community-scale renewable energy prioritization. *Sustainability, 15*(2), 1250. https://www.mdpi.com/2071-1050/15/2/1250.

Yu, W. (1992). *ELECTRE TRI: Aspects méthodologiques et manuel d'utilisation. Université Paris-Dauphine, Thèse de doctorat.*

Chapter 97

PROMETHEE: Preference ranking organisation method for enrichment evaluations for multi-attribute decision-making

Yushuo Cao and Ling Zhang
College of Economics and Management, Nanjing University of Aeronautics and Astronautics, Nanjing, P.R. China

97.1 Introduction

In the domain of decision-making, precisely evaluating and combining multiple attributes, especially under conditions marked by uncertainty and subjectivity, presents a substantial challenge (Zhang et al., 2025). The multi-attribute decision-making (MADM) method provides a valuable methodology for this process. The MADM method has undergone significant methodological evolution, incorporating various approaches to tackle the inherent complexities and uncertainties characterizing real-world decision contexts (Fu et al., 2024). The MADM method plays a pivotal role in structuring decision processes and strategic planning, particularly when evaluating complex criteria that influence optimal choice selection based on expert preferences (Zia et al., 2024).

Preference Ranking Organisation MeTHod for Enrichment Evaluations (PROMETHEE) is a prominent MADM technique that provides systematic solutions for ranking finite alternatives against conflicting criteria. As an outranking approach first proposed by Brans et al. in 1986, it employs six well-defined preference functions to conduct pairwise comparisons, which enables rigorous deviation analysis for selecting the appropriate alternatives (Akram et al., 2023). The PROMETHEE method determines preferences through pairwise comparisons of alternatives (Smet, 2016). For each criterion, the difference between the evaluations of the two alternatives is calculated. When this difference is small, the preference given to the better alternative is slight or possibly zero. As the difference increases, so does the strength of preference. These preferences are represented numerically on a scale of 0 to 1. Each criterion uses a specific function to convert performance differences into preference values. The PROMETHEE method has been applied in various fields, including environmental management (Bakas et al., 2024), energy (Sotiropoulou et al., 2024), transportation (Oubahman & Duleba, 2024), supply chain management (Liang et al., 2024), risk management (Mir et al., 2024), agricultural management (Zobeidi et al., 2024), and education (Oubahman & Duleba, 2024).

This chapter aims to introduce the method of PROMETHEE by proposing a novel T-spherical fuzzy (T-SF) PROMETHEE framework. The motivations and contributions of the chapter are shown as follows.

- This chapter presents a novel information fusion method for constructing the group evaluation matrix, the T-spherical fuzzy weighted geometric (T-SF WG) operator, which incorporates a distance-based similarity measure. Compared to conventional fuzzy sets, the T-spherical fuzzy set (T-SFS) framework employs a three-dimensional evaluation system that better captures uncertain information while enabling flexible characterization through adjustable parameters.
- This chapter develops a novel T-SF PROMETHEE method for ranking alternatives. First, the T-SF Cronbach's measure assesses the weights of competing criteria. This approach evaluates expert rating consistency through similarity analysis in its formulation. The measure quantifies expert hesitation during the rating elicitation process. Additionally, the T-SF PROMETHEE method enables alternative ranking through pairwise comparisons and models preferences using simplified preference functions.

Encyclopedia of Multi-Attribute Decision-Making (MADM). DOI: https://doi.org/10.1016/B978-0-443-33275-3.00059-2

- To demonstrate the practical applicability of the proposed framework, this chapter conducts two numerical examples. Furthermore, a comprehensive analysis is conducted to evaluate the proposed method's availability in comparison to existing T-SF MADM methods. A sensitivity analysis is presented to examine how the parameter t variations impact the results.

This chapter is structured into six sections. Section 97.2 provides an overview of relevant literature. Section 97.3 details the proposed methodology, comprising three key stages. Sections 97.4 and 97.5 present numerical examples, incorporating sensitivity and comparative analyses. Finally, Section 97.6 concludes this chapter.

97.2 Literature review

This section reviews the application of the PROMETHEE method. The PROMETHEE method can evaluate pairwise deviations among alternatives, making it a widely adopted approach in research applications. For example, Akram et al. (2023) developed the fuzzy PROMETHEE method to evaluate the Fangcang shelter hospital. Seikh & Mandal (2023) employed the PROMETHEE method under interval-valued Fermatean fuzzy settings to assess the optimal organization for biomedical waste management. Oubahman & Duleba (2024) developed an innovative model utilizing the fuzzy PROMETHEE method to evaluate public transport mode selection. Akram et al. (2024) introduced the multipolar fuzzy N-soft PROMETHEE approach to enhance digital economic growth. Mohammed et al. (2025) presented a hybrid decision-making framework integrating the PROMETHEE method with spherical cubic fuzzy sets to analyze cloud fault tolerance mechanisms. Mir et al. (2024) employed the PROMETHEE methodology to assess the disaster risk associated with educational infrastructure in mountainous geographies. Oubahman et al. (2024) applied the PROMETHEE method to evaluate the mode choice preferences for university students. Xu & Li (2025) employed the PROMETHEE methodology to enhance the efficiency of information aggregation and feature selection. Li, Xiang et al. (2025) extended the PROMETHEE method to Z-number settings and examined its ordering mechanisms. Bakas et al. (2024) employed the fuzzy PROMETHEE method to manage the water resources of the Mediterranean Basin. Liu et al. (2025) introduced a hybrid framework based on the PROMETHEE method and applied it to managing water resource conflicts.

Furthermore, some researchers have focused on agricultural management using the PROMETHEE method. Zobeidi et al. (2024) employed the PROMETHEE method to evaluate climate change adaptation alternatives for farm management. Bakshi et al. (2025) employed the fuzzy PROMETHEE method to evaluate the location of migrating swarms, ensuring agricultural stability and crop security. Tuesta-Trauco et al. (2025) assess the suitability of land for pitahaya cultivation via the PROMETHEE method. Biswas et al. (2025) utilized the PROMETHEE method to identify the most appropriate conservation agricultural practices. Some researchers applied the PROMETHEE method for supply chain management. Wang et al. (2024)a established a PROMETHEE-based decision-making framework for identifying the barriers to the resilient food supply chain. Liang et al. (2024) developed a robustness PROMETHEE methodology for enhancing the supply chain resilience. And some of them applied the PROMETHEE method to energy management. Sotiropoulou et al. (2024) introduced a hybrid PROMETHEE approach for assessing the optimal locations for onshore wind farms. Papapostolou et al. (2024) developed the fuzzy PROMETHEE method for promoting the production of renewable energy sources.

97.3 Research methodology

97.3.1 Preliminaries

This section recalls some fundamental concepts and operational rules of T-SFSs.

Definition 1. (Mahnaz et al., 2022): For any universal set R, the T-SFS is defined as follows:

$$P = \{(l, \mu(l), \nu(l), \gamma(l))|l \in R\}, \tag{97.1}$$

where $\mu(l) \in [0, 1]$, $\nu(l) \in [0, 1]$, $\gamma(l) \in [0, 1]$ denote the membership, neutral, and nonmembership degrees, respectively, satisfying $0 \le \mu^t(l) + \nu^t(l) + \gamma^t(l) \le 1$. The refusal degree is defined as $\pi(l) = \sqrt[t]{1 - (\mu^t(l) + \nu^t(l) + \gamma^t(l))}$.

Definition 2. (Mahnaz et al., 2022): Let $P_1 = (\mu_{P_1}, \nu_{P_1}, \gamma_{P_1})$ and $P_2 = (\mu_{P_2}, \nu_{P_2}, \gamma_{P_2})$ be two T-spherical fuzzy numbers (T-SFNs), then:

$$P_1 \oplus P_2 = \left\{ \left(\mu_{P_1}^t + \mu_{P_2}^t - \mu_{P_1}^t \mu_{P_2}^t\right)^{\frac{1}{t}}, \nu_{P_1}\nu_{P_2}, \gamma_{P_1}\gamma_{P_2} \right\}, \tag{97.2}$$

$$P_1 \otimes P_2 = \left\{ \mu_{P_1}\mu_{P_2}, \left(\nu_{P_1}^t + \nu_{P_2}^t - \nu_{P_1}^t \nu_{P_2}^t\right)^{\frac{1}{t}}, \left(\gamma_{P_1}^t + \gamma_{P_2}^t - \gamma_{P_1}^t \gamma_{P_2}^t\right)^{\frac{1}{t}} \right\}, \tag{97.3}$$

$$\lambda \cdot P_1 = \left\{ \left(1 - \left(1 - \mu_{P_1}^t\right)^{\lambda}\right)^{\frac{1}{t}}, \nu_{P_1}^{\lambda}, \gamma_{P_1}^{\lambda} \right\}, \lambda > 0, \tag{97.4}$$

$$P_1^{\lambda} = \left\{ \mu_{P_1}^{\lambda}, \left(1 - \left(1 - \nu_{P_1}^t\right)^{\lambda}\right)^{\frac{1}{t}}, \left(1 - \left(1 - \gamma_{P_1}^t\right)^{\lambda}\right)^{\frac{1}{t}} \right\}, \lambda > 0. \tag{97.5}$$

Definition 3. (Yang & Pang, 2022): Let $P = (\mu_P, \nu_P, \gamma_P)$ be a T-SFN, the score and accuracy functions are defined as follows:

$$S(P) = \frac{1}{2}\left(1 + \mu_P^t - \nu_P^t - \gamma_P^t\right), \tag{97.6}$$

$$A(P) = \mu_P^t + \nu_P^t + \gamma_P^t, \tag{97.7}$$

where $S(P) \in [0, 1]$ and $A(P) \in [0, 1]$.

Definition 4. (Liu et al., 2024): For two T-SFNs $P_1 = \left(\mu_{P_1}, \nu_{P_1}, \gamma_{P_1}\right)$ and $P_2 = \left(\mu_{P_2}, \nu_{P_2}, \gamma_{P_2}\right)$, the distance measures are defined as follows:

$$D(P_1, P_2) = \sqrt{\left|\left(\mu_{P_1}\right)^t - \left(\mu_{P_2}\right)^t\right|^2 + \left|\left(\nu_{P_1}\right)^t - \left(\nu_{P_2}\right)^t\right|^2 + \left|\left(\gamma_{P_1}\right)^t - \left(\gamma_{P_2}\right)^t\right|^2}, \tag{97.8}$$

where $D(P) \in [0, 1]$.

Definition 5. (Yang & Pang, 2022): For two T-SFNs $P_1 = \left(\mu_{P_1}, \nu_{P_1}, \gamma_{P_1}\right)$ and $P_2 = \left(\mu_{P_2}, \nu_{P_2}, \gamma_{P_2}\right)$, then:

1. If $S(P_1) > S(P_2)$, then $P_1 > P_2$.
2. If $S(P_1) = S(P_2)$, then
  (1) If $A(P_1) > A(P_2)$, then $P_1 > P_2$.
  (2) If $A(P_1) = A(P_2)$, then $P_1 \sim P_2$.

Definition 6. (Mahnaz et al., 2022): Let $P_\tau (\tau = 1, \cdots, q)$ be a collection of T-SFNs, then the T-SF WG operator is defined as follows:

$$\begin{aligned} & T - SFWG\left(P_{ij}^1, P_{ij}^2, \cdots, P_{ij}^q\right) \\ & = ш^1 P_{ij}^1 \oplus ш^2 P_{ij}^2 \oplus \cdots \oplus ш^q P_{ij}^q \\ & = \left\{ \Pi_{\tau=1}^q \mu_{P_{ij}^\tau}^{ш^\tau}, \left(1 - \Pi_{\tau=1}^q \left(1 - \nu_{P_{ij}^\tau}^t\right)^{ш^\tau}\right)^{\frac{1}{t}}, \left(1 - \Pi_{\tau=1}^q \left(1 - \gamma_{P_{ij}^\tau}^t\right)^{ш^\tau}\right)^{\frac{1}{t}} \right\}; \tau = 1, \cdots, q. \end{aligned} \tag{97.9}$$

where $ш = \left(ш^1, ш^2, \cdots, ш^q\right)^T$ is the weight vector of $\left(P_{ij}^1, P_{ij}^2, \cdots, P_{ij}^q\right)$, $ш^\tau \in [0, 1]$, and $\Sigma_{\tau=1}^q ш^\tau = 1$.

97.3.2 The T-spherical fuzzy preference ranking organisation method for enrichment evaluations method

This chapter proposes a novel T-SF MADM framework that integrates PROMETHEE and Cronbach's measure. The proposed framework begins by constructing a group decision matrix through the WG operator to determine expert weights. Subsequently, the T-SF Cronbach's measure method calculates criterion weights by systematically assessing both data consistency and experts' hesitation characteristics. Finally, the methodology employs the T-SF PROMETHEE approach to rank alternatives through pairwise comparison analysis and preference modeling, as shown in Fig. 97.1.

Step 1. Construction of the group evaluation matrix based on the distance-based similarity measure method and the WG operator.

First, the distance-based similarity measure is used to compute the weights of the experts (Wang et al., 2020). Then, we employ the WG operator to construct the group evaluation matrix.

Step 1.1. Generate the individual evaluation matrix of experts. Let $A = \{a_i | a_1, a_2, \cdots, a_m\}$ be the set of alternatives, $C = \left\{Є_j | Є_1, Є_2, \cdots, Є_n\right\}$ be the set of criteria, and $E = \left\{\backepsilon_\tau \middle| \backepsilon_1, \backepsilon_2, \cdots, \backepsilon_q\right\}$ be the set of experts. Then, the expert $\backepsilon_\tau$ provides the evaluation information about the alternative a_i concerning the criteria $Є_j$ within the linguistic scale shown in

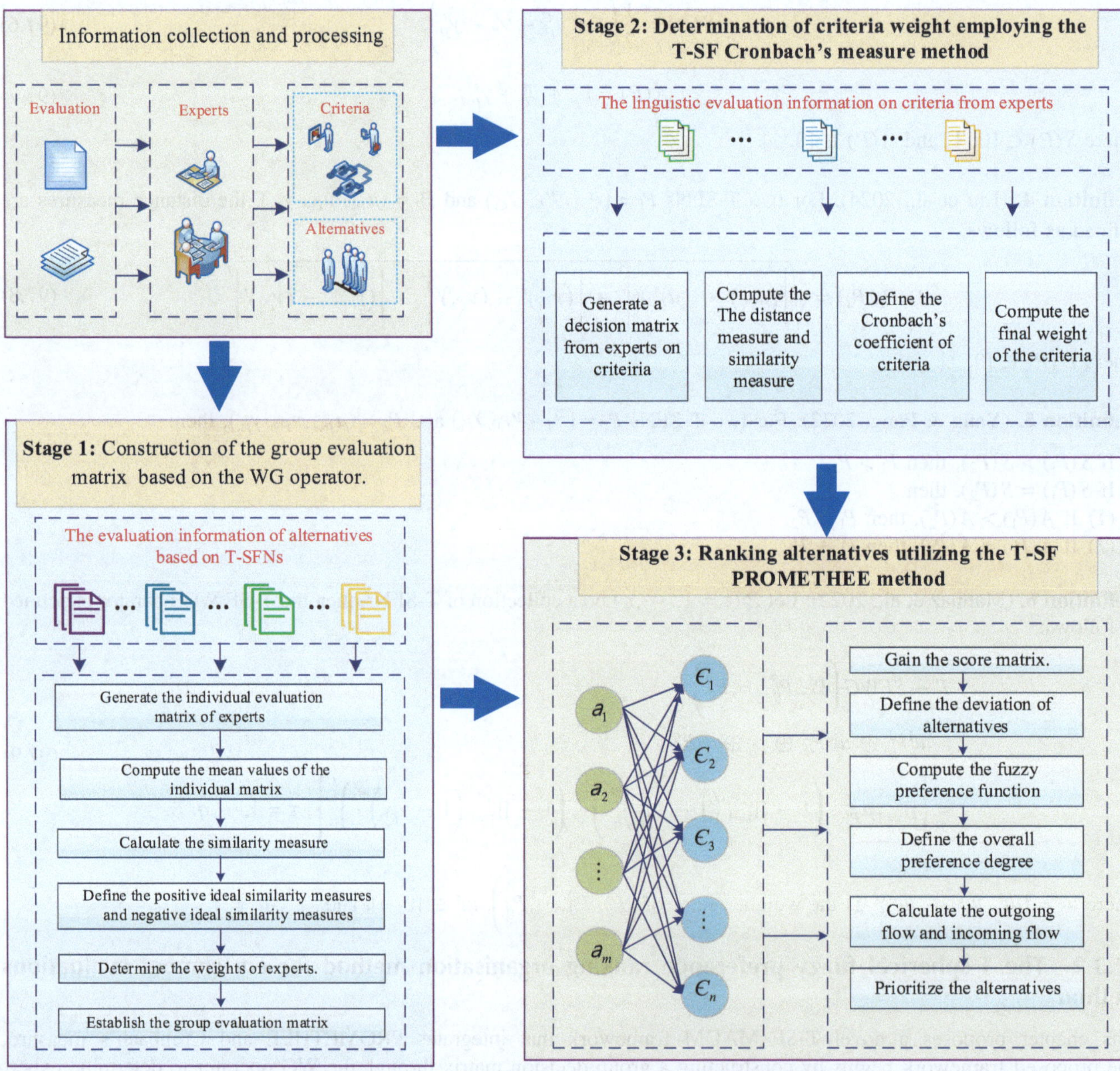

FIGURE 97.1 The flowchart of the T-spherical fuzzy (T-SF) PROMETHEE method.

Table 97.1. The individual evaluation matrix $I^{\tau} = \left[I_{ij}^{\tau}\right]$ of the τth expert is exhibited as follows:

$$I^{\tau} = \begin{matrix} a_1 \\ a_2 \\ \vdots \\ a_m \end{matrix} \overset{\begin{matrix} \epsilon_1 & \epsilon_2 & \cdots & \epsilon_n \end{matrix}}{\begin{bmatrix} \left(\mu_{I_{11}^{\tau}}, \nu_{I_{11}^{\tau}}, \gamma_{I_{11}^{\tau}}\right) & \left(\mu_{I_{12}^{\tau}}, \nu_{I_{12}^{\tau}}, \gamma_{I_{12}^{\tau}}\right) & \cdots & \left(\mu_{I_{1n}^{\tau}}, \nu_{I_{1n}^{\tau}}, \gamma_{I_{1n}^{\tau}}\right) \\ \left(\mu_{I_{21}^{v}}, \nu_{I_{21}^{\tau}}, \gamma_{I_{21}^{\tau}}\right) & \left(\mu_{I_{22}^{\tau}}, \nu_{I_{22}^{\tau}}, \gamma_{I_{22}^{\tau}}\right) & \cdots & \left(\mu_{I_{2n}^{\tau}}, \nu_{I_{2n}^{\tau}}, \gamma_{I_{2n}^{\tau}}\right) \\ \vdots & \vdots & \ddots & \vdots \\ \left(\mu_{I_{m1}^{\tau}}, \nu_{I_{m1}^{\tau}}, \gamma_{I_{m1}^{\tau}}\right) & \left(\mu_{I_{m2}^{\tau}}, \nu_{I_{m2}^{\tau}}, \gamma_{G_{m2}^{\tau}}\right) & \cdots & \left(\mu_{I_{mn}^{\tau}}, \nu_{I_{mn}^{\tau}}, \gamma_{I_{mn}^{\tau}}\right) \end{bmatrix}_{m \times n}}.$$

where $I_{ij}^{\tau} = \left(\mu_{I_{ij}^{\tau}}, \nu_{I_{ij}^{\tau}}, \gamma_{I_{ij}^{\tau}}\right)$ is a T-SFN, representing the evaluation information of the ith alternative concerning the jth criteria given by the expert $\ni_{\tau}$.

Step 1.2. Compute the mean values of the individual matrix.

The mean values of the individual matrix $\overline{I_{ij}^{\tau}}$ is computed as follows:

$$\overline{I_{ij}^{\tau}} = \frac{1}{q}\Sigma_{\tau=1}^{q} I_{ij}^{\tau} = \frac{1}{q}\left(I_{ij}^{1} + I_{ij}^{2} + \cdots + I_{ij}^{q}\right)$$
$$= \left\{\left(1 - \Pi_{\tau=1}^{q}\left(1 - \mu_{I_{ij}^{\tau}}^{t}\right)^{\frac{1}{q}}\right)^{\frac{1}{t}}, \Pi_{\tau=1}^{q} \nu_{I_{ij}^{\tau}}^{\frac{1}{q}}, \Pi_{\tau=1}^{q} \gamma_{I_{ij}^{\tau}}^{\frac{1}{q}}\right\}; \tau = 1, \cdots, q \quad (97.11)$$

Step 1.3. Calculate the similarity measure.

The similarity measure between $\overline{I_{ij}^{\tau}}$ and I_{ij}^{τ} can be calculated as follows:

$$B(I_{ij}^{\tau}, \overline{I_{ij}^{\tau}}) = 1 - \frac{D(I_{ij}^{\tau}, \overline{I_{ij}^{\tau}})}{\Sigma_{\tau=1}^{q} D(I_{ij}^{\tau}, \overline{I_{ij}^{\tau}})}. \quad (97.12)$$

where $D\left(I_{ij}^{\tau}, \overline{I_{ij}^{\tau}}\right) = \sqrt{\left|\left(\mu_{I_{ij}^{\tau}}\right)^{t} - \left(\mu_{\overline{I_{ij}^{\tau}}}\right)^{t}\right|^{2} + \left|\left(\nu_{I_{ij}^{\tau}}\right)^{t} - \left(\nu_{\overline{I_{ij}^{\tau}}}\right)^{t}\right|^{2} + \left|\left(\gamma_{I_{ij}^{\tau}}\right)^{t} - \left(\gamma_{\overline{I_{ij}^{\tau}}}\right)^{t}\right|^{2}}$.

Step 1.4. Define the positive ideal similarity measures and negative ideal similarity measures.

$$B^{+}(I_{ij}^{\tau}, \overline{I_{ij}^{\tau}}) = \left[I_{ij}^{+}\right]_{m \times n}, \; I_{ij}^{+} = \frac{1}{q}\sum_{\tau=1}^{q} B(I_{ij}^{\tau}, \overline{I_{ij}^{\tau}}). \quad (97.13)$$

TABLE 97.1 T-spherical fuzzy number (T-SFN)-based rating scale (Han et al., 2025).

Linguistic scale	Importance weights	T-SFNs
Significantly low (SL)	Extremely unimportant (EU)	(0.1,0.9,0.1)
Very low (VL)	Very unimportant (VU)	(0.2,0.8,0.2)
Low (L)	Unimportant (U)	(0.3,0.7,0.3)
Moderate low (ML)	Slightly unimportant (SU)	(0.4,0.6,0.4)
Moderate (M)	Medium (M)	(0.5,0.5,0.5)
Moderate good (MG)	Moderate important (MI)	(0.6,0.4,0.4)
Good (G)	Important (I)	(0.7,0.3,0.3)
Very good (VG)	Very important (VI)	(0.8,0.2,0.2)
Significantly good (SG)	Significantly important (SI)	(0.9,0.1,0.1)
Exceptionally good (EG)	Exceptionally important (EI)	(0.99,0.01,0.01)

$$B^-(I_{ij}^{\tau}, \overline{I_{ij}^{\tau}}) = \left[I_{ij}^- \right]_{m\times n}, \ I_{ij}^- = \min_{1\le\tau\le q} \left(B(I_{ij}^{\tau}, \overline{I_{ij}^{\tau}}) \right). \tag{97.14}$$

Step 1.5. Determine the weights of experts.

$$\mathcal{U}^{\tau} = \frac{\sqrt{\sum_{i=1}^{m}\sum_{j=1}^{n}\left(B(I_{ij}^{\tau}, \overline{I_{ij}^{\tau}}) - B^-(I_{ij}^{\tau}, \overline{I_{ij}^{\tau}}) \right)^2}}{\sqrt{\sum_{i=1}^{m}\sum_{j=1}^{n}\left(B(I_{ij}^{\tau}, \overline{I_{ij}^{\tau}}_{ij}) - B^+(I_{ij}^{\tau}, \overline{I_{ij}^{\tau}}_{ij}) \right)^2} + \sqrt{\sum_{i=1}^{m}\sum_{j=1}^{n}\left(B(I_{ij}^{\tau}, \overline{I_{ij}^{\tau}}) - B^-(I_{ij}^{\tau}, \overline{I_{ij}^{\tau}}) \right)^2}}. \tag{97.15}$$

Step 1.6. Establish the group evaluation matrix. The group evaluation matrix $G = \left[G_{ij} \right]_{m\times n}$ is formed by using the WG operator and experts' weights, which is represented as follows:

$$\begin{aligned} & T - SFWG\left(I_{ij}^1, I_{ij}^2, \cdots, I_{ij}^q \right) \\ & = \mathcal{U}^1 I_{ij}^1 \oplus \mathcal{U}^2 I_{ij}^2 \oplus \cdots \oplus \mathcal{U}^q I_{ij}^q \\ & = \left\{ \Pi_{\tau=1}^{q} \mu_{I_{ij}^{\tau}}^{\mathcal{U}^{\tau}}, \left(1 - \Pi_{\tau=1}^{q}\left(1 - \nu_{I_{ij}^{\tau}}^{t} \right)^{\mathcal{U}^{\tau}} \right)^{\frac{1}{t}}, \left(1 - \Pi_{\tau=1}^{q}\left(1 - \gamma_{I_{ij}^{\tau}}^{t} \right)^{\mathcal{U}^{\tau}} \right)^{\frac{1}{t}} \right\}; \tau = 1, \cdots, q, \end{aligned} \tag{97.16}$$

where $\mathcal{U}^{\tau} \in [0, 1]$, and $\sum_{\tau=1}^{q} \mathcal{U}^{\tau} = 1$.

Step 2. Determination of criteria weight employing the T-SF Cronbach's measure method.

Step 2.1. Generate a decision matrix of order $q \times n$ according to linguistic scales for q experts to provide their evaluations on the n criteria.

Step 2.2. Compute the distance measure and similarity measure.

$$D_j(\vartheta^{\tau}, \vartheta^{\tau'}) = \sum_{\vartheta^{\tau}, \vartheta^{\tau'} \in \frac{q(q-1)}{2}} \left| \eta_{\vartheta^{\tau}} - \eta_{\vartheta^{\tau'}} \right|, \tag{97.17}$$

where $D(\vartheta^{\tau}, \vartheta^{\tau'})$ represents the distance measure for any two experts ϑ^{τ} and $\vartheta^{\tau'}$, $\eta_{\vartheta^{\tau}}$ denotes the criteria importance evaluation from the τ th expert.

$$\rho_j(\vartheta^{\tau}, \vartheta^{\tau'}) = 1 - D_j(\vartheta^{\tau}, \vartheta^{\tau'}), \tag{97.18}$$

where $\rho_j(\vartheta^{\tau}, \vartheta^{\tau'})$ denotes the similarity measure between ϑ^{τ} and $\vartheta^{\tau'}$ for criterion j.

Step 2.3. The Cronbach's coefficient of criteria is defined as follows:

$$\varsigma_j = \frac{q \cdot \overline{\rho_j(\vartheta^{\tau}, \vartheta^{\tau'})}}{1 + (q-1) \cdot \overline{\rho_j(\vartheta^{\tau}, \vartheta^{\tau'})}}. \tag{97.19}$$

where $\overline{\rho_j(\vartheta^{\tau}, \vartheta^{\tau'})}$ represents the mean of similarity values for the criterion j.

Step 2.4. The final weight of the criteria is computed as follows:

$$\iota_j = \frac{\varsigma_j}{\sum_{j=1}^{n} \varsigma_j}, \tag{97.20}$$

where ι_j represents the weight of the criterion j.

Step 3. Ranking alternatives utilizing the T-SF PROMETHEE method.

Step 3.1. Gain the score matrix. According to the score function in Eq. (97.6) and the group decision matrix, we can gain the score matrix $S = \left[S_{ij} \right]_{m\times n}$.

Step 3.2. Define the deviations of alternatives.

$$d_j(a_a, a_b) = S_j(a_a) - S_j(a_b). \tag{97.21}$$

Step 3.3. Compute the fuzzy preference function. Let a_a and a_b be two alternatives of the set A. The fuzzy preference function $\chi_j(a, b)$ is donated as follows:

$$\chi_j(a, b) = \begin{cases} 0, \; d_j(a_a, a_b) \le 0, \\ S_j(a_a) - S_j(a_b), \; d_j(a_a, a_b) > 0, \end{cases} j = 1, \cdots n, \tag{97.22}$$

where $\chi_j(a, b)$ is the outranking intensity representing that a is superior to b.

Step 3.4. The overall preference degree $\Gamma(a, b)$ is defined as follows:

$$\Gamma(a, b) = \sum_{j=1}^{n} \iota_j \chi_j(a, b). \tag{97.23}$$

TABLE 97.2 Evaluation of alternatives for the experts.

	∂_1				∂_2				∂_3			
	ϵ_1	ϵ_2	ϵ_3	ϵ_4	ϵ_1	ϵ_2	ϵ_3	ϵ_4	ϵ_1	ϵ_2	ϵ_3	ϵ_4
a_1	VG	M	MG	G	SG	ML	G	MG	G	VL	MG	VG
a_2	EG	ML	MG	EG	EG	L	VG	VG	VG	L	M	G
a_3	G	VG	MG	L	VG	G	EG	ML	SG	EG	VG	SL
a_4	L	SL	VL	M	ML	VL	L	MG	M	SL	VL	VL
a_5	MG	MG	M	VL	G	M	G	L	VG	VG	SG	M

TABLE 97.3 The mean values of the individual matrix.

	a_1	a_2	a_3	a_4	a_5
ϵ_1	(0.823,0.182,0.182)	(0.974,0.027,0.027)	(0.823,0.182,0.182)	(0.418,0.594,0.391)	(0.717,0.288,0.288)
ϵ_2	(0.406,0.621,0.342)	(0.341,0.665,0.330)	(0.924,0.084,0.084)	(0.149,0.865,0.126)	(0.674,0.342,0.342)
ϵ_3	(0.639,0.363,0.363)	(0.674,0.342,0.342)	(0.919,0.093,0.093)	(0.243,0.765,0.229)	(0.773,0.247,0.247)
ϵ_4	(0.717,0.288,0.288)	(0.924,0.084,0.084)	(0.314,0.723,0.229)	(0.494,0.543,0.342)	(0.380,0.654,0.311)

TABLE 97.4 The positive and negative ideal similarity measures.

	$B^+(I_{ij}^r, \overline{I}_{ij}^r)$				$B^-(I_{ij}^r, \overline{I}_{ij}^r)$			
	ϵ_1	ϵ_2	ϵ_3	ϵ_4	ϵ_1	ϵ_2	ϵ_3	ϵ_4
a_1	0.667	0.667	0.667	0.667	0.501	0.402	0.535	0.512
a_2	0.667	0.667	0.667	0.667	0.182	0.543	0.586	0.507
a_3	0.667	0.667	0.667	0.667	0.501	0.507	0.447	0.375
a_4	0.667	0.667	0.667	0.667	0.474	0.543	0.547	0.382
a_5	0.667	0.667	0.667	0.667	0.512	0.586	0.511	0.526

TABLE 97.5 Group decision matrix.

	a_1	a_2	a_3	a_4	a_5
ϵ_1	(0.809,0.217,0.217)	(0.939,0.126,0.126)	(0.784,0.237,0.237)	(0.380,0.626,0.405)	(0.684,0.331,0.331)
ϵ_2	(0.365,0.650,0.419)	(0.334,0.668,0.344)	(0.802,0.237,0.237)	(0.130,0.871,0.154)	(0.602,0.420,0.420)
ϵ_3	(0.636,0.369,0.369)	(0.639,0.390,0.390)	(0.780,0.297,0.297)	(0.233,0.768,0.248)	(0.658,0.388,0.388)
ϵ_4	(0.683,0.332,0.332)	(0.837,0.214,0.214)	(0.254,0.759,0.327)	(0.426,0.608,0.419)	(0.293,0.716,0.358)

TABLE 97.6 The original criteria importance evaluation matrix.

	ϵ_1	ϵ_2	ϵ_3	ϵ_4
$\backepsilon_1$	G	VG	MG	SG
$\backepsilon_2$	VG	M	EG	G
$\backepsilon_3$	MG	G	SG	VG

TABLE 97.7 The distance measure between $\backepsilon^\tau$ and $\backepsilon^{\tau'}$.

	ϵ_1	ϵ_2	ϵ_3	ϵ_4
$D_j(\backepsilon^1, \backepsilon^2)$	0.171	0.421	0.760	0.388
$D_j(\backepsilon^1, \backepsilon^3)$	0.137	0.171	0.521	0.217
$D_j(\backepsilon^2, \backepsilon^3)$	0.306	0.258	0.241	0.171
$D_j(\backepsilon^2, \backepsilon^1)$	0.171	0.421	0.760	0.388
$D_j(\backepsilon^3, \backepsilon^1)$	0.137	0.171	0.521	0.217
$D_j(\backepsilon^3, \backepsilon^2)$	0.306	0.258	0.241	0.171
.				

TABLE 97.8 The value of $\overline{\rho_j(\backepsilon^\tau, \backepsilon^{\tau'})}$, ς_j, and ι_j.

	$\overline{\rho_j(\backepsilon^\tau, \backepsilon^{\tau'})}$	ς_j	ι_j
ϵ_1	0.795	0.921	0.267
ϵ_2	0.717	0.884	0.256
ϵ_3	0.493	0.745	0.216
ϵ_4	0.741	0.896	0.260

TABLE 97.9 Fuzzy preference values.

	ϵ_1	ϵ_2	ϵ_3	ϵ_4		ϵ_1	ϵ_2	ϵ_3	ϵ_4
$\chi_j(1, 2)$	0.000	0.001	0.007	0.000	$\chi_j(2, 1)$	0.157	0.000	0.000	0.161
$\chi_j(1, 3)$	0.027	0.000	0.000	0.350	$\chi_j(3, 1)$	0.000	0.395	0.132	0.000
$\chi_j(1, 4)$	0.383	0.181	0.307	0.233	$\chi_j(4, 1)$	0.000	0.000	0.000	0.000
$\chi_j(1, 5)$	0.131	0.000	0.000	0.317	$\chi_j(5, 1)$	0.000	0.185	0.006	0.000
$\chi_j(2, 3)$	0.184	0.000	0.000	0.511	$\chi_j(3, 2)$	0.000	0.396	0.139	0.000
$\chi_j(2, 4)$	0.540	0.180	0.300	0.394	$\chi_j(4, 2)$	0.000	0.000	0.000	0.000
$\chi_j(2, 5)$	0.288	0.000	0.000	0.478	$\chi_j(5, 2)$	0.000	0.186	0.013	0.000
$\chi_j(3, 4)$	0.356	0.576	0.439	0.000	$\chi_j(4, 3)$	0.000	0.000	0.000	0.117
$\chi_j(3, 5)$	0.104	0.210	0.127	0.000	$\chi_j(5, 3)$	0.000	0.000	0.000	0.034
$\chi_j(4, 5)$	0.000	0.000	0.000	0.084	$\chi_j(5, 4)$	0.252	0.366	0.312	0.000

TABLE 97.10 The overall preference degrees.

	ϵ_1	ϵ_2	ϵ_3	ϵ_4		ϵ_1	ϵ_2	ϵ_3	ϵ_4
$\Gamma_j(1, 2)$	0.000	0.000	0.002	0.000	$\Gamma_j(2, 1)$	0.042	0.000	0.000	0.042
$\Gamma_j(1, 3)$	0.007	0.000	0.000	0.091	$\Gamma_j(3, 1)$	0.000	0.101	0.029	0.000
$\Gamma_j(1, 4)$	0.102	0.047	0.066	0.061	$\Gamma_j(4, 1)$	0.000	0.000	0.000	0.000
$\Gamma_j(1, 5)$	0.035	0.000	0.000	0.082	$\Gamma_j(5, 1)$	0.000	0.047	0.001	0.000
$\Gamma_j(2, 3)$	0.049	0.000	0.000	0.133	$\Gamma_j(3, 2)$	0.000	0.102	0.030	0.000
$\Gamma_j(2, 4)$	0.144	0.046	0.065	0.102	$\Gamma_j(4, 2)$	0.000	0.000	0.000	0.000
$\Gamma_j(2, 5)$	0.077	0.000	0.000	0.124	$\Gamma_j(5, 2)$	0.000	0.048	0.003	0.000
$\Gamma_j(3, 4)$	0.095	0.148	0.095	0.000	$\Gamma_j(4, 3)$	0.000	0.000	0.000	0.031
$\Gamma_j(3, 5)$	0.028	0.054	0.027	0.000	$\Gamma_j(5, 3)$	0.000	0.000	0.000	0.009
$\Gamma_j(4, 5)$	0.000	0.000	0.000	0.022	$\Gamma_j(5, 4)$	0.067	0.094	0.068	0.000

TABLE 97.11 Results of outgoing flow and incoming flow.

	$\Upsilon^+(a)$	$\Upsilon^-(a)$
a_1	0.123	0.066
a_2	0.206	0.046
a_3	0.177	0.080
a_4	0.013	0.300
a_5	0.084	0.112

TABLE 97.12 Definition of criteria.

Dimension	Criteria	Definition	Reference
Digital strategic vision	Digital leading insight (ϵ_1)	Actively explore emerging opportunities and anticipate potential challenges in digital transformation, while carefully assessing the impact of digital trends on organizational development.	Memon and Ooi (2023)
	Digital vision (ϵ_2)	Evaluate current conditions and industry dynamics to formulate forward-looking strategic plans that drive organizational growth in the digital era.	Shahzad (2024)
	Digital strategic deployment (ϵ_3)	Develop strategic roadmaps that closely align with the enterprise's digital transformation goals and evolving business needs.	Lin (2024)
	Digital environment control (ϵ_4)	Identify potential digital transformation risks in advance and establish robust strategies for effective risk management and uncertainty absorption.	Wang et al. (2024b)
Digital technologies learning	Digital knowledge learning (ϵ_5)	Enhance employees' digital capabilities through comprehensive learning resources, including technical manuals, expert lectures, and cutting-edge digital courses.	Shahzad (2024)
	Digital technology choosing (ϵ_6)	Select and deploy appropriate digital technologies that precisely match the organization's operational requirements and business objectives.	Zhang and Zheng (2023)
	Digital technology implementation (ϵ_7)	Design, implement, and scale new digital business models while enhancing operational efficiency through strategic technology adoption.	Wang et al. (2024b)
	Review and iteration of digital technology (ϵ_8)	Regularly review and update digital tools and applications based on performance metrics and evolving business needs.	Lin (2024)
Digital team construction	Digital communication and socialization (ϵ_9)	Facilitate effective organizational communication through digital platforms while maintaining team cohesion in remote work environments.	Wang et al. (2024b)
	Digital talent development (ϵ_{10})	Prioritize the cultivation of digital knowledge and technical competencies across all business teams and functional units.	Lin (2024)
	Digital empowerment ϵ_{11})	Foster technological proficiency through targeted resource investment, incentive mechanisms, and empowerment strategies that encourage innovation and experimentation.	Memon and Ooi (2023)
	Form the digital operation team (ϵ_{12})	Establish new teams or augment existing units with members possessing complementary digital and business expertise.	Xia et al. (2023)
Digital ethical awareness	Digital empathy ability (ϵ_{13})	Demonstrate understanding of employee perspectives and provide personalized support to facilitate their digital transformation journey.	Li, Seah et al. (2025)
	Humanized communication and decision-making (ϵ_{14})	Complement digital directives with thoughtful offline interactions, carefully considering timing and employee circumstances.	Zhang and Zheng (2023)
	Digital inclusive counseling (ϵ_{15})	Provide consistent guidance and encouragement to all employees, regardless of their current digital proficiency level, to reduce adoption resistance.	Zhang and Zheng (2023)
	Emotional balance (ϵ_{16})	While leveraging data-driven assessment methods, remain attentive to employees' emotional responses and personal experiences throughout the transformation process.	Li, Seah et al. (2025)

TABLE 97.13 Evaluation of alternatives for the expert $\ni_1$.

	$\in_1$	$\in_2$	$\in_3$	$\in_4$	$\in_5$	$\in_6$	$\in_7$	$\in_8$
a_1	MG	MG	M	G	EG	SG	VG	VG
a_2	VG	SG	G	MG	G	M-G	G	MG
a_3	ML	M	ML	MG	MG	M	G	G
a_4	G	VG	G	EG	VG	SG	EG	SG
a_5	EG	SG	EG	VG	VG	SG	EG	EG
a_6	VG	SG	VG	G	EG	SG	VG	G
	$\in_9$	$\in_{10}$	$\in_{11}$	$\in_{12}$	$\in_{13}$	$\in_{14}$	$\in_{15}$	$\in_{16}$
a_1	G	VG	G	VG	MG	G	MG	G
a_2	EG	SG	EG	SG	EG	EG	SG	EG
a_3	MG	M	G	MG	G	VG	G	VG
a_4	VG	VG	VG	EG	SG	SG	EG	SG
a_5	SG	EG	SG	EG	VG	SG	VG	SG
a_6	MG	EG	SG	VG	G	VG	SG	EG

TABLE 97.14 Evaluation of alternatives for the expert $\ni_2$.

	$\in_1$	$\in_2$	$\in_3$	$\in_4$	$\in_5$	$\in_6$	$\in_7$	$\in_8$
a_1	ML	ML	ML	M	G	G	MG	MG
a_2	MG	G	MG	G	MG	M	M	ML
a_3	L	ML	L	ML	ML	ML	M	M
a_4	MG	G	MG	VG	G	MG	G	G
a_5	VG	VG	SG	G	MG	G	G	VG
a_6	SG	VG	EG	VG	SG	VG	EG	VG
	$\in_9$	$\in_{10}$	$\in_{11}$	$\in_{12}$	$\in_{13}$	$\in_{14}$	$\in_{15}$	$\in_{16}$
a_1	ML	M	ML	M	ML	M	ML	M
a_2	VG	G	G	MG	G	VG	G	VG
a_3	L	ML	M	ML	M	MG	M	MG
a_4	MG	MG	MG	G	VG	G	VG	G
a_5	G	VG	G	VG	MG	G	MG	G
a_6	G	SG	VG	EG	VG	SG	VG	EG

Step 3.5. Calculate the outgoing flow and incoming flow.

$$\Upsilon^{+}(a) = \frac{1}{m-1} \sum_{b=1}^{m} \Gamma(a, b). \tag{97.24}$$

TABLE 97.15 Evaluation of alternatives for the expert $\mathfrak{z}_3$.

	$\mathcal{E}_1$	$\mathcal{E}_2$	$\mathcal{E}_3$	$\mathcal{E}_4$	$\mathcal{E}_5$	$\mathcal{E}_6$	$\mathcal{E}_7$	$\mathcal{E}_8$
a_1	ML	M	ML	MG	VG	VG	G	G
a_2	G	VG	G	G	MG	M	MG	M
a_3	L	ML	L	ML	M	ML	M	MG
a_4	MG	G	MG	VG	G	G	VG	VG
a_5	SG	VG	EG	G	G	VG	VG	SG
a_6	SG	VG	EG	G	VG	SG	VG	MG
	$\mathcal{E}_9$	$\mathcal{E}_{10}$	$\mathcal{E}_{11}$	$\mathcal{E}_{12}$	$\mathcal{E}_{13}$	$\mathcal{E}_{14}$	$\mathcal{E}_{15}$	$\mathcal{E}_{16}$
a_1	M	MG	M	MG	ML	MG	M	MG
a_2	EG	VG	SG	VG	SG	EG	VG	EG
a_3	L	ML	MG	M	MG	G	MG	G
a_4	G	G	G	VG	VG	VG	SG	VG
a_5	VG	SG	VG	EG	G	VG	G	VG
a_6	G	EG	SG	VG	VG	SG	EG	SG

$$\Upsilon^-(a) = \frac{1}{m-1}\sum_{b=1}^{m}\Gamma(b, a). \tag{97.25}$$

Step 3.6. Prioritize the alternatives according to the net flow. First, the T-SF PROMETHEE method can determine the partial preorders (P^+, I^+), and (P^-, I^-).

$$\begin{cases} a_a P^+ a_b \text{iff} \Upsilon^+(a) > \Upsilon^+(b) \\ a_a I^+ a_b \text{iff} \Upsilon^+(a) = \Upsilon^+(b) \end{cases}. \tag{97.26}$$

$$\begin{cases} a_a P^- a_b \text{ iff } \Upsilon^-(a) < \Upsilon^-(b) \\ a_a\ I^-\ a_b \text{ iff } \Upsilon^-(a) = \Upsilon^-(b) \end{cases}. \tag{97.27}$$

Then, the final partial preorder can be obtained by Eqs. (97.28–97.30). The alternative a_a outranks the alternative a_b if and only if the three conditions are satisfied.

$$a_a\ P\ a_b (a_a \text{ outranks } a_b) \text{ iff } \begin{cases} a_a\ P^+\ a_b \text{ and } a_a\ P^-\ a_b; \\ a_a\ P^+\ a_b \text{ and } a_a\ I^-\ a_b; \\ a_a\ I^+\ a_b \text{ and } a_a\ P^-\ a_b. \end{cases} \tag{97.28}$$

The alternative a_a is indifferent to the alternative a_b if and only if the following condition is satisfied:

$$a_a\ I\ a_b (a_a \text{ is indifferent to } a_b) \text{ iff } a_a\ I^+\ a_b \text{ and } a_a\ I^-\ a_b. \tag{97.29}$$

The alternative a_a is incomparable to the alternative a_b if the following condition is satisfied:

$$a_a\ R\ a_b\ (a_a \text{ is incomparable to } a_b) \text{ iff } a_a\ P^+\ a_b \text{ and } a_b\ P^-\ a_a. \tag{97.30}$$

97.4 Numerical example 1

Assessing renewable energy is critical for ensuring a sustainable and secure energy future. As fossil fuel reserves are finite and contribute significantly to greenhouse gas emissions, transitioning to renewable sources is necessary to meet long-term energy demands while mitigating climate change. Effective evaluation of renewable energy potential enables the

TABLE 97.16 The mean values of the individual matrix.

	a_1	a_2	a_3	a_4	a_5	a_6
ϵ_1	(0.490,0.524,0.400)	(0.717,0.288,0.288)	(0.341,0.665,0.330)	(0.639,0.363,0.363)	(0.944,0.058,0.058)	(0.875,0.126,0.126)
ϵ_2	(0.516,0.493,0.431)	(0.823,0.182,0.182)	(0.439,0.565,0.431)	(0.740,0.262,0.262)	(0.843,0.159,0.159)	(0.843,0.159,0.159)
ϵ_3	(0.439,0.565,0.431)	(0.672,0.330,0.330)	(0.341,0.665,0.330)	(0.639,0.363,0.363)	(0.979,0.022,0.022)	(0.974,0.027,0.027)
ϵ_4	(0.616,0.391,0.391)	(0.672,0.330,0.330)	(0.490,0.524,0.400)	(0.931,0.074,0.074)	(0.740,0.262,0.262)	(0.740,0.262,0.262)
ϵ_5	(0.924,0.084,0.084)	(0.639,0.363,0.363)	(0.516,0.493,0.431)	(0.740,0.262,0.262)	(0.717,0.288,0.288)	(0.944,0.058,0.058)
ϵ_6	(0.823,0.182,0.182)	(0.539,0.464,0.464)	(0.439,0.565,0.431)	(0.784,0.229,0.229)	(0.823,0.182,0.182)	(0.875,0.126,0.126)
ϵ_7	(0.717,0.288,0.288)	(0.616,0.391,0.391)	(0.589,0.422,0.422)	(0.924,0.084,0.084)	(0.924,0.084,0.084)	(0.931,0.074,0.074)
ϵ_8	(0.717,0.288,0.288)	(0.516,0.493,0.431)	(0.616,0.391,0.391)	(0.823,0.182,0.182)	(0.944,0.058,0.058)	(0.717,0.288,0.288)
ϵ_9	(0.571,0.448,0.391)	(0.974,0.027,0.027)	(0.456,0.581,0.330)	(0.717,0.288,0.288)	(0.823,0.182,0.182)	(0.672,0.330,0.330)
ϵ_{10}	(0.674,0.342,0.342)	(0.823,0.182,0.182)	(0.439,0.565,0.431)	(0.717,0.288,0.288)	(0.944,0.058,0.058)	(0.979,0.022,0.022)
ϵ_{11}	(0.571,0.448,0.391)	(0.938,0.067,0.067)	(0.616,0.391,0.391)	(0.717,0.288,0.288)	(0.823,0.182,0.182)	(0.875,0.126,0.126)
ϵ_{12}	(0.674,0.342,0.342)	(0.809,0.200,0.200)	(0.516,0.493,0.431)	(0.924,0.084,0.084)	(0.974,0.027,0.027)	(0.931,0.074,0.074)
ϵ_{13}	(0.490,0.524,0.400)	(0.938,0.067,0.067)	(0.616,0.391,0.391)	(0.843,0.159,0.159)	(0.717,0.288,0.288)	(0.773,0.229,0.229)
ϵ_{14}	(0.616,0.391,0.391)	(0.974,0.027,0.027)	(0.717,0.288,0.288)	(0.823,0.182,0.182)	(0.823,0.182,0.182)	(0.875,0.126,0.126)
ϵ_{15}	(0.516,0.493,0.431)	(0.823,0.182,0.182)	(0.616,0.391,0.391)	(0.944,0.058,0.058)	(0.717,0.288,0.288)	(0.944,0.058,0.058)
ϵ_{16}	(0.616,0.391,0.391)	(0.974,0.027,0.027)	(0.717,0.288,0.288)	(0.823,0.182,0.182)	(0.823,0.182,0.182)	(0.979,0.022,0.022)

TABLE 97.17 The similarity measure for the expert ∂_1.

	ϵ_1	ϵ_2	ϵ_3	ϵ_4	ϵ_5	ϵ_6	ϵ_7	ϵ_8	ϵ_9	ϵ_{10}	ϵ_{11}	ϵ_{12}	ϵ_{13}	ϵ_{14}	ϵ_{15}	ϵ_{16}
a_1	0.586	0.633	0.522	0.573	0.799	0.603	0.566	0.566	0.613	0.597	0.613	0.597	0.586	0.573	0.633	0.573
a_2	0.566	0.603	0.767	0.467	0.535	0.547	0.573	0.633	0.909	0.603	0.801	0.632	0.801	0.909	0.603	0.909
a_3	0.543	0.522	0.543	0.586	0.633	0.522	0.580	0.573	0.641	0.522	0.573	0.633	0.573	0.566	0.573	0.566
a_4	0.535	0.540	0.535	0.785	0.540	0.626	0.799	0.603	0.566	0.566	0.566	0.799	0.572	0.603	0.776	0.603
a_5	0.776	0.572	0.882	0.540	0.566	0.603	0.799	0.776	0.603	0.776	0.603	0.909	0.566	0.603	0.566	0.603
a_6	0.426	0.572	0.182	0.730	0.776	0.787	0.607	0.921	0.467	0.882	0.787	0.607	0.460	0.426	0.802	0.882

TABLE 97.18 The positive ideal similarity measures.

	ϵ_1	ϵ_2	ϵ_3	ϵ_4	ϵ_5	ϵ_6	ϵ_7	ϵ_8	ϵ_9	ϵ_{10}	ϵ_{11}	ϵ_{12}	ϵ_{13}	ϵ_{14}	ϵ_{15}	ϵ_{16}
a_1	0.667	0.667	0.667	0.667	0.667	0.667	0.667	0.667	0.667	0.667	0.667	0.667	0.667	0.667	0.667	0.667
a_2	0.667	0.667	0.667	0.667	0.667	0.667	0.667	0.667	0.667	0.667	0.667	0.667	0.667	0.667	0.667	0.667
a_3	0.667	0.667	0.667	0.667	0.667	0.667	0.667	0.667	0.667	0.667	0.667	0.667	0.667	0.667	0.667	0.667
a_4	0.667	0.667	0.667	0.667	0.667	0.667	0.667	0.667	0.667	0.667	0.667	0.667	0.667	0.667	0.667	0.667
a_5	0.667	0.667	0.667	0.667	0.667	0.667	0.667	0.667	0.667	0.667	0.667	0.667	0.667	0.667	0.667	0.667
a_6	0.667	0.667	0.667	0.667	0.667	0.667	0.667	0.667	0.667	0.667	0.667	0.667	0.667	0.667	0.667	0.667

TABLE 97.19 The negative ideal similarity measures.

	ϵ_1	ϵ_2	ϵ_3	ϵ_4	ϵ_5	ϵ_6	ϵ_7	ϵ_8	ϵ_9	ϵ_{10}	ϵ_{11}	ϵ_{12}	ϵ_{13}	ϵ_{14}	ϵ_{15}	ϵ_{16}
a_1	0.586	0.543	0.522	0.492	0.507	0.501	0.512	0.512	0.604	0.586	0.604	0.586	0.586	0.492	0.543	0.492
a_2	0.512	0.501	0.467	0.467	0.535	0.547	0.492	0.543	0.182	0.501	0.333	0.401	0.333	0.182	0.501	0.182
a_3	0.543	0.522	0.543	0.586	0.543	0.522	0.580	0.492	0.641	0.522	0.492	0.543	0.492	0.512	0.492	0.512
a_4	0.535	0.540	0.535	0.607	0.540	0.585	0.507	0.501	0.512	0.512	0.512	0.507	0.572	0.501	0.422	0.501
a_5	0.422	0.572	0.237	0.540	0.512	0.501	0.507	0.422	0.501	0.422	0.501	0.182	0.512	0.501	0.512	0.501
a_6	0.426	0.572	0.182	0.540	0.422	0.426	0.607	0.512	0.467	0.237	0.426	0.607	0.460	0.426	0.422	0.237

TABLE 97.20 Group decision matrix.

	a_1	a_2	a_3	a_4	a_5	a_6
ϵ_1	(0.464,0.547,0.400)	(0.707,0.310,0.310)	(0.333,0.669,0.344)	(0.635,0.370,0.345)	(0.904,0.134,0.134)	(0.862,0.153,0.153)
ϵ_2	(0.505,0.504,0.444)	(0.807,0.218,0.218)	(0.218,0.568,0.443)	(0.735,0.272,0.310)	(0.835,0.176,0.176)	(0.835,0.176,0.176)
ϵ_3	(0.434,0.568,0.443)	(0.673,0.332,0.332)	(0.332,0.669,0.344)	(0.635,0.370,0.345)	(0.966,0.064,0.064)	(0.915,0.143,0.143)
ϵ_4	(0.606,0.406,0.406)	(0.661,0.344,0.344)	(0.344,0.547,0.400)	(0.865,0.172,0.270)	(0.735,0.272,0.272)	(0.724,0.281,0.281)
ϵ_5	(0.836,0.215,0.215)	(0.635,0.370,0.370)	(0.370,0.504,0.444)	(0.735,0.272,0.310)	(0.707,0.310,0.310)	(0.892,0.148,0.148)
ϵ_6	(0.807,0.218,0.218)	(0.535,0.469,0.469)	(0.469,0.568,0.443)	(0.738,0.301,0.301)	(0.807,0.218,0.218)	(0.873,0.141,0.141)
ϵ_7	(0.707,0.310,0.310)	(0.606,0.406,0.406)	(0.406,0.448,0.448)	(0.836,0.215,0.332)	(0.836,0.215,0.215)	(0.845,0.181,0.181)
ϵ_8	(0.707,0.310,0.310)	(0.505,0.504,0.444)	(0.444,0.406,0.406)	(0.807,0.218,0.333)	(0.904,0.134,0.134)	(0.684,0.331,0.331)
ϵ_9	(0.534,0.487,0.420)	(0.937,0.127,0.127)	(0.127,0.631,0.344)	(0.707,0.310,0.272)	(0.807,0.218,0.218)	(0.661,0.344,0.344)
ϵ_{10}	(0.636,0.392,0.392)	(0.807,0.218,0.218)	(0.218,0.568,0.443)	(0.707,0.310,0.310)	(0.904,0.134,0.134)	(0.966,0.064,0.064)
ϵ_{11}	(0.534,0.487,0.420)	(0.874,0.195,0.195)	(0.195,0.406,0.406)	(0.707,0.310,0.359)	(0.807,0.218,0.218)	(0.873,0.141,0.141)
ϵ_{12}	(0.636,0.392,0.392)	(0.776,0.272,0.272)	(0.272,0.504,0.444)	(0.836,0.215,0.270)	(0.937,0.127,0.127)	(0.845,0.181,0.181)
ϵ_{13}	(0.464,0.547,0.400)	(0.874,0.195,0.195)	(0.195,0.406,0.406)	(0.835,0.176,0.333)	(0.707,0.310,0.310)	(0.762,0.247,0.247)
ϵ_{14}	(0.606,0.406,0.406)	(0.937,0.127,0.127)	(0.127,0.310,0.310)	(0.807,0.218,0.272)	(0.807,0.218,0.218)	(0.862,0.153,0.153)
ϵ_{15}	(0.505,0.504,0.444)	(0.807,0.218,0.218)	(0.218,0.406,0.406)	(0.904,0.134,0.324)	(0.707,0.310,0.310)	(0.905,0.134,0.134)
ϵ_{16}	(0.606,0.406,0.406)	(0.937,0.127,0.127)	(0.127,0.310,0.310)	(0.807,0.218,0.272)	(0.807,0.218,0.218)	(0.955,0.072,0.072)

TABLE 97.21 The original criteria importance evaluation matrix.

	ϵ_1	ϵ_2	ϵ_3	ϵ_4	ϵ_5	ϵ_6	ϵ_7	ϵ_8	ϵ_9	ϵ_{10}	ϵ_{11}	ϵ_{12}	ϵ_{13}	ϵ_{14}	ϵ_{15}	ϵ_{16}
$э_1$	VG	SG	EG	G	ML	SG	EG	MG	L	VG	M	EG	VL	MG	SL	ML
$э_2$	VG	EG	SG	ML	L	EG	VG	M	VL	EG	MG	SG	SL	ML	L	VL
$э_3$	SG	VG	EG	EG	MG	EG	SG	G	L	EG	M	SG	VL	VG	SL	ML

optimization of technologies, such as energy storage and grid integration, ensuring a consistent and reliable supply. Furthermore, systematic assessment supports policy formulation and investment decisions, accelerating the development of infrastructure needed for large-scale adoption. According to Hussain et al. (2024), this chapter examines the practicality of the methodology by the following experimental case study. It includes five energy resources used in producing energy or electricity: wind energy (a_1), solar energy (a_2), hydropower energy (a_3), biomass energy (a_4), and geothermal energy (a_5). Furthermore, three experts were invited to evaluate the five energy resources according to the following criteria: friendly environment (ϵ_1), energy storage (ϵ_2), rate of the economic benefits (ϵ_3), and availability of parts and easy installation (ϵ_4). Two experts are from academia, and one is from an energy enterprise. The calculation results of numerical example 1 are shown as follows.

Step 1. Construction of the group evaluation matrix.

Step 1.1–1.6. First, three experts are invited to provide their evaluation of renewable energies according to the criteria shown in Table 97.2. Then, we transform the individual matrix into the T-SFN-based individual evaluation matrix according to the linguistic scale shown in Table 97.1. Next, the mean values of the individual matrices are calculated using Eq. (97.11), shown in Table 97.3. Further, the positive and negative ideal similarity measures are computed using Eqs. (97.12)–(97.14), shown in Table 97.4. The expert's weight is determined using Eq. (97.15), namely, $(0.370, 0.379, 0.250)^T$. Finally, the group decision matrix is obtained using Eq. (97.16) and shown in Table 97.5.

Step 2. Determination of criteria weight.

Steps 2.1–2.4. First, the importance evaluation matrix is provided by experts and presented in Table 97.6. Then, it can be transformed into a T-SFN-based evaluation matrix. Further, the distance measure between experts can be computed using Eq. (97.17), shown in Table 97.7. The similarity measure can be computed using Eq. (97.18). The criteria weights can be calculated using Eqs. (97.19) and (97.20), shown in Table 97.8.

Step 3. Renewable energy ranking.

Steps 3.1–3.4. The score matrix is obtained according to Eq. (97.6) and the group decision matrix. Then, the fuzzy preference values for any two renewable energies are calculated using Eqs. (97.21) and (97.22), shown in Table 97.9. Next, the overall preference degree for any pair of renewable energies is calculated using Eq. (97.23), shown in Table 97.10.

Steps 3.5–3.6. The outgoing and incoming flows are calculated using Eqs. (97.24) and (97.25), shown in Table 97.11. According to the laws in Eqs. (97.26–97.30), the appropriate renewable energy is a_2.

97.5 Numerical example 2

97.5.1 Background

The rapid advancement of the four new modernizations in the automotive industry necessitates a corresponding evolution in leadership approaches within manufacturing enterprises to drive digital transformation effectively. This chapter examines this critical transition through an empirical analysis of a leading Chinese automobile manufacturer that is currently undergoing digital transformation. The chapter focuses specifically on the company's selection process for a middle management position in its passenger vehicle subsidiary, where six candidates from distinct operational departments (one from R&D, one from marketing, one from manufacturing, one from quality control, and two from strategic operations) are being considered for promotion. The evaluation framework incorporates 16 criteria derived from the literature review, as presented in Table 97.12. Further, three experts are engaged in the evaluation process.

97.5.2 Experimental results of the T-spherical fuzzy Preference Ranking Organisation MeTHod for Enrichment Evaluations approach

According to the proposed method, the calculation results are as follows.

TABLE 97.22 The distance measure between ϑ^{τ} and $\vartheta^{\tau'}$.

	ϵ_1	ϵ_2	ϵ_3	ϵ_4	ϵ_5	ϵ_6	ϵ_7	ϵ_8	ϵ_9	ϵ_{10}	ϵ_{11}	ϵ_{12}	ϵ_{13}	ϵ_{14}	ϵ_{15}	ϵ_{16}
$D_j(\vartheta^1, \vartheta^2)$	0.000	0.241	0.241	0.339	0.137	0.241	0.458	0.125	0.171	0.458	0.125	0.241	0.217	0.215	0.388	0.306
$D_j(\vartheta^1, \vartheta^3)$	0.217	0.217	0.000	0.628	0.215	0.241	0.241	0.137	0.000	0.458	0.000	0.241	0.000	0.306	0.000	0.000
$D_j(\vartheta^2, \vartheta^3)$	0.217	0.458	0.241	0.934	0.339	0.000	0.217	0.258	0.171	0.000	0.125	0.000	0.217	0.497	0.388	0.306
$D_j(\vartheta^2, \vartheta^1)$	0.000	0.241	0.241	0.339	0.137	0.241	0.458	0.125	0.171	0.458	0.125	0.241	0.217	0.215	0.388	0.306
$D_j(\vartheta^3, \vartheta^1)$	0.217	0.217	0.000	0.628	0.215	0.241	0.241	0.137	0.000	0.458	0.000	0.241	0.000	0.306	0.000	0.000
$D_j(\vartheta^3, \vartheta^2)$.	0.217	0.458	0.241	0.934	0.339	0.000	0.217	0.258	0.171	0.000	0.125	0.000	0.217	0.497	0.388	0.306

TABLE 97.23 The value of $\overline{\rho_j(\vartheta^{\tau}, \vartheta^{\tau'})}$, ς_j, and ι_j.

	$\overline{\rho_j(\vartheta^{\tau}, \vartheta^{\tau'})}$	ς_j	ι_j
ϵ_1	0.855	0.947	0.066
ϵ_2	0.694	0.872	0.061
ϵ_3	0.839	0.940	0.065
ϵ_4	0.366	0.634	0.044
ϵ_5	0.770	0.909	0.063
ϵ_6	0.839	0.940	0.065
ϵ_7	0.694	0.872	0.061
ϵ_8	0.826	0.935	0.065
ϵ_9	0.886	0.959	0.067
ϵ_{10}	0.694	0.872	0.061
ϵ_{11}	0.916	0.970	0.067
ϵ_{12}	0.839	0.940	0.065
ϵ_{13}	0.855	0.947	0.066
ϵ_{14}	0.661	0.854	0.059
ϵ_{15}	0.742	0.896	0.062
ϵ_{16}	0.796	0.921	0.064

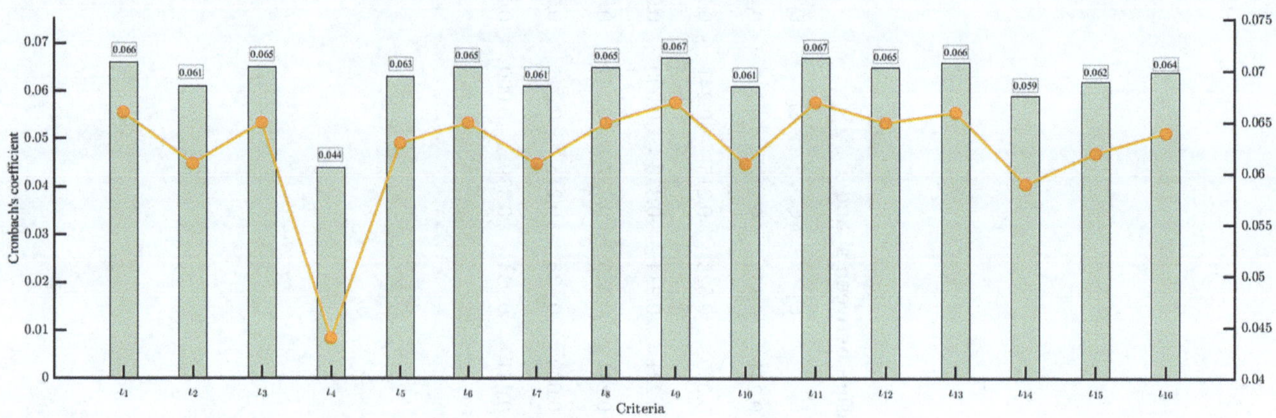

FIGURE 97.2 The weights of competencies.

Step 1. Construction of the group evaluation matrix.

Step 1.1. The three experts provide their evaluation of candidates according to the criteria shown in Tables 97.13–97.15. Then, according to the linguistic scale shown in Table 97.1, we transform the individual matrix into the T-SFN-based individual evaluation matrix (Tables 97.16 and 97.17).

Steps 1.2–1.5. First, we calculate the mean values of the individual matrices using Eq. (97.11), as shown in Table 97.16. Subsequently, take the expert ϑ_1 for example, the similarity measure for the expert ϑ_1 can be calculated using Eq. (97.12), shown in Table 97.18. Next, the positive ideal similarity measures and negative ideal similarity measures can be computed using Eqs. (97.13) and (97.14), shown in Tables 97.18 and 97.19. Finally, the weights of the experts can be determined using Eq. (97.15), namely, $(0.405, 0.197, 0.398)^T$.

TABLE 97.24 The score matrix.

	ϵ_1	ϵ_2	ϵ_3	ϵ_4	ϵ_5	ϵ_6	ϵ_7	ϵ_8	ϵ_9	ϵ_{10}	ϵ_{11}	ϵ_{12}	ϵ_{13}	ϵ_{14}	ϵ_{15}	ϵ_{16}
a_1	0.436	0.457	0.406	0.544	0.782	0.753	0.647	0.647	0.481	0.569	0.481	0.569	0.436	0.544	0.457	0.544
a_2	0.647	0.753	0.616	0.604	0.577	0.473	0.544	0.457	0.910	0.753	0.826	0.714	0.826	0.910	0.753	0.910
a_3	0.349	0.370	0.348	0.407	0.418	0.416	0.443	0.477	0.355	0.370	0.437	0.402	0.437	0.471	0.438	0.471
a_4	0.582	0.674	0.582	0.811	0.674	0.674	0.769	0.739	0.652	0.647	0.638	0.777	0.770	0.748	0.852	0.748
a_5	0.867	0.786	0.951	0.679	0.647	0.753	0.782	0.867	0.753	0.867	0.753	0.910	0.647	0.753	0.647	0.753
a_6	0.817	0.786	0.881	0.668	0.851	0.830	0.796	0.623	0.604	0.951	0.830	0.796	0.706	0.817	0.868	0.935

TABLE 97.25 Fuzzy preference values.

	ϵ_1	ϵ_2	ϵ_3	ϵ_4	ϵ_5	ϵ_6	ϵ_7	ϵ_8	ϵ_9	ϵ_{10}	ϵ_{11}	ϵ_{12}	ϵ_{13}	ϵ_{14}	ϵ_{15}	ϵ_{16}
$\chi_j(1, 2)$	0.000	0.000	0.000	0.000	0.205	0.279	0.102	0.190	0.000	0.000	0.000	0.000	0.000	0.000	0.000	0.000
$\chi_j(1, 3)$	0.088	0.087	0.057	0.138	0.365	0.336	0.204	0.170	0.127	0.199	0.045	0.166	0.000	0.073	0.018	0.073
$\chi_j(1, 4)$	0.000	0.000	0.000	0.000	0.108	0.079	0.000	0.000	0.000	0.000	0.000	0.000	0.000	0.000	0.000	0.000
$\chi_j(1, 5)$	0.000	0.000	0.000	0.000	0.135	0.000	0.000	0.000	0.000	0.000	0.000	0.000	0.000	0.000	0.000	0.000
$\chi_j(1, 6)$	0.000	0.000	0.000	0.000	0.000	0.000	0.000	0.023	0.000	0.000	0.000	0.000	0.000	0.000	0.000	0.000
$\chi_j(2, 3)$	0.298	0.383	0.267	0.197	0.160	0.057	0.101	0.000	0.555	0.383	0.390	0.311	0.390	0.439	0.314	0.439
$\chi_j(2, 4)$	0.065	0.079	0.034	0.000	0.000	0.000	0.000	0.000	0.258	0.106	0.188	0.000	0.056	0.162	0.000	0.162
$\chi_j(2, 5)$	0.000	0.000	0.000	0.000	0.000	0.000	0.000	0.000	0.157	0.000	0.074	0.000	0.180	0.157	0.106	0.157
$\chi_j(2, 6)$	0.000	0.000	0.000	0.000	0.000	0.000	0.000	0.000	0.306	0.000	0.000	0.000	0.120	0.093	0.000	0.000
$\chi_j(3, 4)$	0.000	0.000	0.000	0.000	0.000	0.000	0.000	0.000	0.000	0.000	0.000	0.000	0.000	0.000	0.000	0.000
$\chi_j(3, 5)$	0.000	0.000	0.000	0.000	0.000	0.000	0.000	0.000	0.000	0.000	0.000	0.000	0.000	0.000	0.000	0.000
$\chi_j(3, 6)$	0.000	0.000	0.000	0.000	0.000	0.000	0.000	0.000	0.000	0.000	0.000	0.000	0.000	0.000	0.000	0.000
$\chi_j(4, 5)$	0.000	0.000	0.000	0.133	0.027	0.000	0.000	0.000	0.000	0.000	0.000	0.000	0.124	0.000	0.205	0.000
$\chi_j(4, 6)$	0.000	0.000	0.000	0.144	0.000	0.000	0.000	0.116	0.048	0.000	0.000	0.000	0.064	0.000	0.000	0.000
$\chi_j(5, 6)$	0.051	0.000	0.070	0.011	0.000	0.000	0.000	0.244	0.149	0.000	0.000	0.114	0.000	0.000	0.000	0.000
	ϵ_1	ϵ_2	ϵ_3	ϵ_4	ϵ_5	ϵ_6	ϵ_7	ϵ_8	ϵ_9	ϵ_{10}	ϵ_{11}	ϵ_{12}	ϵ_{13}	ϵ_{14}	ϵ_{15}	ϵ_{16}
$\chi_j(2, 1)$	0.210	0.296	0.210	0.059	0.000	0.000	0.000	0.000	0.428	0.184	0.345	0.145	0.390	0.365	0.296	0.365
$\chi_j(3, 1)$	0.000	0.000	0.000	0.000	0.000	0.000	0.000	0.000	0.000	0.000	0.000	0.000	0.000	0.000	0.000	0.000
$\chi_j(4, 1)$	0.146	0.217	0.177	0.267	0.000	0.000	0.122	0.093	0.170	0.078	0.157	0.209	0.334	0.203	0.395	0.203
$\chi_j(5, 1)$	0.431	0.329	0.545	0.134	0.000	0.000	0.135	0.221	0.271	0.299	0.271	0.341	0.210	0.208	0.190	0.208
$\chi_j(6, 1)$	0.380	0.329	0.475	0.123	0.069	0.077	0.149	0.000	0.123	0.382	0.349	0.227	0.270	0.272	0.412	0.391
$\chi_j(3, 2)$	0.000	0.000	0.000	0.000	0.000	0.000	0.000	0.020	0.000	0.000	0.000	0.000	0.000	0.000	0.000	0.000
$\chi_j(4, 2)$	0.000	0.000	0.000	0.207	0.096	0.200	0.225	0.283	0.000	0.000	0.000	0.064	0.000	0.000	0.099	0.000
$\chi_j(5, 2)$	0.221	0.033	0.335	0.075	0.069	0.279	0.238	0.411	0.000	0.115	0.000	0.196	0.000	0.000	0.000	0.000

$\chi_j(6, 2)$	0.170	0.033	0.265	0.064	0.274	0.357	0.251	0.167	0.000	0.198	0.004	0.082	0.000	0.000	0.116	0.025
$\chi_j(4, 3)$	0.233	0.304	0.234	0.405	0.256	0.258	0.326	0.263	0.297	0.277	0.202	0.375	0.333	0.277	0.413	0.277
$\chi_j(5, 3)$	0.519	0.416	0.602	0.272	0.229	0.336	0.339	0.391	0.398	0.498	0.316	0.507	0.210	0.281	0.208	0.281
$\chi_j(6, 3)$	0.468	0.416	0.532	0.261	0.434	0.414	0.352	0.146	0.249	0.581	0.393	0.393	0.269	0.345	0.430	0.464
$\chi_j(5, 4)$	0.285	0.112	0.368	0.000	0.000	0.079	0.013	0.128	0.101	0.221	0.114	0.132	0.000	0.005	0.000	0.005
$\chi_j(6, 4)$	0.234	0.112	0.298	0.000	0.177	0.156	0.027	0.000	0.000	0.304	0.192	0.018	0.000	0.069	0.017	0.187
$\chi_j(6, 5)$.	0.000	0.000	0.000	0.000	0.204	0.077	0.013	0.000	0.000	0.083	0.077	0.000	0.059	0.064	0.222	0.183

TABLE 97.26 The overall preference degrees.

	ϵ_1	ϵ_2	ϵ_3	ϵ_4	ϵ_5	ϵ_6	ϵ_7	ϵ_8	ϵ_9	ϵ_{10}	ϵ_{11}	ϵ_{12}	ϵ_{13}	ϵ_{14}	ϵ_{15}	ϵ_{16}
$\Gamma_j(1, 2)$	0.000	0.000	0.000	0.000	0.013	0.018	0.006	0.012	0.000	0.000	0.000	0.000	0.000	0.000	0.000	0.000
$\Gamma_j(1, 3)$	0.006	0.005	0.004	0.006	0.023	0.022	0.012	0.011	0.008	0.012	0.003	0.011	0.000	0.004	0.001	0.005
$\Gamma_j(1, 4)$	0.000	0.000	0.000	0.000	0.007	0.005	0.000	0.000	0.000	0.000	0.000	0.000	0.000	0.000	0.000	0.000
$\Gamma_j(1, 5)$	0.000	0.000	0.000	0.000	0.009	0.000	0.000	0.000	0.000	0.000	0.000	0.000	0.000	0.000	0.000	0.000
$\Gamma_j(1, 6)$	0.000	0.000	0.000	0.000	0.000	0.000	0.000	0.002	0.000	0.000	0.000	0.000	0.000	0.000	0.000	0.000
$\Gamma_j(2, 3)$	0.020	0.023	0.017	0.009	0.010	0.004	0.006	0.000	0.037	0.023	0.026	0.020	0.026	0.026	0.020	0.028
$\Gamma_j(2, 4)$	0.004	0.005	0.002	0.000	0.000	0.000	0.000	0.000	0.017	0.006	0.013	0.000	0.004	0.010	0.000	0.010
$\Gamma_j(2, 5)$	0.000	0.000	0.000	0.000	0.000	0.000	0.000	0.000	0.010	0.000	0.005	0.000	0.012	0.009	0.007	0.010
$\Gamma_j(2, 6)$	0.000	0.000	0.000	0.000	0.000	0.000	0.000	0.000	0.020	0.000	0.000	0.000	0.008	0.006	0.000	0.000
$\Gamma_j(3, 4)$	0.000	0.000	0.000	0.000	0.000	0.000	0.000	0.000	0.000	0.000	0.000	0.000	0.000	0.000	0.000	0.000
$\Gamma_j(3, 5)$	0.000	0.000	0.000	0.000	0.000	0.000	0.000	0.000	0.000	0.000	0.000	0.000	0.000	0.000	0.000	0.000
$\Gamma_j(3, 6)$	0.000	0.000	0.000	0.000	0.000	0.000	0.000	0.000	0.000	0.000	0.000	0.000	0.000	0.000	0.000	0.000
$\Gamma_j(4, 5)$	0.000	0.000	0.000	0.006	0.002	0.000	0.000	0.000	0.000	0.000	0.000	0.000	0.008	0.000	0.013	0.000
$\Gamma_j(4, 6)$	0.000	0.000	0.000	0.006	0.000	0.000	0.000	0.008	0.003	0.000	0.000	0.000	0.004	0.000	0.000	0.000
$\Gamma_j(5, 6)$	0.003	0.000	0.005	0.000	0.000	0.000	0.000	0.016	0.010	0.000	0.000	0.007	0.000	0.000	0.000	0.000
	ϵ_1	ϵ_2	ϵ_3	ϵ_4	ϵ_5	ϵ_6	ϵ_7	ϵ_8	ϵ_9	ϵ_{10}	ϵ_{11}	ϵ_{12}	ϵ_{13}	ϵ_{14}	ϵ_{15}	ϵ_{16}
$\Gamma_j(2, 1)$	0.014	0.018	0.014	0.003	0.000	0.000	0.000	0.000	0.029	0.011	0.023	0.009	0.026	0.022	0.018	0.023
$\Gamma_j(3, 1)$	0.000	0.000	0.000	0.000	0.000	0.000	0.000	0.000	0.000	0.000	0.000	0.000	0.000	0.000	0.000	0.000
$\Gamma_j(4, 1)$	0.010	0.013	0.012	0.012	0.000	0.000	0.007	0.006	0.011	0.005	0.011	0.014	0.022	0.012	0.025	0.013
$\Gamma_j(5, 1)$	0.028	0.020	0.036	0.006	0.000	0.000	0.008	0.014	0.018	0.018	0.018	0.022	0.014	0.012	0.012	0.013
$\Gamma_j(6, 1)$	0.025	0.020	0.031	0.005	0.004	0.005	0.009	0.000	0.008	0.023	0.023	0.015	0.018	0.016	0.026	0.025
$\Gamma_j(3, 2)$	0.000	0.000	0.000	0.000	0.000	0.000	0.000	0.001	0.000	0.000	0.000	0.000	0.000	0.000	0.000	0.000
$\Gamma_j(4, 2)$	0.000	0.000	0.000	0.009	0.006	0.013	0.014	0.018	0.000	0.000	0.000	0.004	0.000	0.000	0.006	0.000
$\Gamma_j(5, 2)$	0.014	0.002	0.022	0.003	0.004	0.018	0.014	0.027	0.000	0.007	0.000	0.013	0.000	0.000	0.000	0.000
$\Gamma_j(6, 2)$	0.011	0.002	0.017	0.003	0.017	0.023	0.015	0.011	0.000	0.012	0.000	0.005	0.000	0.000	0.007	0.002

$\Gamma_j(4, 3)$	0.015	0.018	0.015	0.018	0.016	0.017	0.020	0.017	0.020	0.017	0.014	0.024	0.022	0.016	0.026	0.018
$\Gamma_j(5, 3)$	0.034	0.025	0.039	0.012	0.014	0.022	0.021	0.025	0.026	0.030	0.021	0.033	0.014	0.017	0.013	0.018
$\Gamma_j(6, 3)$	0.031	0.025	0.035	0.011	0.027	0.027	0.021	0.010	0.017	0.035	0.026	0.026	0.018	0.020	0.027	0.030
$\Gamma_j(5, 4)$	0.019	0.007	0.024	0.000	0.000	0.005	0.001	0.008	0.007	0.013	0.008	0.009	0.000	0.000	0.000	0.000
$\Gamma_j(6, 4)$	0.015	0.007	0.019	0.000	0.011	0.010	0.002	0.000	0.000	0.018	0.013	0.001	0.000	0.004	0.001	0.012
$\Gamma_j(6, 5)$	0.000	0.000	0.000	0.000	0.013	0.005	0.001	0.000	0.000	0.005	0.005	0.000	0.004	0.004	0.014	0.012

TABLE 97.27 Results of outgoing flow and incoming flow.

	$\Upsilon^{+}(a)$	$\Upsilon^{-}(a)$
a_1	0.041	0.175
a_2	0.132	0.075
a_3	0.000	0.294
a_4	0.117	0.060
a_5	0.175	0.030
a_6	0.188	0.020

Step 1.6. The group decision matrix is constructed using Eq. (97.16), as presented in Table 97.20.

Step 2. Determination of criteria weight.

Steps 2.1–2.4. First, we acquire the criteria importance evaluation matrix provided by experts, shown in Table 97.21. Then, we transform it into the T-SFN-based evaluation matrix according to Table 97.1. Next, the distance measure can be computed using Eq. (97.17), shown in Table 97.22. The similarity measure can be calculated using Eq. (97.18). Finally, the results of the criteria weights can be computed using Eqs. (97.19) and (97.20), shown in Table 97.23 and Fig. 97.2.

Step 3. Candidate ranking.

Steps 3.1–3.4. First, we obtain the score matrix according to Eq. (97.6) and the group decision matrix, shown in Table 97.24. Then, we compute the deviation of the candidates using Eq. (97.21). Next, we compute the fuzzy preference values between any two candidates using Eq. (97.22), shown in Table 97.25. Furthermore, we calculated the overall preference degree for each pair of candidates using Eq. (97.23), as shown in Table 97.26.

Steps 3.5–3.6. We calculate the outgoing and incoming flows using Eqs. (97.24) and (97.25), shown in Table 97.27. Finally, the appropriate candidate can be acquired according to the laws in Eqs. (97.26–97.30). Namely, the appropriate one among the alternatives is candidate a_6.

97.5.3 Sensitivity analysis

This subsection presents a sensitivity analysis to evaluate the methodological robustness and validate the proposed approach systematically. The various parameters t allow experts to express their preferences and extend their decision-making spaces. Different parameters t represent different situations. In this subsection, we conduct a sensitivity analysis to examine how parameter t variations influence the final results. We generate twenty situations for changing the value of the parameter t, and the results are shown in Table 97.28. According to Table 97.28, the parameter t will affect the final values of the outgoing and incoming flows.

97.5.4 Comparative analysis

In this subsection, we conduct a comparative analysis employing various T-SFN-based MADM approaches to validate the reliability of the presented method. We select the existing T-SFN-based MADM methods, including the complex proportional assessment (COPRAS) (Fan et al., 2022), technique for order of preference by similarity to ideal solution (TOPSIS) (Qiao & Qi, 2025), and weighted aggregated sum product assessment (WASPAS) (Anjum et al., 2024). The results of the comparative analysis are shown in Table 97.29 and Fig. 97.3.

According to Table 97.29 and Fig. 97.3, the priority of the candidates calculated by T-SF TOPSIS and T-SF COPRAS is similar, which is $a_3 > a_1 > a_2 > a_4 > a_5 > a_6$ and $a_3 > a_1 > a_4 > a_2 > a_5 > a_6$. It is significantly different from the proposed methodology. Moreover, the priority of candidates acquired by the T-SF WASPAS method is $a_6 > a_5 > a_4 > a_2 > a_1 > a_3$, where the appropriate candidate is consistent with the proposed method. Therefore the presented model is reliable for assessing the leadership competency of manufacturing enterprises undergoing digital transformation. Compared with the above T-SF-based models, the proposed methodology has the following advantages.

- The proposed methodology determines the ranking of candidates by establishing the priority function. The T-SF TOPSIS method, in contrast, only calculates the distances of the positive and negative ideal solutions for each candidate.

TABLE 97.28 Calculation results of the sensitivity analysis.

		$\Upsilon^+(a)$	$\Upsilon^-(a)$		$\Upsilon^+(a)$	$\Upsilon^-(a)$		$\Upsilon^+(a)$	$\Upsilon^-(a)$		$\Upsilon^+(a)$	$\Upsilon^-(a)$		$\Upsilon^+(a)$	$\Upsilon^-(a)$
a_1	$t = 1$	0.090	0.022	$t = 5$	0.087	0.023	$t = 9$	0.087	0.027	$t = 13$	0.086	0.036	$t = 17$	0.082	0.052
a_2		0.100	0.009		0.097	0.009		0.101	0.013		0.106	0.018		0.110	0.024
a_3		0.000	0.465		0.000	0.447		0.000	0.443		0.000	0.434		0.000	0.418
a_4		0.098	0.008		0.098	0.006		0.103	0.007		0.108	0.010		0.111	0.015
a_5		0.106	0.004		0.103	0.003		0.109	0.004		0.117	0.006		0.124	0.008
a_6		0.115	0.000		0.104	0.002		0.101	0.009		0.102	0.014		0.107	0.017
a_1	$t = 2$	0.089	0.023	$t = 6$	0.087	0.023	$t = 10$	0.087	0.029	$t = 14$	0.085	0.040	$t = 18$	0.080	0.056
a_2		0.098	0.009		0.098	0.010		0.102	0.014		0.107	0.019		0.112	0.026
a_3		0.000	0.457		0.000	0.446		0.000	0.441		0.000	0.431		0.000	0.413
a_4		0.098	0.006		0.099	0.006		0.104	0.008		0.109	0.011		0.112	0.016
a_5		0.104	0.003		0.104	0.003		0.111	0.004		0.118	0.006		0.126	0.009
a_6		0.111	0.000		0.103	0.004		0.101	0.010		0.103	0.015		0.108	0.018
a_1	$t = 3$	0.088	0.021	$t = 7$	0.087	0.024	$t = 11$	0.087	0.031	$t = 15$	0.084	0.043	$t = 19$	0.079	0.061
a_2		0.097	0.008		0.099	0.011		0.103	0.015		0.108	0.021		0.113	0.027
a_3		0.000	0.452		0.000	0.445		0.000	0.439		0.000	0.427		0.000	0.407
a_4		0.098	0.005		0.101	0.006		0.106	0.009		0.110	0.013		0.113	0.018
a_5		0.102	0.003		0.106	0.003		0.113	0.005		0.120	0.007		0.128	0.010
a_6		0.106	0.001		0.102	0.005		0.101	0.011		0.104	0.016		0.110	0.019
a_1	$t = 4$	0.087	0.022	$t = 8$	0.087	0.025	$t = 12$	0.087	0.033	$t = 16$	0.083	0.047	$t = 20$	0.077	0.065
a_2		0.097	0.009		0.100	0.012		0.105	0.016		0.109	0.022		0.114	0.029
a_3		0.000	0.449		0.000	0.444		0.000	0.437		0.000	0.423		0.000	0.402
a_4		0.098	0.005		0.102	0.007		0.107	0.009		0.111	0.014		0.114	0.019
a_5		0.102	0.003		0.108	0.004		0.115	0.005		0.122	0.008		0.129	0.011
a_6		0.105	0.001		0.101	0.007		0.101	0.013		0.105	0.017		0.112	0.019

TABLE 97.29 Results of the comparative analysis.

	T-SF TOPSIS		T-SF COPRAS		T-SF WASPAS		Proposed methodology		
	Utility degree	Ranking	Utility degree	Ranking	Utility degree	Ranking	$\Upsilon^{+}(a)$	$\Upsilon^{-}(a)$	Ranking
a_1	0.326	2	0.756	2	7.968	5	0.041	0.175	-
a_2	0.500	3	0.585	4	8.171	4	0.132	0.075	-
a_3	0.011	1	1.000	1	7.774	6	0.000	0.294	-
a_4	0.604	4	0.585	3	8.178	3	0.117	0.060	-
a_5	0.760	5	0.531	5	8.261	2	0.175	0.030	-
a_6	0.772	6	0.517	6	8.284	1	0.188	0.020	1

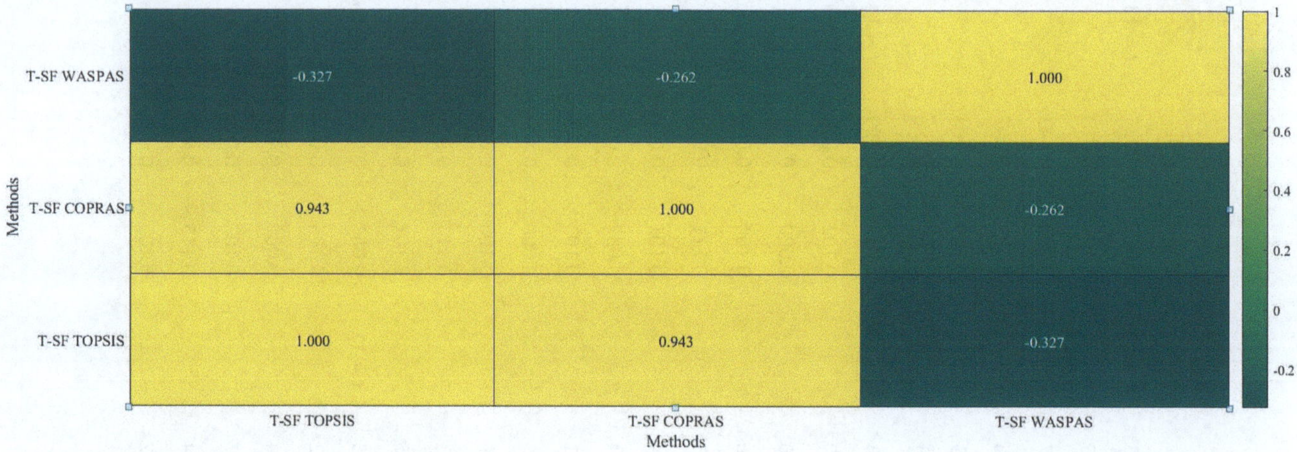

FIGURE 97.3 Results of the comparative analysis.

Furthermore, the T-SF PROMETHEE methodology offers a simpler calculation procedure and demonstrates a more robust capacity to rank candidates than the aforementioned method.

- Compared with the T-SF COPRAS method, the proposed methodology can adjust the calculation process without needing external variables. Moreover, it can also solve situations that involve only cost criteria or benefit criteria, as well as both.

97.6 Conclusion

The MADM method excels in systematically addressing multicriteria evaluation challenges under uncertainty and subjectivity, offering a robust framework for complex decision-making scenarios. The PROMETHEE method employs six well-defined preference functions to conduct pairwise comparisons, enabling precise alternative ranking through rigorous deviation analysis. Therefore this chapter presents an integrated MADM method, the T-SF PROMETHEE methodology, to introduce this method. First, the T-SF WG operator is utilized to construct the group decision matrix. Compared with existing fuzzy sets, the T-SFS describes more uncertain information using a flexible parameter t. Second, the T-SF Cronbach's measure is applied to compute the criteria weights, evaluating both data consistency and experts' hesitation in the decision-making process. The T-SF PROMETHEE method employs an efficient pairwise comparison mechanism for ranking alternatives. This approach quantifies performance deviations between pairs of alternatives through a streamlined counting procedure, significantly reducing computational complexity while maintaining assessment accuracy. In the numerical example 1, "Solar energy (a_2)" is the appropriate renewable energy. In the numerical example 2, "Digital empower ($\mathcal{C}_{11}$)" with a value of 0.067 is the main criterion that influences the competency evaluation of candidate leadership in digital transformation. Next, a sensitive analysis is conducted by generating 20 scenarios of the parameter t to demonstrate the robustness of the proposed methodology. Furthermore, a comparative analysis is presented to examine the availability of this study in relation to existing T-SF MADM methods.

Future studies can focus on the following points. First, expanding the expert panel while developing consensus mechanisms would enhance the reliability of the evaluation. Second, the operator could be used to consider the interrelationship of experts, such as the weighted heronian mean aggregation operator. Third, implementing complex fuzzy sets, particularly complex spherical fuzzy sets, would consider the 2D characteristic of information.

References

Akram, M., Sultan, M., & Deveci, M. (2024). An integrated multi-polar fuzzy N-soft preference ranking organization method for enrichment of evaluations of the digitization of global economy. *Artificial Intelligence in Medicine, 57*(3), 74.

Akram, M., Zahid, K., & Kahraman, C. (2023). A PROMETHEE based outranking approach for the construction of Fangcang shelter hospital using spherical fuzzy sets. *Artificial Intelligence in Medicine, 135*, 102456.

Anjum, M., Simic, V., Alrasheedi, M. A., & Shahab, S. (2024). T-Spherical Fuzzy-CRITIC-WASPAS model for the evaluation of cooperative intelligent transportation system scenarios. *Ieee Access, 12*, 61137–61151.

Bakas, T., Papadopoulos, C., Latinopoulos, D., Kagalou, I., & Spiliotis, M. (2024). Extended intuitionistic fuzzy PROMETHEE II group decision making for mediterranean basin management. *Water Resour. Manage.* https://doi.org/10.1007/s11269-11024-03999-11262.

Bakshi, S., Molla, M. U., & Giri, B. C. (2025). Neutrosophic hesitant fuzzy PROMETHEE and its application to location selection of migrating swarm. *Applied Soft Computing, 180*, 113290.

Biswas, T., Ishizaka, A., Majumder, A., Mandal, B., Dey, S., Mukherjee, S., Baishya, A., Kanthal, S., Ghosh, S., Mandal, A., Chatterjee, R., Ray, S., Bhunia, S., Duary, S., Bhattacharjee, S., Mishra, P., & Acharya, S. K. (2025). The PROMETHEE-GAIA: A multi-criteria decision-making method for identifying best conservation agricultural practices. *Soil Tillage Research, 245*, 106315.

Fan, J., Han, D., & Wu, M. (2022). T-spherical fuzzy COPRAS method for multi-criteria decision-making problem. *Journal of Intelligent & Fuzzy Systems, 43*(3), 2789–2801.

Fu, C., Qin, K., Pang, K., Wu, J., & Zhao, E. (2024). BTWM-HF: A behavioral three-way multi-attribute decision-making method with hesitant fuzzy information. *Expert Systems with Applications, 249*, 123733.

Han, X., Cao, Y., Yu, G., Han, Q., & Wang, W. (2025). An integrated fine-kinney framework based on a T-spherical fuzzy CPT-CRADIS model for estimating occupational risk in the coal mine industry. *Int. J. Fuzzy Syst.* https://doi.org/10.1007/s40815-40025-02025-w.

Hussain, A., Yin, S., Ullah, K., Waqas, M., Senapati, T., Esztergár-Kiss, D., & Moslem, S. (2024). Enhancing renewable energy evaluation: Utilizing complex picture fuzzy frank aggregation operators in multi-attribute group decision-making. *Sustainable Cities Soc, 116*, 105842.

Li, J., Xiang, Y., Peng, H., & Wang, J. (2025). An extended multi-criteria group decision-making method based on preference ranking under Z-number environments. *Engineering Applications of Artificial Intelligence, 149*, 110573.

Li, X., Seah, R. Y. T., & Yuen, K. F. (2025). Mental wellbeing in digital workplaces: The role of digital resources, technostress, and burnout. *Technology in Society, 81*, 102844.

Liang, D., Fu, Y., & Garg, H. (2024). A novel robustness PROMETHEE method by learning interactive criteria and historical information for blockchain technology-enhanced supplier selection. *Expert Systems with Applications. 235*, 121107.

Lin, Q. (2024). Digital leadership: A systematic literature review and future research agenda. *European Journal of Innovation Management.* https://doi.org/10.1108/EJIM-1107-2023-0522.

Liu, P., Khan, Q., Jamil, A., Haq, I. U., Sikandar, W., & Hussain, F. (2024). A novel fuzzy TOPSIS method based on T-spherical fuzzy Aczel–Alsina power Heronian mean operators with applications in pharmaceutical enterprises' selection. *Complex & Intelligent Systems, 10*(2), 2327–2386.

Liu, P., Qiu, X., Pan, Q., & Wu, X. (2025). Graph model for conflict resolution with hybrid information based on prospect theory and PROMETHEE method and its application in water resources conflict. *Inform Sciences, 689*, 121498.

Mahnaz, S., Ali, J., Malik, M. G. A., & Bashir, Z. (2022). T-spherical fuzzy frank aggregation operators and their application to decision making with unknown weight information. *Ieee Access, 10*, 7408–7438.

Memon, K. R., & Ooi, S. K. (2023). Identifying digital leadership's role in fostering competitive advantage through responsible innovation: A SEM-neural network approach. *Technology in Society, 75*, 102399.

Mir, S., Shah, S. A., Bhat, M. S., Akhter, S., Ahad, F., Rashid, H., & Jeelani, P. (2024). Disaster risk assessment of educational infrastructure in mountain geographies using PROMETHEE-II. *International Journal of Disaster Risk Reduction, 107*, 104489.

Mohammed, M. T., Shubber, M. S., Qahtan, S., Alsattar, H. A., Mourad, N., Zaidan, A. A., & Zaidan, B. B. (2025). Determining the superiority of a robust cloud fault tolerance mechanism using a spherical cubic fuzzy set-based decision approach. *Engineering Applications of Artificial Intelligence, 148*, 110402.

Oubahman, L., & Duleba, S. (2024). Fuzzy PROMETHEE model for public transport mode choice analysis. *Evolving Systems, 15*(2), 285–302.

Oubahman, L., Duleba, S., & Esztergár-Kiss, D. (2024). Analyzing university students' mode choice preferences by using a hybrid AHP group-PROMETHEE model: Evidence from Budapest city. *European Transport Research Review, 16*(1), 8.

Papapostolou, A., Karakosta, C., Mexis, F.-D., Andreoulaki, I., & Psarras, J. (2024). A Fuzzy PROMETHEE method for evaluating strategies towards a cross-country renewable energy cooperation: The cases of Egypt and Morocco. *in: Energies*.

Qiao, L., & Qi, X. (2025). Hybrid multi-criteria decision-making algorithm for music composition evaluation using T-spherical fuzzy sets. *International Journal of Information and Communication Technology, 26*(12), 49–69.

Seikh, M. R., & Mandal, U. (2023). Interval-valued Fermatean fuzzy Dombi aggregation operators and SWARA based PROMETHEE II method to bio-medical waste management. *Expert Systems with Applications, 226*, 120082.

Shahzad, M. U. (2024). Core competencies for digital leadership development: A perspective from the lens of paradox theory. *The Bottom Line, 37*(4), 454–472.

Smet, J.-P. B. Y. D. (2016). PROMETHEE methods. In S. Greco, M. Ehrgott, & J. R. Figueira (Eds.). *Multiple Criteria Decision Analysis*. New York, New York: Springer.

Sotiropoulou, K. F., Vavatsikos, A. P., & Botsaris, P. N. (2024). A hybrid AHP-PROMETHEE II onshore wind farms multi-criteria suitability analysis using kNN and SVM regression models in northeastern Greece. *Renewable Energy, 221*, 119795.

Tuesta-Trauco, K. M., Salas López, R., Barboza, E., Zabaleta-Santisteban, J. A., Medina-Medina, A. J., Rivera-Fernandez, A. S., Sánchez-Vega, J. A., Noriega-Salazar, N. M., Oliva-Cruz, M., Tariq, A., & Silva-López, J. O. (2025). Land suitability for Pitahaya (*Hylocereus megalanthus*) cultivation in Amazonas, Perú: Integrated use of GIS, RS, F-AHP, and PROMETHEE. *Remote Sensing*.

Wang, W., Wang, Y., Chen, Y., Deveci, M., Kadry, S., & Pedrycz, W. (2024a). Analyzing the barriers to resilience supply chain adoption in the food industry using hybrid interval-valued fermatean fuzzy PROMETHEE-II model. *J. Ind. Inf. Integr.Journal of Industrial Information Integration, 40*, 100614.

Wang, w, Xi, Y., & Liu, P. (2024b). The connotation, composition and emergence mechanisms of digital leadership under complex adaptive systems theory. *Chinese Jurnal of Mnagement (in Chinese), 21*(4), 475–483 +526.

Wang, W.-Z., Liu, X.-W., & Liu, S.-L. (2020). Failure mode and effect analysis for machine tool risk analysis using extended gained and lost dominance score method. *IEEE Trans. Reliab. 69*(3), 954–967.

Xia, Y., Liu, X., Wang, X., Deng, H., Han, C., Liu, Z., & Tsai, S.-B. (2023). The power of role models in a team: The impact of lead entrepreneur's digital leadership on digital entrepreneurial success. *Information Processing & Management, 60*(6), 103498.

Xu, W., & Li, Y. (2025). Enhancing information fusion and feature selection efficiency via the PROMETHEE method for multi-source dynamic decision data sets. *Knowl-Based Syst, 309*, 112781.

Yang, W., & Pang, Y. (2022). T-spherical fuzzy Bonferroni mean operators and their application in multiple attribute decision making. *Mathematics*.

Zhang, Y., Hao, Z., Gong, Z., & Zhang, R. (2025). Context-dependent probabilistic linguistic multi-attribute decision-making methods. *Appl IntellApplied Intelligence, 55*(7), 681.

Zhang, Z., & Zheng, X. (2023). Digital leadership: Structural dimensions and scale development. *Business and Management Journal (in Chinese), 45*(11), 152–168.

Zia, M. D., Yousafzai, F., Abdullah, S., & Hila, K. (2024). Complex linear Diophantine fuzzy sets and their applications in multi-attribute decision making. *Engineering Applications of Artificial Intelligence, 132*, 107953.

Zobeidi, T., Yazdanpanah, M., Komendantova, N., Löhr, K., & Sieber, S. (2024). Evaluating climate change adaptation options in the agriculture sector: A PROMETHEE-GAIA analysis. *Environmental Sustainability Indicators*. 22, 100395.

Chapter 98

PROMETHEE II: The preference ranking organization method for enrichment evaluation II for multi-attribute decision-making

Zhengyan Yang[1], Weizhong Wang[1], Yu Chen[1], and Muhammet Deveci[2]
[1]*School of Economics and Management, Anhui Normal University, Wuhu, Anhui Province, P.R. China,* [2]*Department of Industrial Engineering, Turkish Naval Academy, National Defence University, Istanbul, Türkiye*

98.1 Introduction

Multi-attribute decision-making (MADM) techniques play a vital role in achieving reliable sustainability evaluations (Palczewski & Sałabun, 2019). In such assessments, MADM approaches are used to rank alternative options according to their performance across selected criteria. Among these methods, the preference ranking organization method for enrichment evaluations (PROMETHEE-II) stands out as one of the most effective tools for ranking available alternatives, thereby reducing potential decision-making errors (Agrawal, 2022). The PROMETHEE-II method relies on an outranking relationship that enables the incorporation of data and preference imprecision within the model (Wątróbski, 2023). Moreover, it allows for limited linear compensation among evaluation criteria, aligning well with the principles of strong sustainability assessment (Harjanti et al., 2023). By utilizing threshold parameters, the method effectively manages uncertainty in preferences and data. In addition to these unique characteristics that distinguish PROMETHEE-II from other MADM techniques with full criteria compensation, it also offers a quantitative assessment outcome, providing valuable analytical insights for decision-makers (Ziemba, 2022). Consequently, PROMETHEE-II has been widely applied in diverse domains, including hospital resource management (Amaral & Costa, 2014), industrial robot selection (Sen et al., 2015), tool steel material evaluation (Maity & Chakraborty, 2015), and hybrid power system design (Chisale et al., 2023), etc.

The remaining structure of this paper is organized as follows: Section 2 reviews the existing literature on the PROMETHEE-II method. Section 3 introduces its key concepts and computational procedures. Sections 4 and 5 provide simple and complex numerical examples to demonstrate its implementation. Section 6 compares PROMETHEE-II with other MADM methods and discusses its advantages. Finally, Section 7 presents the conclusions and outlines future research directions.

98.2 Literature review

The PROMETHEE method, a well-established and comprehensive MADM approach, was initially developed by Brans et al. (1986) and has since evolved into multiple versions. Among them, PROMETHEE-II stands out as an interactive model capable of classifying and ranking complex alternatives that are often difficult to compare (Amaral & Costa, 2014). In recent years, the PROMETHEE framework has been further extended to handle various uncertain and ambiguous decision-making contexts. For instance, Tian et al. (2020) combined an improved analytic hierarchy process (AHP) with the picture fuzzy PROMETHEE-II to evaluate the environmental impacts of tourism. Torbacki (2021) proposed a hybrid MADM framework that integrates decision-making trial and evaluation laboratory based analytic network process and

Encyclopedia of Multi-Attribute Decision-Making (MADM). DOI: https://doi.org/10.1016/B978-0-443-33275-3.00036-1

PROMETHEE-II for assessing cybersecurity readiness in Industry 4.0 environments. Similarly, Samanlioglu and Ayağ, 2021 integrated the analytic network process with hesitant fuzzy PROMETHEE-II to assess the concepts and determine the best. Seikh & Mandal (2023) developed an integrated multi-attribute group decision-making model by combining PROMETHEE-II with the stepwise weight assessment ratio analysis method, while Aruchsamy et al. (2024) introduced a Fermatean fuzzy PROMETHEE-II framework for selecting the most suitable green supplier in the construction sector. More recently, Tang et al. (2025) presented an interval type-2 fuzzy PROMETHEE-II decision model for evaluating medical waste treatment technologies.

Furthermore, the simplicity, transparency, and adaptability of the PROMETHEE-II method in producing reliable ranking outcomes have led to its widespread adoption across various disciplines. Numerous studies have employed both the original and modified versions of PROMETHEE-II to solve practical decision-making problems. For example, Tong et al. (2020) applied an extended fuzzy PROMETHEE-II method to evaluate sustainable maintenance supplier performance in the petrochemical industry. Yu et al. (2023) proposed a novel failure mode and effects analysis-based risk assessment model for submarine pipelines using interval-valued intuitionistic fuzzy rough number and Tomada de decisao interativa e multicritévio with PROMETHEE-II. Sotiropoulou et al. (2024) developed a hybrid geographic information system-based spatial decision framework that integrates AHP, PROMETHEE-II, and machine learning algorithms to identify optimal onshore wind farm sites. Mir et al. (2024) utilized PROMETHEE-II to evaluate disaster risk in educational infrastructure across mountainous regions. Lastly, Wang et al. (2024) introduced an integrated interval-valued fermatean fuzzy-criteria importance through intercriteria correlation PROMETHEE II approach to assess barrier levels influencing alternative participation in food supply chains, while Ghorbani et al. (2025) applied PROMETHEE-II alongside weighted aggregated sum product assessment (WASPAS) and combined compromise abbreviations expanded solution models for geotechnical hazard assessment in tunnel boring machine projects.

98.3 Methodology

The PROMETHEE-II method represents a widely used MADM technique designed for ranking and prioritizing alternative options. The general procedure for applying the PROMETHEE-II method can be outlined as follows:

Step 1. Construction of the initial decision matrix.

Let $\mathbb{Z} = \{Z_i | i = 1, 2, \cdots, m\}$ represent the set of alternatives, and $\Upsilon = \{r_j | j = 1, 2, \cdots, n\}$ denote the set of evaluation criteria. Let $\Theta = \{w_j | j = 1, 2, \cdots, n\}$ be the vector of criteria weights, where $w_j \in [0, 1]$ and $\Sigma_{j=1}^{n} w_j = 1$. The decision matrix $A = (a_{ij})_{m \times n}$ is defined as follows.

$$A = \begin{bmatrix} a_{11} & a_{12} & \cdots & a_{1n} \\ a_{21} & a_{22} & \cdots & a_{2n} \\ \vdots & \vdots & \ddots & \vdots \\ a_{m1} & a_{m2} & \cdots & a_{mn} \end{bmatrix} \tag{98.1}$$

Where a_{ij} i denotes the performance value of the alternative Z_i under the criterion r_j. The elementa_{ij} can be expressed as a fuzzy number, a linguistic assessment, or a precise numerical value, depending on the nature of the decision problem.

Step 2. Normalization of the decision matrix.

In the classical PROMETHEE-II method, six types of preference functions are defined to compare alternatives across both benefit and cost criteria. The availability of multiple preference functions makes normalization an essential step in ensuring comparability among criteria. In this study, the pairwise difference is adopted as the preference function, which requires all criteria to be expressed on a uniform scale. Therefore, normalization is a necessary and fundamental procedure within the PROMETHEE-II framework (Palczewski & Sałabun, 2019).

The decision matrix is normalized using a linear normalization process, expressed as $A_{norm} = [\widetilde{a}_{ij}]_{m \times n}$, according to the following equations:

$$\widetilde{a}_{ij} = \begin{cases} \dfrac{a_{ij} - \min\limits_{i \in n}\{a_{ij}\}}{\max\limits_{i \in n}\{a_{ij}\} - \min\limits_{i \in n}\{a_{ij}\}}, & j \in B \\[2ex] \dfrac{\max\limits_{i \in n}\{a_{ij}\} - a_{ij}}{\max\limits_{i \in n}\{a_{ij}\} - \min\limits_{i \in n}\{a_{ij}\}}, & j \in C \end{cases} \tag{98.2}$$

where B represents the set of benefit criteria and C denotes the set of cost criteria.

Step 3. Obtain the preference index.

For each criterion $j \in m$, the preference index $h_j(Z_i, Z_{i'})$ between alternatives Z_i, and $Z_{i'}$ $(i, i' \in n, i \neq i')$, is computed as follows:

$$h_j(Z_i, Z_{i'}) = \begin{cases} 0 & \text{if } \tilde{a}_{ij} \leq \tilde{a}_{i'j} \\ \tilde{a}_{ij} - \tilde{a}_{i'j} & \text{otherwise} \end{cases} \quad (98.3)$$

Here, $h_j(Z_i, Z_{i'})$ represents the degree of preference of alternative Z_i over $Z_{i'}$ with respect to criterion r_j. For a given alternative Z_i, the preference indices $h_j(Z_i, Z_{i'})$ are calculated only for those criteria corresponding to the maximum evaluation values of Z_i.

Step 4. Derive the relative preference.

Compute the relative preference index $\pi(Z_i, Z_{i'})$, for $i, i' \in n, i \neq i'$, as follows:

$$\pi(Z_i, Z_{i'}) = \sum_{j=1}^{n} w_j h_j(Z_i, Z_{i'}) \quad (98.4)$$

Step 5. Determine the outgoing and incoming flows.

The PROMETHEE-II method defines two types of preference flows, outgoing (positive) and incoming (negative), to assess the dominance relationships among alternatives.

The leaving (or positive) flow for alternative Z_i is given as:

$$\psi^+(Z_i) = \frac{1}{m-1} \sum_{\substack{i'=1 \\ i \neq i'}}^{m} \pi(Z_i, Z_{i'}) \quad (98.5)$$

and the entering (or negative) flow for alternative Z_i is calculated as:

$$\psi^-(Z_i) = \frac{1}{m-1} \sum_{\substack{i'=1 \\ i \neq i'}}^{m} \pi(Z_{i'}, Z_i) \quad (98.6)$$

where m is the total number of alternatives. Each alternative is compared with the remaining $(m-1)$ alternatives. The leaving flow indicates how strongly an alternative dominates others, whereas the entering flow reflects the extent to which it is dominated by the remaining alternatives.

Step 6. Ranking the alternatives.

The final ranking of alternatives in the PROMETHEE-II method is based on the **net flow value**, which is defined as the difference between the leaving and entering flows:

$$\psi(Z_i) = \psi^+(Z_i) - \psi^-(Z_i) \quad (98.7)$$

Alternatives are ordered according to their corresponding $\psi(Z_i)$ values; the higher the net flow, the better the alternative. In other words, an alternative with a higher leaving flow and a lower entering flow achieves a larger $\psi(Z_i)$ and is therefore considered superior. The alternative with the maximum $\psi(Z_i)$ value is identified as the best choice among all considered options.

98.4 Numerical example 1

In this section, a simple numerical example is introduced to demonstrate the application of the PROMETHEE-II method in the context of smartphone selection. With the rapid iteration of consumer electronics, especially smartphones, users are frequently faced with the challenge of choosing from a wide array of devices released each year. Each smartphone differs in terms of features, cost, and performance, making the decision-making process complex and multidimensional. Smartphone selection is inherently a multi-attribute problem, as consumers typically consider multiple factors such as camera quality, battery life, performance, and price. To address this challenge, decision-making techniques can be applied to help users select the most suitable option based on their preferences.

In this example, six smartphone models released in 2024 were selected, namely: Samsung Galaxy S24 (Z_1), Apple iPhone 16 Pro (Z_2), Xiaomi 14 Ultra (Z_3), Google Pixel 9 Pro (Z_4), OnePlus 13 (Z_5), Huawei Mate 70 Pro (Z_6). Each smartphone is evaluated based on eight criteria, including five benefit-type criteria (r_1, r_2, r_4, r_6, r_7) and three cost-type criteria (r_3, r_5, r_8), as shown below: battery life (r_1), camera performance (r_2), price (r_3), processing power (r_4), weight (r_5), screen quality (r_6). Then, the PROMETHEE-II method can be conducted as follows.

Step 1. Construct an initial decision matrix.

In this step, the positive integers {1, 2, 3, 4, 5, 6, 7} are utilized to represent the evaluation information. Then, experts are invited to evaluate each smartphone under each criterion, and the detailed evaluation information is shown in Table 98.1.

Step 2. Normalization of the decision matrix.

As shown in Table 98.1, criteria r_1, r_2, r_4, r_6, r_7 are the beneficial criteria and criteria r_3, r_5, r_8 are the cost criteria. Based on these values, the decision matrix can be normalized by referring to Eq. (98.2). For instance, the maximum evaluation value of the alternative Z_1 with respect to the beneficial criterion r_1 and the cost criterion r_3 can be derived by using Eq. (98.8) and Eq. (98.9). The normalized decision matrix is shown in Table 98.2.

$$\tilde{a}_{11} = \frac{a_{11} - a_{i\ \min}}{a_{i\ \max} - a_{i\ \min}} = \frac{6 - 5}{7 - 5} = 0.50 \tag{98.8}$$

$$a_{13} = \frac{a_{1\ \max} - a_{13}}{a_{1\ \max} - a_{1\ \min}} = \frac{6 - 3}{6 - 2} = 0.75 \tag{98.9}$$

Step 3. Obtain the preference index.

According to Eq. (98.3), the preference index $h_j(Z_i, Z_{i'})$ can be obtained. For instance, we can know $\tilde{a}_{11} > \tilde{a}_{12}$, so the $h_1(Z_1, Z_2)$ can be derived by using Eq. (98.10). The results are shown in Table 98.3.

$$h_1(Z_1, Z_2) = \tilde{a}_{11} - \tilde{a}_{12} = 0.50 - 0.00 = 0.50 \tag{98.10}$$

Step 4. Derive the relative preference.

Let the weight of eight criteria be $w_1 = 0.125$, $w_2 = 0.17$, $w_3 = 0.2$, $w_4 = 0.18$, $w_5 = 0.175$, and $w_6 = 0.15$. According to Eq. (98.4), the related preference can be derived. For instance, the weight of criterion r_1 is $w_1 = 0.125$, and the weight of criterion r_4 is $w_4 = 0.1$. The relative preference $\pi(Z_1, Z_2)$ can be obtained by using Eq. (98.11). The relative preference $\pi(Z_i, Z_{i'})$ is shown in Table 98.4.

TABLE 98.1 The detailed evaluation information of each smartphone.

	r_1	r_2	r_3	r_4	r_5	r_6
Z_1	6	6	3	7	4	6
Z_2	5	7	2	6	3	7
Z_3	7	6	5	6	5	6
Z_4	6	6	4	5	4	5
Z_5	6	5	6	6	6	5
Z_6	7	6	4	6	4	6

TABLE 98.2 The normalized decision matrix.

	r_1	r_2	r_3	r_4	r_5	r_6
Z_1	0.50	0.50	0.75	1.00	0.67	0.50
Z_2	0.00	1.00	1.00	0.50	1.00	1.00
Z_3	1.00	0.50	0.25	0.50	0.33	0.50
Z_4	0.50	0.50	0.50	0.00	0.67	0.00
Z_5	0.50	0.00	0.00	0.50	0.00	0.00
Z_6	1.00	0.50	0.50	0.50	0.67	0.50

$$\pi(Z_1, Z_2) = \sum_{j=1}^{8} w_j h_j(Z_1, Z_2) = 0.50 \times 0.125 + 0.50 \times 0.18 = 0.1525 \tag{98.11}$$

Step 5. Determine the outgoing and incoming flows.

The outgoing and incoming flows of each alternative can be derived by using Eqs. (98.5) and (98.6). For instance, as shown in Table 98.4, the outgoing and incoming flows of the alternative Z_1 can be calculated by using Eqs. (98.12) and (98.13). The outgoing and incoming flows of each alternative are displayed in Table 98.5.

$$\begin{aligned}\psi^+(Z_1) &= \frac{1}{m-1}\sum_{\substack{i'=1\\ i\neq i'}}^{m} \pi(Z_1, Z_{i'})\\ &= \frac{1}{6-1}(0.1525 + 0.2483 + 0.3050 + 0.5167\\ &\quad + 0.1400)\\ &= 0.2725\end{aligned} \tag{98.12}$$

$$\begin{aligned}\psi^-(Z_1) &= \frac{1}{m-1}\sum_{\substack{i'=1\\ i\neq i'}}^{m} \pi(Z_{i'}, Z_1)\\ &= \frac{1}{5}(0.2683 + 0.0625 + 0 + 0\\ &\quad + 0.0625)\\ &= 0.0787\end{aligned} \tag{98.13}$$

Step 6. Ranking the alternatives.

Based on the results shown in Table 98.5, the net flow of each alternative can be obtained by referring to Eq. (98.7), and accordingly, the ranking of each alternative can be determined. The net flow and ranking of each alternative are shown in Table 98.6. To present the results more intuitively, we have created Fig. 98.1 to illustrate the sorting outcome.

According to Fig. 98.1, we can find that the Apple iPhone 16 Pro (Z_2) is the best option among other phones. And the ranking order is $Z_2 \succ Z_1 \succ Z_6 \succ Z_3 \succ Z_4 \succ Z_6$.

98.5 Numerical example 2

To effectively illustrate the practical applicability of the PROMETHEE-II method in real-world decision-making, this chapter presents a complex numerical example focusing on the selection of alternatives. In real practice, each participant plays an indispensable role within an integrated logistics system; however, their level of criticality and functional contribution may vary considerably across different contexts. To ensure the stable operation of the food supply chain amid various external disruptions, this chapter employs quantitative analytical methods to comprehensively examine how different food supply chain participants respond to obstructive factors during the process of resilience formation. Accordingly, a T-spherical fuzzy PROMETHEE-II approach is proposed to evaluate both the obstructive factors and the performance of supply chain participants in enhancing the resilience of the food supply chain.

As discussed above, the identification and prioritization of barriers faced by each participant in the resilient supply chain (RSC) is a crucial step toward successful implementation in the food industry. In this illustrative example, six major participants within the food supply chain are selected for analysis, each playing a distinct yet interdependent role:

- Food supplier (Z_1): Responsible for providing raw materials, goods, and services to enterprises and their partners, suppliers play a vital role in ensuring the stability and continuity of the entire supply chain.
- Food manufacturer (Z_2): Tasked with transforming raw materials into finished food products, manufacturers are accountable for product design, production efficiency, quality control, and cost management throughout the production process.
- Food distributors (Z_3): Distributors serve as intermediaries, transferring products from manufacturers to consumers through extensive sales networks and marketing channels that connect multiple markets and customer groups.
- Food logistics distribution partner (Z_4): Representing third-party logistics enterprises, these partners collaborate with both production and sales entities to achieve optimal resource allocation and improve supply chain responsiveness.
- Food retailer (Z_5): Retailers directly provide products and services to end consumers, ensuring product availability, customer satisfaction, and brand loyalty.

TABLE 98.3 The preference indices.

	r_1	r_2	r_3	r_4	r_5	r_6
$h(Z_1, Z_2)$	0.50	0	0	0.50	0	0
$h(Z_1, Z_3)$	0	0	0.50	0.50	0.33	0
$h(Z_1, Z_4)$	0	0	0.25	1.00	0	0.50
$h(Z_1, Z_5)$	0	0.50	0.75	0.50	0.67	0.50
$h(Z_1, Z_6)$	0	0	0.25	0.50	0	0
$h(Z_2, Z_1)$	0	0.50	0.25	0	0.33	0.50
$h(Z_2, Z_3)$	0	0.50	0.75	0	0.67	0.50
$h(Z_2, Z_4)$	0	0.50	0.50	0.50	0.33	1.00
$h(Z_2, Z_5)$	0	1.00	1.00	0	1.00	1.00
$h(Z_2, Z_6)$	0	0.50	0.50	0	0.33	0.50
$h(Z_3, Z_1)$	0.50	0	0	0	0	0
$h(Z_3, Z_2)$	1.00	0	0	0	0	0
$h(Z_3, Z_4)$	0.50	0	0	0.5	0	0.50
$h(Z_3, Z_5)$	0.50	0.50	0.25	0	0.33	0.50
$h(Z_3, Z_6)$	0	0	0	0	0	0
$h(Z_4, Z_1)$	0	0	0	0	0	0
$h(Z_4, Z_2)$	0.50	0	0	0	0	0
$h(Z_4, Z_3)$	0	0	0.25	0	0.33	0
$h(Z_4, Z_5)$	0	0.50	0.50	0	0.67	0
$h(Z_4, Z_6)$	0	0	0	0	0	0
$h(Z_5, Z_1)$	0	0	0	0	0	0
$h(Z_5, Z_2)$	0.50	0	0	0	0	0
$h(Z_5, Z_3)$	0	0	0	0	0	0
$h(Z_5, Z_4)$	0	0	0	0.50	0	0
$h(Z_5, Z_6)$	0	0	0	0	0	0
$h(Z_6, Z_1)$	0.50	0	0	0	0	0
$h(Z_6, Z_2)$	1	0	0	0	0	0
$h(Z_6, Z_3)$	0	0	0.25	0	0.33	0
$h(Z_6, Z_4)$	0.50	0	0	0.50	0	0.50
$h(Z_6, Z_5)$	0.50	0.50	0.50	0	0.67	0.50

- End use (Z_6): As the ultimate consumer of the food supply chain, the end user satisfies personal needs and expectations through the purchase and consumption of products or services.

To analyze the challenges these participants face, 10 key barriers to RSC implementation are identified as follows:

◆ High investment cost (r_1): Implementing supply chain resilience requires substantial capital for infrastructure development, technology upgrades, and system transformation, leading to high investment and operational costs.

TABLE 98.4 The relative preference $\pi(Z_i, Z_{i'})$.

The value of relative preference					
$\pi(Z_1, Z_2) = 0.1525$	$\pi(Z_2, Z_1) = 0.2683$	$\pi(Z_3, Z_1) = 0.0625$	$\pi(Z_4, Z_1) = 0.0000$	$\pi(Z_5, Z_1) = 0.0000$	$\pi(Z_6, Z_1) = 0.0625$
$\pi(Z_1, Z_3) = 0.2483$	$\pi(Z_2, Z_3) = 0.4267$	$\pi(Z_3, Z_2) = 0.1250$	$\pi(Z_4, Z_2) = 0.0625$	$\pi(Z_5, Z_2) = 0.0625$	$\pi(Z_6, Z_2) = 0.1250$
$\pi(Z_1, Z_4) = 0.3050$	$\pi(Z_2, Z_4) = 0.4833$	$\pi(Z_3, Z_4) = 0.2275$	$\pi(Z_4, Z_3) = 0.1083$	$\pi(Z_5, Z_3) = 0.0000$	$\pi(Z_6, Z_3) = 0.1083$
$\pi(Z_1, Z_5) = 0.5167$	$\pi(Z_2, Z_5) = 0.6950$	$\pi(Z_3, Z_5) = 0.3308$	$\pi(Z_4, Z_5) = 0.3017$	$\pi(Z_5, Z_4) = 0.0900$	$\pi(Z_6, Z_4) = 0.2275$
$\pi(Z_1, Z_6) = 0.1400$	$\pi(Z_2, Z_6) = 0.3183$	$\pi(Z_3, Z_6) = 0.0000$	$\pi(Z_4, Z_6) = 0.0000$	$\pi(Z_5, Z_6) = 0.0000$	$\pi(Z_6, Z_5) = 0.4392$

TABLE 98.5 The outgoing and incoming flows of each alternative.

	$\psi^+(Z_i)$	$\psi^-(Z_i)$
Z_1	0.2725	0.0787
Z_2	0.4383	0.1055
Z_3	0.1492	0.1783
Z_4	0.0945	0.2667
Z_5	0.0305	0.4567
Z_6	0.1925	0.0917

TABLE 98.6 The net flow and ranking of each alternative.

	Z_1	Z_2	Z_3	Z_4	Z_5	Z_6
$\psi(Z_i)$	0.1938	0.3328	-0.0292	-0.1722	-0.4262	0.1008
Ranking	2	1	4	5	6	3

- Pollution emissions in supply chain (r_2): Increasing environmental regulations and penalties for emissions create additional pressure on firms striving for both resilience and sustainability.
- Limit of monetary resources (r_3): Many organizations, especially small and medium-sized enterprises, face financial constraints that limit their ability to invest in resilience measures.
- Insufficient bank loan affordability (r_4): Difficulty in obtaining adequate financing from banks restricts the implementation of resilience-oriented projects.
- Immaturity of technology (r_5): The lack of advanced and practical technologies hinders industries from developing innovative solutions to enhance supply chain resilience.
- Policy enforcement (r_6): Inconsistent implementation of existing policies by certain suppliers undermines the collective effort toward RSC practices.
- Lack of refined policy support (r_7): The absence of detailed and supportive legal frameworks complicates the adoption and enforcement of resilience-related initiatives.

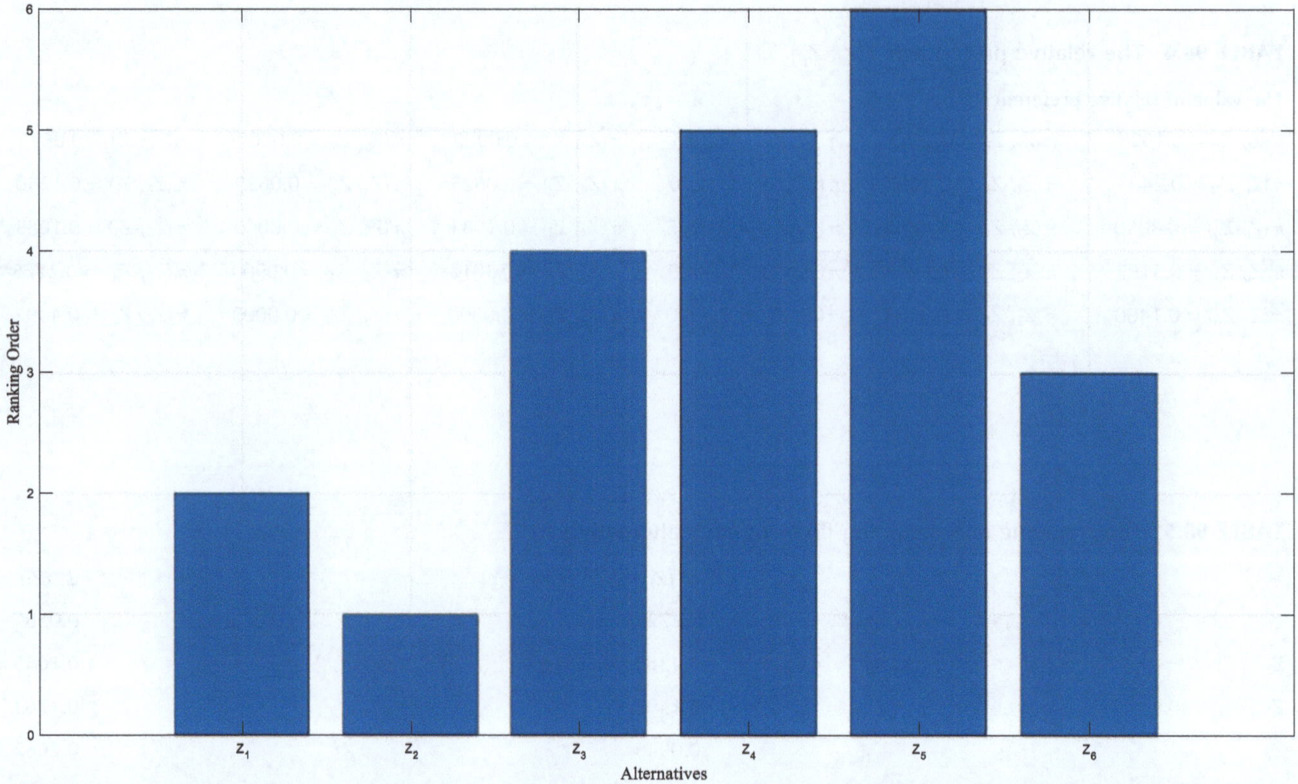

FIGURE 98.1 The ranking order of each alternative.

- Resistive culture (r_8): Organizational inertia, fear of change, and insufficient learning culture often prevent employees from adopting new resilience strategies or technologies.
- Lack of resilient design aspect (r_9): Traditional supply chain designs neglect circularity and reusability, which are essential for resilience-oriented operations.
- Legal uncertainties (r_{10}): The lack of clear legal definitions and regulatory standards for resilience introduces uncertainty and risk for both suppliers and customers.

In this case study, four domain experts participate in the decision-making process. The PROMETHEE-II method is then applied to obtain a comprehensive ranking of the six food supply chain participants with respect to the 10 identified barriers. The relationships between the barriers and participants are illustrated in Fig. 98.2, providing a conceptual overview of the evaluation framework.

Step 1. Construct an initial decision matrix.

In this step, four experts are invited to evaluate the barriers of RSC implementation to different participants in the food industry by linguistic terms, which are shown in Table 98.7. Then, the linguistic evaluation information can be transferred to the T-spherical fuzzy number according to Table 98.7. The linguistic evaluation information of four experts is shown in Tables 98.8-98.11.

Step 2. Fusion of individual preferences.

Let the experts' weights be $\omega_1 = 0.2$, $\omega_2 = 0.3$, $\omega_3 = 0.25$, and $\omega_4 = 0.25$. We use the T-spherical fuzzy ordered weighted averaging operator to integrate individual evaluating matrix by Eq. (98.14). Let $t = 3$, then, the group evaluating matrix are displayed in Table 98.12.

$$
\begin{aligned}
T-SFOWA(T_1, T_2, \cdots, T_k) &= \oplus_{\tau=1}^{k}(\omega_\tau T_k) \\
&= \left(\sqrt[t]{1 - \Pi_{\tau=1}^{k}(1-\mu_\tau^t)^{\omega_\tau}},\ \prod_{\tau=1}^{k} \nu_\tau^{\omega_\tau},\ \prod_{\tau=1}^{k} o_\tau^{\omega_\tau} \right)
\end{aligned}
\tag{98.14}
$$

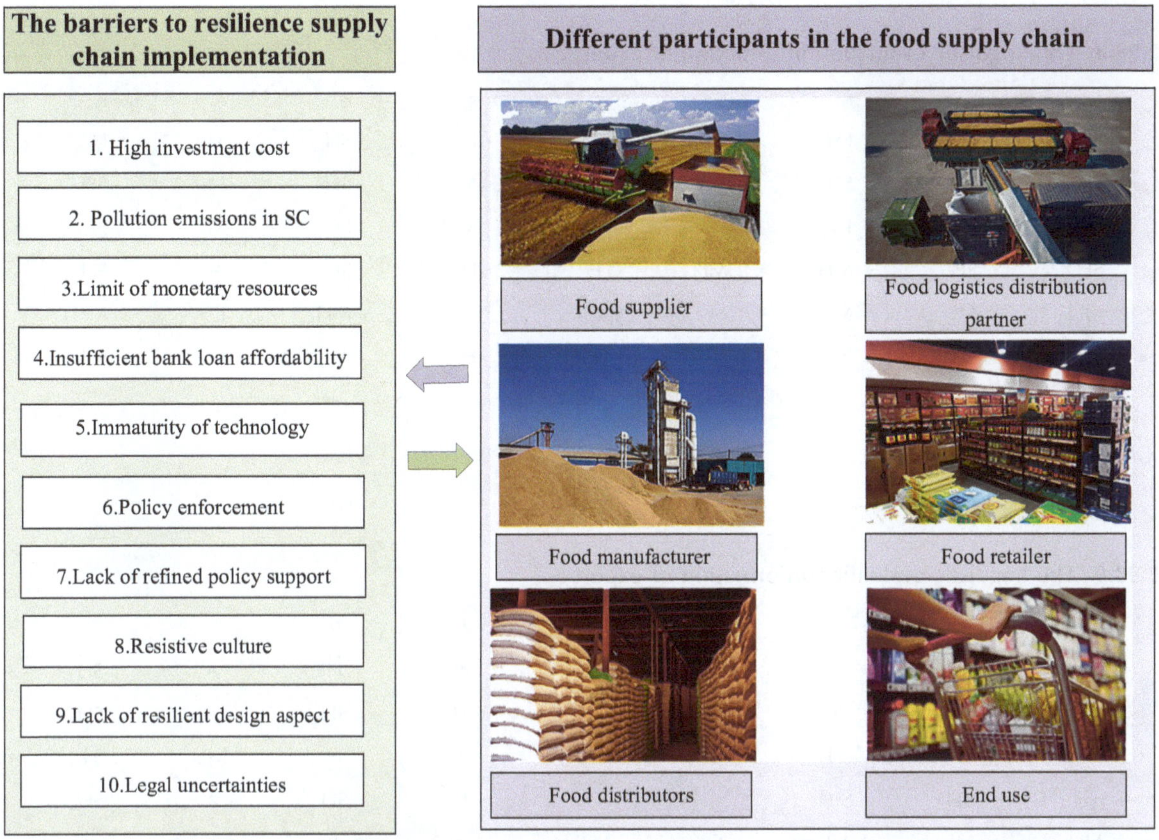

FIGURE 98.2 Different participants in food supply chain (FSC) and barriers to resilient supply chain implementation.

TABLE 98.7 The linguistic terms and their corresponding T-spherical fuzzy numbers (TSFNs).

Linguistic term	TSFNs
Exceptionally low (EL)	(0.10, 0.90, 0.10)
Significantly low (SL)	(0.20, 0.80, 0.20)
Relatively low (RL)	(0.30, 0.70, 0.30)
Moderately low (ML)	(0.40, 0.60,0.40)
Average (A)	(0.50, 0.50, 0.50)
Moderately high (MH)	(0.60, 0.40, 0.40)
High (H)	(0.70, 0.30, 0.30)
Significantly high (SH)	(0.80, 0.20, 0.20)
Exceptionally high (EH)	(0.90, 0.10, 0.10)
Fantastically high (FH)	(0.99, 0.01, 0.01)

TABLE 98.8 The linguistic evaluation information of expert e_1.

	r_1	r_2	r_3	r_4	r_5	r_6	r_7	r_8	r_9	r_{10}
Z_1	SH	H	EH	SH	SH	H	SH	ML	H	EH
Z_2	EH	H	SH	SH	H	MH	SH	ML	SH	SH
Z_3	H	MH	H	H	MH	MH	H	ML	H	H
Z_4	SH	SH	MH	MH	H	H	SH	A	SH	H
Z_5	MH	ML	ML	ML	ML	A	MH	L	MH	H
Z_6	FH	MH	H	SH	H	H	A	SH	SH	EH

TABLE 98.9 The linguistic evaluation information of expert e_2.

	r_1	r_2	r_3	r_4	r_5	r_6	r_7	r_8	r_9	r_{10}
Z_1	SH	SH	H	SH	H	MH	H	A	SH	SH
Z_2	SH	H	SH	EH	SH	H	SH	ML	SH	EH
Z_3	H	MH	H	H	MH	MH	H	ML	H	SH
Z_4	SH	SH	MH	MH	H	H	SH	A	SH	SH
Z_5	MH	ML	ML	ML	ML	A	MH	L	MH	H
Z_6	SH	MH	H	MH	MH	H	MH	ML	H	SH

TABLE 98.10 The linguistic evaluation information of expert e_3.

	r_1	r_2	r_3	r_4	r_5	r_6	r_7	r_8	r_9	r_{10}
Z_1	SH	SH	SH	A	SH	H	FH	MH	SH	SH
Z_2	FH	SH	EH	SH	H	MH	H	A	SH	SH
Z_3	SH	MH	H	H	MH	MH	MH	ML	H	H
Z_4	SH	SH	MH	H	SH	H	H	A	SH	SH
Z_5	H	ML	ML	ML	ML	A	H	ML	H	MH
Z_6	EH	SH	H	EH	SH	MH	SH	ML	FH	EH

TABLE 98.11 The linguistic evaluation information of expert e_4.

	r_1	r_2	r_3	r_4	r_5	r_6	r_7	r_8	r_9	r_{10}
Z_1	SH	MH	MH	MH	SH	H	SH	ML	SH	H
Z_2	EH	SH	SH	EH	SH	H	SH	ML	FH	EH
Z_3	SH	H	MH	H	H	MH	MH	ML	H	SH
Z_4	SH	SH	SH	MH	SH	SH	FH	A	SH	SH
Z_5	MH	ML	ML	ML	ML	A	MH	L	MH	MH
Z_6	MH	ML	A	ML	ML	A	MH	ML	MH	H

TABLE 98.12 The group preference matrix.

	r_1	r_2	r_3	r_4	r_5	r_6	r_7	r_8	r_9	r_{10}
Z_1	(0.79,0.20,0.20)	(0.84,0.26,0.26)	(0.81,0.23,0.23)	(0.86,0.30,0.30)	(0.81,0.23,0.23)	(0.88,0.33,0.33)	(0.64,0.11,0.11)	(0.96,0.51,0.43)	(0.80,0.22,0.22)	(0.78,0.19,0.19)
Z_2	(0.57,0.07,0.07)	(0.83,0.24,0.24)	(0.75,0.17,0.17)	(0.71,0.14,0.14)	(0.82,0.24,0.24)	(0.89,0.34,0.34)	(0.81,0.22,0.22)	(0.97,0.57,0.42)	(0.62,0.09,0.09)	(0.71,0.14,0.14)
Z_3	(0.83,0.24,0.24)	(0.91,0.37,0.37)	(0.88,0.32,0.32)	(0.87,0.30,0.30)	(0.91,0.37,0.37)	(0.92,0.40,0.40)	(0.90,0.35,0.35)	(0.98,0.60,0.40)	(0.87,0.30,0.30)	(0.82,0.24,0.24)
Z_4	(0.79,0.20,0.20)	(0.79,0.20,0.20)	(0.89,0.34,0.34)	(0.91,0.37,0.37)	(0.83,0.24,0.24)	(0.85,0.27,0.27)	(0.64,0.10,0.10)	(0.96,0.50,0.50)	(0.79,0.20,0.20)	(0.80,0.22,0.22)
Z_5	(0.91,0.37,0.37)	(0.98,0.60,0.40)	(0.98,0.60,0.40)	(0.98,0.60,0.40)	(0.98,0.60,0.40)	(0.96,0.50,0.50)	(0.91,0.37,0.37)	(0.99,0.67,0.32)	(0.91,0.37,0.37)	(0.90,0.35,0.35)
Z_6	(0.65,0.11,0.11)	(0.90,0.37,0.34)	(0.89,0.34,0.34)	(0.83,0.27,0.25)	(0.89,0.35,0.32)	(0.90,0.37,0.37)	(0.89,0.35,0.35)	(0.94,0.48,0.35)	(0.67,0.13,0.13)	(0.74,0.16,0.16)

TABLE 98.13 The score function value matrix.

	r_1	r_2	r_3	r_4	r_5	r_6	r_7	r_8	r_9	r_{10}
Z_1	0.7360	0.7744	0.7542	0.7911	0.7552	0.8114	0.6313	0.8320	0.7487	0.7265
Z_2	0.5927	0.7684	0.7059	0.6740	0.7651	0.8159	0.7520	0.8282	0.6203	0.6740
Z_3	0.7684	0.8235	0.8098	0.8015	0.8235	0.8280	0.8173	0.8280	0.8015	0.7651
Z_4	0.7360	0.7360	0.8101	0.8235	0.7684	0.7850	0.6294	0.8125	0.7360	0.7487
Z_5	0.8235	0.8280	0.8280	0.8280	0.8280	0.8125	0.8235	0.8123	0.8235	0.8173
Z_6	0.6342	0.8191	0.8133	0.7682	0.8136	0.8197	0.8124	0.8339	0.6471	0.6975

Based on the group preference matrix, the value of the score function can be calculated by Eq. (98.15). The score function value matrix is shown in Table 98.13.

$$sco(\mathrm{P}) = \frac{1 + \mu^t - \nu^t - o^t}{2} \tag{98.15}$$

Step 3. Normalization of the decision matrix.

First, all the criteria are cost-type. Then, the score function value matrix can be normalized by referring to Eq. (98.2). The normalized decision matrix is displayed in Table 98.14.

TABLE 98.14 The normalization matrix.

	r_1	r_2	r_3	r_4	r_5	r_6	r_7	r_8	r_9	r_{10}
Z_1	0.3790	0.5829	0.6042	0.2394	1.0000	0.3863	0.9903	0.0855	0.3679	0.6336
Z_2	1.0000	0.6476	1.0000	1.0000	1.0000	0.2822	0.3684	0.0000	1.0000	1.0000
Z_3	0.2386	0.0491	0.1487	0.1721	0.0719	0.0000	0.0319	0.0097	0.1082	0.3642
Z_4	0.3790	1.0000	0.1463	0.0294	0.9474	1.0000	1.0000	0.9862	0.4307	0.4783
Z_5	0.0000	0.0000	0.0000	0.0000	0.0000	0.3608	0.0000	1.0000	0.0000	0.0000
Z_6	0.8203	0.0963	0.1204	0.3884	0.1978	0.1934	0.0570	0.0000	0.8682	0.8364

TABLE 98.15 The preference index $h_j(Z_i, Z_{i'})$.

	r_1	r_2	r_3	r_4	r_5	r_6	r_7	r_8	r_9	r_{10}
$h(Z_1, Z_2)$	0.0000	0.0000	0.0000	0.0000	0.1356	0.1041	0.6219	0.0000	0.0000	0.0000
$h(Z_1, Z_3)$	0.1405	0.5337	0.4554	0.0674	0.9379	0.3863	0.9584	0.0000	0.2597	0.2694
$h(Z_1, Z_4)$	0.0000	0.0000	0.4578	0.2101	0.1811	0.0000	0.0000	0.0000	0.0000	0.1552
$h(Z_1, Z_5)$	0.3790	0.5829	0.6042	0.2394	1.0000	0.0254	0.9903	0.0000	0.3679	0.6336
$h(Z_1, Z_6)$	0.0000	0.4866	0.4837	0.0000	0.8022	0.1929	0.9333	0.0855	0.0000	0.0000
$h(Z_2, Z_1)$	0.6210	0.0648	0.3958	0.7606	0.0000	0.0000	0.0000	0.1790	0.6321	0.3664
$h(Z_2, Z_3)$	0.7614	0.5985	0.8513	0.8279	0.8023	0.2822	0.3364	0.0000	0.8918	0.6358
$h(Z_2, Z_4)$	0.6210	0.0000	0.8537	0.9706	0.0455	0.0000	0.0000	0.0000	0.5693	0.5217
$h(Z_2, Z_5)$	1.0000	0.6476	1.0000	1.0000	0.8644	0.0000	0.3684	0.0000	1.0000	1.0000
$h(Z_2, Z_6)$	0.1797	0.5513	0.8796	0.6116	0.6666	0.0888	0.3113	0.2645	0.1318	0.1636
$h(Z_3, Z_1)$	0.0000	0.0000	0.0000	0.0000	0.0000	0.0000	0.0000	0.1862	0.0000	0.0000
$h(Z_3, Z_2)$	0.0000	0.0000	0.0000	0.0000	0.0000	0.0000	0.0000	0.0072	0.0000	0.0000
$h(Z_3, Z_4)$	0.0000	0.0000	0.0024	0.1427	0.0000	0.0000	0.0000	0.0000	0.0000	0.0000
$h(Z_3, Z_5)$	0.2386	0.0491	0.1487	0.1721	0.0621	0.0000	0.0319	0.0000	0.1082	0.3642
$h(Z_3, Z_6)$	0.0000	0.0000	0.0283	0.0000	0.0000	0.0000	0.0000	0.2717	0.0000	0.0000
$h(Z_4, Z_1)$	0.0000	0.4171	0.0000	0.0000	0.0000	0.6137	0.0097	0.9044	0.0628	0.0000

(Continued)

TABLE 98.15 (Continued)

	r_1	r_2	r_3	r_4	r_5	r_6	r_7	r_8	r_9	r_{10}
$h(Z_4, Z_2)$	0.0000	0.3524	0.0000	0.0000	0.0000	0.7178	0.6316	0.7253	0.0000	0.0000
$h(Z_4, Z_3)$	0.1405	0.9509	0.0000	0.0000	0.7568	1.0000	0.9681	0.7182	0.3225	0.1142
$h(Z_4, Z_5)$	0.3790	1.0000	0.1463	0.0294	0.8189	0.6392	1.0000	0.0000	0.4307	0.4783
$h(Z_4, Z_6)$	0.0000	0.9037	0.0259	0.0000	0.6211	0.8066	0.9430	0.9899	0.0000	0.0000
$h(Z_5, Z_1)$	0.0000	0.0000	0.0000	0.0000	0.0000	0.0000	0.0000	0.9145	0.0000	0.0000
$h(Z_5, Z_2)$	0.0000	0.0000	0.0000	0.0000	0.0000	0.0786	0.0000	0.7355	0.0000	0.0000
$h(Z_5, Z_3)$	0.0000	0.0000	0.0000	0.0000	0.0000	0.3608	0.0000	0.7283	0.0000	0.0000
$h(Z_5, Z_4)$	0.0000	0.0000	0.0000	0.0000	0.0000	0.0000	0.0000	0.0101	0.0000	0.0000
$h(Z_5, Z_6)$	0.0000	0.0000	0.0000	0.0000	0.0000	0.1675	0.0000	1.0000	0.0000	0.0000
$h(Z_6, Z_1)$	0.4413	0.0000	0.0000	0.1490	0.0000	0.0000	0.0000	0.0000	0.5003	0.2028
$h(Z_6, Z_2)$	0.0000	0.0000	0.0000	0.0000	0.0000	0.0000	0.0000	0.0000	0.0000	0.0000
$h(Z_6, Z_3)$	0.5817	0.0471	0.0000	0.2164	0.1357	0.1934	0.0251	0.0000	0.7600	0.4722
$h(Z_6, Z_4)$	0.4413	0.0000	0.0000	0.3591	0.0000	0.0000	0.0000	0.0000	0.4375	0.3580
$h(Z_6, Z_5)$	0.8203	0.0963	0.1204	0.3884	0.1978	0.0000	0.0570	0.0000	0.8682	0.8364

TABLE 98.16 The relative preference $\pi(Z_i, Z_{i'})$.

The value of relative preference					
$\pi(Z_1, Z_2) = 0.0557$	$\pi(Z_2, Z_1) = 0.2861$	$\pi(Z_3, Z_1) = 0.0279$	$\pi(Z_4, Z_1) = 0.2544$	$\pi(Z_5, Z_1) = 0.1372$	$\pi(Z_6, Z_1) = 0.1172$
$\pi(Z_1, Z_3) = 0.3878$	$\pi(Z_2, Z_3) = 0.5914$	$\pi(Z_3, Z_2) = 0.0011$	$\pi(Z_4, Z_2) = 0.2507$	$\pi(Z_5, Z_2) = 0.1166$	$\pi(Z_6, Z_2) = 0.0000$
$\pi(Z_1, Z_4) = 0.1014$	$\pi(Z_2, Z_4) = 0.3281$	$\pi(Z_3, Z_4) = 0.0103$	$\pi(Z_4, Z_3) = 0.5232$	$\pi(Z_5, Z_3) = 0.1381$	$\pi(Z_6, Z_1) = 0.2168$
$\pi(Z_1, Z_5) = 0.4595$	$\pi(Z_2, Z_5) = 0.6693$	$\pi(Z_3, Z_5) = 0.1005$	$\pi(Z_4, Z_5) = 0.5232$	$\pi(Z_5, Z_4) = 0.0015$	$\pi(Z_6, Z_1) = 0.1331$
$\pi(Z_1, Z_6) = 0.3046$	$\pi(Z_2, Z_4) = 0.4178$	$\pi(Z_3, Z_6) = 0.0443$	$\pi(Z_4, Z_6) = 0.5232$	$\pi(Z_5, Z_6) = 0.1634$	$\pi(Z_6, Z_1) = 0.2983$

Step 4. Obtain the preference index.
According to Eq. (98.3), the preference index $h_j(Z_i, Z_{i'})$ can be obtained. The results are shown in Table 98.15.
Step 5. Derive the relative preference.
Let the weight of 10 barriers be $w_1 = 0.1$, $w_2 = 0.15$, $w_3 = 0.125$, $w_4 = 0.07$, $w_5 = 0.12$, $w_6 = 0.08$, $w_7 = 0.05$, $w_8 = 0.15$, $w_9 = 0.105$, and $w_{10} = 0.05$. According to Eq. (98.4), the related preference can be derived. The relative preference $\pi(Z_i, Z_{i'})$ is shown in Table 98.16.
Step 6. Determine the outgoing and incoming flows.
The outgoing and incoming flows of each alternative can be derived by using Eqs. (98.5) and (98.6). The results are shown in Table 98.17.
Step 7. Ranking the alternatives.
Based on the results shown in Table 98.17, the net flow of each alternative can be obtained by referring to Eq. (98.7), and the ranking of each alternative can be determined. The results are shown in Table 98.18.

TABLE 98.17 The outgoing and incoming flows of each alternative.

	$\psi^+(Z_i)$	$\psi^-(Z_i)$
Z_1	0.2618	0.1646
Z_2	0.4585	0.0848
Z_3	0.0368	0.3715
Z_4	0.3957	0.1149
Z_5	0.1114	0.4009
Z_6	0.1531	0.2807

TABLE 98.18 The net flow and ranking of each alternative.

	Z_1	Z_2	Z_3	Z_4	Z_5	Z_6
$\psi(Z_i)$	0.0972	0.3737	-0.3347	0.2808	-0.2895	-0.1276
Ranking	3	1	6	2	5	4

According to the results shown in Table 98.18, food manufacturer (Z_2) performed best in eliminating the barrier of implementing resilience in FSC.

98.6 Comparative analysis

This section presents a comparative analysis to evaluate the efficiency and effectiveness of the PROMETHEE-II method. For this purpose, several classical MADM methods are employed for comparison, including compromise ranking of alternatives from distance to ideal solution (CRADIS), technique for order preference by similarity to ideal solution (TOPSIS), WASPAS, and simple additive weighting (SAW). The results derived from these methods are summarized in Table 98.19, while the corresponding ranking outcomes are visually illustrated in Fig. 98.3.

According to Table 98.19 and Fig. 98.3, we can observe that the proposed method has high consistency with other MADM methods. The ranking results of alternatives determined by the PROMETHEE-II method are the same as those determined by CRADIS, TOPSIS, and SAW method. This indicates that the proposed method is highly homogeneous with the other three methods. However, the ranking of alternatives obtained by TOPSIS method is $Z_1 \succ Z_3 \succ Z_5 \succ Z_4 \succ Z_2 \succ Z_6$. This ranking order has a little different with our method. This is because the calculation steps and principles of the two methods are different. Through the comparative analysis, this demonstrates our method is reliable and effective to evaluate alternatives.

First, CRADIS is a typical utility value-based MADM technique that ranks alternatives by measuring their distances from the positive and negative ideal solutions. In contrast, PROMETHEE-II is an outranking-based MADM method that determines the ranking of alternatives through pairwise comparisons. Consequently, PROMETHEE-II can better capture complex preference structures and provide more detailed ranking information, whereas CRADIS lacks this capability.

Second, TOPSIS and SAW represent relatively simplified evaluation models, as they fail to incorporate preference uncertainty and rely on linear compensation among criteria. Compared with these two methods, PROMETHEE-II, through its preference function and net flow calculation, can more flexibly handle nonlinear and intricate preference relationships, thereby offering a more realistic representation of decision-makers' judgments.

Lastly, in facilitating the modeling of complex decision-maker preferences, PROMETHEE-II explicitly incorporates preference information through the use of preference functions. This feature allows decision-makers to express their

TABLE 98.19 The results obtained by different methods.

	CRADIS method		TOPSIS method		WASPAS method		SAW method		The proposed method
	$CR(r_i)$	Ranking	$TO(r_i)$	Ranking	$WP(r_i)$	Ranking	$SAW(r_i)$	Ranking	Ranking
Z_1	0.6116	3	0.6678	1	0.4510	3	0.5012	3	3
Z_2	1.0000	1	0.1597	5	0.6900	1	0.7316	1	1
Z_3	0.2528	6	0.5729	2	0.0706	6	0.1412	6	6
Z_4	0.8352	2	0.2229	4	0.5668	2	0.6541	2	2
Z_5	0.2857	5	0.4112	3	0.0894	5	0.1789	5	5

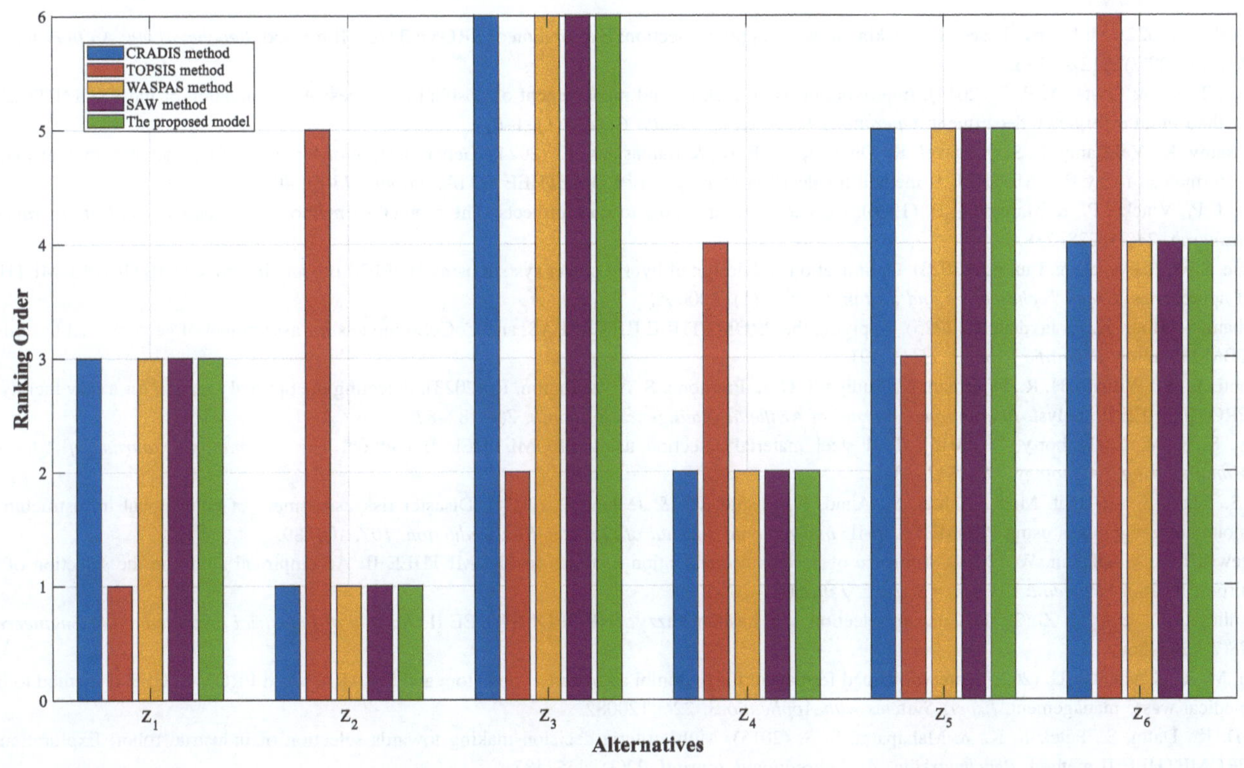

FIGURE 98.3 The ranking results of alternatives by different methods.

subjective judgments directly in the evaluation process, which enhances the interpretability of results. By contrast, WASPAS does not employ explicit preference modeling and instead relies solely on weighted aggregation. While WASPAS can partially address interactions among criteria through weighting, it lacks PROMETHEE-II's ability to reveal and analyze intercriteria relationships via outranking flows.

Overall, while PROMETHEE-II often yields rankings consistent with those generated by other classical MADM methods, it offers greater flexibility, robustness, and analytical depth through its distinctive preference functions and net flow analysis. Particularly in scenarios involving heterogeneous data or where decision-maker preferences play a crucial role, PROMETHEE-II demonstrates clear methodological superiority. This comparison thus underscores the effectiveness and practical applicability of PROMETHEE-II as a comprehensive decision-making tool.

98.7 Conclusions

In this chapter, the PROMETHEE-II method has been introduced as a powerful tool to assist decision-makers in ranking and selecting among multiple alternatives. First, the background and fundamental characteristics of the PROMETHEE-II method were presented in detail. Second, an extensive literature review was conducted to summarize the major extensions of PROMETHEE-II and its wide-ranging applications across various domains. Third, a step-by-step description of the PROMETHEE-II procedure was provided to clarify its computational process. Subsequently, a simple numerical example on smartphone recommendation was employed to demonstrate the basic application and interpret the key equations of the method. Following this, a more complex case study related to RSC implementation was developed to showcase the method's capability in addressing intricate MADM problems. In this context, a TSF-PROMETHEE-II approach was proposed to evaluate the performance of different participants in overcoming obstacles during RSC implementation. Finally, a comparative analysis was carried out to emphasize the strengths and limitations of the PROMETHEE-II method, confirming its flexibility, robustness, and practical value in real-world decision-making scenarios.

References

Agrawal, N. (2022). Multi-criteria decision-making toward supplier selection: Exploration of PROMETHEE II method. *Benchmarking: An International Journal, 29*(7), 2122–2146.

Amaral, T. M., & Costa, A. P. C. (2014). Improving decision-making and management of hospital resources: An application of the PROMETHEE II method in an emergency department. *Operations Research for Health Care, 3*(1), 1–6.

Aruchsamy, R., Velusamy, I., Sanmugavel, K., Dhandapani, P. B., & Ramasamy, K. (2024). Generalization of fermatean fuzzy set and implementation of fermatean fuzzy PROMETHEE II method for decision making via PROMETHEE GAIA. *Axioms, 13*(6), 408.

Brans, J. P., Vincke, P., & Mareschal, B. (1986). How to select and how to rank projects: The promethee method. *European Journal of Operational Research, 24*(2), 228–238.

Chisale, S. W., Eliya, S., & Taulo, J. (2023). Optimization and design of hybrid power system using HOMER pro and integrated CRITIC-PROMETHEE II approaches. *Green Technologies and Sustainability, 1*(1), 100005.

Ghorbani, S., Bour, K., & Javdan, R. (2025). Applying the PROMETHEE II, WASPAS, and CoCoSo models for assessment of geotechnical hazards in TBM tunneling. *Scientific Reports, 15*(1), 491.

Harjanti, T. W., Widjaja, H. R., Nofirman, N., Sudipa, I. G. I., Pramono, S. A., & Rahim, R. (2023). Selecting the optimal location for a new facility: A PROMETHEE II analyst. *International Journal of Artificial Intelligence Research, 7*(1), 82–87.

Maity, S. R., & Chakraborty, S. (2015). Tool steel material selection using PROMETHEE II method. *The International Journal of Advanced Manufacturing Technology, 78*, 1537–1547.

Mir, S., Shah, S. A., Bhat, M. S., Akhter, S., Ahad, F., Rashid, H., & Jeelani, P. (2024). Disaster risk assessment of educational infrastructure in mountain geographies using PROMETHEE-II. *International Journal of Disaster Risk Reduction, 107*, 104489.

Palczewski, K., & Sałabun, W. (2019). Influence of various normalization methods in PROMETHEE II: An empirical study on the selection of the airport location. *Procedia Computer Science, 159*, 2051–2060.

Samanlioglu, F., & Ayağ, Z. (2021). Concept selection with hesitant fuzzy ANP-PROMETHEE II. *Journal of Industrial and Production Engineering, 38*(7), 547–560.

Seikh, M. R., & Mandal, U. (2023). Interval-valued fermatean fuzzy dombi aggregation operators and SWARA based PROMETHEE II method to bio-medical waste management. *Expert Systems with Applications, 226*, 120082.

Sen, D. K., Datta, S., Patel, S. K., & Mahapatra, S. S. (2015). Multi-criteria decision making towards selection of industrial robot: Exploration of PROMETHEE II method. *Benchmarking: An International Journal, 22*(3), 465–487.

Sotiropoulou, K. F., Vavatsikos, A. P., & Botsaris, P. N. (2024). A hybrid AHP-PROMETHEE II onshore wind farms multicriteria suitability analysis using kNN and SVM regression models in northeastern Greece. *Renewable Energy, 221*, 119795.

Tang, J., Liu, X., & Wang, W. (2025). An integrated interval type-2 fuzzy PROMETHEE-II decision model for the selection of medical waste treatment techniques. *International Journal of Information Technology & Decision Making, 24*(04), 1035–1065.

Tian, C., Peng, J., Zhang, W., Zhang, S., & Wang, J. (2020). Tourism environmental impact assessment based on improved AHP and picture fuzzy PROMETHEE II methods. *Technological and Economic Development of Economy, 26*(2), 355–378.

Tong, L., Pu, Z., Chen, K., & Yi, J. (2020). Sustainable maintenance supplier performance evaluation based on an extend fuzzy PROMETHEE II approach in petrochemical industry. *Journal of Cleaner Production, 273*, 122771.

Torbacki, W. (2021). A hybrid MCDM model combining DANP and PROMETHEE II methods for the assessment of cybersecurity in industry 4.0. *Sustainability, 13*(16), 8833.

Wang, W., Wang, Y., Chen, Y., Deveci, M., Kadry, S., & Pedrycz, W. (2024). Analyzing the barriers to resilience supply chain adoption in the food industry using hybrid interval-valued fermatean fuzzy PROMETHEE-II model. *Journal of Industrial Information Integration, 40*, 100614.

Wątróbski, J. (2023). Temporal PROMETHEE II—New multi-criteria approach to sustainable management of alternative fuels consumption. *Journal of Cleaner Production, 413*, 137445.

Yu, Y., Yang, J., & Wu, S. (2023). A novel FMEA approach for submarine pipeline risk analysis based on IVIFRN and ExpTODIM-PROMETHEE-II. *Applied Soft Computing, 136*, 110065.

Ziemba, P. (2022). Energy security assessment based on a new dynamic multi-criteria decision-making framework. *Energies, 15*(24), 9356.

Chapter 99

ORESTE: Organization Rangement et synthese de ronnees relationnelles for multi-attribute decision-making

Ibrahim Yilmaz and Babek Erdebilli
Department of Industrial Engineering, Ankara Yldrm Beyazt University, Ankara, Turkey

99.1 Introduction

Multi-criteria decision-making (MCDM) techniques are frequently employed to address challenging selection and assessment issues. When there are multiple criteria to take into account, they provide decision-makers with an organized and methodical way to compare various options (Ayyildiz & Taskin Gumus, 2020; Haseli & Sheikh, 2022). The primary objective of the majority of conventional MCDM approaches is to ascertain the weight of each criterion and then use these weights to assess the alternatives in order to produce an objective ranking or make a final decision. These techniques aid in bringing consistency and clarity to the decision-making process, particularly when there are numerous criteria and some of them contradict one another. However, a well-known drawback of traditional MCDM approaches is that they fail to directly consider the behavioral aspect of actual decision-making. Human judgments are rarely entirely objective in real life. They are impacted by various responses to gains and losses, cognitive biases, and individual attitudes toward risk. For instance, a decision-maker may exhibit risk-seeking behavior in one situation but risk-averse behavior in another, or they may be more affected by a loss than by a comparable gain. Although behavioral economics has a wealth of evidence supporting these kinds of patterns, standard MCDM approaches typically do not explicitly model them. The decision model and the actual decision-making process may therefore diverge.

99.2 Literature review

The MCDM literature includes a wide range of methods, each with its own mathematical structure, data needs, and typical areas of application. Cardinal methods such as the analytic hierarchy process (AHP), analytic network process (ANP), technique for order preference by similarity to ideal solution (TOPSIS), and VIseKriterijumska Optimizacija I Kompromisno Resenje (VIKOR) work with numerical performance values and often rely on normalization and distance-based calculations. Outranking methods such as elimination and choice translating reality and preference ranking organization method for enrichment evaluation (PROMETHEE) allow decision-makers to express partial preferences and to handle situations where some alternatives cannot be clearly compared with others. This feature is useful when trade-offs between criteria are complex and not all options can be ranked in a strict order.

On the other hand, ordinal approaches such as organization Rangement et synthese de ronnees relationnelles for multi-attribute decision-making (ORESTE) do not require precise numerical scores; instead, they rely solely on the decision-makers rankings. Because of this, they work well in situations where quantitative data is insufficient or untrustworthy, or where experts are more at ease expressing their opinions in terms of better or worse than exact numbers. First put forth by Roubens in 1982, the ORESTE method is a ranking-based MCDM technique created especially to effectively handle ordinal data. Its comparatively straightforward process and minimal data requirements are its key advantages. The decision-maker in ORESTE offers two primary kinds of rankings: (i) a performance ranking of the alternatives for each criterion and (ii) a ranking of the criteria based on their relative importance.

Encyclopedia of Multi-Attribute Decision-Making (MADM). DOI: https://doi.org/10.1016/B978-0-443-33275-3.00050-6

These ordinal inputs are then converted into an overall preference order. This is achieved by calculating Besson distances, which indicate how far the rank of each alternative is from an ideal rank. The distances are then combined with the weights of the criteria to obtain a global dissimilarity index for each alternative. Finally, the alternatives are sorted from the smallest to the largest dissimilarity index, and this ordering gives the final ORESTE ranking.

ORESTE offers several practical advantages. It does not require detailed numerical performance data, which can be difficult, costly, or even impossible to collect in many real-world settings. It also reduces the mental effort for decision-makers by asking them to compare and rank options instead of assigning exact scores. In addition, the steps of the method are relatively easy to follow and to explain to nontechnical stakeholders, which can help to build confidence in the decision-making process and in the resulting ranking. There are, however, some important limitations. Since ORESTE works only with ordinal data, it cannot reflect how large or small the differences between alternatives actually are; a small gap in performance and a very large gap are treated in the same way in the ranking. In addition, the quality and reliability of the final results depend strongly on how consistent the decision-makers are when they provide their rankings.

The ORESTE method, therefore, uses ordinal information: it ranks the criteria by importance, and the alternatives by performance, and in this way offers a practical solution when precise numerical evaluations are not available. It builds global preference structures from rankings rather than from exact values, which helps to reduce redundancy, limit inconsistencies in the data, and simplify the overall decision process. The method is relatively easy to learn and apply, and it does not require advanced technical skills, which makes it accessible in many different decision-making settings (Chatterjee & Chakraborty, 2012; De Leeneer & Pastijn, 2002). Supplier selection is one of the most common fields where MCDM methods are used in industrial engineering. Choosing suitable suppliers has a direct impact on product quality, cost efficiency, delivery reliability, and the long-term competitiveness of a firm. Popular methods for supplier selection include AHP, TOPSIS, PROMETHEE, VIKOR, and various integrated approaches that combine MCDM with fuzzy logic in order to deal with uncertainty. In these approaches, suppliers are usually evaluated according to criteria such as cost, quality, delivery performance, flexibility, technological capability, and environmental performance. These techniques are powerful, but they typically require numerical performance scores, which may not be available or reliable, especially when the suppliers are new, or when the criteria concern qualitative aspects such as trust, cooperation, or relationship quality. In such situations, ORESTE becomes a strong alternative. Because it is rank-based, it is especially suitable in supplier selection problems where decision-makers can clearly compare suppliers with each other but cannot provide precise numbers. For instance, a procurement team may know that Supplier A is better than Supplier B in terms of delivery reliability, but may not be able to say how much better in percentage terms. ORESTE can work with this kind of qualitative comparison and still produce a mathematically sound ranking of suppliers. In addition, since ORESTE requires only relative rankings, it can be applied quickly and with limited data collection effort, which makes it attractive in fast-moving procurement environments. In summary, ORESTE fills a useful niche within the broader family of MCDM methods. For supplier selection problems where numerical data are missing or uncertain, expert opinions play a major role, and decisions must be made quickly, ORESTE offers a structured, transparent, and efficient decision-support tool. In the next parts of this chapter, the mathematical formulation of the ORESTE method will be explained, followed by a detailed supplier selection case study that shows how the method can be applied in an industrial context.

The ORESTE method treats decision problems in two main stages. In the first stage (ORESTE I), a complete preliminary ranking of the alternatives is obtained by considering both their performance on the criteria and the relative importance order of those criteria. In the second stage (ORESTE II), this initial ranking is examined in more detail: contradictions and indifferences are analyzed, and as a result, a partial preranking of the alternatives is produced (Ana et al., 2009). This chapter demonstrates the usefulness of the ORESTE approach through a numerical example, with a particular focus on manufacturing settings where decision support systems depend strongly on systematic supplier evaluation.

99.3 Methodology

Roubens (1982) first presented the ORESTE method, a qualitative MCDM technique that employs ordinal data rather than precise numerical values. To put it simply, rankings are used instead of exact scores. ORESTEs primary benefit is that it can still be applied in situations where trustworthy numerical data are unavailable. In these situations, experts are only able to express which criterion or alternative they believe to be superior or more significant without providing precise figures. As a result, ORESTE is a good fit for a variety of industrial decision-making tasks, such as selecting a supplier, deciding where to locate a facility, or assessing new technologies. Expert opinions in these circumstances are frequently subjective and challenging to convert into exact numerical values. The ORESTE methods fundamental steps can be summed up as

Step 1. Problem definition and identification of alternatives and criteria

Clearly defining the decision problem is the first step in the process. At this point, the decision-maker determines the set of evaluation criteria and the set of alternatives. Let C = {C1, C2,, Cn} be the set of n criteria and A = {A1, A2,, Am} be the set of m alternatives. Before any assessment starts, this first step makes sure that the problems scope and the analysiss goals are clearly defined.

Step 2. Ordinal ranking of criteria by importance

Next, the person making the decision ranks the criteria based on how important they think they are. The most important criterion gets a rank of 1, and the least important one gets a rank of *n*. These simple ordinal ranks are then converted into numerical weights. For this purpose, the rank-sum weighting method is often used, as given in Eq. (99.1), so that more important criteria receive higher weights in the subsequent steps of the ORESTE procedure.

$$wk = n - rk + 1j = 1nn - rj + 1 \quad (99.1)$$

In Eq. (99.1), *rk* is the ordinal rank of criterion *Ck*, and *wk* is the normalized weight assigned to that criterion. The denominator in the formula acts as a scaling factor so that the sum of all weights is equal to 1. In this way, the transformation keeps the original ranking information but also produces numerical weights that can be used to combine and compare criteria in a common scale.

Step 3. Ordinal ranking of alternatives for each criterion

In the next step, the alternatives are ranked separately for each criterion *Ck*. For every criterion, the decision-maker orders the alternatives from best (rank 1) to worst (rank *m*), and these rankings form an ordinal performance matrix *R* = [*rik*]. Here, *rik* denotes the position of alternative *Ai* under criterion *Ck* in the preference ordering of the decision-maker.

Step 4. Determination of the ideal rank and calculation of Besson distances

The ORESTE method then identifies the ideal rank as *r**=1, which corresponds to the most preferred position under any criterion. The deviation of each alternative from this ideal situation is measured by means of the Besson distance, given in Eq. (99.2). This distance shows how far the observed rank of an alternative is from the best possible rank for a given criterion.

$$dik = rik - r^* \quad (99.2)$$

Step 5. Weighted distance calculation

In the following step, the Besson distances are adjusted according to the importance of each criterion. The weighted Besson distance *Dik* is obtained by multiplying the distance *dik* by the weight *wk* of criterion *Ck*, as shown in Eq. (99.3).

$$Dik = wk \cdot dik \quad (99.3)$$

This weighted distance reflects both the deviation from the ideal ranking and the relative significance of the criterion in the overall evaluation.

This weighted distance captures both how far the alternative is from the ideal rank and how important that criterion is in the overall evaluation.

Step 6. Aggregation of weighted distances

To obtain a single composite measure of dissimilarity for each alternative, the weighted distances *Dik* are summed over all criteria. This aggregation leads to the global dissimilarity index for alternative *Ai*, as defined in Eq. (99.4).

$$Di = \Sigma k = 1nwk \cdot rik - 1 \quad (99.4)$$

A smaller value of D_i indicates that the alternative is closer to the ideal profile. The final ranking of alternatives is obtained by ordering them in ascending D_i values.

99.4 Numerical example

99.4.1 Supplier selection using the organization, rangement et synth de r relationnelles method

Supply chain management (SCM) is very important for companies that want to stay competitive, because it has a direct effect on market performance by lowering production costs and shortening production times. To focus on their core activities, many firms buy raw materials and components from external suppliers. This makes supplier selection a critical decision, and MCDM approaches play an important role in this process, since a poor choice of supplier can lead to serious operational and financial problems (Erdebilli et al., 2023). Since the 1980s, the main aim of SCM has been to coordinate the flow of materials and information from suppliers to end users in an efficient way, and to create value through better process integration. Decision-making is at the center of SCM, and MCDM methods help managers make informed and transparent choices by handling conflicts and trade-offs, especially in areas such as inventory management and supplier selection (Erdebilli & Scakyz, 2024; Pinar et al., 2021; Rouyendegh et al., 2014).

For handling such complicated decisions, MCDM techniques offer an organized and transparent framework. They enable decision-makers to assess options more thoroughly by accounting for both quantitative and qualitative factors. Among these techniques, the ORESTE approach is especially well-suited for supplier selection issues where decision-makers prefer to work with ordinal (rank-based) data or where exact numerical performance data are unavailable. ORESTEs reliance on relative rankings makes it compatible with expert-based evaluations and lessens the mental strain of assigning precise performance scores.

Step 1. Problem definition and identification of alternatives and criteria

In this case study, five potential suppliers, denoted as T_1, T_2, T_3, T_4, and T_5, are evaluated with respect to five decision criteria: cost (C), quality (C), delivery reliability (C), flexibility (C), and sustainability (C).

Step 2. Ordinal ranking of criteria importance

The decision-maker ranked the criteria in order of importance as follows: quality (C) rank 1, delivery reliability (C) rank 2, cost (C) rank 3, sustainability (C) rank 4, and flexibility (C) rank 5. These ordinal ranks were converted into weights using the rank-sum method from Eq. (99.1). Table 99.1 presents the priority ranks, calculated scores, and normalized weights for each criterion.

Step 3. Ordinal ranking of alternatives for each criterion

For each criterion *Ck*, the suppliers were ranked from best (1) to worst (5) based on expert judgment. The resulting ordinal performance matrix R = [*rik*] is shown in Table 99.2.

Step 4. Determination of the ideal rank and calculation of Besson distances

Using Eq. (99.2), the deviation of each suppliers rank from the ideal rank $r^*= 1$ was calculated. The absolute differences, representing the Besson distances, are shown in Table 99.3.

Step 5. Weighted distance calculation

Each Besson distance was multiplied by the corresponding criterion weight (Eq. (99.3)), resulting in the weighted distance matrix shown in Table 99.4.

TABLE 99.1 The priority ranks, calculated scores, and normalized weights for each criterion.

Criterion	Priority rank	Score	Weight
Cost (C_1)	3	3.0	0.200
Quality (C_2)	1	5.0	0.333
Delivery reliability (C_3)	2	4.0	0.267
Flexibility (C_4)	5	1.0	0.067
Sustainability (C_5)	4	2.0	0.133

TABLE 99.2 Ordinal performance matrix R.

Supplier	Cost (C_1)	Quality (C_2)	Delivery reliability (C_3)	Flexibility (C_4)	Sustainability (C_5)
*T*1	1	3	2	4	3
*T*2	3	1	1	2	2
*T*3	2	2	3	1	1
*T*4	4	4	4	3	4
*T*5	5	5	5	5	5

TABLE 99.3 Besson distances *dik*.

Supplier	Cost (C_1)	Quality (C_2)	Delivery reliability (C_3)	Flexibility (C_4)	Sustainability (C_5)
*T*1	0	2	1	3	2
*T*2	2	0	0	1	1
*T*3	1	1	2	0	0
*T*4	3	3	3	2	3
*T*5	4	4	4	4	4

TABLE 99.4 Weighted distances and global dissimilarity index D_i.

Supplier	Cost (C_1)	Quality (C_2)	Delivery reliability (C_3)	Flexibility (C_4)	Sustainability (C_5)	Index
*T*1	0.0000	0.6667	0.2667	0.2000	0.2667	1.4000
*T*2	0.4000	0.0000	0.0000	0.0667	0.1333	0.6000
*T*3	0.2000	0.3333	0.5333	0.0000	0.0000	1.0667
*T*4	0.6000	1.0000	0.8000	0.1333	0.4000	2.9334
*T*5	0.8000	1.3333	1.0667	0.2667	0.5333	4.0000

TABLE 99.5 Final supplier ranking.

Index	Total weighted distance *Di*	Final rank
T2	0.6000	1
T3	1.0667	2
T1	1.4000	3
T4	2.9333	4
T5	4.0000	5

Step 6. Aggregation of weighted distances

The weighted distances were summed across all criteria using Eq. (99.4) to obtain the global dissimilarity index D_i for each supplier. The results are presented in Table 99.4 along with the aggregated D_{ic} values.

Step 7. Final ranking

Suppliers were ranked in ascending order of D_i values, with lower values indicating alternatives closer to the ideal ranking profile. The final ranking is shown in Table 99.5.

Supplier T2 achieved the best ranking across multiple high-priority criteria, particularly quality (C) and delivery reliability (C), which were ranked as the two most important factors by the decision-maker. This strong performance in the most heavily weighted criteria drove its lowest D_i value and 1st place ranking. Supplier T3 ranked first in flexibility (C) and sustainability (C), but these criteria had lower weights compared to quality and delivery reliability. Nevertheless, solid performance in cost and competitive scores in other areas placed T3 in second position overall. Supplier T1 had the best score in cost (C) but performed less strongly in the higher-priority quality and delivery reliability criteria, resulting in a middle ranking. This illustrates how ORESTE appropriately balances all criteria rather than overvaluing a single strong attribute. Supplier T4 and T5 had consistently lower ranks across most criteria, with T5 in particular ranking last in all but one category. These consistently poor rankings resulted in the highest D_i values and lowest overall positions in the final ranking.

99.5 Conclusion

The application of the ORESTE method to the supplier selection problem produced a global dissimilarity index (D_i) for each supplier, which measures how far each alternatives ranking is from the ideal ranking profile across all criteria. A lower value means that a supplier consistently outperforms other suppliers and is closer to the ideal ranking across all criteria. On the other hand, a higher value indicates that a supplier performs comparatively worse and is farther from the ideal in a number of criteria. From the results, supplier achieved the best ranking across multiple high-priority criteria, particularly quality (C) and delivery reliability (C), which were ranked as the two most important factors by the decision-maker. This strong performance in the most heavily weighted criteria drove its lowest value and first-place ranking. Supplier ranked first in flexibility (C) and sustainability (C), but these criteria had lower weights compared to quality and delivery reliability. Nevertheless, solid performance in cost and competitive scores in other areas placed it in second position overall. The supplier had the best score in cost (C) but performed less strongly in the higher-priority quality and delivery reliability criteria, resulting in a middle ranking. This illustrates how ORESTE appropriately balances all criteria rather than overvaluing a single strong attribute. Suppliers and had consistently lower ranks across most criteria, with T5 in particular ranking last in all but one category. These consistently poor rankings resulted in the highest values and lowest overall positions in the final ranking. From a strategic perspective, if the companys purchasing strategy focuses mainly on quality and delivery reliability, Supplier T is the most suitable option. If flexibility and sustainability are expected to become more important in the near future, Supplier T may be a more attractive choice, because it shows competitive performance on most criteria. Supplier T is still a reasonable option in cost-focused situations, but it would need to improve its performance on nonprice criteria to become the best alternative. Suppliers T and T would need major improvements in several areas to be truly competitive; in their current state, they are better candidates for backup roles or for very specific, niche needs.

The ORESTE method can be developed in a number of ways in the future. First, a more accurate representation of uncertainty and ambiguity in expert opinions may be possible with hybrid models that incorporate ORESTE with fuzzy logic or interval-based techniques. Second, a better understanding of ORESTEs advantages and disadvantages may come from comparative studies that evaluate it against other MCDM techniques in various application domains, such as TOPSIS, VIKOR, and PROMETHEE. Third, by automatically gathering and analyzing ordinal data from numerous users, the application of ORESTE in digital procurement platforms could be investigated. Lastly, ORESTE would become even more applicable and helpful for contemporary industrial engineering practice if it were modified to support real-time decisions in unstable environments, like global supply chains.

References

Ana, E., Bauwens, W., & Broers, O. (2009). Quantifying uncertainty using robustness analysis in the application of ORESTE to sewer rehabilitation projects prioritizationBrussels case study. *Journal of Multi-Criteria Decision Analysis, 16*, 111–124.

Ayyildiz, E., & Taskin Gumus, A. (2020). A novel spherical fuzzy AHP-integrated spherical WASPAS methodology for petrol station location selection problem: A real case study for stanbul. *Environmental Science and Pollution Research*. https://doi.org/10.1007/s11356-020-09640-0.

Chatterjee, P., & Chakraborty, S. (2012). Material selection using preferential ranking methods. *Materials & Design, 35*, 384–393.

De Leeneer, I., & Pastijn, H. (2002). Decision aiding: Selecting land mine detection strategies by means of outranking MCDM techniques. *European Journal of Operational Research, 139*, 327–338.

Erdebilli, B., & Scakyz, . (2024). An integrated Q-rung orthopair fuzzy (Q-ROF) for the selection of supply-chain management. *Sustainability, 16*, 4901. https://doi.org/10.3390/su16124901.

Erdebilli, B., Yilmaz, ., Aksoy, T., Hacoglu, U., Yksel, S., & Diner, H. (2023). An interval-valued pythagorean fuzzy AHP and COPRAS hybrid methods for the supplier selection problem. *International Journal of Computational Intelligence Systems, 16*, 124.

Haseli, G., & Sheikh, R. (2022). Base criterion method (BCM). In *Multiple criteria decision making: Techniques, analysis and applications*. Singapore: Springer Nature Singapore, 17–38.

Pinar, A., Rouyendegh, B. D., & Ozdemir, Y. S. (2021). Q-rung orthopair fuzzy TOPSIS method for green supplier selection problem. *Sustainability, 13*, 985.

Roubens, J. P. (1982). Preference relations on actions and criteria in multicriteria decision making. *European Journal of Operational Research, 10*(1), 51–55.

Rouyendegh, B. D., Ba, U., & Erkan, T. E. (2014). Sector selection for ERP implementation to achieve most impact on supply chain performance by using AHP-TOPSIS hybrid method. *Tehnicki Vjesnik-Technical Gazette*.

Further reading

Alinezhad, A., & Khalili, J. (2019). *New methods and applications in multiple attribute decision making (MADM)*. Cham: Springer, 199–203 Vol. 277.

Besson, J., et al. (1977). *Analyse et traitement des donnes relationnelles*. Paris: Masson.

Delhaye, C., Teghem, J., & Kunsch, P. (1991). Application of the ORESTE method to a nuclear waste management. *International Journal of Production Economics, 24*(1-2), 29–39.

Figueira, J., Greco, S., & Ehrgott, M. (2005). *Multiple criteria decision analysis: state of the art surveys*. Springer.

Givescu, O. (2007). The ORESTE s method in the multicriteria s decision process for the management of tourism field. *Faculty of Management, Academy of Economic Studies, Journal Economia Management, 10*(1), 37–51.

Kaya, T., & Kahraman, C. (2011). Fuzzy ORESTE approach for military personnel selection. *Expert Systems with Applications, 38*(8), 9307–9313.

Liu, Z., Wang, X., Wang, W., Wang, D., & Liu, P. (2022). An integrated TOPSISORESTE-based decision-making framework for new energy investment assessment with cloud model. *Computational and Applied Mathematics, 41*(1), 42.

Verme, B. K., & Toplama, S. (2022). Oreste method In Fuzzy decision-making problems and a solution proposal. *Journal of Optimization & Decision Making, 1*(2), 123–133.

Voogd, H. (1983). *Multicriteria evaluation for urban and regional planning*. London: Pion Ltd.

Further reading

Alinezhad, A., & Khalili, J. (2019). *New methods and applications in multiple attribute decision making (MADM)*. Cham: Springer, 199–203. Vol. 277.

[illegible], L. et al. (1977). [illegible] *Traitement des données relationnelles*. Paris: Masson.

Delhaye, C., Teghem, J., & Kunsch, P. (1991). Application of the ORESTE method to a nuclear waste management problem. *International Journal of Production Economics*, 24(1-2), 29-39.

Figueira, J., Greco, S., & Ehrgott, M. (2005). *Multiple criteria decision analysis: State of the art surveys*. Springer.

[illegible], G. (2007). The ORESTE method in the multicriteria's decision process for the measurement of tourism [illegible]. [illegible] *Journal Economic Management*, 10(1), 57-[illegible].

Kaya, T., & Kahraman, C. (2011). Fuzzy ORESTE approach for [illegible] personnel selection. *Expert Systems with Applications*, 38(8), 9207-9214.

Liao, Z., Wang, X., Wang, W., Wang, D., & Liu, P. (2022). An integrated TOPSIS-ORESTE-based decision-making framework for new energy investment assessment with cloud model. *Computational and Applied Mathematics*, 41(1), 42.

[illegible], B. K., & Fontana, S. (2022). Oreste method in fuzzy decision-making problems and extension proposal. *Journal of Operations & [illegible]*, 1(1), 124-131.

Voogd, H. (1983). *Multicriteria evaluation for urban and regional planning*. London: Pion Ltd.

Chapter 100

GLDS: Gained and lost dominance score for multi-attribute decision-making

Xingli Wu and Huchang Liao
Business School, Sichuan University, Chengdu, Sichuan Province, P.R. China

100.1 Introduction

Multiple attribute decision-making (MADM) problems represent a class of complex decision-making challenges, with the core research question being how to select, rank, or sort alternatives amidst conflicting attributes (Greco et al., 2025). The theoretical foundation of this field lies in the effective aggregation of attribute performance into comprehensive alternative evaluations. Mainstream MADM methods can be categorized into three types (Wu & Liao, 2023a): utility/value-based methods, decision rule-based methods, and outranking methods. Utility/value-based methods quantify decision-makers' preferences across multiple attributes through utility functions, ultimately aggregating them into an overall utility for decision support (Wallenius et al., 2008). Decision rule-based methods utilize decision rules, like rough set theory, to build decision models (Greco et al., 2001). Outranking methods establish preference (P), indifference (I), and incomparability (R) relations through pairwise comparisons (Govindan & Jepsen, 2016), offering two key advantages: they assess relative superiority without relying on absolute utilities, addressing whether one alternative is fundamentally better than another, and can identify dilemma scenarios where two alternatives exhibit similar overall performance but differ greatly in individual attributes.

There are two classical outranking methods: (1) The elimination and choice expressing the reality (ELECTRE) (elimination et choix traduisant larealité in French) family, a pioneering outranking method introduced by Roy (1968). This family includes several versions (I-IV and Tri), designed for different decision-making contexts such as selection, ranking, and sorting. ELECTRE works by establishing concordance and discordance sets to filter alternatives. While it is effective at identifying optimal alternatives, it produces partial orders that prevent full ranking, can result in nontransitive preference relations, and requires expert-dependent parameter settings for critical thresholds. (2) The preference ranking organization method for enrichment evaluations (PROMETHEE) family, introduced by Brans and Vincke (1985), uses preference functions to combine positive and negative outranking flows. Despite its ease of use and wide applicability, PROMETHEE requires complete rankings, which can hide the inherent incomparability among alternatives. Additionally, a key point in MADM practice is that decision-makers have different risk tolerance attitudes to poor attribute performance (Wu & Liao, 2023b). They often want both exceptional overall performance and the avoidance of severely weak attributes in their choices. However, traditional outranking methods include a compensation mechanism that allows full trade-offs among attributes, which can lead to selecting an alternative with poor performance in critical areas. Such an alternative does not meet the needs of risk-averse decision-makers.

To address these challenges, Wu and Liao (2019, 2022) proposed an outranking method called the gained and lost dominance score (GLDS) method. It consists of two phases: the basic ranking phase and the conflict analysis phase. The basic ranking phase determines dominance relations through pairwise comparisons of alternatives, allowing for an initial ranking. Its strengths include considering two key aspects simultaneously: introducing an attribute compensation mechanism to assess the overall performance of alternatives and quantifying each alternative's performance on its worst attribute to identify weaknesses. Implementing this phase involves normalizing attribute values, calculating partial dominance scores of one alternative over another across attributes, deriving global dominance scores through attribute aggregation, and summing these scores to get each alternative's gained dominance score. At the same time, the dominance scores of other alternatives over the target one are evaluated, with the highest score taken as the lost dominance score.

Encyclopedia of Multi-Attribute Decision-Making (MADM). DOI: https://doi.org/10.1016/B978-0-443-33275-3.00073-7

These are combined to produce a collective score used for ranking. The conflict analysis phase identifies the preference, indifference, and incomparability (PIR) relations through pairwise comparisons. A preference relation is established when one alternative's collective score significantly exceeds another's; an indifference relation occurs when their collective scores and attribute performances are comparable; and an incomparability relation arises when their collective scores are close but differ substantially in at least one attribute. The GLDS method offers notable advantages. The basic ranking phase is efficient and suitable for large-scale MADM problems; the conflict analysis phase accurately identifies PIR relations; threshold settings provide clear practical guidance, reducing subjective bias; explicitly recognizing incomparability avoids risks associated with forced ranking; and it supports decision-makers' tendency to be risk-averse.

This chapter further improves the GLDS framework by simplifying computation and increasing practical convenience.

The rest of this chapter is organized as follows: Section 100.2 reviews the extensions and applications of the GLDS method. Section 100.3 introduces the framework of the GLDS method in a generalized context with precise attribute values. Sections 100.4 and 100.5 present a numerical example, respectively. Finally, Section 100.6 summarizes the conclusions.

100.2 Literature review

The GLDS method, as an outranking approach, develops through three stages: theoretical foundation, method extension, and application. In the theoretical foundation stage, Wu and Liao (2019) proposed the basic framework of GLDS, systematically calculating the gained and lost dominance scores of alternatives through pairwise comparisons to rank them. Subsequently, Wu and Liao (2022) refined the method by adding a conflict analysis framework, accurately identifying PIR relations between alternatives, marking the establishment of GLDS's comprehensive theoretical system.

In the extension phase, scholars systematically expanded the GLDS method across three dimensions. In behavioral decision-making, Liao, Liao et al. (2020) developed a prospect theory-based version of the GLDS method, defining a new dominance score function to measure decision-makers' psychological behavior traits. Similarly, Wan et al. (2021) assigned individual prospect gained and lost dominance scores to alternatives based on prospect theory. Liao et al. (2023) incorporated cumulative prospect theory into the GLDS framework, improving its suitability for group decision-making scenarios. In handling uncertainty, Zheng et al. (2024) introduced a projection-based measurement technique for calculating dominance scores in qualitative environments, while Liu et al. (2023a) addressed MADM problems with incomplete or unknown attribute weights by applying the sample average approximation method within the GLDS framework. Regarding the expression of evaluation information for attribute performance, researchers created various GLDS variants, including those based on probabilistic linguistic term sets (Wu & Liao, 2019), generalized probabilistic linguistic term sets (Fang et al., 2021), probabilistic interval-valued hesitant fuzzy sets (Liang & Wang, 2021), probabilistic reliable linguistic term sets (Hong et al., 2021), continuous interval-valued linguistic term sets (Liang et al., 2020), continuous interval-valued double hierarchy linguistic term sets (Wang et al., 2022), linguistic Z-numbers (Liu et al., 2023a; Xiao et al., 2024), linguistic Z-number preference relations (Zhan & Li, 2025), 2-tuple linguistic variables (Zheng & Liu, 2025), hesitant fuzzy linguistic sets (Fu et al., 2018), double hierarchy hesitant fuzzy linguistic term sets (Tianle et al., 2022), generalized linguistic term sets (Fu, 2023), (Pythagorean fuzzy sets (Zhai et al., 2023), intuitionistic fuzzy sets (Hezam et al. 2023, 2024; Mao et al., 2024), picture fuzzy sets (Wu et al., 2025), q-rung orthopair fuzzy sets (Liao, Zhang et al., 2020; Liu et al., 2020), interval type-2 fuzzy sets (Wang et al., 2022), interval-valued T-spherical fuzzy sets (Wang, Wang et al., 2024), rough sets (Liao, Chang et al., 2020), hesitant fuzzy sets (Liang et al., 2022), probabilistic hesitant fuzzy sets (Liao et al., 2023; Zheng et al., 2025), and spherical Z-numbers (Wu et al., 2024).

In the application stage, the GLDS method shows significant practical value, mainly concentrating on two areas. In risk management, it has been widely used in failure modes and effects analysis, including risk analysis of breast cancer treatments (Mandal et al., 2024), risk assessment of ammonia storage facilities (Zheng, Tang et al., 2024), risk analysis of loader-transport-dumper systems (Liu et al., 2021), risk management and control in healthcare systems (Jiang et al., 2023), fault diagnosis in machine tools (Wang et al., 2019), failure mode identification in stereotactic radiotherapy for lung cancer patients (Liu et al., 2023b), submarine pipeline integrity management (Zhan & Li, 2025). In decision support, GLDS has been successfully applied to site selection for wind-solar shared energy storage projects (Gao et al., 2022), medical service quality assessment (Ming et al., 2020), resident satisfaction evaluation after disasters (Liao et al., 2019), Investment decisions for wind power integrated energy storage stations (Wang et al., 2024), choosing metaverse-related education solutions in higher education (Wang et al., 2024), investment analysis in agricultural supply chains (Zhai et al., 2023), performance assessment of internet hospitals (Liu et al., 2023a), energy source selection for offshore vessel charging stations (Mao et al., 2024), and decision-making in underground mining methods (Fu et al., 2018). These applications not only confirm the practicality and effectiveness of the GLDS method but also offer valuable experience for future research.

100.3 Methodology

A typical MADM problem can be characterized as follows. Given a finite set of alternatives $A = \{a_1, a_2, \ldots, a_m\}$, we aim to establish a systematic decision framework for alternative selection or ranking based on a predefined set of attributes $C = \{c_1, c_2, \ldots, c_n\}$. Notably, we adopt a deterministic decision-making assumption where $\forall\, a_i \in A$ and $\forall\, c_j \in C$, the performance value $g_{ij} \in \mathbb{R}$ of alternative a_i with respect to attribute c_j is precisely specified. The relative importance of attributes is quantified through weights. The weight w_j of c_j satisfies $w_j \geq 0$ and $\sum_{j=1}^{n} w_j = 1$, $\forall\, c_j \in C$. Each attribute is associated with a predefined target value (denoted as g_j^*, $\forall\, j \in \{1, 2, \ldots, n\}$) representing the decision-maker's optimal performance requirement. For benefit-type attributes, g_j^* is typically set to the maximum observed value, while for cost-type attributes, it is set to the minimum. Alternatively, g_j^* may represent an intermediate value or range, depending on the decision context.

The framework of the GLDS method to solve the MADM problem is shown in Fig. 100.1. It consists of two phases: ranking alternatives and conflict analysis. Detailed introductions to these two phases are provided in Sections 100.3.1 and 100.3.2, respectively.

100.3.1 Phase 1: ranking alternatives

Step 1.1. Normalization. To address dimensional inconsistency among attributes in MADM, we should normalize their performance values. The linear normalization method (as shown in Eq. (100.1)) is used, where performance values are scaled to [0, 1] based on their relative positions within their respective ranges, thus removing the effects of units of measurement (Liao & Wu, 2020). Other normalization methods (e.g., vector normalization) can be applied depending on the specific problem. When available or estimable, the marginal utility/value functions of attributes can be included to better capture decision-makers' preferences regarding attribute performance.

$$u_{ij} = 1 - \frac{|g_{ij} - g_j^*|}{\max\{\max_i g_{ij}, g_j^*\} - \min\{\min_i g_{ij}, g_j^*\}} \tag{100.1}$$

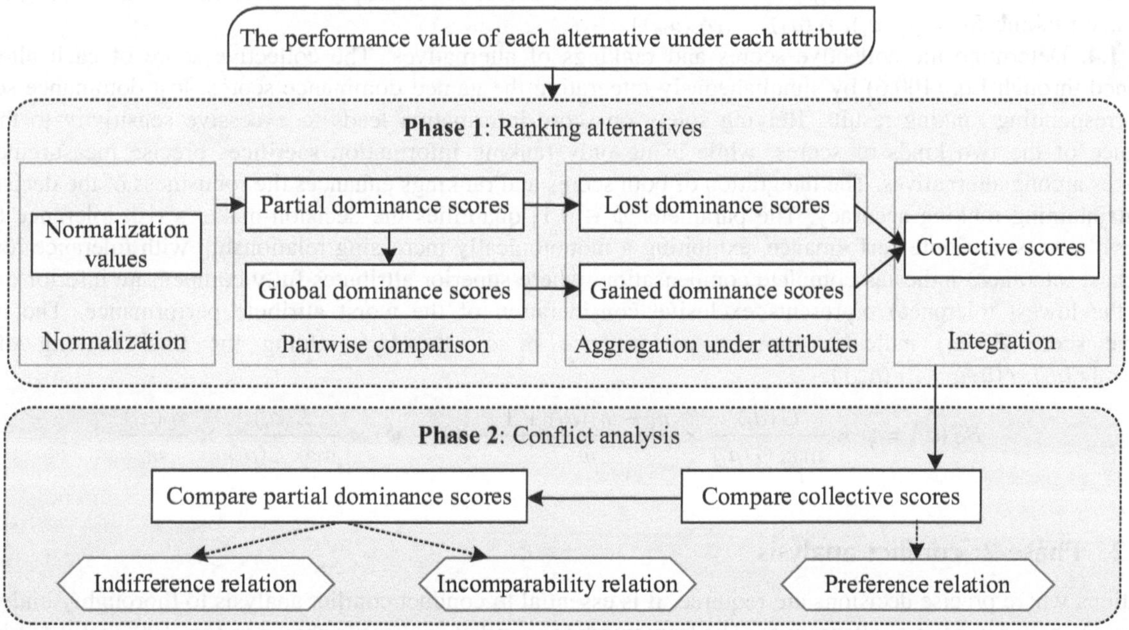

FIGURE 100.1 The framework of the gained and lost dominance score method.

Step 1.2. Determine the dominance score of one alternative over another. The partial dominance score $df_j(a_i, a_v)$ of alternative a_i over a_v with respect to attribute c_j is calculated using Eq. (100.2), $\forall\, a_i, a_v \in A$ and $c_j \in C$. This score measures the relative dominance by directly comparing the performance difference (u_{ij}-u_{vj}) on a single attribute. Specifically, a larger and positive performance difference (u_{ij}-u_{vj}) yields a higher dominance score $df_j(a_i, a_v)$, indicating a_i 's stronger dominance over a_v on this attribute. Correspondingly, $df_j(a_i, a_v) = 0$ if $u_{ij} < u_{vj}$, which confirms a_i 's nondominance relative to a_v in this attribute. The global dominance score $df(a_i, a_v)$ of a_i over a_v is obtained by aggregating the partial dominance scores $df_j(a_i, a_v)$ across all attributes through the weighted aggregation operator specified in Eq. (100.3).

$$df_j(a_i, a_v) = \max(u_{ij} - u_{vj}, 0) \tag{100.2}$$

$$df(a_i, a_v) = \sum_{j=1}^{n} (w_j \times df_j(a_i, a_v)) \tag{100.3}$$

Step 1.3. Determine the gained dominance score and the lost dominance score of each alternative. The gain dominance score $G(a_i)$ of alternative a_i, as defined in Eq. (100.4), is computed by aggregating its global dominance scores $df(a_i, a_v)$ over all other $m-1$ alternatives (where $v = 1, 2, \ldots, m$ and $v \neq i$). This complete compensatory aggregation operator allows full trade-offs between attributes, where superior performance on one attribute (*i.e.*, significant dominance over others) can fully compensate for inferior performance on another attribute (*i.e.*, significant dominance by others). The lost dominance score $L(a_i)$ of alternative a_i, defined in Eq. (100.5), quantifies its worst attribute performance through a two-step calculation. First, it computes the average dominance score of other alternatives over a_i for each attribute c_j (where $j = 1, 2, \ldots, n$), where higher values indicate poorer performance of a_i on c_j. Second, it identifies a_i 's weakest attribute performance by taking the maximum value among these average dominance scores across all attributes.

$$G(a_i) = \frac{1}{m-1} \sum_{v=1}^{m} df(a_i, a_v) \tag{100.4}$$

$$L(a_i) = \max_j \left(\frac{1}{m-1} \sum_{v=1}^{m} (w_j \times df_j(a_v, a_i))\right) \tag{100.5}$$

The gained dominance score $G(a_i)$ exhibits a positive correlation with alternative performance. Higher scores indicate better overall performance, yielding the first subordinate ranking $R_G = \{r_G(a_1), r_G(a_2), \ldots, r_G(a_m)\}$. Conversely, the lost dominance score $L(a_i)$ shows a negative correlation. Lower scores reflect superior performance, generating the second subordinate ranking $R_L = \{r_L(a_1), r_L(a_2), \ldots, r_L(a_m)\}$.

Step 1.4. Determine the collective scores and rankings of alternatives. The collective score of each alternative is determined through Eq. (100.6) by simultaneously integrating the gained dominance scores, lost dominance scores, and their corresponding ranking results. Relying solely on score information leads to excessive sensitivity to the relative importance of the two kinds of scores, while using only ranking information sacrifices precise measurement of the differences among alternatives. The integration of both scores and rankings enhances the robustness of the decision model while maintaining ranking accuracy. The parameter $\psi \in [0,1]$ quantifies the decision-maker's risk tolerance toward an alternative's worst attribute performance, exhibiting a monotonically increasing relationship with tolerance level. $\psi = 1$ (the highest tolerance) indicates complete compensation, where superior attributes fully compensate inferior ones, while $\psi = 0$ (the lowest tolerance) represents exclusive consideration of the worst attribute performance. The higher the collective score $BS(a_i)$ indicates superior performance of a_i, thereby yielding the final ranking of alternatives $R = \{r(a_1), r(a_2), \ldots, r(a_m)\}$.

$$BS(a_i) = \psi \times \frac{G(a_i)}{\max_i G(a_i)} \times \frac{m - r_G(a_i) + 1}{m} - (1 - \psi) \times \frac{L(a_i)}{\max_i L(a_i)} \times \frac{r_L(a_i)}{m} \tag{100.6}$$

100.3.2 Phase 2: conflict analysis

In situations where precise decisions are required, it is essential to conduct conflict analysis to thoroughly understand the PIR relations between pairs of alternatives. The framework for conflict analysis is shown in Fig. 100.2 (Wu & Liao, 2022). Specifically, it first checks whether the difference in collective scores between two alternatives exceeds the preference threshold. If it does, a clear preference relation exists, indicating that one alternative is significantly better than the other. If not, they might be indifferent or incomparable. It is important to note that the original conflict analysis distinguishes

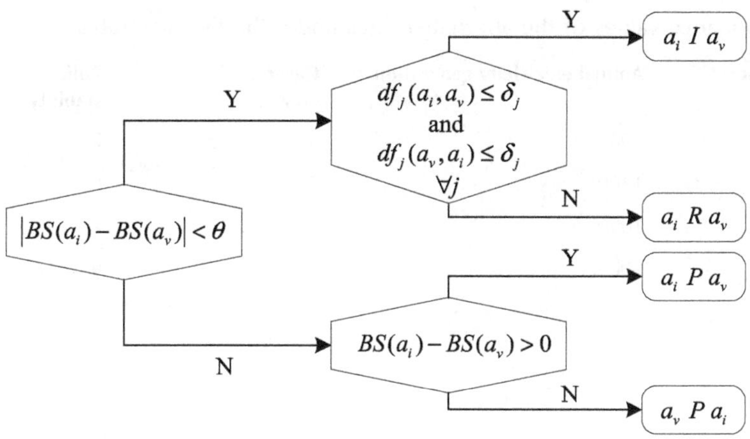

FIGURE 100.2 The conflict analysis framework of the gained and lost dominance score method.

indifference and incomparability relations based on global dominance scores. To make it easier to compare performance differences between alternatives across various attributes, this paper directly uses partial dominance scores to identify these two relations. If the performance differences between two alternatives for each attribute are small (*i.e.*, all partial dominance scores between them are below the indifference threshold), it shows an indifference relation. If they have significant differences in at least one attribute (*i.e.*, some partial dominance scores are above the indifference threshold), they are considered incomparable. Two alternatives that are in an indifference relation can generally be treated as interchangeable since choosing either has little impact on the result. However, for two incomparable alternatives, no substitution is possible; selecting one over the other may overly emphasize the importance of the superior attributes of the chosen alternative, which can lead to decision biases. Therefore, it is necessary to perform a deeper evaluation and trade-off analysis when selecting between two incomparable alternatives.

The indifference threshold, $\delta_j \in [0, 1]$, $\forall j$, for each attribute can be determined by decision-makers based on actual circumstances. Decision-makers can initially evaluate the range within which differences between two alternatives for an attribute are considered insignificant. For example, they might regard a price difference of no more than $4,000 between two cars as insignificant enough. Afterwards, this difference in performance values should be converted into the discrepancy between their normalization values, and this discrepancy is then established as the indifference threshold for the attribute. If decision-makers take a cautious approach when establishing indifference relations, they may tend to set a smaller indifference threshold; otherwise, they might select a larger one. Based on the definition of collective scores, we can further specify the preference threshold as $\theta = 0.5\bar{\delta}/n + 0.5/m$, where $\bar{\delta}$ represents the average indifference threshold across all attributes. The preference threshold is positively related to the indifference threshold but negatively related to the number of alternatives and attributes.

100.4 Numerical example 1: site selection

A multinational energy corporation plans to construct a novel renewable energy power station in the Asia-Pacific region, seeking the optimal site among four alternatives (a_1, a_2, a_3, a_4). Specific decision attributes encompass investment cost (in millions of USD, cost-oriented, lower is better), annual electricity generation (in gigawatt-hour (GWh), benefit-oriented, higher is better), carbon emissions (in tons of CO_2 per GWh, cost-oriented, lower is better), policy stability (on a 10-point scale, benefit-oriented, higher is better), and social acceptance (as a percentage of public support, benefit-oriented, higher is better). The performance values of each alternative site under each attribute are shown in Table 100.1. The target values for the five attributes are 80, 1200, 3, 10, and 95, respectively. The weights of the five attributes are 0.3, 0.3, 0.15, 0.15, and 0.1, respectively.

We present the solving process of the GLDS method below. Firstly, the performance values of alternatives under each attribute are normalized based on Eq. (100.1). The results are shown in Table 100.2. Secondly, we conduct pairwise comparisons between alternatives using Eq. (100.2) to calculate the partial dominance scores for each alternative relative to others under each attribute. Subsequently, these partial dominance scores across attributes are aggregated using Eq. (100.3) to obtain the global dominance score for one alternative over another. The results are shown in Table 100.3. Based on this, Eq. (100.4) is used to compute the weighted sum of global dominance scores for each alternative against all others, yielding the gained dominance score and its subordinate rank for each alternative.

TABLE 100.1 The performance values of the alternative sites under the five attributes.

Sites	Investment cost	Annual electricity generation	Carbon emissions	Policy stability	Social acceptance
a_1	95	1080	4	7	88
a_2	110	1200	7	6	95
a_3	85	1050	5	7	91
a_4	120	900	6	9	75

TABLE 100.2 The normalization values of the alternative sites under the five attributes.

Sites	Investment cost	Annual electricity generation	Carbon emissions	Policy stability	Social acceptance
a_1	0.625	0.6	0.75	0.25	0.65
a_2	0.25	1	0	0	1
a_3	0.875	0.5	0.5	0.25	0.8
a_4	0	0	0.25	0.75	0

Meanwhile, Eq. (100.5) is utilized to assess the extent to which each alternative is dominated by others across attributes, identifying its worst attribute performance, and thus determining the lost dominance score and corresponding subordinate rank for each alternative. Finally, Eq. (100.6) integrates the gained dominance score, lost dominance score, and subordinate ranks to derive a collective score for each alternative. The parameter is set to $\psi = 0.5$. Table 100.4 details the scores and rankings of the alternative sites. The results indicate that a_3 is the optimal choice.

Next, we conduct conflict analysis to determine the PIR relations among the alternative sites. Assuming that when the performance values of two alternatives differ by 10, 50, 1, 1, and 5 or less across the five attributes, respectively, they can be considered indifferent to each other. Converting these differences to normalization values, they roughly correspond to a gap of around 0.25. Therefore, we set the indifference threshold at 0.25. Based on this, the preference threshold can be set at 0.15 (i.e., $0.5\bar{\delta}/n + 0.5/m$). By comparing the collective scores of each alternative with the preference threshold, we draw the following conclusions. Alternative a_1 outperforms a_2 and a_4, a_3 outperforms a_2 and a_4, a_2 outperforms a_4, while there may be an indifference or incomparability relation between a_1 and a_3. The partial dominance scores of a_1 over a_3 under the five attributes are 0, 0.1, 0.25, 0, and 0, respectively, while the partial dominance scores of a_3 over a_1 under the five attributes are 0.25, 0, 0, 0, and 0.15, respectively. All these scores are below the indifference threshold of 0.25, indicating an indifference relation between a_1 and a_3. In summary, both a_1 and a_3 can be considered as the optimal site selection. Choosing either site will not pose additional risks.

100.5 Numerical example 2: electric SUVs selection

A consumer plans to purchase a luxury electric sport utility vehicles (SUV), considering the top 10 series ($a_1 \sim a_{10}$), identified by Edmunds, a prestigious information service platform within the U.S. automotive industry. In the selection process, the consumer focuses on the following attributes: "national market price" (in USD, a cost attribute, c_1) reflecting the purchase cost, "all-electric range" (in miles, a benefit attribute, c_2) measuring driving capability per charge, and "consumer review" (on a 5-star scale, a benefit attribute, c_3) indicating market satisfaction based on average consumer

TABLE 100.3 The global dominance score for one alternative over another.

Sites	a_1	a_2	a_3	a_4
a_1	0.00	0.16	0.09	0.08
a_2	0.26	0.00	0.30	0.15
a_3	0.07	0.17	0.00	0.08
a_4	0.51	0.48	0.53	0.00

TABLE 100.4 The scores and rankings of the alternative sites.

Sites	Gained		Lost		Collective	
	Score	Rank	Score	Rank	Score	Rank
a_1	0.28	2	0.04	1	0.32	2
a_2	0.27	3	0.10	3	0.04	3
a_3	0.31	1	0.06	2	0.43	1
a_4	0.10	4	0.21	4	-0.46	4

ratings. Additional attributes include performance (c_4), comfort (c_5), interior (c_6), technology (c_7), storage (c_8), range and efficiency (c_9), value (c_{10}), and wildcard (c_{11}), all rated on a 10-star scale with higher ratings indicating better performance. The performance values of these eight attributes are sourced from Edmunds' professional team after rigorous 500,000-mile/year tests on test tracks and real roads. The data was collected in July 2025. The consumer's ideal attribute values are \$50,000 for price, 350 miles for all-electric range, 4.5 for consumer review, and 9 for the last eight attributes. Table 100.5 presents detailed performance values of each SUV across these attributes. The consumer assigned weights of 0.14, 0.13, 0.09, 0.08, 0.08, 0.08, 0.08, 0.08, 0.08, 0.08, and 0.08 to the eleven attributes, respectively.

Firstly, the performance values of each attribute are normalized using Eq. (100.1), with the results presented in Table 100.6. Subsequently, each pair of alternatives is compared across all attributes. This process involved calculating partial dominance scores and global dominance scores using Eqs. (100.2) and (100.3), respectively, with the global dominance scores shown in Table 100.7. Furthermore, based on Eqs. (100.4), (100.5), and (100.6) (with $\psi = 0.5$), the gained dominance score, lost dominance score, and overall score for each alternative are computed, respectively, and all results are summarized in Table 100.8. Ultimately, the optimal choice can be identified as the third SUV (a_3) based on its collective score.

Assuming that value differences do not exceed 4,000 and 30 for the first two attributes, respectively, and are within 0.5 for the last nine, we consider these alternatives as nonsignificantly different. Based on this, the indifference thresholds for the first three attributes are set at 0.11, 0.33, and 0.24, respectively, with a unified indifference threshold of 0.33 for the remaining attributes. The average indifference threshold for all attributes is 0.3. The preference threshold can be determined by $0.5\overline{\delta}/n + 0.5/m = 0.06$. After analyzing the collective scores of alternative SUVs, we find that the difference between a_1 and a_3 does not exceed this preference threshold. Therefore, they are considered indifferent or incomparable at the comprehensive level, and both exhibit superiority compared to other SUVs. This implies that the consumer should choose between these two SUVs. Furthermore, when comparing the partial dominance scores of a_1 and a_3 across attributes, we find that their performance differs beyond the indifference threshold in several attributes, including "national market price," "storage," "range and efficiency," and "value." This

TABLE 100.5 The performance values of the alternative SUVs under each attribute.

SUVs	c_1	c_2	c_3	c_4	c_5	c_6	c_7	c_8	c_9	c_{10}	c_{11}
a_1	70,729	290	4.4	8.5	8.5	8.5	9.0	8.5	9.0	8.0	8.0
a_2	62,911	236	3.7	8.5	9.0	8.5	8.0	8.0	7.5	8.0	8.5
a_3	50,700	294	4.2	8.5	9.0	8.0	8.5	7.5	7.5	9.0	8.0
a_4	75,900	258	2.4	8.5	8.5	8.0	7.5	9.0	7.5	8.0	9.0
a_5	71,016	302	4.5	7.5	8.0	8.0	9.0	8.5	8.5	8.0	7.5
a_6	67,500	342	2.4	8.0	8.5	8.5	8.0	7.5	7.5	7.5	9.0
a_7	84,990	329	3.3	8.0	8.0	8.0	7.0	8.5	8.0	8.0	9.0
a_8	73,841	315	4.5	8.5	8.5	8.0	7.5	7.5	9.0	7.5	8.5
a_9	57,556	326	3.4	7.5	8.0	7.5	9.0	8.0	7.5	8.0	8.0
a_{10}	50,388	296	3.3	8.0	7.5	8.0	8.5	7.5	7.5	8.0	8.0

TABLE 100.6 The normalization values of the alternative SUVs under each attribute.

SUVs	c_1	c_2	c_3	c_4	c_5	c_6	c_7	c_8	c_9	c_{10}	c_{11}
a_1	0.41	0.47	0.95	0.67	0.67	0.67	1.00	0.67	1.00	0.33	0.33
a_2	0.63	0.00	0.62	0.67	1.00	0.67	0.50	0.33	0.00	0.33	0.67
a_3	0.98	0.51	0.86	0.67	1.00	0.33	0.75	0.00	0.00	1.00	0.33
a_4	0.26	0.19	0.00	0.67	0.67	0.33	0.25	1.00	0.00	0.33	1.00
a_5	0.40	0.58	1.00	0.00	0.33	0.33	1.00	0.67	0.67	0.33	0.00
a_6	0.50	0.93	0.00	0.33	0.67	0.67	0.50	0.00	0.00	0.00	1.00
a_7	0.00	0.82	0.43	0.33	0.33	0.33	0.00	0.67	0.33	0.33	1.00
a_8	0.32	0.69	1.00	0.67	0.67	0.33	0.25	0.00	1.00	0.00	0.67
a_9	0.78	0.79	0.48	0.00	0.33	0.00	1.00	0.33	0.00	0.33	0.33
a_{10}	0.99	0.53	0.43	0.33	0.00	0.33	0.75	0.00	0.00	0.33	0.33

suggests that although a_1 and a_3 are similar in overall performance, they have clear advantages and disadvantages in specific attributes, and thus do not constitute a direct substitution relationship but should be regarded as incomparable. In summary, to select the optimal SUV between a_1 and a_3, the consumer needs to conduct a more detailed evaluation and comparison of these two SUVs.

TABLE 100.7 The global dominance score for one alternative SUV over another.

n	a_1	a_2	a_3	a_4	a_5	a_6	a_7	a_8	a_9	a_{10}
a_1	0.00	0.08	0.16	0.08	0.02	0.13	0.10	0.06	0.09	0.09
a_2	0.24	0.00	0.21	0.11	0.23	0.15	0.19	0.20	0.16	0.14
a_3	0.19	0.08	0.00	0.13	0.15	0.13	0.17	0.14	0.08	0.00
a_4	0.31	0.18	0.34	0.00	0.27	0.18	0.15	0.24	0.25	0.22
a_5	0.16	0.22	0.27	0.19	0.00	0.22	0.14	0.17	0.11	0.14
a_6	0.31	0.18	0.30	0.13	0.26	0.00	0.15	0.20	0.18	0.15
a_7	0.32	0.25	0.37	0.14	0.21	0.18	0.00	0.22	0.19	0.20
a_8	0.18	0.17	0.24	0.13	0.15	0.13	0.12	0.00	0.19	0.16
a_9	0.28	0.20	0.25	0.21	0.15	0.18	0.16	0.26	0.00	0.08
a_{10}	0.31	0.20	0.20	0.21	0.21	0.19	0.20	0.26	0.11	0.00

TABLE 100.8 The scores and rankings of the alternative SUVs.

SUVs	Gained		Lost		Collective	
	Score	Rank	Score	Rank	Score	Rank
a_1	0.255	2	0.029	1	0.425	2
a_2	0.175	5	0.080	9	-0.235	9
a_3	0.259	1	0.033	2	0.460	1
a_4	0.148	9	0.058	7	-0.189	8
a_5	0.185	4	0.050	5	0.096	4
a_6	0.164	6	0.058	7	-0.088	6
a_7	0.152	8	0.082	10	-0.412	10
a_8	0.196	3	0.038	3	0.232	3
a_9	0.153	7	0.039	4	0.024	5
a_{10}	0.132	10	0.050	5	-0.128	7

100.6 Conclusions

This chapter reviewed the GLDS method and developed a generalized framework with precise attribute values. Two numerical examples confirmed its effectiveness and practicality. The GLDS method demonstrates high flexibility. For MADM problems that only need a rough understanding of alternative rankings, simply executing the first phase of the GLDS method and ranking based on collective scores is enough. However, for a detailed exploration of the best alternative or a thorough understanding of the relationships among alternatives, additional conflict analysis is necessary. Especially in selection problems, the key is to carefully analyze the PIR relations among top-ranked alternatives to determine the best choice.

Compared to other outranking methods, GLDS offers two key advantages. First, GLDS thoroughly assesses the comprehensive performance of alternatives while paying particular attention to their weakest attributes. This dual focus guarantees that the chosen alternative not only performs well overall but also avoids obvious flaws, which aligns well with the needs of risk-averse decision-makers. Second, GLDS includes a conflict analysis framework that accurately identifies PIR relations between alternatives through a simple pairwise comparison process. The threshold settings are meaningful rather than arbitrary, reducing the cognitive load on decision-makers.

References

Brans, J. P., & Vincke, P. (1985). Note—a preference ranking organisation method: (The PROMETHEE method for multiple criteria decision-making). *Management Science, 31*(6), 647–656.

Fang, R., Liao, H. C., Yang, J. B., & Xu, D. L. (2021). Generalised probabilistic linguistic evidential reasoning approach for multi-criteria decision-making under uncertainty. *Journal of the Operational Research Society, 72*(1), 130–144.

Fu, Z. G. (2023). A generalized linguistic gained and lost dominance score method for landslide hazard treatment. *Applied Soft Computing, 145*, 110567.

Fu, Z. G., Wu, X. L., Liao, H. C., & Herrera, F. (2018). Underground mining method selection with the hesitant fuzzy linguistic gained and lost dominance score method. *IEEE Access, 6*, 66442–66458.

Gao, J. W., Wang, Y. P., Huang, N. B., Wei, L. L., & Zhang, Z. X. (2022). Optimal site selection study of wind-photovoltaic-shared energy storage power stations based on GIS and multi-criteria decision making: A two-stage framework. *Renewable Energy, 201*, 1139–1162.

Govindan, K., & Jepsen, M. B. (2016). ELECTRE: A comprehensive literature review on methodologies and applications. *European Journal of Operational Research, 250*(1), 1–29.

Greco, S., Matarazzo, B., & Słowiński, R. (2001). Rough sets theory for multicriteria decision analysis. *European Journal of Operational Research, 129*(1), 1–47.

Greco, S., Słowiński, R., & Wallenius, J. (2025). Fifty years of multiple criteria decision analysis: From classical methods to robust ordinal regression. *European Journal of Operational Research, 323*(2), 351–377.

Hezam, I. M., Basua, D., Mishra, A. R., Rani, P., & Cavallaro, F. (2024). Intuitionistic fuzzy gained and lost dominance score based on symmetric point criterion to prioritize zero-carbon measures for sustainable urban transportation. *Kybernetes, 53*(10), 3816–3847.

Hezam, I. M., Rani, P., Mishra, A. R., & Alshamrani, A. (2023). An intuitionistic fuzzy entropy-based gained and lost dominance score decision-making method to select and assess sustainable supplier selection. *Applied Mathematics for Modern Challenges, 8*(5).

Hong, N., Wang, X. X., & Xu, Z. (2021). Probabilistic reliable linguistic term sets applied to investment project selection with the gained and lost dominance score method. *International Journal of Machine Learning and Cybernetics, 12*(8), 2163–2183.

Jiang, J., Liu, X. W., Wang, W. Z., & Deveci, M. (2023). Assessing the impact of healthcare service risks on healthcare demand under evolving economic and social structures: An improved GLDS decision making method considering risk attitudes. *Structural Change and Economic Dynamics, 67*, 459–479.

Liang, W., & Wang, Y. M. (2021). A probabilistic interval-valued hesitant fuzzy gained and lost dominance score method based on regret theory. *Computers & Industrial Engineering, 159*, 107532.

Liang, W., Wang, J. Y., & Deng, Z. (2022). HFGLDS: Hesitant fuzzy gained and lost dominance score method based on hesitant fuzzy utility function for multi-criteria decision making. *IEEE Access, 10*, 20407–20419.

Liang, X. D., Wu, X. L., & Liao, H. C. (2020). A gained and lost dominance score II method for modelling group uncertainty: Case study of site selection of electric vehicle charging stations. *Journal of Cleaner Production, 262*, 121239.

Liao, H. C., & Wu, X. L. (2020). DNMA: A double normalization-based multiple aggregation method for multi-expert multi-criteria decision making. *Omega, 94*, 102058.

Liao, H. C., Chang, J. Y., Zhang, Z. Y., Zhou, X., & Al-Barakati, A. (2020). Third-party cold chain medicine logistics provider selection by a rough set-based gained and lost dominance score method. *International Journal of Fuzzy Systems, 22*(6), 2055–2069.

Liao, H. C., Yu, J. Y., Wu, X. L., Al-Barakati, A., Altalhi, A., & Herrera, F. (2019). Life satisfaction evaluation in earthquake-hit area by the probabilistic linguistic GLDS method integrated with the logarithm-multiplicative analytic hierarchy process. *International Journal of Disaster Risk Reduction, 38*, 101190.

Liao, H. C., Zhang, H. R., Zhang, C., Wu, X. L., Mardani, A., & Al-Barakati, A. (2020). A q-rung orthopair fuzzy GLDS method for investment evaluation of BE angel capital in China. *Technological and Economic Development of Economy, 26*(1), 103–134.

Liao, N. N., Cai, Q., Garg, H., Wei, G. W., & Xu, X. R. (2023). Novel gained and lost dominance score method based on cumulative prospect theory for group decision-making problems in probabilistic hesitant fuzzy environment. *International Journal of Fuzzy Systems, 25*(4), 1414–1428.

Liao, Z. Q., Liao, H. C., Tang, M., Al-Barakati, A., & Llopis-Albert, C. (2020). A Choquet integral-based hesitant fuzzy gained and lost dominance score method for multi-criteria group decision making considering the risk preferences of experts: Case study of higher business education evaluation. *Information Fusion, 62*, 121–133.

Liu, F., Liao, H. C., Wu, X. L., & Al-Barakati, A. (2023a). Evaluating Internet hospitals by a linguistic Z-number-based gained and lost dominance score method considering different risk preferences of experts. *Information Sciences, 630*, 647–668.

Liu, F., Liao, H. C., Wu, X. L., & Al-Barakati, A. (2023b). Consensus-based failure mode and effect analysis in group decision-making with incomplete weights of risk factors: Case study of stereotactic body radiation therapy for lung cancer. *Applied Soft Computing, 142* 110322.

Liu, L., Wu, J., Wei, G. W., Wei, C., Wang, J., & Wei, Y. (2020). Entropy-based GLDS method for social capital selection of a PPP project with q-rung orthopair fuzzy information. *Entropy, 22*(4), 414.

Liu, Z., Mou, X., Liu, H. C., & Zhang, L. (2021). Failure mode and effect analysis based on probabilistic linguistic preference relations and gained and lost dominance score method. *IEEE Transactions on Cybernetics, 53*(3), 1566–1577.

Mandal, P., Samanta, S., & Pal, M. (2024). Failure mode and effects analysis in consensus-based GDM for surface-guided deep inspiration breath-hold breast radiotherapy for breast cancer under the framework of linguistic Z-number. *Information Sciences, 658*, 120016.

Mao, Q., Fan, J., Imtiaz, S., Munir, H. M., Alsenani, T. R., & Alharbi, M. (2024). Prioritization of renewable energy for offshore ship charging stations based on intuitionistic fuzzy GLDS method: A case of China. *Heliyon, 10*(18).

Ming, Y., Luo, L., Wu, X. L., Liao, H. C., Lev, B., & Jiang, L. (2020). Managing patient satisfaction in a blood-collection room by the probabilistic linguistic gained and lost dominance score method integrated with the best-worst method. *Computers & Industrial Engineering, 145*, 106547.

Roy, B. (1968). Classement et choix en presence de points de vue multiples (La methode ELECTRE). *Revue Francaise D Informatique de Recherche Operationnelle, 2*(8), 57–75.

Tianle, Y. A. O., Weili, W. A. N. G., Run, M. I. A. O., Qiwei, H. U., Jun, D. O. N. G., & Xuefei, Y. A. N. (2022). Warhead power assessment based on double hierarchy hesitant fuzzy linguistic term sets theory and gained and lost dominance score method. *Chinese Journal of Aeronautics, 35*(4), 362–375.

Wallenius, J., Dyer, J. S., Fishburn, P. C., Steuer, R. E., Zionts, S., & Deb, K. (2008). Multiple criteria decision making, multiattribute utility theory: Recent accomplishments and what lies ahead. *Management Science, 54*(7), 1336–1349.

Wan, S. P., Zou, W. C., Dong, J. Y., & Martínez, L. (2021). A probabilistic linguistic dominance score method considering individual semantics and psychological behavior of decision makers. *Expert Systems with Applications, 184*, 115372.

Wang, W. Z., Jiang, W. J., Han, X., & Liu, S. L. (2022). An extended gained and lost dominance score method based risk prioritization for Fine-Kinney model with interval type-2 fuzzy information. *Human and Ecological Risk Assessment: An International Journal, 28*(1), 154–183.

Wang, W. Z., Liu, X. W., & Liu, S. L. (2019). Failure mode and effect analysis for machine tool risk analysis using extended gained and lost dominance score method. *IEEE Transactions on Reliability, 69*(3), 954–967.

Wang, W. Z., Wang, Y., Hu, Y., Zhang, T. L., & Wu, Q. (2024). Assessment of metaverse integration options in the higher education institution using interval-valued T-spherical fuzzy-WHMA-CEM-GLDS framework. *Applied Soft Computing, 156*, 111514.

Wang, X. D., Gou, X. J., & Xu, Z. S. (2022). A continuous interval-valued double hierarchy linguistic GLDS method and its application in performance evaluation of bus companies. *Applied Intelligence, 52*(4), 4511–4526.

Wang, Y. P., Gao, J. W., Wei, L. L., Wu, H. Y., & Zhao, S. T. (2024). Geographic information system-based multi-criteria decision-making analysis for investment assessment of wind-photovoltaic-shared energy storage power stations: A case study of shanxi province. *Environmental Science and Pollution Research, 31*(15), 22604–22629.

Wu, J., Fu, C., Zhao, E. L., Sun, S. L., & Wang, S. Y. (2025). What makes a better hotel selection? A hybrid approach considering tourists' preference and review helpfulness. *Current Issues in Tourism, 28*(10), 1570–1594.

Wu, M. Q., Ma, S. N., & Fan, J. P. (2024). A spherical Z-number multi-attribute group decision making model based on the prospect theory and GLDS method. *Complex & Intelligent Systems, 10*(6), 8501–8524.

Wu, X. L., & Liao, H. C. (2019). A consensus-based probabilistic linguistic gained and lost dominance score method. *European Journal of Operational Research, 272*(3), 1017–1027.

Wu, X. L., & Liao, H. C. (2022). A gained and lost dominance score method with conflict analysis for green economy development evaluation. *Annals of Operations Research, 316*(1), 623–655.

Wu, X. L., & Liao, H. C. (2023a). Value-driven preference disaggregation analysis for uncertain preference information. *Omega, 115* 102793.

Wu, X. L., & Liao, H. C. (2023b). A compensatory value function for modeling risk tolerance and criteria interactions in preference disaggregation. *Omega, 117* 102836.

Xiao, Y., Liao, H. C., Jin, X. W., & Zhan, J. M. (2024). A linguistic Z-number-based sorting method for three-way multi-criterion decision-making in ecological function zoning. *Information Sciences, 673*, 120706.

Zhai, T., Wang, D. Q., Zhang, Q., Saeidi, P., & Raj Mishra, A. (2023). Assessment of the agriculture supply chain risks for investments of agricultural small and mediumsized enterprises (SMEs) using the decision support model. *Economic Research-Ekonomska Istraživanja, 36*(2).

Zhan, M., & Li, Y. L. (2025). Risk evaluation of submarine pipelines using improved FMEA model based on social network analysis and extended GLDS method under a linguistic Z-number preference relation environment. *Journal of Loss Prevention in the Process Industries, 96*, 105611.

Zheng, J., Wang, Y. M., & Zhang, K. (2024). A case-driven emergency decision-making model based on probabilistic linguistic bidirectional projection. *Computers & Industrial Engineering, 187*, 109844.

Zheng, J., Wang, Y. M., & Zhang, K. (2025). A decision-making model with similarity measurement for case selection in public health treatment. *International Journal of Machine Learning and Cybernetics, 16*(1), 337–360.

Zheng, Q. H., & Liu, X. W. (2025). A consensus-based multi-criteria decision making method integrating GLDS method and quantum probability theory for risk analysis of human errors. *Computers & Industrial Engineering, 200*, 110847.

Zheng, Q. H., Tang, J., Wang, W. Z., Deveci, M., & Mardani, A. (2024). Analyzing the risk of the ammonia storage facility using extended FMEA model based on probabilistic linguistic GLDS method with consensus reaching. *International Journal of Hydrogen Energy, 62*, 1231–1244.

Index

Note: Page numbers followed by "*f*" and "*t*" refer to figures and tables, respectively.

B

C

F

G

H

J

K

L

P

S

T

U

Y

Z